Tolley's Corporation Ta

This edition gives the position as at 1 July 2021 and covers all legislation, HMRC's published guidance and other relevant sources of information including the provisions of Finance Act 2021.

Tolley's Corporation Tax 2021–22

by

Kevin Walton MA

Tolley®

LexisNexis® UK & Worldwide

United Kingdom — RELX (UK) Limited trading as LexisNexis®, 1–3 Strand, London WC2N 5JR and 9–10 St Andrew Square, Edinburgh EH2 2AF

LNUK Global Partners — LexisNexis® encompasses authoritative legal publishing brands dating back to the 19th century including: Butterworths® in the United Kingdom, Canada and the Asia-Pacific region; Les Editions du Juris Classeur in France; and Matthew Bender® worldwide. Details of LexisNexis® locations worldwide can be found at www.lexisnexis.com

Published by LexisNexis®
This is a Tolley title

A CIP Catalogue record for this book is available from the British Library.

ISBN for this volume: 9780754557647

Printed and bound by CPI Group (UK) Ltd, Croydon, CR0 4YY

Visit LexisNexis UK at www.lexisnexis.co.uk

About This Book

The text of this work includes full coverage of the corporation tax provisions in the *Finance Act 2021* together with all other relevant material to 1 July 2021 such as statutes, statutory instruments, court cases, Tribunal decisions, press releases, Extra Statutory Concessions and Statements of Practice.

We welcome all comments and suggestions for improvement to this work. You can contact us in this respect by e-mailing the Editor, Gemma Murray at gemma.murray@lexisnexis.co.uk. Any technical queries will be passed on to the author.

Contents

Abbreviations and References

Abbreviations

ACT	Advance Corporation Tax.
APRT	Advance Petroleum Revenue Tax.
APRTA 1986	Advance Petroleum Revenue Tax Act 1986.
art	Article.
CAA	Capital Allowances Act.
CA	Court of Appeal.
CCA	Court of Criminal Appeal.
CCAB	Consultative Committee of Accountancy Bodies.
Ch D	Chancery Division.
CES	Court of Exchequer (Scotland).
Cf.	compare.
CFC	Controlled Foreign Company.
CGT	Capital Gains Tax.
CGTA 1979	Capital Gains Tax Act 1979.
CIR	Commissioners of Inland Revenue ('the Board').
CJEC	Court of Justice of the European Communities.
CRCA	Commissioners for Revenue and Customs Act.
CT	Corporation Tax.
CTA	Corporation Tax Act.
CTT	Capital Transfer Tax.
EC	European Communities.
ECJ	European Court of Justice.
EEC	European Economic Community.
EU	European Union.
Ex D	Exchequer Division.

FA	Finance Act.
FII	Franked Investment Income.
FTT	First Tier Tribunal.
FY	Financial Year.
HC(I)	High Court (Ireland).
HL	House of Lords.
HMRC	Her Majesty's Revenue and Customs
ICAEW	Institute of Chartered Accountants in England and Wales.
ICTA	Income and Corporation Taxes Act.
IHTA 1984	Inheritance Tax Act 1984.
IR	Inland Revenue.
ITA	Income Tax Act 2007.
ITEPA 2003	Income Tax (Earnings and Pensions) Act 2003.
ITTOIA 2005	Income Tax (Trading and Other Income) Act 2005
KB	King's Bench Division.
NI	Northern Ireland.
OTA	Oil Taxation Act.
PC	Privy Council.
PDA	Probate, Divorce and Admiralty Division (now Family Division).
POCA 2002	Proceeds of Crime Act 2002
QB	Queen's Bench Division.
RI	Republic of Ireland (Eire).
s	Section.
SCS	Scottish Court of Session.
Sch	Schedule.
SI	Statutory Instrument.
SP	HMRC Statement of Practice.
Sp C	Special Commissioners.
SR&O	Statutory Rules and Orders.
TCGA 1992	Taxation of Chargeable Gains Act 1992.
TMA 1970	Taxes Management Act 1970.
VAT	Value Added Tax.

VATA 1994	Value Added Tax Act 1994.

References

(*denotes a series accredited for citation in court).

All E R	*All England Law Reports, (LexisNexis, Lexis House, 30 Farringdon Street, London EC4A 4HH).
AC or App Cas	*Law Reports, Appeal Cases, (Incorporated Council of Law Reporting for England and Wales).
Ch	*Law Reports, Chancery Division.
Ex D	*Law Reports, Exchequer Division (see also below).
IR	*Irish Reports, (Law Reporting Council).
LR Ex	*Law Reports, Exchequer Division.
SFTD	Simon's First Tier Decisions.
SSCD	Simon's Tax Cases Special Commissioners' Decisions, (LexisNexis as above).
STC	*Simon's Tax Cases, (LexisNexis as above).
STI	Simon's Tax Intelligence, (LexisNexis as above).
TC	*Official Reports of Tax Cases.
WLR	*Weekly Law Reports, (Incorporated Council of Law Reporting).

The first number in the citation refers to the volume, and the second to the page, so that [1999] 1 All ER 15 means that the report is to be found on page fifteen of the first volume of the All England Law Reports for 1999. Where no volume number is given, only one volume was produced in that year. Some series have continuous volume numbers.

Where legal decisions are very recent and in the lower courts, it must be remembered that they may be reversed on appeal.

In English cases, Scottish and Northern Irish decisions (unless there is a difference of law between the countries) are generally followed but are not binding, and Republic of Ireland Decisions are considered (and vice versa).

1

Introduction — Charge to Tax, Rates and Profits

Simon's Taxes. See **D1.1, D1.12, D1.1308.**

The charge to corporation tax

[1.1] Corporation tax is charged on any company which is resident in the UK in respect of all its 'profits' *wherever arising, worldwide.* A non-resident company is charged to corporation tax only if:

(1) (for disposals of land on or after 5 July 2016) it carries on a trade of dealing in or developing UK land (see **71.2** TRANSACTIONS IN UK LAND);

(2) it carries on a trade (other than a trade within (1) above) in the UK through a permanent establishment (see **64.6** RESIDENCE);

(3) (for disposals on or after 6 April 2019) it disposes of any interests in UK land (see **11.25** CAPITAL GAINS) or assets deriving at least 75% of their value from UK land where the company has a substantial indirect interest in that land (see **11.26**);

(4) with effect from 6 April 2020 (subject to the transitional provisions at **64.7** RESIDENCE) it carries on a UK property business; or

(5) with effect from 6 April 2020 (subject to the transitional provisions at **64.7** RESIDENCE) it has other UK property income.

Where (1) above applies, the company is chargeable to corporation tax on all its profits from the trade wherever arising. Where (2) above applies, the company is liable to corporation tax on the income and gains of the permanent establishment. Where (3) above applies, the company is chargeable to corporation tax on gains from such disposals.

Where (4) above applies, the company is chargeable to corporation tax on all its profits from the business and from loan relationships or derivative contracts that the company is a party to for the purposes of the business. Where (5) above applies, the company is chargeable to corporation tax on all its profits that consist of that income and any profits arising from loan relationships or derivative contracts to which the company is a party for the purposes of enabling it to generate the income. Other UK property income is rent receivable in connection with a *CTA 2009, s 39* concern (mines, quarries etc. — see **60.18** PROPERTY INCOME), rent receivable for electricline wayleaves (see **60.18**) and post-cessation receipts from a UK property business (see **60.4**).

[*CTA 2009, ss 2(1), 5; TCGA 1992, ss 2B, 10B; FA 2019, Sch 1 paras 2, 110, 120, Sch 5 paras 2–5, 35*].

See **21** CONTROLLED FOREIGN COMPANIES for treatment of interests in certain non-resident companies.

Members of a group of companies are each dealt with independently, but there are a number of special provisions relating to the taxation of such members. Similar rules apply to the members of a consortium. See **35** GROUP RELIEF.

'*Company*' for corporation tax purposes means 'any body corporate or unincorporated association' (including an authorised unit trust as defined in *CTA 2010, s 617*). It does not include a partnership, a local authority or a local authority association. [*CTA 2010, s 1121*]. See *Conservative and Unionist Central Office v Burrell* CA 1981, 55 TC 671 (in which the Conservative Party was held not to be an unincorporated association) and *Blackpool Marton Rotary Club v Martin* Ch D 1988, 62 TC 686 (Rotary Club was held to be an unincorporated association and not a partnership). For the treatment of income arising to certain unit trusts for the benefit of individuals, see **46.8** INVESTMENT FUNDS.

For the meaning of '*profits*' see **1.7** below.

Corporation tax is charged on the profits of 'financial years', which run from 1 April, e.g. the 'financial year 2020' or 'FY 20' means the year from 1 April 2020 to 31 March 2021. [*CTA 2009, s 8(1); FA 2017, s 5; FA 2018, s 2; FA 2019, s 2*].

The profits of a company are calculated (and assessments are made) by reference to its ACCOUNTING PERIODS (**2**). The charge is on the full amount of profits arising in the accounting period. [*CTA 2009, s 8(2)(3)*].

Different rates of corporation tax apply to companies with ring fence profits; see **1.4** below.

A special regime applies to certain restitution interest payable to a company. The interest is charged to corporation tax at a special rate of 45% instead of the main rate. See **1.6** below.

Anything to be done by a company under the Taxes Acts must be done by the 'proper officer of the company' (usually the company secretary, except where a liquidator or an administrator has been appointed) or by any person having express, implied or apparent authority to act on its behalf (again, unless a liquidator or administrator has been appointed). [*TMA 1970, s 108(1)(3)*]. See also **58.17** PAYMENT OF TAX.

Simon's Taxes. See **D1.101**, **D1.102** and **D1.108**.

Rates of corporation tax

[1.2] The rate of corporation tax for each financial year is enacted by Parliament and set out in the following table.

	Rate
Financial year 2021	19%
Financial year 2020	19%
Financial year 2019	19%
Financial year 2018	19%
Financial year 2017	19%

Special rates apply to 'ring fence profits'. See **1.4** below.

A special rate of 45% applies to certain restitution interest. See **1.6** below.

The main rate will be 19% for financial year 2022. See **1.3** below for the rates for financial year 2023 onwards.

[*CTA 2010, s 3; FA 2020, ss 5, 6; FA 2021, s 6*].

Rates of corporation tax for financial year 2023 onwards

[1.3] For financial year 2023 onwards, there are two rates of corporation tax which may apply to UK companies, depending on the amount of their profits. Special rates continue to apply to 'ring fence profits'; see **1.4** below.

For financial year 2023, the main rate of corporation tax is **25%** and the standard small profits rate is **19%**. See the table below.

Accounting periods which straddle 1 April 2023 are treated for these purposes as if the different parts of the period falling in different financial years were separate accounting periods and any necessary apportionments must be made. Where an accounting period falls partly in any later financial year, the provisions at **2.3** ACCOUNTING PERIODS apply to apportion profits between financial years.

The standard small profits rate applies to the taxable total profits (see **1.7** below) of a UK resident company for an accounting period if its 'augmented profits' do not exceed a 'lower limit'. Marginal relief (see further below) applies where the augmented profits fall between the lower limit and an 'upper limit'. The standard small profits rate does not apply to close investment-holding companies (see further below).

For an accounting period of 12 months, the '*lower limit*' is normally £50,000 and the '*upper limit*' £250,000. The lower and upper limits for an accounting period are reduced if:

(i) the company has one or more 'associated companies'; or
(ii) the accounting period is less than 12 months.

Where (ii) above applies, the lower and upper limits are reduced (after any reduction under (i) above) proportionately (on a time basis). Where (i) above applies, the limits are in effect shared with the associated companies. This is achieved by dividing the amount of each limit by 1+N, where N is the number of associated companies. Therefore, if a company has two associated companies for a 12-month accounting period, its lower and upper limits are divided by three, becoming £16,667 and £83,333 respectively.

Standard rates of CT	Financial year
	2023
Main rate	25%
Standard small profits rate	19%
Lower limit	£50,000
Upper limit	£250,000
Standard marginal relief fraction	3/200

Augmented profits

'*Augmented profits*' comprise the company's taxable total profits and any 'exempt qualifying distribution' income that is not:

- from a '51% subsidiary' or from a fellow 51% subsidiary of a parent company; or
- from a 'trading company' or 'holding company' owned by a consortium of which the recipient company is a member and which is not itself a '75% subsidiary' of any other company or capable of becoming so by virtue of any existing arrangements.

'*Exempt qualifying distributions*' are distributions within **29.2**(a), (b), (f) or (g) DISTRIBUTIONS which are exempt from corporation tax.

A '*51% (75%) subsidiary*' is a body corporate more than 50% (at least 75%) of the 'ordinary share capital' of which is beneficially owned directly or indirectly by another body corporate. However, in determining whether one company is a 51% subsidiary of another for the purposes of excluding exempt qualifying distribution income:

- a company is not treated as the owner of any share capital which it owns indirectly if that share capital is owned directly by a company (C) and a profit on the sale of the share capital by C would be a trading receipt; and
- a company is not treated as a 51% subsidiary unless the parent company would be beneficially entitled to more than 50% of any profits available for distribution to equity holders and of any assets available for distribution to equity holders on a winding up.

'Ordinary share capital' means all the issued share capital of the company except non-participating shares carrying a fixed-rate dividend, though 'issued share capital' does not include founder members' deposits in a company limited by guarantee (*South Shore Mutual Insurance Co Ltd v Blair* [1999] STC (SCD) 296).

A 'trading company' is a company the business of which consists wholly or mainly of the carrying on of a trade or trades. A 'holding company' is a company the business of which consists wholly or mainly in holding shares or securities of trading companies which are its '90% subsidiaries' (ie in which it holds directly not less than 90% of the ordinary share capital). A company is owned by a consortium if at least 75% of its ordinary share capital is beneficially owned by two or more companies ('members of the consortium'), each owning at least 5% and beneficially entitled to at least 5% of any profits available for distribution to equity holders and of any assets so available on a winding-up.

Associated companies

A company is an 'associated company' of another at any time if one of the two has 'control' of the other or both are under the control of the same person or persons. An associated company is treated as associated even if it was associated only for part of the accounting period. This applies to each of two or more associated companies even if they were associated for different parts of the accounting period.

However, an associated company which has not carried on any trade or business at any time in the accounting period (or the part when it was associated) is disregarded. A non-trading 'passive company' which has one or more 51% subsidiaries and which carries on a business of making investments is treated for this purpose as not carrying on a business (and so disregarded in the count of associated companies).

A company is a '*passive company*' if it has no assets other than shares in 51% subsidiaries, has no income other than dividends which are exempt qualifying distributions, has no chargeable gains, incurs no management expenses and makes no qualifying charitable donations. If the company receives dividends in an accounting period it must itself pay dividends in that period of an amount at least equal to the dividends received. Exempt qualifying distributions, assets representing them and rights to receive them are not treated as assets of the company.

'Control' is as defined in *CTA 2010, ss 450, 451*, see **16.6** CLOSE COMPANIES. That definition, however, is modified as follows:

(a) In determining whether two companies which do not have substantial commercial interdependence are associated, no attribution of the rights and powers of associates within **16.2**(i)–(iv) CLOSE COMPANIES is made. The Treasury has the power to make regulations prescribing the factors to be taken into account in determining whether two companies have substantial commercial interdependence.

(b) Fixed-rate preference shares (as defined) held by a company are ignored in determining if one company is under the control of another if the company holding the shares is not a close company, takes no part in the management or conduct of the issuing company or of its business, and subscribed for the shares in the ordinary course of a business which includes the provision of finance.

(c) A company is not under the control of another company if the only connection (past or present) between the two is that one company is a loan creditor (within *CTA 2010, s 453*) of the other and either the creditor company is not a close company or the creditor relationship arose in the ordinary course of the creditor company's business.
Likewise, where two companies are controlled by the same person which is a loan creditor of each company, that person's rights as loan creditor are ignored in determining whether the two companies are associated. There must be no other connection (past or present) between the two companies, and the loan creditor must either not be a close company or the creditor relationship with each company must arise in the ordinary course of the creditor's business.

(d) Where two companies are controlled by the same person by virtue of rights or powers held in trust by that person, those rights or powers are ignored in determining whether the two companies are associated, where there is no other connection (past or present) between the two companies.

In (c) and (d) above, the circumstances in which two companies have a connection include where there are any dealings between them.

Marginal relief

Where a company's augmented profits for an accounting period exceed the lower limit but do not exceed the upper limit then, if its augmented profits do not include any ring fence profits, the corporation tax charged (at the main rate) on its taxable total profits is reduced by an amount equal to:

$$F \times (U - A) \times \frac{N}{A}$$

where:

F is the standard marginal relief fraction (ie 3/200 for financial year 2023);
U is the upper limit;
N is the amount of the taxable total profits;
A is the amount of the augmented profits.

See **1.4** below for the calculation of marginal relief where a company's augmented profits include ring fence profits.

Information powers

HMRC have powers to obtain information from shareholders and companies issuing bearer securities in order to identify the beneficial owners of shares etc for the purposes of the associated companies provisions.

Close investment-holding companies

As indicated above, the standard small profits rate does not apply to 'close investment-holding companies'. A close company (C) is a '*close investment-holding company*' in an accounting period unless throughout the period it exists wholly or mainly for one of more of the following purposes:

(1) carrying on trade(s) on a commercial basis;
(2) making investments in land, or estates or interests in land, let, or intended to be let, other than to CONNECTED PERSONS (**19**) of the company or to certain individuals related to such connected persons;
(3) holding shares in and securities of, or making loans to, one or more companies each of which is either:
- a 'qualifying company', or
- a company under the control (within *CTA 2010, s 450*) of C or under the same control as C, which itself exists for the purpose of holding shares in or securities of, or making loans to, one or more qualifying companies;

(4) co-ordinating the administration of two or more qualifying companies;
(5) the making of investments within (2) above by one or more qualifying companies or by a company which controls C;
(6) a trade or trades carried on a commercial basis by one or more qualifying companies or by a company which controls C.

A '*qualifying company*' is a company which is under the control of C or of a company which has control of C and which exists wholly or mainly for either or both of the purposes in (1) and (2) above.

A company is not treated as a close investment-holding company in the accounting period beginning at the commencement of its winding-up if it was not such a company in the immediately preceding accounting period.

[*CTA 2010, ss 3, 18A–18N, 1154; FA 2021, ss 6, 7, Sch 1 paras 2, 3, 34*].

Rates of corporation tax on ring fence profits

[1.4] Corporation tax is charged at two rates on ring fence profits (i.e profits from oil extraction and oil rights in the UK and the UK Continental Shelf). The 'main ring fence profits rate' is fixed at 30% and the small ring fence profits rate is 19%. The small ring fence profits rate applies to the ring fence profits of a company if it is a UK resident company with 'augmented profits' below a 'lower limit' (currently £300,000). Marginal relief applies where ring fence profits fall between the lower limit and an 'upper limit' (currently £1,500,000): see further below. For financial year 2023 onwards, the small ring fence profits rate does not apply if the company is a close investment-holding company (see **1.3** above).

For financial year 2023 onwards, the lower and upper limits are reduced to £50,000 and £250,000, respectively.

Ring fence rates of CT	Financial year	
	2022 and earlier	2023
Main ring fence rate	30%	30%
Small ring fence profits rate	19%	19%
Lower limit	£300,000	£50,000
Upper limit	£1,500,000	£250,000
Standard marginal relief fraction	11/400	11/400

For financial year 2023 onwards, 'augmented profits' are defined as at **1.3** above. For earlier years, '*augmented profits*' comprise the company's 'adjusted taxable total profits' and any 'exempt ABGH distribution' income that is not:

- from a '51% subsidiary' or from a fellow 51% subsidiary of a parent company; or
- from a 'trading or holding company' owned by a 'consortium' of which the recipient company is a member and which is not itself a '75% subsidiary' of any other company or capable of becoming so by virtue of any existing arrangements

A '*51% (75%) subsidiary*' is a body corporate more than 50% (at least 75%) of the 'ordinary share capital' of which is beneficially owned directly or indirectly by another body corporate. However, in determining whether one company is a 51% subsidiary of another for the purposes of excluding exempt ABGH distribution income:

- that other is not treated as the owner of any share capital which it owns indirectly and which is owned directly by a company that holds it as trading stock; and
- a company is not treated as a 51% subsidiary unless the parent company would be beneficially entitled to more than 50% of any profits available for distribution to equity holders and of any assets available for distribution to equity holders on a winding up.

'Ordinary share capital' means all the issued share capital of the company except non-participating shares carrying a fixed-rate dividend, though 'issued share capital' does not include founder members' deposits in a company limited by guarantee (*South Shore Mutual Insurance Co Ltd v Blair* [1999] STC (SCD) 296).

A 'trading or holding company' means a trading company (ie a company the business of which consists wholly or mainly of the carrying on of a trade or trades) or a company the business of which consists wholly or mainly in holding shares or securities of trading companies which are its '90% subsidiaries' (ie in which it holds directly not less than 90% of the ordinary share capital). A company is owned by a 'consortium' if at least 75% of its ordinary share capital is beneficially owned amongst them by companies, each owning at least 5% and beneficially entitled to at least 5% of any profits available for distribution to equity holders and of any assets so available on a winding-up. Such companies are the 'members of the consortium'.

'*Exempt ABGH distributions*' are distributions within **29.2**(a), (b), (f) or (g) DISTRIBUTIONS which are exempt from corporation tax.

A company's '*adjusted taxable profits*' are its profits chargeable to corporation tax as if no part of its chargeable gains and allowable losses were chargeable to (or relievable for) capital gains tax before 6 April 2019 under *TCGA 1992, s 2B* (ATED-related gains — see **11.23** CAPITAL GAINS).

The lower and upper limits are reduced for companies which have related 51% group companies (see **58.3** PAYMENT OF TAX) and, on a time basis, where the accounting period is of less than 12 months. For financial year 2023 onwards, the reduction is for companies with associated companies (as at **1.3** above) rather than related 51% group companies. In many cases, this change will be no more than a change in terminology, but there are differences in the meaning of the two expressions.

Marginal relief

Where the ring-fence profits chargeable to corporation tax fall between the lower and upper limit, marginal relief is available. This provides a transition from the lower rate of 19% to the main rate of 30%. Where a company has ring fence and other profits, the marginal relief is applied only to the ring fence profits.

Where a company's augmented profits consist exclusively of ring fence profits, marginal relief operates by reducing the amount charged to corporation tax (at the main rate) by an amount calculated in accordance with the formula:

$$R \times \ (U - A) \times \frac{N}{A}$$

where:

R is the ring fence marginal relief fraction (ie 11/400);
U is the upper limit;
N is the amount of the taxable total profits (the profits chargeable to corporation tax);
A is the amount of the augmented profits.

Where the augmented profits include both ring fence profits and other profits, marginal relief operates by reducing the amount charged to corporation tax (at the main rates) on the company's taxable total profits by an amount calculated in accordance with the formula:

$$R \times \ (UR - AR) \times \frac{NR}{AR}$$

where:

R is the ring fence marginal relief fraction (ie 11/400);
UR is the upper limit multiplied by AR/A;
AR is the amount of ring fence profits that form part of the augmented profits;
NR is the amount of ring fence profits that form part of the taxable total profits (the profits chargeable to corporation tax);
A is the amount of the augmented profits.

For financial year 2023 onwards, the amount charged to corporation tax is also reduced by an amount calculated in accordance with the formula:

$$F \times \ (UZ - AZ) \times \frac{NZ}{AZ}$$

where:

F is the standard marginal relief fraction (ie 3/200 for financial year 2023);
UZ is the upper limit multiplied by AZ/A;
AZ is the amount of profits other than ring fence profits that form part of the augmented profits;
NZ is the amount of profits other than ring fence profits that form part of the taxable total profits (the profits chargeable to corporation tax);
A is the amount of the augmented profits.

In applying the changes above for financial year 2023 onwards, accounting periods which straddle 1 April 2023 are treated as if the different parts of the period falling in different financial years were separate accounting periods and any necessary apportionments must be made. Where an accounting period falls partly in any later financial year, the provisions at 2.3 ACCOUNTING PERIODS apply to apportion profits between financial years.

[*CTA 2010, ss 279A–279EA, 279F–279H, 1154; FA 2021, Sch 1 paras 4–11, 34*].

Tax powers in Northern Ireland

[1.5] The *Corporation Tax (Northern Ireland) Act 2015* (*CTNIA 2015*) devolves the power to set the rate of corporation tax in Northern Ireland to the Stormont Assembly in relation to such financial year as HM Treasury may appoint and subsequent financial years. The Act sets out a mechanism for setting the rate which will be charged on the profits of certain trades and activities of Northern Ireland companies by inserting a new *Part 8B* into *CTA 2010*. The new provisions will come into force on a day to be appointed by order. The government has indicated it will not implement the provisions until the Northern Ireland Executive's finances are on a 'sustainable footing'. [*CTNIA 2015, ss 1, 5*].

The devolved rate will apply to trading profits only and primarily to certain micro, small or medium-sized enterprises. It will also apply to large companies and corporate partners to the extent that profits are attributable to a Northern Ireland trading presence. Non-trading profits, such as income from property, are excluded and remain chargeable at the main rate of corporation tax.

The rate for a financial year may be set by the Northern Ireland Assembly at any level, higher, lower or the same as the UK main rate. If a rate is not set by resolution for a financial year, the rate for that year will be the rate set for the previous financial year. Until the Northern Ireland Assembly exercises the power to set a rate for the first time, the Northern Ireland rate will be the UK main rate. Any reduction in the corporation tax take must, under EU State aid regulations, be offset by a reduction in the province's block grant from Westminster. The UK parliament will retain power over the corporation tax base, including reliefs and allowances.

The '*Northern Ireland profits*' that will be chargeable at the Northern Ireland rate instead of the UK rate are broadly:

(i) all of the trading profits of a company (an '*SME (NI employer) company*') that is a micro, small or medium-sized enterprise ('SME') if the company's workforce time and costs fall largely in Northern Ireland;
(ii) a corporate partner's share of the trade profits of a partnership (an '*NI Chapter 6 firm*'), if that company and partnership are both SMEs and the partnership's workforce time and costs fall largely in Northern Ireland;
(iii) the profits of a large company or an SME company which has made the necessary election (an '*NIRE company*') that are attributable to a 'Northern Ireland regional establishment'; and
(iv) a corporate partner's share of the profits of a partnership (an '*NI Chapter 7 firm*') that are attributable to a Northern Ireland regional establishment where either:

- the partnership is either a large partnership or an SME which has made the necessary election; or
- the partnership is an SME whose workforce time and costs fall largely in Northern Ireland and the corporate partner is not an SME.

A company may make the election mentioned in (iii) above for an accounting period if it is an SME which does not fall within (i) above but has a Northern Ireland regional establishment for the period. A partnership may make the election mentioned in (iv) above if it is an SME which does not fall within (ii) above but has a Northern Ireland regional establishment. A close company or a partnership may not make an election if it has its Northern Ireland regional establishment as a result of tax avoidance arrangements and certain additional workforce requirements are not met.

A company or partnership has a '*Northern Ireland regional establishment*' if it has a fixed place of business (as defined) in Northern Ireland through which it wholly or partly carries on its business or if a dependent agent acting on its behalf has and habitually exercises in Northern Ireland authority to do business on its behalf.

The rate applies only to profits of a '*qualifying trade*', i.e. a trade in relation to which the company is within the charge to corporation tax and which is not an 'excluded trade', or a '*qualifying partnership trade*', i.e. a trade carried on by a partnership which is not an excluded trade. '*Excluded trades*' are broadly oil industry ring-fence trades, certain lending activities and investment activities regulated under *FISMA 2000*, investment management, long-term insurance business and reinsurance. A company or partnership carrying on an excluded trade within the lending and investment, investment management or reinsurance categories can elect for the trade to be treated as a qualifying trade or qualifying partnership trade. By election, the Northern Ireland rate may apply to the proportion of the trade profits which relate to back-office activities (as defined).

If a company has both Northern Ireland losses and mainstream losses in a single period, relief is available separately for each. A Northern Ireland loss is to be relieved first, so far as possible, against Northern Ireland profits before relief is given against mainstream profits. Likewise, a mainstream loss is to be relieved first so far as possible against mainstream profits before being relieved against Northern Ireland profits. If a Northern Ireland loss is to be set against mainstream profits and at any time during the accounting period the Northern Ireland rate is lower than the main rate, that loss will be taken into account by reference to a formula in order to reflect the difference between the Northern Ireland rate and the main corporation tax rate. The loss carry forward, group and consortium relief rules are similarly modified.

Special rules will apply to attribute capital allowances according to whether an asset is used for activities of either the UK and/or NI rate regimes. A number of other rules will be amended to reflect the new circumstances. For example, if there is a lower rate of tax in Northern Ireland, then research and development tax credits, capital allowances and creative reliefs for the film, TV, computer game, theatre, orchestra and museum and gallery industries will be adjusted to ensure that they continue to be broadly equivalent in value to those in Great Britain.

[*CTA 2010, Pt 8B; CTNIA 2015, Sch 1; FA 2016, Sch 8 paras 13, 14, 18; F(No 2)A 2017, s 25, Sch 4 paras 93–105, Sch 6 paras 16, 17, Sch 7; FA 2018, s 29(5); FA 2021, Sch 4*].

Rate of corporation tax on restitution interest

[1.6] The following provisions apply to charge restitution interest received by a company to corporation tax at a special rate of 45%. The rate does not apply to charitable companies.

Where tax has been overpaid by a company as a result of a mistake in law or following unlawful collection of tax by HMRC a restitution award may be made. Where the award is made, as a result of a judgment or an agreement between the parties, the interest element of the award (i.e the element which represents compensation for the time value of money) is chargeable to corporation tax at a special rate of 45% instead of the main rate (currently 19%).

The rate does not apply to any element of the award that represents the repayment of the overpaid tax.

The tax on the restitution interest is deducted at source by HMRC provided the interest is: in relation to a company's claim for restitution for a payment of tax made under a mistake of law or for the unlawful collection of tax; and not limited to simple interest at a statutory rate. The amount deducted is treated as being paid by the company on account of its liability to the charge to corporation tax on the restitution interest.

If however, it subsequently transpires that the payment is or should not have been treated as restitution interest and the company is entitled to keep the gross payment, then HMRC must repay the amount withheld to the company. If the company is not entitled to keep the gross payment, then it must repay the net amount to HMRC. HMRC must give written notice to the company stating the amount of the gross payment and the amount of tax deducted. Any interest payments made under these provisions are excluded from the definition of a company's total profits, and are effectively ring-fenced in that they cannot be reduced by reliefs, allowances or set-offs available against the company's other chargeable profits, (past, present or future).

The rationale behind the special rate is to ensure that the rate of corporation tax applicable to payments of restitution interest made by HMRC reflects both the rates of corporation tax over the period to which typical awards relate.

Definition of restitution interest

Interest is defined as 'restitution interest' if it satisfies three conditions:

(A) the interest is paid/payable by HMRC in respect of a company's right (or possible right) to restitution for tax paid under a mistake of law or for tax collected unlawfully by HMRC (the circumstances of the payment are immaterial in that it can be paid/payable, for example, as an interim payment, pursuant to a judgement or agreement etc);

(B) the claim for interest has been finally determined in court or settled by agreement between HMRC and the company; and
(C) the interest determined in condition B is not limited to simple interest payable under a statutory provision for tax purposes. Note though that this condition does not prevent an award of interest calculated by reference to simple interest at a statutory rate from falling within the definition of restitution interest.

Interest that has been paid as simple interest at a statutory rate before the date of the final judgment or settlement (in condition B above) does not fall within the definition of restitution interest. Interest that is paid before the final judgement or settlement in B above will fall within the definition of restitution interest if condition A above applies and the interest is not limited to simple statutory interest.

The interest that is brought into account as restitution interest is the amount that is, in accordance with GAAP recorded (or ought to have been recorded) in the company's accounts. Where any necessary adjustments to the accounts are required as a result of this provision, any time limits are disregarded.

Anti-avoidance

There is a targeted anti-avoidance rule to counteract relevant avoidance arrangements where the main purpose or one of the main purposes of the arrangement is to obtain a tax advantage. Any tax advantage which arises from relevant avoidance arrangements is to be counteracted by the making of just and reasonable adjustments.

'*Relevant avoidance arrangements*' are defined broadly as arrangements with the main purpose being to obtain a tax advantage in relation to the charge on restitution interest. However, specifically excluded from this definition are commercial arrangements. The legislation goes on to list some examples which would not be considered to be commercial arrangements, such as delaying the recognition of the restitution interest or treating the receipt of the interest in a different way than it would have been in the absence of the arrangements.

If the right to the restitution interest is transferred by a company (other than a charitable company) which is within the scope of corporation tax to a person which is either not a company or is a non-UK resident or charitable company, and the purpose of the transfer was to secure a tax advantage for any person, any restitution interest which subsequently arises is deemed to be that of the transferor. If the transferor no longer exists or has been wound up when the restitution interest arises, HMRC may give a notice to a 'related company' deeming the interest to arise to that company. For this purpose a company is a 'related company' if it was a member of the same group as the transferor at any time in the period beginning 12 months before the winding up or dissolution and ending when the interest is paid or becomes payable (whichever is later). Two companies are members of the same group if one is a 51% subsidiary of the other or both are 51% subsidiaries of another company.

If a UK resident company had accrued rights to the entitlement to restitution interest at the time it changed its residence to become non-UK resident and the main purpose for the change in residence was to secure a tax advantage for any person, then the company is to be treated as a UK resident company in relation to the amount of restitution interest which is attributable to the accrued rights. Further, the company is treated as if it had not made a deemed disposed of the right to receive restitution interest under *TCGA 1992, ss 185, 187* (see **64.9** RESIDENCE).

Administration

Where restitution interest is chargeable to tax under these rules, and an assessment is raised by HMRC (with the amount of tax withheld credited against the liability), the company must pay the amount assessed within 30 days of the date of the assessment. If the amount withheld exceeds the tax liability, statutory interest is payable on the excess from the date on which the tax was withheld until the date of repayment.

Interest that is charged to tax under these rules is not chargeable to corporation tax under any other provision (the restitution charge has priority over any other corporation tax provisions). In addition the corporation tax on restitution payments is disregarded for the purposes of the instalment payments regime.

There is a right of appeal against the deduction by HMRC of the tax withheld from the restitution interest. Where a final court judgment in favour of a company is reversed on a late appeal, with the effect that HMRC are no longer required to make any payment, HMRC are not required to repay any tax it may have deducted from any payment when first made, and the tax deducted does not rank as a payment of corporation tax by the claimant.

The Treasury has the power to amend the above provisions by statutory instrument. But such regulations may not widen the scope of the charge, remove or prejudice any right of appeal, or increase the rate of tax. Nor can the provisions apply to any claim that has been fully determined prior to 21 October 2015.

[*CTA 2010, ss 357YA–357YW; SI 2017 No 364*].

Profits

[1.7] For corporation tax purposes, 'profits' are defined as income and chargeable gains, other than, for disposals before 6 April 2019, gains chargeable to capital gains tax under *TCGA 1992, s 2B* (ATED-related gains — see **11.23** CAPITAL GAINS) or under *TCGA 1992, ss 14D, 188D* (gains on the disposal of UK residential property interests by non-residents — see **11.24** CAPITAL GAINS). [*CTA 2009, s 2(2)(2A); FA 2015, Sch 7 para 58; FA 2019, Sch 1 paras 109, 120*].

Profits include:

- profits arising in the winding-up of a company [*CTA 2009, s 6(2)*] (see **76** WINDING UP); and
- profits accruing to the company's benefit under any trust, or arising from a PARTNERSHIP (**56**), which would be chargeable if they accrued to the company directly [*CTA 2009, s 7*].

Profits do not include those accruing to the company in a fiduciary or representative capacity and in which it has no beneficial interest. [*CTA 2009, s 6(1)*].

For treatment of profits arising from underwriting business of a corporate member of Lloyd's, see *FA 1994, ss 219–230, Sch 21* (as amended).

The profits of an accounting period on which corporation tax is chargeable (the '*taxable total profits*') are found by adding together the amount chargeable under the charge to corporation tax on income (after any reductions required for reliefs) and the amount to be included in respect of chargeable gains (after reductions) to give the '*total profits*' of the period and then deducting any amounts which can be relieved against the total profits. [*CTA 2010, s 4*].

Profits within the charge to corporation tax on income are computed *separately for each source*. The main sources of income are:

Source	See
Trading income	68 TRADING INCOME, 69 TRADING INCOME — DEDUCTIONS
Property income	61 PROPERTY INCOME
Non-trading loan relationships income (including non-trading income from derivative contracts)	27 DERIVATIVE CONTRACTS, 50 LOAN RELATIONSHIPS
Non-trading intangible assets income	42 INTANGIBLE ASSETS
Distributions (if not exempt)	29 DISTRIBUTIONS
Miscellaneous income	53 MISCELLANEOUS INCOME

For computation of chargeable gains see **11** CAPITAL GAINS, **12** CAPITAL GAINS — GROUPS and **13** CAPITAL GAINS — SUBSTANTIAL SHAREHOLDINGS.

Simon's Taxes. See **D1.302.**

Example

[1.8]

A Ltd, incorporated on 1 June 2016, commences business on 1 January 2021. The accounts for the year ended 31 December 2021 show the following.

	£		£
Wages and salaries	178,400	Gross trading profit	2,274,760
Directors' remuneration	82,200	Income from property	8,000
Rent, rates and insurance	49,200	Government securities	340
Motor expenses	38,000	UK company dividends	1,500
Bad debts	8,200	Profit on sale of shares	64,000
Research and development	36,000		
General expenses	94,000		
Legal and professional costs	16,000		
Overdraft interest	6,000		
Debenture finance charges	3,500		
Audit and accountancy	16,000		
Depreciation of fixed assets	82,000		
Loss on sale of fixed assets	6,000		
Net profit	1,733,100		

	£	£
	£2,348,600	£2,348,600

The following further information is available.

(a)	Capital allowances for the year are:		£
	Plant and machinery (including advertising sign)		48,000
	Research and development		24,000

(b)	Bad debts consist of:		£
	Trade debts written off		6,100
	Reserve created	— general impairment	1,800
		— specific impairment	300
			£8,200

(c)	General expenses include:		£
	Advertising — erection of permanent sign (see (a) above)		1,050
	Defalcations by junior staff		1,280
	Entertaining	— small promotional gifts	1,400
		— customers	4,100
		— staff Christmas party	450
	Gifts, donations	— wines, etc. on exhibition stand	800
		— trade protection society	250
		— Oxfam (within *CTA 2010, s 190*)	500
		— political party	500
	Inducement to planning official		750
	Interest on unpaid tax		500
	New premises — rehabilitation costs		3,000
	Share sale — commission and fees		1,500
	VAT — penalty for late return		400

(d) The company qualifies as a small and medium-sized enterprise for the purpose of research and development expenditure. The £36,000 is qualifying expenditure (see 63 RESEARCH AND DEVELOPMENT EXPENDITURE) of which £24,000 relates to the cost of a dedicated research employee and £8,000 to consumable items (which do not form part of an item produced in the course of the research and development).

(e)	Legal and professional costs consist of:	
	Company secretarial services	6,150
	Debenture issue (see (f) below)	1,800
	Debt collection	2,100
	Industrial tribunal representation	750
	Lease variation	1,000
	Patent infringement claim work	3,400
	Preparation of staff service agreements	800
		£16,000

(f) Debenture finance charges relate to £50,000 nominal stock issued on 1 January 2021 for trade finance at £96 per £100, carrying interest at 6.6% payable annually in arrears, for redemption 31 December 2030. The charge to profit and loss comprises interest of £3,300 and redemption reserve costs of £200. As these are arrived at under an amortised cost basis of accounting, the charges are allowable for tax purposes. The issue costs included in legal and professional costs (see (e) above) are directly incurred in bringing the debentures into existence and are also allowable.
The overdraft interest charge is similarly on an amortised cost basis and allowable.
The £340 Government securities credit relates to £9,000 4% Treasury Stock acquired in March 2017 at £9,080 with four years to redemption. It represents gross interest £360 less £20 premium amortisation charge. It is thus properly chargeable as income from non-trading loan relationships. The interest was received on 7 March and 7 September.

(g) Chargeable gain on share sale 30 September 2021, £51,100.

(h) Twenty-six-year lease on new premises, at annual rent £22,500, purchased on 1 January 2017 at a premium of £200,000.
Rates, etc. incurred before 1 January 2021, £20,000.

The computation for *year ended 31 December 2021* is as follows.

		£	£
Net profit			1,733,100
Add: Bad debts — general impairment reserve (see **69.5** TRADING INCOME — DEDUCTIONS)		1,800	
Advertising — sign erection (note 1)		1,050	
Entertaining customers (see **69.40**)		4,100	
Gifts, donations (see **69.46**)	— wines, etc.	800	
	— Oxfam	500	
	— political party	500	
Inducement (note 2)		750	
INTEREST ON OVERDUE TAX (see **43.2**)		500	
Share sale commission and fees (note 3)		1,500	
VAT penalty (see **69.55**)		400	
Lease variation expenses		1,000	
Depreciation		82,000	
Loss on sale of fixed assets		6,000	100,900
			1,834,000
Less: PROPERTY INCOME (see **60**)		8,000	
Government securities		340	
Dividends received		1,500	
Profit on share sale		64,000	73,840
			1,760,160
Less: Plant and machinery allowances (see **10** CAPITAL ALLOWANCES ON PLANT AND MACHINERY)		48,000	
Research and development allowances (see **9** CAPITAL ALLOWANCES)		24,000	
Research and development relief		46,800	
Lease premium allowance (note 4) $200,000\ (1 - {}^{25}/_{50}) \div 26$		3,846	
Pre-trading expenditure (rent and rates) (note 5)		110,000	232,646

	£	£
		£1,527,514
Trading income		1,527,514
Income from property	8,000	
		8,000
Chargeable gain		51,100
Total profits		1,586,614
Less: Non-trading loan relationship deficit (interest on unpaid tax £500 *less* interest on securities £340)		160
		1,586,454
		1,586,454
Less: Charitable donation		500
Taxable Total Profits (TTP)		£1,585,954
Tax chargeable:		
FY 2020 @ 19% on ¼ × 1,585,954		75,332.81
FY 2021 @ 19% on ¾ × 1,585,954		225,998.44
		£301,331.25

Notes

(1) The costs of erecting the advertising sign is capital and has been included in calculating the capital allowances.

(2) The inducement payment is a bribe and as such illegal see **69.49**.

(3) The share sale commission and fees have been included in calculating the capital gain at (g).

(4) The proportion of the lease premium allowable is calculated under *CTA 2009, ss 217–220* see **69.59**.

(5) Pre-trading expenditure in the seven years before a company starts to carry on a trade is allowable, subject to conditions, under *CTA 2009, s 61* see **69.57**.

2

Accounting Periods

Simon's Taxes. See D1.108, D1.309.

Introduction to accounting periods

[2.1] Corporation tax is charged on the full amount of profits arising in an accounting period. There are specific rules which determine when an accounting period starts and when it is treated as coming to an end.

An accounting period often, but not always, coincides with a company's period of account, i.e. the period for which a company makes up its accounts. The end of the period of account is the company's accounting date.

A self-assessment return for the company is prepared for each accounting period.

[*CTA 2009, s 8(2), (3)*].

The start of an accounting period

[2.2] An accounting period of a company begins:

- when the company comes within the charge to corporation tax; or
- immediately after the end of the previous accounting period, if the company is still within the charge to corporation tax;
- when the company goes into administration;
- in the case of a company being wound up, when the winding up starts.

[*CTA 2009, ss 9(1), 12(3)*].

A UK resident company, if not otherwise within the charge to corporation tax, is treated as coming within the charge when it starts to carry on business.

[*CTA 2009, s 9(2)*].

If a company accrues a chargeable gain or allowable loss which is not otherwise in an accounting period, an accounting period then begins when the gain or loss accrues and it falls into that period.

[*CTA 2009, s 9(3)*].

As regards whether a company is 'within the charge to corporation tax' in the absence of income or gain, see *Walker (Inspector of Taxes) v Centaur Clothes Group Ltd* [2000] 2 All ER 589, [2000] 1 WLR 799, HL, where the court held that the legislation dealt with potential income producing sources, and not just actual ones.

These rules are subject to any provision in the Corporation Tax Acts which provide for accounting periods to begin at a different time.

[*CTA 2009, ss 9(5), 12(6)*].

Apportionment

[2.3] Although assessments to corporation tax are made on the basis of accounting periods, the tax rate is fixed by reference to financial years (which run from 1 April to 31 March in any year — see **1.1** INTRODUCTION). The financial year will therefore not always coincide with the accounting period. Where these periods do not coincide, apportionment is necessary to calculate the tax payable.

Apportionment is on a time basis, between the financial years which overlap the accounting period. Corporation tax is then charged on each proportion so computed at the rate fixed for the financial year concerned. [*CTA 2009, s 8(5)*].

Example

[2.4]

For the year ended 30 June 2017, the following information is relevant to A Ltd, a company with no associated companies.

	£
Trading income	2,600,000
Property income	250,000
Income from non-trading loan relationships	300,000

The rate of corporation tax for the financial year 2016 is 20% and the rate for the financial year 2017 is 19%.

The corporation tax computation of A Ltd for the 12-month accounting period ended on 30 June 2017 is as follows:

		£	
Trading income		2,600,000	
Property income		250,000	
Income from non-trading loan relationships		300,000	
		3,150,000	
Total profits apportioned			
1.7.16 – 31.3.17	9/12 ×	£3,150,000	£2,362,500
1.4.17 – 30.6.17	3/12 ×	£3,150,000	£787,500

Tax chargeable	
20% × £2,362,500	472,500
19% × £787,500	149,625
Total tax chargeable	£622,125

The end of an accounting period

[2.5] An accounting period of a company ends on the first occurrence of any of the following:

(a) the expiration of twelve months from the beginning of the accounting period;
(b) an accounting date of the company;
(c) if there is a period for which the company does not make up accounts, the end of that period;
(d) the company's beginning or ceasing to trade;
(e) if the company carries on a single trade, its coming, or ceasing to be, within the charge to corporation tax in respect of that trade;
(f) if the company carries on more than one trade, its coming, or ceasing to be, within the charge to corporation tax in respect of all the trades;
(g) the company's becoming, or ceasing to be, UK resident;
(h) the company's ceasing to be within the charge to corporation tax;
(i) the company's entering administration (in which case the accounting period is treated as ending immediately before the day on which the company enters into administration); or
(j) the company's ceasing to be in administration under *Insolvency Act 1986, Sch B1* (or any corresponding event otherwise than under that Act).

[*CTA 2009, s 10*].

In addition an accounting period of a company ends immediately before a winding up starts and a new one begins when the winding up starts. Once the winding up has started then an accounting period ends after 12 months, or if earlier, when the winding up has been completed. [*CTA 2009, s 12*].

Where more than one trade is carried on with different accounting dates and the company does not prepare a set of accounts for the whole of its activities, the company may choose which of those accounting dates is to be used for the purpose of (b) above. HMRC may, however, select another of those dates if they think, on reasonable grounds, that the date selected by the company is inappropriate. [*CTA 2009, s 11*].

Uncertainty

[2.6] Where the beginning or end of an accounting period is uncertain, HMRC may choose such period (not exceeding twelve months) as appears appropriate. If further facts come to their knowledge, HMRC may revise that period, but the company has rights of appeal. See *R v Ward, R v Special Commr (ex* *p Stipplechoice Ltd) (No 3)* QB 1988, 61 TC 391, where determination of an appeal was quashed because the company did not receive notification that HMRC intended to seek confirmation of the assessment under appeal after revision of the terminal date.

[*ICTA 1988, s 12(8)*].

The validity of extended time limit assessments made by virtue of the predecessor to *s 12(8)*, and subsequently varied by HMRC, was challenged in *Kelsall v Stipplechoice Ltd* CA 1995, 67 TC 349. It was held that the question of whether there was doubt as to the beginning or end of an accounting period at the time the assessment was made (so that the dates could subsequently be revised) is to be determined subjectively by reference to the state of mind of the inspector at that time. This reversed the decision in the High Court, where it was also held that no further leave of the General or Special Commissioners was required for the revision of an extended time limit assessment made by virtue of that section where the original leave to assess was given on the footing that it would be open to the company to contend for a different accounting date on appeal. The Court of Appeal expressed no view on this aspect of the decision.

Accounts for periods in excess of twelve months

[2.7] Where accounts are made up for a period in excess of twelve months, apportionments of profits or gains to different periods are, except where otherwise provided, made on a time basis [*CTA 2010, s 1172*]. In the case of trading profits or miscellaneous profits it is specifically provided that apportionment is to be made on the basis of the number of days falling in each period.

[*CTA 2009, ss 52, 1307*].

Where, however, a more satisfactory basis of arriving at the profit of each accounting period is available, HMRC may apply that basis instead (*Marshall Hus & Partners Ltd v Bolton* Ch D 1980, 55 TC 539).

Income from an overseas property business (see **60** PROPERTY INCOME) is computed as if it were a property business (so that trading income principles apply).

[*CTA 2009, ss 206, 210*].

Interest is taxable as recognised in an accounting period in accordance with generally accepted accounting practice, under the loan relationship rules. Thus any charge in respect of non-trading credits on loan relationships is calculated by reference to accounting periods (see **50.4**, **50.8** LOAN RELATIONSHIPS).

[*CTA 2009, ss 297, 301*].

Chargeable gains are apportioned on an arising basis.

[*TCGA 1992, s 2A; FA 2019, Sch 1 paras 2, 120*].

Qualifying charitable donations are included in the period in which they are paid.

[*CTA 2010, s 189*].

Example

[2.8]

B Ltd prepares accounts for 16 months ending on 30 April 2021. The following information is relevant:

	£
Profit for 16 months	800,000
Income (in respect of non-trading loan relationships) received on 1 March and 1 September each year	50,000
Capital gain (after indexation) arising on 1.6.20	100,000
Tax written down value of plant pool at 1.1.20	40,000
Plant purchased 1.5.20	160,000
Plant purchased 1.2.21	46,000
Proceeds of plant sold 31.12.20 (less than cost)	4,000

B Ltd is chargeable to corporation tax as follows.

	Accounting period 12 months to 31.12.20	Accounting period 4 months to 30.4.21
	£	£
Adjusted profits (apportioned 12:4)	600,000	200,000
Capital allowances (see note)	(167,200)	(47,728)
Trading income	432,800	152,272
Income from non-trading loan relationship	100,000	50,000
Chargeable gain	100,000	—
Chargeable profits	632,800	202,272

Note

Capital allowances are calculated as follows. It is assumed that B Ltd is entitled to the full amount of annual investment allowance.

12 months to 31.12.20

	AIA	Pool	Allowances
	£	£	£
WDV b/f		40,000	
Additions	160,000		
AIA	(160,000)		160,000
WDA at 18%		(7,200)	7,200
Total allowances			£167,200
WDV c/f		£32,800	

4 months to 30.4.21

	AIA	Pool	Allowances
	£	£	£
WDV b/f		32,800	
Additions	46,000		
AIA	(46,000)		46,000
Disposals		(4,000)	
		28,800	
WDA at 18% × 4/12		(1,728)	1,728
Total allowances			£47,728
WDV c/f		£27,072	

Accounts made up to varying dates

[2.9] Where accounts are made up to slightly varying dates (eg the last Saturday in a specified month), provided the variation is not more than four days from a mean date, HMRC will (if the taxpayer agrees in writing) normally accept treatment of each period of account as if it were a twelve-month accounting period ending on the mean date. (HMRC Company Taxation Manual, CTM01560.)

See HMRC Extra-Statutory Concession, C12 for concessionary yearly accounting periods where a retail co-operative society prepares half-yearly or quarterly accounts. The concession has been withdrawn with effect from 1 April 2018.

Key points on accounting periods

[2.10] Points to consider are as follows.

- An accounting period is usually the period for which a company makes up a set of accounts.
- An accounting period begins immediately after the end of the last accounting period or when the company comes within the charge to corporation tax. An accounting period also commences when a company enters liquidation or commences a winding up.
- An accounting period generally ends on the earliest of twelve months after the beginning of an accounting period or the company's accounting reference date. Accounting periods also come to an end when a company begins or ceases to trade; ceases to be within the charge to UK corporation tax; ceases to be UK resident or ceases to be in administration.
- An accounting period cannot exceed twelve months.
- If accounts are prepared for a period in excess of twelve months, profits and gains are required to be apportioned between the relevant accounting periods. Generally, profits (including trading income, property income and miscellaneous income) are required

to be apportioned on a time basis. However, in some cases, a different apportionment is prescribed. For example, chargeable gains are included in the accounting period in which the disposal takes place.

- For accounts covering a period of more than twelve months, it may be possible to apportion profits and gains on a just and reasonable basis if time apportionment would operate unjustly or unreasonably.

3

Alternative Finance Arrangements

Cross references. See **8** BUILDING SOCIETIES, **41.2** INCOME TAX IN RELATION TO A COMPANY, **46.6** INVESTMENT FUNDS, **50** LOAN RELATIONSHIPS, **65.11** RETURNS.

Simon's Taxes. See B5.6.

Introduction to alternative finance arrangements

[3.1] The provisions set out in this chapter provide for the taxation of finance arrangements that do not involve the receipt or payment of interest and respond to the development of financial products that embody such arrangements.

Customers who want access to the type of product referred to above include, in particular, individuals for whom it is important to adhere to Islamic law ('Shariah'). The Quran prohibits Muslims from the practice of 'riba' which is generally understood to mean the receipt or payment of interest. As a result, Muslims have devised other financing structures to facilitate commercial transactions such as:

- 'murabahah' (sale on deferred payment terms discussed in 3.3 below);
- 'diminishing musharaka' (co-ownership where one partner gradually buys out the other covered in 3.4 below);
- 'mudarabah' (providing finance to a venture in exchange for a share of the profits in 3.5 below);
- 'wakala' (an agent makes investments on behalf of a principal covered in 3.6 below).

The legislation described in 3.3–3.7 below sets out a definite tax treatment for certain specific types of contract used in Islamic finance, with economic returns equivalent to interest being treated in the same way as interest for all tax purposes.

It is a fundamental policy requirement that UK tax law apply equally to all taxpayers, irrespective of religion, and that the tax treatment of a transaction cannot depend on whether or not it is Shariah compliant. Accordingly, the legislation is applicable to all financing arrangements which fall within its definitions, regardless of whether undertaken by Muslims, non-Muslims, Islamic or conventional banks, and regardless of whether they are compliant with Shariah or not. For example it sets out a tax regime for a structure called an 'investment bond' (see **3.7** below) which corresponds to an Islamic finance structure called sukuk. However, to decide whether any particular transaction qualifies for the legislated tax treatment, one need consider only the tax law definition.

The legislation does not change the legal nature of the financial arrangements, nor does it deem interest to arise where there is none. Instead, it brings certain types of finance arrangements, and the returns from those arrangements, within the pre-existing tax regime for receipts and payments of interest.

The Treasury have wide powers to make provisions by statutory instrument. These include the power to designate arrangements further to those in **3.3–3.7** below as alternative finance arrangements and the introduction of new provisions relating to alternative finance arrangements. The provisions at **3.3–3.7** below are subject to the financial arrangements being entered into on an arm's length basis (see **3.9** below).

[*CTA 2009, ss 508–520; TIOPA 2010, s 366*].

Definition

[3.2] A '*financial institution*' for the purposes of alternative finance arrangements is:

- a bank (within *CTA 2010, s 1120*);
- a building society (within the meaning of the *Building Societies Act 1986*);
- a wholly-owned subsidiary of either of the above;
- a person authorised by a licence under the *Consumer Credit Act 1974, Pt 3* to carry on consumer credit business or consumer hire business within the meaning of that Act;
- a person authorised in a non-UK jurisdiction to receive deposits or other repayable funds from the public and to grant credits for its own account;
- an insurance company as defined by *FA 2012, s 65*;
- a person who is authorised in a jurisdiction outside the United Kingdom to carry on a business which consists of effecting or carrying out contracts of insurance or substantially similar business but not an insurance special purpose vehicle as defined in *FA 2012, s 139(1)*;
- a bond-issuer but only in relation to any bond assets which are rights under purchase and resale arrangements, diminishing shared ownership arrangements and profit share agency arrangements.

In this context, a company is a wholly-owned subsidiary of another where it has no members apart from the parent, its wholly-owned subsidiaries and a person acting on their behalf.

[*CTA 2009, s 502*].

Alternative finance return

Purchase and re-sale

[3.3] A finance arrangement can, as an alternative to payment of interest, be structured as a purchase of an asset and its onward sale at a higher deferred price. This is illustrated in the following diagram, where the customer obtains the equivalent of a 24 month loan with all interest being paid on the repayment of the loan.

Purchase and resale — murabahah

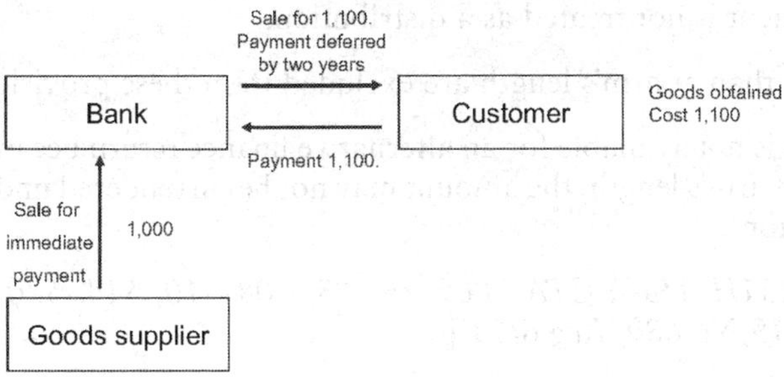

For these provisions to apply, arrangements must be entered into fulfilling the following conditions:

- the transaction must be between two persons;
- at least one of the persons must be a financial institution as defined — see 3.2 above;
- one person buys an asset and sells it to the other person, either immediately or in the case of a non-immediate sale where the seller is a financial institution which purchased the asset for the purposes of entering into purchase and resale arrangements;
- the consideration is deferred (or partly deferred);
- the consideration is greater than the purchase price; and
- the difference equates, in substance, to the return on an investment of money at interest.

Where the whole of the sale price is paid on one day, the alternative finance return is taken to be equal to the return included within the sale price. Where the sale price is to be paid by instalments, each instalment is taken to include alternative finance return equal to an amount of interest that would have been included in the instalment if:

(i) the effective return were interest payable on a loan equal to the first purchase price of the asset;
(ii) the total interest payable on the loan is equal to the amount by which the second purchase price exceeds the first purchase price;

(iii) the instalment were a part repayment of the principal with interest; and
(iv) the loan were made on arm's length terms and accounted for under generally accepted accounting practice.

In either case, the arrangements are treated for corporation tax purposes as a loan relationship to which the company is a party (see **50** LOAN RELATIONSHIPS). The amount of the purchase price is treated as if it were a loan made to the company from the other party (or by the company to the other party as the case may be) and the alternative finance return is treated as if it were interest payable under the loan relationship. The effective return is ignored in determining the consideration for the purchase or sale of the asset for corporation tax or capital gains purposes. However, this does not override any corporation tax or capital gains provisions which provide for the consideration to be other than the actual consideration.

Alternative finance return in the form of an additional payment or any part of a redemption payment is not treated as a distribution.

Transactions other than at arm's length are excluded from these provisions.

Where a deduction is not available for an alternative finance return because the transaction is not at arm's length, the amount may not be surrendered under the group relief provisions.

[*TCGA 1992, ss 151H–151Y; CTA 2009, ss 503, 508–510, 514, 520; CTA 2010, s 110; SI 2019 No 689, Reg 6(13)*].

Diminishing shared ownership

[3.4] This is often used as a Shariah compliant alternative to a mortgage. It requires arrangements under which both a financial institution (see 3.2) and another person (called the 'eventual owner') together acquire a beneficial interest in an asset. The eventual owner occupies the entire property, paying rent on the proportion not owned, and buys out the interest of the financial institution over time, either on a fixed schedule (corresponding to a repayment mortgage) or when desired (corresponding to an interest only mortgage.) It is illustrated below on the assumption that the eventual owner has 25% of the purchase price available.

Diminishing shared ownership — diminishing musharaka

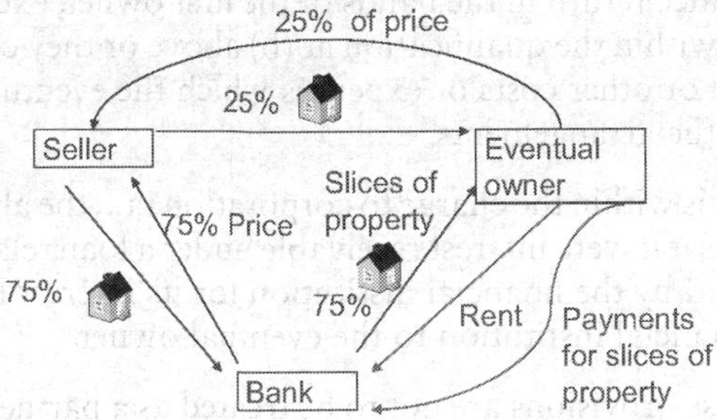

Eventual owner has sole occupancy and pays rent to Bank on proportion owned by Bank.

The requirements are that a financial institution (see **3.2** above) acquires a beneficial interest in an asset and another person ('the eventual owner'):

(a) also acquires a beneficial interest in the asset;
(b) is to make a series of payments to the financial institution amounting in total to the amount paid to acquire its beneficial interest;
(c) is to acquire (in stages or otherwise) the financial institution's beneficial interest as a result of those payments;
(d) is to make additional payments to the financial institution (whether under a lease or otherwise);
(e) has the exclusive right to occupy or otherwise use the asset; and
(f) is exclusively entitled to any income, profit or gain arising from or attributable to the asset, including, in particular, any increase in its value.

It is immaterial whether or not:

- the financial institution acquires its beneficial interest from the eventual owner (for example, in a case where there is an initial conveyance of real property to the eventual owner followed by a sub-sale from the eventual owner to the financial institution);
- whether the eventual owner (or another person other than the financial institution) also has a beneficial interest in the asset; or
- whether or not the financial institution has a legal interest in the asset.

The condition in (e) above does not preclude the eventual owner granting an interest or right in the asset to someone else, e.g. he may sub-let the asset. However, the person to whom the interest or right is granted cannot be the financial institution, a person controlled by the financial institution or a person controlled by a person who also controls the financial institution, and the grant must not be required by the financial institution or by arrangements to which the financial institution is a party.

The condition in (f) above does not prohibit arrangements under which the financial institution may bear any loss (or a share of any loss) resulting from a decrease in the asset's value.

The consideration paid by the first owner is treated as if it were the amount of a loan. Payments made by the eventual owner under these arrangements are treated as alternative finance return in the hands of the first owner, except in so far as they are payments within the qualification at (b) above or they constitute arrangement fees or legal or other costs or expenses which the eventual owner is required to pay under the arrangements.

If the financial institution is within the charge to corporation tax, the alternative finance return is treated as if it were interest receivable under a loan relationship and the consideration paid by the financial institution for its interest is treated as a loan made by the financial institution to the eventual owner.

Arrangements within these provisions are not to be treated as a partnership for tax purposes.

If these arrangements involve the sale of an asset by one party to the arrangements to another, the alternative finance return is excluded in determining the consideration for corporation tax or capital gains purposes (this not overriding any tax or capital gains provisions which provide for the consideration to be other than the actual consideration).

Where a deduction is not available for an alternative finance return because the transaction is not at arm's length, the amount may not be surrendered under the group relief provisions.

[*TCGA 1992, ss 151H–151Y; CTA 2009, ss 504, 508–510, 512, 514, 515, 520; CTA 2010, s 110; SI 2019 No 689, Reg 6(13)*].

Capital allowances

In HMRC Brief 26/07, HMRC state that where diminishing shared ownership ('DSO') arrangements are entered into to acquire assets which would qualify for capital allowances, then the buyer or lessee is entitled to claim capital allowances on capital payments for those assets when they are brought into use.

Capital gains

In HMRC Brief 26/07, HMRC state that, subject to there being any unusual conditions in the DSO arrangements, the buyer will be treated as acquiring the asset in full when unconditional contracts are entered into to acquire a beneficial interest. Indexation allowance is computed accordingly.

Deposit arrangements

[3.5] These are arrangements under which a person deposits money with a financial institution (see **3.2** above), which is invested by that institution, usually together money from other depositors, with a view to profit. The financial institution does not pay any interest to the depositors, but instead pays them a proportion of the profits it earns from investing their money.
This is illustrated in the diagram below.

Deposit — mudarabah

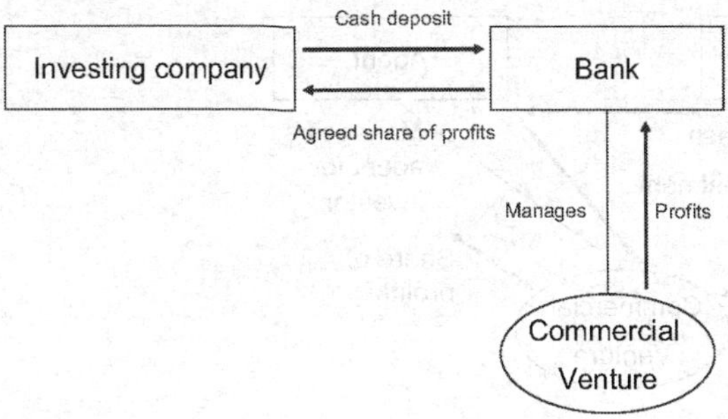

The amounts which the financial institution pays to its depositors equate in substance to the return on an investment of money at interest and constitutes alternative finance return.

The arrangements are treated for corporation tax purposes as a loan relationship to which the company is a party (see 50 LOAN RELATIONSHIPS). The amount of the deposit is treated as if it were a loan made by the company to the financial institution and the alternative finance return is treated as if it were interest payable under the loan relationship. The alternative finance return is not to be treated as a distribution.

Where a deduction is not available for an alternative finance return because the transaction is not at arm's length, the amount may not be surrendered under the group relief provisions.

[*CTA 2009, ss 505, 509, 510, 513, 520; CTA 2010, ss 110, 1019*].

Profit share agency arrangements

[3.6] In the case of a 'profit share agency' as illustrated below, one party acts as agent of the other (the investor) and the agent uses the money provided by the principal with a view to producing a profit.

Profit share agency — wakala

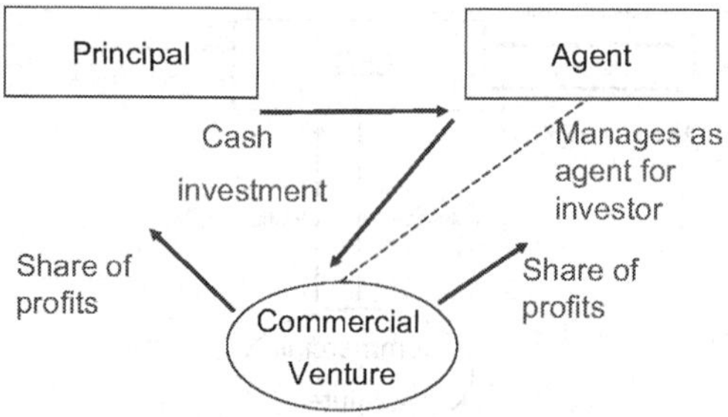

Whereas in most principal/agent relationships the principal is entitled to most of the rewards (and risks), in the case of a profit share agency the principal is entitled to the profits to a specified extent, while the agent is entitled to any additional profits (and may also be entitled to a fee). The provisions require the payments to the principal under his profit entitlement to equate, in substance, to the return on an investment of the money at interest.

If the above conditions are met, the profit share amounts paid to the principal are alternative finance return, while the principal is not taxable on the profits to which the agent is entitled.

The arrangements are treated for corporation tax purposes as a loan relationship to which the company is a party (see 50 LOAN RELATIONSHIPS). Any amount provided under the arrangements is treated as a loan by the principal to the agent and the alternative finance return is treated as interest.

Alternative finance return in the form of a payment under a profit share agency is not treated as a distribution.

Where a deduction is not available for an alternative finance return because the transaction is not at arm's length, the amount may not be surrendered under the group relief provisions.

[*CTA 2009, ss 506, 509, 510, 513, 516, 520, 521; CTA 2010, ss 110, 1019*].

Investment bond arrangements

[3.7] 'Sukuk' (plural of 'sakk' which is Arabic for 'certificate') are a form of tradable Islamic financial instrument that replicate the characteristics of conventional corporate bonds. They are usually structured by creating a special purpose vehicle to acquire assets, financing the acquisition by issuing participation certificates to investors. The assets so acquired are then used for the sponsoring group's business to generate income which is then paid out to the investors. The diagram below illustrates the most common structure, where land is sold to a special purpose vehicle and then rented back.

Alternative finance investment bond — sukuk

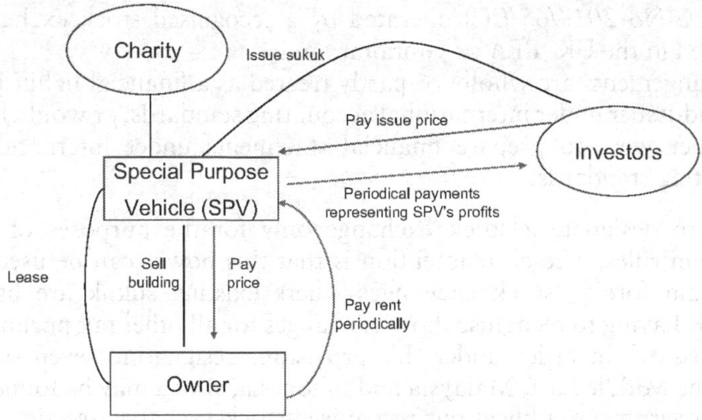

Specific legislation ensures that UK issuers of, and investors in, sukuk receive a tax treatment which equates to the tax treatment of conventional bond issuers and investors.

There is a regulatory provision in *The Financial Services and Markets Act 2000 (Regulated Activities) (Amendment) Order 2010, SI 2010 No 86* intended to exclude sukuk from constituting collective investment schemes. This order contains its own definition of an 'alternative finance investment bond' (AFIB) which, although similar to the definition of an investment bond in *CTA 2009, s 507* is not identical to it. Accordingly there is the risk that an instrument might fall within the tax provisions without falling within the regulatory provisions, or vice versa.

The arrangements covered involve the bond-holder paying a sum of money (the '*capital*') to a bond-issuer, where the assets or class of assets to be acquired to generate income or gains, and the period of the arrangement, are specified. The bond-issuer undertakes to sell the assets at the end of the term, or any that are still in his possession at that time, repay the capital either during the term or at its end, in one or more amounts and make other payments ('*additional payments*') to the bond-holder at one or more times during, or at the end of the bond term. Additional payments under arrangements falling within the definition of an investment bond are alternative finance return. Alternative finance return in the form of an additional payment or any part of a redemption payment is not treated as a distribution.

The other conditions are:

(a) the additional payments represent a reasonable commercial return on a loan of the capital;
(b) the bond-issuer undertakes to manage the assets to produce income to repay the capital at the end of the term and make additional payments;
(c) the bond-holder is entitled to transfer his rights to another person (who becomes the bond-holder);

(d) the arrangements are listed on a recognised stock exchange or, for accounting periods beginning on or after 1 April 2018, admitted to trading on a multilateral trading facility (within *Article 4.1.22* of *EU Directive No 2014/65/EU*) operated by a recognised stock exchange regulated in the UK, EEA or Gibraltar; and

(e) the arrangements are wholly or partly treated as a financial liability of the bond-issuer under international accounting standards, or would be if the issuer were to prepare financial statements under international accounting standards.

It is possible to designate a stock exchange only for the purposes of the investment bond rules. The clear intention is that this power can be used to designate certain foreign stock exchanges where existing sukuk are listed without the UK having to recognise those exchanges for all other tax purposes. HMRC have issued an order under this provision, designating seven stock exchanges in the Middle East, Malaysia and Indonesia, which may be found at www.gov.uk/government/publications/recognised-stock-exchanges-section-48a-finance-act-2005.

Flexibility is allowed for in the terms of the 'arrangements', for example the bond-issuer may acquire the assets before or after the arrangements are in place, the arrangements may include provision for them to be terminated before the end of the term and the termination payment may be reduced should the value of the bond assets fall or the income on them be reduced.

For corporation tax purposes, the effect of the arrangements is that the bond-holder is not treated as having the legal or beneficial interest in the bond assets, as trustee or otherwise, and any profits or gains arising on them is the income of the bond-issuer (otherwise than in a fiduciary capacity) not the bond-holder.

Redemption or additional payments to the bond-holder by the bond-issuer are treated for tax purposes as not made by him in a fiduciary capacity. The bond-holder is not entitled to tax relief on capital expenditure on the bond assets.

Investment bond arrangements are securities for the purpose of the Corporation Tax Acts. A bond-issuer is not a securitisation company for the purpose of the special tax regime applicable to securitisation companies, unless it is one as a result of arrangements which are not investment bond arrangements. Provisions are made in *CTA 2009, s 519* as regards the treatment of a bond-holder for the close company and group relief provisions. The alternative finance return payable under the arrangements is treated as interest on a loan.

Where a deduction is not available for alternative finance return because the transaction is not at arm's length, the amount may not be surrendered under the group relief provisions.

[*TCGA 1992, ss 151H–151Y; ITA 2007, s 564G; CTA 2009, ss 507, 510, 513, 514, 517–520; CTA 2010, ss 110, 1019; FA 2018, s 34(2)(4); SI 2019 No 689, Regs 6(13), 16(10)*].

Other provisions concerning alternative finance arrangements

Non-residents

[3.8] Where a non-resident company is party to an alternative finance arrangement as in 3.3 or 3.6 above, the company is not treated as having a UK permanent establishment by virtue of anything done in relation to the arrangement.

[*ITA 2007, s 835J; CTA 2010, s 1144*].

Equally, where a UK-resident person is a party to or acts for a non-resident person, who is party to an alternative finance arrangement, that person is not regarded as the UK representative of the non-resident in relation to the arrangement.

[*ITA 2007, s 835J*].

See **64.6** RESIDENCE.

Arrangements not at arm's length

[3.9] The arrangements at 3.3–3.7 above are not treated as alternative finance arrangements if:

- they are not entered into at arm's length;
- the transfer pricing rules under in *TIOPA 2010, s 147* (which apply for corporation tax as well as income tax) require the alternative finance or profit share return (or amount representing it) to be recomputed on an arm's length basis;
- the affected person or persons is entitled to a return (the relevant return) which would be an alternative finance return or an amount representing an alternative finance return if the arrangements were alternative finance arrangements (the latter covers the situation where there is an intermediary in back to back arrangements); and
- the party receiving the return is not subject to income or corporation tax, or a corresponding tax under a foreign jurisdiction, on the return.

In this case, the person paying the return is not entitled to any deduction in respect of the return in computing profits or gains for corporation tax purposes or to any deduction against total income or profits. Nor can the prohibited deduction be surrendered by way of group relief.

[*ITA 2007, s 564H; CTA 2009, ss 508, 520; CTA 2010, s 110; TIOPA 2010, s 147*].

Community investment tax relief

[3.10] References to a loan in the community investment tax relief ('CITR') legislation are taken to include references to alternative finance arrangements that involve purchase and re-sale, deposit or a profit share agency within the definitions given above. See **17** COMMUNITY INVESTMENT TAX RELIEF.

[*CTA 2010, ss 256–259; ITA 2007, ss 372A–372D*].

4

Anti-Avoidance

Cross references. See **9.9**(i) CAPITAL ALLOWANCES for 'control' and 'main benefit' transactions, **11.13–11.15** CAPITAL GAINS for value-shifting provisions, **11.4–11.8** CAPITAL GAINS in respect of close investment holding companies, **21** CONTROLLED FOREIGN COMPANIES in relation to the apportionment of profits of controlled foreign companies in 'low tax' jurisdictions, **29.21**, **29.25** DISTRIBUTIONS in respect of dual resident investing companies and exempt distributions, **36.19**, **36.20** HMRC — ADMINISTRATION for publication of tax strategies by large businesses and the special measure regime, **50.34** LOAN RELATIONSHIPS in relation to loan relationships for unallowable purposes, **51.16**, **51.32**, **51.33** LOSSES in respect of company reconstructions, farming and market gardening and leasing, **56.13** PARTNERSHIPS in relation to the realisation of capital from a partnership in a non-taxable form, and **72** TRANSFER PRICING.

Introduction to anti-avoidance

[4.1] This chapter outlines a number of anti-avoidance provisions which apply to corporation tax. Anti-avoidance provisions which are targeted at a specific area of legislation, or regime, are included in the relevant chapters of this annual.

For example, the anti-avoidance provisions with regard to risk transfer schemes, and group mismatch schemes, can be found at **50** LOAN RELATIONSHIPS, the anti-avoidance provisions with regard to the sale of lessors can be found at **49** LEASING.

Before outlining the different provisions, the approach of the Courts with regard to anti-avoidance transactions is considered and the general anti-abuse rule (GAAR) is described.

HMRC have powers, by way of a 'follower notice', to require a person using an avoidance scheme which is defeated in the courts in relation to another taxpayer to concede their position to reflect the court's decision. See **4.29** onwards below. Powers to enable HMRC to issue an 'accelerated payment notice' which requires a user of an avoidance scheme to pay tax upfront before the success or failure of the scheme has been finally determined have also been introduced. See **4.33** onwards below.

There is a regime of warnings and escalating sanctions for taxpayers ('serial avoiders') who persistently engage in tax avoidance schemes that are defeated by HMRC. See **4.37–4.45** below.

In March 2020, HMRC published a new approach to tackling promoters of mass-marketed avoidance schemes. See www.gov.uk/government/publications/tackling-promoters-of-mass-marketed-tax-avoidance-schemes/tackling-promoters-of-mass-marketed-tax-avoidance-schemes.

Anti-avoidance case law

[4.2] For the **general approach of the Courts** to transactions entered into solely to avoid or reduce tax liability, the leading cases are:

Duke of Westminster v CIR [1936] AC 1, (1935) 19 TC 490, HL; *W T Ramsay Ltd v CIR, Eilbeck v Rawling* [1982] AC 300, 54 TC 101, HL; *CIR v Burmah Oil Co Ltd* [1982] STC 30, 54 TC 200, HL; *Furniss v Dawson (and related appeals)* [1984] AC 474, 55 TC 324, HL; *Countess Fitzwilliam v CIR* [1993] 3 All ER 184, 67 TC 614, HL; and *CIR v McGuckian* [1997] NI 157, 69 TC 1, HL. See also *Cairns v MacDiarmid* [1983] STC 178, 56 TC 556, CA; *Ingram v CIR* [1986] Ch 585, [1985] STC 835; *Craven v White, CIR v Bowater Property Developments Ltd*, and *Baylis v Gregory* [1989] AC 398, 62 TC 1, heard together in the HL; *Shepherd v Lyntress Ltd* [1989] STC 617, 62 TC 495; *Moodie v CIR and Sinnett* [1993] 2 All ER 49, 65 TC 610, HL; *Hatton v CIR* [1992] STC 140, 67 TC 759; *Ensign Tankers (Leasing) Ltd v Stokes* [1992] 1 AC 655, 64 TC 617, HL; *Pigott v Staines Investment Co Ltd* [1995] STC 114, 68 TC 342; *MacNiven v Westmoreland Investments Ltd* [2001] UKHL 6, [2003] 1 AC 311, (2001) 73 TC 1, HL; *Barclays Mercantile Business Finance Ltd v Mawson* [2004] UKHL 51, [2005] 1 AC 684, [2005] STC 1 and *CIR v Scottish Provident Institution* [2004] UKHL 52, [2005] 1 All ER 325, [2005] STC 15, HL (hear together); and *Revenue and Customs Comrs v Tower MCashback LLP 1* [2011] UKSC 19, [2011] 2 AC 457, [2011] STC 1143.

The classical interpretation of the constraints upon the Courts in deciding cases involving tax avoidance schemes is summed up in Lord Tomlin's statement in the *Duke of Westminster* case that '. . . every man is entitled if he can to order his affairs so that the tax attaching . . . is less than it otherwise would be'. The case concerned annual payments made under covenant by a taxpayer to his domestic employees, which were in substance, but not in form, remuneration. The judgment was thus concerned with the tax consequences of a single transaction, but in *Ramsay*, and subsequently in *Furniss v Dawson*, the Courts have set bounds to the ambit within which this principle can be applied in relation to modern sophisticated and increasingly artificial arrangements to avoid tax.

Ramsay concerned a complex 'circular' avoidance scheme at the end of which the financial position of the parties was little changed, but it was claimed that a large capital gains tax loss had been created. It was held that where a preconceived series of transactions is entered into to avoid tax, and with the clear intention to proceed through all stages to completion once set in motion, the *Duke of Westminster* principle does not compel a consideration of the individual transactions and of the fiscal consequences of such transactions taken in isolation.

The House of Lords' opinions in *Furniss v Dawson* are of outstanding importance, and establish, inter alia, that the *Ramsay* principle is not confined to 'circular' devices, and that if a series of transactions is 'preordained', a particular transaction within the series, accepted as genuine, may nevertheless be ignored if it was entered into solely for fiscal reasons and without any commercial purpose other than tax avoidance, even if the series of transactions as a whole has a legitimate commercial purpose.

In *Craven v White* the House of Lords indicated that for the *Ramsay* principle to apply all the transactions in a series have to be preordained with such a degree of certainty that, at the time of the earlier transactions, there is no practical likelihood that the transactions would not take place. It is not sufficient that the ultimate transaction is simply of a kind that was envisaged at the time of the earlier transactions.

However, the decision in this case was distinguished in the *Scottish Provident Institution* case (which was heard with the *Barclays Mercantile Business Finance* case) where the HL held that 'it would destroy the value of the *Ramsay* principle' if the composite effect of transactions 'had to be disregarded simply because the parties had deliberately included a commercially irrelevant contingency, creating an acceptable risk that the scheme might not work as planned' and that 'the composite effect of such a scheme should be considered as it was intended to operate and without regard to the possibility that, contrary to the intention and expectations of the parties, it might not work as planned'.

In *Barclays Mercantile (BMBF)* Lord Nicholls held that the capital allowances legislation granted allowances if the expenditure on purchasing plant, etc. was made by the taxpayer claiming the allowances, irrespective of whether or not it was done in the wider context of a scheme with other objectives.

That decision has subsequently been distinguished by the Supreme Court in *Revenue and Customs Comrs v Tower MCashback LLP 1*, which also concerned a claim to capital allowances. Two limited liability partnerships had claimed capital allowances in respect of capital expenditure on computer software. 75% of the purchase price of the software was funded by 'non-recourse loans', which were indirectly made available by the vendor of the software. HMRC initially rejected the claims on the grounds that the expenditure had been incurred 'with a view to granting to another person a right to use or otherwise deal with any of the software in question', within *CAA 2001, s 45(4)*. They issued closure notices, against which the partnerships appealed. At the hearing of the appeals, HMRC abandoned their original contention with regard to *s 45(4)*, but defended the closure notices on alternative grounds. The Supreme Court held that, on the facts found by the Special Commissioner, the partnerships were only entitled to 25% of the allowances which they had claimed, applying the 1992 decision in *Ensign Tankers (Leasing) Ltd v Stokes* case and distinguishing the 2004 decision in BMBF. The case was heard by seven Supreme Court judges, rather than the usual five. Lord Walker delivered the leading judgment, with which all of his colleagues agreed. On the facts of the *Tower MCashback* case, he commented:

> 'One of the lessons of BMBF is that it is not enough for HMRC, in attacking a scheme of this sort, to point to the money going round in a circle. Closer analysis is required . . .
>
> ' . . . In the present case, by contrast [to the BMBF case], the borrowed money did not go to MCashback, even temporarily; it passed, in accordance with a solicitor's undertaking, straight to R&D where it produced no economic activity (except a minimal spread for the two Guernsey banks) until clearing fees began to flow from MCashback to the LLPs (in an arrangement comparable, though not closely similar, to the arrangements between LPI and VP in *Ensign*) . . .

> '. . . The composite transactions in this case, like that in Ensign (and unlike that in BMBF) did not, on a realistic appraisal of the facts, meet the test laid down by the Capital Allowances Act, which requires real expenditure for the real purpose of acquiring plant for use in a trade. Any uncertainty that there may be will arise from the unremitting ingenuity of tax consultants and investment bankers determined to test the limits of the capital allowances legislation.'

The inheritance tax case *Fitzwilliam v CIR* appears to further restrict the application of the *Ramsay* principle, in that the HL found for the taxpayer in a case in which all their Lordships agreed that, once the scheme was embarked upon, there was no real possibility that the later transactions would not be proceeded with. There is, however, some suggestion that a decisive factor was that the first step in the transactions took place before the rest of the scheme had been formulated. Again, in the case of *MacNiven v Westmoreland Investments Ltd* it was held that the *Ramsay* principle did not apply where a company loaned money to a subsidiary to enable it to pay up outstanding interest and thus crystallise tax losses. The interest had been paid within the meaning of the legislation and the manner in which the payment was funded was irrelevant.

In *Chappell v HMRC* CA, [2016] STC 1980, the taxpayer had entered into a marketed scheme under which manufactured payments were made under a loan of securities. The CA found there was no commercial or other purpose to the arrangements except avoiding tax through a deduction for the manufactured payments. The loan notes, interest paid and manufactured payments were all created for the purposes of the scheme and were self-cancelling with no practical significance. This was held to be sufficient to deprive them of their essential characteristics for the purposes of the legislation and so this resulted in no deduction for the taxpayer.

In *Steven Price v HMRC* [2015] UKUT 164 (TCC) the Upper Tribunal found that a capital loss scheme failed under the *Ramsay* principle. The success of the scheme relied on the participants having spent large sums on acquiring assets and then realising very small amounts on their disposal. In its judgment the Upper Tribunal referred to *Collector of Stamp Revenue v Arrowtown Assets Ltd* [2003] HKCFA 46 and stressed the requirements to 'construe statutory provisions purposively' and to 'view transactions realistically'. The Upper Tribunal approved of the lower tribunal's approach when asking the question: what did the taxpayer pay for? He had not outlaid £6 million for some 'worthless shares'. The Upper Tribunal also agreed with the lower tribunal's conclusion that the subscription for shares in this case had not been an isolated transaction, but had formed part of a composite and pre-planned series of steps.

In a criminal prosecution, *R v Quillan* [2015] EWCA Crim 538, the Court of Appeal considered whether a scheme to defraud HMRC was a 'sham'. The allegations against the defendants were that two schemes were set up with the dishonest intention of securing payment of income tax relief at source from HMRC by paying the same amount into pension schemes repeatedly, each time triggering a payment. This was achieved by arranging for the pension schemes to borrow and lend circularly. The Court noted that the claims for income tax relief had been properly made in accordance with the appropriate procedure, and that the contributions had in fact been made. The fact they had been funded by loans was irrelevant. Mere invocation of the concept of 'sham' by the prosecutor was not enough. The Court undertook a detailed analysis of the concept of 'sham' and considered that it required evidence, to the criminal standard of proof, that the contributions lacked any true legal substance. In this respect establishing the common intention of all parties was the key.

Simon's Taxes. See **A2.122.**

General anti-abuse rule

[4.3] The general anti-abuse rule ('GAAR') is intended to counteract the 'tax advantages' arising from 'tax arrangements' which are 'abusive'. Adjustments under the GAAR do not generally take effect until HMRC have referred the case to an independent GAAR Advisory Panel established by the Commissioners for HMRC. Before 22 July 2020, HMRC were generally required to refer the case to the Panel before making an adjustment, subject to the right to make a provisional counteraction before referral to the Panel where, for example, assessing time limits were about to expire. With effect from 22 July 2020, provisional counteraction is replaced with a system of protective GAAR notices. A GAAR Advisory Panel opinion allows HMRC to apply the GAAR to equivalent arrangements used by other taxpayers without further referral.

[*FA 2013, s 206*].

The GAAR applies to a range of taxes including corporation tax.

HMRC do not give formal or informal clearances that the GAAR does not apply. As part of their engagement with large businesses and wealthy individuals, however, HMRC do discuss commercial arrangements and confirm where appropriate that they don't regard particular arrangements as tax avoidance. See www.gov.uk/government/collections/seeking-clearance-or-approval-for-a-transaction.

For published opinions of the GAAR Advisory Panel, see www.gov.uk/government/collections/tax-avoidance-general-anti-abuse-rule-gaar.

Definitions

Arrangements are '*tax arrangements*' if, having regard to all the circumstances, it would be reasonable to conclude that the obtaining of a tax advantage was the main purpose, or one of the main purposes, of the arrangements. For this purpose, '*arrangements*' include any agreement, understanding, scheme, transaction or series of transactions, whether or not legally enforceable.

Tax arrangements are '*abusive*' if entering into them or carrying them out cannot reasonably be regarded as a reasonable course of action in relation to the relevant tax provisions, having regard to all the circumstances. Those circumstances include:

- whether the substantive results of the arrangements are consistent with any express or implied principles on which the provisions are based and their policy objectives;
- whether the means of achieving the results of the arrangements involve one or more contrived or abnormal steps; and

- whether the arrangements are intended to exploit any shortcomings in the provisions.

Where the tax arrangements form part of other arrangements regard must be had to those other arrangements.

The legislation gives the following non-exhaustive examples of what might indicate that tax arrangements are abusive.

- The arrangements result in taxable income, profits or gains significantly less than the economic amount.
- The arrangements result in a tax deduction or loss significantly greater than the economic amount.
- The arrangements result in a claim for repayment or crediting of tax, including foreign tax, that has not been, and is unlikely to be, paid.

The legislation also gives an example of what might indicate that arrangements are not abusive: the arrangements accord with established practice accepted by HMRC.

A '*tax advantage*' includes relief or increased relief from tax, repayment or increased repayment of tax, avoidance or reduction of a charge or assessment to tax, avoidance of a possible assessment to tax or of an obligation to deduct or account for tax, deferral of a payment of tax, and advancement of a repayment tax.

[*FA 2013, ss 207, 208, 214(1)*].

Effect of the GAAR

The GAAR operates by counteracting the tax advantage under the tax arrangements by the making of adjustments that are just and reasonable, whether by HMRC or anyone else (the taxpayer or a responsible partner – see **4.7** below). Adjustments can be made by assessment, modification of an assessment, amendment or disallowance of a claim or otherwise. An adjustment can impose a tax liability where there would not otherwise be one or can increase an existing liability. Adjustments may be made in respect of the tax in question or any other tax to which the GAAR applies. Adjustments have effect for all tax purposes. The normal time limits for making assessments etc. apply to the making of GAAR adjustments.

The effects of an adjustment under the GAAR are normally suspended until HMRC have followed the appropriate procedures at **4.4**, **4.6** or **4.7** below. Before 22 July 2020, HMRC had to follow the appropriate procedures *before* making an adjustment under the GAAR, subject to the right to make a provisional counteraction before referral to the Panel where, for example, assessing time limits were about to expire (see **4.5** below). With effect from 22 July 2020, provisional counteraction is replaced with a system of protective GAAR notices (see **4.5** below).

Where a matter is referred to the GAAR Advisory Panel (see **4.4**(4) or (6) and **4.7**(5) and (7) below), adjustments to counteract the tax advantage cannot be made in the '*closed period*' beginning with the 31st day after the end of the 45-day period for making representations (see **4.4**(2) and **4.7**(2) below) and ending immediately before the day on which notice is given of HMRC's final decision after considering the opinion of the Panel. Similarly, adjustments cannot be made in the closed period following the issue of a pooling notice or notice of binding (see **4.6**, **4.7** below). For this purpose, the 'closed period' is as defined at **4.6** below.

[*FA 2013, s 209; FA 2020, Sch 14, paras 2, 10, 15; FA 2021, Sch 32, para 3*].

Consequential adjustments

Where the counteraction of a tax advantage is final and, if the counteraction was not made as a result of an HMRC final counteraction notice, the taxpayer or responsible partner (see **4.7** below) has notified HMRC of it, a person (not necessarily the taxpayer or responsible partner) has 12 months, beginning with the day the counteraction becomes final, to make a claim for one or more consequential adjustments to be made in respect of any tax to which the GAAR applies. For this purpose, counteraction of a tax advantage is final when the adjustments made and any amounts resulting from them can no longer be varied, on appeal or otherwise.

Consequential adjustments can be made for any period and may affect any person, whether or not a party to the tax arrangements. Adjustments are made on a just and reasonable basis but cannot increase a person's liability to any tax. HMRC must notify the person who made the claim of any adjustments made in writing. Consequential adjustments can be made by assessment, modification of an assessment, amendment of a claim or otherwise. There are no time limits for making such an adjustment.

The procedure for claims made outside a return in *TMA 1970, Sch 1A* (see **15.7** CLAIMS) applies to claims for consequential adjustments for corporation tax purposes. See *FA 2013, s 210(6)* for the procedure rules for other taxes.

[*FA 2013, s 210; FA 2021, Sch 32, para 6*].

See **59.16** PENALTIES for the 60% penalty which applies to arrangements which are counteracted by the GAAR.

Court and Tribunal proceedings

In any court or Tribunal proceedings in connection with the GAAR, HMRC must show both that the tax arrangements are abusive and that the adjustments made to counteract the tax advantage are just and reasonable.

In making a decision in connection with the GAAR a court or Tribunal must take into account any HMRC guidance on the GAAR which was approved by the GAAR Advisory Panel at the time the tax arrangements were entered into and also any relevant opinion of the sub-panel (see **4.4**(9) and **4.6** below) about the arrangements in question.

[*FA 2013, s 211*].

Priority rules

The GAAR can override any priority rule in tax legislation, i.e. any rule to the effect that particular provisions have effect to the exclusion of, or otherwise in priority to, anything else. [*FA 2013, s 212*].

Procedure

[4.4] The normal procedure which HMRC must follow under the GAAR is set out below. See **4.5** below for alternative procedures where a protective GAAR notice is issued or, before 22 July 2020, a provisional counteraction notice was issued. See **4.6** below for alternative procedures in respect of equivalent arrangements. See **4.7** below for the modified normal procedure which applies with effect from 10 June 2021 to counteract tax advantages included in partnership returns.

(1) An HMRC officer designated by the Commissioners for HMRC for the purpose of the GAAR must give the taxpayer a written notice specifying:
- the arrangements and the tax advantage;
- why the officer considers that a tax advantage has arisen from abusive tax arrangements;
- the counteraction which the officer considers should be taken;
- the period within which the taxpayer can make representations (see (2) below); and
- the effect of the rules in (3)–(5) below and of the PENALTIES (**59.17**) which may apply if the proposed counteraction takes effect.

The notice may set out steps that the taxpayer may take to avoid the application of the GAAR.

Where a notice is given on or after 22 July 2020, the adjustments specified in it have effect as if they were made under *FA 2013, s 209* (see **4.3** above under 'Effects of the GAAR'). This rule does not apply if a protective GAAR notice or a provisional counteraction notice have already been given in respect of the specified adjustments (see **4.5** below). The notice must normally be given within the normal time limits for assessments applicable to the proposed adjustments, but if the taxpayer's return is under enquiry and the adjustments relate to matters included in the return, the notice can be given at any time until the time the enquiry is completed.

If no appeal is made in respect of the adjustments or an appeal is withdrawn or determined by agreement, and no final counteraction notice is given under (10) below or the provisions at **4.6** below, the notice has effect as if it were a final counteraction notice (and therefore as if the procedural requirements had been met). A penalty under *FA 2013, s 212A* (see **59.17** PENALTIES) cannot, however, be charged. In any other case, the specified adjustments have no effect unless they (or lesser adjustments) are subsequently specified in a final counteraction notice. The time limits for making the final counteraction notice are treated as met by the giving of the original notice.

(2) The taxpayer has 45 days starting with the day on which HMRC's notice is given to send written representations in response to the notice to the designated HMRC officer. The designated officer may extend the period if the taxpayer makes a written request.

(3) Where a person who has been given a notice under (1) takes 'corrective action' before the beginning of the closed period (see **4.3** above under 'Effect of the GAAR'), the matter is not referred to the GAAR Advisory Panel under (4) or (6) below. A person takes '*corrective action*' for this purpose only if he amends a return or claim to counteract the tax

advantage or relinquishes the tax advantage by entering into a written agreement with HMRC to do so. A person can amend a return or claim for this purpose during an enquiry even if the normal time limits have expired. No appeal may then be made against any enquiry closure notice (see **65.17** RETURNS) to the extent that it takes into account an amendment made as corrective action. The person must notify HMRC of the action taken and the additional tax amount which has or will become due. Where a person takes corrective action in this way no penalty can be charged under the provisions at **59.17** PENALTIES.

(4) If the taxpayer makes no representations and, where relevant, does not take corrective action, a designated HMRC officer must refer the matter to the GAAR Advisory Panel. The officer must at the same time notify the taxpayer that the matter is being referred.
The notice must inform the taxpayer of the period for making representations under (7) below and of the requirement to send any such representations to the officer. The officer must provide the Panel with a copy of the notice given to the taxpayer at step (1) above and the notice informing the taxpayer that the matter has been referred to the Panel.

(5) If the taxpayer does make representations but, where relevant, does not take corrective action, the representations must be considered by a designated HMRC officer.

(6) If the designated HMRC officer in (5) above still considers that the GAAR should apply, he must refer the matter to the GAAR Advisory Panel, together with a copy of the taxpayer's representations and any comments he has on those representations. The officer must notify the taxpayer of his decision on whether or not to refer the matter to the GAAR Advisory Panel as soon as is reasonably practicable.
The same requirements for the officer to notify the taxpayer and to provide information to the Panel apply as at step (4) above. The notice to the taxpayer must, however, also include a copy of any comments on the taxpayer's representations sent by the officer to the Panel.

(7) The taxpayer has 21 days to send written representations to the Panel and the designated HMRC officer about the notice given at step (1) above and any comments made by HMRC on the taxpayer's original representations. The Panel may extend the period for making representations if the taxpayer makes a written request.

(8) If the taxpayer makes representations at step (7) above but did not make representations at step (2) above, the designated HMRC officer may provide the Panel and the taxpayer with comments on the step (7) representations.

(9) A sub-panel of three members of the Panel will consider the matter in question. The sub-panel may invite the taxpayer of the designated HMRC officer to supply further information within a specified period. Information supplied to the sub-panel must also be sent to the other party.
The sub-panel must produce an opinion notice stating their joint opinion as to whether or not the entering into and carrying out of the tax arrangements was a reasonable course of action in relation to the relevant tax provisions, having regard to the circumstances outlined at **4.3** above. An opinion notice may indicate that the sub-panel consider

that it is not possible to reach a view on the information available. Alternatively, the sub-panel may produce two or three opinion notices which taken together state the opinions of all the members. An opinion notice must include the reasons for the opinion and is given both to the designated HMRC officer and the taxpayer.

(10) The designated HMRC officer must, having considered the sub-panel's opinion or opinions, give the taxpayer a written notice (a final counteraction notice) setting out whether or not the tax advantage under the arrangements is to be counteracted under the GAAR. It should be noted that HMRC are not bound by the decision of the sub-panel and may proceed with the application of the GAAR even if the sub-panel's opinion is that the GAAR ought not to apply.
If the GAAR is to apply, the final counteraction notice must specify the adjustments required and any steps that the taxpayer must take to give effect to them.

HMRC are not required to know for certain that a tax advantage has arisen before they embark on this procedure. A designated HMRC officer may carry out the above steps where he considers that a tax advantage might have arisen. Any notice he gives may be expressed to be given on the assumption that a tax advantage arises.

[*FA 2013, ss 209AB, 209AC, Sch 43; FA 2020, Sch 14 paras 4, 12, 15; FA 2021, Sch 32 para 10*].

Protective GAAR notices

[4.5] With effect from 22 July 2020, regardless of when the tax arrangements were entered into, an HMRC officer may issue a protective GAAR notice, stating that a tax advantage might have arisen from abusive arrangements and that, if so, it ought to be counteracted under the GAAR. Such a notice will, for example, be issued to protect against loss of tax where an assessing time limit is about to expire. A notice must:

- specify the arrangements and tax advantage concerned; and
- specify the adjustments (as in **4.3** above) which, on the assumption that the advantage does arise from abusive tax arrangements, the officer proposes should be made.

A notice must normally be given within the normal time limits for assessments applicable to the proposed adjustments. If, however, the taxpayer's return is under enquiry and the return relates to the tax in respect of which the adjustments in the notice are to be made, the notice can be given at any time until the time the enquiry is completed.

A protective notice may not be given if a provisional counteraction notice was given before 22 July 2020 in respect of the same adjustments.

The adjustments specified in a protective notice have effect as if they were made under *FA 2013, s 209* (see **4.3** above under 'Effects of the GAAR').

An appeal can be made by notice against the specified adjustments but is stayed for a period of 12 months beginning with the day on which the protective notice was given. If a final counteraction notice under **4.4** (10) or **4.7**(11) below above or under the provisions at **4.6** below is given before the end of the 12-month period, the stay on the appeal ends when that notice is given.

If no appeal is made or an appeal is withdrawn or determined by agreement, and no final counteraction notice is given, the protective GAAR notice has effect as if it were a final counteraction notice (and therefore that the procedural requirements in **4.4** above or **4.6** below had been met). A penalty under *FA 2013, s 212A* or *212B* (see **59.17** PENALTIES) cannot, however, be charged. In any other case, the specified adjustments have no effect unless they (or lesser adjustments) are subsequently specified in a final counteraction notice. The time limits for making the final counteraction notice are treated as met by the giving of the protective notice.

[*FA 2013, ss 209AA, 209AC; FA 2020, Sch 14 paras 3, 11, 15; FA 2021, Sch 32, para 5*].

Provisional counteraction notices before 22 July 2020

Before 22 July 2020, an HMRC officer could issue a provisional counteraction notice under the GAAR. Notices made before 22 July 2020 continue to operate on and after that date. A notice must:

- specify adjustments (as in **4.3** above) which the HMRC officer reasonably believes may be required to counteract a tax advantage that would (apart from the GAAR) arise to the recipient from tax arrangements;
- detail the arrangements and tax advantage concerned; and
- explain the appeals procedure and the circumstances in which the notice may be cancelled.

Adjustments specified in a notice which are made by HMRC are treated as effecting a valid counteraction of the tax advantage under the GAAR. The taxpayer may appeal against adjustments, stating the grounds of appeal, within the 30 days beginning with the date he receives the notice. If the taxpayer appeals the adjustments are treated as cancelled after 12 months from the date on which the provisional counteraction notice is given, unless, before that time (and whether before or after the issue of the provisional counteraction notice), an HMRC officer gives a notice to the taxpayer:

(1) cancelling the adjustments or withdrawing the notice (without cancelling the adjustments);
(2) issuing a notice within **4.4**(1) above in respect of the same arrangements and tax advantage and specifying the same or lesser adjustments as the counteraction which should be taken;
(3) issuing a pooling notice or notice of binding (see **4.6** below) in respect of the same arrangements and tax advantage and specifying the same or lesser adjustments as the counteraction which should be taken; or
(4) issuing a generic referral notice (see **4.6** below) in respect of the same arrangements and tax advantage and specifying the same or lesser adjustments as the counteraction which should be taken.

Where a notice within (2)–(4) above specifies lesser adjustments, the provisional counteraction notice must be amended accordingly (unless it was issued after the notice in (2)–(4) above).

If a notice within (2) above is given and the matter is not referred to the GAAR Advisory Panel or if a notice within (2)–(4) above is given and subsequently the taxpayer is given a notice stating that the tax advantage is not to be counteracted under the GAAR, the adjustments in the provisional counteraction notice are treated as cancelled unless HMRC has the power to make the adjustments under provisions other than the GAAR and they state that the adjustments are therefore not cancelled. If a notice within (4) above is withdrawn, the adjustments in the provisional counteraction notice are likewise treated as cancelled, subject to the same exception.

Where a notice within (2)–(4) above is given and subsequently the taxpayer is given a notice stating that the tax advantage is to be counteracted, the adjustments in the provisional counteraction notice are confirmed so far as specified in the notice as adjustments required to give effect to the counteraction and are otherwise treated as cancelled.

[*FA 2013, ss 209A–209F; FA 2020, Sch 14 paras 6, 13, 15*].

Counteraction of equivalent arrangements

[4.6] There are provisions to enable the counteraction of 'equivalent' arrangements entered into by other taxpayers. The provisions enable HMRC to issue a 'pooling notice'.

A designated HMRC officer may issue a '*pooling notice*' to a taxpayer (R), where:

(a) a person (P) has been given a notice under **4.4**(1) above or **4.7**(1) below in relation to tax arrangements ('*lead arrangements*');
(b) the 45-day period for representations in **4.4**(2) above or **4.7**(2) below has expired but no final counteraction notice under **4.4**(10) above, **4.7**(11) below or the generic referral provisions below has been given in respect of the matter;
(c) the officer considers that a tax advantage has arisen, or may have arisen, to R from tax arrangements which are abusive;
(d) the officer considers that those arrangements are equivalent to the lead arrangements; and
(e) the officer considers that the advantage should be counteracted.

The notice places R's arrangements in a pool comprising all the arrangements in relation to which pooling notices have been served in respect of the lead arrangements (whether under these provisions or those for partnerships at **4.7** below). Before 5 December 2017, the lead arrangements were themselves in the pool along with the equivalent arrangements. A pooling notice may not be given if R has already been given a notice under **4.4**(1) above.

A designated HMRC officer may issue a '*notice of binding*' to a taxpayer (R), where:

(i) a person has been given a final counteraction notice under **4.4**(10) above, **4.7**(11) below or the generic referral provisions below in relation to tax arrangements ('*counteracted arrangements*') which are in a pool;

(ii) the officer considers that a tax advantage has arisen, or may have arisen, to R from tax arrangements which are abusive;
(iii) the officer considers that those arrangements are equivalent to the counteracted arrangements; and
(iv) the officer considers that the advantage should be counteracted.

A notice of binding may not be given if R has already been given a pooling notice or a notice under **4.4**(1) above or **4.7**(1) below.

A pooling notice or notice of binding must be given as soon as is reasonably practicable after HMRC become aware of the relevant facts. The notice must specify the tax arrangements and tax advantage concerned; explain why the officer considers them to be equivalent to the lead arrangements or the counteracted arrangements and why a tax advantage is considered to have arisen from abusive arrangements; set out the counteraction that the officer considers should be taken; and the effects of the notice. It may, but is not required to, set out steps which could be taken to avoid the proposed counteraction.

Where a pooling notice or notice of binding is given on or after 22 July 2020, the adjustments specified in it have effect as if they were made under *FA 2013, s 209* (see **4.3** above under 'Effects of the GAAR'). This rule does not apply if a protective GAAR notice or a provisional counteraction notice have already been given in respect of the specified adjustments (see **4.5** below). The notice must normally be given within the normal time limits for assessments applicable to the proposed adjustments but if the taxpayer's return is under enquiry and the adjustments relate to matters included in the return, the notice can be given at any time until the time the enquiry is completed.

If no appeal is made in respect of the adjustments or an appeal is withdrawn or determined by agreement, and no final counteraction notice (see **4.7**(11) below and **4.4** (10) above) is given, the notice has effect as if it were a final counteraction notice (and therefore as if the procedural requirements had been met). A penalty under *FA 2013, s 212A* or *212B* (see **59.17** PENALTIES) cannot, however, be charged. In any other case, the specified adjustments have no effect unless they (or lesser adjustments) are subsequently specified in a final counteraction notice. The time limits for making the final counteraction notice are treated as met by the giving of the pooling notice or notice of binding.

Arrangements are '*equivalent*' if they are substantially the same as one another, having regard to their results, the means of achieving those results, and the characteristics on the basis of which it could reasonably be argued in each case that the arrangements are abusive tax arrangements under which a tax advantage has arisen.

Where a person who has been given a pooling notice or a notice of binding takes 'corrective action' before the beginning of the 'closed period', he is treated as not having been given the notice and the arrangements are accordingly no longer in the pool. A person takes '*corrective action*' for this purpose only if he amends a return or claim to counteract the tax advantage or relinquishes the tax advantage by entering into an agreement with HMRC to determine an appeal. A person can amend a return or claim for this purpose during an enquiry even if the normal time limits have expired. No appeal may then be made against any enquiry closure notice (see **65.17** RETURNS) to the extent that it takes into account an amendment made as corrective action. The person must notify HMRC of the action taken and the additional tax amount which has or will become due. The '*closed period*' begins on the thirty-first day after the day on which the pooling notice or notice of binding was given. In the case of a pooling notice, the closed period ends immediately before the day on which notice is given of HMRC's final decision after considering the opinion of the GAAR Advisory Panel (see below). In the case of a notice of binding, the period is treated as ending at the same time as it begins. Where a person takes corrective action in this way no penalty can be charged under the provisions at **59.17** PENALTIES.

Before 5 December 2017, if P in (a) above takes corrective action within the 75-day period beginning with the day on which the notice under **4.4**(1) above was given, the lead arrangements are treated as ceasing to be in the pool. (On and after that date, the lead arrangements are not pooled in any case.)

Where, after a pooling notice has been issued to a person, the GAAR Advisory Panel issue an opinion notice (see **4.4**(9) above) in respect of another set of arrangements in the pool (the '*referred arrangements*'), the HMRC officer must give the person a '*pooled arrangements opinion notice*' setting out a report of the opinion and the person's right to make representations. Only one such notice may be given to a person about the same arrangements. The taxpayer has 30 days from the date of the notice to make representations that no tax advantage has arisen to him or that his arrangements are materially different from the referred arrangements.

The HMRC officer must consider any opinion of the GAAR Advisory Panel about the referred arrangements, together with any representations made, and issue a written notice with his decision as to whether the tax arrangements under consideration are to be counteracted under the GAAR. If so, the notice must set out the adjustments required to give effect to the counteraction and any steps that the taxpayer must take to give effect to it.

Where an HMRC officer gives a notice of binding, he must at the same time give a '*bound arrangements opinion notice*' setting out a report of any opinion of the GAAR Advisory Panel about the counteracted arrangements and the person's right to make representations. The taxpayer has 30 days from the date of the notice to make representations that no tax advantage has arisen to him or that his arrangements are materially different from the counteracted arrangements.

The HMRC officer must then consider any opinion of the GAAR Advisory Panel about the counteracted arrangements, together with any representations made, and issue a written notice (a final counteraction notice) with his decision as to whether the tax arrangements under consideration are to be counteracted under the GAAR. If so, the notice must set out the adjustments required to give effect to the counteraction and any steps that the taxpayer must take to give effect to it.

See **4.7** below for modifications to these provisions which apply with effect from 10 June 2021 to counteract tax advantages included in partnership returns.

[*FA 2013, ss 209(9), 209AB, 209ABA, 209AC, Schs 43A, 43D, para 12; FA 2020, Sch 14, paras 4, 8, 12, 15; FA 2021, Sch 32, paras 1, 3(4), 4, 5, 11; SI 2017 No 1090, Regs 1–10*].

Generic referral of equivalent arrangements to the GAAR Advisory Panel

There are provisions for HMRC to make a generic referral to the GAAR Advisory Panel of arrangements in a pool.

Where:

(A) (on or after 5 December 2017) further to pooling notices given as above, two or more sets of arrangements are in a pool relating to any lead arrangements, and P in (a) above took corrective action within the 75-day period beginning with the day on which the notice under **4.4**(1) was given (or within such longer period as P and HMRC may have agreed); or

(B) (before 5 December 2017) pooling notices had placed one or more sets of arrangements in a pool with lead arrangements, and those lead arrangements ceased to be in the pool,

then, provided none of the pooled arrangements have been referred to the GAAR Advisory Panel (see **4.4**(4), (6) above and **4.7**(5) and (7) below) a designated HMRC officer may give to each of the taxpayers whose arrangements are in the pool a notice of a proposal to make a generic referral to the Panel in respect of the arrangements in the pool. The notices must specify the arrangements and the tax advantage and the period within which the taxpayer can make a proposal (see below).

A person who has been given a notice has 30 days beginning with the day the notice was given to propose to HMRC that it should give him a notice under **4.4**(1) above or **4.7**(1) below and should not proceed with the generic referral.

If none of the notified taxpayers makes such a proposal within the 30-day period, the HMRC officer must make a referral (a '*generic referral*') to the GAAR Advisory Panel. If at least one of the recipients makes a proposal within the 30-day period, the officer must, after that period ends, decide whether to give one of the taxpayers a notice under **4.4**(1) above or **4.7**(1) below or to make a generic referral. On and after 5 December 2017, the officer must make a generic referral if a taxpayer is duly given a notice under **4.4**(1) above or **4.7**(1) below but the matter is not referred to the GAAR Advisory Panel.

Where HMRC make a generic referral to the GAAR Advisory Panel, the designated HMRC officer must provide the Panel with a general statement of the material characteristics of the arrangements together with a declaration that this is applicable to *all* the arrangements and that nothing material to the panel's consideration has been omitted. The general statement must contain a factual description as well as HMRC's opinion, and a copy must be provided to the taxpayers.

A sub-panel of three members of the Panel will consider the referral. The sub-panel must produce an opinion notice stating its collective opinion as to whether or not the entering into and carrying out of the tax arrangements described in the general statement was a reasonable course of action in relation to the relevant tax provisions. An opinion notice may indicate that the sub-panel considers that it is not possible to reach a view on the information available. Alternatively, the sub-panel may produce two or three opinion notices which, taken together, state the opinions of all the members. An opinion notice must include the reasons for the opinion and is given to the designated HMRC officer.

The HMRC officer must then provide a copy of the opinion notice (or notices) to each taxpayer, any one of whom may then, within 30 days, make representations that:

- no tax advantage has arisen to him;
- he has already been given a bound arrangements opinion notice in relation to the arrangements concerned (see above); or
- a matter set out in HMRC's general statement is materially incorrect.

The officer must then, for each taxpayer, consider any opinion of the GAAR Advisory Panel, together with any representations made, and send a written notice (a final counteraction notice) with his decision as to whether the tax arrangements under consideration are to be counteracted under the GAAR. If so, the notice must set out the adjustments required to give effect to the counteraction and the steps that the taxpayer must take to give effect to it.

[*FA 2013, s 214(3), Sch 43B; FA 2021, Sch 32, para 12; SI 2017 No 1090, Regs 1, 11–14*].

Application of the GAAR to partnerships

[4.7] *FA 2021* introduced provisions intended to enable the GAAR procedures to operate in the same way as that in which HMRC conduct enquiries into partnerships, allowing notices to be given via the representative partner, making amendments to the partnership return and feeding counteraction through to each partners' tax returns. The provisions apply with effect from 10 June 2021, regardless of when the tax arrangements were entered into and apply where a partnership return has been made under *TMA 1970, s 12AA*. They will also apply where a partnership return is made under the making tax digital provisions of *TMA 1970, Sch A1, para 10*. [*FA 2013, Sch 43D, para 1; FA 2021, s 124, Sch 32, para 1*].

For the purposes of the provisions, the '*responsible partner*' is the person who delivered the partnership return or, where that person has ceased to be available, the person nominated by the partners as their successor or, in the case of a return under *TMA 1970, Sch A1*, the nominated partner. A partnership return is treated as made on the basis that a particular tax advantage arises to a partner from particular arrangements if it is made on the basis that an increase or decrease in any amounts included in the partnership statement result from the arrangements and that increase or decrease results in a tax advantage for the partner. [*FA 2013, Sch 43D paras 2, 3; FA 2021, Sch 32, para 1*].

Protective GAAR notice

An HMRC officer may issue a protective GAAR notice to the responsible partner, stating that a return was made on the basis that a tax advantage might have arisen to one or more partners from abusive tax arrangements and that, if so, it ought to be counteracted under the GAAR. Where such a notice is given, the provisions relating to protective GAAR notices at **4.5** above apply, with necessary modifications. In particular, where the notice has effect as if it were a final counteraction notice, a penalty under *FA 2013, s 212B* (see **59.17** PENALTIES) cannot be charged. [*FA 2013, Sch 43D para 4; FA 2021, Sch 32, para 1*].

Modification of normal procedure

The provisions apply the normal GAAR procedure outlined at **4.4** above, modified to apply as follows.

(1) A designated HMRC officer must issue a notice of proposed counteraction to the responsible partner, stating that a return was made on the basis that a tax advantage arises to one or more partners from abusive tax arrangements and that it ought to be counteracted under the GAAR. A notice must:

- specify each of the partners in question ('*relevant partners*'), the arrangements and the tax advantage;
- explain why the officer considers that a tax advantage has arisen to each partner from the abusive arrangements;
- set out the counteraction that the officer considers ought to be taken;
- inform the responsible partner of the period for making representations (see (2) below); and
- explain the effect of the rules in (3)–(6) below and of the PENALTIES (**59.17**) which may apply if the proposed counteraction takes effect.

A notice may set out steps that could be taken to avoid the application of the GAAR.

If it subsequently appears to HMRC that the tax advantage has in fact not arisen to a particular partner, they must amend the notice accordingly and may take such other steps as they consider appropriate.

The adjustments specified in a notice have effect as if they were made under *FA 2013, s 209* (see **4.3** above under 'Effects of the GAAR'). This rule does not apply if a protective GAAR notice has already been given in respect of the specified adjustments (whether to the responsible partner as above or as in **4.5** above). The notice must normally be given within the normal time limits for assessments applicable to the proposed adjustments, but if the partnership return is under enquiry and the adjustments relate to matters included in the return, the notice can be given at any time until the time the enquiry is completed.

If no appeal is made in respect of the adjustments or an appeal is withdrawn or determined by agreement, and no final counteraction notice is given under (11) below or the provisions at **4.6** above, the notice has effect as if it were a final counteraction notice (and, therefore, as if the procedural requirements had been met). A penalty under *FA 2013, s 212B* (see **59.17** PENALTIES) cannot, however, be charged. In any other case, the specified adjustments have no effect unless they (or lesser adjustments) are subsequently specified in a final counteraction notice. The time limits for making the final counteraction notice are treated as met by the giving of the original notice.

(2) The responsible partner has 45 days starting with the day on which HMRC's notice is given to send written representations in response to the notice to the designated HMRC officer. The designated officer may extend the period if the responsible partner makes a written request.

(3) Where the responsible partner amends the partnership return or a claim to counteract the tax advantage, and notifies HMRC accordingly, before the beginning of the closed period (see **4.3** above under 'Effect of the GAAR'), the matter is not referred to the GAAR Advisory Panel under (5) or (7) below. The responsible partner can amend a return or claim for this purpose during an enquiry even if the normal time limits have expired. No appeal may then be made against any enquiry closure notice to the extent that it takes into account such an amendment. Where a responsible partner takes corrective action in this way no penalty can be charged under the provisions at **59.17** PENALTIES.

(4) Where a relevant partner takes all necessary action to enter into a written agreement with HMRC to relinquish the tax advantage before the beginning of the closed period, that partner ceases to be treated as a relevant partner. HMRC must amend the original notice accordingly as soon as practicable after the closed period begins. If the partner then fails to enter into the written agreement, HMRC may proceed as if the partner continues to be a relevant partner (but without needing to amend the notice).

(5) If the responsible partner makes no representations, a designated HMRC officer must refer the matter to the GAAR Advisory Panel if the partner has not made the amendments in (3) above before the closed period begins and there remains at least one relevant partner.

The officer must at the same time notify the responsible partner that the matter is being referred. The notice must inform the responsible partner of the period for making representations under (8) below and of the requirement to send any such representations to the officer. The officer must provide the Panel with a copy of the notice given to the responsible partner at step (1) above and the notice informing the responsible partner that the matter has been referred to the Panel.

(6) If the responsible partner does make representations but has not made the amendments in (3) above before the closed period begins, then if there is at least one remaining relevant partner, the representations must be considered by a designated HMRC officer.

(7) If the designated HMRC officer in (6) above still considers that the GAAR should apply, he must refer the matter to the GAAR Advisory Panel, together with a copy of the responsible partner's representations and any comments he has on those representations. The officer must notify the responsible partner of his decision on whether or not to refer the matter to the GAAR Advisory Panel as soon as is reasonably practicable.

The same requirements for the officer to notify the responsible partner and to provide information to the Panel apply as at step (5) above. The notice to the responsible partner must, however, also include a copy of any comments on the responsible partner's representations sent by the officer to the Panel.

(8) The responsible partner has 21 days to send written representations to the Panel and the designated HMRC officer about the notice given at step (1) above and any comments made by HMRC on the partner's original representations. The Panel may extend the period for making representations if the responsible partner makes a written request.

(9) If the responsible partner makes representations at step (8) above but did not make representations at step (2) above, the designated HMRC officer may provide the Panel and the responsible partner with comments on the step (8) representations.

(10) A sub-panel of three members of the Panel will consider the matter in question. The sub-panel may invite the responsible partner or the designated HMRC officer to supply further information within a specified period. Information supplied to the sub-panel must also be sent to the other party.

The sub-panel must produce an opinion notice stating its collective opinion as to whether or not the entering into and carrying out of the tax arrangements was a reasonable course of action in relation to the relevant tax provisions, having regard to the circumstances outlined at **4.3** above. An opinion notice may indicate that the sub-panel considers that it is not possible to reach a view on the information available. Alternatively, the sub-panel may produce two or three opinion notices which, taken together, state the opinions of all the members. An opinion notice must include the reasons for the opinion and is given to both the designated HMRC officer and the taxpayer.

(11) The designated HMRC officer must, having considered the sub-panel's opinion or opinions, give the responsible partner a written notice (a final counteraction notice) setting out whether or not the tax advantage under the arrangements is to be counteracted under the GAAR. It should be noted that HMRC are not bound by the decision of the sub-panel and may proceed with the application of the GAAR even if the sub-panel's opinion is that the GAAR ought not to apply.

If the GAAR is to apply, the final counteraction notice must specify the adjustments required and any steps that the responsible partner must take to give effect to them.

HMRC are not required to know for certain that a tax advantage has arisen before they embark on this procedure. They may carry out the above steps where a designated officer considers that a tax advantage might have arisen to a relevant partner. Any notice may be expressed to be given on the assumption that a tax advantage arises.

[*FA 2013, ss 209ABA, 209AC, Schs 43, 43D, paras 5–9; FA 2021, Sch 32, paras 1, 4, 5*].

Pooling notice or notice of binding given to responsible partner

If a designated HMRC officer considers that a partnership return has been made on the basis that a tax advantage has arisen to a partner (R) or to R and one or more other partners, and that officer has the power to give R a pooling notice or a notice of binding (see **4.6** above) in respect of the tax advantage, the notice may instead be given to the responsible partner. A pooling notice may not be given if a notice has been given under (1) above. A notice of binding may not be given if a pooling notice or a notice under (1) above has already been given.

The provisions at **4.6** above apply to a pooling notice or notice of binding given under the above provisions, with any necessary modifications.

In particular, a notice given under the above provisions must also specify the partners (the 'relevant partners') to which it applies. If it subsequently appears to HMRC that the tax advantage has in fact not arisen to a particular relevant partner, they must amend the notice accordingly and may take such other steps as they consider appropriate.

Where a responsible partner who has been given a pooling notice or a notice of binding amends the partnership return or a claim to counteract the tax advantage before the beginning of the 'closed period' (see **4.6** above), the partner is treated as not having been given the notice and the arrangements are accordingly no longer in the pool. A responsible partner can amend a return or claim for this purpose during an enquiry even if the normal time limits have expired. No appeal may then be made against any enquiry closure notice to the extent that it takes into account such an amendment. The responsible partner must notify HMRC of the action taken.

Where a relevant partner takes all necessary action to enter into a written agreement with HMRC to relinquish the tax advantage before the beginning of the closed period, that partner ceases to be treated as a relevant partner. HMRC must amend the original notice accordingly as soon as practicable after the closed period begins. If the partner then fails to enter into the written agreement HMRC may proceed as if the partner continues to be a relevant partner (but without needing to amend the notice).

Where, further to pooling notices given as above, two or more sets of arrangements are in a pool relating to any lead arrangements, and corrective action has been taken within the 75-day period beginning with the day on which the notice was given (or within such longer period as HMRC may have agreed) then, provided none of the pooled arrangements have been referred to the GAAR Advisory Panel individually, a designated HMRC officer may give to each of the taxpayers whose arrangements are in the pool a notice of a proposal to make a generic referral to the Panel in respect of the arrangements in the pool. The consequences of such a notice are the same as for a notice given under the provisions described under the heading 'Generic referral of equivalent arrangements to the GAAR Advisory Panel' at **4.6** above.

HMRC are not required to know for certain that a tax advantage has arisen before they give a notice, or do anything else, under these provisions. Any notice may be expressed to be given on the assumption that a tax advantage arises.

[*FA 2013, Sch 43D, paras 10–14; FA 2021, Sch 32, para 1*].

Land sold and leased back — payments connected with transferred land

[4.8] The provisions outlined below were designed to counter tax-avoidance arrangements where land owned by a trader is transferred and leased back to him for use in his trade. The common method of transaction is where a trader grants a long lease (i.e. over 50 years) of his land (including business premises) to a property-dealing company at a nominal rent in consideration of a large premium but the legislation is not confined to long leases. The company then grants a lease back to the trader at an excessive rent for the early years of the lease which, in effect, repays the premium plus interest and profit, the rent falling to a nominal one for the remainder of the term of the lease.

Without anti-avoidance provisions, the excessive rent payable by the trader would be an allowable deduction in computing his profits in return for which he would obtain a lump sum in the form of a large premium. As far as the property-dealing company is concerned, the excessive rent it receives is a trading receipt on which it pays tax but against which it can set off the diminishing value of the lease which is part of its stock-in-trade falling to be valued year by year at cost or market value whichever is the lower. The lease, moreover, can be determined prematurely and the transaction repeated with the same property.

Where these provisions apply the tax deduction is limited to the commercial rent.

Specifically, where land (or any interest or estate in land) is transferred (by sale, lease, surrender or forfeiture of lease etc.) and, as a result of:

- a lease of the land, or any part of it, granted at the time of transfer or subsequently by the transferee to the transferor; or
- another transaction or transactions affecting the land or interest or estate,

the transferor, or a company associated (see below) with the transferor, becomes liable to make a payment of rent under a lease of the land or part of it (including any premium treated as rent — see **60.10** PROPERTY INCOME), or any other payment connected with the land or part of it (whether it is a payment of rentcharge or other payment under some other transaction), which would be allowable as a deduction:

- in computing trading profits; or
- in computing the profits of a UK property business; or
- in computing profits or income under any of the provisions listed at *CTA 2010, s 1173* (miscellaneous income) or in computing losses for which relief is available under *CTA 2010, s 91* (see **51.12** LOSSES); or
- under *CTA 2009, s 1219* (management expenses of a company's investment business — see **45.3** INVESTMENT COMPANIES AND INVESTMENT BUSINESS); or
- under *FA 2012, s 76* (expenses of insurance companies); then

the deduction for tax purposes in respect of the rent or other payment is limited to the 'commercial rent' of the land to which it relates for the period for which the payment is made. In fact, the position is judged on a cumulative basis.

A transfer of an estate or interest in land above includes:

(a) the granting of a lease or another transaction involving the creation of a new estate or interest in the land;
(b) the transfer of the lessee's interest under a lease by surrender or forfeiture of the lease; and
(c) a transaction or series of transactions affecting land or an estate or interest in land, such that some person is the owner (or one of the owners) before and after the transaction(s) but another person becomes or ceases to be one of the owners.

With regard to (c), a person is to be regarded as a transferor for the purposes of these provisions if the person is an owner before the transaction(s) and is not the sole owner afterwards.

For any accounting period, amount E (which may be nil) is the expense or total expenses to be brought, in accordance with generally accepted accounting practice (GAAP), into account in the period in respect of the payments made (excluding any just and reasonable portion which relates to services, tenant's rates, or the use of assets other than land). Take the amount of E for the current accounting period and for every previous accounting period ending on or after the date of the transfer. Subtract from the aggregate amount the total deductions given for every such previous accounting period. What remains is the cumulative unrelieved expenses for the current period, and it is this figure which is then compared to the commercial rent for the period and restricted if necessary.

The cumulative unrelieved expenses cannot, however, be carried forward to an accounting period beginning after the payments have ceased; no deduction is available under these provisions for any such expenses. Different rules apply to expenses of insurance companies (see *CTA 2010, ss 839–842*).

In the case of a lease, '*commercial rent*' means the open-market rent, at the time the actual lease was created, under a lease whose duration and maintenance/repair terms are the same as under the actual lease but stipulating a rent payable at uniform intervals at a uniform rate, or progressively increasing proportionately to any increases provided by the actual lease. For other transactions, it is the open market rent which would be payable under a tenant's repairing lease (as defined by *CTA 2010, s 845(3)*) for the period over which payments are to be made (subject to a maximum of 200 years).

In these provisions, 'lease', as well as having its normal meaning, includes (i) an underlease, sublease, tenancy or licence, (ii) an agreement for a lease, underlease, sublease, tenancy or licence, and (iii) in the case of land outside the UK, an interest corresponding to a lease. 'Rent' includes any payment under a lease.

For the purposes of these provisions, the following persons are associated with one another:

(i) the transferor in an 'affected transaction' and the transferor in another affected transaction, if the two persons are acting in concert or if the two transactions are in any way reciprocal;
(ii) any person who is an associate of either of the associated transferors in (i);

(iii) two or more bodies corporate if they participate in, or are incorporated for the purposes of, a scheme the reconstruction, or amalgamation, of a body corporate or bodies corporate.

In addition, persons are associated with one another if they are associates as defined in *CTA 2010, s 882* (see **49.4** below). In (i) above, an '*affected transaction*' is a transfer within these provisions or within the corresponding income tax provisions.

[*CTA 2010, ss 834–848*].

Simon's Taxes. See **B5.247**.

Land sold and leased back — new lease of land after assignment or surrender

[4.9] These provisions apply to certain assignments (sales) or surrenders of leaseholds (but not freeholds) under lease back arrangements, whether or not the rent under the new lease exceeds the commercial rent. Although in form the lump sum received in these instances is consideration for assigning the lease, and the lease back is at an increased rent, in substance the lump sum is a loan and the additional rent represents the repayment of principal and interest.

Where this provision applies, a proportion of the consideration for the assignment or surrender of the first lease is treated as taxable income of the recipient and not as a capital receipt, but there is no restriction on the amount of the deduction for rent payable under the new lease. For these purposes a lease includes an agreement for a lease and any tenancy, but does not include a mortgage. A reference to a lessee or lessor should be read accordingly and includes a reference to the successors in title of a lessee or lessor. Rent includes a payment by a tenant for maintenance or repair not required by the lease.

Specifically, these provisions apply where all of the following conditions are met:

(a) a company (L) is a lessee of land under a lease which has 50 years or less to run ('the original lease') and is entitled to corporation tax relief on the rent;
(b) L assigns the original lease to another person or surrenders it to the landlord, and the consideration for the assignment or surrender would not be taxable except as capital in L's hands;
(c) another lease ('the new lease') for a term of 15 years or less is granted, or assigned, to L (or to a person linked to L);
(d) the new lease comprises or includes all or part of the land which was the subject of the original lease; and
(e) neither L (nor a person linked to L) had, before 22 June 1971, a right enforceable at law or in equity to the grant of the new lease.

The reference in (a) to corporation tax relief is to any of the allowable deductions listed in **4.8** above. For the purposes of (c) and (e), a person is linked to L if he is a partner of L, an associate of L or an associate of a partner of L. Persons are associated with one another if they are associates as defined in *CTA 2010, s 882* (see **49.4** LEASING).

Appropriate proportion

A proportion of the consideration mentioned in (b) above (the 'appropriate proportion') is taxed as income (and not treated as a capital receipt). If it is received by L in the course of a trade and the rent payable under the new lease is allowable as a deduction in calculating the profits or losses of a trade, profession or vocation for tax purposes, the appropriate proportion is treated as a receipt of the trade. If not, it is treated as being within the charge to corporation tax on income. The '*appropriate proportion*' is the proportion of the consideration found by applying to it the formula:

$$\frac{16 - N}{15}$$

where:

N = the term of the new lease expressed in years (taking part of a year as an appropriate proportion of a year).

If the consideration is paid in instalments, the formula is applied to each instalment. If the term of the new lease is one year or less, the appropriate proportion of the consideration or instalment is the whole of it. If the property which is the subject of the new lease does not include all the property which was the subject of the original lease, the consideration must be reduced as is reasonable before applying the formula.

Deductions

Provided the rent under the new lease is payable by a company within the charge to corporation tax, all provisions of *CTA 2009* or *ICTA 1988* providing for deductions or allowances by way of corporation tax relief in respect of payments of rent apply in relation to the rent payable under the new lease.

Relevant definitions

In these provisions, 'lease', as well as having its normal meaning, includes (i) an agreement for a lease, and (ii) any tenancy, but does not include a mortgage.

'Rent' includes a payment by a tenant for work to maintain or repair leased land or premises which the lease does not require the tenant to carry out.

There are provisions (see *CTA 2010, ss 854–858*) whereby for the above purposes the term of the new lease is deemed to end (i) on an earlier date if the rent is reduced or (ii) if the lessor or lessee has power to determine the lease or the lessee has power to vary its terms, on the earliest date on which it can be so determined or varied.

Not all conditions met

If conditions (a)–(d) above are met but condition (e) is not (such that the above provisions do not apply), and the rent under the new lease is payable by a person within the charge to corporation tax:

- no part of the rent paid under the new lease is to be treated as a payment of capital, and
- all provisions of *CTA 2009* providing for deductions or allowances by way of corporation tax relief in respect of payments of rent apply accordingly in relation to that rent.

Certain variations of a lease

Consequences ensue if all of the following conditions are met:

(A) a company (M) is a lessee of land under a lease which has 50 years or less to run ('the original lease') and is entitled to corporation tax relief on the rent;
(B) M varies the original lease by agreement with the landlord;
(C) under the variation, M agrees to pay a rent greater than that payable under the original lease and, does so in return for a consideration which would not be taxable except as capital in M's hands; and
(D) under the variation, the period during which the greater rent is to be paid ends not more than 15 years after the date on which the consideration is paid to M (or, where applicable, the final instalment of the consideration is paid to M).

The consequences are that M is treated as having surrendered the original lease for the consideration mentioned in (C) and as having been granted a new lease for a term of 15 years or less but otherwise on the terms of the original lease varied as mentioned in (B). The provisions described above are then applied accordingly.

[*CTA 2010, ss 849–862*].
Simon's Taxes. See **B5.248.**

Transfers of income streams

[4.10] A principles-based provision applies to tax lump sums received for the transfer of an income stream (i.e. a right to receive income) in the same way as the income would have been taxed. The provision applies where the income stream (which would have been charged to, or brought into account in calculating profits for the purposes of, corporation tax) is sold without the asset from which the income derives.

A sale and repurchase agreement is not regarded as the sale of an asset and is therefore within the provision. The provision also applies where the transfer of the income stream is a consequence of the transfer of all rights under an agreement for annual payments.

The amount of the consideration or market value (where consideration is substantially less than market value) for the transfer is treated as the transferor's income for corporation tax in the same way and to the same extent as if the company had received the income stream i.e. as if no transfer had taken place.

The income is treated as arising either when recognised under generally accepted practice, or, where market value is substituted for consideration, at the time it would have been so recognised if full market value had been received. If at any time it becomes reasonable to assume that the income would not be so treated as arising in an accounting period, it is treated as arising immediately before that time.

Exceptions

The above provision does not apply if the deemed income is otherwise charged to tax as income of the transferor, brought into account in calculating its profits or under *CAA 2001*. It also does not apply where the consideration for the transfer is an advance within the factoring of income provisions.

The following transfers are treated as transfers of an asset and therefore outside the provision:

- the transfer of all or part of a share in the profits or losses of a partnership;
- the grant, surrender or renunciation of a lease of land;
- the disposal of an interest in an oil licence;
- the grant or disposal of an interest in intellectual property which constitutes a pre-*FA 2002* asset; and
- any transactions which are to be treated as transfers of assets under a Treasury order.

[*CTA 2010, ss 752–757*].

Treatment of transferee

The following applies to a company which is the recipient of an income stream as a result of a transfer to which the above provision or the equivalent income tax provision (see *ITA 2007, Pt 13 Ch 5A*) applies.

The consideration paid by the company for the transfer is treated as a money debt owed to it by the person who is due to pay the income stream and the transfer itself is treated as a transaction for the lending of money from which that debt arises. The loan relationship rules (see **50** LOAN RELATIONSHIPS) apply accordingly.

[*CTA 2009, ss 486F, 486G*].

Simon's Taxes. See **D9.301–D9.301B.**

Factoring of income receipts etc.

[4.11] The provisions described below are intended to counter the situation in which a person enters into financing arrangements that equate in substance to his taking out a loan but which are structured in such a way as to effectively give him tax relief for repayment of principal as well as for finance charges.

Say, for example, a borrower (B) has the opportunity to take out a loan of £50,000, under which B would repay the loan to the lender (L) over five years together with total interest of £5,000. Tax relief might be available for the

£5,000 interest but not for the repayment of the £50,000 principal. As an alternative, B transfers to L for £50,000 an asset that is fully expected to produce income of £55,000 over the next five years, at the end of which the asset will be transferred back to B for nothing. L receives £55,000 for an outlay of £50,000. B then claims that the transfer of the asset to L either gives rise only to a chargeable gain (which may be relatively small due to high base cost and available reliefs) or is not taxable at all, and that he is not chargeable on the income of £55,000 which is received not by him but by L. B effectively obtains tax relief on £55,000 (less any CGT payable).

Sometimes, instead of the borrower forgoing income, the arrangements generate a tax deduction for the borrower. Say B grants a long lease of freehold property to L for a premium of £50,000. L then grants a five-year sub-lease back to B at a rent of £11,000 per year. The arrangements will provide for the benefits of ownership to revert to B at the end of the five years. Again, L receives £55,000 for an outlay of £50,000. B obtains tax relief for rent payments of £55,000.

Type 1 finance arrangements: arrangements involving disposals of assets

The anti-avoidance provisions below apply where there is a '*type 1 finance arrangement*'. Such an arrangement exists where:

(i) under the arrangement a person ('the borrower') receives from another person ('the lender') any money or other asset ('the advance') in any period;
(ii) in accordance with generally accepted accounting practice (GAAP) the accounts of the borrower for that period record a financial liability in respect of the advance;
(iii) the borrower (or a person connected with the borrower) disposes of an asset ('the security') under the arrangement to or for the benefit of the lender (or a person connected with the lender);
(iv) the lender (or a person connected with the lender) is entitled under the arrangement to payments in respect of the security; and
(v) in accordance with GAAP those payments reduce the amount of the financial liability recorded in the borrower's accounts.

For the purposes of (ii) above it has to be assumed that the period in which the advance is received ended immediately after the receipt of the advance.

For these purposes, the provisions at **19** CONNECTED PERSONS applies to determine whether persons are connected, except that the lender cannot be regarded as a person connected with the borrower and *vice versa*. If the borrower is a partnership (of which a company is a member), references above to accounts are to the accounts of any member of the partnership as well as the partnership itself. References to accounts also include consolidated group accounts of a group of which the borrower is a member. 'Arrangement' is widely defined for the purposes of these provisions to include any agreement or understanding (whether or not legally enforceable). 'Payments' is also widely defined to include any obtaining of value or benefit. Where it is not the case, these provisions apply as if the accounts in question had been prepared in accordance with GAAP.

Effect of provisions

If an arrangement is a type 1 finance arrangement as above, then:

(a) if, as a result of the arrangement, an amount of otherwise chargeable income would escape tax in the hands of the borrower (or a person connected with the borrower), it does not escape tax;
(b) if, as a result of the arrangement, any amount which would otherwise fall to be taken into account in computing income of the borrower (or a person connected with the borrower) for corporation tax purposes, is not so brought into account, that amount shall be so brought into account; and
(c) if, as a result of the arrangement, the borrower (or a person connected with the borrower) becomes entitled to a deduction in computing any taxable income, or a deduction from total profits, there shall be no such entitlement.

If the borrower is a partnership (of which a company is a member), the above have effect by reference to any member of the partnership.

If the arrangement would not in any event have had any of the effects in (a)–(c) above the payments in (iv) above are treated for corporation tax purposes as income of the borrower, provided that the borrower is a company within the charge to corporation tax or a partnership of which a member is such a company. This applies whether or not the payments are also taxable income of another person.

The advance is treated as a money debt owed by the borrower company and the arrangement as a loan relationship of the company (as a debtor relationship). Any amount which, in accordance with GAAP, is recorded in the accounts as a finance charge in respect of the advance is to be treated as interest payable under that relationship. The intended effect is to place the borrower in the same position for tax purposes as if he had taken out a loan instead of entering into the structured finance arrangement. (If the borrower is a partnership, it is the partnership itself that is deemed to be paying interest, even if the finance charge appears in the accounts of a member.) The time at which this notional interest is to be treated as having been paid depends on the timing of the payments made to the lender in respect of the security; each such payment is treated as if it were part repayment of principal and part interest.

[*CTA 2010, ss 758–762, 774–776*].

See also below under Exceptions.

Simon's Taxes. See **D1.793.**

Arrangements involving partnership changes

More complex types of arrangement might be involved where the borrower (B) is a partnership. For example, B might transfer an income-producing asset ('the security') to a partnership of which it is a member. The lender (L) then joins the partnership for a capital contribution of £50,000 in return for the right to receive partnership profits of £55,000 over the next five years but no profits beyond that period. B claims not to be taxable on the £55,000 of partnership profits diverted to L. In another scenario, an established partnership may already hold an income-producing asset and the above steps then follow without the need for the initial transfer of an asset by B. In this case, the members of the partnership whose profits are thereby reduced claim not to be taxable on the partnership profits diverted to L.

There are similar anti-avoidance provisions to catch this type of arrangement. See *CTA 2010, ss 763–769*. The provisions apply to 'Type 2 finance arrangements', where the security is transferred to the partnership under the arrangement and 'Type 3 finance arrangements' where the security is already held by the partnership. Broadly, the partnership change is treated for tax purposes as if it had not occurred. For this purpose, the partnership change might be the admission of the lender as a partner or a change in profit-sharing ratios affecting the lender's share. The provisions are widely drawn so as also to catch changes made indirectly and/or involving a person connected with the lender. Again, as above, there is provision for a finance charge to be treated as if it were interest paid on a loan.

See also below under Exceptions.

Asset backed pensions anti-avoidance

There is an interaction between these structured finance provisions, being the Type 2 and Type 3 arrangement outlined above, and the asset backed pension contributions anti-avoidance legislation. See **69.24** TRADING INCOME — DEDUCTIONS.

Exceptions

The above provisions are disapplied if the whole of the advance under the finance arrangement falls to be brought into account in determining the taxable income of a 'relevant person'. This includes a case where the advance falls to be brought into account as a disposal receipt or proceeds from a balancing or disposal event, for capital allowances purposes, but not if a balancing charge results and would fall to be restricted under the capital allowances legislation. In respect of amounts brought into account before 6 March 2007 under arrangements made before that date, a '*relevant person*' was a person otherwise affected by the provisions. A '*relevant person*' means the borrower under the arrangements or a person connected with the borrower or, if the borrower is a partnership, another partner.

The provisions are also disapplied if the whole of the advance under the structured finance arrangement is a debtor relationship of the borrower under the loan relationship rules or would be if the borrower were a company within the charge to corporation tax. A debtor relationship in this case does not include a non-lending relationship within *CTA 2009, Pt 6 Ch 2* (see **50.3** LOAN RELATIONSHIPS).

There are also exclusions in cases where certain other statutory provisions do in any case result in the arrangement being taxed as intended. These include, for example, certain repo and stock lending arrangements (see **50.45** LOAN RELATIONSHIPS), ALTERNATIVE FINANCE ARRANGEMENTS (3) and certain sale and finance leaseback transactions. In relation to periods of account beginning on or after 1 January 2019, there is an additional exclusion where the arrangement is a right-of-use lease (see **10.52**(5) CAPITAL ALLOWANCES ON PLANT AND MACHINERY) and the borrower etc. is a lessee who would not have accounted for the arrangement as a finance lease or loan if required to do so under GAAP. The Treasury have power to specify further exclusions by statutory instrument, and any such exclusions may be given retrospective effect.

[*CTA 2010, ss 770–773; FA 2019, Sch 14 paras 4(9), 6(1)*].

The lease premium rules at *CTA 2009, ss 217–221* (see **60.10** PROPERTY INCOME) are disapplied where the grant of the lease constitutes the disposal of an asset for the purposes of these provisions.

See *TCGA 1992, s 263E* as regards the chargeable gains consequences of structured finance arrangements.

Simon's Taxes. See **D1.793** and **D1.794**.

International movements of capital

[4.12] Where a company is a 'reporting body' when a 'reportable event' takes place or when it carries out a 'reportable transaction' it must make a report to HMRC within six months of the transaction. *SI 2009 No 2192, para 3* lays down the information to be provided in the report. The purpose of the report is to enable HMRC to judge if there is a tax advantage to any person.

The following transactions or events that are of a value in excess of £100 million are reportable:

(1) an issue of shares or debentures by a foreign subsidiary;
(2) a transfer by (or one caused or permitted by) the reporting body of shares or debentures of a foreign subsidiary in which the reporting body has an interest;
(3) a transfer by (or one caused or permitted by) a party to a 'single nomination arrangement' of a foreign subsidiary in which that party has an interest. There is no requirement that the transfer be by the reporting body; it must only be by a party to the single nomination arrangement which includes the reporting body;
(4) a transaction/event which results in the foreign subsidiary becoming or ceasing to become a controlling partner in a partnership (as defined); or
(5) any transaction/event specified in regulations.

In general, the transaction value is market value. For the detailed provisions see *SI 2009 No 2192, para 4*.

A transaction is excluded if it is carried out in the ordinary course of trade, all parties are resident in the same country when the transaction is carried out, it is within regulations laid down by HMRC, it is the granting of security to a bank for borrowings of a foreign subsidiary obtained in the ordinary course of business or it consists of a foreign subsidiary giving an insurance company security in the course of a transaction entered into by that subsidiary in the ordinary course of business of investment of its funds.

An arrangement (a '*single nomination arrangement*') may be entered into when there is more than one UK corporate parent company for one of them to be the nominated reporting body for the purposes of these provisions. HMRC has laid down the requirements for such an arrangement in *SI 2009 No 2192, para 6*.

A failure to report a transaction will give rise to a penalty (under *TMA 1970, s 98*) of £300 plus £60 per day of default.

Definitions

A UK resident company is a '*reporting body*' if one of the following conditions is met:

(A) the company is not controlled by a non-UK resident company;
(B) it is controlled by a non-UK resident company and no other relevant UK company is controlled by that parent;
(C) the company is controlled by a non-resident company as are one or more other UK parent companies are controlled by the foreign parent and the company is not party to an arrangement (see below);
(D) the company is controlled by non-resident company as are one or more other UK parent companies and the company is party to arrangement (see below) in respect of which it is the nominated reporting body.

'*Control*' means the person's power to manage the company in accordance with that person's wishes, whether by a shareholding, voting or other powers (e.g. in the articles of association). Two or more persons may be taken together to have control. In a partnership, a right to more than 50% of the assets or income is treated as control.

See HMRC International Manual, INTM700000.

[*FA 2009, s 37, Sch 17; SI 2009 No 2192*].

Simon's Taxes. See **D6.502–D6.504.**

Company becoming non-resident. See **64.9, 64.10** RESIDENCE.

Hybrid and other mismatches

[4.13] There are provisions which implement the rules agreed under the OECD Base Erosion and Profit Shifting (BEPS) project for addressing international and domestic hybrid arrangements under which either a tax deduction is generated in circumstances where there is no corresponding taxable income or more than one tax deduction is generated.

The provisions operate to counteract, by making corporation tax adjustments, the following types of mismatch:

(1) 'deduction/non-inclusion mismatches' arising from 'payments' or 'quasi-payments' and involving hybrid transfer arrangements (see **4.15** below);
(2) deduction/non-inclusion mismatches arising from payments or quasi-payments under, or in connection with, financial instruments (see **4.16** below);

(3) deduction/non-inclusion mismatches arising from payments or quasi-payments in relation to which the payer is a 'hybrid entity' (see **4.17** below);
(4) deduction/non-inclusion mismatches arising in relation to internal transfers of money or money's worth made, or treated as made, by a multinational company's permanent establishment in the UK to the territory in which the company is resident for tax purposes (see **4.18** below);
(5) deduction/non-inclusion mismatches arising from payments or quasi-payments in relation to which a payee is a hybrid entity (see **4.19** below);
(6) deduction/non-inclusion mismatches arising from payments or quasi-payments in relation to which a payee is a multinational company (see **4.20** below);
(7) 'double deduction mismatches' arising from a company being a hybrid entity (see **4.21** below); and
(8) double deduction mismatches involving dual resident companies or multinational companies (see **4.22** below).

A '*deduction/non-inclusion mismatch*' arises where an amount is deductible from a person's income and either there is no corresponding amount of 'ordinary income' arising to another person or such income does arise to another person but is under taxed. A '*double deduction mismatch*' arises where an amount is deductible from more than one person's income or from a single person's income for the purposes of more than one tax.

The provisions (or any corresponding provision under the law of a non-UK territory) apply in the order shown above, so that (1) above is considered before (2) above, and so on.

There are also provisions to counteract imported mismatches, where there is an attempt to circumvent the main provisions by transferring a mismatch into a third jurisdiction. See **4.23** below. See **4.24** below for the reallocation of surplus dual inclusion income between companies in a group. See **4.25** below for adjustments required as a result of later events.

[*TIOPA 2010, s 259A*].

Partnerships

The hybrid mismatch provisions apply as follows where a person is a member of a partnership. References to income, profits or an amount of the person include a reference to his share of income, profits or an amount of the partnership, determined on a just and reasonable basis. This rule applies to a non-UK entity of a similar character to a partnership. [*TIOPA 2010, s 259NE*].

Securitisation companies

No adjustments can be made to the tax treatment of a securitisation company (within the meaning of *SI 2006 No 3296*) under the hybrid mismatch provisions. This rule was introduced by *FA 2021* but is deemed to have applied since the inception of the provisions. [*TIOPA 2010, s 259NEZA; FA 2021, Sch 7, paras 34, 36*].

Transparent funds

Special rules apply to 'transparent funds'. They were introduced by *FA 2021* but are deemed to have applied since the inception of the provisions. [*FA 2021, Sch 7, para 36*].

A '*transparent fund*' is a collective investment scheme or alternative investment fund whose profits or income would be profits or income of its participants for tax purposes if all of its profits or income arose in the UK and all of the participants were chargeable to income tax.

Broadly, the rules disregard certain mismatches which are attributable to investors in the fund with less than a 10% interest in the payment received by the fund (in payee cases) or, in cases within **4.21** below, whose deduction is less than 10% of the maximum that could have been available to participants. Mismatches are not disregarded if there are 'structured arrangements' (as defined).

See *TIOPA 2010, ss 259MA–259MD*.

Priority

The hybrid mismatch provisions take priority over the CORPORATE INTEREST RESTRICTION **24** which is taken to be of no effect for the purposes of these provisions. [*TIOPA 2010, s 259NEA; F(No 2)A 2017, Sch 5 para 20*].

Anti-avoidance

The following applies where there are 'avoidance arrangements' as a result of which any person (whether or not party to the arrangements) would otherwise obtain a 'tax advantage' under the hybrid mismatch or equivalent non-UK provisions. If the person is within the charge to corporation tax or would be but for the arrangements, adjustments must be made on a just and reasonable basis to his treatment for corporation tax purposes. Adjustments may be made by assessment, modification of an assessment, amendment or disallowance of a claim, or otherwise.

A '*tax advantage*' is obtained if the person avoids a restriction on whether or how a deduction may be made, avoids, to any extent, an amount being treated as his income or, for payments made on or after 10 June 2021 and for quasi-payments for which the payment period begins on or after that date, does anything which, to any extent, increases the amount of his dual inclusion income (as variously defined throughout the hybrid mismatch provisions). '*Avoidance arrangements*' are arrangements the main purpose of which is to enable any person to avoid a restriction or having an amount treated as income as above. Arrangements are excluded if the tax advantage can reasonably be regarded as consistent with the principles on which the hybrid mismatch provisions are based and the policy objectives of those provisions (having regard to the BEPS Final Report on Neutralising the Effects of Hybrid Mismatch Arrangements).

For the purpose of the change to the above provisions applying by reference to payment periods beginning on or after 10 June 2021, payment periods straddling that date are treated as two separate periods, the second of which starts on that date. Any necessary apportionments must be made on a time basis or, if a time basis would produce a result that is not just or reasonable, on a just and reasonable basis.

[*TIOPA 2010, s 259M; FA 2021, Sch 7, paras 14, 37, 38*].

FA 2021 changes: retrospection election

A number of changes are made to the hybrid mismatch provisions. Some of the changes are deemed to have applied from the inception of the provisions, but others apply with effect by reference to 10 June 2021. In certain cases, as indicated in the relevant paragraphs below, it is possible for a company to elect for *FA 2021* changes which would otherwise take effect in 2021 to be treated as having applied from the inception of the provisions. Such an election (a '*retrospection election*') must be made on or before 31 December 2021. Any resulting adjustments to claims, returns or elections made before the retrospection election must also be made on or before that date (but subject to this, the normal time limits are disapplied). If those claims include a claim to group relief or group relief for carried-forward losses, the surrendering company may make corresponding adjustments required as a result of any changes to the claim. Again, such adjustments must be made on or before 31 December 2021 (with the normal time limits disapplied). [*FA 2021, Sch 7, para 39*].

Definitions

[4.14] The following definitions apply for the purposes of the hybrid mismatch provisions.

'*Tax*' means income tax, corporation tax on income, diverted profits tax, the controlled foreign companies (CFC) charge, foreign tax on income which corresponds to income tax or corporation tax on income or a foreign charge similar to the CFC charge (a 'foreign CFC charge'). Provincial and local foreign taxes are excluded from the definition with effect, broadly, from 13 July 2017. Foreign taxes on income are excluded from the definition with effect, broadly, from 10 June 2021, to the extent that they are charged on income arising to an entity which is not subject to the tax in question but is to be brought into account for the purposes of the tax by a different entity. Payment of any withholding tax in respect of any amount is ignored. [*TIOPA 2010, s 259B(1)–(4); F(No 2)A 2017, s 24(2)(10)–(12); FA 2018, Sch 7, paras 2, 19(4); FA 2021, Sch 7, paras 1, 37, 38*].

Provisions under the law of a non-UK territory are equivalent to the UK mismatch provisions (or a particular part of the provisions) if it is reasonable to suppose that the non-UK provisions are based on the BEPS final report on mismatches (or later supplement or replacement) and have the same or similar purposes as the UK provisions. [*TIOPA 2010, s 259BA*].

A '*payment*' is a transfer of money or money's worth directly or indirectly from one person to one or more other persons where (ignoring the UK mismatch provisions or any equivalent foreign provisions) an amount (a '*relevant deduction*') may be deducted from the payer's income for a taxable period (the '*payment period*') in calculating the taxable profits. The '*payee*' is any person to whom the transfer is made or to whom an amount of ordinary income arises as a result of the payment.

There is a '*quasi-payment*' in relation to a taxable period (the '*payment period*') of a person (the payer) if, ignoring the UK mismatch provisions or any equivalent foreign provisions, an amount (a '*relevant deduction*') may be deducted from the payer's income for the period in calculating taxable profits and it would be reasonable to expect an amount of ordinary income to arise to one or more other persons as a result of the circumstances giving rise to the deduction. A quasi-payment does not arise if the payer's deduction is an amount deemed under the law of the 'payer jurisdiction' to arise for tax purposes and the circumstances giving rise to it do not include any economic rights between the payer and any of the other persons. In deciding whether it is reasonable to expect ordinary income to arise, the following assumptions must be made: that whether an entity is a distinct and separate person from the payer is determined under the law of the payer jurisdiction and that any person to whom amounts arise or potentially arise adopt the same accounting approach as the payer, are resident in the payer jurisdiction under its tax law and carry on a business (in connection with which the circumstances arise) there. Any person to whom it would be reasonable to expect ordinary income to arise or to whom an amount of ordinary income actually arises as a result of the quasi-payment is a '*payee*'. The payer is also the payee if it would be reasonable to expect ordinary income to arise to an entity which is not a distinct and separate person from the payer for the purposes of UK tax law but is a distinct and separate person under the law of the payer jurisdiction. The '*payer jurisdiction*' for this purpose is the jurisdiction under which the deduction may be deducted.

The '*payee jurisdiction*' is a territory in which a payee is resident for tax purposes under that territory's law or a territory in which the payee has a permanent establishment.

[*TIOPA 2010, s 259BB*].

'*Ordinary income*' is income brought into account, before deductions, in calculating income or profits ('*taxable profits*') on which a tax is charged other than under the CFC charge or a foreign CFC charge. Income is excluded if it is subject to an exclusion, relief or credit applying specifically to it or which arises in connection with the payment or quasi-payment giving rise to the income or (for payments on or after 1 January 2018 or, as the case may be, for accounting periods or payment periods beginning on or after that date (treating periods straddling that date as two separate periods)) if it is charged to the relevant tax at a nil rate. To the extent that tax on profits falls to be refunded other than as a result of a loss relief, any income brought into account in calculating that income is not ordinary income.

Income is treated as ordinary income if it would be brought into account in calculating taxable profits of a person but for that person being a 'qualifying institutional investor' (on the assumption that the territory in question had a tax on income). Where the qualifying institutional investor is an investment trust, this rule is treated as applying from the inception of the hybrid mismatch provisions. In all other cases, the rule applies to payments made on or after 10 June 2021 and quasi-payments for which the payment period begins on or after that date. For this purpose, payment periods straddling 10 June 2021 are treated as two periods, the second beginning on that date. Any necessary apportionments must be made on a time basis or, if a time basis would not give a just and reasonable result, on a just and reasonable basis.

[*TIOPA 2010, s 259BC; FA 2018, Sch 7, paras 3, 19; FA 2021, Sch 7, paras 26, 36–38*].

'*Qualifying institutional investor*' has the same meaning as at **13.7** CAPITAL GAINS — SUBSTANTIAL SHAREHOLDING EXEMPTION. A qualifying institutional investor is 'based' in a territory if it is resident for tax purposes there or, if it is not resident for tax purposes anywhere, if it is established there. [*TIOPA 2010, s 259NDA; FA 2021, Sch 7, para 29*].

Special rules apply to determine whether income of an entity which is a CFC (under UK or non-UK law) which is not ordinary income of the entity under these rules or which is ordinary income but is under taxed is treated as ordinary income of a company subject to the CFC charge or a foreign CFC charge. See *TIOPA 2010, s 259BD*.

An entity which is regarded as being a person for tax purposes under the law of any territory is a '*hybrid entity*' if either:

- some or all of its income or profits are treated for tax purposes under the law of any territory as the income or profits of another person or persons ('*investors*'); or
- under the law or another territory it is not regarded as a distinct and separate person to an entity or entities ('*investors*') that are distinct and separate persons under the law of the first territory.

Any territory under the law of which an investor is within the charge to tax is an '*investor jurisdiction*' of that investor.

[*TIOPA 2010, s 259BE*].

A '*permanent establishment*' is one within **64.6** RESIDENCE or within any similar concept under a non-UK law. [*TIOPA 2010, s 259BF; FA 2016, Sch 10 para 1*].

A '*financial instrument*' is:

- an arrangement the profits or deficits from which would, assuming that the person to whom they arise is within the charge to corporation tax, be brought into account under the loan relationships provisions;
- a contract the profits or losses from which would, assuming that the person to whom they arise is within the charge to corporation tax, be brought into account under the derivative contracts provisions;
- a type 1, type 2 or type 3 finance arrangement within **4.11** above;
- a share forming part of a company's issued share capital or an arrangement providing a person with corresponding rights; or
- anything else which is a financial instrument under UK generally accepted accounting practice.

Hybrid transfer arrangements (see **4.15** below) are excluded.

Instruments meeting the conditions set out in paragraphs (i)–(iv) of point (b) of paragraph 4 of Article 9 of Council Directive (EU) 2016/1164 are also excluded in relation to payments made on or after 1 January 2020 and before 1 January 2023, and quasi-payments for which the payment period begins on or after 1 January 2020 and ends before 1 January 2023.

Additional Tier 1 instruments and Tier 2 instruments within *Banking Act 2009, s 3(1)* and certain instruments which are Tier 1 or Tier 2 items under EU law are also excluded in relation to payments made on or after 1 January 2019 before 1 January 2020 and quasi-payments for which the payment period begins on or after 1 January 2019 and ends before 1 January 2020.

Previously, regulatory capital securities within *SI 2013 No 3209* were excluded from being financial instruments (and the revocation of *SI 2013 No 3209* is ignored for this purpose).

Payment periods which straddle 1 January 2019, 1 January 2020 or 1 January 2023 are treated as two separate taxable periods for this purpose, the second of which starts on that date. Any necessary apportionments must be made on a time basis or, if a time basis would not give a just and reasonable result, on a just and reasonable basis.

[*TIOPA 2010, s 259N; FA 2019, s 19(4)(8)(9); SI 2019 Nos 1251, 1345*].

Two persons are '*related*' on a day that they are in the same 'control group' or one has a 25% investment in the other or a third person has a 25% investment in each of them. A person is in the same '*control group*' as another if throughout any period their financial results for the period are, or are required to be, comprised in group accounts or would be so required by for an exemption or if one has a 50% investment in the other or a third person has a 50% investment in each of them. A person is also in the same control group as another on any day if, within the six months beginning on that day one directly or indirectly participates in the management, control or capital of the other or the same person or persons directly or indirectly participate in the management, control or capital of each of them. 25% investment and 50% investment are defined by reference to share capital, voting rights etc. — see *TIOPA 2010, s 259ND*. [*TIOPA 2010, ss 259NB–259ND; FA 2021, Sch 7, para 24*].

A '*relevant investment fund*' is an open-ended investment company, an authorised unit trust of an offshore fund which meets the appropriate genuine diversity of ownership condition (see **46.13** INVESTMENT FUNDS and **55.4** OFFSHORE FUNDS). [*TIOPA 2010, s 259NA*].

Hybrid transfer deduction/non-inclusion mismatches

[4.15] The counteraction below applies where:

(1) there is a 'hybrid transfer arrangement' in relation to an 'underlying instrument';
(2) a payment or quasi-payment (see **4.14** above) is made under or in connection with the arrangement or instrument;
(3) either the payer is within the charge to corporation tax for the payment period or a payee is within the charge for an accounting period which falls wholly or partly within the payment period;

(4) it is reasonable to suppose that, in the absence of the UK mismatch provisions or equivalent non-UK provisions, there would be a hybrid transfer deduction/non-inclusion mismatch in relation to the payment of quasi-payment; and
(5) either the payer and payee are related (see **4.14** above) at any time in the period beginning on the day the arrangement is made and ending on the last day of the payment period; the arrangement is a 'structured arrangement'; or, in the case of a quasi-payment, the payer is also a payee.

In (1) above, a '*hybrid transfer arrangement*' is a repo, stock lending arrangement or other arrangement which provides for, or relates to, the transfer of a financial instrument (the 'underlying instrument'). Either the arrangement must one which is regarded for tax purposes (including the purposes of a 'qualifying capital tax' — see below) as a transaction equivalent to the lending of money at interest in the hands of one of the parties but not the other (i.e. the arrangement provides for '*dual treatment*') or the arrangement must be one under which a 'substitute payment' could be made. A '*substitute payment*' is a payment or quasi-payment the amount or benefit of which is representative of a return on the underlying instrument but which is paid or given to a person other than the one to whom the return arises (for example a manufactured dividend). A transfer, for these purposes, includes an arrangement under which a financial instrument ceases to be owned by one person and another person comes to own another financial instrument with substantially the same rights and liabilities.

There is a '*hybrid transfer deduction/non-inclusion mismatch*' if the relevant deduction (see **4.14** above) exceeds the sum of the amounts of ordinary income arising from the payment or quasi-payment to each payee for a 'permitted' taxable period and all or part of the excess arises because of dual treatment or a substitute payment (whether or not it arises also for another reason). The amount of the mismatch is equal to that excess. An excess is taken to arise because of dual treatment or a substitute payment (so far as would not otherwise be the case) if it could arise on making certain assumptions about a payee: that the payee does not benefit from any tax exclusion, exemption or relief; that payments and quasi-payments are made in connection with a business carried on by the payee in the payee jurisdiction; and that, if the payee is not within the charge to tax anywhere, it is a company carrying on a business and within the charge to tax in the UK. If the last of these assumptions applies to a payee, the following provisions are disregarded in making that assumption: *CTA 2009, s 441* (LOAN RELATIONSHIPS (**50.34**) for unallowable purposes), the TRANSFER PRICING (**72**) provisions, the hybrid mismatch provisions generally, and the provisions in **25** CORPORATE INTEREST RESTRICTION.

There is also a '*hybrid transfer deduction/non-inclusion mismatch*' if there are one or more amounts of ordinary income (see **4.14** above) that arise from the payment or quasi-payment to a payee for a permitted taxable period which are under taxed because of dual treatment or a substitute payment (whether or not also for another reason).The amount of the mismatch is sum of the proportion of each under-taxed amount equal to the payee's full marginal rate less the highest rate at which tax is charged on taxable profits in which the under-taxed amount is charged (taking account of any credit for underlying tax), divided by the full marginal rate.

Where a hybrid transfer deduction/non-inclusion mismatch arises in both of the above circumstances, the amount of the mismatch is the sum of the amount for each.

A payee's taxable period is '*permitted*' for these purposes if it begins before the end of 12 months after the payment period ends or if it begins later and it is just and reasonable for the ordinary income to arise for that period rather than an earlier one.

Any excess or under-taxed amount is ignored for these purposes if it arises as a result of a payee being a relevant investment fund (see **4.14** above) or if, broadly, it arises because the payment or quasi-payment is a substitute payment and both the underlying return and the substitute payment are brought into account by a financial trader as trading income.

A 'qualifying capital amount' arising to a payee is treated for these purposes as an amount of ordinary income of a payee, and 'tax' includes any 'qualifying capital tax'. A qualifying capital amount arising to a payee for a permitted period is under taxed if the highest rate of tax charged on it (taking into account any credit for underlying tax) is less than the payee's full marginal rate (calculated by including the qualifying capital amount in the taxable profits). If the rate at which a qualifying capital tax is charged on a qualifying capital amount of a payee exceeds the rate which would be charged on an amount of income of the payee, the excess is ignored. A '*qualifying capital amount*' is a capital amount on which a qualifying capital tax is charged but, for this purpose, a qualifying capital tax is treated as not charged on an amount so far as it falls to be refunded or so far as the amount is excluded, reduced or offset by an exemption, relief or credit which applies specifically to the amount or arises as a result of, or in connection with, a payment or quasi-payment giving rise to the amount. A '*qualifying capital tax*' is capital gains tax, corporation tax on chargeable gains or an overseas equivalent, but does not include any tax chargeable at a nil rate.

In (5) above, a '*structured arrangement*' is one which it is reasonable to suppose is designed to secure a hybrid transfer deduction/non-inclusion mismatch (whether or not also designed to secure any other objective) or an arrangement the terms of which share the economic benefit of the mismatch between the parties or otherwise reflect the fact that the mismatch is expected to arise.

Counteraction

Where the payer is within the charge to corporation tax for the payment period, the relevant deduction is reduced by the amount of the mismatch.

If it is reasonable to suppose that the mismatch is not counteracted under the above provision or an equivalent non-UK provision, or that a non-UK provision applies but does not fully counteract the mismatch, the following applies to any payee who is within the charge to corporation tax for an accounting period some or all of which falls within the payment period.

If the payee is the only payee, the 'relevant amount' is treated as income for the accounting period coinciding with the payment period or, if there is no such accounting period, the first accounting period falling wholly or partly within the payment period. The income is chargeable to corporation tax as MISCELLANEOUS INCOME (**53.15**). If there is more than one payee, the relevant amount is divided between them. Each payee's share is determined on a just and reasonable basis with particular regard to any profit sharing arrangements between any of them, to whom any under-taxed amounts arise and to whom any ordinary income would have arisen if it would be reasonable to expect it to arise from the payment or quasi-payment.

The '*relevant amount*' is, where there is no counteraction applicable to the payer, the amount of the mismatch. Where a non-UK provision applies to the payer but does not fully counteract the mismatch, the relevant amount is the amount by which the mismatch exceeds the amount by which it is reasonable to suppose the relevant deduction is reduced by the non-UK provision (but not so as to reduce the relevant deduction below zero).

[*TIOPA 2010, ss 259D–259DG; F(No 2)A 2017, s 24(4), Sch 5 para 19; FA 2018, Sch 7 paras 9, 10, 19(4)*].

Hybrid and other mismatches from financial instruments

[4.16] The counteraction below applies where:

(1) a payment or quasi-payment (see **4.14** above) is made under or in connection with a financial instrument;
(2) either the payer is within the charge to corporation tax for the payment period or a payee is within the charge for an accounting period which falls wholly or partly within the payment period;
(3) it is reasonable to suppose that, in the absence of these provisions and those at **4.17–4.22** below or equivalent non-UK provisions, there would be a hybrid or otherwise impermissible deduction/non-inclusion mismatch in relation to the payment of quasi-payment; and
(4) either the payer and payee are related (see **4.14** above) at any time in the period beginning on the day any arrangement is made in connection with the financial instrument by the payer or a payee and ending on the last day of the payment period; the financial instrument or any arrangement connected with it is a 'structured arrangement'; or, in the case of a quasi-payment, the payer is also a payee.

There is a '*hybrid or otherwise impermissible deduction/non-inclusion mismatch*' if the relevant deduction (see **4.14** above) exceeds the sum of the amounts of ordinary income arising from the payment or quasi-payment to each payee for a 'permitted' taxable period and all or part of the excess arises by reason of the terms, or any other feature, of the financial instrument (whether or not it arises also for another reason). The amount of the mismatch is equal to that excess. An excess is taken to arise by reason of the terms or other feature of the financial instrument (so far as would not otherwise be the case) if it could arise on making certain assumptions about a payee: that the payee does not benefit from any tax exclusion, exemption or relief; that payments and quasi-payments are made in connection with a business carried on by the payee in the payee jurisdiction; and that, if the payee is not within the charge to tax anywhere, it is a company carrying on a business and within the charge to tax in the UK. If the last of these assumptions applies to a payee, the following provisions are disregarded in making that assumption: *CTA 2009, s 441* (LOAN RELATIONSHIPS (**50.34**) for unallowable purposes), *CTA 2009, s 690* (DERIVATIVE CONTRACTS (**27.19**) for unallowable purposes), the TRANSFER PRICING (**72**) provisions, the hybrid mismatch provisions generally, and the provisions in **25** CORPORATE INTEREST RESTRICTION. An excess is taken not to arise by reason of the terms or other feature of the financial instrument so far as it arises by reason of a debt relief provision or an 'interest distribution designation' or in 'relevant debt relief circumstances' (whether or not it would have arisen by reason of the terms or other feature of the financial instrument regardless). The following debt relief provisions are taken into account for this purpose: *CTA 2009, ss 322, 358, 359, s 357* (see **50.25**), *ss 361C, 361D*, and *s 362A*.

There is also a '*hybrid or otherwise impermissible deduction/non-inclusion mismatch*' if there are one or more amounts of ordinary income (see **4.14** above) that arise from the payment or quasi-payment to a payee for a permitted taxable period which are under taxed because of the terms, or another feature, of the financial instrument (whether or not also for another reason).The amount of the mismatch is the sum of the proportion of each under-taxed amount equal to the payee's full marginal rate less the highest rate at which tax is charged on taxable profits in which the under-taxed amount is charged (taking account of any credit for underlying tax), divided by the full marginal rate.

Where a hybrid or otherwise impermissible deduction/non-inclusion mismatch arises in both of the above circumstances, the amount of the mismatch is the sum of the amount for each.

Any excess or part of an excess, and any under-taxed amount is disregarded for these purposes if it arises as a result of a payee being a 'relevant investment fund (see **4.14** above).

A payee's taxable period is '*permitted*' for these purposes if it begins before the end of 12 months after the payment period ends or if it begins later and it is just and reasonable for the ordinary income to arise for that period rather than an earlier one.

In (4) above, a '*structured arrangement*' is one which it is reasonable to suppose is designed to secure a hybrid or otherwise impermissible deduction/non-inclusion mismatch (whether or not also designed to secure any other objective) or an arrangement the terms of which share the economic benefit of the mismatch between the parties or otherwise reflect the fact that the mismatch is expected to arise.

A 'qualifying capital amount' arising to a payee is treated for these purposes as an amount of ordinary income of a payee, and 'tax' includes any 'qualifying capital tax'. A qualifying capital amount arising to a payee for a permitted period is under taxed if the highest rate of tax charged on it (taking into account any credit for underlying tax) is less than the payee's full marginal rate (calculated by including the qualifying capital amount in the taxable profits). If the rate at which a qualifying capital tax is charged on a qualifying capital amount of a payee exceeds the rate which would be charged on an amount of income of the payee, the excess is ignored. A '*qualifying capital amount*' is a capital amount on which a qualifying capital tax is charged but, for this purpose, a qualifying capital tax is treated as not charged on an amount so far as it falls to be refunded or so far as the amount is excluded, reduced or offset by an exemption, relief or credit which applies specifically to the amount or arises as a result of, or in connection with, a payment or quasi-payment giving rise to the amount. A 'qualifying capital tax' is capital gains tax, corporation tax on chargeable gains or an overseas equivalent, but does not include any tax chargeable at a nil rate.

An '*interest distribution designation*' is a designation under the *SI 2009 No 2034, Reg 5(2)* (see **47.10** INVESTMENT TRUSTS).

Excess arises in '*relevant debt relief circumstances*' if the payment or quasi-payment comprises the release of a liability to pay an amount under a debtor relationship and any of the following applies:

(i) an amortised cost basis of accounting is used for the debtor relationship and:
- the release is part of a statutory insolvency arrangement (see **76.5** WINDING UP); or
- the release is not a release of 'relevant rights' (ie rights within **50.25**(ii) LOAN RELATIONSHIPS) but is in consideration of shares (or an entitlement to shares) forming part of the ordinary share capital of a payee; or
- where the debtor company is in one of the forms of insolvency procedure noted at **50.25**(a) LOAN RELATIONSHIPS, the debtor relationship is not a 'connected companies relationship' (see **50.23**); or
- the release occurs as a result of the making of a mandatory reduction instrument or a third country instrument or the application of any of the stabilisation powers contained in the *Banking Act 2009, Pt 1*; or
- the release is neither a deemed release (within **50.25**(i) LOAN RELATIONSHIPS) nor a release of relevant rights (within **50.25**(ii)) and immediately before the release it is reasonable to assume that, without the release and any arrangements of which the release forms part, there would be a material risk that at some time in the next 12 months, a payee would be unable to pay its debts. A company is regarded as being unable to pay its debts if it is unable to pay its debts as they fall due or the value of its assets is less than the amount of its liabilities, taking into account its contingent and prospective liabilities;

(ii) an amortised cost basis of accounting is used for the debtor relationship and the relationship is a connected companies relationship and the release is neither a deemed release nor a release of relevant rights;

(iii) an amortised cost basis of accounting is used for the debtor relationship, the payer is in one of the forms of insolvency procedure noted at **50.25**(a) LOAN RELATIONSHIPS and the relationship between the parties immediately before but not immediately after the payer enters into the insolvency procedure, is a connected companies relationship; or

(iv) the release takes place within 60 days of the payer and payee becoming connected, the payers' acquisition of its rights under the loan relationship is an arm's length transaction and, immediately before the payer became a party to the relationship, it is reasonable to assume that, without the release and any arrangements of which the release forms part, there would be a material risk that at some time in the next 12 months, the payee would be unable to pay its debts.

Counteraction

Where the payer is within the charge to corporation tax for the payment period, the relevant deduction is reduced by the amount of the mismatch.

If it is reasonable to suppose that the mismatch is not counteracted under the above provision or an equivalent non-UK provision, or that a non-UK provision applies but does not fully counteract the mismatch, the following applies to any payee who is within the charge to corporation tax for an accounting period some or all of which falls within the payment period.

If the payee is the only payee, the 'relevant amount' is treated as income for the accounting period coinciding with the payment period or, if there is no such accounting period, the first accounting period falling wholly or partly within the payment period. The income is chargeable to corporation tax as MISCELLANEOUS INCOME (**53.15**). If there is more than one payee, the relevant amount is divided between them. Each payee's share is determined on a just and reasonable basis with particular regard to any profit sharing arrangements between any of them, to whom any under-taxed amounts arise and to whom any ordinary income would have arisen if it would be reasonable to expect it to arise from the payment or quasi-payment.

The '*relevant amount*' is, where there is no counteraction applicable to the payer, the amount of the mismatch. Where a non-UK provision applies to the payer but does not fully counteract the mismatch, the relevant amount is the amount by which the mismatch exceeds the amount by which it is reasonable to suppose the relevant deduction is reduced by the non-UK provision (but not so as to reduce the relevant deduction below zero).

[*TIOPA 2010, ss 259C–259CE; F(No 2)A 2017, s 24(3), Sch 5, para 18; FA 2018, Sch 7, paras 8, 19(4); FA 2021, Sch 7, paras 2–8, 36*].

Hybrid payer deduction/non-inclusion mismatches

[4.17] The counteraction below applies where:

(1) a payment or quasi-payment (see **4.14** above) is made under or in connection with an arrangement;
(2) the payer is a hybrid entity (the '*hybrid payer*');
(3) either the hybrid payer is within the charge to corporation tax for the payment period or a payee is within the charge for an accounting period which falls wholly or partly within the payment period (see **4.14** above);
(4) it is reasonable to suppose that, in the absence of these provisions and those at **4.18–4.22** below or equivalent non-UK provisions, there would be a hybrid payer deduction/non-inclusion mismatch in relation to the payment of quasi-payment; and

(5) either the hybrid payer and payee are in the same control group (see **4.14** above) at any time in the period beginning on the day the arrangement is made and ending on the last day of the payment period; the arrangement is a 'structured arrangement'; or, in the case of a quasi-payment, the hybrid payer is also a payee.

There is a '*hybrid payer deduction/non-inclusion mismatch*' if the relevant deduction (see **4.14** above) exceeds the sum of the amounts of ordinary income arising from the payment or quasi-payment to each payee for a 'permitted' taxable period and all or part of the excess arises by reason of the hybrid payer being a hybrid entity (whether or not it arises also for another reason). The amount of the mismatch is equal to that excess. An excess is taken to arise by reason of the hybrid payer being a hybrid entity (so far as would not otherwise be the case) if it could arise on making certain assumptions about a payee: that the payee does not benefit from any tax exclusion, exemption or relief; and that payments and quasi-payments are made in connection with a business carried on by the payee in the payee jurisdiction. There is, however, no hybrid payer deduction/non-inclusion mismatch to the extent that the relevant deduction is a debit for amortisation under the intangible assets regime (see **42.5** INTANGIBLE ASSETS) or under equivalent foreign provisions.

No excess is taken to arise so far as it is attributable to a qualifying institutional investor based in a territory in which the income or profits of the hybrid entity are treated as income and profits of the investor or the hybrid entity is not regarded as a distinct and separate person to the investor. For this purpose, excess is attributable to a qualifying institutional investor based in a territory to the extent that ordinary income arising from the payment or quasi-payment would be brought into account by it if the income or profits of the hybrid entity were not treated as income and profits of the investor in that territory or the hybrid entity was regarded as a distinct and separate person to the investor in that territory. This rule applies to payments made on or after 10 June 2021 and to quasi-payments for which the payment period begins before that date, subject to the transitional rules below. Note, however, that a retrospection election cannot be made in respect of this change.

A payee's taxable period is '*permitted*' for these purposes if it begins before the end of 12 months after the payment period ends or if it begins later and a claim has been made for it to be permitted. Such a claim can only be made if it is just and reasonable for the ordinary income to arise for that period rather than an earlier one.

In (5) above, a '*structured arrangement*' is one which it is reasonable to suppose is designed to secure a hybrid payer deduction/non-inclusion mismatch (whether or not also designed to secure any other objective) or an arrangement the terms of which share the economic benefit of the mismatch between the parties or otherwise reflect the fact that the mismatch is expected to arise.

Counteraction

Where the hybrid payer is within the charge to corporation tax for the payment period, the relevant deduction so far as it does not exceed the mismatch (the '*restricted deduction*') may not be deducted from the hybrid payer's income for the payment period unless it is deducted from 'dual inclusion income' for that period. Any amount of the restricted deduction which cannot be deducted for the payment period is carried forward for deduction against future dual inclusion income.

'*Dual inclusion income*' for an accounting period is income which is both ordinary income of the payer for that period for corporation tax purposes and ordinary income of an investor in the payer for a 'permitted' taxable period for the purposes of any tax of an investor jurisdiction. For payments made before 10 June 2021 and for quasi-payments for which the payment period begins before that date (see further below), only income arising in connection with the arrangement is included in dual inclusion income. For later payments and quasi-payments, amounts are also included in the ordinary income of an investor in the payer if they are not deductible in computing the taxable profits of any person in any territory for a 'relevant taxable period' (and would not be so deductible in computing the taxable profits of a person 'resident' in a territory in which they are outside the charge to tax or chargeable to tax at a nil rate if that person were UK-resident). It is an additional requirement that the non-deductibility of the amount would not have arisen but for the investor jurisdiction classifying the hybrid entity as transparent. A taxable period is 'relevant' for this purpose, if it begins before the end of 12 months after the accounting period ends or if it begins later and it is just and reasonable for the deductibility of the amount to be determined by reference to that period rather than an earlier one. A person is treated as 'resident' in a territory which has no concept of residence for tax purposes if they are resident there under the general law of the territory.

A payer's taxable period is '*permitted*' for these purposes if it begins before the end of 12 months after the accounting period ends or if it begins later and a claim has been made for it to be permitted. Such a claim can only be made if it is just and reasonable for the ordinary income to arise for that period rather than an earlier one.

If it is reasonable to suppose that the mismatch is not counteracted under a non-UK provision equivalent to the above provision, or that a non-UK provision applies but does not fully counteract the mismatch, the following applies to any payee who is within the charge to corporation tax for an accounting period some or all of which falls within the payment period.

If the payee is the only payee, the 'relevant amount' less any 'dual inclusion income' (see below) is treated as income for the accounting period coinciding with the payment period or, if there is no such accounting period, the first accounting period falling wholly or partly within the payment period. The income is chargeable to corporation tax as MISCELLANEOUS INCOME (**53.15**). If there is more than one payee, the relevant amount is divided between them and a proportion of any dual inclusion income is deducted from that share. Each payee's share is determined on a just and reasonable basis with particular regard to any profit sharing arrangements between any of them and to whom any ordinary income would have arisen if it would be reasonable to expect it to arise from the payment or quasi-payment. Any dual inclusion income is apportioned in the same way.

'*Dual inclusion income*' is income which is both ordinary income of the payer for the payment period and ordinary income of an investor in the payer for a 'permitted' taxable period for the purposes of any tax of an investor jurisdiction. For payments made before 10 June 2021 and for quasi-payments for which the payment period begins before that date, only income arising in connection with the arrangement is included in dual inclusion income.

A payer's taxable period is '*permitted*' for these purposes if it begins before the end of 12 months after the payment period ends or if it begins later and a claim has been made for it to be permitted. Such a claim can only be made if it is just and reasonable for the ordinary income to arise for that period rather than an earlier one.

The '*relevant amount*' is, where there is no counteraction applicable to the payer, the amount of the mismatch. Where a non-UK provision applies to the payer but does not fully counteract the mismatch, the relevant amount is the amount by which the mismatch exceeds the amount of the relevant deduction which it is reasonable to suppose is prevented from being deducted for the payment period from income of the payer other than dual inclusion income by the non-UK provision (but not so as to reduce the relevant deduction that may still be deducted below zero).

For the purposes of the changes to the above provisions applying by reference to payment periods beginning on or after 10 June 2021, payment periods straddling that date are treated as two separate periods, the second of which starts on that date. Any necessary apportionments must be made on a time basis or, if a time basis would produce a result that is not just or reasonable, on a just and reasonable basis. Alternatively, a retrospection election can be made on or before 31 December 2021 to treat the changes as having had effect from the inception of the hybrid mismatch provisions. See **4.13** above.

[*TIOPA 2010, ss 259B(5), 259E–259ED; F(No 2)A 2017, s 24(5); FA 2021, Sch 7, paras 10, 27, 37–39*].

Deduction/non-inclusion mismatches relating to transfers by permanent establishments

[4.18] The counteraction below applies where:

(1) a company is a '*multinational company*', i.e. it is resident in a territory outside the UK (the '*parent jurisdiction*') for tax purposes and is also within the charge to corporation tax because it carries on a business in the UK through a permanent establishment there;

(2) disregarding these provisions and those at **4.19–4.22** below or equivalent non-UK provisions, there is an amount (the '*PE deduction*') that may (in substance) be deducted from the company's income in calculating its taxable profits for an accounting period (the '*relevant PE period*') for corporation tax purposes, that is in respect of a transfer of money or money's worth from the company in the UK to the company in the parent jurisdiction that is actually made or is (in substance) treated as being made for corporation tax purposes and is not in respect of the financing cost of loan capital which the permanent establishment is assumed to have under *CTA 2009, s 21* (see **64.6** RESIDENCE); and

(3) it is reasonable to suppose that, disregarding these provisions and those at **4.19–4.22** below or equivalent non-UK provisions, either the circumstances giving rise to the PE deduction will not result in an increase in the taxable profits of, or a reduction of a loss made by, the company for a 'permitted' taxable period for the purposes of a parent jurisdiction tax or those circumstances will result in such an increase or reduction for one or more permitted taxable periods, but the PE deduction exceeds the aggregate effect on taxable profits of any such increases and reductions. For relevant PE periods beginning on or after 1 January 2018, any increase in taxable profits or reduction of losses is ignored for this purpose where tax is charged at a nil rate under the law of the parent jurisdiction.

In (3) above, periods which straddle 1 January 2018 are treated as two separate taxable periods, the second of which starts on that date. Any necessary apportionments must be made on a time basis or, if a time basis would not give a just and reasonable result, on a just and reasonable basis. The PE deduction in (2) above does not include a debit for amortisation under the intangible assets regime (see **42.5** INTANGIBLE ASSETS) or under equivalent foreign provisions.

In (3) above, a company's taxable period is '*permitted*' for these purposes if it begins before the end of 12 months after the relevant PE period ends or if it begins later and a claim has been made for it to be permitted. Such a claim can only be made if it is just and reasonable for the circumstances giving rise to the PE deduction to affect the profits or loss made for that period rather than an earlier one.

Counteraction

The 'excessive PE deduction' may not be deducted from the company's income for the period unless it is deducted from 'dual inclusion income' for the period. Any amount of the excessive deduction which cannot be deducted for the relevant PE period is carried forward for deduction against future dual inclusion income. The '*excessive PE deduction*' is so much of the PE deduction as exceeds the aggregate effect on taxable profits within (3) above. '*Dual inclusion income*' for an accounting period is income which is both ordinary income of the company for that period for corporation tax purposes and ordinary income of the company for a 'permitted' taxable period for the purposes of any tax of the parent jurisdiction.

In relation to excessive deductions for which the payment period begins on or after 10 June 2021 (see further below), ordinary income of the company for a permitted taxable period is taken to include any 'excessive PE inclusion income' of the company. '*PE inclusion income*' means an amount meeting the following conditions:

(a) the amount is in respect of a transfer of money or money's worth from the company in the parent jurisdiction to the company in the UK that is actually made or (in substance) is treated as made for corporation tax purposes; and
(b) it is reasonable to suppose that either: (i) the circumstances giving rise to the amount will not reduce the taxable profits, or increase a loss, of the company for a 'relevant taxable period' for the purposes of a tax in the

parent jurisdiction; or (ii) that those circumstances will result in such a reduction or increase for one or more relevant taxable periods but the amount exceeds the aggregate effect on taxable profits of such reductions and increases.

'*Excessive PE inclusion income*' means, where (b)(i) above applies, all of the company's PE inclusion income. Where (b)(ii) above applies, it means the PE inclusion income to the extent that it is reasonable to suppose that it exceeds the aggregate effect of the reductions in taxable profits and increases in losses. Any increase in taxable profits or reduction of losses is ignored for this purpose where tax is charged at a nil rate under the law of the parent jurisdiction. A taxable period is 'relevant' for this purpose, if it begins before the end of 12 months after the accounting period ends or if it begins later and it is just and reasonable for any reduction in profits or increase in a loss to be determined by reference to that period rather than an earlier one.

A company's taxable period is '*permitted*' for these purposes if it begins before the end of 12 months after the accounting period ends or if it begins later and a claim has been made for it to be permitted. Such a claim can only be made if it is just and reasonable for the amount of ordinary income to arise for that period rather than an earlier one.

For the purposes of the change to the above provisions applying by reference to payment periods beginning on or after 10 June 2021, payment periods straddling that date are treated as two separate periods, the second of which starts on that date. Any necessary apportionments must be made on a time basis or, if a time basis would produce a result that is not just or reasonable, on a just and reasonable basis. Alternatively, a retrospection election can be made on or before 31 December 2021 to treat the changes as having had effect from the inception of the hybrid mismatch provisions. See **4.13** above.

[*TIOPA 2010, ss 259F–259FC; F(No 2)A 2017, s 24(6); FA 2018, Sch 7, paras 4, 19; FA 2021, Sch 7, paras 11, 17, 36–39*].

Hybrid payee deduction/non-inclusion mismatches

[4.19] The counteraction below applies where:

(1) a payment or quasi-payment (see **4.14** above) is made under or in connection with an arrangement;
(2) a payee is a hybrid entity (a '*hybrid payee*');
(3) either the payer is within the charge to corporation tax for the payment period, an investor in a hybrid payee is within the charge for an accounting period which falls wholly or partly within the payment period, or a hybrid payee is a limited liability partnership;
(4) it is reasonable to suppose that, in the absence of these provisions and those at **4.20–4.22** below or equivalent non-UK provisions, there would be a hybrid payee deduction/non-inclusion mismatch in relation to the payment of quasi-payment; and
(5) either the payer and a hybrid payee are in the same control group (see **4.14** above) at any time in the period beginning on the day the arrangement is made and ending on the last day of the payment period; the arrangement is a 'structured arrangement'; or, in the case of a quasi-payment, the payer is also a hybrid payee.

There is a '*hybrid payee deduction/non-inclusion mismatch*' if the relevant deduction (see **4.14** above) exceeds the sum of the amounts of ordinary income arising from the payment or quasi-payment to each payee for a 'permitted' taxable period and all or part of the excess arises by reason of one or more payees being a hybrid entity (whether or not it arises also for another reason). The amount of the mismatch is equal to that excess. There is, however, no hybrid payee deduction/non-inclusion mismatch to the extent that the relevant deduction is a debit for amortisation under the intangible assets regime (see **42.5** INTANGIBLE ASSETS) or under equivalent foreign provisions. A 'relevant amount' of an excess is taken to arise by reason of one or more payees being a hybrid entity (so far as would not otherwise be the case) if a payee is a hybrid entity, there is no territory in which that payee is resident for purposes of a tax charged under the law of the territory at a higher rate than nil or is chargeable to tax on ordinary income arising by reason of the payment or quasi-payment by virtue of having a permanent establishment there, and that payee is not a CFC for UK or foreign tax purposes. The '*relevant amount*' is equal to the excess or, if less, the amount of ordinary income it is reasonable to suppose would, by reason of the payment or quasi-payment, arise to the payee if it were a company and the payment or quasi-payment were made in connection with a business carried on by it in the UK through a permanent establishment there. If the payee is a partnership, it must be supposed that no amount of ordinary income arises to the payee by reason of the payment or quasi-payment if one of the partners is entitled to the amount and, having regard only to the law of the territory in which the partnership is established and the law of the territory where the partner is resident for tax purposes (or, if not so resident anywhere, where the partner is established), the payee would not be regarded as a hybrid entity. For payments before 1 January 2018, the reference above to there being no territory in which a payee is resident for purposes of a tax charged under the law of the territory at a higher rate than nil was simply a reference to there being no territory in which a payee is resident for tax purposes. This applied also to quasi-payments in relation to which the payment period began before that date (treating straddling periods for this purpose as two separate periods, the second of which started on that date). Any necessary apportionments must be made on a time basis or, if a time basis would not give a just and reasonable result, on a just and reasonable basis.

No excess is taken to arise so far as it is attributable to a qualifying institutional investor based in a territory in which the income or profits of the hybrid entity are treated as income and profits of the investor or the hybrid entity is not regarded as a distinct and separate person to the investor. For this purpose, excess is attributable to a qualifying institutional investor based in a territory to the extent that ordinary income arising from the payment or quasi-payment would be brought into account by it if the income or profits of the hybrid entity were not treated as income and profits of the investor in that territory or the hybrid entity was regarded as a distinct and separate person to the investor in that territory. This rule applies to payments made on or after 10 June 2021 and to quasi-payments for which the payment period begins before that date. Payment periods straddling 10 June 2021 are treated for this purpose as two separate periods, the second of which started on that date. Any necessary apportionments must be made on a time basis or, if a time basis would not give a just and reasonable result, on a just and reasonable basis.

A payee's taxable period is '*permitted*' for these purposes if it begins before the end of 12 months after the payment period ends or if it begins later and a claim has been made for it to be permitted. Such a claim can only be made if it is just and reasonable for the ordinary income to arise for that period rather than an earlier one.

In (5) above, a '*structured arrangement*' is one which it is reasonable to suppose is designed to secure a hybrid payee deduction/non-inclusion mismatch (whether or not also designed to secure any other objective) or an arrangement the terms of which share the economic benefit of the mismatch between the parties or otherwise reflect the fact that the mismatch is expected to arise.

Counteraction

Where the payer is within the charge to corporation tax for the payment period, the relevant deduction is reduced by the amount of the mismatch.

If it is reasonable to suppose that the mismatch is not counteracted under the above provision or an equivalent non-UK provision, or that a non-UK provision applies but does not fully counteract the mismatch, the following applies to any investor in a payee who is within the charge to corporation tax for an accounting period some or all of which falls within the payment period.

If the investor is the only investor in the payee, the 'appropriate proportion' of the 'relevant amount' is treated as income for the accounting period coinciding with the payment period or, if there is no such accounting period, the first accounting period falling wholly or partly within the payment period. The income is chargeable to corporation tax as MISCELLANEOUS INCOME (53.15). If there is more than one investor, the appropriate proportion of the relevant amount is divided between them. Each investor's share is determined on a just and reasonable basis with particular regard to any profit sharing arrangements between any of them.

The '*relevant amount*' is, where there is no counteraction applicable to the payer, the amount of the mismatch. Where a non-UK provision applies to the payer but does not fully counteract the mismatch, the relevant amount is the amount by which the mismatch exceeds the amount by which it is reasonable to suppose the relevant deduction is reduced by the non-UK provision (but not so as to reduce the relevant deduction below zero). The '*appropriate proportion*' of the relevant amount is, if the hybrid payee is the only hybrid payee, all of the relevant amount. If there is more than one investor, the relevant amount is divided between them. Each hybrid payer's share is determined on a just and reasonable basis with particular regard to any profit sharing arrangements between them and the extent to which it is reasonable to suppose that the mismatch arises by reason of each hybrid payee being a hybrid entity.

If it is reasonable to suppose that the mismatch is not counteracted under the either of the above provisions or an equivalent non-UK provision, or that any of those UK or non-UK provisions applies but does not fully counteract the mismatch, the following applies to any hybrid payee which is a limited liability partnership.

If the hybrid payee is the only hybrid payee, the 'relevant amount' is treated as income on the last day of the payment period. The income is chargeable to corporation tax as MISCELLANEOUS INCOME (**53.15**); the rule treating a trade carried on by a limited liability partnership as carried on by its members (see **49.14** PARTNERSHIPS) is disapplied for this purpose. If there is more than one hybrid payee, the relevant amount is divided between them. Each hybrid payee's share is determined on a just and reasonable basis with particular regard to any profit sharing arrangements between any of them and the extent to which it is reasonable to suppose the mismatch arises by reason of each hybrid payee being a hybrid entity.

The '*relevant amount*' is, where there is no counteraction under either of the above provisions or an equivalent non-UK provision, the amount of the mismatch. Where one of those provisions applies but does not fully counteract the mismatch, the relevant amount is the amount by which the mismatch exceeds the amount by which it is reasonable to suppose the relevant deduction is reduced by the provision (but not so as to reduce the relevant deduction below zero).

[*TIOPA 2010, ss 259G–259GE; F(No 2)A 2017, s 24(7); FA 2018, Sch 7, paras 5, 11, 19; FA 2021, Sch 7, paras 28, 37, 38*].

Multinational payee deduction/non-inclusion mismatches

[4.20] The counteraction below applies where:

(1) a payment or quasi-payment (see **4.14** above) is made under or in connection with an arrangement;

(2) a payee is a '*multinational company*', i.e. it is resident in a territory (the '*parent jurisdiction*') for tax purposes and it is regarded as carrying on a business in another territory (the '*PE jurisdiction*') through a permanent establishment (whether it is so regarded under the law of the parent or PE jurisdiction or any other territory);

(3) either:
   (i) the payer is within the charge to corporation tax for the payment period; or
   (ii) the multinational company is UK resident for the payment period and is treated under the law of the parent jurisdiction as carrying on a business in the PE jurisdiction through a permanent establishment but is not so treated under the law of the PE jurisdiction;

(4) it is reasonable to suppose that, in the absence of these provisions and those at **4.21–4.22** below or equivalent non-UK provisions, there would be a multinational payee deduction/non-inclusion mismatch in relation to the payment of quasi-payment; and

(5) either the payer and multinational company are in the same control group (see **4.14** above) at any time in the period beginning on the day the arrangement is made and ending on the last day of the payment period; the arrangement is a 'structured arrangement'; or, in the case of a quasi-payment, the payer is also a payee.

For payments before 1 January 2020 and for quasi-payments in relation to which the payment period began before that date, the condition in (3) above was that the payer was within the charge to corporation tax for the payment period (and (3)(ii) above did not apply).

In (3) above, payment periods which straddle 1 January 2020 are treated as two separate taxable periods, the second of which starts on that date. Any necessary apportionments must be made on a time basis or, if a time basis would not give a just and reasonable result, on a just and reasonable basis.

There is a '*multinational payee deduction/non-inclusion mismatch*' if the relevant deduction (see **4.14** above) exceeds the sum of the amounts of ordinary income arising from the payment or quasi-payment to each payee for a 'permitted' taxable period and all or part of the excess arises by reason of one or more payees being multinational companies (whether or not it arises also for another reason). The amount of the mismatch is equal to that excess.

Where the law of a PE jurisdiction in relation to a payee that is a multinational company makes no provision for charging tax on any companies, so much of the excess as arises as a result is taken not to arise by reason of that payee being a multinational company. For payments made on or after 1 January 2018, or quasi-payments in relation to which the payment period begins on or after that date, if it would not otherwise be the case, the excess is taken to arise by reason of a payee being a multinational company so far as it would not arise on the assumption that the company is not regarded and the law of any territory as carrying on a business in the PE jurisdiction through a permanent establishment there and that, for tax purposes under the law of the parent jurisdiction, all amounts of ordinary income arising, by reason of the payment or quasi-payment, to the company are treated as arising in that jurisdiction and nowhere else. (Payment periods straddling 1 January 2018 are treated for this purpose as two separate periods, the second of which begins on that date. Any necessary apportionments between the two must be made on a time basis or, if that would produce an unjust or unreasonable result, a just and reasonable basis.)

There is, however, no multinational payee deduction/non-inclusion mismatch to the extent that the relevant deduction is a debit for amortisation under the intangible assets regime (see **42.5** INTANGIBLE ASSETS) or under equivalent foreign provisions.

In (2) above, for payments made on or after 1 January 2018, or quasi-payments in relation to which the payment period begins on or after that date, where a person is resident in a territory under the general law of that territory but the territory has no legal concept of residence for tax purposes, the person is nevertheless treated as resident in that territory for tax purposes. (Payment periods straddling 1 January 2018 are treated for this purpose as two separate periods, the second of which begins on that date. Any necessary apportionments between the two must be made on a time basis or, if that would produce an unjust or unreasonable result, a just and reasonable basis.)

A payee's taxable period is '*permitted*' for these purposes if it begins before the end of 12 months after the payment period ends or if it begins later and a claim has been made for it to be permitted. Such a claim can only be made if it is just and reasonable for the ordinary income to arise for that period rather than an earlier one.

In (5) above, a '*structured arrangement*' is one which it is reasonable to suppose is designed to secure a multinational payee deduction/non-inclusion mismatch (whether or not also designed to secure any other objective) or an arrangement the terms of which share the economic benefit of the mismatch between the parties or otherwise reflect the fact that the mismatch is expected to arise.

Counteraction

Where (3)(ii) above applies, the amount of the mismatch is treated as income of the multinational company arising in the UK (and nowhere else) for the payment period. In any other case, the relevant deduction is reduced by the amount of the mismatch.

[*TIOPA 2010, ss 259B(5), 259H–259HC; F(No 2)A 2017, s 24(8); FA 2018, Sch 7 paras 2, 12, 19; FA 2019, s 19(2)(3)(5)–(7)*].

Hybrid entity double deduction mismatches

[4.21] The counteraction below applies where:

(1) it is reasonable to suppose that, disregarding these provisions and those at **4.22** below or equivalent non-UK provisions, there is an amount (the '*hybrid entity double deduction amount*') that could be deducted from the income of a hybrid entity (see **4.14** above) in calculating its taxable profits for a taxable period (the '*hybrid entity deduction period*') and could also be deducted, under the law of an investor jurisdiction (see **4.14** above), from the income of an investor in calculating its taxable profits for a taxable period (the '*investor deduction period*');

(2) either the investor is within the charge to corporation tax for the investor deduction period or the hybrid entity is within the charge for the hybrid entity deduction period;

(3) either the hybrid entity and any investor in it are related (see **4.14** above) at any time in the hybrid entity deduction period or the investor deduction period or an arrangement, to which the hybrid entity or an investor in it is a party, is a 'structured arrangement'.

In (3) above, a '*structured arrangement*' is one which it is reasonable to suppose is designed to secure the hybrid entity double deduction amount (whether or not also designed to secure any other objective) or an arrangement the terms of which share the economic benefit of the amount being deductible by both the hybrid entity and the investors between the parties to the arrangement or otherwise reflect the fact that the amount is expected to arise.

Counteraction

Where the investor is within the charge to corporation tax for the investor deduction period, the hybrid entity double deduction amount may not be deducted from the investor's income for that period unless it is deducted from 'dual inclusion income' or, for accounting periods beginning before 10 June 2021 (see further below), 'section 259ID income' for that period. Any amount of the deduction amount which cannot be so deducted is carried forward for deduction against future dual inclusion income. If HMRC are satisfied that the investor will have no dual inclusion income for an accounting period after the investor deduction period (the '*relevant period*') nor any subsequent accounting period, so much of the deduction amount as has not been deducted from dual inclusion income in previous accounting periods may be deducted against the investor's total profits for the relevant period (see **1.7** INTRODUCTION) or, to the extent that those profits are insufficient, against total profits of subsequent accounting periods. earliest first.

If it is reasonable to suppose that all or part of the hybrid entity double deduction amount is (in substance) deducted for a taxable period under a non-UK provision from income of any person which is not dual inclusion income of the investor for an accounting period, in determining how much of the deduction amount may be deducted for the accounting period of the investor in which that taxable period ends and any subsequent accounting period, the amount deducted under the non-UK provision is treated as having been deducted under the above provisions for a previous accounting period of the investor.

'*Dual inclusion income*' for an accounting period is income which is both ordinary income of the investor for that period for corporation tax purposes and ordinary income of the hybrid entity for a 'permitted' taxable period for the purposes of any non-UK tax.

A hybrid entity's taxable period is '*permitted*' for these purposes if it begins before the end of 12 months after the accounting period of the investor ends or if it begins later and a claim has been made for it to be permitted. Such a claim can only be made if it is just and reasonable for the ordinary income to arise for that period rather than an earlier one.

If the hybrid entity is within the charge to corporation tax for the hybrid entity deduction period and it is reasonable to suppose that no provision equivalent to the above provisions applies in the investor jurisdiction or that such a provision applies but the hybrid entity double deduction amount exceeds the amount that cannot be deducted from income other than 'dual inclusion income' of the hybrid entity for that period (see below) under that provision, then the following applies to the hybrid entity if the secondary counteraction condition below is met.

The secondary counteraction condition is met if the hybrid entity and any investor in it are in the same control group (see **4.14** above) at any time in the hybrid entity deduction period or the investor deduction period or an arrangement, to which the hybrid entity or an investor in it is a party, is a structured arrangement.

The 'restricted deduction' may not be deducted from the hybrid entity's income for the hybrid entity deduction period unless it is deducted from dual inclusion income or 'section 259ID income' for that period. Any amount of the restricted deduction which cannot be so deducted is carried forward for deduction against future dual inclusion income. If HMRC are satisfied that the hybrid entity will have no dual inclusion income for an accounting period after the hybrid entity deduction period (the '*relevant period*') nor any subsequent accounting period, so much of the restricted deduction as has not been deducted from dual inclusion income in previous accounting periods may be deducted against the entity's total profits for the relevant period (see **1.7** INTRODUCTION) or, to the extent that those profits are insufficient, against total profits of subsequent accounting periods, earliest first.

If it is reasonable to suppose that all or part of the hybrid entity double deduction amount is (in substance) deducted for a taxable period under a non-UK provision from income of any person (other than, for accounting periods beginning on or after 10 June 2021, an investor in the hybrid entity) which is not dual inclusion income of the hybrid entity for an accounting period (see below), in determining how much of the restricted deduction may be deducted for the accounting period of the hybrid entity in which that taxable period ends and any subsequent accounting period, the amount deducted under the non-UK provision is treated as having been deducted under the above provisions for a previous accounting period of the hybrid entity. See below for the treatment of accounting periods straddling 10 June 2021 and note that a retrospection election cannot be made in respect of this change.

The '*restricted deduction*' is, where there is no counteraction applicable to the investor, the hybrid entity double deduction amount. Where a non-UK provision applies to the investor but the hybrid entity double deduction amount exceeds the amount that cannot be deducted from income other than dual inclusion income of the hybrid entity for the hybrid entity deduction period, the restricted deduction is the amount that it is reasonable to suppose is the excess.

'*Dual inclusion income*' for an accounting period is income which is both ordinary income of the hybrid entity for that period for corporation tax purposes and ordinary income of an investor in the hybrid entity for a 'permitted' taxable period for the purposes of any tax in an investor jurisdiction. An investor's taxable period is '*permitted*' for these purposes if it begins before the end of 12 months after the accounting period ends or if it begins later and a claim has been made for it to be permitted. Such a claim can only be made if it is just and reasonable for the ordinary income to arise for that period rather than an earlier one.

For accounting periods beginning on or after 10 June 2021 (see further below), amounts are also included in the ordinary income of an investor in the hybrid entity if they are not deductible in computing the taxable profits of any person in any territory for a 'relevant taxable period' (and would not be so deductible in computing the taxable profits of a person 'resident' in a territory in which they are outside the charge to tax or chargeable to tax at a nil rate if that person were UK-resident). It is an additional requirement that the non-deductibility of the amount would not have arisen but for the investor jurisdiction classifying the hybrid entity as transparent. A taxable period is 'relevant' for this purpose, if it begins before the end of 12 months after the accounting period ends or if it begins later and it is just and reasonable for the deductibility of the amount to be determined by reference to that period rather than an earlier one. A person is treated as 'resident' in a territory which has no concept of residence for tax purposes if they are resident there under the general law of the territory.

'*Section 259ID income*' arises where:

- the restricted deduction exceeds the dual inclusion income of the hybrid entity (if any) for the hybrid entity deduction period;

- the investor makes a payment to the hybrid entity in respect of which no amount is deductible from the investor's income under the law of the investor jurisdiction;
- as a result of the payment, ordinary income arises to the hybrid entity for the hybrid entity deduction period;
- the payment is made in direct consequence of another payment made to the investor by a person who is not related to the investor or the hybrid entity; and
- as a result of that other payment, ordinary income arises to the investor.

The amount of the section 259ID income is an amount of income of the hybrid entity equal to the lesser of the amount of the payment by the investor and the amount of the payment by the unrelated party.

For the purposes of the changes to the above provisions applying by reference to accounting periods beginning on or after 10 June 2021, accounting periods straddling that date are treated as two separate periods, the second of which starts on that date. Any necessary apportionments must be made on a time basis or, if a time basis would produce a result that is not just or reasonable, on a just and reasonable basis. Alternatively, except where noted, a retrospection election can be made on or before 31 December 2021 to treat the changes as having had effect from the inception of the hybrid mismatch provisions. See **4.13** above.

[*TIOPA 2010, ss 259B(5), 259I–259IC; FA 2018, Sch 7, paras 13, 14, 19(4); FA 2021, Sch 7, paras 12, 18, 37–39*].

Dual territory double deduction cases

[4.22] The counteraction below applies where:

(1) a company is a 'dual resident company' or a 'multinational company'; and

(2) it is reasonable to suppose that, disregarding these provisions and any equivalent non-UK provisions, there is an amount (the '*dual territory double deduction amount*') that could, by reason of the company being within (1) above, be deducted from the company's income for an accounting period (the '*deduction period*') for corporation tax purposes and could also be deducted from the company's income for the purposes of non-UK tax for a taxable period (the '*foreign deduction period*').

A company is a '*dual resident company*' if it is UK resident and is also within the charge to a tax under the law of a non-UK territory because either it derives its status as a company from that law, its place of management is in that territory or it is for some other reason treated as resident there for the purposes of that tax. A company is a '*multinational company*' if it is within the charge to tax in a territory in which it is not resident (the '*PE jurisdiction*') because it carries on a business there through a permanent establishment and either the PE jurisdiction is the UK or the territory in which the company is resident for tax purposes (the '*parent jurisdiction*') is the UK.

Counteraction

Where the dual territory double deduction arises by reason of the company being a dual resident company, the dual territory double deduction amount may not be deducted from the company's income for the deduction period unless it is deducted from 'dual inclusion income' for that period. Any amount of the deduction amount which cannot be so deducted is carried forward for deduction against future dual inclusion income. If HMRC are satisfied that the company has ceased to be a dual resident company, so much of the deduction amount as has not been deducted from dual inclusion income in previous accounting periods may be deducted against the company's total profits for the accounting period of cessation or, to the extent that those profits are insufficient, against total profits of subsequent accounting periods, earliest first.

If it is reasonable to suppose that all or part of the dual territory double deduction amount is (in substance) deducted for a taxable period under a non-UK provision from income of any person (other than, for accounting periods beginning on or after 10 June 2021, the company) which is not dual inclusion income of the company for an accounting period, in determining how much of the deduction amount may be deducted for the accounting period of the company in which that taxable period ends and any subsequent accounting period, the amount deducted under the non-UK provision is treated as having been deducted under the above provisions for a previous accounting period of the company. See below for the treatment of accounting periods straddling 10 June 2021 and note that a retrospection election cannot be made in respect of this change.

'*Dual inclusion income*' for an accounting period is income which is both ordinary income of the company for that period for corporation tax purposes and ordinary income of the company for a 'permitted' taxable period for the purposes of any non-UK tax. A company's taxable period is '*permitted*' for these purposes if it begins before the end of 12 months after the accounting period ends or if it begins later and a claim has been made for it to be permitted. Such a claim can only be made if it is just and reasonable for the ordinary income to arise for that period rather than an earlier one.

If the dual territory double deduction amount arises as a result of the company being a multinational company for which the UK is the parent jurisdiction, the following applies. If some or all of that amount is (in substance) deducted, for the purposes of a non-UK tax, from the income of any person, for any period, that is not 'dual inclusion income' of the company, the amount of the dual territory double deduction amount that may be deducted from the company's income for the deduction period is reduced by the amount so deducted for the purposes of the non-UK tax. Just and reasonable adjustments may be made to give effect to the reduction, whether by assessment, modification of an assessment, amendment or disallowance of a claim or otherwise and despite any time limit having expired.

'*Dual inclusion income*' is income which is both ordinary income of the company for an accounting period for corporation tax purposes and ordinary income of the company for a 'permitted' taxable period for the purposes of any non-UK tax. A company's taxable period is '*permitted*' for these purposes if it begins before the end of 12 months after the accounting period ends or if it begins later and a claim has been made for it to be permitted. Such a claim can only be made if it is just and reasonable for the ordinary income to arise for that period rather than an earlier one.

If the dual territory double deduction amount arises as a result of the company being a multinational company for which the UK is the PE jurisdiction and it is reasonable to suppose that no provision equivalent to the above provision for multinational companies applies in the parent jurisdiction, then the following applies to the company.

The dual territory double deduction amount may not be deducted from the company's income for the deduction period unless it is deducted from dual inclusion income for that period. Any part of that amount which cannot be so deducted is carried forward for deduction against future dual inclusion income. If HMRC are satisfied that the company has ceased to be a multinational company, so much of the dual territory double deduction amount as has not been deducted from dual inclusion income in previous accounting periods may be deducted against the company's total profits for the accounting period of cessation or, to the extent that those profits are insufficient, against total profits of subsequent accounting periods, earliest first.

If it is reasonable to suppose that all or part of the dual territory double deduction amount is (in substance) deducted for a taxable period under a non-UK provision from income of any person (other than, for accounting periods beginning on or after 10 June 2021, the company) which is not dual inclusion income of the company for an accounting period, in determining how much of the dual territory double deduction amount may be deducted for the accounting period of the company in which that taxable period ends and any subsequent accounting period, the amount deducted under the non-UK provision is treated as having been deducted under the above provisions for a previous accounting period of the company. See below for the treatment of accounting periods straddling 10 June 2021 and note that a retrospection election cannot be made in respect of this change.

'*Dual inclusion income*' for an accounting period is income which is both ordinary income of the company for that period for corporation tax purposes and ordinary income of the company for a 'permitted' taxable period for the purposes of any non-UK tax. A company's taxable period is '*permitted*' for these purposes if it begins before the end of 12 months after the accounting period ends or if it begins later and a claim has been made for it to be permitted. Such a claim can only be made if it is just and reasonable for the ordinary income to arise for that period rather than an earlier one.

For accounting periods beginning on or after 10 June 2021 (see further below), ordinary income of the company for a permitted taxable period for the purposes of a non-UK law is taken to include any 'excessive PE inclusion income' of the company. '*PE inclusion income*' means an amount meeting the following conditions:

(a) the amount is in respect of a transfer of money or money's worth from the company in the parent jurisdiction to the company in the UK that is actually made or (in substance) is treated as made for corporation tax purposes; and

(b) it is reasonable to suppose that either: (i) the circumstances giving rise to the amount will not reduce the taxable profits, or increase a loss, of the company for a 'relevant taxable period' for the purposes of a tax in the parent jurisdiction; or (ii) that those circumstances will result in such a reduction or increase for one or more relevant taxable periods but the amount exceeds the aggregate effect on taxable profits of such reductions and increases.

'*Excessive PE inclusion income*' means, where (b)(i) above applies, all of the company's PE inclusion income. Where (b)(ii) above applies, it means the PE inclusion income to the extent that it is reasonable to suppose that it exceeds the aggregate effect of the reductions in taxable profits and increases in losses. Any increase in taxable profits or reduction of losses is ignored for this purpose where tax is charged at a nil rate under the law of the parent jurisdiction. A taxable period is 'relevant' for this purpose, if it begins before the end of 12 months after the accounting period ends or if it begins later and it is just and reasonable for any reduction in profits or increase in a loss to be determined by reference to that period rather than an earlier one.

For the purposes of the changes to the above provisions applying by reference to accounting periods beginning on or after 10 June 2021, accounting periods straddling that date are treated as two separate periods, the second of which starts on that date. Any necessary apportionments must be made on a time basis or, if a time basis would produce a result that is not just or reasonable, on a just and reasonable basis. Alternatively, except where noted, a retrospection election can be made on or before 31 December 2021 to treat the changes as having had effect from the inception of the hybrid mismatch provisions. See **4.13** above.

[*TIOPA 2010, ss 259J–259JE; FA 2021, Sch 7, paras 13, 18, 37–39*].

Imported mismatches

[4.23] The counteraction below applies where:

(1) a payment or quasi-payment (see **4.14** above) is made, under or in connection with an arrangement (the '*imported mismatch arrangement*');
(2) the payer (P) of the payment or quasi-payment (the '*imported mismatch payment*') is within the charge to corporation tax for the payment period;
(3) the imported mismatch arrangement is one of a '*series of arrangements*' (i.e. a number of arrangements each of which is entered into (whether or not one after another) in pursuance of, or in relation to, an '*over-arching arrangement*');
(4) under an arrangement in the series other than the imported mismatch arrangement, either:
    (i) there is or will be an 'excessive PE deduction'; or
    (ii) there is a payment or quasi-payment (the '*mismatch payment*') in relation to which it is reasonable to suppose that there is or will be a mismatch within any of **4.15–4.17**, **4.19** or **4.20** or a double deduction within **4.21** or **4.22**;

(5) it is reasonable to suppose that the mismatch in (4) above is not capable of counteraction;

(6) (for payments made before 10 June 2021 and quasi-payments for which the payment period began before that date – see further below) one of the provisions at **4.15–4.22** above or any equivalent non-UK provision would apply to the tax treatment of P if P were the payer or a payee of the mismatch payment or (where the mismatch is a hybrid payee deduction/non-inclusion mismatch or a hybrid entity double deduction amount) if P were an investor in the hybrid entity, or if, in the case of an excessive PE deduction, the deduction arose in relation to P; and

(7) either P is in the same control group (see **4.14** above) as a payee (or, for payments made before 10 June 2021 and quasi-payments for which the payment period began before that date (see further below), the payer) in relation to the mismatch payment at any time in the period beginning on the day the over-arching arrangement is made and ending on the last day of the payment period for the imported mismatch payment; P is in the same control group as the company to whom the excessive PE deduction arises at any time in that period; or the imported mismatch arrangement or the over-arching arrangement is a 'structured arrangement'.

In (4) above, a '*PE deduction*' is an amount that may (in substance) be deducted from a company's income in calculating its taxable profits for a taxable period for the purposes of a tax under the law of a territory (the '*PE jurisdiction*') by virtue of the company having a permanent establishment there and which is in respect of a transfer of money or money's worth from the company in the PE jurisdiction to the company in another territory (the '*parent jurisdiction*') in which it is resident for tax purposes which is either actually made or (in substance) treated as made for tax purposes. A PE deduction does not include a debit for amortisation under the intangible assets regime (see **42.5** INTANGIBLE ASSETS) or under equivalent foreign provisions.

For payments made on or after 1 January 2018, or quasi-payments in relation to which the payment period begins on or after that date, where a person is resident in a territory under the general law of that territory but the territory has no legal concept of residence for tax purposes, the person is nevertheless treated as resident in that territory for tax purposes. (Payment periods straddling 1 January 2018 are treated for this purpose as two separate periods, the second of which begins on that date. Any necessary apportionments between the two must be made on a time basis or, if that would produce an unjust or unreasonable result, a just and reasonable basis.)

A PE deduction is '*excessive*' so far as it exceeds the sum of any increases in the taxable profits of the company and any reductions in losses made by the company as a result of the circumstances giving rise to the PE deduction, for the purposes of a parent jurisdiction tax for any 'permitted' taxable period. A company's taxable period is '*permitted*' for these purposes if it begins before the end of 12 months after the taxable period in which the PE deduction is made ends or if it begins later and a claim has been made for it to be permitted. Such a claim can only be made if it is just and reasonable for the circumstances giving rise to the PE deduction to affect the profits or loss for that period rather than an earlier one. For payments made on or after 1 January 2018, or quasi-payments in relation to which the payment period begins on or after that date, any increase in taxable profits or reduction of losses is ignored for this purpose where tax is charged at a nil rate under the law of the parent jurisdiction. (Payment periods straddling 1 January 2018 are treated for this purpose as two separate periods, the second of which begins on that date. Any necessary apportionments between the two must be made on a time basis or, if that would produce an unjust or unreasonable result, a just and reasonable basis.)

In (5) above, a mismatch is capable of counteraction to the extent that it is capable of being considered under the law of a territory which is OECD mismatch compliant for the purposes of determining the tax treatment of a person other than P. If only part of a mismatch is not capable of counteraction, the condition in (5) above is treated as met in relation to that part. The extent to which a mismatch is not capable of counteraction must be determined on a just and reasonable basis. A territory is OECD mismatch compliant if it has introduced provisions equivalent to the hybrid mismatch provisions to give effect to the BEPS Final Report on Neutralising the Effects of Hybrid Mismatch Arrangements.

For payments made before 10 June 2021 and quasi-payments for which the payment period began before that date (see further below), the condition in (5) above was that it was reasonable to suppose that none of the provisions at **4.15–4.22** above nor any equivalent non-UK provision applied, or would apply, in relation to the tax treatment of any person in respect of the mismatch payment or of the company to which the excessive PE deduction arose.

In (7) above, a '*structured arrangement*' is one which it is reasonable to suppose is designed to secure the mismatch in question (whether or not also designed to secure any other objective) or an arrangement the terms of which share the economic benefit of the mismatch between the parties to the arrangement or otherwise reflect the fact that the mismatch is expected to arise.

Counteraction

If, in addition to the imported mismatch payment, there are, or will be, one or more 'relevant payments' in relation to the mismatch in (4) above, the relevant deduction otherwise deductible from P's income for the payment period is reduced by P's share of that mismatch. P's share is determined by apportionment between P and every payer of a relevant payment on a just and reasonable basis (see further *TIOPA 2010, s 259KB(4)–(6)*). A payment or quasi-payment (other than the imported mismatch payment or any mismatch payment) is a '*relevant payment*' if it is made under any arrangement in the series of arrangements and it funds the mismatch payment. Where the mismatch is an excessive PE deduction and the transfer of money or money's worth referred to above is actually made, a relevant payment is a payment or quasi-payment that funds the transfer. If the transfer is only deemed to be made, a relevant payment is one that would have funded it had the transfer actually been made. For payments made on or after 10 June 2021 and quasi-payments for which the payment period begins on or after that date, if the deduction for the imported mismatch payment is reduced by a TRANSFER PRICING (72) adjustment, the mismatch in (4) above is taken to be the amount it would have been on an arm's length basis and P's share is determined accordingly.

If the above provisions do not apply, the relevant deduction otherwise deductible from P's income for the payment period is reduced by the amount of the mismatch in (4) above. For payments made on or after 10 June 2021 and quasi-payments for which the payment period begins on or after that date, if the deduction for the imported mismatch payment is reduced by a transfer pricing adjustment, the amount of the mismatch in (4) above is treated as reduced in the same proportion as the transfer pricing reduction.

In any court or tribunal proceedings, it is for P to show that there are any relevant payments to be taken into account.

If (4)(ii) above applies by virtue of a mismatch within any of **4.17**, **4.19** or **4.20** above or a double deduction within **4.21** or **4.22** or (4)(i) above applies, the reduction in the relevant deduction cannot exceed the appropriate net amount, i.e:

- any amount which could not have been deducted from a person's income in respect of a mismatch payment if counteraction under any of **4.17**, **4.19**, **4.20** or **4.21** above had applied directly (ignoring the effect of any provisions for the carry-forward of amounts);
- (where (4)(ii) above applies by virtue of **4.22** above) the amount by which the dual territory double deduction of the company for a period exceeds its dual inclusion income for that period; or
- (where (4)(i) above applies) the amount by which the excessive PE deduction of the company for the permitted taxable period exceeds its dual inclusion income for that period.

For payments made on or after 10 June 2021 and quasi-payments for which the payment period begins on or after that date, the reduction in the relevant deduction also cannot exceed the amount that the mismatch in (4) above would have been if the amount of the mismatch payment had been equal to the amount of the imported mismatch payment.

For the purposes of the changes above which apply by reference to 10 June 2021, payment periods straddling 10 June 2021 are treated as two separate periods, the second of which starts on that date. Any necessary apportionments must be made on a time basis or, if a time basis would produce a result that is not just or reasonable, on a just and reasonable basis.

[*TIOPA 2010, ss 259B(5), 259K–259KC; F(No 2)A 2017, s 24(9); FA 2018, Sch 7 paras 2, 6, 15–17, 19; FA 2021, Sch 7, paras 21–23, 33, 37, 38*].

Allocation of surplus dual inclusion income within a group

[4.24] There are provisions which enable companies in a group to allocate surplus 'dual inclusion income' to other group members so that it is treated as dual inclusion income of the members to which it is allocated. The provisions apply for accounting periods of claimant companies beginning on or after 1 January 2021. Accounting periods which straddle that date are treated for this purpose only as two separate accounting periods, the second of which begins on 1 January 2021. Any necessary apportionments to the two notional periods must be made on a time basis or, if a time basis would produce an unreasonable or unjust result, on a just and reasonable basis.

Two companies are members of the same group if one is a 75% subsidiary of the other or both are 75% subsidiaries of a third company. '75% subsidiary' has the same meaning as at **35.3** GROUP RELIEF. The provisions at **35.14** apply, with necessary modifications to deny allocation where there are arrangements for a company to leave the group.

Surplus dual inclusion income of one company (company A) can be treated as dual inclusion income of another company (company B) where:

- company A has a 'DII surplus' for an accounting period (the '*surplus period*') (ie its 'dual inclusion income' for the period exceeds its 'counteraction amount');
- company B has a 'DII shortfall' for an accounting period (the '*shortfall period*') (ie its counteraction amount for the period exceeds its dual inclusion income);
- there is an '*overlapping period*' common to both accounting periods;
- there is a time in the overlapping period when both companies are within the charge to corporation tax;
- there is a time in the overlapping period when both companies are members of the same group.

If, during a part of the overlapping period, either company is not within the charge to corporation tax or either company is not a member of the group, that part is treated as not forming part of the overlapping period.

'Dual inclusion income' means any amount that is dual inclusion income under any of the provisions at **4.17**, **4.18**, **4.21–4.23** above. Any amount which is included in dual inclusion income under more than one provision is only counted once. The 'counteraction amount' is the total of the following amounts:

- where **4.17** above applies, the restricted deduction, relevant amount or, where there is more than one payee, the payee's share of the relevant amount;
- where **4.18** above applies, the excessive PE deduction;
- where **4.21** above applies, the hybrid entity double deduction amount or restricted deduction;
- where **4.22** above applies, the dual territory double deduction amount, reduced by any impermissible overseas deduction;
- where **4.23** above applies, the dual territory double deduction or the excessive PE deduction.

Making a claim

Company B can make a claim for all or part of the 'unused part' of company A's DII surplus for an overlapping period to be allocated to it for the shortfall period if it has 'matchable income' for the period. '*Matchable income*' is the ordinary income for the shortfall period which is not dual inclusion income and is equal to or exceeds the amount of the DII surplus identified in the claim for allocation.

The maximum amount that can be allocated is the amount so identified, but this cannot exceed the unused part of company B's DII shortfall for the shortfall period.

Company A must consent to the claim.

Calculating the unused part of the DII surplus

The 'unused part' of company A's DII surplus for the overlapping period is equal to the DII surplus for the period less the amount of any prior allocations for the period.

The DII surplus for the overlapping period is a proportion of the DII surplus for the whole surplus period, calculated on a time basis. The amount of prior allocations for the overlapping period is calculated by taking the following steps.

(1) Identify any prior allocation claims. These are allocation claims made by a company in respect of company A's DII surplus for the surplus period which were made before the current claim (and which have not been withdrawn).

(2) Identify the overlapping period for each prior claim.

(3) For each prior claim, identify any period common to the overlapping period for the current claim and that for the prior claim. If there is no common period, there is no prior allocation for purposes of the current claim. If there is a common period, proceed to step 4.

(4) For each remaining prior claim, determine the previously allocated amount of the DII surplus. This is a proportion of the DII surplus allocated by the prior claim, calculated by reference to the proportion of the overlapping period for the prior claim that is included in the common period in step 3. The determination is made on the basis that an amount is allocated to an earlier claim before a later claim.

(5) The amount of prior allocations for the overlapping period for the current claim is the total of any amounts found in step 4.

If two or more claims are made at the same time, they are taken in the order that the companies making them elect. If no election is made, HMRC may choose in which order to take the claims. If any time basis apportionments would produce an unjust or unreasonable result, the proportion can be modified to produce a just and reasonable result.

Calculating the unused part of the DII surplus

The 'unused part' of company B's DII shortfall for the shortfall period is equal to the DII shortfall for the period less the amount of any prior matches for the period.

The amount of prior matches for the shortfall period is calculated as follows.

(i) Identify any prior allocation claims. These are allocation claims made by company B for the shortfall period which were made before the current claim (and which have not been withdrawn).

(ii) For each prior claim, determine the previously matched amount of the DII shortfall. This is the amount treated as dual inclusion income of company B as a result of the claim. The determination is made on the basis that an amount is matched to an earlier claim before a later claim.

(iii) The amount of prior matches for the shortfall period for the current claim is the total of any amounts found in (ii) above.

Effect of a claim

The amount of company A's dual inclusion income for the surplus period is reduced by the amount claimed and that amount is treated in the hands of company B as if anything done by or to company A in relation to the amount was done by or to company B and all other factual circumstances (or circumstances deemed to exist under the hybrid mismatch provisions) were unchanged.

Procedure

A claim under these provisions must be included in company B's tax return for the shortfall period, whether in the original return or by amendment. A claim can only be withdrawn by amendment of the return. A claim cannot be amended (but must instead be withdrawn and replaced by a new claim).

A claim can be made or withdrawn at any time up to the latest of:

- the first anniversary of the filing date for the return;
- 30 days after the completion of an enquiry into the return;
- 30 days after a notice of amendment to the return is issued by HMRC following the completion of an enquiry into the return;
- 30 days after the final determination of an appeal against such an amendment; and
- such later date as HMRC allow.

Enquiries which are restricted to amendments to the return consisting of making or withdrawing a claim under these provisions do not count as enquires in determining the time limit.

Company A must consent to the claim by notice in writing to HMRC at or before the time the claim is made by company B. A copy of the notice must accompany company B's claim. The notice must include the names of the companies, the amount of the DII surplus to be allocated to company B and the accounting period of company A which is the surplus period. A notice may not be amended but may be withdrawn (by notice) and replaced by a new notice. A withdrawal notice is ineffective unless accompanied by notice of company B's consent to the withdrawal. If company A's consent is withdrawn company B must (so far as it can) amend its return accordingly.

If company A gives notice of consent after filing its tax return for the relevant accounting period, it must amend its return to take account of the consent. It is not prevented from doing so by the normal time limits for amending returns.

If, after company A has given one or more notices of consent, the unused part of its DII surplus is reduced to an amount less than that stated in the notices, it must, within 30 days, withdraw so many of the notices as are required to bring the total claims down to the revised unused part. Company A can then give new notices of consent if needed to make full use of the revised unused part. The company must give notice in writing of the withdrawal of consent, and send a copy of any new notice of consent, to each affected company and to HMRC. If company A fails to act, HMRC may gave a direction as they think fit as to which notice or notices are to be ineffective or reduced (but only to reduce the total amount stated in the consent notices to the revised unused part of company A's DII surplus). HMRC must notify the affected companies accordingly. Company A may appeal against HMRC's directions by notice in writing within 30 days after the notice containing the directions was issued. Any company affected by withdrawal of a consent notice, the issue of a new consent notice or by an HMRC direction must, so far as it can, amend the affected tax return. If a company (company C) becomes liable to tax as a result and any of it remains unpaid six months after company C's time limit for allocation claims, HMRC may assess the tax on any other company that has benefited as a result of the consents given by company A. The amount assessed is restricted to the amount of tax that other company has saved as a result of the consents. That other company may recover the tax from company C, together with any interest on overdue tax it has paid. An assessment must be made not more than two years after the expiry of company C's time limit for allocation claims.

If an HMRC officer discovers that any amount which is the subject of a claim is or has become excessive, the officer may make an assessment in the amount which, in the officer's opinion, ought to be charged. This power is without prejudice to the normal discovery assessment powers at **6.3** ASSESSMENTS and the making of any necessary adjustments by way of discharge or repayment. If an assessment is made because a company affected by the withdrawal of a consent notice, the issue of a new consent notice or an HMRC direction following a reduction in company A's unused DII surplus fails, or is unable to, amend its tax return, the assessment is not out of time if is made within one year from the date company A sent the company the notice of withdrawal or new consent notice or the date HMRC sent the company a copy of the notice containing their directions.

The Treasury may, by statutory instrument, provide for simplifying the procedure for making, and consenting to, claims. It is likely that these will be on the same lines as the simplified arrangements for GROUP RELIEF (**35.12**).

[*FA 1998, Sch, 18 paras 77B–77L; TIOPA 2010, ss 259ZM–259ZMF, 259ZME; FA 2021, Sch 7, paras 15, 16, 40*].

Adjustments for subsequent events

[4.25] Where a reasonable supposition has been made for the purposes of the hybrid mismatch rules and it subsequently turns out to be mistaken or otherwise stops being reasonable, any just and reasonable adjustments may be made by assessment, modification of an assessment, amendment or disallowance of a claim or otherwise. Normal time limits for the making of assessments etc. apply.

An adjustment under the above provision cannot be made on the basis that ordinary income arises after the last permitted taxable period. Instead the following provision applies where:

(1) a relevant deduction is reduced under any of **4.16**, **4.17**, **4.19** or **4.20** above or more than one of them;
(2) no other hybrid mismatch rule, nor any equivalent non-UK provision, applies or will apply to the tax treatment of any person in respect of the payment or quasi-payment;

(3) the rule or rules in (1) above applied because it was reasonable to suppose that the relevant deduction exceeded, or would exceed, the sum or the amounts of ordinary income arising from the payment or quasi-payment to each payee for a permitted taxable period (defined as in **4.16**, **4.17**, **4.19** or **4.20** above or, where more than one rule applies, any permitted taxable period under the rules in question); and

(4) an amount of ordinary income arises by reason of the payment or quasi-payment to a payee for a taxable period that is not a permitted taxable period (and does not arise as a result of any of the hybrid mismatch provisions or any equivalent non-UK provision).

Where these conditions are met, an amount equal to the late ordinary income may be deducted in calculating the payer's taxable total profits for the accounting period in which the taxable period of the payee in which the ordinary income arises ends. If the amount otherwise deductible exceeds the taxable total profits the excess may be carried forward for deduction in subsequent accounting periods, earliest first. The total deduction may not exceed the amount by which the relevant deduction is reduced (as in (1) above).

Where a payment or quasi-payment gives rise to a debit of a company which is recognised for accounting purposes and a relevant deduction of the company in respect of all or part of the debit is reduced under the hybrid mismatch rules, then if there is a reversal of all or part of the debit by a credit recognised for accounting purposes after the end of the accounting period and the credit is brought into account for corporation tax purposes, the amount of the reduction in the deduction in respect of the debit must be adjusted. The adjustment must be made on a just and reasonable basis and may be made by assessment, modification of an assessment, amendment or disallowance of a claim or otherwise. An adjustment can be made regardless of any normal time limits.

[*TIOPA 2010, ss 259L–259LB; FA 2018, Sch 7 paras 18, 19(4)*].

Change in ownership of a shell company

[4.26] Anti-avoidance provisions apply to restrict the carry forward of non-trading loan relationship debits and deficits and non-trading losses on intangible assets after a change of ownership of a '*shell company*', i.e. a company that is not carrying on a trade or UK property business and is not a company with investment business. See **51.17** LOSSES for the circumstances in which there is a change in ownership for these purposes.

Apportionment between accounting periods

For the purposes of the provisions only, the accounting period in which the change occurs is treated as two separate accounting periods, the first ending with the change and the second consisting of the remainder of the period.

The amounts listed below are then apportioned as specified below between those periods. The amounts are:

(A) any adjusted non-trading loan relationship profits for the accounting period being divided (as defined);

(B) any adjusted non-trading loan relationship deficit for that period (as defined);
(C) any non-trading debit falling to be brought into account for that period in respect of any debtor relationship;
(D) any non-trading loan relationship deficit carried forward to that period;
(E) any non-trading intangible fixed assets credits or debits for that period (other than any amount within (F) below);
(F) any non-trading loss on intangible fixed assets carried forward to that period;
(G) any other amounts by reference to which the profits or losses of that period would (apart from these provisions) be calculated.

The basis of apportionment of amounts within (A)–(G) above is as follows.

- Amounts within (A), (B) and (G) above are apportioned on a time basis.
- Amounts within (C) above, where an amortised cost basis applies, are apportioned by reference to the time of accrual of the amount to which the debit relates *except* in the case of certain late interest payments where interest is brought into account when paid, or where an adjustment is required under *CTA 2009, ss 407, 409* (certain debits relating to discounted securities to be brought into account on redemption), where the debit is apportioned to the pre-change part of the period in full.
- Amounts within (D) and (F) above are apportioned to the pre-change part of the period in full.
- Amounts within (E) above are apportioned in accordance with generally accepted accountancy principles as if accounts were drawn up for each part of the period.

If in any case such apportionment would work unreasonably or unjustly, a just and reasonable method of apportionment may be substituted.

Restrictions applicable

The following restrictions apply to the various debits and expenses identified:

(i) **Loan relationship debits.** 'Relevant non-trading debits' may not be carried forward beyond the change of ownership date to the extent to which the aggregate of those debits (including any amounts brought into account for any previous period ending after the change in ownership) exceed the total taxable profits for the notional accounting period ending with the change in ownership.

'*Relevant non-trading debits*' are non-trading debits which are determined on an amortised cost basis of accounting (see **50.1** LOAN RELATIONSHIPS) to which one of the following applies:

(I) *CTA 2009, ss 407 or 409* (postponement until redemption of debits for connected or close companies' deeply discounted securities) applies and, were it not for those sections, the debit would have been brought into account for an accounting period ending before or with the change in ownership;

(II) *CTA 2009, s 373* (late interest not treated as accruing until paid — see **50.11** LOAN RELATIONSHIPS) applies and, were it not for that section, the debit would have been brought into account for an accounting period ending before or with the change in ownership; or

(III) the debit is not within (I) or (II) above but is in respect of a debtor relationship and relates to an amount which accrued before the change in ownership.

(ii) **Non-trading loan relationship deficits.** A brought-forward non-trading loan relationship deficit which is apportioned to the notional accounting period ending at the time of the change in ownership under (D) above cannot be carried forward to any accounting period ending after the change.

(iii) **Non-trading loss on intangible fixed assets.** Relief for such a loss (see **42.9** INTANGIBLE ASSETS) against the total profits of the same accounting period is available only in relation to each of the notional accounting periods considered separately. A loss for an accounting period beginning before the change in ownership cannot be carried forward to an accounting period ending after the change or treated as if it were a non-trading debit of that period.

[*CTA 2010, ss 705A–705G, 730; F(No 2)A 2017, Sch 4 paras 170, 171*].

Disposal of income streams and assets through a partnership

[4.27] Certain avoidance schemes have sought to use the flexibility of partnerships to reduce tax by exploiting the different tax treatments of the members. There is legislation designed to counter such schemes involving the transfer of assets and income streams through or by partnerships. The transferor and transferee members may have different tax attributes, such as: the transferee being a company and the transferor an individual; the transferee has losses to use where the transferor does not; the transferee and transferor are subject to tax at different rates; or the transferor and transferee are subject to different tax computational rules with regard to the asset or income stream.

Where there is a disposal of an asset or income stream through or by a partnership and a main purpose is to secure an income tax or corporation tax advantage, the provisions impose a tax charge as income on the person making the disposal. The legislation amends *ITA 2007* and *CTA 2010* to cover the situation where an individual is the transferor, and the charge imposed is to income tax, and the situation where a company is the transferor and the charge imposed is to corporation tax. The following considers only the provisions which relate to companies that are transferors and the charge to corporation tax, which are found at *CTA 2010, Pt 16 Ch 1A* and *Ch 4.*

The provisions apply where, either directly or indirectly in consequence of, or otherwise in connection with, arrangements, a company (the transferor) disposes, actually or in substance, to another person (the transferee) either a right to relevant receipts, or, an asset (the transferred asset), and:

(i) the disposal is effected (wholly or partly) by or through a partnership (which includes a limited liability partnership);
(ii) the transferor and transferee are, at any time, members of that partnership, or of an associated partnership (which is a member of that partnership, or of another associated partnership); and
(iii) the main purpose, or one of the main purposes, of the disposal (or any of the steps by which the disposal is effected) is to secure a tax advantage for any person.

References to the transferor and transferee above include persons connected with them.

Where these conditions are met (including the further condition below for asset transfers) then the 'relevant amount' is brought into account as income of the transferor chargeable to corporation tax, in the same way and to the same extent as such income would have been brought within the charge to tax but for the disposal.

The '*relevant amount*' is the amount of consideration received by the transferor for the disposal of either the rights to relevant receipts (as in the transfer of income streams legislation at *CTA 2010, s 753(2)–(4)*) or the asset. If no consideration is received, or the consideration is substantially less than the market value of the asset or right transferred, then the market value (as at the time of the disposal) is used instead.

In addition, with regard to the disposal of an asset a further condition must be met, being: it is reasonable to assume that, had the transferred asset been disposed of directly by the transferor to the transferee, the relevant amount (or any part of it) would have been chargeable to corporation tax as income of the transferor, or would have been brought into account as income in calculating profits of the transferor for corporation tax purposes.

The transferor and transferee do not need to be members of the partnership as mentioned at the same time. A disposal includes anything that is a disposal for the purposes of *TCGA 1992*, and in particular such disposal might be undertaken by an acquisition or disposal, or an increase or decrease, in the partnership profit or asset share, or interest in such a share.

Where a disposal could be treated as both a disposal of rights to relevant receipts, and as a disposal of an asset, then these provisions apply in the manner which gives rise to the greater amount of income chargeable to corporation tax.

'*Relevant receipts*' means any income which would be charged to corporation tax as income of the transferor or which would be brought into account as income in calculating the profits of the transferor for corporation tax purposes, whether directly or as a member of a partnership. '*Tax advantage*' means a tax advantage (per *CTA 2010, s 1139*), in relation to income tax or corporation tax on income. '*Arrangements*' is broadly drafted and includes any agreement, understanding, scheme, transaction or series of transactions.

[*CTA 2010, ss 757A, 757B, 779A, 779B*].

Profit fragmentation

[4.28] *FA 2019* introduced anti-avoidance provisions to counter arrangements ('profit fragmentation arrangements') under which UK businesses seek to treat some or all of their profits as arising in the hands of an offshore entity in a jurisdiction where there is significantly lower tax than in the UK. Such arrangements may involve the UK business purporting that business receipts have been earned by the offshore entity when that entity does not have the substance to earn the profits, or the payment of fees and expenses to the offshore entity that are much higher than is justified by the work done by the entity. The provisions counteract the arrangements by requiring just and reasonable adjustments to the expenses, income, profits or losses of the UK business. They apply to value transferred by a UK business on or after 6 April 2019 (for income tax purposes) or 1 April 2019 (for corporation tax purposes). [*FA 2019, Sch 4 para 12*].

For HMRC guidance, see International Manual INTM610000 onwards.

Meaning of 'profit fragmentation arrangements'

'*Profit fragmentation arrangements*' involve:

(i) a resident party (i.e. a person resident in the UK);
(ii) an overseas party (i.e. a person or entity not resident in the UK); and
(iii) a related individual who is either the resident party, a member of a partnership in which the resident party is a partner or a participator in a company which is the resident party.

In (ii) above, the person or entity must be a person resident outside the UK (including trustees of a non-resident settlement and personal representatives treated as non-resident under *ITA 2007, s 834(4)*), an individual domiciled outside the UK or a company, partnership, trust or other entity or arrangements established or having effect under the law of a country or territory outside the UK (whether or not it has legal personality as a body corporate). In (iii) above, 'participator' is defined as at **16.7** CLOSE COMPANIES. A partnership includes a non-UK entity of a similar character to a UK partnership. A trust includes arrangements under non-UK law under which persons acting in a fiduciary capacity hold and administer property on behalf of others.

Subject to the exclusion below, arrangements (as widely defined) are profit fragmentation arrangements if the following four conditions are met.

(a) Provision (the '*material provision*') is made or imposed between the resident party (or a partnership of which the resident party is a member) and the overseas party under the arrangements.
(b) As a result of that provision, value is transferred from the resident party to the overseas party which derives directly or indirectly from the profits of a business (including a trade, profession or vocation) chargeable to income tax or corporation tax. In determining whether this is the case, account must be taken of any method, however indirect, by which property or a right is transferred or transmitted or by which the value of any property is enhanced or diminished. In particular, this includes sales, contracts etc. other than for full consideration (or for more than full

consideration), assignments of shares or rights in a company, rights in a partnership or interest in settled property, the creation of options, requirements for consent or embargoes in the disposition of property or rights and the giving of consideration for their grant or release and the disposal of property or rights on the winding-up, dissolution or termination of a company, partnership or trust. Value may be traced for this purpose through any number of individuals, entities or arrangements. Property held by a company, partnership, trust or other entity or under any arrangements must be attributed to the shareholders, partners etc. on a just and reasonable basis.

(c) The value transferred is greater than it would have been if it had resulted from provision made or imposed between independent parties at arm's length.

(d) It is reasonable to conclude that some or all of the value transferred relates to something done by, or any property or purported right of, a related individual (or a person connected with a related individual) and either:

  (1) under the arrangements, one of the following conditions applies:
  - any part of the value transferred is dealt with by any person in a way calculated to enure for the individual's benefit (or that of a person connected with him) at some time;
  - any part of the value transferred increases the value of any assets held by the individual (or connected person) or held for his benefit (or that of a person connected with him);
  - the individual (or connected person) receives or is entitled to receive any benefit provided or to be provided out of any part of the value transferred;
  - the individual (or connected person) may become entitled to the beneficial enjoyment of any part of the value transferred if powers are exercised, or successively exercised (by any person and whether or not consent is required from another person); or
  - the individual or connected person (alone or acting with others) is able in any way to control directly or indirectly the application of any part of the value transferred; or

  (2) it is reasonable to conclude that the individual or connected person (alone or acting with others) procured the transfer of value in such a way as to avoid the conditions in (1) above being met.

In determining whether any of the conditions in (1) above are met, all benefits which may accrue at any time to a person as a result of the transfer of value must be taken into account, irrespective of nature or form or of legal or equitable rights. In (d) above whether a person is connected with a related individual is determined by applying *ITA 2007, s 993* (with certain modifications) but an individual is also treated as connected with a person or entity if he or a connected person (alone or acting with others) is able to secure that the person or entity acts in accordance with their wishes; is able to acquire rights enabling them to secure that the person or entity so acts; or is able to exercise significant influence over the person or entity, whether or not as a result of legal entitlement. An individual is also treated as connected with a person or entity if that person or entity can reasonably be expected to act, or typically does act, in accordance with his wishes or those of a connected person.

Arrangements are not, however, profit fragmentation arrangements if the material provision does not result in a 'tax mismatch' for a tax period (i.e. a tax year or accounting period) of the resident party or it is not reasonable to conclude that a main purpose of entering into the arrangements was to obtain a 'tax advantage'.

A '*tax mismatch*' occurs in a tax period if, in that period, the material provision results in an increase in expenses of the resident party which are deductible in calculating its liability to a 'relevant tax' or a decrease in its income which would have been taken into account in calculating its liability. It must be reasonable to conclude that the 'resulting reduction' in tax liability exceeds the 'resulting increase' in relevant taxes payable by the overseas party for the period corresponding to the resident party's tax period and that the overseas party's increase is less than 80% of the resident party's decrease. It is irrelevant whether the excess of the reduction in the liability of the resident purpose over the increase in the overseas party's liability arises from different tax rates, the operation of a relief, the exclusion of any amount from a charge to tax or otherwise.

If the overseas party does not have an actual period for the purposes of relevant taxes which coincides with the resident party's tax period, the period corresponding to the tax period is a notional coinciding period. Just and reasonable apportionments must be made to determine the income or tax liability of the overseas party for the notional period.

The '*resulting reduction*' in the resident party's liability to a relevant tax for a tax period is the amount given by:

$$A \times TR$$

where:

A = the sum of (i) the lower of any increase in expenses of the resident party resulting from the material provision and any increase in the deduction allowable as a result of the increase in expenses; and (ii) the amount of any decrease in income of the resident party resulting from the material provision.

TR = the highest tax rate that would apply to profits equal to A chargeable to the relevant tax for the tax period if those profits were added to the resident party's total income.

The '*resulting increase*' in the overseas party's liability to relevant taxes for the period corresponding to the tax period of the resident party is any increase in the total relevant taxes payable by that party (and not refunded) on the assumptions that:

- the overseas party's income for the period, as a result of the material provision, is equal to A;

- account is taken of any deduction or relief (other than a 'qualifying deduction' or 'loss relief') taken into account in determining the overseas party's actual liability to any relevant taxes as a result of the material provision; and
- all further reasonable steps (including claiming reliefs, deductions etc. and making tax elections) are taken under UK and non-UK law, and under any double tax arrangements, to minimise the tax payable by the overseas party in the country or territory in question, other than steps to secure the benefit of any qualifying deduction or loss relief.

For these purposes, withholding tax on payments to the overseas party is treated as tax payable by that party (unless refunded) and not by the person making the payment. Tax payable by an overseas party is treated as refunded if a repayment or payment of a credit is made to any person which derives directly or indirectly from the tax, but tax is not treated as refunded to the extent that it results from loss relief obtained by the overseas party.

A '*qualifying deduction*' is one made in respect of actual expenditure by the overseas party which does not arise directly from the arrangements, but limited to the amount which would have been deductible for income tax or corporation tax purposes if the expenditure had been incurred by the resident party. A '*loss relief*' is any means by which a loss might be used to reduce the amount on which the overseas party is liable to tax on the profits of a business.

If some or all of the overseas party's income is treated for the purposes of a non-UK relevant tax as the income of other persons, the overseas party's liability to any tax includes the liabilities of those persons to the relevant tax, tax payable by that party includes the relevant tax payable by those persons, and loss relief obtained by that party includes loss relief obtained by those persons. This rule will apply where the overseas party is a transparent or hybrid entity so that the tax mismatch test can take account of tax paid by members of the overseas party.

There is no tax mismatch if one would otherwise occur solely by reason of:

- contributions by an employer to a registered pension scheme or overseas pension scheme in respect of any individual;
- a payment to a charity;
- a payment to a person with sovereign immunity from all relevant taxes; or
- a payment to an offshore fund or authorised investment fund which meets the genuine diversity of ownership conditions at **55.4** OFFSHORE FUNDS or **46.13** INVESTMENT FUNDS (whether or not a clearance has been given) or at least 75% of the investors in which are, throughout the period, pension schemes, charities or persons with sovereign immunity from all relevant taxes.

'*Relevant taxes*' are income tax, corporation tax on income and any non-UK tax on income (plus bank surcharge and ring-fence supplementary charge treated as corporation tax). A 'tax advantage' includes relief or increase relief from, or repayment of or increased repayment of, income tax or corporation tax, avoidance or reduction of a charge or assessment, avoidance of an assessment to income tax or corporation tax, deferral of payment, or advancement of repayment of tax and avoidance of an obligation to deduct or account for tax.

[*FA 2019, Sch 4 paras 1–6, 11*]

Counteraction of profit fragmentation arrangements

Just and reasonable adjustments must be made to counteract the tax advantages that would otherwise arise from the arrangements. The adjustments must relate to the expenses, income, profits or losses of the resident party for the tax period in which value is transferred as a result of the material provision and must be based on what the value transferred would have been if the material provision had been between independent parties acting at arm's length.

If the adjustments result in a double payment of tax calculated by reference to the same income or profits (including where the double payment is of non-UK tax) by the resident party or another person, the resident party may make a claim in writing for consequential adjustments to be made to the tax payable as a result of the original adjustments. The consequential adjustments must be just and reasonable and cannot be more than the lesser of the tax paid as a result of the original adjustments and the other tax paid in respect of the same income or profits. Consequential adjustments can be made in respect of any tax period by way of assessment, modification of an assessment, amendment of a claim or otherwise and regardless of any time limit.

No account is taken for tax purposes of any payment made by a person to meet or reimburse the cost of tax charged on the resident party under these provisions.

[*FA 2019, Sch 4 paras 7–9*]

Application to partners

The provisions apply to a member of a partnership by reference to his share of any expenses, income, profits or losses. A member's share, for this purpose, is determined by apportioning the amount in question between the members on a just and reasonable basis. [*FA 2019, Sch 4 para 10*].

Follower notices

[4.29] Users of avoidance schemes which have been defeated in a Tribunal or court hearing in another taxpayer's case can be required to concede their position to reflect the Tribunal's or court's decision. HMRC can issue a follower notice requiring such users for whom there is an open enquiry or appeal to amend their tax return or agree to resolve their appeal in accordance with the decision.

The taxes covered by the provisions are income tax, capital gains tax, corporation tax (including amounts chargeable as if they were corporation tax or treated as if they were corporation tax), inheritance tax, stamp duty land tax and annual tax on enveloped dwellings. The Treasury may extend the provisions to other taxes by order. [*FA 2014, ss 200, 232*]. The provisions are described below only to the extent that they relate to income tax, capital gains tax and corporation tax.

An application for judicial review of follower notices was unsuccessful in *R (oao Broomfield) v HMRC* QB, [2018] STC 1790.

An application was, however, successful in *R (oao Haworth) v HMRC* CA, [2019] STC 1063. The court found that HMRC had misdirected themselves as to the statutory test, by proceeding on the basis that a *likelihood* that the principles applied to the defeated scheme would also apply to the taxpayer, was sufficient for a follower notice to be issued. The court ruled that HMRC had to be of the opinion that the principles *would* apply. An application was also successful in *R (oao Locke) v HMRC* CA, [2019] STC 2543. The taxpayer was a partner in an Eclipse Film Partnership, Eclipse 10, and HMRC had contended that his circumstances were the same as those in *Eclipse Film Partners No 35 v HMRC* CA, [2015] STC 1429. The court held, however, that the decision in that case was focused on whether the partnership carried on a trade, which was not relevant to Mr Locke's case.

For HMRC guidance see www.gov.uk/government/publications/follower-notices-and-accelerated-payments and HMRC Factsheets CC/FS25a — Tax avoidance schemes — follower notices and accelerated payments and CC/FS25b — Tax avoidance schemes — partnership follower notices and accelerated partner payments.

Definitions

Arrangements are '*tax arrangements*' if, having regard to all the circumstances, it would be reasonable to conclude that the obtaining of a 'tax advantage' was their main purpose or one of the main purposes of them. '*Arrangements*' include any agreement, understanding, scheme, transaction or series of transactions, whether or not legally enforceable.

A '*tax advantage*' includes relief or increased relief from tax, repayment or increased repayment of tax, avoidance or reduction of a charge or assessment to tax, avoidance of a possible assessment to tax, deferral of a payment, or advancement of a repayment, of tax and avoidance of an obligation to deduct or account for tax.

An '*enquiry*' means an enquiry under *TMA 1970, ss 9A* or *12AC* (personal and partnership returns), *TMA 1970, Sch 1A para 5* (see **15.7** CLAIMS) or *FA 1998, Sch 18 para 24* (see **65.14** RETURNS). An enquiry is '*in progress*' in the period beginning with the day on which the notice of enquiry is given and ending on the day on which the enquiry is completed.

An '*appeal*' means an appeal or further appeal against an assessment, amendment of a self-assessment, closure notice, amendment of a partnership return or a counteraction notice under *ITA 2007, s 705* or *CTA 2010, s 750* (transactions in securities).

A '*judicial ruling*' means a ruling of a court or Tribunal on one or more issues. Such a ruling is relevant to particular tax arrangements if it relates to tax arrangements, it is a 'final ruling' and the principles laid down, or reasoning given, in it would, if applied to the arrangements in question, deny the asserted tax advantage or part of it. A judicial ruling is a '*final ruling*' if it is a decision of the Supreme Court, if no further appeal can be made (including where a time limit for further action by the appellant has expired) or if a further appeal was abandoned or otherwise disposed of before it was determined. If a ruling becomes final because of the passing of a time limit or because a further appeal is abandoned or otherwise disposed of before being determined, the ruling is treated as made at the time when the time limit expired or the appeal was abandoned or disposed of.

[*FA 2014, ss 201–203, 205*].

Giving of follower notice

[4.30] HMRC may give a follower notice to a person if:

(a) an enquiry into a return or claim made by that person is in progress or that person has made an appeal which has not been finally determined, abandoned or otherwise disposed of;
(b) the return, claim or appeal is made on the basis that a particular tax advantage results from particular tax arrangements;
(c) HMRC are of the opinion that there is a judicial ruling which is relevant to those arrangements; and
(d) no previous follower notice has been given to the same person (and not withdrawn) by reference to the same tax advantage, tax arrangements, judicial ruling and tax year or accounting period.

A follower notice must identify the judicial ruling, explain why HMRC consider that the ruling is relevant to the tax arrangements and explain the effects of the notice. A notice may not be given after the end of the twelve-month period beginning with the later of the date of the judicial ruling and the date the return or claim was received by HMRC or the appeal was made.

The recipient of a follower notice has 90 days beginning with the date the notice is given to send written representations to HMRC objecting to the notice on the grounds that any of (a), (b) or (d) above are not satisfied, that the judicial ruling is not relevant to the arrangements or that the notice was not given within the time limit. Having considered the representations HMRC will notify the recipient of whether they have decided to confirm the notice or withdraw it.

Partnerships

A follower notice may be given to a partnership in respect of a partnership return or an appeal relating to such a return. The notice is given to the representative partner (i.e. the partner responsible for dealing with the return) or to the successor of that partner. For the purposes of (b) above, a return or appeal is made on the basis that a particular tax advantage results from particular tax arrangements if the arrangements increase or reduce any of the items required to be included in the return and they result in a tax advantage for at least one of the partners. Where a partnership follower notice is given to a person as representative partner or to the successor of that partner, (d) above does not prevent a follower notice from being given to that person in another capacity. All notices given to the representative partner and any successor, in that capacity, are treated as given to the same person for the purposes of (d) above.

[*FA 2014, ss 204, 206, 207, 217, Sch 31 paras 2, 3*].

Action required following giving of follower notice

[4.31] Where a person is given a follower notice and it is not withdrawn, he (or, in the case of a partnership notice given to a representative partner who is no longer available, his successor) must take the following corrective action before the time specified below. Where an enquiry is in progress, the person must amend the return or claim to counteract the tax advantage denied by principles laid down, or reasoning given, in the judicial ruling. If an appeal is open, the person must take all necessary action to enter into a written agreement with HMRC for the purpose of relinquishing the denied advantage. After carrying out the necessary action the person must, before the specified time, notify HMRC that he has done so, including details of the denied advantage and (except in the case of a partnership follower notice) any additional amount of tax that has or will become due and payable.

If no representations were made following the giving of the notice, the specified time is the end of the period of 90 days beginning with the day on which the notice was given. If representations were made and the notice confirmed, the specified time is the later of the end of that 90-day period and the end of the period of 30 days beginning with the day on which the person is notified of HMRC's decision to confirm the notice.

No appeal may be brought against an amendment made by an enquiry closure notice to the extent that it takes into account an amendment to a return or claim resulting from corrective action under the above provision. Where the corrective action requires an amendment to a return or claim, such an amendment is not prevented by any time limit.

Where a person fails to take the necessary corrective action before the specified time, a penalty arises. See **59.14** PENALTIES.

[*FA 2014, s 208, Sch 31 para 4*].

Late appeal against a judicial ruling

[4.32] Where a final judicial ruling is reopened because a court or Tribunal grants leave to appeal out of time, and a follower notice has been given based on that ruling, the notice is suspended until HMRC notify the taxpayer that the appeal has resulted in a final judicial ruling or has been abandoned or otherwise disposed of. HMRC must notify the taxpayer that the follower notice has been suspended. No new follower notice may be issued in respect of the original ruling unless the new appeal is abandoned or disposed of without being determined by a court or Tribunal, but this does not prevent a follower notice from being issued in respect of a new final ruling resulting from the appeal. Where the appeal is abandoned or so disposed of, the period beginning when leave to appeal out of time was granted and ending when the appeal is disposed of does not count towards the twelve-month time limit for issuing follower notices in respect of the original ruling (see **4.30** above).

If a new final ruling results from the appeal and it is not relevant to the tax arrangements in question, a suspended follower notice ceases to have effect. In any other case it continues to have effect after the suspension ends and, if there is a new final ruling, the notice is treated as if it were in respect of that ruling. HMRC's notification to the taxpayer that the suspension has ended must indicate which of these outcomes applies. If there is a new final ruling, the notification must also make any amendments to the follower notice needed to reflect the new ruling.

The period during which a follower notice is suspended does not count in determining the specified time by which corrective action must be taken (see **4.31** above).

[*FA 2014, s 216*].

Accelerated payment notices

[4.33] Users of avoidance schemes may be required to pay tax upfront before the success or failure of the scheme has been finally determined. HMRC may issue an 'accelerated payment notice' in certain cases which may override any postponement of tax pending an appeal or, where there is no appeal, require the payment of disputed tax within a specified time. The provisions also prevent the surrender as group relief of corporation tax losses etc. arising from an avoidance scheme. There are special provisions for partnerships.

The taxes covered by the provisions are income tax, capital gains tax, corporation tax (including amounts chargeable as if they were corporation tax or treated as if they were corporation tax), inheritance tax, stamp duty land tax and annual tax on enveloped dwellings. The Treasury may extend the provisions to other taxes by order. [*FA 2014, ss 200, 232*]. The provisions are described below only to the extent that they relate to income tax, capital gains tax and corporation tax.

Where relevant, the definitions at **4.29** above apply for the purposes of these provisions.

HMRC have published a list of disclosed avoidance schemes likely to be subject to accelerated payment notices. See gov.uk/government/publications/tax-avoidance-schemes-on-which-accelerated-payments-may-be-charged-by-hmrc. Updated lists are to be published quarterly.

For HMRC guidance see www.gov.uk/government/publications/follower-notices-and-accelerated-payments and HMRC Factsheets CC/FS25a — Tax avoidance schemes — follower notices and accelerated payments, CC/FS25b — Tax avoidance schemes — partnership follower notices and accelerated partner payments and CC/FS28 — Tax avoidance schemes — accelerated payments for corporation tax and group relief.

Attempts to have the giving of an accelerated payment notice declared unlawful were unsuccessful in *Walapu v HMRC* QB, [2016] EWHC 658 (Admin); 2016 STI 1336 and *R (oao Graham) v HMRC* QB, [2016] EWHC 1197 (Admin);

2016 STI 1653. Judicial review applications were unsuccessful in *R (oao Sword Services Ltd) v HMRC* QB 2016, [2017] STC 596, *R (oao Dickinson) v HMRC* CA 2018, [2019] STC 319, *R (oao Rowe) v HMRC* CA 2017, [2018] STC 462 and *R (oao Carlton) v HMRC* QB, [2018] STC 589.

In *Beadle v HMRC* CA, [2020] STC 1058, the CA confirmed that the FTT has no jurisdiction to consider a challenge to the validity of a notice on appeal against a penalty for late payment of the tax charged by the notice.

Giving of accelerated payment notice

[4.34] HMRC may give an accelerated payment notice to a person if:

(a) an enquiry into a return or claim made by that person is in progress or that person has made an appeal which has not been finally determined, abandoned or otherwise disposed of;
(b) the return, claim or appeal is made on the basis that a particular tax advantage results from particular arrangements;
(c) either HMRC has given a follower notice (see **4.29** above) in relation to the same return, claim or appeal by reason of the same tax advantage and the arrangements, the tax arrangements are 'DOTAS arrangements' or a final counteraction notice under the general anti-abuse rule (see **4.4** and **4.6** above) has been given for the tax advantage (or part of it) and the arrangements in circumstances in which at least two members of the sub-panel of the GAAR Advisory Panel which considered the case concluded that entering into the tax arrangements (or the equivalent arrangements the Panel considered) was not a reasonable course of action (see **4.4**(9) and **4.6** above).

In (c) above, '*DOTAS arrangements*' are arrangements to which HMRC has allocated a reference number under the provisions for DISCLOSURE OF TAX AVOIDANCE SCHEMES (**28**), arrangements implementing a proposal where HMRC has allocated a reference number to the proposed arrangements or arrangements in respect of which a person must provide prescribed information by reason of the arrangements being substantially the same as such arrangements. Arrangements are excluded if HMRC have given notice that the reference number need not be notified to clients.

A notice must specify which of the requirements in (c) above applies and must explain its effects. If the notice is given whilst an enquiry is in progress, it must specify the accelerated payment required (if any); if an appeal is open it must state the amount of the disputed tax, if any (see **4.35** below). If the notice prevents the surrender of an amount as group relief, it must specify that amount and any action required to be taken.

The recipient of an accelerated payment notice has 90 days beginning with the date the notice is given to send written representations to HMRC objecting to the notice on the grounds that any of (a)–(c) above are not satisfied or objecting to the amount specified. Having considered the representations HMRC will notify the recipient of whether they have decided to confirm the notice, to withdraw it or to amend it. In *Rai v HMRC* FTT, [2017] UKFTT 467 (TC); 2017 STI 1870, HMRC's argument that representations must include a statement by the taxpayer of what they consider to be the correct amount are and why, was rejected. The Tribunal criticised HMRC for attempting to set their own rules about what should be in representations.

[*FA 2014, ss 219, 220(2), 221(2), 222; FA 2021, Sch 31, para 43(2)*].

Partnerships

Where a partnership return has been made, no accelerated payment notice may be given to the representative partner (i.e. the partner responsible for dealing with the return) or to the successor of that partner if an enquiry is in progress into that return or an appeal has been made against an amendment of that return or, following an enquiry into that return, a conclusion stated in a closure notice. Instead, a '*partner payment notice*' may be given to each person who was a partner at any time in the period to which the return relates if:

(1) the return or appeal is made on the basis that a particular tax advantage results from particular arrangements;
(2) either HMRC has given a follower notice (see **4.29** above) to the representative partner or successor in relation to the same return or appeal by reason of the same tax advantage and the arrangements, the tax arrangements are DOTAS arrangements or the partner in question has been given a final counteraction notice under the general anti-abuse rule (see **4.4** and **4.6** above) for the tax advantage (or part of it) and the arrangements in circumstances in which at least two members of the sub-panel of the GAAR Advisory Panel which considered the case concluded that entering into the tax arrangements (or the equivalent arrangements the Panel considered) was not a reasonable course of action (see **4.4**(9) and **4.6** above).

For the purposes of (1) above, a return or appeal is made on the basis that a particular tax advantage results from particular tax arrangements if the arrangements increase or reduce any of the items required to be included in the return and they result in a tax advantage for at least one of the partners.

There are provisions as to the contents of a notice and as to representations by the recipient which are similar to those applicable to accelerated payment notices (see above).

[*FA 2014, Sch 32 paras 1–3, 4(1), 5*].

Withdrawal, modification or suspension

HMRC may withdraw a notice at any time and if they do so the notice is treated as never having had effect and any accelerated payments (and penalties) paid must be repaid. Any notice giving consent to the surrender of an amount of group relief specified in the accelerated payment notice is not, however, revived. If a notice is given as a result of more than one of the requirements in (c) or (2) above, they may at any time withdraw it to the extent that it is given by one of those requirements (leaving it effective to the extent it was given by virtue of the remaining requirements). HMRC may also reduce the amount of the accelerated or partner payment required or the disputed tax or amount which may not be surrendered as group relief specified in the notice (and, where an accelerated payment has already been made in excess of the reduced amount, that excess must be repaid). Where the amount which may not be surrendered is reduced, a claim for group relief may be made in respect of the released amount within 30 days after the date on which the notice is amended or withdrawn (and the normal time limits are where necessary extended to facilitate such a claim).

An accelerated or partner payment notice given by virtue of a follower notice must be withdrawn if the follower notice is withdrawn (to the extent that it is given by virtue of the follower notice). If a follower notice is suspended following a late appeal against a judicial ruling (see **4.32** above), the accelerated or partner payment notice is similarly suspended and the period of suspension does not count towards the 30-day and 90-day periods in **4.35** below. A notice is not so suspended if it was also given (and not withdrawn) by virtue of either of the other requirements in (c) or (2) above. If a follower notice is amended following such a late appeal, HMRC may by notice make consequential amendments to the accelerated payment notice.

HMRC must withdraw a notice to the extent that it is given by virtue of DOTAS arrangements if they withdraw the scheme reference number or they give notice under *FA 2004, s 312(6)* or *312ZA(4)* with the result that notification to clients of the reference number is no longer required (see **28.11** DISCLOSURE OF TAX AVOIDANCE SCHEMES). Before 10 June 2021, HMRC were only required to withdraw the notice if they gave notice under *FA 2004, s 312(6)* that promoters were no longer required to notify clients of the reference number.

Where a notice is given by virtue of more than one of the requirements in (c) or (2) above and is withdrawn to the extent that it was given by virtue of one of those requirements and that requirement was the one stated in the notice to apply to determine the accelerated payment required, disputed tax etc. (see **4.35** below), HMRC must modify the notice to specify one of the remaining requirements as the one which applies for that purpose (and to reduce the payment or tax or amount which may not be surrendered as group relief where necessary). This rule also applies where a follower notice by virtue of which the accelerated payment notice was given is suspended as if the follower notice were withdrawn, but any change made only applies during the period of suspension.

Where a notice prevents the recipient from surrendering an amount as group relief or makes such a surrender ineffective and a 'final determination' establishes that the recipient may surrender all or part of that amount, a claim for group relief may be made in respect of the amount so allowed within 30 days after the 'relevant time' (and the normal time limits are where necessary extended to facilitate such a claim). For this purpose, a 'final determination' is a conclusion stated in a closure notice against which no appeal is made or the final determination of an appeal. The 'relevant time' is the end of the period in which an appeal could have been made against the closure notice or the day of the final determination of the appeal as appropriate.

Where a partnership return to which a notice relates is amended under *TMA 1970, s 12ABZB* (amendment following tribunal determination of partners' shares), HMRC may (by notice) make consequential amendments to the notice. If the amount payable under the notice is increased, the amount of the increase must be paid within the 30 days beginning with the day on which the notice of the amendments was given (if that is later than the normal due date within **4.35** below). If the amount payable is decreased, HMRC must repay any excess amount paid.

[*FA 2014, ss 227, 227A, Sch 32, para 8; FA 2021, Sch 31, paras 43(3), 44*].

Effects of accelerated payment notice

[4.35] If an accelerated payment notice is given whilst an enquiry is in progress or a partner payment notice is given and the notice specifies an amount which must be paid, the recipient of the notice must make the specified payment. If no representations were made following the giving of the notice, the payment must be made within the period of 90 days beginning with the day on which the notice was given. If representations were made and the notice confirmed or amended, the payment must be made by the later of the end of that 90-day period and the end of the period of 30 days beginning with the day on which the person is notified of HMRC's decision to confirm or amend the notice.

The amount of the payment required is (subject to any representations) the amount which a designated HMRC officer determines, to the best of his information and belief, as the 'understated tax' (disregarding any partnership dispute referred to the tribunal under *TMA 1970, s 12ABZB* (determination by tribunal of partners' shares) but not yet determined). The 'understated tax' is:

(1) where the notice is given as a result of a follower notice, the additional amount that would be due and payable if the necessary corrective action under the follower notice were taken in respect of what the designated HMRC officer determines, to the best of his information and belief, as the tax advantage denied by the judicial ruling (see **4.31** above);
(2) where the notice is given because the tax arrangements are DOTAS arrangements, the additional amount that would be due and payable if adjustments were made to counteract what the designated HMRC officer determines, to the best of his information and belief, as so much of the asserted tax advantage as is not a tax advantage which results from the arrangements or otherwise; and
(3) where the notice is given as a result of a GAAR counteraction notice, the additional amount that would be due and payable if the adjustments set out in that notice which counteract the asserted tax advantage were made.

Where more than one of (1)–(3) above would apply, the notice must stipulate which of them applies and the payment required must be determined accordingly. Where any of the tax included in the accelerated payment required under the notice has already been paid, the payment required is treated as having been paid at the time of the earlier payment. HMRC's recovery powers apply to the required payment as they apply to payments of tax (see **58** PAYMENT OF TAX).

If an accelerated payment notice is given (and not withdrawn) whilst an appeal is open, any understated tax, understated partner tax or disputed tax (see below) cannot be postponed (see **58.13** PAYMENT OF TAX) pending the outcome of the appeal. Any additional tax arising from the amendment of an accelerated payment notice as a result of the amendment of a partnership return under *TMA 1970, s 12ABZB* (amendment following tribunal determination of partners' shares) also cannot be postponed. If the notice specifies an amount which cannot be surrendered as group relief and an assessment has been made on the claimant company under *FA 1998, Sch 18 para 76* (see **35.12** GROUP RELIEF) to recover group relief already given in respect of that amount, the amount cannot be postponed pending the outcome of the appeal. If an amount of disputed tax is postponed immediately before the giving of an accelerated payment notice, it ceases to be postponed at that time and becomes due and payable on or before the last day of the 90-day period beginning with the day the notice is given. If representations are made against the notice (see **4.34** above), the tax becomes due and payable on or before the later of that 90-day period and the last day of the 30-day period beginning on the day on which HMRC notify their decision about the representations. If additional tax arising from the amendment of an accelerated payment notice following amendment of a partnership return under *TMA 1970, s 12ABZB* is postponed immediately before the giving of the notice amending the accelerated payment notice, it ceases to be postponed at that time. The additional tax becomes due and payable on or before the last day of the 30-day period beginning with the day the notice is given or, if later, the last day on which it would have been payable had it been disputed tax included in the accelerated payment notice as originally issued.

The 'disputed tax' is so much of the tax which is the subject of the appeal as the designated HMRC officer determines, to the best of his information and belief, as the amount required to counteract what that officer so determines to be the tax advantage in dispute (calculated in the same way as the understated tax in (1)–(3) above). Where more than one of (1)–(3) above would apply, the notice must stipulate which of them applies and the tax advantage in dispute must be determined accordingly.

Where an accelerated payment notice is in force in relation to an open appeal and a court or Tribunal decides against HMRC but they seek permission to appeal against the decision, they may apply to the court or Tribunal from which they are seeking permission to appeal to disapply the rule requiring repayment of tax in accordance with the decision. If the court or Tribunal considers it necessary for the protection of the revenue, it may give permission to withhold the affected repayment or to require the provision of adequate security before repayment is made.

If an accelerated payment notice is given (and not withdrawn) and the notice specifies an amount which cannot be surrendered as group relief, the recipient of the notice may not consent to any claim for group relief in respect of the amount so specified. If the recipient has already consented to the surrender of the amount, *FA 1998, Sch 18 para 75* (withdrawal of consent following reduction in amount available for surrender — see **35.12** GROUP RELIEF) applies as if the specified amount ceased to be available for surrender at the time the notice was given. If no representations were made following the giving of the notice, the recipient must so withdraw the notice of consent to surrender within the period of 90 days beginning with the day on which the notice was given. If representations were made and the accelerated payment notice confirmed or amended, the withdrawal must be made by the later of the end of that 90-day period and the end of the period of 30 days beginning with the day on which the person is notified of HMRC's decision to confirm or amend the notice. The amount specified in the notice is (subject to any representations) the amount which a designated HMRC officer determines, to the best of his information and belief, as the amount which would not be a surrenderable loss (within 35.5(a)–(g) GROUP RELIEF) if the position were as in (1)–(3) above and which is not the subject of a claim by the recipient for corporation tax relief which is reflected in any understated tax also specified in the notice. Where more than one of (1)–(3) above would apply, the notice must stipulate which of them applies and the amount specified must be determined accordingly.

The normal time limits are disapplied as necessary to allow the company claiming the group relief to amend its return following receipt of a withdrawal notice or, where consent is not withdrawn as required, following receipt of an HMRC direction. Where a company makes such an amendment to its return but, because an enquiry is in progress, the amendment does not take effect until the enquiry is completed (see **65.15** RETURNS), HMRC may issue an accelerated payment notice to the company as if:

- for the purposes of **4.34**(b) above, the amendment had not been made;
- that one of the requirements at **4.34**(c) above were that the company has made such an amendment to its return which does not take effect until the completion of the enquiry; and
- the understated tax is the additional amount that would be due and payable if the company had never made the claim to group relief.

[*TMA 1970, ss 55(8B)–(8E), 56(4)–(6); FA 2014, ss 220(3)–(7), 221(3)–(5), 223, 224(1), 225(1), Sch 32 paras 4(2)–(5), 6, 6A; FA 2018, Sch 6 paras 10(8), 13(2)(5)*].

See **59.15** PENALTIES for the penalties chargeable for failure to make an accelerated payment.

Schemes involving the transfer of corporate profits

[4.36] Anti-avoidance provisions apply to schemes involving the transfer of corporate profits between two companies that are members of the same group.

The provisions apply where:

(a) two companies, company A and company B, that are members of the same group, are party to any arrangements (whether or not at the same time);
(b) the arrangements result in what is, in substance, a payment (directly or indirectly) from company A to company B of all, or a significant part, of the profits of the business of company A, or of a company which is a member of the same group as company A or company B (or both); and
(c) the main purpose, or one of the main purposes, of the arrangements is to secure a tax advantage for any person involving the profit transfer.

Where these conditions are met then company A's profits are calculated as if the profit transfer had not occurred.

If company A would have deducted the transferred amount, or any part of it, from its profit calculation then that deduction is not allowed. If no deduction would have been brought into account in respect of the payment, or any part of it, then company A's profits are increased by that amount of the transfer, whether or not the profits transferred would be the company's profits apart from the arrangements.

A company is treated as a member of the same group as another company if it is or has been a member of the same group at a time when the arrangements have effect. '*Group*' is defined as for the patent box provisions at *CTA 2010, s 357GD*. See further **57.2** PATENT INCOME.

'*Arrangements*' includes any scheme, arrangement or understanding of any kind, whether or not legally enforceable, involving one or more transactions.

These profit transfer restrictions do not apply to any arrangement falling within *CTA 2009, s 695A*, a targeted anti-avoidance provision which relates specifically to disguised distribution arrangements involving derivative contracts. However, these restrictions do apply to arrangements that have been put in place to circumvent that provision.

'*Tax advantage*' is widely defined, under *CTA 2010, s 1139*, and includes any relief or increased relief from tax, any repayment or increased repayment of tax, and the avoidance or reduction of a charge to tax.

[*CTA 2009, s 1305A*]

Serial avoiders regime

[4.37] A regime of warnings and escalating sanctions applies to taxpayers who persistently engage in tax avoidance schemes that are successfully counteracted ('*defeated*') by HMRC. Following the first defeat of a scheme, HMRC will place the taxpayer on a warning (see **4.38**, **4.39** below). The taxpayer has to annually provide HMRC with information during a five-year warning period (see **4.40** below). If the taxpayer uses any such avoidance scheme while under warning, penalties of up to 60% of the understated tax will be charged (see **59.18** PENALTIES) if the scheme is defeated. If three avoidance schemes which exploit reliefs are used while under warning and are defeated, the taxpayer is denied further benefit of reliefs until the warning period expires (see **4.41**). If HMRC defeat three avoidance schemes while the taxpayer is on warning, the taxpayer's details can be published (see **4.45**). See **4.42** for the application of the regime to partnerships.

The regime applies to a number of direct and indirect taxes and also national insurance contributions (see *FA 2016, Sch 18 para 4* for the full list). It is described below in terms of its application to capital gains tax and corporation tax on chargeable gains, but it should be noted that the regime does not operate independently for each type of tax but embraces all avoidance schemes that a person uses which cover any tax on the list.

In relation to taxes other than VAT, '*tax advantage*' is defined widely by *FA 2016, Sch 18 para 7* for the purposes of these provisions.

For HMRC technical guidance, see www.gov.uk/government/collections/serial-tax-avoidance-regime.

Warning notices

[4.38] Where a person has incurred a 'relevant defeat' (see **4.39** below) in relation to any arrangements (as widely defined), HMRC must give that person a written notice (a '*warning notice*') within the 90 days beginning with the day on which the defeat is incurred. The warning notice must specify the defeat in question, state when the 'warning period' begins and ends and explain the statutory consequences of the notice. The '*warning period*' is the five years following the day on which the warning notice is given. If a person incurs a relevant defeat during a warning period, that period is extended to the end of the five years following the day on which the defeat occurs. [*FA 2016, Sch 18 paras 2, 3*].

Associated persons

Where a person (P) incurs a relevant defeat in relation to any arrangements, any person who is 'associated' with P at the time when P is given the warning notice is also treated for the above purposes as having incurred that relevant defeat, unless both persons are companies in the same group. However, a warning notice thus given to an associated person is disregarded for the purposes of **4.41** below (restriction of relief notices) and see **59.18** PENALTIES. For these purposes, two persons are '*associated*' with one another only if one of them is a body corporate which is controlled (as defined) by the other or if they are bodies corporate under common control (as defined). [*FA 2016, Sch 18 paras 47, 48*].

Meaning of 'relevant defeat'

[4.39] For the purposes of taxes other than VAT, a person (P) incurs a '*relevant defeat*' in relation to arrangements if any of conditions A–C below is met in relation to P and the arrangements. The relevant defeat is incurred when the condition in question is first met.

- Condition A is that a tax advantage has arisen to P from the arrangements and this has been counteracted as in **4.3** above (the GAAR), with the counteraction having become final.
- Condition B is that (in a case not falling within Condition A) a follower notice (see **4.29** above) has been given to P by reference to the arrangements (and not withdrawn) and either the necessary corrective action has been taken (see **4.31** above) or the denied tax advantage has been otherwise counteracted, with the counteraction having become final (determined in the same manner as under **4.3** above).
- Condition C is that (in a case not falling within Condition A or B) the arrangements are 'DOTAS arrangements' (see below) on which P has relied, and the arrangements have been counteracted, with the counteraction having become final. The time at which it falls to be determined whether or not the arrangements are DOTAS arrangements is when the counteraction becomes final.

Condition B applies also where the follower notice is a partnership follower notice in connection with a partnership return and is given to a partnership in which P was a partner in the period covered by the return.

For the purposes of Condition C, P relies on the arrangements if he makes a return, claim or election, or a partnership return is made, on the basis that a 'relevant tax advantage' arises, or if P fails to discharge a 'relevant obligation' and there is reason to believe that the failure is connected with the arrangements. A '*relevant tax advantage*' is one which the arrangements might be expected to enable P to obtain. An obligation is a '*relevant obligation*' if the arrangements might be expected to have the result that the obligation does not arise.

Arrangements are counteracted for the purposes of Condition C if P's tax position is adjusted (other than at his own behest), or an HMRC assessment is made on P, or any other action is taken by HMRC, on the basis that the whole or part of the relevant tax advantage does not arise or that the relevant obligation does arise. Contract settlements (see **6.8** ASSESSMENTS) are treated as assessments for this purpose. P's tax position is adjusted at his own behest if he makes the adjustment at a time when he had no reason to believe that an HMRC enquiry was in the offing (regarding the tax in question) or if HMRC make the adjustment as a result of a full and explicit disclosure by P which is made at such a time.

A counteraction is final for the purposes of Condition C when the assessment, adjustments or action in question, and any amounts thereby arising, can no longer be varied on appeal or otherwise.

[*FA 2016, Sch 18 paras 11–14, 49*].

Meaning of 'DOTAS arrangements'

For the purposes of the serial avoiders regime, arrangements are '*DOTAS arrangements*' at any time if they are 'notifiable arrangements' at that time and a person has provided information in relation to them under *FA 2004, s 308(3)* (obligation of promoter in relation to notifiable arrangements), *s 309* (obligation of person dealing with non-UK promoter) or *s 310* (obligation of parties to notifiable arrangements not involving a promoter) or has failed to comply with any of those provisions in relation to the arrangements. They do not include arrangements in respect of which HMRC has given notice that promoters are not under a duty to notify clients of the reference number. However, they do include arrangements which are excepted from the notification requirement for the reason only that they either had been notified as proposed arrangements or are substantially the same as arrangements already notified.

For the meaning of 'notifiable arrangements' and more on the above-mentioned *FA 2004* provisions, see **28.2** DISCLOSURE OF TAX AVOIDANCE SCHEMES. For the above purposes, a person fails to comply with any of those provisions if (and only if) the Tribunal has determined this to be the case (or has determined against a reasonable excuse), and their determination can no longer be appealed, or the person has made a written admission of such failure to HMRC.

[*FA 2016, Sch 18 paras 8, 10*].

Requirement of annual information notices

[4.40] A person (P) who has been given a warning notice (as in **4.38** above) must give HMRC a written notice (an '*information notice*') in respect of each 'reporting period' within the warning period. The information notice must be given within 30 days after the end of the reporting period to which it relates. Groups of companies may give a combined information notice. The first '*reporting period*' begins with the first day of the warning period and ends with a day specified by HMRC. The remainder of the warning period is divided into further reporting periods of 12 months duration, though the final reporting period ends at the same time as the warning period, even if that results in a reporting period of less than 12 months.

An information notice must state whether, in the reporting period, P:

(a) has made a return, claim or election on the basis that a 'relevant tax advantage' arises (and this includes a return made on that basis since the reporting period ended if the return was due in the reporting period); or
(b) has failed to take action which he would be required to take under, or by virtue of, any tax enactment if it were not for particular DOTAS arrangements (see **4.39** above) or 'disclosable VAT arrangements' (within *FA 2016, Sch 18 para 9*) to which he is a party; or
(c) has become a party to arrangements relating to a supplier's VAT position which might be expected to enable P to obtain a relevant tax advantage in connection with the supplies,

and whether or not P has failed to make any return that he was required to make by a date falling in the reporting period.

A '*relevant tax advantage*' is a tax advantage which particular DOTAS arrangements or disclosable VAT arrangements enable, or might be expected to enable, P to obtain. If (a) above is in point, P must include in the information notice an explanation of how the tax advantage arises and its amount. If (b) is in point, P must similarly explain how the arrangements result in there being no requirement to take the action in question and state the amount of any resulting tax advantage. If (c) is in point, P must state whether it is his view that the relevant tax advantage arises to him and, if so, he must explain how the arrangements enable him to obtain the advantage and state its amount.

If the due date for a return falls within the reporting period and P fails to make the return in that period, HMRC may require from P a supplementary information notice setting out any matters which he would have been required to include in the original information notice if it had not been for that failure. Any such HMRC requirement must be notified in writing and must state the period allowed for compliance.

If P fails to provide a notice (whether an information notice or a supplementary information notice) or provides a notice that is defective, HMRC may by written notice extend the warning period to the end of the five years beginning with the day by which the notice should have been given, or the day on which the defective notice was given. The warning period cannot thus be extended by more than five years from what would otherwise have been its expiry date.

[*FA 2016, Sch 18 para 17*].

Restriction of reliefs

[4.41] HMRC must give a person a written notice (a '*restriction of relief notice*') if:

- the person incurs a relevant defeat (see **4.39** above) in relation to arrangements which he has used whilst in a warning period (see **4.38** above);
- he has been given at least two warning notices in respect of other relevant defeats of arrangements used in that same warning period;
- all the relevant defeats are by virtue of Condition A, B or C in **4.39** (as opposed to conditions relating to VAT that are not reproduced here);
- all the relevant defeats relate to the misuse of a relief; and
- in the case of each of the relevant defeats, either the counteraction was made on the basis that a particular 'avoidance-related rule' applied in relation to a person's affairs or the misused relief in question was a relief for losses under *ITA 2007, Pt 4* or *CTA 2010, Pts 4, 5*.

If a person has been given a single warning notice in relation to two or more relevant defeats, he is treated for the above purposes as having been given a separate warning notice in relation to each defeat. The time at which, for the purposes of the serial avoiders regime, a person has 'used' arrangements is determined by *FA 2016, Sch 18 para 48* in terms of the filing date for returns (meaning the earlier of the actual filing date and the due date), the dates on which claims and elections are made and the date of any failure to comply with an obligation (meaning the date on which the person is first in breach of the obligation).

A relevant defeat relates to the misuse of a relief if the tax advantage in question (or part of it), results from a relief (or an increased relief) or it is reasonable to conclude that the making of a particular claim for relief, or the use of a particular relief, is a significant component of the arrangements in question. A relief means any relief from tax (however described) which must be claimed; management expenses of a company's investment business; any relief for losses under *ITA 2007, Pt 4* or *CTA 2010, Pts 4, 5*; or any other relief listed in *ITA 2007, s 24* (reliefs deductible at Step 2 of the calculation of income tax liability).

'*Avoidance-related rule*' is defined by *FA 2016, Sch 18 para 25*, which also includes an example of such a rule. A statutory rule to the effect that the avoidance of tax must not be a main object or an expected benefit of a transaction or arrangements, or that an action must be carried out for commercial reasons, would be an avoidance-related rule.

The restricted period

A restriction of relief notice must explain its effect (see below) and state when the 'restricted period' begins and ends. The '*restricted period*' is the three years beginning with the day on which the restriction of relief notice is given. If during the restricted period the person to whom a restriction of relief notice has been given incurs a further relevant defeat, HMRC must give him a written notice (a '*restricted period extension notice*'); this extends the restricted period to the end of the three years beginning with the day on which the further defeat occurs. A further defeat is taken into account for this purpose only if it is incurred by virtue of Condition A, B or C in relation to arrangements which the person used in the warning period and relates to the misuse of a relief. If a person to whom a restriction of relief notice has been given incurs a further defeat after the restricted period has ended but during a warning period which at some time ran concurrently with the restricted period, HMRC must give that person a restriction of relief notice.

Effect of restriction of relief notice

A person to whom a restriction of relief notice has been given may not, in the restricted period, make any claim for relief nor surrender group relief. (For the purposes of the serial avoiders regime, 'claim for relief' includes any election or similar action which is in substance a claim for relief.) Claims for relief under a double tax treaty are excluded. Management expenses, trade losses brought forward and property business losses may not be deducted for any accounting period the first day of which is in the restricted period. No losses may be deducted in calculating the total amount of ATED-related gains or NRCGT gains, for any tax year the first day of which is in the restricted period. Further restrictions are listed in *FA 2016, Sch 18 para 20*.

Mitigation, reasonable excuse and appeals

The Commissioners for HMRC may mitigate, in any way they think appropriate, the effect of a restriction of relief notice insofar as it appears to them that there are exceptional circumstances such that it would otherwise have an unduly serious impact with respect to the tax affairs of the taxpayer concerned or another person.

If a person (P) who has incurred a relevant defeat satisfies HMRC or, on appeal, the Tribunal that he had a reasonable excuse for the matters to which the defeat relates, he is treated for the purposes of the restriction of relief provisions as not having incurred that defeat, and any warning notice given to him in relation to that defeat is treated as not having been given. Reasonable excuse does not include insufficiency of funds (unless attributable to events outside P's control), reliance on another person to do anything (unless P took reasonable care to avoid the failure or inaccuracy in question) or reliance on advice if that advice is addressed to, or was given to, a person other than P or takes no account of P's individual circumstances. A person with a reasonable excuse is treated as having continued to have it if the failure or inaccuracy in question was remedied without unreasonable delay after the excuse ceased.

A person may appeal against a restriction of relief notice or a restricted period extension notice within 30 days beginning with the day on which the notice is given. The appeal is to be treated in the same way as an appeal against an income tax assessment. The Tribunal, on an appeal brought before it, may cancel or affirm HMRC's decision to issue the notice. It may also mitigate the effect of a notice to the same extent as HMRC (see above) or to a different extent, but in the latter case only if the Tribunal regards HMRC's decision on mitigation as flawed.

[*FA 2016, Sch 18 paras 19–29, 55*].

Partnerships

[4.42] The consequences described below apply in relation to a partnership tax return under *TMA 1970, s 12AA* if:

- the return has been made on the basis that a tax advantage arises to a partner from any arrangements and that partner has incurred, in relation to that tax advantage and those arrangements, a relevant defeat by virtue of Condition A or Condition C in **4.39** above; or
- a person has incurred a relevant defeat by virtue of Condition B in **4.39** above and the follower notice in question is a partnership follower notice.

A partnership return is regarded as made on the basis that a particular tax advantage arises to a partner from particular arrangements if it is made on the basis that an increase or reduction in any of the items to be included in the partnership statement results from those arrangements and that increase or reduction results in that tax advantage for the partner. Limited liability partnerships are within these rules in the same way as other partnerships. For the above purposes a relevant defeat does not include one which an associated person is treated as having incurred (see **4.38** above).

Each 'relevant partner' is treated for the purposes of the serial avoiders regime as having also incurred the relevant defeat in question. A '*relevant partner*' is any person who was a member of the partnership at any time during the period covered by the partnership return.

The appropriate partner (meaning a partner nominated by HMRC for this purpose) must give HMRC a written notice (a '*partnership information notice*') in respect of each sub-period in the 'information period'. The '*information period*' is the five years following the day of the relevant defeat. If a new information period (relating to another partnership return) begins during an existing information period, those periods are treated as a single period. An information period ends if the partnership ceases. The partnership information notice must be given within 30 days after the end of the sub-period to which it relates. The first sub-period begins with the first day of the information period and ends with a day specified by HMRC. The remainder of the information period is divided into further sub-periods of 12 months duration, though the final sub-period ends at the same time as the information period, even if that results in a sub-period of less than 12 months. A partnership information notice must state (i) whether or not any partnership return which was, or was required to be, delivered in the sub-period has been made on the basis that a 'relevant tax advantage' arises; and (ii) whether or not there has been a failure to deliver a partnership return in the sub-period. A '*relevant tax advantage*' is a tax advantage which particular DOTAS arrangements (see **4.39** above) enable, or might be expected to enable, a member of the partnership to obtain. Where relevant, the information notice must go on to explain how the DOTAS arrangements enable the tax advantage to be obtained and describe any variation in the amounts required to be stated in the partnership statement included in the return. There is similar provision to require supplementary information notices as in **4.40** above, and similar consequences for failure to provide an accurate information notice.

There is provision to the effect that if a partnership return is amended, whether by the partnership itself or by HMRC following an unprompted disclosure, then, for the purpose of applying Condition C in **4.39** above, each affected partner is treated as having simultaneously amended his own return so as to give effect to the amendment of the partnership return.

[*FA 2016, Sch 18 paras 49–53, 58(1)(4)*].

Groups of companies

[4.43] Where HMRC have a duty to give a warning notice (see **4.38** above) to a company (C) which is a member of a 'group', that duty has effect as a duty to give such a notice to every other company which is then a member of the group. HMRC may fulfil that duty by delivering the notice to C (and if it does so may combine warning notices in a single notice). Any warning notice previously given to a current group member is treated as having been given to each current group member.

Where a group company incurs a relevant defeat, however, the provisions for restriction of relief notices (see **4.41** above) and penalties (see **4.44** below) apply by reference only to warning periods of the company which would be warning periods if the above provisions did not apply.

Any warning notice which applies to a company only as a result of the above provisions ceases to apply to it when it leaves the group.

Two companies are members of the same group for this purpose if one is a 75% subsidiary (within *CTA 2010, s 1154*) of the other or both are 75% subsidiaries of a third company.

The warning period rules at **4.39** above apply as if successive representative members of a VAT group were a single person, but the serial avoiders regime applies in general to any company as if the company acting in its capacity as representative member were a different person from the company acting in any other capacity.

[*FA 2016, Sch 18 paras 45, 46*].

Penalties

[4.44] See **59.18** PENALTIES which apply where a person incurs a relevant defeat in relation to any arrangements used during a warning period.

Publishing taxpayer's details

[4.45] The Commissioners for HMRC may publish information about a person if he incurs a relevant defeat (see **4.39** above) in relation to arrangements which he has used in a warning period and has been given at least two warning notices (see **4.38** above) in respect of other defeats of arrangements which were used in the same warning period. If a person has been given a single warning notice in relation to two or more relevant defeats, he is treated for these purposes as having been given a separate warning notice in relation to each of those defeats.

The Commissioners can publish the person's name (including trading name, previous name or pseudonym), address or registered office, the nature of any business carried on, information about the fiscal effect of relevant defeated arrangements (had they not been defeated), e.g. the amount of tax understated, the amount of any penalty, the periods in which or times when relevant defeated arrangements were used, and any other information which they consider appropriate in order to make the person's identity clear. In the case of a person carrying on a trade or business in partnership, the information which may be published includes any trading name of the partnership and the names and addresses of the partners. In the case of a company which is a member of a group, the information which may be published includes any trading name of the group and the name, address or registered office and nature of business of any other group member. Defeated arrangements are relevant if the person used them in the said warning period and has been given a warning notice in respect of them. The information may be published in any manner the Commissioners consider appropriate. It can only be first published in the period of one year beginning with the giving of the most recent of the warning notices in question, and information cannot continue to be published for more than a year. Before publishing the information, the Commissioners must inform the person that they are doing so and provide a reasonable opportunity to make representations about whether it should be published.

[*FA 2016, Sch 18 para 18*].

Key points on anti-avoidance

[4.46] Points to consider are as follows.

- The approach of the courts to tax avoidance has developed over many years. Early cases, such as the *Duke of Westminster* case, dealt with the consequences of a single transaction, and the principle arising from that case was that a person is entitled to arrange his affairs so as to reduce his tax burden.
- Subsequent cases, such as *Furniss v Dawson* and *Craven v White*, have dealt with the treatment of transactions involving a number of steps, and whether circularity or steps inserted for no commercial purpose go beyond simply arranging one's affairs in a tax efficient manner.
- Latterly, HMRC have been active in introducing specific legislation to stop avoidance mechanisms, which has given rise to an enormous growth in anti-avoidance legislation.
- A General Anti-Abuse Rule has been introduced.
- The avoidance rules counteract the treatment of income streams where they are sold for cash lump sums without the asset from which the income derives.
- International movements of capital, such as the issue of shares or debt by overseas subsidiaries, is subject to a reporting requirement, where such transactions are valued over £100 million and do not fall into one of the excluded categories.

- Anti-avoidance provisions apply to restrict the carry forward of non-trading loan relationship debits and deficits and non-trading losses on intangible assets after a change of ownership of a '*shell company*', being a company that is not carrying on a trade or UK property business and is not a company with investment business.
- Provisions apply to counter arrangements where there is a disposal of an asset or income stream through or by a partnership, and a main purpose is to secure an income tax or corporation tax advantage — a tax charge is imposed on the person making the disposal.
- Provisions apply to restrict allowable deductions where, in certain circumstances, a scheme has been entered into involving the transfer of corporate profits between group members.
- *FA 2019* introduced, with effect from April 2019, anti-avoidance provisions to counter arrangements ('profit fragmentation arrangements') under which UK businesses seek to treat some or all of their profits as arising in the hands of an offshore entity in a jurisdiction where there is significantly lower tax than in the UK.

5

Appeals

Cross-references. See 38 HMRC INVESTIGATORY POWERS; 43 INTEREST ON OVERDUE TAX as regards interest on tax becoming due where an appeal is made or determined; 59 PENALTIES.

Simon's Taxes. See A5.3, A5.5, A5.6.

Introduction to appeals

[5.1] This chapter outlines the appeals process, first to HMRC and then the procedure for appeals to the First-tier Tribunal, the Upper Tribunal, and finally considers when Judicial Review of a decision might be appropriate.

A taxpayer who disagrees with an assessment or other decision made by HMRC can appeal against it. This is done by giving notice in writing to HMRC, stating the grounds of appeal. The notice must normally be given within 30 days after the date of issue of the assessment or decision, although late appeals can be made in some circumstances (see 5.4 below).

After a taxpayer appeals there are three main options:

- a different HMRC officer can carry out a review of the decision;
- the taxpayer can ask the Tribunal to decide the matter in dispute;
- the appeal can be settled by agreement at any time.

Reviews are not compulsory, and where HMRC carry out a review but the taxpayer still disagrees with the decision, he can ask the Tribunal to decide the issue (or continue negotiations with HMRC in order to settle the appeal by agreement).

For HMRC reviews, see 5.8 below and for settlement by agreement, see 5.12 below.

Where the taxpayer asks the Tribunal to decide the appeal, the case is usually dealt with by the First-tier Tribunal. The appeal is allocated to one of four categories, default paper, basic, standard or complex, and the process differs according to the category. Basic, standard and complex cases are normally decided at a hearing at which the taxpayer (or his representative) and HMRC are able to present their cases.

Default paper cases can also be decided at a hearing where one of the parties requests a hearing. Complex cases may be transferred for hearing by the Upper Tribunal.

For the First-tier Tribunal process, see 5.16–5.28 below.

If either the taxpayer or HMRC disagree with a decision of the First-tier Tribunal, there is a further right of appeal to the Upper Tribunal, but only on a point of law. Permission to appeal must be obtained from the First-tier Tribunal, or where it refuses permission, from the Upper Tribunal.

For the Upper Tribunal process, see 5.29–5.37 below. Where either party disagrees with an Upper Tribunal decision, there is a similar right of appeal to the Court of Appeal. See 5.40 below.

Where there is no right of appeal or a taxpayer is dissatisfied with the exercise by HMRC or the Tribunal of administrative powers, he may in certain circumstances seek a remedy by way of application for judicial review. See 5.40 below.

Costs can be awarded to or against a taxpayer in cases dealt with by either tribunal or by the courts. See **5.28**, **5.37** and **5.41** below.

HMRC's Litigation and Settlement Strategy is discussed at **5.2** below, and the Alternative Dispute Resolution scheme is discussed at **5.10**.

See generally HMRC Appeals, Reviews and Tribunals Guide.

Coronavirus (COVID-19)

A number of temporary changes have been made to the provisions in this chapter as a result of the lockdown beginning in March 2020 due to the coronavirus pandemic. The main changes are as follows.

- HMRC will allow an extra three months on top of the normal 30-day time limit (see **5.4** below) for making an appeal against a decision dated February 2020 or later where the taxpayer has been affected by coronavirus. See www.gov.uk/tax-appeals/decision.
- The First-tier Tribunal issued a general stay on all proceedings on 24 March 2020 for 28 days until 21 April 2020. Any time limits in those proceedings (such as to comply with a direction, to apply for a decision to be set aside or for permission to appeal to the Upper Tribunal) were extended by 28 days. See www.judiciary.uk/wp-content/uploads/2020/03/200326-COVID-19-FTT-Tax-Chamber-Amended-General-Stay.pdf.
- Appeals received by the First-tier Tribunal before 24 March 2020 and categorised as standard or complex (see **5.21**, **5.22** below) before 21 April 2020 were subject to a further stay on proceedings until 30 June 2020. Any time limits in those proceedings were extended by a further 70 days. See www.judiciary.uk/coronavirus-covid-19-advice-and-guidance/#tribunals.
- The existing limit of £2,000 for allocation by the First-tier Tribunal of penalty appeals to the default paper category (see **5.19** below) is temporarily increased to £20,000. The increase was initially for six months but it has been extended until 30 June 2020. See www.judiciary.uk/wp-content/uploads/2020/03/2020_03_23-Practice-Statement-on-Categorisation-in-Tax-Chamber.pdf and www.judiciary.uk/wp-content/uploads/2021/03/210322-Extension-of-Practice-Statement-on-Categorisation.pdf.
- With effect from 10 April 2020, if a party objects to an appeal being decided on the papers, the First-tier Tribunal may nevertheless decide that it should be decided in that way. However, the Tribunal can only take that step if the matter is urgent, it is not reasonably practicable for there to be a hearing (including one conducted wholly or partly by telephone or by video) and it is in the interests of justice to make that direction. This rule is expressed to expire at the same time as the *Coronavirus Act 2020*, i.e on 24 March 2022 unless that date is either brought forward or extended. [*SI 2009 No 273, Rule 5A; SI 2020 No 416, Rules 1(2), 7(2)*]. Similar provisions apply to hearings in the Upper Tribunal. [*SI 2008 No 2698, Rule 5A; SI 2020 No 416, Rule 5(2)*].

- Hearings will be heard remotely (by telephone or video) where it is reasonably practicable and in accordance with the overriding objective to do so until 18 September 2021. A tribunal may decide to conduct a 'hybrid' hearing, where some participants are in a physical hearing room and others are attending remotely. See www.judiciary.uk/wp-content/uploads/2021/03/Annex-A-Amended-General-Pilot-Practice-Direction-March-2021-FINAL.pdf.
- With effect from 10 April 2020, the First-tier Tribunal may direct that a telephone or video hearing be heard in private if it is not possible for a media representative to listen to or watch the hearing at the time it is taking place and it is in the interests of justice for the hearing to be in private. If a hearing is held in private under this rule, it must be recorded. A hearing must also be recorded if it is public only by virtue of a media representative being able to access the proceedings remotely while they are taking place. These provisions expire at the same time as the *Coronavirus Act 2020*, i.e on 24 March 2022 unless that date is either brought forward or extended. [*SI 2009 No 273, Rules 32(2A), 32A; SI 2020 No 416, Rules 1(2), 7(3)(4); SI 2020 No 651, Rule 7(3)*]. Similar provisions apply to hearings in the Upper Tribunal. [*SI 2008 No 2698, Rules 37(2ZA), 37A; SI 2020 No 416, Rule 5(3)(4); SI 2020 No 651, Rule 5(11)*].
- If a party fails to attend a telephone or video hearing without making an application for it to be adjourned, wins the appeal and then applies for the decision to be set aside on the basis of non-attendance, the Tribunal is unlikely to allow that application. See www.judiciary.uk/wp-content/uploads/2021/03/Annex-A-Amended-General-Pilot-Practice-Direction-March-2021-FINAL.pdf.

The Tax Chamber of the FTT has published a set of frequently asked questions on the impact of coronavirus. See www.judiciary.uk/wp-content/uploads/2020/06/200612-COVID-19-FTT-Tax-Chamber-FAQ.pdf.

Litigation and Settlement Strategy

[5.2] HMRC's Litigation and Settlement Strategy (LSS) is a framework within which HMRC seeks to resolve tax disputes through civil procedures consistent with the law, whether by agreement with the taxpayer or through litigation. The strategy sets out principles for bringing tax disputes to a conclusion, and the relevant factors for HMRC to consider in deciding whether to agree a settlement with the taxpayer or to proceed to litigation, i.e. statutory appeal to the tribunals or the courts. For the text of the LSS, and commentary, see www.gov.uk/government/publications/litigation-and-settlement-strategy-lss. See also HMRC's 'Code of governance for resolving tax disputes' at www.gov.uk/government/publications/resolving-tax-disputes and HMRC Compliance Handbook CH40000 et seq.

Right of appeal

[5.3] Companies have similar rights to individuals with regard to an appeal made under the self-assessment regime. A taxpayer can appeal against:

(a) any assessment other than a self-assessment;
(b) any HMRC amendment of a company tax return following completion or partial completion of an enquiry;
(c) any HMRC amendment (of a self-assessment) made, during an enquiry, to prevent potential loss of tax to the Crown (see **65** RETURNS);
(d) any discovery determination (i.e. a determination by HMRC of an amount included in a company tax return which affects the tax payable for another accounting period or by another company).

An appeal within (d) above cannot be taken forward until the enquiry has been completed.

[*TMA 1970, s 31(1)(2); FA 1998, Sch 18 paras 30(3), 34(3), 48(1), 49*].

An appeal against an assessment to corporation tax is an appeal against the total amount of profits charged to tax in the assessment (*Owton Fens Properties Ltd v Redden* Ch D 1984, 58 TC 218).

It is notable that in *Hannigan v HMRC* FTT, [2009] UKFTT 334 (TC), 2010 SWTI 439, the First-tier Tribunal found that it did not have jurisdiction to hear appeals against income tax assessments that had been withdrawn.

Specific rights of appeal against HMRC decisions, notices or determinations are also included in a number of other provisions, for example: the refusal or removal of gross payment status in CIS cases; the imposition of a penalty or an interest or penalty determination; a determination relating to an employer's failure to operate PAYE; and certain information notices, such as those under *FA 2008, Sch 36 para 1* (except those approved in advance by the Tribunal). Where relevant, such rights are referred to at the appropriate place in this work.

In *Adam Mather v HMRC* FTT, [2014] UKFTT 1062 (TC), the First-tier Tribunal found that a refusal by HMRC to give a ruling (in relation to the application of a VAT provision) was not an appealable decision. The Tribunal stated *Earlsferry Thistle Golf Club* UT, [2014] UKUT 250 (TCC) as authority for the proposition that 'decision' should not be given an unnaturally wide definition in such cases.

In *Couldwell Concrete Flooring v HMRC* FTT, [2015] UKFTT 135 (TC), the First-tier Tribunal noted that it could not hear an appeal against a notice requiring statutory records (however vague and ambiguous) but it could hear an appeal against a penalty for non-compliance with that notice. Additionally the Tribunal could vary a request for information.

In *B & K Lavery Property Trading Partnership v HMRC* UT 2016, [2017] STC 829, the Upper Tribunal upheld the First-tier Tribunal's conclusion that it had jurisdiction to hear issues not specifically identified in the closure notice. In *Dr Vasiliki Raftopoulou v HMRC* UT, [2015] UKUT 579 (TCC), the Upper Tribunal suggested that a single letter could constitute both the opening and closing of an enquiry therefore making it possible for the taxpayer to appeal, and remitted the matter back to the First-tier Tribunal.

Unless otherwise stated or required by context, the remainder of this chapter applies to all appeals and all matters treated as appeals, and not only to appeals within (a)–(d) above. [*TMA 1970, s 48*].

Making an appeal

[5.4] An appeal is made by giving notice in writing, to the officer of Revenue and Customs concerned and specifying the grounds of appeal. Notice must normally be given within 30 days after the date of issue of the assessment or determination, the closure notice or the notice of amendment. [*TMA 1970, s 31A(1)–(5); FA 1998, Sch 18 paras 30(3)(4), 34(3)(4), 48(2), 92(2)*].

See **5.1** above for the extension of the time limit in certain cases for taxpayers affected by the coronavirus.

Late appeals

[5.5] If a taxpayer fails to make an appeal within the normal time limit, an appeal can still be made if HMRC agree or, where HMRC do not agree, the Tribunal gives permission.

HMRC must agree to a written request for a late appeal if they are satisfied that there was a reasonable excuse for not making the appeal within the time limit and that the request was made without unreasonable delay after the reasonable excuse ceased.

[*TMA 1970, s 49*].

In the event of refusal to accept a late appeal, the decision is not subject to further appeal (*R v Special Commrs (ex p. Magill)* QB (NI) 1979, 53 TC 135), but is subject to judicial review (see *R v Hastings and Bexhill General Commrs and CIR (ex p. Goodacre)* QB 1994, 67 TC 126, in which a refusal was quashed and the matter remitted to a different body of Commissioners).

In *R (oao Browallia Cal Ltd) v General Commissioners of Income Tax* QB 2003, [2004] STC 296, it was held that the Appeal Commissioners had a wider discretion than HMRC in considering a late appeal. The court held that the Commissioners in that case had misunderstood their powers and that the lack of any reasonable excuse was 'potentially relevant' but was 'not conclusive'. The decision was followed in *R (oao Cook) v General Commissioners of Income Tax* [2007] EWHC 167 (Admin), [2007] STC 499, [2007] All ER (D) 247 (Jan) in which the General Commissioners' refusal of a late appeal application was quashed because they had only considered the lack of a reasonable excuse and did not consider the possible merits of the appeal itself. When the case was remitted to the General Commissioners, however, they again refused the late appeal, and the court upheld their decision — see *R (oao Cook) v General Commissioners of Income Tax (No. 2)* [2009] EWHC 590 (Admin), [2009] SWTI 683, [2009] STC 1212.

The First-tier Tribunal considered whether a fax stating intention to appeal was a valid notice of appeal in the case of *Greenoaks Pharmacy Ltd v HMRC* (TC01118) [2011] UKFTT 254 (TC). HMRC had commenced an enquiry into a company (G) which operated several retail pharmacies. On 23 July 2009 they issued jeopardy amendments to G's self-assessments, increasing its tax liability by more than £1,000,000. On 21 August G's accountant sent HMRC a fax stating that he would 'be sending appeal and postponement applications to those amendments in due course'. The HMRC officer dealing with the case treated this as an expression of intention rather than a formal appeal. Subsequently HMRC began action to collect the debt, and G sent a further fax indicating that it was appealing against the amendments. HMRC treated this as an application to make a late appeal, and rejected it on the grounds that there was no reasonable excuse for the delay. G lodged an application with the First-Tier Tribunal, contending firstly that the fax which it had sent on 21 August had been a valid notice of appeal (and was within the statutory time limit), and alternatively that it had a reasonable excuse for not having appealed with the statutory limit. The First-Tier Tribunal accepted these contentions and allowed the applications, finding that 'the fax of 21 August 2009 was sufficient to amount to a valid appeal against the amendments made'.

In *Pytchley Ltd v HMRC* (TC01139) [2010] UKFTT 277 (TC), the Tribunal considered the question of prejudice to the taxpayer's position with regard to a late appeal. A company (P) failed to respond to queries from HMRC concerning its tax return. In January 2009 HMRC issued an amendment to the return. In June 2009 P applied to lodge a late appeal against the amendment. HMRC opposed the application but the First-Tier Tribunal granted it. Judge Brannan held that 'the prejudice to the Appellant of being unable to advance an arguably meritorious appeal outweighed its dilatoriness and any prejudice to HMRC'.

In *Data Select Ltd v HMRC* [2012] UKUT 197 (TCC), [2012] SWTI 2185 (Upper Tribunal — 13 June), a company (D) had applied to lodge a late appeal against the disallowance of a substantial claim for repayment of input tax. The First-tier Tribunal rejected the application and the Upper Tribunal dismissed D's appeal against this decision, and held the First-tier tribunal was entitled to decline to admit an application for late appeal, applying the principles laid down in *Smith v Brough* CA [2005] EWCA Civ 261, and *HMRC v Church of Scientology Religious Education College Inc* [2007] EWHC 1329 (Ch), [2007] STC 1196. In *Citipost Mail v HMRC* [2015] UKFTT 252 the First-Tier Tribunal chose to follow the *Data Select* approach which requires that all the circumstances be considered and balanced: it found that the taxpayer should not be granted permission to make a late appeal against post-clearance demand notes, noting the very significant length of delay, the lack of any good reason for not appealing within the time limit, and the need to ensure fairness as between taxpayers. The principles set out in *Data Select* were similarly followed in *Odunlami v HMRC* [2015] UKFTT 688 where an application for a late appeal was refused.

In *Folarin Bamgbopa v HMRC* [2013] UKFTT 664(TC) the tribunal denied permission to notify a late appeal under *TMA 1970, s 49*, noting no good explanation for the two year delay had been given and also that the degree of prejudice to the taxpayer could be off set by a claim for damages against his accountants if they were responsible for the delay. In *Chauhan v HMRC* [2014] UKFTT 851 whilst the Tribunal held it had no jurisdiction to review

HMRC's decision not to allow losses out of time, it did note that the persistent malfunction of computer equipment over a three year period would not be a reasonable excuse.

Permission to appeal was granted by the Tribunal in *Rezaee v HMRC* FTT, [2018] UKFTT 302 (TC), 2018 SWTI 1548. A company officer sought permission to make a late appeal against a notice of personal liability to a penalty for incorrect returns made by the company.

Withdrawing an appeal

[5.6] An appeal once made cannot, strictly, be withdrawn unilaterally (see *R v Special Commissioners (ex p. Elmhirst)* CA 1935, 20 TC 381 and *Beach v Willesden General Commissioners* Ch D 1981, 55 TC 663). If, however, a taxpayer or his agent gives HMRC oral or written notice of his desire not to proceed with an appeal, the appeal is treated as if settled by agreement, so that the provisions at **5.12** below apply (and the appeal is settled without any variation). Agreement is effective from the date of the taxpayer's notification.

This does not apply if HMRC give written notice of objection to such withdrawal within 30 days of the taxpayer's notice, in which case the proceedings will continue.

It was held in the case of *St Anne's Distributors v Revenue and Customs Comrs* [2010] UKUT 458 (TCC), [2011] STC 708, [2011] NLJR 102 that notification by email does not satisfy the 'written notice' requirement.

[*TMA 1970, s 54(4)(5)*].

For postponement of tax pending appeal and for payment of tax on determination of the appeal, see respectively **58** PAYMENT OF TAX, and further **5.27** herein.

The appeal process

[5.7] When an appeal to HMRC is made, there are four options for the appeal to proceed:

(a) the appellant can require HMRC to review the matter in question;
(b) HMRC can offer to review the matter in question;
(c) the appellant can notify the appeal to the Tribunal for it to decide the matter in question; or
(d) the appeal can be settled by agreement between HMRC and the appellant.

Where the appellant requires an HMRC review, he can still notify the appeal to the tribunal if he disagrees with the review's conclusions or HMRC fail to complete a review within the required time.

If HMRC offer a review and the appellant does not accept the offer, he can likewise notify the appeal to the tribunal. Taking any of options (a) to (c) above does not prevent the appeal from being settled by agreement at any time.

[*TMA 1970, s 49A*].

For details of the review process, see **5.8** below; for notifying an appeal to the tribunal, see **5.11** below; and for settlement of appeals by agreement, see **5.12** below.

All notices given under the appeal provisions must be made in writing. Notifications by the appellant can be made by a person acting on his behalf, but all HMRC notifications must be made directly to the appellant (although copies can be sent to his agent).

[*TMA 1970, s 49I*].

HMRC review

[5.8] HMRC implemented a new review procedure at the same time as the overhaul to the Tribunal system was being undertaken. As note above, the taxpayer has a statutory right to request an initial review of an HMRC decision, as a way of attempting to reach an agreement without the need to go to the Tribunal. A taxpayer is not obliged to request a review, and requesting a review does not stop the taxpayer from making an appeal to the Tribunal, as noted above.

As noted in HMRC's Appeals, Reviews and Tribunals Manual at ARTG4050, the following decisions are not reviewable:

(a) decisions where there is no right of appeal;
(b) decisions about whether to allow a late review;
(c) decisions about whether to allow late appeals;
(d) refusals to allow postponement or hardship applications; and
(e) conclusions of a review.

In addition there are a number of matters that the Tribunal considers on application or referral, for example applications for closure notices, information notice applications, applications for daily penalties (the latter two under *FA 2008, Sch 36*). Although these are considered by the Tribunal they are not appeals and they are not within the scope of the review provisions.

Where an appellant notifies HMRC that he requires them to review the matter in question, HMRC must first notify him of their view of the matter. They must do this within the 30 days beginning with the day on which they receive the notification from the appellant, or within such longer period as is reasonable. They must then carry out a review of the matter in question, as described at **5.9** below.

The appellant cannot request a second review of the matter in question and neither can he request a review if he has already notified the appeal to the tribunal.

If it is HMRC who offer to review the matter in question, they must, when they notify the appellant of the offer, also notify the appellant of their view of the matter. The appellant then has 30 days beginning with the date of the document notifying him of the offer to notify HMRC of acceptance of it. If the appellant does so, HMRC must then carry out a review of the matter in question, as described at **5.9** below. Alternatively, the appellant can, within the same 30-day period, notify the appeal to the tribunal for it to decide the matter in question.

If the appellant does not either accept the offer of review or notify the appeal to the tribunal within the 30-day period, then HMRC's view of the matter in question is treated as if it were contained in a written agreement for the settlement of the appeal, so that the provisions at **5.12** below apply (and the appeal is settled on the basis of HMRC's view). The appellant's normal right to withdraw from such agreements does not apply to the deemed agreement. The tribunal may, however, give permission for the appellant to notify the appeal to it after the 30-day period has ended.

HMRC cannot make a second offer of a review or make an offer if the appellant has already required a review or has notified the appeal to the tribunal.

[*TMA 1970, ss 49B, 49C, 49H*].

Conduct of the review

[5.9] The nature and extent of HMRC's review will be determined by them as seems appropriate in the circumstances, but they must take into account the steps taken before the start of the review both by them in deciding the matter in question and by anyone else seeking to resolve the disagreement. They must also take into account representations made by the appellant, provided that these are made at a stage which gives HMRC a reasonable opportunity to consider them.

The review must be completed and HMRC's conclusions notified to the appellant in writing within 45 days beginning with:

- where the appellant required the review, the day HMRC notified him of their view of the matter in question; or
- where HMRC offered the review, the day HMRC received notification of the appellant's acceptance of the offer.

HMRC and the appellant can, however, agree any other period for completion of the review.

If HMRC fail to notify the appellant of their conclusions within the required period, the review is treated as if the conclusion was that HMRC's original view of the matter in question were upheld. HMRC must notify the appellant in writing accordingly.

[*TMA 1970, s 49E*].

HMRC's notice stating the conclusions to the review is treated as a written agreement for the settlement of the appeal, so that the provisions at **5.12** below apply (and the appeal is settled on the basis of those conclusions). The appellant's normal right to withdraw from such agreements does not apply to the deemed agreement.

The appellant does, however, have a further opportunity to notify the appeal to the tribunal for them to determine the matter in question. This must normally be done within the period of 30 days beginning with the date of the document notifying the conclusions of the review. Where, however, HMRC have failed to notify the conclusions within the required period, the time limit is extended to

30 days after the date of the document notifying the appellant that the review is to be treated as if concluded on the basis of HMRC's original opinion. The tribunal may give permission for an appeal to be notified to them after the time limits have expired.

[*TMA 1970, ss 49F, 49G*].

HMRC practice

Reviews are carried out by HMRC officers who have experience of the subject matter of the appeal but are independent of the decision maker and the decision maker's line management.

The review officer will consider whether the case is one which HMRC would want to defend before the tribunal, and in particular will consider:

- whether the facts have been established, and whether there is disagreement about the facts;
- the technical and legal merits of the case;
- whether it would be an efficient or desirable use of resources to proceed with an appeal that will cost more than the sum in dispute;
- the likelihood of success; and
- whether the appeal raises unusual questions of law or general policy or may in some other way potentially have an effect on future decisions.

(HMRC Appeals, Reviews and Tribunals Guide, ARTG4080).

Review officers are instructed generally to avoid discussing the case with the caseworker during the review in order to ensure that the review remains independent. If exceptionally it is necessary discuss a case with the caseworker in any depth during the review the review officer will tell the appellant and offer equivalent telephone or face to face contact with him or his agent, so the appellant has an equal opportunity to make representations. (HMRC Appeals, Reviews and Tribunals Guide, ARTG4620).

See further HMRC Appeals, Reviews and Tribunals Guide, ARTG4000–4860.

Alternative Dispute Resolution

[5.10] Companies (and individuals) can apply to HMRC to use alternative dispute resolution (ADR) to seek to settle tax disputes, whether or not an appealable tax decision or assessment has been made by HMRC. The ADR process was introduced nationwide following a two year trial under which certain taxpayers had been invited by HMRC to use it. Entering into the ADR process does not affect the taxpayer's existing review and appeal rights.

ADR involves an independent person from HMRC (called a 'facilitator'), who has not previously been involved in the dispute, working with both the taxpayer and the HMRC case owner to try to broker an agreement between them. The process does not guarantee resolution of the dispute. Entering into the ADR process does not affect the taxpayer's existing review and appeal rights. See www.gov.uk/guidance/tax-disputes-alternative-dispute-resolution-adr.

Taxpayers can apply to use ADR by following the link from the above web page and completing the online form.

With effect from 15 June 2020, the FTT will allow a stay on proceedings of 150 days to allow for ADR if the hearing has not yet been listed. If the hearing has been listed the FTT will only stay proceedings if both taxpayer and HMRC confirm that they can go ahead on the hearing date if ADR fails. (First-tier Tribunal (Tax Chamber) Practice Statement 15 June 2020). Previously, once an appeal had notified to the FTT and HMRC's statement of case had been served, the FTT would only allow ADR in exceptional circumstances.

Appeal to the Tribunal

[5.11] A taxpayer who has appealed to HMRC can notify the appeal to the Tribunal without requesting an HMRC review first. If he does so, HMRC cannot then make an offer of a review. [*TMA 1970, s 49D*].

The aim of this two step approach (appeal to HMRC, then to the Tribunal) is to facilitate the resolution of issues with HMRC wherever possible, so the Tribunal considers only appeals which cannot be agreed by negotiation.

An appellant can also notify an appeal to the tribunal if he does not wish to accept an HMRC offer of a review or if he disagrees with the conclusions of a review. In both cases there are short time limits within which notification must be made, although the tribunal can give permission for notification to be made outside those limits: see **5.8** and **5.9** above.

There is no provision for HMRC to notify an appeal to the Tribunal.

Notice of appeal must include the appellant's details, details of the decision etc. appealed against, the result the appellant is seeking and the grounds of appeal. The notice must be accompanied by a copy of any written record of the decision and the reasons for it that the appellant has or can reasonably obtain. If the notice is made late it must also include a request for extension of time and the reason for lateness. [*SI 2009 No 273, Rule 20*].

Appeals should be notified to the tribunal online at www.gov.uk/tax-tribunal/appeal-to-tribunal; by e-mail to taxappeals@justice.gov.uk or by post to the HM Courts and Tribunals Service, First-tier Tribunal (Tax Chamber), PO Box 16972, Birmingham B16 6TZ. A Notice of Appeal form (T240) can be downloaded from www.gov.uk/government/publications/notice-of-appeal-ask-a-tax-judge-to-examine-a-dispute-form-t240 or obtained from the Tribunals Service by phoning 0300 123 1024.

With regard to a late appeal, in *G Lupson v HMRC* (TC00976) [2011] UKFTT 100 (TC), the First-tier Tribunal allowed an application to lodge a late appeal in a case where a former publican (L) had suffered brain damage following a heart attack, and had been evicted from the public house which he ran. The tribunal observed that there was serious doubt whether L had received some letters which HMRC had posted to him, and held that, in view of his medical history, it would be in the interests of justice to allow this application.

With regard to the jurisdiction of the tribunal, in the recent case of *HMRC v Hok Ltd* (Upper Tribunal, 25 October 2012) the Upper Tribunal (UT) considered the jurisdiction of the FTT and allowed HMRC's appeal against the controversial First-tier Tribunal (FTT) decision of Judge Geraint Jones.

Hok Ltd had only one employee, who ceased employment during 2009/10. The company did not submit its P35 for 2009/10 by the due date of 19 May. On 27 September HMRC imposed a penalty of £400 (at £100 per month for four months). The company appealed, contending that the amount of the penalty was unreasonable because HMRC should have warned it earlier that it was still required to submit a P35 even though its only employee had left. The FTT allowed the appeal in part but the UT reversed this decision and restored the penalty. The UT held that 'the First-tier Tribunal does not have any judicial review jurisdiction', and specifically disapproved the reasoning of Judge Geraint Jones in *Foresight Financial Services Ltd v HMRC*, FTT [2011] UKFTT 647 (TC) TC01489. The UT held that the FTT could not 'give effect to common law principles in order to override the clear words of a statute', and could not 'arrogate to itself a jurisdiction which Parliament has chosen not to confer on it. Parliament must be taken to have known, when passing the 2007 Act, of the difference between statutory, common law and judicial review jurisdictions. The clear inference is that it intended to leave supervision of the conduct of HMRC and similar public bodies where it was, that is in the High Court, save to the limited extent it was conferred on this tribunal. It follows that in purporting to discharge the penalties on the ground that their imposition was unfair, the tribunal was acting in excess of jurisdiction, and its decision must be quashed.'

See **5.13** onwards below for the process by which an appeal notified to the tribunal is decided.

Settlement by agreement

[5.12] At any time before an appeal is determined by the tribunal, it may be settled by agreement between HMRC and the appellant or his agent. Where such an agreement is reached, in writing or otherwise, the assessment or decision as upheld, varied, discharged, or cancelled by that agreement, is treated as if it had been determined on appeal. Oral agreements are, however, effective only if confirmed in writing by either side (the date of such confirmation then being the effective date of agreement).

The taxpayer may withdraw from the agreement by giving written notice within 30 days of making it.

[*TMA 1970, s 54(1)–(3)(5)*].

The agreement must specify the figure for assessment or a precise formula for ascertaining it (*Delbourgo v Field* CA 1978, 52 TC 225).

The agreement only covers the assessments (or decisions) which are the subject of the appeal, and does not bind HMRC for subsequent years, for example where relievable amounts are purported to be carried forward from the year in question (*MacNiven v Westmoreland Investments Ltd* HL 2001, 73 TC 1 and see also *Tod v South Essex Motors (Basildon)* Ltd Ch D 1987, 60 TC 598).

The issue of an amended notice of assessment cannot in itself constitute an offer for the purposes of a *s 54* agreement; nor can a lack of response by the taxpayer constitute acceptance of an offer (*Schuldenfrei v Hilton* CA 1999, 72 TC 167).

An agreement based on a mutual mistake of fact was as a result invalid, so that the taxpayer could proceed with his appeal (*Fox v Rothwell* [1995] STC (SCD) 336).

See *Gibson v General Commissioners for Stroud* Ch D 1989, 61 TC 645 for a case where there was held not to have been a determination and *R v Inspector of Taxes, ex p. Bass Holdings Ltd; Richart v Bass Holdings Ltd* QB 1992, 65 TC 495 for one where rectification of an agreement was ordered where a relief had been deducted twice contrary to the intention of Revenue and taxpayer.

See *CIR v West* CA 1991, 64 TC 196 for a case where the taxpayer was unsuccessful in seeking leave to defend a Crown action for payment of tax on the ground that the accountant who had entered into an agreement had no authority to do so given him by the taxpayer.

The 30-day period for withdrawal from an agreement cannot be extended on the grounds of reasonable excuse (*Bull v HMRC* FTT, [2019] SFTD 911).

The Tribunal

[5.13] Under the unified tribunal system established by the *Tribunals, Courts and Enforcement Act 2007*, there are two tribunals; the First-tier Tribunal and the Upper Tribunal. The Tribunals are presided over by a Senior President of Tribunals. [*TCEA 2007, s 3*].

The Tribunal Procedure Rules which govern the operation of the Tribunals include an explicit statement of their overriding objective, which is to deal with cases fairly and justly. The Tribunals are required to deal with each case in ways proportionate to its importance, its complexity and the anticipated costs and resources of the parties to the appeal etc. They must avoid unnecessary formality and delay and seek flexibility in the proceedings. They must ensure that the parties are able to participate fully in the proceedings.

The parties to the appeal etc. are in turn required to help the Tribunal to further the overriding objective and to co-operate with the Tribunal generally.

[*SI 2008 No 2698, Rule 2; SI 2009 No 273, Rule 2*].

The Tribunals also have an explicit duty to point out to the parties the availability of any alternative procedure for resolving the dispute and to facilitate the use of the procedure if the parties wish. [*SI 2008 No 2698, Rule 3; SI 2009 No 273, Rule 3*]. See **5.10** above for HMRC's alternative dispute resolution process.

Both the First-tier and Upper Tribunal consist of judges who have particular legal qualifications or experience, and other members who are not legally qualified but meet specified selection criteria. Judges of the Upper Tribunal are appointed by the Crown on the recommendation of the Lord Chancellor. Judges and members of the First-tier Tribunal, and members of the Upper Tribunal, are appointed by the Lord Chancellor. See *TCEA 2007, ss 4, 5, Schs 2, 3*.

The First-tier Tribunal

[5.14] Tax appeals notified to the Tribunal are in most cases initially heard and decided by the First-tier Tribunal. [*TMA 1970, s 47C; SI 2009 No 56, Sch 1 para 27*].

The First-tier Tribunal is organised into separate chambers each with responsibility for different areas of the law and with its own Chamber President. This ensures the panel for any particular appeal has the relevant level of expertise.

With certain exceptions, the Tax and Chancery Chamber is responsible for all appeals, applications, references or other proceedings in respect of the functions of HMRC. It is also responsible for appeals etc. in respect of the exercise of HMRC functions by the National Crime Agency (see **36.16** HMRC — ADMINISTRATION). The exceptions relate to certain tax credit and national insurance matters and to matters for which the Upper Tribunal is responsible. [*TCEA 2007, s 7; SI 2008 No 2684, Arts 2, 5A; SI 2009 No 129, Arts 3, 5*].

The Upper Tribunal

[5.15] The Upper Tribunal is a superior court of record, so that its decisions create legally binding precedents. [*TCEA 2007, s 3(5)*].

It is similarly divided into chambers, including the Tax and Chancery Chamber. The Chamber is responsible for:

(a) further appeals against decisions by the First-tier Tribunal Tax Chamber (see **5.31** below);
(b) applications by HMRC for a tax-related penalty under *FA 2008, Sch 36 para 50* in respect of failure to comply with an information notice or obstruction of an inspection (see **59** PENALTIES);
(c) complex appeals, applications or references transferred from the First-tier Tribunal (see **5.16** below); and
(d) matters referred to the Upper Tribunal following a decision by the First-tier Tribunal Tax Chamber to set aside its own original decision (see **5.33** below).

[*SI 2008 No 2684, Arts 6, 8*].

First-tier Tribunal procedure

Case management

[5.16] The Tribunal has wide powers to regulate its own procedures and to give (and amend) directions about the conduct or disposal of cases. In particular it can, by direction:

- consolidate or hear two or more cases together or treat a case as a lead case (see *SI 2009 No 273, Rule 18*);
- permit or require a party to the case or another person to provide documents, information or submissions to the tribunal or another party;
- hold a hearing to consider any matter, including a case management hearing;
- decide the form of any hearing;
- require a party to produce a bundle of documents for a hearing.

The Tribunal can also substitute a party to a case where necessary or add a person to the case as a respondent. A person who is not a party to the case can apply to the Tribunal to be added as a party.

Either party to a case can apply for the Tribunal to make a direction, either in writing or orally at a hearing, or the Tribunal can make a direction on its own initiative. Applications for a direction must include the reason for making it. Directions can be challenged by applying for a further direction.

In *Tricor plc (formerly PNC Telecom plc) v HMRC* (TC02022) [2012] UKFTT 336 (TC) the appellant company applied for the judge hearing the appeal to be recused, contending that decisions which he had reached in similar cases indicated that he was biased in favour of HMRC. The recusal application was heard by a different judge (Judge Berner) who dismissed it, finding that 'there is nothing in the conduct of the proceedings to suggest otherwise than that the Judge has acted with scrupulous fairness throughout'.

In *Peel Investments (UK) Ltd v HMRC* FTT, [2013] UKFTT 404 (TC) the appellant company applied for the proceedings at the First-tier Tribunal to be stayed pending judgment on another case. The Tribunal granted the stay and repeated the following two stage test with regard to such applications: firstly would the decision of another court be of 'material assistance (not necessarily determinative) in resolving issues before the tribunal or court in question'; and secondly, would it be 'expedient' to state the appeal. In this case the Tribunal decided both tests were met and stayed proceedings.

In *General Healthcare Group v HMRC* [2014] UKFTT 1087 the First-tier Tribunal sets out the considerations to apply when deciding whether a case which is subject to a lead case direction, should be bound by the lead case. Only material factual differences will lead to a departure, and the Tribunal found that the case was bound by the lead case of *Nuffield* [2013] UKFTT 291. Certain questions of law were for the Upper Tribunal to ascertain on appeal.

Any action required to be done in relation to a case on or by a particular day must be done before 5pm on that day (or, if that day is not a working day, by 5pm on the next working day).

[*SI 2009 No 273, Rules 5, 6, 9, 12*].

Administration of cases referred to the Tribunal, including the categorisation of cases (see **5.18** below), is carried out by the Tribunals Service.

Starting proceedings

See **5.11** above for how to notify an appeal to the Tribunal. There are also rules for proceedings to be determined without notice to a respondent (*Rule 19*), and for proceedings started by originating application or reference (*Rule 21*).

Representation

A party to a case can appoint a representative to represent him in the proceedings. The representative does **not** need to be a lawyer or legal representative. The party has to notify the Tribunal and the other parties of the appointment of a representative and they will then treat the representative as authorised until notified otherwise.

Where no such person has been appointed, a party can, with the Tribunal's permission, nevertheless be accompanied at a hearing by another person who can act as a representative or assist in presenting the case.

[*SI 2009 No 273, Rule 11*].

Withdrawal from a case

Subject to any legislation relating to withdrawal from or settlement of particular proceedings, a party can notify the Tribunal of the withdrawal of its case, or part of it. This can be done in writing or orally at a hearing.

A party who has withdrawn its case can, however, apply (in writing) to the Tribunal to reinstate it. The application must be received by the Tribunal within 28 days after it received the withdrawal notice or the date of the hearing. It was held in the case of *St Annes Distributors v HMRC* [2010] UKUT 458 (TCC), [2011] STC 708, [2011] NLJR 102 (and indirect tax case) that notification by email does not satisfy the 'written notice' requirement.

[*SI 2009 No 273, Rule 17*].

Failure to comply with rules

[5.17] An irregularity resulting from any failure to comply with the Tribunal Procedure Rules, a practice direction or a direction by the Tribunal does not in itself make the proceedings void.

Where a party fails to comply with the Rules etc. the Tribunal can take such action as it considers just. This could be to require compliance or waive the requirement, to strike the case out (see below) or, in certain cases, to refer the failure to the Upper Tribunal.

The Tribunal can refer to the Upper Tribunal any failure to:

- attend a hearing, or otherwise be available, to give evidence;
- to swear an oath in connection with giving evidence;
- to give evidence as a witness;
- to produce a document; or
- to facilitate the inspection of a document or other thing (including premises).

The Upper Tribunal then has the same powers as the High Court to deal with the failure (which may include financial penalties).

In *BPP Holdings Ltd v HMRC* CA, [2016] STC 841 HMRC had not complied with an order to give proper particulars of its pleaded case and had not given any reason for its failure. The Court debarred HMRC from further participation in the relevant proceedings.

[*TCEA 2007, s 25; SI 2009 No 273, Rule 7*].

Striking out a case

A case will automatically be struck out if the appellant fails to comply with a direction which states that failure to comply will lead to striking out.

The Tribunal can also strike out a case if the appellant fails to comply with a direction which states that failure to comply may lead to striking out, if the appellant has failed to co-operate with the Tribunal to such an extent that the case cannot be dealt with fairly and justly, or if the Tribunal considers that there is no reasonable prospect of the appellant's case succeeding. In the last two cases, however, the Tribunal must first give the appellant an opportunity to make representations.

If the case is struck out because of the appellant's failure to comply with a direction, the appellant can apply for the case to be reinstated. This must be done in writing within 28 days after the date the Tribunal sent the notification of the striking out.

The above rules also apply to respondents except that, instead of the case being struck out, the respondent is barred from taking any further part in the case.

An appeal against three determinations under *TMA 1970, s 28C* was struck out in *Bartram v HMRC* [2012] UKUT 184 (TCC).

However, the First-Tier Tribunal rejected such an application by HMRC in *RE Clark v HMRC* FTT, [2011] UKFTT 302 (TC) where the appellant sought to appeal against a form P800. Judge Redston held that it was arguable that a form P800 was a notice of assessment giving rise to a right to appeal under *TMA 1970, s 31*, and directed that the case should be relisted for further hearing. However the question of whether a form P800 was a notice of assessment giving rise to a right to appeal was considered in more detail in *Prince v HMRC* FTT, [2012] SFTD 786 where Judge Bishopp accepted HMRC's contentions that a P800 was not a notice of assessment, and struck out three notices of appeal. In *Spring Capital Ltd v HMRC* FTT, [2013] SFTD 570, the Tribunal rejected the approach taken in *Clark*, concluding that, 'it is not open to the tribunal, having concluded that there is an arguable case on jurisdiction, to refuse to strike out the appeal: it must resolve the issue. It must decide whether there is jurisdiction or not and, in the latter case, the appeal must be struck out.'

In *Jack Dyson v HMRC* [2015] UKFTT 131 the First-tier Tribunal struck out an appeal made on behalf of a partnership against a late filing penalty for the partnership return, on the basis that under *FA 2009, Sch 55* only the representative partner or his successor has a right of appeal against such penalty, and Mr Dyson was not that partner.

A struck-out appeal was reinstated in *B Nowroozi v HMRC* FTT, [2019] UKFTT 533 (TC); 2019 SWTI 1586. The taxpayer had relied on his accountants to deal with directions of the Tribunal at a time when he had been diagnosed with stage four cancer.

An attempt to have HMRC barred from taking any part in a case was unsuccessful in *Foulser v HMRC* FTT 2011, [2012] SFTD 94. On appeal to the Upper Tribunal, however, the case was remitted for rehearing by the FTT ([2013] STC 917). An attempt to have HMRC barred also failed in *Ritchie v HMRC* [2016] UKFTT 509 (TC), 2016 STI 2753.

[*SI 2009 No 273, Rule 8*].

Categorisation of cases

[5.18] When an appeal, application or reference is notified to the Tribunal, the Tribunals Service allocate it to one of four categories of case:

(a) default paper;
(b) basic;
(c) standard; or
(d) complex.

Cases may be re-categorised by the Tribunal at any time either on the application of one of the parties or on the Tribunal's own initiative.

Cases involving MP's expenses and financial restrictions civil penalty cases (under *Sch 7* of the *Counter Terrorism Act 2008* and CAA cases (under *CAA 2001, s 563*), are categorised as either standard or complex.

[*SI 2009 No 273, Rule 23(1)–(3)*].

The process by which the appeal etc. will be decided varies according to the category to which the case is allocated as described below.

Default paper cases

[5.19] The following types of cases must normally be categorised as default paper cases:

(a) appeals against fixed penalties of not more than £2,000 for late self-assessment tax returns (see **53.4–53.6** PENALTIES) and certain other late returns or notifications;
(b) appeals against penalties of not more than £2,000 for late payment of tax (see **43.7** LATE PAYMENT INTEREST AND PENALTIES).

Cases can be allocated to a different category if the Tribunal considers it appropriate to do so.

(Tribunals Practice Statement, 29 April 2013).

See **5.1** above for the temporary increase in the above limits during the coronavirus pandemic.

In a default paper case, the respondent (i.e., in an appeal, HMRC) must provide a statement of case to the Tribunal, the appellant and any other respondents to be received within 42 days after the Tribunal sends it notice of the proceedings (or by such time as the Tribunal directs). The statement must state the legislation under which the decision in question was made and set out the respondent's position. If the statement is late it must also include a request for a time extension and give the reason for lateness.

The statement can also contain a request for the case to be dealt with either at or without a hearing.

Once such a statement has been given to the appellant, he may send a written reply to the Tribunal. The reply must be received within 30 days after the date on which the respondent sent its statement to the appellant and must be sent also to each respondent. The reply may include the appellant's response to the respondent's statement of case, provide any further relevant information and contain a request for the case to be dealt with at a hearing. If the reply is late it must also include a request for a time extension and give the reason for lateness.

The Tribunal must hold a hearing before determining a case if any party has requested one in writing. Otherwise, on receipt of the appellant's reply or the expiry of the time limit for such a reply, the Tribunal will determine the case without a hearing, unless it directs otherwise.

[*SI 2009 No 273, Rules 25, 26*].

See **5.1** above for the temporary power for the Tribunal to direct that a case be determined on the papers despite the objections of any party during the coronavirus pandemic.

Default paper cases are decided by one judge or other member of the First-tier Tribunal. (Tribunals Practice Statement, 10 March 2009).

Basic cases

[5.20] The following types of cases must normally be allocated as basic cases (unless they must be allocated as default paper cases):

(a) appeals against penalties for late filing and late payment, including daily penalties;
(b) appeals against penalties under *FA 2007, Sch 24* (errors in documents and failure to notify HMRC of errors in assessments — see **59** PENALTIES);
(c) appeals against indirect tax penalties on the basis of reasonable excuse and certain construction industry scheme decisions;
(d) appeals against information notices (including those at **38** HMRC INVESTIGATORY POWERS and **65** RETURNS);
(e) applications for permission to make a late appeal (see **5.3** above);
(f) applications for the postponement of tax pending an appeal (see **58** PAYMENT OF TAX); and
(g) applications for a direction that HMRC close an enquiry (see **65** RETURNS).

Appeals against penalties for deliberate action or where an appeal is also brought against the assessment to which the penalty relates are excluded from (b) above (as are indirect tax cases).

Cases can be allocated to a different category if the Tribunal considers it appropriate to do so.

(Tribunals Practice Direction, 10 March 2009).

Basic cases normally proceed directly to a hearing, without the need for the respondent to produce a statement of case. Where, however, the respondent intends to raise grounds at the hearing of which the appellant has not been informed, the appellant must be notified of those grounds as soon as is reasonably practicable. The respondent must include sufficient detail to enable the appellant to respond to the grounds at the hearing. [*SI 2009 No 273, Rule 24*].

A decision in a basic case that disposes of proceedings or determines a preliminary issue made at, or following, a hearing must be made by either one, two or, where the Chamber President so decides, three members. The members can be judges or other members as the Chamber President decides, and he will choose one of them to be the presiding member. Any other decision will be made by one judge or other member. (Tribunals Practice Statement, 10 March 2009).

Standard cases

[5.21] In a standard case, the respondent (i.e., in an appeal, HMRC) must provide a statement of case to the tribunal, the appellant and any other respondents to be received within 60 days after the Tribunal sends it notice of the proceedings (or by such time as the Tribunal directs). The statement must state the legislation under which the decision in question was made and set out the respondent's position. If the statement is late it must also include a request for a time extension and give the reason for lateness.

The statement can also contain a request for the case to be dealt with either at or without a hearing.

Within 42 days after the date on which the respondent sent the statement of case, each party to the case must send to the Tribunal and each other party a list of documents of which that party has possession (or the right to take possession or make copies) and on which the party intends to rely or to produce in the proceedings. The other parties must then be allowed to inspect or copy those documents, except for any which are privileged.

The case will then normally proceed to a hearing (see **5.23** below).

[*SI 2009 No 273, Rules 25, 27*].

In *Addo v HMRC* FTT 2018, [2019] SFTD 168, the Tribunal held that the obligation to disclose documents was subject to the duty of all parties to help the Tribunal to further the overriding objective to deal with cases fairly and justly. If the level of disclosure, whilst abiding by the strict terms of the rules, fell short of the level that would be required to further the overriding objective, further disclosure could be required by the making of orders or directions by the Tribunal.

A decision in a standard case that disposes of proceedings or determines a preliminary issue made at, or following, a hearing must be made by one judge or by one judge and one or two members as determined by the Chamber President. The judge will be the presiding member, unless one or more of the other members is also a judge, in which case the Chamber President will choose the presiding member. Any other decision will be made by one judge. (Tribunals Practice Statement, 10 March 2009).

Complex cases

[5.22] A case can be classified as a complex case only if the Tribunal considers that it will require lengthy or complex evidence or a lengthy hearing, involves a complex or important principle or issue, or involves a large financial sum. [*SI 2009 No 273, Rule 23(4)*].

However, in complex cases the costs rule applies — so if the taxpayer loses they may be ordered to pay HMRC's costs of appeal as well as their own. The taxpayer may opt out of the costs regime by informing the Tribunal in writing (*SI 2009 No 273 Rule 10(1)(c)(ii)*). See further **5.28** below.

The procedures in a complex case are the same as those described at **5.21** above for standard cases. The same rules regarding the membership of the Tribunal also apply.

In *JSM Construction v HMRC* [2015] UKFTT 474 the First-tier Tribunal considered such categorisation. A key consideration was whether the appeal 'raised a complex or important principle or issue'. It found that the question of whether a taxpayer was entitled to deduct input VAT was the type of issue considered by the tribunals on a regular basis and in addition, the amount at stake was not a 'large financial sum'. The case was therefore not to be categorised as complex.

Transfer to Upper Tribunal

The Tribunal can, with the consent of the parties, refer a complex case to the Chamber President of the First-tier Tribunal with a request for transfer to the Upper Tribunal. The Chamber President can then, with the agreement of the President of the Tax and Chancery Chamber of the Upper Tribunal, direct that the case be so transferred. [*SI 2009 No 273, Rule 28*].

Costs

See **5.28** below for the taxpayer's option to request that a complex case be excluded from potential liability for costs.

The hearing

[5.23] Basic, standard and complex cases normally require a hearing before they are decided (and see **5.19** above for hearings in default paper cases).

This does not apply, however, if all of the parties consent to a decision without a hearing and the Tribunal considers that it is able to make a decision without a hearing. Hearings are also not required for the correction, setting aside, review or appeal of a tribunal decision (see **5.24–5.26** below) or where the Tribunal strikes out a party's case (see **5.17** above).

Each party to the proceedings is normally entitled to attend the hearing and the Tribunal must give reasonable notice of its time and place. Where the hearing is to consider disposal of the proceedings, at least 14 days' notice must be given except in urgent or exceptional circumstances or with the consent of the parties.

Hearings are normally held in public. The Tribunal may, however, direct that a hearing should be private if it considers that restricting access is justified in the interests of public order or national security, to protect a person's right to respect for their private and family life, to maintain the confidentiality of sensitive information, to avoid serious harm to the public interest or because not to do so would prejudice the interest of justice.

[*SI 2009 No 273, Rules 29–32*].

Failure to attend hearing

If a party fails to attend a hearing, the Tribunal can nevertheless proceed with the hearing if it considers that it is in the interests of justice to do so. The Tribunal must be satisfied that the party was notified of the hearing or that reasonable steps were taken to notify the party. [*SI 2009 No 273, Rule 33*].

The following cases were decided under the rather different provisions applicable before 1 April 2009 to failure to attend a hearing of the General Commissioners, but may be relevant to the above provision. Determinations in the absence of the taxpayer or his agent were upheld where notice of the meeting was received by the appellant (*R v Tavistock Commrs (ex p. Adams) (No 1)* QB 1969, 46 TC 154; *R v Special Commr (ex p. Moschi)* [1981] STC 465, CA, and see *Fletcher v Harvey (Inspector of Taxes)* [1990] STC 711, 63 TC 539, CA), but Commissioners were held to have acted unreasonably in refusing to re-open proceedings when the taxpayer's agent was temporarily absent when the appeal was called (*R & D McKerron Ltd v CIR* [1979] STC 815, 53 TC 28, Ct of Sess). Where the taxpayer was absent through illness, a determination was quashed because the Commissioners, in refusing an adjournment, had failed to consider whether injustice would thereby arise to the taxpayer (*R v Sevenoaks Commrs (ex p. Thorne)* QB 1989, 62 TC 341 and see *Rose v Humbles* CA 1971, 48 TC 103). See also *R v O'Brien (ex p. Lissner)* [1984] STI 710 where the determination was quashed when the appellant had been informed by the inspector that the hearing was to be adjourned.

Evidence and submissions

The Tribunal has wide powers to make directions as to issues on which it requires evidence or submissions, including the nature of such evidence or submissions, the way in which and time at which it must be provided and the need for expert evidence. It may also limit the number of witnesses whose evidence a party can put forward.

The Tribunal can accept evidence whether or not it would be admissible in a civil trial and can exclude evidence provided late or not in accordance with a direction.

[*SI 2009 No 273, Rule 15(1)(2)*].

With regard to admissible evidence, in the recent case *Foulser v HMRC* UT, [2013] UKUT 33 (TCC), the taxpayers had appealed against refusals to allow holdover relief on gifts of shares they had made. The amount of tax was to be determined by the FTT. After the start of the hearing, the taxpayers' tax advisor was arrested on suspicion of cheating the public revenue and false accounting, and documents were seized by HMRC which included information about the taxpayers' affairs. The taxpayers applied to the FTT not to admit any further evidence from HMRC. The FTT considered that it did not have jurisdiction to make such an order. Allowing the taxpayers' appeal, the Upper Tribunal remitted the case to the FTT, holding that the FTT had jurisdiction to determine the appeal and that it was for the FTT to make appropriate directions if the information which HMRC had obtained had produced a risk of unfairness.

The following cases relate to evidence given at hearings of the General Commissioners before 1 April 2009, but may be relevant to the above provision. A party to the proceedings could not insist on being examined on oath (*R v Special Commrs (in re Fletcher)* CA 1894, 3 TC 289). False evidence under oath would be perjury under criminal law (*R v Hood Barrs CA*, [1943] 1 All ER 665). A taxpayer was held to be bound by an affidavit he had made in other proceedings (*Wicker v Fraser* Ch D 1982, 55 TC 641). A remission to Commissioners to hear evidence directed at the credit of a witness was refused in *Potts v CIR* Ch D 1982, 56 TC 25. Rules of the Supreme Court under which evidence can be obtained from a witness abroad could not be used in proceedings before the Commissioners (*Leiserach v CIR* CA 1963, 42 TC 1). As to hearsay evidence under *Civil Evidence Act 1968*, see *Forth Investments Ltd v CIR* Ch D 1976, 50 TC 617 and *Khan v Edwards* Ch D 1977, 53 TC 597.

The Commissioners were under no obligation to adjourn an appeal for the production of further evidence (*Hamilton v CIR* CS 1930, 16 TC 28; *Noble v Wilkinson* Ch D 1958, 38 TC 135), and were held not to have erred in law in determining assessments in the absence abroad of the taxpayer (*Hawkins v Fuller* Ch D 1982, 56 TC 49).

HMRC were prohibited by the First-tier Tribunal from citing an unpublished Special Commissioners' decision in *Ardmore Construction Ltd v HMRC* FTT, [2014] UKFTT 453 (TC); 2014 STI 2585.

Witnesses

The Tribunal, on the application of any party to the proceedings or its own initiative, can issue a summons (in Scotland, a citation) requiring any person either to attend the hearing of those proceedings to give evidence or to produce any relevant document in his possession or control. A witness required to attend a hearing must be given 14 days notice or a shorter period if the Tribunal so directs and, if the witness is not a party, the summons or citations must make provision for necessary expenses of attendance and state who is to pay them. If, before the summons or citation was issued, the witness did not have an opportunity to object, he may apply to the Tribunal for the summons to be varied or set aside. The application must be made as soon as reasonably practicable after the summons or citation is received.

A witness cannot be compelled to give evidence or produce documents which he could not be compelled to give or produce in an action in a court of law.

[*SI 2009 No 273, Rule 16*].

The Tribunal's decision

[5.24] In an appeal case, if the Tribunal decides:

(a) that the appellant is overcharged or undercharged by a self-assessment;
(b) that the appellant is overcharged or undercharged by an assessment other than a self-assessment,

the assessment or amounts are reduced or increased accordingly, but otherwise the assessment or statement stands good. The Tribunal is given the power to vary the extent to which a claim or election included in a tax return is disallowed following an enquiry. (Separate rules apply to claims and elections made outside returns.) In a case within (c) above, the Tribunal can normally only reduce or increase the amount assessed, and this determines the appeal; the Tribunal is not obliged to determine the revised tax payable.

The Tribunal's decision is final and conclusive, subject to:

(i) the correction of clerical mistakes etc. (see **5.25** below);
(ii) the setting aside of a decision (see **5.25** below); and
(iii) a further appeal against the decision (see **5.26** below).

[*TMA 1970, s 50(6)–(11)*].

See **59** PENALTIES for the Tribunal's options in an appeal against a surcharge or a late filing penalty, which turns on the question of whether the appellant had a 'reasonable excuse' for his non-compliance.

The Tribunal can give its decision orally at a hearing or in writing. In either case it will give each party a decision notice in writing within 28 days after making a decision which finally disposes of all the issues in the case or as soon as practicable. The notice will also inform the party of any further right of appeal.

Unless each party agrees otherwise the notice should also include a summary of the findings of fact and the reason for the decision. If it does not, any party to the case can apply for full written findings and reasons, and must do so before applying for permission to appeal (see **5.26** below). The application must be made in writing so that the Tribunal receives it within 28 days after the date it sent the decision notice.

[*SI 2009 No 273, Rule 35*].

An application for a decision to be anonymised was rejected in *Reddleman Properties Ltd v HMRC* [2011] UKFTT 395 (TC). Judge Barton observed that the Tribunal Rules 'do not contain any specific provision relative to the publication of a decision', and held that 'it is not enough that a taxpayer wishes to conceal his private affairs from others'.

The following cases relate to decisions of the General Commissioners before 1 April 2009, but may be relevant to the above provisions.

In reaching their decision, the Commissioners could not take into account matters appropriate for application for judicial review (*Aspin v Estill* CA 1987, 60 TC 549). They did not generally have the power to review on appeal the exercise of a discretion conferred on HMRC by statute (see *Slater v Richardson & Bottoms Ltd* Ch D 1979, 53 TC 155; *Kelsall v Investment Chartwork Ltd* Ch D 1993, 65 TC 750).

The onus is on the appellant to displace an assessment. *See Brady v Group Lotus Car Companies plc* CA 1987, 60 TC 359 where the onus of proof remained with the taxpayer where the amount of normal time limit assessment indicated contention of fraud.

The general principle emerges in appeals against estimated assessments in 'delay cases', which, before self-assessment, made up the bulk of appeals heard by the General Commissioners. For examples of cases in which the Commissioners have confirmed estimated assessments in the absence of evidence that they were excessive, see *T Haythornthwaite & Sons Ltd v Kelly* CA 1927, 11 TC 657; *Stoneleigh Products Ltd v Dodd* CA 1948, 30 TC 1; *Rosette Franks (King St) Ltd v Dick* Ch D 1955, 36 TC 100; *Pierson v Belcher* Ch D 1959, 38 TC 387. In a number of cases, the courts have supported the Commissioners' action in rejecting unsatisfactory accounts (e.g. *Cain v Schofield* Ch D 1953, 34

TC 362; *Moll v CIR* CS 1955, 36 TC 384; *Cutmore v Leach* Ch D 1981, 55 TC 602; *Coy v Kime* Ch D 1986, 59 TC 447) or calling for certified accounts (e.g. *Stephenson v Waller* KB 1927, 13 TC 318; *Hunt & Co v Joly* KB 1928, 14 TC 165; *Wall v Cooper* CA 1929, 14 TC 552). In *Anderson v CIR* CS 1933, 18 TC 320, the case was remitted where there was no evidence to support the figure arrived at by the Commissioners (which was between the accounts figure and the estimated figure assessed), but contrast *Bookey v Edwards* Ch D 1981, 55 TC 486. The Commissioners were entitled to look at each year separately, accepting the appellant's figures for some years but not all (*Donnelly v Platten* CA(NI) 1980, [1981] STC 504). Similarly, the onus is on the taxpayer to substantiate his claims to relief (see *Eke v Knight* CA 1977, 51 TC 121; *Talib v Waterson* Ch D, [1980] STC 563).

For the standard of proof required in evidence, see *Les Croupiers Casino Club v Pattinson* CA 1987, 60 TC 196.

Consent orders. The case can also be settled by the Tribunal making a consent order where the parties have reached agreement. Such an order is made at the request of the parties but only if the Tribunal considers it appropriate to do so. No hearing is necessary if such an order is made. [*SI 2009 No 273, Rule 34*].

Amendment of a decision

[5.25] The Tribunal can correct any clerical mistake or other accidental slip or omission (such as spelling mistakes, or omitted words) in a decision at any time by notifying the parties of the amended decision. This rule applies also to directions and any other document produced by the Tribunal. [*SI 2009 No 273, Rule 37*].

The Tribunal can set aside a decision disposing of a case and re-make the decision if it considers that to do is in the interests of justice and one of the following applies:

- a relevant document was not sent to, or was not received at an appropriate time by, a party or his representative;
- a relevant document was not sent to the Tribunal at a relevant time;
- there was some other procedural irregularity; or
- a party or representative was not present at a hearing.

A party to a case can apply for a decision to be set aside. The application must be in writing and must be received by the Tribunal within 28 days after the date on which the Tribunal sent the decision notice.

[*SI 2009 No 273, Rule 38*].

The Tribunal used this procedure in the case of *Wright v HMRC* FTT, [2009] UKFTT 227 (TC) where it granted an application to set aside a decision of the Special Commissioner on procedural grounds. An application for a decision to be set aside was rejected in *Fraser v HMRC* FTT, [2012] UKFTT 189 (TC) where Judge Poole considered the position of a taxpayer who wanted to rely on further evidence not put before the tribunal at the hearing. Judge Poole commented that 'the function of the Tribunal is to provide efficient resolution of disputes between taxpayers and HMRC. Whilst some latitude may be allowed for taxpayers who are inexperienced in presenting their case, it would completely undermine the Tribunal's function if it were routinely to allow losing parties (whether taxpayers or HMRC) to relitigate appeals on the basis that they did not feel they had put sufficient evidence before the Tribunal when it first heard the appeal'. These principles were applied in *Rosenbaum's Executor v HMRC (No 2)* FTT, [2013] UKFTT 495 (TC) where the Tribunal rejected an application by HMRC for a decision to be set aside.

Appeal against the Tribunal's decision

[5.26] A further appeal to the Upper Tribunal can be made against the First-tier Tribunal's decision. The appeal can be made only on a point of law. No appeal can be made against a decision on whether or not to review a decision (see below), to set aside a decision (see **5.25** above) or to refer a matter to the Upper Tribunal. With regard to what amount to a 'point of law' see the comments of Lord Carnwath in the VAT case *HMRC v Pendragon* [2015] UKSC 37 which challenge the orthodox understanding of the extent of the jurisdiction of the Upper Tribunal, with a view to widen its authority, by allowing a broader interpretation of the reference to 'law' for this purpose.

A person wishing to appeal must make a written application to the First-tier Tribunal for permission to appeal. Such an application must be received by the Tribunal no later than 56 days after the date the Tribunal sent full reasons for the decision to that person. The tribunal may also direct that the 56 days in the latter instance alternatively runs from the date of the decision disposing of all issues in the proceedings.

Where a decision has been amended or corrected following a review (see below) or an application (other than a late application) for a decision to be struck out has been unsuccessful (see **5.25** above), the 56 day limit runs from the date on which the Tribunal sent the notification of amended reasons or correction of the decision or of the failure of the striking out application.

The application must identify the alleged errors in the decision and state the result sought. Late applications must include a request for extension of time and the reason for lateness.

On receiving an application, the Tribunal will first consider whether to review the decision. It can do so only if satisfied that there was an error in law in the decision. Unless it decides to take no action following the review, the Tribunal will notify the parties of the outcome and must give them an opportunity to make representations before taking any action.

If the Tribunal decides not to review the decision or, following a review, decides to take no action, it will then consider whether to give permission to appeal to the Upper Tribunal. It will send a record of its decision to the parties as soon as practicable together with, where it decides not to give permission, a statements of its reasons for refusal and details of the right to apply directly to the Upper Tribunal for permission to appeal (see **5.31** below). The Tribunal's permission can be in respect of part only of the decision or on limited grounds.

[*TCEA 2007, s 11; SI 2009 No 273, Rules 39–41*].

Payment of tax pending further appeal

[5.27] Tax is payable or repayable in accordance with the decision of the Tribunal even if a party appeals to the Upper Tribunal. If the amount charged in the assessment concerned is subsequently altered by the Upper Tribunal, any amount undercharged is due and payable at the end of the thirty days beginning with the date on which HMRC issue the appellant a notice of the amount payable in accordance with the Upper Tribunal's decision. Any amount overpaid will be refunded along with such interest as may be allowed by the decision. See **4.35** ANTI-AVOIDANCE for applications to the court or Tribunal by HMRC to disapply the requirement to repay tax where an accelerated payment notice is in force.

This provision applies equally to any further appeal from a decision of the Upper Tribunal to the Courts.

[*TMA 1970, s 56; FA 2014, s 225(1)*].

Award of costs

[5.28] The Tribunal can make an order awarding costs (or, in Scotland, expenses):

(a) under *TCEA 2007, s 29(4)* ('wasted costs'), and as from 1 April 2013 costs incurred in applying for such costs (*SI 2013 No 477*);
(b) where it considers that a party or representative has acted unreasonably in bringing, defending or conducting the case; and
(c) in a complex case (see **5.22** above), where the taxpayer has not sent a written request that the case be excluded from potential liability for costs or expenses.

A request within (c) above must be sent within 28 days of the taxpayer receiving notice that the case has been allocated as a complex case.

'*Wasted costs*' are any costs incurred by a party because of an improper, unreasonable or negligent act or omission by any representative or employee of a representative, which the Tribunal considers it unreasonable for the party to pay. In *Deluca v HMRC* [2011] UKFTT 579 (TC) the First-Tier Tribunal held that HMRC had acted unreasonably, and directed that they should pay 50% of the appellant's costs.

In *Southwest Communications Group Ltd v HMRC* [2012] UKFTT 701 (TC) HMRC had received the appellant company's witness statements in June 2011. In January 2012, shortly before the case was scheduled for hearing, they decided not to contest the appeal. The company applied for costs, contending that HMRC had acted unreasonably in not settling the case sooner. The First-tier Tribunal accepted this contention. Judge Raghavan held that HMRC should have settled the case within 28 days of receiving the witness statements, and directed that HMRC should pay the company's costs from 20 July 2011.

Before making an order for costs, the Tribunal must give the person who will have to pay them the chance to make representations. If the payer is an individual, it must consider his financial means.

The Tribunal can make an order on its own initiative or on an application from one of the parties. Such an application must be sent both to the Tribunal and to the person from whom costs are sought, together with a schedule of the costs claimed. An application must be made no later than 28 days after the date on which the Tribunal sends a notice recording the decision which finally disposes of all the issues or notice of a withdrawal which ends the case.

The amount of costs will be decided either by agreement of the parties, by summary assessment by the Tribunal or, if not agreed, by assessment. This includes the costs of the assessment. Where the amount is to be decided by assessment, either the payer or the person to whom the costs are to be paid can apply to a county court, the High Court or the Costs Office of the Supreme Court for a detailed assessment of the costs on the standard basis or, where the tribunal's order so specifies, the indemnity basis. Upon making an order for the assessment of costs, the Tribunal may order an amount to be paid on account before the costs or expenses are assessed.

The power of the Tribunal to award costs does not include a power to direct, before the conclusion of an appeal, that the costs of complying with a direction should be borne by one party rather than the other, or by both (*Eclipse Film Partners No. 35 LLP v HMRC* SC, [2016] STC 1385).

In *Darrell Healey v HMRC* [2016] FTT 44 (TC) the First-tier Tribunal dismissed HMRC's application for costs in relation to a case management hearing which HMRC submitted was unnecessary. The Tribunal held that although they would have expected further engagement with the appeals process on the part of the taxpayer, nevertheless it was not considered the hearing was unnecessary and it was not an unreasonable request.

An application for costs where HMRC had withdrawn their case during the hearing was unsuccessful in *Elliott Knight Ltd v HMRC* FTT, [2018] SFTD 818.

Partially successful appellants were ordered to pay two-thirds of HMRC's costs in *Bastionspark LLP v HMRC* UT, [2016] STC 2549.

[*TCEA 2007, s 29(4); SI 2009 No 273, Rule 10*].

Upper Tribunal procedure

[5.29] The powers of the Upper Tribunal to regulate its own proceedings are broadly the same as the powers of the First-tier Tribunal. See *SI 2008 No 2698, Rules 5, 6, 9, 12* and **5.16** above.

Simon's Taxes. See **A5.611–A5.617**.

Representation

The same rights to representation in a case before the Upper Tribunal apply as in a case before the First-tier Tribunal. In addition it can also: (i) suspend the effect of a decision where a party has made an application for permission to appeal or whilst an appeal is on-going; and (ii) ask the First-tier Tribunal to provide documents in relation to any decision and the reasons for that decision. This power enables the Upper Tribunal to have all the information and reasons for decisions before it when it considers appeals and permissions to appeal.

The Upper Tribunal may give a direction itself or on written application by either or all of the parties (unless the application is made orally on the day of the hearing). Written notification of any directions will usually be sent to all parties, and any party may then ask for the direction to be amended, suspended or set aside.

See *SI 2008 No 2698, Rules 5, 6, 9, 12* and **5.16** above.

Withdrawal from a case

A party can notify the Upper Tribunal of the withdrawal of its case, or part of it. This can be done in writing or orally at a hearing. If the case is to be settled without a hearing, written notice must be given before the Tribunal disposes of the case. The withdrawal only takes effect, however, if the Tribunal consents (but this requirement does not apply to the withdrawal of an application for permission to appeal).

A party who has withdrawn its case can, however, apply (in writing) to the Tribunal to reinstate it. The application must be received by the Tribunal within one month after it received the withdrawal notice or the date of the hearing. As noted above, it was held in the case of *St Annes Distributors v HMRC* [2010] UKUT 458 (TCC), [2011] STC 708, [2011] NLJR 102 (an indirect tax case) that notification by email does not satisfy the 'written notice' requirement.

[*SI 2008 No 2698, Rule 17*].

Failure to comply with rules

[5.30] An irregularity resulting from any failure to comply with the Tribunal Procedure Rules, a practice direction or a direction by the Upper Tribunal does not in itself make the proceedings void.

Where a party fails to comply with the Rules etc. the Upper Tribunal can take such action as it considers just. This could be to require compliance or waive the requirement, to strike the case out (see below) or to restrict a party's participation in the case.

The Upper Tribunal has the same powers as the High Court to deal with the failure (which may include financial penalties).

[*TCEA 2007, s 25; SI 2008 No 2698, Rule 7*].

The Upper Tribunal has similar powers to strike out a case as the First-tier Tribunal. See *SI 2008 No 2698, Rule 8* and **5.17** above. Note, however, that the Upper Tribunal cannot strike out an appeal from the decision of another tribunal or judicial review proceedings on the grounds that there is no reasonable prospect of the appellant's case succeeding.

Appeal against decisions of the First-tier Tribunal

Application for permission to appeal

[5.31] A party to a case who disagrees with a decision of the First-tier Tribunal can apply for permission to appeal against it. Applications must first be made to the First-tier Tribunal (see **5.26** above), but if that Tribunal refuses permission a further application can be made to the Upper Tribunal.

Applications to the Upper Tribunal must be in writing and must be received no later than one month after the date on which the First-tier Tribunal sent the notice refusing permission to appeal. An application must include the grounds for appeal and state whether the appellant wants the application to be dealt with at a hearing. It must be accompanied by copies of any written record of the decision being challenged, any statement of reasons for that decision, and the notice of the First-tier Tribunal's refusal of permission to appeal. Late applications must include a request for extension of time and the reason for lateness.

If the application to the First-tier Tribunal for permission to appeal was refused because it was made out of time, the application to the Upper Tribunal must include the reason for the lateness of the first application. The Upper Tribunal can then admit the application only if it considers that it is in the interests of justice to do so.

If the Tribunal refuses permission to appeal it will notify the appellant of its decision and its reasons. If the refusal is made without a hearing the appellant can apply in writing for the decision to be reconsidered at a hearing. The application must be received by the Tribunal within 14 days after the date that written notice of its decision was sent. This rule applies also where the Tribunal gives permission on limited grounds or subject to conditions without a hearing.

If the Tribunal grants permission, the application for permission is then normally treated as a notice of appeal, and the case will proceed accordingly. If all the parties agree, the appeal can be determined without obtaining any further response.

In *Carmel Jordan v HMRC* [2015] UKUT 218 the Upper Tribunal held that any decision of the First-tier Tribunal relating to information notices issued under *FA 2008 Sch 36* cannot be appealed. The Tribunal explained the purpose of the legislation was to restrict judicial scrutiny to one stage in order to avoid undue delays to HMRC's information gathering process.

[*SI 2008 No 2698, Rules 21, 22; SI 2009 No 274, Rule 14*].

See also the reference above at **5.26** with regard to the comments of Lord Carnwath in the VAT case *HMRC v Pendragon* [2015] UKSC 37 which would provide for a wider jurisdiction of the Upper Tribunal, with a view to keeping appeals in tax and other specialist fields within the specialist tribunals and limiting the extent to which such appeals come before the Court of Appeal.

Notice of appeal

[5.32] If the First-tier Tribunal gives permission to appeal to the Upper Tribunal (or the Upper Tribunal gives permission but directs that the application for permission should not be treated as a notice of appeal) an appellant can appeal to the Upper Tribunal by providing a notice of appeal. This must be received by the tribunal within one month after the notice giving permission to appeal was sent.

The notice must include the grounds for appeal and state whether the appellant wants the application to be dealt with at a hearing. If, the First-tier Tribunal gave permission to appeal, the notice must be accompanied by copies of any written record of the decision being challenged, any statement of reasons for that decision, and the notice of permission to appeal. Late applications must include a request for extension of time and the reason for lateness.

A copy of the notice and the documents provided will then be sent by the Upper Tribunal to the respondents who can provide a written response. The response must be received by the Tribunal not later than one month after the copy of the notice of appeal was sent. (Where an application for permission to appeal stands as the notice of appeal (see **5.31** above), the response must be received not later than one month after the Tribunal sent to the respondent notice that if had granted permission to appeal.)

The response must indicate whether the respondent opposes the appeal, and if so, the grounds for opposition (which can include grounds which were unsuccessful before the First-tier Tribunal) and whether the respondent wants the case to be dealt with at a hearing. Late responses must include a request for extension of time and the reason for lateness.

A copy of the response and any documents provided will then be sent by the Tribunal to the appellant and any other parties to the case who can, in turn, provide a written reply. The reply must be received by the Tribunal within one month of the date the tribunal sent the copy of the respondent's response.

[*SI 2008 No 2698, Rules 23–25*].

An application by HMRC for the Tribunal to accept a late notice of appeal was rejected in *HMRC v McCarthy and Stone (Developments) Ltd* UT, [2014] STC 973.

Other cases before the Upper Tribunal

[5.33] Where a case has been transferred or referred to the Upper Tribunal from the First-tier Tribunal (see **5.3** above) or where a case is started by direct application to the Upper Tribunal, the Upper Tribunal will determine by direction the procedure for considering and disposing of the case.
[*SI 2008 No 2698, Rule 26A*].

The hearing

[5.34] The Upper Tribunal can make any decision with or without a hearing, but in deciding whether to hold a hearing, it must have regard to any view expressed by any party to the case.

See **5.1** above for the temporary power for the Tribunal to direct that a case be determined on the papers despite the objections of any party during the coronavirus pandemic.

Each party is normally entitled to attend the hearing and the Upper Tribunal must give reasonable notice of its time and place. At least 14 days' notice must normally be given except in urgent or exceptional circumstances or with the consent of the parties. In application for permission to bring judicial review cases, the notice period must normally be at least two days.

Hearings are normally held in public, but the Tribunal can direct that a hearing, or part of it, should be held in private.

[*SI 2008 No 2698, Rules 34–37*].

If a party fails to attend a hearing, the Upper Tribunal can nevertheless proceed with the hearing if it considers that it is in the interests of justice to do so. The Tribunal must be satisfied that the party was notified of the hearing or that reasonable steps were taken to notify the party. [*SI 2008 No 2698, Rule 38*].

Similar rules apply in relation to evidence, submission and witnesses as apply to the First-tier Tribunal. See *SI 2008 No 2698, Rules 15, 16* and **5.23** above.

The Upper Tribunal's decision

[5.35] If the Upper Tribunal decides that the First-tier Tribunal's decision involved an error on a point of law it can set aside that decision and either remit the case back to the First-tier Tribunal or remake the decision itself.

If it remits the case to the First-tier Tribunal, the Upper Tribunal can direct that the case is reheard by different members.

If it decides to remake the decision itself, the Upper Tribunal is free to make any decision that the First-tier Tribunal could make if it were rehearing the case (see **5.25** above) and can make such findings of fact as it considers appropriate.

[*TCEA 2007, s 12*].

The Upper Tribunal can give its decision orally at a hearing or in writing. In either case it will give each party a decision notice in writing as soon as practicable. The notice will include written reasons for the decision unless the decision was made with the consent of the parties or the parties have consented to the tribunal not giving written reasons. The notice will also inform the party of any further right of appeal. [*SI 2008 No 2698, Rule 40*].

The case can also be settled by the Upper Tribunal making a consent order where the parties have reached agreement. Such an order is made at the request of the parties but only if the Tribunal considers it appropriate to do so. No hearing is necessary if such an order is made. [*SI 2008 No 2698, Rule 39*].

Identical provisions to those applicable to decisions by the First-tier Tribunal apply to decisions of the Upper Tribunal. See *SI 2008 No 2698, Rule 42* and **5.25** above — amendments of a decision. With regard to setting aside a decision — virtually identical provisions to those applicable to decisions by the First-tier Tribunal apply to decisions of the Upper Tribunal. An application for a decision to be set aside must be received by the Upper Tribunal no later than one month after the date on which the Tribunal sent the decision notice. See *SI 2008 No 2698, Rule 43* and **5.25** above.

Appeal against the Tribunal's decision

[5.36] A further appeal to the Court of Appeal (in Scotland, the Court of Session) can be made against the Upper Tribunal's decision. The appeal can be made only on a point of law and the Tribunal will give permission to appeal only if the appeal would raise some important point of principle or practice or there is some other compelling reason for the Court to hear it.

A person wishing to appeal must make a written application to the Tribunal for permission to appeal. Such an application must be received by the Tribunal within one month after the date the Tribunal sent written reasons for the decision to that person. Where a decision has been amended or corrected following a review (see below) or an application (other than a late application) for a decision to be struck out has been unsuccessful (see **5.30** above), the one month limit runs from the date on which the tribunal sent the notification of amended reasons or correction of the decision or of the failure of the striking out application.

The application must identify the alleged errors of law in the decision and state the result sought. Late applications must include a request for extension of time and the reason for lateness.

On receiving an application, the Upper Tribunal will first consider whether to review the decision. It can do so only if either it overlooked a legislative provision or binding authority which could have affected the decision or if a court has subsequently made a decision which is binding on the Upper Tribunal and could have affected the decision.

The Tribunal will notify the parties of the outcome of a review. If it decides to take any action following a review without first giving every party an opportunity to make representations, the notice must state that any party not given such an opportunity can apply for the action to be set aside and for the decision to be reviewed again.

If the Tribunal decides not to review the decision or, following a review, decides to take no action, it will then consider whether to give permission to appeal. It will send a record of its decision to the parties as soon as practicable together with, where it decides not to give permission, a statements of its reasons for refusal and details of the right to apply directly to the court for permission to appeal (see **5.38** below). The Tribunal's permission can be in respect of part only of the decision or on limited grounds.

[*TCEA 2007, s 13; SI 2008 No 2698, Rules 44–46; SI 2008 No 2834*].

See **5.27** above for the payment of tax pending an appeal from a decision of the Upper Tribunal.

Award of costs

[5.37] The Upper Tribunal can make an order awarding costs (or, in Scotland, expenses):

(a) in proceedings on appeal from the Tax Chamber of the First-tier Tribunal;
(b) in judicial review cases (see **5.40** below);
(c) in cases transferred from the Tax Chamber of the First-tier Tribunal;
(d) under *TCEA 2007, s 29(4)* (wasted costs including costs incurred in applying for such costs — see **5.28** above); or
(e) where the Tribunal considers that a party or representative has acted unreasonably in bringing, defending or conducting the case.

Before making an order for costs, the Tribunal must give the person who will have to pay them the chance to make representations. If the payer is an individual, it must consider his financial means.

The Tribunal can make an order on its own initiative or on an application from one of the parties. Such an application must be sent both to the tribunal and to the person from whom costs are sought, together with a schedule of the costs claimed. An application must be made no later than one month after the date on which the Tribunal sends the notice recording the decision which finally disposes of all the issues in the case.

The amount of costs will be decided either by agreement of the parties, by summary assessment by the Tribunal or, if not agreed, by assessment (including the costs and expenses of the assessment). Where the amount is to be decided by assessment, either the payer or the person to whom the costs are to be paid can apply to a county court, the High Court or the Costs Office of the Supreme Court for a detailed assessment of the costs on the standard basis or, where the Tribunal's order so specifies, the indemnity basis. From 1 April 2013, upon making an order for assessment of costs the Tribunal may make an order for an amount to be paid on account.

The Upper Tribunal has recently considered the matter of excessive costs claim. Following the Upper Tribunal decision in *HMRC v Taylor & Haimendorf (No 2)* [2010] UKUT 417 (TCC), [2011] STC 126, HMRC applied for costs of £17,990, including a claim for £8,010 in respect of 38 hours' attendance on documents. The shareholders objected to HMRC's claims, and in *HMRC v Taylor & Haimendorf (Costs) (No 3)* (UT 4 March 2011, FTC/43/2010) the Upper Tribunal held that HMRC were entitled to reasonable costs but that the claim for £8,010 was excessive and reduced the amount in question to £925. The tribunal therefore awarded HMRC total costs of £10,905.

[*SI 2008 No 2698, Rule 1*].

Appeal to the Court of Appeal

[5.38] As noted at 5.36 above, a party who disagrees with a decision of the Upper Tribunal can ask the Tribunal for permission to appeal to the Court of Appeal (in Scotland, the Court of Session). The appeal can be made only on a point of law.

If the Tribunal refuses permission, the party can seek permission to appeal directly from the Court. The Court will give permission only if the appeal would raise some important point of principle or practice or there is some other compelling reason for the Court to hear it.

[*TCEA 2007, s 13; SI 2008 No 2834*].

There are no tax-specific rules governing the making of applications for permission to appeal or for notifying appeals where permission has been given by the Court or Upper Tribunal. The *Civil Procedure Rules 1998, SI 1998 No 3132* therefore apply.

The Court's decision

If the Court finds that the decision of the Upper Tribunal involved an error on a point of law it can set aside the decision. It must then either remake the decision itself or remit the case back to either the Upper Tribunal or the First-tier Tribunal, with directions for its reconsideration. Those directions can include a direction that the case is to be re-heard by different tribunal members.

Where the case is remitted to the Upper Tribunal, it can itself decide to remit the case to the First-tier Tribunal.

If the Court decides to remake the decision itself, it can make any decision that the Upper Tribunal or first-tier Tribunal could have made, and can make such findings of fact as it considers appropriate.

[*TCEA 2007, s 14*].

Case law

The following cases relate to the pre-1 April 2009 appeal process (which involved initial appeal to the High Court rather than the Court of Appeal) but remain relevant to the new process.

Withdrawal etc.

Once set down for hearing, a case cannot be declared a nullity (*Way v Underdown* CA 1974, 49 TC 215) or struck out under *Order 18, Rule 19 of the Rules of the Supreme Court* (*Petch v Gurney (Inspector of Taxes)* [1994] 3 All ER 731, [1994] STC 689, 66 TC 743, CA), but the appellant may withdraw (*Hood Barrs v CIR (No 3)* CA 1960, 39 TC 209, but see *Bradshaw v Blunden (No 2)* Ch D 1960, 39 TC 73). Where the appellant was the inspector and the taxpayer did not wish to proceed, the Court refused to make an order on terms agreed between the parties (*Slaney v Kean* Ch D 1969, 45 TC 415).

Remission of cases to tribunal

In *Consolidated Goldfields plc v CIR* Ch D 1990, 63 TC 333, the taxpayer company's request that the High Court remit a case to the Commissioners for further findings of fact was refused. Although the remedy was properly sought, it would only be granted if it could be shown that the desired findings were:

(a) material to some tenable argument;
(b) reasonably open on the evidence adduced; and
(c) not inconsistent with the findings already made.

However, in *Fitzpatrick v CIR* CS 1990, [1991] STC 34, a case was remitted where the facts found proved or admitted, and the contentions of the parties, were not clearly set out, despite the taxpayer's request for various amendments and insertions to the case, and in *Whittles v Uniholdings Ltd (No 1)* [1993] STC 767n, remission was appropriate in view of the widely differing interpretations which the parties sought to place on the Commissioners' decision (and the case was remitted a second time (see [1993] STC 767) to resolve misunderstandings as to the nature of a concession made by the Crown at the original hearing and apparent inconsistencies in the Commissioners' findings of fact). If a case is remitted, the taxpayer had the right to attend any further hearing by the Commissioners (*Lack v Doggett* CA 1970, 46 TC 497) but the Commissioners could not, in the absence of special circumstances, admit further evidence (*Archer-Shee v Baker* CA 1928, 15 TC 1; *Watson v Samson Bros* Ch D 1959, 38 TC 346; *Bradshaw v Blunden (No 2)* Ch D 1960, 39 TC 73), but see *Brady v Group Lotus Car Companies plc* CA 1987, 60 TC 359 where the Court directed the Commissioners to admit further evidence where new facts had come to light suggesting the taxpayers had deliberately misled the Commissioners. Errors of fact in the case may be amended by agreement of the parties prior to hearing of the case (*Moore v Austin* Ch D 1985, 59 TC 110). See *Jeffries v Stevens* Ch D 1982, 56 TC 134 as regards delay between statement of case and motion for remission.

Appeal restricted to point of law

Many court decisions turn on whether the Commissioners' decision was one of fact supported by the evidence, and hence final. The courts will not disturb a finding of fact if there was reasonable evidence for it, notwithstanding that the evidence might support a different conclusion of fact. The leading case is *Edwards v Bairstow & Harrison* HL 1955, 36 TC 207, in which the issue was whether there had been an adventure in the nature of trade. The Commissioners' decision was reversed on the ground that the only reasonable conclusion from the evidence was that there had been such an adventure. For a recent discussion of the application of this principle, see *Milnes (Inspector of Taxes) v J Bean Group Ltd* [1975] STC 487, 54 ATC 156.

A new question of law may be raised in the courts on giving due notice to the other parties (*Muir v CIR* CA 1966, 43 TC 367) but the courts will neither admit evidence not in the stated case (*Watson v Samson Bros* Ch D 1959, 38 TC 346; *Cannon Industries Ltd v Edwards* Ch D 1965, 42 TC 625; *Frowd v Whalley* Ch D 1965, 42 TC 599, and see *R v Great Yarmouth Commrs (ex p. Amis)* QB 1960, 39 TC 143) nor consider contentions of which evidence in support was not produced before the Commissioners (*Denekamp v Pearce* Ch D 1998, 71 TC 213).

Use of Parliamentary material

Following the decision in *Pepper v Hart* HL 1992, 65 TC 421, the courts are prepared to consider the parliamentary history of legislation, or the official reports of debates in Hansard, where all of the following conditions are met.

- Legislation is ambiguous or obscure, or leads to an absurdity.
- The material relied upon consists of one or more statements by a Minister or other promoter of the Bill together if necessary with such other parliamentary material as is necessary to understand such statements and their effect.
- The statements relied upon are clear.

Any party intending to refer to an extract from Hansard in support of any argument must, unless otherwise directed, serve copies of the extract and a brief summary of the argument intended to be based upon the extract upon all parties and the court not less than five clear working days before the first day of the hearing (Supreme Court Practice Note, 20 December 1994) (1995 STI 98).

Status of decision

A court decision is a binding precedent for itself or an inferior court except that the House of Lords, while treating its former decisions as normally binding, may depart from a previous decision should it appear right to do so. For this see

Fitzleet Estates Ltd v Cherry HL 1977, 51 TC 708. Scottish decisions are not binding on the High Court but are normally followed. Decisions of the Privy Council and of the Irish Courts turning on comparable legislation are treated with respect. A court decision does not affect other assessments already final and conclusive but may be followed, if relevant, in the determination of any open appeals against assessments and in assessments made subsequently irrespective of the years of assessment or taxpayers concerned (*Waring, Re, Westminster Bank Ltd v Burton-Butler* [1948] Ch 221, [1948] 1 All ER 257; *Gwyther v Boslymon Quarries Ltd* [1950] 2 KB 59, [1950] 1 All ER 384; *Bolands Ltd v CIR* SC(I) 1925, 4 ATC 526). Further, a court decision does not prevent the Crown from proceeding on a different basis for other years (*Hood Barrs v CIR (No 3)* CA 1960, 39 TC 209).

For joinder of CIR in non-tax disputes, see In *re Vandervell's Trusts* HL 1970, 46 TC 341.

Restrictions on interim payments in tax proceedings

[5.39] There are provisions restricting the power of a court to grant an interim remedy requiring the Commissioners for HMRC or an officer of HMRC to pay any sum to any claimant (however described) in tax proceedings. The rules apply to applications for an interim remedy (however described), made in any court proceedings relating to a 'taxation matter' (which means anything other than national insurance contributions), if the application is based (wholly or partly) on a point of law which has yet to be determined.

The court may only grant the interim remedy if it is shown to the satisfaction of the court that:

(a) taking account of all sources of funding (including borrowing) reasonably likely to be available to fund the proceedings, the interim payment is necessary to enable proceedings to continue; or
(b) the circumstances of the claimant are exceptional and such that the granting of the remedy is necessary in the interests of justice.

[*FA 2013, s 234*].

Judicial review

[5.40] Principles have been developed by the Courts for the review of the **legality** of decisions made by public bodies and tribunals, which include HMRC, the First-tier Tribunal and Upper Tribunal. On the basis that a decision by HMRC will generally be of a public law nature, then judicial review (at the High Court) is the correct procedure, save in cases where the Upper Tribunal would itself have jurisdiction to hear an appeal.

TCEA 2007, s 18 states that the Upper Tribunal can determine applications for judicial review in specific circumstances where four conditions are satisfied:

(1) the application must solely be seeking relief that could be granted in judicial review proceedings;
(2) the application does not call into question anything done in a Crown Court;

(3) the application falls within the classes proscribed in directions. On 29 October 2008, the Lord Chief Justice made a direction stating that challenges could be made in relation to any decision of the First-tier Tribunal, unless the Lord Chancellor had made an order that the decision was an excluded decision for the purposes of *s 11(5)(f)*. However, the direction states that it does not apply to an application for a declaration of incompatibility under *HRA 1998, s 4*;

(4) the application must be heard by a High Court or Court of Appeal judge or a person authorised by the Lord Chief Justice.

In any other case the Upper Tribunal must transfer the application to the High Court.

Thus, a taxpayer who is dissatisfied with the exercise of administrative powers may in certain circumstances (e.g. where HMRC has exceeded or abused its powers or acted contrary to the rules of natural justice, or where the Tribunal has acted unfairly or improperly) seek a remedy in a mandatory or prohibiting order or a quashing order.

For example, judicial review can be used to consider cases where:

(a) HMRC's decision is in relation to a discretionary matter, for example a decision on whether a late claim should be accepted, or the application of an Extra-Statutory Concession;

(b) the taxpayer believes that an HMRC officer is not carrying out, or is delaying in carrying out his duties or has assumed powers to which he is not entitled;

(c) a taxpayer is not disputing that HMRC's decision is technically correct, but claims that he was misdirected and in consequence suffered disadvantage, for example a return is wrong because he relied on incorrect advice received from HMRC;

(d) the taxpayer believes that an HMRC officer has not listened properly to his representations or has acted in a way that appears to be unfair; or

(e) there is no appeal on a point of law against a Tribunal decision, for example where the Tribunal has refused a late appeal or refused to review its previous decision.

As noted, this is done by way of application for judicial review to the High Court under *Supreme Court Act 1981, s 31* and *Part 54 of the Civil Procedure Rules*. The High Court can in certain cases transfer an application for judicial review or for leave to apply for judicial review to the Upper Tribunal (see *Supreme Court Act 1981, s 31A*).

The issue on an application for leave to apply for judicial review is whether there is an arguable case (*R v CIR (ex p Howmet Corpn)* [1994] STC 413n). The procedure is generally used where no other, adequate, remedy, such as a right of appeal, is available. See *R v Special Commr (ex p. Stipplechoice Ltd) (No 1)* CA, [1985] STC 248 and *(No 3)* QB 1988, 61 TC 391, *R v HMIT (ex p. Kissane and Another)* QB, [1986] STC 152, *R v CIR (ex p. Goldberg)* QB 1988, 61 TC 403 and *R v Dickinson (ex p. McGuckian)* CA(NI) 1999, 72 TC 343.

The case of *R (oao UK Uncut Legal Action Ltd) v HMRC* QB, [2013] STC 2357 follows on from the widely publicised case of *Goldman Sachs International v HMRC (No 2)* [2010] UKFTT 205 (TC), [2010] SFTD 930, [2010]

SWTI 2200 which had ultimately been settled by an agreement between GSI and HMRC which attracted considerable adverse publicity for reportedly waiving the interest which was legally chargeable on the unpaid NICs, and was strongly criticised by the House of Commons Public Accounts Committee for being unduly lenient. Another company (UKU) subsequently applied to the QB for judicial review of the agreement, contending that the settlement breached HMRC's duty of fairness to the general body of taxpayers. The QB dismissed the application. Nicol J found that 'the settlement with (GS) was not a glorious episode in the history of the Revenue. The HMRC officials who negotiated it had not been briefed by the lawyers who were litigating against (GS). They relied on their belief or recollection that there was a barrier to the recovery of interest on the unpaid NICs. That was erroneous. HMRC now accepts that there was no such barrier.' However, 'maladministration and illegality are separate issues', and the settlement had not been unlawful.

There is a very long line of cases in which the courts have consistently refused applications where a matter should have been pursued through the ordinary channels as described earlier in this chapter. See, for example, *R v Special Commrs (ex p. Morey)* CA 1972, 49 TC 71; *R v Special Commrs (ex p. Emery)* QB 1980, 53 TC 555; *R v Walton General Commrs (ex p. Wilson)* CA, [1983] STC 464; *R v Special Commrs (ex p. Esslemont)* CA, 1984 STI 312; *R v Brentford General Commrs (ex p. Chan and Others)* QB 1985, 57 TC 651; *R v Special Commr (ex p. Napier)* CA 1988, 61 TC 206; *R v North London General Commrs (ex p. Nii-Amaa)* QB 1999, 72 TC 634.

See, however, *R v HMIT and Others (ex p. Lansing Bagnall Ltd)* CA 1986, 61 TC 112 for a successful application where the inspector issued a notice under a discretionary power on the footing that there was an obligation to do so, and *R v CIR (ex p. J Rothschild Holdings plc)* CA 1987, 61 TC 178 where the Revenue were required to produce internal documents of a general character relating to their practice in applying a statutory provision.

See also *R v CIR (ex p. Taylor) (No 1)* CA 1988, 62 TC 562 where an application for discovery of a document was held to be premature, and *R v Inspector of Taxes, Hull, ex p. Brumfield and others* QB 1988, 61 TC 589, where the court was held to have jurisdiction to entertain an application for judicial review of a failure by the Revenue to apply an established practice not embodied in an extra-statutory concession (cf. *R v Inspector of Taxes, Reading, ex p Fulford-Dobson* [1987] QB 978, [1987] 3 WLR 277 at **36.3** HMRC — ADMINISTRATION, which see for 'care and management' powers of the Revenue). It was held that there had been no unfairness by the Revenue when it refused to assess on the basis of transactions that would have been entered into by the applicants had a Revenue Statement of Practice been published earlier (*R v CIR, ex p. Kaye* QB 1992, 65 TC 82). A similar view was taken in *R v CIR (ex p. S G Warburg & Co Ltd)* QB 1994, 68 TC 300 where the Revenue declined to apply a previously published practice because not only was it not clear that the taxpayer's circumstances fell within its terms but also the normal appeal procedures were available.

The underlying facts in *Carvill v CIR (No 2); R (oao Carvill) v CIR* Ch D, [2002] STC 1167 were that in two separate appeals relating to different tax years, income from an identical source had been held liable to tax for some years (the earlier years) but not others; an application for judicial review of the Revenue's refusal to refund tax, and interest on tax, paid for the earlier years was rejected; the assessments for those years were valid assessments which the Sp C in question had had jurisdiction to determine, and the taxpayer the right to challenge, and those assessments had not been set aside. See also *Davies and another v HMRC* CA, [2008] STC 2813, in which an application for judicial review was to be heard before any appeal to the Special Commissioners as it related to whether the taxpayers had a legitimate expectation that they would be treated in accordance with HMRC's published guidance.

The first step is to obtain leave to apply for judicial review from the High Court. Application for leave is made ex parte to a single judge who will usually determine the application without a hearing. The Court will not grant leave unless the applicant has a sufficient interest in the matter to which the application relates. See *CIR v National Federation of Self-Employed and Small Businesses Ltd* HL 1981, 55 TC 133 for what is meant by 'sufficient interest' and for discussion of availability of judicial review generally.

Applications must be made **within three months** of the date when the grounds for application arose. The Court has discretion to extend this time limit where there is good reason, subject to conditions, but is generally very reluctant to do so. Grant of leave for review does not amount to a ruling that application is made in good time (*R v Tavistock Commrs (ex p. Worth)* QB 1985, 59 TC 116).

Simon's Taxes. See A5.3 and A5.702.

Costs awarded in appeals

[5.41] See 5.29 and 5.37 for the award of costs by the First-tier and Upper Tribunals.

Costs may be awarded by the courts in the usual way. In suitable cases, e.g. 'test cases', HMRC may undertake to pay the taxpayer's costs.

Interest is payable on any costs awarded to or against the Crown in the High Court, unless the court orders otherwise (*Crown Proceedings Act 1947, s 24(2)*). The rate is that payable upon judgment debts.

Costs awarded by the courts may include expenses connected with the drafting of the case stated (*Manchester Corporation v Sugden* CA 1903, 4 TC 595). Costs of a discontinued application for judicial review were refused where the Revenue were not informed of the application (*R v CIR (ex p. Opman International UK)* QB 1985, 59 TC 352).

Legal costs of appeals are not allowable for tax purposes generally (*Allen v Farquharson* KB 1932, 17 TC 59; *Smith's Potato Estates Ltd v Bolland* HL 1948, 30 TC 267; *Rushden Heel Co v Keene* HL 1948, 30 TC 298; *Spofforth & Prince v Golder* KB 1945, 26 TC 310).

With regard to the costs involved in pursuing judicial review proceedings which had been withdrawn, in *R (on the application of Valentines Homes & Construction Ltd) v HMRC* [2010] EWCA Civ 345, [2010] STC 1208, the Court of Appeal held that the taxpayer company should be awarded the costs of pursuing an application for judicial review.

A married couple were the sole directors of the taxpayer company, which was in the construction industry. Following a serious injury on the part of a director, the company failed to account for PAYE for the four months from May to August 2007. HMRC issued notices requiring payment of the deemed tax due under the PAYE regulations and instituted proceedings in the county court. The taxpayer calculated it owed less tax than was deemed due, but HMRC would not amend their figures. Agreement was not reached and the taxpayer applied for judicial review. The parties subsequently agreed to the withdrawal of the county court proceedings and the application for judicial review, but the taxpayer pursued the application for review when HMRC refused to pay the costs of the application. In the event, the taxpayer was ordered to pay to HMRC, the costs of preparation of the acknowledgment of service summarily assessed at £500, on the basis that it was not justified in pursuing the application for permission to apply for judicial review once the county court proceedings had been settled. The taxpayer appealed.

Allowing the appeal, the Court of Appeal held that it was not an abuse of process of the court or unreasonable for the appellant to resort to a public law claim. Despite the good sense and relevance of the equitable liability practice, HMRC had initiated, and despite all reasonable efforts by the taxpayer to settle for the sum actually due, persisted in their statutory claim for the amount deemed to be due. HMRC failed to respond to the appellants' proposals for over four months, notwithstanding reminders. They were then supplied with detailed and, it appears, scrupulous, calculations of the sum actually due but persisted in a claim for the sum deemed to be due. The taxpayer would be awarded £6,000 for the costs of commencing the judicial review.

Key points on appeals

[5.42] Points to consider are as follows.

- HMRC provide the option of internally reviewing decisions made by its officers. A finite timeframe is given for providing the independent review decision. The benefits of an internal review are that an independent officer reviews the decision and how it was made, the quantum (where appropriate) and the risk to HMRC of losing the appeal. There is no material cost to the client in the majority of cases in opting for internal review.
- Any appeal or referral for internal review must accurately and clearly state the grounds for the appeal, as these are normally the points considered by the Tribunal.
- Data released by HMRC of internal reviews undertaken in 2013/14 shows that 84% of all internal reviews related to penalties and taxpayers had the most success in connection with VAT penalties where 60% of cases were cancelled or varied. The data also indicates that 82% of appeals to the First-tier tribunal were decided wholly or partially in HMRC's favour.

- HMRC also operate an alternative dispute resolution process to settle disputes. This allows a facilitator (from HMRC) to mediate between the two parties. See 5.10 above.
- The Tribunals Service manages the appeal and the system is formal and structured so it is essential that the adviser is disciplined and organised to avoid damaging their client's case. If you are not happy with the categorisation of the appeal, you can ask for the appeal to be moved to another category, if you believe this will be beneficial.
- HMRC will often appoint Counsel to represent them so the adviser needs to consider seriously whether to appoint Counsel where a hearing is scheduled.
- In the majority of cases, the burden of proof rests with the company. However, in cases where HMRC suspects that the company deliberately omitted or failed to report income or gains, the burden of proof is on HMRC to demonstrate that the omission or failure was deliberate.
- HMRC is guided by its Litigation and Settlement Strategy. If the dispute is over a point of law, then it is not normally possible to negotiate a settlement for a proportion of the disputed figure.
- Taking matters before the Tribunal is costly in terms of time and money so the client needs to be made fully aware of these two factors when deciding whether to take an appeal before the Tribunal. What are the chances of success? Is the client prepared to pay the tax on top of the professional costs and to suffer the disruption the process will cause?

6
Assessments

Cross references. See **5** APPEALS; **15.8** CLAIMS; **56.3** PARTNERSHIPS; **56.21** PARTNERSHIPS with regard to European Economic Interest Groupings; **64.6** RESIDENCE; **65.14**, **65.18** RETURNS for determination of tax liability where no return is delivered.

Simon's Taxes. See A4.3.

Introduction to assessments

[6.1] Self-assessment for corporation tax was introduced for accounting periods ending on or after 1 July 1999. Companies self-assess their profits chargeable to corporation tax by submitting returns which are processed by HMRC on receipt, with any queries being dealt with later by way of opening an enquiry (see **65.14** RETURNS with regard to enquiries, now part of the compliance check process).

However, HMRC may also make assessments or determinations where necessary, for example where no return has been delivered, or where HMRC discover that profits have not been assessed. The following chapter provides details of the circumstances surrounding such assessments by HMRC, the discovery process, applicable time limits, and relevant case law with regard to fraudulent and negligent conduct.

Assessments

[6.2] A company must submit a return detailing its chargeable profits and including a self-assessment to tax. In addition to the self-assessment procedure, HMRC has retained the power to raise assessments in certain circumstances, for example, where no return has been made, or where it is considered profits have been under-declared. In the latter case HMRC is able to raise a 'discovery' assessment, relating to further facts or circumstances which have come to light with regard to the self-assessment within a return (see **6.3** below).

An assessment is made by an officer of HMRC by raising a notice of assessment for the relevant accounting period of the company. The notice must be served on the person assessed (normally by post) and must state its date of issue and the time limit for giving notice of appeal (**5.3** APPEALS). Where any statutory provision gives the Commissioners for HMRC the power to make an assessment then such an assessment is also made by an officer in the same manner as above.

[*TMA 1970, s 30A(1)–(3)(5); FA 1998, Sch 18 para 47(1)*].

See **36.4** HMRC—ADMINISTRATION for the exercise of functions of an HMRC officer by automated process.

Where the company does not deliver a company tax return following the issue of a return notice, an HMRC officer may make a determination to the best of his information and belief of the amount of tax payable. See further **65.18** RETURNS — determinations where no return delivered. Tax is payable as if the determination were a self-assessment, with no right of appeal, and the determination can only be displaced by the filing of a return and the making of a self-assessment based thereon.

[*FA 1998, Sch 18 paras 36–40*].

Case law has had an impact on the various requirements as to an assessment, for example, an assessment must include a statement of the tax actually payable (*Hallamshire Industrial Finance Trust Ltd v CIR* (1978) 53 TC 631). An assessment defective in form or containing errors may be validated by *TMA 1970, s 114(1)*, or in some cases the court may choose to use its powers under *TMA 1970, s 56(6)* to alter an assessment on appeal (*Pickles v Foulsham* (1925) 9 TC 261, HL; *Bath & West Counties Property Trust Ltd v Thomas* (1977) 52 TC 20). However, *s 114(1)* does *not* extend to integral fundamental parts of the assessment such as an error in the year of assessment for which it is made (*Baylis v Gregory* (1988) 62 TC 1, HL).

Further, an officer's power of assessment is not limited to persons (or sources of income) within the area of his tax office (*R v Tavistock Commrs (ex p Adams) (No 2)* (1971) 48 TC 56, CA).

In *Gunn v HMRC* [2011] UKUT 59 (TCC), the First-Tier Tribunal had dismissed appeals by a company director, who then appealed to the Upper Tribunal, contending that the notices of assessment were invalid because they did not give details of the statutory provisions under which they were raised. The Upper Tribunal dismissed the appeal, holding that the notices of assessment were 'in substance and effect' in conformity with the Taxes Acts, and were therefore authorised by *TMA 1970, s 114*.

A taxpayer may authorise HMRC (on form 64-8) to automatically provide his agent with a copy of any assessment made on him. If an assessment is not dealt with promptly, interest (or additional interest) may arise on unpaid tax, and any appeal may be out of time.

See **6.7** below for the normal time limits within which an assessment may be made, including extended time limits.

See 32.6 EUROPEAN UNION LEGISLATION regarding the application of the corporation tax provisions where a company ceases to be UK-resident in the course of the formation of an SE or where an SE becomes non-UK resident.

Discovery

Discovery assessments and determinations

[6.3] Under corporation tax self-assessment, if HMRC have any queries in respect of a return, they will open an enquiry as part of the compliance check process (see **65.14** RETURNS). Once the time limit for an enquiry has passed, or an enquiry has been closed, then the only way HMRC can examine a chargeable period is by using the discovery process. Thus 'discovery' is the right of HMRC to re-open earlier periods which are otherwise considered closed.

However this right can only be used in specific instances — a 'discovery assessment' may be made where HMRC consider that an amount which ought to have been assessed to tax has not been assessed, or that an assessment has become insufficient, or that relief has been given which is, or has become, excessive. For example, this would occur where certain facts, or circumstances, which would have an impact on the tax payable have not been declared or disclosed, and HMRC discover this to be the case.

This additional assessment is made in the amount (or further amount) which HMRC consider, in their opinion, should be charged in order to make good the loss of tax.

Similarly, if HMRC discover that a return for an accounting period incorrectly states an amount that affects, or may affect, the tax payable for another accounting period or by another company, they may make a 'discovery determination' of the amount which, in their opinion, ought to have been stated in the return. For a case discussing what constitutes a 'discovery determination' for the purposes of this provision, see *Nijjar Dairies Ltd v HMRC* [2013] UKFTT 434 (TC).

Notice of a discovery assessment or determination must be served on the company, stating the date of issue and the time limit for any appeal, and the assessment or determination may be altered after the notice has been served only under express provisions.

A *discovery assessment* will thus be appropriate where, for example, a discovery leads to an additional tax liability on the company for the period. A *discovery determination* would be appropriate where there is a discovery that losses carried forward or surrendered as group relief have been overstated. If such a determination reduces losses, etc. available for another period or to another company, and the time allowed for the required amendment has expired, a discovery assessment would be appropriate. (HMRC Company Taxation Manual, CTM95520 and CTM95530).

In practice, where a return has been filed and the time limit for opening an enquiry has not expired (nor an enquiry already been closed), HMRC normally deal with matters by opening an enquiry rather than by issuing a discovery assessment or determination. (HMRC Company Taxation Manual, CTM95520). For the limited circumstances in which a discovery assessment may be made even though the deadline for opening an enquiry has not passed, see HMRC Enquiry Manual EM3255 and HMRC Tax Bulletin August 2001 pp 875, 876.

In *Easinghall Ltd v HMRC* UT, [2016] STC 1476 an officer had opened a discovery assessment for a year, regarding a possible understatement of profits. Easinghall Ltd appealed the assessment. On review a second officer decided to withdraw the assessment. Shortly afterwards the first officer had written to the company and opened an enquiry into the same year. Easinghall Ltd applied for a closure notice. The Upper Tribunal concluded that HMRC were bound by the letter from the second officer and this should be read as cancelling the discovery assessment, so that the enquiry into the return should be closed.

Required circumstances

Subject to the exceptions below, a discovery assessment for an accounting period for which the company has delivered a return, or a discovery determination, may only be made in the following circumstances:

(a) where the discovery arose from a situation brought about carelessly or deliberately by the company, a person acting on behalf of the company, or a partner of the company at the relevant time; or

(b) where the time limit to open an enquiry into the return has expired (see **65.14** RETURNS) or, where HMRC have opened an enquiry into the return, they have either issued a partial closure notice dealing with the issue to which the discovery relates or issued a final closure notice and they could not reasonably have been expected, on the basis of the information made available to them before that time, to be aware of the situation giving rise to the discovery.

Information is for this purpose regarded as 'made available' to HMRC if it is contained:

(i) in the company's returns (or accompanying documentation) for the period or the two immediately preceding accounting periods; or

(ii) in a claim (or accompanying documentation) made by the company as regards the period; or

(iii) in any documents, accounts or information produced to, or provided for, HMRC for the purposes of an enquiry into a return (as in (i)) or claim (as in (ii)),

or if it is information the existence and relevance of which are notified in writing to HMRC by the company (or a person acting on its behalf) or could reasonably be expected to be inferred by HMRC from information falling within (i)–(iii) above.

As regards (b) above, there is an onus on the company to draw attention to any important information relevant to a tax liability, particularly if there is some doubt as to the interpretation which could be placed on that information. Information made available by the company's agent on its behalf is made available by the company. However, where information is made available by, or on behalf of, someone other than the company, e.g. in the return of another member of the group, then HMRC may still make a discovery assessment or determination on the company. (HMRC Company Taxation Manual, CTM95550).

The above restrictions do not apply where a discovery assessment or determination gives effect to a discovery determination duly made in relation to another company's return.

Nor do these restrictions apply in relation to any income or gains in respect of which HMRC have given notice after completing an enquiry (so far as it dealt with the matters to which the notice relates) under certain anti-avoidance provisions, such as *TIOPA 2010, ss 81, 82* (schemes and arrangements designed to increase double taxation relief), *TCGA 1992, s 184G* or *s 184H* (avoidance utilising losses — see **11.4** CAPITAL GAINS).

A discovery assessment or determination may in any event not be made if the discovery arose from a situation attributable to a mistake in the return as to the basis on which the company's liability ought to have been computed, and the return was in fact made on the basis of, or in accordance with, the practice generally prevailing at the time the return was made.

Any objection to a discovery assessment or determination on the grounds that the above conditions have not been complied with can only be made on an appeal against the assessment or determination.

[*FA 1998, Sch 18 paras 41–45*].

Whilst the following case law relates to individuals and partnerships, the provisions of *FA 1998, Sch 18 paras 41–45* operate in the same way.

The case of *DW Hankinson v HMRC (No 3)* [2012] STC 485 considered the interpretation of the similar income and capital gains tax provisions for discovery assessments found at *TMA 1970, s 29*. It is interesting to note that the Upper Tribunal rejected the taxpayer appellant's attempt to apply a restrictive interpretation to the discovery provisions. The Court of Appeal upheld the Upper Tribunal decision. See also the case *M Jones v HMRC* (TC01023) [2011] UKFTT 149 (TC) (16 March 2011) below.

In *Charlton v HMRC* UT 2012, [2013] STC 866 the taxpayer had entered into an avoidance scheme and included the scheme's reference number under the DISCLOSURE OF TAX AVOIDANCE SCHEMES (**28**) rules in his return. HMRC issued a discovery assessment and the taxpayer appealed. The Upper Tribunal held that HMRC had made a discovery but that the conditions at (b) above were not satisfied. The information which had been provided with the return was such that an HMRC officer would have been reasonably expected to have been aware of the insufficiency of tax shown by the return. This can be contrasted with the case *Sanderson v HMRC* CA 2016, [2016] STC 638 where the taxpayer noted participation in a capital loss scheme in his 1998/99 tax return but did not provide details. A discovery assessment was raised in 2004. The court held that whilst the tax return might have alerted a hypothetical officer to the implementation of the scheme, it did not contain enough information to make the officer aware of an 'actual insufficiency' of tax for the purposes of *TMA 1970, s 29*, so that the assessment was valid.

In *Freeman v HMRC* [2013] UKFTT 496(TC) the tribunal held that a discovery assessment raised by HMRC under *TMA 1970, s 29* was invalid because HMRC could have been reasonably expected, on the basis of information available to it at the relevant time to have been aware of the loss of tax. The tribunal decided that a document provided to HMRC in April 2000, in the context of an enquiry into the taxpayer's 1997/98 return, was 'information available' in relation to the 2002/03 tax year. Thus the tribunal's conclusion is that there is no temporal restriction in relation to *TMA 1970, s 29(6)(d)(ii)*.

Similarly, in *HMRC v Lansdowne Partners Ltd Partnership* CA 2011, [2012] STC 544 an amended assessment was issued out of time on the basis that certain rebated fees were not allowable. The partnership appealed that firstly the fees were deductible, and alternatively that HMRC's amendment was outside the statutory time limit. The General Commissioners found for the taxpayer. The Court of Appeal dismissed HMRC's appeal. Whilst the Court accepted the fees were not deductible, the court agreed the amendment was out of time. The amendment could only have been valid if the relevant officer could not have been reasonably expected on the information available to him before that time, to be aware that the partnership statement was wrong. All relevant information had been submitted, and a hypothetical officer should have been aware of the case law relating to the tax treatment of such fees.

In *Pattullo v HMRC* UT, [2016] STC 2043 a discovery assessment was issued in respect of tax planning which was the subject of a different case progressing through the courts. The Tribunal held that a discovery could only occur once that similar case's appeal was final, because it was only at that point in time that what had only been a suspicion on the part of the tax officer was converted to the positive view that there was an insufficiency of tax. In *Michael Yin v HMRC* FTT, [2014] UKFTT 865 (TC) the Tribunal held that HMRC were correct to wait until the expiry of the appeal period for the direction notice before issuing the discovery assessments (which was the only way of assessing the taxpayer's income). The amount of under-assessed income was only 'discovered' at that point.

In *Terence Lynch v NCA* FTT, [2014] UKFTT 1088 (TC) the First-tier Tribunal found that the National Crime Agency (NCA) had been entitled to raise discovery assessments. The Tribunal found that the NCA had reasonable grounds to suspect there was a charge to income tax as a result of criminal conduct (under the *Proceeds of Crime Act 2002*); and that the conditions for a discovery assessment under *TMA 1970, s 29* were met: unexplained bank deposits were missing from the tax return, which the tax officer would not have been aware of at the end of the enquiry period, and the 20 year time limit applied (in cases of such deliberate concealment). In *John Martin v HMRC* [2015] UKUT 161 the Upper Tribunal found that the issue of a confiscation order (under the Proceeds of Crime Act 2002) did not preclude HMRC from raising a discovery assessment on the basis of what HMRC believed to have been Mr Martin's profits to build and maintain a house and his lifestyle.

In *Tooth v HMRC* SC, [2021] STC 1049, the SC held that a discovery assessment which relied on the extended time limits for 'deliberate conduct' was invalid, because the taxpayer's conduct had not been deliberate. The court held that a deliberate inaccuracy means a statement which, when made, was deliberately inaccurate, and not a deliberate statement which is (in fact) inaccurate. The accuracy of a statement should be determined in the light of the whole tax return. The court also ruled that there was no concept of 'staleness' in the statutory scheme for raising discovery assessments. This concept had been used in a number of cases to rule that a discovery assessment was invalid. In *Beagles v HMRC* [2018] UKUT 380 (TCC), [2019] STC 54, for example, there was a two and a half year gap between HMRC making a discovery and issuing an assessment. There was no ongoing litigation at the time of the discovery. The Upper Tribunal held that the discovery had become 'stale' and had lost its quality of newness before the assessment was made, and that the assessment was, therefore, invalid. The SC has now ruled that staleness cannot prevent HMRC raising a valid assessment.

In *Cussens v HMRC* FTT, [2019] UKFTT 542 (TC); 2019 SWTI 1555, discovery assessments were held not to be valid because they had not been made using best judgement. HMRC had made assessments on an uncooperative taxpayer by taking an estimate of sales and deducting 50% for expenses. The Tribunal found that it was 'unthinkable' that such a high net profit could be achieved and there was no evidence that HMRC had undertaken any research into the margins achieved by similar businesses.

Appeals

An appeal may be brought against any discovery assessment or determination by written notice to HMRC within 30 days after issue of the notice of the assessment or determination.

In *Burgess and Brimheath Developments Ltd v HMRC* [2015] UKUT 578 (TC) the Upper Tribunal confirmed that in appeals against discovery assessments (issued pursuant to *TMA 1970 s 29*, or *FA 1998 Sch 18 para 41*) HMRC bears the burden of demonstrating the assessments are valid, regardless of whether the appellant has raised the issue.

SP1/06 — providing HMRC with sufficient information

HMRC's Statement of Practice SP 1/06 on 'Self-Assessment: Finality and Discovery' clarifies how much information a taxpayer needs to provide in the tax return to remove the possibility of a discovery assessment.

The Statement is intended to provide more certainty for both individuals and companies following the decision in the case of *Langham v Veltema* (2004) 76 TC 259, CA, where it was held that a discovery assessment could be made once the enquiry window was closed even though HMRC was made aware of the possibility that a property valuation might have been insufficient.

The Statement provides three examples of where the taxpayer can rely on information in the tax return to provide against protection from a later discovery assessment provided the information is reasonable and true.

- In a valuation case, the information should state that a valuation has been used, by whom it has been carried out, that it was carried out by a named independent and suitably qualified valuer and, if that was the case, the appropriate basis of the valuation.

- In the case of an exceptional item in the accounts, for example concerning repairs, the information should state that a programme of work has been carried out, what it included, the total cost allocated to revenue and capital and the particular basis of allocation.
- In a case where the taxpayer adopts a different view of the law from that published as HMRC's view, the tax return should indicate that a different view had been adopted by providing comments to the effect that HMRC guidance has not been followed or that no adjustment has been made to take account of it.

The Statement stresses that only the minimum information necessary to make disclosure of an insufficiency should be submitted:

> 'Information will not be treated as being made available where the total amount supplied is so extensive that an officer "could not have been reasonably expected to be aware" of the significance of particular information and the officer's attention has not been drawn to it by the taxpayer or taxpayer's representative.'

It further states that the *Veltema* judgment does not require the provision of enough information to quantify the effect on the assessment.

The decision in *Langham v Veltema* has been applied in several subsequent cases including *Agnew v HMRC* [2010] UKFTT 272 (TC) and *Tetley v HMRC* [2010] UKFTT 118 (TC) but has been distinguished in *HMRC v Lansdowne Partners Limited Partnership* [2011] EWCA Civ 1578, [2012] STC 544 (see above) and *Charlton v HMRC* [2011] UKFTT 467 (TC), [2011] SFTD 1160 (see above).

William Blumenthal v HMRC [2012] UKFTT 497 (TC) was a decision of the FTT involving a more complicated capital loss planning scheme, where the FTT made the points that: the disclosure needs to be sufficient to enable an officer to determine whether or not an insufficiency exists; the adequacy of the disclosure depends on the arrangements and must make clear the facts and the position taken by the taxpayer on those facts; where the facts and law are complex disclosure needs to include some brief explanation of the main tax issues and the position taken on those issues, and not just the facts. On this basis it would then be reasonable to expect an officer to be aware of an insufficiency.

[*FA 1998, Sch 18 paras 41–45, 48, 49; F(No 2)A 2017, Sch 15 paras 31, 32*].

Simon's Taxes. See **A6.7**.

Over-repayments

[6.4] The discovery assessment provisions at **6.3** above also apply to an amount paid to a company by way of repayment of tax, INTEREST ON OVERPAID TAX (**43**), 'land remediation tax credit' (see **59.14** PENALTIES), research and development (and vaccine research) tax credits, above the line R&D expenditure credits (see **63** RESEARCH AND DEVELOPMENT EXPENDITURE), first-year tax credits (see **10.25** CAPITAL ALLOWANCES ON PLANT AND MACHINERY) or any of the creative industry credits (see **26** CREATIVE INDUSTRIES RELIEFS), to the extent that it ought not to have been paid, unless it is recoverable under *ICTA 1988, s 826(8A)* (interest recoverable as if it were INTEREST ON OVERDUE TAX (**43**)).

Any such assessment is on miscellaneous income, and INTEREST ON OVERDUE TAX (**42**) runs from the date when the payment being recovered was made. For these purposes amounts allowed by way of set-off are treated as paid, and an intended repayment which exceeds the tax paid is nonetheless treated as a repayment. In the case of an assessment to recover tax repaid in respect of an accounting period (or interest thereon), income tax repaid in respect of a payment received in an accounting period (or interest thereon), or land remediation or research and development tax credits paid for an accounting period, the assessment is treated as being for the accounting period in respect of which the repayment or credit was made.

Except in cases of careless or deliberate error (previously fraud or negligence) (for which the time limit is 20 years, see also **6.7** below), the time limit for a discovery assessment by virtue of these provisions is (where relevant) extended to the later of the end of the accounting period following that in which the amount assessed was paid and the expiry of three months from the day on which HMRC complete an enquiry into a relevant company tax return (see **65.17** RETURNS).

[*FA 1998, Sch 18 paras 46, 52, 53; F(No 2)A 2017, Sch 6 para 5*].

Double assessment

[6.5] Where a company makes a written claim to HMRC that it has been assessed (including self-assessment) more than once for the same cause and for the same accounting period, and HMRC are satisfied, then HMRC must take the necessary steps to eliminate the double charge.

If the company does not agree with HMRC's decision on a claim then they may appeal to the Tax Tribunal against the refusal of a claim. The appeal must be made in writing to HMRC within 30 days after the notice of refusal of the claim is given.

[*FA 1998, Sch 18 para 50*].

See also 5 APPEALS.

Finality of assessments

[6.6] An assessment cannot be altered after the notice has been served except in accordance with the express provisions of the *Taxes Acts* (for example where the taxpayer appeals — see 5 APPEALS).

[*FA 1998, Sch 18 paras 47(2), 49*].

Where over-assessment results from an *error or mistake* in a return, see **15.10** CLAIMS, now with regard to overpayment relief (as from 1 April 2010).

Where an amount required to be included in a company tax return may affect tax payable for another accounting period or by another company, and that amount can no longer be altered (for which see *FA 1998, Sch 18 para 88(3)–(5)*), it is taken as conclusively determined in relation to the other period or company (without affecting HMRC's power to make assessments).

The above rule does not prevent the company making a claim for overpayment relief. It also has no effect on the operation of the CORPORATE INTEREST RESTRICTION 25.

[*FA 1998, Sch 18 para 88; F(No 2)A 2017, Sch 5 para 4, Sch 15 para 34*].

Time limits

[6.7] Except where specifically provided, the normal time limit for assessments is four years after the end of the accounting period.

[*FA 1998, Sch 18 para 46(1), Sch 19 para 17*].

In certain cases, however, as described below, extended limits apply to assessments for the purpose of making good a loss of tax.

An objection to the making of any assessment on the grounds that it is out of time can only be made on an appeal against the assessment. [*FA 1998, Sch 18 para 46(3)*].

An assessment may be made on tax lost through:

(a) deliberate action of the company or a person related to the company;
(b) careless action not appropriately remedied;
(c) failure to comply with the tax avoidance schemes legislation (see **28.1** DISCLOSURE OF TAX AVOIDANCE SCHEMES); or
(d) arrangements which were expected to result in a tax advantage in respect of which the taxpayer was under an obligation to notify HMRC of a monitored promoter's reference number under the high-risk promoters of avoidance schemes provisions (see **28.26** DISCLOSURE OF TAX AVOIDANCE SCHEMES) but failed to do so.

In the case of carelessness, the assessment may be made not more than six years after the accounting period to which it relates.

In the case of deliberate action, the assessment may be up to 20 years from the end of the accounting period to which the loss of tax relates. The latter time limit applies where there is a failure to notify chargeability or where (c) or (d) above apply.

[*FA 1998, Sch 18 para 46(2)–(2B)*].

An objection to the making of any assessment on the grounds that it is out of time can only be made on an appeal against the assessment. [*FA 1998, Sch 18 para 46(3)*].

Simon's Taxes. See **A4.320, A4.325.**

Contract settlements and closure notices

[6.8] Enquiries or compliance checks into company tax returns may be settled by either contract settlement or by formal closure notice.

Contract settlement

If the company taxpayer is prepared to agree with the officer's findings, then they might agree to enter into a contract settlement, which is a contract between HMRC and the taxpayer to pay any additional tax resulting from the enquiry or investigation, together with interest and, where appropriate, penalties, without a formal assessment of all the tax. This may be particularly appropriate where HMRC's enquiry has been more extensive and covered several accounting periods.

A monetary offer may be made by the company taxpayer to HMRC in consideration for no formal proceedings being taken for any irregularities arising from the enquiry or investigation. If the offer is accepted by HMRC, it forms the basis of a binding contract under which proceedings can be taken for recovery of the amount offered. Such an agreement formally brings the enquiry or investigation to an end and HMRC are not able to make any further enquiries for the years concerned unless there is a new discovery.

Where a contract settlement is agreed, HMRC will usually not issue a closure notice, and it has been confirmed that the contract settlement will be treated for all purposes as a closure notice. (HMRC Enquiry Manual EM6001).

Where appropriate, contract settlements are used as a way of closing a civil investigation of fraud under Code of Practice 9 (COP 9 — HMRC Investigations where we suspect tax fraud), avoiding the need to proceed to formal prosecution. See **38.16** HMRC INVESTIGATORY POWERS.

See *CIR v Nuttall* CA, (1989) 63 TC 148 for confirmation of power to enter into such agreements. Amounts due under such an agreement which are unpaid may be pursued by an action for a debt, but the Crown does not rank as a preferential creditor in respect of the sums due (*Nuttall* above; *CIR v Woollen* CA, [1992] STC 944, 65 TC 229).

The importance of clarifying exactly what liabilities are to be included in a settlement can be seen in the case *S Hughes v HMRC* [2010] UKFTT 589 (TC). In this instance the taxpayer agreed a settlement covering personal income tax and Class 4 national insurance contributions. The officer conducting the enquiry noted payments were also required under the Construction Industry Scheme and HMRC subsequently issued determinations. The taxpayer appealed arguing these should have been included in the agreed settlement. The First Tier Tribunal dismissed the appeal noting the wording of the negotiated settlement stated specifically which taxes were being dealt with and that this would therefore not preclude HMRC from taking further action with regard to liabilities arising under a wholly separate regime which had not been the subject of the enquiry or the negotiations.

Closure notice

In the case of a formal closure notice, HMRC amend the return to make the adjustments they consider to be necessary.

If, during the course of the enquiry, the company considers that it should be brought to an end, it may apply to the tribunal for a direction that the officer should issue a closure notice within a specified period. Such an application is heard in the same way as an appeal, and, unless it considers that the officer has reasonable grounds for continuing the enquiry beyond the specified period, the tribunal must give the direction applied for.

If, during the course of the enquiry, the taxpayer company has made amendments to the return, they are taken into account in the closure notice.

See also **59.27** PENALTIES for mitigation of penalties.

7

Banks

Cross-reference. **31.18** DOUBLE TAX RELIEF.

Simon's Taxes. See D7.7.

Introduction to banks

[7.1] In general, the term 'bank' is defined by reference to the carrying on of a *bona fide* banking business, but for certain purposes it is specially defined as:

(a) the Bank of England;
(b) a person who has permission under *Financial Services and Markets Act 2000 (FISMA 2000), Pt 4A* to accept deposits (excluding building and friendly societies, credit unions and insurance companies);
(c) (before the end of the Brexit implementation period (11pm on 31 December 2020)), an EEA firm within *FISMA 2000, Sch 3 para 5(b)* which has permission under *para 15* of that Schedule (as a result of qualifying for authorisation under *para 12(1)*) to accept deposits;
(d) an international organisation of which the UK is a member and which is designated as a bank for the particular purpose by Treasury order; or
(e) the European Investment Bank.

For what constitutes a bona fide banking business, see *Hafton Properties Ltd v McHugh* Ch D 1986, 59 TC 420.

HMRC operate a code of practice on taxation for banks to which many of the major banks have signed up to. See **7.10** below.

[*ITA 2007, s 991; CTA 2010, s 1120; SI 2019 No 689, Regs 1, 15(12), 17(12); European Union (Withdrawal Agreement) Act 2020, Sch 5 para 1(1)*].

See also HMRC Banking Manual.

Simon's Taxes. See **D7.701**.

Liability of banks to corporation tax

[7.2] Banking businesses are assessable on their profits under normal taxation provisions with interest on advances to customers included in trading profits. The profits continue to be taxable as trading income where changes in the fair value of securities (held for the purpose of carrying on a banking or insurance business or a business consisting of dealing in securities) are accounted for in reserves (either in the statement of recognised gains and losses or statement of changes in equity). See **7.3** below for the bank surcharge. For the charge to corporation tax on income on certain net receipts arising during compulsory liquidation, see *CTA 2010, ss 634–641; ITA 2007, ss 837A–837H*. See also **Simon's Taxes D7.725**.

[*CTA 2009, s 128*].

Bank loss relief restriction

The proportion of a banking company's annual taxable profit that can be offset by carried-forward losses is restricted to 25%. The restriction applies in addition to the restriction for companies generally at **51.13** LOSSES (broadly for accounting periods beginning on or after 1 April 2017).

The restriction applies to trading losses (*CTA 2010, s 45*), non-trading loan relationship deficits (*CTA 2009, s 457*) and management expenses (*CTA 2009, ss 63, 1223*) carried forward from accounting periods ending before 1 April 2015 (a 'pre-2015 loss'). Where a company's accounting period begins before and ends on or after 1 April 2015, the accounting period is split into two notional periods and profits, losses etc. apportioned on a time basis or any other just and reasonable basis. The rationale behind this restriction is to prevent banks that had built up exceptionally large losses as a result of the financial crisis of 2008 from using the losses to eliminate tax on recovering profits.

The restriction applies to a banking company which is UK resident, or which carries on a trade in the UK through a PE, which is an authorised person per *FISMA 2000* and carries on a relevant regulated activity (such as deposit taking, see *CTA 2010, s 269BB*) in the course of a trade, and is not excluded; or which is a member of a partnership which undertakes such activity. The provisions also apply to building societies, which for this purpose include savings banks established under the *Savings Bank (Scotland) Act 1819*. Excluded entities include insurance companies, investment trusts, and certain entities which do not carry on a relevant regulated activity. There are exclusions for losses arising before the company began a 'regulated activity' and for certain start-up losses (see below). It is possible also for building societies and banking companies within the building society's group (which have been allocated an amount of carried-forward loss allowance by the building society), to designate relevant carried-forward losses as unrestricted. See **8** BUILDING SOCIETIES.

For the purposes of this restriction a group is defined as the group under international accounting standards or, where appropriate, United States generally accepted accounting practice. Joint ventures are brought into the same groups as the companies that jointly control it relying on international accounting standards definitions.

Trading losses

To calculate the restriction, it is necessary to firstly calculate the company's 'relevant trading profits' for an accounting period. The '*relevant trading profits*' are calculated as at **51.14** LOSSES. The restriction does not apply if the amount given by **51.14**(1) is not greater than nil.

Any deduction in respect of a pre-2015 trading loss cannot exceed 25% of the relevant trading profits.

Non-trading loan relationships

For non-trading loan relationships, it is necessary to calculate the company's 'total relevant non-trading profits' or, for accounting periods beginning before 1 April 2020 (treating periods straddling that date as two separate periods, the second of which begins on that date), its 'relevant non-trading profits'. 'Total relevant non-trading profits' are calculated as at **51.14** LOSSES. The '*relevant non-trading profits*' are also calculated as at **51.14** LOSSES. The restriction does not apply if the amount given by **51.14**(1) is not greater than nil.

Any deduction in respect of a pre-2015 non-trading loan relationship deficit cannot exceed 25% of the relevant trading profits.

Management expenses

For management expenses, it is necessary to calculate the company's 'relevant profits' (i.e. the sum of its relevant trading profits and its relevant non-trading profits). All that can be relieved is the 'relevant maximum'. This is 25% of the relevant profits after reduction by carried-forward trading losses and pre-1 April 2017 non-trading deficits (within **50.7** LOAN RELATIONSHIPS).

Exclusions

The above provisions do not apply to any carried forward reliefs that arose in an accounting period ending before the accounting period in which a company began to carry on relevant regulated activity. The statutory definition of a relevant regulated activity is not the same as the full definition of a banking company. A relevant regulated activity includes activity of a type that would be regulated under *FISMA 2000* even if the company carrying on the activity is not regulated under that Act.

Losses arising in a company's start-up period are also excluded where they have arisen in the first five years of a company beginning to undertake relevant regulated activity. This five-year rule may be curtailed when a company changes group/partnerships under certain circumstances. Reliefs generated in the start-up period are assumed to have been used before any reliefs that arose after the start-up period, so that (unrestricted) start-up losses are taken to have been used before (restricted) relief that arose after the start-up period when establishing what relevant carried forward losses remain to a company at 1 April 2015. Where a company's accounting period begins before and ends after the last day of its start-up period, the accounting period is split into two notional periods and profits, losses etc. apportioned on a time basis or any other just and reasonable basis.

Anti-avoidance

Anti-avoidance provisions remove profits from the calculation of relevant profits (and so deny the use of any pre-2015 restricted reliefs against such profits) where they arise from arrangements that: create profits in a company with restricted reliefs that could otherwise be used against those profits; where the main benefit, or one of the main benefits, of the arrangement is to secure a tax advantage for the company, or the company and connected companies; and, the value of the tax advantage is greater than the value of any other economic benefit of the arrangements to the company, or the company taken with companies connected with it. The definition of group is not relied upon for this anti-avoidance rule; instead a test of connection (read in accordance with *CTA 2010, s 1122*) is relied upon.

[*CTA 2010, ss 269B, 269BA, 269BB, 269BD, 269C–269CR; F(No 2)A 2017, Sch 4 paras 17–22; FA 2019, Sch 10 paras 13, 14; FA 2020, Sch 4 paras 36–38, 42–46*].

Simon's Taxes. See **D7.705.**

Compensation payments

Certain types of compensation payments made by banking companies to their customers (as defined) are not deductible for the purposes of calculating the trade profits of the company chargeable to corporation tax. In addition, in the same accounting period, the company is deemed to have received a trading receipt equal to 10% of the expenses disallowed (in effect disallowing administrative and other costs associated with the making of the compensation payment). These rules apply to banking companies wherever they are located, subject to meeting certain conditions. The provisions apply also to corporate partners in a partnership.

The provisions apply where compensation is paid or payable to, or for the benefit of a customer of the banking company or of a company that is associated with the banking company at the time when the expenses in question are recognised for accounting purposes (unless paid under arrangements between the two companies made on arm's length terms).

The disclosure condition must be met in relation to the compensation expense; broadly, the company must have made reference to a known liability in documents such as statutory accounts, statutory reports etc. in the current or the previous accounting periods. A disclosure is disregarded for this purpose if it applies to a single error affecting a single customer. Disclosures made more than five years before the period of account in which a compensation expense is recognised for accounting purposes are also disregarded.

Compensation for administrative error, computer failures or losses caused by a third party acting independently of the bank is excluded.

[*CTA 2009, ss 133A–133N; FA 2021, s 134(1); SI 2019 No 689, Reg 16(2)*].

Bank surcharge

[7.3] An 8% surcharge is levied on a banking company's 'surcharge profits'. Each banking company (or group of companies) is entitled to a £25 million annual allowance against the surcharge ('*surcharge allowance*'), which effectively reduces the profits liable to the surcharge. Broadly, a company's 'surcharge profits' are its taxable total profits without the deduction of any non-banking group relief or group relief for carried-forward losses, non-banking loss relief or relief for losses arising before 2016. Adjustments are also made for any chargeable gains or allowable losses transferred from or to other group companies (see **12.6** CAPITAL GAINS — GROUPS) and for research and development expenditure credits (see **63.10** RESEARCH AND DEVELOPMENT EXPENDITURE).

The bank surcharge is generally treated as if it were corporation tax (but not for the purposes of the shadow ACT rules (see **29.30** DISTRIBUTIONS). The surcharge is payable on the usual corporation tax due date for a company.

[*CTA 2010, ss 269D–269DO; F(No 2)A 2017, Sch 4 paras 161–163; FA 2020, s 33; SI 2016 No 566*].

Agreements to forgo tax reliefs

[7.4] If part of any arrangements entered into are an agreement to forgo a right to tax relief (e.g. on losses), and the Treasury designates the arrangements as such, no tax relief is to be given to the company or any other party under the Corporation Taxes Acts. These rules were introduced in connection with the Asset Protection Scheme packages which the Government entered into with, principally, banks (although the provision is wide enough to cover other companies) during the financial crisis of 2008–2009.

[*FA 2009, s 25*].

Overseas issues

Overseas debts

[7.5] There is relief for certain receipts and debts the proceeds of which cannot be remitted to the UK but which form part of profits (see **69.70** TRADING INCOME — DEDUCTIONS). This relief applies to unremittable interest accrued on a loan made in the normal course of trade by a bank or other financial institution. It does not apply to the principal, or to a loan made in a currency other than the local currency of the country imposing currency restrictions where the interest is paid in the local currency and is available to be re-lent in that currency. [*CTA 2009, ss 172–179*].

Simon's Taxes. See B2.117.

Non-resident central banks

[7.6] Non-resident central banks as specified by Order in Council are exempt from tax on interest, public annuities and dividends paid out of UK public revenue (but may be taxable thereon if carrying on business in the UK) and also on chargeable gains. Profits, income and chargeable gains of the issue departments of the Reserve Bank of India and the State Bank of Pakistan are exempt.

[*TCGA 1992, s 271(8); ITA 2007, ss 839, 840; CTA 2010, s 988*]

Simon's Taxes. See **D1.231, D1.232.**

UK banking business carried on by non-residents

[7.7] Where a banking business is carried on in the UK by a person not resident or not ordinarily resident in the UK, it cannot deduct interest on money borrowed for investment in 3½% War Loan.

See also **64.11** RESIDENCE.

[*ITTOIA 2005, s 154A; CTA 2009, s 405*].

Gross payment of interest

[7.8] The requirement to deduct tax under *ITA 2007, s 874* (see **41.2** INCOME TAX IN RELATION TO A COMPANY) does not apply to a payment of interest by a bank made in the ordinary course of its business. This exclusion also does not apply to payments of interest to an individual in respect of compensation or to any payment in respect of a 'regulatory capital security' (see **50.28** LOAN RELATIONSHIPS) before 12 February 2019 or, in the case of a transitional qualifying instrument, 1 January 2024. [*ITA 2007, s 878; SI 2013 No 3209, Regs 2, 9; FA 2019, Sch 20 paras 1, 16*].

The requirement to deduct tax under *ITA 2007, s 874* also does not apply to a payment of interest on an advance to a bank if, at the time the payment is made, the person beneficially entitled to the interest is within the charge to corporation tax on the interest or is a bank which would be so within the charge to corporation tax but for the foreign permanent establishments exemption (see **31.15** DOUBLE TAX RELIEF). [*ITA 2007, s 879*].

Bank Levy

[7.9] The Bank Levy is a tax charge on specified liabilities reported in banks' balance sheets (excluding the first £20 billion). The levy is not an allowable deduction for corporation tax purposes.

The Bank Levy rates are as follows:

	Short-term chargeable liabilities	Long-term chargeable equity and liabilities
1.1.21 onwards	0.100%	0.050%
1.1.20–31.12.20	0.140%	0.070%
1.1.19–31.12.19	0.150%	0.075%
1.1.18–31.12.18	0.160%	0.080%
1.1.17–31.12.17	0.170%	0.085%
1.1.16–31.12.16	0.180%	0.090%

Transitional provisions apply on the reduction in rates from 1 January 2016, so that instalment payments due before that date are payable as if the reduction had not been made (with a corresponding reduction made to the first post-1 January 2016 payment).

For periods of account ending on or after 1 January 2021, bank levy will be chargeable only on equity and liabilities recognised on the UK balance sheets of banks and building societies.

[*FA 2011, s 73, Sch 19; FA 2018, s 33, Sch 9; FA 2021, s 134(5)–(7); SI 2011 No 1785; SI 2016 No 874*].

Simon's Taxes. See D7.707–D7.711.

Code of Practice on Taxation for Banks and Governance Protocol

[7.10] The Code of Practice on Taxation for Banks ('the Code') is part of a strategy designed to change the attitudes and behaviour of banks towards avoidance given their unique position as potential users, promoters and funders of tax avoidance. The Code describes the approach expected of banks with regard to governance, tax planning and engagement with HMRC and it aims to encourage banks, building societies and organisations providing banking services operating in the UK to adopt best practice in relation to their tax affairs. HMRC operate the Code under a published Governance Protocol.

The Commissioners for HMRC (the 'Commissioners') must publish a report on the operation of the Code, which will list the groups or entities which have unconditionally adopted the Code at the date of the report as well as those groups or entities which have not adopted the Code. In addition, if the Commissioners conclude that a group or entity has breached the Code during a reporting period they may separately name the group or entity within that report.

[*FA 2014, ss 285–288*].

The Code is at www.gov.uk/government/publications/code-practice-taxation-banks.

The Governance Protocol can be found at www.gov.uk/government/publications/code-of-practice-on-taxation-for-banks-governance-protocol.

8

Building Societies

Simon's Taxes. See D7.8.

Introduction to building societies

[8.1] A building society is one within the meaning of the *Building Societies Act 1986*. The tax treatment of such societies is outlined below.

[*CTA 2010, s 1119; Building Societies Act 1986, s 120, Sch 2*].

Liability to corporation tax

[8.2] A building society is liable to corporation tax on its profits. For the purposes of computing the taxable profits a building society is treated as though it were a company except with regard to dividends and interest payable to investors (and income tax thereon). Such interest, dividends or alternative finance return under ALTERNATIVE FINANCE ARRANGEMENTS (3), are treated as arising under a loan relationship, and so relievable under the LOAN RELATIONSHIPS (50) provisions. Interest under 'SAYE savings arrangements' within *ITTOIA 2005, s 702* and as defined by *ITTOIA 2005, s 703* are treated in the same way as dividends, and dividends and interest are not treated as distributions of the society.

Bank levy applies to building societies as well as banks. See 7.9 BANKS.

[*CTA 2009, ss 498, 1326; CTA 2010, s 1054*].

Bank surcharge

The 8% surcharge on the profits of banking companies applies equally to building societies. See 7.3 BANKS.

Compensation payments

The restrictions on deductions for certain types of compensation payments paid or payable by a banking company to its customers are also applicable to building societies (which fall within the definition of 'banking company' for the purposes of those provisions). See 7.2 BANKS.

Loss relief restriction

The loss relief restriction for banking companies (see **7.2** BANKS) applies equally to qualifying building societies (including savings banks established under the *Savings Bank (Scotland) Act 1819*). Additional relief is however provided to building societies (or banking companies in the same group as the building society) in that they are able to designate certain pre-2015 losses as unrestricted. Where the losses are designated as unrestricted, they are treated as if they were not a 'relevant carry forward loss' and can be relieved in full. A building society can designate losses either to itself or a banking company in the same group as the building society.

For the purposes of this restriction a group is defined as the group under international accounting standards or, where appropriate, United States generally accepted accounting practice. Joint ventures are brought into the same groups as the companies that jointly control it relying on international accounting standards definitions.

[*CTA 2010, ss 269B(1), 269CH(1)–269CH(5), 269BD, 269CM, 269CN*].

A building society has an initial £25 million carried-forward loss 'allowance' against which it can use to designate pre-2015 losses as unrestricted. This is a cumulative amount and is reduced where a building society designates an amount of carried-forward losses as unrestricted, or where a building society allocates an amount of the allowance to another company in its group. For companies in the building society's group, the amount of allowance is the amount allocated and is reduced when the company designates an amount of carried-forward losses as unrestricted.

To the extent a banking company's allowance is not used through designation in one accounting period it is available in any other accounting period. The allowance is not tied to an accounting period, so once a company has an amount of allowance allocated to it, it may designate losses as unrestricted in any original return or by amendment under the normal rules for amendment of a return.

[*CTA 2010, s 269CH(6)–(9)*].

Where the loss allowance is allocated to other group companies a statement of allocation must be submitted at or before the time when a company submits a tax return, or an amendment is made to a tax return, which makes a designation following the allocation made under this section. HMRC may accept a statement as valid after the return is submitted. The loss allowance can be re-allocated, providing it has not already been designated. A revised statement of allocation must be submitted at or before the time when a company submits a tax return, or an amendment is made to a tax return, which makes a designation following the allocation made under this section. HMRC may accept a statement as valid after the return is submitted.

[*CTA 2010, ss 269CI, 269CJ*].

Where losses are designated as unrestricted they must be identified in a company tax return for the accounting period for which the company makes a deduction in respect of the losses. This may be the original return, or an amended return. The return must specify the amount of the loss and whether it is a pre-2015 trading loss, loan relationship deficit or management expense. A designation can be amended or withdrawn by an amended tax return.

[*FA 1998, Sch 18 paras 83Y–83YC*].

Simon's Taxes. See D7.820–D7.825.

Mergers and transfers

General rules

[8.3] There are various provisions that apply where there is a transfer of the whole of a building society's business to a successor company in accordance with the *Building Societies Act 1986*. A society can merge/transfer its business in a number of ways, as follows:

(a) in an amalgamation (under the *Building Societies Act 1986, s 93*) where two or more societies combine to establish a single new society which succeeds to their trades;
(b) in a transfer of engagements (under the *Building Societies Act 1986, s 94*) where one society transfers all or part of its business to another society; or
(c) on a transfer of its business (under the *Building Societies Act 1986, s 97*) where, with the consent of its members, a building society transfers its business to a commercial successor company; (either one specially formed for the purpose or an existing company) or a mutual society.

The tax implications of such relevant transfers are set out in regulations and can be summarised as follows:

(i) for capital allowances purposes a trade will not be treated as ceasing and recommencing; all allowances etc that were available to the transferor will continue to be available to the transferee on the same basis;
(ii) loss relief that would have been available to the transferor if he had continued to carry on the trade, will generally continue to be available to the transferee on the same basis;
(iii) if the transferee carries on the transferred trade as part of its existing trade, the transferred trade will be treated as a separate trade carried on by the transferee. Similarly if part of a trade is transferred and the transferee carries on the transferred trade as part of its existing trade, the transferor is treated as having carried on the transferred trade as a separate trade. In both situations, apportionments of expenses etc are to be made on a just and reasonable basis;
(iv) where a transferee replaces a transferor building society as a party to a loan relationship or a derivative contract and the closing value in the accounts of the building society in relation to the loan relationship or derivative contract is different from the opening value in the accounts of the transferee, the debits or credits in respect of the difference are to be brought into account; and
(v) where a loan relationship or derivative contract has been transferred intra-group to a company before a relevant transfer, the relevant transfer will not cause the degrouping provisions to apply (although they will

apply if the company ceases to be a member of the same group as the transferee within six years whilst still a party to the relevant loan relationship or derivative contract).

In addition special rules apply where the relevant transfer is:

(1) within (c) above and there is a disposal of an asset (including an intangible fixed asset) by the transferor to the transferee. In such situations the disposal is treated as taking place on a no gain no loss basis;

(2) one that falls within (a) above, a transfer of all of a business within (b) above or a transfer within (c) above, which includes a transfer of assets (including intangible fixed assets) and:
   - the transferor and the recipient of the assets are not members of the same group at the time of the relevant transfer and, as a result of the transfer, a company leaves the transferor's chargeable gains group. In such situations, the degrouping provisions do not apply for any asset acquired by the company that leaves the group from the transferor or any other member of the transferor's group;
   - the transferor and recipient of the assets become members of the same chargeable gains group but later cease to be members of the same group. In such situations the degrouping provisions do not apply for any asset acquired by the transferee (or any other member of the same group as the transferee) as a consequence of the relevant transfer from the transferor or any other group company. Also, this regulation deals with the case where a company which was a member of the transferors group becomes a member of the transferee's group and subsequently ceases to be a member of that group. In these situations, the degrouping provisions apply to assets acquired from the transferor (or any other group company of the transferor) when the company ceases to be a member of the same group as the transferee;

(3) one that falls within (c) above and rights are conferred on members of a society to acquire shares in the successor company. In such situations, no capital gains liability arises in respect of rights, the issue of such shares to trustees on behalf of the members and the subsequent disposal of such shares to members, or on the disposal by the society of shares in the successor company;

(4) one that falls within (c) above and distributions are made in connection with the transfer. In such situations, no liability to income tax (either on the society, the successor company or the members) arises in respect of the distributions, although such distributions may be capital receipts within *TCGA 1992, s 122*.

[*SI 2009 No 2971; FA 1988, Sch 12; TCGA 1992, s 216*].

Simon's Taxes. See **D7.827–D7.830.**

SAYE savings arrangements

The disregarding of certain sums payable under SAYE schemes (for income tax and capital gains tax purposes) within *ITTOIA 2005, s 702* continues to apply to payments after the transfer under a scheme which was within that section in relation to the society immediately before the transfer, notwithstanding that it ceased to be so by reason of the transfer.

[*FA 1988, Sch 12 para 7*].

Costs of conversion

In *Halifax plc v Davidson (Inspector of Taxes)* [2000] STC (SCD) 251, (and associated cases), costs incurred by a building society on conversion to a public limited company were disallowed as capital expenditure to the extent that they related to payment of statutory cash bonuses to non-voting members of the society, but otherwise allowed.

Core capital deferred shares and permanent interest bearing shares

[8.4] Under the Capital Requirements Directive IV, building societies issue a type of share known as a 'core capital deferred share' ('CCDS'), which qualify as Common Equity Tier 1 capital. Building societies can also issue a type of perpetual share known as a 'permanent interest bearing share' ('PIBS'), which do not so qualify (but which did qualify before 2014).

Core capital deferred shares

Core capital deferred shares are treated for tax purposes as shares and are not dealt with under the provisions applicable to PIBSs. Payments in respect of CCDSs are treated as a distribution by the society and are not treated as interest for income tax purposes or as payments in respect of a loan relationship. CCDSs are not loan capital, qualifying corporate bonds or restricted preference shares (see **35.4** GROUP RELIEF). [*SI 2013 No 460*].

Permanent interest bearing shares

The main tax implications relevant to PIBS (referred to in the legislation as 'qualifying shares') are summarised below.

Capital gains exemption

Building society shares which are qualifying shares expressed in sterling (and which are not convertible into, or redeemable in, a currency other than sterling) are *for purposes other than those of corporation tax* (and subject to *TCGA 1992, s 117(2)*) 'qualifying corporate bonds' within *TCGA 1992, s 117*, and hence exempt from capital gains tax. Gains and losses on disposals by corporate holders are dealt with under the LOAN RELATIONSHIPS (**50**) provisions.

[*TCGA 1992, s 117(A1)(4)–(6)(11)–(13)*].

Accrued income scheme

'Securities' for the purposes of *ITA 2007, ss 616–677* includes building society shares which are qualifying shares.

[*ITA 2007, s 619(1)*].

Incidental costs of issue

A deduction is allowed, in computing the trading income of a building society for corporation tax purposes, for the incidental costs of obtaining finance by the issue of qualifying shares, provided that the amount of any dividend or interest on the shares is an allowable deduction. However, a deduction is not allowed where such costs are brought into account as debits under the LOAN RELATIONSHIPS (50) rules. The incidental costs allowed are expenditure (including abortive expenditure) on fees, commissions, advertising, printing and other incidental matters (but not stamp duty) wholly and exclusively for the purpose of obtaining the finance or of providing security for it or repaying it. Costs in consequence of, or for protection against, exchange rate losses, or of repayment of the shares that are attributable to their issue at a discount or repayment at a premium, are excluded.

[*CTA 2009, s 131*].

Preferential rights of acquisition

Where a building society confers on members or former members priority rights to acquire shares in the society which are qualifying shares, the rights are regarded, for capital gains tax purposes, as options acquired for no consideration and having no value when acquired.

[*TCGA 1992, s 149*].

Simon's Taxes. See **D7.803**.

9
Capital Allowances

Cross-reference. See **10** CAPITAL ALLOWANCES ON PLANT AND MACHINERY.

Simon's Taxes. See Part B3.

Other sources. See Tolley's Capital Allowances.

Introduction to capital allowances

[9.1] Capital allowances (balancing charges) are a deduction from (addition to) the profits etc. of trades and other qualifying activities in arriving at the taxable amount. The amount of depreciation charged in the accounts of a business is not so allowed. Allowances are generally treated as trading expenses (receipts) of the period of account (see **9.2**(i) below) to which they relate. [*CAA 2001, ss 2, 6; SI 2019 No 1087, Reg 3(3)*]. The law relating to capital allowances is in *Capital Allowances Act 2001* (*CAA 2001*).

Certain allowances are given in relation to trades, some only in relation to particular kinds of trade, and some additionally given against particular sources of non-trading income — details are given in the relevant section of the chapter.

Capital allowances are available in respect of expenditure on plant and machinery, which is a sufficiently large and important subject to warrant its own chapter — see **10** CAPITAL ALLOWANCES ON PLANT AND MACHINERY. They are also available in respect of certain other types of expenditure as detailed in **9.3–9.26** below.

For commentary on devolution of the power to set the corporation tax rate in Northern Ireland to the Stormont Assembly and consequential modification of the capital allowance rules, see **1.1** INTRODUCTION: CHARGE TO TAX, RATES AND PROFIT COMPUTATIONS.

A structures and buildings allowance has been introduced for expenditure on the construction of commercial buildings and structures. The allowance is available on eligible construction costs incurred on or after 29 October 2018 and is given at an annual rate on a straight-line basis. See **9.22–9.26**.

Matters of general application

[9.2] The following matters are pertinent to more than one type of capital allowance.

(i) **Meaning of 'chargeable period'.** For corporation tax purposes, a '*chargeable period*' is an accounting period. [*CAA 2001, s 6(1)*].

(ii) **Claims.** A capital allowance claim under self-assessment must be included in the company tax return (or amended return) (see **65.4, 65.6** RETURNS) for the accounting period for which the claim is made. It must specify the amount claimed, which must be expressed in figures at the time the claim is made.

The claim must be made (and may be amended or withdrawn) at any time up to the latest of:

(a) the first anniversary of the filing date for the company tax return;

(b) 30 days after closure of any enquiry into that return (unless the enquiry, being otherwise out of time, was limited, as referred to in **65.15** RETURNS, to matters to which a previous amendment making or withdrawing a capital allowance claim relates, or which are affected by the amendment);

(c) 30 days after notice of any amendment of that return by HMRC following such an enquiry; and

(d) 30 days after determination of any appeal against an amendment, or at a later time if HMRC allow it (for which see **51.3** LOSSES).

These time limits override the normal time limits for amendment of a company tax return. Amendments or withdrawals of claims must be made by amending the return.

If the effect of a claim is to reduce the available capital allowances for another accounting period for which a return has already been made, the company has 30 days to make the necessary amendments of that return.

If it fails to do so, HMRC may, by written notice and subject to a right of appeal within 30 days of the issue of the notice, amend the return to correct the position (notwithstanding any time limit otherwise applicable).

[*CAA 2001, s 3; FA 1998, Sch 18 paras 78–83*].

In *Dundas Heritable Ltd v HMRC* UT, [2019] STC 1612, the company claimed capital allowances in returns submitted more than 12 months after the filing date (and therefore after the date in (a) above). HMRC opened enquiries into the returns, which were restricted only to the capital allowances claims. The company argued that, following the opening of the enquiry, the capital allowances claims were not out of time as they were made before the date in (b) above. The Upper Tribunal agreed with the company and confirmed the First-tier Tribunal's decision to allow its appeal.

(iii) **Capital expenditure and receipts.** References in the capital allowances legislation to the incurring of capital expenditure and the paying of capital sums exclude any sums allowed as deductions in computing the payer's profits or earnings and sums payable under deduction of tax. Corresponding rules apply as regards the receipt of such sums. [*CAA 2001, s 4, Sch 3 para 9*].

(iv) **Time expenditure incurred.** Capital expenditure (other than that constituted by an 'additional VAT liability' — see (viii) below) is generally treated, for capital allowances purposes, as incurred as soon as there is an unconditional obligation to pay it, even if all or part of it is not required to be paid until some later date.

However, expenditure is treated as incurred on a later date in the following circumstances.

- Where any part of the expenditure is not required to be paid until a date more than four months after the date determined as above, it is treated as incurred on that later date.
- Where an obligation to pay becomes unconditional earlier than in accordance with normal commercial usage, with the sole or main benefit likely to be the bringing forward of the chargeable period in which the expenditure would otherwise be treated as incurred, it is instead treated as incurred on the date on or before which it is required to be paid.

Where, as a result of an event such as the issuing of a certificate, an obligation to pay becomes unconditional within one month after the end of a chargeable period, but at or before the end of that chargeable period the asset concerned has become the property of, or is otherwise attributed under the contract to, the person having the obligation, the expenditure is treated as incurred immediately before the end of that chargeable period.

The above provisions do not override any specific rule under which expenditure is treated as incurred later than the relevant time given above.

[*CAA 2001, s 5*].

Simon's Taxes. See **B3.104.**

(v) **Exclusion of double allowances.** No allowance under any of the codes covered in this chapter (business premises renovation, research and development etc.) can be made in respect of any expenditure that has been allocated to a plant and machinery pool (see **10.26** CAPITAL ALLOWANCES ON PLANT AND MACHINERY), and on which a plant or machinery allowance (or balancing charge) has consequently been given (or made). No allowance under any of those codes can be made in respect of the provision of any asset to which the allocated expenditure related. Expenditure which has attracted an allowance under any of those codes (and any asset to which that expenditure related) cannot be allocated to a plant and machinery pool.

Additional rules apply under *CAA 2001, s 9* to prevent double allowances in relation to plant or machinery treated as fixtures (as at **10.36** *et seq.* CAPITAL ALLOWANCES ON PLANT AND MACHINERY). These do not prevent a person making a fixtures claim in respect of capital expenditure if the only previous claim was for industrial buildings allowances (now abolished), research and development allowances or business premises renovation allowances, but see **10.45** CAPITAL ALLOWANCES ON PLANT AND MACHINERY for restrictions on the amount of expenditure on which plant and machinery allowances can be claimed.

[*CAA 2001, ss 7–10, Sch 3 para 10; SI 2019 No 1087, Reg 3(6)*].

Where an item of expenditure qualifies for more than one type of capital allowance, it is the taxpayer's choice as to which to claim, but the choice cannot be altered in later years. (HMRC Capital Allowances Manual CA16000).

Simon's Taxes. See **B3.114.**

(vi) **Expenditure met by another's contributions.** Subject to the exceptions below, a person is not regarded as incurring expenditure for capital allowances purposes to the extent that it is met, or will be met, directly or indirectly by another person or by a '*public body*', i.e. the Crown or any government or public or local authority (whether in the UK or elsewhere). For the scope of 'public authority', see *McKinney v Hagans Caravans (Manufacturing) Ltd* CA(NI) 1997, 69 TC 526. There is an exception where the expenditure is met by a Regional Development Grant or NI equivalent. In practice, applications for Regional Development Grants were no longer accepted after 31 March 1988, but NI equivalents did continue to be available until 31 March 2003. Expenditure met by insurance or other compensation money due in respect of a destroyed, demolished or defunct asset is not excluded from allowances. The above rule is disapplied, and allowances are thus available, if the contributor is not a public body and can obtain neither a capital allowance on his contribution by virtue of (vii) below nor a deduction against profits of a trade, profession or vocation or any qualifying activity within **10.4**(iii)–(vi) CAPITAL ALLOWANCES ON PLANT AND MACHINERY. This does not apply for the purposes of structures and buildings allowance (see **9.22** below).

[*CAA 2001, ss 532–536, Sch 2 para 19, Sch 3 paras 106–108; SI 2019 No 1087, Reg 3(9)*].

Simon's Taxes. See **B3.111.**

(vii) **Contribution allowances.** Contributors towards another person's capital expenditure on an asset may receive allowances ('*contribution allowances*') where the contribution is for the purposes of a trade or 'relevant activity' carried on (or to be carried on) by the contributor (C), and where the expenditure would otherwise have entitled the other person (assuming him not to be a public body) to structures and buildings allowance or mineral extraction allowances. Contribution allowances are not available where C and the other person (R) are CONNECTED PERSONS (**19**). A '*relevant activity*' is a profession or vocation or an activity within **10.4**(iii)–(vi) CAPITAL ALLOWANCES ON PLANT AND MACHINERY.

In the case of mineral extraction, contribution allowances are such as would have been made if the contribution had been expended on the provision for C's trade etc. of a similar asset and as if the asset were at all material times used for the purposes of C's trade etc. (so that, for mineral extraction allowances, balancing adjustments do not apply to such contributions). On a transfer of the trade etc., or part thereof, the allowances (or part) are subsequently made to the transferee.

In the case of structures and buildings allowance, the contribution must be to expenditure which is qualifying expenditure for SBAs purposes (see **9.18** below), and must be made for the purposes of a qualifying activity carried on (or to be carried on) by a tenant of land in which C has an interest or, if R is a public body (whether in the UK or elsewhere), by either C or any such tenant. C is treated for the purposes of SBAs as if:

(a) the contribution were expenditure incurred by C on the construction or acquisition of the building or structure;

(b) the building etc. were brought into qualifying use on the day on which R brought it into qualifying use; and

(c) the day on which the qualifying expenditure is incurred were the day on which C made the contribution.

If R is a public body, the day referred to in (b) above is, if earlier, the day on which R first brought the building etc. into *non-residential* use. This applies in relation to contributions made on or after 11 March 2020.

If, at any time in the period beginning with the making of the contribution and ending with the bringing of the building into non-residential use, C does not have a relevant interest, C is treated for SBAs purposes as having had a relevant interest in the building at the beginning of that period, and is not treated as ceasing to have that interest on any subsequent sale of R's relevant interest in the building. In relation to contributions made before 11 March 2020, C is treated as having had a relevant interest in the building etc. on the day on which R brought it into qualifying use.

In determining, for the above purposes, the day on which R first brings a building etc. into non-residential use, any use of it which is insignificant is ignored.

[*CAA 2001, ss 537, 538A–542, Sch 3 para 110; FA 2020, Sch 5 paras 3, 9; SI 2019 No 1087, Reg 3(10)(11)*].

Capital contributions towards expenditure on dredging are treated as expenditure incurred by the contributor on that dredging. [*CAA 2001, s 543*].

Simon's Taxes. See **B3.112.**

(viii) **VAT capital goods scheme.** Under the VAT capital goods scheme, the input tax originally claimed on the acquisition of certain capital assets is subject to amendment within a specified period of adjustment in accordance with any increase or decrease in the extent to which the asset is used in making taxable, as opposed to exempt, supplies for VAT purposes.

The items covered by the scheme are limited to land and buildings (or parts of buildings) worth at least £250,000, computers (and items of computer equipment) worth at least £50,000, and aircraft, ships, boats or other vessels worth at least £50,000. See Tolley's Value Added Tax under Capital Goods Scheme for a full description.

Special capital allowances provisions apply where a VAT adjustment is made under the capital goods scheme.

'*Additional VAT liability*' and '*additional VAT rebate*' mean, respectively:

- an amount which a person becomes liable to pay, or
- an amount which he becomes entitled to deduct,

by way of adjustment under the VAT capital goods scheme in respect of input tax. Generally (but see below), such a liability or rebate is treated as incurred or made on the last day of the period:

- which is one of the periods making up the applicable VAT period of adjustment under the VAT capital goods scheme, and
- in which occurred the increase or decrease in use giving rise to the liability or rebate.

However, for the purpose of determining the chargeable period (see (i) above) in which it accrues, an additional VAT liability or rebate is treated as accruing on whichever is the relevant day below.

- Where the liability or rebate is accounted for in a VAT return, the last day of the period covered by that return.
- If, before the making of a VAT return, HMRC assess the liability or rebate, the day on which the assessment is made.
- If the trade (or other qualifying activity — see **10.4** CAPITAL ALLOWANCES ON PLANT AND MACHINERY) is permanently discontinued before the liability or rebate has been accounted for in a VAT return and before the making of an assessment, the last day of the chargeable period in which the cessation occurs.

Where an allowance or charge falls to be determined by reference to a proportion only of the expenditure incurred or a proportion only of what that allowance or charge would otherwise have been, a related additional VAT liability or rebate is similarly apportioned.

[*CAA 2001, ss 546–551; SI 2019 No 1087, Reg 3(13)*].

Simon's Taxes. See **B3.103, B3.104.**

(ix) **Composite sales** may be apportioned by the Tribunal regardless of any separate prices attributed in the sale agreement. [*CAA 2001, ss 562–564*]. See *Fitton v Gilders & Heaton* Ch D 1955, 36 TC 233, and *Wood v Provan* CA 1968, 44 TC 701.

Simon's Taxes. See **B3.110.**

(x) **Finance leasing.** See **69.43** TRADING INCOME — DEDUCTIONS as regards restrictions on capital allowances where certain finance leasing arrangements are involved. These are disapplied in relation to long funding leases. See also **10.47** *et seq.*, **10.57, 10.61, 10.62** CAPITAL ALLOWANCES ON PLANT AND MACHINERY.

(xi) **Recovery of assets under *Proceeds of Crime Act 2002, Pt 5*.** *Proceeds of Crime Act 2002, Pt 5 Ch 2* provides for the recovery, in civil proceedings before the High Court (or, in Scotland, the Court of Session), of property which is, or represents, property obtained through 'unlawful conduct' (as defined in the Act). If the Court is satisfied that any property is recoverable under the provisions, it will make a '*recovery order*', vesting the property in an appointed trustee for civil recovery. Alternatively, the Court may make an order under *s 276* of the *Act* staying (or, in Scotland, sisting) proceedings on terms agreed by the parties. The vesting of property in a trustee for civil recovery or any other person, either under a recovery order or in pursuance of a *s 276* order, is known as a *Pt 5* transfer. A '*compensating payment*' may in some cases be made to the person who held the property immediately before the transfer. If the order provides for the creation of any interest in favour of that person, he is treated as receiving (in addition to any other compensating payment) a compensating payment equal to the value of the interest. [*Proceeds of Crime Act 2002, ss 240(1), 266(1)(2), 276, 316(1), 448, Sch 10 para 2*].

Where the property in question is plant or machinery, the relevant interest in an industrial building or in a flat (within **9.6** below), or an asset representing qualifying expenditure on research and development (within **9.20** below), there are provisions to ensure that the *Pt 5* transfer has a tax-neutral effect, unless a compensating payment is made to the transferor in which case its amount and/or value must be brought into account as a disposal value or, as the case may be, as proceeds from a balancing event. [*Proceeds of Crime Act 2002, Sch 10 paras 12–29*].

(xii) **Avoidance affecting proceeds of balancing event.** There is an anti-avoidance rule to prevent a balancing allowance being created or increased by means of any tax avoidance scheme that depresses an asset's market value and thus the amount to be brought into account on a balancing event (e.g. a sale) or as a disposal value. The rule denies entitlement to a balancing allowance, though the unrelieved balance of expenditure immediately after the event must be computed as if the allowance had been made. The rule applies to allowances for industrial buildings, agricultural buildings, business premises renovation, flat conversion expenditure, dwelling-houses let on assured tenancies and mineral extraction. It applies in relation to any event that would otherwise occasion a balancing allowance, except where it occurs in pursuance of a contract entered into on or before that date and is not consequent upon the exercise after that date of any option or right. [*CAA 2001, s 570A*]. **Simon's Taxes.** See **B3.108C**.

Business premises renovation (abolished)

[9.3] For expenditure incurred on or after 11 April 2007 and **before 1 April 2017**, subject to the conditions below, 100% capital allowances (known as business premises renovation allowances) are available for qualifying expenditure (see below) incurred by individuals and companies (whether as landlords or tenants) on the conversion or renovation of vacant business premises in designated development areas of the UK for the purpose of bringing those premises back into business use. The premises must have been unused for at least one year before the date the work begins. Certain trades are excluded. [*CAA 2001, ss 360A–360Z4; SI 2007 No 945, Reg 2A*].

Business premises renovation allowances are available to the person (including a company) who incurred the qualifying expenditure and has the 'relevant interest' in the 'qualifying building'. [*CAA 2001, s 360A(2)*].

Relevant interest

In its simplest form, the '*relevant interest*' is the interest (freehold or leasehold) in the qualifying building to which the person incurring the qualifying expenditure was entitled when it was incurred. If there is more than one such interest, and one was reversionary on all the others, the reversionary interest is the relevant interest. The creation of a subordinate interest (e.g. leasehold out of freehold) does not transfer the relevant interest. An interest arising on, or as a result of completion of, construction is treated as having been held when the expenditure was incurred. If a leasehold relevant interest is extinguished by surrender, or by the person entitled to it acquiring the interest reversionary on it, the interest into which it merges becomes the relevant interest. [*CAA 2001, ss 360E, 360F*].

Leases

'*Lease*' is defined (as are related expressions accordingly), and in particular includes an agreement for a lease whose term has begun and a tenancy. [*CAA 2001, s 360Z4*].

Termination of leases

The following apply if a lease is terminated.

- Where a lease ends and the lessee, with the lessor's consent, remains in possession without a new lease being granted, the lease is treated as continuing.
- A new lease granted on the termination of an old lease on exercise of an option available under the old lease is treated as a continuation of the old lease.
- If on termination of a lease the lessor pays any sum to the lessee in respect of a building comprised in the lease, the lease is treated as surrendered in consideration of the payment.
- If, on the termination of a lease, a lessee who is granted a new lease makes a payment to the lessee under the old lease, the two leases are treated as the same lease, the old lessee having assigned it to the new lessee for payment.

[*CAA 2001, s 360Z3*].

Providing of State aid information

A claim made on or after 1 July 2016 for business premises renovation allowances must include any information required by HMRC for the purpose of complying with certain EU State aid obligations. This may include information about the claimant (or its activities), information about the subject matter of the claim and other information relating to the grant of State aid through the provision of the allowances. See **36.13** HMRC — ADMINISTRATION as regards the publishing by HMRC of State aid information. [*FA 2016, s 180(1)–(4)(10), Sch 24 Pt 1*].

Qualifying expenditure

Qualifying expenditure means capital expenditure incurred before 1 April 2017 on, or in connection with:

- the conversion of a 'qualifying building' into 'qualifying business premises';
- the renovation of a 'qualifying building' if it is, or will be, 'qualifying business premises'; or
- repairs to a 'qualifying building' (or to a building of which the 'qualifying building' forms part), to the extent that they are incidental to either of the above (and for this purpose repairs are treated as capital expenditure if disallowable in computing the taxable profits of a property business (see **60.2** PROPERTY INCOME) or of a trade, profession or vocation),

In addition to the above, in relation to expenditure incurred on or after 1 April 2014, such expenditure must meet further conditions. To be qualifying expenditure it must also be incurred on:

- building works;
- architectural or design services;
- surveying or engineering services;
- planning applications; or
- statutory fees or statutory permissions.

Additional expenditure on unspecified activities (for example, project management services) is allowed up to a limit (for the total of such costs) of 5% of the qualifying expenditure incurred in respect of the first three bullet points above (being the building and architectural, design, surveying and engineering costs).

Certain expenditure is excluded from qualifying, being expenditure incurred on, or in connection with:

- the acquisition of, or of rights in or over, land;
- the extension of a qualifying building (except to the extent necessary to provide access to 'qualifying business premises');
- the development of adjoining or adjacent land; or
- the provision of plant and machinery, unless it is, or it becomes, a fixture as in **10.36** *et seq.* CAPITAL ALLOWANCES ON PLANT AND MACHINERY.

For expenditure incurred on or after 1 April 2014, the final bullet point above is amended such that a fixture, which is not to be excluded, must be on a specific list of fixtures which are acceptable:

- integral features within the meaning of *CAA 2001, s 33A* (taking account of s *33A(6)* and *(7)*) see further **10.10** CAPITAL ALLOWANCES ON PLANT AND MACHINERY;
- automatic control systems for opening and closing doors, windows and vents;
- window cleaning installations;
- fitted cupboards and blinds;
- protective installations such as lightening protection, sprinkler and other fire fighting or containing equipment, fire alarm systems and fire escapes;
- building management systems;
- cabling in connection with telephone, audio visual data installations and computer networking facilities, which are incidental to the occupation of the building;
- sanitary appliances and bathroom fittings which are hand driers, counters, partitions, mirrors or shower facilities;
- kitchen and catering facilities (for food and drink for the occupants of the building);
- signs;
- public address systems;
- intruder alarm systems.

Variation, addition or removal of a description of fixture on this list may be made by regulation.

Expenditure is also excluded if (and to the extent that) it exceeds what would have been a normal and reasonable amount to incur on such works, services, or other matters in prevailing market conditions, assuming an arm's length transaction. Expenditure is also excluded if the qualifying building was used at any time during the period of 12 months ending with the day on which the expenditure is incurred. Additionally, where the works, services or other matters are not completed or provided within 36 months of the incurring of qualifying expenditure, the expenditure will be treated as incurred when the works, services or other matters are completed or provided. If a person who has made a tax return subsequently becomes aware that it has become incorrect due to this last provision, the person has three months to give notice to HMRC specifying the amendment required.

There is a ceiling of 20 million euros on the amount of expenditure on a single project that can be qualifying expenditure. In determining whether the ceiling has been reached, current expenditure must be aggregated with any expenditure incurred by any person on that project in the immediately preceding three years on which business premises renovation allowances have been made. Expenditure is incurred on a single project if it would be treated as part of a single investment project for the purposes of *Article 14 para 13* of the *EU General Block Exemption Regulation (No 651/2014)*. A single project might be the renovation of a single building involving one or a number of participants, or groups of buildings where the outcome of the project is closely linked, due, for example, to their proximity.

[*CAA 2001, ss 360B(1)–(5), 360BA; SI 2007 No 945, Reg 5(2)(3)(5)*].

A '*qualifying building*' is any building or structure (or part of a building or structure) which:

(A) is situated in an area which, on the date the conversion or renovation work begins, is a 'disadvantaged area';
(B) was unused for at least one year before the date the work begins;
(C) was last in use for the purposes of a trade, profession or vocation or as an office or offices;
(D) was not last in use as a dwelling or part of a dwelling; and
(E) (in the case of part of a building or structure) had not last been occupied and used in common with another part of the building or structure which was last in use as a dwelling or which does not meet itself the one-year rule in (B) above.

A '*disadvantaged area*' is an area designated as such for these purposes by Treasury regulations or, in the absence of such regulations, an area for the time being designated as a disadvantaged area for stamp duty land tax purposes. Any such regulations may designate an area for a limited time only. If a building or structure is situated partly in a designated area and partly outside it, expenditure is to be apportioned on a just and reasonable basis in determining how much of it is qualifying expenditure. The areas designated are areas designated as development areas by the *Assisted Areas Order 2014 (SI 2014 No 1508)* (previously the *Assisted Areas Order 2007 (SI 2007 No 107)*) plus NI.

Expenditure incurred on or after 11 April 2012 is not qualifying expenditure if the qualifying building in question is not in a disadvantaged area on the date the expenditure is incurred.

[*CAA 2001, s 360C(1)–(6); SI 2007 No 945, Regs 3, 5(1)(4)*].

For any premises (i.e. a building or structure or part thereof) to be '*qualifying business premises*';

- they must be a qualifying building as above;
- they must be used, or available and suitable for letting for use, for '*qualifying purposes*', i.e. the purposes of a trade, profession or vocation or as an office or offices; and
- they must not be used, or available for use, as a dwelling or part of a dwelling.

Once premises are qualifying business premises, they do not cease to be so by reason only of *temporary* unsuitability for use, or for letting, for qualifying purposes.

[*CAA 2001, s 360D(1)–(3)*].

The above definitions of qualifying expenditure, qualifying building and qualifying business premises may be amended by Treasury regulations. [*CAA 2001, ss 360B(5), 360C(7), 360D(4)*]. Consequently, it is provided that premises are not qualifying business premises if they are converted or renovated by, or used by, a business engaged in any of the following trades.

For expenditure incurred on or after 22 July 2014, the trades excluded are any trade (or part of a trade):

(a) in the fishery and aquaculture sector;
(b) in the coal, steel, shipbuilding or synthetic fibres sectors;
(c) in the transport sector or in related infrastructure;
(d) relating to the development of broadband networks;
(e) relating to energy generation, distribution and infrastructure;
(f) in the primary agricultural production sector; or
(g) carried on by any undertaking (as defined) which is either subject to an outstanding recovery order made under Treaty on the Functioning of the European Union, Article 108(2) or which it is reasonable to assume would be regarded as a firm in difficulty for the purposes of the EU General Block Exemption Regulation (651/2014).

For expenditure incurred on or after 11 April 2012 and before 22 July 2014, the trades excluded are any trade (or part of a trade) in any sector to which *Commission Regulation (EC) No 800/2008* (on State aid) does not apply by virtue of *Article 1 para 3*. For expenditure incurred before 11 April 2012, the trades excluded were any trade (or part of a trade) in any sector to which *Commission Regulation (EC) No 1628/2006* (on State aid) did not apply by virtue of *Article 1 para 2*. Broadly, these are trades within (a), (b) or (f) above, (for expenditure incurred on or after 11 April 2012) trades consisting of the processing and marketing of certain agricultural products and (for expenditure incurred before 11 April 2012) the manufacture and marketing of products which imitate or substitute for milk and milk products. Trades within (g) above are also excluded, but by reference to the Community Guidelines on State Aid for Rescuing and Restructuring Firms in Difficulty rather than the General Block Exemption Regulation.

[*SI 2007 No 945, Reg 4*].

Initial allowances

The initial allowance is **100%** of the qualifying expenditure, may be claimed in whole or in part, and is made for the chargeable period (see **9.2**(i) above) in which the expenditure is incurred. The initial allowance is not available if the qualifying building is not qualifying business premises at the 'relevant time'; any initial allowance already made is withdrawn in such circumstances, and is also withdrawn if the person to whom the allowance was made has sold the relevant interest before the 'relevant time'. The '*relevant time*' is the time the premises are first used by the person with the relevant interest or, if not so used, are first suitable for letting for qualifying purposes. [*CAA 2001, ss 360G, 360H*].

Writing-down allowances

Writing-down allowances (WDAs) are available where the expenditure has not been wholly relieved by an initial allowance. The annual WDA is **25%** of the qualifying expenditure, on a straight line basis, proportionately reduced or increased if the chargeable period is less or more than a year, and may be claimed in whole or in part. The WDA cannot exceed the residue, i.e. the unrelieved balance, of the qualifying expenditure. The person who incurred the expenditure is entitled to a WDA for a chargeable period if *at the end of that period*:

- he is entitled to the relevant interest (see above) in the qualifying building;

- he has not granted, out of the relevant interest, a long lease (exceeding 50 years) of the qualifying building for a capital sum; and
- the qualifying building is qualifying business premises.

There is nothing to prevent a WDA being given in the same chargeable period as an initial allowance for the same expenditure.

[*CAA 2001, ss 360I–360K, 360Q, 360R*].

Effect of grants on entitlement to allowances

No initial allowance or WDA is available for qualifying expenditure if a 'relevant grant or payment' is made towards the expenditure or any 'related expenditure'. '*Related expenditure*' means any other expenditure incurred by any person in respect of the same qualifying building and on the same 'single investment project' as the qualifying expenditure. Any allowance already made is withdrawn if a relevant grant or payment is subsequently made towards the qualifying expenditure or if within the three years beginning when that expenditure was incurred, a relevant grant or payment is made towards any related expenditure. If a person who has made a return becomes aware that anything in it has become incorrect because of this rule, he must give notice to an officer of HMRC specifying how the return needs to be amended; the notice must be given within three months beginning with the day on which he first becomes aware of the inaccuracy.

A '*relevant grant or payment*' means an EU State aid or any other grant or subsidy nominated by Treasury order for this purpose. 'EU state aid' is not for this purpose limited to State aid required to be notified to and approved by the European Commission. '*Single investment project*' has the same meaning as in Commission Regulation (EU) No 651/2014 (General Block Exemption Regulation). Following Brexit, the definition applies by reference to the Regulation as it had effect immediately before 11pm on 31 December 2020 (IP completion day).

[*CAA 2001, s 360L; SI 2020 No 1499*].

Balancing allowances and charges

If a 'balancing event' occurs, a balancing adjustment, i.e. a balancing allowance or balancing charge, is made to or on the person who incurred the qualifying expenditure and for the chargeable period in which the event occurs. If more than one balancing event occurs, a balancing adjustment is made only on the first of them. **No balancing adjustment** is made in respect of a balancing event occurring more than five years after the time the premises were first used, or suitable for letting, for qualifying purposes. For expenditure incurred before 6 April 2014, the stipulated period is seven years rather than five. Any of the following is a '*balancing event*':

(i) the sale of the relevant interest (see above) in the qualifying building;
(ii) the grant, out of the relevant interest, of a long lease (exceeding 50 years) of the qualifying building for a capital sum;
(iii) (where the relevant interest is a lease) the coming to an end of the lease otherwise than on the person entitled to it acquiring the reversionary interest;

(iv) the death of the person who incurred the qualifying expenditure;
(v) the demolition or destruction of the qualifying building;
(vi) the qualifying building's otherwise ceasing to be qualifying business premises.

The proceeds of a balancing event depend upon the nature of the event and are as follows.

(1) On a sale of the relevant interest, the net sale proceeds receivable by the person who incurred the qualifying expenditure.
(2) On the grant of a long lease, the capital sum involved or, if greater, the premium that would have been paid in an arm's length transaction.
(3) In an event within (iii) above, where the persons entitled to, respectively, the lease and the superior interest are CONNECTED PERSONS (**19**), the market value of the relevant interest in the qualifying building at the time of the event.
(4) On death, the residue (see below) of qualifying expenditure.
(5) On demolition or destruction, the net amount received for the remains by the person who incurred the qualifying expenditure, plus any insurance or capital compensation received by him.
(6) On the qualifying building's otherwise ceasing to be qualifying business premises, the market value of the relevant interest in the qualifying building at the time of the event.

If the residue, i.e. the unrelieved balance, of qualifying expenditure immediately before the event exceeds the proceeds of the event (including nil proceeds), a balancing allowance arises, equal to the excess. (This is subject to the anti-avoidance rule at **9.2**(xi) above.) If the proceeds exceed the residue (including a nil residue), a balancing charge arises, normally equal to the excess but limited to the total initial allowances and WDAs previously given to the person concerned in respect of the expenditure.

[*CAA 2001, ss 360M–360P*].

Note that, by virtue of *CAA 2001, s 572*, a surrender for valuable consideration of a leasehold interest is treated as a sale (for equivalent proceeds), and thus falls within (1) above (if not caught by (3) above).

Any proceeds of sale of the relevant interest or other proceeds of a balancing event are, if attributable to both, apportioned on a just and reasonable basis between assets representing qualifying expenditure and other assets, and only the first part taken into account as above. [*CAA 2001, s 360Z2*].

Demolition costs

Where a qualifying building is demolished, the net cost (after crediting any money received for remains) of demolition borne by the person who incurred the expenditure is added to the residue of qualifying expenditure immediately before the demolition, and is thus taken into account in computing the balancing adjustment; no amount included in gross demolition costs can then be included for any capital allowances purposes as expenditure on replacement property. [*CAA 2001, s 360S*].

Making of allowances and charges

If the person entitled to allowances or liable to charges under these provisions carries on a trade or occupies the qualifying building for the purposes of a trade, profession or vocation, the allowances/charges are treated as expenses/receipts of the trade, profession or vocation.

If the taxpayer's interest in the qualifying building is an asset of a property business (see **60.2** PROPERTY INCOME) carried on by him at any time in the chargeable period (see **9.2**(i) above) in question, allowances/charges under these provisions are treated as expenses/receipts of that business. If the above is not the case but his interest in the building is nevertheless subject to a lease or a licence, he is deemed to be carrying on a property business anyway, and allowances/charges given effect accordingly. [*CAA 2001, ss 360Z, 360Z1*].

Additional VAT liabilities and rebates

See **9.2**(viii) above as regards these generally. The initial allowance above is also available in respect of any additional VAT liability incurred at a time when the qualifying building is, or is about to be, qualifying business premises; the allowance is made for the chargeable period in which the liability accrues. For the purposes of WDAs, the residue of qualifying expenditure is treated as increased by the amount of an additional VAT liability at the time it accrues. The making of an additional VAT rebate is a balancing event, but it does not give rise to a balancing allowance and gives rise to a balancing charge only if it exceeds the residue (including a nil residue) of qualifying expenditure at the time the rebate accrues; otherwise the residue is treated as reduced by the amount of the rebate at the time it accrues. [*CAA 2001, ss 360T–360Y*].

Connected persons and other anti-avoidance provisions

Special provisions apply to sales of property where:

(a) the sale results in no change of control; or
(b) the sole or main benefit which might be expected is the obtaining of a capital allowance.

Paragraph (a) also covers sales between CONNECTED PERSONS (**19**), and (b) includes cases where the anticipated benefit is a reduction in a charge or the increase of an allowance. Where these provisions apply, market value is substituted for purchase price (if different), and this also applies to transfers other than by way of sale. [*CAA 2001, ss 567, 568, 570(1), 573, 575, 575A, 577(4)*].

Simon's Taxes. See **B3.11.**

Dredging

[9.4] Writing-down and balancing allowances may be claimed for capital expenditure on **dredging** incurred for the purposes of a *qualifying trade* (provided that plant and machinery allowances (see **10** CAPITAL ALLOWANCES ON PLANT AND MACHINERY) are not available in respect of the same expenditure).

'*Dredging*' must be done in the interests of navigation, and either:

(i) the qualifying trade must consist of the maintenance or improvement of navigation of a harbour, estuary or waterway; or
(ii) the dredging must be for the benefit of vessels coming to, leaving or using docks or other premises used in the qualifying trade.

It includes removal, by any means, of any part of, or projections from, any sea or inland water bed (whether then above water or not), and the widening of any inland waterway.

A '*qualifying trade*' is:

- a trade within (i) above; or
- a trade consisting of:
  - the manufacture, processing, maintaining or repairing of goods or materials; or
  - the storage of raw materials for manufacture, goods to be processed, goods manufactured or processed but not yet delivered to a purchaser, or (d) goods on arrival in the UK from a place outside the UK; or
  - agricultural contracting; or
  - the catching of fish or shellfish; or
  - the working of a source of mineral deposits; or
- an undertaking that is an electricity, water, hydraulic power, sewerage, transport, highway, tunnel, bridge, inland navigation or dock undertaking.

Expenditure only partly for a qualifying trade is apportioned as may be just and reasonable, and for this purpose, where part only of a trade qualifies, the qualifying and non-qualifying parts are treated as separate trades.

[*CAA 2001, ss 484, 485*].

Writing-down allowances

Writing-down allowances of 4% p.a. (although a lesser amount may be claimed) are given to the person for the time being carrying on the trade during a writing-down period of 25 years beginning with the first day of the chargeable period in which the expenditure was incurred, subject to an overall limit equal to the amount of the expenditure. No allowance is given for a chargeable period in which a balancing allowance arises (see below).

[*CAA 2001, ss 487, 489, Sch 3 para 103*].

Expenditure incurred for a trade before it is carried on attracts allowances as if it were incurred on the first day on which the trade was carried on. Similarly, expenditure incurred in connection with a dock etc. with a view to occupying it for the purposes of a qualifying trade other than one within (i) above attracts allowances as if it were incurred when the dock etc. is first so occupied. [*CAA 2001, s 486*].

Balancing allowances

A balancing allowance is given for the chargeable period of *permanent discontinuance* of the trade, equal to expenditure incurred less writing-down allowances given, to the person last carrying on the trade. The allowance includes expenditure incurred before 6 April 1956, but in relation to such expenditure, all possible allowances are deemed to have been given in respect of 1955/56 and earlier years as if the provisions introduced by *FA 1956* had always been in force.

Permanent discontinuance includes sale of the business (unless it is a sale between CONNECTED PERSONS (**19**), or without change of control, or one the sole or main benefit of which appears to be a capital allowance advantage), but not deemed discontinuance under **68.15** TRADING INCOME.

[*CAA 2001, s 488, Sch 3 para 104*].

Contributions to expenditure

See **9.2**(vi)(vii) above.

Simon's Taxes. See **B3.8**.

Example

[9.5]

D Ltd is the proprietor of an estuary maintenance business preparing accounts to 30 June. Expenditure qualifying for dredging allowances is incurred as follows.

	£
Year ended 30.6.19	4,000
Year ended 30.6.20	5,000

On 2 January 2021, D Ltd sells the business to an unconnected third party.

The allowances available are

Date of expenditure	Cost	Residue brought forward	Allowances WDA 4%	Residue carried forward
	£	£	£	£
Year ended 30.6.19				
2019	4,000		160	£3,840
Year ended 30.6.20				
2019	4,000	3,840	160	3,680
2020	5,000		200	4,800
			£360	£8,480
Six months ending 2.1.21				
Balancing allowance			£8,480	

Flat conversion (abolished)

[9.6] Flat conversion allowances are **abolished** with effect for expenditure incurred on or after **1 April 2013**. Writing-down allowances on earlier expenditure also cease to be available for chargeable periods (as in 9.2(i) above) beginning on or after 1 April 2013. However, notwithstanding the abolition of flat conversion allowances, balancing adjustments continue to apply for chargeable periods beginning on or after 1 April 2013 in relation to expenditure incurred before that date.

Balancing adjustments

If a 'balancing event' occurs, a balancing adjustment, i.e. a balancing allowance or balancing charge, is made to or on the person who incurred the qualifying expenditure and for the chargeable period in which the event occurs. If more than one balancing event occurs, a balancing adjustment is made only on the first of them. No balancing adjustment is made in respect of a balancing event occurring **more than seven years** after the time the flat was first suitable for letting as a dwelling. Any of the following is a '*balancing event*':

(i) the sale of the 'relevant interest' (see below) in the flat;
(ii) the grant, out of the relevant interest, of a long lease (exceeding 50 years) of the flat for a capital sum;
(iii) (where the relevant interest is a lease) the coming to an end of the lease otherwise than on the person entitled to it acquiring the reversionary interest;
(iv) the death of the person who incurred the qualifying expenditure;
(v) the demolition or destruction of the flat;
(vi) the flat's otherwise ceasing to be a qualifying flat.

The proceeds of a balancing event depend upon the nature of the event and are as follows.

(1) On a sale of the relevant interest, the net sale proceeds receivable by the person who incurred the qualifying expenditure.
(2) On the grant of a long lease, the capital sum involved or, if greater, the premium that would have been paid in an arm's length transaction.
(3) In an event within (iii) above, where the persons entitled to, respectively, the lease and the superior interest are CONNECTED PERSONS (**19**), the market value of the relevant interest in the flat at the time of the event.
(4) On death, the residue (see below) of qualifying expenditure.
(5) On demolition or destruction, the net amount received for the remains by the person who incurred the qualifying expenditure, plus any insurance or capital compensation received by him.
(6) On the flat's otherwise ceasing to be a qualifying flat, the market value of the relevant interest in the flat at the time of the event.

If the residue, i.e. the unrelieved balance, of qualifying expenditure immediately before the event exceeds the proceeds of the event (including nil proceeds), a balancing allowance arises, equal to the excess. (This is subject to the anti-avoidance rule at 9.2(xii) above.) If the proceeds exceed the residue (including a nil residue), a balancing charge arises, normally equal to the excess but limited to the total initial and writing-down allowances previously given to the person concerned in respect of the expenditure.

[*CAA 2001, ss 393M–393P*].

Note that, by virtue of *CAA 2001, s 572*, a surrender for valuable consideration of a leasehold interest is treated as a sale (for equivalent proceeds), and thus falls within (1) above (if not caught by (3) above).

Any proceeds of sale of the relevant interest or other proceeds of a balancing event are, if attributable to both, apportioned on a just and reasonable basis between assets representing qualifying expenditure and other assets, and only the first part taken into account as above. [*CAA 2001, s 393U*].

The '*relevant interest*' is determined in similar manner, with appropriate modifications, as for business renovation allowances (see **9.3** above). In its simplest form, the relevant interest is the interest in the flat to which the person who incurred the expenditure was entitled when it was incurred. [*CAA 2001, ss 393F, 393G*]. As regards termination of leases, provisions similar to those in **9.3** above apply. [*CAA 2001, s 393V*]. '*Lease*' is defined (as are related expressions accordingly), and in particular includes an agreement for a lease whose term has begun and a tenancy. [*CAA 2001, s 393W*].

Demolition costs

Where a qualifying flat is demolished, the net cost (after crediting any money received for remains) of demolition borne by the person who incurred the expenditure is added to the residue of qualifying expenditure immediately before the demolition, and is thus taken into account in computing the balancing adjustment; no amount included in gross demolition costs can then attract capital allowances of any kind. [*CAA 2001, s 393S*].

Making of allowances and charges

If the company's interest in the flat is an asset of a UK property business (see **60.2** PROPERTY INCOME) carried on by it at any time in the chargeable period (see **9.2**(i) above) in question, allowances/charges under these provisions are treated as expenses/receipts of that business. If the above is not the case, the company is deemed to be carrying on a UK property business anyway, and allowances/charges given effect accordingly. [*CAA 2001, s 393T*].

Simon's Taxes. See **B3.10.**

Enterprise zone building allowances

[9.7] Advantageous provisions applied before 1 April 2011 to expenditure on the construction of an 'industrial building', 'qualifying hotel' or 'commercial building', which was incurred (or contracted for) within ten years of the inclusion of the site in an 'enterprise zone'. An '*enterprise zone*' was an area designated as such by the Secretary of State (or by Scottish Ministers, the National Assembly for Wales or, for NI, the Department of the Environment). [*CAA 2001, ss 271(1)(b), 298*]. Areas that were designated are listed in HMRC Capital Allowances Manual at CA37600; in all cases the ten-year life of the zone expired earlier than 1 April 2007. For definitions of '*industrial building*', '*qualifying hotel*' and '*commercial building*', see respectively HMRC Capital Allowances Manual CA32000, CA32401 and CA37200. For full coverage of enterprise zone allowances, see HMRC Capital Allowances Manual CA37000–37760.

Transitional

Despite the abolition of enterprise zone allowances with effect on and after 1 April 2011, a balancing charge can still arise in a chargeable period (see **9.2**(i) above) beginning on or after that date on the disposal of a building on which enterprise zone allowances had been claimed. This will be the case if an event occurs within seven years after the building is first used, and the event is such that, disregarding the abolition, it would have been a balancing event giving rise to a balancing charge. Similarly, if an initial allowance falls to be withdrawn by virtue of *CAA 2001, s 307*, it will be withdrawn notwithstanding the abolition, but only if the event giving rise to the withdrawal occurs within seven years after the end of the chargeable period for which the initial allowance was made. See further below.

Initial and writing-down allowances

An initial allowance of 100% was available on the expenditure but the full amount did not have to be claimed. If any part of the initial allowance was not claimed, then writing-down allowances at 25% p.a. of cost on the straight line basis were given on the unclaimed balance. [*CAA 2001, ss 306(1)(2), 310(1)(a)*]. For a chargeable period straddling 1 April 2011, any writing-down allowance to which a company would otherwise have been entitled (were it not for abolition) was apportioned by reference to the number of days in the chargeable period which fell before 1 April 2011 and the total number of days in the chargeable period. [*FA 2008, s 86*].

Withdrawal of an initial allowance

An initial allowance which has been made in respect of a building which is to be a qualifying building is withdrawn if, when the building is first used, it is not a qualifying building. An initial allowance which has been made in respect of a building which has not yet been used is withdrawn if the company to whom it was made sells its interest in the building prior to first use. [*CAA 2001, s 307*]. Notwithstanding the abolition of enterprise zone allowances, there will be a withdrawal under these rules if, within seven years after the end of the chargeable period for which the initial allowance was made, an event occurs which, if *CAA 2001, s 307* remained in force, would result in that allowance being withdrawn. [*FA 2008, Sch 27 paras 32, 35*].

Balancing charges

Notwithstanding the abolition of enterprise zone allowances, a balancing charge arises if a balancing event occurs on or after 1 April 2011 and within seven years after the building is first used. [*FA 2008, Sch 27 paras 31, 35*].

The amount of a balancing charge is the excess (if any) of the proceeds of the balancing event over the amount of unrelieved qualifying expenditure on the building immediately before the event. However, the amount of a balancing charge made on any company cannot exceed the aggregate amount of enterprise zone allowances made to that company in respect of the building. A balancing event occurs when a building is sold or is destroyed or is permanently put out of use or when the company's interest in the building is lost on the termination of a lease or foreign concession. The proceeds of a balancing event are the net proceeds of sale or any insurance, salvage or compensation monies received as a result of the event. [*CAA 2001, ss 314–316, 320*].

A balancing event can also occur upon the receipt of capital value attributable to a subordinate interest in the building. This is to prevent taxpayers avoiding a balancing charge by disposing of the commercial substance of their interest in the building while retaining the interest itself. It normally applies only where the payment of capital value is made (or an agreement to make it is made) seven years or less after the making of the agreement under which the qualifying expenditure was incurred (or, if that agreement was conditional, seven years or less after it became unconditional); however, this restriction does not have effect in certain cases involving guaranteed exit arrangements. [*CAA 2001, ss 327–331, Sch 3 para 71*]. For details, see HMRC Capital Allowances Manual CA37700.

For companies carrying on a trade, a balancing charge is given effect as a receipt in calculating profits. [*CAA 2001, s 352*]. The timing of the charge is by reference to events occurring in a period of account (see **9.2**(i) above). As regards lessors and licensors, a balancing charge is treated as a receipt of a UK property business or, if the lease or licence is an asset of an overseas property business, as a receipt of that business. Where the building is not an asset of any property business, the charge is treated as a receipt of a notional UK property business. [*CAA 2001, s 353*]. The timing of the charge is by reference to events occurring in an accounting period.

Simon's Taxes. See **B3.281**.

'Know-how'

[9.8] For corporation tax purposes, 'know-how' created or acquired from an unrelated party on or after 1 April 2002 or from any party on or after 1 July 2020 generally falls within the intangible assets regime. The following applies where know-how does not fall within that regime.

Subject to the above, expenditure on acquiring 'know-how' (so far as not otherwise deductible for income tax purposes) gives rise to writing-down and balancing allowances (and balancing charges) where the person acquiring it either:

(i) is then carrying on a trade for use in which it is acquired; or
(ii) subsequently commences such a trade (in which case the expenditure is treated as incurred on commencement); or
(iii) acquires it with a trade (or part) in which it was used, and either the parties to the acquisition make the appropriate joint election under *CTA 2009, s 178* (see **68.45** TRADING INCOME), or corporation tax equivalent, or the trade was carried on wholly outside the UK before the acquisition.

The same expenditure may not be taken into account in relation to more than one trade.

Expenditure is, however, *excluded* where the buyer and seller are bodies of persons (which includes partnerships) under common control.

[*CAA 2001, ss 452(1), 454, 455*].

'*Know-how*' means any industrial information and techniques of assistance in (a) manufacturing or processing goods or materials, (b) working, or searching etc. for, mineral deposits, or (c) agricultural, forestry or fishing operations. [*CAA 2001, s 452(2)(3)*]. For expenditure on offshore divers' training courses treated as on know-how, see HMRC Capital Allowances Manual CA74000.

All qualifying expenditure of a trade is pooled, and:

(1) if the 'available qualifying expenditure' exceeds the 'total disposal value', a writing-down allowance is available of **25%** of the excess, proportionately reduced or increased where the period is less or more than one year, or if the trade has been carried on for part only of a chargeable period (and subject to any lesser amount being claimed), *except that* if the chargeable period is that of permanent discontinuance of the trade, a balancing allowance of **100%** of the excess is available;
(2) if the 'total disposal value' exceeds the 'available qualifying expenditure', a balancing charge arises of **100%** of the excess.

'*Available qualifying expenditure*' in a pool for a chargeable period consists of qualifying expenditure allocated to the pool for that period and any unrelieved qualifying expenditure brought forward in the pool from the previous chargeable period (usually referred to as the written-down value brought forward). In allocating qualifying expenditure to the pool, rules identical to those for patent rights at **9.9**(i) and (ii) below must be observed.

The '*total disposal value*' is the aggregate of any disposal values to be brought into account for the period, i.e. the net sale proceeds (being capital sums) from any disposal of know-how on which qualifying expenditure was incurred (but excluding any sale the consideration for which is treated as a payment for goodwill under *CTA 2009, s 178* (see **68.45** TRADING INCOME) or income tax equivalent).

The allowances and charges are given effect as deductions or receipts of the relevant trade.

[*CAA 2001, ss 456–463*].

For receipts arising from sales of know-how, see also **68.45** TRADING INCOME.

Simon's Taxes. See B3.615, B3.616.

Mineral extraction

[9.9] Mineral extraction allowances are available in respect of qualifying expenditure (see **9.10** below) incurred by a person carrying on a 'mineral extraction trade'. A '*mineral extraction trade*' is a trade consisting of or including the working of a source of '*mineral deposits*', i.e. such deposits of a wasting nature including any natural deposits or geothermal energy capable of being lifted or extracted from the earth, but only to the extent that profits are within the charge to UK tax (or would be if there were any profits). A '*source of mineral deposits*' includes a mine, an oil well and a source of geothermal energy.

[*CAA 2001, s 394*]. A *share* in an asset may qualify for mineral extraction allowances. [*CAA 2001, s 435*]. Special rules apply to companies carrying on a ring fence trade (within *CTA 2010, s 277*); those rules are not covered in this work.

If an election is made under *CTA 2009, s 18A* (see **31.15** DOUBLE TAX RELIEF) to exempt from UK corporation tax, the profits arising from foreign permanent establishments of a UK company, then a business which consists of, or includes, the working of a source of mineral deposits carried on through one or more such permanent establishments is treated as an activity separate from any other activity of the company. For the above purposes, that activity is regarded as an activity the profits from which (if any) are *not* within the charge to UK tax. [*CAA 2001, s 431A*].

Simon's Taxes. See **B3.4**.

Qualifying expenditure

[9.10] '*Qualifying expenditure*' means capital expenditure, incurred for the purposes of a mineral extraction trade, on:

(a) '*mineral exploration and access*' (i.e. searching for or discovering and testing the mineral deposits of any source, or winning access to any such deposits);
(b) acquisition of a '*mineral asset*' (i.e. any mineral deposits or land comprising mineral deposits, or any interest in or right over such deposits or land) (subject to the limitations in **9.11** below);
(c) construction of works, in connection with the working of a source of mineral deposits, which are likely to become of little or no value when the source ceases to be worked;
(d) construction of works which are likely to become valueless when a foreign concession under which a source of mineral deposits is worked comes to an end;
(e) net expenditure incurred on the restoration of the site of a source of mineral deposits (or land used in connection with working such a source) within three years after the cessation of the trade, unless relieved elsewhere. In this case, the expenditure is treated as incurred on the last day of trading.

Included in (a) above is abortive expenditure (including appeal costs) on seeking planning permission for the undertaking of mineral exploration and access or the working of mineral deposits. All expenditure (including appeal costs) on seeking such planning permission is included in (a) above. Such expenditure is not to be treated as expenditure on the acquisition of a mineral asset.

Expenditure on the acquisition of, or of rights over, mineral deposits or the site of a source of mineral deposits falls into (b) rather than (a) above, subject to the position above with regard to expenditure on planning permission.

However, the following are *not* qualifying expenditure:

- expenditure on the provision of plant or machinery (except certain pre-trading expenditure — see below), and see **9.17** below;

- expenditure on acquisition of, or of rights in or over, the *site* of any works in (c) or (d) above;
- expenditure on works constructed wholly or mainly for processing the raw products, unless the process is designed to prepare the raw products for use as such;
- (subject to *CAA 2001, s 415* — see below) expenditure on buildings and structures for occupation by, or welfare of, workers;
- expenditure on a building constructed *entirely* for use as an office;
- expenditure on the office part of a building or structure constructed *partly* for use as an office, where such expenditure exceeds 10% of the capital expenditure on construction of the whole building;
- expenditure incurred at a time when a person is carrying on the trade but it is not at that time a mineral extraction trade, which as defined only includes activities within the charge to UK tax (ignoring the reference to commencement of a trade at *CAA 2001, s 577(2)*);
- the person has not begun to carry on the trade when the expenditure is incurred, and when the trade is commenced it is not a mineral extraction trade, which as defined only includes activities within the charge to UK tax (ignoring the reference to commencement of a trade at *CAA 2001, s 577(2)*).

[*CAA 2001, ss 395–399, 400(1), 403(1)(2), 414, 416*].

Qualifying expenditure also includes capital contributions, for the purposes of a mineral extraction trade carried on outside the UK, to the cost of accommodation buildings, and certain related utility buildings and welfare works, for employees engaged in working a source, provided that the buildings or works are likely to be of little or no value when the source ceases to be worked, that the expenditure does not result in the acquisition of an asset, and that relief is not due under any other tax provision. [*CAA 2001, s 415*].

Pre-trading expenditure

Pre-trading expenditure for the purposes of a mineral extraction trade is treated as incurred on the first day of trading. This applies equally to pre-trading expenditure on mineral exploration and access, but in determining whether such expenditure is qualifying expenditure within (a) above, the following limitations apply.

(i) In the case of pre-trading expenditure on plant or machinery which is used at a source but is sold, demolished, destroyed or abandoned before commencement of the mineral extraction trade, qualifying expenditure is limited to net expenditure after taking account of sale proceeds, insurance money or capital compensation.

(ii) In the case of pre-trading exploration expenditure other than on plant or machinery, qualifying expenditure is limited to net expenditure after taking into account any reasonably attributable capital sums received before the first day of trading.

In either case, if mineral exploration and access is not continuing at the source on the first day of trading, qualifying expenditure is further limited to net expenditure incurred in the six years ending on that day.

[*CAA 2001, ss 400(2)–(5), 401, 402, 434*].

Simon's Taxes. See B3.405–B3.410.

Limitations on qualifying expenditure

[9.11] Qualifying expenditure within **9.10**(b) above (acquisition of mineral asset) is limited in the following circumstances.

If the mineral asset is an interest in land, an amount equal to the 'undeveloped market value' of the interest is excluded. '*Undeveloped market value*' is the market value of the interest at the time of acquisition ignoring the mineral deposits and assuming that development of the land (other than that already lawfully begun or for which planning permission has already been granted) is, and will remain, unlawful. Where the undeveloped market value includes the value of buildings or structures which, at any time after acquisition, permanently cease to be used, their value at acquisition (exclusive of land and after deducting any net capital allowances received in respect of them) is treated as qualifying expenditure incurred at the time of cessation of use. These provisions operate by reference to the actual time of acquisition, regardless of any different time given by the pre-trading expenditure provisions at **9.10** above. They do not apply where an election is made under *CAA 2001, s 569* or its forerunner (election to treat connected persons transactions as made at written-down value). [*CAA 2001, ss 403(3), 404, 405, Sch 3 para 84*].

Where a deduction has been allowed under *ITTOIA 2005, ss 60–67* in respect of a premium under a lease, the qualifying expenditure allowable in respect of the acquisition of the interest in land to which the premium relates is correspondingly reduced. [*CAA 2001, s 406*].

Simon's Taxes. See B3.410.

Second-hand assets

[9.12] Where:

(a) an asset is acquired from another person; and
(b) either that person or any previous owner incurred expenditure on it in connection with a mineral extraction trade,

the buyer's qualifying expenditure is restricted to the seller's qualifying expenditure on the asset less net allowances given to him. If an oil licence (or an interest therein) is acquired, the buyer's qualifying expenditure is limited to the amount of the original licence fee paid (or such part of it as it is just and reasonable to attribute to the interest). However, these restrictions do not affect amounts treated under rules below as qualifying expenditure on mineral exploration and access.

Where:

(i) the purchased asset above is a mineral asset; and
(ii) part of its value is properly attributable to expenditure on mineral exploration and access incurred as in (b) above,

so much if any of the buyer's expenditure as it is just and reasonable to attribute to the part of the value in (ii) above (not exceeding the amount of original expenditure to which it is attributable) is treated as qualifying expenditure on mineral exploration and access, with the remainder treated as expenditure on acquisition of a mineral asset. Expenditure deducted by a previous owner in computing taxable profits is excluded for these purposes from the original expenditure.

Where:

- capital expenditure is incurred in acquiring assets for a mineral extraction trade from a person (the seller) who did *not* carry on a mineral extraction trade; and
- the assets represent expenditure on mineral exploration and access incurred by the seller,

the buyer's qualifying expenditure is limited to the amount of the seller's expenditure. Assets include any results obtained from any search, exploration or inquiry on which the expenditure was incurred. This restriction does not apply if the asset is an interest in an oil licence acquired by the buyer; in this case, so much if any of the buyer's expenditure as it is just and reasonable to attribute to the part of the value of the licence attributable to the seller's expenditure (but limited to the amount of that expenditure) is treated as qualifying expenditure on mineral exploration and access, with the cost of the oil licence being reduced by the buyer's expenditure so attributable (without limitation).

[*CAA 2001, ss 407–409, 411, Sch 3 paras 85–87*].

Simon's Taxes. See **B3.411, B3.412.**

Writing-down allowances and balancing adjustments

[9.13] For each item of qualifying expenditure (see **9.10** above), a writing-down allowance (WDA) is available for each chargeable period (see **9.2**(i) above) and is equal to a set percentage (as below) of the amount (if any) by which 'unrelieved qualifying expenditure' exceeds the total of any disposal values falling to be brought into account as in **9.14** below. The WDA is proportionately reduced or increased if the chargeable period is less or more than a year, or if the mineral extraction trade has been carried on for part only of the chargeable period.

In the circumstances listed at **9.15** below, a balancing allowance is available, instead of a WDA, equal to the excess (if any) of (1) 'unrelieved qualifying expenditure' over (2) total disposal values. (This is subject to the anti-avoidance rule at **9.2**(xi) above.) If, for any chargeable period, (2) exceeds (1), there arises a liability to a balancing charge, normally equal to that excess but limited to net allowances previously given. A claim for a WDA *or* a balancing allowance may require it to be reduced to a specified amount.

Rates of WDA are as follows:

Acquisition of a mineral asset (see **9.10**(b) above)	10% p.a.

Other qualifying expenditure	25% p.a.

'*Unrelieved qualifying expenditure*' means qualifying expenditure (other than first-year qualifying expenditure) incurred in the chargeable period and the tax written-down value brought forward (i.e. net of allowances and any disposal values) of qualifying expenditure (including first-year qualifying expenditure) incurred in a previous chargeable period.

[*CAA 2001, ss 417–419*].

The net demolition costs (i.e. the excess, if any, of demolition costs over money received for remains) of an asset representing qualifying expenditure is added to that expenditure in determining the amount of any balancing allowance or charge for the chargeable period of demolition, and is not then treated as expenditure incurred on any replacement asset. [*CAA 2001, s 433*].

There is no provision for pooling expenditure (in contrast to plant and machinery at **10.26** CAPITAL ALLOWANCES ON PLANT AND MACHINERY). In practice, HMRC do not object to the grouping together of assets for computational convenience, provided individual sources are kept separate and assets attracting different rates of WDA are not grouped with each other. However, where a disposal value falls to be brought into account or a balancing allowance arises, it will sometimes be necessary to reconstruct separate computations for individual items of expenditure previously grouped. (HMRC Capital Allowances Manual CA50410).

Simon's Taxes. See **B3.419–B3.422**.

Disposal events and values

[9.14] A disposal value must be brought into account (by deduction from unrelieved qualifying expenditure — see **9.13** above), for the chargeable period in which the event occurs, on the occurrence of any of the following events.

(i) An asset representing qualifying expenditure (see **9.10** above) is disposed of or permanently ceases to be used for the purposes of a mineral extraction trade (whether because of cessation of trade or otherwise).

(ii) A mineral asset begins to be used (by the trader or another person) in a way which constitutes development which is neither 'existing permitted development' nor development for the purposes of a mineral extraction trade. Development is '*existing permitted development*' if, at the time of acquisition, it had already lawfully begun or the appropriate planning permission had already been granted.

(iii) In a case not within (i) or (ii) above, a capital sum is received which, in whole or in part, it is reasonable to attribute to qualifying expenditure.

The amount to be brought into account depends upon the nature of the event.

(a) On an event within (i) or (ii) above, it is an amount determined in accordance with the list at **10.27**(a)–(g) CAPITAL ALLOWANCES ON PLANT AND MACHINERY (disregarding (f), the reference to abandonment at (d) and the text immediately following the list). However, if the asset is an interest in land, the amount so ascertained is then restricted by excluding the '*undeveloped market value*', determined as in **9.11** above but by reference to the time of disposal.

(b) On an event within (iii) above, it is so much of the capital sum as is reasonably attributable to the qualifying expenditure.

[*CAA 2001, ss 420–425*].

In relation to sales at other than market value, the connected person and other anti-avoidance provisions, and election potential, of *CAA 2001, ss 567–570* (and forerunners) apply with appropriate modifications for mineral extraction allowances as they do for industrial buildings allowances (see **9.9**(i) above).

Simon's Taxes. See **B3.420**.

Balancing allowances

[9.15] A person is entitled to a balancing allowance (instead of a writing-down allowance) for a chargeable period if:

- the chargeable period is that in which the first day of trading falls, and either the qualifying expenditure is pre-trading expenditure on plant or machinery within **9.10**(i) above or it is pre-trading exploration expenditure within **9.10**(ii) above where mineral exploration and access is not continuing at the source on the first day of trading; or
- the qualifying expenditure was on mineral exploration and access, and in that chargeable period he gives up the exploration, search or inquiry to which the expenditure related, without subsequently carrying on a mineral extraction trade consisting of or including the working of related mineral deposits; or
- in that chargeable period he permanently ceases to work particular mineral deposits, and the qualifying expenditure was on mineral exploration and access relating solely to those deposits or on the acquisition of a mineral asset consisting of those deposits or part of them; but where two or more mineral assets are comprised in, or derive from, a single asset, the above applies only when *all* the relevant mineral deposits cease to be worked; or
- the qualifying expenditure falls within *CAA 2001, s 415* (capital contributions to certain buildings or works for benefit of employees abroad — see **9.10** above), and in that chargeable period, the buildings or works permanently cease to be used for the purposes of or in connection with the mineral extraction trade; or
- the qualifying expenditure was on the provision of any assets, and in that chargeable period any of those assets is disposed of or otherwise permanently ceases to be used for purposes of the trade; or
- the qualifying expenditure is represented by assets, and in that chargeable period those assets are permanently lost or cease to exist (due to destruction, dismantling or otherwise) or begin to be used wholly or partly for purposes other than those of the mineral extraction trade; or
- the mineral extraction trade is permanently discontinued in that chargeable period.

[*CAA 2001, ss 426–431*].

Simon's Taxes. See **B3.421**.

Making of allowances and charges

[9.16] Mineral extraction allowances (or balancing charges) are given (or made) as trading expenses (or trading receipts) in calculating the profits of the mineral extraction trade. [*CAA 2001, s 432*].

Simon's Taxes. See B3.423.

Plant and machinery allowances

[9.17] Plant and machinery is normally excluded from relief under the current provisions, but certain pre-trading expenditure may qualify (see **9.10** above). The normal plant and machinery rules (see **10** CAPITAL ALLOWANCES ON PLANT AND MACHINERY) apply to plant and machinery provided for mineral exploration and access in connection with a mineral extraction trade. However, this does not apply to expenditure incurred either at a time when a person is carrying on the trade but it is not at that time a mineral extraction trade or when the person has not begun to carry on the trade and when the trade is commenced it is not a mineral extraction trade. This rule covers the position when a mineral extraction activity enters or ceases to be within the charge to UK tax. The reference to commencement of a trade at *CAA 2001, s 577(2)* is ignored for these purposes. [*CAA 2001, ss 159, 160*].

Where such expenditure is incurred prior to the date of commencement of a mineral extraction trade and the plant or machinery is still owned at that date, and there is no prior time when the person carried on that trade and the trade was not within the charge to UK tax, it is treated as if sold immediately before that date and re-acquired on that date. The capital expenditure on re-acquisition is deemed to be equal to the actual expenditure previously incurred. [*CAA 2001, s 161*].

Example

[9.18]

X Ltd has for some years operated a mining business with two mineral sources, G and S. Accounts are prepared to 30 September. On 31 December 2020, the mineral deposits and mineworks at G are sold at market value to Z for £80,000 and £175,000 respectively. A new source, P, is purchased on 30 April 2021 for £170,000 (including land with an undeveloped market value of £70,000) and the following expenditure incurred before the end of the period of account ended on 30 September 2021.

	£
Plant and machinery	40,000
Construction of administration office	25,000
Construction of mining works which are likely to have little value when mining ceases	50,000
Staff hostel	35,000
Winning access to the deposits	150,000
	£300,000

During the year to 30 September 2021, X Ltd also incurred expenditure of £20,000 in seeking planning permission to mine a further plot of land, Source Q. Permission was refused.

Residue of expenditure brought forward (based on accounts to 30 September 2020)		£
Mineral exploration and access	– Source G	170,000
	– Source S	200,000
Mineral assets	– Source G	95,250
	– Source S	72,000

The mineral extraction allowances due for the year ending 30 September 2021 are as follows:

		£	£
Source G			
Mineral exploration and access			
WDV b/f		170,000	
Proceeds		175,000	
Balancing charge		£5,000	(5,000)
Mineral assets			
WDV b/f		95,250	
Proceeds		80,000	
Balancing allowance		£15,250	15,250
Source S			
Mineral exploration and access			
WDV b/f		200,000	
WDA 25%		(50,000)	50,000
WDV c/f		£150,000	
Mineral assets			
WDV b/f		72,000	
WDA 10%		(7,200)	7,200
WDV c/f		£64,800	
Source P			
Mineral exploration and access			
Expenditure		150,000	
WDA 25%		(37,500)	37,500
WDV c/f		£112,500	
Mineral assets			
Expenditure	note (c)	100,000	
WDA 10%		(10,000)	10,000
WDV c/f		£90,000	
Mining works			
Expenditure		50,000	
WDA 25%		(12,500)	12,500
WDV c/f		£37,500	
Source Q			
Mineral exploration and access			
Expenditure	note (b)	20,000	

WDA 25%	(5,000)	5,000
WDV c/f	£15,000	
Total allowances (net of charges)		£132,450

Notes

(a) Allowances are not due on either the office or staff hostel. The plant and machinery qualify for plant and machinery allowances (see **10** CAPITAL ALLOWANCES ON PLANT AND MACHINERY) rather than for mineral extraction allowances (see **9.17** above).

(b) Abortive expenditure on seeking planning permission is qualifying expenditure as if it were expenditure on mineral exploration and access (see **9.10** above).

(c) The undeveloped market value of land is excluded from qualifying expenditure (see **9.11** above).

Patent rights

[9.19] Subject to the application of the regime for INTANGIBLE ASSETS (**42**), allowances are available, and balancing charges made, in respect of 'qualifying expenditure' on the purchase of patent rights, i.e. the right to do or authorise the doing of anything which would, but for that right, be a patent infringement. The obtaining of a right to acquire future patent rights and the acquisition of a licence in respect of a patent are each treated for these purposes as a purchase of patent rights. '*Qualifying expenditure*' may be either:

- '*qualifying trade expenditure*', i.e. capital expenditure incurred by a person on purchase of patent rights for the purposes of a trade carried on by him and within the charge to UK tax; or
- '*qualifying non-trade expenditure*', i.e. capital expenditure incurred by a person on purchase of patent rights if the above does not apply but any income receivable by him in respect of the rights would be liable to tax.

Expenditure incurred by a person for the purposes of a trade he is about to carry on is treated as if incurred on the first day of trading, unless all the rights in question have been sold before then. The same expenditure cannot be qualifying trade expenditure in relation to more than one trade.

The grant of a licence in respect of a patent is treated as a sale of part of patent rights. The grant by a person entitled to patent rights of an exclusive licence, i.e. a licence to exercise the rights to the exclusion of the grantor and all others for the remainder of their term, is, however, treated as a sale of the whole of those rights.

[*CAA 2001, ss 464–469*].

Qualifying expenditure is pooled for the purpose of determining entitlement to writing-down allowances and balancing allowances and liability to balancing charges. A separate pool applies for each separate trade and for all qualifying non-trade expenditure.

For each pool of qualifying expenditure, a writing-down allowance (WDA) is available for each chargeable period (see **9.2**(i) above) other than the 'final chargeable period' and is equal to a maximum of **25%** of the amount (if any) by which 'available qualifying expenditure' exceeds the total of any disposal values falling to be brought into account. The WDA is proportionately reduced or increased if the chargeable period is less or more than a year, or if (where relevant) the trade has been carried on for part only of the chargeable period. A claim for a WDA may require it to be reduced to a specified amount. For the 'final chargeable period', a balancing allowance is available, equal to the excess (if any) of (1) 'available qualifying expenditure' over (2) total disposal values. If, for *any* chargeable period, (2) exceeds (1), there arises a liability to a balancing charge, equal to that excess.

The '*final chargeable period*', as regards a pool of qualifying trade expenditure, is the chargeable period in which the trade is permanently discontinued. As regards a pool of non-qualifying trade expenditure, it is the chargeable period in which the last of the patent rights in question either comes to an end (without any such rights being revived) or is wholly disposed of.

'*Available qualifying expenditure*' in a pool for a chargeable period consists of qualifying expenditure allocated to the pool for that period and any unrelieved qualifying expenditure brought forward in the pool from the previous chargeable period (usually referred to as the written-down value brought forward).

In allocating qualifying expenditure to a pool, the following must be observed.

(i) Qualifying expenditure can be allocated to a pool for a chargeable period only to the extent that it has not been included in available qualifying expenditure for an earlier chargeable period. (There is now nothing to prohibit the allocation of *part only* of a particular amount of qualifying expenditure for a particular chargeable period.)
(ii) Qualifying expenditure cannot be allocated to a pool for a chargeable period earlier than that in which it is incurred.
(iii) Qualifying expenditure cannot be allocated to a pool for a chargeable period if in any earlier period the rights in question have come to an end (without any of them being revived) or have been wholly disposed of.

[*CAA 2001, ss 470–475*].

A *disposal value* falls to be brought into account for a chargeable period in which a person sells the whole or part of any patent rights on the purchase of which he has incurred qualifying expenditure. The disposal value is equal to the net sale proceeds (limited to *capital* sums), except that:

(1) it cannot exceed the qualifying expenditure incurred on purchase of the rights in question; and
(2) where the rights were acquired as a result of a transaction between CONNECTED PERSONS (19) (or a series of such transactions), (1) above shall have effect as if it referred to the greatest capital expenditure incurred on the purchase of those rights by any of those connected persons.

[*CAA 2001, ss 476, 477*].

Connected persons and other anti-avoidance

Where a person incurs capital expenditure on the purchase of rights either from a connected person (see **19** CONNECTED PERSONS), or so that it appears that the sole or main benefit from the sale and any other transactions would have been the obtaining of an allowance under these provisions, the amount of that expenditure taken into account as qualifying expenditure may not exceed an amount determined as follows:

(a) where a disposal value (see above) falls to be brought into account, an amount equal to that value;
(b) where no disposal value falls to be brought into account, but the seller receives a capital sum chargeable under *CTA 2009, s 912* (see **42.43** INTANGIBLE ASSETS), an amount equal to that sum;
(c) in any other case, an amount equal to the smallest of
- market value of the rights;
- the amount of capital expenditure, if any, incurred by the seller on acquiring the rights;
- the amount of capital expenditure, if any, incurred by any person connected with the seller on acquiring the rights.

[*CAA 2001, s 481*].

Making of allowances and charges

An allowance (or balancing charge) in respect of qualifying *trade* expenditure is given effect as a trading expense (or trading receipt). [*CAA 2001, s 478*].

An allowance in respect of qualifying *non-trade* expenditure is set against the person's 'income from patents' for the same accounting period, with any excess being carried forward without time limit against such income for subsequent accounting periods. A balancing charge is charged as taxable income. For these purposes, '*income from patents*' embraces royalties and similar sums, balancing charges under these provisions, and receipts from the sale of patent rights taxable under *CTA 2009, s 912* or *918* (see **59.27** PENALTIES). [*CAA 2001, ss 479, 480, 483*].

Trading partnerships and successions

Trading partnerships and successions are treated in the same way as for industrial buildings allowances (see **9.9**(iii)(iv)).

Simon's Taxes. See B3.601–B3.609.

Research and development

[9.20] 'Qualifying expenditure' incurred by a trader on 'research and development' (R & D) attracts an allowance equal to **100%** of the expenditure. A claim for an allowance may require it to be reduced to a specified amount (but the part of the allowance thus forgone cannot be claimed for a later chargeable period).

'*Qualifying expenditure*' is capital expenditure incurred by a trader on R & D related to the trade and undertaken directly or on his behalf (i.e. by an agent or other person in a similar contractual relationship, see *Gaspet Ltd v Elliss CA*

1987, 60 TC 91). It includes such expenditure incurred before commencement of the trade (pre-commencement expenditure). Expenditure potentially leading to or facilitating an extension of the trade is related to that trade, as is expenditure of a medical nature specially related to the welfare of workers in the trade. A just and reasonable apportionment may be made of capital expenditure only partly qualifying.

Expenditure on the acquisition of, or of rights in or over, land cannot be qualifying expenditure, except insofar as, on a just and reasonable apportionment, such expenditure is referable to a building or structure already constructed on the land, or to plant or machinery which forms part of such a building or structure, and otherwise qualifies as R & D expenditure.

Expenditure on R & D includes all expenditure incurred for carrying out (or providing facilities for carrying out) R & D. Expenditure on the acquisition of rights in, or arising out of, R & D is, however, excluded. Also excluded is expenditure on provision of a *dwelling*, except where not more than 25% of the expenditure (disregarding any 'additional VAT liability' or 'rebate' — see **9.2**(viii) above) on a building consisting partly of a dwelling and otherwise used for R & D is attributable (on a just and reasonable apportionment) to the dwelling, in which case the dwelling can be ignored and the whole of the building treated as used for R & D.

An 'additional VAT liability' (see **9.2**(viii) above) incurred in respect of qualifying expenditure is itself qualifying expenditure, provided the same person still owns the asset in question and it has not been demolished or destroyed.

In *Vaccine Research Limited Partnership v HMRC* [2014] UKUT 389, the Upper Tribunal considered whether a partnership had incurred 'qualifying expenditure'. A payment of £193m was made by the partnership to a company, Numology, which then subcontracted the research out to another company, Pep Tcell, for £14m. The Tribunal accepted that the partnership's activities of funding and supervising Pep Tcell amounted to a trade and were commercial, as their objective was the development of vaccines to generate royalties. However the quantum of the payment was questioned, and the circulatory of the funding between Numology and the partnership was considered. The Tribunal concluded that only £14m of the partnership payment was 'qualifying expenditure'.

In *Brain Disorders Research Ltd Partnership v HMRC* CA, [2018] STC 2382, the court found that schemes designed to obtain capital allowances did not work. The partnership had set up, and paid, a special purpose vehicle (SPV) to undertake scientific research. The SPV in turn used a sub-contractor who could perform the research at a fraction of the price; however, the partnership claimed allowances for the full amount paid to the SPV. Applying *CA 2001, s 437* purposively, and analysing the facts realistically, it was impossible to conclude that capital expenditure had been incurred on any scientific research in any amount greater than that paid by the SPV to the sub-contractor. The court further held that the partnership was not trading at all and therefore even the latter amount was not qualifying expenditure.

Meaning of research and development

'*Research and development*' means activities that fall to be treated as such in accordance with generally accepted accounting practice (see **68.18** above) and includes oil and gas exploration and appraisal. However, this is subject to Treasury regulations which narrow the definition by reference to guidelines issued by the Department of Trade and Industry (DTI). [*CAA 2001, s 437(2)(3)*]. The latest regulations refer to Government guidelines issued on 5 March 2004 and updated by the Department for Business, Innovation and Skills on 6 December 2010 (see www.gov.uk/government/publications/guidelines-on-the-meaning-of-research-and-development-for-tax-purposes). [*SI 2004 No 712*].

For special provisions relating to oil licences, see *CAA 2001, ss 552–556* as amended.

Making of allowances

The allowance is given as a trading expense of the chargeable period (see **9.2**(i) above) in which the expenditure is incurred (or, in the case of pre-commencement expenditure, the chargeable period in which the trade commences). An allowance in respect of an additional VAT liability is similarly given, but by reference to the time the *liability* is incurred.

[*CAA 2001, ss 437(1), 438–441, 447, 450, Sch 3 paras 89, 90*].

Disposal events and balancing charges

If a disposal value (see below) falls to be brought into account for the same chargeable period as that for which the related allowance falls to be given, the allowance is given on the excess (if any) of the expenditure over the disposal value.

If a disposal value falls to be brought into account for the chargeable period after that for which the related allowance is given, liability to a balancing charge arises for that later chargeable period. Effect is given to the charge by treating it as a trading receipt. The charge is equal to disposal value (or, where a reduced allowance was claimed, the excess, if any, of disposal value over unrelieved expenditure), except that it cannot exceed the allowance given (less any earlier balancing charges arising from 'additional VAT rebates' — see below).

A disposal value falls to be brought into account for a chargeable period in which a disposal event occurs, or, if such an event occurs later, for the chargeable period in which the trade is permanently discontinued. If, exceptionally, a disposal event occurs *before* the chargeable period for which the related allowance falls to be given, it is brought into account for the later chargeable period.

Either of the following is a disposal event (unless it gives rise to a balancing charge under the rules for industrial buildings or plant and machinery allowances).

(a) The trader ceases to own the asset representing the qualifying expenditure;

(b) An asset representing the qualifying expenditure is demolished or destroyed before the trader ceases to own it.

On the sale of an asset, the seller is treated for these purposes as ceasing to own it at the earlier of the time of completion and the time when possession is given.

The amount of the disposal value depends on the nature of the disposal event, as follows.

- If the event is a sale of the asset at not less than market value, it is the net sale proceeds.
- If the event is the demolition or destruction of the asset, it is the net amount received for the remains, plus any insurance or capital compensation received (but see below as regards demolition costs).
- In any other event, it is the market value of the asset at the time of the event.

An 'additional VAT rebate' (see **9.2**(viii) above) made in respect of qualifying expenditure, before the asset in question ceases to belong to the trader or has been demolished or destroyed, must be brought into account as a disposal value (or as an addition to a disposal value otherwise arising) for the chargeable period in which the rebate accrues or, if later, the chargeable period in which the trade commences.

[*CAA 2001, ss 441(1), 442–444, 448, 449–451*].

Demolition costs

On demolition of an asset (within (b) above), the disposal value is reduced (or extinguished) by any demolition costs incurred by the trader. If the demolition costs exceed the disposal value, then, provided the asset had not begun to be used for non-qualifying purposes, the excess is itself treated as qualifying R & D expenditure, incurred at time of demolition (or, if earlier and where relevant, immediately before cessation of the trade). The demolition costs cannot be treated for any capital allowances purposes as expenditure on any replacement asset.

[*CAA 2001, s 445*].

Connected persons and other anti-avoidance

Connected persons and other anti-avoidance provisions apply to substitute market value for sale consideration on certain 'sole or main benefit' transactions, sales without change of control and sales between connected persons. For most sales, the election referred to at **9.9**(i) above is available, with the result that an asset representing expenditure for which an R & D allowance has been made as above will be treated as transferred for nil consideration. [*CAA 2001, ss 567–570, 575, 575A*].

Simon's Taxes. See B3.7.

Example

[9.21]

C Ltd is in business manufacturing and selling cosmetics, and it prepares accounts annually to 30 June. For the purposes of this trade, the company built a new laboratory adjacent to its existing premises, incurring the following expenditure.

		£
April 2019	Laboratory building	50,000
June 2019	Technical equipment	3,000
March 2020	Technical equipment	4,000
July 2020	Plant	2,500
August 2021	Extension to existing premises comprising 50% further laboratory area and 50% sales offices	30,000

In September 2020 a small fire destroyed an item of equipment originally costing £2,000 in June 2019; insurance recoveries totalled £3,000. In March 2021, the plant costing £2,500 in July 2020 was sold for £1,800.

The allowances due are as follows.

		£
Y/e 30.6.19		
Laboratory building		50,000
Technical equipment		3,000
		£53,000
Y/e 30.6.20		
Technical equipment		4,000
		£4,000
Y/e 30.6.21		
Net allowance on plant sold	(note (a))	£700
Balancing charge on equipment destroyed	(note (b))	(£2,000)
Y/e 30.6.22		
Extension (qualifying R&D expenditure only)		£15,000

Notes

(a) As the plant is sold in the period of account in which the expenditure is incurred, the disposal value of £1,800 is set against the expenditure of £2,500, resulting in a net allowance of £700.

(b) The destruction of the equipment in the year to 30 June 2021 results in a balancing charge limited to the allowance given. The charge accrues in the accounting period in which the event occurs.

Structures and buildings allowances

[9.22] A structures and buildings allowance (SBA) is available for expenditure on the construction of commercial (non-residential) buildings and structures. The relief extends to capital expenditure on the improvement of existing structures and buildings, including converting existing premises to qualifying business use. The detailed rules are contained in regulations made by statutory instrument under powers conferred on the Treasury by *FA 2019, s 30*.

SBA is available on eligible construction costs incurred on or after **29 October 2018**, at an annual rate on a straight-line basis. On and after 1 April 2020, the standard annual rate is **3%**; it was previously 2%. A higher annual rate of **10%** has been introduced by *FA 2021* for 'freeport qualifying expenditure' (broadly, where the building or structure is constructed in a 'freeport tax site'). There is no system of balancing charges or balancing allowances on a subsequent disposal of the asset. Instead, a purchaser will continue to claim the allowance at the annual rate on the original cost. The amount eligible for relief is not increased where a structure or building is purchased, or where it has appreciated in value, as this does not represent the cost of construction. Relief is available for UK and overseas structures and buildings, where the business is within the charge to UK tax. The cost of land or rights over land, and the costs of obtaining planning permission, is not eligible for relief. Relief is not available for structures or buildings where a contract for the construction works was entered into before 29 October 2018.

See also HMRC Capital Allowances Manual CA90000 onwards.

Throughout this commentary, references to a 'building' include a structure, unless the context demands otherwise.

The entitlement conditions

An SBA is potentially available for 'qualifying expenditure' (see **9.23** below) incurred, on or after 29 October 2018 on the construction or acquisition of a building whose construction commenced on or after that date, provided the building is not in 'residential use' (see **9.24** below). A person carrying on a 'qualifying activity' is entitled to an SBA for a chargeable period (see **9.2**(i) above) if, on any day in that period, he has the 'relevant interest' in the building in relation to the expenditure (see **9.25** below) and the building is in 'non-residential use' (see **9.24** below), provided the beginning of that day falls:

- on or after the later of the day on which the building is first brought into 'qualifying use' by the person and the day on which the qualifying expenditure is incurred (and in either case, whether the day is in the same or an earlier chargeable period); and
- either:
  - in the case of freeport qualifying expenditure (see **9.23** below), within the ten years beginning with the later of the day on which the building is first brought into non-residential use and the day on which the qualifying expenditure is incurred; or
  - in the case of other qualifying expenditure, within the 33⅓ years beginning with the later of the day on which the building is first brought into non-residential use and the day on which the qualifying expenditure is incurred.

A person ceases to be entitled to an SBA if the building is demolished.

[*CAA 2001, s 270AA(1)–(4)(6); FA 2020, s 29(2)(6)(7), Sch 5 paras 4, 10; FA 2021, Sch 22 para 7(2)(3); SI 2019 No 1087, Reg 2*].

The construction of a building is treated as having commenced before 29 October 2018 (with the result that no SBA is available) if any contract for works to be carried out in the course of the construction of that particular building (whether or not the contract also relates to the construction of other buildings or structures) was entered into before that date. [*CAA 2001, s 270AB; SI 2019 No 1087, Reg 2*].

A claim for an SBA must be separately identified as such in the tax return in which it is made and, where it relates to freeport qualifying expenditure, must include such information as HMRC may require. [*CAA 2001, s 3(2ZA); FA 2021, Sch 22 para 15(3); SI 2019 No 1087, Reg 3(4)*].

Rate of allowance and length of writing-down period

With effect on and after 1 April 2020, regardless of when the qualifying expenditure was incurred, the SBA for a chargeable period of one year is, except where the expenditure is freeport qualifying expenditure, 3% of the qualifying expenditure, such that the expenditure is fully relieved only over a writing-down period of 33⅓ years. Before 1 April 2020, the rate was 2%, and the writing-down period was 50 years.

Where the qualifying expenditure is freeport qualifying expenditure, the SBA for a chargeable period of one year is 10% of the expenditure. The writing-down period is ten years.

The allowance is proportionately increased or reduced for chargeable periods of more or less than one year. It is also proportionately reduced if the above conditions for entitlement to an SBA are met for only part of the chargeable period (including where the writing-down period ends part way through the chargeable period) or if that entitlement ceases due to demolition (see above) at some time during the period.

For the purpose only of computing the allowance for a chargeable period straddling 1 April 2020, that period is split into two separate notional chargeable periods, the second beginning on that date. So, for example, for an accounting period covering the year to 31 December 2020, the allowance for expenditure meeting the entitlement conditions throughout the year will be based on 91 days at 2% and 275 days at 3%.

The reduction from 50 to 33⅓ in the number of years comprised in the writing-down period applies equally to qualifying expenditure which had already attracted an allowance at the old 2% rate before 1 April 2020. This is achieved by enabling the shortfall in allowances to be claimed in the chargeable period in which the writing-down period of 33⅓ years comes to an end. It applies only if the person entitled to the allowance on 31 March 2020 does not dispose of the relevant interest in the building before the time that the writing-down period ends and continues to be entitled to an allowance in respect of the expenditure at that time.

[*CAA 2001, ss 270AA(2)(5)(6), 270EA, 270GD; FA 2020, s 29(2)(3)(5)–(7); FA 2021, Sch 22 para 7(4)(5); SI 2019 No 1087, Reg 2*].

Buildings in multiple use

A person may meet the above entitlement conditions by reference to a building which is put to multiple uses in a chargeable period. A building is put to multiple uses if:

- it is used for the purposes of two or more qualifying activities;
- part of it is in use for the purposes of a qualifying activity and part of it for the purposes of another activity; or
- part of it is used both for the purposes of a qualifying activity and for those of another activity (but the part of the building in question must not be an area within a dwelling-house).

In relation to any particular qualifying activity, the SBA for a chargeable period of one year is 3% (2% before 1 April 2020) or 10% (for freeport qualifying expenditure) of the appropriate proportion of the qualifying expenditure. The appropriate proportion is arrived at by apportioning the qualifying expenditure between all the activities for which the building is used. This apportionment must be carried out on a just and reasonable basis and with particular regard to the extent to which the building is used for each activity in the chargeable period.

[*CAA 2001, s 270EB; FA 2020, s 29(4)(6)(7); FA 2021, Sch 22 para 11; SI 2019 No 1087, Reg 2*].

Disposal of the building

It should be noted that the above entitlement conditions do not require the qualifying expenditure to have been incurred by the person who currently has the relevant interest. If the relevant interest in the building is sold at any time after the building is brought into use, the potential entitlement to the SBA passes from seller to purchaser, but only in relation to the historical qualifying expenditure and not to the amount paid for the interest by the purchaser. See also the definition of 'qualifying expenditure' at **9.23** below. The sale does not give rise to any balancing charge or balancing allowance, but the seller ceases to be entitled to the SBA as regards any time falling after the sale.

An adjustment is made for capital gains purposes where a person disposes of an interest in a building by reference to which he has obtained an SBA. If the expenditure by reference to which the SBA has been made is allowable as a deduction in computing the gain or loss on disposal, the consideration for the disposal is treated as increased by the amount of the SBA given to the seller. [*TCGA 1992, s 37B; SI 2019 No 1087, Reg 4(4)*].

Where a person who is, or has been, the lessor under a lease of a building or structure subject to the rules for leases granted for 35 years or more disposes of the building or structure or an interest in it to a connected person, any expenditure by reference to which an allowance has been made to the lessee is not an allowable deduction in computing the gain or loss on disposal. [*TCGA 1992, s 39A; SI 2019 No 1087, Reg 4(6)*].

Demolition of the building

As stated above, entitlement to an SBA ceases if the building in question is demolished. Demolition generally counts as a disposal for capital gains purposes by virtue of *TCGA 1992, s 24* (see Tolley's Capital Gains Tax). In the computation of a gain or loss accruing to a person making a disposal, there is normally excluded from the sums allowable as a deduction any expenditure to the extent to which a capital allowance has been made in respect of it. [*TCGA 1992, ss 39, 41*]. This rule is disapplied in the case of the SBA to enable a person to obtain relief from CGT for so much of the capital expenditure on a building as has failed to attract SBAs as a result of its demolition (but see above regarding disposals by a lessor to a connected person). [*TCGA 1992, ss 39(3B), 41(4A); SI 2019 No 1087, Reg 4(5)(7)*].

Under the normal chargeable gains rules, land and buildings (or structures) may be treated for the purposes of *TCGA 1992, s 24* as separate assets and, if they are so treated, the land is treated as if it were also sold and immediately reacquired at market value (see *TCGA 1992, s 24(3)*).Where the asset is a leasehold interest in a building or structure by reference to which a person is entitled to a structures and buildings allowance, *s 24(3)* is disapplied. The land and building or structure are still treated as separate assets but there is no deemed disposal of the land. An irrevocable election can be made to disapply the special treatment (so that there is a deemed disposal of the land under *s 24(3)*). Such an election must be made by the person deemed to dispose of the building or structure by notice to HMRC by the first anniversary of 31 January following the tax year of the deemed disposal (or, for corporation tax purposes, within two years of the end of the accounting period of the deemed disposal). [*TCGA 1992, s 24(3A)–(3F); SI 2019 No 1087, Reg 4(2)*].

Where a person (P) makes a deemed disposal under *TCGA 1992, s 24* of an interest in a building or structure and another person (the contributor) has received a contribution allowance in relation to the building or structure (see **9.2**(vii) above), the contributor may claim an allowable loss equal to the 'unclaimed allowance amount'. This applies only if the contributor does not have an interest in the building or structure which is an interest in UK land (within *TCGA 1992, s 1C*). A claim must identify the building or structure and quantify the unclaimed allowance amount.

The '*unclaimed allowance amount*' is the difference between the amount in respect of which the contribution allowance was originally available (so far as not allowable as a deduction in computing the gain on the deemed disposal by P) and the total contribution allowances to which the contributor was entitled before the deemed disposal (on the assumption that the allowance was available at all times since an entitlement to the allowance first arose).

[*TCGA 1992, s 24A; SI 2019 No 1087, Reg 4(3)*].

Disuse of the building

A building which, immediately before falling into disuse, was in non-residential use is treated, for the purposes of the above entitlement conditions as continuing to be in non-residential use. [*CAA 2001, s 270AA(3); SI 2019 No 1087, Reg 2*]. Thus, allowances remain available in periods of disuse.

Qualifying activities

Each of the following is a '*qualifying activity*' for the purposes of the SBA:

- a trade, profession or vocation;
- a UK property business or overseas property business (see **60.2** PROPERTY INCOME), excluding (in both cases) so much of the business as consists of furnished holiday lettings;
- any of the concerns listed in *CTA 2009, s 39(4)* (mines, quarries and sundry other undertakings); and
- managing the investments of a company with investment business (see **45** INVESTMENT COMPANIES AND INVESTMENT BUSINESS),

but to the extent only that the profits therefrom are within the charge to UK tax (or would be if there were any profits).

If, for the purposes of a qualifying activity, a person incurs expenditure before the date on which he starts to carry on the activity (but on or after 29 October 2018), the expenditure is treated as if it were incurred on the date on which he starts to carry on the activity.

Foreign permanent establishments

If an election is made under *CTA 2009, s 18A* (see **31.15** DOUBLE TAX RELIEF) to exempt from UK corporation tax the profits arising from foreign permanent establishments of a UK company, then a business carried on through one or more such permanent establishments is treated as an activity separate from any other activity of the company. For the above purposes, that activity is regarded as an activity the profits from which (if any) are *not* within the charge to UK tax.

[*CAA 2001, ss 270CA–270CD, 270BN; SI 2019 No 1087, Reg 2*].

Making of allowances

An SBA is given effect by treating the allowance as a deductible expense in calculating profits or losses of the qualifying activity for the chargeable period. Where the qualifying activity is managing the investments of a company with investment business, SBAs are given by deduction from any income of the business. Any excess allowances is treated as in **45.4** INVESTMENT COMPANIES AND INVESTMENT BUSINESS. [*CAA 2001, ss 270HA–270HE*].

Structures and buildings allowance — qualifying expenditure

[9.23] '*Qualifying expenditure*' for the purposes of the SBA is expenditure which is 'qualifying capital expenditure' on the construction or purchase of a building, and which is not 'excluded expenditure'.

Capital expenditure incurred on construction is '*qualifying capital expenditure*' if the 'relevant interest' in the building (see **9.25** below) has not been sold or has been sold only after the building was brought into 'non-residential use' (see **9.24** below).

As regards capital expenditure on the purchase of a building, the question of whether (and to what extent) the expenditure is qualifying capital expenditure depends firstly on whether or not the building is purchased from a developer. If not, the capital sum paid by the purchaser for the relevant interest in the building is potentially qualifying capital expenditure only if that relevant interest was sold to the purchaser before the building was first used. The portion of the capital sum that is '*qualifying capital expenditure*' cannot be greater than the capital expenditure incurred on the construction. It may be that the building is sold unused on more than one occasion, in which case only the capital sum paid on the last such sale is potentially qualifying capital expenditure.

If the construction expenditure was incurred by a developer (i.e. a person carrying on a trade consisting wholly or partly in the construction of buildings with a view to their sale), and the relevant interest in the building is sold by the developer in the course of the development trade before the building is first used, the following rules apply. If the sale of the relevant interest by the developer was the only sale of the relevant interest before the building is first used, any capital sum paid by the purchaser for that interest is '*qualifying capital expenditure*'. If the sale of the relevant interest by the developer was not the only such sale of the relevant interest before the building is first used, any capital sum paid by the purchaser for that interest on the last such sale is potentially qualifying capital expenditure. The portion of the capital sum that is '*qualifying capital expenditure*' cannot be greater than the sum paid for the relevant interest on the earlier sale by the developer.

In each case, the qualifying expenditure is treated as incurred by the purchaser when the capital sum in question is paid.

The following applies if the construction expenditure is incurred by a developer, and the relevant interest in the building is sold in the course of the development trade after the building is first used. In relation to the person to whom the relevant interest is sold (and any person who subsequently acquires that interest), the expenditure on the construction of the building is treated as if it had been '*qualifying capital expenditure*', with the result that the person concerned can potentially claim the SBA.

Any expenditure whose amount cannot be provably quantified does not count as expenditure on the construction of a building. If an item of expenditure falls to be apportioned between expenditure for which and SBA can be made and other expenditure, the apportionment is to be made on a just and reasonable basis. An apportionment must similarly be made if the sum paid for the sale of the relevant interest in a building is attributable partly to assets representing expenditure for which an SBA can be made and partly to assets representing other expenditure.

It should be noted that the transfer of the relevant interest otherwise than by way of sale is treated as a sale of the relevant interest at market value. [*CAA 2001, s 573; SI 2019 No 1087, Reg 3(14)*].

Freeport qualifying expenditure

Qualifying expenditure is '*freeport qualifying expenditure*' if it meets the following conditions:

(i) construction begins at a time when the building is situated in a 'freeport tax site';

(ii) the building is first brought into qualifying use by the person entitled to the SBA at a time before 1 October 2026 when the building is situated in a freeport tax site;
(iii) the qualifying expenditure is incurred before 1 October 2026 and at a time when the building is situated is in a freeport tax site;
(iv) the person who incurs the qualifying expenditure is within the charge to income tax or corporation tax when it is incurred; and
(v) the allowance statement (see **9.26** below) made by the person who incurred the qualifying expenditure and relied on for the first valid SBA claim states that that person wants the expenditure to be freeport qualifying expenditure.

In (i) above, construction of the building begins when the first contract for construction works is entered into.

A '*freeport tax site*' means an area designated as such by Treasury regulations. At the time the regulations are made, the area must be situated in a 'freeport' or the Treasury must consider that the area is in use (or likely to be used) for purposes connected with activities carried on (or likely to be carried on) in a freeport. A '*freeport*' is an area identified as such in a document published by the Treasury or with its consent (and not withdrawn). The Government announced at Budget 2021 that eight freeports in England will begin operations from late 2021. These are East Midlands Airport, Felixstowe and Harwich, Humber, Liverpool City Region, Plymouth and South Devon, Solent, Teesside and Thames.

Where a building is only partly in a freeport tax site, the qualifying expenditure is apportioned, so that only that part of it which, on a just and reasonable basis is attributable to the part situated in the site is treated as freeport qualifying expenditure. This test is applied by reference to the later of the day on which the building is first brought into non-residential use and the day on which the qualifying expenditure is incurred. A similar apportionment is required where the building is only partly first brought into qualifying use before 1 October 2026.

The Treasury can amend the conditions for qualifying expenditure to be freeport qualifying expenditure by statutory instrument.

Excluded expenditure

For the above purposes, expenditure is '*excluded expenditure*' if it is expenditure:

(a) on the acquisition of land (including fees, stamp duty land tax, land and buildings transaction tax, land transaction tax and other incidental costs);
(b) on the '*alteration of land*', i.e. land reclamation, land remediation (as defined), or landscaping (other than so as to create a structure);
(c) on, or in connection with, the seeking of planning permission (including fees and related costs);
(d) of a capital nature on the provision of plant or machinery (as in **10** CAPITAL ALLOWANCES ON PLANT AND MACHINERY); or
(e) in excess of market value.

The market value rule in (e) above excludes any expenditure in excess of:

- (in a case where the qualifying capital expenditure is the capital sum paid for the relevant interest in the building), the market value of the relevant interest; and
- (in any other case) the *'market value amount'* of the works, services and other matters to which it relates, i.e. the amount of expenditure which it would have been normal and reasonable to incur on the works etc. in the prevailing market conditions on the assumption that the transaction giving rise to that expenditure was on arm's length terms in the open market.

Expenditure treated as expenditure on construction

Expenditure incurred on the renovation or conversion of a part of a building, or on repairs to a part of a building that are incidental to the renovation or conversion of that part, is treated as if it were expenditure on the construction for the first time of that part of the building. Such expenditure is to be treated as capital expenditure if it is not deductible in computing the taxable profits or losses of the qualifying activity.

What this means in practice is that the renovation etc. expenditure is treated as entirely separate from the original construction expenditure for the building. The renovation etc. expenditure has its own writing-down period, which continues after the expiry of the writing-down period for the original expenditure. See also below under Expenditure incurred on different days.

In relation to a building that was brought into use before 29 October 2018 any such renovation or conversion of, or repairs to, a part of the building are treated as if they represented the construction of that part for the first time (so that they are not disbarred from qualifying for SBAs).

A similar rule applies in relation to a building that was brought into use at a time when it was not in a freeport tax site. Any renovation or conversion of, or repairs to, a part of the building are treated as if they represented the construction of that part for the first time, so that, if the site is then in a freeport tax site, the enhanced rate of SBA can apply.

If a person incurs capital expenditure, other than alteration expenditure within (b) above, for the purposes of preparing land as a site for the construction of a building, this counts as capital expenditure on the construction of the building.

Expenditure incurred on different days

Capital expenditure may be incurred on the construction of a building after it has been brought into 'non-residential use' (see **9.24** below) and on different days (whether or not in the same chargeable period). This may, for example, apply to expenditure on renovation, conversion and repairs as above. For ease of administration, e.g. to avoid having a separate writing-down period for every such item of expenditure, the expenditure can be treated for SBA purposes as having been incurred:

- on the latest day on which any qualifying capital expenditure on the construction is incurred (Day L); or

- on the first day of the chargeable period following that in which Day L falls; or
- on the first day of the chargeable period following that in which falls the day on which the expenditure in question is actually incurred.

[*CAA 2001, ss 270BA–270BM, 270BNA–270BNC, 573A; FA 2020, Sch 5 paras 5, 6, 10; FA 2021, s 113, Sch 22 paras 8–10, 17; SI 2019 No 1087, Reg* 2].

Structures and buildings allowance — qualifying use

[9.24] A building or structure is in '*qualifying use*' for the purposes of the SBA if it is in 'non-residential use' (see below) for the purposes of a qualifying activity (see **9.22** above) carried on by the person who has the relevant interest (see **9.25** below) in the building. The extent to which a building is in use for the purposes of a particular activity is to be determined on a just and reasonable basis. A building is treated as not being in use for the purposes of a particular activity if such use is insignificant.

A building is treated as being used for the purposes of a property business during any period if the person with the relevant interest is entitled, under the terms of a lease or otherwise, to rents, or other receipts, of such amounts as may reasonably have been expected to have been payable if the transaction had been between two persons on arm's length terms in the open market.

HMRC consider that 'insignificant' takes its ordinary meaning as 'too small or unimportant to be worth consideration' (HMRC Capital Allowances Manual CA92200).

Residential and non-residential use

A building is in '*residential use*' if it is used as (or for purposes ancillary to use as) a dwelling-house, residential accommodation for school pupils, student accommodation (as defined), residential accommodation for members of the armed forces, a home or other institution providing residential accommodation for children or adults (but not where that accommodation is provided together with personal care for persons in need of it by reason of old age, disability, alcohol or drug dependence or mental disorder), or a prison or similar establishment. Any part of a building that is used as a dwelling house (whether or not it is also used for any other purposes) is not in qualifying use.

A building situated on land that is (or is intended to be) occupied or enjoyed (together with a building in residential use) as a garden or grounds is automatically treated as being in residential use.

A building is in '*non-residential use*' if it is in use which is not residential use.

[*CAA 2001, ss 270CE–270CG; SI 2019 No 1087, Reg* 2].

Structures and buildings allowance — the relevant interest

[9.25] The relevant interest in relation to any 'qualifying expenditure' (as in **9.23** above) is the interest in the building to which the person who incurred the expenditure on its construction was entitled when the expenditure was incurred. If that person was entitled to more than one interest in the building at that time, and one of those interests was reversionary on all the others, the reversionary interest is the relevant interest.

Subject to the rules below on leases granted for 35 years or more, an interest does not cease to be the relevant interest merely because of the creation of a lease or other interest to which that interest is subject. Thus, on the grant of a lease, the relevant interest, and potential entitlement to the SBA, remains with the lessor.

If the relevant interest is a leasehold interest which is extinguished upon the person entitled to it acquiring the interest which is reversionary upon it, the interest into which the leasehold interest merges becomes the relevant interest. In determining the relevant interest, a person who incurs expenditure on the construction of a building, and is entitled to an interest in it upon completion of construction, is treated as having had that interest when the expenditure was incurred.

On the sale of the relevant interest, the seller (and not the purchaser) is treated for the purposes of the entitlement conditions at **9.22** above as the person who has the relevant interest on the day of transfer.

Leases granted for 35 years or more

The following rule applies if:

- 'qualifying capital expenditure' (as in **9.23** above) has been incurred on the construction or acquisition of a building;
- a lease of the building is granted out of the interest which is the relevant interest in relation to the qualifying expenditure; and
- the effective duration of the lease (see below) is at least 35 years.

If the market value of the retained interest in the building is less than one-third of the capital sum given as consideration for the lease (see below):

- the lessee is treated as acquiring the relevant interest upon the grant of the lease; and
- the lessor is treated as acquiring the relevant interest from the lessee upon the expiry or surrender of the lease.

The relevant interest, and potential entitlement to the SBA, is thus transferred to the lessee.

For this purpose, the capital sum given as consideration for the lease is treated as excluding the amount, in respect of any premium required to be paid under the lease, that is brought into account as a receipt in calculating the lessor's profits (see **60.10** PROPERTY INCOME).

[*CAA 2001, ss 270DA–270DE; SI 2019 No 1087, Reg 2*].

CTA 2009, s 243 contains rules for ascertaining the effective duration of a lease, which is not necessarily the same as its contractual duration; in particular, any rights the tenant has to extend the lease, or any entitlement of his to a further lease of the same premises, may be taken into account.

Structures and buildings allowance — miscellaneous

[9.26] The following miscellaneous provisions apply for the purposes of the SBA.

Requirement for an allowance statement

In determining the amount of an SBA due to a person (P), the amount of the qualifying expenditure is treated as nil unless, before P first makes a claim for an SBA by reference to the building, the 'allowance statement requirement' is met. The '*allowance statement requirement*' is met if:

- in a case where P incurred the qualifying expenditure, P makes an 'allowance statement'; and
- in any other case, P obtains an allowance statement (or a copy of it) from any person previously entitled to a relevant interest in the building.

An '*allowance statement*' is a written statement, identifying the building to which it relates, of:

- the date of the earliest contract (written or oral) for the construction of the building;
- the amount of qualifying expenditure (see **9.23** above) incurred on its construction or purchase; and
- the date on which it is first brought into non-residential use.

If the qualifying expenditure includes any freeport qualifying expenditure (see **9.23** above), an allowance statement must state the amount of that expenditure.

[*CAA 2001, s 270IA; FA 2020, Sch 5 paras 7, 10; FA 2021, Sch 22 para 12; SI 2019 No 1087, Reg 2*].

Where capital improvement or renovation costs that qualify for SBA are incurred on a building that already qualifies for SBA and an allowance statement for the building exists, for administrative ease, HMRC advise that a taxpayer can add those costs to the existing allowance statement. The relevant parts of expenditure must be clearly identified. (HMRC Capital Allowances Manual CA94650).

Buildings qualifying for research and development allowances

There are provisions to deal with cases in which expenditure on a building potentially qualifies for both SBAs and the research and development (R & D) allowance at **9.20** above.

Sale of relevant interest on or after 11 March 2020

If, on or after 11 March 2020, a person sells the relevant interest in a building to another person (P), the total SBAs available to P are reduced (but not below nil) by the amount of any R & D allowance available to P by reference to the building.

Additionally, if the sale in question, or a sale of the relevant interest at an earlier time, is by a person entitled to an R & D allowance by reference to the building *and* the amount paid on any of those sales is less than the total remaining SBAs available at the time of sale, the total SBAs available to the buyer cannot exceed the 'permitted maximum'. The '*permitted maximum*' is:

- the lowest sum paid for the relevant interest on the sale in question or any of the earlier such sales, less
- the total SBAs arising since the earliest such sale.

In applying these provisions, reference to the total SBAs is to the total to which an entitlement has arisen or would have arisen if the building had been in continuous qualifying use since first brought into non-residential use.

Sale of relevant interest before 11 March 2020

Different provisions applied where the relevant interest was sold before 11 March 2020. If the purchaser (P) was entitled to an R & D allowance in respect of expenditure incurred on the acquisition of the building, the *total* amount of SBAs available to P by reference to the building was limited to the excess of the qualifying expenditure (as in **9.23** above) over the aggregate of:

- the total SBAs that could have been claimed in respect of it before the sale on the assumption that it had been in continuous qualifying use (see **9.24** above) since it was first brought into non-residential use; and
- the amount of R & D allowance to which P is entitled.

If the seller of the relevant interest was entitled to an R & D allowance in respect of his expenditure on the acquisition of the building, but the purchaser (P) is not entitled to an R & D allowance, the total amount of SBAs available to P by reference to the building is limited to the lower of:

- the excess of the qualifying expenditure over the total SBAs that could have been claimed in respect of it before the sale on the assumption that it had been in continuous qualifying use since first being brought into non-residential use; and
- the capital sum paid by P for the relevant interest.

[*CAA 2001, s 270EC; FA 2020, Sch 5 paras 2, 8; SI 2019 No 1087, Reg 2*].

Anti-avoidance

If, at any time, tax avoidance arrangements exist in relation to a building (whether or not a person with a relevant interest in the building is party to them), and a person would obtain an SBA-related tax advantage as a result, the advantage is to be counteracted by the making of such adjustments as are just and reasonable. Adjustments thus made may affect the tax treatment of persons other than the person in relation to whom the advantage is counteracted. An SBA-related tax advantage includes obtaining an SBA that is in any way more favourable to a person than the one that would otherwise be obtained. [*CAA 2001, s 270IB; SI 2019 No 1087, Reg 2*].

Additional VAT liabilities and rebates

The following applies if a person is entitled to an SBA by reference to qualifying expenditure (as in **9.23** above) that he has incurred, and he incurs an 'additional VAT liability' (see **9.2**(viii) above) in respect of that expenditure. For the purpose of calculating SBAs the qualifying expenditure is increased, at the beginning of the chargeable period (see **9.2**(i) above) in which the additional VAT liability accrues, by the amount of the liability. If, at the end of the writing-down period, the person who is entitled to an SBA by reference to qualifying expenditure is the person who incurred that expenditure, that person is entitled to an additional amount of SBA for the chargeable period in which the writing-down period ends. That amount is equal to the excess of the additional VAT liability over the total amount of SBAs to which the person has been entitled during the writing-down period in respect of that liability. In a case where an additional VAT rebate has also made to that person in respect of the qualifying expenditure, this additional amount is subject to the restriction below on the total amount of SBAs available.

The following applies if a person is entitled to an SBA by reference to qualifying expenditure that he has incurred, and an 'additional VAT rebate' (see **9.2**(viii) above) is made to that person in respect of that expenditure. For the purpose of calculating SBAs the qualifying expenditure is reduced, at the beginning of the chargeable period in which the additional VAT rebate accrues, by the amount of the rebate. The *total* amount of SBAs available by reference to the qualifying expenditure incurred by that person is restricted to the excess of the qualifying expenditure (including any additional VAT liability as above) over the additional VAT rebate.

[*CAA 2001, ss 270GA–270GC; SI 2019 No 1087, Reg 2*].

Co-ownership authorised contractual schemes (CoACS)

A CoACS (see **46.25** INVESTMENT FUNDS) is broadly transparent for tax purposes, i.e. the scheme itself incurs no tax liability. This means that its investors are treated as if they had invested directly in the underlying assets of the scheme and are subject to personal taxation accordingly. Provisions similar to those at **10.73** CAPITAL ALLOWANCES ON PLANT AND MACHINERY apply in relation to the SBA. This includes the making of an election whereby the operator of a CoACS carrying on a qualifying activity can elect to compute SBAs and allocate them to the investors.

An election under **10.73** (a plant and machinery election) made on or after 4 July 2019 automatically has effect for SBAs as well. If a plant and machinery election had already been made under the provisions at **10.73** CAPITAL ALLOWANCES ON PLANT AND MACHINERY, and an SBA is available by reference to a building which is subject to the scheme, the scheme operator has the option of withdrawing that election.

[*CAA 2001, ss 262AEA, 270IC–270IF; SI 2019 No 1087, Reg 2*].

Highway undertakings

For the purposes of the SBA, the carrying on of a highway undertaking (as defined) is treated as the carrying on of an undertaking by way of trade; and a person carrying on a highway undertaking is treated as occupying, for the purposes of the undertaking, any road in relation to which it is carried on. *CAA 2001, ss 270FA–270FC* deal with aspects of the SBA peculiar to highway undertakings.

Leases

A lease includes an agreement for a lease if the term to be covered by the lease has begun, a tenancy and, in the case of land outside the UK, an interest corresponding to a lease. There are rules that treat a lease as continuing in various circumstances, for example if it is renewed, extended or replaced. There are also rules dealing with certain events that may occur on the termination of a lease. For example, if another lease is then granted to a different lessee (B) and, in connection with the transaction, B pays a sum to the previous lessee (A), then the two leases are to be treated as if they were the same lease which had been assigned by A to B in consideration of the payment. [*CAA 2001, ss 270IK, 270IL; SI 2019 No 1087, Reg 2*].

Example

[9.27]

BM Ltd is an established company trading as car mechanics and preparing accounts to 31 March each year. In its 12-month period of account to 31 March 2021, the company incurs qualifying expenditure of £180,000 on the construction of a building on freehold land it holds in the UK, which it intends to use for the purposes of the trade. It begins to use the building for those purposes on 1 June 2021. BM Ltd can claim structures and buildings allowances as follows.

Y/e 31.3.21)

No allowance is due as the building has not been brought into qualifying use before the end of the accounting period.

Y/e 31.3.22)

The building is brought into qualifying use on 1 June 2021. The allowance is therefore due for the period 1 June 2021 to 31 March 2022 (304 days).

The allowance (to be deducted as an expense of the trade) is £180,000 × 3% × 304/365 = £4,498.

Y/e 31.3.23)

The allowance is £180,000 × 3% = £5,400

If BM Ltd continues to own the freehold and to carry on a qualifying activity, and the building is not demolished or brought into residential use, the company will continue to be entitled to an allowance of £5,400 for each accounting period up to and including the year ended 31 March 2054. For the year ended 31 March 2055, only the period up to 30 September 2054 falls within the period of 33⅓ years from first use, so the allowance will be £180,000 × 3% × 183/365 = £2,702. Allowances will then have been given on the full expenditure of £180,000 ((£5,400 x 32 years) + £4,498 + £2,702).

10

Capital Allowances on Plant and Machinery

Cross-references. See **9** CAPITAL ALLOWANCES for allowances on items other than plant or machinery.

Simon's Taxes. See B3.3.

Other sources. See Tolley's Capital Allowances.

Introduction to capital allowances on plant and machinery

[10.1] The law relating to capital allowances was consolidated in *Capital Allowances Act 2001* (*CAA 2001*) as part of the Tax Law Rewrite programme.

Capital allowances (balancing charges) are a deduction (addition) in computing the profits of trades and other qualifying activities for a 'chargeable period' (as in **10.2**(i) below). [*CAA 2001, s 2; SI 2019 No 1087, Reg 3(3)*].

For a full list of qualifying activities in relation to which plant and machinery allowances are available, see **10.4** below.

For commentary on devolution of the power to set the corporation tax rate in Northern Ireland to the Stormont Assembly and consequential modification of the capital allowance rules, see **1.1** INTRODUCTION: CHARGE TO TAX, RATES AND PROFIT COMPUTATIONS.

Matters of general application

[10.2] The following matters are pertinent to capital allowances generally.

(i) **Meaning of 'chargeable period'.** For corporation tax purposes, a '*chargeable period*' is an accounting period. [*CAA 2001, s 6(1)*].

(ii) **Claims.** A capital allowance claim under self-assessment must be included in the company tax return (or amended return) (see **65.4**, **65.6** RETURNS) for the accounting period for which the claim is made. It must specify the amount claimed, which must be expressed in figures at the time the claim is made.

The claim must be made (and may be amended or withdrawn) at any time up to the latest of:

- the first anniversary of the filing date for the company tax return;
- 30 days after closure of any enquiry into that return (unless the enquiry, being otherwise out of time, was limited, as referred to in **65.15** RETURNS, to matters to which a previous amendment making or withdrawing a capital allowance claim relates, or which are affected by the amendment);
- 30 days after notice of any amendment of that return by HMRC following such an enquiry; and
- 30 days after determination of any appeal against an amendment, or at a later time if HMRC allow it (for which see **51.3** LOSSES).

These time limits override the normal time limits for amendment of a company tax return. Amendments or withdrawals of claims must be made by amending the return.

If the effect of a claim is to reduce the available capital allowances for another accounting period for which a return has already been made, the company has 30 days to make the necessary amendments of that return. If it fails to do so, HMRC may, by written notice and subject to a right of appeal within 30 days of the issue of the notice, amend the return to correct the position (notwithstanding any time limit otherwise applicable).

[*CAA 2001, s 3; FA 1998, Sch 18 paras 78–83*].

In *Dundas Heritable Ltd v HMRC* UT, [2019] STC 1612, the company claimed capital allowances in returns submitted more than 12 months after the filing date (and therefore after the date in (a) above). HMRC opened enquiries into the returns, which were restricted only to the capital allowances claims. The company argued that, following the opening of the enquiry, the capital allowances claims were not out of time as they were made before the date in (b) above. The Upper Tribunal agreed with the company and confirmed the First-tier Tribunal's decision to allow its appeal.

(iii) **Capital expenditure and receipts.** References in the capital allowances legislation to the incurring of capital expenditure and the paying of capital sums exclude any sums allowed as deductions in computing the payer's profits or earnings and sums payable under deduction of tax. Corresponding rules apply as regards the receipt of such sums. [*CAA 2001, s 4, Sch 3 para 9*].

(iv) **Time expenditure incurred.** Capital expenditure (other than that constituted by an 'additional VAT liability' — see (viii) below) is generally treated, for capital allowances purposes, as incurred as soon as there is an unconditional obligation to pay it, even if all or part of it is not required to be paid until some later date.

However, expenditure is treated as incurred on a later date in the following circumstances.

- Where any part of the expenditure is not required to be paid until a date more than four months after the date determined as above, it is treated as incurred on that later date.
- Where an obligation to pay becomes unconditional earlier than in accordance with normal commercial usage, with the sole or main benefit likely to be the bringing forward of the chargeable period in which the expenditure would otherwise be treated as incurred, it is instead treated as incurred on the date on or before which it is required to be paid.

Where, as a result of an event such as the issuing of a certificate, an obligation to pay becomes unconditional within one month after the end of a chargeable period, but at or before the end of that chargeable period the asset concerned has become the property of, or is otherwise attributed under the contract to, the person having the obligation, the expenditure is treated as incurred immediately before the end of that chargeable period.

The above provisions do not override any specific rule under which expenditure is treated as incurred later than the relevant time given above.

[*CAA 2001, s 5*].

Simon's Taxes. See B3.104, B3.107.

(v) **Exclusion of double allowances.** No allowance under any of the codes covered in **9** CAPITAL ALLOWANCES (business premises renovation, research and development etc.) can be made in respect of any expenditure that has been allocated to a plant and machinery pool (see **10.26** below), and on which a plant or machinery allowance (or balancing charge) has consequently been given (or made). No allowance under any of those codes can be made in respect of the provision of any asset to which the allocated expenditure related. Expenditure which has attracted an allowance under any of those codes (and any asset to which that expenditure related) cannot be allocated to a plant and machinery pool.

Additional rules apply under *CAA 2001, s 9* to prevent double allowances in relation to plant or machinery treated as fixtures (as at **10.36** *et seq.* below). These do not prevent a person making a fixtures claim in respect of capital expenditure if the only previous claim was for industrial buildings allowances (now abolished), research and development allowances or business premises renovation allowances (now abolished), but see **10.45** below for restrictions on the amount of expenditure on which plant and machinery allowances can be claimed. [*CAA 2001, ss 7–10, Sch 3 para 10; SI 2019 No 1087, Reg 3(6)*].

Where an item of expenditure qualifies for more than one type of capital allowance, it is the taxpayer's choice as to which to claim, but he cannot alter his choice in later years. (HMRC Capital Allowances Manual CA16000, HMRC Brief 12/09, 31 March 2009).

Simon's Taxes. See **B3.114.**

(vi) **Expenditure met by another's contributions.** Subject to the exceptions below, a person is not regarded as incurring expenditure for capital allowances purposes to the extent that it is met, or will be met, directly or indirectly by another person or by a '*public body*', i.e. the Crown or any government or public or local authority (whether in the UK or elsewhere). For the scope of 'public authority', see *McKinney v Hagans Caravans (Manufacturing) Ltd* CA(NI) 1997, 69 TC 526. There is an exception where the expenditure is met by a Regional Development Grant or NI equivalent. In practice, applications for Regional Development Grants were no longer accepted after 31 March 1988, but NI equivalents did continue to be available until 31 March 2003. Expenditure met by insurance or other compensation money due in respect of a destroyed, demolished or defunct asset is not excluded from allowances. The above rule is disapplied, and allowances are thus available, if the contributor is not a public body and can obtain neither a capital allowance on his contribution by virtue of (vii) below nor a deduction against profits of a trade, profession or vocation or any qualifying activity within **10.4**(iii)–(vi) below. This does not apply for the purposes of structures and buildings allowance (see **9.22** CAPITAL ALLOWANCES). [*CAA 2001, ss 532–536, Sch 2 para 19, Sch 3 paras 106–108; SI 2019 No 1087, Reg 3(9)*].

Simon's Taxes. See **B3.111.**

(vii) **Contribution allowances.** Contributors towards another person's capital expenditure on plant or machinery may receive allowances ('*contribution allowances*') where the contribution is for the purposes of a trade or 'relevant activity' carried on (or to be carried on) by the contributor, and where the expenditure would otherwise have entitled the other person (assuming him not to be a public body) to plant and machinery allowances. Contribution allowances are not available where the contributor and the other person are CONNECTED PERSONS (**19**). A '*relevant activity*' is a profession or vocation or an activity within **10.4**(iii)–(vi) below.

Contribution allowances are such as would have been made if the contribution had been expended on the provision for the contributor's trade etc. of similar plant or machinery and as if the plant or machinery were at all material times used for the purposes of the contributor's trade etc. (so that balancing adjustments do not apply to such contributions). The contributor's deemed expenditure can only be allocated to a single asset pool (see **10.26** below). On a transfer of the trade etc., or part thereof, the allowances (or part) are subsequently made to the transferee.

[*CAA 2001, ss 537, 538, Sch 3 para 109*].

Capital contributions towards expenditure on dredging are treated as expenditure incurred by the contributor on that dredging. [*CAA 2001, s 543*].

Simon's Taxes. See **B3.112.**

(viii) **VAT capital goods scheme.** Under the VAT capital goods scheme, the input tax originally claimed on the acquisition of certain capital assets is subject to amendment within a specified period of adjustment in accordance with any increase or decrease in the extent to which the asset is used in making taxable, as opposed to exempt, supplies for VAT purposes.

The items covered by the scheme are limited to land and buildings (or parts of buildings) worth at least £250,000, computers (and items of computer equipment), aircraft, ships, boats or other vessels worth at least £50,000. See Tolley's Value Added Tax under Capital Goods Scheme for a full description.

Special capital allowances provisions apply where a VAT adjustment is made under the capital goods scheme.

'*Additional VAT liability*' and '*additional VAT rebate*' mean, respectively:

- an amount which a person becomes liable to pay, or
- an amount which he becomes entitled to deduct,

by way of adjustment under the VAT capital goods scheme in respect of input tax. Generally (but see below), such a liability or rebate is treated as incurred or made on the last day of the period:

- which is one of the periods making up the applicable VAT period of adjustment under the VAT capital goods scheme, and
- in which occurred the increase or decrease in use giving rise to the liability or rebate.

However, for the purpose of determining the chargeable period (see (i) above) in which it accrues, an additional VAT liability or rebate is treated as accruing on whichever is the relevant day below.

- Where the liability or rebate is accounted for in a VAT return, the last day of the period covered by that return.
- If, before the making of a VAT return, HMRC assess the liability or rebate, the day on which the assessment is made.
- If the trade (or other qualifying activity — see **10.4** below) is permanently discontinued before the liability or rebate has been accounted for in a VAT return and before the making of an assessment, the last day of the chargeable period in which the cessation occurs.

Where an allowance or charge falls to be determined by reference to a proportion only of the expenditure incurred or a proportion only of what that allowance or charge would otherwise have been, a related additional VAT liability or rebate is similarly apportioned.

[*CAA 2001, ss 546–551; SI 2019 No 1087, Reg 3(13)*].

Simon's Taxes. See **B3.103, B3.104.**

(ix) **Composite sales** may be apportioned by the Appeal Tribunal regardless of any separate prices attributed in the sale agreement. [*CAA 2001, ss 562–564*]. See *Fitton v Gilders & Heaton* Ch D 1955, 36 TC 233, and *Wood v Provan* CA 1968, 44 TC 701.
Simon's Taxes. See **B3.110.**

(x) **Finance leasing.** See **69.43** TRADING INCOME — DEDUCTIONS as regards restrictions on capital allowances where certain finance leasing arrangements are involved. These are disapplied in relation to long funding leases. See also **10.47** *et seq.*, **10.57**, **10.61**, **10.62** below.

(xi) **Recovery of assets under *Proceeds of Crime Act 2002, Pt 5*.** *Proceeds of Crime Act 2002, Pt 5 Ch 2* provides for the recovery, in civil proceedings before the High Court (or, in Scotland, the Court of Session), of property which is, or represents, property obtained through 'unlawful conduct' (as defined in the Act). If the Court is satisfied that any property is recoverable under the provisions, it will make a '*recovery order*', vesting the property in an appointed trustee for civil recovery. Alternatively, the Court may make an order under *s 276* of the *Act* staying (or, in Scotland, sisting) proceedings on terms agreed by the parties. The vesting of property in a trustee for civil recovery or any other person, either under a recovery order or in pursuance of a *s 276* order, is known as a *Pt 5* transfer. A '*compensating payment*' may in some cases be made to the person who held the property immediately before the transfer. If the order provides for the creation of any interest in favour of that person, he is treated as receiving (in addition to any other compensating payment) a compensating payment equal to the value of the interest. [*Proceeds of Crime Act 2002, ss 240(1), 266(1)(2), 276, 316(1), 448, Sch 10 para 2*].
Where the property in question is plant or machinery, the relevant interest in an industrial building or in a flat (within **9.6** CAPITAL ALLOWANCES), or an asset representing qualifying expenditure on research and development (within **9.20** CAPITAL ALLOWANCES), there are provisions to ensure that the *Pt 5* transfer has a tax-neutral effect, unless a compensating payment is made to the transferor in which case its amount and/or value must be brought into account as a disposal value or, as the case may be, as proceeds from a balancing event. [*Proceeds of Crime Act 2002, Sch 10 paras 12–29*].

Plant and machinery — qualifying expenditure

[10.3] Allowances are available in respect of 'qualifying expenditure' incurred by a person carrying on a trade or other 'qualifying activity' (see **10.4** below). Subject to **10.6–10.11** below and to other specific exclusions, expenditure is '*qualifying expenditure*' if it is 'capital expenditure' (see **10.2**(iii) above) incurred on the provision of plant or machinery wholly or partly for the purposes of the qualifying activity carried on by that person, and as a result of which that person owns the plant or machinery (for which see the paragraph on 'Ownership' in **10.16** below). [*CAA 2001, s 11*]. See **10.32** below as regards partial use for other purposes. Provided these tests are met (but subject to specific restrictions — see, for example, **10.61** below), it is irrelevant whether or not the object of the person incurring the expenditure was, or included, the obtaining of capital allowances (see the CA judgment in *Barclays Mercantile Business Finance Ltd v Mawson* HL 2004, 76 TC 446, a case involving complex finance leasing arrangements).

A scheme which sought to give a company capital allowances on an amount which was nearly double the expenditure which was actually incurred failed in *Cape Industries Ltd v HMRC* FTT (unreported). The company entered into a complex series of transactions involving a sale and leaseback of plant and machinery together with an option to repurchase. Following a detailed analysis of the line of cases beginning with *WT Ramsay Ltd v CIR* HL, [1981] STC 174, the Tribunal decided that, on a composite approach, CIS made no real disposals of the assets. (Note that the scheme would not now succeed, even if the *Ramsay* approach was disregarded, as a result of changes made by *FA 2011* to the long funding lease provisions.)

Expenditure incurred for the purposes of, and prior to the commencement of, a qualifying activity is treated as incurred on the first day on which the activity is carried on. [*CAA 2001, s 12*].

Expenditure incurred on the provision of plant or machinery for long funding leasing is excluded from being qualifying expenditure in the hands of the lessor (see **10.50** below). See **10.36** *et seq.* below as regards fixtures which become part of land or buildings.

Whether plant or machinery is acquired new or second-hand is generally irrelevant (but see **10.61** below as regards certain sales between connected persons etc.). A *share* in plant or machinery can qualify for allowances [*CAA 2001, s 270*].

See also Eligible expenditure at **10.6–10.11** below.

Simon's Taxes. See **B3.305.**

Plant and machinery — qualifying activities

[10.4] Any of the following is a '*qualifying activity*':

(i) a trade, profession or vocation;
(ii) an employment or office;
(iii) a UK property business or overseas property business (see **60** PROPERTY INCOME);
(iv) a UK furnished holiday lettings business or overseas furnished holiday lettings business (see **60.7** PROPERTY INCOME);
(v) any of the concerns listed in *CTA 2009, s 39(4)* (mines, quarries and sundry other undertakings);
(vi) managing the investments of a company with investment business (see **45** INVESTMENT COMPANIES AND INVESTMENT BUSINESS);
(vii) special leasing, i.e. the hiring out of plant or machinery otherwise than in the course of another qualifying activity (see **10.54** below),

but (other than for the purposes of **10.55** and **10.59** below) to the extent only that the profits therefrom are within the charge to UK tax (or would be if there *were* any profits).

Foreign permanent establishments

If an election is made under *CTA 2009, s 18A* to exempt from UK corporation tax the profits arising from foreign permanent establishments of a UK company, then a business carried on through one or more such permanent establishments is treated as an activity separate from any other activity of the company. For the above purposes, that activity is regarded as an activity the profits from which (if any) are *not* within the charge to UK tax. However, neither of these rules applies insofar as the business consists of a plant or machinery lease under which the company is a lessor if any profits or losses arising from the lease are to be left out of account by virtue of *CTA 2009, s 18C*. See **31.15** DOUBLE TAX RELIEF for details.

[*CAA 2001, ss 15–17, 17A, 17B, 18, 19(1), 20*].

Dwelling-houses

As regards (iii) and (vii) above, expenditure in providing plant or machinery for use in a dwelling-house (or flat — see HMRC Capital Allowances Manual CA20020, 20040) is not qualifying expenditure. Expenditure on plant or machinery partly for such use is apportioned as is just and reasonable. [*CAA 2001, s 35*]. See HMRC Brief 45/10, 22 October 2010 as regards the meaning of 'dwelling-house' generally and university halls of residence in particular.

Simon's Taxes. See B3.304.

Making of allowances and charges

[10.5] Where the qualifying activity is within **10.4**(i) or (iii)–(v) above, plant and machinery allowances are treated as expenses of, and balancing charges are treated as receipts of, the qualifying activity. [*CAA 2001, ss 247–250, 250A, 252*].

Allowances and charges are computed for corporation tax purposes by reference to events in accounting periods (see **10.2**(i) above). [*CAA 2001, ss 2(1), 6(1)*].

As regards **10.4**(vi) above, see **45.4** INVESTMENT COMPANIES AND INVESTMENT BUSINESS. As regards a qualifying activity of special leasing (as in **10.4**(vii) above), see **10.54** below.

See **10.2**(ii) above as regards the *claiming* of capital allowances.

Simon's Taxes. See B3.380.

Eligible expenditure

[10.6] The capital expenditure eligible for allowances includes that on alteration of existing buildings incidental to the installation of plant or machinery for the purposes of a trade or other qualifying activity [*CAA 2001, s 25*] and on demolition of plant or machinery which it replaces [*CAA 2001, s 26(1)(2)*]. There is, however, a distinction between alterations incidental to the installation of plant or machinery and alterations consequential upon the installation of plant or machinery (*J D Wetherspoon plc v HMRC* UT, [2012] UKUT 42 (TCC)); the Tribunal report includes detailed consideration of the application of *CAA 2001, s 25* in the context of a public house.

Costs of moving plant from one site to another and re-erecting it, so far as not deductible in computing profits, qualify for allowances (HMRC Capital Allowances Manual CA21190). Capital expenditure on animals and other living creatures kept for the purposes of farming or any other trade, or on shares in such animals etc., is excluded. [*CAA 2001, s 38*].

Depreciation

Where it appears that any sums, not otherwise taxable, are to be payable, directly or indirectly, to the owner of plant or machinery in respect of, or to take account of, the *whole* of the depreciation of that plant or machinery, the expenditure incurred in providing that plant or machinery for the purposes of the qualifying activity is not qualifying expenditure. [*CAA 2001, s 37*]. As regards subsidies towards *partial* depreciation, see **10.74** below.

Simon's Taxes. See **B3.305–312**.

Meaning of plant or machinery

[10.7] 'Plant' and 'machinery' are not statutorily defined; instead case law is heavily relied upon. '*Machinery*' is given its ordinary meaning, but '*plant*' has been considered in many cases before the courts and tribunals.

Plant includes apparatus kept for permanent employment in the trade etc., but a line is drawn between that which performs a function in the business operations (which may be plant) and that which provides the place or setting in which these operations are performed (which is not). See *Cole Bros Ltd v Phillips* HL 1982, 55 TC 188 (electric wiring and fittings in department store held not to be plant) and *St. John's School v Ward* CA 1974, 49 TC 524 (prefabricated school buildings held not to be plant) and contrast *CIR v Barclay, Curle & Co Ltd* HL 1969, 45 TC 221 (dry docks, including cost of excavation, held to be plant) and *CIR v Scottish & Newcastle Breweries Ltd HL* 1982, 55 TC 252 (lighting and decor of licensed premises held to be plant). If an item used for carrying on a business does not form part of the premises and is not stock-in-trade, then it is plant (*Wimpy International Ltd v Warland* CA 1988, 61 TC 51).

Permanent employment in the trade

Permanent employment demands some degree of durability, see *Hinton v Maden & Ireland Ltd* HL 1959, 38 TC 391 (shoe manufacturer's knives and lasts, average life three years, held to be plant). In practice, a life of two years or more is sufficient, and this applies equally as regards animals functioning as apparatus with which a trade is carried on (see HMRC Capital Allowances Manual CA21100, 21220).

Held to be plant

Movable office partitions (*Jarrold v John Good & Sons Ltd* CA 1962, 40 TC 681); mezzanine platforms installed in a warehouse (but not ancillary lighting) (*Hunt v Henry Quick Ltd* Ch D 1992, 65 TC 108); swimming pools for use on caravan site (*Cooke v Beach Station Caravans Ltd* Ch D 1974, 49 TC 514); grain silos (*Schofield v R & H Hall Ltd* CA(NI) 1974, 49 TC 538); barrister's books (*Munby v Furlong* CA 1977, 50 TC 491); Building Society window screens (*Leeds Permanent Building Society v Proctor* Ch D 1982, 56 TC 293); light fittings (*Wimpy International Ltd v Warland* CA 1988, 61 TC 51; *J D Wetherspoon plc v HMRC* UT, [2012] UKUT 42 (TCC)); synthetic grass football pitch (*CIR v Anchor International Ltd* CS 2005, 77 TC 38); wooden gazebo placed in garden of public house to provide shelter (*Andrew v HMRC* FTT (TC 799), [2011] SFTD 145).

Held not to be plant

Stallions (*Earl of Derby v Aylmer* KB 1915, 6 TC 665); wallpaper pattern books (*Rose & Co Ltd v Campbell* Ch D 1967, 44 TC 500); canopy over petrol-filling station (*Dixon v Fitch's Garage Ltd* Ch D 1975, 50 TC 509); ship used as floating restaurant (*Benson v Yard Arm Club Ltd* CA 1979, 53 TC 67); false ceilings (*Hampton v Fortes Autogrill Ltd* Ch D 1979, 53 TC 691); a football stand (*Brown v Burnley Football Co Ltd* Ch D 1980, 53 TC 357); an inflatable tennis court cover (*Thomas v Reynolds* Ch D 1987, 59 TC 502); shop fronts, wall and floor coverings, suspended floors, ceilings and stairs etc. (*Wimpy International Ltd v Warland, Associated Restaurants Ltd v Warland* CA 1988, 61 TC 51); permanent quarantine kennels (allowances having been granted for movable kennels) (*Carr v Sayer* Ch D 1992, 65 TC 15); lighting ancillary to mezzanine platform installation qualifying as plant (*Hunt v Henry Quick Ltd* Ch D 1992, 65 TC 108); a planteria (a form of glasshouse — see also **10.8** below) (*Gray v Seymours Garden Centre (Horticulture)* CA 1995, 67 TC 401); access site and wash hall containing car wash equipment (*Attwood v Anduff Car Wash Ltd* CA 1997, 69 TC 575); housing for underground electricity sub-station (*Bradley v London Electricity plc* Ch D 1996, 70 TC 155); golf putting greens (*Family Golf Centres Ltd v Thorne* (Sp C 150), [1998] SSCD 106); an all-weather horse racing track (*Shove v Lingfield Park 1991 Ltd* CA 2004, 76 TC 363); decorative wood panelling and toilet cubicle walls and doors in a public house (*J D Wetherspoon plc v HMRC* UT, [2012] UKUT 42 (TCC)); valeting bay used by garage to apply glasscoat finishes to cars (*Rogate Services Ltd v HMRC* FTT, [2014] UKFTT 312(TC); 2014 STI 2092); the cost of launching leased satellites into orbit (*Inmarsat Global Ltd v HMRC* UT, [2021] STC 713); underground gas storage cavities (*Cheshire Cavity Storage 1 Ltd and another v HMRC* UT, [2021] STC 675).

In *McVeigh v Arthur Sanderson & Sons Ltd* Ch D 1968, 45 TC 273, held that cost of blocks etc. of a wallpaper manufacturer (admitted to be plant) should include something for the designs but the designs, following *Daphne v Shaw* KB 1926, 11 TC 256, were not plant. (*Daphne v Shaw* has since been overruled by *Munby v Furlong* above.)

Borrowings

Interest etc. on money borrowed to finance purchases of plant and charged to capital, held not eligible for capital allowances (*Ben-Odeco Ltd v Powlson* HL 1978, 52 TC 459 and cf *Van Arkadie v Sterling Coated Materials Ltd* Ch D 1982, 56 TC 479). In *HMRC v Tower MCashback LLP 1 and another* SC, [2011] STC 1143, by virtue of an arrangement involving 75% of the purchase price being funded by the making of non-recourse loans (on extreme terms) to the partners, the price ostensibly paid by an LLP for software was vastly in excess of its true market value. The CA concluded that the terms of the borrowing should be considered in relation to the fundamental question of whether the taxpayer suffered the economic burden of paying the full amount and that on this basis capital allowances were available on the full price. The Supreme Court disagreed, holding that the LLPs were entitled only to 25% of the allowances which they had claimed. Lord Walker held that the composite transactions in this case 'did not, on a realistic appraisal of the facts, meet the test laid down by the Capital Allowances Act, which requires real expenditure for the real purpose of acquiring plant for use in a trade'.

Buildings

[10.8] See **10.10** below for allowances for expenditure on integral features (as defined) of buildings and structures.

See **10.11** below for provisions restricting allowances for certain expenditure on buildings and structures.

Certain expenditure on buildings, as below, is treated for capital allowance purposes as being on plant and machinery (unless tax relief could otherwise be obtained). On any disposal, the disposal value (see **10.27** below) in respect of expenditure within (i) and (ii) below is taken as nil [*CAA 2001, s 63(5)*].

(i) Expenditure on *thermal insulation of existing building* by a person occupying the building for the purposes of a trade carried on by him or letting the building in the course of a UK property business or overseas property business (other than a furnished holiday lettings business). This measure is subject to the overriding rule, where the building is let, that expenditure incurred in providing plant or machinery for use in a *dwelling-house* cannot be qualifying expenditure (see **10.3** above); in addition, expenditure is not qualifying expenditure if a deduction is available for it under the rules for landlord's expenditure on energy-saving items at **60.4** PROPERTY INCOME or would be so available if the expenditure did not potentially attract capital allowances. Expenditure incurred within this category qualifies for writing-down allowances at the special rate (see **10.28** below); expenditure incurred on or before that date qualified for the normal writing-down allowances at **10.26** below. [*CAA 2001, ss 27, 28*].

(ii) *Hotels and restaurants.* HMRC regard as eligible for capital allowances expenditure on *apparatus* to provide electric light or power, hot water, central heating, ventilation or air conditioning, alarm and sprinkler systems. Also on cost of hot water pipes, baths, wash basins etc. (CCAB Statement, 9 August 1977.) See now *Cole Bros Ltd v Phillips* HL 1982, 55 TC 188 and *CIR v Scottish & Newcastle Breweries Ltd* HL 1982, 55 TC 252.

See generally HMRC Capital Allowances Manual CA21000 *et seq.*

Professional fees

Fees such as survey fees, architects' fees, quantity surveyors' fees, structural engineers' fees, service engineers' fees or legal costs, only qualify as expenditure on the provision of plant or machinery if they relate directly to the acquisition, transport and installation of the plant or machinery. Where professional fees are paid in connection with a building project that includes the provision of plant or machinery, only the part, if any, which relates to services that can properly be regarded as on the provision of plant or machinery can be qualifying expenditure for plant or machinery allowances.

Preliminary expenses

The same applies to preliminary expenses, e.g. site management, insurance, general purpose labour, temporary accommodation and security, in connection with a building project. (HMRC Capital Allowances Manual CA20070). Where preliminary expenses are allocatable or apportionable to expenditure on alterations to a building incidental to the installation of plant or machinery they can rank as eligible expenditure so long as the cost of the alterations is eligible expenditure (*J D Wetherspoon plc v HMRC* UT, [2012] UKUT 42 (TCC)).

Cable television

The cost of provision and installation of ducting in connection with construction of cable television networks is regarded as expenditure on plant or machinery (Revenue Press Release 15 March 1984).

Glasshouses and polytunnels

Glasshouses are likely to be accepted as plant only where, during construction, sophisticated environmental control systems are permanently installed, incorporating e.g. a computer system controlling heating, temperature and humidity control, automatic ventilation systems and automatic thermal or shade screens (HMRC Capital Allowances Manual CA22090). See, for example, *Gray v Seymours Garden Centre (Horticulture)* CA, 67 TC 401, where a 'planteria' was held to be premises. See also **10.11** below and, as regards whether glasshouses are 'long-life assets', **10.34** below.

As regards polytunnels, used mainly by the farming and horticulture industry, see HMRC Capital Allowances Manual CA22090, and see HMRC Brief 32/12, December 2012.

Pig industry

HMRC have published guidance illustrating the range of assets on which the pig industry might claim plant and machinery capital allowances (HMRC Brief 03/10, February 2010).

Slurry storage systems

Slurry storage systems, used for the temporary storage of slurry, qualify as plant or machinery, but any building or structure which is part of a slurry storage facility does not qualify (HMRC Brief 66/08, 29 December 2008).

Simon's Taxes. See **B3.308, B3.310.**

Computer software

[10.9] Where capital expenditure is incurred on the acquisition of computer software for the purposes of a trade or other qualifying activity, the software, if it would not otherwise be plant, is treated as such for capital allowances purposes. Similarly, where capital expenditure is incurred after that date in acquiring for such purposes a right to use or otherwise deal with computer software, both the right and the software are treated as plant provided for the purposes of the qualifying activity and (so long as entitlement to the right continues) as belonging to the person incurring the expenditure.

Where a right is granted to another person to use or deal with the whole or part of software or rights which are treated as plant, and the consideration for the grant consists of (or would if it were in money consist of) a capital sum, a disposal value (see **10.27** below) has to be brought into account (unless the software or rights have previously begun to be used wholly or partly for purposes other than those of the qualifying activity, or the activity for which they were used has been permanently discontinued). The amount of the disposal value to be brought into account is the net consideration in money received for the grant, plus any insurance moneys or other capital compensation received in respect of the software by reason of any event affecting that consideration. However, market value is substituted where the consideration for the grant was not, or not wholly, in money, or where:

- no consideration, or money consideration less than market value, was given for the grant;
- there is no charge under *ITEPA 2003* (i.e. on employment, pension or social security income); and
- the grantee cannot obtain plant and machinery or research and development allowances for his expenditure or is a dual resident investing company connected with the grantor.

Where a disposal value falls to be calculated in relation to software or rights, then for the purpose of determining whether it is to be limited by reference to the capital expenditure incurred (see **10.27** below), that disposal value is increased by any disposal value previously falling to be brought into account as above in respect of the same person and the same plant.

[*CAA 2001, ss 71–73, Sch 3 para 18*].

See **42.4** INTANGIBLE ASSETS for the extent to which computer software may be included in that regime (and hence excluded from the above provisions).

Simon's Taxes. See **B3.341.**

Integral features of buildings and structures

[10.10] Where a person incurs expenditure on the provision of an 'integral feature' of a building or structure used by him for the purposes of a qualifying activity (see **10.4** above) that he carries on, that expenditure is treated for the purposes of plant and machinery allowances as qualifying expenditure on plant or machinery. Expenditure so treated qualifies for writing-down allowances at the special rate (see **10.28** below). No deduction is then available for the expenditure in calculating income from the activity (whether or not such a deduction would be available under general principles).

For these purposes, an '*integral feature*' is any of the following:

- an electrical system (including a lighting system);
- a cold water system;
- a space or water heating system, a powered system of ventilation, air cooling or air purification, and any floor or ceiling comprised in such a system;
- a lift, escalator or moving walkway; or
- external solar shading.

The above list is not, however, to be taken as including any asset whose principal purpose is to insulate or enclose the interior of a building or to provide an interior floor, wall or ceiling which is intended to remain permanently in place. The Treasury may vary the above list by statutory instrument, but they can add an asset only if it would not otherwise qualify for plant and machinery allowances and can remove an asset only if it would thereby qualify for plant and machinery allowances at a rate other than the special rate.

Expenditure incurred on the *replacement* of an integral feature also qualifies as above. For this purpose, an integral feature is treated as replaced if the amount of the expenditure is more than half the cost of replacing the feature at the time the expenditure is incurred. If a person incurs expenditure which does not meet this test but, within twelve months, incurs further expenditure on the integral feature, the test is again applied but by reference to the aggregate expenditure. If the aggregate amount is more than half the cost of replacing the feature at the time the initial expenditure was incurred, both the initial expenditure and the further expenditure qualifies. It is not a requirement that the further expenditure be incurred in the same chargeable period as the initial expenditure; the tax return covering the earlier chargeable period can be amended if necessary.

[*CAA 2001, ss 33A, 33B*].

Simon's Taxes. See **B3.345**.

Restrictions on eligible expenditure

[10.11] Certain expenditure is excluded from the definition of plant and machinery for capital allowances purposes.

General exceptions

Expenditure falling within any of *CAA 2001, ss 28–32, 71* (relating to thermal insulation and computer software — see **10.6–10.9** above) is not affected by the legislation described below. The same applies to expenditure within *CAA 2001, s 33A* (integral features of buildings and structures — see **10.10** above). [*CAA 2001, s 23(1)(2)*].

Expenditure on buildings which does not qualify for allowances

Expenditure on the construction or acquisition of a building does not qualify for plant and machinery allowances (subject to the general exceptions above and the specific exceptions listed at (1)–(32) below). For these purposes the expression 'building' includes:

- any assets incorporated in the building;
- any assets which, although not incorporated in the building (because they are movable or for some other reason), are nevertheless of a kind which are normally incorporated into buildings; and
- any of the following:
  - (i) walls, floors, ceilings, doors, gates, shutters, windows and stairs;
  - (ii) mains services, and systems, of water, electricity and gas;
  - (iii) waste disposal systems;
  - (iv) sewerage and drainage systems;
  - (v) shafts or other structures in which lifts, hoists, escalators and moving walkways are installed; and
  - (vi) fire safety systems.

[*CAA 2001, s 21; FA 2019, s 35*].

Expenditure on structures which does not qualify for allowances

'*Structure*' means a fixed structure of any kind, other than a building. A structure is 'any substantial man-made asset' (see Revenue Press Release 17 December 1993).

Expenditure on the construction or acquisition of a structure or any other asset listed immediately below, or on any works involving the alteration of land, does not qualify for plant and machinery allowances (subject to the general exceptions above and the specific exceptions listed at (1)–(32) below).

(a) A tunnel, bridge, viaduct, aqueduct, embankment or cutting.
(b) A way, hard standing (such as a pavement), road, railway, tramway, a park for vehicles or containers, or an airstrip or runway.
(c) An inland navigation, including a canal or basin or a navigable river.
(d) A dam, reservoir or barrage (including any sluices, gates, generators and other equipment associated with it).
(e) A dock, harbour, wharf, pier, marina or jetty, or any other structure in or at which vessels may be kept or merchandise or passengers may be shipped or unshipped.
(f) A dike, sea wall, weir or drainage ditch.
(g) Any structure not included above, except:
  - (i) a structure (other than a building) within the definition of an 'industrial building';
  - (ii) a structure in use for the purposes of a gas undertaking; or
  - (iii) a structure in use for the purposes of a trade consisting in the provision of telecommunications, television or radio services,

  and see *CIR v Anchor International Ltd CS 2005, 77 TC 38*, in which a synthetic football pitch was held not to be within this exclusion.

[*CAA 2001, s 22, Sch 3 para 13; FA 2019, s 35*].

In the context of item (a), in *HMRC v SSE Generation Ltd* CA, [2021] STC 369, the Court of Appeal held that a tunnel was something along which people or vehicles are intended to travel and not simply any subterranean passage, and an aqueduct was a bridge or viaduct-like structure which carries a canal.

Specific exceptions

The above exclusions do not affect the question as to whether expenditure on any of the items listed in (1)–(32) below qualifies for plant and machinery allowances. Note that items (1)–(15) below do not include any asset whose principal purpose is to insulate or enclose the interior of a building or to provide an interior wall, floor or ceiling which (in each case) is intended to remain permanently in place.

(1) Any machinery (including devices for providing motive power) not within any other item in this list.
(2) Gas and sewerage systems provided mainly to meet the particular requirements of the qualifying activity, or provided mainly to serve particular plant or machinery used for the purposes thereof.
(3) Manufacturing or processing equipment; storage equipment, including cold rooms; display equipment; and counters, checkouts and similar equipment.
(4) Cookers, washing machines, dishwashers, refrigerators and similar equipment; washbasins, sinks, baths, showers, sanitary ware and similar equipment; and furniture and furnishings.
(5) Hoists.
(6) Sound insulation provided mainly to meet the particular requirements of the qualifying activity.
(7) Computer, telecommunication and surveillance systems (including their wiring or other links).
(8) Refrigeration or cooling equipment.
(9) Fire alarm systems; sprinkler and other equipment for extinguishing or containing fires.
(10) Burglar alarm systems.
(11) Strong rooms in bank or building society premises; safes.
(12) Partition walls, where movable and intended to be moved in the course of the qualifying activity.
(13) Decorative assets provided for the enjoyment of the public in hotel, restaurant or similar trades.
(14) Advertising hoardings; signs, displays and similar assets.
(15) Swimming pools (including diving boards, slides and structures on which such boards or slides are mounted).
(16) Any glasshouse constructed so that the required environment (namely, air, heat, light, irrigation and temperature) for the growing of plants is provided automatically by means of devices forming an integral part of its structure; see also below.
(17) Cold stores.
(18) Caravans provided mainly for holiday lettings. (Under *CAA 2001, s 23(5)*, 'caravan' includes, in relation to a holiday caravan site, anything treated as such for the purposes of the *Caravan Sites and Control of Development Act 1960* (or NI equivalent).

(19) Buildings provided for testing aircraft engines run within the building.
(20) Movable buildings intended to be moved in the course of the qualifying activity.
(21) The alteration of land for the purpose only of installing plant or machinery (and see below).
(22) The provision of dry docks.
(23) The provision of any jetty or similar structure provided mainly to carry plant or machinery.
(24) The provision of pipelines, or underground ducts or tunnels with a primary purpose of carrying utility conduits.
(25) The provision of towers provided to support floodlights.
(26) The provision of any reservoir incorporated into a water treatment works or any service reservoir of treated water for supply within any housing estate or other particular locality.
(27) The provision of silos provided for temporary storage; or storage tanks.
(28) The provision of slurry pits or silage clamps.
(29) The provision of fish tanks or fish ponds.
(30) The provision of rails, sleepers and ballast for a railway or tramway.
(31) The provision of structures and other assets for providing the setting for any ride at an amusement park or exhibition.
(32) The provision of fixed zoo cages.

[*CAA 2001, s 23(3)–(5)*].

However, for capital allowances claims made on or after 29 October 2018, nothing in the above list (1)–(32) enables allowances to be claimed on costs relating to plant or machinery which is itself ineligible under *CAA 2001, s 21* or *s 22* above. [*CAA 2001, ss 21(4), 22(4); FA 2019, s 35*]. In particular, this seeks to ensure that expenditure on the alteration of land (item 21 above) will be eligible for capital allowances only where the alteration is made for the purpose of installing *eligible* plant or machinery. This partly reverses a decision of the FTT in *SSE Generation Ltd v HMRC* FTT (TC 6618), [2018] UKFTT 416 (TC). (Note that the decision of the Court of Appeal (see above) was on different grounds.)

As regards expenditure on *glasshouses* (item 16 above), see **10.8** above for the HMRC approach to allowances for such expenditure, and **10.34** below as to whether glasshouses are 'long-life assets'.

In *May v HMRC* FTT, [2019] UKFTT 32 (TC), 2019 SWTI 510, a facility built on a farm for drying, conditioning and storing grain after harvest was held to be a silo within (27) above.

Interests in land

Expenditure on the provision of plant or machinery does not include expenditure incurred on the acquisition of an interest in land, but this restriction does not apply to any asset which is so installed or otherwise fixed in or to any description of land as to become, in law, part of that land. 'Land' does not include buildings or other structures but is otherwise as defined in *Interpretation Act 1978, Sch 1*. 'Interest in land' for these purposes has the same meaning as in *CAA 2001, s 175* (allowances for fixtures — see **10.36** *et seq.* below). [*CAA 2001, s 24*].

Simon's Taxes. See B3.308.

Annual investment allowance

[10.12] A person is entitled to an annual investment allowance (AIA) for a chargeable period (see **10.2**(i) above) in respect of any 'AIA qualifying expenditure' which he incurs in that period on plant or machinery which he owns at some time during that period. Subject to the exclusions below, qualifying expenditure (see **10.3** above) is '*AIA qualifying expenditure*' if it is incurred by a company (or by an individual or a partnership made up entirely of individuals, as regards which see the corresponding chapter of Tolley's Income Tax). In determining whether expenditure is AIA qualifying expenditure, any effect of *CAA 2001, s 12* (pre-commencement expenditure — see **10.3** above) on the time at which it is to be treated as incurred is disregarded. As regards ownership of plant or machinery, see **10.16** below under *Ownership*.

Amount of the AIA

The maximum AIA is as follows.

For expenditure incurred on and after 1 January 2022	£200,000
For expenditure incurred on and after 1 January 2019 and before 1 January 2022	**£1,000,000**
For expenditure incurred on and after 1 January 2016 and before 1 January 2019.	£200,000

The increased maximum of £1,000,000 was originally intended to come to an end on 31 December 2020, but *FA 2021* has extended it for a further year.

The amount of the AIA available is either the maximum as above or the actual amount of the AIA qualifying expenditure, whichever is the lower. A company may choose to claim less than the full AIA available. The above maximum is proportionately increased, or reduced, if the chargeable period is more than, or less than, twelve months.

Periods straddling 1 January 2022

Where a chargeable period straddles 1 January 2022, the maximum for that period is the sum of:

- the entitlement, based on the previous £1 million maximum, for the portion of the chargeable period ending on 31 December 2021, and
- the entitlement, based on the new £200,000 maximum, for the portion of the chargeable period beginning on 1 January 2022,

as if those portions were separate chargeable periods.

Thus, if exactly half of the chargeable period fell before 1 January 2022, the maximum for the full chargeable period would be £600,000 (half of £1 million plus half of £200,000) or, if lower, the amount of the AIA qualifying expenditure. This is subject to an overriding rule, as regards expenditure incurred in the part of the chargeable period falling after 31 December 2021, that no more than the appropriate proportion of £200,000 can qualify for the AIA. So if the business in this example incurred, say, £550,000 of AIA qualifying expenditure in the chargeable period but all of it was incurred in the second half of that period, the AIA for the chargeable period would be restricted to £100,000 (half of £200,000).

Periods straddling 1 January 2019

Where a chargeable period straddles 1 January 2019, the maximum for that period is the sum of:

- the entitlement, based on the previous £200,000 maximum, for the portion of the chargeable period ending on 31 December 2018, and
- the entitlement, based on the new £1 million maximum, for the portion of the chargeable period beginning on 1 January 2019,

as if those portions were separate chargeable periods.

Thus, if exactly one-quarter of a chargeable period fell before 1 January 2019, the maximum for the full chargeable period would be £800,000 (one-quarter of £200,000 plus three-quarters of £1 million) or, if lower, the amount of the AIA qualifying expenditure. This is subject to an overriding rule that no more than £200,000 of expenditure incurred in the part of the chargeable period falling before 1 January 2019 can qualify for the AIA. So if the business in this example incurred, say, £700,000 of AIA qualifying expenditure in the chargeable period but all of it was incurred in the first quarter of that period, the AIA for the chargeable period would be restricted to £200,000.

Basic rules

The AIA is made for the chargeable period in which the AIA qualifying expenditure is incurred. (See **10.2**(iv) above as regards the date on which expenditure is treated as having been incurred.)

The taxpayer is free to decide how to allocate the AIA between different classes of AIA qualifying expenditure; he might, for example, choose to allocate it to expenditure qualifying for writing-down allowances at the special rate in priority to expenditure qualifying at the normal rate.

An AIA and an FYA cannot be claimed in respect of the same expenditure (see **10.14** below).

If expenditure is incurred partly for the purposes of a qualifying activity and partly for other purposes, any resultant AIA must be reduced as is just and reasonable.

See **10.26** below for how the AIA interacts with writing-down allowances.

Exclusions

Expenditure is not AIA qualifying expenditure in any of the following circumstances.

(i) The expenditure is incurred in the chargeable period in which the qualifying activity is permanently discontinued.

(ii) The expenditure is incurred on the provision of a '*car*', defined for these purposes (by *CAA 2001, s 268A*) as a mechanically propelled road vehicle which is neither (1) of a construction primarily suited for the conveyance of goods or burden of any description nor (2) of a type not commonly used as a private vehicle and unsuitable for such use. Motor cycles do qualify for the AIA. It is confirmed on page 12 of an HMRC Technical Note published in December 2008 ('Modernising tax relief for business expenditure on cars') that the above definition means that black hackney cabs (e.g. London taxis) are not regarded as cars for this purpose. A double cab pick-up may also qualify as a car — see HMRC Employment Income Manual EIM23150, and see **10.76** below.

As regards (2), see employee benefits case of *Gurney v Richards* Ch D, [1989] STC 682 (fire brigade car equipped with flashing light held within excluded class), decided on similarly worded legislation (see **21.23** CONTROLLED FOREIGN COMPANIES). See also *Bourne v Auto School of Motoring* Ch D 1964, 42 TC 217 (driving school cars) and *Roberts v Granada TV Rental Ltd* Ch D 1970, 46 TC 295 (mini-vans etc.).

(iii) The provision of the plant or machinery is connected with a change in the nature or conduct of a trade or business carried on by a person other than the person incurring the expenditure on its provision, and the obtaining of an AIA was the main benefit, or one of the main benefits, which could reasonably be expected to arise from the making of the change.

(iv) The provision of the plant of machinery is by way of gift (see **10.68** below).

(v) The plant or machinery was previously used by the owner for purposes other than those of the qualifying activity (see **10.69** below), which includes the purposes of long funding leasing (see **10.50** below).

In addition, if an arrangement is entered into and a main purpose of it is to enable a person to claim an AIA to which he would not otherwise be entitled, the AIA is not made or, if already made, is withdrawn.

See also the anti-avoidance rules at **10.61** below which restrict a buyer's entitlement to AIAs in certain types of transaction.

Restrictions

Restrictions apply as set out below. Where more than one chargeable period ends in the same financial year (i.e. a year beginning on 1 April), each such period must be considered separately, i.e. as if it were the only chargeable period ending in that year, in determining if any of restrictions 2 to 4 apply.

Restriction 1: single companies

Only one AIA is available to a company for a chargeable period for all qualifying activities carried on by it. The AIA may be allocated to the qualifying expenditure as the company sees fit.

Restriction 2: groups of companies

Where a 'group' of companies subsists in any financial year, only one AIA is available to the group. The AIA may be allocated, as the group sees fit, to qualifying expenditure incurred by group companies for chargeable periods ending in the financial year in question. For this purpose, a '*group*' comprises a parent company (as defined in *Companies Act 2006, s 1162*) and its subsidiaries. A company (P) is the parent of another company (C) in a financial year if P is a parent of C at the end of C's chargeable period ending in that financial year.

Restriction 3: groups of companies under common control

Where, in a financial year, two or more groups are under common 'control' and 'related' to one another, only one AIA is available to the companies that are members of those groups. The AIA may be allocated, as the companies see fit, to qualifying expenditure incurred by those companies for chargeable periods ending in the financial year in question. A '*group*' is defined similarly as for restriction 2 above.

For this purpose, a company is controlled by a person in a financial year if it is controlled by that person at the end of its chargeable period ending in that financial year. A group of companies is controlled by a person in a financial year if the parent company is controlled by that person at the end of its chargeable period ending in that financial year. '*Control*' of a company means the power of a person to secure, by means of shareholding or voting control or as a result of any powers conferred by the articles of association or other regulatory document, that the affairs of the company are conducted in accordance with that person's wishes.

A company (C1) is '*related*' to another company (C2) in a financial year if they meet either of the two conditions below (or both of them). If C1 is thereby related to C2, C1 is also related to any other company to which C2 is related. A group of companies (G1) is related to another group of companies (G2) in a financial year if a company which is a member of G1 is related to a company which is a member of G2. If G1 is related to G2, G1 is also related to any other group of companies to which G2 is related.

The conditions are as follows.

(1) The shared premises condition. This condition is met in relation to two companies in a financial year if, at the end of the 'relevant chargeable period' of one or both companies, the companies carry on qualifying activities from the same premises.

(2) The similar activities condition. This condition is met in relation to two companies in a financial year if:
  - more than 50% of the turnover of one company for the 'relevant chargeable period' is derived from qualifying activities within a particular NACE classification; and
  - more than 50% of the turnover of the other company for the 'relevant chargeable period' is derived from qualifying activities within that same NACE classification.

  NACE classification means the first level of the common statistical classification of economic activities in the EU established by Regulation (EC) No 1893/2006 of the European Parliament and the Council of 20 December 2006. NACE is a well established statutory industry classification system. The first level divides activities into 17 main classifications. A list of these classifications is included at HMRC Capital Allowances Manual CA23090.

The '*relevant chargeable period*' means the chargeable period ending in the financial year.

Restriction 4: other companies under common control

Where, in a financial year, two or more companies are under common control and related to one another (both defined as for restriction 3 above), but neither of restrictions 2 and 3 above is in play, only one AIA is available to those companies. The AIA may be allocated, as the companies see fit, to qualifying expenditure incurred by them for chargeable periods ending in the financial year in question.

Operation of AIA where restrictions apply

This following rules apply where, due to any of restrictions 1 to 4 above, a person is (or persons between them are) entitled to a single annual investment allowance in respect of the AIA qualifying expenditure incurred.

- If the AIA qualifying expenditure is less than or equal to the maximum AIA (disregarding the length of any chargeable period), the person is (or the persons between them are) entitled to an AIA in respect of all the AIA qualifying expenditure.
- If the AIA qualifying expenditure is more than the maximum AIA (disregarding the length of any chargeable period), the person is (or the persons between them are) entitled to an AIA in respect of so much of the AIA qualifying expenditure as does not exceed the maximum AIA.

The amount of AIA allocated to AIA qualifying expenditure cannot exceed the maximum amount that would have been available in respect of that expenditure if none of restrictions 1 to 4 above had applied. Any person may still choose to claim less than the full AIA available to him.

Periods straddling 1 January 2019 or 2022

If any of the chargeable periods straddle either 1 January 2019 or 1 January 2022, the general rules above for periods straddling those dates apply in determining the maximum AIA to be shared between qualifying activities/companies sharing the AIA. If there is more than one such period, only that period which gives rise to the greatest maximum allowance is taken into account.

Additional VAT liabilities

In general, where expenditure was AIA qualifying expenditure, any 'additional VAT liability' (see **10.2**(viii) above), incurred in respect of that expenditure at a time when the plant or machinery in question is provided for the purposes of the qualifying activity, is also AIA qualifying expenditure — for the chargeable period in which the liability accrues. An additional VAT liability incurred at a time when the plant or machinery is used for overseas leasing other than protected leasing (see **10.55** below) is not AIA qualifying expenditure.

[*CAA 2001, ss 38A, 38B, 51A–51G, 51K, 51L, 205, 218A, 236, 237, 268A, 574(2); FA 2019, s 32, Sch 13; FA 2021, s 15; SI 2019 No 689, Reg 10(2)*].

Simon's Taxes. See B3.329.

Super-deduction and SR allowance

[10.13] *FA 2021* introduced temporary enhanced first-year allowances (FYAs) for certain qualifying expenditure incurred by companies in the period 1 April 2021 to 31 March 2023 inclusive. Although technically FYAs, the enhanced allowances are described separately here because different rules apply on disposal of the plant and machinery.

Expenditure incurred, by a company within the charge to corporation tax, on or after 1 April 2021 and before 1 April 2023 qualifies for an enhanced FYA if it falls within one of three categories.

(i) **Super-deduction.** Expenditure ('*super-deduction expenditure*') on unused (not second-hand) plant and machinery qualifies for an FYA of **130%** if it is not special rate expenditure (see **10.28** below) or expenditure on plant or machinery for use wholly or partly for the purposes of a ring fence trade within *CTA 2010, s 330(1)* (oil extraction activities).

(ii) **SR allowance.** Special rate expenditure ('*SR allowance expenditure*') on unused (not second-hand) plant and machinery qualifies for an FYA of 50% if it is not expenditure on plant or machinery for use wholly or partly for the purposes of a ring fence trade.

(iii) Expenditure on the provision of plant or machinery (whether or not unused) for use partly for the purposes of a ring fence trade and partly for the purposes of another qualifying activity qualifies for an FYA of **100%** if it is not special rate expenditure. The FYA must be allocated between the ring fence trade and the other qualifying activity on a just and reasonable basis. For the permanent FYA on expenditure wholly for use for the purposes of a ring fence trade, see **10.14**(e) below.

Expenditure does not qualify for any of these FYAs if it is within any of the exclusions at **10.15** below, except that the exclusion at **10.15**(iv) does not apply to expenditure within (i) or (ii) above if the plant or machinery is leased under an 'excluded lease of background plant or machinery for a building (see **10.49**(1)(B) below).

In determining for these purposes the time at which expenditure is incurred, *CAA 2001, s 12* (pre-commencement expenditure – see **10.3** above) is disregarded. In determining whether expenditure qualifies for an FYA within (i) or (ii) above, the normal rules determining when expenditure is incurred in *CAA 2001, s 5* (see **10.2**(iv) above) do not apply if the expenditure is incurred under a contract entered into before 3 March 2021. Instead, the expenditure is treated as if it were incurred when the contract was entered into (so that the expenditure will not qualify for the FYA). Subject to this rule, the normal rules for determining when expenditure under a hire purchase agreement is incurred apply as at **10.57** below but only if under the agreement:

- the plant or machinery must be delivered to the company incurring the expenditure without transfer of ownership ('bailed' or in Scotland 'hired') in return for periodical payments by that company; and

- ownership of the plant and machinery will pass to the company if the terms of the agreement are complied with and one or more of the following occurs:
  - the exercise of an option to purchase by the company;
  - the doing of another specified act by any party to the agreement; or
  - the happening of another specified event.

A super-deduction or SR allowance cannot be postponed under the provisions for ships at **10.16** below.

It is specifically provided that the amount to be allocated to the relevant pool in respect of expenditure on which a super-deduction has been given (see **10.26** below) is to be treated as nil. This rule is intended to prevent the allocation of a negative balance to the pool because the allowance given is greater than the amount of the expenditure. It does not prevent the allocation of the remaining part of expenditure to the pool where a super-deduction is claimed only on part of the expenditure.

[*FA 2021, ss 9, 12(9)*].

Reduced super-deduction

Where a company incurs super-deduction expenditure (i.e. expenditure within (i) above) in an accounting period beginning before and ending on or after 1 April 2023, the rate of the super-deduction is reduced. The percentage rate is determined by taking the following steps.

(1) Divide the number of days in the accounting period before 1 April 2023 by the total number of days in the period.
(2) Multiply the result by 30.
(3) Add 100.

For example, where a company's accounting period ends on 30 September 2023, the result is a rate of 115%. (182/365 multiplied by 30 equals 15. 15 + 100 = 115.)

The rate of a super-deduction due in respect of an additional VAT liability (see **10.24** below) is also reduced where the company becomes entitled to it in an accounting period ending on or after 1 April 2023. If the company became entitled to the super-deduction before 1 April 2023, the percentage rate is found using steps (1)–(3) above. Otherwise, the percentage rate is 100%.

[*FA 2021, s 11*].

Disposal of assets

Super-deduction

A balancing charge arises in an accounting period in which a disposal event (see **10.27** below) occurs to the extent that a super-deduction has been given in respect of the expenditure in question. The amount of the balancing charge is determined as follows.

(a) Find the proportion of the disposal value that relates to the super-deduction. The proportion is found by dividing the amount on which a super-deduction has been given by the total expenditure on which capital allowances have been claimed (as a super-deduction, another FYA or by allocation to a pool (including allocation in the period of the disposal event)) and multiplying the result by the amount of the disposal value. If a super-deduction has been given in respect of the entire expenditure on the plant and machinery in question, this means that the whole of the disposal value relates to the super-deduction.

(b) If the disposal event is in an accounting period beginning on or after 1 April 2023, the balancing charge is simply the proportion of the disposal value found in (a) above.

(c) If the disposal event is in an accounting period ending before 1 April 2023, the balancing charge is the proportion of the disposal value multiplied by 1.3.

(d) If the disposal event is in an accounting period straddling 1 April 2023, the balancing charge is the proportion of the disposal value multiplied by a factor calculated as follows:

 (I) Divide the number of days in the accounting period before 1 April 2023 by the total number of days in the period.

 (II) Multiply the result by 0.30.

 (III) Add 1.

 For example, where a company's accounting period ends on 30 September 2023, the result is a factor of 1.15. (182/365 multiplied by 0.3 equals 0.15. 0.15 + 1 = 1.15.)

The disposal value to be brought into account in the relevant pool is reduced by the proportion found in (a) above. Where a super-deduction has been claimed in respect of the full amount of the expenditure, the amount so brought into account will therefore be nil. If a balancing charge arises only in respect of part of the expenditure, the remainder must be brought into account in the pool.

A balancing charge arising under these provisions cannot be postponed under the provisions for ships at **10.16** below.

[*FA 2021, s 12*].

SR allowance

A balancing charge arises in an accounting period in which a disposal event (see **10.27** below) occurs to the extent that an SR allowance has been given in respect of the expenditure in question. The amount of the balancing charge is determined as follows.

(A) Divide the amount of the expenditure in respect of which an SR allowance has been given by 2.

(B) Find the proportion of the disposal value that relates to the SR allowance. The proportion is found by dividing the amount found in (A) above by the total expenditure on which capital allowances have been claimed (see further below) and multiplying the result by the amount of the disposal value.

(C) The balancing charge is the proportion of the disposal value found in (B) above. If an SR allowance has been given in respect of the entire expenditure on the plant and machinery in question, this means that the balancing charge will be 50% of the disposal value.

In (B) above, the total expenditure on which capital allowances have been claimed is taken to be the sum of:

- (i) the expenditure in respect of which an SR allowance has been given (i.e. the full amount of the expenditure and not the amount of the 50% SR allowance);
- (ii) any expenditure in respect of which another FYA has been given; and
- (iii) any expenditure not within (i) which has been allocated to a pool (including in the accounting period of the disposal event).

The disposal value to be brought into account in the special rate pool is reduced by the amount of the balancing charge. Where an SR allowance has been claimed in respect of the full amount of the expenditure, the amount so brought into account will therefore be 50% of the disposal value.

A balancing charge arising under these provisions cannot be postponed under the provisions for ships at **10.16** below.

[*FA 2021, s 13*].

Anti-avoidance

Any tax advantage connected with a super-deduction or SR allowance that would otherwise be obtained as a result of certain arrangements is to be counteracted by the making of just and reasonable adjustments (by way of an assessment, amendment of an assessment, amendment or disallowance of a claim or otherwise).

The circumstances in which a tax advantage is connected with a super-deduction or SR allowance include, but are not restricted to, the obtaining of such an allowance or the avoidance of a balancing charge).

Arrangements are subject to this provision if they have a main purpose of obtaining such a tax advantage and either it is reasonable to conclude that they are abnormal or include steps that are abnormal, contrived or lacking in a genuine commercial purpose or it is reasonable to regard them as circumventing the intended reliefs under *CAA 2001* or otherwise exploiting shortcomings in that Act. All of the relevant circumstances must be taken into account for this purpose.

[*FA 2021, s 14*].

Example 1

A Ltd prepares trading accounts to 31 December each year. In the two years ending on 31 December 2022 and 31 December 2023, it incurs expenditure on new plant and machinery of £1,000,000 and £800,000, respectively. All of the expenditure is super-deduction expenditure. The written-down value in the main pool at 1 January 2022 was £365,000.

The capital allowances are as follows.

A Ltd's capital allowances are as follows.

	Super-deduction Expenditure	Main Pool	Allowances
	£	£	£
Accounting period 1.1.22–31.12.22			
WDV b/f		365,000	
Additions	1,000,000		
Super-deduction 130%	(1,300,000)		1,300,000
WDA 18%		(65,700)	65,700
WDV c/fwd		299,300	
Total allowances			£1,365,700
Accounting period 1.1.23–31.12.23			
Additions	800,000		
Super-deduction 107.4% — note (a)			859,200
WDA 18%		(53,874)	53,874
WDV c/fwd		245,426	
Total allowances			£913,074

Note

(a) The rate of super-deduction for the year ended 31 December 2023 is calculated as follows.
   (1) Divide the number of days in the accounting period before 1 April 2023 by the total number of days in the period: 90/365 = 0.246573.
   (2) Multiply the result by 30: 30×0.246573=7.4.
   (3) Add 100: 100+7.4=107.4.

Example 2

B Ltd makes up accounts to 30 September. On 1 July 2021, it incurs super-deduction expenditure on an item of plant of £1,500,000 and claims a super-deduction for the year ended 30 September 2021 of £1,950,000. On the assumption that B Ltd sells the asset for £750,000 on (i) 31 August 2022, (ii) 31 August 2023 or (iii) 31 August 2024, B Ltd must bring into account a balancing charge as follows.

(i) Sale on 31 August 2022. As the accounting period (to 30 September 2022) ends before 1 April 2023, the balancing charge is £750,000×1.3=£975,000.

(ii) Sale on 31 August 2023. As the accounting period (to 30 September 2023) straddles 1 April 2023, the balancing charge is found by multiplying the disposal value by the amount found by taking the following steps:

(1) Divide the number of days in the accounting period before 1 April 2023 by the total number of days in the period: 182/365=0.5.
(2) Multiply the result by 0.30: 0.5×0.3=0.15.
(3) Add 1: 0.15+1=1.15.

The amount of the balancing charge is, therefore, £750,000×1.15=£862,500.

(iii) Sale on 31 August 2024. As the accounting period (to 30 September 2024) begins on or after 1 April 2023, the balancing charge is equal to the disposal value, i.e. £750,000.

First-year allowances

[10.14] A person is entitled to a first-year allowance (FYA) for a chargeable period (see **10.2**(i) above) in respect of any 'first-year qualifying expenditure' which he incurs in that period on plant or machinery which he owns (see **10.16** below under *Ownership*) at some time during that period. He may claim the allowance in respect of the whole or a part of the first-year qualifying expenditure. In determining for these purposes the time at which expenditure is incurred, *CAA 2001, s 12* (pre-commencement expenditure — see **10.3** above) is disregarded. Otherwise, see **10.2**(iv) above as regards the date on which expenditure is treated as having been incurred.

FYAs used to be widely available. For expenditure on or after 1 April 2008, however, they remain available only for expenditure within (a)–(i) below and were replaced more generally by the AIA at **10.12** above. See also **10.13** above for the temporary super-deduction and SR allowance, which are also, strictly speaking, FYAs.

An FYA and an AIA cannot be claimed in respect of the same expenditure; where both allowances are possible, the taxpayer can choose which, if any, to claim.

Subject to the exclusions at **10.15** below, qualifying expenditure (as in **10.3** above) is '*first-year qualifying expenditure*' if it is incurred:

(a) **before 1 April 2020** by any person on **'energy-saving plant or machinery'** (see **10.17** below) which is unused and not second-hand, in which case the maximum FYA is **100%**;

(b) **before 1 April 2020** by any person on **'environmentally beneficial plant or machinery'** (see **10.18** below), unused and not second-hand, in which case the maximum FYA is **100%** (but long-life asset expenditure, see **10.34** below, does not qualify);

(c) **before 1 April 2025** by any person on cars first registered after 16 April 2002 which are either **'electrically-propelled'** or have **'low CO_2 emissions'** (see **10.19** below), and which are unused and not second-hand, in which case the maximum FYA is **100%**;

(d) **before 1 April 2025** by any person on plant or machinery, unused and not second-hand, installed at a **'gas refuelling station'** (see **10.20** below) for use solely for or in connection with refuelling vehicles with natural gas, biogas or hydrogen fuel, in which case the maximum FYA is **100%**;

(e) by a company on plant or machinery for use wholly for the purposes of a 'ring fence trade' within *CTA 2010, s 330(1)* (**petroleum extraction activities**), in which case the maximum FYA is **100%**; (the FYA is withdrawn where the plant etc. is not used in such a trade, or is used for some other purpose, within the five years after the expenditure is incurred — see *CAA 2001, s 45G*);

(f) **before 1 April 2025** by any person on **'zero-emission goods vehicles'**, unused and not second-hand, in which case the maximum FYA is **100%**; this is subject to exclusions and to a monetary limit on the total FYAs of this type that can be claimed by any person; see **10.21** below. The Treasury may by order extend this period of availability;

(g) **after 31 March 2012** by a company on the provision of unused (not second-hand) plant or machinery for use primarily in an area which (at the time the expenditure is incurred) is a 'designated assisted area', in which case the maximum FYA is **100%**. The expenditure must be incurred in the period beginning with the date on which the area is (or is treated as) designated and ending with the later of the day immediately before the eighth anniversary of that date or 31 March 2021, and there are exclusions and a monetary limit on the total FYAs of this type that can be claimed by any person in respect of any one investment project in any area; see **10.22** below;

(h) **after 22 November 2016 and before 1 April 2023** by any person on unused (not second-hand) plant or machinery installed solely for the purpose of charging electric road vehicles, in which case the maximum FYA is **100%**;

(i) **before 1 October 2026** by a company on the provision of unused (not second-hand) plant or machinery for use primarily in an area which (at the time the expenditure is incurred) is in a 'freeport tax site', in which case the maximum FYA is **100%**. See **10.23** below for exclusions and the withdrawal of the FYA where the plant etc. is not used primarily in a freeport tax site at any time in the five years after first use.

[*CAA 2001, ss 39, 45A, 45AA, 45B–45D, 45DA, 45DB, 45E–45R, 50, 52, 52A, 268A–268C; F(No 2)A 2017, s 38; FA 2019, ss 33(1)(2)(5), 34; FA 2021, Sch 22 paras 2, 3, 5; SI 2017 No 1304; SI 2020 No 260; SI 2021 No 120, Arts 3–5*].

Simon's Taxes. See **B3.320–325, B3.330.**

Exclusions from FYAs

[10.15] FYAs are not available under *any* of **10.13**(i)–(iii) or **10.14**(a)–(i) above in the circumstances listed below (and note also the exclusion of long-life assets from **10.14**(b)).

(i) The expenditure is incurred in the chargeable period in which the qualifying activity is permanently discontinued.

(ii) The expenditure is incurred on the provision of a '*car*' (defined as in **10.12**(ii) above).
This exclusion does *not* apply as regards **10.14**(c) above, in relation to which the above-mentioned definition of 'car' applies but with the specific inclusion of any mechanically-propelled road vehicle of a type commonly used as a hackney carriage. Motor cycles have always been excluded from the definition of car for the purposes of **10.14**(c) above.

(iii) The plant or machinery would be a long-life asset but for the transitional provisions of *CAA 2001, Sch 3 para 20* (see **10.34** below).

(iv) The expenditure is on plant or machinery for leasing (whether or not in the course of a trade). For this purpose, 'leasing' expressly includes the letting of a ship on charter or of any other asset on hire. This exclusion does *not* apply as regards expenditure within **10.13**(i) or (ii) above or **10.14**(a) or, (b) above, but only if the plant or machinery is leased under an 'excluded lease of background plant or machinery for a building' (see **10.49**(1)(B) below). This exclusion does not apply as regards expenditure within **10.14**(c) above where that expenditure was incurred before 1 April 2013.
Expenditure by a company on plant and machinery to be used by its subsidiary in return for an annual charge fell within the exclusion (*M F Freeman (Plant) Ltd v Jowett* (Sp C 376), [2003] SSCD 423).
Where a business supplies plant or machinery with an operator, and the equipment is to be operated solely by the operator thus provided, HMRC accept that this is the provision of a service and not merely plant hire. FYAs are not excluded. HMRC similarly accept that the provision of building access services by the scaffolding industry (but not simply the supply of scaffolding poles etc. for use by others) is the provision of a service. (HMRC Capital Allowances Manual CA23115).

(v) The provision of the plant or machinery is connected with a change in the nature or conduct of a trade or business carried on by a person other than the person incurring the expenditure on its provision, and the obtaining of an FYA was the main benefit, or one of the main benefits, which could reasonably be expected to arise from the making of the change.

(vi) The provision of the plant of machinery is by way of gift (see **10.68** below).

(vii) The plant or machinery was previously used by the owner for purposes other than those of the qualifying activity (see **10.69** below), which includes the purposes of long funding leasing (see **10.50** below).

For exclusions from **10.14**(f) above, see **10.21** below.

[*CAA 2001, s 46; F(No 2)A 2017, s 38(4); FA 2021, s 9(9), Sch 22 para 4*].

See also the anti-avoidance rules at **10.61** below which restrict a buyer's entitlement to FYAs in certain types of transaction.

First-year allowances — miscellaneous matters

[10.16] *Partial use for non-trade etc. purposes* results in FYAs being scaled down as is just and reasonable. [*CAA 2001, s 205*]. See **10.32** below as regards writing-down allowances in such cases.

See **10.74** below for the scaling down of FYAs where it appears that a *partial depreciation subsidy* will be payable.

See **10.72** below for the denial of FYAs on plant and machinery treated as changing hands by virtue of certain partnership changes and other *successions*.

Ownership

Before *CAA 2001* came into effect (see **10.1** above), the question of whether a person *owns* plant and machinery at some time in the chargeable period in which the expenditure is incurred was expressed in terms of whether it *belonged* to him at some time during the chargeable period related to the incurring of the expenditure. [*CAA 1990, s 22(1)*]. 'Belongs' has its ordinary meaning and normally entails a right of disposition over the thing possessed. See also *Bolton v International Drilling Co Ltd* Ch D 1982, 56 TC 449, *Ensign Tankers (Leasing) Ltd v Stokes* HL 1992, 64 TC 617, *Melluish v BMI (No 3) Ltd* HL 1995, 68 TC 1 and *BMBF (No 24) Ltd v CIR* Ch D, [2002] STC 1450. Following the decision in *Stokes v Costain Property Investments Ltd* CA 1984, 57 TC 688, specific provisions were introduced to determine entitlement to allowances for plant or machinery which are fixtures (see **10.36** *et seq.* below). See **10.57** below as regards plant and machinery acquired on hire-purchase, and **10.75** below as regards certain expenditure incurred by a lessee under the terms of a lease. For ownership of certain assets transferred under oil production sharing contracts to the government or representative of the production territory, see *CAA 2001, s 171*. The change in terminology in *CAA 2001* was not intended to be a change in the law.

Ships (postponement of FYAs)

Where a ship qualifies for an FYA (other than a super-deduction or SR allowance – see **10.13** above), the person entitled may, by written notice, *postpone* all or part of the allowance. The amount to be postponed must be specified in the notice. Where an FYA is claimed in respect of part only of the qualifying expenditure, the above applies in respect of the FYA claimed. The notice must be given no later than the first anniversary of 31 January following the tax year in which ends the chargeable period for which the allowance is due. Available qualifying expenditure for writing-down allowances (see **10.26** below) is computed as if the postponed FYA had, in fact, been made. Postponed FYAs may be claimed over one or more subsequent chargeable periods. [*CAA 2001, s 130(1)(3)–(6), s 131(1)(2)(4)(7); CTA 2010, Sch 1 para 337*]. See **10.31** below for postponement of writing-down allowances and deferment of balancing charges.

Additional VAT liabilities

See **10.24** below.

Energy-saving plant or machinery

[10.17] '*Energy-saving plant or machinery*', for the purposes of **10.14**(a) above, is plant or machinery which, either at the time the expenditure is incurred or at the time the contract for its provision is entered into, is of a description specified by Treasury order *and* meets the energy-saving criteria specified by Treasury order for plant or machinery of that description. See below as regards the impact of receiving feed-in tariffs or renewable heat incentive payments.

The Treasury Order currently giving effect to these provisions (the *Capital Allowances (Energy-saving Plant and Machinery) Order 2018, SI 2018 No 268*) operates by giving statutory authority to the energy technology lists issued by the Department for Business, Energy and Industrial Strategy (formerly the Department of Energy and Climate Change) and HMRC. Plant or machinery qualifies as energy-saving plant or machinery, therefore, if:

(a) it falls within a technology class specified in the Energy Technology Criteria List;
(b) it meets the energy-saving criteria set out in that List; and
(c) in the case of classes (4) to (15) below, it is of a type specified in (and not removed from) or which has been accepted for inclusion in, the Energy Technology Product List. In the case of solar thermal systems, either the system itself or the solar collector included in the system must meet this requirement. In the case of automatic monitoring and targeting equipment, the automatic monitoring and targeting system need not meet the requirement. Similarly, air source split and multi-split (including variable refrigerant flow) heat pumps do not need to meet the requirement.

The Energy Technology Criteria List specifies the following technology classes:

(1) combined heat and power;
(2) lighting;
(3) pipework insulation;
(4) boilers;
(5) motors and drives;
(6) refrigeration;
(7) heat pumps;
(8) radiant and warm air heaters;
(9) compressed air equipment;
(10) solar thermal systems and collectors;
(11) automatic monitoring and targeting equipment;
(12) air-to-air energy recovery equipment;
(13) heating, ventilation and air conditioning equipment (for expenditure incurred before 4 August 2009, air conditioning zone controls);
(14) uninterruptible power supplies;
(15) high speed hand air dryers; and
(16) (for expenditure incurred on or after 2 July 2015) waste heat to electricity conversion equipment.

The Energy Technology Criteria and Product Lists can be viewed on the enhanced capital allowances website at www.gov.uk/guidance/energy-technology-list.

The Treasury have the power to provide that, in specified cases, a 100% first-year allowance cannot be made unless a 'certificate of energy efficiency' issued by, or by a person authorised by, the Secretary of State, the Scottish Ministers, the National Assembly for Wales, or the Department of Enterprise, Trade and Investment in Northern Ireland as appropriate, is in force. A '*certificate of energy efficiency*' certifies that particular plant or machinery, or plant or machinery of a particular design, meets the energy-saving criteria specified as in (ii) above. Currently, the Treasury Order requires a certificate of energy efficiency to be in force in the case only of plant and machinery falling within the 'combined heat and power' technology class.

If one or more components of an item of plant and machinery qualify under these provisions, but the whole item does not, normal apportionment rules are disapplied, and instead the first-year qualifying expenditure under **10.14**(a) above is limited to the amount (or aggregate amount) specified in the ETPL for that component (or those components); where relevant, each *instalment* of expenditure falls to be apportioned in the same way as the whole.

Feed-in tariffs and renewable heat incentives

Expenditure on plant or machinery is to be treated as never having qualified for FYAs as energy-saving plant or machinery if:

(a) a payment is made, or another incentive is given, under a scheme established by virtue of *Energy Act 2008, s 41* (feed-in tariffs) (or under a corresponding NI scheme) in respect of electricity generated by the plant or machinery; or

(b) a payment is made, or another incentive is given, under a scheme established by regulations under *Energy Act 2011, s 113* (renewable heat incentives in NI) in respect of heat generated, or gas or fuel produced, by the plant or machinery.

FYAs already given will be withdrawn by means of an assessment or amended assessment.

If a person who has made a tax return subsequently becomes aware that anything in it has become incorrect as a result of the above, he must give notice to HMRC specifying how the return needs to be amended. The notice must be given within three months of his becoming so aware.

[*CAA 2001, ss 45A, 45AA, 45B, 45C; FA 2019, s 33(1)(4)(5); SI 2018 No 268; SI 2019 No 501*].

See also first-year tax credits at **10.25** below.

Simon's Taxes. See B3.324.

Environmentally beneficial plant or machinery

[10.18] '*Environmentally beneficial plant or machinery*', for the purposes of **10.14**(b) above, is plant or machinery which, either at the time the expenditure is incurred or at the time the contract for its provision is entered into, is of a description specified by Treasury order *and* meets the environmental criteria specified by Treasury order for plant or machinery of that description. A Treasury order may identify qualifying plant or machinery by reference to technology lists or product lists issued by the relevant Secretary of State. The intention is to promote the use of technologies, or products, designed to remedy or prevent damage to the physical environment or natural resources (Revenue Press Release BN 26, 9 April 2003); the Treasury orders refer, in fact, to the Water Technology Product List (WTPL) available at www.gov.uk/government/

publications/water-efficient-enhanced-capital-allowances. An order may provide that, in specified cases, no FYA is to be given under **10.14**(b) above unless a '*relevant certificate of environmental benefit*' is in force, i.e. a certificate issued by the Secretary of State, the Scottish Ministers, the Welsh Assembly or the relevant NI department, or by persons authorised by them, to the effect that a particular item, or an item constructed to a particular design, meets the relevant environmental criteria. If a certificate is revoked, it is treated as having never been in issue, with the result that FYAs under **10.14**(b) above will not have been available. Subject to penalty under *TMA 1970, s 98* for non-compliance, a person who has consequently made an incorrect tax return must give notice to HMRC, specifying the amendment required to the return, within three months of his becoming aware of the problem. Technology classes currently included in the WTPL, subject to the appropriate criteria or product approval, are listed below:

- flow controllers;
- leakage detection equipment;
- meters and monitoring equipment;
- efficient taps;
- efficient toilets;
- rainwater harvesting equipment;
- water reuse systems (see also below);
- cleaning in place equipment;
- efficient showers;
- efficient washing machines;
- (before 29 March 2019) small scale slurry and sludge dewatering equipment;
- (before 29 March 2019) vehicle wash waste reclaim units;
- water efficient industrial cleaning equipment;
- water management equipment for mechanical seals; and
- greywater recovery and reuse equipment.

Expenditure on the following items falling within the category of 'water reuse systems' will qualify only if a relevant certificate of environmental benefit (see above) is in force:

- efficient membrane filtration systems for the treatment of wastewater for recovery and reuse; and
- efficient wastewater recovery and reuse systems.

If one or more components of an item of plant and machinery qualify under these provisions, but the whole item does not, normal apportionment rules are disapplied, and instead the first-year qualifying expenditure under **10.14**(b) above is limited to the amount (or aggregate amount) specified in the WTPL for that component (or those components); where relevant, each *instalment* of expenditure falls to be apportioned in the same way as the whole.

[*CAA 2001, s 45H–45J; FA 2019, s 33(1)(3)(5); SI 2003 No 2076; SI 2019 No 499*].

See also first-year tax credits at **10.25** below.

Simon's Taxes. See **B3.324D.**

Energy-efficient cars

[10.19] For the purposes of **10.14**(c) above, a car has 'low CO_2 emissions' if it is first registered on the basis of a qualifying emissions certificate (see *CAA 2001, s 268C*) and has CO_2 emissions (see *CAA 2001, s 268C*) of 0g/km (50g/km or less for expenditure incurred before 1 April 2021; 75g/km for expenditure incurred before 1 April 2018). A car is '*electrically-propelled*' if it is propelled solely by electrical power derived from an external source or from a storage battery not connected to any source of power when the car is in motion. See also HMRC Capital Allowances Manual CA23153. [*CAA 2001, s 45D; FA 2013, s 68(1)(5); SI 2021 No 120, Arts 1, 3*].

Simon's Taxes. See **B3.324A**.

Gas refuelling stations

[10.20] For the purposes of **10.14**(d) above, a '*gas refuelling station*' is any premises (or part) where mechanically-propelled road vehicles are refuelled with natural gas, biogas or hydrogen fuel. Plant or machinery installed for use solely for or in connection with such refuelling includes any storage tank for such fuels, any compressor, pump, control or meter used in the refuelling and any equipment for dispensing such fuels to vehicles' fuel tanks. [*CAA 2001, s 45E*].

Simon's Taxes. See **B3.324B**.

Zero-emissions goods vehicles

[10.21] A '*zero-emissions goods vehicle*', for the purposes of **10.14**(e) above, is a 'goods vehicle' which cannot in any circumstances emit CO_2 by being driven. A '*goods vehicle*' is a mechanically propelled road vehicle which is of a design primarily suited for the conveyance of goods or burden of any description. The vehicle must be registered but it does not matter whether it is first registered before or after the expenditure is incurred. [*CAA 2001, s 45DA*].

Exclusions

Expenditure does not qualify if, at the time the claim for the FYA is made, the person who incurred the expenditure is, or forms part of, an undertaking that is:

- an 'undertaking in difficulty' (for the purposes of the General Block Exemption Regulation (EU) No 651/2014); or
- subject to an outstanding recovery order made by virtue of *Art 108(2)* of the Treaty on the Functioning of the European Union (Commission Decision declaring aid illegal and incompatible with the common market).

Following Brexit, the meaning of 'undertaking in difficulty' for this purpose is the meaning for the purposes of the General Block Exemption Regulation as it had effect immediately before 11pm on 31 December 2020 (IP completion day).

Also excluded is expenditure incurred:

(a) for the purposes of a qualifying activity in the fishery or aquaculture sector or relating to the management of waste of other undertakings; or
(b) taken into account for the purposes of a 'relevant grant or payment' made towards that expenditure.

For the purposes of (b) above, a grant or payment is a *'relevant grant or payment'* if it is either a State aid (other than a capital allowance under *CAA 2001, Pt 2*) or if it is declared by Treasury Order to be relevant. If a relevant grant or payment is made *after* the making of an FYA on a zero-emission goods vehicle, the allowance is to be withdrawn. An assessment or tax adjustment to withdraw the FYA can be made at any time no later than three years after the end of the chargeable period in which the grant or payment was made.

[*CAA 2001, s 45DB; SI 2020 No 1499*].

Cap on first-year allowances

No one person can claim FYAs of more than 85 million euros on zero-emission goods vehicles. This is not an annual limit but an aggregate limit over the five-year period during which these FYAs are available. If expenditure on a vehicle exceeds the limit or takes the aggregate spending on such vehicles over the limit, the excess does not qualify for these FYAs. For this purpose, expenditure incurred in sterling or any other currency is to be converted into euros using the spot rate of exchange for the day on which the expenditure is incurred.

The 85 million euro limit applies to expenditure per 'undertaking'. An *'undertaking'* means an 'autonomous enterprise' or an 'enterprise' together with its 'partner enterprises' (if any) and its 'linked enterprises' (if any). All these expressions have the meaning given by Annex 1 to the Commission Regulation (EU) No. 651/2004 (General Block Exemption Regulation). Following Brexit, the definitions apply by reference to Annex 1 as it had effect immediately before 11pm on 31 December 2020 (IP completion day).

There are rules to take account of the fact that an individual enterprise could be an autonomous, linked or partner enterprise at different times during the five-year period for which these FYAs are available. For the purpose of applying the cap, the historic expenditure incurred by a person whilst an undertaking in his/her/its own right, or part of a larger linked or partner enterprise, is added to the historic expenditure incurred by any other undertaking of which that person becomes part. The rules also ensure that the original undertaking (assuming it still exists) is still required to take into account the historic expenditure incurred by a person who was, but is no longer, part of that undertaking.

Scenario 1

X is an autonomous enterprise and has claimed FYAs of 20 million euros on zero-emission goods vehicles. X then becomes part of a linked enterprise (Y) which has already claimed FYAs of 50 million euros on zero-emission goods vehicles. For the purpose of applying the cap going forward, Y is now deemed to have claimed FYAs of 70 million euros on zero-emission goods vehicles.

Scenario 2

W was part of a linked enterprise Z but subsequently becomes autonomous. At that time, Z had already claimed FYAs of 25 million euros on zero-emission goods vehicles. For the purpose of applying the cap going forward, both W and Z are now deemed to have claimed FYAs of 25 million euros on zero-emission goods vehicles.

[*CAA 2001, s 212T; SI 2020 No 1499*].

Providing of State aid information

A claim made on or after 1 July 2016 for FYAs on zero-emissions goods vehicles must include any information required by HMRC for the purpose of complying with certain EU State aid obligations. This may include information about the claimant (or his activities), information about the subject-matter of the claim and other information relating to the grant of State aid through the provision of the FYAs. See **36.13** HMRC — ADMINISTRATION as regards the publishing by HMRC of State aid information. [*FA 2016, s 180(1)–(4)(10), Sch 24 Pt 1*].

Simon's Taxes. See **B3.324F.**

Plant and machinery for use in designated assisted areas

[10.22] For the purposes of **10.14**(g) above, '*designated assisted area*' means an area designated as such by Treasury order and falling wholly within an 'assisted area'. An area may be so designated only if, at the time the order is made, it falls wholly within an 'enterprise zone' and the Treasury and the responsible local authority have entered into a memorandum of understanding relating to the availability of the first-year allowances. An order designating an area may provide for it to be treated as having been a designated assisted area before the making of the order. The areas which have been so designated are listed in *SI 2014 No 3183*, *SI 2015 No 2047*, *SI 2016 No 751* and *SI 2018 No 485*. Note that certain areas are designated with retrospective effect, so that certain areas are treated as having been designated on 1 April 2012. For maps showing designated areas (updated to 17 April 2018) see www.gov.uk/government/publications/enterprise-zones.

An '*assisted area*' is an area specified as a development area under *Industrial Development Act 1982, s 1* or Northern Ireland. An '*enterprise zone*' is an area recognised by the Treasury as an area in respect of which there is special focus on economic development and identified on a map published by the Treasury for the purposes of the first-year allowances. The responsible local authority is the local authority for all or part of the area or two or more such authorities or, where relevant, the Scottish Ministers, the Welsh Ministers or the Department of Enterprise, Trade and Investment in Northern Ireland. The Treasury may by order amend the definition of 'assisted area' in certain circumstances.

In order for expenditure to qualify for FYAs under **10.14**(g) above, the following further conditions must be met:

(i) the company must be within the charge to corporation tax;
(ii) the expenditure must be incurred for the purposes of a trade or a concern within *CTA 2009, s 39(4)*;

(iii) the expenditure must be incurred for the purposes of a business of a kind not previously carried on by the company, expanding a business carried on by the company or starting up an activity which relates to a fundamental change in a product or production process of, or service provided by, a business carried on by the company;

(iv) the plant or machinery must be unused (not second-hand) and the expenditure must not be 'replacement expenditure'.

With regard to the third bullet point and expenditure incurred on starting up an activity which relates to a fundamental change in a product, process or service, this condition is met only if the amount of expenditure incurred on the plant and machinery required for such change exceeds the amount by which the plant or machinery which is being replaced (or modernised) is depreciated in the three years prior to the chargeable period in which such expenditure is incurred.

For this purpose, '*replacement expenditure*' is expenditure on providing plant or machinery intended to perform the same or a similar function as plant or machinery on which the company had previously incurred qualifying expenditure and which is superseded by the new plant or machinery. If the new plant or machinery is capable of and intended to perform a significant additional function which enhances the capacity or productivity of the qualifying activity, then to the extent that the expenditure is attributable to that function it is not replacement expenditure. The part of the expenditure attributable to the additional function must be determined on a just and reasonable basis.

Exclusions

The general exclusions at **10.15** above apply, along with the following additional exclusions. If, at the time the company incurs the expenditure, it intends the plant or machinery to be used partly in an area which is not a designated assisted area, no FYA can be claimed if a main purpose for which any person is a party to the transaction under which the expenditure is incurred (or any scheme or arrangements of which that transaction is part) is to obtain an FYA or a greater FYA in respect of the part of the expenditure attributable (on a just and reasonable basis) to the intended use in the non-designated area.

Allowances also cannot be claimed where the person incurring the expenditure is, or forms part of, an 'undertaking' which is:

- an undertaking in difficulty for the purposes of the General Block Exemption Regulation (EU) 651/2014; or
- subject to an outstanding recovery order following an EC decision declaring an aid illegal.

Expenditure is also excluded if it is incurred for the purposes of a qualifying activity:

(a) in the fishery or aquaculture sectors as covered by Regulation (EU) No 1379/2013 of the European Parliament and of the Council;

(b) in the coal, steel, shipbuilding or synthetic fibres sectors;

(c) in the transport sector or related infrastructure, or relating to energy generation, distribution or infrastructure, or relating to the development of broadband networks;

(d) relating to the management of waste for other undertakings (such as a waste collector contracting with a local authority or large retail business to provide an integrated waste management service); or

(e) relating to the primary production of agricultural products, on-farm activities necessary for preparing an animal or plant product for first sale or the first sale of agricultural products by a primary producer to wholesalers, retailers or processors, in circumstances where the sale does not take place on separate premises reserved for that purpose.

With regard to (b) and (c) the expressions take their meaning from the General Block Exemption Regulation (EU) No 651/2014. Following Brexit, the definitions apply by reference to the Regulation as it had effect immediately before 11pm on 31 December 2020 (IP completion day).

Expenditure is also excluded if a grant or payment is made towards the expenditure or any other expenditure incurred by any person in respect of the same designated assisted area and the same 'single investment project', if the grant or payment is either a State Aid (whether or not notified) or of a type specified by Treasury order. If such a grant or payment is made towards the expenditure after a first-year allowance has already been given, the allowance is withdrawn. An allowance is similarly withdrawn if such a grant or payment is made towards any other expenditure incurred by any person in respect of the same designated assisted area and on the same single investment project, but only if the grant or payment is made within three years of the incurring of the original expenditure. Expenditure incurred in respect of a designated assisted area includes, for this purpose, expenditure incurred on the provision of things for use primarily in that area or on services to be provided primarily in that area.

Expenditure incurred by large enterprises in enterprise zones that fall within assisted areas that are classified by the European Commission as being *TFEU Art 107(3)(c)* areas the condition in (iii) above is met only if the expenditure relates to 'a business of a kind not previously carried on by the company'.

Except in relation to the first exclusion noted above, if a person who has made a return becomes aware that anything in it has become incorrect because of the above exclusions, he must give notice to HMRC, within three months of first becoming aware of the incorrectness, specifying how the return needs to be amended.

For these purposes, an '*undertaking*' means an 'autonomous enterprise' or an enterprise and its 'partner enterprises' and 'linked enterprises', if any (all terms as defined in Annex 1 to EC Regulation 800/2008, from 17 July 2014, (EU) No 651/2014). 'Agricultural product' and 'single investment project' have the meanings given in the EU Regulation No 651/2014. In (c) above, 'management' and 'waste' have the meanings given in Article 1 of Directive 2006/12/EC. '*TFEU*' refers to the Treaty on the Functioning of the European Union.

The Treasury may amend the above provisions by order to give effect to changes in the relevant EU Regulations.

Withdrawal of first-year allowances

There are provisions for the withdrawal of FYAs if, within the period of five years beginning with the day the plant of machinery is first brought into use for the purposes of a qualifying activity carried on by the company or, if earlier, the day on which it is first held for such use, either:

- the primary use to which the plant or machinery is put is **not** in an area which was a 'relevant area' at the time the expenditure was incurred; or
- the plant or machinery is held for use otherwise than primarily in an area which was a 'relevant area' at that time.

'*Relevant area*' means: for expenditure by large companies (not SMEs under the General Block Exemption Regulation) which falls within *CAA 2001, s 45K(8)(b) or (c)*, a *TFEU Art 107(3)(a)* area; for all other expenditure a designated assisted area within the meaning of *s 45K*, see first paragraph at **10.22** above.

Where the plant or machinery ceases to be owned by the company or any person connected with it at a time before the end of the five-year period, the provisions for withdrawal apply only up to that time. Any person whose return becomes incorrect as a result of the provisions must give notice to HMRC, specifying how the return needs to be amended, within three months of becoming aware that it has become incorrect.

Cap on first-year allowances

The allowance is limited to expenditure of 125 million euros by any person in respect of any single investment project in a particular designated assisted area. In applying the limit, expenditure incurred in a different currency is to be converted into euros using the spot rate of exchange for the day on which it is incurred. Note that the limit is on allowances for expenditure incurred in respect of a single project and not expenditure incurred by a single company. The Treasury can increase the limit by statutory instrument. '*Single investment project*' has the same meaning as in the General Block Exemption Regulation (EU) No 651/2014. Following Brexit, the definition applies by reference to the Regulation as it had effect immediately before 11pm on 31 December 2020 (IP completion day).

[*CAA 2001, ss 39, 45K–45N, 52, 212U; SI 2014 No 3183; SI 2020 No 1499*].

Providing of State aid information

A claim made on or after 1 July 2016 for FYAs under these provisions must include any information required by HMRC for the purpose of complying with certain EU State aid obligations. This may include information about the claimant (or his activities), information about the subject-matter of the claim and other information relating to the grant of State aid through the provision of the FYAs. See **36.13** HMRC — ADMINISTRATION as regards the publishing by HMRC of State aid information. [*FA 2016, s 180(1)–(4)(10), Sch 24 Pt 1*].

Plant and machinery for use in freeport tax sites

[10.23] For the purposes of **10.14**(i) above, a '*freeport tax site*' means an area designated as such by Treasury regulations. At the time the regulations are made, the area must be situated in a 'freeport' or the Treasury must consider that the area is in use (or likely to be used) for purposes connected with activities carried on (or likely to be carried on) in a freeport. A '*freeport*' is an area identified as such in a document published by the Treasury or with its consent (and not withdrawn).

The government announced at Budget 2021 that eight freeports in England will begin operations from late 2021. These are East Midlands Airport, Felixstowe and Harwich, Humber, Liverpool City Region, Plymouth and South Devon, Solent, Teesside, and Thames.

For expenditure to qualify for FYAs under **10.14**(i) above, the following further conditions must be met:

(i) the company must be within the charge to corporation tax;
(ii) the expenditure must be incurred for the purposes of a trade or a concern within *CTA 2009, s 39(4)*;
(iii) the plant or machinery must be unused (not second-hand).

The Treasury has the power to amend the conditions for FYAs under **10.14**(i) above by statutory instrument.

A claim for an FYA under these provisions must include such information as HMRC may require.

Exclusions

The general exclusions at **10.15** above apply, along with the following further exclusion. If, at the time the company incurs the expenditure, it intends the plant or machinery to be used partly in an area which is not a freeport tax site, no FYA can be claimed in respect of the 'non-freeport part' of the expenditure if a main purpose for which any person is a party to the transaction under which the expenditure is incurred (or any scheme or arrangements of which that transaction is part) is to obtain an FYA or a greater FYA in respect of that part. The 'non-freeport part' of the expenditure is the part attributable, on a just and reasonable basis, to the intended use in an area which is not a freeport tax site.

Withdrawal of first-year allowances

There are provisions for the withdrawal of FYAs if, within the period of five years beginning with the day the plant of machinery is first brought into use for the purposes of a qualifying activity carried on by the company or, if earlier, the day on which it is first held for such use, either:

- the primary use to which the plant or machinery is put is **not** in an area which was a freeport tax site at the time the expenditure was incurred; or
- the plant or machinery is held for use otherwise than primarily in an area which was a freeport tax site at that time.

Where the plant or machinery ceases to be owned by the company or any person connected with it at a time before the end of the five-year period, the provisions for withdrawal apply only up to that time. Any person whose return becomes incorrect as a result of these provisions must give notice to HMRC, specifying how the return needs to be amended, within three months of becoming aware that it has become incorrect.

[*CAA 2001, ss 3(2ZZA), 45O–45R, 573A; FA 2021, s 113, Sch 22 paras 3, 15(2), 17*].

Additional VAT liabilities

[10.24] In general, where expenditure has qualified for an FYA, any 'additional VAT liability' (see **10.2**(viii) above), incurred in respect of that expenditure at a time when the plant or machinery in question is provided for the purposes of the qualifying activity, also qualifies — at the same rate and for the chargeable period in which the liability accrues. An additional VAT liability incurred at a time when the plant or machinery is used for overseas leasing other than protected leasing (see **10.55** below) does not qualify for an FYA. However, there is nothing to prevent an FYA in respect of an additional VAT liability from being available in the chargeable period in which the qualifying activity is permanently discontinued, notwithstanding exclusion **10.15**(i) above, where the liability (but not the original expenditure) is incurred in that period. [*CAA 2001, ss 236, 237, Sch 3 paras 46–50*].

See **10.13** above for the rate of a super-deduction in respect of an additional VAT liability.

Simon's Taxes. See **B3.393.**

First-year tax credits

[10.25] A company can surrender a loss attributable to first-year allowances on energy-saving or environmentally-beneficial plant and machinery (see **10.14**(a) and (b) above) in exchange for a cash payment (a '*first-year tax credit*') from the Government. Expenditure incurred on or after 1 April 2008 and before 1 April 2020 can qualify for first-year tax credits as described below. There are certain excluded organisations (co-operative housing associations, self-build societies, charities and scientific research organisations) to which first-year tax credits are not available.

A company can claim a first-year tax credit for an accounting period if it:

(a) incurs 'relevant first-year expenditure' for a qualifying activity (see **10.4** above) the profits of which are within the charge to corporation tax;
(b) claims and receives a first-year allowance (FYA) on that expenditure;
(c) makes a loss in carrying on the qualifying activity; and
(d) is not an excluded organisation (see above).

The amount the company may surrender (the '*surrenderable loss*') in exchange for a first-year tax credit is the lesser of:

(i) the amount of the FYA in (b) above; and
(ii) so much of the loss in (c) above as is unrelieved (see below).

The amount of loss surrendered in exchange for a first-year tax credit is not available for relief in any other way, and any loss carried forward to future accounting periods is reduced accordingly.

Relevant first-year expenditure

'*Relevant first-year expenditure*' in (a) above means first-year qualifying expenditure under **10.14**(a) or (b) above (energy-saving plant or machinery or environmentally beneficial plant or machinery) incurred **on or after 1 April 2008 and before 1 April 2020** (see above). Any effect of *CAA 2001, s 12* (pre-commencement expenditure — see **10.3** above) on the time expenditure is treated as incurred is disregarded for this purpose. The Treasury have power to defer the latter date by statutory instrument.

An additional VAT liability (see **10.24** above) cannot be relevant first-year expenditure.

Amount of the tax credit

The amount of a first-year tax credit is the 'applicable percentage' of the amount of the surrenderable loss, but this is subject to an upper limit equal to the company's total PAYE and NICs liabilities for 'payment periods' ending in the accounting period or, if greater, £250,000. A company can claim the whole or only part of the available tax credit.

For this purpose, the '*applicable percentage*' is equal to two-thirds of the rate of corporation tax chargeable on profits of the qualifying activity for the chargeable period (or, if there is more than one rate, the average over the period), rounded up to the nearest second decimal place. Slightly different rules apply where the qualifying activity is a ring fence trade. For chargeable periods beginning before 1 April 2018, the applicable rate was 19%, but for this purpose, chargeable periods straddling that date are treated as two separate chargeable periods, the second of which starts on that date. The surrenderable loss for the actual chargeable period is then apportioned between the two notional periods on a just and reasonable basis.

A company's PAYE liability for a payment period is the amount of income tax for which it is required to account to HMRC under the PAYE regulations for that period, ignoring deductions for child tax credit and working tax credit. A company's NICs liability for a payment period is the Class 1 national insurance contributions for which it is required to account to HMRC for that period, ignoring deductions for statutory sick pay, statutory maternity pay, child tax credit and working tax credit. A '*payment period*' is a period, ending on the fifth day of a month, for which the company is liable to account to HMRC for income tax and national insurance contributions.

Giving effect to the tax credit

Where a valid tax credit claim is made, the amount is normally paid to the company by HMRC. Alternatively, the amount, and any interest for late payment, can be applied to discharge the company's corporation tax liability. If HMRC open an enquiry into the company's tax return for the period concerned, they are not required to pay the tax credit until the enquiry is completed, but they may make a payment on a provisional basis as they think fit. HMRC are likewise not required to pay a tax credit for an accounting period until the company has paid its PAYE and NICs liabilities for payment periods ending in the accounting period. A payment of tax credit is not income of the company for tax purposes.

Unrelieved losses

For the purposes of (ii) above, the precise extent (if any) to which a loss is unrelieved depends upon the qualifying activity (see *CAA 2001, Sch A1 paras 11–16*). Generally speaking though, the loss incurred is reduced by:

- any relief that was *or could have been* obtained under *CTA 2010, s 37* (see **51.3, 51.4** LOSSES) or *CTA 2010, s 42* (carry-back of loss of ring fence trade),
- any amount that was *or could have been* surrendered as group relief (see **35** GROUP RELIEF),
- any amount surrendered under another tax credit provision, i.e. those for research and development, vaccine research, remediation of contaminated land and films, television, video games, theatrical productions, orchestral concerts and museum and gallery exhibitions,
- (for property businesses) any relief that was *or could have been* claimed under *CTA 2010, s 62(1)–(3)* (loss relieved against profits of same accounting period — see **60.9** PROPERTY INCOME), and
- any amount set off against the loss under *CTA 2010, ss 92–96* (write-off of government investment — see **51.36** LOSSES),

and what remains is the unrelieved loss. No account is taken of any losses brought forward from an earlier period or carried back from a later period, or any loss incurred on a leasing contract in circumstances to which *CTA 2010, s 53* (see **51.33** LOSSES) applies.

Clawback

First-year tax credits are clawed back if the plant and machinery in question (the '*tax-relieved plant and machinery*') is disposed of within four years after the end of the accounting period for which the tax credit was paid.

The appropriate part (the '*restored loss*') of the loss surrendered is treated as if it were not a surrenderable loss, and the tax credit paid in respect of the restored loss is treated as if it should never have been paid. For this purpose, the tax credit paid in respect of the restored loss is taken to be the applicable percentage (see above) of the restored loss.

For these purposes, a company disposes of an item of plant or machinery if a disposal event occurs (see **10.27** below) or if there is a change in ownership of the item in circumstances such that a provision (a '*continuity or business provision*' applies under which, for the purposes of plant and machinery allowances, anything done to or by the company is treated as having been done to or by the person becoming the owner of the item.

The restored loss is found by the formula:

$$(LS - OERPM) - (OE - DV) - ARL$$

where:

LS = the loss surrendered;
OERPM = the amount of original expenditure less the amount attributable to the plant or machinery disposed of;

OE = the aggregate of the original expenditure on the item disposed of and any other tax-relieved plant and machinery which the company has previously disposed of;
DV = the aggregate of the disposal values of the item disposed of and any other tax-relieved plant and ma-chinery which the company has previously disposed of; the disposal value of the item taken to its normal disposal value except that where either the company disposes of the item to a connected person for less than its market value or there is a change in ownership to which a continuity of business provision applies, the disposal value is taken to be the market value of the item; and
ARL = the aggregate of any restored losses calculated on a previous clawback.

If a company which has made a tax return becomes aware that, as a result of these clawback provisions, the return has become incorrect, it must notify HMRC within three months of so becoming aware, specifying how the return needs to be amended.

Anti-avoidance

A transaction is disregarded in determining the amount of any first-year tax credit if it is attributable to arrangements (as wifely defined) a main object of which is to enable a company to obtain a first-year tax credit to which it would not otherwise be entitled or a first-year tax credit of a greater amount than that to which it would otherwise be entitled.

Penalties

A fraudulent or negligent incorrect claim to a first-year tax credit attracts a penalty not exceeding the excess amount claimed. A similar penalty applies where a company discovers that a claim which was not made fraudulently or negligently is incorrect and does not remedy the error without unreasonable delay.

[*CAA 2001, s 262A, Sch A1; FA 1998, Sch 18 para 83ZA; F(No 2)A 2017, Sch 4 para 126, Sch 6 para 7; FA 2018, s 29; FA 2019, s 33(1)(2)(5)*].

Pooling, writing-down allowances and balancing adjustments

[10.26] Qualifying expenditure (as in **10.3** above) is *pooled* for the purpose of determining entitlement to writing-down allowances and balancing allowances and liability to balancing charges. In addition to the *main pool* for each qualifying activity, there may be a *single asset pool* and/or a *class pool*, and qualifying expenditure falling to be allocated to either of the latter (see **10.29–10.34**, **10.74** below) cannot be allocated to the main pool.

For each pool of qualifying expenditure, a **writing-down allowance (WDA)** is available for each chargeable period (see **10.2**(i) above) other than the 'final chargeable period' and is equal to a maximum of **18%** of the amount (if any) by which 'available qualifying expenditure' exceeds the total of any disposal values (see **10.27** below) falling to be brought into account. See **10.28** below (special rate expenditure) for an exception to the normal rate. The WDA is proportionately reduced if the chargeable period is less than a year, or if the qualifying activity has been carried on for part only of the chargeable period. A claim for a WDA may require it to be reduced to a specified amount. For the 'final chargeable period', a **balancing allowance** is available, equal to the excess (if any) of (1) 'available qualifying expenditure' over (2) total disposal values. If, for *any* chargeable period, (2) exceeds (1), there arises a liability to a **balancing charge,** equal to that excess.

See **10.13** above for special rules for bringing disposal values into account where a super-deduction or SR allowance has been given.

The maximum rate of WDA in a main pool or a special rate pool is increased to 100% if the balance of the pool (i.e. 'available qualifying expenditure' less total disposal values) is £1,000 or less (proportionately reduced or increased if the chargeable period is less or more than a year, or if the qualifying activity has been carried on for part only of the chargeable period). This figure may be amended in future by Treasury order made by statutory instrument.

The '*final chargeable period*', as regards the main pool, is the chargeable period in which the trade or other qualifying activity is permanently discontinued. As regards a single asset pool, it is normally the first chargeable period in which a disposal event (see **10.27** below) occurs. As regards class pools, see **10.28** (special rate expenditure) below.

Available qualifying expenditure

'*Available qualifying expenditure*' in a pool for a chargeable period consists of qualifying expenditure allocated to the pool for that period and any unrelieved qualifying expenditure brought forward in the pool from the previous chargeable period (usually referred to as the written-down value brought forward). There are rules requiring an allocation to a pool in specific circumstances, for example where an item falls to be transferred from one type of pool to another, and prohibiting the allocation of certain excluded expenditure. These are listed in *CAA 2001, s 57(2)(3)*, and are covered elsewhere in this chapter where appropriate. See **10.59** below as regards restrictions under connected persons and other anti-avoidance provisions.

In allocating qualifying expenditure to the appropriate pool, the following rules must be observed (and see below for interaction with first-year allowances).

(a) Qualifying expenditure can be allocated to a pool for a chargeable period only to the extent that it has not been included in available qualifying expenditure for an earlier chargeable period. (There is nothing to prohibit the allocation of *part only* of a particular amount of qualifying expenditure for a particular chargeable period.)

(b) Qualifying expenditure cannot be allocated to a pool for a chargeable period earlier than that in which it is incurred.

(c) Qualifying expenditure can be allocated to a pool for a chargeable period only if the company concerned *owns* the plant or machinery at some time in that period.

Where an 'additional VAT liability' (see **10.2**(viii) above) is incurred in respect of qualifying expenditure, at a time when the plant or machinery in question is provided for the purposes of the qualifying activity, it is itself expenditure on that plant or machinery and may be taken into account in determining available qualifying expenditure for the chargeable period in which it accrues.

The net cost of demolition of plant and machinery demolished during a chargeable period, and not replaced, is allocated to the appropriate pool for that chargeable period.

Interaction with annual investment allowance

If an annual investment allowance (AIA) (see **10.12** above) is made in respect of an amount of AIA qualifying expenditure, the expenditure is nevertheless added to the appropriate pool (or pools). Such allocation is necessary to enable a disposal value to be properly brought into account when a disposal event occurs in relation to the item in question. Following the allocation, the available qualifying expenditure in the pool (or in each pool) is reduced by the amount of the AIA on the expenditure allocated. It follows that any excess of the AIA qualifying expenditure over the AIA made will qualify for WDAs beginning with the chargeable period in which the expenditure is incurred.

Interaction with first-year allowances

If a first-year allowance (FYA) (see **10.13**, **10.14** above) is made in respect of an amount of first-year qualifying expenditure, none of that amount can be allocated to a pool for the chargeable period in which the expenditure is incurred, and only the balance (after deducting the FYA) can be allocated to a pool for a subsequent chargeable period.

However, expenditure which qualifies for an FYA for a chargeable period is not excluded from being allocated to a pool for that period if either (1) the FYA is not claimed or (2) it is claimed in respect of part only of the expenditure (in which case the remaining part can be so allocated).

If an FYA is made in respect of an amount of qualifying expenditure, at least some of the balance (after deducting the FYA) must be allocated to a pool for a chargeable period no later than that in which a disposal event (see **10.27** below) occurs in relation to the item in question. It will usually be beneficial to choose to allocate the whole balance. A nil balance (following a 100% FYA) is deemed to be so allocated. Such allocation is necessary to enable a disposal value to be properly brought into account. See **10.13** above for allocation where a super-deduction is claimed.

[*CAA 2001, ss 26(3)–(5), 53–56, 56A, 57–59, 65, 235*].

See the Examples at **10.35** below.

Simon's Taxes. See **B3.331–333**, **B3.393**.

Disposal events and values

[10.27] Where a person has incurred qualifying expenditure (see **10.3** above) on plant or machinery, a **disposal value** must be brought into account for a chargeable period (see 10.2(i) above) in which any one of the following **disposal events** occurs (but normally only in relation to the first such event to occur in respect of that plant or machinery).

(i) The person ceases to own the plant or machinery.
(ii) The person loses possession of it, and it is reasonable to assume the loss is permanent.
(iii) It has been in use for 'mineral exploration and access' (see **9.10**(a) CAPITAL ALLOWANCES) and the person abandons it at the site where it was so in use.
(iv) It ceases to exist as such (by reason of its destruction, dismantling or otherwise).
(v) It begins to be used wholly or partly for purposes other than those of the qualifying activity.
(vi) It begins to be leased under a long funding lease (see **10.50** below).
(vii) The qualifying activity is permanently discontinued.

The amount to be brought into account depends upon the nature of the event.

(a) On a sale (other than one within (b) below), it is the net sale proceeds plus any insurance or capital compensation received (by the person concerned) by reason of any event affecting the sale price obtainable.
(b) On a sale at less than market value, it is market value, unless:
    (i) the buyer (not being a dual resident investing company connected with the seller) can claim plant or machinery or research and development allowances for his expenditure; or
    (ii) the sale gives rise to a charge to tax under *ITEPA 2003* (i.e. on employment, pension or social security income),

    in which case (a) above applies.
(c) On demolition or destruction, it is the net amount received for the remains, plus any insurance or capital compensation received.
(d) On permanent loss (otherwise than within (c) above), or on abandonment as in (iii) above, it is any insurance or capital compensation received.
(e) On commencement of a long funding lease, it is as stated in **10.50** below.
(f) On permanent discontinuance of the qualifying activity preceding an event in (a)–(e) above, it is whatever value would otherwise have applied on the occurrence of that event.
(g) On a gift giving rise to a charge to tax on the recipient under *ITEPA 2003* (i.e. on employment, pension or social security income), it is nil. See also HMRC Capital Allowances Manual CA23250.
(h) On any other event, it is market value at the time of the event.

However, the disposal value is in all cases limited to the qualifying expenditure incurred on the plant or machinery by the person in question. In addition, there is no requirement to bring a disposal value into account if none of the qualifying expenditure in question has been taken into account in determining the person's available qualifying expenditure (see **10.26** above) for any chargeable period up to and including that in which the disposal occurs. As regards both these rules, see also **10.60** below as regards certain transactions between connected persons.

See **10.13** above for special rules for bringing disposal values into account where a super-deduction or SR allowance has been given.

See **10.48** below for a further disposal event in the case of long funding leasing, and for the appropriate disposal value.

Additional VAT rebates

Where an 'additional VAT rebate' (see **10.2**(viii) above) is made in respect of an item of qualifying expenditure, a disposal value of an equivalent amount must be brought into account (on its own or as an addition to any other disposal value brought into account for that item) for the chargeable period in which the rebate accrues. Any disposal value brought into account for a subsequent chargeable period is limited to the original qualifying expenditure less all additional VAT rebates accrued in all chargeable periods up to (but not including) that chargeable period. If the disposal value is itself the result of an additional VAT rebate, it is limited to the original qualifying expenditure less *any* disposal values brought into account as a result of earlier events.

[*CAA 2001, ss 60, 61, 62(1), 63(1), 64(1)(5), 238, 239*].

Anti-avoidance

The disposal value is restricted on an event within (a), (b) or (h) above where:

- the plant or machinery is subject to a lease, and
- arrangements have been entered into that have the effect of reducing the disposal value in so far as it is attributable to rentals payable under the lease.

The disposal value is to be determined as if the arrangements had not been entered into. This does not apply where the arrangements take the form of a transfer of relevant receipts as in **4.10** ANTI-AVOIDANCE such that an amount has been treated as taxable income.

[*CAA 2001, s 64A*].

See **10.60** below for other anti-avoidance rules.

Simon's Taxes. See **B3.331, B3.334, B3.335, B3.393.**

Special rate expenditure

[10.28] Certain expenditure qualifies for writing-down allowances (WDAs) at a special rate of **6%** of the amount (if any) by which available qualifying expenditure (see **10.26** above) exceeds the total of any disposal values (see **10.27** above) falling to be brought into account. This is known as '*special rate expenditure*'. The special rate was 8% before 1 April 2019 (see also below under Hybrid rate for periods straddling 1 April 2019). Special rate expenditure comprises the following:

(i) expenditure on thermal insulation within **10.8**(i) above;
(ii) expenditure on integral features of buildings and structures (see **10.10** above);
(iii) long-life asset expenditure within **10.34** below;
(iv) expenditure on certain cars (see below);
(v) expenditure on the provision of cushion gas, i.e. gas that functions, or is intended to function, as plant in a particular gas storage facility; and
(vi) expenditure on the provision of solar panels.

Hybrid rate for periods straddling 1 April 2019

Where a chargeable period begins before and ends on or after 1 April 2019, the special rate is a hybrid rate computed as follows and rounded up, if necessary, to two decimal places:

$$R = \left(8 \times \frac{BD}{PA}\right) + \left(6 \times \frac{AD}{PA}\right)$$

where:

R = the hybrid special rate;
BD = the number of days in the period of account falling before 1 April 2019;
AD = the number of days in the period of account falling on or after 1 April 2019; and
PA = the number of days in the period of account.

Cars

A car is within (iv) above if it is not one of the following:

- a car with 'low CO_2 emissions';
- an electrically-propelled car (as defined by *CAA 2001, s 268B*); or
- a car first registered before 1 March 2001.

A car has '*low CO2 emissions*' if, when first registered, it was registered on the basis of a qualifying emissions certificate (as defined by *CAA 2001, s 268C*) and its CO_2 emissions (see *CAA 2001, s 268C*) do not exceed 50g/km. For expenditure incurred before 1 April 2021, the limit was 110g/km. For expenditure incurred before 1 April 2018, the limit was 130g/km. '*Car*' is as defined by *CAA 2001, s 268A* (see **10.12**(ii) above) and excludes a motor cycle.

Supplementary

If only a part of the expenditure on any item is special rate expenditure, the part which is and the part which is not are treated as if they were separate items of plant or machinery; any necessary apportionments must be made on a just and reasonable basis.

If special rate expenditure is incurred wholly and exclusively for the purposes of the qualifying activity, and does not fall to be allocated to a single asset pool, it is allocated to a class pool known as the '*special rate pool*'. Even if allocated to a single asset pool, the special rate of WDAs still applies. As regards the special rate pool, see **10.26** above for the 100% rate of WDAs where the balance of the pool is no more than £1,000. The special rate WDA is proportionately reduced or increased if the chargeable period is less or more than a year, or if the qualifying activity has been carried on for part only of the chargeable period. A claim for a WDA can require it to be reduced to a specified amount. The final chargeable period (see **10.26** above) of a special rate pool is that in which the qualifying activity is permanently discontinued.

[*CAA 2001, ss 65(1), 104A, 104AA, 104B–104D, 104G; FA 2019, s 31; SI 2021 No 120, Arts 1, 6*].

Connected persons transactions — transitional

If, on or after 1 April 2008, there is a sale between CONNECTED PERSONS (**19**) of an integral feature (see **10.10** above) on which expenditure was incurred on or before that date and the buyer's expenditure would otherwise be special rate expenditure, the buyer's expenditure is qualifying expenditure only if the original expenditure was qualifying expenditure or if the buyer's expenditure would have been qualifying expenditure if incurred at the time the original expenditure was incurred. If expenditure is thereby prevented from being qualifying expenditure, this rule is again applied if there is a further sale between connected persons, but reference to the original expenditure is always to the pre-1 April 2008 expenditure. [*FA 2008, Sch 26 para 15*]. This rule is designed to prevent allowances being claimed on or after 1 April 2008 on an integral feature if allowances would not have been available for that feature on or before that date (Treasury Explanatory Notes to the 2008 Finance Bill).

Other anti-avoidance

Where a disposal value less than the 'notional written-down value' would otherwise fall to be brought into account in respect of special rate expenditure which has attracted restricted allowances as above, an adjustment may be required. Where the event giving rise to the disposal value is part of a scheme or arrangement a main object of which is the obtaining of a tax advantage under the plant and machinery allowances provisions, the 'notional written-down value' is substituted for the disposal value. The '*notional written-down value*' is qualifying expenditure on the item in question less maximum allowances to date, computed on the assumptions that the item was the only item of plant or machinery, that the expenditure (if on a long-life asset) was not excluded from being long-life asset expenditure by the operation of a monetary limit and that all allowances have been made in full. [*CAA 2001, s 104E*].

Simon's Taxes. See **B3.331**.

Exclusions from the main pool

[10.29] The majority of items excluded from the main pool of qualifying expenditure are set out in **10.30–10.34** below. In addition to those, the following items are excluded:

- special rate expenditure (see **10.28** above);
- plant and machinery in respect of which a partial depreciation subsidy is received (see **10.74** below);

- plant and machinery used for overseas leasing (see **10.55** *et seq.* below).

Cars

[10.30] Expenditure on cars used exclusively for the purposes of the qualifying activity goes into the main pool unless the expenditure is special rate expenditure. Cars with an element of non-business use are not pooled but attract only the special rate of writing-down allowances if the expenditure is special rate expenditure. See **10.28** above for details of those cars the expenditure on which is special rate expenditure. A 'car' excludes a motor cycle, which means that a motor cycle is treated like any other item of plant or machinery.

See **68.33** TRADING INCOME as regards expenditure on *hiring* a car.

Simon's Taxes. See **B3.342**.

Ships

[10.31] Qualifying expenditure (see **10.3** above) on the provision of a ship for the purposes of a trade or other qualifying activity can only be allocated to a *single asset pool* (see **10.26** above), known as a *single ship pool*. This does not apply if:

- an election is made to exclude such treatment (see below); or
- the qualifying activity is one of special leasing (see **10.54** below); or
- the ship is otherwise provided for leasing (which expressly includes letting on charter), *unless* it is not used for 'overseas leasing' (other than 'protected leasing') at any time in the 'designated period' *and* it appears that it will be used only for a 'qualifying purpose' in that period (see **10.55** *et seq.* below for meaning of expressions used here).

When a disposal event occurs in relation to a single ship pool, the available qualifying expenditure (see **10.26** above) in that pool for the chargeable period in question is transferred to the '*appropriate non-ship pool*' (i.e. the pool to which the expenditure would originally have been allocated in the absence of the single ship pool rules), and the single ship pool is brought to an end with no balancing allowance or charge. The disposal value is brought into account in the pool now containing the qualifying expenditure. In addition to the circumstances at **10.27** above, a disposal event occurs if a ship is provided for leasing or letting on charter and begins to be used otherwise than for a 'qualifying purpose' at some time in the first four years of the 'designated period' (see **10.55** onwards below as regards expressions used).

If the ship ceases to be used by the person who incurred the qualifying expenditure, without his having brought it into use for the purposes of the qualifying activity, then, in addition to any adjustments required as above, any writing-down allowances (WDAs) previously made (or postponed — see below) are withdrawn, and the amount withdrawn is allocated to the 'appropriate non-ship pool' (see above) for the chargeable period in question.

A person who has incurred qualifying expenditure on a ship may elect, for any chargeable period, to disapply the single ship pool provisions in respect of:

- all or part of any qualifying expenditure that would otherwise be allocated to a single ship pool in that period; or
- all or part of the available qualifying expenditure (see **10.26** above) already in a single ship pool,

with the result that the amount in question is allocated to the 'appropriate non-ship pool' (see above). The election must be made no later than the first anniversary of 31 January following the tax year in which ends the chargeable period in question.

Postponement of WDAs

A person entitled to a WDA for a chargeable period in respect of a single ship pool may, by written notice, postpone all or part of it to a later period. The amount to be postponed must be specified in the notice. Where a reduced WDA is claimed, all or part of the reduced amount may be postponed. The time limits for giving notice are the same as for the election referred to immediately above. Available qualifying expenditure (see **10.26** above) is computed as if the postponed WDA had, in fact, been made. Postponed WDAs may be claimed over one or more subsequent chargeable periods. See **10.16** above for postponement of first-year allowances.

[*CAA 2001, ss 127–129, 130(2)(7), 131(1)(3)–(7), 132, 133, 157(1)*].

Deferment of balancing charges on qualifying ships

Balancing charges on ships may be deferred and set against subsequent expenditure on ships for a maximum of six years from the date of disposal. A claim for deferment of the whole or part of a balancing charge may be made by the shipowner where a disposal event within **10.27**(i)–(iv) above occurs after 20 April 1994 in relation to a 'qualifying ship' (the old ship). A '*qualifying ship*' is, broadly, a ship of a sea-going kind of 100 gross registered tons or more, excluding offshore installations (as defined by *ITA 2007, s 1001*) and ships of a kind used or chartered primarily for sport or recreation (but passenger ships and cruise liners are not so excluded). The provisions also apply to ships of less than 100 tons in cases where the old ship is totally lost or is damaged beyond worthwhile repair. A ship brought into use in the trade on or after 20 July 1994 must within three months of first use (unless disposed of during those three months) be registered in the UK, the Channel Islands, Isle of Man, a colony (as to which see Revenue Tax Bulletins April 1995 p 208, June 1998 p 553), a European Union State or a European Economic Area State and must continue to be so until at least three years from first use or, if earlier, until disposed of to an unconnected person. It is a further condition that no amount in respect of the old ship has been allocated to an overseas leasing pool (see **10.55** below), a 'partial use' single asset pool (see **10.32** below), a 'partial depreciation subsidy' single asset pool (see **10.74** below) or a pool for a qualifying activity consisting of special leasing (see **10.54** below).

The balancing charge on the old ship is in effect calculated as if allowances had been granted, and the charge arises, in a single ship pool, with appropriate assumptions where that is not, in fact, the case (see *CAA 2001, s 139*).

Deferment is achieved by allocating the amount deferred to the 'appropriate non-ship pool' (see above) for the chargeable period in question, so that it is effectively set against the disposal value brought into account in that pool (see above) as a result of the disposal event concerned. The *maximum deferment* is the *lowest* of (i) the amount treated as brought into account in respect of the old ship under *CAA 2001, s 139* (see above), (ii) the amount to be expended on new shipping (see below), so far as not already set against an earlier balancing charge, in the six years starting with the date of disposal of the old ship, (iii) the amount which, in the absence of a deferment claim, would have been the total balancing charge for the chargeable period in question in the appropriate non-ship pool, and (iv) the amount needed to reduce the profit of the trade or other qualifying activity to nil (disregarding losses brought forward), no deferment being possible if no such profit has been made. If the amount actually expended within (ii) above turns out to be less than the amount deferred, the amount of the deficiency is reinstated as a balancing charge for the chargeable period to which the claim relates.

Where an amount is expended on new shipping within the six-year period allowed and is attributed by the shipowner, by notice to HMRC, to any part of an amount deferred, an amount equal to the amount so matched is brought into account as a disposal value, for the chargeable period in which the expenditure is incurred, in the single ship pool to which the expenditure is allocated, thus reducing the amount on which allowances may be claimed on the new ship. No amount of expenditure can be attributed to a deferment if there is earlier expenditure on new shipping within the said six-year period which has not been attributed to that or earlier deferments. An attribution may be varied by the trader by notice to HMRC within a specified time (see *CAA 2001, s 142*).

For the purposes of these provisions, an amount is expended on new shipping if it is qualifying expenditure, incurred by the claimant wholly and exclusively for the purposes of a qualifying activity, on a ship (the new ship) which will be a qualifying ship (see above) for at least three years from first use or, if earlier, until disposed of to an unconnected person. Expenditure is treated as incurred by the claimant if it is incurred by a successor following a partnership change or company reconstruction in consequence of which the qualifying activity was not treated as discontinued. Expenditure incurred on a ship which has belonged to either the shipowner or a connected person within the previous six years or which is incurred mainly for tax avoidance reasons does not qualify. The expenditure must be allocated to a single ship pool. If an election is made to disapply the single ship pool provisions, the expenditure is deemed never to have been expenditure on new shipping (but must nevertheless be treated as such in matching expenditure with deferments, so that the election prevents further matching of amounts already deferred). Expenditure does not qualify if the overseas leasing provisions at **10.55** below come to apply to the new ship.

For income tax purposes, the claim for deferment must be made within two years after the end of that chargeable period. Where a claim for deferment is found to be erroneous as a result of subsequent circumstances, the shipowner must, within three months after the end of the chargeable period in which those circumstances first arise, notify HMRC accordingly (failure to do so incurring a penalty under *TMA 1970, s 98*); consequential assessments may be made within twelve months after notice is given, notwithstanding normal time limits.

[*CAA 2001, ss 134–158, Sch 3 para 24; F(No 2)A 2017, Sch 4 para 125*].

Simon's Taxes. See **B3.350–351.**

Plant and machinery partly used for non-trade etc. purposes

[10.32] Qualifying expenditure (see **10.3** above) incurred partly for the purposes of the trade or other qualifying activity and partly for other purposes can only be allocated to a *single asset pool* (see **10.26** above). (See **10.16** above as regards first-year allowances.) Where in other cases plant or machinery *begins to be used* partly for other purposes, such that a disposal value falls to be brought into account (see **10.27**(v) above) in a pool, an amount equal to the disposal value is allocated to a single asset pool for the chargeable period in question. In respect of a single asset pool under these provisions, writing-down allowances and balancing allowances and charges are reduced to such amount as is just and reasonable (though the full amount is deducted in arriving at any unrelieved qualifying expenditure carried forward).

Where, circumstances change such that the proportion of use for purposes other than those of the qualifying activity increases during a chargeable period, and the market value of the plant or machinery at the end of the period exceeds the available qualifying expenditure (see **10.26** above) in the pool for that period by more than £1 million, then if no disposal value would otherwise fall to be brought into account for the period, a disposal value must be brought into account (equal to market value — see **10.27**(g) above) and, in the next or a subsequent chargeable period, an equivalent amount may be allocated to a new single asset pool as if it were qualifying expenditure newly incurred.

[*CAA 2001, ss 206–208, Sch 3 para 42*].

See also *Kempster v McKenzie* Ch D 1952, 33 TC 193 and *G H Chambers (Northiam Farms) Ltd v Watmough* Ch D 1956, 36 TC 711 and HMRC Capital Allowances Manual CA 23530, 27100 as regards further adjustment for any element of personal choice.

Simon's Taxes. See **B3.359.**

Short-life assets

[10.33] A person who has incurred qualifying expenditure (see **10.3** above) on an item of plant or machinery may elect for it to be treated as a short-life asset, provided it is not an excluded item (see list below). There is no requirement as to the expected useful life of the item, but short-life asset treatment will be of no practical benefit where the item remains in use for more than eight years. The election is irrevocable and must be made within two years after the end of the chargeable period in which the expenditure (or earliest expenditure) is incurred.

Identification

In general, HMRC will require sufficient information in support of an election to minimise the possibility of any difference of view at a later date (e.g. on a disposal) about what was and was not covered by the election, and to ensure that it does not incorporate any excluded items (see list below). Where separate identification of short-life assets acquired in a chargeable period is either impossible or impracticable, e.g. similar small or relatively inexpensive items held in very large numbers, perhaps in different locations, then the information required in support of the election may be provided by reference to batches of acquisitions. (HMRC SP 1/86).

Exclusions

Each of the following items of plant or machinery is excluded from being a short-life asset.

(i) A car, defined as at **10.12**(ii) above with the exception of cars hired out to disabled persons in receipt of certain disability allowances, independence payments or mobility supplements. Note that motor cycles are excluded from the definition of 'car' and are thus not excluded from being short-life assets.
(ii) A ship.
(iii) An item which is the subject of special leasing (see **10.54** below).
(iv) An item acquired partly for the purposes of a trade or other qualifying activity and partly for other purposes.
(v) An item which is the subject of a partial depreciation subsidy (see **10.74** below).
(vi) An item received by way of gift or whose previous use by the person concerned did not attract capital allowances (see **10.68, 10.69** below and, as regards long funding leasing, **10.50** below).
(vii) An item the expenditure on which is long-life asset expenditure (see **10.34** below).
(viii) An item the expenditure on which is special rate expenditure (see **10.28** above) unless it is a car hired out to persons receiving certain disability allowances or mobility supplements.
(ix) An item provided for leasing, unless it will be used within the 'designated period' for a 'qualifying purpose' (see **10.55** *et seq.* below as regards these expressions), and with the exception in any case of cars hired out to persons receiving certain disability allowances or mobility supplements.
(x) An item leased overseas such that it attracts only a 10% writing-down allowance (see **10.55** below).
(xi) An item leased to two or more persons jointly such that *CAA 2001, s 116* applies.

Treatment of short-life assets

Qualifying expenditure in respect of a short-life asset can only be allocated to a *single asset pool* (see **10.26** above), known as a *short-life asset pool.* If no disposal event within **10.27**(i)–(vi) above occurs in any of the chargeable periods ending on or before the 'relevant anniversary' (referred to below as the '*cut-off date*'), the short-life asset pool is brought to an end on the cut-off date but with no balancing allowance or charge and no denial of a writing-down allowance for the final period. The item ceases to be a short-life asset and the available qualifying expenditure in the pool is allocated to the main pool for the first chargeable period ending *after* the cut-off date. (If the item is a car the expenditure on which was special rate expenditure (see **10.28** above), it is allocated to the special rate pool rather than the main pool.)

The '*relevant anniversary*' (and thus the cut-off date) is the eighth anniversary of the end of the chargeable period in which the expenditure was incurred (or the first such period in which any of it was incurred).

The following applies where short-life asset treatment has been claimed on the basis that the item has been provided for leasing, but will be used within the 'designated period' for a 'qualifying purpose' (so is not excluded by (ix) above). (See **10.55** onwards below as regards expressions used here.) If, at any time in a chargeable period ending on or before the cut-off date (as above), the item begins to be used otherwise than for such a purpose, and that time falls within the first eight years of the 'designated period', the short-life asset pool is brought to an end at that time but with no balancing allowance or charge and no denial of a writing-down allowance for the final period. The item ceases to be a short-life asset and the available qualifying expenditure in the pool is allocated, for the chargeable period in which that time falls, to the main pool.

If at any time before the cut-off date (as above), a short-life asset is disposed of to a connected person (within **19** CONNECTED PERSONS), short-life asset treatment continues in the connected person's hands (though the original cut-off date remains unchanged). If both parties so elect (within two years after the end of the chargeable period in which the disposal occurs), the disposal is treated as being at a price equal to the available qualifying expenditure (see **10.26** above) then in the short-life asset pool, and certain anti-avoidance provisions on transactions between connected persons are disapplied. If no election is made, the anti-avoidance provisions at **10.59** below apply in full, and the exception at **10.27**(b)(i) above is disapplied (so that market value can be substituted for a lesser sale price even where the buyer is entitled to capital allowances).

If a disposal event occurs in respect of a short-life asset pool such that the pool ends and a balancing *allowance* arises (see **10.26** above), and an 'additional VAT liability' (see **10.2**(viii) above) is subsequently incurred in respect of the item concerned, a further balancing allowance of that amount is given for the chargeable period in which the additional VAT liability accrues.

HMRC accept that it may not be practicable for individual pools to be maintained for every short-life asset, especially where they are held in very large numbers. Statement of Practice SP 1/86 sets out examples of acceptable bases of computation where the inspector is satisfied that the actual life in the business of a distinct class of assets with broadly similar average lives, before being sold or scrapped, is likely to be less than five years.

[*CAA 2001, ss 83–89, 240, 268D*].

See *Example (A)* at **10.35** below.

Simon's Taxes. See **B3.343**.

Long-life assets

[10.34] There are special provisions relating to certain '*long-life asset expenditure*', i.e. qualifying expenditure (as in **10.3** above) incurred on the provision of a 'long-life asset' for the purposes of a qualifying activity (but see below for exclusions by reference to a monetary limit).

Subject to below, a '*long-life asset*' is plant or machinery which it is reasonable to expect will have a useful economic life of at least 25 years (or where such was a reasonable expectation when the plant or machinery was new, i.e. unused and not second-hand). For these purposes, the useful economic life of plant or machinery is the period from first use (by any person) until it ceases to be, or to be likely to be, used by anyone as a fixed asset of a business. As an introduction to a detailed discussion of what constitutes a long-life asset (including 12 examples), HMRC have stated that they 'will generally accept the accounting treatment as determining whether an asset is long-life provided it is not clearly unreasonable' (Revenue Tax Bulletin August 1997 pp 445–450). For whether glasshouses (for which see generally **10.8** and **10.11**(16) above) are long-life assets, see Revenue Tax Bulletin June 1998 p 552. For aircraft, see Revenue Tax Bulletin June 1999 pp 671, 672, April 2000 pp 739, 740 and December 2003 pp 1074, 1075.

The following *cannot* be long-life assets.

(i) Fixtures (see **10.36** below) in, or plant or machinery provided for use in, a building used wholly or mainly as a dwelling-house, showroom, hotel, office or retail shop or similar retail premises, or for purposes ancillary to such use.
(ii) Cars, as defined at **10.12**(ii) above.
(iii) Motor cycles.

Long-life asset expenditure which is incurred wholly and exclusively for the purposes of a qualifying activity, and which does not require allocation under other rules to a single asset pool, can only be allocated to the special rate pool in **10.28** above. Writing-down allowances for a chargeable period in respect of long-life asset expenditure (whether in the special rate pool or a single asset pool) are therefore given at the special rate (currently 6%).

A claim for a writing-down allowance may require it to be reduced to a specified amount. Where plant and machinery allowances have been claimed for long-life asset expenditure, any earlier or later expenditure on the same asset for which allowances are subsequently claimed, unless excluded by (i)–(iii) above, is treated as also being long-life asset expenditure if it would not otherwise be so. This over-rides the exclusion of expenditure within the monetary limit referred to below.

Monetary limit

Expenditure is not long-life asset expenditure if it is expenditure to which the monetary limit (see below) applies and it is incurred in a chargeable period for which that limit is not exceeded. The monetary limit does not apply to the following types of expenditure:

- expenditure on a share in plant or machinery; or
- a contribution treated as plant or machinery expenditure under *CAA 2001, s 538* (see **10.2**(vii) above); or
- expenditure on plant or machinery for leasing (whether or not in the course of a trade).

The monetary limit is £100,000, proportionately reduced or increased for chargeable periods of less or more than a year and, as regards a company, divided by one plus the number of its 'related 51% group companies' (within *CTA 2010, s 279F* — see **58.3** PAYMENT OF TAX). For accounting periods beginning on or after 1 April 2023, the division is by reference to associated companies (defined as at **1.3** INTRODUCTION: CHARGE TO TAX, RATES AND PROFIT COMPUTATIONS) rather than related 51% group companies. In many cases, this change will be no more than a change in terminology, but there are differences in the meaning of the two expressions. For the purpose of applying the monetary limit, all expenditure under a contract is treated as incurred in the first chargeable period in which any expenditure under the contract is incurred.

Transitional rule for second-hand assets

A second-hand asset is excluded from the long-life asset provisions if:

- the previous owner properly claimed plant and machinery allowances for expenditure on its provision;
- his expenditure did not fall to be treated as long-life asset expenditure; and
- his expenditure would have fallen to be so treated if the long-life asset rules (apart from this transitional rule) had always been law.

A provisional claim to normal writing-down allowances may be made by a purchaser on this basis, before the vendor has made the appropriate return, provided that reasonable steps have been taken to establish that entitlement will arise, and that the appropriate revisions will be made, and assessments accepted, if entitlement does not in the event arise (Revenue Tax Bulletin August 1997 p 450).

[*CAA 2001, ss 56(5), 65(1), 90–104, 268A, Sch 3 para 20; CTA 2010, s 115; FA 2021, Sch 1 paras 16, 33*].

Simon's Taxes. See **B3.344.**

Examples of capital allowances on plant and machinery

[10.35] The following examples illustrate a number of matters detailed above.

(A) Short-life assets

A Ltd prepares trading accounts to 30 September each year, and buys and sells machines, for use in the trade, as follows.

	Cost	Date of acquisition	Disposal proceeds	Date of disposal
Machine X	£40,000	30.1.12	£13,000	1.12.13
Machine Y	£25,000	1.3.12	£4,000	1.12.20

A Ltd also buys other plant and machinery for use in the trade for £100,000 in the year ended 30 September 2012. A Ltd elects under *CAA 2001, s 83* for machines X, and Y to be treated as short-life assets. The main pool of qualifying expenditure brought forward at the beginning of the accounting period 1.10.11–30.9.12 is £80,000.

A Ltd's capital allowances are as follows.

	Main Pool	Machine X	Machine Y	Total Allowances
		Short-life asset pools		
	£	£	£	£
Accounting period 1.10.11–30.9.12				
WDV b/f	80,000			
Additions	100,000	40,000	25,000	
AIA 100%	(100,000)			100,000
WDA 19% — note (c)	(15,200)	(7,600)	(4,750)	27,550
	64,800	32,400	20,250	£127,550
Accounting period 1.10.12–30.9.13				
WDA 18%	(11,664)	(5,832)	(3,645)	£21,141
	53,136	26,568	16,605	
Accounting period 1.10.13–30.9.14				
Disposal		(13,000)		
Balancing allowance		£13,568		13,568
WDA 18%	(9,564)		(2,989)	12,553
				£26,121
	43,572		13,616	
Accounting period 1.10.14–30.9.15				
WDA 18%	(7,842)		(2,450)	£10,292
	35,730		11,166	
Accounting period 1.10.15–30.9.16				
WDA 18%	(6,431)		(2,010)	£8,441
	29,299		9,156	
Accounting period 1.10.16–30.9.17				
WDA 18%	(5,274)		(1,648)	£6,922
	24,025		7,508	
Accounting period 1.10.17–30.9.18				
WDA 18%	(4,325)		(1,351)	£5,676
	19,700		6,157	

Accounting period 1.10.18–30.9.19			
WDA 18%	(3,546)	(1,108)	£4,654
	16,154	5,049	
Accounting period 1.10.19–30.9.20			
WDA 18%	(2,907)	(909)	£3,816
	13,247	4,140	
Accounting period 1.10.20–30.9.21			
Transfer to pool	4,140	(4,140)	
	17,387	—	
Disposal	(4,000)		
	13,387		
WDA 18%	(2,410)		£2,410
WDV c/f	£10,977		

Notes

(a) The eighth anniversary of the end of the chargeable period in which the expenditure on Machine Y is incurred is 30.9.20 (the cut-off date). The balance of expenditure on Machine Y is thus transferred to the main pool in the period of account 1.10.20–30.9.21, this being the first chargeable period ending after the cut-off date.

(b) The hybrid rate of WDA for the year to 30 September 2012 is 19.03%, computed as follows (where 183 is the number of days from 1 October 2011 to 31 March 2012, 183 is the number of days from 1 April 2012 to 30 September 2012 and 366 is the total number of days in the period of account).

$$R = \left(20 \times \frac{183}{366}\right) + \left(18 \times \frac{183}{366}\right) = 19$$

(B) Special rate pool

B Ltd begins trading on 1 January 2021 and makes up accounts to 31 December. In the year ending 31 December 2021, the company incurs capital expenditure on plant and machinery of £2,000,000, of which £1,500,000 is special rate expenditure and the remainder falls to be allocated to the main pool. All of the expenditure is incurred before 1 April 2021. B Ltd carries on no other qualifying activity and none of the restrictions at **10.14** above apply to restrict the maximum annual investment allowance. None of the capital expenditure qualifies for first-year allowances.

B Ltd's plant and machinery allowances for the year ended 31 December 2021, assuming it claims all allowances to which it is entitled, will be calculated as follows.

	Main pool of expenditure	*Special rate pool*	*Total allowances*
	£	£	£
Additions	500,000	1,500,000	
AIA (note (a))		(1,000,000)	1,000,000
		500,000	
WDA (18% p.a.)	90,000		90,000
WDA (6% p.a.)		30,000	30,000
WDV c/fwd	£410,000	£470,000	
Total allowances claimed			£1,120,000

Note

(a) The company is free to choose how to allocate the annual investment allowance to expenditure. In this example the allowance has been allocated to special rate expenditure as this maximises the writing-down allowances available.

Fixtures

[10.36] There are special provisions to determine entitlement to allowances on fixtures, i.e. plant or machinery which, by law, becomes part of the building or land on which it is installed or otherwise fixed, including any boiler or water-filled radiator installed as part of a space or water heating system. A dispute may arise as to whether fixtures have, in law, become part of a building or land. Where two or more persons' tax liabilities are affected by the outcome of such a dispute, the question is determined for tax purposes by the Tribunal, and each of the parties concerned is entitled to be a party to the proceedings. [*CAA 2001, ss 172(1)(2), 173, 204(1)–(3)*].

In *J C Decaux (UK) Ltd v Francis* (Sp C 84), [1996] SSCD 281, automatic public conveniences and other street furniture such as bus shelters were held to be fixtures forming part of the land (and see **10.37** below).

These provisions determine ownership for capital allowances purposes of plant or machinery that is (or becomes) a fixture and determine entitlement to allowances in each of the various circumstances described at **10.37–10.42** below. See **10.51** below for the disapplication of these provisions in cases involving long funding leases of plant or machinery that is (or becomes) a fixture. The provisions do not affect the entitlement of a contributor towards capital expenditure (see **10.2**(vii) above). [*CAA 2001, s 172(1)(2)(5)*]. The availability of capital allowances to the purchaser is conditional upon (a) previous business expenditure on fixtures being pooled by the seller before their transfer to the purchaser, and (b) the seller and purchaser, within two years of the transfer, fixing their agreement on the value of the fixtures transferred. See **10.46** below for details. See, respectively, **10.43**, **10.44** and **10.45** below for provisions determining cessation of ownership (and consequent disposal values), acquisition of ownership in certain cases and restrictions of qualifying expenditure where allowances previously claimed.

Although the rules apply strictly on an asset-by-asset basis, HMRC accept that in practice they may be applied to groups of assets provided that this does not distort the tax computation (Revenue Tax Bulletin June 1998 p 552).

For the purposes of the fixtures provisions, an '*interest in land*' means:

(i) the fee simple estate in the land;
(ii) in Scotland, in the case of feudal property prior to abolition of feudal tenure, the estate or interest of the proprietor of the *dominium utile*, and in any other case, the interest of the owner;
(iii) a lease (defined for these provisions in relation to land as any leasehold estate in (or, in Scotland, lease of) the land (whether a head-lease, sub-lease or under-lease) or any agreement to acquire such an estate (or lease));
(iv) an easement or servitude;
(v) a licence to occupy land,

and any agreement to acquire an interest as in (i)–(iv) above. Where an interest is conveyed or assigned by way of security subject to a right of redemption, the interest is treated as continuing to belong to the person having the redemption right. [*CAA 2001, ss 174(4), 175, Sch 3 para 29*]. As regards (v) above, for the HMRC view of when a licence to occupy land exists for these purposes, see Revenue Tax Bulletin June 2000 p 761.

See generally HMRC Capital Allowances Manual CA26000 *et seq.*

Finance leasing

See **69.43** TRADING INCOME — DEDUCTIONS as regards restrictions on capital allowances where certain finance leasing arrangements are involved. See also **10.47**, **10.57**, **10.61**, **10.62** below.

Simon's Taxes. See **B3.355–358.**

Expenditure incurred by holder of interest in land

[10.37] Where a person having an interest in land incurs capital expenditure on plant or machinery which becomes a fixture in relation to that land, for the purposes of a trade or other qualifying activity, then, subject to the election in **10.38** or **10.42** below, the fixture is treated as belonging to that person. If there are two or more such persons, with different interests, the only interest to be taken into account for this purpose is:

(i) an easement or servitude, or any agreement to acquire same;
(ii) if (i) does not apply to any of those interests, a licence to occupy the land;
(iii) if neither (i) nor (ii) applies to any of those interests, that interest which is not directly or indirectly in reversion on any other of those interests in the land (in Scotland, that of whichever of those persons has, or last had, the right of use of the land).

[*CAA 2001, s 176*].

In *J C Decaux (UK) Ltd v Francis* (Sp C 84), [1996] SSCD 281, suppliers to local authorities of automatic public conveniences and other street furniture such as bus shelters, which were held to be fixtures forming part of the land, were held not to have an interest in the land.

Expenditure incurred by equipment lessor

[10.38] An 'equipment lease' exists where:

- a person incurs capital expenditure on an item of plant or machinery for leasing;
- an agreement is entered into for the lease, directly or indirectly from that person (the '*equipment lessor*'), of the item to another person (the '*equipment lessee*');
- the item becomes a fixture; and
- the item is not leased as part of the land in relation to which it is a fixture.

Such an agreement, or a lease entered into under such an agreement, is an '*equipment lease*'. Provided that:

(i) under the equipment lease, the plant or machinery is leased for the purposes of a trade or other qualifying activity carried on (or to be carried on in future) by the equipment lessee;

(ii) it is not for use in a dwelling-house;

(iii) the equipment lessor and equipment lessee are not CONNECTED PERSONS (**19**);

(iv) if the expenditure on the fixture had been incurred by the equipment lessee, he would have been entitled to allowances under **10.37** above,

the equipment lessor and equipment lessee may jointly elect for the fixture to be treated, from the time the expenditure is incurred by the equipment lessor (or, if later, from the commencement of the lessee's qualifying activity), as owned by the lessor and not the lessee.

Where the following conditions are met, (i) and (iv) above do not have to be satisfied (and the potentially later start date of the election is not relevant):

(1) the plant or machinery becomes a fixture by being fixed to land which is neither a building nor part of a building;

(2) the lessee has an interest in that land when he takes possession of the plant or machinery under the equipment lease;

(3) under the terms of the equipment lease the lessor is entitled, at the end of the lease period, to sever the plant or machinery from the land to which it is then fixed, whereupon it will be owned by the lessor;

(4) the nature of the plant or machinery and the way it is fixed to the land are such that its use does not, to any material extent, prevent its being used, after severance, for the same purposes on different premises; and

(5) the equipment lease is such as falls under generally accepted accounting practice (see **68.18** TRADING INCOME) to be treated in the accounts of the equipment lessor as an operating lease.

The election must be made within two years after the end of the equipment lessor's chargeable period in which the expenditure is incurred.

[*CAA 2001, ss 174(1)–(3), 177–180, 203, Sch 3 paras 30–33*].

See **10.42** below as regards expenditure incurred by an energy services provider.

Expenditure included in consideration for acquisition of existing interest in land

[10.39] Where a person acquires a pre-existing interest in land to which a fixture is attached, for a consideration in part treated for capital allowance purposes as being expenditure on provision of the fixture, the fixture is treated as belonging to the person acquiring the interest. This applies equally where the fixture in question was previously let under an 'equipment lease' (see**10.38** above) and, in connection with the acquisition, the purchaser pays a capital sum to discharge the equipment lessee's obligations under that lease. It also applies where the fixture was provided under an energy services agreement (see **10.42** below) and, in connection with the acquisition, the purchaser pays a capital sum to discharge the client's obligations under that agreement.

[*CAA 2001, ss 181(1)(4), 182(1), 182A(1), Sch 3 paras 34, 35*].

Where the above provisions would otherwise apply, they are treated as not applying (and as never having applied) where the following conditions are met:

(i) a person is treated as the owner of the fixture (other than under *CAA 2001, s 538* (contributions to expenditure — see **10.2**(vii) above)) immediately before the time of the above acquisition, in consequence of his having incurred expenditure on its provision; and
(ii) that person is entitled to, and claims, an allowance in respect of that expenditure.

Where any person becomes aware that a return of his has become incorrect because of the operation of this provision, the necessary amendments to the return must be notified to HMRC within three months of his becoming so aware, subject to penalties for failure.

[*CAA 2001, ss 181(2)(3), 182(2)(3), 182A(2)(3), 203*].

Expenditure incurred by incoming lessee — election to transfer lessor's entitlement to allowances

[10.40] Where a person with an interest in land to which a fixture is attached grants a lease and he would (or if chargeable to tax would) be entitled, for the chargeable period in which the lease is granted, to capital allowances in respect of the fixture, and the consideration given by the lessee falls, in whole or in part, to be treated for plant and machinery allowances purposes as expenditure on the provision of the fixture, an election is available to the lessor and lessee. They may jointly elect (by notice to HMRC within two years after the date on which the lease takes effect) that, from the grant of the lease, the fixture is treated as belonging to the lessee and not to the lessor. No such election is available if lessor and lessee are CONNECTED PERSONS (**19**. These provisions apply to the entering into of an agreement for a lease as they apply to a grant of a lease. [*CAA 2001, ss 174(4), 183, Sch 3 para 36*].

Expenditure incurred by incoming lessee — lessor not entitled to allowances

[10.41] Where:

- a person with an interest in land to which a fixture is attached grants a lease;
- the provisions at **10.40** above do not apply, because the lessor is not entitled to capital allowances in respect of the fixture;
- before the lease is granted, the fixture has not been used for the purposes of a trade or other qualifying activity by the lessor or a person connected with him (see **19** CONNECTED PERSONS); and
- the consideration given by the lessee includes a capital sum falling, in whole or in part, to be treated for plant and machinery allowances purposes as expenditure on the provision of the fixture,

the fixture is treated as belonging to the lessee from the time the lease is granted.

Rules similar to those of *CAA 2001, s 181(2)(3), s 182(2)(3), s 182A(2)(3), s 203* at **10.39** above apply (by reference to the time of grant).

[*CAA 2001, s 184, Sch 3 para 37*].

Expenditure incurred by energy services provider

[10.42] An '*energy services agreement*' is an agreement entered into by an 'energy services provider' and his client that provides, with a view to the saving or more efficient use of energy, for:

- the design of plant or machinery or of systems incorporating it;
- the obtaining and installation of the plant or machinery; and
- its operation and maintenance,

and under which any payment by the client in respect of the operation of the plant or machinery is wholly or partly linked to the energy savings or increased energy efficiency. An '*energy services provider*' is a person carrying on a qualifying activity consisting wholly or mainly in providing energy management services. [*CAA 2001, s 175A*].

Where:

- an energy services agreement is entered into;
- the energy services provider incurs capital expenditure under the agreement on an item of plant or machinery;
- the item becomes a fixture;
- at the time the item becomes a fixture, the client has an interest in the land in relation to which it is a fixture but the provider does not;
- the item is neither leased nor used in a dwelling-house;
- the operation of the item is carried out wholly or substantially by the provider or a person connected with him; and
- provider and client are not CONNECTED PERSONS (**19**),

the energy services provider and the client may jointly elect for the fixture to be treated, from the time the expenditure is incurred, as owned by the former and not the latter. This opens the way for the energy services provider to claim

100% first-year allowances where his expenditure is within **10.14**(a) above. The election must be made no later than two years after the end of the chargeable period in which the expenditure is incurred. If the client would not have been entitled to allowances under **10.37** above if he had incurred the expenditure himself, the election is available only if the item belongs to the technology class 'Combined Heat and Power' in the Energy Technology Criteria List (see **10.17** above). The intention is that, in such specified cases, allowances to the provider are not to be denied only because the client is a non-taxpayer. [*CAA 2001, s 180A*]. See also HMRC Capital Allowances Manual CA23150.

Cessation of ownership

[10.43] The following points apply.

(A) If a person is treated as owning a fixture under *CAA 2001, s 176* (see **10.37** above) *s 181, 182* or *182A* (see **10.39** above), *s 183* (see **10.40** above) or *s 184* (see **10.41** above), he is treated as ceasing to be the owner if and when he ceases to have the 'qualifying interest'. The '*qualifying interest*' is the interest in the land in question, except that where **10.40** or **10.41** apply it is the lease there referred to. There are rules (see *CAA 2001, s 189*) for identifying the qualifying interest in special cases.

(B) Where, under **10.40** above, the lessee begins to be treated as owning the fixture, the lessor is treated as ceasing to own it at that time.

(C) Where a fixture is permanently severed from the building or land, such that it is no longer owned by the person treated as owning it, he is treated as ceasing to own it at the time of severance.

(D) Where an equipment lessor is treated as owning a fixture (see **10.38**) above) and either he assigns his rights under the equipment lease or the financial obligations of the equipment lessee (or his assignee etc.) are discharged, the equipment lessor is treated as ceasing to own the fixture at that time (or the earliest of those times).

(E) Where an energy services provider is treated as owning a fixture (see **10.38** above) and either he assigns his rights under the energy services agreement or the financial obligations of the client (or his assignee etc.) are discharged, the energy services provider is treated as ceasing to own the fixture at that time (or the earliest of those times).

[*CAA 2001, ss 188–192A*].

The *disposal value* to be brought into account in relation to a fixture depends upon the nature of the event.

(1) On cessation of ownership under (A) above due to a sale of the qualifying interest (other than where (2) below applies), and subject to the election below, it is that part of the sale price that falls (or would, if there were an entitlement, fall) to be treated for plant and machinery allowances purposes as expenditure by the purchaser on the provision of the fixture.

(2) On cessation of ownership under (A) above due to a sale of the qualifying interest at less than market value (unless the buyer (not being a dual resident investing company connected with the seller) can claim

plant or machinery or research and development allowances for his expenditure, in which case (1) above applies), it is the amount that, if that interest were sold at market value (determined without regard to the disposal event itself) at that time, would be treated for plant and machinery allowances purposes as expenditure by the purchaser on provision of the fixture.

(3) On cessation of ownership under (A) above where neither (1) or (2) above applies but the qualifying interest continues (or would do so but for being merged with another interest), it is an amount determined as in (2) above.

(4) On cessation of ownership under (A) above due to the expiry of the qualifying interest, it is any capital sum received by reference to the fixture, or otherwise nil.

(5) On cessation of ownership under (B) above, and subject to the election below, it is that part of the capital sum given by the lessee for the lease as qualifies for plant and machinery allowances as the lessee's expenditure on the fixture.

(6) On cessation of ownership under (C) above, it is market value at time of severance.

(7) On cessation of ownership under (D) above, it is the consideration for the assignment or, as the case may be, the capital sum, if any, paid to discharge the equipment lessee's financial obligations.

(8) On cessation of ownership under (E) above, it is the consideration for the assignment or, as the case may be, the capital sum, if any, paid to discharge the client's financial obligations.

(9) On permanent discontinuance of the trade or other qualifying activity followed by the sale of the qualifying interest, it is an amount determined as in (1) above.

(10) On permanent discontinuance of the qualifying activity followed by demolition or destruction of the fixture, it is the net amount received for the remains, plus any insurance or capital compensation received.

(11) On permanent discontinuance of the qualifying activity followed by permanent loss (other than as in (10) above) of the fixture, it is any insurance or capital compensation received.

(12) On the fixture's beginning to be used wholly or partly for purposes other than those of the qualifying activity, it is that part of the sale price that would fall to be treated for plant and machinery allowances purposes as expenditure by the purchaser on the provision of the fixture if the qualifying interest were sold at market value.

[*CAA 2001, s 196, Sch 3 para 41*].

Fixtures are treated as disposed of at their 'notional written-down value' (if greater than would otherwise be the case) where the disposal event is part of a scheme or arrangement having tax avoidance (whether by increased allowances or reduced charges) as a main object. The '*notional written-down value*' is qualifying expenditure on the item in question less maximum allowances to date, computed on the assumption that all allowances have been made in full. [*CAA 2001, s 197*].

A special election is available where the disposal value of fixtures falls to be determined under (1), (5) or (9) above. Subject as below and to *CAA 2001, ss 186, 186A, 187* (see **10.45** below) and *s 197* (above), the seller and purchaser (or, where (5) above applies, the lessor and lessee under **10.40** above) may jointly elect under *CAA 2001, s 198* to fix the amount so determined. Where (5) above applies, the lessor and lessee under **10.40** above may make a similar election under *CAA 2001, s 199*. The election fixes the amount at a figure not exceeding either the capital expenditure treated as incurred on the fixtures by the seller (or lessor) or the actual sale price (or capital sum). The remainder (if any) of the sale price (or capital sum) is attributed to the other property included in the sale.

The notice of election must (subject to below) be given within two years after the interest is acquired (or the lease granted), and is irrevocable. A copy must also accompany the return of the persons making the election. The notice must contain prescribed information and must quantify the amount fixed by the election, although if subsequent circumstances reduce the maximum below that fixed, the election is treated as being for that reduced maximum amount. There are provisions for the determination of questions relating to such elections by the Tribunal. Where any person becomes aware that a return of his has become incorrect because of such an election (or because of subsequent circumstances affecting the election), the necessary amendments to the return must be notified to HMRC within three months of his becoming so aware, subject to penalties for failure.

If **10.46**(A) below applies, and the application to the Tribunal is not determined before the end of the two-year period for making the above election, that period is extended until such time as the application is determined or withdrawn.

[*CAA 2001, ss 198–201, 203, 204(4)–(6)*].

In practice, HMRC normally accept an election covering a group of fixtures, or all the fixtures in a single property, but not one covering fixtures in different properties (e.g. where a portfolio of properties is sold) (Revenue Tax Bulletin June 1998 p 552).

Acquisition of ownership in certain cases

[10.44] If, on the termination of a lease, the outgoing lessee is treated under **10.43**(A) above as ceasing to own a fixture, the lessor is thereafter treated as the owner. This applies in relation to a licence as it does in relation to a lease. [*CAA 2001, s 193*].

The following apply where an election is made under **10.38** above (election to treat fixture as owned by equipment lessor), and either:

- the equipment lessor assigns his rights under the equipment lease; or
- the equipment lessee's financial obligations under the lease (or those of his assignee etc.) are discharged (on the payment of a capital sum).

If the former applies, then, from the time of the assignment, the fixture is treated as belonging to the assignee for capital allowance purposes, and the consideration for the assignment treated as consideration given by him on provision of the fixture. If the assignee makes any further assignment, he is treated under this provision as if he were the original lessor.

If the latter applies, the capital sum is treated as consideration for the fixture, and the fixture is treated from the time of the payment as belonging to the equipment lessee (or to any other person in whom his obligations under the lease have become vested).

[*CAA 2001, ss 194, 195*].

The same applies, with appropriate modifications, where the election in question was under **10.42** above (election to treat fixture as owned by energy services provider). [*CAA 2001, ss 195A, 195B*].

Restriction of qualifying expenditure where allowance previously claimed

[10.45] Where:

(i) a fixture is treated under these provisions as belonging to any person (the current owner) in consequence of his incurring capital expenditure on its provision; and
(ii) the plant or machinery is treated (other than under *CAA 2001, s 538* — contributions to expenditure, see **10.2**(vii) above) as having belonged at a 'relevant earlier time' to a person (who may be the same as the person within (i) above) in consequence of his incurring expenditure other than that within (i) above; and that person, having claimed a plant and machinery allowance for that expenditure, must bring a disposal value into account,

so much (if any) of the expenditure referred to in (i) above as exceeds the 'maximum allowable amount' is left out of account in determining the current owner's qualifying expenditure or, as the case may be, is taken to be expenditure which should never have been so taken into account.

A '*relevant earlier time*' is any time before the earliest time when the plant or machinery is treated as belonging to the current owner in consequence of the expenditure referred to in (i) above. The relevant earlier time does not, however, include any time before an earlier sale of the plant or machinery other than as a fixture and other than between CONNECTED PERSONS (**19**).

The '*maximum allowable amount*' is the sum of the disposal value referred to in (ii) above and so much (if any) of the expenditure referred to in (i) above as is deemed under *CAA 2001, s 25* (installation costs, see **10.6** above) to be on provision of the plant or machinery. Where (ii) above is satisfied in relation to more than one disposal event, only the most recent event is taken into account for this purpose.

Where any person becomes aware that a return of his has become incorrect because of the operation of this provision, the necessary amendments to the return must be notified to HMRC within three months of his becoming so aware, subject to penalties for failure.

[*CAA 2001, ss 185, 203, Sch 3 para 38*].

Previous claim for industrial buildings allowances

Where:

(a) a person has claimed industrial buildings allowances for expenditure partly on the provision of plant or machinery, and transfers the relevant interest in the building concerned; and
(b) the transferee, or any other person to whom the plant or machinery is subsequently treated under these provisions as belonging, claims plant and machinery allowances for expenditure incurred thereon when it is a fixture in the building,

the claim in (b) above may not exceed the '*maximum allowable amount*', i.e. an amount equal to the proportion of the 'notional residue' that the part of the consideration for the transfer attributable to the fixture bears to the total consideration.

The '*notional residue*' is the residue of expenditure which would have been attributable to the relevant interest immediately after the transfer (calculated on the assumption that the transfer was a sale), if the transfer had occurred immediately before the abolition of industrial buildings allowance on 1 April 2011. If, however, the consideration for the transfer does not exceed that notional residue, the '*maximum allowable amount*' is restricted to the part of the consideration that is attributable to the fixture.

[*CAA 2001, s 186, Sch 3 para 39*].

Previous claim for research and development allowances

Where:

- a person ('*the past owner*') has claimed research and development allowances (see **9.20** CAPITAL ALLOWANCES) on expenditure ('*the original expenditure*');
- an asset representing the whole or part of that expenditure has ceased to be owned by that person;
- the asset was, or included, plant or machinery; and
- the new owner (i.e. the person who acquired the asset, or any other person who is subsequently treated as the owner of the plant or machinery) claims plant and machinery allowances for expenditure incurred thereon when it is a fixture,

the new owner's qualifying expenditure cannot exceed the 'maximum allowable amount'. The '*maximum allowable amount*' is:

$$\frac{F}{T} \times A$$

where:

F = the part of the consideration for the past owner's disposal of the asset that is attributable to the fixture;
T = the total consideration for that disposal; and
A = the smaller of (i) the disposal value of the asset when the past owner ceased to own it and (ii) so much of the original expenditure as related to the asset.

[*CAA 2001, s 187, Sch 3 para 40*].

Previous claim for business premises renovation allowances

Where:

- a person ('*the past owner*') has claimed business premises renovation allowances (see **9.3** CAPITAL ALLOWANCES) on expenditure ('*the original expenditure*');
- there has been a balancing event as a result of which an asset representing the whole or part of the original expenditure ceased to be owned by the past owner;
- the asset was, or included, plant or machinery; and
- the new owner (i.e. the person who acquired the asset, or any other person who is subsequently treated as the owner of the plant or machinery) claims plant and machinery allowances for expenditure incurred thereon when it is a fixture,

the new owner's qualifying expenditure cannot exceed the 'maximum allowable amount'. If the proceeds from the balancing event exceed R (see below), the '*maximum allowable amount*' is:

$$\frac{F}{T} \times R$$

where:

F = so much of the proceeds from the balancing event as are attributable to the fixture;
T = the total proceeds from the balancing event; and
R = the qualifying expenditure incurred by the past owner on the asset less the net business premises renovation allowances (i.e. total allowances less any balancing charges) in respect of that asset.

If the proceeds from the balancing event do not exceed R, the '*maximum allowable amount*' is so much of the proceeds from the balancing event as are attributable to the fixture.

[*CAA 2001, s 186A*].

Effect of changes in ownership of a fixture

[10.46] The availability of capital allowances to the purchaser is conditional upon previous business expenditure on fixtures being pooled by the seller before their transfer to the purchaser, and the seller and purchaser, within two years of the transfer, fixing their agreement on the value of the fixtures transferred. These provisions apply where:

(a) a fixture is treated under these provisions as belonging to any person ('*the current owner*') in consequence of his incurring capital expenditure ('*new expenditure*') on its provision;

(b) the plant or machinery is treated (other than under *CAA 2001, s 538* — contributions to expenditure, see **10.2**(vii) above) as having belonged at a 'relevant earlier time' to any person (who may be the same as the person within (a) above) in consequence of his incurring expenditure other than that within (a) above ('*historic expenditure*'); and

(c) a person within (b) above was entitled to claim plant and machinery allowances on his expenditure.

Where (c) above is satisfied in relation to more than one amount of historic expenditure, only the most recently incurred expenditure is taken into account for these purposes. A '*relevant earlier time*' in (b) above is any time before the earliest time when the plant or machinery is treated as belonging to the current owner in consequence of his incurring the new expenditure. A relevant earlier time does not, however, include any time before an earlier sale of the plant or machinery other than as a fixture and other than between CONNECTED PERSONS (**19**). Where the past owner's period of ownership was entirely before 1 April 2012, that period of ownership is treated as not occurring at a relevant earlier time, so that these provisions do not apply in relation to such ownership.

In determining the current owner's qualifying expenditure where these provisions apply, the new expenditure is treated as nil (and thus no allowances are due) in the following circumstances:

- the 'pooling requirement' is not met in relation to the past owner (i.e. the person within (c) above); or
- the 'fixed value requirement' applies in relation to the past owner but is not met; or
- the 'disposal value statement requirement' applies in relation to the past owner but is not met.

None of the above affects the disposal value (if any) which falls to be brought into account by the past owner as a result of his having claimed allowances on the historic expenditure. It is up to the current owner to show whether either of the fixed value or disposal value statement requirements applies and, if so, whether the requirement is met. For this purpose, he must provide an officer of HMRC, on request, with a copy of any Tribunal decision, election or statement by reason of which the requirement in question is met.

The pooling requirement

The '*pooling requirement*' is that the historic expenditure must have been allocated to a pool in a chargeable period beginning on or before the day on which the past owner ceases to be treated as the owner of the fixture. The pooling requirement is also treated as met if a first-year allowance was claimed on the historic expenditure or any part of it.

The fixed value requirement

The fixed value requirement *applies* if the past owner is or has been required (as a result of having claimed allowances on the historic expenditure) to bring the disposal value of the plant or machinery into account in accordance with **10.43**(1), (5) or (9) above.

In a case falling within **10.43**(1) or (9) above, the '*fixed value requirement*' is that either:

(i) a 'relevant apportionment' of the sale price has been made; or

(ii) the case is one where the person who purchased the fixture from the past owner was not entitled to claim a plant and machinery allowance, and the current owner has obtained both:
- a written statement made by that person that (i) above has not been satisfied and is no longer capable of being satisfied; and
- a written statement made by the past owner of the amount of disposal value that he brought into account.

For the purposes of (i) above, a '*relevant apportionment*' of the sale price is made if:

(A) the Appeal Tribunal determines the part of the sale price that constitutes the disposal value, on an application made by either the past owner or the person who purchased the fixture from him, before the end of the two years beginning with the date when the purchaser acquires the qualifying interest (see **10.43** above); or

(B) an election in respect of the sale price is made under *CAA 2001, s 198* (see **10.43** above), jointly by the two persons mentioned in (A) above. For this purpose, the election must be made either before the end of the two years beginning with the date when the purchaser acquires the qualifying interest or, if an application is made as mentioned in (A) above and not determined or withdrawn by the end of that two-year period, before the application is determined or withdrawn.

In a case falling within **10.43**(5) above (incoming lessee paying a capital sum for the lease), the '*fixed value requirement*' is as above except that: references to the sale price are to the capital sum given by the lessee for the lease; references to the person who purchased the fixture from the past owner are to the lessee; references to the two years beginning with the date when the purchaser acquires the qualifying interest are to the two years beginning with the date when the lessee is granted the lease; and the reference to an election under *CAA 2001, s 198* is to an election under *CAA 2001, s 199*.

The disposal value statement requirement

The disposal value statement requirement *applies* if the past owner is or has been required (as a result of having claimed allowances on the historic expenditure) to bring the disposal value of the plant or machinery into account in accordance with **10.43**(2) or (3) above or **10.27**(h) above. This is designed to cater for a small subset of disposal events that may occur other than by virtue of an immediate sale of, or grant of a lease of, the fixtures. Say, for example, a past owner had previously ceased his qualifying activity and had brought the market value of the fixtures into account in accordance with **10.27**(h). If, some years later, he sells his former business premises with its fixtures, the disposal value statement requirement will apply on that sale.

The '*disposal value statement requirement*' is that the past owner has, no later than two years after he ceased to own the plant or machinery, made a written statement of the amount of disposal value that he was required to bring into account. The current owner must obtain that statement, directly or indirectly, from the past owner.

Miscellaneous

Amounts specified in a statement by the past owner of the amount of disposal value that he brought into account have effect in place of any apportionment that could have been made under *CAA 2001, ss 562–564* (see **10.2**(ix) above).

[*CAA 2001, ss 187A, 187B*].

Long funding leasing

[10.47] The rules on leasing of plant and machinery were reformed as set out at **10.48–10.52** below with effect from, broadly, 1 April 2006 (and see **10.53** below for commencement and transitional provisions). For 'long funding leases', the new regime grants entitlement to capital allowances to the lessee rather than to the lessor as previously. There are corresponding changes to the tax treatment of lease rentals, to ensure that the lessor is no longer taxed on, and the lessee does not obtain a deduction for, the capital element of rentals (see **69.52** TRADING INCOME — DEDUCTIONS). The new regime applies only to leases which are essentially financing transactions, known as '*funding leases*', comprising mainly finance leases but also some operating leases. Leases of no more than five years' duration are excluded from the regime, as are pre-1 April 2006 leases (subject to transitional rules). There are transitional rules to enable leases finalised on or after 1 April 2006 to remain within the pre-existing regime in appropriate circumstances. The coverage below is divided into sections on lessees (**10.48**), relevant definitions (**10.49**), lessors (**10.50**), fixtures (**10.51**), miscellaneous (**10.52**) and commencement/ transitional provisions (**10.53**).

See also HMRC Business Leasing Manual BLM20000 *et seq.* (defining long funding leases), HMRC Business Leasing Manual BLM 40000 *et seq.* (taxation of income and expenditure under long funding leases) and HMRC Capital Allowances Manual CA23800 *et seq.* (capital allowances aspects of long funding leases).

Simon's Taxes. See **B3.340Y–340ZC.**

Lessees

[10.48] Where a person carrying on a qualifying activity (see **10.4** above) incurs expenditure (whether or not capital expenditure) on the provision of plant or machinery for the purposes of that activity under a 'long funding lease' (see **10.49**(1) below), the plant or machinery is treated as owned by him at all times whilst he is the lessee. He is then treated as having incurred *capital expenditure* on the provision of the plant or machinery, of an amount determined as below depending on whether the lease is a 'long funding operating lease' (see **10.49**(3) below) or a 'long funding finance lease' (see **10.49**(4) below), at the 'commencement' (see *CAA 2001, s 70YI(1)*) of the term of the lease. The combined effect is to treat that capital expenditure as qualifying expenditure (as in **10.3** above) of the lessee for the purposes of plant and machinery capital allowances and, where appropriate, as first-year qualifying expenditure (as in **10.14** above) for the purposes of first-year allowances.

If the lease is a 'long funding operating lease' (see **10.49**(3) below), the capital expenditure is equal to the market value of the plant or machinery as at the commencement of the term of the lease or, if later, the date on which the plant or machinery is first brought into use for the purposes of the qualifying activity.

If the lease is a 'long funding finance lease' (see **10.49**(4) below), then, subject to the possible addition and restriction described below, the capital expenditure is equal to the present value, as at the commencement of the term of the lease or, if later, the date on which the plant or machinery is first brought into use for the purposes of the qualifying activity, of the 'minimum lease payments' (see **10.49**(6) below). Present value is computed as it would be if accounts were prepared in accordance with generally accepted accounting practice (GAAP) on the date on which that value is first recognised in the lessee's books or other financial records. The present value of any 'relievable amount' included in the minimum lease payments must be excluded. An amount (amount X) is a '*relievable amount*' if:

- an arrangement is in place under which all or part of any residual amount (see **10.49**(5) below) is guaranteed by the lessee or a person connected with him;
- amount X is within the minimum lease payments because of that arrangement; and
- it is reasonable to assume that, were amount X to be incurred under the arrangement, relief would be available as a result (other than relief which would in any case be available due to amount X being within the minimum lease payments). In deciding whether relief would be available as a result, no account is taken of any part of the arrangement other than the part providing the guarantee or any other arrangement connected with the arrangement or forming part of a set of arrangements that includes the arrangement.

If the lessee paid rentals under the lease before its term commenced, the capital expenditure also includes the amount of any such rentals for which tax relief is otherwise unavailable (and would still have been unavailable even if the plant or machinery had been used pre-commencement). If a main purpose of entering into the lease (or arrangements that include the lease) was to obtain capital allowances on an amount materially greater than the market value of the leased asset at the commencement of the term of the lease, the capital expenditure is restricted to that market value.

If the *lessor* under the long funding finance lease subsequently incurs additional expenditure such that the lease rentals increase (disregarding any increase attributable to a 'relievable amount' as above), the *lessee* is treated as incurring further capital expenditure on the plant or machinery. The further expenditure is equal to the increase (if any) in the present value of the minimum lease payments and is treated as incurred on the date it is first recognised in the lessee's books or other financial records.

As regards long funding finance leases, the same principles apply whether the lease is accounted for as a lease or as a loan.

Consequences ensue where plant or machinery is the subject of a 'transfer and long funding leaseback'. A '*transfer and long funding leaseback*' occurs if:

- a person (S) transfers (see *CAA 2001, s 70Y(3)*) plant or machinery to another person (B); and
- at any time after the date of the transfer, the plant or machinery is available to be used by S, or by a person (other than B) who is connected (within **19** CONNECTED PERSONS) with S (CS), under a long funding plant or machinery lease.

The consequences are that no annual investment allowance (see **10.12** above) or first-year allowance (see **10.14** above) is available in respect of the expenditure of S or CS under the lease. Also, in determining the qualifying expenditure of S or CS, there is disregarded any excess of his expenditure over the disposal value to be brought into account by S. Where no such disposal value falls to be brought into account, the qualifying expenditure of S or CS (if otherwise greater) is restricted to the lesser of the market value of the plant or machinery, the capital expenditure (if any) incurred on it by S before the transfer and any capital expenditure incurred on it before the transfer by any person connected with S.

A further restriction applies if S is not required to bring a disposal value into account because of the transfer, and at any time before that transfer S or a linked person acquired the plant and machinery without incurring either capital expenditure or qualifying revenue expenditure. In such cases the qualifying expenditure of S or CS under the lease is restricted to nil. A '*linked person*' is a person that has been connected with S at any time between when the person first acquired the plant or machinery and the transfer by S. '*Qualifying revenue expenditure*' is expenditure of a revenue nature on the provision of plant or machinery that is at least equal to the amount of expenditure that would reasonably be expected to have been incurred on the provision of the plant or machinery in a transaction between persons dealing with each other at arm's length in the open market, or that is incurred by the manufacturer of the plant or machinery and is at least equal to the amount that it would have been reasonable to expect to have been the normal cost of manufacturing the plant or machinery.

Disposal events and values

Any of the following events is a disposal event, and a disposal value (see **10.27** above) must be brought into account by the lessee for the chargeable period in which that event occurs:

- the termination of the lease;
- the plant or machinery beginning to be used wholly or partly for purposes other than those of the qualifying activity; and
- the permanent discontinuance of the qualifying activity.

The disposal value is (QE – QA) + R where:

QE is the person's qualifying expenditure on the provision of the plant or machinery;
QA is the 'qualifying amount' (see below); and
R is any 'relevant rebate' (see below) plus any other 'relevant lease-related payment' (see below).

If the event in question would also give rise to a disposal event within **10.27** above in the case of the lessee, that disposal event is ignored.

Meaning of 'qualifying amount'

If the lease is a 'long funding operating lease', the '*qualifying amount*' is the aggregate amount of the reductions made under *CTA 2010, s 379* (see **69.52** TRADING INCOME — DEDUCTIONS under Lessees) (and its income tax equivalent) for periods of account in which the person concerned was the lessee.

If the lease is a 'long funding finance lease', the '*qualifying amount*' is the aggregate of the payments made to the lessor by the lessee (including any initial payment and any payment under a guarantee of any 'residual amount' — see **10.49**(6) below) other than any 'relievable payment' (see below). It excludes so much of any payment as, in accordance with GAAP, falls (or would fall) to be shown in the lessee's accounts as finance charges, or interest expenses, in respect of the lease. Any payment representing charges for services or representing 'taxes' (as in **10.49**(6) below) to be paid by the lessor is also excluded. If the long funding finance lease is not an arm's length transaction, the qualifying amount is reduced to so much of the aggregate payments (net of exclusions) as would reasonably be expected to have been made if the lease had been an arm's length transaction.

Meaning of 'relevant rebate'

If the disposal event is the termination of the long funding operating or finance lease, '*relevant rebate*' means any amount payable to the lessee (or a person connected with him) that is calculated by reference to 'termination value' (as defined by *CAA 2001, s 70YH*), e.g. lease rental refunds. In any other case, '*relevant rebate*' means any such amount that would have been so payable if, when the relevant event occurred, the lease had terminated and the plant or machinery had been sold for its then market value. In all cases, if the lease is not an arm's length transaction, 'relevant rebate' includes any amount that would reasonably be expected to have been so payable if the lease had been such a transaction.

Meaning of 'relievable payment'

A payment (payment X) is a '*relievable payment*' if:

- an arrangement is in place under which all or part of any residual amount (see **10.49**(6) below) is guaranteed by the lessee or a person connected with him;
- payment X is within the 'minimum lease payments' (see **10.49**(6) below) because of that arrangement; and
- it is reasonable to assume that relief would be available as a result of making payment X (other than relief which would in any case be available due to payment X being within the minimum lease payments). In deciding whether relief would be available as a result, no account is taken of any part of the arrangement other than the part providing the guarantee or any other arrangement connected with the arrangement or forming part of a set of arrangements that includes the arrangement.

Meaning of 'relevant lease-related payment'

'*Relevant lease-related payment*' means any payment which:

- is payable at any time for the benefit (directly or indirectly) of the lessee or a person connected with him,
- is connected with the long funding lease, or with any arrangement connected with that lease, and
- is not within the exclusions provided for by *CAA 2001, s 70E(2FA)(c)*,

if, and to the extent that, the payment is not otherwise brought into account for tax purposes as income or a disposal receipt by the person for whom the benefit is payable (or would not be if that person were within the charge to tax). 'Payment' includes the provision of any benefit, the assumption of any liability and any other transfer of money's worth. If the lease is not an arm's length transaction, 'relevant lease-related payment' includes any amount that would reasonably be expected to have been so payable if the lease had been such a transaction.

[*CAA 2001, ss 70A–70D, 70DA, 70E; FA 2019, Sch 14 paras 1(3), 6(1)*].

Meaning of 'long funding lease' and other definitions

[10.49] The following definitions apply for these purposes.

(1) A '*long funding lease*' is a 'funding lease' (as in (2) below) that is not a 'short lease' (see (A) below), is not an 'excluded lease of background plant or machinery for a building' (see (B) below) and is not excluded under the *de minimis* provision at (C) below for plant or machinery leased with land. Where, at the 'commencement' (see *CAA 2001, s 70YI(1)*) of the term of a plant or machinery lease (as widely defined by *CAA 2001, s 70K*), the plant or machinery is not being used for the purposes of a qualifying activity, but subsequently is so used, the lease is a long funding lease if it would otherwise have been a long funding lease at its 'inception' (see *CAA 2001, s 70YI(1)*); this covers, for example, the situation where either the lessor or the lessee is originally non-UK resident and subsequently becomes UK resident. However, the treatment of a lease as a long funding lease as regards the *lessee* is always subject to the following two conditions.

- The lessee must treat the lease as a long funding lease in his first tax return (and thus his first accounts) the profits declared by which are affected by the question of whether or not the lease is a long funding lease. Once a lease has or has not been so treated in a return, no tax can be recovered on a claim within **15.10** CLAIMS, due to the return having made on that basis.

  A lessee cannot use the above to turn what would otherwise be a long funding lease into a non-long funding lease if:

  (i) at any time in the 'relevant period', he the lessee himself is a sub-lessor of any of the same plant or machinery under a long funding lease. The 'relevant period' is the period from inception of the first-mentioned lease to (i) the making of the said tax return or (ii) where relevant, the making of the final amendment to that tax return; or

(ii) the lease is the leaseback in a 'transfer and long funding leaseback' (see above).

- A lease is not a long funding lease as regards the lessee if either the lessor or any superior lessor under a chain of leases (as defined) is entitled, at the commencement of the term of the lease, to any capital allowance (not necessarily a plant or machinery allowance) in respect of the leased plant or machinery. This also applies if such entitlement would have arisen but for *CAA 2001, s 70V* (see **10.52** below under Tax avoidance involving international leasing). It also applies if the entitlement arose at an earlier time but no requirement has yet arisen to bring into account a disposal value as described in **10.50** below. These conditions are applied on the assumption that the lessor in question is within the charge to UK tax, even if that is not, in fact, the case. However, where the inception of the lease is before 28 June 2006 and the lessor remains entitled to capital allowances by virtue only of the exception under (2)(iii) below the lease is still regarded as a long funding lease as regards the lessee.

[*CAA 2001, ss 70G, 70H, 70Q*].

The above-mentioned exclusions from long funding lease treatment are defined in (A)–(C) below.

(A) A '*short lease*' is defined as a lease whose term is seven years or less (five years or less for leases entered into before 1 January 2019). The 'term' of a lease is defined by *CAA 2001, s 70YF* (as amended by *FA 2019, Sch 14 paras 8(2), 10*). There is an anti-avoidance rule at *section 70I(9)* aimed at preventing arrangements between CONNECTED PERSONS (**19**) being used to create artificially short leases.

A lease entered into before 1 January 2019 whose term is more than five years but no more than seven is nevertheless a short lease if three conditions are met. The first two conditions are that (i) the lease falls to be treated under GAAP as a finance lease, and (ii) the residual value of the plant or machinery implied in the terms of the lease is not more than 5% of its market value at commencement of the lease term. The third condition compares the lease rentals due in each year of the lease term (ignoring any variations resulting from changes in published interest rates); the total rentals due in Year 1 must not be more than 10% less than those due in Year 2, and the total rentals due in any of Years 3 to 7 must not be more than 10% greater than those due in Year 2. The finance lease in a sale and finance leaseback caught by *CAA 2001, s 221* (see **10.61** below) is excluded from being a 'short lease' (if it otherwise would be) where the sale etc. part of the arrangement occurs after 8 October 2007. Where the sale etc. occurs after 11 March 2008, this treatment extends to *any* finance lease that is part of the leaseback arrangement. However, if certain conditions are satisfied, a joint (irrevocable) election may be made by the seller (or assignor) and the lessor (within two years of the sale etc.) to disapply the exclusion. The conditions are the same as those relating to the similar election in *CAA 2001,* *s 227* (see **10.61** below), in particular that the sale etc. takes place not more than four months after the plant or machinery is first brought into use; the effect of the election is also the same as that of the *CAA 2001, s 227* election.

The finance lease in a lease and finance leaseback caught by *CAA 2001, s 228A* (see **10.62** below) is excluded from being a 'short lease' (if it otherwise would be) where the original lease is granted after 11 March 2008. This treatment extends to any other finance lease that is part of the lease and finance leaseback arrangements except for the original lease.

[*CAA 2001, s 70I; FA 2019, Sch 14 paras 8(1), 10*].

(B) An '*excluded lease of background plant or machinery for a building*' occurs where 'background plant or machinery' is affixed to (or otherwise installed in or on) land that consists of (or includes) a building and is leased with that land under a 'mixed lease' (as defined by *CAA 2001, s 70L* — broadly a lease of plant or machinery plus other assets — see also **10.52** below under Mixed leases). '*Background plant or machinery*' is plant or machinery of such description as might reasonably be expected to be installed in various buildings and whose sole or main purpose is to contribute to the functioning of the building or its site as an environment in which activities can be carried on. There is provision for the Treasury to supplement this definition by statutory instrument and to similarly designate particular types of plant or machinery as being, or as not being, background plant or machinery — see now *SI 2007 No 303*. There are anti-avoidance provisions to prevent this exclusion from applying if a main purpose of the mixed lease (or of transactions of which it is part) is to entitle the lessor to capital allowances on the background plant or machinery or if the rentals vary according to the value of allowances available to the lessor. [*CAA 2001, ss 70R–70T; SI 2007 No 303*].

(C) The *de minimis* provision referred to above applies in a case in which relatively small amounts of plant and machinery are leased with land and the exclusion at (B) above would have applied but for the plant or machinery not being 'background plant or machinery'. The lease is excluded from long funding lease treatment if, at commencement of its term, the aggregate market value of all such plant or machinery does not exceed 10% of the aggregate market value of any 'background plant or machinery' leased with the land *and* does not exceed 5% of the market value of the land (including buildings and fixtures and assuming an absolute interest). [*CAA 2001, s 70U*].

See also HMRC Business Leasing Manual BLM20000 *et seq.*

(2) A '*funding lease*' is a plant or machinery lease (as widely defined by *CAA 2001, s 70K*) which meets the 'finance lease test', the 'lease payments test' or the 'useful economic life test' (see bullet points below) (or meets more than one of these tests) and does not fall within either of the exceptions below. A plant or machinery lease whose inception is on or

after 1 April 2010 is automatically a funding lease if the plant or machinery is cushion gas, i.e. gas that functions, or is intended to function, as plant in a particular gas storage facility.

- A lease meets the '*finance lease test*' as regards any person if it is one that, under GAAP, falls (or would fall) to be treated in that person's accounts as either a finance lease or a loan. A lease also meets the finance lease test as regards *the lessor* if is one that, under GAAP, falls (or would fall) to be so treated in the accounts of a person connected with him (within **19** CONNECTED PERSONS). The Treasury has power to vary the finance lease test by statutory instrument.
- A lease meets the '*lease payments test*' if the present value of the 'minimum lease payments' (see (6) below) is not less than 80% of the 'fair value' of the leased plant or machinery. Present value is calculated using the interest rate implicit in the lease. The latter is arrived at by applying normal commercial criteria including GAAP. If it cannot be so arrived at, it is taken to be the incremental borrowing rate (defined as for accounting purposes); for leases, the inception of which was before 1 January 2022, it is taken to be 1% above LIBOR (as defined by *CAA 2001, s 70O(5)*); for leases entered into before 1 January 2019, it is the temporal discount rate for the purposes of *FA 2005, s 70*. '*Fair value*' means market value less any grants receivable towards the purchase or use of the plant or machinery.
- A lease meets the '*useful economic life test*' if the term of the lease exceeds 65% of the remaining useful economic life (see *CAA 2001, s 70YI(1)*) of the leased plant or machinery. (The 'term' of a lease is defined by *CAA 2001, s 70YF* (as amended by *FA 2019, Sch 14 paras 8(2), 10*).)

Exceptions.

(i) A contract within **10.57** below (hire-purchase contracts etc.) is not a funding lease.

(ii) A lease is not a funding lease if, before the 'commencement' (see *CAA 2001, s 70YI(1)*) of its term, the lessor has leased the same plant or machinery under one or more other plant or machinery leases, none of which were funding leases, and the aggregate term of those other leases exceeds 65% of the remaining useful economic life of the plant or machinery at the commencement of the earliest lease; for this purpose only, any person who was a lessor under a pre-1 April 2006 lease is treated as the same person as the lessor under the first post-1 April 2006 lease.

(iii) A lease is not a funding lease as regards the lessor if, before 1 April 2006, the plant or machinery had, for a period or periods totalling at least ten years, been the subject of one or more leases and the lessor was also the lessor of the plant or machinery on the last day before 1 April 2006 on which it was leased.

[*CAA 2001, ss 70J, 70N–70P, 70YJ; FA 2019, Sch 14 paras 9, 10; FA 2021, s 132(1)(4)*].

(3) A '*long funding operating lease*' is any long funding lease that is not a long funding finance lease within (4) below. [*CAA 2001, s 70YI(1)*].

(4) A '*long funding finance lease*' is a long funding lease that meets the *finance lease test* at (2) above (disregarding the connected persons rule). In relation to periods of account beginning on or after 1 January 2019, and in relation only to a lessee, a '*long funding finance lease*' is additionally defined as a right-of-use lease (see (5) below) which is a long funding lease that meets the lease payments test or useful economic life test in (2) above but which was not previously classified as a long funding operating lease. This means that there is no change in the tax treatment of a long funding operating lease following a lessee's adoption of IFRS 16 (see **49.2** LEASING). [*CAA 2001, s 70YI(1); FA 2019, Sch 14 paras 1(5), 6(1)*].

(5) A '*right-of-use lease*', in relation to a lessee, is a lease in respect of which, under GAAP, a right-of-use asset falls (or would fall) at the commencement date of the lease to be recognised in the lessee's accounts (which will be the case if the lessee has adopted IFRS 16 — see **49.2** LEASING), or a right-of-use asset would fall to be so recognised but for the lessee's subleasing the asset. In determining whether a lease meets this definition at any time in an accounting period, it is to be assumed that the accounting policy applied for the period also applied at the commencement date of the lease. [*CAA 2001, s 70YI(1); FA 2019, Sch 14 paras 1(5), 6(1)*].

(6) The '*minimum lease payments*' are the minimum payments under the lease over the term of the lease (including any initial payment). In the case of the lessee, they also include so much of any 'residual amount' as is guaranteed by him or a person connected with him. In the case of the lessor, they also include so much of any 'residual amount' as is guaranteed by the lessee or a person who is not connected with the lessor. Any payment representing charges for services or representing 'taxes' to be paid by the lessor must be excluded from 'minimum payments' for the purposes of this definition. ('*Taxes*' means UK or foreign taxes or duties, but not income tax, corporation tax or foreign equivalents.) '*Residual amount*' means so much of the 'fair value' (see the 'lease payments test' in (2) above) of the plant or machinery subject to the lease as cannot reasonably be expected to be recovered by the lessor from the payments under the lease. [*CAA 2001, s 70YE*]. This definition of 'minimum lease payments' is based on GAAP (Treasury Explanatory Notes to Finance Bill 2006).

(7) For the purposes of these provisions, the *market value* of any plant or machinery at any time is to be determined on the assumption of a disposal by an absolute owner free from all leases and other encumbrances. [*CAA 2001, s 70YI(2)*].

Lessors

[10.50] Expenditure incurred on the provision of plant or machinery for leasing under a long funding lease is not qualifying expenditure for the purposes of plant and machinery capital allowances. [*CAA 2001, s 34A*].

Where expenditure on plant or machinery is already included in qualifying expenditure and the plant or machinery begins to be leased under a long funding lease, a disposal event then occurs and a disposal value must be brought into account as follows.

- If the lease is a 'long funding operating lease' (see **10.49**(3) above), the disposal value is the market value of the plant or machinery at commencement of the lease.
- If the lease is a 'long funding finance lease' (see **10.49**(4) above), the disposal value depends on the date of the 'inception' (see *CAA 2001, s 70YI(1)*) of the lease.
  Where the inception of the lease is on or after 13 November 2008, the disposal value is the greater of the market value of the plant or machinery at commencement of the lease and the 'qualifying lease payments'. The '*qualifying lease payments*' means the minimum payments under the lease, including any initial payment but excluding so much of any payment as falls (or would fall) under GAAP to be treated as the gross return on investment, i.e. the interest element. Any payment representing charges for services or representing 'taxes' (as in **10.49**(6) above) to be paid by the lessor must also be excluded.
  Where the inception of the lease was before 13 November 2008, the disposal value was the amount that would have fallen to be recognised as the lessor's net investment in the lease if accounts had been prepared in accordance with GAAP on the date (the '*relevant date*') on which the lessor's net investment in the lease was first recognised in his books or other financial records. In relation to leases granted after 12 December 2007, any rentals made (or due) under the lease on or before the relevant date were treated for these purposes as made (and due) on the day after the relevant date. In relation to leases granted after 11 March 2008, the lessor's net investment in the lease was calculated for these purposes as if he had no liabilities of any kind at any time on the relevant date, but only if the effect of doing so was to increase the disposal value.

[*CAA 2001, s 61(1)(ee), (2), (6)–(9)*]. (See **10.27** above as regards disposal events and disposal values generally.)

Where the owner of plant or machinery has been leasing it under a long funding lease and ceases to do so but continues to use it for the purposes of a qualifying activity (see **10.4** above), writing-down allowances are available to him as if he had, on the day after the cessation, incurred capital expenditure on the acquisition of that plant or machinery and as if he owned it as a result of that notional capital expenditure. The plant or machinery is thereafter treated as if it were not the same plant or machinery that existed previously. The amount of the notional capital expenditure is equal to the 'termination amount' in relation to the long funding lease under which the plant or machinery was last leased. [*CAA 2001, s 13A*]. However, neither an annual investment allowance (see **10.12** above) nor a first-year allowance (see **10.14** above) is available on the notional capital expenditure, and nor can it qualify for short-life asset treatment as in **10.33** above. The *termination amount*' is determined as follows.

- If that lease terminated as a result of a disposal event or if a disposal event is triggered by the termination, the termination amount is the disposal value that would have fallen to be brought into account by the lessor on the fictional assumptions that he had been entitled to capital allowances on the plant or machinery and had claimed his full entitlement. 'Disposal event' is itself to be construed in accordance with those assumptions. See generally **10.27** above as regards disposal events and disposal values.

- If the above does not apply and the lease is a 'long funding operating lease' (see **10.49**(3) above), the termination amount is the market value of the plant or machinery immediately after the termination.
- If the above does not apply and the lease is a 'long funding finance lease' (see **10.49**(4) above), the termination amount is the value at which, immediately after the termination, the plant or machinery is recognised in the lessor's books or other financial records.

[*CAA 2001, s 70YG*].

Note that where plant or machinery either begins or ceases to be leased under a long funding lease, there is also, by virtue of *TCGA 1992, s 25A*, as amended, a deemed disposal and reacquisition, at similar values as above, for CGT purposes. See Tolley's Capital Gains Tax.

Election available to lessors

The Treasury has made regulations enabling a lessor to elect for his plant and machinery leases to be treated as long funding leases if they would not otherwise be so treated; the election cannot be made on an individual lease by lease basis. For guidance, see the HMRC Technical Note referred to in **10.47** above. See also HMRC Business Leasing Manual BLM24005 et seq. The election (a 'long funding lease election') applies to all the lessor's 'eligible leases' (as defined by *SI 2007 No 304, Reg 3*) and 'qualifying incidental leases' that are finalised on or after the effective date, but does not affect the lessees' position. The election must be made within two years of the end of the accounting period in which falls the date from which the election is to take effect; it must be made in a tax return or an amended tax return. It can be revoked, by means of an amended return, within the permitted time for making it but is thereafter irrevocable. The election must specify the effective date, which cannot precede the period of account or (as the case may be) the tax year to which it relates. Leases of less than twelve months' duration (except as below) and leases finalised before 1 April 2006 are excluded from being eligible leases for these purposes, as are certain other leases. A '*qualifying incidental lease*' is a plant or machinery lease that is wholly incidental to an eligible lease and which would itself have been an eligible lease if its term were twelve months or more. [*FA 2006, Sch 8 para 16; SI 2007 No 304*].

Fixtures

[10.51] The fixtures rules at **10.36** onwards above do not apply, to determine either ownership or entitlement to allowances of either the lessee or the lessor, where plant or machinery that is (or becomes) a fixture is the subject of a long funding lease. If the lessee under the long funding lease himself leases out all or any of the plant or machinery under a lease that is not a long funding lease, the provisions at **10.36** onwards are similarly disapplied as regards both the lessor and the lessee under that sub-lease. [*CAA 2001, ss 172(2A), 172A*]. Thus, the allowances (for expenditure on fixtures) available to any such lessors and lessees are to be determined under the rules applicable to long funding leases, rather than the rules applicable to fixtures.

Miscellaneous

[10.52] The following matters are relevant.

Mixed leases

There is provision for a situation where plant or machinery is leased with other types of asset (whether plant or machinery or not). In such case, different leases are deemed to exist so that the above rules can be applied to each such notional lease (known as a '*derived lease*' — see, for example, **10.49**(1)(B) above). [*CAA 2001, ss 70L, 70M*].

Transfers, assignments etc.

Where a *lessor* of plant or machinery transfers it to a new lessor (other than by granting him a lease), it is treated for the purposes of these provisions (as regards lessors) as the termination of the existing lease and the creation of a new lease commencing at the date of transfer (which may or may not be the case in reality). Provided there is effectively no change to the term of the original lease or to the payments due under it, then, as regards the new lessor, the new lease retains the classification of the original lease (i.e. as a long funding lease or as a lease other than a long funding lease, as the case may be) and, as regards the lessee, the old and new leases are treated as a single continuing lease. [*CAA 2001, s 70W*].

The above also applies, with the appropriate modifications, where a *lessee* of plant or machinery transfers it to a new lessee. [*CAA 2001, s 70X*].

Extension of the term of a lease

Where the term of a *long funding operating lease* (see **10.49**(3) above) is extended as a result of one or more specified events (involving variations to the provisions of the lease, the granting or exercise of options etc.), a new lease is deemed to begin. [*CAA 2001, s 70YB; FA 2021, s 17(2)*].

Where the term of a lease that is *not* a long funding lease is extended as a result of one or more specified events (as above), it is necessary to consider whether or not it thereby becomes a long funding lease. If, were it to be assumed that the lease has then terminated and a new lease commenced, the new lease would be a long funding lease, or at least that assumption is made, and the 'new' lease is a long funding lease as regards the lessor. If not, the term of the lease is taken to be the term as extended. [*CAA 2001, s 70YC; FA 2021, s 17(3)*].

Neither of these provisions apply where:

- on or after 1 January 2020 there is a change in the payments under a lease that would have been payable on or before 30 June 2021;
- the effect of the change is that the lease is extended;
- the change would not have been made but for CORONAVIRUS (see **23.2**);
- after the change, the consideration for the lease is substantially the same as (or less than, the consideration before the change;
- there is no other substantive change to the lease terms; and
- the lessor and lessee have not made any arrangement in connection with any changes to capital allowances arising as a result of the change in payments.

Either the lessee or lessor may, however, elect irrevocably for this exclusion not to apply (so that either *CAA 2001, s 70YB* or *70YC* applies to the extension). An election must be made within the 21 months beginning with the day after the day on which the change in payments occurs. The maker of the election must notify the other party to the lease and include a copy of that notification with the election notice. A notice of election must also include any information specified by HMRC.

The normal procedural rules for claims and elections (see **15** CLAIMS) do not apply to an election under these provisions.

A copy of the election must be included by each party to the lease in their tax return (or amended return) for the period in which the change in payments occurred.

[*CAA 2001, ss 70YCA, 70YCB; FA 2021, s 17(4)*].

Tax avoidance involving international leasing

There are anti-avoidance rules aimed at arrangements made to lease plant and machinery into the UK, and then lease it back out again (other than under a long funding lease) in order to obtain the benefit of UK capital allowances. The rules deem the leasing by the UK resident to be long funding leasing, so that capital allowances are not available to him. They apply where the provision of the asset by the non-UK resident is itself long funding leasing as regards the UK resident or is under a contract within **10.57** below (hire-purchase contracts etc.), such that the UK resident would otherwise be entitled to capital allowances. They are not aimed at normal commercial arrangements (see also Treasury Explanatory Notes to Finance Bill 2006). [*CAA 2001, s 70V*].

Sale and leaseback/lease and leaseback arrangements

Where an existing long funding lessor transfers (e.g. by selling or leasing) the plant or machinery that is the subject of the existing lease to another person and leases the plant or machinery back from him, the leaseback is a long funding lease as regards both of them. Similar treatment is applied where the leaseback is via a series of leases. [*CAA 2001, s 70Y*].

Change in the accountancy classification of a long funding lease

There are rules to cater for changes in generally accepted accounting practice (GAAP) such that an operating lease falls to be reclassified as a finance lease for accounting purposes or *vice versa*. In relation to periods of account beginning on or after 1 January 2019, these rules are disapplied where a long funding lease is thus reclassified upon the adoption of a different accounting standard or a change to an accounting standard, but at the same time are extended to cover the case where a right-of-use lease (see **10.49**(5) above) which is a 'long funding finance lease' (see **10.49**(4) above begins to be accounted for as an operating lease. [*CAA 2001, s 70YA; FA 2019, Sch 14 paras 1(4), 6(1)*].

Increase in proportion of residual amount guaranteed

The following applies as regards the lessor if, in the case of a lease other than a long funding lease and as a result of arrangements, there is an increase in the proportion of the residual amount that is guaranteed by the lessee (or by a person not connected with the lessor) (as to which see **10.49**(6) above) and the lease would have been a long funding lease if those arrangements had been made before its 'inception' (see *CAA 2001, s 70YI(1)*). The lease is treated as terminated, and a new lease treated as commenced, as at the time of the arrangement (or the latest arrangement if more than one). [*CAA 2001, s 70YD*].

Commencement/transitional provisions

[10.53] The long funding leasing rules above (and those at **69.52** TRADING INCOME) apply in respect of a lease where one of the conditions at (a) and (b) below is met. However, regardless of these conditions, a lease 'finalised' (see below) before 21 July 2005 cannot be a long funding lease (but this let-out is itself disapplied if the lessor does not come within the charge to UK tax until after 17 May 2006).

(a) Condition 1 is that the lease is not an 'excepted lease' and that it is 'finalised' on or after 1 April 2006 or the 'commencement' (see *CAA 2001, s 70YI(1)*) of its term is on or after that date.
(b) Condition 2 applies if the commencement of the term of the lease was before 1 April 2006 but the plant or machinery is not brought into use by the person concerned for the purposes of a qualifying activity (see **10.4** above) until on or after that date. (This covers, for example, the situation where the person concerned becomes UK resident on or after that date, such that his activity becomes a qualifying activity.) The person concerned may be the lessor or the lessee depending on from whose point of view one is applying the provisions.

There are regulations enabling a *lessor* to elect for a lease to be treated, as regards him only, as a long funding lease if it would not otherwise be such a lease, but the election cannot be made on an individual lease by lease basis. See **10.50** above.

For these purposes, a lease is '*finalised*' when there is a written contract for it between lessor and lessee, the contract is unconditional (or any conditions have already been met) and there are no terms still to be agreed.

For the purposes of (a) above, a lease is an '*excepted lease*' if it meets *all* the following conditions.

(i) Condition 1 is that before 21 July 2005 there was written evidence of an agreement or common understanding (the '*pre-existing heads of agreement*') between (or effectively between) lessor and lessee as to the 'principal terms of the lease' (as defined).
(ii) Condition 2 is that the leased plant or machinery was 'under construction' (as defined) before 1 April 2006.
(iii) Condition 3 is that the lease is 'finalised' (see above) before 1 April 2007 (but see below).
(iv) Condition 4 is that the commencement of the term of the lease is before 1 April 2007 (but see below).
(v) Condition 5 is that the lessee is the person(s) identified as such in the 'pre-existing heads of agreement' (within (i) above).

(vi) Condition 6 is that the principal terms of the lease are not materially different from those in the 'pre-existing heads of agreement' (within (i) above).

The date in (iii) and (iv) above is deferred to 1 April 2009 if construction of the asset proceeds continuously from 1 April 2006 (and at the normal pace for an asset of its type) and the lease commences as soon as is practicable after construction is substantially complete. There is provision to treat this condition as satisfied if it is failed only by reason of unforeseen events beyond the control of the parties (including the main constructor).

There are rules (see *FA 2006, Sch 8 paras 20, 25*) as to how these transitional provisions are to be applied in a case where the 'pre-existing heads of agreement' (see (i) above) relates to two or more assets.

If a person incurs expenditure before 19 July 2006 for leasing under a long funding lease which does not meet all the conditions in (i)–(vi) above, but in respect of which there was a 'pre-existing heads of agreement' before 21 July 2005 (as in (i) above), such expenditure (the '*old expenditure*') is treated as separate from any expenditure incurred on or after date (the '*new expenditure*'). *FA 2006, Sch 8 para 22* provides rules, for this purpose only, as to the time at which an amount of expenditure is treated as being incurred. The old and new expenditure are treated as if incurred on separate assets leased under separate leases; the notional lease relating to the old expenditure is then deemed to be an excepted lease. The lease rentals are apportioned between the two notional leases in a just and reasonable manner. These splitting provisions apply in determining the income tax or corporation tax liability of anyone who is at any time the lessor or the lessee under the actual lease.

Mixed leases

Where a lease is a mixed lease (see **10.52** above), it is first necessary to consider whether the mixed lease is itself an 'excepted lease' for the purposes of these transitional provisions. If it is not, one can then consider separately, in the case of each derived lease, whether that lease is an 'excepted lease'.

Transfers

There is provision to ensure that a lease that is outside the long funding leasing regime (by virtue of the commencement/transitional provisions) remains outside that regime if it is transferred from one lessor to another or from one lessee to another. For this to have effect, there must be no effective change to the term of the lease or to the payments due under it, and the lessor or lessee (as the case may be) must be within the charge to UK tax immediately before the transfer.

[*FA 2006, Sch 8 paras 15–27*].

Special leasing

[10.54] '*Special leasing*' is the hiring out of plant or machinery otherwise than in the course of a trade or other qualifying activity. It is itself a qualifying activity for the purpose of claiming plant and machinery allowances. However, plant or machinery provided for use in a dwelling-house or flat is excluded from being qualifying expenditure. See **10.3** above. See HMRC Brief 45/10, 22 October 2010 as regards the meaning of 'dwelling-house'.

Where a person hires out more than one item of plant and machinery, he has a *separate qualifying activity* in relation to each item. A qualifying activity of special leasing begins when the plant or machinery is first hired out. It is permanently discontinued if the lessor permanently ceases to hire it out. [*CAA 2001, s 19(2)–(4)*].

Manner of making allowances and charges for special leasing

For corporation tax purposes, a plant and machinery allowance is given effect by deducting it from the company's income for the current accounting period from any qualifying activity it has of special leasing. If, however, the plant or machinery was not used for the whole (or for a part) of the current accounting period for the purposes of a qualifying activity carried on by the *lessee*, the allowance (or a proportionate part) can only be set against the lessor's income from that particular qualifying activity of special leasing. A balancing charge is taxed as income from special leasing.

Excess allowances

Where the deductible allowances exceed the income against which they may be set, the excess is deducted from the company's income of the same description for the next accounting period (and so on for subsequent accounting periods). The company may, however, make a claim to deduct the excess from any profits of the current accounting period and of any previous accounting period ending within the 'carry-back period'. (This does not apply where, as above, the deduction can be made only against income from a particular qualifying activity of special leasing, and group relief is similarly restricted in such circumstances — see **35.5**(b) GROUP RELIEF.) The '*carry-back period*' is a period of equal length to the current accounting period which ends at the start of the current accounting period. If the preceding accounting period began before the start of the carry-back period, the total amount of deductions that may be made from the profits of that accounting period are proportionately reduced. A claim must be made within two years after the end of the current accounting period; if the claim is a carry-back claim, it need not be made in a return.

Leasing partnerships

A company may carry on a business of leasing plant or machinery in partnership with others. If the company's share of the business profits for an accounting period is not the same (in percentage terms) as its share of the capital allowances for that accounting period, excess allowances cannot be set against profits of the current and preceding accounting periods as above.

[*CAA 2001, ss 3(5), 259, 260, 261A*].

Simon's Taxes. See **B3.380.**

Overseas leasing (obsolescent)

[10.55] Special rules apply to qualifying expenditure incurred on the provision of plant or machinery used for overseas leasing (as defined). These include the reduction of allowances and, in some cases, the prohibition of allowances. They are, however, in the course of being phased out; in determining for the purposes of these rules whether plant or machinery is used for overseas leasing, no account is to be taken of any lease finalised on or after 1 April 2006. [*CAA 2001, s 105(2A)*]. See the 2018/19 and earlier editions of this work for these provisions.

Simon's Taxes. See **B3.340T**.

Miscellaneous issues concerning capital allowances on plant and machinery

[10.56] The matters discussed at **10.57–10.75** below apply for the purposes of capital allowances on plant and machinery.

Hire-purchase and similar contracts

[10.57] The following applies where a person incurs capital expenditure, on the provision of plant or machinery for the purposes of a trade or other qualifying activity, under a contract providing that he will (or may) become the owner of it on performance of the contract. One example of such a contract is a hire-purchase agreement. That person is treated for the purposes of plant and machinery allowances as the sole owner of the plant or machinery for as long as he is entitled to the benefit of the contract. When the plant or machinery is brought into use for the purposes of the qualifying activity, the full outstanding capital cost (i.e. excluding the hire or interest element) attracts capital allowances immediately. Any such capital payments made before it is brought into use attract allowances as they fall due.

As regards any such contract that, in accordance with generally accepted accounting practice (GAAP), falls to be treated as a lease (or would so fall if the person prepared accounts), the person mentioned above is treated as owning the plant or machinery only if the contract falls (or would fall) under GAAP to be treated by that person as a *finance lease*. In relation to periods of account beginning on or after 1 January 2019, this rule also has effect if the person is a lessee under a right-of-use lease (see **10.49**(5) above) and the contract would fall to be treated in his accounts as a finance lease *if* he were required under GAAP to determine whether it falls to be so treated; this applies to a lessee who has adopted IFRS 16 (see **49.2** LEASING) and is thus not required in his accounts to distinguish between finance leases and operating leases. At any time at which, by virtue only of the preceding rule, the lessee is *not* treated as owning the plant or machinery, no-one else is treated as owning it either; so, in these circumstances, neither lessee nor lessor are entitled to capital allowances.

These provisions are extended so as to apply where the plant or machinery is used for the purposes of any overseas activity that would be a qualifying activity within **10.4** above if the person carrying it on were UK resident.

Any two or more agreements (or undertakings) are treated for these purposes as a single contract if, when taken together, they have the effect that the person concerned will (or may) become the owner of the plant or machinery on performance of the 'contract'.

If the person mentioned above is treated as owning the plant or machinery but the contract is not completed, so that he does not, in fact, become the owner of the plant or machinery, he is treated as ceasing to own it when he ceases to be entitled to the benefit of the contract. The resulting disposal value (see **10.27** above) depends on whether the plant or machinery has been brought into use for the purposes of the qualifying activity. If it has, the disposal value is

(i) the total of any capital sums received by way of consideration, compensation, damages or insurance in respect of the person's rights under the contract or the plant or machinery itself, plus
(ii) the capital element of all instalments treated as paid (see above) but not, in fact, paid.

This is subject to the overriding rule that the disposal value cannot exceed the qualifying expenditure brought into account (see **10.27** above).

If the plant or machinery has not been so brought into use, the disposal value is the total in (i) above (but see below as regards assignments).

[*CAA 2001, ss 67, 68, Sch 3 para 15; FA 2019, Sch 14 paras 1(2), 6(1)*].

The above rules do not apply to expenditure incurred on 'fixtures' within *CAA 2001, ss 172–204* (see **10.36** onwards above), and if plant or machinery which has been treated under the above rules as owned by a person becomes such a fixture, he is treated as ceasing to own it at that time (unless it is treated as belonging to him under *sections 172–204*). [*CAA 2001, s 69, Sch 3 para 16*].

The above rules similarly do not apply (except in relation to deemed ownership of the asset concerned) if the person mentioned above acquires the plant or machinery for leasing under a 'finance lease' (as defined in **10.61** below, and note the exclusion of long funding leases from that definition). [*CAA 2001, s 229(3), Sch 3 para 44*]. See also **10.61**, **10.62** below and **69.43** TRADING INCOME — DEDUCTIONS as regards finance lease allowance restrictions. See **10.47** above as regards long funding leasing.

If the person entitled to the benefit of a hire-purchase or similar contract assigns that benefit before the plant or machinery is brought into use, and the assignee's allowances fall to be restricted under the anti-avoidance provisions at **10.61** below, both the disposal value and the expenditure against which it is set are increased by the capital expenditure he would have incurred if he had wholly performed the contract. The same applies in finance lease cases. This is to protect the assignee against an undue repression of qualifying expenditure by reference to the assignor's disposal value (see **10.61** below). [*CAA 2001, s 229*].

Consequences ensue where:

- a person (S) transfers (see *CAA 2001, s 70Y(3)*) plant or machinery to another person (B);
- at any time after the date of the transfer, the plant or machinery is available to be used by S or by a person (other than B) who is connected (within **19** CONNECTED PERSONS) with S (CS);

- it is available to be so used under a contract which provides that S or CS will (or may) become the owner of the plant or machinery on the performance of the contract (e.g. a hire-purchase agreement); and
- S or CS incurs capital expenditure on the provision of the plant or machinery under that contract.

The consequences are that no annual investment allowance (see **10.12** above) or first-year allowance (see **10.14** above) is available in respect of the expenditure of S or CS under the contract. Also, in determining the qualifying expenditure of S or CS, there is disregarded any excess of his expenditure over the disposal value to be brought into account by S. Where no such disposal value falls to be brought into account, the qualifying expenditure of S or CS (if otherwise greater) is restricted to the lesser of the market value of the plant or machinery, the capital expenditure (if any) incurred on it by S before the transfer and any capital expenditure incurred on it before the transfer by any person connected with S. *CAA 2001, ss 214, 215* (see **10.61** below) do not then apply in relation to the contract.

A further restriction applies if S is not required to bring a disposal value into account because of the transfer, and at any time before that transfer S or a linked person acquired the plant and machinery without incurring either capital expenditure or qualifying revenue expenditure. In such cases the qualifying expenditure of S or CS under the lease is restricted to nil. A 'linked person' is a person that has been connected with S at any time between when the person first acquired the plant or machinery and the transfer by S. 'Qualifying revenue expenditure' is expenditure of a revenue nature on the provision of plant or machinery that is at least equal to the amount of expenditure that would reasonably be expected to have been incurred on the provision of the plant or machinery in a transaction between persons dealing with each other at arm's length in the open market, or that is incurred by the manufacturer of the plant or machinery and is at least equal to the amount that it would have been reasonable to expect to have been the normal cost of manufacturing the plant or machinery.

[*CAA 2001, s 229A*].

For a further anti-avoidance rule, see **10.52** above under Tax avoidance involving international leasing.

Simon's Taxes. See **B3.340A, B3.340D.**

Abortive expenditure

[10.58] The rules at **10.57** above for hire-purchase and similar contracts can equally be applied to expenditure under other contracts which proves to be abortive. A disposal value falls to be brought into account as in **10.57** above when the contract fails to be completed. Thus, for example, plant and machinery allowances can be obtained in respect of a non-refundable deposit paid on an item of plant or machinery which is never actually supplied, notwithstanding the fact that the item is never owned by the person incurring the expenditure.

Connected persons, leasebacks and other anti-avoidance measures

[10.59] Anti-avoidance measures are described in **10.60–10.65** below. See **19** CONNECTED PERSONS for the definition of that term for these purposes.

See also **10.57** above and **69.42** TRADING INCOME — DEDUCTIONS as regards finance lease allowance restrictions. See **10.47** above as regards long funding leasing.

See **10.72** below as regards succession to a trade or other qualifying activity carried on by a connected person.

Simon's Taxes. See B3.311A, B3.334, B3.340H–340S, B3.342, B3.365.

Restrictions on disposal values

[10.60] For disposals of plant or machinery acquired as a result of transaction(s) between connected persons, the limit on the disposal value (see **10.27** above) is to the greatest amount of qualifying expenditure incurred on it by any of the participants in the transaction(s) (after deducting any 'additional VAT rebates' made — see **10.2**(viii) above).

The normal absence of any requirement to bring a disposal value into account if none of the qualifying expenditure in question has been taken into account in determining available qualifying expenditure (see **10.27** above) does not apply if the person concerned acquired the plant or machinery as a result of such transaction(s) as are mentioned above *and* any earlier participant was required to bring a disposal value into account. Instead, the current participant's qualifying expenditure is deemed to be allocated (if this is not actually the case), for the chargeable period in which the current disposal event occurs, to whichever pool is appropriate, thus requiring the bringing into account of a disposal value (which is then subject to the above-mentioned limit).

[*CAA 2001, ss 62(2)–(4), 64(2)–(5), 239(5)(6)*].

Restrictions on allowances

[10.61] Where plant or machinery is purchased:

(i) from a connected person, or
(ii) in a 'sale and leaseback transaction',

no annual investment allowance (AIA) or first-year allowances (FYAs) (see **10.12**, **10.14** above) are available. Also, in determining the buyer's qualifying expenditure, there is disregarded any excess of his expenditure (including any 'additional VAT liability' incurred in respect thereof — see **10.2**(viii) above) over the disposal value to be brought into account by the seller.

Where, in the circumstances in (i) or (ii) above, the seller is not required to bring a disposal value into account because of the transfer, and at any time before that transfer the seller or a linked person acquired the plant and machinery without incurring either capital expenditure or qualifying revenue expenditure, then the qualifying expenditure of the buyer (if otherwise greater) under the lease is restricted to nil. A '*linked person*' is a person that has been connected with S at any time between when the person first acquired the plant or machinery and the transfer by the seller. '*Qualifying revenue expenditure*' is expenditure of a revenue nature on the provision of plant or machinery that is at least equal to the amount of expenditure that would reasonably be expected to have been incurred on the provision of the plant or machinery in a transaction between persons dealing with each other at arm's length in the open market, or that is incurred by the manufacturer of the plant or machinery and is at least equal to the amount that it would have been reasonable to expect to have been the normal cost of manufacturing the plant or machinery.

For expenditure which does not fall into the case above, the buyer's qualifying expenditure (if otherwise greater) is restricted to the lesser of:

(a) market value at time of sale; and
(b) the capital expenditure, if any, incurred by the seller or any person connected with him,

with modifications to the expenditure incurred by the buyer, and by the seller or any person connected with him, to allow for 'additional VAT liabilities' and 'rebates' — see *CAA 2001 s 242*, and **10.2**(viii) above.

These provisions apply to contracts for future delivery, hire-purchase etc. contracts, and assignments of hire-purchase etc. contracts as they do to direct sales.

See also below under Transactions to obtain tax advantages.

For the above purposes, a sale is a '*sale and leaseback transaction*' if the plant or machinery:

- continues to be used for the purposes of a 'qualifying activity' carried on by the seller (or by a connected person other than the buyer); or
- is used at some time after the sale for the purposes of a 'qualifying activity' carried on by the seller (or by a connected person other than the buyer) without having been used in the meantime for the purposes of any other 'qualifying activity' except that of leasing the plant or machinery.

For the purposes of these provisions, a '*qualifying activity*' is any activity within **10.4**(i)–(vii) above regardless of whether or not profits therefrom are within the charge to UK tax.

The 'sole or main benefit' restrictions referred to above do not generally apply to straightforward finance leasing transactions (*Barclays Mercantile Industrial Finance Ltd v Melluish* Ch D 1990, 63 TC 95).

Supply in the ordinary course of business

Neither the restriction to the buyer's qualifying expenditure nor the denial of AIA and FYAs has effect in relation to the sale (or the supply for future delivery or on hire-purchase) of unused plant or machinery in the ordinary course of the seller's business.

Both the restriction to the buyer's qualifying expenditure and the denial of AIA and FYAs do apply in these circumstances, however, if the transaction in question falls within the provisions described below under Transactions to obtain tax advantages.

Election available in sale and leasebacks

In the case of sale and leaseback transactions, a joint (irrevocable) election under *CAA 2001, s 228* may be made by the seller (or assignor) and the lessor (within two years of the sale etc.) provided that:

- the seller (or assignor) incurred capital expenditure on acquiring the plant or machinery unused (and not second-hand) and not under a transaction itself within the above provisions;
- the sale etc. takes place not more than four months after the plant or machinery is first brought into use for any purpose; and
- the seller (or assignor) has not claimed capital allowances for the expenditure or included it in a pool of qualifying expenditure.

The effect of the election is that no allowances are made to the seller (or assignor) in respect of the expenditure, and that allowances which are accordingly available to the lessor are given by reference to the smaller of his expenditure and the amount in (b) above, i.e. disregarding the current market value at the time of the sale etc.

[*CAA 2001, ss 213(1)(2), 214–218, 227, 228, 230–233, 241, 242, 244, 245, 268E*].

Transactions to obtain tax advantages

Capital allowances are restricted if plant or machinery is purchased in a transaction that has an 'avoidance purpose' or is part of, or occurs as a result of, a scheme or arrangement that has an 'avoidance purpose'. This applies whether the scheme or arrangement was made before or after the transaction was entered into and whether or not the scheme or arrangement is legally enforceable. The provisions apply to contracts for future delivery, hire-purchase etc. contracts, and assignments of hire-purchase etc. contracts as they do to direct sales, and the references below to the buyer should be read accordingly.

A transaction, scheme or arrangement has an '*avoidance purpose*' if a main purpose of a party in entering into it is to enable any person to obtain a tax advantage under the plant and machinery allowances code that would not otherwise be obtained. This includes *inter alia*:

- the obtaining of an allowance that is in any way more favourable than the one that would otherwise be obtained; and
- avoiding liability for the whole or part of a balancing charge to which liability would otherwise arise.

The consequences depend on the nature of the tax advantage, as set out in (1), (2) and (3) below. If a transaction, scheme or arrangement involves more than one kind of tax advantage, the rules below operate separately in relation to each.

(1) If the nature of the tax advantage is:
   - that an allowance to which the buyer is entitled for a chargeable period is calculated using a percentage rate that is higher than the one that would otherwise be used; or
   - that the buyer is entitled to an allowance sooner than he would otherwise be entitled to it,

the consequences are as follows. Firstly, no AIA or FYAs are available to the buyer. Secondly (under *CAA 2001, s 218ZA*), the tax advantage is negated, i.e. the percentage rate of any allowance or (as the case may be) the timing of the buyer's entitlement to any allowance is presumed to be what it would be if no tax advantage had been obtained.

The above applies whether or not the buyer's qualifying expenditure falls to be restricted as a result of (i) or (ii) above or as a result of an election under *CAA 2001, s 228* (sale and leasebacks — see above) or as a result of the election mentioned in **10.49**(1)(A) above (long funding leasing).

(2) If the nature of the tax advantage is something other than the above, and the tax advantage is not within (3) below, the consequences are as follows. Firstly, no AIA or FYAs are available to the buyer. Secondly (under *CAA 2001, s 218ZA*), all or part of the buyer's capital expenditure on the plant or machinery is to be left out of account in determining his available qualifying expenditure. Subject to below, the amount of expenditure to be left out of account is such amount as would, or would in effect, cancel out the tax advantage (whether that advantage is obtained by the buyer or by another person and whether it relates to the transaction in question or to something else). If that amount would exceed the whole of the buyer's expenditure under the transaction, the whole of that expenditure is left out of account.

If the buyer's qualifying expenditure also falls to be restricted as a result of (i) or (ii) above or as a result of an election under *CAA 2001, s 228* (sale and leasebacks — see above) or as a result of the election mentioned in **10.49**(1)(A) above (long funding leasing), the amount of expenditure to be left out of account is the greater of the two restrictions.

(3) The following consequence ensues (under *CAA 2001, s 218ZB*) where:

- the tax advantage relates to the disposal value of the plant or machinery under the transaction (whether the advantage is the obtaining of a more favourable allowance or the avoidance of all or part of a balancing charge); and
- a 'payment' is made (or is to be made) to any person under the transaction, scheme or arrangement, some or all of which would not be taken into account in determining the disposal value of the plant or machinery.

The disposal value is to be adjusted in a just and reasonable manner so as to include an amount representing so much of the payment as would cancel out the tax advantage. 'Payment' extends here to the providing of any benefit, the assuming of any liability and any other transfer of money or money's worth.

[*CAA 2001, ss 213, 215, 217, 218ZA, 218ZB, 268E*].

See further **Simon's Taxes** at **B3.366**.

Sale and finance leasebacks

The above restrictions (other than those under *CAA 2001, s 218ZA*) on the buyer's qualifying expenditure and on his entitlement to AIA and FYAs do not apply if plant or machinery is the subject of a 'sale and finance leaseback'. However, where the finance lessor in a sale and finance leaseback has substantially divested himself of any risk that the lessee will default, the lessor's expenditure does not qualify for plant and machinery allowances at all (and this applies regardless of the election generally available in sale and leasebacks — see above).

A '*sale and finance leaseback*' is a transaction:

- in which the plant or machinery continues to be used for the purposes of an activity carried on by the seller or by a connected person other than the buyer; or
- in which the plant or machinery is used at some time after the sale for the purposes of a qualifying activity carried on by the seller (or by a connected person other than the buyer) without having been used in the meantime for the purposes of any other qualifying activity except that of leasing the plant or machinery; or
- in which the plant or machinery is used at some time after the sale etc. for the purposes of a non-qualifying activity carried on by the seller (or by a connected person other than the buyer) without having been used in the meantime for the purposes of a qualifying activity except that of leasing the plant or machinery,

where the availability of the plant or machinery for the use in question is a direct or indirect consequence of its having been leased under a 'finance lease'.

'*Finance lease*' means any arrangements for plant or machinery to be leased or made available such that the arrangements (or arrangements in which they are comprised) would fall, in accordance with generally accepted accounting practice (see **68.18** TRADING INCOME), to be treated in the accounts of one or more of those companies as a finance lease or as a loan.

[*CAA 2001, ss 219, 221, 225, 230, Sch 3 para 45*].

Sale and finance leasebacks are generally excluded from 'short lease' treatment and are thus within the scope of the long funding leasing rules at **10.47** above (see **10.49**(1)(A) above).

Plant or machinery subject to further operating lease

The following rules apply where plant or machinery, whilst continuing to be the subject of a sale and finance leaseback, is leased to the original owner, or a person connected with him, under an operating lease. In computing the income/profits of the lessee (i.e. the lessee under the operating lease), the deduction for operating lease rentals is restricted to the 'relevant amount'. In computing the income/profits of the lessor (i.e. the lessor under the operating lease), amounts receivable by him under the operating lease are included as income without netting off any amounts due by the lessor to the lessee. However, amounts receivable are not included as income to the extent that they exceed the 'relevant amount'. In each case, the '*relevant amount*' is the maximum amount of finance lease rentals deductible in computing the finance lessee's income/profits (see above). In applying these rules, such apportionments are to be made as are just and reasonable where only some of the plant or machinery subject to the sale and finance leaseback is also subject to the operating lease. For the above purposes, an operating lease is a lease that does not fall under GAAP to be treated in the lessee's accounts as a finance lease or, for periods of account beginning on or after 1 January 2019 in the case of a lessee using IFRS 16 (see **49.2** LEASING), would not fall to be so treated if the accounts were required to distinguish between finance leases and operating leases.

[*CAA 2001, s 228J; FA 2019, Sch 14 paras 1(6), 6(1)*].

Cars

A special rule applies where a disposal value is required to be brought into account on a sale (or on the performance of a contract) within any of the provisions above, and the asset is a car the expenditure on which is allocated to a single asset pool due to non-business use. If allowances fall to be restricted as above, the disposal value is equal to the lesser of market value at the time of the disposal event and the capital expenditure incurred (or treated as incurred) on the car by the person disposing of it. The new owner is treated as having incurred capital expenditure on the car of the same amount. [*CAA 2001, s 208A*].

Lease and finance leasebacks

[10.62] A '*lease and finance leaseback*' occurs if a person ('L') leases plant or machinery to another ('F') in circumstances such that, had it been a sale, the transaction would have been a sale and finance leaseback as defined in **10.61** above (except that the availability of the plant or machinery for the use in question must in this case be a *direct* consequence of its having been leased under a finance lease). For this purpose, a person is regarded as leasing an item of plant or machinery to another person only if he grants him rights over the item for consideration and is not required to bring all of that consideration into account under the plant and machinery capital allowances code.

In calculating L's income or profits for a period of account, the amount deductible in respect of finance lease rentals cannot exceed the 'permitted maximum'. Normally, the '*permitted maximum*' is the amount of the finance charges shown in the accounts, but relation to a period of account during which the leaseback terminates it also includes a proportion of the net book value of the item immediately before the termination, such proportion to be computed in accordance with a formula in *CAA 2001, s 228B(4)*.

If the use of the plant or machinery under the leaseback includes use by a person other than L or F, but who is connected with L, the above applies in relation to that person as it does in relation to L.

In the period of account in which the leaseback terminates, L's income/profits from the qualifying activity for the purposes of which the leased item was used immediately before the termination are increased by a proportion of the original consideration for the lease, such proportion to be computed in accordance with a formula in *CAA 2001, s 228C(3)*. The above restriction on deductible finance lease rentals does not apply to any refund of finance lease rentals on the termination of a leaseback.

The above rules do not apply to a person who becomes the finance lessee by means of an assignment of the lease.

For the above purposes, a '*termination*' of a leaseback includes an assignment of L's interest, the making of any other arrangements under which a person other than L becomes liable to make payments under the leaseback and any variation as a result of which the leaseback ceases to be a finance lease.

Special provision is made for cases in which accounts are not drawn up in accordance with generally accepted accounting practice (GAAP). Additionally, the above rules are adapted in a case where the leaseback does not fall under GAAP to be treated in L's accounts as a finance lease but does fall to be so treated in the accounts of a person connected with L. If the leaseback falls to be so treated in the accounts of neither L nor a person connected with him, those rules are disapplied. In that case, however, L's income/profits for the period of account during which the term of the leaseback begins are increased by the consideration payable to L for the grant of the original lease.

For the above purposes, the consideration given for the lease do not include rentals payable under that grant. Nor does it include any 'relevant capital payment' within **49.6** LEASING; if some but not all of the consideration is a relevant capital payment, the above provisions have effect subject to such modifications as are just and reasonable.

[*CAA 2001, ss 228A–228C, 228G–228H*].

Finance leases in lease and finance leasebacks are generally excluded from 'short lease' treatment and are thus within the scope of the long funding leasing rules at **10.47** above (see **10.49**(1)(A) above).

Plant or machinery subject to further operating lease

CAA 2001, s 228J (see **10.61** above) applies equally where plant or machinery is the subject of a lease and finance leaseback.

Transitional provisions

In relation to any leasebacks whose term commenced before 17 March 2004, transitional rules seek to preserve the pre-existing treatment of lease rentals payable before that date or in respect of any period ending before that date and a time proportion of lease rentals payable for periods straddling that date. For the effect on L's lease rental deductions, see *FA 2004, Sch 23 paras 2, 3*.

The increase in L's income/profits for the period of account in which the leaseback terminates is capped, in accordance with a formula in *FA 2004, Sch 23 para 5*, if a pre-17 March 2004 leaseback terminates early, i.e. other than by expiry of its term.

The increase in L's income/profits for the period of account in which the leaseback terminates is abated if a pre-17 March 2004 leaseback terminates early, L reacquires ownership of the plant or machinery and L's capital expenditure on reacquisition is itself restricted under **10.61** above. If the restriction equals or exceeds the increase in profits/income, the increase is cancelled; in other cases, the increase is reduced by the restriction. However, the increase is reinstated in modified form if a disposal event (see **10.27** above) occurs in relation to the whole or part of the plant or machinery within six years after the leaseback terminates. See *FA 2004, Sch 23 para 6*.

Where a pre-17 March 2004 lease and finance leaseback terminates and L then disposes of the plant or machinery, there is provision for his chargeable gain to be reduced for capital gains tax purposes. See *FA 2004, Sch 23 para 10.*

Leasing — restriction of lessor's qualifying expenditure

[10.63] See **49.8** LEASING for the restriction of a lessor's qualifying expenditure for the purposes of plant and machinery allowances to the 'value of the asset to the lessor' (as defined) where there are arrangements intended to reduce that value. The legislation was a response to identified avoidance schemes. There should be no need to consider whether the applies in the case of a normal commercial lease as the value of the asset to the lessor would not normally be less than the capital expenditure incurred by him.

Allocation of expenditure to chargeable periods

[10.64] The following applies only where a company that is a member of a group has a period of account which does not coincide with that of the group's principal company. If the company incurs at any time in its chargeable period capital expenditure on the provision of plant or machinery for leasing under a finance lease (as defined in (ii) above) or under a 'qualifying operating lease', the expenditure must be time-apportioned. The amount that can be included in qualifying expenditure for that chargeable period is restricted to the amount time-apportioned to the period beginning on the date the expenditure is incurred and ending at the same time as the chargeable period itself. The balance of the expenditure can, however, be included in qualifying expenditure for the next chargeable period. The restriction does not apply to a chargeable period if a disposal event occurs in that period in respect of the plant or machinery in question. A '*qualifying operating lease*' is a plant or machinery lease that is a funding lease, is not a finance lease and has a term of between four and five years. [*CAA 2001, s 220*].

Transfers of trade to obtain balancing allowance

[10.65] The following provision applies to the transfer of a trade which fulfils the following conditions:

(i) a company ceases to carry on a trade or part of a trade;
(ii) another company begins to carry on the trade or part;
(iii) the first company would be entitled to a balancing allowance (where the whole trade is transferred only);
(iv) the cessation of the trade or part is part of a scheme or arrangement the main purpose, or one of the main purposes of which is to entitle the first company to an allowance.

In the case of a transfer within *CTA 2010, Pt 22, Ch 1*, the trade or part discontinued is treated as a separate trade for both companies, with apportionment of expenses, assets and liabilities so far as just.

The trade is treated as continuing and no balancing adjustment arises. For transfers of trade without a change in ownership see **11.16** CAPITAL GAINS, and between such companies on the formation of an SE or SCE by merger under *CAA 2001, s 561A*.

This anti-avoidance provision does not apply where there is a company reconstruction within *CTA 2010, Pt 22 Ch 1* with no change in ownership of the assets. [*CTA 2010, ss 954–957*].

Anti-avoidance — capital allowance buying

[10.66] There are provisions to prevent the use by companies of schemes to, in effect, transfer an entitlement to capital allowances on plant or machinery where the written-down value is greater than the balance sheet value. The provisions apply where the following four conditions are met:

(a) a company carries on a qualifying activity either alone or in partnership;
(b) there is a 'qualifying change' in relation to the company on any day (the '*relevant day*');
(c) the company or, where the qualifying activity (or trade) is carried on in partnership, the partnership had an 'excess of allowances' in relation to the activity (or trade); and
(d) the qualifying change meets one of the 'limiting conditions'.

[*CAA 2001, s 212B*].

Definitions

There is a '*qualifying change*' in relation to the company on the relevant day if any one or more of the following conditions is satisfied.

(A) Either the 'principal company' or principal companies of the taxpayer company at the start of the day is not, or are not, the same as at the end of the day, or there is no such principal company at the start of the day but there is one or more at the end of the day.
(B) Any principal company of the taxpayer company is a 'consortium principal company' and its 'ownership proportion' at the end of the day is more than at the start of the day.
(C) The qualifying activity is a trade and the company ceases to carry on the whole or part of the trade on the relevant day and it begins to be carried on in partnership by two or more companies in circumstances to which *CTA 2010, ss 938–953* (company reconstructions without change in ownership — see **51.16** LOSSES) apply.
(D) The qualifying activity is carried on by the company in partnership at the start of the relevant day and its percentage share in the profits or losses of the activity (or trade) at the end of the day is less than at the start of the day (or is nil). A company's percentage share is determined on a just and reasonable basis, but regard must be had to anything which would be taken into account in allocating profits between partners under *CTA 2009, s 1262*.

A company (U) is a '*principal company*' of another company (C) if C is a qualifying 75% subsidiary of U and U is not a qualifying 75% subsidiary of another company. If U is a qualifying 75% subsidiary of another company (V) then V, but not U, is a principal company of C if V is not a qualifying 75% subsidiary of another company, and so on.

A company (X) is a principal company of C and also a '*consortium principal company*' of C if C is 'owned' by a consortium of which X is a member or C is a qualifying 75% subsidiary of a company owned by the consortium and, in either case, X is not a qualifying 75% subsidiary of another company. If X is a qualifying 75% subsidiary of another company (Y), then Y, but not X, is a principal company (and consortium principal company) of C if Y is not a qualifying 75% subsidiary of another company, and so on. For this purpose, a company is '*owned*' by a consortium if it is not a qualifying 75% subsidiary of another company but at least 75% of its ordinary share capital is beneficially owned between them by other companies, each of which owns no less that 5% of the capital. Those other companies are the members of the consortium.

A consortium principal company's '*ownership proportion*' is the lowest of:

- the percentage of the subsidiary company's ordinary share capital that it beneficially owns;
- the percentage to which it is beneficially entitled of any profits available for distribution to equity holders of the subsidiary company; and
- the percentage to which it would be beneficially entitled of any assets of the subsidiary company available to equity holders on a winding-up.

The expression 'equity holder' is interpreted, and the amounts available for distribution are determined, under the rules for GROUP RELIEF (**35**) and where the subsidiary has no ordinary share capital those rules are applied as if its members were equity holders.

A company is a '*qualifying 75% subsidiary*' of another company if either of the first two of the following conditions is satisfied and the third condition is also satisfied. The first condition is that the subsidiary has ordinary share capital and at least 75% of that capital is beneficially owned directly or indirectly by the parent. The second condition is that the subsidiary does not have ordinary share capital and the parent has control of it. The third condition is that the parent is beneficially entitled to at least 75% of any profits available for distribution to equity holders of the subsidiary and of any assets of the subsidiary available for distribution to equity holders on a winding-up.

For the purposes of (c) above, a company or partnership has an '*excess of allowances*' if the 'tax written-down value' is greater than the 'balance sheet value'. In computing each of these amounts, plant or machinery is excluded if it is provided for leasing under a long funding lease or if it is treated as owned by someone other than the company or partnership under *CAA 2001, s 67* (hire purchase etc. — see **10.57** above).

The '*tax written-down value*' is the total of amount 1 and amount 2. Amount 1 is the total of any unrelieved qualifying expenditure in respect of plant and machinery in the main pool and any class or single asset pools which is available to be carried forward from the 'old period' (i.e. the accounting period which ends on the relevant day — see below). The unrelieved expenditure in each pool at the end of the old period is calculated for this purpose on the assumption that all qualifying expenditure that could have been allocated to the pool has been so allocated, including any balance of first-year qualifying expenditure remaining after the giving of first-year allowances for the period. The assumption is also made that any transaction on the relevant day which would reduce the unrelieved expenditure has not taken place.

Amount 2 is the total of any qualifying expenditure on the provision of a ship for the purposes of the qualifying activity which is in any pool and is unrelieved at the end of the old period as a result of a notice under *CAA 2001, s 130* (postponement of allowances — see **10.31** above).

Where the qualifying change is within (C) above, amounts 1 and 2 are taken to be what they would have been but for the change. Plant and machinery expenditure on which is included in amounts 1 and 2 is referred to below as '*relevant plant and machinery*'.

The '*balance sheet value*' is that of the relevant plant and machinery and is found by adding together any amounts shown in respect of it in a balance sheet of the company or partnership drawn up in accordance with generally accepted accounting practice at the beginning of the relevant day, but adjusted to reflect the disposal of any of the relevant plant and machinery on that day. The amounts to be added together are the amounts shown as the net book value or carrying amount of the relevant plant and machinery plus any amounts shown as the net investment in finance leases of it. Just and reasonable apportionments are to be made where any of the plant or machinery is a fixture in land (defined as at **10.36** above) and the amount to be shown in the balance sheet in respect of the land would include an amount in respect of the fixture and where any of the plant or machinery is subject to a finance lease and any land or other asset is also subject to the lease.

For the purpose of (d) above, the '*limiting conditions*' are that:

(I) the excess of allowances is £50 million or more;
(II) the excess of allowances is £2 million or more but less than £50 million and is not insignificant as a proportion of the total amount or value of the benefits derived, as a result of the qualifying change or any 'arrangements' made to bring about the change or any arrangements otherwise connected with the change, by any person who is a 'relevant person' at the end of the relevant day;
(III) the excess of allowances is less than £2 million and the qualifying change has an unallowable purpose; and
(IV) the main purpose, or one of the main purposes of, any arrangements is to procure that condition (I), (II) or (III) is not met.

A '*relevant person*' means a principal company of the taxpayer company, a person carrying on the qualifying activity in partnership or a person connected (within *CTA 2010, s 1122*) with such a company or person.

A qualifying change has an '*unallowable purpose*' if the main purpose, or one of the main purposes, of any arrangements made to bring about the change or any arrangements otherwise connected with the change is for any person to become entitled to a reduction in corporation tax profits or an increase in losses resulting from a claim to allowances for qualifying expenditure on the relevant plant or machinery or qualifying expenditure which would fall within amount 2 above. '*Arrangements*' include any agreement, understanding, scheme, transaction or series of transactions, whether or not legally enforceable.

[*CAA 2001, ss 212C–212M*].

Effect of provisions

Where the provisions above apply, the accounting period of the taxpayer company which is current on the relevant day ends with that day and a new accounting period starts the next day. Where (A), (B) or (D) apply and the qualifying activity is carried on in partnership at the start of the relevant day it is the accounting period of the partnership which comes to an end with that day, and an accounting period of either the partnership or company which is carrying on the activity after the qualifying change which starts the next day. The accounting period which ends on the relevant day is the '*old period*' below, and the accounting period starting on the next day is the '*new period*'.

Where the taxpayer company or the partnership carrying on the qualifying activity at the beginning of the relevant day has an 'excess of allowances' (see below) at the end of the old period in any single asset, class or main pool the following apply in relation to each pool.

(1) The unrelieved qualifying expenditure in the pool is reduced at the start of the new period by the amount of the excess allowances (see below). Where (C) applies, this rule applies from the time of the qualifying change rather than the start of the new period.

(2) The amount of the excess allowances is treated from the beginning of the new period as qualifying expenditure in a new pool of the same type. Where (C) applies, this rule applies from the time of the qualifying change rather than the start of the new period.

(3) Where, following the qualifying change, a person ceases to carry on a qualifying activity and the taxpayer company begins to carry it on as part of its trade or business, in claiming allowances on expenditure in the new pool the transferred activity is treated as a separate trade or business. This rule applies equally where only part of an activity is transferred or where the taxpayer company starts to carry on the activity in partnership.

(4) A loss attributable to an allowance claimed on expenditure in the new pool cannot be set off under *CTA 2010, ss 37, 45A* (relief for trade losses — see **51.3, 51.6** LOSSES), *CTA 2010, ss 62 or 66* (relief for property business losses — see **51.10** LOSSES) or *CAA 2001, ss 259, 260(3)* (special leasing — see **10.54** above) except against profits of a qualifying activity carried on by the company, or a company which is a member of the partnership, at the start of the relevant day. For this purpose, any activity not carried on by the company or member at the start of the relevant day is not treated as forming part of a qualifying activity carried on by them at that time even if it would otherwise be so treated for corporation tax purposes.

(5) The amount of such a loss that can be so used by any person cannot exceed the amount which would have been available for use by that person but for the qualifying change.

(6) Similarly, a loss attributable to an allowance claimed on expenditure in the new pool cannot be claimed as group relief or group relief for carried forward losses unless it could have been claimed but for the qualifying change, and the amount of any such loss that can be claimed cannot exceed the amount which could have been claimed but for the qualifying change.

A company or partnership has an '*excess of allowances*' in a pool if 'PA' is greater than 'BSVP' and the amount of the excess is the difference between the two. For this purpose, 'PA' is the amount in relation to the pool used in calculating amount 1 above, and 'BSVP' is so much of the balance sheet value as it is appropriate to attribute to the pool on a just and reasonable apportionment. If, however, PA is less than BSVP for any other pool, the amount of the excess of allowances for the pool in question is reduced by the difference between the two amounts for the other pool (or where a reduction under this rule has already been made in respect of any other pools or a reduction under the equivalent rule for postponed allowances below has already been made, by so much of the difference as is left).

Where there is a disposal event in respect of any of the relevant plant and machinery, the disposal proceeds must be apportioned between the new pool and the original pool on a just and reasonable basis.

Where amount 2 is an amount other than nil (i.e. where the company or partnership has postponed allowances), provisions similar to those at (3) to (6) above apply by reference to the postponed allowances. If PA is less than BSVP for any pool, the amount of the postponed allowances is reduced by the difference between the two amounts for the pool (or where a reduction under the equivalent rule for pools above has already been made, by so much of the difference as is left).

If any plant or machinery is transferred on the relevant day and would, but for the requirement to ignore such transfers, reduce the tax written-down value as defined above, no person other than the company or partnership can claim an allowance in respect of that plant or machinery after the transfer.

[*CAA 2001, ss 212N–212S; F(No 2)A 2017, Sch 4 para 124*].

Anti-avoidance — disposal of plant or machinery subject to lease where income retained

[10.67] The following provisions apply where a lessor company carrying on a business of leasing plant or machinery (see **49.10** LEASING), whether alone or in partnership, sells or otherwise disposes of any plant or machinery which it acquired wholly or partly for the purposes of the business and which is at the time of disposal subject to a 'lease' to another person. For this purpose, a '*lease*' includes an underlease, sublease, tenancy or licence or any agreement for any of those things.

If the lessor remains entitled immediately after the disposal to some or all of the rentals under the lease which are payable on or after the day of the disposal then the amount of any disposal value (see **10.27** above) which the company is required to bring into account is determined as follows.

Where the amount or value of the consideration for the disposal exceeds the limit that would otherwise be imposed by *CAA 2001, s 62* (disposal value not to exceed qualifying expenditure incurred by the company (see **10.27** above) or that incurred by a CONNECTED PERSON (**19**)) or *CAA 2001, s 239* (limit on disposal value where additional VAT rebate received — see **10.27** below) that limit does not apply. Instead, the disposal value is the amount or value of the consideration.

In any other case the disposal value is the sum of the amount or value of the consideration and the total of the net present values (see below) of the rentals under the lease in respect of the plant or machinery which are payable during the 'term' of the lease (as defined) and on or after the day of the disposal and to which the lessor remains entitled immediately after the disposal. In this case the disposal value remains subject to the limit imposed by *CAA 2001, s 62* or *s 239*. Where the lease includes any land or other asset which is not plant or machinery, the net present value of rentals in respect of the plant or machinery is taken to be so much of the amount of the net present value of the rentals as, on a just and reasonable basis, relates to the plant or machinery.

To the extent that rentals are taken into account in the disposal value as above they are left out of account in calculating the income of the lessor's business for corporation tax purposes. Any apportionment required for this purpose is to be made on a just and reasonable basis.

The net present value of a rental is calculated by applying the formula

$$\frac{RI}{(1+T)^i}$$

where:

RI = the amount of the rental payment,

T = the temporal discount rate (i.e. 3.5% or such other rate as may be specified in regulations made by the Treasury), and

i = the number of days in the period beginning with the day of the disposal and ending with the day on which the payment is due, divided by 365.

Where the above provisions apply, any rentals receivable by the lessor before 22 March 2006 are left out of account in calculating the income of its business for corporation tax purposes.

[*CAA 2001, ss 228K–228M*].

Plant or machinery received by way of gift

[10.68] Where plant or machinery received by way of gift is brought into use for the purposes of a trade or other qualifying activity carried on by the donee, the donee is entitled to writing-down allowances as if he had purchased it from the donor at the time it is brought into use and at its market value at that time. The deemed expenditure cannot qualify for the annual investment allowance (see **10.12** above) or first-year allowances (see **10.14** above). [*CAA 2001, ss 14, 213(3), Sch 3 paras 12, 43*]. **Simon's Taxes.** See **B3.303.**

Previous use outside the business

[10.69] Where a person brings into use, for the purposes of a trade or other qualifying activity carried on by him, plant or machinery which he previously owned for purposes not entitling him to plant and machinery allowances in respect of that activity, writing-down allowances are calculated as if the trader etc. had, at the time of bringing it into use, incurred expenditure on its acquisition equal to its market value at that time. If, however, actual cost is less than market value, the actual cost is used instead. The actual cost for this purpose is reduced to the extent that it would have been reduced under the anti-avoidance provisions of *CAA 2001, s 218* or (prior to its repeal) *CAA 2001, s 224* (see **10.61** above) had it been expenditure on plant or machinery for use in the qualifying activity.

The deemed expenditure cannot qualify for the annual investment allowance (see **10.12** above) or first-year allowances (see **10.14** above).

[*CAA 2001, s 13, Sch 3 para 11*].

Simon's Taxes. See **B3.303**.

See also **10.50** above as regards an asset ceasing to be used for long funding leasing but being retained by the lessor for use in a qualifying activity.

Plant or machinery moving between property businesses

[10.70] A special rule applies where a person carrying on any of the four types of property business uses an item of plant or machinery in rotation between the different types whilst retaining ownership throughout. The four types are: an ordinary UK property business, an ordinary overseas property business, a UK furnished holiday lettings business or an EEA furnished holiday lettings business. See **60.7** PROPERTY INCOME for furnished holiday lettings. The rule recognises that a single letting may move in and out of furnished holiday lettings status from one tax year to another depending on whether or not all the conditions for that status are met for a particular year.

The rule applies where the person acquired the item for the purposes of one business (Business A) and has begun to use it for the purposes of a second business (Business B). If he then ceases to use the item for the purposes of Business B and recommences to use it for the purposes of Business A, he is treated as having incurred capital expenditure on the day following the cessation on the provision of the item of plant or machinery for the purposes of Business A. The amount of that notional capital expenditure is the lower of the market value of the item on the date of cessation and the original expenditure on the item. The item is then regarded as an item of plant or machinery distinct from the original item.

It would appear that on the initial movement of the item from Business A to Business B, a full disposal value (see **10.27** above) is required to be brought into account. The above rule operates only where the item reverts to being used in Business A.

[*CAA 2001, s 13B*].

Partnerships

[10.71] Partnerships are entitled to allowances in respect of an item of plant or machinery used for the trade or other qualifying activity carried on by the partnership, and owned by one or more partners without being partnership property. Any transfer of the item between partners, whilst it continues to be so used, does not require a disposal value to be brought into account. These provisions do not apply if such an item is *let* by one or more partners to the partnership or otherwise made available to it in consideration of a tax-deductible payment. [*CAA 2001, s 264*].

Following a change in the persons carrying on a trade or other qualifying activity, other than one resulting in the activity being treated as permanently discontinued, allowances are subsequently given and balancing charges subsequently made as if the new partnership etc. had carried on the activity before the change. For this purpose, a '*qualifying activity*' does not include an office or employment but otherwise includes any of the activities at **10.4**(i)–(vii) above regardless of whether or not the profits therefrom are within the charge to UK tax. [*CAA 2001, s 263*]. See **10.72** below as regards partnerships treated as discontinued and successions to trades generally.

Simon's Taxes. See B3.390.

Successions

[10.72] Following a change in the persons carrying on a trade or other qualifying activity, such that the activity is treated as permanently discontinued, any plant or machinery transferred, without being sold, to the new owner for continuing use in the qualifying activity is treated as sold at market value on the date of change, although no annual investment allowance or first-year allowance (where otherwise applicable) is available to the new owner. For this purpose, a '*qualifying activity*' does not include an office or employment but otherwise includes any of the activities at **10.4**(i)–(vii) above regardless of whether or not the profits therefrom are within the charge to UK tax. These provisions apply equally to plant or machinery not in use but provided and available for use for the purposes of the qualifying activity. [*CAA 2001, s 265; CTA 2009, Sch 1 para 496*].

If a beneficiary succeeds to a 'qualifying activity' (as above) under a deceased proprietor's will or intestacy, he may elect for written-down value to be substituted (if less) for market value. [*CAA 2001, s 268, Sch 3 para 53*].

Where a person succeeds to a trade or other qualifying activity carried on by a person 'connected' with him, each is within the charge to UK tax on the profits, and the successor is not a dual resident investing company, they may jointly elect, within two years after the date of change, for plant or machinery to be treated as transferred at a price giving rise to neither a balancing allowance nor a balancing charge. This applies to plant or machinery which immediately before and after the succession is owned by the person concerned and either in use, or provided and available for use, for the purposes of the qualifying activity, and regardless of any actual sale by the predecessor to the successor. Allowances and charges are subsequently made as if everything done to or by the predecessor had been done to or by the successor. Where *CAA 2001* has effect, it is expressly provided that the deemed sale takes place when the succession takes place.

For this purpose, persons are '*connected*' if:

(a) they are CONNECTED PERSONS (**19**); or
(b) one of them is a partnership in which the other has the right to a share of assets or income, or both are partnerships in both of which some other person has the right to such a share; or
(c) one of them is a body corporate over which the other has control (within *CAA 2001, s 574*), or both are bodies corporate, or one a body corporate and one a partnership, over both of which some other person has control.

The above election precludes the application of *CAA 2001, s 104E* (disposal value in connection with special rate expenditure in avoidance cases — see **10.28** above), *CAA 2001, s 104* (disposal value of long-life assets in avoidance cases — see **10.34** above), *CAA 2001, s 265* (see above) and the similar provisions in *CAA 2001, s 108* (see **10.55** above), and their forerunners. Annual investment allowances and first-year allowances are precluded by **10.61** above.

[*CAA 2001, ss 266, 267, Sch 3 para 52; SI 2019 No 689, Reg 10(3)*].

Simon's Taxes See **B3.390.**

Co-ownership authorised contractual schemes (CoACS)

[10.73] A CoACS (see **46.25** INVESTMENT FUNDS) is broadly transparent for tax purposes, i.e. the scheme itself incurs no tax liability. This means that its investors are treated as if they had invested directly in the underlying assets of the scheme and are subject to personal taxation accordingly. Where the participants in a CoACS together carry on a qualifying activity, then from 16 November 2017 each participant in the scheme is regarded as carrying on the qualifying activity to the extent that the profits arising to the participant from the activity are, or (if there were any) would be, chargeable to tax.

For scheme accounting periods beginning on or after 1 April 2017, the operator of a CoACS carrying on a qualifying activity can elect to compute plant and machinery capital allowances and allocate them to the investors. The election is made by notice to an HMRC officer and must specify an accounting period of the scheme as the first such period for which the election has effect. That first accounting period must not exceed twelve months. The election then has effect for that first accounting period and all subsequent accounting periods of the scheme and is, subject to the exception below, irrevocable. An election made on or after 4 July 2019 applies also to structures and buildings allowances (see **9.26** CAPITAL ALLOWANCES).

Where an election has effect for a scheme accounting period, the operator of the scheme must calculate the capital allowances that would be available to the scheme on the basis of various assumptions, e.g. that the scheme is a person, that the accounting period is a chargeable period and that the qualifying activity carried on by the participants is carried on by the scheme. It is assumed that property which was subject to the scheme at the beginning of the first accounting period for which the election has effect was acquired by the scheme at that time at its tax written-down value. Property which ceases to be subject to the scheme at any time is treated as if it ceased to be owned by the scheme, and a disposal value at tax written-down value must be brought into account. There is no entitlement to annual investment allowances or first-year allowances on any expenditure. The operator must allocate to each participant a proportion (which may be zero) of the capital allowances calculated. The allocation is to be on the basis of what is just and reasonable. Regard may be had in particular to the relative size of each participant's holding of scheme units, but no regard is to be had to circumstances relating to a participant's tax liability. If there is more than one qualifying activity, the calculation and allocation of allowances are to be made separately for each activity.

A participant cannot claim capital allowances other than those allocated to him by the operator. A participant is treated as ceasing to own his interest in the property subject to the scheme at the beginning of the first scheme accounting period for which the election has effect, and must bring in a disposal value equal to tax written-down value.

Where property consisting of a fixture ceases to be subject to the scheme at any time when an election has effect and a person (the '*current owner*') is subsequently treated as the owner of the fixture as a result of incurring capital expenditure on its provision (the '*new expenditure*'):

(a) the new expenditure is treated as nil if the 'disposal value statement requirement' is not met; and
(b) in any other case the new expenditure is treated as equal to the disposal value that the operator brought into account as above on the fixture's ceasing to be subject to the scheme.

The '*disposal value statement requirement*' is that the operator has, within two years after the fixture's ceasing to be property subject to the scheme, made a written statement of the disposal value in (b) above, and that the current owner has obtained that statement or a copy of it. The provisions at **10.45** and **10.46** above are disapplied in relation to the new expenditure.

Where an election was made before 4 July 2019 and a structures and buildings allowance is available by reference to a building or structure which is subject to the CoACS, the operator can make a separate election in respect of structures and buildings allowances. This allows the scheme to apply the two codes of allowances in the same way. Alternatively, the operator can withdraw the plant and machinery election, so that again, both codes operate in the same way. The election may be withdrawn by notice no more than twelve months after the end of the accounting period in which the building or structure is first brought into qualifying use. The election then ceases to apply for the accounting period in which the notice is given and all subsequent periods.

If an election is withdrawn, property which was subject to the scheme at the beginning of the accounting period in which the notice of withdrawal is given is treated as ceasing to be owned by the scheme, and as acquired by the participants in just and reasonable proportions, at that time. The disposal value for that disposal is the tax written-down value (i.e. the amount which, on the assumption that the expenditure in question is in its own pool, results in there being neither a balancing allowance nor a balancing charge).

[*CAA 2001, ss 262AA–262AF; F(No 2)A 2017, s 40; SI 2019 No 1087, Reg 3(7)(8)*].

Partial depreciation subsidies

[10.74] Partial depreciation subsidies, i.e. sums, not otherwise taxable on the recipient, are payable to him, directly or indirectly, by any other person in respect of, or to take account of, *part* of the depreciation of plant or machinery resulting from its use in the recipient's trade or other qualifying activity.

Where it appears that a partial depreciation subsidy will be payable, an annual investment allowance or first-year allowance (where available — see **10.12**, **10.14** above) can nevertheless be given, but must be scaled down as is just and reasonable (though the full amount is deducted in arriving at the balance of expenditure available for writing-down allowances).

Qualifying expenditure (see **10.3** above) which has been the subject of a partial depreciation subsidy can only be allocated to a *single asset pool* (see **10.26** above). Where qualifying expenditure has otherwise been allocated to a pool and a partial depreciation subsidy is received for the first time in respect of it, it must be transferred to a single asset pool. This is achieved by bringing in a disposal value (equal to market value — see **10.27**(g) above) in the original pool for the chargeable period in which the subsidy is paid and allocating an equivalent amount to the single asset pool. Writing-down allowances and balancing allowances and charges in respect of the single asset pool are reduced to such amounts as are just and reasonable (though the full amount is deducted in arriving at any unrelieved qualifying expenditure carried forward).

[*CAA 2001, ss 209–212*].

See **10.6** above as regards subsidies towards the whole of such depreciation. See **10.2**(vi)(vii) above as regards contributions by others towards *expenditure* qualifying for plant and machinery and other capital allowances.

Simon's Taxes. See B3.360.

Lessee required to provide plant or machinery

[10.75] A lessee required to provide plant or machinery under the terms of the lease (including any tenancy), and using it for the purposes of a trade or other qualifying activity, is treated as if he owned it (for as long as it is used for those purposes), but is not required to bring in a disposal value (see **10.27** above) on termination of the lease. If:

- the plant or machinery continues to be so used until termination of the lease;
- the lessor holds the lease in the course of a qualifying activity; and
- on or after termination, a disposal event occurs at a time when the lessor owns the plant or machinery,

the *lessor* is required to bring in a disposal value, for the chargeable period in which the disposal event occurs, in the pool to which the expenditure would have been allocated if incurred by the lessor. These rules do not, however, apply where the plant or machinery becomes, by law, part of the building in which it is installed or attached (see **10.36** above) under a lease. [*CAA 2001, s 70, Sch 3 para 17*].

Simon's Taxes. See B3.340B.

Key points on capital allowances on plant and machinery

[10.76] Points to consider are as follows:

- For capital allowance purposes expenditure is incurred when there is an unconditional obligation to pay for it. This may be earlier than the payment or invoice date and could therefore present planning opportunities. Where payment is made more than four months after the unconditional obligation, however, that date becomes the date expenditure is incurred and there is also anti-avoidance legislation where the rules are manipulated to reduce tax.
- There is a time limit for claiming capital allowances (broadly one year after the due filing date) so for returns submitted late the tax liability may be higher than predicted. The capital allowances can be claimed in a later return but this may still lead to higher than expected interest payments and penalties.
- Plant and machinery is not defined in the legislation. It is therefore necessary to look to case law which can be difficult to interpret. The basic starting point is whether the item in question performs a function in the business rather than merely being part of the setting.
- Many of the items which have been the subject of well-known cases e.g. lighting in *CIR v Scottish & Newcastle Breweries Ltd* are now classified as integral features. Where, however, that item still performs a function — e.g. lighting adding to the ambience in a pub toilet, or a drainage system in a garden centre — it may still qualify as general plant and machinery.
- Where repairs on an integral feature total more than 50% of the cost to replace that item (at the time the repairs are incurred) over a twelve-month period the repairs are not fully deductible as revenue expenditure. Instead they are treated as an addition to the special rate pool and attract a 6% writing down allowance. Where possible it may be worth obtaining quotes before repairs are undertaken.
- Correct classification of expenditure is important. Significant repairs to a lift, for example, are likely to be classified as an integral feature whereas the same repairs to a hoist should qualify as revenue expenditure and be fully tax deductible.
- First-year allowances, where available, can only be claimed in the period in which the expenditure is incurred. This may mean that even if a company is loss making it is still advantageous to claim a first-year allowance to build up additional losses to carry forward. The super-deduction, SR allowance and annual investment allowance are also 'use it or lose it' reliefs.

- Anti-avoidance legislation applies to prevent companies with large capital allowance pools being acquired only to make use of the future capital allowances.
- The annual investment allowance should be allocated first to the special rate pool as this attracts the lowest writing-down allowances.
- Where a main pool or special rate pool has a balance below £1,000 allowances can be claimed in one year to bring the balance to nil.
- Where it is considered that a capital item which qualifies for capital allowances is likely to have a useful economic life of less than eight years, a short life asset election should be considered in order to claim balancing allowances on its disposal/scrappage. In order to make the most of short life asset elections a company should ensure that it tracks all disposals thoroughly to match them to the short life assets. It is not possible to elect for cars to be treated as short-life assets.
- In order to claim capital allowances on fixtures the owner of the qualifying asset is generally required to have an interest in the land on which it is affixed. Elections may be possible where, for example, expenditure is incurred by an equipment lessor and in the absence of such an election nobody would be entitled to the allowances.
- Where fixtures are disposed of it is often advisable for the seller and purchaser to enter into a joint election (*CAA 2001, s 198*) to fix the disposal proceeds for capital allowance purposes. Such an election clarifies the situation and should reduce the likelihood of questions from HMRC. Elections can be entered into between connected parties but there is anti-avoidance legislation to prevent values being set only for the purpose of mitigating tax and where there are no bona fide commercial reasons.
- Partnerships are also entitled to capital allowances. Each partner is entitled to its corresponding share of the allowances based on the profit share ratio. A partnership is only entitled to an annual investment allowance if all of the members are individuals.
- Where plant and machinery is transferred to a connected party a joint election may be entered into to treat the asset, for tax purposes, as being transferred at tax written down value rather than market value.

11

Capital Gains

Cross-references. See also 12 CAPITAL GAINS — GROUPS; 13 CAPITAL GAINS — SUBSTANTIAL SHAREHOLDING EXEMPTION; 33 EXEMPT ORGANISATIONS.

Other sources. See Tolley's Capital Gains Tax.

Simon's Taxes. See **D1.9.**

Introduction to capital gains

[11.1] This chapter considers the application of the capital gains legislation to a company in respect of capital transactions which might be undertaken. The following chapter considers the capital gains position with regard to groups of companies (see **12** CAPITAL GAINS — GROUPS). The exemption for substantial shareholdings in trading companies is at **13** CAPITAL GAINS — SUBSTANTIAL SHAREHOLDING EXEMPTION. For comprehensive guidance on the computation of capital gains of companies see Tolley's Capital Gains Tax.

Companies are liable to corporation tax on their chargeable gains. These gains are included in their profits liable to corporation tax as described in **11.2** below.

UK-resident companies are chargeable to corporation tax on gains on assets situated in the UK or overseas. Non-resident companies are chargeable to corporation tax only on chargeable gains on the disposal of:

(a) UK-situated assets with a connection to the company's UK permanent establishment (see **64.6** RESIDENCE);
(b) (for disposals on or after 6 April 2019) interests in UK land (see **11.25** below); and
(c) (for disposals on or after 6 April 2019) assets deriving at least 75% of their value from UK land where the company has a substantial indirect interest in that land (see **11.26** below).

Companies accordingly do not pay 'capital gains tax' as such, but for disposals before 6 April 2019, there were two exceptions to this rule. The exceptions were for the capital gains tax charges on high value disposals of dwellings and non-resident disposals of UK residential property interests (see **11.24** below). For later disposals, the charge on high value disposals of dwellings is abolished and the charge on UK residential property interests is replaced by the corporation tax charge in (b) above.

[*TCGA 1992, ss 1(2), 2B; CTA 2009, ss 4, 19; FA 2019, Sch 1 paras 2, 112, 120*].

Simon's Taxes. See **D1.104, D1.901.**

Chargeable gains and allowable losses are nevertheless computed in accordance with provisions relating to capital gains tax, except that:

(i) computations are made by reference to accounting periods instead of years of assessment [*TCGA 1992, s 2D (previously TCGA 1992, s 8(3))*];
(ii) provisions in the legislation confined solely to individuals do not apply to companies [*TCGA 1992, ss 2E, 2F (previously TCGA 1992, s 8(4)(5))*];
(iii) indexation allowance is available to companies but has now been frozen at its December 2017 level (see further below) [*TCGA 1992, s 53; FA 2018, s 26(2)*];

(iv) special provisions apply after 31 March 1996 to gilts, loan stock etc. acquired by companies (see **50** LOAN RELATIONSHIPS);
(v) identification rules for shares and securities are different for companies;
(vi) gains and losses on **42** INTANGIBLE ASSETS created or acquired by companies after 31 March 2002 are taxed as income (under the intangible fixed assets regime, see *CTA 2009, Pt 8*) rather than under the chargeable gains regime; and
(vii) as further indicated below.

No indexation allowance is available in respect of expenditure incurred after 31 December 2017, and for expenditure incurred on or before that date and falling to be deducted on a disposal after that date, indexation allowance is computed up to and including December 2017 only. [*TCGA 1992, s 54(1)(1B); FA 2018, s 26(3)*].

There are a number of provisions specific to cross-border transactions carried out by UK companies. In general, these are designed to ensure that there isn't a tax charge on transactions where no cash is involved and there is no effective change of ownership, or they are designed to comply with EU legislation.

See *TCGA 1992, ss 284A, 284B* for anti-avoidance legislation bringing into charge certain gains deferred under extra-statutory concessions.

Rate of corporation tax on capital gains

[11.2] The whole of the chargeable gains (less allowable losses under **11.3** below) of a company is included in the profits chargeable to corporation tax (i.e. the '*taxable total profits*'). This does not apply, however, to gains arising before 6 April 2019 and chargeable under *TCGA 1992, s 2B, 14D,* or *188D* to capital gains tax (see **11.23; 11.24** below).

The rate of corporation tax applicable will either be the full rate as in **1.2** INTRODUCTION AND RATES OF TAX or, for financial year 2023 and subsequent years, the small profits rate, with marginal relief as appropriate. The rate so determined applies to both income and chargeable gains included in the chargeable profits.

If the company's accounting period straddles different financial years, chargeable profits are apportioned on a time basis between the years.

[*CTA 2009, s 8(5); CTA 2010, ss 4, 18–33*].

See **8** BUILDING SOCIETIES and **46** INVESTMENT FUNDS for special provisions in relation to these organisations.

Capital losses

[11.3] The amount of chargeable gains assessable for an accounting period is the total chargeable gains accruing to the company in that period less allowable losses in that period and allowable losses brought forward from any previous period. The resulting net figure is treated as chargeable to corporation tax as in **11.2** above.

Allowable losses include short-term losses accruing under *Schedule D, Case VII* for years before 1971/72 which remain unrelieved. This is the only instance where losses incurred before 6 April 1965 can be carried forward.

A special rule applies for financial year 2020 and subsequent years where a company has two or more accounting periods falling wholly within the same financial year, is chargeable to corporation tax for each period only because of a chargeable gain (or allowable loss) arising on the disposal of an asset, and during any gaps between those periods is not chargeable to corporation tax. So far as not otherwise deducted, losses arising in one of the periods can be deducted from gains arising in any of the other periods. The effect is that a loss arising in a later period can be carried back to an earlier period and a loss in an earlier period can be carried forward. To the extent that the loss is carried forward to an accounting period falling wholly within the same financial year, it can be deducted without the application of the restriction on deduction of losses rules at **51.13** LOSSES. The restriction will apply to its deduction in any later accounting period. This provision will be relevant in particular to non-UK resident companies making direct or indirect disposals of UK land (see **11.25** below).

[*TCGA 1992, s 2A(1)(3)(4), Sch 11 para 12; FA 2019, Sch 1 paras 2, 120, 121; FA 2020, Sch 4 paras 39, 42*].

Note that, for disposals before 6 April 2019, the legislation for these provisions was at *TCGA 1992, s 8(1), Sch 11 para 12*.

For corporation tax on chargeable gains purposes an allowable loss does not include:

(a) any loss which, if it had been a gain, would have been exempt from corporation tax in the hands of the company; or

(b) any loss accruing on a disposal directly or indirectly in consequence of, or otherwise in connection with, any 'arrangements' the main purpose of which, or one of the main purposes of which, is to secure a 'tax advantage'.

For the purposes of (b) above, it does not matter whether the loss accrues at a time when there are no chargeable gains against which it could be set or whether the tax advantage would be secured for the company incurring the loss or for another company.

'*Arrangements*' include any agreement, understanding, scheme, transaction or series of transactions, whether or not legally enforceable.

'*Tax advantage*' means relief or increased relief from, or repayment or increased repayment of, corporation tax or the avoidance or reduction of a charge or assessment to corporation tax or the avoidance of a possible assessment to corporation tax.

[*TCGA 1992, ss 2A(2), 16A, 184D*].

Note that, for disposals before 6 April 2019, the legislation for these provisions was at *TCGA 1992, ss 8(2), 16A, 184D*.

Simon's Taxes. See **D1.925**.

HMRC consider that whether a transaction forms part of a series of transactions, or a scheme, or arrangements in general is a question of fact, but this conclusion will follow in any case where one transaction would not have taken place without another transaction, or would have taken place on different terms without that other transaction. They do not, however, consider it necessary for transactions to depend on each other in this way for them to form part of a scheme or arrangements. In their view, if, on the facts, any participant in arrangements is found to have a main purpose of achieving a tax advantage, that is sufficient to demonstrate that one of the main purposes of the arrangements is the securing of a tax advantage. (HMRC Capital Gains Manual CG40242, 40243).

Where there is more than one way of achieving a commercial objective and a course of action is chosen on commercial grounds, any incidental tax advantage is not relevant. However, where the tax advantage was material to the choice, the anti-avoidance legislation may be in point, but HMRC have indicated that this is unlikely to be the case unless there is evidence of additional, complex or costly steps included solely for tax reasons. (HMRC Capital Gains Manual CG40245).

Allowable capital losses cannot normally be offset against trading profits or other income (but see **51.27** LOSSES). However, trading losses can be offset against chargeable gains within the same accounting period and, if unexhausted, against chargeable gains arising in earlier periods (**51.3**, **51.4** LOSSES). Management expenses of a company with investment business may be offset against chargeable gains within the same or a succeeding accounting period (**45** INVESTMENT COMPANIES AND INVESTMENT BUSINESS).

[*CTA 2010, s 37; CTA 2009, ss 1219, 1223*].

Capital losses are generally computed in the same way as capital gains. A capital loss is not an allowable loss unless it is claimed in a quantified amount. The time limit for such claims is four years after the end of the accounting period in which the loss was incurred. Where unused losses are brought forward and set against chargeable gains in a later accounting period, losses incurred after the start of self-assessment are used before earlier ones.

[*TCGA 1992, s 16; FA 2019, Sch 1 para 24*].

See **51.13** LOSSES for the inclusion of capital losses in the corporate loss restriction regime for accounting periods beginning on or after 1 April 2020 (subject to transitional rules for straddling periods).

Avoidance utilising losses

[11.4] There are a number of anti-avoidance provisions relating specifically to corporate capital losses. In particular, there are three targeted provisions attacking arrangements entered into which have as a main purpose the obtaining of a tax advantage.

For details of the provisions, see this paragraph, **11.7** and **11.8** below and **12.24** CAPITAL GAINS — GROUPS.

See also **12.25** CAPITAL GAINS — GROUPS for the restriction (where the provisions at **12.20–12.24** CAPITAL GAINS — GROUPS do not apply) on the set-off of pre-entry losses where a company joins a group.

As part of a general initiative countering various avoidance schemes (see **11.3** above) provisions were introduced by *FA 2006* to ensure that capital losses cannot be used against income profits.

Two strategies to utilise capital losses are targeted by the provisions. The first is to turn an income receipt into capital (see **11.7** below). The second is to generate a deduction from income as part of arrangements to crystallise a capital gain (see **11.8** below). The effect is to restrict the use of capital losses. In both cases, the provisions apply only where HMRC issue a notice to the company concerned (see below).

Both sets of provisions require that there be 'arrangements', the main purpose, or one of the main purposes, of which is to secure a 'tax advantage' (although each contains a qualification of the definition of tax advantage given below — see **11.7** and **11.8** below). [*TCGA 1992, ss 184G(2)(5), 184H(2)(4)*].

'*Arrangements*' for this purpose include any agreement, understanding, scheme, transaction or series of transactions, whether or not legally enforceable.

A '*tax advantage*' means obtaining or increasing relief from, or repayment of, corporation tax, the avoidance or reduction of a corporation tax charge or assessment or the avoidance of a possible assessment to corporation tax. [*TCGA 1992, ss 184D, 184G(10), 184H(10)*].

For HMRC's view on the application of the terms 'arrangements', 'tax advantage' and 'main purpose', see **11.3** above and HMRC Capital Gains Manual CG44100 onwards.

HMRC notices

[11.5] As noted above, the application of the provisions is contingent upon the issue of a notice to the company by HMRC. Such a notice may be issued if HMRC have reasonable grounds for considering that the statutory conditions triggering the legislation are present. It must specify the arrangements in question, the accounting period (or periods) involved and the effect of the anti-avoidance provisions.

If the company has not yet made a return for the accounting period it may, if it makes a return within the 90-day period beginning with the day on which the notice is given, make the return disregarding the notice and make any necessary amendment later within the same 90-day period.

If the company has already made a return for the accounting period, HMRC may only issue a notice if a notice of enquiry (see **65.14** RETURNS) has been given in respect of that return. The company may amend its return in light of the notice at any time within the 90-day period beginning with the day on which the notice is given. A closure notice in respect of the enquiry may not be issued before the earlier of the company amending its return or the end of the 90-day period.

If enquiries into the return have been completed, HMRC's power to issue a notice is subject to two requirements, both of which must be met:

(1) at the time enquiries were completed HMRC could not, on the basis of information made available to them (within *FA 1998, Sch 18 para 44(2)(3)* — see **6.3** ASSESSMENTS) before that time, reasonably have been aware of circumstances indicating that a notice could have been issued; and

(2) a request for information was made during the enquiry which, if duly complied with, would have resulted in a reasonable expectation that HMRC would issue a notice.

If a notice is issued in these circumstances no discovery assessment may be made before the earlier of the company amending its return or the end of the 90-day period beginning with the day on which the notice is given. However, the normal restrictions on making discovery assessments in *FA 1998, Sch 18 paras 43, 44* do not apply (see **6.3** ASSESSMENTS).

On receiving a notice containing HMRC's view of the position, it is up to the company to decide if it needs to amend its self-assessment. If it fails to make an amendment which ought to have been made its return will be incorrect (with all the resulting implications for penalties, etc.).

[*TCGA 1992, ss 184G(6)(8)(9), 184H(6)(8)(9), 184I*].

Clearances

[11.6] HMRC operate an informal clearance procedure and will give advice on actual or proposed transactions. Applications for clearance should be addressed to BAI Clearance, HMRC, BX9 1JL (ensure the application is marked as 'Market sensitive' or 'Non-market sensitive', as applicable).

HMRC will aim to give a response within 30 days of receipt of a clearance application. A clearance will state the terms on which it has been given and HMRC will regard itself bound by a clearance provided that all relevant facts are accurately given. Where the clearance is sought in advance, the transaction must be executed in accordance with the proposals set out in the clearance application. Where a clearance cannot be given HMRC will state the reasons, but taxpayers are not bound by their decision.

Schemes converting income into capital

[11.7] HMRC may issue a notice (see **11.5** above) invoking anti-avoidance measures where it has reasonable grounds for considering that the following four conditions are, or may be, satisfied:

- any receipt or other amount arises to a company (the '*relevant company*') on the disposal of an asset and that receipt arises directly or indirectly in consequence of, or otherwise in connection with, any arrangements (see **11.4** above);
- that amount is taken into account in calculating a chargeable gain (the '*relevant gain*') accruing to a company (the '*relevant company*') and losses arise (or have arisen) to that company (whether before or after or as part of the arrangements);

- but for the arrangements an amount would have been taken into account wholly or partly instead of the amount in (a) above as income of the relevant company (or as the income of a company in the same capital gains tax group (see **12.2** CAPITAL GAINS — GROUPS) at any time in the period beginning with the time at which the arrangements were made and ending when the matters, other than the tax advantage, intended to be secured by the arrangements are secured); and
- the main purpose, or one of the main purposes, of the arrangements was the obtaining of a tax advantage (see **11.4** above) involving the deduction of the capital losses from the relevant gain.

If all these conditions are satisfied when the HMRC notice is given, the relevant company may not deduct any loss from the relevant gain.

[*TCGA 1992, s 184G(1)–(5)(7)(10)*].

Schemes securing deductions

[11.8] HMRC may issue a notice (see **11.5** above) invoking anti-avoidance measures where it has reasonable grounds for considering that the following four conditions are, or may be, satisfied:

- a chargeable gain (the '*relevant gain*') accrues to a company (the '*relevant company*') directly or indirectly in consequence of, or otherwise in connection with, any arrangements (see **11.4** above) and that company has capital losses available;
- the relevant company, or a company connected with it, becomes entitled to an 'income deduction' directly or indirectly in consequence or, or otherwise in connection with, the arrangements;
- the main purpose, or one of the main purposes, of the arrangements was the obtaining of a tax advantage (see **11.4** above) involving both the income deduction and the deduction of losses from the relevant gain; and
- the arrangements are not 'excluded arrangements' (see below).

It does not matter whether the tax advantage is secured for the relevant company or any other company.

'*Excluded arrangements*' are certain arm's length sale and leaseback transactions involving land within *CTA 2010, s 835(1)* or *s 835(1)* (previously *ICTA 1988, s 779(1)(2)* — see **4.8** ANTI-AVOIDANCE) where there is no connection between the lessor and the lessee. An '*income deduction*' means a deduction in calculating income for corporation tax purposes or a deduction from total profits.

If all the above conditions are satisfied when the HMRC notice is given, the relevant company may not deduct any loss from the relevant gain.

[*TCGA 1992, s 184H(1)–(5)(7)(10)(11)*].

Liquidation

[11.9] The vesting of a company's assets in a liquidator is disregarded. All the acts of the liquidator in relation to such assets are treated as acts of the company. [*TCGA 1992, s 8(6)*].

Simon's Taxes. See **D1.914.**

See also **76** WINDING UP.

Recovery from shareholders

[11.10] Where a person connected with a UK resident company (see **19** CONNECTED PERSONS):

- receives, or becomes entitled to receive, in respect of shares in that company;
- a capital distribution which is not a reduction of capital but which constitutes, or is derived from, a disposal of assets from which a chargeable gain accrues to the company; and
- the company does not pay, within a specified time (see below), the corporation tax due from it for the accounting period in which the gain accrues,

the recipient of the distribution may, by assessment within two years of the due date, be required to pay so much of that corporation tax as relates to chargeable gains but not exceeding the lesser of:

(i) a part of that tax, at the rate in force when the gain accrued, proportionate to his share of the total distribution made by the company; and
(ii) the value of the distribution he received or became entitled to receive.

The person then has a right of recovery against the company, including any interest charged on him under *TMA 1970, s 87A* (see **43.2** INTEREST ON OVERDUE TAX).

The time specified (as above) is the date the tax became payable by the company or, if later, the date the assessment was made on the company.

[*TCGA 1992, s 189*].

See also **58.14** PAYMENT OF TAX as regards recovery of tax from third parties generally.

Simon's Taxes. See **D1.904.**

Interest charged to capital

[11.11] In relation to interest referable to an accounting period ending **before 1 April 1996**, before the introduction of the LOAN RELATIONSHIPS (**50**) provisions, interest on money borrowed by a company for the construction of any building, structure or works, and referable to a period before disposal, could be added to the expenditure allowable as a deduction under *TCGA 1992, s 38* in computing the gain on the disposal by the company of the building etc. This was subject to the proviso that the expenditure on the construction itself was allowable, and that the interest was neither allowable as a deduction in computing any profits or gains for corporation tax purposes (nor would have been so but for an insufficiency of profits or gains) nor a charge on income. [*TCGA 1992, s 40*].

Government securities and QCBs

[11.12] See the general taxation provisions relating to LOAN RELATIONSHIPS (50).

Value-shifting

[11.13] The following provisions apply to the disposal of an asset (the *s 30* disposal) if a scheme has been effected or arrangements have been made (whether before or after the disposal) whereby the value of the asset has been materially reduced and a 'tax-free benefit' is conferred at any time on:

(a) the person making the disposal or a person connected with him (see **19** CONNECTED PERSONS); or

(b) any other person, except in a case where tax avoidance was not a main purpose of the scheme or arrangements.

Where the disposal of an asset precedes its acquisition, references to a reduction include references to an increase. See *Land Securities Plc v HMRC* FTT 2011, [2012] SFTD 215 for the application of this rule to shares etc. treated as acquired following disposal.

The provisions do not apply if the disposal of the asset is a disposal by a company of shares in, or securities (within *TCGA 1992, s 132*) of another company. Instead the provisions at **11.14** below apply.

Any allowable loss or chargeable gain accruing on the *s 30* disposal is to be calculated as if the consideration were increased by such amount as is 'just and reasonable' having regard to the scheme or arrangements and the tax-free benefit. Where such an increase of consideration has been made for one asset and the tax-free benefit was an increase in value of another asset, the consideration for the first subsequent disposal of that other asset is to be reduced by such amount as is 'just and reasonable' in the circumstances. (There is no provision for the acquirer's cost of the asset to be correspondingly increased or reduced.)

These provisions do not apply to disposals between companies in a group (see **12.2** CAPITAL GAINS — GROUPS).

[*TCGA 1992, s 30(1)(2)(4)–(7)(9)*].

A '*tax-free benefit*' arises to a person if he becomes entitled to money or money's worth or his interest in the value of any asset is increased or he is wholly or partly relieved from any liability to which he is subject *and* none of the foregoing benefits when conferred is otherwise liable to income tax, capital gains tax or corporation tax. [*TCGA 1992, s 30(3)*].

HMRC do not regard ordinary commercial group relief transactions (e.g. the purchase of group relief) as falling within *TCGA 1992, s 30*.

Where a disposal within *TCGA 1992, s 30* would otherwise form the basis for a claim for loss relief against income under *CTA 2010, Pt 4 Ch 5* these provisions apply if *any* benefit is conferred, whether tax-free or not. [*TCGA 1992, s 125A*].

Simon's Taxes. See **C2.116.**

Certain disposals of shares by companies

[11.14] The following provision applies (and those at 11.13 above do not apply) for corporation tax purposes to the disposal by a company of shares in, or securities (within *TCGA 1992, s 132*) of, another company if:

(a) 'arrangements' have been made under which the value of the shares or securities, or any 'relevant asset' is materially reduced (or, where the disposal precedes the acquisition of the shares or securities, is materially increased);

(b) the main purpose, or one of the main purposes, of the arrangements is to avoid a liability to corporation tax on chargeable gains (of the disposing company or any other person); and

(c) the arrangements do not consist solely of the making of an 'exempt distribution'.

In calculating the chargeable gain or allowable loss on the disposal, the consideration is increased by an amount which is just and reasonable having regard to the arrangements and any charge to or relief from corporation tax that would have arisen from the disposal or arrangements but for this provision.

In (a) above, '*arrangements*' include any agreement, understanding, scheme, transaction or series of transactions, whether or not legally enforceable. An asset is a '*relevant asset*' if it is owned by a member of the disposing company's group (within *TCGA 1992, s 170* — see **12.2** CAPITAL GAINS — GROUPS) at the time of the disposal. In (c) above, an '*exempt distribution*' is one within the exempt class under *CTA 2009, s 931H* (see **29.16**(d) DISTRIBUTIONS) or which would be within that class but for the recipient being a small company (within *CTA 2009, s 931S*).

The following applies where there are arrangements (as above) under which the value of shares or securities is materially reduced and the main purpose, or one of the main purposes of the arrangements is to avoid a liability to corporation tax on chargeable gains (of the company carrying out the transaction concerned or any other person). If, but for the arrangements, a transaction would be treated as a disposal of shares by a company under *TCGA 1992, s 29(2)* (value passing out of shares in company), the transaction is to be treated as such a disposal.

[*TCGA 1992, s 31*].

Close company transferring asset at undervalue

[11.15] Where, after 5 April 1965 (31 March 1982 where, on the ultimate disposal after 5 April 1988, market value at that date is substituted for cost), a close company transfers an asset to any person otherwise than at arm's length for a consideration less than market value, the difference is apportioned among the issued shares of the company so as to reduce the deductible cost in the capital gains tax computation on disposal of those shares; but this does not apply to transfers within a group. [*TCGA 1992, s 125*].

By concession, *s 125* is not applied where the transferee is a participator (or associate) and the transfer is treated as an income distribution under *CTA 2010, ss 1000, 1020* (see **29.7** DISTRIBUTIONS) or as a capital distribution under *TCGA 1992, s 122* (see Tolley's Capital Gains Tax under Shares and Securities), or where the transferee is an employee and is assessed as employment income on the excess of the market value of the asset over any amount paid for it. (HMRC Extra-Statutory Concession, D51).

Where the transfer is to a trust for the benefit of the employees of the transferring company, the difference that is apportioned is limited (where it would otherwise be greater) to any excess of allowable expenditure over the transfer consideration. [*TCGA 1992, s 239*].

Simon's Taxes. See **D1.919**.

Transfer of assets to non-resident company

[11.16] A UK resident company may be trading overseas through a permanent establishment. If the company decides to transfer this trade to a non-UK resident company, *TCGA 1992, s 140* gives relief with regard to chargeable gains which might arise — the provisions allow the UK company to postpone the gains arising on the transfer.

Certain conditions need to be met, as follows:

(a) a UK resident company has to have been carrying on a trade outside the UK through a permanent establishment;
(b) the whole or part of that trade together with its assets (excluding cash) are transferred to a company that is not UK resident;
(c) the transfer is wholly or partly in exchange for securities (shares or shares and loan stock) issued by the transferee to the transferor;
(d) following the issue of the shares, the transferor holds at least 25% of the ordinary share capital of the transferee; and
(e) a net chargeable gain arises on the assets transferred.

Where these conditions are met, the proportion of the resulting net chargeable gains relating to the shares (and not any cash received — thus in proportion that the market value of the shares at the time of the transfer bears to the market value of the whole consideration received) may be claimed by the transferor company as being deferred.

The gain will only be treated as arising when one of the following events occurs:

(i) The transferor company disposes of all or any of the shares received. The 'appropriate proportion' of the deferred gain (insofar as not already charged under this specific provision or under (ii) below) is then treated as a chargeable gain arising at that time. In determining whether a gain is deemed to arise under this provision, for disposals on or after 22 November 2017, the disapplication of *TCGA 1992, s 127* (reorganisations of share capital etc. — see **62.1** REORGANISATIONS AND RECONSTRUCTIONS) under the provisions at **13.13** CAPITAL GAINS — SUBSTANTIAL SHAREHOLDING EXEMPTION is ignored (so that a reorganisation etc. within *s 127* is treated as not being a disposal of the shares). The gain is in addition to any gain or loss actually arising on the disposal of the shares. The '*appropriate proportion*' is the proportion in which the market value of the shares disposed of bears to the market value of the shares held immediately before the disposal. However, no addition to the consideration is made under this provision if its application would be directly attributable to the disposal of an asset before 1 April 1982.

(ii) The *transferee company disposes*, within six years of the transfer, of the whole or part of the assets on which chargeable gains were deferred. The gain chargeable (in so far as it has not already been charged under this provision or under (i) above) is the proportion which the deferred gain on the assets disposed of bears to the total deferred gains on assets held immediately before the disposal.

The following disposals are disregarded.

- For the purposes of (i) above, intra-group transfers within *TCGA 1992, s 171* (see **12.2** onwards CAPITAL GAINS — GROUPS). A charge will arise when a subsequent owner makes a disposal outside the group.
- For the purposes of (i) above, securities transferred by a transferor as part of the process of a merger to which *TCGA 1992, s 140E* applies (see **11.31** below). In relation to a subsequent disposal of the shares or disposal by the transferee company of assets within (ii) above, the transferee is treated as if it were the transferor company.
- For the purposes of (i) above, securities transferred by a transferor company as part of the process of the transfer of a business to which **11.18** below applies. In relation to a subsequent disposal of the securities or disposal by the transferee company of assets within (ii) above, the transferee is treated as if it were the transferor company.
- For the purposes of (ii) above, intra-group transfers which would be within *TCGA 1992, s 171* if for those purposes a group included (without qualification) non-UK resident companies. A charge will arise when a subsequent owner makes a disposal outside the group.

No claim may be made under these provisions as regards a transfer in relation to which a claim is made under *TCGA 1992, s 140C*.

[*TCGA 1992, s 140, Sch 4 para 4; FA 2018, s 27*].

For the interaction between (i) above and the substantial shareholdings exemption, see **13.9** CAPITAL GAINS — SUBSTANTIAL SHAREHOLDING EXEMPTION.

Simon's Taxes. See D6.523.

Transfers, divisions and mergers within the European Union

Effect of Brexit

[11.17] The reliefs at **11.18** below give effect in UK law to the EU Mergers Directive *2009/133/EC*. After the end of the Brexit implementation period, i.e. after IP completion day (11pm on 31 December 2020), the Directive no longer applies to the UK. *SI 2019 No 689, Reg 6*, however, provides for the retention of the reliefs as they apply to UK corporation tax. The effect of a transfer, division or merger in the home state of the companies involved (where that is not the UK) will depend on the tax laws of that state and any double tax treaties.

For the purposes of the reliefs a '*relevant state*' is an EU member state or, after IP completion day, the UK or an EU member state. [*TCGA 1992, s 140L(1)(ba); SI 2019 No 689, Regs 1, 6(12); European Union (Withdrawal Agreement) Act 2020, Sch 5 para 1(1)*].

Transfer or division of UK business between companies in different EC member states

[11.18] The following reliefs apply to transfers or divisions of UK businesses between companies resident in different relevant states (see **11.17** above).

Transfer of UK business

A special relief may be claimed where a company resident in one relevant state transfers the whole or part of a business carried on by it in the UK to a company resident in another relevant state wholly in exchange for shares or debentures in the latter company, provided that the further conditions below are satisfied.

A company is regarded as resident in a relevant state under the laws of which it is chargeable to tax because it is regarded as so resident (unless it is regarded under DOUBLE TAX RELIEF (**31.3**) arrangements entered into by the relevant state as resident in a territory not within any of the relevant states).

Division of UK business

The relief may also be claimed where a company resident in one relevant state transfers part of its business to one or more companies at least one of which is resident in another relevant state. The part of the transferor's business which is transferred must be carried on by the transferor in the UK and the transferor must continue to carry on a business after the transfer.

The transfer must be made in exchange for the issue of shares in or debentures of each transferee to the holders of shares in or debentures of the transferor, except where, and to the extent that, a transferee is prevented from meeting this requirement by reason only of *Companies Act 2006, s 658* (rule against limited company acquiring its own shares) or a corresponding provision in another member state.

The further conditions below must also be satisfied.

Further conditions

A claim for relief must be made by both the transferor and the transferee (or each of the transferees). The anti-avoidance provision below must not apply, and either:

(i) if the transferee company is, or each of the transferee companies are, non-UK resident immediately after the transfer, any chargeable gain accruing to it, or them, on a disposal of the assets included in the transfer would form part of its, or their, corporation tax profits under *TCGA 1992, s 2B(3)* (previously *s 10B*); or

(ii) if it is, or they are, UK resident at that time, none of the assets included in the transfer is exempt from UK tax on disposal under double tax relief arrangements.

Effect of relief

Any assets included in the transfer are treated for the purposes of corporation tax on chargeable gains as transferred for a no gain/no loss consideration, and *TCGA 1992, s 25(3)* (deemed disposal by non-resident on ceasing to trade in the UK through a permanent establishment or a branch or agency) does not apply to the assets by reason of the transfer.

In the case of a division of a UK business, where the transfer is not made wholly in exchange for the issue of shares in or debentures of each transferee, neither *TCGA 1992, s 24* (deemed disposal where asset lost, destroyed or becoming of negligible value) nor *TCGA 1992, s 122* (capital distributions) apply to the transfer.

Also in the case of a division of a UK business, where the transferor and transferee (or each of the transferees) are all resident in relevant states, but are not all resident in the same state, the transfer of assets is treated as if it were a scheme of reconstruction within *TCGA 1992, s 136* if it would not otherwise be so treated. Where *s 136* applies as a result of this provision, the anti-avoidance provision at *s 136(6)* does not apply (and neither does *s 137* (restrictions on company reconstructions).

Anti-avoidance

The above provisions do not apply unless the transfer is effected for *bona fide* commercial reasons and not as part of a scheme or arrangement, a main purpose of which is avoidance of income, corporation or capital gains taxes. Advance clearance may be obtained from HMRC on the application of the companies, to the same address and subject to the same conditions and appeal procedures as apply to clearances under *TCGA 1992, s 138* (see Tolley's Capital Gains Tax under Anti-avoidance).

[*TCGA 1992, ss 140A, 140B, 140DA, 140L(2); FA 2019, Sch 1 para 50; SI 2019 No 689, Regs 1, 6(2)(4)(12); European Union (Withdrawal Agreement) Act 2020, Sch 5 para 1(1)*].

Capital allowances

Where the above provisions apply and, immediately after the transfer, either the transferee or one or more of the transferees, is resident in the UK, or at that time carries on a business in the UK through a permanent establishment (or branch or agency), consisting of, or including, the business (or part) transferred, then the transfer or division does not give rise to any allowances or charges in respect of *CAA 2001*.

Furthermore, in relation to the assets included in the transfer, anything done by or to the transferor before the transfer is treated, after the transfer, as having been done to or by the transferee or each transferee.

This treatment does not apply if the successor is a dual resident investing company (as defined) in the accounting period in which the transfer takes place.

The provisions of *CTA 2010, ss 948, 949* (see **51.16** LOSSES) do not apply where a claim is made under these provisions.

[*CAA 2001, s 561*].

Transfer or division of non-UK business between companies in different EC member states

[11.19] The following reliefs apply to the transfer or division of a non-UK business between companies in different relevant states (see **11.17** above).

Transfer of non-UK business

Special provisions apply, on a claim, where a company resident in the UK transfers to a company resident in another relevant state the whole or part of a business carried on by the UK company immediately before the transfer through a permanent establishment in a relevant state other than the UK. The transfer must be wholly or partly in exchange for shares or debentures in the non-UK transferee company and the further conditions below must be satisfied.

A company is not regarded as resident in the UK if it were regarded under any DOUBLE TAX RELIEF (**31.3**) arrangements to which the UK is a party as resident in a territory not within any of the relevant states. A company is regarded as resident in another relevant state under the laws of which it is chargeable to tax because it is regarded as so resident (unless it is regarded under a double tax relief arrangement entered into by the relevant state as resident in a territory not within any of the relevant states).

Division of non-UK business

The provisions may also apply where a company resident in the UK transfers part of its business to one or more companies at least one of which is resident in another relevant state other than the UK. The part of the transferor's business which is transferred must be carried on by the transferor immediately before the transfer in a relevant state other than the UK through a permanent establishment and the transferor must continue to carry on a business after the transfer.

The transfer must be made in exchange for the issue of shares in or debentures of each transferee to the holders of shares in or debentures of the transferor, except where, and to the extent that, a transferee is prevented from meeting this requirement by reason only of *Companies Act 2006, s 658* (rule against limited company acquiring its own shares) or a corresponding provision in another relevant state.

The further conditions below must also be satisfied.

Further conditions

The transfer must include all the UK company's assets used in the business or part (with the possible exception of cash) and the anti-avoidance provision below must be satisfied. The aggregate of the chargeable gains accruing to the UK company on the transfer must exceed the aggregate of the allowable losses so accruing.

The UK company must make a claim for the provisions to apply. No claim may, however, be made where a claim is made under *TCGA 1992, s 140* at **11.16** above in relation to the same transfer.

Effect of provisions

The transfer is treated as giving rise to a single chargeable gain of the excess of the aggregate of the chargeable gains accruing to the UK company on the transfer over the aggregate of the allowable losses so accruing.

In the case of a division of a non-UK business, where the transferor and transferee (or each of the transferees) are all resident in relevant states, but are not all resident in the same state, the transfer of assets is treated as if it were a scheme of reconstruction within *TCGA 1992, s 136* if it would not otherwise be so treated. Where *s 136* applies as a result of this provision, the anti-avoidance provision at *s 136(6)* does not apply (and neither does *s 137* (restrictions on company reconstructions).

Anti-avoidance

The transfer must be effected for *bona fide* commercial reasons and not as part of a scheme or arrangement a main purpose of which is avoidance of income, corporation or capital gains taxes. Advance clearance may be obtained from HMRC on the application of the UK company, to the same address and subject to the same conditions and appeal procedures as apply to clearances under *TCGA 1992, s 138* (see Tolley's Capital Gains Tax under Anti-avoidance).

[*TCGA 1992, ss 140C, 140D, 140DA, 140L; SI 2019 No 689, Regs 1, 6(3)(4)(12); European Union (Withdrawal Agreement) Act 2020, Sch 5 para 1(1)*].

Double tax relief

Where the above provisions apply, where gains accruing to the UK company would have been chargeable to tax under the law of the member state in which the trade was carried on immediately before the transfer but for the Mergers Directive, the amount of tax is treated for double tax relief purposes as tax paid in that other member state. In calculating the amount of the tax so treated it is assumed that, so far as permitted under the law of the member state, any losses arising on the transfer are set against the gains, and that the UK company claims any available reliefs.

These provisions apply also where *TCGA 1992, s 140F* (European cross-border merger: assets not left within UK tax charge — see **11.20** below) applies.

[*TIOPA 2010, s 122*].

European cross-border mergers

[11.20] The following provisions apply to:

(a) (before Brexit IP completion day (11pm on 31 December 2020)) the formation of an SE (see **32.6** EUROPEAN UNION LEGISLATION) by the merger of two or more companies in accordance with *Council Regulation (EC) No 2157/2001, Arts 2(1), 17(2)*;

(b) (before Brexit IP completion day) the formation of an SCE (see **32.6**) by the merger of two or more 'co-operative societies', at least one of which is a registered society within *Co-operative and Community Benefit Societies Act 2014* or NI equivalent (previously, a society registered under *Industrial and Provident Societies Act 1965*), in accordance with *Council Regulation (EC) No 1435/2003*;

(c) a merger effected by the transfer by one or more companies or co-operative societies of all their assets and liabilities to a single existing company or co-operative society; and

(d) a merger effected by the transfer by two or more companies of all their assets to a single new company (which is not an SE or SCE) in exchange for the issue by the transferee company of shares or debentures to each person holding shares in or debentures of a transferee company.

From Brexit IP completion day, no new SEs or SCEs can be formed in the UK.

For the purposes of (b) and (c) above, a '*co-operative society*' is a registered society within *Co-operative and Community Benefit Societies Act 2014* or NI equivalent (previously, a society registered under the *Industrial and Provident Societies Act 1965*) or a similar society established under the law of a relevant state (see **11.17** above) other than the UK.

Each of the merging companies or co-operative societies must be resident in a relevant state but they must not all be resident in the same state. A company resident in a relevant state for this purpose if it is within a charge to tax under the law of the State as being resident for that purpose and it is not regarded, for the purposes of any DOUBLE TAX RELIEF (**31**) arrangements to which the state is a party, as resident in a territory not within a relevant state.

Treatment of securities issued on merger

If it does not constitute or form part of a scheme of reconstruction within the meaning of *TCGA 1992, s 136*, the merger is nevertheless treated as if it were a scheme of reconstruction for the purposes of that section, but the anti-avoidance provision at *section 136(6)* does not apply (and neither does *s 137* (restrictions on company reconstructions — see Tolley's Capital Gains Tax under Anti-avoidance). See, however, the anti-avoidance provision below.

Assets left within UK tax charge

If:

(i) *TCGA 1992, s 139* (reconstruction involving transfer of business — see **62.15** REORGANISATIONS AND RECONSTRUCTIONS) does not apply to the merger;

(ii) where the merger is within (a), (b) or (c) above, the transfer of assets and liabilities is made in exchange for the issue of shares in or debentures of the transferee to the holders of shares in or debentures of a transferor, except where, and to the extent that, the transferee is prevented from meeting this requirement by reason only of *Companies Act 2006, s 658* (rule against limited company acquiring its own shares) or a corresponding provision in another relevant state; and

(iii) where the merger is within (d) above, in the course of the merger each transferor ceases to exist without being in liquidation (within the meaning of *Insolvency Act 1986, s 247*), then any 'qualifying transferred assets' are treated for chargeable gains purposes as acquired by the transferee (i.e. the SE, SCE or merged company) for a consideration resulting in neither gain nor loss for the transferor company or co-operative society.

For this purpose, an asset transferred to the transferee as part of the merger process is a '*qualifying transferred asset*' if:

- either the transferor was resident in the UK at the time of the transfer or any gain accruing on disposal of the asset immediately before that time would have been a chargeable gain forming part of the transferor's chargeable profits by virtue of *TCGA 1992, s 2B(3)* (previously *s 10B*); trade carried on via UK permanent establishment — see **64.6** RESIDENCE above); and
- either the transferee is resident in the UK at the time of the transfer or any gain accruing to it on disposal of the asset immediately after the transfer would have been a chargeable gain forming part of its chargeable profits by virtue of *TCGA 1992, s 2B(3)* (previously *s 10B*).

Where the condition at (ii) above applies, but the transfer is not made wholly in exchange for the issue of shares in or debentures of each transferee, neither *TCGA 1992, s 24* (deemed disposal where asset lost, destroyed or becoming of negligible value) nor *TCGA 1992, s 122* (capital distributions) apply to the transfer.

Assets not left within UK tax charge

If:

- in the course of the merger, a company or co-operative society resident in the UK (company A) transfers to a company or co-operative society resident in another member state all the assets and liabilities relating to a business carried on by company A in a member state other than the UK through a permanent establishment;
- the aggregate chargeable gains accruing to company A on the transfer exceed the aggregate allowable losses;
- where the merger is within (a), (b) or (c) above, the transfer of assets and liabilities is made in exchange for the issue of shares in or debentures of the transferee to the holders of shares in or debentures of a transferor, except where, and to the extent that, the transferee is prevented from meeting this requirement by reason only of *Companies Act 2006, s 658* or *Companies Act 1985, s 143* (rule against limited company acquiring its own shares) or a corresponding provision in another member state; and
- where the merger is within (c) or (d) above, in the course of the merger each transferor ceases to exist without being in liquidation (within *Insolvency Act 1986, s 247*),

the allowable losses are treated as set off against the chargeable gains and the transfer is treated as giving rise to a single chargeable gain equal to the excess. See **11.19** above for special double tax relief provisions applying where this provision applies.

Anti-avoidance

The above provisions do not apply if the merger is not effected for *bona fide* commercial reasons or if it forms part of a scheme or arrangements of which the main purpose, or one of the main purposes, is avoiding liability to UK tax. The advance clearance provisions of *TCGA 1992, s 138* apply, with any necessary modifications, for this purpose as they apply for the purposes of *TCGA 1992, s 137*.

Subsidiary merging with parent

Where a merger is effected by the transfer by a company or all its assets and liabilities to a single company which holds the whole of its ordinary share capital and *TCGA 1992, s 139* does not apply, then, if, in the course of the merger, the transferor ceases to exist without being in liquidation, neither *TCGA 1992, s 24* nor *TCGA 1992, s 122* apply to the transfer.

[*TCGA 1992, ss 140E–140GA, 140L; FA 2019, Sch 1 para 51; SI 2019 No 689, Regs 1, 6(5)–(8)(12); European Union (Withdrawal Agreement) Act 2020, Sch 5 para 1(1)*].

Capital allowances

Where there is a merger leaving assets within the charge to UK tax to which the above provisions apply (or would apply but for *TCGA 1992, s 139* applying), the transferee takes over the capital allowance position of the transferor company in relation to any 'qualifying assets' transferred as part of the merger, so that no allowances or charges arise from the transfer in respect of the *Capital Allowances Act 2001*.

Any necessary apportionments are made in a reasonable manner. *CTA 2010 s 948* (see **51.16** LOSSES) does not apply where this provision applies. An asset is a '*qualifying asset*' if it is transferred to the transferee as part of the merger, either the transferor is resident in the UK at the time of transfer or the asset is an asset of the transferor's UK permanent establishment, and either the transferee is resident in the UK on formation or the asset is an asset of the transferee's UK permanent establishment on formation.

[*CAA 2001, s 561A*].

Transparent entities

[11.21] Certain of the rules at **11.18–11.20** above do not apply where one of the parties is a 'transparent entity'. For the rules applying in such circumstances, see Tolley's Capital Gains Tax under Overseas Matters.

A '*transparent entity*' for this purpose is an entity which is resident in a relevant state (see **11.17** above) other than the UK and is listed as a company in the Annex to the Mergers Directive, but which does not have an ordinary share capital and, if resident in the UK, would not be capable of being registered as a company under *Companies Act 2006*.

[*TCGA 1992, ss 140H–140L*].

Assets subject to EU exit charge

[11.22] The following applies where an asset becomes a chargeable asset of a company on or after 1 January 2020 because either the company becomes resident in the UK or the asset begins to be held for the purposes of a trade carried on by the company in the UK through a permanent establishment. If, at the time the asset becomes a chargeable asset, it is also subject to an 'EU exit charge', it is treated for chargeable gains purposes as if the company had acquired it for its market value at that time.

For this purpose, an asset is a chargeable asset of a company if its disposal would give rise to a UK chargeable gain or allowable loss. An '*EU exit charge*' is a charge to tax under the law of a member state in accordance with the EU Anti Tax Avoidance Directive (Directive (EU) 2016/1194, Art 5(1)).

[*TCGA 1992, s 184J; FA 2019, Sch 8 para 11*].

This provision relieves any potential double taxation at the time of the disposal of the asset by exempting from UK tax any gain or loss arising before the asset came within the scope of UK tax on chargeable gains.

Capital gains tax charge on high value disposals of dwellings

[11.23] Companies are chargeable to capital gains tax on 'high value disposals' on or after 6 April 2013 of dwellings that are subject to the annual tax on enveloped dwellings ('ATED') in *FA 2013, ss 94–174*. The charge is abolished for disposals after 5 April 2019 but, for earlier disposals, is one of the two exceptions to the rule that companies are not subject to capital gains tax but pay corporation tax on their chargeable gains (see **11.1** above). It applies whether or not the company is resident in the UK. [*TCGA 1992, ss 2(7A), 2B(1); FA 2019, Sch 1 paras 2, 120*].

An 'EEA UCITS' (within *Financial Services and Markets Act 2000, s 237*) which is neither a unit trust scheme nor an open-ended investment company is exempt from the charge. [*TCGA 1992, s 100A; FA 2019, Sch 1 para 46*].

The charge is abolished with effect for disposals on or after 6 April 2019. See **11.24** below.

The charge

A company is charged to capital gains tax on the total amount of 'ATED-related chargeable gains' accruing to it in a tax year before 2019/20 on high value disposals, after deducting 'ATED-related allowable losses' accruing in the tax year on high value disposals and any such losses for previous tax years (2013/14 onwards) which have not been allowed as a deduction from gains of any previous tax year. No other deductions are allowable from ATED-related gains. The gains are chargeable to capital gains tax at a rate of 28%.

Losses cannot be carried back to be set against gains of an earlier tax year. Relief in respect of a loss may be given only once by deduction from ATED-related gains, and may not be given at all if relief has been or may be given under any other provision. Losses unrelieved at 6 April 2019 can be carried forward as if they were corporation tax allowable losses.

A disposal is a '*high value disposal*' if:

(a) the disposal is of the whole or part of a 'chargeable interest';
(b) the disposed of interest has, at any time in the 'ownership period' been or formed part of a 'single-dwelling interest';
(c) the company has been within the charge to annual tax on enveloped dwellings with respect to the single-dwelling interest on one or more days in the ownership period which are not 'relievable days' (or would have been so within the charge if ATED had commenced on 31 March 1982); and
(d) the consideration for the disposal exceeds the 'threshold amount'.

Where the disposed of interest is a partnership asset, it is the 'responsible partners' who must be within the charge to ATED for the purposes of (c) above. Where the disposed of interest was held for the purposes of certain collective investment schemes, the person with day-to-day control over the management of its property must be within the charge.

The expressions 'chargeable interest', 'dwelling', 'single-dwelling interest' and 'responsible partners' have the same meaning for these purposes as for the annual tax on enveloped dwellings.

The '*ownership period*' is the period beginning with the date on which the company acquired the chargeable interest or, if later, the 6 April in the relevant year, and ending on the day before the disposal. The 'relevant year' depends on whether the property being sold was held on 5 April 2013, 2015 or 2016, and whether ATED was payable before the relevant date. The relevant year is 2016 if the interest disposed of was held on 5 April 2016 and no other single-dwelling interest was within the charge to ATED on one or more days, or would have been in the charge but for it being relievable, in the period ending with 31 March 2016 during which the company held the interest disposed of (*Case* 3). If it is not 2016, then the relevant year is 2015 if the interest disposed of was held on 5 April 2015 and no other single-dwelling interest was within the charge to ATED, or would have been in the charge but for it being relievable, in the period ending with 31 March 2015 during which the company held the interest disposed of (*Case* 2). If the relevant year is not 2015 nor 2016, then it is 2013 (*Case* 1).

If the company has made an election under *TCGA 1992, Sch 4ZZA para 5*, the ownership period starts on the day on which the company acquired the chargeable interest or, if later, 31 March 1982. A '*relievable day*' is one for which any of the ATED reliefs in *FA 2013, s 132* has been claimed (or, for days falling before 1 April 2013, would have been claimable if ATED had then been in force).

In (d) above, the '*threshold amount*' is, subject to the following, £1 million for disposals on or after 6 April 2015 (£2 million for disposals in tax years 2013–14 and 2014–15). If the disposal is a part disposal or the company has made any 'related disposals', the threshold amount is:

£1 million (tax year 2015–16, £2 million for earlier years) x C/TMV

where C is the consideration for the disposal and TMV is what would be the market value of a notional asset consisting of the disposed of interest, any undisposed of part of the chargeable interest, any chargeable interest (or part) which was the subject of a related disposal and any chargeable interest (or part) held by the company at the time of the disposal which, if the company had disposed of it at that time, would have been the subject of a related disposal.

If the disposed of interest is a fractional share of the whole of a chargeable interest (or part), these rules apply by reducing the £1 million (for tax year 2015–16, £2 million for earlier years) amount by reference to the company's fractional share.

The threshold amount will be reduced to £500,000 for disposals on or after 6 April 2016.

A disposal made by the company in the six years ending with the day of the disposal in question (but not before 6 April 2013) is a '*related disposal*' if it meets conditions (a)–(c) above and the single-dwelling interest in (c) above is either the same interest or another single-dwelling interest in the same dwelling.

[*TCGA 1992, ss 2B–2D, 4(3A); FA 2019, Sch 1 paras 2, 18, 120, 121*].

Restriction of losses

A disposal which would not otherwise be a high value disposal only because it does not meet condition (d) above is treated as a high value disposal if:

- an ATED-related loss would accrue in a tax year on the disposal if it were a high value disposal; and
- the total allowable deductions under *TCGA 1992, s 38* exceeds the threshold amount.

In such a case, the ATED-related loss is restricted to the amount which would have been the loss if the consideration had been £1 greater than the threshold amount. This rule does not restrict the amount of any loss which is not ATED-related nor does it affect any gain arising on the disposal.

[*TCGA 1992, s 2E; FA 2019, Sch 1 para 2*].

Tapering of gains

The amount of an ATED-related gain is reduced where the capital gains tax chargeable would otherwise leave the company worse off than it would have been had it sold the interest for less than the threshold amount. The gain is reduced by so much of it as exceeds five thirds of the difference between the consideration and the threshold amount. Where only a part of the gain is an ATED-related gain, the amount excluded from charge in this way is reduced by the same proportion.

This rule does not restrict the amount of any gain which is not ATED-related nor does it affect any loss arising on the disposal.

[*TCGA 1992, s 2F; FA 2019, Sch 1 para 2*].

Computation of gains and losses

Special rules apply to determine whether or not an ATED-related gain or loss accrues on a disposal. The calculation of an ATED-related gain or loss differs according to whether or not the interest was held by the company on 5 April 2013, 5 April 2015 or 5 April 2016 (Cases 1, 2 or 3, as above).

Interest held on 5 April 2013, 5 April 2015 or 5 April 2016

Where the interest disposed of was held by the company on 5 April 2013, 5 April 2015 or 5 April 2016, the ATED-related gain or loss is an amount equal to the 'relevant fraction' of the gain or loss, computed using capital gains tax rules, which (apart from the current provisions) would have accrued on the disposal if the company had acquired the interest on 5 April 2013, 5 April 2015 or 5 April 2016 (as appropriate) at market value.

The '*relevant fraction*' is the number of days in the relevant ownership period which are 'ATED chargeable days', divided by the total number of days in that period. The '*relevant ownership period*' begins on 6 April in the relevant year (as above) and ends the day before the disposal. '*ATED chargeable days*' are days by reference to which condition (c) above is met. If there is a change in the number of ATED chargeable days as a result of a claim under *FA 2013, s 105(3)* (adjustment of chargeable amount under ATED), any necessary adjustments can be made by assessment etc. to give effect to any resulting change to the capital gains tax liability.

If there is no ATED-related gain or loss after applying the above rules, the gain or loss on the disposal is calculated according to normal principles ignoring the current provisions, unless there is a non-resident CGT disposal (see **11.24** below) which is or involves a relevant high value disposal on or after 6 April 2015. For the detailed provisions see Tolley's Capital Gains Tax under Land.

If there is an ATED-related gain or loss, a non-ATED-related gain or loss (which remains within the charge to corporation tax on chargeable gains) must be calculated using the following steps:

(1) Compute, using corporation tax rules, the gain or loss which would have accrued on 5 April 2013, 5 April 2015 or 5 April 2016 (as appropriate) if the company had disposed of the interest at market value;

(2) if step (1) gives rise to a gain, deduct the ATED-related gain (as calculated above) and adjust the remaining gain by notional indexation allowance (see below);

(3) if step (1) gives rise to a loss, deduct the ATED-related loss (as calculated above);

(4) add the amount in (1) above to the amount in (2) or (3) above together (treating any amount which is a loss as a negative amount).

The notional indexation allowance in (2) above is a fraction of the difference between the indexation allowance which would, but for the current provisions, be due on the disposal and the indexation allowance given in computing the gain in (1) above. The fraction is the number of days in the ownership period beginning on 6 April in the relevant year and ending with the day before the disposal which are **not** ATED chargeable days, divided by the total number of days in that period.

A company can make an irrevocable election to disapply the above rules for a particular interest. If it makes such an election, the ATED-related gain or loss is computed using the rules for instances where Cases 1, 2 or 3 do not apply. The election must be made in a return (or amendment to a return).

Cases 1, 2 or 3 do not apply, or election made

Where Cases 1, 2 or 3 do not apply, or an election is made (as above) then the ATED-related gain or loss is computed using the following steps:

(i) Compute the gain or loss on the disposal using capital gains tax principles (and ignoring the current provisions).

(ii) The ATED-related gain or loss is the proportion of the gain or loss that the number of days in the period beginning on the day the company acquired the interest (or 31 March 1982 if later) and ending with the day before the disposal which are 'ATED chargeable days' bears to the total number of days in that period.

The gain or loss which is not ATED-related (and remains within the charge to corporation tax on chargeable gains) is computed as follows. Deduct the ATED-related gain from the gain in (i) above and adjust the remaining gain by notional indexation allowance. Where there is a loss in (i) above, deduct from it the ATED-related loss.

The notional indexation allowance for this purpose is a fraction of the indexation allowance which would, but for the current provisions, be due on the disposal. The fraction is the number of days in the period beginning on the day the company acquired the interest (or 31 March 1982 if later) and ending with the day before the disposal which are **not** ATED chargeble days, divided by the total number of days in that period.

Interaction with non-resident CGT disposals

The above rules for calculating the ATED-related gain or loss are replaced by the following rules when certain conditions are met:

(a) the relevant high value disposal is a non-resident CGT disposal, or is one of two or more disposals which are treated as comprised in a non-resident CGT disposal; and

(b) the interest disposed of by the high value disposal was held by the company on 5 April 2015, neither Case 2 nor Case 3 applies (see above), and no election has been made for the retrospective basis of computation based on the entire period of ownership (see above).

The following steps should be applied in such instances:

(i) Compute the relevant fraction of the gain or loss (as calculated using capital gains tax principles) which would have accrued on the disposal if the company acquired the interest on 5 April 2015 at its market value (the 'post-April 2015 ATED-related gain or loss'). The relevant fraction is the number of ATED chargeable days in the period beginning on 5 April 2015 and ending the day before disposal, divided by the total number of days in that period.

(ii) Compute the relevant fraction of the 'notional pre-April 2015 gain or loss' (see below), as calculated using capital gains tax principles. The relevant fraction to apply is the number of ATED chargeable days in the period beginning on the day the company acquired the interest, or 6 April 2013 if later, and ending on 5 April 2015, divided by the total number of days in that period.

(iii) Add the results of (i) and (ii) together, treating a loss as a negative amount, which will result in either an ATED-related gain, or loss.

If the company did not hold the interest disposed of on 5 April 2013, the 'notional pre-April 2015 gain or loss' is that which would have accrued on 5 April 2015 if the interest had been disposed of at market value on that date. Otherwise it is that which would have accrued on 5 April 2015 if the company has acquired it on 5 April 2013 at market value and disposed of it on 5 April 2015 at market value.

For the calculation of the non-ATED-related gain or loss which accrues where a non-resident CGT disposal is, or involves, one or more relevant high value disposals, and for details on the non-resident CGT disposals, see Tolley's Capital Gains Tax under Land.

[*TCGA 1992, s 57A, Sch 4ZZA; FA 2019, Sch 1 paras 6, 18*].

Charge to capital gains tax on disposal of UK residential property by non-UK resident

[11.24] For disposals on or after 6 April 2015 and before 6 April 2019, capital gains tax is extended to disposals of UK residential property by non-residents, including certain companies.

The main features of the current provisions are as follows:

- Capital gains tax is charged on gains ('*NRCGT gains*') accruing on a disposal before 6 April 2019 of a UK residential property interest by a non-resident person (other than a disposal within **71.2–71.4** TRANSACTIONS IN UK LAND.
- Tax is charged on the total amount of the NRCGT gains arising in a tax year after deduction of any allowable losses on disposals of UK residential property interests (whether or not NRCGT losses) of the same tax year, and any unused such losses brought forward from previous years.
- Gains and losses by companies are calculated as for corporation tax purposes but there are special rules for property interests held on 5 April 2015. Unless an election is made, only the gain arising after that date is charged. Alternatively an election can be made for time apportionment or, particularly where a loss arises, for the whole of the gain to be charged.
- There are special provisions for calculating the gain or loss where the disposal is, or includes, a disposal chargeable under the provisions for high-value disposals of dwellings (see **11.23** above).
- Relief for losses arising on non-resident CGT disposals can generally only be obtained against NRCGT gains but unused NRCGT losses can be carried forward and set against general chargeable gains of a later tax year for which the taxpayer is resident in the UK (or operates through a UK-permanent establishment).
- Companies are charged to capital gains tax (and not corporation tax) on the chargeable gains at 20%.
- A person who makes a non-resident CGT disposal must, in most cases, make a special return reporting the disposal to HMRC within the 30 days following the day of the completion of the disposal. See **65** RETURNS.

- Tax on NRCGT gains is generally due 30 days after completion of sale (i.e. on the date the return reporting the disposal is due), except where the company is registered for self-assessment, in which case payment may be made on the normal payment date for CGT, though the disposal must still be reported in a return within 30 days.
- Qualifying members of a group of companies may make an election to be treated as an NRCGT group. Disposals of UK-residential property interests between members of the group are disregarded, and the charge to tax applies as if the members of the group were a single body.
- Diversely-held companies as well as certain unit trust schemes and open-ended investment companies are not chargeable under the provisions if they make a claim to that effect.
- NRCGT losses of a company which are unrelieved at 6 April 2019 can be carried forward as if they were ordinary allowable losses.

For the detailed provisions see Tolley's Capital Gains Tax under Land.

Disposals of UK land by non-residents

[11.25] For disposals on or after 6 April 2019, non-UK resident companies are chargeable to corporation tax on gains on interests in UK land (but interests with a connection to the company's UK permanent establishment are charged under the provisions at **64.6** RESIDENCE).

An '*interest in UK land*' is an estate, interest, right or power in or over land in the UK, or the benefit of an obligation, restriction or condition affecting the value of such, but not including:

- any interest or right (other than a rentcharge or, in Scotland, a feu duty) held to secure payment of money or performance of any other obligation;
- a licence to use or occupy land;
- in England, Wales or Northern Ireland, a tenancy at will or an advowson, franchise (i.e. a grant from the Crown, such as the right to hold a market or fair, or the right to take tolls) or manor; or
- any other interest or right specified in Treasury regulations.

'*Land*' includes buildings and structures and any land under the sea or otherwise covered by water.

The grant of an option binding the grantor to sell an interest in land is treated for these purposes as the disposal of an interest in land.

[*TCGA 1992, ss 1C, 2B(4)(a)(5); FA 2019, Sch 1 paras 2, 120*].

These provisions replace and extend the provisions at **11.24** above for non-resident disposals of UK residential property, and are subject to the rebasing rules at **11.31** below.

Rollover relief

Rollover relief under *TCGA 1992, s 152* is available if the old asset is an interest in UK land and any gain would otherwise be chargeable under the above provisions only if the new asset is also an interest in UK land (provided that any other necessary conditions for relief are satisfied).

For this purpose, references to the acquisition of new assets include references to acquisition of an interest in them or to entering into an unconditional contract for the acquisition of them. The reference to a disposal of an old asset includes the disposal of an interest in the old asset.

[*TCGA 1992, s 159A; FA 2019, Sch 1 para 53*].

Disposals of assets deriving 75% of value from UK land by non-residents

[11.26] For disposals on or after 6 April 2019, a non-UK resident company is chargeable to corporation tax on gains the disposal of assets deriving at least 75% of their value from UK land if it has a 'substantial indirect interest' in that land. Gains on assets with a connection to the company's UK permanent establishment are, however, charged under the provisions at **64.6** RESIDENCE).

These provisions are subject to the rebasing rules at **11.31** below.

[*TCGA 1992, s 2B(4)(b)(6); FA 2019, Sch 1 paras 2, 120*].

For HMRC guidance, see HMRC Capital Gains Manual CG73930–73952. For a worked example of how these provisions apply, see CG73932.

An asset derives at least 75% of its value from UK land if it is a right or interest in a company and at least 75% of the market value of the company's 'qualifying assets' derives, directly or indirectly, from interests in UK land (defined as at **11.25** above) at the time of the disposal. For this purpose, market value can be traced through any number of companies, partnerships, trusts and other entities or arrangements (whether or not established under UK law), but not through a normal commercial loan (as defined by *CTA 2010, ss 158(1)(b)* or *159(4)(b)* — see **35.4** GROUP RELIEF). In tracing market value in this way, the assets held by a company, partnership etc. must be attributed to the shareholders, partners, beneficiaries etc. in whatever way is appropriate.

Normal valuation principles apply in determining market value but HMRC accept that formal valuation may not always be necessary. They expect the basis of valuation to be appropriate to the value and complexity of the situation. Sources of information that would allow a taxpayer to conclude with strong confidence whether the company was UK property rich (i.e. it meets the 75% test above) or not might include informal valuations undertaken shortly before the disposal for other commercial purposes to report to independent parties (such as shareholders, banks and other similar creditors) or formal valuations undertaken for a recent balance sheet. (HMRC Capital Gains Manual CG73934).

'*Qualifying assets*' are all assets of the company other than any assets so far as they are matched to a 'related party liability'. Interests in UK land, however, remain qualifying assets even if so matched. An asset is matched to a 'related partly liability' if the asset consists of a right under a transaction (including, but not restricted to, a right under a loan relationship or derivative contract) which entitles the company to require another person to meet a liability (including a contingent liability) under the transaction and that other person is relevant to the market value tracing exercise or is a 'related party' (defined, broadly, as under *CTA 2010, Pt 8ZB* — see **71.8** TRANSACTIONS IN **UK** LAND) of the company on the day of the disposal. A person is relevant to the market value tracing exercise if he has assets which are taken into account in that exercise or has obligations (as trustee or otherwise) in relation to the holding of assets in any trust or other arrangement which are taken into account.

These provisions do not apply to a disposal of a right or interest in a company if it is reasonable to conclude that, so far as the market value of the company's qualifying assets derives from interest in UK land, all of those interests are used for trading purposes. Interests in UK land not used for trading purposes can, however, be ignored for this purpose provided that they have a total market value of no more than 10% of the total market value of interests used for trading purposes. An interest in UK land is used for trading purposes only if it is being used, or has been acquired for use, in or for the purposes of a 'qualifying trade'. A '*qualifying trade*' is one which has been carried on by the company or a connected person through the year ending with the disposal in question on a commercial basis with a view to the realisation of profits. It must be reasonable to conclude that the trade will continue to be so carried on for more than an insignificant period of time.

The provisions also do not apply to two or more disposals of rights or interests in companies if the disposals are 'linked' and:

- some but not all of the disposals would be disposals of assets deriving at least 75% of their value from UK land; but
- if one of the companies included all of the assets of the others, a disposal of an interest or right in it would not be a disposal of an asset deriving at least 75% of its value from UK land (on the assumption that all of the other companies are related parties of that company on the day of disposal).

For this purpose, disposals are '*linked*' if they are made under the same arrangements by the same person or connected persons and are made to the same person or to persons connected with each other. Additionally, the person making each disposal must be connected with the company in which the right or interest is disposed of. Whether or not two persons are connected is determined for this purpose immediately before the arrangements are entered into. '*Connected persons*' are defined as in **19** CONNECTED PERSONS, except that partners are treated as connected with each other and with each other's spouses, civil partners and relatives in all circumstances.

A person disposing of an asset deriving at least 75% of its value from UK land has a '*substantial indirect interest*' in that land if, at any time in the two years ending with the disposal, it has a '25% investment' in the company. A company's 25% investment is, however, ignored if it is only held for a period or periods forming an insignificant proportion of that part of his period of ownership of the interest or right in the company which is within the two-year period. As a general rule, HMRC consider 'insignificant' to be 10% or less than of the time (HMRC Capital Gains Manual CG73936). See further below for disposals which have an appropriate connection with a collective investment vehicle.

A person (P) has a '25% *investment*' in a company (C) if:

- P possess or is entitled to acquire 25% or more of the voting power in C;
- P would receive 25% or more of the proceeds of a disposal of the whole of the equity in C;
- P would receive 25% or more of the amount distributed if the income in respect of the equity of C were distributed among the equity holders; or
- P would receive 25% or more of the assets available for distribution to the equity holders on a winding-up of C.

The equity in C is made up of shares (including stock and any other members' interests) in C other than restricted preference shares (within *CTA 2010, s 160*), and loans to C other than normal commercial loans. If C does not have share capital, the definitions of 'normal commercial loan' and 'restricted preference share' are modified as necessary. Receiving any proceeds, amounts or assets includes both direct and indirect receipt and the direct or indirect application of the proceeds, amount or assets for a person's benefit (but not so as to give a person a 25% investment in a company due only to the existence of a normal commercial loan). It does not matter whether the receipt or application is at the time of the disposal, distribution etc. or subsequently.

If a person (A) directly receives any proceeds, amount or assets, or any proceeds etc. are directly applied for A's benefit, and another person (B) directly or indirectly owns a percentage of A's equity, B is treated as indirectly receiving that percentage of the proceeds etc. (or that percentage of the proceeds etc. are treated as indirectly applied for B's benefit). The percentage ownership for this purpose is determined by applying *CTA 2010, ss 1155–1157*, modified as necessary.

A person's entitlement to proceeds, amounts or assets includes, for these purposes, his share of the proceeds, amounts or assets of any partnership of which he is a member, determined on a just and reasonable basis. A person is also taken to have all of the rights and interests of any person connected with him (as defined).

For examples demonstrating situations in which a taxpayer has a 25% investment, see HMRC Capital Gains Manual CG73940.

Anti-avoidance

An anti-avoidance rule applies where a person enters into arrangements with a main purpose of obtaining a capital gains tax or corporation tax advantage as a result of any of the above provisions applying or not applying or as a result of 'treaty shopping' (i.e. where double tax arrangements apply despite the above provisions in circumstances where the advantage is contrary to the object and purpose of the double tax arrangements). The rule applies to arrangements entered into on or after 22 November 2017 in a treaty shopping case or to arrangements entered into on or after 6 July 2018 in any other case. Where the rule applies, just and reasonable adjustments are to be made to counteract the advantage, by way of assessment, modification of an assessment, amendment or disallowance of a claim or otherwise. The legislation specifically states that, in a treaty shopping case, the adjustments are to be made regardless of the effect of the double tax arrangements.

[*TCGA 1992, Sch 1A; FA 2019, Sch 1 paras 14, 120*].

Impact of double tax agreements

Where the UK has a double tax agreement with the territory in which the taxpayer is resident, the above provisions apply subject to the terms of that agreement. See **31** DOUBLE TAX RELIEF for agreements generally.

The OECD Model Agreement contains a 'securitised land provision', which gives the source state (the state where the immovable property is situated) the primary right to tax gains on indirect disposals. This is formulated as disposals of shares or similar interests in companies, partnerships and trusts, where more than 50% of the value is derived, directly or indirectly, from immovable property in the source state. Not all UK agreements contain a comparable provision, however, and those that do are frequently on different terms due to changes in the OECD Model and the preferences of both the UK and the treaty partner. See HMRC Capital Gains Manual CG73948.

Units in an authorised contractual scheme

A unit in an authorised contractual scheme which is a co-ownership scheme (a CoACS) and is treated as an asset for chargeable gains purposes (see **46.25** INVESTMENT FUNDS) is treated for the purposes of the above provisions as if it were a share in a company. [*TCGA 1992, Sch 5AAA para 5; FA 2019, Sch 1 para 21*].

Disposals with a connection to a collective investment vehicle

Where a person disposes of an asset deriving at least 75% of its value from UK land and the disposal has an 'appropriate connection' to a 'collective investment vehicle', it is treated as having a substantial indirect interest in the UK land at the time of the disposal, even if not satisfying the 25% investment requirement above.

For this purpose, a 'collective investment vehicle' is defined as at **11.27** below. A disposal has an '*appropriate connection*' to a collective investment vehicle if:

(i) the asset disposed of consists of a right or interest in a collective investment vehicle;
(ii) the asset disposed of consists of a right or interest in a company at least half of whose market value derives from being a direct or indirect participant in one or more collective investment vehicles;
(iii) the vehicle is constituted by two or more persons carrying on a trade or business in partnership and the disposal is made by a person as a participant in the vehicle;
(iv) the vehicle is a company and the disposal is made by it; or
(v) a company (not the vehicle) makes the disposal and the vehicle and one or more other collective investment vehicles that are 'UK property rich' have a 50% investment in the company.

In (v) above, a collective investment vehicle is '*UK property rich*' if, on the assumption that it was a company, a disposal of a right or interest in it would be a disposal of an asset deriving at least 75% of its value from UK land but ignoring, with effect from 10 April 2020, the exceptions for interests in land used for trading purposes and for linked disposals. Whether collective investment vehicles have a 50% investment in a company is determined by treating them as a single person and applying the above 25% investment test by replacing references to 25% with references to 50% (and disregarding the requirement to attribute rights and interests of connected persons).

A disposal does not have an appropriate connection to a collective investment scheme if it would otherwise fall within (i), (ii), (iv) or (v) above and the vehicle or vehicles concerned each meet two conditions.

The first condition (the non-UK real estate condition) is that, at the time of the disposal, by reference to the vehicle's prospectus, no more than 40% of the expected market value of its investments is intended to derive from investments consisting of UK land or rights or interests in UK property rich companies.

The second conditions depends on whether or not the vehicle is a company. If the vehicle is a company, the second condition (the non-close condition) is that the company must not be a close company or must be a close company only because it has a 'qualifying investor' (as defined to include various types of institutional investor) as a direct or indirect participator. If the vehicle is not a company, the second condition (the genuine diversity of ownership condition) is that the vehicle must, broadly, fulfil the genuine diversity of ownership condition applicable to certain offshore funds under *SI 2009 No 3001, Reg 75* (as modified; see **55.4** OFFSHORE FUNDS). Where (v) above would otherwise apply, and the vehicle in question is constituted by two or more persons carrying on a trade or business in partnership, the second condition is taken to be met if the company in (v) above meets the non-close condition.

[*TCGA 1992, Sch 5AAA paras 3, 6, 7; FA 2019, Sch 1 para 21; SI 2020 No 315, Regs 4–6*].

Disposals of interests in UK land — collective investment vehicles

[11.27] The provisions at **11.25** and **11.26** above are subject to the following special rules relating to collective investment vehicles.

For HMRC guidance see HMRC Capital Gains Manual APP15 and APP 16.

Offshore collective investment vehicles treated as companies

An 'offshore collective investment vehicle' which is neither a company nor a partnership is treated for the purposes of the provisions at **11.25** and **11.26** above as if it were a company, and the rights of its 'participants' as if they were shares in that company. Accordingly, such vehicles are chargeable to corporation tax on direct and indirect disposals of UK land and non-resident participants may be subject to the charge in **11.26** above. This rule applies to authorised contractual schemes but does not displace the calculation rules on a disposal of units at **46.25** INVESTMENT FUNDS. For a unit trust scheme, however, the rule applies instead of *TCGA 1992, s 99* (see **46.5**). This rule does not apply where an election for transparency has effect (see **11.28** below).

[*TCGA 1992, s 103DB, Sch 5AAA para 4; FA 2019, Sch 1 paras 8, 21*].

Meaning of offshore collective investment vehicle

An '*offshore collective investment vehicle*' is a 'collective investment vehicle':

- constituted as a body corporate (other than a limited liability partnership) resident outside the UK;
- under which property is held on trust for the participants where the trustees are not UK-resident; or
- constituted by other arrangements that create rights in the nature of 'co-ownership' (defined so as not to be restricted to its meaning under UK law) which take effect as a result of the law of a territory outside the UK.

A '*collective investment vehicle*' is:

(i) a collective investment scheme (see **46.2** INVESTMENT FUNDS);
(ii) an alternative investment fund (within the *Alternative Investment Fund Managers Regulations 2013, Reg 3*);
(iii) a company which is a UK real estate investment trust (see **47.11** INVESTMENT TRUSTS) or, for disposals on or after 10 April 2020, the principal company of a group UK real estate investment trust;
(iv) a company resident outside the UK which is not a member of a group and meets the property income conditions below;
(v) a company resident outside the UK which is the principal company of a group, which is not a 'close company' only because it has a 'qualifying investor' (as defined to include various types of institutional investor) as a direct or indirect participator, and meets the property income conditions below; or
(vi) a company resident outside the UK which is a member of a group but not the principal company, which is not a close company only because it has a qualifying investor or a company wholly (or almost wholly) owned by qualifying investors as a direct or indirect participator, and meets the property income conditions below.

Before 10 April 2020, (iv)–(vi) above did not apply, but a company resident outside the UK which met the property income conditions was a collective investment vehicle.

For a company within (iv) above, the property income conditions are that:

- the company is not a close company (or is only a close company because it has a qualifying investor as a direct or indirect participator);
- at least half of its income derives directly or indirectly from long-term property investments (i.e. direct or indirect investments in land or estates, interests or rights in or over land which are made on a long-term basis);
- it distributes all (or substantially all) of its 'profits' (excluding capital profits) from long-term property investments on an annual basis; and
- it is not liable to tax on its profits in any territory in which it is resident so far as the profits derive directly or indirectly from long-term property investments.

For a company within (v) or (vi) above, the property income conditions are that:

- at least half of the group's income derives directly or indirectly from long-term property investments;
- the group distributes all (or substantially all) of its profits from long-term property investments on an annual basis; and
- the company is not liable to tax on its profits in any territory in which it is resident so far as the profits derive directly or indirectly from long-term property investments.

Before 10 April 2020, the property income conditions were that:

- the company is not a close company (or is only a close company because it has a qualifying investor as a direct or indirect participator);
- at least half of its income is property income from long-term investments (i.e. income from direct or indirect investments in land or estates, interests or rights in or over land which are made on a long-term basis);
- it distributes all (or substantially all) of such property income on an annual basis; and
- it is not liable to tax on that income in any territory in which it is resident.

For this purpose, '*close company*' is defined, with certain modifications, in accordance with *CTA 2010, Pt 10 Ch 2* (see **16.2** CLOSE COMPANIES), but includes non-UK resident companies.

A '*participant*' in a collective investment vehicle is, in the case of a company, a shareholder in the company, or in other cases, a person who takes part in the arrangements or undertaking, whether by becoming the owner of any part of the property that is the subject of or held by the arrangements or undertaking or otherwise. A '*unit*' of a collective investment vehicle is either a share in the company or the rights or interests (however described) of the participant.

[*TCGA 1992, Sch 5AAA paras 1, 2, 46; FA 2019, Sch 1 para 21; SI 2020 No 315, Regs 1–3, 15*].

Election for transparency

[11.28] The manager of an offshore collective investment vehicle (see **11.27** above) which is UK property rich and is transparent for income tax purposes (otherwise than as a result of being constituted by two or more persons carrying on a trade or business in partnership) may make an election to be treated for all purposes relating to chargeable gains as a partnership. Partnership treatment will then apply to all times on and after the vehicle's constitution (but not for disposals before 6 April 2019).

For this purpose, a vehicle is '*UK property rich*' if, on the assumption that it was a company, a disposal of a right or interest in it would be a disposal of an asset deriving at least 75% of its value from UK land as in **11.26** above but ignoring, with effect from 10 April 2020, the exceptions for interests in land used for trading purposes and for linked disposals. A vehicle is transparent for income tax purposes if UK-resident individual participants in it would be chargeable to income tax on part of the income of the vehicle under any of the provisions listed in *ITTOIA 2005, s 830(2)* (foreign income) or would have been so chargeable if the assets from which the income is derived were outside the UK.

An election can apply whether or not the vehicle would otherwise be chargeable to UK tax on chargeable gains. Where an election has effect, neither *TCGA 1992, s 103D* (tax transparent funds — see **46.25** INVESTMENT FUNDS) nor *TCGA 1992, s 99* (unit trust schemes — see **46.5**) apply to the vehicle. Neither do the provisions at **11.27** above. An election has no effect in relation to any units held by an insurance company for the purposes of its long-term business.

Where an election has effect and either the second or third sets of rebasing rules at **11.31** below would otherwise apply on a disposal, the first rebasing rule (for indirect disposals and direct disposals not chargeable before 6 April 2019) applies instead.

A notice requiring a partnership return may be given to the manager of the vehicle. Such a notice does not oblige the reporting of information other than to determine the capital gains liability of each partner, but a notice may require a return to be submitted whether or not any partnership property has been disposed of in the year in question.

An election requires the consent of the participants in the vehicle and must be made by notice to HMRC within the twelve months beginning with the earliest date on which an interest in UK land (defined as at **11.25** above) or a right or interest in a UK property rich company becomes part of the vehicle's property or, if later, before 1 October 2020. An election made on or after 10 April 2020 must include each participants' name, unique taxpayer reference, place of residence or business and, where relevant, date of birth. The election is irrevocable. If the vehicle was constituted before 6 April 2019, the election applies to disposals on or after 6 April 2019 and can be made at any time before 1 October 2020. For participants on 6 April 2019, the making of the election is not treated as a disposal of their units, and when any units are subsequently disposed of, any gains or losses of the participant are determined as if the election had applied throughout the vehicle's existence.

[*TCGA 1992, Sch 5AAA paras 3, 8–11, 49, 49A; FA 2019, Sch 1 para 21; SI 2020 No 315, Regs 1, 4, 8, 18, 19*].

Election for exemption from charge on interests in UK land

[11.29] An offshore collective investment vehicle (see **11.27** above) can make an election to be exempt from corporation tax on chargeable gains under the provisions at **11.25** and **11.26** above if:

- it is a company or is treated as a company under **11.27** above;
- it is 'UK property rich';
- in the case of an alternative investment fund (within the *Alternative Investment Fund Managers Regulations 2013, Reg 3*), it would also meet the definition of a collective investment vehicle for another reason; and
- either:
  - — it is a collective investment scheme and meets the 'genuine diversity of ownership condition';
  - — it is a collective investment scheme, it meets the 'UK tax condition' and is wholly, or almost wholly, owned by one or more other collective investment schemes each of which meets the genuine diversity of ownership condition;

- — it is a company (but not a vehicle treated as a company under **11.27** above) and it meets the 'recognised stock exchange condition' and the 'non-close condition'; or
- — it is a collective investment vehicle of any kind and meets both the 'UK tax condition' and the 'non-close condition'.

A company (wherever resident) which is not a collective investment vehicle can make an election with similar effect if:

- it is wholly (or almost wholly) and, for elections made on or after 10 April 2020, directly owned by a collective investment scheme which is either constituted by two or more persons carrying on a trade or business in partnership or is constituted by an authorised contractual scheme which is a co-ownership scheme (a 'CoACS' — see **46.25** INVESTMENT FUNDS);
- the company or, where the collective investment scheme is a CoACS, the CoACS is UK property rich; and
- either:
  - — the company meets both the 'UK tax condition' and the 'non-close condition'; or
  - — the collective investment scheme directly owning the company meets the 'genuine diversity of ownership condition' or is wholly (or almost wholly) and directly owned by one or more 'qualifying partnerships', each of which meets the genuine diversity of ownership condition.

A vehicle or company in respect of which an election has been made is referred to as a '*qualifying fund*' or a '*qualifying company*'.

A company or a collective investment vehicle is '*UK property rich*' if (on the assumption, in the latter case, that the vehicle was a company) a disposal of a right or interest in it would be a disposal of an asset deriving at least 75% of its value from UK land as in **11.26** above but ignoring, with effect from 10 April 2020, the exceptions for interests in land used for trading purposes and for linked disposals.

The '*genuine diversity of ownership condition*' is, broadly, that the scheme must fulfil the genuine diversity of ownership condition applicable to certain offshore funds under *SI 2009 No 3001, Reg 75* (as modified). The '*recognised stock exchange condition*' is that the company must have ordinary share capital which is regularly traded on a recognised stock exchange. The '*non-close condition*' is that the company must not be a close company (defined as at **11.27** above) or must be a close company only because it has a 'qualifying investor' (as defined to include various types of institutional investor) as a direct or indirect participator. The '*UK tax condition*' is that the person making the election must reasonably consider that, if all of the company's shares were disposed of at market value, no more than 25% of the total proceeds would be left out of account for chargeable gains purposes as a result solely of double tax arrangements. If any of the proceeds would arise to a company wholly, or almost wholly, owned by investors within **11.30**(a)–(c) below, that company is treated for this purpose as if it were exempt from corporation tax on chargeable gains otherwise than as a result of double tax arrangements.

A company is wholly, or almost wholly, owned by a person if it is wholly owned by that person or if that person has a 99% investment in it. A company is wholly owned by a person if that person has a 100% investment in it. Whether a person has a 100% or 99% investment in a company is determined by applying the 25% investment test at **11.26** above by replacing references to 25% with references to 100% or 99% and making certain additional modifications (see *TCGA 1992, Sch 5AAA paras 40(3), 41(3)*).

A company is directly owned by a collective investment scheme or partnership if it is owned by the scheme or partnership otherwise than through a company, partnership, trust or other entity or arrangements. A '*qualifying partnership*' is a collective investment scheme constituted by two or more persons carrying on a trade or business in partnership.

[*TCGA 1992, Sch 5AAA paras 3, 12, 13, 40, 41, 46; FA 2019, Sch 1 para 21; SI 2020 No 315, Regs 1, 4, 9, 10*].

Effects of election

In addition to the exemptions noted above, the following rules apply where a qualifying fund or company has made an election under the above provisions.

If a person in which the qualifying fund or company has a 40% investment makes a direct disposal of any interests in UK land by reference to which the fund or company is UK property rich, a proportion of that person's gain is not a chargeable gain (and a proportion of a loss is not an allowable loss). This applies also where the person makes an indirect disposal within **11.26** above and the fund or company has a 40% investment in the company rights or an interest in which are disposed of. The proportion is that which so much of the consideration for the disposal as forms part (directly or indirectly) of the assets of the qualifying fund or company bears to the total consideration. Whether a qualifying fund or company has a 40% investment in a person is determined by applying the 25% investment test at **11.26** above by replacing references to 25% with references to 40% (and disregarding the requirement to attribute rights and interests of connected persons). If HMRC consider that the proportion of the gain which would otherwise be exempt would exceed the total gain, they may make just and reasonable adjustments to the exempt proportion to prevent that result. [*TCGA 1992, Sch 5AAA para 16; FA 2019, Sch 1 para 21*].

The exceptions for interests in land used for trading purposes and for linked disposals at **11.26** above do not apply to a disposal on or after 10 April 2020 of units in a vehicle in respect of which an election has been made. Likewise, in the case of an election by a qualifying company, those exemptions do not apply on a disposal of units in the relevant fund to the extent that the disposal constitutes the disposal of a right or interest in the company. [*TCGA 1992, Sch 5AAA para 33A, SI 2020 No315, Reg 14*].

If a company (the 'investing company') which has ordinary share capital owned by one or more qualifying institutional investors within *TCGA 1992, Sch 7AC* (see **13.7** CAPITAL GAINS — SUBSTANTIAL SHAREHOLDINGS) makes a gain or loss part of which is not chargeable or allowable under these provisions and some or all of the ownership (determined as at **66.5**) of those investors in the investing company is through the qualifying company, that ownership is ignored for the purposes of the exemption at **13.7**.

The following provisions apply where a participant (see **11.27** above) in the 'relevant fund' becomes entitled to receive an amount representing, in substance, value derived directly or indirectly from a disposal of UK land within **11.25** or **11.26** above if the amount is revenue in nature and is not subject to income tax or corporation tax on income(on the participant or anyone else). In the case of a qualifying fund, the participant is deemed for chargeable gains purposes to have sold all its units in the relevant fund at market value immediately before the time it became entitled to the amount, and to have reacquired the units at their market value immediately after that time. Likewise, in the case of a qualifying company, the participant is deemed to have sold, and immediately reacquired its rights and interests in the company or, where the relevant fund is a CoACS and the disposal is on or after 10 April 2020, the CoACS. For the calculation and treatment of gains arising from the deemed disposal see further below. This provision cannot result in a deemed gain arising to an investor within **11.30**(a)–(c) below other than an insurance company or to a company which is wholly (or almost wholly) owned by one or more such investors (none of which is an insurance company).

The '*relevant fund*' is the qualifying fund or, in the case of a qualifying company, the collective investment scheme which owns the company.

[*TCGA 1992, Sch 5AAA paras 21, 33(3), 34, 39; FA 2019, Sch 1 para 21; SI 2020 No 315, Regs 1, 11, 13*].

Disposal of company covered by election

Where a qualifying fund or company which has made an election, or a company covered by the election, disposes of all of its rights and interests in another company (company C) which is UK property rich and also covered by the election, company C is treated for chargeable gains purposes as selling and immediately reacquiring, at that time, the 'appropriate proportion' of every 'qualifying asset' the actual disposal of which would be a disposal of UK land within **11.25** or **11.26** above, at market value.

For this purpose, a company is covered by an election in respect of a disposal if the disposal would be wholly or partly exempt under *TCGA 1992, Sch 5AAA para 16* (see above). A '*qualifying asset*' is an asset held by company C, any other company covered by the election or by the qualifying fund or company throughout the period of one year ending on the day of the disposal. The '*appropriate proportion*' of a qualifying asset is equal to the proportion that would not be a chargeable gain under *para 16* on a sale of the asset for total consideration resulting in a gain of £100 immediately before the actual disposal of the rights and interests in company C.

[*TCGA 1992, Sch 5AAA para 31; FA 2019, Sch 1 para 21*].

Making an election

An election must be made by the manager of the relevant fund. It must be made by notice to HMRC and must specify the date from which it is to take effect. That date can be before the date the election is made, but can only be a date more than twelve months earlier with HMRC consent (whether general or particular).

An election must be accompanied by such information as may be specified by HMRC about disposals made by participants in the relevant fund in the two years ending the day before the election is made (or, if shorter, the period beginning with the constitution of the fund). If information has already been provided to HMRC it is sufficient for the election to set out when it was provided. Information about disposals before 6 April 2019 is not required.

[*TCGA 1992, Sch 5AAA paras 14, 17, 39, 50; FA 2019, Sch 1 para 21*].

Information requirements following the making of an election

The qualifying fund or company must provide HMRC with information and documents in accordance with conditions specified by HMRC for each period of account ending at a time when the election is in force. Such information or documents must be provided within twelve months from the end of the period. For this purpose, a period of account is any period for which accounts of the relevant fund are drawn up, but a period of account cannot exceed twelve months (so that where accounts are drawn up for a longer period, the period is divided into two periods of account, the first of which is twelve months long (and so on)). [*TCGA 1992, Sch 5AAA para 15(1)–(3)(7)(8); FA 2019, Sch 1 para 21*].

Election ceasing to have effect

An HMRC officer designated by the Commissioners for HMRC for the purpose may revoke an election if, in his opinion, there has been a breach of the above information requirements without reasonable excuse, HMRC can, however, waive a breach which is insignificant, having regard to the number and seriousness of any previous breaches.

A designated HMRC officer may also revoke an election if he considers it appropriate to do so in order to safeguard the public revenue.

Revocation of an election by HMRC must be made by notice by the designated officer to the manager of the relevant fund.

The manager of the relevant fund may also revoke an election by notice to HMRC.

A revocation notice must specify the date on which the election will cease to have effect; the election then no longer applies to disposals made on or after that day. Where the revocation is by the fund manager, the date specified may be before the date the notice is given if HMRC consent (whether by way of a general consent or consent in the particular case).

If HMRC revoke an election they must specify the grounds, and the manager of the relevant fund may appeal against the decision. An appeal must be made by notice to the designated HMRC officer within 30 days of the notice. The Tribunal cannot allow an appeal unless it considers that a designated HMRC officer could not reasonably have been satisfied that there were grounds for revocation.

If a qualifying fund or company ceases to meet the applicable exemption conditions, the election ceases to have effect automatically for disposals on or after the time at which the conditions cease to be met. This rule is subject to the following exceptions.

(i) If the fund or company ceases to meet the conditions otherwise than as a result of ceasing to be UK property rich and the manager of the relevant fund expects that all of the conditions will be met within 30 days of the failure, then if the conditions are in fact met within those 30 days, the failure is ignored. This exception can apply no more than four times in any twelve-month period.

(ii) If the fund or company ceases to meet the conditions for any reason and the manager expects the failure to last for a temporary period of no more than nine months, then the conditions are treated as continuing to be met during that period, provided that they are in fact met within the nine-month period. This exception does not, however, disapply the provisions below for a deemed disposal to arise when an election ceases to have effect (so that a deemed disposal will arise at the beginning of the temporary period).

(iii) If the fund or company ceases to meet the conditions for any reason at a time when the manager is taking steps to dispose of all of the relevant fund's assets so that it can be wound up, then the conditions are treated as continuing to be met until the relevant fund is wound up. This exception does not, however, disapply the provisions below for a deemed disposal to arise when an election ceases to have effect (so that a deemed disposal will arise at the time the qualifying fund or company actually ceases to meet the conditions).

Where an election ceases to have effect (or where (ii) or (iii) above apply) in the case of a qualifying fund, each participant in the relevant fund is deemed for chargeable gains purposes to have sold its units in the relevant fund immediately before that time, and to have immediately reacquired them, at market value. Likewise, in the case of a qualifying company, each participant in the relevant fund is deemed to have sold its rights and interests in the company or, where the relevant fund is a CoACS and the disposal is on or after 10 April 2020, the CoACS, immediately before the election ceased to have effect, and to have immediately reacquired them, at market value. For the calculation and treatment of gains arising from the deemed disposals see further below.

[*TCGA 1992, Sch 5AAA paras 15(5)(6), 18–20, 22, 27, 28, 30, 38, 42; FA 2019, Sch 1 para 21; SI 2020 No 315, Regs 1, 12*].

Deemed disposals of UK land by company or fund

If an election which has been in effect continuously for at least five years ceases to have effect (otherwise than in 'disqualifying circumstances') or the manager of the relevant fund starts taking steps to dispose of all of the assets of the relevant fund so it can be wound up, the qualifying fund or company is treated for chargeable gains purposes as selling and immediately reacquiring, at that time, every asset the actual disposal of which would be a disposal of UK land within **11.25** or **11.26** above, at market value. In the case of any asset covered by the election for twelve months and held by a company at the time the election ceases to have effect or the steps are first taken, the company is deemed to have sold at that time, and immediately reacquired, the 'appropriate proportion' of the asset at its market value.

For this purpose, an election ceases to have effect in 'disqualifying circumstances' if it is revoked by a designated HMRC officer either because in his opinion there has been at least three serious breaches of the information requirements above or to safeguard the public revenue. An asset is covered by an election for twelve months if a disposal of it would be wholly or partly exempt under *TCGA 1992, Sch 5AAA para 16* (see above under 'Effect of election'). The '*appropriate proportion*' of an asset is equal to the proportion that would not be a chargeable gain under *para 16* on a sale of the asset for total consideration resulting in a gain of £100.

An election made by a fund or company is taken, for this purpose, to be the same election as a subsequent election made by another fund or company which owns the first fund or company.

[*TCGA 1992, Sch 5AAA para 32; FA 2019, Sch 1 para 21*].

Calculation and treatment of gains of participants on deemed disposals

The following provisions apply where a person is deemed to make a disposal of units in a qualifying fund or of rights or interests in a qualifying company either on becoming entitled to receive an amount not otherwise taxable where the value derives from a disposal of UK land or when an election ceases to have effect.

In calculating the deemed gain, a deduction is allowed for any allowable incidental costs which the person would reasonably have been expected to have incurred if the deemed sale had been an actual sale. [*TCGA 1992, Sch 5AAA para 24; FA 2019, Sch 1 para 21*].

A proportion of any deemed gain is deemed to arise only when, at the time of the deemed disposal or subsequently, the person actually disposes of a unit in the relevant fund or actually receives any part of the otherwise non-taxable amount. The proportion charged is equal to the consideration for the actual disposal or the amount of the receipt but not so as to exceed the amount of the deemed gain. Where part of a deemed gain becomes chargeable on more than one occasion, the total proportions brought into charge cannot be more than the total deemed gain. In the case of a deemed gain arising because of entitlement to an otherwise non-taxable amount, if not all of the gain has been charged when the relevant fund is wound up, the remaining part is treated as arising at that time. In the case of an election ceasing to have effect (but not where (ii) above applies), any part of the deemed gain not already charged is treated as arising three years after the deemed disposal or, if earlier, when the relevant fund is wound up. If the deemed gain arises as a result of (ii) above, any part of the gain not already charged is treated as arising when the relevant fund is wound up. If the deemed disposal arises because the election has ceased to have effect, these provisions apply only if the election ceased to have effect because the exemption conditions have ceased to be met. A deemed gain arising when an election is revoked is chargeable immediately. [*TCGA 1992, Sch 5AAA paras 23, 29; FA 2019, Sch 1 para 21*].

The manager of a relevant fund must notify any person in writing where:

- that person is deemed to have made a disposal on becoming entitled to an otherwise non-taxable amount;

- that person is deemed to have made a disposal as a result of the revocation of an election; or
- the remaining part of a deemed gain becomes chargeable as a result of the relevant fund being wound up or at the end of the three-year period after a deemed disposal.

Notice must be given within 30 days beginning with the event in question. If a manager fails to give notice he is liable to a penalty of up to £3,000. If the duty to notify applies to two or more managers, the total penalties cannot be more than £3,000. HMRC must assess a penalty under these provisions and notify the manager within twelve months of first becoming aware of the failure. An appeal can be made to HMRC against a decision to impose a penalty within 30 days after the penalty was notified. The appeal must be in writing and must specify the grounds of appeal.

The penalty must be paid within thirty days of the day on which the manager was notified of the penalty or, if an appeal is made, within 30 days of the day on which the appeal is finally determined or withdrawn.

[*TCGA 1992, Sch 5AAA paras 25, 26; FA 2019, Sch 1 para 21*].

UK real estate investment trusts

None of the above exemptions apply to gains made by a company which is, or is a member of, a UK real estate investment trust so far as the gain is exempt under *CTA 2010, s 535* or *s 535A* (see **47.29** INVESTMENT TRUSTS) otherwise than as a result of a notice under *CTA 2010, s 586(1)* or *s 587(1)* (joint venture elections).

Where a gain is made by a company which is a member of a UK group real estate investment trust and the gain is exempt under *CTA 2010, s 535* or *s 535A* as a result of a notice under *CTA 2010, s 586(1)* or *s 587(1)* and both the company and the principal company of the group are covered by an election in respect of a qualifying fund, the exemption provided under the above provisions is reduced by the exemption under the real estate investment trust rules. For this purpose, a company is covered by an election in respect of a disposal if the disposal would be wholly or partly exempt under *TCGA 1992, Sch 5AAA para 16* (see above under 'Effects of election').

[*TCGA 1992, Sch 5AAA paras 35, 36; FA 2019, Sch 1 para 21*].

General

Where a person disposes of a right or interest in a company and parts of the gain or loss are not chargeable as a result of the operation of more than one exemption provision, then subject to any rules above which provide for a different basis, each exemption must be applied separately, without regard to the others, to the whole of the gain or loss. The total proportion which is exempt is then the total of the exempt proportions separately found (but not so as to exceed the total gain or loss). The exemption provisions to which this rule applies are any of the above exemptions, *TCGA 1992, Sch 7AC para 3* (see **66.5** SUBSTANTIAL SHAREHOLDINGS OF COMPANIES) and any provision of *CTA 2010, Pt 12* (real estate investment trusts). [*TCGA 1992, Sch 5AAA para 37; FA 2019, Sch 1 para 21*].

The Treasury has power to make regulations to amend the above provisions and to allow managers of collective investment vehicles to report information and make payments of tax on behalf of participants. [*TCGA 1992, Sch 5AAA paras 43–45, 48; FA 2019, Sch 1 para 21*].

Exemption for disposals of interests in companies owned by certain investors

[11.30] A gain arising to a company which is wholly (or almost wholly) owned by one or more investors within (a)–(c) below) is not a chargeable gain if it arises on the disposal of a right or interest in a company whose assets consist wholly of units in:

(i) a collective investment vehicle in respect of which an election for transparency has been made (see **11.28** above);

(ii) a qualifying fund or company in respect of which an election for exemption has been made (see **11.29** above);

(iii) a company which is a UK real estate investment trust or the principal company of a group UK real estate investment trust; or

(iv) a property authorised investment fund which is 'UK property rich' (as defined at **11.29** above).

The investors in question are:

(a) a qualifying institutional investor within TCGA 1992 Sch 7AC (substantial shareholdings exemption — see **13.7** CAPITAL GAINS — SUBSTANTIAL SHAREHOLDINGS);

(b) certain companies carrying on life assurance business or long-term business;

(c) a qualifying fund or company in respect of which an election under the provisions at **11.29** above is in force.

[*TCGA 1992, Sch 5AAA para 33; SI 2020 No 315, Reg 13*].

Rebasing for non-residents of interests in UK land held on 5 April 2019

[11.31] Subject to the following provisions, the normal corporation tax rules apply in calculating gains and losses charged under the provisions at **11.25** and **11.26** above. Broadly, only the part of the gain arising after 5 April 2019 is chargeable, unless the provisions at **11.24** above (non-resident CGT disposals of UK residential property) would have applied to a disposal of the asset on or before that date, in which case the part of the gain arising after 5 April 2015 is chargeable. Special rules are therefore needed to calculate the chargeable amount where the asset was held before 6 April 2019. The legislation divides assets into one of three separate categories, and for each category, provides a default method of calculation, rebasing the cost of the asset to its value at 5 April 2019 and/or 5 April 2015, and allowing elections to be made for an alternative method or methods of calculation.

Where the interest disposed of results from interests which have been acquired at different times, the date of acquisition of the first interest is taken, for these purposes, as the date on which all the interests were acquired. [*TCGA 1992, s 36A, Sch 4AA para 22(2); FA 2019, Sch 1 paras 4, 17*].

The application of any of the rebasing rules which treat an asset as acquired on a different date to the date of its actual acquisition is ignored in determining whether or not the asset is a wasting asset. In calculating a gain or loss on a disposal where a rebasing rule has applied, *TCGA 1992, s 41* (restriction of losses by reference to capital allowances) and *TCGA 1992, s 47* (wasting assets qualifying for capital allowances) apply in relation to any capital or renewals allowance made in respect of the expenditure actually incurred in acquiring or providing the asset as if that allowance were made in respect of the expenditure treated as incurred on the deemed acquisition date. [*TCGA 1992, Sch 4AA paras 19, 20; FA 2019, Sch 1 para 17*].

Indirect disposals and direct disposals not chargeable before 6 April 2019

The following rules apply to:

(i) all indirect disposals of UK land (i.e. disposals of assets within **11.26** above);
(ii) direct disposals of UK land (i.e. disposals of interests in UK land within **11.25** above) that were not fully residential before 6 April 2019; and
(iii) direct disposals of UK land by persons who were not chargeable before 6 April 2019.

In (ii) above, a disposal is not fully residential if there was no time in the period from date of acquisition (or 6 April 2015 if later) to 5 April 2019 inclusive at which the land in question consisted of, or included, a dwelling. An interest in UK land which subsists at any time before 6 April 2019 under a contract for an off-plan purchase of a dwelling (i.e. a contract for acquisition of land consisting of, or including, a building or part of a building that is to be constructed or adapted as a dwelling) is treated as fully residential before that date.

In (iii) above, a disposal is made by a person who was not chargeable before 6 April 2019 if, immediately before that date, the person was:

- a company other than a 'closely-held company' (for this purpose a divided company is treated as a closely-held company if the gain or loss is primarily or wholly attributable to a particular division of the company and, if that division were a separate company, it would be closely-held);
- a unit trust scheme, or open-ended investment company (or non-UK equivalent), which is 'widely-marketed' (as defined) throughout the period from the date the scheme acquired the interest in land which is the subject of the disposal to the date of disposal, or if shorter, throughout the period of five years ending on the date of disposal;
- a unit trust scheme, or open-ended investment company (or non-UK equivalent), which has as an investor an offshore fund, open-ended investment company or authorised unit trust (the '*feeder fund*'), where the scheme and the feeder fund have the same manager, and the scheme is widely-marketed, after taking account of scheme documents for the

feeder fund and the intended investors of the feeder fund, throughout the shortest of: the period from the date the scheme acquired the interest in land which is the subject of the disposal to the date of disposal; the period of five years ending on the date of disposal; and the period from the date the feeder fund first became an investor to the date of disposal; or

- a company carrying on life assurance business if immediately before 6 April 2019 the interest in land which is the subject of the disposal is held to provide benefits to policyholders in the course of that business.

Arrangements (as defined) with a main purpose of obtaining a tax advantage as a result of a person not being a closely-held company or being a widely-marketed scheme are ignored for these purposes.

Default rule — rebasing

In calculating the gain or loss on the disposal, the asset is treated as having been acquired at its market value on 5 April 2019.

Election for retrospective computation

Where the company so elects, rebasing does not apply and the gains or losses are computed (as for CGT or corporation tax) on the basis of the position over the whole period of ownership. Such an election may be beneficial where a loss arises, but in the case of an indirect disposal of UK land, such a loss is not an allowable loss.

[*TCGA 1992, Sch 4AA paras 1(3), 2–5; FA 2019, Sch 1 para 17*].

Direct disposals of pre-April 2015 assets fully chargeable before 6 April 2019

The following rules apply to any direct disposal of UK land if the company held the interest in the land in question throughout the period from 6 April 2015 to the date of disposal and the land consisted of a dwelling on every day in the period from 6 April 2015 to 5 April 2019 inclusive. The rules do not apply if the disposal is of an interest subsisting under a contract for the acquisition of land that, at any time in that period, did not consist of a building to be constructed or adapted for use as a dwelling if the company was not chargeable before 6 April 2019 (see above).

Default rule — rebasing

In calculating the gain or loss on the disposal, the asset is treated as having been acquired at its market value on 5 April 2015.

Election for retrospective computation

Where the taxpayer so elects, rebasing does not apply and the gains or losses are computed (as for CGT or corporation tax) on the basis of the position over the whole period of ownership. Such an election may be beneficial where a loss arises.

Election for straight-line time apportionment

Where the taxpayer so elects, rebasing does not apply and the gains or losses are computed (as for CGT or corporation tax) on the basis of the position over the whole period of ownership and then apportioned so that only the post-5 April 2015 part of it is treated as arising on the disposal. That part is found by multiplying the gain or loss by the number of days in the period beginning on 6 April 2015 and ending on the day of disposal, and dividing the result by the number of days in the period beginning on the day the taxpayer acquired the interest disposed of (or 31 March 1982 if later) and ending on the day of disposal.

[*TCGA 1992, Sch 4AA paras 6–11; FA 2019, Sch 1 para 17*].

Direct disposals of pre-April 2015 assets partly chargeable before 6 April 2019

The following rules apply to any direct disposal of UK land if none of the above provisions apply and the interest being disposed of was not a post-April 2015 asset (i.e. one acquired after 5 April 2015) which was 'fully residential before 6 April 2019'. For this purpose, an interest subsisting under a contract for the acquisition of land that, at any time in that period, did not consist of a building to be constructed or adapted for use as a dwelling is treated as not fully residential before 6 April 2019. An asset was *'fully residential before 6 April 2019'* if the land in question consisted of a dwelling throughout the period from acquisition to 5 April 2019.

Default rule — rebasing

In calculating the gain or loss on the disposal, the asset is treated as having been acquired at its market value on 5 April 2015 and then sold and immediately reacquired at its market value on 5 April 2019. The gain or loss arising on the deemed disposal on 5 April 2019 (under the non-resident disposal rules at **42.28** onwards below) is treated as a gain or loss arising on the actual disposal (in addition to the actual gain or loss). If the asset was in fact acquired after 5 April 2015, the assumption that it was acquired on that day does not apply.

Election for retrospective computation

Where the taxpayer so elects, rebasing does not apply and the gains or losses are computed (as for CGT or corporation tax) on the basis of the position over the whole period of ownership. Such an election may be beneficial where a loss arises.

[*TCGA 1992, Sch 4AA paras 12–15; FA 2019, Sch 1 para 17*].

Making an election

An election for the retrospective or time-apportionment basis of computation can only be made in a self-assessment tax return for the accounting period in which the disposal is made or in the UK land disposal return for the disposal (or in an amendment to either type of return). An election made in a UK land disposal return can be revoked in the self-assessment return (or amendment), provided that the latter return is delivered by the filing date. Otherwise, an election is irrevocable. Note that UK land disposal returns have not yet been introduced for companies. [*TCGA 1992, Sch 4AA para 21; FA 2019, Sch 1 para 17*].

Companies becoming, or ceasing to be, UK resident on or after 6 April 2019

If a company becomes UK-resident on or after 6 April 2019 and subsequently makes a direct or indirect disposal of UK land, the above provisions apply if they would otherwise have applied but for the fact that the disposal is made when the company is UK-resident. [*TCGA 1992, Sch 4AA para 16; FA 2019, Sch 1 para 17*].

The above provisions do not apply where a company ceases to be resident in the UK after 5 April 2019 and disposes of an asset held on that date which is a direct or indirect disposal of UK land (instead the gain or loss is chargeable or allowable in full). The asset disposed of is, however, excepted from the application of *TCGA 1992, s 185(2)(3)* (deemed disposal on company ceasing to be UK-resident). [*TCGA 1992, Sch 4AA para 18; FA 2019, Sch 1 para 17*].

Registration and payment of tax by non-resident companies on disposals of interests in UK land

[11.32] A non-resident company or offshore collective investment vehicle which is not otherwise within the charge to UK corporation tax becomes chargeable when it makes a direct or indirect disposal of UK land on or after 6 April 2019. Accordingly, HMRC consider that the company or vehicle must register with HMRC within three months of the date of the disposal (see **65.2** RETURNS). This does not apply if the company is registered with Companies House or, in the case of a collective investment vehicle, if it has made an election for transparent or exempt treatment (see **11.29** above). Dormant companies which have previously been registered with HMRC will need to register again.

HMRC consider that, where a company holds no other interests in UK land after the disposal, it will stop being chargeable to corporation tax. The company will therefore have a one-day accounting period. See **58.3** PAYMENT OF TAX for the application of the instalment payment rules for large companies to such accounting periods. See also **11.4** above for the treatment of losses where a company has two or more accounting periods falling wholly within the same financial year and is chargeable to corporation tax for each period only because of a chargeable gain (or allowable loss).

See www.gov.uk/guidance/register-a-non-resident-company-for-corporation-tax.

Key points on capital gains

[11.33] Points to consider are as follows.

- Where it is intended that a capital loss will be used, ensure that the claim to use the loss is submitted on time.
- There are a number of restrictions on the use of capital losses. Where a company is to rely upon the use of losses, ensure that the losses have been identified and their availability for use analysed before they are needed.
- When analysing the likely availability of capital losses, consider carefully the targeted anti-avoidance rules. The broad meaning of the term 'arrangements' and the purpose test are designed to give these provisions a relatively low threshold for application.
- Where anti-avoidance provisions are potentially in point (whether in relation to capital losses, value shifting or otherwise), the taxpayer should consider taking advice to limit potential penalties.
- Make use of the clearance regime for reorganisations and reconstructions, but remember that the statutory regime is only concerned with the question of whether the transactions involved are being carried out for bona fide commercial reasons. Where there is doubt as to a technical issue, the HMRC non-statutory business clearance service may be used. In each case, submit the clearance application as soon as possible once the likely structure is settled, to allow time to deal with any questions HMRC raises.
- Bear in mind the potential for secondary chargeable gains liabilities. It may be prudent to consider the need for indemnities if external investors are involved or all or part of a business is to be sold.
- If assets are to be transferred to a non-resident company under *TCGA 1992, s 140* or *s 140A et seq*, ensure that the relevant claim is made on time. Remember also that a claim made under one such provision may preclude a claim being made under a similar provision (as is the case with, for example, *ss 140* and *140C*).
- If a transaction within *TCGA 1992, s 140* is in contemplation, consider carefully the events that could bring the deferred gain into charge. In particular, while there is a six-year period during which the disposal of the relevant assets can crystallise the gain (with exceptions for certain intra-group disposals), the disposal of the shares issued in consideration for the transfer of the business will bring the gain into charge at any time in the future. Therefore, care must be taken to ensure that a disposal of those shares is not triggered, even accidentally, in the future.
- Non-UK resident companies are chargeable to UK tax on gains on disposals of interests in UK land and on disposals of assets deriving at least 75% of their value from UK land. The charges apply to disposals on or after 6 April 2019 and replace the narrower CGT charge on UK residential property interests that previously applied.
- Special rules applied for ATED-related gains for disposals before 6 April 2019.

12

Capital Gains — Groups

Cross-references. See also 13 CAPITAL GAINS — SUBSTANTIAL SHAREHOLDING EXEMPTION, 33 EXEMPT ORGANISATIONS.

Other sources. See Tolley's Capital Gains Tax.

Simon's Taxes. See D2.3.

Introduction to capital gains — groups

[12.1] Groups of companies are able to benefit from beneficial reliefs with regard to capital gains. For example, a key relief allows the transfer of assets between group companies to happen without giving rise to a chargeable gain. In addition, rollover relief (see further Tolley's Capital Gains Tax) is extended to other members of a capital gains group, so a gain in one company can be 'rolled over' into the acquisition of an appropriate asset made by another group company.

In addition to the various reliefs described below, there are certain anti-avoidance provisions applicable to transactions between companies within a capital gains group. For example, the provisions restricting the use of losses (or set off of gains) arising before a company joins a group, the application of a charge when an asset which has been transferred intra-group is sold to a third party, the rules regarding appropriations to and from stock, and transactions undertaken which lead to an artificial reduction in the value of a group member's shares before a share sale.

This chapter outlines the rules regarding membership of a capital gains group, the reliefs available to such members, and the anti-avoidance provisions applicable. A more detailed analysis of capital gains provisions in general can be found in Tolley's Capital Gains Tax.

Definitions relating to capital gains — groups

[12.2] For the purposes of the capital gains provisions relating to groups of companies, the following definitions are applicable.

Definition of company

'*Company*' for the purposes of the capital gains group provisions means one within the meaning of the *Companies Act 2006* or the corresponding enactment in Northern Ireland or which is constituted under any other Act, Royal Charter, or letters patent (other than a limited liability partnership) or under the law of a country outside the UK. It also includes a registered society within *Co-operative and Community Benefit Societies Act 2014*, a building society (see **8.2** BUILDING SOCIETIES) and (from 17 March 1998) an incorporated friendly society. [*TCGA 1992, s 170(9)*].

Residence

Any company, whatever its country of residence, can be a member of a group and can be taken into account in establishing the existence of a group for the purposes of corporation tax on chargeable gains. See **35.2** GROUP RELIEF for the corresponding group relief provisions.

[*TCGA 1992, s 170(1A)(9)*].

Definition of group

The definition of a group for capital gains purposes is found at *TCGA 1992, s 170*.

A '*group*' comprises:

(a) a company ('*the principal company of the group*'); and
(b) that company's '75% subsidiaries' (i.e. where not less than 75% of the 'ordinary share capital' is beneficially owned directly or indirectly by the principal company), and those subsidiaries' 75% subsidiaries (and so on), except that any 75% subsidiary which is not 'an effective 51% subsidiary' of the principal company is excluded. Beneficial ownership is not affected by the existence of an option which may require disposal of shares at a future date (see *J Sainsbury plc v O'Connor* (1991) 64 TC 208, CA).

This definition is subject to the following rules.

(i) A company ('the subsidiary') which is a 75% subsidiary of another company cannot be a principal company of a group, unless:
 (A) because of the exclusion in (b) above (with regard to the 51% subsidiary requirement), the two companies are not in the same group;
 (B) the requirements of the definition of a group in (a) and (b) are otherwise satisfied; and
 (C) no further company could, under this provision, be the principal company of a group of which the subsidiary would be a member.
(ii) A company can only be a member of one capital gains group. Therefore if a company would otherwise belong to more than one group (the principal company of each of which is below called the '*head of a group*'), it belongs only to the group which can first be determined under the following tests.
 (A) The group to which it would belong if the exclusion of a company which is not an 'effective 51 per cent subsidiary' in (b) above were applied without the inclusion of any amount to which the head of a group:
  (a) is entitled of any profits available for distribution to equity holders of a head of another group; or
  (b) would be entitled of any assets of a head of another group available for distribution to its equity holders on a winding-up.
 (B) The group the head of which is entitled to a greater percentage than any other head of a group of its profits available for distribution to equity holders.
 (C) The group the head of which would be entitled to a greater percentage than any other head of a group of its assets available for distribution to equity holders on a winding-up.
 (D) The group the head of which owns (as in *CTA 2010, s 1154(2)*) directly or indirectly more of its ordinary share capital than any other head of a group.

The provisions of *CTA 2010, Pt 5 Ch 6* (group relief: equity holders and profits or assets available for distribution, see **35.4** GROUP RELIEF) apply with minor modification for (ii) and (A) and (B) above. One modification to the *CTA 2010* provisions for these purposes disapplies the requirement that certain arrangements for changes in profit or asset shares are assumed to take place in applying the 50% test. The anti-avoidance measures of *CTA 2010, ss 171(1)(b)(3), 173, 174* and *ss 176–178* (see **35.4** GROUP RELIEF) do **not** apply for these purposes.

[*TCGA 1992, s 170(2)–(8)*].

> ***Example***
>
> A Ltd owns 75% of the ordinary share capital of B Ltd, which in turns owns 75% of the ordinary share capital of C Ltd. C Ltd owns 75% of the ordinary share capital of D Ltd and D Ltd owns 75% of the ordinary share capital of E Ltd.
>
> For group capital gains purposes, the 'A' group is formed with A Ltd being the principal company. A Ltd owns 75% of B Ltd and 56.25% (75% x 75%) of C Ltd so both B Ltd and C Ltd can be included in A Ltd's gains group.
>
> However, A Ltd only owns 42% of D Ltd (75% x 75% x 75%), and therefore as this is below 50%, D Ltd is not part of A Ltd's group. Consequently, the A Ltd's capital gains group comprises companies A Ltd, B Ltd and C Ltd.
>
> C Ltd and D Ltd cannot be linked for group gains purposes. The reason for this is that a company which is a 75% subsidiary of another company cannot be a principal company unless it fails the effective subsidiary test. In other words a company cannot be a member of more than one group for group gains purposes — as in (ii) above.
>
> However, D Ltd can be a principal company in its own right and form its own group with E Ltd.
>
> Thus for group gains, there are two groups:
>
> (a) the A group comprising A Ltd, B Ltd and C Ltd; and
>
> (b) the D group, comprising D Ltd and E Ltd.

Open-ended investment companies

An open-ended investment company (see **46** INVESTMENT FUNDS) cannot be the principal company of a group [*TCGA 1992, s 170(4A) treated as inserted by SI 2006 No 964, Reg 107*] or a member of a group (see HMRC Capital Gains Manual CG45110).

Ordinary share capital

'*Ordinary share capital*' means all issued share capital of a company except shares carrying a fixed rate of dividend only. [*CTA 2010, s 1119*]. Any share capital of a registered society within *Co-operative and Community Benefit Societies Act 2014* (previously, a registered industrial and provident society) is treated as ordinary share capital. 'Issued share capital' does not include founder members' deposits in a company limited by guarantee (*South Shore Mutual Insurance Co Ltd v Blair* [1999] STC (SCD) 296).

HMRC Company Taxation Manual CTM00515, 00516 set out HMRC's interpretation of 'ordinary share capital' in *CTA 2010, s 1119*, with special regard to foreign entities.

When looking at overseas companies, a number of factors may be taken into account in deciding if a foreign 'company' has 'issued share capital'. As an essential, the foreign 'company' must be a distinct legal entity, separate from its members and able to hold assets. If this condition is met, other factors to be considered are:

- whether the member's interest is like shares in share capital (a portion of the capital of the corporate body) or debt (money owed by the body corporate to its members);
- what proprietary rights characteristic of shares attach to them, both economic and voting, and what responsibilities;
- how they are legally evidenced in accordance with local law;
- whether they are denominated in a stated fixed value;
- whether the members' interests compose a fixed and certain amount measuring the company's capital which creditors may look to as security; and
- whether the members' interests are capable of transfer and if so, whether such a transfer would amount to transferring of a portion of the capital of the company, with attendant proprietary rights and responsibilities (rather than a claim as creditor).

Simon's Taxes. See **D2.305–D2.307**.

Companies deemed not to change group

Principal becomes member of another group

[12.3] A group remains the same group so long as the same company remains the principal company of the group. If at any time the principal company of a group becomes a member of another group, the first group and the other group are regarded as the same, and the question whether or not a company has ceased to be a member of a group is determined accordingly. [*TCGA 1992, s 170(10)*].

Becoming a European Company — Societas Europaea

Where the principal company of a group:

- becomes an SE by reason of being the acquiring company in the formation of an SE by merger by acquisition (in accordance with *Council Regulations (EC) No 2157/2001, Arts 2(1), 17(2) and 29(1)*);
- becomes a subsidiary of a holding SE; or
- is transformed into an SE (in accordance with *Art 2(4)*),

the group and any group of which the SE is a member on formation are regarded as the same, and the question whether or not a company has ceased to be a member of a group is determined accordingly. [*TCGA 1992, s 170(10A)*].

From Brexit IP completion day (11pm on 31 December 2020), no new SEs can be formed in the UK. From IP completion day, every SE that is registered in the United Kingdom immediately before that day is automatically converted into a 'UK Societas'.

Winding up

The passing of a resolution, or the making of an order, or any other act for the winding-up of a member of a group is not treated as an occasion on which any company ceases to be a member of the group. [*TCGA 1992, s 170(11)*].

Transfers within a group

[12.4] A key benefit from being in a capital gains group is that transfers of chargeable assets between members of the same group are treated as no gain, no loss transfers. Thus the transfer happens at the disposing company's base cost plus indexation allowance to the date of transfer. (See further Tolley's Capital Gains Tax under Indexation). This rule applies automatically and is mandatory for such transfers (assuming the conditions for it to apply are met).

The conditions for intra-group transfers of assets to be treated as no gain, no loss disposals are:

(a) that either the transferor company is UK resident at the time of disposal or the asset is a 'chargeable asset' in relation to that company immediately before that time; and
(b) that either the transferee company is UK resident at that time or the asset is a 'chargeable asset' in relation to that company immediately after that time.

For these purposes, an asset is a '*chargeable asset*' in relation to a company at a particular time if, on a disposal by the company at that time, any gain would be a chargeable gain and within the charge to corporation tax under **11.1**(a)–(c) CAPITAL GAINS (non-resident companies).

For disposals on or after 6 April 2019, a previous deemed disposal by the transferor company under *TCGA 1992, s 25(3)* (deemed disposal on asset ceasing to be chargeable asset) is ignored in applying the no gain/no loss rule to the transferee company if no gain or loss was deemed to arise on the deemed disposal (as a result of *TCGA 1992, s 25ZA(2)*).

[*TCGA 1992, s 171; FA 2019, Sch 1 paras 61, 120*].

In *Gallaher Ltd v HMRC* FTT, [2019] UKFTT 207 (TC), the FTT found that the exclusion from *TCGA 1992, s 171* of an intra-group disposal to a transferee which is outside the UK tax net but located within an EU member state was a disproportionate restriction on the freedom of establishment. The tax charge arising on such a disposal was therefore disapplied. The Upper Tribunal ([2021] STC 247), however, has referred the issue to the CJEU. See now **58.20** PAYMENT OF TAX for CT payment plans for transactions with EEA resident group members which allow for payment by instalments where *s 171* is disapplied. The facility for such plans was introduced to prevent the disapplication of a tax charge in accordance with the FTT's decision in *Gallaher*.

Example

A Ltd owns 100% of B Ltd. In September 1993 A Ltd purchased a property at a cost of £500,000. In January 2022, A Ltd decided to transfer the property to B Ltd. This transaction is automatically treated as taking place at no gain/no loss.

If it is assumed that the indexation allowance due up to December 2017 is £250,000, the proceeds of the transaction are deemed to be £750,000, in order to give rise to no gain no loss, as follows.

	£
Proceeds	750,000
Cost	(500,000)
Indexation	(250,000)
Gain/loss	NIL

After the transfer B Ltd has a base cost of this particular property of £750,000.

Intra-group transfers are subject to anti-avoidance provisions where the company which acquired the asset leaves the group within six years of the transfer; see **12.15** below.

Note to the example

Indexation allowance is frozen at its December 2017 level. No indexation allowance is available in respect of expenditure incurred after 31 December 2017, and for expenditure incurred on or before that date and falling to be deducted on a disposal after that date, indexation allowance is computed up to and including December 2017 only.

Exceptions to no gain no loss transfer

[12.5] There are various exceptions to the intra group 'no gain no loss' transfer relief at **12.4** above. The relief does not apply to:

(i) *assumed* (as opposed to actual) transfers;
(ii) a disposal of a *debt* due from a group member effected by satisfying it (or part of it);
(iii) a disposal on redemption of *redeemable shares*;
(iv) a disposal of an interest in shares in consideration of a *capital distribution*;
(v) the receipt of *compensation* for destruction etc. of assets (in that the disposal is treated as being to the insurer or other person who ultimately bears the burden of furnishing the compensation);
(vi) a disposal by or to an investment trust (and see **12.19** below);
(vii) a disposal to a 'dual resident investing company' (see **35.23** GROUP RELIEF);
(viii) a disposal by or to a real estate investment trust (see **47.8** INVESTMENT TRUSTS);
(ix) a disposal by one member of a group to another in fulfilment of its obligations under an option granted to that other member at a time when the two companies were not members of the same group;
(x) a disposal by or to an incorporated friendly society entitled to tax exemptions under *FA 2012, s 165*;
(xi) a disposal by or to a venture capital trust (and see **12.19** below);
(xii) a high value disposal on which an ATED-related gain is chargeable to (or an ATED-related loss is allowable for the purposes of) capital gains tax (see **11.23** CAPITAL GAINS).

[*TCGA 1992, s 171(2)*].

As regards (iv), the assets acquired in the capital distribution are nevertheless treated as transferred at a 'no gain, no loss' price (see *Innocent v Whaddon Estates Ltd* Ch D 1981, 55 TC 476). Where an exchange of securities for those in another company is, under *TCGA 1992, ss 127, 135*, not treated as involving a disposal of the original shares or the acquisition of a new holding, it is not treated as a 'no gain, no loss' transfer as above. [*TCGA 1992, s 171(3)*]. Where the consideration given for shares consists of qualifying corporate bonds, see Revenue Tax Bulletin December 1996 p 372 for an analysis of the consequences.

Where it is assumed, for any purpose, that a group member has acquired or sold an asset, it is also assumed that it was not prima facie a sale to, or acquisition from, a group member. [*TCGA 1992, s 171(6)*].

Simon's Taxes. See **D2.314–D2.316.**

Election for deemed intra-group transfers

[12.6] Where two companies, X and Y, are members of a group, and a chargeable gain or allowable loss accrues to X, X and Y may make a joint election to transfer the gain or loss, or a specified part of it, from X to Y. The effect of the election is that, for the purposes of corporation tax on chargeable gains:

- the gain or loss, or specified part, is treated as accruing to Y (and not to X) at the time that, but for the election, it would have accrued to X; and
- if Y is not resident in the UK, the transferred gain or loss is taken to accrue in respect of a chargeable asset (i.e. an asset a gain on the disposal of which would be a chargeable gain forming part of Y's chargeable profits under **11.1**(a)–(c) CAPITAL GAINS).

An election will be disregarded if, taken together with any earlier elections, it would have the effect of transferring more than the total gain or loss. An election cannot be made in respect of a degrouping charge within **12.14** below (but see **12.31** below for the intra-group transfer of a degrouping charge).

The election must be made in writing to an HMRC officer on or before the second anniversary of the end of the accounting period of X in which the gain or loss accrued (or actual disposal was made). It can be made only if an actual transfer of the asset (or part) from X to Y would have been a no gain/no loss disposal within *TCGA 1992, s 171*. For this purpose, the condition at **12.4**(b) above is that, at the time of the deemed transfer, company Y is resident in the United Kingdom, or carrying on a trade in the United Kingdom through a permanent establishment or the asset is a chargeable asset in relation to company Y.

This provision is intended to facilitate the bringing together of chargeable gains and allowable losses within one group company. Any payment made by X to Y, or vice versa, in connection with the election is not to be taken into account in computing profits or losses of either company or treated as a distribution, *provided* it does not exceed the chargeable gain or allowable loss deemed to accrue to Y on the disposal.

An election cannot be made to transfer a gain made on the disposal of an interest in an oil field within *TCGA 1992, s 197* (or treated as so made under *TCGA 1992, s 197(4)*) from a company carrying on a 'ring fence trade' (as defined) to a company not carrying on such a trade.

[*TCGA 1992, ss 171A, 171B; FA 2019, Sch 1 paras 62, 63*].

Simon's Taxes. See **D2.329**.

Appropriation to or from trading stock

[12.7] Companies may transfer assets between group members which were not held as trading stock in one company, but will be so held by the other company (and vice versa). Provisions are in place to prevent such transfers from happening without giving rise to an appropriate chargeable gain, or trading profits or loss (as applicable), when the intra-group transfer occurs.

Thus, where a company ('company A') acquires an asset as trading stock of a trade from another member of the group ('company B'), and the asset did not form part of the trading stock of a trade carried on by company B, company A is treated as acquiring the asset otherwise than as trading stock and immediately appropriating it as trading stock (for the purposes of *TCGA 1992, s 161* or *Sch 7AC para 36*).

The effect is that, subject to an election being made under *s 161(3)*, a chargeable gain or allowable loss accrues to company A based on the difference between market value and the no gain, no loss transfer value (which applies to the transfer of the asset from B to A, before A then appropriates the asset to stock) (see **12.4** above).

Similarly, where a company ('company C') disposes of an asset forming part of the trading stock of a trade to another member of the group ('company D'), and the asset is acquired by company D otherwise than as trading stock of a trade carried on by it, company C is treated as appropriating the asset immediately before the disposal for a purpose other than use as trading stock (for the purposes of *TCGA 1992, s 161* or *Sch 7AC para 36*).

The effect is that company C is treated as making a disposal from trading stock at market value prior to the transfer and is then deemed to have acquired the asset (for capital gains purposes) at that time at the amount brought into the accounts of the trade for tax purposes on the deemed appropriation. Company D will then receive the asset at that market value, and indexation will run from the date the property is transferred.

Although a non-UK resident company can be a member of a group (see **12.2** above), references above to a trade do not include a trade carried on by a non-UK resident company unless it is carried on in the UK through a permanent establishment (see **64.6** RESIDENCE).

[*TCGA 1992, s 173*].

Acquisition 'as trading stock' implies a commercial justification for the acquisition, see *Coates v Arndale Properties Ltd* (1984) 59 TC 516, HL, *Reed v Nova Securities Ltd* (1985) 59 TC 516, HL, *N Ltd v Inspector of Taxes* [1996] STC (SCD) 346 and *Property Dealing Company v Inspector of Taxes* [2003] STC (SCD) 233.

Simon's Taxes. See D2.313.

Rollover relief

[12.8] Rollover relief on the *replacement of business assets* is granted under *TCGA 1992, ss 152–158* (see Tolley's Capital Gains Tax under Rollover Relief) is extended to groups such that a gain made by one company can be rolled over into the purchase of an appropriate asset by another group company.

With regard to the requirements for the application of rollover relief and groups:

(i) all the trades carried on by group members are treated as a single trade (except as regards intra-group transfers);
(ii) *TCGA 1992, s 154* (special rules for depreciating assets) applies as if all group members were the same person.

A disposal by a company when it is a member of a group, and an acquisition by another company when it is a member of the same group, are treated as made by the same person.

Claims to relief must be made by both companies concerned. It is not necessary for the companies making the disposal and acquisition to be members of the group throughout the period between the transactions, as long as each is a member at the time of its own transaction.

Where a non-trading group member disposes of or acquires assets used only for the trades within (i) above (ie. trades of other group members), relief is given as if it were carrying on a trade.

The relief is not available in respect of consideration applied in the acquisition of new assets by a 'dual resident investing company' (see **35.23** GROUP RELIEF).

Relief is also denied where the acquisition of the new asset is one to which any of the no gain/no loss provisions applies (generally this is to prevent rollover relief where the new asset has been acquired from another group member) or where the new asset is a chargeable intangible asset.

In determining whether a company is a member of a group for the these purposes with regard to either the acquisition or the disposal (or both), see **12.2** above.

However, the reference above to 'trade' does not include a trade carried on by a non-UK resident company otherwise than through a permanent establishment in the UK (see **64.6** RESIDENCE).

Where the disposal or the acquisition, or both are made by different group companies:

(i) either the company making the disposal must be UK resident at the time of the disposal or the assets must be 'chargeable assets' in relation to that company immediately before that time; and
(ii) either the company making the acquisition must be UK resident at the time of the acquisition or the assets must be chargeable assets in relation to that company immediately after that time.

For these purposes, an asset is a 'chargeable asset' in relation to a company at a particular time if, on a disposal by that company at that time, any gain would be a chargeable gain and would be within the charge to corporation tax by virtue of *TCGA 1992, s 2B(3)* (previously *TCGA 1992, s 10B*); non-UK resident company trading in the UK through a permanent establishment — see **50.3** OVERSEAS MATTERS.

[*TCGA 1992, s 175; FA 2019, Sch 1 para 64*].

Compulsory acquisitions of land

[12.9] For the purposes of the rollover relief under *TCGA 1992, s 247* (see Tolley's Capital Gains Tax under Land), a disposal by a company when it is a member of a group, and an acquisition by another company when it is a member of the same group, are treated as made by the same person, provided that relief is claimed by both companies. Relief is, however, denied where the acquisition of the new land is one to which any of the no gain/no loss provisions applies.

[*TCGA 1992, ss 175, 247(5A)*].

Where (i) above applies in a case where one member of a group makes the disposal and a second the acquisition, it may happen that the disposal takes place after the first company has ceased to trade, or the acquisition takes place before the second company commences trading. Relief will then be restricted in respect of the period during which the assets disposed of were not used for business purposes, and will be conditional on the replacement assets not being used or leased for any purpose prior to the second company's commencing trading, and being taken into use for the purposes of the trade on its commencement. (HMRC Statement of Practice, SP 8/81).

For the interaction of rollover relief with the exemption for substantial shareholdings, see **13.18** CAPITAL GAINS — SUBSTANTIAL SHAREHOLDINGS.

Simon's Taxes. See **C3.302B**.

Assets held on 31 March 1982

[12.10] See Tolley's Capital Gains Tax under Assets held on 31 March 1982 for details of these provisions generally, and in particular for the election under *TCGA 1992, s 35(5)* for all disposals by a person after 5 April 1988 of assets held on 31 March 1982 to be subject to the general re-basing rule of *TCGA 1992, s 35(1)(2)*. This election is subject to the following special provisions in relation to groups of companies.

Election by principal company

No group member other than the 'principal company' of a group (for which see *TCGA 1992, s 170* as in **12.2** above) may make an election under *TCGA 1992, s 35(5)* unless the company did not become a group member until after the 'relevant time'.

An election by the principal company does, however, have effect as an election by any other company which is a group member at the 'relevant time', except that this does not apply to a company which, in some period after 5 April 1988 and before the 'relevant time', makes a disposal, at a time when it is not a group member, of an asset held on 31 March 1982, and does not itself make the election within the prescribed time limit.

The time limit for the making of the election by the principal company is two years (or such longer time as HMRC may allow) from the end of the accounting period in which occurs the first disposal after 5 April 1988 of an asset held on 31 March 1982 by a company which is a group member (other than an 'outgoing company' in relation to the group) or which is an 'incoming company' in relation to the group.

See, however, HMRC Statement of Practice, SP 4/92 as regards certain disposals which are ignored for this purpose. See HMRC Capital Gains Manual CG46374 for the circumstances in which a late election may be accepted.

An election by the principal company of a group continues to apply to a company leaving the group after the 'relevant time', unless it is an 'outgoing company' in relation to the group and the principal company election is made after it ceases to be a group member.

The '*relevant time*' is the earliest of:

(i) the first time when a group member (other than an 'outgoing company' in relation to the group) makes a disposal after 5 April 1988 of an asset held on 31 March 1982;
(ii) the time immediately after the first occasion on which an 'incoming company' in relation to the group becomes a group member; and
(iii) the time when the principal company makes the election.

An '*outgoing company*', in relation to a group, is a company which ceases to be a group member before the end of the period during which an election could be made which would apply to it, and at a time when no such election has been made.

An '*incoming company*', in relation to a group, is a company which makes its first disposal after 5 April 1988 of an asset held on 31 March 1982 at a time when it is not a group member, and which becomes a group member before the expiry of the time limit for making an election which would apply to it without that election having been made.

In relation to a determination as to whether a company is a member, or the principal member, of a group, see **12.2** above.

[*TCGA 1992, s 35(5), Sch 3 paras 8, 9*].

Collection of unpaid tax from group members and directors

[12.11] Where a chargeable gain accrues to a company (the 'taxpayer company') and either:

(i) that company is UK resident at the time the gain accrues; or
(ii) the gain is within the charge to corporation tax by virtue of *TCGA 1992, s 2B(3)(4)* (non-UK resident company — see **11.1**(a)–(c) CAPITAL GAINS) or, for disposals before 6 April 2019, *TCGA 1992, s 10B* (non-UK resident company trading in the UK through a permanent establishment — see **64.6** RESIDENCE),

the following rules apply where all or part of the corporation tax assessed on the taxpayer company for the accounting period in which the gain accrues remains unpaid six months after it became payable.

HMRC may serve on any of the following persons a notice requiring that person to pay, within 30 days, the unpaid tax or, if less, an amount equal to corporation tax on the chargeable gain at the rate in force when the gain accrued:

(a) if the taxpayer company was a member of a 'group' at the time when the gain accrued, the 'principal company' of the 'group' at that time and any other company which was, at any time in the twelve months before the gain accrued, a member of the same 'group' and owned the asset disposed of, or any part of it, or where that asset is an interest or right in or over another asset, owned either asset or any part of either asset;
(b) if the taxpayer company was not UK-resident when the gain accrued, any person who is, or during the twelve months before the gain accrued was, a 'controlling director' of the taxpayer company or of a company which has, or within that twelve-month period had, 'control' over the taxpayer company.

For the purpose of (a) above, '*group*' and '*principal company*' are as defined as in **12.2** above but as if references there to 75% subsidiaries were to 51% subsidiaries. In determining whether a company is a member of a group at any time in the twelve-month period referred to in (a) and (b) above, see **12.2** above. As regards (b) above, '*control*' is as under *CTA 2010, ss 450, 451* (see **16.6** CLOSE COMPANIES), and a '*controlling director*' is a 'director' (within the extended meaning under the employment income benefits legislation and *CTA 2010, s 452(1)* (see **16.8** CLOSE COMPANIES) with such control.

The notice must state the amount of tax assessed, the original due date and the amount required from the person on whom it is served. It has effect, as regards collection, interest and appeals, as if it were a notice of assessment on that person. The notice must be served within three years beginning with the date on which the liability of the taxpayer company for the accounting period in question was finally determined (including a determination under *FA 1998, Sch 18 para 36* or *37* in the absence of a full return, see **65.18** RETURNS). In the case of a self-assessed liability, including one superseding a determination, the date of determination of the liability is taken as the last date on which notice of an enquiry into the return may be given (see **65.14** RETURNS), or, if such notice is given, 30 days after the action which concludes the enquiry process. In the case of a discovery assessment (see **6.3** ASSESSMENTS), it is the due and payable date or (if there is an appeal against the assessment) the date the appeal is finally determined.

A person paying an amount under these provisions may recover it from the taxpayer company, but such an amount is not deductible for any tax purpose.

[*TCGA 1992, s 190; FA 2019, Sch 1 paras 69, 120*].

See also **64.6** RESIDENCE as regards tax unpaid by non-resident companies.

Simon's Taxes. See D2.345.

Depreciatory transactions

[12.12] Where two or more members of a group of companies are parties to a 'disposal of assets' at other than market value which has the effect of materially reducing the value of the shares or 'securities' of one of those companies ('a depreciatory transaction'), any loss arising on the ultimate disposal of those shares or securities by a member or a former member of the group (having been a member when the transaction took place) is to be allowable only so far as is 'just and reasonable'. Account may be taken of any other post-30 March 1982 transaction which has:

(i) enhanced the value of the assets of the company the shares in which are being disposed of; and
(ii) depreciated the assets of any other group member.

Where the ultimate disposal of the shares or securities takes place on or after 22 November 2017 (or is treated as taking place before 22 November 2017 as a result of a negligible value claim (see **45.11** LOSSES) made on or after that date), any depreciatory transactions occurring on or after 31 March 1982 are taken into account. Previously, only depreciatory transactions occurring in the six years ending with that disposal were taken into account.

The restriction is applied to the allowable loss after indexation, rather than to the unindexed loss before indexation (*Tesco plc v Crimmin* (1997) 69 TC 510), and in arriving at the amount by which it was 'just and reasonable' to reduce the allowable loss, indexation should be applied to the value of the depreciatory transaction(s) from the date(s) of the transaction(s) to the date of the ultimate disposal (*Whitehall Electric Investments Ltd v Owen* [2002] STC (SCD) 229).

Where such a reduction is made, any chargeable gain accruing on the disposal within six years of the transaction of the shares etc. in any other party thereto is to be reduced as is 'just and reasonable' (but not so as to exceed the reduction in the allowable loss). Regard may also be had to the effect of the depreciatory transaction on the value of the shares at the date of disposal.

A 'depreciatory transaction' also includes any other transaction where:

(a) the company, the shares or securities in which are the subject of the ultimate disposal, or any 75% subsidiary of that company, was party to that transaction; and
(b) the parties to the transaction were, or included, two or more companies which, when the transaction occurred, were in the same group.

A transaction is not depreciatory to the extent that it is a payment which is brought into account in computing a chargeable gain or allowable loss of the company making the ultimate disposal. Cancellation within *Companies Act 2006, s 641* of shares or securities of one group member which are owned by another is deemed to be a depreciatory transaction unless it falls within this exemption.

Claims under *TCGA 1992, s 24(2)* that shares or securities have become of negligible value also come within this section.

References to the disposal of assets include appropriation by one member of a group of the goodwill of another.

'*Securities*' includes loan stock or similar securities, whether secured or unsecured.

'*Group of companies*' includes non-resident companies.

[*TCGA 1992, s 176; FA 2018, s 28*].

As regards distributions out of post-acquisition profits, see HMRC Capital Gains Manual, CG46540.

Simon's Taxes. See **D2.350.**

Distributions as depreciatory transactions

[12.13] The restriction on capital losses because of depreciatory transactions (see **12.12** above) also applies where a first company has a holding in a second company which amounts (with or without the addition of holdings by CONNECTED PERSONS (**19**)) to 10% of all the holdings of the same class in the second company (and the first company is not a dealing company in relation to the holding) and a distribution is, or has been, made in respect of the holding which materially reduces the value of the holding. Distributions brought into account in computing a chargeable gain or allowable loss accruing to the ultimate disponor are ignored. [*TCGA 1992, s 177*].

Simon's Taxes. See **D2.352.**

Degrouping charge

[12.14] A degrouping charge applies where a company ceases to be a member of a group at a time when it owns an asset previously transferred to it by another group member.

Note that these provisions do not apply if, before the chargeable company leaves the group (or leaves a second group — see below), it has become an investment trust or a venture capital trust and triggered the provisions at **12.18** or **12.19** below. [*TCGA 1992, s 179(2C)(2D)*].

The provisions apply where a company (the transferee company) has acquired an asset from another company (the transferor company) at a time when both companies are members of the same group and the transferee company ceases to be a member of the group within six years after the time of the acquisition. It is also a requirement that the asset be within the charge to UK corporation tax both before and after the transfer, the precise conditions being similar to those for intra-group transfers at **12.4** above.

If, when the transferee leaves the group it, or an 'associated' company also leaving the group, owns (not as trading stock) the asset, replacement property to which a gain on the disposal of the original asset has been carried forward under rollover relief (see Tolley's Capital Gains Tax under Rollover relief) or an asset the value of which is wholly or partly derived from the original asset, the transferee is treated as if, immediately after its acquisition of the asset (subject to **12.16** below), it had sold, and immediately reacquired, the asset at its then market value. There will thus be a gain or loss by reference to the market value of the asset at that time and its 'no gain/no loss' acquisition consideration under **12.4** above. The gain or loss on the deemed sale is normally treated as accruing immediately after the beginning of the accounting period in which (or at the end of which, if that be the case) the company ceases to be a member of the group. This will apply in most cases but it is subject to the proviso that the time of accrual cannot be earlier than the time of transfer of the asset. Companies are '*associated*' for this purpose if one is a 75% subsidiary (as defined in **12.2** above) of the other or both are 75% subsidiaries of another company.

CTA 2010, ss 138–142 (limits on GROUP RELIEF (**35.6**)) have effect as if the actual circumstances were as they are treated above as having been.

[*TCGA 1992, s 179(1)(1A)(3)(4)(10)(10A); FA 2019, Sch 1 para 65*].

Simon's Taxes. See **D2.330–D2.334**.

Companies leaving the group at the same time

There is an exception to the degrouping charge where both the transferee and the transferor companies leave the group at the same time and either:

- the companies are both 75% subsidiaries and effective 51% subsidiaries (as defined in **12.2** above) of another company on the date of acquisition of the asset and continue to be so until immediately after they cease to be members of the group; or
- one of the companies is both a 75% subsidiary and an effective 51% subsidiary of the other on the date of acquisition and continues to be so until immediately after the companies cease to be members of the group.

Where either condition is satisfied, the above provision does not apply.

However, the degrouping charge will nevertheless apply in certain circumstances where a company in a group transfers an asset intra-group and both transferor and transferee then leave that group to form a second group which, at the time the transferee leaves the first group, is 'connected' with the first. If the transferee company leaves the second group, the charge will apply (in relation to the departure from the second group) if the intra-group transfer, which is deemed for this purpose to have taken place in the second group, occurred within the preceding six years. Where the two groups cease to be connected (without the transferee having left the second group), the transferee company and any associated company are treated as having left the second group at that time and the provision applies accordingly. Where the above exception would otherwise apply in relation to the departure from the second group it does not do so if the transferee leaving the first group was part of arrangements a main purpose of which was the avoidance of a corporation tax liability. The two groups are '*connected*' at a particular time for this purpose if, broadly, at that time the second group is under the control of the first group or both groups are under the common control of a person or persons who control or have controlled the first group at any time since the chargeable company left the first group. The general definitions of *CTA 2010, ss 450, 451* (meaning of 'control') apply for this purpose (except for banking businesses).

[*TCGA 1992, s 179(2)–(2B)(9A)*].

Company leaving group due to share disposal

Where the conditions listed below are satisfied, a degrouping gain or loss under the above provisions is not treated as a separate gain or loss, but instead the gain or loss accruing on a 'group disposal' (see below) is adjusted to take account of the degrouping gain or loss. The conditions are as follows:

(A) the transferee company ceases to be a member of the group as a result of one or more disposals ('*group disposals*') by a group member of the transferee's shares or those of another group member;

(B) either:

  (i) the company making the group disposal (or, if there is more than one such disposal, at least one of them) is UK resident at the time of disposal, the shares are within the charge to corporation tax (or would be but for the substantial shareholdings exemption — see **13** CAPITAL GAINS — SUBSTANTIAL SHAREHOLDINGS), or any part of the gains or loss on the disposal (or at least one of them) is treated as accruing to a person under *TCGA 1992, s 13(2)* (attribution of gains to members of non-resident companies), or

  (ii) had (i) above applied to the group disposal or to each of them, any gain arising would not have been a chargeable gain as a result of the substantial shareholdings exemption; and

(C) *CTA 2010, s 535* (UK real estate investment trusts: exemption of gains — see **47.29** INVESTMENT TRUSTS) would not apply to the degrouping gain or loss.

For these purposes, *TCGA 1992, s 127* (share reorganisations etc. treated as not involving disposal — see **62.3** onwards REORGANISATIONS AND RECONSTRUCTIONS) is ignored in determining whether there has been a disposal.

Where the conditions are satisfied, a chargeable gain or allowable loss on a single group disposal is calculated by adding any degrouping gain which would have arisen but for these provisions to the consideration for the group disposal. Any degrouping loss which would have been allowable but for these provisions is treated as an allowable deduction in computing the gain or loss on the group disposal.

Where the group disposal is within *TCGA 1992, s 127* so that there is no disposal for chargeable gains purposes, the adjustments in respect of the degrouping gain or loss are made to any gain or loss on a disposal of the 'new holding' (see **62.3** REORGANISATIONS AND RECONSTRUCTIONS) or a part of it. Where there is a degrouping gain, the amount of the gain reduces the allowable expenditure and any excess over the amount of that expenditure is treated as an additional gain on the new holding disposal. If the disposal is of only part of the new holding, only that part of the excess of the degrouping gain over the allowable expenditure that corresponds to the part of the new holding disposed of is treated as an additional gain in this way. Where there is a degrouping loss, it is added to the allowable expenditure.

If there is more than one group disposal, the degrouping profit or loss is apportioned to the group disposals as the companies making them jointly elect or, if no election is made, by dividing it equally between the group disposals. An election must be made to HMRC no later than two years after the end of the accounting period in which the first group disposal is made.

If a group disposal consists of shares of more than one class, the company can apportion any increase or deduction to be made under these provisions between the classes as it considers appropriate.

[*TCGA 1992, s 179(3A)–(3H)*].

Company ceasing to be group member on principal company joining another group

Where the transferee company ceases to be a member of a group only because the principal company becomes a member of another, second, group (e.g. it is not an 'effective 51% subsidiary' of the principal company of the other group as in **12.2** above) the following provisions apply.

(I) The transferee company is not treated under the above provisions as selling the asset at that time.

(II) If:

- (i) within six years of that time the company ceases at any time ('*the relevant time*') to satisfy the following conditions: namely that it is a '75% subsidiary' (as defined in **12.2** above) of one or more members of the other group mentioned in (a) above and an 'effective 51% subsidiary' (as defined in **12.2** above) of one or more of those members; and
- (ii) at the relevant time the company or a company in the same group, owns (otherwise than as trading stock) the asset, or property to which a chargeable gain has been rolled over from the asset, or an asset the value of which is wholly or partly derived from the original asset,

the transferee company is treated as if, immediately after acquiring the asset (subject to **12.16** below), it had sold and reacquired it at its market value at the time of acquisition.

(III) (II) above does not apply if:

- (i) the transferee company ceases at the relevant time to the conditions in (II)(i) above as a result of one or more disposals by a member of the second group of the transferee's shares or those of another group member;
- (ii) either:
  - the company making the share disposal (or, if there is more than one such disposal, at least one of them) is UK resident at the time of disposal, the shares are within the charge to corporation tax (or would be but for the substantial shareholdings exemption — see **13**), or any part of the gains or loss on the disposal (or at least one of them) is treated as accruing to a person under *TCGA 1992, s 13(2)* (attribution of gains to members of non-resident companies); or

– had those conditions applied to the share disposal or to each of them, any gain arising would not have been a chargeable gain as a result of the substantial shareholdings exemption; and

(iii) in the absence of this provision *CTA 2010, s 535* (UK real estate investment trusts: exemption of gains — see **47.29** INVESTMENT TRUSTS) would not apply to the gain or loss in (II) above.

Instead the provisions above applying to a company leaving a group as a result of a share disposal (i.e. *TCGA 1992, s 179(3C)–(3H)*) apply (with appropriate modifications).

(IV) Any gain or loss on the deemed sale in (II) above is treated as arising immediately before the relevant time.

[*TCGA 1992, s 179(5)–(8)*].

Supplementary provisions

Ceasing to be a member of a group

Where a company ceases to be a member of a group in consequence of another member of the group ceasing to exist the company is not treated as ceasing to be a group member for the purposes of the degrouping charge provisions. [*TCGA 1992, s 179(1)*]. HMRC consider that this let out only applies to the case of a parent company ceasing to be a member of a group on the occasion of its only subsidiary ceasing to exist on dissolution (or all its subsidiaries ceasing to exist simultaneously on dissolution). HMRC has confirmed it does not apply the deemed sale and reacquisition where the company receiving the asset ceases to be a group member as a result of its only subsidiary leaving the group (HMRC Capital Gains Manual CG45410 and see *Dunlop International AG v Pardoe* CA 1999, 72 TC 71).

Where, as part of a process of merger to which *TCGA 1992, s 140E* (European cross-border merger: assets left within UK tax charge) applies, a company which is a member of a group ceases to exist and as a consequence assets, or shares in one or more companies which were also members of the group, are transferred to the transferee, the company which has ceased to exist and any company whose shares have been transferred to the transferee are, for the purposes of these provisions, not treated as having left the group. The transferee and the company which ceased to exist are treated as the same entity and, if the transferee is itself a member of a group following the merger, any company which was a member of the first group and became a member of the transferee's group as a result of the merger is treated as if the two groups were the same. [*TCGA 1992, s 179(1B)–(1D)*].

Where shares in a company are transferred as part of the process of the transfer of a business to which *TCGA 1992, s 140A* (see **11.18** CAPITAL GAINS) or *TCGA 1992, s 140C* applies, and as a result, the company ceases to be a member of a group, it is treated as not having left the group. If the company becomes a member of a second group, of which the transferee company is a member, as a result of the transfer, the company is treated as if the two groups were the same. [*TCGA 1992, s 179(1AA)*].

Value shifting

If under these provisions a deemed sale arises at any time, and if on an actual sale at market value at that time any loss or gain would, under the value shifting provisions (see **11.13** CAPITAL GAINS), have been calculated as if the consideration were increased by an amount, the market value at the time of the deemed sale is treated as having been greater by that amount. [*TCGA 1992, s 179(9)*].

Assessments etc.

Any adjustment of tax or recomputation of liability on a disposal may be made by assessment or otherwise as a result of any deemed disposal and reacquisition mentioned above. [*TCGA 1992, s 179(13)*].

Example

C Ltd had the following transactions.

1.3.88	Purchased a freehold property £20,000.
1.12.15	Sold the freehold to D Ltd (a wholly-owned subsidiary) for £40,000 (market value £100,000).
31.5.21	Sold its shareholding in D Ltd (at which time D Ltd continued to own the freehold property).

Both C Ltd and D Ltd prepare accounts to 30 April.

The consideration for the sale of the shares is £1 million, and C Ltd purchased the shares in March 1986 for £120,000.

Relevant values of the RPI are: March 1986 96.73, March 1988 104.1, December 2015 260.6, December 2017 278.1.

(i) C Ltd's disposal of the property to D Ltd is to be treated as one on which, after taking account of the indexation allowance, neither gain nor loss arises (see **12.4** above).

Indexation factor 260.6 – 104.1/104.1 = 1.503

	£
Cost to C Ltd	20,000
Indexation allowance £20,000 × 1.503	30,060
Deemed cost to D Ltd	£50,060

(ii) On the sale of C Ltd's shares in D Ltd on 31.7.21 (i.e. within six years after the transaction in (i) above), *C Ltd* will have a deemed disposal as follows.

Deemed disposal by D Ltd on 1.12.14	
	£
Market value at 1.12.14	100,000
Cost (as above)	50,060
Degrouping gain	£49,940
D Ltd's new base cost for future gains	£100,000

C Ltd's chargeable gain on disposal of D Ltd shares on 31.7.21

	£
Consideration	1,000,000
Add degrouping gain	49,940
	1,049,940
Less acquisition cost	120,000
Uninexed gain	929,940
Indexation allowance (278.1 – 96.73/96.73) × £120,000	225,000
Chargeable gain subject to CT	£704,940

Note to the example

(1) Indexation allowance is frozen at its December 2017 level. No indexation allowance is available in respect of expenditure incurred after 31 December 2017, and for expenditure incurred on or before that date and falling to be deducted on a disposal after that date, indexation allowance is computed up to and including December 2017 only.

Deferral of degrouping charge

[12.15] Where a company is treated as making a gain under the degrouping charge provisions in **12.14** above or such a gain is taken into account in calculating a gain on a disposal of shares under those provisions a claim can be made to defer part of the gain.

Where the degrouping gain is taken into account in calculating a gain on a disposal of shares, the claim can be made by the company making the share disposal or, if there is more than one such disposal, the companies making those disposals acting jointly. In any other case the claim is to be made by the company to whom the degrouping gain is deemed to accrue. The effect is to reduce the amount of the gain by the amount specified in the claim. The reduction must be just and reasonable with regard, in particular, to any transaction as a direct or indirect result of which the asset to which the gain relates was acquired.

Where a gain is reduced in this way, the consideration for the deemed reacquisition of the asset (see **12.14** above) is taken to be its market value less the amount of the adjustment to the gain. In effect the part of the gain excluded is deferred until final disposal of the asset.

[*TCGA 1992, s 179ZA*].

Exemption for substantial shareholdings

[12.16] Where a company ceases to be a member of a group and is deemed under *TCGA 1992, s 179* to have sold and immediately reacquired at market value an asset transferred to it by another group member, then normally the time of the deemed sale is immediately after the transfer (see **12.14** above). However, where:

- a degrouping charge (as in **12.14** above) arises in relation to an asset, and

- a gain on a disposal of that asset (by the company then owning it) immediately before the time of degrouping would have been exempt under the provisions at **13** CAPITAL GAINS — SUBSTANTIAL SHAREHOLDING EXEMPTION,

the deemed sale and reacquisition is instead treated as taking place immediately before the time of degrouping.

A comparable rule applies where the degrouping charge arises under *TCGA 1992, s 179(5)–(8)*. In this case, the rule applies by reference to the 'relevant time' (see **12.14** above) rather than the 'time of degrouping'.

[*TCGA 1992, Sch 7AC para 38*].

Exemption for mergers

[12.17] *Taxation of Chargeable Gains Act 1992, s 179* in **12.14** above does not apply, subject to conditions, where, as part of a 'merger', a company (Company A) ceases to be a member of a group ('the A group'), and it is shown that the merger was carried out for bona fide reasons and that the avoidance of a liability to tax was not the main or one of the main purposes of the merger.

'*Merger*', in broad terms, means an arrangement whereby one or more companies ('the acquiring compan(y)(ies)') not in the A group acquire interests in the business previously carried on by Company A, and one or more members of the A group acquire interests in the business or businesses previously carried on either by the acquiring company or companies or by a company at least 90% of the ordinary share capital of which is owned by two or more of the acquiring companies. For this purpose a group member is treated as carrying on as one business the activities of that group. 25% of the value of the interests acquired must take the form of ordinary share capital, whilst the remainder of the interests acquired by the A group must consist of share capital or debentures or both. The value of the interests acquired must be substantially the same, and the consideration for the interests acquired by the acquiring companies must substantially consist of the interests acquired by the A group.

For these purposes, references to a company include a non-UK resident company.

[*TCGA 1992, s 181*].

See HMRC Capital Gains Manual CG45463 for examples on the operation of these provisions. See also **13.11** COMPANIES regarding demergers.

Company becoming an investment trust after acquiring asset intra-group

[12.18] Similar treatment as in **12.14** above (company leaving group) applies where a company (the '*acquiring company*') becomes an investment trust (within *CTA 2010, s 1158* — see **47.3** INVESTMENT TRUSTS) not more than six years after the company acquired an asset from another company in its group, the disposal by which it acquired the asset (the corresponding disposal) having been treated by virtue of *TCGA 1992, s 171* (intra-group transfers — see **12.4** above) as a no gain/no loss disposal. The provisions apply where at the beginning of the said accounting period, the acquiring company owns, otherwise than as trading stock, either the asset itself or replacement property, i.e. property into which a chargeable gain on disposal of the asset has been rolled over, whether directly (i.e. as a result of a single rollover relief claim) or indirectly (where two or more such claims have been made). For the purposes of these provisions, an asset acquired is deemed to be the same as an asset owned subsequently if the value of the latter asset is derived, wholly or partly, from the original asset (in particular where the original was a leasehold and the lessee has acquired the freehold reversion). The provisions do not apply if the acquiring company was an investment trust at the time of the corresponding disposal (in which case the no gain/no loss treatment would not have applied — see **12.5**(vi) above) nor if it has been an investment trust for any intervening accounting period.

The acquiring company is treated as if, immediately after the corresponding disposal, it had sold and immediately reacquired the asset at its market value at that time. The resulting chargeable gain or allowable loss is treated as accruing immediately before the end of the acquiring company's accounting period which immediately preceded that in which it became an investment trust. Notwithstanding normal time limits, any consequential corporation tax assessment may be made at any time within six years after the end of the accounting period in which the company became an investment trust. These provisions are disapplied if, prior to the company becoming an investment trust, the above treatment has already applied to the asset by virtue either of **12.14** above or **12.19** below (company becoming a venture capital trust).

[*TCGA 1992, s 101A*].

Company becoming a venture capital trust after acquiring asset intra-group

[12.19] The same treatment as in **12.18** above (company becoming an investment trust) applies where the acquiring company becomes a venture capital trust (VCT) (within *ITA 2006, Pt 6* — see **74** VENTURE CAPITAL TRUSTS) not more than six years after it acquired the asset intra-group by means of a no gain/no loss disposal under *TCGA 1992, s 171* (see **12.4** above). For this purpose, a company becomes a VCT at the time of the coming into effect of HMRC's approval (the time of approval). The provisions apply where, at the time of approval, the acquiring company owns, otherwise than as trading stock, either the asset itself (with the same rules as in **12.18** above as to derivation of assets) or replacement property (as in **12.18** above). The provisions do not apply if the acquiring company was a VCT at the time of the intra-group disposal (see **12.5**(xi) above) and do not apply if it has been a VCT at any time in the intervening period. Nor do they apply if, prior to the company becoming a VCT, the said treatment has already applied to the asset by virtue either of **12.18** above or **12.14** above (company leaving group).

The chargeable gain or allowable loss resulting from the deemed disposal at market value immediately after the intra-group transfer is treated as accruing to the acquiring company immediately before the time of approval. Notwithstanding normal time limits, any consequential corporation tax assessment may, in a case in which HMRC's approval has effect as from the beginning of an accounting period, be made at any time within six years after the end of that accounting period.

[*TCGA 1992, s 101C*].

Buying gains or losses

[12.20] There are two sets of anti-avoidance provisions designed to prevent groups of companies buying and selling companies in order to make use of capital losses suffered by another company or group.

The first set of provisions, introduced in 1993 and described at **12.25** below, applies to prevent 'loss buying' where a group of companies with unrealised gains would acquire a company with realised or unrealised losses. The assets in question would then be transferred to the new group company at no gain/no loss as in **12.4** above, and the gain would then realised by that company, thus enabling the losses to be utilised against the gain. The provisions now operate by restricting the deduction of losses accruing to a company before the time it becomes a member of a group.

These provisions were supplemented in 1998 by provisions countering 'gain buying', where a group of companies with unrealised capital losses would acquire a company with a realised gain. The provisions were repealed on the introduction of the third set of provisions.

The third set of provisions was introduced in *FA 2006* as part of a package of anti-avoidance provisions relating to capital losses of companies (see **11.3** and **11.4** CAPITAL GAINS). The provisions restrict the use of losses in both loss buying and gain buying situations where there is a change of ownership of a company as a result of arrangements with a tax avoidance purpose and are described below. The provisions apply in priority to the original loss buying provisions and replace the original gain buying provisions, which are repealed. The provisions are wide in scope and can apply in certain cases where there is no group of companies involved (see (c) below).The stated intention of the provisions is to ensure that relief for a company's capital losses should only be available against its own capital gains or those of companies that were under the same economic ownership both when the capital loss was realised and when the loss is used to reduce other gains. (Treasury Explanatory Notes to the Finance Bill 2006).

Simon's Taxes. See D2.4.

Tax avoidance schemes

[12.21] The provisions described below to restrict loss buying and gain buying apply where:

(A) there is a 'qualifying change of ownership' of a company (the '*relevant company*'); and
(B) the change occurs directly or indirectly in consequence of, or otherwise in connection with, any 'arrangements' the main purpose, or one of the main purposes, of which is to secure a 'tax advantage'.

For this purpose, there is a '*qualifying change of ownership*' of a company if any of the following occur.

(a) The company joins a group of companies. Whether a company is a member of a group is determined as in **12.2** above except that nothing in *TCGA 1992, s 170(10)* or *(10A)* is treated as preventing all the companies of one group from being regarded as joining another group when the principal company of the first group becomes a member of the other group at any time unless:
   (i) the same persons own the 'shares' of the principal company of the first group immediately before that time and the shares of the principal company of the other group immediately after that time;
   (ii) the principal company of the other group was not the principal company of any group immediately before that time; and
   (iii) immediately after that time the principal company of the other group had assets consisting entirely (or almost entirely) of shares of the principal company of the first group.

   References above to '*shares*' of a company are to the shares comprised in the company's issued share capital.
(b) The company ceases to be a member of a group.
(c) The company becomes subject to different control, i.e. one or more of the following occur:
   (i) a person who did not previously have control (within *CTA 2010, s 450*) of the company (whether alone or together with one or more others) comes to have control;
   (ii) a person who previously had control of the company alone comes to have control of the company together with one or more others; or
   (iii) a person ceases to have control of the company (whether the person had control alone or together with one or more others).

   A company is not, however, treated as becoming subject to different control where it joins a group of companies in circumstances in which (a)(i)–(iii) above apply or where, although there is a change in the direct ownership of the company, it continues to be a 75% subsidiary of the same company.

'*Arrangements*' include any agreement, understanding, scheme, transaction or series of transactions, whether or not legally enforceable.

'*Tax advantage*' means relief or increased relief from, or repayment or increased repayment of, corporation tax or the avoidance or reduction of a charge or assessment to corporation tax or the avoidance of a possible assessment to corporation tax.

[*TCGA 1992, ss 184A(1)(4), 184B(1)(4), 184C, 184D, 288(1)*].

For HMRC's views on the application of the terms 'arrangements', 'tax advantage' and 'main purpose', see **11.4** CAPITAL GAINS and HMRC Capital Gains Manual CG47024–47029. For HMRC's views generally, see HMRC Capital Gains Manual CG47020–47338.

Loss buying

[12.22] The loss buying provisions apply where conditions (A) and (B) above are met and the tax advantage under the arrangements involves the deduction from any chargeable gains of a loss (a '*qualifying loss*') accruing to the relevant company on a disposal of a 'pre-change asset' (see below).

In these circumstances, the qualifying loss is not deductible from a company's chargeable gains.

It is immaterial whether the loss accrues before, after or at the time of the qualifying change of ownership, whether the loss accrues at a time when there are no gains from which it could be deducted, whether the tax advantage also involves something other than the deduction of a qualifying loss or whether the advantage would be secured for the company to which the loss accrues or any other company.

[*TCGA 1992, s 184A(1)(2)(5)*].

> *Example*
>
> A Ltd is a company with realised by unrelieved capital losses. It has an issued share capital of 600 shares.
>
> A Ltd issues 400 new shares with limited rights to X. The original shareholders sell their shares in A Ltd to group B, but because of the holding of X, A Ltd does not become a member of the B group.
>
> The B group has just acquired assets that are expected to rise in value. The assets are transferred at cost to A Ltd in the expectation that when the assets are sold the gains arising will be reduced by the losses in A Ltd.
>
> The issue of shares with limited rights and the sale of the remaining shares to the B group is an arrangement designed to obtain a tax advantage. The loss is a qualifying loss and therefore cannot be deducted from the post-change gains.

Gain buying

[12.23] The gain buying provisions apply where conditions (A) and (B) above are met and the tax advantage under the arrangements involves the deduction of a loss from a gain (a '*qualifying gain*') accruing to the relevant company or any other company of a pre-change asset. In these circumstances, only a loss arising on a disposal before 21 March 2007 of a pre-change asset can be deducted from a qualifying gain.

It is immaterial whether the gain accrues before, after or at the time of the qualifying change of ownership, whether the gain accrues at a time when there are no losses which could be deducted from it, whether the tax advantage also involves something other than the deduction of a loss from a qualifying gain or whether the advantage would be secured for the company to which the gain accrues or any other company. [*TCGA 1992, s 184B(1)(2)(5)*].

For HMRC examples of the operation of the provisions, see HMRC Guidance at CG47020 onwards.

Pre-change assets

[12.24] For the purposes of the above provisions, a '*pre-change asset*' is an asset held by the relevant company before the qualifying change of ownership occurs.

An asset ceases to be a pre-change asset on disposal by a company other than the relevant company if, after the qualifying change of ownership, it has been disposed of otherwise than by an intra-group no gain/no loss transfer within **12.4** above. If the company making the latter disposal retains an interest in or over the asset, that interest continues to be a pre-change asset.

If the relevant company or any other company holds an asset ('*the new asset*') at or after the time of the qualifying change of ownership, the value of which derives in whole or in part from a pre-change asset, the new asset is also treated as a pre-change asset provided that the company concerned did not acquire the asset as a result of a transfer other than an intra-group no gain/no loss transfer. For this purpose, the cases in which the value of an asset is derived from another asset include any case where assets have been merged or divided or have changed their nature and where rights or interests in or over assets have been created or extinguished.

Where a pre-change asset is the 'old asset' for the purposes of *TCGA 1992, s 116*, (reorganisation of share capital involving qualifying corporate bonds (see Tolley's Capital Gains Tax)) the 'new asset' under that section is also a pre-change asset. Where a pre-change asset is the 'original shares' for the purposes of *TCGA 1992, ss 127–131* (reorganisation of share capital — see Tolley's Capital Gains Tax under Shares and Securities), the 'new holding' under those provisions is also a pre-change asset.

Where one of the deferral provisions listed below applies to defer a gain on the disposal of a pre-change asset, so much of any gain or loss accruing on a subsequent occasion as accrues in consequence of the application of the deferral provision is treated as a gain or loss on the disposal of a pre-change asset. The provisions are:

- *TCGA 1992, s 139* (reconstruction involving transfer of business — see **62.15** REORGANISATIONS AND RECONSTRUCTIONS);
- *TCGA 1992, s 140* (transfer of assets to non-resident company — see **11.16** CAPITAL GAINS);
- *TCGA 1992, s 140A* (transfer or division of UK business between companies in different EC member states — see **11.18** CAPITAL GAINS);
- *TCGA 1992, s 140E* (cross-border merger leaving assets within UK tax charge);
- *TCGA 1992, ss 152, 153* (rollover relief on the replacement of business assets — see **12.8** CAPITAL GAINS — GROUPS); and
- *TCGA 1992, s 187* (postponement of charge on deemed disposal on company ceasing to be UK resident before 1 January 2020 — see **64.9** RESIDENCE).

If a pre-change asset is transferred by the relevant company to another company directly or indirectly in consequence of, or in connection with the arrangements in (A) above, and any of *TCGA 1992, ss 139, 140A* or *140E* apply to the transfer, the asset is a pre-change asset in the hands of the transferee company. The above provisions for determining when an asset ceases to be a pre-change asset then apply as if the transferee company were the relevant company.

Pooled assets

Special identification rules apply where a pre-change asset (whether held by the relevant company or, as a consequence of an intra-group no gain/no loss transfer, by another company) consists of a 'section 104 holding' or '1982 holding' (see Tolley's Capital Gains Tax under Shares and securities — identification rules) of shares, securities or other assets dealt in without identifying the particular asset disposed of or acquired.

Such a holding (a '*pre-change pooled asset*') cannot be added to as a result of any disposal or acquisition taking place after the qualifying change of ownership. Any shares etc. that would otherwise be added to the pre-change pooled asset instead form or are added to a separate *s 104* holding (the '*other pooled asset*').

Shares etc. of the same class as those comprised in the other pooled asset which are disposed of at or after the time of the qualifying change of ownership are identified:

- first with shares etc. forming part of the other pooled asset;
- next with shares etc. forming part of the pre-change pooled asset; and
- finally, in accordance with the normal identification rules (see Tolley's Capital Gains Tax under Shares and securities — identification rules).

These identification rules apply even if some or all of the assets disposed of are separately identified by the disposal or by a transfer or delivery giving effect to it. Shares etc. disposed of by a company in one capacity are not identified with shares etc. which are held, or which can only be disposed of, in some other capacity. Shares or securities of a company are not treated as being of the same class unless they are so treated by the practice of a recognised stock exchange or would be if dealt with on such an exchange.

[*TCGA 1992, ss 184A(3), 184B(3), 184E, 184F*].

Restriction on set-off of pre-entry losses where a company joins a group

[12.25] Where the loss buying provisions at **12.19** above do not apply, *TCGA 1992, Sch 7A* restricts the deduction of allowable losses ('pre-entry losses') which accrue to a company before the time it becomes a member of a group of companies (the '*relevant group*'). The restriction is described in detail at **12.26–12.30** below.

The restriction does not apply where the loss buying provisions at **12.19** above apply.

[*TCGA 1992, s 177A, Sch 7A para 1(1)*].

Before 19 July 2011, the provisions also applied to losses accruing to a company after the time at which it became a member of a group on assets held by it at that time. The restrictions on the use of such losses were removed by *FA 2011* as they are now considered unnecessary because of *TCGA 1992, s 184A* (see **12.19** above). The restrictions do, however, continue to apply to such losses realised before 19 July 2011 as if they had accrued immediately before the company became a member of the group. See the 2016/17 or earlier edition of this work for details.

Definitions

[12.26] A '*pre-entry loss*', in relation to a company, means any allowable loss that accrued to it at a time before it became a member of the relevant group. [*TCGA 1992, Sch 7A para 1(2)*].

If:

(a) the principal company of a group of companies ('*the first group*') has at any time become a member of another group ('*the second group*') so that the two groups are treated as the same under *TCGA 1992, s 170(10)* or *(10A)* (see **12.2** above); and
(b) the second group, together in pursuance of *TCGA 1992, s 170(10)* or *(10A)* with the first group, is the relevant group,

then, except where the circumstances are as listed below, the members of the first group are treated for the purposes of *Sch 7A* as having become members of the relevant group at that time, and not by virtue of *TCGA 1992, s 170(10)* or *(10A)* at the times when they became members of the first group. The circumstances are where:

(1) the persons who immediately before the time when the principal company of the first group became a member of the second group owned the shares comprised in the issued share capital of the principal company of the first group are the same as the persons who, immediately after that time, owned the shares comprised in the issued share capital of the principal company of the relevant group; and
(2) the company which is the principal company of the relevant group immediately after that time
   (i) was not the principal company of any group immediately before that time; and
   (ii) immediately after that time had assets consisting entirely, or almost entirely, of shares comprised in the issued share capital of the principal company of the first group.

[*TCGA 1992, Sch 7A para 1(6)(7)*].

For discussion of *Sch 7A para 1(6)(7)* see *Five Oaks Properties Ltd v HMRC (and related appeals)* (Sp C 563), [2006] SSCD 769, *HMRC v Prizedome Ltd; HMRC v Limitgood Ltd* CA, [2009] STC 980 and *ANO (No 1) Ltd v HMRC* FTT, [2019] SFTD 1147.

Where an allowable loss accrues to a company under *TCGA 1992, s 116(10)(b)* (gain or loss on shares exchanged on reorganisation, conversion or reconstruction for qualifying corporate bonds to crystallise when bonds sold), that loss is deemed to accrue at the time of the reorganisation etc. for the purposes of deciding whether a loss accrues before a company becomes a member of the relevant group. [*TCGA 1992, Sch 7A para 1(9)*]. Likewise, the annual deemed disposals of unit trust etc. holdings of a life assurance company's long-term insurance fund under *TCGA 1992, s 212* are deemed to occur for this purpose without regard to the 'spreading' provisions of *TCGA 1992, s 213*. [*TCGA 1992, Sch 7A para 1(10)*].

Restrictions on the deduction of pre-entry losses

[12.27] In the calculation of the amount to be included in respect of chargeable gains in any company's total profits for any accounting period:

(a) if in that period there is any chargeable gain from which the whole or any part of any pre-entry loss accruing in that period is deductible in accordance with the provisions in **12.28** below, the loss or, as the case may be, that part of it is deducted from that gain;
(b) if, after all the deductions in (a) above have been made, there is in that period any chargeable gain from which the whole or any part of any pre-entry loss carried forward from a previous accounting period is deductible in accordance with the provisions in **12.28**, the loss or, as the case may be, that part of it is deducted from that gain;
(c) the total of chargeable gains (if any) remaining after all the deductions in (a) or (b) above is subject to deductions in accordance with *TCGA 1992, s 2A(1)* (previously *TCGA 1992, s 8(1)*; chargeable gains less allowable losses of company to be included in chargeable profits; see **11.2** CAPITAL GAINS) in respect of any allowable losses that are not pre-entry losses; and
(d) any pre-entry loss which has not been the subject of a deduction under (a) or (b) above (as well as any other losses falling to be carried forward under *section 2A(1)*) are carried forward to the following accounting period of that company.

[*TCGA 1992, Sch 7A para 6(1); FA 2019, Sch 1 para 91; FA 2020, Sch 4 para 18(2)(3)*].

Further restrictions on the deduction of pre-entry losses may apply for accounting periods beginning on or after 1 April 2020 (subject to transitional rules for accounting periods straddling that date (see **51.13** LOSSES under 'Deductions from chargeable gains')). Where the company's chargeable gains for the period exceed the amount of allowable losses arising in the period (including any pre-entry losses deductible under (a) above):

(1) deductions under (b) above cannot exceed the total of:
    (i) the amount of carried-forward pre-entry losses that would be so deductible on the assumption that such losses were subject to the restriction on deduction of carried-forward losses at **51.13** LOSSES; and
    (ii) the amount of other carried-forward losses that would be deductible from gains in the period on the same assumption;
(2) deductions under (c) above cannot exceed the difference (if any) between the total in (1) above and the pre-entry losses actually deducted under (b) above.

[*TCGA 1992, Sch 7A para 6(1A)–(1C); FA 2020, Sch 4 paras 18, 42–46*].

Subject to (a)–(d) above, any question as to which or what part of any pre-entry loss has been deducted from any particular chargeable gain is decided in accordance with such elections as may be made by the company to which the loss accrued. An election must be made by notice to HMRC before the end of the period of two years beginning with the end of the company's accounting period in which the gain in question accrued. [*TCGA 1992, Sch 7A para 6(2)(3)*].

For the purposes of *Sch 7A* where any matter falls to be determined under the above provisions by reference to an election but no election is made, it is assumed, so far as consistent with any elections that have been made that losses are set against gains in the order in which the losses accrued, and that the gains against which they are set are also determined according to the order in which they accrued with losses being set against earlier gains before they are set against later ones. [*TCGA 1992, Sch 7A para 6(4)*].

Gains from which pre-entry losses are to be deductible

[12.28] A pre-entry loss that accrued to a company before it became a member of the relevant group is deductible from a chargeable gain accruing to that company if the gain is one accruing:

(a) on a disposal made by that company before the date on which it became a member of the relevant group ('*the entry date*');

(b) on the disposal of an asset which was held by that company immediately before the entry date; or

(c) on the disposal of any asset which:
  (i) was acquired on or after the entry date by the company to whom the loss accrued ('company A') or a company which, at the time of the acquisition, was a group company of company A (i.e. a member of the same group as company A), from a person who was not a member of the relevant group at the time of the acquisition; and
  (ii) since its acquisition from that person has not been used or held for any purposes other than those of a trade or business which was being carried on by company A immediately before the entry date and which continued to be carried on by company A, or a company which, when it carried on the trade or business, was a group company of company A, until the disposal.

Where the company subsequently becomes a member of another group, the above provision continues to apply to any loss which accrued before the company joined the relevant group by reference to the date it joined the relevant group (and does not apply separately to the loss by reason of it being a pre-entry loss in relation to the company becoming a member of the second group).

[*TCGA 1992, Sch 7A para 7(1)–(1C)*].

Where two or more companies become members of the relevant group at the same time and those companies were all members of the same group of companies immediately before they became members of the relevant group, then:

(I) an asset is treated for the purposes of (b) above as held, immediately before it became a member of the relevant group, by the company to which the pre-entry loss in question accrued if that company is one of those companies and the asset was in fact so held by another of those companies; and

(II) the acquisition of an asset is treated for the purposes of (c) above as an acquisition by the company to which the pre-entry loss in question accrued if that company is one of those companies and the asset was in fact acquired (whether before or after they became members of the relevant group) by another of those companies.

[*TCGA 1992, Sch 7A para 7(3)*].

An asset is not treated as a '*pre-entry asset*' (i.e. as held by a company immediately before the entry date) if the company which held the asset on the entry date is not the company making the disposal and since the entry date the asset has been disposed of in circumstances in which *TCGA 1992, s 171* (intra-group transfers at no gain/no loss — see **12.4** above) does not apply, except where the company making the disposal retains an interest in or over the asset (when the interest is treated as a pre-entry asset).

An asset ('*the second asset*') which derives wholly or partly its value from another asset ('*the first asset*') acquired or held by a company at any time, is treated as the same asset if the second asset is held subsequently by the same company, or by any company which is or has been a member of the same group of companies as that company (e.g. a freehold derived from a leasehold where the lessee acquires the reversion). Where this treatment applies, whether under this provision or otherwise, the second asset is treated as a pre-entry asset in relation to a company if the first asset would have been.

[*TCGA 1992, Sch 7A para 7(4)–(4C)*].

Subject to *Sch 7A para 7(6)* below, where a gain accrues on the disposal of the whole or any part of:

(1) any asset treated as a single asset but comprising assets only some of which were held at the time mentioned in (b) above; or

(2) an asset which is treated as held at that time by virtue of a provision requiring an asset which was not held at that time to be treated as the same as an asset which was so held (see **12.26** above),

a pre-entry loss is deductible under (b) above from the amount of that gain to the extent only of such proportion of that gain as is attributable to assets held at that time or, as the case may be, represents the gain that would have accrued on the asset so held. [*TCGA 1992, Sch 7A para 7(5)*].

Where:

(A) a chargeable gain accrues under *TCGA 1992, s 116(10)* on the disposal of a qualifying corporate bond which has been exchanged for shares etc. (see **12.26** above);

(B) that bond was not held as required by (b) above at the time mentioned in (b); and

(C) the whole or any part of the asset which is the 'old asset' for the purposes of *TCGA 1992, s 116* was so held, the question whether that gain is one accruing on the disposal of an asset, the whole or any part of which was held by a particular company at that time, is determined for the purposes of *Sch 7A para 7* as if the bond were deemed to have been so held to the same extent as the old asset. [*TCGA 1992, Sch 7A para 7(6)*].

Change of a company's nature

[12.29] If:

(a) within any period of three years, a company becomes a member of a group of companies and there is (either earlier or later in that period, or at the same time) 'a major change in the nature or conduct of a trade or business' carried on by that company immediately before it became a member of that group, or

(b) at any time the scale of the activities in a trade or business carried on by a company has become small or negligible, and before any considerable revival of the trade or business, that company becomes a member of a group of companies,

the trade or business carried on before that change, or which has become small or negligible, is disregarded for the purposes of **12.28**(c) above in relation to any time before the company became a member of the group in question.

'*A major change in the conduct of a trade or business*' includes a reference to a major change in services or facilities provided or a major change in customers or, in the case of a company with investment business, a major change in the nature of investments held. Regard will also be had to appropriate changes in other factors such as the location of the company's business premises, the identity of the company's suppliers, management or staff, the company's methods of manufacture, or the company's pricing or purchasing policies to the extent that these factors indicate that a major change has occurred. Efficiency changes and technological advancements would not in themselves indicate that a major change in the nature or conduct of a trade or business has occurred.

HMRC will compare any two points in three years which include the date of change of ownership of the company. This applies even if the change is the result of a gradual process which began outside the period of three years mentioned in (a) above. HMRC take note of both qualitative and quantitative issues as discussed in the cases *Willis v Peeters Picture Frames Ltd* CA (NI) 1982, 56 TC 436 and *Purchase v Tesco Stores Ltd* Ch D 1984, 58 TC 46 respectively (HMRC Statement of Practice 10/91).

Where the operation of the above provisions depends on circumstances or events at a time after the company becomes a member of any group of companies (but not more than three years after), an assessment to give effect to the provisions may be made within six years from that time or the latest such time.

[*TCGA 1992, Sch 7A para 8*].

Miscellaneous

[12.30] Where, but for an election under *TCGA 1992, s 161(3)* (appropriation of asset to trading stock), there would be deemed to have been a disposal at any time by a company of an asset the amount by which the market value of it may be treated as increased under the election does not include the amount of any pre-entry loss that would have accrued on that disposal, and *Sch 7A* has effect as if the pre-entry loss of the last mentioned amount had accrued to the company at that time. [*TCGA 1992, Sch 7A para 10*].

The provisions of *Sch 7A* are prevented from applying where a loss arises, or a company joins a group, as a result of any enactment under which transfers of property etc. are made from a statutory body, a subsidiary of such a body or a company wholly owned by the Crown. [*TCGA 1992, Sch 7A para 11*]. Note, however, that with effect for appropriations of assets to trading stock made on or after 8 March 2017, the election is not permitted where appropriation at market value would give rise to an allowable loss. See **69.63** TRADING INCOME — DEDUCTIONS.

For the purposes of *Sch 7A*, and without prejudice to the provisions in *Sch 7A para 11* above, where:

(a) a company which is a member of a group of companies becomes at any time a member of another group of companies as the result of a disposal of shares in or other securities of that company or any other company; and

(b) that disposal is one within the no gain/no loss provisions,

Sch 7A has effect in relation to the losses that accrued to that company before that time and the assets held by that company at that time as if any time when it was a member of the first group were included in the period during which it is treated as having been a member of the second group. [*TCGA 1992, Sch 7A para 12*].

Key points on capital gains — groups

[12.31] Points to consider are as follows.

- When assessing the position of a chargeable gains group, the status of overseas entities can be important. In particular, consider whether such entities are likely to be respected as companies and whether ownership interests in those entities will be treated as ordinary share capital.
- Bear in mind the priority rules where transactions have more than one potential interpretation. For example, a reorganisation under *TCGA 1992, s 135* will take priority over the no-gain/no-loss rules in *s 171*.
- If reliance is to be placed on relief under *TCGA 1992, s 171A*, ensure that an election is made on time.

- Where a company is to rely upon the use of losses, ensure that the losses have been identified and their availability for use analysed before they are needed.
- Where anti-avoidance provisions are potentially in point (for example in relation to capital losses), the taxpayer should consider taking advice to limit potential penalties.
- If roll-over relief is to be claimed on the replacement of business assets, ensure that the transactions take place within the time scales required by the legislation and claims are submitted by the parties on time.
- Consider the potential for secondary chargeable gains liabilities. It may be prudent to consider the need for indemnities if external investors are involved or all or part of a business is to be sold.
- Remember that degrouping charges for the purposes of corporation tax on chargeable gains can crystallise losses as well as gains.
- Bear in mind that all degrouping charges are not the same. Where the substantial shareholding exemption applies, the timing of the deemed disposal and reacquisition is altered to the time immediately before the time of the degrouping. Also, while the intangible fixed asset regime rules are similar to the capital gains provisions, the loan relationships and derivative contracts rules are different in some important respects, not least timing and the inability to realise a loss.

13

Capital Gains — Substantial Shareholding Exemption

Simon's Taxes. See D1.10.

Introduction to capital gains — substantial shareholding exemption

[13.1] Under the substantial shareholding exemption (or 'SSE'), a gain on a disposal by a company of shares is exempt (and a loss is not allowable) where, throughout a continuous 12-month period beginning not more than six years before the disposal, the company (the '*investing company*') held a 'substantial shareholding' (broadly, at least a **10%** interest) in the company (the '*investee company*') whose shares are the subject of the disposal. The exemption extends to assets related to shares (as in **13.5** below).

The investee company must be a trading company or the holding company of a trading group (or subgroup). Shares held by members of a worldwide group are aggregated in determining whether a company holds a substantial shareholding.

A specific additional exemption (see **13.7** below) applies where the investee company is not a trading company but the *investing company* is owned by qualifying institutional investors (as defined). In such a case a full or partial exemption may apply depending on the level of ownership by such investors, and the substantial shareholding condition may be met if the investing company's shareholding is below a 10% interest but cost more than £20 million.

[*TCGA 1992, s 192A, Sch 7AC; F(No 2)A 2017, ss 27, 28*].

See generally HMRC Capital Gains Manual, CG53000–53240.

Application of the exemptions under the SSE

[13.2] It should first be noted that where the disposal does not give rise to a chargeable gain (or an allowable loss) by virtue of some other enactment, then the exemptions described in this chapter are of no application.

Neither do they apply to a disposal which, by virtue of any chargeable gains enactment, is a 'no gain/no loss' disposal.

[*TCGA 1992, Sch 7AC para 6(1)*].

Definition of company and group

[13.3] For the purposes of the SSE provisions, a '*company*' is as defined at **12.2** CAPITAL GAINS — GROUPS.

A '*group of companies*' is also as defined at **12.2** but as if each reference there to '75%' were a reference to '51%'. Thus, subject to the detailed rules there, a '*group*' comprises a company and its 'effective 51% subsidiaries' (within *CTA 2010, s 1154*), and may include non-UK resident companies.

A '*holding company*' of a group is the principal company of the group (within the meaning given in **12.2**).

A '*subgroup*' is a number of companies that *would* form a group were it not for the fact that one of them (the '*holding company*' of the subgroup) is itself a 51% subsidiary.

Shares held by members of a worldwide group are aggregated in determining whether a company holds a substantial shareholding — see further **13.9** below.

[*TCGA 1992, Sch 7AC para 26*].

The exemptions

Exemptions for shares — the main SSE

[13.4] A gain accruing to a company (the '*investing company*') on a disposal of shares (or an 'interest in shares' — see **13.20** below) in another company (the '*investee company*') is not a chargeable gain if:

(a) the investing company held a 'substantial shareholding' (see **13.9** below) in the investee company throughout any continuous period of twelve months beginning not more than six years prior to the disposal (see **13.10** below); and
(b) the requirements at **13.11** below are met in relation to the investee company.

See also the anti-avoidance rule at **13.8** below.

[*TCGA 1992, Sch 7AC paras 1, 7, 28; F(No 2)A 2017, s 27(2)(3)(6)*].

By virtue of *TCGA 1992, s 16(2)* (see **11.3 CAPITAL GAINS**), a loss on a disposal is not an allowable loss if a gain on that disposal would not have been a chargeable gain.

The nature of the condition at (a) above is such that part disposals out of a once-substantial shareholding can continue to attract the exemption for up to five years after the shareholding has ceased to be substantial (i.e. has dropped below the 10% threshold).

The exemption is available even where the shares disposed of are not the shares that meet the substantial shareholding requirement at (a) above. If (a) above is met in relation to ordinary shares (and (b) is also met), a disposal of a holding of, say, fixed-rate preference shares in the investee company will qualify for the exemption, irrespective of the size and duration of that holding. (HMRC Capital Gains Manual, CG53155).

The exemption is automatic and does not require the making of a claim.

Exemption for assets related to shares

[13.5] *Schedule 7AC para 2* includes a subsidiary exemption, which allows the SSE to be extended to cover assets which are 'related to shares', such as share options or convertible securities, where the main exemption conditions are met.

A gain accruing to a company (company A) on a disposal of an asset 'related to shares' in another company (company B) is not a chargeable gain (and a loss is not an allowable loss) if:

(i) at the time of the disposal, company A holds shares (or an 'interest in shares' — see **13.20** below) in company B; and
(ii) any gain on a disposal at that time of those shares (or that interest) would be exempt under **13.4** above (disregarding **13.2** above).

This exemption also applies where:

(a) the shares etc. are held not by company A itself but by another member of a group of companies (see **13.3** above) of which company A is a member; and
(b) any gain on a disposal at that time of those shares etc., on the assumption that they were held by company A, would be exempt under **13.4** above (disregarding **13.2** above).

Where assets of a company are vested in a liquidator, the above applies as if they were vested in the company and as if the acts of the liquidator were the acts of the company (disposals by the company to the liquidator, and *vice versa*, being disregarded).

See also the anti-avoidance rule at **13.8** below.

[*TCGA 1992, Sch 7AC paras 2, 6(2)*].

The exemption is automatic and does not require the making of a claim.

For this purpose, an asset is '*related to shares*' in a company if it is:

(1) an option to acquire or dispose of shares (or an 'interest in shares' — see **13.20** below) in that company; or
(2) (broadly) a security that is convertible or exchangeable into shares (or an interest in shares) in that company, or into an option within (1) above, or into another security within this definition; or
(3) an option to acquire or dispose of a security within (2) above (or an interest in any such security); or
(4) an interest in, or option over, any option or security within (1)–(3) above; or
(5) an interest in, or option over, any interest or option within (4) above (or an interest in, or option over, any interest or option within this sub-paragraph).

As regards (2) above, a convertible or exchangeable security is not an asset related to shares if, when the conversion etc. rights were granted, there was no more than a negligible likelihood that they would be exercised to any significant extent. It is therefore not possible to bring a security within the scope of the exemption by attaching some spurious or extremely remote rights to convertibility in the event of some unlikely occurrence. (HMRC Capital Gains Manual, CG53010).

Certain securities, options etc. are outside the scope of corporation tax on chargeable gains, and thus outside the exemptions in this chapter, due to their falling within the LOAN RELATIONSHIPS (**49**) or DERIVATIVE CONTRACTS (**27**) rules. (HMRC Capital Gains Manual, CG53010).

An '*interest*' in a security or option has a similar meaning to an 'interest in shares' at **13.20** below.

[*TCGA 1992, Sch 7AC para 30*].

Exemption where main conditions previously met

[13.6] A further possibility of exemption under the SSE is provided under *Sch 7AC para 3* where the exemption at either **13.4** or **13.5** above does not apply because some of the conditions were not satisfied at the time of the disposal even though they had been satisfied at a time in the two years immediately preceding the disposal.

If the conditions at either **13.4** or **13.5** above are not fully met (with the result that a chargeable gain or allowable loss would arise on the disposal), then a gain accruing to a company (company A) on a disposal of shares (or an interest in shares — see **13.20** below), or an asset 'related to shares' (see **13.5** above), in another company (company B) is still not a chargeable gain (and a loss is not an allowable loss) where *all* of the following conditions *are* met:

(a) At the time of disposal, company A had held a 'substantial shareholding' (see **13.9** below) in company B throughout any continuous period of 12 months beginning not more than six years prior to the disposal (see also **13.10** below).

(b) At the time of disposal, either company A is UK-resident or any chargeable gain accruing to it on the disposal would form part of its corporation tax profits by virtue of *TCGA 1992, s 2B(3)(4)* (non-resident companies — see **11.1**(a)–(c) CAPITAL GAINS) or, for disposals before 6 April 2019, *TCGA 1992, s 10B* (trade carried on through UK permanent establishment — see **64.6** RESIDENCE).

(c) There was a time within the two years ending with the disposal (the '*relevant period*') when a gain on a hypothetical disposal by:
  - (i) company A; or
  - (ii) a company that at any time in the relevant period was a member of the same group (see **13.3** above) as company A,

  being a disposal of shares (or an interest in shares) in company B that the disposing company then held, would have been exempt under **13.4** above (disregarding **13.2** above, and see also below).

(d) If, at the time of disposal, the requirements at **13.11** below as to the investee company are not met in relation to company B, there was a time within the relevant period (as defined at (c) above) when company B was controlled by:
  - (i) company A; or
  - (ii) company A together with any persons connected with it (within *TCGA 1992, s 286* — see **19.4** CONNECTED PERSONS); or
  - (iii) a company that at any time in the relevant period was a member of the same group (see **13.3** above) as company A; or
  - (iv) any such company together with persons connected with it.

'Control' is to be construed in accordance with *CTA 2010, ss 450, 451* — see **16.6** CLOSE COMPANIES.

For the purpose only of determining the 'relevant period' for the purposes of (c) or (d) above, the time of disposal is taken as the time the contract is made, notwithstanding that the contract may be conditional. In determining whether the gain on the hypothetical disposal in (c) above would have attracted the exemption at **13.4** above, the requirements at **13.11**(b) below as to the status of the investee company immediately after the time of disposal are taken to be satisfied.

See also the anti-avoidance rule at **13.8** below.

[*TCGA 1992, s 288(1), Sch 7AC paras 3(1)–(4)(7)(8), 6(2); F(No 2)A 2017, s 27(2)(6); FA 2019, Sch 1 paras 92, 120*].

Thus, for example, where the investee company ceases to trade on being put into liquidation, so that it can no longer meet the requirements at **13.11** below, disposals by the investing company (including capital distributions) can continue to attract the exemption for a further two years.

Anti-avoidance

It should be noted, however, that the above exemption also contains an anti-avoidance element in that if, for example, the investee company's trade is transferred elsewhere (within a group, for instance) and the conditions above are all met, a loss on a disposal by the investing company within the two years following the transfer will not be an allowable loss.

A further anti-avoidance measure applies as follows to prevent the exemption from applying to a gain (but not a loss) where value has been transferred into the investee company within the said two-year period and a claim made for gift relief. Otherwise it would be possible to put a valuable asset into a company, which had ceased trading, under the protection of a gift relief hold-over claim, then dispose of the shares and claim no chargeable gain arises under the SSE rules.

Thus, where the above exemption would otherwise apply but:

(1) immediately before the disposal by company A, company B holds an asset, and

(2) the allowable expenditure attributable to that asset has been reduced by a claim for gifts hold-over relief under *TCGA 1992, s 165* (see Tolley's Capital Gains Tax under Hold-Over Reliefs) on an earlier disposal of the asset within the relevant period (as defined above),

a gain on the disposal by company A does not attract the exemption *but* a loss on the disposal is not an allowable loss. (Where assets of company B are vested in a liquidator, (1) above applies as if they were vested in the company.)

[*TCGA 1992, Sch 7AC para 3(5)(6)*].

The exemption is automatic and does not require the making of a claim.

Example

Swallow Ltd acquired 1,500 shares in Summer Ltd in April 1999. Swallow Ltd holds no other investments in any company, has been a trading company throughout its existence, and is not a member of a group. Summer Ltd has 10,000 issued shares and has been a trading company since its formation. Swallow Ltd makes the following disposals of Summer Ltd shares.

31 May 2017	600 shares
30 April 2022	400 shares
30 June 2022	500 shares

The effect of the disposals for the purpose of corporation tax on chargeable gains is as follows:

31 May 2017 disposal

Swallow Ltd held at least 10% of the ordinary share capital of Summer Ltd throughout the six years prior to the disposal. The disposal is therefore part of a substantial shareholding and no chargeable gain or allowable loss arises on the disposal.

30 April 2022 disposal

Although Swallow did not hold at least 10% of the shares in Summer Ltd immediately before the disposal (the minimum holding being only 900 of 10,000 shares), there is a 12-month period beginning within six years prior to the disposal throughout which it did hold at least 10%. The period is 1 June 2016 to 31 May 2017. Accordingly, the substantial shareholding exemption applies and no chargeable gain or allowable loss arises on the disposal.

30 June 2022 disposal

Swallow Ltd holds only 5% of the share capital of Summer Ltd immediately before the disposal. In the six-year period prior to the disposal, from 1 July 2016 to 30 June 2022, the company held at least 10% of Summer Ltd's shares only from 1 July 2016 to 31 May 2017. This is not a continuous 12-month period beginning six years prior to the disposal, and therefore the substantial shareholding exemption will not apply. A gain on the disposal of 500 shares will be a chargeable gain, and a loss an allowable loss.

Exemption where investing company owned by qualifying institutional investors

[13.7] A full or partial exemption (see below) applies under the SSE in respect of a gain accruing to an investing company on the disposal of shares in an investee company, if the *investing company* is fully or partially owned by 'qualifying institutional investors' and if:

(a) the investing company held a substantial shareholding (as modified for this exemption) in the investee company throughout a period of 12 months beginning not more than six years prior to the disposal;
(b) the investee company does *not* meet the requirements at **13.11** below; and
(c) the investing company is not a 'disqualified listed company'.

This exemption gives relief to certain bodies which would be exempt from tax if they had owned shares in a non-trading investee company directly where such shares are held indirectly through an investing company. For this purpose, a '*qualifying institutional investor*' is any of the following:

(a) the trustee or manager of a registered pension scheme (other than an investment-regulated scheme within *FA 2004, Sch 29A*) or an overseas pension scheme (other than one which would be an investment-regulated scheme if it were a registered pension scheme);
(b) a company carrying on life assurance business within *FA 2012, s 56*, where immediately before the disposal, the company's shareholding in the investing company is part of the company's long-term business fixed capital (as defined by *FA 2012, s 137*);
(c) a person not liable for corporation tax or income tax because of sovereign immunity (sovereign wealth funds etc);
(d) a charity;
(e) an investment trust;
(f) an authorised investment fund (defined as in *SI 2006 No 964*) meeting the genuine diversity of ownership condition in *SI 2006 No 964, reg 9A*;

(g) the trustees of an exempt unauthorised unit trust meeting the genuine diversity of ownership condition.

The Treasury may amend the list by regulations.

A company is a '*disqualified listed company*' if any of its ordinary share capital is listed on a recognised stock exchange, it is not a qualifying institutional investor itself, and it is not a 'qualifying UK REIT'. A '*qualifying UK REIT*' for these purposes is a UK real estate investment trust (see **47.11** INVESTMENT TRUSTS) which is not treated as a close company because it is controlled by or on behalf of the Crown (*CTA 2010, s 443*), or is a close company only because it has an institutional investor (within *CTA 2010, s 528(4A)*) as a participator.

In determining the proportion of the investing company's ordinary shares owned by qualifying institutional investors, both direct and indirect holdings are taken into account, applying *CTA 2010, ss 1155–1157* with the following modifications. It is not possible to trace ownership through a disqualified listed company but it is possible to trace ownership through an exempt unauthorised unit trust (as per *SI 2013 No 2819*), which is treated as a body corporate for these purposes. Shares subject to a repurchase agreement or stock lending arrangements (see **13.10** below) are treated as owned by the original owner. Shares held by a partnership are treated as being owned by each partner in accordance with that partner's proportionate interest in the shares.

Amount of the exemption

The exemption applies in full i.e. no chargeable gain or allowable loss accrues to an investing company on the disposal of shares in an investee company, if qualifying institutional investors own 80% or more of the ordinary share capital of the investing company immediately before the disposal.

If qualifying institutional investors own at least 25% but less than 80% of the ordinary share capital of the investing company immediately before the disposal, the amount of the chargeable gain or loss is reduced by the percentage owned by such investors. For example, if two qualifying institutional investors together own 75% of the investing company, the latter's gain on disposing of a holding in the investee company is reduced by 75% i.e. the investing company pays tax on only 25% of the gain.

[*TCGA 1992, Sch 7AC paras 3A, 3B, 30A; F(No 2)A 2017, s 28(2)(5)(7)*].

General anti-avoidance and the SSE

[13.8] *Schedule 7AC para 5* excludes the application of the SSE where arrangements have been put in place from which the sole or main benefit is obtaining the exemption from chargeable gains.

Therefore none of the exemptions in **13.4–13.7** above are available where:

(a) an 'untaxed' gain accrues to an investing company (Company A) on a disposal of shares (or an interest in shares, see **13.20** below), or an asset related to shares (see **13.5** above), in another company (Company B);
(b) before the accrual of that gain, either:

(i) Company A acquired control of Company B, or the same person(s) acquired control of both companies; or

(ii) there was a 'significant change of trading activities affecting Company B' at a time when it was controlled by Company A or when both companies were controlled by the same person(s); and

(c) these circumstances occur in pursuance of arrangements (including any scheme, agreement or understanding, whether or not legally enforceable) from which the sole or main benefit that could be expected is that the gain would be exempt under any of **13.4–13.6** above.

For the above purposes:

(A) a gain is '*untaxed*' if it (or all but an insubstantial part of it) represents profits that have not been brought into account (in the UK or elsewhere) for the purposes of tax on profits for a period ending on or before the date of the disposal. Profits in respect of which an amount is apportioned to a UK resident company under the CONTROLLED FOREIGN COMPANIES (**21**) rules are brought into account for this purpose. '*Profits*' means income or gains (whether or not realised);

(B) 'control' is to be construed in accordance with *CTA 2010, ss 450, 451* — see **16.6** CLOSE COMPANIES; and

(C) there is a '*significant change of trading activities affecting Company B*' if:

(i) there is a 'major change in the nature or conduct of a trade' carried on by Company B or a '51% subsidiary' (within *CTA 2010, s 1154*) of Company B; or

(ii) there is a major change in the scale of the activities of a trade carried on by Company B or a 51% subsidiary; or

(iii) Company B or a 51% subsidiary begins to carry on a trade.

By virtue of *CTA 2010, s 672 et seq*, a '*major change in the nature or conduct of a trade*' includes a major change in the type of property dealt in or services or facilities provided, or in customers, outlets or markets. See **51.17** LOSSES.

[*TCGA 1992, s 288(1), Sch 7AC para 5; CTA 2010, ss 450, 451*].

HMRC expect cases where this anti-avoidance rule is in point to be unusual and infrequent. It is a question of fact as to whether a gain wholly (or wholly but for an insubstantial part — interpreted by HMRC as 20% or less) represents untaxed profits; this involves looking at how the consideration obtained for the disposal by Company A is derived from assets held directly or indirectly by Company B. Profits are not 'untaxed' if they are simply covered by a specific relief or if they represent dividends which are themselves paid out of taxed profits. If a gain represents both taxed and untaxed profits, it should be taken as first representing taxed profits, with only any remaining balance representing untaxed profits. (HMRC Statement of Practice SP 5/02).

'Substantial shareholding' requirement

Meaning of substantial shareholding

[13.9] For the purposes of these provisions, a company holds a '*substantial shareholding*' in another company if it holds shares (or 'interests in shares' — see **13.20** below) in that company by virtue of which:

(a) it holds **at least 10%** of the company's ordinary share capital;
(b) it is beneficially entitled to at least 10% of the profits available for distribution to equity holders of the company; and
(c) it would be beneficially entitled on a winding-up to at least 10% of the assets of the company available for distribution to equity holders.

CTA 2010, Pt 5 Ch 6 (s 157 et seq) applies, with suitable modifications, to define an 'equity holder' and to determine the profits or assets available for distribution (see **35.4**, GROUP RELIEF).

[*TCGA 1992, Sch 7AC para 8*].

Additionally, where qualifying institutional investors own at least 25% of the ordinary share capital of the investing company (see **13.7** above), the investing company also holds a substantial shareholding if it holds ordinary shares (or interests in ordinary shares) in the investee company that cost it at least £20 million (acquired in a single or over several acquisitions), whether representing a 10% interest or not. The shares (or any other shares in the investee company) must give the investing company beneficial entitlement to a percentage of profits and assets on a winding up at least equal to the percentage of ordinary shares held by the investing company, although this condition is treated as met if a shortfall is insignificant.

[*TCGA 1992, Sch 7AC para 8A; F(No 2)A 2017, s 28(3)(7)*].

For the purposes of deciding whether the 'substantial shareholding' test is satisfied, holdings of shares (and interests in shares) by members of the same group of companies (which may be a worldwide group — see **13.3** above) are aggregated. [*TCGA 1992, Sch 7AC para 9(1)*].

When a company goes into liquidation it loses beneficial interest of its assets as a result of those assets being vested in the liquidator. However, the SSE rules protect an investing company from this outcome (as far as the SSE rules are concerned) so that it can continue to satisfy the necessary conditions for exemption.

Therefore where assets of the investing company, or of a member of the same group as the investing company, are vested in a liquidator, they are treated for the purposes of the substantial shareholding requirement (and those of **13.14**, **13.15** below) as if they were vested in the company and as if the acts of the liquidator were the acts of the company (disposals by the company to the liquidator, and *vice versa*, being disregarded). [*TCGA 1992, Sch 7AC para 16*].

Insurance companies

Special rules apply in relation to assets of long-term insurance funds where the investing company is an insurance company, or in certain cases a 51% subsidiary of an insurance company, or a member of the same group as an insurance company. [*TCGA 1992, Sch 7AC paras 9(2), 17*].

Holding period

[13.10] As stated at 13.4(a) above, the investing company must have held a substantial shareholding in the investee company throughout a continuous period of twelve months beginning not more than six years prior to the disposal. Shares are treated as having been held for such a period if, for example, they were acquired at any time on 15 June 2020 and sold at any time on 14 June 2021; they do not have to be held on the anniversary of the acquisition. (HMRC Capital Gains Manual, CG53008).

With regard to the holding period, the following special rules apply.

No gain/no loss transfers

Where the investing company acquired any shares from another company by means of a 'no gain/no loss' transfer, i.e. under any chargeable gains enactment that states that a disposal is to be treated as made for such consideration that no gain or loss accrues, the period during which it is treated as holding those shares is extended to include the period during which the previous owner held them.

The period is further extended back through any series of no gain/no loss transfers by which the shares arrived in the hands of the present owner. The present owner is thus treated as having had the same entitlements, to shares and to any rights enjoyed by virtue of holding shares, as the company or companies by which they were held at any earlier time in the extended period.

These include any entitlements etc. arising from the aggregation rule for groups of companies in **13.9** above. These rules also cover 'interests in shares' (see **13.20** below), and the extension also covers any period during which the asset held by any of the previous companies concerned in the no gain/no loss series consisted of shares (or an interest in shares) from which the current shares (or interest) are 'derived'.

For the above purposes, any transfer which, by virtue of *TCGA 1992, s 171(3)*, is not treated as a no gain/no loss transfer (intra-group share exchanges, see **12.4** CAPITAL GAINS — GROUPS), and which would otherwise have been so, is treated as if it had been a no gain/no loss transfer. A transfer between non-UK resident group companies is treated as a no gain/no loss transfer even where the shares are not chargeable assets of the transferor company immediately before transfer or of the transferee company immediately after transfer if it would otherwise have been a no gain/no loss transfer within *TCGA 1992, s 171*.

Shares (or interests in shares) are '*derived*' from other shares (or interests) only where:

(a) a company becomes co-owner of shares previously owned by it alone, or *vice versa*;
(b) a company's interest in shares as co-owner changes (but co-ownership continues);
(c) a shareholding is treated by virtue of *TCGA 1992, s 127* (including its application by virtue of another enactment) as the same asset as another shareholding; or
(d) there is a sequence of two or more of the above occurrences.

[*TCGA 1992, Sch 7AC para 10; F(No 2)A 2017, s 27(4)(6)*].

Deemed disposals and reacquisitions

Where, under any corporation tax enactment, shares have been deemed to be disposed of and immediately reacquired by a company, the company is regarded as not having held the shares during any part of the holding period falling before the deemed disposal and reacquisition. This rule extends to 'interests in shares' (see **13.20** below) and to shares (or interests) from which the current shares (or interest) are 'derived' (as above).

[*TCGA 1992, Sch 7AC para 11*].

Sale and repurchase agreements (repos)

Where the company that holds shares transfers them under a repo (as defined), such that, by virtue of *FA 2007, Sch 13 para 6* or *TCGA 1992, s 263A* (see Tolley's Capital Gains Tax under Shares and Securities), the disposal falls to be disregarded, it is similarly disregarded for the purposes of the provisions in this chapter.

Thus, during the period covered by the repo, the ownership of the shares, and the entitlement to any rights attached to them, rests with the original owner and not the interim holder.

If, at any time during that period, the original owner, or a member of the same group as the original owner, becomes the *actual* holder of any of the shares transferred (or any shares directly or indirectly representing them), this rule ceases to have effect at that time in relation to the shares concerned.

[*TCGA 1992, Sch 7AC para 12*].

Stock lending arrangements

Rules identical to those above for repos apply where shares are transferred under a stock lending arrangement (as defined), such that, by virtue of *TCGA 1992, s 263B(2)* (see Tolley's Capital Gains Tax under Shares and Securities), the disposal falls to be disregarded. [*TCGA 1992, Sch 7AC para 13*].

Transfer of trading assets within a group

The period in which the investing company is treated as holding a substantial shareholding in the investee company is extended if the following conditions are met:

(1) immediately before the disposal the investing company holds a substantial shareholding in the investee company;
(2) an asset which, at the time of the disposal, is being used for the purposes of a trade carried on by the investee company was transferred to it by the investing company or another company;
(3) at the time of the transfer company the investee company, the investing company and, where relevant, the company transferring the asset were all members of the same group (as in **13.3** above); and

(4) the asset was previously used by a member of the group, other than the investee company, for the purposes of a trade carried on by it at a time when it was such a member.

Where these conditions are satisfied, the investing company is treated as having held the substantial shareholding at any time during the twelve months ending with the time of disposal when the asset was used as in (2) above if it did not otherwise hold a substantial shareholding at that time.

'Trade' in (2) and (4) includes oil and gas exploration and appraisal (within *CTA 2010, s 1134*).

[*TCGA 1992, Sch 7AC para 15A*].

The extended holding period provided by these provisions was held not to apply in a case where a stand-alone company created a new subsidiary and then hived-down its trade and assets before selling the share in the subsidiary (*M Group Holdings Ltd v HMRC* FTT, [2021] UKFTT 69 (TC), 2021 SWTI 1407). As the company, M Ltd, only owned the subsidiary, MCS Ltd, for a period of just under 11 months, it relied on the extension to the substantial shareholding exemption provided by the above provisions. HMRC argued that the extension did not apply here because it applied only to any period in which the assets were held and used for the purposes of a trade by a company that was at the time of such use 'a member of the group' (see (4) above). As there had been no group prior to the incorporation of MCS Ltd there could be no extended period of ownership. M Ltd argued that the requirement was only that the assets should have been used for the purposes of a trade prior to the transfer. The Tribunal was unable to determine any purpose pointing either way from the wording of the legislation but considered that the natural or ordinary meaning was the one put forward by HMRC. The judge acknowledged that this produced an 'oddity or arbitrariness' of the exemption applying depending on whether or not there has been a separate, possibly dormant, subsidiary for the whole 12 months. In the absence of an obvious intention behind the legislation, this arbitrariness was, however, insufficient to justify departing from the natural meaning. The Tribunal, therefore, dismissed the company's appeal.

Requirements for investee company

[13.11] The requirements to be met in relation to the investee company for the purposes of the exemption at **13.4** above are that:

(a) it must have been a 'qualifying company' (see below) throughout the period:
  (i) beginning with the start of the latest twelve-month period for which the substantial shareholding requirement (see **13.4**(a) above) was met; and
  (ii) ending with the time of the disposal; and

(b) if either the disposal is to a person connected with the investing company or if the substantial shareholding holding requirement is met because of the transfer of trading assets within the group provisions in **13.10** above, the investee company must be a 'qualifying company' immediately after the time of the disposal.

A '*qualifying company*' is a 'trading company' or the 'holding company' (as in **13.3** above) of a 'trading group' or 'trading subgroup' (see **13.12** below).

Where the disposal is made under a contract and, by virtue of *TCGA 1992, s 28* (see Tolley's Capital Gains Tax under Disposal), the time of disposal for tax purposes precedes the conveyance or transfer of the asset disposed of, the requirements at both (a) and (b) above must be met by reference to the time of the conveyance or transfer as well as the time of the disposal.

See also the position outlined at **13.6** with regard to the subsidiary exemptions where the condition at (b) above is not satisfied.

[*TCGA 1992, Sch 7AC para 19; F(No 2)A 2017, s 27(5)(6)*].

[13.12] For the purposes of this chapter, a '*trading subgroup*' is a 'subgroup' (as in **13.3** above), one or more of whose members carries on 'trading activities' and the activities of whose members, taken together, do not include to a 'substantial' extent activities other than 'trading activities'.

'*Trading activities*' are defined in relation to a subgroup as they are in relation to a group (for which see **13.12** above), with the appropriate modifications. [*TCGA 1992, Sch 7AC para 22*]. Thus intra-subgroup activities are disregarded in the same way as intra-group activities when determining whether there is a 'trading subgroup'. However, intra-group activities between a member of a subgroup and another group company that is not within the subgroup are not disregarded in considering the status of the subgroup.

See **13.16** below as regards the treatment of holdings in joint venture companies.

Share reorganisations etc.

Treatment of certain events as disposals

[13.13] Without the special rules below, the exemptions at **13.4–13.7** above would be of no relevance to any of the following events (in relation to shares held by the investing company in the investee company).

(a) A reorganisation of share capital, company take-over/reconstruction or conversion of securities which, by virtue of *TCGA 1992, s 127*, does not constitute a disposal (see Tolley's Capital Gains Tax under Shares and Securities), the 'new holding' standing in the shoes of the original shares.

(b) An event which would have been within (a) above but for the fact that the 'new asset' consists of a qualifying corporate bond and which, by virtue of *TCGA 1992, s 116(10)* (see Tolley's Capital Gains Tax under Qualifying Corporate Bonds), is not treated as a disposal.

(c) A tax-exempt distribution on a demerger which, by virtue of *TCGA 1992, s 192* (see **29.24** DISTRIBUTIONS), does not constitute a capital distribution.

To the extent that a gain would thereby be exempt (or a loss non-allowable) under **13.4–13.6** above, the enactment mentioned in (a), (b) or (c) above, whichever is relevant, is disapplied, so that an event in (a) or (b) is treated as a disposal, a distribution in (c) is treated as a capital distribution and the new shares or securities are normally treated as acquired at market value. Where this disapplication has effect, the provisions at **25.9** CORPORATE VENTURING SCHEME, where relevant, are modified accordingly.

[*TCGA 1992, Sch 7AC para 4*].

Example

A Ltd owns 35% of B Ltd. Both are trading companies. X plc intends to take over B Ltd; X plc offers all the shareholders in B Ltd three X plc shares for each B Ltd share that they own. As a result of this offer A Ltd will receive 10,500 X plc shares which have a market value of £126,000. A Ltd acquired the B Ltd shares for £3,500 in January 2000. Following the share exchange there is a total of 500,000 X plc shares in issue.

The take over above falls within the reorganisation provisions at *TCGA 1992, s 135* and thus *TCGA 1992, s 127* operates such that the shares in B Ltd will not be treated as being disposed of and the X plc shares will not be treated as being acquired — instead the B Ltd and X plc shares will be treated as the same asset with the X plc shares taking on the base cost of the B Ltd shares (of £3,500) and the original acquisition date (January 2000).

Thus A Ltd has a relief from tax at this point, which applies until the X plc shares are sold. However, if *TCGA 1992, ss 135/127* were disapplied, the disposal of the B Ltd shares would give rise to a chargeable gain, which would qualify for SSE under the exemptions at **13.4–13.6** above.

Therefore, under *TCGA 1992, Sch 7AC para 4*, the reorganisation provisions are not used and the disposal of the B Ltd shares is treated as giving rise to a chargeable gain, which is covered by the SSE. This means that A Ltd acquires the X plc shares on the day it receives them in exchange for the B Ltd shares, with a base cost of £126,000.

Effect of earlier company reconstruction etc.

[13.14] The following applies where:

(a) shares held by the investing company in the investee company were acquired as a result of either:
   (i) an exchange of securities within *TCGA 1992, s 135*; or
   (ii) a scheme of reconstruction within *TCGA 1992, s 136*; and

(b) *TCGA 1992, s 127* applied, such that the event was not treated as a disposal and the 'new holding' stood in the shoes of the original shares; and

(c) *TCGA 1992, s 127* did not fall to be disapplied by **13.13** above (because, for example, the conditions for the exemptions at **13.4–13.6** above were not satisfied or the event took place before 1 April 2002).

The question of whether, at any time *before* the event in (a)(i) or (ii) above, the substantial shareholding requirement at **13.9** above was met, or the requirements relating to the investee company at **13.11** above were met, is determined by reference to the shares held by the investing company at that time. This rule can apply more than once, i.e. where there has been more than one event within (a)(i) or (ii) above, and it can apply in combination with the rule at **13.15** below where there have been one or more transfers within that paragraph as well as one or more events within (a)(i) or (ii) above.

[*TCGA 1992, Sch 7AC paras 14, 25*].

Effect of earlier demerger

[13.15] The following applies where:

(a) shares held by the investing company in the investee company were acquired as a result of a transfer by a parent company of shares in its subsidiary; and
(b) the demerger provisions of *TCGA 1992, s 192* (see **29.24** DISTRIBUTIONS) applied, such that the transfer was not treated as a capital distribution and the transferred shares in the subsidiary fell to be treated as received as a result of a reorganisation of share capital and thus (by virtue of *TCGA 1992, s 127*) as standing in the shoes of the shares previously held in the parent company.

The question of whether, at any time *before* the transfer, the substantial shareholding requirement at **13.9** above was met, or the requirements relating to the investee company at **13.11** above were met, is determined by reference to the shares held by the investing company at that time. This rule can apply more than once, i.e. where there has been more than one such transfer, and it can apply in combination with the rule at **13.14** above where there have been one or more events within that paragraph as well as one or more transfers within this paragraph.

[*TCGA 1992, Sch 7AC paras 15, 25*].

Treatment of holdings in joint venture companies

[13.16] The legislation sets out rules for disregarding and looking through shares where a company has a qualifying shareholding in a joint venture company, as detailed below.

For the following purposes, a company is a '*joint venture company*' ('JVC') if (and only if):

(i) it is a 'trading company' or the 'holding company' (as in **13.3** above) of a 'trading group' or 'trading subgroup' (see **13.12** below); and
(ii) there are five or fewer persons who between them hold **75% or more** of its ordinary share capital (within *ICTA 1988, s 832(1)*, see **12.2** CAPITAL GAINS — GROUPS) (counting members of a group of companies, as in **13.3** above, as if they were a single company).

The following provisions apply only where a company has a 'qualifying shareholding' in a JVC. A company has a '*qualifying shareholding*' in a JVC if (and only if):

(a) it is a sole company (i.e. not a member of a group) and it holds shares, or an 'interest in shares' (see **13.20** below), in the JVC by virtue of which it holds **10% or more** of the JVC's ordinary share capital; or

(b) it is a member of a group, the group members between them hold 10% or more of the ordinary share capital of the JVC and the company itself holds part of that ordinary share capital.

Where the above conditions are satisfied, definitions of 'trading company', 'trading group' and 'trading subgroup' have effect with the modifications in (1)–(3) below. Where the JVC is itself a 'holding company' (as in **13.3** above), the references in (1), (2) and (3) below to its activities are to the activities (other than intra-group activities) of the JVC and its '51% subsidiaries' (within *CTA 2010, s 1154*). Each reference below to a holding of shares in a JVC includes securities of the JVC or an interest in shares in, or securities of, the JVC.

(1) In determining whether a company with a qualifying shareholding in a JVC is a 'trading company', its holding of shares in the JVC is disregarded. It is treated as carrying on a share of the JVC's activities proportionate to its percentage shareholding in the JVC. This does not apply if the company and the JVC are members of the same group of companies.

(2) In determining whether a group, of which a company with a qualifying shareholding in a JVC is a member or is the holding company, is a 'trading group', there is disregarded any holding of shares in the JVC by any member of the group which has a qualifying shareholding in the JVC. Each such member is treated as carrying on a share of the JVC's activities proportionate to its percentage shareholding in the JVC. This does not apply if the JVC is itself a member of the group.

(3) In determining whether a company with a qualifying shareholding in a JVC is the holding company of a 'trading subgroup' (see **13.12** above), there is disregarded any holding of shares in the JVC by the company and by any of its 51% subsidiaries which itself has a qualifying shareholding in the JVC. The company and each such subsidiary is treated as carrying on a share of the JVC's activities proportionate to its percentage shareholding in the JVC. This does not apply if the JVC is a member of the same group as the company.

[*TCGA 1992, Sch 7AC paras 23, 24, 26(4)*].

Consequential rules

Degrouping charge

[13.17] See **12.19** CAPITAL GAINS — GROUPS for interaction between the exemptions in this chapter and the charge where a company ceases to be a member of a 75% group of companies and has had an asset transferred to it by another group member within the preceding six years.

Negligible value claims

Where:

(a) a company makes a negligible value claim under *TCGA 1992, s 24(2)* (see Tolley's Capital Gains Tax under Losses) in respect of an asset; and
(b) by virtue of the provisions in this chapter, a loss on a disposal of that asset at the time of the claim would not be an allowable loss,

the consequent deemed disposal and reacquisition is regarded as taking place at the time of the claim and cannot be backdated to an earlier time. Thus, in these circumstances, a negligible value claim cannot result in an allowable loss. [*TCGA 1992, Sch 7AC para 33*].

Reorganisation involving qualifying corporate bond

Where, on a reorganisation of share capital, the 'new asset' consists of a qualifying corporate bond (see Tolley's Capital Gains Tax under Qualifying Corporate Bonds), the exemptions in this chapter do not apply to or affect the chargeable gain or allowable loss deemed to accrue under *TCGA 1992, s 116(10)(b)* on a subsequent disposal of the whole or part of the new asset. This does not apply if the 'reorganisation' was, in fact, a deemed disposal and reacquisition in a period of account beginning before 1 January 2005 within *FA 1996, s 92(7)* (asset ceasing to be a 'convertible security' but continuing to be a creditor relationship of the company). [*TCGA 1992, Sch 7AC para 34*].

Note that the above is of no application where the reorganisation has itself been treated as an exempt disposal by virtue of **13.13** above.

Appropriation of asset to trading stock

Where an asset acquired by a company otherwise than as trading stock is appropriated by the company for the purposes of its trade as trading stock (whether on the commencement of the trade or otherwise) and, if the company had then sold the asset for its market value, a chargeable gain or allowable loss would have accrued to the company but for the exemption under the current provisions, the company is treated for chargeable gains purposes as if it had thereby disposed of the asset for its market value. *TCGA 1992, s 173* applies for this purpose as it does for the purposes of *TCGA 1992, s 161* (see **12.7** CAPITAL GAINS — GROUPS). [*TCGA 1992, Sch 7AC para 36*].

Held-over gains on gifts of business assets

[13.18] Where:

(a) a company disposes of an asset;
(b) the allowable expenditure attributable to that asset would have been greater were it not for a claim for gifts hold-over relief under *TCGA 1992, s 165* (see Tolley's Capital Gains Tax under Hold-Over Reliefs) having been made in respect of an earlier disposal; and
(c) by virtue of the provisions in this chapter, any gain on the disposal in (a) above would not be a chargeable gain,

the amount of the held-over gain is treated as a gain accruing to the company at the time of the disposal in (a) above and as being a gain which is outside the exemptions in this chapter. If the disposal in (a) above is a part disposal, only an appropriate proportion of the held-over gain becomes chargeable on that occasion. [*TCGA 1992, Sch 7AC para 37*].

FOREX matching regulations

No gain or loss is treated as arising under *SI 1994 No 3227* on a disposal on which any gain would be exempt under the provisions in this chapter. [*TCGA 1992, Sch 7AC para 39*].

Miscellaneous matters concerning capital gains — substantial shareholding exemption

[13.19] The question of whether an asset is a chargeable asset for the purposes of corporation tax on chargeable gains generally is to be determined without regard to the availability, or potential availability, of the exemptions covered in this chapter, and references elsewhere to 'chargeable assets' should be read accordingly.

For the purposes of this chapter, an '*interest in shares*' is an interest as a co-owner of shares (whether they be owned jointly or in common and whether the interests of the co-owners are equal or disparate). [*TCGA 1992, Sch 7AC para* 29].

Clearance for transactions can be obtained from HMRC. Applications are handled by specialist teams in the Large Business Office ('LBO'). Where a company's affairs are not dealt with by an LBO, they should send the application to their usual HMRC officer in the first instance. Those companies whose affairs are dealt with by an LBO should send the application to the officer who deals with their affairs. Applications should be marked on the envelope and the covering letter with 'compliance – Code of Practice 10 application – substantial shareholding exemption'. See HMRC Brief 41/2007 1 June 2007.

The First-tier Tribunal decision in *Williamson Tea Holdings Ltd v HMRC* [2010] SFTD 1101 looked at whether the consideration given in a transaction was wholly in respect of the sale of shares, to which the substantial shareholdings exemption could apply. The case arose because part of the consideration was described in the contract as a payment for a non-competition agreement and HMRC sought to tax that element as a disposal of goodwill. The Tribunal found as a fact that the whole sum paid was for the disposal of shares but this case emphasises the practical importance of being able to demonstrate that consideration is clearly paid for the disposal of shares, to which the exemption can apply.

Key points on capital gains — substantial shareholding exemption

[13.20] Points to consider are as follows.

- Each case must be analysed in detail, working through the various conditions for the substantial shareholding exemption (SSE) to apply; the legislation is very complex and can give rise to some odd and unexpected results.
- The grouping provisions for SSE purposes cover companies which are incorporated and/or resident outside the UK as well as UK companies. Take particular care when dealing with overseas entities; they may not be treated as companies for UK tax purposes, or may be respected as companies but may not be treated as having ordinary share capital. If that is the case, UK companies within the group may not qualify for the SSE.

- The requirement that the substantial shareholding condition be met by virtue of the holding of shares or interests in shares can cause difficulties. An example might be where a company has issued ordinary shares and convertible loan notes to its parent company but the rights of the parent under the loan notes swamp its rights under the shares. It is possible that such a loan note holding could dilute the parent's rights by virtue of its shareholding to less than 10%.
- The trading conditions often give rise to questions in practice; the legislation does not clearly indicate when non-trading activities will be regarded as 'substantial' and reliance must be placed on the guidance given by HMRC in its Capital Gains Manual. If there is doubt, it is possible to ask HMRC to confirm the position under its non-statutory business clearance procedure.
- Where a scenario appears to lend itself to the application of the SSE, ensure that no other chargeable gains reliefs may apply instead. The interaction between the SSE and other such reliefs (for example, no-gain/no-loss transfers under *TCGA 1992, s 171* and no disposal fictions such as *TCGA 1992, s 135*) must always be considered carefully.
- Where a disposal of shares is thought to qualify for the SSE but the consideration for the sale includes deferred consideration, bear in mind that the deferred consideration will not qualify for the SSE (on the basis that an earn-out right is a separate capital gains asset, per *Marren (Inspector of Taxes) v Ingles* [1979] STC 58). Consider whether it may be possible commercially to structure the consideration in a different way to enable the seller to benefit more fully from the application of the SSE.

14

Charities

Cross-references. See **33** EXEMPT ORGANISATIONS and **69.46** TRADING INCOME — DEDUCTIONS.

Other sources. See Tolley's Charities Manual.

Simon's Taxes. See **B5.8, D7.2.**

Introduction to charities

[14.1] UK charitable tax reliefs are generally available to organisations equivalent to charities in the EU and the EEA countries. The definition of a 'charity' for tax purposes takes the form of a four stage test. The stages are:

- The company must be established for charitable purposes only (as in (a)–(o) below);
- It must be located in the UK or an EU member state or a territory specified in HMRC regulations (currently Iceland, Norway and Liechtenstein);
- If the body or trust is a charity within the meaning of *Charities Act 2011, s 10* (previously of *Charities Act 1993*), it must have complied with any requirement to be registered in the register of charities kept under

Charities Act 2011, s 29 (previously *Charities Act 1993, s 3*). In any other case, the body or trust must have complied with any requirement under the law of a territory outside England and Wales to be registered in a corresponding register;

- All persons with control or management responsibilities must be fit and proper persons. HMRC have issued guidance on how this test will be applied — see www.gov.uk/government/publications/charities-fit-and-proper-persons-test.

HMRC may publish a list of charities names and addresses that appear to be eligible for relief, but this is a guide only, not definitive.

[*FA 2010, Sch 6; Charities Act 2011, ss 2, 3; SI 2010 No 1904; SI 2019 No 689, Reg 19*].

The following are '*eligible bodies*' which qualify as charities:

- the Trustees of the National Heritage Memorial Fund;
- the Historic Buildings and Monuments Commission for England;
- the Trustees of the British Museum, and
- the Trustees of the National History Museum.

[*CTA 2010, s 468*].

The Commonwealth War Graves Commission and the Imperial War Graves Endowment Fund, which provides investment income for the Commonwealth War Graves Commission, are also treated as charities for tax purposes. [*FA 2015, s 123*].

A '*charitable purpose*' is one which is for the public benefit and which is within one of the following categories:

(a) the advancement of education;
(b) the prevention or relief of poverty;
(c) the advancement of religion;
(d) the advancement of health or the saving of lives;
(e) the advancement of citizenship or community development;
(f) the advancement of the arts, culture, heritage or science;
(g) the advancement of amateur sport;
(h) the advancement of human rights, conflict resolution or reconciliation or the promotion of religious or racial harmony or equality and diversity;
(i) the advancement of environmental protection or improvement;
(j) the relief of those in need by reason or youth, age, ill-health, disability, financial hardship or other disadvantage;
(k) the advancement of animal welfare;
(l) the promotion of the efficiency of the armed forces of the Crown, or of the efficiency of the police, fire and rescue services or ambulance services;
(m) any other purposes, not within (a)–(l) above but recognised as charitable purposes under *Charities Act 2011, s 5*;
(n) any purposes that may reasonably be regarded as analogous to, or within the spirit of, any purposes falling within (a) to (m) above; and
(o) any purposes that may reasonably be regarded as analogous to, or within the spirit of, any purposes which have been recognised under charity law as falling within (n) above or this category.

[*Charities Act 2011, ss 2, 3*].

Charities are regulated by the Charities Commission, and in Scotland by the Office of the Scottish Charities Regulator. Under *Charities Act 2011, ss 54–59*, HMRC may disclose information regarding charities to the Charity Commission.

Charities can register with HMRC online, see www.gov.uk/charity-recognition-hmrc.

Simon's Taxes. See **B5.801–B5.814**.

Specific exemptions and reliefs from tax

[14.2] Apart from the exemptions at **14.3–14.8** below, charities are subject to tax on investment and rental income and gains and on profits from trades carried on in order to raise funds. The exemptions at **14.3, 14.4** and **14.5** below are not general exemptions. Therefore, they do not extend to trades not falling within **14.5** below or to miscellaneous income generally (cf. *Grove v Young Men's Christian Association* (1903) 4 TC 613 and *Governors of Rotunda Hospital, Dublin v Coman (Surveyor of Taxes)* (1920) 7 TC 517, HL).

The exemptions are subject to the restrictions at **14.9** below.

Claims must be made for exemptions to apply, generally within four years of the end of the accounting period to which they relate.

Simon's Taxes. See **B5.823–B5.840**.

Rents

[14.3] UK or overseas rents or other receipts from an estate, interest or right in or over any land vested in any person for charitable purposes, and otherwise chargeable to corporation tax as property or trading income (or to income tax under *ITTOIA 2005, Pt 2* (trading income) or *Pt 3* (property income)), are exempt to the extent they are applied for charitable purposes only.

Distributions from real estate investment trusts which are liable to corporation tax, are exempt to the extent that they arise in respect of a person who holds them for charitable purposes and the income is applied for those purposes.

[*CTA 2009, Pts 3, 4; CTA 2010, s 485*].

Interest, distributions, etc.

[14.4] Income of a charitable company, or applicable for charitable purposes under an Act of Parliament, charter, decree, deed of trust or will, is exempt so far as applied for charitable purposes and consisting of:

- income from non-trading loan relationships; or
- distributions from exempt unauthorised unit trusts (before 6 April 2014, all unauthorised unit trusts);
- dividends from UK or overseas resident companies.

To qualify for exemption, the income must be applied for charitable purposes only, and a claim is required.

Exemption for corporation tax also applies to tax in respect of non-trading gains of companies on intangible fixed assets under *CTA 2009, ss 745–753* (see **42.9** INTANGIBLE ASSETS).

Income of trustees arising from public revenue dividends, and which is applicable towards repairs of any cathedral, college, church, chapel etc., being income otherwise chargeable to corporation tax on trading profits (or to income tax under *ITTOIA 2005, Pt 4 Ch 2* (interest)), is also exempt so far as applied to those purposes only.

[*CTA 2010, ss 486, 487*].

Trading profits

[14.5] A charitable trade is a trade carried on by a charitable company where:

(a) the trade is exercised in the course of carrying out a primary purpose of the charity; or
(b) the work is mainly carried on by its beneficiaries.

Profits of a charitable trade carried on by a charitable company or post-cessation receipts of such a trade which it receives or to which it is entitled are exempt from corporation tax provided that the profits or receipts are applied for charitable purposes only and that a claim is made.

Where the trade is exercised partly in the course of carrying out a primary purpose of the charity and partly otherwise, each part is treated as a separate trade. Where the work is carried out partly but not mainly by beneficiaries, the part carried on by the beneficiaries and the other part are treated as separate trades. Expenses and receipts are to be apportioned on a just and reasonable basis between the separate trades.

[*CTA 2010, ss 478, 479*].

For trades held to fall within the exemption, see *Glasgow Musical Festival Association* (1926) 11 TC 154, Ct of Sess; *Royal Choral Society v CIR* (1943) 25 TC 263, CA, and *Dean Leigh Temperance Canteen Trustees v CIR* (1958) 38 TC 315. For regular trading see *British Legion, Peterhead Branch Remembrance and Welcome Home Fund v CIR* (1953) 35 TC 509, 32 ATC 302, Ct of Sess. (In practice, HMRC may in such cases allow a reasonable deduction for services etc. provided free.) For annual shows of agricultural societies, see **33.2** EXEMPT ORGANISATIONS.

Other exemptions

Small trades and certain miscellaneous income

[14.6] Subject to the following conditions, a tax exemption applies, on a claim being made to HMRC, to trading profits and other income which is chargeable to corporation tax as miscellaneous income under any of the provisions listed in *CTA 2010, s 1173*.

The conditions are that it is not otherwise exempted from tax and the income is applied solely for the purposes of the charity and either:

(a) the trading incoming resources do not exceed the 'requisite limit'; or
(b) the charity had, at the beginning of the chargeable period, a reasonable expectation that the requisite limit would be met.

The '*requisite limit*' is 25% of the charitable company's total incoming resources for the accounting period, but cannot be less than £8,000 or more than £80,000. For accounting periods beginning before 1 April 2019, the monetary limits were £5,000 and £50,000.

The monetary limits are proportionately reduced for chargeable periods of less than twelve months. The extension of the exemption to miscellaneous income is intended to cover miscellaneous fund-raising activities not being trading activities (or treated as trading). Certain specified tax charges on miscellaneous income (listed in *CTA 2010, s 481(2)*) are excluded from the exemption.

[*CTA 2010, ss 480–482; FA 2019, s 41(3)–(6)*].

HMRC's guidance is that they will consider any evidence to satisfy the reasonable expectation test in (b) above. Such evidence may include minutes of meetings at which the expectations were discussed, copies of cash-flow forecasts and business plans prepared for these meetings and copies of the previous year's accounts.

Small-scale fund-raising events

Profits from events such as bazaars, jumble sales, gymkhanas, carnivals etc., arranged by voluntary organisations or charities, held for, and promoted as being held for, the purpose of raising funds for charity, are not taxed if a claim is made and:

(a) the organisation or charity is not regularly carrying on these trading activities;
(b) it is not competing with other traders; and
(c) the profits are transferred to charities or otherwise applied for charitable purposes.

The exemption covers up to 15 of each type of event in any one location in any financial year of the charity etc. and includes events accessed electronically. Small events, e.g. jumble sales or coffee mornings, do not count toward the limit to the extent that the gross takings from these events do not exceed £1,000 in any week. The limit of 15 is increased or reduced proportionately for financial years of more or less than twelve months.

The exemption corresponds with the VAT exemption for fund-raising events, for which see the corresponding chapter of Tolley's Value Added Tax. Any event meeting the criteria for the VAT exemption will automatically qualify for the corporation tax exemption if the condition at (c) above is satisfied.

[*CTA 2010, s 483*].

Lotteries

Lottery profits applied solely to the charity's purposes, being profits otherwise chargeable to corporation tax as trading income (or to income tax under *ITTOIA 2005, Pt 2* (trading income) or *Pt 5* (miscellaneous income)), are exempt, provided that the lottery is an exempt lottery within *Gaming Act 2005, Pts 1, 4* or *Sch 11* or is promoted and conducted in accordance with *Gaming Act 2005, Pt 5* (or NI equivalent).

[*CTA 2010, s 484*].

Property income

Property income, whether chargeable as trading or property income, is exempt from corporation tax if the income is vested in any person for charitable purposes. REIT distributions are also exempt to the extent the shares from which they derive are similarly held for charitable purposes. In each case a claim must be made.

[*CTA 2010, s 485*].

Estate income

Where a charitable company is liable to corporation tax on estate income, that income is not brought into account in calculating total profits of that company, provided that the estate income is applied for charitable purposes only and a claim is made.

[*CTA 2010, s 489*].

Investment income and non-trading profits from loan relationships

Such income is exempt from corporation tax if it is income of a charitable company or it is required by legislation, court judgment, charter, trust deed or will be used for charitable purposes only and is so used. A claim is required.

Where public revenue dividends are received on securities by trustees and the income is applicable and applied only for the repair of a cathedral, college, church, chapel or other building used for divine worship, the income is exempt from corporation tax provided a claim is made.

[*CTA 2010, ss 486, 487, Sch 2 para 71*].

Miscellaneous income

Where income is received by a charitable company or is required by statute to be applied for charitable purposes only and is so applied, it is exempt provided a claim is made. The income covered by this provision is non-trading gains on intangible fixed assets, annual payments and qualifying income from intangible fixed assets.

[*CTA 2010, s 488, Sch 2 para 72*].

Capital gains

[14.7] Charities are exempt from corporation tax on capital gains applicable, and applied, for charitable purposes. Where property held on charitable trusts ceases to be subject to those trusts without actually being disposed of, the trustees are deemed to have disposed of, and immediately reacquired, the property at its market value at that time. The notional gain arising is taxable. To the extent that the property represents, directly or indirectly, gains which have accrued to the trustees from disposals made during the currency of the charity, tax is chargeable as if the exemption had never applied. Tax on such gains may be assessed within three years after the year of assessment or accounting period in which the cessation occurs.

[*TCGA 1992, ss 256, 256A–256D*].

The exemption applies to capital payments made to UK charities as beneficiaries of an offshore settlement, in respect of which a chargeable gain would be treated as accruing to the trust under *TCGA 1992, s 87*. The exemption applies only to the extent that the payment is applicable and is applied for charitable purposes. (HMRC Tax Bulletin Issue 36, August 1998 pp 573, 574).

See also *TCGA 1992, s 257* as regards gifts to charities treated as made for a 'no gain, no loss' consideration.

As regards the time at which charitable purposes arise, see *Guild and Others (as Trustees of the William Muir (Bond 9) Ltd Employees' Share Scheme) v CIR* (1993) 66 TC 1, Ct of Sess (trustees of share scheme required to repay loans out of proceeds of distribution and to apply balance to charitable purposes; held not to apply proceeds of distribution for charitable purposes).

See, however, **14.9** below as regards restrictions on relief.

Simon's Taxes. See **B5.840**

Miscellaneous

[14.8] Offshore income gains accruing to a charitable trust are not taken into account in calculating total income. 'Offshore income gain' has the same meaning as in *Chapter 5 of Pt 2* of the *Offshore (Tax) Funds Regulations 2009 (SI 2009 No 3001)* (see **55** OFFSHORE FUNDS).

[*ITA 2007, ss 535(1), (2), 538(2)*].

Charitable unit trust schemes are excluded from the normal income tax treatment of unauthorised unit trusts, and are thus able to pass on their income to participating charities without deducting tax.

[*SI 1988 No 267*].

Employee secondment

For a deduction in arriving at trading profits for employees seconded by companies to charities, see **69.46** TRADING INCOME — DEDUCTIONS.

Restrictions on exemptions

[14.9] If a charity incurs (or is treated as incurring) 'non-charitable expenditure' (a 'non-exempt amount') in a chargeable period, relief for 'attributable income' is restricted to the amount by which it exceeds the non-charitable expenditure.

If a charity's non-charitable expenditure exceeds its 'total income and gains', the excess is treated as non-charitable expenditure of the previous period for this purpose. Excess non-charitable expenditure may arise in a chargeable period wholly or partly as result of the carry back in which case the excess is to be carried back to the previous period and so on, but only to chargeable periods ending not more than six years before the end of the period in which the expenditure was actually incurred. Any necessary adjustments are to be made accordingly by assessment or otherwise. Where a charity's attributable income and gains are so restricted, the charity may specify (by notice to HMRC) which items of income or gains are to be disallowed. If such a notice is required by HMRC and the charity fails to comply within 30 days from the date the requirement is imposed, HMRC will determine which items to disallow.

A charity has a '*non-exempt amount*' for an accounting period if it has both non-charitable expenditure for the period and attributable income and gains and it is the lesser of these amounts.

'*Attributable income*' for an accounting period is exempt income and attributable gains are those which are not chargeable.

[*CTA 2010, ss 492–495*].

Where a charitable company has a non-exempt amount, attributable gains of that company for the period may be allocated to the non-exempt amount, so far as not already used up. Attribution may be by specification by the charitable company or determination by an officer of HMRC.

Non-charitable expenditure

'*Non-charitable expenditure*' is expenditure falling into one of the following categories:

(a) any trading loss other than in charitable trade or it qualifies under the small trade, fund raising or lotteries exemptions;
(b) any loss relating to land where income from the land would not qualify for exemption;
(c) any miscellaneous loss not arising as a result of charitable activities;
(d) expenditure not incurred for charitable purposes only and not required to be taken into account in calculating the profits of a trade or property business carried on by the charitable company or the profit or loss on any miscellaneous transaction carried on by such a company;
(e) the amount of the charitable company funds invested in an investment other than an approved charitable investment;
(f) loans made by the company in an accounting period which are neither investments nor approved charitable loans.

When expenditure is treated as incurred depends on UK GAAP.

[*CTA 2010, ss 496–501*].

Where the investment or loan is realised or repaid in whole or in part in the chargeable period in which it was made, any further investment or lending of the sum realised or repaid in that period is, to the extent that it does not exceed the sum originally invested or lent, ignored in arriving at non-charitable expenditure of the period.

'*Approved charitable investments and loans*' are the following:

(A) investments in securities:
  (a) issued or guaranteed by the UK government or an EU government;
  (b) issued or guaranteed by the government or a governmental body of any territory or part;
  (c) issued by an international entity listed in the Annex to Council Directive 2003/48/EC or an entity meeting the four criteria set out at the end of that Annex;
  (d) issued by a building society;
  (e) issued by a mutual credit institution authorised by the appropriate governmental body in the territory in which the securities are issued;
  (f) issued by an open ended investment trust;
  (g) issued by an open-ended investment company;
  (h) issued by a company and listed on a recognised stock exchange; or
  (i) issued by a company but not listed on a recognised stock exchange,

(B) an investment in a common investment fund established under *Charities Act 1960, s 22* (or NI equivalent), *Charities Act 1993, s 24* or *Charities Act 2011, s 96*;

(C) an investment in a common deposit fund established under *Charities Act 1960, s 22A, Charities Act 1993, s 25* or *Charities Act 2011, s 100*;

(D) an investment in a fund which is similar to those in (i) or (ii) above, which is established for the exclusive benefit of charities or class of charities;

(E) Northern Ireland Treasury bills;

(F) deposits with a banks (as defined in *CTA 2010, s 1120*) in respect of which interest is payable at a commercial rate, but excluding a deposit made as part of an arrangement whereby the bank, etc. makes a loan to a third party;

(G) an interest in land, other than as security;

(H) certificates of deposit including uncertificated eligible debt security units as defined in *ITA 2007, s 986;*

(I) units in a unit trust scheme or in a recognised scheme within *FISMA 2000, s 237*;

(J) loans or other investments as to which HMRC are satisfied, on a claim, that the loans or other investments are made for the benefit of the charity and not for the avoidance of tax (whether by the charity or by a third party);

(K) a deposit with the National Savings Bank, a building society or a credit institution operating on mutual principles and duly authorised in the territory in which the deposit is taken;

(L) bills, certificates of tax deposit, savings certificates and tax reserve certificates issued by the UK government.

(A)(a), (b) or (c) do not apply to an investment unless:

(i) the securities are traded or quoted on a recognised investment exchange or an exchange being the principal or only market in a territory where the securities are listed; and

(ii) (if the securities are shares or debenture stock):
- the securities are fully paid up or the terms of issue require them to be fully paid up within nine months of issue; or
- the shares do not have a nominal value.

In the case of an investment in a company which is incorporated, (A) above does not apply unless conditions (i) and (ii) above are met and throughout the last business day before the investment day the company has issued and paid up share capital of at least £1 million (or its equivalent in some other currency) and dividends were paid in every year from 5 years before the calendar year in which the investment day falls on all shares in issue at that time.

[*CTA 2010, ss 511–513; Charities Act 2011, Sch 7 para 142; SI 2019 No 689, Reg 17(7)*].

'Approved charitable loans'

A loan which is not made by way of investment is a qualifying loan if it is one of the following:

(1) A loan made to another charity for charitable purposes only.

(2) A loan to a beneficiary of the charity which is made in the course of carrying out the purposes of the charity.

(3) Money placed on a current account with a recognised bank or licensed institution (as in (F) above) otherwise than under arrangements under which a loan is made to another person.

(4) A loan, not within (1) to (3) above, as to which HMRC are satisfied, on a claim, that the loan is made for the benefit of the charity and not for the avoidance of tax (whether by the charity or by a third party).

[*CTA 2010, s 514*].

Payments between charities

Any payment received by one charity from another, other than in return for full consideration, which would otherwise not be chargeable to tax (and which is not of a description within any of the relieving provisions of *CTA 2010, s 515*, see **14.2** *et seq.* above), is chargeable to corporation tax as income from non-trading loan relationships, but is eligible for relief, on making a claim, if it is applied for charitable purposes only.

[*CTA 2010, s 474*].

Simon's Taxes. See **B5.850–B5.852.**

Tainted donations

[14.10] There are anti-avoidance provisions which remove entitlement to tax reliefs and counteract tax advantages where a person makes a relievable charitable donation which is a 'tainted donation' (see below, but broadly a donation linked to arrangements for the donor to obtain a financial advantage). The provisions apply equally to donations to community amateur sports clubs (see **75.2** VOLUNTARY ASSOCIATIONS).

The following reliefs can be denied under the provisions:

(a) gifts of chargeable assets (*TCGA 1992, s 257* — see **14.7** above);
(b) gifts of plant and machinery (*CAA 2001, s 63(2)* — see **68.32** TRADING INCOME);
(c) payroll giving (*ITEPA 2003, Pt 12*);
(d) gifts of trading stock (*ITTOIA 2005, s 108; CTA 2009, s 105*);
(e) gift aid donations by individuals (*ITA 2007, Pt 8 Ch 2*);
(f) gifts of shares and real property (*ITA 2007, Pt 8 Ch 3; CTA 2010, Pt 6 Ch 3* — see **14.16** below);
(g) cash gifts by companies (*CTA 2010, Pt 6 Ch 2* — see **14.11** below); and
(h) any other gift or disposal in respect of which a charity is entitled to claim a repayment of tax.

An amount of income arising under a UK settlement (within *ITTOIA 2005, s 628*) to which a charity is entitled under the settlement's terms is treated for these purposes as an amount gifted to the charity by the trustees.

[*CTA 2010, ss 939A, 939B, 939I(1)*].

Meaning of 'tainted donation'

A donation is a '*tainted donation*' if each of the following three conditions is satisfied.

(1) The donor or a person connected with the donor (a '*linked person*') enters into 'arrangements' (before or after the donation is made) and it is reasonable to assume from the likely effects of the donation and the arrangements or of the circumstances in which they are made that neither would have been made independently of one another. Where it is a connected person who enters into the arrangements, he must be connected (see below) with the donor at a time in the period beginning with the earliest, and ending with the latest, of the time the arrangements are made, the time the donation is made, and the time when the arrangements are first materially implemented.
(2) The main purpose, or one of the main purposes, of the linked person entering into the arrangements is to obtain a financial advantage directly or indirectly from the charity or a connected charity for one or more linked persons.
(3) The donor is neither a 'qualifying charity-owned company' nor a 'housing provider' linked with the charity. A housing provider is linked with a charity if one is wholly owned or subject to control by the other or both are wholly owned or subject to control by the same person.

For the above purposes, '*arrangements*' include any scheme, arrangement or understanding of any kind, whether or not legally enforceable, involving a transaction or transactions. *CTA 2010, s 1122* applies to determine whether two persons are '*connected*', but in addition, a beneficiary is treated as connected with a person in the capacity as trustee and with the settlor. In applying those sections for the purposes of these provisions, persons living together as husband and wife or as if they were civil partners are treated as if they were in fact husband and wife or civil partners of each other and 'close company' includes a company which would be close if it were UK-resident. Two charities are connected for the purposes of (2) above if they are connected in a matter relating to the structure, administration or control of either of them.

A '*qualifying charity-owned company*' is a company which:

(i) is wholly owned by one or more charities (within *CTA 2010, s 200*), at least one of which is the charity to whom the donation is made or a connected charity; and
(ii) has not previously been under the control of, and does not carry on a trade previously carried on by, any of the linked persons potentially financially advantaged by the arrangements or any person (other than a charity) connected with such a linked person at any time in the four years ending on the day on which (i) above was first satisfied.

A '*housing provider*' is a body which is a non-profit provider of social housing or is entered on a register maintained under *Housing Act 1996, s 1, Housing (Scotland) Act 2001, s 57, Housing (Scotland) Act 2010, s 20* or NI equivalent.

[*CTA 2010, ss 939C, 939G, 939H, 939I(1); SI 2019 No 1458, Sch 3 para 31*].

Financial advantage

The following applies where the arrangements involve a 'transaction' to which the linked person entering into them or any other linked person ('X') and another person ('Y') are parties. X is treated as obtaining a financial advantage within (2) above if the terms of the transaction are less beneficial to Y or more beneficial to X (or both) than those reasonably to be expected in a transaction at arm's length or if the transaction is not of a kind which a person acting at arm's length and in Y's place might reasonably be expected to make. This rule is not, however, intended to limit the circumstances in which a person is treated as obtaining a financial advantage. '*Transaction*' includes, for example, the sale, letting or exchange of property, the provision of services or of a loan, or other form of financial assistance, and investment in a business.

A financial advantage is ignored for the purposes of the above provisions in the following circumstances:

- where the advantage is applied by the person obtaining it for charitable purposes only;
- where the advantage is a benefit associated with a gift aid donation (within *ITA 2007, s 417*) or with a payment within (g) above;
- where the donation is within (f) above and the advantage is a benefit of value which would be taken into account in determining the relievable amount for the purposes of the reliefs in (f) above; and
- where the donation is within (d) above and the advantage would be brought into account under *ITTOIA 2005, s 109* or *CTA 2009, s 108* (receipt of benefits by donor or connected person).

[*CTA 2010, ss 939D, 939E*].

Effect of provisions

Where the provisions apply, any relief that would otherwise have been available in respect of the tainted donation or an 'associated donation' under (a) to (h) above is not available. For the purposes of tax on chargeable gains, *TCGA 1992, s 257* (disapplication of market value rule for gifts of assets to charities — see **14.7** above) does not apply to the tainted donation or any associated donation.

An '*associated donation*' is an otherwise relievable donation made under the arrangements by a person other than a company which is a qualifying charity-owned company (see above) in relation to the donation or a housing provider (see above) linked with the charity to which the donation is made.

[*TCGA 1992, s 257A; CTA 2010, s 939F*].

Charitable donations relief

[14.11] A company may claim relief by deduction from total profits (after all other deductions other than group relief and group relief for carried-forward losses) of the period in which the donation is made for a 'qualifying charitable donation'. However, the donation cannot create a loss. Relief under these provisions applies also to donations to Community Amateur Sports Clubs ('CASCs') (see also **75** VOLUNTARY ASSOCIATIONS).

A '*qualifying charitable donation*' for corporation tax purposes is a qualifying payment i.e. one which is:

- a payment of a sum of money;
- a sum which is not repayable (but see below for exception);
- not made by a company which is a charity;
- not disqualified as an 'associated acquisition, etc.' by the charity;
- not disqualified as a certain distribution;
- not disqualified as having an 'associated benefit'.

Where the company is wholly owned by the charity, or that charity and a number of others, the payment was designed to reduce the company's taxable profits to nil and a repayment by the charity is made within the year after the end of the period in which the donation was made and is intended to make such adjustment as necessary to reduce the taxable profits to nil, the payment is not treated as a repayment of the original donation. The repayment is not treated as non-charitable expenditure (see **14.9** above) or, in the case of a CASC, non-qualifying expenditure (which expenditure may be chargeable to tax for a CASC under *CTA 2010, s 666*).

An '*associated acquisition*' is a donation which is conditional on an acquisition of property by the charity from the donor company or an associate and the donation and the acquisition are associated or form part of an arrangement. Where the acquisition is for no consideration (i.e. it is a gift) it is to be ignored for this purpose.

In the case of *Noved Investment Co v Revenue and Customs Comrs* [2006] STC (SCD) 120, the Special Commissioners held that what is now *CTA 2010, s 1000(1)G* was not restricted to bilateral transactions and that transfers of assets or liabilities by a company to its members at an undervalue can include cash. Accordingly, such cash transfers could be qualifying donations. See HMRC's Corporate Tax Manual CTM15250 and 15350.

'*Charity*' for this purpose is as defined in **14.1** above. The Trustees of the National Heritage Memorial Fund, The Historic Buildings and Monuments Commission for England and the National Endowment for Science, Technology and the Arts are treated as established for charitable purposes only. The definition also includes CASCs.

A payment is not a qualifying donation if the company, or a connected person (**19** CONNECTED PERSONS), or a person connected with such a person, receives a benefit in consequence of the gift, and either:

(A) the aggregate value of the benefits received in relation to the gift exceeds the variable limit, which is:
  - where the gift is £100 or less, 25% of the amount of the gift;
  - where the gift is greater than £100, £25 plus 5% of the excess over £100; or

(B) the sum of the total value of the benefits received in relation to the gift and the total value of any other benefits (if any) received in relation to qualifying donations made by the company to the charity earlier in the accounting period exceeds £500.

For payments before 6 April 2019, the limits in (A) above were:

- where the gift was £100 or less, 25% of the amount of the gift;
- where the gift was greater than £100 but not more than £1,000, £25;
- where the gift was greater than £1,000, 5% of the amount of the gift.

Where (A) above applies, the treatment of a payment is modified if (i) to (iv) below applies. These are:

(i) the related benefit applies to a period of less than a year;
(ii) the benefit relates to a right to receive payments at intervals over less than a year;
(iii) the benefit is one of a series received at intervals over less than a year;
(iv) the payment is not associated with benefits received at intervals, but is one of a series of payments made at intervals of less than a year.

In the cases of (i) to (iii), the benefit and the payment are annualised and for (iv) the payment is annualised. The annualised amount, in the case of (i) and (ii) (where (iii) and (iv) do not also apply) is found by multiplying the amount by 365 and dividing the result by the number of days in the period of time referred to in (i) or (ii). Where (iii) or (iv) applies, the denominator is the average number of days in the intervals of less than a year.

Where a benefit:

(1) consists of the right to receive a benefit or benefits at intervals over a period of less than twelve months;
(2) is an associated benefit which relates to a period of less than twelve months;
(3) is one of a series of benefits, received at intervals, in consequence of making a series of gifts at intervals of less than twelve months; or

(4) the benefit is not received at intervals, but the payment is one of a series of payments made at intervals of less than twelve months,

the value of the benefit and the amount of the gift are 'annualised' for the purposes of (ii) above. Where a one-off benefit is received in consequence of making a gift which is one of a series of gifts made at intervals of less than twelve months, the amount of the gift is likewise 'annualised'. Acknowledgement of a donor in the charity's literature does not amount to a benefit *provided that* it does not take the form of an advertisement for the donor's business (see para 3.27 of the HMRC guide referred to below).

Charity trading subsidiaries and companies owned by a CASC

Where a qualifying payment is made by a company that is wholly owned by a charity, the company can claim that the donation, or any part of it, is to be treated as made in an earlier accounting period falling wholly or partly within the nine months prior to the date of the donation. A claim to have the payment treated as paid in an earlier accounting period must be made within two years from the end of the accounting period in which the payment is made, or such longer period as HMRC may allow.

A company is treated as wholly owned by a charity if all its ordinary share capital is directly or indirectly owned by one or more charities, or if it is limited by guarantee and every person beneficially entitled to participate in its divisible profits, or to share in the net assets available for distribution in a winding-up, is a charity or a company wholly owned by a charity. The ordinary share capital of a company is treated as owned by a charity where a CASC beneficially owns the share capital.

Where a charity-owned company makes an estimated gift aid payment, which subsequently proves to exceed its profits for the accounting period in which the payment is made, so that a repayment is made within twelve months, solely as adjustment, the donation is not made 'subject to a condition as to repayment' and such repayment is not treated as non-charitable expenditure for corporation tax purposes.

Restrictions on relief apply where a qualifying payment is made by a company which is wholly owned, or controlled, by a CASC, or a number of charities which include the CASC, where 'inflated member-related expenditure' is incurred by such company in that period.

Under these provisions where a company which is owned or controlled by a CASC incurs 'inflated member-related expenditure' the amount of the qualifying payment paid by the company that qualifies for tax relief is reduced (but not below nil). The amount of the reduction is the total amount of the inflated member-related expenditure, or, if less, the amount of the qualifying payment. Thus the amount of the inflated member-related expenditure is effectively brought back into the charge to tax.

If, in the same accounting period, the amount of inflated member-related expenditure is greater than the qualifying payment, then the qualifying payment is reduced to nil and any excess inflated member-related expenditure is carried back (for up to six years) to adjust qualifying payments in earlier years, the most recent year first (after any reductions under these provisions for that year, and any other amounts already carried back).

The definition above (company wholly owned by a charity) applies for these purposes. In addition the club controls the company it if has the power to secure that the affairs of the company are conducted in accordance with the club's wishes, either: through voting power or the holding of shares in the company (or another company); or as a result of powers conferred by the articles of association (or other regulating document) of the company or any other company. Two or more charities, including the club, will also control the company if, acting together, they have such power to secure the affairs of the company are so conducted.

'*Inflated member-related expenditure*' occurs in two cases, where the company:

(a) incurs expenditure on the employment of a member of the club and this is not at arm's length – the Treasury may by order specify what expenditure is, and is not, to be treated as employment expenditure in such instances; or
(b) incurs expenditure on a supply of goods and services to the club by either a member of the club, or a member-controlled body, in each case otherwise than on arm's length terms.

However, where the expenditure taken as a whole is beneficial to the company, rather than to the third party, then that expenditure will not fall within the definition above.

'*Member of the club*' for these purposes includes a reference to a person connected with a member of the club. A company is '*member-controlled*' if a member of the club has (or two or more members of the club acting together have) the power to secure that the affairs of the company are conducted in accordance with the wishes of the member(s), either: through voting power or the holding of shares in the company (or another body corporate); or as a result of powers conferred by the articles of association (or other regulating document) of the company or any other body corporate. A partnership is '*member-controlled*' if a member of the club has (or two or more members of the club acting together have) the right to a share of more than half the assets, or more than half the income, of the partnership.

Further details on the tax treatment of CASCs can be found at 75 VOLUNTARY ASSOCIATIONS.

[*CTA 2010, ss 189–202, 202A–202C, Sch 2 paras 56–58; F(No 2)A 2017, Sch 4 para 160; FA 2019, s 40(3)(4)*].

Simon's Taxes. See **D1.321**.

Gift aid donation to charity

[14.12] When a charitable company receives a donation under the gift aid scheme, it is treated as receiving an amount under deduction of tax at the basic rate for the tax year in which it is made. Therefore, its income is the grossed up amount of the gift. This amount is exempt from corporation tax to the extent that it is applied for charitable purposes only. A claim must be made for this exemption.

[*ITA 2007, ss 429, 472*].

Gifts of money to charities

[14.13] Cash payments, when made by non-charities, are exempt from corporation tax in the hands of the charity if they are used for charitable purposes only and a claim is made.

Where cash payments are made to a charity by a company, the gift is not liable to corporation tax, provided a claim is made.

Where there is a gift of money to a scientific research association in an accounting period for which the exemption is claimed, the payment is exempt from corporation tax provided a claim is made.

HMRC publish a gift aid and payroll giving guide for school charities. The guide contains information and simple examples specifically related to funds received by school charities to help make the most of these donations. The guide is available on the HMRC website at http://www.hmrc.gov.uk/charities/gift_aid/rules/school-charities.htm.

[*CTA 2010, ss 473, 475–477*].

Gift Aid Small Donations Scheme

[14.14] The Gift Aid Small Donations Scheme enables eligible charities and Community Amateur Sports Clubs to claim gift aid style top-up payments on small cash donations (less than £30 (£20 before 6 April 2019)) without requiring the donor to provide a gift aid declaration. The amount of small donations on which the new top-up repayment can be claimed is capped at, broadly, £8,000 per tax year, per charity.

In order to qualify for the repayment charities will need to have been in existence for at least two years, and have made successful gift aid claims in two of the last four years. The link with successful gift aid claims is intended to reduce the risk of fraud inherent in the breaking of the link to donors through a declaration. Regulations provide for the administration of such top-up claims, payments and overpayments, and apply the main information gathering provisions relating to tax in *FA 2008, Sch 36*.

[*Small Charitable Donations Act 2012; SI 2013 No 938; SI 2019 No 337*].

Other gifts

[14.15] Where the payment is made by another charity other than for full consideration and it is not chargeable to corporation tax apart from *CTA 2010, s 474*, if the amount is applied for charitable purposes only and a claim is made the company may claim exemption.

[*CTA 2010, s 474*].

Gifts of shares, securities and real property

[14.16] Relief is available to companies other than charities which dispose of the whole of the beneficial interest in the 'qualifying investments' listed below, otherwise than at market value and which make a claim. For this purpose, a charity must fall within one of the following categories:

(i) a body of persons or trust established for charitable purposes only;
(ii) the Trustees of the National Heritage Memorial Fund;
(iii) the Historic Buildings and Monuments Commission for England; or
(iv) the National Endowment for Science, Technology and the Arts.

'*Qualifying investments*' are:

(a) shares and securities listed or dealt in on a recognised stock exchange or on or after 6 April 2007 dealt in on any designated market in the UK;
(b) units in authorised unit trusts (see **46.3** INVESTMENT FUNDS);
(c) shares in open-ended investment companies (see **46.2** INVESTMENT FUNDS);
(d) interests in offshore funds (see **55** OFFSHORE FUNDS); and
(e) a 'qualifying interest in land'.

Where a valid claim is made, relief for the 'relievable amount, ' is available as a qualifying charitable donation for the accounting period in which the disposal is made. Where relief is claimed under *CTA 2010, s 205*, no relief can be claimed under *CTA 2009, s 105* (see **69.46** TRADING INCOME — DEDUCTIONS) or any other provision for the same disposal.

For disposals to a charity, the '*relievable amount*' is the value of the 'net benefit to the charity' either at the time the disposal is made or immediately after that time (whichever gives the lower value), plus 'incidental costs' of the disposal minus the total value of any benefits by the company as a result of the disposal, or (where the disposal is at an undervalue) the excess (if any) of that value over any consideration given for the disposal.

'*Incidental costs*' are defined as:

(A) payments for services of a surveyor, valuer, auctioneer, accountant, agent or legal adviser, incurred wholly and exclusively by the company for the purposes of the disposal;
(B) costs wholly and exclusively incurred by the company in connection with transfer or conveyance;
(C) costs of advertising to find a buyer; and
(D) reasonable costs of valuation or apportionment required for these provisions.

The '*net benefit to the charity*' is normally the market value of the investment. Where, however, the charity is, or becomes, subject to a 'disposal-related obligation' to any person (whether or not the donor or a connected person), the net benefit is the market value of the investment reduced by the aggregate 'disposal-related liabilities' of the charity.

An obligation is a '*disposal-related obligation*' if it is reasonable to suppose that the disposal would not have been made in its absence or if it relates to, or is framed by reference to, or is conditional upon the charity receiving, the investment in question or a related investment.

A charity's '*disposal-related liability*' is its liability under the disposal-related obligation. Contingent obligations are taken into account if the contingency actually occurs.

The market value of the investment is determined as for capital gains tax purposes. In computing the amount deductible, any consideration receivable at a future time, contingently or otherwise, is brought fully into account as it is for capital gains tax purposes (see Tolley's Capital Gains Tax under Disposal).

The amount deductible is reduced by the value of any benefits received by the donor company or any connected person (see **19** CONNECTED PERSONS). The amount deductible is increased by any incidental costs of disposal (construed as for capital gains tax purposes) incurred by the person making it. Where consideration is received for the disposal, this increase is limited to the excess, if any, of the deemed consideration for capital gains tax purposes (disposal deemed to be at no gain/no loss) over the actual consideration. The cost of the asset to the charity for capital gains tax purposes is reduced by the amount deductible as above, or, if it is less than that amount, is reduced to nil.

[*CTA 2010, ss 203–212*].

A payment made, or to be made to a foreign charity is non-charitable expenditure if it is incurred for charitable purposes only but a charity has not taken such steps as are reasonable in the circumstances to ensure that the payment will be applied for charitable purposes.

[*CTA 2010, s 500*].

Gifts of pre-eminent property to the nation

[14.17] A company making a 'qualifying gift' of 'pre-eminent property' to be held for the benefit of the public or the nation qualifies for a reduction in tax liability equal to a percentage of the value of the property. A gain accruing on a qualifying gift is not a chargeable gain (and a loss is not an allowable loss). [*TCGA 1992, s 258(1A)*].

It is explicitly provided that nothing in the following provisions gives rise to any right or expectation that an offer to make a qualifying gift will be accepted. [*FA 2012, Sch 14 para 25*].

Qualifying gift

A person makes a '*qualifying gift*' if:

(a) the person offers to give pre-eminent property to be held for the benefit of the public or nation;
(b) the person is legally and beneficially entitled to the property and the property is not owned jointly or in common with others;
(c) the offer is in accordance with a scheme set up for this purpose by the Secretary of State;
(d) the offer is registered in accordance with the scheme;
(e) the offer, or part of it, is accepted in accordance with the scheme; and
(f) the gift is made pursuant to the offer, or part, accepted.

In the following paragraphs, the '*agreed terms*' means the terms on which acceptance of the offer is agreed, as recorded in the way required by the scheme, and the '*offer registration date*' means the date the offer was registered under (d) above.

[*FA 2012, Sch 14 para 1*].

Pre-eminent property

'*Pre-eminent property*' means:

(1) any picture, print, book, manuscript, work of art, scientific object or other thing that the relevant Minister (i.e. the Secretary of State and/or Scottish, Welsh or Northern Irish equivalent as applicable — see *FA 2012, Sch 14 para 23*) is satisfied is pre-eminent for its national, scientific, historic or artistic interest;

(2) any collection or group of pictures, prints, books, manuscripts, works of art, scientific objects or other things if the relevant Minister is satisfied that the collection or group taken as a whole is pre-eminent for its national, scientific, historic or artistic interest; or

(3) any object that is or has been kept in a significant building (within *IHTA 1984, s 230(3)(a)–(d)*) if it appears to the relevant Minister desirable for the object to remain associated with the building.

For this purpose, '*national interest*' includes interest within any part of the UK. In determining whether an object or collection or group of objects is pre-eminent, regard must be had to any significant association which they have with a particular place.

[*FA 2012, Sch 14 paras 22, 23*].

The relief

Relief is given by way of a reduction of the company's corporation tax liability for the accounting period in which the offer registration date falls. A portion of the liability is treated as satisfied, as if the company had paid that portion when it became due (or on the offer registration date, if the portion became due before that date). The portion so treated as satisfied is the smaller of:

- 20% of the value set out in the agreed terms as the agreed value of the property (or such lower figure as may be specified in the agreed terms); and
- the company's corporation tax liability for the accounting period, less any amount treated as satisfied in respect of a previous qualifying gift.

If the company's corporation tax liability is revised at any time, the relief given must be recalculated (but revision of the agreed terms is not permitted).

If a qualifying gift is set aside or declared void, the tax reduction is withdrawn and the company is required to pay the portions of its liabilities no longer treated as satisfied under the above provisions, together with any late payment interest and penalties in respect of them by the later of the end of the period of 30 days beginning with the day on which the gift was set aside or declared void and the date by which the company would have been required to pay those amounts but for the relief.

Effect on interest and penalties

Any liability to pay late payment interest or late payment penalties (and interest on such penalties) arising in the period beginning with the offer registration date and ending with the date the qualifying gift is made ceases when the gift is made, and is treated as if it had never arisen, to the extent that the tax concerned is treated as satisfied under the above provisions. In determining whether or to what extent interest or a penalty is attributable to that tax, any attribution or apportionment is to be done so as to minimise the interest and penalties payable by the company. This provision does not affect any interest that accrued, or penalty to which the company became liable, before the offer registration date.

The effect of this provision is negated if the qualifying gift is set aside or declared void.

Suspension of tax pending negotiations

Where a company makes an offer within (a) above and:

(A) the offer is registered in accordance with the scheme;
(B) the offer includes a proposal of what should be the agreed terms;
(C) the company will be required to pay an amount of, or on account of, corporation tax for an accounting period for which a tax reduction is proposed by a certain date; and
(D) the negotiation of the terms is not expected to conclude before that date,

the company may make a request that the obligation to pay the amount by the due date be suspended until the negotiations conclude. Such a request must be made in writing to HMRC at least 45 days before the due date in question, and must be accompanied by a copy of the donor's proposal within (B) above and such other information as HMRC may reasonably require. The running total of amounts for which suspension can be requested in respect of the same offer and the same accounting period must not exceed the proposed tax reduction figure for that accounting period. For these purposes, negotiations conclude when the qualifying gift is made or when the offer is withdrawn or rejected.

Suspension of an amount stops the donor from becoming liable to late payment penalties for failing to pay that amount but does not stop late payment interest from accruing.

In considering whether or to what extent to agree to a request, HMRC must have regard to all the circumstances of the case (including the creditworthiness of the potential donor), and they may impose conditions on their agreement to the suspension. HMRC may by notice in writing to the potential donor, withdraw their agreement to a suspension with effect from the date specified in the notice. If they do so, the potential donor must pay the suspended amount, together with any late payment interest, by the end of the period of 30 days beginning with the specified date. The last day of that period is then treated for the purposes of late payment penalties as the date on or before which the amount must be paid.

When the negotiations conclude, then, if the offer is withdrawn or rejected, the potential donor must pay the amount suspended, together with any late payment interest, within 30 days. The last day of the 30-day period is treated for the purposes of late payment penalties as the date on or before which the amount must be paid. If the negotiations conclude because a qualifying gift is made, the potential donor is only required to pay so much as is not treated as satisfied under the above provisions. If the negotiations conclude in relation only to part of the offer, these provisions take effect as far as reasonably practicable in relation to that part and, on receipt of a revised copy of the donor's proposal, HMRC may agree to a further suspension in relation to the part still under negotiation.

[*FA 2012, Sch 14 paras 12–20*].

Treasury powers to amend provisions

The Treasury has the power by order made by statutory instrument to change the percentages specified for determining the amount of the tax reduction. [*FA 2012, Sch 14 paras 14(4), 21*].

Special rules applicable to gifts of real property

[14.18] A '*qualifying interest in land*' is a freehold interest (or a leasehold interest which is for a term of years absolute) in UK land (but not an agreement to acquire freehold land or for a lease). The following two circumstances are additionally brought within the relief.

(i) Where there is a disposal of the beneficial interest in a qualifying interest in land to a charity, and there is also a disposal to the charity of any easement, servitude, right or privilege so far as benefiting that land, the disposal of the easement etc. is regarded as a separate disposal from the disposal of the land.
[*CTA 2010, s 205(2)(3)*].

(ii) Where a person with a freehold or leasehold interest in UK land grants to a charity a lease, for (except in Scotland) a term of years absolute, of the whole or part of that land, this is regarded as a disposal for which the relief is available.

In the application of the above in Scotland:

(1) references to a freehold interest in land are to the interest of the owner;
(2) references to a leasehold interest in land which is a term of years absolute are to a tenant's right over or interest in a property subject to a lease; and
(3) references to an agreement for a lease do not include missives of let that constitute an actual lease.

[*CTA 2010, s 205(6)*].

The following supplementary provisions apply to disposals of qualifying interests in land.

(A) Where two or more persons are entitled jointly or in common to a qualifying interest in land, the relief applies only if each person disposes of the whole of his beneficial interest in the land to the charity. Relief is then allowed to each of those persons, being apportioned between or amongst them as they may agree.

(B) The relief is dependent on the receipt by the person disposing of the interest of a certificate given by or on behalf of the charity specifying the description of the interest concerned and the date of the disposal, and stating that the charity has acquired the interest.

(C) If a 'disqualifying event' occurs at any time in the period from the date of the disposal to the sixth anniversary of the end of the accounting period of the disposal (*'the provisional period'*), the person (or each of the persons) making the disposal is treated as never having been entitled to the relief in respect of the disposal (and HMRC has the necessary assessment, etc. powers). A *'disqualifying event'* occurs if the person (or any one of the persons) who made the disposal, or any connected person (see **19** CONNECTED PERSONS), either becomes entitled to an interest or right in relation to all or part of the land to which the disposal relates, or becomes party to an arrangement under which he, or a person connected with him, enjoys some right in relation to all or part of that land, otherwise than for full consideration in money or money's worth. This does *not* apply if the person became so entitled as a result of a disposition of property on death, whether by will, by intestacy or otherwise.

[*CTA 2010, ss 203–216*].

A payment made, or to be made, to a body situated outside the UK is non-charitable expenditure under *CTA 2010, s 496(1)(d)* if it is incurred for charitable purposes only, but the charitable company has not taken such steps as HMRC consider are reasonable in the circumstances to ensure that the payment will be applied for charitable purposes.

Foreign charities are currently excluded from *CTA 2010, s 496(1)(d)* by virtue of *CTA 2010, s 500*.

[*CTA 2010, ss 213–217*].

Expenditure on grassroots sport

[14.19] Certain contributions made by a company to grassroots sport are allowed as a deduction from total profits for the accounting period in which the payment is made. The deduction does not apply if relief is available under the qualifying charitable donation provisions (see **14.11** above), or would be but for the inflated member-related expenditure provisions for CASCs at **14.11** above.

The amount of the deduction depends on whether the contribution is by or to a 'qualifying sports body' or it is a direct payment to grassroots sport, as follows.

(a) Qualifying sport body payments. An unlimited deduction equal to the amount of expenditure is allowed if, at the time of payment, the company making or receiving the payment is a qualifying sport body.
(b) Direct payments. A deduction up to a maximum of £2,500 per 12-month accounting period is permitted if the payment is made by a company which is not a qualifying sport body directly to grassroots sport (i.e. not through a qualifying sport body). If an accounting period is less than 12 months long the limit is reduced proportionately. The Treasury may increase the limit by statutory instrument. No deduction is allowed for payments in excess of the maximum.

A *'qualifying sport body'* is a or a body which is wholly owed by a recognised sport governing body. A *'recognised sport governing body'* is a body included in a list maintained by the UK Sports Council or one of the Sports Councils of

England, Scotland, Wales or Northern Ireland of governing bodies recognised by them. The Treasury may by statutory instrument amend the meaning of 'qualifying sport body' or designate particular bodies to be treated as such.

To be eligible for the deduction, the payment must be 'qualifying expenditure' and must not have been refunded. It can only be deducted from the company's total taxable profits once all other corporation tax reliefs other than relief for qualifying charitable donations, group relief, and group relief for carried forward losses have been given for the relevant accounting period. A deduction cannot reduce the company's total profits for the accounting period below nil. Any allowable amount that cannot be deducted because of this rule may potentially be surrendered as GROUP RELIEF (35.5) for the same accounting period.

If a company receives a payment for charitable purposes which are for facilitating participation in amateur eligible sport, it is only able to claim a deduction under these provisions for any expenditure that exceeds so much of the income as does not have to be brought into account for corporation tax purposes. This rule operates across accounting periods such that an amount received in one period may have be taken into account in considering whether a payment made in a later period is allowable.

Qualifying expenditure

A payment is 'qualifying expenditure' if:

(a) it is incurred for charitable purposes which are for facilitating participation in amateur eligible sport. It is specifically provided that paying a person to play does not fall within the scope of this condition, but paying coaches or officials may qualify. The definition of 'eligible sport' is the same as that in the CASC legislation (see 75.2 VOLUNTARY ASSOCIATIONS);

(b) no deduction from total profits or in computing profits is otherwise available for the payment.

A just and reasonable apportionment is made where expenditure is partly for the above purposes and partly for other purposes.

[*CTA 2010, ss 217A–217D; F(No 2)A 2017, s 22(5)–(7)*].

Key points on charities

[14.20] Points to consider are as follows:

- Does the body fall within the definition of a charity for tax purposes?
- Does company law permit the company to make the charitable gift?
- Exemptions from tax on charities' income are specific, not general. Therefore if a charity has income not within the specific exemptions it will be liable to tax on that income.

- Companies receive relief for charitable donations against profits of the year in which they are made, except where the donor is owned by the charity, in which case the donation may be made up to nine months after the end of the accounting period to which it relates.
- Charities should avoid making investments in or substantial loans to their trading companies from which they have received donations financed by trading profits.

15

Claims

Cross references. See **9.2**(ii) CAPITAL ALLOWANCES; **11.3** CAPITAL GAINS for requirement to notify loss; **31.6** DOUBLE TAX RELIEF.

Simon's Taxes. See **A4.204, D1.1345.**

Introduction to claims

[15.1] A claim for relief, an allowance or repayment must be quantified at the time it is made and, subject to any special provision, must be made within four years of the end of the accounting period to which it relates, unless a different time limit is prescribed within the legislation for that particular claim or election.

Amendments may be made to claims within the same time limit for the original claim or election. All claims must be expressed in figures at the time the claim is made.

Certain claims must be made in the tax return of the company in question, such as claims with regard to group relief, capital allowances, research and development tax credits (including the above the line R&D expenditure credit), film tax and creative industries relief, land remediation tax credits and vaccine research tax credits. Other claims do not need to be made in the return but may not be made before the return for the period to which the claim relates is delivered.

This chapter examines these claims in more detail and considers appeals and other relief in respect of such claims.

Claims and elections

[15.2] Generally claims or elections should be made in writing (whether within the tax return, or otherwise). *CTA 2009* and *CTA 2010* specifically state this is to be the case with regard to claims and elections made under those acts. [*FA 1998, Sch 18 paras 54–56; CTA 2009, s 1315; CTA 2010, s 1175*].

Subject to any express provision to the contrary:

(a) claims and elections affecting only one accounting period, and which are made after notice has been given requiring the delivery of a company tax return for that period, must be made in the return, or by amendment of the return, if they can be so made. This requirement does not apply with regard to a claim for an amount to be exempt from tax under the provisions for gifts qualifying for gift aid relief in respect of charitable companies and certain eligible bodies (within *CTA 2010, ss 472, 475*). [*FA 1998, Sch 18 para 57*].
A claim, etc. made after the return has been delivered is treated as an amendment of the return (as under **65.8** RETURNS).
Group relief, group relief for carried-forward losses, first-year tax credit and capital allowance claims (see further below) and claims to research and development tax credits, including RDEC, and film and creative industry credits (such as television, video games and theatrical production credits), (see **63** RESEARCH AND DEVELOPMENT EXPENDITURE; **26** CREATIVE INDUSTRIES RELIEFS) may only be made by inclusion in a tax return;
(b) claims and elections which affect an accounting period (or periods) other than that in which the event or occasion giving rise to the claim (etc.) occurs are treated as amending the return for that period (or for the period affected), as under **65.8** RETURNS, where that return has already been delivered and can be so amended [*FA 1998, Sch 18 para 58*];
(c) otherwise, *TMA 1970, Sch 1A* (as amended by *FA 1998, Sch 19 para 42*) provides the procedure for claims etc. (see **15.7** below).

(a)–(c) above do not, however, affect the time limit or any other condition for making a claim or election.

Certain claims not required to be made in a company tax return may not be made before the return for the period to which the claim relates is delivered. This applies to certain claims for income tax repayments.

In *Spring Salmon & Seafood v HMRC* [2015] UKFTT 616 the First-tier Tribunal found that the company had made a valid claim in its tax return, so that the closure notice issued by HMRC was valid, and was therefore effective in denying the claim (for terminal loss relief). In the two returns in question the section to be completed for trading losses had been left blank, but the Tribunal noted that the tax properly chargeable in the year to which the returns related could only be understood when considering the computation, letter and financial documents supplied by the company. The claim was therefore included in the return.

As noted at (c) above a claim not included in a company tax return must be in such form as HMRC require and must contain a declaration that the particulars in it are correct to the best of the information and belief of the claimant. See further **15.7** below.

Consequential claims

For consequential claims, elections etc. arising out of HMRC assessments or amendments to self-assessments, see **15.6** below.

[*TMA 1970, Sch 1A para 2; FA 1998, Sch 18 paras 9, 10(2), 57–60*].

Simon's Taxes. See **D1.1345** *et seq.*

Claims and elections are covered in HMRC Company Taxation Manual CTM90602 onwards.

Group relief

[15.3] For special rules relating to group relief claims, see **35.12** GROUP RELIEF.

Capital allowances

[15.4] For special rules relating to capital allowances claims, see **9.2** CAPITAL ALLOWANCES, **10.2** CAPITAL ALLOWANCES ON PLANT AND MACHINERY.

Other claims

[15.5] For claims for payment of research and development tax credits or RDEC, see **63** RESEARCH AND DEVELOPMENT EXPENDITURE. For claims for payment of tax credits for film or TV production, video game development and theatrical or orchestral concert production, see **26** CREATIVE INDUSTRIES RELIEFS. For claims for first-year tax credits, see **10.25** CAPITAL ALLOWANCES ON PLANT AND MACHINERY. For the election for the patent box rules to apply, which can be made in the tax computation accompanying the return, or separately in writing, see **57** PATENT INCOME.

For consequential claims, elections etc. arising out of HMRC assessments or amendments to self-assessments (which may generally be made within one year from the end of the accounting period in which the assessment was made or the enquiry into the relevant return closed), or where an assessment is made in a case involving a loss of tax brought about carelessly or deliberately, see **15.6** below.

Consequential claims

[15.6] Where:

(a) a company tax return is amended by HMRC under *FA 1998, Sch 18 para 34(2A)* (i.e. an amendment, following completion or partial completion of an enquiry, to a return other than the return which was the subject of the enquiry) so that the tax payable is increased; or
(b) a discovery assessment (see **6.3** ASSESSMENTS) is made; or
(c) an assessment to recover excessive group relief or group relief for carried-forward losses (see **15.2** above) is made,

the following provisions apply to allow certain claims, elections, applications and notices to be made, given, revoked or varied.

However, where an assessment is made in a case involving careless or deliberate conduct (see **6.3** ASSESSMENTS), the more restricted relief described in the final paragraph below applies instead.

A claim or election, as above, which:

- relates to the accounting period in respect of which the amendment or assessment was made; or
- was made or given by reference to an event occurring in that period,

and the making of which has or could have the effect of reducing a 'relevant liability' of the company, may be made or given at any time within one year from the end of the '*relevant accounting period*', i.e. that in which the partial or final closure notice was issued or the assessment made.

Similarly, if previously made or given, it may be varied or (unless irrevocable) revoked in the same manner as it was made or given, and by or with the consent of the same person(s) who made it, gave it or consented to it (or their personal representatives).

A '*relevant liability*' is the increased liability arising from the amendment or assessment, or any other liability of the company for the accounting period to which the amendment or assessment relates or any subsequent accounting period ending not later than one year after the end of the relevant accounting period.

If the effect of a consequential claim, etc. as above would be to alter the tax liability of another person, the written consent of that person (or their personal representative) to the claim, etc. is required. If the effect is to increase that person's liability, neither the above provisions nor *TMA 1970, s 43A* (the corresponding income and capital gains tax provisions) apply in relation to any amendment or assessment made because of the increased liability.

Where one or more claims etc. as above are made in consequence of an amendment or assessment, the combined tax liability of the company and any other persons affected cannot be reduced by more than the additional tax liability resulting from that amendment or assessment which allowed the claim to be made. Where this limitation involves more than one period or more than one person, the limited amount available is apportioned between the periods or persons concerned. The manner in which the apportionment is to be made is specified by HMRC by written notice to the person(s) concerned, who may, however, within 30 days from the date of the notice (where more than one person is concerned, the last notice), give (or jointly give) written notice substituting a different manner of apportionment.

The claims appeals provisions are appropriately modified in relation to revocations or variations of claims under the above provisions.

Assessments involving loss of tax brought about carelessly or deliberately

Where an assessment is made in a case involving a loss of tax brought about carelessly or deliberately, the above provisions for consequential claims are disapplied. Instead, the company may require that in arriving at the tax assessed, any relief or allowance is given to which the company would have been entitled for the accounting period had a claim or application been made within the normal time limits. The claims or applications must be made either before the assessment is made or within the time provided for an appeal against the assessment (see HMRC Company Taxation Manual, CTM90665).

[*FA 1998, Sch 18 paras 61–65; F(No 2)A 2017, Sch 4 para 108, Sch 15 para 33*].

Simon's Taxes. See D1.1345.

Claims etc. not included in returns

[15.7] A claim or election not included in a company tax return must be in such form as required by HMRC and must contain a declaration that the particulars contained therein are correct to the best information and belief of the claimant. HMRC do not generally provide a standard form for claims but may set certain requirements for any such claims.

For example, subject to any specific provision otherwise, a claim or election made otherwise than in a return must be made to an officer of HMRC. As noted, the claim etc. must include a declaration by the claimant that all particulars are correctly stated to the best of his information or belief. No claim requiring a tax repayment can be made unless the claimant has documentary proof that the tax has been paid or deducted. The claim must be made in a form determined by HMRC and may require, *inter alia*, a statement of the amount of tax to be discharged or repaid and (except as below) supporting information and documentation.

In practice, HMRC do not generally determine the particular form in which a claim must be made. In the case of a claim by or on behalf of a person who is not resident in the UK, HMRC may require a statement or declaration in support of the claim to be made by affidavit.

A person who may wish to make a claim must keep all records that may be required for the purpose and must preserve them until such time as HMRC may no longer enquire into the claim or such enquiries are treated as completed. HMRC have the power to make regulations specifying records which are required to be kept. There is a maximum penalty of £3,000 for non-compliance in relation to any claim *actually made*. Similar provisions and exceptions apply as in **65.13** RETURNS as to the preservation of the information contained in documents and other records instead of originals and the exception from penalty for non-compliance in relation to dividend vouchers, interest certificates etc.

A claimant may, at any time within twelve months of making a claim, amend the claim by notice to an officer of HMRC. An officer of HMRC may similarly, at any time within nine months of the claim being made, amend the claim to correct any obvious errors or mistakes (including errors of principle and arithmetical mistakes).

No such amendments may, however, be made while the claim is under enquiry (see below). HMRC have powers to enquire into a claim etc. (or amendment thereof) similar to those relating to company tax returns (see **65.14** RETURNS), but these powers are to be replaced by the unified powers at **38.3–38.10** HMRC INVESTIGATORY POWERS with effect from a date to be appointed. Notice of intention to enquire must be given by the first anniversary of the end of the accounting period to which the claim relates or, if later, by the quarter day (meaning 31 January, 30 April etc.) next following the first anniversary of the date of claim etc. In the event of such an enquiry, they have powers to call for documents, etc. similar to those relating to enquiries into company tax returns. Where an enquiry is in progress, an officer of HMRC may give provisional effect to the claim etc. (or amendment thereof) to such extent as he thinks fit.

An enquiry is complete when HMRC's officer issues a closure notice informing the claimant of his conclusions. If the claim is for discharge or repayment of tax, the notice must either state that, in the officer's opinion, no amendment of the claim is required or amend the claim so as to make good or eliminate any deficiency or excess which in the officer's opinion has arisen (the latter only applying, in the case of an enquiry into an amendment of a claim, so far as the deficiency or excess is attributable to that amendment). In the case of any other claim, the notice must either allow the claim or disallow it wholly or to the extent the officer considers appropriate. The claimant may apply to the Tribunal for a direction to issue a closure notice in the same way as applies to enquiries into returns (see **65.17** RETURNS).

HMRC must give effect to such an amendment, by assessment if necessary, within 30 days after issue of the closure notice.

An appeal may be made against an amendment by HMRC to a claim following an enquiry, written notice of appeal to be given normally within 30 days after the amendment is made (extended to three months where questions of residence of the company are involved). If an amendment is varied on appeal, HMRC have a further 30 days to give effect to the variation. Where a claim etc. does not give rise to a discharge or repayment of tax (for example, a claim to carry forward trading losses), there are provisions as to disallowance of such claims on completion of the enquiry, with appeal procedures similar to those above.

Appeals against amendments to claims are made to HMRC and may also be notified to the First-tier Tribunal.

Where these provisions apply to a claim, etc. which results in an increase in the tax payable, all necessary adjustments, by way of assessment or otherwise, may be made so as to give effect to it.

[*TMA 1970, s 42(11), Sch 1A; FA 1998, Sch 18 para 60(3)*].

Simon's Taxes. See **D1.1345**.

Time limits

[15.8] Unless otherwise specified, claims for relief from corporation tax must be made within four years of the end of the accounting period to which they relate.

[*FA 1998, Sch 18 para 55*].

See **67** TIME LIMITS and Tolley's Income Tax under Time Limits — Fixed Dates and Time Limits — Miscellaneous. See also **15.11** below with respect to recovery of tax paid under mistake of law.

Appeals in respect of claims

[15.9] Appeals have to be made in writing within 30 days of the issue of:

- a notice of amendment to a self-assessment; or
- a notice of an assessment which is not a self-assessment.

HMRC will allow an extra three months on top of the normal 30-day time limit for making an appeal against a decision dated February 2020 or later where the taxpayer has been affected by coronavirus. See www.gov.uk/tax-appeals/decis ion.

See **5.3** APPEALS and **6.3** ASSESSMENTS.

As regards claims etc. to which *TMA 1970, Sch 1A* applies (see below), appeals against amendments to claims etc. must be made within 30 days of the amendment being made, extended to three months where the appeal relates to certain residence etc. claims or to pension funds for overseas employees.

Any notice of appeal in connection with the self-assessment provisions must state the grounds of appeal.

[*TMA 1970, Sch 1A para 9; FA 1998, Sch 18 para 92*].

TMA 1970, Sch 1A deals with all aspects of claims not within *FA 1998, Sch 18 paras 57, 58* (mainly those not included in the company tax return (or amended return), see **15.1** above).

[*FA 1998, Sch 18 para 59*].

TMA 1970, s 46D has effect as respects the Tribunal to which an appeal under *Sch 1A* lies.

In *Dr Vasiliki Raftopoulou v HMRC* [2015] UKUT 579 the Upper Tribunal found that the First-tier Tribunal had jurisdiction to decide whether the taxpayer had a reasonable excuse for the lateness of a claim for repayment. The Tribunal concluded that if the taxpayer had had a reasonable excuse for not filing her claim within the time limit and had made the claim without unreasonable delay after the excuse had ceased, then *TMA 1970, s 118(2)* would deem her claim to have been filed within the relevant time limit so that the appeal could fall within *TMA 1970, Sch 1A*.

Claim for recovery of overpaid tax

[15.10] Where a company has paid an amount of corporation tax and believes that the tax is not due, it can make a claim to HMRC for repayment of the tax. Where a company has been assessed as liable to pay an amount of tax, or there has been a determination or direction to that effect, it can likewise make a claim for the amount to be discharged if it believes that the tax is not due. For these purposes, tax paid by one company on behalf of another is treated as paid by the other company.

HMRC will not give effect to such a claim in the following circumstances:

(a) the amount is excessive because of:
- a mistake in a claim;
- a mistake consisting of making, or failing to make, an election, claim or notice;
- a mistake in allocating expenditure to a capital or a mistake consisting of making, or failing to make, such an allocation; or
- a mistake in bringing in a capital allowances disposal value into account or a mistake consisting of bringing, or failing to bring, such a value into account;

(b) the claimant can seek relief by taking other steps under tax legislation;
(c) the claimant could have sought relief by taking such steps within a period which has expired by the time the claim is made, if it knew, or ought reasonably to have known, before the end of that period that such relief was available;
(d) the claim is made on grounds that have been put to a court or tribunal in the course of an appeal relating to the amount or grounds that have been put to HMRC in the course of such an appeal settled by agreement;
(e) the claimant knew, or ought reasonably to have known, of the grounds for the claim before the latest of: the date an appeal relating to the amount was determined by a court or tribunal, the date on which such an appeal was withdrawn by the claimant, and the end of the period in which the claimant could have appealed;
(f) the amount was due as a result of proceedings by HMRC against the claimant, or under an agreement between the claimant and HMRC settling such proceedings; and
(g) the amount is excessive because of a mistake in calculating the claimant's liability where the liability was calculated in accordance with the practice generally prevailing at the time.

The exclusion in (g) above does not apply where a claim to relief relates to tax charged contrary to EU law. For this purpose, an amount is charged contrary to EU law if it is contrary to the provisions of the Treaty on the Functioning of the European Union relating to the free movement of goods, persons, services or capital (or replacement provisions under any subsequent treaty). See also **15.11** below with regard to the time limits for restitution claims where tax has been charged contrary to EU law.

[*FA 1998, Sch 18 paras 51, 51A*].

Making a claim

A claim must be made within four years after the end of the accounting period concerned. Where the claim relates to tax overpaid, that accounting period is the period in respect of which the payment was made or, where the amount paid is excessive due to a mistake in a tax return or returns, the period to which the return (or if more than one, the first return) relates. Where the claim relates to an assessment, determination or direction, the accounting period concerned is that to which that assessment etc. relates or, where the amount due is excessive due to a mistake in a tax return or returns, the period to which the return (or if more than one, the first return) relates.

A claim cannot be made in a tax return.

Where, under the construction industry scheme or other tax legislation, one person (P) is accountable to HMRC for corporation tax payable by another person or for any other amount that has been or is to be set off against another person's liability, a claim in respect of the amount can only be made by that other person. If, however, P has paid such an amount but was not in fact accountable to HMRC for it, P, and only P, can make a claim in respect of that amount. Effect will not be given to such a claim by P to the extent that the amount has been repaid to, or set against amounts payable by, the other person.

Partnerships

A claim in respect of an amount paid or due by one or more partners in accordance with a self-assessment which is excessive because of a mistake in a partnership return must be made by a nominated partner (or his personal representative). The partner must have been a partner at some time in the period for which the return was made.

[*FA 1998, Sch 18 paras 51B–51D*].

Discovery assessment etc. following claim

Where the grounds for a claim also provide grounds for HMRC to make a discovery assessment or determination (see **6.3** ASSESSMENTS) for any period and such an assessment or determination could not otherwise be made as a result of one of the restrictions noted below, those restrictions are disregarded and an assessment or determination is not out of time if made before the final determination of the claim (i.e. before the time at which the claim can no longer be varied). The restrictions concerned are those at **6.3**(b) ASSESSMENTS and the expiry of a time limit for making a discovery assessment or determination (see **6.7** ASSESSMENTS).

Similar provisions apply in relation to amendments of partnership returns.

[*FA 1998, Sch 18 paras 51E, 51F*].

Contract settlements

The above provisions apply also to amounts paid under a contract settlement (see **6.8** ASSESSMENTS). If the person who paid the amounts due under the settlement (the '*payer*') was not the person from whom the tax concerned was due (the '*taxpayer*'), then the provisions are modified accordingly. If an amount is repayable to the payer as a result of a claim, HMRC can set the amount repayable against any amount payable by the taxpayer under any discovery assessment or determination made as a result of the claim.

[*FA 1998, Sch 18 para 51G*].

Special relief

A claim can be made for discharge or repayment of tax charged in an HMRC determination (under *FA 1998, Sch 18 paras 36, 37* — see **65.4** RETURNS) if the following apply:

(1) the claimant believes the tax is not due or, if already paid, was not due;
(2) relief under the above provisions would have been available but for (c) above or because the tax is due as a result of proceedings by HMRC against the claimant (see (f) above) or because more than four years have passed since the end of the tax year or accounting period; and
(3) where the claim would fail because the tax is due as a result of proceedings by HMRC, the claimant was neither present nor legally represented during the proceedings.

HMRC will not give effect to the claim unless:

(i) in HMRC's opinion it would be unconscionable to seek to recover the tax or withhold repayment of it;
(ii) the taxpayer's affairs (in matters concerning HMRC) are otherwise up to date or satisfactory arrangements have been put in place to bring them up to date as far as possible; and
(iii) either the taxpayer has not previously made a claim for relief or relief under HMRC's equitable liability practice or, where such a claim has been made, the exceptional circumstances of the case mean that the present claim should be allowed.

For the purposes of (iii) above, it does not matter whether the previous claim succeeded. A claim must include information and documentation which is reasonably required to determine whether (i)–(iii) above apply.

The jurisdiction of the Tribunal in determining whether (i) above applies is limited to deciding whether the opinion of HMRC was 'unreasonable' in the judicial review sense. The Tribunal cannot consider afresh whether it would be unconscionable to seek to recover the tax or withhold repayment. See *Currie v HMRC* FTT, [2014] UKFTT 882 (TC); 2014 STI 3362.

[*FA 1998, Sch 18 para 51BA*].

Restitution — tax paid under mistake of law

[15.11] It was confirmed in *R v CIR (ex p. Woolwich Equitable Building Society)*, HL 1990, 63 TC 589 that a claim can be made through the courts, under common law, for restitution of tax payments made to the Revenue under an unlawful statutory demand and that interest is payable from the dates of the payments. In *Deutsche Morgan Grenfell Group plc v CIR* HL 2006, [2007] STC 1 the company successfully sought to obtain this remedy in respect of tax paid under a mistake of law. In making its claim, the company contended that under *Limitation Act 1980, s 32(1)(c)* it could make the claim for restitution within six years of the time it discovered the mistake (or could with reasonable diligence have discovered it), rather than within the normal time limit of six years from the time of payment under *Limitation Act 1980, s 5*. In upholding the company's claim, the House of Lords held that the effect of *Limitation Act 1980, s 32(1)(c)* was that the limitation period had not begun until 8 March 2001 (the date of the CJEC decision in *Metallgesellschaft Ltd v CIR* CJEC 2001, [2001] STC 452). The Supreme Court overruled this part of the decision, however, in *Test Claimants in the FII Group Litigation v HMRC* SC, [2020] STC 2387. It held that the correct approach was that time begins to run under *Limitation Act 1980, s 32(1)(c)* when the claimant discovers, or could with reasonable diligence discover, his mistake 'in the sense of recognising that a worthwhile claim arises' with sufficient confidence to justify obtaining legal advice and collecting evidence with a view to commencing a claim.

Following the High Court decision in *Deutsche Morgan Grenfell*, provisions were included in *FA 2004* to prevent the application of the extended time limit of *Limitation Act 1980, s 32(1)(c)* to taxation matters. Accordingly, *s 32(1)(c)* (and the NI equivalent) does not apply in relation to any action or claim for relief from the consequences of a mistake of law relating to a taxation matter under the care and management of HMRC brought after 7 September 2003, whether the action or claim is expressed to be brought on the grounds of mistake or on some other ground (such as unlawful demand or *ultra vires*). [*FA 2004, s 320(1)(6)*]. The effect of this provision is that court actions for restitution based on mistake of law must generally be brought within six years of the tax having been paid. *FA 2004, s 321* makes a similar change to Scottish law, so that claims for relief for tax paid under an error of law must generally be made within five years of the tax having been paid.

FA 2004, s 320 also includes provisions to prevent a claim to amend an existing action, seeking to introduce claims for a different payment, transaction, period or other matter, from being treated by the courts under *Limitation Act 1980, s 35* as being a separate action commenced on the same date as the original action (and thereby, in some cases, potentially circumventing the above provisions). This applies to amendment claims made after 19 November 2003, and for this purpose, such a claim is treated as made before 20 November 2003 if the Revenue consented to the making of it in writing before that date or if, immediately before that date, the Revenue's consent had been sought and not refused or an application to the court for permission to make the claim had been made and not refused. [*FA 2004, s 320(2)(5)*].

The above provisions take legal effect only on 22 July 2004 (the date of Royal Assent to *FA 2004*). *FA 2004, s 320(3)* therefore deems an action begun before that date but after 7 September 2003, or a claim to amend an existing action made before 22 July 2004 but after 19 November 2003 to be discontinued on 22 July 2004 and provides for the recovery (with interest) of any amount paid out by the Revenue in relation to such an action or amendment.

These provisions are extended by *FA 2007, s 107* to prevent the application of *Limitation Act 1980, s 32(1)(c)* in relation to actions brought before 8 September 2003 as well as those brought on or after that date. This is subject to the following exceptions:

(a) where the action, or cause of action, has been the subject of a House of Lords judgment or order before 6 December 2006 as to the application of *s 32(1)(c)*;
(b) where the parties to the action are bound, under a group litigation order, by a House of Lords judgment or order before 6 December 2006 in another action as to the application of *s 32(1)(c)*; and
(c) where the action, or cause of action, relates to the charging of tax contrary to European Union law.

The extended provisions take legal effect only on 19 July 2007 (the date of Royal Assent to *FA 2007*). Any court judgment or order given or made before that date but after 5 December 2006 is therefore deemed to have been what it would have been had the extended provisions been in force at all times since the action was brought and any available defence of limitation had been raised. Any payment made under the judgment that is accordingly taken not to have been imposed is repayable with interest.

In *Test Claimants in the FII Group Litigation v HMRC* CJEU, [2014] STC 638 *FA 2007, s 107* above was held to breach European Community law because it does not incorporate any transitional provisions. The exception in (c) above was introduced by *FA 2014, s 299* to amend *FA 2007, s 107* to comply with that decision. Although the exception takes legal effect on 17 July 2014 (the date of Royal Assent to *FA 2014*), it applies to actions brought, and causes of action arising, before, on or after that date. See also *United Kingdom v European Commission* CJEU, (C-640/13), which confirmed that *FA 2007, s 107* breached EU law (but note that the decision did not consider the changes made by *FA 2014*).

In *Wallace v HMRC* Ch D, [2018] STC 790, it was held that a common law claim for restitution cannot be made where a claim for recovery of overpaid tax under **15.10** above can be made.

Restitution interest paid to a company as a result of a mistake in law or following unlawful collection of tax by HMRC, as a result of a judgment or an agreement which became final on or after 21 October 2015, is chargeable to corporation tax at a special rate of 45%. See **1.7** INTRODUCTION: CHARGE TO TAX, RATES AND PROFITS.

Simon's Taxes. See A1.706.

16

Close Companies

Simon's Taxes. See Part D3.

Introduction to close companies

[16.1] There are many UK resident companies that are defined as 'small' for various parts of the Corporation Taxes Acts. In addition, many private limited companies are owner managed businesses and are controlled by a limited number of individuals. These companies may therefore be defined as 'close'. There are special tax rules that apply to 'close' companies. This stems from the fact that the directors and shareholders are often the same people, and there are concerns that, because of this link, it is easier for the company's affairs to be arranged to give tax advantages to the company, its directors and shareholders.

The following paragraphs describe these special rules and the effects that may arise as a result.

For HMRC's guide to close companies see CTM60000 *et seq.*

Close company — definition

[16.2] Subject to the exceptions at 16.3 below, a company is a '*close company*' if *either* Condition A or Condition B below is met.

Condition A is that the company:

- is under the 'control' (**16.6** below) of five or fewer 'participators' (**16.7** below); or
- is under the control of participators who are 'directors' (**16.8** below).

Condition B is that five or fewer participators, or participators who are directors, together possess or are entitled to acquire:

(a) such rights as would, in the event of a winding-up, entitle them to receive the greater part of the assets available for distribution among participators; or

(b) such rights as would, in the event of a winding-up, so entitle them if one were to disregard any rights which any of them (or any other person) has as a loan creditor (**16.11** below), whether of that company or any other company.

For the purpose of applying Condition B, participators in and directors of any company (a 'company participator') entitled to receive assets in the notional winding-up are themselves treated as participators in or directors of the company under consideration. Company participators are disregarded for that purpose, unless acting in a fiduciary or representative capacity.

[*CTA 2010, ss 439, 441*].

CTA 2010, s 440 determines the part of the assets available for distribution among the participators which a person is treated as being entitled to receive in the notional winding-up envisaged by Condition B above. In particular, the assumption is made that any company participator will also be wound up and that the assets distributed to it will be distributed onwards to its own participators.

For the purposes of Condition B, a person is treated as entitled to acquire anything which he is entitled to acquire at a future date or will, at a future date, be entitled to acquire, with reference to both contractual rights and any rights under a trust deed, for example. See further CTM60120.

If a person (B) possesses any rights or powers on behalf of another person (A), or may be required to exercise any rights or powers on A's direction or on A's behalf, those rights or powers are to be attributed to A. There can also be attributed to a person (P) all the rights and powers:

(i) of any company of which P has control, or of which P and his 'associates' (**16.9** below) have control;

(ii) of any two or more companies within (a) above;

(iii) of any associate of P; or

(iv) of any two or more associates of P.

Any rights or powers already attributed to A, where A is a company or an associate of P, may in turn be attributed to P under any of (i)–(iv) above. However, any rights or powers attributed under (i)–(iv) to an associate cannot consequently be attributed under (i)–(iv) to another associate.

Any such attributions that *can* be made under (i)–(iv) above *will* be made if they result in the company being treated as under the control of five or fewer participators and thus a close company.

[*CTA 2010, s 451*].

The first-mentioned holder of shares in joint ownership is treated as able alone to exercise the rights attaching thereto (*Harton Coal Co Ltd* [1960] Ch 563, [1960] 3 All ER 48). For circumstances in which HMRC are bound to attribute rights and powers as in (a)–(d) above, see *R v CIR (ex p Newfields Developments Ltd)* [2001] UKHL 27, [2001] 4 All ER 400, [2001] 1 WLR 1111.

Exceptions

[16.3] Notwithstanding **16.2** above, none of the following can be a close company.

- (a) A non-UK resident company.
- (b) A registered society within **22.1** CO-OPERATIVE AND COMMUNITY BENEFIT SOCIETIES (previously a registered industrial and provident society (within *CTA 2010, s 1119*)).
- (c) A building society.
- (d) A company controlled by the Crown or by persons acting on behalf of the Crown and independently of any other person. But this exception applies only for the purposes of Condition A at **16.2** above. It does not apply at all if the company is a close company as a result of its being under the control of persons acting independently of the Crown.
- (e) A company 'involved' with a non-close company (see below).
- (f) Subject to the conditions set out at **16.4** below, a quoted company.

For the purposes of (e) above, a company is '*involved*' with a non-close company if:

- (i) it is controlled by one or more non-close companies and cannot be treated as a close company except by taking, as one of its five or fewer participators, a non-close company; or
- (ii) it would not be a close company were it not for **16.2**(a) above or **16.6**(d) below and would still not be a close company if the term 'participators' did not include loan creditors (**16.11** below) which are non-close companies.

For the purposes only of applying (i) and (ii) above, the term 'close company' includes a company that would be a close company if it were UK resident; and 'non-close company' must be construed accordingly. If shares in a company (C) are held on trust for a registered pension scheme, the persons holding the shares are generally treated as the beneficial owners, so that the shares are held by a non-close company. However, this is not the case if the scheme is established for the benefit of (or for the benefit of dependants of) present or former directors or employees of C or of certain companies related to C (for which see *CTA 2010, s 445(3)*).

[*CTA 2010, ss 442–447*].

Quoted companies

[16.4] The circumstances under which a quoted company cannot be a close company at a particular time are summarised below. All three of conditions (a)–(c) must be met.

(a) Shares carrying at least 35% of the voting power in the company must have been allotted unconditionally to, or acquired unconditionally by, and at that time be beneficially held by, the public. For this purpose, 'shares' include stock but do not include shares entitled to a fixed rate of dividend. See below as regards 'voting power' and see **16.5** below as regards shares 'beneficially held by the public'.

(b) Such shares must, within the twelve months before that time, have been dealt in on, and listed on, a 'recognised stock exchange'.

(c) The voting power possessed by 'principal members' of the company must not at that time exceed 85% of the total voting power in the company.

In determining for these purposes the voting power which a person possesses, there is to be attributed to the person any voting power that would be attributed to him if the attribution rules at **16.2** above applied.

A '*principal member*' of a company is a person possessing more than 5% of the voting power. If, however, there are more than five such persons, a person is a principal member of the company only if he is one of the five persons possessing the greatest percentages. If there are no such five persons because two or more persons possess equal percentages, a person is a principal member of the company only if he is one of the six or more persons (including the two or more who are equal) who possess the greatest percentages.

[*CTA 2010, s 446*].

Example

A holds 10% of the voting power of X Ltd. B and C hold 8% each, D and E hold 7% each and F holds 6%. No other member holds more than 5%. A, B, C, D and E each hold more than 5% and are principal members of the company, as they are the five persons holding the greatest percentages. F is not a principal member, as he does not meet the latter requirement. If G acquires a 10% holding, he will also become a principal member of the company. Since D and E have equal shareholdings, both will remain principal members, making six in total.

A '*recognised stock exchange*' means:

- any market of a recognised investment exchange designated by HMRC; and
- any market outside the UK which is designated by HMRC.

HMRC publish a current list of recognised stock exchanges at www.gov.uk/guidance/recognised-stock-exchanges.

[*CTA 2010, s 1137*].

HMRC issued a guidance note on 29 March 2007 on the treatment of AIM shares and the designation of recognised investment exchanges as recognised stock exchanges — see SWTI Issue 14, 13 April 2007.

Shares beneficially held by the public

[16.5] For the purposes of **16.4**(a) above, shares are beneficially held by the public if:

- they are beneficially held by a UK resident company which is not a close company, or by a non-UK resident company which would not be a close company if it were UK resident; or
- they are held on trust for a registered pension scheme; or
- they are not comprised in the holding of a 'principal member' (see **16.4** above).

A principal member's holding consists of the shares which carry the voting power possessed by him.

But shares in a company (C) are *not* beneficially held by the public if they are held:

(a) by a director (**16.8** below) of C;
(b) by an associate (**16.9** below) of a director of C;
(c) by a company which is under the control (**16.6** below) of one or more persons each of whom is such a director or associate;
(d) by an associated company (**16.10** below) of C; or
(e) as part of a fund the capital or income of which is applicable or applied wholly or mainly for the benefit of:
    - individuals who are employees, directors, past employees or past directors of C or of any company within (c) or (d) above, or
    - dependants of any such individuals.

In determining (a)–(e) above, if a person (B) (a nominee) possesses any rights or powers on behalf of another person (A), or may be required to exercise any rights or powers on A's direction or on A's behalf, any shares to which those rights or powers are attached are attributed to A.

[*CTA 2010, s 447*].

Control

[16.6] A person (P) is treated as having '*control*' of a company (C) if P exercises, is able to exercise, or is entitled to acquire, direct or indirect control over C's affairs. It includes the possession of, or right to acquire:

(a) the greater part of the share capital or issued share capital of C; or
(b) the greater part of the voting power of C; or
(c) so much of the issued share capital of C as would give the right to receive the greater part of the company's income, were all that income distributed; or
(d) rights to the greater part of C's assets in a distribution on a winding-up or in any other circumstances.

Any rights that P or any other person has as a loan creditor (**16.11** below) are disregarded for the purposes of the assumption inherent in (c) above.

If two or more persons together satisfy any of the above conditions, they are treated as having control of C.

For the above purposes, a person is treated as entitled to acquire anything which he is entitled to acquire at a future date or will, at a future date, be entitled to acquire. The attribution rules at **16.2** above also apply for these purposes.

It should be noted that the control test found at (d) above with regard to a winding-up is distinct from the winding-up test found at *s 439(3)* described at **16.2** above.

[*CTA 2010, ss 450, 451*].

Participator

[16.7] '*Participator*' means a person having a share or interest in the capital or income of the company and includes:

(a) any person possessing, or entitled to acquire, share capital or voting rights;
(b) any 'loan creditor' (**16.11** below);
(c) any person possessing a right to receive, or to participate in, distributions or any amount payable by the company (in cash or in kind) to loan creditors by way of premium on redemption;
(d) any person entitled to acquire such a right as in (c) above; and
(e) any person entitled to ensure that present or future income or assets of the company will be applied directly or indirectly for his benefit.

In (c) above, with reference to the definition of participator, 'distribution' is not to be given the extended meaning explained in **29.13** DISTRIBUTIONS.

For the above purposes, a person is treated as entitled to do anything which he is entitled to do at a future date or will, at a future date, be entitled to do.

It should be noted that for the purposes of determining whether a company is controlled by five or fewer participators the definition of 'participator' is effectively widened by the attribution to such a persons of the rights and powers of their associates, etc. see **16.2** above. Thus a person may be treated as a participator even though they do not fall into any of the categories (a) to (e) above by virtue of being an associate of a participator — see **16.9** below.

[*CTA 2010, s 454*].

A recognised money broker is not treated as a participator in a stock-jobbing company solely by reason of short-term loans or advances arising in the ordinary course of their respective trades. (HMRC ESC C8).

Director

[16.8] '*Director*' includes any person:

(a) who occupies the position of director (by whatever name called); or
(b) in accordance with whose directions or instructions the directors are accustomed to act; or
(c) who is a manager of the company (or otherwise concerned in the management of the company's trade or business) and who is the beneficial owner of, or able directly or indirectly to control, at least 20% of the ordinary share capital of the company. For this purpose, the holdings and powers of his associates (**16.9** below) may be attributed to him.

[*CTA 2010, s 452*].

As regards (b) above, whilst not specifically stated for the purposes of this definition, HMRC do not normally regard a professional adviser as a director merely because the directors act on advice given by that person in a professional capacity. See, for example, *ITEPA 2003, s 67(2)*.

Associate

[16.9] '*Associate*' in relation to a person (P) means:

(a) any spouse or civil partner of P, any parent or remoter forebear of P, any child or remoter issue of P, or any brother or sister of P;
(b) any partner of P;
(c) the trustee(s) of any settlement of which P, or any relative (as in (a) above) of P (living or dead), is or was a settlor; see **19.2** CONNECTED PERSONS for the definitions of 'settlement' and of 'settlor';
(d) if P has an interest in any shares or obligations of a company which are subject to a trust, the trustee(s) concerned;
(e) if P is itself a company and has an interest in any shares or obligations of a company which are subject to a trust, any other company which has an interest in those shares or obligations;
(f) if P has an interest in any shares or obligations of a company which are part of a deceased person's estate, the personal representatives of the deceased; and
(g) if P is itself a company and has an interest in any shares or obligations of a company which are part of a deceased person's estate, any other company which has an interest in those shares or obligations.

[*CTA 2010, s 448*].

Note that (a) above also does not include the spouse or civil partner of another relative of P; this is in contrast to the definition of 'connected person' (see **19.1** CONNECTED PERSONS). Trustees have an interest in shares comprised in the settlement (*CIR v J Bibby & Sons Ltd* [1945] 1 All ER 667, 29 TC 167, HL).

Associated company

[16.10] A company is an '*associated company*' of another company at a particular time if, at that time or at any other time within the preceding twelve months:

- one of them has control of the other, or
- both are under the control of the same person or persons.

[*CTA 2010, s 449*].

Loan creditor

[16.11] A '*loan creditor*' is a person to whom money is owed by the company in respect of:

- any money borrowed by the company; or
- any capital assets acquired by the company; or

- any right to receive income created in the company's favour; or
- any redeemable loan capital issued by the company; or
- any debt the value of which (to the company) at the time the debt was incurred (including any premium thereon) substantially exceeded the consideration given for it.

The definition is extended to include any person, other than the creditor himself, who has a beneficial interest in the debt or loan capital.

A person carrying on a banking business is not deemed to be a loan creditor in respect of any loan capital issued or debt incurred by the company for money lent by him to the company in the ordinary course of that business.

[*CTA 2010, s 453*].

As to what constitutes a *bona fide* banking business, see *Hafton Properties Ltd v McHugh* (1986) 59 TC 420.

Example

A plc is a quoted company whose ordinary share capital is owned as follows.

		%
B	a director	10
C	wife of B	5
D	father of B	4
E		17
F	business partner of E	2
G	a director	10
H		8
I Ltd	a non-close company	30
J		7
100	other shareholders	7
		100

It can be shown that A plc is a close company by considering the following three steps.

(i) Is A plc controlled by five or fewer participators or by its directors?

		%	%
I Ltd			30
B	own shares	10	
	C's shares	5	
	D's shares	4	
			19
E	own shares	17	
	F's shares	2	
			19
			68

As A plc is controlled by three participators, the initial conclusion is that the company is close.

(ii) Is A plc a quoted company, with at least 35% of the voting power owned by the public?

	%
I Ltd	30
J	7
100 other shareholders	7
	44

As at least 35% of the share capital is owned by the public it appears that A plc is exempt from close company status, subject to step (iii).

(iii) Is more than 85% of the voting power in A plc owned by its principal members?

	%
I Ltd	30
B	19
E	19
G	10
H	8
	86

Although J owns more than 5% of the share capital, he is not a principal member because five other persons each hold more than J's 7% and so themselves constitute the principal members.

Because the principal members own more than 85% of the share capital A plc is a close company.

Loans and certain benefits provided to participators

[16.12] A tax charge arises under *CTA 2010, s 455* if a close company makes any loan or advances any money to an individual who is either:

- a 'participator' in the company; or
- is an 'associate' of a participator.

There is due from the company, as if it were an amount of corporation tax chargeable on the company for the accounting period in which the loan or advance is made, an amount equal to the percentage of the loan or advance at the income tax upper dividend rate (32.5% for 2016/17 to 2020/21).

The charge also applies when the close company makes a loan or advance to:

- the trustees of a settlement in which at least one trustee or beneficiary (or potential beneficiary) is a participator in the close company, or an associate of such participator; or

- a limited liability partnership or other partnership where at least one of the partners is an individual and that individual is a participator in the close company or is an associate of a participator in the close company.

A similar charge to tax applies to arrangements which confer a benefit on the participator.

This charge applies if, during an accounting period, a close company is party to tax avoidance arrangements under which a benefit is directly or indirectly conferred on an individual who is a participator in the close company, or an associate of such participator. In such instances there is due from the company, as if it were an amount of corporation tax chargeable on the company for the accounting period in which the benefit is conferred, an amount equal to the percentage of the benefit at the income tax upper dividend rate (currently 32.5%).

'*Tax avoidance arrangements*' are arrangements (broadly defined to include any kind of arrangement, scheme or understanding) where the main purpose, or one of the main purposes, is:

(a) to avoid or reduce, or obtain relief from a *s 455* charge to tax (above); or
(b) to obtain a tax advantage for the participator or associate.

'*Tax advantage*' is as broadly defined in *CTA 2010, s 1139*.

However, this charge does not apply if or to the extent that the conferral of the benefit gives rise to a charge to tax under *s 455*, or a charge to income tax on the participator or associate.

With regard to both the charge under *s 455* and that under *s 464A*, the tax is due and payable in accordance with *TMA 1970, s 59D* (see **58.2** PAYMENT OF TAX) on the day following the end of the period of nine months from the end of the accounting period in which the loan or advance was made (for companies not within the instalment payment regime — see **58.3**), and that is the date from which interest is chargeable for late payment. However, the rules relating to interest on unpaid tax are modified to ensure that the repayment, release or writing off of a loan, or repayment of a benefit conferred, does not result in the repayment of interest charged because of late payment (see **43.2** INTEREST ON OVERDUE TAX).

'*Participator*' and '*associate*' are generally as defined in **16.7** and **16.9** above. If, however, a company (C) controls another company (D), a participator in C is to be treated for these purposes as being also a participator in D.

These provisions apply to a loan or advance made by a close company to a company receiving it in a fiduciary or representative capacity as they do to a loan or advance made to an individual.

[*CTA 2010, s 455(1)–(3), (5)(6), s 464A; TMA 1970, s 109(3)*].

See **16.13** below as regards circumstances in which a close company is to be *treated* as making a loan, and **16.14** below for exceptions to the above provisions. See **16.15** below as to what happens when the loan or advance (or part of it) is repaid, released or written off, or a benefit conferred is repaid.

HMRC do not accept that separate accounts with the same participator may be aggregated or 'netted off' for these purposes (HMRC Company Taxation Manual, CTM61550).

HMRC's information gathering powers apply with regard to the charges and reliefs underthese provisions (see **37 HMRC** INVESTIGATORY POWERS), and HMRC have appropriate information powers under *CTA 2010* with regard to bearer securities. It is notable that bearer shares have been abolished as from 26 May 2015, and all such issued shares must be converted into registered shares (*The Small Business, Enterprise and Employment Act 2015*). [*CTA 2010, s 465; FA 2013, Sch 30*].

In *Earlspring Properties Ltd v Guest* (1995) 67 TC 259, CA, it was held that a failure to notify liability under these provisions constituted neglect and gave rise to a liability to interest and penalties. See also *Joint v Bracken Developments Ltd* (1994) 66 TC 560.

Simon's Taxes. See **D3.401–D3.402.**

Example

A is an individual and a participator in a close company, X Ltd. X Ltd and A are also partners in a partnership. Under the partnership agreement 75% of the profits are allocated to X Ltd and charged on X Ltd at the corporation tax rate. X Ltd leaves its profits undrawn on capital account in the partnership and A draws on them.

The effect of these transactions is that there is a benefit conferred on A which is subject to the *s 464A* charge. This is because A has received funds from X Ltd, and there was no charge under *s 455* on X Ltd, and no income tax charge on A. If the funds had been transferred directly from X Ltd to A then they would have been chargeable to income tax (if transferred as remuneration or a dividend) or a *s 455* charge would have arisen (if they had been transferred as a loan).

Matters treated as loans

[16.13] The circumstances in which, for the purposes of these provisions, a close company is to be *treated* as making a loan to a person are listed below.

(a) The person incurs a debt to the close company. This does not apply if the debt is for goods or services supplied by it in the ordinary course of the company's trade or business and on credit not exceeding six months and no longer than that normally given to the company's customers.

(b) A debt due from the person to a third party is assigned to the close company.

(c) Under arrangements made by any person:
- a close company makes a loan or advance not otherwise within **16.12** above; and
- some person other than the close company makes a payment or transfers property to, or releases or satisfies (in whole or in part) a liability of, an 'individual' who is a participator, or the associate of a participator, in the lending company. ('*Individual*' includes fiduciary or representative companies as mentioned in **16.12** above.)

The above does not apply if:
- the arrangements are made in the ordinary course of a business carried on by the person making them; or

- an amount not less than the loan or advance falls to be included for tax purposes in the total income of the participator or associate.

If a company (C) controls another company (D), a participator in C is to be treated for the above purposes as being also a participator in D.

(d) A company (C) which is controlled by a close company makes a loan or advance not otherwise within **16.12** above; the provisions apply as if the loan or advance had been made by the close company. If C is not controlled by a close company at the time of making the loan or advance but a close company subsequently acquires control of it, the provisions apply as if the loan or advance had been made by the close company immediately after the time it acquired control. See also below.

[*CTA 2010, ss 455(4), 456(2), 459, 460(1)–(3)*].

As regards (a) above, in *Grant v Watton (Inspector of Taxes)* [1999] STC 330, 71 TC 333, the company supplied services to a partnership in which it was a limited partner, and of which its controlling director was the general partner, under an agreement for reimbursement of the amounts charged in the company's accounts (plus a mark up), but with no formal or implied agreement as to the time payment would be made. It was held that, for these purposes, the debt was incurred when the debtor became legally committed to expenditure in relation to the services supplied to the partnership.

The misappropriation of a close company's money by a participator may give rise to a debt within (a) above (*Stephens (Inspector of Taxes) v T Pittas Ltd* [1983] STC 576, 56 TC 722).

The interpretation of 'makes any loan or advances any money' (now in *CTA 2010, s 455*) was discussed in *Potts' Executors v IRC* [1951] AC 443; [1951] 1 All ER 76; 32 TC 211, HL. This case in turn was discussed in *Aspect Capital Ltd v HMRC* UT, [2014] STC 1360, where the First-tier Tribunal specifically declined to follow obiter dicta of Lord Simonds in Potts' Executors. In *Aspect Capital* the company entered into a facility agreement with employees whereby the company agreed to purchase shares on the employee's behalf from a trust, using its own funds, and the employee agreed to repay the company at a later date. This was held to be a loan.

Aspect Capital was distinguished in *RKW Ltd v HMRC* FTT, [2014] UKFTT 151 (TC). In 2000 a US citizen (G) agreed to subscribe for a controlling shareholding in a UK company (R), paying in four annual instalments. G failed to make these payments. HMRC issued an assessment charging tax under what is now *CTA 2010, s 455*. R appealed, contending that *s 455* should not be treated as applying to a subscription for shares by someone who was not already a 'participator' in the company. Judge Connell accepted this contention and allowed the appeal, distinguishing the decision in *Aspect Capital* because that case concerned the grant of additional shares to existing participators, and holding that 'securing control of a close company is not within the contextual or purposive meaning of incurring a "debt"'.

It was held in *Mirror Image Contracting Ltd v HMRC* (TC02350, 20 November 2012), that when a shareholder unilaterally withdraws money from a company then this is an advance which gives rise to a charge to tax under what is now *CTA 2010, s 455*. In that case an unmarried couple (S and J) had incorporated a company to carry out construction work. S and J separated. S, the minority shareholder (49%) withdrew more than £110,000 from the company's bank accounts. He also sold the company van and used the proceeds to buy a car which he registered in his own name. HMRC issued an amendment to the company's self-assessment for the year ended March 2009, charging tax under what is now *CTA 2010, s 455*. The judge upheld the amendment and also observed that the effect of the decision in *Bamford v ATA Advertising Ltd*, Ch D (1972) 48 TC 359 was that the company was not entitled to a deduction for the amounts which had been withdrawn.

The rules in (d) above apply equally where two or more close companies control, or acquire control of, C. The loan is apportioned between them in proportion to the nature and amount of their respective interests in C. [*CTA 2010, s 460(4)*].

References in (d) above to a company making a loan or advance include the company being treated under (a) or (b) above as making a loan or advance. [*CTA 2010, s 460(7)*].

The rules at (d) above *do not apply* if it is shown that there are no arrangements (otherwise than in the ordinary course of business) connecting the making of the loan with:

- the acquisition of control; or
- the making of any payment or the transfer of any property (whether directly or indirectly) by the close company to C; or
- the releasing or satisfying by the close company (in whole or in part) of any liability of C.

[*CTA 2010, s 461*].

Exceptions

[16.14] The charge in **16.12** above does not apply to a loan or advance made in the ordinary course of a business carried on by a company if the business includes the lending of money. [*CTA 2010, s 456(1)*]. For a case in which a loan by an investment company to its chairman was held not to have been made in the ordinary course of its business, so that the charge to tax applied, see *Brennan v Deanby Investment Co Ltd* (2001) 73 TC 455, CA(NI).

The charge also does not apply to a debt incurred for the supply of goods or services by a close company in the ordinary course of its trade or business unless the credit given exceeds six months or is longer than that normally given to the company's customers.

Loans and advances are excluded from the charge in **16.12** above if they are made to a director (**16.8** above) or employee of a close company (or of an associated company (**16.10** above) of the close company) and:

(a) the loan or advance does not exceed £15,000;
(b) the loan/advance and any other outstanding loans/advances from the close company and any of its associated companies to the borrower do not together exceed £15,000;

(c) the borrower works 'full-time' for the close company or any of its associated companies; and

(d) the borrower does not have a 'material interest' in the close company or in any of its associated companies. If the borrower acquires a material interest whilst any part of the loan or advance remains outstanding, the company is to be regarded as making to him at that time a loan or advance equal to the amount outstanding.

The reference in (b) above to other outstanding loans/advances does not include one made before 31 March 1971 unless it was made for the purpose of purchasing an only or main residence. The condition in (b) is not to be treated as met if any such outstanding pre-31 March 1971 loans/advances together exceed £10,000. The reference in (d) above to an outstanding loan or advance does not include one made before 31 March 1971.

A '*material interest*' is defined by *CTA 2010, s 457* and broadly means a 5% interest. The interests of any associates (**16.9** above) of the borrower must be taken into account in determining whether the borrower has a material interest.

Loans or advances made to a trustee of a charitable trust are excluded from the charge in **16.12** above if the loan or advance is applied only to the purposes of the charitable trust.

[*CTA 2010, ss 456(2)–(7), 457, Sch 2 para 69*].

For the above purposes, a director or employee is treated as working '*full-time*' if his hours are at least three-quarters of the company's normal working hours (HMRC Company Taxation Manual CTM61540).

Loan repaid, released or written off and return payment of benefit

[16.15] If a close company has made a loan/advance which gave rise to a charge to tax under *s 455* as at **16.12** above, relief is given from that tax (i.e. by repayment, discharge or set-off), or a proportionate part of it, if the whole or part of the loan/advance is repaid, released or written off. The relief is given on a claim, which must be made no later than four years after the end of the financial year in which the repayment is made or the release or writing off occurs.

Similarly with regard to a charge arising under *s 464A*, relief is given from that tax (i.e. by repayment, discharge or set-off), or a proportionate part of it, if a payment ('the return payment') is made to the close company in respect of the benefit, and no consideration is given for the return payment. The relief is given on a claim, which must be made no later than four years after the end of the financial year in which the return payment is made to the company.

If the event giving rise to the relief occurs after the tax has become due and payable, the relief cannot be given before the end of the period of nine months after the end of the accounting period in which that event occurred.

TMA 1970, Sch 1A (claims etc. not included in returns — see **15.7** CLAIMS) applies to the above claim unless it is included (by amendment or otherwise) in the return for the period in which the loan/advance was made, or the benefit conferred, *and* the relief is capable of being given at the time the claim is made.

If a loan/advance is repaid, released or written off, or benefit repaid, any INTEREST ON OVERDUE TAX (**42**) in respect of the related tax ceases to accrue from the date of the repayment, release or writing off, or return payment. However, any liability to interest accrued up to that date still stands.

[*CTA 2010, ss 458, 464B; TMA 1970, s 109(1)(3A)(3B)(4)*].

As long as the company was a close company at the time of making the loan/advance, the above treatment is followed even if the company is not a close company when the loan/advance etc is released or written off (HMRC Company Taxation Manual CTM61655).

Where, under the terms of a deed, a company accepted the replacement of the participator by a third party as its debtor, this amounted to the release of the debt (*Collins v Addies*; *Greenfield v Bains* (1992) 65 TC 190, CA).

It should be noted that the company cannot claim a debit under the loan relationship provisions for the amount released or written off on a loan to a participator.

[*FA 2010, s 43*].

Effect on the borrower

[16.16] Where a close company that has made a loan/advance which gave rise to a charge to tax under *s 455* as at **16.12** above releases or writes off the debt, the amount released or written off is treated as income of the borrower under *ITTOIA 2005, ss 415–420*. See Tolley's Income Tax under Savings and Investment Income.

Where the borrower is also an employee (or a relative of an employee), this charge to tax takes priority over any potential charge under the beneficial loan provisions of *ITEPA 2003, s 188* (see Tolley's Income Tax under Employment Income), so that the same amount will not give rise to a charge under both sets of rules (HMRC Company Taxation Manual CTM61655).

The person liable for a charge to income tax under *ITTOIA 2005, s 417* on the release of a loan or advance is: where the loan was made to a partnership, any partner who is an individual, and if more than one person is liable then the liability is apportioned between them on a just and reasonable basis; and in any other case, the person to whom the loan or advance was made.

In *Stewart Fraser Ltd v HMRC* FTT 2010, TC00923, a close company waived a loan to its director. It was accepted the waiver gave rise to a charge to income tax under the above provisions and that this took precedence over the employment income charge at *ITEPA 2003, s188*. However, the FTT held that the waiver was in respect of the director's employment and not his shareholding, on the basis the shareholders had not been consulted on the waiver, and was therefore remuneration which was subject to Class 1 National Insurance contributions.

In *Esprit Logistics Management Ltd v HMRC* FTT, [2018] UKFTT 287 (TC), the company released sums owed by a director by way of a bonus for his services to the company. The Tribunal held that the transaction amounted to a repayment of the loan and there was no release of the loan for the purposes of the *ITTOIA 2005, s 415* charge.

If:

- a company (X) was chargeable to tax under **16.12** above in respect of a loan/advance made to the trustees of a settlement;
- X releases or writes off the whole or part of the debt;
- the person from which the debt was due at the time of the release or writing off is a company (Y); and
- the release or writing off takes place after the settlement has ended,

Y is treated as receiving (at the time of the release or writing off) an amount within the charge to corporation tax on income. That amount is the amount released or written off.

[*CTA 2010, ss 463, 464*].

Example

T is a participator in V Ltd, a close company. V Ltd loaned T £100,000 on 10 May 2020. On 2 March 2021, T repays £73,000 and on 11 February 2022, V Ltd agrees to waive the balance of the loan. V Ltd has a year end of 31 March and is not a large company for instalment payment purposes.

The effect of these transactions is as follows.

V Ltd		
On 1.1.22	The company becomes liable to pay corporation tax of (£100,000 – £73,000 =) £27,000 × 32.5%	£8,775
On 1.1.23	The company is due a repayment of £27,000 × 32.5%	£8,775
T		
On 11.2.22	T's 2021/22 taxable income is increased by	£27,000
	If T pays tax at the higher rate and has utilised his dividend allowance for 2021/22 against other dividends, the deemed income will be subject to tax at the dividend upper rate of 32.5% on £27,000	£8,775

Restrictions on relief — order of set off

[16.17] There are restrictions on the relief which may be claimed under *CTA 2010, ss 458, 464B*.

Rule One: the 30-day rule

This is found at *s 464C(1)*. Where a close company has amounts outstanding, being either a loan or advance or the conferral of a benefit, which gives rise to a tax charge under either *s 455* or *s 464A*, and within any period of 30 days:

(a) the company receives a 'qualifying amount' of repayments (being repayments not previously the subject of matching under this section) totalling at least £5,000 in respect of one or more chargeable payments made to a person; and

(b) the company makes 'relevant chargeable payments' (defined as payments which are not repaid within the 30-day period under consideration) totalling at least £5,000 to the same person or an associate of the person (and such payments have not previously been the subject of matching under this section); and

(c) the relevant chargeable payments are made in a later accounting period to the original chargeable payments being repaid at (a);

then the repayments at (a) are matched with the relevant chargeable payments at (c) (instead of the original chargeable payments), and are treated as a repayment of those chargeable payments, to the extent that such repayments do not exceed such chargeable payments. Where there is an excess of repayments then these can be set off against the original chargeable payments.

'*Chargeable payments*' means a loan or advance made by the close company which gives rise to a charge to tax under *CTA 2010, s 455*, or the conferral of a benefit on an individual in circumstances which gives rise to a charge to tax under *CTA 2010, s 464A*. Where a chargeable payment falls into the latter category then the conferral of the benefit is treated for the purposes of *s 464C* as a loan made by the close company to the individual to the value of the benefit conferred, and any payment for which relief would be due to the company is treated (for these purposes) as a repayment of the loan.

The effect is that the original amount which gave rise to the charge to tax is treated as if it had not been repaid for the purposes of the relief provisions, to the extent a further chargeable payment has been made by the company. This restriction does not apply to any repayments which are chargeable to income tax on the participator or their associate (by reference to whom the loan, advance, or benefit was a chargeable payment). For example, where a dividend is declared by the close company which is equal in amount to that of the loan outstanding, and the participator is charged to income tax on this amount, then the restriction at *s 464C* would not apply.

Example

B is an individual and a participator in a close company, Y Ltd, which has a year end of 31 March 2021. On 25 March 2021, Y Ltd lends £20,000 to B. If the loan is not repaid before 1 January 2022, then Y Ltd must pay a *s 455* tax charge of £6,500, being 32.5% of the loan amount outstanding. On 1 December 2021, a dividend of £13,000 is declared by Y Ltd on which B is chargeable to income tax. On the same day, B repays the remaining £7,000. Then on 10 December 2021, B borrows £4,500 from the company, and on 15 December 2021, B borrows a further £2,000.

For the purposes of the 30-day rule, there was a loan of £20,000 outstanding and of that:

- £13,000 was repaid (by way of the application of a chargeable dividend towards the amount of the loan) which leaves a loan outstanding of £7,000. B repays £7,000 which is greater than the £5,000 de minimis limit for repayments.
- Nine days and then fourteen days later, respectively, so within the 30-day period, and in the subsequent accounting period to the original loan, B withdraws a further £6,500 (£4,500 plus £2,000) which is also in excess of the £5,000 de minimis for chargeable payments.

- The amount redrawn by B of £6,500 is matched with the same amount of repayments made within the 30-day period and is treated as repaid. The excess £500 of repayments is treated as a repayment of the original borrowing, leaving £6,500 of the original borrowing outstanding (and subject to the *s 455* charge). The amount repaid by dividend is not considered for these purposes as an income tax charge arose on it.

Rule Two: Arrangements

This is found at *s 464C(3)*. Irrespective of the 30-day rule at *s 464C(1)* above, where:

(a) immediately before a repayment is made to the company there is an outstanding amount of at least £15,000, in respect of one or more chargeable payments made to a person (which give rise to a tax charge under *s 455* or *s 464A*); and
(b) at the time the repayment is made, arrangements had been made for one or more chargeable payments to be made by the company to replace some or all of the amount repaid; and
(c) under the arrangements the company makes chargeable payments totalling at least £5,000 to the same person or an associate of the person (and such payments have not previously been treated as repaid under this section or the 30-day rule at *s 464(C)(1)*);

then the repayments at (a) (where they have not already been treated as a repayment under *s 464C*) are matched with the chargeable payments made under the arrangements at (c) (instead of the original chargeable payments), to the extent that such repayments do not exceed such chargeable payments. The chargeable payments at (c) are treated as having been repaid to that extent. Where there is an excess of repayments then these can be set off against the original chargeable payments.

'*Chargeable payment*' is as outlined above. Similarly to the 30-day rule this restriction does not apply to any repayments which are chargeable to income tax on the participator or their associate (by reference to whom the loan, advance, or benefit was a chargeable payment).

Example

Arrangements to withdraw

P is a participator in close company Q Ltd. P borrows £30,000 from the company on 1 June 2021 during the year ended 30 June 2021. P then borrows £30,000, on terms of a 40-day loan, from the bank and repays the loan to Q Ltd on 20 March 2022. 40 days after the repayment to the close company P withdraws £35,000 from the company as a new loan and repays the bank.

At the time of the repayment, P had made arrangements to withdraw a new payment (in order to repay the bank loan) and so the original loan from the company would be treated as not repaid and the *s 455* tax would become due and payable on 1 April 2022. The £30,000 repaid is matched with the second loan from the company (used to repay the bank) and is treated as a repayment of such loan. A further £5,000 would still be outstanding on this additional loan from the company, and any *s 455* tax in respect of this would be due and payable on 1 April 2023.

If a person who has made a tax return becomes aware that, after making it, anything in it has become incorrect because of the operation of the rules in *CTA 2010, s 464C* then that person must give notice to an HMRC officer specifying how the return needs to be amended. Such notice must be given within three months beginning with the day on which the person became aware that anything in the return had become incorrect because of the operation of that section.

The Treasury have the power to vary the de minimis limits by statutory instrument.

[*CTA 2010, ss 464C, 464D*].

Additional items treated as distributions

[16.18] As regards certain benefits provided by close companies to participators and/or directors, which are classed as distributions, see **29.8, 29.10, 29.12** DISTRIBUTIONS. See also **29.15**(g)(i) DISTRIBUTIONS for items *not* treated as distributions.

Close company transferring assets at undervalue

[16.19] See **11.15** CAPITAL GAINS.

Demergers

[16.20] For treatment of certain 'chargeable payments' made following an 'exempt distribution', see **29.25** DISTRIBUTIONS.

Key points on close companies

[16.21] Points to consider are as follows.

- The majority of owner managed companies will fall within the definitions of a close company so for most practitioners the points in this chapter will be of direct relevance to their clients.
- Only UK resident companies can be close companies. If a company is not UK resident the rules for close companies cannot apply.
- Close companies under common control are treated as associated for the purposes of the small profits rate. The effect is to divide the profit limits between the number of associated companies.
- The attribution of rights to and from associates can result in a person controlling a company where they are associated in the current period.

- A close company owning a property which is only let to connected parties will be treated as a close investment holding company (CIHC) and will be taxed at the full corporate tax rates.
- Where loans are made to participators a tax charge of 32.5% will be payable by the company if the loan is still outstanding nine months following the end of the accounting period. Payments by the company to a trust (where one of the trustees or beneficiaries is a participator, or associate of such participator) and to partnerships (where one or more of the partners is an individual who is a participator, or an associate of a participator) are also within the tax charge. Where the loan is released/repaid the tax is refunded/relieved but not before the end of the period of nine months following the accounting period in which it is released/repaid. The refund/relief must be claimed no later than four years from the end of the accounting period in which the loan is released/repaid. A similar tax charge applies with regard to benefits conferred as part of tax avoidance arrangements on participators or associates of participators.
- The charge on a loan to a participator cannot be avoided by routing the loan through another person or entity. There are specific provisions to catch this.
- Where there are two separate loans with a shareholder they are treated separately in determining the tax due. Care should be exercised in dealing with the bookkeeping.
- Where the repayment of a loan is dealt with via book entries the repayment date is the date the book entries are made.
- If there are a number of loans and a repayment is made it can be offset against a particular debt. If no assignment is made the repayment is set against the earliest debt first.
- There are limitations on relief from the 32.5% tax charge, providing an order of set off where a further loan, advance or benefit is provided by the close company to the participator, or associate of such participator.
- Where a bed and breakfast arrangement is carried out in relation to a loan HMRC will scrutinise the arrangement closely so care should be exercised to ensure all the transactions are carried out in the right order on the correct dates, subject to the provisions which provide an order of set off for relief.

17

Community Investment Tax Relief

Introduction to community investment tax relief

[17.1] The Community Investment Tax relief scheme provides tax relief to companies and individuals investing in Community Development Finance Institutions ('CDFIs') which have been accredited by the Government under the rules of the scheme. The intention is that CDFIs will use investors' funds to finance small businesses and social enterprises in disadvantaged communities.

The relief takes the form of a reduction in the investor's corporation tax or income tax liability. The quantum of the relief is a maximum of 25% of the amount invested (which may be by way of loan or by subscription), spread over five years, (although note that the investment term need not be limited to five years). Relief cannot in any year exceed the amount needed to reduce the investor's tax liability to nil.

[*CTA 2010, ss 218–269, Sch 2 para 59; ITA 2007, ss 333–382; SI 2003 No 96*].

No exemption is provided for chargeable gains on disposals of investments in CDFIs.

This chapter deals with the relief due to investors who are companies. For coverage of the relief due to individual investors, see the corresponding chapter of Tolley's Income Tax.

References in this chapter to the '*investment date*' are to the day on which the investment in the CDFI is made, and references to the '*five-year period*' are to the five years beginning with that day.

[*CTA 2010, s 223; ITA 2007, s 338*].

HMRC guidance is available in HMRC Community Investment Tax Relief Manual.

The relief

Eligibility for relief

[17.2] Relief will be available to a qualifying investor (see **17.3** below) who makes a qualifying investment (see **17.4** below) in a body that is accredited as a CDFI at the time the investment is made.

[*CTA 2010, s 219; ITA 2007, s 334*].

Qualifying investor

No control of CDFI by investor

[17.3] The investor must not control the CDFI at any time in the five-year period. 'Control' is construed in accordance with *CTA 2010, s 1124* where the CDFI is a body corporate, with similar rules applying in other cases, with any potential future rights and powers of the investor, and any rights and powers held or exercisable by another on his behalf, taken into account. References to 'the investor' include any person connected with it (within **19** CONNECTED PERSONS).

Beneficial ownership

The investor must be the sole beneficial owner of the investment when it is made (which in the case of a loan means sole beneficial entitlement to repayment).

Investor not to be accredited

The investor must not itself be accredited as a CDFI as at the investment date. See **17.11** below as regards denial of relief where an investor company subsequently becomes a CDFI.

No acquisition of share in partnership

Where the CDFI is a partnership, the investment must not consist of or include any capital contributed by the investor on becoming a member of the partnership. This includes the provision of loan capital treated as partners' capital in the partnership accounts.

No tax avoidance purpose

The investment must not be made as part of a scheme or arrangement a main purpose of which is the avoidance of tax.

[*CTA 2010, ss 231–235*].

Qualifying investment

[17.4] An investment is a '*qualifying investment*' in a CDFI if:

(a) the investment consists of a loan, securities or shares satisfying the conditions at **17.5** or, as the case may be, **17.6** below;
(b) the investor receives from the CDFI a valid tax relief certificate (see **17.20** below); and
(c) the conditions at **17.7** below (no pre-arranged protection against risks) are met.

[*CTA 2010, s 225*].

For implications for alternative finance arrangements see **3.10** ALTERNATIVE FINANCE ARRANGEMENTS.

Conditions to be satisfied in relation to loans

[17.5] There are three such conditions.

(1) Either the CDFI receives from the investor, on the investment date, the full amount of the loan or, in the case of a loan made under a drawdown facility, the loan agreement provides for the CDFI to receive the full amount of the loan within 18 months after the investment date. Where a loan agreement authorises the body to draw down amounts of the loan over a period of time, the loan is treated as made when the first amount is drawn down.
(2) The loan must not carry any present or future right to be converted into, or exchanged for, a loan, securities, shares or other rights, any of which are redeemable within the five-year period.
(3) The loan must not be made on terms that allow any person to require:
    (a) repayment within years one and two (of the five-year period) of any of the loan capital advanced during those two years; or
    (b) repayment within year three of more than 25% of the balance of loan capital outstanding at the end of year two; or
    (c) repayment before the end of year four of more than 50% of the balance of loan capital outstanding at the end of year two; or
    (d) repayment before the end of year five of more than 75% of that balance.

    Any of the above percentages may be altered by Treasury order, but only in relation to loans made on or after a date specified in the order. For the above purposes, there is disregarded any requirement to repay that may arise as a consequence of certain standard commercial default provisions in the loan agreement.

[*CTA 2010, s 226*].

Conditions to be satisfied in relation to securities or shares

[17.6] There are two such conditions.

(1) The securities or shares must be subscribed for wholly in cash and fully paid for (in the case of shares, fully paid up) on the investment date and with no undertaking for any further payment in connection with the acquisition.

(2) The second is that they must not carry:
  - (a) any present or future right to be redeemed within the five-year period; or
  - (b) any present or future right to be converted into, or exchanged for, a loan, securities, shares or other rights, any of which are redeemable within the five-year period.

[*CTA 2010, ss 227, 228*].

Pre-arranged protection against risks

[17.7] Any arrangements (as very broadly defined) under which the investment in the CDFI is made (or arrangements preceding the investment but relating to it) must not include arrangements a main purpose of which is to provide (by means of any insurance, indemnity, guarantee or otherwise) complete or partial protection for the investor against the normal risks attaching to the investment. Arrangements are, however, allowed if they do no more than provide the kind of commercial protection, e.g. the use of property as security for a loan, that might be expected if the investment were made by a bank. [*CTA 2010, s 230*].

Form of corporation tax relief

[17.8] Subject to the State aid limit below, where a company which is eligible for relief makes a claim for relief for any one of the 'relevant accounting periods', its corporation tax liability for that period is reduced by 5% of the 'invested amount' (see **17.10** below) in respect of the investment in question (and see below for carry-forward of unused relief).

The reduction in corporation tax liability is made after any reduction in respect of investment relief under the CORPORATE VENTURING SCHEME (**25**) but before any double tax relief.

The '*relevant accounting periods*' are the accounting period in which the investment date falls, and each of the accounting periods in which the subsequent four anniversaries of that date fall.

Carry-forward of unused relief

Any tax reduction available as above for a relevant accounting period is carried forward to the extent (if any) that it is not fully deducted for that year at Step 2 of the calculation of corporation tax liability at **65.7** RETURNS. For each subsequent relevant accounting period for which the investor is entitled to a tax reduction for the same investment, he can claim to have the reduction increased by the amount of any of the relief brought forward that remains unused. Relief cannot be carried forward beyond the five-year investment period.

State aid limit

The amount of the tax reduction for an accounting period (including any reduction for carried-forward relief) may be limited as follows. The sum of the amounts listed below must not exceed €200,000:

- so far as it represents State aid granted to the investor, the total of the tax reductions made in the current accounting period or any earlier accounting period ending in the three years ending at the end of the current accounting period (but excluding any tax reductions in respect of investments made before 1 April 2013); and
- the total of any other 'de minimis aid' (within the meaning of Commission Regulation (EC) No. 1998/2006, Article 2) granted to the investor during the three years ending at the end of the current accounting period.

Claims

The company is entitled to make a claim for relief for a relevant accounting period if it appears to the company that the conditions for the relief are for the time being satisfied. The company *must* also have received a tax relief certificate from the CDFI. In general claims cannot be made before the end of the accounting period to which it relates. Otherwise, by default, the general time limit for making claims applies. See **17.11** below for specific circumstances in which no claim for relief can be made.

[*CTA 2010, ss 220–220B*].

Attribution of relief

[17.9] Community investment tax relief is 'attributable' to any investment in respect of an accounting period if relief as in **17.8** above has been obtained in respect of that investment and has not been withdrawn (as opposed to reduced).

Where for any accounting period relief has been obtained by reason of a single investment (i.e. one loan, or securities or shares comprised in one issue), the relief attributable to it is the reduction made in the investor's tax liability. Where the relief has been obtained by reason of two or more investments, it is attributed to those investments in proportion to the invested amounts (see **17.10** below) for the period in which relief is due (not, in the case of carried-forward relief, the year in which it is given).

Relief attributable to any one issue of securities or shares is attributed *pro rata* to each security or share in that issue, and any reduction of relief is similarly apportioned between the securities or shares in question. For these purposes, any bonus shares, issued in respect of the original shares and being shares in the same company, of the same class and carrying the same rights, are treated as if comprised in the original issue, and relief is apportioned to them accordingly. This applies only if the original shares have been continuously held (see **17.25** below) by the investor (as sole beneficial owner) since their issue, and, where it does apply, the bonus shares are themselves treated as having been continuously held since the time of the original issue.

[*CTA 2010, ss 240, 241, 269(1)(2)*].

Meaning of the 'invested amount'

[17.10] For the purposes of **17.8** above, in respect of a **loan**, the '*invested amount*' is as follows.

(a) In the accounting period in which the investment date falls, it is the 'average capital balance' (see below) for the first year of the five-year period (see **17.1** above).
(b) In each subsequent accounting period (subject to (c) below), it is the average capital balance for the one year beginning with the anniversary of the investment date falling in that tax year.
(c) For any accounting period after that in which the first anniversary of the investment date falls, it is initially determined as in (b) above but is restricted to, if less, the average capital balance for the six-month period beginning eighteen months after the investment date.

For the purposes of (a)–(c) above, the '*average capital balance*' of a loan for any period of time is the mean of the daily balances of capital outstanding during that period.

In respect of **securities or shares**, the '*invested amount*' for any accounting period is the amount subscribed for them (not necessarily in that accounting period).

[*CTA 2010, s 222*].

See **17.12** below as regards receipt of value which may lead to restriction of the invested amount.

Circumstances in which no claim for relief can be made

[17.11] In the circumstances listed below, no claim for community investment tax relief can be made.

Loans — disposals and excessive repayments/receipts of value

No claim can be made for an accounting period in respect of a loan if:

(a) the investor disposes of all or any part of the loan (disregarding any repayment of the loan) before the 'qualifying date' relating to that period; or
(b) at any time after the investment is made but before that 'qualifying date', the amount of the capital outstanding on the loan is reduced to nil; or
(c) before that 'qualifying date', cumulative loan repayments (or receipts of value treated as repayments) trigger the withdrawal of relief provisions (see **17.12** below).

The '*qualifying date*' relating to an accounting period is the anniversary of the investment date next occurring after the end of that period.

[*CTA 2010, s 236*].

Securities or shares — disposals and excessive receipts of value

No claim can be made for an accounting period in respect of any securities or shares other than those held by the investor (as sole beneficial owner) continuously (see **17.25** below) throughout the period beginning when the investment is made and ending immediately before the 'qualifying date' (as in (a) above) relating to that period. In addition, no claim can be made for an accounting period if, before the 'qualifying date' (as above) relating to that period, cumulative receipts of value trigger the withdrawal of relief provisions (see **17.12** below). [*CTA 2010, s 237*].

Loss of accreditation by the CDFI

Where the CDFI ceases to be accredited as such during the first year of the five-year period, no claim for relief can be made. Where accreditation is lost at any later time within the five-year period, no claim can be made for the accounting period in which falls the most recent anniversary of the investment date preceding (or coinciding with) the date the accreditation is lost, or for any subsequent accounting period. (There is no withdrawal of relief for any earlier accounting period). [*CTA 2010, s 238*].

Accreditation of the investor

Provisions similar to those applying on loss of CDFI accreditation (as above) apply if the investor becomes accredited as a CDFI within the five-year period. [*CTA 2010, s 239*]. This does not apply to individual investors.

Withdrawal or reduction of relief

[17.12] Community investment tax relief may fall to be withdrawn or reduced on:

(a) a disposal of the investment (see **17.13** below);
(b) a repayment of an investment consisting of a loan (see **17.15** below);
(c) a return of value to the investor in respect of the investment (see **17.16–17.19** below); or
(d) relief subsequently being found not to have been due.

Where relief given falls to be withdrawn or reduced, and also where it is found not to have been due in the first place, the withdrawal etc. is achieved by means of an assessment to corporation tax for the accounting period for which the relief was obtained. An assessment to recover relief may be made up to six years after the end of the accounting period for which the relief was obtained (without prejudice to powers of recovery where loss of tax has been brought about deliberately). [*CTA 2010, ss 254, 255*].

Disposals

[17.13] An investment is regarded as being disposed of if it is so regarded for the purposes of tax on chargeable gains, and see also **17.24** below (certain company reconstructions treated as disposals). [*CTA 2010, s 266*].

Loans

Where the investment consists of a loan, and the investor disposes of the whole of it within the five-year period (see **17.1** above), otherwise than by way of a 'permitted disposal', or disposes of part of it during that period, any relief attributable to the investment (see **17.9** above), for any accounting period, is withdrawn. Repayment of the loan does not count as a disposal. A disposal is a '*permitted disposal*' if it is:

(a) by way of a distribution in the course of dissolving or winding up the CDFI; or
(b) a disposal within *TCGA 1992, s 24(1)* (entire loss, destruction etc. of asset — see Tolley's Capital Gains Tax under Computation of Gains and Losses); or
(c) a deemed disposal under *TCGA 1992, s 24(2)* (assets of negligible value — see Tolley's Capital Gains Tax under Losses); or
(d) made after the CDFI has ceased to be accredited as such.

[*CTA 2010, s 243*].

Securities or shares

Where the investment consists of securities or shares, and the investor disposes of the whole or any part of the investment within the five-year period, any relief attributable to the investment (see **17.9** above), for any accounting period, is withdrawn or reduced. This does not apply if the CDFI has ceased to be accredited before the disposal or if the disposal arises from the repayment, redemption or repurchase by the CDFI of any of the securities or shares.

In the case of a 'permitted disposal' (defined as for Loans above) or a disposal by way of a bargain made at arm's length, the relief attributable to the investment for any accounting period (including any carried forward to a subsequent period) is withdrawn, or is reduced by 5% of the disposal consideration (if such reduction would not amount to full withdrawal). Where relief has been carried forward, relief given in a later accounting period is reduced in priority to relief given in an earlier period. If the relief initially obtained for any accounting period (plus any obtained by carry-forward) is less than 5% of the invested amount (see **17.8** above), i.e. because the investor's tax liability is insufficient to fully absorb the available relief, the reduction is correspondingly restricted. In the case of any other disposal, the relief for all accounting periods is withdrawn.

[*CTA 2010, s 244*].

Identification rules on disposal of securities or shares

[17.14] Special rules apply on the disposal of shares if community investment tax relief is attributable (see **17.9** above) to the shares disposed of and they have been held continuously (see **17.25** below) since the time of issue. The rules apply for the purposes of **17.13** above and this chapter generally and for the purposes of taxing chargeable gains. The rules apply to securities as they apply to shares.

Where shares comprised in the holding have been acquired on different days, a disposal is identified with acquisitions on a first in/first out basis. In matching the shares disposed of with shares acquired on a particular day, shares to which relief is attributable, and which have been held continuously since issue, are treated as being disposed of after any other shares included in the holding and acquired on that day. If, on a reorganisation of share capital (e.g. a scrip issue), a new holding falls, by virtue of *TCGA 1992, s 127* (or any other chargeable gains enactment which applies that section — see Tolley's Capital Gains Tax under Shares and Securities, and see also **17.23** below), to be equated with the original shares, shares comprised in the new holding are deemed for these purposes to have been acquired when the original shares were acquired.

[*CTA 2010, ss 264, 269(2); TCGA 1992, s 151BA*].

Excessive repayments of loan capital

[17.15] Where the investment consists of a loan, and the 'average capital balance' for the third, fourth or final year of the five-year period (see **17.1** above) is less than the 'permitted balance' for the year in question (other than by an amount of 'insignificant value'), any relief attributable to the investment (see **17.9** above), for any accounting period, is withdrawn.

For these purposes, the '*average capital balance*' of the loan for any period of time is the mean of the daily balances of capital outstanding during that period, disregarding any 'non-standard repayments' made in that period or at any earlier time. The '*permitted balance*' of the loan is as follows:

(a) for the third year of the five-year period, 75% of the average capital balance for the six months beginning eighteen months after the investment date;
(b) for the fourth year, 50% of that balance; and
(c) for the final year, 25% of that balance.

For these purposes, an amount is of '*insignificant value*' if it does not exceed £1,000 or if it is insignificant in relation to the average capital balance for whichever year of the five-year period is under consideration.

'*Non-standard repayments*' are repayments made:

(i) at the choice or discretion of the CDFI and not under any obligation under the loan agreement; or
(ii) as a consequence of certain standard commercial default provisions in the loan agreement.

[*CTA 2010, s 245*].

Value received by investor — loans

[17.16] Where the investment consists of a loan, and the investor 'receives value' (see **17.18** below), other than an amount of 'insignificant value', from the CDFI during the 'six-year period', (i.e. the period of six years beginning one year before the investment date) the investor is treated as having received a repayment equal to the amount of value received.

This may have consequences for **17.10** above (determination of invested amount) and **17.15** above (withdrawal of relief where excessive repayments made). Where the value is received in the first or second year of the six-year period, the repayment is treated as made at the beginning of that second year. Where the value is received in a later year, the repayment is treated as made at the beginning of the year in question. The repayment is not treated as a 'non-standard repayment' for the purposes of **17.15** above.

An amount is of '*insignificant value*' if it does not exceed £1,000 or if it is insignificant in relation to the 'average capital balance' for the year of the six-year period in which the value is received (treating any value received in the first year as received at the beginning of the second). There are provisions to aggregate a receipt of value, whether insignificant or not, with amounts of insignificant value received previously, and treating that aggregate, if it is not itself an amount of insignificant value, as an amount of value received at the time of the latest actual receipt. The '*average capital balance*' of the loan for any year is the mean of the daily balances of capital outstanding during that year, disregarding the receipt of value in question.

[*CTA 2010, ss 246, 248*].

These provisions apply equally to receipts of value by and from persons connected (within **19** CONNECTED PERSONS), at any time in the six-year period, with the investor or, as the case may be, the CDFI. [*CTA 2010, s 253*].

Value received by investor — securities or shares

[17.17] Any relief attributable (see **17.9** above) to the 'continuing investment' (see (b) below), is withdrawn where the investment consists of securities or shares, and the following circumstances are present, for any accounting period:

(a) the investor 'receives value' (see **17.18** below), other than an amount of 'insignificant value', from the CDFI during the six-year period (defined as in **17.16** above);

(b) the investment or a part of it has been continuously held (see **17.25** below) by the investor (as sole beneficial owner) since the investment was made (the '*continuing investment*'); and

(c) the receipt wholly or partly exceeds the permitted level of receipts (see below) in respect of the continuing investment (other than by an amount of insignificant value).

The permitted level of receipts is exceeded where:

(i) any value is received by the investor (disregarding any amounts of insignificant value) in the first three years of the six-year period; or

(ii) the aggregate value received by the investor (disregarding any amounts of insignificant value) exceeds:
   (A) before the beginning of the fifth year of the six-year period, 25% of the amount subscribed for the securities or shares comprising the continuing investment;
   (B) before the beginning of the final year of that period, 50% of that amount;
   (C) before the end of that period, 75% of that amount.

Where a receipt of value in (a) above is not an amount of 'insignificant value' but is nevertheless insufficient to trigger any withdrawal of relief under the above rules, any tax relief subsequently due is computed as if the amount subscribed for the securities or shares comprising the continuing investment (and thus the invested amount at **17.10** above) were reduced by the amount of value received. This restriction applies for accounting periods ending on or after the anniversary of the investment date falling immediately before (or coinciding with) the receipt of value.

For the above purposes, an amount is of '*insignificant value*' if it does not exceed £1,000 or if it is insignificant in relation to the amount subscribed by the investor for the securities or shares comprising the continuing investment.

There are provisions to aggregate a receipt of value, whether insignificant or not, with amounts of insignificant value received previously, and treating that aggregate, if it is not itself an amount of insignificant value, as an amount of value received at the time of the latest actual receipt.

[*CTA 2010, ss 247, 248, 252*].

These provisions apply equally to receipts of value by and from persons connected (within **19** CONNECTED PERSONS), at any time in the six-year period, with the investor or, as the case may be, the CDFI. [*CTA 2010, s 253*].

Meaning of, and amount of, value received

[17.18] For the purposes of **17.16** and **17.17** above, the investor may '*receive value*' from the CDFI in a number of situations, as follows (and see **17.16, 17.17** above re connected persons):

Type of value received	Quantification of value received
Repayment, redemption or repurchase by the CDFI of any securities or shares included in the investment	The amount received
Release or waiver by the CDFI of any liability of the investor to the CDFI (which it is deemed to have done if discharge of the liability is twelve months or more overdue) or discharge (or agreement to discharge) of any liability of the investor to a third party	The amount of the liability
Making of a loan or advance by the CDFI to the investor which has not been repaid in full before the investment is made; for this purpose a loan includes any debt incurred, other than an ordinary trade debt (as defined), and any debt due to a third party which is assigned to the CDFI	The amount of the loan etc. less any amount repaid before the making of the investment
Provision of a benefit or facility by the CDFI for the investor, or for any associates (as defined) of the investor — except in circumstances such that, if a payment had been made of equal value, it would have been a 'qualifying payment'	The cost to the CDFI of providing the benefit etc. (net of any consideration given for it by the investor, its associate, a director or employee or an associate of a director or employee)
Disposal of an asset by the CDFI to the investor for no consideration or for consideration less than market value (as defined), or acquisition of an asset from the investor for consideration exceeding market value	The difference between market value and the consideration received (if any)
Making of a payment by the CDFI to the investor other than a 'qualifying payment'	The amount of the payment

References above to a debt or liability do not include one which would be discharged by making a qualifying payment. References to a benefit or facility do not include one provided in circumstances such that, had a payment been made of an amount equal to its value, that payment would have been a qualifying payment. References to a payment or disposal include one made indirectly to, or to the order of, or for the benefit of, the person in question.

Each of the following is a 'qualifying payment':

(i) a reasonable (in relation to their market value) payment for any goods, services or facilities provided by the investor in the course of trade or otherwise;
(ii) the payment of interest at no more than a reasonable commercial rate on money lent;
(iii) the payment of a dividend or other distribution which represents no more than a normal return on investment;
(iv) a payment to acquire an asset at no more than its market value;
(v) a payment not exceeding a reasonable and commercial rent for property occupied;
(vi) a payment discharging an ordinary trade debt.

[*CTA 2010, ss 249, 250, 268, 269(3)*].

Value received where more than one investment

[17.19] Where the investor makes more than one investment in the CDFI for which relief is claimed, any value received (other than value within **17.18** above, in the first row of the table) is apportioned between the investments by reference to the average capital balances of loans and the amounts subscribed for securities or shares. [*CTA 2010, s 251*].

Administration

Tax relief certificates

[17.20] Before an investment in a CDFI can qualify for tax relief, the CDFI must issue to the investor a tax relief certificate (see **17.8**, **17.4**(b) above) in a specified form. In relation to an accreditation period, a CDFI may issue tax relief certificates in respect of investments made in it within that period of an aggregate value of up to £20 million in the case of a 'wholesale CDFI' (i.e. one whose objective is to finance other, generally smaller, CDFIs) or £10 million in the case of a 'retail CDFI' (i.e. one whose objective is to invest directly in enterprises). The Treasury may substitute other figures by order but not so as to reduce them for periods beginning before the order takes effect. Any tax relief certificate issued wholly or partly in contravention of these limits is invalid (and thus the investment in question does not satisfy **17.4**(b) above and does not attract tax relief). A CDFI is liable to a penalty of up to £3,000 for the issue of a tax relief certificate made fraudulently or negligently. [*CTA 2010, s 229*].

Disclosure

Notification to HMRC

[17.21] Certain events giving rise to withdrawal or reduction of investment relief must be notified to HMRC by the investor. Such notice must be given no later than twelve months after the end of the accounting period in which the event occurs. If the requirement arises from the receipt of value by a connected person, the above deadline is extended to, if later, the end of the period of 60 days beginning when the investor comes to know of the event. The penalty provisions of *TMA 1970, s 98* apply in the event of non-compliance. [*CTA 2010, s 260*].

Exchange of information

[17.22] There are provisions for the exchange of information between the Secretary of State and HMRC in so far as this is necessary to enable them both to discharge their functions appertaining to community investment tax relief. Information thus obtained cannot be further disclosed except for the purposes of legal proceedings arising out of those functions. [*CTA 2010, s 261*].

Miscellaneous matters concerning community investment tax relief

Company restructuring

[17.23] For the attribution of relief to any loan, securities or shares for these purposes, see **17.9** above.

Reorganisations of share capital

The following apply where the CDFI is a company and the investment consists of shares or, in the case of **17.24** below, shares or securities.

Rights issues etc.

The share reorganisation rules of *TCGA 1992, ss 127–130* are disapplied where:

(a) a reorganisation (within *TCGA 1992, s 126*) involves an allotment of shares or debentures in respect of, and in proportion to, an existing holding of shares of the same class in the CDFI held by the investor in a single capacity;
(b) community investment tax relief is attributable to the shares in the existing holding or to the allotted shares; and
(c) if the relief is attributable to the shares in the existing holding, those shares have been held continuously (see **17.25** below) by the investor since they were issued.

The effect is that the allotted shares are treated as a separate holding acquired at the time of the reorganisation. This does not, however, apply in the case of bonus shares where these are issued in respect of shares comprised in the existing holding and are of the same class and carry the same rights as those shares. (For *TCGA 1992, ss 126–130*, see Tolley's Capital Gains Tax under Shares and Securities.)

Reorganisation involving issue of QCB

The general deferral treatment on a reorganisation involving an issue of QCBs is disapplied if, in a case otherwise within *TCGA 1992, s 116(10)* (see Tolley's Capital Gains Tax under Qualifying Corporate Bonds):

(i) the old asset consists of shares to which community investment tax relief is attributable and which have been held continuously (see **17.25** below) by the investor since they were issued; and
(ii) the new asset consists of a qualifying corporate bond.

The effect is that the investor is deemed to have disposed of the shares at the time of the reorganisation, and the resulting chargeable gain or allowable loss crystallises *at that time.*

[*TCGA 1992, s 151BB*].

Company reconstructions

[17.24] *TCGA 1992, s 135* (exchange of securities for those in another company) and *s 136* (schemes of reconstruction involving issue of securities), which normally equate the new holding with the original shares, are disapplied in the following circumstances:

(a) an investor holds shares in or debentures of a company (company A);
(b) community investment tax relief is attributable to those shares;
(c) those shares have been held continuously (see **17.25** below) by the investor since they were issued; and
(d) there is a reconstruction whereby another company issues shares or debentures in exchange for, or in respect of, company A shares or debentures.

The result is that the transaction is treated, both for the purposes of this chapter and for the purposes of taxing chargeable gains, as a disposal of the original securities or shares (and an acquisition of a new holding). (For *TCGA 1992, ss 135, 136*, see Tolley's Capital Gains Tax under Shares and Securities.)

[*TCGA 1992, s 151BC; CTA 2010, s 266*].

Circumstances in which investment not held 'continuously'

[17.25] An investor is not treated as having held an investment (or a part of an investment) continuously throughout a period if:

(a) under any provision of *TCGA 1992*, the investment (or part) has been deemed to be disposed of and immediately reacquired by the investor at any time in that period; or
(b) there has been at any time in that period a transaction treated, by virtue of **17.24** above (company reconstructions etc.), as a disposal by the investor.

[*CTA 2010, s 267*].

Nominees and bare trustees

[17.26] For the purposes of this chapter, actions of a person's nominee or bare trustee in relation to loans, shares or securities are treated as actions of that person. [*CTA 2010, s 262*].

18
Compensation and Damages

Simon's Taxes. See B2.204, B2.204A, B2.213, B2.417, B2.419, C2.5.

Introduction to compensation and damages

[18.1] The following paragraphs deal with the treatment of all types of compensation received or paid with the exception of capital sums received as compensation for damage or injury to, or the destruction or depreciation of, assets and compensation for loss of office.

These issues are dealt with in Tolley's Capital Gains Tax under Capital Sums Derived from Assets and Tolley's Income Tax under Compensation for Loss of Employment.

Paragraphs 18.2–18.8 cite case law which determines whether compensation and damages received or paid in various situations is treated:

- as a trading receipt/expense;
- on capital account; or
- under a different basis e.g. as employment income.

Compensation for compulsory acquisition

[18.2] Following *Stoke-on-Trent City Council v Wood Mitchell & Co Ltd* [1979] STC 197, any element of compensation, paid by an authority possessing compulsory purchase powers for the acquisition of property used for a trade or profession, representing temporary loss of profits, will be treated as a trading receipt.

Compensation for losses on trading stock and to reimburse revenue expenditure, such as removal expenses and interest, will be similarly treated. (HMRC Statement of Practice, SP 8/79. See HMRC Capital Gains Manual CG72150.)

Cancellation or variation of trading agreements

[18.3] Compensation etc. received on the cancellation or variation of contracts which, if completed, would have given rise to trading receipts, is normally also treated as a trading receipt of the accounting period in which the cancellation or variation took place.

See *Short Bros Ltd v CIR* (1927) 12 TC 955, CA (cancellation of shipbuilding contract); *CIR v Northfleet Coal & Ballast Co Ltd* (1927) 12 TC 1102 (cancellation of contract for minerals extraction); *Jesse Robinson & Sons v CIR* (1929) 12 TC 1241 and *Creed v H & M Levinson Ltd* (1981) 54 TC 477 (cancellation of contract for sale of goods); *Greyhound Racing Association (Liverpool) Ltd v Cooper* (1936) 20 TC 373 (surrender of hiring agreement); *Bush, Beach & Gent Ltd v Road* (1939) 22 TC 519 (cancellation of merchanting franchise); *Shove v Dura Manufacturing Co Ltd* (1941) 23 TC 779 (cancellation of commission agreement); *Shadbolt v Salmon Estate (Kingsbury) Ltd* (1943) 25 TC 52 (withdrawal of building rights); *Sommerfelds Ltd v Freeman* (1966) 44 TC 43 (breach of contract for sale of goods — rights assigned).

For further cases on this point, see Tolley's Tax Cases. See also **18.6** below.

Termination of agencies

[18.4] Compensation received on the termination of agencies is a trading receipt (unless the agency, by reason of its relative size, etc., is part of the 'whole structure of the recipient's profit-making apparatus', see **18.7** below).

See *Kelsall Parsons & Co v CIR* (1938) 21 TC 608, CS (manufacturers' agency); *Fleming v Bellow Machine Co Ltd* (1965) 42 TC 308 (distributors' sub-agency); *Anglo-French Exploration Co Ltd v Clayson* (1956) 36 TC 545, CA, and *Blackburn v Close Bros Ltd* (1960) 39 TC 164 (provision of agency, managerial and secretarial services).

In all these cases, compensation was held to be a trading receipt, but compare *Ellis v Lucas* (1966) 43 TC 276 where a certified accountant, who was auditor to a number of companies and carried out related accountancy work, was paid compensation on his agreeing to relinquish his post as auditor. In the absence of a finding by the Commissioners that the auditorship did not constitute an asset of the taxpayer's profession, except in so far as it included general accountancy work, so much of the payment as did not relate to general accountancy work was compensation for loss of office and therefore within the charge to tax as employment income (although exempt under what is now *ITEPA 2003, Pt 6 Ch 3*) (see Tolley's Income Tax under Compensation for Loss of Employment and Damages) and only the balance constituted a trading receipt.

For further cases on this point, see Tolley's Tax Cases. See also **18.5** below.

For payments received on termination of building society agencies, see HMRC Capital Gains Tax Manual, CG13050 *et seq*.

Ex gratia payments

[18.5] In *Walker v Carnaby, Harrower, Barham & Pykett* (1969) 46 TC 561, a sum equivalent to the audit fee was paid to a firm of accountants as a solatium on their agreeing not to seek re-election as auditors to a group of companies. It was held that, but for being voluntary, the payment would have been taken into account as part of the firm's profits, but that 'ordinary commercial principles' did not require the bringing into account of a voluntary payment not made as consideration for past services, but in recognition of such services or by way of consolation for the termination of a contract.

Voluntary payments were also held not to be assessable as trading receipts in *Brander & Cruickshank* [1971] 1 All ER 36, [1971] 1 WLR 212, HL (loss of company secretaryships by firm of advocates); *Chibbett v Joseph Robinson & Sons* (1924) 9 TC 48 (loss of office as ship-managers on liquidation); *Simpson v John Reynolds & Co (Insurances) Ltd* (1975) 49 TC 693, CA (loss of client by insurance brokers) and *Murray v Goodhews* (1977) 52 TC 86, CA (termination of caterers' tenancies).

However, ex gratia payments to an estate agent who, contrary to local custom, had not been given an agency which he expected were held to be assessable as additional remuneration for work already carried out (*McGowan v Brown & Cousins* (1977) 52 TC 8), and a non-contractual payment to a diamond broker by a fellow-broker, as compensation for transfer of a client's business after substantial work had been done on the client's behalf but before any corresponding benefit had been gained from purchases by the client, was held to be a trading receipt (*Rolfe v Nagel* (1981) 55 TC 585, CA).

See also *Falkirk Ice Rink Ltd* [1975] STC 434, 51 TC 42, Ct of Sess, where the payment related to future services, and for further cases on this point, see Tolley's Tax Cases.

Other receipts chargeable as income

[18.6] Damages awarded to producers for breach of a sole licence to perform a play were held assessable in *Vaughan v Parnell & Zeitlin Ltd* (1940) 23 TC 505 as was statutory compensation for the restriction of development rights (*Johnson v W S Try Ltd* (1946) 27 TC 167, CA). Retrospective compensation for requisitioned trading stock was held to be a trading receipt of the year of requisition in *Newcastle Breweries Ltd* (1927) 12 TC 927, HL, as were compensation to a shipping company for delay in the overhaul of a ship (*Burmah Steam Ship Co v CIR* (1930) 16 TC 67, Ct of Sess) and to a jetty owner for loss of use (*London & Thames Haven Oil Wharves Ltd v Attwooll* (1966) 43 TC 491, CA). For further cases on this point, see Tolley's Tax Cases. See also 18.7 below.

Compensation relating to capital assets

[18.7] An agreed sum received on the termination of 'pooling agreements' between two companies was held to be a capital receipt on the ground that the agreements *'related to the whole structure of the appellants' profit-making* *apparatus*' in *Van Den Berghs v Clark* (1935) 19 TC 390, HL. This was followed in *Barr, Crombie & Co Ltd v CIR* (1945) 26 TC 406, 1945 SC 271, Ct of Sess (terminating ship-managers' agreement) and *Sabine v Lookers Ltd* (1958) 38 TC 120, CA (variation of car distributor's agreement). See also *British-Borneo Petroleum Syndicate Ltd v Cropper* (1968) 45 TC 201 (cancellation of royalty agreement).

Compensation paid to a company making fireclay goods for refraining from working a fireclay bed was held to be capital in *Glenboig Union Fireclay Co Ltd v CIR* (1922) 12 TC 427, HL, but cf. *Waterloo Main Colliery Co Ltd v CIR (No 1)* (1947) 29 TC 235 where compensation for the requisition of part of a mining area was held to be a trading receipt. Reimbursement for restoration expenditure on a ship which had deteriorated whilst requisitioned was held to be a capital receipt in *CIR v West* (1950) 84 Ll L Rep 284, 31 TC 402, Ct of Sess, but compensation for loss of use of a requisitioned ship was assessable as a trading receipt in *Ensign Shipping Co Ltd v CIR* (1928) 12 TC 1169, CA. For further relevant cases, see Tolley's Tax Cases. See also **18.6** above.

Payment of compensation

[18.8] Payment of compensation is treated as follows:

(a) Deductible as revenue expenditure. A substantial payment by a principal for the cancellation of an expensive agency agreement was held deductible in *Anglo-Persian Oil Co Ltd v Dale* (1931) 16 TC 253, CA, on the grounds that it was made not only to commute revenue expenditure but also to rationalise the principal's working arrangements. The decision was applied in *Croydon Hotel & Leisure Co Ltd v Bowen* [1996] STC (SCD) 466, in which a payment for the termination of a hotel management agreement was held to be allowable.
Contrast *Mallett v Staveley Coal & Iron Co Ltd* (1928) 13 TC 772, CA, where a payment to surrender certain onerous mining leases was held to secure an advantage for the enduring benefit of the trade and therefore to be capital expenditure. For other items held to be revenue expenditure, see *Commr of Taxes v Nchanga Consolidated Copper Mines Ltd* [1964] AC 948, PC, and *United Steel Companies* (below), *BW Noble Ltd v Mitchell (Inspector of Taxes)* 11 TC 372, 43 TLR 102, CA (payment to get rid of director), and *O'Keeffe v Southport Printers Ltd* (1984) 58 TC 88 (payments on cessation in lieu of notice). See also *G Scammell & Nephew v Rowles* (1939) 22 TC 479, CA.

(b) Capital expenditure. A payment by the operator of a single ship for cancelling an order for a second was held to be on capital account (*'Countess Warwick' Steamship Co Ltd v Ogg* (1924) 8 TC 652) as were payments by a steel company to secure the closure of railways steelworks (*United Steel Companies Ltd v Cullington (Inspector of Taxes)* [1940] AC 812, [1940] 2 All ER 170, HL, which also involved payments by sub-contractors on revenue account); for cessation of mining to prevent subsidence (*Bradbury v The United Glass Bottle Manufacturers Ltd* (1959) 38 TC 369, CA); for the cancellation of an electricity agreement on the closure of a quarry (*William Sharp & Son* (1959) 38 TC 341, Ct of Sess) and as compensation on the termination of tied tenancies by a brewery company (*Watneys London Ltd v Pike* (1982) 57 TC 372).

(c) Other expenditure not deductible. Damages paid by a brewery to a hotel guest injured by a falling chimney were held to have been incurred as a property owner and not as a trader (*Strong & Co of Romsey Ltd v Woodifield* (1906) 5 TC 215, HL). Penalties for the breach of war-time regulations (and associated costs) were disallowed in *Alexander von Glehn & Co Ltd* (1920) 12 TC 232, CA, and damages for breach of American anti-trust law (but **not** the associated legal expenses) in *Cattermole v Borax & Chemicals Ltd* (1949) 31 TC 202. See also *Fairrie v Hall* (1947) 28 TC 200 (damages for libel) and *Knight v Parry* (1972) 48 TC 580 (damages for breach of contract of employment).

(d) Date of payment. Where damages awarded by a court against a solicitor were later compounded, the compounded amount (accepted as allowable) was held to be an expense of the year in which the court award was made (*Simpson v Jones* (1968) 44 TC 599). See also *CIR v Hugh T Barrie Ltd* (1928) 12 TC 1223, CA (NI).

For further relevant cases, see Tolley's Tax Cases.

Key points on compensation and damages

[18.9] Points to consider are as follows.

- As a general rule, where compensation is in respect of a trade it will usually be taxed as a trading receipt. This includes compensation for loss of profits, cancellation of trading contracts etc. Compensation for the permanent loss of a capital asset is a capital receipt but compensation for the temporary loss of a capital asset is an income receipt. A compensation receipt can be apportioned between capital and income elements.
- Where the payment is voluntary there may be scope for it not to be treated as a trading receipt.
- For the payer the payment is usually tax deductible where it relates to the trade or business and is not a capital payment. The question is whether the payment is made wholly and exclusively for business purposes.

[illegible]

[illegible] by way of payment [illegible]

[illegible]

19

Connected Persons

Introduction to connected persons

[19.1] Transactions between connected persons are deemed to be made other than by way of an arm's length bargain. Therefore, the transaction is deemed to be made for consideration equal to market value.

This chapter sets out the definition of 'connected persons' under the general provision of *CTA 2010, s 1122*. Reference is made to this section throughout the Corporation Taxes Acts. It should be noted that a modified definition may be applied in relation to any specific legislation. In these cases, reference is made as appropriate in the text describing that legislation.

Simon's Taxes. See **A1.156, C2.110.**

Definition of connected persons

[19.2] **An individual** (P) is connected with:

- P's spouse or civil partner;
- any 'relative' of P or of P's spouse or civil partner; and
- with the spouse or civil partner of any such relative.

'*Relative*' means brother, sister, ancestor or lineal descendant.

It appears that a widow or widower is no longer a spouse (*Vestey's Exors and Vestey v CIR* HL 1949, 31 TC 1). Spouses divorced by decree nisi remain connected persons until the divorce is made absolute (*Aspden v Hildesley* Ch D 1981, 55 TC 609).

A trustee of a 'settlement', in the capacity of a trustee, is connected with:

(a) the 'settlor' (if an individual) (see below); and
(b) any person connected with the settlor (if within (a)); and
(c) a 'body corporate connected with the settlement' (see below).

Partners are connected with each other and with each other's spouses or civil partners and relatives except in connection with acquisitions and disposals of partnership assets made 'pursuant to *bona fide* commercial arrangements'.

A **'company'** (see below) is connected with another company if:

(a) the same person 'controls' both;
(b) one is controlled by a person (P) who has control of the other in conjunction with persons connected with P;
(c) a person (P) controls one company and persons connected with P control the other;
(d) the same group of persons controls both; or
(e) the companies are controlled by separate groups which can be regarded as the same by interchanging connected persons.

A company is connected with a person who (either alone or with persons connected with him) has control of it. It is understood that HMRC will accept that a partnership and a company under common control are connected in relation to the treatment for capital allowances of assets transferred on a succession.

Persons acting together to secure or exercise control of a company are treated in relation to that company as connected with each other and with any other person acting on the direction of any of them to secure or exercise such control. For the meaning of 'acting together to secure or exercise control', see *Steele v EVC International NV (formerly European Vinyls Corp (Holdings) BV)* CA 1996, 69 TC 88. Control may be 'exercised' passively. (See *Floor v Davis* HL 1979, 52 TC 609).

Interpretation of definitions

[19.3] '*Company*' includes any body corporate, unincorporated association or unit trust scheme. It does not include a partnership.

'*Control*' is as defined in *CTA 2010, ss 450, 451* (see **16.6** CLOSE COMPANIES).

'*Settlement*' includes any disposition, trust, covenant, agreement, arrangement or transfer of assets (but not a charitable loan arrangement).

[*ITTOIA 2005, s 620*].

'*A body corporate connected with the settlement*' is a close company (or one which would be close if resident in the UK) the participators in which include the trustees of the settlement, or a company of which such a close company etc. has control (as defined by *CTA 2010, s 1124*).

[*ITTOIA 2005, s 637(8); CTA 2010, s 1122(6)*].

'*Settlor*' is any person by whom the settlement was made or who has directly or indirectly (or by a reciprocal arrangement) provided, or undertaken to provide, funds for the settlement.

[*ITTOIA 2005, s 620*].

Group of companies

[19.4] The same definitions are applied for the purposes of corporation tax on chargeable gains by *TCGA 1992, s 286*. In a 2009 case, *Kellogg Brown & Root Holdings Ltd v HMRC* ChD [2009], the taxpayer company was a subsidiary of a US parent. In the course of a re-organisation, two of the company's subsidiaries were transferred to another group company and the shares were subsequently distributed in kind. The company claimed that the loss on transfer of the subsidiaries was available for set off against subsequent gains. It was held that the effect of *TCGA 1992, s 286(5)(b)* was that the companies were connected at the time of the sale of the shares.

20

Construction Industry Scheme

HMRC guidance on the Construction Industry Scheme can be found in the HMRC Construction Industry Reform Manual, which is available on the gov.uk website. Guidance on the scheme is also available on the website at www.gov.uk/government/publications/construction-industry-scheme-cis-340.

Simon's Taxes. See E5.5.

Introduction to the construction industry scheme

[20.1] The construction industry scheme (CIS) sets out how payments to sub-contractors by contractors in the construction industry for construction work are treated for tax purposes. In the main, the CIS applies to sub-contractors and contractors engaged in mainstream construction work. However, its remit also extends to businesses in other sectors that have a high annual spend on construction.

The present scheme is predominantly designed to deal with the issue of false self-employment in the construction industry. In principal, the scheme works on the assumption that construction workers will be deemed to be in receipt of employment income unless certain conditions were met.

Overview of the CIS

[20.2] The legal framework for the current scheme is provided for in *FA 2004*, but much of the detail is contained in regulations (see *Income Tax (Construction Industry Scheme) Regulations 2005 (SI 2005 No 2045)*). HMRC are given wide powers to make regulations governing the scheme as they consider necessary or expedient.

[*FA 2004, ss 73, 76, 77(1), Sch 12 para 9*].

Outline of the scheme

The purpose of the CIS is to target tax evasion by sub-contractors working in construction who are unknown to HMRC. Under the scheme payments made to sub-contractors suffer deduction of tax at one of two rates. The amount deducted must be paid over by the contractor to HMRC. A sub-contractor can only be paid gross if certain conditions are met. Key features of the scheme include:

- a verification service to enable contractors to check whether sub-contractors are registered for gross or net payment (see **20.10** below); and
- periodic returns by contractors, which replaced the former voucher system (see **20.10** below).

The scheme imposes various obligations on both sub-contractors and contractors. Sub-contractors must register with HMRC. Sub-contractors who do not register with HMRC are subject to a higher rate of deduction. Sub-contractors who registered are automatically registered for net payment. However, where a sub-contractor can show that the eligibility conditions for gross payment have been met, HMRC will grant gross payments status, allowing payments to the sub-contractor to be made gross without deduction of tax.

Contractors are obliged to verify their sub-contractors with HMRC and to ensure that sub-contractors are paid correctly in accordance with their deduction status. Amounts deducted from sub-contractors must be paid over to HMRC by the contractor. Penalties apply where payments are made late more than once during the tax year. The penalty rate depends on the number of late payments during the year. The contractor must also make periodic returns to HMRC concerning contract payments, as well as providing information about such payments to the sub-contractor.

In *David Crossman v HMRC* [2016] UKFTT 4 the taxpayer appealed against tax and penalty assessments raised under the CIS scheme. The First-tier Tribunal found that some payments assessed by HMRC under the CIS scheme were not within its scope: employees are excluded, as well as parties who are not sub-contractors, because they are not answerable to the main contractor.

Definitions

[20.3] The CIS scheme applies to payments under a '*construction contract*'. This is a contract relating to 'construction operations' and involving a 'sub-contractor' and a 'contractor'. A contract of employment is specifically excluded from the definition of a construction contract. [*FA 2004, s 57(2)*]. For a discussion of the indicators of employment status, see Tolley's Income Tax under Employment Income.

Construction operations

The following operations are '*construction operations*':

(a) construction, alteration, repair, extension, demolition or dismantling of buildings or structures, including offshore installations and temporary structures;
(b) construction, alteration, repair, extension or demolition of works forming part of the land, and this specifically includes walls, roadworks, power-lines, electronic communications apparatus, aircraft run ways, docks and harbours, railways, inland waterways, pipe-lines, reservoirs, water-mains, wells, sewers, industrial plant and installations for purposes of land drainage, coast protection or defence;
(c) installation of heating, lighting, air-conditioning, ventilation, power supply, drainage, sanitation, water supply or fire protection;
(d) internal cleaning if carried out during construction, alteration, repair, extension or restoration; and
(e) painting or decorating (internal and external).

Operations which are an integral part of operations in the above list are also included; for instance, site clearance, earth-moving, excavation, tunnelling and boring, laying of foundations, erection of scaffolding, site restoration, landscaping and the provision of roadways and other access works.

Specifically excluded from the definition of construction operations are:

(i) operations outside the UK and its territorial sea;
(ii) drilling for, or extraction of, oil or natural gas, and extraction of minerals;
(iii) manufacture of building or engineering components or equipment and delivery of these to site;
(iv) manufacture of components for heating, ventilation etc. systems and delivery to site;
(v) the work of architects, surveyors and consultants;
(vi) making, installing or repairing artistic works;
(vii) signwriting and erecting, installing or repairing signboards and advertisements;
(viii) installation of seating, blinds and shutters;
(ix) installation of security systems and public address systems.

The Treasury may, by order, amend the definition of construction operations.

[*FA 2004, s 74*].

Sub-contractor

A person is a 'sub-contractor' if the contract imposes on him a duty to:

(A) carry out construction operations; or
(B) furnish his own labour or the labour of others in carrying out construction operations; or
(C) arrange for the labour of others to be furnished in carrying out construction operations.

Alternatively, a person may be a sub-contractor if, under the construction contract, he is answerable to the contractor for construction operations carried out by others who are working for him (whether under a contract or other arrangements).

[*FA 2004, s 58*].

Contractor

The term '*contractor*' in relation to a construction contract includes someone who is, at the same time, a party to that contract and a sub-contractor in another construction contract relating to any or all of the same construction operations. [*FA 2004, s 57(2)(b)*]. This would include, for instance, a gang-leader.

Other than that, the definition of a '*contractor*' may be divided into three categories.

(i) Persons who are automatically classed as contractors. These are:
   (a) any person carrying on a business which includes construction operations; and
   (b) the Secretary of State if the contract is made by him under *Housing Associations Act 1985, s 89*.

(ii) Persons carrying on a business which exceeds a set level of expenditure on construction operations.
   Thus, for 2021/22 onwards, a person (P) carrying on a business at any time is a contractor if, in the period of one year ending with that time, P's expenditure on construction operations exceeds £3 million. Where that condition is met at any time, P may elect for it to be treated as no longer being met if, at that time, P is not expected to have any further expenditure on construction operations. Where the condition ceases to be met, P may elect for it to be treated as continuing to be met until such time as P is not expected to have any further expenditure on construction operations. Neither circumstance prevents the condition from being met again subsequently in relation to P.
   For 2020/21 and earlier years, P was a contractor if P's expenditure on construction operations exceeded:
   - £1 million per year on average over the period of three years ending at the same time as the last period of account; or
   - where the business was not being carried on at the beginning of that three-year period, £3 million over the whole of the truncated period.

   Once thus defined as a contractor, P was deemed to continue to be a contractor until HMRC were satisfied that expenditure on construction operations had been less than £1 million for each of three successive years beginning in or after the period of account in which contractor status was acquired.
   Where P was a contractor immediately before the start of 2021/22 due to P's expenditure on construction operations having exceeded the set level but would otherwise have ceased to be a contractor due to the increased set level for 2021/22 onwards, P is treated as continuing to meet the set level of expenditure condition and thus as continuing to be a contractor. This continues to be the case until such time as P is not expected to have any further expenditure on construction operations.

(iii) Specified bodies or persons specified, provided their expenditure on construction operations for the one year up to the time the matter is being judged exceeds £3 million (for 2021/22 onwards). The same elections are available as are available to P in (ii) above. For 2020/21 and earlier years, the equivalent condition was that, in any period of three years, the body or person had an average annual expenditure on construction operations of more than £1 million. Contractor status then ceased to apply if, subsequently, there were three successive years in which expenditure on construction operations was less than £1 million. The same transitional rule applies as in (ii) above where the body or person was a contractor immediately before the start of 2021/22 due to their expenditure on construction operations having exceeded the set level but would otherwise have ceased to be a contractor due to the increased set level for 2021/22 onwards.

The bodies or persons specified are:

- any public office or department of the Crown (including any NI department and any part of the Scottish Administration);
- the Corporate Officer of the House of Lords, the Corporate Officer of the House of Commons, and the Scottish Parliamentary Corporate Body;
- any local authority;
- any development corporation or new town commission;
- the Commission for the New Towns;
- the Housing Corporation, a housing association, a housing trust, Scottish Homes, and the Northern Ireland Housing Executive;
- any NHS trust;
- any Health and Social Services trust.

For the purposes of all the above limits, where a trade is transferred from one company to another and *CTA 2010, Pt 22 Ch 1* (no change of ownership) applies, the transferor's expenditure is treated as having been incurred by the transferee, with apportionment by HMRC (subject to appeal) when only part of the trade is transferred.

Under *FA 2004, s 73A*, the Treasury may designate any international organisation of which the UK is a member as being outside the above definition of a contractor.

[*FA 2004, s 59; FA 2021, Sch 6 paras 2, 3, 8(1)*].

Simon's Taxes. See E5.542.

Contract payments

'*Contract payments*' are payments under a construction contract from the contractor to:

- a sub-contractor;
- a nominee of the sub-contractor or the contractor; or
- a nominee of a person who is a sub-contractor under another construction contract relating to the construction operations.

Where the contractor makes a payment to a third party which discharges his obligation to pay a person within the above list, that payment is deemed to have been made directly to that person.

However, the following are not contract payments.

(I) Payments to agency workers (i.e. earnings under *ITEPA 2003, Pt 2 Ch 7*).

(II) Payments where the recipient is registered for gross payment (see **20.5** below) when the payment is made (but see below for certain qualifications in the case of nominees and partnerships).

(III) Payments excepted by regulations as follows:

- small payments, i.e. payments made by contractors within **20.3** (1)(b), (2) or (3) above and approved for this purpose, in a case where the total payments under the construction contract (excluding direct cost of materials to the sub-contractor) do not, or are not likely to, exceed £1,000;
- payments made by a contractor within **20.3**(1)(a) above, and approved for this purpose, to a body or person for work carried out on land owned by that body or person or on agricultural property (as defined) of which that body or person is a tenant, in a case where the total payments under the construction contract (excluding direct cost of materials to the sub-contractor) do not, or are not likely to, exceed £1,000;
- reverse premiums (within the meaning of *CTA 2009, s 96* — see **68.53** TRADING INCOME — as modified for this purpose);
- payments by local authority maintained schools under devolved budgets;
- payments made by contractors within **20.3**(2) above in respect of construction operations relating to property used (as defined) in their own or another group company's business;
- payments made by public bodies within **20.3**(1)(b) or (3) above under a private finance transaction (as defined); and
- payments made by any body of persons or trust established for charitable purposes only.

The qualifications to the exception at (II) above are as follows:

(a) where the recipient is a nominee, then the nominee, the person who nominated him and the person for whose labour the payment is made (employee's labour in the case of a company) must all be registered for gross payment when the payment is made;

(b) where the recipient is registered for gross payment as a partner in a firm, the exception only applies to payments under contracts where the firm is a sub-contractor or, where the firm has been nominated to receive payments, the person who nominated the firm is a sub-contractor. Note that, in such a case, the person nominating the firm must also be registered for gross payment;

(c) where the recipient is registered for gross payment other than as a partner in a firm but is or becomes a partner in a firm, the exception does not apply to payments under contracts where the firm is a sub-contractor or, where the firm has been nominated to receive payments, the person who nominated the firm is a sub-contractor.

For a case where the Upper Tribunal upheld a finding that an Isle of Man company was a 'nominated person' within these provisions, so that payments which it received from an associated UK company were 'contract payments', see *Island Contract Management (UK) Ltd v HMRC* UT [2016] STC 715.

[*FA 2004, s 60; SI 2005 No 2045, Regs 18–24; SI 2021 No 321, Regs 1, 6, 7*].

Payments from which tax must be deducted

[20.4] A key feature of the CIS is the deduction of tax from payments made to sub-contractors who are not registered for gross payment status.

Where a contractor makes a contract payment to a sub-contractor, the contractor must make a deduction on account of tax. Tax is deducted at the 'relevant percentage' of the contract payment after excluding the cost of materials (exclusive of VAT) used (or to be used) in carrying out the construction operation. For 2021/22 onwards, the legislation makes clear that it is only the cost of materials to the sub-contractor that can be excluded here; previously, the legislation provided that the cost of materials to any person other than the contractor. The 'relevant percentage', is set by *SI 2007 No 46* and depends on the registration status of the contractor:

Registration status of sub-contractor	Relevant percentage
Registered under deduction	20%
Not registered	30%
Registered for gross payment	Nil

The amount deducted from a contract payment by the contractor must be paid to HMRC. The sub-contractor's income for tax purposes includes any deduction made under the CIS.

Example

A contractor makes payment of £5,400 to a sub-contractor. The sub-contractor is registered under deduction. The sub-contractor spends £1,500 on materials in carrying out the construction contract.

The amount paid to the sub-contractor excluding materials is £3,900 (£5,400 – £1,500).

The contractor must deduct £780, being 20% of £3,900, and pay the amount deducted over to HMRC.

Where a person becomes a contractor by virtue of **20.3**(ii) above, i.e. by virtue of exceeding a set level of expenditure on construction operations, that person may be afforded a period of grace to enable them to set up the required procedures to enable them to operate the deduction scheme under the CIS. For 2021/22 onwards, an HMRC officer may, if they consider it appropriate to do so, exempt the contractor (by written notice) from the requirement to deduct sums from contract payments for a specified period, which cannot be more than 90 days (although the period can be extended by one or more further such notices). The notice may also treat the contractor as if such an exemption had applied to specified contract payments made before the date of the notice or to contract payments made during a specified period before the date of the notice. For 2020/21 and earlier years, a period of grace operated on a non-statutory basis (see HMRC Construction Industry Scheme Reform Manual CISR12060).

[*FA 2004, s 61; FA 2021, Sch 6 paras 4, 5, 8(1); SI 2007 No 46*].

Treatment of tax deducted

Where the sub-contractor is not a company, the amounts deducted are treated as income tax paid in respect of the profits of the trade, with any excess being treated as Class 4 National Insurance contributions.

Where the sub-contractor is a company, the amount deducted is applied in the following order:

(1) against payment due under the contractor's obligations as an employer or contractor in respect of PAYE, Class 1 NIC, deductions under the CIS or student loan deductions, whether arising before or after the deduction in question;
(2) against corporation tax,

and any excess is repaid.

HMRC have extensive powers to make regulations governing the treatment of sums deducted.

Generally, where a sub-contractor is a company, no repayment of any amount deducted and paid over to HMRC by a contractor can be made to the sub-contractor until after the end of the tax year of the deduction. However, in certain cases, for example where a sub-contractor is subject to a winding up under the *Insolvency Act 1986* and has ceased trading (or has ceased to make payments from which deductions should be made, or both), where the amount deducted by the contractor is excessive a repayment can be made during the year.

Restriction on set-off claims

HMRC had become aware that the above set-off facility was being abused by some employers to reduce their monthly employer liabilities or to create spurious repayment claims. In relation to any set-off claim contained in an employer return submitted on or after 6 April 2021, and made in respect of 2021/22 or a subsequent tax year, regulations enable HMRC officers to correct or remove set-off claims made on PAYE RTI returns where such claims are made on the basis of an error or omission, and also prohibit sub-contractors, in some cases, from making further set-off claims for the remainder of the tax year.

If an HMRC officer reasonably believes that there may be an error relating to a set-off claim made by a company claimant which is a sub-contractor either registered for payment under deduction or not registered for either payment under deduction or gross payment, the officer may give a notice to the claimant requiring production of evidence, normally within 14 days, to support entitlement to the claim or the amount of the set-off. The notice can be given in relation to a set-off claim made in respect of a tax period falling within the current tax year or any of the three preceding tax years (but not 2020/21 or any earlier year). There is provision for the claimant to apply for an extension of time in which to comply, though not beyond 42 days.

Where either the notice is not complied with or the evidence provided leads the officer to reasonably conclude that the set-off claim contains an error or was made in error, the officer must, by notice, require the claimant to correct or remove (whichever is applicable) the set-off claim. The claimant must comply within 14 days; again, the claimant can apply for an extension, but not beyond 42 days. In the absence of compliance, officers may themselves correct or remove the set-off claim.

An HMRC officer may, in any case, remove a set-off claim where the claimant was not entitled to make such claims due to the claimant not being a sub-contractor or not being a company or being registered for gross payment and thus not having suffered any tax deductions. This power of removal can be exercised in relation to a set-off claim made in respect of a tax period falling within the current tax year or any of the preceding three tax years or, where the claimant is not a sub-contractor, any year (but not 2020/21 or any earlier year).

Where an officer has removed or corrected a set-off claim, that officer must give notice of that fact to the claimant within seven days after the removal or correction. Where the removal or correction results in an additional amount becoming due under PAYE, the notice must warn the claimant that late payment interest will apply. For the purpose of applying late payment interest, the additional amount is due and payable on the date on which the employer return containing the set-off claim was submitted. Where the removal or correction does not have that result, the notice must specify the amount of CIS deductions available to the claimant to set off against relevant liabilities in future tax periods.

Once a set-off claim has been removed or corrected, the HMRC officer has power to give notice prohibiting the claimant from making any further set-off claims for the remainder of the tax year in which the set-off claim was made.

A claimant can appeal to the Tribunal against a removal or correction but only on the ground that HMRC failed to take due account of evidence provided or, where applicable, that HMRC were wrong to conclude that the claimant was not a sub-contractor. A claimant can similarly appeal against a prohibition notice but only on the ground that the claimant had a reasonable excuse for failing to timeously correct or remove the set-off claim which led to the prohibition. All such appeals must be made by notice to HMRC within 30 days. If, on appeal, a removal or correction is set aside, any accompanying prohibition notice is automatically set aside also.

[*FA 2004, s 62; FA 2021, Sch 6 paras 6, 8(1); SI 2005 No 2045, Regs 24A–24M; SI 2021 No 321, Regs 1, 10*].

Registration

[20.5] Sub-contractors are required to register with HMRC. Those who fail to register suffer a higher rate of deduction. The registration requirement aims to tackle tax avoidance by ensuring sub-contractors are 'known' to HMRC.

A sub-contractor can register under deduction of tax or, if the gross payment conditions are met, for gross payment.

In order to be registered, an applicant must provide sufficient documents, records and information to establish, to the satisfaction of HMRC, his identity and address. If HMRC are not satisfied with the information provided, they may refuse to register the person and issue a refusal notice advising him of this decision. Where a refusal notice is issued, a person can appeal against the decision to refuse registration (see below).

Where the sub-contractor wishes to register for gross payment (see **20.6** below), he must also supply sufficient evidence that gross payment registration conditions are met.

An application by a company for registration under the scheme may be made online on form CIS305. See www.gov.uk/government/publications/construction-industry-scheme-company-registration-cis305. HMRC also produce extensive guidance for contractors and sub-contractors in booklet CIS340 (www.gov.uk/government/publications/construction-industry-scheme-cis-340). Where an application for gross payment is refused (or gross payment registration cancelled), the sub-contractor has a right of appeal (see below).

There is a penalty of up to £3,000 for knowingly or recklessly making a statement, or supplying a document, which is false in a material particular for the purpose of becoming registered for gross payment or for payment under deduction. See HMRC factsheet CC/FS41 at www.gov.uk/government/publications/compliance-checks-construction-industry-scheme-penalties-for-false-registration-ccfs41. For 2021/22 onwards (but not so as to affect any statement made, or document furnished, before 6 April 2021), this penalty can equally be charged on a person (A) who exercises influence or control over another (B) or is in a position to do so, where A makes any such statement or supplies any such document, for the purpose of enabling or facilitating B to become registered for gross payment or for payment under deduction. The same applies if A instead encourages B to make the statement or supply the document.

[*FA 2004, ss 63, 72; FA 2021, Sch 6 paras 7, 8*].

Registration for gross payment

A sub-contractor who meets certain conditions can register for gross payment. This enables the contractor to pay the sub-contractor gross without making a deduction on account of tax.

The requirements for registration for gross payment vary, depending upon whether the applicant is:

(a) an individual (see **20.6** below);
(b) a company (see **20.7** below); or
(c) an individual or company applying as a partner in a firm (see **20.8** below).

The rules governing the documents, records and information that must be provided to HMRC in support of an application for registration are set out in *SI 2005 No 2045*. The regulations also provide for appeals against a notice of cancellation of, or a refusal to grant, registration. The Treasury is specifically empowered to alter, by order, the conditions relating to registration for gross payment.

[*FA 2004, s 64, Sch 11 para 13; SI 2005 No 2045, Regs 25, 26*].

Cancellation of registration for payment under deduction

Where a person has registered for payment under deduction, HMRC can issue a determination cancelling that registration where they have reasonable grounds to suspect that the person:

- has provided incorrect information in support of the application for registration;
- has fraudulently made an incorrect return or provided incorrect information under the CIS scheme, whether as a contractor or a sub-contractor; or
- knowingly failed to comply with any provision of the CIS, whether as a contractor or as a sub-contractor.

Where such a determination is made, the registration is cancelled with immediate effect by issuing a cancellation notice to the person stating the reasons for the cancellation.

[*SI 2005 No 2045, Reg 25(4)*].

Cancellation of gross payment registration

A person's registration may be cancelled where that person fails to comply with the requirements of the construction industry scheme. HMRC have the power to make a determination cancelling a person's registration for gross payment where it appears to them that:

- if an application for gross payment registration were to be made by a sub-contractor at that time, HMRC would refuse to register him;
- an incorrect return has been made or incorrect information provided by that person under the CIS, whether as a contractor or a sub-contractor; or
- he has failed to comply with any provision of the CIS, whether as a contractor or a sub-contractor.

Where such a determination is made, a person's registration is cancelled with effect from 90 days after the date of notice of cancellation (see below). However, the effective date may be delayed by an appeal (see below). Where an appeal is made, the cancellation date is the latest of:

- the abandonment of the appeal;
- determination of the appeal by the Tribunal; or
- determination of the appeal by the Upper Tribunal or a court.

Where a person's gross payment registration is cancelled, that person becomes registered under deduction of tax (and is liable to deduction at the rate of 20%).

More seriously, HMRC can also make a determination cancelling a person's gross payment registration where they have reasonable grounds to suspect that the person:

- became registered for gross payment on the basis of false information;
- fraudulently made an incorrect return or provided incorrect information under the CIS scheme; or
- knowingly failed to comply with any provision of the CIS scheme, whether as a contractor or a sub-contractor.

Where a determination is made in these circumstances, the person's gross payment registration is cancelled with immediate effect. Where gross payment registration is cancelled, HMRC must issue without delay a notice stating the reasons for the cancellation. It is up to HMRC's discretion whether that person is then registered for payment under deduction.

The person whose gross payment registration is cancelled may not re-apply for gross payment registration for at least a year after the cancellation takes effect.

Numerous cases have reached the tax tribunals and courts concerning the granting or withdrawal of gross payment status. The case of *Westview Rail Ltd* (TC00215) [2009] UKFTT 269 (TC) tested whether there were grounds for an appeal against cancellation of gross payment status. *Enderby Properties Ltd* (TC00396) [2010] UKFTT 85 (TC) and *GC Ware Electrics* (TC00499) [2010] UKFTT 197 tested whether insufficient funds constituted a reasonable excuse for late payments. *Grosvenor* (TC00227) [2009] UKFTT 283 (TC), *Ductaire Fabrications Ltd* (TC00288) [2009] UKFTT 350 (TC), *Pollard* (TC00563) [2010] UKFTT 269 (TC) and *Burns (t/a TK Fabrications)* (TC00371) [2010] UKFTT 58 (TC) are further examples of cases where HMRC cancelled gross payment status.

The financial consequences of cancellation of gross payment registration are not a relevant factor to be taken into account by HMRC when deciding how to exercise their discretion to cancel registration (*HMRC v J P Whitter (Waterwell Engineers) Ltd* SC 2018, [2018] STC 1394).

[*FA 2004, ss 66, 67(5), 68; SI 2005 No 2045, Regs 25, 26*].

Appeals

A right of appeal exists against:

- the refusal to register a person for payment under deduction (appeal against a refusal notice);
- the cancellation of registration for payment under deduction (appeal against a cancellation notice);
- the refusal to register a person for gross payments;
- the cancellation of gross payment registration; or
- the refusal to register a person for payment under deduction where gross payment registration has been cancelled.

As far as appeals against a refusal to register for payment under deduction (whether after cancellation of a gross payment registration or otherwise) and the cancellation of registration for payment under deduction, the appeal must be made within 30 days of the 'timing event' stating the reason for the appeal. The 'timing event' in relation to each type of appeal is, respectively:

- the issue of the refusal notice;
- the issue of the cancellation notice; and
- the cancellation of the gross payment registration.

The following table summarises the position for each type of appeal.

Nature of appeal	Deadline for making appeal	Reason for appeal
Appeal against a refusal notice	30 days from issue of the refusal notice	Reasons for believing that the application should not have been refused
Appeal against a cancellation notice	30 days from the issue of the cancellation notice	Reasons for believing that the registration should not have been cancelled
Refusal to register for payment under deduction after cancellation of gross payment registration	30 days from cancellation of gross payment registration	Reasons for believing that the person should have been registered for payment under deduction

[*SI 2005 No 2045, Reg 25(5)*].

Where the appeal concerns the refusal to register for gross payment or the cancellation of gross payment registration, it must be made by giving notice to HMRC within 30 days of the decision. The notice must state the reasons why the decision is believed to be unjustified. Appeal is to the Tribunal.

[*FA 2004, ss 67, 68; SI 2005 No 2045, Reg 25*].

Registration for gross payment — individuals

[20.6] For an individual to qualify for registration for gross payment, he must satisfy three tests:

- the business test;
- the turnover test; and
- the compliance test.

The business test

In order to meet the business test, the individual must satisfy HMRC that he or she is carrying on a business in the UK that:

- consists of or includes the carrying out of construction operations or the furnishing of labour or arranging for the furnishing of labour for the carrying out of construction operations; and
- that the business is, to a substantial extent, be carried on using an account with a bank.

The individual must provide the following evidence to HMRC to demonstrate that the business test is met:

- the business address;
- invoices, contracts or purchase orders for construction work;
- the books and accounts of the business; and
- details of the business bank account, including bank statements.

[*FA 2004, Sch 11, para 2; SI 2005 No 2045, Reg 27*].

The turnover test

To pass the turnover test, the individual must satisfy HMRC that the likely receipt of 'relevant payments' in the year following the application is not less than the relevant turnover threshold. For individuals, the turnover threshold is set at £30,000.

Relevant payments' for this purpose are payments under contracts relating to 'construction operations' (see **20.3** above) or contracts relating to the work of individuals in the carrying out of construction operations. Payments representing the cost of materials are excluded.

The following evidence is required to satisfy the turnover test:

(a) evidence of the turnover during the twelve months prior to the application (the '*qualifying period*') (this is the net turnover excluding VAT and cost of materials);
(b) evidence of relevant payments which may include bank statements and paid cheques;
(c) evidence that total relevant payments received in the 12 months prior to the application equalled or exceeded the relevant turnover threshold (£30,000) (or, for the purposes of cancellation of registration for gross payment (under *FA 2004, s 66*), evidence that the relevant payments in the qualifying period equalled or exceeded the relevant turnover threshold, or the average amount of relevant payments received in the qualifying period and two previous years equalled or exceeded the relevant turnover threshold);
(d) documentary evidence that construction operations were carried out during the qualifying period.

A business that does not meet the turnover test can be treated as if it did if:

(i) the business does not consist mainly of construction operations;
(ii) overall turnover in the year prior to making the application exceeds the relevant turnover threshold; and
(iii) any relevant payments likely to be received in the year following the application will relate to construction operations which are an ancillary part of the business.

This is designed to cover the situation where overall turnover exceeds the threshold but relevant payments derive from an ancillary part of the business and are less than the threshold.

[*FA 2004, Sch 11 para 3; SI 2005 No 2045, Reg 29*].

The compliance test

In the twelve months prior to the application (the '*qualifying period*') the individual must have complied with specified tax compliance obligations concerning payment of tax and submission of returns (or, before 6 April 2016, *all* his tax compliance obligations). Over the same period, the applicant must have supplied any requested information and accounts concerning any business of his (i.e. not just the business relating to the application). These requirements also apply to a company controlled by the applicant. Compliance must be within any required time limits or at the required time. That is to say, late compliance is no compliance at all for the purposes of this test.

The above compliance requirements are relaxed in two respects, as follows:

- HMRC are of the opinion that the applicant or company had a reasonable excuse for the failure and that the failure has been remedied without unreasonable delay after the excuse ceased to apply; or

- the obligation or request is of a kind prescribed in column 2 of Table 3 in *SI 2005 No 2045, Reg 32*.

In the event that an applicant was not subject to any compliance obligations because of absence abroad, unemployment, or being in full-time education, HMRC require evidence in support of this. In the case of absence abroad, the applicant must also show evidence of compliance with comparable obligations under the tax laws of the country of residence.

The applicant must have paid any National Insurance contributions as they fell due. This is not subject to the 'reasonable excuse' defence.

Finally, there must be reason to expect that the applicant will continue to comply with compliance obligations and requests for documents etc., and continue to pay his national insurance contributions, after the qualifying period.

[*FA 2004, s 64, Sch 11 paras 1–4, 14; SI 2005 No 2045, Regs 27–29, 31–37*].

Registration for gross payment — partners

[20.7] An individual applying for registration for gross payment as a partner in a firm must first meet the compliance test laid down for individuals (see **20.6** above). A company applying for such registration must first meet all the tests for companies (see **20.8** below) as appropriate. In addition, the firm itself must meet the following business, turnover and compliance tests.

The business test

The firm's business must be carried on in the UK. It must include either the carrying out of construction operations, or the furnishing of, or arranging for the furnishing of, labour for construction operations. It must, to a substantial extent, be carried on using an account with a bank. The evidence required to satisfy HMRC that these conditions are satisfied is as prescribed for individuals by *SI 2005 No 2045*, see **20.6** above.

The turnover test

The partners must satisfy HMRC that the likely receipt of relevant payments (see **20.6** above) in the year following the application is not less than the smaller of:

(a) the relevant turnover threshold which, in the case of partnerships, is £100,000; and
(b) the 'multiple turnover threshold'.

The '*multiple turnover threshold*' is obtained by adding together:

(i) the number of individuals in the partnership multiplied by the threshold for individuals (£30,000, see **20.6** above); and
(ii) in respect of each company (if any) in the partnership, the threshold that would obtain were the company to be applying in its own behalf (see **20.8** below).

Where the number of partners in (i) above has fluctuated over the twelve-month period prior to the application, the number is taken to be the maximum number of partners at any one time in that period. In calculating the figure in (ii) above, it is necessary to ignore companies whose only shareholders are other companies which are limited by shares and registered for gross payment.

The evidence required to satisfy the turnover test (prescribed by *SI 2005 No 2045, Reg 29*) includes the evidence as prescribed for individuals in **20.6** above by reference to the above turnover threshold for partnerships. In the case of a new business carried on by the firm where there is no evidence as prescribed in (a), (c) or (d) in **20.6** above, the following evidence can be given instead, but only in relation to one application for registration for gross payment:

(A) evidence of relevant payments which may include bank statements and paid cheques;
(B) evidence of turnover of partners during the qualifying period;
(C) evidence of construction contracts entered into by the firm including payment schedules where the aggregate value of contracts exceeds £100,000 and payments have been made of at least £30,000.

A firm that does not meet this test may be treated as if it did (as in the case of individuals — see **20.6** above).

The compliance test

Each of the partners at the time of the application must, during the qualifying period (i.e. the twelve months prior to the application), have complied with tax compliance obligations (as in **20.6** above) in relation to any income tax or corporation tax charge which was computed by reference to the firm's business. Over the same period, each partner must have supplied all requested information and accounts concerning the firm's business or his share of the profits of that business. Compliance must be within any required time limits or at the required time.

There are similar 'reasonable excuse' and regulatory relaxations as for individuals (see **20.6** above). There must be reason to expect that, following the qualifying period, each of the persons who are from time to time partners in the firm will continue the record of compliance.

Where a firm is already registered for gross payment and it enters into a joint venture with another firm or company, the joint venture does not need to satisfy the compliance test if the partners in the firm have a right to a share of at least half the assets or half the income of the joint venture.

[*FA 2004, s 64, Sch 11 paras 5–8, 14; SI 2005 No 2045, Regs 27–37*].

Registration for gross payment — companies

[20.8] In order to register for gross payment, a company must pass the business, turnover and compliance tests described below. However, HMRC may, in addition to these tests, make a direction applying the conditions relating to individuals (see **20.6** above) to the directors of the company. If the company is a close company, this is extended to include the beneficial owners of shares in the company. Rather than apply all the conditions to all of the directors or shareholders, the direction may specify which conditions are to apply, and to which directors or shareholders.

In particular, HMRC may make such a direction where there has been a change in control (within *CTA 2010, s 1124(1)–(3)*) of a company that either is, or is applying to be, registered for gross payment. HMRC are empowered to make regulations requiring the submission of information concerning changes in control of such companies.

The business test

The company's business must be carried on in the UK. It must include either the carrying out of construction operations, or furnishing of, or arranging for the furnishing of labour for construction operations. It must, to a substantial extent, be carried on using an account with a bank. The evidence required to satisfy HMRC that these conditions are satisfied is prescribed for individuals by *SI 2005 No 2045* in **20.6** above.

The turnover test

A company may pass this test by:

(a) satisfying HMRC that its only shareholders are companies limited by shares and registered for gross payment; or

(b) providing HMRC with evidence that relevant payments (see **20.6** above) received in the year following the application are likely to equal or exceed a set threshold.

The set threshold is the smaller of:

(i) the relevant turnover threshold which, in the case of companies, is £100,000; and

(ii) the individual threshold (£30,000, see **20.6** above) multiplied by the number of 'relevant persons'. A '*relevant person*' is a director (within *ITEPA 2003, s 67*) or, for close companies, a director or a beneficial owner of shares. Where the number of relevant persons has fluctuated over the 12-month period prior to the application, the number is taken to be the maximum number of such relevant persons at any one time in that period.

The evidence required to satisfy the turnover test (prescribed by *SI 2005 No 2045, Reg 29*) includes the evidence as prescribed for individuals in **20.6** above but by reference to the above set threshold for companies. In the case of a new business carried on by the company where there is no evidence as prescribed in (a), (c) or (d) in **20.6** above, the following evidence may be given instead, but only in relation to one application for registration for gross payment:

(A) evidence of relevant payments which may include bank statements and paid cheques;

(B) evidence of turnover of relevant persons during the qualifying period;

(C) evidence of construction contracts entered into by the company including payment schedules where the aggregate value of contracts exceeds £100,000 and payments have been made of at least £30,000;

(D) where the business was acquired from another person, firm or company, similar evidence as above in relation to the transferor.

A company that does not meet this test may be treated as if it did (as in the case of individuals — see **20.6** above).

The compliance test

The provisions relating to companies mirror those relating to individuals (see **20.6** above). However, in addition to this a company must have complied with certain *Companies Act 2006* (or the Northern Ireland equivalent) obligations during the qualifying period. Those obligations are under:

- *sections 394, 395, and 437–451* (contents, laying and delivery of annual accounts);
- *sections 167(1) and (2), and 276(1) and (2)* (return of directors and secretary and notification of changes therein);
- *sections 854–859* (annual returns);
- *Part 34* (accounts of overseas company).

Where a member of a joint venture company is already registered for gross payment, the company does not need to satisfy the compliance test if the member owns at least 50% of its share capital or voting power.

[*FA 2004, s 64, Sch 11 paras 9–12, 14; SI 2005 No 2045, Regs 27–37*].

Charities

[20.9] For the purposes of the CIS, a payment under a construction contract is not regarded as a contract payment if the payment is made by a charity.

[*SI 2006 No 2045, Reg 24*].

CIS procedures and administration

[20.10] Detailed procedures and administrative arrangements for the operation of the scheme are contained in *SI 2005 No 2045*. There are detailed provisions governing verification by contractors of sub-contractors' registration status, monthly returns by contractors, payments and recovery of tax deducted, electronic communications and methods of payment, and HMRC powers to inspect records. See **20.11** below for the late filing penalty for returns.

Multiple contractors

A contractor may elect to be treated as different contractors in relation to different groups of sub-contractors. The election must be made (or revoked) by notice to an officer of HMRC before the beginning of the tax year for which it is to have effect. There are special provisions which apply where a contractor acquires the business of another contractor. [*SI 2005 No 2045, Reg 3*].

Verification of status of sub-contractors

Anyone making contract payments must verify with HMRC the registration status of the recipient, which, for 2017/18 onwards with minor exceptions, must be done electronically. HMRC will confirm whether the payment should be made gross or under deduction. Verification is not necessary if the recipient has been included in the contractor's returns (see below) in the current or previous two tax years. Where the contractor is a company, the return could be one made by another company in the same group and, where a multiple contractors election has been made (see above), the return could be one made in relation to a different group of sub-contractors. If the contractor acquired the contract under which the payment is to be made in a transfer of a business as a going concern and the transferor satisfied these conditions, the contractor does not need to verify if he has notified HMRC of the transfer. HMRC must notify a contractor if a person registered for gross payment becomes registered for payment under deduction, or vice versa, or if a registered person has ceased to be registered. Once a person has been verified or notified as being registered (whether for gross payment or payment under deduction) the contractor is entitled to assume that the person has not subsequently ceased to be so registered. [*FA 2004, s 69; SI 2005 No 2045, Reg 6*].

HMRC automatically notify affected contractors when a sub-contractor changes status.

Monthly returns by contractors

There are detailed provisions for monthly returns by contractors of payments made to sub-contractors. A contractor must make monthly returns to HMRC within 14 days after the end of every tax month and written information must also be provided to sub-contractors who are registered for payment under deduction or who are not registered. There is no statutory obligation to make a nil return, but HMRC encourage contractors to make voluntary nil returns. Contractors' monthly returns are subject to the late filing penalty at **20.11** below. With minor exceptions, returns must be made electronically. [*FA 2004, ss 70, 76, Sch 12 paras 7, 8; SI 2005 No 2045, Reg 4; SI 2021 No 321, Regs 1, 5*].

Scheme representative

A contractor company may appoint another company in the same group ('a scheme representative') to act on its behalf in relation to the requirement to make a return or other such requirements under the regulations. [*SI 2005 No 2045, Reg 5*].

Collection and recovery of sums deducted

The arrangements for accounting for tax deductions, late payment and repayment interest and penalties for late in-year payments broadly follow those for PAYE (see Tolley's Income Tax under Pay as You Earn and HMRC Explanatory Booklet CIS340). However, Real Time Information does not apply to the CIS. There are detailed provisions governing methods of payment, including electronic payment. [*FA 2004, s 71; FA 2009, Sch 56; SI 2005 No 2045, Regs 7, 7A, 8–17, 44–49, 58, 59*].

Late filing penalty

[20.11] Where a contractor fails to file a monthly return of payments made to sub-contractors (see **20.10** above) on time, the following penalties will be charged. An initial penalty of £100 is payable for failure to make a return on or before the filing date. A further penalty of £200 is payable where the contractor's failure to make the return continues after the end of two months beginning with the day on which the initial penalty is triggered; this is the day after the filing date and is known as the '*penalty date*'.

If the failure continues after the end of a six-month period beginning with the penalty date, the contractor is liable to a penalty equal to the *greater* of £300 and 5% of any liability to make tax payments which would have been shown in the return in question.

A second tax-geared penalty is payable if the failure continues after the end of a twelve-month period beginning with the penalty date. The amount of this second penalty depends on whether or not, by failing to make the return, the contractor is deliberately withholding information that would enable or assist HMRC to assess the tax due, as shown below.

	Penalty is the *greater* of		
	Fixed amount	and	% of liability
Deliberate and concealed withholding of information	£3,000		100%
Deliberate but not concealed withholding of information	£1,500		70%
In any other case	£300		5%

If the failure continues after the end of a twelve-month period beginning with the penalty date and the information required in the return relates only to persons registered for gross payment, the two higher penalties in the table above apply (by reference to the fixed amounts only) if, by failing to make the return, the contractor is deliberately withholding information which relates to such persons.

For the first return that a contractor makes (together with any return with an earlier filing date than that return), the total fixed penalties (£100 and £200) cannot exceed an upper limit of £3,000. Also, where a tax-geared penalty arises that would otherwise be the greater of £300 and 5% of the payments due, it is instead 5% of the payments due.

For the above purposes, the withholding of information by a contractor is concealed if the contractor makes arrangements to conceal that it has been withheld.

The same rules apply as in **59.3** PENALTIES under the heading 'Unified code' as regards reasonable excuse, reduction for disclosure, reduction in special circumstances, reduction for other penalties and double jeopardy. The same rules apply as regards assessment of penalties and appeals against penalty assessments as for other penalties under *FA 2009, Sch 55* — see respectively **59.23** and **59.24** PENALTIES.

[*FA 2009, Sch 55 paras 1, 7–13, 27*].

Late payment interest (see **43.4** INTEREST ON OVERDUE TAX) is chargeable on late paid penalties, and repayment interest (**44.3** INTEREST ON OVERPAID TAX) arises on overpaid penalties.

Key points on the construction industry scheme

[20.12] The key points are as follows:

- The scheme sets out how payments by contractors to sub-contractors are treated for tax purposes.
- Although the scheme applies predominantly to those in main-stream construction work, its remit also extends to businesses in other sectors with a high annual spend on construction.
- The scheme aims to tackle tax evasion in the construction industry by sub-contractors who are not known to HMRC.
- Sub-contractors must register with HMRC, either for payment under deduction or, if certain conditions are met, for gross payment status.
- Unless a sub-contractor is registered for gross payment status, the contractor must make a deduction on account of tax when making a payment to a sub-contractor under a construction contract.
- The rate of deduction depends on whether the sub-contractor is registered with HMRC. Contractors registered under deduction with HMRC suffer deduction at a rate of 20%. A higher rate of deduction of 30% applies to unregistered sub-contractors.
- Contractors must verify the registration status of sub-contractors they engage with HMRC.
- Contractors must make monthly returns to HMRC and pay over amounts deducted on account of tax. Penalties are charged for late returns.

21

Controlled Foreign Companies

Cross-references. See also **31.13** DOUBLE TAX RELIEF; **34** FOREIGN CURRENCY.

Simon's Taxes. See **D4.4**.

Introduction to controlled foreign companies

[21.1] The controlled foreign company (CFC) provisions are anti-avoidance legislation which aims to prevent UK resident companies setting up subsidiaries abroad with a view to keeping low taxed profits outside the UK tax net. The legislation brings these profits back within the charge to UK tax by attributing such overseas profits to the UK company, in certain circumstances.

The main features of the regime are as follows.

- A CFC is a company which is not resident in the UK and is controlled by UK resident persons.

- A number of statutory exemptions apply to exclude many CFCs from the CFC charge. See **21.6–21.11** below.
- If none of the exemptions apply, then the profits of the CFC are potentially subject to the CFC charge, but only to the extent that they pass through the CFC charge gateway, i.e. they fall within one of the five individual gateways (see **21.14–21.19** below). An exemption, full or partial, can be claimed for finance company profits which derive from qualifying loan relationships (see **21.20** below).
- Profits which pass through the CFC charge gateway are chargeable profits and are apportioned between persons with an interest in the CFC. If certain conditions apply, the apportionment is made on a formulaic basis; if not, a just and reasonable apportionment is made. Where at least 25% of the profits are apportioned to a UK resident company, that company is liable to the CFC charge. See **21.21–21.25** below.
- The CFC's creditable tax is apportioned on the same basis as the chargeable profits. The creditable tax is the sum of any double tax relief which would be available in respect of any income included or represented in the chargeable profits, UK income tax deducted at source or charged on the CFC's income and UK corporation tax charged on the CFC's income.
- The amount of the CFC charge is equal to the corporation tax rate of the chargeable company applied to the apportioned profits, less the creditable tax apportioned to the chargeable company.
- The CFC charge is treated as though it were an amount of corporation tax and therefore all the compliance provisions which apply generally to corporation tax also apply to the CFC charge. Companies are required to include details of significant interests in CFCs in their tax returns and to self-assess any CFC tax due.

For HMRC guidance on the current regime see HMRC International Manual, INTM190000 onwards.

Simon's Taxes. See **D4.4.**

Clearances

Clearances can be obtained under the non-statutory clearance procedure which enables HMRC to provide certainty to a UK company as to the application of the CFC legislation to a particular set of facts and also to resolve areas of doubt or difficulty before the company has to complete its self-assessment return. HMRC aim to reply to a clearance application within 28 days if all the relevant information is provided.

A clearance will state the terms on which it is given and will normally apply indefinitely so long as the circumstances and the legislation are unchanged. All UK resident interest holders in a CFC may apply for a clearance, and if there is more than one such interest holder then one of them may apply on behalf of the others. Clearance is not available on matters that are only indirectly related to the CFC legislation, such as the computation of assumed taxable total profits.

All CFC applications and supporting documentation should be sent to HMRC and the UK group's Customer Relationship Manager or Customer Co-ordinator or electronically to cfcs.mailbox@hmrc.gov.uk. No paper copies are needed. Alternatively, paper applications can be sent to the following address: HMRC, Business, Assets and International, Base Protection Policy Team, NE98 1ZZ.

See HMRC International Manual, INTM251900 onwards.

Meaning of controlled foreign company

[21.2] A CFC is defined as a company which is not resident in the UK and is controlled by UK resident persons. [*TIOPA 2010, s 371AA(3)*].

For accounting periods beginning on or after 1 January 2019, a non-resident company is also taken to be a CFC (if it otherwise would not be) if a UK-resident company has (directly or indirectly and alone or with any 'associated enterprises') more than a '50% investment' in it. For this purpose, accounting periods straddling 1 January 2019 are treated as two separate accounting periods, the second of which starts on that date. Where any amounts need to be apportioned between the two notional periods, a time basis must be used, unless it would be unjust or unreasonable, in which case a just and reasonable basis must be used.

A person is an '*associated enterprise*' of a UK-resident company if one has, directly or indirectly, a '25% investment' in the other or a third person has, directly or indirectly, a 25% investment in both. A '50% investment' and a '25% investment' are both defined in *TIOPA 2010, s 259ND* (as modified).

[*TIOPA 2010, s 371RG; FA 2019, s 20(4)–(6)*].

Cell companies

Both unincorporated and incorporated cells are treated as if they were non-UK resident companies. An '*unincorporated cell*' is an identifiable part (by whatever name known) of a non-UK resident company where the assets and liabilities of the relevant company may be wholly or mainly allocated to the unincorporated cell, such that the cell's liabilities are met wholly or mainly out of its assets and there are members of the company whose rights are wholly or mainly limited to the cell's assets. An '*incorporated cell*' is an entity (by whatever name known) established under the articles of association or other document regulating a non-UK resident company which has a legal personality distinct from that of the non-UK resident company, but is not itself a company.

[*TIOPA 2010, s 371VE*].

Therefore the legislation should apply to entities such as 'Protected Cell Companies' and 'Incorporated Cell Companies' found within the company law of jurisdictions such as Guernsey and Jersey.

Control

[21.3] For the purposes of **21.2** above, a company is controlled by persons resident in the UK if they have the power to secure that the affairs of the company are conducted in accordance with their wishes. This may be obtained through shares or voting power, or by powers in the articles of association or some other document.

The definition of control also includes persons who hold the majority of rights (more than 50%) to the CFC's income on distribution or assets on a winding up or the disposal proceeds on the sale of any shares in the CFC.

If two or more persons, taken together, would have control over the company as described above, then they are taken to control the company. The persons who are 'taken together' do not have to be connected in any way; they need only be resident in the UK.

A company is also deemed to be controlled by UK resident persons (and is therefore a CFC) where:

- there are two persons (A and B) who taken together control the company;
- one of those persons (A) is resident in the UK and holds at least 40% of the interests, rights and powers with regard to the company, and in respect of which A and B are considered as controlling the company; and
- the other (B) is not resident in the UK and holds at least 40% but not more than 55% of the interests, rights and powers with regard to the company, and in respect of which A and B are considered as controlling the company.

[*TIOPA 2010, ss 371RB, 371RC*].

Example 1

T SA is a non-UK resident company, whose shares are owned as follows.

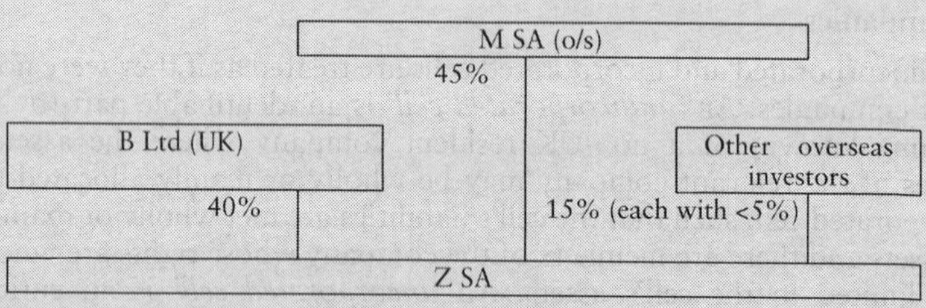

As B Ltd only owns 40% it looks as if the company could not be controlled by UK-resident persons. In addition, the other major shareholder only controls 45%. However, applying the 40% test there are two companies (B Ltd and M SA (overseas)) who taken together control T SA. Both own at least 40% and M SA does not own more than 55%. Thus T SA is deemed to be controlled by UK-resident persons.

Example 2

Z SA is a non-UK resident company, whose shares are owned as follows.

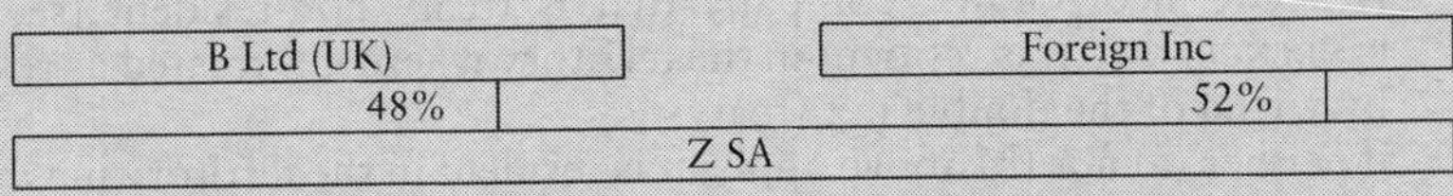

Looking at the control test, irrespective of the fact Foreign Inc owns 52% of the shares, applying the 40% test: one party is UK resident, both parties own at least 40% and Foreign Inc does not hold more than 55%, thus Z SA is deemed to be controlled by UK-resident persons.

In determining whether a person or persons control (or are deemed to control) a company the following rights and powers are attributed to each person:

- rights and powers which a person is entitled to acquire (or will be entitled to acquire) at a future date; or
- rights and powers which may be exercised by other persons on his behalf (now or in the future); or
- if the person is UK resident the rights and powers of UK resident CONNECTED PERSONS (**19**).

[*TIOPA 2010, ss 371RD, 371VF*].

A person also controls an overseas company where that person is the company's parent (defined as the person that would be required to prepare consolidated financial statements under FRS 102, whether they are actually prepared or not) and the 50% condition is met. The 50% condition means essentially that if, on the assumption that the subsidiary is a CFC, at least 50% of the CFCs chargeable profits would be apportioned to the parent company and its UK resident subsidiaries.

The Treasury have the power to provide, by regulations, that if specified conditions are met then a company will not be taken to be a CFC under the accounting standards test, or any equivalent test provided by regulations.

[*TIOPA 2010, ss 371RE, 371RF*].

Territory of residence

[21.4] A *territory* includes a jurisdiction which may not have full independent status (such as the Channel Islands) but not individual states of a federal state (such as the USA). See HMRC International Manual, INTM242300.

In determining the territory of residence of a CFC (for the purposes of determining that a company is not UK resident and for the purposes of the exemptions at **21.8** and **21.11** below), the following rules apply:

(a) the CFC is taken to be resident in the territory where it is liable to tax by reason of domicile, residence or place of management. A company's domicile is taken to be its territory of incorporation (*Gasque v CIR* 23 TC 210). Tax means a tax on profits of a similar nature to UK income tax or corporation tax and does not include turnover or payroll taxes; however it is not necessary that the company should actually pay tax in that territory (e.g. if its profits are covered by reliefs), provided that it would pay if it had sufficient profits;

(b) if (a) above does not determine a territory of residence and the company is a UK incorporated company that is treaty non-resident (see **64.2** RESIDENCE) then it is resident in the territory where it is treated as resident by virtue of the double tax treaty;

(c) if neither (a) nor (b) above apply, it is resident in the territory in which it is incorporated or formed.

For the purposes of (a) above, where there are two or more territories in which the CFC is liable to tax by reason of domicile, residence or place of management, the following steps need to be followed (in order) to determine the place of residence; if two or more steps apply then the earliest takes precedence:

(i) where an election for, or an HMRC designation of, a specific territory of residence for a previous accounting period continues in force (see further below), the elected/designated territory is its place of residence (see further below);

(ii) where the CFC's place of effective management is in only one of the eligible territories, the territory of effective management is its place of residence;

(iii) where the CFC's place of effective management is in two or more of the eligible territories and, immediately before the end of the accounting period in question, over 50% of the CFC's assets are situated in one of those eligible territories, the territory where 50% of the CFC's assets are is its place of residence;

(iv) where immediately before the end of the accounting period in question, over 50% of the CFC's assets are situated in one of the eligible territories, the territory where 50% of the CFC's assets are is its place of residence;

(v) where an election for a territory of residence is made, the elected territory is the CFC's place of residence;

(vi) where a determination of a territory of residence is made by HMRC, on a just and reasonable basis, the determined territory is its place of residence.

For tests (iii) and (iv) the amount of the CFC's assets is determined by reference to market value immediately before the end of the CFC's accounting period.

[*TIOPA 2010, ss 371TA, 371TB*].

Elected or designated residence

An irrevocable election for a territory of residence can be made by one or more persons who have a majority interest in the CFC in the accounting period concerned. For this purpose, a person (or persons together) have a majority interest if their apportioned percentage of the CFC's chargeable profits represent more than half of the total percentage of the CFC's chargeable profits for the accounting period which would be likely to be apportioned to chargeable companies (see **21.25** below).

An election must be made by notice to an HMRC officer within twelve months of the end of the CFC's accounting period to which it relates, and must state, in respect of each person, the amount of the CFC's chargeable profits for the accounting period which would be likely to be apportioned to him and must be signed by the persons making it.

Alternatively, HMRC may make an irrevocable designation of the territory of residence. HMRC must give a notice of such a designation to every UK company which the officer considers would be likely to be a chargeable company were the CFC charge to apply, setting out the date of the designation, the name of the CFC concerned, the accounting period and the territory designated.

The election or designation has effect for the accounting period for which it is made and for each succeeding accounting period in which there is no change in the territories in which the CFC might be resident; it will not apply for an accounting period in which one of the eligible territories ceases to be eligible or a further territory becomes eligible. The election or designation has effect irrespective of any change in the persons having interests in the company or any change in those interests.

[*TIOPA 2010, s 371TC*].

Scope of the CFC charge

[21.5] A charge (the '*CFC charge*') applies to a UK resident company which has an interest in a controlled foreign company (CFC) in relation to an accounting period of the CFC if (and only if) the CFC has 'chargeable profits' (see **21.12** below) for the accounting period and none of the exemptions in **21.6–21.11** below applies for the period. [*TIOPA 2010, ss 371AA(1), 371BA(1)(2)*].

As a result of the exemptions, in practice only a small proportion of CFCs are affected by the CFC rules.

Exemptions from charge

[21.6] Many companies resident outside the UK will fall within the broad definition of a CFC outlined above. However, the legislation provides that where specified conditions are satisfied, no assessment or apportionment of the chargeable profits of the CFC can be made.

The exemptions are as follows:

(A) the exempt period exemption (see **21.7** below);
(B) the excluded territories exemption (see **21.8** below);
(C) the low profits exemption (see **21.9** below);
(D) the low profit margin exemption (see **21.10** below); and
(E) the tax exemption (see **21.11** below).

The exempt period exemption

[21.7] There is a temporary exemption period of twelve months during which a foreign subsidiary may be exempted from the CFC rules, provided that at any time during an accounting period of the CFC (the '*relevant time*'):

(i) the CFC was, immediately before the relevant time, carrying on a business, or if the relevant time is the date of incorporation or formation of the CFC, it was formed with the intention of controlling one or more companies which will qualify for the exempt period (the 'initial condition');

(ii) without this exemption there would be one or more chargeable companies (see **21.25** below) liable to the CFC charge (the 'charging condition'); and
(iii) at no time during the 12 months ending immediately before the relevant time was the charging condition met.

This exemption is available provided that: the foreign subsidiary does not restructure to avoid a CFC charge in subsequent periods (so it must have at least one accounting period which begins after the end of the exempt period during which it is a CFC) and, throughout the period from the end of the exempt period to the end of the CFC's first accounting period beginning after the exempt period the charging condition is met and each chargeable company would have been a chargeable company at the start of the exempt period (or is connected to such a company).

HMRC may extend the 12-month period if a chargeable company gives notice to HMRC before the end of the exempt period.

There are anti-avoidance rules which prevent this exemption from applying where arrangements are entered into at any time and the main purpose, or one of the main purposes, of the arrangements is to secure a tax advantage under this exemption.

[*TIOPA 2010, ss 371JA–371JF*].

The excluded territories exemption

[21.8] A CFC will be excluded from the CFC rules if it meets all of the following conditions:

(i) it is resident and carries on business in an excluded territory (specified in regulations — see *SI 2012 No 3024, Sch*). For the purpose of this exemption, a company's residency is determined as above. However, it is specifically provided that with regard to treaty-non resident companies, and companies resident by incorporation, that they must be actually liable to tax in the relevant territory. If as a result of this test, there is no territory of residence for the CFC, the excluded territories exemption cannot apply;
(ii) the total of the CFC's 'relevant income' is no more than 10% of its accounting profits, excluding transfer pricing adjustments, for the accounting period in question or £50,000 (reduced proportionately for short accounting periods);
(iii) no intellectual property has been transferred to the CFC from 'related' parties in the UK within the previous six years, where the transfer had a significant impact on the assumed total profits of the CFC, the total intellectual property held by the CFC, or the value of intellectual property held by the transferor (if only part of the intellectual property is transferred then it must form a significant part of the CFC's intellectual property, or significantly increase the CFC's assumed total profits); and
(iv) the CFC is not involved in an arrangement, the main purpose or one of the main purposes of which is to obtain a tax advantage (as defined at *CTA 2010, s 1139*) for any person at any time during the accounting period.

In addition, if at any time during the accounting period the CFC carries on insurance business in relation to which the CFC is regulated in any territory, the business must not be carried on in Luxembourg at that time.

Subject to further conditions (see *SI 2012 No 3024, Reg 4*), the requirements in (ii) and (iii) above do not have to be satisfied in order for the excluded territories exemption to apply where the CFC is resident in Australia, Canada, France, Germany, Japan or the USA.

In (ii) above, *'relevant income'* consists of the total of the following types of income. Income which falls into more than one category is only counted once.

- Category A income: the gross amount of income which is either exempt from tax in the territory or subject to a reduced tax rate in specified circumstances which include a tax holiday or other investment incentive and tax repayment schemes. Where a CFC has a permanent establishment in an excluded territory, the same category A income conditions apply to the income from the permanent establishment as apply to the income from the CFC's territory.
- Category B income: the CFC's non-trading income which benefits from a notional deduction for interest expense in the CFC's territory so that the income is effectively subject to a reduced tax rate, and where that deduction would not be available for such amounts when determining the CFCs assumed taxable profits for an accounting period.
- Category C income: amounts from a settlement in relation to which the CFC is a settlor or beneficiary and the CFC's share of any partnership income where the CFC is a partner.
- Category D income: amounts arising in circumstances in which a CFC has related party transactions which result, following the application of transfer pricing rules, in its income being reduced in the CFC's territory and where there is no corresponding increase in any other territory so that the income is effectively subject to a reduced tax rate. This category also includes income which is taxed at a reduced rate by virtue of any ruling, other decision or arrangement by the territory's governmental authorities.

A person is *'related'* to a CFC if:

- they are connected or associated with the CFC;
- at least 25% of the CFC's chargeable profits would be apportioned to that person if a CFC charge were applicable; or
- the person is connected with either or both of the controllers of the CFC (under the 40% test of control (see **21.3** above)).

[*TIOPA 2010, ss 371KA–371KJ, 371VF(3); SI 2012 No 3024*].

The low profits exemption

[21.9] A CFC with low profits is exempt from the CFC charge. Low profits are defined as:

- accounting profits or assumed total taxable profits (see **21.12** below) of no more than £50,000; or

- accounting profits or assumed total taxable profits of no more than £500,000 (of which no more than £50,000 represents non-trading income).

The above amounts are reduced proportionately if the accounting period is less than twelve months.

'Accounting profits' are the amount of pre-tax profits of the CFC determined in accordance with generally accepted accounting practice but excluding amounts that would be exempt distributions in the hands of the CFC if it were a UK tax resident company, property business profits or losses and capital profits or losses. There are also various adjustments that must be made to the accounting profits; in particular an adjustment must be made to take account of the transfer pricing rules unless the difference made by the application of the rules to the measure of profits is not more than £50,000.

This exemption does not apply:

(i) where arrangements have been entered into at any time with the main purpose (or one of the main purposes) being to secure the low profit exemption for either the relevant accounting period or one or more accounting periods of the CFC;
(ii) where at any time in the relevant accounting period, the CFC's business is, wholly or mainly, the provision of 'UK intermediary services' being the provision of services of a UK resident individual to the UK resident client of the CFC;
(iii) for a CFC that falls within this exemption by virtue of the accounting profits limits if, in determining the CFC's assumed taxable total profits (see **21.12** below) the group mismatch scheme provisions (see **50.36** LOAN RELATIONSHIPS) apply so as to exclude an amount from being brought into account as a debit or credit for the purposes of the loan relationship or derivative contracts rules.

[*TIOPA 2010, ss 371LA–371LC, 371VC, 371VD*].

The low profits margin exemption

[21.10] A CFC is exempt from the CFC charge if its accounting profits are no more than 10% of its relevant operating expenditure.

Accounting profits (see **21.9** above) are those profits before deduction of interest. Relevant operating expenditure is the operating expenditure brought into account in determining accounting profits, excluding the cost of goods purchased unless they are actually used in the CFC's territory of residence. The cost of any expenditure which gives rise directly or indirectly to income of a connected person is also excluded.

Anti-avoidance rules prevent the exemption from applying where an arrangement is entered into which has a main purpose of securing that the exemption applies.

[*TIOPA 2010, ss 371MA–371MC*].

The tax exemption

[21.11] A CFC is exempt from the CFC charge if the 'local tax amount' is at least 75% of the corresponding UK tax.

The '*local tax amount*' is the tax paid in the CFC's territory for that accounting period in respect of the CFC's local chargeable profits (subject to any specific deductions required). The corresponding UK tax is the amount of corporation tax which would be charged in respect of the CFC's assumed taxable total profits for the accounting period (see **21.12** below) but without taking into account any double taxation relief in respect of the local tax paid by the CFC in its territory of residence. Chargeable gains and losses are ignored.

Deductions must be made for any UK tax actually charged in respect of any income included in the CFC's assumed taxable total profits and any UK income tax suffered by deduction which could be set off against the corporation tax liability and which has not been repaid. For example, this will arise where the company has rents arising in the UK subject to deduction of tax at source or where the CFC is trading through a permanent establishment in the UK and paying corporation tax.

This exemption does not apply if it is not possible to determine residency by reason of domicile, residency or place of management (see **21.4** above), or if the local tax amount is determined under 'designer rate' tax provisions (i.e. under tax regimes which appear to HMRC to be designed to in effect allow companies to pay just the right amount of tax to circumvent the 75% rule and which are specified as such in regulations). The tax laws of Guernsey, Jersey, Isle of Man and Gibraltar have been specified as designer rate tax provisions under this rule.

[*TIOPA 2010, ss 371NA–371NE; SI 2000 No 3158*].

The CFC's chargeable profits

[21.12] For the purposes of **21.5** above, a CFC's '*chargeable profits*' for an accounting period are its 'assumed taxable total profits' for the period determined on the basis:

(1) that the 'assumed total profits' are limited to only so much of them as pass through one of the CFC charge gateways (see **21.14–21.19** below); and
(2) amounts are to be deducted from the assumed total profits under *CTA 2010, s 4(2)* (see **1.7** INTRODUCTION) only to the extent that is just and reasonable having regard to (1) above.

The CFC's '*assumed taxable total profits*' are the taxable total profits, as calculated in accordance with UK corporation tax rules, making certain assumptions (see **21.13** below).

Chargeable gains are ignored, but income arising to trustees where a CFC is a settlor or beneficiary of a settlement are included.

The CFC's '*assumed total profits*' for an accounting period are its assumed taxable total profits for the period, but before deducting any of the usual reliefs against total profits under *CTA 2010, s 4*.

[*TIOPA 2010, ss 371BA(3), 371SB*].

Simon's Taxes. See **D4.420.**

Assumptions to be made in computing profits

[21.13] The following assumptions must be made when determining the CFC's assumed taxable total profits (see **21.12** above), the corresponding UK tax (within **21.11** above), and the creditable tax (see **21.23** below):

(a) the CFC is UK resident at all times during the accounting period, has been UK resident from the beginning of the its first accounting period and will continue to be UK resident until it ceases to be a CFC;
(b) the CFC is, has been and will continue to be, within the charge to UK corporation tax;
(c) a determination of the CFC's assumed taxable total profits has been made for all previous accounting periods back to (and including) the CFC's first accounting period; this assumption applies in particular for the purposes of applying any relief which is relevant to two or more accounting periods;
(d) the CFC is not a close company;
(e) the CFC has made all relevant claims and elections sufficient to obtain the maximum amount of relief (with the exception of the foreign permanent establishment exemption election (see **31.15** DOUBLE TAX RELIEF), claims for unremittable overseas income (see **64.4** RESIDENCE), the designated currency election for investment companies (see **34.4** FOREIGN CURRENCY), and the election for a lease to be treated as long funding lease (see **10.53** CAPITAL ALLOWANCES ON PLANT AND MACHINERY). Additionally it is assumed that a claim in respect of reinvestment relief for intangible fixed assets (see **42.14** INTANGIBLE ASSETS) has not nor will be made by the CFC. This assumption can (if notice is given to HMRC within given time limits and in the required form) be varied such that it can be assumed the CFC has made, not made or has disclaimed/postponed a specified claim or election otherwise assumed.
Notice can only be given by a company or companies that either alone or together would have more than 50% of the chargeable profits of the CFC apportioned to them were the CFC charge to be applied. In particular:
    - notice of a designated currency election can be given. The designated currency election can apply where the CFC does not prepare its accounts in accordance with generally accepted accounting practice;
    - notice of a long funding lease election being made (or withdrawn) by the CFC, can be given. Where such a notice is made the assumed taxable total profits of the CFC are calculated taking into account the election;
    - an unremittable overseas income claim cannot be made unless it is not possible to remit the income either to the UK or to any of the territories overseas in which the CFC is resident. It follows that income arising in a territory of residence of the CFC can never be excluded from the taxable profits calculation even if it is not possible to remit it to the UK;

(f) any intangible fixed asset created or acquired by the CFC before its first accounting period is brought into account in that period at its value as recognised for accounting purposes at that time. For these purposes there is a requirement to assume that rollover relief has not been claimed nor will be claimed by the CFC in respect of the identified intangible fixed asset (see (e) above);

(g) for the purposes of the restriction on deductions for carried-forward losses at **51.13** LOSSES, the CFC's deductions allowance, trading profits deductions allowance and non-trading profits deductions allowance are all nil. If those amounts would be increased because of a reversal of an onerous lease provision, the allowances are taken to be equal to that increase;

(h) the CFC is neither a member of a group nor a member of a consortium for the purposes of any provision of the Tax Acts (see **35** GROUP RELIEF). The main effect of this assumption is to prevent the group loss relief provisions from applying;

(i) for the purposes of the CORPORATE INTEREST RESTRICTION **25**, the CFC is a member of a worldwide group for a period of account for which it would be a member if (g) above were ignored and is the only UK group company in the period;

(j) if the CFC incurs any capital expenditure on plant or machinery for the purposes of its trade before the first accounting period in which it falls within the CFC regime it is assumed that the expenditure was incurred for purposes wholly other than those of the trade, and was not brought into use for the purposes of the trade until the beginning of the CFC's first accounting period. This has the effect of bringing in a value equal to the market value of the plant and machinery employed in the trade at the beginning of the CFC's first accounting period;

(k) where the application of the Corporation Tax Acts is dependent upon a purpose test which considers whether a purpose of an arrangement or other conduct is to obtain a tax advantage, the provisions also apply where the arrangement or other conduct has as one of its main purposes the avoidance or reduction of a CFC charge;

(l) the double tax relief anti-avoidance provisions apply in computing the creditable tax of a CFC.

For assumptions (a) and (b) it is not necessary to assume that there is any change in the location in which the CFC carries on its activities; this means that for the UK tax computation of profits, the CFC will be treated as undertaking its trading or business activities outside the UK. Additionally it is assumed that the CFC does not get the benefit of the exemption for FOTRA securities.

[*TIOPA 2010, ss 371SC–371SR; F(No 2)A 2017, Sch 4 paras 180, 181, Sch 5 para 23; FA 2018, s 31(5)*].

The CFC charge gateway

[21.14] The assumed total profits of a CFC are liable to the CFC charge only to the extent that they pass through the CFC charge gateway (see **21.12** above).

Profits pass through the CFC charge gateway for this purpose to the extent that they pass through any of the following five gateways:

(1) profits attributable to UK activities (see **21.15** below);
(2) non-trading finance profits (see **21.16** below);
(3) trading finance profits (see **21.17** below);
(4) captive insurance business (see **21.18** below); and
(5) solo consolidation (see **21.19** below).

[*TIOPA 2010, s 371BB*].

In addition there are certain exemptions for profits from qualifying loan relationships which apply when the CFC's profits would otherwise fall within (2) above. See **21.20** below.

For each gateway it is necessary first to establish whether the test applies and then, if it does, the extent to which profits pass through the gateway and are therefore chargeable profits of the CFC.

Gateway 1 — profits attributable to UK activities

[21.15] This gateway test applies to all CFCs which do not fall within any of the exemptions at **21.7–21.11** above, unless any of the following apply:

- the CFC does not hold any assets or bear risks under an arrangement, the main purpose of which is to reduce or eliminate any liability to UK tax and as a result of the arrangement the CFC expects its business to be more profitable than it would otherwise be; or
- the CFC does not have any UK managed assets and bears no UK managed risks at any time during the accounting period; or
- the CFC has itself the capability throughout the accounting period to ensure that its business would be commercially effective if its UK managed assets and risks were to stop being UK managed; or
- the CFC's assumed total profits only consist of (one or both of) non-trading finance profits (see **21.16** below) or property business profits (as defined).

[*TIOPA 2010, s 371CA*].

Profits which pass through the gateway

This test excludes from the CFC charge the profits from subsidiaries where the significant people function or key entrepreneurial risk-taking function (referred to as the 'SPF') is outside the UK.

The concept of SPF is defined by reference to the OECD report on the Attribution of profits to a Permanent Establishment of July 2010. SPFs are functions that lead to the assumption of risk, the ownership of assets, or the on-going management of risks and assets. SPFs are not considered to be the provision of an advisory function or supervisory function (for example, saying yes or no to a proposal) or governance arrangements. It is likely in applying these new rules a company would need to use transfer pricing specialists, who are familiar with these concepts, and with examining the relative values and importance of differing functional profiles.

The following steps need to be taken to establish the profits which pass through the gateway:

(a) identify the relevant assets and risks from which the CFC assumed total profits have arisen (excluding any asset or risk if the CFC's assumed total profits are only negligibly higher than they have been if the CFC had not held that asset or borne that risk to any extent at all).

(b) identify the SPFs which are relevant to the economic ownership etc. of the relevant assets and risks.

(c) identify which of these SPFs are carried on in the UK (either by the CFC or by a company connected with the CFC), so UK SPFs, and which are non-UK SPFs.
- If the SPFs are all non-UK, the gateway test is not met and the assumed total profits of the CFC will not be liable to the CFC charge;
- If there are any UK SPFs, assume that they are carried out by a UK permanent establishment of the CFC and then determine the extent to which the relevant assets and risks identified would be attributed to that permanent establishment.

(d) exclude from the relevant assets those which reduce gross income, or increase expenses by less than half of the amount that would follow if the assets or risks were not owned or borne by the CFC at all (so where the UK activities are a minority of the total activities).

(e) In addition the following amounts are **excluded:**
  (i) profits where substantial economic value, other than tax savings, arises from the CFC's holding of assets or its bearing of risks;
  (ii) profits where they arise from arrangements that independent companies would have entered into;
  (iii) all trading profits if the following 'safe harbour' conditions are met:
    (1) at all times during the relevant accounting period, the CFC has in its territory of residence, premises which it intends to use with a reasonable degree of permanence for the carrying on of its activities;
    (2) no more than 20% of the CFCs relevant trading income derives (directly or indirectly) from UK resident persons, or UK resident permanent establishments. Relevant trading income is trading income excluding income arising from the sale of goods in the UK that were produced by the CFC in its territory of residence, but disregarding income if a corresponding expense is exempt under an overseas permanent establishment election per *CTA 2009, s 18A* (special conditions apply to banking CFCs);
    (3) the 'UK related management expenditure' is no more than 20% of 'total related management expenditure'. UK related management expenditure is management expenditure which relates to staff or other individuals who carry out relevant management functions in the UK. Total related management expenditure is the total expenditure incurred by the CFC in relation to staff or other individuals who carry out 'relevant management functions' in relation to managing or controlling any of the relevant assets or risks of the CFC;

(4) there has been no transfer of intellectual property to the CFC from related parties (see **21.8** above) in the UK within the previous six years which significantly reduced the value of intellectual property held by the transferor. If any part of the CFC's intellectual property was so transferred to it, the transfer must not have significantly reduced the value of intellectual property held by the transferor and either the property transferred must not form a significant part of the total intellectual property of the CFC or, as a result of the transfer, the CFCs assumed total profits must not be significantly higher than they would have otherwise been; and

(5) no more than 20% of the total trading income of the CFC arises from goods exported from the UK. However, goods which are exported from the UK into the CFC's territory of residence are disregarded.

If the 20% condition in (3) above is not met, but all the other safe harbour conditions are, then where the UK related management expenditure for any given asset or risk is not more than 50% of the total related management expenditure for that asset or risk, then the condition is met (and the trading profits arising from that asset or risk are excluded from charge).

In (4) above, the legislation does not define 'significant' and the facts and circumstances of each case should be taken into account. However, as a rule of thumb, 'significant' can be taken to mean 10% or more. (HMRC International Manual, INTM200840).

Any remaining profits after taking the above steps pass through the gateway and fall within the CFC charge.

Anti-avoidance provisions apply where arrangements have taken place which involved the organisation or reorganisation of the business in order to fall within one of the safe harbours.

[*TIOPA 2010, ss 371DA–371DL*].

Gateway 2 — non-trading finance profits

[21.16] This gateway test applies if the CFC has certain non-trading finance profits (see below).

[*TIOPA 2010, s 371CB(1)*].

But it does not apply if:

(i) the CFC has trading or property business profits (or both) and/or exempt distribution income, and it is a holding company of 51% subsidiaries; and

(ii) the CFC's non-trading finance profits are no more than 5% of:
- the total of trading or property business profits;
- the total of the CFC's exempt distribution income; or
- the sum of the two totals (where all the conditions in (i) above are met).

Where the 5% threshold in relation to trading or property business profits in (ii) above is breached and all the conditions detailed in (i) above are met, the gateway test will still not apply if the CFC's adjusted non-trading finance profits (as defined) do not exceed 5% of the total of the CFC's exempt distribution income.

[*TIOPA 2010, ss 371CC, 371CD*].

Non-trading finance profits

'*Non-trading finance profits*' are amounts included in the CFC's assumed total profits (see **21.12** above) which are non-trading profits from loan relationships and non-exempt distributions, or which arise from a 'relevant finance lease' but are not trading profits. For the purposes only of this gateway test, profits which arise from the investment of funds held for the purposes of a trade are excluded, if that trade is carried on by a CFC and no profits of that trade for the accounting period pass through the CFC charge gateway. Profits which arise from the investment of funds held by the CFC for the purposes of its UK or overseas property business are similarly excluded. These exclusions do not apply to non-trading finance profits arising from funds held: because of a prohibition or restriction on the payment of dividends imposed under the law of the CFC's territory of incorporation, its articles of association or any arrangement entered into by the CFC; with a view to paying dividends or other distributions at a time after the end of the relevant accounting period; with a view to acquiring shares in any company, or making a capital contribution to a person; with a view to investing in land at a time after the end of the relevant accounting period; only or mainly for contingencies; or, in order to reduce or eliminate a tax or duty imposed by any territory.

Trading finance profits of a group treasury company can also to be treated as non-trading finance profits where a notice is given to HMRC.

A '*relevant finance lease*' is either an arrangement providing for an asset to be made available by one person to another which falls to be treated in accordance with generally accepted accounting practice (GAAP) as a finance lease or loan in the accounts of the lessor or a connected person or a hire-purchase, conditional sale or other arrangement of a similar character. Where accounts for a period are not prepared under either international accounting standards or UK GAAP then any question relating to GAAP for that period is to be determined with regard to international accounting standards. Loan relationships cannot be relevant finance leases.

[*TIOPA 2010, ss 371CB(2)–(8), 371VG, 371VIA*].

Profits which pass through the gateway

Where the gateway test applies, any non-trading finance profits that are included within the CFC's assumed total profits for the accounting period pass through the gateway, if they fall within one or more of the following categories:

(a) non-trading finance profits that are attributable to UK activities (as defined);

(b) non-trading finance profits so far as they arise from the investment of UK monetary and non-monetary assets. However, funds or other assets received by the CFC either in exchange for goods or services, or by way of a loan, are not included;

(c) non-trading finance profits to the extent that they arise from an arrangement (including a relevant finance lease), directly or indirectly with a UK resident company (or UK PE) connected with the CFC, where it is reasonable to assume that the arrangement is made as an alternative to the CFC paying dividends or making any other distribution to the other company (and the main reason for the arrangement is to do with any tax liability);

(d) non-trading finance profits where they arise from the direct or indirect finance lease of an asset to a UK resident company or UK permanent establishment of a non-UK company that is connected to the CFC, where the alternative is that the other company could have purchased the asset (the 'relevant asset'), or could have made (directly or indirectly) an arrangement (not being a relevant finance lease, and/or not involving a CFC) whereby the other company would, directly or indirectly, purchase rights to use the relevant asset (and the main reason for either lease arrangement is to do with any tax liability).

[*TIOPA 2010, ss 371EB–371EE*].

Example

During its accounting period CFC X has exempt trading profits before interest and tax of 1,000. CFC X also receives exempt dividend income from its wholly owned subsidiary Y of 1,000. Y has no non-trading finance profits arising in the period. During the accounting period CFC X accrues non-trading finance profits of 80.

CFC X meets the requirements for trading profits, and exempt distributions (from 51% subsidiaries) and so the amount we need to consider is 2,000.

5% of 2,000 is 100 and so all of CFC X's non-trading finance profits of 80 will be exempt. Therefore CFC X will not need to consider Gateway 2.

Simon's Taxes. See **D4.427.**

Gateway 3 — trading finance profits

[21.17] This gateway test applies if the CFC has 'trading finance profits' and funds or other assets which derive from UK connected capital contributions (as defined).

Trading finance profits of a group treasury company (as defined) can be treated as non-trading finance profits where a notice is given to HMRC.

'*Trading finance profits*' are profits from trading loan relationships, distributions treated as trading income and trading profits from a relevant finance lease (see **21.16** above).

[*TIOPA 2010, ss 371CE, 371CEA, 371VG(4); F(No 2)A 2017, Sch 5 para 21*].

Profits which pass through the gateway

Where the gateway test applies, the profits that pass through this gateway are those which represent trading finance profits arising from the use or investment of an excess of 'free capital' for the CFC, during the accounting period.

'*Free capital*' is funding that does not give rise to any debits when determining the CFC finance profits, so loan relationship or other finance income deductions. The likelihood is that such funding would be provided by a connected or associated party, such as a parent entity. So this gateway operates by comparing the CFC's free capital position with what it would be if the CFC had been a company which was not a 51% subsidiary of any other company, but carrying on the same business with the same amount of funding. The difference is the 'excess' of free capital.

There are special rules for calculating the excess of free capital which apply to CFCs that carry on insurance business.

In addition the value of free capital is increased where: the CFC is the ultimate debtor to a qualifying loan relationship of another CFC or where the CFC is the debtor under a loan relationship and the creditor has made an overseas permanent establishment election and also a claim for exemption of intra-group non-trading finance profits (see **21.20** below).

[*TIOPA 2010, ss 371FA–371FD*].

The *Controlled Foreign Companies (Excluded Banking Business Profits) Regulations SI 2012 No 3041* provide an exclusion from a CFC charge for certain profits of finance trading companies, including banks, where certain conditions are met.

If the conditions are met then no CFC charge arises under this gateway in respect of trading finance profits where they arise from banking business carried on by the CFC in relation to which the CFC is regulated in the territory in which it is resident. The conditions are that:

(i) the CFC is a member of a UK banking group (its 'parent group') which is required by the Prudential Regulation Authority to prepare consolidated financial information;

(ii) the CFC's tier one capital ratio at the end of the relevant accounting period does not exceed 125% of its parent group's tier one capital ratio; and

(iii) it is reasonable to suppose that the CFC's average tier one capital ratio during the relevant accounting period did not exceed 125% of its parent group's tier one capital ratio.

See *SI 2012 No 3041, Reg 5* for formulae for calculating a CFC's tier one capital ratio and its parent group's tier one capital ratio.

[*SI 2012 No 3041*].

Gateway 4 — captive insurance business

[21.18] This gateway test applies if, at any time during the accounting period, the main part of the CFC's business is insurance business and the CFC's assumed total profits include amounts which derive from insurance contracts entered into with:

- a connected UK resident company;
- a connected non-UK resident company, acting through a UK permanent establishment; or
- a UK resident person and the contract is linked to the provisions of goods or services to the UK resident person. This is targeted at in-house warranty insurance situations. For example, a UK retail group may establish a captive insurance company offshore. It may then market warranty plans, written by the captive insurance company, to UK resident persons at the point of sale of its retail goods.

[*TIOPA 2010, s 371CF*].

Profits which pass through the gateway

CFC profits that pass through this gateway are amounts included in the CFC's assumed total profits that arise from insurance business which derives from relevant insurance contracts (as above).

Profits from an EEA resident captive insurance CFC will pass through this gateway (and be chargeable CFC profits) where they are derived from an insurance contract for which the insured has no significant UK non-tax reason for entering.

[*TIOPA 2010, s 371GA*].

Gateway 5 — solo consolidation

[21.19] This gateway applies to banking subsidiaries, of UK resident banks, which have applied to the Prudential Regulation Authority for a solo consolidation waiver. Under these arrangements an unregulated subsidiary is treated as if it were a division of the regulated financial company.

It also applies where the CFC is controlled by a UK resident bank which holds CFC shares and any fall in the value of those shares would be (wholly or mainly) ignored for the purpose of determining whether the UK bank meets the requirements of the PRA handbook in relation to the bank's capital, where the main purpose, or one of the main purposes, of holding the shares is to obtain a tax advantage for itself or a connected company.

[*TIOPA 2010, s 371CG*].

Profits which pass through the gateway

The profits which pass through the gateway are the CFC's assumed total profits which would **not** be treated as exempt profits under an overseas permanent establishment election, if the CFC were deemed to be an overseas permanent establishment.

[*TIOPA 2010, s 371HA*].

Exemption for profits from qualifying loan relationships

[21.20] A chargeable company (i.e. a UK resident shareholder company which will suffer the CFC charge — see **21.25** below) or companies, may make a claim for exemption of certain 'qualifying loan relationships profits' that would otherwise pass through the CFC charge gateway because they fall within the non-trading finance profits gateway (see **21.16** above). The CFC must have a business premises at its disposal from which it carries out its activities on a permanent basis.

Any such claim cannot include profits that:

- arise from the investment of funds held by the CFC for trading purposes or for the purposes of a property business;
- fall within the solo consolidation gateway (see **21.19** above); or
- arise from a relevant finance lease (see **21.16** above).

The effect of the claim is that (for the claimant chargeable company only) qualifying loan relationship profits which are **not** exempt under these provisions are within the CFC charge.

For accounting periods beginning on or after 1 January 2019, '*qualifying loan relationships profits*' are so much of the CFC's profits from its 'qualifying loan relationships' taken together which are non-trading finance profits falling within **21.16**(b) above and not falling within **21.16**(a) (i.e., broadly, they must derive from UK capital investment but not be generated by UK activity). Previously, '*qualifying loan relationships profits*' were all of the CFC's profits from its qualifying loan relationships taken together. For this purpose, accounting periods straddling 1 January 2019 are treated as two separate accounting periods, the second of which starts on that date. Where any amounts need to be apportioned between the two notional periods, a time basis must be used, unless it would be unjust or unreasonable, in which case a just and reasonable basis must be used.

[*TIOPA 2010, s 371IA; FA 2019, s 20(2)(5)(6)*].

See also **31.6** DOUBLE TAX RELIEF for restrictions on relief where a claim has been made under these provisions.

Qualifying loan relationship

A '*qualifying loan relationship*' is, broadly, a loan relationship where the CFC is the creditor and the ultimate debtor is a company connected with the CFC and controlled by the same UK resident persons who control the CFC. The following exclusions apply:

(i) if the ultimate debtor is a non-UK resident company, the creditor relationship cannot be treated as a qualifying loan relationship if some or all of the company debits are being bought into account either as profits of a UK permanent establishment of the non-UK resident company or as property income of a UK property business;

(ii) if the ultimate debtor is a UK resident company a credit can only be brought into account as a credit in respect of a qualifying loan relationship if a foreign profits election is in place (see **31.15** DOUBLE TAX RELIEF) and all the company's debits are bought into account for the purposes of determining exemption adjustment;

(iii) if the ultimate debtor is another CFC, the creditor relationship cannot be treated as a qualifying loan relationship so long as some or all of the other CFC's debits are relevant to the application of the charge gateway or the low profits exemption (see **21.9** above) and as a result there is no CFC charge for the accounting period concerned or the charge is reduced. The loan relationship is only disqualified to the extent that the debits on the loan give rise to a more beneficial result under the gateway rules or low profits exemption rules, compared to where no such loan would have been entered into;

(iv) the creditor relationship cannot be treated as a qualifying loan relationship if the loan relationship is connected to an arrangement, the main purpose of which is to provide funding for a loan to another person from the ultimate debtor (this exclusion also covers transactions that are economically equivalent to the provision of a loan relationship). This exclusion is targeted at complex artificial arrangements designed to conceal the true identity of the ultimate debtor;

(v) the creditor relationship cannot be a qualifying loan relationship where it is sourced to any extent from relevant UK funds (other than a loan) which originate directly or indirectly from a UK resident company which has a main business of banking or insurance; or where the loan relationship was created as part of an arrangement which gives rise to a taxable deduction for a UK connected bank or insurance company;

(vi) the creditor relationship cannot be a qualifying loan relationship where third-party debt of a non-UK resident group company is repaid (in whole or in part), and effectively replaced with new UK debt under or in connection with an arrangement the main purpose or one of the main purposes of which is to obtain a tax advantage for any person. This provision catches arrangements that give rise to an increase in net interest expense in the UK whether paid to unconnected persons or to non-UK connected persons. If a loan is made to a UK group company, which in turn lends to another UK group company then the UK to UK element is ignored. The test of purpose must be applied to the whole of the arrangement, not just to particular loans which form part of the arrangement. The fact that the existing external debt was used for a commercial purpose is not conclusive as to the question of what the main purpose of an arrangement is. The events mentioned in this provision (namely the loan to the UK resident connected party, funding of the CFC and use of those funds to enable a non-UK resident connected company to repay external debt) must occur under the same arrangement. The restriction applies where the relevant loan is used to any extent (other than a negligible one) to repay wholly or partly another loan;

(vii) the creditor relationship cannot be a qualifying loan relationship where the loan is made by a UK company to a connected non-UK debtor company and subsequently an arrangement is made in connection with the loan relationship with the purpose of securing a reduction in relevant UK credits or increase in relevant UK debits of a UK connected company in comparison to what credits or debits would have been if the relevant arrangement had not been made. A UK connected company is a UK resident company which is either connected with the CFC, or was connected with a company with which the CFC is connected.

[*TIOPA 2010, ss 371IG, 371IH*].

Amount of exempt profits

In order to establish the amount of profits which get the exemption:

(a) either the qualifying resources rule, or the 75% exemption rule, is applied; and
(b) then the matched interest rule (if relevant).

The qualifying resources rule

The chargeable company can elect for this rule to apply to all (or part of) of the profits of the qualifying loan relationships (the 'relevant profits').

The '*relevant profits*' are determined by applying the following steps to each qualifying loan relationship:

(I) Step 1 is to determine the credits from the qualifying loan relationship that are brought into account for the purposes of determining the CFC's non-trading finance profits for the accounting period. The amount determined is 'the Step 1 credits';
(II) Step 2 is to add to or subtract from the Step 1 credits such debits or credits as arise from derivative contracts or other arrangements that are a hedge of interest rate or FOREX risk relating to the qualifying loan relationship. The amount determined is 'the Step 2 credits';
(III) Steps 3 and 4 are further steps for bringing into account debits and credits (so far as not reflected in the Step 2 credits) for the purposes of determining the CFC's non-trading finance profits for the accounting period. This is done by subtraction from or addition to the Step 2 credits of a just and reasonable proportion of debits or credits to give the CFC's qualifying loan relationship profits for the qualifying loan relationship in question.

Such profits (or a proportion of such profits) are exempt if it is shown that throughout the period the principal outstanding on the relevant loan is funded by the CFC out of 'qualifying resources' and that the ultimate debtor (i.e. borrower of the funds) was resident in the same territory at all times during the period.

This exclusion does not apply if:

- the debt is repaid within 48 hours of it being made (provided the loan repayment does not occur under an arrangement which has as its main purpose, or one of its main purposes, the aim of ensuring the initial restriction does not apply); or
- an amount of short-term debt is repaid within six months out of the proceeds of the issue of ordinary non-redeemable shares by the parent company to persons who are not members of the CFC group (and it was the intention that the loan would be repaid out of the funds from the issue of the shares).

'*Qualifying resources*' are a source of funds that place no demands on group resources outside the ultimate debtor's territory of residence (the 'relevant territory'). They are defined as profits of the CFC so far as they consist of the making of loans to members of the CFC group which are used solely for the purpose of the CFC business in the relevant territory.

Qualifying resources are also funds (or other assets) received by the CFC in relation to shares held by the CFC in members of the CFC group, where those funds generally derive from profits that have been earned in the relevant territory by members of the CFC group. See further *s 371IC(1)–(7)*.

The requirement that the relevant territory be the territory where the ultimate debtor (of the qualifying loan relationship) is resident means that those qualifying resources have to be derived from the same territory in which the borrower (in respect of the qualifying loan relationship) is resident. In situations such as this there are further limitations to qualifying resources so that: loans made to persons outside the relevant territory are not treated as being for the purpose of the business carried on in that relevant territory; and, profits earned outside of the relevant territory that are distributed to or arise to a company resident in the relevant territory are not treated as earned in the relevant territory.

Where the qualifying loan relationship is part of an arrangement that results in an increase in debt in the UK of members of the group then there is a limitation on the amount of qualifying resources treated as a source for the qualifying loan relationship, such limitation being the amount of that debt.

The amount of loan may vary during the year.

[*TIOPA 2010, ss 371IB, 371IC, 371IF; F(No 2)A 2017, Sch 4 para 179*].

Example

A £100 million loan is funded at the beginning of an accounting period entirely out of qualifying resources and this loan is increased to £200 million half way through the year with the balance of the loan being funded out of non-qualifying resources. Throughout the period the percentage of the loan funded from qualifying resources is 100% for the first six months and 50% for the second six months so that over the year it would appear that the percentage of profits that are exempt should be 75%. However, the exemption only applies to a minimum proportion of the loan that, at all times during the period, is funded from qualifying resources. In this case only 50% of the loan was funded from qualifying resources for the whole period.

C's claim should therefore specify in its claim for the first accounting period that 50% of the profits are exempt. In the second accounting period if the loan remains at £200 million throughout the period C's claim should again specify 50% as exempt. In this scenario a claim under the 75% exemption rule (see below) would be more advantageous for the company.

The 75% exemption rule

This applies to a qualifying loan relationship where a claim has not been made under the qualifying resources rule. It provides that 75% of the profits of the qualifying loan relationship is exempt.

[*TIOPA 2010, s 371ID*].

Matched interest rule

This rule applies if there are 'leftover profits' which are not exempt after applying the qualifying resources rule or the 75% exemption rule and the leftover profits would otherwise be included in the CFC's chargeable profits.

If the 'aggregate net tax-interest expense' of the worldwide group for the period of account coinciding with or overlapping the company's accounting period is nil, the 'matched interest profits' are exempt. Otherwise a more limited exemption applies if the 'relevant proportion' of the matched interest profits apportioned to the company or other chargeable companies exceeds the aggregate net tax-interest expense. The '*relevant proportion*' of the matched interest profits is calculated by adding together the amount for each company found by multiplying the matched interest profits by the percentage of the CFC's chargeable profits apportioned to it. The limited exemption is given effect by treating the matched interest profits as equal to the amount they would otherwise be multiplied by E/RPMIP. 'E' for this purpose is the amount of the excess of the apportioned matched interest profits over the aggregate net tax-interest expense and RPMIP is the relevant proportion.

For these purposes, the '*matched interest profits*' are the leftover profits after leaving out of account 'excluded debits' and 'excluded credits'. For the meaning of 'aggregate net tax-interest expense', 'excluded debits' and 'excluded credits' see **24.5** CORPORATE INTEREST RESTRICTION. In computing the aggregate net tax-interest expense for the purpose of these provisions, debits, credits and other amounts arising from banking or insurance business carried on by a company within the charge to corporation tax are ignored.

Before the introduction of the corporate interest restriction (broadly with effect from 1 April 2017), this rule applied in conjunction with the worldwide debt cap provisions. The rule applied if there were 'leftover profits' which were not exempt after applying the qualifying resources rule or the 75% exemption rule and the charging of the CFC charge would result in the chargeable company having a financing income amount (under *TIOPA 2010, s 314A*).

The leftover profits were exempt if the 'tested income amount' (TIA) exceeds the 'tested expense amount' (TEA). Otherwise a percentage (Z%) of the leftover profits were exempt if the CFC charge caused the TIA to exceed the TEA. The percentage is calculated using the following formula:

$Z\% = 100\% \times (E / (I + R))$

where:

- E is the amount of the excess which would be caused by the finance income amounts;
- I is the amount of any increase in the TIA which would be caused by the finance income amounts; and
- R is the amount of any reduction in the TEA which would be caused by the finance income amounts.

Necessary modifications were made to the worldwide debt cap rules but only for the purposes of applying this section. It required that a calculation of TIA and TEA to be made for a UK group, if one had not already been made. This includes banking and insurance groups and groups that are not large groups. Further, there was a specific limitation that excluded debits, credits and other amounts that arose from banking or insurance business in determining what the finance income amount would be for any company and what the TIA and TEA would be.

[*TIOPA 2010, s 371IE; F(No 2)A 2017, Sch 5 para 22*].

Claims

A claim for this exemption to apply must be made in the chargeable company's tax return for the period within the usual time limits (or, later, if allowed by HMRC). A claim may also be varied or withdrawn outside of the usual time limits where there are changes to the aggregate net tax-interest expense (previously, the tested income and expense amounts), provided that claim is made within 12 months of such a change and the claim is made to take account of that change (and not for another purpose).

[*TIOPA 2010, s 371IJ; F(No 2)A 2017, Sch 5 para 22, Sch 15 para 43*].

Calculating the CFC charge

[21.21] Where profits of a CFC pass through the CFC charge gateway, the CFC charge is determined in accordance with a series of steps. These are used to work out whether or not a charge arises and, if it does, which UK resident companies are chargeable. In outline the steps are as follows:

Step 1: determine the persons (the '*relevant persons*') who have 'relevant interests' in the CFC during the accounting period (see **21.22** below). The CFC charge only applies to companies that are UK resident during the accounting period when it has a relevant interest in the CFC.

Step 2: determine the CFC's creditable tax for the accounting period (see **21.23** below).

Step 3: apportion the CFC's chargeable profits and creditable tax among the relevant persons (see **21.24** below).

Step 4: determine which companies are chargeable companies (see **21.24** below).

Step 5: calculate the CFC charge that applies to each chargeable company. The charge is levied on the percentage of the CFC's chargeable profits apportioned to the chargeable company. The amount of the charge is reduced by the percentage of the CFC's creditable tax apportioned to the chargeable company.

The rate of the CFC charge is simply the rate of corporation tax applicable to the chargeable company for the relevant accounting period (if there is more than one rate, the average rate is used). The CFC charge is treated as if it were an amount of corporation tax charged on the company for the relevant accounting period (see **21.26** below).

Where the chargeable company is a banking company subject to the bank surcharge (see **7.3** BANKS), the surcharge is likewise chargeable on the profits apportioned from the CFC. All or part of the company's (or group's) surcharge allowance can, however, be allocated against the apportioned profits, effectively reducing the surcharge element of the CFC charge. Anti-avoidance provisions apply to prevent transfer of profits out of the CFC to avoid the surcharge.

[*TIOPA 2010, ss 371BC, 371BI*].

Relevant interests

[21.22] The following rules apply to determine which persons have a relevant interest in a CFC for the purposes of Step 1 at **21.21** above.

A UK resident company's 'interest' in a CFC is a *'relevant interest'* except to the extent that it is an indirect interest held through another UK resident company. This ensures that the relevant interest will be held by the UK resident company which is at the bottom of a chain of two or more UK companies.

Where a UK resident company has a relevant interest in a CFC, any interests in the CFC held by a person, other than a UK resident company, who is connected or associated with that company are also relevant interests. Indirect interests held by virtue of an interest in a UK resident company or another person who is connected or associated with the company which has a relevant interest are excluded.

Any other person (P) with a direct interest in the CFC also has a relevant interest except to the extent that the interest is the same as another person's relevant interest by virtue of the other person having an interest in P.

The following have an '*interest*' in a company:

- any person who has, or is entitled to acquire, share capital or voting rights in the company;
- any person who has, or is entitled to acquire, a right to receive or participate in distributions of the company;
- any person who is entitled to direct how the company's income or assets are to be applied, to have such income or assets applied on their behalf or to secure that such income is applied (directly or indirectly) for their benefit; and
- any other person who alone or together with other persons, controls the company.

Rights of a loan creditor are ignored other than rights arising from an embedded derivative under a loan relationship.

In determining whether a person has an interest in a CFC by virtue of a loan relationship with embedded derivatives in a situation where accounts have not been prepared under either UK generally accepted accounting practice or international accounting standards, then the issue will be determined by assuming accounts have been prepared in accordance with international accounting standards.

[*TIOPA 2010, ss 371OB(2), 371OC, 371OD, 371OE, 371VH*].

Creditable tax

[21.23] The profits to be apportioned are calculated together with the creditable tax claimable.

Creditable tax is the **sum of:**

(1) the amount of any double taxation relief which would be available in respect of any income included or represented in the CFC's chargeable profits for the accounting period;
(2) UK income tax deducted at source or charged on the CFC's income; and
(3) UK corporation tax charged on the CFC's income.

[*TIOPA 2010, s 371PA*].

Apportionment to relevant persons

[21.24] The rules require indirect interests in a chain of companies to be multiplied together to arrive at the correct apportionment percentage. If there is more than one chain leading to the same CFC then the relevant interests through each chain are aggregated.

The following conditions must be met in order for the CFC's chargeable profits and creditable tax to be apportioned among the relevant persons using the formulaic approach below:

(a) the relevant persons all have their relevant interests by virtue only of their holding, directly or indirectly, ordinary shares in the CFC;
(b) each relevant person is either only UK resident or only non-UK resident at all times during the accounting period;
(c) a company with an intermediate interest in the CFC only has that interest from holding, directly or indirectly, ordinary shares in the CFC.

When these conditions are met the chargeable profits and creditable tax of the CFC are apportioned to the relevant persons in proportion to their ordinary shareholdings in the CFC. HMRC may however direct another just and reasonable apportionment be used (which may be challenged on appeal).

If the conditions for the above approach are not met then a just and reasonable approach is to be applied. If arrangements are entered into at any time, the main purpose or one of the main purposes of which is to obtain for any person a tax advantage, then not only must a just and reasonable approach be applied to the apportionment, but the apportionment must counteract the effects of the arrangement so far as it is practicable to do so.

[*TIOPA 2010, ss 371QC, 371UC*].

Indirect shareholdings

Where a relevant person ('R') has an interest in a CFC by virtue of indirectly holding ordinary shares in the CFC the apportionment is made using the following formula:

$$P \times S$$

where:

P is the product of the appropriate fractions of R and each of the companies through which R indirectly holds the relevant shares, other than the company which directly holds the relevant shares; and

S is the percentage of issued ordinary shares in the CFC which the relevant shares represent.

[*TIOPA 2010, s 371QE*].

Where the holding varies throughout the period then the relevant interest is the sum of the relevant percentages for each holding period, weighted on the basis of the number of days in the holding period in relation to the number of days in the accounting period. See *TIOPA 2010, s 371QF*.

Chargeable company

[21.25] A *'chargeable company'* is one which has at least 25% of the CFC's chargeable profits apportioned to it, due to its relevant interest. The 25% includes any chargeable profits apportioned to relevant persons connected or associated with it at any time during the accounting period.

Certain companies are excluded from this definition, including: a manager of offshore funds that holds a relevant interest in a CFC in order to 'seed' a fund (under certain conditions); a company which is a participant in an offshore fund where the CFC is the offshore fund (where it is reasonably believed the 25% threshold will not be met); and where the CFC shares are held as trading assets. There are special rules for insurance companies carrying on a BLAGAB business.

[*TIOPA 2010, ss 371BD, 371BE, 371BF, 371BG*].

Example

X Ltd, a UK company, has profits of £600,000 in the year to 31 March 2022. It has two wholly-owned subsidiaries, one in the UK, the other, Zero Ltd, resident in Ruritania. Zero Ltd has an accounting period ending on 28 February 2022. It has interest income from Utopia of £150,000 and it paid tax in Utopia of £4,000 on this income. It paid tax on this income in Ruritania, where it is resident, of £15,000. The Utopian tax is not creditable against the Ruritanian tax.

The tax computation for X Ltd will show:

	£	£
Taxable total profits		600,000
UK tax at 19%		114,000
s 371BC charge 150,000 × 19%	28,500	
Creditable tax	(19,000)	9,500
Total UK tax bill		123,500

In this example all of the overseas tax is claimable in full, as it is less than 19% of the income source.

The accounting period of Zero Ltd (to 28 February 2022) falls to be assessed in X Ltd's accounting period to 31 March 2022.

Interaction with group relief rules

See 35.5 GROUP RELIEF.

Administration of CFCs

[21.26] The CFC charge is treated as though it were an amount of corporation tax and therefore all statutory provisions which apply generally to corporation tax also apply to the CFC charge. This includes provisions relating to returns, accounts statements and reports, assessment, collection and receipt of corporation tax, rights of appeal, and administration, penalties, interest on unpaid tax and priority of tax in insolvency cases. [*TIOPA 2010, s 371UB*].

An appeal against an HMRC amendment to a return or against a discovery assessment involving CFC tax is heard by the Tribunal. If the appeal involves a question likely to affect the liability to CFC tax of more than one person, each of those persons is entitled to appear and be heard or to make representations in writing. The question must then be determined separately from any other matters in the appeal and a decision on that question is binding on all the persons concerned. [*TIOPA 2010, s 371UE*].

Where the CFC charge is not fully paid on the date it is due and payable, HMRC can give notice of liability to another UK resident company when it holds or has held (directly or indirectly) the whole or any part of the same interest in the CFC concerned as is or was held by the defaulting company. If any sum remains unpaid after three months of such a notice, the outstanding amount may be recovered from the original defaulting company and/or the company on which notice has been served. [*TIOPA 2010, s 371UF*].

Key points on CFCs

[21.27] Points to consider are as follows.

- The controlled foreign company (CFC) rules seek to cancel any tax advantage from placing subsidiaries into low tax jurisdictions. If a UK holding company has a subsidiary in, say, Jersey, which has a zero rate of tax, any profits diverted to that company would escape UK corporation tax. In order to negate this possible leakage of tax the CFC rules impute these profits back to the UK parent company. Many of the more sophisticated jurisdictions operate similar rules for the same reasons.
- A CFC is a company which is not resident in the UK and is controlled by UK resident persons.
- A number of statutory exemptions apply to exclude many CFCs from the CFC charge. See **21.6–21.11** below.
- If none of the exemptions apply, then the profits of the CFC are potentially subject to the CFC charge, but only to the extent that they pass through the CFC charge gateway, i.e. they fall within one of the five individual gateways. Before it is considered whether profits fall within a gateway it must first be determined whether a gateway applies. There are certain exclusions that apply which will mean a gateway will only apply in certain instances. However the first gateway is of more general application, for profits attributable

to UK activities. Each gateway should be considered, however, some are specific, such as the captive insurance gateway, or the banking subsidiary gateway (solo consolidation).

- An exemption can be claimed for finance company profits which derive from qualifying loan relationships — either full or partial.
- Profits which pass through the CFC charge gateway are chargeable profits and are apportioned between persons with an interest in the CFC. If certain conditions apply, the apportionment is made on a formulaic basis; if not, a just and reasonable apportionment is made. Where at least 25% of the profits are apportioned to a UK resident company, that company is liable to the CFC charge. See **21.21–21.25** below.
- The CFC's creditable tax is apportioned on the same basis as the chargeable profits. The creditable tax is the sum of any double tax relief which would be available in respect of any income included or represented in the chargeable profits, UK income tax deducted at source or charged on the CFC's income and UK corporation tax charged on the CFC's income.
- The amount of the CFC charge is equal to the corporation tax rate of the chargeable company applied to the apportioned profits, less the creditable tax apportioned to the chargeable company.
- The CFC charge is treated as though it were an amount of corporation tax and therefore all the compliance provisions which apply generally to corporation tax also apply to the CFC charge. Companies are required to include details of significant interests in CFCs in their tax returns and to self-assess any CFC tax due.

22

Co-operative and Community Benefit Societies

Cross-references. **40** HOUSING ASSOCIATIONS; **54.1** MUTUAL COMPANIES.

Simon's Taxes. See **D7.625–D7.630**.

Introduction to co-operative and community benefit societies

[22.1] The provisions described in this chapter apply to societies registered under *Co-operative and Community Benefit Societies Act 2014*, registered NI industrial and provident societies and credit unions, and European Co-operative Societies.

[*CTA 2010, s 1119*].

Share or loan interest paid

[22.2] Share or loan interest paid by a society within **22.1** above is not a distribution (see **29** DISTRIBUTIONS).

Dividends, bonuses, interest payments etc. payable to a shareholder by a society are treated as interest under a loan relationship (see **50.2** LOAN RELATIONSHIPS). The society must make a return to HMRC within three months of the end of the relevant accounting period. The return must show the name and place of residence of every recipient of more than £15 and the amount paid to him.

The shareholder is treated as holding the loan relationship for trading or non-trading purposes according to the purpose for which his holding in the society is held.

Interest is paid by a society without deduction of income tax (unless paid to a person whose usual place of abode is abroad, when income tax is deductible under *ITA 2007, ss 449, 899, 901, 903*).

Note this treatment applies equally to co-operative associations (see **22.5** below) established and resident in the UK provided the primary objective of the association is to assist their members in the carrying on of agricultural or horticultural businesses on land occupied by them in the UK or of fishery businesses.

[*CTA 2009, ss 499, 500; CTA 2010, ss 1055, 1056;*].

Deductions in computing trading profits

[22.3] Certain deductions are available in computing the profits of a trade carried on by a society which either does not sell to non-members or does not by its rules or practice limit the number of shares in the society. A deduction is allowed if:

(a) it represents a discount, rebate, dividend or bonus granted by the society to a member or non-member in connection with his transactions with the society. The transactions must be taken into account in computing the society's trading profit; and
(b) the sum is calculated by reference to the size of the transaction or the amounts paid or payable by or to the person concerned. It must not be calculated by reference to any share or interest in the capital of the society.

If a dividend or bonus is deductible under these provisions it is not treated as a distribution (see **29** DISTRIBUTIONS).

[*CTA 2009, s 132*].

Amalgamations, transfers etc.

[22.4] Where one of a number of transactions takes place in relation to a society within **22.1** above (e.g. amalgamation and transfer to a new society or transfer of a society's whole business to another society) the transaction is a 'relevant transfer' and *SI 2009 No 2971 Mutual Societies (Transfers of Business) (Tax) Regulations* applies. Assets disposed of by one society to another on a union, amalgamation or transfer of engagements are treated as disposed of, for the purpose of capital gains computations, at such a consideration as would secure that no gain or loss accrues on the disposal.

Note this treatment applies equally to co-operative associations (see **22.5** below) established and resident in the UK provided the primary objective of the association is to assist their members in the carrying on of agricultural or horticultural businesses on land occupied by them in the UK or of fishery businesses.

[*TCGA 1992, s 217D*].

Co-operative associations

[22.5] A '*co-operative association*' is a body of persons with a written constitution which the Secretary of State (or the Department of Agriculture and Rural Development for Northern Ireland, as the case may be) is satisfied is 'in substance' a co-operative association.

The provisions outlined in **22.2**, **22.4** above apply to co-operative associations established and resident in the UK provided the primary objective of the association is to assist their members in the carrying on of agricultural or horticultural businesses on land occupied by them in the UK or of fishery businesses.

[*CTA 2009, s 499(3); CTA 2010, s 1058*].

See also HMRC Extra-Statutory Concession C12.

Trading losses

[22.6] Trading losses brought forward under *CTA 2010, s 45* or *s 45B* (see **51.6**, **51.7** LOSSES) may be set off against:

(a) non-trading loan relationship profits; and
(b) amounts assessable as overseas income (other than from an overseas trade).

[*CTA 2010, s 47; F(No 2)A 2017, Sch 4 para 149*].

23

Coronavirus (COVID-19)

Introduction to coronavirus (COVID-19)

[23.1] In response to the coronavirus (COVID-19) pandemic, the UK Government introduced lockdown and social distancing measures in March 2020. As a result, many businesses were unable to continue operating. Over the succeeding weeks and months, a number of coronavirus support schemes were introduced to relieve the impact of the pandemic. These included, in particular, the Coronavirus Job Retention Scheme (CJRS) under which employers could furlough employees and apply for Government funding to cover a proportion of their pay (see www.gov.uk/guidance/claim-for-wage-costs-through-the-coronavirus-job-retention-scheme), and the Self-Employment Income Support Scheme (SEISS) under which the self-employed could claim a Government grant based on a percentage of average monthly trading profits (see www.gov.uk/guidance/claim-a-grant-through-the-coronavirus-covid-19-self-employment-income-support-scheme). There are also various coronavirus business support grant schemes, a non-exclusive list of which is given at **23.2** below.

Although full lockdown was lifted on 4 July 2020, a number of businesses were still unable to operate, and those that were able could operate only with the imposition of restrictions based on a continuing need for social distancing and hygiene measures. Further lockdowns were subsequently put in place in England, running from 31 October to 1 December 2020 and from 4 January to 21 June 2021. In between lockdowns, multi-tier systems often operated, under which restrictions were put in place according to locality. The devolved administrations introduced their own largely equivalent rules.

FA 2020, s 106, Sch 16 confirms that coronavirus support payments made to businesses/employers are within the scope of corporation tax on income, and sets out the rules for applying this (see **23.2** onwards). It also imposes a charge to income tax (see **23.6**) on a recipient of certain coronavirus support payments who was not entitled to the payment in accordance with the scheme under which it was made, which includes the case where a payment under the CJRS is not used for the purposes for which it was made.

A number of tax measures have also been taken, by primary or secondary legislation or by concession, to relieve the impact of the COVID-19 pandemic. See 23.7 below.

Taxation of coronavirus support payments

[23.2] For the purposes of the provisions on taxation of coronavirus support payments in *FA 2020, s 106, Sch 16*, a '*coronavirus support payment*" means a payment made (whether before or after Royal Assent to *FA 2020*) under any of the following schemes:

(a) the coronavirus job retention scheme (CJRS);
(b) the self-employment income support scheme (SEISS);
(c) any other scheme that is the subject of a Treasury direction given under *Coronavirus Act 2020, s 76* (HMRC functions in relation to coronavirus or coronavirus disease);
(d) the coronavirus statutory sick pay rebate scheme;
(e) a coronavirus business support grant scheme (see below);
(f) any other scheme that may be specified or described in Treasury regulations under these provisions. The following have been specified: the Test and Trace Support Payment Scheme (www.gov.uk/test-and-trace-suppo rt-payment), the Self-Isolation Support Grant in Scotland (www.mygov. scot/self-isolation-grant), and the Self-Isolation Support Scheme in Wales (https://gov.wales/self-isolation-support-scheme).

'*Coronavirus*' means severe acute respiratory syndrome coronavirus 2 (SARS-CoV-2), and '*coronavirus disease*' means COVID-19 (the official designation of the disease caused by coronavirus). [*Coronavirus Act 2020, s 1; FA 2020, s 106(5)*].

Items (a) and (d) are referred to collectively as '*employment-related schemes*'.

The Treasury can make regulations further providing about (or modifying) the application of the taxation of coronavirus support payments provisions to a scheme within (b)–(f) above; any such provision may have retrospective effect.

A coronavirus business support grant scheme in (e) above is any scheme (whenever announced), other than a scheme within subsection (a) to (d) above, under which a public authority makes grants to businesses with the object of providing support to those businesses in connection with any effect or anticipated effect (direct or indirect) of COVID-19. Examples of such schemes include:

- the small business grant fund (SBGF) (www.gov.uk/guidance/check-if-y oure-eligible-for-the-coronavirus-small-business-grant-fund);
- the retail, hospitality and leisure grant fund (RHLGF) (www.gov.uk/gu idance/check-if-youre-eligible-for-the-coronavirus-retail-hospitality-an d-leisure-grant-fund);
- the local authority discretionary grants fund (www.gov.uk/guidance/ap ply-for-the-coronavirus-local-authority-discretionary-grants-fund;

- any scheme corresponding to any of those above in Scotland, Wales and Northern Ireland.

[*FA 2020, s 106; FA 2021, s 32(1); SI 2021 No 92, Regs 1, 2*].

For the purposes of the taxation of coronavirus support payments provisions, a business includes a trade, profession or vocation, a UK or overseas property business or a business consisting wholly or partly of the making of investments. [*FA 2020, Sch 16 para 1(6)*].

The Treasury can make regulations to modify the application of any provisions of the Tax Acts that affect the treatment of amounts taxable under the provisions at **23.3–23.5** below. [*FA 2020, Sch 16 para 7*].

Taxation of coronavirus support payments referable to a business

[23.3] The following applies if a company carrying on a business (see **23.2** above), either alone or in partnership, receives a coronavirus support payment (see **23.2**) that is referable to the business (see further below). So much of the support payment as is referable to the business is a receipt of a revenue nature for corporation tax purposes and is to be brought into account in calculating the profits of that business for tax purposes. If an amount of the support payment is referable to more than one business or business activity, the amount is to be allocated between those businesses or activities on a just and reasonable basis.

If the recipient of a coronavirus support payment is a company which used to carry on a business, so much (if any) of the payment as is referable to the business but which is not referable to activities of the business undertaken while it was being carried on by the recipient is to be treated for corporation tax purposes as follows:

- an amount referable to a trade, profession or vocation is to be treated as a post-cessation receipt (see **68.16** TRADING INCOME); and
- an amount referable to a UK property business or an overseas property business is to be treated (in either case) as a post-cessation receipt from a UK property business (see **60.4** PROPERTY INCOME).

In any case not within the above, the recipient of the amount is to be treated as if carrying on, at the time of receipt of the amount, the business to which the amount is referable. That amount is to be treated as if it were referable to activities undertaken by the business at that time, and is thus brought into account under the main rule above. Where the recipient incurred expenses that are referable to that amount and would be deductible in calculating the profits of the business if it were being carried on at the time of receipt of that amount, those expenses are deductible from that amount; but this does not apply to expenses arising directly or indirectly from the company ceasing to carry on business.

[*FA 2020, Sch 16 paras 1, 2*].

A coronavirus support payment made under an employment-related scheme (see **23.2** above) is referable to the business of the person entitled to the payment as an employer (even if that person is not the employer of the employee to whom the payment relates for other purposes) and to no other business. No deduction for any expenses in respect of the same employment costs which are the subject of the payment is allowable in calculating the profits of any other business or the liability of any other person to tax on post-cessation receipts. There are also rules for determining when a payment under the self-employed income support scheme is referable to a business (not relevant to companies).

A payment under a coronavirus business support grant scheme (see **23.2** above) or a scheme within **23.2**(f) is referable to the business of the person to whom the payment relates. Where such payment is made in respect of a partner of a firm and is retained by the partner, rather than being distributed amongst the partners, it is not to be treated as a receipt of the partnership.

[*FA 2020, Sch 16 para 3; FA 2021, s 32(2)(4); SI 2021 No 92, Regs 1, 3*].

Exemptions and reliefs

A coronavirus support payment which relates to mutual activities of a business carrying on a mutual trade is not taxable.

A payment is ignored in calculating a charity's incoming resources for the purpose of the exemption for small trades and miscellaneous income (at **14.6** CHARITIES) and a payment under an employment-related scheme is ignored in calculating the receipts of a community amateur sports club for the purpose of the exemptions from corporation tax on UK trading income and property income (at **75.2** VOLUNTARY ASSOCIATIONS).

CTA 2009, s 61 (which provides for pre-trading expenditure to be deducted in the first period of trading; see **69.57** TRADING INCOME — DEDUCTIONS) does not apply to employment costs where a coronavirus support payment made under an employment-related scheme relates to those costs.

[*FA 2020, Sch 16 para 4*].

Taxation of coronavirus support payments where employment costs deductible by another person

[23.4] A company which receives a coronavirus support payment under an employment-related scheme (see **23.2** above) to which it is entitled as an employer is chargeable to **income tax** on the payment to the extent that:

- the payment is not taxable under the provisions at **23.3** above; and
- expenses incurred by another person on the same employment costs which are the subject of the payment are deductible in calculating the taxable profits of a business carried on by that person or in calculating that person's liability to tax on post-cessation receipts in respect of a trade, profession or vocation or UK property business.

[*FA 2020, Sch 16 para 5*].

Taxation of coronavirus support payments where no business carried on

[23.5] A company which receives a coronavirus support payment (other than under an employment-related scheme or the self-employment income support scheme) is charged to corporation tax on the payment if:

- the payment is not taxable under the provisions at **23.3** above; and
- at the time of receipt, the company did not carry on a business the profits of which are charged to tax and to which the payment could be referable.

If the company is a charity, the payment is treated as miscellaneous income under a provision listed in *CTA 2010, s 1173* for the purposes of the exemption for small trades and miscellaneous income (at **14.6** CHARITIES).

[*FA 2020, Sch 16 para 6*].

Income tax charge to recover coronavirus support payments

[23.6] A company which receives a coronavirus support payment to which it is not entitled is subject to recovery of the payment by way of an **income tax** charge. This does not apply to payment made under a coronavirus business support grant scheme, the coronavirus statutory sick pay rebate scheme or a scheme within **23.2**(f) above. The charge is equal to the whole amount to which the company is not entitled (less any amount actually repaid). In effect, income tax is charged at 100% of the payment. No loss, deficit, expense or allowances can be taken into account in calculating the amount of income tax and no deduction is allowed for the tax in calculating profits or losses for corporation tax purposes.

The circumstances in which a company is treated as not entitled to a payment include, in the case of the coronavirus job retention scheme, cases where the company ceases to be entitled to retain the payment after receipt because of a change in circumstances or because it has not used the payment to pay the costs it was intended to reimburse within a reasonable period.

The charge does not apply to payments made under a coronavirus business support grant scheme or the coronavirus statutory sick pay rebate scheme.

The tax becomes chargeable when the payment is received, unless the company was entitled to receive it but subsequently ceases to be entitled to retain it, in which case it becomes chargeable at that later time.

If a charge arises under these provisions, the tax charges at **23.3–23.5** above are disapplied and the original payment is not income of the company for tax purposes.

These provisions apply also to payments under the self-employed income support scheme made on or after 6 April 2021 (not relevant to companies).

[*FA 2020, Sch 16 para 8; FA 2021, s 32(3)(4); SI 2021 No 92, Regs 1, 3*].

Administration

The provisions of *FA 1998, Sch 18* (company self-assessment returns, enquiries etc. — see **65** RETURNS) apply to income tax under these provisions as if it were corporation tax. See below, however, for the requirement to notify chargeability.

The income tax is added to the corporation tax for the accounting period in which it becomes chargeable (as above) and payment is due nine months and one day after the end of the period. The instalment payment rules for large companies do not apply. Payments can be made under a group payment arrangement (see **58.3** PAYMENT OF TAX).

If an HMRC officer considers (whether or not on the basis of information or documents obtained by virtue of the exercise of **HMRC** INVESTIGATORY POWERS (38) under *FA 2008, Sch 36*) that a company has received a coronavirus support payment to which it is not entitled, the officer may make an assessment of the income tax which ought in the officer's opinion to be charged. The normal and extended time limits at **6.7** ASSESSMENTS apply to the making of such assessments. The normal provisions as to assessments, appeals, payment of tax and recovery of tax unpaid apply.

Where the income tax is chargeable in relation to a payment received by a partnership:

- an assessment may be made on any of the partners in respect of the total amount of tax chargeable on the partnership;
- each of the partners is jointly and severally liable for the tax assessed; and
- if the total amount of tax chargeable is included in a self-assessment tax return made by one of the partners, the other partners are not required to include the tax in their own tax return.

Interest on overdue tax is payable as if the tax were corporation tax.

[*FA 2020, Sch 16 paras 9, 11(1)–(5)*].

Notification of liability

A company chargeable to income tax under these provisions must notify HMRC that it is so chargeable by the later of 20 October 2020 or the 90th day after the income tax becomes chargeable (as above). If the coronavirus support payment was received by a partnership, all of the partners are treated as meeting this requirement if one of them has done so.

Where the time limit for raising an assessment would otherwise be extended to 20 years, due specifically to a failure to notify chargeability (see **6.7** ASSESSMENTS), this applies to income tax chargeable under these provisions only if the company knew at the time the tax first became chargeable that they were not entitled to the coronavirus support payment.

A penalty under *FA 2008, Sch 41* (failure to notify chargeability — see **59.2** PENALTIES) applies for failure to meet this requirement as if the tax were corporation tax for the accounting period in which it becomes chargeable. If the company knew that it was not entitled to the coronavirus support payment at the time the income tax first became chargeable, the failure is automatically treated as deliberate and concealed and the 'potential lost revenue' is the amount of income tax which would have been assessable on the last day of the period in which notification should have been given.

Where the failure to notify chargeability is by a member of a partnership that received the coronavirus support payment in question, each partner is taken to know anything that any of the other partners knows. Where a partner would otherwise be liable to a penalty under *FA 2008, Sch 41*, the partner is instead jointly and severally liable with the other partners to a single penalty under those provisions for the failures by each of them to notify. In a case other than one in which at least one partner knew that the partnership was not entitled to the coronavirus support payment at the time the income tax first became chargeable, if the failure of at least one of the partners was deliberate and concealed, the single penalty is treated as a penalty for a deliberate and concealed failure. If the failure of at least one of the partners was deliberate but not concealed, the single penalty is treated as a penalty for a deliberate but not concealed failure. The potential lost revenue is treated as being the amount of income tax which would have been assessable on any one of the partners at the end of 31 January following the tax year in which the coronavirus support payment was received by the partnership. If at least one partner knew that the partnership was not entitled to the coronavirus support payment at the time the income tax first became chargeable, the potential lost revenue is the amount of income tax which would have been assessable on any one of the partners on the last day of the period in which notification should have been given.

[*FA 2020, Sch 16 paras 11(6)(7), 12–14*].

Company directors etc.

An HMRC officer can give a notice making an individual jointly and severally liable to HMRC for the income tax if it appears to him that:

- the company is, or there is a serious possibility of it becoming, subject to an insolvency procedure (as defined at **58.18** PAYMENT OF TAX);
- the individual was responsible for the management of the company at the time the income tax first became chargeable and the individual knew at that time that the company was not entitled to the coronavirus support payment; and
- there is a serious possibility that some or all of the tax will not be paid.

For this purpose, directors, shadow directors and other individuals concerned (directly or indirectly) in, or who take part in, the company's management are taken to be responsible for the management of the company.

The effect of the notice is to make the individual jointly and severally liable with the company and any other individual to whom a notice is given for the income tax. The notice must specify the company to which it relates, set out the reasons that the officer considers that the conditions are met, specify the amount of the tax and state the effect of the notice. It must also offer the individual a review of the notice and explain the right of review and appeal. The provisions of *FA 2020, Sch 13 paras 10–15, 17* (governing reviews, appeals, withdrawal of notices and cases where the company no longer exists) apply, with modifications, to notices under these provisions as they apply to the provisions for joint and several liability of directors etc. at **58.18** PAYMENT OF TAX.

[*FA 2020, Sch 16 para 15*].

Temporary measures to relieve impact of coronavirus

[23.7] A number of tax measures have also been taken, by primary or secondary legislation or by concession, to relieve the impact of the coronavirus (COVID-19) pandemic.

Appeals

A number of temporary changes have been made to the provisions relating to appeals. The main changes are as follows.

- HMRC will allow an extra three months on top of the normal 30-day time limit for making an appeal against a decision dated February 2020 or later where the taxpayer has been affected by coronavirus.
- The First-tier Tribunal issued a general stay on all proceedings on 24 March 2020 for 28 days until 21 April 2020.
- Appeals received by the First-tier Tribunal before 24 March 2020 and categorised as standard or complex before 21 April 2020 were subject to a further stay on proceedings until 30 June 2020.
- The existing limit of £2,000 for allocation by the First-tier Tribunal of penalty appeals to the default paper category is temporarily increased to £20,000. The increase was initially for six months but it has been extended until 30 June 2021.
- With effect from 10 April 2020, if a party objects to an appeal being decided on the papers, the First-tier Tribunal or Upper Tribunal may nevertheless decide that it should be decided in that way. However, the Tribunal can only take that step if the matter is urgent, it is not reasonably practicable for there to be a hearing (including one conducted wholly or partly by telephone or by video) and it is in the interests of justice to make that direction. This rule is expressed to expire at the same time as the *Coronavirus Act 2020*, i.e. on 24 March 2022 unless that date is either brought forward or extended.
- Hearings will be heard remotely (by telephone or video) where it is reasonably practicable and in accordance with the overriding objective to do so until 18 September 2021. A tribunal may decide to conduct a 'hybrid' hearing, where some participants are in a physical hearing room and others are attending remotely.
- With effect from 10 April 2020, the First-tier Tribunal or Upper Tribunal may direct that a telephone or video hearing be heard in private if it is not possible for a media representative to listen to or watch the hearing at the time it is taking place and it is in the interests of justice for the hearing to be in private. If a hearing is held in private under this rule, it must be recorded. A hearing must also be recorded if it is public only by virtue of a media representative being able to access the proceedings remotely while they are taking place. These provisions expire at the same time as the *Coronavirus Act 2020*, i.e. on 24 March 2022 unless that date is either brought forward or extended.
- If a party fails to attend a telephone or video hearing without making an application for it to be adjourned, wins the appeal and then applies for the decision to be set aside on the basis of non-attendance, the Tribunal is unlikely to allow that application.

See **5.1** APPEALS.

Corporate Interest Restriction

HMRC have indicated that they will temporarily accept elections (see **24.6**, **24.8** CORPORATE INTEREST RESTRICTION) by email when they cannot be posted or included with a Corporate Interest Restriction return (see **65.21** RETURNS). Emails should be sent to the customer compliance manager or to msbcorporateinterest.restrictionmailbox@hmrc.gov.uk.

Where a group has missed the deadline for appointing a reporting company and now wish to do so, HMRC may appoint a reporting company. They will not routinely do so but will consider doing so where there is an unforeseeable change in circumstances or other reason outside the group's control. This could be because of coronavirus or some other reason.

See **24.1** CORPORATE INTEREST RESTRICTION.

Non-statutory clearances

HMRC have been unable to accept clearance applications in the post due to the situation with coronavirus, so applications should instead be made by email to nonstatutoryclearanceteam.hmrc@hmrc.gsi.gov.uk.

Residence

HMRC consider that existing legislation and guidance in relation to company residence and permanent establishments already provides sufficient flexibility to deal with changes in business activities necessitated by the response to the pandemic. HMRC do not consider that a company will necessarily become resident in the UK because a few board meetings are held here because of the pandemic, or because some decisions are taken in the UK over a short period of time. HMRC take a holistic view of the facts and circumstances of each case.

HMRC do not consider that a non-resident company will automatically have a taxable presence by way of permanent establishment after a short period of time owing to the presence of an employee in the UK during the pandemic. While the habitual conclusion of contracts in the UK would create a taxable presence in the UK, it is a matter of fact and degree as to whether that habitual condition is met. Furthermore, the existence of a UK PE does not in itself mean that a significant element of the profits of the non-resident company would be taxable in the UK.

(HMRC International Manual INTM120185, 261010).

Trading income: crisis-driven changes to trading activities

HMRC have published guidance on the possible implications for the taxation of trading income arising from changes in normal business activities caused by crisis situations such as coronavirus. The guidance does not introduce any relaxations to the rules but summaries existing law and practice that might be relevant to affected companies. These include consideration of whether changes result in a new trade being carried on, the effect of temporary breaks in trading activity, donations and expenditure. See HMRC Business Income Manual BIM48000.

Long funding leases

See **10.52** CAPITAL ALLOWANCES ON PLANT AND MACHINERY for the easement of the provisions applicable to certain plant and machinery leases which are extended due to coronavirus.

24

Corporate Interest Restriction

Simon's Taxes. See **D1.14**.

Introduction to the corporate interest restriction

[24.1] *F(No 2)A 2017* introduced provisions which place a limit on the amount of interest and certain other financing costs that large worldwide groups of companies can deduct when calculating their profits subject to corporation tax. The provisions are a response to the recommendations of the G20/OECD project to tackle Base Erosion and Profit Shifting (BEPS). The provisions apply, subject to the detailed commencement and transitional provisions at **24.13** below, to periods of account of groups beginning on or after 1 April 2017 (with periods straddling that date treated as two distinct periods, the second of which begins on 1 April 2017). The main features of the provisions are as follows.

- The provisions operate in relation to worldwide groups (see **24.2** below) and by reference to periods of account of the group for which consolidated financial statements are prepared.
- The effect of the provisions is to disallow certain loan relationship and derivative contract debits and financing expenses (tax-interest expense amounts) in calculating the taxable profits of UK group companies where the group's aggregate net tax-interest expense for a period of account exceeds its interest capacity for the period. That excess is the disallowed amount. See **24.3** below.

- The interest capacity of a group for a period of account cannot be less then £2 million. Therefore, any group with aggregate net tax-interest expense in the UK below the £2 million de minimis limit will not be subject to the restriction.
- The restriction is given effect by allocating the disallowed amount to companies in the group that are within the charge to corporation tax and which have a net interest expense in the period of account. A disallowance allocated to an individual company reduces that company's deductions for debits in the accounting period or accounting periods that overlap the period of account.
- Amounts that are disallowed under the corporate restriction are carried forward indefinitely for relief as a deduction in a later period in which there is sufficient capacity for the deduction to be made. This is known as 'interest reactivation'. See **24.4** below.
- The group's aggregate net tax-interest expense for a period of account is calculated, firstly, by taking, for each group company, the tax-interest amounts which are (or would, but for these provisions, be) brought into account for corporation tax purposes in an accounting period falling wholly or partly within the period of account and deducting any 'tax-interest income amounts' (broadly, certain loan relationship credits, derivative contract credits and financing income which would be brought into account for corporation tax purposes) to find the company's net tax-interest expense or net tax-interest income. Amounts for accounting periods not falling wholly within the period of account are apportioned. The aggregate of the net tax-interest income amounts for all of the group companies with such an amount is then deducted from the aggregate of the net tax-interest expense amounts. The excess is the aggregate net tax-interest expense (and a negative amount is the aggregate net tax-interest income). See **24.5** below.
- The 'interest capacity' of a worldwide group for a period of account is the group's 'interest allowance' for the period plus any unused interest allowances for earlier periods to the extent that they are unexpired (see below). The 'interest allowance' for the period is the sum of the 'basic interest allowance' for the period and the amount of any aggregate net tax-interest income for the period. See **24.6** below.
- A group's 'basic interest allowance' is calculated by applying either the fixed ratio method or (where the group makes an election) the group ratio method. Both methods require the calculation of two separate limits or caps and it is the lower of the two in the period which operates to limit deductions.
- Under the fixed ratio method, the first cap is the fixed ratio restriction, which is a fixed ratio (30%) of the group's UK earnings before interest, tax, depreciation and amortisation (EBITDA), measured using UK tax principles ('tax-EBITDA'). The second cap is the fixed ratio debt cap, which is equal to the 'adjusted net group-interest expense' of the group for the period plus the group's excess debt cap brought forward. The adjusted net group-interest expense is calculated by taking the external net group interest expense of the worldwide group (including any

specified interest-like amounts) based on the consolidated financial statements and then subjected it to a series of further complicated adjustments, to align the result more closely with UK tax principles.

- Under the group ratio method, the first cap is the group ratio restriction, which is a variable ratio (the group ratio percentage) of tax-EBITDA. The group ratio percentage reflects the proportion that the qualifying net group-interest expense (the adjusted net group-interest expense reduced by certain downward adjustments) of the worldwide group bears to its EBITDA ('group-EBITDA'). The second cap is the group ratio debt cap equal to the qualifying net group-interest expense of the group for the period plus the group's excess debt cap brought forward.
- Unused interest allowance may be carried forward in certain circumstances. It can then be used to shelter an increased amount of deductions for net interest expense in a future period against the interest disallowance. Unused interest allowance is a cumulative calculation and it can only be carried forward for five years before expiring.
- 'Excess debt cap' arises in a period (the 'generating period') where the fixed ratio debt cap or group ratio debt cap is not the limiting factor when computing the group's basic interest allowance for that period. The excess debt cap is available for carry forward to later periods but subject to a carry-forward limit. This limit is the sum of the excess debt cap generated in the period of account of the group immediately preceding the generating period (if any), and the total disallowed amount of the group in the generating period.
- A number of additional elections are available which modify the calculation of the interest allowance for the purposes of the corporate interest restriction in certain circumstances. See **24.8** below.
- The corporate interest restriction provisions operate with certain modifications to particular types of company. See **24.9** below. In particular there is an exemption for certain public infrastructure companies. See **24.10** below.
- There are provisions to prevent groups from circumventing the corporate interest restriction. They apply where there are arrangements that have a main purpose of enabling a company to obtain a tax advantage resulting from eliminating, or reducing the amount of, any interest restriction, reactivating, or reactivating an increased amount of, carried forward disallowed interest or changing the timing of any restriction or reactivation. See **24.11** below.
- Worldwide groups must appoint a reporting company which is responsible for making an interest restriction return for each period of account. See **24.12** below and **65.21** RETURNS. HMRC have powers, similar to those for company tax returns, to enquire into interest restriction returns and to issue determinations where a return is not submitted. Penalties apply for failure to make a return, incorrect or uncorrected returns, for companies which supply false information to the group's reporting company and for failure to keep and preserve records. See **59.22** PENALTIES.

HMRC have various regulation-making powers to amend the provisions of the corporate interest restriction where different members of a group deal with any matter in a different way to the treatment in the group's financial statements, where a member of the group is party to a capital market arrangement or to take account in a change in accounting standards. [*TIOPA 2010, ss 495–498; F(No 2)A 2017, Sch 5 para 1*].

The following anti-avoidance provisions take priority over the corporate interest restriction (so that the restriction is treated as of no effect for the purposes of those provisions): hybrid and other mismatches (see **4.13** ANTI-AVOIDANCE), risk transfer schemes (see **50.20** LOAN RELATIONSHIPS), group mismatch schemes (see **50.36**) and tax mismatch schemes (see **50.37**).

The corporate interest restriction replaces the previous worldwide debt cap provisions, for which see the 2020/21 edition of this work.

For HMRC guidance on the restriction generally, see HMRC Corporate Finance Manual CFM95000 onwards.

See also **60.17** PROPERTY INCOME for an election available to agents of non-resident company landlords to apply a simplified restriction on the deduction of financing costs in calculating income tax to be deducted from rental income.

Coronavirus (COVID-19)

HMRC have indicated that, due to measures put in place to stop the spread of coronavirus, they will temporarily accept elections (see **24.6**, **24.8** below) by email when they cannot be posted or included with a Corporate Interest Restriction return (see **65.21** RETURNS). Emails should be sent to the customer compliance manager or to msbcorporateinterest.restrictionmailbox@hmrc.gov.uk.

Where a group has missed the deadline for appointing a reporting company and now wish to do so, HMRC may appoint a reporting company. They will not routinely do so but will consider doing so where there is an unforeseeable change in circumstances or other reason outside the group's control. This could be because of coronavirus or some other reason.

See HMRC Guidance Note 1 July 2020.

Meaning of 'worldwide group'

[24.2] The following definitions apply for the purposes of the corporate interest restriction.

A '*worldwide group*' consists of an 'ultimate parent' and its 'consolidated subsidiaries'. If the ultimate parent has no such subsidiaries then the group is a '*single-company worldwide group*'. Otherwise, the group is a '*multi-company worldwide group*'. The ultimate parent must be a company or be a non-corporate entity whose shares or other interests are listed on a recognised stock exchange with no participator owning more than 10% by value of those shares or interests. It must not be a consolidated subsidiary of any other entity that could itself be an ultimate parent. The Crown, Ministers of the Crown, government departments, Northern Ireland departments and foreign sovereign powers cannot be ultimate parents. A worldwide group retains its identity so long as the ultimate parent continues to be the ultimate parent.

A '*consolidated subsidiary*' is a subsidiary (as defined by international accounting standards (IAS)) which is not a non-consolidated subsidiary (i.e. a subsidiary in respect of which, if its parent entity would be required under IAS to measure its investment, it would be required to do so using fair value accounting or, for periods of account beginning on or after 1 January 2018 (subject to the transitional rule at **24.13** below), on the basis that the subsidiary were an asset held for sale or distribution to owners). Specific provisions deal with 'stapled' entities (as defined) and dual listed group structures and there are also provisions which modify the definition of a group in the case of certain portfolio investments made by insurance entities.

[*TIOPA 2010, ss 453, 473–478; F(No 2)A 2017, Sch 5 para 1; FA 2018, Sch 8 paras 13, 22*].

The '*financial statements*' of a worldwide group for a period (a '*period of account*') are the consolidated financial statements of the ultimate parent and its subsidiaries for that period. Financial statements which are not drawn up on an acceptable basis are ignored and instead IAS financial statements (as defined) are deemed to have been drawn up. Financial statements are drawn up on an acceptable basis for this purpose if they are IAS financial statements, are not materially different from IAS financial statements or are drawn up in accordance with generally accepted accounting practice of the UK, Canada, China, India, Japan, South Korea or the USA. Similar provisions apply to replace actual financial statements with deemed IAS consolidated financial statements where the actual statements consolidate the wrong subsidiaries or cover more than one worldwide group, where no actual consolidated financial statements are drawn up or where the consolidated financial statements are for a period exceeding 19 months or are not drawn up until more than 30 months after the beginning of the period. If no financial statements are drawn up the ultimate parent may in certain cases make an election to determine when a period of account is deemed to end (but this may be no more than 18 months after the start of the period).

Amounts recognised in financial statements in a currency other than sterling are translated for the purposes of these provisions into the sterling equivalent, using the average exchange rate for the period of account calculated using daily spot rates.

A '*UK group company*' is a member of the worldwide group which is within the charge to corporation tax.

[*TIOPA 2010, ss 479–489; F(No 2)A 2017, Sch 5 para 1*].

Disallowance of interest etc.

[24.3] The corporate interest restriction applies to a worldwide group in a period of account if its 'aggregate net tax-interest expense' (see **24.5** below) for the period exceeds its 'interest capacity' (see **24.6** below). The excess is disallowed for corporation tax purposes. Because the interest capacity cannot be less than £2 million, the restriction can only apply if the aggregate net tax-interest expense is greater than that amount.

Where the group has made a full interest restriction return (see **65.21** RETURNS) for the period, each company to which part of the total disallowance has been allocated in the return must leave out of account for corporation tax purposes 'tax-interest expense amounts' (broadly loan relationship debits, certain derivative contract debits and the financing element of payments under finance leases etc. — see **24.5** below) which in total equal the allocated disallowance. Where a company's accounting periods do not exactly coincide with the group's period of account, the return will apportion the company's allocated disallowance between its accounting periods.

A company which is 'non-consenting' may, however, make a revocable election (see **65.21** RETURNS) to disapply this rule and instead to leave out of account tax-interest expense amounts that in total equal its pro-rata share of the total disallowed amount. The pro-rata share is calculated by reference to the company's proportionate share of the group's aggregate net tax-interest expense. This rule allows individual group companies to avoid excessive and disproportionate disallowances.

If a group is subject to interest restriction in a period of account but either no reporting company (see **65.21** RETURNS) has been appointed or no full interest restriction return has been submitted, UK group companies are required to leave their pro-rata share of the total disallowed amount out of account for accounting periods falling wholly or partly within the period of account.

Where a company has to leave an amount out of account under these provisions, the legislation specifies a default order in which its tax-interest expense amounts must be so left out:

(1) non-trading loan relationship debits;
(2) non-trading derivative contract debits;
(3) any amounts included within the extended definition of tax-interest expense amounts that applies only to banking companies;
(4) trading loan relationship debits;
(5) trading derivative contract debits;
(6) debits in respect of finance leases, debt factoring and service concession arrangements.

The company may, however, make a revocable election substituting its own allocation. See **65.21** RETURNS.

[*TIOPA 2010, ss 373(1)(2), 375–377, 450(3), Sch 7A paras 23, 24; F(No 2)A 2017, Sch 5 paras 1, 2*].

Non-consenting companies

A company is a '*non-consenting*' company in relation to a particular interest restriction return if it is not a consenting company. A company is a consenting company in relation to a return if, before the return is submitted, it has notified HMRC and the group's reporting company that it wishes to be a consenting company in relation to such returns (and has not subsequently given notice that it no longer wishes to be a consenting company). A company which was one of the companies which authorised the appointment of the reporting company is automatically treated as a consenting company unless it was listed as a company wishing to be a non-consenting company in the notice of appointment (or it subsequently gives notice that it no longer wishes to be a consenting company). See **65.21** RETURNS. [*TIOPA 2010, Sch 7A paras 10, 11; F(No 2)A 2017, Sch 5 para 2*].

Reactivation of disallowed amounts

[24.4] Tax-interest expense that is disallowed under the provisions at **24.3** above is carried forward and 'reactivated' (i.e. claimed as a deduction) in a later accounting period as if it were tax-interest expense of that later period, where the group's interest allowance for the related period of account exceeds its aggregate net tax-interest expense for that period. Disallowed amounts are carried forward at the individual company level, so that they may be capable of reactivation even where the company has joined a different group (subject to anti-avoidance provisions — see **24.11** below).

Where disallowed interest would (but for being disallowed) have been brought into account in calculating the profits or losses of a trade, and the company later ceases to carry on that trade, its trading activities become small or negligible or the trade becomes uncommercial and non-statutory (as defined), the disallowed interest will no longer be available for carry forward and reactivation. Similar provisions apply where disallowed interest would (but for being disallowed) have been brought into account in computing the profits of an investment business carried on by the company.

Reactivation applies where:

(i) for a period of account a group's interest allowance exceeds its aggregate net tax-interest expense;

(ii) at least one company in the group is within the charge to corporation tax;

(iii) at least one such company has carried forward disallowed interest that is 'available' for reactivation; and

(iv) a full interest restriction return is submitted for that period and it contains a statement that the group is subject to interest reactivation in the period.

The group must reactivate the maximum possible amount of the available disallowed interest. The total amount reactivated in a period of account must not be greater than the excess in (i) above (referred to in the legislation as the 'interest reactivation cap'). Each company to which part of the total reactivation has been allocated in the return must bring into account for corporation tax purposes tax-interest expense amounts (see **24.5** below) which in total equal the allocated reactivation. Where the company's accounting periods do not exactly coincide with the group's period of account, the reactivation must be brought into account for the first accounting period which overlaps the period of account. If the company joined the group during the period of account, it must bring the reactivation into account for the first accounting period in which it is a member.

Reactivated amounts are treated as expense amounts of the current accounting period of the same type as the expense amount previously disallowed. If not all of the expense amounts brought forward are to be used in an accounting period, the amounts so used are identified in the following order:

(1) non-trading loan relationship debits;
(2) non-trading derivative contract debits;
(3) any amounts included within the extended definition of tax-interest expense amounts that applies only to banking companies;
(4) trading loan relationship debits;
(5) trading derivative contract debits;
(6) debits in respect of finance leases, debt factoring and service concession arrangements.

The company may, however, make a revocable election substituting its own allocation. See **65.21** RETURNS.

In certain circumstances, a company could be subject to both a reactivation and a disallowance in the same accounting period. In such cases, only the net disallowance, or net reactivated amount, is left out of account, or brought into account, as appropriate. This situation can arise where an accounting period straddles two group periods of account or where the company joins a different group during an accounting period.

[*TIOPA 2010, ss 373(3)–(5), 378–381, 450(3), Sch 7A paras 25, 26; F(No 2)A 2017, Sch 5 paras 1, 2; FA 2018, Sch 8 para 18*].

Aggregate net tax-interest expense

[24.5] For the purposes of the corporate interest restriction, a worldwide group's '*aggregate net tax-interest expense*' for a period of account of the group is calculated by:

(a) adding together the 'net tax-interest expense' amounts of each company that was a member of the group at any time in the period and that has such an amount in that period, and
(b) subtracting the sum of the 'net tax-interest income' amounts of each group company that has such an amount in that period.

Where this gives a negative figure, the aggregate net tax-interest expense is nil and instead the group has '*aggregate net tax-interest income*' (calculated by deducting the amount in (a) above from that in (b) above).

[*TIOPA 2010, s 390; F(No 2)A 2017, Sch 5 para 1*].

A company has '*net tax-interest expense*' in a period of account where its 'tax-interest expense amounts' for the period exceed its 'tax-interest income amounts'. The amount of the company's net tax-interest expense for that period is equal to the amount of the excess. Where the tax-interest income amount exceeds the tax-interest expense amounts, the company has '*net tax-interest income*' for the period equal to the excess. Net tax-interest expense or income for a period of account is referable to a company's accounting period to the extent that it comprises amounts that are (or would be apart from these provisions) brought into account in the accounting period.

[*TIOPA 2010, s 389; F(No 2)A 2017, Sch 5 para 1*].

A company's '*tax-interest expense amounts*' for a group period of account comprise the amounts which are (or would, but for these provisions, be) brought into account for corporation tax purposes in an accounting period falling wholly or partly within the period of account which are:

(i) loan relationship debits other than 'excluded debits';
(ii) derivative contract debits, other than excluded debits, where the underlying subject matter consists only of one or more of: interest rates, an index determined by reference to income or retail prices, currency, an asset or liability representing a loan relationship or any other underlying subject matter which, at the time the company entered into or acquired the contract, is subordinate to any of the others or is of small value compared to the value of the whole underlying subject matter; or
(iii) the financing element of amounts payable under finance leases, on debt factoring, or on service concession arrangements accounted for as a financial liability.

For periods of account beginning on or after 1 January 2019, *CTA 2009, s 906(1)* (which gives priority to the INTANGIBLE ASSETS (**42**) rules) does not apply for the purpose of determining whether an amount is a tax-interest expense amount (or a tax-interest income amount). Accordingly, amounts capitalised in the carrying value of an intangible asset may be included to the extent that they would otherwise fall within (i)–(iii) above.

Where a company's accounting periods do not exactly coincide with the group's period of account, or where a company joins or leaves a group part way through a period of account, its tax-interest expense amount for the period of account is reduced, on a just and reasonable basis, by any amounts referable to parts of the accounting period or periods which do not fall in the period of account or by any amounts referable to a time when the company was not a member of the group. Where an amount would be a tax-interest expense amount but is disallowed under other rules (for example, under the hybrid mismatch rules at **4.13** ANTI-AVOIDANCE), where it, or part of it, subsequently becomes deductible it, or that part, is treated as a tax-interest expense amount at that later time (even if it does not meet the above conditions at that time).

'*Excluded debits*' are debits in respect of an exchange loss or an 'impairment loss' or, in the case of a derivative contract, in respect of a risk arising in the ordinary course of a trade (other than a financial trade) where the contract was entered into wholly for reasons unrelated to the capital structure of the worldwide group (or any of its members). For this purpose, a debit is in respect of a risk arising in the ordinary course of a financial trade only to the extent that the risk relates to an amount which is, or is likely to be a tax-interest expense amount or income amount of the company. For periods of account beginning before 1 January 2018 (subject to the transitional rule at **24.13** below), '*excluded debits*' are debits in respect of an exchange loss or an 'impairment loss' or in respect of a derivative contract which hedges risks arising in the ordinary course of a trade where the contract was entered into wholly for reasons unrelated to the capital structure of the worldwide group or any of its members. An '*impairment loss*' is a loss in respect of the impairment of a financial asset, but a debit in respect of an impairment loss does not include a debit in respect of an asset for which fair value accounting is used.

Interest distributions made by an authorised investment fund are not tax-interest expense amounts of the fund. Similar rules apply to interest distributions by property authorised investment funds, tax elected funds and investment trusts. Special provisions apply to calculate the tax-interest expense amounts of a securitisation company (see *SI 2006 No 3296, Reg 22*).

Similar provisions apply to determine a company's '*tax-interest income amounts*', but by reference to loan relationship credits, derivative contract credits and financing income. Income receivable from another company in consideration of the provisions of a guarantee of that company's borrowing is also included. '*Excluded credits*' are credits in respect of an exchange gain or the reversal of an impairment loss or, in the case of a derivative contract, in respect of a risk arising in the ordinary course of a trade (other than a financial trade) where the contract was entered into wholly for reasons unrelated to the capital structure of the worldwide group (or any of its members). For this purpose, a credit is in respect of a risk arising in the ordinary course of a financial trade only to the extent that the risk relates to an amount which is, or is likely to be a tax-interest expense amount or income amount of the company. For periods of account beginning before 1 January 2018 (subject to the transitional rule at **24.13** below), '*excluded credits*' are credits in respect of an exchange gain or the reversal of an impairment loss or in respect of a derivative contract which hedges risks arising in the ordinary course of a trade where the contract was entered into wholly for reasons unrelated to the capital structure of the worldwide group or any of its members. Where a company claims double tax credit relief in respect of a tax-interest income amount so that the corporation tax in respect of it is reduced, the amount is reduced to take account of the foreign tax credit by deducting an amount equal to the credit divided by the rate of corporation tax.

A company can make an irrevocable election to apply the amortised cost basis of accounting to its creditor loan relationships instead of applying the fair value basis for the purposes of calculating tax-interest expense amounts and tax-interest income amounts. Where a company makes such an election and a loan relationship which is fair valued in the company's accounts is hedged with a derivative that would qualify as a fair value hedge, the loan relationship can be revalued for movements in value of the hedged risk when applying the amortised cost basis. An election must be made within 12 months of the end of the first accounting period in which the company has a fair-value creditor relationship and is subject to these provisions and has effect for that accounting period and all subsequent periods.

[*TIOPA 2010, ss 382–388, 391, 391A, 456, 457; F(No 2)A 2017, Sch 5 para 1; FA 2018, Sch 8 paras 2, 3, 22; FA 2019, Sch 11 paras 2, 22; SI 2006 No 964, Regs 18(2A), 69Z16(2A), 69Z61(2A); SI 2009 No 2034, Reg 12A; SI 2017 No 1227, Regs 2, 5*].

See **49.2** LEASING for transitional provisions which exclude certain receipts or expenses arising on a change of accounting basis to apply IFRS 16 from being tax-interest income amounts or tax-interest expense amounts.

Interest capacity and interest allowance

[24.6] The '*interest capacity*' of a worldwide group for a period of account is the group's 'interest allowance' for the period plus any 'unused' interest allowances for earlier periods to the extent that they are 'unexpired' in the current period (see below). Where the interest capacity would otherwise be less than £2 million it is taken to be equal to £2 million. If the period of account is more or less than a year the £2 million is increased or decreased proportionately.

Unused interest allowance cannot be carried forward in this way if an abbreviated return election (see **65.21** RETURNS) has effect for the period in which it originated, the receiving period or any period in between or if no interest restriction return (see **65.21**) is made for any such period.

A group's interest allowance is not fully '*used*' in a period where the group's interest allowance for the period exceeds the aggregate net tax-interest expense of the group in that originating period plus the sum of any carried forward disallowed tax-interest amounts that are reactivated in that period (see **24.4** above). When unused interest allowance is carried forward, amounts for earlier periods are used before amounts for later periods.

Interest allowance of an earlier period is '*unexpired*' in a later period where the later period begins five years or less after the earlier period begins and ends five years or less after the earlier period ends. If the later period:

- begins more than five years after the earlier period begins but ends within five years of the earlier period ending;
- begins less than five years after the earlier period begins, but ends more than five years after the earlier period ends; or
- begins more than five years after the earlier period begins (but less than five years after the earlier period ends) and ends more than five years after the earlier period ends,

a proportionate amount of the unused interest allowance of the earlier period is regarded as unexpired and available for use in the later period.

Where, as a result of a change in ownership on or after 29 October 2018 which is disregarded for the purposes of the provisions at **51.17** LOSSES (restrictions on carry-forward of losses) as a result of *CTA 2010, s 724A*, one company ceases to be the ultimate parent of a worldwide group and another company becomes the ultimate parent of a new worldwide group, the interest allowance of the new group is calculated as if periods of account of the old group ending before the change in ownership were periods of account of the new group. Unused interest allowance of the old group can then be carried forward by the new group.

The '*interest allowance*' of a worldwide group for a period of account is the sum of the 'basic interest allowance' for the period and the amount of any aggregate net tax-interest income (see **24.4** above) for the period. A group's '*basic interest allowance*' is calculated by applying either the fixed ratio method or (where the group makes an election) the group ratio method.

[*TIOPA 2010, ss 392–396; F(No 2)A 2017, Sch 5 para 1; FA 2018, Sch 8 para 19; FA 2019, Sch 11 paras 3, 23*].

Transitional adjustments for group mismatches

Transitional rules apply in computing certain amounts for the purpose of calculating the basic interest allowance. The amounts affected are the net group-interest expense, the adjusted net group-interest expense, the qualifying net group-interest expense and the group-EBITDA. See below for the meaning of these amounts.

Where, on 1 April 2017, a company is a party to a loan relationship which is dealt with in its accounts on an amortised cost basis but in the worldwide group's financial statements on a fair value basis, then in calculating the amounts listed above, the group's financial statements are treated, in relation to the loan relationship, as having been drawn up on an amortised cost basis. This rule applies also where the loan relationship is dealt with in the group's financial statements as a hedged item in a designated fair value hedge where the carrying value of the hedged item is adjusted for changes in fair value attributable to the hedged risk.

Where on 1 April 2017 a loan relationship exists between two worldwide group members and:

- the loan relationship was previously recognised in the group's financial statements but was derecognised when a group member became the creditor under the loan relationship or the creditor company became a member of the group;
- neither *CTA 2009, s 361* nor *s 362* applied on the derecognition, but a gain or loss was recognised in the group's financial statements,

then, in calculating the amounts listed above, an amount equal to the gain or loss is treated as brought into account on a just and reasonable basis over the remaining term of the loan.

Where a finance charge arises in relation to a company in respect of an acceptable structured finance arrangement under a registered pension scheme and that finance charge is treated as interest payable under a transaction or loan relationship under *CTA 2010, ss 761(3), 762(3), 766(3)* or *769(3)*, then if the charge is a tax-interest expense amount of the company, then (if it is not otherwise the case), in calculating the amounts listed above, an amount equal to the charge is treated as brought into account as if it were a relevant expense amount recognised in the group's financial statements.

[*SI 2017 No 1224*].

Calculation of the basic interest allowance

Fixed ratio method

Applying the fixed ratio method, a group's basic interest allowance for a period of account is equal to the lower of:

- 30% of the 'aggregate tax-EBITDA' of the group for the period; and

- the 'fixed ratio debt cap' of the group for the period.

The '*aggregate tax-EBITDA*' of a worldwide group for a period of account is the sum of the tax-EBITDAs for the period of each company which was a member of the group at any time in the period, but cannot be less than nil. The tax-EBITDA of a company for a period of account of the group is the total of the 'adjusted corporation tax earnings' for each accounting period falling wholly or partly in the period of account. Where a company's accounting period does not exactly coincide with the group's period of account, or where a company joins or leaves a group part way through an accounting period, its adjusted corporation tax earnings for the accounting period are reduced, on a just and reasonable basis, to exclude any amounts referable to parts of the accounting period which do not fall in the period of account or by any amounts referable to a time when the company was not a member of the group.

A company's '*adjusted corporation tax earnings*' equals the sum of all the amounts the company brings into account when determining its taxable total profits for the accounting period plus any amounts the company would have brought into account when determining taxable profits had the company made profits, or more profits, in that period. The following amounts are excluded:

- tax-interest expense amounts and tax-interest income amounts;
- claimed capital allowances (including balancing allowances) and balancing charges;
- certain amounts that are deductible and taxable under the rules for intangible fixed assets (see *TIOPA 2010, s 408*);
- any losses brought forward or carried back (other than capital losses actually brought into account);
- loan relationship deficits for any accounting period other than the period in question;
- management expenses referable to any accounting period other than the period in question;
- any group relief or group relief for carried forward losses to the extent that it consists of surrenderable amounts arising at a time when the surrendering company was a member of the worldwide group;
- certain tax reliefs, including under the regimes for creative industries, contaminated land, patent box, research and development expenditure and gift aid; and
- unutilised capital losses.

Where a company claims double tax credit relief in respect of an amount of income which forms part of its adjusted corporation tax earnings so that the corporation tax in respect of it is reduced, the amount is reduced to take account of the foreign tax credit by deducting an amount equal to the credit divided by the rate of corporation tax.

A group's '*fixed ratio debt cap*' for a period of account is equal to the 'adjusted net group-interest expense' of the group for the period plus the group's 'excess debt cap' brought forward. The '*adjusted net group-interest expense*' is the 'net group-interest expense' after certain upward and downward adjustments (which align it with UK tax principles — see below). A negative total is taken to be nil. The '*net group-interest expense*' is the sum of all relevant expense amounts recognised in the group's financial statements as items of profit or loss less the sum of all relevant income amounts so recognised. The relevant expense amounts and relevant income amounts are:

- profits and losses (including interest and ancillary expenses (as defined) arising from loan relationships and related transactions;
- interest payable or receivable in respect of a money debt not arising from the lending of money (within **50.3** LOAN RELATIONSHIPS);
- alternative finance return payable or receivable under alternative finance arrangements;
- manufactured interest payable or receivable;
- financing charges or financing income in respect of the advance under a repo or quasi-repo;
- financing charges or financing income treated as interest payable or receivable under a structured finance arrangement (or which would be were the company in question within the charge to corporation tax);
- dividends payable or receivable in respect of preference shares accounted for as a financial liability/asset;
- profits and losses (including ancillary expenses) arising from derivative contracts and related transactions where the underlying subject matter consists only of one or more of: interest rates, an index determined by reference to income or retail prices, currency, an asset or liability representing a loan relationship or any other underlying subject matter which, at the time the company entered into or acquired the contract, is subordinate to any of the others or is of small value compared to the value of the whole underlying subject matter;
- financing charges and financing income implicit in payments made or received under finance leases;
- financing charges and financing income relating to debt factoring or any similar transaction; and
- financing charges and financing income implicit in payments made or received under a service concession arrangement if and to the extent that it is accounted for as a financial liability/asset.

Exchange gains and losses, impairment losses and reversals of impairment losses in respect of loan relationships and derivative contracts are excluded. Amounts arising under a derivative contract in respect of risks arising in the ordinary course of a trade where the contract was entered into wholly for reasons unrelated to the capital structure of the worldwide group or any of its members are also excluded. For periods of account beginning on or after 1 January 2018 (subject to the transitional rule at **24.13** below), this exclusion does not apply where the risk arises in the ordinary course of a financial trade and, for this purpose, an amount is in respect of a risk arising in the ordinary course of a financial trade only to the extent that the risk relates to an amount which is, or is likely to be a tax-interest expense amount or income amount of the worldwide group. Amounts payable or receivable under a pension scheme are also excluded.

Where an amount in respect of a derivative contract is recognised in the group consolidated financial statements as an item of profit or loss in a period of account and:

- that amount (the '*excluded derivative contract amount*') would, if all members of the group were within the charge to corporation tax and subject to certain other assumptions, be excluded from being brought into account for corporation tax purposes under any of *Regs 7* (currency contracts), *8* (commodity or debt contracts) or *9* (interest rate contracts) of the *Disregard Regulations* (see **27.13** DERIVATIVE CONTRACTS); and
- one or more amounts (the 'replacement derivative contract amounts') would, on the basis of those same assumptions, be brought into account for corporation tax purposes in respect of those derivative contracts under *Regs 9* or *10* of the *Disregard Regulations* in relevant accounting periods of group companies,

the group's financial statements are to be treated as if the replacement derivative contract amounts were recognised in the group financial statements for that period instead of the excluded derivative contract amount. Where a company's accounting period does not exactly coincide with the group's period of account, or where a company joins or leaves a group part way through an accounting period, its replacement derivative contract amounts for the accounting period are reduced, on a just and reasonable basis, to exclude any amounts referable to parts of the accounting period which do not fall in the period of account or by any amounts referable to a time when the company was not a member of the group.

Where a relevant expense amount or relevant income amount is recognised in group financial statements in determining the carrying value of an asset or liability, the legislation provides that the amount is included in the calculation of net group-interest expense when the carrying value is written down or, in the case of an income amount, when the amount written down is reduced. This does not apply if the asset in question is a '*relevant asset*', i.e. plant, property or equipment, an investment property, an intangible asset, goodwill, shares in a company or an interest in an entity which entitles the holder to a share of the profits in the entity. For periods of account beginning on or after 1 January 2019, where, on the assumption that the exclusion of relevant assets does not apply, this provision would apply to an amount attributable to a capitalised expense or capitalised income, it is expressly provided that that amount is not included in the calculation of net group-interest expense.

To find the adjusted net group-interest expense, the net group-interest expense is adjusted as follows. Upward adjustments are made for:

- relevant expense amounts brought into account in group financial statements in determining the carrying value of a non-financial asset or non-financial liability (for periods of account beginning before 1 January 2019, any asset or liability);
- amounts included in the net group-interest expense calculation on the reduction of an amount written down in respect of the carrying value of a non-financial asset (for periods of account beginning before 1 January 2019, any asset);
- relevant expense amounts recognised in the group financial statements for the period in equity or shareholders' funds which are brought into account for corporation tax purposes by a member of the group under

CTA 2009, s 321 or *s 605* or *CTA 2009, s 320B* or *SI 2013 No 3209, Reg 3A* (see **50.28** LOAN RELATIONSHIPS), or would be if the member were within the charge to corporation tax;

- relevant income amounts which relate to debt releases or modifications that would not be brought into account for corporation tax purposes under *CTA 2009, s 322* or *s 323A* or, for periods of account beginning on or after 1 January 2019, *CTA 2009, s 358* or *s 359*.

Downward adjustments are made for:

- relevant income amounts brought into account in group financial statements in determining the carrying value of a non-financial asset or non-financial liability (for periods of account beginning before 1 January 2019, any asset or liability);
- amounts included in the net group-interest expense calculation as an amount written down in respect of the carrying value of a non-financial asset (for periods of account beginning before 1 January 2019, any asset);
- relevant expense amounts recognised in the group financial statements for the period in equity or shareholders' funds which are brought into account for corporation tax purposes by a member of the group under *CTA 2009, s 321* or *s 605* or *SI 2013 No 3209, Reg 3A*, or would be if the member were within the charge to corporation tax;
- relevant expense amounts which relate to debt releases or modifications that would not be brought into account for corporation tax purposes under *CTA 2009, s 322* or *s 323A* or, for periods of account beginning on or after 1 January 2019, *CTA 2009, s 354*;
- relevant expense amounts any amounts recognised in profit or loss in respect of dividends payable on preference shares which are recognised as a financial liability in the financial statements.

An asset is a non-financial asset if it is not a financial asset for accounting purposes or it is a share in a company. Similarly, a liability is a non-financial liability if it is not a financial liability for accounting purposes or it is in respect of a share issued by a company.

Where the fixed ratio method is applied in a period of account, '*excess debt cap*' arises in that period (the '*generating period*') where the fixed ratio debt cap is not the limiting factor when computing the group's basic interest allowance for that period; i.e. where 30% of aggregate tax-EBITDA is less than the adjusted net group-interest expense. The amount of the excess debt cap is the difference between the two amounts. If 30% of aggregate tax-EBITDA is greater than the adjusted net group-interest expense, the excess debt cap for the period is nil.

The amount of excess debt cap that can be carried forward from the generating period and used in later periods (to increase the fixed ratio debt cap or the group ratio debt cap, as applicable) is limited, if it would otherwise be greater, to an amount equal to any excess debt cap previously generated (as at the period immediately before the generating period) plus the total amount disallowed under the corporate interest restriction for the generating period.

[*TIOPA 2010, ss 397, 400(1)(3)(5)–(7), 405–413, 417(5)(6), 420, 421, 494(1); F(No 2)A 2017, Sch 5 para 1; FA 2018, Sch 8 paras 4, 5, 20–23; FA 2019, Sch 11 paras 5, 6, 8, 19, 20, 22, Sch 20 para 8*].

Group ratio method

A group can make a (revocable) election to calculate its basic interest allowance using the group ratio method in its interest restriction return for a period of account. Such an election may be beneficial where a UK sub-group's interest deductions exceed the limit given by the fixed ratio rule but its leverage reflects the external gearing of the worldwide group overall. Applying the group ratio method, a group's basic interest allowance for a period of account is equal to the lower of:

- the 'group ratio percentage' of the aggregate tax-EBITDA of the group for the period; and
- the 'group ratio debt cap' of the group for the period.

The '*group ratio percentage*' is the proportion, expressed as a percentage, found by dividing the group's 'qualifying net group-interest expense' for the period by its 'group-EBITDA' for the period. The percentage cannot exceed 100% (so that the basic interest allowance cannot be more than its aggregate tax-EBITDA) and is treated as 100% where the calculation would otherwise give a negative percentage or where group-EBITDA is zero.

The '*qualifying net group-interest expense*' is the adjusted net group-interest expense reduced by certain downward adjustments. These are for relevant expense amounts which are upward adjustments in calculating the adjusted net group-interest expense and amounts recognised as items of profit and loss in the group's financial statement but which are not downward adjustments in calculating the adjusted net group-interest expense. The amounts must relate to:

(i) a transaction with, or a financial liability owed to, a person who, at any time in the period, is a 'related party' (see **24.7** below) of a group member;

(ii) results-dependent securities (i.e. securities issued by an entity where the payments made under the instrument depend on the results of the entity's business or the business of any other entity in the group (or any part of it), but excluding securities where the payments are inversely correlated to business performance, securities in respect of alternative finance arrangements and regulatory capital securities); or

(iii) equity notes within *CTA 2010, s 1016*, but excluding regulatory capital securities within **50.28** LOAN RELATIONSHIPS (before repeal of those provisions).

The qualifying net group-interest expense cannot be less than nil. In (i) above, where the person is not a related party of the group member throughout the period, the amount of the adjustment is reduced on a just and reasonable basis.

For the purposes of (i) above, a person is not treated as a related party of a group member if they would otherwise be so treated only because of the rule treating parties to a loan relationship as related by virtue of financial assistance provided by a related party (see **24.7** below) and either:

- the financial assistance was provided before 1 April 2017 or by a member of the group, or it consists of a non-financial guarantee (as defined) or relates only to an undertaking in relation to shares in the ultimate parent of the group or loans to a group member; or

- the group member in question is a company that has not been UK-resident at any time before 29 October 2018 and the financial assistance is provided before that date and is in respect of a loan relationship, derivative contract, finance lease, debt factoring or service concession arrangement accounted for as a financial liability to which the member is a party for the purposes of its UK property business.

A group's '*group-EBITDA*' for a period of account is the sum of its profit before tax, its net group-income expense (as above) and its 'depreciation and amortisation adjustment'. Each of these amounts may be a negative amount for this purpose. Profit before tax equals the sum of all income amounts less the some of all expenses amounts that are recognised as items of profit and loss in the group financial statements (excluding any amounts of tax income or tax expense, as defined for accounting purposes). R&D expenditure credit (within **63.10** RESEARCH AND DEVELOPMENT EXPENDITURE) or any amount relating to it is excluded from the profit before tax. Note that this exclusion applies to all periods of account but was not included in the legislation as originally enacted. The reporting company of a worldwide group for any period of account beginning before 1 January 2018 may therefore make an election for the exclusion not to apply for the period of account. Such an election must be made (or revoked) in the interest restriction return for the period.

The '*depreciation and amortisation adjustment*' consists of the aggregate of the following three separate adjustments.

- The capital (expenditure) adjustment—this consists of any amounts factored into the calculation of profit before tax reflecting depreciation, amortisation and certain other amounts of capital expenditure (e.g. provision for future capital expenditure) on 'relevant assets' (as above).
- The capital (fair value movement) adjustment—this consists of any fair value movements on relevant assets brought into account in calculating profit before tax.
- The capital (disposals) adjustment—this consists of any losses taken into account in the profit before loss figure on a disposal of relevant assets less any losses so taken into account plus profits on disposal recalculated on the assumption that the asset in question was not depreciated, amortised or revalued. See **24.8** below for the election to apply a different basis to the recalculation of capital profits.

In calculating group-EBITDA, the same adjustment must be made in respect of excluded derivative contract amounts as must be made in calculating net group-interest expense (see above).

A group's '*group ratio debt cap*' for a period of account is equal to the qualifying net group-interest expense of the group for the period plus the group's 'excess debt cap' brought forward.

Where the group ratio method is applied in a period of account, '*excess debt cap*' arises in that period (the '*generating period*') where the group ratio debt cap is not the limiting factor when computing the group's basic interest allowance for that period; i.e. where the amount given by applying the group ratio percentage to aggregate tax-EBITDA is less than the qualifying net group-interest expense. The amount of the excess debt cap is the difference between the two amounts. If a negative figure results, the excess debt cap for the period is nil.

The amount of excess debt cap that can be carried forward from the generating period and used in later periods (to increase the fixed ratio debt cap or the group ratio debt cap, as applicable) is limited, if it would otherwise be greater, to an amount equal to any excess debt cap previously generated (as at the period immediately before the generating period) plus the total amount disallowed under the corporate interest restriction for the generating period.

[*TIOPA 2010, ss 398, 399, 400(2)(4)–(7), 414–421; F(No 2)A 2017, Sch 5 para 1; FA 2018, Sch 8 paras 6, 23; FA 2019, Sch 5 para 33, Sch 20 para 8*].

New holding company

Where, as a result of a change in ownership on or after 29 October 2018 which is disregarded for the purposes of the provisions at **51.17** LOSSES (restrictions on carry-forward of losses) as a result of *CTA 2010, s 724A*, one company ceases to be the ultimate parent of a worldwide group and another company becomes the ultimate parent of a new worldwide group, in determining the fixed ratio debt cap or group ratio debt cap for the new group's first period of account, its excess debt cap generated in the immediately preceding period of account is taken to be that of the old group for the period of account ending with the change in ownership. [*TIOPA 2010, s 400A; FA 2019, Sch 11 paras 4, 23*].

Meaning of 'related party'

[24.7] For the purposes of the corporate interest restriction, a person is a '*related party*' of another person:

(i) throughout any period for which their financial results are, or are required to be, included in group accounts (or would be but for an exemption);
(ii) on any day where, within the period of six months beginning or ending with that day, one directly or indirectly participates (within the meaning of *TIOPA 2017, ss 155, 157*) in the management, control or capital of the other, or another person participates in the management, control or capital of them both; or
(iii) on any day where one has a 25% investment in the other, or a third person has a 25% investment in them both.

In (iii) above, a person (P) has a 25% investment in another person (C) if P possesses, or is entitled to acquire, 25% or more of the voting power in C, or P would be entitled to least 25% of the proceeds, amount or assets: (a) on a disposal of the whole of the equity in C, (b) on an income distribution to equity holders in C, or (c) on a distribution of assets to equity holders (as defined) on a winding up of C. P's rights to proceeds, amounts or assets include not only any direct or indirect rights, but also any direct or indirect application of such rights for P's benefit (which can include a receipt or application of proceeds, amounts or assets for the benefit of a person in which P owns a direct or indirect equity interest). Where any rights are held in partnership, P's share of such rights is apportioned on a just and reasonable basis. P is taken, for this purpose, to have the rights and interests of any person connected with P, or who is a member of a partnership (or connected with such a member) of which P is a member (or of which a person connected with P is a member). Two persons are not, however, regarded as related under this rule merely as a result of their being parties to a normal commercial loan (as defined). P is also taken to have the rights and interests of a person (T) with whom P acts together in relation to the investment in C (broadly, where T acts in accordance with P's wishes, or vice versa, for the purpose of influencing the conduct of C's affairs, they are both party to an arrangement designed to affect the value of any equity T holds in C, or the same person manages any or all of any equity P and T hold in C (except where that person does so as the operator of different collective investment schemes)). Finally, P is also taken to have the rights and interests of a person or persons with whom P has entered into a 'qualifying arrangement' in relation to C (broadly, an arrangement involving shares in C held by P or any of those persons, by reference to which they can reasonably be expected to be acting together in relation to C to exert greater influence than would have been possible by any one of them acting alone, or to achieve an outcome that would have been significantly more difficult to achieve by any one of them acting alone).

In certain circumstances, where a loan or other financial liability of a group company (D) is owed to an unrelated party, that loan or liability is nevertheless treated as being between related parties where an entity which is related to D provides a guarantee, indemnity or other kind of financial assistance in respect of D's liability. See **24.6** for an exception to this rule for the purpose of calculating qualifying net group-interest expense where the guarantee etc. was provided before 1 April 2017. A liability is regarded as if it were owed to a related party where a related party indirectly stands in the position of creditor to that liability, for example via a series of back-to-back loans.

Where shareholders in a company lend money on exact (or very similar) terms and in proportion to their shareholdings or voting power in the company and the lenders together have a 25% investment in the company, the loans are treated as made between related parties. Where rights under such a loan are transferred, the transferee is treated as a related party of the company even if it holds no shares or voting power.

Where related parties hold less than 50% of a particular debt issuance (i.e. debt that is issued at the same time and conferring the same rights), no part of that debt is regarded as being made between related parties. Where parties to a loan become related as a result of a release of debt in circumstances where, without the release, it would be reasonable to conclude that the debtor would be unable to pay its debts within the next 12 months, they are not regarded as being related parties in relation to the loan. A loan provided by a person to a related party that is not made directly or indirectly in consequence of, or otherwise in connection with, any of the circumstances that cause those parties to be related is not treated as being made between related parties. Where a public body (as defined) lends money to a related party the loan is be regarded as being between related parties if the making of a profit is merely incidental to the making of the loan. Where a finance lease is granted prior to 1 April 2017, the parties to that lease are not treated as related parties in relation to the lease. In the case of a securitisation company, parties are not regarded as being related under (ii) above where that condition is met simply because the securitisation company is held by a trustee of a settlement and the other party is a settlor of that settlement.

[*TIOPA 2010, ss 462–472, 491(1); F(No 2)A 2017, Sch 5 para 1*].

Elections

[24.8] In addition to the group ratio election at **24.6** above, a number of additional elections are available which modify the calculation of the interest allowance for the purposes of the corporate interest restriction. Each election must be made in the interest restriction return.

Interest allowance (alternative calculation) election

An interest allowance (alternative calculation) election allows a group to make certain modifications to its accounts-based calculations in order to bring those calculations more into line with UK tax principles of recognition and measurement. Specifically, the election results in:

(i) an alternative method of calculating amounts relating to capitalised interest when calculating adjusted net group-interest expense which, broadly, aligns the recognition of such amounts with UK tax principles of recognition where they arise on assets that are taxed in accordance with GAAP;
(ii) adjustments to net group-interest expense in respect of amounts recognised on a change in accounting policy (and see **49.2** LEASING for transitional provisions relating to the adoption of IFRS 16);
(iii) adjustments to the group's profits before tax for a period of account beginning on or after 1 January 2019 to exclude any employee remuneration not paid within nine months of the end of the period (and to include such excluded remuneration in a subsequent period of account in which it is paid); and
(iv) amounts in respect of employer pension contributions and employee share options being replaced with amounts that better align accounting profits with the calculation of taxable profits when calculating profit before tax for the purposes of the calculation of group-EBITDA.

An interest allowance (alternative calculation) election is irrevocable. Where, however, an election was made before 7 November 2018 and had effect for any period of account ending before that date, a temporary window is available for the election to be revoked to avoid a group being disadvantaged by the introduction of the rule in (iii) above. The reporting company may revoke the election so that it does not apply to the first period of account beginning on or after 7 November 2018 and subsequent periods. The revocation must be made by notice in writing to HMRC before 12 May 2019.

[*TIOPA 2010, ss 423–426; F(No 2)A 2017, Sch 5 para 1; FA 2019, Sch 11 paras 7, 9, 10, 22, 27, Sch 14 para 18*].

Interest allowance (non-consolidated investment) election

An interest allowance (non-consolidated investment) election allows a group to modify its calculation of qualifying net group-interest expense and group-EBITDA to include within that calculation an appropriate amount of the group-interest of specified non-consolidated associates and joint ventures of the group. Essentially, this allows a group to 'consolidate' an associate or joint venture. Where a group makes such an election it must, as a consequence, also leave out of account any interest or other profits from transactions between members of the main group and those associates or joint ventures. An interest allowance (non-consolidated investment) election may be made on a period-by-period basis. [*TIOPA 2010, ss 427–429; F(No 2)A 2017, Sch 5 para 1; FA 2019, Sch 11 para 11*].

Interest allowance (consolidated partnerships) election

An interest allowance (consolidated partnerships) election allows a group to modify its calculation of qualifying net group-interest expense and group-EBITDA to exclude amounts relating to consolidated partnerships by treating them as if they were accounted for using the equity method in the group accounts. Such an election is irrevocable. [*TIOPA 2010, s 430; F(No 2)A 2017, Sch 5 para 1*].

Group-EBITDA (chargeable gains) election

Where a group makes a group-EBITDA (chargeable gains) election, in computing the capital (disposals) adjustment, it will recalculate amounts recognised on disposals of relevant assets (that are not shares or other interests in another member of the group) so that the calculation of such amounts is more in line with the way UK tax rules determine chargeable gains. Equivalent recalculations must also be made where a relevant asset-owning company leaves the group. In such a case, provisions deem a disposal of the relevant asset immediately before the company ceases to be a member of the group. Such an election is irrevocable (but will only have effect for periods where a group has elected to apply the group ratio method). [*TIOPA 2010, s 422; F(No 2)A 2017, Sch 5 para 1*].

Group ratio (blended) election

A group ratio (blended) election allows an alternative method of calculating the group ratio percentage where a group is held by a number of investors and a related party investor is a member of a different worldwide group. Broadly, the alternative method calculates a weighted, blended average of each investor's applicable group ratio percentage which, in the case of a related party investor, is the group ratio of its (other) worldwide group. A group ratio (blended) election can be made on a period-by-period basis and could be advantageous where, for example, a joint venture has a relatively low group ratio, but its investors have high group ratios. The election also includes an alternative group ratio debt cap calculation. [*TIOPA 2010, ss 401–404; F(No 2)A 2017, Sch 5 para 1*].

Particular types of company or business

[24.9] The effect of the corporate interest restriction is modified in relation to certain types of companies, businesses and transactions, as follows.

Oil and gas

Any amounts taken into account in calculating the ring fence income of a company within *CTA 2010, s 275* or the aggregate gain or loss under *TCGA 1992, s 197(3)* are ignored for the purposes of the restriction. Adjustments are to be made accordingly on a just and reasonable basis. [*TIOPA 2010, s 451; F(No 2)A 2017, Sch 5 para 1*].

Real estate investment trusts

Real estate investment trusts are, subject to certain modifications, within the corporate interest restriction rules but specific provisions deal with the treatment of any interest restriction as between the exempt and residual part of the business. [*TIOPA 2010, s 452; F(No 2)A 2017, Sch 5 para 1; FA 2019, Sch 11 paras 14, 22, 24; FA 2021, s 38(2)(3)*].

Insurance groups

Provisions set out how the amortised cost basis of calculation should apply to an insurer who elects to use that basis for its creditor relationships instead of fair value accounting. In addition, certain consolidated investments held by insurance groups are treated as outside the insurance group's worldwide group for corporate interest restriction purposes. [*TIOPA 2010, ss 453, 456; F(No 2)A 2017, Sch 5 para 1*].

Members of Lloyd's

The definition of tax-interest income and expense is adapted to cover certain loan relationship and derivative amounts that corporate members of Lloyds bring into account for corporation tax purposes. [*TIOPA 2010, s 454; F(No 2)A 2017, Sch 5 para 1*].

Investment managers

If an entity (S) is a member of a worldwide group as a result of one or more other members managing S and holding rights or interests in S, the entity managing S does so in the ordinary course of carrying on a business of providing investment management services and the management of S is not coordinated to any extent with the management by any person of any other entity, the group does not include any subsidiaries of S (i.e. they are not consolidated subsidiaries of any group member).

Note that this provision applies to all periods of account but was not included in the legislation as originally enacted. The reporting company of a worldwide group for any period of account beginning before 1 January 2018 may therefore make an election for the exclusion not to apply for the period of account. Such an election must be made (or revoked) in the interest restriction return for the period.

[*TIOPA 2010, s 454A; FA 2018, Sch 8 paras 12, 23*].

Shipping companies

Tonnage tax profits for an accounting period are treated as nil for the purpose of calculating the company's adjusted corporation tax earnings for the period. [*TIOPA 2010, s 455; F(No 2)A 2017, Sch 5 para 1*].

Cooperative and community benefit societies

The definition of tax-interest income or expense excludes certain distributions made by cooperative and community benefit societies which are treated as interest for corporation tax purposes under *CTA 2009, s 499*.

Charities

Interest payments on loans made by a charity to its trading, or non-charitable wholly-owned subsidiary are excluded from the concept of tax-interest expense where donations made by the subsidiary to the charity would be eligible for gift aid relief. [*TIOPA 2010, s 459; F(No 2)A 2017, Sch 5 para 1*].

Securitisation vehicles

Draft regulations have been published under which all amounts which fall within the permanent securitisation regime are included in the concept of tax-interest, and when applying the group ratio method the results-dependency test will be disapplied for instruments issued by a securitisation company within that regime. Groups will be able to treat any tax liability arising from an interest restriction in a company that is party to a capital market arrangement as if it were a liability of another group company.

Leases

Certain modifications are made to the calculation of tax-EBITDA in respect of long funding operating leases and finance leases that are not long funding finance leases to ensure that the calculation aligns with accounting classification. Equivalent adjustments are also made for the purposes of the group ratio method to ensure that amounts of 'depreciation' in respect of an asset held under a finance lease are included in the capital (expenditure) adjustment. [*TIOPA 2010, s 460; F(No 2)A 2017, Sch 5 para 1*].

Banking companies

So far as the activities of a banking company's trade consist of, or include, dealing in 'financial instruments', tax-interest expense amounts and tax-interest income amounts also include any amounts arising directly from dealing in such instruments. '*Financial instruments*' include, for this purpose, loan relationships, derivative contracts and shares and other securities. Impairment losses and the reversal of an impairment loss are excluded. Equivalent modifications are also made when calculating net group-interest expense (and, thereby, adjusted net group-interest expense, qualifying net group-interest and group-EBITDA). [*TIOPA 2010, s 450; F(No 2)A 2017, Sch 5 para 1*].

Public infrastructure companies

[24.10] An optional partial exemption from the corporate interest restriction applies to certain companies which provide public infrastructure assets. The exemption is intended to ensure that private investment in public infrastructure is not deterred by the restriction, particularly as such companies are usually highly geared. (HMRC Corporate Finance Manual CFM97110 (Draft)). In summary, the exemption operates as follows. A company (a '*qualifying infrastructure company*') qualifies for the exemption for an accounting period if:

(i) it is fully taxed in the UK in the period (i.e. all of its sources of income are within the charge to corporation tax (disregarding any source the income from which can be reasonably regarded as insignificant for the period) and it has not made an election for the foreign permanent establishments exemption or a claim for double tax relief);

(ii) all, or all but an insignificant proportion, of its income derives from 'qualifying infrastructure activities' carried on by the company, shares in a qualifying infrastructure company or loan relationships or other financing arrangements to which the only other party is a qualifying infrastructure company; and

(iii) all, or all but an insignificant proportion, of the total value of its assets derives from tangible assets that are related to qualifying infrastructure activities, service concession arrangements in respect of assets that are related to qualifying infrastructure activities, financial assets to which the company is a party for the purpose of qualifying infrastructure activities carried on by the company or another associated qualifying infrastructure company, assets held under a pension scheme for persons employed for the purpose of qualifying infrastructure activities carried on by the company or another associated qualifying infrastructure company, assets in respect of deferred tax attributable to qualifying infrastructure activities carried on by the company or another associated qualifying infrastructure company, shares in a qualifying infrastructure company or loan relationships or other financing arrangements to which the only other party is a qualifying infrastructure company; and

(iv) it has made an election that has effect for the period. An election must be made before the accounting period for which it is to have effect ends and applies until such time as a company no longer meets these conditions or until it is revoked. An election for an accounting period beginning before 1 April 2018 may be made at any time before that date. An election is only revocable after five years however, and a new election cannot be made for another five years following a revocation. A company may not make an election for the foreign permanent establishments exemption or a claim for double tax relief for any period for which an election under these provisions has effect. There is provision for two or more members of a group to make a joint election modifying certain conditions for the exemption.

If a company does not meet the requirements in (ii) and (iii) above for an accounting period beginning before 1 April 2018 but would do so for a notional accounting period ending on that date which is at least three months long, the company is treated as meeting the requirements for the actual period, but certain just and reasonable adjustments must be made in calculating the exemption.

A company carries on a '*qualifying infrastructure activity*' for this purpose if it provides a public infrastructure asset or carries on any other activity that is ancillary to or facilitates the provision of a public infrastructure asset. '*Public infrastructure assets*' are:

- tangible assets forming part of the infrastructure (as defined, but including, for example water, electricity or telecommunication facilities, railways, health or educational facilities, prisons) of the UK, which are, or to be procured by a public body or used in the course of an activity regulated by an 'infrastructure authority' (as defined, but including those for airports, the environment, utilities, harbours, roads and railways);
- buildings (or part of buildings) that are part of a UK property business and are let (or sub-let) on a short-term basis (broadly where the lease is for less than 50 years) to unrelated parties.

Provision of an asset for this purpose includes its acquisition, design, construction, conversion, improvement, operation, repair or decommissioning.

Both types of asset must have, have had, or be likely to have an expected economic life of at least ten years, and be recognised on the balance sheet of a member of the company's group (which is itself fully taxed in the UK, disregarding any source the income from which can be reasonably regarded as insignificant).

In (iii) above, assets are related to qualifying infrastructure activities if they are public infrastructure assets or other assets used in the course of a qualifying infrastructure activity carried on by the company or an associated qualifying infrastructure company. A company is taken to meet the conditions in (ii) and (iii) above if it has no income or, as appropriate, no assets.

Where the above conditions are met for an accounting period:

(1) amounts are excluded from being tax-interest expense amounts to the extent that the creditor is not a related party of the company or it is itself a qualifying infrastructure company and the creditor's recourse is, broadly, limited to the income and assets of the company or another qualifying infrastructure company;
(2) amounts are similarly excluded if they are in respect of certain pre-13 May 2016 loan relationships;
(3) the company is treated as having no tax-interest income amounts in the period;
(4) the company is treated as having tax-EBITDA of nil for the period;
(5) amounts within (1)–(3) are ignored in computing the group's adjusted net group-interest expense and qualifying net group-interest expense;
(6) the group-EBITDA for the period is calculated as if the group did not include the company;
(7) the £2 million de minimis limit is not taken into account in calculating the group's interest capacity. If, however, the interest restriction would otherwise be greater than it would if the public infrastructure rules did

not apply, the interest capacity is taken to be £2 million and the public infrastructure rules are disapplied. For periods of account beginning on or after 1 January 2018 (subject to the transitional rule at **24.13** below), this exception applies only where qualifying infrastructure companies in the group do not receive significant tax-interest amounts from qualifying infrastructure companies outside the group that are related parties.

These provisions apply with modifications to joint venture companies and to companies which are members of a partnership or other transparent entity.

[*TIOPA 2010, ss 432–449, 494(1); F(No 2)A 2017, Sch 5 paras 1, 32, 33; FA 2018, Sch 8 paras 7–11, 22–24; FA 2019, Sch 5 para 34, Sch 11 paras 12, 13, 20, 24*].

Anti-avoidance

[24.11] There are provisions to prevent groups from circumventing the corporate interest restriction. They apply where there are arrangements that have a main purpose of enabling a company to obtain a tax advantage resulting from eliminating, or reducing the amount of, any interest restriction, reactivating, or reactivating an increased amount of, carried forward disallowed interest or changing the timing of any restriction or reactivation. Where the provisions apply, HMRC may make such adjustments as are just and reasonable to counteract the advantage, whether by assessment, amendment or disallowance of a claim or otherwise. A tax advantage for these purposes may relate to all taxes chargeable as, or treated as if they are, corporation tax such as the CFC charge, bank levy and banking surcharge or to diverted profits tax.

These provisions apply to arrangements whenever entered into, but arrangements are excluded to the extent that they secure that an amount paid before 1 April 2017 is brought into an accounting period ending before that date and, as a direct consequence, there is a reduction in the tax-interest expense amounts which could otherwise have been left out of account by the corporate interest restriction. For this purpose, an accounting period which straddles 1 April 2017 is treated as two separate accounting periods, the second of which begins on that date.

Arrangements are also excluded if the obtaining of any tax advantages that would arise from them can reasonably be regarded as arising wholly from commercial restructuring (as defined) entered into because of the introduction of the corporate interest restriction.

[*TIOPA 2010, s 461; F(No 2)A 2017, Sch 5 paras 1, 34*].

Returns and compliance

[24.12] Worldwide groups must appoint a reporting company which is responsible for making an interest restriction return for each period of account. See **65.21** RETURNS.

Penalties apply for failure to make a return, incorrect or uncorrected returns, for companies which supply false information to the group's reporting company and for failure to keep and preserve records. See **59.22** penalties.

The reporting company has the power to require UK group companies to provide it with the information necessary to comply with its obligations. Where no reporting company is in place for a period of account, or no return has been made within the time limit, each UK group company has the power to require other such companies to provide it with information it needs to determine whether, or the extent to which, it must leave amounts out of account or bring them into account under the corporate interest restriction. [*TIOPA 2010, Sch 7A paras 60(1)–(3), 61; F(No 2)A 2017, Sch 5 para 1*].

Commencement and transitional provisions

[24.13] The corporate interest restriction applies to periods of account of worldwide groups beginning on or after 1 April 2017. Where a period of account of no more than 18 months straddles that date and the financial statements for the period are drawn up before the end of the 30 months beginning with the start of the period, the period of account is treated for the purposes as two separate periods for which financial statement have been drawn up, the second starting on 1 April 2017. Any necessary apportionments must be made on a time basis unless that basis would work unjustly or unreasonably, in which case the apportionment must be made on a just and reasonable basis. [*F(No 2)A 2017, Sch 5 para 25*].

A similar rule applies to the changes at **24.2**, **24.5**, **24.6** and **24.10** above which apply for periods of account beginning on or after 1 January 2018, but by reference to that date rather than 1 April 2017. [*FA 2018, Sch 8 para 22*].

Certain credits and debits are ignored for the purposes of the restriction as follows:

- debits or credits brought into account under *SI 2004 No 3271* (change in accounting practice — see **27.8** DERIVATIVE CONTRACTS and **50.16** LOAN RELATIONSHIPS) where the later period in relation to the change begins before 1 April 2017; and
- debits or credits brought into account under *F(No 2)A 2015, Sch 7 paras 115, 116, 119, 120* (transitional provisions for derivative contracts and loan relationships following change to UK GAAP);

A UK group company can make an election to be treated as if it had made a disregard election under the *Disregard Regulations* (*SI 2004 No 3256, Reg 6A*) (see **27.13** DERIVATIVE CONTRACTS) in relation to derivative contracts entered into before 1 April 2020. Where such an election has effect, the fair value movements on certain hedging derivative contracts are disregarded in the tax-interest and tax-EBITDA figures. Instead those amounts are brought into account in line with the hedged item. For a company's election to have effect, all of the companies which were UK group companies of the group on 1 April 2017 must make an election. Elections must be made before 1 April 2018 and are irrevocable.

[*F(No 2)A 2017, Sch 5 paras 29–31*].

Key points on the corporate interest restriction

[24.14] Points to consider are as follows.

- The corporate interest restriction was introduced in 2017 as a response to the recommendations of the G20/OECD project to tackle Base Erosion and Profit Shifting (BEPS) to place a limit on the amount of interest and certain other financing costs that large worldwide groups of companies can deduct when calculating their profits subject to corporation tax. The provisions replace the narrower provisions of the worldwide debt cap. The rules for both sets of provisions are very complex but must not be ignored.
- Any group with aggregate net tax-interest expense in the UK below the £2 million de minimis limit will not be subject to the restriction. As a consequence, it is estimated that most small and medium-sized groups are unlikely to be affected.
- Where a company close to the de minimis limit requires funds, it may be worth considering raising equity finance as an alternative as the benefit of any tax relief on loan finance must be set against the large potential compliance costs of this regime. Clearly, all other legal, regulatory and commercial factors would need to be evaluated.
- The corporate interest restriction includes an entirely separate compliance regime. Worldwide groups must appoint a reporting company which is responsible for making an interest restriction return for each period of account. See **65.21** RETURNS. HMRC have powers, similar to those for company tax returns, to enquire into interest restriction returns and to issue determinations where a return is not submitted. Penalties apply for failure to make a return, incorrect or uncorrected returns, for companies which supply false information to the group's reporting company and for failure to keep and preserve records. See **59.22** penalties.

25

Corporate Venturing Scheme

Simon's Taxes. See D8.3.

Introduction to the corporate venturing scheme

[25.1] The corporate venturing scheme provided tax relief for shares issued before 1 April 2010. Under the scheme, certain trading companies were able to obtain corporation tax relief at 20% ('*investment relief*') on corporate venturing investments, i.e. acquisitions (by cash subscription) of minority shareholdings in 'small higher risk' trading companies. Despite the abolition of the scheme, the following capital gains issues may continue to be relevant to companies who made investments under it:

- an allowable capital loss on the disposal of a corporate venturing investment, computed net of investment relief, can be relieved against *income* of the accounting period in which the loss arises and accounting periods ending in the previous 12 months (or can be relieved against chargeable gains in the normal way); and
- investing companies were able to postpone chargeable gains ('*deferral relief*') on disposals of corporate venturing investments where they reinvested in other shares attracting investment relief. Such deferred gains are brought back into charge on disposal of the shares.

This chapter deals with these two issues, but the provisions relating to investment relief itself are no longer covered. See the 2019/20 or earlier edition of this work for full coverage.

See generally HMRC Venture Capital Schemes Manual, VCM90000 *et seq*.

Chargeable gains and allowable losses

[25.2] A gain on the disposal at any time by the investing company of shares to which investment relief is attributable is a chargeable gain, though see 25.6 below as regards deferral relief. A loss on such a disposal is an allowable loss — see 25.4 below as to the computation of the loss and 25.5 below as regards possibility of setting the loss against income rather than gains. For the rules for identifying disposals with acquisitions, see 25.3 below.

Investment relief is 'attributable to shares' if investment relief was obtained in respect of those shares and has not been withdrawn. Where for any one accounting period relief was obtained by reason of more than one issue of shares, the relief is attributed to those issues in proportion to the amounts subscribed. Relief attributable to any one issue of shares is attributed *pro rata* to each share in that issue, and any reduction of relief is similarly apportioned between the shares in question. For these purposes, any bonus shares, issued in respect of the original shares and being shares in the same company, of the same class and carrying the same rights, are treated as if comprised in the original issue, and relief is apportioned to them accordingly. This applies only if the original shares have been held continuously since issue, and, where it does apply, the bonus shares are themselves treated as having been held continuously since the time of the original issue. [*FA 2000, Sch 15 para 45*].

Identification rules

[25.3] The rules below apply, for the purpose of identifying shares disposed of, where a company makes a part disposal of a holding of shares of the same class in the same company, and the holding includes shares to which investment relief is attributable (see 25.2 above) and which have been held continuously (see 25.5(a) below) since the time of issue. The rules apply for the purposes of the corporate venturing scheme and for the purposes of corporation tax on chargeable gains generally. As regards the latter, the normal rules (see Tolley's Capital Gains Tax under Shares and Securities) were disapplied.

Where shares comprised in the holding have been acquired on different days, a disposal was identified with acquisitions on a first in/first out basis. In matching the shares disposed of with shares acquired on a particular day, shares to which investment relief was attributable and which have been held continuously were treated as being disposed of *after* any other shares acquired on that day.

If, on a reorganisation of share capital (e.g. a scrip issue), a new holding falls, by virtue of *TCGA 1992, s 127*, to be equated with the original shares (see Tolley's Capital Gains Tax under Shares and Securities, and see also 25.7 below), shares comprised in the new holding were deemed for the above purposes to have been acquired when the original shares were acquired.

[*FA 2000, Sch 15 para 93; FA 2006, s 72(2)(e)*].

Computation of allowable loss

[25.4] If a loss would otherwise accrue on a disposal by the investing company of shares to which investment relief is attributable, and the investment relief does not fall to be withdrawn (as opposed to reduced) as a result of the disposal, the company's acquisition cost for the purposes of corporation tax on chargeable gains is reduced by the amount of investment relief attributable to the shares immediately after the disposal, but not so as to convert the loss into a chargeable gain. This applies only if the condition at 25.5(a) below (shares held continuously) has been met from issue to disposal.

[*FA 2000, Sch 15 para 94*].

Set-off of allowable loss against income

[25.5] Subject to all the conditions at (a)–(c) below being satisfied and a claim being made, an allowable loss, on a disposal by the investing company of shares to which investment relief is attributable (see **25.2** above), can be set against *income* (as an alternative to setting it against chargeable gains in the normal way — see **11.3** CAPITAL GAINS). The loss is as computed after applying the reduction at **25.4** above. The conditions are as follows.

(a) The shares must have been held continuously by the company from time of issue to time of disposal. If, during any period:
  (i) the company was deemed under any provision of *TCGA 1992* to have disposed of and immediately reacquired the shares; or
  (ii) following a scheme of reconstruction or amalgamation within *TCGA 1992, s 136* (or which would have been within that *section* but for the provisions of *TCGA 1992, s 137(1)*, which excludes schemes effected other than for *bona fide* commercial reasons or for tax avoidance), the company was deemed by virtue of **25.8** below to have made a disposal of shares which it retained under the scheme,

  it was not treated for the purposes of the corporate venturing scheme provisions as having held the shares continuously throughout that period.

(b) The investment relief must not fall to be withdrawn in full as a result of the disposal. For the circumstances in which relief could be withdrawn, see the 2019/20 or earlier edition of this work.

(c) The disposal has to be either:
  (i) by way of bargain at arm's length for full consideration; or
  (ii) by way of a distribution on a dissolution or winding-up of the issuing company; or
  (iii) a disposal within *TCGA 1992, s 24(1)* (entire loss, destruction etc. of asset); or
  (iv) a deemed disposal under *TCGA 1992, s 24(2)* (assets of negligible value).

The set-off is against income of the accounting period in which the loss was incurred. As regards any unrelieved balance, the claim can be extended to income of accounting periods ending within the 12 months immediately preceding the accounting period in which the loss is incurred. Income of an accounting period beginning before, and ending within, that 12 months is apportioned on a time basis so as to exclude income thereby deemed to have accrued prior to that 12-month period. The income of each accounting period included in the claim is treated as reduced by the loss, or by so much of it as cannot be relieved in a later accounting period. Where claims are made to relieve two or more losses, they are relieved in the order in which they were incurred. Relief is given before any relief claimed under *CTA 2010, Pt 4, Ch 5 (ss 68–90)* (loss incurred by investment company on disposal of unlisted shares — see **51.27** LOSSES) and before any deduction for charges on income or other amounts which could be deducted from or set against or treated as reducing profits of any description. Once relief has been obtained under these provisions for an amount of loss, that amount cannot be relieved under *s 70* or against chargeable gains.

Claims must be made within two years after the end of the accounting period in which the loss is incurred.

Where a claim is made under these provisions, *TCGA 1992, s 30* (value shifting to give tax-free benefit, see **11.13** CAPITAL GAINS) has effect in relation to the disposal if *any* benefit was conferred, whether tax-free or not. No loss relief against income is available if the disposal is the result of a scheme of reconstruction effected for tax avoidance rather than commercial reasons.

[*FA 2000, Sch 15 paras 67–72, 97*].

Deferral relief

[25.6] Deferral relief was available where a chargeable gain would otherwise accrue to the investing company:

(a) on a disposal of shares to which investment relief was attributable (see **25.2** above) immediately before the disposal and which satisfy the condition at **25.5**(a) above (shares held continuously) from issue to disposal; or
(b) on the occurrence of a chargeable event under these provisions (see below),

and the company made a 'qualifying investment'. A '*qualifying investment*' was a subscription for shares ('*qualifying shares*') on which investment relief was obtained under the corporate venturing scheme, other than shares issued by a 'prohibited company'. The qualifying shares had to be issued to the investing company within the one year immediately preceding or the three years immediately following the time the chargeable gain in question accrues. If the qualifying shares were issued *before* the gain accrued, they had to have been held continuously (see **25.5**(a) above) by the investing company from issue until the time the gain accrues, and investment relief had to still be attributable to them. A '*prohibited company*' means either:

(i) the company whose shares were disposed of (as in (a) above) or, or as the case could be, in relation to whose shares the chargeable event occurred (as in (b) above); or
(ii) a company which, when the gain accrues or when the qualifying shares were issued, was a member of the same group as the company in (i) above.

Deferral relief was 'attributable to shares' if expenditure on those shares has been used to defer the whole or part of a chargeable gain and no chargeable event has occurred resulting in the deferred gain being brought back into charge.

The following themselves become qualifying shares:

(A) any bonus shares, issued in respect of the qualifying shares and being shares in the same company, of the same class and carrying the same rights;

(B) any shares issued on a company reconstruction within **25.9** below in exchange for qualifying shares.

Postponement of the original gain

On a claim by the investing company, the whole or part of the chargeable gain could be deferred. The amount to be deferred was the lower of:

(I) the amount of the gain (or the amount remaining in charge after any previous deferral relief claim);

(II) the amount subscribed for the qualifying shares (to the extent that it has not been used in previous deferral relief claims); and

(III) the amount specified by the company in the claim.

No time limit was specified for making a claim, so the general six-year time limit applies as in **15.8** claims.

Deferred gain becoming chargeable

The deferred gain will become chargeable on the occurrence of, *and at the time of*, one of the following chargeable events:

(1) a disposal of qualifying shares by the investing company; or

(2) any other event giving rise to a withdrawal of, or reduction in, the investment relief attributable to qualifying shares.

If the qualifying investment was made before the gain accrues, there was disregarded for the purposes of (2) above any reduction made by reason of an event occurring before the gain accrues.

The chargeable gain accruing to the investing company at the time of the chargeable event was equal to so much of the deferred gain as was attributable to the shares in relation to which the chargeable event occurs. For these purposes, a proportionate part of the net deferred gain (i.e. the deferred gain less any amount brought into charge on an earlier chargeable event, e.g. a part disposal) was attributed to each of the qualifying shares held immediately before the chargeable event. Thus, a part disposal of qualifying shares brought into charge a proportionate part of the deferred gain.

Provision is made to ensure that a previously deferred gain accruing as above is brought into charge under *TCGA 1992, s 2B(3)* (previously *s 10B*; see **64.6** RESIDENCE) in the case of a non-UK resident company carrying on a trade or vocation through a permanent establishment in the UK.

[*FA 2000, Sch 15 paras 73–79*].

Company restructuring

Reorganisations of share capital

[25.7] The following applies where a company holds shares in another company, being shares of the same class, held in the same capacity and forming part of the ordinary share capital of that other company, and there is a reorganisation within the meaning of *TCGA 1992, s 126*. If the shares fall within two or more of the categories below, *TCGA 1992, s 127*, or, where appropriate, *TCGA 1992, s 116*, applies separately to each category. (This is subject to the disapplication of those provisions in the circumstances set out below.) The categories were:

(a) shares to which deferral relief is attributable (see **25.6** above);
(b) shares to which investment relief, but not deferral relief, is attributable (see **25.2** above) and which have been held continuously (see **25.5**(a) above) by the company since they were issued; and
(c) shares in neither of the categories above.

[*FA 2000, Sch 15 para 80*].

Rights issues etc. Where:

(i) a reorganisation (within *TCGA 1992, s 126*) involves an allotment of shares or debentures in respect of and in proportion to an existing holding;
(ii) investment relief is attributable (see **25.2** above) to the shares in the existing holding or to the allotted shares; and
(iii) if investment relief is attributable to the shares in the existing holding, those shares have been held continuously (see **25.5**(a) above) by the company since they were issued,

the share reorganisation rules of *TCGA 1992, ss 127–130* are disapplied. The effect is that the allotted shares are treated as a separate holding acquired at the time of the reorganisation. This does not apply in the case of bonus shares where these are issued in respect of shares comprised in the existing holding and are of the same class and carry the same rights as those shares.

If, in a case otherwise within *TCGA 1992, s 116(10)* (see Tolley's Capital Gains Tax under Qualifying Corporate Bonds):

(A) the old asset consists of shares to which investment relief is attributable and which have been held continuously (see **25.5**(a) above) by the company since they were issued; and
(B) the new asset consists of a qualifying corporate bond,

the usual treatment is disapplied. The effect was that the company is deemed to have disposed of the shares at the time of the relevant transaction, and the resulting chargeable gain or allowable loss crystallises *at that time*.

[*FA 2000, Sch 15 para 81*].

Company reconstructions and amalgamations

[25.8] Subject to **25.9** below, *TCGA 1992, s 135* and *s 136*, which equate the new holding with the original shares, are disapplied in the following circumstances:

(a) a company holds shares in another company (Company A);
(b) investment relief is attributable (see **25.2** above) to those shares;
(c) those shares have been held continuously (see **25.5**(a) above) by the investing company since they were issued; and

(d) there is a reconstruction or amalgamation whereby a third company issues shares or debentures in exchange for, or in respect of, Company A shares or debentures.

The result is that the transaction was treated, both for the purposes of the corporate venturing scheme provisions and for the purposes of corporation tax on chargeable gains generally, as a disposal of the original shares (and an acquisition of a new holding).

[*FA 2000, Sch 15 paras 82, 96*].

Issuing company becoming wholly-owned subsidiary of new holding company

[25.9] Notwithstanding **25.8** above, *TCGA 1992, s 135* is not disapplied (and there is thus no disposal and acquisition) where, by means entirely of an exchange of shares, all the shares in one company (the '*old shares*') are acquired by another company, and the conditions below are satisfied. Following such a share exchange, the shares thereby issued by the acquiring company (the '*new shares*') stand in place of the old shares, so that:

(i) any investment relief or deferral relief attributable to the old shares (see, respectively, **25.2**, **25.6** above) is attributed to the new shares for which they were exchanged;
(ii) the new shares are treated as having been issued at the time the old shares were issued and as having been held continuously (see **25.5**(a) above) by the investing company since that time (provided the old shares had been so held);
(iii) generally speaking, anything done, or required to be done, by or in relation to the acquired company is treated as having been done etc. by or in relation to the acquiring company.

The conditions to be satisfied are as follows.

(a) The consideration for the old shares consists entirely of the issue of the new shares.
(b) New shares are issued only at a time when the issued shares in the acquiring company consist entirely of subscriber shares (and any new shares already issued in consideration of old shares).
(c) The consideration for new shares of each description consists entirely of old shares of the 'corresponding description'.
(d) New shares of each description are issued to holders of old shares of the 'corresponding description' in respect of, and in proportion to, their holdings.
(e) Before any exchange of shares takes place, HMRC have given an 'approval notification'.

For the purposes of (c) and (d) above, old and new shares are of a '*corresponding description*' if, assuming they were shares in the same company, they would be of the same class and carry the same rights. All references above to 'shares' (other than to 'subscriber shares') include references to 'securities'. An '*approval notification*' (see (e) above) is given by HMRC, on an application by either company involved, if they are satisfied that the share exchange will be effected for commercial reasons and does not form part of a scheme or arrangements to avoid liability to corporation tax or capital gains tax.

The provisions of *FA 2000, Sch 15 para 80* (see **25.7** above) apply to a reconstruction within the above provisions where a company's holding of 'old shares' fell within more than one of the categories there mentioned.

[*FA 2000, Sch 15 paras 83–87*].

For interaction between these provisions and the exemptions relating to substantial company shareholdings, see **13.13** CAPITAL GAINS — SUBSTANTIAL SHAREHOLDING EXEMPTION.

26

Creative Industries Reliefs

Simon's Taxes. See **D7.12.**

Introduction to creative industries reliefs

[26.1] This chapter considers the special regimes applicable, and the reliefs available, to the creative industries. Specifically it examines the reliefs for high-end television and animation programme production, and for video games development, the relief for film production, theatrical productions relief, orchestral concerts relief and museum and gallery exhibitions relief.

Although the regimes are all quite similar, this chapter describes each regime and relief separately. Claims cannot be made under more than one of the regimes for the same expenditure, and there is a similar restriction with regard to duplicate claims for the various R&D reliefs; see **63** RESEARCH AND DEVELOPMENT EXPENDITURE.

For commentary on devolution of the power to set the corporation tax rate in Northern Ireland to the Stormont Assembly and consequential modification of the creative industries reliefs, see **1.5** INTRODUCTION: CHARGE TO TAX, RATES AND PROFIT COMPUTATIONS.

HMRC has a specialist unit to deal with claims for relief; the Creative Industries Unit, Manchester Incentives and Reliefs Team, HMRC S0733, Newcastle NE98 1ZZ. It can be contacted by email at creative.industries@hmrc.gov.uk.

Providing of State aid information

A claim for relief under the creative industries regimes must include any information required by HMRC for the purpose of complying with certain EU State aid obligations. This may include information about the claimant (or his activities), information about the subject-matter of the claim and other information relating to the grant of State aid through the provision of the FYAs. See **36.13** HMRC — ADMINISTRATION as regards the publishing by HMRC of State aid information. [*FA 2016, s 180(1)–(4)(10), Sch 24 Pt 1; F(No 2)A 2017, Sch 6 para 19; SI 2018 No 28*].

Staff furloughed during coronavirus (COVID-19) pandemic

Staffing costs in respect of an employee on furlough (i.e. who ceased work) are not considered by HMRC to constitute production expenditure for the purposes of the various creative industries reliefs. This applies equally to all furlough payments, whether or not they are reimbursed by the CJRS, and includes any 'top-up' element. If an employee has been placed on flexible furlough, then any payment in respect of the furloughed time will not be eligible. Holiday pay and sick pay are statutory requirements and HMRC consider them to be a necessary cost of employing staff and part of the cost of their working time. Any period during furlough which is taken as annual leave or recorded as sick leave is potentially eligible for relief, and should be apportioned in line with work done. See the relevant HMRC Manual at APC50130, FPC50130, MGET60120, OTR60120, TPC50130, TTR50130 and VGDC50130.

High-end television, animation, children's television and video games tax relief

[26.2] There are tax reliefs for the production of high-end television, animation and video games.

Eligible companies that are engaged in the making of qualifying television productions intended for release to the general public, or qualifying video games productions are able to claim an additional deduction in computing their taxable profits. Where that additional deduction results in a loss, the companies can surrender those losses for a payable tax credit.

Both the additional deduction and the payable credit are calculated on the basis of UK core expenditure up to a maximum of 80% of the total core expenditure by the qualifying company. The additional deduction is 100% of qualifying core expenditure and the payable tax credit is 25% of losses surrendered.

The credit in the case of each relief is based on the company's qualifying expenditure on the production of qualifying television programmes or video games. For television programmes, at least 10% of the qualifying expenditure must be on goods or services used or consumed in the UK. For video games, at least 25% of the qualifying expenditure must be provided from within the EEA.

Productions must be certified by the Department of Culture, Media & Sport (DCMS) as culturally British in order to qualify for the relief.

Claims are not allowed to be made for the same expenditure under these provisions and the film tax relief provisions below, or the provisions for R&D relief at *CTA 2009, Pt 13* (enhanced relief and R&D tax credits) and *Pt 3 Ch 6A* (above the line R&D expenditure tax credit). Similarly relief under the Intangible Fixed Assets (IFA) regime at *CTA 2009, Pt 8* does not apply to assets representing production expenditure on television programmes to which the taxation provisions below apply, nor to assets representing core expenditure on a video game to which the taxation provisions below apply. Such expenditure represents 'excluded assets' for the purposes of the IFA regime.

High-end television, animation and children's television production

[26.3] *CTA 2009, Pt 15A* provides for the reliefs for television production. There are five Chapters in this Part covering: an introduction to the reliefs including key definitions and basic concepts; how the activities are to be taxed; the tax relief itself, including details of British programmes, certification, qualifying expenditure; losses; and, entitlement to the relief.

The Chapters are dealt with in turn below.

Definitions and basic concepts

[26.4] Key definitions and points of interpretation are as follows:

'Television programme' means any programme (with or without sounds) which is produced to be seen on television, and consists of moving or still images or of legible text (or a combination of these), including the internet. Where qualifying programmes are commissioned as an individual series or serial that series or serial is treated as a single television programme. A single qualifying programme commissioned separately (for example a pilot programme) is treated as a single programme. A programme is treated as being complete when it is first in a form in which it can be reasonably regarded as ready for broadcast to the general public.

A 'relevant programme' for the purposes of the relief is one which meets certain conditions: being A and B, and in the case of a television programme which is neither animation nor a children's programme, also C and D.

Condition A — the programme is: a drama, a documentary, animation or a children's programme. A programme is a 'drama' if it consists: wholly or mainly of a depiction of events; the events are depicted (wholly or mainly) by one or more persons performing; and, the whole or major proportion of what is done by the person or persons performing, whether by way of speech, acting, singing, or dancing, involves the playing of a role. It also includes comedy. A relevant programme is to be treated as animation if at least 51% of total core expenditure is on animation. A programme is a children's programme if, when production begins, it is reasonable to expect that the programme's primary audience will be under the age of 15.

Condition B — the programme is not an excluded programme (see below).

Condition C — a programme slot length (being the period of time which the programme is commissioned to fill) must be greater than 30 minutes (this does not apply to animation or children's programmes).

Condition D — the average core expenditure (see below), per hour of slot length, is not less than £1 million (one million pounds sterling) (this does not apply to animation or children's programmes).

A 'qualifying relevant programme' is a relevant programme for which the conditions for television tax relief, see below, are met.

A television programme is an 'excluded programme' (and not within the scope of the reliefs) if it falls within any of these categories:

- any advertisement or other promotional programme;
- any news, current affairs or discussion programme;
- quiz shows, game shows, panel shows, variety shows, chat shows or similar entertainment;
- any programme consisting of or including a competition or contest, or the results of a competition or contest;
- any broadcast of a live event or of a theatrical or artistic performance given otherwise than for the purpose of being filmed;
- any programmes produced for training purposes.

Certain children's programmes are not, however, excluded programmes, as follows:

- the programme is a quiz show or game show; or
- the programme consists of or includes a competition or contest, or the results of such; and

- the prize total does not exceed £1,000.

The prize total is the total of each money prize and the amount spent on other prizes by the provider. HM Treasury may increase this limit by regulation.

With regard to a 'television production company', there can only be one television production company in relation to a relevant programme. In order to be a television production company in relation to a relevant programme the company must be responsible for pre-production, principal photography and post production of the relevant programme, as well as for delivery of the completed programme. The company must be actively engaged in planning and decision-taking during those stages of a programme's production; and it must directly negotiate, contract and pay for rights, goods and services.

There is a special rule for qualifying co-productions, which are relevant programmes eligible to be certified as British (within these rules) as a result of an agreement between the British government and any other government, international organisation or authority, with a co-producer as detailed within such agreement. A company which is such a co-producer must make an effective creative, technical and artistic contribution to the programme (so long as it does not do this in partnership). Co-producers who only provide finance are excluded.

Where there is more than one company meeting these conditions the company most directly engaged in the activities referred to is the 'television production company' in relation to the relevant programme. It is also possible that there may not be a television production company associated with a relevant programme. A company may elect (in its tax return for a period) to **not** be regarded as a 'television production company'. That election has effect in relation to relevant programmes which commence principal photography in that or any subsequent accounting period.

'Television production activities' includes work on development, pre-production, principal photography and post production of the programme. Where any of the programme is computer generated, references to principal photography include computer generation of the images. HM Treasury may amend this definition by regulation in particular to provide that certain activities are not television production activities.

'Production expenditure' means expenditure on television production activities in connection with the relevant programme.

'Core expenditure' means production expenditure on pre-production, principal photography and post production of the relevant programme.

'UK expenditure' means expenditure on goods or services that are used or consumed in the United Kingdom. The nationality of those providing the goods and services has no bearing on whether the expenditure qualifies. The 'used or consumed' test does not focus on the supplier of goods and services, but instead concentrates on the recipient or customer as the means of determining UK qualifying expenditure. Any apportionment between non-UK expenditure and UK expenditure is made on a just and reasonable basis.

[*CTA 2009, ss 1216A–1216AJ, 1216B*].

Taxation of activities of television production company

[26.5] The activities of a television production company in relation to each qualifying relevant programme (being a programme which meets the conditions for relief for which a claim is made) will be treated as a separate trade, ('the separate programme trade') so that where a television production company makes more than one programme that it claims relief for it will have more than one trade (save where the programmes are commissioned together, as above with regard to a single television programme).

A trade is treated as starting when pre-production begins or when any income is received from the relevant programme, whichever is earlier. The legislation provides the basic rules for the computation of amounts to be brought into account for the purposes of determining a profit or a loss for the separate programme trade.

For the first period of account: a debit is brought in for the costs of the relevant programme incurred; and a credit is brought in for the proportion of the income determined by a set formula (see below).

The calculation is cumulative, so for subsequent periods of account the additional amounts for that year (being the difference in costs and income incurred to date from the amounts used in the previous year) are brought into account. Therefore: a debit is brought in for the difference between the costs incurred to date and the corresponding amount for the previous period; and a credit is brought in for the difference between the proportion of total estimated income treated as earned at the end of the period and the corresponding amount for the previous period.

The formula for calculating the proportion of total estimated income treated as earned at the end of the period of account is: $(C / T) \times I$

Where:

C = total to date of the costs incurred (and represented in the work done);

T= the estimated total cost of the relevant programme;

I = the estimated total income from the relevant programme.

'Income from a relevant programme' constitutes any receipts in connection with its making or from its exploitation. This includes:

- receipts from the sale of the programme or rights in it;
- royalties or other payments for use of the programme or aspects of it (for example characters or music);
- payments for rights to produce games or other merchandise;
- receipts received by the company by way of a profit share agreement; and
- income from relevant programmes held as capital assets (the income will be treated as revenue in nature).

Costs on the relevant programme are taken to be incurred where they are costs on the production activities or activities undertaken with a view to exploiting the programme. However, expenditure that is prohibited or limited by the Corporation Taxes Acts is excluded (such as capital expenditure). Further, where a company is making a relevant programme that is treated as a capital asset in its hands (normally this would be capital and a deduction prohibited) then such expenditure in respect of the programme is treated as being of a revenue nature.

Costs are incurred when they are represented in the state of completion of the work in progress. Payments in advance are ignored until the work is done and deferred payments are recognised to the extent that work is represented in the state of completion. Only amounts for which there is an unconditional obligation to pay can be treated as incurred and where this obligation is linked to income being earned, then the cost can only be included when an appropriate amount of income has been brought into account.

With regard to pre-trading expenditure, where a company incurs expenditure on development of the relevant programme which pre-dates the commencement it is treated as if it were expenditure incurred immediately after the company begins to carry on the trade. The company should amend its tax return if it has previously taken such expenditure into account. Such an amendment may be made regardless of the normal time limits.

Any estimates for the purposes of these provisions at the balance sheet date for each period of account must be on a just and reasonable basis and must also take into consideration all relevant circumstances.

[*CTA 2009, ss 1216A, 1216B–1216BF*].

The television tax reliefs

[26.6] The company may claim an additional deduction and a payable tax credit (based on its qualifying expenditure on the relevant programme) if it meets the relevant conditions (see below). The additional deduction is taken into account in calculating its profit or loss from its separate programme trade. The additional deduction and the payable tax credit together make up the new tax relief.

'Qualifying expenditure' is core expenditure on the relevant programme that is taken into account in calculating the profits and losses of the separate programme trade (as above). The Treasury may, by regulation, amend this definition to provide that particular sorts of expenditure are or are not qualifying expenditure.

The additional deduction

The amount of the additional deduction is calculated as follows:

For the first period of account in which the trade of producing the relevant programme is carried out the additional deduction is given by: E

Where E is the lesser of the amount of:

- qualifying expenditure which is UK expenditure (see above); or
- 80% of the total qualifying expenditure.

In subsequent periods of account the additional deduction is: E – P

Where E is the lesser of:

- the amount of qualifying expenditure to date (i.e. the sum for the current period and all subsequent periods) which is UK expenditure; and
- 80% of that amount.

P is the total amount of additional deduction for all previous periods. These provisions may be amended by regulations.

The tax credits

A television production company may claim a television tax credit in an accounting period for which it has a surrenderable loss.

'Surrenderable loss' is the lesser of: the available loss for the trade for the period; and, the available qualifying expenditure for the period.

The 'available loss' for an accounting period is: L + RUL

Where: L is the amount of the company's loss for the period and RUL is the amount of any relevant unused loss.

RUL – the 'relevant unused loss' of a company – is that part of a loss neither surrendered for tax credit nor carried forward under *CTA 2010, s 45* or *s 45B*.

The 'available qualifying expenditure' for these purposes, for the first period of account during which the trade is carried on, is the same as above, so is amount 'E'.

The available qualifying expenditure for subsequent periods is: E – S

Where:

- E is the amount defined above; and
- S is the aggregate of the amounts surrendered for television tax credit in previous periods (see below).

Any necessary apportionments can be made where a period of account of the separate programme trade does not coincide with an accounting period.

A company may surrender all or part of its surrenderable loss for a period and thus be entitled to a payable tax credit in respect of the surrender.

The payable tax credit rate is 25%.

Where a part of the loss is surrendered the company's available loss will be reduced by the surrendered amount.

Where a company is entitled to a television tax credit for a period, and it claims that credit, HMRC will pay the credit to the company. An amount of credit that is payable, or an amount of interest payable on such credit under *ICTA 1988, s 826*, may be set against any corporation tax that the company owes (which satisfies the obligation to pay the credit).

When the company's tax return is the subject of an enquiry then no payment need be made to the company until the enquiry is completed (although HMRC may make such provisional payments as it deems fit).

However, when the company owes HM Revenue and Customs any amount of PAYE, Class 1 National Insurance contributions or any amount due for visiting performers (*ITA 2007, s 966*), no payment need be made to the company until the company has paid any amounts due.

A payment of a television tax credit is not income for the company for any tax purpose.

In determining the amount of costs incurred on a programme for a period no amount is to be included if it is still unpaid four months after the period ends (although this does not override the normal consideration of when costs are taken to be incurred as detailed above).

[*CTA 2009, 1216CF–1216CK; F(No 2)A 2017, Sch 4 para 140*].

Conditions to be met for the reliefs to apply

The relief is available to the television production company if the relevant programme satisfies a number of criteria as follows:

- it is intended for broadcast;
- it is a British programme; and
- the required level of core expenditure is met.

'Intended for broadcast' means the programme is intended for broadcast to the general public. This is determined when the television production activities begin, so where a programme starts out being intended for broadcast but subsequently the intention changes, it still meets this condition. However, where the original intention is not to broadcast the programme to the general public then the condition is not met.

To prevent double claims, relief is not available under these provisions for animation or high-end television where relief has already been given for R&D on the same expenditure(under *CTA 2009, Pt 13* or *Pt 3 Ch 6A*).

A programme (other than qualifying co-productions) needs to obtain a certificate that it is a British programme. A television production company must apply to the Secretary of State for a relevant programme to be certified as British and certain conditions must be met to satisfy the 'cultural test'. Documentation should be provided as required, and further information may be requested by the Secretary of State in order to determine whether a certificate should be provided. The detailed conditions to be met with regard to the 'cultural test' are contained in the *Cultural Test (Television Programmes) Regulations, SI 2013 No 1831*.

Applications may be made for an interim or final certificate. An 'interim' certificate is granted before the programme is completed and states that if completed according to the proposals it will be British. A 'final' certificate is granted after the programme is completed. The Secretary of State may, by regulations, amend the application process, particulars required etc. The Secretary of State shall certify a relevant programme if he is satisfied that it meets the requirements for an interim or final certificate. However, if the Secretary of State is not so satisfied, he must not certify the relevant programme. An interim certificate may be given subject to certain conditions and it may have an expiry date. In any case an interim certificate expires when a corresponding final certificate is issued. The Secretary of State must revoke a certificate if it becomes clear that it should not have been issued. A revoked certificate is treated as never having been issued (unless the Secretary of State provides otherwise).

A further condition for the relief is that not less than 10% of the core production expenditure on the relevant programme must be UK expenditure. HM Treasury may vary this minimum percentage of UK expenditure by regulations.

[*CTA 2009, ss 1216C–1216CE; SI 2013 No 1831; SI 2017 No 1138*].

Anti-avoidance and disclosure

A general anti avoidance provision is provided which denies television production tax relief to the extent that it arises from artificially inflated claims.

Where a transaction is attributable to arrangements entered into (wholly or partly) for a disqualifying purpose, that transaction is disregarded in determining the amount of additional deduction or television tax credit due. Arrangements are entered into for a disqualifying purpose when their main object, or one of their main objects, is to enable a company to obtain an additional deduction or a television tax credit that it would not otherwise be entitled to, or a larger deduction or greater amount of television tax credit than it would otherwise be entitled to.

'Arrangements' is broadly defined to include any scheme, agreement or understanding, whether or not legally enforceable.

HMRC may disclose information to the Secretary of State for the purposes of his functions and also allows for the same information to be disclosed to the British Film Institute. Otherwise a duty of confidentiality is imposed on any person to whom the information is disclosed and a person commits an offence if he discloses information about an identifiable person in contravention of this. Such information can only be disclosed as authorised by enactment, in pursuance of a court order, for the purposes of a criminal investigation (or other legal proceedings connected with the operation of the television and video games relief), with the consent of HMRC, or with the consent of each person to whom the information relates.

A defence for a person charged with such an offence is provided, for example, where he believed the disclosure to be lawful, or the information had already lawfully been made public. The penalties for a person convicted of wrongful disclosure are: on conviction on indictment to imprisonment for a term not exceeding two years or a fine or both; or on summary conviction to imprisonment for a term not exceeding 12 months or a fine (not exceeding the statutory maximum), or both.

A prosecution may only be brought in England and Wales by or with the consent of the Director of Public Prosecutions. A prosecution may only be brought in Northern Ireland by HMRC or with the consent of the Director of Public Prosecutions for Northern Ireland.

[*CTA 2009, ss 1216CL–1216CN*].

Programme losses

[26.7] There is a restriction on carry forward relief for losses arising whilst a programme is in production to the extent that such losses may only be carried forward under *CTA 2010, s 45* or *s 45B* (see **51.7**, **51.6** LOSSES) to be set against profits of the same trade in a later period. Where a loss is set against such profits, the set off is ignored for the purposes of *CTA 2010, s 269ZB* (restriction on deductions for carried-forward losses from trading profits — see **51.13** LOSSES).

For the accounting period during which a qualifying programme is completed or abandoned, and for any subsequent accounting periods if the trade continues, any trading loss carried forward from a pre-completion accounting period to a later accounting period (that is not attributable to television tax relief) is to be treated as a loss arising in that later period, for the purposes of *CTA 2010, s 37* (see **51.3, 51.4** LOSSES) and GROUP RELIEF (35). The amount which can be set sideways against other profits of the same or an earlier period, or be surrendered as group relief, is restricted to the amount (if any) that is not attributable to television tax relief.

The loss that is 'attributable to television tax relief' is the amount of the total loss less the amount of loss that there would have been without the additional deduction for television tax relief. The purpose of this provision is to restrict loss relief to 'real' losses, and not those created or increased by the television tax relief. However, this does not apply to losses carried forward or surrendered under the terminal loss provisions.

A 'terminal loss' arises where a television production company ceases to carry on a separate trade in relation to a relevant programme and has an amount of loss that remains to be carried forward.

Where a television production company with a terminal loss carries on another trade in relation to another qualifying programme it can, by election, treat such a loss as being a loss brought forward for that other qualifying programme trade in the next accounting period following the cessation.

Where a company with a terminal loss is in a group relationship with another company at the time of the cessation then the company with the terminal loss may surrender this loss to another television production company within the same group (in relation to a qualifying programme) provided that company makes a claim for the loss.

Where a terminal loss is set off against profits of the same company or another group member, the set off is ignored for the purposes of *CTA 2010, s 269ZB*.

A 'qualifying programme' means a relevant programme in relation to which the conditions for television tax relief are met.

'Completion period' means the accounting period of the company in which the relevant programme is completed or if not completed, in which it is abandoned. 'Pre-completion period' means an accounting period of the company before the completion period.

'The separate programme trade' means the company's separate trade in relation to the relevant programme.

[*CTA 2009, ss 1216D–1216DC; F(No 2)A 2017, Sch 4 paras 32–34*].

Entitlement to relief

[26.8] Entitlement to relief for any period is dependent on having the appropriate certification and also meeting the UK expenditure condition.

A company is entitled to relief with regard to a completion period, and the company tax return for this period must be accompanied by a final certificate. This final certificate then covers both the final period and any interim periods. However, if no such final certificate is provided the company loses eligibility for all periods and must amend its return(s) accordingly. The company must report in its tax return for the completion period (see above) whether a relevant programme has been completed or abandoned. The UK expenditure condition also applies, see further below.

With regard to claims during interim accounting periods, which are periods prior to the completion period during which production activities are undertaken for the relevant programme, a company is entitled to relief only if an interim certificate (see above) accompanies its company tax return for that period (see below the further condition as to statement of expenditure). If an interim certificate is revoked the company loses eligibility for any period in respect of which the interim certificate has been provided and must amend its return(s) accordingly.

However, if the company abandons television production activities its tax return for the final accounting period may be accompanied by an interim certificate. The company does not lose entitlement to any earlier relief.

If a final certificate is revoked, the company loses eligibility for all periods and must amend its return(s) accordingly.

In addition to the provision of an interim certificate, the company is only entitled to relief in an interim accounting period where it includes, in its company tax return for that period, a statement of the planned amount of UK expenditure on the relevant programme (and that amount indicates that the condition as to UK expenditure being at least 10% of core expenditure (see above) will be met on completion).

Where this condition is met but it subsequently becomes apparent that the amount of UK expenditure on completion will be too low, the company loses eligibility for all periods and must amend its company tax return(s) accordingly.

If the relevant programme is completed or abandoned, its company tax return for the final accounting period must be accompanied by a statement that it has been completed or abandoned, as the case may be, and by a final statement of UK core expenditure on the relevant programme. If the company tax return shows that the amount of UK core expenditure is too low and no such final statement is provided, the company loses eligibility for all period(s) and must amend its company tax return(s) accordingly.

The normal time limits for amendments of assessments are overridden as necessary in order to allow these provisions to have effect.

[*CTA 2009, ss 1216E–1216EC*].

Video games development relief

[26.9] *CTA 2009, Pt 15B* provides for reliefs for video games development. There are five Chapters in this Part covering: an introduction to the two reliefs including key definitions and basic concepts; how the activities are to be taxed; the tax relief itself, including details of British video games, certification, qualifying expenditure; losses; and, entitlement to the relief.

See also HMRC Video Games Development Company Manual.

The Chapters are dealt with in turn below.

Definitions and basic concepts

[26.10] 'Video game' does not include anything produced for advertising or promotional purposes or gambling, and references to a video games includes the game's soundtrack. A video game is regarded as being 'completed' when copies of it can be made and these are made available to the general public.

A 'video games development company' in relation to a video game is the company which is responsible for developing the game. It must be actively engaged in planning and decision-making during the design, production and testing of the game and it must directly negotiate, contract and pay for rights, goods and services. There can only be one video games development company in relation to a video game.

There may be more than one company meeting these conditions, and where this is the case, the company most directly engaged in the activities referred to is the video games development company in relation to the relevant game. It is possible that there may be no video games development company in relation to the relevant game.

A company may elect in its tax return for an accounting period not to be regarded as a video games development company. That election has effect in relation to relevant games which begin to be produced in that or any subsequent accounting period.

'Video game development activities' include work involved in designing, producing and testing the video game. Regulations may provide that certain activities are or are not video game development activities.

'Core expenditure' in relation to the video game means expenditure on designing, producing and testing the video game. However, any expenditure incurred in designing the initial concept for the video game (e.g. setting out the business case for making a game) and on further debugging a completed video game or carrying out maintenance in connection with a video game is not regarded as core expenditure.

Any apportionment between non-European expenditure and European expenditure (i.e. expenditure on goods and services provided from within the UK or EEA) is made on a just and reasonable basis. This definition may be amended by regulation.

[*CTA 2009, ss 1217AA–1217AF; SI 2019 No 689, Reg 16(22)*].

Taxation of activities of video games development company

[26.11] The activities of a video games development company in relation to each qualifying video game (being a video game which meets the conditions for relief for which a claim is made) will be treated as a separate trade ('the separate video game trade') so that where a video games development company makes more than one game it will have more than one trade.

A company is treated as beginning a video game trade on the earlier of when income is received, or the design starts.

The legislation provides the basic rules for the computation of amounts to be brought into account for the purposes of determining a profit or a loss for the separate video game trade.

For the first period of account: a debit is brought in for the costs of the video game incurred; and a credit is brought in for the proportion of the estimated income determined by a set formula (see below).

The calculation is cumulative, so for subsequent periods of account the additional amounts for that year (being the difference in costs and income incurred to date from the amounts used in the previous year(s)) is brought into account. Therefore: a debit is brought in for the difference between the costs incurred (and represented in work done) to date and the corresponding amount for the previous period; and a credit is brought in for the difference between the proportion of total estimated income treated as earned at the end of the period and the corresponding amount for the previous period.

The formula for calculating the proportion of total estimated income treated as earned at the end of the period of account is: $(C / T) \times I$

Where:

C = total to date of the costs incurred (and represented in the work done);

T= the estimated total cost of the video game;

I = the estimated total income from the video game.

'Income from the video game' constitutes any receipts in connection with its production or from its exploitation. This includes:

- receipts from the sale of the video game or rights in it;
- royalties or other payments for use of the video game or aspects of it (for example characters or music);
- payments for rights to produce games or other merchandise;
- receipts received by the company by way of a profit share agreement; and
- income from video games held as capital assets (the income will be treated as revenue in nature).

Costs of the video game are taken to be incurred where they are costs on the development activities or activities undertaken with a view to exploiting the programme. However, expenditure that is prohibited or limited by the Corporation Taxes Acts is excluded (such as capital expenditure). Further, where a company is making a video game that is treated as a capital asset in its hands (normally this would be capital and a deduction prohibited) then such expenditure in respect of the programme is treated as being of a revenue nature.

Costs are incurred when they are represented in the state of completion of the work in progress. Payments in advance are ignored until the work is done and deferred payments are recognised to the extent that work is represented in the state of completion. Only amounts for which there is an unconditional obligation to pay can be treated as incurred and where this obligation is linked to income being earned, then the cost can only be included when an appropriate amount of income has been brought into account.

Any estimates for the purposes of these provisions at the balance sheet date for each period of account must be on a just and reasonable basis and must also take into consideration all relevant circumstances.

[*CTA 2009, ss 1217B–1217BE*].

Video games tax relief

[26.12] The company may claim an additional deduction and a payable tax credit (based on its qualifying expenditure on the video game) if it meets the relevant conditions (see below). The additional deduction is taken into account in calculating its profit or loss from its separate video game trade. The additional deduction and the payable tax credit together make up the new video games tax relief.

'Qualifying expenditure' is core expenditure on the video game that is taken into account in calculating the profits and losses of the separate video game trade (as above). However, if the core expenditure on the video game includes sub-contractor payments which (in total) exceed £1 million, the excess is not 'qualifying expenditure'. A sub-contractor payment means a payment made by the company to another person in respect of work on design, production or testing of the video game that is contracted out.

The Treasury may, by regulation, amend this definition to provide that particular sorts of expenditure are or are not qualifying expenditure.

The additional deduction

The amount of the additional deduction is calculated as follows:

For the first period of account in which the separate video game trade is carried out the additional deduction is given by: E

Where E is the lesser of the amount of:

- qualifying expenditure which is European expenditure (see above); or
- 80% of the total qualifying expenditure.

In subsequent periods of account the additional deduction is: E – P

Where E is the lesser of:

- the amount of qualifying expenditure to date (i.e. the sum for the current period and all subsequent periods) which is European expenditure; and
- 80% of the total amount of qualifying expenditure to date.

P is the total amount of additional deductions for all previous periods. These provisions may be amended by regulations.

The tax credits

A video games development company may claim a video games tax credit in an accounting period for which it has a surrenderable loss.

'Surrenderable loss' is the lesser of: the available loss of the separate video game trade for the period; and, the available qualifying expenditure for the period.

The 'available loss' for an accounting period is: L + RUL

Where: L is the amount of the company's loss for the period in the separate video game trade and RUL is the amount of any relevant unused loss.

RUL – the 'relevant unused loss' of a company – is that part of a loss neither surrendered for tax credit nor carried forward under *CTA 2010, s 45* or *s 45B*.

The 'available qualifying expenditure' for these purposes, for the first period of account during which the trade is carried on, is the same as above, so is amount 'E'.

For any periods of account following the first a separate calculation is made. The available qualifying expenditure for these subsequent periods is: E – S

Where:

- E is the amount defined above (for the additional deduction); and
- S is the aggregate of the amounts surrendered for video games tax credit in previous periods (see below).

Any necessary apportionments can be made where a period of account of the separate video game trade does not coincide with an accounting period.

A company may surrender all or part of its surrenderable loss for a period and thus be entitled to a payable tax credit in respect of the surrender.

The payable tax credit rate is 25%.

Where a part of the loss is surrendered the company's available loss will be reduced by the surrendered amount.

Where a company is entitled to a video games tax credit for a period, and it claims that credit, HMRC will pay the credit to the company. An amount of credit that is payable, or an amount of interest payable on such credit under *ICTA 1988, s 826*, may be set against any corporation tax that the company owes (which satisfies the obligation to pay the credit).

When the company's tax return is the subject of an enquiry then no payment need be made to the company until the enquiry is completed (although HMRC may make such provisional payments as it deems fit).

However, when the company owes HM Revenue and Customs any amount of PAYE, Class 1 National Insurance contributions or any amount due for visiting performers (*ITA 2007, s 966*), no payment need be made to the company until the company pays any amounts due.

A payment of a video games tax credit is not income for the company for any tax purpose.

In determining the amount of costs incurred on a video game for a period no amount is to be included if it is still unpaid four months after the period ends (although this does not override the normal consideration of when costs are taken to be incurred as detailed above).

[*CTA 2009, 1217CF–1217CK; F(No 2)A 2017, Sch 4 para 141; SI 2019 No 689, Reg 16(25)*].

Conditions to be met for the reliefs to apply

The relief is available to the television production company if the relevant programme satisfies a number of criteria as follows:

- it is intended for supply;
- it is a British video game; and
- the required level of core expenditure is met.

'Intended for supply' means the video game is intended for supply to the general public. This is determined when the video game production activities begin, so where a video game starts out being intended for broadcast but subsequently the intention changes, it still meets this condition. However, where the original intention is not to supply the video game to the general public then the condition is not met.

To prevent double claims, relief is not available under these provisions for video game development where relief has already been given for R&D on the same expenditure (under *CTA 2009, Pt 13* or *Pt 3 Ch 6A*).

A video game needs to obtain a certificate that it is a British video game. A video games development company must apply to the Secretary of State for a relevant video game to be certified as British and certain conditions must be met to satisfy a points-based 'cultural test'. Documentation should be provided as required, and further information may be requested by the Secretary of State in order to determine whether a certificate should be provided. The detailed conditions for satisfying the cultural test are set out in *SI 2014 No 1958*. To pass the test, a video game must achieve a total of 16 points awarded on the basis of the setting, content, language and British cultural aspects of the game, where certain work on the game is carried out, and the residence or nationality of the personnel involved in the making of the game.

Applications may be made for an interim or final certificate. An 'interim' certificate is granted before the video game is completed and states that if completed according to the proposals it will be British. A 'final' certificate, stating that it is a British video game, is granted after the video game is completed. The Secretary of State may, by regulations, amend the application process, particulars required etc. The Secretary of State shall certify a relevant video game if he is satisfied that it meets the requirements for an interim or final certificate. However, if the Secretary of State is not so satisfied, he shall not certify the relevant video game. An interim certificate may be given subject to certain conditions and it may have an expiry date. In any case an interim certificate expires when a corresponding final certificate is issued. The Secretary of State shall revoke a certificate if it becomes clear that it should not have been issued. A revoked certificate is treated as never having been issued (unless the Secretary of State provides otherwise).

A further condition for the relief is that not less that 25% of the core expenditure on the video game must be European expenditure (see above). HM Treasury may vary this minimum percentage of European expenditure by regulations.

[*CTA 2009, ss 1217C–1217CE; SI 2014 No 1958; SI 2019 No 689, Reg 16(23)(24)*].

Anti-avoidance and disclosure

A general anti-avoidance provision is provided which denies video games tax relief to the extent that it arises from artificially inflated claims.

Where a transaction is attributable to arrangements entered into (wholly or partly) for a disqualifying purpose, that transaction is disregarded in determining the amount of additional deduction or video game tax credit due. Arrangements are entered into for a disqualifying purpose when their main object, or one of their main objects, is to enable a company to obtain an additional deduction or a video game tax credit that it would not otherwise be entitled to, or a larger deduction or greater amount of video game tax credit than it would otherwise be entitled to.

'Arrangements' is broadly defined to include any scheme, agreement or understanding, whether or not legally enforceable.

HMRC may disclose information to the Secretary of State for the purposes of his functions and also allows for the same information to be disclosed to the British Film Institute. Otherwise a duty of confidentiality is imposed on any person to whom the information is disclosed and a person commits an offence if he discloses information about an identifiable person in contravention of this. Such information can only be disclosed as authorised by enactment, in pursuance of a court order, for the purposes of a criminal investigation (or other legal proceedings connected with the operation of the television and video games relief), with the consent of HMRC, or with the consent of each person to whom the information relates.

A defence for a person charged with such an offence is provided, for example, where he believed the disclosure to be lawful, or the information had already lawfully been made public. The penalties for a person convicted of wrongful disclosure are: on conviction on indictment to imprisonment for a term not exceeding two years or a fine or both; or on summary conviction to imprisonment for a term not exceeding 12 months or a fine (not exceeding the statutory maximum), or both.

A prosecution may only be brought in England and Wales by or with the consent of the Director of Public Prosecutions. A prosecution may only be brought in Northern Ireland by HMRC or with the consent of the Director of Public Prosecutions for Northern Ireland.

[*CTA 2009, ss 1217CL–1217CN*].

Video game losses

[26.13] There is a restriction on carry forward relief for losses arising whilst a video game is in development. Such losses may only be carried forward under *CTA 2010, s 45* or *s 45B* (see **51.7**, **51.6** LOSSES) to be set against profits of the same trade in a later period. Where a loss is set against such profits, the set off is ignored for the purposes of *CTA 2010, s 269ZB* (restriction on deductions for carried-forward losses from trading profits — see **51.13** LOSSES).

For the accounting period during which a video game is completed or abandoned, and for any subsequent accounting periods if the trade continues, any trading loss carried forward from a pre-completion accounting period to a later accounting period (that is not attributable to video games tax relief) is to be treated as a loss arising in that later period and may be deducted from total profits of the same or an earlier period under *CTA 2010, s 37* (see **51.3**, **51.4** LOSSES) or surrendered as GROUP RELIEF (35). The amount which can so be set sideways against other profits of the same or an earlier period, or be surrendered as group relief, is restricted to the amount (if any) that is not attributable to video games tax relief.

The loss that is 'attributable to video games tax relief' is the amount of the total loss less the amount of loss that there would have been without the additional deduction for tax relief. The purpose of this provision is to restrict loss relief to 'real' losses, and not those created or increased by the video games tax relief. However, this does not apply to losses carried forward or surrendered under the provisions on terminal losses (*s 1217DC*).

A 'terminal loss' arises where a video games development company ceases to carry on a separate trade in relation to a qualifying video game and has an amount of loss that remains to be carried forward.

Where a video games development company with a terminal loss carries on another trade in relation to another qualifying video game it can, by election, treat such a loss as being a loss brought forward for that other qualifying video game trade in the next accounting period following the cessation.

Where a company with a terminal loss is in a group relationship with another company at the time of the cessation then the company with the terminal loss may surrender this loss to another video games development company within the same group (in relation to a qualifying video game) provided that company makes a claim for the loss.

Where a terminal loss is set off against profits of the same company or another group member, the set off is ignored for the purposes of *CTA 2010, s 269ZB*.

A 'qualifying video game' means a video game in relation to which the conditions for video games tax relief are met.

'Completion period' means the accounting period of the company in which the video game is completed or if not completed, in which video game activities are abandoned in relation to the video game. 'Pre-completion period' means an accounting period of the company before the completion period.

'The separate video game trade' means the company's separate trade in relation to the video game.

[*CTA 2009, ss 1217D–1217DC; F(No 2)A 2017, Sch 4 paras 36–38*].

Entitlement to relief

[26.14] Entitlement to relief for any period is dependent on having the appropriate certification and also meeting the European expenditure condition (see above).

If the video game is completed a video games development company is entitled to relief with regard to a completion period, and the company tax return for this period must be accompanied by a final certificate. This final certificate then covers both the final period and any interim periods. However, if no such final certificate is provided the company loses eligibility for all periods and must amend its return(s) accordingly. The company must report in its tax return for the completion period (see above) whether a video game has been completed or its development abandoned. The European expenditure condition also applies, see further below.

With regard to claims during interim accounting periods, which are periods prior to the completion period during which video game development activities are undertaken for the relevant video game, a company is entitled to relief only if an interim certificate (see above) accompanies its company tax return for that period (see below the further condition as to statement of expenditure). If an interim certificate is revoked the company loses eligibility for any period in respect of which the interim certificate has been provided and must amend its return(s) accordingly.

However, if the company abandons video game development activities its tax return for the final accounting period may be accompanied by an interim certificate. The company does not lose entitlement to any earlier relief.

If a final certificate is revoked, the company loses eligibility for all periods and must amend its return(s) accordingly.

In addition to the provision of an interim certificate, the company is only entitled to relief in an interim accounting period where it includes, in its company tax return for that period, a statement of the planned amount of European expenditure on the video game (and that amount indicates that the condition as to European expenditure being at least 25% of core expenditure (see above) will be met on completion).

Where this condition is met but it subsequently becomes apparent that the amount of European expenditure on completion will be too low, the company loses eligibility for all periods and must amend its company tax return(s) accordingly.

If the video game is completed or its development abandoned, its company tax return for the final accounting period (the completion period) must be accompanied by a statement that it has been completed or abandoned, as the case may be, and by a final statement of European core expenditure on the relevant programme. If the company tax return shows that the amount of European core expenditure is too low and no such final statement is provided, the company loses eligibility for all period(s) and must amend its company tax return(s) accordingly.

The normal time limits for amendments of assessments are overridden as necessary in order to allow these provisions to have effect.

[*CTA 2009, ss 1217E–1217EC; SI 2019 No 689, Reg 16(26)*].

Claims and overpayments

[26.15] A claim for either of the *CTA 2009, Pt 15A* or *Pt 15B* reliefs above must be made in a company tax return (or amended return) (see **65.4**, **65.8** RETURNS) for the accounting period for which the claim is made, within one year of the filing date for that return or by such later time as HMRC may allow. It can similarly only be amended or withdrawn by amendment of the company tax return within the same time limit. It must specify the quantum of the amount claimed. An election not to be a television production company or not to be a video games development company can only be made by being included in the return. The provisions of *FA 2007, Sch 24* with regard to penalties for errors applies, see **59** PENALTIES.

[*FA 1998, Sch 18 paras 10(4)(6)(7), 83S–83X; FA 2007, Sch 24 para 28(fa)*].

For recovery of overpayments of television and video games tax credits the provisions at *FA 1998, Sch 18 para 52* apply, see **6.4** ASSESSMENTS.

Films

[26.16] A special regime applies to film production companies.

The regime is discussed at **26.17–26.26** below.

A company is not able to claim film tax relief under *CTA 2009, Pt 15* and any of the television tax reliefs or video games tax relief in relation to the same expenditure. Similarly a company is not able to claim enhanced R&D relief under *CTA 2009, Pt 13*, or under *Pt 3 Ch 6A* (R&D expenditure tax credit) as well as film tax relief under *Pt 15*. Similarly relief under the Intangible Fixed Assets (IFA) regime at *CTA 2009, Pt 8* does not apply to assets representing production expenditure on a film to which the taxation provisions below apply. Such expenditure represents 'excluded assets' for the purposes of the IFA regime.

See HMRC Film production Company Manual.

Films and film production companies

[26.17] Corporation tax relief is available for expenditure on a 'film' that qualifies for relief.

A '*film*' includes any record, however made, of a sequence of visual images that is capable of being used as a means of showing that sequence as a moving picture. Each part of a series of films is treated as a separate film, unless the films form a series of not more than 26 parts, have a combined playing time of not more than 26 hours and the series is a self-contained work or is a documentary series with a common theme.

A film is completed when it is in such a condition that copies can be taken and distributed for presentation to the general public.

[*CTA 2009, s 1181; SI 2006 No 3399*].

A film qualifies for relief if all the following conditions are met.

(A) The film must be 'intended' for '*theatrical release*' (i.e. release to the paying public at the commercial cinema with the intention of obtaining the significant proportion of earnings from the release). A film is '*intended*' for theatrical release throughout an accounting period if it is intended for release at the end of that period. If it is not intended for release at the end of an accounting period, the condition is treated as not being met throughout that accounting period or in any subsequent accounting period but this does not affect any earlier accounting period where the condition was met.

(B) The film must be a '*British*' film, i.e. certified by the Secretary of State under the *Films Act 1985, Sch 1A*. Films may also be designated as British films by Order in Council if made in accordance with the terms of any agreement between the UK and any other government, international organisation or authority. The *Films Co-Production Agreements Order 1985, SI 1985 No 960*, as variously amended, lists the countries with such agreements.

(C) At least 10% of the 'core expenditure' on the film incurred by the 'film production company' (or in the case of a 'qualifying co-production', by the 'co-producers') must be on '*UK expenditure*' (goods or services used or consumed in the UK). Any apportionment between UK and non-UK expenditure is to be made on a fair and reasonable basis. '*Core expenditure*' is the 'production expenditure' on pre-production, principal photography and post production. '*Production expenditure*' is expenditure on the film-making activities in connection with the film which are the activities involved in the development, pre-production, principal photography and post production of the film. The term 'principal photography' can include the generation of computer images in the film.

There can be only one 'film production company' in relation to the film. A 'film production company' is widely defined for this purpose to ensure the company has an active involvement in the film production and that its participation is not restricted to the provision or arrangement of finance. A '*film production company*' in relation to a film is the company that (otherwise than in partnership):

- is responsible for the pre-production, principal photography and the post-production of the film and is actively engaged in planning and decision-making during these stages;
- is responsible for delivery of the completed film;
- directly negotiates, contracts and pays for rights, goods and services in relation to the film.

A company may elect out of the regime, i.e. not to be treated as a film production company. The election must be made in the company's corporation tax return (either in the original return or by amendment to the original return). Similarly, the election may be withdrawn only by amending its return for the period. The election applies to films commencing principal photography in the accounting period in respect of which the return containing the election was made or any subsequent accounting periods.

In the case of a '*qualifying co-production*' (a film treated as a national film in the UK by virtue of an agreement between the UK government and any other government, international organisation or authority, as noted above), the film production company is a company that (otherwise than in partnership) is a co-producer and makes an effective creative, technical and artistic contribution to the film. A '*co-producer*' is a person who is a co-producer for the purposes of the qualifying co-production agreement. If there is more than one company that fits the description of a film production company in relation to a film, the company most directly engaged in the activities referred to is the film production company.

[*CTA 2009, ss 1180–1189, 1197; FA 1998, Sch 18 para 10*].

Computation of profits and gains

[26.18] In relation to films certified by the Secretary of State, under the *Films Act 1985, Sch 1*, as British films for the purpose of film tax relief and intended for theatrical release at the time principal photography commences, the production activities of the film production company in relation to the film are treated as a trade separate from any of its other activities. Such trade, '*the separate film trade*' is treated as commencing when pre-production of the film begins or, if earlier, when any income from the film is received by the company.

'*Film-making activities*' means activities involved in the development, pre-production, principal photography and post-production of the film and includes computer generation of images. The Treasury may (by regulation) amend this definition. Expenditure incurred by the company on film-making activities in connection with the film or on activities with a view to exploiting the film ('*costs of the film*') is deductible as revenue expenditure subject to the normal restrictions under the Corporation Taxes Acts. Expenditure is treated as revenue if it would otherwise be regarded as capital by reason only of being incurred on the creation of the film.

'*Income*' means any receipts by the company in connection with the making or exploitation of the film. For this purpose, capital receipts are treated as revenue. '*Income from the film*' includes receipts from the sale of the film or rights in it, royalties or other payments for use of the film or aspects of it, payments for rights to produce games or other merchandise, and receipts by way of a profit share agreement.

Pre-trading expenditure is treated as having been incurred immediately after the company began the separate film trade. Estimates must be made at the balance sheet date for each period of account on a just and reasonable basis taking into account all relevant circumstances. If such expenditure has already been taken into account for other tax purposes, the company tax return must be amended accordingly (notwithstanding any limitation on the time within which an amendment may normally be made).

In determining the profit or loss for the first period of account, the costs of the film incurred in that period are brought into account as a debit and the proportion of estimated total income from the film treated as earned in the period is brought into account as a credit. For any subsequent period of account, the difference between the costs of the film incurred to date and the corresponding amount for the previous period is brought into account as a debit. Similarly, the difference between the proportion of estimated total income from the film treated as earned at the end of that period and the corresponding amount for the previous period is brought into account as a credit.

The proportion of estimated total income from the film treated as earned at the end of any period of account is determined by the formula C/T × I where C is the total costs incurred to date, T is the estimated total cost of the film and I is the estimated total income from the film. Estimates are to be made as at the balance sheet date for each period of account, on a fair and reasonable basis and considering all relevant circumstances.

Costs are treated as incurred when they are represented in the state of completion of the work in progress. Accordingly, payments in advance are to be ignored until work has been represented in the state of completion. Unpaid amounts are included in costs only if there is an unconditional obligation to pay them but if the obligation is linked to income being earned from the film, the costs can be included only when the appropriate amount of income is or has been taken into account.

[*CTA 2009, ss 1190–1200*].

Enhanced relief

[26.19] Film tax relief is available for expenditure on a film that qualifies for film tax relief (as above) and where a claim is made. The film production company can claim an enhanced deduction in respect of '*qualifying expenditure*' on the film, such expenditure being defined as 'core expenditure' (see above). The rate of enhancement is 100%.

For the first period of account during which the trade is carried on, the additional deduction is the relevant enhancement rate above multiplied by the lower of:

- the amount of the qualifying UK expenditure; or
- 80% of the total amount of qualifying expenditure.

For any subsequent period of account the additional deduction is:

- the relevant enhancement rate above multiplied by the lower of the amount of the qualifying UK expenditure incurred to date or 80% of the total amount of qualifying expenditure incurred to date;
- less the amount of the additional deduction (or aggregate amount of additional deductions) given in the previous period (or periods).

Film tax credits

[26.20] A film production company may claim a payable film tax credit for an accounting period in which it has a '*surrenderable loss*' which is equal to the lower of the amount of the trading loss for that period and the 'available qualifying expenditure', see further below. The trading loss is accordingly reduced for any amount so surrendered. The credit is not treated as income for tax purposes. The amount of the credit is 25% of the amount of the loss surrendered.

The surrenderable loss is the lower of:

(i) the company's trading loss for that period in the separate film trade, plus any unsurrendered loss brought forward (its 'available loss'); and

(ii) the available qualifying expenditure.

For the first period of account during which the trade is carried on, the '*available qualifying expenditure*' is the lower of:

- the amount of the qualifying UK expenditure; or
- 80% of the total amount of qualifying expenditure.

For any subsequent period of account the '*available qualifying expenditure*' is:

- the lower of the amount of the qualifying UK expenditure incurred to date or 80% of the total amount of qualifying expenditure incurred to date;
- less the amount of the loss surrendered (or aggregate amounts surrendered) in the previous period (or periods).

In determining the amount of the available qualifying expenditure for tax credit purposes, no account is taken of costs still unpaid four months after the end of the period of account in question.

Where a company is entitled to a film tax credit and makes a claim, the credit will be paid by HMRC but any amount payable in respect of the credit or interest thereon may be applied in discharging the company's liability to corporation tax. HMRC need not pay the credits (or may pay as much as they think fit) until the completion of enquiries into the company's tax return. Nor need they pay the credits before the company has settled its liabilities in an accounting period for PAYE, Class 1 National Insurance contributions or tax for foreign entertainers under *ITA 2007, s 966*. Relief is denied to the extent it arises from artificially inflated claims (as defined).

[*CTA 2009, ss 1201, 1202; F(No 2)A 2017, Sch 4 para 139*].

Claims and overpayments

[26.21] A claim for film tax relief must be made in a company tax return (or amended return) (see **65.4, 65.8** RETURNS) for the accounting period for which the claim is made, within one year of the filing date for that return or by such later time as HMRC may allow. It can similarly only be amended or withdrawn by amendment of the company tax return within the same time limit. It must specify the quantum of the amount claimed. Penalties are dealt with under *FA 2007, Sch 24* (penalties for errors), see **58** PENALTIES.

For the purposes of a claim to tax credit an amount unpaid four months after the end of the accounting period is not taken into account. There is an anti-avoidance provision which applies when a transaction is part of transactions for a 'disallowable purpose'. A '*disallowable purpose*' is one which aims to give the company an additional deduction or a higher tax credit.

[*CTA 2009, ss 1201–1205; FA 1998, Sch 18 paras 10(4), 83S–83X*].

For recovery of overpayments of film tax credit, see **6.4** ASSESSMENTS.

Entitlement to relief

[26.22] Entitlement to the above relief is further conditional on the film continuing to meet the requirements for certification as a 'British film', the minimum percentage on UK expenditure and status (where a claim is made on that basis) as a limited-budget film.

In the company's '*completion period*', in which the film is completed or abandoned, the company tax return for that period must state that the film has been completed or abandoned and be accompanied by:

- a final certificate (from the Secretary of State under the *Films Act 1985, Sch 1*) (such a certificate also having effect for previous periods). Without the certificate, or if the certificate is revoked, entitlement to relief is withdrawn for any period and the company tax return must be amended for any period for which relief was claimed. If the film is abandoned, the return may be accompanied by an interim certificate in which case the company would still be entitled to relief in that or any previous period; and
- a final statement of the amount of core expenditure that is UK expenditure. If the condition for UK expenditure is not met, entitlement to relief is withdrawn for any period and the company tax return must be amended for any period for which relief was claimed.

In any earlier accounting period ('interim accounting period') of the company the company tax return must:

(i) be accompanied by an interim certificate (similarly from the Secretary of State under the *Films Act 1985, Sch 1*). If an interim certificate ceases to be in force or is revoked then, unless a final certificate is provided as above, entitlement to relief is withdrawn for any period for which relief depended on the certificate and the company tax return for any such period must be amended accordingly; and

(ii) state the amount of planned core expenditure that is UK expenditure and that the UK expenditure condition will be met on completion of the film. If it subsequently appears that the UK expenditure condition will not be met, relief is withdrawn for any period for which its entitlement depended on such a statement and the company tax return for any such period must be amended accordingly.

The normal time limits for amendments or assessments do not apply in this case.

[*CTA 2009, ss 1212–1216*].

Confidentiality

[26.23] *CRCA 2005, s 18(1)* does not prevent HMRC disclosing information to the Secretary of State or the UK Film Council in relation certification of films as British films for the purposes of film tax relief. There are restrictions on whom such information disclosed can in turn be disclosed to and provisions for prosecution for wrongful disclosure.

[*CTA 2009, ss 1206, 1207*].

Losses

[26.24] In the accounting periods of the film production company before that in which the film is completed or abandoned, relief for a trading loss is available only to the extent that it can be carried forward under *CTA 2010, s 45* or *s 45B* (see **51.6**, **51.7** LOSSES) to be set against profits of the same trade in a later period. Where a loss is set against such profits, the set off is ignored for the purposes of *CTA 2010, s 269ZB* (restriction on deductions for carried-forward losses from trading profits — see **51.13** LOSSES). Any such loss as is not attributable to film tax relief is treated as a loss incurred in the period to which it is carried forward.

To the extent they are not attributable to film tax relief, losses in later periods may be set against the profits of the same or earlier period under *CTA 2010, s 37*, carried forward for set-off against total profits under *CTA 2010, s 45A* (post-1 April 2017 losses only) or surrendered as GROUP RELIEF (**35**). The amount of a trading loss attributable to film tax relief is the total loss less the amount of the loss there would have been had there been no additional deduction for enhanced relief in that or in any earlier period. The amount of the trading loss attributable to film tax relief may be carried forward for set-off against profits of the same trade in a later period under *CTA 2010, s 45* or *s 45B*. Where a loss is set against such profits, the set off is ignored for the purposes of *CTA 2010, s 269ZB*. These provisions do not apply to a loss to the extent it is carried forward or surrendered as a terminal loss (as below).

If a film production company ceases to carry on the trade, it can elect to surrender part or all of any remaining losses (which could otherwise be carried forward as above) to another of its trades in relation to a qualifying film. The loss would be treated as a loss brought forward by that other trade in the accounting period following that at the end of which the cessation takes place. Part or all of such a loss can also be surrendered to a trade in relation to a qualifying film of another company in the same group (defined as for GROUP RELIEF (**35**) purposes). That company may elect for the surrendered loss to be treated as a loss brought forward by it for set off against profits of its accounting period beginning after the cessation.

Where a terminal loss is set off against profits of the same company or another group member, the set off is ignored for the purposes of *CTA 2010, s 269ZB*.

[*CTA 2009, ss 1208–1211; F(No 2)A 2017, Sch 4 paras 28–30*].

Terminal loss relief

[26.25] A loss claim by a claimant (which is also a film production company) in respect of a terminal loss incurred by another group company (see **26.24** above) must be included in the claimant company's corporation tax return for the accounting period of the claim, either when the return is filed or by amending the self assessment within the required time limit. The claim must state the surrendering company's name and the amount of relief, which must be quantifiable at the time the claim is made.

The claim must also give details of any group company not resident in the UK for tax purposes either in the surrendering company's accounting period of claim or the claimant's corresponding accounting period.

The amount available for surrender is calculated by taking the surrendering company's loss under *CTA 2009, s 1211* and deducting all amounts for which that company has given, and not withdrawn, notices of consent. There are rules to determine which claims and withdrawals are to be matched. The surrendering company's written consent ('notice of consent') is required to the claim, which must state:

(A) the surrendering company's name, tax reference and its accounting period to which the claim relates;
(B) the claimant company's name, tax reference and its accounting period to which the claim relates; and
(C) the amount of the terminal loss being surrendered.

A notice may not be amended, but can be withdrawn (by notice to the officer who had received the original notice of consent) and replaced. The notice of withdrawal must contain the consent of the surrendering company, unless the reason for the withdrawal is that the loss available for relief has been reduced. The surrendering company must also submit an amended corporation tax return or returns, if the return or returns for the periods in question have already been filed. If it does not do so, the notice is not effective.

A claim may be withdrawn until the latest of:

(a) a year from the claimant company's filing date for the accounting period of claim;
(b) where an enquiry has been opened, 30 days after the enquiry is closed;
(c) where a return is amended following an enquiry, 30 days after the amendment is issued; and
(d) where an amendment is appealed, 30 days after the appeal is settled,

but HMRC may agree to a later time limit.

There are provisions requiring the surrendering company to withdraw the notice or notices of consent where the amount available for surrender is reduced.

HMRC are given power to assess any other company which benefited from a loss relief claim where the tax due by the claimant company after a notice has been withdrawn remains unpaid six months after the surrendering companies time limit for claims, provided that the assessment must not be made more than two years after the time limit expires. The company so assessed has a right of recovery against the claimant company. There is also a power to assess where the relief given is found to be excessive.

[*SI 2007 No 678*].

Treasury powers

[26.26] The Treasury have powers to make provision, by order (approved by a resolution of the House of Commons) to make various amendments. They may provide that certain activities are not film-making activities, amend the definition or vary the minimum percentage of UK expenditure, provide that particular sorts of expenditure are not qualifying expenditure or amend the percentage of qualifying expenditure used to calculate the enhanced deduction. They may also, by order, vary the way in which surrenders and claims of losses are made.

[*CTA 2009, ss 1183, 1198–1200, 1211*].

Simon's Taxes. See **division D7.12.**

Theatrical productions relief

[26.27] Theatrical productions relief provides relief for a production company by giving an additional deduction for certain qualifying expenses and by providing a payable theatre tax credit when a company surrenders certain losses arising in its trade, in a similar way as for film, television, animation and video games tax relief (as above).

See also HMRC Theatre Tax Relief Manual.

Definitions and basic concepts

[26.28] Key definitions and points of interpretation are as follows:

'*Theatrical production*' means a dramatic production or ballet. A '*dramatic production*' is a production of a play, opera, musical or other dramatic piece (which may include improvisation, and may include a circus show) which meets the following conditions: the actors, singers, dancers or other performers give their performance through roles; each performance in the proposed run is live (meaning the performers are actually present in front of the audience); and the presentation of a live performance is the main object (or one of the main objects) of the company's activities with regard to the production. As indicated in the explanatory notes to the *Finance Bill 2014*, a circus may be considered a dramatic piece where, for example, the performance is scripted and the performers play roles as opposed to something like a pure high-wire trapeze performance which is generally regarded as an indoor sport.

A dramatic production or ballet is not regarded as a theatrical production if any of the following apply:

- the main purpose, or one of the main purposes, for which it is made is to advertise or promote any goods or services;
- the performance includes a competition or contest;
- a wild animal (being an animal which is not commonly domesticated in the British Isles) is to be used (in that it performs or is shown) in any performance;
- the performance is of a sexual nature (meaning that it would be reasonable to assume such content is included solely or principally for the purpose of sexually stimulating any member of the audience, verbally or otherwise); or
- the making of a recording of the performance as a film (as defined in *CTA 2009, s 1181*, for film relief, see above), or part of a film, for exhibition to the paying general public at the cinema, or for broadcast to the general public (by any means, including television, radio or the internet), is the main object, or one of the main objects, of the company's activities with regard to the production.

There can only be one production company in relation to a theatrical production. In order to be a '*production company*' in relation to a theatrical production the company (not being in a partnership) must be responsible for producing, running and closing the theatrical production and be actively engaged in decision-making during those phases. The company must also make an effective creative, technical and artistic contribution to the production and directly negotiate, contract and pay for rights, goods and services in relation to the production.

Where there is more than one company meeting these conditions the company most directly engaged in the activities referred to is the production company. It is also possible that there may not be a production company associated with a theatrical production if no company meets the criteria.

'*Core expenditure*' means expenditure on activities involved in producing and closing the production, such as the costs of the costumes, and the final striking of the set. This does not include expenditure on any matters not directly involved in producing the production, so this will exclude financing, marketing, legal services, or storage, and it does not include expenditure on the ordinary running of the production. However, expenditure on or after the first performance with regard to a substantial recasting, or a substantial redesign of the set may be treated as core expenditure.

The '*costs of a theatrical production*' means expenditure incurred on the activities in developing, producing, running and closing the production, or activities with a view to exploiting the production. This is subject to the trade profit calculation rules in the Corporation Tax Acts which may prohibit or restrict a deduction, save that capital expenditure incurred on the creation of an asset, here the theatrical production, is treated as being of a revenue nature.

HM Treasury may amend the above definitions of core expenditure and production costs by regulation in particular to provide that certain activities are, or are not, activities involved in developing, or producing, running or closing a theatrical production.

'*European expenditure*' means expenditure on goods or services that are provided from within the UK or European Economic Area. This may be amended by regulation. Any apportionment between non-European expenditure and European expenditure is made on a just and reasonable basis.

[*CTA 2009, ss 1217F–1217FC, 1217GB(2)(3), 1217GC, 1217O; SI 2019 No 689, Reg 16(27)(28)*].

Companies qualifying for the reliefs

[26.29] A company qualifies for theatrical production relief if it is the production company in relation to the production and it meets the commercial purpose condition and the European expenditure condition (subject to the tax avoidance provisions, see further **26.31** below). There are further conditions to be met with regard to accounting periods which are not the final accounting period of the theatrical trade, see further **26.33** below.

The commercial purpose condition is that at the beginning of the production phase the company must intend that all the live performances (or a high proportion) will be to paying members of the general public (thus private events will not be eligible unless those attending are charged with a view to making a profit). Educational performances also meet this condition. This allows for a charitable theatrical production company, whose main charitable aim is educational, to present to schools. However, a performance is not regarded as provided for educational purposes if the production company is, or is associated with, a person who has responsibility for the persons who will benefit from the performance provided, or is otherwise connected with such persons (by being their employer, for example). A production company is associated with a person where such person controls the production company, or where such person is a subsidiary company controlled by the production company, or another company under common control. Control is as defined in *CTA 2010, s 450* — see **16.6** CLOSE COMPANIES.

The European expenditure condition is that at least 25% of the core expenditure on the theatrical production is European expenditure (see above for definitions). The Treasury may amend this percentage by regulation.

A company which qualifies for relief may make a claim for the additional deduction in calculating the profit or loss of the separate theatrical trade (see below), and theatre tax credit where it has surrenderable losses. Such claim is made under the provisions of *FA 1998, Sch 18*. See further **26.31** below and **15.5** CLAIMS.

Taxation of the production company with a separate theatrical trade

[26.30] Where a production company makes a claim for an accounting period for the additional deduction with regard to a production, then the activities of such company in relation to the theatrical production are treated as a separate trade (distinct from any other activities of the company). Therefore if a production company were involved in more than one theatrical production it would have more than one trade.

The separate trade is treated as starting when the production phase begins or at the time when any income is first received from the production, whichever is earlier. Where the company tax return (per *FA 1998, Sch 18 para 3(1)*) in which the claim is made is for an accounting period later than the one in which the separate trade commenced, then the company must make any amendments to tax returns for earlier periods that may be necessary. The normal time limits for amendments and assessments are overridden as necessary in order to allow this provision to have effect.

Where, at any point, the company fails to meet the definition of '*production company*' in relation to the production (see above), then it is treated as ceasing to carry on the separate trade at that time.

The legislation provides the basic rules for the computation of amounts to be brought into account for the purposes of determining a profit or a loss for the separate trade of the production company.

For the first period of account: a debit is brought in for the costs of the theatrical production incurred (representing work done) to date; and a credit is brought in for the proportion of the estimated total income from the production, treated as earned at the end of that period (such income is determined by a set formula — see below).

The calculation is cumulative, so for subsequent periods of account the additional amounts for a particular year, being total costs and income incurred to date less the amounts used in previous years, are brought into account. Therefore: a debit is brought in for the difference between the costs incurred to date and the corresponding amount for the previous period; and a credit is brought in for the difference between the proportion of total estimated income treated as earned at the end of the period and the corresponding amount for the previous period.

The formula for calculating the proportion of total estimated income treated as earned at the end of a period of account is: (C / T) x I

Where:

C = total to date of the costs incurred (and represented in the work done);

T= the estimated total cost of the theatrical production; and

I = the estimated total income from the theatrical production.

'*Income from a theatrical production*' constitutes any receipts in connection with the making or exploitation of the production, and includes:

- receipts from the sale of tickets or of rights in the theatrical production;
- royalties or other payments for use of aspects of the theatrical production (for example characters or music);
- payments for rights to produce merchandise; and
- receipts received by the company by way of a profit share agreement.

Receipts which would be regarded as being of a capital nature are treated as being of a revenue nature under these provisions.

Costs of the production are as defined above. Costs are incurred at a given time when they are represented in the state of completion of the work in progress. Payments in advance are ignored until the work is done and deferred payments are recognised to the extent that the goods or services in question are represented in the state of completion of the work in progress. Only amounts for which there is an unconditional obligation to pay can be treated as incurred and where this obligation is linked to income being earned from the production, then the cost can only be included when an appropriate amount of income has been brought into account. Any amount that has not been paid four months after the end of the period of account is ignored.

With regard to pre-trading expenditure, where a company incurs expenditure on the 'costs of a theatrical production' which pre-dates the commencement of the separate trade, then it is treated as if it were expenditure incurred immediately after the company begins to carry on the trade. The company should amend its tax return if it has previously taken such expenditure into account. Such an amendment may be made regardless of the normal time limits.

Any estimates for the purposes of these provisions must be made as at the balance sheet date for each period of account on a just and reasonable basis, and must take into consideration all relevant circumstances.

[*CTA 2009, ss 1217H, 1217I–1217IF*].

The theatrical production tax reliefs

[26.31] Where a company which qualifies for the relief (as above) has made a claim for an accounting period then the company is entitled to make an additional deduction (which is essentially 100% of qualifying expenditure — but see below for details) in calculating its profit or loss from its separate trade for the accounting period concerned. It may then also claim a payable theatre tax credit where it has a surrenderable loss in that period. Both reliefs are based on the company's qualifying expenditure in relation to the theatrical production.

'*Qualifying expenditure*' is core expenditure (defined above) in relation to a theatrical production that is taken into account in calculating the profits and losses of the separate theatrical trade. To prevent double claims for relief certain expenditure is excluded: expenditure for which the company is entitled to an R&D expenditure credit under the RDEC provisions at *CTA 2009, Pt 3, Ch 6A*; and expenditure for which the company has obtained relief under *CTA 2009, Pt 13* (additional relief for R&D expenditure); see further **63** RESEARCH AND DEVELOPMENT EXPENDITURE.

Similarly relief under the Intangible Fixed Assets (IFA) regime at *CTA 2009, Pt 8* does not apply to assets held by a theatrical production company which represent expenditure on a theatrical production that is treated as a separate trade under these provisions. Such expenditure represents 'excluded assets' for the purposes of the IFA regime.

The additional deduction

The amount of the additional deduction is calculated as follows:

For the **first period of account** during which the separate theatrical trade is carried out the additional deduction is given by: E

Where 'E' is the lesser of the amount of:

- qualifying expenditure which is European expenditure (see above); or
- 80% of the total qualifying expenditure incurred to date.

In **subsequent periods of account** the additional deduction is: E – P

Where 'E' is the lesser of:

- the amount of qualifying expenditure incurred to date which is European expenditure; and
- 80% of the total amount of qualifying expenditure incurred to date.

'P' is the total amount of additional deductions for all previous periods.

These provisions may be amended by regulations.

[*CTA 2009, ss 1217H, 1217J–1217JA; SI 2019 No 689, Reg 16(29)*].

Theatre tax credits

A production company which is treated as carrying on a separate trade may claim a theatre tax credit of either 25% (touring production — see below) or 20% (non-touring production) of the surrenderable loss for an accounting period.

The '*surrenderable loss*' in an accounting period is the lesser of: the available loss for the separate theatrical trade for the period; and, the available qualifying expenditure for the period.

The '*available loss*' for an accounting period is: L + RUL

Where: L is the amount of the company's loss for the period in the separate theatrical trade; and RUL is the amount of any 'relevant unused loss' which is that part of the available loss for the previous accounting period that has neither been surrendered for tax credit nor carried forward under *CTA 2010, s 45* or *s 45B* and set against profits of the separate theatrical trade.

The '*available qualifying expenditure*' for these purposes, for the **first period of account** during which the trade is carried on, is the same as above, so is amount 'E'.

The '*available qualifying expenditure*' for **subsequent periods** is expenditure incurred to date less any amounts previously surrendered for credits as given by: E – S

Where: 'E' is the amount defined above (so as incurred to date); and, 'S' is the aggregate of the amounts surrendered for theatre tax credits in previous periods.

Any necessary apportionments (on a day count basis) can be made where a period of account of the separate theatrical trade does not coincide with an accounting period.

A company may surrender all or part of its surrenderable loss for a period and thus be entitled to a payable tax credit in respect of the surrender.

As noted, the payable tax credit rate is:

- 25% for touring theatrical productions; or
- 20% if the theatrical production is not touring.

A theatrical production is a '*touring*' production only if the company intends at the beginning of the production phase that the performances will be presented in six or more separate premises, or, that the performances will be presented in at least two separate premises and that there will be at least 14 performances.

Where a part of the loss is surrendered the company's available loss will be reduced by the surrendered amount.

Where a company is entitled to a theatre tax credit for a period, and it claims that credit, HMRC must pay the credit to the company. An amount of credit that is payable, or an amount of interest payable on such credit under *ICTA 1988, s 826*, may be set against any corporation tax that the company owes (which satisfies the obligation to pay the credit).

When the company's tax return is the subject of an enquiry then no payment need be made to the company until the enquiry is completed (*FA 1998, Sch 18 para 32*), although HMRC may make such provisional payments as it deems fit.

However, when the company owes HMRC any amount of PAYE, Class 1 National Insurance contributions or any amount due for visiting performers (*ITA 2007, s 966*), no payment need be made to the company until any such amounts due are paid.

A payment of a theatre tax credit is not income for the company for any tax purpose.

The total amount of any theatre tax credits payable for any undertaking is capped at Euro 50 million per year under EU State Aid limitations. '*Undertaking*' is as defined in the *General Block Exemption Regulation* (in force per *Art 1* of *Council Regulation (EC) No 994/98*). Following Brexit, the definition applies by reference to the Regulation as it had effect immediately before 11pm on 31 December 2020 (IP completion day).

[*CTA 2009, ss 1217K–1217KC; F(No 2)A 2017, Sch 4 para 142; SI 2020 No 1499*].

Anti-avoidance

Anti-avoidance provisions deny theatrical production tax relief where there are any tax avoidance arrangements in place relating to the production.

'*Tax avoidance arrangements*' are arrangements entered into where their main object, or one of their main objects, is to enable a company to obtain a tax advantage. '*Arrangements*' is broadly defined to include any scheme, agreement or understanding, whether or not legally enforceable. '*Tax advantage*' is as defined in *CTA 2010, s 1139*.

In addition, a transaction (other than tax avoidance arrangements) which is not entered into for genuine commercial reasons is ignored for determining the additional deduction and tax credit reliefs.

[*CTA 2009, ss 1217LA–1217LB*].

Losses of the theatrical trade

[26.32] Where a loss arises in the separate theatrical trade in any accounting period before that in which the trade ceases (the '*completion period*') the only loss relief that is available in respect of it is to carry forward the loss under *CTA 2010, s 45* or *s 45B* (see **51.6**, **51.7** LOSSES) to be set against profits of the same trade in a later period. Where a loss is set against such profits, the set off is ignored for the purposes of *CTA 2010, s 269ZB* (restriction on deductions for carried-forward losses from trading profits — see **51.13** LOSSES). If a loss is carried forward to the completion period, so much of it as is not attributable to the additional deduction in **26.31** above may be treated for loss relief purposes as if it were a loss made in the completion period.

A loss made in the completion period (or treated as so made) may, to the extent that it is not attributable to the additional deduction, be deducted from total profits of the same or an earlier period under *CTA 2010, s 37* (see **51.3**, **51.4** LOSSES) or surrendered as GROUP RELIEF (**35**).

Terminal loss relief

A company may make a claim for a loss, which would (had the separate exhibition trade not ceased) have been carried forward against future profits of the trade, to be treated as a loss brought forward to be set against the profits of another separate theatrical trade carried on by it for the first accounting period beginning after the cessation. Alternatively, the company may surrender all or part of the loss to another company ('company B') in the same group (defined as for GROUP RELIEF (35) purposes) which also carries on a separate theatrical trade. On the making of a claim by company B the surrendered loss is treated as a loss brought forward to be set against the profits of that trade for the first accounting period beginning after the cessation.

Where a terminal loss is set off against profits of the same company or another group member, the set off is ignored for the purposes of *CTA 2010, s 269ZB*.

The Treasury may by statutory instrument make administrative rules for the surrender of losses and resulting claims.

[*CTA 2009, ss 1217M–1217MC; F(No 2)A 2017, Sch 4 paras 40–42*].

Entitlement to relief

[26.33] As noted at **26.29** above, a company will qualify for theatrical production relief if it is the production company in relation to the production and it meets the commercial purpose condition and the European expenditure condition. However, a company is not entitled to relief (be it a claim for an additional deduction, theatre tax credits, or terminal loss relief) for an interim accounting period unless: its company tax return (per *FA 1998, Sch 18 para 3(1)*) for the period states the amount of planned core expenditure on the theatrical production that is European expenditure; and, that amount is such that the European expenditure condition will be met in relation to the production. If these requirements are met, then the company is provisionally treated for that period as if the European expenditure condition is met (provisional relief).

An '*interim accounting period*' with regard to a company means any accounting period that is one in which the company carries on the separate theatrical trade, and which precedes the accounting period in which the trade ceases.

Where the company has made such a statement in its tax return and is entitled to provisional relief, and it subsequently appears that the European expenditure condition will not be met on the company ceasing to carry on the separate theatrical trade, then the company is not entitled to provisional relief (as above) for any period which depended on that statement, and must amend its company tax return for such period.

Where a company ceases to carry on the separate theatrical trade the company tax return for the period in which cessation occurs must state that the company has ceased to so trade, and be accompanied by a final statement of the amount of core expenditure on the theatrical production that is European expenditure. If that statement shows that the European expenditure condition is not met then the company:

- is not entitled to any theatrical tax relief (be it a claim for an additional deduction, theatre tax credits, or terminal loss relief) for any period;
- is not treated as if the theatrical production is a separate trade for corporation tax purposes for any period; and

- therefore the provisions above with regard to the use of losses do not apply in relation to the theatrical production for any period.

The company must then amend its company tax return accordingly for any period in which it was treated as carrying on a separate theatrical trade. The normal time limits for amendments and assessments are overridden as necessary in order to allow these provisions to have effect.

[*CTA 2009, ss 1217N–1217NA; SI 2019 No 689, Reg 16(30)(31)*].

Claims and overpayments

[26.34] A claim for the theatrical tax reliefs above must be made in a company tax return (or amended return) (see **65.4**, **65.8** RETURNS) for the accounting period for which the claim is made, within one year of the filing date for that return or by such later time as HMRC may allow. It can similarly only be amended or withdrawn by amendment of the company tax return within the same time limit. It must specify the quantum of the amount claimed. The provisions of *FA 2007, Sch 24* with regard to penalties for errors applies, see **59** PENALTIES.

For recovery of overpayments of theatre tax credits the provisions at *FA 1998, Sch 18 para 52* apply, see **6.4** ASSESSMENTS.

[*FA 1998, Sch 18 paras 10(4), 83S–83X; FA 2007, Sch 24 para 28(fa)*].

Orchestral concerts

[26.35] The main features of the special regime for orchestral concert production companies are as follows.

- Orchestra tax relief applies to companies which are responsible for the production of orchestral concerts, i.e. concerts by an orchestra, ensemble, group or band consisting wholly or mainly of instrumentalists who are the primary focus of the event. Companies qualify for relief for single concerts or, by election, a series of concerts. See below.
- To qualify a company must intend that the concert (or all, or a high proportion of, the concerts) should be performed 'live' before the paying public or for educational purposes. See **26.36** below.
- At least 25% of the core expenditure (as defined) by the company on the production of the concert or series of concerts must be on goods or services provided from within the UK or European Economic Area. See **26.36** below.
- Where a production company qualifies for orchestra tax relief on the production of a concert or series, the company's activities in relation to the concert's, or series', production are treated as a trade separate from any of its other activities. Special rules apply to compute the profits or losses of the separate orchestral trade. See **26.37** below. Losses are ring-fenced so that they can only be set against future profits of the separate trade. When the trade ceases, any remaining losses can be set against the profits of another separate orchestral trade or surrendered to another company in the same group which also carries on a separate orchestral trade. See **26.40** below.

- A company which qualifies for orchestra tax relief may claim an additional deduction for each accounting period in calculating the profit or loss of the separate orchestral trade. Broadly, the additional deduction for an accounting period is the core expenditure for the period which is European expenditure or, if less, 80% of the core expenditure. Only expenditure incurred before 1 April 2022 qualifies. See **26.38** below.
- If the company makes a loss in the separate trade it may surrender the whole or part of its surrenderable loss (as defined) for the accounting period. The amount of the credit is 25% of the loss surrendered. The total tax credits payable to any undertaking must not exceed 50 million euros per year in accordance with EU State aid limitations. See **26.44** below.
- A claim for orchestra tax relief must be made in a company tax return (or amended return) for the accounting period for which the claim is made, within one year of the filing date for that return or by such later time as HMRC may allow.

See also HMRC Orchestra Tax Relief Manual.

Definitions

An '*orchestral concert*' is a concert by an orchestra, ensemble, group or band consisting wholly or mainly of instrumentalists who are the primary focus of the event. A concert is, however, excluded from the regime if:

- a main purpose of the concert is to advertise or promote goods or services;
- it consists of or includes a competition or contest; or
- the main object of the production company's activities in relation to the concert is making a recording for broadcast or release to the public, for use as a soundtrack to a tv, radio, theatre, video game or similar production for broadcast, exhibition or release or for use in a film for exhibition at the commercial cinema.

A '*qualifying orchestral concert*' is an orchestral concert where there are at least 12 instrumentalists and none of the instruments, or only a minority of them, are electronically or directly amplified. A '*qualifying orchestral concert series*' is two or more orchestral concerts, all or a high proportion of which are qualifying orchestral concerts.

A '*production company*' in relation to a concert is the company that (otherwise than in partnership) is responsible for putting on the concert from the start of the production process to the finish, including employing or engaging the performers. The company must be actively engaged in decision-making for the concert and must make an effective creative, technical and artistic contribution to the concert and directly negotiate, contract and pay for rights, goods and services in relation to it. There can only be one production company for a concert and where there is more than one company meeting the conditions the company most directly engaged in the activities referred to is the production company. It is also possible that there may not be a production company in relation to a concert if no company meets the criteria.

[*CTA 2009, ss 1217PA, 1217PB, 1217RA(3)(5)*].

Companies qualifying for relief

[26.36] A company which is the production company of a single qualifying orchestral concert (see **26.35** above) qualifies for orchestra tax relief in relation to the concert if:

(i) it intends that the concert should be performed 'live' before the paying public or for educational purposes; and

(ii) at least 25% of the 'core expenditure' by the company on the production of the concert is '*European expenditure*' (i.e. expenditure on goods or services provided from within the UK or the European Economic Area ('EEA')). Any necessary apportionment of expenditure must be made on a just and reasonable basis.

A company which is the production company of a qualifying orchestral concert series (see **26.35** above) qualifies for orchestra tax relief in relation to the series if it makes the election at **26.37** below and:

(a) it intends that all, or a high proportion of, the concerts should be performed live before the paying public or for educational purposes; and

(b) at least 25% of the core expenditure by the company on the production of the series is European expenditure. Any necessary apportionment of expenditure must be made on a just and reasonable basis.

In (i) and (a) above a concert is '*live*' if it is to an audience before whom the musicians are actually present. A concert is not for educational purposes if the production company is, or is associated with, a person who has responsibility for, or is otherwise connected with, the persons for whose benefit the concert is to be performed. A company is associated with a person if that person controls (within *CTA 2010, s 450*) the company or if that person is a company controlled by the production company or by a person who also controls the production company.

'*Core expenditure*' is expenditure on the activities involved in producing the concert or series, including on travel to and from a venue which is not a usual venue for concerts produced by the company. Expenditure (such as financing, marketing, legal services or storage) on any matters not directly involved with, and speculative expenditure on activities not involved with, putting on the concert or series is excluded. Expenditure on the actual performances (such as payments to the musicians) is also excluded.

The Treasury may amend the conditions in (ii) and (b) above by statutory instrument.

[*CTA 2009, ss 1217RA–1217RC; SI 2019 No 689, Reg 16(33)(34)*].

Computation of profits

[26.37] Where a production company qualifies for orchestra tax relief on the production of a concert, the company's activities in relation to the concert's production are treated as a trade separate from any of its other activities. That trade, '*the separate orchestral trade*' is treated as commencing at the beginning of the pre-performance stage of the concert or, if earlier, when the first income from the production of the concert is received.

A company which is the production company of a qualifying orchestral concert series (see **26.35** above) may make an election so that the company's activities in relation to the production of the whole series are treated as a single trade separate from any of its other activities (including activities relating to any concerts which are not part of the series). An election is irrevocable and must be made by notice in writing to HMRC before the first concert in the series. The notice must specify the concerts to be included in the election and indicate if any of them will not be qualifying orchestral concerts. The election may apply to concerts in more than one accounting period. The trade, '*the separate orchestral trade*' is treated as commencing at the beginning of the pre-performance stage of the first concert or, if earlier, when the first income from the production of the series is received.

In computing the profits of the separate orchestral trade, income from a production of a concert or series means any receipts by the company in connection with the production or exploitation of the concert or series, including receipts from the sale of tickets or rights in the concert or series, royalties or other payments for use of the concert or series, payments for rights to produce merchandise, and receipts by way of a profit share agreement. Capital receipts are treated as revenue.

The costs of a production of a concert or series means expenditure incurred by the company on activities involved in developing and putting on the concert or series or activities with a view to exploiting the concert or series. Deduction of such costs is subject to the normal restrictions in calculating the taxable profits of a trade, but expenditure is treated as revenue if it would otherwise be capital by reason only of being incurred on the creation of the concert or series. The costs that have been incurred at a given time do not include any unpaid amount unless it is subject to an unconditional obligation to pay. An obligation to pay an amount which is linked to income being earned from the production of the concert or series is not treated as unconditional unless the appropriate income has been brought into account under the provisions below.

Pre-trading expenditure is treated as having been incurred immediately after the company began the separate orchestral trade. If such expenditure has already been taken into account for other tax purposes, the company tax return must be amended accordingly (regardless of the normal time limits for making amendments).

In determining the profit or loss for the first period of account, the costs of the production of the concert or series incurred in that period are brought into account as a debit and the proportion of estimated total income from that production treated as earned in the period is brought into account as a credit. For any subsequent period of account, the difference between the costs of the production of the concert or series incurred to date and the corresponding amount for the previous period is brought into account as a debit. Similarly, the difference between the proportion of estimated total income from the production of the concert or series treated as earned at the end of that period and the corresponding amount for the previous period is brought into account as a credit.

The proportion of estimated total income from the production of the concert of series treated as earned at the end of any period of account is determined by the formula C/T × I where C is the total costs incurred to date, T is the estimated total cost of the production of the concert or series and I is the estimated total income from the concert or series. Estimates are to be made as at the balance sheet date for each period of account, on a fair and reasonable basis and considering all relevant circumstances.

[*CTA 2009, ss 1217Q–1217QG*].

Orchestra tax relief

[26.38] A company which qualifies for orchestra tax relief (see **26.36** above) may claim an additional deduction for an accounting period in calculating the profit or loss of the separate orchestra trade (see **26.37** above) for the period. It may also claim an orchestra tax credit for an accounting period in which it has a 'surrenderable loss' (see below).

For the purposes of the two reliefs, in determining the amount of costs incurred on a production of a concert or series at the end of a period of account, any amount which is unpaid four months after the end of the period is ignored.

Additional deduction

The amount of the additional deduction for an accounting period is calculated as follows. For the first period of account during which the separate orchestra trade is carried on, the deduction is so much of the 'qualifying expenditure' incurred in the period as is European expenditure or, if less, 80% of the total qualifying expenditure incurred in the period.

For any subsequent period of account the deduction is equal to:

- the total of the qualifying expenditure incurred to date as is European expenditure or, if less, 80% of the total qualifying expenditure incurred to date; *less*
- the total additional deductions given for pervious periods.

'*Qualifying expenditure*' for this purpose is core expenditure (see **26.36** above) on the production of the concert or series which is taken into account in computing the profits or losses of the separate orchestral trade other than expenditure which is otherwise relievable under any of the other reliefs in this chapter (i.e. the reliefs for films, tv, video games or theatrical productions).

Where a claim for the additional deduction is made in a return for an accounting period later than that in which the separate orchestra trade commenced, the company must make any necessary amendments to earlier returns (without regard to any time limits which would otherwise prevent any such amendments).

The Treasury may amend the 80% figure specified above by statutory instrument.

Orchestra tax credits

A company which claims an orchestra tax credit may surrender the whole or part of its surrenderable loss for the accounting period. The amount of the credit is 25% of the loss surrendered. The total tax credits payable to any undertaking must not exceed 50 million euros per year in accordance with EU State aid limitations.

The '*surrenderable loss*' for an accounting period is the 'available loss' for the period in the separate orchestra trade or, if less, the 'available qualifying expenditure' for the period. The '*available loss*' is the loss for the period plus so much of any available loss for the previous accounting period as has not been surrendered as tax credit or carried forward under *CTA 2010, s 45* or *s 45B* (see **51.6, 51.7** LOSSES) and set off against profits of the separate orchestral trade. The '*available qualifying expenditure*' for a period of account is the total of the qualifying expenditure incurred to date as is European expenditure or, if less, 80% of the total qualifying expenditure incurred to date, less, for any but the first period of account, the total amount previously surrendered as tax credit. If a period of account does not coincide with an accounting period, any necessary apportionments needed to find the available qualifying expenditure for the accounting period must be made by reference to the number of days in the periods concerned.

Tax credits are normally paid by HMRC to the company but they may instead apply the credit, together with any interest on it, to discharge any liability of the company to corporation tax. HMRC are not required to pay any tax credit in respect of an accounting period whilst an enquiry into the return for the period is open (but may do so on a provisional basis). If the company owes HMRC any amount of PAYE or Class 1 NICs or any amount due under *ITA 2007, s 966* (visiting performers) for any payment period ending in the accounting period, HMRC are not required to make a payment of tax credit until any such amounts are paid.

The available loss for the period is reduced by the amount surrendered. Orchestra tax credits are not income of the recipient for any tax purposes.

Anti-avoidance

A company does not qualify for orchestra tax relief if there are any tax avoidance arrangements relating to the production of the concert or series. Arrangements (as widely defined) are tax avoidance arrangements if they have as a main purpose the obtaining of a tax advantage (within *CTA 2010, s 1139*).

A transaction is ignored in determining any orchestra tax relief to the extent that it is attributable to arrangements entered into otherwise than for genuine commercial reasons.

[*CTA 2009, ss 1217R–1217RM; F(No 2)A 2017, Sch 4 para 143; SI 2019 No 689, Reg 16(34)(35); SI 2020 No 1499*].

Claims and overpayments

[26.39] A claim for orchestra tax relief must be made in a company tax return (or amended return) (see **65.4, 65.8** RETURNS) for the accounting period for which the claim is made, within one year of the filing date for that return or by such later time as HMRC may allow. It can similarly only be amended or withdrawn by amendment of the company tax return within the same time limit. It must specify the amount claimed.

[*FA 1998, Sch 18 paras 10(4), 83S–83X*].

For recovery of overpayments of orchestra tax credit, see **6.4** ASSESSMENTS.

Provisional entitlement to relief

Where a company claims orchestra tax relief for any accounting period before that in which it ceases to carry on the separate orchestral trade, its return for the period must state the amount of planned core expenditure on the production of the concert or concert series that is European expenditure. That amount must indicate that the European expenditure condition at **26.36**(ii) or (b) above will be met. If it subsequently appears that the condition will not be met, relief for any period which depended on such a statement is withdrawn and the company must amend its returns accordingly.

The company's return for the accounting period in which the separate orchestral trade ceases must state that the trade has ceased and must be accompanied by a final statement of the amount of the core expenditure that is European expenditure. If the statement shows that the European expenditure condition is not met, the company is not entitled to any orchestra tax relief or to transfer its terminal losses and must amend its returns accordingly.

Amendments or assessments to give effect to these provisions can be made regardless of the normal time limits.

[*CTA 2009, ss 1217T, 1217TA; SI 2019 No 689, Reg 16(36)(37)*].

Losses

[26.40] Where a loss arises in the separate orchestral trade in any accounting period before that in which the trade ceases (the '*completion period*') the only loss relief that is available in respect of it is to carry forward the loss under *CTA 2010, s 45* or *s 45B* (see **51.6**, **51.7** LOSSES), to be set against profits of the same trade in a later period. Where a loss is set against such profits, the set off is ignored for the purposes of *CTA 2010, s 269ZB* (restriction on deductions for carried-forward losses from trading profits — see **51.13** LOSSES). If such a loss is carried forward to the completion period, so much of it as is not attributable to the additional deduction in **26.38** above may be treated for loss relief purposes as if it were a loss made in the completion period.

A loss made in the completion period (or treated as so made) may, to the extent that it is not attributable to the additional deduction, be deducted from total profits of the same or an earlier period under *CTA 2010, s 37* (see **51.3**, **51.4** LOSSES) or surrendered as GROUP RELIEF (**35**).

Terminal loss relief

A company may make a claim for a loss, which would (had the separate orchestral trade not ceased) have been carried forward against future profits of the trade, to be treated as a loss brought forward to be set against the profits of another separate orchestral trade carried on by it for the first accounting period beginning after the cessation. Alternatively, the company may surrender all or part of the loss to another company ('company B') in the same group (defined as for GROUP RELIEF (35) purposes) which also carries on a separate orchestral trade. On the making of a claim by company B the surrendered loss is treated as a loss brought forward to be set against the profits of that trade for the first accounting period beginning after the cessation.

Where a terminal loss is set off against profits of the same company or another group member, the set off is ignored for the purposes of *CTA 2010, s 269ZB*.

The Treasury may by statutory instrument make administrative rules for the surrender of losses and resulting claims.

[*CTA 2009, ss 1217S–1217SC; F(No 2)A 2017, Sch 4 paras 44–46*].

Museum and gallery exhibitions

[26.41] The special regime for museum and gallery exhibition production companies applies for accounting periods beginning on or after 1 April 2017. For this purpose, an accounting period which straddles that date is treated as two separate accounting periods, the second of which starts on 1 April 2017. Any necessary apportionments between the two notional periods must be made on a just and reasonable basis. [*F(No 2)A 2017, Sch 6 para 21*].

The main features of the regime are as follows.

- Exhibition tax relief applies to companies which are responsible for the production of public exhibitions, i.e. curated public displays of an organised collection of objects or works of scientific, historic, artistic or cultural interest. Where the exhibition is produced at a single venue only one production company qualifies. If the exhibition is produced at more than one venue, however, additional companies may qualify if they are responsible for the production of the exhibition at one or more of the venues. See below.
- To qualify a company must either be a charitable company which maintains a museum or gallery or wholly owned by a company or local authority which maintains a museum or gallery. See **26.42** below.
- At least 25% of the core expenditure (as defined) by the company on the production of the exhibition must be on goods or services provided from within the UK or the European Economic Area. See **26.42** below.
- Where a production company qualifies for exhibition tax relief on the production of an exhibition, the company's activities in relation to the exhibition's production are treated as a trade separate from any of its other activities. Special rules apply to compute the profits or losses of the separate exhibition trade. see **26.43** below. Losses are ring-fenced so that they can only be set against future profits of the separate trade. When the trade ceases, any remaining losses can be set against the profits of another separate exhibition trade or surrendered to another company in the same group which also carries on a separate exhibition trade. See **26.46** below.

- A company which qualifies for exhibition tax relief may claim an additional deduction for each accounting period in calculating the profit or loss of the separate exhibition trade. Broadly, the additional deduction for an accounting period is the core expenditure for the period which is European expenditure or, if less, 80% of the core expenditure. Only expenditure incurred before 1 April 2022 qualifies. See **26.44** below.
- If the company makes a loss in the separate trade it may surrender the whole or part of its surrenderable loss (as defined) for the accounting period. If the exhibition is a touring exhibition, the amount of the credit is 25% of the loss surrendered, subject to a maximum of £100,000. Otherwise the amount of the credit is 20% of the loss surrendered, subject to a maximum of £80,000. The total tax credits payable to any undertaking must not exceed 50 million euros per year in accordance with EU State aid limitations. See **26.44** below.
- A claim for exhibition tax relief must be made in a company tax return (or amended return) for the accounting period for which the claim is made, within one year of the filing date for that return or by such later time as HMRC may allow.

See also HMRC Museums and Galleries Exhibition Tax Relief Manual.

Definitions

An '*exhibition*' is a curated public display of an organised collection of objects or works (or of a single object or work) which are considered to be of scientific, historic, artistic or cultural interest. A display is public for this purpose if the general public are admitted to it. It does not matter whether or not the public are charged for admission or if a single opening session or a small number of sessions are restricted to visitors other than the general public. A display is excluded if:

- it is organised in connection with a competition of any kind;
- a main purpose of the display is selling anything displayed or advertising or promoting any goods or services;
- it includes a live performance by any person (other than one which is merely incidental to, or forms a merely incidental part of, the collection displayed);
- anything displayed is for sale; or
- anything displayed is alive.

An exhibition is a '*touring exhibition*' if:

(a) there is a primary production company (see below) for the exhibition which is within the charge to corporation tax;
(b) when planning the exhibition, the company intends that (c)–(e) below will be satisfied;
(c) the exhibition is held at two or more venues;
(d) at least 25% of the object or works displayed at the first venue are also displayed at every subsequent venue; and
(e) there is no more than six months between deinstallation of the exhibition at one venue and installation at the next.

A company is the '*primary production company*' for an exhibition if it makes an effective creative, technical or artistic contribution to the exhibition and directly negotiates for, contracts for and pays for rights, goods and services in relation to it. If the exhibition is held at only one venue the company must be responsible for the production of the exhibition there. If the exhibition is held at two or more venues, the company must be responsible for the production of the exhibition at (at least) the first venue. The company must not be acting in partnership. If more than one company meets these conditions, the company that most directly meets them is the primary production company. If no company meets the conditions there is no primary production company.

A company is responsible for the production of an exhibition at a venue if it is responsible for producing, running and, if the exhibition is temporary, deinstalling and closing it there and the company is actively engaged in decision-making in relation to the exhibition at the venue.

If an exhibition is held at more than one venue then there may be one or more secondary production companies for it. A company is a '*secondary production company*' for an exhibition at a venue if it is not the primary production company but is responsible for the production of the exhibition at the venue. The company must not be acting in partnership. If more than one company meets these conditions for a particular venue, the company that most directly meets them is the secondary production company for the exhibition at that venue. If no company meets the conditions there is no such secondary production company.

[*CTA 2009, ss 1218ZAA–1218ZAD; F(No 2)A 2017, Sch 6 para 1*].

Companies qualifying for relief

[26.42] A company which is the primary production company or a secondary production company for an exhibition (see **26.41** above) qualifies for exhibition tax relief in relation to the exhibition if:

(i) either it is a charitable company which maintains a museum or gallery or it is wholly owned by a company or local authority (see further below) which maintains a museum or gallery;
(ii) it intends that the exhibition should be public (see **26.41** above); and
(iii) at least 25% of the 'core expenditure' by the company on the production of the exhibition is '*European expenditure*' (i.e. expenditure on goods or services provided from within the UK or the European Economic Area (EEA)). Any necessary apportionment of expenditure must be made on a just and reasonable basis.

In (i) above, 'museum or gallery' includes a library, archive or an outdoor exhibition site. A company which has an ordinary share capital is wholly owned by a charity which maintains a museum or gallery if every part of that share capital is owned by one or two charities, each of which maintains a museum or gallery. A company which is limited by guarantee is wholly owned by a charity which maintains a museum or gallery if there are no more than two 'beneficiaries' of the company and each of them is either a charity which maintains a museum or gallery or a company wholly owned by such a charity. A company is wholly owned by a local authority if its entire ordinary share capital is owned by the local authority or, where the company is limited by guarantee, the local authority is the sole beneficiary. for these purposes, ordinary share capital is treated as owned by a charity or local authority if it directly or indirectly owns the share capital within the meaning of *CTA 2010, ss 1154–1156* (taking the references in those sections to bodies corporate to include a charity or local authority). A '*beneficiary*' of a company is a person who is beneficially entitled to participate in the company's divisible profits or who will be so entitled to share in the company's net assets on its winding up.

'*Core expenditure*' is expenditure on the activities involved in producing, deinstalling and closing the exhibition at each venue for which the company's activities form part of its separate exhibition trade (see **26.43** below). Expenditure on deinstalling and closing the exhibition at a venue is only core expenditure if the exhibition is open at the venue for no more than 12 months. Expenditure on storage of the exhibits for a single venue exhibition is excluded. In the case of an exhibition held at more than one venue, only expenditure incurred on storage of the exhibits between deinstallation at one venue and the opening of the exhibition at the next is included, and only where storage is at a location other than an exhibition venue. Only storage expenditure for a period not exceeding four months is included. The following types of expenditure are excluded:

- expenditure (such as financing, marketing, legal services or promotional events) on any matters not directly involved with putting on the exhibition;
- speculative development expenditure on initial concepts and feasibility;
- expenditure on the ordinary running of the exhibition and on further development while it is running;
- expenditure relating to any live performance;
- expenditure on purchasing the exhibits; and
- expenditure on infrastructure, unless incurred solely for the exhibition.

The Treasury may amend the condition in (iii) above by statutory instrument. It may similarly amend the meaning of 'core expenditure' to provide that specified activities are not to be treated as activities in developing, producing, running, deinstalling or closing an exhibition or an exhibition of a specified type.

[*CTA 2009, ss 1218ZCA–1218ZCD, 1218ZF; F(No 2)A 2017, Sch 6 para 1; SI 2019 No 689, Reg 16(39)(40)*].

Computation of profits

[26.43] Where a primary or secondary production company qualifies for exhibition tax relief on the production of an exhibition, the company's activities in relation to the exhibition's production are treated as a trade (the'*separate exhibition trade*') separate from any of its other activities (including producing any other exhibition). In the case of a primary production company, the trade is treated as commencing at the beginning of the production stage of the exhibition at its first venue or, if earlier, when the first income from the production of the exhibition is received. The trade is treated as ceasing when the exhibition closes at its last venue. In the case of a secondary production company, the trade is treated as commencing at the beginning of the production stage of the exhibition at the first venue for which the company is the secondary production company or, if earlier, when the first income from the production of the exhibition is received by the company. The trade is treated as ceasing when the exhibition closes at the last venue for which the company is the secondary production company.

In computing the profits of the separate exhibition trade, income from a production of an exhibition means any receipts by the company in connection with the production or exploitation of the exhibition, including receipts from the sale of tickets or rights in the exhibition, royalties or other payments for exploitation of the exhibition or aspects of it, payments for rights to produce merchandise, grants made for the purposes of the exhibition and receipts by way of a profit share agreement.

The costs of a production of an exhibition means expenditure incurred by the company on activities involved in developing, producing, running, deinstalling and closing the exhibition or activities with a view to exploiting the exhibition. Deduction of such costs is subject to the normal restrictions in calculating the taxable profits of a trade. The costs that have been incurred at a given time do not include any unpaid amount unless it is subject to an unconditional obligation to pay. An obligation to pay an amount which is linked to income being earned from the production of the exhibition is not treated as unconditional unless the appropriate income has been brought into account under the provisions below.

Pre-trading expenditure is treated as having been incurred immediately after the company began the separate exhibition trade. If such expenditure has already been taken into account for other tax purposes, the company tax return must be amended accordingly (regardless of the normal time limits for making amendments).

In determining the profit or loss for the first period of account, the costs of the production of the exhibition incurred in that period are brought into account as a debit and the proportion of estimated total income from that production treated as earned in the period is brought into account as a credit. For any subsequent period of account, the difference between the costs of the production of the exhibition incurred to date and the corresponding amount for the previous period is brought into account as a debit. Similarly, the difference between the proportion of estimated total income from the production of the exhibition treated as earned at the end of that period and the corresponding amount for the previous period is brought into account as a credit.

The proportion of estimated total income from the production of the exhibition treated as earned at the end of any period of account is determined by the formula $C/T \times I$ where C is the total costs incurred to date, T is the estimated total cost of the production of the exhibition and I is the estimated total income from the concert or series. Estimates are to be made as at the balance sheet date for each period of account, on a fair and reasonable basis and considering all relevant circumstances.

The Treasury may by statutory instrument amend the meaning of the costs of production of an exhibition to provide that specified activities are not to be treated as activities in developing, producing, running, deinstalling or closing an exhibition or an exhibition of a specified type.

[*CTA 2009, ss 1218ZB–1218ZBF, 1218ZF; F(No 2)A 2017, Sch 6 para 1*].

Exhibition tax relief

[26.44] A company which qualifies for exhibition tax relief (see **26.42** above) may claim an additional deduction for an accounting period in calculating the profit or loss of the separate exhibition trade (see **26.43** above) for the period. It may also claim an exhibition tax credit for an accounting period in which it has a 'surrenderable loss' (see below).

For the purposes of the two reliefs, in determining the amount of costs incurred on a production of an exhibition at the end of a period of account, any amount which is unpaid four months after the end of the period is ignored.

Additional deduction

The amount of the additional deduction for an accounting period is calculated as follows. For the first period of account during which the separate exhibition trade is carried on, the deduction is so much of the 'qualifying expenditure' incurred in the period as is European expenditure or, if less, 80% of the total qualifying expenditure incurred in the period.

For any subsequent period of account the deduction is equal to:

- the total of the qualifying expenditure incurred to date which is European expenditure or, if less, 80% of the total qualifying expenditure incurred to date; *less*
- the total additional deductions given for previous periods.

Where a period of account does not coincide with an accounting period, any apportionments needed to determine the additional deduction for the accounting period must be made by reference to the number of days in the periods concerned.

'*Qualifying expenditure*' for this purpose is core expenditure (see **26.42** above) incurred on or before 31 March 2022 on the production of the exhibition which is taken into account in computing the profits or losses of the separate exhibition trade, other than expenditure which is otherwise relievable under any of the other reliefs in this chapter (i.e. the reliefs for films, tv, video games, theatrical productions or orchestral concerts) or the reliefs for RESEARCH AND DEVELOPMENT EXPENDITURE (**63**).

Where a claim for the additional deduction is made in a return for an accounting period later than that in which the separate exhibition trade commenced, the company must make any necessary amendments to earlier returns (regardless of the normal time limits for making amendments).

The Treasury may amend the 80% figure specified above or substitute a later date than 31 March 2022 by statutory instrument.

Exhibition tax credits

A company which claims an exhibition tax credit may surrender the whole or part of its surrenderable loss for the accounting period. If the exhibition is a touring exhibition (see **26.41** above), the amount of the credit is 25% of the loss surrendered, subject to a maximum of £100,000. Otherwise the amount of the credit is 20% of the loss surrendered, subject to a maximum of £80,000. The total tax credits payable to any undertaking must not exceed 75 million euros per year in accordance with EU State aid limitations.

The '*surrenderable loss*' for an accounting period is the 'available loss' for the period in the separate exhibition trade or, if less, the 'available qualifying expenditure' for the period. The '*available loss*' is the loss for the period plus so much of any available loss for the previous accounting period as has not been surrendered as tax credit or carried forward under *CTA 2010, s 45* or *s 45B* (see **51.7, 51.6** LOSSES) and set off against profits of the separate exhibition trade. The '*available qualifying expenditure*' for a period of account is the total of the qualifying expenditure incurred to date which is European expenditure or, if less, 80% of the total qualifying expenditure incurred to date, less, for any but the first period of account, the total amount previously surrendered as tax credit. If a period of account does not coincide with an accounting period, any necessary apportionments needed to find the available qualifying expenditure for the accounting period must be made by reference to the number of days in the periods concerned.

Tax credits are normally paid by HMRC to the company but they may instead apply the credit, together with any interest on it, to discharge any liability of the company to corporation tax. HMRC are not required to pay any tax credit in respect of an accounting period whilst an enquiry into the return for the period is open (but may do so on a provisional basis). If the company owes HMRC any amount of PAYE or Class 1 NICs for any payment period ending in the accounting period, HMRC are not required to make a payment of tax credit until any such amounts are paid.

The available loss for the period is reduced by the amount surrendered. Exhibition tax credits are not income of the recipient for any tax purposes.

Anti-avoidance

A company does not qualify for exhibition tax relief if there are any tax avoidance arrangements relating to the production of the exhibition. Arrangements (as widely defined) are tax avoidance arrangements if they have as a main purpose the obtaining of a tax advantage (within *CTA 2010, s 1139*).

A transaction is ignored in determining any exhibition tax relief to the extent that it is attributable to arrangements entered into otherwise than for genuine commercial reasons.

[*CTA 2009, ss 1218ZC, 1218ZCE–1218ZCN; F(No 2)A 2017, Sch 6 para 1; SI 2019 No 689, Reg 16(41)*].

Claims and overpayments

[26.45] A claim for exhibition tax relief must be made in a company tax return (or amended return) (see **65.4, 65.8** RETURNS) for the accounting period for which the claim is made, within one year of the filing date for that return or by such later time as HMRC may allow. It can similarly only be amended or withdrawn by amendment of the company tax return within the same time limit. It must specify the amount claimed.

[*FA 1998, Sch 18 paras 10(4), 83S–83X; FA 2016, Sch 8 paras 4, 6; F(No 2)A 2017, Sch 6 paras 4, 6*].

For recovery of overpayments of exhibition tax credit, see **6.4** ASSESSMENTS.

Provisional entitlement to relief

Where a company claims exhibition tax relief for any accounting period before that in which it ceases to carry on the separate exhibition trade, its return for the period must state the amount of planned core expenditure on the production of the exhibition that is European expenditure. That amount must indicate that the European expenditure condition at **26.42**(iii) above will be met. If it subsequently appears that the condition will not be met, relief for any period which depended on such a statement is withdrawn and the company must amend its returns accordingly.

The company's return for the accounting period in which the separate exhibition trade ceases must state that the trade has ceased and must be accompanied by a final statement of the amount of the core expenditure that is European expenditure. If the statement shows that the European expenditure condition is not met, the company is not entitled to any exhibition tax relief or to transfer its terminal losses (see **26.46** below) and must amend its returns accordingly.

Amendments or assessments to give effect to these provisions can be made regardless of the normal time limits.

[*CTA 2009, ss 1218ZE, 1218ZEA; F(No 2)A 2017, Sch 6 para 1; SI 2019 No 689, Reg 16(42)(43)*].

Losses

[26.46] Where a loss arises in the separate exhibition trade in any accounting period before that in which the trade ceases (the '*completion period*') the only loss relief that is available in respect of it is to carry forward the loss under *CTA 2010, s 45* or *s 45B* (see **51.7**, **51.6** LOSSES) to be set against profits of the same trade in a later period. Where a loss is set against such profits, the set off is ignored for the purposes of *CTA 2010, s 269ZB* (restriction on deductions for carried-forward losses from trading profits — see **51.13** LOSSES). If a loss is carried forward to the completion period, so much of it as is not attributable to the additional deduction in **26.44** above may be treated for loss relief purposes as if it were a loss made in the completion period.

A loss made in the completion period (or treated as so made) may, to the extent that it is not attributable to the additional deduction, be deducted from total profits of the same or an earlier period under *CTA 2010, s 37* (see **51.3**, **51.4** LOSSES) or surrendered as GROUP RELIEF (**35**).

Terminal loss relief

A company may make a claim for a loss, which would (had the separate exhibition trade not ceased) have been carried forward against future profits of the trade, to be treated as a loss brought forward to be set against the profits of another separate exhibition trade carried on by it for the first accounting period beginning after the cessation. Alternatively, the company may surrender all or part of the loss to another company ('company B') in the same group (defined as for GROUP RELIEF (35) purposes) which also carries on a separate exhibition trade (in respect of the same or another exhibition). On the making of a claim by company B the surrendered loss is treated as a loss brought forward to be set against the profits of that trade for the first accounting period beginning after the cessation.

Where a terminal loss is set off against profits of the same company or another group member, the set off is ignored for the purposes of *CTA 2010, s 269ZB*.

The Treasury may by statutory instrument make administrative rules for the surrender of losses and resulting claims.

[*CTA 2009, ss 1218ZD–1218ZDC; F(No 2)A 2017, Sch 6 para 1*].

27

Derivative Contracts

Cross references. See **25** CORPORATE INTEREST RESTRICTION; **64.6** RESIDENCE for the charge to corporation tax on non-UK resident companies in respect of derivative contracts to which a company is a party for the purposes of a UK property business or to generate other UK property income; **50** LOAN RELATIONSHIPS.

Other sources. See generally, HMRC Corporate Finance Manual.

Simon's Taxes. See **D1.8**.

Introduction to derivative contracts

[27.1] The derivative contracts legislation applies to tax the profits and losses which companies make in respect of derivatives such as options, futures and swaps. The general rule is that amounts, including exchange gains and losses, are brought into account for tax purposes on the basis that they are recognised in a company's accounts in accordance with generally accepted accounting practice as items of profit or loss. Certain derivative contracts over shares are excluded from the derivative contracts legislation. See **27.3** below.

Special rules apply for recognising the profits and losses arising on derivative contracts that are used for hedging purposes and are contained in the *Loan Relationships and Derivative Contracts (Disregard and Bringing into Account of Profits and Losses) Regulations 2004 (SI 2004 No 3256)*, commonly referred to as the *Disregard Regulations*. The rules are considered at **27.12–27.14** below.

Where an embedded derivative is separated from a contract other than a loan relationship the bifurcation of the contract is generally ignored for tax purposes and thus profits and losses arising on the embedded derivative are generally disregarded for the purposes of the derivative contracts legislation. This is considered further at **27.2** below.

A number of anti-avoidance provisions apply including cases where a company is a party to a derivative contract for an unallowable purpose. These provisions are considered further at **27.16**, **27.17**, **27.19**, **27.23**, **27.26** and **27.27** below.

Generally, any profits and losses arising on a derivative contract are treated either as trading or as non-trading profits and losses depending on whether or not a company is a party to the derivative contract for the purposes of its trade. Non-trading credits and debits are treated as if they were non-trading credits or debits arising under the LOAN RELATIONSHIPS (**50**) rules, and effectively aggregated with other non-trading loan relationship credits and debits, the net amount being chargeable as non-trading income or relievable as a non-trading deficit, as the case may be. In certain cases, any profits and losses arising on a derivative contract are treated as giving rise to chargeable gains or allowable losses for the purposes of the *TCGA 1992*. The circumstances in which such treatment applies are considered at **27.40** below.

Except where otherwise indicated, the derivative contracts rules take priority over other legislation. This includes, e.g. priority over the capital gains rules in *TCGA 1992* and the provisions dealing with financial futures and commodities in *CTA 2009, s 981*.

The loan relationship rules take precedence over the derivative contract rules except where:

(a) an embedded derivative has been bifurcated from a loan relationship (in this case the derivative contracts legislation applies to the embedded derivative); and

(b) an amount only falls to be dealt with under the loan relationships legislation as it represents interest or discount arising on a money debt that has not arisen as a result of a transaction for the lending of money.

[*CTA 2009, ss 699, 700, 981*].

The deduction of debits in respect of certain derivative contracts may be subject to restriction by the CORPORATE INTEREST RESTRICTION (**25**).

Treasury power to amend legislation

The Treasury may, by order, amend most provisions of the derivative contracts legislation, and such amendment may have effect for statutory accounting periods beginning at any time in the calendar year in which the order is made. In addition, the Treasury has the power to amend the derivative contracts legislation by regulation where there is a change in accounting standards, which affects the way in which profits and losses arising on a derivative contract are recognised in a company's accounts. Such changes may be made with retrospective effect to the date that a company began to apply the new accounting treatment if the change in accounting treatment takes effect before the necessary legislative changes have been made. [*CTA 2009, ss 701, 701A*].

Interest rate hedging products redress payments

HMRC have published guidance on the tax treatment of compensation payments made by certain banks as redress for the mis-selling of interest rate hedging products. Where the swap was taken out for the purposes of the company's trade, the redress payment should be treated as a trading receipt. See www.gov.uk/government/publications/tax-interest-rate-hedging-products-i rhp.

Simon's Taxes. See D1.8.

Meaning of 'derivative contract'

[27.2] An instrument is a '*derivative contract*' of a company for an accounting period if:

- it is a 'relevant contract';
- it meets the accounting condition for the accounting period; and
- it is not excluded because of its underlying subject matter (see 27.3 below) or under any other corporation tax provision.

See also 27.34 below for contracts where the underlying subject matter is wholly or partly comprised of a holding in an open-ended investment company, unit trust or an offshore fund.

Relevant contracts

A '*relevant contract*' is:

(a) an 'option';
(b) a 'future'; or
(c) a 'contract for differences'.

A company becomes a party to a relevant contract when it enters into or acquires such a contract. It acquires a relevant contract on becoming entitled to the rights, and subject to the liabilities, under the contract, whether by assignment or otherwise.

[*CTA 2009, ss 577, 578*].

Meaning of option, future and contract for differences

An '*option*' includes a 'warrant'. A '*warrant*' is an instrument which gives the holder a right to subscribe for shares or loan stock in a company, whether or not the shares or assets exist or are identifiable. However, the term '*option*' does not include a contract which provides that, after setting off their obligations to each other under the contract, a cash payment of the difference is made by one party to the other or each party has a duty to make a cash payment to the other in respect of all their obligations under the contract and no property passes. These conditions do not prevent a contract with currency as the subject matter from being an option.

[*CTA 2009, ss 580, 710*].

A '*future*' is a contract for the sale of property under which delivery is to be made at a future date agreed when the contract is made, and at a price so agreed. A price is taken to be so agreed whether it is for a determined amount, or left to be determined by reference to a future market or exchange price, or so expressed as to allow for variations to take account of changes in quality and quantity on delivery. As in the case of an option, a future that can only be cash settled (except where the underlying subject matter of the future is currency) is treated as a contract for differences.

[*CTA 2009, s 581*].

A '*contract for differences*' is a contract which has the purpose or pretended purpose of securing a profit or avoiding a loss by reference to fluctuations in the value or price of property described in the contract or in an index or in other factors designated in the contract. Also included are 'investment contracts' and 'contracts for difference' within *Energy Act 2013, s 6* and *Sch 2 para 1(1)*. A contract for differences does not include a future or option, an insurance contract, a capital redemption policy effected in the course of a capital redemption business as defined in *FA 2012, s 56(3)*, a contract of indemnity, a guarantee, a warranty or a loan relationship. As noted above, however, where an option or a future can only be cash settled (i.e. there is no provision for physical settlement to take place) and the underlying subject matter of the option or future is not currency, the option or future is treated as a contract for differences for the purposes of the derivative contracts legislation.

[*CTA 2009, s 582*].

The accounting condition

The accounting condition is that the relevant contract is treated as a derivative for the purposes of the relevant accounting standard for the accounting period in question or would be so treated for accounting purposes were the relevant accounting standard used.

The '*relevant accounting standard*' is:

- FRS 25 issued in December 2004 (now superseded); or
- for any accounting period for which it is required or permitted to be used, any subsequent accounting standard dealing with transactions which are derivatives.

[*CTA 2009, s 579(1)(a), (3), (5)*].

As IAS 39, IFRS 9, FRS 26 and FRS 102 all define derivative in essentially the same way, a contract that is a derivative within one of those standards will satisfy the accounting test (HMRC Corporate Finance Manual CFM50220).

A relevant contract, which did not satisfy the accounting test solely because it failed to satisfy the requirements of FRS 26, para 9(b) (essentially, this prevented prepaid or substantially prepaid contracts from falling within the definition of a derivative for the purposes of FRS 26) was brought within the derivative contracts legislation. The profits and losses arising on the derivative contract for the purposes of the derivative contracts legislation have to be determined using a fair value basis of accounting.

[*CTA 2009, ss 579(1)(b), (4), 600*].

Contracts that do not satisfy the accounting condition

Where a relevant contract does not satisfy the accounting condition it is nevertheless brought within the derivative contracts legislation if:

(a) the underlying subject matter of the contract is commodities; or
(b) the contract is a contract for differences whose underlying subject matter is: land; tangible movable property other than commodities which are tangible assets; intangible fixed assets; weather conditions; or creditworthiness.

[*CTA 2009, s 579(2)*].

Embedded derivatives that are separated from loan relationships

An embedded derivative which is separated ('bifurcated') from a loan relationship in a company's accounts is brought within the derivative contracts legislation (see also **50.48** LOAN RELATIONSHIPS). According to its characteristics, the embedded derivative is treated as an option, future or contract differences. For example, where an option to acquire shares is separated from a convertible security the embedded derivative will be treated as an option. In the case of an index-linked loan relationship where the embedded derivative is separated from the loan relationship, the embedded derivative will, typically, be treated as a contract for differences.

See also **27.43** below for special treatment for options to acquire shares and contracts for differences linked to movements in the value of shares.

[*CTA 2009, s 585*].

Embedded derivatives that are separated from other contracts, including derivative contracts

An embedded derivative which is separated ('bifurcated') from a derivative contract or from a non-financial contract is brought within the derivative contracts legislation. Typically, such bifurcation is ignored for tax purposes and, instead, the profits and losses arising on the contract (including a derivative contract) have to be determined using an amortised cost basis of accounting.

It is possible in certain cases for a company to elect for the bifurcation of the contract to be respected for tax purposes. No such an election, however, can be made if the contract is a contract of long-term insurance or the underlying subject matter of the embedded derivative is, or includes, commodities. Such an election must be made before the end of the first accounting period in which the contract is bifurcated in the company's accounts. Where such an election is made it continues to apply if the derivative contract is later transferred to another company in the same CGT group.

The bifurcation of a contract is not ignored for tax purposes where *SI 2004 No 3256, Reg 9* (see **27.14** below) applies to the embedded derivative. The reason for this is to enable a company to use an embedded derivative to hedge an asset or liability to which the company is a party.

It is also not possible for a company to elect to disregard the bifurcation where *CTA 2009, s 592* applies. This section applies where an embedded derivative is separated from a derivative contract and the underlying subject matter of the embedded derivative consists, or is treated as consisting wholly, of shares in a company. In such cases under *CTA 2009, s 592*, the embedded derivative is excluded from the derivative contracts legislation and is treated as being a chargeable asset while the host contract is taxed under the provisions of the loan relationships legislation.

[*CTA 2009, ss 584, 586, 616–618*].

Excluded contracts

[27.3] A relevant contract is not a derivative contract if its underlying subject matter (see further below) consists wholly of, or is treated as consisting wholly of, any one or more of the following types of excluded property. '*Excluded property*' is intangible fixed assets or shares in a company, (but, in the former case, only for relevant contracts which are options or futures). In the case of shares, the exclusion applies only where any of the conditions A to E below apply and the transaction is not designed to produce a return equating in substance to a return on a money investment at a commercial rate of interest.

Further the exclusion for shares does not apply to shares in an open ended investment company or units in a unit trust which are treated for tax purposes as being creditor relationships under *CTA 2009, s 490*.

The conditions are as follows:

(A) the relevant contract is a 'plain vanilla contract' entered into or acquired by a company carrying on long-term business or is an approved derivative for the purposes of Rule 3.2.5 of the Prudential Sourcebook for Insurers and is not prevented from being treated as a derivative for the purposes of FRS 26 because it has been prepaid in whole or in part; or

(B) the relevant contract is entered into or acquired otherwise than in the course of a trade, as part of a hedging transaction where shares or rights of a unit holder or the company's share capital or a liability related to the share capital of the company are the subject matter of the contract, and the company is not treated as a party to a derivative contract under the loan relationships with embedded derivatives rules (see **27.40**); or

(C) the relevant contract is entered into or acquired otherwise than in the course of a trade and is a quoted option to subscribe for shares in a company; or

(D) the contract, an option or future, is entered into or acquired otherwise than as an integral part of a company's trade, *CTA 2009, s 585(2)* does not require the company to be treated as a party to an embedded derivative and the shares to be acquired or delivered under the terms of the option or future amount to 10% or more of the ordinary share capital of the company (as defined for the purposes of *CTA 2010, s 1119*), or would do so if acquired or delivered; or

(E) the company has a hedging relationship between the derivative contract and a loan relationship that has been bifurcated in the company's accounts into a host contract and an embedded derivative and one of *CTA 2009, ss 645, 648, 653–655, 658* apply to the embedded derivative.

A '*plain vanilla contract*' is a contract which is a relevant contract that has not been separated from another contract (see **27.2**).

[*CTA 2009, ss 589, 591, 708*].

Underlying subject matter

The underlying subject matter of a relevant contract is:

(1) in the case of an option, the property to be delivered on the exercise of the option;

(2) in the case of a future, the property which, if the future were to run to delivery, would fall to be delivered at the date and price agreed when the contract was made;

(3) in the case of a contract for differences, where the contract relates to fluctuations in the value or price of property described in the contract, it is the property so described, and where an index or factor is designated in the contract, it is the matter by reference to which the index or factor is determined. This may for example include interest rates, weather conditions or creditworthiness.

As regards (1) and (2) above, there is no requirement that the property actually has to be delivered, and if the property to be delivered is itself a derivative contract, the underlying subject matter is the underlying subject matter of that other contract. As regards (3) above, interest rates are not the underlying subject matter of a contract where they are used merely in a formula to determine the amount of the payment where the date of payment may vary and the amount varies according to the date of payment.

Where the underlying subject matter of a relevant contract consists of or includes income from shares in a company or rights of unit trust holder or unit trust scheme (for example dividends), the underlying subject matter is not to be treated as shares by reason only of that income.

[*CTA 2009, s 583*].

Mixed derivatives

[27.4] Special provisions apply where the underlying subject matter of a relevant contract consists of any one or more of the excluded types of property within 27.3 above in addition to property which is not so excluded, and which satisfies the accounting test.

Where the non-excluded property is not 'subordinate' or 'small', then in the case of a derivative contract which is an option or a future, it is to be treated as two separate contracts using a just and reasonable apportionment, i.e. a relevant contract whose underlying subject matter consists of one or more of the excluded properties and a relevant contract whose underlying subject matter consists of the non-excluded property. In the case of a contract for differences where the non-excluded subject matter is not 'subordinate' or 'small', the entire contract will not be excluded from the derivatives contracts legislation.

[*CTA 2009, ss 590, 593*].

Contract which becomes or ceases to be a relevant contract

[27.5] This provision applies if a company is a party to a chargeable asset which becomes a derivative contract, the company must bring into account a chargeable gain or allowable loss for the period during which it ceases to be a party to the contract, for example where the contract ceases to satisfy the necessary conditions for it to be excluded from the derivative contracts legislation. The gain or loss is calculated on the assumption that the company disposed of the contract immediately before the time when the contract became a derivative contract and the consideration was the notional carrying value of the contract at that time.

[*CTA 2009, s 661*].

Where a relevant contract ceases to fall within the derivative contracts legislation the company is treated as having become a party to the contract for chargeable gains purposes for a consideration equal to the value at which it would have been carried in the company's accounts had a period of account ended immediately before that time.

[*CTA 2009, s 662*].

Taxation of derivative contracts

[27.6] In general, all profits arising from a company's derivative contracts are chargeable to corporation tax as income in accordance with the following rules (but see **27.40** below for an exception to this rule which charges certain derivative contracts under the capital gains regime). Credits and debits (computed as below) are brought into account as follows.

- **Trading credits and debits.** Where the company enters into a derivative contract for trading purposes, credits or debits arising from the contract are treated as receipts or expenses of the trade for that period (in the case of expenses, overriding anything to the contrary in *CTA 2009, ss 53, 54 or 59* (allowable deductions).
- **Non-trading credits and debits.** Any credits or debits arising from derivative contracts *not* entered into for trading purposes are treated as if they were non-trading credits or debits arising under the LOAN RELATIONSHIPS (**50**) rules, and effectively aggregated with other non-trading loan relationship credits and debits, the net amount being chargeable as non-trading income or relievable as a non-trading deficit, as the case may be.

A non-UK resident company carrying on a trade in the UK through a permanent establishment must bring into account debits and credits to the extent they are attributable to the permanent establishment, in accordance with the rules at **64.6** RESIDENCE. With effect from 6 April 2020 (subject to the transitional provisions at **64.7** RESIDENCE), non-resident companies must also bring into account non-trading debits and credits from contracts to which the company is a party for the purposes of a UK property business or to enable it to generate other UK property income.

[*CTA 2009, ss 571–574; FA 2019, Sch 5 paras 18, 35; FA 2020, Sch 6 paras 2, 10*].

Credits and debits to be brought into account

The general rule is that the amounts which are brought into account in computing a company's profits for the purposes of the derivative contracts legislation are:

(i) profits and losses of the company which arise to it from its derivative contracts and related transactions (excluding expenses); and

(ii) expenses incurred by the company under or for the purposes of those contracts and transactions.

The expenses which may be taken into account are those the company incurs directly:

(a) in bringing a derivative contract into existence;
(b) in entering into or giving effect to a related transaction;
(c) in making payments under the terms of a derivative contract or in pursuance of a related transaction;
(d) in taking steps for ensuring the receipt of payments under a derivative contract or in respect of a related transaction; or
(e) any expenses incurred in respect of a derivative contract or related transaction into which the company may enter (but does not enter), provided that if the company had entered into the derivative contract or related transaction, the charges or expenses would have qualified for relief under heads (a)–(d) above.

Where a company is considering entering a derivative contract or related transaction but has not done so, and it incurs expenses in connection with entering the contract or regarding a liability which may arise under it, the debits may be brought into account in the same way as they would be taken in had the contract been completed.

A '*related transaction*' is any acquisition or disposal (in whole or part) of rights or liabilities under the contract, including where such rights or liabilities are transferred or extinguished by a sale, gift, surrender or release, and where the contract is discharged by performance in accordance with its terms.

[*CTA 2009, ss 594A, 596, 607*].

A special rule applies with effect from 6 April 2020 where a non-UK resident company has debits under a derivative contract to which it is party for the purposes of its UK property business which are referable to any time within the seven years before commencement of the business. Such debits (net of certain credits) can be brought into account in the first accounting period in which the company carries on the business, provided that they have not otherwise been brought into account for tax purposes. It is a further requirement that the debits would have been brought into account in computing the profits or losses of the company if it had been carrying on the business at the time to which the debits are referable. The credits which must be set off against the debits are those which would have been brought into account at any time in the seven-year period if the company had then been carrying on the business and which would not otherwise have been brought into account. This rule is subject to the transitional rule at *FA 2019, Sch 5 para 40* (see **64.7** RESIDENCE).

The above rule applies also to a non-UK resident company which is party to a derivative contract for the purpose of enabling it to generate other UK property income (i.e. rent receivable in connection with a *CTA 2009, s 39* concern (mines, quarries etc. — see **60.18** PROPERTY INCOME), rent receivable for electric-line wayleaves (see **60.18**) or post-cessation receipts from a UK property business (see **60.4**)).

[*CTA 2009, s 607ZA; FA 2020, Sch 6 paras 4, 10*].

In *Union Castle Mail Steamship Co Ltd v HMRC* CA, [2020] EWCA Civ 547, a debit arising from the derecognition of a financial asset was disallowed on the grounds that the loss did not arise from the derivative contracts in question.

Credits and debits where a company is not, or has ceased to be, party to derivative contract

Provisions apply to include in computing a company's derivative contract credits and debits amounts that are recognised in its accounts in respect of a derivative contract, even though for some all of the relevant accounting period the company is not a party to the derivative contract. The cases in which such amounts are included in computing a company's derivative contract profits are:

(a) where the company was a party to the derivative contract, amounts in respect of the derivative contract were recognised in the company's accounts as an item of profit or loss when it was a party's contract and any amounts in respect of the contract continue to be recognised in its accounts as an item of profit or loss after it has ceased to be a party to the contract;

(b) where the amounts that are recognised in the company's accounts are recognised as a result of a transaction which has effect of transferring to the company all or part of the risk or reward relating to the derivative contract without a corresponding transfer of rights or obligations under the contract;

(c) where profits or losses arising in respect of the disposal of a derivative contract continue to be recognised in the company's accounts after the company has ceased to be a party to the contract; or

(d) where amounts are recognised in the company's accounts because the company may enter into a derivative contract but has not yet done so and the amounts are not amounts that fall to be brought into account under *CTA 2009, s 607* (pre-contract or abortive expenses).

Debits that would be recognised under this provision are not brought into account in computing a company's derivative contract profits to the extent that an amount is:

(i) brought into account as a debit under these provisions by another company;

(ii) brought into account so as to reduce the assumed taxable total profits of another company for the purposes of the CFC legislation in *TIOPA 2010, Pt 9A*; or

(iii) allowable as a deduction by a person for the purposes of income tax.

An anti-double charge provision also applies in the case of credits and this applies in respect of an amount:

(i) which is brought into account as a credit under these provisions by another company;

(ii) which is brought into account in determining the assumed taxable total profits of another company the purposes of the CFC legislation that is contained in *TIOPA 2010, Pt 9A*; or

(iii) on which a person is chargeable to income tax.

In order to avoid a double tax charge in the case of a credit a company is required to make a claim for one or more consequential adjustments to be made in respect of the amount brought into account as a credit and on receipt of the claim HMRC are required to make such of the consequential adjustments claimed as are just and reasonable. Consequential adjustments can be made in respect of any period, by way of an assessment, the modification of an assessment, the amendment of a claim or otherwise and despite any time limit imposed by or under any enactment.

[*CTA 2009, ss 607A, 607B, 607C*].

Computation in accordance with generally accepted accounting practice

[27.7] The amounts to be brought into account as credits and debits in respect of derivative contracts are amounts that, in accordance with generally accepted accounting practice, are recognised in the company accounts for the relevant period as an item of profit or loss. This includes amounts that were previously recognised as an item of other comprehensive income and have been transferred to become an item of profit or loss in determining the company's profit or loss for the accounting period in question. The terms 'item of profit or loss' and 'item of other comprehensive income' each has the meaning that it has for accounting purposes.

Where a company's period of account does not coincide with an accounting period, so that it overlaps two accounting periods, the normal rule is that the profit or loss recognised in the company's accounts in respect of derivative contracts for the relevant period of account is apportioned between the two accounting periods on a time basis unless such apportionment would work unreasonably or unjustly. In the latter case, the company's derivative contract profits and losses that are attributable to each of the two accounting periods are determined by reference to the amounts that would have been recognised in determining the company's accounting profit or loss in accordance with generally accepted accounting practice, had it drawn up accounts for each of the two periods.

Transitional provisions apply where amounts were included in other comprehensive income for an accounting period beginning before 1 January 2016 and were taken into account in computing the company's derivative contract profits. In such cases a transitional adjustment applies in respect of the net debits or credits that have been so taken into account and which have not been transferred from other comprehensive income to become an item of profit or loss before the start of a company's first accounting period beginning on or after 1 January 2016. The transitional adjustment is equal and opposite to the net amount of such credits or debits. The transitional adjustment is required to be brought into account on a weighted basis over a five year period, as follows: year 1 – 40%; year 2 – 25%; year 3 – 15%; year 4 – 10%; year 5 – 10% (see further *F(No 2)A 2015, Sch 7, paras 120–124*).

There is provision to ensure that an amount which has been recognised in other comprehensive income, and that has not been recycled to profit or loss at the time that a company ceases to recognise the derivative contract in its accounts, is brought into account in computing the company's derivative contract profits, if at the time that the company ceases to be a party to the derivative contract, or at any later time, it is not expected that such amount will in future be recycled to profit or loss. In such cases, the amount is required to be included in computing the company's derivative contract profits for the accounting period in which the relevant time falls. This provision also applies in the same way where part of a contract ceases to be recognised in a company's accounts and amounts in respect of that part of the contract have been recognised in other comprehensive income and have not been transferred to become an item of profit or loss.

[*CTA 2009, ss 595, 597, 604A*].

Change of accounting policy

[27.8] The following provisions apply where a company changes the basis of accounting on which credits or debits are calculated from one period (the '*earlier period*') to the next (the '*later period*') if the basis in each period is in accordance with the law and practice applicable to that period and the change is not made to comply with amending legislation not applicable to the earlier period. The change in basis may result from a change in accounting policy (such as the company switching from UK generally accepted accounting practice to international accounting standards or vice versa) or made to comply with a requirement under the derivative contracts provisions for credits and debits to be determined on a particular basis.

Any difference between the closing 'tax-adjusted carrying value' of a derivative contract in the earlier period and the opening 'tax-adjusted carrying value' in the later period, is treated as a debit or credit (as the case may be).

Where the change in basis is to comply with a requirement for credits and debits to be determined on a particular basis, the debit or credit is brought into account in the later period. Where the change in basis results from a change in accounting policy, the debit or credit is spread over a ten-year period beginning with the later period. One-tenth of the debit or credit is brought into account in each year, but if the company ceases to be within the charge to corporation tax before the end of the ten-year period, any remaining amount is brought into account in the final accounting period.

Where the company ceases to be party to a derivative contract in an accounting period (the '*cessation period*') and *CTA 2009, s 607A* (see **27.6** above) applies to the cessation, then any difference between 'the amount outstanding' in respect of the contract at the end of the earlier period and 'the amount outstanding' at the beginning of the later period is treated as a debit or credit (as the case may be) in the later period.

The '*tax-adjusted carrying value*' means the carrying value of the contract recognised for accounting purposes and includes accruals, prepayments and impairment losses (including provisions for bad and doubtful debts), as adjusted for certain provisions as they apply for the purpose of determining derivative contracts debits and credits.

The '*amount outstanding*' means so much of the amount recognised in the company's balance sheet as deferred income or loss arising in the cessation period as has not yet brought into account.

These provisions do not apply if the differences as detailed above are otherwise brought into account in computing a company's loan relationship profits.

The provisions are subject to the provisions at **27.13** below.

[*CTA 2009, ss 613–615, 702; SI 2004 No 3271, Regs 1, 3, 3A, 4*].

There are a number of cases where additional adjustments arising as a result of the change in accounting treatment are not brought into account for tax purposes. These are:

(a) where the derivative contract is an embedded derivative which is separated from a contract other than a loan relationship and the embedded derivative is not brought within the scope of the derivative contracts legislation (see **27.2** above). In this case, any transitional adjustment arising in respect of the embedded derivative is ignored for tax purposes;
(b) where the derivative contract is an interest rate contract to which *SI 2004 No 3256, Reg 9* applies (see **27.14** below), any transitional adjustment arising in respect of the derivative contract is ignored for tax purposes. This is because such contracts are required to be brought into account for tax purposes using an appropriate accruals basis which is designed to track the way in which the contract would previously have been accounted for under former UK GAAP. The effect of such treatment is that all profits and losses arising on the contract should be brought into account for tax purposes over its life;
(c) were recognised in other comprehensive income for accounting periods beginning before 1 January 2016, and were not subsequently transferred to become items of profit or loss in an accounting period beginning before that date;
(d) any exchange gains or losses arising to a company in respect of a derivative contract, the underlying subject matter of which consists of currency, are disregarded where those exchange gains or losses represent the reversal of exchange gains or losses arising to the company in periods of account before the later period, and such exchange gains or losses had not been brought into account for corporation tax.

[*SI 2004 No 3271, Regs 3A(7A), 3C(2)*].

Exchange gains and losses

[27.9] Exchange gains and losses that arise in respect of a derivative contract that are recognised in a company's accounts as an item of profit and loss are included in computing its profits and losses under the derivative contracts regime.

Any exchange gains or losses that arise as a result of the translation of the assets, liabilities, income and expenses of all or part of a company's business from the functional currency of the business, or that part of the business, into another currency are disregarded for the purposes of the derivative contracts legislation where such amounts are recognised in the company's accounts as an item of other comprehensive income. Exchange movements arising as a result of the change to the functional currency of an investment company are also disregarded in computing the company's derivative contract profits. The functional currency of a business or part of business is defined as the currency of the primary economic environment in which the business or part operates and the terms assets, liabilities, income and expenses and item of other comprehensive income, each has the meaning that it has for accounting purposes. This exclusion does not apply, however, to any exchange movements arising as a result of a change in the designated currency of an investment company where an election under *CTA 2010, s 9A* has effect (under *CTA 2010, s 9A* the designated currency of an investment company is treated in the same way as if it were the company's functional currency).

Where:

(a) a derivative contract is a designated hedge of a net investment in a foreign operation (e.g. a branch) of the company; and

(b) amounts representing exchange gains and losses in respect of the derivative contract have, in accordance with generally accepted accounting practice been recognised in the company's accounts as items of other comprehensive income,

such amounts are to be disregarded in computing the company's profits for corporation tax. Further, there is no provision for such amounts to be taxed if they are recycled from other comprehensive income to profit or loss.

Exchange movements arising on a derivative contract are also disregarded for the purposes of the derivative contracts legislation where the derivative is used to hedge an investment in shares, ships or aircraft or to hedge shares that the company has issued. See **27.10** below.

[*CTA 2009, s 606; SI 2004 No 3256, Reg 5A*].

Derivative contract carried at fair value — determination of exchange gains and losses

Where a derivative contract is carried at fair value in a company's accounts, exchange movements arising on the contract would not be separately recognised in its accounts. In such cases, the exchange movement arising on the contract is determined for tax purposes by comparing the spot value of the contract, as translated into the currency by reference to which the company's taxable profits (excluding chargeable gains) are computed, at the start of the accounting period in question (or, if later, the date that it became a party to the contract) and the spot value of the currency or currencies covered by the contract, again as translated into the company's functional currency, at the end of the accounting period (or if earlier, the date that it ceased to be a party to the contract).

[*SI 2005 No 3422, Reg 7*].

Matching of exchange gains and losses (the 'Disregard Regulations')

[27.10] There are provisions which enable companies to bring into (or leave out of) account foreign exchange movements which are matched with certain items in computing its derivative contracts profits. The provisions are contained in *SI 2004 No 3256*, usually known as the 'Disregard Regulations'. See also **27.12** onwards below for hedging generally.

Matching shares, ships or aircraft

Exchange movements arising on a derivative contract that is used to hedge exchange movements on shares, ships or aircraft are disregarded in computing derivative contract profits where certain conditions are satisfied. This rule does not apply, however, to the extent that movements in the fair value of, or in profits or losses arising on the disposal of the shares, ships, or aircraft are taken into account in computing the company's profits for the purposes of a trade carried on by it where this trade consists of, or includes, dealing in shares, ships or aircraft.

Where a company acquires the shares, ship or aircraft after it has become a party to the contract, exchange movements arising on the contract in the accounting period in which the asset is acquired are only treated as matched to the extent that the exchange movements are attributable, on a just and reasonable basis, to the period for which the company held the asset (and if appropriate, to the extent that the contract is treated as matched against the asset).

Shares, ships or aircraft are treated as matched to the greatest possible extent first with derivative contracts which have been designated as a hedge of that asset (see condition 1 below) and then with contracts within condition 2 below.

Condition 1 is satisfied if, for the accounting period in question, the shares, ships or aircraft are a hedged item under a designated hedge of exchange rate risk in which the derivative contract is the hedging instrument. This is designed to cover cases where a contract is designed as a fair value hedge of the relevant asset in the company's individual (as opposed to consolidated) accounts.

Condition 2 is that the currency in which the liability is expressed is such that the company intends, by entering into and continuing to be a party to that liability, to eliminate or substantially reduce the economic risk of holding the asset, or part of the asset, which is attributable to fluctuations in exchange rates. In this case, a derivative contract is treated as matched with an asset only to the extent that the value of the obligation under the contract does not exceed the unmatched carrying value of the asset at the time at which the company becomes a party to the contract or, if later, the time at which the asset is acquired. The carrying value of the liability is its value as shown in the company's accounts. The unmatched carrying value of the asset is normally its 'relevant value' to the extent that it has not previously been matched. The 'relevant value' of an asset is the value shown in the company's accounts. In the case of shares this is subject to the election below.

Where a derivative contract is treated as matched by virtue of condition 2 and only part of the debtor relationship could be regarded as matching an investment in shares, ships or aircraft, matching treatment will only apply to the relevant portion of the contract.

[*SI 2004 No 3256, Regs 4(1)–(4)(5), 4A(1), 4B, 5(2)*].

Election to match net asset value of shares

A company can make an election at any time for shares held by it to be treated as being matched at the higher of the carrying value of the shares in its accounts and the net asset value underlying such shares (as defined). An election is made by notice in writing to HMRC, and has effect from a date specified in the notice. The election can be revoked before it has taken effect, or from a date specified in the revocation notice, which must be at least 12 months after the election was made. The election has effect for all shares of the company which are matched under condition 2 above or the equivalent rule for matching of debtor relationships. A review period (see below) must be specified. Where the date specified for the election to take effect is not the first day of an accounting period, then the accounting period is split into separate periods falling before and after the date the election takes effect.

Where a company makes such an election, it has to designate a review period. The company may choose the length of its review periods, provided that a review period starts with the start of an accounting period (or if later the date when a contract (or liability) is first matched with shares) and a review period ends with the end of an accounting period. The company is required to determine the net asset value underlying the shares in question at the start of each review period and this becomes the value which is eligible to be treated as matched during that period. Where during a review period (current review period) there is an increase or decrease of 10% or more in the net asset value underlying any shares that the company is matching, a new review period is deemed to start in respect of those shares at that time and will end at the end of the current review period. This is to permit a company to vary its hedging in respect of the shares in question at the time that the variation in the net asset value occurs.

[*SI 2004 No 3256, Regs 4A, 4B, 4C*].

Currency contract matched with share capital

Provision is also made for exchange movements arising on a derivative contract which is matched with the whole or part of a company's share capital that is denominated in a foreign currency to be disregarded in computing derivative contracts profits. Exchange movements on contracts are also disregarded where matched with the whole or part of any hybrid capital instrument (previously any regulatory capital security – see **50.28** LOAN RELATIONSHIPS) issued by the company or, in the case of a building society, any deferred shares issued by the society. In the latter two cases, the disregard applies only to the extent that the instrument or shares are accounted for as equity instruments in accordance with GAAP. The regulations do not specify any other conditions which have to be satisfied in order for such treatment to apply. HMRC provide guidance in the Corporate Finance Manual at CFM62850 as to the circumstances in which they consider that this provision will apply. They suggest that this is most likely where share capital is treated as a financial liability in a company's accounts.

[*SI 2004 No 3256, Reg 4(4A)(4B); FA 2019, Sch 20 para 9(4)*].

Identification rules

Where a company holds a number of assets in the same currency and has debtor relationships or derivative contracts which are eligible to be treated as matched against such assets, identification rules apply to determine the extent to which an asset is to be treated as matched.

The extent to which an asset is matched is determined in accordance with the following rules:

- Rule 1: Debtor relationships and currency contracts are regarded as matched to the greatest extent possible with assets which are ships or aircraft;
- Rule 2: Subject to Rule 1, debtor relationships and currency contracts are regarded as matched to the greatest possible extent with assets on the disposal of which a chargeable gain would accrue if a disposal were made on a date falling more than 12 months after the date of acquisition of the asset. This is designed to exclude shares and assets related to shares which are eligible for substantial shareholding relief (*TCGA 1992, Sch 7AC*);
- Rule 3: Subject to Rules 1 and 2, debtor relationships and currency contracts are regarded as matched with assets on the disposal of which no chargeable gain would be treated as accruing by virtue of the substantial shareholding legislation.

[*SI 2004 No 3256, Reg 5*].

Risk transfer schemes

See **50.20** LOAN RELATIONSHIPS for anti-avoidance legislation which counters so-called risk transfer or over hedging transactions and applies to both derivative contracts and loan relationships.

Bringing into account of matched exchange gains and losses

[27.11] Any matched exchange gains and losses are only brought into account for tax purposes when a company ceases to own the matched asset. The treatment that applies depends on the nature of the asset.

Shares

In the case of shares, the matched exchange movement is dealt with under capital gains rules. The consideration for the disposal of the shares is increased where a net gain has arisen and is reduced where a net loss has arisen. If the amount of the net loss exceeds the consideration (before adjustment under these provisions), the excess is treated as additional consideration for the acquisition of the shares. The net forex gain or loss must be calculated using the company's 'relevant currency' (see **34.6** FOREIGN CURRENCY) at the time of the disposal. Where there has been a change in the relevant currency, the net gain or loss is to be re-translated from the previous currency into the new currency based on the spot rate of exchange for the day of the change in currency.

[*SI 2002 No 1970, Regs 2, 4, 5*].

It is possible for the time of recognition of the matched exchange movements to be deferred where a company disposes of shares and the disposal is treated as a no gain no loss disposal for the purposes of *TCGA 1992*.

[*SI 2002 No 1970, Reg 8*].

Loan relationships, ships and aircraft

Where the matched asset is a ship or an aircraft, the matched exchange gain or loss is brought into account as a loan relationship debit or credit when the company disposes of the asset in question. Where the currency contract is matched against a creditor loan relationship, any exchange gain or loss arising on the derivative contract is brought into account as a credit or debit for the purposes of the loan relationship legislation in the accounting period in which the company ceases to be a party to the creditor loan relationship.

[*SI 2002 No 1970, Reg 6*].

Net investment in a branch

Where the matched asset is a net investment in a branch, the matched exchange movement is not brought into account for tax purposes. This is because there is no provision to bring such deferred exchange movements within the charge to tax.

[*SI 2002 No 1970, Reg 2(1), 4(4)*].

Derivative contracts and hedging

[27.12] Under IFRS and UK GAAP, all derivatives are measured on the balance sheet at their fair value even if they are accounted for as a hedge of one or more risks of an asset, liability or transaction. Hedge accounting is only possible where certain conditions, such as the nature of the hedging instrument and the documentation of the hedge, are met. As a consequence, companies could, in the absence of special rules, be exposed to considerable volatility in their taxable profits because of fair value changes in derivatives.

Special provisions therefore apply to modify the tax treatment of derivative contracts which function as a hedge. The provisions are contained in *SI 2004 No 3256*, usually known as the 'Disregard Regulations'. See also **27.10** above for matching of exchange gains and losses.

The provisions may apply where a company enters into:

(1) a currency contract to hedge a forecast transaction or a firm commitment (*Reg 7*; see **27.13** below);
(2) a commodity contract or a debt contract to hedge a forecast transaction or a firm commitment (*Reg 8*; see **27.13** below); or
(3) a derivative contract whose underlying subject matter includes interest rates to hedge an underlying transaction (*Reg 9*; see **27.14** below).

The terms '*forecast transaction*' and '*firm commitment*' are defined as having the meaning that they have for accounting purposes. [*SI 2004 No 3256, Reg 2(2)*].

For the provisions to apply, an election must normally be made. The provisions also apply, however, without the need for an election, where the contract in question is a designated fair value hedge; where the hedged item is a loan relationship in relation to which the company uses fair value accounting; or where the contract is part of an arrangement (as widely defined) with a main purpose of obtaining a tax advantage which would not arise if the provisions applied.

[*SI 2004 No 3256, Reg 6*].

See also **27.15** below for contracts hedging the proceeds of a rights issue or an open offer of shares (*Reg 7A*); those provisions apply automatically, without the need for an election.

Meaning of hedging relationship

A company has a hedging relationship between a derivative contract (hedging instrument) and an asset, liability, receipt or expense (the hedged item) if and to the extent that:

(a) the hedging instrument and the hedged item are designated by the company as a hedge;

(b) in any other case, the hedging instrument is intended to act as a hedge of:
- the exposure to changes in fair value of a hedged item which is a recognised asset or liability or an unrecognised firm commitment, or an identified portion of such an asset, liability or commitment that is attributable to a particular risk and could affect profit or loss of the company;
- the exposure to variability in cash flows that is attributable to a particular risk associated with a hedged item that is a recognised asset or liability or a forecast transaction and could affect profit or loss of the company; or
- a net investment in a foreign operation of the company.

[*SI 2004 No 3256, Reg 2(5)*].

Making an election

An election is made by notice in writing to HMRC and applies all of the provisions in (1)–(3) above, unless the notice states which of those provisions is to apply. For a company adopting fair value accounting for the first time on or after 1 January 2015 (a '*new adopter*'), the election has effect for derivative contracts held in the first accounting period in which fair value accounting is used and subsequent periods provided that it is made before the latest of:

- six months after the start of the first period in which fair value accounting is used;
- six months after first entering into a derivative contract for which fair value accounting is used; or
- for companies which are not 'qualifying companies' under the senior accounting officer provisions at **36.18 HMRC—Administration**) 12 months after the end of that period.

In other cases, the election has effect for derivative contracts entered into on or after the date specified in the election notice (which must be later than the date of the election itself). If a new adopter does not make the election within the above time limits, an election cannot take effect before two years after the end of the first accounting period in which fair value accounting is used.

An election can be amended or revoked by notice in writing before the election takes effect (for a new adopter, before the later of the time limits above where they apply), or at a later time. If notice is given after the election has effect, then this will apply for derivative contracts entered into on or after the date specified in the notice (but cannot be before the date of the notice). However, new adopters will be subject to an initial lock-in period of three years (being two years after the end of the period in which fair value accounting was first used).

In determining which period is the first accounting period in which fair value accounting is used, an accounting period of a non-UK resident company is ignored if it begins solely as a result of a direct or indirect interest in UK land (see **11.25, 11.26** CAPITAL GAINS) on or after 6 April 2019.

HMRC published guidance for companies to help them to decide whether to elect into the *Disregard Regulations* for hedging of derivative contracts from 1 January 2015. The guidance and worked examples can be found at:

www.gov.uk/government/publications/corporation-tax-hedging-derivative-contracts-and-disregard-regulations.

[*SI 2004, No 3256, Reg 6A; FA 2020, Sch 6 paras 8, 11*].

Hedging forecast transactions and firm commitments

[27.13] The following provisions apply under the *Disregard Regulations* where a company has a currency contract (*Reg 7*) or a commodity contract or debt contract (*Reg 8*) and:

(a) there is a hedging relationship (see **27.12** above) between the contract or part of the contract and a forecast transaction or firm commitment (the hedged item); and
(b) any fair value profits or losses arising on the hedged item are not brought into account for corporation tax purposes.

For the provisions to apply, either an election must be made or one of the other requirements at **27.12** above must be met.

A currency contract is one whose underlying subject matter consists wholly of currency. This in effect means that the scope of *Reg 7* is limited to contracts for the forward purchase and sale of foreign currency (including contracts which are settled by a cash payment equal to the difference between the contract rate and the exchange rate between the two currencies covered by the contract at the date of settlement). It does not extend to cross currency swaps since these also involve periodic payments over the life of the contract that are determined by reference to interest rates. Where a company uses a cross currency swap as a hedge the swap will normally fall within the scope of *Reg 9* (interest rate contracts — see **27.14** below). *Reg 7* does not apply to a currency contract to which *Reg 4* applies (see **27.10** above).

A commodity contract is defined as a derivative contract whose underlying subject matter is commodities. Where the underlying subject matter of a derivative contract also includes interest rates the contract will normally fall within *Reg 9* where the contract is used as a hedge.

A debt contract is defined as a derivative contract whose underlying subject matter is an asset or liability representing a loan relationship. Where the underlying subject matter of the contract also includes interest rates the derivative will normally fall within *Reg 9* of the *Disregard Regulations* (interest rate contracts — see below) where the contract is used as a hedge.

Recognition of profits and losses for tax purposes

Where the above requirements are satisfied, the normal rule is that any profits or losses arising on the contract in an accounting period (including any arising on a change of accounting basis and prior period adjustments) are excluded from the company's derivative contracts credits and debits for the period. Instead, all such profits and losses are brought into account for tax purposes on the earlier of:

(i) the time that the company ceases to be a party to the contract; or
(ii) the time when the hedged item begins to affect the company's profit or loss.

If there is a hedging relationship between only part of the contract and the hedged item, these provisions apply only to a proportion of the profits or losses, calculated by reference to the value of that part of the contract compared to the value of the whole contract.

If, when the company ceases to be a party to the contract, it enters into a replacement contract to hedge the same forecast transaction or firm commitment, the profits or losses under the old contract are deferred and treated as profits and losses of the new contract.

The above rules are modified where the forecast transaction or firm commitment is a transaction or commitment in relation to expenditure which would be taken into account for tax purposes in computing the profits of a trade or a property business, or which would be so deducted but for a provision prohibiting the deduction of capital expenditure in relation to the depreciation of an asset. In such cases the net profit or loss arising on the contract is brought into account for tax purposes in the accounting period in which the expenditure falls, or would fall, to be deducted. Where the forecast transaction or firm commitment represents expenditure on a capital asset that is to be used in the trade or property business, the amount of the net profit or loss on the contract that is to be brought into account for any accounting period is calculated on the same basis as the fixed asset is depreciated in the company's accounts by applying the formula in *Reg 10(3A)*.

Where a company partially terminates a contract, or where part of the hedged item is recognised in determining the company's profit or loss, a proportionate amount of the net profit or loss that has arisen on the contract is brought into account for tax purposes.

Intra-group transfers

Where the above provisions apply to a contract and the contract is transferred to another company in the same group (as in **27.24** below), the following rules apply. If the transferee meets the requirements for the above provisions to apply and the hedged item remains the same, the normal intra-group transfer provisions at **27.24** below do not apply. Instead, the above provisions apply to the transferee and the profits or losses which have not been brought into account in computing the transferor's taxable profits are transferred to the transferee and treated as its profits and losses.

Where a company has not made an election to apply the above provisions to the contract but the transferee has made such an election, the election is deemed not to have effect in relation to the transferred contract.

[*SI 2004 No 3256, Regs 6B, 6D, 7, 8, 10*].

Hedging using interest rate contracts

[27.14] The following provisions apply under the *Disregard Regulations* (*Reg* 9) where a company has an interest rate contract and:

(a) there is a hedging relationship between the contract, or a portion of the contract, and any of the risks arising in respect of an asset, liability, receipt or expense (the hedged item); and
(b) the fair value profits or losses arising on the hedged item or in relation to any of the risks, in relation to which the contract was intended to act as a hedge, arising in respect of the hedged item, or any portion of the hedged item, are not brought into account for the purposes of corporation tax for that period.

The intention of the wording in (b) above is that the provisions do not apply where:

(i) a derivative contract is designated as a fair value hedge in a company's accounts and revaluations of the hedged item are taken into account for corporation tax purposes; or
(ii) the hedged item is accounted for on a fair value basis and such fair value profits and losses are brought into account in computing the company's taxable profits.

For the provisions to apply, either an election must be made or one of the other requirements at **27.12** above must be met.

An interest rate contract is defined as:

(i) a derivative contract whose underlying subject matter is, or includes, interest rates. It will thus be noted that the definition goes far wider than what would generally be considered to be an interest rate contract, for example an interest rate swap, forward rate agreement or an interest rate future; or
(ii) in a case not falling within (i) above, a swap contract in which payment falls to be made by reference to a rate of interest or to an index determined by reference to income or retail prices (e.g. an RPI swap).

Recognition of profits and losses for tax purposes

Where the above requirements are met, any fair value profits or losses arising in respect of the contract (or the relevant portion of such fair value profits or losses where a derivative contract is only partially used for hedging purposes) as recognised in the company accounts are disregarded for the purposes of the derivative contracts legislation. Instead, any profits and losses arising in respect of the interest rate contract, or where the contract is only partially used for hedging purposes, the relevant proportion of the contract, are recognised for tax purposes on an appropriate accruals basis.

An appropriate accruals basis is one where:

(a) the contract is shown in the company's accounts at cost (which may be nil) and the cost is adjusted for any cumulative amortisation of any premium or other amount falling to be recognised in arriving at the cost of the contract; and
(b) the aggregate of:
   (i) the amount of periodical payments under the contract, or in the case of a swap contract under which only a single payment is to be made, the value of the payment; and
   (ii) the credits and debits representing interest arising, on the assumption that an effective interest method is used, in respect of the asset or liability representing a loan relationship which is a hedged item,

   represent the credits or debits that would be given by generally accepted accounting practice in relation to an asset or liability representing a loan relationship whose terms include those of both the hedged item and the interest rate contract;
(c) exchange gains and losses are recognised as a result of the translation of the contract at the balance sheet date. This means, in the case of a currency contract, that the contract has to be revalued by translating the currency or currencies to which the contract relates into the company's functional currency (defined as 'the currency of the primary environment in which the company operates'), or in the case of an investment company that has elected for a currency to be its designated currency for tax purposes, that currency, using the relevant spot rate of exchange at the end of the accounting period in question; and
(d) profits or losses which arise as a result of the contract coming to an end before its stated maturity date are amortised and brought into account over the unexpired term of the hedged item.

Where an interest rate contract begins or ceases to fall within these provisions, an adjustment is required for tax purposes to reflect the fact that the taxable profits have been determined on an appropriate accruals basis, whereas otherwise they would have been determined on a fair value basis. The amount of this adjustment has to be determined on a just and reasonable basis with a view to ensuring that as a result of the change, no amounts are double counted or are left out of account for tax purposes and with regard to the unexpired term of the hedged item. This may apply where, for example, a company ceases to use the derivative contract as a hedge but it continues to be a party to the contract.

Intra-group transfers

Where the above provisions apply to a contract and the contract is transferred to another company in the same group (as in **27.24** below), the following rules apply. If the transferee meets the requirements for the above provisions to apply and the hedged item remains the same, the normal intra-group transfer provisions at **27.24** below apply (despite the normal prohibition on their application where the transferor uses fair value accounting) and the above provisions apply to determine the carrying value of the derivative contract in the hands of the transferor immediately before the transfer takes place. The above provisions then apply to the transferee whether or not it has made an election.

Where a company has not made an election to apply the above provisions to the contract but the transferee has made such an election, the election is deemed not to have effect in relation to the transferred contract.

[*SI 2004 No 3256, Regs 6C, 6D, 9*].

Hedging proceeds of a rights issue or an open offer of shares

[27.15] The following provisions apply under the *Disregard Regulations* (*Reg 7A*), where a company has a derivative contract where the underlying subject matter consists wholly of currency (i.e. a currency forward contract) and there is a hedging relationship between the contract and the anticipated or future proceeds of an announced or proposed rights issue or open offer of shares. There is such a relationship to the extent that:

- the contract (or part of the contract) is intended to hedge the economic risk to future capital raised under the share issue; and
- the economic risk is attributable to fluctuations in exchange rates between the currency in which the share issue is denominated and the company's functional currency.

A rights issue or open offer of shares is defined as an offer or invitation to existing shareholders to subscribe for or purchase further shares in proportion to (or nearly as may be in proportion to) their current holdings.

If these requirements are met, the provisions apply automatically without the need for an election.

If there is a hedging relationship between only part of the contract and the hedged item, the provisions apply only to a proportion of the profits or losses, calculated by reference to the value of that part of the contract compared to the value of the whole contract.

The provisions do not apply where a company (C) enters into a derivative with a person (A) with which it is connected unless a person that is connected with C enters into a derivative contract with a person that is not connected with C and the contract confers rights or imposes liabilities which are equivalent to those of A under the contract which A has entered with C. The effect of this wording is that A itself does not have to enter into the contract with the third-party, all that is necessary is that a connected company enters into such a contract.

Recognition of profits and losses for tax purposes

Exchange gains or losses that arise on the forward contract are disregarded in computing the company's derivative contract profits to the extent that the contract is hedging the proceeds of the rights issue or open offer. The company is, however, liable to tax on any exchange gains arising on the forward contract where such gains are distributed to its shareholders and the gains are brought into account in the accounting period in which the distribution is made. In the Corporate Finance Manual, HMRC have said that they will treat any exchange gains as forming the bottom tranche of a company's profits and thus, a tax charge will only arise if and to the extent that a company's distributable profits at any time are less than the amount of the exchange gain that has been disregarded under this provision (CFM57170).

[*SI 2004 No 3256, Regs 7A, 10A*].

Special computational provisions

Amounts not fully recognised for accounting purposes

[27.16] An anti-avoidance provision applies where profits and losses arising on a derivative contract are not fully recognised in a company's accounts in accordance with generally accepted accounting practice as a result of tax avoidance arrangements to which the company is at any time a party. For these purposes arrangements are tax avoidance arrangements if the main purpose, or one of main purposes, of any party to the arrangements, in entering into them, is to obtain a tax advantage within *CTA 2010, s 1139*). Arrangements in turn are defined as including any arrangements, scheme or understanding of any kind, whether or not legally enforceable, involving a single transaction or two or more transactions. Where this provision applies the company is required to recognise the full amount of the credits arising on the derivative for an accounting period in computing its derivative contract profits and a fair value basis has to be used to determine those credits. It is not permitted to bring any debits into account in respect of the derivative contract.

Where the company is a party to the derivative contract at the start of the first accounting period to which the provisions apply and the fair value of the contract is greater that its tax-adjusted carrying-value (defined in *CTA 2009 s 702*) in the company's accounts at that time, the company is required to recognise a credit equal to the difference in computing its derivative contract profits for that period.

[*CTA 2009, ss 599A, 599B*].

Debits arising from the derecognition of derivative contracts

[27.17] A company cannot bring into account in computing its derivative contract profits any debits it recognises in its accounts in respect of the derecognition of a derivative contract if the company remains a party to the contract and the derecognition is a result of tax avoidance arrangements to which the company is a party. Arrangements are tax avoidance arrangements if the main purpose, or one of the main purposes, of any party to the arrangements, in entering into them, is to obtain a tax advantage (within *CTA 2010, s 1139*). Arrangements in turn are defined as including any arrangements, scheme or understanding of any kind, whether or not legally enforceable, involving a single transaction or two or more transactions.

[*CTA 2009 s 698A*].

Special provision for a release of a liability under a derivative contract

[27.18] Where a company's liability to pay an amount under the contract is released, no credit is required to be brought into account in respect of the release if it is part of a statutory insolvency arrangement within the meaning given by *CTA 2009, s 1319*. [*CTA 2009, s 611*].

Unallowable purposes

[27.19] Where, in any accounting period, a derivative contract of a company has an unallowable purpose, any '*exchange credits*' (i.e. credits attributable to exchange gains arising on the contract) and any debits in respect of the contract which, on a just and reasonable apportionment, are attributable to the unallowable purpose are not to be brought into account for that period, except as detailed below.

A derivative contract has an unallowable purpose where at any time during the accounting period the company is a party to, or enters into a related transaction in respect of, the contract:

(a) otherwise than for its business or other commercial purposes;
(b) in respect of activities for which it is not within the charge to corporation tax;
(c) for a tax avoidance purpose.

For this purpose, a related transaction is defined as at **27.6** above but also includes anything that equates in substance to an acquisition or disposal in whole or in part of rights and liabilities under the derivative contract.

A company will be regarded as being a party to a derivative contract for a tax avoidance purpose where the main purpose, or one of the main purposes, for which the company was a party to the contract at that time, or for which it entered into the related transaction, was to secure a tax advantage for itself or any other person. '*Tax advantage*' is defined by reference to *CTA 2010, s 1139*.

A debit disallowed under this rule cannot be allowed as a deduction for corporation tax purposes under any other provision. Where the amount of a debit that would fall to be disallowed under this provision has been reduced by being offset against a derivative contract credit, the amount that is disallowed is to be increased by the amount that has been so offset.

Where, in the case of a derivative contract, the debits relating to the unallowable purpose for an accounting period exceed the exchange credits relating to it in the same accounting period (i.e. there is a '*net loss*'), the '*excess accumulated net losses*' are brought into account as a debit for that period.

The '*excess accumulated net losses*' on a contract for an accounting period is found as follows:

(I) find the sum of net losses for the period and any preceding period;
(II) deduct any part of l which has been brought into account in previous periods;

(III) find the sum of credits (others than exchange credits) for the period and any previous periods which are referable, on a just and reasonable basis, to the unallowable purpose;

(IV) deduct from III (but not to reduce it below nil) any debits for the period or any previous period which were not excluded as a result of the unallowable purpose and any amounts brought into account in any previous periods;

(V) compare the result of II with that of IV — the lower amounts gives the amount of the excess accumulated net losses for the period.

[*CTA 2009, ss 690–692*].

Capitalised expenditure

[27.20] A relieving measure applies where amounts that would otherwise have been included in computing a company's derivative contract profits for an accounting period are included in determining the carrying value of an asset or liability. In such cases where the profits or losses on the asset or liability are not determined for corporation tax purposes by reference to the amounts that are recognised in the company's accounts in accordance with generally accepted accounting practice, the amounts which are so included are included in computing the company's derivative contract profits for that accounting period. Such treatment does not apply to amounts included as part of the cost of an intangible fixed asset where the company has made an election to write down the cost of that asset on a fixed-rate basis (see **41** INTANGIBLE ASSETS). Where this provision applies and relief has been obtained for a debit that has been capitalised, no debit in respect of the writing down, amortisation or depreciation of the asset or liability is to be brought into account to the extent that such debit is attributable to the debit that has been capitalised.

Where relief has been claimed under this provision in respect of debits that have been capitalised no debit in respect of the writing down, amortisation, or depreciation may be claimed to the extent that such amount is attributable to the debit for which relief has been obtained.

[*CTA 2009, s 604*].

Counteracting effect of avoidance arrangements

[27.21] Anti-avoidance provisions apply to counter any derivative-related tax advantages that would (in the absence of the provisions) arise from relevant avoidance arrangements. Where the provisions apply, adjustments are to be made on a just and reasonable basis to the debits and credits that are brought into account for the purposes of the derivative contracts legislation to counteract the effect of the avoidance arrangements. Adjustments may be made by way of an assessment, the modification of an assessment, amendment or disallowance of a claim, or otherwise. Arrangements are defined in the usual way as including any agreement, understanding, scheme, transaction or series of transactions (whether or not legally enforceable).

Arrangements are relevant avoidance arrangements if their main purpose, or one of their main purposes, is to enable a company to obtain a derivative-related tax advantage. A company will obtain a derivative-related tax advantage if:

(a) it brings into account a debit in computing its profits for the purposes of the derivative contracts legislation to which it would not otherwise be entitled;

(b) it brings into account a debit in computing's its profits for the purposes of the derivative contracts legislation which exceeds that to which it would otherwise be entitled;

(c) it avoids having to bring a credit into account in computing its profits for the purposes of the derivative contracts legislation;

(d) the amount of any credits brought into account by the company in computing its profits for the purposes of the derivative contracts legislation is less than it would otherwise be; or

(e) it brings a debit or credit into account earlier or later than it otherwise would in computing its profits for the purposes of the derivative contracts legislation.

Arrangements are not relevant avoidance arrangements if the obtaining of any derivative-related tax advantages that would (in the absence of the provision) arise from them can reasonably be regarded as consistent with any principles on which the provisions of the derivative contracts legislation that are relevant to the arrangements are based (whether expressed or implied) and the policy objectives of those provisions.

Examples are provided of circumstances which might indicate that this exclusion is not applicable. These are:

(i) the elimination or reduction, for the purposes of corporation tax, profits of a company arising from any of its derivative contracts, where for economic purposes profits, or greater profits, arise to the company from that contract;

(ii) the creation or increase, for the purposes of corporation tax, of a loss or expense arising from a derivative contract, where for economic purposes no loss or expense, or a smaller loss or expense, arises from that contract;

(iii) preventing or delaying the recognition as an item of profit or loss of an amount that would apart from the arrangements be recognised in the company's accounts as an item of profit or loss, or be so recognised earlier;

(iv) ensuring that a derivative contract is treated for accounting purposes in a way in which it would not have been treated in the absence of some other transaction forming part of the arrangements;

(v) enabling a company to bring into account a debit in respect of an exchange loss, in circumstances where a corresponding exchange gain would not give rise to a credit or would give rise to a credit of a small amount;

(vi) enabling a company to bring into account a debit in respect of a fair value loss in circumstances where a corresponding fair value gain would not give rise to a credit or would give rise to a credit of a smaller amount.

In such cases the exclusion is only not available if it is reasonable to assume that such a result was not the anticipated result when the provisions of the derivative contracts legislation that are relevant to the arrangements were enacted.

[*CTA 2009, ss 698B, 698C, 698D*].

Transfers of value to connected companies

[27.22] Where a company fails to exercise in full its rights under an option which was a derivative contract and there is a transfer of value by the company which held the option (the 'transferor') to a connected company (the 'transferee') which is not otherwise chargeable to corporation tax, a credit is brought into account by the transferor. The credit has to be brought into account in the accounting period in which the option expires, or would have expired had the rights under it been exercised. The amount of the credit is, where the option expired, the amount paid by the transferor for it and where any of the rights were exercised, an amount representing a just and reasonable proportion of the amount paid. In determining whether or not there is a transfer of value, it is assumed that if there had not been a connection between the companies, all rights would have been exercised in full on the latest date they could be exercised.

An option is within these provisions if it falls within the definition in 27.2 above, but without the exclusion of cases involving cash settlement.

Companies are '*connected*' for these purposes in an accounting period if, at any time in that period, one company controls the other or both companies are under the control of the same person. Control has the meaning given at **50.24** LOAN RELATIONSHIPS).

[*CTA 2009, s 695*].

For transfers of value in general, see 72 TRANSFER PRICING.

Exchange gains and losses where derivative contract not at arm's length

[27.23] Where, in an accounting period, a company is party to a derivative contract the provisions of which are not at arm's length, so that the transfer pricing provisions (see 72 TRANSFER PRICING) apply to treat the company as not being party to the contract, any exchange gains and losses arising in that accounting period as regards the derivative contract are to be left out of account in determining the related credits and debits. Where the contract in question is to any extent 'matched', the above provisions apply to leave out of account exchange gains or losses only to the extent that they are unmatched.

Where the transfer pricing provisions instead require profits and losses to be computed as if the contract had been on arm's length terms, any such exchange gain or loss is instead adjusted for those purposes to the amount which would have arisen if the contract had been on such terms. Again, this provision applies only to the extent that the contract is unmatched.

A derivative contract is '*matched*' for this purpose if and to the extent that it is in a matching relationship with another derivative contract or loan relationship (i.e. one is intended to eliminate or substantially reduce the risk of the other from exchange rate fluctuations) or exchange gains or losses arising in relation to an asset or liability representing the loan relationship are excluded from being brought into account under the disregard regulations (see **27.10** above).

Apart from these provisions, nothing in the transfer pricing provisions is to require exchange gains and losses from derivative contracts to be computed as though the contracts had been on arm's length terms.

[*CTA 2009, s 694*].

Transactions within groups

[27.24] There are provisions requiring adjustments to ensure that intra-group transactions under the derivative contracts regime are tax neutral. The provisions apply where, as a result of a related transaction (see **27.6** above) between two members of a group (both being within the charge to corporation tax in respect of the transaction), one of those companies (the 'transferee company') directly or indirectly replaces the other (the 'transferor company') as a party to a derivative contract, or becomes party to a contract equivalent to one to which the other company has ceased to be party. The provisions similarly apply where a series of transactions, having the same effect as a related transaction between two companies each of which has been a member of the same group at some time in the course of those transactions, results in such a replacement.

In determining the credits and debits to be brought into account, the transferor company is treated as having entered into the transaction (or the first of a series of transactions, as the case may be) in the accounting period in which the transaction takes place for a consideration equal to the 'notional carrying value' of the derivative contract. The transferee is treated as having acquired the contract for a consideration equal to that amount for any accounting period in which it is party to the contract. (This means that where the transferee uses fair value accounting the movement in fair value in the accounting period of transfer will be the difference between the fair value at the end of that period and the carrying value to the transferor of the contract and where the transferee uses an amortised cost, then the carrying value of the transferor will be used as the cost to the transferee.) The '*notional carrying value*' is the amount that would have been the tax-adjusted carrying value (see **27.8** above) of the contract in the transferor's accounts had a period of account ended immediately before the company ceased to be party to the contract.

Where:

(a) payment of the transfer consideration is deferred;
(b) the amount payable exceeds the amount which would have been payable had payment been made at the time of the transfer; and
(c) some or all of the excess can reasonably regarded as representing a return on an investment of money at interest (and thus as a discount arising on the money debt),

the transferor's disposal consideration is increased by the amount of the discount. No adjustment, however is made to the price at which the transferee is deemed to have acquired the derivative contract.

The transfer pricing provisions in *TIOPA 2010, Pt 4* (see **72** TRANSFER PRICING) do not apply to debits or credits determined as above.

'Group' for these purposes is as under *TCGA 1992, s 170* (see **12.2** CAPITAL GAINS — GROUPS).

The circumstances in which a company replaces another as party to derivative contract include a company becoming a party to a derivative contract which confers rights, imposes liabilities or does both, equivalent to those held or owed by the original party to the contract.

See **58.20** PAYMENT OF TAX for CT payment plans for transactions with EEA resident group members which allow for payment by instalments which result in the company being replaced as a party to a derivative contract by a company resident outside the UK in an EEA state, where the transaction would have been within the above provisions if the transferee were UK-resident. Plans can be entered into in respect of transactions occurring in accounting periods ending on or after 10 October 2018.

Fair value accounting

The above provisions do not apply where the transferor's profits and losses arising on the contract are determined for the purposes of the derivative contracts legislation using a fair value basis of accounting.

Instead, the amount to be brought into account by the transferor company is the fair value (as defined by *CTA 2009, s 710*) of the contract as at the date the transferee company becomes a party to the contract. The transferee is treated as acquiring the contract at its fair value at that date.

As above, where:

(a) payment of the transfer consideration is deferred;
(b) the amount payable exceeds the amount which would have been payable had payment been made at the time of the transfer; and
(c) some or all of the excess can reasonably be regarded as representing a return on an investment of money at interest (and thus as a discount arising on the money debt),

the transfer is consideration is increased by the amount of the discount. No adjustment, however, is made to the price at which the transferee is deemed to acquire the derivative contract.

[*CTA 2009, ss 624–628*].

See **27.13**, **27.14** above for the interaction of these provisions with *Regs 7, 8* and *9* of the *Disregard Regulations.*

In *HBOS Treasury Services plc (now HBOS Treasury Services Ltd) v HMRC* FTT 2009, [2010] SFTD 134, the bank entered a scheme to monetise interest rate swaps by a transfer to a subsidiary followed by a later sale of the subsidiary (at a time before a degrouping charge applied). The scheme involved the novation of the swaps. The Tribunal Judge held that in order for the intra-group transfer provisions to apply in the case of a novation there must not be any amendments to the terms of the contract as a result of the novation that have any meaningful financial consequences. In the present case there were amendments to the terms of the contract and, accordingly, the Tribunal Judge concluded that what is now *CTA 2009, s 625* did not apply to the novation of the contract.

Degrouping charge

[27.25] A degrouping charge applies where after replacing the transferor company as party to a derivative contract as in **27.24** above, the transferee company ceases within the 'relevant six-year period' to be a member of the group. The '*relevant six-year period*' is the period of six years following the related transaction or the last of the series of transactions.

In this case, the transferee company is treated (subject to the conditions below) as having assigned the rights and liabilities under the derivative contract immediately before degrouping for consideration equal to their fair value at that time and as having immediately reacquired them for the same amount. Thus, any gain or loss is brought into charge to tax under the derivative contract provisions immediately before the transferee leaves the group.

The degrouping charge does not apply where the transferee company ceases to be a member of the group by reason only of an exempt distribution within *CTA 2010, s 1075*. However, if there is a chargeable payment (within the meaning of *CTA 2010, s 1088(1)*) within five years after making the exempt distribution, a degrouping charge arises as above but the transferee company is treated as having assigned the rights and liabilities under the derivative contract immediately before making the chargeable payment for a consideration equal to their fair value at the time that it left the group.

[*CTA 2009, ss 630–632*].

Company ceasing to be UK-resident etc.

[27.26] Where a company ceases to be UK-resident, it is deemed to have assigned its rights and liabilities under its derivative contracts immediately before and to have reacquired them immediately after it ceased to be UK-resident, at their fair value. (Thus, any profit or loss on the rights or liabilities will be brought into account as a derivative contract credit or debit.)

This provision does not apply to a derivative contract that has been transferred to the transferee under the group transfer provisions in *CTA 2009, s 625* within the previous six years and the time at which the transferee migrates from the UK is the same as that at which it leaves the group. There is no requirement that a degrouping charge arises.

It also does not apply if, immediately after the company ceases to be UK-resident, the contract is held for the purposes of the company's UK permanent establishment, its trade of dealing in or developing UK land, or (with effect from 6 April 2020, subject to the transitional provisions at **64.7** RESIDENCE) its UK property business or (with effect from 6 April 2020, subject to those transitional provisions) for the purpose of enabling the company to generate other UK property income.

If a contract held by a non-UK resident company ceases to be held for one of the above purposes (and does not then become held for any other of those purposes), it is treated as if the company had assigned, and immediately reacquired, it immediately before the cessation for its fair value at that time. This does not apply, however, if the provisions in *CTA 2009, s 625* apply and the company leaves the group under those provisions at the same time as it ceases to hold the asset for any of the above purposes.

[*CTA 2009, ss 609, 610; FA 2019, Sch 5 paras 19, 20, 35*].

See **58.19** PAYMENT OF TAX for exit charge payment plans under which a company may pay corporation tax under these provisions by instalments or defer payment.

Derivative contracts with non-residents

[27.27] Special provisions apply (except as below) where either:

(a) a company and a non-resident both become party to a derivative contract; or
(b) a company becomes party to a derivative contract to which a non-resident is party or *vice versa.*

For each accounting period for any part of which the company and a non-resident are both parties to a derivative contract which makes provision for 'notional interest payments' (e.g. interest-based payments under an interest rate or currency swap), no 'excluded debits' arising to the company from the derivative contract may be brought into account by the company.

An '*excluded debit*' is the excess of the aggregate of 'notional interest payments' made by the company to the non-resident while they are both party to the contract over the aggregate of such payments made by the non-resident to the company. A '*notional interest payment*' is any payment of an amount determined (wholly or mainly) by applying a rate equal to a specified rate of interest to a specified notional principal amount for a specified period.

These special provisions do not apply:

(i) to a company which is a bank, a building society, a financial trader (see below) or a recognised clearing house (within *Financial Services and Markets Act 2000, s 285*) holding the derivative contract (otherwise than as agent or nominee) solely for the purposes of a UK trade (or part);
(ii) with effect from 6 April 2020 (subject to the transitional provisions at **64.7** RESIDENCE) where the non-resident holds the derivative contract (otherwise than as agent or nominee) and is chargeable to corporation tax on income arising from the contract, or would be if there were any such income;
(iii) (before 6 April 2020) where the non-resident holds the derivative contract (otherwise than as agent or nominee) solely for the purposes of a *UK* trade (or part) carried on through a permanent establishment (or branch or agency — see **64.6** RESIDENCE); or
(iv) where arrangements made under *TIOPA 2010, s 2(1)* (see **31.3** DOUBLE TAX RELIEF) with the government of the territory in which the non-UK resident is resident (or, if the non-resident is party to the contract as agent or nominee of another person, with the government of the territory in which that other person is resident) make provision, whether for relief or otherwise, in relation to interest.

As regards (i) above, for the guidelines used by HMRC in deciding whether a company should be approved as a financial trader, see HMRC Statement of Practice SP 4/02, 30 September 2002.

[*CTA 2009, ss 696, 697; FA 2019, Sch 5 paras 21, 35*].

Provisions not at arm's length — amounts imputed

[27.28] Where, under the TRANSFER PRICING (70) rules, any amounts fall to be treated as profits or losses arising to, or expenses incurred by, a company in respect of any of its derivative contracts or related transactions, those provisions will have effect so as to require credits or debits relating to the deemed amounts to be brought into account to the same extent as if they were actual amounts.

No credit is to be brought into account to the extent that it corresponds to an amount which has not previously been brought into account as a debit as a result of the above rule.

[*CTA 2009, s 693*].

Disguised distribution arrangements

[27.29] Legislation applies to counteract the use of avoidance schemes that utilise total return swaps linked to company profits. The measures target schemes involving two companies in the same group (as defined in *CTA 2010, s 357GD* – the patent box provisions) and negate any debits and certain credits which would arise from certain derivative arrangements the effect of which is to transfer profits of a company to other group companies.

Where two group companies, company A and B, are a party to arrangements involving one or more derivative contracts (whether or not they are a party at the same time) and the arrangements result in what is, in substance, a payment (directly or indirectly) from company A to company B of all or a significant part of the profits of the business of A (or of a company which is a member of the same group as A or B), then no debits for a specified contract (see below) which relates to the profit transfer, and which would otherwise be taxable under the derivative provisions, are to be brought into account by A or B.

These provisions only apply to arrangements which are not of a kind that companies carrying on the same kind of business as company A would enter into in the ordinary course of business.

The derivative contracts included in the arrangements are each referred to as a '*specified contract*'.

Where one or more debits of a specified contract are not brought into account, then no credits arising from the same contract, which relate to the same profit transfer and which would otherwise be taxable, are to be brought into account by A or B, to the extent the total credits do not exceed the total debits. However, a credit can be brought into account if it arises (directly or indirectly) from arrangements the main purpose of which, or one of the main purposes, is to secure a tax advantage (per *CTA 2010, s 1139*) for any person.

A company is a member of the same group as another company, for these purposes, if it is (or has been) a member of the same group at a time when the arrangements have effect.

'*Arrangements*' is widely defined to include any scheme, arrangement or understanding of any kind, whether or not legally enforceable, involving a single or two or more transactions.

[*CTA 2009, s 695A*].

Group mismatch and tax mismatch schemes

[27.30] The group mismatch scheme legislation described at **50.36** LOAN RELATIONSHIPS and the tax mismatch scheme legislation described at **50.37** LOAN RELATIONSHIPS apply for the purposes of both the loan relationships and the derivative contracts regimes.

European cross-border mergers

[27.31] The following provisions apply to:

(a) (before Brexit IP completion day (11pm on 31 December 2020)) the formation of an SE by the merger of two or more companies in accordance with *Council Regulation (EC) No 2157/2001, Arts 2(1), 17(2)*;

(b) (before Brexit IP completion day) the formation of an SCE by the merger of two or more 'co-operative societies', at least one of which is a registered society within **22.1** CO-OPERATIVE AND COMMUNITY BENEFIT SOCIETIES, in accordance with *Council Regulation (EC) No 1435/2003*;

(c) a merger effected by the transfer by one or more companies or co-operative societies of all their assets and liabilities to a single existing company or co-operative society; and

(d) a merger effected by the transfer by two or more companies of all their assets to a single new company (which is not an SE or SCE) in exchange for the issue by the transferee company of shares or debentures to each person holding shares in or debentures of a transferor company.

From Brexit IP completion day, no new SEs or SCEs can be formed in the UK.

Each of the merging companies must be resident in a relevant state, but not all can be resident in the same state. A company is resident in a relevant state for this purpose if it is within a charge to tax under the law of the State as being resident for that purpose and it is not regarded, for the purposes of any DOUBLE TAX RELIEF (**31**) arrangements to which the State is a party, as resident in a territory not within a relevant state. In the case of merger under (c) or (d) above, the transferor must cease to exist without being in liquidation.

A '*relevant state*' is an EU member state or, after Brexit IP completion day, the UK or an EU member state.

For the purposes of (b) and (c) above, a '*co-operative society*' is a registered society within **22.1** CO-OPERATIVE AND COMMUNITY BENEFIT SOCIETIES or a similar society established under the law of a member state other than the UK.

Where:

(i) immediately after the merger the transferee is either resident in the UK and within the charge to corporation tax or is not resident in the UK but is within the charge to corporation tax as a consequence of carrying on a trade in the UK through a permanent establishment; and

(ii) for mergers within (a), (b) or (c) above, the transfer of assets and liabilities is made in exchange for the issue of shares in or debentures of the transferee to the holders of shares in or debentures of a transferor, except where, and to the extent that, the transferee is prevented from meeting this requirement by reason only of *Companies Act 2006, s 658* (rule against limited company acquiring its own shares) or a corresponding provision in another member state,

then, in determining the debits and credits to be brought into account in respect of a derivative contract, if the rights and liabilities under the contract are transferred in the course of the merger, the transfer is treated as having been made for a consideration equal to the notional carrying value (see **27.24** above). This does not apply where the transferor uses fair value accounting for the contract. Instead, the transfer must be treated by both companies as being at fair value.

Where:

(A) in the course of the merger, a company resident in the UK transfers all the assets and liabilities relating to a business it carries on through a permanent establishment in a member state other than the UK to a company resident in the another member state;
(B) the transfer includes the transfer of rights and liabilities under a derivative contract; and
(C) for mergers within (a), (b) or (c) above, the transfer of assets and liabilities is made in exchange for the issue of shares in or debentures of the transferee to the holders of shares in or debentures of a transferor, except where, and to the extent that, the transferee is prevented from meeting this requirement by reason only of *Companies Act 2006, s 658* (rule against limited company acquiring its own shares) or a corresponding provision in another member state,

then, if tax would have been chargeable under the law of the other member state in respect of the transfer of rights or liabilities under the derivative contract but for the Mergers Directive (*90/434/EEC*), double tax relief (whether unilateral or by agreement) is available as if the amount of tax which would have been so payable but for the Directive were payable. For this purpose, it is to be assumed that, to the extent permitted by the law of the other member state, losses arising on the transfer are set against gains so arising and that any relief due to the UK company under that law is claimed.

The above provisions do not apply unless the merger is effected for *bona fide* commercial reasons and is not part of a scheme or arrangements of which the main purpose or one of the main purposes is avoiding a liability to tax. Advance clearance can be obtained that this condition is met.

[*CTA 2009, ss 682–686; SI 2019 No 689, Regs 1, 16(14); European Union (Withdrawal Agreement) Act 2020, Sch 5 para 1(1)*].

Cross border transfers of business

[27.32] Where a UK resident company transfers the whole or part of a business that it previously carried on through a permanent establishment in another relevant state (see **27.31** above) and a derivative contract is included as part of the assets that are transferred, and certain conditions are satisfied, the UK resident company is able to claim double tax credit relief for the overseas tax that would have been payable in respect of the merger, but for the operation of the mergers directive.

[*TIOPA 2010, ss 118, 119; SI 2019 No 689, Reg 18(3)(4)*].

Transparent entities

[27.33] The cross border merger and cross border transfer of business provisions at **27.31** and **27.32** above are varied apply where one of the parties is a 'transparent entity'. See *CTA 2009, s 687 and TIOPA 2010, ss 120, 121.*

A '*transparent entity*' for this purpose is an entity which is resident in a member state other than the UK and is listed as a company in the Annex to the Mergers Directive, but which does not have an ordinary share capital and, if resident in the UK, would not be capable of being registered as a company under *Companies Act 2006*. [*CTA 2009, ss 687, 688; TIOPA 2010, s 120(6); SI 2019 No 689, Reg 16(15)(16)*].

Derivative whose underlying subject matter is an interest in a unit trust, open ended investment company or offshore fund

[27.34] Special provisions apply in relation to such schemes, broadly as follows.

Where a contract does not otherwise qualify as a derivative contract, it is to be treated as such if its underlying subject matter is wholly or partly comprised of a holding in an open ended investment company, unit trust or an offshore fund and that company, unit trust or offshore fund does not satisfy the 'qualifying investments' test.

[*CTA 2009, ss 587, 601*].

Where a company has, for two successive years, a relevant contract which is a contract relating to a holding in an OEIC, unit trust or offshore fund that does not satisfy the qualifying investments test for the second year but not the first and immediately before the beginning of the second period it was a chargeable asset, any chargeable gain or allowable loss has to be brought in by the company in the year in which it ceases to be a party to the contract, using the following assumptions:

(i) the company disposed of the relevant contract immediately before the beginning of the second accounting period;
(ii) the consideration for the disposal was the accounting value (if any) according to the company's accounts at the end of the first year.

[*CTA 2009, s 660*].

Investment trusts and venture capital trusts

[27.35] Any capital profits or losses arising to an investment trust or a venture capital trust from a derivative contract must not be brought into account in determining derivative contract credits or debits. Capital profits or losses in this case are those which, in preparing accounts in accordance with UK generally accepted accounting practice, are carried to or sustained by a capital reserve in accordance with the relevant Statement of Recommended Practice (SORP). The relevant SORP is that relating to the Financial Statements of Investment Trust Companies issued by the Association of Investment Trust Companies in January 2003 as from time to time modified or revised.

The excess of relevant credits over relevant debits from derivative contracts is to be treated as income from shares and securities for the purposes of determining whether or not a company may be approved as an investment trust or a venture capital trust under *CTA 2010, s 1160(3)* or *ITA 2007, s 276(3)* respectively. (See generally **47.2** INVESTMENT TRUSTS and **73** VENTURE CAPITAL TRUSTS.)

Treasury powers

The Treasury may by order amend the above provisions so as to alter the definition of capital profits or losses following the modification, amendment, revision or replacement of a SORP.

[*CTA 2009, ss 637, 638*].

Authorised unit trusts and open ended investment companies

[27.36] Capital profits, gains or losses arising to authorised unit trusts and open ended investment companies in respect of derivative contracts to which they are a party are excluded in computing their profits chargeable to corporation tax. These are defined as such profits, gains or losses that fall to be dealt with under the heading 'net gains/losses', in the statement of total return for the accounting period. This is in turn defined as the statement of total return which, in accordance with the Statement of Recommended Practice (SORP) used for the accounting period, must be included in the accounts contained in the annual report of the authorised investment fund. The SORP is in turn defined as, in relation to any accounting period for which it is required or permitted to be used, the SORP relating to authorised investment funds issued by the Investment Management Association in November 2008.

It is not possible for an authorised unit trust or open ended investment company to carry back a loss on a derivative contract that is not excluded in calculating its taxable profits for set off against its taxable profits of earlier periods.

[*SI 2006 No 964, Regs 10–14*].

Miscellaneous provisions related to derivative contracts

Partnerships involving companies

[27.37] Where any of the partners in a partnership which carries on a trade, profession or business, and which is a party to a derivative contract, is a company, no account is taken of debits or credits in relation to the contract in calculating the profits of the partnership for corporation tax purposes. Each company partner is instead required to bring into account a share of the credits and debits in respect of the contract as follows. The credits and debits are determined separately for each company partner as if the contract was entered into or acquired by the company for the purposes of its own trade or business, and as if any transactions carried out by the firm in relation to the contract were carried out by the company. To the extent that any exchange gains or losses are recognised in the firm's statement of recognised gains and losses or statement of changes in equity, they are treated as recognised in the corresponding statement of the company partner (such that they fall to be disregarded in computing the derivative contract profits of that company partner). The company is then required to bring into account a share of the credits and debits so determined corresponding to its share in partnership profits.

Where the company partner uses fair value accounting in relation to its interest in the firm the credits and debits determined as above must be determined on a fair value basis of accounting.

[*CTA 2009, ss 620, 621*].

Prevention of deduction of income tax

[27.38] A company is not required to deduct income tax from any payment made under a derivative contract to which these provisions apply. [*ITA 2007, s 980*].

Index-linked gilt-edged securities with embedded contracts for differences

[27.39] Credits and debits arising on a derivative contract are not to be brought into account where:

(a) the rights and liabilities arising under a contract are split into two parts as set out in 27.40 below, with respect to a creditor relationship;
(b) the creditor relationship is an index-linked gilt-edged security giving rise to non-trading credits and debits in respect of the equivalent deemed loan relationship; and
(c) the 'embedded derivative' contract is a contract for differences.

[*CTA 2009, s 623*].

Derivative contracts and chargeable gains basis

[27.40] For the purpose of these provisions, a '*chargeable asset*' is any asset on which a gain would be a chargeable gain. '*Asset*' includes any obligations under futures contracts which are regarded as assets under *TCGA 1992, s 143*.

In four circumstances, a derivative contract is charged under the capital gains regime. These are:

(a) the contract relates to land or certain tangible moveable property;

(b) the company has a creditor relationship with an embedded derivative which is an option;
(c) the company has a creditor relationship with an embedded derivative which is an exactly tracking contract for differences, the underlying subject matter of which is certain shares;
(d) the contract is a property based total return swap.

Any profits or losses that are recognised in the company's accounts in respect of such derivatives in accordance with generally accepted accounting practice are treated as chargeable gains or allowable losses for the purposes of corporation tax on chargeable gains and are brought into account for tax purposes in the accounting period in which they are so recognised. There are two exceptions to this rule. The first is that special computational rules apply to property based total return swaps — see *CTA 2009, s 659(3)–(4A)*. The second is where, were the embedded derivative an actual option which was disposed at the end of that accounting period, any gain arising on the option would be ignored for tax purposes under the substantial shareholding legislation in *TCGA 1992, Sch 7AC* (see **13.5** CAPITAL GAINS — SUBSTANTIAL SHAREHOLDINGS). In such cases any gains or losses arising on the embedded derivative contract are ignored in computing the company's profits for the purposes of derivative contracts legislation.

[*CTA 2009, ss 640–642*].

Carry back of losses

[27.41] Where there is a 'net loss' under the provisions in 27.40 above in an accounting period (the '*loss period*') and, in a previous accounting period falling wholly or partly within 24 months immediately preceding the start of the loss period, there is a 'net gain' under the above provisions, a claim can be made for the loss to be wholly or partly carried back and set against part or all of the gain (but not so as to reduce either the loss or the gain below nil). The claim must be made within two years of the end of the period in which the net loss arose. Losses must be set against gains of a later period before those of an earlier period. Where a gain period falls partly before the 24-month period mentioned above, the loss can only be offset against the proportion of the gain falling within the 24-month period (time-apportioned based on the number of days).

A '*net loss*' in this case is the sum of any allowable losses arising under *CTA 2009, s 641* in a period less the sum of any chargeable gains arising under the above provisions in the same period, in both cases in respect of the company's derivative contracts. A '*net gain*' is the excess of *CTA 2009, s 641* gains over *s 641* losses, further reduced by any non-*s 641* allowable losses. Any non-*s 641* allowable losses must be set against any non-*s 641* gains before the remainder is deducted from *s 641* gains.

[*CTA 2009, ss 663–664*].

Derivative contracts relating to land etc.

[27.42] Non-trading increases and decreases in the value of derivative contracts are not treated as non-trading credits and debits under the derivative contracts regime but instead are treated as chargeable gains or allowable losses within the capital gains regime where the following conditions are met:

(A) the underlying subject matter relates to land (wherever situated) or tangible movable property other than commodities which are tangible assets;
(B) the company is not a party to the derivative contract at any time in the accounting period for trading purposes;
(C) the company is not an excluded body; and
(D) no two or more of the parties to the contract are connected persons (within **19** CONNECTED PERSONS).

Where the derivative includes income from land or tangible moveable property (see above) and that income is subordinate income, it is left out of account. Whether or not income is subordinate is determined at the time the company enters into or acquires the contract. There are also special provisions allowing carry back losses (see below).

[*CTA 2009, ss 643, 644*].

Creditor relationships — embedded derivatives which are options to acquire shares

[27.43] Where in a company's accounts in accordance with generally accepted accounting practice a derivative contract is separated from a creditor relationship:

(i) the contract is treated as an option by *CTA 2009, s 585(3)*;
(ii) the underlying subject matter is qualifying ordinary shares or mandatorily convertible preference shares;
(iii) the creditor relationship is not a trading relationship at any time in the accounting period;
(iv) the company is not an open ended investment company, investment trust, venture capital trust or a unit trust; and
(v) the company was not a party to the loan relationship immediately before the start of its first statutory accounting period beginning on or after 1 January 2005.

the asset representing the creditor relationship is not treated as a qualifying corporate bond, under *TCGA 1992, s 117(A1)* and so is not prevented from falling within the chargeable gains rules by virtue of the exemption for QCBs under *TCGA 1992, s 115(1)(b)*. Therefore, gains and losses on a disposal of the loan relationship are subject to capital gains tax rules. This treatment does not apply if either:

(a) the creditor relationship provides that the shares to be acquired on conversion or exchange will have a specified cash (i.e. market) value at the time of conversion or exchange or:
    (i) the rights and liabilities in the derivative contract are such that the company is entitled or obliged to accept cash instead of the underlying shares; and
    (ii) the amount of the payment differs by a not insignificant amount from the value of the shares which it would be entitled or obliged to acquire under the contract.

'*Mandatorily convertible preference shares*' are shares which represent the creditor relationship, are not qualifying ordinary shares and are issued on terms that stipulate they must be converted into or exchanged for qualifying ordinary shares within 24 hours after the time that they are acquired.

'*Qualifying ordinary shares*' are listed shares or those in a holding company or a trading company, where the shares form all or part of the issued share capital (other than, in either case, capital which carries a right to a fixed rate dividend but no other right to share in profits or capital where the holders have no right to dividends or to share in profits in any other way).

[*CTA 2009, ss 645–647*].

Prevention of double counting

Where the option to acquire shares is exercised and the transaction is treated as a no gain/no loss reorganisation for the purposes of *TCGA 1992, s 127* in order to avoid any double counting an adjustment will be made on the subsequent disposal of the shares that are acquired. The adjustment is determined on a formula basis and, very broadly, is designed to secure that the base cost of the shares is increased by any chargeable gains that have been brought into charge to tax in respect of the embedded derivative and any profits that have been brought into account in respect of the host contract (including any discount that is recognised in the company accounts) and is reduced by any allowable losses that are brought into account in respect of the embedded derivative.

A further adjustment applies where an exchangeable security is exchanged for shares or a convertible security is disposed of otherwise than for shares. In such cases, the acquisition cost of the security is increased to the extent that the sum of the discount that has been brought into account in respect of the loan relationship host contract and any chargeable gains that have been brought into account in respect of the embedded derivative exceed any allowable losses that have been so brought into account. The acquisition cost of the security is reduced to the extent that the allowable losses that have been brought into account in respect of the embedded derivative exceed the sum of any chargeable gains that have been so brought into account and any discount that has been recognised in respect of the host contract. Where the amount of this adjustment exceeds the cost of the asset the excess is added to the disposal consideration.

[*CTA 2009, ss 670, 671*].

Embedded derivatives — exactly tracking contracts for differences

[27.44] In certain cases where a company holds an index-linked loan or loan note that is bifurcated in its accounts into a host debt contract and an embedded derivative which falls to be treated as a contract for differences for the purposes of the derivative contracts legislation, any profits or losses arising on the embedded derivative will be treated as giving rise to chargeable gains or allowable losses for the purposes of corporation tax on chargeable gains on the basis on which such profits or losses are recognised in the company's accounts.

For such treatment to apply the following conditions have to be satisfied:

(a) the company must not be a party to the underlying creditor relationship for the purposes of its trade, unless the company is a mutual trading company or it is a party to the creditor relationship for the purposes of its life assurance business;

(b) the company is not an authorised unit trust, investment trust, open ended investment company or venture capital trust;

(c) the underlying subject matter of the derivative contract is qualifying ordinary shares which are listed on a recognised stock exchange. '*Qualifying ordinary shares*' are defined as shares other than those which entitle the holder to a dividend at a fixed rate and to no other right to share the profits of the company or which do not entitle the holder to receive dividends or to otherwise share in the profits of the company;

(d) the contract must be an exactly tracking contract. This means that the amount which must be paid to discharge the non-bifurcated loan or loan note must be exactly linked to movements in the value of the relevant index or asset from the time at which the loan or loan note came into existence until its redemption. It is permissible however for there to be a very slight variation to the period for which the indexation applies provided that such deviation is only required for valuation purposes.

[*CTA 2009, ss 633, 634, 635, 648, 649*].

As the loan relationship as a whole is not treated as a QCB in such cases anti-double counting provisions apply for the purposes of the *TCGA 1992* on a disposal of the security. In such cases the disposal proceeds of the security are reduced to the extent that the discount that has been brought into account in respect of the host contract and the chargeable gains that have been brought into account in respect of the embedded derivative exceed the allowable losses that have been so brought into account. Where the amount of the allowable losses exceeds the amount of the discount and the chargeable gains, the cost of the asset is reduced by this amount and to the extent that the amount of the reduction exceeds the cost of the asset, the disposal consideration of the asset is increased by the excess.

[*CTA 2009, ss 672–673*].

Property-based total return swaps

[27.45] Taxation on a capital gains basis (see **27.40** above) applies to a contract for differences where:

- one or more indices are specified in the contract;
- at least one of those indices is an index of changes to the value of land;
- the underlying subject matter also includes interest rates;
- the contract is not at any time in the accounting period in question held by the company for trading purposes;
- the company is not an excluded body;
- no two or more of the parties to the contract are connected persons (within **19** CONNECTED PERSONS); and
- securing a tax advantage is not the main purpose (nor one of the main purposes) for which the company is a party to the contract.

[*CTA 2009, s 650*].

Special treatment for derivatives that are separated from a debtor loan relationship

[27.46] The following transactions are not to be brought into account for corporation tax under the derivative contract rules.

Debtor relationships with embedded derivatives — options

Where a debtor relationship is bifurcated in a company's accounts into a host contract and an embedded option, any gains or losses that the company recognises in its accounts in respect of the embedded option are left out of account for the purposes of the derivative contracts legislation where the following conditions are satisfied:

(a) the embedded derivative is separated from the host loan relationship and is treated as an option;
(b) the underlying subject matter is shares;
(c) either the company was not carrying on a banking or securities business or the contract was not entered into in the ordinary course of such business;
(d) the company is not an open ended investment company, investment trust, venture capital trust or a unit trust.

Where profits or losses arising in respect of an embedded option are disregarded for the purposes of the derivative contracts legislation and the option is an option to acquire shares in the issuer and the option is exercised, *TCGA 1992, s 144(2)* will apply so that the grant of the option and the issue of the shares are treated as a single transaction. Since the issue by a company of its own shares is not a disposal for the purposes of the *TCGA 1992*, this means that no chargeable gain or allowable loss will arise as a result of the exercise of the option.

When the option is exercised and the issuer makes a cash payment to discharge its obligations in respect of the option, in essence, the issuer will be treated as realising a chargeable gain to the extent that the amount of the payment made to redeem the security that is attributed to the embedded option is less than the initial tax-adjusted carrying value of the option and as realising an allowable loss where the payment that is attributed to the embedded option exceeds the initial tax-adjusted carrying value of the option The payment made to redeem the security is split as follows. An amount equal to the fair value of the loan relationship host contract (i.e. the loan relationship after the option has been separated from it) at the date that the option is exercised is allocated to the loan relationship host contract with the balance being deemed to be payable in respect of the embedded derivative. This follows the accounting treatment that a company would adopt in its accounts.

[*CTA 2009, s 654*].

Where a loan relationship is redeemed in circumstances where the option is not exercised, in essence, the same approach is followed as discussed in the preceding paragraph to determine whether a chargeable gain or an allowable loss arises in respect of the redemption or novation of the security.

[*CTA 2009, s 655*].

Debtor relationships with embedded derivatives — contracts for differences

Any debits or credits that a company recognises in its accounts in respect of a contract for differences that has been separated from a debtor relationship are left out of account for the purposes of the derivative contracts legislation where the following conditions are satisfied:

(A) the contract is a relevant contract and the company is a party to it because of a debtor relationship;
(B) the contract is treated as a contract for differences and is not a deemed option under *CTA 2009, s 652*;
(C) the contract is an exactly tracking contract;
(D) the underlying subject matter is shares;
(E) when the company became a party to the contract, it was not trading as a bank or securities house, or, if it was, it did not become a party to the contract in the ordinary course of such business;
(F) the company is not an open ended investment company, investment trust, venture capital trust or a unit trust.
(G) the company was not a party to the underlying debtor relationship immediately before the start of its first statutory accounting period beginning on or after 1 January 2005.

In such cases a chargeable gain or allowable loss can arise for the purposes of the *TCGA 1992* when a company ceases to be a party to the loan relationship. A chargeable gain will arise if the amount paid to redeem the loan relationship is less than its issue price whereas if the redemption amount exceeds the issue price an allowable loss will arise.

An '*exactly tracking contract*' means a contract where the amount to be paid to discharge the rights and liabilities is equal to R% of C where R% is the percentage change (if any) over the relevant period in the value of the underlying subject matter and the consideration, determined using generally accepted accounting practice, being the proceeds of the issue giving rise to the debtor relationship. The '*relevant period*' is usually the time between the issue of the securities and their redemption, or otherwise the relationship comes to an end but this can change if there is a delay in obtaining the valuation of the rights and liabilities under the liability representing the debtor relationship. Where the debtor relationship comes to an end and an amount is paid to discharge the company's obligations under the relationship (discharge amount), the gain or loss is treated as a capital gain or loss and the following assumptions are made:

(i) the derivative contract is an asset of the company;
(ii) there is a disposal at the time the relationship ends;
(iii) the consideration is equal to the 'relevant amount'; and
(iv) the cost of the asset is equal to the discharge amount.

For this purpose, the '*relevant amount*' means the proceeds of issue of the security representing the loan relationship or, if the company was not a party to the original loan relationship, the tax-adjusted carrying value of the host contract when the company became a party. The '*host contract*' means the loan relationship to which the company is a party because of a debtor relationship.

A '*securities house*' means a person authorised under *FISMA 2000* and whose business consists wholly or mainly of dealing, as a principal, in financial instruments within the meaning of *ITA 2007*.

[*CTA 2009, ss 656–658, 709*].

Loan relationship bifurcated into a host contract and an equity instrument

Where a debtor relationship is bifurcated in a company's accounts in accordance with generally accepted accounting practice into a host contract and an equity instrument, the equity instrument will fall outside the derivative contracts legislation. Any profits and losses arising on the host contract will be dealt with under the loan relationships legislation.

Where a company ceases to be a party to the debtor relationship it is possible for the company to claim an allowable loss for the purposes of the *TCGA 1992* to the extent that the amount that it pays to redeem the loan relationship as a whole (i.e. ignoring the bifurcation), as reduced by an amount equal to the fair value of the host contract at that date, exceeds the initial tax-adjusted carrying value of the equity instrument. The initial tax-adjusted carrying value of the equity instrument is the value at the time at which it was separated from the loan relationship. Where an embedded option is treated as an equity instrument it is never revalued for accounting purposes.

[*CTA 2009, ss 665, 666*].

Plain vanilla options and futures over shares — prevention of double counting

Anti-double counting provisions apply where a company is a party to a plain vanilla (or stand alone) option or future, i.e. an option or future that has not been separated from another contract, and it acquires shares under the terms of the option or future. In such cases an adjustment is made to the base cost of the shares for the purposes of the *TCGA 1992*. The base cost of the shares is increased for any net gain that has arisen to the company on the option or future and which has been brought into account in computing its derivative contract profits. Where a net loss has arisen on the option or future the base cost of the shares acquired is reduced. Where the amount of the net loss exceeds the base cost of the shares acquired the excess is added to the disposal proceeds of the shares on a subsequent disposal of the shares.

[*CTA 2009, ss 667–669*].

Power to amend by regulation

[27.47] The Treasury may by order amend most provisions of the derivative contracts legislation and such amendment may have effect for statutory accounting periods beginning at any time in the calendar year in which the order is made. For further information see *CTA 2009, s 701*. In addition the Treasury has the power to amend the derivative contracts legislation by regulation where there is a change in accounting standards which affects the way in which profits and losses arising on a derivative contract are recognised in a company's accounts. Such changes may be made with retrospective effect to the date that a company began to apply the new accounting treatment if the change in accounting treatment takes effect before the necessary legislative changes have been made.

[*CTA 2009, ss 701, 701A*].

Key points on derivative contracts

[27.48] Points to consider are as follows:

- The derivative contracts legislation covers virtually all derivative contracts to which a company is a party. There are certain limited cases where derivative contracts the underlying subject matter of which consists, or is deemed to consist wholly of shares, are excluded from the derivative contracts legislation (see **27.3**).
- The credits or debits for an accounting period are brought into account as follows.
  - Where the company enters into a derivative contract for trading purposes, credits or debits arising from the contract are treated as receipts or expenses of the trade for that period.
  - Any credits or debits arising from derivative contracts *not* entered into for trading purposes are treated as if they were non-trading credits or debits arising under the LOAN RELATIONSHIPS (**50**) rules and effectively aggregated with other non-trading loan relationship credits and debits, the net amount being chargeable as non-trading income or relievable as a non-trading deficit, as the case may be.
- Subject to exceptions, exchange movements in respect of derivative contracts that are recognised as an item of profit or loss in a company's accounts in accordance with generally accepted accounting practice are brought into account in computing its derivative contracts profits in the accounting period in which they are so recognised. Where a company accounts for a derivative contract on a fair value basis, exchange movements are, in effect, determined for tax purposes by comparing the spot value of the currency or currencies covered by the contract at the start of the accounting period in question (or, if later, the date that it became a party to the contract) and the spot value at the end of the accounting period (or if earlier, the date that it ceased to be a party to the contract). See **27.9** above. There are provisions which enable companies to bring into (or leave out of) account foreign exchange movements which are matched with certain items in computing its derivative contracts profits. See **27.10** above.
- Special provisions apply to modify the tax treatment of derivative contracts which function as a hedge. They may apply where a company enters into:

(1) a currency contract to hedge a forecast transaction or a firm commitment;
(2) a commodity contract or a debt contract to hedge a forecast transaction or a firm commitment; or
(3) a derivative contract whose underlying subject matter includes interest rates to hedge an underlying transaction.

For the provisions to apply, an election must normally be made. See **27.13–27.15** above.

- Where a company is a party to an interest rate swap, a cross currency swap or any other contract which provides for payments to be made by the company that are based on applying a specified interest rate to a notional principal amount, the company will need to ensure that the counterparty to the contract meets one of the following conditions:
  (a) it is a UK resident company;
  (b) it is chargeable to corporation tax on income arising from the contract, or would be if there were any such income; or
  (c) it is resident for tax purposes in a territory that has a double tax treaty with the UK that contains an interest article (see **27.27**).

  Where these conditions are not satisfied, the UK company will be denied tax relief for any net interest-based payments that it makes under the terms of the contract unless it is a bank, building society or financial trader. It is normal for companies to cover against this exposure by requiring representations to be given by the counterparty to the contract that it will satisfy one of the above conditions and by providing that the counterparty may only transfer or novate the contract to a person who satisfies one of these conditions.
- There are a number of anti-avoidance rules applicable to the derivative contracts provisions. These include the unallowable purpose rule which applies where a company is a party to a derivative contract, or a related transaction in respect of the derivative contract, otherwise than for its business or other commercial purposes, in respect of activities for which it is not within the charge to corporation tax or for a tax avoidance purpose. See **27.19** above.
- Where it is desired to transfer a derivative contract from one group company to another under the intra-group transfer provisions of *CTA 2009, s 625* (see **27.24**), and the transfer is taking place by way of a novation, it will be important to ensure that there are no changes to the terms of the contract as a result of the novation which might have material financial consequences. If this is not the case, such changes might prevent the transfer from falling within *CTA 2009, s 625* based on the Tribunal's decision in *HBOS Treasury Services plc (now HBOS Treasury Services Ltd) v Revenue and Customs Comrs* [2009] UKFTT 261 (TC), [2010] SFTD 134.

- The deduction of debits in respect of certain derivative contracts may be subject to restriction by the CORPORATE INTEREST RESTRICTION (24).

28

Disclosure of Tax Avoidance Schemes

Introduction to disclosure of tax avoidance schemes

[28.1] There are obligations on promoters of certain tax avoidance schemes, and in some cases on persons entering into transactions under such schemes, to disclose those schemes to HMRC. The rules are designed to give HMRC early intelligence on marketed tax-avoidance schemes, so that the schemes can be challenged and/or closed down early. They also incorporate a requirement for scheme users to disclose the use of the scheme in the relevant tax returns, to reduce the potential for taxpayers to escape detection in cases where HMRC staff are otherwise unable to spot the use of the scheme. This also has the effect of discouraging the use of such strategies by taxpayers who do not want to jeopardise their relationships with HMRC.

The provisions cover the whole of income tax, capital gains tax, corporation tax, inheritance tax and annual tax on enveloped dwellings. The disclosure requirements are triggered where arrangements feature one of eight hallmarks.

Disclosure can be made online via gov.uk (www.gov.uk/guidance/forms-to-disclose-tax-avoidance-schemes) or alternatively forms for making disclosures can be completed and printed from the same location and sent to HMRC by post.

For HMRC guidance on the disclosure regime see www.gov.uk/government/publications/disclosure-of-tax-avoidance-schemes-guidance.

HMRC have also published a list of points with regard to the responsibilities of operating the scheme: www.gov.uk/government/publications/ten-things-about-disclosing-a-tax-avoidance-scheme/ten-things-about-disclosing-a-tax-avoidance-scheme.

A special compliance regime applies to certain high-risk promoters of tax avoidance schemes. With effect from 10 June 2021, HMRC can issue a 'stop notice' requiring a promoter to stop marketing a particular scheme if it satisfies certain conditions. This power can apply even if the scheme in question has not been defeated before a tribunal or court. HMRC's other powers under the regime are aimed at promoters who satisfy one or more 'threshold conditions' relating to previous behaviour or who promote a series of avoidance schemes which are defeated. The regime provides for the issuing of a 'conduct notice' requiring the person to whom it is given to comply with specified conditions as to the information they provide to clients, compliance with any disclosure requirements and not promoting schemes which rely on contrived or abnormal steps to produce a tax advantage. Promoters who fail to comply with a conduct notice may be issued with a monitoring notice. Names of promoters subject to such a notice may be published by HMRC, including details of how the conduct notice was breached, and promoters are required to notify their monitored status to clients. Information powers and penalties apply to promoters subject to a conduct notice and to promoters subject to a monitoring notice and their clients and intermediaries. See **28.18** onwards below.

Arrangements requiring disclosure

[28.2] '*Notifiable arrangements*' requiring disclosure under the provisions are 'arrangements' which:

- fall within any description prescribed by Treasury regulations (see below);
- enable, or might be expected to enable, any person to obtain an 'advantage' in relation to any tax (which may include capital gains tax and corporation tax) that is so prescribed in relation to arrangements of that description;
- are such that the main benefit, or one of the main benefits, that might be expected to arise from the arrangements is the obtaining of that advantage; and

- it is a hallmarked scheme.

The provisions also require disclosure of '*notifiable proposals*', i.e. proposals for arrangements which would be notifiable arrangements if entered into, whether the proposal relates to a particular person or to any person who may seek to take advantage of it.

For these purposes, '*arrangements*' include any scheme, transaction or series of transactions. An '*advantage*', in relation to any tax, means:

- relief or increased relief from, or repayment or increased repayment of, that tax;
- the avoidance or reduction of a charge or assessment to that tax;
- the avoidance of a possible assessment to that tax;
- the deferral of any payment of tax;
- the advancement of any repayment of tax; or
- the avoidance of any obligation to deduct or account for any tax.

[*FA 2004, ss 306, 318(1)*].

Simon's Taxes. See **A7.205, A7.206.**

Any arrangements which fall within any of the descriptions (or '*hallmarks*') listed below are prescribed by the Treasury for the purposes of these provisions.

The hallmarks are as follows.

(1) **Confidentiality in cases involving a promoter.** Arrangements fall within this hallmark if it might be reasonably expected that a promoter would wish the way in which the arrangements secure a tax advantage (or might secure a tax advantage) to be kept confidential from any other promoter at any time following the event which triggers the disclosure. Arrangements also fall within this hallmark if:
   - it might reasonably be expected that a promoter would, but for these provisions, wish to keep the way in which the arrangements secure or might secure) a tax advantage confidential from HMRC for some or all of that period, and a reason for doing so is to facilitate repeated or continued use of the element of the arrangements which secure the advantage or of substantially the same element; or
   - where there is no promoter by virtue only of the provision relating to legal professional privilege in **28.4**(C) below, or the promoter is not UK resident, it might reasonably be expected that the user of the arrangements would wish to keep confidential from HMRC the way that the arrangements secure a tax advantage for some or all of that period.

(2) **Confidentiality in cases not involving a promoter.** Arrangements fall within this hallmark if there is no promoter and:
   (a) the intended user of the arrangements is a business (as defined) which is not a '*small or medium-sized enterprise*' (broadly, a micro, small or medium-sized enterprise as defined in the Commission Recommendation of 6 May 2003);

(b) it might reasonably be expected that the user would wish the way in which the arrangements secure a tax advantage to be kept confidential from HMRC at any time following the event triggering the disclosure; and

(c) a reason for doing so is to facilitate repeated or continued use of the element of the arrangements which secure the advantage or of substantially the same element or to reduce the risk of HMRC opening an enquiry into a return or account.

Arrangements also fall within this hallmark if there is no promoter and (a) above applies and, if there had been a promoter, it might reasonably be expected that they would wish to have kept the way in which the arrangements secure a tax advantage to be kept confidential from HMRC at any time following the event triggering the disclosure and a reason for doing so would be to facilitate repeated or continued use of the element of the arrangements which secure the advantage or of substantially the same element.

(3) **Premium fee.** Arrangements fall within this hallmark if they are such that it might reasonably be expected that a promoter or a person connected with a promoter of arrangements that are the same as, or substantially similar to, the arrangements in question, would, but for these provisions, be able to obtain a 'premium fee' from a person experienced in receiving services of the type being provided. Arrangements where there is no promoter or where the tax advantage is intended to be obtained by an individual, or business that is a small or medium-sized enterprise, are excluded. A '*premium fee*' for this purpose is one chargeable by virtue of any element of the arrangements from which the tax advantage is expected to arise and which is to a significant extent attributable to, or to any extent contingent on the obtaining of, that advantage. The premium fee must be so attributable on the obtaining of the tax advantage as a matter of law (rather than upon other factors such as the take up of an employment scheme by a certain number of employees).

(4) **Standardised tax products**. Arrangements fall within this hallmark if they are made available by a promoter for implementation by more than one person and an informed observer who had studied the arrangements could reasonably be expected to conclude that:

- the arrangements have substantially standardised documentation to enable implementation, the form of that documentation is determined by the promoter and the substance of the documentation does not need to be tailored to any material extent;
- a person implementing the arrangements must enter into a specific transaction or series of transactions;
- the transaction or series of transactions are substantially standardised in form; and
- either the main purpose of the arrangements is to enable a person to obtain a tax advantage or the arrangements would be unlikely to be entered into but for the expectation of obtaining a tax advantage.

Arrangements consisting solely of one or more plant or machinery leases (see (6) below) are excluded, as are an enterprise investment scheme or ISA, arrangements using the CORPORATE VENTURING SCHEME (25) or VENTURE

CAPITAL TRUSTS (74), arrangements qualifying for community investment tax relief, specified employee share schemes, certain pension schemes; schemes to which *ITTOIA 2005, s 731* (periodical payments of personal injury damages) applies and arrangements which would fall within (8) below but for the exclusions from that hallmark.

(5) **Loss schemes.** Arrangements are within this hallmark if the promoter expects more than one individual to implement them or to implement arrangements which are substantially the same and an informed observer, having studied them, could reasonably be expected to conclude that:

(a) the main benefit or one of the main benefits of the arrangements for some or all of the participants is the provision of losses;

(b) the arrangements (including the way they are structured) contain an element or elements unlikely to have been entered into but for the provision of those losses; and

(c) the participants would be expected to use the losses to reduce their liability to income tax or capital gains tax.

(6) **Leasing arrangements.** This hallmark applies to high-value plant or machinery leases which are not short-term leases where one of three additional conditions are met as set out below.

Arrangements falling within this hallmark include a high value plant or machinery lease.

A '*plant or machinery lease*' for this purpose is:

- any agreement or arrangement which, in accordance with generally accepted accounting practice, falls (or would fall) to be treated as a lease under which the lessor grants to the lessee the right to use the plant or machinery for a period;
- any other agreement or arrangement to the extent that, in accordance with generally accepted accounting practice, it conveys or falls (or would fall) to be regarded as conveying the right to use the plant or machinery; or
- a finance lease under *CAA 2001, s 221(1)(c)* where the plant or machinery is the subject of a sale and finance leaseback as defined under that section.

The lease is a '*high value*' lease if the lower of the cost to the lessor, or the market value, of either:

- any one asset forming part of the plant or machinery leased or to be leased under the arrangements is at least £10 million; or
- the aggregate of all the assets forming part of the plant or machinery leased or to be leased under the arrangements is at least £25 million.

The lease is a '*short-term lease*' if it has a term not exceeding two years. It will not be a short-term lease if the lessee can extend the term beyond two years by the exercise of an option or by some other arrangement entered into at the inception of the lease. Nor will it be a short-term lease if arrangements are entered into, at or about the time of the inception of the lease, for the assets to be leased to one or more other persons under one or more other leases and the aggregate of the terms of the lease to the lessee and to such other persons as are connected with the lessee exceed two years.

The three additional conditions, one of which must also be met, are as follows.

- Condition 1 is that the arrangements are designed such that one or more of the leases comprised in the arrangements are, or would be, entered into by one party who has the right to claim capital allowances on expenditure incurred on the plant or machinery and by another party (ignoring guarantors) who is not, or would not be, chargeable to corporation tax (whether or not there are other parties to the lease who satisfy neither of those conditions).
- Condition 2 is that the arrangements are designed to remove the whole or greater part of any risk of a loss which would otherwise fall directly or indirectly upon the lessor if the payments due under the lease are not made in accordance with its terms and the risk is so removed by the provision of money or a money debt (as defined in *ITEPA 2003, s 702(6)*).
- Condition 3 is that the arrangements are designed to consist of, or include, a sale and finance leaseback arrangement (within *CAA 2001, s 221*) or a lease and finance leaseback (within *CAA 2001, s 228F(5); CAA 2001, s 228A* for leases entered into on or after 9 October 2007). This does not apply where assets leased, or to be leased, under sale and finance leaseback arrangements are, or will be, unused and not second-hand at the time when the assets are acquired or created and where the interval between the acquisition or creation of the assets and their sale under the arrangements is not more than four months.

Condition 3 does not apply if the plant or machinery is, or the promoter expects it to become, a fixture (as defined by *CAA 2001, s 173(1)*) which is leased with relevant land (as defined by *CAA 2001, s 173(2)*) unless it is used for storage or production (as defined). It will, however, apply if the qualifying expenditure incurred on that fixture amounts or will amount to more than 50% of the aggregate value of assets subject to the lease and the rent payable under the lease is directly or indirectly dependent on the availability of capital allowances on expenditure on any plant or machinery comprised in the lease. In determining the value of the assets subject to the lease, the value of the land is the market value of the lessor's interest and the value of plant or machinery is to be determined in the same manner as for a 'high value' lease above.

(7) **Employment income provided through third parties.** See Tolley's Income Tax for further details.

(8) **Financial products.** Arrangements are within the hallmark if they include at least one 'specified financial product' and it would be reasonable to expect an informed observer (having studied the arrangements and having regard to all relevant circumstances) to conclude that:

(a) one of the main benefits of including a specified financial product in the arrangements is to give rise to a tax advantage; and

(b) either:

(i) a specified financial product included in the arrangements contains at least one term unlikely to have been entered into were it not for the tax advantage; or

(ii) the arrangements involve one or more contrived or abnormal steps (other than certain specified steps which are deemed not to be contrived or abnormal) without which the tax advantage could not be obtained.

The condition at (b)(i) is treated as not met if it would otherwise be met only because the specified financial product includes a term requiring that it be held for a minimum period before it is redeemed and *TCGA 1992, s 135* (exchange of securities) or *s 136* (schemes of reconstruction) applies to it. The condition is also treated as not met if it would otherwise be met only because the specified financial product includes a term under which the issuing company can secure that the redemption date falls before the end of the 'permitted period' and but for that term, the specified financial product would be an 'equity note'. 'Permitted period' and 'equity note' are defined for this purpose by *CTA 2010, s 1016*. Both of the conditions at (b) above are treated as not met if they would otherwise both be met only because the specified financial product includes a term providing for conversion into, or redemption in, a currency other than sterling.

The '*specified financial products*' are loans, shares, derivative contracts, certain repos and quasi-repos, stock lending arrangements, alternative finance arrangements and contracts which, whether alone or in combination with other contracts, are required under generally accepted accounting practice to be treated as a loan, deposit or other financial asset or obligation or would be if the person entering into the arrangements were a company. Financial products held in an individual savings account are excluded.

Arrangements are excluded from the hallmark if a promoter is a participating entity or part of a participating group in the Code of Practice on Taxation for Banks and HMRC had confirmed or could reasonably be expected to confirm to the promoter that the arrangements are acceptable transactions under the Code.

For the purpose only of determining whether arrangements are prescribed by (1)–(3) or (6) above, **28.4**(C) below is disregarded.

[*SI 2006 No 1543*].

Simon's Taxes. See A7.215–A7.224A.

Who is required to disclose

Disclosure by promoter

[28.4] A 'promoter' must provide HMRC with specified information on any notifiable proposal within five business days of the 'relevant date' (i.e. the earliest of the date he first makes a firm approach to another person; the date on which he makes the proposal available for implementation by any person; and the date he first becomes aware of any transaction forming part of arrangements implementing the proposal).

There is a separate requirement for a promoter to provide HMRC with specified information relating to notifiable arrangements and to do so within five business days of the date on which he first becomes aware of any transaction forming part of those arrangements; but this does not apply if the arrangements implement a proposal which has been notified as above.

The disclosure under these provisions must provide sufficient information as might be reasonably expected to enable an HMRC officer to comprehend the manner in which the proposal or arrangements are intended to operate, including the details specified in *SI 2012 No 1836, Reg 4.*

Where a promoter has complied with the above requirements and another person is a promoter in relation to the same proposal or arrangements or to a proposal or arrangements that are substantially the same (whether they relate to the same or different parties), the notification obligation of that other promoter is discharged if:

- the promoter who made the disclosure has notified the identity and address of the other promoter to HMRC or the other promoter holds the reference number allocated to the arrangements; and
- the other promoter holds the information included in the disclosure.

Previously, where two or more persons were promoters in relation to the same proposal or arrangements, notification by one promoter discharged the obligations of the others.

If a promoter has discharged his obligations in relation to a proposal or arrangements, he is not required to notify proposals or arrangements which are substantially the same as those already notified (whether or not they relate to the same parties).

Details of clients

A further disclosure requirement applies where a promoter of notifiable arrangements provides services to any client in connection with the arrangements and either the promoter is subject to the requirement to provide the client with the reference number allocated under **28.11**(a) below or would be subject to that requirement if he had not failed to make the necessary disclosure of the proposal or arrangements. The requirement also applies to a provider of services who is subject to the requirement to provide a client with specified information relating to a reference number under **28.11**(b) below. Unless HMRC have withdrawn the obligation to notify the reference number to the client, the promoter or provider must provide HMRC with specified information about the client within 30 days of the end of each calendar quarter (i.e. 31 March etc.) during which the promoter or provider is subject to the requirement in question. The specified information is the scheme reference number (if there is one), the name, address, unique taxpayer reference number and national insurance number of the client, the promoter or provider's name and address and the end date of the quarter in relation to which the information is provided. In certain circumstances, the 30-day limit is extended to 60 days to the extent that the specified information consists of the client's unique taxpayer reference number and national insurance number.

HMRC have a further power which applies where a promoter or provider has provided HMRC with the specified information but HMRC suspect that a person other than the client to whom the information relates is or is likely to be a party to the arrangements. HMRC may by written notice require the promoter or provider to provide specified information about any person they might reasonably be expected to know is or is likely to be a party to the arrangements. The promoter or provider must comply with the requirement within ten days of receiving the notice or such longer period as HMRC direct. The specified information is the name and address of, and any identification number allocated by HMRC to, any person other than the client who is or is likely to be a party to the arrangements (but only those who will, or are likely to, either sell the arrangements to another person or achieve a tax advantage by implementing the arrangements), together with sufficient information as might be reasonably expected to enable HMRC to comprehend how such a person is involved in the arrangements. Only information held by the promoter or provider at the time of receipt of the notice can be required.

Meaning of promoter

A '*promoter*' is a person who conducts a 'relevant business' and who in the course of that business:

(a) in relation to a notifiable proposal:
   (i) is to any extent responsible for the design of the proposed arrangements; or
   (ii) makes a 'firm approach' to another person with a view to making the proposal available for implementation by that person or any other person; or
   (iii) makes a notifiable proposal available for implementation by another person; or
(b) in relation to notifiable arrangements:
   (i) is a promoter by virtue of (a)(ii) or (iii) above in relation to a notifiable proposal which is implemented by the arrangements;
   (ii) is to any extent responsible for the design of the arrangements; or
   (iii) is to any extent responsible for the organisation or management of the arrangements.

A person is not, however, a promoter by reason of anything done in circumstances prescribed in regulations.

A '*relevant business*' for this purpose is a trade, profession or business which involves the provision to other persons of services relating to taxation or which is carried on by a bank (within *CTA 2010, s 1120*) or securities house (within *CTA 2010, s 1009(3)*). Anything done by a company which is a member of the same 51% group (as defined) as a bank or securities house is taken to be done in the course of a relevant business if it is done for the purposes of the trade etc. of the bank or securities house.

For the purposes of (a)(ii) above, a person makes a '*firm approach*' to another person if he makes a 'marketing contact' with that person when the proposed arrangements have been 'substantially designed'. A promoter makes a '*marketing contact*' with another person if he provides information about the proposal, including an explanation of the tax advantage to be obtained, with a view to that person or any other person entering into transactions forming part of the proposed arrangements. Arrangements have been '*substantially designed*' when it would be reasonable to believe that a person wishing to obtain the tax advantage might use the scheme or a scheme which is not substantially different.

The following exclusions apply.

(A) A company providing services within (a) or (b) above to a company which is a member of the same group (as defined) is not a promoter.

(B) An employee of (or of a person connected (within **19** CONNECTED PERSONS) with) either a promoter or a person entering into any transaction forming part of the proposed arrangements is also excluded from being a promoter. This exception is amended with effect from 17 April 2015 to ensure that employees of a promoter resident outside the UK (in the event the employer does not make a disclosure), or any person who is to any extent responsible for the organisation or management of notifiable arrangements, are not excluded from being treated as a promoter.

(C) A person is not treated as a promoter where his involvement in the proposal or arrangements is such that he is not required to provide all of the required information because of the legal professional privilege rules above.

(D) A person is not treated as a promoter by virtue of (a)(i) or (b)(ii) above where:
- in the course of providing tax advice, he is not responsible for the design of any element of the proposed arrangements or arrangements from which the tax advantage expected to be obtained arises;
- his relevant business is the provision of tax services but he does not provide tax advice in the course of carrying out his responsibilities in relation to the proposed arrangements or arrangements; or
- he is not responsible for the design of all the elements of the proposed arrangements or arrangements from which the tax advantage is expected to be obtained arises and could not reasonably be expected to have sufficient information to comply with the disclosure requirements or to know whether a disclosure is required.

[*FA 2004, ss 307, 308, 310A, 310B, 313ZA, 313ZB, 319(3); FA 2021, Sch 31 paras 3, 11, 12; SI 2004 No 1864, Regs 1, 3(1)(2), 4(1)–(3), 5, 6; SI 2012 No 1836, Regs 4(1), 5(1)(4)(5), 13, 18*].

Simon's Taxes. See **A7.210, A7.230, A7.231.**

Introducers

[28.5] Where HMRC suspect that a person (P) is an 'introducer' of a proposal which may be notifiable, they can by notice require P to provide them with the name and address of each person who has provided him with information about the proposal (usually a promoter or another introducer). On and after

26 March 2015, HMRC may also, or alternatively, require P to provide them with specified information in relation to each person with whom P has made a 'marketing contact' (see **28.4** above) in relation to the proposal (including their name and address). The notice must be in writing and must specify the proposal concerned. P must comply with the notice within ten days or such longer time as HMRC direct.

A person is an 'introducer' of a notifiable proposal if he makes a marketing contact with another person about the proposal. A person is not, however, an introducer by reason of anything done in circumstances prescribed in regulations.

[*FA 2004, ss 307, 313C; SI 2012 No 1836, Reg 15*].

Simon's Taxes. See **A7.245.**

Disclosure by person dealing with non-UK promoter

[28.6] A person who enters into any transaction forming part of notifiable arrangements in relation to which there is a non-UK resident promoter (and no UK resident promoter) must himself provide HMRC with specified information relating to those arrangements. He must do so within five business days after entering into the first such transaction. The information to be supplied to HMRC is similar to that which promoters must provide (see above). This obligation is discharged if a promoter makes disclosure of the notifiable arrangements in question.

[*FA 2004, ss 309, 319(4); SI 2004 No 1864, Regs 1, 3(3), 4(4)(7), 6; SI 2012 No 1836, Regs 4(2)(4), 5(6)*].

Simon's Taxes. See **A7.211, A7.230, A7.231.**

Disclosure by parties to notifiable arrangements not involving a promoter

[28.7] A person who enters into any transaction forming part of notifiable arrangements in respect of which neither he nor any other person in the UK has an obligation as above must himself provide HMRC with specified information (similar to that which a promoter must provide) relating to those arrangements. Such disclosure must normally be made within 30 days beginning with the day after the day in which he enters into the first transaction forming part of the arrangements. Reasonable and proportionate measures should be put in place to ensure that the date of the first transaction is identified and that notification is made within the time limit. However, if disclosure is made as soon as possible and there is a reasonable excuse for failing to notify in time, no penalty will be charged.

However, where a person is not to be treated as a promoter in relation to notifiable arrangements by virtue of legal professional privilege (see below under legal professional privilege), the disclosure must be made within five business days after entering into the transaction.

[*FA 2004, ss 310, 319(4); SI 2004 No 1864, Regs 1, 3(4), 4(5)(5A), 6; SI 2012 No 1836, Regs 4(3)(4), 5(7)(8)*].

Simon's Taxes. See A7.212, A7.230, A7.231.

Duty to provide further information as requested by HMRC

[28.8] Where a person provides prescribed information about notifiable proposals or arrangements pursuant to *FA 2004, s 308* (with regard to the duty of a promoter), *s 309* (with regard to the duty of a person dealing with a non-UK promoter), or *s 310* (with regard to persons in arrangements with no promoter) then HMRC have powers to request further information. This applies where a person has provided such prescribed information, or where the person has provided information in purported compliance with *ss 309, 310* but HMRC believe that the person has not provided all the prescribed information. HMRC may require the person to provide further specified information, and documents, relating to the notifiable proposals or arrangements. The person then has ten working days to comply with the request (beginning with the day HMRC imposed the requirement), or such longer period as may be directed.

Where such a request has been made and HMRC believe that the person has failed to provide the information or documents required, then HMRC may apply to a tribunal for an order requiring such person to provide such information or documents. The tribunal may make an order only if they are satisfied that HMRC have reasonable grounds for suspecting that the information or documents will assist them in considering the notifiable proposals or arrangements. The person must comply with an order of the tribunal within ten working days, or such longer period as HMRC may direct. 'Working day' means a day which is not a weekend, bank holiday, Christmas Day or Good Friday. Where a person has failed to provide information or documents required under this section penalties are provided under *TMA 1970, s 98C* (see **59.10** PENALTIES).

[*FA 2004, s 310A*].

Duty to provide updated information

[28.9] Where, in compliance with the main obligations at **28.4** above, information has been provided to HMRC about notifiable arrangements, or proposed notifiable arrangements, and a reference number has been allocated to the arrangements (see **28.11** below), the promoter must inform HMRC of:

(a) any change in the name by which the notifiable arrangements are known; and
(b) any change in the name or address of any person who is a promoter in relation to the notifiable arrangements or the notifiable proposal.

The promoter must give HMRC the updated information (on the prescribed form) within 30 days after the change occurs. If there is more than one promoter, the obligation to inform HMRC of a change within (b) above falls on the promoter whose details have changed. Once a promoter has informed HMRC of a change within (a) or (b), the duty of any other promoter to inform HMRC of that change is discharged.

[*FA 2004, ss 310C, 316; FA 2021, Sch 31 para 14*].

Mechanics of disclosure

[28.10] The correct forms must be used (see above). The following information must be given:

- notifier's name and address;
- notifier's and promoter's name and address where non-UK promoter involved;
- details of the reason for the notification (normally the hallmark(s)) which apply;
- a summary of the scheme and its name;
- details of the steps involved and how the tax advantage arises;
- the statutory provisions on which the tax advantage is based.

Where more than one hallmark applies, it is only necessary to mention one, although HMRC would prefer that the main applicable hallmark was indicated.

The explanation of the scheme must be such that an HMRC officer may understand how the tax advantage arises. It should identify the steps and the applicable law. Common terms need not be explained in depth. It may be useful to provide any prospectus or scheme diagrams (anonomysed if necessary), but form AAG1 must still be completed. If any co-promoters are involved, they may be detailed in the application and they will not then have to disclose the scheme themselves.

Simon's Taxes. See A7.230.

Reference numbers allocated to arrangements

[28.11] HMRC may allocate a reference number (sometimes referred to as a 'scheme reference number' or SRN) to arrangements or proposed arrangements in the following circumstances:

(a) *Disclosure made.* Where a person has made a disclosure as above, HMRC may allocate a reference number to the arrangements in question within 90 days after the disclosure. HMRC may allocate a reference number even if the disclosure is incomplete or defective.

(b) *Notice of potential allocation not complied with.* HMRC may also allocate a reference number to arrangements or proposed arrangements where:

    (i) they become aware that, on or after 10 June 2021, a transaction forming part of the arrangements has been entered into, a firm approach has been made with a view to making a proposal for arrangements available for implementation or a proposal has been so made available;

    (ii) HMRC have issued a notice explaining that, unless the recipient can satisfy them, before the end of the 'notice period', that the arrangements or proposal are not notifiable, they may allocate a reference number to them;

(iii) the recipient has failed to satisfy HMRC before the expiry of the notice period.

In this case, HMRC may allocate the reference number within the year beginning the day after the end of the notice period. The '*notice period*' is the 30 days beginning with the day on which the notice in (ii) above is issued, or a longer period if HMRC so direct.

HMRC must issue a notice to anyone they reasonably suspect to be a promoter of the arrangements or proposal. They may, but are not required to, issue a notice to any other person they reasonably suspect to be involved in the supply of the arrangements or proposed arrangements. A notice cannot be issued until 15 days after HMRC become aware that a condition within (i) has been met.

HMRC may withdraw a reference number allocated under this provision at any time.

The allocation of a reference number does not in itself indicate that HMRC accept that the arrangements could as a matter of law result in the obtaining by any person of a tax advantage.

Where a reference number is allocated under (a) above, HMRC must then notify the number to the person making the disclosure and to any co-promoter whose identity and address has been notified to HMRC by that person. Where a reference number is allocated under (b) above, HMRC must notify the number to any person they reasonably suspect to be a promoter or involved in the supply of the arrangements or proposed arrangements (whether or not the notice in (b)(ii) above was given to that person).

Appeal against allocation of number

A person who has been notified, as above, of a reference number allocated under (b) above may appeal to the Tribunal against HMRC's decision to allocate it. Notice of appeal must be given to the Tribunal in writing within the 30 days beginning with the day of notification, stating the grounds of appeal. The Tribunal may, however, accept a late appeal. An appeal can be brought on the grounds that HMRC did not act in accordance with the requirements in (b) above or that the arrangements or proposal are not notifiable.

If the Tribunal cancels HMRC's decision, HMRC must withdraw the number. Making an appeal does not, however, prevent the powers and duties deriving from the allocation of the number from applying during the appeal process.

Further information requested by HMRC

Where HMRC have allocated a reference number under (b) above, they may require any person they reasonably suspect to be, or to have been, a promoter of, or otherwise involved in the supply of, the arrangements or proposed arrangements to provide specified information or documents. HMRC must have reasonable grounds for suspecting that the information or documents will assist them in considering the arrangements or proposed arrangements. The information or documents must be provided to HMRC within the ten working days beginning with the day on which HMRC imposed the requirement (or by a later date if HMRC so direct).

Duty to provide number to clients and other parties

A promoter who is providing services to a client in connection with notifiable arrangements must pass on to the client any reference number allocated under (a) above for those arrangements or for arrangements which are substantially the same as those arrangements. He must do so within 30 days after the date he first becomes aware of any transaction forming part of the arrangements or, if later, the date on which the reference number is notified to him (by HMRC or a co-promoter).

The duty of a promoter to notify the reference number to the client is discharged where he has provided the client with prescribed information relating to the reference number allocated to a notifiable proposal for the arrangements, provided that the proposal and the arrangements are substantially the same.

Where a reference number is allocated under (b) above, a person (a '*provider*') who provides services on or after 10 June 2021 to a client in connection with the arrangements or proposed arrangements must provide prescribed information relating to the number to the client. The provider must do so within the 30 days beginning with the date of notification of the number (whether the notification was by HMRC or another person).

HMRC may, by notice, withdraw the obligation to provide information to clients.

A client who has been notified of a reference number or prescribed information must notify the reference number or information to any other person that he might reasonably be expected to know is, or is likely to be, a party to the arrangements and who might reasonably be expected to gain a tax advantage under the arrangements. He must do so within 30 days beginning with the date he first becomes aware of any transaction forming part of the arrangements or, if later, the date on which the reference number is notified to him.

Where client is an employer

Where the client is an employer and receives, or might reasonably be expected to receive, by reason of the notifiable arrangements, a tax advantage covered by the DOTAS regime in relation to the employment of any of the client's employees, the client must, within 30 days, provide (on the prescribed form) the reference number to each of the employees in question. For this purpose, 'employee' includes an office holder and a former employee. Regulations may exempt a client from complying with this duty in prescribed circumstances.

HMRC may give notice that, in relation to notifiable arrangements or a notifiable proposal specified in that notice, clients do not have to pass on reference numbers after the date specified in the notice.

Duty to report number to HMRC

A company which is a party to any notifiable arrangements giving rise to a corporation tax or capital gains tax advantage must quote the allocated reference number in its company tax return for the accounting period in which the company is notified of the number (or, if earlier, the accounting period in which the tax advantage is expected to arise) or on form AAG4 (see below). If disclosure is made in the company's return, the number must be given in all subsequent returns until the advantage ceases to apply to the company. Form AAG4 should be used where the company is a party to a scheme but is not required to complete a return, or the return does not have a box for the information, or there are more numbers to be notified than there are spaces on the return. In the latter case, AAG4 should only be used to notify numbers which do not fit on the return. These duties are disapplied for employees in cases where an employer provides information about them under **28.12** below.

Where an AAG4 is used, it must be filed not later than twelve months from the end of the accounting period in which the number is notified or, if earlier, the period in which the tax advantage is expected to arise. Where a scheme number has been notified to a company, but no tax advantage is expected (e.g. because it does not intend to use the scheme) the number does not need to be returned to HMRC. The company must also quote the accounting period in which, or the date on which, the advantage is expected to arise.

Comparable provisions apply for income tax. For arrangements under which a tax advantage is expected to arise by reason of a person's employment, the obligation falls on the employer to quote the reference number etc. on a return in such form as HMRC may specify (AAG4). HMRC have the power to remove, by notice, from a specified date a person's obligation to notify them of the avoidance scheme disclosure number.

A client of a promoter is obliged to pass on the reference number to third parties when there is sufficient commercial connection with that party to have a reasonable expectation that they will gain a tax advantage from the scheme.

Where a promoter has provided the reference number to a client under the above provisions, the client must, within a specified period, provide the promoter with specified information. The information required, as detailed by *SI 2013 No 2592*, is the client's unique tax reference number or national insurance number, or confirmation that the individual has neither. The regulations also impose the obligation on the promoter to include this information in its quarterly reports to HMRC (permitting a 60 day reporting requirement instead of a 30 day reporting requirement in respect of the UTR or NI number requirement where the user's 10 days have not expired).

Duty of client to provide information

Where a promoter or other person has provided the reference number to a client under the above provisions, the client must provide that person with specified information. The client must provide the information within ten days of the later of the date the client receives the reference number and the date the client first enters into a transaction forming part of the notifiable arrangements. The information required is the client's unique tax reference number or national insurance number or confirmation that he does not have such a number.

Duty to provide additional information to clients or other parties

Where, as above, a promoter or provider is required to pass on to the client the referencc number for arrangements, or a client is required to pass on the reference number to other parties, HMRC may specify additional information which must be simultaneously passed on in each case. This is confined to information supplied by HMRC relating to proposals or arrangements in general. HMRC may specify the form and manner in which such additional information is to be provided.

[*FA 2004, ss 310D–313, 316, 316A; FA 2021, Sch 31 paras 4–10, 14, 15, 44, 45(1); SI 2012 No 1836, Regs 8A–12*].

Simon's Taxes. See **A7.233**.

Duty of client to provide employee details

[28.12] The following applies if a promoter of notifiable arrangements or a notifiable proposal or another person provides services to any client in connection with the arrangements or proposal and the following conditions are met:

(a) the client receives from the promoter or provider the reference number allocated to the arrangements (or proposed arrangements) as in **28.11** above; and

(b) the client is an employer, and, as a result of the arrangements (or proposed arrangements):
  (i) one or more of the client's employees receive, or might reasonably be expected to receive, in relation to their employment, an advantage in relation to any tax covered by the DOTAS regime; or
  (ii) the client receives, or might reasonably be expected to receive, any such advantage in relation to the employment of one or more of the client's employees.

Where an employee is within subsection (b)(i) above, or is an employee within (b)(ii), the client must provide HMRC with prescribed information relating to the employee at a time or times to be prescribed by regulations. The information is the name, address and reference number of the employer; the name and any NI number of the employee; the scheme reference number; the tax year in which the employee obtains or expects to obtain the tax advantage (or confirmation it is nil); and the name and address of the promoter and the name of the arrangements. For this purpose, 'employee' includes an office holder and a former employee. Regulations may exempt a client from complying with this duty in prescribed circumstances.

The information to be provided as above must be provided in the prescribed form and manner or the duty will not be regarded as complied with. If, as in **28.11** above, HMRC have given notice, in relation to specified arrangements, that promoters no longer have to pass on reference numbers, or that parties do not have to report such numbers to HMRC, the client is discharged from the above obligation in relation to those arrangements.

[*FA 2004, ss 313ZC, 316; FA 2021, Sch 31 paras 13, 14; SI 2012 No 1836, Reg 13B*].

Voluntary disclosure of information to HMRC

[28.13] No duty of confidentiality or other restriction on disclosure (however imposed) prevents the voluntary disclosure by any person to HMRC of information or documents which the person has reasonable grounds for suspecting will assist HMRC in determining whether there has been a breach of any requirement imposed as above under the DOTAS regime. [*FA 2004, s 316B*].

A disclosure by an independent financial advisor of information relating to tax avoidance schemes was held to meet these requirements in *R (oao Emblin) v HMRC* QB, [2018] STC 934.

Legal professional privilege

[28.14] These provisions do not require the disclosure of privileged information, i.e. information with respect to which a claim to legal professional privilege (or Scottish equivalent) could be maintained in legal proceedings. [*FA 2004, s 314*]. Where a person is not to be treated as a promoter for this reason, the party to the notifiable arrangements or notifiable proposals (the taxpayer making use of the scheme) must make the appropriate disclosure.

Simon's Taxes. See A7.225–A7.228.

Compliance

[28.15] The following compliance powers apply.

Pre-disclosure enquiries

If HMRC suspects that a person is the introducer of a proposal, or the promoter of a proposal or arrangements, which may be notifiable under the above provisions, they may, by written notice, require that person to state whether in his opinion notification is required, and if not, the reasons for his opinion. In giving those reasons, it is not sufficient to indicate that a lawyer or other professional has given an opinion. The recipient of a notice must comply with it within the ten days beginning on the day after that on which the notice is issued.

If HMRC receive a statement (whether or not in response to a notice) giving reasons why a proposal or arrangements are not notifiable, they may apply to the Tribunal for an order requiring specified further information or documents to be provided in support of the reasons. The information or documents must be provided within the 14 days beginning on the day after that on which the order is made.

[*FA 2004, ss 313A, 313B; SI 2004 No 1864, Reg 8A; SI 2012 No 1836, Reg 14*].

Order to disclose

HMRC can apply to the Tribunal for an order that a proposal or arrangements are notifiable under the above provisions. The application must specify both the proposal or arrangements concerned and the promoter. [*FA 2004, s 314A*].

They can also apply to the Tribunal for an order that a proposal or arrangements be treated as notifiable. Again, the application must specify both the proposal or arrangements concerned and the promoter. Before making such an order, the Tribunal must be satisfied that HMRC have taken all reasonable steps (which need not include making use of the pre-disclosure enquiry provisions above) to establish whether the proposal or arrangements are notifiable and have reasonable grounds for suspecting that they may be notifiable. Grounds for suspicion may include an attempt by the promoter to avoid or delay providing information or documents under the pre-disclosure enquiry provisions and failure to comply with a requirement under those provisions in relation to other proposals or arrangements. The disclosure required as a result of an order under this provision must be made within the ten days beginning on the day after that on which the order is made. [*FA 2004, s 306A; SI 2004 No 1864, Reg 4(1A)*].

HMRC made a successful application for an order that arrangements were notifiable in *EDF Tax Ltd (in creditor's voluntary liquidation) v HMRC* FTT 2019, [2020] SFTD 161.

Supplementary information

Where HMRC believe that a disclosure by a promoter has not included all the information required to be disclosed they can apply to the Tribunal for an order requiring the promoter to provide specified information or documents. Before making an order, the Tribunal must be satisfied that HMRC have reasonable grounds for suspecting that the information or documents form part of, or will support or explain, the required information. Information or documents required by an order under this provision must be provided within the ten days beginning on the day after that on which the order is made. [*FA 2004, s 308A; SI 2004 No 1864, Reg 4(3A)*].

Publication of information by HMRC

[28.16] HMRC may publish specified information about arrangements (or proposed arrangements) to which a reference number is allocated (see **28.11** above), any person who is a promoter in relation to them and, where the number is allocated under **28.11**(b) above, any person otherwise involved, on or after 10 June 2021, in their supply. This can include information identifying a person as a promoter or other person involved in the supply of the arrangements, but in this case, HMRC must first inform him that they are considering publishing that information and give him reasonable opportunity to make representations about whether it should be published. No information can be published that identifies a person who enters into a transaction forming part of the arrangements (unless he is identified as a promoter or other person involved in the supply of the arrangements). No information may be published about a person involved in the supply of the arrangements if there are reasonable grounds for believing that their involvement is limited to activities subject to legal professional privilege.

Where the reference number is allocated under **28.11**(b) above, information identifying a promoter or other person involved in the supply of the arrangements can only be published for the first time within one year of the day on which the number is allocated. The information may not continue to be published for more than one year after its first publication. In determining the one-year periods, no account is taken of any period during which HMRC are prohibited from publishing the information because of court of tribunal proceedings.

Once any such information has been published about arrangements, HMRC must also publish information about any ruling of a court or tribunal that is made in relation to arrangements intended to secure a tax advantage if, in HMRC's opinion, the ruling is relevant to the arrangements in question. A ruling is relevant to the arrangements if it is final and if the principles laid down, or reasoning given, in the ruling would, if applied to the arrangements, allow the purported tax advantage arising from those arrangements.

[*FA 2004, ss 316C, 316D; FA 2021, Sch 31 paras 16, 17, 44, 45(3)*].

Penalties concerning the disclosure of tax avoidance schemes

[28.17] Penalties are chargeable for failures to comply with requirements under the disclosure provisions. See **59.10** PENALTIES.

High-risk promoters of avoidance schemes

[28.18] A special compliance regime (sometimes referred to as the 'POTAS' regime) applies to certain promoters of tax avoidance schemes. With effect from 10 June 2021, HMRC can issue a 'stop notice' requiring a promoter to stop marketing a particular scheme if it satisfies certain conditions. This power can apply even if the scheme in question has not been defeated before a tribunal or court. Names and other details of promoters subject to such a notice may be published. HMRC's other powers under the regime are aimed at promoters who satisfy one or more 'threshold conditions' relating to previous behaviour or who promote a series of avoidance schemes which are defeated. HMRC can issue a 'conduct notice' (see **28.24** below) requiring the recipient to comply with specified conditions as to the information they provide to clients, compliance with any disclosure requirements under the provisions at **28.2** onwards above and not promoting schemes which rely on contrived or abnormal steps to produce a tax advantage. Promoters who fail to comply with a conduct notice may be issued with a monitoring notice (see **28.25** below). Names of promoters subject to such a notice may be published by HMRC, including details of how the conduct notice was breached, and promoters are required to notify their monitored status to clients. Information powers and penalties apply to promoters subject to a stop notice or a conduct notice and to promoters subject to a monitoring notice and their clients and intermediaries. Clients who fail to comply with their duty to provide HMRC with a monitored promoter's reference number are subject to extended time limits for assessment (see **6.7** ASSESSMENTS). Special rules apply to partnerships — see **28.31** below.

The taxes covered by the provisions are income tax, capital gains tax, corporation tax, petroleum revenue tax, inheritance tax, stamp duty land tax, stamp duty reserve tax and annual tax on enveloped dwellings. The provisions applicable to promoters who promote a series of avoidance schemes which are defeated also apply to VAT. [*FA 2014, ss 281A, 283(1)*].

For HMRC guidance on the provisions see www.gov.uk/government/uploads/system/uploads/attachment_data/file/454865/POTAS.pdf.

Simon's Taxes. See **A7.301–A7.313**.

POTAS—definitions

[28.19] Arrangements are subject to the provisions if they enable, or might be expected to enable, any person to obtain a 'tax advantage' and the main benefit, or one of the main benefits, that might be expected to arise from the arrangements is the obtaining of that advantage. '*Arrangements*' include any agreement, scheme, arrangement or understanding of any kind, whether or not legally enforceable, involving one or more transactions.

A proposal is subject to the provisions if it is a proposal for arrangements which, if entered into, would be subject to the provisions (whether the proposal relates to a particular person or to any person who may seek to use it).

A '*tax advantage*' includes relief or increased relief from tax, repayment or increased repayment of tax, avoidance or reduction of a charge or assessment to tax, avoidance of a possible assessment to tax, deferral of a payment, or advancement of a repayment, of tax and avoidance of an obligation to deduct or account for tax.

A person carrying on a business in the course of which he is, or has been, a promoter in relation to a proposal or arrangements carries on that business 'as a promoter'. A person is a '*promoter*' in relation to a proposal if he:

(i) is to any extent responsible for the design of the proposed arrangements; or
(ii) makes a 'firm approach' to another person with a view to making the proposal available for implementation by that, or any other, person; or
(iii) makes the proposal available for implementation by other persons.

A person is a '*promoter*' in relation to arrangements if he:

(a) is a promoter by virtue of (ii) or (iii) above in relation to a proposal which is implemented by the arrangements; or
(b) is to any extent responsible for the design, organisation or management of the arrangements.

A company is not, however, a promoter if the only persons to whom it provides services in connection with a proposal or arrangements are companies in the same group, provided that it has not provided such services to any person other than a group member during the three previous years. If the company subsequently provides such services to a person other than a group member, this rule is deemed not to have applied during the previous three years. Companies are members of the same group for this purpose if one is a 51% subsidiary of the other or both are 51% subsidiaries of a third company.

A person is not a promoter on account of (i) above or by virtue of being responsible for the design of arrangements within (b) above, if either he does not provide any tax advice in connection with the arrangements or could not reasonably be expected to know that the arrangements or proposal are subject to the provisions.

With effect from 10 June 2021, a person who is a member of a 'promotion structure' is treated as carrying on a business as a promoter, whether or not that person actually carries on a business. A person (P) is a member of a promotion structure in any of the following four scenarios:

(1) *Multiple entity promoter*. P and one or more others carry out activities between them that would, if carried out by a single person, cause that person to be a promoter and each of the persons carrying out those activities is 'closely related' to at least one other of them. For this purpose, a person (A) is '*closely related*' to another (B) if:
   (i) A can secure that B act's in accordance with A's wishes or vice versa;
   (ii) B typically acts, or it is reasonable to expect B to act, in accordance with A's wishes;
   (iii) a third person is able to secure that A and B act in accordance with that person's wishes;
   (iv) A and B typically act, or it is reasonable to expect A and B to act, in accordance with a third person's wishes;
   (v) A has a 50% investment (as defined) in B (or vice versa); or
   (vi) a third person has a 50% investment in A and B.

(2) *Acting for a non-resident promoter*. P acts under the instruction or guidance of a non-UK resident person (C) who carries on a business as a promoter and:
   - under that guidance or instruction, P is a promoter or facilitates any activity which would make another person a promoter; or
   - P receives remuneration of any kind from C in connection with C's business.

   For this purpose, a person is a promoter if they satisfy the definition of a promoter above, whether or not they carry on a business. Receiving remuneration includes receiving any payment or benefit as a consequence of C's instructions, whether or not C is the source of it. Also included are payments or benefits received as a consequence of any arrangements made by C (or in the making of which C participated) that are referable to C's business.

(3) *Control of another promoter*. P is an individual who controls or has significant influence (see **28.24** below) over a body corporate or partnership that carries on a business as a promoter and either of the following conditions is met:
   - at any time after first controlling or having significant influence over the body corporate or partnership, P was subject to an order disqualifying them as a company director or subject to insolvency or debt-related proceedings (as widely defined); or

- at any time P controlled or had significant influence over another body corporate or partnership that carried on a business as a promoter which was dissolved or became dormant or insolvent (as widely defined).

(4) *Transfer of promotion business.* There has been a 'relevant transfer' to P or to a body corporate or partnership that P controls or has significant influence over. A '*relevant transfer*' is the transfer of the whole of the business of a person carrying on business as a promoter, the transfer of any part of such a business that relates to the promotion of arrangements or proposals for arrangements or the transfer of property, rights or liabilities of such a business that are connected with the promotion of arrangements or proposals for arrangements. It does not matter whether or not the transfer is formal or for consideration or whether it is direct or indirect.

A person's activities as a promoter include:

- where (1) above applies, the activities carried out by that person and others which result in their treatment as a multiple entity promoter;
- where (2) above applies, activities carried out under the instruction or guidance of a person carrying on a business as a promoter;
- where (3) above applies, the activities of the body corporate or partnership; and
- where (4) above applies to a transfer to a body corporate or partnership, the activities of the body corporate or partnership.

Where a promoter (a '*monitored promoter*') of a proposal is subject to a monitoring notice (see **28.25** below), the proposal is a '*monitored proposal*' if the promoter, on or after the date the notice takes effect:

- first makes a firm approach to another person about the proposal;
- first makes the proposal available for implementation by another person; or
- first becomes aware of any transaction forming part of the proposed arrangements being entered into by any person.

Where a promoter of arrangements is a monitored promoter, the arrangements are '*monitored arrangements*' if:

- the promoter is a promoter of a proposal implemented by the arrangements by virtue of (ii) or (iii) above and, on or after the date the notice takes effect:
  - he first makes a firm approach to another person about the proposal;
  - he first makes the proposal available for implementation by another person;
  - he first becomes aware of any transaction forming part of the proposed arrangements being entered into by any person;
- the date on which the promoter first takes part in designing, organising or managing the arrangements is on or after the date on which the notice takes effect; or

- the arrangements enable, or are likely to enable, the person entering into the transactions forming them to obtain the tax advantage on or after the date the notice takes effect.

A person makes a '*firm approach*' to another person if he provides information about the proposal, including an explanation of the expected tax advantage, at a time when the proposed arrangements have been 'substantially designed', with a view to that, or any other, person entering into transactions forming part of the proposed arrangements. Arrangements have been '*substantially designed*' when it would be reasonable to believe that a person wishing to obtain the tax advantage might use the scheme or a scheme which is not substantially different.

A person is an '*intermediary*' in relation to a proposal if he is not a promoter of it but he communicates information about it to another person in the course of a business with a view to that, or any other, person entering into transactions forming part of the proposed arrangements.

'*Prescribed*' means prescribed, or of a description prescribed, in regulations made by HMRC by statutory instrument.

A person ('P') is a '*controlling member*' of a partnership (see **28.31** below) at any time when P has a right to a share of more than half the assets or income of the partnership. Any interests or rights of any individual who is connected with P (if P is an individual) and of any body corporate controlled by P are attributed to P for this purpose. The following are connected with P: P's spouse or civil partner; P's relatives (i.e. a brother, sister, ancestor or lineal descendant); the spouse or civil partner of P's relatives; relatives of P's spouse or civil partner; and the spouse or civil partner of a relative of P's spouse or civil partner. P controls a body corporate if P has power to secure that its affairs are conducted in accordance with P's wishes either by means of holding shares or voting power in a body corporate (whether or not the body corporate in question) or as a result of powers under the articles of association or other document regulating a body corporate.

A '*managing partner*' of a partnerships is a member of the partnership who directs, or is on a day to day level in control of, the management of the partnership's business.

The Treasury may amend the definitions of 'controlling member' and 'managing partner' by statutory instrument.

An '*authorised HMRC officer*' is an HMRC officer who is, or is a member of a class of officers who are, authorised by the Commissioners for HMRC for the purposes of the high-risk promoter provisions.

[*FA 2014, ss 234–236, 254, 282, 283, Sch 33A, Sch 36 paras 19–21; FA 2021, Sch 30 paras 9, 10, 18; SI 2015 No 130*].

Threshold conditions

[28.20] A person meets a threshold condition if:

(a) HMRC publish information about the person under the deliberate tax defaulter provisions in *FA 2009, s 94* (see **38.17** HMRC INVESTIGATORY POWERS);

(b) the person is named in a report under *FA 2014, s 285* because HMRC have determined that the person has breached the Code of Practice on Taxation for Banks by promoting arrangements which they cannot reasonably have believed achieved a tax result intended by Parliament;

(c) the person has been given a conduct notice under the dishonest conduct of tax agents provisions in *FA 2012, Sch 38 para 4* (see **38.18** HMRC INVESTIGATORY POWERS) and either the time limit for making an appeal against the notice has expired or an appeal has been made and rejected by the Tribunal;

(d) the person fails to comply with disclosure requirements under *FA 2004, ss 308–310, 313ZA* (see **28.4–28.7** above) or, with effect from 10 June 2021, *FA 2004, ss 310C, 312(2)* or *316A* (see **28.9, 28.12** above) or *F(No 2)A 2017, Sch 17 paras 11(1), 21(3, 23(2), 27(3)* or *33* (duties under VAT disclosure rules), including where the person had a reasonable excuse for non-compliance (see also below);

(e) the person is charged with a specified criminal offence (but such a charge is disregarded for this purpose if it has been dismissed, if the proceedings have been discontinued or following final acquittal);

(f) arrangements of which the person is a promoter have been referred to the GAAR Advisory Panel (see **4.4** ANTI-AVOIDANCE and **59.21** PENALTIES) or are in a pool (see **4.6** ANTI-AVOIDANCE) in respect of which a generic referral has been made or, with effect from 10 June 2021, are equivalent (see **4.6** ANTI-AVOIDANCE) to arrangements which have been referred to the Panel; the referral has been subject to one or more opinion notices of the sub-panel considering the case that the arrangements are not reasonable; and those notices, taken together, state the opinion of at least two of the members of the sub-panel;

(g) the person carries on a trade or profession that is regulated by a specified professional body, is found guilty of misconduct of a type prescribed for this purpose, has prescribed action taken against him, and has a prescribed penalty imposed on him (see below);

(h) the Financial Conduct Authority, Financial Services Authority or another prescribed regulatory body imposes a prescribed sanction for misconduct (including a fine or suspension of approval);

(i) the person fails to comply with an information notice under *FA 2008, Sch 36 paras 1, 2, 5* or *5A* (see **38.4** HMRC INVESTIGATORY POWERS) or, with effect from 10 June 2021, with DOTAS information requirements under *FA 2004, ss 308A, 310A, 313ZB, 313A* or *313B* (see **28.4, 28.15** above) or VAT equivalents;

(j) the person ('P') enters into an agreement with another person ('C') which relates to a proposal or arrangements of which P is the promoter on terms which imposes certain contractual obligations on C (see further below); or

(k) the person is subject to a stop notice (see **28.22** below) and fails to comply with the requirement not to promote arrangements or proposals of the type described in the notice, fails to make a quarterly return or fails to comply with an obligation arising from HMRC's information and inspection powers. For stop notices issued before 10 June 2021, this condition was that the person had been given a 'stop notice' and, after the end of the period of 30 days beginning on the day the notice was given, made a firm approach to another person with a view to making an 'affected proposal' (i.e. a proposal which is in substance the same as the proposal specified in the stop notice) available for implementation by that person or another or made an affected proposal available for implementation by other persons.

As regards (d) above, with effect for the purposes of determining whether a person meets this threshold condition in a three-year period, a failure to comply with a said requirement occurs only at the time (if any) that:

- the 'appeal period' ends following a determination by the Appeal Tribunal that such a failure occurred, or that it would have occurred but for the person's having a reasonable excuse, and it has ended without the determination being overturned; or
- the person admits in writing to HMRC that he has failed to comply with the requirement in question.

The 'appeal period' is the period during which an appeal could have been made or, where an appeal has been made, the period during which it has not yet been finally determined, withdrawn or otherwise disposed of.

For the purposes of (e) above, the following offences are specified:

- a common law offence of cheating the public revenue;
- in Scotland, an offence of fraud or uttering;
- an offence under *Theft Act 1968, s 17* (false accounting) or NI equivalent;
- an offence under *TMA 1970, s 106A* (fraudulent evasion of income tax);
- an offence under *TMA 1970, s 107* (false statements: Scotland);
- an offence under *Customs and Excise Management Act 1979, s 50(2)* (improper importation of goods with intent to defraud or evade duty), *s 167* (untrue declarations etc.), *s 168* (counterfeiting documents etc.), *s 170* (fraudulent evasion of duty) or *s 170B* (taking steps for the fraudulent evasion of duty);
- an offence under *VATA 1994, s 72(1)* (being knowingly concerned in the evasion of VAT), *s 72(3)* (false statement etc.), or *s 72(8)* (conduct involving commission of other offence);
- an offence under *Fraud Act 2006, s 1*;
- an offence under *CRCA 2005, s 30* (impersonating a Commissioner or officer of HMRC), *s 31* (obstruction of HMRC officer etc.) or *s 32* (assault of HMRC officer);
- an offence under *SI 2007 No 2157, Reg 45(1)* (money laundering); and
- an offence under *Criminal Justice and Licensing (Scotland) Act 2010, s 49(1)* (possession of articles for use in fraud).

For the purposes of (g) above, the type of misconduct prescribed is conduct by a person which a professional body describes as misconduct or which is a breach of a rule or condition imposed by such a body and which is relevant to the provision of tax advice or tax-related services. Prescribed action means any action by a professional body which results in any claim of misconduct being referred to a disciplinary process or a conciliation, arbitration or similar settlement process. A prescribed penalty means a fine or financial penalty greater than £5,000 and/or a condition or restriction attached to, or the suspension, withdrawal or non-renewal of, a practising certificate, or suspension, expulsion or exclusion from membership of the professional body, whether it be temporary or permanent. In (f) above, the specified professional bodies are the Institutes of Chartered Accountants in England and Wales and of Scotland, the General Council of the Bar, the Faculty of Advocates, the General Council of the Bar in Northern Ireland, the Law Society, the Law Societies of Scotland and Northern Ireland, the Association of Accounting Technicians, the Association of Chartered Certified Accountants, the Association of Taxation Technicians, the Chartered Institute of Taxation and Chartered Accountants Ireland. With effect for the purposes of determining whether a person meets this threshold condition in a three-year period, the threshold condition is not confined to decisions and actions taken by the professional body itself and may thus take account of decisions and actions by independent bodies in matters of relevant forms of professional misconduct.

The threshold condition in (j) above is met if the contractual obligation prevents or restricts the disclosure by C to HMRC of information about the proposals or arrangements, whether or not by referring to a wider class of persons, or if the obligation requires C to impose a similar contractual obligation on any tax adviser to whom C discloses information. The condition is also met if contractual obligations require C:

- to meet the whole or part of the costs of, or contribute to a fund to meet the costs of, any 'proceedings' relating to arrangements promoted by C (whether or not implemented by C) or, where C implements the arrangements, to take out an insurance policy to insure against the risk of having to meet such costs; and
- to obtain P's consent before making any agreement with HMRC regarding arrangements promoted by P or withdrawing or discontinuing any appeal against a decision about such arrangements.

'*Proceedings*' for this purpose include any sort of proceedings for resolving disputes (i.e. not just court proceedings) which are commenced or contemplated.

Note that, where the threshold condition in question is within (i) above, it is treated as met when the time limit for compliance with the information notice expires without the promoter complying with it.

[*FA 2014, Sch 34 paras 1–12, 14; F(No 2)A 2017, Sch 16 para 61; FA 2021, Sch 30 paras 7, 29–31; SI 2015 No 131*].

Relevant defeat

[28.21] For the purposes of the high-risk promoter regime, a '*defeat*' of arrangements occurs in any of the following circumstances.

(A) A tax advantage arising from the arrangements is counteracted (partly or wholly) by HMRC under the general anti-abuse rule ('GAAR'; see **4.3** ANTI-AVOIDANCE) and the counteraction is 'final'.

(B) A follower notice (see **4.29** ANTI-AVOIDANCE) has been given by reference to the arrangements (and not withdrawn) and either the taxpayer takes corrective action or the denied tax advantage is counteracted (partly or wholly) and the counteraction is final.

(C) A tax advantage arising from 'DOTAS arrangements' is counteracted and the counteraction is final. '*DOTAS arrangements*' are arrangements which a person has disclosed to HMRC under *FA 2004, s 308, 309* or *310* (see **28.4, 28.6, 28.7** above) or in respect of which a person has 'failed to comply' (as defined) with a requirement to do so. Arrangements which a person would be so required to disclose but for certain specified exceptions are treated for this purpose as having been disclosed. A tax advantage is counteracted if 'adjustments' are made to the taxpayer's position on the basis that the whole or part of the advantage does not arise. Arrangements in respect of which HMRC have given notice that the reference number need no longer be notified to clients (see **28.11** above) are excluded.

(D) A tax advantage arising from 'disclosable VAT arrangements' (as defined) is counteracted and the counteraction is final.

(E) A final judicial ruling holds that a particular 'avoidance-related rule' applies to counteract the whole or part of a tax advantage arising from the arrangements. An '*avoidance-related rule*' is a rule falling within category 1 or category 2. A rule falls within category 1 if it refers to the purpose or main purpose or purposes of a transaction, arrangements or other action or matter and to whether or not the purpose is or involves the avoidance of tax or obtaining an advantage in relation to tax. A rule is also in category 1 if it refers to expectations as to what are, or may be, the expected benefits (whether or not the sole or main benefits) of a transaction, arrangements or any other action or matter and to whether or not the avoidance of tax or obtaining an advantage in relation to tax is such a benefit. A rule falls within category 2 if it results in a person being treated differently for tax purposes depending on whether or not purposes referred to in the rule are commercial purposes.

A counteraction is '*final*' for these purposes when the assessment or adjustments made to effect it, and any amounts arising as a result, can no longer be varied, on appeal or otherwise. A judicial ruling is '*final*' if it is a Supreme Court ruling or a ruling of any other tribunal or court against which no further appeal can be made. '*Adjustments*' are any adjustments, by assessment, modification of an assessment or return, amendment or disallowance of a claim, entering into a contract settlement or otherwise.

A defeat of arrangements entered into by any person which are 'promoted arrangements' of a promoter is a '*relevant defeat*' in relation to that promoter if either:

(i) the arrangements are not 'related' to any other promoted arrangements of the promoter; or

(ii) they are related to other promoted arrangements of the promoter and any of cases 1–3 below applies (in which case there is a relevant defeat of the arrangements in question and of each of the related arrangements).

If there has been a relevant defeat in relation to promoted arrangements of a promoter there can be no further relevant defeat of those arrangements or of any related arrangements.

For the purpose of (ii) above, case 1 applies if any of (A)–(D) above are met in relation to any of the arrangements and the decision to make the counteraction in question has been upheld by a judicial ruling which is final. Case 2 applies if (E) above is met in relation to any of the arrangements. Case 3 applies if at least 75% of the 'tested arrangements' have been defeated and no final judicial ruling has upheld a corresponding tax advantage under any of the arrangements. The '*tested arrangements*' are any of the arrangements in respect of which: there has been an enquiry or investigation by HMRC into a return, claim or election; HMRC has assessed a taxpayer on the basis that the tax advantage (or part of it) does not arise; a final counteraction notice under the GAAR (see **4.4–4.6** ANTI-AVOIDANCE) has been given in relation to the tax advantage (or part of it); or HMRC have taken any other action on the basis that a tax advantage does not arise under the arrangements.

Arrangements are '*promoted arrangements*' in relation to a promoter if they are arrangements to which the high-risk promoter regime applies or would apply if that regime applied generally to VAT. Separate arrangements are '*related*' to each other if they are substantially the same. For this purpose, arrangements which have been allocated the same reference number under **28.11** above or the equivalent VAT provisions are treated as substantially the same (if they would not otherwise be so treated). Arrangements which are subject to follower notices by reference to the same judicial ruling are likewise treated as substantially the same. Where a notice of binding under the GAAR has been given (see **4.5** ANTI-AVOIDANCE, the bound arrangements are treated as being substantially the same as the lead arrangements and any other arrangements otherwise treated as substantially the same as the lead arrangements.

Attribution of relevant defeat

A relevant defeat in relation to a person (Q) is treated as a relevant defeat in relation to another person (P), whether or not it is also treated as a relevant defeat of Q, if either:

(1) where P is not an individual:
- at a time when the defeated arrangements were promoted arrangements in relation to Q either P was a body corporate or partnership controlled by Q or Q was a body corporate or partnership controlled by P; and
- at the time of the relevant defeat, P was a body corporate or partnership controlled by Q, Q was a body corporate or partnership controlled by P or both were bodies corporate or partnerships controlled by a third person; or

(2) where P and Q are both bodies corporate or partnerships, at a time when the defeated arrangements were promoted arrangements in relation to Q, a third person (C) controlled Q and C controls P at the time of the relevant defeat.

This rule applies even if Q has ceased to exist or if P did not exist at any time when the defeated arrangements were promoted arrangements in relation to Q. For the purposes of the rule, in determining whether arrangements are promoted arrangements in relation to Q, the definition of 'promoter' applies as if the word 'design' were omitted at **28.4**(b) above.

A person controls a body corporate if he has power to secure that the affairs of the body corporate are conducted in accordance with his wishes, whether by means of the holding of shares, the possession of voting power or the articles of association or other document or by means of his controlling a partnership. A person controls a partnership if he is a 'controlling member' or 'managing partner' of the partnership (as defined).

The Treasury may amend the above provisions by statutory instrument.

[*FA 2014, s 237D(6), Sch 34A paras 1–17, 19, 24–31*].

Defeat notices

An authorised HMRC officer (or another officer acting with the approval of an authorised officer) may give a person carrying on a business as a promoter a '*defeat notice*' if:

(a) he becomes aware of one (and only one) relevant defeat in relation to the promoter in the previous three years (in which case the notice is a '*single defeat notice*'); or

(b) he becomes aware of two (but not more than two) relevant defeats in relation to the promoter in the previous three years (a '*double defeat notice*').

If, after a single defeat notice has ceased to have effect because of a judicial ruling (see below), the officer becomes aware of a further relevant defeat in relation to the promoter which occurred whilst the notice was in effect, he may issue a further single defeat notice (even if the further defeat did not occur in the three years preceding the issuing of the notice).

A defeat notice must be given before the end of the 90 days beginning with the date on which the defeat in question first came to an authorised HMRC officer's attention. Before 10 June 2021, the 90-day period began when the defeat came to the attention of HMRC in general. The notice must state the 'look-forward period', explain the effect of the notice (see **28.24** below) and include any further information which HMRC have specified must be included in such notices. A notice given to a partnership must state that it is a partnership defeat notice. A defeat notice has effect throughout the look-forward period unless it ceases to have effect because the relevant defeat is 'overturned'. The '*look-forward period*' is the five years beginning the day after the notice is given or, in the case of a further single defeat notice, the period beginning the day after the notice is given and ending five years from the day on which the further relevant defeat occurred.

A single defeat notice ceases to have effect if, and on and after the day that, the relevant defeat is overturned. If one (and only one) of the relevant defeats on which a double defeat notice is based is overturned, the notice is treated as if it had always been a single defeat notice based on the other relevant defeat. If both the relevant defeats on which a double defeat notice is based are overturned on the same date, the notice ceases to have effect on that date. HMRC must notify the promoter accordingly.

Only a relevant defeat to which case 3 above applies can be overturned. Such a defeat is '*overturned*' if, before the notice was given, less than 100% of the tested arrangements had been defeated and, at a time when the notice has effect, a court or tribunal upholds a tax advantage arising under any of the arrangements taken into account in determining the case 3 relevant defeat. The relevant defeat is overturned on the day on which the judicial ruling becomes final. For this purpose, a court or tribunal upholds a tax advantage if it makes a ruling that no part of the advantage is to be counteracted and that ruling is final.

Deemed defeat notices

Provision is made for a defeat notice to be deemed to have been given to a person (P) who is carrying on a business as a promoter when certain conditions are met in respect of 'third party defeats'. This applies where an authorised officer becomes aware at any time (the '*relevant time*') that a relevant defeat has occurred in relation to P and in the preceding three years there have been one or two third party defeats. A '*third party defeat*' is a relevant defeat which has occurred in relation to a person other than P.

Where there has been one such third party defeat, then if:

- a conduct notice or single or double defeat notice has been given to the other person in respect of the third party defeat; at the time of that defeat, HMRC would have been able to give a defeat notice to P under the rules for attributing relevant defeats above if they had been aware that the defeat was also a relevant defeat in relation to P; and so far as the HMRC officer is aware, the conditions for giving P a defeat notice in respect of the defeat have never otherwise been met; and
- had a defeat notice in respect of the third party defeat been given to P at the time of that defeat, the defeat notice would still have effect at the relevant time,

the high-risk promoter provisions apply as if the officer had, with due authority, given P a single defeat notice at the time of the third party defeat.

Where there have been two third party defeats, then if:

- a conduct notice or single or double defeat notice has been given to the other person in respect of each, or both, of the third party defeats; at the time of the second defeat, HMRC would have been able to give a double defeat notice to P under the rules for attributing relevant defeats above if they had been aware that either of the defeats was also a relevant defeat in relation to P; and so far as the HMRC officer is aware, the conditions for giving P a defeat notice in respect of either or both of the defeats have never otherwise been met; and
- had a defeat notice in respect of the two third party defeats been given to P at the time of the second defeat, the defeat notice would still have effect at the relevant time,

the high-risk promoter provisions apply as if the officer had, with due authority, given P a single defeat notice at the time of the third party defeat.

[*FA 2014, ss 241A, 241B, Sch 34A para 18, Sch 36 para 4A; FA 2021, Sch 30 para 26*].

Stop notices

[28.22] The first type of notice that HMRC may issue under the POTAS regime is the 'stop notice'. *FA 2021* has expanded both the circumstances in which, and the effect of, stop notices with effect from 10 June 2021. Previously, such notices could be given only where a follower notice had been given in respect of the avoidance scheme in question and the effect of the notice was indirect, in that the giving of the notice was the first leg of a threshold condition for giving a conduct notice. Stop notices given on or after 10 June 2021 can be given at an earlier stage, to stop the marketing of schemes before they have been defeated. Promoters subject to such a stop notice are required, subject to penalties, not to market the scheme and have to provide quarterly returns to HMRC confirming their compliance with the notice or giving details of clients to whom they have, despite the notice, marketed the scheme. HMRC may publish details of persons subject to such a notice.

Stop notices issued on or after 10 June 2021

An authorised HMRC officer may issue a stop notice if the officer suspects that the recipient 'promotes', or has promoted, arrangements or proposals for arrangements which the officer considers meet conditions A and B, conditions A and C or conditions B and D.

(A) Condition A is that arrangements of the type specified in the notice:
- would, if implemented before 5 April 2019, have been likely to cause a person to be treated as taking a 'relevant step' for the purposes of the employment income loan charge provisions or to cause a relevant benefit to arise under the trading income loan charge provisions;
- would be the same as, or similar to, arrangements or proposed arrangements ('reference arrangements') to which a scheme reference number has been allocated under DOTAS (see **28.11** above);
- would be the same as, or similar to, arrangements in respect of which any person has been issued with a follower notice (see **4.29** ANTI-AVOIDANCE); or
- would be the same as, or similar to, arrangements of a type specified in regulations made by HMRC.

(B) Condition B is that arrangements or proposals of the type specified in the notice have been, or are likely to be, marketed (by the recipient of the notice or otherwise) as capable of enabling a particular tax advantage but it is more likely than not that they are not so capable.

(C) Condition C is that condition A is met as a result of the allocation of a scheme reference number and either:
- HMRC have required a person to provide further information or documents (under *FA 2004, s 310A* or *s 311C* — see **28.4, 28.11** above) about the reference arrangements and that person has failed to do so; or
- HMRC have made an application to the Tribunal for an order under *FA 2004, s 308A* (see **28.15** above) requiring the provision of information or documents about the reference arrangements.

(D) Condition D is that arrangements or proposals of the type specified in the notice would be within the meaning of those terms for the purposes of the POTAS regime (see **28.19** above) and the recipient of the notice is subject to a conduct notice (see **28.24** below) or a monitoring notice (see **28.25** below).

A person (P) '*promotes*' arrangements or a proposal for arrangements if P does anything in connection with them that would cause that person to be carrying on a business as a promoter (or to be treated as such) under the POTAS regime if the arrangements or proposal were within the meaning of those terms for the purposes of the regime (see **28.19** above).

A stop notice must specify the arrangements in question.

[*FA 2014, s 236A; FA 2021, Sch 30 para 1*].

Withdrawal of a stop notice

A person (P) subject to a stop notice may make a request to HMRC in writing for the notice to cease to apply to them if they have not promoted arrangements of the type specified in the notice and do not intend to do so, if they consider that the conditions for making the notice are not met or if they consider that there are other reasons for the notice to cease to apply. Such a request must be made within the period of 30 days beginning with the day on which the notice was given. It must contain an explanation of the basis for the request and be accompanied by such evidence to support that explanation as is reasonable in the circumstances.

The authorised HMRC officer to whom the request has been made then has 45 days from receipt of the request to decide whether or not the notice should cease to apply to P and to give P a notice (a 'decision notice') setting out their decision. If HMRC fail to give a decision notice within the time limit, the stop notice automatically ceases to apply to P.

An authorised HMRC officer may also determine that a stop notice should cease to apply to a person who has not made a request by giving that person a withdrawal notice.

A notice that provides for a stop notice to cease to apply to a person must include the date on which it ceases to apply (which may be earlier or later than the date of the decision notice or withdrawal notice).

Where a stop notice is given on the basis that a scheme reference number has been allocated (see Condition A above) and that number is withdrawn, the stop notice ceases to apply to every person who is subject to it from the time of withdrawal. HMRC must notify every person to whom the notice was given or that they are aware is subject to it. The notice must state the reason for the withdrawal of the scheme reference number and may contain any further explanation HMRC consider appropriate (such as their view of the arrangements or proposal in question).

The recipient of an HMRC decision notice refusing a request for a stop notice to cease to apply can appeal against the decision. The appeal must be made by notice in writing within the 30-day period beginning with the day on which the decision notice is given and must state the grounds of appeal (which are restricted to the same grounds as those which can be relied on to make a request for a notice to cease to apply).

A person (P) making an appeal can also make a request for the stop notice to be suspended until the appeal is determined, withdrawn or otherwise disposed of. Such a request must be made in writing and must contain an explanation of the basis for the request and be accompanied by such evidence to support that explanation as is reasonable in the circumstances. There is no time limit for making a request (subject to the determination etc. of the appeal) and a request can be made at the same time as, or after, making the appeal.

The authorised HMRC officer to whom the request has been made then has 30 days beginning with day of receipt of the request to decide whether or not to suspend the notice and to notify P accordingly. If HMRC fail to give a suspension decision notice within the time limit, the stop notice is suspended automatically until either HMRC do give a suspension decision notice or the appeal is determined, withdrawn or otherwise disposed of.

[*FA 2014, ss 236D–236G; FA 2021, Sch 30 para 1*].

Stop notices issued before 10 June 2021

An authorised HMRC officer may give a person ('P') a '*stop notice*' if:

- a person has been given a follower notice (see **4.29** ANTI-AVOIDANCE) relating to particular arrangements;
- P is a promoter of a proposal implemented by those arrangements; and
- 90 days have passed since the follower notice was given, the notice has not been withdrawn and, if representations objecting to the notice were made, HMRC have confirmed the notice.

A stop notice must specify the arrangements which are the subject of the follower notice, specify the court or tribunal ruling identified in that notice, specify the proposal implemented by those arrangements and explain the effect of the stop notice. An authorised HMRC officer may notify P in writing that a stop notice is to cease to have effect from a specified date (which may be before the notice is given).

See **28.20**(k) above for the effect of a stop notice issued before 10 June 2021.

[*FA 2014, Sch 34 para 12*].

Effects of a stop notice issued on or after 10 June 2021

[28.23] A person subject to a stop notice must not promote the arrangements or any proposal for arrangements specified in the notice or any arrangements or proposals with a similar form or effect. This applies not just to the recipient of the notice but also to any body corporate or partnership controlled by the recipient or over which the recipient has significant influence (where the recipient is a body corporate or partnership), any person with control or significant influence over the recipient or any person to whom the recipient makes a 'relevant transfer' (see **28.19**(4) above).

A recipient of a stop notice who controls or has significant influence over a body corporate or partnership must give a copy of the notice to that body corporate or partnership within five days of the giving of the notice and must provide HMRC with its name, business address or registered office and any name, previous name or pseudonym under which it has carried on a business, within 15 days of the giving of the notice. Similar requirements apply where the recipient is itself a body corporate or partnership with respect to any person which it controls or has significant influence over. A recipient who makes a 'relevant transfer' must give a copy of the notice to the transferee and provide HMRC with its name, business address or registered office and any name, previous name or pseudonym under which it has carried on a business, within 15 days of the transfer.

HMRC may give a copy of the notice to any person if they consider that the original recipient is obliged to give that person a copy. This does not affect the obligation of the original recipient to do so.

For the meaning of 'control' and 'significant influence' see **28.24** below.

Quarterly returns

A person (P) subject to a stop notice must give HMRC a return for each three-month period falling within the three years starting on the day the notice was given. Each return must contain the following information:

(a) the number of clients to which, in that period, P has made a firm approach relating to a proposal for arrangements of the type specified in the notice, has made the proposal available for implementation or has provided services in relation to such arrangements or a proposal;
(b) the name and address of any such clients, together with their unique taxpayer reference and national insurance number (if any); and
(c) any name by which the arrangements or proposal are known or marketed.

The return for the first three-month period must also include the details in (a) and (b) above for any time before that period. A return is still required even if the number of clients in (a) above is nil. If P does not have the unique taxpayer reference or national insurance number of any of the clients, the return must include a statement of that fact.

A return must be submitted within the 15-day period beginning with the last day of the three-month period to which it relates.

HMRC can notify a person required to submit returns that they are no longer required to do so. The obligation to make returns will then cease from the time specified in the notice.

[*FA 2014, ss 236B, 236C; FA 2021, Sch 30 para 1*].

Disclosure to clients and intermediaries

A person (P) subject to a stop notice who has at any time promoted arrangements or a proposal of the type specified in the notice must notify any clients to whom P has made a firm approach relating to such a proposal, any clients to whom P has made the proposal available for implementation and to any clients to whom P has provided services in relation to such arrangements or a proposal. P must also notify anyone who they could reasonably be expected to know is an intermediary in relation to such a proposal. The notice must set out that P is subject to a stop notice and that the arrangements or proposal are of the type specified in the notice. It must be accompanied by a copy of the stop notice.

Existing clients and intermediaries must be notified within five days of the day on which P becomes aware that they are subject to the notice. Where P subsequently becomes aware of an intermediary, the notification must be given within five days of P becoming so aware.

[*FA 2014, s 236J; FA 2021, Sch 30 para 1*].

Publication by HMRC

HMRC may publish the name (including business name and any previous name or pseudonym) of a person subject to a stop notice together with the business address or registered office, any other information which they consider appropriate to publish to make clear the person's identity and details of the arrangements or proposal in question. Publication may not take place before the end of the period in which a request for the notice to be withdrawn. If such a request is made, publication may not take place before the end of the period in which an appeal against HMRC's decision not to withdraw the notice could be made. If such an appeal is made, publication may not take place before the proceedings on that appeal to the Tribunal are determined, withdrawn or otherwise disposed of. Publication is not, however, delayed by any further appeal from the tribunal.

HMRC may, however, publish details of the arrangements or proposal and the fact that a stop notice applies to them as soon as the notice is issued, regardless of the above time limits.

If, following publication, the stop notice is withdrawn because of the withdrawal of a scheme reference number, HMRC must publish the fact that the notice no longer has effect, the reason why the reference number was withdrawn and any other explanation they consider appropriate. HMRC may also publish information about the persons who were subject to the notice.

[*FA 2014, s s236H, 236I; FA 2021, Sch 30 para 1*].

Notification of interested persons

If a person subject to a stop notice fails to comply with it (i.e. they continue to promote the arrangements or proposal), an authorised HMRC officer may send a copy of the notice to anyone that might be affected by it (including clients and anyone else making use of the arrangements). The officer may also provide the name of the person who has failed to comply, their business address or registered office and any other information needed to make clear that person's identity, together with details of the arrangement or proposal, an explanation of the effect of the stop notice and of why it was given. [*FA 2014, s 236K; FA 2021, Sch 30 para 1*].

Information etc.

See **28.27** below for the application of HMRC's information and inspection powers under *FA 2008, Sch 36* to persons subject to a stop notice.

Conduct notices

[28.24] A '*conduct notice*' is a notice requiring the person to whom it is given to comply with specified conditions. HMRC must issue such a notice in any of the four situations described below.

A conduct notice has effect from the date specified in it and may be amended at any time by an authorised HMRC officer. A notice ceases to have effect at the end of the relevant period (see below). Notices issued before 10 June 2021 ceased to have effect after two years or on an earlier date specified in the notice. A notice also ceases to have effect if a monitoring notice (see **28.25** below) takes effect. A notice may also be withdrawn by an authorised HMRC officer. With effect from 10 June 2021, instead of amending a conduct notice, an authorised HMRC officer may withdraw it and issue a replacement notice. A provisional notice may cease to have effect as a result of a judicial decision (see further below).

The relevant period is determined on the basis of the following table.

Conditions met	*Maximum relevant period (years)*
1 ordinary condition	2
2 ordinary conditions	4
3 or more ordinary conditions	5
1 significant condition	3
1 significant condition and 1 or more other significant conditions or ordinary conditions	5

The HMRC officer issuing a conduct notice must notify the relevant period to the recipient. If an officer subsequently becomes aware that the recipient has met additional conditions, the relevant period may be recalculated and the recipient notified accordingly.

Significant conditions are the threshold conditions in **21.10**(a)–(c), (e) or (f) above and, where an HMRC officer has made a determination that they should be regarded as significant, any of the conditions in (I)–(III) below. The remaining threshold conditions are ordinary conditions.

If a replacement notice is issued with a commencement date later than 12 months before the end of the relevant period for the original notice, the new notice ceases to have effect at the end of that period.

Any day on all or part of which the conduct notice is suspended by an HMRC officer does not count towards the relevant period. The officer must notify the promoter of the suspension, and of the resumption, of the notice as soon as practicable. If the promoter is given an information notice under the provisions at **28.26** below and fails to comply with the notice within the time limit for doing so, any days falling after the expiry of the time limit and before the information or documents are provided also do not count towards the relevant period. Where the relevant period needs to be recalculated, HMRC must notify the promoter of the number of days left out of account and of the revised end date for the relevant period as soon as practicable.

Threshold condition satisfied

An authorised HMRC officer must issue a conduct notice if he becomes aware at any time that a person (P) carrying on a business as a promoter has, in the previous three years and at a time when he was carrying on such a business, met one or more of the threshold conditions (see **28.20** above) and the officer determines that the meeting of the condition or conditions should be regarded as significant in view of the purposes of the POTAS regime. For this purpose, meeting any of the threshold conditions in **28.20**(a)–(c), (e) or (f) is automatically treated as significant. With effect from 10 June 2021, meeting a threshold condition or conditions is also automatically treated as significant if P is a member of a promotion structure under the multiple entity promoter scenario (see **28.19**(1) above). No conduct notice need be issued if the officer determines that it is inappropriate to do so, having regard to the extent of the impact that P's activities are likely to have on the collection of tax. A conduct notice cannot be issued if P is already subject to such a notice or to a monitoring notice (see **28.25** below). A conduct notice given to a partnership must state that it is a partnership conduct notice.

Related companies and partnerships — threshold conditions

An authorised HMRC officer must also issue a conduct notice if he becomes aware at any time (the 'relevant time') that:

(i) a person (P1) has, in the previous three years, met one or more of the threshold conditions;
(ii) at the relevant time another person (P2) is treated as meeting one or more of the threshold conditions by virtue of the 'control or influence rules' described below;
(iii) P2 is, at the relevant time, carrying on a business as a promoter; and

the officer determines that the meeting of the condition(s) by either P1 or P2 should be regarded as significant in view of the purposes of the POTAS regime. Before 10 June 2021, the requirement was for the meeting of the condition(s) by both P1 and P2 to be regarded as significant.

The officer must issue the conduct notice to P2, unless he determines that it is inappropriate to do so, having regard to the extent of the impact that P2's activities are likely to have on the collection of tax. The giving of a conduct notice to P2 does not prevent the giving of such a notice to P1 in his own right.

The '*control or influence rules*' referred to in (ii) above treat persons under the control or significant influence of one or more others, persons in control of, or with significant influence over, others and persons controlled by, or under the significant influence of, the same person or persons as meeting a threshold condition at the relevant time as set out below.

For these purposes a person controls a body corporate if he has power to secure that its affairs are conducted in accordance with his wishes, whether by means of the holding of shares, the possession of voting power or the articles of association or other document or by means of his controlling a partnership. Two or more persons together control a body corporate if together they have the power to secure by any of those means that its affairs are conducted in accordance with their wishes.

A person controls a partnership if he is a member of the partnership and either has the right to a share of more than half its assets or income or directs, or (on a day-to-day level) is in control of, the management of its business. Two or more persons together control a partnership if they are members of the partnership and together meet one of those conditions. For these purposes, the interests or rights of any individual who is connected with a person (if the person is an individual) and of any body corporate controlled by the person are attributed to the person; see **28.19** above (under the definition of 'controlling member') for more details.

A person has '*significant influence*' over a body corporate or partnership if, whilst not controlling it, he exercises, or is able to exercise, significant influence over it (whether or not as the result of a legal entitlement). Two or more persons together have significant influence over a body corporate or partnership if together they meet that condition.

Persons under another's control or influence

Where P2 is a body corporate or partnership, P2 is treated as meeting a threshold condition at the relevant time if P1 controls or has significant influence over P2 at that time and P1 met the threshold condition at a time when either P1 was carrying on a business as a promoter or P2 was carrying on a business as a promoter and P1 controlled or had significant influence over P2. However, where P1 is an individual (other than one who is a member of a promotion structure within **28.19**(3) or (4) above), this treatment applies only where the threshold condition in question is one within **28.20**(a) or (c) or any of (e)–(i) above.

P2 is also treated as meeting a threshold condition at the relevant time if two or more persons together controlled or had significant influence over it at a time when one of those persons met the threshold condition, P2 was a promoter at that time and those persons also controlled or had significant influence over P2 at the relevant time.

Persons in control of, or with significant influence over, others

P2 is treated as meeting a threshold condition at the relevant time if P1 is a body corporate or partnership and met the threshold condition at a time (the 'earlier time') when it was carrying on a business as a promoter and was controlled by P2 or P2 had significant influence over it. This applies additionally if at the earlier time it was another body corporate or partnership controlled by, or under the significant influence of, P2 that was carrying on a business as a promoter.

Persons under common control or influence

Where P2 is a body corporate or partnership, P2 is treated as meeting a threshold condition at the relevant time if:

- P2 or another body corporate or partnership met the threshold condition at a time (the 'earlier time') when P1 controlled or had significant influence over P2;
- at the earlier time there was a body corporate or partnership which P1 controlled or had significant influence over which carried on a business as a promoter; and

- P1 controls or has significant influence over P2 at the relevant time.

P2 is also treated as meeting a threshold condition at the relevant time if:

- P2 or another body corporate or partnership met the threshold condition at a time (the 'earlier time') when two or more persons together controlled or had significant influence over P2;
- at the earlier time there was a body corporate or partnership which those persons together controlled or had significant influence over which carried on a business as a promoter; and
- those persons together control or have significant influence over P2 at the relevant time.

Defeat of promoted arrangements

An authorised HMRC officer must issue a conduct notice if he becomes aware at any time (the '*relevant time*') that a person who is carrying on a business as a promoter meets any of the following conditions and the officer determines that the meeting of the condition(s) should be regarded as significant in view of the purposes of the POTAS regime. The conditions are that:

(I) in the previous three years, at least three 'relevant defeats' have occurred in relation to the promoter; or

(II) at least two relevant defeats have occurred in relation to the promoter at times when he was subject to a single defeat notice; or

(III) at least one relevant defeat has occurred in relation to the promoter at a time when he was subject to a double defeat notice.

With effect from 10 June 2021, meeting any of the conditions is automatically treated as significant if the promoter is a member of a promotion structure under the multiple entity promoter scenario (see **28.19**(1) above).

A determination that either of the conditions at (II) or (III) above is met can only be made while the relevant defeat notice is still in effect on or before the 90th day after that on which it ceased to have effect. No conduct notice need be issued if the officer determines that it is inappropriate to do so, having regard to the extent of the impact that the promoter's activities are likely to have on the collection of tax.

A conduct notice cannot be issued in these circumstances if the promoter is already subject to a conduct notice or a monitoring notice. If an HMRC officer is considering at the same time whether or not a conduct notice must be made because of a threshold condition, the meeting of a condition in (I)–(III) above is treated as meeting a threshold condition and any conduct notice must be given on that basis.

An authorised HMRC officer must give a further conduct notice to a promoter if:

(1) a conduct notice has ceased to have effect otherwise than because of a judicial ruling or because it is withdrawn or a monitoring notice is given, and the notice was 'provisional';

(2) the officer determines that the promoter had failed to comply with one or more conditions in the conduct notice;

(3) the conduct notice relied on a case 3 relevant defeat (see **28.21** above) but less than 100% of the tested arrangements had been defeated before the notice was given;

(4) after the conduct notice ceased to have effect, one or more case 1 or 2 relevant defeats has occurred in relation to the promoter and any arrangements to which the case 3 relevant defeat also relates; and

(5) had that defeat or defeats occurred before the conduct notice ceased to have effect, HMRC would have had to notify the promoter that it was no longer provisional.

A further conduct notice cannot be issued in these circumstances if the promoter is already subject to a conduct notice or a monitoring notice and need not be issued if the HMRC officer determines that it is inappropriate to do so, having regard to the extent of the impact that the promoter's activities are likely to have on the collection of tax.

A conduct notice is '*provisional*' if (3) above applies to it, unless an authorised HMRC officer notifies the promoter that is no longer provisional. A notice ceases to be provisional if:

(A) (i) two, or all three, of the relevant defeats by reference to which the notice is given would not have been relevant defeats if case 3 in **28.21** above had required 100% of the tested arrangements to have been defeated, and (ii) the same number of 'full relevant defeats' occur in relation to the promoter; or

(B) where (A)(i) above does not apply, a full relevant defeat occurs in relation to the promoter.

A '*full relevant defeat*' is either a relevant defeat other than one under case 3 or a case 3 relevant defeat where all of the tested arrangements are defeated. For this purpose, the rule that there can be only one relevant defeat of particular arrangements and any related arrangements does not prevent a full relevant defeat from occurring in respect of arrangements in relation to which a relevant defeat under case 3 has previously occurred.

A provisional conduct notice ceases to have effect if a court or tribunal upholds a tax advantage arising under any of the arrangements taken into account in determining the case 3 relevant defeat. For this purpose, a court or tribunal upholds a tax advantage if it makes a ruling that no part of the advantage is to be counteracted and that ruling is final. HMRC must notify the promoter accordingly.

Related companies and partnerships — defeat of promoted arrangements

An authorised HMRC officer must also issue a conduct notice if he becomes aware at any time (the '*relevant time*') that:

(a) a person (P1) meets any of conditions (I)–(III) above;

(b) at the relevant time another person (P2) meets that condition by virtue of the 'control or influence rules' described below;

(c) P2 is, at the relevant time, carrying on a business as a promoter; and the officer determines that the meeting of these conditions by either P1 or P2 should be regarded as significant in view of the purposes of the POTAS regime. Before 10 June 2021, the requirement was for the meeting of the conditions by both P1 and P2 to be regarded as significant.

The officer must issue the conduct notice to P2, unless he determines that it is inappropriate to do so, having regard to the extent of the impact that P2's activities are likely to have on the collection of tax. The giving of a conduct notice to P2 does not prevent the giving of such a notice to P1 in his own right.

A conduct notice cannot be issued in these circumstances if P2 is already subject to a conduct notice or a monitoring notice. If an HMRC officer is considering at the same time whether or not a conduct notice must be made because of a threshold condition, P2's meeting of the condition in (ii) above is treated as P2 meeting a threshold condition and any conduct notice must be given on that basis.

The '*control or influence rules*' referred to in (b) above treat persons under the control or significant influence of one or more others, persons in control of, or with significant influence over, others and persons controlled by, or under the significant influence of, the same person or persons as meeting a condition within (I)–(III) above at the relevant time as set out below. See above under Related companies and partnerships — threshold conditions for as to when a person controls, or has significant influence over, a body corporate or partnership.

Persons under another's control or influence

Where P2 is a body corporate or partnership, P2 is treated as meeting a condition at the relevant time if P1 controls or has significant influence over P2 at that time and P1 met the condition at a time when either P1 was carrying on a business as a promoter or P2 was carrying on a business as a promoter and P1 controlled of had significant influence over P2. However, this rule does not apply where P1 is an individual.

P2 is also treated as meeting a condition at the relevant time if two or more persons together controlled or had significant influence over it at a time when one of those persons met the condition, P2 was a promoter at that time and those persons also controlled or had significant influence over P2 at the relevant time.

Persons in control of, or with significant influence over, others

P2 is treated as meeting a condition at the relevant time if P1 is a body corporate or partnership and met the condition at a time (the 'earlier time') when it was carrying on a business as a promoter and was controlled by P2 or P2 had a significant influence over it. This applies additionally if at the earlier time it was another body corporate or partnership controlled by, or under the significant influence of, P2 that was carrying on a business as a promoter.

Persons under common control or influence

Where P2 is a body corporate or partnership, P2 is treated as meeting a condition at the relevant time if:

- another body corporate or partnership met the condition at a time ('time T') when P1 controlled or had significant influence over P2;
- at time T there was a body corporate or partnership which P1 controlled or had significant influence over and which carried on a business as a promoter; and
- P1 controls or has significant influence over P2 at the relevant time.

P2 is also treated as meeting a condition at the relevant time if:

- P2 or another body corporate or partnership met the condition at a time (the 'time T') when two or more persons together controlled or had significant influence over P2;
- at time T there was a body corporate or partnership which those persons together controlled or had significant influence over which carried on a business as a promoter; and
- those persons together control or have significant influence over P2 at the relevant time.

Terms of a conduct notice

The terms of a conduct notice are determined by the officer giving it, but are limited to conditions that it is reasonable to impose to ensure that the promoter:

(a) provides adequate information (as defined, and including an assessment of the risk that the expected tax advantage will not be achieved) to clients (as defined) about proposals and arrangements of which he is a promoter;
(b) provides adequate information to intermediaries about proposals of which he is a promoter;
(c) does not fail to comply with any specified duties under the disclosure of tax avoidance schemes provisions (see **28.2** above) or under *FA 2008, Sch 36 paras 1–9* (see **38.4** HMRC INVESTIGATORY POWERS);
(d) does not discourage others from complying with any specified disclosure obligation;
(e) does not enter into an agreement which imposes on another person contractual obligations within **28.20**(j) above;
(f) does not promote proposals or arrangements which rely on, or involve a proposal to rely on, one or more contrived or abnormal steps to produce a tax advantage;
(g) does not fail to comply with any stop notice (see **28.22** above); and
(h) (with effect from 10 June 2021) provides information or documents to HMRC for the purposes of monitoring compliance with any conditions in the notice.

In the case of a partnership conduct notice, conditions may be imposed relating to the persons who are partners when the notice is given and to persons who subsequently become partners.

Before deciding on the terms of a notice, the officer must provide an opportunity for the promoter to comment on the proposed terms.

Transfer of promoter's business, assets or liabilities

If an authorised HMRC officer becomes aware that a person (P) to whom a conduct notice has been given has, on or after 10 June 2021, made a relevant transfer (see **28.19**(4) above) to another person (T), the officer may give T a conduct notice. If the terms of the proposed notice are the same as those of the existing notice, there is no requirement for the officer to provide an opportunity for T to comment on them. If the proposed terms are different, the opportunity for comment is restricted to the differences. If a person given a notice under this provision considers that no relevant transfer was made to them, representations can be made to that effect, and HMRC must withdraw the notice if, in the light of the representations, they no longer consider that the provision applies.

[*FA 2014, ss 237, 237A–237D, 238–241, Sch 34 paras 13, 13A–13D, 14, Sch 34A paras 17–23, Sch 36 paras 4, 5, 20, 21; FA 2017, s 24; FA 2021, Sch 30 paras 11, 12, 19, 20, 22–25*].

Information

See **28.27** below for the application of HMRC's information and inspection powers in *FA 2008, Sch 36* to persons subject to a conduct notice. Those powers apply with effect from 10 June 2021. Previously, there was a specific information power under which HMRC could (as often as is necessary) by notice in writing require a person subject to a conduct notice to provide information or produce a document which was reasonably required for the purpose of monitoring compliance with the notice. [*FA 2014, s 262; FA 2021, Sch 30 para 3*].

Monitoring notices

[28.25] Where a conduct notice applies to a promoter and an authorised HMRC officer determines that:

(i) the promoter has failed to comply with one or more conditions in the notice; or
(ii) (where the conduct notice is in effect on or after 10 June 2021) the promoter has provided false or misleading information in relation to the notice,

the officer must apply to the Tribunal for approval to give the promoter a 'monitoring notice'. This does not apply if the conditions in (i) above were imposed under **28.24**(a)–(c) above and the officer considers the failure to comply to be such a minor matter that it should be disregarded.

Where the conduct notice is in effect on or after 10 June 2021, the application must be made within the 12 months of the officer's determination.

An authorised officer may (but is not required to) apply to the Tribunal for approval to give a promoter (P) a monitoring notice if, within the six years after a conduct notice ceases to apply on or after 10 June 2021, the officer makes a determination within (i) or (ii) above and could not reasonably have been expected to make the determination while the conduct notice was in force. If, within the same period, P has made a relevant transfer (see **28.19**(4) above) on or after 10 June 2021 to another person (D), the officer may apply to the

Tribunal for approval to give D a monitoring notice instead. Such an application can only be made if the officer could not reasonably be expected to have applied to the Tribunal to give P a monitoring notice, or to have given P such a notice, before the relevant transfer. It does not matter whether the relevant transfer took place before or after the conduct notice ceased to apply. An application to give a monitoring notice to P or D must be made within 12 months of the officer's determination within (i) or (ii) above. (In the following commentary, in respect of an application to give a monitoring notice to D, references to 'the promoter' can be taken to be references to D.)

An application for approval must include a draft notice and the officer must also notify the promoter of the application. The notice to the promoter must state which conditions have not been complied with and the officer's reasons for determining that there has been a failure to comply.

No application can be made to the Tribunal in respect of a conduct notice which is provisional. Any failure to comply with a condition in such a notice can, however, be taken into account in determining whether to make an application if the notice ceases to be provisional.

The Tribunal may approve the giving of a monitoring notice only if it is satisfied that the officer would be justified in giving it and that the promoter has been given a reasonable opportunity to make representations to the Tribunal. If the promoter's representations include a statement that it was not reasonable to include a particular condition in the conduct notice and the Tribunal is satisfied that it was not so reasonable, the Tribunal must assume that there was no failure to comply with the condition (and must refuse to approve HMRC's application if this applies to all the conditions which HMRC consider have not been complied with). If the Tribunal gives approval it may amend the draft notice. A promoter may appeal against the decision of the Tribunal in the usual way (see 5 APPEALS).

A monitoring notice must explain its effect and specify the date from which it takes effect (which cannot be earlier than the date the notice is given). It must also inform the recipient of the right to request its withdrawal (see further below). The notice must state the conditions of the conduct notice which HMRC have determined that the promoter has failed to comply with and the reasons for that determination. A notice given to a partnership must state that it is a partnership monitoring notice. If the notice is a replacement notice given to a former partner of a partnership itself subject to a monitoring notice (see **28.31** below) it must also state the date of that notice and the name of the partnership.

Withdrawal of a monitoring notice

An authorised HMRC officer may withdraw a notice if he thinks it is no longer necessary, taking into account matters including the promoter's behaviour and compliance whilst the notice has had effect and likely future behaviour.

A person subject to a monitoring notice (a '*monitored promoter*') may make a request in writing to an authorised HMRC officer that the notice should cease to apply. Such a request can be made at any time after the twelve months beginning with the end of the period in which an appeal against the Tribunal's decision to approve the giving of the notice could have been made or, where such an appeal was made, the twelve months beginning with the date on which the appeal was finally determined, withdrawn or otherwise disposed of. If the notice is a replacement notice, the twelve-month period applies by reference to appeals against the Tribunal's decision about the original notice. HMRC must determine whether or not the notice should cease to apply within the 30 days beginning with the date on which the request is received and must notify the promoter of their determination specifying the date from which the notice is to cease to apply (and whether or not a follow-on conduct notice – see below – is to be given) or their reasons for refusal of the request.

A monitored promoter can appeal against a refusal by HMRC by notice in writing within 30 days beginning with the date on which the refusal notice was given, stating the grounds of appeal.

If HMRC decide to withdraw a notice or, following a request from the promoter, decide that a notice should cease to apply, they may issue a follow-on conduct notice to take effect immediately after the monitoring notice ceases to have effect.

Transfer of promoter's business, assets or liabilities

If an authorised HMRC officer becomes aware that a person (P) to whom a monitoring notice has been given has, on or after 10 June 2021, made a relevant transfer (see **28.19**(4) above) to another person (T), the officer may give T a monitoring notice. If a person given a notice under this provision considers that no relevant transfer was made to them, representations can be made to that effect, and HMRC must withdraw the notice if, in the light of the representations, they no longer consider that the provision applies.

The monitoring notice must explain its effect and specify the date from which it takes effect (which cannot be earlier than the date it is given). It must also inform T of the right to request its withdrawal. The notice must state the conditions of the conduct notice which HMRC have determined that P has failed to comply with and the reasons for that determination.

[*FA 2014, ss 242–247, Sch 36 para 6; FA 2021, Sch 30 paras 2, 21, 27*].

Effects of a monitoring notice

[28.26] A monitoring notice has the following effects.

Publication by HMRC

HMRC may publish the name (including business name and any previous name or pseudonym) of a monitored promoter together with the business address or registered office, the nature of the business carried on, a statement of the conditions in a conduct notice with which the promoter has failed to comply and any other information which they consider appropriate to publish to make clear the promoter's identity. Where the monitored promoter is a partnership, it is the details of the partnership which may be published (and not those of particular partners). Publication may not take place before the end of the period in which an appeal against the Tribunal's decision to approve the giving of the notice can be made or, where such an appeal is made, before the appeal is finally determined, withdrawn or otherwise disposed of. If the notice is a replacement notice (see **28.31** below), the restriction applies by reference to appeals against the Tribunal's decision about the original notice. If HMRC publish details of a monitored promoter they must publish the fact of a withdrawal of the notice in the same way. [*FA 2014, s 248, Sch 36 para 14; FA 2021, Sch 30 para 21*].

Publication by monitored promoter

The monitored promoter must give a notice stating that he is a monitored promoter and which conduct notice conditions have not been complied with to anyone who is a client (as defined) at the time the monitoring notice takes effect and to anyone who becomes a client whilst the notice has effect. The notice must also identify the original monitoring notice if the monitoring notice in question is a replacement notice (see **28.31** below). The information in the notice must also be published in a prominent position on the promoter's website and any other websites promoting, or providing information on, the activities of the promoter. The requirement to give such notices does not apply until ten days after the end of the period in which an appeal against the Tribunal's decision to approve the giving of the notice can be made or, where such an appeal is made, ten days after the appeal is finally determined, withdrawn or otherwise disposed of. If the notice is a replacement notice (see **28.31** below), the requirement applies by reference to appeals against the Tribunal's decision about the original notice. In the case of someone becoming a client whilst the monitoring notice has effect, the promoter must give them the required notice within ten days of their first becoming a client.

The information, together with the promoter's reference number (see below), must also be included in certain publications and correspondence with clients and intermediaries and in correspondence with professional bodies and regulatory authorities.

[*FA 2014, s 249; SI 2015 No 549, Regs 2, 3*].

Reference number

Once all rights to appeal against the decision of the Tribunal to approve the giving of the monitoring notice (or original notice) are exhausted, HMRC will allocate a reference number to the monitored promoter. HMRC then notify the number to the promoter if and, if the promoter is non-UK resident, to any person who HMRC know is an intermediary in relation to a proposal of the promoter and (with effect from 10 June 2021) to any person who HMRC know is a member of a promotion structure within **28.19**(2) as a result of acting under the instruction or guidance of the promoter. A promoter so notified must in turn notify the number to anyone who becomes a client while the monitoring notice has effect or who is an intermediary whilst the notice has effect and to any person who is a member of a promotion structure within **28.19**(2) as a result of acting under the instruction or guidance of the promoter. Unless the monitoring notice is a replacement notice, he must also notify the number to any person he can reasonably be expected to know has entered into arrangements, in the period in which the conduct notice preceding the monitoring notice had effect, which are likely to enable that person to obtain a tax advantage whilst the monitoring notice has effect if the monitored promoter is a promoter of those arrangements or of a proposal implemented by those arrangements. Notification must be given within 30 days of HMRC's notification of the number or later event triggering the requirement to notify.

An intermediary who is notified by HMRC of a reference number or a person so notified by a promoter must, within 30 days of being so notified, provide the number to any other person they might reasonably be expected to know has become, or is likely to have become, a client of the monitored promoter whilst the monitoring notice has had effect. An intermediary or (with effect from 10 June 2021) other notified person who is a member of a promotion structure within **28.19**(2) above as a result of acting under the instruction or guidance of the promoter must also, within 30 days, provide the number to any person to whom he has communicated, in the course of a business and since the monitoring notice took effect, information about a proposal of the monitored promoter and to any person who he might reasonably be expected to know has, since the notice took effect, entered into, or is likely to enter into, transactions forming part of arrangements of which the monitored promoter is a promoter. An intermediary or other person notified of a reference number by the promoter does not have to provide the number to a person if he reasonably believes that that person has already been provided with the number.

A person who has been notified of a reference number under any of the above provisions must report it to HMRC if he expects to obtain a tax advantage from arrangements of which the promoter to whom the number relates is a promoter. The report must normally be made in each tax return for any period which includes a period for which the tax advantage is obtained (irrespective of whether the return relates to the tax affected). If no tax return has to be made for such periods or if a tax return is not submitted by the filing date, a separate report must be made by 31 January following the end of each tax year in which a tax advantage may arise (or, for corporation tax purposes, not later than twelve months from the end of each accounting period in which a tax advantage may arise) to HMRC, Counter Avoidance Directorate CA Intelligence SO528, PO Box 194 Bootle L69 9AA. If the arrangements give rise to a claim under *TCGA 1992, s 261B* (trade loss treated as CGT loss) and that claim is made outside of a tax return, the claim must include the reference number.

[*FA 2014, ss 250–253; FA 2021, Sch 30 paras 13–15; SI 2015 No 549, Regs 5, 6, Sch 2*].

Information

The following information powers apply where a monitoring notice has effect. See also **28.27** below for the application of HMRC's information and inspection powers under *FA 2008, Sch 36* apply to persons subject to a monitoring notice.

Information and documents

HMRC may by notice in writing require a monitored promoter or a person who is an intermediary in relation to a monitored proposal (see **28.19** above) to provide information or produce a document which is reasonably required by HMRC for:

- considering the possible consequences of implementing a monitored proposal for the tax positions of those implementing it;
- checking the tax position of any person that HMRC believe has implemented a monitored proposal;
- checking the tax position of any person that HMRC believe has entered into transactions forming monitored arrangements.

A notice can be given to an intermediary only after he has been notified of the promoter's reference number. A notice given for the purpose of checking the tax position of a person cannot be given more than four years after that person's death. '*Checking*' and '*tax position*' are defined as for HMRC's general information powers (see **38.3** HMRC INVESTIGATORY POWERS) but a person's tax position also includes his position as regards deductions or repayments of tax, or sums representing tax, that he is required to make under PAYE regulations or other provisions and the withholding by him of another person's PAYE income (within *ITEPA 2003, s 683*).

Information or a document required under a notice must be provided or produced within ten days beginning with the day the notice is given or within such longer period as HMRC direct.

The giving of a notice under the above provisions must be approved by the Tribunal if it requires a promoter or intermediary to provide information or produce a document relating (wholly or partly) to a person who is not that promoter or intermediary and not an 'undertaking' of which the promoter or intermediary is the 'parent undertaking'. The promoter or intermediary must normally have been told that the information or documents are required and have been given a reasonable opportunity to make representations to HMRC, but is not entitled to be present at the hearing. The Tribunal must be given a summary of any representations made. Where the Tribunal is satisfied that informing the promoter or intermediary would prejudice the assessment or collection of tax, it can approve the giving of the notice without the taxpayer having been informed. There is no right of appeal against a decision of the Tribunal. '*Undertaking*' and '*parent undertaking*' are defined as in *Companies Act 2006, ss 1161, 1162, Sch 7*.

[*FA 2014, ss 255, 256*].

Ongoing duty to provide information

HMRC may give a notice to a monitored promoter requiring him to provide prescribed information and produce prescribed documents relating to all monitored proposals and monitored arrangements of which he is a promoter at the time of the notice or which he becomes a promoter after that time but before the monitoring notice ceases to have effect. A notice must specify the time within which information must be provided or a document produced. [*FA 2014, s 257*]. See *SI 2015 No 549, Reg 7* for the prescribed information and documents.

Person dealing with non-resident monitored promoter

Where a non-UK resident monitored promoter fails to comply with a duty to provide information under either of the above powers, HMRC may issue a notice requiring the information from:

(1) a person who is an intermediary in relation to the monitored proposal concerned;
(2) a person to whom the promoter has made a firm approach with a view to making the proposal available for implementation by a third person;
(3) (with effect from 10 June 2021) any person who is a member of a promotion structure within **28.19**(2) above as a result of acting under the instruction or guidance of the promoter;
(4) where HMRC are not aware of any person within (1), (2) or (3) above to whom a notice could be given, a person who has implemented the proposal in question; or
(5) where the duty in question relates to monitored arrangements, a person who has entered into any transaction forming part of those arrangements.

The HMRC officer giving the notice must reasonably believe that the person to whom the notice is given is able to provide the information. Information required under a notice must be provided within ten days beginning with the day the notice is given or within such longer period as HMRC direct.

[*FA 2014, s 258; FA 2021, Sch 30 para 16*].

Duty to provide information about clients

HMRC may give notice to a monitored promoter under which the promoter must give HMRC, for each 'relevant period', the name, address and any additional prescribed information (see *SI 2015 No 549, Reg 8*) for each client (as defined) for whom such information has not been given for a previous relevant period. Each of the following is a 'relevant period':

(a) the 'calendar quarter' in which the notice is given (but excluding any time before the monitoring notice takes effect);
(b) any period from the time the monitoring notice takes effect until the start of the period in (a) above; and
(c) each subsequent calendar quarter (excluding any time after the monitoring notice ceases to have effect).

A '*calendar quarter*' is a period of three months beginning on 1 January, 1 April, 1 July or 1 October.

Information must be provided within the 30 days beginning with the end of each relevant period or, for a relevant period within (b) above, within the 30 days beginning with the day on which the notice is given, if later.

A similar notice may be given to a person who is an intermediary in relation to a monitored proposal or (with effect from 10 June 2021) a person who is a member of a promotion structure within **28.19**(2) above as a result of acting under the instruction or guidance of the promoter.

Where a promoter or intermediary has provided information under the above provisions in connection with a particular proposal or particular arrangements but an authorised HMRC officer suspects that a person for whom such information has not been provided has been, or is likely to be, a party to transactions implementing the proposal or is a party to a transaction forming the whole or part of the arrangements, the officer may by notice in writing require the promoter or intermediary to provide the information about any such person together with the reason why the information was not provided as required. Information required under a notice must be provided within ten days beginning with the day the notice is given or within such longer period as HMRC direct. A notice does not require information to be provided if it has already been provided under the above provisions.

[*FA 2014, ss 259–261, 283(1); FA 2021, Sch 30 para 17; SI 2015 No 549, Regs 8–10*].

Duty to notify HMRC of address

A monitored promoter must inform HMRC of its address within 30 days of the end of any calendar quarter at the end of which the monitoring notice applies. [*FA 2014, s 263*].

Duty of client or intermediary to provide information to promoter

An intermediary or client who is informed of a monitored promoter's reference number must within ten days notify the promoter of his national insurance number and unique taxpayer reference number. If he has neither of those numbers he must inform the promoter of that fact within ten days. There is no need to provide the information if the client or intermediary has previously provided it to the promoter. [*FA 2014, s 265*].

Information and inspection powers

[28.27] With effect from 10 June 2021, HMRC's information and inspection powers under *FA 2008, Sch 36* (see **38.3** HMRC INVESTIGATORY POWERS) apply, with necessary modifications, to persons subject to a stop notice, conduct notice or monitoring notice for the purposes listed below as they apply for the purpose of checking a person's tax position. The powers also apply to a person if an HMRC officer suspects that:

- the person carries on, or has carried on, a business as a promoter in relation to a proposal or arrangements and the officer suspects that the person has met a threshold condition or could be given a defeat notice or that a stop notice could be given in respect of the proposal or arrangements; or
- the person made a relevant transfer (see **28.19**(4) above) or is a person to whom a relevant transfer was made.

The purposes for which the powers can be used are:

- determining whether a person (P) within the above categories carries on a business as a promoter or has done so in the past;
- determining whether P has met a threshold condition;
- determining whether P could be given a defeat notice;
- determining whether P has provided false or misleading information or documents in relation to a stop notice, conduct notice or monitoring notice;
- determining whether arrangements or a proposal which HMRC suspect are promoted by P could be specified in a stop notice;

- enabling HMRC to understand how arrangements or proposals, which HMRC suspect P promotes, operate;
- identifying any other person with a connection to P that results in P being a member of a promotion structure;
- determining whether P made a relevant transfer and, if so, to whom;
- determining whether a relevant transfer was made to P and, if so, by whom;
- monitoring compliance with any stop notice, conduct notice or monitoring notice to which P is subject.

The penalty provisions in *FA 2008, Sch 36* are disapplied, but see **59.13** PENALTIES for penalties for failures etc. arising from the application of *Sch 36* under the above provisions.

These powers are in addition to those for monitored promoters at **28.26** above, but replace the previous information powers for conduct notices at **28.24** above.

[*FA 2014, s 272A; FA 2021, Sch 30 para 4*].

Information powers — further provisions

Failure to provide information

[28.28] Where a person has provided information or produced a document in purported compliance with any of the information powers at **28.26** or (prior to their repeal) **28.24** above (other than those under *FA 2014, s 263* or *s 265*), HMRC may apply to the Tribunal for an order for the person to provide further specified information or produce further specified documents which they have reasonable grounds for suspecting are required by the information power in question or will support or explain information required by the power.

If the Tribunal grants such an order the information or documents must be provided or produced within ten days or such later date as HMRC direct. The duty to provide information or produce a document under such a notice is treated as part of the duty under the original information power (for the purposes of penalties etc.).

[*FA 2014, s 264*].

Appeals

A person given a notice under any of the information powers at **28.24** or **28.26** above (other than those under *FA 2014, s 263* or *s 265*) may appeal against the notice as a whole or against any particular requirement in the notice. There is, however, no right of appeal where the information or documents form part of the person's 'statutory records' or where the Tribunal has approved the giving of the notice (see **28.26** above under 'Information and documents').

Notice of appeal must be given in writing to the HMRC officer who gave the notice within the period of 30 days beginning with the date on which the notice was given and must state the grounds of appeal. A decision on an appeal by the Tribunal is final (so that there is no further right of appeal to the Upper Tribunal or Court of Appeal). Where the Tribunal confirms or varies the notice or a requirement in it, the person to whom the notice was given must comply with the notice or requirement within the period specified by the Tribunal. If the Tribunal does not specify such a period, compliance must be within such period as an HMRC officer reasonably specifies in writing.

Subject to the above, the appeal provisions of *TMA 1970, Pt 5* (see 5 APPEALS) apply to an appeal against a notice.

For this purpose, '*statutory records*' are information and documents which a taxpayer is required to keep and preserve under any enactments relating to any of the taxes to which the high-risk promoter provisions apply. Information and documents cease to be statutory records when the period for which they must be kept and preserved ends.

[*FA 2014, s 266*].

Compliance with a notice

HMRC may specify the form and manner in which information must be provided or documents produced. Documents must be produced for inspection either at a place agreed to by the recipient of the notice and an HMRC officer or at a place (other than one used solely as a dwelling) that an HMRC officer reasonably specifies. Copies of documents can be produced unless the notice requires the production of the original document or an HMRC officer in writing subsequently requests the original document. Where a copy is produced, it must be an exact copy of the original document, which must be retained and unaltered (except for the redaction of any privileged information). Where an officer makes a request for the original document, it must be produced within the period and at the time and by the means reasonably requested by the officer.

The production of a document under these provisions does not break any lien (i.e. any right) claimed on it.

[*FA 2014, ss 267, 268; SI 2015 No 549, Reg 11*].

Restrictions on information powers

The recipient of a notice under any of the information powers at **28.24** or **28.26** above is not required to:

(i) produce a document if it is not in his possession or power;
(ii) provide or produce information that relates to the conduct of a pending tax appeal or any part of a document containing such information;
(iii) provide journalistic material (within *Police and Criminal Evidence Act 1984, s 13*) or information contained in such material;
(iv) subject to the exceptions below, provide or produce 'personal records' (within *Police and Criminal Evidence Act 1984, s 12*); or
(v) produce a document the whole of which originates more than six years before the giving of the notice.

With regard to (iv) above, a notice may require a person to produce documents that are personal records, omitting any personal information (i.e. information whose inclusion in the documents makes them personal records) and to provide any information in personal records that is not personal information.

[*FA 2014, ss 269, 270*].

Legal professional privilege

A notice cannot require a person to provide information in respect of which a claim to legal professional privilege (or, in Scotland, a claim to confidentiality of communications) could be maintained in legal proceedings. [*FA 2014, s 271*].

Tax advisers

A notice under **28.26**(3) or (4) above does not require a 'tax adviser' to provide information about, or to produce documents which are his property and which consist of, communications between him and a person in relation to whose tax affairs he has been appointed or between him and any other tax adviser of such a person, the purpose of which is the giving or obtaining of advice about any of those tax affairs. For this purpose, a '*tax adviser*' is a person appointed (directly or by another tax adviser) to give advice about the tax affairs of another person.

This restriction does not apply to any information, or any document containing information, which explains any information or document which the tax adviser has, as tax accountant, assisted any client in preparing for, or delivering to, HMRC. The restriction is not disapplied if the information concerned, or a document containing the information, has already been provided or produced to an HMRC officer. [*FA 2014, s 272*].

Confidentiality

No duty of confidentiality or other restriction on disclosure (however imposed) prevents the voluntary disclosure to HMRC by a client or intermediary of information or documents about a person subject to a stop notice issued on or after 10 June 2021 or proposals or arrangements of a type specified in such a notice, or about a monitored promoter or monitored proposals or arrangements. With effect from 10 June 2021, it is made explicit that this rule does not authorise disclosures which contravene data protection legislation. [*FA 2014, s 273; FA 2021, Sch 30 para 5*].

Concealing, destroying or disposing of documents

[28.29] A person must not conceal, destroy or otherwise dispose of, or arrange for the concealment, destruction or disposal of, a document that is subject to a requirement under the information powers in *FA 2014, s 262* (see **28.24** above) or *FA 2014, ss 255, 257* (see **28.26** above) or *FA 2008, Sch 36* as applied by *FA 2014, s 272A* (see **28.27** above). This does not apply if he does so after the document has been produced to HMRC in accordance with the notice, unless an HMRC officer has notified him in writing that the document must continue to be available for inspection (and has not withdrawn the notification). It also does not apply if a copy of the document was produced in compliance with the notice and the destruction, etc. takes place after the end of the period of six months beginning with the day on which the copy was produced unless within that period an HMRC officer makes a request for the original document.

Similarly, where a person has been informed that a document is, or is likely to be, the subject of such a notice addressed to him, he must not conceal, destroy or otherwise dispose of, or arrange for the concealment, destruction or disposal of, the document. This does not apply if he acts more than six months after he was so informed (or was last so informed).

A person who conceals, destroys or otherwise disposes of, or arranges for the concealment, destruction or disposal of, a document in breach of the above provisions is treated as having failed to comply with the duty to produce the document under the provision in question. If more than one provision is in question the person is treated as only having failed to comply with the duty under *FA 2014, s 255* or, if that section is not in question, with the duty under *FA 2014, s 257*.

[*FA 2014, Sch 35 paras 6, 7; FA 2021, Sch 30 para 8(6)(7)*].

Failure to comply with the above provisions may be a criminal offence. See **28.30** below.

Offences and penalties

[28.30] For penalties under the high-risk promoters provisions, see **59.13** PENALTIES.

It is an offence for a person required to produce a document by a notice under *FA 2014, s 255* (see **28.26** above) which has been approved by the Tribunal to conceal, destroy or otherwise dispose of the document or to arrange for its concealment, destruction or disposal. This does not apply if he does so after the document has been produced to HMRC in accordance with the notice, unless an HMRC officer has notified him in writing that the document must continue to be available for inspection (and has not withdrawn the notification). It also does not apply if a copy of the document was produced in compliance with the notice and the destruction, etc. takes place after the end of the period of six months beginning with the day on which the copy was produced unless within that period an HMRC officer makes a request for the original document.

It is also an offence for a person to conceal, destroy or otherwise dispose of, or to arrange for the concealment, destruction or disposal of, a document after an HMRC officer has informed him in writing that the document is, or is likely to be, the subject of such a notice and approval for giving the notice is to be obtained from the Tribunal. This does not apply if the person so acts more than six months after he was so informed (or was last so informed).

On summary conviction of either of the above offences the offender is liable to a fine. On conviction on indictment the punishment is imprisonment for a maximum of two years and/or a fine.

[*FA 2014, ss 278–280*].

Partnerships

[28.31] Persons carrying on a business in partnership (within the meaning of *Partnership Act 1890*) are treated as a person for the purposes of the high-risk promoter provisions. A partnership is treated as continuing to be the same partnership (and the same person) regardless of a change in membership, provided that a person who was a member before the change remains a member after the change. Accordingly, a partnership is taken to have done any act which bound the members (restricted, in the case of a limited partnership, to the general partners) and to have failed to comply with any obligation of the firm (within the meaning of *Partnership Act 1890*) which the members failed to comply with. Where, however, a member has done, or failed to do, an act at any time, the partnerships is not treated at any later time as having done or failed to do that act if at that later time neither that member nor any other person who was a member at the earlier time is still a member.

A 'partnership' does not include, for the purposes of the high-risk promoter provisions, a body of persons forming a legal person that is distinct from themselves.

Responsibility of partners

A notice under the high-risk promoter provisions given to a partnership has effect at any time in relation to the persons who are members of the partnership at that time (the '*responsible partners*'). This does not, however, affect any liability of a member who has left the partnership for anything that the responsible partners did or failed to do before he left. Anything which must be done by the responsible partners must be done by all of them (but see below regarding 'nominated partners'). References in the provisions to a right of a person (such as a right of appeal) must be interpreted accordingly.

The responsible partners are jointly and severally liable to any penalty under **59.13** PENALTIES and to any interest on such a penalty, but no amounts can be recovered from a person who did not become a responsible partner until after the act or omission which led to the penalty occurred or, in the case of a daily penalty or interest accruing for a particular day, until after the beginning of that day.

A notice given to a partnership by HMRC must be served either on all of the current partners or on a 'representative partner'. For this purpose a '*representative partner*' is a nominated partner or, if there is no nominated partner, a partner designated by an authorised HMRC officer as a representative partner and notified to the partnership as such.

Anything which must be done by the responsible partners can instead be done by a '*nominated partner*', i.e. a partner nominated by the majority of the partners to act as the partnership's representatives for the purposes of the high-risk promoter provisions. The partnership must notify HMRC of a nomination or its revocation.

Partnership changes

Where the business of a partnership subject to a defeat notice, conduct notice or monitoring notice starts to be carried on by one of the partners but not in partnership (i.e. where the other partners leave the partnership), the notice continues to apply to the continuing partner.

Where a controlling member of a partnership subject to a defeat notice leaves the partnership and carries on a business as a promoter, an authorised HMRC officer may give that person a replacement defeat notice. If the business is conducted by a partnership of which that person is a controlling member the replacement notice may be given to the partnership, but the notice will cease to have effect if that person leaves the partnership. Similar provisions apply to allow the giving of replacement conduct notices and monitoring notices.

Where a partner in a partnership which is subject to a defeat notice, conduct notice or monitoring notice ceases to carry on the partnership's business but continues to carry on a part (but not the whole) of the business, an authorised HMRC officer may give that partner a replacement notice. If the departing partner carries on the part of the business in partnership, a replacement notice may be given to that partnership, but the notice will cease to have effect if the partner leaves the partnership. These rules apply whether it is one, some or all of the partners in the original partnership who carry on a part of the business.

A replacement conduct notice ceases to have effect on the date on which the original notice would have ceased to have effect and must state that date as its expiry date. Such a notice may not be given after the expiry of the original notice. The look-forward period for a replacement defeat notice begins on the day after that on which the notice is given and ends at the end of the look-forward period of the original notice. Such a notice cannot be given after the end of the look-forward period of the original notice. A replacement conduct or monitoring notice may not be given to a person if a conduct or monitoring notice previously given to that person still has effect.

[*FA 2014, Sch 36 paras 1–3, 7–13, 15–18*].

29

Distributions

Cross-references. See **8.3** BUILDING SOCIETIES; **35** GROUP RELIEF and **61** PURCHASE BY A COMPANY OF ITS OWN SHARES.

Simon's Taxes. See Part D5.

Introduction to distributions

[29.1] The term 'distribution' is widely drawn for corporation tax purposes and includes some payments and other transactions which would not normally be treated as 'distributions' within the normal meaning of the term — for example, some payments of interest on securities of a company may be treated as distributions in certain circumstances. Although distributions received by companies are in principle chargeable to corporation tax, in practice most fall within one of the exemptions at **29.16** below and are exempt from corporation tax.

This chapter considers the scope and corporation tax treatment of distributions. See **29.30** onwards below for the system of 'shadow ACT' under which relief can be obtained in respect of surplus advance corporation tax paid on distributions made before 6 April 1999.

Scope of distributions

[29.2] The term 'distribution' is widely defined in *CTA 2010, s 1000*. Subject to the exceptions listed at **29.15** below, it includes any of the items listed below as follows. See also **29.12 – 29.14** below for benefits provided to participators in close companies which are treated as distributions.

(a) Dividends (including capital dividends). [*CTA 2010, s 1000(1)A*].
(b) Any distribution 'in respect of shares' (except for repayments of share capital or where there is equivalent 'new consideration'). The distribution may be in cash or otherwise. [*CTA 2010, s 1000(1)B*].
(c) Issue of redeemable share capital or any 'security' (otherwise than for new consideration) (see **29.3** below). [*CTA 2010, s 1000(1)C, D*].
(d) Interest or other distribution exceeding a reasonable commercial return in respect of non-commercial securities of the company and any such amount which exceeds the principal secured by the security. No amount is regarded as part of the principal of a security in so far as it exceeds new consideration received by the borrowing company (see **29.4** and **29.7** below). [*CTA 2010, s 1000(1)E*].
(e) Interest or other distribution paid in respect of 'special securities' except to the extent it represents repayment of principal or falls within (d) above (see **29.5** and **29.7** below). [*CTA 2010, s 1000(1)F*].
(f) The excess over new consideration arising on transfers of assets or liabilities by a company to its shareholders or to a company by its shareholders. [*CTA 2010, ss 1000(1)G, 1020*].
(g) Where a company makes a bonus issue following a repayment of share capital, it may be treated as having made a distribution. [*CTA 2010, ss 1000(1)H, 1022*].

See **29.11** below for the meaning of 'in respect of shares', 'shares', 'security' and 'new consideration'.

See also HMRC Tax Bulletin Issue 76, April 2005 p 1199 for HMRC's view that, in the majority of cases, where goodwill is transferred by a sole trader (or partnership) to a company on the incorporation of a business, before the company has commenced trading, at a value higher than its market value, the excess is to be treated as a distribution. If it is clear that there was no intention to transfer the goodwill at excess value and that reasonable efforts were made to carry out the transfer at market value by using a professional valuation, the distribution can be 'unwound'. For discussion of valuation of goodwill of property-based business (e.g. public houses, hotels, care homes etc.) see 'Taxation' 23 October 2008 p 445.

In *First Nationwide v R&CC* [2011] STC 1540 it was noted that a dividend includes dividends paid by non-UK entities, even if that payment would not have been a lawful dividend under UK company law.

> 'The fact that since 1948 English company law prevented distributions out of a share premium account from being made by way of dividend did not change the ordinary meaning of the word "dividend". If the law in a different jurisdiction permitted distributions to be made out of a share premium account as dividends, those distributions remained dividends within the ordinary meaning of that word. There was nothing to suggest that a dividend payable out of a share premium account was not a dividend as ordinarily understood in England by a commercial man or company lawyer. In construing the word "dividend" it was right to consider what the relevant company was actually permitted to do under its governing law rather than what the company would be able to do with its share premium account were it an English company. It followed that a distribution out of the share premium account of a Cayman company which was made by the procedure or mechanism of payment of a dividend, was a "dividend"'.

[*CTA 2010, ss 1000, 1006, 1019, 1064, 1072*].

Simon's Taxes. See D5.1.

Issue of redeemable share capital or any security

[29.3] A distribution includes the issue in respect of shares in the company of redeemable share capital in so far as it is not referable to 'new consideration', see **29.11** below. It also includes the issue of securities only partly for new consideration. The value of any redeemable share capital (or security) is the amount of the share capital (or principal) together with any premium payable on redemption (or maturity), or in a winding-up, or in any other circumstances. The paying-up of issued share capital by the company also falls under this head.

[*CTA 2010, ss 1003–1004*].

Interest or other distribution exceeding a reasonable commercial return

[29.4] With reference to 29.2(d) above a non-commercial security is one where the consideration given by the company for the use of the principal represents more than a reasonable commercial return for its use. Thus a distribution includes any interest or other distribution borne by the company in respect of securities (except any part representing principal), to the extent that the interest etc. exceeds a reasonable commercial return for the use of the principal secured. A distribution is not treated as representing the principal of the security to the extent it exceeds new consideration.

[*CTA 2010, ss 1005, 1006*]. See also **29.7** below.

Where a company issues a security at a premium representing new consideration, references to the part of the distribution representing principal secured on the security are to be taken as a reference to the sum of the part of the distribution which represents the principal and the part representing the premium. The reasonable commercial return for this purpose is taken as the sum of the part of the distribution representing a reasonable commercial return for the use of the principal and that for the use of the premium. [*CTA 2010, s 1007*].

Where a security is issued by a company for new consideration in excess of the amount of the principal secured by the security, the amount of the principal so secured is treated for this purpose as increased to the amount of the new consideration, subject to the further provisions below. *CTA 2010, s 1007* does not apply to the security. [*CTA 2010, s 1008*].

Link to shares of company or associated company (i.e. where one company 'controls' the other or both are under common control)

CTA 2010, s 1008 does not apply where the security is one which to a significant extent reflects dividends or other distributions in respect of, or fluctuations in the value of, shares in one or more companies each of which is either the issuing company or an associated company.

There is, however, an exception (so that *CTA 2010, s 1008* does apply) if the security is issued in the ordinary course of its business by a bank (within *CTA 2010, s 1120*, see **7.1** BANKS) or 'securities house' (as defined) and the link to shares is by reason only that the security reflects fluctuations in an index whose underlying subject matter is shares in other companies as well as the issuing company (or associated companies — as defined in *CTA 2010, s 1010*), those other companies' shares representing a significant proportion of the underlying market value.

'Control' for this purpose is held by a person who exercises, is able to exercise or who is entitled to acquire control over a company's affairs, whether directly or indirectly. In particular, there is control where the greater part of issued share capital, voting power, income on a distribution or assets on a winding up is held by a company. Rights held as a loan creditor are ignored and two or more companies together may satisfy the conditions and have control.

Shares held by a company (and voting or other powers arising from such shares) are left out of account for this purpose if a profit on sale of the shares would be treated as a trading receipt of the company's trade and the shares are not assets of an insurance company's long-term insurance fund.

[*CTA 2010, ss 450, 451, 1009–1011*].

Hedging arrangements

CTA 2010, s 1008 also does not apply at any time at which there are or have been 'hedging arrangements' (as defined in *CTA 2010, s 1010*) relating to some or all of the issuing company's liabilities under the security. There is, however, an exception (so that *CTA 2010, s 1008* does apply) where each of the following four conditions are met at that time *and* at all earlier times after 16 April 2002 when there have been such hedging arrangements.

(i) The hedging arrangements must not constitute, include or form part of any scheme or arrangement a main purpose of which is avoidance of tax, stamp duty or stamp duty land tax.
(ii) They must be such that where, at any time, a corporation tax deduction falls to be made by the issuing company in respect of the security, then at that time (or within a reasonable time before or after it) any offsetting amounts under the arrangements arise to the issuing company or to a fellow group member (see 35.3 GROUP RELIEF).
(iii) The whole of every offsetting amount under (ii) above must be brought into charge to corporation tax by a company (or together by companies) within (ii) above.
(iv) Any corporation tax deduction for expenses of establishing or administering the hedging arrangements must be reasonable in proportion to the amounts required to be brought into charge under (iii) above.

'Hedging arrangements' means any scheme or arrangement for the purpose of securing that an offsetting amount of income or gain accrues or is received/receivable.

[*CTA 2010, ss 1012–1014*].

Distribution paid in respect of 'special securities'

[29.5] For the purpose of 29.2(e) above, 'special securities' are such securities as fulfil any of the following conditions:

(a) they are issued otherwise than for new consideration;
(b) the securities are (i) convertible, directly or indirectly into shares or securities; or (ii) carry a right to receive shares in or securities of the company; and (iii) are not quoted or issued on terms comparable to listed securities;
(c) the return on the security depends to any extent on the results of the company's business or any part of it (but not merely if the return increases if results deteriorate or decreases if results improve);
(d) the securities are 'connected with' shares in the company;
(e) the securities are 'equity notes' held by a company associated with the issuing company or which is a 'funded company'.

HMRC consider that a security does not fall within (c) above by virtue only of it being subject to a statutory bail-in under *Financial Services (Banking Reform) Act 2013*. See HMRC Brief 24/14.

For this purpose, an '*equity note*' is a security in respect of which any of the following tests are satisfied so far as the whole or part of the principal is concerned:

(1) no redemption date is given;
(2) the redemption date, or the latest date for redemption, falls more than 50 years after the issue date of the security;
(3) the redemption date is after a particular event occurs and it is probable or certain that the event will occur;
(4) the issuing company can secure that there is no specified redemption date and that the redemption date falls more than 50 years after the issue date of the security.

A company is a '*funded company*' if there are arrangements involving the company being put in funds (directly or indirectly) by the issuing company or a company associated with the issuing company.

Relevant alternative finance return is not treated as a distribution under the above provisions. Hybrid capital instruments (see **50.28** LOAN RELATIONSHIPS) are not treated as special securities by virtue of (e) above.

Shares issued before 6 April 1965 or securities issued before 6 April 1972 are treated as not meeting the condition at (a) above. Similarly, securities issued before 6 April 1972 do not meet condition (b)(ii) above.

See also the exception at **29.7** below.

[*CTA 2010, ss 1015–1017, Sch 2 para 103; FA 2019, Sch 20 para 4*].

In *HBOS Treasury Services plc v HMRC* [2009] UKFTT 261 (TC) the bank entered a scheme to remonetise interest rate swaps in such a way as to avoid the normal incidence of tax on such a transaction. The scheme involved the novation of the swaps. It was held that the scheme did not work.

Exceptions with regard to certain securities, and to 'special securities'

[29.6] Any interest or other distribution on 'special securities' which are not 'non-commercial' securities (see **29.5** above) issued by a company to another company within the charge to corporation tax is not treated as a distribution provided that the recipient company is neither exempt from tax in respect of the interest, etc. nor (where **29.5** above applies) otherwise outside the matters in respect of which that company is within the charge to corporation tax.

These provisions do not apply where the securities are 'special securities' within **29.5**(c) above, and:

(a) the principal does not exceed £100,000;
(b) the principal and interest must be repaid within five years of the principal being paid to the borrower; and
(c) the obligation was entered into before 9 March 1982, or was entered into before 1 July 1982 pursuant to negotiations in progress on 9 March 1982, the borrower having before that date applied for the loan and supplied any documents required in support of his application.

Where the repayment period of either principal or interest is extended after 8 March 1982 (but is still within (b) above), **29.5** above does not apply to any interest etc. paid after the repayment period in force at that date.

[*CTA 2010, s 1032, Sch 2 para 107*].

In HMRC Brief 47/2008, reissued as Brief 100/2009, HMRC set out their policy on deduction of tax at source from interest which is treated as a distribution. In their view, income tax is only deductible from payments that have the character of interest, i.e. which fall to be treated as interest under UK tax rules. If the payments are classed as a distribution, that test is no longer satisfied and therefore no withholding tax is required. This will mainly apply to companies that issue securities.

See HMRC Tax Bulletin May 1993 p 68 as regards the definition of an equity note.

See also **29.7** below.

'Principal'

[29.7] As regards **29.4** and **29.5** above:

(i) no amount is regarded as representing principal secured by a security in so far as it exceeds 'new consideration' (see **29.11** below) received by the company for its issue; and
(ii) where a security is issued at a premium consisting of 'new consideration', references to the principal represented by a distribution are taken as referring to the aggregate of the principal and the premium represented by the distribution (and a similar rule applies as regards **29.4** above in relation to the reasonable commercial return for the use of principal represented by a distribution).

[*CTA 2010, ss 1007, 1008, 1018*].

Transfer of assets or liabilities between company and members

[29.8] The transfer of assets or liabilities between a company and its members is treated as a distribution in so far as the market value of any benefit received by a member exceeds that of any 'new consideration' (see **29.11** below) given by him.

[*CTA 2010, s 1020*].

In *Noved Investment Co v HMRC* (2006) Sp C 521, the Special Commissioners held that transfers of assets or liabilities by a company to its members at an undervalue can include cash.

Repayment of share capital followed by a bonus issue

[29.9] Where a company repays share capital (and see **29.10** below), and at the same time or later issues any share capital as paid up (otherwise than by the receipt of 'new consideration', see **29.11** below), the amount so paid up is treated as a distribution.

Such a distribution is treated as made in respect of the bonus shares and is limited to the total amount of share capital repaid less any amount previously treated as a distribution under this provision.

Where the bonus share capital is issued after 5 April 1973, this provision only applies if the issue is made within ten years of the repayment or is of redeemable share capital unless the company is under the control of not more than five persons or is unquoted (disregarding debentures and preference shares), unless it is under the control of a company (or companies) which is (or are) neither controlled by five or fewer persons nor unquoted.

'Control' is as defined in **16.6** CLOSE COMPANIES.

> *Example*
>
> In 2011 X Ltd, a close company, redeemed £50,000 worth of variable-rate preference shares. In 2014, it made a bonus issue of one ordinary share of £1 for every ten held, which amounted to £20,000. In 2016, it made a further bonus issue of ordinary shares on a 1:11 basis, which also amounted to £20,000. X Ltd is treated as having made a distribution of £20,000 in each of the financial years 2014 and 2016. If X Ltd makes a similar bonus issue of 1:12 in 2021, the amount treated as a distribution (assuming that there has been no further repayment of share capital) will be limited to £10,000, being the balance of the £50,000 repaid in 2011.

These provisions do not apply to the repayment of fully-paid 'preference shares' which:

(i) existed as such on 6 April 1965, or
(ii) were issued as such after 6 April 1965 wholly for 'new consideration not derived from ordinary shares'

and in either case remained fully-paid preference shares until the date of repayment.

'Preference shares' are defined for this purpose as shares carrying the right to a dividend at a fixed percentage of the nominal value only and such other rights in respect of dividends and capital as are comparable with those general for fixed-dividend shares listed in the Official List of the Stock Exchange. Thus variable-rate preference shares (as in the example above) are outside this definition.

'New consideration not derived from ordinary shares' means 'new consideration' (see **29.11** below) except in so far as it consists of:

(a) the surrender, transfer or cancellation of 'ordinary shares' in the company or any other company;
(b) the variation of rights in such shares; or
(c) consideration derived from a repayment made in respect of such shares.

'*Ordinary shares*' are all shares except preference shares as defined above.

[*CTA 2010, ss 1022, 1023, Sch 2 para 105*].

Repayment of share capital

[29.10] Where a company issues (or has issued at any time after 6 April 1965) any 'share capital' as paid up (otherwise than by the receipt of 'new consideration', for example a bonus issue, and the amount 'paid up' is not treated as a distribution), then any subsequent distribution in respect of that share capital is not treated as a repayment of share capital up to the amount treated as 'paid up' (so that the exclusion from distribution treatment in **29.2**(b) above does not apply). This does not apply to that part of the repayment which exceeds the amount so 'paid up' — the excess is generally a distribution as under **29.3** above.

'Share capital' for this purpose includes:

(a) all the shares of the same class;
(b) shares issued in respect of any shares under (a) above;
(c) shares exchanged for any shares under (a) above (whether directly or indirectly);
(d) shares into which any shares under (a) above have directly or indirectly been converted.

Where shares have been issued at a premium representing new consideration, the premium (less any amount that has been applied in paying up share capital) is treated as part of the share capital in determining whether any repayment is to be treated as a distribution. Subject to this, premiums paid on the redemption of share capital are not to be treated as repayments of share capital.

A distribution is outside these provisions if it is made:

(i) more than ten years after an issue of shares within that subsection;
(ii) otherwise than in respect of redeemable share capital; and
(iii) by a company which is neither under the control of five or fewer persons nor unquoted (disregarding debentures and preference shares), or which is controlled by a company (or companies) which is or are neither controlled by five or fewer persons nor unquoted.

In determining whether a distribution is treated as a repayment of share capital, a distribution made out of a reserve arising from a reduction of share capital (as defined) is treated as if it were made out of profits available for distribution otherwise than by virtue of the reduction. For this purpose, 'share capital' includes any premium on issue representing new consideration.

[*CTA 2010, ss 1024–1027A*].

HMRC guidance for dividends paid to individuals and other non-corporates following a share capital reduction can be found at HMRC Company Taxation Manual, CTM15440.

Definitions

[29.11] A company is a '75% subsidiary' if not less than 75% of its ordinary share capital is owned directly or indirectly by another.

A company is a '51% subsidiary' if not less than 51% of its ordinary share capital is owned directly or indirectly by another.

[*CTA 2010, s 1154*].

'New consideration' means consideration provided otherwise than out of the assets of the company (i.e. where the cost does not fall on the company). Amounts retained by the company by way of capitalising a distribution do not constitute new consideration, but a premium paid on the issue of shares which is later applied in paying up further share capital may be treated as new consideration (except in so far as it has been taken into account to enable a distribution to be treated as a repayment of share capital (see **29.10** above)).

Consideration derived from the value of any share capital or security of, or from voting or other rights in, a company is new consideration only if it represents:

(i) money or value received from the company as a 'non-CD distribution' (see below);

(ii) money received from the company which, for the purposes of *CTA 2010, Pt 23*, constitute a repayment of share capital (see **29.10** above) or of the principal of the security; or

(iii) the giving up of the right to the share capital or security on its cancellation, extinguishment or acquisition by the company.

But in so far as any amount under (ii) or (iii) exceeds any payment made to the company for the issue of the share capital or security or, in the case of share capital which constituted a non-CD distribution, exceeds the nominal value of that share capital, it is not to be treated as new consideration.

A '*non-CD distribution*' is a distribution other than one within **29.2**(c) above.

[*CTA 2010, s 1115*].

'Shares' includes stock and any other interest of a member in a company.

'Security' includes securities not creating or evidencing a charge on assets. Interest paid, or other consideration given, by a company for money advanced without the issue of a security is nevertheless treated as if paid or given in respect of a security issued for that advance by the company. Where securities are issued at a discount, and are not listed on a recognised stock exchange, the principal secured is to be taken as not exceeding the issue price, unless the terms of issue are reasonably comparable with those of securities so listed.

[*CTA 2010, s 1117*].

A thing is to be regarded as done 'in respect of' shares or securities if it is done to the holder or former holder thereof (as such), or in pursuance of a right granted or offer made in respect of a share. Anything so done by reference to shareholdings at a particular time is regarded as done to the then holder or his personal representatives. If arrangements are entered into among companies to make distributions to each other's members, the acts of one may be attributed to another. In relation to a group of companies, anything done to a UK resident 90% member of the group is treated as being in respect of securities of that company or any other company in the group.

[*CTA 2010, ss 1112, 1114*].

Close companies — additional distributions

[29.12] Certain payments made and benefits given to participators and their associates by close companies are treated as distributions, see **29.13** below. Unless otherwise stated, terms used at **29.13** below have the same meaning as in **16.2–16.9** CLOSE COMPANIES. The exceptions listed in **29.15** below apply.

Benefits to participators and their associates

[29.13] Where a close company incurs expense in, or in connection with, the provision for any 'participator' (or an associate of his) of living or other accommodation, entertainment, domestic or other services, or of other benefits or facilities of whatever nature, so much of that expense as is not made good by the participator is treated as a distribution.

The distribution treatment does not apply to benefits provided to a participator who is an employee to whom the earnings and benefit code under *ITEPA 2003, Pt 3* applies in the case of: the provision of benefits given, on that person's death or retirement, to the spouse, children or dependants; the provision of living accommodation (under *ITEPA 2003, ss 97–113*) and the benefits under *ITEPA 2003, ss 114–215* (cars and vans, loans, etc.) and *s 223* (payments of director's tax) ignoring the exclusion for lower paid employees in *s 216*. (See HMRC Company Taxation Manual CTM60510).

'Participator' includes an associate of a participator and a participator in a company which controls the company providing the benefit.

Arrangements whereby each of a number of companies makes a payment etc. to a participator in another are included.

The measure of the distribution is the cash equivalent of the benefit or expense as defined in the employment benefits legislation (see Tolley's Income Tax under Employment Income) less any amount made good to the company.

These provisions do not apply where the company and the participator are resident in the UK and:

(a) one is a '51% subsidiary' of the other or both are 51% subsidiaries of a third company so resident; and
(b) the benefit arises on or in connection with the transfer of assets or liabilities between the company and the participator.

'51% subsidiary' is as defined in **29.8** above.

[*CTA 2010, ss 1064–1069*].

Simon's Taxes. See **D3.410.**

Example

[29.14]

R is a participator in S Ltd, a close company, but he is neither a director nor an employee. For the whole of 2021/22, S Ltd provided R with a new car of which the 'price' for tax purposes (i.e. under *ITEPA 2003, ss 122–124*) was £25,675, and which had a carbon dioxide emissions figure of 210 g/km. R was required to, and did, pay S Ltd £500 a year for the use of the car. The cost of providing the car, charged in S Ltd's accounts for its year ended 31 March 2022, was £5,000.

Deemed distribution

If the benefit of the car had been assessable as employment income, the cash equivalent would have been:

	£
£25,675 @ 37%	9,500
Less contribution	500
	£9,000

S Ltd is treated as making a distribution of £9,000 to R and R is treated as receiving dividend income for 2021/22 of £9,000.

S Ltd's taxable profits

In computing S Ltd's profits chargeable to corporation tax, the actual expenditure charged (£5,000) must be added back.

Items which are not distributions

[29.15] Items which are treated as not being distributions are:

(a) Distributions made in respect of share capital on winding up (see **76** WINDING UP). [*CTA 2010, s 1030*].

(b) Distributions made in respect of share capital in anticipation of dissolution under *Companies Act 2006, ss 1000 or 1003*. The maximum distributions are £25,000, otherwise all the distributed profits will be distributions. Further conditions apply. [*CTA 2010, s 1030A*].

(c) A distribution as part of a merger to which *TCGA 1992, s 140E* or *s 140F* applies (cross border mergers) where the company ceases to exist as a result of the merger without being wound up, is treated as a distribution in respect of share capital in a winding up. [*CTA 2010, s 1031*].

(d) Small distributions to members on dissolution of an unincorporated association which is of a social or recreational nature and has not carried on a trade or investment business. (HMRC Extra-Statutory Concession, C15).

(e) Payments for group relief (see **35.16** GROUP RELIEF), except in so far as they exceed the amount surrendered. [*CTA 2010, s 183*].

(f) *Share or loan interest* paid by registered societies within **22.1** CO-OPERATIVE AND COMMUNITY BENEFIT SOCIETIES (previously registered industrial and provident societies) or certain co-operative associations. [*CTA 2010, s 1055*].

(g) *Dividends or bonuses* deductible in computing the income of registered societies within **22.1** CO-OPERATIVE AND COMMUNITY BENEFIT SOCIETIES (previously registered industrial and provident societies) or MUTUAL COMPANIES (**54**). [*CTA 2010, s 1056*].

(h) *Dividends or interest* payable in respect of shares in, deposits with, or loans to, BUILDING SOCIETIES (**8**). [*CTA 2010, s 1054*]. However, this exemption does not apply to core capital deferred shares. [*SI 2013 No 460, Reg 3*].

(i) *Stock dividends* (see Tolley's Income Tax under Savings and Investment Income). [*CTA 2010, ss 1049–1053*].

For this purpose, a stock dividend is either one issued in lieu of cash, or a bonus issue of shares in respect of shares of a 'qualifying class'. In both cases, the issuing company must be UK-resident. In the case of bonus shares, shares are of a 'qualifying class' if shares of that class carry the right to bonus shares of that or another class under the terms of original issue or those terms as subsequently amended. There are special rules for the situation where bonus share capital (as defined) is converted into or exchanged for shares of a different class. 'Bonus share capital' means the share capital or part of it not issued for new consideration.

There is provision for returns to be made to HMRC where stock dividends or bonus issues are made and rules for determining the return periods.

(j) *Interest on securities* not within **29.4–29.7** above i.e. interest etc. paid in respect of certain securities, provided the securities are 'special securities', both companies are within the charge to corporation tax and the terms are commercial. However, this exemption does not apply to securities falling within the exceptions outlined at **29.7** above, for securities within *CTA 2010, Sch 2 para 107*. [*CTA 2010, s 1032*].

(k) Money provided by a close company for the purchase of its shares by trustees of its profit sharing scheme. (CCAB Memorandum TR 308, June 1978).

(l) Certain *purchases by a company of its own shares* (see **61** PURCHASE BY A COMPANY OF ITS OWN SHARES). [*CTA 2010, s 1033–1047*].

(m) Any 'relevant alternative finance' return within *CTA 2009, ss 507* or *513* is not treated as a distribution for corporation tax purposes. (See **3.7** ALTERNATIVE FINANCE ARRANGEMENTS.) [*CTA 2009, ss 507, 513*].

(n) The transfer of a building society's business to a company. [*FA 1998, Sch 12 para 6*].

(o) Interest and share dividends paid by a UK agricultural or fishing co-operative. [*CTA 2009, s 1057*].

(p) The surrender to another group member of an amount in respect of an RDEC (see **63** RESEARCH AND DEVELOPMENT EXPENDITURE). [*CTA 2009, ss 104O, 104R*].

(q) A payment in respect of a regulatory capital security, before the repeal of the provisions relating to such securities (see **50.28** LOAN RELATIONSHIPS). Anti-avoidance provisions apply if there are arrangements in place the main purpose, or one of the main purposes, of which is to obtain a tax advantage (within *CTA 2010, s 1139*) as a result of the application of this provision, such that the payment would not benefit from the exemption from being a distribution. [*SI 2013 No 3209, Reg 5; SI 2015 No 2056; FA 2019, Sch 20 paras 1, 10, 11*].

(r) A qualifying amount payable in respect of a hybrid capital instrument (see **50.28** LOAN RELATIONSHIPS). [*CTA 2009, s 420A; FA 2019, Sch 20 para 2*].

A bonus issue of non-redeemable share capital does not constitute a distribution unless it follows a repayment of share capital (see **29.9** above).

The Treasury has the power to introduce regulations to deal with the tax consequences of financial sector regulation, with regard to securities of any EU or UK regulatory requirement, see further **7.1** BANKS.

Corporation tax treatment of distributions

[29.16] The charge to corporation tax on income applies to any dividend or other distribution of a company unless it falls within one of the exemptions detailed below. [*CTA 2009, s 931A*]. In practice, most dividends, whether received from a UK company or a foreign company, are exempt from UK corporation tax. Different treatment applies to distributions received by different categories of company — small and medium-sized or large.

A company is a 'small company' for this purpose if it is a micro or small enterprise as defined in the Annex to *Commission Recommendation 2003/361/EC* of 6 May 2003. However, a company is not small for this purpose if at any time in an accounting period it is an open-ended investment company, an authorised unit trust scheme, an insurance company or a friendly society. [*CTA 2009, s 931S*].

Small companies

A distribution received by a small company is exempt if:

(i) the paying company is a UK resident or resident in a 'qualifying territory' at the time the small company receives the distribution;
(ii) the distribution is not interest that is treated as a distribution by *paras E* or *F* of *CTA 2010, s 1000(1)*, see **29.2** above;
(iii) the receipt is a dividend in respect of which no tax deduction is given for the distribution outside the UK;
(iv) the distribution is not made as part of a tax advantage scheme; and
(v) the distribution is received from a CFC in an accounting period of a recipient in which the recipient is a small company and the whole or part of the distributions is from chargeable CFC profits (apportioned to chargeable companies under the CFC rules — see **21** CONTROLLED FOREIGN COMPANIES).

Definitions

For the purposes of the small companies' exemption, a country is a '*qualifying territory*' if the UK has a double tax agreement containing a non-discrimination provision with the territory.

However, the Treasury may, by statutory instrument, provide that a country fulfilling these conditions is not a qualifying territory or that a country not fulfilling these conditions is a qualifying territory. *SI 2009 No 3314*, issued under this power, provides that a territory which would otherwise qualify, is not a qualifying territory if the payer of the distribution is an 'excluded company'. An '*excluded company*' is one excluded from one or more benefits of any double taxation relief arrangements in force in relation to that territory.

A '*non-discrimination provision*' is a clause in a double taxation agreement which provides that a national of one state is not to be less favourably treated in tax matters than a national of the other contracting state.

For this purpose, a company is '*resident*' if, under the laws of a state, it is resident because of its domicile, residence or place of management but not only on its income from sources in that territory or capital situated there.

Wide powers are given to the Treasury to amend these provisions by statutory instrument.

[*CTA 2009, ss 931B–931CA*].

Companies that are not small

A distribution received by a large or medium-sized company is exempt if it falls into an exempt class, is not interest treated as a distribution (within para E or F of *CTA 2010, s 1000(1)*) and no tax deduction is given for the distribution outside the UK.

[*CTA 2009, s 931D*].

The following five classes of distribution are exempt:

(a) **Distributions from controlled companies:** a distribution is exempt where the recipient, or the recipient together with another person controls the payer company and, in the latter case, one of the parties holds at least 40% and not more than 55% of the share capital, rights and powers. However, the dividend is not exempt if it is paid as part of a tax avoidance scheme one of the purposes of which is to arrange for the dividend to fall into an exempt class and the dividend is paid out of pre-control profits. [*CTA 2009, ss 931E, 931J*].

(b) **Distributions in respect of non-redeemable, ordinary shares:** a distribution on an ordinary, non-redeemable share is exempt. There is an anti-avoidance provision which provides that if a dividend is paid as part of an avoidance scheme and the shares are not true ordinary shares or are in fact redeemable shares, they do not fall into the exempt class. [*CTA 2009, ss 931F, 931K*].

(c) **Distributions in respect of portfolio holdings:** a dividend on a holding (a portfolio holding) carrying a right to less than 10% of the profits, or assets on a winding up of all the share capital of that class of share (if more than one). Where not all shares in a class are paid up to the same extent, the shares are not all of one class (share premiums being disregarded for this purpose). There is an anti-avoidance provision which attacks schemes to manipulate holdings so as to come within this exempt class. [*CTA 2009, ss 931G, 931L*].

(d) **Dividends derived from transactions not designed to reduce tax:** a distribution made in respect of 'relevant profits' is exempt. 'Relevant profits' means any profits available for distribution when the distribution was made, other than profits from avoidance transactions. [*CTA 2009, s 931H*].

    Where a distribution falls under another exempt class, it is treated as made first out of relevant profits, any other dividend is treated as made out of profits other than relevant profits (i.e. it is non-exempt) and when those profits are exhausted, the balance is treated as paid out of relevant profits.

(e) **Dividends in respect of shares accounted for as liabilities:** a dividend is exempt if it fulfils the conditions to be accounted for as a liability under *CTA 2009, s 521C* except for condition (1)(f) of that section, not being a share held for an unallowable purpose. If such share is held for an unallowable purpose it would be treated as within the loan relationship rules. [*CTA 2009, s 931I*].

Where a distribution is not exempt under (a) above, but would qualify under one of the other exemptions and it is paid as part of a tax avoidance scheme, is part of the return for such a scheme, the return is economically equivalent to interest and there is a connection between the payer and recipient, then the distribution is not treated as exempt. [*CTA 2009, s 931M*].

In addition to the specific anti-avoidance provisions identified for certain exemptions above, there are four further general anti-avoidance provisions, not specifically linked to the exempt classes, which apply to prevent a distribution from falling into an exempt class if it would otherwise do so. The main aim of these provisions is to ensure that dividends paid as part of a tax avoidance scheme remain taxable in the UK. These are that the distribution is part of a tax advantage scheme and:

(i) a non-UK resident receives a tax deduction in respect of it [*CTA 2009, s 931N*];
(ii) the scheme involves making a payment or giving up a right to income and all or part of the consideration is the distribution and *CTA 2009, s 1301(2), (4)* to *(7)* applies to the payment [*CTA 2009, s 931O*];
(iii) the scheme involves the giving up of a right to payment for goods or services, and in return the receipt of the income given up as a distribution. This provision does not apply when the transfer pricing provisions apply [*CTA 2009, s 931P*];
(iv) the scheme has diverted a payment which would be trading income of a company to another person and one of the main purposes of the scheme was to achieve exemption on the distribution [*CTA 2009, s 931Q*].

It is open to a company to elect, within two years of the end of the accounting period in which the distribution is received, for the distribution not to be exempt [*CTA 2009, s 931R*].

Capital distributions

The fact that a distribution is exempt does not prevent it from being taken into account in the calculation of chargeable gains. [*CTA 2009, s 931RA*].

Definitions

A 'relevant person' in relation to a distribution is the company which receives the distribution and any person connected with that company [*CTA 2009, s 931T*].

A 'scheme' includes any scheme, arrangements or understanding of any kind whatever, whether or not legally enforceable, involving a single transaction or two or more transactions.

A 'tax advantage scheme' is a scheme with a main purpose of obtaining a tax advantage (other than a negligible tax advantage).

[*CTA 2009, s 931V*].

The provisions *of CTA 2009* dealing with trading profits and property income take priority over the above. [*CTA 2009, s 931W*].

Mutual companies

[29.17] Payments made to members of MUTUAL COMPANIES (54) (other than those carrying on life assurance business) are within the provisions of this chapter only if made out of income chargeable to corporation tax or out of income of the company consisting of 'exempt ABGH distributions'. '*Exempt ABGH distributions*' are distributions within **29.2**(a), (b), (f) or (g) above which are exempt from corporation tax (see **29.16** above).

[*CTA 2010, s 1070*].

Companies not carrying on a business

[29.18] Where a company:

(i) does not carry on, and has never carried on a trade, or a business of holding investments;
(ii) does not hold, and has never held, an office; and
(iii) is not established for purposes which include either carrying on a trade, carrying on a business of holding investments, or holding an office,

then the provisions of this chapter apply to distributions made by the company only to the extent that they are made out of profits of the company which are within the charge to corporation tax or which are income of the company consisting of 'exempt ABGH distributions'. '*Exempt ABGH distributions*' are distributions within **29.2**(a), (b), (f) or (g) above which are exempt from corporation tax (see **29.16** above).

[*CTA 2010, s 1071*].

Discretionary payments from trusts

[29.19] Where trustees of a settlement make a discretionary distribution to a company, other than a charity (within *CTA 2010, s 467*), an eligible body within *CTA 2010, s 468* or a scientific research association (within *CTA 2010, s 469*) the payment is disregarded in calculating the company's income for corporation tax purposes, and no credit is given, or repayment made, of the tax deducted at the trust income tax rate. In the case of non-UK resident companies, this applies to so much (if any) of the payment as is income of the company for corporation tax purposes.

[*CTA 2010, s 610*].

Demergers

[29.20] There are three main ways for a group to carry out a demerger: the statutory route (which is examined further below); via liquidation; and by way of a Companies Act reconstruction (which requires court approval).

The statutory route depends on *CTA 2010, ss 1073–1099* which are intended to facilitate the breaking-up of large companies and groups of companies by exempting certain distributions of assets from the normal tax treatment (see **29 DISTRIBUTIONS**).

General enquiries concerning the demerger legislation should be addressed to BAI Clearance, HMRC, BX9 1JL. Market sensitive issues should be addressed to the Team Leader.

Simon's Taxes. See **D6.420–D6.424**.

Exempt distributions — demergers

[29.21] Generally, in a demerger the holding company transfers its subsidiaries, either directly to its shareholders, or indirectly to new companies set up by the shareholders. Such a transfer by the holding company would normally be treated as a distribution of its assets to its shareholders. However, if the conditions for an exempt demerger are met, no distribution will arise.

Subject to **29.25** below, the following are exempt distributions.

(a) The transfer is to all or any of its 'members' by a company ('the distributing company') of 'shares' in a '75% subsidiary' which:
   (i) are irredeemable;
   (ii) constitute the whole or 'substantially the whole' of the distributing company's holding of the subsidiary's 'ordinary share capital';
   (iii) confer the whole or 'substantially the whole' of the distributing company's voting rights in the subsidiary;
   (iv) unless the distributing company is a 75% subsidiary after the distribution, the distributing company must be a trading company or the holding company of a trading group; and
   (v) similarly unless the transfer relates to two or more 75% subsidiaries and the distributing company is dissolved without having any residual net assets for distribution on a winding up or otherwise then the distributing company must be a trading company or the holding company of a trading group.
   [*CTA 2010, ss 1076, 1082*].

(b) The transfer is by the distributing company to another company or companies of:
   (i) a 'trade' or trades (provided that no, or only a minor, interest in any such trade is retained); or
   (ii) shares in one or more of its 75% subsidiaries. (In this case, the shares may be redeemable, but must otherwise meet the requirements set out in (a) above.)

   To qualify for exemption, the transfer must be coupled with the issue by the transferee company (or companies) to all or any of the members of the distributing company of shares which:
   (A) are irredeemable;
   (B) constitute the whole or 'substantially the whole' of the transferee company's issued ordinary share capital; and
   (C) confer the whole or 'substantially the whole' of the voting rights in that company.

   The distributing company must not retain more than a minor interest in the transferred trade.

   Shares issued by the transferee must be irredeemable, constitute the whole or substantially the whole of the issued ordinary share capital and confer the whole or substantially the whole of the voting rights in the company. After the making the distribution, the distributing company must be a trading company or a holding company of a trading group — however this condition does not apply if the distributing company is dissolved without making a further distribution (and having no assets).

[*CTA 2010, ss 1077, 1083*].

The carrying on of the transferred trade or trades or the holding of the transferred shares must constitute the only or main activity of each and every transferee company after the distribution. This is not construed as meaning 'for ever after', but an intention that the conditions should cease to be satisfied at some later time would require consideration under the anti-avoidance provisions (see below). (HMRC Statement of Practice, SP 13/80 as revised).

The group, or the largest group must be a trading group after the transfer.

All companies must be resident in a member state and must either be a trading company or a member of a trading group at the time the distribution is made.

The distribution must be made wholly or mainly to benefit some or all of the trading activities carried on before the distribution by a single company or group and afterwards by two or more companies or groups.

The distribution must not be part of a scheme or arrangement for a prohibited purpose.

The distribution must be made wholly or mainly for the purpose of benefiting some or all of the 'trading activities' which before the distribution are carried on by a single company or 'group' and after the distribution will be carried on by two or more companies or groups.

[*CTA 2010, ss 1074, 1081*].

A distribution cannot be exempt if it forms part of a scheme or arrangements the main purpose or one of the main purposes of which is:

(i) the avoidance of tax (including stamp duty or stamp duty land tax);
(ii) the making of a 'chargeable payment' (see **29.25** below) (or what would be a chargeable payment if any of the companies were an unquoted company);
(iii) the acquisition (other than by members of the distributing company) of 'control' of that or of any other 'relevant company' or of any company in the same group as a relevant company;
(iv) the cessation of a trade; or
(v) the sale of a trade after the distribution.

[*CTA 2010, s 1081*].

HMRC's interpretation of several of these requirements is contained in HMRC Statement of Practice, SP 13/80 as revised. In brief:

(i) the question of whether what is transferred constitutes a trade is considered from the transferee's point of view, and without regard to minor assets linked with trading assets. Whether only a part of the transferor's trade, or merely some of his assets, are transferred is not conclusive;
(ii) a 'minor interest in a trade' means around 10% or less, and does not include indirect involvement conferring no measure of control;
(iii) 'substantially the whole' means 90% or more;

(iv) the concurrent transfer of ordinary share capital to ordinary shareholders for consideration, or to preference shareholders, or of other shares or securities to ordinary shareholders, does not prevent relief being given under these provisions;

(v) 'after' in (5) means 'at any time after'.

For the treatment for income and capital gains tax purposes of trustees and beneficiaries where the trustees hold shares in a company which carries out an exempt distribution, see HMRC Tax Bulletin October 1994 pp 162–165 and HMRC Capital Gains Tax Manual, CG33900 onwards.

Simon's Taxes. See **D6.421, D6.422.**

Transactions involving entities in EU member states

[29.22] The following is also an exempt distribution if:

(a) it is a distribution consisting of:
  (i) the transfer of part of a business by a company to one or more other companies; and
  (ii) the issue of shares by the transferees to the members of the transferor; and

(b) the requirements of either *TCGA 1992, s 140A(1A) or s 140C(1A)* (See **11.21** CAPITAL GAINS) are satisfied.

[*CTA 2010, s 1078*].

Definitions

[29.23] 'Distributing company' means the company which makes the transfer of shares or trade in **29.21**(a) or (b) above. [*CTA 2010, s 1079*].

A 'member' of a company means a holder of ordinary share capital of that company. 'Shares' includes stock.

In determining whether a company the shares in which are transferred by the distributing company is a '75% subsidiary' of that company, shares therein owned indirectly by the distributing company are to be disregarded. The subsidiary must, at the time of transfer, be either a trading company or the holding company of a trading group.

'Trade' does not include dealing in shares, securities, land, trades or commodity futures, and '*trading activities*' are to be construed accordingly. [*CTA 2010, s 1099*].

A 'group', except for the purposes of **29.21**(3) above, means a company and its 75% subsidiaries.

In **29.21**(3) above, the term means a company and its 51% subsidiaries.

See also below regarding a 'trading company'.

'Control' is as defined in *CTA 2010, s 1099*, see **16.6** CLOSE COMPANIES.

A 'trading company' is one the business of which consists wholly or mainly in the carrying on of a trade or trades, and a 'trading group' is a group the business of the members of which (taken together) consists wholly or mainly in the carrying on of a trade or trades.

A '*holding company*' means a company the business of which (disregarding any trade that it carries on) consists wholly or mainly in the holding of shares or securities of one or more companies which are its 75% subsidiaries.

[*CTA 2010, s 1099*].

'Ordinary share capital' is all the issued share capital of the company except that carrying a fixed dividend only. [*CTA 2010, s 1119*]. 'Issued share capital' does not include founder members' deposits in a company limited by guarantee (*South Shore Mutual Insurance Co Ltd v Blair (Inspector of Taxes)* [1999] STC (SCD) 296). See **12.2** CAPITAL GAINS — GROUPS.

'Unquoted company'. A company is unquoted if no class of shares or securities therein (disregarding debenture or loan stock or preferred shares) is listed in the Stock Exchange Official List and dealt in on the Stock Exchange. A company under the sole control of one or more companies which are not unquoted is outside this definition. [*CTA 2010, s 1098*].

Relief from tax on capital gains

[29.24] Any exempt distribution within **29.21**(a) above is not a capital distribution for the purposes of *TCGA 1992, s 122*, and will not, therefore, give rise to a deemed disposal.

The distribution is treated as if it were a reorganisation of the distributing company's share capital for the purposes of *TCGA 1992, ss 126–130*. [*TCGA 1992, s 192(2)*]. See Tolley's Capital Gains Tax under Shares and Securities.

Where a company ceases to be a member of a group solely because of an exempt distribution (within **29.21**(a) or (b) above), no charge arises under *TCGA 1992, s 179* (see **12.15** CAPITAL GAINS — GROUPS). This relief is withdrawn if a chargeable payment (see **29.25** below) is made within five years after the exempt distribution; the time limit for making assessments is extended (where necessary) to three years after the making of the chargeable payment. [*TCGA 1992, s 192(3)(4)*].

For the treatment of trustees and beneficiaries where the trustees hold shares in a company which carries out an exempt distribution, see HMRC Capital Gains Manual CG33900.

Chargeable payment connected with exempt distribution

[29.25] If within five years after an exempt distribution there is a 'chargeable payment', it is treated as:

(a) miscellaneous income (chargeable to corporation tax);
(b) an annual sum payable otherwise than out of profits or gains chargeable to income tax for the purposes of *ITA 2007, ss 449, 901, 946, 962–964* (requiring the payer to deduct and account for income tax at the basic rate) unless it is a transfer of money's worth; and
(c) a distribution for the purposes of *CTA 2009, s 1305(1)* (distributions not deductible in computing income).

In no case is the payment to be treated as a repayment of capital for the purposes of **29.9**, **29.10** above.

A '*chargeable payment*' is any 'payment' made by a 'company concerned in an exempt distribution':

(i) directly or indirectly to a member of that company or of any other such company;
(ii) in connection with, or with any transaction affecting, the shares of that or any other such company;
(iii) which is neither a distribution nor an exempt distribution nor made to a member of the same group as the paying company; and
(iv) which is not made for *bona fide* commercial reasons or forms part of a scheme or arrangements a main purpose of which is the avoidance of tax (including stamp duty and stamp duty land tax).

Where a company concerned in an exempt distribution is an 'unquoted company' (see **29.23** above), (i) above is extended to payments made by or to any other person in pursuance of a scheme or arrangements made with the unquoted company. If the unquoted company is:

(A) under the control of five or fewer persons; and
(B) not under the sole control of a company not within (A) above,

payments made in pursuance of a scheme or arrangements made with any of the persons referred to in (A) above are chargeable payments.

'*Payment*' includes a transfer of money's worth including the assumption of a liability.

A '*company concerned in an exempt distribution*' includes every relevant company and any company connected with a relevant company (or with any other company which is so connected) at any time between the exempt distribution and the chargeable payment. In establishing connection, *CTA 2010, s 1122;* (see **19** CONNECTED PERSONS) applies.

Where a chargeable payment is made within five years of an exempt distribution, the chargeable payment is treated as a distribution within *CTA 2009, s 1305* therefore it does not qualify for a corporation tax deduction.

[*CTA 2010, ss 1087–1089*].

See also **29.24** above.

Simon's Taxes. See **D6.423**.

Consequences of demerger

[29.26] The types of demerger detailed at **29.21**(a) and (b)(ii) above result in a change of ownership of the subsidiary company demerged.

If this is accompanied by a major change in the nature or conduct of the trade (which may result from those management changes the legislation is designed to bring about), the provisions of *CTA 2010, ss 673–676* (see **51.17** LOSSES), and *CTA 2010, ss 704, 705* (see **60** PROPERTY INCOME) may be triggered.

Briefly, these act to prohibit the carry-forward of losses arising before the change of ownership to be used in periods after the change of ownership. Since such restrictions contradict the intention of the demerger legislation, HMRC will consider sympathetically the application of *CTA 2010, ss 673–676* where they apply as a result of an exempt distribution, and the underlying ownership of the trade is unchanged.

Winding-up etc.

[29.27] The requirement for a distributing company to be a trading company or the holding company of a trading group after the distribution (see **29.23** above) is removed in the following circumstances.

(a) Distributions within **29.21**(a) above.
Where the transfer relates to two or more 75% subsidiaries of the distributing company which is then dissolved without there having been, after the exempt distribution, net assets of the company available for distribution in a winding-up or otherwise. A company will, concessionally, not be regarded as failing to meet these conditions merely because it retains, after the distribution, sufficient funds to meet the cost of liquidation and to repay a negligible amount (i.e. £5,000 or less) of share capital remaining. (HMRC Extra-Statutory Concession, C 11).

(b) Distributions within **29.21**(b) above.
Where there are two or more transferee companies, each of which receives a trade or shares in a separate 75% subsidiary of the distributing company, and the distributing company is dissolved without there having been, after the exempt distribution, net assets of the company available for distribution in a winding-up or otherwise.

[*CTA 2010, s 1082*].

Returns

[29.28] Within 30 days after an exempt distribution, the distributing company must make a return to HMRC giving particulars of the distribution and the reasons why it is exempt. Where a clearance (see **29.29** below) has been given in respect of the distribution, the return need only refer to the clearance notification and confirm that the distribution is precisely that for which clearance application was made. (HMRC Statement of Practice, SP 13/80 as revised).

If a chargeable payment is made consisting of the transfer of money's worth, the payer must, within 30 days of the payment, make a return to HMRC giving particulars of:

(a) the transaction effecting the transfer;
(b) the name and address of each and every recipient and the value of what is transferred to him; and
(c) any chargeable payment in money which accompanied the transfer.

In the case of a payment which is not a chargeable payment solely because it is made for genuine commercial reasons and otherwise than for tax avoidance purposes (see **29.25** above), a return must be made within 30 days of the payment giving particulars of:

(i) in the case of a transfer of money's worth, the transaction by which it is effected;
(ii) the name and address of each and every recipient and the value of the payment made to him; and
(iii) the circumstances by reason of which the payment is not a chargeable payment.

[*CTA 2010, ss 1095, 1096*].

See, however, **29.29** below.

Clearance

[29.29] Application may be made for advance determination that a distribution is exempt or that a payment is not chargeable.

Applications for clearance should be addressed to BAI Clearance, HMRC, BX9 1JL (or, if market-sensitive information is included, to Team Leader at that address). Applications may be emailed to reconstructions@hmrc.gsi.gov.uk. Application may be made in a single letter to the same address for clearance under *CTA 2010, ss 1091–1094* and under any one or more of *CTA 2010, ss 1044, 1045* (see **61.9** PURCHASE BY A COMPANY OF ITS OWN SHARES), *CTA 2010, ss 748, 749* (transactions in securities, see **70.1** TRANSACTIONS IN SECURITIES), *TCGA 1992, s 138(1)* (share exchanges, see Tolley's Capital Gains Tax under Anti-Avoidance), *TCGA 1992, s 139(5)* (reconstructions involving the transfer of a business, see **62.15** REORGANISATIONS AND RECONSTRUCTIONS), *TCGA 1992, s 140B* (transfer of a UK trade between EU member states, see **11.18** CAPITAL GAINS), *TCGA 1992, s 140D* (transfer of non-UK trade between EU member states, see **11.19** CAPITAL GAINS) and *CTA 2009, s 832* (see **42.30** INTANGIBLE ASSETS).

The application must fully and accurately disclose all facts and circumstances material for the decision of HMRC, failing which any clearance granted is void. In general, it should include the following.

(i) The name of each relevant company (see **29.23** above), its tax reference, residence status, whether it is a distributing, subsidiary or transferee company (see **29.21** above) in relation to the proposed transactions, and whether it is a trading company or holding company (see **29.23** above) under the demerger provisions definitions, or some other type of company.
(ii) Details of the group structure where appropriate.
(iii) A statement of the reasons for the demerger, the trading activities to be divided, the anticipated trading benefits and any other benefits expected to accrue.
(iv) A detailed description of all the proposed transactions, including any prior transactions or rearrangements in preparation for the demerger, making it clear why it is considered that all the relevant conditions are satisfied.
(v) Confirmation, together with all relevant information, that the distribution is not excluded from relief as part of a scheme (see **29.21** above), and a statement of the circumstances (if any) in which it is envisaged that

control of a relevant company might be acquired by someone other than a member of the distributing company, or that a trade carried on by one of those companies before or after the demerger might cease or be sold.

(vi) The latest available balance sheets and profit and loss accounts of the existing companies (as listed at (i) above), and, where appropriate, a consolidated group balance sheet and profit and loss account, with a note of any material relevant changes between balance sheet date and the proposed demerger.

Where, exceptionally, it is not possible to explain the purpose of a demerger adequately in writing, HMRC will invite the applicants to an interview.

(HMRC Statement of Practice, SP 13/80 as revised).

HMRC may call for further particulars within 30 days of the receipt of the application, or of particulars previously requested, and if these are not supplied within a further 30 days (or such longer period as HMRC may allow) HMRC need not proceed further on the application. Subject to this, HMRC must notify its decision to the applicant within 30 days of the receipt of the application or of the particulars last requested. If the decision is unfavourable, or not communicated to him within the time limit, the applicant may, within 30 days after the receipt of the decision or after the expiry of the time limit, require HMRC to place the matter before the tribunal. The decision of the tribunal is then treated as that of HMRC.

Where a clearance has been given in respect of a payment which would otherwise be a chargeable payment, there is no obligation to make a return under these provisions (see **29.28** above).

A company which becomes or ceases to be connected (see **19** CONNECTED PERSONS and **29.25** above) with another company may seek clearance for any payment which may be made at any time after it became, or ceased to be, so connected (whether or not there is any present intention to make any payment). No payment to which a clearance relates is to be treated as chargeable merely by reason of the company's being, or having been, connected with the other company.

[*CTA 2010, ss 1091–1094*].

Simon's Taxes. See **D6.429.**

Shadow advance corporation tax

[29.30] Where a company resident in the UK made a qualifying distribution before 6 April 1999, it became liable to pay advance corporation tax (ACT) (subject to relief for qualifying investment income received). [*ICTA 1988, s 14(1)*]. The ACT could then be offset against the company's liability to 'mainstream' corporation tax on its profits for that accounting period subject to a maximum set-off. ACT was abolished from 6 April 1999.

Following the abolition of ACT, a system of 'shadow ACT' was introduced to enable surplus ACT (see **29.33** below) as at 5 April 1999 to be relieved broadly in accordance with companies' expectations prior to abolition. The system, introduced under the enabling provisions of *FA 1998, s 32*, operates as set out at **29.31** onwards. An accounting period straddling 5 April 1999 is treated as two separate accounting periods, ending on and commencing immediately after that date, with profits being time-apportioned between those accounting periods. Following the abolition of tax credits from 6 April 2016, changes were made to the system for distributions made in accounting periods beginning on or after that date. An accounting period straddling 5 April 2016 is treated as two separate accounting periods, ending on and commencing immediately after that date. Changes described below as applying with effect from 6 April 2016 have effect subject to this transitional rule.

[*SI 1999 No 358, Reg 3; SI 2017 No 454, Reg 1*].

Computation of shadow ACT

[29.31] Shadow ACT is computed for an accounting period on a similar basis and at the same rate as applied before 6 April 1999. For the financial year 1999 onwards, shadow ACT is treated as having been paid at the rate of 25% of the amount or value of the 'relevant distributions' (i.e. 20% of the dividend etc. plus the shadow ACT).

'*Relevant distributions*'. The distributions in respect of which the shadow ACT computation is made include all distributions made on or after 6 April 1999 within *CTA 2010, Pt 23* (see **29.2–29.6** above), and also certain deemed distributions arising in respect of benefits provided to participators in close companies (see **29.13** above), but *excluding* manufactured dividends within *CTA 2010, Pt 17* (see **52** MANUFACTURED PAYMENTS) and most intra-group distributions.

[*SI 1999 No 358, Regs 3, 11; SI 2017 No 454, Reg 5*].

Reduction for qualifying investment income

[29.32] Where 'qualifying investment income' (QII) is received in an accounting period, or surplus QII is brought forward (including a surplus arising before 6 April 1999), shadow ACT is *not* treated as having been paid in that period except to the extent that '*franked distributions*' (i.e. distributions plus the shadow ACT thereon) exceed the sum of nine-eighths of the QII received and the amount of any surplus QII brought forward.

With effect from 6 April 2016, '*qualifying investment income*' means 'exempt ABGH distributions' of a company grossed up by ten-ninths. '*Exempt ABGH distributions*' are distributions within **29.2**(a), (b), (f) or (g) above which are exempt from corporation tax (see **29.16** above).

Before 6 April 2016, 'qualifying investment income' means '*franked investment income*' (FII), i.e. the sum of the amount or value of dividends and other qualifying distributions (see **29.7** above) received by a UK resident company from another UK resident company and such proportion of each distribution as corresponds to the 'tax credit fraction' in force when the distribution is made. From 6 April 1999 to 5 April 2016 inclusive, the tax credit fraction is one-ninth of the amount or value of the relevant distribution (i.e. 10% of the dividend etc. plus the tax credit). Thus, a dividend of £360 amounts to QII in the hands of a UK recipient company of £400.

The definition of QII is subject to a number of restrictions in relation to replacement of interest income by income consisting of distributions, arrangements to pass on the value of FII, distributions received by dealers, intra-group distributions and abnormal dividends.

[*CTA 2010, ss 1109, 1126; SI 1999 No 358, Regs 3, 3A, 6A, 7–10A, 11; SI 2010 No 669; SI 2017 No 454, Regs 4, 5*].

Utilisation of shadow ACT and surplus ACT

[29.33] Shadow ACT which is treated as having been paid by a company in respect of any relevant distribution made by it in an accounting period is set against its liability to corporation tax on any profits charged to corporation tax for that accounting period, but no actual corporation tax relief is given for such amounts of shadow ACT. The capacity for offset against corporation tax available (see below) is allocated first to the shadow ACT so computed. Any balance of the offset capacity available for an accounting period is then allocated to surplus ACT brought forward at 6 April 1999, for which actual corporation tax relief is then given.

The *maximum* set-off is the amount of shadow ACT that would have been payable in respect of a franked distribution equal to the profits and made at the end of the accounting period (i.e. 20% of profits chargeable to corporation tax).

[*SI 1999 No 358, Regs 3, 12, 14, 15*].

Surplus shadow ACT

If the shadow ACT exceeds the offset capacity for the period, it is treated as 'surplus shadow ACT', to be carried back and treated as shadow ACT in respect of distributions made in accounting periods beginning in the previous six years (but not before 6 April 1999), with any unused balance being carried forward to the next accounting period. Surplus shadow ACT is, however, not carried back so as to displace actual surplus ACT relieved in an earlier period except in the period beginning 24 months before the *end* of the accounting period in which the surplus shadow ACT arose and ending the day before the commencement of that period.

[*SI 1999 No 358, Regs 3, 12, 14*].

For cases turning on whether there was an accounting period in relation to surplus ACT, see *Walker (Inspector of Taxes) v Centaur Clothes Group Ltd* [2000] 2 All ER 589, [2000] 1 WLR 799, HL, and *Aproline Ltd v Littlejohn* [1995] STC (SCD) 201.

Withdrawal from shadow ACT system

[29.34] A company may opt out of the shadow ACT system by notifying HMRC that it will not seek, or will cease to seek, recovery of unrelieved surplus ACT. Where such notice was given in the accounting period beginning on 6 April 1999 (as in **29.30** above) and related to that period, the company was thereby excluded from the shadow ACT arrangements from the start. Where it is given in any accounting period and indicates that the company wishes that accounting period to be the last for which it will seek recovery of unrelieved surplus ACT (the 'final accounting period'), then no further recovery will be possible after that period. In those circumstances, and also in relation to the accounting period in which all surplus ACT is exhausted, the shadow ACT computation continues to be made for (normally) the following accounting period, with any surplus shadow ACT arising in that period being carried back to displace surplus ACT relieved as under **29.33** above in the final accounting period (and in that case the accounting period from which the surplus shadow ACT is carried back becomes the final accounting period, i.e. the last period for which surplus ACT relief may be obtained). (These displacement provisions are more complex where accounting periods are not of 12 months' duration.) The latter prevents excessive relief being obtained by the restriction of dividends, and consequent ability to reclaim unrelieved surplus ACT, in the final period within the arrangements, followed by the payment of exceptional dividends in (normally) the following accounting period. There are special rules in relation to determination of the final accounting period for these purposes in the case of groups of companies (see generally **29.35** below).

[*SI 1999 No 358, Regs 4, 5*].

Intra-group allocation of shadow ACT

[29.35] Special rules determine when and how shadow ACT generated within a group of companies is to be allocated, and the allocation of group surplus shadow ACT. Broadly, no company in a group gets relief for surplus ACT until all group shadow ACT has been offset.

Where a group member generates shadow ACT in excess of its maximum capacity to utilise it in the period in which it is generated, the excess is to be allocated by the parent company to another or other group member(s), but not so as to displace their own shadow ACT or to exceed their maximum capacity for using shadow ACT in the same period.

Where the total group shadow ACT exceeds the group capacity to use it, the balance remaining after the allocation to other group companies is to remain in the company in which it arose and to be carried forward.

Where the total group shadow ACT does not exceed the group capacity, the parent company determines which other group members are to receive the allocation and the amounts to be allocated to them, in accordance with their capacity to use that amount. HMRC may allocate the excess in accordance with the regulations where the company fails to do so, but such allocation can subsequently be overridden by an allocation made by the parent company.

There are also provisions dealing with a company joining or leaving a group, or being a member of more than one group. 'Group' for these purposes is broadly a company resident anywhere in the EEA and its 51% subsidiaries, but is specially defined to take into account certain special rights.

[*SI 1999 No 358, Regs 6, 13*].

Changes in ownership of a company

[29.36] The provisions relating to changes in ownership of companies under the pre-April 1999 rules (at *ICTA 1988, ss 245–245B*) were imported, with appropriate modifications, into the shadow ACT rules.

Major change in business

If a 'major change in the nature or conduct of a trade or business' takes place within three years of (or at the same time as) a change in ownership of a company (see **51.17** LOSSES), a new accounting period is deemed to commence at the time of the change in ownership. This applies for the purposes of setting off unrelieved surplus ACT against the company's liability to corporation tax on any profits charged to corporation tax for an accounting period ending after the change of ownership. For this purpose the profits of the company charged to corporation tax for the accounting period is to be apportioned to the revised accounting periods on a time basis.

In this case, unrelieved surplus ACT may not be carried forward from the accounting period ending with the change in ownership (such surplus ACT accordingly being lost). The prohibition on the carry forward of unrelieved surplus ACT also applies to ACT which had been surrendered to the company.

'*Major change in the nature or conduct of a trade or business*' includes:

(a) a major change in the type of property dealt in or services or facilities provided;
(b) a major change in customers, outlets or markets;
(c) the company's ceasing to be a 'trading company' and becoming an 'investment company' (or vice versa);
(d) where the company is an investment company, a major change in the nature of its investments.

The change may be the result of a gradual process which began outside the relevant period. See **51.17** LOSSES for HMRC practice as regards what constitutes a major change in the nature or conduct of a trade or business.

'*Trading company*' means a company the business of which consists wholly or mainly of the carrying on of a trade or trades.

'*Investment company*' means a company (other than a 'holding company'), the business of which consists wholly or mainly of making investments whence the principal part of its income is derived.

'*Holding company*' means a company the business of which consists wholly or mainly in the holding of shares or securities of companies which are its 90% subsidiaries and which are trading companies.

Revival of business

Similar consequences ensue if, once the scale of the activities in its trade or business has become small or negligible, there is a change in the ownership of the company before any considerable revival of that trade or business.

Surrendered ACT

Where there is a change in the ownership of a company (see **51.17** LOSSES) to which ACT had been surrendered in respect of a distribution made before the change, and in the period from three years before to three years after the change there is 'a major change in the nature or conduct of a trade or business' (see above) of the surrendering company, any unrelieved surplus ACT which had been so surrendered may not be carried forward to an accounting period ending after the change (the accounting period in which the change occurred being treated as two separate accounting periods, up to and after the change, for this purpose).

Assets acquired after change

Where there is a change in the ownership of a company (see **51.17** LOSSES) which carries forward unrelieved surplus ACT of an accounting period beginning before the change to an accounting period ending after the change, and:

(i) after the change the company acquires an asset from a fellow group member under the no gain, no loss provisions of *TCGA 1992, s 171* (see **12.4** CAPITAL GAINS — GROUPS); and
(ii) within three years of the change in ownership, a chargeable gain accrues to the company on its disposal of that asset (or of an asset deriving its value in whole or part from that asset),

the ACT set-off limit (in **29.33** above) for the period in which the chargeable gain arises is reduced by an amount equal to 20% of the gain.

Application of losses provisions

The provisions restricting the carry forward of losses following a change in ownership of a company are applied as if the benefit of losses were a reference to the benefit of unrelieved surplus ACT. For those provisions, see **51.17** LOSSES.

[*SI 1999 No 358, Regs 16–18*].

In the case of *CIR v Aberdeen Milk Co Ltd* [1999] STC 787, 73 TC 563, Ct of Sess, surplus ACT arising to a successor company on privatisation could not be carried back to the period before the transfer.

Other provisions

[29.37] The profits against which unrelieved surplus ACT may be set include amounts chargeable on the company in respect of CONTROLLED FOREIGN COMPANIES (**21**). The following calculations are required:

(i) Ascertain the amount of profits of a CFC apportioned to the company for the relevant accounting period (E) and the corresponding amount of creditable tax (D).
(ii) Ascertain the amount of available relevant allowances (see above) for the accounting period (F), whether or not a claim for relief in respect of them is made.
(iii) Calculate the notional shadow ACT (C) which would have been treated as payable on a distribution by the company of an amount which, when added to C would equal E – F.

(iv) The amount C – D is called the relevant maximum. Any shadow ACT on actual distributions (S) which has not been set off against corporation tax liability is set off against the CFC tax to the extent that it does not exceed the relevant maximum, but does not reduce the amount of liability.

(v) Any surplus unrelieved ACT is set off against the CFC tax (and reduces the amount of tax payable) to the extent that it does not exceed the amount C – D – S.

In effect, surplus unrelieved ACT only reduces CFC tax to the extent that the tax exceeds the creditable tax, tax on all available relevant allowances and shadow ACT.

Where the whole of a company's surplus shadow ACT has not been set off under (iv) above and the company is a member of a group, the excess may be allotted to another company in the group which has liability to CFC tax.

[*SI 1999 No 358, Reg 20*].

Where relief is available for a foreign tax credit, the income or gain subject to the foreign tax is excluded from profits for the purpose of determining the maximum shadow ACT set-off and the foreign tax credit is deducted from the corporation tax liability. Shadow ACT can be set against the corporation tax liability relating to the foreign income or gain limited to the maximum ACT credit that would have applied had the foreign income or gain been the only income or gain for the accounting period or, if lower, the corporation tax liability as reduced by the foreign tax credit (see *SI 1999 No 358, Reg 12(4)(5)*).

Any necessary assessment may be made to recover tax which ought to have been paid (including interest thereon) as a result of an excessive set-off of ACT, and to restore the tax position of those concerned (see *SI 1999 No 358, Reg 19*).

Key points on distributions

[29.38] Points to consider are as follows.

- A distribution from a company can take many forms, and can include not only normal dividends in respect of shares in the company, but also interest on securities that exceeds a normal commercial return. Most types of payment in respect of shares are likely to be treated as a distribution.
- A return of capital will usually not be treated as a distribution. This is important in the context of a purchase of own shares or a capital reduction. For this to apply it is important to check that the shares were acquired for valuable consideration. A bonus issue created out of distributable reserves will not be regarded as having been acquired for valuable consideration.
- Care must be taken where a purchase of own shares follows or is followed by a bonus issue, as this could give rise to a distribution. It is important to look at the history of a company before proceeding with a purchase of own shares or other capital reduction.

- Where a close company provides benefits to shareholders, and those benefits are not taxed as benefits arising from employment, they can be taxed on the shareholders as distributions.
- Bonus shares in the form of stock dividends are taxed on the shareholder as distributions. These occur usually where the shareholder is offered a choice between receiving a cash dividend or additional shares of broadly equivalent value.

30

Diverted Profits Tax

Simon's Taxes. See Part D2.7.

Introduction to diverted profits tax

[30.1] The diverted profits tax was introduced by *FA 2015*. The Government's stated intention in introducing the tax was to counter 'the use of aggressive tax planning techniques used by multinational enterprises to divert profits from the UK'.

The main features of the tax are as follows.

- The tax is charged on taxable diverted profits of a company for an accounting period if any of three situations apply.
- The first situation applies to a UK-resident company where provision is made or imposed between the company and a related person as a result of which the company achieves a tax reduction significantly greater than any tax increase for the other person (i.e. there is a tax mismatch), and it is reasonable to assume that the provision was designed to secure the tax reduction. See **30.5** below.

- The second situation applies to a non-UK resident company trading in the UK through a permanent establishment where the first situation would apply to that permanent establishment if it were a UK-resident company. See **30.6** below.
- The third situation applies to a non-UK resident company where a person is carrying on activity in the UK in connection with supplies of goods, services or other property by the company, it is reasonable to assume that any of the activity of that person or the company (or both) is designed to ensure that the company does not carry on a trade in the UK for corporation tax purposes and, in connection with the supplies of services etc., either the main purpose of the arrangements put in place is to avoid corporation tax, or a tax mismatch is secured such that the total tax derived from UK activities is significantly reduced. There is an exception from the charge where UK-related sales or expenses are below £10,000,000 and £1,000,000 respectively. See **30.7** below.
- Diverted profits tax for an accounting period is generally charged at a rate of 25% of the amount of the taxable diverted profits. The rate is 55% for certain oil industry profits. The rate is 33% for certain banking company profits. The 25% rate is to increase to 31% for accounting periods beginning on or after 1 April 2023 (subject to transitional rules for straddling periods). The 55% and 33% rates will remain unchanged.
- A company within the charge to diverted profits tax must notify HMRC within three months of the end of the accounting period (see **30.14** below). There is, however, no duty to self-assess.
- The tax is imposed by HMRC issuing a charging notice (see **30.16** below) to the company.
- Before issuing a charging notice, HMRC must issue a preliminary notice setting out the details of the proposed charge. The company may make representations to HMRC about the preliminary notice. See **30.15** below.
- The diverted profits tax must be paid within 30 days after the date on which the charging notice is issued. There are provisions enabling the tax to be collected from a company's UK representative or from certain related companies. See **30.18** below.
- Following the issue of the charging notice there is then a 15-month review period (previously one year) in which HMRC must review the notice at least once. If the company has paid the tax, HMRC may issue one or more amending notices reducing the amount charged. If HMRC consider that the charge is insufficient they may issue one supplementary charging notice imposing an additional charge. The review period starts immediately after the date on which the tax is due and payable and can be brought to an early end by agreement between HMRC and the company or by the company alone following the issuing of a supplementary charging notice. See **30.16** below.
- After the end of the review period the company has 30 days to appeal against the charging notice and any supplementary charging notice. See **30.16** below.

HMRC are responsible for the collection and management of diverted profits tax. [*FA 2015, s 103*].

HMRC guidance is in their International Manual at INTM480000 onwards.

HMRC will not provide formal statutory or non-statutory clearances in respect of diverted profits tax but, following informal discussions, a company may seek further comfort about the DPT position. HMRC will not usually provide a view on whether transactions are likely to fall within the scope of DPT as it would require a considerable amount of resource from the company and HMRC to obtain the necessary assurance about the level of risk. (HMRC International Manual INTM489848).

Compliance facility

HMRC have introduced a disclosure facility for companies that are within the scope of diverted profits tax but have failed to notify HMRC for one or more accounting periods. A company can register for the facility and is then required to make a full and accurate disclosure of the facts for all in-date accounting periods, use reasonable endeavours to determine the correct amount of tax payable, pay all outstanding liabilities and fully cooperate throughout the process. Where this process is carried out, HMRC will:

- not start an investigation into potential corporation tax, DPT or other liabilities arising from the company's profit diversion arrangements during the period HMRC allows for completion of the review and disclosure report;
- accept the proposal to pay additional tax, interest, and where applicable, penalties due and agree to take no further action with respect to transfer pricing or DPT for the periods covered, provided that HMRC are satisfied that the disclosure is based on appropriate evidence and changes to the transfer pricing policy proposed are reasonable and consistent with the arm's length principle;
- treat the disclosure as 'unprompted' for the purposes of considering penalties;
- not charge penalties for inaccuracies in returns or failure to notify for DPT if the company taken reasonable care or it has a reasonable excuse respectively
- in certain circumstances, not charge penalties for inaccuracies in returns or failure to notify for DPT if the company has been careless in filing its returns and/or non-deliberately failed to notify for DPT if it registers for the facility before 31 December 2019 and goes on to fully meet the requirements of the facility;
- treat the timing of the disclosure, for penalties purposes, as when the company registers to use the facility; and
- where a deliberate inaccuracy is being disclosed, not publish details of the company in line with the deliberate defaulters' legislation.

For full details of the facility see www.gov.uk/government/publications/hmrc-profit-diversion-compliance-facility.

Definitions

[30.2] The following definitions apply for the purposes of diverted profits tax.

A '*transaction*' includes arrangements, understandings and mutual practices, whether or not legally enforceable or intended to be so. '*Arrangements*' means any scheme or arrangement of any kind, whether or not legally enforceable or intended to be so. A series of transactions includes a number of transactions each entered into under the same arrangement, whether or not one after the other. The following do not prevent a series of transactions from being treated as one by means of which provision has been made or imposed between any two persons (as in **30.5**(a) and **30.7** below):

- that there is no transaction in the series to which both of those persons are parties;
- that the parties to any arrangement under which the series of transactions are entered into do not include either or both of those persons; and
- that there is one or more transactions in the series to which neither of those persons is a party.

'*Connected*' has the same meaning as in **19** CONNECTED PERSONS.

For diverted profits tax purposes, a company's accounting periods are the same as its accounting periods for corporation tax purposes. Where a non-UK resident company is not within the charge to corporation tax and the conditions at **30.7**(b) and (d) below apply, the company is assumed to have such accounting periods for corporation tax purposes as it would have had if it had carried on a trade in the UK through a UK permanent establishment by reason of the activity of the avoided PE. Where HMRC have insufficient information to identify the accounting periods of such a company, they will determine them to the best of their information and belief. Where a company (C1) does not have an accounting period which coincides with an accounting period of another company (C2), references to the '*corresponding accounting period*' of C1 in relation to an accounting period of C2 are to a notional accounting period that would coincide with C2's accounting period. Just and reasonable apportionments are to be made to determine the income or tax liability of C1 for the corresponding accounting period.

[*FA 2015, ss 111, 113*].

Partnerships

[30.3] Where a person is a member of a partnership, references in this chapter to the expenses, income or revenue of, or a reduction in the income of, that person include that person's share of the expenses etc. of the partnership. '*Partnership*' includes a limited liability partnership to which **56.11** PARTNERSHIPS applies and an entity established under the law of a territory outside the UK which is of a similar character to a partnership. [*FA 2015, ss 112, 114(1)*].

When diverted profits tax may apply

[30.4] A company may be liable to diverted profits tax for an accounting period only if it falls within one or more of the following categories:

- UK companies — involvement of entities or transactions lacking economic substance;

- non-UK companies — involvement of entities or transactions lacking economic substance;
- non-UK companies avoiding a UK taxable presence.

[*FA 2015, s 77(2)*].

Involvement of entities or transactions lacking economic substance — UK companies

[30.5] A company (C) which is UK resident in an accounting period may be liable to diverted profits tax for that period if:

(a) provision (the '*material provision*') has been made or imposed between C, or a partnership of which C is a member, and another person (P) (whether or not that person is UK resident) by means of a transaction or series of transactions;
(b) at the time of the making or imposition of the material provision or, so far as the provision relates to 'financing arrangements', within the six months beginning with that time, either:
  (i) C or P was directly or indirectly participating in the management, control or capital of the other; or
  (ii) the same person or persons were directly or indirectly participating in the management, control or capital of both C and P;
(c) the material provision results in an 'effective tax mismatch outcome' (see below) between C and P for the accounting period;
(d) the effective tax mismatch outcome does not wholly arise from a loan relationship or from a loan relationship and a derivative contract taken together, where the derivative contract is entered into entirely to hedge a risk in connection with the loan relationship;
(e) the insufficient economic substance condition below is met; and
(f) C and P are not both small or medium-sized enterprises (as defined for TRANSFER PRICING purposes (see **72.6**)) for the accounting period.

In (b) above, '*financing arrangements*' are arrangements made for providing or guaranteeing, or otherwise in connection with, any debt, capital or other forms of finance. Whether a person is directly or indirectly participating in the management, control or capital of another is determined according to the same rules as apply for TRANSFER PRICING (see **72.2**).

Effective tax mismatch outcome

The material provision results in an '*effective tax mismatch outcome*' between C and P for an accounting period of C if:

(1) in the accounting period it results in expenses of C for which a deduction has been taken into account in computing tax payable by C and/or a reduction in C's income which would otherwise have been taken into account in computing tax payable by C;
(2) the resulting reduction in tax payable by C is greater than the resulting increase in tax payable by P for its corresponding accounting period; and
(3) the resulting increase in tax payable by P is less than 80% of the resulting reduction in tax payable by C.

It does not matter whether or not the overall '*tax reduction*' (i.e. the excess of C's tax reduction over the increase in P's tax liability) results from the application of different tax rates, the operation of a relief, the exclusion of an amount from a charge to tax, or otherwise.

The following taxes are taken into account in (1) and (2) above: corporation tax on income; sums chargeable under *CTA 2010, s 269DA* (bank surcharge — see 7.3 BANKS); ring fence trade supplementary charge under *CTA 2010, s 330(1)*; income tax; and any non-UK tax on income. Withholding tax on payments made to P is treated as tax payable by P unless it is refunded.

There is no effective tax mismatch outcome if the results in (1) above arise solely from employer contributions to a registered pension scheme or overseas pension scheme (as defined) in respect of any individual; from a payment to a charity or a person who cannot be liable to any of the relevant taxes because of sovereign immunity; or from a payment to an offshore fund or authorised investment fund which meets the genuine diversity of ownership condition (see **46.13** INVESTMENT FUNDS and **55.4** OFFSHORE FUNDS) or at least 75% of the investors in which are registered or overseas pension schemes, charities or persons who cannot be liable to any of the relevant taxes because of sovereign immunity. Where HMRC consider that these exemptions are being exploited in order to facilitate profit diversion HMRC will seek to deny the benefit of the exemption, including through use of the general anti-abuse rule (see **4.3** ANTI-AVOIDANCE). (HMRC International Manual INTTM489750).

For the purposes of (2) and (3) above, the resulting reduction in tax payable by C for an accounting period is:

A × TR

where A is the sum of any reduction in income within (1) above and, where there are expenses within (1) above, the lower of the expenses and the deduction taken into account in respect of them; and TR is the rate at which C would be chargeable to the tax in question for the accounting period on profits equal to A.

For the purposes of (2) and (3) above, the resulting increase in tax payable by P for the corresponding accounting period is any increase in tax that would be paid by P (and not refunded) on the following assumptions:

(A) P's income for the period as a result of the material provision is an amount equal to A;

(B) account is taken of any deduction or relief (other than a qualifying deduction or loss relief (see below)) taken into account by P in computing its actual liability to tax in consequence of the material provision; and

(C) all further reasonable steps are taken under UK law, the law of any country or territory outside the UK or double tax arrangements to minimise the amount of tax paid by P in the country or territory concerned (other than steps to secure the benefit of a qualifying deduction or loss relief). Such steps include claiming, or obtaining the benefit of, relief, deductions, reductions or allowances and making tax elections.

In (B) and (C) above, a qualifying deduction is one which is made in respect of actual expenditure by P; which does not arise directly from the making or imposition of the material provision; which is of a kind for which C would have obtained a tax deduction if it had incurred the expenditure for which the deduction is given; and which does not exceed the deduction C would have so obtained. A qualifying loss relief is any means by which a loss might be used for corporation tax purposes to reduce P's tax liability and, in the case of a non-UK resident company, any corresponding means by which a loss corresponding to a corporation tax loss might be used for the purposes of a non-UK tax corresponding to corporation tax to reduce P's tax liability.

Tax payable by P is refunded for these purposes only to the extent that any repayment of, or credit for, tax is made to any person directly or indirectly in respect of all or part of the tax payable by P. An amount refunded is, however, ignored to the extent that it results from qualifying loss relief obtained by P.

Partnerships

Where P is a partnership, references to P's tax liability and to tax payable by P above are taken to include the tax liabilities of, and tax payable by, all members of the partnership. References to loss relief obtained by P are taken to include loss relief obtained by any member. Withholding tax on payments made to a member is treated as tax payable by the member unless it is refunded.

Insufficient economic substance

The insufficient economic substance condition is met if the effective tax mismatch outcome is referable either to a single transaction or any one or more of the transactions in a series of transactions and it is reasonable to assume that the transaction or transactions were designed to secure the tax reduction. This does not apply, however, if at the time of making or imposing the material provision it was reasonable to assume that, for C and P taken together and taking account of all accounting periods for which the transaction or series would have effect, their non-tax financial benefits would exceed the financial benefits of the tax reduction.

The condition is also met if a person is party to the transaction, or one or more of the transactions in the series of transactions, in (a) above and it is reasonable to assume that their involvement was designed to secure the tax reduction. This does not apply, however, if at the time of making or imposing the material provision it was reasonable to assume that, for C and P taken together and taking account of all accounting periods for which the transaction or series would have effect, the non-tax financial benefits from the contribution made to the transaction or series by that person, in terms of the functions or activities of their 'staff', would exceed the financial benefits of the tax reduction. The condition is also not met if, in the accounting period, the income attributable to the ongoing function or activities of the person's staff in terms of their contribution to the transactions or transactions exceeds the other income attributable to the transaction or transactions. For this purpose, functions or activities which relate to holding, maintaining or protecting any asset from which income attributable to the transaction or transactions derives is ignored.

A person's '*staff*' include directors and other officers of the person and any externally provided workers (as defined at **63.5** RESEARCH AND DEVELOPMENT EXPENDITURE, but substituting references to 'company' with 'person'). If the person is a partnership, individual members of the partnership are staff. '*Tax*' includes non-UK tax.

In determining for the above purposes whether an assumption is reasonable, regard must be had to all the circumstances, including any additional liability for tax arising from the transaction or transactions. A transaction or transactions, or a person's involvement in them, may be designed to secure the tax reduction even if they are also designed to secure a commercial or other objective.

[*FA 2015, ss 80, 106–110*].

Involvement of entities or transactions lacking economic substance — non-UK companies

[30.6] A company which is non-UK resident in an accounting period may be liable to diverted profits tax for that period if:

(i) the company carries on a trade in the UK through a UK permanent establishment (which is subject to corporation tax under the provisions at **64.6** RESIDENCE); and
(ii) the provisions at **30.5** above would apply to the UK permanent establishment for the period if it were treated as:
  - a distinct and separate person from the company (whether or not it would otherwise be so treated);
  - as a UK resident company under the same control (within *CTA 2010, s 1124*) as the foreign company; and
  - as having entered into any transaction or series of transactions entered into by the foreign company, but only to the extent that it is relevant to the permanent establishment. For this purpose, a transaction or series of transactions is relevant to the permanent establishment only to the extent that it is relevant in determining the corporation tax profits under the provisions at **64.6** RESIDENCE.

Where a non-UK company operates on the UK continental shelf and the profits are treated for corporation tax purposes (by *CTA 2009, s 1313(2)*) as the profits of a trade carried on in the UK through a UK permanent establishment, the above provisions apply as if the company did in fact trade in the UK through that permanent establishment.

[*FA 2015, s 81*].

Non-UK companies avoiding a UK taxable presence

[30.7] A company (FC) which is non-UK resident in an accounting period may be liable to diverted profits tax for that period if:

(a) it carries on a trade during all or part of the period;
(b) a person (the '*avoided PE*'), whether or not UK resident, carries on activity in the UK in the period in connection with supplies of services, goods or other property made by FC in the course of its trade;

(c) the exception below for companies with limited UK-related sales or expenses does not apply;
(d) it is reasonable to assume that any of the activity of the avoided PE or FC (or both) is designed to ensure that, as a result of the avoided PE's activity, FC does not carry on the trade in the UK for corporation tax purposes (whether or not it is also designed to secure any commercial or other objective);
(e) the mismatch condition below and/or the tax avoidance condition below are met;
(f) the avoided PE is not 'excepted' (see below); and
(g) the avoided PE and FC are not both small or medium-sized enterprises (as defined for TRANSFER PRICING purposes (see **72.6**)) for the accounting period

In (d) above, '*activity*' includes any limitation imposed or agreed in respect of that activity.

In (f) above, the avoided PE is '*excepted*' if its activity is such that FC would not be treated as carrying on a trade in the UK through a permanent establishment as a result of the activity because of either the exclusion for agents of independent status or that for alternative finance arrangements (see **64.6**(i)(iii) RESIDENCE); and, where the avoided PE is not an agent of independent status only because of the rules for brokers, investment managers and members or managing agents at Lloyd's, the company and the avoided PE are not connected at any time in the accounting period.

Where FC is a member of a partnership, a trade carried on by the partnership is treated for the purposes of the above provisions as carried on by FC and supplies made in the course of the trade are treated as made by FC in the course of the trade.

The mismatch condition

The mismatch condition in (e) above is that:

(i) in connection with the supply of services etc. in (b) above (or in connection with those and other supplies), arrangements are in place under which provision (the '*material provision*') is made or imposed between FC, or a partnership of which FC is a member, and another person (A) by means of a transaction or series of transactions;
(ii) at the time of the making or imposition of the material provision or, so far as the provision relates to 'financing arrangements', within the six months beginning with that time, either:
    (i) FC or A was directly or indirectly participating in the management, control or capital of the other; or
    (ii) the same person or persons were directly or indirectly participating in the management, control or capital of both FC and A;
(iii) the material provision results in an 'effective tax mismatch outcome' (see below) between FC and A for the accounting period;
(iv) the effective tax mismatch outcome does not wholly arise from a loan relationship or from a loan relationship and a derivative contract taken together, where the derivative contract is entered into entirely to hedge a risk in connection with the loan relationship;

(v) the insufficient economic substance condition below is met; and
(vi) FC and A are not both small or medium-sized enterprises for the accounting period.

In (ii) above, '*financing arrangements*' are arrangements made for providing or guaranteeing, or otherwise in connection with, any debt, capital or other forms of finance. Whether a person is directly or indirectly participating in the management, control or capital of another is determined according to the same rules as apply for TRANSFER PRICING (see **72.2**). In (iii) above, 'effective tax mismatch outcome' has the same meaning as at **30.5** above, but substituting FC for C and A for P. Similarly, the insufficient economic substance condition is as at **30.5** above, making the same substitutions. 'Arrangements' include any agreement, understanding, scheme, transaction or series of transactions (whether or not legally enforceable).

The tax avoidance condition

The tax avoidance condition is that, in connection with the supplies of services etc in (b) above (or in connection with those and other supplies), arrangements are in place a main purpose of which is to avoid or reduce a charge to corporation tax.

Limited UK-related sales or expenses

FC is not liable to diverted profits tax under the above provisions if its 'UK-related sales revenues' and the UK-related sales revenues of companies connected with it for the accounting period do not exceed £10,000,000 in total.

FC is also not liable to diverted profits tax if the total expenses relating to the activity in (b) above incurred by it and any companies connected with it do not exceed £1,000,000.

For accounting periods of less than twelve months, the £10,000,000 and £1,000,000 amounts are reduced proportionately. The amounts may be amended by Treasury regulations.

'*UK-related sales revenues*' of FC are its sales revenues from supplies of services, goods or other property which relate to the activity in (b) above. '*UK-related sales revenues*' of a company connected with FC are its sales revenues to the extent that they are from supplies of services, goods or other property which relate to the activity in (b) above and are trading receipts not taken into account in calculating the company's corporation tax profits.

'*Revenues*' and '*expenses*' for these purposes are those recognised in accordance with generally accepted accounting practice (GAAP) in the company's profit and loss account or income statement for the period (or which would be so recognised if the company drew up accounts for the period in accordance with GAAP).

[*FA 2015, ss 86, 87, 106–110*].

The charge to diverted profits tax

[30.8] Diverted profits tax for an accounting period is imposed by HMRC issuing a charging notice (see **30.16** below) to the company. The tax is generally charged at a rate of 25% of the amount of the 'taxable diverted profits' specified in the charging notice. The rate is 55%, however, to the extent that the diverted profits are within the oil industry ring fence or would be if they were chargeable to corporation tax. The rate is 33% to the extent that the diverted profits are 'surcharge profits' within the bank surcharge (see **7.3** BANKS) or would be if they were chargeable to corporation tax. For this purpose, surcharge profits or profits which would be surcharge profits if they were chargeable to corporation tax, to the extent that they are determined by reference to notional PE profits (see **30.10** below), do not include any amount included in notional PE profits under **30.10**(2) below.

If the charging notice is issued more than six months after the end of the accounting period, a further amount of tax is added representing interest for the period beginning six months after the end of the period and ending on the day the notice is issued. The rate of interest is 2.5% per annum (3% per annum for the period 1 October 2015 to 5 April 2017).

The 25% rate is to increase to 31% for accounting periods beginning on or after 1 April 2023. Accounting periods which straddle 1 April 2023 are treated for this purpose only as two separate periods, the second of which begins on that date. Any necessary apportionments must be made on a time basis. The 55% and 33% rates will remain unchanged.

[*FA 2015, s 79; FA 2019, s 88(4)(5); FA 2021, s 8; SI 1989 No 1297, Reg 5A*].

The '*taxable diverted profits*' for an accounting period are determined by applying the rules at **30.9** below where **30.5** or **30.6** above apply (i.e. where there is involvement of entities or transactions lacking economic substance) and by applying the rules at **30.10** below where **30.7** above applies (i.e. where a non-UK company avoids a UK taxable presence).

Taxable diverted profits — involvement of entities or transactions lacking economic substance

[30.9] Where **30.5** or **30.6** above apply (i.e. where there is involvement of entities or transactions lacking economic substance) the taxable diverted profits for an accounting period are determined by applying the rules described below.

For the purpose of those rules, the '*actual provision condition*' is met if:

(i) the material provision (see **30.5** above) results in expenses of the company for which (ignoring any adjustment required under the TRANSFER PRICING (72) rules) a deduction would be allowed in computing the company's corporation tax liability (where **30.5** above applies) or in computing its chargeable profits attributable to the UK permanent establishment (where **30.6** above applies); and

(ii) the 'alternative provision' would also have resulted in allowable expenses of the same type and for the same purposes (whether or not payable to the same person) as so much of the expenses in (i) above as result in the effective tax mismatch outcome (see **30.5** above), but would not have resulted in 'taxable income' of a 'connected company' for its corresponding accounting period.

In (ii) above, the '*alternative provision*' is the provision which it is just and reasonable to assume would have been made or imposed between the company and one or more companies connected with it instead of the material provision if tax on income (including any non-UK tax) had not been a consideration. For this purpose, making or imposing no provision is treated as making or imposing an alternative provision. '*Taxable income*' of a company is income which would have resulted from the alternative provision and which would have been with the charge to corporation tax, less any allowable expenses which it is just and reasonable to assume would have been incurred in earning the income. A '*connected company*' is a company which is or, if the alternative provision had been made, would have been connected with the company in question.

'*Diverted profits*' for an accounting period are the amount chargeable to corporation tax as a result of any adjustments required to be made under the TRANSFER PRICING (72) provisions to the result of the material provision and, where **30.6** above applies, which is attributable to the UK permanent establishment. For this purpose (and for the purposes of the provisions below), for accounting periods beginning on or after 29 October 2018, an adjustment required to be made to the result of any provision under any tax rule other than the TRANSFER PRICING (72) rules is treated as required to be made under the transfer pricing rules to the extent that an adjustment under those rules would have been required if not for the adjustment actually required.

No taxable diverted profits

No taxable diverted profits arise to a company for an accounting period from a particular material provision if:

(a) the actual provision condition is met; and
(b) either there are no diverted profits of the company for the period; or all of the company's diverted profits for the period are taken into account in a corporation tax assessment included in the company's return for the period before the end of the review period (see **30.16** below).

Taxable diverted profits calculated by reference to actual provision

If the actual provision condition is met, but (b) above does not apply, the taxable diverted profits from a particular material provision for an accounting period are an amount equal to so much of the diverted profits as are not taken into account in a corporation tax assessment included in the company's return for the period before the end of the review period (see **30.16** below). For accounting periods beginning before 29 October 2018, the taxable diverted profits from a material provision are the amount which is:

(1) chargeable to corporation tax as a result of the application of the TRANSFER PRICING (72) provisions to the results of the material provision;
(2) where **30.6** above applies, attributable to the UK permanent establishment; and
(3) not taken into account in a corporation tax assessment included in the company's return for the period before the end of the review period (see **30.16** below).

Taxable diverted profits calculated by reference to alternative provision

If the actual provision condition is not met, the taxable diverted profits from a particular material provision for an accounting period are:

(A) if the actual provision condition would have been met but for the fact that taxable income of a connected company for its corresponding accounting period would have resulted from the alternative provision, the sum of so much of the diverted profits as are not taken into account in a corporation tax assessment included in the company's return for the period before the end of the review period (for accounting periods beginning before 29 October 2019, the amount given by applying (1)–(3) above) and the amount of any such taxable income; or

(B) in any other case, the sum of the notional 'additional amount' arising from the alternative provision and any taxable income of a connected company, for that company's corresponding accounting period, which would have resulted from the alternative provision.

The '*additional amount*' is the additional amount on which the company would have been chargeable to corporation tax for the period had the alternative provision been made or imposed instead of the material provision (ignored any adjustment required to the results of the material provision under the TRANSFER PRICING (72) provisions) less the amount which is:

- chargeable to corporation tax as a result any adjustment required to be made under the TRANSFER PRICING (72) provisions to the results of the material provision;
- where **30.6** above applies, attributable to the UK permanent establishment; and
- taken into account in a corporation tax assessment included in the company's return for the period before the end of the review period (see **30.16** below).

[*FA 2015, ss 82–85, 111A; FA 2019, Sch 6 paras 2–5, 7, 8*].

Taxable diverted profits — non-UK company avoiding UK taxable presence

[30.10] Where 30.7 above applies (i.e. where a non-UK company avoids a UK taxable presence) the taxable diverted profits for an accounting period are determined by applying the rules described below.

For the purpose of those rules, the '*actual provision condition*' is met if:

(i) the material provision (see **30.7** above) results in expenses of FC for which (ignoring any adjustment required to the results of the material provision under the TRANSFER PRICING (72) rules) a deduction would be allowed in computing what would have been the 'notional PE profits' for the accounting period; and

(ii) the 'alternative provision' would also have resulted in allowable expenses of the same type and for the same purposes (whether or not payable to the same person) as so much of the expenses in (i) above as result in the effective tax mismatch outcome (see **30.7** above), but would not have resulted in 'taxable income' of a 'connected company' for its corresponding accounting period.

For this purpose (and those below), for accounting periods beginning on or after 29 October 2018, an adjustment required to be made to the result of any provision under any tax rule other than the TRANSFER PRICING (72) rules is treated as required to be made under the transfer pricing rules to the extent that an adjustment under those rules would have been required if not for the adjustment actually required.

In (i) above, the '*notional PE profits*' are the sum of:

(1) the profits which would have been the profits of FC for the accounting period, attributable for corporation tax purposes to the avoided PE (see **30.7** above) if the avoided PE had been a UK permanent establishment through which FC carried on the trade; and
(2) the total of royalties or other sums paid by FC during the period in connection with the trade in circumstances where the payment avoids the application of *ITA 2007, s 906* (duty to deduct tax — see **41.2**(d) INCOME TAX IN RELATION TO A COMPANY). For this purpose, a payment avoids the application of *ITA 2007, s 906* if that section does not apply to it but would have applied had the avoided PE been a UK permanent establishment.

For accounting periods beginning on or after 29 October 2018, in calculating the notional PE profits, no account is taken of any adjustment required to be made under the TRANSFER PRICING (72) rules to the results of any provision made or imposed between FC and the avoided PE if it is only taken into account in a corporation tax assessment included in a return of the avoided PE after the end of the review period (see **30.16** below).

In (ii) above, the '*alternative provision*' is the provision which it is just and reasonable to assume would have been made or imposed between FC and one or more companies connected with it instead of the material provision if tax on income (including any non-UK tax) had not been a consideration. For this purpose, making or imposing no provision is treated as making or imposing an alternative provision. '*Taxable income*' of a company is income which would have resulted from the alternative provision and which would have been with the charge to corporation tax, less any allowable expenses which it is just and reasonable to assume would have been incurred in earning the income. A '*connected company*' is a company which is or, if the alternative provision had been made, would have been connected with FC.

Only tax avoidance condition met

Where the tax avoidance condition at **29.4** above is met, but the mismatch condition at **29.4** above is not, FC's taxable diverted profits for the accounting period in question are the notional PE profits for the period.

Mismatch and actual provision conditions met

Where the mismatch and actual provision conditions are both met, FC's taxable diverted profits for the accounting period in relation to the material provision concerned are the notional PE profits for the period.

Only mismatch condition met

Where the mismatch condition is met but the actual provision condition is not, FC's taxable diverted profits for the accounting period in relation to the material provision in question are as follows:

- if the actual provision condition would have been met but for the fact that taxable income of a connected company for its corresponding accounting period would have resulted from the alternative provision, the sum of the notional PE profits for the period and the amount of any such taxable income; or
- in any other case, the sum of what would have been the notional PE profits had the alternative provision been made instead of the material provision and any taxable income of a connected company, for that company's corresponding accounting period, which would have resulted from the alternative provision.

[*FA 2015, ss 88–91, 111A; FA 2019, Sch 6 paras 6–8*].

Credit for UK or foreign tax

[30.11] A credit is allowed against a liability to diverted profits tax for certain UK and foreign tax paid in respect of the same profits. Credits are given on a just and reasonable basis.

Where a company has paid corporation tax or a corresponding foreign tax (including where the tax is imposed by a province, state or other part of a country or on behalf of a municipality or other local body) in respect of particular profits, a credit is allowed against that company's liability to diverted profits tax in respect of the same profits or against another company's liability to diverted profits tax which is calculated by reference to the same profits. No credit is allowed against the other company's liability to diverted profits tax if or to the extent that the liability arises under **30.10**(2) above. Withholding tax paid (and not refunded) on payments made to a person are treated for this purpose as corporation tax or a corresponding foreign tax paid by the recipient.

Where a company has paid a controlled foreign companies (CFC) charge or a similar non-UK charge which is calculated by reference to profits of another company (the '*CFC profits*'), a credit is allowed against any liability which a company has to diverted profits tax in respect of taxable diverted profits of that company which are calculated by reference to amounts which also constitute all or part of the CFC profits.

Where a company's notional PE profits for an accounting period include an amount within **30.10**(2) above and the company's liability to diverted profits tax for the period is determined by reference to the rules applicable where only the mismatch condition is met (see **30.10** above), a credit is allowed against the company's liability to diverted profits tax equal to the amount which is both included in taxable income for the purposes of those rules and in the notional PE profits under **30.10**(2) above.

Where by reason of payment of a royalty or other sum paid to a non-UK resident a company's liability to diverted profits tax for an accounting period includes liability arising under **30.10**(2) above and double tax relief or exemption under *ITTOIA 2005, s 758* (prior to its repeal; see **41.6** INCOME TAX IN RELATION TO A COMPANY) would have been due to the payee had the avoided PE been a UK permanent establishment, a credit is allowed against the company's diverted profits tax liability, calculated having regard to the amount of the relief or exemption.

No credit is allowed for an amount paid after the end of the review period (see **30.16** below) in respect of the charging notice in question or, where the diverted profits tax was imposed by a supplementary charging notice, after the end of the review period in which that notice was issued.

[*FA 2015, ss 100, 114(2); FA 2021, s 34(5)*].

Relief from corporation tax

[30.12] Where a charge to diverted profits tax has become final (i.e., where, following the review period, no appeal has been made against a charging notice or supplementary charging notice or an appeal has been withdrawn or finally determined otherwise than by the notice being cancelled — see **30.16** below), the taxable diverted profits are not chargeable to corporation tax.

Note that this provision was introduced by *FA 2019* but has retrospective effect from the introduction of diverted profits tax from 1 April 2015.

Procedures and compliance for diverted profits tax

[30.13] The procedure under which diverted profits tax is charged is described in summary below. For the detailed provisions see the paragraphs indicated in the list.

(1) A company within the charge to diverted profits tax must notify HMRC within three months of the end of the accounting period (six months for periods ending before 1 April 2016) (see **30.14** below).

(2) HMRC must issue a preliminary notice to a company for an accounting period if they have reason to believe that a charge to diverted profits tax applies, and taxable diverted profits arise, in the period, setting out the details of a proposed charge to diverted profits tax. A notice issued on the basis that **30.5** or **30.6** above apply must be issued within six months after the normal time limit for amending the tax return for the accounting period. A notice issued on the basis that **30.7** above applies must be issued within two years of the accounting period. In either case, where no notification under (1) above has been given, a notice must be issued within four years of the accounting period. See **30.15** below.

(3) The company then has 30 days to make representations to HMRC about the preliminary notice. See **30.15** below.

(4) Within 60 days of the issuing of the preliminary notice HMRC must either issue a charging notice, containing a charge to diverted profits tax, or notify the company that no such notice will be issued. See **30.16** below.

(5) The diverted profits tax must be paid within 30 days after the date on which the charging notice is issued. There are provisions enabling the tax to be collected from a company's UK representative or from certain related companies. See **30.18** below.

(6) Following the issue of the charging notice there is then a 15-month review period (previously one year) in which HMRC must review the notice at least once. If the company has paid the tax, HMRC may issue one or more amending notices reducing the amount charged. If HMRC consider that the charge is insufficient they may issue one supplementary charging notice imposing an additional charge. The review period starts immediately after the date on which the tax is due and payable and can be brought to an early end by agreement between HMRC and the company or by the company alone following the issuing of a supplementary charging notice. See **30.16** below.

(7) After the end of the review period the company has 30 days to appeal against the charging notice and any supplementary charging notice. See **30.16** below.

Duty to notify HMRC

[30.14] A company must notify HMRC if:

- it is within **30.5** or **30.6** above for an accounting period and in that period the financial benefit of the tax reduction (see **30.5** above) is significant compared to the non-tax financial benefits of the material provision; or
- it is within **30.7** above for an accounting period and, where the mismatch condition is met, in that period the financial benefit of the tax reduction is significant compared to the non-tax financial benefits of the material provision.

In determining for this purpose whether a company is within **30.5** or **30.6** above, the insufficient economic substance condition at **30.5**(e) above is ignored. In determining whether a company is within **30.7** above:

- the condition at **30.7**(d) above is taken to be that FC is not, as a result of the avoided PE's activity, within the charge to corporation tax by reason of carrying on a trade in the UK;
- the insufficient economic substance condition at **30.7**(v) is ignored; and
- the tax avoidance condition at **30.7** above is taken to be that, in connection with the supplies of services etc in **30.7**(b) above (or in connection with those and other supplies), arrangements are in place that result in the reduction of a charge to corporation tax as a result of which there is an overall reduction in the amount of tax (including non-UK tax) payable in respect of the UK activity.

Notification must be made in writing within the three months beginning at the end of the accounting period. For accounting periods ending before 1 April 2016, the three month notification period is extended to six months. A notification must state which of the provisions at **30.5**, **30.6** or **30.7** apply and, where relevant, the name of the avoided PE (see **30.7** above). Where **30.5** or **30.6** above apply, or where **30.7** above applies and the mismatch condition is met, the notification must also include a description of the material provision and the parties to it.

Notification is not required where:

(i) at the end of the period allowed for notifying HMRC (the '*notification period*') it is reasonable, ignoring the possibility of future TRANSFER PRICING (72) adjustments, for the company to conclude that no charge to diverted profits tax will arise for the accounting period;

(ii) HMRC confirm before the end of the notification period that notification is not required because the company, or a company connected with it, has already provided enough information for HMRC to decide whether or not to issue a preliminary notice (see **30.15** below) and HMRC has examined that information;

(iii) at the end of the notification period it is reasonable for the company to conclude that it, or a company connected with it, has already provided enough information for HMRC to decide whether or not to issue a preliminary notice and that HMRC has examined that information;

(iv) either a notification was given for the immediately preceding accounting period or a notification for that period was not required because (ii) or (iii) above applied and it is reasonable for the company to conclude at the end of the notification period of the accounting period in question that there has been no material change in circumstances; or

(v) HMRC make a direction that notification is not required in other specified circumstances.

The fact that notification is not required does not mean that a charge to diverted profits tax cannot arise.

HMRC recommend that notification should be sent to the diverted profits tax email address: divertedprofits.notification@hmrc.gsi.gov.uk . Companies may, however, send notifications to Diverted Profits Tax Unit, Large Business, S0791, Newcastle, NE98 1ZZ. Companies should also send a copy to their customer relationship managers. (HMRC International Manual INTM489898).

Failure to make a notification under these provisions may result in a penalty under *FA 2008, Sch 41* (see **59.2** PENALTIES).

[*FA 2015, ss 92, 116(3)*].

Preliminary notices

[30.15] If an HMRC officer designated for the purpose has reason to believe that a charge to diverted profits tax applies, and taxable diverted profits arise, to a company in an accounting period he must give the company a preliminary notice for the period. A notice can be given whether or not a notification under **30.14** above has been given. The notice must state the accounting period to which it applies and:

- set out the basis on which the officer has reason to believe that a charge to diverted profits tax applies;
- include details of the proposed charge and explain how the charge has been calculated, including how the taxable diverted profits have been determined; where relevant, details of the alternative provision used to determine the profits; and how the interest element of the tax would be calculated;
- state who would be liable to pay the tax; and

- explain how late payment interest under *FA 2009, s 101* (see **43.4** INTEREST ON OVERDUE TAX) will apply if the tax is not paid.

Where the HMRC officer has insufficient information to determine the above details, it is enough for them to be determined to the best of the officer's information and belief. See **30.17** below for how taxable diverted profits are estimated.

A preliminary notice issued on the basis that **30.5** or **30.6** above apply must be issued within six months after the time limit for amending the tax return for the accounting period (see **65.8** RETURNS), ignoring any exceptions to that time limit. A preliminary notice issued on the basis that **30.7** above applies must be issued within 24 months after the accounting period. The 24-month time limit previously also applied to notices issued on the basis that **30.5** or **30.6** above apply, where the 24 months expired before 12 February 2019.

If the company has not notified HMRC under **30.14** above within the notification period and HMRC believe that an amount of diverted profits tax which ought to have been charged has not been charged, a notice may be issued within four years after the accounting period.

Where relevant, a copy of the notice must be given to the UK permanent establishment (see **30.6** above) or the avoided PE (see **30.7** above).

[*FA 2015, s 93; FA 2019, Sch 6 para 9*].

Representations by the company

A company to which a preliminary notice has been issued may make written representations to the HMRC officer who issued it within the 30 days beginning with the day the notice is issued. The officer will consider representations only if they are made on the following grounds:

(i) that there is an arithmetical error in calculating the profits or the tax or an error in a figure on which an assumption in the notice is based;

(ii) that the small or medium-sized enterprise requirement at **30.5**(f) or **30.7**(g) or (vi) above is not met;

(iii) where the notice states that **30.5** or **30.6** above applies, that any of the requirements at **30.5**(b), (d) or (3) above are not met;

(iv) where the notice states that **30.7** above applies, that the exception for companies with limited UK-related sales or expenses applies or that the avoided PE is excepted; or

(v) where the notice states that **30.7** above applies and that the mismatch condition is met, that that condition is not met because the requirements at **30.7**(ii) or (iv) or that at **30.5**(3) (as applied for the purposes of **30.7** above) are not met.

Unless there are representations about arithmetical errors, nothing in the above list requires the HMRC officer to consider representations about any TRANSFER PRICING (**72**) provision or the attribution of profits to a UK permanent establishment through which a company carries on a trade (including any notional attribution as in **30.10** above).

[*FA 2015, s 94*].

Charging notice

[30.16] Having considered any representations following the issue of a preliminary notice (see **30.15** above), the HMRC officer must either issue a charging notice to the company or notify the company that such a notice will not be issued (in pursuance of the preliminary notice in question — HMRC are not prevented from issuing a charging notice in pursuance of another preliminary notice for the same accounting period). The officer must take either action within the sixty days beginning with the date of issue of the preliminary notice. Where relevant, a copy of the notice must be given to the UK permanent establishment (see **30.6** above) or the avoided PE (see **30.7** above). The notice must state the accounting period to which it applies and:

- set out the basis on which the officer considers that a charge to diverted profits tax applies;
- state the amount of the charge imposed by the notice and explain how it has been calculated, including how the taxable diverted profits have been determined; where relevant, details of the alternative provision used to determine the profits; and how the interest element of the tax has been calculated;
- state who is liable to pay the tax and when the tax is due and payable; and
- explain how late payment interest under *FA 2009, s 101* (see **43.4** INTEREST ON OVERDUE TAX) will apply if the tax is not paid.

See **30.17** below for how taxable diverted profits are estimated.

[*FA 2015, s 95*].

HMRC review of notice

Following the issuing of a charging notice an HMRC officer must carry out a review of the amount of diverted profits tax charged on the company for the accounting period (and may carry out more than one such review). The review must be carried out within the period (the '*review period*') of 15 months beginning immediately after the date on which the tax is due and payable. The review period may be brought to an end early if the company and the HMRC officer agree (in writing) or if, following the issuing of a supplementary charging notice (see below) the company notifies HMRC that it is terminating the period. The review period was previously 12 months; the longer 15-month period applies where the period would otherwise have expired on or after 29 October 2018.

If an HMRC officer is satisfied that the diverted profits tax charged on a company for an accounting period is insufficient he may, during the review period, issue a supplementary charging notice imposing an additional charge to tax. Only one such notice may be issued in respect of a charging notice. A supplementary charging notice may not be issued during the last thirty days of the review period. Such a notice must contain the same information as a charging notice

If the company has paid the tax charged by a charging notice or a supplementary charging notice in full and the officer is satisfied that the amount of the tax is excessive, he may, during the review period, issue an amending notice to reduce the amount of the taxable diverted profits and the tax charged in the charging notice. Any tax overpaid will then be repaid. More than one amending notice may be issued in respect of a charging notice or supplementary charging notice.

In determining whether the taxable diverted profits for an accounting period are excessive or insufficient, the HMRC officer must not take any account of the provisions at **30.17** below. The restrictions on the type of representations which may be considered following the issuing of a preliminary notice (see **30.15** above) do not apply to restrict the representations which the officer may consider during the review period.

Where relevant, copies of any amending or supplementary charging notices must be given to the UK permanent establishment (see **30.6** above) or the avoided PE (see **30.7** above).

[*FA 2015, s 101; FA 2019, Sch 6 para 11*].

In *R (oao Glencore Energy UK Ltd) v HMRC* CA 2017, [2018] STC 51, the court held that HMRC were required to consider both the amount of the liability and whether or not any liability arose in their review. The company's application for judicial review was refused on the basis that the review process was an adequate alternative remedy.

Amendment of CT return during review period

With effect from 12 February 2019, the company or, where relevant, the avoided PE, may amend a company tax return made by it to reduce the taxable diverted profits at any time during the first twelve months of the review period. [*FA 2015, ss 101A, 101B; FA 2019, Sch 6 para 12*].

Appeals

A company may appeal against a charging notice or supplementary charging notice in writing, specifying the grounds of appeal, within 30 days after the end of the review period. On an appeal, the Tribunal may confirm, amend or cancel the charging or supplementary charging notice. The provisions at **30.17** below are ignored in determining for this purpose whether the taxable diverted profits have been correctly calculated. The appeal provisions which apply for corporation tax purposes apply for diverted profits tax purposes as if a charging notice or supplementary charging notice were an assessment. See **5 APPEALS**. Diverted profits tax may not, however, be postponed pending an appeal. [*FA 2015, s 102*].

Estimating profits for preliminary and charging notices

[30.17] The taxable diverted profits which are specified in a preliminary notice (see **30.15** above) or a charging notice (see **30.16** above) must be determined on the basis of the best estimate that can reasonably be made at the time applying the rules at **30.9** or **30.10** above as appropriate. This is subject to the following rules.

Involvement of entities or transactions lacking economic substance

Where taxable diverted profits would fall to be determined under the rules at **30.9** above and the HMRC officer issuing the notice considers that:

(i) the material provision results in expenses of the company for which a deduction has been taken into account in computing its corporation tax liability or, where **30.6** above applies, its chargeable profits attributable for corporation tax purposes to the UK permanent establishment;

(ii) the expenses (or part of them) result in the effective tax mismatch outcome (see **30.5** above);

(iii) the part of the expenses which result in the effective tax mismatch outcome might be greater than they would have been if they had resulted from provision made or imposed at arm's length between independent persons; and

(iv) it is reasonable to assume that either the actual provision condition at **30.9** above is met or it would have been met but for the fact that taxable income of a connected company for its corresponding accounting period would have resulted from the alternative provision;

the best estimate must be made on the assumption that so much of the deduction in (i) above as relates to any part of the expenses which result in the effective tax mismatch outcome is reduced by 30% and that the TRANSFER PRICING (72) provisions are ignored in relation to those expenses. The amount of the reduction is itself reduced where the deduction has already been reduced by a transfer pricing adjustment. The 30% reduction figure can be amended by Treasury regulations.

Non-UK company avoiding UK taxable presence

Where taxable diverted profits would fall to be determined under the rules at **30.10** above and the HMRC officer issuing the notice considers that:

(a) the mismatch condition (see **30.7** above) is met;

(b) the material provision results in expenses of FC for which (ignoring TRANSFER PRICING (72)) a deduction for allowable expenses would be allowed in computing the notional PE profits of FC for the accounting period;

(c) the expenses (or part of them) result in the effective tax mismatch outcome;

(d) the part of the expenses which result in the effective tax mismatch outcome might be greater than they would have been if they had resulted from provision made or imposed at arm's length between independent persons; and

(e) it is reasonable to assume that either the actual provision condition at **30.10** above is met or it would have been met but for the fact that taxable income of a connected company for its corresponding accounting period would have resulted from the alternative provision;

the best estimate must be made on the assumption that so much of the deduction in (i) above as relates to any part of the expenses which result in the effective tax mismatch outcome is reduced by 30% and that the TRANSFER PRICING (72) provisions are ignored in relation to those expenses. The 30% reduction figure can be amended by Treasury regulations.

[*FA 2015, ss 96, 97*].

Payment of tax

[30.18] Diverted profits tax charged by a charging notice or supplementary charging notice issued to a company must be paid by the company within 30 days after the day the notice is issued. Payment may not be postponed on any grounds: the tax remains due and payable despite any review or appeal (see **30.16** above). [*FA 2015, s 98*]. Failure to pay tax on time may result in a penalty under *FA 2009, Sch 56* (see **59.7** PENALTIES).

No deduction or other relief is allowed for diverted profits tax, and no account is taken of any amount paid for the purposes of meeting or reimbursing the cost of the tax, in computing income, profits or losses for any tax purposes. [*FA 2015, s 99*].

Recovery of tax payable by non-resident company

Where a company liable to diverted profits tax is not UK-resident, *CTA 2010, ss 969–972* (see **64.6** RESIDENCE) apply to enable recovery of the tax from the company's UK representative. For this purpose, an avoided PE (see **30.7** above) is treated as if it were a permanent establishment of the company (and therefore as its UK representative).

Where diverted profits tax charged on a non-UK resident company remains unpaid in whole or part at the end of the due date, the following companies may be served notice by HMRC requiring them to pay the tax.

(1) Any company which was, at any time in the 'relevant period', a 51% subsidiary (by reference to ordinary share capital) of the non-resident company, or of which the non-resident company was a 51% subsidiary, or where both were 51% subsidiaries of a third company.

(2) Any company which was, at any time during the 'relevant period', a member of a consortium which owned (see **35.19** GROUP RELIEF) the non-resident company at that time.

(3) Any company which was, at any time during the 'relevant period', a member of the same group (as for group relief purposes, see **35.3** GROUP RELIEF) as a company which was at that time a member of a consortium which owned (see **35.19** GROUP RELIEF) the non-resident company.

The '*relevant period*' is the period beginning twelve months before the start of the accounting period in question and ending when the unpaid tax became payable.

The notice may require payment, within 30 days of service, of the overdue tax or (in the case of a company within either or both of (2) and (3) above but not within (1) above) of an appropriate proportion of it (see *FA 2015, Sch 16 para 7*). A payment made in pursuance of a notice is not an allowable deduction in computing income, profits or losses for any tax purposes, but the paying company may recover the amount from the non-resident company. The notice must state the amount of the unpaid tax, the date it first became payable and the amount required to be paid by the recipient. For recovery and appeals purposes, the notice has effect as if it were a charging notice and the amount charged by it were an amount of diverted profits tax charged on the recipient.

HMRC have three years beginning with the date on which the charging notice or supplementary charging notice was issued in which to serve notice under these provisions.

[*FA 2015, Sch 16 paras 2–8*].

31

Double Tax Relief

Cross-references. See **21** CONTROLLED FOREIGN COMPANIES; **29.16** DISTRIBUTIONS **35.23** GROUP RELIEF; **64** RESIDENCE.

Simon's Taxes. See **D4.8, D4.9, D4.10, E6.4, F1, F2.**

Introduction to double tax relief

[31.1] This chapter considers the provisions within UK tax law that provide relief for double taxation suffered (as a tax charge in the UK and overseas) by a UK company on the same source of income.

The double tax relief provisions in this chapter do not apply to overseas income in the form of a distribution or dividend where the dividend exemption applies (see further **29.16** DISTRIBUTIONS). The provisions do apply to overseas dividends that are not exempt.

Where the same income is liable to be taxed in both the UK and another country, relief may be available in the following ways:

(a) under the specific terms of a double tax agreement between the UK and that other country — see **31.3** below [*TIOPA 2010, s 2*];

(b) under special arrangements with Ireland — see Tolley's Income Tax under Double Tax Relief; or
(c) under the unilateral double tax relief provisions contained in UK tax legislation — see **31.2** below. [*TIOPA 2010, s 18*].

An exemption from UK tax is available for the profits of foreign permanent establishments of UK resident companies. Companies can make an irrevocable election for the exemption to apply to their overseas permanent establishments. See further **31.7** below.

Unilateral relief

[31.2] Unilateral relief applies to taxes other than those for which credit is available under the bilateral double tax agreements in **31.17** below. The taxes are those payable under the law of any territory outside the UK and computed by reference to income or gain arising in that territory. They are allowed (to the extent defined below) as a credit against UK income tax or corporation tax paid on that income or gain by UK residents. Unilateral relief is not available if relief is available under a double tax agreement or in cases or circumstances in which such an agreement specifically prohibits relief.

Relief is only available against UK tax chargeable under the same category of income or gain under which the foreign income is chargeable (*George Wimpey International Ltd v Rolfe* (1989) 62 TC 597). Where appropriate an apportionment must be made to determine what part of income may be regarded as 'arising in' the overseas territory, and in making that apportionment it is the principles of UK tax law which are to be applied (see *Yates (Inspector of Taxes) v GCA International Ltd* [1991] STC 157, 64 TC 37 and HMRC Statement of Practice, SP 7/91, 16 July 1991).

The machinery and limits (with modifications as below) are substantially the same as those under which the bilateral agreements operate and the credit given is, basically, such as would be allowable were a double taxation agreement in force with the territory concerned.

A limit is placed on relief available for corporation tax where a non resident incurs overseas tax on the profits or capital gains of a UK permanent establishment. Relief is limited to the amount which would have been relieved if the permanent establishment had been a UK resident liable to tax on the income or gains.

[*TIOPA 2010, ss 8, 9, 11, 18, 25, 30*].

Unilateral relief under *TIOPA 2010, ss 8–18* is available on dividends received from overseas companies (which do not fall within the exemption regime) with regard to:

(a) overseas tax directly charged on the dividend which would not have been charged if the dividend had not been paid; and
(b) tax in respect of the overseas company's profits paid under the law of the country in which it is resident where:
    (i) the dividend is paid by a company resident overseas to a company resident in the UK, or to a company resident outside the UK but forming part of the profits of a UK permanent establishment (see **64.6** RESIDENCE) of the company; and

(ii) the recipient company (or a company of which it is a 'subsidiary') controls (directly or indirectly) at least 10% of the voting power in the overseas company (but see also **31.10** below).

In (b)(i) above, in the case of a company resident outside the UK but forming part of the profits of a UK permanent establishment, relief is limited to the amount which could be claimed in the same circumstances by a UK-resident company. The taxes concerned must correspond to income tax, capital gains tax or corporation tax on income or capital gains. Municipal taxes qualify, provided they meet these criteria.

'*Subsidiary*' means a company of which 50% or more of the voting power is controlled, directly or indirectly, by the other.

[*TIOPA 2010, ss 12–17*].

A credit for tax on income or gains which is paid under the other territory's law and corresponds to UK tax is available as a credit against UK tax unless a credit is available for tax on those income or gains under a double taxation agreement.

[*TIOPA 2010, ss 9, 18*].

For the scope of 'dividends', see *Memec plc v CIR* (1998) 71 TC 77, CA (in which receipts under a silent partnership agreement were held not to attract relief). See also HMRC Tax Bulletin June 2006 p 1295 for an article on the classification of foreign entities for UK tax purposes and for a list of overseas business entities on whose classification for UK tax purposes HMRC has been asked to express a view. See also Revenue Interpretation (RI) 279 with regard to entity classification.

Where no credit is available for foreign tax, relief is available by deduction of foreign tax paid on the non-UK source income from that income, in computing the income liable to UK corporation tax. See **31.4** below.

See *Yates (Inspector of Taxes) v GCA International Ltd* [1991] STC 157, 64 TC 37 where a tax imposed on gross receipts less a fixed 10% deduction was held to correspond to UK income tax or corporation tax. Following that decision, HMRC amended their practice. (HMRC Statement of Practice, SP 7/91, as revised.) Foreign taxes are examined to determine whether, in their own legislative context, they serve the same function as UK income and corporation taxes in relation to business profits, and are thus eligible for unilateral relief. As regards those overseas taxes which HMRC consider admissible (or inadmissible) for relief, these are listed by country in HMRC Double Taxation Relief Manual, DT2100 *et seq*. See also HMRC Business Income Manual, BIM45905. Current information may be obtained from the HMRC website (http://www.hmrc.gov.uk/international).

In *Aozora GMAC Investments Ltd v HMRC* FTT, [2021] UKFTT 99 (TC), 2021 SWTI 1517, the prohibition on unilateral relief in cases where the relevant double tax agreement prohibits relief was held not to apply even though the USA tax authority had denied relief to the company under the agreement.

Simon's Taxes. See **D4.803**.

Relief by agreement

[31.3] Relief from double taxation may be available under the provisions of an applicable double taxation agreement. A list is given in **31.17** below of the bilateral agreements made by the UK which are currently operative. Subject to the following general provisions, the extent of such relief depends on the terms of the relevant double tax agreement, which should be carefully studied.

Arrangements under such an agreement may provide for:

(i) relief from income or corporation tax in respect of income or chargeable gains;
(ii) charging UK income to non-UK residents;
(iii) determining income to be attributed to non-UK residents or their agencies, etc., or to UK residents who have special relationships with non-UK residents; or
(iv) exchange of information concerning taxes covered by the agreement, particularly in relation to the prevention of fiscal evasion.

[*TIOPA 2010, ss 6, 18; FA 2006, ss 173, 175*].

The ECJ, in *Test Claimants in Class IV of the ACT Group Litigation v CIR: C-374/04* ([2006] ECR I-11673, [2007] All ER (EC) 351, [2010] All ER (D) 247) held that EC Treaty (as was, now TFEU) Articles 43 and 56 did not preclude a member state from granting a tax credit to a company resident within it on dividends received from other resident companies, although no such credit was available on dividends from companies resident in other member states. The granting of the tax credit was linked with a charge to tax on the dividend and therefore the non-resident company (that did not receive the tax credit but equally did not suffer UK tax on the dividend) was not in a comparable position to the resident company. Where the two states have a double taxation agreement in force between them and a third state does not, granting of a tax credit on a dividend paid by a company in the first state to one in the second state, but not to one in the third state, is not precluded. The case was returned to the UK courts and judgment in the most recent appeal was handed down on 21 December 2010. The Court of Appeal ruled that the judge in the lower court had been entirely correct to grant the claimant groups of companies only a partial tax credit and in finding that the claimants were not entitled to a repayment of the 5% income tax charge.

In *Hill Samuel Investments Ltd v Revenue and Customs Comrs* [2009] STC (SCD) 315, 11 ITLR 734 the point at issue was to what extent was the UK claimant required to take reasonable steps to reduce the foreign tax on the transaction. It was held that 'taking reasonable steps' did not involve entering an entirely different transaction whether or not it had the same economic effect.

In the case of *Bayfine UK v HMRC* [2011] EWCA Civ 304, [2010] EWHC 609 (Ch), [2010] STC 1379, where more than one state taxes the same profits, which state is to give credit is determined according to the state of source, which has the primary taxing right. This involved a UK recipient of US source income, which had 'checked the box' in the US and so its income was included in the US profits of its parent. In the High Court it was held that the US was the state of source and had the primary taxing rights, thus the UK had to give relief under the US-UK treaty. However this was overturned in the Court of Appeal and it was held the UK had primary taxing rights and that HMRC was not obliged to give relief for US tax either under the treaty or unilaterally.

As regards the concept of 'permanent establishment' on which taxation rights are based under most treaties, HMRC take the view that a website, or a server on which e-commerce is conducted through a website, is not of itself a permanent establishment. (See HMRC International Manual, INTM266100 and **64.6** RESIDENCE).

For the circumstances in which HMRC will certify that a company is UK resident for the purposes of double tax agreements, see Revenue Tax Bulletin December 2002 pp 989–991. See also INTM120130 for guidance on when HMRC will not review a company's residence, and also INTM120070 for guidance on the operation of the residence tie-breaker clause in double tax treaties, and a list of treaties with the UK which have such a clause.

For the scope of 'dividends' attracting treaty relief, see *Memec plc v CIR* (1998) 71 TC 77, CA (in which receipts under a silent partnership agreement were held not to attract relief). As above at **31.2**, see RI 279 on entity classification, and a list of overseas entities HMRC have already considered.

In *Next Brand Ltd v HMRC* [2015] SFTD 606 the First-tier Tribunal considered the nature of a dividend payment with regard to double tax treaty relief. The Tribunal observed that the relevant provisions refer to income, gains and profits and therefore cover 'dividends representing the payment of profit not dividends with some other purpose'. It held that the dividends in this instance represented the repayment of a loan and not a distribution of profit, and therefore treaty relief was not available.

In *R v CIR (ex p Commerzbank AG)* (1991) 68 TC 252, interest on unpaid tax was held not to fall within the scope of double tax agreements, but on a reference to the European Court of Justice (see 68 TC 264), the Court upheld the view that, in the case of EU member states, such discrimination against non-UK resident companies was prevented by the relevant Articles of the EC Treaty (now TFEU).

In *HMRC v FCE Bank plc* (Upper Tribunal 14 October 2011), the Upper Tribunal upheld the First Tier Tribunal decision that the non-discrimination article in a treaty applied in the case where HMRC refused a group relief claim of two UK subsidiaries, on the basis the holding company of the two UK resident sister subsidiaries was in the US. Such a claim would not have been denied in the case of a UK resident holding company, and this was the only difference, thus this was discrimination under the Treaty provision.

In *GE Financial Investments v HMRC* FTT, [2021] UKFTT 210 (TC), 2021 SWTI 1715, the company was not entitled to relief under the UK-USA double tax treaty despite being taxable in the USA on its worldwide income. The company (GEFI) was a UK-resident member of the GE group and was the limited partner in a Delaware limited partnership (LP). The general partner in LP was a USA-resident group member (GEFI Inc). GEFI and GEFI Inc were 'stapled entities' for the purposes of the US federal income tax because the shares in one could not be transferred without the shares in the other also being transferred to the same transferee. The effect was that GEFI was subject to US tax on its worldwide income. The FTT held, however, that GEFI was neither resident in the UK nor did it carry on a business there through a permanent establishment so that relief under the treaty was not available.

See HMRC Double Taxation Relief Manual, DT1950 onwards. for HMRC's approach to non-discrimination claims generally.

Mutual agreement procedure

Double tax agreements normally contain a 'mutual agreement procedure' (MAP) provision enabling a taxpayer who considers that the action of a tax authority has resulted, or will result, in taxation not in accordance with the agreement to present his case to the competent authority in his state of residence.

The UK competent authority is HMRC, and the address to which all relevant facts and contentions should be sent is CTIAA Business International, 100 Parliament Street, London SW1A 2BQ. For the presentation of such cases, and for giving effect to solutions and agreements reached under such procedures, see *TIOPA 2010, ss 124, 125*. Details of the procedures can be found in the HMRC Double Taxation Relief Manual. See also HMRC Statement of Practice SP1/18 which sets out HMRC's approach to the operation of the MAP, in particular with reference to transfer pricing disputes (see **72.16** TRANSFER PRICING).

In *McCabe v HMRC* FTT, [2019] SFTD 1007, the taxpayer's application for disclosure of documents held by HMRC relating to a MAP agreement between HMRC and the Belgian tax authorities concerning his residence status was refused.

See also **31.5** below for double tax dispute resolution in the EU.

Anti-avoidance

The case of *Bayfine UK v HMRC* [2011] EWCA Civ 304, has been highlighted above. In that case two UK resident companies (both subsidiaries of a US company) entered forward contracts. One made a loss and the other a profit of the same amount. Group relief was claimed on the loss and double tax relief on the profit. It was found by the Special Commissioners that no DTR was due as the profit arose in the UK. The High Court did not agree, but the decision of the Commissioners was upheld in the Court of Appeal on 23 March 2011 who applied a purposive construction to the interpretation of the treaty. Arden LJ commented (at para 40) that the primary purpose of double tax treaties is both to eliminate double taxation and 'to prevent fiscal evasion which would include the avoidance of taxation' and thus the Treaty should be interpreted to avoid the grant of double relief as well as to confer relief against double taxation.

An anti-avoidance provision applies to prevent the use of double taxation agreements to obtain a tax advantage. A double tax agreement may provide that the trading profits of a non-resident company which is controlled or managed outside the UK are not taxable in the UK except to the extent that they are attributable to a permanent establishment in the UK. Where this clause is included, nonetheless, the UK profits will be taxable on any company resident in the UK which is entitled to those profits. Residence is determined according to the relevant double tax agreement. This provision does not apply to partnership profits chargeable to tax in the UK.

[*TIOPA 2010, s 130*].

The OECD's Multilateral Convention to Implement Tax Treaty Related Measures to Prevent Base Erosion and Profit Shifting is brought into effect, from 1 October 2018, by *SI 2018 No 630*. The Convention modifies existing double tax agreements between signatory jurisdictions which have agreed to apply it. It includes arbitration provisions to help resolve disputes. The Convention applies in the UK from 1 April 2019 for corporation tax.

Simon's Taxes. See **D4.803, D4.803A.**

Specific matters

Relief by deduction

[31.4] An election can be made not to claim relief by way of credit (see **31.6** below), for example where there is no or insufficient UK tax payable on the foreign income against which the foreign tax can be credited. Where such an election is made or where a credit for foreign tax is not taken under treaty or unilateral relief, or is not otherwise allowable in respect of foreign income (see also **31.6** below under 'Relief for disallowed credit'), any foreign tax paid on that income is generally deductible from that income for purposes of UK assessment. If the income of a person is reduced by an amount paid in foreign tax on that income source and a payment is made by a tax authority (by reference to the foreign tax) to that person (or any person connected with them, as determined by *CTA 2010, s 1122*) then that person's income is increased by the amount of the payment.

This does not apply to underlying tax excluded from a claim for relief under *TIOPA 2010, s 60* (to prevent the application of the 'mixer' cap in certain cases — see **31.12** below) and applies subject to the reduction of foreign tax paid on profits of an overseas permanent establishment under *TIOPA 2010, s 71B* (see **31.7** below). Where foreign tax for which such a deduction has been given is subsequently adjusted, the UK tax charge may be revised within six years from date of the foreign tax adjustment. Where, by reason of the adjustment, relief has become excessive, written notice of that fact must be given to HMRC within one year of the date of the adjustment subject to a penalty for failure to comply not exceeding the amount of the additional UK tax payable.

A person may only deduct foreign tax from any foreign income where he has not already reduced his income by reference to the foreign tax. The amount of a deduction is reduced where a payment is made by a tax authority in respect of the foreign tax to another person, directly or indirectly, in consequence of a scheme (which includes any scheme, arrangement or understanding of any kind) that has been entered into.

[*TIOPA 2010, ss 27, 79, 80, 112; FA 2018, s 30(4)*].

Simon's Taxes. See **D4.803.**

Prevention of double relief

Credit may not be given for foreign tax for which relief is available in the territory in which it would otherwise be payable, either under double tax arrangements or under the law of that territory in consequence of any such arrangements. It is also made clear that unilateral relief will not be allowed where credit could be claimed under a double tax agreement, or in cases or circumstances in which such an agreement made after 20 March 2000 specifically prohibits relief.

[*TIOPA 2010, s 25*].

Tax sparing relief

Under *TIOPA 2010, ss 4, 20* it may be provided in a double tax agreement that any tax which would have been payable in a foreign country but for a relief under the law of that territory given with a view to promoting industrial, commercial, scientific, educational or other development therein is nevertheless treated for purposes of credit against UK tax as if it had been paid. (It is not available for unilateral relief or where relief is given by way of deduction from dividend income).

See, for example, HMRC Double Taxation Relief Manual at DT12758 in the case of Malaysia.

Matching credit for tax spared below immediate overseas subsidiary

Where:

(a) an amount of tax would, but for a relief, have been payable by a company ('company A'), in respect of any of its profits, under the law of its territory of residence;
(b) company A pays a dividend out of those profits to another company ('company B') resident in the same territory;
(c) company B, out of profits consisting of or including all or part of that dividend, pays a dividend to a UK-resident company ('company C'); and
(d) had company B been UK resident, it would have been entitled under a double tax agreement with its actual territory of residence to relief for the spared tax,

then the spared tax is taken into account for the purposes of unilateral relief for underlying tax as if it had been payable and paid. If these conditions are not fulfilled, unilateral relief is not available for spared tax in respect of any dividend paid by a non-UK resident company to a UK-resident company, notwithstanding any double tax agreement with the territory concerned providing any relief for spared tax.

Without prejudice to the above specific relief, treaty relief for underlying tax which is spared below the level of the immediate non-resident subsidiary is denied unless it is specifically provided for in a double tax agreement.

[*TIOPA 2010, ss 4, 17, 20*].

Simon's Taxes. See **D4.936.**

Acquisitions and disposals of loan relationships

Special provision is made for the relief of foreign tax relating to accrued interest in relation to which a non-trading credit is brought into account (see **50.4** LOAN RELATIONSHIPS), and for foreign tax to be disregarded where it is attributable to interest accruing under a loan relationship (see **50.2** LOAN RELATIONSHIPS) at a time when the company concerned was not a party to the relationship (unless it ceased to be a party under certain repo or stock-lending arrangements).

Foreign tax attributable to 'notional interest payments' within *TIOPA 2010, s 107(3)* are to be disregarded where it is attributable to a time when the company was not a party to the derivative contract concerned.

[*TIOPA 2010, s 107*].

Where shares are treated as loan relationships, the above provisions have effect for share distributions as they would for interest under a loan relationship.

With regard to loan relationships, the foreign tax is disregarded where it is attributable to the distribution accruing in respect of such shares, or to interest accruing under a loan relationship, at a time when the company does not hold the shares, or is not a party to the relationship (unless it ceased to hold the shares under certain repo or stock-lending arrangements).

[*TIOPA 2010, s 108*].

Simon's Taxes. See **D4.807**.

Special arrangements — interest

Double tax agreements under *TIOPA 2010, s 6* making provision in relation to interest may also have a provision dealing with cases where, owing to a special relationship, the amount of interest paid exceeds the amount which would have been paid in the absence of that relationship, and requiring the interest provision to be applied only to that lower amount.

Any such special relationship provision has to be construed:

(a) as requiring account to be taken of all factors, including whether, in the absence of the relationship, the loan would have been made at all, or would have been in a different amount, or a different rate of interest and other terms would have been agreed. This does not apply, however, where the special relationship provision expressly requires regard to be had to the debt on which the interest is paid in determining the excess interest, and accordingly expressly limits the factors to be taken into account, and in the case of a loan by one company to another, the fact that it is not part of the lending company's business to make loans generally is disregarded; and

(b) as requiring the taxpayer either to show that no special relationship exists or to show the amount of interest which would have been paid in the absence of that relationship.

[*TIOPA 2010, s 131*].

With regard to (a) above, see HMRC International Manual, INTM501010 for a further discussion of the tax considerations of intra-group funding, the special relationship provision and transfer pricing.

Special relationships — royalties

Double tax agreements may make similar provision in relation to royalties. Any special relationship provision, unless it expressly requires regard to be had to the use, right or information for which royalties are paid in determining the excess royalties, has to be construed as requiring account to be taken of all factors. These include:

(A) in the absence of the relationship, whether the royalty agreement would have been made at all, or the rate or amount of royalties and other terms which would have been agreed; and
(B) if the asset in respect of which the royalties are paid (or any asset which it represents or from which it is derived) had previously been in the beneficial ownership of:
  (i) the person liable to pay the royalties;
  (ii) a person who has at any time carried on a business which, when the royalties fall due, is carried on in whole or part by the person liable to pay the royalties; or
  (iii) a person who is or has been an 'associate', as specially defined, of a person within (i) or (ii),

the amounts paid under the transaction(s) which resulted in the asset falling into its present beneficial ownership, the amounts which would have been so paid in the absence of the special relationship, and the question as to whether the transaction(s) would have taken place at all in the absence of that relationship.

The taxpayer must also show either that no special relationship exists, or the amount of royalties which would have been paid in the absence of the relationship, and if he cannot show that (B) above does not apply, he must show that the transaction(s) mentioned therein would have taken place in the absence of a special relationship, and the amounts which would then have been paid under those transaction(s).

The taxpayer must also show either that no special relationship exists, or the amount of royalties which would have been paid in the absence of the relationship, and if he cannot show that (B) above does not apply, he must show that the transaction(s) mentioned therein would have taken place in the absence of a special relationship, and the amounts which would then have been paid under those transaction(s).

[*TIOPA 2010, ss 132, 133*].

Royalties and 'know how' payments

Notwithstanding that credit for overseas tax is ordinarily given only against income which arises (or is deemed to arise) in the overseas territory concerned, HMRC treatment (per ESC B8) as regards this class of income is as follows.

Income payments made by an overseas resident to a UK trader for the use, in that overseas territory, of any *copyright, patent, design, secret process or formula, trade mark etc.*, may be treated, for credit purposes (whether under double tax agreements or by way of unilateral relief) as income arising outside the UK — *except* so far as they represent consideration for services (other than merely incidental) rendered in the UK by the recipient to the payer (HMRC Extra Statutory Concession B8).

For the treatment of sales of 'know-how' etc., see 68.45 TRADING INCOME and 42.43 INTANGIBLE ASSETS.

Bank Levy

In calculating profits or losses for income tax or corporation tax purposes no deduction is allowed in respect of any tax which is imposed by a territory outside the UK and corresponds to the bank levy, and in addition no account is taken of any amount paid (directly or indirectly) by a member of a group to another member for the purposes of meeting or reimbursing the cost of such a tax charged.

The legislation also ensures that where a company makes a claim for double taxation relief for a foreign bank levy against the charge to the UK bank levy, none of that foreign bank levy will be an allowable deduction for income tax or corporation tax purposes.

[*FA 2011, Sch 19 para 69A*].

Double tax dispute resolution in the EU

[31.5] Before Brexit, the UK was subject to Council Directive (EU) 2017/1852 on tax dispute resolution mechanisms in the EU which applies a framework for resolving double tax disputes between member states. It features a binding procedure for resolving disputes within two years, with a framework for further time-limited arbitration proceedings. Taxpayers faced with tax treaty disputes can initiate a procedure whereby the member states in question must try to resolve the dispute amicably within two years. If at the end of this period, no solution has been found, the member states must set up an Advisory Commission to arbitrate. If member states fail to do this, the taxpayer can bring an action before the national court (in the UK, the Upper Tribunal) to do so. The Advisory Commission will be comprised of three independent members and representatives of the competent authorities in question. It will have six months to deliver an opinion leading to a final, binding decision. This decision will be immediately enforceable and must resolve the dispute.

The UK legislation which implemented the Directive, *SI 2020 No 51*, applied to questions in dispute relating to income or capital earned in a tax period commencing on or after 1 January 2018. The UK legislation is revoked with effect from IP completion day (11pm GMT on 31 December 2020) by *SI 2020 No 1383*.

Secrecy requirements under any enactment do not prevent HMRC or certain other persons from disclosing information required to be disclosed under any instrument, agreement or arrangement covered by the regulations. [*TIOPA 2010, s 128C; FA 2019, s 83*].

Relief by way of credit

[31.6] Relief is to be allowed by way of credit against attributable corporation tax (i.e. UK tax otherwise chargeable) on any income or chargeable gain ('the relevant income or gain') up to the amount of that tax (see below in relation to trade receipts). The foreign tax on the overseas income can only be set against the corresponding UK tax in respect of the same income (see **31.8** below). The credit for tax must not exceed corporation tax at the rate payable by the company on the income or gain which is the subject of the claim after allowing for general deductions, earlier year deficits on loan relationships, debits on loan relationships, current year deficits on loan relationships and debits on intangible fixed assets. In determining for this purpose how much of the UK resident company's profits is attributable to the company's permanent establishment outside the UK, the following assumptions must be made:

- the permanent establishment is treated as a distinct and separate enterprise engaged in the same or similar activities under the same or similar conditions and dealing wholly independently with the company of which it is a permanent establishment;
- the permanent establishment has the same credit rating as the company of which it is part;
- regardless of any allocation in the books of the company, the permanent establishment has the equity and loan capital it would have on an allocation made on a just and equitable basis of the company's capital amongst its foreign permanent establishments, on the basis they were distinct and separate entities from the company, subject to the provisions of any full double taxation treaty, in force between the UK and the state in which the permanent establishment is situated; and
- any 'free assets' (as defined) of an insurance company are to be attributed to its permanent establishment on this same basis.

For credit relief purposes the tax on non-trading loan relationships is taken as tax on income from total non-trading credits with regard to the period, and not the company's non-trading profits it has on its non-trading loan relationships. Similarly, with regard to intangible fixed assets. The relief for foreign tax on each non-trading credit from a loan relationship, derivative contract or intangible fixed asset is restricted to the amount of UK tax on the net amount of that non-trading credit after deducting non-trading debits of the same loan relationship, contract or asset (taking account of any deductions already made against other non-trading credits from the same relationship, contract or asset in the same period).

[*TIOPA 2010, ss 18, 42, 43, 49B, 50, 51; CTA 2009, Pt 2 Ch 4*].

This applies both to unilateral relief and to relief by agreement, though it is confined in the latter case to those UK taxes which are covered by the agreement. Relief is only available against UK tax chargeable under the same class of income as that under which the foreign tax was chargeable on the foreign income. (*George Wimpey International Ltd v Rolfe* (1989) 62 TC 597).

Both reliefs apply to corporation tax on chargeable gains as they do to income.

[*TIOPA 2010, ss 2, 18*].

Relief for overseas tax paid is available against UK tax on chargeable gains provided that both liabilities relate to the same source, i.e. notwithstanding that they may arise at different times or be charged on different persons. (HMRC International Manual, INTM161040 and HMRC Statement of Practice, SP 6/88).

Relief under an agreement is limited to that which would be allowed if all reasonable steps had been taken, including all relevant claims, elections, etc., under the law of the territory concerned or under double tax arrangements with that territory, to minimise the foreign tax payable.

[*TIOPA 2010, s 33*].

As regards what HMRC considers taxpayers can and cannot reasonably be expected to do, the former is likely to include appeals against excessive assessments, claims for reliefs generally known to be available, and selection of any option which produces a lower tax liability, and the latter is likely to include claims to reliefs whose availability is uncertain, and where disproportionate expenditure would be required to pursue a claim, substituting carry-forward claims for carry-back claims and *vice versa*, and attempting to exercise influence the taxpayer does not have on the underlying tax paid by a subsidiary.

Trade income

The following restriction applies in relation to a credit for foreign tax in connection either with a payment of foreign tax or with income received in respect of which foreign tax has been deducted at source.

The meaning of 'relevant income or gain' under *TIOPA 2010, s 42* (see above) is amended in relation to 'trade income' to refer only to so much of the income arising or gains accruing out of transactions in connection with which the foreign tax arises.

For this purpose, '*trade income*' includes:

(a) income or profits chargeable as UK or overseas trading income (see **68** TRADING INCOME); or
(b) of a property business (see **60.4** PROPERTY INCOME); or
(c) post-cessation receipts chargeable to corporation tax (see **68.16** TRADING INCOME); or
(d) income arising outside the UK which is charged to tax as income not otherwise charged (under *CTA 2009, s 979*); and
(e) any other instance where the trading rules are used to calculate profits (but this does not apply to income of an insurance company to which *TIOPA 2010, s 99* applies).

In determining the corporation tax attributable to any income or gain, account is to be taken of deductions or expenses etc. that would be allowable and are directly attributable to the income and also a reasonable proportion of expenses etc. that are only partly attributable, e.g. overheads. Connected company (within *CTA 2010, ss 1122, 1123*) expenses are also to be taken into account in so far as they are reasonably attributable to the income or gain. There are anti-avoidance provisions the purpose of which is to catch arrangements which divert income for credit relief purposes to other persons.

[*TIOPA 2010, ss 44, 45*].

Special cases

Where a foreign tax payment is made in connection with an asset which is in a 'hedging relationship' (as defined) with a derivative contract, the reference to 'relevant income or gain' (or 'income or gain' in *TIOPA 2010*) for these purposes is extended to include the income arising out of the assets and the derivative contract taken together (but only so as to include the income or loss from the derivative contract as is reasonably attributable to the hedging relationship).

Where royalties from different non-UK jurisdictions are paid in respect of the same asset, the royalty income in an accounting period (before 1 April 2010 — in a year of assessment) in respect of that asset is to be treated as arising from a single transaction and the foreign tax credits in respect of such income are to be aggregated.

Where a person ('A') carrying on a trade enters into a scheme or arrangement with another person ('B') in order to circumvent the above provisions in relation to A, any income received in pursuance of the scheme or arrangement is to be treated as trade income of B.

Where there is a series or group of transactions, arrangements or assets (a 'portfolio') and a number of tax credits arise in respect of that portfolio, the income or gains arising from the portfolio or part of the portfolio may be aggregated and apportioned in a fair and reasonable manner. This is provided it is not reasonably practicable to prepare separate computations for each transaction etc. or separate computations would not, when compared with an aggregate computation, make a material difference to the amount of allowable credit for foreign tax.

Relief under *TIOPA 2010, s 44(2)* is restricted in the case of a bank or a company connected with a bank.

[*TIOPA 2010, ss 44–49*].

See also **31.18** below in relation to banks and other financial traders regarding the case of *Legal & General Assurance Society Ltd v HMRC* [2006] STC 1763 (which preceded the above changes made by *FA 2005*).

Relief for disallowed credit

Where an amount of credit for foreign tax is disallowed because of the application of *TIOPA 2010, s 42* above, relief may be available instead as a deduction in computing taxable profits.

This has effect notwithstanding the general rule in *TIOPA 2010, s 31* that relief may be by credit or deduction but not a mixture of the two.

The amount that can be deducted is the lower of the disallowed credit and the amount of any loss, *after* deducting foreign tax, that is attributable to the income in respect of which the foreign tax was paid; if there is no such loss, no deduction is available.

[*TIOPA 2010, s 35*].

Anti-avoidance

Wide-ranging anti-avoidance provisions apply to certain schemes or arrangements in relation to relief by way of credit under a double tax agreement where the main purpose or one of the main purposes of which is the avoidance of tax.

The legislation applies in relation to any credit for foreign tax which is connected either with a payment of foreign tax or with income received from which foreign tax has been deducted (or treated as deducted) at source. 'Foreign tax' includes UK tax treated as foreign tax by *TIOPA 2010, s 63(5)*. The provisions apply where:

(a) relief by way of credit against UK tax is available under a double tax agreement for the foreign tax suffered on the income or gain;
(b) there is a scheme or arrangement, which is a 'prescribed scheme or arrangement' within (i) to (vi) below, the main purpose, or one of the main purposes, of which is to provide for an amount of foreign tax to be taken into account;
(c) the aggregate amount of credit relief which can be or has been claimed for the foreign tax by the company, and by any connected persons in a corresponding chargeable period (where the chargeable periods in question have at least one day in common), is more than a minimum amount i.e. at least £100,000 (see HMRC International Manual INTM170120);
(d) the scheme or arrangement is either not a scheme or arrangement relating to underlying-tax and one or more of the six following conditions apply or it is an underlying-tax scheme or arrangement and, if it were assumed that the taxpayer company were resident in the UK, one of the six conditions would apply.

For returns due on or after 1 April 2018, where the conditions are satisfied, the provisions apply automatically and operate by requiring the making of any adjustments (by the taxpayer or, if the taxpayer fails to make the adjustments, by HMRC) necessary to counteract the effects of the scheme or arrangement. The adjustments may be made by way of assessment, modification of an assessment, amendment or disallowance of a claim or otherwise.

Previously, if HMRC considered, on reasonable grounds, that the above conditions were or may have been satisfied in relation to any person they could give that person a notice (a '*counteraction notice*') informing him of their view and that as a consequence he would be required, in his tax return for the period concerned, to make such adjustments as were necessary to counteract the effects of the scheme or arrangement that were referable to the purpose in (b) above. The notice could (but was not required to) specify the adjustments required.

The six conditions for a scheme or arrangement are as follows:

(i) A scheme enables foreign tax which is properly attributable to one source of income or gain to be shifted to a different source of income or gain.
(ii) It enables any scheme participant to claim credit for a payment of foreign tax that increases the total amount of foreign tax paid by all the scheme participants by less than the amount which that person can claim (for example, because the payment made by the claimant is matched by a tax saving for another scheme participant).
(iii) It involves a scheme participant making a claim or election etc. or omitting to make a claim or election etc. which in either case has the effect of increasing the credit for foreign tax available to any scheme

participant. References here to claims and elections or suchlike are to claims etc. made under the law of any territory or under the terms of a double tax agreement.

(iv) It has the effect of reducing the total UK tax liability on income and chargeable gains of a scheme participant and (in relation to a credit for foreign tax which relates to a payment of foreign tax on or after 22 November 2017) any person connected with that participant to less than it would have been in the absence of the transactions made under the scheme. This will be the case, for example, where the credit for foreign tax on the scheme income covers not only the UK tax on that income but at least some of the UK tax on other income, thereby reducing total liability.

(v) Under the scheme, a tax deductible payment is made by a person, in return for which that person or a connected party (within the meaning of *CTA 2010, s 1122*) receives consideration which is taxable in a foreign territory (and thus on which credit relief can be obtained in respect of the foreign tax).

(vi) Under a scheme involving deemed foreign tax, see below.

Where one of the main purposes of the scheme is to obtain relief for underlying tax in respect of a dividend paid by a foreign company, the above schemes are treated as prescribed schemes of the foreign company if they would be treated as such if the company were UK resident (without assuming its activities are carried on in a different place).

It is immaterial whether a pre-execution step was under a scheme or arrangement — a step taken or not taken by a participant in a scheme or arrangement can be a step taken or omitted from being taken before a scheme or arrangement comes into existence. In addition, the reason for taking or not taking the step does not matter provided the effect is to increase, or give rise to, a credit claim by a participant.

Schemes involving deemed foreign tax

Further anti-avoidance legislation applies generally to counter certain schemes entered into by financial traders. The provisions:

(i) prevent the use of manufactured payments instead of real overseas dividends in order to sidestep existing anti-avoidance defences in the double tax relief legislation. These changes prevent credits for notional overseas tax from being treated more favourably than tax credits on real dividends. This will not result in the automatic denial of relief in relation to deemed overseas tax, since it will still be necessary for that tax to arise as part of a scheme or arrangement one of the main purposes of which is to cause that tax to be taken into account for double tax relief purposes;

(ii) ensure that a person may only deduct foreign tax from any foreign income where he has not already reduced his income by reference to the foreign tax.

The provisions apply to a scheme or arrangement where there is an amount of deemed foreign tax and either condition A or condition B is met.

Condition A is met where it could reasonably be expected that, under the scheme or arrangement, no real foreign tax would be paid or payable by a participant in the scheme or arrangement.

Condition B is met where it could reasonably be expected that, under the scheme or arrangement, real foreign tax would be paid or payable by a participant in the scheme or arrangement but the increase in the foreign tax total would be less than the amount allowable to the claimant as a credit in respect of the deemed foreign tax.

'*Real foreign tax*' is defined as including, in relation to *TIOPA 2010, s 10* (accrued income profits), the foreign tax chargeable in respect of the interest payable on the securities referred to in *s 10(1)(c)* and, in relation to the manufactured overseas dividend (MOD) rules, the foreign tax chargeable on the overseas dividend of which the MOD is representative. These provisions have effect for foreign tax paid or payable on or after 21 October 2009.

HMRC have confirmed that they will not use this legislation to prevent participants taking advantage of pricing arbitrage opportunities in the foreign equities market.

See HMRC International Manual INTM170040

Counteraction notice

Where a person received a counteraction notice and the conditions at (a)–(d) above were in fact satisfied, that person had to make, in his tax return for the period concerned, such adjustments as were necessary to counteract the effects of the scheme or arrangement that were referable to the purpose in (b) above.

If the counteraction notice was given before the person has made his return for the chargeable period concerned then, if the return was made in the period of 90 days beginning with the day on which the notice was given, it could disregard the notice, and at any time before the end of the 90 days the person could amend the return in order to comply with the notice.

If no counteraction notice had been given before the person's return was made, a notice could only be given if the person had been given a notice of enquiry (see **65.14** RETURNS) in respect of the return. After an enquiry had been completed, a counteraction notice could only be given if:

- at the time the enquiry was completed HMRC could not have reasonably been expected, on the basis of the information made available (see **6.3** ASSESSMENTS) to them before that time, to have been aware that the circumstances were such that a notice could have been given; and
- the person was requested to provide information during the enquiry and, if it had been so provided, HMRC could reasonably have been expected to give the person a notice.

If the counteraction notice was given after the person had made his return, he could amend the return to comply with the notice within 90 days beginning with the day on which the notice was given. If the notice was given after an enquiry into the return had started, a final closure notice (see **65.17** RETURNS) could not be issued until the end of the period of 90 days beginning with the issue of the notice or, if earlier, an amendment was made to the return complying with the notice (though this did not prevent the issue of a partial closure notice that was unrelated to any matter to which the counteraction notice related). If the notice was given after the completion of an enquiry, a discovery assessment (see **6.3** ASSESSMENTS) in relation to the gains or income to which it related could not be made until the end of the period of 90 days beginning with the issue of the notice or, if earlier, an amendment was made to the return complying with the notice.

Where a notice was issued and no amendment was made to the return for the purpose of complying with it, the above provisions did not prevent a return becoming incorrect if such an amendment should have been made.

[*TIOPA 2010, ss 81–95; F(No 2)A 2017, Sch 15 paras 38, 39; FA 2018, s 31*].

See generally HMRC International Manual INTM170010–170140.

Simon's Taxes. See **D4.812.**

CFC provisions — double tax relief for qualifying loan relationships

There are provisions which restrict the double taxation relief given by way of credit or deduction in certain circumstances, where a claim has been made in respect of qualifying loan relationships under the CONTROLLED FOREIGN COMPANIES (**21.20**) rules.

The provisions apply when one or more UK companies form part of an arrangement whereby a loan is made from one CFC to another CFC that is the ultimate debtor in relation to that loan. Where one or more UK companies form part of a conduit in such an arrangement the double tax relief which the UK resident company (the 'relevant UK company') may claim either by credit or deduction will be limited to the amount of corporation tax that would be due in respect of the UK corporation tax profits that arise from that arrangement.

This cap is given by the formula: R × S

where 'R' is the rate of corporation tax payable by the relevant UK company and 'S' is the UK company's share of the relevant profit amount, or the proportion of such relevant profit amount which arises in the period.

This is in addition to the usual limitation found at the existing *TIOPA 2010, s 42* (see **30** DOUBLE TAX RELIEF). If the amount given by the formula is nil then no credit is allowed.

Steps are provided at *s 49A(4)* for the calculation of the relevant UK company's share of the relevant profit amount. Loan relationships credits are as defined within the loan relationship rules at *CTA 2009, Pt 5* and the definition is extended to persons in the lending chain who are not within the charge to corporation tax by assuming they are. The explanatory notes provide an example:

CFC A (Creditor CFC) lends (loan A) to UK company (relevant UK company) that in turn lends (loan B) to CFC B (ultimate debtor CFC). In the relevant period UK company has interest receivable of 100 on loan B from CFC B and CFC A has interest receivable of 90.

The steps undertaken are:

(1) ascertain the total amount of the loan relationship credits arising from loan B (to the person who made loan B);

(2) establish loan relationship credits for the creditor CFC (CFC A) for the qualifying loan relationship (at (1)) and deduct from amount ascertained at (1); and

(3) allocate this profit amount between all persons in the lending chain on a just and reasonable basis.

References to loan B above do not include any part of that loan which is not funded by loan A, or any amounts where loan B is used to make a further loan to another person.

In the example the relevant profit amount is 10, which would be apportioned to the UK company. The double tax relief (by way of credit) would thus be capped at 10 ('S') × the corporation tax rate of the relevant UK company ('R').

With regard to the restriction on a deduction of foreign tax, new *ss 112(3A)* and *(3B)* are inserted. They apply in the same circumstances as for the credit cap (above, found at *s 49A(1)(a)–(c)*), and include a third condition to be met which modifies the amount of foreign tax that can be deducted to take into account any repayment of the foreign tax. This is done by defining 'Z' as that net amount (being the foreign tax less any repayment) and comparing this figure to the cap at *s 49A*, R × S. If there is an excess then a deduction can be made, and this is limited (under new *s 112(3B)*) by reference to the R × S formula.

By way of example, if Z were nil (as all the foreign tax had been repaid) then Z would not exceed R × S and so the third condition would not be met, therefore no foreign tax can be deducted. However, if Z equals the amount of foreign tax deducted (as there is no repayment of foreign tax) then the third condition would be met: a deduction would be permitted but would be limited by reference to R × S.

[*TIOPA 2010, ss 49A, 112(3A)(3B)*].

Claims

Relief must be claimed within six years after the end of the accounting period for which the income or gains are chargeable or, if later, within one year after the end of the accounting period in which the foreign tax is paid. Where the amount of foreign tax payable is adjusted subsequent to a claim for relief, with the result that the tax credit becomes excessive, the taxpayer must give written notice to HMRC of this fact within one year of the date on which the adjustment is made, subject to a penalty for failure to comply which may not exceed the excess relief. Certain cases where the adjustment is taken into account under regulations relating to Lloyd's underwriters are excluded from this requirement. For this, and for HMRC view of what constitutes an 'adjustment', see HMRC International Manual, INTM162120.

[*TIOPA 2010, ss 79, 80*].

Where a company claimed double tax relief arising from two US partnerships, HMRC denied the relief on the grounds that the company had not taken 'all reasonable steps' to minimise the US tax. The Special Commissioners found there were no other reasonable steps open to the company which would reduce the US tax, therefore there was no restriction on the ability to claim relief. *Hill Samuel Investments Ltd v HMRC* [2009] STC (SCD) 315, 11 ITLR 734.

A further anti-avoidance provision applies when a company qualifies for a credit for foreign tax and it, or a person connected with it, receives a payment from a tax authority by reference to the foreign tax. The credit is reduced by the amount of the payment. The *CTA 2010, s 1122* definition of a connected person is adopted for this purpose. The provision applies whether the relief is under treaty or unilateral. The credit allowed or the deduction given (under *TIOPA 2010, s 112* see **31.4** above) is also reduced where a payment is made by a foreign tax authority to another person (directly or indirectly) as a consequence of a scheme (which includes any scheme, arrangement or understanding of any kind) that has been entered into.

[*TIOPA 2010, s 34*].

Simon's Taxes. See **D4.901**.

Utilisation of unrelieved foreign tax on profits of overseas permanent establishments

[31.7] For UK resident companies, any 'unrelieved foreign tax' can be carried back or forward (see further below) if it arises in respect of any of the company's 'qualifying income' from an 'overseas permanent establishment' of the company. This does not apply where an election for exemption of the overseas PE profits under *CTA 2009, s 18A* has been made — see **31.15** below.

'*Unrelieved foreign tax*' on any income is the excess of the amount of the credit for foreign tax which would (disregarding the limitation to corporation tax on that income under *TIOPA 2010, s 42* — see **31.6** above) be available against corporation tax in respect of the income over the amount which is actually so allowed.

An '*overseas permanent establishment*' for this purpose is a 'permanent establishment' through which a company carries on a trade in a territory outside the UK, and '*permanent establishment*' has the meaning given by any double tax agreement with that territory or, in the absence of such a definition, the meaning given by *CTA 2010, s 1141* (see **64.6** RESIDENCE).

'*Qualifying income*' of a permanent establishment is those of its profits which are chargeable as arising from a trade carried on partly, but not wholly, outside the UK, under *CTA 2009, Pt 3 Ch 2*.

Where an amount of unrelieved foreign tax arises in respect of any qualifying income, the unrelieved foreign tax may, on a claim, be treated as if it were paid in respect of, and computed by reference to, income of the same description and from the same source in either:

(a) the next accounting period (and successive accounting periods), whether or not there is any income from that source in that accounting period; or
(b) such one or more preceding accounting periods, beginning not more than three years before that in which the unrelieved foreign tax arises, as results from applying the rules described below. Set off is against the latest year first (and current years credits are set off first),

or partly in one way and partly in the other (i.e. a mix of (a) and (b)).

Where the company ceases to have a permanent establishment, no further relief is given for any balance of excess.

The rules referred to in (b) above require that the unrelieved foreign tax must be so treated that:

(1) credit for it (or for any remaining balance) is allowed against corporation tax in respect of income of a later period before an earlier one; and
(2) before allowing credit for it against corporation tax in respect of any income of an accounting period, credit for foreign tax must be allowed first for foreign tax in respect of the income of that period (other than unrelieved foreign tax of another period), and then for unrelieved foreign tax arising in an earlier accounting period before a later one.

The claim must be made not more than four years after the end of the accounting period in which the excess arose or, if later, one year after the end of the accounting period in which the foreign tax concerned is paid and must specify the amounts to be dealt with under each of (a) and (b) above.

Where unrelieved foreign tax of an accounting period is treated as paid in respect of income of another accounting period, no further application of these provisions may be made in relation to that tax.

Where there is more than one permanent establishment in the same territory and their profits are charged to tax together, such establishments are treated as if they were a single establishment for these purposes. However, where there was one establishment, which has ceased, and a new establishment is started in the same territory, they are treated as separate establishments.

If a particular permanent establishment ceases in an accounting period, unrelieved foreign tax relating to it may not be carried forward from that period. If the company subsequently in the same period has a permanent establishment in the same territory, it is treated as a new and different source. However, two or more overseas permanent establishments in the same territory which are taxed as one under the law of that territory are treated for the purposes of these provisions as a single permanent establishment.

[*TIOPA 2010, ss 72–78; FA 2018, s 30(3)*].

Adjustment of foreign tax on profits of overseas permanent establishments

There are provisions to restrict the amount of credit relief under **31.6** above where an overseas permanent establishment (defined as above) of a UK-resident company has made a loss which has been relieved against income other than that of the permanent establishment or the company. The provisions apply for any accounting period beginning on or after 22 November 2017 where in that or any earlier accounting period, either:

(1) a loss or other amount attributable to the permanent establishment is deducted from or otherwise allowed against amounts of any person other than the company under the tax law of the territory in which the permanent establishment is situated and as a result there is a decrease in the foreign tax chargeable for a period ending in the accounting period; or

(2) tax is chargeable in the territory in which the permanent establishment is situated on the aggregate profits, or aggregate profits or gains, of the permanent establishment and other persons (other than the company), a loss or other amount attributable to the permanent establishment is deducted from or otherwise allowable against, or is brought into account as a deduction or allowance in calculating, amounts other than amounts of the permanent establishment, and as a result there is a decrease in the foreign tax chargeable for a period ending in the accounting period.

For this purpose, accounting periods which straddle 22 November 2017 are treated as two separate accounting periods, the first ending on 21 November 2017 and the second commencing on 22 November 2017. Any amounts taken into account in calculating the company's credit relief are apportioned between the two notional periods on a time basis or, if a time basis would produce an unjust or unreasonable result, on a just and reasonable basis. In determining whether or not these provisions apply to an accounting period it must be assumed that they were in force for all previous accounting periods beginning on or after 22 November 2011. No account can be taken of any accounting period beginning before that date.

If the above conditions apply, then, in computing the amount of credit relief, the amount of foreign tax paid in respect of the company's 'qualifying income' from the overseas permanent establishment in the accounting period is reduced (but not below nil) by the total of:

(a) the decrease in the foreign tax in (1) or (2) above; and
(b) any amount by which the total for the previous accounting period exceeded the foreign tax paid for that period.

In calculating the total in (a) and (b) above, a deduction or allowance of the kind referred to in (1) or (2) above is ignored if it results in a deduction or other allowance that is reduced under *TIOPA 2010, s 259JC* (counteraction of mismatch in dual territory double deduction cases — see **4.22** ANTI-AVOIDANCE). If it becomes necessary to adjust the total for an accounting period an adjustment may be made, whether or not by HMRC, by way of assessment, modification of an assessment, amendment or disallowance of a claim or otherwise and notwithstanding any time limit.

'*Qualifying income*' of a permanent establishment is those of its profits which are chargeable as a trade carried on partly, but not wholly, outside the UK, under *CTA 2009, Pt 3 Ch 2*.

[*TIOPA 2010, ss 71A, 71B; FA 2018, s 30(2)(5)–(7)*].

Simon's Taxes. See **D4.809**.

Allocation of deductions

[31.8] For the purpose of determining the amount of any credit relief (see **31.6** above), in arriving at corporation tax attributable to the relevant income or gain for a relevant accounting period, the following is to be taken into account.

(i) Any amount that for corporation tax purposes is deductible from or allowable against profits of more than one description may be allocated as the company thinks fit.
[*TIOPA 2010, s 52*].
Charges so allocated may not, however, exceed the income against which they are set (*Commercial Union Assurance Co plc v Shaw* (1999) 72 TC 101, CA).

(ii) Where a non-trading credit is brought into account as regards a loan relationship (see **50.4** LOAN RELATIONSHIPS), special provision is made for the attribution of corporation tax to such credits for the purposes of relief of any foreign tax on the item. A similar provision applies in relation to non-trading credits on intangible fixed assets (see **42.9** INTANGIBLE ASSETS). Non-trading deficits brought forward may only be set against subsequent non-trading loan relationship gains, but may be allocated among such gains as the company thinks fit.
Where, as regards loan relationships, this does not apply, and there is a non-trading deficit (see **50.7** LOAN RELATIONSHIPS) on the company's loan relationships, the deficit is allocated for foreign tax relief purposes in the same way as relief is claimed or is available under *CTA 2009, Pt 5 Ch 16, s 456 et seq*.
[*TIOPA 2010, ss 42, 50–55; F(No 2)A 2017, Sch 4 paras 176, 177*].

(iii) Where there are non-trading debits on intangible assets, these have to be analysed for double tax relief purposes. The amount eligible for double tax relief is the excess of the total amount of the company's non-trading deficits for the period less those carried forward (if any) [*TIOPA 2010, s 56*].

(iv) *CTA 2009, ss 19–32* (profits attributable to permanent establishments — see **64.6** RESIDENCE), and regulations thereunder, apply (with the necessary modifications) for these purposes. [*TIOPA 2010, s 43*].

Simon's Taxes. See **D4.806, D4.807**.

Example

The following information about A Ltd (which owns 20% of the voting power of B Ltd, a non-resident company) for the year ended 31 March 2022 is relevant.

	£
UK income	1,200,000
UK chargeable gains	300,000
Overseas income (tax rate 40%) from B Ltd (gross)	300,000
Qualifying charitable donations	15,000

A Ltd may allocate the charitable donations as it wishes in order to obtain maximum double tax relief. The following calculation shows how this is best done.

	UK income and gains	Overseas income	Total
	£	£	£
Income and gains	1,500,000	300,000	1,800,000
Deduct charitable donations	15,000	—	15,000
	£1,485,000	£300,000	£1,785,000
CT at 19%	282,150	57,000	339,150
Deduct Double tax relief	—	(57,000)	(57,000)
CT liability	£282,150	—	£282,150

Shadow ACT

[31.9] Where relief is available for a foreign tax credit, the income or gain subject to the foreign tax is excluded from profits for the purpose of determining the maximum set-off of shadow ACT and surplus ACT (from accounting periods beginning before 6 April 1999, see **29.30** onwards DISTRIBUTIONS) and the foreign tax credit is deducted from the corporation tax liability. Shadow ACT can be set against the corporation tax liability relating to the foreign income or gain limited to the maximum ACT credit that would have applied had the foreign income or gain been the only income or gain for the accounting period or, if lower, the corporation tax liability as reduced by the foreign tax credit (see *SI 1999 No 358, Reg 12(4)(5)*).

Underlying tax

Underlying tax attributable to dividends

[31.10] Where a non-exempt dividend is paid to a UK resident company or to a non-resident company but forming part of the profits of a UK permanent establishment (see **64.6** RESIDENCE) by a 'related company' in the circumstances set out in **31.2**(b) above (ie. the recipient controls at least 10% of the voting power of the overseas company), relief is given for the following taxes payable by the overseas company in respect of its profits:

(a) any UK income or corporation tax; and
(b) any tax imposed by the law of any other territory,

being underlying tax, which is any tax not chargeable directly on, or by deduction from, the dividend.

Where the overseas company has received a dividend from a third company similarly related to the overseas company, relief may similarly be claimed (subject to certain restrictions on the taxes to be taken into account) for underlying tax payable by the third company, to the extent that it would have been taken into account had it been paid (at the time when the relevant dividend was received) direct to a UK-resident company entitled to relief.

Dividends payable through a chain of related companies may similarly be relieved. While relief is given only for underlying tax (and not withholding tax), it is given for withholding tax arising on dividends paid between foreign companies in a chain, which is treated as part of the underlying tax charge, under (b) above, in the recipient companies.

For this purpose, the 'related company' criteria in **31.2**(b) above (where companies are treated as related where one company, or a company of which it is a subsidiary, controls at least 10% of the voting power in the other company) are amended. The companies in this case are also related where one company, or a company of which it is a subsidiary, controls at least 10% of the ordinary share capital of the other company.

See, however, **31.12** below as regards a general restriction on the amount of relief applicable where dividends are paid through so-called 'mixer' companies. See also **29.11** below as regards a restriction on the relief applicable where the overseas company is a controlled foreign company which is exempt from apportionment by virtue of an acceptable distribution policy.

[*TIOPA 2010, ss 57, 62*].

Simon's Taxes. See **D4.905–D4.907**.

Restriction of relief

Where an 'avoidance scheme' is involved, and underlying tax relating to a dividend includes an amount in respect of tax payable (by reference to the profits which bear that tax) at a rate in excess of the full corporation tax rate in force at the time the dividend was paid, relief is restricted as if tax had been payable at the corporation tax rate.

An '*avoidance scheme*' for this purpose is a scheme or arrangement of any kind, a main purpose of which is to claim relief for an amount of underlying tax, and the parties to which include the company claiming the relief (or a related company or a connected person within *CTA 2010, s 1122*) and a person not under the control (as specially defined) of that company at any time before anything is done in relation to the scheme etc. [*TIOPA 2010, ss 67, 68*].

Example — TIOPA 2010, ss 67, 68

T Ltd, a UK-resident company liable to corporation tax at the full 19% rate for the year ended 31 March 2022, receives a non-exempt dividend on 1 June 2021 of £18,000 gross (tax withheld £770) from X inc, a non-UK resident company in which it holds 20% of the voting power. It claims relief for underlying tax of £4,000 as follows.

£1,600 tax at 10% on profits of £16,000 out of which a £14,400 dividend paid.

£2,400 tax at 40% on profits of £6,000 of Y pty (a subsidiary of X inc) from whom a dividend was received by X Inc, out of which a £3,600 dividend was paid.

T Ltd computes relief as follows (ignoring mixer cap — see below).

	£	£
Gross dividend received		18,000
plus underlying tax		4,000
		£22,000
Tax thereon at 19%		4,180
less underlying tax	4,000	
tax withheld	770	4,180
Corporation tax payable		£nil

It transpires, however, that the dividend from Y pty was bought in as part of a tax avoidance scheme, so that the provisions of *TIOPA 2010, ss 67, 68* apply. The computation is therefore revised as follows.

	£	£
Gross dividend received		18,000
plus underlying tax (see below)		2,500
		£20,500
Tax thereon at 19%		3,895
less underlying tax	2,444	
tax withheld	770	3,214
Corporation tax payable		£681

Underlying tax

The relief for underlying tax in respect of the dividend from Y pty is recalculated as if the tax rate on the underlying profits had been the corporation tax rate of 19% applicable at the time of receipt of the dividend from X inc by T Ltd.

£3,600 × $^{100}/_{81}$ = £4,444 on which 19% tax is £844.

The total underlying tax is thus (£844 + £1,600 =) £2,444.

Simon's Taxes. See **D4.940.**

Foreign mergers

In relation to dividends received by a UK-resident company from an overseas company, relief for underlying tax also includes cases where profits of an overseas company ('company A'), which have borne foreign tax, become profits of another overseas company ('company B') other than by payment of a dividend (e.g. following a merger), and company B then pays a dividend to another company out of those profits.

For the purposes of underlying tax relief, company B is treated as having paid the tax paid by company A in respect of those of its profits which have become profits of company B. However, the amount of relief accordingly available to a

UK-resident company is limited to that which would have been available had the profits been transferred from company A to company B by way of dividend. [*TIOPA 2010, s 69*].

Simon's Taxes. See D4.929.

Group treated as a single entity

There are provisions enabling two or more overseas companies which are taxed as a single entity in the country or territory in which they are resident to be treated as a single company for underlying tax relief purposes in relation to the payment of a dividend to another company by any one of the overseas companies. [*TIOPA 2010, s 71*].

See HMRC International Manual INTM164150. For the implications of the application of the provisions in various countries, see Revenue Tax Bulletins February 2002 pp 911–913, February 2003 p 1007 and October 2003 pp 1063–1064.

Simon's Taxes. See D4.928.

Calculation of underlying tax relief

[31.11] The underlying tax is calculated in accordance with *TIOPA 2010, ss 57–60*, by reference to the paying company's 'relevant profits'.

Thus the underlying tax is:

(a) if a relevant dividend is received in an accounting period of the recipient in which it is a medium-sized or large company (ie. where the dividend exemption rules apply), the foreign tax borne on the appropriate proportion of 'relevant profits', which, for these purposes, are those profits out of which the dividend is treated as being paid under *CTA 2009, s 931H* (being profits out of which a non exempt dividend is paid) [*TIOPA 2010, s 59(2),(3)*];

(b) when (a) above does not apply, the foreign tax attributable to the proportion of the 'relevant profits' represented by the dividend;

(c) in both (a) and (b) above, such foreign tax as does not exceed the formula of M% × (D+PA) (prior to *TIOPA 2010* the formula was M% x (D+U)), this being the corporation tax rate applicable to the profits of the recipient in the accounting period in which the dividend is paid (M) (or the average rate over the period) applied to the sum of the dividend (D) and the underlying tax (PA) (as calculated per (a) and (b) above — formerly (U)). The formula has come to be known as the 'mixer cap' formula (see **31.12** below).

'*Small company*' is as defined at **29.15** DISTRIBUTIONS.

A '*relevant dividend*' is a dividend paid other than on 'relevant profits' per *CTA 2009, s 931H*.

No relief for underlying tax is given if a deduction is allowed in a foreign jurisdiction in respect of an amount determined by reference to the dividend.

The meaning of '*relevant profits*' was considered, in the case of *Bowater Paper Corporation Ltd v Murgatroyd* (1969) 46 TC 37, HL, to be the profits available for distribution as shown by the accounts and not as computed for foreign tax purposes. This is added to any tax chargeable directly on, or deducted from, the dividend, and the total is deducted from the UK tax as under **31.6** above.

'*Relevant profits*' are specifically defined in *TIOPA 2010, s 59(8)* as profits of any period shown as available for distribution in the accounts of the company paying the dividend. The 'accounts' in this case are those drawn up in accordance with the law of the country or territory in which the distributing company is incorporated or formed, with no provision for reserves, bad debts, impairment losses or contingencies except as required under that law.

The '*relevant profits represented by the dividend*' are the profits of the specified period covered by the dividend or, if not paid for a specified period, the profits of the last period of account made up to the date before the dividend became payable. Where the total dividend exceeds the profits available for distribution of that period, the relevant profits are the profits of that period plus so much of the profits remaining available for distribution of preceding periods equal to the excess, taking the most recent preceding period before the next most recent preceding period and so on.

[*TIOPA 2010, ss 57–59*].

Where the paying company has *accumulated losses*, HMRC consider that the 'relevant profits' for this purpose are the undistributed profits of the most recent period available at the time of payment.

Rates of underlying tax are calculated by HMRC, Revenue Policy International (Underlying Tax Group), PO Box 46, Fitz Roy House, Nottingham NG2 1BD (tel. 0115–974 2033) in accordance with the following formula.

$$\frac{\text{actual tax paid} \times 100}{\text{actual tax paid} + \text{relevant profit}}$$

This formula automatically takes into account any deferred taxation charged plus under- and over-provisions for tax in previous years. (CCAB Memorandum 19 October 1979).

Example

A Ltd, a company resident in the UK, receives a dividend in the year ended 31 March 2022 of £1,000 gross from B Ltd, an overseas company in which it controls 10% of the voting power. Overseas tax of £50 is deducted from the dividend on payment. The underlying tax rate for the dividend is agreed at 16%.

	£
Gross dividend	1,000
Underlying tax @ 16%	190
Underlying assessable income	£1,190

			£
Corporation tax thereon @ 19%			226
Overseas tax suffered:	Direct tax	50	
	Underlying tax	190	
Tax credit relief due (restricted)			226
Corporation tax payable			£nil

The underlying tax for which relief is given is limited in certain cases to the amount of the tax actually paid by the overseas company on the particular profits out of which the dividend is paid. This applies in particular to dividends declared by and from a company resident in Belize, the Gambia, Malaysia, Malta or Singapore (where relief is given under an agreement) or Guernsey or Jersey (where the relief is unilateral), each of which operates a 'company tax deducted' system whereby tax is deducted from the dividend at the standard corporate rate and accounted for to the tax authorities, but subject to subsequent adjustment. In so far as that tax is refunded or found not to be due, double tax relief is denied. (SP 12/93, 27 July 1993). But note further the changes to the tax systems in Guernsey and Jersey applicable from 2008 and 2009 respectively.

Credit for underlying tax along a chain of shareholdings is concessionally given to portfolio shareholders (where relief is given under the relevant double tax agreement for underlying tax).

(HMRC Extra-Statutory Concession, C1 — see also INTM167420, it is notable per HMRC guidance that the only countries where this applies are Burma (Myanmar) and St Kitts-Nevis).

For HMRC guidance on computing an underlying rate and information about underlying tax in overseas countries, see HMRC International Manual, INTM 164100 *et seq*. and INTM164400 *et seq*. For calculation of relief for tax in overseas countries, see HMRC Double Taxation Manual, DT2140 onwards (for example, for the calculation of relief for Californian corporate franchise tax, see DT19855).

For underlying tax generally see *Barnes v Hely-Hutchinson* (1939) 22 TC 655, HL; *Canadian Eagle Oil Co Ltd v R* (1945) 27 TC 205, HL; *Brooke Bond & Co Ltd v Butter* (1962) 40 TC 342.

Split rate taxes

Where foreign tax on profits is dependent on how much of the profits is distributed, HMRC consider that the underlying tax in relation to a dividend should reflect the rate of tax on distributed profits rather than the average rate. For dividends paid between 31 March 2000 and 31 December 2001 inclusive, however, HMRC will in practice accept computations on either basis. (SP 3/01, 27 November 2001 and Annex D to Technical Note 'An Exemption for Substantial Shareholdings').

Simon's Taxes. See D4.905–D4.910.

Mixing and onshore pooling

Restriction of relief — 'mixer' companies

[31.12] There are provisions which effectively eliminate the tax advantage of routing overseas dividends through 'mixer' companies in favourable foreign jurisdictions (such as the Netherlands).

Where the credit is to be given to a company, the rate of corporation tax to be used is the rate paid by the recipient of the dividend in the accounting period in which the dividend was received or, if relevant, the average rate for that period.

The relievable underlying tax in respect of any dividend paid up through an overseas subsidiary (including a lower-tier subsidiary) is restricted by the formula of M% × (D+PA) (see also **31.11**(c) above), the restriction being to the rate of corporation tax determined as above (M), applied to the sum of the dividend (D) and the underlying tax (PA) to be taken into account (apart from these provisions).

The claim for relief may, however, be so framed as to exclude any specified amounts of underlying tax from being taken into account for this purpose (which may prevent the application of the cap in certain cases).

The 'mixer cap' restriction does not, however, apply where the overseas companies paying and receiving the dividend are 'related' (in the circumstances described at **31.2**(b) above). Neither does it apply where the companies are both resident in the same overseas territory (subject to Treasury regulations which may prescribe cases where this exclusion will not apply, for which see *SI 2001 No 1156* which prevents certain dual-resident companies resident in the same overseas territory from obtaining the benefit of mixing).

Like other income, dividends are apportioned on a time basis between financial years with different rates of corporation tax. The effect is that profits are taxed for the whole period at an average rate. Therefore the rate above which relief will cut off will be lower as a result of a rate cut. This difference may not be covered by eligible unrelieved foreign tax (if any is applicable to that period).

[*TIOPA 2010, ss 57, 58, 60*].

See HMRC International Manual at INTM164220, 164230 and 164235 for a summary (with examples) of these provisions.

In *Peninsular & Oriental Steam Navigation Company v HMRC* CA, [2016] STC 2001 the CA held that a scheme devised to enhance double tax relief artificially by manipulating dividend payments to increase the amount of underlying tax did not work (without the need to consider recharacterisation under the *Ramsay* principle — see **4.2** ANTI-AVOIDANCE).

Simon's Taxes. See D4.915.

Dividends, interest, etc. paid to non-residents

Dividends

[31.13] There is generally no withholding tax deducted on payments of dividends made by a UK company to another company, whether resident within the UK or overseas.

The European 'Parent-Subsidiary' Directive 2011/96/EU applied before Brexit where the parent company holds a specified minimum of the capital of a company in another member state (or, by bilateral agreement, a specified minimum of the voting rights). The *Directive* ceased to have effect in relation to the UK from IP completion day (11pm on 31 December 2020). As a result, some EU countries may start to deduct tax from dividends paid by EU subsidiaries to UK parent companies. The amount deducted will depend upon the relevant domestic laws of each company involved and the double tax treaties that are in place.

The *Directive* provides that dividends paid to such a parent company are to be exempt from withholding tax in the country of the paying company, that the country of the parent company is equally not to charge withholding tax on the dividend received, and that the recipient country must either exempt the dividend from corporation tax or give credit for the proportion of the subsidiary's corporation tax relating to the dividend. Where the *Directive* applies and gives more favourable treatment than the dividends article in a double taxation agreement, the *Directive* is to take precedence over the agreement.

The *Directive* applies where the parent company holds a minimum of 10% of the capital of a company in another member state. A member state can instead, by means of a bilateral agreement, substitute a voting power test such as the 10% test used by the UK (see **31.2** above).

Interest etc.

[31.14] Where payments required or authorised to be made under deduction of UK income tax are made to non-UK residents, the payer may be authorised by HMRC, by a notice under *SI 1970 No 488*, to make payments without deduction of tax, or under deduction of tax at a specified or maximum rate. Payments may normally only be so made once the notice has been given by HMRC following application by the overseas recipient, and there may be a substantial delay in HMRC being in a position to issue a notice in response to such an application. HMRC have therefore introduced the following schemes to simplify the process.

Provisional treaty relief for syndicated loans

For syndicated loans where the overseas lending members are corporations, and a syndicate manager acts on behalf of all the members of the syndicate, HMRC are prepared to accept a single composite claim for treaty relief made by the syndicate manager on behalf of all the syndicate members eligible to claim the relief, subject to certain conditions, including that the overseas syndicate members should be normal corporate entities and are not transparent entities. For full details see www.gov.uk/government/publications/double-taxation-relief-interest-paid-to-overseas-company-syndicates/double-taxation-relief-loans-from-overseas-company-syndicates.

Double tax treaty passport scheme

Broadly under this scheme any overseas corporate entity and certain overseas transparent entities may apply for a double taxation treaty passport from HMRC. If a passport is granted by HMRC, the holder is entered onto the public register with a unique passport number. If a UK borrower enters into a loan agreement with a lender who is registered as a passport holder, the lender will notify them of their passport holder status and reference number. The UK borrower should then notify HMRC at least 30 days before the first interest payment is due on the loan (using form DTTP2). HMRC will use the DTTP2 notification details to issue a direction to the UK borrower to pay the interest with tax deducted at the rate set out in the relevant double tax treaty. A syndicate as such cannot be a treaty passport holder (the provisional treaty relief scheme applying instead). For loans taken out before 6 April 2017 the passport regime was only available in relation to overseas corporate lenders and UK corporate borrowers. See www.gov.uk/government/uploads/system/uploads/attachment_data/file/606556/Double_Taxation_Treaty_Passport_Scheme_-_Terms_and_Conditions_and_Guidance.pdf.

European member states

For exemption from income tax for certain payments of interest and royalties between associated companies of different EU member states before 1 June 2021, see **41.5** INCOME TAX IN RELATION TO A COMPANY.

Beneficial ownership

One of the most important conditions for treaty relief is that the recipient must be the 'beneficial owner' of the interest or dividend, etc.

In determining whether the recipient of dividends, interest or royalties is the 'beneficial owner', HMRC will, as far as UK double taxation conventions are concerned, interpret 'beneficial ownership' using the 'international fiscal meaning'.

In *Indofood International Finance Ltd v JP Morgan Chase Bank* CA, [2006] EWCA Civ 158, the Court of Appeal supported the view (in the OECD Model Convention on Income and on Capital) that, under an 'international fiscal meaning', beneficial ownership is to be determined by reference to a test which requires that the recipient 'enjoy the full privilege to directly benefit from the income'. It added that where recipients are bound in commercial and practical terms to pass on the income, they will not be the beneficial owner of the income and so not entitled to treaty relief. HMRC guidance provided in their Internet Statement of 9 October 2006 followed the *Indofood* case and discussed their practice in relation to existing treaty clearances.

Simon's Taxes. See **E6.461**.

Exemption for foreign permanent establishment profits

[31.15] A company can make an election for profits arising from its foreign permanent establishments to be exempt from corporation tax (and for losses from those permanent establishments to be excluded). An election can be made UK-resident companies or non-UK resident companies which expect to become UK resident and will apply to all accounting periods of the company beginning on or after the 'relevant day'.

For this purpose, where the election is made by a UK-resident company, the '*relevant day*' is the day on which, at the time of the election, the next (or first) accounting period is expected to begin. In the case of an election by a non-UK resident company, the '*relevant day*' is the day on which the company becomes UK resident. If an accounting period begins before and ends on or after the relevant day, then for corporation tax purposes that period is treated as two accounting periods, the first ending immediately before the relevant day and the second starting on that day. Profits and losses are to be apportioned to the two periods on a just and reasonable basis. An election can only be revoked by the company which made it before the relevant day, but it is revoked automatically where the company ceases to be UK resident. Otherwise the election is irrevocable.

[*CTA 2009, s 18F*].

Effects of election

For each accounting period to which an election applies appropriate adjustments are made in calculating the company's total taxable profits to secure that profits and losses making up the 'foreign permanent establishments amount' are left out of account. Profits and losses are not, however, left out of account if they are:

(1) profits or losses of a trade of dealing in or developing UK land (see **71.2** TRANSACTIONS IN UK LAND) or would be such profits or losses if the company were non-UK resident;

(2) (for disposals on or after 6 April 2019) gains or losses which would be, were the company non-UK resident, gains or losses on disposals on or after 6 April 2019 within **11.25** or **11.26** CAPITAL GAINS (disposals of direct and indirect interests in UK land);

(3) with effect from 6 April 2020 (subject to the transitional provisions at **64.7** RESIDENCE) profits or losses of a UK property business;

(4) with effect from 6 April 2020 (subject to the transitional provisions at **64.7** RESIDENCE) profits consisting of other UK property income; or

(5) with effect from 6 April 2020 (subject to the transitional provisions at **64.7** RESIDENCE) profits or losses arising from loan relationships or derivative contracts to which the company is a party for the purposes of its UK property business or to generate other UK property income.

The '*foreign permanent establishments amount*' is the aggregate of the 'profits amount' for each territory outside the UK in which the company carries on, or has carried on, business through a permanent establishment, less the aggregate of the 'losses amount' for each such territory.

The calculation of the profits amount and losses amount differs depending on whether or not there is a double tax treaty between the territory and the UK which includes a provision (a '*non-discrimination provision*') that a permanent establishment of an enterprise of a contracting state is not to be taxed less favourably in the other state than an enterprise of that other state carrying on the same activities. Where there is such a treaty, the '*profits amount*' is the profits which would be taken to be attributable to the permanent establishment in ascertaining the amount of any credit relief for foreign tax). The '*losses amount*' is calculated on the same basis. If an amount of credit relief does not depend on the profits taken to be attributable to the permanent establishment because, under the treaty, the foreign tax is not charged by reference to such profits, then only profits which would be taken to be attributable to the permanent establishment if the foreign tax were charged by reference to such profits are included in the profits amount (and only such losses are included in the losses amount).

Where there is no such treaty, the profits amount and losses amount are the amounts which would be taken to be so attributable to the permanent establishment if there were such a treaty and it was in the terms of the OECD model tax convention.

If a treaty does not include provisions for a credit to be allowed against tax computed by reference to the same profits as those by reference to which the tax was computed in the foreign territory concerned, it is assumed, for the above purposes, to do so.

All claims and elections (other than those for capital allowances, see below) that would reduce any profits amount, or increase a losses amount, are assumed to have been made.

Special rules apply to the calculation of the adjustments to the company's total taxable profits in relation to chargeable gains and gains taken into account in computing income, capital allowances, income from immovable property, profits and losses from investment business, payments subject to deduction of tax and certain employee share acquisitions. See below.

[*CTA 2009, ss 18A, 18C(5), 18R, 18S; FA 2019, Sch 1 paras 111, 120, Sch 5 paras 12, 35*].

If, at any time in an accounting period to which an election applies, the company is a 'small company' then there is no profits amount or losses amount for that period for any permanent establishment in a territory which does not have a double tax treaty with a non-discrimination provision. A '*small company*' is a micro or small enterprise within the Annex to Commission Recommendation 2003/361/EC.

If the company is a close company (within *CTA 2010, s 439*) at any time during such an accounting period, so much of the company's profits which are derived from chargeable gains are not profits amounts or losses amounts. This exclusion does not apply to gains on the disposal of assets used only for the purposes of a trade carried on through the permanent establishment concerned or to gains on the disposal of foreign currency or a debt within *TCGA 1992, s 252(1)* where the currency or debt is or represents money in use for the purposes of such a trade.

The exemption does not apply to any profits or losses arising from basic life assurance and general annuity business.

[*CTA 2009, ss 18P, 18Q, 18S*].

Chargeable gains

The adjustments to be made under these provisions include adjustments to remove the effect of any gains or losses relating to the disposal of assets taken into account in computing the foreign permanent establishments amount, so that, in appropriate cases, a gain may be increased to reflect a loss so taken into account or a loss increased to reflect a gain.

The profits to be taken into account in computing the 'profits amount' for a permanent establishment above include any gains in respect of immoveable property which has been used for the purposes of the business carried on through the permanent establishment, to an extent which is appropriate having regard to the extent which it has been so used. This also applies to the 'losses amount' and losses in respect of such property. Gains and losses which would be taken to be attributable to the permanent establishment for the purposes of ascertaining credit relief in respect of foreign tax payable before the election takes effect are excluded from the profits and losses amounts.

[*CTA 2009, s 18B*].

Where a company to which an election applies makes a no gain/no loss disposal (including a disposal within *TCGA 1992, s 152* (rollover relief)), the amount of the deemed consideration which results in that no gain/no loss, is to be arrived at after taking account of any adjustments under these provisions (so that the consideration includes the amount which would be the foreign permanent establishments amount attributable to the disposal for the accounting period in which it was made if the disposal were not a no gain/no loss disposal). [*TCGA 1992, s 276A*].

Example 1

An asset is acquired for £300 in 2017 and used exclusively in a foreign permanent establishment until 2021 when it is transferred back to the UK head office to be used there. At the time of the transfer its market value is £2,100 and the other state taxes a gain of £1,800. The asset is eventually sold to an unconnected party in 2025 for £4,300.

Ignoring indexation allowance, the gain in the corporation tax computation will be £4,000 but this will be reduced to £2,200 by the exemption adjustment of £1,800 in relation to the gain arising in 2021.

The legislation does not prescribe how the adjustment is calculated and HMRC guidance on the matter states time apportionment would also be an appropriate method.

Example 2

An asset costing £2,000 is used in the exempt permanent establishment of group company X. It is transferred to group company Y when its value is £2,400. *TCGA 1992, s 171* applies such that this is a no gain/ no loss transfer. However, ignoring indexation allowance, *TCGA 1992, s 276A* requires the no gain/ no loss value to be £2,400 rather than £2,000.

If company Y then used the asset in the UK before disposing of it for £3,000 its chargeable gain would be £600 (instead of £1,000) which preserves the value of the exemption for the transferee company — which is not taxed on company X permanent establishment's £400 gain.

Capital allowances

Where a company carries on a business through a permanent establishment outside of the UK and an election for exemption is made the business carried on through the permanent establishment is treated for plant and machinery allowances purposes as a separate activity whose profits and gains are not chargeable to tax. No actual capital allowances can therefore be claimed by the company for capital expenditure on assets used for the purposes of the business of the permanent establishment. Instead, notional allowances or charges are required to be taken into account in calculating the profit or loss amount. At the beginning of the first accounting period to which the exemption applies, each such asset is treated for this purpose as being transferred to the permanent establishment at its tax-written down value. However, the normal disposal value (see **10.27** CAPITAL ALLOWANCES ON PLANT AND MACHINERY) is used if the asset, or group of assets, has a historic cost greater than £5 million, and the company has used (or is treated as if it had used) the plant or machinery other than for the purposes of the foreign permanent establishment activity at any time in the six years prior to the first exemption period (excluding (where the expenditure does not exceed £50 million) any accounting period that ends earlier than 12 months before 19 July 2011). A balancing charge or balancing allowance may therefore arise.

Similar provisions apply for the purposes of mineral extraction allowances.

Profits or losses from plant or machinery leases are disregarded in the calculation of profits or losses amounts where any allowance (other than a notional allowance as above) has been claimed on the expenditure by the company (or a connected company) as lessor (see *CAA 2001, s 70K*).

[*CAA 2001, ss 15(2A), 431A–431C; CTA 2009, s 18C(1)–(4)*].

Income arising from immovable property

Income from immovable property used for the business carried on through the permanent establishment is included in the profits amount.

[*CTA 2009, s 18CA*].

Profits and losses from investment business

Profits or losses attributable to the investment part of the permanent establishment's business are to be left out of account in determining any profits losses amount unless the profits or losses are generated by assets which are 'effectively connected' with a part of the permanent establishment that carries out a trade or overseas property business. 'Effectively connected' takes the same meaning that it has in the OECD Model Tax Convention on Income and on Capital. This means that if a permanent establishment carries on only investment business, its profits or losses will not be exempt from corporation tax.

[*CTA 2009, s 18CB*].

Payments subject to deduction

Profits or losses of a permanent establishment are excluded from profits and losses amounts where they are referable to any transaction between a UK resident person and an exempt permanent establishment and the UK resident would be required to deduct income tax from payments in respect of the transaction if those payments were made to a company resident in the permanent establishment's territory, having regard to any relevant treaty provisions.

This does not apply to banks unless the transaction is part of arrangements the main purpose (or one of the main purposes) of which is to avoid such a withholding obligation.

[*CTA 2009, s 18D*].

Employee share acquisitions

Any corporation tax relief for employee share acquisitions as provided for under *CTA 2009, Pt 12, Chs 2* or *3* is taken into account in determining the profits or losses amounts of the exempt foreign permanent establishment in a relevant territory to the extent that the relief is linked to the business carried on by the permanent establishment in that territory.

The extent to which any relief is so linked must be determined on a just and reasonable basis having regard to the extent to which the work of the employees concerned contributes to the purposes of the permanent establishment's business.

[*CTA 2009, s 18E*].

Pre-entry losses

Where losses have arisen in any of the company's foreign permanent establishments in the six-year period ending at the end of the accounting period in which the election is made and those losses have not been eliminated by profits from those establishments before the end of that period then the company will have an 'opening negative amount' and no adjustments can be made to the company's total taxable profits until that amount has been eliminated.

The '*opening negative amount*' is ascertained by calculating the foreign permanent establishments amount (excluding chargeable gains and allowable losses) for each accounting period ending less than six years before the end of the accounting period in which the election is made and for that accounting period. The earliest negative amount is carried forward to the next period where it is either increased by another negative amount or reduced or eliminated by a positive amount, but not so as to cause the result to be positive. This process continues through each accounting period and if there is a negative amount remaining after applying it to the last period, that amount is the opening negative amount. The period for which this process must be carried out is extended if there is a losses amount of more than £50 million in an accounting period beginning within the six-year period ending on 18 July 2011, if that period would not otherwise fall within the normal six-year period. Where the period is extended in this way, the process must be carried out for the period of the losses amount and each subsequent accounting period up to and including that in which the election is made.

In each subsequent accounting period (starting with the first to which the election applies) the total opening negative amount is then reduced by the aggregate of any profits amounts for the period. In the first accounting period in which that aggregate exceeds the remaining opening negative amount, adjustments can be made to the company's total taxable profits under the above provisions of an amount equal to the excess and the company can specify which profits are to be adjusted in its tax return for that period.

Alternatively, the company can elect for the opening negative amount to be streamed. If such an election is made then, in effect, the above provisions are applied separately to losses in a particular territory so that they do not delay the application of the exemption to other permanent establishments which would otherwise have no, or a shorter, transitional period. The election must be made at the same time as the exemption election and can only be revoked before the first accounting period to which the exemption election applies. It must specify the territories which are to be streamed. Where not all of the negative opening amount is streamed in this way, the residual amount must be eliminated against the residual profits amounts (i.e. for each accounting period, the total profits amount less the streamed profits amounts) in the same way.

Where a business carried on through a foreign permanent establishment is transferred to a connected company and the business has a 'transferred total opening negative amount', adjustments are made to ensure, broadly, that the above provisions apply to the same extent as they would have been had the business been carried on by the transferee throughout. Where the transferee makes an exemption election which takes effect after the transfer day and the accounting period of the transfer is to be taken into account in calculating its opening negative amount (as above), the transferred total opening negative amount is added to the foreign permanent establishments amount for that period, but only to the extent that it is attributable to the period by reference to which the opening negative amount is calculated. If the effect of this rule would be to exclude a losses amount of more than £50 million arising in an accounting period beginning within the six-year period ending on 18 July 2011 which would otherwise be taken into account as above, that amount is added to the foreign permanent establishments amount of the transferee for the accounting period of the transfer. If the transferee's exemption election took effect before the transfer, the transferred total opening negative amount is treated as the transferee's opening negative amount (in addition to any such actual amount). A separate streaming election can be made in respect of the transferred amount, which does not have to be made at the same time as the exemption election. The transferred total opening negative amount is disregarded in applying the above provisions to the transferor after the day on which the transfer takes place.

If the transferor has not made an election for exemption before the transfer day, the '*transferred total opening negative amount*' is the amount that would have been that company's opening negative amount if it had carried on no business other than the transferred business, there had been no transfer and the company had made an election which took effect from the day after the transfer day. If the transferor made an election which took effect before the transfer day, the transferred opening negative amount is the remaining part of the transferor's opening negative amount insofar as it is attributable to the transferred business.

[*CTA 2009, ss 18J–18O; FA 2011, Sch 13 paras 34, 35*].

Example 3

The overseas permanent establishment of Zed Ltd has the following results for the six years prior to the operation of the election:

Year	Profit/(loss)	Loss carried forward (if any)
-6	2,000	0
-5	(1,000)	1,000
-4	4,000	0
-3	(5,000)	5,000
-2	1,500	3,500
-1	1,000	2,500

The total opening negative amount is 2,500.

Example 4

A company with three foreign permanent establishments makes an election under *CTA 2009, s 18A* which takes effect for the accounting period ending 31 December 2021. The profits amounts and losses amounts (excluding chargeable gains and allowable losses) for the three territories in the preceding six years are as follows.

Year ended 31 December	Territory 1	Territory 2	Territory 3	Foreign permanent establishments amount
2015	2,000	0	(6,000)	(4,000)
2016	1,000	(2,000)	1,000	0
2017	(5,000)	(2,000)	2,000	(5,000)
2018	2,000	4,000	(3,000)	3,000
2019	(10,000)	1,000	2,000	(7,000)
2020	2,000	2,000	2,000	6,000
Opening negative amount				£7,000

The opening negative amount must be extinguished by matching with the aggregate profits amount for each subsequent accounting period, starting with the first period for which the election takes effect (i.e. the year ended 31 December 2021). No adjustments can be made to the company's total taxable profits under *CTA 2009, s 18A* until the opening negative amount has been so extinguished.

Alternatively, the company could have elected for the opening negative amount for Territory 1 to be streamed, so that it need be matched only with profits amounts for that territory. The opening negative amount is calculated as follows.

Year ended 31 December	Territory 1	Loss carried forward
2015	2,000	0
2016	1,000	0
2017	(5,000)	5,000
2018	2,000	3,000
2019	(10,000)	13,000
2020	2,000	11,000
Total negative amount for Territory 1		11,000

The streamed negative amount for that territory is the lower of £11,000 and the aggregate total opening negative amount, i.e. £7,000. The company streams no other territory, so the residual negative amount is the difference between the aggregate negative amount £7,000 and the streamed negative amount £7,000, i.e. nil. The profits amounts for Territory 1 must therefore be matched with the negative amount £7,000 before exemption can apply (i.e. the first £7,000 of such amounts are not exempt), but there is no restriction on exemption for profits amounts of Territories 2 and 3.

Anti-diversion

The exemption cannot apply to 'diverted profits' that are included within the adjusted relevant profits (ie profits computed without reference to chargeable gains or losses).

In such situations the diverted profits are left out of account.

Diverted profits are those profits that pass through what is referred to as the 'diverted profits' gateway, which is determined (with necessary modifications) using essentially the same principles as those that apply to the CFC gateways (see **21.14** CONTROLLED FOREIGN COMPANIES), with the exception of the solo consolidation rules, on the assumption that references to the 'CFC charge gateway' were references to the 'diverted profits gateway'. See HMRC International Manual, INTM286320 onwards.

This 'anti-diversion' rule does not however apply if any of the full CFC exemptions apply (modified, as necessary to reflect that fact that the provisions relate to a PE). These exemptions, being the excluded territories exemption, low profits exemption, low profit margin exemption, and tax exemption (where the profits are not subject to a lower level of tax), are outlined at **21.6** CONTROLLED FOREIGN COMPANIES.

[*CTA 2009, ss 18G, 18H–18HE, 18I–18IDE*].

European cross-border transfers of business

[31.16] This provision applies either where a UK resident company transfers the whole or part of a business carried on by it in another relevant state and a loan relationship, derivative contract or intangible fixed asset is part of the transfer. A '*relevant state*' is an EU member state or, after the end of the Brexit implementation period (11pm on 31 December 2020), the UK or an EU member state.

Or it applies if a UK resident company transfers part of its business to one or more companies. The transfer must be for genuine commercial reasons and must not be part of tax avoidance arrangements. At least one of the transferees must be resident in a relevant state other than the UK. The transferee must continue to carry on a business after the transfer. The transfer must be made in exchange for shares or debentures, unless this is precluded by UK or other country's legal prohibition on purchase of own shares.

In these cases, notional tax is treated as having been incurred and is eligible for double tax relief. Any losses or reliefs are assumed to be claimed in calculating the notional tax charge.

Similar rules apply for mergers of SEs or SCEs, subject to an additional condition which is that, in the course of the merger, each transferor ceases to exist without going into liquidation.

[*TIOPA 2010, ss 116–121, 123; SI 2019 No 689, Regs 1, 18; European Union (Withdrawal Agreement) Act 2020, Sch 5 para 1(1)*].

Simon's Taxes. See **D1.663, D1.770, D1.8104.**

Agreements in force

[31.17] A list is given below of the double tax agreements made by the UK which are currently operative. The agreements have effect to the extent, and as from the operative dates, specified therein (SI numbers in round brackets). Additional notes for certain agreements are given after the list, together with details of agreements made but not yet in force.

Albania (2013/3145), **Algeria** (2015/1888), **Antigua and Barbuda** (1947/2865; 1968/1096), **Argentina** (1997/1777), **Armenia** (2011/2722), **Australia** (1968/305; 1980/707; 2003/3199), **Austria** (1970/1947; 1979/117; 1994/768; 2010/2688), **Azerbaijan** (1995/762),

Bahrain (2012/3075), **Bangladesh** (1980/708), **Barbados** (2012/3076), **Belarus** (2018/778), **Belgium** (1987/2053; 2010/2979), **Belize** (1947/2866; 1968/573; 1973/2097), **Bolivia** (1995/2707), **Bosnia-Herzegovina** (see note below), **Botswana** (2006/1925), **British Virgin Islands** (2009/3013), **Brunei** (1950/1977; 1968/306; 1973/2098; 2013/3146), **Bulgaria** (2015/1891; 1987/2054), **Burma** (see Myanmar below),

Canada (1980/709; 1980/1528; 1985/1996; 2003/2619; 2014/3274; 2015/2011), **Cayman Islands** (2010/2973), **Chile** (2003/3200), **China** (2011/2724; 2013/3142), **Colombia** (2018/377), **Croatia** (2015/2011), **Cyprus** (2018/839; 2019/1113), **Czech Republic** (see note below),

Denmark (1980/1960; 1991/2877; 1996/3165),

Egypt (1980/1091), **Estonia** (1994/3207), **Ethiopia** (2011/2725),

Falkland Islands (1997/2985), **Faroe Islands** (2007/3469), **Fiji** (1976/1342), **Finland** (1970/153; 1980/710; 1985/1997; 1991/2878; 1996/3166), **France** (2009/226),

Gambia (1980/1963), **Georgia** (2004/3325; 2010/2972), **Germany** (2010/2975; 2014/1874), **Ghana** (1993/1800), **Gibraltar** (2020/298), **Greece** (1954/142), **Grenada** (1949/361; 1968/1867), **Guernsey** (2018/1345), **Guyana** (1992/3207),

Hong Kong (2010/2974), **Hungary** (2011/2726),

Iceland (2014/1879; 1991/2879), **India** (1981/1120; 1993/1801; 2013/3147), **Indonesia** (1994/769), **Ireland** (1976/2151; 1976/2152; 1995/764; 1998/3151), **Isle of Man** (2018/1347), **Israel** (1963/616; 1971/391; 2019/1111), **Italy** (1990/2590), **Ivory Coast** (1987/169),

Jamaica (1973/1329), **Japan** (2006/1924; 2014/1881), **Jersey** (2018/1348), **Jordan** (2001/3924),

Kazakhstan (1994/3211; 1998/2567), **Kenya** (1977/1299), **Kiribati** (as per Tuvalu), **Korea, Republic of (South)** (1996/3168), **Kosovo** (2015/2007), **Kuwait** (1999/2036),

Latvia (1996/3167), **Lesotho** (2018/376), **Libya** (2010/243), **Liechtenstein** (2012/3077), **Lithuania** (2001/3925; 2002/2847), **Luxembourg** (1968/1100; 1980/567; 1984/364; 2010/237),

Macedonia (2007/2127), **Malawi** (1956/619; 1964/1401; 1968/1101; 1979/302), **Malaysia** (1997/2987; 2010/2971), **Malta** (1995/763), **Mauritius** (1981/1121; 1987/467; 2003/2620; 2011/2442; 2018/840), **Mexico** (1994/3212; 2010/2686), **Moldova** (2008/1795), **Mongolia** (1996/2598), **Montserrat** (1947/2869; 1968/576; 2011/1083), **Morocco** (1991/2881), **Myanmar** (1952/751),

Namibia (1962/2352; 1962/2788; 1967/1490), **Netherlands** (2009/227; 1980/1961; 1983/1902; 1990/2152; 2013/3143), **New Zealand** (1984/365; 2004/1274; 2008/1793), **Nigeria** (1987/2057), **Norway** (2013/3144; 1985/1998; 2000/3247),

Oman (1998/2568; 2010/2687),

Pakistan (1987/2058), **Panama** (2013/3149), **Papua New Guinea** (1991/2882), **Philippines** (1978/184), **Poland** (2006/3323), **Portugal** (1969/599),

Qatar (2010/241; 2011/1684),

Romania (1977/57), **Russia** (1994/3213),

Saudi Arabia (2008/1770), **St. Christopher (St. Kitts) and Nevis** (1947/2872), **Senegal** (2015/1892), **Serbia and Montenegro** (see note below), **Sierra Leone** (1947/2873; 1968/1104), **Singapore** (1997/2988; 2010/2685; 2012/3078), **Slovak Republic (Slovakia)** (see note below), **Slovenia** (2008/1796), **Solomon**

Islands (1950/748; 1968/574; 1974/1270), **South Africa** (1969/864; 2002/3138; 2011/2441), **Spain** (2013/3152), **Sri Lanka** (1980/713), **Sudan** (1977/1719), **Swaziland** (1969/380), **Sweden** (2015/1891; 1984/366), **Switzerland** (1978/1408; 1982/714; 1994/3215; 2007/3465; 2010/2689; 2018/627),

Taiwan (2002/3137), **Tajikistan** (2014/3275), **Thailand** (1981/1546), **Trinidad and Tobago** (1983/1903), **Tunisia** (1984/133), **Turkey** (1988/932), **Turkmenistan** (2016/1217), **Tuvalu** (1950/750; 1968/309; 1974/1271),

Uganda (1952/1213; 1993/1802), **Ukraine** (1993/1803; 2018/779), **United Arab Emirates** (2016/754), **Uruguay** (2016/753), **U.S.A.** (1980/568; 2002/2848), **Uzbekistan** (1994/770; 2018/628; 2018/628),

Venezuela (1996/2599), **Vietnam** (1994/3216),

Yugoslavia (1981/1815 and see note below),

Zambia (2014/1876; 1972/1721; 1981/1816), **Zimbabwe** (1982/1842).

Shipping & Air Transport only—Algeria (Air Transport only) (1984/362), Brazil (1968/572), Cameroon (Air Transport only) (1982/1841), Hong Kong (Air Transport) (1998/2566), Hong Kong (Shipping Transport) (2000/3248), Iran (Air Transport only) (1960/2419), Jordan (1979/300), Lebanon (1964/278), Saudi Arabia (Air Transport only) (1994/767), Zaire (1977/1298).

Czechoslovakia

The Agreement published as *SI 1991 No 2876* between the UK and Czechoslovakia is treated as remaining in force between the UK and, respectively, the Czech Republic and the Slovak Republic. (HMRC Statement of Practice 5/93).

Yugoslavia

The Agreement published as *SI 1981 No 1815* between the UK and Yugoslavia is regarded as remaining in force between the UK and, respectively, Bosnia-Herzegovina, and Serbia and Montenegro (and, prior to the implementation of new agreements, Croatia, Slovenia and Macedonia). (HMRC Statements of Practice 3/04, 3/07).

Copies of double tax agreements and other statutory instruments published from 1987 onwards are available on the Stationery Office website at www.hmso.gov.uk/stat.htm.

Agreements not yet in force

A protocol to the agreement with Belgium was signed on 14 March 2014 (see *SI 2014 No 1875*). A comprehensive agreement with Kyrgyzstan was signed on 13 June 2017 (see *SI 2018 No 525*). A protocol to the agreement with Germany was signed on 12 January 2021 (see *SI 2021 No 634*). A protocol to the agreement with Sweden was signed on 23 February 2021 (see *SI 2021 No 633*).

Banks and other financial traders

Restriction of credit relief

[31.18] Special provisions restrict the amount of double taxation relief which can be claimed by banks or other financial concerns involved in overseas lending. Where there is a payment of foreign tax or income received in respect of which foreign tax has been deducted at source, see **31.6** above for the restrictions which apply to credit relief for foreign tax in connection with trade income.

Provisions also restrict underlying tax which a UK bank (or a company connected with the bank) can claim on dividends received from a foreign related company. The restriction applies where the underlying tax is (or includes) foreign tax on interest or dividends earned or received by the foreign related company (or by a third, fourth or successive company); and where the restrictions set out in **31.6** above in relation to trade income would have applied to that company if it were UK resident.

The credit for underlying tax is not to exceed the UK corporation tax, at the rate in force at the time when the foreign tax was chargeable, on the amount of interest or dividends less the company's 'relevant expenditure' which is properly attributable to the earning of the interest or dividends.

Banks have to include the 'notional funding costs' in calculating the credit, where this is significantly different from the funding costs used in the calculation. '*Notional funding costs*' means the funding costs that the bank would incur in order to wholly fund the transaction (on the basis of the bank's average funding costs).

[*TIOPA 2010, ss 36, 37, 42, 44–49*].

See *Legal & General Assurance Society Ltd v Revenue and Customs Comrs* [2006] STC 1763 (which preceded the changes made by *FA 2005*), where the High Court confirmed (in dismissing HMRC's appeal) that the legislation did not require the identification of the UK profit which corresponded exactly with the foreign taxable income for the purpose of determining the credit available for foreign tax paid.

See Revenue Tax Bulletin April 1996 p 306.

The bank levy charge provides a framework for double tax relief with respect to the bank levy and similar levies that may be imposed by foreign territories. Double tax relief can be provided either bilaterally or unilaterally, as follows:

(a) bilaterally — existing double tax treaties will not provide relief for the bank levy (and similar other levies). Where arrangements are made with a view to affording relief from double taxation in relation to the bank levy and any equivalent foreign levy then such arrangements can take effect where the Treasury makes an order for them to do so. Regulations can be made to remove or reduce the amount of double taxation relief in cases where a scheme is in place.;

(b) unilaterally — rather than envisaging bilateral arrangements with regard to the bank levy and similar overseas levies, regulations can be issued unilaterally by the UK to allow for relief. Regulations have been issued which allow relief for the French bank levy.

[*SI 2012 No 458*].

See further 7 BANKS.

Simon's Taxes. See **D4.1003**.

Foreign residents

Non-UK resident persons (whether companies or individuals) trading in the UK through permanent establishments (or branches or agencies) may claim tax credit relief for tax withheld by a third country from interest on a loan to a resident of that country where the unilateral relief arrangements in their state of residence allow for such relief.

[*TIOPA 2010, s 30*].

See *CIR v Commerzbank AG*; *CIR v Banco Do Brasil* (1990) 63 TC 218 for a case on interest exemption under the UK/USA Agreement.

See also **51.37** losses.

Simon's Taxes. See **D4.1001–D4.1008**.

Key points on double tax relief

[31.19] Points to consider are as follows.

- Where a treaty is in force the treaty relief must be taken. Before any income is received from an overseas jurisdiction or any payments are made from the UK the taxpayer should ensure that the necessary clearances have been obtained from the appropriate Fiscal Authorities. This process may vary between jurisdictions. For example when receiving income from a US payer the completion of the form W-8BEN by the recipient and its subsequent filing with the payer of the income in the US is sufficient to operate treaty rates. However in the UK it is necessary for HMRC forms to be completed. These forms normally require the overseas recipient to obtain confirmation of their fiscal residence status in the other territory by having their home tax authorities certify their residence status. Once completed, HMRC will ratify to the UK payer operation of the treaty rate.
- Relief for foreign taxes in excess of the treaty rate are not allowed; instead a repayment must be sought from the overseas authority. It is recommended that this situation is avoided (if possible) as obtaining these refunds can be a difficult process including filing foreign tax returns leading to delays.
- Foreign taxes suffered but not credited against UK tax liabilities, for example, because there is no UK liability, cannot be carried forward.
- By election foreign taxes may be claimed as a deduction from income rather than a credit. This offers some relief from the loss of credit relief. For example if a taxpayer has UK trading losses to

cover their foreign income so that there is no UK tax liability then the foreign taxes are lost. By electing to deduct the foreign taxes from the overseas income as an 'expense' the losses required to offset that income is reduced by an amount equal to the foreign tax. This loss is then available for relief in future years. This effectively gives an indirect partial carry forward of the foreign taxes suffered.

- There is an elective exemption from UK tax for the profits of foreign permanent establishments of UK resident companies. It is considered the PE exemption regime will be most beneficial to industry sectors which have to operate overseas through branches due to regulatory reasons, such as the banking and insurance sectors (save for long term business which is excluded). Companies with loss making branches overseas would not make the election (it is an opt-in regime) and would therefore be able to continue with the existing treatment.
- The local tax treatment of some entities as against HMRC's treatment can give rise to double taxing even in treaty countries. A typical example of this is US Limited Liability Corporations (LLCs). With LLCs the US treat them as transparent entities and tax the income and gains as if they were the shareholder's income and gains, thus paying US tax on these sources. However, if the shareholder is UK resident then they are treated as only receiving a dividend on actual distributions. HMRC take the view that the US tax paid has been paid on behalf of the LLC and not as the shareholder's own liability and deny any form of double tax relief. This leads to a double charge on effectively the same income. In *Anson v HMRC* SC, [2015] STC 1777, however, the Supreme Court did not agree with HMRC's view. On examining the relevant Delaware law and the LLC's members' agreement the Supreme Court held that the taxpayer was entitled to his share of the profits as they arose, and it was this income which was taxable in the UK (as well as in the US), therefore double tax relief was allowed. HMRC have, however, announced that they will continue with their existing practice to treat US LLCs as companies. This is on the basis that the decision was specific to the facts and findings determined by the First-tier Tribunal. See HMRC Brief 15/15.

32

European Union Legislation

Simon's Taxes. See **Division A2.2.**

Introduction to European Union Legislation

[32.1] The UK became a member of the European Economic Community (EEC) (now the European Union) in 1972, on ratification of the Treaty of Rome (termed the 'EC Treaty'), and with the commencement of the *European Communities Act 1972* and left on 31 January 2020 (see **32.2** below).

The main purpose of the EC Treaty was to bring about the gradual integration of the states within Europe and to establish a common market founded on the four freedoms of movement (for goods, services, people and capital). In order to pursue these goals the member states surrendered part of their sovereignty and gave the Community institutions (now institutions of the Union) the power to adopt legislation that would be directly applicable in the member states and take precedence over national law.

During the period in which it was an EU member state, the UK, along with the other member states, entered into various additional treaties, which developed the role of the Community and its institutions, the most recent being the Treaty of Lisbon. Post this treaty the European Community became the European Union, and the areas where the Union has competence to legislate have been widened. In addition, the old treaties of the Communities were consolidated. The EC Treaty is now the Treaty on the Functioning of the European Union ('TFEU') and, along with the Treaty on European Union ('TEU'), it establishes the Union, the internal market, the fundamental freedoms, and the Union's institutions, functions and legislative powers.

The following chapter provides an overview of EU Law as it applies to direct tax matters, and highlights some key issues relevant to company taxation.

The judgments of the Court of Justice of the European Union (commonly known as the European Court of Justice — 'ECJ') are extensive and wide ranging. They examine the principles and application of EU Law, and there is a considerable body of case law dealing with the application of EU Law to direct tax matters. Such case law is not considered herein, however, it should be noted when considering cross border EU tax issues. Relevant ECJ case law is referred to throughout this annual, where appropriate.

Brexit and retained EU law

[32.2] On 29 March 2017, the then Prime Minister invoked Article 50 of the TFEU and gave notice to the European Council of the UK's intention to withdraw from the EU. The UK negotiated a Withdrawal Agreement and left the EU on 31 January 2020 with an 11-month implementation period up to 31 December 2020. *FA 2019, s 90* gives the Treasury powers to make regulations by statutory instrument to maintain the effect of tax legislation affected by the UK's withdrawal from the EU and EEA.

On 24 December 2020, the European Commission and UK Government announced an agreement in principle on the legal terms of the future EU-UK relationship – the (draft) EU-UK Trade and Cooperation Agreement (TCA). The TCA was signed by UK and EU leaders and then approved by the UK Parliament on 30 December 2020 and applied provisionally until full ratification by the European Parliament with effect from 1 May 2021. The UK has enacted the *EU (Future Relationship) Act 2020*, which makes provision to implement the TCA in the UK.

The majority of key domestic tax changes associated with Brexit take effect from the end of the implementation period (specifically, 11pm (GMT) on 31 December 2020, referred to as 'IP completion day'), including the full repeal of the *European Communities Act 1972*, incorporation of retained EU law (see below) into the UK domestic legal regime, and the commencement of associated Brexit legislation and statutory instruments.

Retained EU law is a collective term given to the body of EU-derived laws preserved and converted into domestic UK law at IP completion day when the repeal of the *European Communities Act 1972* took effect. As with other domestic law, it can be amended or repealed in the future. EU law that was not retained ceased to apply in relation to the UK following the end of the transition period. Retained EU law falls into three categories:

(1) EU-derived domestic legislation – ie UK legislation which was enacted to give effect to EU legislation – for example, the mergers legislation (*TCGA 1992, s 140* onwards) which was introduced to implement the Mergers Directive;
(2) direct EU legislation – ie English language versions of EU regulations, EU decisions and EU tertiary legislation; and
(3) other rights, powers etc – these can include rights arising under Directives, but only if they are of a kind recognised by the Court of Justice in a case decided before IP completion day, or by a UK court or tribunal in a case begun before IP completion day.

[*EUWA 2018, ss 2, 3, 4*].

Judgments of the CJEU made before IP completion day are binding on the First-tier Tribunal, the Upper Tribunal and the High Court, in relation to disputes about the validity, meaning or effect of retained EU law. There is an exception if the law has been modified since IP completion day and it would be inconsistent with the intention of the modifications for the court or tribunal to follow the EU judgment. The Supreme Court, and the UK's higher appeals courts including the Court of Appeal in England and Wales, the Court of Appeal in Northern Ireland, and the Inner House of the Court of Session (in Scotland), are not bound by any judgments of the CJEU, whether made before or after IP completion day. In deciding whether to depart from a pre-IP completion day EU judgment, these courts must apply the same test as the Supreme Court applies in deciding whether to depart from its own case law, namely, whether it appears right to do so. Judgments of the Court of Justice made after IP completion day are not binding on UK tribunals or courts, but they may 'have regard' to those judgments if they are relevant to the matter being litigated. [*EUWA 2018, s 6; SI 2020 No 1525*].

EU Jurisdiction

[32.3] European Union law is effective in the UK by virtue of *European Communities Act 1972, s 2*. The *European Union (Withdrawal) Act 2018* repealed the *European Communities Act 1972* in its entirety on 'exit day' (31 January 2020) subject to its continuing effect during the withdrawal agreement implementation period which ended on 'IP completion day' (11pm GMT on 31 December 2020). See **32.2** above for the continuing effect of retained EU law.

EU law consists of the Treaties (the TEU and the TFEU), Regulations, Directives and Decisions made under delegated powers, together with the general principles of interpretation developed by the ECJ. The primacy of EU law is one of the general principles underpinning the foundation of the EU, and the ECJ has ruled that national courts must apply EU law 'in its entirety . . . and must accordingly set aside any provision of national law which may conflict with it, whether prior or subsequent to the community rule' (*Simmenthal* (C-106/77) [1978] ECR 629).

With regard to the application of a Directive, similarly the ECJ has held that 'wherever the provisions of a Directive appear . . . to be unconditional and sufficiently precise, those provisions may . . . be relied upon as against any national provision which is incompatible with the Directive in so far as the provisions define rights which individuals are able to assert against the State' (*Becker v Finanzamt Munster-Innenstadt* [1982] 1 CMLR 499).

Under these principles judgments of the ECJ have supremacy over domestic decisions, even if the proceedings commenced in another member state.

Whilst indirect taxes, such as VAT, are specifically within the competence of the EU, direct taxes are not. However, under the provisions as to the approximation of laws, Directives which have an impact on direct tax matters can be adopted, where they are necessary to ensure the functioning of the internal market.

In addition, notwithstanding that direct tax is not within the competence of the EU, Member States' domestic tax laws should not infringe EU law. Thus an extensive body of case law has developed in relation to direct tax, which deals with instances where such matters contravene or infringe a fundamental freedom enshrined in the Treaties. Direct tax matters are generally referred to the ECJ by the national courts, or by the Commission.

There are various cases dealing with the UK's group relief rules, for example, such as *Marks & Spencer plc v Halsey* ECJ Case C-446/03, [2006] STC 237, and more recently *Philips Electronics UK Ltd v HMRC* ECJ Case C-18/11. See also **35.2** GROUP RELIEF.

The Commission plays a key role with regard to direct tax matters — as guardian of the Treaties the Commission keeps the tax regimes of the Member States under review, to ensure they do not infringe the provisions of the Treaties. For example, in October 2011 the ECJ ruled on a case brought by the Commission with regard to the withholding tax regime in Germany on outbound dividends — it found that the German rules, which treated dividends paid to non-resident companies differently to those paid to domestic companies, were an unjustified restriction of the free movement of capital (*European Commission v Germany C-284/09* [2012] 1 CMLR 1207, [2011] STC 2392, ECJ).

In addition the Commission ensures that Member States' tax provisions do not amount to unlawful State Aid (in contravention of Articles 107 and 108 of the TFEU). Member States must notify the Commission in advance of bringing in new provisions that could amount to such. For example, approval from the Commission was sought for the 2011 changes to the UK's research and development tax relief for small and medium enterprises.

EU Statements

[32.4] The primary law consists of the EU Treaties and the general principles, as highlighted in **32.3** above. Secondary law is made up of laws which give effect to the aims of primary law. Secondary legislation comprises statements of the European Council and European Commission and are graded under the EU Treaties as follows.

(a) **Regulations** are binding in their entirety and have general effect in all member states. They are directly applicable in the legal systems of member states and do not have to be implemented by national legislation.

(b) **Directives** are binding as to result but their general effect is specific to named member states. The form and methods of compliance are left to individual member states, which are normally given a specific period in which to implement the necessary legislation.

(c) **Decisions** are binding in their entirety and are specific to a member state, commercial enterprise or private individual. They take effect on notification to the addressee.

(d) **Recommendations and opinions** are not binding and are directed to specific subjects on which the Council's or Commission's advice has been sought.

Applicable Regulations and Directives

[32.5] As highlighted above, in contrast to the extensive application of EU legislation in the VAT sphere, as direct taxes are not within the competency of the EU, the Union only has limited powers to issue legislation in this sphere, such powers being based on ensuring the correct functioning of the internal market. Therefore direct taxes are subject to only the following specific measures.

(a) *Council Regulation 2137/85* concerning European Economic Interest Groupings.
(b) *Directive 2009/133/EC* concerning deferral of tax on income and gains on mergers, divisions, transfers of assets and exchanges of shares between companies of different member states.
(c) *Directive 2011/96/EU* concerning distributions of profits to parent companies.
(d) *Directive 2003/49/EC* as amended by Directive 2004/76/EC (29 April 2004) concerning interest and royalty payments.
(e) *Directive 2016/1164/EU* concerning tax avoidance. The Directive entered into force on 8 August 2016 and must be implemented by member states by 31 December 2018 (or 31 December 2019 in respect of the exit tax rules).

In addition, the two directives on mutual assistance in tax matters also apply, the most recent updated versions being: the *Directive 2011/16/EU*, on administrative cooperation in the field of taxation, as most recently amended by *Directive 2018/822/EU* to introduce new disclosure and reporting rules for intermediaries such as tax advisers, accountants and lawyers involved in the design and promotion of 'aggressive' cross-border tax planning schemes (see **36.15** HMRC — ADMINISTRATION); and, *Directive 2010/24/EU* ('MARD') concerning mutual assistance for the recovery of claims relating to taxes, duties and other measures.

EU Directives are not themselves within the scope of retained EU law (see **32.2** above) and so cease to apply with effect from Brexit IP completion day (11pm on 31 December 2020). However, UK domestic legislation that implements EU directives is within the scope of retained EU law and so continues to have effect until amended or repealed.

As regards (a), see the related UK legislation at **56.21** PARTNERSHIPS. From IP completion day, the ability to form an EEIG within the UK was removed. Any EEIGs that were registered in the UK immediately before IP completion day were automatically converted into 'UK Economic Interest Groupings' or 'UKEIGs'. As regards (b), see **11.18, 11.19** CAPITAL GAINS. As regards (c), see **31.13** DOUBLE TAX RELIEF.

As regards (d), the UK legislation implementing the Directive is repealed with effect for payments on or after 1 June 2021 (subject to anti-forestalling rules which may apply to payments made on or after 3 March 2021); see **41.5** INCOME TAX IN RELATION TO A COMPANY.

As regards MARD, the UK legislation is amended (with effect from IP completion day) to reflect the fact that MARD is extended to the UK as a third country by the EU Withdrawal Agreement and to ensure that the legislation continues to give effect to MARD. MARD will apply to the UK for the five years following IP completion day for amounts that became due or transactions that occurred before that day and, if the debt falls under the Northern Ireland Protocol, for as long as that Protocol remains in force. See **36.14** HMRC — ADMINISTRATION.

For a case on the application of *Directive 90/434/EEC* (Mergers Directive), see *Leur-Bloem v Inspecteur der Belastingdienst/Ondernemingen Amsterdam 2: C-28/95* [1998] QB 182, [1997] ECR I-4161, ECJ. For a case on the application of *Directive 90/435/EEC* (Parent-Subsidiary Directive) see joined cases *Denkavit International BV: C-283/94, VITIC Amsterdam BV: C-291/94 and Voormeer BV v Bundesamt fur finanzen: C-292/94* [1996] ECR I-5063.

In addition to the above, *Convention 90/436/EEC* (23 July 1990), concerning arbitration in double taxation disputes arising from transfer pricing adjustments, came into force on 1 January 1995. See **72.16** TRANSFER PRICING. This is supplemented by Council Directive 2017/1852/EU (10 October 2017) regarding tax dispute resolution mechanisms in the EU. The UK legislation implementing the Directive is revoked with effect from IP completion day. See **31.5** DOUBLE TAX RELIEF.

The European Company/Cooperative

[32.6] *Council Regulation (EC) No 2157/2001* provides for the formation of a company as a European Company or *Societas Europaea* ('SE'). It permits the formation of new SEs and also allows for the 'transformation' of existing companies into SEs and for the merger between two (or more) companies in different member states into an SE. For most tax purposes, an SE based in the UK is treated like a UK-resident plc, but special provisions are required to deal with, among other matters, the formation of SEs by cross-border merger. The provisions are intended to be broadly tax-neutral. (Revenue Technical Note, 'Implementation of the European Company Statute', January 2005).

Council Regulation 1435/2003/EC together with an associated Directive 2003/72/EC allows for the creation of European Cooperative Societies — 'Societas Cooperative Europaea' (SCE). Similarly to an SE, the SCE is a capital company limited by shares. The SCE provisions were implemented in the UK by the *European Cooperative Society Regulations 2006 (SI 2006 No 2078)*.

From Brexit IP completion day (11pm on 31 December 2020), no new SEs or SCEs can be formed in the UK. From IP completion day, every SE that is registered in the United Kingdom immediately before that day is automatically converted into a 'UK Societas'.

The SE and SCE Council Regulations do not contain any provisions relating to the taxation of an SE/SCE, nor do the applicable Directives. Therefore the direct tax position of the SE/SCE should be no different from the direct tax position of a plc or cooperative under national law, save for any specific requirements under the direct tax directives, such as the deferral of tax required under the *Mergers Directive 2009/133/EC* (see **32.5** above).

CTA 2009 includes the provisions dealing with the tax consequences of the formation of an SE by merger of two or more companies resident in different member states, and an SCE by merger of two or more cooperative societies, one of which is a registered society within **22.1** CO-OPERATIVE AND COMMUNITY BENEFIT SOCIETIES (previously a society registered under the Industrial and *Provident Societies Act* 1965).

The provisions cover the deferral of tax charges on the formation of the SE/SCE that would otherwise arise in respect of:

- capital gains and capital allowances (see **11.20** CAPITAL GAINS);
- intangible assets (see **42.27**, **42.28** INTANGIBLE ASSETS);
- loan relationships (see **50.42** LOAN RELATIONSHIPS); and
- derivative contracts.

Anti-avoidance provisions ensure that the rules apply only to the formation of an SE/SCE by merger effected for *bona fide* commercial reasons and which is not part of a scheme or arrangements of which the main purpose (or one of the main purposes) is avoiding a liability to tax and where the merging parties (one or more of them) are not transparent for tax purposes.

There are provisions for obtaining advance clearance from HMRC that the transactions satisfy the anti-avoidance provision. The provisions have effect in relation to the formation of SEs occurring on or after 1 April 2005, or for SCEs occurring on or after 18 August 2006.

[CTA 2009, *merger provisions within Part 5 Loan Relationships, Part 7 Derivatives, Part 8 Intangible Assets*; TCGA 1992, ss 140E–140G].

Residence

For the residence for tax purposes of an SE/SCE transferring its registered office to the UK, see **64.2** RESIDENCE.

Continuity on ceasing to be UK resident

If at any time a company ceases to be resident in the UK in the course of the formation of an SE by merger (whether or not the company continues to exist following the merger), FA 1998, *Sch 18* (company RETURNS (**64**), ASSESSMENTS (**6**), APPEALS (**5**), etc.) applies after that time in relation to liabilities accruing and other matters arising before that time as if the company were still UK-resident and, if the company has ceased to exist, as if the SE were the company.

Where an SE transfers its registered office outside the UK before IP completion day and ceases to be UK-resident, FA 1998, *Sch 18* applies after that time in relation to liabilities accruing and other matters arising before that time as if the SE were still UK-resident.

[FA 1998, *Sch 18 paras* 87A–87C].

Non-resident central banks

[33.3] Non-resident central banks as specified by Order in Council are exempt from tax on certain classes of income. The issue departments of the Reserve Bank of India and the State Bank of Pakistan are exempt from corporation taxes.

[*CTA 2010, s 988; TCGA 1992, s 271(8)*].

See 7.6 BANKS.

The British Museum, The Natural History Museum

[33.4] The British Museum and The Natural History Museum are defined as 'eligible bodies' within the charities provisions and are, on a claim, exempt from tax, including in respect of chargeable gains, as CHARITIES (14).

[*CTA 2010, ss 468, 475–477A, 490; TCGA 1992, s 271(6); Museums and Galleries Act 1992, Sch 8 para 1(8)(9)*].

Charities

[33.5] CHARITIES (14) are generally exempt.

The Crown

[33.6] The Crown is not within the taxing Acts. In addition it is specifically not subject to tax in respect of stock or dividends belonging to it (*ICTA 1988, s 49(2)*) see relevant case law *Bank voor Handel v Administrator of Hungarian Property* HL 1954, 35 TC 311, and *Boarland v Madras Electric Supply Corpn Ltd* HL 1955, 35 TC 612. But see also *ITA 2007 s 978* as to instances of assessment, deduction and payment of tax by public offices and departments of the Crown.

International organisations

[33.7] International organisations (e.g. the United Nations (*SI 1974 No 1261*)) may be specified by Order in Council as exempt from certain taxes (*International Organisations Act 1968*), as may certain financial bodies under the *Bretton Woods Agreement Act 1945* (e.g. the International Monetary Fund (*SI 1946 No 36*)) and other bodies under the *European Communities Act 1972* (e.g. the North Atlantic Salmon Conservation Organisation (*SI 1985 No 1773*)).

The International Development Association is exempt [*International Development Association Act 1960, s 3 and SI 1960 No 1383*] as is the International Finance Corporation [*International Finance Corporation Act 1955, s 3 and SI 1955 No 1954*], and the International Monetary Fund [*International Monetary Fund Act 1979, s 5*].

The Treasury may also designate any of the international organisations of which the UK is a member (e.g. The European Bank for Reconstruction and Development (*SI 1991 No 1694*)) for the purpose of exemption from various requirements for the deduction of tax from payments made in the UK. [*ITA 2007, s 979(1)*].

Friendly societies

[33.8] For the exemptions which apply to friendly societies see *FA 2012, ss 150–179, Schs 18, 19*.

The Historic Buildings and Monuments Commission for England

[33.9] The Historic Buildings and Monuments Commission for England is exempt from tax as an 'eligible body' under the charities provisions, on a claim, as if it is a charity the whole of whose income is applied only for charitable purposes. It is also exempt from tax on chargeable gains (without claim).

[*CTA 2010, ss 468, 475–477A, 490; TCGA 1992, s 271(7)*].

Housing Associations and self-build societies

[33.10] Housing Associations and self-build societies have certain exemptions. See **39** HOUSING ASSOCIATIONS.

Local authorities, etc.

[33.11] The income and gains of local authorities, local authority associations and health service bodies (as defined by *CTA 2010, ss 984–987*) are exempt from corporation tax. The Treasury may by order disapply the exemption for a specified activity, or class of activity, of an NHS foundation trust.

[*CTA 2010, s 984; TCGA 1992, s 271(3); National Health Service and Community Care Act 1990, s 61(1)*].

For payments of interest by local authorities, see **41.12** INCOME TAX IN RELATION TO A COMPANY.

National Heritage Memorial Fund

[33.12] The National Heritage Memorial Fund is classed as an 'eligible body' under the charities provisions and has the same exemptions as CHARITIES (**14**). A claim must be made, except in relation to chargeable gains.

[*CTA 2010, ss 468, 475–477A, 490; TCGA 1992, s 271(7)*].

Simon's Taxes. See **D1.238**.

Scientific research associations

[33.13] A body qualifies as a scientific research association for an accounting period if it is an association which:

(a) has as its object the undertaking of (within *CTA 2010, s 1138* — see **63.1** RESEARCH AND DEVELOPMENT EXPENDITURE) which may lead to or facilitate an extension of any class(es) of trade; and

(b) is prohibited by its memorandum of association or similar instrument from distribution of its income or property, in any form, to its members (other than as reasonable payments for supplies, labour, power, services, interest and rent).

For further requirements which must be met see *SI 2007 No 3426*.

A scientific research association which meets the above conditions is exempt from corporation tax on capital gains.

[*CTA 2010, ss 469–470; TCGA 1992, s 271(6)(b); SI 2007 No 3424; SI 2007 No 3426*].

See also **14.13** CHARITIES for the exclusion of gifts of money from the profits of a scientific research association and **69.61** TRADING INCOME — DEDUCTIONS as regards relief for contributions to scientific research organisations.

Simon's Taxes. See **C5.135**.

Statutory bodies

[33.14] Some STATUTORY BODIES (**66**) receive a measure of exemption.

Pension schemes

[33.15] A registered pension scheme is exempt from income tax on income derived from investments (including futures contracts and option contracts) or deposits held for the purposes of the scheme. [*FA 2004, s 186; FA 2006, s 158, Sch 21 para 7*]. In addition a gain accruing on a disposal of scheme investments by a registered pension scheme or, for disposals on or after 6 April 2013, an overseas pension scheme is not a chargeable gain for capital gains tax purposes. [*TCGA 1992, s 271(1A); FA 2013, Sch 25 paras 14, 20*]. This is subject to exceptions where income is derived from certain property held by self-directed schemes or where gains are realised from such property.

For details of registered pension schemes and overseas pension schemes, including charges made on scheme administrators and charges and surcharges for unauthorised payments, see Tolley's Income Tax under Pension Provision.

Pension Protection Fund

The Pension Protection Fund (PPF) (set up by *Pensions Act 2004* to assume responsibility for final salary occupational pension schemes (and other pension schemes with defined benefit elements) whose sponsoring employers have become insolvent, leaving insufficient assets in the scheme) is given broadly equivalent tax treatment to that of a registered pension scheme.

Simon's Taxes. See E7.1–E7.5.

Trade Unions

[33.16] Registered trade unions which are precluded from assuring more than £4,000 by way of gross sum or £825 p.a. by way of annuity for any one person and which make a claim, are exempt from corporation tax on qualifying income or gains. An annuity contract which is a registered pension scheme is ignored for these purposes, as is an annuity contract issued and held in connection with a registered pension scheme (other than an occupational scheme). The limits may be increased by Treasury order.

The exemption is granted in respect of non-trading income and chargeable gains which are applicable and applied for the purpose of 'providing benefits', i.e. sickness, injury and superannuation payments, payments for loss of tools, etc. This includes legal expenses incurred in representing members at Industrial Tribunal hearings of cases alleging unfair dismissal, or in connection with a member's claim in respect of an accident or injury he has suffered, and general administrative expenses of providing such benefits. (HMRC Statement of Practice, SP 1/84).

The exemption also applies to employers' associations registered as trade unions and to the Police Federations for England and Wales, Scotland, and Northern Ireland, and other police organisations with similar functions.

[*CTA 2010, ss 981–983*].

Simon's Taxes. See D7.635.

Unit trusts, investment trusts and VCTs

[33.17] Unit trusts (46.5 INVESTMENT FUNDS) and investment trusts (47.2 INVESTMENT TRUSTS) and VENTURE CAPITAL TRUSTS (73) are exempt from corporation tax on their capital gains.

[*TCGA 1992, s 100(1)*].

Clubs and societies

[33.18] For the principle that a person cannot derive a taxable profit from trading with itself, see 54 MUTUAL COMPANIES.

Major sporting events: power to provide for tax exemptions

[33.19] *FA 2014* introduces a power, as from 17 July 2014, for the Treasury to make regulations providing for exemption from income tax and corporation tax in relation to major sporting events to be held in the UK. Regulations made under this power must be approved by a resolution of the House of Commons.

The regulations may, in particular: exempt specified classes of person, profit, income or activity from income or corporation tax; provide for specified classes of activity to be disregarded in determining whether a person has a permanent establishment in the UK; disapply a duty to deduct income tax from a payment. Classes of person may be specified wholly or partly by reference to residence outside the UK, or documents issued or authority given by persons exercising functions in connection with the sporting event.

[*FA 2014, s 48*].

34

Foreign Currency

Simon's Taxes. See D4.2.

Introduction to foreign currency

[34.1] Companies do not always prepare their accounts in the same currency as they operate in, and in addition neither of these may be sterling. The Taxes Acts make provision for the translation of these amounts into sterling for the purposes of UK corporation tax.

This chapter also includes HMRC's views on the tax implications of the use of Bitcoin and other cryptocurrencies. See 34.7 below.

Corporation tax currency provisions

Basic rule

[34.2] For corporation tax purposes, a company's income and chargeable gains for an accounting period must be computed and expressed in sterling. This basic rule is subject to the exceptions outlined at 34.3, 34.5 and 34.6 below. The position with regard to losses is also outlined therein.

[*CTA 2010, s 5*].

Operating and accounting currencies

[34.3] The application of the rule in 34.2 above is modified with regard to its application to certain profits or losses falling to be computed in accordance with generally accepted accounting practice (chargeable gains and losses do not fall into such category).

The rules consider three main circumstances:

(a) **Company operating in sterling and preparing accounts in another currency.** Where for a period of account a UK-resident company (other than a UK resident investment company — see **34.4** below), in accordance with generally accepted accounting practice, prepares its accounts in a currency other than sterling but identifies sterling as its 'functional currency' in those accounts, then, for corporation tax purposes, sterling must be used to compute its profits or losses which fall to be calculated in accordance with generally accepted accounting practice as if the company prepared its accounts in sterling. [*CTA 2010, s 6*].

(b) **Company operating in currency other than sterling and preparing accounts in another currency.** Where for a period of account a UK-resident company (other than a UK resident investment company — see **34.4** below), in accordance with generally accepted accounting practice, prepares its accounts in one currency but identifies another currency other than sterling as its 'functional currency', then, for corporation tax purposes, sterling must be used to compute its profits or losses which fall to be calculated in accordance with generally accepted accounting practice by:
   (i) computing those profits or losses in the functional currency as if the company prepared its accounts in that currency; and
   (ii) taking the sterling equivalent of those profits or losses (see **34.5** below). [*CTA 2010, s 7*].

(c) **Company preparing accounts in currency other than sterling.** If, for a period of account a UK-resident company prepares its accounts in a currency other than sterling (the '*accounts currency*') and neither (a) nor (b) above applies, then, for corporation tax purposes, sterling must be used to compute its profits or losses which fall to be calculated in accordance with generally accepted accounting practice by:
   (i) computing those profits or losses in the accounts currency; and
   (ii) taking the sterling equivalent of those profits or losses (see **34.5** below).

   This also applies to a non-UK resident company within the charge to corporation tax, if for a period of account the company prepares the accounts of its UK PE in a currency other than sterling. [*CTA 2010, ss 8, 9*].

'*Functional currency*' means the currency of the primary economic environment in which the company operates. For periods of account beginning on or after 1 January 2016 this definition refers to the functional currency of a company or part of a company's business as meaning the currency of the primary economic environment in which the company or part of its business operates.

Where (b) above applies, it is assumed that any sterling amount mentioned in any other provision is its equivalent expressed in the company's functional currency. Where (c) above applies, it is assumed that any such sterling amount is its equivalent expressed in the company's accounts currency.

[*CTA 2010, ss 6–9, 17(4); FA 2019, Sch 5 para 29*].

Simon's Taxes. See **D4.202A.**

UK resident investment companies

[34.4] Separate rules apply for UK resident investment companies, which can elect prospectively for a different functional currency (the designated currency) for tax purposes other than that used in the accounts.

Where a company makes such an election, then the designated currency is treated as if it were the functional currency and no part of its business can be regarded, in accordance with generally accepted accounting practice, as having another currency as its functional currency. In order for an election to take effect from the date specified therein, at that date the company must be a UK resident investment company and either Condition A or Condition B must be met.

Condition A is that a significant proportion of the company's assets and liabilities are denominated in that currency.

Condition B is that the currency is the functional currency of another company and it is reasonable to assume both companies meet the consolidation condition. The consolidation condition is met where the financial results of the UK resident investment company are required to be consolidated into accounts prepared under acceptable accounting practice by the other company, being the ultimate parent of the worldwide group of which the UK company is a member, or would be so required if such accounts were prepared.

Period for which election has effect

The election has effect from the day specified within it, until: the end of the period of account where the company makes another election; or, a revocation event occurs, whichever is first to occur.

A revocation event will occur in a period of account if, at any time during the period: it is no longer the case that a significant proportion of the assets and liabilities of the company are denominated in its designated currency; and, the currency is no longer the functional currency of another company which met the consolidation condition during the immediately preceding period of account.

For a newly incorporated company, where an election was made after incorporation and before the start of its first accounting period, a revocation event will occur in respect of its first period of account where condition A and not condition B above is satisfied at the beginning of its first accounting period, and at any time after the beginning of that accounting period a significant proportion of the company's assets and liabilities are not denominated in its designated currency.

A revocation event will also occur in a period of account (including in the company's first accounting period) if at any time during that period the company ceases to be a UK resident investment company.

Effects of election

CTA 2010, ss 6(1A) and *7(1A)* allow for the designated currency as elected for by the UK resident investment company to be used for tax purposes.

Under *s 6(1A)*, where the company has prepared its accounts in a currency other than sterling and has elected for sterling to be its designated currency, or where no election has been made has identified sterling as its functional currency in its accounts, then the profits or losses for the period are calculated in sterling.

Under *s 7(1A)*, where the company has prepared its accounts in one currency and had elected for a different non-sterling currency to be its designated currency, or where no election has been made has identified such different non-sterling currency as its functional currency in its accounts, then the profits or losses for the period are first calculated in the designated or identified currency and the sterling equivalent then taken.

Straddle periods

Where an election begins or ceases to have effect during a period of account of the company (the straddling period of account) it is assumed that the straddling period of account consists of two separate periods of account. The first period is treated as ending immediately before the date on which the election (or the revised election) takes effect (or a revocation event occurs), and the second beginning with that day and ending with the end of the straddling period. For these purposes it is assumed that the company prepares its accounts for each of the two periods in the same currency and otherwise on the same basis as it prepares its accounts for the straddling period of account. If the accounts for the straddling period of account, in accordance with generally accepted accounting practice, identify a currency as the company's functional currency, then it is assumed the accounts for each of the two deemed periods do so likewise.

An '*investment company*' is defined as a company whose business consists wholly or mainly in the making of investments and the principal part of whose income is derived from those investments.

[*CTA 2009, ss 6(1A), 7(1A), 9A, 9B, 17(3A); FA 2018, Sch 8 paras 27, 28*].

Simon's Taxes. See **D4.202B.**

Sterling equivalents

[34.5] Where an amount is to be translated into its sterling equivalent as required by **34.3**(b) or (c), or **34.4** above or a sterling amount is to be translated into its equivalent in another currency, the translation is made as follows. The translation must be made:

- by reference to the average exchange rate for the accounting period; or
- if the amount to be translated relates to a single transaction, an appropriate spot exchange rate; or
- where the amount to be translated relates to more than one transaction, an exchange rate derived on a just and reasonable basis from appropriate spot exchange rates for those transactions.

This provision is subject to special rules where a translation into sterling is made for the purposes of calculating carried-forward or carried-back amounts: see **51.26** LOSSES.

[*CTA 2010, ss 10, 11*].

Chargeable gains

[34.6] Special rules apply where a company disposes of a ship, aircraft, stocks or shares or an interest in stocks or shares if at any time in the company's period of ownership of the asset its 'relevant currency' is not sterling. If the company incurs allowable expenditure within *TCGA 1992, s 38(1)(a)–(c)* before it acquires the asset, the period of ownership is treated for this purpose as beginning at the time the first such expenditure was incurred.

For this purpose 'ship' and 'aircraft' include the benefit of a finance lease or hire purchase contract to which *CAA 2001, s 67* applies and which relates to plant or machinery which is a ship or aircraft.

A company's *'relevant currency'* at any time is its functional currency (see **34.3** above) at that time or, where the company is a UK resident investment company which has made an election under *CTA 2010, s 9A* (see **34.4** above), the currency designated in the election.

If the company's relevant currency when it disposes of the ship etc. is not sterling, the gain or loss is calculated in the relevant currency at the time of the disposal and then translated into sterling by reference to the spot rate of exchange on the day of the disposal. In all cases where the special rules apply (whether or not the relevant currency is sterling at the date of disposal), the following computational rules must be followed.

(a) Where any allowable expenditure within *TCGA 1992, s 38(1)(a)–(c)* is incurred in a currency other than the company's then relevant currency, it must be translated into the relevant currency using the spot rate of exchange for the day on which it is incurred.
(b) Where there is a change in the company's relevant currency before the asset is disposed of, allowable expenditure incurred before the change must be translated into the new relevant currency using the spot rate for the day of the change.
(c) Any disposal consideration given in a currency other than the company's relevant currency must be translated into the relevant currency using the spot rate or the day of the disposal.

Any translation of expenditure under (a) above must be done before any translation of the expenditure under (b) above. If there is more than one change in a company's relevant currency, (b) above must be applied to each change in order, earliest first. If the acquisition of the asset was treated either as a no gain/no loss transaction or was treated as made at market value, the deemed expenditure is treated for these purposes as incurred at the time of the acquisition.

[*CTA 2010, s 9C*].

Bitcoin and other cryptocurrencies

[34.7] HMRC have published guidance on the potential tax liabilities for businesses, including companies, in respect of cryptoassets, which has now been incorporated into a Cryptoassets Manual. Broadly, cryptoassets are cryptographically secured digital representations of value or contractual rights which can be transferred, stored and traded electronically. All cryptoassets use some form of distributed ledger technology (blockchain) but there are different types which work in different ways. The main types include: exchange tokens (intended as a method of payment, but also becoming popular as an investment, for example, cryptocurrencies such as bitcoin), utility tokens (which provide access to particular goods or services on a platform), security tokens (which provide the holder with particular interests in a business) and stablecoins (which minimise volatility as they may be pegged to a stable asset such as a fiat currency or precious metal) (HMRC Cryptoassets Manual CRYPTO10100).

HMRC consider that cryptoassets are not money or currency and do not normally consider the buying and selling of cryptoassets to be the same as gambling (CRYPTO10100, 10450). Cryptoassets are chargeable assets for capital gains purposes if they are both capable of being owned and have a value that can be realised (CRYPTO22050). Cryptoassets held by companies may, however, fall within the intangible fixed assets rules if they are intangible assets for accounting purposes and meet the definition of an intangible fixed asset (which requires them to have been created or acquired for use on a continuing basis) (CRYPTO41150). The acquisition of exchange tokens does not generally involve entering into a loan relationship (CRYPTO41100).

Only in exceptional circumstances would HMRC expect businesses to buy and sell exchange tokens with such frequency, level of organisation and sophistication that the activity amounts to a financial trade in itself. If the activity does not amount to a trade, the company must still consider if other legislation applies, such as miscellaneous income or chargeable gains (CRYPTO40150). Mining of cryptoassets (i.e. generating new cryptoassets as a reward for verifying additions to the blockchain) is likely either to amount to trading or to give rise to miscellaneous income (CRYPTO40200).

A disposal of a cryptoasset may occur where the asset is sold for money, where it is exchanged for another cryptoasset, where it is used to pay for goods or services or where it is given to another person. Using a mixer, tumbler or similar service so that the company receives the same type of tokens they put into the transaction is not a disposal (CRYPTO41250). Where cryptoassets are fungible, the share identification rules apply to them. See CRYPTO41350. Difficulties may arise where there is a 'hard fork' in the blockchain for a cryptoasset which results in new tokens coming into existence. Where as a result of a fork a company holds both original assets and new assets, the two must be held in separate pools and the allowable costs for the old assets split between them on a just and reasonable basis (CRYPTO41600).

There is no disposal of a cryptoasset if a company loses its private key so that it cannot access the asset. If, however, it can be shown that there is no prospect of recovering the key or accessing the assets, a negligible value claim can be made (CRYPTO41500).

For the requirement to establish the pound sterling value of transactions (such as where, say, bitcoin is exchanged for ether), see CRYPTO40100.

35

Group Relief

Cross-references. See 4.33 ANTI-AVOIDANCE; 12.2–12.19 CAPITAL GAINS — GROUPS; 21 CONTROLLED FOREIGN COMPANIES; 76.4 WINDING UP; 58.3 PAYMENT OF TAX.

Simon's Taxes. See D2.1, D2.2.

Introduction to group relief

[35.1] There are certain benefits afforded groups of companies under UK tax law. In some respects this means a group of companies is treated in a similar fashion to one corporate entity, as the intention of the legislation is to minimise or extinguish certain tax charges on transactions between group entities, and to allow losses within a group to be used in the most tax efficient manner (subject to any appropriate anti-avoidance provisions).

One of the main tax advantages of membership of a group is that certain losses etc. of one company within the group may be relieved against the profits of another (**35.2–35.4** below). This is known as group relief, or, where a consortium exists, it may be consortium relief.

F(No 2)A 2017 introduced an additional form of group relief, known as '*group relief for carried-forward losses*', which provides for the surrender of losses and other amounts carried forward to an accounting period beginning on or after 1 April 2017 by one company within a group to another member company.

The following types of losses can be transferred as group relief:

(a) Trading losses.
(b) Non-trading deficits on loan relationships.
(c) Capital allowance excess (from special leasing of plant and machinery only).
(d) Qualifying charitable donations.
(e) Qualifying expenditure on grassroots sport.
(f) Excess UK property business losses.
(g) Excess management expenses of companies with investment business.
(h) Excess non-trading losses on intangible fixed assets.

The following types of losses can be transferred as group relief for carried-forward losses:

(a) Trading losses.
(b) Non-trading deficits on loan relationships.
(c) UK property business losses.
(d) Management expenses of companies with investment business.
(e) Non-trading losses on intangible fixed assets.

Scope of group relief

[35.2] Where companies form part of a group (as defined below) then losses and other amounts for an accounting period may be surrendered by one company to another within this same group — this is known as '*group relief*'. Where companies are part of a consortium, then certain relief is available as between the consortium company and the consortium member. This is known as 'consortium' relief — see further **35.19**.

Relief from corporation tax may be obtained by surrendering the items specified in **35.5** below (in whole or in part) by one member of a group (the 'surrendering company') and claimed by another (the 'claimant company') against its own profits chargeable to corporation tax. The relief is also available to and from certain consortium companies, see **35.19** below.

Claims may be made:

(a) for trading losses and other amounts eligible for corporation tax relief (as set out in **35.5** below) where both the claimant and surrendering companies are within the charge to corporation tax (see further **35.6** below); or

(b) for losses and other amounts not eligible for corporation tax relief (effectively for 'qualifying overseas losses', see further the 'EEA amount', as set out in **35.10** below) arising to an 'EEA company'. An '*EEA company*' is a non-resident company within the charge to tax under the law of any European Economic Area (EEA) territory and which is either resident in any EEA territory or not so resident but carrying on a trade through a permanent establishment in any EEA territory. An EEA territory is a territory outside the UK that is within the EEA or, after the end of the Brexit implementation period (11pm on 31 December 2020), Gibraltar.

[*CTA 2010, s 99; F(No 2)A 2017, Sch 4 para 157; SI 2019 No 689, Regs 1, 17(3); European Union (Withdrawal Agreement) Act 2020, Sch 5 para 1(1)*].

Losses of EEA group members

The inclusion of (b) above was made in response to the case of *Marks and Spencer plc v Halsey (Inspector of Taxes): C-446/03* [2006] STC 237 (see below), in which the UK company claimed group relief in respect of losses incurred by its European subsidiaries.

The ECJ ruled (on 13 December 2005) that, although *Articles 43 EC* and *48 EC* on freedom of establishment and discrimination do not preclude the residence requirements, which prevent resident parent companies from deducting losses of non-resident subsidiaries, it is an infringement of those EC Treaty rights to deny group relief to a resident parent company where the non-resident subsidiary has exhausted all possibilities in its member state of residence of utilising the losses in question. This followed the referral to the ECJ of the case by the High Court which stayed proceedings on the appeal of the company against the decision of the Special Commissioners (*Marks and Spencer plc v Halsey (Inspector of Taxes)* [2003] STC (SCD) 70, 5 ITLR 536).

The High Court then ruled (in *Marks and Spencer plc v Halsey (Inspector of Taxes)* [2006] STC 1235) that, on the basis of the ECJ judgment, group relief was not available in the case of the French subsidiary. Claims in respect of the German and Belgian subsidiaries were remitted to the Special Commissioners to hear further evidence and submissions and to determine the appeals in light of this and the ECJ decision.

Both parties appealed to the Court of Appeal, which ruled that the UK group relief rules should not be struck out in their entirety, that what was meant by 'no possibility of use of losses locally' was 'a real possibility' rather than 'no real likelihood' and that that test can be met at or up to the time when the claimant company makes its claim for group relief. (*Marks and Spencer plc v Halsey (Inspector of Taxes)* [2007] EWCA Civ 117, [2007] 2 CMLR 499, [2008] STC 526.)

The case was then heard by the First-tier Tribunal, which had to consider if Marks & Spencer fulfilled the requirements for relief laid down by the ECJ. The point at issue concerned the 'no possibility of relief' in the member state of residence test. The Tribunal held that this test was satisfied in the respect of all claims made while the overseas company was in liquidation or had been dissolved. The Tribunal also considered the correct method to be used to compute the losses relievable. One of the methods put forward by the company was accepted. Under this method, a UK tax computation was prepared, based on the local accounting loss per the annual accounts. The case went to the Upper Tribunal and judgment was given on 21 June 2010 where the losses of the foreign subsidiaries were allowed, except with regard to the years where the 'no possibility' test of other set off were not satisfied at the date of the original claims and the later claims were outside the time limits. Both parties applied for leave to appeal. In 2011 the Court of Appeal considered the matter of the 'no possibilities test' and held that it must be satisfied by the time the actual claim for relief is made, and not at the end of the accounting period in which the losses crystallised. The Court held that successive claims were allowed in respect of the same loss, and agreed with the UT that a proportion of the loss which satisfies the test could be allowed, even if all the loss does not. The matter came before the Supreme Court which handed down judgment in May 2013 in favour of the taxpayer — the 'no possibilities' test should be applied when the group relief claim was made, on the basis that the alternative approach, evaluating at the time of the losses, was so restrictive as to make it virtually impossible to benefit from the relief, which would frustrate rather than give effect to the ECJ's judgment. (*Marks & Spencer plc v HMRC* [2013] STC 1262; [2013] UKSC 30; [2014] UKSC 11.) Following this decision, the Supreme Court held a further hearing to consider three further issues in the case, and unanimously upheld the Court of Appeal decision on all three points, upholding the manner in which the company had computed its losses, but holding that some of its claims (the 'pay and file claims', rather than the 'self-assessment claims') had been lodged outside the statutory time limits. (*HMRC v Marks & Spencer plc (No 4) (and cross-appeal)* SC, [2014] STC 819.)

The decision in this case was followed by the ECJ in *A Oy C-123/11* 2013 STI 485. A Finnish company merged with a Swedish subsidiary and claimed that the prior year losses of that subsidiary (which had ceased activity) should be deductible from its profits taxed in Finland, as would have been the case if the subsidiary had been Finnish. The Finnish tax authority rejected the claim and the company appealed. The matter was referred to the ECJ which held that whilst the freedom of establishment did not preclude such national legislation as justified on the grounds of the balanced allocation of taxing powers between member states (considered together with the risk of double use of losses and tax avoidance), it would be incompatible with EU law if the losses were not allowed to be deducted where the parent company was able to show that the non-resident subsidiary had exhausted the possibilities of taking those losses into account, and that there was no possibility of the losses being taken into account in its State of residence either by itself or by a third party.

In *Philips Electronics UK Ltd v Revenue and Customs Comrs* [2009] UKFTT 226 (TC), [2010] 1 CMLR 511, [2009] SFTD 629 the First Tier Tribunal accepted the company's claim that *ICTA 1988, ss 403D* and *406(2)* (which restricted consortium relief with regard to UK resident investors in joint ventures, and UK branches of overseas companies) contravened EU law and therefore could not prohibit the taxpayer company from claiming consortium relief. The Upper Tribunal referred the case to the ECJ (case C-18/11). The Court held in its judgment of 6 September 2012 that the UK legislation which imposes conditions on the surrender of the losses of a UK PE of a company in another member state (restricting the surrender of such losses within the UK group if the losses could potentially be used or off-set against any non-UK tax of any person) is contrary to the freedom of establishment and could not be justified by overriding reasons in the public interest. See further **35.8** below) which highlights the *FA 2013* changes to the legislation in response to this case.

As noted above, following the *Marks & Spencer* case the UK amended its legislation to allow for loss relief from EEA territories, in limited circumstances. In *European Commission v UK* CJEU (C-172/13), [2015] STC 1055, the ECJ held that it was lawful under EU law for the UK to apply the 'no possibilities' test under the revised legislation immediately after the accounting period in which the losses arose. It appears this judgment contradicts the ruling of the Supreme Court in *Marks & Spencer*, in which it was held that the no possibilities test was to be applied at the point of making the claim. It should be remembered, however, that the latter case related to periods before the introduction of the revised legislation.

In *Esso Exploration and Production UK Ltd v HMRC* FTT, [2020] SFTD 628, the FTT rejected a claim for cross-border group relief by seven UK companies in respect of losses of £228 million incurred by a Danish company in the same worldwide group. The only link between the surrendering company and the appellants was that their ultimate parent was a US corporation. The surrendering company's immediate parent was a company resident in Luxembourg. The FTT followed the decision of the CJEU in *Skatteverket v Holmen AB*, Case C-608/17, in which it was held that the concept of 'final losses' in *Marks and Spencer* does not apply where, as in this case, an intermediate parent is in a different EU Member State from the Member State where the loss-making subsidiary exists.

Simon's Taxes. See **D2.2.**

Group companies

Definition of a 'group'

[35.3] Companies are members of a 'group' of companies if one is a '75% subsidiary' of the other or both are 75% subsidiaries of a third company. This requires 75% of the company's ordinary share capital to be beneficially held directly or indirectly, and entitlement to 75% of the profits on a distribution and 75% of the assets available to equity holders on a winding up (see below with regard to 'equity holders').

[*CTA 2010, ss 151, 152, 1154*].

The residence of the companies constituting the group is not relevant although only UK-resident companies and companies carrying on a UK trade through a permanent establishment may claim group relief (see **35.2** above). See, however, **35.8** below as regards limitation of the application of the definition of 'group'.

Illustration of a group for group relief purposes:

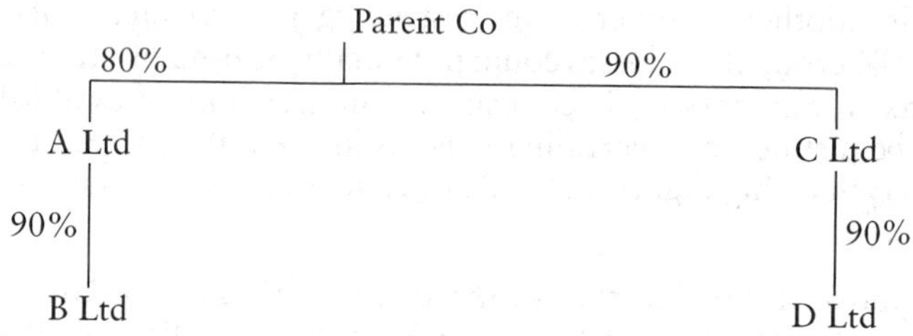

In the above scenario Parent Co and A Ltd are in a 75% group.

However, Parent Co and B Ltd are not in the same group for group relief purposes, as Parent Co holds 80% of the shares in A Ltd, which in turn holds 90% of the shares in B Ltd – which gives an indirect shareholding to Parent Co of only 72% (80% of 90% gives 72%). This is less than the required 75% so a group is not formed by Parent Co, A Ltd and B Ltd, therefore B Ltd is not able to surrender losses to Parent Co, or vice versa.

B Ltd and A Ltd are within a 75% group, so trading losses can be surrendered between them.

There are thus two group relief groups in the above scenario:

Parent Co + A Ltd + C Ltd + D Ltd

and

A Ltd + B Ltd

It can therefore be seen that a company can participate in more than one group for group relief purposes.

For the purposes of group relief, however, a company is treated as not owning:

(a) any share capital held as trading stock; or
(b) any share capital which it owns indirectly and which is directly held by another body corporate as trading stock.

[*CTA 2010, s 151(3)*].

Any share capital of registered societies within **22.1** CO-OPERATIVE AND COMMUNITY BENEFIT SOCIETIES (previously industrial and provident societies) is treated as ordinary share capital. [*CTA 2010, s 151(2)*].

As noted above, the company owning the shares must also be beneficially entitled to **at least** 75% of profits available for distribution to equity holders as such of the subsidiary **and** of assets similarly available in a winding-up. [*CTA 2010, s 151(4)*]. There are various provisions which provide the rules with regard to an analysis of these two additional conditions, and these are considered further in detail below.

It is provided that an open-ended investment company or authorised unit trust (see **45** INVESTMENT FUNDS) can not be treated as a member of a group.

Simon's Taxes. See D2.205–D2.207.

'Equity holders'

Definition of 'equity holder' with regard to a 'group'

[35.4] There are complex provisions within the legislation which deal with the definition of an 'equity holder'.

An 'equity holder' of a company is a holder of its 'ordinary shares' or a 'loan creditor' in respect of a loan other than a 'normal commercial loan'. The latter applies to any redeemable loan capital where the money is borrowed or capital assets transferred in return for any right of the company to receive income or in return for consideration, the value to the creditor company being at the time of transfer substantially less than the amount of the debt (including any debt premium).

The Treasury has the power to introduce regulations to deal with the tax consequences of financial sector regulation, with regard to securities of any EU or UK regulatory requirement, see further **7.1** BANKS.

A regulatory capital security within the provisions at **50.28** LOAN RELATIONSHIPS (before their revocation) is treated as a normal commercial loan for equity holder purposes, subject to certain anti-avoidance and transitional provisions.

[*CTA 2010, s 158; SI 2013 No 3209, Reg 4; FA 2019, Sch 20 paras 1, 10, 11*].

Definition of 'ordinary shares' with regard to an 'equity holder'

'*Ordinary shares*' means, for this purpose, all shares other than certain preference shares: special provision was necessary to prevent companies (in particular banks), which received funding in exchange for shares, failing the test for a group for group relief purposes.

Ordinary shares do not include 'restricted preference shares', defined as follows:

(i) issued for consideration, which is or includes new consideration, received by the company in respect of the issue of the shares;
(ii) carrying no rights to conversion into other shares or securities (subject to certain exclusions);
(iii) carrying no rights to acquire shares or securities;
(iv) not carrying rights to dividends, or carrying a restricted right to dividends; and
(v) not carrying a right to repayment of more than the consideration given for the shares, except in so far as the rights are comparable to those attaching to fixed interest shares quoted on the Stock Exchange.

Dividends carry a 'restricted right' to dividends if the dividends are no more than a reasonable commercial return on the new consideration; and one of the following applies:

(1) the dividends are fixed as to amount or rate of the nominal value of the shares and the company has no entitlement to reduce or not pay any of the dividends;

(2) the rate of dividend on the nominal value of the shares is a standard published rate or varies with RPI or similar index and the company has no entitlement to reduce or not pay any of the dividends; or

(3) (1) or (2) would be met but for the requirement that the company has no entitlement to reduce or not pay any of the dividends and either the company is only entitled to reduce the dividend 'in relevant circumstances' or having regard to all circumstances it is only likely that the company will reduce the amount of or fail to pay dividends if the company is in severe financial difficulties or does not pay on the recommendation of a regulatory body.

The Treasury may prescribe the circumstances in which a company is to be treated as in severe financial difficulties.

[*CTA 2010, ss 158–164*].

As regards (ii) above, rights of conversion into shares or securities of the company's 'quoted parent company' are disregarded, as are rights of conversion into shares satisfying (i), (iii), (iv) and (v) above, or securities satisfying (iii) and (iv) below (with regard to '*loan creditor*'), not themselves carrying conversion (other than into shares or securities in the 'quoted parent company') or acquisition rights.

A company is another company's '*quoted parent company*' for these purposes if and only if:

(A) the other company is its 75% subsidiary (see **35.3** above), for which purpose it is assumed that the company is the 'quoted parent company' of the other;

(B) the parent is not itself a 75% subsidiary; and

(C) the parent's ordinary shares (or each class thereof) are listed on a recognised stock exchange or dealt in on the Unlisted Securities Market.

[*CTA 2010, s 164; ITA 2007, s 1005*].

Definition of 'loan creditor'

As highlighted above, an 'equity holder' of a company is also a 'loan creditor' in respect of a loan other than a 'normal commercial loan'.

'*Loan creditor*' is as defined in *CTA 2010, s 453* (see **16.7** CLOSE COMPANIES) except that banks are specifically included.

[*CTA 2010, ss 158, 453*].

'*Normal commercial loan*' is one representing (in whole or in part) new consideration (as defined in *CTA 2010, s 1115*) and:

(i) which carries no right of conversion into other shares or securities or acquisition of additional shares or securities;

(ii) which carries no right to acquisition of additional shares or securities;

(iii) the interest on which is dependent neither on the results of the company's business (or part thereof) nor on the value of its assets, and represents no more than a reasonable commercial return on the new consideration lent; and

(iv) on which any repayment right is limited to such consideration or is reasonably comparable with the amount generally repayable (in respect of an equal amount of new consideration) under the terms of issue of listed securities.

As regards (i) above, rights of conversion into shares or securities of the company's quoted parent company (as above) or, for loans made on or after 21 March 2012, of a quoted unconnected company (as defined) are disregarded, as are rights of conversion into shares satisfying (i), (iii), (iv) and (v) of 'restricted preference shares' definition above, or securities satisfying (iii) and (iv) above, not themselves carrying conversion (other than into shares or securities in the quoted parent company) or acquisition rights.

A loan is not within (iii) above by reason only of the fact that:

(I) the terms of the loan provide for a reduction in the rate of interest in the event of an improvement in that business (or part) or an increase in the value of any of those assets, or for an increase in the rate of interest in the event of a deterioration in the business (or part) or a diminution in the value of any of those assets; or

(II) where the loan was to be applied in the acquisition of land other than with a view to resale at a profit (or to incidental loan costs), and was secured only on that land, the terms of the loan are such that the only way the loan creditor can enforce payment is by exercising rights granted as security over that land.

A loan on which the amount of interest depends to an extent on the results of the company's business as above, covers a limited recourse loan. (HMRC Company Taxation Manual, CTM81010.)

A hybrid capital instrument or (before the repeal of the relevant provisions) a regulatory capital security within **50.28** LOAN RELATIONSHIPS is a normal commercial loan for these purposes.

[*CTA 2010, ss 162, 163, 164A; FA 2019, Sch 20 paras 1, 6; SI 2013 No 3209, Reg 4*].

Where any person has, directly or indirectly, provided new consideration for shares or securities in the company and that person (or any person connected with him, see **19** CONNECTED PERSONS) uses in his trade assets belonging to the company which have been the subject of certain capital allowances, that person and no other is treated as an equity holder in respect of those shares or securities and as beneficially entitled to any distribution of profits or assets attributable to those shares or securities.

Where this provision applies to a bank which has provided new consideration solely by way of a normal commercial loan in the normal course of its banking business, and the cost of the assets so used is less than such new consideration, the bank is treated as a loan creditor for an amount equal to that cost and therefore as an equity holder in respect of that amount.

[*CTA 2010, ss 159, 1122, 1123*].

Definition of 'profits available for distribution'

Profits available for distribution represent the total profits of the subsidiary for the 'accounting period' or, if there is no such profit, £100 (the 'profit distribution'). It does not matter that there are no profits. All payments not otherwise treated as DISTRIBUTIONS (**29**) are included. In the case of a non-resident company trading through a UK permanent establishment (or branch or agency) (see **35.2** above), the total profits are determined as if it were UK-resident.

[*CTA 2010, s 165*].

'Profits' for this purpose are the 'commercial' distributable profits (having regard to company law requirements), rather than those computed for tax purposes (see HMRC Company Taxation Manual, CTM81035) and only the company's interest as an equity holder is taken into account. The percentage of the profits or assets to which an equity-holding company is, or would be, beneficially entitled includes any indirect entitlement through another body corporate. [*CTA 2010, s 167*].

Assets available on a winding up

The assets available for distribution in a winding-up comprise any excess of assets over liabilities as shown in the subsidiary's balance sheet at the end of the accounting period, or (if there is no such excess or the balance sheet is prepared to a different date) £100. Any such asset received by the equity holder on a winding-up is treated as a distribution to him, notwithstanding that it would not otherwise be so treated.

[*CTA 2010, s 166*].

Any new consideration provided by an equity holder for its shares which is then loaned to, or used to acquire shares in, that equity holder or any person connected with it (see **19** CONNECTED PERSONS) is to be deducted from the total distributable assets and from those distributable to that equity holder.

[*CTA 2010, s 166*].

'*Relevant accounting period*' means any which is current at a time relevant to the group relief claim.

[*CTA 2010, s 168*].

There are detailed anti-avoidance provisions relating to the calculation of the relevant percentages in relation to equity holders of shares or securities with restricted or terminable rights. There are special rules where the surrendering or claimant company is non-UK resident.

[*CTA 2010, ss 169–182*].

See **35.14** below for HMRC's interpretation of 'option arrangements'.

Kinds of group relief

[35.5] The following can be surrendered as group relief by a company for an accounting period:

(a) Trading losses computed as under *CTA 2009, s 47* except losses:
   (i) from trades carried on wholly overseas;
   (ii) from trades not carried on on a commercial basis and with a view to the realisation of gain (with an exception for statutory functions) (*CTA 2010, s 44*; see **51.2** LOSSES); and
   (iii) which are denied relief by *CTA 2010, s 48* (losses from farming or market gardening) (see **51.32** LOSSES).

(b) Capital allowance excess — refers to the excess allowances which have been deducted from or set against income from special leasing of plant and machinery. Such excess allowances may be surrendered in so far as they exceed such income for an accounting period (before deduction of losses or capital allowances brought forward) and the machinery or plant is not used by the lessee for a non-qualifying purpose (*CTA 2010, s 101*). See **51.3** LOSSES.

(c) Non-trading deficits on loan relationships (see **50.7** LOAN RELATIONSHIPS), these include non-trading debits on derivative contracts.

(d) Amounts allowable as charitable donations.

(e) Amounts allowable as qualifying expenditure on grassroots sport (see **14.19** CHARITIES).

(f) Losses in a UK property business, excluding losses brought forward from earlier periods and losses incurred in a property business which was not carried on either on a commercial basis or in the exercise of statutory functions (*CTA 2010, s 102*, see **59** PROPERTY INCOME).

(g) Management expenses of companies with investment business (not brought forward from an earlier accounting period) (*CTA 2010, s 103* and see **44** INVESTMENT COMPANIES AND INVESTMENT BUSINESS).

(h) Non-trading losses on intangible fixed assets (*CTA 2010, s 104*, see **42.9** INTANGIBLE ASSETS), excluding any brought forward from an earlier accounting period.

Amounts within (a) to (c) above are eligible for surrender regardless of whether the surrendering company has other profits of the same accounting period against which they could be set.

Amounts within (d)–(h) above ('*relevant amounts*') can be surrendered only to the extent that the total relevant amounts for the accounting period exceed the 'profit-related threshold' for the period. The order of set off for surrender purposes is taken to consist first of qualifying charitable donations, then of grassroots sport expenditure, then of losses in a UK property business, then of management expenses and finally of non-trading losses on intangible assets.

The '*profit-related threshold*' is the sum of the surrendering company's 'gross profits' and the amount of any CFC chargeable profits apportioned to the company (where the company is a chargeable company for CFC purposes).The CFC profits which are included within the profit-related threshold are the chargeable profits for an accounting period of the CFC ending in the surrender period, as apportioned to the surrendering company.

The company's '*gross profits*' are its profits without any deduction in respect of amounts within (a)–(g) above or of any losses, allowances or other amounts of other periods. This does not include capital losses brought forward from a previous period and deducted as part of the computation of chargeable gains. (*Taylor v MEPC Holdings Ltd* [2003] UKHL 70, [2004] 1 All ER 536, [2004] STC 123, HL).

See also **21** CONTROLLED FOREIGN COMPANIES.

See **35.8** below for UK losses of non-UK resident companies and **35.9** below for overseas losses of UK-resident companies.

The availability of group relief as above is subject to restriction in the case of dual resident investing companies (see **35.23** below), certain ring-fenced activities, certain transactions in relation to the sale of lessor companies (see **49.9** LEASING) and certain transactions by leasing partnerships (**49.3** LEASING).

[*CTA 2010, ss 97–105; CAA 2001, s 260(7), Sch 2 para 36; F(No 2)A 2017, s 22(3)(4), Sch 4 paras 157, 158; SI 2004 No 2310, Arts 14, 15*].

Simon's Taxes. See **D2.215–D2.225**.

Limits on group relief

[35.6] In order for a valid claim for group relief to be made both the surrendering and claimant company must apply to HMRC: a company may surrender its surrenderable amounts for the surrender period; the claimant company may make a claim for group relief for the claim period for all or part of the amounts.

The following conditions must be met:

(i) the surrendering company must consent to the claim (see **35.12** below);
(ii) there is a common period (the 'overlapping period'); and
(iii) the surrendering and the claimant companies are members of the same group (**35.3**) and both are 'UK related'.

The amount for which group relief may be claimed against total profits may not exceed the lesser of:

(a) the 'unused part of the surrenderable amount for the overlapping period'; and
(b) the 'unrelieved part of the claimant company's total profits for the overlapping period'.

The amount referred to in (a) above is so much of the total amount available for surrender for the accounting period of the surrendering company as is attributable (see below) to the 'overlapping period' and has not been the subject of any prior surrenders attributable to the 'overlapping period'.

The amount referred to in (b) above is so much of the total profits of the claimant company for the accounting period of the claim as is attributable (see below) to the 'overlapping period', reduced by any previously claimed group relief attributable to the 'overlapping period'.

A company is '*UK related*' if it is UK resident or, if it is not UK resident, it is within the charge to corporation tax. This definition is as amended by *FA 2019*, but applies, with retrospective effect, from 5 July 2016 (when the corporation tax charge on TRANSACTIONS IN UK LAND (**71**) by non-resident companies was introduced). Previously, a company was UK related if it was either UK resident or carried on a trade through a permanent establishment in the UK. Where a claim to group relief becomes possible as a result of the change, the time limit for making the claim (see **35.12** below) is extended to 31 December 2019 if it would otherwise be earlier.

The '*overlapping period*' is the period common to the accounting periods of both the claimant company and the surrendering company to which the claim relates, but excluding any part of the common period when:

- those companies are not both members of the same group and in the case of a non-UK resident company, carrying on a UK trade through a permanent establishment (or branch or agency); or
- in the case of a 'qualifying overseas loss' (see **35.10** below), the surrendering company is not a member of the same group as the claimant company (as defined for this purpose in **35.3** above) and is not resident or not carrying on a trade through a permanent establishment within an EEA territory.

There are detailed rules for determining the surrenderable amount for the overlapping period and the unrelieved part of the claimant company's total profits.

Claims which would otherwise be treated as having been made at the same time are deemed to have been made in such order as the company or companies making them elect or jointly elect, or in the absence of such an election in such order as HMRC may direct. See the example at **35.7** below.

See also **4.35** ANTI-AVOIDANCE for the effect on group relief claims where an accelerated payment notice has been issued.

Attribution to overlapping periods

Where an apportionment falls to be made as above, to determine how much of an amount for a period falls to be attributed to a part of the period, the apportionment is generally made on a time basis according to how much of the whole period coincides with the part.

However, if some or all of the apportionments to be made in any particular case would lead to an unjust or unreasonable result, in relation to any person, the apportionments are to be made in such other manner as may be just and reasonable.

[*CTA 2010, ss 129–131, 134, 135, 138–141; FA 2019, s 24(1)(3)(4)*].

For 'just and reasonable' apportionment, see HMRC Company Taxation Manual, CTM80260.

De-grouping charge

See **12.15** CAPITAL GAINS — GROUPS for the effect on *CTA 2010, ss 138–142* of the application of the de-grouping provisions of *TCGA 1992, s 179*.

Consortia

The above rules apply with appropriate modifications to consortium group relief claims. Limitations also apply with regard to such relief claims. See further 35.19 below.

Example

[35.7]

X Ltd incurs a trading loss in the year ending 31 December 2021 of £120,000. Throughout that period, it has two wholly-owned subsidiaries Y Ltd and Z Ltd. Y Ltd prepares accounts to 31 March, and has profits of £100,000 in the year ending 31 March 2021. Z Ltd prepares accounts to 30 September and has profits of £400,000 in the year ending 30 September 2021. No group relief claims or surrenders have been made other than those referred to below.

Y Ltd claims the maximum relief for the year ending 31 March 2021 by surrender from X Ltd.

Overlapping period three months to 31 March 2021

Maximum loss available for surrender

$^3/_{12}$ × £120,000 = £30,000

Maximum profits against which loss surrendered may be set

$^3/_{12}$ × £100,000 = £25,000

Thus X Ltd surrenders losses of £25,000 to Y Ltd.

Z Ltd then claims the maximum relief for the year ending 30 September 2021 by surrender from X Ltd.

Overlapping period nine months to 30 September 2021

Maximum loss available for surrender

	£
$^9/_{12}$ × £120,000 =	90,000
less amount previously surrendered (note (a))	25,000
	£65,000

Maximum profits against which loss surrendered may be set

$^9/_{12}$ × £400,000 = £300,000

Thus X Ltd surrenders losses of £65,000 to Z Ltd.

The balance of X Ltd's loss (£30,000) may be surrendered against losses of subsequent periods of Y Ltd and Z Ltd which overlap with X Ltd period to 31 December 2021 or subsequent periods as group relief for carried-forward losses.

Note

(a) As the overlapping period in relation to the surrender to Y Ltd falls entirely within the overlapping period in relation to the surrender to Z Ltd, the whole of the loss surrendered in relation to the earlier period is deducted from that available for the later period.

Overseas losses

UK losses of non-resident companies

[35.8] In relation to group relief for UK losses of non-resident companies within the charge to UK corporation tax, relief is broadly restricted as follows. Amounts available for surrender under these provisions, in addition to any losses or other amounts available for surrender by non-resident companies, are as set out in **35.10** below.

As highlighted above, losses, etc. available for surrender by the non-resident company for an accounting period are those which:

(i) are attributable to activities the income or gains from which for that period are or (if there were any) would be brought into account in computing chargeable profits for corporation tax purposes;
(ii) are not attributable to activities which are exempt under any double taxation relief arrangements (see **31.17** DOUBLE TAX RELIEF), disregarding any claim requirement; and
(iii) do not correspond to, or are represented by, an amount which is deductible or otherwise allowable for foreign tax purposes against any 'non-UK profits' of any person, although this does not apply to amounts which are, or are an element in computing, profits exempted from that foreign tax.

The restriction at (iii) above does not apply where the surrendering company is established in a 'relevant territory' (but not elsewhere). For such a company, a further restriction applies. For such a company, in addition to meeting (i) and (ii), no amounts can be surrendered as group relief in the UK if the losses (or any amount brought into account in calculating them) are, in any period, deducted from or otherwise allowed against the non-UK profits of any person.

A company is established in a relevant territory for this purpose if it is constituted under the law of the UK or a relevant territory and has its registered office, central administration or principal place of business within the EEA or, after the end of the Brexit implementation period (11pm on 31 December 2020), Gibraltar. A 'relevant territory' is a territory outside the UK but within the EEA or Gibraltar.

The difference is thus, for non-EEA companies the UK losses cannot be used in the UK if they could potentially be used against non-UK profits, whereas for EEA companies the losses have to be actually used against non-UK profits.

'*Foreign tax*' for this purpose means any tax corresponding to income or corporation tax (including local and regional taxes), and any foreign tax provision by virtue of which the deductibility of an amount is dependent on whether or not it is deductible for UK tax purposes is disregarded.

'*Non-UK profits*' are amounts (or elements in computing amounts) charged to foreign tax and not included in corporation tax total profits of any person for any accounting period.

Similarly the total profits for an accounting period against which relief may be claimed by a non-resident company are restricted to amounts comprised in the company's corporation tax chargeable profits for the period and not arising from activities exempt from corporation tax under any double taxation relief arrangements (and this restriction on the scope of total profits applies also for the purposes of the definition of 'non-UK profits' as above).

For these purposes, amounts are exempt under double tax relief arrangements if their effect is to cause any income or gains arising from the activities to be disregarded in computing chargeable profits.

[*CTA 2010, ss 107, 108, 186, 187; FA 2019, Sch 5 para 30; SI 2019 No 689, Regs 1, 17(2); European Union (Withdrawal Agreement) Act 2020, Sch 5 para 1(1)*].

Overseas losses of UK-resident companies

[35.9] A loss, etc. of a UK-resident company is not available for surrender by way of group relief if it is 'attributable' to a permanent establishment through which the company carries on a trade outside the UK, and all or any part of it is, or represents, an amount allowable against 'non-UK profits' (as above) of any other person for the purposes of 'non-UK tax' under the law of the territory where the permanent establishment is situated. 'Non-UK tax' for this purpose means any tax corresponding to income or corporation tax (including local and regional taxes.

A loss, etc. is 'attributable' to a permanent establishment for this purpose if it would be available for surrender by way of group relief if it were computed only by reference to that permanent establishment and by the application of the same principles as apply to a permanent establishment through which a non-UK resident company carries on a trade in the UK (as above).

[*CTA 2010, ss 106, 187*].

Simon's Taxes. See **D2.261.**

The EEA amount which may be surrendered

[35.10] Five steps have to be taken in order to determine the amount which may be surrendered. The steps are:

(1) find out how much is eligible for corporation tax relief (ignoring these provisions). Only the eligible amount will be available for relief — it is called the EEA amount;
(2) determine the 'qualifying part of the EEA amount' by finding out the extent to which the EEA amount satisfies the equivalence, EEA tax loss, qualifying loss and precedence conditions (see below);
(3) recalculate the EEA amount using the certain assumptions (see below). This will produce the recalculated EEA amount. The recalculation is done using corporation tax computational rules for determining losses or other amounts. (The Treasury has power to amend these rules for this purpose.)
(4) determine the amount which may be surrendered i.e. the lesser of the EEA amount and the 'relevant proportion' of the recalculated EEA amount. The relevant proportion is the qualifying part of the EEA

amount to the EEA amount. There is an anti-avoidance provision which applies if there are arrangements with the main purpose, or one of the main purposes, of obtaining group relief;

(5) if any of this amount is excluded as mentioned below, deduct the excluded amount.

The conditions mentioned in (2) above are as follows:

(a) **the equivalence condition** is met to the extent that the EEA amount is made up of items which would be surrenderable if the company had been UK resident, i.e. items within **35.5** (see also (a) at **35.10** above).

(b) **the tax loss condition** differs according to whether the companies are resident in the EEA country or not. In the former case, this condition is met by identifying the EEA amount as the amount calculated under the overseas tax law. However, amounts attributable to permanent establishments in the UK are excluded. Where the company is not resident in an EEA country but is carrying on trade through a permanent establishment within the EEA, the EEA amount is the amount determined for tax purposes in an EEA territory. However, there are exclusions to the extent that the EEA amount is subject to 'relieving arrangements'.
'*Relieving arrangements*' are double tax relief arrangements which have such effect that the income of gains would be ignored for UK tax purposes.

(c) **the qualifying loss condition** is fulfilled to the extent that the surrendering company or any other company cannot relieve the EEA amount in an EEA territory for overseas tax purposes by:
   (I) the EEA amount cannot be relieved in the EEA territory or any territory outside the UK in calculating profits of any person (not just the surrendering company);
   (II) the EEA amount is not relievable in calculating profits of any person (not just the surrendering company) in any future period. This test must be applied immediately after the end of the period in which the loss arises; and
   (III) the EEA amount is not relievable in calculating profits of any person (not just the surrendering company) in the current or any previous period. If there is any possibility at all of the company or any other person obtaining relief, even if they forget or fail to do so, then the loss is not a qualifying loss.

   In *European Commission v UK* CJEU (C-172/13); [2015] STC 1055, the ECJ held that it was lawful under EU law for the UK to apply the 'no possibilities' test in (II) above immediately after the accounting period in which the losses arose. It appears this judgment contradicts the ruling of the Supreme Court in *HMRC v Marks & Spencer plc (No 3)* SC, [2013] STC 1262, in which it was held that the no possibilities test was to be applied at the point of making the claim. It should be noted, however, that the latter case related to periods before the introduction of the timing rule in (II) above.

(d) **the precedence condition** addresses the situation where relief could be claimed in more than one country because there is an intermediate overseas company. It is met to the extent that no relief can be given for the EEA amount in a territory (outside the UK and which is not the EEA territory) in which a company which owns (directly or indirectly) ordinary share capital in the surrendering company is resident, where a UK resident company owns (directly or indirectly) ordinary share capital in the company resident in the territory and the surrendering company is a 75% subsidiary of that UK resident company, otherwise than as a result of it being a 75% subsidiary of another UK resident company.

In recalculating the EEA amount using UK tax rules, four assumptions have to be made. These are:

(i) *residence* — the surrendering company is assumed to become UK resident at the beginning of the EEA accounting period and to remain UK resident throughout that period. This does not involve assuming that there is a change in residence for the purpose of assumption (ii) below, or that it loses UK residence at the end of the EEA accounting period;

(ii) *place the activities carried on* — a trade is assumed to be carried on in the UK, as is any property business. Regarding interests in property, they have to be treated as being, so far as possible, the UK equivalents;

(iii) *accounting periods* — the UK accounting period is treated as beginning at the beginning of the EEA accounting period and ending at the earlier of the end of the EEA accounting period and twelve months after the beginning. Thereafter, if the EEA accounting period continues, it ends at the earlier of twelve months or when the EEA accounting period ends;

(iv) *capital allowances* — if the EEA company incurred any capital expenditure on the provision of plant or machinery for the purposes of any activity before the beginning of the loss period, it is treated as incurred for a non-qualifying activity and then brought into use for a qualifying activity at the beginning of the loss period under *CAA 2001, s 13* (see **10.65** CAPITAL ALLOWANCES ON PLANT AND MACHINERY).

[*CTA 2010, ss 111–128; SI 2019 No 689, Reg 17(3)*].

See HMRC Company Taxation Manual, CTM81502 onwards which details how the extension to the group relief rules work.

Unallowable overseas losses of non-resident companies

[35.11] There are anti-avoidance provisions to prevent losses arising in EEA territories from being available for group relief in the UK where they have been purposefully created for such relief.

In the case of a non-resident company that is resident in any EEA territory, or if not resident is carrying on a trade in such territory through a permanent establishment, where a loss or other amount (as set out in **35.10** above) arising to that company is not attributable for corporation tax purposes to any UK permanent establishment, then it is not available for surrender by way of group relief under the provisions identified at **35.10** above if:

(a) it qualifies for group relief or arises to the non-resident company by reason only of 'arrangements'; and

(b) the main purpose or one of the main purposes of the relevant arrangements was to secure that the amount would qualify for group relief.

'*Arrangements*' includes any agreement, understanding, scheme, transaction or series of transactions (whether or not legally enforceable) made. See Company Tax Manual, CTM81502.

[*CTA 2010, s 127; Sch 2 para 52*].

Claims

[35.12] The provisions below apply for the purposes of group relief and group relief for carried-forward losses (see **35.24** onwards below), and references below to group relief should be read accordingly. For certain additional requirements in relation to claims to group relief for carried-forward losses see **35.29** below.

Claimant company

A claim for group relief under self-assessment must be included in the company tax return (or amended return) (see **65.4**, **65.8** RETURNS) for the accounting period for which the claim is made. It must specify the amount claimed (which must be expressed in money at the time the claim is made) and the surrendering company. The time limit for making a claim is extended to 31 December 2019 in certain cases where relief became available only because of the extension of the meaning of 'UK related' at **35.6** above.

It must also state whether any of the following:

(a) the claimant company;
(b) the surrendering company; or
(c) any other company by reference to which either those companies are members of the same group or the conditions for consortium relief are satisfied,

was not UK resident in either or both of the surrendering company's accounting period to which the surrender relates or the corresponding accounting period of the claimant company.

[*FA 1998, Sch 18 para 68*].

The claim must be made (and may be withdrawn) at any time up to the latest of:

(i) the first anniversary of the filing date for the claimant company tax return;
(ii) 30 days after closure of any enquiry into that return (unless the enquiry, being otherwise out of time, was limited (see **65.15** RETURNS) to matters to which a previous amendment making or withdrawing a group relief claim relates, or which are affected by the amendment);
(iii) 30 days after notice of any amendment of that return by HMRC following such an enquiry; and
(iv) 30 days after determination of any appeal against an amendment within (iii),

or at a later time if HMRC allow it (for which see **51.3** LOSSES).

[*FA 1998, Sch 18 para 74*].

These time limits override the normal time limits for amendment of a company tax return. Withdrawals of claims must be made by amending the return, and a claim can only be amended by withdrawal and replacement by another claim.

A claim may be made after the surrendering company has left the group (*A W Chapman Ltd v Hennessey* (1981) 55 TC 516).

In *R (oao Bampton Group Ltd) v King (HMRC) (and related applications)* [2012] EWHC 361 the claimant companies had submitted claims to group relief which were excessive in amount, because the relevant profits and losses had been time-apportioned incorrectly. They subsequently made a late claim for some of the relief to be set against the profits of another company in the group. HMRC rejected the claim and the High Court dismissed an application for judicial review. Blair J held that 'in a commercial setting such as this, the responsibility for formulating a claim for group relief correctly must lie with the group'. The Court of Appeal unanimously upheld this decision [2012] EWCA Civ 1744. Arden LJ held that 'none of the passages in Code of Practice 14 relied on by the appellants imposed an obligation on HMRC to disclose a matter which had been spotted prior to the enquiry but which was not present to the minds of the officials of HMRC handling the affairs of the taxpayer during the enquiry. To hold otherwise would indeed without justification shift the responsibility for those errors from those who had caused the error, namely the taxpayer and its advisers, to HMRC.'

A claim may be made for less than the full amount available for surrender at the time of the claim, but is ineffective if it is for more than that amount. The amount available for surrender at any time is the total amount available (see **35.5** above) on the basis of the surrendering company's tax return, disregarding any amendment whose effect is deferred pending completion of an enquiry (see **65.15** RETURNS), *less* all amounts for which notices of consent (see below) have been given and not withdrawn. Withdrawals are given effect before any claims made on the same day.

Where claims are made on the same day for an aggregate amount in excess of the amount available for surrender, HMRC determines which of the claims is to be ineffective to prevent an excess arising.

Claims may be made by more than one company in respect of the same surrendering company accounting period. [*CTA 2010, s 135*].

In *LINPAC Group Holdings Ltd v HMRC* FTT, [2020] SFTD 575, the FTT held that group relief claims remained valid even though subsequent claims were made (and then withdrawn) in respect of the same profits. The company claimed group relief for the years ended 31 December 2006 and 2008 in its tax returns, utilising losses of other UK group companies (the 'domestic claims'). It subsequently made further claims for group relief for those years (the 'cross-border claims'), this time using losses of group members resident in other EU member states. The company later accepted that the cross-border claims did not meet the criteria for entitlement and sought to revert to the domestic claims. HMRC argued that the domestic claims were no longer open to the company because its making of the cross-border claims involved the withdrawal of the domestic claims by virtue of *FA 1998, Sch 18 para 73* and it was too late to make those claims afresh. The FTT rejected this argument. In *Marks &*

Spencer plc v HMRC SC, [2014] STC 819, the Supreme Court had held that a later claim could be valid even if an earlier claim had not been withdrawn. It therefore followed that earlier and later claims could coexist and that an earlier claim could remain valid after the making of a later claim. Although the cross-border claims did not expressly keep the domestic relief claims open, the FTT decided that there was no implicit withdrawal. Instead, the cross-border claims were being advanced as preferred alternatives to the domestic claims, conditionally upon their proving to be well-founded.

[*FA 1998, Sch 18 para 69*].

Consent — surrendering company

A claim requires the written consent of the surrendering company (and a consortium claim also that of each member of the consortium), which must be given to the officer of HMRC to whom the company makes its tax returns at or before the time the claim is made, and a copy of which must accompany the claim.

The consent notice must give the names and tax reference numbers of the surrendering company and the company to which relief is being surrendered, the amount of the relief, and the surrendering company accounting period to which the surrender relates. It may not be amended, but may be withdrawn (by notice to the officer to whom the consent was notified) and replaced within the normal time limits (as above). Notice of withdrawal must be accompanied by the written consent of the claimant company, unless the withdrawal is the result of a reduction in the amount available for surrender (for which see below), and the claimant company must, so far as it may do so, amend its return accordingly.

See, however, below as regards simplified claim and surrender procedures.

Where the consent relates to a loss or other amount in respect of which corporation tax relief has already been given to the surrendering company for any accounting period, the company must (notwithstanding any time limits otherwise applicable), at the same time as giving its consent, amend the return for that period.

Where there is a reduction in the total amount available for surrender (as above) below the amount for which consent to surrender has already been given, the company must, within 30 days, withdraw its consent (and may issue new notices of consent) so as to bring the total of amounts for which consent is given within the total amount available. Copies of the withdrawal notices and any new consents must be sent to the companies affected and to HMRC.

If the company fails to take such corrective action, HMRC may by written notice to the company give directions as to which consents are to be treated as reduced or eliminated to the extent necessary to achieve that objective (subject to appeal in writing by the company within 30 days of the notice to the officer by whom it was given), and must copy the notice to any claimant company affected by those directions. A claimant company notified of any withdrawal or new consent or HMRC direction must, so far as it may do so, amend its return for the period in question accordingly.

[*FA 1998, Sch 18 paras 70–75*].

Unpaid tax and HMRC assessments

Where a claimant company becomes liable to tax in consequence of receiving a notice of withdrawal or new consent or HMRC direction (as above), and any of the tax is unpaid six months after the company's 'time limit for claims' (see below), HMRC may, up to two years after that time limit, make an assessment in the name of the claimant company on any other company which has obtained group relief as a result of the surrender. The amount of the assessment is limited to the lesser of the amount of the unpaid tax and the amount of tax the other company saves by virtue of the surrender. The other company may recover the tax (and any interest thereon) from the claimant company.

The company's 'time limit for claims' for this purpose is the latest of the dates in (i)–(iv) above on which the company could make or withdraw a group relief claim for the accounting period for which the claim in question was made.

An assessment may be made to recover group relief which in the opinion of HMRC is or has become excessive. This is without prejudice to the making of a discovery assessment (see **6.3** ASSESSMENTS) or to the making of adjustments by way of discharge or repayment of tax. As regards notices of assessment, time limits and appeals, the same conditions apply as in relation to discovery assessments. Where a claimant company fails, or is unable, to amend its return following receipt of a notice of withdrawal or new consent or HMRC direction (as above), an assessment may be made (if otherwise out of time) up to one year after the date of the notice (the date of the new notice if a new notice of consent follows a withdrawal notice).

[*FA 1998, Sch 18 paras 49, 75A–76*].

Simplified group relief procedures

The *Corporation Tax (Simplified Arrangements for Group Relief) Regulations 1999* (*SI 1999 No 2975*) (as amended) provide for a group of companies all, or substantially all, of whose tax returns are made to the same tax office to enter into special arrangements enabling an authorised company within the group to act for the group in relation to group relief claims. The authorised company may then, in a form provided or authorised by HMRC, provide a written statement containing the information necessary for the amendment of company tax returns of the companies covered by the arrangements for the purpose of making or withdrawing group relief claims and surrenders.

Group companies are liable for any incorrect claim or return arising from the authorised company's statement. Consortium companies which can claim or surrender group relief may be included in the arrangements (and the authorised company may be a consortium company).

The simplified arrangements may apply also to group relief for carried-forward losses — see **35.24** below.

For the detailed requirements as to the making of an application by an authorised company, and the consequences of entering into such arrangements, see *SI 1999 No 2975* (as amended) and HMRC Company Taxation Manual, CTM97600 onwards. Note that it is not necessary for all the companies included in the arrangements to have identical accounting periods.

[*FA 1998, Sch 18 para 77; SI 1999 No 2975*].

Losses of non-resident companies

Overseas losses of non-resident companies

The above provisions apply to claims in respect of overseas losses of non-resident companies (see **35.2**(b) and **35.10** above) with the following modifications. References to the relief being surrendered is to the EEA amount. References to the surrendering company's accounting period are to its deemed accounting period under **35.10**(iii) above. Notice of consent of the surrendering company is to be given by the claimant company to the officer of HMRC to whom that company makes its returns and the requirement for the notice to contain details of tax district reference does not apply.

Notice of withdrawal of consent is to be given by the claimant company and not the surrendering company. A notice of withdrawal and any new notice of consent under *FA 1998, Sch 18 para 75* (reduction in amount available for surrender) is to be sent to an officer of HMRC by the claimant rather than the surrendering company and any notice containing directions by an officer of HMRC is to be given to the claimant company. The claimant company rather than the surrendering company can appeal against such directions and the rest of *Sch 18* is to be similarly read with appropriate modifications.

Where a notice to produce documents is given to the claimant company for the purposes of an enquiry, the notice may require the claimant company to explain why the EEA amount meets the conditions for it to be treated as a qualifying loss and to provide details of the recalculation required (see **35.10** above). The claimant company may also be required to explain why the EEA amount is not prevented from being surrendered by virtue of the unallowable losses provision in **35.11** above.

[*FA 1998, Sch 18 para 77A*].

A claim may be made after the surrendering company has left the group (*A W Chapman Ltd v Hennessey* (1981) 55 TC 516).

See **35.5** above as regards amounts available for relief.

Simon's Taxes. See **D2.240–D2.244**.

Claims by non-UK resident companies trading in the UK

[35.13] As noted at 35.6 above, non-UK resident companies who are within the charge to corporation tax and who fulfil the conditions for group relief may make a claim for such relief.

Such claims must fulfil the following conditions:

- the surrendering company must consent to the claim;
- there must be an overlapping period;
- either, the surrendering company is a 75% subsidiary of the claimant and the latter is UK resident; or both the claimant and surrendering companies are 75% subsidiaries of a third company and that company is UK resident.

[*CTA 2010, ss 135, 136*].

Arrangements for transfer of company to another group or consortium

[35.14] Relief is denied where two companies are members of a group and 'arrangements' are in existence by virtue of which one company could leave the group and join another group, or any person could gain control of one company but not the other, or a third company could succeed to the trade of one of the companies.

Similar restrictions apply to consortium relief (see **35.19** below). There are also provisions to cover the situation where there are arrangements under which the consortium-owned company could leave the group or where the company could come under the control of a third company.

[*CTA 2010, ss 154, 155*].

Definition of 'arrangements'

'*Arrangements*' for this purpose are those of any kind, whether in writing or not. The following, however, are not arrangements:

- the power of a Minister of the Crown, the Scottish Ministers or a Northern Ireland department to direct a statutory body as to the disposal of its (or any subsidiary's) assets; and
- a condition imposed by, or agreed with a Minster of the Crown, the Scottish Ministers or a Northern Ireland department or a statutory body.

A '*statutory body*' is specifically defined to mean a body (other than a company within the meaning of *Companies Act 2006, s 1(1)*) established by or under a statutory provision for the purposes of carrying out functions conferred on it by or under a statutory provision. The Treasury may, by order, specify that a particular body is or is not to be treated as a statutory body for this purpose.

[*CTA 2010, s 156(2)*].

Arrangements which are in existence during the relevant period are within the definition irrespective of when they came into existence (*Pilkington Bros Ltd v CIR* (1982) 55 TC 705, HL) and without regard to the extent of their implementation (*Irving v Tesco Stores (Holdings) Ltd* (1982) 58 TC 1, HL).

Arrangements which could not legally be carried out without variation of the underlying agreement were ineffective for these purposes (*Scottish and Universal Newspapers Ltd v Fisher* [1996] STC (SCD) 311).

The appointment of a receiver constitutes arrangements for these purposes (*Farnborough Airport Properties Co Ltd v HMRC* CA, [2019] STC 517).

The restriction of relief applies only to accounting periods or parts thereof during which the arrangements subsisted (*Shepherd v Law Land plc* (1990) 63 TC 692, HL).

Exception for joint venture companies

Agreements between the companies holding shares or securities in a joint venture company, which allow or require remaining members to acquire the holding of a departing company (and which allow or require a departing company to transfer its shares to remaining members) are not regarded as arrangements (or option arrangements — see **35.4** above) for the purposes of the above provisions until one of the following specified events occurs:

(a) the voluntary departure of a member;
(b) the commencement of liquidation, administration or receivership of a member;
(c) a serious deterioration in the financial condition of a member;
(d) a change in the control or ownership of a member;
(e) a default by a member in performing its obligations under the terms of an agreement between the members or with the joint venture company, including its articles of association;
(f) an external change in the commercial circumstances in which the undertaking operates such that its viability is seriously threatened;
(g) unresolved disagreement among the members;
(h) any contingency of a similar kind provided against, but not intended to happen, when the agreement in question was entered into.

A provision in the articles of a joint venture company providing for the suspension of a member's voting rights on the occurrence of a specified event is not regarded as bringing arrangements into existence until the specified event actually occurs. These provisions do not apply if the persons who would acquire shares, securities or control of the joint venture company in consequence of the occurrence of a specified event could (alone or with connected persons) dictate the timing of the acquisition in advance of the specified event. The definition of 'connected persons' in *CTA 2010, s 1122* applies for this purpose, but persons are not regarded as connected solely by virtue of their interest in the joint venture company.

[*CTA 2010, ss 155A, 174A*].

Exception for mortgage of securities

If shares or securities in a company are used as security for a mortgage, the mortgage is not in itself regarded as constituting arrangements (or options arrangements) until a default or other event occurs which enables the mortgagee to exercise his rights against the mortgagor (unless the default is remedied before the mortgagee exercises his rights). [*CTA 2010, ss 155B, 174B*].

Exceptions under SP 3/93

'Arrangements' (and 'option arrangements') are the subject of an HMRC Statement of Practice. The special rules relating to 'arrangements' are not applied to the following cases:

(I) Straightforward negotiations for the disposal of shares or securities in a company, before the point at which an offer is accepted subject to contract or on a similar conditional basis.
(II) An offer to the public at large of shares in a business, unless there are exceptional features.
(III) Operations leading towards the disposal of shares or securities in a company, until any necessary approval by shareholders has been given, or the company's directors become aware that it will be given.

(IV) Where, following negotiations with a number of potential purchasers, the vendor concentrates on one, unless there were an understanding between them in the character of an option, e.g. if the offer, whether or not formally made, were allowed to remain open for an appreciable period, allowing the potential purchaser to choose the moment to create a bargain.

(V) Company reconstructions requiring the approval of shareholders, until the necessary approval is given or the directors are aware that it will be given.

'Arrangements' (but not 'option arrangements') may exist even though not enforceable. If an agreement provides for the creation of specified option rights exerciseable at some future time, 'option arrangements' come into existence when the agreement is entered into.

(HMRC Statement of Practice, SP 3/93).

See also HMRC Company Taxation Manual, CTM80165–CTM80205.

Simon's Taxes. See **D2.251, D2.252.**

Transfer of deductions

[35.15] Anti avoidance provisions restrict amounts within group relief claims made by a company where there has been a qualifying change in relation to the company. A '*qualifying change*' is defined as for the capital allowance buying provisions at *CAA 2001, s 212C*, and is aimed at certain changes in ownership of a company, or changes in profit ratios of a partnership or changes in ownership ratios for a consortium. For further details see **51.23** LOSSES.

[*CTA 2010, Part 14A*].

Payment for group relief

[35.16] Payments may be made for group relief and, in certain circumstances, will be tax neutral. If, by agreement, the claimant company pays the surrendering company an amount equal to, or less than, the relief surrendered by it as above, that payment is ignored in the corporation tax computations of both payer and payee and is not treated as a distribution (see **59.11** PENALTIES).

[*CTA 2010, s 183*].

Other limitations on relief

[35.17] Relief may not be given more than once in respect of the same amount. [*CTA 2010, s 137(7)*].

In the case where it is discovered that too much relief has been given, see **35.12** above.

See also 35.5 above.

No group relief is available for a deduction which is denied for the relevant return under alternative finance arrangements where the provision is not at arm's length and *CTA 2009, s 520* applies.

[*CTA 2010, s 110*].

Relationship to other reliefs

[35.18] Group relief is deducted from the claimant company's total profits (see 35.5 above) before reduction by any of the losses etc. listed below, but as reduced by any other relief from tax (including relief in respect of qualifying charitable donations under *CTA 2010, Pt 6* or in respect of non-trading deficits on loan relationships (see **50.7** LOAN RELATIONSHIPS). Total profits for this purpose are calculated on the assumption that the company makes all relevant claims to set trading losses and capital allowances against total profits under *CTA 2010, s 37* and *CAA 2001, s 260(3)* respectively. See **51.3** LOSSES and **10.54** CAPITAL ALLOWANCES ON PLANT AND MACHINERY.

The losses etc. referred to above are trade losses carried back under *CTA 2010, s 37*, capital allowances carried back under *CAA 2001, s 260(3)*, non-trading deficits carried back under *CTA 2009, s 389* (see **50.4** LOAN RELATIONSHIPS) or a deficit under *CTA 2009, ss 459, 463B* for a later year than the year of claim and, for accounting periods beginning on or after 1 April 2021, brought forward losses and other amounts of a type which are subject to the restriction on deduction of carried-forward LOSSES (**51.13**). For accounting periods beginning before 1 April 2021, group relief for carried-forward losses under *CTA 2010, s 188CK* (see **35.24** below) was also included.

[*CTA 2010, s 137; F(No 2)A 2017, Sch 4 para 159; FA 2021, Sch 8 paras 4, 17*].

Example

A Ltd (a group member) has the following, for the accounting periods shown.

	To 31 December 2020	To 31 December 2021
Trading (loss) brought forward (pre-April 2017)	(£500)	—
Trading income/(loss)	£1,000	(£1,000)
Income from non-trading loan relationships	£500	£500
Qualifying charitable donations	(£200)	(£200)

Group relief available to A Ltd will be subject to the following options and restrictions.

(a) *For the accounting period ended 31 December 2020*

(i) The loss brought forward and the qualifying charitable donations must be relieved in priority to group relief. The maximum amount of group relief claimable will accordingly be the amount of profits on which corporation tax would otherwise be borne, i.e. £800.

(ii) If relief for this period is claimed under *CTA 2010, s 37(3)(b)* for so much of the trading loss of the following period as cannot be relieved in that period, i.e. £500, such relief would be displaced by a group relief claim, and would then be available for carrying forward.

(b) *For the accounting period ending 31 December 2021*
Whether or not the company claims relief under *CTA 2010, s 37*, no group relief may be claimed.

Simon's Taxes. See D2.202.

Consortia

[35.19] Consortium relief is a variation of group relief where losses of a consortium company can be transferred to consortium members and vice versa. The transfer of losses will be in proportion to the consortium member's interest in the consortium.

Definition of consortium

A consortium company is a company which is owned, to the extent of 75% (at least) by consortium members (each of which owns at least 5% of the shares of the consortium company). There are other requirements, see further below.

Available consortium relief

Group relief is available where either the surrendering company or the claimant company is a member of a consortium and the other company (the consortium company) is:

(a) a 'trading company' which is 'owned by the consortium' and which is not a 75% subsidiary (see **35.3** above) of any company, or
(b) a trading company which:
  (i) is a '90% subsidiary' of a 'holding company' which is owned by the consortium, and
  (ii) is not a 75% subsidiary of any other company, or
(c) a holding company which is owned by the consortium and which is not a 75% subsidiary of any company;

and both companies are UK related, i.e. each is UK resident or a non-resident company carrying on a trade in the UK through a permanent establishment (see **35.6** above).

Consortium relief is also available where the claimant or the surrendering company is not a member of a consortium, but is a member of the same group as a third company (the link company) which itself is a member of the consortium and the claimant and surrendering companies are UK related. There are no requirements with regard to the location of the link company.

[*CTA 2010, ss 132, 133, 134A, 153*].

Where the surrendering company consents to the claim, there is an overlapping period and one of the undernoted conditions applies, then consortium relief is available. More than one company may make a claim against a surrenderable amount.

The conditions are:

(1) either (when surrendering up) the surrendering company is a trading company or a holding company which is owned by a consortium and the claimant is a member of the consortium and both are UK related (see above), or (when surrendering down) the claimant company is a trading or holding company owned by a consortium, the surrendering company is a member of the consortium and both are UK related;
(2) the above similarly applies where the consortium company is surrendering and there is a link company, which is a member of the consortium, but the claimant company is not;
(3) the above similarly applies where the consortium company is the claimant company and there is a link company, which is a member of the consortium, but the surrendering company is not.

No claim may be made where the shares in the other company (or its holding company) are held by the member of the consortium as trading stock.

[*CTA 2010, ss 130, 132, 133*].

The residence of the companies is not relevant in determining whether the consortium relationship requirement is satisfied (and see further below), although the claimant and surrendering companies must each either be resident in the UK or carry on a UK trade through a permanent establishment.

[*CTA 2010, s 134*].

Relief may also be restricted by reference to the surrendering company's losses, and the claimant company's profits, of the corresponding accounting period (see below for more details).

Relief may also be restricted where a company which is a consortium member claims consortium group relief and also claims bad debt relief in respect of a loan to the consortium company. See **50.22** LOAN RELATIONSHIPS.

See also **63.6** RESEARCH AND DEVELOPMENT EXPENDITURE for a restriction on surrendering losses by a small or medium-sized company which is owned by a consortium and is entitled to research and development relief.

A '*holding company*' is a company the business of which consists wholly or mainly in the holding of shares or securities in trading companies which are its 90% subsidiaries. [*CTA 2010, s 185*]. A single subsidiary will constitute its parent a holding company.

A '*trading company*' is a company the business of which consists wholly or mainly of the carrying on of a trade or trades or the holding company of a trading group. [*CTA 2010, s 90*].

A company is '*owned by a consortium*' if at least 75% of its 'ordinary share capital' is directly and beneficially owned amongst them by companies each owning at least one-twentieth, which are the 'members of the consortium'. [*CTA 2010, s 154*].

For this purpose, '*ordinary share capital*' means all the issued share capital of a company other than restricted preference shares. Restricted preference shares are those fulfilling all the following conditions:

- shares issued for, or which include, new consideration;

- no conversion rights attached to loan stock or shares or stock in the parent company;
- no right to acquisition of shares or securities attached to the shares;
- no right to dividends or restricted right to dividends;
- no right to repayment in excess of new consideration, except so far as the rights are reasonably comparable with those generally carried by fixed dividend shares listed on a recognised stock exchange.

'*Issued share capital*' does not include founder members' deposits in a company limited by guarantee (*South Shore Mutual Insurance Co Ltd v Blair (Inspector of Taxes)* [1999] STC (SCD) 296).

A company is the '*90% subsidiary*' of another if not less than 90% of its ordinary share capital is directly owned by that other. The definition of 'ordinary share capital' given above applies. The parent company must also be beneficially entitled to at least 90% of profits available for distribution to the equity holders as such of the subsidiary and of assets similarly available in a winding-up.

[*CTA 2010, ss 154–157*].

See **35.4** above, and note that a holder of 'ordinary share capital' of a company may not qualify as an 'equity holder', for which a different definition of 'ordinary shares' applies. [*CTA 2010, ss 153, 1154*].

For the definition of a 75% subsidiary, see **35.3** above.

A claim for group relief requires the consent of all other members of the consortium.

[*FA 1998, Sch 18 para 70(2)*].

Restrictions on consortium relief

Claims for consortium relief are restricted as follows:

(i) Where the claimant company is a member of a consortium, the amount which may be set off against its total profits for the overlapping period is the lowest in that period of the following percentages of the surrenderable amount:
   (A) the percentage (or average percentage) of the surrendering company's ordinary share capital which is beneficially owned by the claimant company;
   (B) the percentage (or average percentage) of any profits available for distribution to the surrendering company's equity holders to which the claimant company is beneficially entitled;
   (C) the percentage (or average percentage) of any assets of the surrendering company available for distribution to its equity holders on a winding-up to which the claimant company would be beneficially entitled; and
   (D) the percentage (or average percentage) of the voting power in the surrendering company that is directly possessed by the claimant company.

(ii) Where the surrendering company is a member of a consortium, the amount which may be set off against the total profits of the claimant company for the overlapping period is the lowest in that period of the following percentages of those total profits:
   (A) the percentage (or average percentage) of the claimant company's ordinary share capital which is beneficially owned by the surrendering company;
   (B) the percentage (or average percentage) of any profits available for distribution to the claimant company's equity holders to which the surrendering company is beneficially entitled;
   (C) the percentage (or average percentage) of any assets of the claimant company available for distribution to its equity holders on a winding-up to which the surrendering company would be beneficially entitled; and
   (D) the percentage (or average percentage) of the voting power in the claimant company that is directly possessed by the surrendering company.

(iii) Where the claimant (or surrendering) company is a subsidiary of a holding company owned by a consortium, (i) (or (ii)) above applies by reference to the holding company rather than the claimant (or surrendering) company.

Terms used in (i)–(iii) are defined as above and as in **35.3–35.4** above.

In determining the average percentage of a member's interest in a consortium, a weighted average taking into account the length of time involved will be used. (HMRC Company Taxation Manual, CTM80540).

In *BUPA Insurance Ltd v HMRC* UT, [2014] STC 2615, a public company (B) acquired a large shareholding in a company (C) which carried on a reinsurance business and had incurred losses. Under the share purchase agreement, B was required to pay the vendor (T) an 'earn-out consideration' equal to any distribution made by C. One of B's subsidiaries (BI) subsequently claimed consortium relief in respect of losses incurred by C. HMRC rejected the claim on the grounds that B's contractual obligation to pay an 'earn-out consideration' to T affected its 'beneficial entitlement' to any distribution made by C (see (i)(B) and (ii)(B) above). BI appealed. The UT allowed the appeal, holding that B's contractual obligations 'to pay earn-out consideration to (T) did not deprive (B) of "beneficial entitlement" to any distribution (actual or notional) made by (C)'. The Tribunal held, that for the purposes of the legislation dealing with consortium relief, '"beneficial entitlement" is a wider concept than "equitable ownership"'.

Where a claimant company or link company would control the surrendering company (being the consortium company), but for the existence of arrangements which prevent such control (either by those companies alone, or together with other consortium members), then the available relief is halved. Similarly with regard to the position of a surrendering company or link company which might control the claimant company, but for the existence of arrangements which prevent such control. The provisions apply where those arrangements are part of a scheme, the main purpose, or one of the main purposes, of which is to enable the claimant company to obtain a tax advantage (within *CTA 2010, s 1139*). The provisions were considered in *Eastern Power Networks plc and others v HMRC* CA, [2021] STC 568.

[*CTA 2010, ss 143, 144, 146A, 146B*].

Simon's Taxes. See **D2.208, D2.230, D2.231.**

Examples

(A) Loss by company owned by consortium

[35.20]

On 1 April 2021, the share capital of E Ltd was owned as follows.

	%
A Ltd	40
B Ltd	40
C Ltd	20
	100

All the companies were UK resident for tax purposes.

During the year ended 31 March 2022 the following events took place.

On 1.7.21 D Ltd bought 20% from A Ltd

On 1.10.21 C Ltd bought 10% from B Ltd

The companies had the following results for the year ended 31 March 2022.

		£
A Ltd	Profit	40,000
B Ltd	Profit	33,000
C Ltd	Profit	10,000
D Ltd	Profit	18,000
E Ltd	Loss	(100,000)

None of the companies have any carried-forward losses or other unrelieved amounts.

Consortium relief for the loss sustained by E Ltd would be available as follows.

	A Ltd	B Ltd	C Ltd	D Ltd
	£	£	£	£
Profits for the year ended 31.3.22	40,000	33,000	10,000	18,000
Deduct Loss surrendered by E Ltd	(25,000)	(33,000)	(10,000)	(13,500)
Chargeable profits	£15,000	—	—	£4,500

E Ltd		Losses
	£	£
Loss for the year ended 31.3.22		100,000
Deduct Loss surrendered to A Ltd	(25,000)	
B Ltd	(33,000)	
C Ltd	(10,000)	
D Ltd	(13,500)	(81,500)
Not available for consortium relief		£18,500

Notes

(a) Loss relief for each member of the consortium is the lower of its share of the loss and its own profit for the overlapping period.

(b) The maximum share of losses of E Ltd appropriate to each member is:

	%	£
A Ltd 40% × 3/12 + 20% × 9/12	25	25,000
B Ltd 40% × 6/12 + 30% × 6/12	35	35,000
C Ltd 20% × 6/12 + 30% × 6/12	25	25,000
D Ltd 20% × 9/12	15	15,000
	100	£100,000

(B) Loss by consortium member

A Ltd, B Ltd, C Ltd and D Ltd have for many years held 40%, 30%, 20% and 10% respectively of the ordinary share capital of E Ltd. All five companies are UK resident and have always previously had taxable profits. However, for the year ended 30 June 2021, D Ltd has a tax loss of £100,000, followed by taxable profits of £40,000 for the subsequent year. E Ltd's taxable profits are £80,000 and £140,000 for the two years ending 31 December 2020 and 31 December 2021 respectively.

With the consent of A Ltd, B Ltd and C Ltd, D Ltd can (if it wishes) surrender the following part of its loss of £100,000 to E Ltd.

	£
Common period 1.7.20 to 31.12.20	
E Ltd's profit 6/12 × £80,000 × 1/10	4,000
D Ltd's loss 6/12 × £100,000	(50,000)
Common period 1.1.21 to 30.6.21	
E Ltd's profit 6/12 × £140,000 × 1/10	7,000
D Ltd's loss 6/12 × £100,000	(50,000)

The lower common figures for the two periods are £4,000 and £7,000.

Therefore, E Ltd can claim £4,000 of D Ltd's loss against its own profits for the year ended 31.12.20 and £7,000 against its profits for the year ending 31.12.21.

Group/consortium relief interaction

[35.21] Special provisions apply where both consortium group relief ('consortium relief') (see **35.19** above) and other group relief ('group relief') (see **35.2** onwards above) may be claimed in respect of the same losses, etc, i.e. where either the member of a consortium (consortium member) or a company owned by a consortium (consortium company) is a member of a group, or both are members of separate groups. Restrictions apply to the consortium relief available as follows.

Company owned by consortium also a member of a group

(i) Consortium relief is available on the ownership proportion to consortium members in respect of losses, etc. of the consortium company only after deduction of all possible group relief claims thereon (but taking into account any claims made by group companies in respect of other losses within the group).

(ii) The profits of the consortium company against which (or against a fraction of which) relief for losses, etc. of consortium members may be claimed are first reduced by any group relief claims it could make in respect of losses, etc. of other companies in the consortium company's group (but taking into account any claims made by other group companies in respect of such losses).

(iii) the ownership proportion is the lowest of:
   (A) the proportion of the ordinary share capital of the surrendering company which is beneficially owned by the claimant company;
   (B) the proportion of profits of the surrendering company available for distribution to equity holders of that company to which the claimant is beneficially entitled;
   (C) the proportion of the surrendering company's assets available for distribution to such equity holders on winding up to which the claimant would be beneficially entitled.

   The proportions are those for the overlapping period, and if they vary during that period, the average is taken.

Similar rules apply where the claimant company is the consortium company and where there is a link company (see below).

An '*equity holder*' for this purpose is any person holding ordinary shares in the company or is a loan creditor in respect of a loan which is not a normal commercial loan. For this purpose, loan creditor and ordinary shares are specially defined (*CTA 2010, ss 158(1)(b)–160*).

[*CTA 2010, ss 143–147, 157–168*].

Member of consortium also a member of a group (referred to as the 'link company')

(a) Any consortium relief claim the link company could make (disregarding any deficiency of profits) may be made by any other company in the link company's group (provided that it is not itself a consortium member).

The provisions at **35.6** above (which limit relief by reference to overlapping periods of the claimant and surrendering companies) apply as if any period during which the claimant company was not a group member were not comprised in the overlapping period and were a part of the claimant company's accounting period which did not coincide with any part of the surrendering company's accounting period. The total consortium relief of the link company and other companies in the same group may not exceed that claimable by the link company (but disregarding any deficiency of profits in the link company).

(b) Consortium relief may be claimed by a consortium company in respect of losses, etc. of members of the same group as the link company, which are not themselves consortium members, as if the surrendering company were a member of the consortium at all times at which the link company is a member. The fraction of the profits against which the losses, etc. may be claimed is determined by reference to the consortium member's share in the claimant consortium company, in the surrendering company's overlapping period of loss, etc. The provisions at **35.6** above (which limit relief by reference to overlapping periods of the claimant and surrendering companies) apply as if any period during which the surrendering company was not a group member were not comprised in the overlapping period and were a part of the claimant company's accounting period which did not coincide with any part of the surrendering company's accounting period. The total relief which may be claimed by the consortium company in an accounting period from the link company and other members of the same group may not exceed what it could have claimed from the link company if the link company's accounting period was the same as that of the consortium company.

Where a *consortium company* has trading losses and other profits against which the losses could be set under *CTA 2010, s 37* (see **51.3** LOSSES), the losses, etc. available for consortium relief are reduced by the amount of any such set-off which could be claimed. This operates in priority to (i) above where applicable.

Amounts available for a claim are reduced by the group's potential relief, i.e. the maximum group relief (other than consortium relief) that could be given if every group relief claim in respect of the surrenderable amounts that could have been made were in fact made.

There are no location requirements with regard to the link company.

[*CTA 2010, ss 133, 147–149*].

Simon's Taxes. See **D2.232**.

Example

[35.22]

A Ltd owns 100% of the share capital of B Ltd

B Ltd owns 40% of the share capital of D Ltd

C Ltd owns 60% of the share capital of D Ltd

D Ltd owns 100% of the share capital of E Ltd

D Ltd owns 100% of the share capital of F Ltd

There are two groups, A and B, and D, E and F.

D is a consortium company owned by a consortium of B and C. This relationship has existed for a number of years with all companies having the same accounting periods. None of the companies has any losses brought forward.

The companies have the following results for year ended 31 July 2021.

A Ltd	£100,000	profit
B Ltd	£(30,000)	loss
C Ltd	£Nil	
D Ltd	£(20,000)	loss
E Ltd	£10,000	profit
F Ltd	£(3,000)	loss

E Ltd claims group relief as follows.

		£	£
Profit			10,000
Deduct Group relief: loss surrendered by F Ltd	note (a)	3,000	
Group relief: loss surrendered by D Ltd	note (a)	7,000	(10,000)
			—

A Ltd can claim group relief and consortium relief as follows.

		£	£
Profit			100,000
Deduct Group relief: loss surrendered by B Ltd	note (b)	30,000	
Consortium relief: loss surrendered by D Ltd	note (c)	5,200	(35,200)
Chargeable profit			£64,800

Notes

(a) Where a loss of a consortium company or of a company within its group may be used both as group relief and consortium relief, group relief claims take priority. In determining the consortium relief available, it is assumed that the maximum possible group relief is claimed after taking account of any other actual group relief claims within the consortium company's group. As F Ltd has surrendered losses of £3,000 to E Ltd, D Ltd can only surrender £7,000 to E Ltd. Consortium relief is restricted to the balance of D Ltd's loss, i.e. £13,000. If E Ltd had not claimed £3,000 group relief for F Ltd's loss, D Ltd could have surrendered £10,000 to E Ltd by way of group relief and this would have reduced D Ltd's loss for consortium relief purposes to £10,000.

(b) Group relief available to A Ltd is the lower of £100,000 and £30,000.

(c) Consortium relief available to A Ltd is the lower of £70,000 (its profit as reduced by group relief) and £5,200 (40% of £13,000, see note (a) above). The relief available to A Ltd is the same as that which B Ltd could have claimed if it had had sufficient profits. A Ltd could also have claimed consortium relief in respect of F Ltd's loss if that had exceeded the £10,000 necessary to cover E Ltd's profit.

Dual resident investing companies

[35.23] Group relief is not available for a loss, etc. of the company which would otherwise have been the surrendering company, if that company is a 'dual resident investing company'.

A UK resident company is a '*dual resident company*' if it is within the charge to tax under the laws of a territory outside the UK, whether it derives its company status under those laws, or because its place of management is in that territory, or because it is for any other reason regarded as resident in that territory, for the purposes of that charge. A dual resident company is a '*dual resident investing company*' in an accounting period if either:

(a) throughout that period it is not a '*trading company*', i.e. a company whose business consists wholly or mainly of the carrying on of a trade or trades; or

(b) although it is a trading company in that period, either:
  - (i) it carries on in that period a trade of which a main function is:
    - (A) acquiring and holding, directly or indirectly, investments of any kind, including interests in companies which are CONNECTED PERSONS (**19**) within *CTA 2010, ss 1122, 1123*; or
    - (B) making payments which are similar to those in (C) below but which are deductible in computing the surrendering company's profits for corporation tax; or
    - (C) making payments which are qualifying charitable donations; or
    - (D) making payments in relation to which debits fall to be brought into account under the LOAN RELATIONSHIPS (**49**) provisions as regards loan relationships; or
    - (E) obtaining funds in connection with any activity within (A)–(D) above; or
  - (ii) although not within (i) above, it carries on any of the activities within (i)(A)–(E) above:
    - (A) to an extent which does not appear justified by any trade which it does carry on; or
    - (B) for a purpose which does not appear to be appropriate to any such trade.

[*CTA 2010, s 109*].

Certain capital allowance restrictions apply to transactions between CONNECTED PERSONS (**19**) one of which is a dual resident investing company, as above. See also **10** CAPITAL ALLOWANCES ON PLANT AND MACHINERY, **12.4**, **12.8** CAPITAL GAINS — GROUPS, and **51.16** LOSSES.

Simon's Taxes. See **D4.133**.

Group relief for carried-forward losses

[35.24] *F(No 2)A 2017* introduced an additional form of group relief, known as '*group relief for carried-forward losses*', which provides for the surrender of losses and other amounts carried forward to an accounting period beginning on or after 1 April 2017 by one company within a group to another member company.

For these purposes, an accounting period which straddles 1 April 2017 is treated as if it were two separate accounting periods, the first ending on 31 March 2017 and the second beginning on 1 April 2017. Any necessary apportionments between the two periods must be made on a time basis unless that would produce an unjust or unreasonable result, in which case a just and reasonable basis must be used. Special rules apply, however, where the amount to be apportioned is either an amount chargeable to corporation tax which would have been less but for the CORPORATE INTEREST RESTRICTION (**25**) provisions or an amount for which relief is available which would have been greater but for the restriction. An amount chargeable to corporation tax which would not have arisen at all but for the restriction provisions is apportioned entirely to the second period.

[*CTA 2010, s 188AA; F(No 2)A 2017, Sch 4 paras 23, 190–192*].

For the purposes of the relief, a '*group*' is defined as at **35.3** above. A '*trading company*' means a company whose business consists wholly or mainly in the carrying on of a trade, and a '*holding company*' is a company whose business consists wholly or mainly in holding share or securities of in trading companies which are its 90% subsidiaries. [*CTA 2010, ss 188FB, 188FC; F(No 2)A 2017, Sch 4 para 23*].

A payment by the claimant company to the surrendering company in respect of the surrender of amounts under these provisions is not taken into account in determining the profits or losses of either company for corporation tax purposes and is not treated as a distribution provided that it does not exceed the amounts surrendered. [*CTA 2010, s 188FA; F(No 2)A 2017, Sch 4 para 23*].

For restrictions on group relief for carried-forward losses where there is a change in ownership of a company see **35.30–35.32** below.

Simon's Taxes. See **D2.209, D2.234–D2.236A.**

Amounts which may be surrendered

[35.25] Subject to the commencement rules at **35.24** above, a company may surrender certain losses and other amounts ('*surrenderable amounts*') carried forward to an accounting period (the '*surrender period*') so far as that loss or other amount is eligible for corporation tax relief. The losses and amounts are:

(i) post-1 April 2017 non-trading loan relationship deficits carried forward against total profits (see **50.6** LOAN RELATIONSHIPS);

(ii) non-trading losses on intangible fixed assets (see **42.9** INTANGIBLE ASSETS) other than any part of such a loss that is made up of an amount previously carried forward from an accounting period beginning before 1 April 2017;

(iii) management expenses carried forward and treated as management expenses of the accounting period (see **45.3** INVESTMENT COMPANIES AND INVESTMENT BUSINESS) other than expenses first deductible for an accounting period beginning before 1 April 2017;
(iv) trade losses carried forward for set-off against total profits (see **51.6** LOSSES); and
(v) UK property business losses of accounting periods beginning on or after 1 April 2017 carried forward and treated as a loss of the period (see **51.10** above) or as management expenses of the period (see **45.6** INVESTMENT COMPANIES AND INVESTMENT BUSINESS).

In (ii), (iii) and (v) above, the transitional rule at **35.24** above applies for accounting periods straddling 1 April 2017. A qualifying charitable donation carried forward as management expenses (see **45.3** INVESTMENT COMPANIES AND INVESTMENT BUSINESS) may not be surrendered.

An amount within (ii), (iii) or (v) above cannot be surrendered if the surrendering company's investment business became small or negligible before the beginning of the surrender period.

For accounting periods beginning on or after 1 April 2021, no carried-forward amount may be surrendered to the extent that it could be deducted from the company's total profits for the period. Previously, the rule was that, where *CTA 2010, s 269ZD* applied to a company for an accounting period (restriction on the amount of deductions for carried-forward amounts — see **51.13** LOSSES), no amounts could be surrendered unless the carried-forward amounts were used against the company's profits up to the permitted maximum. For all accounting periods, no amounts may be surrendered if the company has no assets capable of producing income at the end of the surrender period.

A company surrenders a loss or other amount by consenting to one or more claims for group relief for carried-forward losses (see **35.26** below) in respect of the loss or amount.

[*CTA 2010, ss 188BB–188BF; F(No 2)A 2017, Sch 4 para 23; FA 2021, Sch 8 paras 6, 17*].

Overseas losses of UK company

A loss or other amount of a company which was UK-resident in the loss-making period is not available for surrender so far as it is 'attributable' to a permanent establishment through which the company carried on a trade outside the UK in that period and it is, or represents, an amount which is or has been allowable against 'non-UK profits' of any other person for the purposes of 'non-UK tax' under the law of the territory where the permanent establishment is situated. If, in order to determine whether an amount is or has been so allowable, it is necessary under the law of the territory to know if it is or has been allowable in the UK, the amount is taken to be or to have been allowable for the purposes of the non-UK tax if, and only if, the company is treated as resident in the territory for the purposes of the non-UK tax.

'*Non-UK profits*' are amounts (or elements in computing amounts) charged to foreign tax and not included in corporation tax total profits of any person for any accounting period. '*Non-UK tax*' means any tax corresponding to income or corporation tax (including local and regional taxes).

A loss or other amount is '*attributable*' to a permanent establishment for this purpose if it would be available for surrender if it were computed only by reference to that permanent establishment alone and by the application of the same principles as apply to a permanent establishment through which a non-UK resident company carries on a trade in the UK.

[*CTA 2010, s 188BH; F(No 2)A 2017, Sch 4 para 23; SI 2019 No 689, Regs 1, 17(2); European Union (Withdrawal Agreement) Act 2020, Sch 5 para 1(1)*].

UK losses of non-resident company

A loss or other amount of a company which was not UK-resident in the loss-making period but was within the charge to UK corporation tax can be surrendered so far as:

(i) they are attributable to activities of the company in respect of which it is within the charge to corporation tax for the loss-making period;
(ii) they are not attributable to activities which are exempt under any double taxation relief arrangements (see **31.17** DOUBLE TAX RELIEF), disregarding any claim requirement, for the loss-making period; and
(iii) where the company was not established in a relevant territory during the loss-making period, they do not correspond to, and are not represented by, an amount which is or has been deductible or otherwise allowable for non-UK tax purposes against any non-UK profits of any person.

A company is established in a relevant territory for this purpose if it is constituted under the law of the UK or a relevant territory and has its registered office, central administration or principal place of business within the EEA or, after the end of the Brexit implementation period (11pm on 31 December 2020), Gibraltar. A '*relevant territory*' is a territory outside the UK but within the EEA or Gibraltar.

No amounts can be surrendered by a company established in a relevant territory during the loss-making period if the losses (or any amount brought into account in calculating them) are, in any period, deducted from or otherwise allowed against the non-UK profits of any person, although this does not apply to amounts which are, or are an element in computing, profits exempted from that non-UK tax. If, in order to determine whether an amount is or has been so allowable, it is necessary under the law of the territory to know if it is or has been allowable in the UK, the amount is taken to be or to have been allowable for the purposes of the non-UK tax.

For these purposes, amounts are exempt under double tax relief arrangements if their effect is to cause any income or gains arising from the activities to be disregarded in computing chargeable profits.

[*CTA 2010, s 188BI; F(No 2)A 2017, Sch 4 para 23; FA 2019, Sch 5 para 31; SI 2019 No 689, Regs 1, 17(4); European Union (Withdrawal Agreement) Act 2020, Sch 5 para 1(1)*].

Dual resident company

A company may not surrender a loss or other amount which it was not eligible to surrender as group relief under the provisions at **35.23** above. [*CTA 2010, s 188BJ; F(No 2)A 2017, Sch 4 para 23*].

Eligibility to claim group relief for carried-forward losses

[35.26] Subject to the commencement rules at 35.24 above, a company may make a claim for group relief for carried-forward losses for an accounting period (the '*claim period*') in respect of all or part of another company's surrenderable amounts (see 35.25 above) if:

(i) the surrendering company consents to the claim;
(ii) there is a period (the '*overlapping period*') which is common to the surrender period (see 35.25 above) and the claim period; and
(iii) at a time in the overlapping period, one of the following conditions is met: the group condition, consortium condition 1 or consortium condition 2.

A company may make a claim for group relief for carried-forward losses for an accounting period in respect of all or part of another company's surrenderable amounts which are attributable to a specified loss-making accounting period of the surrendering company if:

(1) the surrendering company consents to the claim;
(2) there is an overlapping period; and
(3) either consortium condition 3 or consortium condition 4 is met throughout a period beginning before or during the specified loss-making period and ending during or after the overlapping period.

In (iii) above, the group condition is met if both companies are members of the same group and both are 'UK related'.

A company is '*UK related*' if it is UK resident or, if it is not UK resident, it is within the charge to corporation tax. This definition is as amended by *FA 2019*, but applies, with retrospective effect, from the introduction of group relief for carried-forward losses. (Before the change was made, a non-UK resident company would have been UK related only if it carried on a trade through a permanent establishment in the UK.) Where a claim to group relief for carried-forward losses becomes possible as a result of the change, the time limit for making the claim (see 35.12 above) is extended to 31 December 2019 if it would otherwise be earlier.

Consortium condition 1 is met if the claimant company is a trading company or holding company which is owned by a consortium of which the surrendering company is a member and both companies are UK related.

Consortium condition 2 is met if the claimant company is a trading company or holding company which is owned by a consortium of which the surrendering company is not a member but the surrendering company is a member of the same group as a third company (the '*link company*') which is a member of the consortium and both the surrendering and claimant companies are UK related. The conditions are not met, however, if a profit on the sale of the surrendering company's or link company's shares in the claimant company (or, where the consortium owns the claimant company through a holding company, on the sale of its shares in the holding company) would be a trade receipt.

In (3) above, consortium condition 3 is met if the surrendering company is a trading company or holding company which is owned by a consortium of which the claimant company is a member and both companies are UK related.

Consortium condition 4 is met if the surrendering company is a trading company or holding company which is owned by a consortium of which the claimant company is not a member but the claimant company is a member of the same group as a third company (the '*link company*') which is a member of the consortium and both the surrendering and claimant companies are UK related. The conditions are not met, however, if a profit on the sale of the claimant company's or link company's shares in the surrendering company (or, where the consortium owns the claimant company through a holding company, on the sale of its shares in the holding company) would be a trade receipt.

A claim for relief for an accounting period cannot be made if an amount carried forward to the period by the clamant company that is within **35.25**(i)–(v) above is not deducted in full from the total profits of the period. A claim also cannot be made if the company claims to not set off brought forward trade losses against profits of the same trade or brought forward non-trading loan relationship deficits against non-trading profits.

[*CTA 2010, ss 188CB–188CJ; F(No 2)A 2017, Sch 4 para 23; FA 2019, s 24(2)–(4)*].

Amount of relief

[35.27] Relief is given by deduction from the claimant company's total profits of the claim period. The amount of relief is subject to the provisions for restricting deductions for carried-forward losses (see **51.13** LOSSES).

Where the conditions in **35.26**(i)–(iii) above are met, the amount of relief is the amount of the surrenderable amounts or, if lower, the part of the amounts claimed, but the relief may not exceed the lesser of:

(a) the unused part of the surrenderable amounts for the overlapping period; and
(b) the difference between the claimant company's 'relevant maximum' for the overlapping period and the amount of previously claimed relief for the overlapping period.

The amount referred to in (a) above is so much of the total amounts available for surrender for the accounting period of the surrendering company as are attributable to the overlapping period and have not been the subject of any prior surrenders attributable to the overlapping period. The total surrenderable amounts for the overlapping period are found by apportioning the surrenderable amounts for the surrender period on a time basis. Prior surrenders are identified using the following steps.

(1) Identify any claims ('prior claims') made by any company before the current claim which have not been withdrawn and which relate to the same amounts.
(2) For each prior claim, identify the overlapping period.
(3) Identify any period that is common to the overlapping periods for the current claim and the prior claim. If there is no common period there is no previously used amount for the prior claim.

(4) Determine the previously used amount for the prior claim. This is the proportion of the amount of relief given on the prior claim equal to the proportion of the overlapping period for the prior claim that falls within the common period in (3) above. It is assumed for this purpose that relief is given on the prior claim before relief on any later claim.

(5) The amount of the prior surrenders attributable to the overlapping period is the sum of the amounts determined at (4) above for each prior claim.

In (b) above, the claimant company's '*relevant maximum*' for the overlapping period is found using the following steps:

(i) Calculate the relevant maximum for the purposes of the provisions for restricting the amount of deductions for carried-forward losses (see **51.13** LOSSES) for the claim period.

(ii) Deduct from that amount any deductions for the claim period for trade losses carried forward and set off against profits of the same trade (other than deductions that would be ignored for the purposes of the restriction under *CTA 2010, s 269ZB* (deductions from trading profits: see **51.13**) by reason of the CREATIVE INDUSTRIES RELIEFS **26** provisions or the provisions for UK and EEA furnished holiday lettings), non-trading loan relationship deficits carried forward and set off against non-trading profits and any amounts carried forward and set off against total profits within **51.13**(1)–(8).

(iii) Apportion the amount found in (ii) above to the overlapping period on a time basis.

If the company's 'qualifying profits' for the claim period is less than its 'deductions allowance' for that period, the amount in (i) above is taken to be those qualifying profits. See **51.13** for the meaning of 'qualifying profits' and 'deductions allowance'.

The amount of previously claimed relief for the overlapping period is identified using the following steps.

(A) Identify any claims ('prior claims') for group relief for carried-forward losses made for the claim period by the claimant company before the current claim which have not been withdrawn and which relate to the same amounts.

(B) For each prior claim, identify the overlapping period;

(C) Identify any period that is common to the overlapping periods for the current claim and the prior claim. If there is no common period there is no previously claimed amount for the prior claim.

(D) Determine the previously claimed amount for the prior claim. This is the proportion of the amount of relief given on the prior claim equal to the proportion of the overlapping period for the prior claim that falls within the common period in (C) above. It is assumed for this purpose that relief is given on the prior claim before relief on any later claim.

(E) The amount of previously claimed relief for the overlapping period is the sum of the amounts determined at (D) above for each prior claim.

If any of the time apportionments required under these provisions would give a result which is unjust or unreasonable, the apportionment must be modified to produce a just and reasonable result.

Further limitations apply to restrict the amount of relief where the claim relies on one of the consortium conditions in **35.26**(iii) as follows.

(I) If the claim relies on consortium condition 1, the relief is limited to the 'ownership proportion' of the claimant company's relevant maximum for the overlapping period. This is the lowest of: the proportion of the ordinary share capital of the claimant company beneficially owned by the surrendering company; the proportion of any profits available for distribution to equity holders of the claimant company to which the surrendering company is entitled; the proportion of any assets of he claimant company available to such equity holders on a winding-up to which the surrendering company would be entitled; and the proportion of the voting power in the claimant company directly possessed by the surrendering company. If any of these proportions changes during the overlapping period, the average is used. If the claimant company is owned by a consortium of which the surrendering company is a member the proportions are calculated by reference to the holding company rather than the claimant company.

(II) If the claim relies on consortium condition 2, the limit in (I) above applies as if references to the surrendering company were to the link company.

(III) If the claim relies on consortium condition 2, the total relief for the claim period for losses and other amounts surrendered by the link company and members of its group is limited to the limit that would apply in (I) above to amounts surrendered by the link company, on the assumption that the link company is UK related and that the accounting period of the link company is the same as that of the claim company.

(IV) If the claim relies on consortium condition 1 and during any part of the overlapping period arrangements are in place enabling a person to prevent the surrendering company, either alone or with other consortium members, from controlling the claimant company, relief is given as if the claimant company's relevant maximum for the overlapping period were 50% of what it would otherwise be. The arrangements must form part of a scheme with a main purpose of enabling the claimant company to obtain a tax advantage under these provisions. This restriction applies also to claims which rely on consortium conditions 2 where the arrangements prevent the link company, alone or with other consortium members, from controlling the claimant company.

(V) If the claim relied on either consortium condition and the claimant company is a member of a group, in determining that company's relevant maximum for the overlapping period, the amount found at (i) above is reduced by the sum of the maximum group relief for carried-forward losses that could be claimed for the period on the basis of the group condition in **35.26**(iii) above and the maximum group relief that could be claimed for the period under **35.6** above. Before determining the maximum amounts, it is necessary to take account of any previous claims by other group members.

The overlapping period for these purposes excludes any part of the common period when the condition in **35.26**(iii) is not met. Instead that part is treated as a part of both the surrender period and the claim period which is not part of the overlapping period.

Claims which would otherwise be treated as having been made at the same time are deemed to have been made in such order as the company or companies making them elect or jointly elect, or in the absence of such an election in such order as HMRC may direct.

[*CTA 2010, ss 188CK(1)–(3), 188DB–188DL; F(No 2)A 2017, Sch 4 para 23; FA 2019, Sch 10 paras 2, 24, 32; FA 2021, Sch 8 paras 7, 18*].

Similar provisions apply where a claim relies on the conditions in **35.26**(1)–(3) above. The amount of relief is the amount of the surrenderable amounts attributable to the specified loss-making period or, if lower, the part of the amounts claimed, but the relief may not exceed the lesser of:

- (aa) the unused part of those surrenderable amounts for the overlapping period;
- (bb) the difference between the claimant company's 'relevant maximum' for the overlapping period and the amount of previously claimed relief for the overlapping period; and
- (cc) the potential group relief amount.

The amount in (aa) above is calculated in the same way as the amount in (a) above, except that, where a prior claim relied on the conditions in **35.26**(i)–(iii) above, only a fraction of the previously used amount for that claim is taken into account at (4) above. That fraction is equal to the sum of the surrenderable amounts attributable to the specified loss-making period divided by the sum of all the surrenderable amounts. The amount in (bb) above is calculated in the same way as the amount in (b) above. The amount in (cc) above is calculated using the following steps.

- (AA) Calculate the maximum group relief which could have been given to the claimant company for amounts within **35.5** above which the surrendering company had for the specified loss-making period (ignoring any lack of profits from which the relief could have been deducted).
- (BB) Deduct from that amount any such group relief actually given.
- (CC) Multiply the amount found in (BB) above by the fraction equal to the sum of the amounts within **35.5**(a), (c), (f)–(h) above which were eligible for surrender divided by the total amounts within **35.5** eligible for surrender.
- (DD) Deduct from that amount any group relief for carried-forward losses previously given to the claimant company on claims where the surrendering company and the specified loss-making period are the same.

The overlapping period for these purposes excludes any part of the common period when the condition in **35.26**(3) is not met. Instead that part is treated as a part of both the surrender period and the claim period which is not part of the overlapping period.

Further limitations apply to restrict the amount of relief as follows.

- If the claim relies on consortium condition 4, the total relief on claims by the link company and members of its group in respect of the same surrender period and specified loss-making period of a surrendering company cannot exceed the relief that could be given to the link company, on the assumption that the link company is UK related and no other such claims were made by other members of the group based on consortium condition 4 and ignoring any lack of profits of the link company from which the relief could be deducted.

- If the claim relies on consortium condition 3 and during any part of the overlapping period arrangements are in place enabling a person to prevent the claimant company, either alone or with other consortium members, from controlling the surrendering company, relief is given as if the total surrenderable amounts for the overlapping period were 50% of what they would otherwise be. The arrangements must form part of a scheme with a main purpose of enabling the claimant company to obtain a tax advantage under these provisions. This restriction applies also to claims which rely on consortium conditions 4 where the arrangements prevent the link company, alone or with other consortium members, from controlling the surrendering company.
- If the claim relied on either consortium condition and the surrendering company is a member of a group, the surrendering company's surrenderable amounts for the surrender period which are attributable to the specified loss-making period are reduced by the fraction of the group's potential relief equal to the sum of the surrenderable amounts attributable to the specified loss-making period divided by the sum of all the surrenderable amounts. The group's potential relief is the maximum group relief for carried-forward losses that could be claimed on the basis of the group condition in **35.26**(iii) above in respect of the surrenderable amounts of the surrender period. and the maximum group relief that could be claimed for the period under **35.6** above. Before determining the group's potential relief, it is necessary to take account of any previous claims based on the group condition in respect of amounts surrendered by a member of the group other than the surrendering company.

[*CTA 2010, ss 188CK(4)(5), 188EB–188EK; F(No 2)A 2017, Sch 4 para 23; FA 2019, Sch 10 paras 3, 25, 32*].

Order of deductions

A deduction for group relief for carried-forward losses is made before deductions from total profits in respect of a trade loss, excess special leasing capital allowance (see **10.54** CAPITAL ALLOWANCES ON PLANT AND MACHINERY) or non-trading loan relationship deficit carried back from a later accounting period but after all other deductions. Total profits are calculated for this purpose on the assumption that the company makes all relevant claims to set trading losses or capital allowances against total profits.

Relief may not be given more than once in respect of the same amount.

[*CTA 2010, ss 188CK(6)–(9); F(No 2)A 2017, Sch 4 para 23*].

Example

[35.28]

A Ltd has a subsidiary company, B Ltd, in which it owns 75% of the ordinary share capital. The companies commence trading on 1 April 2020 and have the following results for the two years ending 31 March 2021 and 31 March 2022.

		Year ended 31.3.21	Year ended 31.3.22
		£	£
A Ltd	Trade profits/(loss)	(20,000)	110,000
	Property income	—	30,000
B Ltd	Trade profits/(loss)	(150,000)	10,000

Group relief for carried-forward losses may be claimed for B Ltd's carried-forward trade loss as follows.

	Year ended 31.3.21	Year ended 31.3.22
	£	£
A Ltd		
Trade profit/(loss)	(20,000)	110,000
Property income	—	30,000
	—	140,000
Deduct trade loss carried forward	—	(20,000)
Trade loss surrendered by B Ltd	—	(120,000)
Total taxable profits	£Nil	£Nil
B Ltd		
Trade profit/(loss)	(150,000)	10,000
Deduct trade loss carried forward		(10,000)
Total taxable profits	£Nil	£Nil
B Ltd loss memoranda		
Trade loss	150,000	
Carried forward against total profits of y/e 31.3.22	(10,000)	
Surrendered to A Ltd for y/e 31.3.22	(120,000)	
Unrelieved loss c/fwd to y/e 31.3.23	£20,000	

Claims for relief

[35.29] The provisions at **35.12** above (including those providing for simplified arrangements) apply to group relief for carried-forward losses as they apply to group relief. There are certain additional requirements for group relief for carried-forward losses, however, as follows.

A claim which relies on **35.26**(i)–(iii) above must state whether or not, in the accounting period of the surrendering company to which the claim relates or the corresponding accounting period of the claimant company, any of the following companies were not resident in the UK: the claimant company, the surrendering company and any company by reference to which those companies are members of the same group or consortium condition 1 or 2 is met.

A claim which relies on **35.26**(1)–(3) above must state whether or not, in the accounting period of the surrendering company to which the claim relates, the specified loss-making period of the surrendering company or the corresponding accounting period of the claimant company, any of the following companies were not resident in the UK: the claimant company, the surrendering company and any company by reference to which consortium condition 3 or 4 is met.

[*FA 1998, Sch 18 para 68(5)–(8); F(No 2)A 2017, Sch 4 para 112*].

A notice of surrender must identify the particular losses and other amounts to be surrendered by specifying the provision under which it was carried forward and, where the surrendering company is owned by a consortium, its accounting period to which the loss or amount is attributable. A notice of surrender where the claim relies on **35.26**(1)–(3) above must also state which accounting period of the surrendering company is the specified loss-making period. [*FA 1998, Sch 18 paras 71(1A), 71A; F(No 2)A 2017, Sch 4 paras 115, 116*].

Restriction on relief following change in ownership

[35.30] Where there is a 'change in ownership' of a company (the '*transferred company*') on or after 1 April 2017, then (subject to the exceptions below) group relief for carried-forward losses is not available to a claimant company for accounting periods ending after the change in respect of 'pre-acquisition losses' surrendered by the transferred company or a 'co-transferred company'.

For these purposes only, an accounting period of the transferred company or co-transferred company which straddles the date of the change is treated as two separate accounting periods, ending with the date of the change and beginning with the following date respectively. The profits or losses of the whole period are apportioned to each on a time basis, or by such other method as is just and reasonable.

There is a '*change in ownership*' of a company (C) in the circumstances described at **51.17**(i)(ii) losses and also where, as a result of the acquisition by a person of a holding of the ordinary share capital of C, the group condition in **35.26** above is met in relation to C and another company which was not a member of the same group as C before the acquisition.

A '*co-transferred company*' is any company which is 'related' to the transferred company both immediately before and after the change in ownership. Two companies are '*related*' if, assuming either was the claimant company and the other the surrendering company, the group condition or any of the consortium conditions at **35.26** above are satisfied.

'*Pre-acquisition losses*' are:

(i) post-1 April 2017 non-trading loan relationship deficits for an accounting period beginning before the change in ownership carried forward against total profits (see **50.6** LOAN RELATIONSHIPS);
(ii) non-trading losses on intangible fixed assets (see **42.9** INTANGIBLE ASSETS) carried forward from one or more accounting periods beginning before the change;
(iii) management expenses carried forward (see **45.3** INVESTMENT COMPANIES AND INVESTMENT BUSINESS) which were first deductible for an accounting period beginning before the change;
(iv) trade losses made in an accounting period beginning before the change and carried forward for set-off against total profits (see **51.6** LOSSES); and
(v) UK property business losses of accounting periods beginning before the change and carried forward as a loss of subsequent periods (see **51.10** above) or as management expenses (see **45.6** INVESTMENT COMPANIES AND INVESTMENT BUSINESS).

If consortium condition 3 or consortium condition 4 (see **35.26** above) were met throughout the period beginning before or during the specified loss-making period and ending with or after the time of the change in ownership, the above provisions do not prevent a company from claiming relief for carried-forward losses for amounts surrendered by the transferred company which are attributable to the loss-making period.

Where the transferred company *claims* group relief for carried forward losses for an accounting period ending after the change in respect of pre-acquisition losses and consortium condition 1 or consortium condition 2 (see **35.26** above) was met immediately before the change in relation to the transferred company (as the company owned by the consortium) and the surrendering company, the amount of relief cannot exceed the maximum that would be available if the claim relied on the relevant consortium condition (see **35.27**(I) and (II) above) and the ownership proportion (see **35.27**(I) above) is taken to be what it would be immediately before the change. For this purpose, the accounting period of the surrendering company in which the change takes place is treated as two separate accounting periods, ending with the date of the change and beginning with the following date respectively. The profits or losses of the whole period are apportioned to each on a time basis.

None of the above provisions prevent the giving of relief against total profits of a claimant company which arise more than five years after the end of the accounting period of the transferred company in which the change in ownership occurs. For these purposes only, an accounting period of the claimant company which straddles the end of the five years is treated as two separate accounting periods, ending with the date of the end of the period and beginning with the following date respectively. The profits or losses of the whole period are apportioned to each on a time basis, or by such other method as is just and reasonable.

None of the above provisions prevent the giving of relief if immediately before the change in ownership the group condition in **35.26** above was met by the transferred company and the claimant company.

If, however, certain other provisions which restrict losses on a 'major change' following a change in ownership also apply in relation to the change in ownership, the company in relation to which the major change has occurred cannot claim relief for pre-acquisition losses in accounting periods ending after the change in ownership against 'affected profits'. The accounting period in which the change in ownership occurs is treated as two separate accounting periods, ending with the date of the anniversary and beginning with the following date respectively. The profits or losses of the whole period are apportioned to each on a time basis, or by such other method as is just and reasonable.

The provisions in question are those at **51.17**(a), **51.20** LOSSES and **45.9**(b) INVESTMENT COMPANIES AND INVESTMENT BUSINESS. The restriction also applies if the provisions at **51.17**(a) or **45.9**(b) would apply if the extended meaning of 'change in ownership' above applied to them.

Profits arising in accounting periods ending after the change in ownership are '*affected profits*' so far as they arise within five years of the end of the accounting period of the transferred company in which the change in ownership occurred and they can fairly and reasonably be attributed to activities or other sources of income as a result of which (or partly as a result of which) the major change has occurred. Accounting periods which straddle the end of the five-year period are treated for this purpose as two separate notional accounting periods, ending with the end of the five-year period and beginning with the following date respectively. Apportionments between the two notional periods are made on a time basis unless that would be inequitable, in which case a just and reasonable basis is used.

[*CTA 2010, ss 676CA–676CI, 719; F(No 2)A 2017, Sch 4 paras 77, 89*].

Change in ownership: restriction on relief where asset transferred within group

[35.31] Restrictions on group relief for carried-forward losses apply where, on or after 1 April 2017, there is a 'change in ownership' of a company; and either:

(1) after the change the company acquires an asset from another group company so that either *TCGA 1992, s 171* (no gain/no loss transfer; see **12.4** CAPITAL GAINS — GROUPS) or *CTA 2009, s 775* (tax-neutral transfer of INTANGIBLE ASSETS (see **42.13**)) applies and the company realises a chargeable gain or non-trading chargeable realisation gain on the same asset within five years of the change; or
(2) a chargeable gain (or part of such a gain) on a disposal of an asset within five years of the change is treated as arising under *TCGA 1992, s 171A* (notional transfers within a group; see **12.6** CAPITAL GAINS — GROUPS).

The gain, or part, in (1) or (2) above is the '*relevant gain*' for the purposes of these provisions.

There is a '*change in ownership*' of a company (C) for this purpose in the circumstances described at **51.17**(i)(ii) LOSSES and also where, as a result of the acquisition by a person of a holding of the ordinary share capital of C, the group condition in **35.26** above is met in relation to C and another company which was not a member of the same group as C before the acquisition.

In (1) above, an asset acquired by the company is treated as the same as an asset owned by it at a later time if the value of the latter is derived in whole or part from the former. In particular a leasehold is treated as the same asset as a freehold where the lessee has acquired the reversion.

The accounting period in which the change of ownership takes place is treated as two separate accounting periods, ending with the date of the change and beginning with the following date respectively. The profits or losses of the whole period are generally apportioned to each notional period on the same basis as in **45.9** INVESTMENT COMPANIES AND INVESTMENT BUSINESS. In addition, the chargeable gains and the non-trading chargeable realisation gains included, in accordance with *TCGA 1992, s 8(1)* and *Sch 7A* (see **11.3** CAPITAL GAINS, **12.25** CAPITAL GAINS — GROUPS) and *CTA 2009, Pt 8 Ch 6* (see **42.10** INTANGIBLE ASSETS), in the total profits for the period being divided are also apportioned. The total of those amounts, in so far as it exceeds the relevant gain, is apportioned to the pre-change part of the divided period, and an amount equivalent to the relevant gain (or, if less, the total itself) is apportioned to the post-change part of the divided period.

If the total profits of the company for the accounting period in which the relevant gain accrues include, in accordance with *TCGA 1992, s 2A(1)* (previously *s 8(1)*) and *Sch 7A* and *CTA 2009, Pt 8 Ch 6*, an amount in respect of chargeable gains or non-trading chargeable realisation gains, group relief for carried-forward losses may not be given for that period in respect of a 'pre-acquisition loss' against so much of the total profits as represent the relevant gain. The profits which represent a gain for this purpose are found by comparing the amount of the gain (Y) and the amount included in total profits in respect of chargeable gains or non-trading chargeable realisation gains (Z). If Y does not exceed Z, the amount of the profits which represent the gain is equal to Y; otherwise it is Z.

'*Pre-acquisition losses*' are:

(i) post-1 April 2017 non-trading loan relationship deficits for an accounting period beginning before the change in ownership carried forward against total profits (see **50.6** LOAN RELATIONSHIPS);
(ii) non-trading losses on intangible fixed assets (see **42.9** INTANGIBLE ASSETS) carried forward from one or more accounting periods beginning before the change;
(iii) management expenses carried forward (see **45.3** INVESTMENT COMPANIES AND INVESTMENT BUSINESS) which were first deductible for an accounting period beginning before the change;
(iv) trade losses made in an accounting period beginning before the change and carried forward for set-off against total profits (see **51.6** LOSSES); and

(v) UK property business losses of accounting periods beginning before the change and carried forward as a loss of subsequent periods (see **51.10** above) or as management expenses (see **45.6** INVESTMENT COMPANIES AND INVESTMENT BUSINESS).

[*CTA 2010, ss 676DA–676DE, 719; F(No 2)A 2017, Sch 4 paras 76, 89*].

Change in ownership: cases involving the transfer of a trade

[35.32] The following applies where on or after 1 April 2017 there is a change in ownership of a company (see **51.17** above) and the transferred company or a 'co-transferred company' transfers a trade (in circumstances within **51.16** above) to a successor company within the period of eight years beginning three years before the change. Subject to the exceptions below, group relief for carried-forward losses is not available to a claimant company for accounting periods ending after the change in respect of trade losses surrendered by the successor company but originally made by the transferred company or co-transferred company in an accounting period beginning before the change in ownership and carried forward for relief against total profits.

For these purposes only, an accounting period of the transferred company or co-transferred company which straddles the date of the change is treated as two separate accounting periods, ending with the date of the change and beginning with the following date respectively. The profits or losses of the whole period are apportioned to each on a time basis, or by such other method as is just and reasonable.

The above provision does not prevent the giving of relief against total profits of a claimant company which arise more than five years after the end of the accounting period of the transferred company in which the change in ownership occurs. For these purposes only, an accounting period of the claimant company which straddles the end of the five-year period is treated as two separate accounting periods, ending with the date of the end of the period and beginning with the following date respectively. The profits or losses of the whole period are apportioned to each on a time basis, or by such other method as is just and reasonable.

The above provision does not prevent the giving of relief if immediately before the change in ownership the group condition in **35.26** above was met by the transferred company and the claimant company.

A '*co-transferred company*' is any company which is related to the transferred company both immediately before and after the change in ownership. Two companies are '*related*' if, assuming either was the claimant company and the other the surrendering company, the group condition or any of the consortium conditions at **35.26** above are satisfied.

If a trade transferred by the transferred company or co-transferred company is subsequently transferred to another company, that subsequent transfer is treated for the purposes of these provisions as having been made by the transferred company or co-transferred company (rather than the successor company) at the time of the actual transfer. If the actual transfer was within

51.16 above, then the deemed transfer is so treated. These rules apply also where, following the original transfer, the original trade was included in the activities of another composite trade carried on by the successor trade and it is that composite trade that is subsequently transferred.

[*CTA 2010, ss 676EA, 676EC–676EE; F(No 2)A 2017, Sch 4 para 79*].

Key points on group relief

[35.33] Points to consider are as follows.

- For group relief purposes subsidiaries must be effective 75% subsidiaries. It is important to establish which companies are part of a group for group relief, and it is possible to have more than one group within a larger group where shareholdings are complex and fragmented.
- The time limit for making a group relief claim is usually two years from the end of the accounting period of the company using the loss.
- Group relief can be comprised of a number of elements, for example trading losses, non-trading loan relationship deficits, surplus management expenses. Rules differ in terms of the computation of each of these elements, and it may be possible to surrender only certain types of loss.
- Any payment to a fellow subsidiary for the use of surrendered losses is not taxable and no tax deduction is given to the paying company.
- Losses incurred by overseas resident group companies within the EEA can be claimed by UK resident group companies if those losses cannot be used in the overseas territory either in the year of loss or in any other year in which those losses can be claimed. In practice claims for such losses are likely to be rare, but should not be forgotten.
- Groups can be formed relatively easily, but it is harder to split up a group. The exempt distribution demerger provisions allow groups to be split up, but there are a number of requirements that must be met in order to make use of these provisions (see **29.21**). For example, the exempt distribution route cannot be used where the demerger involves investment companies. The shareholders would have to consider more complex methods to separate the activities of the group, for example an *Insolvency Act 1986, s 110* liquidation demerger.
- A 'link' company provides for the interaction between group relief and consortium relief, and for accounting periods commencing on or after 10 December 2014 there are no location requirements for such a company.

- *F(No 2)A 2017* introduced an additional form of group relief, known as '*group relief for carried-forward losses*', which provides for the surrender of losses and other amounts carried forward to an accounting period beginning on or after 1 April 2017 by one company within a group to another member company.
- Group relief for carry-forward losses is subject to restriction where the total set-off of carried-forward amounts in the group exceeds £5,000,000. See **51.13** LOSSES.

36

HMRC — Administration

Introduction to HMRC — administration

[36.1] Her Majesty's Revenue and Customs (HMRC) was formed by the merger of the Inland Revenue and HM Customs and Excise, following the coming into force of the *Commissioners for Revenue and Customs Act 2005* on 7 April 2005.

This chapter examines how HMRC undertakes the administration of tax and provides an outline of the structure and powers of HMRC, the Commissioners and its officers. In addition it provides an overview of various administrative matters including the taxpayer's Charter, how a taxpayer may go about making a complaint when HMRC make an error, electronic communication provisions, HMRC's international obligations, and the requirements as to the duties of senior accounting officers.

Large companies (and partnerships) must publish an annual tax strategy online, outlining their approach to tax risk, tax planning and dealing with HMRC (see **36.19** below). If they have a history of unco-operative behaviour they may become subject to a special measures regime (see **36.20** below).

Structure of HMRC

[36.2] The collection and management of corporation tax is administered by the **Commissioners** for Her Majesty's Revenue and Customs (HMRC). [*TMA 1970, s 1; Commissioners for Revenue and Customs Act 2005, Sch 4 para 12*].

The Commissioners also have the important function of advising the Treasury and the Chancellor of the Exchequer on proposals for new or amending legislation, in particular to stop avoidance of tax, and for alterations in the law deemed advisable in view of adverse decisions of the courts. Therefore the practical day to day administration of tax is undertaken by officers of Revenue and Customs, who are civil servants appointed by the Commissioners.

HMRC officers are responsible for processing returns, making assessments, dealing with claims and allowances, carrying out enquiries and collection and recovery of tax. HMRC officers may issue notices to taxpayers to make returns and notices of appeal have to be given to them. Disputes may be resolved through the Tribunal structure (the vast majority of cases being heard by the First-tier Tribunal) with subsequent appeals limited to points of law being available to the Upper Tribunal and thence to the Court of Appeal (or in Scotland, to the Court of Session) and then the Supreme Court (see further 5 APPEALS).

[*Commissioners for Revenue and Customs Act 2005, ss 2, 6, 7, Sch 1; FA 1998, Sch 18, para 48*].

Criminal prosecutions of tax offences in England and Wales are conducted by the Central Fraud Group of the Crown Prosecution Service.

[*Commissioners for Revenue and Customs Act 2005, ss 34–42, Sch 3*].

In this publication, 'HMRC' means Her Majesty's Revenue and Customs.

Information on many aspects of corporation tax including legislation, forms and publications, and the HMRC Manuals can be found on the gov.uk website.

'Care and management' powers

[36.3] As noted at **36.2** above, the Commissioners for HMRC have responsibility for the 'collection and management' of taxes, including corporation tax. The courts have stated that HMRC's general duties of 'care and management' of the tax system have further ramifications and impose an implied duty to treat taxpayers fairly and to use their discretionary powers to ensure discrimination does not arise. See *R v CIR (ex p National Federation of Self-employed and Small Businesses Ltd)* (1981) 55 TC 133, HL in which the validity of amnesties by the predecessors of the Commissioners, the Board of Inland Revenue, was considered.

These powers and duties have been further considered by the courts on a number of occasions. HMRC extra statutory concessions (**36.5** above) have been the subject of frequent judicial criticism (see Lord Edmund-Davies' opinion in *Vestey v CIR (No 1)* (1979) 54 TC 503, HL, for a review of this and the *Wilkinson* decision above). In *R v Inspector of Taxes, Reading, ex p*

Fulford-Dobson [1987] QB 978, [1987] 3 WLR 277, a claim that the Revenue had acted unfairly in refusing a concession where tax avoidance was involved was rejected, but the taxpayer's right to seek judicial review of a Revenue decision to refuse the benefit of a concession was confirmed in *R v HMIT (ex p Brumfield)* (1988) 61 TC 589.

A decision by the Revenue to revoke its authorisation to pay a dividend gross was upheld in *R v CIR (ex p Camacq Corporation)* (1989) 62 TC 651, CA.

For a general discussion of the HMRC's care and management powers, and an example of a ruling by the Court that HMRC had exercised a discretionary power reasonably, see *Preston v CIR* [1985] 2 All ER 327, [1985] STC 282, HL. Where a discretionary power is given to the Revenue, it is an error in law to proceed on the footing that the power is mandatory (*R v HMIT and Others (ex p Lansing Bagnall Ltd)* (1986) 61 TC 112, CA). See also *R v CIR (ex p J Rothschild Holdings plc)* (1987) 61 TC 178, CA, where the Revenue were required to produce internal documents of a general character relating to their practice in applying a statutory provision.

HMRC policy of selective prosecution for criminal offences in connection with tax evasion did not render a decision in a particular case unlawful or *ultra vires*, provided that the case was considered on its merits fairly and dispassionately to see whether the criteria for prosecution were satisfied, and that the decision to prosecute was then taken in good faith for the purpose of collecting taxes and not for some ulterior, extraneous or improper purpose (*R v CIR (ex p Mead and Cook)* (1992) 65 TC 1).

The making of a 'forward tax agreement', by which the Inland Revenue renounced their right and duty to investigate the true financial and other circumstances of the other party during the period of the agreement in return for payments of money, was not a proper exercise of the Inland Revenue's care and management powers, and was accordingly *ultra vires* and illegal. As such, it was not unfair of the Revenue to end the agreement. (*Al Fayed v A-G for Scotland* [2004] STC 1703).

Exercise of HMRC officer functions by automated process

[36.4] HMRC can use automated processes or other means to perform functions which, under the applicable statute, must be performed by an HMRC officer. These include (but are not restricted to):

- notices to file returns under *FA 1998, Sch 18 para 3* (see **65.4** RETURNS);
- assessment of tax under *TMA 1970, s 30A* (see **6.2** ASSESSMENTS); and
- penalty determinations under *TMA 1970, s 100* (see **59.23** PENALTIES).

This rule was introduced following a number of tribunal decisions, which held that notices issued automatically by computer were not valid. (The UT had, however, already overturned such a decision in *HMRC v Rogers* UT 2019, [2020] STC 220. In that case, the UT held that the requirement for a notice to deliver a return had to be given by an HMRC officer did not mean that a notice had to be given by an identified officer or that the return had to be submitted to that named officer. It was sufficient that the notice had been given under the authority of an officer.)

Although it was enacted by *FA 2020*, the rule is treated as always having been in force. It does not apply, however, to anything done by HMRC if a court or tribunal determined before 11 March 2020 that the act in question was invalid because it was not done by an HMRC officer (provided that the court or tribunal's decision had not been set aside or overturned on appeal before 11 March 2020).

[*FA 2020, s 103*].

HMRC non-statutory clearances

[36.5] HMRC's non-statutory clearance regime is covered at www.gov.uk/guidance/non-statutory-clearance-service-guidance and www.gov.uk/seeking-clearance-or-approval-for-a-transaction. HMRC will provide clarification on guidance or legislation in relation to a specific transaction. Before using HMRC's clearance service, the taxpayer or agent should have first checked that the transaction is not covered by a more appropriate clearance or approval route. The taxpayer/agent can seek clearance only if he has fully considered the relevant HMRC guidance and/or contacted the relevant helpline and has either not been able to find the information needed or remains uncertain about HMRC's interpretation of recent tax legislation. HMRC will then set out their advice in writing within 28 days (or longer if difficult or complicated issues are involved). Further details can be found on the web page, including checklists to help decide what information needs to be provided and details of where to send the clearance application.

Certain types of transaction have statutory clearance procedures. These are covered throughout this work where appropriate; see, for example, **61.9** PURCHASE BY A COMPANY OF ITS OWN SHARES.

For the extent to which taxpayers may rely on guidance given by HMRC, see further the letter from the Deputy Chairman to the various professional bodies following the decision in *Matrix-Securities Ltd v IRC* [1994] 1 All ER 769, [1994] 1 WLR 334, HL. In *R (oao Hely-Hutchinson) v HMRC* [2015] EWHC 3261 (Admin), the Administrative Court held that in principle HMRC should be held to its published guidance, and departure from it may found an action for judicial review if it would result in conspicuous unfairness. Such unfairness may result from the unequal treatment of different taxpayers and from retrospective withdrawal of guidance in relation to past transactions or claims.

HMRC Charter

[36.6] HMRC are required to publish a Charter setting out standards of behaviour and values to which they aspire in dealing with taxpayers. The latest version of the Charter was published in November 2020. See www.gov.uk/government/publications/hmrc-charter/the-hmrc-charter.

The Charter must be regularly reviewed by HMRC and they must publish an annual report detailing the extent to which they have demonstrated the standards and values set out in the Charter. [*CRCA 2005, s 16A*].

HMRC error

[36.7] HMRC factsheet 'Complaints' outlines HMRC's complaints procedure.

If a taxpayer thinks that a tax bill is wrong or that his tax affairs have been handled badly, he may ask for his case to be reviewed by the Customer Relations or Complaints Manager for the office or unit concerned. If the taxpayer is still dissatisfied, he may approach the Area Director with overall responsibility for that office or unit. The taxpayer has further recourse to the Adjudicator (see below), an independent adjudicator appointed to deal with complaints which still have not been settled satisfactorily after reference to the Area Director.

Guidance can also be found in the Complaints and Remedy Guidance Manual with regard to advice on the circumstances in which payment may be claimed from HMRC as a consequence of their mistake or unreasonable delay. These fall into three general categories.

(a) **Claiming back costs.** Any reasonable costs paid as a direct result of HMRC error, such as postage, telephone calls, travelling expenses, professional fees, financial charges, and interest on overpaid tax and national insurance, may be reclaimed. If the extra costs arose because of HMRC delay in dealing with the taxpayer's affairs, interest normally charged on overdue tax or national insurance owed by the taxpayer may be waived, or interest paid on money owed by HMRC, during the unreasonable delay, subject to HMRC internal review. See CRG5350 and CRG5525.

(b) **Compensation for worry and distress.** If HMRC's actions have affected the taxpayer particularly badly, HMRC may pay compensation (usually in the range £25–£500) to acknowledge and apologise for the way the taxpayer was treated. See CRG6075.

(c) **Further mistakes or delays in dealing with complaint.** If HMRC handle a complaint poorly, or take an unreasonable time to deal with it, compensation (usually in the range £25–£500) may be paid, on top of any reasonable costs, to reflect this. See CRG6150.

HMRC Adjudicator

[36.8] A taxpayer who is not satisfied with HMRC's response to a complaint has the option of putting the case to an independent Adjudicator. The Adjudicator's Office considers complaints about HMRC's handling of a taxpayer's affairs, e.g. excessive delays, errors, discourtesy or the exercise of HMRC discretion. Matters subject to existing rights of appeal are excluded.

Complaints normally go to the Adjudicator only after they have been considered by, firstly, the Customer Relations or Complaints Manager and, secondly, a senior officer of the relevant HMRC office, and where the taxpayer is still not satisfied with the response received. The alternatives of pursuing the complaint to an MP, or (through an MP) to the Parliamentary Ombudsman continue to be available.

The Adjudicator reviews all the facts, considers whether the complaint is justified, and, if so, settles the complaint by mediation or makes recommendations as to what should be done. HMRC normally accept the recommendations.

The adjudicator also investigates complaints about the Valuation Office Agency (now part of HMRC).

The address is The Adjudicator's Office, PO Box 10280, Nottingham, NG2 9PF (tel. 0300 057 1111).

The Adjudicator publishes an annual report.

Leave to apply for judicial review of the rejection by the Adjudicator of a complaint concerning the use of information from unidentified informants was refused in *R v Revenue Adjudicator's Office (ex p Drummond)* (1996) 70 TC 235.

See: www.adjudicatorsoffice.gov.uk.

Communications

Open Government

[36.9] Information on HMRC policies and decisions is widely available. Most internal HMRC guidance manuals are available on the HRMC website (at www.gov.uk/government/collections/hmrc-manuals).

Telephone Helplines

[36.10] An employers' telephone helpline on 0300 200 3200 can be used for general enquiries about PAYE, national insurance and value added tax registration. See also **20.8** CONSTRUCTION INDUSTRY SCHEME — the CIS helpline on 0300 200 3210.

A range of other helplines for general and specific enquiries is available on the gov.uk website (at www.gov.uk/contact-hmrc).

Use of electronic communications

[36.11] HMRC have broad powers to make regulations, by statutory instrument, to facilitate two-way electronic communication in the delivery of information, e.g. tax returns and the making of tax payments. [*FA 1999, ss 132, 133*]. The intention is to provide a range of electronic services which taxpayers can use as an alternative to paper if they so wish.

The powers have been used to require the electronic filing of corporation tax returns and the electronic payment of corporation tax (see **58.4** PAYMENT OF TAX).

HMRC disclosure of information

[36.12] HMRC officers are bound by a general duty of confidentiality but this general duty is overridden in many specific circumstances. For example, the Commissioners may instruct HMRC officers to disclose confidential information where it is in the public interest to do so.

There are circumstances when HMRC officials may disclose information to a prosecuting authority, for advice or for the commencement of proceedings. Information disclosed in this way is subject to on-going confidentiality safeguards.

Provisions exist whereby HMRC may provide information to other government departments, for example, in relation to social security.

In addition, HMRC may disclose information, that would otherwise be subject to a legal obligation of confidentiality, to the Financial Conduct Authority, Prudential Regulation Authority or the Secretary of State for the purposes of assisting an investigation.

There are detailed provisions concerning the exchange of information between the tax authorities of member states and there are also provisions for the disclosure of information required under double taxation agreements to foreign tax authorities.

See **36.14** below.

[*CRCA 2005, ss 18, 20, 21; SSAA 1992, ss 121E, 122; FSMA 2000, s 168*].

The information gathering powers of HMRC are outlined in **37 HMRC INVESTIGATORY POWERS.**

Power to publish State aid information

[36.13] The Commissioners for HMRC may publish 'State aid information' to comply with certain EU State aid obligations and obligations under the EU withdrawal agreement (including the NI protocol) requiring such publication. They may also disclose State aid information to another person for the purpose of having it published. '*State aid information*' is information relating to the grant of State aid through the providing of a tax advantage. [*FA 2016, ss 181, 182; SI 2020 No 1499*].

International co-operation

[36.14] Further to global moves to combat fraud and tax evasion the UK has entered into international agreements for mutual assistance in tax enforcement, covering exchange of information foreseeably relevant to the administration, enforcement or recovery of UK or foreign tax, the recovery of debts and the service of documents relating to UK or foreign tax. *FA 2006, ss 173–175* make certain provisions in respect of such arrangements. Many of these information exchange agreements are based on the 2002 OECD model — a list of such agreements can be found at www.gov.uk/government/collections/tax-information-exchange-agreements.

Any information that can be disclosed to another territory under this provision can be disclosed to HMRC by any other Government department. Such information can then be disclosed by HMRC to an authorised officer of any territory with whom arrangements have been made. Information may not, however, be disclosed under any such arrangements unless HMRC are satisfied that the counterparty is bound by, or has undertaken to observe, rules of confidentiality at least as strict as those applying in the UK.

HMRC are able to use their information gathering powers regarding domestic taxes (*FA 2008, Sch 36* — see **38** HMRC INVESTIGATORY POWERS) to obtain information in respect of foreign tax liabilities covered by the international arrangements. For the procedural rules governing recovery of foreign taxes under these provisions, see *SI 2007 No 3507*.

The UK is a signatory to the joint Council of Europe and OECD Convention on Mutual Administrative Assistance in Tax Matters (*SI 2007 No 2126; SI 2011 No 1079*). The convention includes provisions for: exchange of information on request; automatic exchange of information; spontaneous exchange of information; simultaneous tax examinations; tax examination abroad; assistance in recovery of tax; and service of documents.

See generally HMRC's International Exchange of Information Manual.

Co-operation between tax authorities of EU member states

The Administrative Co-operation in the field of taxation Directive (2011/16/EU) provides for the exchange of information between tax authorities of EU member states to enable them to correctly assess liabilities to the taxes covered by the *Directive* (which include taxes on income and capital). This is transposed into UK law by regulations (see *SI 2012 No 3062*). Those regulations remain in force following Brexit (see the *European Union (Withdrawal) Act 2018, s 2*).

See also **36.15** below.

Recovery of taxes etc. due in EU member States (MARD)

Provision is made for the recovery in the UK of amounts in respect of which a request for enforcement has been made in accordance with the Mutual Assistance Recovery Directive (MARD) (*Directive 2010/24/EU*) by an authority in another EU member State. Disclosure of information by a UK tax authority (e.g. the Commissioners for HMRC) for these purposes (or for the purposes of a request for enforcement by the UK) is not generally precluded by any obligation of secrecy.

Broadly, the UK tax authority has the same powers it would have for a corresponding claim in the UK, in particular in relation to penalties and interest. Treasury regulations make provision for procedural and supplementary matters. Regulations may also be made by the UK tax authority for the application, non-application or adaptation of the law applicable to corresponding UK claims.

No proceedings may be taken against a person under these provisions if they show that proceedings relevant to the liability in question are pending (i.e. still open to appeal), or about to be instituted, before a competent body in the member State in question. This does not apply to any steps which could be taken in similar circumstances in the case of a corresponding UK claim or if the foreign proceedings are not prosecuted or instituted with reasonable expedition. If a final decision on the foreign claim (i.e. one against which no further appeal lies or would be in time), or a part of it, has been given in favour of the taxpayer by a competent body in the member State in question, no proceeding may be taken under these provisions in relation to the claim (or part).

Following Brexit, the UK legislation is amended (with effect from IP completion day on 31 December 2020) to reflect the fact that MARD is extended to the UK as a third country by the EU Withdrawal Agreement and to ensure that the legislation continues to give effect to MARD. MARD will apply to the UK for the five years following IP completion day for amounts that became due or transactions that occurred before that day and, if the debt falls under the Northern Ireland Protocol, for as long as that Protocol remains in force.

[*FA 2011, s 87, Sch 25; SI 2011 No 2931; SI 2020 No 996*].

Automatic information exchange with the USA

In 2010 the USA introduced legislation to combat tax evasion by US persons. These provisions, known as the Foreign Accounts Tax Compliance Act (FATCA), require financial institutions outside the USA to pass information about the accounts of US persons to the US Internal Revenue Service (IRS). Any financial institution that fails to comply is subject to a 30% withholding tax on US source income.

On 12 September 2012, the UK and USA entered into an Intergovernmental Agreement (IGA). Under the IGA, if UK financial institutions comply with legislation that meets the terms negotiated between the two countries, and the UK shares this information with the US, those institutions will be deemed to have complied with FATCA and will not be subject to the withholding tax. The financial institutions must register with the IRS but will provide the required information to HMRC, who will in turn provide it to the IRS.

FA 2013, s 222 gave the Treasury power to make regulations giving effect to the IGA, any agreement modifying or supplementing the IGA and any subsequent agreement or arrangements for the exchange of tax information between the UK and another territory which make provision corresponding, or substantially similar, to the IGA (see the Common Reporting Standard at **35.14** below). The regulations implementing the IGA (*SI 2015 No 878*) define the key terms, such as 'reportable account', included in the IGA and set out the required due diligence and reporting requirements of UK financial institutions. They also contain provision for penalties for non-compliance, and an appeals process. As part of the IGA, the US has agreed to provide the UK with reciprocal data on the US accounts of UK persons.

For official guidance, see www.gov.uk/government/publications/uk-us-automatic-exchange-of-information-agreement/uk-us-automatic-exchange-of-information-agreement.

Common Reporting Standard

On 9 April 2013, the governments of the UK, France, Germany, Italy and Spain announced an agreement to develop and pilot multilateral tax information exchange based on the Model Intergovernmental Agreement to Improve International Tax Compliance and to Implement FATCA developed between these countries and the USA (see **35.12** above). Other countries subsequently committed to join this pilot. (Treasury Press Release, 9 April 2013; HMRC Press Release, 28 November 2013.) On 6 May 2014, the Organisation for Economic Co-operation and Development (OECD) Declaration on Automatic Exchange of Information in Tax Matters was endorsed by its member countries and by several non-member countries. On 21 July 2014, the OECD released the full version of a Common Reporting Standard (CRS) (formally known as the Standard for Automatic Exchange of Financial Account Information in Tax

Matters). The CRS calls on governments to obtain detailed account information from their financial institutions and exchange that information automatically with other jurisdictions on an annual basis. Over 100 countries have committed to adopt the CRS, with approximately half of those undertaking to begin exchanging information in 2017 and the remainder in 2018. See generally the OECD website at www.oecd.org/tax/exchange-of-tax-information/automaticexchange.htm for more details. For country-by-country status, see www.oecd.org/tax/automatic-exchange/crs-implementation-and-assistance/crs-by-jurisdiction and www.oecd.org/tax/transparency/AEOI-commitments.pdf. For HMRC guidance for UK account holders in financial institutions, see www.gov.uk/government/uploads/system/uploads/attachment_data/file/386413/Automatic_exchange_of_information_-_account_holders.pdf.

The regulations implementing the CRS in the UK (*SI 2015 No 878*) define key terms, such as 'reportable account', and set out the required due diligence and reporting requirements of financial institutions. They also contain provision for penalties for non-compliance, and an appeals process. The regulations took effect on 1 January 2016.

Under an agreement signed by the EU and Switzerland on 27 May 2015, both sides will automatically exchange information on the financial accounts of each other's residents from 2018. Member States will receive annually the names and addresses etc. of their residents with accounts in Switzerland, as well as other financial and account balance information. The EU has signed similar agreements with Andorra, Liechtenstein, Monaco and San Marino (see ec.europa.eu/taxation_customs/individuals/personal-taxation/taxation-savings-income/international-developments_en).

Client notification requirement

On and after **30 September 2016**, persons who provide professional advice or services in respect of taxation or finance involving overseas income or assets are required to notify their clients about matters including the CRS, the penalties for offshore tax evasion and the opportunities to disclose previous offshore evasion to HMRC. The regulations require a standard notification letter, headed 'If you have money or other assets abroad, you could owe tax in the UK', to be sent to affected clients no later than **31 August 2017**. Affected clients are those to whom the adviser has provided advice or services about income or assets outside the UK, or who the adviser has referred overseas for such advice or services, but disregarding clients for whom the adviser has completed and submitted a personal tax return reflecting such advice or services. The penalty for non-compliance is £3,000. A similar obligation falls upon financial intermediaries. See www.gov.uk/government/publications/client-notification-income-or-assets-abroad for more information, including the text of the standard letter. See also HMRC International Exchange of Information Manual IEIM600000–609000. [*FA 2013, s 222; F(No 2)A 2015, s 50; SI 2015 No 878, Regs 12A–12F, 13, Sch 3; SI 2016 No 899*].

EU disclosure rules for cross-border tax arrangements (DAC 6)

[36.15] *FA 2019, s 84* gave the Treasury the power to make regulations (see now *SI 2020 No 25*) to require disclosure to HMRC of information about certain cross-border tax arrangements to give effect to international rules. This is in response to the EU's sixth Directive on Administrative Co-operation in the field of taxation (EU Directive 2018/822/EU (amending Directive 2011/16/EU)) (DAC 6). DAC 6 requires member States to enact rules obliging 'intermediaries' and in some cases taxpayers, to report information to tax authorities about cross-border arrangements that contain certain hallmarks. '*Cross-border*' means concerning more than one member State, or a member State and a third (non-EU) country.

The UK regulations are amended with effect from Brexit IP completion day (11pm on 31 December 2020), so that they now apply only to arrangements within the hallmarks in (D) below. The Trade and Cooperation Agreement between the UK and the EU requires the UK to abide by OECD rules on exchange of information on cross-border arrangements. The retention of the category D hallmarks enables the UK to comply with the OECD's Mandatory Disclosure Rules (MDR). The Government intends to repeal the remaining UK DAC 6 rules entirely, and replace them with new legislation specifically to implement the OECD MDR. HMRC will consult on the new legislation later in 2021.

The regulations have effect in relation to:

(a) a reportable cross-border arrangement which is, or continues to be, made available for implementation or ready for implementation on or after 1 July 2020;
(b) a reportable cross-border arrangement in respect of which, on or after 1 July 2020, an intermediary provided aid, assistance or advice with respect to designing, marketing, organising, making available for implementation or managing the implementation of the reportable cross-border arrangement; and
(c) a reportable cross-border arrangement the first step in the implementation of which was made on or after 25 June 2018.

Six-month deferral due to COVID-19

However, due to the impact of the COVID-19 (coronavirus) pandemic, the EU gave member States the option to delay implementation. The Government deferred the first reporting deadlines by six months (see *SI 2020 No 713*). Revised dates are as follows:

- For arrangements which were made available for implementation, or which were ready for implementation, or where the first step in the implementation took place between 1 July 2020 and 31 December 2020, reports must now be made within the 30 days beginning on 1 January 2021. Under the original rules, such arrangements would have had to be reported within 30 days of the reporting trigger point being reached.
- For arrangements in respect of which a UK intermediary provided aid, assistance or advice between 1 July 2020 and 31 December 2020, reports must be made within 30 days beginning on 1 January 2021. Again, under the original rules, such arrangements would have had to be reported within 30 days of the aid etc. being provided.
- In a case within (c) above in which the first step is taken before 1 July 2020, the report must be made on or before 28 February 2021 (instead of 31 August 2020 as originally intended).

- Where three monthly reports are required in relation to marketable arrangements (see below), the first such report must be made by 30 April 2021.

Reporting requirements

The reporting obligation applies primarily to intermediaries; however, a secondary one also applies to the taxpayer. An '*intermediary*' is defined as someone with an EU connection who designs, markets, organises or makes available for implementation or manages the implementation of a reportable cross-border arrangement. Such intermediaries are likely to include professional advisers such as lawyers, accountants and tax advisers, as well as banks, financial advisers and, more generally, parties involved in transactions who could be considered to fall under any of the categories above. In addition, intermediary also refers to any person who undertakes to provide aid, assistance or advice in respect of a reportable cross-border arrangement, or any person who could reasonably be expected to know that such aid, assistance or advice relates to a reportable cross-border arrangement.

There is no obligation on a UK intermediary to report if to do so would breach legal professional privilege (LPP). In this case the intermediary must notify another intermediary, or the 'relevant taxpayer', that they are obliged to make a report instead. That report must then be made within 30 days of receiving the notification.

If there is no intermediary, or due to LLP there is no intermediary that can make a report, the obligation to report falls instead on the relevant taxpayer. The '*relevant taxpayer*' is any person to whom a reportable cross-border arrangement is made available for implementation or who is ready to implement a reportable cross-border arrangement, or who has implemented the first step of such an arrangement.

The report must set out the reportable information in relation to the reportable cross-border arrangement that is within the UK intermediary's knowledge, possession or control.

Information on reportable cross-border arrangements must be filed by the UK intermediary with the HMRC within 30 days beginning on the day after the reportable cross-border arrangement is made available for implementation, is ready for implementation, or the first step has been implemented, whichever occurs first. If the intermediary is within these rules because it has provided aid, assistance or advice, it must report within 30 days after giving that aid etc. If the reporting obligation relates to a marketable arrangement, meaning, an arrangement that is designed, marketed, ready for implementation or made available for implementation without a need to be substantially customised, the intermediary must make an updated report every three months.

If the reporting obligation falls on a relevant taxpayer (see above), that person must make a report within 30 days of the first of the following:

(i) the day after the arrangement is made available for implementation to that taxpayer;

(ii) the day after the arrangement is ready for implementation by that taxpayer; and

(iii) the first step in implementing the arrangement is made in relation to that taxpayer.

Where a UK relevant taxpayer participates in a reportable cross-border arrangement, that person must make a return for each of the company accounting periods or tax years or for which they obtain a tax advantage from the arrangement. The due date for the return coincides with that for the company tax return or self-assessment tax return.

In order to determine whether or not the reporting requirements have been complied with, an HMRC officer may require a person, who the officer reasonably suspects is a UK intermediary or UK relevant taxpayer, to provide such information or documents as the officer reasonably requires as specified by written notice. The information or documents must be provided within such period, being not less than 30 days, and by such means and in such form, as is reasonably required by the officer.

Reportable arrangements

An arrangement will be reportable if it meets at least one of five hallmarks. As noted above, only hallmarks within (D) below apply with effect from IP completion day.

The hallmarks are listed in Annex IV to DAC 6 (see https://eur-lex.europa.eu/legal-content/EN/TXT/PDF/?uri=CELEX:32018L0822&from=EN) and are described as presenting an indication of a potential risk of tax avoidance, although there is no requirement for a tax avoidance motive. All of the generic hallmarks, and some of the specific hallmarks, are taken into account for the purposes of DAC 6 only if they fulfil the main benefit test. The main benefit test is fulfilled if a main benefit which, having regard to all relevant facts and circumstances, that a person may reasonably expect to derive from an arrangement is the obtaining of a tax advantage. The hallmarks are very wide and have the potential to catch a large number of transactions that would not normally be regarded as involving tax avoidance.

The hallmarks are as follows:

(A) Generic hallmarks linked to the main benefit test: arrangements that give rise to performance fees or which involve mass-marketed schemes.

(B) Specific hallmarks linked to the main benefit test: this includes certain tax planning features, such as buying a loss-making company to exploit its losses in order to reduce tax liability. Another example would involve arrangements aimed at converting income into capital in order to obtain a tax benefit.

(C) Specific hallmarks related to cross-border transactions; some of these hallmarks are subject to the main benefit test: for example, deductible cross-border payments between associated enterprises where the recipient is essentially subject to no tax, zero or almost zero tax. Another hallmark is about deductions for the same depreciation on an asset claimed in more than one jurisdiction.

(D) Specific hallmarks concerning the automatic exchange of information and beneficial ownership: an arrangement is reportable if it has the effect of undermining the rules on anti-money laundering, transparency of beneficial ownership or the automatic exchange of financial account information.

(E) Specific hallmarks concerning transfer pricing: these include the use of unilateral safe harbours; the transfer of hard-to-value intangible assets when no reliable comparables exist and the projection of future cash flows or income are highly uncertain.

Generic hallmarks

The 'generic' hallmarks are concerned with the conditions under which the arrangements are entered into, as opposed to the specific hallmarks, which describe attributes of the arrangements themselves.

DAC 6 provides that a cross-border arrangement is reportable if it satisfies the main benefit test and one of the following applies:

- **confidentiality**—the relevant taxpayer or another participant in the arrangement agrees to a confidentiality condition relating to not disclosing to other intermediaries or the tax authorities how the arrangement may secure a tax advantage;
- **fee linked to tax savings**—the intermediary is entitled to a fee or other amount by reference to the amount of the tax advantage, or the fee is dependent on the tax advantage being obtained;
- **standardised documentation**—the arrangement has a substantially standardised set of documentation or structure, and is available to more than one relevant taxpayer without a need to be substantially customised.

Specific hallmarks

Under this heading, a cross-border arrangement is reportable if it satisfies the main benefit test and one of the following applies:

- **sale of a loss company**—the arrangement includes contrived steps consisting of acquiring a loss-making company, discontinuing its main activity and using the losses, including by transferring the losses to another jurisdiction or accelerating the use of the losses;
- **income into capital**—the arrangement converts income into capital, gifts or other categories of revenue that are taxed at a lower level or are exempt from tax;
- **circular transactions**—the arrangements involve funds moving in a circle (round-tripping), using interposed entities without other primary commercial function or transactions that offset or cancel each other or have similar features.

Specific hallmarks related to cross-border transactions

This category of hallmark has the potential to catch transactions that are purely commercial, with no tax avoidance motive. Some have a main benefit test and some do not, as set out below.

A cross-border arrangement is reportable if it involves deductible cross-border payments between associated enterprises and one of the following applies:

- the recipient is not tax resident in any jurisdiction;
- the recipient is tax resident in a jurisdiction with no corporation tax, or a corporation tax rate that is almost zero, and the main benefit test is met;
- the recipient is tax resident in a third (non-EU) jurisdiction that is assessed by Member States or the OECD as uncooperative;
- the payment is exempt from tax, or benefits from a preferential tax regime, in the recipient's home state, and the main benefit test is met.

There is a detailed definition of an associated enterprise that refers to ownership of 25% of the votes, capital or profits of another enterprise, or the ability to exercise significant influence over another enterprise.

A cross-border arrangement is also reportable if one of the following applies:

- deductions for the same depreciation on an asset are claimed in more than one jurisdiction;
- double tax relief for the same item of income or capital is claimed in more than one jurisdiction;
- the arrangement includes a transfer of assets and there is a material difference in the amount treated as consideration for the assets in the jurisdictions involved.

There is no main benefit test for these three types of arrangement.

Specific hallmarks concerning automatic exchange of information and beneficial ownership

A further category of reportable cross-border arrangements is designed to catch schemes that undermine, or exploit the absence of, international agreements on the automatic exchange of information on financial accounts. This applies to EU rules but also agreements with third countries, so covers both the DAC and the OECD's Common Reporting Standard (CRS).

For instance, cross-border arrangements would be reportable if they involve the use of an account that has similar features to those of the type of financial account that is subject to information exchange under the DAC or CRS, but that purports not to be such a financial account. The reclassification of income or capital into another product, or the conversion of a financial institution into a different type of financial institution, in a way that avoids the rules on automatic exchange of information, are further examples of arrangements that would be caught under this head.

Cross-border arrangements are also reportable if they involve a non-transparent legal or beneficial ownership chain and contain other features that circumvent the Fourth Money Laundering Directive 2015/849 (EU) (also known as DAC 5).

There is no main benefit test for these hallmarks, and although their primary focus is schemes that are intended to avoid reporting rules, there is no purpose test. They could, therefore, catch commercial arrangements that are not motivated by avoiding reporting requirements.

Specific hallmarks concerning transfer pricing

The final category of reportable cross-border arrangements, for which there is again no main benefit test, concerns transfer pricing and applies to arrangements involving:

- the use of unilateral safe harbour rules (for example, an exemption for small and medium-sized enterprises);
- the transfer of hard-to-value intangibles;
- an intra-group cross-border transfer of functions, risks or assets, if as a result the transferor's profit-making capacity is reduced by more than 50%.

Employees

A person (P) is not to be treated as an intermediary in relation to a reportable cross-border arrangement where P is an employee of another person (E) and E is an intermediary or a relevant taxpayer in relation to the arrangement. Where E is connected to another person (F), P is to be treated as an employee of F as well as being an employee of E. For this purpose, E is connected with F where E is closely bound to F by financial, economic or organisational links.

[*SI 2020 No 25, Regs 1–13; SI 2020 No 1649*].

Penalties

A fixed penalty of up to £5,000 may be levied for failure to comply with the UK reporting requirements. Daily penalties of £600 may also be charged in some cases during the 'initial period' if the fixed penalty appears to an HMRC officer to be inappropriately low after taking into account all relevant considerations (for which see *SI 2020 No 25, Reg 14(3)*). The '*initial period*' is the period beginning when the default occurs and ending with the earlier of the day the daily penalty is determined and the last day before the failure ceases. HMRC must commence proceedings before the First-tier Tribunal if they are to charge this daily penalty. Amongst other options, the Tribunal may increase the maximum penalty to an amount of up to £1 million.

If the failure continues, further penalties of £600 per day may be levied.

In the case of the obligation on a UK relevant taxpayer to make annual returns, there is a fixed penalty £5,000 in respect of each reportable cross-border arrangement to which the failure relates. This is increased to £7,500 if it is the second such failure during the 36 months ending with the date on which the current failure began. The penalty is increased to £10,000 if there have already been two or more such failures during that 36-month period.

SI 2020 No 25, Reg 18 sets out the time limits for charging the above penalties. A penalty is to be treated for all purposes as if it were tax charged in an assessment. A penalty is due and payable at the end of the 30 days beginning with the issue of the notice of determination by HMRC or (as the case may be) the date of the determination of the penalty by the First-tier Tribunal.

UK intermediaries and relevant taxpayers can appeal against penalties. If an HMRC officer thinks it right because of special circumstances, the officer may reduce a penalty. Penalties may be cancelled if a reasonable excuse exists (see *SI*

2020 No 25, Reg 21). HMRC had said that COVID-19 would be a reasonable excuse for a delay in reporting (HMRC International Exchange of Information Manual IEIM800000), but this may have been largely superseded by the subsequent announcement of a six-month deferral of the first reporting deadlines (see above).

[*SI 2020 No 25, Regs 14–21*].

Simon's Taxes. See **A6.1204A.**

Assets Recovery

[36.16] See also 58.7 PAYMENT OF TAX.

The National Crime Agency is an independent government agency and not part of HMRC. Its remit is to use criminal confiscation, civil recovery and taxation functions to recover money and assets that have come from criminal activity, thus depriving criminals of the proceeds of their crime. There are provisions in *Proceeds of Crime Act 2002* (*Pt 6*) in respect of certain serious crimes that allow the functions of HMRC to be undertaken by the NCA.

In order to carry out HMRC functions, the agency must have reasonable grounds to suspect that:

(a) income arising or a gain accruing to a person in respect of a chargeable period is chargeable to income tax or is a chargeable gain and arises or accrues as a result (whether wholly or partly, directly or indirectly) of the 'criminal conduct' of that person or another; or
(b) a company is chargeable to corporation tax on its profits arising in a chargeable period and the profits arise as a result (whether wholly or partly, directly or indirectly) of the criminal conduct of the company or another person,

and must serve a notice on HMRC specifying the person or company, the period or periods concerned, and the functions which they intend to carry out. The periods involved may include periods beginning before the *Act* was passed.

Where the agency is acting in such a capacity it is immaterial that a source cannot be identified for any income. Thus an assessment made by the agency under *TMA 1970, s 29* (discovery assessment) in respect of income charged to tax under *ITTOIA 2005, Pt 5 Ch 8* (income not otherwise charged — see Tolley's Income Tax under Miscellaneous Income) cannot be reduced or quashed only because it does not specify (to any extent) the source of the income.

The agency may cease carrying out the functions specified in the notice (originally served on HMRC) at any time, but *must* so cease where the conditions allowing the original notice to be made are no longer satisfied. Any assessment made under *TMA 1970, s 29* is subsequently invalid to the extent that it does not specify a source for income.

For the above purposes, '*criminal conduct*' is conduct which constitutes an offence anywhere in the UK or which would do so if it occurred there, but does not include conduct constituting an offence relating to a matter under the care and management of HMRC.

It should be noted that the vesting of a function in the agency under these provisions does not divest HMRC or its officers of their functions (so that, for example, HMRC can continue to carry out routine work). Certain functions, as listed in *Proceeds of Crime Act 2002, s 323(3)*, cannot be carried out by the agency. For example, if the agency serves notice in relation to a company and in respect of a chargeable period or periods, the general HMRC functions vested in the agency do not include functions relating to any requirement which is imposed on the company in its capacity as an employer and relates to a tax year which does not fall wholly within the chargeable period(s).

In respect of actions carried out by the agency in the exercise of HMRC functions taxpayers have the same rights of appeal as any other taxpayer, thus appeals may be made to the appropriate tribunal. In hearing such appeals, the tribunal may be assisted by one or more assessors selected for their special knowledge and experience of the matter to which the appeal relates from a panel appointed for the purpose by the Lord Chancellor.

[*Proceeds of Crime Act 2002, ss 317, 318(1)(2), 319, 320(1)–(3), 323(1)(3), 326(1)(2)*].

A company whose tax affairs are being investigated by the agency should check its website (www.nationalcrimeagency.gov.uk) for guidance on how their cases will be dealt with.

See **6.3** ASSESSMENTS for a case involving a discovery assessment raised by the National Crime Agency.

HMRC officers undertaking criminal investigations into direct tax or tax credits offences have powers to seize suspected criminal cash under the *Proceeds of Crime Act 2002* and to exercise search and seizure warrants under that Act.

[*FA 2013, s 224; SI 2016 No 208*].

Confidentiality

[36.17] For the confidential treatment of information supplied to HMRC see Tolley's Income Tax under HMRC — Confidentiality of Information.

Duties of senior accounting officers

[36.18] Senior accounting officers of qualifying companies are required to certify that the company has taken reasonable steps to ensure that it has 'appropriate tax accounting arrangements'.

For HMRC guidance on the provisions see their Senior Accounting Officers Guidance Manual.

For the purpose of these rules, the *Companies Act 2006* definition of company, director and officer are adopted. Charities, mutual societies and dormant companies are all potentially within the scope, if the conditions are fulfilled.

Excluded, or potentially excluded companies are:

- bodies incorporated other than under the *Companies Act 2006*;
- partnerships;
- private equity structures — these will not be held responsible for the tax accounting arrangements of a target;
- foreign companies — only UK incorporated companies are caught. Therefore, CFCs, UK permanent establishments and overseas companies resident in the UK due to the location of central management and control are all outside the SAO provisions;
- companies incorporated in the UK but not resident there — such a company will be within the SAO legislation only to the extent that they are trading in, or have a taxable activity in the UK;
- dormant companies — although strictly within the SAO legislation, they are unlikely to have a tax charge or any tax accounting arrangements. They should be included in the certificate, with a note to the effect that they are dormant.

Foreign branches of UK companies are within the SAO legislation. Provided the responsibility for foreign tax has been delegated to a reasonably competent and qualified individual, reasonable steps would not include an in depth check of the foreign tax position. However, a check that the foreign tax had been paid would be expected.

Where a company or group is in liquidation or is insolvent, there may be no SAO and it was originally indicated that the legislation may not apply. However the latest version of the guidance (see below) highlights that these rules apply in most cases where insolvency procedures are being undertaken.

A qualifying company must, for every financial year, notify HMRC of the name or names of the senior accounting officer for that year in a form laid down by HMRC by the deadline for filing the company's accounts for that year, or such longer period as HMRC may allow. The notification should be sent to the company's Client Relationship Manager at HMRC. A notification may apply to more than one company.

The main duty of the SAO is to take reasonable steps to ensure the company establishes, maintains and monitors appropriate tax accounting arrangements. This involves monitoring the accounting arrangements and identifying the ways in which the arrangements are deficient. As evidence of these steps, the officer must complete a certificate stating that the company had appropriate tax accounting arrangements or give an explanation as to the respects in which it was deficient. Guidance is available as to the extent to which entries and balances in earlier years come within the scope of the provisions. The certificate must be filed within the time limit for filing accounts, or such longer period as HMRC may allow. Certificates may be submitted in any recognised paper or electronic format, including letter, fax or email (HMRC Brief 12/16).

The taxes and duties covered by this legislation are:

- corporation tax (including any amount assessable or chargeable as if it were CT for example in connection with loans to participators);
- VAT;
- PAYE;
- insurance premium tax;

- stamp duty land tax;
- stamp duty reserve tax;
- petroleum revenue tax;
- customs duties;
- excise duties (including air passenger duty);
- bank levy.

Penalties are provided for under these provisions. They are as follows:

(a) failure of the senior accounting officer to take reasonable steps to maintain appropriate tax accounting arrangements, £5,000;
(b) failure of senior accounting officer to provide a certificate or to provide a certificate with a careless or deliberate inaccuracy, £5,000;
(c) failure of a qualifying company to notify name of senior accounting officer for a year, £5,000.

As noted in the guidance, if the SAO changes during a financial year, more than one person will have held the SAO role with the qualifying company.

Where the penalty is for failure to carry out the main duty as in (a) above: if the latest SAO is the one who has failed then the latest SAO is liable to the penalty; if the latest SAO succeeds in the main duty but their predecessor failed then the predecessor is liable to the penalty.

Where the penalty is for failure to provide a certificate as in (b) above, then, irrespective of how many persons were SAO in the financial year and throughout the period up until the time limit for providing the certificate, the person who was the SAO when the time limit for providing the certificate expired is liable.

However, there will be no penalty on that SAO for failing to provide a certificate: if the SAO has suffered a penalty in relation to another group company for a similar failure for a corresponding financial year; or if any other SAO has provided a certificate in respect of that company for that financial year.

If one of the SAOs for a financial year provides a timely certificate then only that SAO is liable to an inaccuracy penalty for that financial year.

No penalty will be charged where HMRC are satisfied that there is reasonable excuse.

In *Castlelaw (No 628) Ltd v HMRC* FTT, [2020] SFTD 491, a penalty was charged in respect of a dormant company whose details were omitted from a notification by a 100 company group. The Tribunal upheld the penalty, holding that the SAO of the company had no reasonable excuse.

HMRC may issue an assessment in respect of the penalty to the person liable, but must do so not more than six months after the behaviour resulting in the penalty first comes to HMRC's notice or more than six years after the filing date. The person then has 30 days during which to appeal. Otherwise the person has 30 days to pay the penalty. Where an appeal is made and determined or withdrawn, the 30 days run from the date of withdrawal or determination. There is provision to avoid double assessment when the senior accounting officer holds that capacity for more than one company in a group. There are provisions for appeals against penalty notices.

Definitions

'*Appropriate tax accounting arrangements*' are arrangements to keep accounting records which enable the company to calculate accurately in all material respects its liability to a specified list of direct and indirect taxes.'

Subject to an overriding power of the Treasury to specify by statutory instrument that a company or class of company is not a qualifying company, a '*qualifying company*' is one which satisfies both or either of the following conditions:

(1) relevant turnover more than £200 million. (Turnover is as defined in *CA 2006, s 474* and shown in the statutory accounts i.e. adjustments in the corporation tax computation are not taken into account.) Where no turnover is shown in the statutory accounts (e.g. in the case of banks and insurance companies) the test at (2) below applies on its own;
(2) relevant '*balance sheet total*' more than £2 billion.

Where the company is a member of a group, these figures relate to the whole group. If the group companies' year ends are not co-terminous, the latest accounts ending before the group's balance sheet date are to be used.

'*Balance sheet total*' is the gross total of assets in the balance sheet.

'*Senior accounting officer*' for a non-group company is the director or officer who, in the company's reasonable opinion, has overall responsibility for the company's financial accounting arrangements. In a group situation, it is the group director or officer with overall responsibility for the accounting function, as above. One person may be senior accounting officer for more than one company. In determining if a group exists, a test of 51% ownership applies.

'*Director*' or '*officer*' are taken to have their *Companies Act 2006* meaning.

[*FA 2009, s 93, Sch 46*].

Publication of tax strategies by large businesses

[36.19] For financial years beginning on or after 15 September 2016, certain large businesses must publish their tax strategy each year. The strategy must be published on the internet before the end of the financial year to which it relates. If the business was required to publish its tax strategy for the previous financial year, the current year's strategy must be published no more than 15 months after the previous strategy was published. The strategy must be freely available to public view free of charge and must remain so until the next year's strategy is published or, if no such strategy need be published, for at least one year. The strategy may be published either as a separate document or as a self-contained part of a wider document.

The requirement to publish a tax strategy applies to the following entities.

(1) The 'head' of a 'UK group' which is a 'qualifying group' for the financial year. A '*UK group*' is a 'group' whose head is a body corporate incorporated in the UK. A '*group*' is either an 'MNE group' (as defined in the OECD Model Legislation in the OECD Country-by-Country

Reporting Implementation Package) or a 'group other than an MNE group' (as defined by reference to 51% subsidiaries and including at least two UK companies or UK permanent establishments). The '*head*' of a group is the member of the group which is not a 51% subsidiary of another member of the group.

A group other than an NME group is a '*qualifying group*' for a financial year if either the aggregate turnover of its UK companies and UK permanent establishments for the preceding year was more than £200 million or the aggregate balance sheet total assets for those companies and permanent establishments for that year exceeded £2 billion. An NME group is a 'qualifying group' for a financial year if there was a mandatory country-by-country reporting requirement under *FA 2015, s 122* for the previous financial year or there would have been if the head of the group were UK-resident for tax purposes.

(2) The 'head' of a 'UK sub-group' of a 'foreign' group' where the foreign group is a qualifying group for the financial year. A '*foreign group*' is a group whose head is a body corporate incorporated outside the UK. A '*UK sub-group*' consists of two or more bodies corporate that would be a UK group but for the fact that they are members of a larger foreign group. The '*head*' of a UK sub-group is the member of the sub-group which is not a 51% subsidiary of another member of the sub-group.

(3) A UK company which is a 'qualifying company' for the financial year. A company is a '*qualifying company*' for a financial year if at the end of the previous financial year it was not a member of a UK group or a UK sub-group and for that year its turnover exceeded £200 million or its balance sheet total assets exceeded £2 billion. If the company was a member of a foreign group at the end of the previous year, the turnover and balance sheet thresholds apply as in (1) above. The requirement to publish the company's tax strategy for a financial year applies even if the company becomes a member of a group or UK sub-group during the year.

A UK permanent establishment of a foreign body corporate is treated as if it were a company for these purposes and, if the foreign body corporate is a member of a group or a UK sub-group, as a member of that group or sub-group.

(4) A 'UK partnership' which is a 'qualifying partnership' for the financial year. A '*UK partnership*' is a UK partnership, limited partnership or limited liability partnership which is carrying on a trade, business or profession with a view to profit. A UK partnership is a 'qualifying partnership' if, for the previous financial year, its turnover exceeded £200 million or its balance sheet total assets exceeded £2 billion.

In relation to a partnership, a '*financial year*' means any period of account for which its representative partner is required to provide a partnership statement in a return.

A tax strategy must set out the following:

- the approach of the group, sub-group, company, permanent establishment or partnership to risk management and governance in relation to UK taxation;

- the attitude of the group etc. towards tax planning affecting UK taxation;
- the level of risk in relation to UK taxation that the group etc. is prepared to accept; and
- the approach of the group etc. towards its dealings with HMRC.

It may include other information relating to taxation (UK or otherwise). In the case of a group or sub-group, the tax strategy may set out the required information by reference to the group or sub-group as a whole or to individual members (or both). Information about activities consisting of the provision of tax advice or related professional services to other persons does not have to be included in the tax strategy. The strategy must make it clear that the group etc. regards its publication as complying with the above requirements.

For HMRC guidance see www.gov.uk/guidance/large-businesses-publish-your-tax-strategy.

Penalty for failure to comply

See **59.19** PENALTIES.

[*FA 2016, s 161(2), Sch 19 paras 1–17, 19, 20, 22, 23, 25*].

Special measures regime for unco-operative large businesses

[36.20] *Finance Act 2016* introduced a special measures regime for large businesses which engage in what HMRC consider to be aggressive tax planning or which do not engage with HMRC in an 'open and collaborative manner' (see HM Treasury Explanatory Notes to the Finance Bill 2016). The regime operates by HMRC first issuing a warning notice which provides the taxpayer with an opportunity to make representations about whether the regime should apply. A warning notice may be followed by a special measures notice, the effect of which is that any inaccuracies in a document given to HMRC are deemed to be at least careless (and therefore subject to a penalty). If a special measures notice is confirmed by a confirmation notice then HMRC may publicly identify the taxpayer as subject to the regime.

The regime is described in the following paragraphs as it applies to UK groups. See below for its application to other types of taxpayer.

Warning notice

An HMRC officer who has been designated for the purpose may give a notice (a '*warning notice*') to the 'head' of a 'UK group' if he considers that the group is a 'qualifying group' that meets the following conditions. The conditions are that:

(1) the group has 'persistently' engaged in 'unco-operative behaviour';
(2) some or all of that behaviour has caused or contributed to two or more 'significant tax issues' in respect of the group or members of it which are unresolved; and

(3) there is a reasonable likelihood of further instances of unco-operative behaviour causing or contributing to significant tax issues in respect of the group or its members.

For this purpose a UK group has engaged in '*unco-operative behaviour*' if a member of the group or two or more members taken together satisfy either or both of the behaviour condition or the arrangements condition. A group has '*persistently*' engaged in such behaviour if a member of the group or two or more members taken together have done so on a sufficient number of occasions for it to be clear that it represents a pattern of behaviour.

A group member, or two or more members taken together, satisfy the behaviour condition if they behave in a way which has delayed or otherwise hindered HMRC in the exercise of their functions in connection with determining the UK tax liability of the group or a member. The extent to which HMRC have used statutory powers to obtain information, the reasons why those powers have been used, the number and seriousness of inaccuracies in and omissions from documents given to HMRC and the extent to which group members (or their agents) have relief on interpretations of UK tax legislation which are 'speculative' are all actors indicative of such behaviour. An interpretation is '*speculative*' for this purpose if it is likely that a court or tribunal would disagree with it.

A member of a UK group satisfies the arrangements condition if it is a party to a '*tax avoidance scheme*': i.e. arrangements in respect of which a final counteraction notice under the general anti-abuse rule (see **4.3** ANTI-AVOIDANCE), arrangements which are notifiable arrangements under the provisions for DISCLOSURE OF TAX AVOIDANCE SCHEMES (**29.2**) other than any arrangements for which the promoter has been notified that clients need no longer be provided with the scheme number) or arrangements notifiable under equivalent VAT provisions.

There is a 'significant tax issue' in respect of a UK group or a group member if there is a disagreement (or reasonable likelihood of a disagreement) between HMRC and a group member about an issue affecting the amount of the UK tax liability of the group or member which has been, or could be, referred to a court or tribunal to determine. The tax at stake must be, or be likely to be, at least £2 million.

'UK group', 'qualifying group' and the 'head' of a UK group are all as defined at **36.19**(1) above. References above to things done by a group member include acts or omissions of former members when they were still members of the group but do not include acts or omissions of current members before they joined.

The warning notice must set out the reasons why the officer considers that the above conditions are met and may be withdrawn at any time by giving a further notice to that effect. If the notice has not been withdrawn it expires after 15 months. Once a warning notice has been given, the notice, and any subsequent special measures notice (see below), continue to have effect even if the group ceases to be a qualifying group, changes its membership or becomes a UK sub-group of a foreign group (see **36.19**(2) above).

If, while the warning notice is in effect, the head of the group becomes a member of a group headed by another body corporate (H), the warning notice is treated as having been given to H on the day it was actually given to the original head of the group. A notice deemed to be given in this way is valid even if H is not the head of a qualifying UK group to which the conditions at (1)–(3) above apply.

Special measures notice

A designated HMRC officer may give the head of a UK group a '*special measures notice*' if:

(a) a warning notice has been given to the head and not withdrawn;
(b) 12 months have passed since the day on which the warning notice was given;
(c) the 15 months beginning with the day on which the warning notice was given have not elapsed; and
(d) the officer considers that the UK group meets the conditions at (1)–(3) above. The officer may take into account any behaviour for this purpose, whether or not mentioned in the warning notice and must consider any representations made by any group member before the end of the 12 months beginning with the day the warning notice was given.

The special measures notice must set out the reasons why the officer considers that the above conditions are met and may be withdrawn at any time by giving a further notice to that effect. If the notice has not been withdrawn it expires after 27 months beginning with the later of the day it was given and the day on which it was last confirmed (see below).

A designated HMRC officer may also give the head of a UK group a special measures notice if:

(A) a warning notice or special measures notice has been given to the head and has expired;
(B) it appears to the officer that in the period of six months since the notice expired the group has engaged in unco-operative behaviour and there is a reasonable likelihood that, if the behaviour had occurred before the notice expired a special measures notice or confirmation notice could have been given;
(C) during the seven months beginning with the day on which the notice expired HMRC have notified the head of the group that a special measures notice may be given; and
(D) no more than nine months have elapsed since the notice expired.

In deciding whether to give such a notice the officer must consider any representations made by any group member within eight months from the day the original notice expired.

If, while a special measures notice is in effect, the head of the group becomes a member of a group headed by another body corporate (H), the notice is treated as having been given to H on the day it was actually given to the original head of the group. A notice deemed to be given in this way is valid even if H is not the head of a qualifying UK group to which the conditions at (1)–(3) above apply.

Confirmation notice

A designated HMRC officer may give the head of a UK group a notice (a '*confirmation notice*') confirming a special measures notice if:

(i) a special measures notice has been given to the head and not withdrawn;
(ii) 24 months have passed since the later of the day on which the special measures notice was given and the day on which it was last confirmed;

(iii) the 27 months beginning with the later of the day the notice was given and the day on which it was last confirmed have not elapsed; and
(iv) the officer considers that the UK group meets the conditions at (1)–(3) above. The officer may take into account any behaviour for this purpose, whether or not mentioned in the warning notice, special measures notice or a previous confirmation notice and must consider any representations made by any group member before the end of the period in (ii) above.

The confirmation notice must set out the reasons why the officer considers that the above conditions are met and may be withdrawn at any time by giving a further notice to that effect. If the notice has not been withdrawn it expires after 27 months beginning with the day on which it was given.

If, while a confirmation notice is in effect, the head of the group becomes a member of a group headed by another body corporate (H), the notice is treated as having been given to H on the day it was actually given to the original head of the group. A notice deemed to be given in this way is valid even if H is not the head of a qualifying UK group to which the conditions at (1)–(3) above apply.

Sanctions

Penalties

For the purposes of the penalty provisions at **59.4** PENALTIES, an inaccuracy in a document given to HMRC by or on behalf of a member of a group whilst the group is subject to a special measures notice is treated as being due to failure by the member to take reasonable care if either:

- the inaccuracy relates to a tax avoidance scheme which was entered into whilst the group member at a time when it was a member of a group and the group was subject to a special measures notice; or
- the inaccuracy is attributable, wholly or in part, to an interpretation of UK tax law which, at the time the document was given, was speculative.

This rule does not, however, apply to treat a deliberate inaccuracy as merely careless. It also does not apply where, during the currency of a special measures notice, the head of the group becomes a member of a group headed by another body corporate (H), and the inaccuracy is in a document given to HMRC by a member of H's group at a time before the head of the group to which the notice was originally given became a member of H's group.

Publication of information

The Commissioners for HMRC may publish certain information about a UK group if a special measures notice given to the head of the group is in force and the notice has been confirmed by a confirmation notice. They may also publish information if a special measures notice confirmed by a confirmation notice has expired but a further special measures notice has been given to the head of the group as a result of the conditions in (A)–(D) above and is in force.

The information which may be published is the name of the group and its address or registered office, the fact that it is subject to a confirmed special measures notice and any other information HMRC consider it appropriate to publish in order to identify the group. When the group ceases to be subject to a special measures notice HMRC must publish a notice stating that it is no longer subject to the notice within the 30 days beginning with that on which the notice is withdrawn or expires.

Before publishing information the Commissioners must inform the head of the group of their intention to do so and allow the head a reasonable opportunity to make representations about whether publication should go ahead.

Application of regime to UK sub-groups, companies and partnerships

The special measures regime applies to UK sub-groups of overseas groups which are qualifying groups (see **36.19**(2) above), qualifying companies (see **36.19**(3) above) and qualifying partnerships (see **36.19**(4) above), the above provisions being modified as necessary. In particular, in the case of a UK sub-group, once a warning notice has been given, the notice, and any subsequent special measures notice, continue to have effect even if the group ceases to be a qualifying group, the sub-group changes its membership or becomes a UK sub-group of another foreign group. In the case of a partnership, references to the head of a UK group should be read as references to the representative partner of the partnership, and references to a member of a group as references to a partner in a partnership acting in his capacity as partner.

[*FA 2016, Sch 19 paras 35–53*].

37

HMRC Extra-Statutory Concessions

Introduction to HMRC Extra-Statutory Concessions

[37.1] Extra Statutory Concessions (ESCs) are relaxations of the strict letter of the law which give taxpayers a reduction in tax liability to which they would not otherwise be entitled. Most ESCs are made to deal with what are, generally, minor or transitory anomalies under the legislation and to meet cases of hardship at the margins of the code where a statutory remedy would be difficult to implement.

ESCs are of general application but it should be borne in mind that in a particular case there may be special circumstances which will require to be taken into account in considering the application of a concession.

A concession will not be given in any case where an attempt is made to use it for tax avoidance.

Following the House of Lords' decision in the *Wilkinson* case ([2006] STC 270) the scope of HMRC's discretion to make ESCs was clarified and since then HMRC has undertaken reviews of its ESCs, with a view to putting them onto a legislative footing where the existing ESC exceeds the scope of its discretion. The provisions of *FA 2008, s 160* allow the tax treatment afforded by existing ESCs to be legislated by Treasury order. A number of concessions have subsequently been replaced by legislation, and have become obsolete. Concessions might also become obsolete where it is superseded by a later concession, where it contained a time limit which has expired, if it is withdrawn, or if the tax or duty referred to no longer applies.

[37.2] The following is a summary of the concessions applicable to companies published by HMRC. The published list of ESCs can be found at www.gov.uk/government/collections/extra-statutory-concessions.

See also **36.3** HMRC — ADMINISTRATION.

Simon's Taxes. See **Part G2**.

A37 **Tax treatment of directors' fees received by partnerships and other companies.** Under certain conditions, such fees could be included in computing partnership profits or in the corporation tax assessment of the other company. With effect from 6 April 2018, the concession has been superseded by an equivalent statutory rule. See **68.27** TRADING INCOME.

B8 **Double taxation relief: income consisting of royalties and know-how payments.** Payments made by an overseas resident to a UK trader for the use of copyright etc. are treated as arising outside the UK except in so far as they represent consideration for services (other than merely incidental services) rendered in the UK by the recipient to the payer. See **31.4** DOUBLE TAX RELIEF.

B41 **Claims to repayment of tax.** Where an over-payment of tax has arisen because of official error, and there is no doubt or dispute as to the facts, claims to repayment of tax are accepted outside the statutory time limit. See Tolley's Income Tax under Claims.

C1 **Credit for underlying tax: dividends from trade investments in overseas companies.** Credit is given along a chain of shareholdings in certain circumstances. See **31.11** DOUBLE TAX RELIEF.

C11 **Demergers.** The conditions imposed following a distribution are relaxed. See **29.27** DISTRIBUTIONS.

C12 A **retail co-operative society** which prepares half-yearly or quarterly accounts can be treated as having yearly accounting periods ending on an agreed date. This concession is withdrawn with effect from 1 April 2018. See generally **2.9** ACCOUNTING PERIODS.

C15 **Dissolution of unincorporated associations: distributions to members.** Small distributions by social or recreational associations which have not carried on a trade or business are not treated as distributions under *ICTA 1988, s 209* (now *CTA 2010, Pt 23*). See **29.15**(b) DISTRIBUTIONS.

D10 **Unquoted shares acquired before 6 April 1965: disposal following reorganisation of share capital.** Where, in consequence of a reorganisation of share capital before 6 April 1965, a valuation at that date is required, or time apportionment is limited, under *TCGA 1992, Sch 2 para 19*, the gain chargeable to corporation tax on a disposal of the entire holding (whether in a single transaction or in separate transactions in the same accounting period) is limited to the actual gain realised. See Tolley's Capital Gains Tax under Assets held on 6 April 1965.

D16 **Relief for the replacement of business assets: repurchase of same asset** will give rise to relief where for purely commercial reasons. See Tolley's Capital Gains Tax under Rollover Relief.

D18 **Default on mortgage granted by vendor.** In such circumstances and where the vendor regains beneficial ownership of the asset and so elects, the chargeable gain is limited to the net proceeds obtained from the transactions and the loan treated as never having existed. See Tolley's Capital Gains Tax under Disposal.

D22 **Relief for the replacement of business assets: expenditure on improvements to existing assets** may attract relief provided that the existing assets are used only for trade purposes, or are so used on completion of the improvements. See Tolley's Capital Gains Tax under Rollover Relief.

D23 **Relief for the replacement of business assets: partition of land on the dissolution of a partnership.** Partitioned assets are treated as new assets provided that the partnership is immediately dissolved. See Tolley's Capital Gains Tax under Rollover Relief.

D24 **Relief for the replacement of business assets: asset not brought immediately into trading use** may attract relief provided that:

(a) it is proposed to incur expenditure on work for the purpose of enhancing its value;

(b) the work begins as soon as possible after acquisition, and is completed within a reasonable time;

(c) on completion of the work, the asset is taken into use for trade purposes only; and

(d) the asset is not let or used for non-trade purposes between acquisition and being taken into use for trade purposes.

See Tolley's Capital Gains Tax under Rollover Relief.

D25 **Relief for the replacement of business assets: expenditure on acquisition of an interest in an asset already used for the purposes of a trade** will attract relief as if the further interest acquired was a new asset taken into use for trade purposes. See Tolley's Capital Gains Tax under Rollover Relief.

D32 **Transfer of a business to a company.** Liabilities taken over on a transfer of business will not be treated as consideration for the rollover provisions of *TCGA 1992, s 162* and no capital gain will arise on the transfer. See Tolley's Capital Gains Tax under Rollover Relief.

D33 **Capital gains tax on compensation and damages.** Damages derived from underlying assets will be treated as exempt where the asset is exempt, and where there is no underlying asset damages will be exempt. Amendments were made to the concession in January 2014. See Tolley's Capital Gains Tax under Assets.

D34 **Rebasing and indexation: shares held at 31 March 1982.** A single holding treatment will apply even if the shares were acquired before 7 April 1965. See Tolley's Capital Gains Tax under Assets held on 31 March 1982.

D39 **Extensions of leases.** Relief is given where a lessee surrenders an existing lease and is granted a new, longer lease at arm's length on the same property at a different rent, but otherwise on the same terms. See Tolley's Capital Gains Tax under Land.

D42 **Mergers of leases.** Indexation allowance may be given on the costs of acquisition of a lease by reference to the date on which it was acquired, even though it ceased to exist on the acquisition of a superior interest in the property, such as the freehold reversion. This replaces an earlier practice for disposals after 28 June 1992. See Tolley's Capital Gains Tax under Land.

D52 **Share exchanges, company reconstructions and amalgamations — incidental costs of acquisition and disposal and warranty payments** may be treated as consideration given for the new holding. See Tolley's Capital Gains Tax under Shares and Securities.

D53 ***TCGA 1992, s 50*: grants repaid.** Government, public or local authority grants for acquiring assets which are then repaid on disposal of the asset will reduce the value of the consideration received for capital gains purposes.

I5 **PRT instalments** may be withheld where production ceases following catastrophic loss or damage.

(b) the work is being done as part of a larger operation which is completed within a reasonable time;

(c) on completion of the work the asset is taken into use for trade purposes or retained;

(d) the asset is not let or used for any purpose other than the trade [illegible] ... and it has not taken into use for the purpose [illegible]

See Tolley's Capital Gains Tax under Rollover Relief.

D24 For the replacement of business assets, acquisition of an interest in an asset already used for trade purposes as a fixed asset by the trader ... interest acquired, where a new asset ... [illegible] ... see Tolley's Capital Gains Tax under Rollover Relief.

D32 Transfer of a business to a company. Liabilities taken over ... business will not be treated as consideration ... [illegible] ... see Tolley's Capital Gains Tax under Rollover Relief.

D33 Capital gains tax on compensation and damages. Damages derived from underlying assets will be treated as exempt where the asset is exempt, and where there is no underlying asset ... will be exempt ... [illegible] ... see Tolley's Capital Gains Tax under Assets.

D34 Rebasing and indexation: shares held at 31 March 1982 ... holding ... even if the shares were acquired before ... April 1982 ... Capital Gains Tax ... 31 March 1982.

D35 Extensions of leases. This applies when a lessee surrenders an existing lease and is granted a new, longer lease at terms ... on the same property at a different rent ... see Tolley's Capital Gains Tax under Land.

D42 Mergers of leases. Indexation allowance may be given on the cost of acquisition of a lease by reference to the date on which it was acquired even though it ceases to exist on the acquisition of a superior interest in the property such as the freehold reversion. This replaces an earlier practice for disposals after 29 March 1982. See Tolley's Capital Gains Tax under Land.

D52 Share exchanges, company reconstructions and amalgamations ... incidental costs of acquisition and disposal and warranty payments may be treated as consideration given for the new holding. See Tolley's Capital Gains Tax under Shares and Securities.

D58 [illegible] grants from a public or local authority ... for acquiring assets ... acquisition and disposal of the asset will reduce the value of the consideration received for capital gains purposes.

[illegible] ... instalments may be withheld where production ceases following catastrophic loss or damage.

38

HMRC Investigatory Powers

Cross-references. See **59** PENALTIES; **65** RETURNS.

Introduction to HMRC investigatory powers

[38.1] HMRC have wide powers to enforce compliance with tax legislation. There is a common set of information and inspection powers covering income tax, capital gains tax, corporation tax and other taxes, including inheritance tax and stamp duty land tax and VAT, enabling HMRC to conduct a single 'compliance check' into a taxpayer's tax position across any or, as relevant, all of those taxes. Evidence can be obtained both directly from the taxpayer and from third parties. The powers are described at **38.3–38.10** below and operate in tandem with those for enquiries into self-assessment returns, for which see **38.2** below and **65.14–65.17** RETURNS. *FA 2021* has extended HMRC's powers to include the issue of information notices for the purpose of collecting tax debts.

For compliance checks generally, see HMRC Factsheets CC/FS1–CC/FS6 and HMRC Compliance Handbook. HMRC have published a statement of the principles governing their litigation and settlements strategy. The statement covers how HMRC enters into, handles and settles disputes about any of the taxes for which they are responsible. See HMRC Compliance Handbook CH40350. See also **38.16** below for HMRC's practice in cases of serious tax fraud.

In addition to the above powers, HMRC can obtain specialist and bulk information from specified 'data holders': see **38.12** below.

HMRC have a cross-tax power to obtain working papers from tax agents who engage in dishonest conduct. See **38.18** below.

HMRC are able to exercise certain powers under the *Police and Criminal Evidence Act 1984* when conducting direct tax criminal investigations. See **38.13** below.

There are special provisions relating to computer records (see **38.14** below).

For a discussion of HMRC's power to conduct an informal investigation outside of the above powers, see *R (oao JJ Management LLP) v HMRC* CA, [2020] STC 1422.

Self-assessment enquiries

[38.2] The self-assessment enquiry procedures are explained at **65.14–65.17** RETURNS; these operate in tandem with the provisions below.

See in particular **38.6** below for restrictions on HMRC's power to issue an information notice where a tax return has been made.

Information and inspection powers

[38.3] *FA 2008, Sch 36* applies a common set of information and inspection powers for HMRC covering income tax, capital gains tax, corporation tax, diverted profits tax and VAT. The powers are covered at **38.4–38.10** below only to the extent that they apply for the purposes of corporation tax.

See also **28.27** DISCLOSURE OF TAX AVOIDANCE SCHEMES for the application of the provisions, with modifications, for the purposes of the POTAS regime.

Simon's Taxes. See **A6.316, A6.610–A6.624.**

Definitions

For the purposes of the provisions at **38.4–38.10** below, the following definitions apply.

'*Checking*' includes carrying out an investigation or enquiry of any kind. '*Document*' includes a part of a document (unless the context requires otherwise).

An '*authorised HMRC officer*' is an HMRC officer who is, or who is a member of a class of officers, authorised by the Commissioners for HMRC for the particular purpose.

The carrying on of a business includes the letting of property and the activities of a charity, a government department, a local authority (within *ITA 2007, s 999*), a local authority association (within *ITA 2007, s 1000*) or any other public authority. HMRC can make regulations specifying activities as businesses.

'*Tax*' means any or all of income tax, capital gains tax, corporation tax, VAT, insurance premium tax, inheritance tax, stamp duty land tax, stamp duty reserve tax, petroleum revenue tax, aggregates levy, climate change levy, annual tax on enveloped dwellings, soft drink industry levy and landfill tax. It also includes taxes of EU member states in respect of which information can be disclosed or, where an information notice is issued for the purpose of collecting a tax debt, which are covered by the EU Directive on mutual assistance for the recovery of taxes (*Directive 2010/24/EU*, as it had effect immediately before 11pm on 31 December 2020 (Brexit IP completion day)) and taxes of territories to which a tax enforcement agreement apply (see **31.2**(c) HMRC — CONFIDENTIALITY OF INFORMATION).

A company's '*tax position*' is its position at any time and in relation to any period as regards any tax, including its position as to past, present and future liability to any tax, penalties and other amounts which have been paid or are, or may be, payable by or to him in connection with any tax, and any claims, elections, applications and notices that have or may be made or given in connection with any tax.

'*Collecting a tax debt*' means taking any steps for, or in connection with, the recovery of an amount of tax or another amount (such as interest or a penalty) in connection with any tax. It does not matter that another person is also, or has been, liable to pay the amount (for example, where the liability has been transferred as part of insolvency proceedings).

'*Parent undertaking*', '*subsidiary undertaking*' and '*undertaking*' have the same meanings as in *Companies Act 2006, ss 1161, 1162, Sch 7*.

[*FA 2008, Sch 36 paras 33(7), 58–60, 63, 63A, 63B, 64; FA 2021, s 127(6)–(8)*].

Responsibility of company officers

Everything to be done by a company under the provisions at **38.4**–**38.10** below must be done by it through the '*proper officer*' (i.e. the secretary of a corporate body, except where a liquidator or administrator has been appointed when the latter is the proper officer, or the treasurer of a non-corporate body) or, except where a liquidator has been appointed, any authorised officer. The service of a notice on a company may be effected by serving it on the proper officer. [*TMA 1970, s 108; FA 2008, Sch 36 para 56*].

Information and documents

[38.4] An HMRC officer may give a notice (an '*information notice*') in writing require a person to provide information or to produce a document if it is reasonably required:

(a) for the purpose of checking that person's tax position or the purpose of collecting a tax debt of that person;
(b) for the purpose of checking the tax position, or collecting a tax debt, of another person whose identity is known to the officer;
(c) for the purpose of checking the UK tax position, or collecting a tax debt, of a person whose identity is not known to the officer or of a class of persons whose individual identities are not known to the officer; or

(d) for the purpose of checking the tax position, or collecting a tax debt, of another person, or class of persons, whose identity or identities are not known by the officer but can be ascertained from information held by the officer.

A notice can only be given for the purpose of collecting a tax debt on or after 10 June 2021, but can be given in respect of a tax debt whenever arising.

A notice may require either specified information or documents or information or documents described in the notice (so that a notice is not restricted to information or documents which HMRC can specifically identify). Where it is given with the approval of the tribunal (see further below), the notice must say so.

The information or documents must be provided or produced within the time period and at the time, by the means and in the form (if any) reasonably specified in the notice.

Documents must be produced for inspection either: at a place agreed to by the recipient of the notice and an HMRC officer; or at a place (other than one used solely as a dwelling) that an HMRC officer reasonably specifies. HMRC may specify in the notice that documents should be sent to them by post or email (*TeING Ltd v HMRC* UT, [2016] UKUT 363 (TCC), 2016 STI 2545).

Subject to any conditions or exceptions set out in regulations made by HMRC, copies of documents can be produced unless the notice requires the production of the original document or an HMRC officer in writing subsequently requests the original document. Where an officer makes such a request, the document must be produced within the period and at the time and by the means reasonably requested by the officer.

An HMRC officer may take copies of, or make extracts from, a document (or copy) produced to him, and if it appears necessary to him, he may remove the document at a reasonable time and retain it for a reasonable period. The officer must, without charge, provide a receipt for a document which is removed where this is requested and must also provide, again without charge, a copy of the document, if the person producing it reasonably requires it for any purpose. Where a document which has been removed is lost or damaged, HMRC are liable to compensate the owner for expenses reasonably incurred in replacing or repairing it.

The production or removal of a document under these provisions does not break any lien (i.e. any right) claimed on it.

[*FA 2008, Sch 36 paras 1–9; FA 2021, s 127(2)–(5)(8)*].

In the case of *P Whight v HMRC* [2011] UK FTT 60 (TC) the First-tier Tribunal held that HMRC have a right to see the original documentation which supported schedules forwarded on behalf of the taxpayer. The case related to capital gains tax on a share disposal, and the determination of residence of the taxpayer, who claimed to have been non-UK resident for five tax years. The tribunal held that the taxpayer in this case had not shown as a matter of fact that the documents were not reasonably required for the purpose of checking the taxpayer's position, and also that the request was not disproportionate or onerous in these particular circumstances.

The requirements of a notice were held not to breach the recipient's human rights in *R (oao Derrin Brothers Properties Ltd) v HMRC* QB, [2014] EWHC 1152 (Admin); 2014 STI 1835. The Court of Appeal later confirmed that the third party notices had been correctly issued in *Derrin Brothers Properties Ltd v HMRC, HSBC and Lubbock Fine* [2016] EWCA Civ 15.

In *Matharu Delivery Service Ltd v HMRC* FTT, [2019] UKFTT 553 (TC); 2019 SWTI 1587, the Tribunal held that HMRC were entitled to a fully itemised, chronological version of a director's loan account with the company.

In *Victor Tee v HMRC* [2014] UKFTT 977 the Tribunal held the notice was too widely drafted and was vague and uncertain. The taxpayer's appeal succeeded.

In *PML Accounting Ltd v HMRC* FTT, [2015] UKFTT 440 (TC) the First-tier Tribunal held that an information notice issued to a suspected 'managed service company provider' did not relate to the tax position of the company but to that of its clients. Therefore the notice should have been issued as a third party notice (see below) and was invalid. However, in *R (oao PML Accounting Ltd) v HMRC* CA 2018, [2019] STC 1, the Court held that the First-tier Tribunal had not had jurisdiction to consider the validity of the information notice, as there had been no appeal against the notice (the original case was an appeal against penalties imposed for failure fully to comply with the notice). Furthermore HMRC were not obliged to destroy any work product created as a result of their access to the documents under the notice or to undertake not to use the information and work product for any future purpose.

The taxpayer was held not to be able to rely on the right of a person not to self-incriminate in order to refuse to comply with a notice under these provisions in *Gold Nuts Ltd v HMRC* FTT, [2016] SFTD 371.

Notices

Taxpayer notice

[38.5] An information notice under **38.4**(a) above can be given without the approval of the tribunal (see **5** APPEALS), but where such approval is obtained the taxpayer has no right of appeal against the notice or a requirement in it.

Where approval is sought from the tribunal, the application for approval must be made by, or with the agreement of, an authorised HMRC officer. The taxpayer must normally have been told that the information or documents are required and have been given a reasonable opportunity to make representations to HMRC, and the tribunal must be given a summary of any such representations. Where, however, the tribunal is satisfied that informing the taxpayer would prejudice the assessment or collection of tax, it can approve the giving of the notice without the taxpayer having been informed.

In *Perfectos Printing Inks Co Ltd v HMRC* FTT, [2020] SFTD 430, the FTT held that it had no power to direct that an application for tribunal approval should be decided at an *inter partes* oral hearing.

Third party notice

Except in the case of a financial institution notice (see further below), a notice within 38.4(b) above cannot be given without either the agreement of the taxpayer (i.e. the person whose tax position is to be checked) or the approval of the tribunal and must normally name the taxpayer. The appeal may be heard without giving notice to the taxpayer i.e. the application will be heard in his absence. Where approval is obtained from the tribunal, there is no right of appeal against the notice or a requirement in it.

Where approval is sought from the tribunal, the application for approval must be made by, or with the agreement of, an authorised HMRC officer. The taxpayer must normally have been given a summary of the reasons why an officer requires the information or documents. The person to whom the notice is to be given must normally have been told that the information or documents are required and have been given a reasonable opportunity to make representations to HMRC and the tribunal must be given a summary of any such representations. These requirements can, however, be disapplied where the tribunal is satisfied that informing the recipient of the notice or giving a summary of reasons to the taxpayer would prejudice the assessment or collection of tax.

The tribunal can also disapply the requirement to name the taxpayer in the notice if it is satisfied that the officer has reasonable grounds for believing that naming him might seriously prejudice the assessment or collection of tax. There is no appeal against the grant of a notice.

A copy of the notice must normally be given to the taxpayer. The tribunal can, however, disapply this requirement if an application for approval is made by, or with the agreement of, an authorised HMRC officer. The tribunal must be satisfied that the officer has reasonable grounds for believing that giving a copy of the notice to the taxpayer might prejudice the assessment or collection of tax.

Where a third party notice is given for the purpose of checking the tax position of a parent undertaking and any of its subsidiary undertakings, the above provisions apply as if the parent undertaking were the taxpayer. The requirement for the notice to name the taxpayer is satisfied by stating in the notice that its purpose is checking the tax position of the parent and subsidiary undertakings and naming the parent undertaking. Where a notice is given to a parent undertaking for the purpose of checking the tax position of one or more subsidiary undertakings, neither the agreement of the parent undertaking or the approval of the tribunal is required and a copy does not have to be given to the parent undertaking.

Where a third party notice is given for the purpose of checking the tax position of more than one of the partners in a business carried on in partnership, in their capacity as such, the above provisions apply as if the taxpayer were at least one of the partners. The requirement for the notice to name the taxpayer is satisfied by stating in the notice that its purpose is checking the tax position of more than one of the partners and giving a name in which the partnership is registered for any purpose. Where a third party notice is given to one of the partners for the purpose of checking the tax position of any of the other partners, neither the agreement of any of the partners nor the approval of the tribunal is required and a copy does not have to be given to any other partners.

In *HMRC v Ex parte a taxpayer* [2014] UKFTT 931 the Tribunal confirmed that all reasons for the third party notice should be summarised by HMRC, not only the most important ones. It is not appropriate to exclude reasons for confidentiality purposes unless application has been made on the basis that informing the taxpayer might prejudice the assessment or collection of tax.

In *Derrin Brothers Properties Ltd v HMRC, HSBC and Lubbock Fine* [2016] EWCA Civ 15 the Court of Appeal explained the scope of the third parties' right to make representations at the Tribunal. They can only make representations to state any practical difficulties with compliance. Therefore, there is no requirement for third parties to be told the reason why the information is required and they cannot argue the taxpayer's case as to the scope or nature of the investigation.

In *X Ltd v HMRC* UT, [2020] STC 454, the UT confirmed that there is no power for the FTT to direct that an application for tribunal approval should be decided at an *inter partes* oral hearing because that would give rise to the risk of delay to, or obstruction of, HMRC investigations. It also held that it was open to the FTT to delay a determination of an application for a closure notice until after HMRC's application for approval of a third-party notice so that it would benefit from knowing whether HMRC had succeeded in the third-party notice application before deciding whether to direct HMRC to close their enquiries.

Third party notices were held to have been validly issued to non-UK resident individuals in *Ex parte PQ* FTT 2019, [2020] STC 1.

Financial institution notices

A notice within **38.4**(b) above can be given to a 'financial institution' without the agreement of the taxpayer or approval of the Tribunal if, in the reasonable opinion of the officer giving the notice, it would not be onerous for the institution to provide the information or produce the documents. Such a notice can only be given by, or with the agreement of, an authorised HMRC officer.

The notice must normally name the taxpayer to which it relates. The Tribunal can, however, disapply this requirement if it is satisfied that the officer has reasonable grounds for believing that naming the taxpayer might seriously prejudice the assessment or collection of tax.

A copy of the notice must normally be given to the taxpayer, together with a summary of why HMRC require the information or documents. These requirements can also, however, be disapplied where the Tribunal is satisfied that giving a copy of the notice or giving a summary of reasons to the taxpayer would prejudice the assessment or collection of tax.

There is no right of appeal against the decision of the Tribunal to disapply any of these requirements.

A financial institution notice can only be given on or after 10 June 2021, but may relate to periods, liabilities or tax debts arising before that date.

A '*financial institution*' is a person treated as such under the OECD's Common Reporting Standard (CRS) or a person who issues credit cards. There is an exclusion for persons (such as family trusts and charities) which are within the CRS definition only because they are an investment entity within *section VIII(A)(6)(b)* of the CRS.

Non-disclosure of notice

With effect from 10 June 2021, where the Tribunal has disapplied the requirement for a copy of a third party notice or a financial institution notice to be given to the taxpayer, the notice can include a requirement that the recipient must not disclose the notice or anything relating to it to the taxpayer or (except for the purpose of complying with the notice) to any other person. The requirement not to disclose usually applies for 12 months beginning on the date the notice is given. HMRC may, however, by notice in writing withdraw a requirement before the normal end date or extend it for a further period of 12 months (and may do so more than once). The notice must be given before the expiry of the 12-month period and must be given by, or with the agreement of, an authorised HMRC officer. A non-disclosure requirement can only be extended if the authorised HMRC officer has reasonable grounds for believing that not doing so might prejudice the assessment or collection of tax.

See **59.11** PENALTIES for the penalty for failure to comply with a requirement under these provisions.

Notice about persons whose identity is not known

The giving of a notice under **38.4**(c) above requires the approval of the Tribunal. The Tribunal can approve the giving of the notice only if it is satisfied that:

- there are reasonable grounds for believing that the person or class of persons to whom the notice relates may have failed, or may fail, to comply with any law relating to tax (including the law of a territory outside the UK);
- any such failure is likely to have led, or to lead, to serious prejudice to the assessment or collection of tax; and
- the information or document is not readily available from another source.

There is no right of appeal against a decision of the Tribunal to grant approval.

The approval of the Tribunal is permitted but not required for a notice to be given to a parent undertaking for the purpose of checking the tax position of one or more subsidiary undertakings whose identities are not known to the HMRC officer giving the notice. Such approval is also permitted but not required for a notice to be given to a partner in a business carried on in partnership for the purpose of checking the tax position of partners whose identities are not known to the officer giving the notice.

Notice about person whose identity can be ascertained

A notice within **38.4**(d) above must be given by an authorised HMRC officer and can only require the recipient to provide all or any of the name, last known address and date of birth of the taxpayer (or class of taxpayer) concerned. The officer must have reason to believe that the recipient of the notice will be able to ascertain the taxpayer's identity (or taxpayers' identities) from the information held by the officer and that the recipient obtained the information required in the course of carrying on a business. A notice cannot be given if the taxpayer's identity (or taxpayers' identities) can be readily ascertained by other means from the information held by the officer.

Inaccurate information and documents in reply to a notice

Where, in complying with an information notice, a company provides inaccurate information or a document carelessly or deliberately and, on later discovering the mistake, does not take reasonable steps to inform HMRC, the company will incur a penalty of £3,000 in respect of each such inaccuracy.

[*FA 2008, Sch 36 paras 4A, 15, 16, 34A, 35, 37, 51A, 61ZA; FA 2021, s 126(1)–(4)(9), Sch 34 para* 2].

For further restrictions on the above powers, see **38.6** below. For appeals against information notices, see **38.8** below.

See HMRC Compliance Handbook CH220000 onwards and, for third party notices, CH225000 onwards.

Restrictions on information notice powers

[38.6] An information notice does not require a person to:

(i) produce a document if it is not in his possession or power;
(ii) provide or produce information that relates to the conduct of a pending tax appeal or any part of a document containing such information;
(iii) provide journalistic material (within *Police and Criminal Evidence Act 1984, s 13*) or information contained in such material;
(iv) subject to the exceptions below, provide or produce 'personal records' (within *Police and Criminal Evidence Act 1984, s 12*); or
(v) produce a document the whole of which originates more than six years before the giving of the notice, unless the notice is given by, or with the agreement of, an authorised officer.

With regard to (iv) above, an information notice may require a person to produce documents (or copies) that are personal records, omitting any personal information (i.e. information whose inclusion in the documents makes them personal records) and to provide any information in personal records that is not personal information.

[*FA 2008, Sch 36 paras 18–20*].

In *Brantjes v HMRC* FTT, [2020] UKFTT 177 (TC); 2020 SWTI 1233, the FTT held that a taxpayer could not be required by a notice to provide bank statements which she did not have and which the bank did not keep in hard copy form. A document which did not exist when the notices were issued was neither in the taxpayer's possession or power, even if it could be created at her instigation.

Notice where tax return made

Where a person has made a tax return under *TMA 1970, ss 8, 8A* or *12AA* or *FA 1998, Sch 18 para 3* (see **65.8** RETURNS) in respect of a tax year or accounting period, a taxpayer notice (see **38.4**(a) above) can be given for the purpose of checking the income tax, capital gains tax or corporation tax position for that year or chargeable period only if:

(a) an enquiry notice under *TMA 1970, ss 9A, 12AC, Sch 1A para 5* or *FA 1998, Sch 18 para 24* (see **65.8** RETURNS) has been given in respect of either the return or a claim or election for the year or period to which the return relates and the enquiry has not been completed so far as relating to the matters to which the taxpayer notice relates;

(b) an HMRC officer has reason to suspect that an amount that ought to have been assessed to tax may not have been assessed, that an assessment for the period may be or have become insufficient or relief from tax for the period may be or have become excessive;

(c) the notice is given for the purpose of obtaining information or a document that is also required to check the taxpayer's position as regards any tax other than income tax, capital gains tax or corporation tax; or

(d) the notice is given for the purpose of obtaining information or a document that is required to check the taxpayer's position as regards his obligation to make deductions or repayments under PAYE, the construction industry scheme or any other provision.

However, this provision does not prevent a notice being given for the provision of information or documents relating to the animals subject to a herd basis election or the products of those animals. In addition, it does not apply where a counteraction provision under *CTA 2010, s 733* or *ITA 2007, s 684* (transactions in securities) applies.

Where a third party notice is given to a parent undertaking for the purpose of checking the tax position of one or more subsidiary undertakings, the above provisions apply as if the notice were a taxpayer notice or taxpayer notices given to the subsidiary undertaking or each of them.

Where a business is carried in partnership and a partnership return (see **62** RETURNS) has been made by one of the partners, the above provisions apply as if the return had been made by each of the partners, and condition (a) above can be met in relation to a partner by reference to either the partnership return or his personal, trustee or company return for the period concerned.

Where it appears to HMRC that there has been a change in ownership of a company (within *CTA 2010, Pt 14 Ch 7*) and, in connection with that change, a person (the '*seller*') may be or become liable to corporation tax under *CTA 2010, ss 710* or *713* (previously *ICTA 1988, ss 767A* or *767AA*) (recovery of unpaid corporation tax from persons controlling company), the above restriction does not apply to a taxpayer notice given to the seller.

[*FA 2008, Sch 36 paras 21, 35(4), 36, 37(1)(2); F(No 2)A 2017, Sch 15 para 36*].

Similar provisions apply to restrict the power to issue a taxpayer notice where a NRCGT return (see **11.24** CAPITAL GAINS) has been made. See *FA 2008, Sch 36 para 21ZA*.

Legal professional privilege

An information notice cannot require a person to provide information, or to produce any part of a document, in respect of which a claim to legal professional privilege (or, in Scotland, a claim to confidentiality of communications) could be maintained in legal proceedings.

HMRC can make regulations providing for the resolution of disputes as to whether information or a document is privileged by the tribunal.

In *R (oao Prudential plc) v Special Commissioner of Income Tax* [2013] STC 376 the Supreme Court confirmed that legal professional privilege cannot be granted to tax accountants. The Supreme Court upheld this decision ([2013] UKSC 1).

The question of the extent to which an engagement letter was covered by legal professional privilege was considered in *Behague v HMRC* FTT, [2013] UKFTT 596 (TC), 2013 STI 3577.

In *Mark Lewis v HMRC* [2013] UKFTT 722 (TC) it was held that legal professional privilege is not transferable between litigations. In that case documents created as part of the negotiations for a compromise agreement were held only to be protected for the purpose of the proceedings they were aimed at avoiding.

See also cases referred to at **38.13**.

[*FA 2008, Sch 36 para 23*].

Auditors

An information notice does not require an auditor (i.e. a person appointed as an auditor for the purpose of an enactment) to provide information held in connection with the performance of his functions under that enactment or to produce documents which are his property and which were created by him, or on his behalf, for or in connection with the performance of those functions.

This restriction does not apply to any information, or any document containing information, which explains any information or document which an auditor has, as tax accountant, assisted any client in preparing for, or delivering to, HMRC. Where the notice is given under **38.4**(c) above, the restriction also does not apply to information giving the identity or address of a person to whom the notice relates or of a person who has acted on behalf of such a person or to a document containing such information. Where the restriction is so disapplied, only that part (or parts) of a document which contains the relevant information has to be produced. The restriction is not disapplied if the information concerned, or a document containing the information, has already been provided or produced to an HMRC officer.

[*FA 2008, Sch 36 paras 24, 26, 27*].

Tax advisers

An information notice does not require a 'tax adviser' to provide information about, or to produce documents which are his property and which consist of, communications between him and a person in relation to whose tax affairs he has been appointed or between him and any other tax adviser of such a person, the purpose of which is the giving or obtaining of advice about any of those tax affairs. For this purpose, a '*tax adviser*' is a person appointed (directly or by another tax adviser) to give advice about the tax affairs of another person.

This restriction is disapplied in the same circumstances as the restriction applying to auditors is disapplied.

[*FA 2008, Sch 36 paras 25–27*].

In a case where the company's auditor was the same legal entity that acted as its tax agent, HMRC were prevented by the above provisions from requiring the production of documents relating to the audit (*Re an Application by Revenue and Customs Comrs to give an information notice under Para 3 of Sch 36 to the Finance Act 2008* FTT, [2019] SFTD 117).

Obtaining contact details for debtors

[38.7] HMRC are given power to issue a written notice requiring a third party which is a company or local authority etc. or otherwise has a business relationship with the debtor named in the notice to provide the address or other contact details for that debtor who owes money to HMRC. The third party has a right of appeal on the grounds that the requirement would be unduly onerous. The penalty for non-compliance is £300, but this amount may be changed by statutory instrument where there is a change in the value of money. [*FA 2009, s 97, Sch 49*].

Appeals against information notices

[38.8] A taxpayer can appeal to the tribunal against a taxpayer notice (see **38.4**(a) above) or any requirement in such a notice unless the notice was given with the approval of the tribunal. No appeal can be made against a requirement to provide information or to produce a document which forms part of his 'statutory records'.

Third party notices

A person given a third party notice (see **38.4**(b) above) can appeal to the tribunal against the notice or any requirement in it on the ground that compliance would be unduly onerous. An 'involved' third party may appeal the notice on any ground. No appeal can be made, however, where the notice was given with the approval of the tribunal or against a requirement to provide information or produce a document forming part of the taxpayer's statutory records.

Where a third party notice is given for the purpose of checking the tax position of a parent undertaking and any of its subsidiary undertakings, no appeal can be made against a requirement to provide information or produce a document forming part of the statutory records of the parent undertaking or any of its subsidiaries. No appeal can be made against a requirement, in a third party notice given to a parent undertaking for the purpose of checking the tax position of one or more subsidiary undertakings, to produce a document forming part of the statutory records of the parent undertaking or any of its subsidiary undertakings.

Where a third party notice is given for the purpose of checking the tax position of more than one of the partners in a business carried on in partnership, no appeal can be made against a requirement to provide information or produce a document forming part of the statutory records of any of the partners. No appeal can be made against a requirement, in a notice given to a partner for the purpose of checking the tax position of other partners, to produce a document forming part of the statutory records of the partner receiving the notice.

A person given a notice about persons whose identity is not known, or a notice to obtain information about a person whose identity can be ascertained, (see **38.4**(c) and (d) above), can appeal to the tribunal against the notice or any requirement in it on the ground that compliance would be unduly onerous. No appeal can be made against a requirement, in a notice given to a parent undertaking for the purpose of checking the tax position of one or more subsidiary undertakings, to produce a document forming part of the statutory records of the parent undertaking or any of its subsidiary undertakings. Likewise, no appeal can be made against a requirement, in a notice given to a partner in a business carried on in partnership for the purpose of checking the tax position of other partners, to produce a document forming part of the statutory records of the partner receiving the notice.

Definitions

For this purpose, '*statutory records*' are information and documents which a taxpayer is required to keep and preserve for tax purposes (see **65.13** RETURNS) and VAT purposes. To the extent that information or documents do not relate to the carrying on of a business and are not required to be kept or preserved for VAT purposes, they only form part of a taxpayer's statutory documents to the extent that the tax year or accounting period to which they relate has ended. Information and documents cease to be statutory records when the period for which they are required to be preserved ends. There is no link between the tax under enquiry and the source of the obligation to keep records so that, for example, records required to be kept for VAT purposes are statutory records even in the context of a notice which relates only to corporation tax (*Gold Nuts Ltd v HMRC* FTT, [2017] UKFTT 354 (TC); 2017 STI 1326).

Time limit for appeal

Notice of appeal under the above provisions must be given in writing to the HMRC officer who gave the information notice within the period of 30 days beginning with the date on which the information notice was given. A decision on an appeal by the tribunal is final (so that no appeal to the Upper Tribunal or Court of Appeal can be made — see *Jordan v HMRC* UT, [2015] STC 2314). Where the tribunal confirms the notice or a requirement in it, the person to whom the notice was given must comply with the notice or requirement within the period specified by the tribunal. If the tribunal does not specify such a period, compliance must be within such period as an HMRC officer reasonably specifies in writing.

It is notable in *Karim Mawji v HMRC* FTT, [2014] UKFTT 899 (TC) that in considering an appeal against an information notice the Tribunal considered the substantive issues to ascertain why HMRC needed the information, as well as the more procedural issues, and the lack of cooperation.

In *Joshy Mathew v HMRC* FTT, [2015] UKFTT 139 (TC) the Tribunal found that most documents requested by HMRC were not statutory records, however, the taxpayer was required to produce them. A notice to produce statutory records cannot be appealed. The Tribunal examined each item in the notice to determine whether such item was a 'statutory record'. With regard to the provision of a schedule of shareholdings the Tribunal noted that as there had been no acquisitions or disposals of shareholdings during the relevant period, the schedule was not relevant to the preparation of the tax return, and so this item could be appealed. Similarly the Tribunal found that loans for purchasing personal assets, and employment contracts, were not 'requisite' for the purpose of completing a tax return and were therefore not statutory records.

In *Couldwell Concrete Flooring v HMRC* UT, [2015] UKUT 135 (TCC) the Tribunal linked the definition of 'statutory records' in *FA 2008, Sch 36* with the obligation to keep records per *FA 1998, s 21(5)*. This provision requires companies to keep all records which are 'necessary to establish, without doubt, that a return is accurate'. If there was a duty to keep the information then it was a statutory record. The Tribunal also noted that it could not hear an appeal against a notice requiring statutory records, but that it could hear an appeal against a penalty for non-compliance with that notice.

In *Carmel Jordan v HMRC* UT, [2015] UKUT 218 (TCC) the Upper Tribunal held that any decision of the First-tier Tribunal relating to information notices issued under *FA 2008, Sch 36* cannot be appealed further. The Tribunal explained the purpose of the legislation was to restrict judicial scrutiny to one stage in order to avoid undue delays to HMRC's information gathering process.

Subject to the above, the appeal provisions of *TMA 1970, Pt 5* (see 5 APPEALS) apply to an appeal against an information notice as they apply to an appeal against an income tax assessment.

[*FA 2008, Sch 36 paras 29–33, 35, 37, 62*].

Concealing, destroying or disposing of documents

[38.9] A person to whom an information notice is addressed must not conceal, destroy or otherwise dispose of, or arrange for the concealment, destruction or disposal of, a document that is the subject of the notice. This does not apply if he does so after the document has been produced to HMRC in accordance with the notice, unless an HMRC officer has notified him in writing that the document must continue to be available for inspection (and has not withdrawn the notification). It also does not apply if a copy of the document was produced in compliance with the notice and the destruction, etc. takes place after the end of the period of six months beginning with the day on which the copy was produced unless within that period an HMRC officer makes a request for the original document.

Similarly, where a person has been informed that a document is, or is likely to be, the subject of an information notice addressed to him, he must not conceal, destroy or otherwise dispose of, or arrange for the concealment, destruction or disposal of, the document. This does not apply if he acts more than six months after he was so informed (or was last so informed).

[*FA 2008, Sch 36 paras 42, 43*].

Failure to comply with the above provisions may be a criminal offence or result in penalties. See **38.11** below.

Inspection of business premises and other property

[38.10] An HMRC officer may enter a person's 'business premises' and inspect the premises and any 'business assets' and 'business documents' that are on the premises if the inspection is reasonably required for the purpose of checking that person's tax position. The officer may not enter or inspect any part of the premises used solely as a dwelling.

HMRC also have the power to enter the business premises on two other occasions. Firstly, where the premises are those of an 'involved third party', defined for corporation tax purposes as a person who is or has been a managing agent at Lloyd's in relation to a Lloyd's syndicate. Secondly, where HMRC need to inspect the premises for the purposes of valuation for the purposes of corporation tax on chargeable gains. In this case, the officer may be accompanied by a person needed to assist with the valuation (e.g. a valuer). In the latter case, the occupier or controller of the premises must agree the time of the inspection and be given written notice of the agreed time or the tribunal must approve the inspection and the occupier, etc. must be given seven days' notice. Evidence of authority must be produced if the occupier etc. requests it.

Agreed time for inspection

An inspection must normally be carried out at a time agreed to by the occupier of the premises. It can, however, be carried out at any reasonable time if:

(i) the occupier has been given at least seven days' notice (in writing or otherwise) of the time of the inspection; or
(ii) the inspection is carried out by, or with the agreement of, an authorised HMRC officer.

Where (ii) above applies, the officer carrying out the inspection must provide a notice in writing stating the possible consequences of obstructing the officer in the exercise of the power. If the occupier is present when the inspection begins, the notice must be given to him. If he is not present, the notice must be given to the person who appears to be the officer in charge of the premises, but if no such person is present, the notice must be left in a prominent place at the premises. The giving of such a notice does not require the approval of the tribunal, but such approval can be applied for by, or with the agreement of, an authorised HMRC officer. No notice of an application for approval of inspection need be given to the taxpayer and there is no appeal against the decision. A penalty for deliberate obstruction of an officer in the course of an inspection can only be charged where such approval has been obtained (see **38.11** below).

An officer may not inspect a business document if or to the extent that an information notice (see **38.4** above) given at the time of the inspection to the occupier of the premises could not require him to produce the document (see **38.6** above).

Marking assets, copying documents etc.

The officer may mark business assets and anything containing business assets to indicate that they have been inspected. He may obtain and record information (electronically or otherwise) relating to the premises, assets and documents inspected. He may take copies of, or make extracts from, a document (or copy) which he inspects, and if it appears necessary to him, he may remove the document at a reasonable time and retain it for a reasonable period. He must, without charge, provide a receipt for a document which is removed where this is requested and must also provide, again without charge, a copy of the document, if the person producing it reasonably requires it for any purpose. Where a document which has been removed is lost or damaged, HMRC are liable to compensate the owner for expenses reasonably incurred in replacing or repairing it.

Definitions

For the above purposes, '*business premises*' are premises (including any land, building or structure or means of transport), or a part of premises, that an HMRC officer has reason to believe are used in connection with the carrying on of a business by or on behalf of the taxpayer concerned.

'*Business assets*' are assets, other than documents, that an HMRC officer has reason to believe are owned, leased or used in connection with the carrying on of any business. They do not include documents, other than documents that are trading stock or plant.

'*Business documents*' are documents, or copies of documents, relating to the carrying on of any business that form part of any person's statutory records.

[*FA 2008, Sch 36 paras 10–17, 32, 62*].

Offences and penalties under *FA 2008, Sch 36*

[38.11] For penalties for failure to comply with an information notice within **38.4** above or deliberately obstructing an HMRC officer in the course of an inspection of business premises under the power at **38.10** above that has been approved by the tribunal, see **59.11** PENALTIES.

It is an offence for a person required to produce a document by an information notice within **38.4** above which has been approved by the tribunal to conceal, destroy or otherwise dispose of the document or to arrange for its concealment, destruction or disposal. This does not apply if he does so after the document has been produced to HMRC in accordance with the notice, unless an HMRC officer has notified him in writing that the document must continue to be available for inspection (and has not withdrawn the notification). It also does not apply if a copy of the document was produced in compliance with the notice and the destruction, etc. takes place after the end of the period of six months beginning with the day on which the copy was produced unless within that period an HMRC officer makes a request for the original document.

It is also an offence for a person to conceal, destroy or otherwise dispose of, or to arrange for the concealment, destruction or disposal of, a document after an HMRC officer has informed him in writing that the document is, or is likely to be, the subject of an information notice approval for which is to be obtained from the tribunal. This does not apply if the person so acts more than six months after he was so informed (or was last so informed).

On summary conviction of either of the above offences the offender is liable to a fine not exceeding the statutory maximum. On conviction on indictment the punishment is imprisonment for a maximum of two years and/or a fine.

[*FA 2008, Sch 36 paras 53–55*].

In the *Parissis* case (TC01083 [2011] UKFTT 218) it is interesting to note that HMRC applied for and got penalties against three individuals with regard to information requests (under the old *TMA 1970, s 20* regime, the forerunner to *Sch 36*), even though the individuals might not in practice be able to obtain the documents sought. The principle established is that it is for the recipients of formal notices to make all reasonable efforts to obtain the information requested. The Tribunal commented that 'it costs very little to ask' but in this case there was no evidence the individuals had asked (the documents related to Guernsey trusts and it was possible an application might have been needed to a Guernsey Court). Merely asserting that a document is not within one's power or possession is not an adequate defence.

Data-gathering powers

[38.12] HMRC have power to obtain specialist and bulk information ('relevant data') from a data-holder falling within one of a list of specified categories. The power applies to all UK taxes and also to foreign taxes covered by the EU Directive for Administrative Cooperation (Directive 2011/16/EU) or by a tax information exchange agreement. The power can be used both for the purposes of risk assessment and for obtaining third-party data in connection with specific tax checks. It may be used to obtain personal data such as names and addresses of individuals. It cannot, however, generally be used to check the tax position of the data-holder to whom the notice is sent. '*Relevant data*' is data of a kind specified for each type of data-holder by Treasury regulations made by statutory instrument (see *SI 2012 No 847*). A data-holder notice under these provisions must specify the data to be provided. The notice can specify only data that HMRC have reason to believe may be relevant to a chargeable or other period ending within the four years ending with the date of the notice.

A notice under these provisions can be given without the approval of the Tribunal, but where such approval is obtained by HMRC the data-holder has no right of appeal against the notice or any requirement in it. If approval is not sought by HMRC the data-holder can appeal against the notice or a requirement in it on the grounds that it would be unduly onerous to comply, that the data-holder is not within the list of specified data-holders or that the data specified in the notice is not relevant data. Appeal cannot be made on the first of those grounds against a requirement to provide data forming part of the data-holder's statutory records (i.e. records required to be kept and preserved under any tax enactment). Data ceases to form part of a data-holder's statutory records when the period for which it is required to be preserved has expired. The procedures for appeals are the same as those for appeals against information notices under *FA 2008, Sch 36* (see **38.8** above).

Where approval is sought from the Tribunal, the application for approval must be made by, or with the agreement of, an authorised HMRC officer. The data-holder must normally have been told that the data is required and have been given a reasonable opportunity to make representations to HMRC. The Tribunal must be given a summary of any representations made. Where the Tribunal is satisfied that informing the data-holder would prejudice any purpose for which the data is required, it can approve the giving of the notice without the data-holder having been informed.

The data required by a notice must be provided by such means and in such form as is reasonably specified in the notice. If the notice requires the data to be sent somewhere, it must be sent to such address and within such period as is reasonably specified in the notice. If documents are to be made available for inspection, they must be so made available either at a place (other than one used solely as a dwelling) and time reasonably specified in the notice or at a place and time agreed between an HMRC officer and the data-holder. A notice requiring the provision of specified documents requires their provision only if they are in the data-holder's possession or power. An HMRC officer may take copies of, or make extracts from, documents provided and, if he thinks it reasonable to do so, may retain documents for a reasonable period. If a document is retained, the data-holder may request a copy of it if he reasonably requires it for any purpose. The retention of a document is not regarded as breaking any lien claimed on the document, and HMRC must compensate the owner if a document is lost or damaged.

[*FA 2011, Sch 23 paras 1–7, 28, 29, 45, 46, 65*].

Responsibility of company officers

Everything to be done by a company under the above provisions must be done by it through the '*proper officer*' (i.e. the secretary of a corporate body, except where a liquidator or administrator has been appointed when the latter is the proper officer, or the treasurer of a non-corporate body) or, except where a liquidator has been appointed, any authorised officer. The service of a notice on a company may be effected by serving it on the proper officer. [*TMA 1970, s 108; FA 2011, Sch 23 para 43*].

Data-holders

The following is a list of the categories of data-holders who are subject to the above provisions. The provisions also apply to persons who previously fell within a category, but no longer do so.

(1) An employer.
(2) A third party making payments to or in respect of another person's employees.
(3) An approved payroll giving agent.
(4) A person carrying on a business (or any other activity carried on by a body of persons) in connection with which certain payments relating to services provided by persons other than employees or in respect of intellectual property rights are made or are likely to be made. For this purpose the making of payments includes the provision of benefits and the giving of any other valuable consideration. There are special rules for services provided under agency contracts (see *FA 2011, Sch 23 para 10*) and certain persons performing in the UK duties of an employment with a non-UK resident employer (see *FA 2011, Sch 23 para 11*).

(5) A person by or through whom interest, building society share dividends, foreign dividends, an amount payable on redemption of a deeply discounted security or an alternative finance return are paid or credited.

(6) A person who is in receipt of money or value of, or belonging to, another.

(7) A person who has a contractual obligation to make payments to retailers in settlement of payment card transactions (a 'merchant acquirer'). The relevant data is, in relation to a retailer, information relating to payment card transactions (including the currency), the reference number of the account into which payments are made and, where necessary to identify the account, the branch where the account is held (see *SI 2012 No 847* as amended by *SI 2013 No 1811*).

(8) A person who provides services by which monetary value is stored electronically for the purpose of payments being made in respect of transactions to which the provider of the services is not a party (often known as a 'digital wallet').

(9) A person who provides services to enable or facilitate transactions between suppliers and customers (other than services solely enabling payments to be made) and receives information about such transactions in doing so (a 'business intermediary').

(10) A person who is the registered or inscribed holder of securities. This category and those at (11)–(13) below apply where HMRC is trying to establish who is the beneficial owner of some shares or securities or beneficially entitled to a particular payment. The limited scope of the information that may be required is set out in *FA 2011, Sch 23 para 14(3)*.

(11) A person who receives a payment derived from securities or would be entitled to do so if a payment were made (and see (10) above).

(12) A person who receives a payment for the purchase by an unquoted company of its own shares (within *CTA 2010, s 1033*) (and see (10) above).

(13) A person who receives a chargeable payment within *CTA 2010, Pt 23 Ch 5* (company distributions: demergers) (and see (10) above).

(14) A person who makes a payment derived from securities that has been received from, or is paid on behalf of, another.

(15) A person by whom a payment out of public funds is made by way of grant or subsidy.

(16) A person by whom licences or approvals are issued or a (local authority or statutory) register is maintained.

(17) A lessee, an occupier of land, a person having the use of land and a person who, as agent, manages land or receives rent or other payments from land. The reference to a person who manages land includes a person who markets property to potential tenants, searches for tenants or provides similar services.

(18) A person who effects, or is a party to, securities transactions (as defined) wholly or partly on behalf of others (whether as agent or principal).

(19) A person who, in the course of business, acts as registrar or administrator in respect of securities transactions.

(20) A person who makes a payment derived from securities to anyone other than the registered or inscribed holder.

(21) A person who makes a payment derived from bearer securities. It is notable that bearer shares have been abolished as from 26 May 2015, and all such issued shares must be converted into registered shares (the *Small Business, Enterprise and Employment Act 2015*).
(22) An accountable person (within *SI 1986 No 1711*) for the purposes of stamp duty reserve tax.
(23) The committee or other person or body managing a clearing house for any terminal market in commodities.
(24) An auctioneer.
(25) A person carrying on a business of dealing in, or of acting as an intermediary in dealings in, tangible movable property.
(26) A Lloyd's syndicate managing agent.
(27) An ISA plan manager or Child Trust Fund account provider.
(28) A licence holder under *Petroleum Act 1998*.
(29) The responsible person (within *Oil Taxation Act 1975, Pt 1*) for an oil field.
(30) A person involved in an insurance business.
(31) A person who makes arrangements for persons to enter into insurance contracts.
(32) A person concerned in a business which is not an insurance business but who has been involved in the entering into of an insurance contract providing cover for any matter associated with the business.
(33) A person involved in subjecting aggregate to exploitation in the UK or connected activities, making or receiving supplies of commodities subject to climate change levy or landfill disposal.
(34) A person who makes a settlement (within *ITTOIA 2005, s 620*), the trustees of a settlement, a beneficiary under a settlement and any other person to whom income is payable under a settlement.
(35) A charity.
(36) (From 16 November 2017 but in relation to relevant data with a bearing on any period whether before, on or after that date) a money service business, i.e. a business providing money transfer, cheque cashing and currency exchange services (other than a credit institution such as a bank or building society).

[*FA 2011, Sch 23 paras 8–27, 49; F(No 2)A 2017, s 69; SI 2019 No 689, Reg 20(3)*].

Penalties

For penalties for failure to comply with a data-holder notice and for the provision of inaccurate information or documents, see **59.12** PENALTIES.

Simon's Taxes. See **A6.330–A6.339**.

Police and Criminal Evidence Act 1984 powers

[38.13] HMRC are able to exercise certain powers under the *Police and Criminal Evidence Act 1984* when conducting direct tax criminal investigations. The powers involved include those concerning search warrants and arrest. Only HMRC officers authorised by the Commissioners for HMRC are able to exercise the powers. Similar powers are available to HMRC in Scotland and Northern Ireland.

The power to seek judicial authority to require the delivery of documents at **38.16** below is restricted to circumstances where the equivalent police power cannot be used because the material concerned is outside its scope.

The existing legislation applying these powers was consolidated by the *Police and Criminal Evidence Act 1984 (Application to Revenue and Customs) Order 2015, SI 2015 No 1783.*

[*Police and Criminal Evidence Act 1984, s 114; SI 2007 Nos 3166, 3175; SI 2015 No 1783*].

See HMRC Technical Note 'Criminal investigation powers and safeguards', 30 November 2007.

Proceeds of Crime Act 2002 powers

[38.14] HMRC are able to exercise certain powers under the *Proceeds of Crime Act 2002* directly when conducting direct tax criminal investigations. The powers involved are those for search and seizure of cash, productions orders, search and seizure warrants, customer information orders and account monitoring orders. Previously these powers could be exercised by the police on behalf of HMRC.

[*Proceeds of Crime Act 2002, Pts 5, 8; FA 2013, s 224, Sch 48*].

Computer records etc.

[38.15] The following applies to any tax provisions requiring a person to produce a document or cause a document to be produced, furnished or delivered, or requiring a person to permit HMRC to inspect a document, to make copies of or extracts from, or remove, a document (i.e. including the provisions at **38.4**, **38.11** and **38.16**).

For the purposes of such provisions, a reference to a document is a reference to anything in which information of any description is recorded, and a reference to a copy of a document is to anything onto which information recorded in the document has been copied, by whatever means and whether directly or indirectly.

Where a document has been, or may be, required to be produced, inspected etc. under any such provisions, a person authorised by the Commissioners for HMRC (previously the Board of Inland Revenue) can obtain access to any computer and associated apparatus or material used in connection with the document at any reasonable time in order to inspect it and check its operation. Reasonable assistance can be required from the person by whom or on whose behalf the computer has been so used or any person in charge of the computer etc. or otherwise concerned with its operation.

A penalty of £300 applies for obstruction of such access or refusal to provide assistance.

[*FA 2008, s 114*].

HMRC's practice in cases of serious tax fraud

[38.16] The policy of the Commissioners for HMRC in cases of suspected tax fraud, as set out in Code of Practice COP 9, is as follows:

- The Commissioners reserve complete discretion to pursue a criminal investigation with a view to prosecution where they consider it necessary and appropriate.
- Where a criminal investigation is not commenced the Commissioners may decide to investigate using the COP 9 procedure.
- The recipient of COP 9 will be given the opportunity to make a complete and accurate disclosure of all his deliberate and non-deliberate conduct that has led to irregularities in his tax affairs.
- Where HMRC suspect that the recipient has failed to make a full disclosure of all irregularities, the Commissioners reserve the right to commence a criminal investigation with a view to prosecution.
- The term 'deliberate conduct' means that the recipient knew that an entry or entries included in a tax return and/or accounts were wrong but submitted it/them anyway, or that the recipient knew that a tax liability existed but chose not to tell HMRC at the right time.
- In the course of the COP 9 investigation, if the recipient makes materially false or misleading statements, or provides materially false documents, the Commissioners reserve the right to commence a criminal investigation into that conduct as a separate criminal offence.

If the Commissioners decide to investigate using the COP 9 procedure the taxpayer will be given a copy of the above statement by an authorised officer.

Under its published Criminal Investigation Policy (see www.gov.uk/government/publications/criminal-investigation/hmrc-criminal-investigation-policy), HMRC reserve complete discretion to conduct a criminal investigation in any case, with a view to prosecution by the Crown Prosecution Service ('CPS') in England and Wales or the appropriate prosecuting authority in Scotland and Northern Ireland. Examples of the kind of circumstances in which HMRC will generally consider commencing a criminal, rather than civil, investigation are, inter alia, cases involving organised or systematic fraud including conspiracy; cases where an individual holds a position of trust or responsibility; cases where materially false statements are made or materially false documents are provided in the course of a civil investigation; cases where deliberate concealment, deception, conspiracy or corruption is suspected; cases involving the use of false or forged documents; cases involving money laundering; cases where there is a link to suspected wider criminality; and repeated offences.

See *R v CIR (ex p Mead and Cook)* QB 1992, 65 TC 1 as regards HMRC discretion to seek monetary settlements or institute criminal proceedings. See *R v CIR (ex p Allen)* QB 1997, 69 TC 442 for an unsuccessful application for judicial review of a Revenue decision to take criminal proceedings. HMRC have an unrestricted power to conduct a prosecution in the Crown Court, there being no requirement for the consent of the Attorney-General (*R (oao Hunt) v Criminal Cases Review Commission* DC, [2000] STC 1110).

The Crown Prosecution Service is not precluded from instituting criminal proceedings in circumstances where HMRC has accepted a monetary settlement (*R v W* CA, [1998] STC 550). However, the Revenue in commenting on this case stated that the CPS will ordinarily bring proceedings that encompass tax evasion charges only where that evasion is incidental to allegations of non-fiscal criminal conduct (Revenue Tax Bulletin June 1998 pp 544, 545).

Statements made or documents produced by or on behalf of a taxpayer are admissible as evidence in proceedings against him notwithstanding that reliance on HMRC's practice above or on their policy for mitigating penalties (see **59.27** PENALTIES) may have induced him to make or produce them. [*TMA 1970, s 105*].

See generally HMRC Fraud Civil Investigation Manual.

Contractual disclosure facility

The contractual disclosure facility (CDF) provides an opportunity offered to taxpayers to tell HMRC about any tax fraud in which they have been involved. See www.gov.uk/guidance/admitting-tax-fraud-the-contractual-disclosure-facility-cdf. HMRC write to taxpayers whom they suspect have committed a tax fraud; their letter will offer a CDF contract and will be accompanied by a copy of COP 9 (see above). Taxpayers have 60 days from date of receipt to either accept or formally reject the offer of a contract. If they accept, they must produce an Outline Disclosure within the same 60-day period; this should contain a brief description of the frauds committed, a formal admission of deliberately bringing about a loss of tax, details of any non-fraudulent irregularities and any proposals for a payment on account. If the Outline Disclosure is accepted, the taxpayer will be required to make progress towards the production of a Certificate of Full Disclosure.

Under the terms of the CDF contract the taxpayer will not be criminally investigated, with a view to prosecution, for matters covered by the Outline Disclosure. The customer's co-operation will have the potential to maximise reductions in penalties. If the taxpayer rejects the offer of a contract or makes no response, HMRC have the option of starting a criminal investigation, though in most cases they will pursue a civil investigation.

See also HMRC Fraud Civil Investigation Manual FCIM200000.

If a taxpayer wishes to own up to a fraud without waiting to be contacted by HMRC, he may complete form CDF1 (www.gov.uk/government/publications/voluntary-disclosure-contractual-disclosure-facility-cdf1); HMRC will then consider the taxpayer for a CDF contract. Alternatively, disclosures, whether under the CDF, one of HMRC's targeted campaigns, or otherwise, may be made online using the digital disclosure service at www.gov.uk/government/publications/hm-revenue-and-customs-disclosure-service. See www.gov.uk/government/publications/hmrc-your-guide-to-making-a-disclosure for HMRC guidance on voluntary disclosures.

Simon's Taxes. See **A6.1007–A6.1014.**

Publishing details of deliberate tax defaulters

[38.17] HMRC have the power to publish, in any manner they think appropriate, information about a company. The power may be exercised where, following an investigation, one or more 'relevant tax penalties' are due and the total lost revenue in respect of all penalties exceeds £25,000 (which amount may be varied by statutory instrument.)

A '*relevant tax penalty*' is one which falls into one of the following categories:

- a penalty in respect of a deliberate inaccuracy in a taxpayer's document;
- a penalty in respect of an inaccuracy in a taxpayer's document due to the deliberate supply of false information or withholding of information; or
- a deliberate failure to notify chargeability.

The details which may be published, in manner at the discretion of HMRC, is intended to be such as to make the taxpayer company's identity clear, including the name of the taxpayer, registered address, and nature of any business.

Before publishing, the company must be informed of HMRC's intention and be given reasonable opportunity to make representations. Publication may only take place after a penalty becomes final. It may not occur more than one year after the day the penalty becomes final. Where the maximum reduction in penalty has been given for unprompted disclosure or the maximum reduction has been given for prompted disclosure (and in this case only, at HMRC discretion having regard to circumstances) publication may not take place. A penalty becomes final when the appeal period has expired, or, if there is a contract settlement, the date of the contract.

From a date to be appointed by statutory instrument, the above applies also where a body corporate or a partnership has incurred a penalty under *FA 2007, Sch 24* in respect of a deliberate inaccuracy involving an offshore matter or an offshore transfer or a penalty under *FA 2008, Sch 41* in respect of a deliberate failure which involves an offshore matter or an offshore transfer. In this case the Commissioners may publish information in respect of any individual who controls the body corporate or partnership ('control' being construed as in *CTA 2010, s 1124*), where the individual has obtained a tax advantage (as in *FA 2013, s 208* — see **4.3** ANTI-AVOIDANCE) as a result of the inaccuracy or failure. This applies regardless of the amount of potential lost revenue, and the let-out applies only if the penalty is reduced, by reason of *unprompted* disclosure, to the full extent permitted.

[*FA 2009, s 94*].

Dishonest tax agents

[38.18] HMRC have a power to obtain 'working papers' from 'tax agents' who engage in 'dishonest conduct' (and to charge penalties on such agents — see below). The power applies across most of the taxes administered by HMRC, including corporation tax.

Tax Agent

A '*tax agent*' is defined as an individual who assists clients with their tax affairs in the course of business. Such assistance includes advising a client with regard to tax, or acting or purporting to act as agent on behalf of a client with regard to tax matters. It also includes assistance with any document that is likely to be relied on by HMRC to determine a client's tax position.

Assistance given for non-tax purposes is also included where it is given in the knowledge that it will be, or is likely to be, used by a client in connection with the client's tax affairs.

'*Tax*' is widely defined to cover most taxes (income tax, corporation tax, CGT, VAT, CIS, IHT, IPT, SDLT, SDRT, PRT, aggregates levy, climate change levy, landfill tax, and any excise duty (other than vehicle excise duty)).

[*FA 2012, Sch 38 paras 2, 37*].

Conduct notices

A '*conduct notice*' will be issued to a tax agent by HMRC where it considers that there is evidence of dishonest conduct on the part of an agent. Such notice will be agreed in advance by a senior authorised officer of HMRC, on review of the evidence.

An individual engages in '*dishonest conduct*' where, in the course of acting as a tax agent, the individual does something dishonest with a view to bringing about a loss of tax revenue (regardless of whether a loss is actually brought about).

A '*loss of tax revenue*' occurs if the agent's clients were to: account for less tax than required to by law; obtain more tax relief than entitled to by law; account for tax later than required to; or obtain tax relief earlier than they would otherwise be entitled to.

The legislation considers the position of the agent themselves, and HMRC will need evidence that the agent knew they were acting dishonestly. A conduct notice must state the grounds on which the determination of dishonest conduct has been made.

The recipient of a notice under these provisions has the right to appeal it to the First-tier Tribunal. Notice of appeal must be given in writing to the officer who gave the conduct notice within 30 days of the date on which the notice was given. Where an appeal is notified to the tribunal, it may confirm or set aside the determination of conduct.

A person commits an offence if they conceal, destroy, or otherwise dispose of a document for which access may be sought under these provisions. A person guilty of such an offence is liable on summary conviction to a fine (up to the statutory maximum) and on indictment to imprisonment for up to two years, or both.

[*FA 2012, Sch 38 paras 3, 4, 5, 6*].

File access notices

Once a conduct notice has been issued, and only after any appeal process has been completed (and found in HMRC's favour) will a 'file access' notice be issued. There are special provisions with regard to tax agents who have been convicted of offences relating to tax that involve fraud or dishonesty (and no appeals are outstanding) within the previous twelve months.

Such notice allows HMRC access to '*relevant documents*' being the working papers of the agent (relating to assisting clients with their tax affairs), including obtaining access from a third-party document-holder. The notice relates to all relevant documentation in the possession or power of the party, or as specified within the notice (where such document is within the holder's possession or power).

First-tier Tribunal approval (conducted under the normal tribunal rules) is required before a file access notice may be issued.

In addition, where the recipient document holder is a person other than the tax agent, such recipient can appeal a file access notice to the tribunal on the basis that compliance would be unduly onerous. Such appeal should be made in writing to the officer within 30 days of file access notice.

Before obtaining Tribunal approval for the issue of such a notice, HMRC must discuss the notice in advance with the document-holder and tax agent before applying for a file access notice, which may highlight areas where documentation may not be available, for example under the third party's documentation retention policy.

A file access notice cannot require production of documents that are privileged, contain personal or journalistic material, relate to a tax appeal or are over 20 years old (unless still relevant for tax).

There is a similar office for concealment or destruction of documents, as above.

[*FA 2012, Sch 38 paras 7–21*].

Penalties

The penalty for failure to comply with a file access notice is £300. If the offence continues are the notification of a penalty a possible daily penalty of £60 may apply. Such penalty may not apply where there is a reasonable excuse, however, an insufficiency of funds, or relying on a third party to do something (unless the person took reasonable care to avoid the failure), are not considered a 'reasonable excuse'.

A tax agent who engages in dishonest conduct is liable to a civil penalty.

The penalties applicable are between £5,000 and £50,000 and the assessment would take into account:

- whether the individual disclosed the dishonest conduct;
- whether that disclosure was prompted or unprompted;
- the quality of that disclosure; and
- the quality of the individual's compliance with any file access notice in connection with the dishonest conduct.

Where there are special circumstances HMRC may reduce the penalty to less than £5,000.

A penalty can be appealed within 30 days of its issue. On notification to the tribunal the penalty assessment may be confirmed or cancelled, and the amount of the penalty may be confirmed or substituted.

A penalty should be paid within 30 days of being issued, or, if notice of appeal has been given, before the end of 30 days from the date the appeal is withdrawn or determined.

A person is not liable under these provisions for anything in respect of which they have been convicted of an offence.

Interest is charged on penalties paid late.

[*FA 2012, Sch 38 paras 22–35; FA 2009, s 101*].

Publishing the details of a dishonest tax agent

If an agent is subject to a penalty, and only after the appeals process has concluded, then HMRC may publish the names of tax agents who have been penalised for dishonest conduct.

Details of a third party (such as an employer, or previous employer) may also be published. In such cases the third party is permitted to make representations about whether their details should be published, and the way their organisation is described.

[*FA 2012, Sch 38 para 28*].

It is envisaged that as a 'tax agent' is defined by reference to being in business, any agents engaged in 'pro bono' work, or as in-house tax advisers, would be excluded.

HMRC guidance on the dishonest tax agent provisions can be found in HMRC Compliance Handbook at CH180000 onwards. Once it is finally established that a member of a professional body has engaged in dishonest conduct it is likely HMRC will report them to such body, where disciplinary action would be taken, as appropriate.

39

HMRC Statements of Practice

Introduction to HMRC Statements of Practice

[39.1] Statements of Practice (SOP) explain HM Revenue and Customs interpretation of legislation and the way HMRC applies the law in practice. They do not affect a taxpayer's right to argue for a different interpretation, if necessary in an appeal to an independent tribunal.

The following is a summary of those Statements of Practice published by HMRC as updated which are relevant to companies and, where applicable, referred to in this book. These can be found at www.gov.uk/government/collections/statements-of-practice. This includes a list of obsolete statements.

Statements are divided into those originally published before 18 July 1978 (which are given a reference letter (according to the subject matter) and consecutive number, e.g. A34) and later Statements (which are numbered consecutively in each year, e.g. SP 6/94).

As regards HMRC internal guidance manuals, see **36.9** HMRC — ADMINISTRATION.

Simon's Taxes. See **Part G1**.

B1	**Treatment of VAT.** Guidance on the general principles applied in dealing with VAT in the computation of corporation tax liabilities. See **73** VALUE ADDED TAX.
B6	**Goods sold subject to reservation of title.** Goods treated as purchases in the accounts of the buyer will be similarly treated for tax purposes. See **69.63** TRADING INCOME — DEDUCTIONS.
C1	**Lotteries and football pools.** Where part of the cost of a ticket is to be donated to a club, etc., that part is, in certain circumstances, not treated as a trading receipt. See **68.5** TRADING INCOME, **75.6** VOLUNTARY ASSOCIATIONS.
C6	**Group relief: *ICTA 1988, s 403C*.** Consortium relief — in determining the average percentage of a consortium member's interest in the consortium company HMRC's position is to take weighted average over the relevant time period. See **35.19** GROUP RELIEF.
C10	**Valuation fees.** Costs related to *Companies Act 1985* compliance are regarded as allowable expenses. See **68.47** TRADING INCOME.
D21	**Capital gains tax — 6 April 1965 valuation time limit: company leaving group: *TCGA 1992, ss 178, 179*.** HMRC will exercise discretion to extend the time limit as appropriate. See **12.15** CAPITAL GAINS — GROUPS.
SP 8/79	**Compensation for acquisition of property under compulsory powers.** Guidance as to the treatment of compensation for temporary loss of profits and expenses. See **18.2** COMPENSATION AND DAMAGES, ETC.

SP 13/80 **Demergers — *ICTA 1988, ss 213–218*.** Guidance on the application of the provisions and on clearance procedures. See **29.20** et seq. DISTRIBUTIONS.

SP 5/81 **Expenditure on farm drainage.** Certain expenditure to restore drainage is permitted as revenue expenditure. See **68.30** TRADING INCOME.

SP 8/81 **Replacement of business assets: groups of companies.** Conditions for relief explained where assets are disposed of or acquired by group companies after cessation or before commencement of trading. See **12.8** CAPITAL GAINS — GROUPS.

SP 12/81 **Construction industry tax scheme — carpet fitting** is considered to be outside the scope of the scheme. See **20.3** CONSTRUCTION INDUSTRY SCHEME.

SP 2/82 **Company purchasing own shares — *ICTA 1988, ss 219–229*.** The conditions for relief are clarified. See **61.5**(2), **61.9** PURCHASE BY A COMPANY OF ITS OWN SHARES.

SP 1/84 **Trade unions — provident benefits: legal and administrative expenses.** See **33.16** EXEMPT ORGANISATIONS.

SP 6/84 **Non-resident lessors — *ICTA 1988, s 830*.** The factors governing liability to tax on profits or gains of such lessors of mobile drilling rigs etc. are outlined. See **64.13** RESIDENCE.

SP 6/88 **Double taxation relief — capital gains tax.** The conditions under which relief is available are clarified. See **31.6** DOUBLE TAX RELIEF.

SP 4/89 **Company purchase of own shares — CGT treatment.** This confirms capital gains treatment for a corporate shareholder where a company buys back shares. See also *Strand Options and Futures Ltd v Vojak* [2003] EWCA Civ 1457, [2004] STC 64, 76 TC 220.

SP 6/89 **Delay in rendering tax returns — interest on overdue tax: *TMA 1970, s 88*.** The circumstances in which interest will be sought are clarified.

SP 1/90 **Company residence.** HMRC's interpretation of the application of the case law on company residence is explained. See **64.2**, **64.3** RESIDENCE.

SP 2/90 **Guidance notes for migrating companies — notice and arrangements for payment of tax.** See **64.10** RESIDENCE.

SP 3/91 **Finance lease rental payments.** See **69.42** TRADING INCOME — DEDUCTIONS.

SP 7/91 **Double taxation — business profits: unilateral relief.** Revenue practice as regards admission of foreign taxes for relief is revised. See **31.2** DOUBLE TAX RELIEF.

SP 10/91 **Corporation tax — a major change in the nature or conduct of a trade.** HMRC's interpretation of that expression is explained. See **12.29** CAPITAL GAINS — GROUPS, **51.17** LOSSES.

SP 4/92 **Capital gains re-basing elections.** Certain disposals are ignored in relation to the time limit for such elections. See **12.10** CAPITAL GAINS — GROUPS.

SP 3/93 **Groups of companies — arrangements.** Guidance on HMRC's interpretation of 'arrangements' for the various purposes of the group legislation. See **35.4, 35.14, 35.19** GROUP RELIEF.

SP 4/93 **Deceased persons' estates — discretionary interests in residue.** Payments out of income of the residue are treated as income of the recipient for the year of payment, whether out of income as it arises or out of income arising in earlier years. See **53.7** MISCELLANEOUS INCOME.

SP 5/93 **UK/Czechoslovakia double taxation Convention.** The Convention is regarded as applying to the Czech and Slovak Republics. See **31.17** DOUBLE TAX RELIEF.

SP 12/93 **Double taxation — dividend income — tax credit relief** for dividends paid under a 'company tax deducted' arrangement may be restricted. See **31.11** DOUBLE TAX RELIEF.

SP 15/93 **Business tax computations rounded to nearest £1,000** will be accepted in certain cases. See **65.20** RETURNS.

SP 8/95 **Venture capital trusts — default terms in loan agreements.** Certain event of default clauses will not disqualify a loan from being a security for the purposes of approval. See **74.2** VENTURE CAPITAL TRUSTS.

SP 3/97 **Investment trusts investing in authorised unit trusts or open-ended investment companies.** The conditions under which such investments may be made are clarified. See **45** INVESTMENT FUNDS and **47.2** INVESTMENT TRUSTS.

SP 4/97 **Taxation of commission, cashbacks and discounts.** HMRC's views are outlined. See **68.26** TRADING INCOME.

SP 3/00 **Enterprise investment scheme, venture capital trusts, corporate venturing scheme, enterprise management incentives and capital gains tax reinvestment relief — location of activity.** The requirement that trade(s) be carried on 'wholly or mainly in the UK' is clarified. See **24.7** CORPORATE VENTURING SCHEME, **74.4**(2)(b) VENTURE CAPITAL TRUSTS.

SP 4/00 **Tonnage tax.** Detailed administrative practice for the entire tonnage tax regime is set out. See **68.66** TRADING INCOME.

SP 3/01 **Relief for underlying tax.** The treatment of foreign dividends paid out of profits subject to variable rates of tax or where there are accumulated losses is clarified. See **31.11** DOUBLE TAX RELIEF.

SP 5/01 **Loss relief, capital allowances and group relief.** The conditions for acceptance of late claims for relief are set out. See **51.3** LOSSES.

SP 1/02 **Corporation tax self-assessment and chargeable gains valuations.** Certain enquiries remaining open solely because of an un-agreed chargeable gains valuation will be limited to outstanding matters relating to the valuation. See **65.14** RETURNS.

SP 3/02 **Tax treatment of transactions in financial futures and options.** Sets out HMRC views on the tax treatment of such transactions as defined in *TCGA 1992, s 143*.

SP 4/02 **Definition of financial trader for the purposes of *FA 2002, Sch 26 para 31*.** The guidelines used by HMRC in deciding whether a company should be approved as a financial trader are explained. See **27.27** DERIVATIVE CONTRACTS.

SP 5/02 **Exemptions for companies' gains on substantial shareholdings: sole or main benefit test — *TCGA 1992, Sch 7AC para 5*.** Revenue guidance is given on the application of the anti-avoidance rule. See **13.8** CAPITAL GAINS — SUBSTANTIAL SHAREHOLDINGS.

SP 1/06 **Self-Assessment — Finality and Discovery.** This clarifies how much information a taxpayer needs to provide in the tax return to remove the possibility of a discovery assessment. See **6.3** ASSESSMENTS.

SP 2/06 **Venture Capital Trusts, Corporate Venturing Schemes.** This clarifies the gross assets rule, valuation of assets and payments in respect of shares and securities. See **25** CORPORATE VENTURING; **73** VENTURE CAPITAL TRUSTS.

SP 3/07 **Double Taxation Relief — Yugoslavia.** See **31.17** DOUBLE TAX RELIEF.

SP 2/10 **Advance pricing agreements (APAs).** Provides up to date details of the administration of the APA scheme relating to transfer pricing issues. It supersedes the earlier SP 3/99. See **72** TRANSFER PRICING.

SP 1/11 **Transfer pricing, mutual agreement procedure and arbitration.** Describes the UK's practice in relation to methods for reducing or preventing double taxation. It is superseded by SP 1/18.

SP1/12 **Advanced Thin Capitalisation Agreements under the APA legislation.** This gives detailed guidance on how HMRC will operate agreements on thin capitalisation in practice. See **72.3** TRANSFER PRICING.

SP1/18 **Transfer pricing, mutual agreement procedure and arbitration.** This statement describes the UK's practice in relation to methods for reducing or preventing double taxation and supersedes SP 1/11. It considers the use of mutual agreement procedure (MAP) under the relevant UK Double Taxation Convention and/or the EU Arbitration Convention and also describes the UK's approach to the use of arbitration where MAP is unsuccessful. See **72.16** TRANSFER PRICING.

40

Housing Associations

Simon's Taxes. See D7.637 *et seq.*

Introduction to housing associations

[40.1] This chapter looks at the tax treatment of housing associations and self-build societies. Housing associations which are approved for the purpose can claim tax exemptions for rent received from its members and for gains made on disposal of their properties. Similar reliefs apply to self-build societies.

'*Housing association*', according to the *Housing Associations Act 1985*, means a society, body of trustees or company:

(a) which is established for the purpose of, or amongst whose objects or powers are included those of, providing, constructing, improving or managing, or facilitating or encouraging the construction or improvement of, housing accommodation; and

(b) which does not trade for profit or whose constitution or rules prohibit the issue of capital with interest or dividend exceeding such rate as may be prescribed by the Treasury, whether with or without differentiation as between share and loan capital.

Further provision may be made, by statutory instrument, for the purposes of the reliefs for housing associations and self-build societies.

[*CTA 2010, ss 649, 657*].

Tax treatment

Rental income

[40.2] Housing associations may claim to have rents, which they are entitled to receive from their members, disregarded for tax purposes, provided that the associations are approved as in 40.5 below.

[*CTA 2010, s 642(1)(2)*].

Interest paid

[40.3] Where an approved housing association claims exemption from tax (see 40.2), interest paid that is attributable to the properties subject to a tenancy is ignored for tax purposes. However, if the interest is attributable to a property not subject to a tenancy, the amount of interest attributable to that property is treated as so paid.

[*CTA 2010, s 642(1)(3)(4)*].

Example

A housing association pays yearly interest of £4,000. It has three properties, two of which are occupied and one vacant. The last rent charged for this latter property was £400 p.a.

Rents		£
Property A		400
Property B		800
Property C (unoccupied)		400
Total rents		£1,600
Interest attributable to		
Property A	$\frac{400}{1,600} \times £4,000$	£1,000
Property B	$\frac{800}{1,600} \times £4,000$	£2,000
Interest attributable to let properties treated as not paid		£3,000

The balance of £1,000 interest paid by the association is treated as so paid for tax purposes.

Chargeable gains

[40.4] An approved housing association within **40.5** may also claim exemption from corporation tax on chargeable gains accruing on the sale of any property which is or has been occupied by a tenant of the association. A claim is made as under **40.6**.

[*CTA 2010, s 643*].

Disposals of land and other assets by a housing association to the Regulator of Social Housing, the Secretary of State or Scottish Homes under a scheme within *Housing Act 1964, s 5* or *Housing Associations Act 1985, Sch 7 para 5*, and subsequent disposals of those assets by the Regulator of Social Housing, etc. to a single housing association, are treated as taking place on a no gain, no loss basis. The same applies to:

(a) transfers of land between the Regulator of Social Housing and relevant housing providers (essentially non-profit registered providers of social housing);
(b) transfers of land between relevant housing providers; and
(c) transfers under a direction from the Regulator of Social Housing of property other than land between relevant housing providers.

Similar relief applies to Northern Ireland housing associations.

[*TCGA 1992, ss 218–220*].

A non-arm's length disposal of an estate or interest in land to a relevant housing provider may, on a joint claim being made, be treated as that of the association on a subsequent disposal. [*TCGA 1992, s 259*].

Approved associations

[40.5] Housing associations are approved, for the purposes of the tax exemptions in this chapter, by the Secretary of State for the Environment, the Scottish Ministers, the Welsh Ministers or the Department for Social Development for Northern Ireland (or under delegated authority). A housing association may only be approved if certain conditions are satisfied:

(a) the association is a housing association within the meaning of the *Housing Associations Act 1985* or its Northern Ireland equivalent;
(b) the association must be (or be deemed to be) a registered society within *Co-operative and Community Benefit Societies Act 2014* (previously a society registered under *Industrial and Provident Societies Act 1965*) or its Northern Ireland equivalent;
(c) membership must be restricted to tenants or prospective tenants, and the grant or assignment of tenancies must be restricted to members; and
(d) the association must satisfy such other requirements and comply with such other conditions as may be laid down by the approving authority.

Approval has effect from the date specified by the approving authority (which may be earlier or later than the date approval is given).

[*CTA 2010, ss 644–646*].

Administration

[40.6] A claim for exemption from tax must be made within two years of the end of the accounting period to which it relates.

A housing association must not make a claim unless the following requirements are substantially complied with for the period to which the claim relates:

(a) none of its properties were occupied other than by a member (or, for a maximum period of six months after a member's death, by another person in accordance with his will or intestacy); and
(b) the association satisfied the conditions at **40.5** above and observed any covenants required under those conditions to be included in grants of tenancies.

If an adjustment to an association's corporation tax liability is required as a result of a claim, the adjustment can be made by assessment, repayment of tax or otherwise. Such adjustments can also be made where, following an enquiry, the association's claim or company tax return is amended.

[*CTA 2010, ss 647, 648*].

Special situations

[40.7] The following are governed by special rules.

Relief by grant

[40.8] Housing associations, which are not approved under **40.5** and do not trade for profit, may claim relief from corporation tax, by means of a grant. The claim must be made to the Secretary of State for the Environment, the Secretary of State for Scotland or the Welsh Assembly. It must show that, throughout the period for which the claim is made, the association provided or maintained houses for letting or hostels, and its other activities were incidental thereto. The form of the claim and its supporting evidence are as required by the Secretary of State from time to time, and HMRC are authorised to disclose information to him. The terms and conditions of the grant are within the Minister's discretion, save that no relief is available for tax attributable to activities other than those specified above. A housing association must be registered to be eligible for relief. Identical provisions (with necessary modifications) apply for Northern Ireland. [*Housing Act 1988, s 54*].

Approved self-build societies

[40.9] A self-build society (within the meaning of *Housing Associations Act 1985* or Northern Ireland equivalent) which is registered (or deemed to be registered) under *Co-operative and Community Benefit Societies Act 2014* and which is approved (see **40.5** above) may claim relief from corporation tax on rent receivable from its members and on chargeable gains arising on the disposal of any land to a member, provided that none of its land is occupied by a non-member. Claims are made as outlined in **40.6** above.

[*CTA 2010, ss 650–656*].

Disposals of land by unregistered self-build societies to the Regulator of Social Housing, the Scottish Housing Regulator, the Secretary of State, Scottish Homes, the Homes and Communities Agency or the Greater London Authority are treated as being for such consideration that no chargeable gain or allowable loss arises.

[*TCGA 1992, s 219*].

41

Income Tax in Relation to a Company

Introduction to income tax in relation to a company

[41.1] This chapter describes the rules which require the deduction of income tax from certain payments made by a company. It also covers the exemptions available, along with special cases such as gilts and local authority securities.

For the charge to income tax on certain UK income of a non-UK resident company which is not chargeable to corporation tax, see **64.8** RESIDENCE.

Deduction of tax at source

[41.2] Certain payments made by a company have income tax deducted from them (i.e. they are paid net of the income tax deducted). The payments in question are listed below. For the making of returns to HMRC and payment of the income tax so deducted see **41.8** below.

Annual payments

Income tax at the basic rate is deductible from annuities, annual payments and patent royalties (and this applies whether the payments are made by a company or any other person, but see below as regards inter-company payments). [*ITA 2007, ss 901, 903*].

Income tax is not required to be deducted from certain annual payments made under a liability incurred for consideration which is non-taxable, or which consists of a dividend. The annual payment must, in the hands of the recipient, be either charged to income tax under *ITTOIA 2005, Pt 5* (miscellaneous income) or to corporation tax under *CTA 2009, Pt 10 Ch 7* (annual payments not otherwise charged — see **53.14** MISCELLANEOUS INCOME) or *SI 2013 No 2819, Reg 15* (income treated as received by unit holders in exempt unauthorised unit trusts — see **46.22** INVESTMENT FUNDS), or be a non-trading credit under the provisions for LOAN RELATIONSHIPS (50). [*ITA 2007, s 904; SI 2013 No 2819, Reg 37*].

Yearly interest

Income tax at the basic rate must be deducted from payments of 'yearly interest' arising in the UK if it is paid:

(i) by a company or local authority (otherwise than in a fiduciary or representative capacity);
(ii) by or for a partnership of which a company is a member; or
(iii) to a person whose usual place of abode is outside the UK (subject to **41.5** below).

[*ITA 2007, s 874*].

The meaning of '*yearly interest*' is derived from case law and refers, broadly, to interest on a debt where the debtor and creditor intend that the debt should exist for more than a year, or where it is mutually accepted that the interest may be paid from year to year. Payments of yearly interest specifically include interest paid by a registered co-operative and community benefit society (previously a registered industrial and provident society) in respect of any mortgage, loan, loan stock or deposit; or any interest, dividend or bonus in respect of a holding in its share capital.

Interest under the *Late Payment of Commercial Debts (Interest) Act 1998* (or under a contractual right but for which that Act would have applied) is *not* 'yearly interest'. (Revenue Tax Bulletin August 1999 pp 686, 687). Statutory interest paid to creditors in a company administration is yearly interest (*Lomas v HMRC* SC, [2019] UKSC 12, 2019 SWTI 705).

A payment of interest which is payable to an individual in respect of *compensation* is to be treated as a payment of yearly interest (irrespective of the period in respect of which the interest is paid). An example of interest paid in respect of compensation is that paid by financial institutions in cases of financial mis-selling. The Commissioners for HMRC may make regulations which disapply this in prescribed circumstances.

In determining for the above purposes whether a payment of interest arises in the UK, no account is to be taken of the location of any deed under which the interest is paid.

[*ITA 2007, s 874(1)(2)(5)(5A)(5B)(6)(6A)*].

For interest paid to a person outside the UK, see HMRC Savings and Investment Manual SAIM9200–9260. As to whether interest arises in the UK, see HMRC Savings and Investment Manual SAIM9090, but see also *Ardmore Construction Ltd v HMRC* CA, [2018] STC 1487.

As regards local authorities, see HMRC Brief 22/08, 9 April 2008. Where all or part of interest paid by the issuer of a security is treated as a distribution for corporation tax purposes and is taxed in the recipient's hands as if it were a dividend, income tax should not be deducted by the company from that payment or part of it. See HMRC Briefs 47/08, 100/09.

For the particular treatment of distributions by authorised investment funds, see **46.9** INVESTMENT FUNDS. [*ITA 2007, s 874(4)*].

Generally, these provisions apply to alternative finance return and profit share return (for which see **3.3–3.7** ALTERNATIVE FINANCE ARRANGEMENTS) as they do to interest. [*ITA 2007, s 564Q*].

Exceptions

For an exception from the duty to deduct tax from certain payments to companies, local authorities etc., see **41.3** below.

The obligation to deduct tax on payments of yearly interest is subject to numerous further exceptions, as listed below:

(a) payments of interest made by a building society; the obligation to deduct tax does apply if the interest is payable to an individual in respect of compensation (see above);
(b) payments of interest by a deposit-taker (e.g a bank) where the investment is a 'relevant investment' (see below);
(c) payments of interest that are public revenue dividends (see below);
(d) payments of interest by a bank if made in the ordinary course of its business; the obligation to deduct tax does apply if the interest is payable to an individual in respect of compensation (see above);
(e) payments of interest on advances from banks or building societies or from the European Investment Bank (providing, in the case of a bank, that the person beneficially entitled to the interest is within the charge to corporation tax, or would be but for an overseas permanent establishment exemption election — see **31.15** DOUBLE TAX RELIEF);
(f) payments of interest on deposits with the National Savings Bank;
(g) dividends from investment trust companies which are designated as interest distributions (see **47.10** INVESTMENT TRUSTS);
(h) interest distributions by authorised unit trusts (see **46.9**, **46.10** INVESTMENT FUNDS);
(i) interest distributions by open-ended investment companies (see **46.9**, **46.10** INVESTMENT FUNDS);
(j) payments of interest on peer-to-peer loans (as defined);
(k) payments of interest on a quoted Eurobond (see HMRC Brief 21/08, 7 April 2008);
(l) payments of interest on loans to buy a life annuity: such loans are already subject to deduction of tax;
(m) payments of interest which are chargeable to income tax as relevant foreign income (as defined);
(n) payments of interest by a person authorised under *Financial Services and Markets Act 2000* whose business consists wholly or mainly of dealing as principal in financial instruments (as defined) and who pays the interest in the ordinary course of that business;
(o) payments of interest by a recognised clearing house or recognised investment exchange (both as defined) which are made in the ordinary course of carrying on the business of providing a central counterparty clearing service (as defined);

(p) payments of yearly interest by a registered co-operative and community benefit society (previously a registered industrial and provident society) in respect of any mortgage, loan, loan stock or deposit, or any interest, dividend or bonus in respect of a holding in its share capital, if made to a person whose usual place of abode is in the UK. The society must make returns of such payments to HMRC;

(q) payments of interest under the *Late Payment of Commercial Debts (Interest) Act 1998* ('statutory interest');

(r) payments in respect of regulatory capital securities (see **50.28** LOAN RELATIONSHIPS) before 12 February 2019 or, in the case of a transitional qualifying instrument, 1 January 2024; and

(s) payments of interest on 'qualifying private placements'; a '*qualifying private placement*' is a form of unlisted debt instrument, issued by a company, in relation to which the conditions set out in *SI 2015 No 2002* are met.

[*ITA 2007, ss 874(3), 875–888, 888A–888E; FA 2019, Sch 20 paras 1, 16; SI 2013 No 3209, Regs 1, 2, 6, 8, 9; SI 2015 No 2002*].

Relevant investments

A '*relevant investment*' (see (b) above) subject to the exclusions below) is, subject to the exclusions in *ITA 2007, ss 863–870* an investment where either:

- the person beneficially entitled to any interest is an individual (or the persons so entitled are all individuals), or is a Scottish partnership all the partners of which are individuals; or
- the person entitled to the interest receives it as the personal representative of a deceased individual; or
- the interest arises to the trustees of a discretionary or accumulation settlement (as defined in *ITA 2007, s 873*).

[*ITA 2007, s 856*].

UK public revenue dividends

A '*UK public revenue dividend*' (see (c) above) is any income from securities which is paid out of the public revenue of the UK or NI, excluding interest on local authority stock. Interest on gilt-edged securities (as defined), securities issued by the National Savings Bank and securities which are the subject of a Treasury direction are payable gross (unless the holder of the security has made a deduction at source application). Otherwise, the person by or through whom the payment is made must deduct tax at the basic rate in force for the year of payment. HMRC have wide powers to make regulations governing the accounting arrangements and modifying the provisions governing the collection of tax deducted at source (see **41.8** below) in their application to UK public revenue dividends. [*ITA 2007, ss 890–895*].

Local authority and statutory corporation stock

Tax is deductible under *ITA 2007, s 874* (see above) except in the circumstances set out in **41.12** below and **66.9** STATUTORY BODIES. [*ITA 2007, s 981*].

Simon's Taxes. See **A4.421–427**.

Manufactured interest

Manufactured interest (see **52.3** MANUFACTURED PAYMENTS) on UK securities paid by UK residents are also subject to deduction at source of income tax at the basic rate. Tax is not to be deducted where the payment is representative of gilt-edged securities or other securities on which interest is payable without deduction of tax. In addition tax need not be deducted where the manufactured interest is paid by a UK resident company in the course of a trade carried on through a permanent establishment which has made an overseas permanent establishment exemption election (see **31.15** DOUBLE TAX RELIEF). This means that manufactured interest paid by an exempted permanent establishment of a UK company is treated in the same way as manufactured interest paid by a non-UK resident.

[*ITA 2007, s 919*].

Intellectual property royalties

Subject to the special rules for inter-company payments (see **41.3** below) and to the exemption for payments between associated companies in EU member states (see **41.5** below), income tax must be deducted at the basic rate from such payments to an owner whose usual place of abode is outside the UK. A paying agent must deduct his commission (if any) before the tax is computed.

Intellectual property for the above purposes means (i) copyright of literary, artistic or scientific works; (ii) patents, trade marks, designs, models, plans and secret formulas or processes; (iii) information concerning industrial, commercial or scientific experience; and (iv) public lending rights as before. The copyright in a cinematographic film or video recording and the sound track of any such film or video (except insofar as it is separately exploited) are excluded.

Copyright royalties payable to an author/originator of a literary, dramatic, musical or artistic work that has been created in the course of his profession are fees for professional services and do not fall within the rules above (HMRC International Manual INTM342590).

[*ITA 2007, ss 906–909*].

Exception for payments to companies, public authorities etc.

[41.3] Certain payments ('*excepted payments*') made by companies and local authorities which would otherwise be subject to the deduction of income tax, can be paid gross where any of (a)–(e) below apply. The types of payment to which this applies are:

- (i) yearly interest (*ITA 2007, s 874(2)*;
- (ii) payments in respect of building society securities (*ITA 2007, s 889(4)*);
- (iii) annual payments by persons other than individuals (*ITA 2007, s 901(4)*);
- (iv) patent royalties (*ITA 2007, s 903(7)*);
- (v) royalty payments where the owner lives abroad (*ITA 2007, s 906(5)*);
- (vi) proceeds of sale of patent rights paid to non-UK residents (*ITA 2007, s 910(2)*);

(vii) manufactured interest on UK securities; payments by UK residents etc. (*ITA 2007, s 919(2)*); and
(viii) chargeable payments connected with exempt distributions (*ITA 2007, s 928(2)*).

Where a company, local authority or partnership which includes a company or local authority makes a payment within (i)–(viii) above and reasonably believes that any one of (a)–(e) below is satisfied at the time the payment is made, then no income tax need be deducted.

(a) The person beneficially entitled to the income in respect of which the payment is made is a UK-resident company.
(b) The person beneficially entitled to the income in respect of which the payment is made is a non-UK resident company which carries on a trade in the UK through a permanent establishment (see **64.6** RESIDENCE) and the payment falls to be brought into account when computing the 'chargeable profits' of such permanent establishment.
(c) The payment is made to one of the following or its nominee:
 (i) a local authority;
 (ii) a health service body within *CTA 2010, s 986*;
 (iii) a public officer or department of the Crown within *ITA 2007, s 978* (other than one within *ITA 2007, s 978(2)*);
 (iv) a charity (see **14.1** CHARITIES);
 (v) a body mentioned in *CTA 2010, s 468* (bodies afforded the same tax exemptions as charities, see **33.9**);
 (vi) a scientific research organisation within *CTA 2010, s 469*;
 (vii) the trustees of a Parliamentary pension fund within *ICTA 1988, s 613(4)*;
 (viii) the persons entitled to receive the income of certain colonial, etc. pension funds within *ICTA 1988, s 614(3)*;
 (ix) scheme administrator of a registered pension scheme (or sub-scheme administrator of a split scheme).
(d) The person to whom the payment is made is (or is the nominee of) the plan manager of an individual savings account under *ITTOIA 2005, Pt 6 Ch 3*, and receives the payment in respect of account investments.
(e) The person beneficially entitled to the income in respect of which the payment is made is a partnership each member of which is either:
 (i) a body within (c) above;
 (ii) a UK-resident company;
 (iii) a non-UK resident company which carries on a trade in the UK through a permanent establishment (or branch or agency) and in computing whose 'chargeable profits' (see **64.6** RESIDENCE) the company's share of the payment falls to be brought into account; or
 (iv) the European Investment Fund.

The Treasury has powers to amend by order the persons and bodies to whom (c) and (e)(ii)–(iv) above apply.

[*ITA 2007, ss 929, 930, 932–937*].

Disapplication of exemption and penalties

Where HMRC have reasonable grounds for believing that none of the relevant conditions above will be satisfied in relation to any payment at the time the payment is made, they may give a direction to the company, local authority or partnership disapplying the exemption in relation to any such payment. The direction may refer to either a particular payment or a specified description of payment, but may not apply to payments made before the giving of the direction. [*ITA 2007, s 931*].

If a company, local authority or partnership makes a payment without deduction of tax because they have a reasonable belief that one of the relevant conditions above applies but none of the relevant conditions was in fact met, then the right to make the payment without deduction of income tax is treated as never having applied to the payment.

Penalties of up to £3,000 (and £600 per day for continuing failure) may be imposed under *TMA 1970, s 98* for failure to deduct and account for tax where the conditions for the exemption described above are not satisfied.

[*ITA 2007, ss 931, 938; TMA 1970, s 98(4A)–(4C)*].

See Revenue Tax Bulletin August 2001 pp 867, 868 for a brief summary of the provisions and an indication of HMRC's approach to the 'reasonable belief' requirement.

For amounts taxable under *ITA 2007, Pt 13 Ch 4* (tax avoidance: sales of occupation income), if the person liable is non-UK resident HMRC may direct that they be subjected to deduction of tax at the basic rate in force for the year in which the payment is made. [*ITA 2007, s 944*]. Such a direction may, however, only be made once there is entitlement to the consideration, i.e. on execution of a contract (*Pardoe v Entergy Power Development Corp* Ch D 2000, 72 TC 617).

Simon's Taxes. See **A4.460.**

Cross-border royalties

[41.4] If a company pays a royalty from which it is required to deduct income tax under *ITA 2007, ss 901–906* and the company reasonably believes that, at the time the payment is made, the 'payee' (i.e. the person beneficially entitled to the income in respect of which the payment is made) is entitled to relief under any double tax arrangements, then the company may calculate the income tax to be deducted from the payment by reference to the rate of income tax applicable under the arrangements (and, if appropriate, pay the interest gross).

If the payee was not in fact so entitled, the company must account for the tax as if the above rule had never applied.

'Royalty' for this purpose includes any payment received as consideration for the use of, or the right to use, any copyright, patent, trade mark, design, process or information, and any proceeds of sale of all or any part of any patent rights. Information about such payments may be required in a company's tax return (subject to a penalty of up to £3,000 under *FA 1998, Sch 18 para 20* for failure). Penalties of up to £3,000 (and £600 per day for continuing failure) may be imposed under *TMA 1970, s 98* for failure to deduct and account for tax where the conditions for the relief described above are not satisfied.

An officer of HMRC may direct a company that it may not deduct by reference to the rate per the arrangements, if that officer is not satisfied that the payee will be entitled to relief under double taxation arrangements in respect of one or more payments to be made by the company. Such a direction may be varied or revoked by a later direction.

[*ITA 2007, ss 911–913; TMA 1970, s 98(4D)*].

See also **41.5** below.

Where a person makes an 'intellectual property royalty' payment (broadly as defined at **41.2**(d) above) to a 'connected' person under 'DTA tax avoidance arrangements', the duty to deduct tax applies without regard to the provisions of any double tax treaty. Payer and payee are '*connected*' for this purpose if the participation condition (as at **72.2** TRANSFER PRICING but suitably modified) is met as between them. '*DTA tax avoidance arrangements*' are arrangements (as widely defined) having as a main purpose the obtaining a 'tax advantage' (as in **4.3** ANTI-AVOIDANCE) by virtue of a double tax treaty where this is contrary to the object and purpose of the treaty. There are provisions whereby arrangements made before 28 June 2016 are regarded as DTA tax avoidance arrangements in relation to payments made on or after that date where a main purpose is to obtain a tax advantage by a virtue of a double tax treaty not involving the UK.

Income tax suffered by a company as a result of this provision cannot be set off against any corporation tax liability under *CTA 2010, s 967* (see **41.9** below) or *s 968* (see **64.5** RESIDENCE).

[*ITA 2007, s 917A*].

Simon's Taxes. See **A4.4**, **A4.445**.

Interest and royalty payments to companies in the EU

[41.5] The provisions at **41.6** and **41.7** below give effect in the UK to EU Directive 2003/49/EC of 3 June 2003 on a common system of taxation applicable to interest and royalty payments made between associated companies of EU member states (the 'Interest and Royalties Directive') as amended. See **32.2** EUROPEAN UNION LEGISLATION for the impact of Brexit.

Following Brexit (see **32.2** EUROPEAN UNION LEGISLATION), the provisions are **repealed.** As a result, the treatment of interest and royalty payments will depend on the terms of any double tax treaty the UK has with the member state concerned.

The repeal of the provisions applies, in most cases, to payments made on or after 1 June 2021. The repeal applies to payments made on or after 3 March 2021, however, if arrangements have been made with a main purpose of securing that the provisions will apply to the payment. Exemption notices issued under **41.6**(d) below are accordingly cancelled. [*FA 2021, s 34(7)–(10)*].

Payments of interest and royalties from the EU to the UK are also no longer subject to the EU Directive following Brexit. As a result, some EU countries may deduct tax from such payments, depending on the relevant double tax treaty.

Exemption from income tax

[41.6] The following provisions are repealed with effect as indication at **41.5** above. Subject to this and except as detailed below, a payment of interest or royalties is not liable to income tax provided that, at the time the payment is made, the following conditions are met:

(a) the payment is made by a UK company or a UK permanent establishment of an EU company (but not a UK company's permanent establishment in a territory other than the UK);
(b) the person beneficially entitled to the income is an EU company (but not such a company's UK or non-EU permanent establishment);
(c) the companies referred to in (a) and (b) above are 25% associates (i.e. one of them holds directly 25% or more of the capital or voting rights in the other or a third company holds directly 25% or more of the capital or voting rights in each of them); and
(d) if the payment is one of interest, HMRC has issued an exemption notice.

For the purposes of (a) above, a payment is treated as made by a permanent establishment in a territory of a company resident in another territory (and not by the company) if and to the extent that it represents a tax-deductible expense for that permanent establishment.

In (b) above, the person beneficially entitled to the income is an EU company's UK or non-EU permanent establishment (rather than the company) if and to the extent that the payment is directly connected to the permanent establishment's business and is subject to corporation tax (or foreign equivalent) in the State where the permanent establishment is situated.

For the procedures governing the issue of exemption notices (see (d) above) see the *Exemption from Tax for Certain Interest Payments Regulations 2004* (*SI 2004 No 2622*). The regulations also make provision for the cancellation of an exemption notice where the conditions are not satisfied and also for the recovery of tax.

The above exemption does not apply to so much of any interest or royalties paid between parties in a 'special relationship' as exceeds the amount that would have been paid in the absence of such a relationship (i.e. payments exceeding an arm's length amount (which may be nil)).

'*Special relationship*' is construed in the same way as under *TIOPA 2010, s 131* (in the case of interest) and *s 132* (in the case of royalties). See **31.4** DOUBLE TAX RELIEF. This provision does not affect any claim for double taxation relief under *TIOPA 2010, s 2* (see **31.3** DOUBLE TAX RELIEF).

The above exemption does not apply to a payment of interest or royalties where the main purpose or one of the main purposes for the creation or assignment of the debt-claim under which the interest is paid, or the right in respect of which the royalties are paid, is to take advantage of the exemption.

[*ITTOIA 2005, ss 758–765; FA 2021, s 34(1), (7)–(10)*].

Payment of royalties without deduction at source

[41.7] The following provisions are repealed with effect as indication at **41.5** above. Subject to this, if a company makes a royalty payment and there would otherwise be a duty to deduct income tax under *ITA 2007, s 903(7)* or *s 906*, then, if the company reasonably believes that, at the time the payment is made, the payment falls within the exemption at **41.6** above, then the company may, if it thinks fit, make the payment without deduction of tax.

If the exemption did not in fact apply to the payment, the company must account for the tax as if the above rule had never applied, and HMRC have powers to direct the company that it is not to apply to a particular payment or payments (and such directions may be varied or revoked by subsequent directions).

If, before the royalty payment is made, the company beneficially entitled to the payment believed the exemption would apply but has subsequently become aware that it would not, it must without delay notify HMRC and the company making the payment.

Where there is a special relationship (see **41.6** above) between the payer and recipient, or between one of them and a third party, which results in the payment exceeding what would have been paid at arm's length, exemption from deduction of tax only applies to the amount which would have been paid at arm's length.

Information about payments may be required in a company's tax return. Penalties of up to £3,000 (and £600 per day for continuing failure) may be imposed under *TMA 1970, s 98* for failure to deduct and account for tax where the exemption does not apply and the company did not believe or could not reasonably have believed that it would apply.

Where the exemption applies but a payment has been made subject to deduction of tax source, a claim for relief may be made to HMRC.

[*ITA 2007, ss 914–917; TMA 1970, s 98(4DA); FA 2021, s 34(1)(2)(8)–(10)*].

Simon's Taxes. See **B5.319**.

Collection of income tax deducted at source

[41.8] A UK-resident company must make a return to HMRC of:

(i) payments from which it was liable to deduct income tax and the income tax for which it is accountable; and

(ii) credits that it claims for income tax deducted from payments received.

Returns (form CT61) must be made for 'return periods' which end on 31 March, 30 June, 30 September, 31 December and at the end of an accounting period of the company. Such returns must be made within 14 days of the end of the return period. If a company's year end is different from any of these dates then there will be five return periods, to the accounting date of the company.

[*ITA 2007, s 949*].

If a relevant payment is made outside an accounting period, a return must be made within 14 days of the payment. [*ITA 2007, s 950*].

If a company becomes aware of an error in a return, it must submit an amended return for the period. [*ITA 2007, s 958*].

Credit can be claimed in a return for income tax deducted from payments received in the accounting period in which the return period falls. Income tax which has been suffered in a return period is refunded to the maximum of income tax deducted and paid by the company in the return periods up to that point. Any excess not repaid is carried forward as a credit to the following return period. At the end of the accounting period if there is a cumulative excess of tax suffered (which has not been repaid) then this can be set off against the company's corporation tax liability.

The company is liable to pay to HMRC the income tax it deducted (or was liable to deduct) from payments (against which it may claim credit for income tax deducted from payments received) at the time by which the return is to be made, i.e. 14 days after the end of the return period (or 14 days after a payment which is not made in an accounting period). An officer of HMRC has power to assess the company if he considers that a return is incorrect, or believes that a payment has not been returned.

See **43.8** INTEREST ON OVERDUE TAX for the position if such income tax is not paid by the due date. The raising of an assessment on the company does not affect the due date of payment of the tax for interest purposes.

[*ITA 2007, ss 946, 949, 951–953*].

Non-UK resident companies (and non-corporates) are directly liable to assessment under *ITA 2007, ss 963, 964*. See **43.8** INTEREST ON OVERDUE TAX as regards interest on late paid tax under such assessments.

Simon's Taxes. See **A4.465**.

Income tax suffered by a company

[41.9] Few UK resident companies receive income under deduction of income tax. Where a company does receive such income, the company may obtain relief by setting off the income tax against its accountability to HMRC for income tax deducted from payments by it in the same accounting period (see **41.8** above). To the extent that relief is not so obtained, the excess income tax suffered is set off against any corporation tax due by the company for the accounting period into which the receipt falls for corporation tax purposes.

Where the receipt is exempt from corporation tax, the income tax is taken into account in the accounting period into which it would have fallen had it been liable to corporation tax.

Payments received by another party on behalf of or in trust for the company are taken into account but receipts by a company on behalf of or in trust for another person are not.

[*CTA 2010, s 967*].

Example

[41.10]

S Ltd prepares accounts each year to 31 October. During the two years ending 31 October 2021 it makes several payments (not being interest) from which basic rate income tax is deducted and receives several sums under deduction of basic rate income tax. The payments are taxable/ deductible for corporation tax purposes.

The following items are shown net.

	Receipts	Payments
	£	£
21.12.19		7,800
4.1.20	3,900	
9.8.20	7,800	
24.10.20	11,700	
25.3.21		7,800
14.8.21		9,360

The adjusted profits (*before* taking account of the gross equivalents of the above amounts) were as follows.

	£
Year ended 31.10.20	630,000
Year ended 31.10.21	860,000

S Ltd will use the following figures in connection with the CT61 returns rendered to HMRC and will also be able to set off against its corporation tax liability the income tax suffered as shown.

Return period	£ Payments	£ Receipts	£ Cumulative payments less receipts	£ Income tax paid/ (repaid) with return
Year ended 31.10.20				
1.11.19 to 31.12.19	7,800		7,800	1,950
1.1.20 to 31.3.20		3,900	3,900	(975)
1.4.20 to 30.6.20 (No return)			3,900	
1.7.20 to 30.9.20		7,800	(3,900)	(975)*
				(975)*
1.10.20 to 31.10.20		11,700	(15,600)	(2,925)
				(3,900)*

Year ended 31.10.21			
1.11.20 to 31.12.20 (No return)			
1.1.21 to 31.3.21	7,800	7,800	1,950
1.4.21 to 30.6.21 (No return)		7,800	
1.7.21 to 30.9.21	9,360	17,160	2,340
1.10.21 to 31.10.21 (No return)		17,160	
			£4,290

* for the period 1.7.20 to 30.9.20 during the year ended 31 October 2020, of the total income tax suffered of £1,950, £975 will be refunded (as £1,950 has been paid to date and £975 repaid so far) and the remaining £975 will be carried forward. As no further income tax is deducted by the company and paid to HMRC during this accounting period no further refunds can be made during the period. At the end of the year the remaining net tax suffered of £3,900 will be set off against the company's corporation tax liability.

Taxable profits

	Year ended 31.10.20	Year ended 31.10.21
	£	£
Adjusted profits as stated	630,000	860,000
Add Cumulative receipts £15,600 + net tax £3,900	19,500	
Deduct Cumulative payments £17,160 + tax of £4,290		21,450
Taxable profits	£649,500	£838,550

Tax payable

	Year ended 31.10.20	Year ended 31.10.21
	£	£
CT @ 19%	123,405	159,324
Deduct Income tax suffered	(3,900)	
Net liability	£119,505	£159,324

Gilt-edged securities

[41.11] See Tolley's Income Tax under Savings and Investment Income for provisions of general application, and in particular for the general availability of gross payment of interest on gilt-edged securities. For the general corporation tax treatment of gilts, see **49** LOAN RELATIONSHIPS.

Local authority securities

[41.12] A local authority (as defined in *ITA 2007, s 999*) must (except as below) deduct income tax from payments of yearly interest at the basic rate for the year in which the payment is made.

[*ITA 2007, s 874*].

Interest on local authority securities issued in a foreign currency is, if the Treasury so directs, paid without deduction of income tax and exempt from income tax (but not corporation tax) in the hands of a non-resident beneficial owner. Where for repayment of the principal amount due under a security there is an option between sterling and one or more foreign currencies, these provisions apply only if that option is exercisable solely by the holder of the security. Income from such securities is not exempt merely because it is deemed to be income of a non-resident.

For securities issued before 6 April 1982, similar provisions apply where the securities were issued in the currency of a country outside the scheduled territories at the time of issue.

[*ITTOIA 2005, ss 755, 756*].

Settlements

[41.13] Discretionary payments by trustees treated as income of the payee are taken as being net after income tax at the rate applicable to trusts. [*CTA 2010, s 610*]. Where this treatment applies to a payment made to a company within the charge to corporation tax, other than a charity (within *CTA 2010, s 467*) or a body treated as a charity under *CTA 2010, s 468*, the payment is disregarded for corporation tax purposes, and no credit is given, or repayment made, of the tax deducted. In the case of non-UK resident companies, this applies to so much (if any) of the payment as is comprised in the company's profits for corporation tax purposes.

[*CTA 2010, s 610*].

Simon's Taxes. See **I5.1306.**

42

Intangible Assets

Cross references. See **4.26** ANTI-AVOIDANCE for restrictions on the carry forward of non-trading losses after a change of ownership of a shell company; **51.23** LOSSES for restrictions on the transfer of deductions after a change of ownership of a company; **50** LOAN RELATIONSHIPS.

Simon's Taxes. See **D1.6.**

Introduction to intangible assets

[42.1] A special regime applies to determine the treatment of expenditure and receipts in respect of intangible assets. The regime applies *only to companies* and only to assets acquired or created on or after 1 April 2002 (subject to transitional arrangements, see **42.42** below). All intangible assets acquired on or after 1 July 2020 are brought within the regime, even if an acquisition before that date would have resulted in exclusion under the transitional rules. Such assets are, however, subject to the restrictions on the amount of debits at **42.7** below if they fall within one of the categories of restricted asset (broadly where they were acquired directly or indirectly from a related party and were previously excluded from the regime).

The regime deals with expenditure on the creation, acquisition and enhancement of intangibles (including abortive expenditure) as well as on their preservation and maintenance. It also applies to payments for the use of such assets, e.g. royalties. Profits on disposal of such assets are taxed as income. Losses on disposal and payments are relievable against income. The tax treatment of amortisation normally follows the accounts treatment. Relief for amortisation of goodwill and customer-related intangible assets is, however, either not available or subject to restriction, depending on when the asset was acquired — see **42.6** below.

A form of rollover relief (similar to, but not to be confused with, capital gains tax rollover relief) is available where realisation proceeds of intangibles are reinvested in new intangibles. See **42.11**. In general, amounts brought into account under the intangible asset regime, are not brought into account for corporation tax under any other provisions unless the legislation expressly states otherwise. See generally HMRC Corporate Intangibles Research and Development (CIRD) Manual, CIRD10000 *et seq.*

[*CTA 2009, s 906*].

For the corporation tax treatment of intellectual property excluded from the intangible assets regime by the commencement rules see **42.43** below.

For the *income tax* charge for 2019/20 onwards which applies to UK derived amounts from intangible property arising to certain non-resident companies see **42.44** below.

For commentary on devolution of the power to set the corporation tax rate in Northern Ireland to the Stormont Assembly and consequential modification of the intangible fixed assets regime, see **1.5** INTRODUCTION: CHARGE TO TAX, RATES AND PROFIT COMPUTATIONS.

Intangible fixed assets

[42.2] Except as otherwise indicated, transactions involving gains or losses in respect of 'intangible fixed assets' are dealt with for corporation tax purposes as described in this chapter. No other charges or reliefs apply in respect of those transactions.

An '*intangible asset*' for this purpose has the meaning it has under 'generally accepted accounting practice'. In particular it includes 'intellectual property', other assets such as agricultural quota, franchises and telecommunication rights and, except as otherwise indicated, is extended to include 'goodwill' (as defined under 'generally accepted accounting practice' and excluding goodwill which appears only in consolidated accounts).

The definition specifically includes internally-generated intangible assets (*CTA 2009, ss 712(1)* and *715(3)*). This followed the case of *Greenbank Holidays Ltd v HMRC* [2010] SFTD 653, confirmed in the Upper Tribunal [2011] STC 1582. All goodwill is treated as created in the course of carrying on the business i.e. for this purpose it cannot be created by purchase. Goodwill is treated as created on or after 1 April 2002, unless the business was carried on at any time before that date by the company or by a related company.

In *Spring Capital Ltd v HMRC (No 3)* [2015] UKFTT 0066 (TC)a company's claim for a large deduction for amortisation of goodwill on a transfer of trade was rejected by the First-tier Tribunal. However, the case is of particular note for its discussion on the valuation of goodwill, with the Tribunal preferring the accepted price/earnings method over the method proposed by HMRC.

In *Bloomberg Inc v HMRC* FTT, [2018] SFTD 1079, the acquisition of partnership units by the UK permanent establishments of US entities did not constitute the acquisition of intangible fixed assets.

Definitions

[42.3] An asset is an '*intangible fixed asset*' if it is acquired or created for use on a continuing basis in the course of the company's activities. This includes an option or other right either to acquire an intangible asset which, if acquired, would be a fixed asset, or to dispose of an intangible fixed asset. It is generally irrelevant whether or not the asset is capitalised in the company's accounts.

'*Intellectual property*' is:

(a) any patent, trade mark, registered design, copyright or design right, plant breeders' rights or rights under *Plant Varieties Act 1997, s 7*, or corresponding or similar right under foreign law;
(b) any economically valuable information or technique not protected by a right within (a); or
(c) any licence or other right in respect of anything within (a) or (b).

As to unregistered trade marks see *Iliffe News and Media Ltd v HMRC* FTT 2012, [2013] SFTD 309, in which a purported transfer of unregistered trade marks consisting of newspaper mastheads was held to be void as a matter of law.

'*Royalty*' means a royalty in respect of the enjoyment or exercise of rights that constitute an intangible fixed asset.

'*Generally accepted accounting practice*' is as defined by *CTA 2010, s 1127*. Accounts drawn up in accordance with generally accepted accounting practice are referred to in this chapter as 'GAAP-compliant accounts'. Where non-

GAAP-compliant accounts are drawn up, or accounts are not drawn up at all, these provisions are applied to amounts as they would have appeared had GAAP-compliant accounts been drawn up. This applies equally to amounts derived from earlier periods with non-GAAP-compliant accounts.

In determining whether a company's accounts are GAAP-compliant, reference may be made to consolidated group accounts as regards the useful life or economic value of any asset. Resort cannot be made to such accounts if prepared under the law of a foreign jurisdiction on a basis that diverges substantially from generally accepted accounting practice in relation to the useful life or economic value of any assets. Nor, for periods of account beginning on or after 1 January 2005, can resort be made to the consolidated accounts if they are drawn up using a different accounting framework from that used for the company's individual accounts and as a result they are prepared on a basis that differs substantially from that of the individual accounts in relation to the useful life or economic value of any assets.

[*CTA 2009, ss 712–719; FA 2019, Sch 9 para 3*].

Excluded assets

[42.4] Where (or to the extent that) an asset is excluded from the intangible fixed assets regime (see below), any option or other right to acquire or dispose of it is similarly excluded. Assets which are partly excluded are treated as two separate assets, one within the current provisions, the other subject to the normal corporation tax provisions, with any necessary apportionments being made on a just and reasonable basis.

The following assets are **excluded entirely** from the regime.

(a) An asset representing rights enjoyed through an estate, interest or right in or over land, or rights in relation to tangible movable property (see *CTA 2009, s 805*).
(b) An asset treated in the company accounts as an intangible asset but which in a previous accounting period was treated as a tangible asset on which capital allowances (on plant and machinery) were claimed (see *CTA 2009, s 804*).
(c) Certain oil licences (see *CTA 2009, s 809*).
(d) Financial assets (including loan relationships, derivative contracts and insurance or capital redemption policies) (see *CTA 2009, s 806*), subject to special provision in relation to finance leases (see **42.40** below).
(e) An asset representing:
    (i) shares or other rights in relation to the profits, governance or winding up of a company;
    (ii) rights under a trust (other than a right which is treated for accounting purposes as representing an interest in trust property which is an intangible fixed asset within these provisions); or
    (iii) the interest of a partner in a partnership (other than an interest which falls, for accounting purposes, to be treated as representing an interest in partnership property which is an intangible fixed asset within these provisions).

(f) An asset to the extent it is held either for a non-commercial purpose or for the purpose of activities in respect of which the company is not within the charge to corporation tax.

(g) An asset held by a film production company to the extent it represents production expenditure on a film under the *FA 2006* regime (see **26.16** and **26.17** CREATIVE INDUSTRIES RELIEFS).

(h) An asset held by a television production company to the extent it represents production expenditure on a television programme under the regime for relief at *CTA 2009, Pt 15A* (see **26.3** CREATIVE INDUSTRIES RELIEFS).

(i) An asset held by a video games development company to the extent it represents core expenditure on a video game under the regime for relief at *CTA 2009, Pt 15B* (see **26.9** CREATIVE INDUSTRIES RELIEFS).

(j) An asset held by a theatrical production company to the extent it represents expenditure on a theatrical production treated as expenditure of a separate trade under the regime for relief at *CTA 2009, Pt 15C* (see **26.27** CREATIVE INDUSTRIES RELIEFS).

(k) An asset held by an orchestral concert production company to the extent it represents expenditure on a concert or concert series treated as expenditure of a separate trade under the regime for relief at *CTA 2009, ss 1217P–1217U* (see **26.35** CREATIVE INDUSTRIES RELIEFS).

(l) An asset held by a museums and galleries exhibition production company to the extent it represents expenditure on an exhibition treated as expenditure of a separate trade under the regime for relief at *CTA 2009, Pt 15E* (see **26.41** CREATIVE INDUSTRIES RELIEFS).

In *Armajaro Holdings Ltd v HMRC* FTT, [2013] UKFTT 571 (TC); 2013 STI 3462, interests in a limited liability partnership acquired by a company were held to fall within (e)(iii) above.

The following assets are excluded except as regards '*royalties*', i.e. any payment in respect of the enjoyment or exercise of rights that constitute an intangible fixed asset.

(i) An asset to the extent that it is held for the purposes of any mutual trade or business (other than life assurance business). See *CTA 2009, s 810*.

(ii) An asset held by a company to the extent that it represents expenditure by the company on:
- the production of the original master version (as defined) of a film that commenced principal photography before January 2007;
- the acquisition before 1 October 2007 of the original master version of a film that commenced principal photography before 1 April 2006; or
- the production or acquisition of a 'master version' (as defined) of a sound recording.

(iii) An asset held by a company to the extent that it represents expenditure by the company on computer software falling to be treated for accounting purposes as part of the costs of the related hardware.

The following assets are excluded to the extent specified.

(A) An asset held by a company to the extent that it represents expenditure by the company on research and development (within *CTA 2009, ss 1039–1142*, see **63** RESEARCH AND DEVELOPMENT EXPENDITURE) is excluded from the provisions as follows.
  (i) The provisions at **42.5**, **42.8** below for the computation of tax debits and credits do not apply, *except for* credits in respect of receipts recognised as they accrue and debits reversing such credits.
  (ii) The provisions at **42.10** below for debits and credits on the realisation of intangible fixed assets apply as if the cost of the asset did not include any of the research and development expenditure.

(B) An asset held by a company to the extent that it represents capital expenditure (as determined for capital allowance purposes) by the company on computer software in respect of which the company has so elected is excluded from the provisions as follows.
  (i) The provisions at **42.5**, **42.8** below for the computation of tax debits and credits do not apply, except *for* credits in respect of receipts recognised as they accrue and debits reversing such credits.
  (ii) The provisions at **42.10** below for debits and credits on the realisation of intangible fixed assets apply as if the cost of the asset did not include any expenditure in respect of which the election was made.
  (iii) A credit is brought in under the current provisions only to the extent that the receipts to which the credit relates do not fall to be taken into account in computing disposal values for capital allowance purposes under *CAA 2001, s 72*.

  Such an election must specify the expenditure to which it relates, must be made in writing to HMRC within two years after the end of the accounting period in which the expenditure was incurred, and is irrevocable.

(C) Goodwill and certain related assets acquired by the company on or after 8 July 2015 (except where the acquisition contract had become unconditional before that date). See **42.6** below for details of the restrictions applying to such acquisitions. Note that different rules apply for assets acquired or created on or after 1 April 2019.

[*CTA 2009, ss 800–816A; F(No 2)A 2017, Sch 6 para 11; FA 2019, Sch 9 para 5*].

Computation of tax debits

[42.5] Debits are brought into account for tax purposes in respect of three types of loss relating to intangible fixed assets. These are:

(a) expenditure on an intangible fixed asset that is written off for accounting purposes as it is incurred;
(b) writing down an intangible fixed asset on an accounting or fixed rate basis; or
(c) reversal of a previous accounting gain,

other than on realisation of intangible fixed assets see **42.10** below.

Expenditure on an asset includes;

- expenditure (including abortive expenditure) incurred to acquire, create or establish title to an asset, as a royalty for use of an asset; or
- in maintaining, enhancing or defending title to it.

Capital expenditure on tangible assets is not taken into account.

Goodwill

See **42.6** below for restrictions on the debits which can be brought into account in respect of goodwill and related assets.

Restricted assets

See **42.7** below for restrictions on the debits which can be brought into account in respect of certain 'restricted assets' acquired on or after 1 July 2020.

Expenditure written off as it is incurred

Where expenditure is recognised in determining the profit or loss (and does not relate to previously capitalised expenditure, see below), a corresponding debit is brought into account for tax purposes. This debit is equal in amount to the accounting debit except in so far as the further provisions described in this chapter otherwise require. This applies to expenditure for the purpose of acquiring, creating, or establishing title to, the asset, by way of royalty in respect of use of the asset, or on maintaining, preserving or enhancing, or defending title to, the asset, and includes abortive expenditure. However, capital expenditure on tangible assets is excluded in determining expenditure on intangible assets.

[*CTA 2009, ss 59, 726–728*].

Writing-down of capitalised cost

Where a loss is recognised in determining the profit or loss in respect of capitalised expenditure, a corresponding debit is brought into account for tax purposes, equal in amount to the accounting debit unless other provisions described in this chapter otherwise require. This is subject to the election described below. The loss may arise though amortisation, or as a result of an impairment review. However, the valuation of an asset to determine the initial amount to be capitalised is not included.

Where the amount of the expenditure on the asset (the 'accounting expenditure') is adjusted for tax purposes (the 'tax expenditure'), e.g. where the cost is reduced as a result of reinvestment relief (see **42.12** below), then for the period of account in which the expenditure is first capitalised the tax debit is the amount which bears the same relation to the accounting debit as the tax expenditure bears to the accounting expenditure. For subsequent periods, the accounting debit is adjusted in the ratio which the 'tax written-down value' immediately before the accounting write-down bears to the accounting value. The '*tax written-down value*' of an asset for this purpose is the expenditure as adjusted for tax purposes *less* the debits previously brought into account (as above) (taking account of any debits brought into account on a change of accounting policy, see **42.41** below). On a part realisation of the asset, the previous written-down value is reduced to the proportion which the carrying values for accounting purposes immediately after the part realisation represent of those immediately before it, and subsequent allowances are based on this amount.

A company may, however, elect instead to write down the cost of an asset at a fixed rate for tax purposes. This applies whether or not the asset is written down for accounting purposes. The election, which is irrevocable, must be made in writing within two years after the end of the accounting period in which the asset was acquired or created by the company. It has effect in relation to all capitalised expenditure on the asset. The debit is at an annual rate of 4% of the capitalised tax expenditure on the asset (see above), but limited to the balance of the 'tax written-down value'. For this purpose this is the expenditure as adjusted for tax purposes less the fixed rate allowances previously given. An adjustment is made as above in the case of a part realisation and taking account of any debits or credits brought into account on a change of accounting policy, see **42.41** below. After a part realisation the allowance is given by reference to the accounting value of the part retained immediately after the part realisation and of any subsequent expenditure (subject to any adjustments required for tax purposes).

See **42.6** below for the 6.5% annual fixed rate applicable to goodwill and related assets acquired or created on or after 1 April 2019.

Reversal of earlier accounting gain

A loss may be recognised in determining the profit or loss which reverses (in whole or part) a gain previously recognised and in respect of which a credit was brought into account for tax purposes (see **42.8** below). In such a case, a corresponding debit is brought into account for tax purposes, the amount bearing the same relation to the accounting loss as the previous tax credit bore to the accounting gain (or part) reversed.

This does not apply to a loss recognised by way of amortisation, or as a result of an impairment review, of an asset previously revalued (see **42.8** below).

[*CTA 2009, ss 726–732, 742–744*].

Example 1

A company acquires an intangible fixed asset in year 1 at a capitalised cost of £2,000, amortised on a straight-line basis over 10 years. As a result of a reinvestment relief claim (see **42.11** below), the cost for tax purposes is reduced to £1,600. The charge in the accounts in each of years 1 to 10 (£200) is thus reduced to a tax debit of (£200 × £1,600/2,000) = £160.

In year 2 further expenditure of £700 on the asset is capitalised. The revised book value of (£2,000 – £200 + £700) = £2,500 is amortised over a further 10 years at £250 a year. The tax written-down value is (1,440 + 700) = £2,140, so that the charge in the accounts becomes (£250 × £2,140/2,500) = £214.

Example 2

A company acquires an intangible fixed asset with an indefinite life for £1,000 in year 1. The company is a UK subsidiary of a multinational group and prepares its accounts under IFRS. There is no amortisation charge in the accounts. It elects for the fixed-rate write-down for tax purposes. No adjustment is required to the cost for tax purposes, and the tax debit is thus £40 a year.

In year 10 the asset is partly realised for £700, £600 of the book value of the asset being set against the disposal in the accounts, giving a profit on disposal of 100 and a revised book value of £400.

The tax written-down value at the end of year 9 is (£1,000 - (9 × 40)) = £640. The remaining tax expenditure set against the disposal proceeds is (£600/1,000 × £640) = £384, resulting in a taxable profit on sale of 316. The tax written-down value is reduced to (£400/1,000 × 640) = £256. The fixed rate deduction is reduced to £400 @ 4%, i.e. 16 over the following 16 years.

Example 3

Writing-down on accounting basis

On 1 April 2018, Oval Ltd purchased an intangible asset from an unrelated company, Edgbaston Ltd, for £100,000. The asset is to be used for trading purposes and has a remaining useful economic life of 15 years. The cost of the asset is capitalised in Oval Ltd's accounts and in accordance with generally accepted accounting practice is amortised on a straight-line basis over the remaining 15 year life. On 1 April 2021, the company sells the asset to another unrelated company, Riverside Ltd, for £150,000.

Oval Ltd will bring into account for tax purposes the following debits and credits in respect of the intangible asset.

	£
Y/e 31.3.19	
Cost of asset	100,000
Debit for year (1/15 of cost)	(6,667)
WDV at 31.3.19	93,333
Y/e 31.3.20	
Debit for year (1/15 of cost)	(6,667)
WDV at 31.3.20	86,666
Y/e 31.3.21	
Debit for year (1/15 of cost)	(6,667)
WDV at 31.3.21	£80,000
Y/e 31.3.22	
Proceeds of realisation	150,000
Less Tax written-down value	80,000
Taxable credit	£70,000

As the asset was held for trading purposes, the debits of £6,667 for each of the years ended 31 March 2019, 2020 and 2021 are allowable trading deductions, and the credit of £70,000 for the year ended 31 March 2022 is a trading receipt.

Example 4

Non-trading loss on intangible assets

A Ltd is an investment company drawing up accounts each year to 31 March. The following figures are relevant for the two years ended 31 March 2021 and 2022.

	Y/e 31.3.21	Y/e 31.3.22
	£	£
Property income	15,000	16,000
Income from non-trading loan relationships	5,000	20,000
Overseas income (foreign tax paid £3,800)	20,000	—
Management expenses	5,000	5,000
Non-trading profit/(loss) on intangible fixed assets	(55,000)	11,000

A Ltd wishes to make the most tax-efficient use of the non-trading loss, and so makes a claim to set off £15,000 against profits of the year ended 31 March 2021 under *CTA 2009, s 753(1)*. The corporation tax computations for the two years ended 31 March 2021 are as follows.

	£
Y/e 31.3.21	
UK Property income	15,000
Income from non-trading loan relationships	5,000
Overseas income	20,000
	40,000
Deduct Management expenses	5,000
Non-trading loss	15,000
Taxable Total Profits	£20,000
Corporation tax: £20,000 @ 19%	3,800
Deduct Double tax relief	3,800
Corporation tax payable	Nil

	£
Y/e 31.3.22	
UK property income	16,000
Income from non-trading loan relationships	20,000
Income from non-trading intangible assets	11,000
	47,000
Deduct Management expenses	5,000
Non-trading loss	40,000
Taxable Total Profits	£2,000
Corporation tax: £2,000 @ 19%	£380

Use of non-trading loss

	£
Loss y/e 31.3.21	55,000

Set-off against profits for y/e 31.3.21	15,000
Set-off against profits for y/e 31.3.22	£40,000
	Nil

Debits for goodwill and related assets

[42.6] The debits which can be brought into account in respect of goodwill and certain goodwill-related assets depend on the date on which the asset was acquired or created. The provisions below apply to:

(i) goodwill in a business or part of a business;
(ii) intangible fixed assets that consist of information which relates to customers or potential customers of a business or part of a business;
(iii) intangible fixed assets that consist of a relationship (whether contractual or not) between a person carrying on a business and one or more customers of that business or part of that business;
(iv) unregistered trademarks or other signs used in the course of a business or part of a business; and
(v) licences or other rights in respect of an asset within (i)–(iv) above.

[*CTA 2009, s 879A; FA 2019, Sch 9 para* 6].

The provisions apply (except where otherwise stated) for accounting periods beginning on or after 1 April 2019. For this purpose, accounting periods straddling that date are treated as two separate periods, the second starting on that date. [*FA 2019, Sch 9 para* 7].

Where a company acquires an asset under an unconditional obligation in a contract, the asset is treated for the purposes of these provisions as acquired on the date when the company became subject to the obligation or, if later, when the obligation became unconditional. An obligation is unconditional for this purpose if it may not be varied or extinguished by exercise of a right, whether under the contract or otherwise. [*CTA 2009, s 879P; FA 2019, Sch 9 para* 6].

Asset acquired or created on or after 1 April 2019

Subject to the following (and in particular the restriction rules below), where a company acquires or creates an asset within (i)–(v) above on or after 1 April 2019, it is treated as having made an election to write down the cost at a fixed rate (see **42.5** above). The fixed rate to be applied is 6.5% (instead of the 4% rate that applies to other assets). The Treasury has the power to change the fixed rate percentage by statutory instrument. [*CTA 2009, s 879B; FA 2019, Sch 9 para* 6].

Where the company's acquisition of the asset on or after 1 April 2019 is not part of the acquisition of a business, no debits may be brought into account in respect of it other than realisation debits (see **42.10** below). Realisation debits are treated as non-trading debits. This rule applies also where the acquisition is part of the acquisition of a business but the company does not acquire any 'qualifying IP assets' as part of the business acquisition for use in its business on a continuing basis.

A '*qualifying IP asset*' is a patent, registered design, copyright or design right, plant breeders' right or right under *Plant Varieties Act 1997, s 7*, an equivalent non-UK right or a licence or other right in respect of any such asset. The asset must not be to any extent an excluded asset within **42.4** above or a pre-FA 2002 asset (see **42.42** below). A licence or other right to use computer software which does not permit its manufacture, adaptation or supply is excluded. The Treasury has the power to amend the meaning of qualifying IP asset by statutory instrument.

[*CTA 2009, ss 879I, 879J; FA 2019, Sch 9 para 6*].

Where the company acquires the asset on or after 1 April 2019 directly or indirectly from an individual or partnership (the 'transferor'), no debits may be brought into account in respect of it other than realisation debits, and realisation debits are treated as non-trading debits, if the 'related party condition' is met but the 'third party acquisition condition' is not met. The '*related party condition*' is met if the transferor is a related party of the company at the time of the transfer. If the transferor is a partnership, it is met where any partner who is an individual is a related party of the company at the time of the transfer. The '*third party acquisition condition*' is met if:

(a) in the case of an asset which is goodwill, the transferor acquired all or part of the 'relevant business' in one or more 'third party acquisitions' as part of which goodwill (the 'previously acquired goodwill') was acquired, and the asset is acquired by the company as part of the acquisition of all of the relevant business; or
(b) in any other case, the transferor acquired the asset in a third party acquisition and it is acquired by the company as part of the acquisition of all of the relevant business.

The '*relevant business*' is the business (or part) mentioned in (i)–(iv) above. A '*third party acquisition*' occurs when the transferor acquires something from a company at a time when the transferor is not a related party of the company or, where the transferor is a partnership, at a time when no individual who is a partner is a related party of the company. A third party acquisition also occurs when the transferor acquires something from a person who is not a company at a time when that person is not connected (see **42.34** below) with the transferor or, where the transferor is a partnership, at a time when no individual who is a partner is connected with the transferor. An acquisition is not, however, a third party acquisition if it has a main purpose of obtaining a tax advantage for any person and it occurs between 8 July 2015 and 31 March 2019 inclusive.

[*CTA 2009, ss 879K, 879L; FA 2019, Sch 9 para 6*].

Partial restriction on debits

Where the above provisions prohibiting debits other than realisation debits do not apply, and the asset is not a pre-FA 2019 asset (see below), the amount of each debit brought into account in respect of an asset within (i)–(v) above is restricted as below in two circumstances.

The first circumstance in which debits are restricted is where the company acquires the asset on or after 1 April 2019 as part of the acquisition of a business, and as a part of that acquisition also acquires qualifying IP assets (as above) for continuing use in the business. The restriction applies if the amount given by the following formula is less than one. The formula is:

$$\frac{(A \times 6)}{B}$$

where:

- A is the 'expenditure' incurred for or in connection with the acquisition of the qualifying IP assets; and
- B is the expenditure incurred for or in connection with the acquisition of the asset in question and any other assets within (i)–(v) above acquired with the business.

In effect, this provision limits the amount of expenditure on assets within (i)–(v) above for which a company receives amortisation relief to six times the company's expenditure on qualifying IP assets.

For this purpose, '*expenditure*' means expenditure which is capitalised for accounting purposes or which is otherwise recognised in determining the company's profit or loss, subject to any adjustments under the intangible assets rules and for TRANSFER PRICING (72). The Treasury can amend the formula by statutory instrument.

The second circumstance in which debits are restricted is where the company acquires the asset on or after 1 April 2019 directly or indirectly from an individual or partnership (the 'transferor') and both the related party condition and the third party acquisition condition are met. The restriction applies if the amount given by the following formula is less than one. The formula is:

$$\frac{A}{B}$$

where:

- A is the 'accounting value' of third party acquisitions; and
- B is the expenditure incurred for or in connection with the acquisition of the asset in question which is capitalised for accounting purposes or which is otherwise recognised in determining the company's profit or loss, subject to any adjustments under the intangible assets rules and for TRANSFER PRICING (72).

The 'accounting value' of third party acquisitions means the notional accounting value of the asset in question, or, where that asset is goodwill, the notional accounting value of the previously acquired goodwill (see (a) above). The notional accounting value of an asset is what its accounting value would have been in GAAP-compliant accounts of the transferor drawn up immediately before the acquisition by the company on the basis that the relevant business (as above) was a going concern.

In either of the above circumstances, the debits of the company in respect of the asset are subject to the restrictions.

(I) Only a proportion of a debit other than a realisation debit can be brought into account. The proportion is found by multiplying the amount of the debit that would otherwise be brought into account by the 'relevant amount'. For this purpose, in calculating the amount of the debit that would otherwise be brought into account, the effect of this restriction on the tax written-down value of the asset is ignored (i.e. the full amount of the debit before restriction is deducted).

(II) In the case of a realisation debit, two separate debits must be brought into account. The first debit is a debit calculated by applying the restriction in (I) above. The second debit, which must be treated as a non-trading debit, is equal to the amount of the overall debit that would otherwise be brought into account less the amount of the first debit. In calculating the second debit, the effect of these provisions on the tax written-down value of the asset is not disregarded.

The '*relevant amount*' is, where only one of the circumstances applies, the amount found by applying the relevant formula above. If both circumstances apply, the relevant amount is found by multiplying the amount found by applying one formula by the amount found by applying the other.

In the first circumstance above, the effect of these provisions is to limit the amount of expenditure on assets within (i)–(v) above for which a company receives relief (other than on realisation) to six times the company's expenditure on qualifying IP assets. In the second circumstance above, the limit is the notional accounting value of the assets acquired from third parties.

[*CTA 2009, ss 879M–879O; FA 2019, Sch 9 para 6*].

Pre-FA 2019 assets: treatment with effect from 1 April 2019

No debits may be brought into account in respect of an asset within (i)–(v) above which is a 'pre-FA 2019 asset' other than realisation debits (see **42.10** below). Realisation debits arising on such assets are treated as non-trading debits. This rule in effect preserves the effect of the pre-*FA 2019* rules below for assets which were subject to those rules. An asset is a '*pre-FA 2019 asset*' of a company (C) if it falls within one of the following four categories.

(1) C acquired or created the asset during the period 8 July 2015 to 31 March 2019 inclusive and the asset was a chargeable intangible asset (see **42.11** below) of C at anytime in the period 29 October 2018 and 31 March 2019 inclusive.

(2) Another company acquired or created the asset during the period 8 July 2015 to 31 March 2019 inclusive, the asset was a chargeable intangible asset of that company at any time in the period 29 October 2018 and 31 March 2019 inclusive and C acquired the asset on or after 1 April 2019 from a 'related party'. An asset is not, however, a pre-FA 2019 asset in this category if:

   (A) C acquired the asset from a company within the charge to corporation tax and the asset was not a pre-FA 2019 asset of that company immediately before the acquisition; or

(B) C acquired the asset from a person (the 'intermediary') who had acquired the asset on or after 1 April 2019 from a third person who was not then a related party of the intermediary (or, if the intermediary is not a company, any company of which the intermediary was a related party) and who is not a related party of C at the time of C's acquisition.

For the meaning of 'related party' see **42.34** below. For these purposes (and in (3) below), a person (including a partnership) is also a related party of another person (or partnership) if the participation condition (see **72.2** transfer pricing) is met between them.

(3) The asset was created on or after 29 October 2018, C acquired it on or after 1 April 2019 from a related party (the 'transferor') and the value of the asset derives in whole or part from another asset which had 'preserved status'. If only part of the asset's value derives from the other asset, the asset is treated for these purposes as two separate assets, one representing the value so derived and the other representing the remaining part of the value, with any necessary apportionments made on a just and reasonable basis. Only the separate asset deriving its value from the other asset is a pre-FA 2019 asset in this category. The circumstances in which the value of an asset may derive from another asset include where assets have been merged or divided or have changed their nature or where rights or interests in or over assets have been created or extinguished. It is immaterial for these purposes who created the asset.

An asset has '*preserved status*' if:

- it was acquired or created by a company during the period 8 July 2015 to 31 March 2019 inclusive and the asset was a chargeable intangible asset (see **42.11** below) of that company at any time in the period 29 October 2018 and 31 March 2019 inclusive when the company and C were related parties or when the company and the transferor were related parties; or
- it was a pre-FA 2019 asset of a company at any time in the period beginning on 1 April 2019 and ending with the acquisition by C when the company and C were related parties or when the company and the transferor were related parties.

(4) C acquired the asset on or after 1 April 2019 directly or indirectly in consequence of, or in connection with, a disposal of an asset within (i)–(v) above by another person and the asset disposed of would have been a pre-FA 2019 asset of the company had it been transferred to C at the time of the disposal. It does not matter whether the asset disposed of is the same as the asset acquire, whether the acquired asset is acquire at the time of the disposal or whether the acquired asset is acquired by merging assets or otherwise.

[*CTA 2009, ss 879C–879H; FA 2019, Sch 9 para 6*].

Treatment of goodwill and related assets before 1 April 2019

For accounting periods beginning on or after 8 July 2015 and before 1 April 2019, no debits may be brought into account in respect of an asset within (i)–(v) above other than realisation debits (see **42.10** below). Realisation debits arising on such assets are treated as non-trading debits.

For this purpose, accounting periods straddling 8 July 2015 or 1 April 2019 are treated as two separate periods, the second starting on either 8 July 2015 or 1 April 2019.

This restriction does not apply where a company acquired the goodwill or related asset before 8 July 2015, or under an obligation under a contract that had become unconditional before 8 July 2015. An obligation is treated as unconditional for these purposes if it could not be varied or extinguished by the exercise of a right (whether under the contract or otherwise).

[*CTA 2009, s 816A; F(No 2)A 2015, s 33; FA 2019, Sch 9 paras 5, 7*].

Goodwill and related assets acquired before 8 July 2015

Acquisitions of assets within (i)–(v) above before 8 July 2015 (or under an obligation under a contract that had become unconditional before that date) are unaffected by the above provisions, so that debits can be brought into account in the normal way, unless the acquisition was from a related party individual in circumstances where the provisions at **42.39** below apply.

Debits for restricted assets

[42.7] Special rules apply to certain assets ('restricted assets') acquired by a company on or after 1 July 2020 directly or indirectly from a related party which were previously excluded from the regime by the commencement rules at **42.42** below. The rules are intended to prevent transactions between related parties being used to obtain a tax advantage by bringing assets into the intangible assets regime at market value. They operate to limit the amount of any debits by restricting the acquisition cost to be taken into account (see Treasury Explanatory Notes to the 2020 Finance Bill).

The rules apply for accounting periods beginning on or after 1 July 2020. Accounting periods straddling that date are treated for this purpose only as two separate periods, the second of which begins on 1 July 2020.

'*Restricted assets*' are intangible fixed assets which fall within one of the following three categories.

(1) an intangible fixed asset of a company (company A) is a restricted asset if the company acquired it on or after 1 July 2020 from a related party and either:
    (a) the asset was a pre-*FA 2002* asset (i.e. it was excluded from the regime by the commencement rules – see **42.42** below) in the hands of any company on 1 July 2020 and it has not, at any time on or after that date, been the subject of a 'relieving acquisition'; or
    (b) the asset was created before 1 April 2002, was held by a person (the 'intermediary') other than a company immediately before 1 July 2020 and has not, at any time on or after that date, been the subject of a relieving acquisition.

    An asset is not within (b) above if the intermediary acquired it on or after 1 April 2002 from a third party which:

- is either not a company or, if it is a company, was not a related party of the intermediary at the time of the intermediary's acquisition;
- at the time of the intermediary's acquisition, was not a related party of any company of which the intermediary was a related party; and
- was not a related party of company A at the time of company A's acquisition.

A 'relieving acquisition' is an acquisition from a person who is not then a related party.

(2) An intangible fixed asset (asset A) of a company is a restricted asset if the company acquired it on or after 1 July 2020 from a related party and:

(i) it was created on or after 1 July 2020 and has not been the subject of a relieving acquisition;

(ii) its value derives in whole or part from another asset (asset B); and

(iii) asset B was a pre-*FA 2002* asset or a restricted asset in the hands of any company on the date asset A was created.

The condition in (iii) above is treated as met if asset B was held by a person other than a company on the date asset A was created, that person was then a related party of a company and asset B would have been a pre-*FA 2002* asset or a restricted asset in the hands of that company on the date asset A was created if that company had acquired asset B from that person immediately before that date.

For the purposes of (ii) above, the circumstances in which the value of an asset is derived from another asset include where assets have been merged or divided, assets have changed their nature or where rights or interests in or over assets have been created or extinguished. This would apply to, for example, the grant of a licence or similar arrangement in respect of an asset.

(3) An intangible fixed asset (asset A) of a company is a restricted asset if the company acquired it on or after 1 July 2020 and:

(I) asset A was acquired by any company on or after 1 July 2020 directly or indirectly as a consequence of, or otherwise in connection with, the realisation by another person of another asset (asset B);

(II) that company and that other person were related parties at the time of the realisation of asset B;

(III) asset B was a pre-*FA 2002* asset or a restricted asset in the hands of any company during the period from 1 July 2020 to the time of the realisation in (I) above;

(IV) asset B was not the subject of a relieving acquisition at any time in that period; and

(V) asset A has not been the subject of a relieving acquisition at any time after the realisation of asset B in (I) above.

For this purpose, it does not matter whether asset B is the same as asset A, whether asset A is acquired at the time of the realisation of asset B or whether asset A is acquired by merging asset or otherwise.

The condition in (III) is treated as met if immediately before 1 July 2020 asset B was held by a person other than a company, that person was then a related party of a company and asset B would have been a pre-*FA 2002* asset in the hands of that company on that date if that company had acquired asset B from that person immediately before that date.

The following rules apply to a restricted asset for the purposes of the provisions at **42.5** above (debits) and **42.41** below (change of accounting policy), and to the determination of tax written-down value for the purposes of those provisions.

(A) If the asset is within (1) above and the company was the first company to acquire it on or after 1 July 2020, the company is treated as acquiring the asset at no cost.

(B) If the asset is within (1) above but the company was not the first company to acquire it on or after 1 July 2020, the company is treated as acquiring the asset for an amount equal to A – B where:
A is the consideration for which the company actually acquired the asset or, if different, the amount which it would otherwise be treated for tax purposes as acquiring it; and
B is the market value on the date the asset was first acquired by any company on or after 1 July 2020.
If the result is negative, the acquisition cost is treated as nil.

(C) If the asset is asset A within (2) or (3) above, the company is treated as acquiring it for an adjusted amount, calculated as follows.
Step 1. Find the amount for which the company actually acquired the asset or, if different, the amount which it would otherwise be treated for tax purposes as acquiring it.
Step 2. Deduct from that amount so much of the 'notional deduction amount' for asset B as is just and reasonable.
Again, if the result is negative, the acquisition cost is treated as nil.
The '*notional deduction amount*' for asset B is:
- where (A) above would have applied if the company had acquired asset B instead of asset A, the market value of asset B at the time asset A was acquired;
- where (B) above would have applied if the company had acquired asset B instead of asset A, the market value of asset B at the time it was first acquired by a company on or after 1 July 2020;
- where the current rule would have applied if the company had acquired asset B instead of asset A, the amount that would have been deducted at step 2 if the company had acquired asset B.

Where fungible assets which are restricted assets are treated as a single asset which is itself a restricted asset (under the transitional rules at **42.42** below), the company is treated as acquiring the single asset for the sum of the amounts which it would be treated as acquiring each of the restricted assets under the above rules.

'*Market value*' for the above purposes means the price the asset might reasonably be expected to fetch on a sale in the open market. For the meaning of 'related party' see **42.34** below. A person (including a partnership) is also a related party for these purposes in relation to another person (or partnership) if the participation condition (see **72.2** TRANSFER PRICING) is met between them.

Where a company acquires an asset under an unconditional obligation in a contract, it is treated as acquiring it on the date on which it became subject to the obligation or, if later, the date on which the obligation became unconditional. An obligation is unconditional for this purpose if it cannot be varied or extinguished by exercising a right (under the contract or otherwise).

[*CTA 2009, ss 900A–900I, 900N; FA 2020, s 31(13)–(15)*].

Computation of tax credits

[42.8] Five types of credits relating to intangible fixed assets are brought into account for tax purposes. Amounts brought into account in connection with the realisation of an intangible fixed asset do not give rise to a credit (see **42.10** below). Where the following provisions require an amount to be a '*recognised amount*' for a period, this is an amount recognised (including prior-year adjustments apart from corrections of fundamental errors) in the company's profit and loss account or income statement, in its statement of recognised gains and losses or statement of changes in equity, or in any other statement of items brought into account in determining the company's profits and losses for that period. It also includes an amount which would have been so recognised if the profit and loss or other such statement as mentioned above had been drawn up in accordance with generally accepted accounting practice (see **42.2** above).

Receipts recognised as they accrue

Where a gain representing a receipt in respect of an intangible asset is recognised in determining the profit or loss, a corresponding credit is brought into account for tax purposes, equal in amount to the accounting gain except in so far as the further provisions described in this chapter otherwise require.

Revaluations

Where the accounting carrying value of an intangible fixed asset is increased on a revaluation (including a valuation of an asset which has a balance sheet value but has not previously been valued, and the restoration of past losses), a credit is brought into account for tax purposes of the lesser of:

(a) an amount bearing the same relation to the increase in value as the tax written-down value immediately before the revaluation bears to the accounting book value by reference to which the revaluation is carried out; or

(b) the 'net total of relevant tax debits' previously brought into account.

The '*net total of relevant tax debits*' is the difference between the total debits (in respect of the writing-down of capitalised cost, see **42.2** above) and total credits (under the current revaluations provision) previously brought into account for tax purposes in respect of the asset concerned. Such debits and credits also take account of any adjustments on a change of accounting policy as described at **42.41** below.

'Revaluation' includes the valuation of an asset shown at a value in the company's balance sheet, but which has previously been valued and a revaluation representing the restoration of past losses.

The above does not apply to an asset in respect of which an election has been made for tax write-down at a fixed rate (see **42.5** above).

Negative goodwill

Where an accounting gain is recognised in determining the profit or loss in respect of negative goodwill arising on an acquisition of a business, a corresponding tax credit is brought into account, equal in amount to so much of the accounting gain as, on a just and reasonable apportionment, is attributable to intangible fixed assets.

See **42.6** above with regard to goodwill and goodwill-related assets.

Reversal of earlier accounting debit

A gain may be recognised in determining the profit or loss which reverses (in whole or part) a loss previously recognised and in respect of which a debit was brought into account for tax purposes (see **42.5** above). In such a case, a corresponding credit is brought into account for tax purposes, the amount bearing the same relation to the accounting gain as the previous tax debit bore to the accounting loss (or part) reversed. This does not apply to a gain on a revaluation (as above).

Receipts in respect of royalties

A credit is to be brought into account for a receipt in respect of a royalty in so far as it does not give rise to a credit which (as above) is taken into account as a receipt recognised as it accrues (whether in the period of account in which it is received or a subsequent period of account). The credit is to equal so much of the amount as does not give rise to such a credit and is to be brought into account in the period the receipt is recognised in the accounts. This provision is deemed to have always had effect in relation to any credits so brought into account. [*CTA 2009, ss 720–725*].

Giving effect to credits and debits

[42.9] Credits and debits under the current provisions are given effect according to the purpose for which the asset concerned is used, as follows, with any necessary apportionment where an asset is held for more than one of the following purposes being made on a just and reasonable basis.

Assets held for trade purposes

Credits and debits are given effect as receipts and expenses of the trade in computing the profits of the trade carried on in that period.

Assets held for property business purposes

Credits and debits are given effect as receipts and expenses of the property business in computing business profits. A '*property business*' for this purpose is a 'UK property business' (other than a 'furnished holiday lettings business' or an 'overseas property business' (see **59** PROPERTY INCOME). Commercial lettings of furnished holiday accommodation which are treated as a trade under *CTA 2009, s 265* are similarly so treated for these purposes.

Assets held for mines, transport undertakings, etc. purposes

Credits and debits are given effect as receipts and expenses of the concern in computing trading profits. This applies to concerns listed in *CTA 2009, s 749*.

Assets held for other purposes

Credits and debits in respect of assets used for purposes other than the above (described as 'non-trading credits and debits') are aggregated, and the aggregate 'non-trading gain' or 'non-trading loss' given effect as follows.

See also **42.6** above with regard to goodwill and goodwill-related assets acquired on or after 8 July 2015.

A non-trading gain is chargeable to corporation tax as income.

Relief for a non-trading loss may be claimed, in whole or part, by set-off against total profits. Such a claim must be made within two years after the end of the accounting period to which it relates, or within such further period as HMRC may allow. To the extent that the loss is neither so relieved nor surrendered by way of GROUP RELIEF (**35**) or group relief for carried forward losses (see **35.26**), it is carried forward as a non-trading loss of the following accounting period. For accounting periods beginning before 1 April 2017 (and subject to the transitional provisions below), an unrelieved loss was carried forward as a non-trading *debit* of the following accounting period. A loss cannot be so carried forward to be treated as a loss of the following accounting period if the company ceased to be a company with investment business in the period in which the loss arose (or is treated as arising).

For these purposes, an accounting period which straddles 1 April 2017 is treated as if it were two separate accounting periods, the first ending on 31 March 2017 and the second beginning on 1 April 2017. Any necessary apportionments between the two periods must be made on a time basis unless that would produce an unjust or unreasonable result, in which case a just and reasonable basis must be used. Special rules apply, however, where the amount to be apportioned is either an amount chargeable to corporation tax which would have been less but for the CORPORATE INTEREST RESTRICTION (**25**) provisions or an amount for which relief is available which would have been greater but for the restriction. An amount chargeable to corporation tax which would not have arisen at all but for the restriction provisions is apportioned entirely to the second period.

[*CTA 2009, ss 745–753; F(No 2)A 2017, Sch 4 paras 5, 190–192; FA 2019, Sch 5 para 22, Sch 9 para 4*].

See **45.9** INVESTMENT COMPANIES AND INVESTMENT BUSINESS for restrictions on relief for non-trading losses following a change of ownership of an investment company.

Realisation of intangible fixed assets

[42.10] '*Realisation*' of an intangible fixed asset for this purpose means a transaction (including any event giving rise to an accounting gain) which results, in accordance with generally accepted accounting practice (see **42.2** above), in its ceasing to be recognised in the balance sheet or in its carrying value being reduced (the latter being referred to as a 'part realisation'). This applies to an asset that has no balance sheet value (or no longer has one) as if it had one.

Where there is a realisation of an intangible fixed asset in respect of which tax debits have been brought into account under *CTA 2009, ss 729, 730* (writing-down of capitalised cost, see **42.5** above), or under *CTA 2009, s 871* (adjustment on change of accounting policy, see **42.41** below) a tax credit (or debit) is brought into account equal to the amount by which the 'proceeds of realisation' (if any) exceed (or are less than) the 'tax written-down value' of the asset (see **42.5** above) immediately before the realisation.

If no tax debits have been brought into account in respect of the asset, the same applies by reference to the cost of the asset recognised for tax purposes, i.e. (subject to any adjustment for tax purposes) the amount of the capitalised expenditure for accounting purposes. Otherwise, a tax credit is brought into account equal to the full amount of the 'proceeds of realisation'. In the case of a part realisation, the tax written-down value (or cost) is for these purposes reduced in the same proportion as that by which the accounting carrying value is reduced as a result of the realisation. Thereafter, the cost of the asset (where no tax debits have been brought into account in respect of it) is that immediately after the part realisation plus any subsequent expenditure.

The '*proceeds of realisation*' are those recognised for accounting purposes reduced by amounts so recognised as incidental realisation costs, subject to any adjustment required for tax purposes (e.g. under transfer pricing rules). But, for realisations on or after 22 November 2017, where the realisation involves the receipt of something other than money, the '*proceeds of realisation*' are the amount that would have been recognised for accounting purposes had the receipt been of a sum of money equal to the price the thing concerned might reasonably have been expected to fetch on a sale in the open market (again reduced by amounts recognised as incidental realisation costs, subject to any adjustment required for tax purposes). This does not apply, however, where the realisation takes place due to an obligation, under a contract, that was unconditional before 22 November 2017.

The above provisions are subject to the reinvestment relief rules in **42.11** below.

See **42.5** above with regard to goodwill and goodwill-related assets acquired on or after 8 July 2015. Where a company disposes of such goodwill or goodwill-related assets, any realisation debits are treated as non-trading debits.

Abortive realisation expenditure

A loss recognised in determining the profit or loss in respect of abortive expenditure on realisation of an intangible fixed asset gives rise to a corresponding tax debit which, subject to any adjustment required for tax purposes, is equal in amount to the accounting loss.

A '*chargeable realisation gain*' is a gain on realisation of an asset which gives rise to a credit to be taken into account as above and a chargeable intangible asset is an asset giving rise to such a gain.

[*CTA 2009, ss 733–741, s 816A; FA 2018, s 20*].

Example

A company realises part of an intangible fixed asset with accounting book value of £5,000 and tax written-down value of £4,000 for £3,750, the book value of the part retained being £1,875. The amount to be set against the sale proceeds in arriving at the credit to be brought into account is (£4,000 × (£5,000 – £1,875)/£5,000) = £2,500, so that the credit is (£3,750 – £2,500) = £1,250.

Relief in case of reinvestment

[42.11] Where a company invests the proceeds of realisation of an intangible asset (the 'old asset') in other such assets, and the proceeds exceed the capitalised cost (if any) for accounting purposes (so far as recognised for tax purposes) of the old asset, it may claim relief as below. In the case of a part realisation, the cost for this purpose is reduced to the same proportion as the reduction in accounting value as a result of the part realisation bears to that value immediately before the part realisation (and so on for subsequent part realisations).

Full relief is available if the old asset was a 'chargeable intangible asset' of the company throughout the period of its ownership by the company, but if this condition was met for a substantial part, but not the whole, of that period (including the time of realisation), relief is available as if a corresponding part of the asset were a separate asset in respect of which the relief is available (any necessary apportionments being made on a just and reasonable basis). The other assets in which the proceeds are invested must also be 'chargeable intangible assets' immediately after the expenditure on them was incurred, and the expenditure must have been incurred in the period beginning one year before, and ending three years after, the date of realisation of the old asset (which period may be extended as HMRC may by notice allow in any particular case), and must be capitalised by the company for accounting purposes. Expenditure is for this purpose treated as incurred when recognised for accounting purposes. Reacquisition of the old asset is treated as acquisition of a different asset for these purposes. Deemed realisations and reacquisitions are disregarded for these purposes (except as detailed in **42.22**, **42.23** below). An asset is a '*chargeable intangible asset*' in relation to a company at any time if, were it to be realised at that time, any gain on realisation would give rise to a credit within **42.10** above (disregarding the availability of relief under this provision or by virtue of the transfer being treated as 'tax-neutral'). References to a transfer being treated as '*tax-neutral*' mean that it is not regarded in

Transfers within a group

[42.13] The transfer intra-group of an intangible fixed asset is treated as 'tax-neutral' (see **42.11** above) provided the asset is a 'chargeable intangible asset' (see also **42.11** above) in relation to the transferor company before and the transferee company after the transfer. This does **not**, however, apply where:

- the transferor or the transferee is an incorporated friendly society within *FA 2012, s 172*;
- the transferee is a dual-resident investing company within *CTA 2010, s 109* (see **35.23** GROUP RELIEF); or
- an election under *CTA 2009, s 18A* (exemption for foreign permanent establishments — see **31.15** DOUBLE TAX RELIEF) applies to the transferor and the asset has at any time been held by it wholly or partly for the purposes of a foreign permanent establishment through which it carries on business.

The provisions of *TIOPA 2010, Pt 4* (see **72** TRANSFER PRICING) do not apply to such intra-group transfers treated as 'tax neutral'.

'*Tax neutral*' in relation to the transfer of an asset means that the transaction is not treated as being either an acquisition or a realisation of the asset. The transferee stands in the shoes of the transferor.

Interaction with treatment of company reconstructions or amalgamations. These rules take precedence over the company reconstruction and amalgamation rules at **42.26** below.

[*CTA 2009, ss 774–776*].

See **58.20** PAYMENT OF TAX for CT payment plans for tax arising from a transfer of an intangible asset to a non-UK resident company which is resident in an EEA state where the transfer would have been tax-neutral under these provisions if the transferee were UK-resident. Plans can be entered into in respect of transactions occurring in accounting periods ending on or after 10 October 2018.

Roll-over relief on reinvestment

Application to group member

[42.14] Rollover relief is not available where the other assets are acquired from another member of the same group. For the purposes of the rules at **42.11** above, where the realisation of the old asset is by one company in a group and the reinvestment in other assets by another (not being a dual resident investing company (see **35.23** GROUP RELIEF)), then provided that the other assets are 'chargeable intangible assets' in relation to the latter company immediately after the expenditure is incurred, and are not acquired from another group member by a 'tax-neutral transfer' (see **42.13** above), the companies may jointly claim to be treated as the same person.

[*CTA 2009, s 777*].

Acquisition of company becoming group member

[42.15] For the purposes of the rules at **42.11** above, expenditure by a company ('A') on the acquisition of a 'controlling interest' in a company ('B'), where company B (or one or more other companies not in the same group as company A before it acquired that interest but which become so immediately after (and as a result of) that acquisition) holds intangible fixed assets (the 'underlying assets'), is treated as equivalent to expenditure on acquiring the assets themselves. The 'chargeable intangible assets' requirement under **42.11** above has then to be met by reference to the company by which they are held immediately after that acquisition.

Company A acquires a '*controlling interest*' in company B by acquiring shares in company B such that they become members of the same group immediately after the acquisition, having not been so immediately before the acquisition. The amount of expenditure treated as incurred by company A on the underlying assets is then the lesser of the 'tax written down value' (see **42.5** above) of the underlying assets immediately before the acquisition and the amount or value of the consideration for the acquisition of the controlling interest. In these circumstances, relief under **42.11** above must be claimed jointly by company A and the company or companies holding the underlying assets, and the tax written down value of the underlying assets in the hands of the company or companies holding the underlying assets is reduced by the amount available for relief (see **42.11** above). Any necessary allocation of the reduction between different underlying assets is made by the company which holds them (or, if there is more than one such company, as they agree between them).

[*CTA 2009, ss 778, 779*].

Degrouping

Company ceasing to be group member

[42.16] Where:

(i) a company which is a member of a group transfers to another company an intangible fixed asset (the 'relevant asset') which is a 'chargeable intangible asset' (see above) in relation to the transferring company before the transfer and the transferee company after the transfer, and

(ii) the transferee company, having been a member of the group at the time of the transfer or having subsequently become so, ceases to be a member after the transfer but within six years after the date of the transfer at a time when it (or an 'associated company' (see **42.18** below) leaving the group at the same time) still holds the relevant asset,

then for the purposes of the current provisions, the transferee company is treated as if, immediately after the relevant asset was transferred to it, it had disposed of and reacquired it at its then market value. Any resulting adjustments to be made for tax purposes by the transferee company (or by a company to which the relevant asset has subsequently been transferred) in relation to the period between the transfer of the relevant asset to the transferee company and that company ceasing to be a group member is made by bringing in the aggregate net credit or debit as if it had arisen immediately before the transferee company left the group.

To determine how effect is to be given to debits and credits in these circumstances (see **42.9** above), it is the purposes for which the relevant asset was held by the transferee company immediately after the transfer which are considered, except that if it was then held by that company for the purposes of a trade, a property business or a mine or transport undertaking, etc. which ceased before it left the group, any debit or credit is instead treated as a non-trading debit or credit.

These provisions are subject to **42.18–42.21** below.

Where a relevant asset is transferred as part of the process of a transfer to which the provisions at **42.27** below apply, then if as a result of the transfer the transferee ceases to be a member of a group, the above provisions are disapplied by deeming the transferee not to have left the group. If, as a consequence of the transfer, the transferee ceases to be a member of one group and becomes a member of another, the two groups are treated as the same group for the purposes of the above provisions.

[*CTA 2009, ss 780–782; FA 2019, s 26(2)*].

In these and the following degrouping provisions:

(a) companies are '*associated*' if, by themselves, they would form a group of companies (see **42.12** above);
(b) an asset acquired by a company is treated as the same as an asset owned at a later time by the company (or by an associated company) if the second asset derives its value in whole or part from the first; and
(c) references to a company leaving a group do not include cases where it does so in consequence of another group member ceasing to exist.

[*CTA 2009, s 788*].

Company leaving group because of a share disposal

[42.17] The provisions in **42.16** above do not apply where a company ceases to be a member of a group on or after 7 November 2018 as a result of a disposal of shares by another company if any gain on the disposal would be exempt under the substantial shareholdings exemption (see **13.4** CAPITAL GAINS — SUBSTANTIAL SHAREHOLDINGS), assuming that the company making the disposal were within the charge to corporation tax. This exemption does not apply if the disposal is part of arrangements under which the recipient of the shares will dispose of them to another person.

Where the company ceases to be a member of a group on or after 21 December 2018, the above exemption still applies where the substantial shareholding exemption does not apply only because the gain is otherwise exempt or the disposal is a no gain/no loss disposal (see **13.2** CAPITAL GAINS — SUBSTANTIAL SHAREHOLDINGS).

[*CTA 2009, s 782A; FA 2019, s 26(3)(5)(6)*]

Associated companies leaving group at same time

[42.18] The provisions in **42.16** above do not apply if either:

- both companies are 75% subsidiaries and effective 51% subsidiaries of another company on the date of the acquisition and both remain 75% subsidiaries and effective 51% subsidiaries of that other company until immediately after they cease to be members of the group; or
- one of the companies is both a 75% subsidiary and an effective 51% subsidiary of another company on the date of the acquisition and remains a 75% subsidiary and effective 51% subsidiary of that other company until immediately after they cease to be members of the group.

Where the transferee company subsequently leaves another group which has a 'relevant connection' with the first (for which see the corresponding capital gains provisions of *TCGA 1992, s 179* at **12.15** CAPITAL GAINS — GROUPS), **42.16** above applies as if it was the second group of which both companies were members at the time of the transfer. This is subject to **42.21** below where a merger was carried out for genuine commercial reasons.

There is a '*relevant connection*' between two groups if, at the time the transferee leaves the second group, the principal company of that group is under the control of the principal company of the first group (at that time or which was the principal company when the transferee ceased to be a member) or of a person or persons who at present, or at any time since the transferee ceased to be a member of the first group had control of it or such a person who would have had control had the company continued to exist. For this purpose, control is as defined in *CTA 2010, ss 450, 451*, subject to limitations where a bank would be treated as having control.

[*CTA 2009, ss 783–784, 788*].

Principal company becoming member of another group

[42.19] The provisions in **42.16** above do not apply where a company leaves a group by reason only of the fact that the 'principal company of the group' (see **12.2** CAPITAL GAINS — GROUPS) joins another group (the 'second group'). If, however, within six years after the transfer to it of the relevant asset, the transferee company at any time ceases to satisfy the 'qualifying condition' (otherwise than as a result of a disposal of shares within **42.17** above) and at that time the asset is held by either the transferee company or another company in the same group, the following applies.

The '*qualifying condition*' is that the company is a 'relevant subsidiary' of one or more members of the second group. Before 7 November 2018, the qualifying condition was that the company was both a '75% subsidiary' and an 'effective 51% subsidiary' (see **12.2** CAPITAL GAINS — GROUPS) of one or more members of the second group. The transferee company is a '*relevant subsidiary*' of a member of the second group (company A) if it would be a member of company A's group if company A were the principal company of a group.

The transferee company is treated for the purposes of the current provisions as if, immediately after the transfer to it of the asset, it had realised and immediately reacquired it at its market value at the time of the transfer. Any resulting adjustments to be made for tax purposes by the transferee company (or by a company to which the relevant asset has subsequently been transferred) in relation to the period between the transfer of the relevant asset to the transferee company and that company ceasing to satisfy the condition referred to above are made by bringing in the aggregate net credit or debit as if it had arisen immediately before the transferee company ceased to satisfy that condition.

To determine how effect is to be given to debits and credits in these circumstances (see **42.9** above), it is the purposes for which the relevant asset was held by the transferee company immediately after the transfer which are considered. However, if it was then held by that company for the purposes of a trade, a property business or a mine or transport undertaking, etc. which ceased before it ceased to satisfy the condition referred to above, any debit or credit is instead treated as a non-trading debit or credit.

These provisions are subject to **42.21** below.

[*CTA 2009, ss 785, 786, 788; FA 2019, s 26(4)(5)*].

Company ceasing to be a member of a group by reason of exempt distribution

[42.20] **42.16** and **42.19** above do not apply where a company ceases to be a member of a group by reason only of an 'exempt distribution' within *CTA 2010, s 1075* (see **29.21** DISTRIBUTIONS), unless there is a 'chargeable payment' within *CTA 2010, s 1088* (see **29.25** DISTRIBUTIONS) within five years after the making of the exempt distribution. (In this case all necessary adjustments for tax purposes may be made within the three years after the making of the chargeable payment.)

For the purposes of the '75% subsidiary' test in **29.23** DISTRIBUTIONS, a company is not treated as owning any share capital in a company if a profit on sale of the shares would be treated as a trading receipt, by the company itself if it owns them directly or, if it owns them indirectly, by the company which owns them directly.

[*CTA 2009, ss 787, 788*].

Merger carried out for bona fide commercial reasons

[42.21] The provisions in **42.16–42.20** above do not apply where the transferee company leaves the group as part of a 'merger' carried out for *bona fide* commercial reasons and not having avoidance of liability to tax as a main purpose. '*Merger*' is specially defined for this purpose in *CTA 2009, ss 789(2)–(6), 790*.

[*CTA 2009, ss 789, 790*].

Application of relief on reinvestment in relation to degrouping charge

[42.22] The provisions described at **42.11** above apply with the following modifications where, under **42.16** or **42.19** above, the transferee company is treated as having realised (and immediately reacquired) an asset immediately after the transfer by the transferor company.

(a) The requirement for the old asset to be a chargeable intangible asset applies in relation to the transferor company.

(b) The period within which expenditure on the other assets must be incurred applies by reference to the date the transferee company ceased to be a group member (in **42.16** above) or ceased to satisfy the requisite condition (in **42.19** above) rather than the date of realisation of the asset.
(c) References to the proceeds of realisation of the old asset are read as referring to the amount (market value) for which the transferee is treated as having realised it.

Any reduction of the deemed realisation proceeds as a result of a claim to reinvestment relief does not, however, affect the deemed cost of reacquisition by the transferee company.

[*CTA 2009, s 791*].

Reallocation of degrouping charge within group

[42.23] Where, by virtue of the provisions in **42.16** or **42.19** above, a realisation gain giving rise to a charge under **42.10** above accrues to a company ('company X'), the gain (or any part of it) may be treated as accruing to any other company ('company Y') which, at the 'relevant time', is a member of the 'relevant group', if both companies jointly so elect, provided that, at the 'relevant time', company Y:

(a) is UK-resident; or
(b) (where (a) above does not apply) carries on a UK trade through a UK permanent establishment (see **64.6** RESIDENCE) in respect of the profits or gains of which it is not exempt from corporation tax under double tax arrangements;
(c) (where (a) and (b) above do not apply) carries on a trade of dealing in or developing UK land of which the profits are not exempt from corporation tax under double tax arrangements; or
(d) (where (a)–(c) above do not apply) with effect from 6 April 2020 (subject to the transitional provisions at **64.7** RESIDENCE), carries on a UK property business the income of which is not exempt from corporation tax under double tax arrangements.

An election may not be made if Y is either an incorporated friendly society within *FA 2012, s 172* or a dual-resident investing company within *CTA 2010, s 109* (see **35.23** GROUP RELIEF).

The gain (or part) is then treated as a non-trading credit (see **42.9** above) accruing to company Y at the 'relevant time' (and as so accruing in respect of an asset held for the purposes of the appropriate UK activity within (b)–(d) above where it is not UK-resident).

The '*relevant time*' is immediately before company X ceased to be a group member (in **42.16** above) or ceased to satisfy the requisite condition (in **42.19** above), and the '*relevant group*' is the group of which it ceased to be a member (in **42.16** above) or the second group (in **42.19** above).

The election must be made by written notice to HMRC within two years after the end of the accounting period (of company X) in which the relevant time falls.

Where such an election has been made, company Y may claim relief on reinvestment (see **42.11** above) as if the deemed realisation had been made by company Y and not company X, the conditions as regards the old asset being treated as met if they would have been had there been no election and had the claim had been made by company X. The proceeds of realisation and the cost of the old asset are similarly what they would have been on a claim by company X. Where the election relates to only part of the gain on the deemed realisation, relief may be claimed as if a corresponding part of the asset had been the subject a separate deemed realisation, with any necessary apportionments being made accordingly.

[*CTA 2009, ss 792–794; FA 2019, Sch 5 paras 23–25, 35*].

Recovery of degrouping charge from another group company or controlling director

[42.24] Where a degrouping charge falls to be brought into account on a company for an accounting period under **42.16** or **42.19** above, or following an election under **42.23** above, and corporation tax assessed on the company for that period remains unpaid six months after the due date, provision is made for recovery from the following persons of the amount referable to the degrouping charge (or the outstanding tax if less).

(a) If the defaulting company was a member of a group at the 'relevant time', a company which was at that time the principal company of the group and any other company which at any time in the period of twelve months ending with the 'relevant time' was a member of that group and owned the asset or part of it in respect of which the degrouping charge arose (or any part of it).

(b) If at the 'relevant time' the defaulting company is non-UK resident (but, with effect before 6 April 2020, carries on a UK trade through a permanent establishment (see **64.6** RESIDENCE)), any person who is, or during the period of twelve months ending with the 'relevant time' was, a 'director' (as widely defined) having 'control' (within *CTA 2010, ss 450, 451*) of the defaulting company or of a company that has, or within that period had, control of the defaulting company.

Somewhat wider definitions of 'group' and 'principal company' apply for these purposes (by reference to 51% subsidiaries rather than 75% subsidiaries). The '*relevant time*' is when the defaulting company ceased to be a group member (in **42.16** above) or ceased to satisfy the requisite condition (in **42.19** above), or whichever of those times would have applied had there been no election (in **42.23** above).

An HMRC notice requiring payment from another person as above (within 30 days from the date of the notice) has effect (as regards recovery, interest and appeals) as if it were a notice of assessment. It must be served within three years after the date of final determination (for which see *CTA 2009, s 798*) of the corporation tax liability of the defaulting company for the accounting period for which the degrouping charge fell to be brought into account. The company paying the tax may recover it from the defaulting company, but the payment is not an allowable deduction for tax purposes.

[*CTA 2009, ss 795–798; FA 2019, Sch 5 paras 26, 35*].

Intra-group payments in respect of reliefs

[42.25] A payment either for group rollover relief (see **42.14**, **42.15** above) or for the reallocation of a degrouping charge (see **42.23** above) is not taken into account for corporation tax purposes as regards the payer or the payee provided that it does not exceed the amount of the relief.

A payment for group rollover relief means a payment made in connection with a claim for relief under **42.11** above by virtue of the provisions in **42.14** or **42.15** above, by the company whose proceeds of realisation are reduced as a result of that claim, to a company whose acquisition costs are thereby reduced (in **42.14** above), or the tax written-down value of whose assets is thereby reduced (in **42.15** above), under an agreement between the companies. The amount of the relief in such a case is the amount of the reduction as a result of the claim in the acquisition costs, or the tax written-down value of the assets, as the case may be, of the company to which the payment is made.

A payment for the reallocation of a degrouping charge means a payment made in connection with an election under the provisions in **42.23** above, by the company to which the chargeable realisation gain accrues to the company to which, as a result of the election, the whole or part of that gain is treated as accruing, under an agreement between the companies. The amount of the relief in such a case is the amount treated as a result of the election as accruing to the company to which the payment is made.

[*CTA 2009, s 799*].

Transfer of business or trade

Company reconstruction involving transfer of business

[42.26] Where a scheme for the reconstruction of any company or companies within *TCGA 1992, s 136*:

(a) involves the transfer of the whole or part of the business of one company to another, and
(b) the transferor company receives no part of the consideration for the transfer (otherwise than by the transferee company taking over liabilities of the business),

the following provisions apply. This is, however, conditional on the reconstruction being effected for genuine commercial reasons and not as part of a scheme or arrangements a main purpose of which is avoidance of liability to income tax, corporation tax or capital gains tax (although advance clearance may be obtained that this condition is met, see **42.30** below).

If:

(i) the assets transferred include intangible fixed assets which are chargeable intangible assets (see **42.11** above) in relation to the transferor company immediately before the transfer, and

(ii) in relation to the transferee company immediately thereafter,

the transfer of those assets is treated for the purposes of the current provisions as tax-neutral (see **42.11** above). This does not, however, apply where the transfer is within a group or either company is an incorporated friendly society within *FA 2012, s 172* or a dual-resident investing company within *CTA 2010, s 109* (see **35.23** GROUP RELIEF).

See **42.13** above for the interaction between these provisions and those dealing with transfers within a group.

[*CTA 2009, s 818*].

Companies resident in different EU member states

[42.27] Special provisions apply where a '*relevant company*' (i.e. a body incorporated under the law of a relevant state) resident in one relevant state transfers the whole or part of a business carried on in the UK to a relevant company resident in another relevant state in exchange for securities (including shares) in the latter company, and both companies make a claim. A '*relevant state*' is an EU member state or, after the end of the Brexit implementation period (11pm on 31 December 2020), the UK or an EU member state.

The provisions also apply where a relevant company transfers part of a business to one or more relevant companies and the following conditions apply. Where the business transferred is carried on in the UK, at least one transferee must be resident in a member state other than that in which the transferor is resident, and the transferor must remain in business after the transfer. A claim must be made by all parties and either the transfer must be made in exchange for an issue of shares or debentures of the transferees to the holders of shares and debentures in the transferor, or the only reason that this is not done is a legal prohibition on purchase of own shares.

The application of the provisions is, however, conditional on the reconstruction or amalgamation being effected for genuine commercial reasons and not as part of a scheme or arrangements a main purpose of which is avoidance of liability to income tax, corporation tax or capital gains tax (although advance clearance may be obtained that this condition is met, see **42.30** below).

A company is regarded for these purposes as '*resident in a relevant state*' under the laws of which it is chargeable to tax because it is regarded as so resident (unless it is regarded under double tax arrangements entered into by the relevant state as resident in a territory not within any of the relevant states).

Where such a claim is made, if the transfer includes intangible fixed assets which are chargeable intangible assets (see **42.11** above) in relation to the transferor company immediately before the transfer and in relation to the transferee company immediately thereafter, the transfer of those assets is treated for the purposes of the current provisions as tax-neutral (see **42.11** above).

These provisions do not apply if the transferor is a 'transparent entity'. [*CTA 2009, ss 819, 820, Sch 2 para 102; SI 2019 No 689, Regs 1, 16(17)(18); European Union (Withdrawal Agreement) Act 2020, Sch 5 para 1(1)*].

Transparent entities

Special provisions apply where one of the parties is a 'transparent entity'. [*TIOPA 2010, ss 120, 121*].

A '*transparent entity*' for this purpose is an entity which is resident in a relevant state other than the UK and does not have an ordinary share capital. [*CTA 2009, 820(4); SI 2019 No 689, Reg 16(18)*].

European cross-border mergers

[42.28] The following provisions were originally introduced to facilitate the tax-neutral formation of SEs (see **32.6** EUROPEAN UNION LEGISLATION) by merger, but have since been extended to apply also to the formation of European co-operative societies (SCEs) by merger and other mergers of companies resident in different EU member states. Accordingly, the provisions apply to:

(a) (before Brexit IP completion day (11pm on 31 December 2020)) the formation of an SE by the merger of two or more companies in accordance with *Council Regulation (EC) No 2157/2001, Arts 2(1), 17(2)*;

(b) (before Brexit IP completion day) the formation of an SCE by the merger of two or more 'co-operative societies', at least one of which is a society registered under *Co-operative and Community Benefit Societies Act 2014*, in accordance with *Council Regulation (EC) No 1435/2003*;

(c) a merger effected by the transfer by one or more companies or co-operative societies of all their assets and liabilities to a single existing company or co-operative society; and

(d) a merger effected by the transfer by two or more companies of all their assets to a single new company (which is not an SE or SCE) in exchange for the issue by the transferee company of shares or debentures to each person holding shares in or debentures of a transferee company.

From Brexit IP completion day, no new SEs or SCEs can be formed in the UK.

Each merging company must be resident in a relevant state, and not all in the same relevant state. A '*relevant state*' is an EU member state or, after the end of the Brexit implementation period (expected to be 31 December 2020), the UK or an EU member state. In the cases of (a), (b) and (c) above either the transfer taking place as part of the merger is in exchange for the issue of shares or debentures by the transferee to each person holding shares in or debentures of a transferor or the only reason this condition is not fulfilled is that purchase of own shares is prohibited by law. In the cases of (c) and (d) it is required that, in the course of the merger, each transferor ceases to exist without being put into liquidation. Where the requisite conditions are fulfilled, the transfer of qualifying assets in the course of a merger is tax-neutral.

For the purposes of (b) and (c) above, a '*co-operative society*' is a society registered under *Co-operative and Community Benefit Societies Act 2014* or a similar society established under the law of a member state other than the UK.

A company is resident in a relevant state for this purpose if it is within a charge to tax under the law of the state as being resident for that purpose and it is not regarded, for the purposes of any DOUBLE TAX RELIEF (30) arrangements to which the state is a party, as resident in a territory not within a relevant state.

The assets must be chargeable intangible assets (see **42.11** above) both in the hands of the transferor immediately before the transfer and in the hands of the transferee immediately afterwards.

These provisions do not apply unless the merger is for genuine commercial reasons and is not part of a scheme or arrangements of which the main purpose or one of the main purposes is avoiding liability to tax. Advance clearance can be obtained that this condition is met (see **42.30** below).

These provisions do not apply if one or more of the parties is a transparent entity and the assets and liabilities of a transparent entity are transferred to another company as a result of the merger.

Transfer of non-UK trade.

(A) Where:
   - (i) in the course of the merger a company or co-operative society resident in the UK (company A) transfers to a company or co-operative society resident in another relevant state all the assets and liabilities relating to a business carried on by company A in a relevant state other than the UK through a permanent establishment; and
   - (ii) the transfer includes intangible fixed assets:
     - (I) which are chargeable intangible assets (see **42.11** above) in relation to the company A immediately before the transfer; and
     - (II) in the case of one or more of which the proceeds of realisation exceed the cost recognised for tax purposes; or

(B) where a UK resident company transfers part of a business (carried on in a relevant state other than the UK through a permanent establishment immediately before the transfer) to one or more companies and at least one transferee is resident in a relevant state other than the UK, the transferor continues to carry on a business after the merger; and

(C) no claim is made under the provisions at **42.29** below in relation to those assets; and

(D) where the merger is within (b) or (c) above, or is within (a) above, the transfer of assets and liabilities is made in exchange for the issue of shares in or debentures of the transferee to the holders of shares in or debentures of a transferor, except where, and to the extent that, the transferee is prevented from meeting this requirement by reason only of *Companies Act 2006, s 658* (rule against limited company acquiring its own shares) or a corresponding provision in another relevant state,

then, if tax would have been chargeable under the law of the other relevant state in respect of the transfer of those assets but for the Mergers Directive (*2009/133/EC*), double tax relief (whether unilateral or by agreement) is available as if the amount of tax which would have been so payable but for the Directive were payable.

These provisions do not apply unless the merger is for genuine commercial reasons and is not part of a scheme or arrangements of which the main purpose or one of the main purposes is avoiding liability to tax. Advance clearance can be obtained that this condition is met (see **42.30** below).

[*CTA 2009, ss 821–825; SI 2019 No 689, Regs 1, 16(19)(20); European Union (Withdrawal Agreement) Act 2020, Sch 5 para 1(1)*].

Transparent entities. Special provisions apply where one of the parties is a 'transparent entity'. See *TIOPA 2010 ss 120, 121*.

A '*transparent entity*' for this purpose is an entity which is resident in a member state other than the UK and is listed as a company in the Annex to the Mergers Directive, but which does not have an ordinary share capital and, if resident in the UK, would not be capable of being registered as a company under *Companies Act 2006*. [*CTA 2009, ss 819, 820; SI 2019 No 689, Regs 1, 16(17)(18)*].

Claims to postpone charge on transfer of assets to non-resident company

[42.29] Special provisions apply where a UK-resident company carrying on a non-UK trade through a permanent establishment (see **64.6** RESIDENCE) transfers the whole or part of that trade together with its assets, or its assets other than cash, to a non-UK resident company in exchange, wholly or partly, for shares (or shares and loan stock) in that company, so that thereafter it holds one-quarter or more of the transferee company's ordinary share capital. This is, however, conditional on the transfer being effected for genuine commercial reasons and not as part of a scheme or arrangements a main purpose of which is avoidance of liability to income tax, corporation tax or capital gains tax (although advance clearance may be obtained that this condition is met, see **42.30** below). For this purpose, transfers within a group are ignored.

If such a transfer includes intangible fixed assets which are chargeable intangible assets (see **42.11** above) in relation to the transferor company immediately before the transfer ('*relevant assets*'), that company may claim as follows.

(a) If the proceeds of realisation of a relevant asset exceed the cost recognised for tax purposes, they are treated as reduced by the excess or, if the securities are not the whole of the consideration for the transfer, by a proportion of the excess corresponding to the proportion that the market value of the securities at the time of the transfer bears to the market value of the whole of the consideration at that time.

(b) If at any time after the transfer the transferor company realises the whole of the securities held by it immediately before that time, it must bring into account for tax purposes a credit equal to the aggregate of the amounts by which proceeds of realisation were reduced under (a) above (so far as not already recovered under this provision or (c) below). If it realises part only of the securities, this applies to a proportion of that aggregate corresponding to the proportion that the market value of the part of the securities disposed of bears to the market value of the securities held immediately before the disposal. Disposals within *TCGA 1992, s 171* (no gain, no loss disposals, see **12.6** CAPITAL GAINS — GROUPS) are disregarded for this purpose, but the first subsequent disposal of the securities not so disregarded is then treated as a disposal by the transferor company.

(c) If at any time within six years after the transfer the transferee company realises all of the relevant assets held by it immediately before that time, the transferor company must bring into account for tax purposes a credit equal to the aggregate of the amounts by which proceeds of realisation were reduced under (a) above (so far as not already recovered under (b) above or under this provision). If only part of the relevant assets so held is disposed of at that time, the credit is reduced to the proportion applicable to the relevant assets disposed of. Intra-group disposals are disregarded for this purpose, but the first subsequent disposal of the relevant assets not so disregarded is then treated as a disposal by the transferee company.

[*CTA 2009, ss 827–830*].

Clearance

[42.30] Application may be made for clearance that the transactions in **42.26** above (reconstruction, transfer or merger) are genuine commercial transactions and not for tax avoidance purposes. The condition is treated as satisfied if, prior to the transaction taking place, the company has applied to HMRC and received clearance. The applicant must be, in the case of transactions within **42.25** or **42.26** above, the transferee, and within **42.27** and **42.28**, the transferor. The provisions are similar to those in *TCGA 1992, s 138* (see **11.16** CAPITAL GAINS and Tolley's Capital Gains Tax under Anti-Avoidance). [*CTA 2009, ss 832, 833, 841*].

A clearance application must be made in writing and details of the transactions must be given. HMRC may request further information by notice issued within 30 days of receipt of the application or of receiving information previously requested. If the company does not provide information within 30 days, HMRC need not proceed with the application.

HMRC must give their decision within 30 days of receiving the application or 30 days of receiving information requested in a notice. The applicant has a right of appeal to the tribunal if clearance is refused or HMRC do not meet the 30 day time limit. The tribunal's decision on clearance is treated as a decision by HMRC under these provisions. Where the information provided by the applicant is not full and accurate, and clearance is granted, it is void.

Applications for clearance should be addressed to BAI Clearance, HMRC, BX9 1JL (or, if market-sensitive information is included, to the Team Leader at that address). Applications may be emailed to reconstructions@hmrc.gsi.gov.uk. Application may be made in a single letter to the same address for other clearances. [*CTA 2009, ss 831–833*].

Transfer of business of building society to company

[42.31] Provisions equivalent to those relating to capital gains in *TCGA 1992, s 216* (see **8.3** BUILDING SOCIETIES) apply in relation to the current provisions to treat the transfer of chargeable intangible assets as tax-neutral (see **42.11** above). [*CAA 2009, ss 824, 825*].

Amalgamation of, or transfer of engagements by, certain societies and associations

[42.32] Provisions equivalent to those relating to capital gains in *TCGA 1992, s 215* (see **8.2** BUILDING SOCIETIES) and *CTA 2010, s 1057* (see **22.4**, **22.5** CO-OPERATIVE AND COMMUNITY BENEFIT SOCIETIES) apply in relation to the current provisions to treat the transfer of chargeable intangible assets as tax-neutral (see **42.11** above) on the amalgamation of, or transfer of engagements by, building societies, co-operative and community benefit societies and co-operative associations. [*CAA 2009, s 826*].

Transactions between related parties

[42.33] The rules described at **42.35–42.39** below deal with transactions involving 'related parties'. For the definition of 'related party', see **42.34** below.

Meaning of 'related party'

[42.34] A person ('B') is a '*related party*' in relation to a company ('A') in the following circumstances:

(a) B is a company, and either A controls or has a major interest in B or *vice versa*;
(b) B is a company and B and A are both under the control of the same person (other than the Crown or certain governmental or international institutions);
(c) A is a close company (see **16** CLOSE COMPANIES) and B is a 'participator' (or an 'associate' of a 'participator') in A or a 'participator' in a company that controls, or has a major interest in, C ('*Associate*' and '*participator*' are as defined at **16.7**, **16.9** CLOSE COMPANIES) except that for these purposes 'participator' excludes certain loan creditors.);
(d) B is a company and A is another company in the same group (see **42.12** above).

For determining whether a party is related to a company, where they would be related under the above rules but for one party (other than an individual) being the subject of 'insolvency arrangements' or equivalent, they are treated as related for the purposes of debits and credits to be brought into account.

For these purposes:

(i) '*control*' in relation to a company is the power of a person to secure that the company's affairs are conducted in accordance with their wishes, either through shareholding or voting power (in or in relation to any company) or through powers conferred by the articles of association or other regulatory document of any company;
(ii) a person has a '*major interest*' in a company if it and any other person together control the company, with each of them having at least 40% of the rights and powers by means of which they have such control;
(iii) insolvency arrangements include arrangements under which a liquidator, provisional liquidator, receiver, administrator or administrative receiver of a company or partnership act.

'*Connected persons*' are specially defined in *CTA 2009, ss 842–843*, broadly as under *CTA 2010, ss 1122, 1123* (see **19** CONNECTED PERSONS) but with the omission of the 'partners' and 'persons acting together' provisions at **19.2**.

The rights and powers of a partner are ignored unless the partner has control of or a major interest in the firm. 'Control' is determined as for a company (see (i) above). Rights and powers held, or to be held, jointly are taken into account.

[*CTA 2009, ss 835–841*].

Transfer between company and related party

[42.35] Where an intangible asset is transferred by a company to a related party (see below) or *vice versa* and the asset is a chargeable intangible asset (see **42.11** above) in relation to the transferor immediately before the transfer or in relation to the transferee immediately thereafter, the transfer of those assets is treated for all tax purposes, as regards both transferor and transferee, as being at market value, *except* in any of the following circumstances.

(a) The transfer pricing provisions of *TIOPA 2010, Pt 4* (see **72** TRANSFER PRICING) apply (whether or not the consideration for the transfer falls to be adjusted under that part). Where, however, the market value of the asset (as determined under *CTA 2009, s 845(5)*) is greater than the value determined under the transfer pricing rules, then the price at which the asset is deemed to be transferred is increased by the amount of the difference (effectively reinstating the market value where this is greater than the transfer pricing amount).
The consideration falls within the transfer pricing provisions without falling to be adjusted in a case where the conditions in *TIOPA 2010, s 148(2)* are met (see **72.2**(a)(b) TRANSFER PRICING) but the actual and arm's length provisions do not differ.

(b) The transfer is tax-neutral under any other provisions in the intangible assets regime (see **42.11** above).

(c) An asset is transferred from the company to a related party at less than market value or to the company by the related party at more than its market value and:
  - the related party is not a company, or is a company in relation to which the asset is not an intangible asset falling within these provisions; and
  - the transfer results in an amount being taken into account (or to an amount which would be taken into account but for the market value rule) in computing any person's taxable income, profits or losses by virtue of *CTA 2010, Pt 23 Ch 2* on distributions (see **29** DISTRIBUTIONS) or *ITEPA 2003, Pt 3* (see Tolley's Income Tax under Employment Income). In this case, the market value rule above does not apply for the purposes of those provisions.

(d) The asset is transferred to the company by a related party who makes a claim for hold-over relief on gifts for business assets under *TCGA 1992, s 165* (see Tolley's Capital Gains Tax under Hold-Over Reliefs). In this case, the transfer is treated as being at market value less the amount of the held-over gain and any necessary adjustments may be made to the company's tax position as a result of the claim.

(e) The asset is held for the purposes of an exempt foreign permanent establishment (see **31.15** DOUBLE TAX RELIEF).
(f) The asset is transferred (before 1 April 2018) under the disincorporation relief rules (see **42.40** below).
(g) The asset is a restricted asset to which the restrictions at **42.7** above apply.

For the meaning of 'related party' see **42.34** above. A person is also a related party for these purposes in relation to a 'company' if the participation condition (see **72.2** transfer pricing) is met between them. For the purpose of determining the profits to be allocated to a corporate partner, a '*company*' includes a partnership. Where a gain on the disposal of an intangible asset by a partnership is to be taken into account for the purpose of determining the amount of profits to be allocated to a corporate partner and for that purpose the reference to a company in the above provisions is to be read as a reference to a partnership, the gain is treated as a chargeable realisation gain (see **42.10** above) and the market value rule applies accordingly.

As regards (c) above, an example was given by the Explanatory Notes to the Finance (No 3) Bill 2005 of a controlling shareholder transferring an intangible asset to the company for £10,000 when the asset is worth only £1,000 where the market value rule does not prevent the shareholder from being taxed on a distribution representing the consideration received for the asset in excess of its value.

[*CTA 2009, ss 844–849A; FA 2020, s 31(3)*].

Grant of licence or other right to related party

[42.36] Where a company grants, on or after 22 November 2017, a licence or other right in respect of an intangible asset to a related party (see below) or a company is granted a licence or other right over an intangible asset held by a related party, then:

- if the grant is at less than market value, it is treated for all tax purposes of the grantor as being at market value (i.e. the price the licence or right might reasonably be expected to fetch on a sale on the open market); or
- if the grant is at more than market value, it is treated for all tax purposes of the grantee as being at market value.

This rule applies only if either the asset is a 'chargeable intangible asset' (see **42.11** above) of the grantor immediately before the grant or it is a chargeable intangible asset of the grantee immediately after the grant. It does not apply where the grant is made pursuant to an obligation, under a contract, that was unconditional before 22 November 2017 (i.e. the obligation could not be varied or extinguished by the exercise of a right, whether under the contract or otherwise).

For the meaning of 'related party' see **42.34** above. For the purposes of these provisions, a person is also a related party for these purposes in relation to a 'company' if the participation condition (see **72.2** TRANSFER PRICING) is met between them. For the purpose of determining the profits to be allocated to a corporate partner, a '*company*' includes a partnership. Where a gain on the grant of a licence or other right by a partnership is to be taken into account for the purpose of determining the amount of profits to be allocated to a corporate partner and for that purpose the reference to a company in the above provisions is to be read as a reference to a partnership, the gain is treated as a chargeable realisation gain (see **42.10** above) and the market value rule applies accordingly.

Where the consideration for a grant would otherwise fall to be adjusted in the hands of one of the parties both under these provisions and under the TRANSFER PRICING (**72**) provisions, only the transfer pricing adjustment applies unless the adjustment under these provisions is greater (in which case the adjustment is made under these provisions and no adjustment is made under the transfer pricing rules).

Where the above provisions apply in circumstances where the grant is either by the company at less than market value or to the company at more than market value and the related party is not a company, the market value rule under these provisions does not apply for the purposes of calculating any person's income, profits or losses under *CTA 2010, Pt 23 Ch 2* (DISTRIBUTIONS (**29**)), except *CTA 2010, s 1000(2)* (expenses of close company treated as distribution — see **29.13**) or under *ITEPA 2003, Pt 3* (employment income). This rule applies also where the related party is a company but the licence or right is not a chargeable intangible asset in its hands either immediately before or after the grant (as the case may be).

The above provisions are also subject to those at **42.7**(C) above where the asset is a restricted asset.

[*CTA 2009, ss 849AB–849AD; FA 2018, s 21; FA 2020, s 31(4)*].

Reinvestment relief in case of part realisation involving related party

[42.37] Reinvestment relief (see **42.11** above) does not apply in relation to the part realisation of an intangible fixed asset by a company if, as a result of or in connection with the part realisation, a related party acquires an interest of any description in the asset or in another asset deriving all or part of its value from that asset.

[*CTA 2009, s 850*].

Delayed payment of royalty to related party

[42.38] Where a royalty (see **42.4** above) payable by a company to or for the benefit of a related party is not paid in full by twelve months after the end of the period of account in which a debit in respect of it is recognised by the company for accounting purposes (see **42.5** above), and credits representing the full amount of the royalty are not brought into account under the current provisions (see **42.8** above) in any accounting period by the person to whom it is payable, the royalty is brought into account under the current provisions only when it is paid.

[*CTA 2009, s 851*].

Goodwill etc. acquired from a related party individual

[42.39] Anti-avoidance provisions apply with regard to certain assets acquired directly or indirectly from related parties (see **42.34** above), on or after 3 December 2014 and **before 8 July 2015** (unless the acquisition took place under a contract which had become unconditional before that date). These provisions are repealed with regard to acquisitions on or after 8 July 2015. From this date the restrictions described at **42.6** above, with regard to goodwill and goodwill-related assets apply instead.

Subject to the above, where a company directly or indirectly acquires goodwill and/or certain other intangible assets (together referred to as relevant assets) from an individual who is related to the company, or from a partnership where any individual partner is related to the company, the company is not permitted to obtain relief for any debits arising in respect of the writing down of such relevant assets.

The other assets referred to above are:

(i) an intangible fixed asset that consists of information which relates to customers or potential customers of the business, or part of the business, carried on by the transferor;

(ii) an intangible fixed asset that consists of a relationship (whether contractual or not) that the transferor has with one or more customers of a business, or part of a business, carried on by the transferor;

(iii) an unregistered trademark or other sign used in the course of a business, or part of a business, carried on by the transferor; and

(iv) a licence or other right in respect of: an asset which is the goodwill for all or part of the business that is transferred; or, an asset falling within (i)–(iii) above.

[*CTA 2009, ss 849B, 849D; FA 2015, s 26*].

These provisions applied to accounting periods beginning on or after 3 December 2014, with straddle periods being treated as two separate accounting periods. The restriction applied to assets that are acquired by a company on or after 3 December 2014, unless the acquisition took place under the contract which had become unconditional before that date. For acquisitions that took place before 24 March 2015 the restriction only applied to acquisitions that took place directly (as opposed to indirectly). The restriction does not apply to an indirect acquisition that took place under a contract which had become unconditional before 24 March 2015.

[*FA 2015, s 26(6)*]

However, a company is permitted to obtain relief as a non-trading debit for any realisation debit that it realises on a subsequent disposal of such relevant assets. [*CTA 2009 s 849D*]. See **42.10** above for a discussion of realisations of IFA assets.

Where some of the goodwill or other assets that the company acquired had in turn been acquired by the transferor from an unrelated third party (acquired third-party assets), then the company is permitted to obtain tax relief for some of the debits that it recognises in its accounts in respect of the amortisation of the acquired third-party assets. To be a third-party acquisition:

- where the transferor acquires the asset from a company then at the time of the acquisition: if the transferor is an individual they should not be a related party to that company; if the transferor is a partnership, no individual who is a partner should be a related party to that company;
- where the transferor acquired the asset from a person who is not a company, then at the time of the acquisition: if the transferor is an individual they should not be connected with that person; if the transferor is a partnership, then no individual who is a partner should be connected with that person.

There is an exception, in that this relaxation with regard to acquired third-party assets does not apply where the main purpose, or one of the main purposes, of the acquisition is for any person to obtain a tax advantage within the meaning of *CTA 2010, s 1139*.

[*CTA 2009, s 849B(9)*].

The proportion of the amortisation debits for which the company is permitted to claim relief is determined by reference to: the accounting value of such acquired third-party assets immediately before they were acquired by the company (determined on the assumption that the transferor had drawn up GAAP-compliant accounts immediately before the acquired third-party assets were acquired by the company); divided by the total expenditure incurred by the company in connection with the acquisition of the relevant assets that it capitalised in its accounts or that were otherwise recognised in determining the company's profit and loss without being capitalised.

Where the company disposes of some or all of the acquired third-party assets and a realisation debit arises the same methodology is applied to determine the proportion of the realisation debit that is to be treated as a trading debit, with the balance being treated as non-trading debit.

As noted above, these provisions have been repealed in relation to acquisitions on or after 8 July 2015.

[*CTA 2009, ss 816A(7), 849B(4),(5),(7), 849C; FA 2015, s 26; F(No 2)A 2015, s 33*].

Supplementary provisions

Research and development

[42.40] Where a deduction is allowed for revenue expenditure on research and development (see 63 RESEARCH AND DEVELOPMENT EXPENDITURE), which is brought into account in determining the value of an intangible asset, no deduction for tax purposes will be allowed in respect of the writing down of so much of the value of the intangible asset as is attributable to that expenditure.

[*CTA 2009, s 1308(4)(5)*].

Treatment of grants etc.

Where a grant or other payment is intended by the payer to meet, directly or indirectly, a company's expenditure on an intangible fixed asset, any gain recognised in determining the company's profit or loss in respect of the grant etc. is treated as representing a receipt in respect of the asset (and hence as within **42.8** above). This does not, however, apply to grants under *Industrial Development Act 1982, Pt 2* or corresponding NI grants, any profit and loss account gain in respect of which is disregarded for the purposes of the current provisions. Where the bringing of such an exempt grant into account by a company results in a reduction in the amount of a loss recognised in determining the profit or loss, or in the amount of expenditure on an intangible fixed asset capitalised for accounting purposes, the amount of the reduction is added back for the purposes of the current provisions.

[*CTA 2009, ss 852, 853*].

Finance leasing etc.

The Treasury has wide regulatory powers to make provision for the application of the current provisions in relation to a company which is a finance lessor of an intangible asset which is the subject of a finance lease. The term 'finance lease' has the meaning for this purpose that it has for accounting purposes, including hire-purchase, conditional sale and other like arrangements, and 'finance lessor' and 'finance lessee' have a corresponding meaning.

[*CTA 2009, ss 854, 855*]. For the initial regulations under this provision, see *SI 2002 No 1967*.

Assets acquired or realised together

Assets acquired of or disposed of in a single bargain are treated as acquired or disposed of together, notwithstanding any separate pricing or separate acquisitions or disposals. Where assets are acquired together, values allocated in accordance with generally accepted accounting practice (see **42.2** above) to particular assets are accepted for the purposes of the current provisions, and in the absence of such allocation a just and reasonable apportionment is made. Where assets are disposed of together, a just and reasonable apportionment of the disposal proceeds is made.

[*CAA 2009, s 856*].

Deemed market value acquisition — adjustment of amounts in case of nil accounting value.

Where a company is treated under the current provisions as acquiring an asset at market value, but the accounting value of the asset transferred, in the hands of the transferee, is nil, then:

- the cost of the asset recognised for accounting purposes;
- the accounting value of the asset; and
- the amount of any loss recognised for accounting purposes in respect of capitalised expenditure on the asset,

are all taken to be such as would have been recognised had the asset been acquired at market value. Any revaluation of the asset (see **42.8** above) is disregarded.

[*CTA 2009, s 857*].

Fungible assets

Assets of a nature to be dealt in without identifying the particular assets involved, and which are of the same kind and held by the same person in the same capacity (*'fungible assets'*), are treated for the purposes of the current provisions as indistinguishable parts of a single asset which grows or diminishes as assets of the same kind are added or realised.

[*CTA 2009, s 900J; FA 2020, s 31(5)(13)*].

Note that the legislation for this rule was previously at *CTA 2009, s 858*.

See also **42.42** below for transitional rules which apply where a company has fungible assets which are pre-*FA 2002* assets and/or restricted assets.

Assets ceasing to be chargeable intangible assets

Where an asset ceases to be a chargeable intangible asset in relation to a company (see **42.11** above) either:

(a) on the company's ceasing to be UK-resident; or
(b) on the asset beginning to be held for the purposes of a mutual trade or business; or
(c) (in the case of a non-UK resident company) in any circumstances not involving the realisation of the asset by the company,

the current provisions have effect as if the company had, immediately before the triggering event, realised and immediately reacquired the asset at its market value at that time. An election may be made for a gain arising before 1 January 2020 by virtue of (a) above to be postponed in certain cases where the asset concerned is held for the purposes of a non-UK trade carried on through a permanent establishment (see **64.6** RESIDENCE).

[*CTA 2009, ss 859–862; FA 2019, Sch 8 para 10*].

See **58.19** PAYMENT OF TAX for exit charge payment plans under which a company may pay corporation tax under (a) or (c) above by instalments or defer payment.

Asset becoming chargeable intangible asset

Where an asset becomes a chargeable intangible asset in relation to a company (see **42.11** above) either:

(i) on the company's becoming UK-resident; or
(ii) on the asset ceasing to be held for the purposes of a mutual trade or business; or
(iii) (in the case of a non-UK resident company) on its beginning to be held for the purposes of a trade carried on in the UK through a permanent establishment (see **64.6** RESIDENCE) or a trade of dealing in or developing UK land or (broadly with effect from 6 April 2020) for the purposes of a UK property business or enabling the company to generate other UK income,

the current provisions have effect as if the company had, immediately after the triggering event, acquired the asset at its book value at that time.

[*CTA 2009, s 863; FA 2019, Sch 5 paras 27, 35*].

Asset subject to EU exit charge

The following applies where an asset becomes a chargeable intangible asset of a company on or after 1 January 2020 because either the company becomes resident in the UK or the asset begins to be held for the purposes of a trade carried on by the company in the UK through a permanent establishment. If, at the time the asset becomes a chargeable intangible asset, it is also subject to an 'EU exit charge', it is treated for the purposes of the current provisions as if the company had acquired it for its market value at that time.

For this purpose, an asset is a chargeable asset of a company if its disposal would give rise to a UK chargeable gain or allowable loss. An '*EU exit charge*' is a charge to tax under the law of a member state in accordance with the EU Anti Tax Avoidance Directive (Directive (EU) 2016/1194, Art 5(1)).

[*CTA 2009, s 863A; FA 2019, Sch 8 para 12*].

This provision relieves any potential double taxation at the time of the disposal of the asset by exempting from UK tax any gain or loss arising before the asset came within the scope of UK tax on chargeable gains.

Tax avoidance

Arrangements (as widely defined) a main object of which are to enable a company to obtain a debit (or a greater debit) under **42.5** above or to avoid (or reduce) a credit under **42.10** above are disregarded in determining such debits and credits.

[*CTA 2009, s 864*].

Expenditure not generally tax-deductible

No debit may be brought in under the current provisions (see **42.5** above) in respect of expenditure which would not be an allowable trade deduction under:

(a) *CTA 2009, s 1298* (business entertainment or gifts);
(b) *CTA 2009, s 1304* (crime-related expenditure);
(c) *CTA 2009, s 56* (hired cars); or
(d) *FA 2004, s 246(2)* (certain retirement benefits).

[*CTA 2009, s 865*].

Delayed payment of pension contributions

Where a company includes in its accounts a debit in respect of pension contributions, but they are not paid until after the end of the period in which the debit is recognised, the contributions are brought into account only when paid. Any necessary allocations must be made on a just and reasonable basis.

[*CTA 2009, s 868*].

Delayed payment of employees' remuneration

Where a debit in respect of employees' remuneration is recognised by a company for accounting purposes but the remuneration is not treated as received as employment income within nine months after the end of the period of account in which the debit is recognised, the remuneration is brought into account under the intangible assets provisions (see **42.5** above) only when it is paid.

This applies equally to '*potential remuneration*', i.e. amounts reserved in the employer's accounts with a view to it becoming remuneration, which is regarded as received when it becomes remuneration so treated as above. Any necessary apportionment for these purposes is made on a just and reasonable basis.

If a tax calculation has to be made before the nine months has expired and when remuneration (as above) has not been paid, it is to be assumed that it will not be paid before the end of the nine-month period. If it is subsequently paid before the end of that period, the calculation can be revised and the tax return amended accordingly. Remuneration is treated as paid when it is treated as received by the employee under *ITEPA 2003*, or would be so treated if it were not exempt income.

[*CTA 2009, ss 866, 867*].

Bad debts etc.

For the purposes of the current provisions, no debit may be brought into account in respect of a debt (monetary or otherwise) except by way of impairment loss or to the extent the debt is released as part of a statutory insolvency arrangement. Any gain brought into account for accounting purposes by the debtor in respect of a release as part of a statutory insolvency arrangement is disregarded. Otherwise, any gain relating to an unpaid debt in respect of an intangible fixed asset which is brought into account for accounting purposes by the debtor is treated as regards credits in respect of receipts recognised as they accrue (see **42.10** above) as a gain in respect of the asset. Any necessary apportionment for these purposes is made on a just and reasonable basis. [*CTA 2009, s 869*].

Disincorporation relief

FA 2013 introduced provisions, applicable to disincorporations with a transfer date on or after 1 April 2013 to 31 March 2018, to allow joint claims to be made by a company and its shareholders to allow qualifying business assets (being goodwill, or an interest in land and buildings used in the business) to be transferred at a reduced value so that no corporation tax will be payable on the transfer of the assets.

The reduced value for the purposes of post-*FA 2002* goodwill under *CTA 2009, s 849A* is:

- where the goodwill has been written down for tax purposes the lower of the tax written down value and its market value;

- where the goodwill is shown in the balance sheet but has not been written down, then the lower of the costs of the goodwill, and its market value; and
- where the asset is not shown in the balance sheet then the proceeds are treated as being nil.

For pre-*FA 2002* goodwill, taxable under the capital gains provisions, the transfer value is the lower of the allowable disposal costs (under *TCGA 1992, s 38*) and market value.

Claims are restricted to those businesses where the market value of the classes of assets allowed for disincorporation relief does not exceed £100,000. Joint claims must be made to HMRC within two years of the date of the transfer of the business assets. In addition to the market value cap the business transferred must be as a going concern, all of the assets of the business are transferred (or all other than cash), the shareholders to whom the business is transferred are individuals, and each of those shareholders held shares in the company for the twelve months ending on the date of the business transfer.

Shareholders to whom the assets are transferred will inherit the transfer value for the purpose of capital gains tax and the shareholders must use this transfer value in subsequent transactions.

[*CTA 2009, s 849A*].

Change of accounting policy

[42.41] Where there is a change in accounting policy in preparing a company's accounts from one period of account to the next in accordance with the law and practice applicable in relation to those periods, then if there is any accounting difference between the closing accounting value of the assets concerned in the earlier period and their opening value in the later period, a corresponding debit or credit (as the case may be) is to be taken into account for tax purposes in the later period. This applies in particular where a company prepares its accounts for one period in accordance with UK generally accepted accounting practice and for the next period in accordance with international accounting standards, or vice versa.

Change of value

Where, as a result of the change of accounting policy, there is a difference between the closing accounting value of an intangible fixed asset in the earlier period and its opening accounting value in the later period, the amount of the debit or credit to be brought into account (subject to the cap as noted below) is the proportion of the accounting difference that the tax written down value of the asset at the end of the earlier period bears to the accounting value at that time.

The tax written down value of the asset at the beginning of the later period is then taken to be the tax written down value at the end of the earlier period as reduced by the debit or increased by the credit (as the case may be). Subsequently, the cost of the asset for tax purposes is the tax written down value (as reduced or increased) together with the cost recognised for tax purposes of any subsequent expenditure that is capitalised for accounting purposes and the tax written down value is to be determined taking account only of subsequent debits and credits.

This does not apply to an intangible fixed asset in respect of which an election for writing down at a fixed-rate has been made (see **42.5** above). Nor does it apply where, in respect of the accounting difference, a debit or credit is brought into account for tax purposes on the reversal of an earlier accounting credit or debit, or in respect of a revaluation gain (see **42.5** and **42.8** above).

Disaggregation

A change of accounting policy may result in an intangible fixed asset that was treated as one asset ('*the original asset*') in the earlier period, being treated as two or more assets ('*the resulting assets*') in the later period. In this case, where, as a result of the change of accounting policy, there is a difference between the closing accounting value of the original asset in the earlier period and the opening accounting value of the resulting assets in the later period, the amount of the debit or credit to be brought into account (subject to the cap noted below) is the proportion of the accounting difference that the tax written down value of the original asset at the end of the earlier period bears to the accounting value of that asset at that time.

The tax written down value of each resulting asset at the beginning of the later period is then taken to be the proportion of the tax written down value of the original asset at the end of the earlier period (as reduced by the debit or increased by the credit as the case may be) that the opening accounting value of that asset in the later period bears to the aggregate opening accounting values of the resulting assets at that time. Subsequently, the cost of each resulting asset for tax purposes is the tax written down value (as above) together with the cost recognised for tax purposes of any subsequent expenditure that is capitalised for accounting purposes and the tax written down value is to be determined taking account only of subsequent debits and credits. However, where a credit is to be taken into account, it must not exceed the excess of debits previously brought into account for tax purposes over previous credits.

This does not apply where an election for writing down at a fixed-rate has been or is subsequently made (see **42.5** above) in respect of the original or resulting assets (see below). Nor does it apply where, in respect of the accounting difference, a debit or credit is brought into account for tax purposes on the reversal of an earlier accounting credit or debit, or in respect of a revaluation gain (see **42.5** and **42.8** above).

Original asset subject to fixed-rate writing down

Where a change in accounting policy results in the disaggregation of assets (as above) and an election for writing down at a fixed-rate (see **42.5** above) has been or is subsequently made in respect of the original asset, the election applies to the original asset for periods up to and including the earlier period, and to the resulting assets for the later and subsequent periods. The tax written down value of each resulting asset at the beginning of the later period is then taken to be the proportion of the tax written down value of the original asset at the end of the earlier period that the opening accounting value of that asset in the later period bears to the aggregate opening accounting values of the resulting assets at that time. Subsequently, the cost of each resulting asset for tax purposes is the tax written down value (as above) together with the cost recognised for tax purposes of any subsequent expenditure that is capitalised for accounting purposes and the tax written down value is to be determined taking account only of subsequent debits and credits.

Resulting assets subject to fixed-rate writing down

Where a change in accounting policy results in the disaggregation of assets (as above) and no election for writing down at a fixed-rate (see **42.5** above) has been made in respect of the original asset, such an election may be made in respect of any of the resulting assets provided it is made within two years after the end of the accounting period in which the original asset was acquired or created.

The effect of the election is that the original asset is treated as consisting of as many assets ('notional original assets') as there are resulting assets, each notional original asset being treated as the same asset as one of the resulting assets (its 'corresponding resulting asset'). An appropriate proportion of every amount falling to be taken into account in relation to the original asset is to be attributed to each notional original asset, the 'appropriate portion' being ascertained by reference to its corresponding resulting asset. The '*appropriate proportion*' in this case is the amount which the opening accounting value of that asset in the later period bears to the aggregate opening accounting values of all the resulting assets at that time. The provisions of this chapter apply to each of the notional original assets and its corresponding resulting asset accordingly.

Cap on credit to be brought into account

Where a change in accounting policy results in a difference between the closing accounting value of the asset (or, in the case of disaggregation, the original asset) in the earlier period and the opening accounting value of the asset (or the resulting assets) in the later period, the amount of any credit to be brought into account for tax purposes is limited to the net aggregate amount of relevant tax debits previously brought into account, this being the total debits previously brought into account in respect of the asset (or, in the case of disaggregation, the original asset at the end of the earlier period) less the total credits previously brought into account in respect of that asset.

Subsequent events

Where there is a further change in accounting policy affecting an asset to which these provisions have already applied, these provisions are to apply again. Where there is a subsequent part realisation affecting an asset to which these provisions have already applied, the provisions of *CTA 2009, s 744* apply. In this case the tax written-down value of the intangible asset immediately after the subsequent part realisation is found by reducing its written-down value immediately before the subsequent part realisation by the fraction equal to its carrying value (for accounting purposes) immediately after the part realisation divided by that immediately before it. Subsequent allowances are based on that amount.

[*CTA 2009, ss 872–879*].

Commencement of the intangible assets regime and transitional provisions

[42.42] Except as below, the intangible assets regime applies only to intangible fixed assets of a company which are:

(a) created by the company after 31 March 2002; or
(b) acquired by the company after 31 March 2002 and before 1 July 2020 from a person who is not a 'related party' (see further below); or
(c) acquired by the company after 31 March 2002 and before 1 July 2020 from a related party in the following cases:
  (i) where the asset is acquired from a company in whose hands the asset fell within the intangible assets regime;
  (ii) where the asset is acquired from an intermediary who acquired the asset after 31 March 2002 from a third party which was not a related party of the intermediary (at the time of the intermediary's acquisition of the asset) or of the company (at the time of the company's acquisition); or
  (iii) where the asset was created by any person after 31 March 2002;
(d) acquired by the company on or after 1 July 2020;
(e) held by the company immediately before 1 July 2020 where at that time, the company is not within the charge to corporation tax in respect of the asset.

Assets within (d) or (e) above are within the regime only for accounting periods beginning on or after 1 July 2020, and for this purpose, an accounting period straddling that date is treated as two separate accounting periods, the second of which begins on that date. Assets within (d) above are subject to special rules restricting debits where they are 'restricted assets' (see **42.7** above).

The condition in (e) above is not met if, at any time in the period 19 March 2020 to 30 June 2020 inclusive, the asset is excluded from the regime by the commencement rules in the hands of any company that is within the charge to corporation tax in respect of it unless after that time, but during that period, the asset is acquired by any other company from a person who at the time of acquisition is not a related party of that other company.

For these purposes (except in the case of certain internally-generated assets, see below) an asset is regarded as acquired or created after 31 March 2002 to the extent that expenditure on its acquisition or creation is so incurred. Similar rules apply to determine whether assets are treated as acquired on or after 1 July 2020, between 1 April 2002 and 30 June 2020 or between 19 March 2020 and 30 June 2020. Acquisition expenditure is generally treated as incurred when it is recognised for accounting purposes. There are, however, two special cases.

(A) Acquisition expenditure which does not qualify for any form of tax relief against income under the law as it was before 1 April 2002, and which would be treated as incurred after commencement under the general rule, is treated as incurred before that date if the asset is (or would be) treated as disposed of and acquired before commencement for chargeable gains purposes.

(B) Creation or acquisition expenditure which under law as it was before 1 April 2002 qualifies for any capital allowance is treated as incurred when an unconditional obligation to pay it comes into being (notwithstanding that all or any part of the expenditure may not be required to be paid until a later date).

Where as a result of these rules the asset would fall within the regime only to a limited extent, the expenditure is treated as being on two separate assets, one within and one outside the current provisions, with any necessary apportionment being made on a just and reasonable basis.

Intangible fixed assets not within (a)–(e) above are referred to as '*pre-FA 2002 assets*'. As regards application of certain of the current provisions to certain pre-*FA 2002* assets, see further below.

For the meaning of 'related party' see **42.34** above. A person (including a partnership) is also a related party for these purposes in relation to another person (or partnership) if the participation condition (see **72.2** transfer pricing) is met between them.

[*CAA 2009, ss 880–883, 887–889; FA 2020, s 30(6)(7)(14)(15)*].

Royalties

A '*royalty*' is defined as any payment in respect of the enjoyment or exercise of rights that are an intangible fixed asset. The intangible assets provisions apply to royalties only where they are recognised for accounting purposes on or after 1 April 2002, and royalties brought into account for tax purposes before that date are not brought into account again on or after that date.

To the extent that royalties would have been brought in before 1 April 2002 had the intangible assets provisions been in force, but were not, they are brought in immediately after commencement. A royalty is brought into account for these purposes if it would have been had the person concerned been within the charge to corporation tax. These rules are not affected by the above rules determining whether assets are within the current provisions.

These rules cannot be interpreted as allowing or requiring an amount to be brought into account in connection with the realisation of an existing asset within **42.10** above. [*CTA 2009, ss 714, 896*].

Internally-generated assets

Internally-generated *goodwill* is regarded as created before (and not after) 1 April 2002 if the business in question was carried on at any time before that date by the company or a related party (see **42.34** above). Other internally-generated assets representing expenditure which under existing law does not qualify for any capital allowance ('*non-qualifying expenditure*') are regarded as created before (and not after) 1 April 2002 if the asset in question was held at any time before that date by the company or a related party (see **42.34** above). If only part of the expenditure on an asset is non-qualifying expenditure, the expenditure is correspondingly treated as being on two separate assets, with any necessary apportionment being made on a just and reasonable basis. [*CTA 2009, ss 884, 885*].

Where a company has acquired a business from a related party, the 'business in question' means the acquired business. A company's argument that the 'business in question' meant the business carried on by it, which was not the same as the business previously carried on by the related party, was rejected in *Armstrong and Haire Ltd v HMRC* FTT, [2020] UKFTT 296 (TC); 2020 SWTI 1802.

Fungible assets

Special commencement provisions also apply in the case of fungible assets. For the purpose of the intangible assets regime, fungible assets of the same kind held by the same person in the same capacity are generally pooled and treated as indistinguishable parts of a single asset (see **42.40** above). For this purpose, however, assets which do not fall within the regime (i.e. pre-*FA 2002* assets), assets which are restricted assets (see above) and other assets which fall within the regime (standard intangible fixed assets) are treated as assets of different kinds. Each type of asset is allocated to a separate pool which is regarded as a single asset of a type determined in accordance with the assets allocated to it (so that the pool to which restricted assets are allocated is treated as a single restricted asset, and so on). Realisations of assets are treated as diminishing the pre-*FA 2002* pool first, then the restricted assets pool, and finally, the standard intangible fixed assets pool. Assets acquired are allocated to the pre-*FA 2002* pool or the restricted assets pool to the extent that they can be identified with assets realised by the company from the pre-*FA 2002* or restricted assets pool in accordance with the following rules.

The rules are that acquisitions are to be identified with pre-*FA 2002* assets or restricted assets realised within the period beginning 30 days before and ending 30 days after the acquisition; assets realised earlier fall to be identified before those realised later, and acquisitions are considered in the date order in which they take place.

Note that only assets acquired on or after 1 July 2020 can be restricted assets (see **42.7** above), so that, for accounting periods beginning before that date, the above rules applied by reference only to two kinds of assets – pre-*FA 2002* assets and standard intangible fixed assets. For this purpose, an accounting period straddling that date is treated as two separate accounting periods, the second of which begins on that date. The rules were previously in *CTA 2009, ss 890, 891*.

[*CTA 2009, ss 900K–900M, 900O; FA 2020, s 31(8)(9)(13)–(15)*].

Assets acquired on transfer of business

Where a pre-*FA 2002* asset (see above) in the hands of a company is transferred to another company, and the transfer is one to which *TCGA 1992, s 139* (company reconstruction or amalgamation), *TCGA 1992, s 140A* (transfer of UK business to company resident in another member state), *TCGA 1992, s 140E* (merger leaving assets within UK tax charge) or, where the transfer is on or after 1 July 2020, *TCGA 1992, s 171* (transfers within a group) applies (see **62.15** REORGANISATIONS AND RECONSTRUCTIONS, **11.18**, **11.20** CAPITAL GAINS, **12.4**

CAPITAL GAINS — GROUPS), so that the transferor company is treated as disposing of the asset for a no gain, no loss consideration, the asset is treated as a pre-*FA 2002* asset in the hands of the transferee company. [*CTA 2009, s 892; FA 2020, s 31(10)*].

Assets treated as pre-FA 2002 assets

Assets whose value derives from pre-FA 2002 assets

This anti-avoidance provision is aimed at the type of scheme which commonly involves the grant of a long-term licence over an intangible asset for a lump sum. Where a company acquires an intangible fixed asset from a related party during the period 1 April 2002 to 30 June 2020 inclusive and the asset was created on or after 1 April 2002, it is treated as a pre-*FA 2002* asset in the hands of the company (and so excluded from the regime) in so far as its value is derived in whole or in part from another asset which:

- has not at any time after 4 December 2005 been a chargeable intangible asset in the hands of the company or related transferor or another related party of the company or transferor; and
- has been a pre-*FA 2002* asset in the hands of the related transferor or in the hands of another related party of the company or transferor.

The value of an asset is derived from another asset where assets have been merged or divided or have changed their nature, or where rights or interests in or over assets have been created or extinguished. Where only part of the value of the acquired asset is derived from the existing asset, it is treated as a separate existing asset to the extent that its value is so derived, any necessary apportionment being made on a just and reasonable basis.

Assets acquired in connection with disposals of pre-FA 2002 assets

Where a company acquires an intangible fixed asset at any time before 1 July 2020 it will be treated as a pre-*FA 2002* asset where the acquisition is made directly or indirectly in consequence of or otherwise in connection with a disposal of a pre-*FA 2002* asset by a person who at the time of the disposal is a related party (see below) in relation to the company. This provision applies where the asset acquired would otherwise be a chargeable intangible asset in the hands of the company at the time of the acquisition, and a disposal of an existing asset can include a part disposal or any other disposal of the asset (under the capital gain tax rules). It does not matter whether the asset disposed of is the same as the one acquired, whether the acquisition and disposal take place at the same time or whether the acquired asset is acquired by the merging of two or more assets or by any other way. This anti-avoidance provision applies to transactions such as where a company grants a licence out of an existing trademark and claims to have made a part-disposal of the trade mark to which the 'no loss, no gain' rule under *TCGA 1992, s 171* applies while the company to whom the licence was granted claims it is a newly created intangible fixed asset.

For the meaning of 'related party' see **42.34** above. A person (including a partnership) is also a related party for these purposes in relation to another person (or partnership) if the participation condition (see **72.2** TRANSFER PRICING) is met between them.

[*CTA 2009, ss 893–895; FA 2020, s 30(11)(12)*].

Where relief is available under these provisions, the consideration for disposal for capital gains purposes is treated as reduced by the amount qualifying for relief. The purchaser is unaffected by this adjustment for tax purposes. [*TCGA 1992, s 156ZA*].

Application of relief on reinvestment in relation to pre-FA 2002 assets

Where a company realises an existing asset after commencement, the rules for relief on reinvestment (see **42.11** above) apply with the necessary modifications. [*CTA 2009, ss 898–900*].

Special provisions

See *CTA 2009, ss 897* for special provisions relating to *telecommunications rights* within *ITTOIA 2005, Pt 2 Ch 10* and *CTA 2009, s 905* with regard to *Lloyd's syndicate capacity*.

Intellectual property excluded from the intangible assets regime

[42.43] The provisions below apply to income from and expenditure on intellectual property not falling within the intangible assets regime as a result of the commencement and transitional rules for that regime at **42.42** above.

See **9.8** and **9.19** CAPITAL ALLOWANCES for allowances on capital expenditure in acquiring know-how and patent rights; **41.2** and **41.5** INCOME TAX IN RELATION TO A COMPANY for patent royalties and other royalties paid to non-residents; **31.4** DOUBLE TAX RELIEF for DTR treatment of royalties from abroad; **33.13** EXEMPT ORGANISATIONS as regards research institution spin-out companies; **68.45**, **68.47**, **68.49** TRADING INCOME and **69.61** TRADING INCOME — DEDUCTIONS for trading receipts and expenses with regard to intellectual property. See also **57** PATENT INCOME.

Simon's Taxes. See **B5.3**.

Income from intellectual property

Subject to the exceptions noted below, the proceeds of disposal of 'know-how' or for certain restrictive covenants relating to the disposal of know-how (whether or not legally enforceable) less expenditure wholly and exclusively incurred in acquiring the know-how are chargeable to corporation tax, provided they are not otherwise charged to tax. The exceptions are where:

(a) the consideration is taken into account for capital allowance purposes;
(b) the consideration is taxed as trading income;
(c) the disposal is of goodwill and the capital sum is taxed as a part or whole disposal of a trade;
(d) the disposal is to a connected person.

'*Know-how*' means any industrial information or techniques likely to assist in manufacturing or processing goods or materials, in working a mine, oil-well or other source of mineral deposits (including searching for, discovery or testing of deposits or winning access to them), or in carrying out any agricultural, forestry or fishing operations. HMRC consider that know-how does not include information about marketing, packaging or distribution (Revenue Tax Bulletin, August 1993 p 86).

[*CTA 2009, ss 907–910*].

Patent income and expenses

The following provisions apply where a company has not elected into the 'patent box' regime, for which see **57** PATENT INCOME.

'*Patent income*' means any royalty or other sum paid in respect of the use of a patent or any amount on which corporation tax is payable in relation to (i) the sale of patent rights under *CTA 2009, ss 912, 918 or 1272* (see below) or (ii) balancing charges under the capital allowances code for patent rights (see **9.19** CAPITAL ALLOWANCES).

Relief can be claimed for expenses incurred by a company, otherwise than for the purposes of a trade, in connection with the grant, maintenance or extension of the term of a patent or in connection with a rejected or abandoned patent application, provided that, if the expenses had been incurred for the purposes of a trade, they would have been allowable in calculating the profits of that trade.

Where a claim is made, the expenses are deducted or set off against the company's patent income for the accounting period in which they are incurred with any unallowed balance being carried forward indefinitely against patent income without further claim, so long as the company remains within the charge to corporation tax. Any CAPITAL ALLOWANCES (**9.19**) must be deducted before relief is given for the expenses.

Where or to the extent that expenditure is funded by a grant or other contribution from a public body, or a contribution by a person other than the company, the company is not regarded as having incurred the expenditure for the purpose of the above provisions. The exception to this is that the company is treated as having incurred the expenditure if the contributor (assuming he is within the charge to tax) is not a public body and the expenditure is not eligible for capital allowances or for relief in arriving at the contributor's trading profits.

[*CTA 2009, ss 924–927*].

Patent royalties may be subject to deduction of tax at source (see **41.2** and **41.5** INCOME TAX IN RELATION TO A COMPANY), as are other royalties paid to non-UK residents.

Spreading of patent royalties

Where royalties are received, less tax, for user of a patent which comprises two or more complete years, the corporation tax liabilities are reducible, on application, to the total that would have been payable if the royalties had been paid by equal instalments (corresponding to the number of complete years concerned, but not exceeding six years) made at yearly intervals ending with the date of actual receipt. [*ICTA 1988, s 527*].

Sales of patent rights

Profits from sales of the whole or part of any patent rights (including receipts for rights for which a patent has not yet been granted), which consist wholly or partly of a capital sum, are chargeable to tax as miscellaneous income. The company is charged to tax if a UK resident or, if not UK resident, where the patent is a UK patent.

In the case of a sale by a non-UK resident, the purchaser may have to deduct tax at source under *ITA 2007, s 901* (see **41.2** INCOME TAX IN RELATION TO A COMPANY) although this may be modified by double tax agreements.

References above to the sale of patent rights include the exchange of patent rights, and in the case of such an exchange, references above and below to the proceeds of sale and the price include the consideration for the exchange, and references to capital sums included in the proceeds include references to so much of the consideration for the exchange as would have been a capital sum if it had been a money payment. Where patent rights are acquired or disposed of together with other property, the acquisition costs or proceeds, as appropriate, must be apportioned on a just and reasonable basis.

'*Patent rights*' means the right to do or authorise the doing of anything which would, but for the right, be an infringement of a patent.

Spreading provisions

In the case of a UK-resident company, the chargeable profits are spread equally over a period of six years, starting with the accounting period in which the proceeds are received. If the proceeds are received in instalments, each instalment is likewise spread over six years. The company may elect, by notice to an officer of HMRC, to disapply spreading, so that the profits (or instalments) are taxed in the accounting period in which they were received. The election must be made within two years after the end of the accounting period in which the profits or instalment were received.

Where the seller is a partnership and the sale is in the course of a trade carried on by the partnership, each amount chargeable to corporation tax under the above spreading provisions is chargeable on the partners for the time being carrying on the trade, unless there is a partnership change such that no corporate partner which carried on the trade before the change continues to do so afterwards. See *CTA 2009, s 1271(4)–(6)* (and, in the event of a subsequent cessation of the partnership trade, *CTA 2009, s 1272*) for the mechanics by which this is achieved.

Where a body corporate commences winding-up during the period over which the charge is spread in that period, no such election can be made and any charge arising under the spreading provisions becomes immediately chargeable in the accounting period in which winding-up commences.

The making of an election for spreading does not affect the amount of income tax to be deducted by the purchaser in the case of a sale by a non-UK resident, and any adjustment required as a result of such an election is made by repayment of tax on a year by year basis.

Similar provision is made for companies not resident in the UK in receipt of a lump sum or instalments for the sale of patent rights. However the obligation to deduct income tax from the payment to the non-UK resident is not affected by the right to spread the tax charge or by the right to claim a deduction for expenditure on the patent rights. Any necessary adjustment is made by repayment of tax.

Licences

The acquisition of a licence in respect of a patent is treated for the purposes of the above provisions as a purchase of patent rights, and the grant of a licence is treated as a sale of part of such rights. Where, however, the licence is a licence to exercise the rights to the exclusion of all other persons (including the grantor) for the whole of the period until the rights come to an end, the grant is treated as a sale of the whole of the rights. The use in certain circumstances of an invention, which is the subject of a patent, by the Crown or a foreign government is treated as use under a licence.

The sale of a right to acquire future patent rights under a patent which has not yet been granted is treated as a sale and purchase of patent rights and, if the purchaser exercises the right to acquire the patent rights, the expenditure on the right to acquire is treated as part of the cost of the patent rights.

[*CTA 2009, ss 912–923, 1271, 1272*].

Simon's Taxes. See **B5.330–B5.335**.

Disposal of know-how

Subject to the exceptions below, profits arising where consideration is received for the disposal of 'know-how' are chargeable to corporation tax as miscellaneous income. Also included within the charge are profits arising where consideration is received for giving, or wholly or partly fulfilling, an undertaking (whether or not legally enforceable) which is given in connection with a disposal of know-how and which restricts or is designed to restrict any person's activities in any way. Sale of know-how includes exchange of know-how. Sale of know-how includes sale of know-how with other property. A sale is regarded as one bargain, even if the consideration specifies separate prices or that the deal comprises separate sales. The consideration and expenditure is allocated on a just and reasonable basis. Where the apportionment or allocation materially affects more than one taxpayer, the rules in *CAA 2001, s 563(2)–(6)* must be used to determine the allocation. The matter '*materially affects*' a taxpayer if it is material to the determination of his tax liability in any period.

Where the know-how disposed of has been used in a trade, and the disposal is part of the disposal of all or part of the trade, the consideration is treated for corporation tax purposes as a capital receipt for goodwill, subject to the exclusions below. If the purchaser is within the charge to corporation tax, the consideration paid is treated as a capital payment for goodwill, unless the trade was carried on wholly outside the UK before the transaction took place. If the seller is within the charge to corporation tax, it may, under *CTA 2009, s 178*, jointly elect with the purchaser within two years of the disposal not to apply these provisions. Where an election is made within the equivalent income tax provision (*ITTOIA 2005, s 194*) and the purchaser is within the charge to corporation tax, the parties are treated as also making an election under *CTA 2009, s 178*.

The charge does not apply if:

- the consideration is brought into account as a revenue receipt under general principles;
- the consideration is brought into account as a disposal value under the capital allowances know-how code — *CAA 2001, s 462* (see **9.8** CAPITAL ALLOWANCES);
- the consideration is treated as a trading receipt (see **68.45** TRADING INCOME);
- the consideration is received as part of the disposal of all or part of a trade and is treated as a capital receipt for goodwill under these provisions (see **68.45** TRADING INCOME); or
- the disposal is by way of a sale and the buyer is a body of persons (including a firm) over which the seller has control, the seller is a body of persons over which the buyer has control or the buyer and seller are both bodies of persons and another person has control over them both.

[*CTA 2009, ss 176–179, 928–931*].

Simon's Taxes. See **B5.345–B5.347**.

Income tax charge on offshore receipts from intangible property

[42.44] For 2019/20 onwards, an *income tax* charge applies to 'UK derived amounts' from intangible property arising to a person (including a company) who is not UK resident and who is not resident in a 'full treaty territory'. The charge is targeted towards large multinational groups holding intangible property in low tax jurisdictions, where the income which arises in relation to that intangible property is referable to the sale of goods or services in the UK.

The charge for a tax year is on the full amount of the UK-derived amounts arising in the year. The person chargeable is the person receiving or entitled to the amounts.

'*UK derived amounts*' are amounts (including capital amounts) in respect of the enjoyment or exercise of rights constituting 'intangible property' where the enjoyment or exercise of the rights, or of rights derived, directly or indirectly, from those rights, enables, facilitates or promotes (directly or indirectly) 'UK sales'. It does not matter if the amounts relate to UK sales in the tax year in question or in a different year. UK-derived amounts are treated for income tax purposes as arising from a source in the UK.

'*UK sales*' are services, goods or other property provided either in the UK or to persons in the UK. Where an amount derives partly from UK sales and partly from other sales or anything else, the amount is treated as a UK derived amount to the extent that is just and reasonable. In the case of an amount derived partly from UK and partly from other sales, this is presumed to be the proportion of the amount that the value of the UK sales bears to the value of the total sales, unless the contrary is shown.

For the purposes of these provisions, a person is resident in a territory if he is liable to tax there by reason of domicile, residence or place of management but not in respect only of income from sources or capital situated there. If a person is resident in a territory outside the UK for general legal purposes but the territory has no provision for a person to be resident there for tax purposes, he is treated as resident there for the purposes of these provisions. A '*full treaty territory*' is one with which the UK has a double tax treaty containing a non-discrimination provision (i.e. a provision under which nationals of one state cannot be subject in the other state to any tax or tax requirement more burdensome or other than those to which nationals of the other state are subject). If a partnership is treated for tax purposes as an entity separate from the partners in a full treaty territory, then if the partnership is resident there, each of the partners is also treated as resident there.

'*Intangible property*' means any property other than tangible property, estates, interests or rights in or over land, rights in respect of tangible property or estates etc. in land, financial assets (within *CTA 2009, s 806* and including loan relationships, derivative contracts and insurance or capital redemption policies), shares or other rights in the profits, governance or winding up of a company or any property prescribed in regulations made by the Treasury.

The Treasury may amend these provisions by statutory instruments, but not after 31 December 2019.

[*ITTOIA 2005, ss 608A–608I; FA 2019, Sch 3 paras 4, 7, 10–14*].

Note that the normal limit on income tax liability for non-resident companies does not apply to tax charged under these provisions — see **64.8** RESIDENCE.

Exemptions

The above provisions do not apply to a person if the total value of the UK sales for the tax year is no more than £10 million. For this purpose, any amount (capital or revenue) which a person, or a person connected with him, receives, or is entitled to receive, which relates (wholly or partly, directly or indirectly) to the provision of goods, service or other property constituting UK sales are treated as that person's UK sales.

The provisions also do not apply if substantially all of the 'relevant activity' relating to the intangible property to which any UK-derived amounts for a tax year relate is, and has at all times been, undertaken in the territory in which the taxpayer is resident throughout the tax year and there is no connection between the intangible property and a 'related person'. The exclusion applies only on a claim.

'*Relevant activity*' is anything done by anyone for the purpose of creating, developing or maintaining any of the intangible property or for the purpose of generating amounts that relate to the enjoyment or exercise of rights constituting any of the intangible property. There is a connection between intangible property and a related person if any of the property has been transferred (directly or indirectly) from a person related to the taxpayer or if the property derives, directly or indirectly, from anything so transferred or from intangible property held by a person related to the taxpayer.

Two persons are related if they are in the same 'control group', one has a '25% investment' in the other or a third person has a 25% investment in both. Two persons are also related at a particular time if at any time in the preceding or following six months one of them directly or indirectly participates in the management, control or capital of the other (within *TIOPA 2010, ss 157, 159, 160* — see **72.2** TRANSFER PRICING) or a third person directly or indirectly participates in the management, control or capital of them both. Two persons are in the same 'control group' if they are consolidated for accounting purposes (i.e. their financial result are, or are required to be, comprised in group accounts prepared under *Companies Act 2006, s 399* (or corresponding overseas provision) or would be but for an exemption), one has a '51% investment' in the other or a third person has a 51% investment in both.

A person has a '*51% investment*' in another (C) if he possesses or is entitled to acquire more than half of the voting power in C; if, in the event of a disposal of all of the equity in C, he would receive more than half of the proceeds; if he would receive more than half of the amount of any income in respect of the equity of C distributed among the equity holders; or if he would receive more than half of the assets of C available for distribution among the equity holders on a winding-up of C. A '*25% investment*' is defined in the same way but by reference to a person having at least a quarter of any of the relevant amounts. See also *TIOPA 2010, s 464(2)–(11)* for the meaning of equity and **24.7** CORPORATE INTEREST RESTRICTION for rules for the attribution of rights and interests which apply also for these purposes.

The provisions also do not apply if the amount of tax paid by the taxpayer in the overseas territory of residence in respect of UK-derived amounts in a tax year (the 'local tax amount') is at least half of the corresponding UK tax. This exclusion does not apply if local tax amount is determined under 'designer tax provisions'. For this purpose, the corresponding UK tax is the amount that would otherwise be chargeable under these provisions on the basis that the taxpayer is not entitled to any relief or allowance for the tax year. '*Designer tax provisions*' are provisions which appear to HMRC to be designed to enable persons to exercise significant control over the amount of tax payable in respect of UK-derived amounts.

In determining the local tax amount, any necessary apportionments must be made on a just and reasonable basis. If any of the overseas tax is repaid to any person, or any credit for tax is paid to any person, and the repayment or payment is directly or indirectly in respect of all or part of the tax on UK-derived amounts, the local tax amount must be reduced by the amount of the repayment or payment. Again, any necessary apportionments must be made on a just and reasonable basis.

The Treasury may amend the above exemptions, or create additional exemption, by statutory instrument.

[*ITTOIA 2005, ss 608J–608N, 608S–608V; FA 2019, Sch 3 paras 4, 7*].

Appeals

There is no provision for the postponement of tax where an appeal is made against an assessment to income tax under these provisions. The provisions at **5.27** APPEALS do apply in the case of a further appeal, although the court or Tribunal may override those provisions on application by HMRC or where it considers it necessary for the protection of the revenue. [*ITTOIA 2005, s 608Y; FA 2019, Sch 3 para 4*].

Recovery of tax from group member

If an amount of income tax assessed on a person under these provisions has not been paid in full (together with any interest arising on it) by the end of six months from the date on which it became due, HMRC may give a notice to any other person who was a member of the taxpayer's control group at any time in the tax year in question, requiring that person to pay any unpaid tax an interest within 30 days of the giving of the notice. Such a notice can be given anywhere in the world but cannot be given more than three years and six months after the due date. (Where the tax is charged in a determination under *TMA 1970, s 28C*, or in a self-assessment included in a return under *TMA 1970, s 8* or *s 8A*, these rules apply by reference to the date on which the determination was issued or the return was delivered rather than the due date.)

Once a notice has been given, the tax is treated as if it had been assessed on the group member and is due and payable when it originally became due and payable. This does not give the group member a right of appeal against the original assessment (and any appeal against the assessment by the original taxpayer does not affect the liability under the notice). The person to whom a notice is given may, however, appeal against the notice itself on the grounds that they were not a group member. An appeal must be made within 30 days beginning with the day the notice is given. Amounts due under the notice remain payable, and the provisions at **5.27** APPEALS apply in the case of a further appeal, although the court or Tribunal may override those provisions on application by HMRC or where it considers it necessary for the protection of the revenue.

A person who makes a payment required by a notice can recover the amount from the original taxpayer. Payments are not deductible for any tax purposes, nor are reimbursements treated as receipts.

[*ITTOIA 2005, ss 608O–608R; FA 2019, Sch 3 paras 4, 7*].

Anti-avoidance

Where a person enters into arrangements (as widely defined) on or after 29 October 2018 with a main purpose of obtaining a tax advantage (as defined) as a result of anything not being chargeable to income tax under the above provisions or of any double tax arrangements where the advantage is contrary to their object and purpose, the tax advantage must be counteracted by the making of just and reasonable adjustments by way of assessment, modification of an assessment, amendment or disallowance of a claim or otherwise. [*ITTOIA 2005, s 608W; FA 2019, Sch 3 paras 4, 8*].

Key points on intangible assets

[42.45] Points to consider are as follows:

Scope

1. The intangible fixed assets legislation applies, with certain limited exceptions (see **42.4**), to assets which are treated as intangible assets for accounting purposes and which are capitalised in a company's accounts. It is specifically provided that the legislation applies to goodwill and intellectual property (see **42.2**). However restrictions apply with regard to goodwill and goodwill-related assets acquired on or after 8 July 2015, see **42.5**.

2. The legislation applies to intangible fixed assets which were acquired or created by a company on or after 1 April 2002, subject to the exclusions in the transitional rules at **42.42**. All intangible assets acquired on or after 1 July 2020 have now been brought within the regime. Such assets are, however, subject to the restrictions on the amount of debits at **42.7** if they fall within one of the categories of restricted asset (broadly where they were acquired directly or indirectly from a related party and were previously excluded from the regime).

3. Anti-avoidance provisions apply to prevent a company from arranging to bring an asset excluded by the commencement and transitional provisions (a pre-*FA 2002* asset) which is held by the company, or a person related with the company, within the intangible fixed assets legislation. Profits or losses arising on a disposal of pre-*FA 2002* assets are normally treated as chargeable gains or allowable losses for the purposes of the *TCGA 1992*.

Relief for expenditure

4. Where an intangible asset is within the intangible fixed assets legislation a company is able to obtain relief for the amortisation which is recognised in its accounts in respect of the intangible fixed asset. Adjustments are made for tax purposes where there is a difference between the expenditure on the asset which is recognised for tax purposes and the amount capitalised in a company's accounts (see **42.5**). Special rules apply to goodwill and related assets. See **42.6**.

5. As an alternative to claiming relief for an intangible fixed asset on the basis on which it is amortised in a company's accounts, a company may elect to claim relief for the expenditure at the rate of 4% per annum on a straight line basis. This election has to be made within two years of the end of the accounting period in which the asset was created or acquired. The

election would be beneficial where expenditure on an asset has been capitalised but the asset is not being written down in the company' accounts for example where the company uses international accounting standards and the asset does not have a finite life (see **42.5**).

6. Where a company does not capitalise expenditure on an intangible fixed asset it is able to obtain relief for expenditure which is charged to profit or loss (e.g. royalties or licence fees for the use of an intangible fixed asset or expenditure that is written off as it is incurred) (see **42.5**).

Non-deductible expenditure

7. No relief may be claimed in respect of expenditure (whether or not it is capitalised) which relates to business entertaining and gifts, crime related expenditure, expensive hired cars or motorcycles or certain retirement benefits — see **42.40** (expenditure not generally deductible).

Revaluations

8. A company is liable to tax on any revaluation gains recognised in its accounts in respect of an intangible fixed asset. The gain which is brought into charge to tax, however, is limited to the amortisation for which the company has claimed tax relief in respect of the asset. A revaluation charge does not arise where a company has elected to write the asset down at 4% per annum on a straight line basis (see **42.8**).

Disposals

9. When an intangible fixed asset is sold a company is liable to tax on the difference between the disposal proceeds of the asset and the tax written down value of the asset. It is possible for a company to elect to roll over the disposal proceeds against the purchase of a replacement asset (otherwise than from another group company) either by it or by another company in its group (the intangible fixed asset legislation group definition tracks the *TCGA 1992, s 170* group definition) that is within the charge to the intangible fixed assets legislation in respect of the replacement asset. A company, however, may only claim rollover relief to the extent that the disposal proceeds exceed the original tax cost of the asset (as opposed to its tax written down value). This thus means that even where rollover relief is claimed that there will be a clawback of the tax relief which has been claimed in respect of the amortisation of the asset (see **42.11**, **42.13** and **42.14**).

10. Where a company in the group acquires a new group member it is possible for an intangible fixed asset gain to be rolled over against the cost of intangible fixed assets held by the new group member where certain conditions are satisfied (see **42.15**).

Intra-group transfers and degrouping charge

11. It is possible for an intangible fixed asset to be transferred between group companies at its tax written down value. The definition of a group for the purposes of the intangible fixed assets legislation tracks the *TCGA*

1992, s 170 definition. A degrouping charge applies if the transferee leaves the group within six years of the transfer and in such cases the transferee is deemed to have disposed of and immediately reacquired the intangible fixed asset at its market value at the time of the transfer (see **42.13**).

12. The taxable profit arises in the accounting period in which the transferee company leaves the group. At the same time the transferee company is entitled to claim additional amortisation from the time of the transfer representing the difference between the amortisation for which relief has been claimed and the amount which would have been claimed had the calculations been based on the market value of the asset at the time of the transfer (see **42.16**).

Anti-avoidance

13. An anti-avoidance provision applies where a company enters into arrangements which have as their main object, or one of the main objects, to increase the debits or to reduce the credits which are taken into account under the intangible fixed assets legislation. Where this provision applies the arrangements are disregarded in determining the debits or credits which are brought into account for the purposes of the intangible fixed assets legislation (see **42.40**).

Treatment of debit and credits

14. Where a company is a party to an intangible fixed asset for the purposes of its trade any debits and credits arising in respect of the asset are included in computing its trading profits.

15. Where an intangible fixed asset is held for a property business any debits and credits are treated as expenses and receipts of the business.

Income tax charge on offshore receipts from intangible property

For 2019/20 onwards, an *income tax* charge applies to 'UK derived amounts' from intangible property arising to a person (including a company) who is not UK resident and who is not resident in a 'full treaty territory'.

43

Interest on Overdue Tax

Cross-reference. See 73.5 VALUE ADDED TAX.

Introduction to interest on overdue tax

[43.1] Interest is charged on overdue corporation tax by virtue of *TMA 1970, s 87A*. The harmonised interest regime for all taxes and duties administered by HMRC under *FA 2009, s 101, Sch 53* does not yet apply to corporation tax.

Corporation tax self assessment periods

[43.2] In relation to accounting periods ending on or after 1 July 1999 to which self-assessment applies, corporation tax carries interest from the due and payable date (nine months and one day after the end of the accounting period, see 58.2 PAYMENT OF TAX), even if it is a non-business day, until payment.

Where corporation tax assessed on a company may be assessed on other persons in certain circumstances, the due and payable date is that which refers to the company's liability.

Interest payable under these provisions is deductible in computing income, profits or losses under the loan relationship rules (see 50.3 LOAN RELATIONSHIPS).

In the case of interest on tax assessable under *ITA 2007, s 945 et seq* these provisions apply in relation to return periods which fall within a self-assessment accounting period.

Details of interest rates are set out at 43.5 below.

Interest on tax subsequently discharged is adjusted or repaid so as to secure that the total is as it would have been had the tax discharged never been charged.

Large companies — instalment payments

In the case of certain 'large' companies which are required to make instalment payments in respect of their corporation tax liabilities (see **58.3** PAYMENT OF TAX), a special rate of interest (see **43.5** below) applies to unpaid instalments until nine months after the end of the accounting period. This is calculated as base rate plus 1%. After this date the normal rate of interest applicable to overdue corporation tax applies, until the tax is paid.

Return to be filed

Interest is not calculated until a return is made or some other charge to tax arises. (HMRC Pamphlet 'A Guide to Corporation Tax Self Assessment' para 5.4.4).

In the case of quarterly instalment payments, interest (and penalties) is only calculated after the company has filed its return (or HMRC have determined the liability in the absence of a return) *and* the normal due date has passed. See HMRC's website at 'Corporation Tax interest charges'.

Carry back of losses etc.

Generally a trading loss of an accounting period can only be carried back twelve months and set against the profits of such a preceding period (*CTA 2010, s 37*). However, in certain situations the trading loss can be set against profits arising up to three years previously (see further **51.4** LOSSES).

Where the losses are set-off in an accounting period falling wholly within that prior twelve-month period, and some or all of the tax for that period is unpaid, interest is calculated on the net amount after set-off.

However, where the losses are carried back to an accounting period not falling wholly within the preceding twelve months, interest on the unpaid tax for that earlier period which is cancelled by the loss relief will run up to the normal due date for payment of tax for the period in which the loss was incurred. Therefore the tax will only be relieved for the period arising after the due date to payment (i.e. the period arising after nine months post the end of the loss making period).

Similar restrictions also apply where a non-trading deficit on a company's loan relationships is carried back on a claim under *CTA 2009, s 389(1)* or *s 459(1)(b)* (see **50.4** LOAN RELATIONSHIPS). Thus the interest will run until the due date for payment for the accounting period in which the deficit arises. Where relief is given by repayment, the amount repaid is, as far as possible, treated as if it were a discharge of the corporation tax charged for that period.

Close companies

Interest on corporation tax charged on certain loans by close companies (see **16.12** *et seq* CLOSE COMPANIES) is not, however, refunded when tax is repaid following repayment, release or writing off of the loan, and any relief from tax under **16.12** is, for the purposes of refund of interest under *TMA 1970, s 91*, set only against tax assessed under **16.12**. Interest ceases to run, however, from the date of the repayment, etc. and for this purpose any tax unpaid at that time is assumed, as far as possible, to be tax under **16.12** (see HMRC Pamphlet 'A Guide to Corporation Tax Self Assessment', para 5.4.2). See now HMRC's website at 'Directors' loan account and Corporation Tax explained'.

[*TMA 1970, ss 87A, 90, 91(1A)(1B)(2A), 109(3A)–(5); SI 1998 No 3175, Reg 7*].

Simon's Taxes. See **A4.623, A4.624, D1.1320.**

Disaster etc. of national significance

No interest is chargeable on unpaid tax where HMRC agree that payment may be deferred by reason of circumstances arising from a disaster or emergency specified by order in a statutory instrument made for the purpose. Where no actual agreement is made, but HMRC are satisfied that one could have been made, this applies as if there were a notional agreement. The period for which interest does not arise is the period beginning with a date specified in the order or, if HMRC direct, a later date from which the agreement for deferred payment has effect and ending with the date on which that agreement ceases to apply or, if earlier, the date on which the order is revoked or amended so that it ceases to apply to the deferred amount. These provisions apply to disasters before as well as after an order is made. If, under the agreement, payment is to be by instalments, the agreement comes to an end if any instalment is not paid by the due date.

[*FA 2008, s 135; FA 2020, s 105*].

Examples

(A) General

[43.3]

S Ltd (which has no associated companies) prepares accounts to 31 July. On 31 May 2021, it makes a payment of £120,000 on account of its corporation tax liability for the year to 31 July 2020, the due date being 1 May 2021. On completing its corporation tax return, the company ascertains its total CT liability for that year to be £142,500 and makes a further payment of £22,500 on 16 July 2021. Following an enquiry by HMRC, various adjustments are made and the final CT liability is agreed at £145,500 on 25 November 2021. The company pays a further £3,000 on 5 January 2022.

It is assumed that interest rates remain unchanged after 7 April 2020.

Interest on overdue tax will be payable as follows.

		£
1.05.21 to 31.05.21	£120,000 × 2.60% × $^{30}/_{366}$ =	255.73
1.05.21 to 16.07.21	£22,500 × 2.60% × $^{76}/_{366}$ =	121.47
1.05.21 to 5.01.22	£3,000 × 2.60% × $^{249}/_{366}$ =	53.06
Total interest charge		£430.26

(B) Refund of interest charged

On 1 November 2021, T Ltd pays CT of £100,000 for its year ended 31 December 2020. The due date for payment was 1 October 2021. The liability is finally agreed at £80,000 and a repayment of £20,000 is made to T Ltd on 1 March 2021.

Assuming that interest rates remain unchanged after 7 April 2020, the interest position will be as follows.

(i) T Ltd will be charged interest on £100,000 for the period 1.10.21 to 1.11.21 (31 days). The charge will be raised following payment of the £100,000 on 1.11.21.

$£100,000 \times 2.60\% \times {}^{31}/_{366} = £220.21$

(ii) The company will be entitled to interest on overpaid tax of £20,000 for the period 1.11.21 (date of payment) to 1.3.22 (date of repayment) (120 days).

$£20,000 \times 0.5\% \times {}^{120}/_{365} = £32.87$

(iii) T Ltd will also receive a refund of interest charged on £20,000 for the period 1.10.21 to 1.11.21.

$£20,000 \times 2.60\% \times {}^{31}/_{366} = £44.04$

(C) Instalment payments

R Ltd has no associated companies and had taxable profits in excess of £1,500,000 for the year ended 31 March 2020.

For the year ended 31 March 2021, R Ltd makes instalment payments of £110,000 (this being equivalent to a quarter of its estimated corporation tax liability of £440,000) on the first three due dates. The last instalment is not paid until 24 July 2021. On 3 September 2021, the tax liability is finally agreed at £524,800. R Ltd pays the balance due of £84,800 on 10 September 2022.

The rates of interest are assumed for the purposes of this example to remain unchanged after 30 March 2020 for quarterly payments and 7 April 2020 otherwise.

The interest on tax unpaid is calculated as follows.

Instalments due on quarter dates £524,800 × $^1/_4$ = £131,200

1st instalment	£
14 October 2020 to 13 January 2021	
131,200 – 110,000 = £21,200 @ 1.10% × $^{92}/_{366}$ =	58.62
1st and 2nd instalment	
14 January 2021 to 13 April 2021	
262,400 – 220,000 = £42,400 @ 1.10% × $^{90}/_{366}$ =	114.68
1st, 2nd and 3rd instalments	
14 April 2021 to 13 July 2021	
393,600 – 330,000 = £63,600 @ 1.10% × $^{91}/_{366}$ =	173.94

1st, 2nd, 3rd and 4th instalments	
14 July 2021 to 23 July 2021	
524,800 – 330,000 = £194,800 @ 1.10% × 10/366 =	58.55
24 July 2021 to 31 December 2021	
524,800 – 440,000 = 84,800 @ 1.10% × 161/366 =	410.33
Normal due date for payment — 1 January 2022	
1 January 2022 to 10 September 2022	
524,800 – 440,000 = 84,800 @ 2.60% × 253/366 =	1,524.08
Interest on unpaid tax	2,340.20

New harmonised regime

[43.4] The harmonised regime applies a consistent interest charge to late payments across a number of taxes and duties. The regime is not yet in effect for corporation tax. If and when the regime is extended to corporation tax, the general rule will remain the same, in that interest on overdue corporation tax ('late payment interest') will run from the due date of payment to the day before the actual date of payment of the tax (or the date it is satisfied by set-off).

There will be a number of exceptions to the general rules and special provisions detail how the charge will apply specific circumstances. With regard to corporation tax special rules will apply with regard to certain loss carry back claims. These are detailed in *F(No 3)A 2010, Sch 9*. The new rules are similar to the previous rules outlined above.

Late payment interest will be charged on such amounts in the earlier period as if no carry back claim had been made, but only up to the normal due date for tax in the later period in which the loss arises (i.e. nine months and one day post the end of the accounting period), with regard to the following loss carry back claims:

(i) non-trading loan relationship deficit claims under *CTA 2009, ss 389(1), 459(1)(b)*;
(ii) loss claims under *CTA 2010, s 37* or *s 42*, which are not wholly carried back to the preceding twelve-month period;
(iii) claim under *TIOPA 2010, s 77* to carry back unrelieved foreign tax for an overseas branch or agency per *TIOPA 2010, s 72*; or
(iv) loss carry back under *CTA 2010, s 37* or *s 42* which generates or increases excess unrelieved foreign tax which is then carried back under a *TIOPA 2010, s 77* claim.

With regard to payment of corporation tax by persons other than the company assessed, under: *TCGA 1992, ss 137(4), 139(7)* or *190; FA 1998 Sch 18 para 75A(2); CTA 2009, s 795(2)*; and *CTA 2010, Ch 7 Pt 22*; the late payment interest start date in respect of such amount is the date when the tax became due and payable.

Under the harmonised regime, where there is a 'common period' then neither late payment interest nor repayment interest will arise. A 'common period' arises where there is an amount of corporation tax payable by the company at the same time there is an amount of corporation tax repayable to the company by HMRC; *FA 2009, Sch 54A*. In addition, this schedule sets out the conditions to apply for HMRC to recover repayment interest which ought not to have been paid as if it were late payment interest.

The harmonised regime applies to income tax self assessment with effect from 31 October 2011 (see *SI 2011 No 701*), to the annual tax on enveloped dwellings with effect from 1 October 2013 (see *SI 2013 No 2472*), and to construction industry scheme deductions with effect from 6 May 2014 (see *SI 2014 No 992*). The commencement date for corporation tax self assessment has not yet been fixed.

Interest rates

[43.5] The interest rate is determined by criteria contained in Treasury regulations made by statutory instrument; see *SI 1989 No 1297, Regs 3ZAA, 3ZB*.

It is understood that a denominator of 366 is used in calculations of such interest regardless of whether or not a leap year is involved.

Self-assessment

Overdue corporation tax payments

[43.6] For underpayments of corporation tax for accounting periods ending on or after 1 July 1999, the following rates of interest apply.

- **2.60% p.a. from 7 April 2020**
- 2.75% p.a. from 30 March 2020 to 6 April 2020
- 3.25% p.a. from 21 August 2018 to 29 March 2020
- 3.00% p.a. from 21 November 2017 to 20 August 2018
- 2.75% p.a. from 23 August 2016 to 20 November 2017
- 3.00% p.a. from 29 September 2009 to 22 August 2016
- 2.50% p.a. from 24 March 2009 to 28 September 2009
- 3.50% p.a. from 27 January 2009 to 23 March 2009
- 4.50% p.a. from 6 January 2009 to 26 January 2009
- 5.50% p.a. from 6 December 2008 to 5 January 2009
- 6.50% p.a. from 6 November 2008 to 5 December 2008
- 7.50% p.a. from 6 January 2008 to 5 November 2008
- 8.50% p.a. from 6 August 2007 to 5 January 2008
- 7.50% p.a. from 6 September 2006 to 5 August 2007
- 6.50% p.a. from 6 September 2005 to 5 September 2006
- 7.50% p.a. from 6 September 2004 to 5 September 2005
- 6.50% p.a. from 6 December 2003 to 5 September 2004
- 5.50% p.a. from 6 August 2003 to 5 December 2003
- 6.50% p.a. from 6 November 2001 to 5 August 2003
- 7.50% p.a. from 6 May 2001 to 5 November 2001
- 8.50% p.a. from 6 February 2000 to 5 May 2001

- 7.50% p.a. from 6 March 1999 to 5 February 2000
- 8.50% p.a. from 7 January 1999 to 5 March 1999

Overdue instalment payments

For accounting periods ending on or after 1 July 1999, a special rate of interest applies in the case of certain 'large' companies, which are required to make instalment payments in respect of their corporation tax liabilities (see 58.3 PAYMENT OF TAX). The special rate of interest applies to any unpaid instalments until nine months after the end of the accounting period (whereafter the normal interest rate (above) applies). Details are as follows.

- **1.10% p.a. from 30 March 2020**
- 1.25% p.a. from 23 March 2020 to 29 March 2020
- 1.75% p.a. from 13 August 2018 to 22 March 2020
- 1.50% p.a. from 13 November 2017 to 12 August 2018
- 1.25% p.a. from 15 August 2016 to 12 November 2017
- 1.50% p.a. from 16 March 2009 to 14 August 2016
- 2.00% p.a. from 16 February 2009 to 15 March 2009
- 2.50% p.a. from 19 January 2009 to 15 February 2009
- 3.00% p.a. from 15 December 2008 to 18 January 2009
- 4.00% p.a. from 17 November 2008 to 14 December 2008
- 5.50% p.a. from 20 October 2008 to 16 November 2008
- 6.00% p.a. from 21 April 2008 to 19 October 2008
- 6.25% p.a. from 18 February 2008 to 20 April 2008
- 6.50% p.a. from 17 December 2007 to 17 February 2008
- 6.75% p.a. from 16 July 2007 to 16 December 2007
- 6.50% p.a. from 21 May 2007 to 15 July 2007
- 6.25% p.a. from 22 January 2007 to 20 May 2007
- 6.00% p.a. from 20 November 2006 to 21 January 2007
- 5.75% p.a. from 14 August 2006 to 19 November 2006
- 5.50% p.a. from 15 August 2005 to 13 August 2006
- 5.75% p.a. from 16 August 2004 to 14 August 2005
- 5.50% p.a. from 21 June 2004 to 15 August 2004
- 5.25% p.a. from 17 May 2004 to 20 June 2004
- 5.00% p.a. from 16 February 2004 to 16 May 2004
- 4.75% p.a. from 17 November 2003 to 15 February 2004
- 4.50% p.a. from 21 July 2003 to 16 November 2003
- 4.75% p.a. from 17 February 2003 to 20 July 2003
- 5.00% p.a. from 19 November 2001 to 16 February 2003
- 5.50% p.a. from 15 October 2001 to 18 November 2001
- 5.75% p.a. from 1 October 2001 to 14 October 2001
- 6.00% p.a. from 13 August 2001 to 30 September 2001
- 6.25% p.a. from 21 May 2001 to 12 August 2001
- 6.50% p.a. from 16 April 2001 to 20 May 2001
- 6.75% p.a. from 19 February 2001 to 15 April 2001
- 7.00% p.a. from 20 April 2000 to 18 February 2001
- 8.00% p.a. from 21 February 2000 to 19 April 2000
- 7.75% p.a. from 24 January 2000 to 20 February 2000
- 7.50% p.a. from 15 November 1999 to 23 January 2000
- 7.25% p.a. from 20 September 1999 to 14 November 1999

- 7.00% p.a. from 21 June 1999 to 19 September 1999
- 7.25% p.a. from 19 April 1999 to 20 June 1999
- 7.50% p.a. from 15 February 1999 to 18 April 1999
- 8.00% p.a. from 18 January 1999 to 14 February 1999
- 8.25% p.a. from 7 January 1999 to 17 January 1999

[*SI 1989 No 1297, Regs 3ZA, 3ZB; SI 1998 No 3175, Reg 7; SI 1998 No 3176, Regs 4–6; SI 2000 No 893*].

Effective date of payment of tax

[43.7] Companies must submit their tax returns online and pay all corporation tax, interest and late-filing penalties electronically. [*SI 2003 No 282, Reg 3*].

Payment can be made by any of the methods listed below. The effective date of payment is given for each method.

(1) *Direct debit.* The effective date of payment is one bank working day before the payment collection date as agreed in the payment plan. Initially, the direct debit must be set up at least five bank working days before the date the company wants to make the payment. For subsequent payments, at least three bank working days should be allowed.
(2) *Faster payment* — by online or telephone banking — the date HMRC receives the payment.
(3) *Electronic funds transfer* — payment by BACS, CHAPS or Government Banking Service — one day prior to receipt by HMRC.
(4) *Debit or credit card over the internet* (HMRC's *BillPay* system) — the date on which payment is made.
(5) *Bank giro or Girobank* — the date on which payment is made at the bank.
(6) *At a Post Office with a scannable payslip* — the date payment is made.

(HMRC Debt Management and Banking Manual DMBM201020).

Payment made in any other manner need not be accepted as payment. However it is specifically provided that if such payments are tendered, accepted and paid by cheque, they will be treated as made on the second business day after the cheque is received. [*SI 2003 No 282, Reg 3A*].

Income tax deducted from payments

[43.8] As regards income tax payable by companies that they have deducted from yearly interest and other payments, interest arises if payment is made after the due date. The interest will run until the date of payment, but see further below where the income tax due for an earlier return period is discharged by items received in a later return period.

The rates of interest for payments due on or after 14 October 1999 (i.e. under self-assessment) are as under **43.2**(ii) above.

[*TMA 1970, s 87; FA 1989, s 178*].

For *UK-resident companies*, the due dates are 14 days after the expiry of the return periods (ending 31 March, 30 June, 30 September, 31 December and with the ending of an accounting period) in which the relevant dividends or other payments were made and interest will run from these dates even if they are non-business days.

[*ITA 2007, s 945 et seq*].

If a payment is made by a company on a date not falling within an accounting period of the company, tax is due 14 days after the payment.

[*ITA 2007, s 956 et seq)*].

Where income tax paid is repaid or discharged following the receipt in a later return period of FII or income suffering tax by deduction, interest will nevertheless be chargeable where the original payment was late. The interest charged in such a case will, cease to run at the earliest of:

- the date the income tax was paid;
- 14 days after the end of the later return period; or,
- if the return for that period was made within those 14 days, from the date of the return.

[*TMA 1970, s 87(2)(3); ITA 2007, s 1025*].

See **41.8** INCOME TAX IN RELATION TO A COMPANY.

The harmonised regime under *FA 2009* replicates these provisions — *FA 2009, Sch 53 para 13*.

For *non-UK resident companies* (and non-corporates), assessment is directly under *ITA 2007, ss 693, 964;* (see **41.8** INCOME TAX IN RELATION TO A COMPANY). Interest under *TMA 1970, s 86* runs from 31 January following the end of the year of assessment. See HMRC Tax Bulletin February 2001 p 827 for the application of these provisions.

In the case of *Mellham Ltd v Burton (Collector of Taxes)* HL [2006] STC 908, interest was held not to be payable on overdue ACT to the extent that, if paid, it would have been repaid or set off against mainstream corporation tax.

With regard to ACT please see earlier versions of this annual.

Simon's Taxes. See **A4.626.**

Exchange restrictions

[43.9] Where corporation tax is payable in respect of income or chargeable gains arising abroad which cannot be remitted to the UK due to action of the foreign government, HMRC may allow the tax to remain uncollected. If so, interest ceases to run from the date on which HMRC were in possession of the information necessary to make their decision. No interest is payable if that date is within three months of the due and payable date.

Where a demand for payment is subsequently made by HMRC, interest begins to run again unless the tax is paid within three months. [*TMA 1970, s 92*]. See **64.4** RESIDENCE.

A claim can be made by the company for such unremitted income not to be taken into account for corporation tax purposes. [*CTA 2009, ss 1274, 1275*].

See HMRC Company Taxation Manual CTM92200.

Interest charge objections

[43.10] HMRC do not have a general power to mitigate interest, ultimately if the tax due is reduced then the interest charged will also be reduced. However, taxpayers can raise an objection to the interest charge by writing to their Corporation Tax Office. HMRC's Interest Review Unit will consider any such objection and decide whether there is a case for the interest to be reduced. HMRC guidance setting out the circumstances when mitigation of interest will be considered can be found in the Debt Management and Banking Manual at DMB404010 and DMB404020.

It is considered that, generally, interest may be mitigated in cases of error or unreasonable delay on the part of HMRC which financially disadvantaged the taxpayer by either imposing an interest charge that would not otherwise have had to be paid, or increasing the amount of an interest charge that already existed or was building up.

Simon's Taxes. See A4.620.

Interest on judgment debts

[43.11] The same rate of interest as under the harmonised interest regime (see 43.4 above; currently 2.60% p.a.) applies to interest payable to HMRC under *Judgments Act 1938, s 17* or under an order under *County Courts Act 1984, s 74* where the debt to which the interest relates arises from court proceedings relating to a tax matter. See *F(No 2)A 2015, s 52*. Similar rules apply in Scotland and Northern Ireland. See *FA 2016, ss 170, 171*.

44

Interest on Overpaid Tax

Introduction to interest on overpaid tax

[44.1] Repayments of corporation tax attract repayment interest under *ICTA 1988, s 826*. Interest runs from the later of the normal due date and the date on which the tax was paid. Separate rules apply to large companies required to pay corporation tax by instalments. Companies that pay tax before the normal due date are entitled to interest ('credit interest') from HMRC, usually (though not at the time of writing) at a higher rate.

The harmonised interest regime for all taxes and duties administered by HMRC under *FA 2009, s 102, Sch 54* does not yet apply to corporation tax.

Restitution interest

Special rules apply to companies awarded restitution interest as a result of a mistake in law or following unlawful collection of tax by HMRC, as a result of a judgment or an agreement which became final on or after 21 October 2015. Such interest is chargeable to corporation tax at a special rate of 45%, generally deducted at source by HMRC (which is then set off against the liability when it is formally assessed). See further **1.7** INTRODUCTION: CHARGE TO TAX, RATES AND PROFIT COMPUTATIONS. [*CTA 2010, ss 357YA–357YW*].

Corporation tax self assessment periods

[44.2] For accounting periods ending on or after 1 July 1999, to which self-assessment applies, a repayment of tax or payment of credit carries interest from the 'material date' until the payment order is issued, where the repayment or payment falls to be made in respect of any of the following:

(a) corporation tax for the period;

(b) income tax in respect of a payment received in the period;
(c) research and development tax credits (see **63** RESEARCH AND DEVELOPMENT EXPENDITURE);
(d) land remediation tax credits (see **59.14** PROFIT COMPUTATIONS) or life assurance company tax credits;
(e) film tax credits (see **26.17** CREATIVE INDUSTRIES RELIEFS);
(f) television tax credits (see **26.6** CREATIVE INDUSTRIES RELIEFS);
(g) video game tax credits (see **26.12** CREATIVE INDUSTRIES RELIEFS);
(h) theatre game tax credits (see **26.31** CREATIVE INDUSTRIES RELIEFS);
(i) orchestra tax credits (see **26.38** CREATIVE INDUSTRIES RELIEFS);
(j) exhibition tax credits (see **26.44** CREATIVE INDUSTRIES RELIEFS);
(k) first-year tax credits payable under *CAA 2001, Sch A1* (see **10.18** CAPITAL ALLOWANCES ON PLANT AND MACHINERY).

Details of the rates, including those for instalment payments by 'large companies', are as set out in **44.4** below.

Interest under these provisions is paid without deduction of tax. Where interest is payable under these provisions to a company within the charge to corporation tax, it is brought into account in computing profits or income under the loan relationship rules (see **50.3** LOAN RELATIONSHIPS).

The '*material date*' is:

(i) for corporation tax, the later of the date the corporation tax was paid and the date on which it became (or would have become) due and payable, i.e. nine months after the end of the accounting period (see **58.2** PAYMENT OF TAX);
(ii) for income tax repayments and payments of tax credit in relation to (b) or (c) above, the day after the end of the accounting period in which the payment was received by the company;
(iii) in the case of a tax repayment on a claim under *CTA 2010, s 458* in respect of repayment, release or writing off of a close company loan or advance (see **16.15** close companies), the later of:
  - the date the entitlement to the tax repayment accrued (i.e. the date nine months after the end of the accounting period in which the loan etc. was made or, if the loan had not been repaid, released or written off at that date, the date nine months after the end of the accounting period in which it was repaid, released or written off); and
  - the actual date of payment of the tax to be repaid;
(iv) in the case of research and development and tax credits within (e)–(k) above, the filing date (see **65.4** RETURNS) for the company tax return for the accounting period for which the credit is claimed (or if later the date of receipt by HMRC of the return (or amended return) containing the claim);
(v) in the case of first-year tax credits, the later of the filing date of the company's return for the chargeable period and the date the return, or amended return is filed with HMRC.

In relation to repayments within (iii) above, the repayment is treated as if it were a repayment of corporation tax for the accounting period in which the loan (or part) was repaid, released or written off.

Corporation tax repayments are as far as possible treated as repayments of tax paid on a later rather than an earlier date.

Large companies — Instalment Payments

In the case of certain 'large' companies, which are required to make instalment payments in respect of their corporation tax liabilities (see **58.3** PAYMENT OF TAX), a special rate (see **44.4** below) applies to any excess instalment payments until nine months after the end of the accounting period concerned and a lower rate applies to repayments made after that time. This is termed 'credit interest'.

The special higher rate also applies to corporation tax payments made by a company, which is *not* a large company, before the day following the expiry of nine months after the end of an accounting period. Interest is payable from the date of payment until that day although not for periods before the first instalment date which would apply if the company were a large company.

Credit interest is normally calculated when the tax charge is recorded or (if later) when the normal due date has passed.

Restrictions on interest

Interest is restricted where losses of an accounting period are carried back under *CTA 2010, s 37* (see **51.4** LOSSES) or under *CTA 2010, s 45F* (see **51.9** LOSSES) to an accounting period not falling wholly within the twelve months preceding the period in which the loss was incurred or, in the case of a claim under *s 45F*, the period in which the trade ceased. Interest on any repayment of corporation tax paid for the earlier period, or on any payment of income tax or tax credit in respect of payments received in that period, is only payable from nine months after the end of the accounting period in which the loss arose or the trade ceased.

Similarly when the carry back of a loan relationship non-trading deficit gives rise to a repayment of corporation tax (or income tax) interest on the repayment runs from the normal due date for payment of tax for the period in which the deficit arose. See **50.4** LOAN RELATIONSHIPS.

Recovery of interest paid

Where, solely as a result of a change in a company's corporation tax liability, it appears to HMRC that any interest paid under these provisions ought not to have been paid, it is recoverable without assessment as if it were INTEREST ON OVERDUE TAX (**43**).

[*ICTA 1988, ss 826, 826A; FA 1989, ss 178, 179(1)(c)(ii), 180(6); CTA 2009, ss 389(1), 459(1)(b); F(No 2)A 2017, Sch 4 para 106, Sch 6 para 2; FA 2019, s 88(1)(2); SI 1998 No 3175, Reg 8*].

Simon's Taxes. See **A4.632–A4.634, D1.1320.**

Repayment supplement is not paid in respect of out of date claims, since the amount repaid is regarded as an *ex gratia* payment made without acceptance of any legal liability. (HMRC Repayment Claims Manual, RM5104).

In the case of *Sempra Metals Ltd v CIR* [2007] UKHL 34, HL, (following the finding by the ECJ that the requirement that both parties to an election under *s 247* be UK-resident contravened EC law), it was held that in providing for compensation, interest should be calculated on a compound basis.

Example 1

X Ltd prepares accounts to 31 December. On 15 June 2021, it submits its tax return for the year ended 31 December 2020 showing a corporation tax liability for the period of £14,000, and accompanied by a payment of £7,000. On 1 October 2021, it makes a further payment of £7,000. It subsequently submits an amended return showing a reduced liability of £12,500, and £1,500 is repaid to the company on 1 December 2021.

It is assumed that interest rates for corporation tax repayments other than by instalment, and for tax paid before the due date, remain unchanged after 29 September 2009 and 21 September 2009 respectively.

X Ltd will be entitled to interest on overpaid tax, calculated as follows.

		£
15.6.21 to 30.9.21	£7,000 × 0.5% × 108/365 =	10.35
1.10.21 to 30.11.21	£1,500 × 0.5% × 61/365 =	1.25
Total interest		£11.60

Example 2 — instalment payments

Z Ltd has no associated companies and had taxable profits in excess of £1,500,000 for the year ended 31 March 2019. For the year ended 31 March 2021, Z Ltd pays £143,000 for the first instalment on 30 September 2020 (early payment of instalment due on 14 October) this being equivalent to a quarter of its estimated corporation tax liability of £572,000.

The same amount is paid on the due dates for the second and third instalments and on 5 July 2021 for the fourth instalment (early). On 3 September 2021, the tax liability is agreed at £506,800 and £65,200 is repaid to the company on 22 September 2022.

As above, the rates of interest are assumed for the purposes of this example to remain unchanged after 29 September and 21 September 2009.

The interest on tax overpaid is calculated as follows.

Instalments due on quarter dates £506,800 × 1/4 = £126,700

	£
1st instalment	
14 October 2020 to 13 January 2021	
143,000 – 126,700 = £16,300 @ 0.5% × 91/365 =	20.32
1st and 2nd instalments	
14 January 2021 to 13 April 2021	
286,000 – 253,400 = £32,600 @ 0.5% × 90/365 =	40.19
1st, 2nd and 3rd instalments	

14 April 2021 to 5 July 2021	
429,000 – 380,100 = £48,900 @ 0.5% × 83/365 =	55.60
Plus early payment 4th instalment	
6 July 2021 to 13 July 2021	
572,000 – 380,100 = £191,900 @ 0.5% × 8/365 =	21.03
14 July 2021 to 31 December 2021	
£572,000–506,800 = £65,200 @ 0.5% × 169/365 =	150.94
Normal due date 1 January 2022	
1 January 2022 to 21 September 2022	
572,000 – 506,800 = £65,200 @ 0.5% × 264/365 =	235.79
Interest on overpaid tax	523.87

Harmonised regime

[44.3] The following provisions do not yet apply for corporation tax purposes. After the provisions have come into force, interest will be paid from the 'start date', as defined, to the date of repayment (including set-off).

The general rule found at *FA 2009, Sch 54* is that the repayment start date is the later of: the date on which the amount was paid to HMRC; and, where the payment is in connection with a liability to make a payment to HMRC and is to be repaid by them, the date payment of the tax became due and payable. For corporation tax purposes the general due and payable date is nine months and one day after the end of the accounting period. [*TMA 1970, s 59D*].

The instalment payment regime is to remain outside the new provisions.

Repayment interest on the corporation tax to be repaid for earlier periods will only arise from the day after the expiry of nine months following the end of the period in which the deficit, loss, or excess arose, with regard to the following:

(i) non-trading loan relationship deficit claims under *CTA 2009, ss 389(1), 459(1)(b)*;
(ii) loss claims under *CTA 2010, s 37, s 42* or *s 45F*, which are not wholly carried back to the preceding twelve-month period;
(iii) claim under *TIOPA 2010, s 77* to carry back unrelieved foreign tax for an overseas branch or agency per *TIOPA 2010, s 72*; or
(iv) loss carry back under *CTA 2010, s 37, s 42* or *s 45F* which generates or increases excess unrelieved foreign tax which is then carried back under a *TIOPA 2010, s 77* claim.

In addition, the provisions clarify the position as to the start date of repayment interest for a repayment of income tax — the date is the day after the end of the accounting period in which the repayment is received.

With regard to close companies, where relief is claimed following the repayment of a loan to a participator, the start date is the later of: (a) nine months after the end of the accounting period in which the loan date falls, or if the loan repayment date is on or after the tax due date, nine months after the end of the accounting period in which the loan is repaid; or (b) the date on which the tax which is to be repaid was paid to HMRC.

Under the new harmonised regime, where there is a 'common period' then neither late payment interest nor repayment interest will arise. A 'common period' arises where there is an amount of corporation tax payable by the company at the same time there is an amount of corporation tax repayable to the company by HMRC. See *FA 2009, Sch 54A*. In addition, this schedule sets out the conditions to apply for HMRC to recover repayment interest which ought not to have been paid as if it were late payment interest.

The harmonised regime applies to income tax self assessment with effect from 31 October 2011 (see *SI 2011 No 701*), to the annual tax on enveloped dwellings with effect from 1 October 2013 (see *SI 2013 No 2472*), and to construction industry scheme deductions with effect from 6 May 2014 (see *SI 2014 No 992*). The commencement date for corporation tax self assessment has not yet been fixed.

[*FA 2009, Sch 54; F(No 2)A 2017, Sch 4 para 182*].

Interest rates

[44.4] Interest rates are based on the official bank rate as determined by the Monetary Policy Committee of the Bank of England. Revisions take effect 13 working days after any change of base rate is announced, and are published on the HMRC website

The standard repayment interest rate is base rate less 1%, subject to a minimum rate of 0.5%.

A special rate applies to quarterly instalment repayment interest — calculated as base rate less 0.25%. However, currently the quarterly instalment payment, and main repayment, rates are the same as the bank interest rate is sufficiently low that the minimum rate applies.

[*FA 1989, ss 178, 179; SI 1989 No 1297; SI 2011 No 2446*].

It is understood that a denominator of 365 is used in calculations of repayment interest regardless of whether or not a leap year is involved.

Self-assessment

Corporation tax repayments

[44.5] For corporation tax repayments for accounting periods ending on or after 1 July 1999, the following rate of interest applies, changes being announced in HMRC Press Releases.

0.50% p.a. from 29 September 2009
0.00% p.a. from 27 January 2009 to 28 September 2009
1.00% p.a. from 6 January 2009 to 26 January 2009
2.00% p.a. from 6 December 2008 to 5 January 2009

3.00% p.a. from 6 November 2008 to 5 December 2008
4.00% p.a. from 6 January 2008 to 5 November 2008
5.00% p.a. from 6 August 2007 to 5 January 2008
4.00% p.a. from 6 September 2006 to 5 August 2007
3.00% p.a. from 6 September 2005 to 5 September 2006
4.00% p.a. from 6 September 2004 to 5 September 2005
3.00% p.a. from 6 December 2003 to 5 September 2004
2.00% p.a. from 6 August 2003 to 5 December 2003
3.00% p.a. from 6 November 2001 to 5 August 2003
4.00% p.a. from 6 May 2001 to 5 November 2001
5.00% p.a. from 6 February 2000 to 5 May 2001
4.00% from 6 March 1999 to 5 February 2000
5.00% p.a. from 7 January 1999 to 5 March 1999

Instalment payments and other tax paid early

For accounting periods ending on or after 1 July 1999, a special rate of interest (credit interest) applies in the case of certain 'large' companies, which are required to make instalment payments in respect of their corporation tax liabilities (see **58.3** PAYMENT OF TAX). The special rate applies to any excess instalment payments until nine months after the end of the accounting period concerned. The lower rate referred to above applies to repayments made after that time.

The special rate also applies to corporation tax payments made early by a company, which is *not* a large company, early being before the day following the expiry of nine months after the end of an accounting period. Interest is payable from the later of: (a) the date on which the tax was paid, and (b) the date on which, if the company had been a large company, the first instalment of tax for the accounting period would have been due; up to the normal due date.

Changes are announced in HMRC Press Releases. Details are as follows.

0.50% p.a. from 21 September 2009
0.25% p.a. from 16 March 2009 to 20 September 2009
0.75% p.a. from 16 February 2009 to 15 March 2009
1.25% p.a. from 19 January 2009 to 15 February 2009
1.75% p.a. from 15 December 2008 to 18 January 2009
2.75% p.a. from 17 November 2008 to 14 December 2008
4.25% p.a. from 20 October 2008 to 16 November 2008
4.75% p.a. from 21 April 2008 to 19 October 2008
5.00% p.a. from 18 February 2008 to 20 April 2008
5.25% p.a. from 17 December 2007 to 17 February 2008
5.50% p.a. from 16 July 2007 to 16 December 2007
5.25% p.a. from 21 May 2007 to 15 July 2007
5.00% p.a. from 22 January 2007 to 20 May 2007
4.75% p.a. from 20 November 2006 to 21 January 2007
4.50% p.a. from 14 August 2006 to 19 November 2006
4.25% p.a. from 15 August 2005 to 13 August 2006
4.50% p.a. from 16 August 2004 to 14 August 2005
4.25% p.a. from 21 June 2004 to 15 August 2004
4.00% p.a. from 17 May 2004 to 20 June 2004

3.75% p.a. from 16 February 2004 to 16 May 2004
3.50% p.a. from 17 November to 15 February 2004
3.25% p.a. from 21 July 2003 to 16 November 2003
3.50% p.a. from 17 February 2003 to 20 July 2003
3.75% p.a. from 19 November 2001 to 16 February 2003
4.25% p.a. from 15 October 2001 to 18 November 2001
4.50% p.a. from 1 October 2001 to 14 October 2001
4.75% p.a. from 13 August 2001 to 30 September 2001
5.00% p.a. from 21 May 2001 to 12 August 2001
5.25% p.a. from 16 April 2001 to 20 May 2001
5.50% p.a. from 19 February 2001 to 15 April 2001
5.75% p.a. from 21 February 2000 to 18 February 2001
5.50% p.a. from 24 January 2000 to 20 February 2000
5.25% p.a. from 15 November 1999 to 23 January 2000
5.00% p.a. from 20 September 1999 to 14 November 1999
4.75% p.a. from 21 June 1999 to 19 September 1999
5.00% p.a. from 19 April 1999 to 20 June 1999
5.25% p.a. from 15 February 1999 to 18 April 1999
5.75% p.a. from 18 January 1999 to 14 February 1999
6.00% p.a. from 7 January 1999 to 17 January 1999

[*SI 1998 No 3175, Reg 8; SI 1998 No 3176, Regs 4, 7, 8*].

Unauthorised demands for tax

[44.6] There is a general right to interest under *Supreme Court Act 1981, s 35A* in a case where a taxpayer submits to such an unauthorised demand, provided that the payment was not made voluntarily to close a transaction. (*Woolwich Equitable Building Society v CIR* HL 1992, 65 TC 265 — the regulation in question was held to be ultra vires).

Simon's Taxes. See **A1.707**.

Value added tax

[44.7] Value added tax repayment supplements under *VATA 1994, s 79* are disregarded for corporation tax purposes. [*CTA 2009, s 1286*].

Over-repayments

[44.8] See **58.24** PAYMENT OF TAX, **6.4** ASSESSMENTS as regards assessment of overpaid interest under these provisions.

Interest on judgment debts

[44.9] A special rate of interest applies to interest payable by HMRC under *Judgments Act 1938, s 17* or under an order under *County Courts Act 1984, s 74* where the debt to which the interest relates arises from court proceedings relating to a tax matter. The annual rate is the Bank of England official rate plus 2%. See *F(No 2)A 2015, s 52*. With effect from 15 September 2016, similar rules apply in Scotland and Northern Ireland. See *FA 2016, ss 170, 171*.

Interest on unlawful ACT

[44.10] *FA 2019* introduced a new non-exclusive statutory remedy to provide an interest return on unlawfully charged advance corporation tax ('ACT'). The remedy entitles a company (including the successor to a company which paid the ACT) to an order requiring HMRC to pay to it an amount representing simple interest at the applicable rates on the ACT for the period from payment to the date the ACT was set off or repaid, together with simple interest on that interest from that date until the interest is repaid. The provisions apply where the company started proceedings against HMRC before 12 December 2012 in respect of ACT if the claim has not been settled, discontinued or finally determined. They apply only to ACT paid on or after 1 January 1996 or in the six years ending immediately before the proceedings were started and which was set off or repaid (wholly or in part) before the proceedings commenced. For the applicable rates of interest see *FA 2019, s 85(4)*.

These provisions are intended to remove uncertainty about the interest position following *Prudential Assurance Co Ltd v HMRC*, SC [2018] UKSC 39.

The provisions do not limit the remedies that a court may award, but only a single remedy can be obtained (so that a court award prohibits an order under these provisions, and vice versa).

Interest paid by HMRC under these provisions is taxable in the accounting period in which it is paid.

[*FA 2019, ss 85, 86*].

45

Investment Companies and Investment Business

Simon's Taxes. See D7.301–D7.324.

Introduction to investment companies and investment business

[45.1] Companies with investment business, and investment companies, should be distinguished from trading companies. Whilst the basic approach to the calculation of their profits within the charge to corporation tax is the same, in that you consider the separate sources of income (each trade for example being such a source), there is key difference with regard to the deductions for expenses which are allowed. Unlike trading companies, companies with investment business can obtain relief for management expenses that are not otherwise relievable, subject to certain restrictions. [*CTA 2009, s 1217(2)(3)*].

The broad definition of what constitutes management expenses is examined further below, along with any restrictions applicable to their deduction.

The position with regard to certain types of receipt is then examined at 45.7, and the specific relief for investment companies with regard to unquoted shares, at 45.8.

The updated anti-avoidance provisions relating to a change in ownership, post the tax law rewrite which was completed with *CTA 2010*, is then considered at 45.9.

Companies with investment business

A '*company with investment business*' is a company whose business consists wholly or partly of making investments. It is not simply a company that holds investments or receives interest income, it must have a business of making investments. A credit union is not a company with investment business. [*CTA 2009, s 1218B*]. However, it will include, for example, a trading company with shares in subsidiary companies, as this is a distinct business of making investments.

'*The making of investments*' does not require turning them over (*Tyre Investment Trust Ltd* (1924) 12 TC 646). For treatment of income from land as investment income, see *Webb v Conelee Properties Ltd* (1982) 56 TC 149.

Investment companies

The expression '*investment company*' is now only relevant when considering which companies may claim relief against income for capital losses on sales of certain shares, see further **45.8** below and for the purposes of foreign currency provisions (see **45.2** below). Broadly, an investment company is a company whose business consists wholly or mainly in the making of investments and the principal part of whose income is derived from such investments.

A company which carries on the business of buying and selling investments with a view to making a profit from such dealing and whose receipt of income from the investments is incidental to the main business is often called an investment dealing company or finance company. This type of company is not an investment company and the profits and losses of such a company are calculated in accordance with the rules for taxing trades. See **1** INTRODUCTION and **67** TRADING INCOME.

Functional currency

[45.2] UK resident investment companies may elect for a different functional currency for tax purposes than the currency used in the accounts. See **34.4** FOREIGN CURRENCY.

Management expenses

[45.3] The ability to claim management expenses includes companies with investment business – not just those qualifying as investment companies – and also includes non UK resident companies. The extension to companies with an investment business is important for companies who hold shares in subsidiaries as well as having their own trade.

Management expenses of a company's investment business which are 'referable' to a particular accounting period (i.e. when they are debited in the accounts, see further below) are allowed as a deduction in computing the company's total profits for corporation tax purposes for that period.

For this purpose, management expenses are management expenses of the company's investment business so far as they are incurred in respect of the business of making investments and so far as the investments concerned are not held for an 'unallowable purpose' during the accounting period. Any apportionment of expenses necessary to meet these requirements is to be made on a just and reasonable basis. See **45.4** below for certain expenses which are treated as management expenses.

No deduction is allowed for expenses which are otherwise deductible from total profits or in computing any component of total profits. Therefore where the expenses relate to a particular source of income, such as UK property income, or debits under the loan relationship rules, then they will be deducted in calculating the profits of such source, and not as a general management expense of the company.

Subject to certain exceptions, no deduction is allowed for expenses of a capital nature. The exceptions are amounts treated as management expenses under:

- *CTA 2009, ss 1232–1246* (see **45.4**(i)–(x) below);
- *CTA 2009, s 985(3)* (share incentive plans);
- *CTA 2009, s 999(4)* (deduction for costs of setting up certain employee share schemes);
- *CTA 2009, s 1000(3)* (deduction for costs of setting up employee share ownership trust);
- *CTA 2009, s 1013(3)* (employee share acquisitions: relief if shares acquired by employee or other person);
- *CTA 2009, s 1021(3)* (employee share acquisitions: relief if employee or other person acquires share option);
- *FA 2004, s 196* (employers' contributions to pension scheme); or
- any other provision of the Corporation Tax Acts.

[*CTA 2009, ss 1219, 1221(1)*].

In *Centrica Overseas Holdings Ltd v HMRC* FTT, [2020] UKFTT 197 (TC); 2020 SWTI 1317, the FTT held that expenditure by a company in connections with a sale of the business of a subsidiary was not management expenses. COHL was an intermediate holding company in the group headed by Centrica plc. It had a Dutch subsidiary, O, and in 2009, Centrica made a strategic decision to sell the businesses of O and its subsidiaries, preferably by way of a sale of O's shares. In the event, there was a partial sale by O in 2011 of the assets of its subsidiaries. Centrica incurred expenses of £3.8 million over the period 2009–2011 paid to three firms for services relating to the transaction, including financial advice, finding a buyer, vendor due diligence and advice on Dutch law. The expenditure was recharged to COHL and the company claimed that £2.5 million of it was expenses of management deductible from its profits. The FTT held that the expenditure did not qualify as expenses of management of COHL's investment business because the company did not itself carry out any of the management activities in relation to which it was incurred. On a realistic view of the facts, it was Centrica that made all of the decisions. The group's central teams (legal, tax, M&A etc.) who worked on the sale did not think of themselves as providing services to COHL but as working to give effect to Centrica's decision to sell the O businesses. To the extent that the directors of COHL participated in managing the process, they did so in their group capacities as Head of Tax and General Counsel and there was no evidence to show that they took any relevant decisions as directors of COHL or that any of the advice for which the company paid was used by them as directors in conducting its investment business.

Accounting period to which management expenses are referable

Where management expenses are debited to a company's accounts (be it charged in the profit and loss account or income statement, the statement of recognised gains or losses or statement of changes in equity, or other statement) in accordance with generally accepted accounting practice ('GAAP') for a period of account which coincides with an accounting period, the expenses are '*referable*' to that accounting period.

Where the company's period of account does not coincide with an accounting period (for example where the company's period of account exceeds twelve months), the expenses are to be apportioned between any accounting periods falling within the period of account on a time basis unless that would give an unjust or unreasonable result in which case a just and reasonable method is to be used.

If a company draws up accounts for a period of account but management expenses are not debited in accordance with GAAP, the expenses are referable to the accounting period to which they would have been referable had they been debited in accordance with GAAP.

Where management expenses are not referable to an accounting period by virtue of the above provisions because the company has not drawn up accounts, or in any other instance where an accounting period does not fall within any period of account, then it has to be assumed that there is a period of account that coincides with it. If, under UK GAAP, the management expenses would be debited in the accounts drawn up for that deemed period, then it is to be assumed that they are so debited and referable to that accounting period.

These provisions do not take precedence over any other provision of the Corporation Tax Acts which provides for amounts to be treated as management expenses referable to an accounting period.

Where the employment costs of a Salaried Member of an LLP are expenses of management, but are not referable to an accounting period, then they are treated as referable to the accounting period in which they are paid. See further **56.11** PARTNERSHIPS, and **45.4** below.

[*CTA 2009, ss 1224–1227A, 1255(1)*].

Simon's Taxes. See **D7.305**.

Unallowable purpose

Investments are held for an '*unallowable purpose*' so far as they are held for a purpose that is not a business or other commercial purpose of the company or for the purpose of activities in respect of which the company is not within the charge to corporation tax. This will therefore exclude investments held for social or recreational purposes and investments of a non resident company with a permanent establishment in the UK, if the investment is not part of the business of that permanent establishment.

Investments are treated as not being held for a business or other commercial purpose if they are held directly or indirectly in consequence of, or otherwise in connection with, 'arrangements' the main purpose, or one of the main purposes, of which is to secure a deduction or increased deduction for management expenses or any other tax advantage (within *CTA 2010, s 1139*).

'*Arrangements*' include any agreement, understanding, scheme, transaction or series of transactions, whether or not legally enforceable. An expense which is only partly allowable must be apportioned on a 'just and reasonable' basis.

[*CTA 2009, s 1220*].

HMRC consider that the test would not be failed solely because the company's investments generate dividends exempt from tax under *CTA 2009, s 1285*, or capital gains covered by the substantial shareholdings exemption or exempt under *TCGA 1992, s 100(1)* (in the case of authorised unit trusts etc.), or because the investment is in a company which itself is not within the charge to corporation tax (for example, a non-UK resident subsidiary). See HMRC Company Taxation Manual CTM08210–08225.

There is a similar restriction for management expense deductions generally, found at *CTA 2009, s 1248*, see **45.5** below.

Reduction for income derived from non-taxable sources

Management expenses must be reduced by any income derived from non-taxable sources (other than 'exempt ABGH distributions') held in the course of a company's investment business or, in the case of a non-UK resident company, non-taxable sources held in the course of its investment business carried on through a UK permanent establishment which is property or rights used by, or held by or for that establishment (see **64.6** RESIDENCE). '*Exempt ABGH distributions*' are distributions within **29.2** (a), (b), (f) or (g) DISTRIBUTIONS which are exempt from corporation tax. [*CTA 2009, s 1222*].

Simon's Taxes. See **D7.307**.

Claw back of relief where credits reverse management expense debits

Accounts prepared in accordance with GAAP could include a deduction for management expenses made for a period of account earlier than that in which payment of the expense is made. This arises where the accounts include a debit for expenses accrued in the period. If some, or all, of the sum represented by the debit is paid, and then wholly or partly repaid (or the sum is never paid) the accounts for a later period of account will include a credit for the amount accrued and not paid. There are rules to deal with such a situation and to claw back any relief given.

Pursuant to such provisions, a claw back of relief for management expenses applies: where a 'credit' is 'brought into account' by a company in a period of account (the '*period of the credit*') that 'reverses' some or all of a 'debit' brought into account in an earlier period of account and that debit represents management expenses deductible for an accounting period ending before, or at the same time as, the period of the credit; and those management expenses are not expenses brought forward to that accounting period from an earlier accounting period.

For this purpose, a credit '*reverses*' a debit if it is made because the sum represented by the debit (i.e. the expenses in question) is paid and then repaid, or is never paid. A credit or debit is '*brought into account*' if it is brought into account in the company's profit and loss account or income statement, the statement of recognised gains or losses or statement of changes in equity, or other statement. A '*credit*' is an amount which increases or creates a profit or reduces a loss, and a '*debit*' is an amount which reduces a profit or increases or creates a loss, for accounting purposes for a period of account.

Where the period of the credit coincides with an accounting period, the 'reversal amount' is applied to reduce any management expenses (excluding any brought forward expenses) deductible for that accounting period. Any amount remaining after reducing those management expenses to nil is treated as a receipt of the company chargeable for that period under the charge to corporation tax on income.

Where the reversal period does not coincide with an accounting period, the reversal amount is apportioned between any accounting periods falling within the reversal period and only that amount apportioned to an accounting period is dealt with for that period in accordance with the above provisions. The apportionment is to be made on a time basis unless that would give an unjust or unreasonable result in which case a just and reasonable method is to be used. Where an accounting period does not coincide with, or fall within, any period of account of the company, a period of account is to be deemed to coincide with that accounting period and it is assumed that, in calculating for accounting purposes the company's profits and losses for that period of account, amounts were brought into account in accordance with UK GAAP.

The '*reversal amount*' is however much of the credit reverses the part of the debit that represents deductible management expenses. Any amount of the credit that represents sums otherwise taken into account in calculating the company's corporation tax profits or losses, whether in the relevant accounting period or any earlier accounting period, is excluded. The '*relevant accounting period*' for this purpose is the latest accounting period of the company falling wholly or partly in the period of the credit.

[*CTA 2009, ss 1228–1230, 1231(1)(2), 1255(2)(3)*].

Simon's Taxes. See **D7.313.**

Carry forward of excess management expenses etc.

Management expenses are automatically set against the investment income and gains in the current accounting period. Where the management expenses exceed the gross income and gains in the current period they are 'excess' and if the company is part of a group these excess management expenses may be transferred to a fellow 75% owned company, upon making the relevant claim (see 35 GROUP RELIEF).

Any management expenses which remain unrelieved in an accounting period may be carried forward and treated as management expenses of the next succeeding accounting period and may continue to be so carried forward until relieved. This includes any brought forward management expenses which are restricted under the bank loss relief restriction (i.e. the expenses fall within *CTA 2010, s 269CC*). For accounting periods beginning on or after 1 April 2017 (subject to the transitional rules below), a claim must be made for carry forward of excess management expenses. Such a claim must be made within two years after the end of the accounting period to which they are to be carried forward or within such later time as HMRC. Management expenses may not be carried forward to the extent that they are surrendered as group relief for carried forward losses (see **35.24** GROUP RELIEF). Management expenses carried forward are not required to be set off before any other deduction against total profits but are subject to the restriction on carried-forward losses at **51.13** LOSSES.

For these purposes, an accounting period which straddles 1 April 2017 is treated as if it were two separate accounting periods, the first ending on 31 March 2017 and the second beginning on 1 April 2017. Any necessary apportionments between the two periods must be made on a time basis unless that would produce an unjust or unreasonable result, in which case a just and reasonable basis must be used. Special rules apply, however, where the amount to be apportioned is either an amount chargeable to corporation tax which would have been less but for the CORPORATE INTEREST RESTRICTION (**25**) provisions or an amount for which relief is available which would have been greater but for the restriction. An amount chargeable to corporation tax which would not have arisen at all but for the restriction provisions is apportioned entirely to the second period.

Any qualifying charitable donations made in the accounting period, to the extent they are paid for the purpose of the company's investment business, may similarly be carried forward as management expenses.

[*CTA 2009, s 1223; F(No 2)A 2017, Sch 4 paras 6, 144, 190–192*]. See also **45.6** below with regard to losses of a property business.

Amounts treated as management expenses

[45.4] Generally expenses will only qualify for a deduction as a management expense to the extent that they are made in respect of the company's investment business and to the extent they are not made for an unallowable purposes, as highlighted above. There has been considerable case law on this subject, some of which is discussed further below.

Certain types of management expenses now have a statutory footing. The amounts listed at (i)–(x) below are treated as management expenses, so far as they would not otherwise be so treated, if they are not otherwise deductible from total profits or in calculating a component of total profits. [*CTA 2009, s 1232*].

(i) **Excess capital allowances.** Capital allowances on structures and buildings or plant and machinery to which a company with investment business is entitled in respect of a qualifying activity consisting of managing its investments (see **9.22** CAPITAL ALLOWANCES, **10.4** CAPITAL ALLOWANCES ON PLANT AND MACHINERY) are treated as management expenses so far as they cannot be deducted from the income of the business. The deemed expenses are referable to the accounting period for which the company is entitled to the allowances. [*CTA 2009, s 1233; SI 2019 No 1087, Reg 7(3)*]. **Simon's Taxes.** See **D7.308.**

(ii) **Payments for restrictive undertakings.** A payment for a restrictive undertaking which is treated as earnings of an employee under *ITEPA 2003, s 225* is treated as a management expense if it is made, or treated under *ITEPA 2003, s 226* (valuable consideration given for restrictive undertaking) as made, by a company with investment business. [*CTA 2009, s 1234*].

(iii) **Employees seconded to charities and educational establishments.** Where a company carrying on a business consisting wholly or partly of making investments makes the services of an employee employed for the purposes of that business available to a charity or educational establishment (within *CTA 2009, s 70*), the company's expenses attributable to the employment during the secondment are treated as management expenses. The secondment must be both stated and intended to be temporary. [*CTA 2009, s 1235*].

(iv) **Payroll deduction scheme — contributions to agents' expenses.** Where a company with investment business withholds sums from payments to an individual under an approved payroll deduction scheme (see *ITEPA 2003, s 714*) and pays those sums to an approved agent (within *ITEPA 2003, s 714(3)*), expenses the company incurs in making a payment to the agent for expenses incurred by him in connection with his scheme functions are treated as management expenses. [*CTA 2009, s 1236*].

(v) **Counselling and outplacement services.** 'Counselling expenses' incurred by a company with investment business in relation to an employee or office-holder of the company are treated as management expenses if certain conditions are met. For this purpose, '*counselling expenses*' are expenses incurred in the provision of services to the employee in connection with the cessation of the office or employment or incurred in the payment or reimbursement of fees for, or travelling expenses in connection with, such provision. The conditions to be met are conditions A–D and, for travelling expenses, condition E in *ITEPA 2003, s 310*. [*CTA 2009, s 1237*].

(vi) **Retraining expenses.** Expenses incurred by a company with investment business in the payment or reimbursement of 'retraining course expenses' (within *ITEPA 2003, s 311(2)*) for an employee or office-holder are treated as management expenses if the conditions in *ITEPA 2003, s 311(3)(4)* and, for travelling expenses, those in *s 311(5)*, are met. If the company's corporation tax liability for an accounting period has been determined on the assumption that a deduction for such expenses is allowable but the deduction is not in fact allowable, the recovery of tax provisions at *CTA 2009, s 75(2)–(6)* (see **69.25** TRADING INCOME — DEDUCTIONS) apply. [*CTA 2009, s 1238*].

(vii) **Redundancy payments etc.** Where a company with investment business makes a 'redundancy payment' or an 'approved contractual payment' to an employee, and management expenses are deductible by the company, then, if the payment is in respect of the employee's employment wholly in the investment business, it is treated as management expenses. In the case of an approved contractual payment, the deduction cannot exceed the amount which would have been due to the employee if a redundancy payment had been payable. If the payment is in respect of employment which is only partly in the investment business, the payment is apportioned on a just and reasonable basis.

Where the payment is referable to an accounting period beginning after the investment business has ceased, it is treated as referable to the last accounting period in which the business was carried on.

For this purpose, a '*redundancy payment*' is a redundancy payment payable under *Employment Rights Act 1996, Pt 11* (or Northern Ireland equivalent) and a '*contractual payment*' is one which, under an agreement, an employer is liable to make to an employee on the termination of his employment contract. Such a payment is '*approved*' if, in respect of the agreement, an order is in force under *Employment Rights Act 1996, s 157* (or Northern Ireland equivalent).

If the company's business, or part of it, permanently ceases and the company makes a payment to the employee in addition to the redundancy payment or, if an approved contractual payment is made, the amount that would have been due if a redundancy payment had been payable, the additional payment is treated as management expenses if it would not otherwise be so treated because of the cessation of the business or part of the business. The deduction is limited to three times the amount of the redundancy payment or, if an approved contractual payment is made, the amount that would have been due if a redundancy payment had been payable. If the additional payment is referable to an accounting period beginning after the investment business, or part of it, has ceased, it is treated as referable to the last accounting period in which the business or part was carried on.

A payment made by the Secretary of State under *Employment Rights Act 1996, s 167* (or an equivalent Northern Ireland payment) is treated as a redundancy payment or approved contractual payment by the company for the purpose of the above provisions to the extent that the company reimburses the government.

[*CTA 2009, ss 1239–1243*].

(viii) **Contributions to local enterprise organisations or urban regeneration companies.** Contributions, in cash or in kind, by a company with investment business to a 'local enterprise organisation' or an 'urban regeneration company' are treated as management expenses. If, however, the company or a connected person receives, or is entitled to receive, a 'disqualifying benefit', whether from the local enterprise organisation, urban regeneration company or anyone else, the management expenses are reduced by the value of the benefit. For this purpose, a '*disqualifying benefit*' is a benefit the expenses of obtaining which, if incurred directly by the company at arm's length, would not be deductible as management expenses. '*Local enterprise organisation*' and '*urban regeneration company*' are defined as for the purposes of *CTA 2009, s 82* — see **69.64** TRADING INCOME — DEDUCTIONS. [*CTA 2009, s 1244*].

(ix) **Payments to Export Credit Guarantee Department.** Sums payable by a company with investment business to the Export Credits Guarantee Department under an agreement entered into under arrangements made under *Export and Investment Guarantees Act 1991, s 2*, or with a view to entering into such an agreement, are treated as management expenses. [*CTA 2009, s 1245*].

(x) **Levies under *Financial Services and Markets Act 2000*.** Sums spent by a company with investment business in paying certain levies, or as a result of an award of costs, under *Financial Services and Markets Act 2000* are treated as management expenses. See *CTA 2009, s 92(2)(3)* for the full list of qualifying payments. [*CTA 2009, s 1246; Financial Services and Markets Act 2000, s 411(2)*].

(xi) **Flood defence relief payments:** contributions to flood and coastal erosion risk management projects. The same rules apply to investment companies that apply to trading companies with necessary modifications to terminology etc. where needed. For details see **69.45** TRADING INCOME — DEDUCTIONS [*CTA 2009, s 1244A*].

Amounts within (i), (iii)–(viii) or (x), (xi) above are deductible as management expenses without having to satisfy the requirement that they be incurred in respect of so much of the company's investment business as consists of making investments and for the investments concerned not to be held for an 'unallowable purpose' (see **45.3** above). But note (vii) above where the employment is only partly in the investment business. This rule applies also to amounts treated as management expenses under *CTA 2009, ss 993–998* (costs related to approved share incentive plans), *CTA 2009, s 999(4)* (deduction for costs of setting up approved employee share option schemes), *s 1000(3)* (deduction for costs of setting up qualifying employee share ownership trusts) or any of *CTA 2009, ss 1001–1038* (tax relief in connection with employee share acquisitions). [*CTA 2009, s 1221(2)(3)*]. Amounts within (ii) or (ix) above, or otherwise treated as management expenses (see the remaining entries in the list at **45.3** above), must satisfy the requirements.

For employee related expenses see **Simon's Taxes, D7.309.**

Costs incurred on an acquisition by merger or takeover of another company were held to be allowable as management expenses in *Camas plc v Atkinson (Inspector of Taxes)* [2004] EWCA Civ 541, [2004] 1 WLR 2392, [2004] STC 860, CA, on the grounds that the activities on which the expenditure was incurred were part of the process of managerial decision-making and it was further held that capital expenditure was not excluded by the legislation in force at the time. In that case the company had incurred substantial expenditure in evaluating a proposed acquisition, which did not go ahead. It should be noted, however, that *CTA 2009, s 1219(3)(a)* specifically excludes expenditure of a capital nature from deduction as management expenses from 1 April 2004 (see **45.3** above). A distinction should be drawn between the costs of a change in a company's investments (including its share portfolio) and the acquisition of share capital of a new subsidiary.

In *Holdings Ltd v CIR* [1997] STC (SCD) 144, a Special Commissioner held that fees for professional advice concerning an investment company's potential liabilities under letters of assurance given to the bankers of a trading subsidiary were allowable. For the interaction of management expenses and double tax relief, see *Jones v Shell Petroleum Co Ltd* (1971) 47 TC 194, HL.

In *Howden Joinery Group plc v HMRC* FTT, [2014] SFTD 1186, a holding company was required to make payments under guarantees for rental payments under leases held by trading subsidiaries. In 2008 M went into administration and H was required to make payments under the lease guarantee agreements. H claimed a deduction for these payments as management expenses. The First-tier Tribunal held that 'the providing of a parent company guarantee is a common core task of a holding company' but held that 'this is essentially expenditure on the assets of the business' which 'falls on the wrong side of the line of deductible management expenses'.

Where an investment company provides relocation packages for its employees who are obliged to relocate, reasonable costs may be allowed as management expenses. However, where the company acquires the beneficial interest in the employee's property, the purchase and subsequent sale of the property will normally fall to be dealt with under the CAPITAL GAINS (**11**) provisions. (Revenue Tax Bulletin May 1994 p 124).

Other items which generally qualify as management expenses include audit and accountancy costs, share register and annual general meeting costs; reasonable salaries and staff costs; premises costs; registered office expenses; stock exchange quotation cost; and valuation costs. Commitment fees and guarantee commissions are part of the cost of raising loans and so will be deductible under the loan relationship rules and not as management expenses.

Where an individual who is a member of an LLP is treated as an employee under *ITTOIA 2005, s 863A(2)* (a Salaried Member) then the costs of employing such a Salaried Member are expenses of earning profits and are allowable deductions in the same way and the same period as expenses in respect of any other employee. If no deduction is made under normal accounting practice for the expenses paid in respect of the Salaried Member's employment, then a specific statutory deduction is allowed in arriving at the profits of the LLP. With regard to an investment business, where such employment costs are expenses of management, but are not referable to an accounting period, then they are treated as referable to the accounting period in which they are paid. The availability of a deduction is then subject to the normal rules for management expenses. See further **56.11** PARTNERSHIPS, and **45.5** below. [*CTA 2009, s 1227A*].

Any expenses relating to specific income must be set against that source only, for example a UK property business. Expenses relating to properties being let out must be set against the UK property business income, and not treated as a management expense.

See generally HMRC Company Taxation Manual, CTM08150 *et seq.*

Restrictions on deductions for management expenses

Unpaid remuneration

[45.5] Employees' 'remuneration' must be paid within the nine months following the end of the period of account for which it is charged in a company's accounts to be deductible as a management expense for that period. Otherwise, the amount is deductible only for the period of account in which it is paid. No deduction is allowable for any amount not paid at all.

It is immaterial whether an amount is charged for particular employments or employments generally. '*Remuneration*' is an amount which is, or is treated as, earnings for the purposes of *ITEPA 2003, Pts 2–7*. It is paid when treated as received by an employee for the purposes of *ITEPA 2003, s 18* or *s 19*, or would be if it were not exempt income. '*Employee*' includes an office-holder.

If the company's profits are calculated before the end of the nine-month period, it must be assumed that any unpaid remuneration will not be paid before the period ends. If the remuneration is then in fact paid before the period ends, this rule does not prevent the revision of the calculation and the amendment of the tax return accordingly.

[*CTA 2009, ss 1249, 1250*].

Car hire

A deduction for management expenses incurred on the hiring of a 'car', not falling into one of the following categories, is reduced by 15%.

For the meaning of 'car', see **69.9** TRADING INCOME — DEDUCTIONS.

Where the above restriction, or a 'corresponding restriction' has applied, any subsequent rental rebate (or debt release other than as part of a statutory insolvency arrangement) is also reduced for tax purposes by 15%. For this purpose, the '*corresponding restrictions*' are those under *CTA 2009, s 56(2)* (see **69.9** TRADING INCOME — DEDUCTIONS), *ITTOIA 2005, s 48(2)* (income tax trading income restriction) and *FA 2012, s 82(4)* (insurance company expenses).

The excepted categories are:

(a) a car first registered before 1 March 2001;
(b) a car with low CO_2 omissions (not more than 110 g/km driven (130 g/km before 1 April 2018));
(c) an electrically propelled car; or
(d) a qualifying hire car.

(b) and (c) are defined as for capital allowances.

The legislation at *CTA 2009, s 1251* states the provisions under *CTA 2009, s 58A* (short term hiring in and long-term hiring out) also apply. The restriction above in deductible hire charges does not apply if A or B applies:

(i) the hire period does not exceed 45 consecutive days; and
(ii) the hire period and any linked period do not together exceed 45 days 'the sub-hire period'
or if:
(i) the company makes the car available to a customer for more than 45 days; or
(ii) a car is so made available and the linked periods exceed 45 days.

Condition B does not apply if the customer is an employee of the taxpayer company, or connected with it and there must be no reciprocal arrangements. The exceptions do not apply if there is an avoidance motive. Where there is a sub-hire period, expenditure must be apportioned between it and the remainder of the period on a time basis. If the contract provides for a replacement car in the event of the original car being unavailable, both cars are treated as if they were the same car.

[*CTA 2009, s 1251*].

Securing a tax advantage

No deduction is given for any particular management expenses (including any amount treated as a management expense — see **45.4** below) if any part of them is incurred directly or indirectly in consequence of, or in connection with, any 'arrangements for securing a tax advantage'. This rule does not apply to an expense if, under *CTA 2010, s 799*, the company is not entitled to a relevant tax relief (within the meaning of that provision) in respect of all or part of the expense.

For this purpose, '*arrangements for securing a tax advantage*' are arrangements (including any agreement, understanding, scheme, transaction or series of transactions, whether or not legally enforceable) the main purpose, or one of the main purposes, of which is to secure a deduction or increased deduction for management expenses or any other tax advantage (within *CTA 2010, s 1139*).

[*CTA 2009, s 1248*].

Other restrictions

In addition to the above provisions, those listed below (and, where relevant, their predecessors) prohibit or restrict the deduction of management expenses:

- *CTA 2009, s 1290* (employee benefit contributions);
- *CTA 2009, s 1298* (business entertaining and gifts);
- *CTA 2009, s 1302* (social security contributions);
- *CTA 2009, s 1303* (penalties, interest and VAT surcharges);
- *CTA 2009, s 1304* (crime-related payments);
- *CTA 2009, s 1305A* (schemes involving the transfer of corporate profits — see further **4.36** ANTI-AVOIDANCE);
- *FA 2004, s 200* (no other relief for employers in connection with pension contributions);
- *FA 2004, s 246* (restriction of deduction for non-contributory pension provision); and
- *FA 2004, s 196A* (power to restrict employer's pension contributions relief).

[*CTA 2009, s 1247*].

Case law

Management expenses do not include an exchange loss on the payment of interest (*Bennet v Underground Electric Railways Co of London Ltd* (1923) 8 TC 475); or brokerage and stamp duty on investment changes (*Capital and National Trust Ltd v Golder* (1949) 31 TC 265, CA); or payments to the guarantor of loan stock capital by the investment company issuing the stock (*Hoechst Finance Ltd v Gumbrell* (1983) 56 TC 594, CA). In *L G Berry Investments Ltd v Attwooll* (1964) 41 TC 547, the Special Commissioners' finding that part of the directors' remuneration was not allowable was upheld.

Miscellaneous

UK property business losses

[45.6] Where a company with investment business continues to carry on an investment business but ceases to carry on a UK property business (see **60** PROPERTY INCOME), any unrelieved losses from that business may be carried forward and treated as management expenses of the following accounting period. For accounting periods beginning on or after 1 April 2017 (subject to transitional provisions for periods straddling that date), this relief must be claimed. A claim may be made for all or part of the unrelieved loss and must be made within two years after the end of the accounting period to which the loss is carried forward or within such later period as HMRC allow. Previously, relief was automatic. [*CTA 2010, s 63; FA 2016, s 55(b); F(No 2)A 2017, Sch 4 para 14*].

Appeals

Appeals on management expense matters can be made under the general rules in *TMA 1970*, and the First Tier Tribunal will adjudicate, see further **5.1** APPEALS.

Claims

Claims may be made to set off unrelieved management expenses of an accounting period (the excess over gross profits of the company) as GROUP RELIEF (**35.5**) under *CTA 2010, ss 99, 103*.

Simon's Taxes. See **D1.1116, D2.220, D7.311.**

Example

XYZ Ltd, an investment company, rents out rooms, halls and equipment to conference providers. It makes up accounts to 31 March.

The following details are relevant.

	31.3.20	31.3.21
	£	£
Rents receivable	38,000	57,000
Interest receivable accrued (gross)	10,000	5,000
Chargeable gains	18,000	15,000
Expenses		
attributable to property	20,000	25,000
attributable to management	50,000	40,000
Capital allowances		
attributable to property	1,000	500
attributable to management	2,000	1,000

The corporation tax computations are as follows.

		£	£
Year ended 31.3.20			
Property income			
Rents			38,000
Deduct	Capital allowances	1,000	
	Expenses	20,000	(21,000)
			17,000
Income from non-trading loan relationships			10,000
Chargeable gains			18,000
			45,000
Deduct	Management expenses	50,000	
	Capital allowances	2,000	(52,000)
			(7,000)
As at 31.3.21			
Unrelieved balance carried forward			£(7,000)

		£	£
Year ended 31.3.21			
Property income			
Rents			57,000
Deduct	Capital allowances	500	
	Expenses	25,000	(25,500)
			31,500
Income from non-trading loan relationships			5,000
Chargeable gains			15,000
			51,500
Deduct	Management expenses	40,000	
	Capital allowances	1,000	
	Unrelieved balance from previous accounting period	7,000	(48,000)
			3,500

On 1 April 2021, XYZ Ltd diversified and began to provide conference services itself.

The following details are relevant for its accounting period ending 31 March 2022.

	31.3.20
	£
Income from conferences	65,000
Rents received	40,000
Interest receivable accrued (gross)	5,000
Conference costs	22,000
Expenses	
attributable to property	20,000
attributable to management	73,000
Capital allowances	
attributable to conferences	2,000
attributable to property	400

attributable to management			800

The corporation tax computations are as follows.

Year ended 31.3.22

		£	£	£
Trading income				65,000
Deduct	Conference costs		22,000	
	Capital allowances		2,000	
				(24,000)
				41,000
Property income				
Rents			40,000	
Deduct	Capital allowances	400		
	Expenses	20,000	(20,400)	
				19,600
Income from non-trading loan relationships				5,000
Deduct	Management expenses	73,000		
	Capital allowances	800		(73,800)
Unrelieved balance carried forward				(8,200)

Receipts

Industrial development grants

[45.7] A grant received by a company with investment business under *Industrial Development Act 1982, ss 7* or *8* (or Northern Ireland equivalent) is an amount to which the charge to corporation tax on income applies.

This rule does not apply if the grant is designated as made towards specified capital expenditure or as compensation for the loss of capital assets, or if the grant is for all or part of a corporation tax liability (including one already paid). It also does not apply if the grant is taken into account in calculating corporation tax profits under another provision.

[*CTA 2009, s 1252*].

Contributions to local enterprise organisations or urban regeneration companies — disqualifying benefits

If a management expenses deduction has been made by a company under **45.4**(viii) above and the company or a connected person receives a 'disqualifying benefit' which is attributable in any way to the contribution, the company is treated as receiving an amount equal to the value of the benefit and to which the charge to corporation tax on income applies.

For this purpose, 'disqualifying benefit' has the same meaning as at **45.4**(viii) above. So far as the value of a benefit is taken into account in determining the amount of the original deduction it is excluded from this provision.

[*CTA 2009, s 1253*].

Repayments under Financial Services and Markets Act 2000

A payment made to a company with an investment business, as a result of a repayment provision made either under *Financial Services and Markets Act 2000, s 136(7)* or *s 214(1)* or by scheme rules (i.e. the rules referred to in *Financial Services and Markets Act 2000, Sch 17 para 14(1)*) for fees to be refunded in certain cases, is treated as an amount to which the charge to corporation tax on income applies. Payments treated as trading or property business receipts are ignored for this purpose.

[*CTA 2009, s 1254*].

Simon's Taxes. See D7.301.

Losses on unquoted shares

[45.8] Where an investment company makes a capital loss on the disposal of shares in certain qualifying companies (unquoted shares in certain trading companies, as defined by the EIS rules) then it may claim to set that loss against income, under *CTA 2010, s 68 et seq*. This relief can only be claimed by investment companies — it does not extend to companies with investment business.

For details see further **51.27** LOSSES.

Change in ownership

Restrictions on relief

Prescribed circumstances

[45.9] Anti-avoidance provisions apply to restrict the carry forward of management expenses, loan relationship and intangible assets deductions where there is a change in the ownership of a company with an investment business, in prescribed circumstances.

The restrictions mirror those for trading losses at **51.17** LOSSES and apply where:

(a) after the change there is a 'significant increase' in the company's capital; or
(b) within the period from three years before to five years after the change there is a major change in the nature or conduct of the company's business. This includes a change in the nature of the company's investments, even if it is the result of a gradual process which began before that period; or
(c) the change occurs after the scale of business activities carried on by the investment company has become small or negligible and before any considerable revival.

Where either the change in ownership or the major change took place before 1 April 2017, (b) above applied by reference to a six-year period beginning three years before the change in ownership.

[*CTA 2010, ss 677, 729; F(No 2)A 2017, Sch 4 para 80*].

As regards (b) above, see further **51.17** LOSSES as regards what constitute a change in ownership of a company and a 'major change' in the nature or conduct of a trade or business.

As regards (a) above, there is a '*significant increase*' in the company's capital if 'amount B' is at least 125% of 'amount A' and also exceeds it by at least £1 million, where:

- 'amount A' is the lower of (I) the amount of its capital immediately before the change and (II) the 'highest 60 day minimum amount' for the year immediately preceding the change; and
- 'amount B' is the highest 60 day minimum amount for the five years beginning with the change (three years where the change took place before 1 April 2017).

The '*highest 60 day minimum amount*' for a period is found by taking the highest of the daily amounts of the company's capital over the period and determining whether there was a period of at least 60 days within the overall period in which there was no daily amount lower than the amount taken. If there was no such period, the next highest of the daily amounts is taken and the same test carried out, and so on until the highest 60 day minimum amount is found.

For this purpose, the amount of the company's capital (expressed in sterling) is the aggregate of (I) its paid up share capital (including any share premium account), (II) any outstanding debts (including interest due) incurred by the company for any money borrowed or capital assets acquired by the company, for any right to receive income created in favour of the company, or for consideration the value of which to the company (at the time the debt was incurred) was substantially less than the amount of the debt (including any premium thereon), and (III) any outstanding redeemable loan capital.

[*CTA 2010, ss 688–691; F(No 2)A 2017, Sch 4 para 83*].

See HMRC's Company Taxation Manual CTM08750.

Apportionment between accounting periods

Where these provisions apply the accounting period in which the change occurs is treated (for the purposes only of the provisions) as two separate accounting periods, up to and after the change.

The amounts listed below are then apportioned as specified below between those periods. The amounts are:

(A) the amount for the accounting period being divided of any adjusted non-trading loan relationship profits (as defined);
(B) any adjusted non-trading loan relationship deficit for that period (as defined);
(C) any non-trading debit falling to be brought into account for that period in respect of any debtor relationship;
(D) any non-trading loan relationship deficit carried forward to that period;
(E) any non-trading intangible fixed assets credits or debits for that period (other than any amount within (F) below;

(F) any non-trading loss on intangible fixed assets carried forward to that period;
(G) any management expenses referable to that period, but excluding any amounts which would be disallowed because of *CTA 2009, s 1219(3)(b)* (expenses otherwise allowable in computing total profits);
(H) any excess management expenses carried forward to that period;
(I) any capital allowances which would (apart from these provisions) be added to the management expenses of that period; and
(J) any other amounts by reference to which the profits or losses of that period would (apart from these provisions) be calculated.

The basis of apportionment of amounts within (A)–(J) above is as follows.

- Amounts within (A), (B), (I) and (J) above are apportioned on a time basis.
- Amounts within (C) above, where an amortised cost basis applies, are apportioned by reference to the time of accrual of the amount to which the debit relates *except* in the case of certain late interest payments where interest is brought into account when paid, or where an adjustment is required under *CTA 2009, ss 407, 409* (certain debits relating to discounted securities to be brought into account on redemption), where the debit is apportioned to the pre-change part of the period in full.
- Amounts within (D), (F) and (H) above are apportioned to the pre-change part of the period in full.
- Amounts within (E) and (G) above are apportioned in accordance with generally accepted accountancy principles as if accounts were drawn up for each part of the period.

If in any case such apportionment would work unreasonably or unjustly, a just and reasonable method of apportionment may be substituted.

[*CTA 2010, ss 678, 685, 686; F(No 2)A 2017, Sch 4 para 82*].

Restrictions applicable

The following restrictions apply to the various debits and expenses identified:

(i) **Loan relationship debits.** 'Relevant non-trading debits' may not be carried forward beyond the change of ownership date to the extent to which the aggregate of those debits (including any amounts brought into account for any previous period ending after the change in ownership) exceed the total taxable profits for the accounting period ending with the change in ownership.
'*Relevant non-trading debits*' are non-trading debits which are determined on an amortised cost basis of accounting (see **50.1** LOAN RELATIONSHIPS) to which one of the following applies:
(I) *CTA 2009, ss 407 or 409* (postponement until redemption of debits for connected or close companies' deeply discounted securities) applies and, were it not for those sections, the debit would have been brought into account for an accounting period ending before or with the change in ownership;

(II) *CTA 2009, s 373* (late interest not treated as accruing until paid — see **50.11** LOAN RELATIONSHIPS) applies and, were it not for that section, the debit would have been brought into account for an accounting period ending before or with the change in ownership: or

(III) the debit is not within (I) or (II) above but is in respect of a debtor relationship and relates to an amount which accrued before the change in ownership.

(ii) **Non-trading loan relationship deficits.** A brought-forward non-trading loan relationship deficit which is apportioned to the notional accounting period ending at the time of the change in ownership under (D) above cannot be carried forward to any accounting period ending after the change.

(iii) **Non-trading loss on intangible fixed assets.** Relief for such a loss (see **42.9** INTANGIBLE ASSETS) against the total profits of the same accounting period is available only in relation to each of the notional accounting periods considered separately. A loss for an accounting period ending before the change in ownership cannot be carried forward to an accounting period ending after the change.

(iv) **Management expenses.** Management expenses and capital allowances which are apportioned to either of the notional accounting periods as in (H) and (I) above, are treated as management expenses referable to that notional period. In computing the taxable total profits of the company for an accounting period ending after the change, no deduction can be made for management expenses deductible, or allowances falling to be made for, an accounting period beginning before the change.

(v) **UK property business losses.** Relief for losses under *CTA 2010, s 62(3)* (relief for loss against total profits of accounting period of loss — see **59** PROPERTY INCOME) is available only in relation to each of the notional accounting periods considered separately. A loss made in an accounting period beginning before the change in ownership cannot be carried forward to an accounting period ending after the change.

(vi) **Overseas property business losses.** A loss made in an accounting period beginning before the change in ownership cannot be carried forward to an accounting period ending after the change.

Where deductions have been restricted because of (i), (ii) or (iv) above, in applying the *CAA 2001* provisions relating to balancing charges by reference to any event after the change, any allowance falling to be made in taxing the company's trade for any period before the change is disregarded in so far as the profits of that and any subsequent chargeable period before the change are insufficient to give effect to it (assuming that it is relieved in priority to any loss not attributable to such an allowance).

[*CTA 2010, ss 679–684, 687, 730; F(No 2)A 2017, Sch 4 para 81; SI 2019 No 1087, Reg 9(2)*].

Assessment

Where these provisions are triggered by circumstances or events at any time in the three years after the change, an assessment to give effect to them may be made within six years of that time (or the latest such time). [*CTA 2010, s 727*].

Information

For the purposes of these provisions HMRC may, by notice in writing, require any person who is the registered owner of shares, stock or securities of a company to state whether he is the beneficial owner thereof and, if not, to supply the name and address of the person(s) on whose behalf he holds them. [*CTA 2010, s 728*].

Asset transferred within group

Where there is a change in ownership of a company with investment business and none of the prescribed circumstances in (a)–(c) above applies, restrictions similarly apply where:

(1) after the change the company acquires an asset from another company in the same group so that *TCGA 1992, s 171* (transaction treated as giving rise to neither gain nor loss, see **12.4** CAPITAL GAINS — GROUPS) or *CTA 2009, s 775* (tax-neutral transfer of intangible fixed asset, see **42.13** INTANGIBLE ASSETS) applies, and
(2) a chargeable gain or a non-trading chargeable realisation gain on an intangible fixed asset (the 'relevant gain') arises to the company on disposal or realisation of the asset (or of an asset deriving its value wholly or partly from that asset — in particular where the original asset was a leasehold, the lessee has acquired the reversion and the freehold is disposed of) within five years of the change (three years where the change took place before 1 April 2017).

Where the change takes place on or after 1 April 2017, the restrictions apply also where a chargeable gain (or part of such a gain) on a disposal of an asset within five years of the change is treated as arising under *TCGA 1992, s 171A* (notional transfers within a group; see **12.6** CAPITAL GAINS — GROUPS). The 'relevant gain' is that gain or part.

[*CTA 2010, s 692; F(No 2)A 2017, Sch 4 para 84*].

See **51.17** LOSSES as regards what constitute a change in ownership of a company.

The accounting period of the change is divided in two as above and the amounts listed at (A) to (J) above are then apportioned as specified above between those periods.

In addition, the chargeable gains and the non-trading chargeable realisation gains included, in accordance with *TCGA 1992, s 8(1)* and *Sch 7A* (see **11.3** CAPITAL GAINS, **12.25** CAPITAL GAINS — GROUPS) and *CTA 2009, Pt 8 Ch 6* (see **42.10** INTANGIBLE ASSETS), in the total profits for the period being divided are also apportioned. The total of those amounts, in so far as it exceeds the relevant gain, is apportioned to the pre-change part of the divided period, and an amount equivalent to the relevant gain (or, if less, the total itself) is apportioned to the post-change part of the divided period.

Management expenses and capital allowances which are apportioned to either of the notional accounting periods as in (H) and (I) above, are treated as management expenses referable to that notional period. [*CTA 2010, ss 694, 695, 699(2)(3), 702, 703; F(No 2)A 2017, Sch 4 para 86; SI 2019 No 1087, Reg 9(3)*].

If the total profits of the company for the accounting period in which the relevant gain accrues include, in accordance with *TCGA 1992, s 2A(1)* (previously *s 8(1)*)and *Sch 7A* and *CTA 2009, Pt 8 Ch 6*, an amount in respect of chargeable gains or non-trading chargeable realisation gains, the following restrictions apply:

- **Loan relationship debits.** The debits which can be brought into account in any accounting period beginning after the change in ownership do not include 'relevant non-trading debits' (see (i) above) to the extent that those debits exceed the 'modified total profits' of the accounting period. If debits are excluded in this way, they can nevertheless be carried forward to the next accounting period, subject to the application of this rule for that period.
  The '*modified total profits*' of an accounting period are the total profits less the relevant gain if it accrues in the period and after deducting any amounts which can be relieved against the profits (other than a non-trading deficit of the period falling to be deducted under *CTA 2009, s 461* or *s 463B* (see **50.6, 50.7** LOAN RELATIONSHIPS)).
- **Non-trading loan relationship deficit.** If a non-trading deficit is apportioned to the first of the notional accounting periods, none of it may be carried forward to a subsequent accounting period.
- **Non-trading loss on intangible fixed assets.** Relief for such a loss (see **42.9** INTANGIBLE ASSETS) against the total profits of the same accounting period is available only in relation to each of the notional accounting periods considered separately. A loss for an accounting period beginning before the change in ownership may not be relieved in the accounting period in which the relevant gain arises against so much of the total profits of that period as 'represent the relevant gain'.
  The amount of any profits that '*represent the relevant gain*' is the amount of the relevant gain or, if less, the amount included in the profits in respect of chargeable gains or, as the case may be, non-trading chargeable realisation gains for the accounting period concerned.
- **Management expenses.** In calculating the taxable total profits for the accounting period in which the relevant gain arises, no deduction for management expenses may be made for such expenses or capital allowances carried forward from an accounting period beginning before the change in ownership from so much of the total profits as represents the relevant gain.
- **UK property business losses.** Relief for losses under *CTA 2010, s 62(3)* (relief for loss against total profits of accounting period of loss — see **59** PROPERTY INCOME) is available only in relation to each of the notional accounting periods considered separately. A loss made in an accounting period beginning before the change in ownership may not be deducted from so much of the profits of an accounting period ending after the change as represents the relevant gain.
- **Overseas property business losses.** A loss made in an accounting period beginning before the change in ownership may not be deducted from so much of the profits of an accounting period ending after the change as represents the relevant gain.

[*CTA 2010, ss 693, 696–701; F(No 2)A 2017, Sch para 85*].

The assessment and information powers relating to the deductions provisions above apply equally under these provisions.

See HMRC's Company Taxation Manual CTM08710 onwards.

Simon's Taxes. See D7.320–D7.324.

FA 2013 anti-avoidance

[45.10] Anti-avoidance provisions were introduced in *FA 2013* to restrict the carry forward of non-trading losses after the change in ownership of a shell company and also with regard to the transfer of deductions and of profits on the change in ownership of a company where arrangements have been undertaken to benefit from such deductions. See further in this regard **4.26** ANTI-AVOIDANCE and **51.23** LOSSES respectively.

Key points on investment companies and investment business

[45.11] Points to consider are as follows.

- The parent company of a group will be a 'company with investment business', regardless of whether it also has trading operations. It will therefore be able to claim as management expenses a deduction for costs it incurs in relation to managing its investments in its subsidiaries.
- Care is needed when considering how unrelieved management expenses for an accounting period can be utilised. It is not possible to carry back management expenses to a prior period. Current year management expenses may only be group relieved to the extent that current period management expenses exceed current period profits of the surrendering company (i.e. profits before offset of losses (current year or brought forward), charges on income and management expenses).
- Management expenses carried forward are treated as management expenses arising in the following accounting period. Expenses first deductible for an accounting period beginning on or after 1 April 2017 (subject to transitional rules) may be surrendered as group relief for carried-forward losses.
- Brought forward management expenses are deductible in the next accounting period in which the company has investment business. Excess management expenses cannot however be carried forward after the company ceases to carry out investment business. In the event that a company has excess management expenses and is to sell all its investments but intends to recommence its business, consideration should be given to maintaining an investment business. Holding surplus cash on deposit does not comprise an investment business.

- It is not possible to claim a management expense deduction for expenses of a capital nature. As a result, expenses incurred in relation to the acquisition or disposal of investments will not be deductible as management expenses, although they may be deductible in calculating any chargeable gain arising on disposal of the investment. It may however be possible to claim a management expense deduction for expenses incurred before a decision to proceed with an acquisition or disposal is made. For example, costs incurred in appraising and investigating investments should generally be deductible.
- Given the broad application of the loss restriction provisions on a change of ownership of a company (see **45.9**), in most cases it is unlikely that a purchaser would ascribe value to tax losses in the target company.

46

Investment Funds

Cross-references. See **11.25** onwards CAPITAL GAINS for offshore collective investment vehicles and disposals of UK land; **12.4**, CAPITAL GAINS — GROUPS; **27.34** DERIVATIVE CONTRACTS; **50.49** LOAN RELATIONSHIPS; **62.15** REORGANISATIONS AND RECONSTRUCTIONS.

Simon's Taxes. See D8.1.

Authorised investment funds

[46.1] The legislation applying to 'authorised investment funds' ('AIFs'), which includes open-ended investment companies ('OEICs') and authorised unit trusts ('AUTs') (see **46.2** and **46.3** below) is contained in *SI 2006 No 964*.

Collective investment schemes

Authorised unit trusts and open-ended investment companies are the most common forms of 'collective investment schemes'. A '*collective investment scheme*' is an arrangement with respect to property of any description, including money, the purpose or effect of which is to enable persons taking part in the arrangements (whether by becoming owners of all or part of the property or otherwise) to participate in or receive profits or income arising from the acquisition, holding, management or disposal of the property or sums paid out of such profits or income. [*Financial Services and Markets Act 2000, s 235; FA 2004, s 118(4); SI 2006 No 964, Regs 6, 8*]. The object of such a scheme is to enable a large number of investors to pool their money by investing in a professionally managed fund of investments, thus spreading risk. A body corporate (other than an open-ended investment company) is not regarded as a collective investment scheme, so that INVESTMENT TRUSTS (**46**), VENTURE CAPITAL TRUSTS (**73**), CO-OPERATIVE AND COMMUNITY BENEFIT SOCIETIES (**22**) and friendly societies are not collective investment schemes.

Individual savings accounts (ISAs)

The *Individual Savings Accounts Regulations 1998* (*SI 1998 No 1870*) enable investments in authorised investment funds to be held in individual savings accounts (see Tolley's Income Tax under Exempt Income).

Open-ended investment companies

[46.2] OEICs are investment companies in which shares are continuously created or redeemed, according to investor demand. An OEIC is defined in *CTA 2010, s 613* as a company incorporated in the UK to which the *Financial Services and Markets Act 2000, s 236* applies.

The taxation of OEICs and their shareholders are covered partly by primary legislation but mainly by *SI 2006 No 964* (the regulations for authorised investment funds) set out in **46.5–46.10** below. See **46.12** below for OEICs which are property authorised investment funds ('PAIFs').

[*CTA 2010, ss 613–615; SI 2006 No 964, Reg 4*].

Authorised unit trusts

[46.3] As defined in *CTA 2010, s 616(1)*, an AUT is a 'unit trust scheme' where the property is held for the beneficiaries by a trustee and it is authorised by the FSA to sell to the public (subject to an order set out in the *Financial Services and Markets Act 2000, s 243*, for the whole or part of an accounting period). The investors are issued with units that represent their entitlement to profit, losses and gains in the AUT. The primary objective of an AUT is to provide income or capital return to the investor by reducing investment risk through holding a range of different investments.

There are some exclusions to the general definition of a 'unit trust scheme' for Capital Gains Tax purposes as outlined in *SI 1988 No 266, SI 1988 No 267, SI 1988 No 268* as amended. These include unit trust schemes which are:

- a limited partnership scheme;
- a profit sharing scheme which has been approved as an approved share option scheme; and
- an employee share ownership plan.

The same exclusions apply for Income Tax purposes but in addition, an enterprise zone property scheme or a charitable unit trust scheme are also excluded.

See also **46.21** below as regards court investment funds.

Umbrella companies and umbrella schemes

[46.4] An '*umbrella company*' is an OEIC which provides for separate pooling of shareholder contributions and of the profits or income out of which payments are made to those shareholders and under which they may exchange rights in one pool for those of another. Each of the parts of an umbrella company is regarded for the purpose of these provisions as an OEIC unless expressly provided for elsewhere in any other tax provisions, but the umbrella company as a whole is not to be regarded as an OEIC nor as a company. [*CTA 2010, s 615; SI 2006 No 964, Reg 7*].

'*Umbrella schemes*' are authorised unit trust schemes which provide for separate pools of contributions and of the profits or income out of which payments are made to the participants and under which they may exchange rights in one pool for those of another. Each of the parts of an umbrella scheme is regarded for the purpose of these provisions as an authorised unit trust but the scheme as a whole is not to be regarded as an authorised unit trust or any other form of collective investment scheme. [*CTA 2010, s 619; SI 2006 No 964, Reg 7*].

Simon's Taxes. See D8.103.

Tax treatment of authorised investment funds

Corporation tax

[46.5] *CTA 2010, s 614* has effect as if the trustees of an AUT were a company resident in the UK, and the rights of unit holders were shares in the company. [*CTA 2010, s 617*].

A special rate of corporation tax applies to OEICs and to the trustees of an AUT, equal to the basic rate of income tax in that financial year (and the standard small profits rate introduced for financial year 2023 onwards does not apply). [*CTA 2010, ss 614, 618; FA 2021, Sch 1 paras 27, 28*].

SI 2006 No 964, Reg 94(2)–(4) makes it clear that AIFs cannot form part of any arrangements for group relief purposes.

Capital gains

For capital gains purposes, any unit trust scheme is treated as if the scheme were a company and the rights of the unit holders were shares in the company and, in the case of an authorised unit trust, as if the company were UK resident and ordinarily resident. For disposals on or after 1 January 2018, this provision does not apply to offshore funds which are transparent funds. [*TCGA 1992, s 99(1)(1A); SI 2017 No 1204, Regs 1, 3*]. Capital gains, accruing to OIECs or AUTs (including umbrella companies or umbrella schemes see **46.4** above), for the benefit of investors, are not chargeable gains. [*TCGA 1992, s 100(1); SI 2006 No 964, Reg 100*]. For company reorganisations involving authorised unit trusts, see **62.15** REORGANISATIONS AND RECONSTRUCTIONS.

The non-resident CGT charge introduced by *FA 2015* (*Sch 7*) for disposals before 6 April 2019 did not apply to, inter alia, authorised unit trusts or OEICs where the following conditions were met: a claim is made in respect of the disposal; and, the unit trust scheme or OEIC is widely marketed throughout the relevant ownership period, or has a qualifying investor. The relevant ownership period begins with the date the interest in the UK land was acquired and ends with the date of disposal, or if shorter, a period of five years ending with the date of disposal. [*TCGA 1992, s 14F*].

See Tolley's Capital Gains Tax under Unit Trusts and Other Investment Vehicles for the capital gains tax treatment of disposals, amalgamation with or conversion of an AUT to an OEIC, accumulation units and monthly savings schemes.

Loan relationships and derivative contracts

'Capital profits, gains or losses' arising to an AIF from a derivative contract or from a debtor or creditor relationship are to be disregarded under these provisions. '*Capital profits, gains or losses*' in this case are those which, in preparing accounts in accordance with UK generally accepted accounting practice, fail to be dealt with in the statement of total return (under the heading of 'net gains/losses on investments during the period' or 'other gains/losses') in accordance with the relevant Statement of Recommended Practice (SORP). Interest distributions (see **46.7** below) paid by an AIF are taxable under the loan relationship rules (see **50** LOAN RELATIONSHIPS) as if they were interest payable on a loan. A deficit on a loan relationship of an AIF cannot be carried back to set against profits of an earlier accounting period under *CTA 2009, ss 456–460.*

[*SI 2006 No 964, Regs 8, 10–12, 13, 14*].

Interest distributions: deduction of expenses

Where an AIF makes an interest distribution for a distribution period, the amount that can be relieved against the total profits of the AIF under *CTA 2010, s 4* (see **1.7** INTRODUCTION) cannot exceed the amount that would reduce the total profits chargeable to corporation tax for the accounting period in which the distribution period ends to below the amount chargeable to corporation tax as property income. [*SI 2006 No 964, Reg 12A*].

Diversely owned AIFs

Tax treatment of diversely owned AIFs

[46.6] An AIF that carries out an 'investment transaction' (see below) and meets the 'genuine diversity of ownership condition' (see **46.13**) in respect of an accounting period is referred to as a 'diversely owned AIF'.

There are provisions which prevent defined financial transactions carried out by diversely owned AIFs from being characterised as trading transactions for tax purposes. The rules give diversely owned AIFs certainty that gains on the realisation of certain types of investments cannot be re-characterised as profits arising from a trade, which would then be taxable as income.

Where an AIF is diversely owned, all capital profits, gains or losses arising from investment transactions are treated as non-trading and the corporation tax provisions under which trading profits and losses are computed and charged do not apply to these transactions.

Capital profits, gains and losses for this purpose are any profits, gains or losses treated as capital for accounting purposes under the Statement of Recommended Practice (SORP) which applies to AIFs.

The regulations prevent capital gains being re-characterised as trading profits (and therefore revenue), but they do not prevent revenue profits from investment transactions being taxable as income. For example, interest receivable in respect of a loan relationship will be taxable as income even where the regulations apply to prevent any capital profit on disposal of the loan relationship being characterised as trading income.

Where the regulations do not apply, it remains a question of fact whether or not activities carried out by an AIF amount to trading for tax purposes. In such cases, the normal principles for determining whether or not there is a trade will apply however, there is no automatic assumption that transactions which are not investment transactions will be trading transactions by default.

Whilst it is possible that some activities carried out by an AIF might, based on the facts, amount to trading, there is a general and prevailing assumption that an AIF will not be conducting a trade.

Meaning of investment transaction

An 'investment transaction' is any transaction:

- in stocks or shares;
- in a 'relevant contract';
- which results in the diversely owned AIF becoming party to a loan relationship or related transaction;
- in units in a collective investment scheme;
- in securities;
- consisting of the buying or selling of foreign currency;
- in a carbon emission trading product; or
- in rights under a life insurance policy.

Any transaction that is not specified in the above list (known as the '*white list*') is not an investment transaction for the purposes of the regulations. However, this does not mean that the transaction will be a trading transaction by default. Such a transaction may still be non-trading on first principles.

Under the regulations, any transaction in a relevant contract is deemed to be an investment transaction, with a 'relevant contract' defined as an option, a future or a contract for differences.

Transactions in a wide range of derivative contracts are encompassed in the regulations. The definitions are widely-drawn and, importantly, there is no requirement for options, futures or contracts for differences to be accounted for as a derivative financial instrument in order to be a relevant contract.

[*SI 2006 No 964, Regs 14F–14N*].

The practical effect of the introduction of the white list is that significant volumes of transactions can be undertaken by the AIFs (in respect of items included in the white list) without the risk of the fund being regarded as trading in these investments. In a situation where an AIF undertakes a transaction which is not on the white list, and is subsequently found to be trading, only that particular transaction would be taxed as a trading item, and it would not result in the entire AIF activity being treated as trading. It is important to note, however, that this certainty would only apply to those AIFs which satisfy a genuine diversity of ownership condition (see **46.13** below).

Distributions made by authorised investment funds

[46.7] The total amount available for distribution to participants is to be shown in the distribution accounts as available for distribution either as dividends (a 'dividend distribution'), or as yearly interest (an 'interest distribution'). These provisions do not apply to an AIF which is a registered pension scheme within the meaning of *FA 2004, Pt 4* or is treated as having become such a scheme under *FA 2004, Sch 36*. They also do not apply for Tax Elected Funds (TEFs) or Property Authorised Investment Funds (PAIFs). [*SI 2006 No 964, Regs 16, 17*].

For these purposes, the making of a distribution includes the investment of an amount on behalf of the participant in respect of his accumulation units (this being subject to the treatment of de minimis amounts — see below). [*SI 2006 No 964, Regs 15, 18(4)(b), 22(4)*].

Interest distributions

An '*interest distribution*' is treated as a payment of yearly interest made on the '*distribution date*' (i.e. the date specified or in accordance with the terms of the trust or instrument of incorporation of the company or, if there is no such date, the last day of the distribution period), to the participants in proportion to their rights, including interest paid to a participant not liable to income tax. No amount may be shown as an interest distribution unless the AIF satisfies a 'qualifying investments test' throughout the distribution period. This requires that, at all times in the period, at least 60% of the market value of the fund's investments are represented by 'qualifying investments'.

'*Qualifying investments*' are funds invested within any of the following categories.

(1) Money placed at interest.
(2) Securities (excluding shares in a company).
(3) Shares in a building society.
(4) Qualifying units in another AIF (which itself satisfies the qualifying investments test in relation to 1–3 above and 5–8 below).

(5) Derivative contracts whose underlying subject matter consists wholly of any one or more of 1–4 above or currency.
(6) Contracts for differences whose underlying matter consists wholly of any one or more of the following; interest rates, creditworthiness or currency.
(7) Derivative contracts not within 5 or 6 above where there is a hedging relationship (as defined) between the derivative contract and an asset within 1–4 above; or
(8) Alternative finance arrangements. Funds invested in alternative finance arrangements are qualifying investments under *SI 2006 No 964, Reg 20*.

[*SI 2006 No 964, Regs 15, 18–21*].

Dividend distributions

A '*dividend distribution*' is treated as a dividend on shares paid on the distribution date (as above), to the participants in proportion to their rights, including dividends paid to a participant not liable to corporation tax. [*SI 2006 No 964, Regs 15, 22*].

De minimis amounts

An AIF is not treated as making an interest or dividend distribution if:

- the fund has (in accordance with FSA rules) an agreed '*de minimis limit*' (an amount in respect of which a distribution of fund income is not required if the amount shown in the fund's distribution accounts as available for distribution does not exceed that limit);
- the fund has a de minimis amount shown in the distribution accounts as available for distribution to participants but waives distribution of that amount and carries it forward as an amount available for distribution in the next distribution period; and
- none of the fund's units in issue on the 'distribution date' (as above) are in bearer form. It is notable that bearer shares have been abolished as from 26 May 2015, and all such issued shares must be converted into registered shares (the *Small Business, Enterprise and Employment Act 2015*).

[*SI 2006 No 964, Reg 23*].

Tax treatment of participants

[46.8] These provisions do not apply to an AIF which is a registered pension scheme within the meaning of *FA 2004, Pt 4* or is treated as having become such a scheme under *FA 2004, Sch 36*. [*SI 2006 No 964, Reg 25*].

Participants chargeable to income tax

Interest distributions

[46.9] Income tax is not deductible at source from interest distributions made on or after **6 April 2017** (see **41.2**(h) INCOME TAX IN RELATION TO A COMPANY).

For 2016/17 and earlier years, basic rate tax is deductible under *ITA 2007, s 874* unless either:

- the participant is a company or the trustee of a unit trust scheme; or
- the 'residence condition' or the 'reputable intermediary condition' is met with respect to the participant on the distribution date; or
- the 'offshore marketing condition' is met with respect to the class of units in relation to which the distribution is made.

However, if the participant is a company which is a trustee of the trust to which (or under which) the distribution is made (or received), the obligation to deduct tax is not excluded by virtue of the fact that the participant is a company and one of the other conditions would have to be satisfied for the exemption to apply. In the case of accumulation units, the obligation to deduct tax is an obligation to deduct a sum out of the amount being credited to scheme capital on the participant's behalf.

[*SI 2006 No 964, Reg 26*].

The '*residence condition*' requires broadly that a valid declaration is made to the legal owner of the AIF, in the prescribed form, that either the participant is not resident in the UK or, if the units are held by the participant as the personal representative of a deceased holder, the deceased was not resident in the UK at the time of his death. [*SI 2006 No 964, Regs 30–33, 75*].

The '*reputable intermediary condition*' requires broadly that the interest distribution is paid on behalf of the participant to a company which is subject to certain money laundering controls, and that the legal owner has reasonable grounds for believing the participant to be not resident in the UK. If it subsequently transpires that the participant was in fact resident, the tax which should have been deducted is payable by the legal owner under *ITA 2007, s 946*.

The '*offshore marketing condition*' extends the instances when interest distributions may be paid without deduction of income tax to cases where the units in a fund are not marketed to investors resident in the UK. For the condition to be met information must be available to investors before they acquire the units stating that income tax will not be deducted from any interest distributions and that an investor must notify HMRC of any distribution if they are chargeable to income tax in the tax year of distribution.

See *TMA 1970, s 98(4E)* for penalty provisions. [*SI 2006 No 964, Regs 27–33A*].

Where interest distributions are made without the deduction of tax, the fund is required to notify HMRC under *SI 2006 No 964, Regs 71–74* within 14 days of the end of the tax year. This notice must be given in writing and has effect for the tax year in which it is given and for subsequent tax years until the notice is withdrawn. Failure to do so will result in the fund being liable to a maximum penalty of £3,000.

HMRC may, by notice, require that a fund provide them with information for the purpose of determining whether interest distributions were properly made without deduction of tax. This information will include copies of any relevant books, documents, residence declarations or other records, and must be provided within the timescale as specified in the notice.

It is specifically provided that annual payments made in respect of a participant's interest in an AIF are not qualifying annual payments if:

(i) at the time of payment the payer had reasonable grounds for believing that the recipient was non-UK resident or the payment is made in respect of a class of unit which meets the 'offshore marketing condition' (see above);
(ii) the payment is referable to and not more than any management fees paid to the manager of the AIF in relation to the participant's interest; and
(iii) the management fees represent a reasonable commercial amount.

Consequently UK payers are not obliged to deduct income tax before making or passing such payments to non-UK resident investors, or where such fund is marketed to non-UK resident investors. The withholding requirements are reapplied if, in fact, the participant, or, in the case of a trust, the beneficial owner is resident in the UK.

[*SI 2013 No 1772*].

Dividend distributions

A dividend distribution from an AIF is treated in the same way as other UK company dividends and bears a notional tax credit of 10% that may be used to reduce the investor's liability to tax on the income.

For non-taxpayers, the fact that the credit is only notional means that they cannot claim a repayment of the credit, and they are in exactly the same position as a basic rate taxpayer.

Participants chargeable to corporation tax

Interest distributions

[46.10] Tax is not deductible at source from interest distributions made on or after **6 April 2017** (see **41.2**(h) INCOME TAX IN RELATION TO A COMPANY). Previously, where, on the distribution date, the participant is within the charge to corporation tax, the obligation to deduct tax does not apply to interest distributions unless the participant is a company which is a trustee of the trust to which (or under which) the distribution is made (or received). In the case of accumulation units, the obligation to deduct tax is an obligation to deduct a sum out of the amount being invested on the participant's behalf.

[*SI 2006 No 964, Reg 47*].

SI 2006 No 964, Regs 71–74 lays out the requirements to notify HMRC in writing within 14 days of the end of the tax year where interest distributions are made before 6 April 2017 without deduction of tax and the powers of HMRC in this respect.

Dividend distributions

Where, on the distribution date, the participant is within the charge to corporation tax, then (unless the participant is the manager of the AIF in the ordinary course of business) for the purpose of computing the unit holder's corporation tax liability, the 'unfranked' part of a dividend distribution is treated as:

(i) an annual payment and not as a dividend distribution or interest distribution; and

(ii) having been received by the participant after deduction of income tax at the basic rate for the tax year in which the distribution date falls, from a corresponding gross amount.

The above treatment does not apply to financial traders (*SI 2006 No 964, Reg 48(2A)*), they are taxed in full on the dividend distribution as trading income. Certain insurance businesses (non-basic life assurance and general annuity businesses) can continue under (i) and (ii) above. This prevents non-taxable policy holders returns from suffering by being taxed in the fund first.

It does not apply to so much of any dividend distribution as on a just and reasonable apportionment is attributable to an unallowable arrangement. An unallowable arrangement is an arrangement the main purpose or one of the main purposes of which is to secure that an amount of tax, or an increased amount of tax, is treated as deducted under (ii). 'Arrangement' includes any arrangement, agreement, scheme, transaction, series of transactions or understanding (whether or not legally enforceable).

If there is any foreign element to the tax treated as deducted in (ii) a corresponding proportionate part of the distribution is treated as if it were income from the respective territory and the tax suffered treated as if it were tax equivalent to UK corporation tax, payable under the law of the territory.

Where tax is deemed to have been deducted under (ii) above, repayment to the participant may not exceed the participant's portion (by reference to the participants' rights in the fund in the distribution period in question) of the legal owner's net liability to corporation tax in respect of that gross income, as reduced by any double tax relief, whether under an agreement or by way of credit under *TIOPA 2010, s 18* (see **31.2, 31.3** DOUBLE TAX RELIEF). In calculating the amount repayable, tax treated as having been deducted by virtue of (ii) above is set off in priority to any other tax subject to deduction under *ITA 2007, Pt 15*. The statement sent to the participant relating to the distribution must show the legal owner's net liability to corporation tax in respect of the gross income.

The '*unfranked*' part of the dividend distribution is found by the formula:

$$U = \frac{A \times C}{D}$$

where:

U is the unfranked part of the dividend distribution to the participant;
A is the amount of the dividend distribution;
C is such amount of the gross income as derives from income in respect of which the legal owner is charged to corporation tax, as reduced by:

(a) any amount carried forward from an earlier accounting period and allowed as a deduction in computing the legal owner's liability to corporation tax for the accounting period in which the last day of the distribution period falls, and

(b) an amount equal to the legal owner's net liability to corporation tax in respect of the gross income.

D is the gross income as in C (and similarly reduced), but including any part deriving from franked investment income.

[*TIOPA 2010, s 18; SI 2006 No 964, Regs 48–52, 70; SI 2006 No 981*].

Qualified investor schemes

[46.11] A 'qualified investor scheme' (QIS) is a fund, authorised by the Financial Services Authority, in which a statement that the fund is a qualified investor scheme is included in the instrument constituting the scheme. [*SI 2006 No 964, Reg 53(3)*]. Only institutional and certain sophisticated investors are eligible to participate in such schemes.

A QIS is treated for tax purposes in the same way as any other open-ended investment company or authorised unit trust provided that it meets the 'genuine diversity of ownership condition' — see **46.13** below).

Property Authorised Investment Funds

[46.12] A Property Authorised Investment Fund (PAIF) can be set up is an AIF that has an investment portfolio primarily comprising of real property or shares in UK REITs or certain other similar entities.

The PAIF regime was introduced to provide an open-ended equivalent of the UK-REIT regime that aims to provide a UK tax efficient vehicle for investments in real estate. It does this by shifting the point of tax for property income from the AIF level to the investor (i.e. the effect is broadly the same as if the investor had owned the property or REIT shares directly).

Entry into and membership of the PAIF regime

[46.13] *SI 2006 No 964, Pt 4A*, which outlines the conditions that are to be met in order to be treated as a PAIF. In order to be within the PAIF regime, an AIF must be constituted as an OEIC. The PAIF regime is an elective regime where an Authorised Corporate Director (ACD), or proposed ACD, must give advance notice in writing to HMRC if it wants the PAIF rules to apply from a given date. For existing OEICs, notice must be given at least 28 days before the beginning of the accounting period for which the PAIF regime is to apply, whilst this notification period is extended to 42 days for new OEICs.

In addition to being an OEIC, to be eligible to be treated as a PAIF there are six conditions that have to be met throughout each accounting period. These conditions are:

- the property investment business condition;
- the genuine diversity of ownership condition;
- the corporate ownership condition;
- the loan creditor condition;
- the balance of business conditions; and

- the notification condition.

[*SI 2006 No 964, Pt 4A, paras 69D–69O*].

The property investment business condition

In order to meet the property investment business condition:

- the OEIC's instrument of incorporation and prospectus (including supplements) must include a statement that the company's investment objectives are to carry on 'property investment business' and to manage cash raised from investors for that purpose; and
- the OEIC must carry on such a business.

The term '*property investment business*' means a business consisting of one or more of the following:

- 'property rental business' (see below);
- owning shares in UK REITs; or
- owning shares or units in foreign entities that are equivalent to UK REITs.

For this purposes a 'property rental business' (as defined in *SI 2006 No 964, Pt 4A, Reg 69H*) is:

- a UK or overseas property business; and
- the relevant business of an intermediate holding vehicle (IHV). An entity is an IHV in an accounting period if:
  - (a) it is a company, trust or partnership and not a collective investment scheme;
  - (b) it is wholly owned either by the PAIF or another IHV or series of IHVs which are wholly owned by the parent, unless this is prohibited by local laws or regulations that require a proportion of local ownership;
  - (c) the function of the IHV is solely to enable the holding of real estate based outside of the UK;
  - (d) the IHV has its accounts consolidated with those of the parent; and
  - (e) all property rental income of the IHV (or the full proportion of that income representing the interest of the parent in the IHV) must be reflected in the distribution accounts of the parent at the same time as the income is reflected in the accounts of the IHV.

The genuine diversity of ownership condition

[*SI 2006 No 964, Reg 9A as amended by SI 2011 No 2192*].

The genuine diversity of ownership condition is met if condition A–C are satisfied:

Condition A

The fund documents (meaning the instrument constituting the fund and its prospectus) must contain a statement that units in the fund will be widely available, must specify the intended categories of investor and must specify that the manager of the fund must market and make available the units in accordance with condition C below.

Condition B

Neither the specification of the intended categories of investor, nor any other terms or conditions governing participation in the fund (whether or not specified in the fund documents), has the effect of limiting investors to a limited number of specific persons or specific groups of connected persons, or deters a reasonable investor within the intended categories of investor from investing in the fund.

Condition C

Units in the fund must be marketed and made available sufficiently widely to reach the intended categories of investor in a manner appropriate to attract those categories of investors. In addition, a person who is an intended category of investor can, upon request to the manager of the fund, obtain information about the fund and acquire units in it.

This condition shall be treated as being met even if, at the relevant time, the fund has no capacity to receive additional investments, unless the capacity of the fund to receive investments in it is fixed by the fund documents, and a pre-determined number of specific persons or specific groups of connected persons make investments in the fund which collectively exhaust all, or substantially all, of that capacity.

A PAIF also meets the genuine diversity of ownership condition if:

- an investor in the fund is a unit trust scheme (a 'feeder fund');
- conditions A–C above are met in relation to the PAIF after taking into account the fund documents relating to the feeder fund and the intended investors in the feeder fund; and
- the PAIF and the feeder fund have the same manager (or proposed manager).

An advance clearance in relation to the genuine diversity of ownership condition may be made in writing to the Tax Tribunal by the manager (or proposed manager) of an AIF. An application for clearance must be accompanied by the fund documents in the form in which it is proposed that those documents will apply at the beginning of the first accounting period of the fund for which clearance is sought.

The corporate ownership condition — the 10% test

[*SI 2006 No 964, Reg 69K*].

The aim of this condition is to prevent a corporate body from owning 10% or more of a PAIF, so ensuring the fund's income from UK property stays within the remit of UK taxation. The corporate ownership condition must be met upon entering the regime, and throughout each accounting period within which the AIF is within the PAIF regime, and is met if conditions A–D are satisfied:

Condition A

No body corporate is beneficially entitled (directly or indirectly) to 10% or more of the net asset value of the fund. This condition is treated as met in cases where the body corporate has taken reasonable steps to prevent it from acquiring a holding of 10% or more and, on becoming aware that it does in fact hold 10% or more, it takes steps to ensure that the holding is reduced;

Condition B

The instrument of incorporation and prospectus of the PAIF must include provisions under which any corporate shareholder must undertake not to acquire 10% or more of the share capital of the PAIF and undertake that should its holding exceed 10%, it would be reduced to below 10%;

Condition C

The instrument of incorporation and prospectus of the PAIF must include provisions under which any company acquiring shares must provide a certificate stating that it holds the shares as beneficial owner or, that it does not hold them as beneficial owner but has obtained undertakings from the beneficial owners; and

Condition D

The investing company must undertake to disclose certain information about its ownership to the manager of the PAIF, if so required.

There are special rules and circumstances that apply to feeder funds.

The loan creditor condition

[*SI 2006 No 964, Reg 69M*].

The purpose of this condition is to restrict the way in which a PAIF can borrow money so as to prevent income, or capital growth of the fund from being extracted through a profit-related loan. A PAIF must meet three conditions throughout each accounting period in respect of any loan relationship in which the PAIF is the debtor party, these being that:

- no interest is due which is calculated by reference to the results of the PAIF business or the value of any of its assets;
- the creditor in respect of any debt is not entitled to interest which exceeds a reasonable commercial return on any amount lent; and
- the amount due to the creditor on repayment does not exceed the amount lent or it is reasonably comparable with the amount generally repayable under the terms of issue of securities listed on a recognised stock exchange.

The balance of business conditions — the 60% test

[*SI 2006 No 964, Reg 69N*].

(a) no less than 60% of a PAIF's net income must come from property investment assets; and

(b) at least 60% of the PAIF's assets, at fair value, must be property investment assets.

Throughout the accounting period, conditions (a) and (b) above are relaxed for those newly set up PAIFs, where a reduced level of at least 40% will be allowed in their first period of account. This relaxation does not apply to PAIFs that are created as a result of a conversion.

For the purposes of the 60% test (or the 40% test if relaxed in the first period of account), assets must be valued in accordance with generally accepted accounting practice. If there is a choice of accounting method, then a fair value option must be used. No account should be taken of liabilities secured against or otherwise relating to assets of any property investment business when determining net assets for the purposes of this condition.

The notification condition

The manager has to elect by giving notice that the PAIF regime will apply or, if it is proposed to incorporate an OEIC, that the person expected to become the manager of the OEIC on its incorporation has given notice for it to apply to the company and such notice has taken effect.

Notice must be given in writing to HMRC. For an existing company, notice must be given at least 28 days before the first accounting period for which the PAIF regime is going to apply, and for a new company notice must be given at least 42 days before the date of expected incorporation and authorisation. The notice may be amended or withdrawn at any time before it takes effect.

HMRC may issue a 'quashing notice' in prescribed circumstances and the procedure for this is laid down in *Reg 69S* of *SI 2006 No 964, Pt 4A, 69S*. There is a right of appeal to the Tax Tribunal against a quashing notice within 28 days beginning with the date of the notice. In this case, the Tax Tribunal will decide whether HMRC's action was just and reasonable and the date from which the PAIF regime is to apply, subject to certain restrictions.

Consequences of entry

On entering the PAIF regime, a new accounting and distribution period begins for the fund (*SI 2006 No 964, Reg 69V*). Any pre-entry property rental business shall be treated for the purposes of corporation tax as ceasing on entry into the regime. The assets of the pre-entry property rental business will be treated as being sold immediately before entry, and reacquired immediately after entry, at their market value at that time. Any property investment business carried on afterwards will be tax exempt.

Under *SI 2006 No 964, Reg 69V* assets which were used in any pre-entry property business are treated, for capital allowances purposes, as being sold immediately after entry at a value which does not give rise to any balancing allowances or charges.

Tax treatment of PAIFs

[46.14] A PAIF is exempt from UK corporation tax on its net Property Investment Business (PIB) income, but the other non-PIB (or 'residual business') is theoretically still subject to tax at the rate applicable to open-ended investment companies (although in practice no tax should apply due to tax deductions being available in respect of distributions made out of this income). UK dividend income receipts are not subject to UK corporation tax in the hands of a PAIF.

To arrive at the net PIB income, the calculation should be made in accordance with the current Statement of Recommended Practice (SORP) as issued by the Investment Management Association (IMA). Essentially the net PIB income computation follows the rules for the computation of property income.

However, loan relationship adjustments, hedging derivative contracts and embedded derivatives are taken into account so far as they relate to the tax-exempt business. Any capital allowances that the tax-exempt business would claim if it were taxable, should be claimed in full.

Residual income comprises of UK dividends and income arising from the residual business. In arriving at the taxable income, the residual income is reduced by any deduction allowable for corporation tax purposes along with PAIF interest distributions.

There is a charge to corporation tax where a PAIF is also a QIS and the net PIB income divided by financing cost of the exempt business gives a figure of less than 1.25.

There may also be a charge to corporation tax if HMRC considers that the arrangements have been designed to obtain a 'tax advantage' that qualifies as tax avoidance.

Where distributions are made to a 'holder of excessive rights' and the PAIF has not taken sufficient care to avoid making such a distribution, it is treated as receiving an amount of income equal to the percentage held by the holder applied to the net tax exempt income of the PAIF. Such income is subject to corporation tax as if it were residual net income arising in the accounting period in which the distribution was made by the company.

A '*holder of excessive rights*' is a company which is a participant in a PAIF and is beneficially entitled to shares representing the right to 10% or more of the net asset value of the PAIF.

Tax compliance

A PAIF must file a corporation tax return complimented by:

- a calculation of its tax exempt net income and residual income; and
- a reconciliation between the net income of the company and the total income shown in the distribution accounts, as attributed to the three different categories of distribution (see distributions made by PAIFs below).

There is an obligation to make a quarterly return (CT61 return) in respect of PIB income or PAIF interest income (relevant income). The return must be filed during a period ending within 14 days of the day immediately following the end of the return period in question, with any tax due payable with the return.

The relevant PAIF must issue a certificate of tax deducted to the recipients. HMRC have the power to assess if payment is not made on the due date or where HMRC think a relevant distribution has been omitted or a return is otherwise incorrect.

Distributions made by PAIFs

PAIFs are required to distribute all their income to investors. Distributions are treated first as coming out of tax exempt income, secondly out of PAIF distributions of interest (up to the pre-distribution amount) and thirdly out of PAIF distributions (dividends). All distributions are treated as paid to fund-holders in proportion to their rights [*SI 2006 No 964, Regs 69Z15(2), 69Z16(2) and 69Z17(2)*].

Tax treatment of participants

Distributions of property income by a PAIF are chargeable to corporation tax as property income in the hands of a company recipient. In the case of a recipient within the charge to income tax, the distributions are treated as profits of a UK property business (within the meaning of *ITTOIA 2005, s 264*).

Where the participant is not resident in the UK, similar charging provisions apply and the non-resident landlords rules do not apply.

There are exclusions for dealers in respect of distributions, e.g. dealers in securities and members of Lloyd's.

For participants within the charge to UK corporation tax, PAIF interest distributions should be treated as though they were payments of yearly interest usually without deduction of tax. Participants are treated as receiving a gross amount of yearly interest arising from a loan relationship.

In the case of participants within the charge to income tax, PAIF interest distributions should be treated as though they were net of tax receipts of yearly interest in the hands of UK income tax payers [*ITTOIA 2005, Pt 4, Ch 2*].

No tax credit is available under *CTA 2010, Pt 23, Ch 7* in respect of interest distributions for corporate recipients and non-corporate recipients [*ITTOIA 2005, s 397*].

PAIF dividend distributions received by participants shall be treated as if they were a dividend on shares (i.e. they are exempt from corporation tax, *SI 2006 No 964, Reg 69Z20(1)*). In the case of participants within the change to UK income tax, PAIF dividend distributions should be treated in the same manner as any other UK company dividend and carry a 1/9 non-repayable tax credit.

Breaches

Where a PAIF becomes aware that it no longer satisfies any one of the PAIF conditions highlighted above (except in the case of excessive rights — see below), it must provide to HMRC the date of the breach and the date the condition became satisfied again (if appropriate). It must also give details of the condition that was breached and what, if anything, the company has done to prevent the breach recurring.

In the event of the excessive rights condition being breached, as soon as it is reasonably practicable, the company must provide the name and address of the person who received the distribution, its value, details of the recipient's interest in the company, the steps the company took to prevent the acquisition of any excessive holdings, and steps the company has taken (or is taking) to ensure there is no longer any excessive holding in the company.

Leaving the PAIF regime

[46.15] An OEIC may leave the PAIF regime in four ways:

- optional exit — a PAIF must notify HMRC in writing specifying the final day on which the regime is to apply, which must be after the date that HMRC receives any notice;

- HMRC have power to issue a termination notice, but only in specified circumstances, and there is a right of appeal against the notice (*SI 2006 No 964, Reg 69Z37*);
- a PAIF may cease to be authorised by the Financial Services Authority, or cease to carry on property investment business;
- the PAIF may be the subject of a merger or take-over.

In these circumstances, the tax exempt property business of the PAIF is treated as ceasing and, immediately before cessation, the assets are deemed to be sold and re-acquired at market value (for corporation tax but not for capital gains tax purposes). The OEIC's accounting period is treated as coming to an end on the date of the cessation and a new one will begin immediately post cessation. For the purposes of capital allowances, the assets are treated as being sold immediately before cessation and re-acquired by the OEIC after the cessation, at the tax written down value. [*SI 2006 No 964, Reg 69Z41(5)*]. No balancing allowance or charge will arise and the provisions for successions (*CAA 2001, ss 198, 199*) do not apply.

Tax elected funds

[46.16] The tax elected funds (TEF) regime is an elective regime which is open to AIFs meeting certain conditions. Similar to the PAIF regime above, the TEF regime moves the point of taxation from the fund to the investor and as such, investors in a TEF will broadly be taxed in the same way as if they owned the underlying assets directly.

Entry into and membership of the TEF regime

[46.17] An AIF that meets the following conditions, contained in *SI 2006 No 964, Regs 9A, 69Z45–69Z48*, may elect to become a TEF:

- the property condition;
- the genuine diversity of ownership condition;
- the loan creditor condition; and
- the scheme documentation condition.

The property condition

The AIF must not have a UK or overseas property business.

The genuine diversity of ownership condition

The three conditions described in **46.13** for PAIFs must be met throughout the accounting period. Similar to the PAIF regime, an advance clearance in relation to the genuine diversity of ownership condition may be made in writing to the Tax Tribunal by the manager (or proposed manager) of the AIF.

The loan creditor condition

The conditions to be met in terms of the loan creditor condition are similar to those described in **46.13** for PAIFs.

The scheme documentation condition

The instrument constituting the AIF and its prospectus must include terms which require the AIF to meet the property condition and the loan creditor condition on entry and throughout each accounting period.

Application process

[46.18] Either the manager, or the prospective manager (where the fund is not yet established), is required to apply in writing to HMRC to enter the TEF regime, at least 28 days before the beginning of the specified accounting period for an existing AIF, and at least 42 days before the expected authorisation date for a new fund.

Before making an application in relation to an existing AIF, shareholder or unit holder approval must be obtained and the fund must have applied for any necessary regulatory approval. The contents of the application are described in *SI 2009 No 2036, Reg 69Z51*.

Tax treatment of TEFs

[46.19] For the purpose of corporation tax, the income arising to a TEF will be categorised under one of the following:

(a) dividend income;
(b) property investment income (e.g. REITs tax-exempt distributions and property income distributions in relation to shares held in a PAIF);
(c) property business income (arising as a result of a breach of the property condition) being profits of a UK property business that are not within (b) above and income from an overseas property business; and
(d) other income.

Distributions made by TEFs

[46.20] Distributions by TElFs shall be attributed as follows:

- TEF distributions (dividends):
  (a) dividend income;
  (b) property investment income; and
  (c) property business income.
- TEF distributions (non-dividends).

Where a distribution is made from TEF distributions (dividends), it is treated as paid to fund-holders in proportion to their rights on the distribution date by the fund (*SI 2009 No 2036, Reg 69Z60*) and subject to a de minimis amount (*SI 2009 No 2036, Reg 69Z66*).

In the case where a distribution is made from TEF distributions (non-dividend), the distributions are treated as being a payment of yearly interest made on the distribution date and subject to the treatment of de minimis amounts.

Breach of TEF conditions

Provisions within *SI 2009 No 2036, Reg 69Z65* apply if one or more of the TEF conditions are breached. Within 28 days of becoming aware of the breach, the fund must provide designated information to HMRC, including the date of the breach, details of the condition that was breached and the steps the fund proposes to take to rectify the breach.

Leaving the TEF regime

Optional exit

In the event that the manager decides to take its AIF outside of the TEF regime, then the manager must give notice to HMRC in writing, specifying the reasons for the fund leaving the TEF regime and the final accounting period for which the regulations are to apply.

Forced exit

HMRC can, in certain circumstances, issue a termination notice to the manager of an OEIC. A TEF may appeal against any termination notice within 28 days, beginning with the day on which the termination notice is given.

[*SI 2009 No 2036, Regs 69Z70, 69Z71, 69Z72*].

Court investment funds

[46.21] Court investment funds (CIFs) are a form of authorised unit trust set up by the Lord Chancellor under the *Administration of Justice Act 1982, s 42(1)*. They are available only for individuals whose money is under control of certain courts, e.g. road accident victims and the mentally incapacitated. The Public Trustee as Accountant General of the Supreme Court holds all units in the fund on the investors' behalf. CIFs are treated for tax purposes as authorised unit trusts, the investment manager being treated as the trustee. Persons whose interests entitle them, as against the Accountant General (or other authorised person), to share in the fund's investments and persons authorised to hold shares in the fund on their own behalf are treated as unit holders.

[*CTA 2010, s 620*].

Unauthorised unit trusts

[46.22] Special provisions apply to the income and gains of a unit trust scheme not within **46.3** above (an 'unauthorised unit trust' (UUT)), the trustees of which are UK resident. Such a trust is outside the rules in **46.5** above (tax treatment of AIFs). There are separate provisions for approved exempt and non-exempt UUTs and their investors.

Exempt UUTs

A UUT is an exempt UUT for a period of account if its trustees are UK resident, all of its unit holders are 'eligible investors', it is approved by HMRC and it is not treated by regulations as not being a unit trust scheme for the purposes of the definition of 'unauthorised unit trust' in *ITA 2001, s 989*. A unit holder is an '*eligible investor*' if any gain on a disposal of its units would be wholly exempt from CGT or corporation tax (otherwise than by reason of residence) or if it holds all of its units pending disposal in the capacity of manager of the UUT. A UUT is not treated as failing to meet the requirement that all unit holders be eligible investors if the managers or trustees become aware that a unit holder is not an eligible investor but could not reasonably be expected to have been so aware previously and the unit holder disposes of its units within 28 days. This relaxation to the requirement can, however, only be relied on twice in any period of ten years.

For the procedure for approval see *SI 2013 No 2819, Regs 4–6*. Once approved the UUT must meet the following continuing requirements for each period of account:

- appropriate arrangements must be in place to ensure that all of the unit holders are eligible investors;
- the period of account must not exceed 18 months;
- accounts for the period must be prepared in accordance with the Investment Management Association's Statement of Recommended Practice for the Financial Statements of Authorised Funds so far as relating to determining revenue and capital and must be audited independently as being so prepared; and
- the managers or trustees must supply a copy of the trust's accounts and a statement that the eligible investors requirement has been met throughout the period with the tax return.

HMRC may withdraw approval where these requirements are not met (or if the managers or trustees ask them to do so). There is a right of appeal against the rejection of an application for approval and against the withdrawal of an approval.

Income of an exempt UUT is treated as income of the trustees and not of the unit holders and is within the charge to income tax. Income tax is charged at the basic rate, with basis periods based on the trust's period of account used to determine the amount chargeable for each tax year. Gains of an exempt UUT are not chargeable gains. Exempt UUTs continue to obtain a full deduction for finance costs when calculating the profits of a residential property business. The restriction with regard to finance cost deductions for property businesses for income tax purposes is specifically disapplied for trustees of exempt UUTs because, as they are subject to income tax at the basic rate only, they can only receive basic rate relief for finance costs.

The basis period for the first tax year that a trust is an exempt UUT begins on the first day of the first period of account in respect of which the trust is approved, and ends with the accounting date in that year. The basis period for a subsequent tax year begins immediately after the end of the basis period for the previous tax year, and ends with the accounting date in the current tax year. The changes address concerns that income may be taxed twice on cessation and ensure that no amount of income falls out of charge.

Tax is charged on unit holders on income treated as received from an exempt UUT in a tax year. For this purpose unit holders are treated as receiving income if an amount is shown in the accounts for a period of account as income available for payment to them or for investment. Income is treated as received by a unit holder for a distribution period and in most cases on a date provided for by the terms of the trust. A period of account may have one or more distribution periods. If income is treated as received by a unit holder in relation to its trade or in relation to its UK property business, the income is taxed under those provisions in priority to the exempt UUT regulations. Where taxable income arises to the unit holders for a period of account, the trustees are treated as making a deemed payment of that amount on the final day of the period. The deemed payment is then deducted in computing the trustees net income for the tax year (but only up to the amount of that income, with any excess carried forward to the following tax year).

Non-exempt UUTs

For the purposes of income and chargeable gains arising to UK resident trustees of a UUT that is not an exempt UUT or is treated by regulations as not being a unit trust scheme for the purposes of the definition of 'unauthorised unit trust' in *ITA 2007, s 989*, the trustees are treated as if they were a UK resident company and the rights of the unit holders are treated as if they were shares in the company. As a non-exempt UUT will be within the charge to corporation tax, such trust may also be within the quarterly instalment payments regime, see further **58.3** PAYMENT OF TAX. Unit holders who receive a distribution from the trustees are treated as if they had received a UK dividend with a tax credit.

[*SI 2013 No 2819; SI 2019 No 689, Reg 34*].

Simon's Taxes. See D8.175.

Pension fund pooling scheme (PFPS)

[46.23] A PFPS is an authorised unit trust where special provisions apply to ensure that certain international pooled pension funds (registered as 'pension fund pooling vehicles') are transparent for UK tax purposes, by disapplying the tax rules for unauthorised unit trusts (as above). An application must be made to HMRC to participate in the scheme. The participants in a PFPS are treated for income tax, capital allowances and capital gains tax purposes as though they themselves own a share of each of the trust assets directly.

There is also relief from stamp duty reserve tax on the transfer of assets by participants into the scheme. Participation in PFPS is restricted to registered pension schemes which are occupational pension schemes, UK-based superannuation funds used primarily by companies employing British expatriates working overseas (as defined in *ICTA 1988, s 615(6)*), and pension funds established outside the UK broadly equivalent to UK registered pension schemes. [*SI 1996 Nos 1583, 1585 as amended*]. The position in the country in which any overseas participator is based will of course be crucial to the operation of such schemes.

Unit trusts for exempt unit holders

[46.24] If, for any reason other than non-residence, any of the holders of units in a unit trust scheme would not be liable to capital gains tax (or to corporation tax on chargeable gains) on a disposal of units, any gains accruing to the trust itself are also not chargeable gains. In determining whether this exemption applies, no account is taken of units which are disposed of by a unit holder and are held by the fund managers pending disposal. Also, no account is to be taken of the possibility of a corporation tax charge on income arising in respect of a gain accruing on a disposal by an insurance company or an incorporated or registered friendly society.

[*TCGA 1992, s 100(2–2B)*].

This exemption applies whenever the gains accrue, and is of practical importance in relation to unit trust schemes which have not been designated as authorised unit trusts (in **46.3** above).

Authorised contractual schemes

[46.25] An '*authorised contractual scheme*' is a type of collective investment scheme authorised by the Financial Conduct Authority. It may take the form of either a co-ownership scheme or a partnership scheme (as defined). [*Financial Services and Markets Act 2000, s 235A*]. Direct investors in a scheme must either invest at least £1 million or be a professional institutional investor. Other investors can invest via a feeder fund. (HMRC Draft Authorised Contractual Schemes Manual ACSM1020). An authorised contractual scheme is transparent for tax purposes, i.e. the scheme itself incurs no tax liability. This means that its investors are treated as if they had invested directly in the underlying assets of the scheme and are subject to personal taxation accordingly.

Participants in co-ownership schemes — disposals of units on or after 1 January 2018

A unit in an authorised contractual scheme which is a co-ownership scheme is treated as an asset for capital gains purposes and, accordingly, a participant's interests in the scheme property is disregarded. In computing the gain on a disposal of units, any amount which represents income from the scheme property and is taken into account as a receipt or other credit of the participant in computing an amount chargeable to income tax is treated as enhancement expenditure within *TCGA 1992, s 38(1)(b)* (see **16.11**(b) COMPUTATION OF GAINS AND LOSSES). The deductions otherwise allowable from the consideration are reduced (but not below nil) by any amounts arising to the participant from the scheme property which is taken into account as an expense or debit of the participant in computing an amount chargeable to income tax or anything paid or transferred to, or anything else of value received by, the participant which is referable to the holding of the units. No reduction is made for CAPITAL SUMS DERIVED FROM ASSETS (**10**). If the amount of the reduction exceeds the otherwise allowable deductions, the excess is added to the consideration. Amounts which reduce the allowable deductions in this way are not also dealt with under the provisions at **40.1** INTERACTION WITH OTHER TAXES.

Any expenditure incurred by the participant in respect of which a capital allowance or renewals allowance has been, or may be, made is excluded from the allowable deductions in computing a loss on a disposal of units.

Units in a scheme are treated as securities for the purposes of the share identification rules.

These provisions do not apply to expenditure incurred before 1 January 2018 nor to any amount arising, paid, transferred or received before that date which would otherwise be treated as enhancement expenditure or excluded from the allowable deductions.

If a person is entitled to a structures and buildings allowance in relation to any scheme property, his interest is not disregarded under these provisions for the purposes of *TCGA 1992, s 37B* (exclusion of certain expenditure: structures and buildings allowance — see **9.22**).

[*TCGA 1992, ss 103D, 103DA; SI 2017 No 1204, Regs 1, 6; SI 2019 No 1087, Reg 4(9)*].

Note that these provisions apply also to interests in a transparent offshore fund (treating the participator's rights or interests in the fund, however described, as units) — see **55.11** OFFSHORE FUNDS.

See also **11.26** CAPITAL GAINS for the treatment of units as shares in a company for the purposes of the charge on non-residents disposing of assets deriving 75% of their value from UK land.

Participants in co-ownership schemes — disposals of units before 1 January 2018

A participant's interests in the property subject to an authorised contractual scheme which is a co-ownership scheme and which is not a 'relevant offshore fund' are disregarded for capital gains purposes. Instead, units in the scheme are treated as assets for those purposes. In computing the gain or loss arising on disposal of a unit, the rules for accumulation units at **70.3** above apply as if the unit were a unit in a unit trust scheme (but not an authorised unit trust) and the participant were a unit holder. An offshore fund is a 'relevant offshore fund' if it is not constituted by a company or a partnership and it is not a unit trust scheme. [*TCGA 1992, s 103D; SI 2013 No 1400, Reg 3*].

Other matters

For scheme accounting periods beginning on or after 1 April 2017, an operator of a CoACS carrying on a qualifying activity can elect to compute plant and machinery capital allowances and allocate them to investors. See **10.73** CAPITAL ALLOWANCES ON PLANT AND MACHINERY.

The Treasury are empowered to make regulations imposing requirements on the operator of a co-ownership authorised contractual scheme (CoACS) in relation to the provision of information to participants in the scheme, to enable them to meet their tax obligations, and to HMRC. The regulations are expected to have effect for scheme accounting periods beginning on or after 1 April 2017. The Treasury may also make regulations providing for how participants in a CoACS are to be treated for corporation tax purposes in relation to scheme investments in an offshore fund. These may require a CoACS to allocate amounts of accumulated income as the income of participants in the accounting period in which the amounts accrue to the CoACS, and for those amounts to be regarded as income of the participants to whom they are allocated. [*F(No 2)A 2017, ss 41, 42*].

Collective Investment Schemes — exchanges, mergers and schemes of reconstruction

[46.26] Regulations are in force with regard to exchanges, mergers and schemes of reconstruction involving collective investment schemes. *TCGA 1992* is amended with regard to such transactions as follows:

- With regard to an authorised contractual scheme, a participant's interest in the property subject to the scheme is disregarded for the purposes of *TCGA 1992* and instead the participant's holding of units issued under the scheme is treated as an asset for the purposes of capital gains tax. [*SI 2013 No 1400, Reg 3*].
- Provisions are introduced to provide relief for insurance companies which transfer assets into a co-ownership scheme or comparable offshore funds. [*SI 2013 No 1400, Regs 4–7*].
- The treatment of umbrella funds under *TCGA 1992, s 99A* is extended to other types of collective investment scheme. [*SI 2013 No 1400, Reg 8*].
- The share reorganisation provisions in *TCGA 1992, ss 127–131* apply with necessary adaptations as if the scheme were a company and the event in question a reorganisation of its share capital, so no disposal of the original holding is treated as occurring and the new holding is treated as the same as the original, where such arrangements have been effected for bona fide commercial reasons. These provisions apply where:
  - units are exchanged for other units in the same collective investment scheme where there is no change in underlying property and where all the units (or units of a certain class) are exchanged;
  - a collective investment scheme acquires the interests in another collective investment scheme and the acquiring scheme issues units to the unit holders in the target scheme;
  - a collective investment scheme is involved in a scheme of reconstruction where units are issued in the successor scheme to unit holders in the original scheme (units can be issued in accordance with the UCITS regulations *SI 2011 No 1613*). *TCGA 1992, Sch 5AZA* defines a scheme of reconstruction for these purposes.

  [*SI 2013 No 1400, Regs 11–15*].

47

Investment Trusts

Cross-references. See **12.2**, **12.19** CAPITAL GAINS — GROUPS; **45.3** INVESTMENT COMPANIES AND INVESTMENT BUSINESS; **50.49** LOAN RELATIONSHIPS; **62.15** REORGANISATIONS AND RECONSTRUCTIONS.

Introduction to investment trusts

[47.1] Investment trusts are companies which are used for collective investment purposes in the UK. Where they meet certain conditions a beneficial tax treatment is applied (such as an exemption from chargeable gains) — see further 47.2 below. Where a company invests in property and carries on a property rental business then they may opt to become a real estate investment trust (REIT) which benefits from a special tax regime, where various conditions are met (including a distribution condition), see further **47.11** *et seq* below.

Investment trusts

[47.2] Investment trust companies are the closed ended form of collective investment schemes available in the UK. Investment trusts are not in fact trusts in any legal sense, but limited companies incorporated under UK company law and listed on the official UK list. Investment trusts are subject to corporate tax legislation, however, they are exempt from tax on chargeable gains provided they are approved by HMRC. In order to obtain approval from HMRC, the company must fulfil certain conditions.

Definition of investment trust

[47.3] A company is an investment trust for an accounting period if it fulfils the following conditions.

(1) Throughout the period substantially all of its business consists of investing its funds in shares, land or other assets with the aim of spreading investment risk and giving its members the benefit of the results of the management of its funds.
(2) Throughout the period the shares making up the ordinary share capital or, if there are such shares of more than one class, those of each class, are admitted to trading on a regulated market (as defined).
(3) Throughout the period the company is neither a venture capital trust (see **68** VENTURE CAPITAL TRUSTS) nor a company UK real estate investment trust (see **67.5** below).
(4) The company is approved for the period by HMRC.

The Treasury has the power to make regulations amending condition (2) above or treating conditions (1) and (2) as satisfied in specified cases. Regulations may also be made specifying the circumstances in which a company can be approved and the process by which approval can be given, refused or withdrawn.

'*Shares*' includes stock.

'*Ordinary share capital*' means all the issued share capital (by whatever name called) of a company, other than that which produces a fixed rate of dividend and is non-participating. For HMRC's interpretation of 'ordinary share capital', see HMRC Brief 54/2007.

[*CTA 2010, ss 1119, 1158, 1159; SI 2019 No 689, Reg 17(13)*].

The application procedure

[47.4] A company may apply to the Commissioners for approval as an investment trust by submitting an application that specifies the first day of an accounting period in respect of which the applicant seeks approval and contains a statement that the applicant meets, or is expected to meet, all of the eligibility conditions and requirements of this statutory instrument. Where the accounting period has not commenced at the time of the application the applicant must specify a provisional date and then confirm in writing as soon a practicable the date of the first day of that accounting period.

The application must contain an undertaking that subsequent accounting periods in respect of which it is or expects to be an investment trust meet the eligibility requirements in the instrument. Also, the applicant must submit its investment policy and provide evidence that the shares making up its ordinary share capital are admitted to trading on a regulated market. If the shares are not admitted to trading at the time of the application the application can contain the applicant's prospectus with a statement of how the applicant will comply with the trading requirement.

The application must be made before the end of 90 days beginning with the last day of the first accounting period for which approval is sought and the applicant may withdraw the application at any time during the period beginning with the day on which the application is made and ending 28 days after the day on which the Commissioners give notice under *Reg 10* accepting the application.

The Commissioners must respond in writing, either accepting, rejecting or seeking further information (which re-sets the clock to accept or reject from when the information is provided) within 28 days from the day on which the application was made and the applicant may appeal to any rejection to tribunal within 42 days.

[*SI 2011 No 2999, Regs 6, 7, 8, 9, 10 and 11*].

Requirements to be met whilst approved

[47.5] In each accounting period in respect of which it is approved as an investment trust the company must meet the following conditions:

(1) It must not be 'close' as defined by *CTA 2010, s 439*.

(2) The maximum amount of income it is permitted to retain is the highest of the following amounts:
   - (i) 15% of its income for the period;
   - (ii) the accumulated revenue losses brought forward from previous accounting periods, in instances where the amount of income the investment trust is permitted to retain under *Regs 19* and *21* (taken together and ignoring this paragraph (ii)) does not exceed the amount of any accumulated revenue losses brought forward from previous periods; and
   - (iii) any amount of income that the investment trust is required to retain in respect of the accounting period under a restriction imposed by law.

In calculating the amount of the investment trusts's income for the purposes of (2) above, the amounts to be brought into account in respect of its loan relationships are to be determined without reference to any debtor relationships of the investment trust; and, income treated as arising under *Reg 18(1)* (the charge to tax: further provisions) of the Offshore Funds Regulations is to be ignored.

The income distribution requirement in (2) above is modified where conditions A–C below are met so that the amount the investment trust may retain is reduced by an amount equal to 85% of the amount refereed to in condition B.

Condition A is that the investment trust is a participant in an offshore reporting fund within the meaning of *Reg 50* (meaning of 'reporting fund') of the Offshore Funds Regulations.

Condition B is that there is an amount which falls to be reported to the investment trust in accordance with *Reg 92(1)(b)* (contents of a report to participants: non-transparent funds) of the Offshore Funds Regulations.

Condition C is that the amount referred to in condition B is accounted for by the investment trust through the capital column of the income statement in accordance with the AIC Statement of Recommended Practice, or would have been so accounted for if that Statement had been applied correctly.

The income distribution requirements do not apply in relation to an accounting period if the amount that the investment trust would be required to distribute in accordance with those regulations, taken together, would be less than £30,000. This limit is proportionately reduced for accounting periods less than 12 months.

An investment trust must notify HMRC of a change in the investment policy and provide a copy of the new policy before the filing date for its company tax return.

Any breach of the eligibility conditions or any requirements of the statutory instrument must be notified to HMRC in writing as soon as practicable after the investment trust becomes aware of any breach and specify steps taken or to be taken to correct the breach.

[*SI 2011 No 2999, Regs 17–24*].

Breach and withdrawal of approval

[47.6] Breaches are defined as either 'minor' or 'serious'.

A minor breach is one that has a reasonable excuse and is inadvertent and corrected as soon as reasonable practicable and without intervention by the Commissioners. Where the Commissioners are notified under *Reg 24* there is no minor breach.

A serious breach is where the company becomes 'close' if it has three minor breaches of the same requirement in ten years or four in relation to one or more requirements.

Breach of the income distribution requirement

(1) There is a breach of the income distribution requirement if:
   (a) there is a difference between:
      (i) the amount that the investment trust is required to distribute in relation to an accounting period; and
      (ii) the amount which the investment trust distributed in relation to that accounting period; and

(b) the amount referred to in paragraph (ii) is less than the amount referred to in paragraph (i).

(2) If the difference between the two amounts specified in paragraph (1) is greater than 1% but less than or equal to 5% of the income of the investment trust for the accounting period then, subject to paragraph (5), the breach is a minor breach.

(3) If the difference between the two amounts specified in paragraph (1) is greater than 5% of the income of the investment trust for the accounting period, the breach is a serious breach.

(4) If the difference between the two amounts specified in paragraph (1) is less than or equal to 1% of the income of the investment trust for the accounting period then, subject to paragraph (5), the investment trust is to be treated as not having breached the income distribution requirement.

(5) Paragraph (4) only applies if the failure to comply with the income distribution requirement was inadvertent.

For the purpose of this regulation, the income of the investment trust includes income that falls to be reported to it in accordance with *Reg 92(1)(b)* (contents of report to participants: non-transparent funds) of the Offshore Funds Regulations.

Consequences of serious breaches

If the investment trust is in breach of a requirement imposed by these Regulations, and the following apply:

- the breach is a serious breach; and
- the Commissioners give notice in writing to the investment trust stating that it is in breach of a requirement imposed by these Regulations and that the breach is a serious breach;

then:

- the investment trust is to be treated as a company which has not been approved as an investment trust for the accounting period in which the serious breach occurred (or, if there is more than one serious breach, the first of them) and for all subsequent accounting periods.

This does not apply where the company to which this regulation applies makes a successful application under *Reg 5* in respect of any accounting period subsequent to the accounting period in which the serious breach occurred.

Breach of the eligibility conditions

If an investment trust is in breach of any of the eligibility conditions:

The investment trust is to be treated as a company which has not been approved as an investment trust for the accounting period in which the breach of the eligibility condition occurred (or, if there is more than one breach, the first of them) and for all subsequent accounting periods. However, the above does not apply where the company to which this regulation applies makes a successful application under *Reg 5* in respect of any accounting period subsequent to the accounting period in which the breach of an eligibility condition occurred.

[*SI 2011 No 2999, Regs 25–30*].

Transactions

[47.7] If an investment trust carries out an investment transaction in an accounting period the transaction is treated as being entered into other than in the course of trade for the purposes of the Corporation Tax Acts.

The following are treated as 'investment transactions' for the purposes of this part:

(a) any transaction in stocks and shares;
(b) any transaction in a relevant contract (see *Regs 34–40*);
(c) any transaction which results in an investment trust becoming a party to a loan relationship or a related transaction in respect of a loan relationship (see *Reg 39*);
(d) any transaction in units in a collective investment scheme (see *Reg 40*);
(e) any transaction in securities of any description not falling within paragraphs (a) to (d);
(f) any transaction consisting in the buying or selling of any foreign currency;
(g) any transaction in a carbon emission trading product (see *Reg 41*); or
(h) (with effect on or after 8 April 2014) any transaction in rights under a life insurance policy.

A relevant contract is, broadly:

(a) an option;
(b) a future; or
(c) a contract for differences.

[*SI 2011 No 2999, Regs 31–41; SI 2014 No 685*].

Investment trusts which have interests in offshore non-reporting funds

[47.8] An investment trust must satisfy a number of conditions in relation to an asset that represents an interest in an offshore non-reporting fund ('the asset') if the disposal of the asset is not to give rise to a charge to tax on the investment trust. Where the conditions below are satisfied the disposal of an asset will not be subject to a charge to tax under the Offshore Funds Regulations, which would otherwise be the case:

(a) the investment trust has access to the accounts of the non-reporting fund;
(b) the investment trust had sufficient information about the non-reporting fund to enable it to prepare computations of reportable income for the non-reporting fund for every accounting period which, if the non-reporting fund were a reporting fund, would be a reporting period during which the investment trust had acquired the asset and ending with the day of disposal;
(c) the investment trust has prepared such computations; and

(d) any excess of the investment trust's share of the reportable income of the non-reporting fund over the investment trust's share of the distributions made by the non-reporting fund is included in the amount available for distribution by the investment trust for each accounting period of the investment trust which falls within the period mentioned in (b).

Where an investment trust holds an asset in relation to which the conditions are not satisfied for the entire period that it holds the asset the investment trust may treat the asset as an interest in a reporting fund if it makes a deemed disposal and reacquisition of the asset representing the interest. In order to do so, the investment trust must reasonably expect to satisfy the conditions from the date of the reacquisition until the date on which it disposes of the asset. If it satisfies the conditions for this period then there will not be a tax charge as above.

[*SI 2011 No 2999, Regs 42, 43, 44*].

Capital gains

[47.9] Investment trusts are exempt from tax on capital gains realised on disposals. [*TCGA 1992, s 100(1)*].

For the treatment of forward currency transactions as being of a capital or revenue nature, and their effect on the test in **47.8**(c) above, see HMRC Company Taxation Manual, CTM47210. For loan relationships of investment trusts, see **50.49** LOAN RELATIONSHIPS.

For company reorganisations involving investment trusts, see **62.15** REORGANISATIONS AND RECONSTRUCTIONS. For the transfer of assets within a group of companies to a company which subsequently becomes an investment trust, see **12.19** CAPITAL GAINS — GROUPS.

Treatment of investment trust interest dividends

[47.10] The tax treatment of investment trust dividends may be altered where three conditions are fulfilled:

- a company is an investment trust or prospective investment trust in the relevant accounting period;
- the company pays a dividend in respect of that period; and
- the dividend is paid on or before the first anniversary of the end of that period of account.

Where a dividend is paid for a period of account containing more than one accounting period, the body must be an investment trust or prospective investment trust for the whole of the accounting period. The trust may designate all or part of the dividend (not to exceed the trust's qualifying interest income for the period) as an 'interest distribution'. The designation is irrevocable once the interest distribution is made.

Where a distribution is paid for a period of account which includes more than one accounting period, the following formula should be applied to attribute the distribution to a particular accounting period:

$$\frac{A \times I}{T}$$

Where A is the amount of 'qualifying interest income' for the accounting period, I is the total distributed as interest distributions for the period of account and T is the total qualifying interest income for all accounting periods in the period of account.

'*Qualifying interest income*' is, broadly, the excess of the company's relevant credits over its relevant debits for a year — e.g. interest income over interest payments. Loan relationship transactions and certain transactions in derivatives and contracts for differences are taken into account. See *SI 2009 No 2034, Regs 8, 9*.

Interest distributions are not treated as dividend distributions for the purposes of the Taxes Acts. The effect on the trust or prospective trust is that the distribution is treated as if it were an interest payment under a loan relationship, and therefore a deduction is allowable in arriving at the company's profits chargeable to corporation tax. However, where the interest distribution exceeds the trust's qualifying interest income for the period, the excess is not allowed as a deduction.

Similarly, the recipient of the interest distribution is treated as interest received.

Tax is not deductible at source from interest distributions (see **41.2**(h) INCOME TAX IN RELATION TO A COMPANY).

[*SI 2009 No 2034; SI 2011 No 2951*].

There is further guidance available in HMRC Corporate Tax Manual, CTM47000 *et seq*.

Real estate investment trusts

[47.11] UK resident property companies or groups which carry on a 'property rental business' may opt to become real estate investment trusts (REITs). UK REITs must distribute at least 90% of net taxable profits on rental income to investors, withholding tax at the basic rate. A REIT must distribute all of any profits derived from investments in other UK REITs, such profits being termed '*UK REIT investment profits*' and treated as separate from the other property rental business of the REIT. Provided a company meets the eligibility criteria for a REIT, the qualifying profits and gains from the 'property rental business' including any UK REIT investment profits will not be subject to corporation tax, but profits on any other business will be subject to corporation tax at the main rate of corporation tax (whether or not the REIT would otherwise qualify for the small profits rate). To the extent that dividends paid by the trust derive from the profits and gains of the 'property letting business' they are taxed in the hands of the recipient as property income rather than as distributions.

Separate, but similar rules are laid down for groups and single companies.

[*CTA 2010, ss 523–609; ITA 2007, ss 973, 974; FA 2019, Sch 1 paras 114–120*].

Property rental business

[47.12] A '*property rental business*' is a business forming part of a UK property business or overseas property business (see **59** PROPERTY INCOME). Where a REIT has receipts and expenses relating to tied premises, these may be regarded as part of a UK property business. [*CTA 2010, s 519*]. However, the following type of business is not a property rental business:

- incidental letting of property (wherever situated) held in connection with a property trade;
- letting of property used for administrative purposes of the property rental business, but temporarily not required for those purposes, where it is let for a term of not more than three years and the space let is comparatively small compared to that occupied for administrative purposes;
- letting of property if the property would fall within generally accepted accounting practice to be described as owner-occupied;
- provision of services in connection with overseas property where the services would not be taxed as property income if provided in connection with a UK property;
- entering into structured finance arrangements in connection with factoring of rent and other income receipts (see **4.11** ANTI-AVOIDANCE).

A business is not a property rental business in so far as it gives rise to the following type of income or profits:

- income in connection with a caravan site treated as trading receipts under *ITTOIA 2005, s 20(1)*;
- rent in respect of an electric-line wayleave;
- rent in respect of the siting of a gas or oil pipeline or of a wind turbine;
- rent in respect of the siting of a mast or similar structure for use in a mobile telephone network or other system of electronic communication; or
- dividends from shares in a company within the REIT regime (but see below); or
- income from an interest in a limited liability partnership on a winding-up under *CTA 2009, s 1273(4)*.

HMRC may, by order, amend the above exclusions.

Income from investments in other UK REITs are included within the REIT's property rental business profits, although the profits derived from such investments (termed 'UK REIT investment profits', see below) are treated as separate from the other property rental business profits of the REIT.

[*CTA 2010, s 605*].

A business carried on by a non-UK group company is a property rental business for REIT purposes if the business would be a property rental business if carried on in the UK. References to a non-UK company's UK property rental business are to the company's property rental business in the UK. Income from such a business would normally be chargeable to income tax. For REIT purposes, however, the income is treated as chargeable to corporation tax.

[*CTA 2010, ss 519(4), 520*].

Qualifying conditions — single companies

[47.13] In order to qualify for REIT status, a number of conditions must be met by the company itself and by the business activities of the company.

Conditions for company

[47.14] A company may give notice to become a UK REIT provided it meets the following conditions:

- (a) the company is a UK company;
- (b) the company is not an open-ended investment company (see **46.2** INVESTMENT FUNDS);
- (c) the company's ordinary share capital is admitted to trading on a recognised stock exchange; this means that REITs can be listed on trading platforms such as AIM, Plus and their foreign equivalents;
- (d) subject to below, the company is not a close company (see **16** CLOSE COMPANIES); for this purpose, a company is treated as a close company if prevented from being close only by *CTA 2010, s 444* or *s 447(a)*;
- (e) there must be no more than one class of ordinary shares issued by the company and issued shares must either form part of the company's ordinary share capital or be non-voting fixed-rate preference shares; and
- (f) in the case of any borrowings, the interest payable to the loan creditor must not exceed a reasonable commercial return nor be contingent upon the results of all or any part of the company's business or on the value of any of its assets. On repayment of the loan, the creditor must not be entitled to an amount exceeding the amount lent, or if repayment is made by way of listed securities, the amount must be reasonably comparable with the amount generally repayable. However, a loan is not treated as dependent on the company's results only due to the interest under the contract being reduced if the results improve or being increased should the results deteriorate.

Condition (d) above does not have to met in relation to any accounting period ending during the first three years after the company enters the regime. As regards any accounting period beginning within that three-year period but ending outside it, the condition does not have to be met during the part of that period preceding the three-year anniversary.

If a company is a close company only because it has an 'institutional investor' (as defined by *CTA 2010, s 528(4A)*) as a participator, condition (d) is regarded as met. Previously, the condition was regarded as met if the company was a close company only because it had as a participator a limited partnership which was a collective investment scheme (see **46.1** INVESTMENT FUNDS).

The effect of the notice is that the company is a UK REIT from the date specified in the notice. The requirements of the notice are laid down in *CTA 2010, s 525*.

Once a company is accepted as a UK REIT, it will remain a UK REIT until notice is given by the company to HMRC, notice is given to the company by HMRC, or there is an automatic termination due to the breach of certain conditions (see below **47.34**).

[*CTA 2010, ss 527(5)–(8), 528, 529*].

Further condition relating to shares

[47.15] It is a further condition that either:

(a) throughout the accounting period the shares forming the company's ordinary share capital meet the requirement of *CTA 2010, s 1137(2)(b)* (definition of 'listed' in relation to shares); or
(b) during the accounting period shares forming part of the company's ordinary share capital are traded on a recognised stock exchange.

The above requirement is, however, relaxed, for the first three accounting periods after a company joins the REIT regime . The condition in (a) is treated as met throughout each of those accounting periods if it is met at the end of the third period. The condition at (b) is met if during the period consisting of those three accounting periods combined, shares forming part of the ordinary share capital are traded on a recognised stock exchange.

CTA 2010, ss 528A, 528B].

Conditions for property rental business

[47.16] In order to qualify for REIT status the company must have a qualifying property rental business (whether or not it has any other business) throughout an accounting period. A property rental business qualifies as such if the conditions (a) and (b) below are met throughout that period and the distribution condition below is met.

(a) The property rental business must involve at least three properties. A property is treated as a single property if it is rented or available for rent as a commercial or residential unit separate from any other such unit (for example, a shop within a shopping complex or a flat within an apartment block).
(b) No one property is to have a value of more than 40% of the total value of all the properties involved in the property rental business.

For these purposes, the property rental businesses of all members of a group are treated as one business.

A property involved in a business includes any estate or interest in land which is exploited in earning income for that business.

Any profits derived from investments in other UK REITs are termed 'UK REIT investment profits'. Whilst these profits are part of the company's overall property rental business carried on in the UK, they are treated as separate from the other property rental business of the REIT.

'*UK REIT investment profits*' are distributions received by the company (or by a member of a group UK REIT), which are 'distributions of exempt profits', from its shareholdings in:

(a) the principal company of a group UK REIT, and it is a distribution of amounts shown in that group UK REIT's financial statements as profits or gains (or both) from UK group members, or from UK property rental income of non-UK members (including a distribution made by the principal company of a post-cessation group); or

(b) a company UK REIT and it is a distribution in respect of profits or gains (or both) of the property rental business of that company (including distributions made by the post-cessation company).

A '*distribution of exempt profits*' means a distribution of profits falling within *s 550(2)(a)(aa)(c)(d)*, being profits that relate to property income distributions. For this purpose this includes distributions made by the principal company of a post cessation group, or by a post cessation company.

[*CTA 2010, ss 529, 549A*].

The distribution condition

The distribution condition is met if at least 90% of the profits of the property rental business (see **47.19** below) arising in the accounting period are distributed by way of dividend on or before the filing date for the company's tax return for that period.

The company must distribute all of any profits derived from investments in other UK REITs, being UK REIT investment profits, as defined above. These profits are part of the company's overall property rental business carried on in the UK, however, they are treated as separate from the other property rental business of the REIT. At least 90% of the rest of the company's profits from its property rental business arising in the period should be distributed as noted.

The distribution condition does not apply to the extent it would be unlawful. Where part of a distribution has been withheld to avoid, or reduce, a tax charge which may be imposed if the REIT makes a distribution to investors with a shareholding of 10% or more (see **47.28** below), it will nevertheless count as having been made.

Where the 90% condition is not satisfied, the REIT regime continues to apply, provided that corporation tax will be charged on an amount calculated as follows, as if it were miscellaneous income:

$$P - D$$

Where:

P = 90% of the profits of the property rental business in the accounting period; and

D = total profits of the property rental business distributed before the filing date for that accounting period.

Corporation tax is charged at the main rate (so that the standard small profits rate introduced for financial year 2023 onwards does not apply).

No deduction is permitted from the taxable amount for this purpose.

[*CTA 2010, ss 530, 549A, 564, 565; FA 2021, Sch 1 para 27; SI 2006 No 2864, Reg 6*].

Increase in profits after tax return filed

The following applies where a REIT has filed its tax return showing the amount of the profits of its property rental business and, on the first date on which the return can no longer be amended, those profits have been increased from the amount originally shown in the return. Any distribution of those profits made before the end of the period of three months beginning with that date is to be treated as having been made by the deadline set above. However, the total amount of profits that can thus be treated as having been distributed by that deadline is limited to 90% of the amount of the increase in profits. A similar rule applies to a REIT group but by reference to the profits originally shown in the financial statement at **47.18**(b) below (group's UK property business).

However, this provision cannot be relied upon to satisfy the requirement to distribute all of the company's UK REIT investment profits.

[*CTA 2010, s 530A*].

Conditions for the balance of business

[47.17] The following conditions must also be met in relation to the proportion of a company's qualifying property rental business relative to its other business.

(a) The 'profits' arising from the company's property rental business in the accounting period must amount to at least 75% of the aggregate of the profits arising from that business and from any other business in that period. '*Profits*' in this case are those before deduction of tax as calculated in accordance with international accounting standards, excluding realised and unrealised gains and losses on property disposals and, excluding changes in the fair value of hedging derivative contracts (as defined) and amounts out of the company's normal business over its history, however they are treated in the accounts. The income used in the calculation of profits and aggregate profits of the property rental business includes any UK REIT investment profits (as defined above, but ignoring the requirement that such profits be exempt profits).

(b) The combined value at the beginning of the accounting period of the assets involved in the property rental business and the assets relating to residual business so far as consisting of cash must be at least 75% of the total value of assets held by the company. The assets relating to the residual business includes cash and '*relevant UK REIT shares*', which are shares held by the company in the principal company of a group UK REIT or in another UK company REIT.

As regards the valuation of assets in (a) and (b) above, they must be valued in accordance with international accounting standards and, where the valuation can be made on either a cost or fair value basis, a fair value basis must be used. Any liabilities secured against or relating to the assets are ignored for this purpose. Where the property is used as security for borrowings, those liabilities are ignored for valuation purposes. If a non-group company holds an interest in a group company, its percentage interest of profits, expenses, gains, losses, assets and liabilities are excluded for REIT purposes. In (b) above, 'cash' includes money held on deposit (whether or not in sterling), gilts and money held in any other way, or any investment of any other form, that may be specified in regulations made by statutory instrument.

[*CTA 2010, ss 531, 533(3)*].

Qualifying conditions — groups

[47.18] A group for these purposes is a company (the principal company) and all of its 75% subsidiaries held directly or indirectly, provided that the principal company has at least a 51% interest in each other company. Insurance companies and open-ended investment companies cannot form part of a REIT group. Subject to the rules for joint ventures (see **47.42** below), a company cannot be a member of more than one group.

The principal company of a group may give notice to become a UK REIT group, provided all of the relevant conditions are fulfilled.

The conditions in **47.14**(a) to (f) must be fulfilled by the principal company. In addition, the group as a whole must have a property rental business which must have at least three properties and no single property must account for more than 40% of the total value of properties in that property rental business. The further condition at **47.15** relating to shares must be met by reference to the shares of the principal company.

Finally, the principal company must produce financial statements for the accounting period and file them with HMRC, showing:

(a) all the group's property rental business;
(b) the group's UK property rental business; and
(c) the group's other (or 'residual') business.

The group's UK property business includes the property rental business of UK members of the group and the UK property rental business of other, non-UK members. For accounting periods beginning on or after 6 April 2019, for the purposes of (a) above, the UK rental business of a non-UK group member is treated as if it were the business of a UK resident group member.

The statements for (a) and (c) above must specify for each member, in accordance with international accounting standards, the income, expenses, profits before tax (excluding gains or losses on property, whether realised or not) and assets (valued at the beginning of the accounting period using fair value, where there is a choice), ignoring liabilities secured against or relating to those assets. The statement in relation to (b) above must specify, for each member, profits calculated in accordance with **47.22** below. Where a subsidiary company is not wholly owned, the income, expenses, gains, losses, assets and liabilities of that subsidiary are to be reduced by the proportion of the subsidiary owned by non-group members. Further provisions in relation to the financial statements are contained in *SI 2006 No 2865*.

[*CTA 2010, ss 528A, 528B, 532, 533, 606; FA 2019, Sch 1 paras 114, 120; SI 2006 No 2865*].

Conditions for business

[47.19] The property rental businesses of the group members are treated as a single business.

With respect to the 90% distribution condition at **47.16** above, at least 90% of the 'UK profits' of the property rental business arising in an accounting period must be distributed by the principal company by way of dividend on or before the filing date for the principal company's tax return for the accounting period. The principal company of a REIT group can issue stock dividends in lieu of cash dividends in order to meet the distribution requirement.

'*UK profits*' for this purpose are those in the financial statements of the property rental businesses in the UK.

As noted above with regard to single company REITs, the principal company of the group must distribute all of any profits derived from investments in other UK REITs, being 'UK REIT investment profits', as defined (see **47.14** above). These profits are part of the group's UK profits, however, they are treated as separate from the other UK property rental business. At least 90% of the rest of the group's UK profits arising in the period should be distributed as noted.

The distribution condition does not apply to the extent that compliance with the condition would be unlawful. Where part of a distribution has been withheld to avoid or reduce a tax charge which may be imposed if the principal company makes a distribution to investors with a shareholding of 10% or more (see **47.28** below), it will nevertheless count as having been made.

With regard to the conditions in relation to the proportion of a company's property rental business relative to its other business in **47.18** above, the income and assets tests are applied to determine the balance of business between the group's property rental business, based on the financial statements for (a) above, and the group's residual business, based on the financial statements for (c) above. The income used in the calculation of profits and aggregate profits of the property rental business (to determine whether the conditions as to the balance of the business have been met) includes any UK REIT investment profits (but ignoring the requirement that such profits be exempt profits). In addition for such periods, assets relating to the residual business includes cash and '*relevant UK REIT shares*', which are shares held by a member of the group UK REIT, in the principal company of another group UK REIT or in a UK company REIT.

[*CTA 2010, ss 530, 531, 532, 552*].

Entry into the regime

Notice of entry

[47.20] A company or a group of companies can enter into the REIT regime from a date specified by written notice to HMRC. Notice must be given to HMRC by the company or principal company of the group before the date specified. The notice must be accompanied by a statement by the company that the conditions set out in **47.14** above for the single company, or **47.18** above for a group of companies, are reasonably expected to be satisfied throughout the specified accounting period.

There is a special facility for new companies or groups seeking to qualify. Where the company or principal company of a REIT group does not expect to satisfy condition (c) in **47.14** on the first day of its accounting period, the statement in the company or principal company's notice must indicate the following:

- that condition (c) is reasonably expected to be satisfied for at least part of the first day of, and throughout the rest of, the accounting period; and
- that the other conditions are reasonably expected to be satisfied throughout the period.

HMRC may prescribe (by order) any other information or documents to be given in or with the notice. Once a company enters the regime, it will remain within the regime until it ceases to be so as a result of a termination event set out in **47.36** below.

[*CTA 2010, ss 523–526*].

Effects of entry

[47.21] On entry into the regime, the company or group's existing property rental business is treated as ceasing to exist at the point of entry and for corporation tax purposes, one accounting period ends immediately before entry and another begins on entry for the new, property rental business. The assets involved in that business are treated for corporation tax purposes as sold immediately before the entry, and reacquired immediately after the entry, at their market value and any gains arising as a result are not chargeable gains. On any subsequent disposal (apart from one following an early exit from the regime — see **47.39** below) of such an asset (whether actual or deemed), that deemed consideration at market value is to be used as its base cost. For capital allowances purposes, the new business is treated as acquiring the assets at their written-down value as though the pre-entry business had not ceased and no election may be made under *CAA 2001, ss 198, 199*.

The reference to the pre-entry business of a group is to be read as a reference to the pre-entry business of the UK property business of the group (or UK pre-entry business of a non-UK resident member of the group). The deemed disposal and re-acquisition of assets has effect in relation to each UK resident member and the UK property business of any non-UK members of the group. References to the pre-entry or post-entry property rental business of the company is to be read as a reference to the company as a group member. The cessation of an accounting period before entry, and the beginning of a new accounting period on entry, applies to each UK resident member.

If a company becomes a member of a REIT group, the effects of entry apply to the company at the time it joins the group. References to the pre-entry business of the company are to be read as references to its business before it joins the group and references to the property rental business of the company as references to the company as a member of the group's property rental business of the group with property rental business.

Where a subsidiary company is not wholly owned, and a proportion of the assets of a group member's property rental business are excluded from a financial statement (see **47.18** above), the excluded amount is to be ignored for the purposes of these provisions.

[*CTA 2010, ss 536, 537*].

Calculation of profits

[47.22] The profits arising from the property rental business (as calculated above, and including any UK REIT investment profits so far as those profits are a distribution of exempt profits (see above)) are not chargeable to corporation tax. The exemption is extended to the profits of a UK property rental business of a non-UK member of a UK REIT group.

Those profits arising from the residual business are chargeable to corporation tax at the main rate of corporation tax (so that the standard small profits rate introduced for financial year 2023 onwards does not apply).

Where a percentage of profits are excluded from the financial statements of a UK REIT group, (see **47.16**), those profits are treated as being profits of the residual business for the relevant member of the group. Such profits may be chargeable to corporation tax in the hands of the member company.

[*CTA 2010, s 534; FA 2021, Sch 1 para* 22].

For the purposes of attributing distributions (in **47.27** below) or determining whether the REIT meets the 90% distribution test (in **47.19** above) or the debt financing ratio (in **47.33** below), profits are calculated as follows.

The profits of a UK property rental business are calculated using the property income rules in *CTA 2009, s 210; ITTOIA 2005, s 272* (see **60** PROPERTY INCOME) whether the profits relate to a UK or a non-UK company.

However, the exclusion for property income purposes relating to debits and credits arising from loan relationships, embedded derivatives and hedging derivative contracts does not apply in respect of loan relationships, certain embedded derivative contracts and certain hedging relationships entered into for the purpose of the property rental business.

Income and expenditure relating partly to the property rental business and partly to the residual business is to be apportioned on a just and reasonable basis. Any capital allowances available will automatically be taken into account in the calculation of profits of the property rental business without the requirement for a claim under *CAA 2001, s 3*. No account is taken of the restriction on deductions for carried-forward losses at **51.13** LOSSES.

[*CTA 2010, s 599; F(No 2)A 2017, Sch 4 para 168*].

Ring-fencing and offset of losses

[47.23] The new business is effectively ring-fenced and treated as a separate business distinct from the pre-entry business, any residual business and the business after cessation of the regime ('the post-cessation business') (see **47.36** below). '*The post-cessation business*' relates to the property rental business after the group or company ceases to be a UK REIT.

A loss incurred by the property rental business cannot be set off against profits of the residual business and vice versa. A loss incurred by the pre-entry business cannot be set off against profits of the property rental business and a loss incurred by the property rental business cannot be set against the profits of any post-cessation business. Receipts accruing after entry to the REIT regime, relating to the pre-entry business, cannot be treated as receipts of the property rental business. '*Loss*' in this case also includes a deficit, expense, charge or allowance.

The provisions regarding ring-fencing and offset of losses apply to the UK property business of a non-UK member of a UK REIT group.

For the purpose of calculating the amount of profits, *CTA 2010, s 66* is disapplied so that losses arising from an overseas part of the property rental business can be set off against the UK part of the business. Also for this purpose, the exemption from the transfer pricing rules for small and medium-sized enterprises (see **72.6** TRANSFER PRICING) does not apply to either the company's property rental or residual business.

[*CTA 2010, ss 66, 541, 542*].

Distributions

Treatment of shareholders' dividends from REITs

[47.24] REITs can offer investors a stock dividend as an alternative to, or in combination with, a cash dividend, in meeting the 90% of profits from tax exempt property business distribution requirement. Distributions made from a REIT, or the principal company of a REIT group, of the property rental business' profits (including gains) are taxable on the shareholder (whether or not UK resident) as income from a UK property business. This rule applies so far as the distribution is a distribution of exempt profits.

However, this does not apply to distributions from one UK REIT to another UK REIT. Such profits are 'UK REIT investment profits' of the recipient UK REIT and are treated as part of the recipient's property rental business profits (and will thus be exempt from tax) so far as the UK REIT investment profits received is a distribution of exempt profits (see above).

In the case of a group REIT, the property rental business' profits includes profits and gains in respect of the UK property rental business of non-UK members (see 47.2).

A non-resident shareholder is not subject to taxation as a non-resident landlord in respect of the distributions. In the case of certain traders where distributions would normally be taxable as trading income, such as financial traders and members of Lloyd's, the REIT distribution will continue to be taxable under those rules.

'*Property income dividends*' (distributions from property rental income of REITs, commonly known as 'PIDs') do not fall to be treated as property income for double tax treaty purposes. They derive from shares, therefore they are dividends and the dividend article applies. However, where a REIT pays a dividend, not derived from property income and with a one-ninth tax credit attached, no tax credit repayment claim may be made (as a UK shareholder would not be entitled to claim a repayment).

The property income treatment applies in the case of companies which are members of a partnership. A tax credit does not apply to these distributions.

Distributions from one or more REITs are treated, in the hands of the shareholder, as the profits of a single business separate from any other UK or overseas property business (so far as they are 'distributions of exempt profits', see above, essentially property income dividends). This applies equally, in the case of a shareholder which is a partnership, to receipts by a partner of a share of any distribution.

The stock dividend income provisions (see now *ITTOIA 2005, ss 409–413A*) do not apply to distributions of profits and gains of a REIT's property rental business so far as it is a distribution of exempt profits (but does not include distributions between REITs which are UK REIT investment profits, see above).

Property income treatment continues to apply to distributions, made by a company or principal company, deriving from the profits of a property rental business after that company or group has left the REIT regime.

[*CTA 2010, ss 548, 549*].

Deduction of tax

[47.25] Where a REIT makes a distribution from its property rental profits (including gains and its UK REIT investment profits), the rules for the assessment, collection and recovery of tax are to be prescribed by Treasury regulations. In particular, the regulations may require the company or principal company of a REIT group to deduct income tax at source at the basic rate and may specify classes of shareholder to whom distributions can be made gross. The regulations may also contain detailed provisions for the calculation and payment of tax, claims and appeals, payment of interest, notices and returns, etc. The regulations may also apply to distributions deriving from the profits of a property rental business after a company or group has left the REIT regime. Regulations covering these matters were laid on 1 November 2006 (*The Real Estate Investment Trusts (Assessments and Recovery of Tax) Regulations 2006, SI 2006 No 2867*) and confirm that a return must be made to HMRC in respect of each quarter in which a property income distribution is paid. The return must include the amount of property income distribution paid and the tax withheld and due to HMRC. In addition the UK REIT must provide with the return, for the return period ending on the last day of the accounting period, a reconciliation statement showing how the dividends payable each year are attributable to each type of profit. See further **47.44** below.

[*ITA 2007, ss 973, 974; CTA 2010, s 548; SI 2006 No 2867*].

Non-residents

[47.26] Double taxation treaties contain a variety of ways for dealing with dividends. It is necessary to consider in each case how the treaty provisions affect PIDs. Details of any relief available to a resident of another country who is paid a PID can be found at www.gov.uk/guidance/double-taxation-relief-for-companies. A claim must be made in respect of each dividend, but any number of PIDs may be included in each claim.

The first claim must be sent for certification to the tax authority in which the claimant is resident. It should then be sent to HMRC. Subsequent claims should be sent direct to HMRC, unless the country of residence is Switzerland, in which case all claims must first be sent to the tax authority there for certification. Some country-specific claim forms will be issued in due course.

Attribution of distributions

[47.27] In identifying which distributions derive from the REIT's property rental business (and which, therefore, are liable to deduction of tax at source and treatment as property income in the hands of the recipient), the distributions are to be attributed in the following order:

(1) first to payments made to meet the full distribution requirement for UK REIT investment profits, then payments made to meet the 90% distribution requirement for other property rental business profits; for earlier accounting periods first to payments made to meet the 90% distribution requirement as in **47.16** above;

(2) to the extent that the company determines, distributions deriving from activities chargeable to corporation tax in relation to income (excluding gains on capital assets);

(3) distributions of profits of the company's property rental business (up to the amount of such profits not yet identified as having been distributed);

(4) distributions of gains arising from the property rental business which, by virtue of **47.29** below, are not chargeable gains;

(5) other distributions.

In determining the amount of gains within (4) above, *TCGA 1992, s 269ZBA* (restriction on deduction of carried forward capital losses — see **51.13** LOSSES) is ignored.

The provisions above dealing with the attribution of distributions applies to the principal company of a group, and in identifying the part of the distribution relating to the property rental business, reference to the company's property rental business is to the group's property rental business.

[*CTA 2010, s 550; FA 2019, Sch 1 para 117; FA 2020, Sch 4 para 21*].

Example

In its first period as a REIT a company has the following profits:

	£000
Property rental business	
Net rental income	5,500
Less: capital allowances	(500)
Property rental income	5,000
Property rental gains on disposal of rental property	250
Residual business	
Investment income	200
Gain on sale of fixed asset	150

The REIT distributes £5,500,000 in respect of that year's profits. This can be attributed to profits in the following ways.

A: Attributing as much as possible to property rental business

		£000
90% distribution requirement	((1) above)	4,500
Balance of property rental income	((3) above)	500
Property rental gain	((4) above)	250
Other activities	((5) above)	250
		5,500

B: Attributing as much as possible to the residual business

		£000
90% distribution requirement	((1) above)	4,500
Investment income	((2) above)	200
Other income*	((2) above)	500
Profits of property rental income	((3) above)	300
		5,500

* £500,000 is the difference between the tax measure of property rental business income (£5m) and the accounting measure (£5.5m) represented by capital allowances.

Distributions to holders of excessive rights

[47.28] A charge may be imposed, by Treasury regulation, on a REIT, or the principal company of a UK REIT group, if it makes a distribution to or in respect of a person who is beneficially entitled (directly or indirectly) to 10% or more of the company's share capital or dividends or controls 10% or more of its voting rights. For these purposes a person is a company, or person treated as a body corporate, in a territory outside the UK.

Where a REIT, or principal company of a UK REIT group, distributes to a person with more than the maximum holding and it has not taken reasonable steps to avoid so doing, the REIT company, or principal company, is treated as receiving an amount of income equivalent to:

$$\left(DO \times SO \times \frac{(BRT)}{(MCT)}\right) + \left(DP \times SP \times \frac{(BRT)}{(MCT)}\right)$$

where:

DO = the total amount of the company's property rental profits distributed in respect of ordinary shares.

SO = is the lesser of:

- excessive shareholder's percentage interest; and
- percentage interest of recipient of distributions.

BRT = the basic rate of tax at the time of the distribution.

DP = the REIT's total property rental profits distributed in respect of preference shares.

SP = the lesser of the percentage of rights:
- in respect of preference shares by the holder of the excessive rights; and
- held by the distribution recipient in respect of which the distribution was made.

MCT = the main UK corporation tax rate on residual profits.

The amount arrived at is charged to corporation tax at the main rate as if it were profits of the residual business of the REIT for the accounting period in which the distribution was made. The standard small profits rate introduced for financial year 2023 onwards does not apply. No loss, deficit, expense or allowance may be offset from the amount chargeable.

There are regulations requiring a REIT which makes a distribution to a holder of excessive rights to provide information to HMRC.

[*CTA 2010, ss 551–554; FA 2021, Sch 1 para 25; SI 2006 No 2864, Regs 10, 11*].

Capital gains

[47.29] Where a company is a REIT or is a member of a UK REIT group, a gain arising on the disposal of an asset used wholly and exclusively for the purpose of the property rental business is not a chargeable gain. Nor is an asset chargeable if it has been used partly for the property rental business and partly for the residual business during one or more periods of which in aggregate amounts to less than one year.

Where an asset has been used partly for the property rental business and partly for the residual business during one or more periods of at least one year in total, the gain is not chargeable to the extent that it can reasonably be attributed to the property rental business. The gain should be attributed on the basis of the length of time and extent to which the asset has been used in each business. Gains arising in respect of the residual business are chargeable to corporation tax at the main rate (so that the standard small profits rate introduced for financial year 2023 onwards does not apply).

Where a proportion of the gains of a group member's property rental business are excluded from a financial statement (see **47.18** above), the excluded amount is to be treated for corporation tax purposes as gains of the relevant member's residual business. With respect to transfers out of the ring-fence (see **47.30** below) in relation to property developed by the company and sold within three years of completion, such property being treated as if it were never part of the property rental business, reference to the company is a reference to the group member.

Where the company (company A) disposes, on or after 6 April 2019, of an asset consisting of a right or interest in another company (company B) which is 'UK property rich', a proportion of the gain is not a chargeable gain and the asset is treated as having been used for the purposes of the property rental business to an extent equal to the same proportion. The proportion is that which, at the start of the accounting period of the disposal, the value of company B's 'PRB assets' bears to the total value of company B's assets. The value of company B's '*PRB assets*' is the value of those assets deriving (directly or indirectly) from assets used for the purposes of UK property rental business. Company B is '*UK property rich*' if the disposal would be of an asset deriving at least 75% of its value from UK land (under the provisions at **11.26** CAPITAL GAINS).

This rule also applies to the disposal of a right or interest in an offshore collective investment scheme which is UK property rich and is transparent for income tax purposes (otherwise than as a result of being constituted by two or more persons carrying on a trade or business in partnership) if no election under *TCGA 1992, Sch 5AAA para 8* has been made (see **11.28** CAPITAL GAINS). The rule does not apply to the extent that the gain is already exempt under the provisions at **13.7** CAPITAL GAINS — SUBSTANTIAL SHAREHOLDINGS. In determining the amount of a gain which is not a chargeable gain under this rule, any unrelieved allowable losses on disposals made before 6 April 2019 and any other deficits or other losses for accounting periods ending before that date which would otherwise have been deducted from profits or gains or any kind of the residual business of the company may be deducted from the gain. In making the determination, *TCGA 1992, s 269ZBA* (restriction on deduction of carried forward capital losses – see **51.13** LOSSES) is ignored. For this purpose, accounting periods straddling 6 April 2019 are treated as two separate periods, the first of which ends on 5 April 2019. Any necessary apportionments between the notional periods must be made on a time basis or, if a time basis would not be just and reasonable, on a just and reasonable basis.

If company B has acquired, directly or indirectly, one or more properties and has subsequently developed them, then if the development costs exceed 30% of the fair value of the property at acquisition (or, if later, on entry) and company A's disposal of the right or interest in company B is made within the three-year period beginning with the completion of the development, the above rule does not apply to so much of any gain on the disposal as relates to the developed property.

[*CTA 2010, ss 533, 535–535B, 556(3A)–(3C); FA 2019, Sch 1 paras 115, 118, 120; FA 2020, Sch 4 para 20; FA 2021, Sch 1 para 23*].

Movement of assets out of ring-fence

[47.30] An asset used wholly and exclusively for the purpose of the property rental business which begins to be used (otherwise than by being disposed of in the course of a trade) wholly and exclusively in the residual business is treated as disposed of by the property rental business and immediately re-acquired by the residual business for a consideration equal to the market value of the asset. On any subsequent disposal (apart from one following an early exit from the regime — see **47.39** below) of such an asset (whether actual or deemed), the deemed consideration at that market value is to be used as its base cost. This treatment excludes assets disposed of in the course of a trade (see below). For capital allowances purposes, the assets are not treated as having been transferred, the residual business being treated as standing in the shoes of the property rental business.

Where a percentage of a gain relating to the property rental business is excluded, that part is treated as a gain of the residual business. These provisions apply to non-UK group members as well as UK group members.

[*CTA 2010, s 555*].

Where an asset which has been used wholly and exclusively for the purpose of the property rental business is disposed of in the course of a trade for the purposes of the residual business (but not where it is disposed of to another company in the same group), there is no deemed sale and re-acquisition but the asset is treated as disposed of in the course of the residual business. This applies in particular where a company develops property, where the cost of development exceeds 30% of the fair value of the property at entry or acquisition, whichever is the later, and where the property is disposed of within three years from the completion of the development. Where an asset held by the property rental business at entry is disposed of in the course of a trade, the company can claim repayment of a proportion of the entry charge (now abolished — see **47.22** above) relating to that asset. The proportion is the market value of the asset at entry divided by the aggregate market value of assets treated as sold and re-acquired on entry, ignoring any assets of negative market value.

[*CTA 2010, s 556; FA 2020, Sch 4 para 22*].

Movement of assets into ring-fence

[47.31] An asset used wholly and exclusively for the purpose of the residual business which begins to be used wholly and exclusively in the property rental business, is treated as disposed of by the residual business and immediately re-acquired by the property rental business for a consideration equal to the market value of the asset. For capital allowances purposes, the assets are not treated as having been transferred, the property rental business being treated as standing in the shoes of the residual business.

Where a percentage of a gain of property rental business is excluded, that part is treated as a gain of the residual business. These provisions apply to non-UK group members as well as UK group members.

[*CTA 2010, s 557*].

Disposal proceeds awaiting re-investment

[47.32] Where

(a) a company or a member of a UK REIT group disposes of an asset used wholly and exclusively for the purposes of the property rental business and holds the proceeds in 'cash', and
(b) the proceeds are used to enter into a loan relationship (such as a bank deposit),

any profits or losses arising from that relationship (such as bank interest) are not treated as part of the profits of the property rental business but are taxable under the loan relationship rules as arising in the residual business.

This rule also applies to proceeds held in cash on a disposal of an asset on or after 6 April 2019 to the extent that a proportion of the gain or loss is not a chargeable gain or allowable loss under *CTA 2010, s 535A* (see **47.29** above).

'*Cash*' in this case includes any currency held on deposit or gilt stocks or bonds or other investments as specified by HMRC regulations. Where the asset disposed of was used partly for the property rental business and partly for the residual business this treatment applies to the proportion of the disposal proceeds that may reasonably be attributed to the property rental business on the basis of the length of time and extent to which the asset has been used in each business.

[*CTA 2010, s 547; FA 2019, Sch 1 paras 116, 120*].

Debt financing

[47.33] A tax charge is imposed on a REIT that does not meet a minimum financing cost ratio. The charge is imposed where, for an accounting period, the profits from the property rental business (or in the case of a REIT group, the sum of the property rental profits for members of the group) as set out in the financial statements (see **47.18** above), divided by the property finance costs is less than 1.25 (but not where it is nil or a negative amount).

In this case, the property rental profits are taken before the offset of capital allowances, losses brought forward from a previous accounting period or the disregarding of debits and credits arising from loan relationships, embedded derivatives and hedging derivative contracts (see **47.22** above).

Finance costs in this case mean the amount of debt financing costs incurred in respect of the property rental business, or in the case of a REIT group, the amount of debt financing costs incurred in respect of the property rental business excluding any financing costs owed by one member of the group to another member. In calculating debt financing costs, the matters to be taken into account are:

- interest payable on borrowing;
- amortisation of discounts relating to borrowing;
- amortisation of premiums relating to borrowing;
- the financing expense implicit in payments made under 'finance leases';
- alternative finance return;
- periodic payments from derivative contracts or other arrangements entered into as a hedge of risk in connection with borrowing so far as they are attributable to the hedge; and
- amortisation of discounts and premiums relating to such a derivative contract or other arrangement.

This list may be amended in future by Treasury regulations made by statutory instrument.

A lease is a '*finance lease*' in relation to a particular person if it falls (or would fall), in accordance with generally accepted accounting practice ('GAAP'), to be treated as a finance lease or loan in that person's accounts. For periods of account beginning on or after 1 January 2019, in relation to a lessee, a right-to-use lease (see **10.49**(5) CAPITAL ALLOWANCES ON PLANT AND MACHINERY) is a finance lease for this purpose if it would have been accounted for as such had the lessee been required, in accordance with GAAP, to determine whether or not it was a finance lease.

Where the ratio of the REIT's financing cost ratio is less than 1.25, the company is charged to corporation tax on the excess of the actual financing costs for the period over the amount of financing costs that would have caused the calculation outlined above to equal 1.25. However, for accounting periods beginning on or after 17 July 2012, the chargeable amount is limited to 20% of the property rental profits brought into the calculation if this gives a lesser figure. The chargeable amount is treated as profits of the residual business of the company, or the principal company in the case of a REIT group. Corporation tax is charged at the main rate (so that the standard small profits rate introduced for financial year 2023 onwards does not apply). No deductions or reliefs may be set against these chargeable profits.

HMRC may waive this charge if they consider that the company was in severe financial difficulties at a time in the accounting period, the financial cost ratio is less than 1.25 for that accounting period because of unexpected circumstances and the company could not reasonably have taken action to avoid the ratio being below 1.25. The Treasury has power to make regulations specifying criteria to be applied in deciding whether to waive a charge.

[*CTA 2010, ss 543, 544, 599; FA 2019, Sch 14 paras 4(8), 6(1); FA 2021, Sch 1 para 24; SI 2014 No 4518, Reg 2*].

Breach of conditions

[47.34] A company or principal company which has given notice of entry into the regime (**47.22** above) must notify HMRC as soon as reasonably practicable if the following conditions cease to be satisfied:

- conditions (c) and (d) of the conditions for the company (see **47.14**);
- the further condition for the company relating to shares (see **47.15**);
- conditions (a) and (b) of the conditions for the business (see **47.16**);
- the distribution condition (see **47.16**); or
- conditions (a) and (b) for the balance of business (see **47.17**).

The company or principal company must provide HMRC with details of the date on which the breach occurred and when the breach was rectified (if at all), a description of the breach and details of the steps taken (if any) to prevent the breach happening again.

Breach of conditions for company

The REIT regime will continue to apply if the breach is the result of a REIT becoming a member of a REIT group or as the result of the principal company of a REIT group becoming a member of another REIT group.

In addition, the REIT regime will also continue to apply in the case of a breach of condition (d) in **47.14** above if the breach is due to the actions (or lack of actions) by a person other then the REIT company or principal company. However, the company must remedy the breach no later then the end of the accounting period after the breach occurred. If the breach is not remedied within that time frame, the company or group will be treated as ceasing to be a REIT or REIT group at the end of the accounting period in which the breach occurred.

In accordance with the relaxation of condition (d) for companies entering the REIT regime (see **47.14**), the above notification does not have to be given if condition (d) ceases to be met during the company's first three years in the regime. If condition (d) is not met at the start of the first day after that three-year period ends, a breach is treated as occurring at that time.

If there is a breach of condition (c) in **47.14** or the further condition relating to shares in **47.15**, and the provisions above do not apply, the company or group will be treated as ceasing to be a REIT or REIT group from the end of the previous accounting period. This applies equally where there is a breach of condition (d) in **47.14** except that the company or group cannot thereby be treated as ceasing to be a REIT or REIT group at any time before the end of the initial three-year period.

As regards the further condition relating to shares, and the relaxation of that condition for the first three accounting periods after a company joins the REIT regime (see **47.14**), the company or group will be treated as ceasing to be a REIT or REIT group at the end of the second accounting period if the condition is not met in relation to those first three accounting periods.

Breach of conditions for the business

The REIT regime will continue to apply if a company or principal company does not meet the conditions throughout the accounting period. However, HMRC may issue a notice of termination where the conditions are breached more than twice in a ten-year period, beginning with the date that the first breach occurred. If a breach of condition (b) is a necessary consequence of a breach of condition (a) in the same accounting period, then the breach of condition (b) is to be ignored. If the breach of either condition lasts for more than one, but not more than two accounting periods, the breach is treated as only occurring once.

HMRC may also issue a notice of termination if there is a breach of conditions (a) and (b) for three consecutive accounting periods (see **47.16**).

Breach of the distribution condition

The REIT provisions will continue to apply if there is a breach of the distribution condition, but the company will be chargeable to corporation tax on an amount determined to be profits of the residual business. The amount is calculated as 90% of the company or group's property rental profits less the amount distributed before the filing date (see **47.16**).

However, no charge to corporation tax will arise if the company or principal company make a dividend distribution within a three-month period (beginning on the date on which the company or group's profits can no longer be altered) which is sufficient to meet the distribution condition.

Breach of balance of business condition

Where a company does not comply with condition (b) in **47.17** at the beginning of its initial accounting period in the REIT regime, that regime will continue to apply provided that condition (b) is met at the beginning of the second accounting period.

The REIT regime will cease to apply if condition (b) is not met at the beginning of the second accounting period and HMRC consider the breach so fundamental that the regime should not apply.

Where conditions (a) or (b) of the balance of business conditions are not satisfied after the initial accounting period, the REIT regime will continue to apply where, in the case of (a), the profits from the property rental business are at least 50% of the total profits for the accounting period and in the case of (b), the value of the assets of the property rental business plus the value of the assets relating to residual business so far as consisting of cash are at least 50% of the total value of assets.

A company or principal company may rely on the relaxation of condition (a) and condition (b) for up to two times in a ten-year period beginning with the first date the relaxation was relied on. (For this purpose, condition (a) is treated as breached on the last day of the accounting period for which the company's profits are assessed for the purposes of that condition.) But, if the conditions are breached in three consecutive accounting periods, the breach will no longer qualify for this relaxation. However, where a breach lasts for one, but not more than two accounting periods, it is treated as one breach.

[*CTA 2010, ss 561, 562, 562A–562C, 563–569; SI 2006 No 2864, Regs 7–7B*].

Cancellation of tax advantage

[47.35] If HMRC consider that a company or a company in a UK REIT group has tried to obtain a 'tax advantage' under these provisions for itself or another person, they may, by notice to the company, counteract the advantage and assess the company to an additional amount of corporation tax equivalent to the value of the tax advantage. The tax advantage may be counteracted by adjustment by way of an assessment, amendment of a tax return, cancellation of a right of repayment or a requirement for the return of a repayment already made. A 'tax advantage' has the meaning given under *CTA 2010, s 1139* and includes, in particular, entering into arrangements to avoid or reduce the entry charge under **47.22** above (now abolished). A tax advantage does not, however, include benefits arising from the REIT regime unless the sole or main purpose of joining the regime is to create or inflate a loss, deduction or expense or to have another effect which may be specified by Treasury regulation. An appeal against a notice to cancel a tax advantage may be made to the tribunal by written notice to HMRC within 30 days from the date of the notice to the company. The tribunal may quash the notice, confirm it or vary it.

[*CTA 2010, ss 545, 546*].

Leaving the regime

Termination by notice

[47.36] A company REIT or the principal company in a REIT group can give notice in writing to HMRC specifying a date (to be later than that on which HMRC receives the notice) at the end of which the REIT regime is to cease to apply to the company or group.

[*CTA 2010, s 571*].

HMRC may give written notification (a '*termination notice*') to a company REIT or to the principal company in a REIT group, giving the reasons for the issue of the notice, that the regime is to cease to apply to it if:

(a) the company has relied on the breach provisions on the specified number of occasions in the specified period (see **47.34** above);
(b) the company has been given two notices in relation to the cancellation of a tax advantage in a specified period (see **47.35** above);
(c) HMRC consider that the breach of the company conditions (see **47.14** above), property rental business conditions (see **47.16**), the balance of business conditions (see **47.17** above) or an attempt by the company to obtain a tax advantage is so great that it no longer qualifies for REIT status;
(d) there is a breach of condition (d) in **47.14** above in certain circumstances within the initial three-year period; or
(e) the company or a member of the group has over-relied in certain circumstances on the relaxation of the further condition relating to shares at **47.15** above.

Except where (d) or (e) above applies, the REIT regime will cease to apply (subject to the early exit provisions below) at the end of the accounting period before that in which the event occurs (or the last event occurs) which caused HMRC to give the notice. Where (d) or (e) applies, the regime will cease to apply from the beginning of the first accounting period within the regime or such later day as may be specified by HMRC in the notice. An appeal against a termination notice may be made to the tribunal, by notice in writing from the company or the principal company to HMRC within 30 days from the date on which the notice is given to the company.

[*CTA 2010, ss 572, 573, 573A, 573B, 574–576*].

HMRC may also give a termination notice where there are multiple breaches of conditions. A termination notice may be issued where there has been a breach of at least two of the conditions at **47.14**, **47.16** and **47.17** above during the ten-year period beginning on the day on which the company first fails to satisfy a condition, at least one of the conditions breached is contained in a different section from that containing another and the company has relied on the breach provisions more then four times in the ten-year period. For this purpose, a company is treated as having first failed to satisfy the condition at **47.16**(a) above on the last day of the accounting period in which its profits are assessed. The following types of breach are not taken into account in determining the number of breaches:

- a breach of either of conditions (c) and (d) at **47.14** above in consequence of a REIT becoming a member of a REIT group;
- a breach of condition (c) at **47.14** above in respect of which the company used the special facility for new companies at **47.20** above;
- a breach of the condition at **47.16**(a) above in the company's initial accounting period within the REIT regime;
- a breach of the condition at **47.16**(b) above at the beginning of the company's initial accounting period within the regime; and

- a breach of condition (d) in **47.14** above which occurs during the initial three-year period.

[*CTA 2010, s 577*].

Automatic termination

[47.37] If any of the company conditions (a), (b), (e) or (f) in **47.14** above are not satisfied in an accounting period, the REIT regime is treated as ceasing to apply to the company at the end of the previous accounting period. The company which gave notice of entry, as set out in **47.20** above, must notify HMRC as soon as is reasonably practicable if any of those conditions cease to be satisfied. [*CTA 2010, s 578*].

Effects of cessation

[47.38] The effect of cessation will apply where a company or group ceases to be a UK REIT or where a company ceases to be a member of a UK REIT group. The effects will apply to each member of a UK REIT group.

On leaving the regime, the company's property rental business is treated as ceasing to exist immediately before the cessation and for corporation tax purposes, an accounting period of the residual business ends on cessation and a new accounting period of the company (in respect of the '*post-cessation*' business) begins.

The assets involved in the property rental business immediately before cessation are treated for corporation tax purposes as sold immediately before cessation by the property rental business and reacquired immediately after cessation by the post-cessation business at their market value. On any subsequent disposal (apart from one following an early exit — see below) of such an asset (whether actual or deemed), the deemed consideration at that market value is to be used as its base cost. Where a subsidiary company is not wholly owned, and a proportion of the profits of a group member's property rental business are excluded from a financial statement (see **47.18** above), the excluded amount is to be ignored for the purpose of these provisions.

For capital allowances purposes, the post-cessation business is treated as acquiring the assets at their written-down value as though the property rental business had not ceased. [*CTA 2010, ss 579, 580, 602*].

Effects of early exit

Notice by the company or group

[47.39] The following rule applies if a company leaves the REIT regime, a company leaves a UK REIT group, or a group leaves the REIT regime by notice from HMRC or automatic termination and that company or group has been within the regime for a continuous period of less than ten years immediately before the cessation.

Where the company disposes of an asset that was part of the property rental business within a period of two years beginning with the date of cessation, any deemed disposals that applied to that asset on entry to the regime (under **47.21** above), on transfer out of the ring fence (under **47.30** above) or on exit from the regime (as above), are ignored in calculating the gain on the disposal.

[*CTA 2010, s 581*].

Notice by HMRC

The following rules apply if the company leaves the REIT regime as a result of an HMRC termination notice or an automatic termination and has been within the regime for a continuous period of less than ten years immediately before the cessation. An HMRC termination notice or an automatic termination may relate to the group as a whole or to one or more members and may, in particular, alter the effects of the provisions relating to groups.

HMRC may direct that:

(i) the effects of a regime provision are modified. In particular, they may alter the time the company or group is treated as leaving the REIT regime as a result of the termination notice or automatic termination and they may disapply or alter the effect of the provisions which exempt the profits and gains of the REIT's property rental business from corporation tax; or
(ii) the effects of other corporation tax provisions are applied, disapplied or modified, in particular to prevent all or part of a loss, deficit or expense from being set off or otherwise used at all or in a specified manner.

An appeal against such a direction may be made by the company or principal company of the group to the tribunal, who may quash HMRC's direction, confirm it or vary it.

[*CTA 2010, s 582; FA 2019, Sch 1 para 119*].

Groups

[47.40] In relation to the following group reliefs, the property rental businesses of the group members are treated as a separate group distinct from the pre-entry businesses of those companies, the residual businesses and the post-cessation businesses:

- actual or notional transfers within a group under *TCGA 1992, ss 171, 171A–171C*;
- reallocation of rolled-over gains within a group under *TCGA 1992, ss 179A, 179B*;
- group relief under *CTA 2010, Pt 5*;
- group relief for carried-forward losses under *CTA 2010, Pt 5A*;
- loan relationships under *CTA 2009, Pt 5 Chs 4, 6–8;*
- derivative contracts under *CTA 2009, Pt 7*; and
- intangible fixed assets under *CTA 2009, Pt 8*.

[*CTA 2010, s 601; F(No 2)A 2017, Sch 4 para 169*].

Demergers

[47.41] Where a REIT leaves a group and either the company, or where the REIT has become a member of a new group, the new group satisfies certain conditions immediately after it leaves the group, the company or principal company of the new group may give notice of entry to HMRC by the day the company leaves the existing REIT group. The conditions to be satisfied are as follows:

- conditions (a) and (b) of the conditions for the company (see **47.14**);
- conditions (a) and (b) of the conditions for the business (see **47.16**);
- the distribution condition (see **47.16**); and
- conditions (a) and (b) of the conditions for the balance of business (see **47.16**).

The date of entry given in the notice must be the day the company leaves the existing group. The company will qualify as a REIT from that date even if it does not expect to satisfy conditions (c), (e) and (f) at **47.14** above throughout the first accounting period. The company has six months to qualify, during which it will be treated as a REIT. If it fails to satisfy all the conditions by the time six months has expired, it will be treated as if it had not been a REIT from the date it left the group.

Where there is a demerger, involving a REIT transferring a property rental business asset to a 75% subsidiary and a subsequent disposal of that subsidiary by the REIT, and the acquiring company subsequently gives a notice of entry (see **47.18**) specifying an accounting period commencing within six months of the date of transfer, the REIT provisions apply to the group that the subsidiary is now a member of from the beginning of that accounting period. The purchasing company may give notice of entry even if conditions (c), (e) and (f) in **47.14** are not complied with throughout the period stated in the notice.

The provisions concerning the effects of entry, the entry charge (now abolished) and the movement of assets out of ring-fence (see **47.21**, **47.22** and **47.30** respectively) do not apply to the transfer of the property rental business asset by the existing REIT provided conditions (c), (e) and (f) in **47.14** are met by the acquiring company within six months of the date of transfer.

[*CTA 2010, ss 558, 559*].

Joint ventures

[47.42] A joint venture for this purpose means a company or group carrying on a property rental business where an interest in the joint venture is held by a REIT or one or more members of a REIT group.

A REIT or principal company of a REIT group, known as the venturing company or group, may apply for a joint venture look through notice to apply to the joint venture company if the following conditions are satisfied:

- the venturing company or group is beneficially entitled to 40% or more of the profits available for distribution; and
- the venturing company or group is beneficially entitled to 40% or more of the assets on a winding up.

The notice must specify the joint venture company, the date from which the notice will apply and be given in writing to HMRC before the date on which the notice will apply.

A REIT or principal company of a REIT group may also give notice for a joint venture look through notice to apply in relation to property rental business carried on by one or more members of a joint venture group. The conditions above will apply in so far as they relate to the principal company of the joint venture group.

[*CTA 2010, ss 583–587*].

Once notice has been given by a venturing company, the property rental business carried on by the joint venture company will be treated as if it had formed a new REIT group with the venturing company. Where notice has been given by a venturing group, the property rental business carried on by the joint venture company will be treated as if it were a member of the venturing group. These provisions apply where a joint venture look through notice has been issued in respect of a joint venture group. For the purposes of 'UK REIT investment profits' the joint venture company and the venturing company, if they are recipients of UK REIT distributions, are treated as a member of a group UK REIT.

The notice will continue to apply until the venturing company or group ceases to fulfil the conditions above as to entitlement to profits or assets. However the early exit rules (see **47.26**) will continue to apply to a joint venture company or group.

The conditions regarding the balance of business (see **47.16**) must be met by the joint venture company or group at the beginning of each accounting period for which the notice has effect.

The venturing company's accounts are prepared in accordance with *SI 2006 No 2865*, as amended for the joint venture situation. The principal company of a joint venture group must prepare accounts for the group for each accounting period in much the same way as for a REIT group (see **47.16**).

It used to be the case that the joint venture company or members of a joint venture group could be chargeable to tax on an entry charge (see **47.22**) in certain circumstances. In particular, this could apply where the venturing company became the principal company of a REIT group and increased its holding in the joint venture company or group or where the venturing company or group increased its shareholding in the joint venture company or group to at least 75%. The charge is abolished with effect on and after 17 July 2012.

Where the principal company of a UK REIT group gives notice in relation to members of a joint venture group, the above apply in relation to a property rental business carried on by the members of the joint venture UK REIT group. Similar provisions apply where a company UK REIT and the members of a joint venture group become members of a new UK REIT group.

[*CTA 2010, ss 549A, 588–597; FSI 2006 No 2865*].

Penalties

[47.43] Penalties under *TMA 1970, s 98* will apply for failure to comply with:

- the requirement to provide a notice of a breach of conditions or with any requirements imposed by regulations in relation to such breaches under **47.34** above;
- requirements imposed by regulations in connection with deduction of income tax from distributions under **47.25** above;
- the requirement to provide notice of a breach of company conditions in relation to automatic termination under **47.37** above; and

- the requirement to meet the company conditions and for the principal company to send in financial statements as part of those conditions under **47.14** and **47.18** above.

An initial penalty will apply of up to £300 and if the failure continues after this penalty has been imposed, a further penalty of up to £60 per day can be imposed for each day the failure continues.

[*TMA 1970, s 98*].

Administration

[47.44] When a company makes a distribution from its property letting business it must deduct tax at the basic rate in force for the year of payment unless the conditions for gross payment are made.

[*SI 2006 No 2867, Regs 2, 3*].

Where a REIT or principal company of a REIT group makes a distribution from property rental income, it must submit a return to HMRC for each quarter in which a distribution is made plus a return to the accounting date if that does not fall on a calendar quarter. The returns should be delivered within 14 days after the end of the period.

A reconciliation of the payments for the year also has to be delivered within 14 days of the accounting date, with the distributions attributed as to source (see 47.20). The tax deducted from the distribution must be paid over to HMRC, without assessment, with the same deadlines as for the returns. The company has to give the recipient a statement showing the gross payment, tax deducted and net amount paid.

No tax is to be deducted if the payee is a company resident or trading through a permanent establishment in the UK, a local authority, NHS Trust, public office or department of the Crown, charity or similarly treated body, the EIF, scientific research organisation, various pension funds, ISAs, CTF, PEP funds which are to apply the payment for permitted purposes or a partnership otherwise qualifying.

[*SI 2006 No 2867, Regs 2, 4, 6, 7*].

HMRC has power to assess where it believes that tax due has not been paid.

[*SI 2006 No 2867, Reg 9*].

Miscellaneous provisions

Manufactured dividends

[47.45] Special provisions apply to dividends that represent payments of distributions of the property rental profits of a REIT or principal company of a REIT group. But note the new provisions with regard to manufactured dividends at **52.2** MANUFACTURED PAYMENTS.

[*CTA 2010, ss 785, 786*].

Charities

For charitable companies and REITs see **14.3** CHARITIES.

Connected persons

The Treasury are given powers to regulate, by statutory instrument, the operation of the REIT legislation in the public interest where there are transactions between connected persons.

[*CTA 2010, ss 598, 600*].

Anti-avoidance

[47.46] *SI 2009 No 3315* introduces anti-avoidance provisions aimed at artificially manipulated commercial arrangements where the purpose or main purpose of the arrangements is to enable the party or parties of the arrangement to meet the conditions to qualify as a REIT, where it or they would not otherwise have qualified.

Key points on investment trusts

[47.47] Points to consider are as follows.

- When calculating the value of assets used in the property rental business of a REIT for the purposes of the asset balance of business test, all assets used in that business should be included, not just properties. For example, the value of company cars used by those who work in the property rental business should be included.
- Note that the 10% test only applies to corporate shareholders.
- Where a UK REIT invests in another UK REIT the income therefrom will be exempt and the UK REIT must distribute all profits derived from that investment, the requirement to distribute 90% of the profits derived from the rest of its property rental business remains the same.
- Where a group of companies wishes to hold more than 10% of a UK REIT, it could do so by fragmenting its shareholding in the UK REIT between a number of sister subsidiaries, each holding less than 10%. This is generally accepted by HMRC as the 10% rule and was introduced to prevent tax treaties removing the withholding tax requirements for dividends paid by UK REITs.
- The non-UK property business of non-UK group members can be taken into account for the purposes of the profit and asset balance of business tests and the property business tests.
- The purpose of the UK REIT regime is to tax shareholders on a similar basis to holding the underlying property directly. The treatment is not directly comparable however as gains arising from the property rental business distributed to shareholders by way of dividend are treated as property income in the hands of shareholders rather than as gains.

- On a takeover of a UK REIT by a non-REIT, the UK REIT will at some point breach the close company condition and the listed company condition, with the result that the UK REIT will leave the regime. A UK REIT is deemed to leave the regime at the end of the accounting period in which the company becomes close or at the end of the accounting period before that in which the company ceased to be listed. In order to maximise the time during which the REIT is within the regime, consideration could be given to amending the accounting reference date of the UK REIT to a date shortly before the company ceases to be listed.
- Where a UK REIT and a non-REIT enter into a joint venture, the UK REIT will need to ensure that profits and losses are shared on a pre-tax basis since the UK REIT's share of the joint venture's income is not subject to tax. If returns are shared equally after tax, the UK REIT will suffer a loss.
- When determining whether profits are required to be distributed as property income distributions, the measure of profits to use is calculated on the same basis as if they were taxable profits. As such, whilst capital allowances are not relevant in reducing a UK REIT's charge to tax, they are relevant in reducing the amount required to be distributed by the UK REIT and taxed as property income in the hands of shareholders.
- Certain conditions for being within the UK REIT regime are required to be met throughout an accounting period, including the company conditions, the property business conditions (being at least three properties with no one property worth more than 40% of the total portfolio value), the profit balance of business test and the profit: financing cost ratio. Compliance with these tests will need to be monitored on an ongoing basis. In particular, UK REIT operations managers will need to assess commercial proposals alongside their internal or external tax advisers to ensure that the proposals do not result in a breach of any of the conditions.

48

Land Remediation

Simon's Taxes. See **D1.501–D1.521.**

Introduction to land remediation

[48.1] Relief is available for companies that acquire contaminated or derelict land for the purposes of their trade or UK property business for capital expenditure incurred on remediation of that land. Companies can elect for capital expenditure to be deducted in computing the profits of the trade or business and may claim an enhanced deduction for allowable expenditure (including such capital expenditure) of 150%. Where the enhanced deduction results in a loss then the loss can be used in the normal way or it can be surrendered in return for a cash payment.

See generally the HMRC Corporate Intangibles Research and Development Manual, CIRD60000 *et seq*.

For commentary on devolution of the power to set the corporation tax rate in Northern Ireland to the Stormont Assembly and consequential modification of the land remediation relief rules, see **1.1** INTRODUCTION: CHARGE TO TAX, RATES AND PROFIT COMPUTATIONS.

Qualifying expenditure

[48.2] '*Qualifying land remediation expenditure*' is expenditure meeting the following six conditions.

(a) It must be on land all or part of which is in a 'contaminated state' or a 'derelict state'.
Land is in a '*contaminated state*' if something in, on or under the land is in such a condition that 'relevant harm' is likely to be caused. '*Relevant harm*' is defined as death of, or significant injury or damage to, living organisms, significant pollution of 'controlled waters', material adverse impact on the ecosystem or structural or other significant damage to buildings or other structures or interference with buildings or other structures that significantly compromises their use.

However land is not contaminated by reason only of the presence in, on or under it of living organisms or decaying matter deriving from living organisms, air or water or anything other than the result of industrial activity. This exclusion does not, however, apply to arsenic, arsenical compounds, radon or Japanese knotweed (but only such part of a site as is contaminated by these items qualifies for relief).

Land is in a '*derelict state*' if it is not in productive use and cannot be put into productive use without the removal of buildings or other structures. A nuclear site is not contaminated or derelict land for the purpose of this relief.

'*Controlled waters*' are as under *Water Resources Act 1991, Pt III* or equivalent Scottish or NI legislation.

These requirements may be varied by statutory instrument. '*Land*' is defined as 'any estate, interest or rights in or over land' and for these purposes, 'land' includes buildings (see HMRC Corporate Intangibles, Research and Development Manual, CIRD60130 and *Interpretation Act 1978, Sch 1*).

(b) It must be expenditure which would not have been incurred had the land not been in a contaminated or derelict state. Any increase in expenditure by reason only of the land being in a contaminated or derelict state is treated as satisfying this condition, as is expenditure on works done, operations carried out or steps taken mainly for the purposes described in (c) below.

(c) It must be on 'relevant contaminated land remediation' or, as the case may be, 'relevant derelict land remediation' undertaken directly by the company or on its behalf.

'*Relevant contaminated land remediation*' in relation to contaminated land in which a major interest has been acquired by the company is the doing of any works, the carrying out of any operations or the taking of any steps in relation to the land (or adjoining or adjacent land) or any controlled waters affected by the state of that land, for the purpose of preventing or minimising, or remedying or mitigating the effects of, any relevant harm by reason of which the land is in a contaminated state. Preparatory activities are included provided that they are for the purpose of assessing the condition of the land or waters concerned and are connected to the remediation activities to be undertaken by the company or on its behalf. The removal of Japanese knotweed to a landfill site and certain activities required by any of the enactments listed in *SI 2009 No 2037, Art 5* are not relevant contaminated land remediation.

'*Relevant derelict land remediation*' in relation to derelict land in which a major interest has been acquired by the company is the doing of any works, the carrying out of any operations or the taking of any steps in relation to the land for purposes specified by order. Currently the specified purposes are the removal of post-tensioned concrete heavyweight construction, building foundations and machinery bases, reinforced concrete pilecaps, reinforced concrete basements, or redundant services which are located below the ground. Preparatory activities are included provided that they are for the purpose of assessing the condition of the land or waters concerned and are connected to the remediation activities to be undertaken by the company or on its behalf.

(d) It must be incurred on 'staffing costs' or on materials employed directly in the remediation or be qualifying expenditure on 'sub-contracted land remediation'.

'Staffing costs' include all employment income (other than benefits in kind), employer NICs and pension contributions paid to, or in respect of, directors or employees directly and actively engaged in the relevant land remediation in (b) above. If between 20% and 80% of a director's or employee's time is spent directly and actively so engaged, an appropriate proportion of costs related to him or her qualify. If less than 20% is so spent, none of the costs qualify, and if more than 80%, all of the costs qualify. Staff providing support services (e.g. secretarial or administrative services) are not thereby treated as engaged in the activities they support.

Qualifying expenditure on '*sub-contracted land remediation*' is expenditure consisting of payments made for sub-contracted land remediation work. Except where the company and the sub-contractor are connected persons (within *CTA 2010, s 1122*), such payments qualify in full. Where the company and the sub-contractor are connected persons, then provided that, in accordance with generally accepted accounting practice (see **68.18** above), the whole of the sub-contractor payment and all of the sub-contractor's 'relevant expenditure' has been brought into account in determining the sub-contractor's profit or loss for a 'relevant period', the whole of the sub-contractor payment (up to the amount of the sub-contractor's 'relevant expenditure') qualifies. '*Relevant expenditure*' is expenditure on staffing costs or materials (as under (c) above), not of a capital nature, which is incurred by the sub-contractor in carrying on, on behalf of the company, the activities to which the sub-contractor payment relates, and which satisfies (e) below. A '*relevant period*' is a period for which the sub-contractor draws up accounts and which ends not more than twelve months after the end of the period of account of the company in which, in accordance with generally accepted accounting practice (see **68.18** above), the sub-contractor payment is brought into account in determining the company's profit or loss. Any necessary apportionment of expenditure for these purposes is made on a just and reasonable basis.

A person has a '*relevant connection*' to a company if he is or was a 'connected person' within *CTA 2010, s 1122* either when the action (or inaction) in question occurred, or when the land in question was acquired by the company, or at any time when the remediation work was undertaken.

(e) It must not be subsidised. For this purpose, expenditure is treated as subsidised to the extent that any grant or subsidy is received in respect of the expenditure, or the expenditure is met directly or indirectly by any person other than the company (any unallocated payment being allocated for this purpose in a just and reasonable manner).

(f) It must not be on landfill tax.

[*CTA 2009, ss 1144–1146A, 1170–1179; SI 2009 No 2037*].

Deduction for capital expenditure

[48.3] Where:

(1) a company acquires, or has acquired, a 'major interest' in land in the UK for the purposes of a trade or UK property business carried on by it;
(2) either the land was in a contaminated state at the time of the acquisition or was in a derelict state throughout the period beginning with the earlier of 1 April 1998 and the date of acquisition by the company or a connected person; and
(3) the company incurs capital expenditure which is qualifying land remediation expenditure (see **48.2** above) in respect of the land,

the company may make an election for the expenditure to be allowed as a deduction in computing the trade or business profits for the period in which it is incurred. For this purpose, expenditure incurred for the purposes of a trade or business about to be carried on is treated as incurred on the first day of trading or business and in the course of carrying on the trade or business. Relief is not available if capital allowances (other than a structures and buildings allowance) are, or may be, given in respect of the expenditure.

The condition at (2) above does not have to be met where the land is in a contaminated state because of the presence in, on or under it, of Japanese knotweed.

A '*major interest*' in land is a freehold interest in the land or a leasehold interest which is either a grant or an assignment of a lease for a term of at least seven years.

An election must be made by notice in writing within two years of the end of the accounting period to which it relates.

[*CTA 2009, ss 1147, 1148, 1178A; SI 2009 No 2037, Art 7; SI 2019 No 1087, Reg 7(2)*].

Additional deduction

[48.4] Where:

(i) a company acquires, or has acquired, a 'major interest' in land in the UK for the purposes of a trade or UK property business carried on by it;
(ii) either the land was in a contaminated state at the time of the acquisition or was in a derelict state throughout the period beginning with the earlier of 1 April 1998 and the date of acquisition by the company or a connected person;
(iii) the company carries on a trade or UK property business in the accounting period in question; and
(iv) the company incurs expenditure which is qualifying land remediation expenditure (see **48.2** above) in respect of the land which is allowable (whether or not as a result of **48.3** above) as a deduction in computing the taxable profits of the trade or business for the period,

the company may make a claim for an additional deduction in calculating the profits of the trade or business of 50% of the qualifying land remediation expenditure (i.e. giving a total deduction of 150% of the expenditure).

The condition at (ii) above does not have to be met where the land is in a contaminated state because of the presence in, on or under it, of Japanese knotweed.

Relief is not available if all or part of the land is in a contaminated or derelict state wholly or partly as a result of the company's own actions or inaction, the actions or inaction of a person with a relevant connection to the company (see **48.2** above) or the actions or inaction of a person with a 'relevant interest' in the land. For this purpose, a person holds a 'relevant interest' in land if he holds any interest in, right over or licence to occupy the land (including an option to acquire such an interest etc.) or has disposed of any estate or interest in the land for a consideration to any extent reflecting the impact or likely impact on the value of the land of the remediation of its contamination or dereliction.

[*CTA 2009, ss 1149, 1150; SI 2009 No 2037, Art 7*].

Land remediation tax credit

[48.5] For an accounting period in which the company has a 'qualifying land remediation loss', it may claim a 'land remediation tax credit' equal to 16% of the amount of that loss. The 16% figure is subject to revision by the Treasury by order. A '*qualifying land remediation loss*' arises for an accounting period in which the company obtains relief under **48.4** above and incurs a loss in the trade or UK property business concerned. The amount of the qualifying land remediation loss is so much of the trading or UK property business loss as is 'unrelieved' or, if less, 150% of the related qualifying land remediation expenditure. A trading or UK property business loss is '*unrelieved*' for this purpose to the extent that the loss has not and could not have been relieved by a claim under *CTA 2010, s 37* (against profits of the same period, see **51.3**, **51.10** LOSSES), and has not otherwise been relieved (including under *CTA 2010, s 37* against profits of earlier periods, see **51.4** LOSSES), and has not been surrendered as GROUP RELIEF (**35**) or group relief for carried-forward losses. Losses carried back or brought forward to the accounting period in question are disregarded for this purpose.

On receiving a claim for land remediation tax credit, HMRC pay to the company the amount of the tax credit, and the amount of the company's trading or UK property business loss available to be carried forward from the period is accordingly reduced by the amount of the qualifying land remediation loss for the period (or by a corresponding proportion of it where the amount of the tax credit claimed was less than 16% of the qualifying land remediation loss). The tax credit payment is not treated as income for any tax purposes, and (together with any interest paid with it — see **48.6** below) may be applied to any corporation tax liability of the company. Where there is an enquiry into the company's tax return for the period (see **65.14** RETURNS), payment need not be made until the enquiry is completed (although HMRC has discretion to make a payment on a provisional basis if they think fit). Similarly payment need not be made until all PAYE and NICs payments for payment periods (i.e. periods ending on the fifth day of each month for which liability to account for PAYE and NICs arises) ending in the accounting period have been made.

Where tax credit is paid in respect of expenditure, the expenditure may not be taken into account in computing a chargeable gain or allowable loss on disposal of the land to which it relates.

[*CTA 2009, ss 1151–1158; F(No 2)A 2017, Sch 4 paras 137, 138*].

Claims and overpayments

[48.6] A claim for payment of a land remediation tax credit within **48.5** above must be made in a company tax return or amended return (see **65.4** RETURNS) for the accounting period for which the credit is claimed, within one year of the filing date for that return (see **65.8** RETURNS) or by such later time as HMRC may allow. It can similarly only be amended or withdrawn by amendment of the company tax return within the same time limit. It must specify the amount claimed. [*FA 1998, Sch 18 paras 10(2A), 83G–83L*]. For recovery of overpayments of land remediation tax credit, see **65.18** RETURNS.

INTEREST ON OVERPAID TAX (43) applies to land remediation tax credit payments from the filing date (see **65.4** RETURNS) for the company tax return for the accounting period for which the credit is claimed (or if later the date of receipt by HMRC of the return (or amended return) containing the claim) until payment. Such interest is recovered (as if it were INTEREST ON UNPAID TAX (42)) where there is a change in the tax credit payable resulting in an assessment (or amendment) to recover an amount of the credit (unless the change in the available credit results in a change in the company's corporation tax liability – see **44.2**(vi) INTEREST ON OVERPAID TAX – or is in whole or part to correct an HMRC error). [*ICTA 1988, s 826(1)(e)(3B)(8A)(8BA)*].

Anti-avoidance

[48.7] Any transaction attributable to arrangements (including any scheme, agreement or understanding, whether or not legally enforceable) whose sole or main object is to enable a company to obtain a relief or payment under any of the above provisions to which it would not otherwise be entitled, or a greater relief or payment than that to which it would otherwise be entitled, is disregarded in determining the amount of any such relief or payment. [*CTA 2009, s 1169*].

49
Leasing

Introduction to leasing

[49.1] Leasing is a very important source of medium and long-term finance for industry. In large value deals the principal reason for leasing is usually cost — leasing can provide a lower after-tax cost to the lessee than alternative sources of finance. This is particularly important where the lessee himself is in a non-tax paying position and cannot take advantage of capital allowances. In broad terms, accounting standards require that lessors and lessees should recognise assets and liabilities arising from lease transactions according to their 'substance' rather than according to legal ownership. As a result, the rules governing the taxation of leases is complex, and given the popularity and potential favourable tax treatment in this area, a wealth of anti-avoidance legislation has been introduced and developed over recent years. This chapter looks at the tax treatment of certain leases and the anti-avoidance provisions currently in operation.

Changes to Lease Accounting Standards

[49.2] *FA 2019* introduced a number of provisions to deal with the tax implications of the adoption of International Financial Reporting Standard 16 (IFRS 16) on Leases. Entities which apply FRS 101 or IFRS are required to adopt IFRS 16 for periods of account beginning on or after 1 January 2019. The Standard removes the existing distinction between finance leases and operating leases for lessees (but not lessors), on which many tax rules depend. The provisions are intended to allow those tax rules to continue to operate as intended and to ensure that the taxation of leases is broadly consistent regardless of which accounting framework is adopted (as, where FRS 102 is applied, the distinction between operating and finance leases continues). (Treasury Explanatory Notes to the 2019 Finance Bill). Leases dealt with under IFRS 16 are referred to for tax purposes as 'right-of-use leases' — for the full definition see **10.49**(5) CAPITAL ALLOWANCES ON PLANT AND MACHINERY. Broadly, in relation to a lessee, a right-to-use lease is treated for tax purposes as a finance lease if it would have been accounted for as such had the lessee been required, in accordance with GAAP, to determine whether or not it was a finance lease.

See **10.47** onwards CAPITAL ALLOWANCES ON PLANT AND MACHINERY, **69.52** TRADING INCOME — DEDUCTIONS for the effect of IFRS 16 on the long funding lease provisions.

The detailed *FA 2019* provisions replace and repeal *FA 2011, s 53* below, subject to the transitional rules below.

FA 2011, s 53 applies for periods of account beginning before 1 January 2019 and requires businesses which account for lease transactions to treat them, for the purposes of the Taxes Acts only, as if any changes to accounting standards had not taken place. This applies to any business, whether as lessee, lessor, or both, that accounts for lease transactions using a lease accounting standard that is newly issued or changed on or after 1 January 2011. Thus where a business prepares accounts using the old standard in their previous accounting period then they should use their old standard for their leasing transactions for the purpose of the Taxes Act instead of using the new standard. Otherwise where a business uses a new standard for the first time in its accounts, then it should use the old standard which corresponds to the new standard with regard to their leasing transactions, for tax purposes. The old standard for these purposes is either IAS disregarding any leasing change, or UK GAAP disregarding any leasing change.

However, this rule did not apply where the change in a leasing standard is a change to UK GAAP that permits or requires businesses to account for a lease, or a transaction accounted for as a lease, in a manner equivalent to that provided for by IFRS for small and medium-sized entities issued by the IAS Board (ignoring any change that may be made to the leasing section of that Standard). HMRC confirmed in their guidance on the UK GAAP provisions in FRS 102, that it was therefore not envisaged that *s 53* would apply to entities on transition to FRS 102 s 20 (the treatment for leases) — see final comments with regard to the guidance for leases in 'FRS 102 Overview Paper, Corporation Tax implications' Part A section 10, HMRC 21 July 2017.

[*FA 2011, s 53; FA 2019, Sch 14 para 11*].

Transitional rules apply where a lessee treats a lease as a right-of-use asset under IFRS 16 and had not previously accounted for the lease as a finance lease to modify the effect of *CTA 2009, ss 261, 262* (change of accounting basis for property business — see **60.4** PROPERTY INCOME).

If the first period of account for which the right-of-use asset is recognised in the accounts of the lessee begins on or after 1 January 2019, any adjustments under the change of basis rules are spread across the average length of the leases giving rise to them (by applying the steps in *FA 2019, Sch 14 para 13*). If the lessee adopted IFRS 16 early, so that the first period of account for which the right-of-use asset was so recognised began before 1 January 2019, the change in basis is nevertheless treated for this purpose as occurring in the first period of account beginning on or after 1 January 2019. If a lease is transferred to a connected party during the period over which the adjustments are spread, the remaining adjustment amounts are treated as arising to the transferee and are spread over the remaining spreading period. Any apportionments needed for this purpose must be made on a just and reasonable basis. This rule does not apply if it is reasonable to suppose that the transfer, or arrangements of which it is part, are designed to avoid tax. If the lessee permanently ceases to carry on activities within the charge to corporation tax before the end of the spreading period (and the remaining adjustment amounts are not treated as arising to a transferee), the remaining amounts are treated as arising to the lessee immediately before the cessation. If the lessee prepares accounts by reference to a portfolio of leases, these provisions apply to the portfolio as they apply to individual leases, subject to any necessary modifications.

[*FA 2019, Sch 14 paras 12–17; FA 2020, s 35*].

Where a receipt or expense arises to a lessee company under *CTA 2009, ss 180–187* (change of accounting basis for trades — see **68.20** TRADING INCOME) or *ss 261, 262* in circumstances where the lease was treated under the old accounting policy as a finance lease and, under the new accounting policy, would be treated as a right-of-use lease but for its short term or the low value of the leased asset, the receipt or expense is not a 'tax-interest income amount' or a 'tax-interest expense amount' for the purposes of the CORPORATE INTEREST RESTRICTION (**24.5**). Where a group has made an interest allowance (alternative calculation) election (see **24.8**) this rule applies to adjustments to the worldwide group's financial statements, so that change of accounting basis adjustments are not treated as 'relevant income amounts' or 'relevant expense amounts' (see **24.6**). [*FA 2019, Sch 14 para 19*].

Simon's Taxes. See B5.403.

Leased trading assets

[49.3] In certain circumstances where a payment is made under a lease of a trading asset, corporation tax relief for the payment is restricted. The provisions apply where:

- a payment is made by a company under a lease of an asset (other than land or an interest in land) created after 14 April 1964;
- a deduction is allowed for the payment in calculating trading profits for corporation tax purposes; and
- at a time before the lease was created the asset was used for the purposes of the trade or for the purposes of another trade carried on by the lessee, and was then owned by the person carrying on the trade in which it was used.

The deduction for the payment is limited to the 'commercial rent' of the asset to which it relates for the period for which the payment is made. In fact, the position is judged on a cumulative basis in similar manner to that described in **4.8** above, taking into account the payments for every previous accounting period ended on or after the date the lease was created. It is the cumulative unrelieved expenses for the current period which is then compared to the commercial rent for the period and restricted if necessary. The cumulative unrelieved expenses cannot, however, be carried forward to an accounting period beginning after the payments have ceased; no deduction is available under these provisions for any such expenses.

The '*commercial rent*' is the rent which might at the time the lease is created be expected to be paid under a lease of the asset if the lease were for the rest of the asset's 'expected normal working life' (as defined), the rent were payable at uniform intervals and at a uniform rate, and the rent gave a reasonable return for the asset's market value at that time, taking account of the terms and conditions of the actual lease. If the asset is used at the same time partly for the purposes of the trade and partly for other purposes, the commercial rent is to be determined by reference to what would be paid for such partial use.

For the above purposes, a lease is an agreement or arrangement under which payments are made for the use of, or otherwise in respect of, the asset. It includes an agreement or arrangement under which the payments (or any of them) represent instalments of, or payments towards, a purchase price.

The above provisions do not apply to payments under a lease which is a long funding finance lease as regards the lessee (see **10.47** CAPITAL ALLOWANCES ON PLANT AND MACHINERY).

[*CTA 2010, ss 863–869*].

Simon's Taxes. See **B5.413**.

Leased assets — capital sums

[49.4] In certain circumstances where a payment is made under a lease of an asset (other than one created on or before 14 April 1964), and a 'capital sum' is obtained in respect of an interest in the asset, corporation tax is chargeable. This does not apply if **49.3** above (or income tax equivalent) applies to the payment or would do so were it not for the exclusion in **49.3** of payments under long funding finance leases. A lease is defined as in **49.3** above.

A '*capital sum*' is any sum of money, or any money's worth, except in so far as it falls to be taken into account as a trading receipt or is chargeable to corporation tax as miscellaneous income.

The provisions apply where a payment is made under a lease of an asset (other than land or an interest in land), the payment is one for which a tax deduction is available (see below) and any one of the following conditions is met:

(a) the person making the payment (P) obtains a capital sum in respect of the lessee's interest in the lease;
(b) 'an associate' (see below) of P obtains a capital sum by way of consideration in respect of the lessee's interest in the lease;

(c) the lessor's interest in the lease, or any other interest in the asset, belongs to an associate of P, and the associate obtains a capital sum in respect of the interest; or
(d) the lessor's interest in the lease, or any other interest in the asset, belongs to an associate of P, and an associate of that associate obtains a capital sum by way of consideration in respect of the interest.

Conditions (a)–(d) may be met before, at or after the time when the payment is made, but can be met only if the person obtaining the capital sum is a company within the charge to corporation tax.

The conditions are not met if the lease is a hire-purchase agreement for plant or machinery and the capital sum has to be brought into account as the whole or part of the capital allowances disposal value of the plant or machinery (and provided, in the case of (c) or (d), that the capital sum is obtained in respect of the lessee's interest in the lease).

The reference above to a tax deduction is to a deduction allowable:

- in computing trading profits for corporation tax purposes; or
- in computing profits or income under any of the provisions listed at *CTA 2010, s 1173* (miscellaneous income) or in computing losses for which relief is available under *CTA 2010, s 91* (see **51.12** LOSSES); or
- under *CTA 2009, s 1219* (management expenses of a company's investment business — see **45.3** INVESTMENT COMPANIES AND INVESTMENT BUSINESS); or
- under *FA 2012, s 76* (expenses of insurance companies); or
- in computing the profits of a trade, profession or vocation for income tax purposes; or
- in computing profits or income under any of the provisions listed at *ITA 2007, s 1016* (miscellaneous income) or in computing losses for which relief is available under *ITA 2007, s 152* (miscellaneous LOSSES); or
- against employment income under *ITEPA 2003, s 336* or in computing losses in an employment for income tax purposes.

The company obtaining the capital sum is treated as receiving, at the time the sum is obtained, an amount to which the charge to corporation tax on income applies.

The amount is equal to the amount(s) of the payment for which the above-mentioned tax deduction is made, but is not to exceed the capital sum. Where the lease is a hire-purchase agreement and the capital sum is obtained in respect of the lessee's interest in the lease, the recipient's capital expenditure on the asset is taken as reducing the capital sum for the purpose of applying this rule (see *CTA 2010, s 875*).

If a payment or part of a payment is taken into account in deciding the chargeable amount in respect of a capital sum, the payment or part must be left out of account in deciding whether a charge arises under these provisions in respect of another capital sum and, if so, the chargeable amount. This rule is applied in the order in which capital sums are obtained. If the capital sum is received before the payment is made, any necessary adjustment to the recipient's tax position can be made within six years after the accounting period in which the payment is made (*CTA 2010, s 876*).

If a company disposes of an interest in an asset to a person who is the company's 'associate' (as below), it is regarded as obtaining the greatest of the actual sum obtained, the open market value and the value of the interest to the person to whom it is transferred.

Reference above to any sum obtained in respect of an interest in an asset includes any insurance money obtained in respect of the interest and any sum representing money or money's worth obtained in respect of the interest by a transaction or series of transactions disposing of it. Reference to any sum obtained in respect of the lessee's interest in a lease of an asset includes any sums representing consideration for a surrender of the interest to the lessor, an assignment of the lease, the creation of a sublease or another interest out of the lease or a transaction or series of transactions under which the lessee's rights are merged in any way with the lessor's rights or with any other rights as respects the asset.

There is provision for payments to be apportioned where made by persons in partnership and for sums to be apportioned where obtained by persons in partnership or by persons jointly entitled to the interest in an asset (see *CTA 2010, ss 880, 881*).

Meaning of 'associates'

For the above purposes, the following are associated with each other:

- an individual and the individual's spouse, civil partner or relative (meaning a brother, sister, ancestor or lineal descendant);
- an individual and a spouse or civil partner of a relative of the individual;
- an individual and a relative of the individual's spouse or civil partner;
- an individual and a spouse or civil partner of a relative of the individual's spouse or civil partner;
- a trustee of a settlement and an individual who is the settlor or any person associated with that individual;
- a person and a body of persons (which may be a partnership) of which he has control (within the meaning of *CTA 2010, s 1124*);
- a person and a body of persons of which persons associated with the person have control;
- a person and a body of persons of which the person and persons associated with the person have control;
- two or more bodies of persons associated with the same person;
- in relation to a disposal by joint owners, the joint owners and any person associated with any of them.

[*CTA 2010, ss 870–886*].

Simon's Taxes. See **B5.410–B5.415A**.

Leasing of plant or machinery

Leasing partnerships — restriction on use of losses

[49.5] Where a 'business of leasing plant or machinery' (as defined in **49.11** below), within the charge to corporation tax, is carried on by a company in partnership, certain losses derived from capital allowances are restricted as set out below. In relation to accounting periods straddling that date, the provision applies only if the company starts to carry on the business in partnership, or a 'relevant change' in the company's interest in the business occurs, on or after that date. A '*relevant change*' in the company's interest in the business is a change to a basis of profit sharing which is not 'allowable'.

Where the company's interest in the leasing business during the accounting period of the partnership is not 'determined on an allowable basis', any loss incurred in its 'notional business' in its accounting period, comprised (wholly or partly) in the partnership accounting period, is restricted to the extent that it derives from any relevant capital allowances. The extent is determined on the basis that any relevant capital allowances are the final amounts to be deducted. The restricted part of the loss may be carried forward but can only be set off against income of the company's notional business deriving from a lease of plant or machinery which was entered into before the end of the accounting period in which the loss in the notional business was incurred. It is not available for group relief, group relief for carried-forward losses or relief against total profits of the company.

The interest of a company in the leasing business during the partnership's accounting period is 'determined on an allowable basis' if (for the purposes of *CTA 2009, ss 1262–1264* — see **56.3** PARTNERSHIPS) the company's share in the profits (excluding chargeable gains) or loss of the leasing business and its share in any 'relevant capital allowances' for that period are both determined by reference to the same single percentage. '*Relevant capital allowances*' are capital allowances in respect of expenditure incurred on the provision of plant or machinery wholly or partly for the purposes of the leasing business. The company's '*notional business*' is the business the profits or losses of which are determined, in relation to the company, under *CTA 2009, s 1259* (see **56.3** PARTNERSHIPS).

For the above purposes, a lease, as well as having its normal meaning, includes an underlease, sublease, tenancy or licence and an agreement for any of those things.

[*CTA 2010, ss 887–889; F(No 2)A 2017, Sch 4 para 173*].

Capital receipts to be treated as income

[49.6] If, under a lease of plant or machinery, there is an unconditional obligation, first arising after 12 December 2007, to make a 'relevant capital payment' or if such a payment is made after that date without obligation, the lessor is treated for corporation tax purposes as receiving income attributable to the lease of an amount equal to the amount of the 'capital payment'. The income is treated as income for the period of account in which the obligation first arose or, as the case may be, income for the period of account in which the payment is made. These provisions apply to long funding leases (see **69.52** TRADING INCOME — DEDUCTIONS) as well as to other plant or machinery leases. The provisions apply equally if the obligation arises, or the payment is made, under an agreement or arrangement relating to a lease of plant or machinery, whether made before, during or after the currency of the lease itself.

For these purposes, a payment includes the provision of value by whatever means. A '*capital payment*' is any payment other than one which, if made to the lessor, would fall to be included in the lessor's income for corporation tax purposes or which would fall to be included were it not for *CTA 2010, s 360* (which determines the amount to be brought into account as taxable income from a long funding finance lease — see **69.52** TRADING INCOME — DEDUCTIONS).

A capital payment is a '*relevant capital payment*' if either:

- it is payable by lessee to lessor in connection with the grant, assignment, novation or termination of the lease or with any provision of the lease or, as the case may be, the agreement or arrangement (including the variation or waiver of any such provision); or
- the lease rentals are less than (or payable later than) they might reasonably be expected to be if there were no obligation to make the capital payment and the capital payment were not made.

However, a capital payment is *not* a '*relevant capital payment*' if, or to the extent that:

- it reduces the lessor's expenditure for the purposes of plant and machinery capital allowances — see the rules on expenditure met by another's contributions at **9.2** CAPITAL ALLOWANCES — or would do so if the circumstances were not such that the contributions rules are disapplied; or
- it represents compensation for damage to, or damage caused by, the plant or machinery in question.

Where a capital payment is an initial payment under a long funding lease (see **10.47** CAPITAL ALLOWANCES ON PLANT AND MACHINERY) and the commencement of the term of the lease is an event that requires the lessor to bring a disposal value into account, the payment is a relevant capital payment but only to the extent (if any) that it exceeds the disposal value.

For these purposes, a lease of plant or machinery includes a lease of plant or machinery together with other property, in which case the payment is apportioned on a just and reasonable basis and only the amount apportioned to the plant or machinery is chargeable under these provisions. It does not, however, include a lease all the lessor's income from which (if any) would be chargeable as PROPERTY INCOME (**59**) or a long funding lease of plant or machinery on which the lessor would have been treated as having incurred qualifying expenditure for the purposes of plant and machinery capital allowances if it were not for *CAA 2001, s 34A* at **10.50** CAPITAL ALLOWANCES ON PLANT AND MACHINERY.

There is bad debt relief if the above provisions have applied by virtue of an unconditional obligation and at any time the lessor reasonably expects that the relevant capital payment will not be paid (or will not be fully paid). The lessor is allowed a deduction for the expected shortfall in computing his profits for the period of account in which that time falls.

For the above purposes, a lease, as well as having its normal meaning, includes a licence and the letting of a ship or aircraft on charter or any other asset on hire.

[*CTA 2010, ss 890–894, Sch 2 paras 96, 97*].

Simon's Taxes. See B5.415A.

Consideration for taking over payment obligations as lessee

[49.7] Where, under any arrangements (as widely defined), a company (C) becomes entitled to tax deductions (whether in calculating income or total profits) as a result of agreeing to take over obligations (by whatever means) of another person (D) as lessee under a lease of plant or machinery, C is chargeable to corporation tax on any consideration received for the agreement. The consideration is treated as income received by C in the period of account in which it takes over the obligations. Consideration includes the provision of any benefit, the assumption of any liability and the transfer of money or money's worth, and includes any payment made (directly or indirectly) in connection with the agreement if the agreement would not have been made had the payment not been provided for. The charge applies equally where a person connected with C (within **19** CONNECTED PERSONS) becomes entitled to tax deductions or is the person to whom consideration is payable. It does not apply to the extent (if any) that the consideration is otherwise taxable as income in the hands of C or a connected person. The charge takes priority over any other charge which might otherwise apply, other than the general anti-abuse rule (see **4.3** ANTI-AVOIDANCE).

[*CTA 2010, s 894A*].

Restrictions with regard to the leasing of plant and machinery

[49.8] There are certain restrictions on capital allowances claimed in respect of plant and machinery which is leased, and also with regard to deductions in respect of rental rebates for leased plant and machinery. The provisions were introduced to combat two specific avoidance schemes which had been disclosed to HMRC.

The first scheme involved arrangements intended to create a company that is taxed on very little income from the leasing of an asset, but which is potentially able to claim capital allowances on the full cost of the asset, creating tax losses where there is a commercial profit. The first scheme may, alternatively or additionally, rely on obtaining a deduction for a rebate of rentals to generate a tax loss where there is a commercial profit.

The second scheme involved arrangements where a lessor that has claimed capital allowances in the initial loss-making phase of a lease of plant or machinery avoids tax on the income that arises once the lease moves into its tax-profitable phase. The intended effect is to turn a tax-timing advantage into a permanent loss of tax on a transaction that is commercially profitable.

Amendments to *CAA 2001*

Where a lessor is treated as incurring capital expenditure under *CAA 2001, s 67* (hire purchase etc.) or under *CAA 2001, s 70A* (long funding leases) then the amount of capital expenditure that is treated as qualifying expenditure is limited where:

(i) there are arrangements under which plant or machinery is to be leased; and

(ii) there are arrangements under which the value of the asset to the lessor is reduced.

The amount of the lessor's qualifying expenditure is restricted to 'V'.

'V' is defined as the aggregate of the amount of the present value of the lessor's income from the asset and the amount of the present value of the residual value of the asset after any rental rebate.

For the purposes of calculating 'V', the lessor's income from the asset includes all amounts that it is reasonable to expect the lessor will receive in connection with the lease and which will be taxed as income (this includes amounts treated as income, for example under *CTA 2010, s 890*). The residual value is the market value (per *CAA 2001, s 577*) of the lessor's interest in the asset immediately after the termination of the lease. The reference to 'lessor's interest' covers the situation where the lessor is the beneficiary of a contract under *CAA 2001, s 67* or a lessee under a long funding lease.

Amounts which have been brought into account as disposal receipts for capital allowances purposes, charges made by the lessor for services supplied in connection with the leased asset and qualifying UK and foreign tax paid by the lessor are all excluded from the lessor's income amounts.

A 'lease' for these purposes includes any arrangements which provide for plant and machinery to be leased or otherwise made available by a person to another person.

[*CAA 2001, s 228MA*].

In the case of both the amounts receivable in connection with the lease and the residual value at the end of the lease term, the present value is calculated based on the interest rate implicit in the lease, but it provides for an alternative (the incremental borrowing rate (as defined for accounting purposes); for leases entered into before 1 January 2022 the London interbank offered rate plus 1%) if the rate cannot otherwise be established. [*CAA 2001, s 228MB; FA 2021, s 132(2)(5)*].

CAA 2001, s 228MC defines rental rebate for the purpose of *s 228MA*. The definition is largely based on the definition in *CAA 2001, s 70YH*.

Rental rebate for corporation tax purposes

Where the avoidance in the first scheme highlighted above is centred on, or includes, the amount of deduction claimed for rental rebate the amended legislation counters this. Broadly the effect of the rules is that the amount of a rental rebate which may be claimed as a deduction in computing profits is limited to the amount receivable in connection with the lease that has been brought into account in computing the lessor's income.

In calculating this amount, however, the finance charge element of rentals paid under a finance lease is excluded, as are any elements that represent charges for service or tax.

[*CTA 2009, s 60A*].

A further anti-avoidance provision applies in respect of arrangements reducing the disposal value of a leased asset. Where plant or machinery is leased and a disposal event occurs which falls within *CA 2001, s 61(2)* items 1, 2 or 7 (sale of plant or machinery) and arrangements have been entered into that have the effect of reducing the disposal value of the asset in so far as it is attributable to rentals payable under the lease, then the disposal value is to be determined as if arrangements had not been entered into.

The provision does not apply where the arrangements fall within the transfer of income stream provisions found at *ITA 2007, s 809AZA* or *CTA 2010, s 752* and the relevant amount has been treated as income under *ITA 2007, s 809AZB* or *CTA 2010, s 753*, respectively.

[*CAA 2001, s 64A*].

Simon's Taxes. See **B3.311A.**

Sale of lessors

[49.9] The provisions at **49.10–49.14** below apply where a company, which carries on a 'business of leasing plant or machinery' on its own or in partnership, changes ownership, or changes its interest in a business carried on in partnership. See also HMRC Business Leasing Manual BLM80000 *et seq*.

The provisions are designed to ensure that on a change of ownership, or interest in a partnership, a charge is borne by the original owner and an equal and opposite relief is granted to the new owner. The charge applies in respect of long-leases where in the early years of a lease the capital allowances available to the lessor are greater than the rental income from the lease, giving rise to losses, the charge broadly equating to the tax benefit of such losses. This prevents the lessor making use of such losses, for example, by way of group relief, where the profits arising in the later years of the lease (when the rental income is greater than the capital allowances) are sheltered on the sale of the lessor company to a group with tax losses. The charge thus counters the losses available to the original owner and the corresponding relief counters the profits passed on to the new owner.

Leasing business carried on by a company alone

[49.10] If on any day (the '*relevant day*'):

- a company carries on a 'business of leasing plant or machinery' otherwise than in partnership;
- the company is within the charge to corporation tax in respect of the business; and
- there is a 'qualifying change of ownership' in relation to the company,

the accounting period of the company ends on the relevant day and a new accounting period begins on the following day. Also, the company is treated as receiving a taxable business receipt in the accounting period ending on the relevant day and as incurring a deductible business expense of an equal amount in the new accounting period. See below as to the amount of the taxable receipt. The expense potentially qualifies for the relief at **49.12** below.

No part of any loss can be deducted under *CTA 2010, s 37(3)(b)* (relief for trade losses against total profits of earlier accounting periods) or *s 45F* (terminal loss relief for carried-forward losses) from so much of the company's total profits as derive from the taxable receipt. In determining how much of the profits derive from the receipt, profits are to be calculated on the basis that the receipt is the final amount to be added.

Business of leasing plant or machinery

A company carries on a '*business of leasing plant or machinery*' for this purpose if either:

(a) at least half of the 'relevant plant or machinery value' relates to 'qualifying leased plant or machinery'; or
(b) at least half the company's income over the twelve months before the relevant day derives from plant or machinery falling within the definition at *CTA 2010, s 387(7)*, see below.

For the purposes of (a) above, '*relevant plant or machinery value*' is the total of (i) the value of plant and machinery in the company's balance sheet as at the start of the relevant day (see *CTA 2010, s 389*) and (ii) any such value which would be shown in the company's balance sheet drawn up at the end of the relevant day and would also have been shown in the balance sheet of an 'associated company' (as defined by *CTA 2010, s 408*) drawn up at the start of that day. The assumptions made as to the amount shown in the company's balance sheet are: that the balance sheet is drawn up in accordance with GAAP; and, that if the company acquired any plant or machinery from a connected person, then it is assumed the company acquired it for the 'ascribed value' as at the relevant day.

In certain circumstances (see *CTA 2010, s 390*) where the company leases the plant or machinery under a long funding lease, the 'ascribed value' of the plant or machinery on the relevant day must be used instead of its balance sheet value.

The '*accounting value*' of the plant or machinery is broadly the amounts recorded in the company's balance sheet at the start of the relevant day together with the value of any plant or machinery transferred to the lessor company on that day by associated companies.

In determining the company's income for the purposes of (b) above, any necessary apportionment is to be made on a time basis or, where this leads to an unjust result, on a just and reasonable basis. The proportion of income that derives from qualifying plant or machinery is to be determined on a just and reasonable basis.

The plant or machinery mentioned in (b) above is that which is or has been leased out in the twelve months prior to the relevant day by the company or a qualifying associate (being a person connected with the company, on the relevant day or at any time in the prior twelve months) where the lease is not an excluded lease of background plant or machinery for a building and if the lessor is a qualifying associate, the lessee under the lease is or was someone other than the company. Where the relevant company is owned by a consortium (or is a 75% subsidiary of such a company) then the reference to 'connected' person above includes any member of the consortium and any person connected with such a member.

For plant and machinery which is subject to a lease at the relevant time, and the relevant company (partnership) is a lessor, and it does not fall into the exclusions, then the '*ascribed value*' of such plant or machinery at the relevant time is the higher of: the market value at the relevant time; and the present value at that time of the lease.

The exclusion referred to is with regard to plant and machinery which is subject to an equipment lease (within the meaning of *CAA 2001, Ch 14 Pt 2* — fixtures), where the relevant company (or partnership) is the equipment lessor, and such lessor is treated at that time as the owner of the plant and machinery per an election made under *CAA 2001, s 177(1)(a)(i)*. In such cases the '*ascribed value*' of the plant and machinery is the present value at the relevant time of the lease.

Where plant and machinery does not fall into either of these categories, then the '*ascribed value*' is the market value. Market value is to be determined on the assumption of a disposal by an absolute owner free from all leases and other encumbrances. If plant and machinery is a fixture then its market value is so much of the market value of the relevant land (as defined in *CAA 2001, s 173(2)*) and the fixture together as is attributable to the fixture, on a just and reasonable apportionment.

The present value of a lease is the present value of: the amounts payable under the lease after the relevant time, and any residual amount. 'Amounts payable under the lease' does not include amounts payable by the lessor, or amounts that represent charges for services or qualifying UK or foreign tax to be paid by the lessor. Where a lessee has an option to continue the lease for a period after the end of its initial term, and it is reasonably certain that the lessee will exercise that option, then amounts payable under the continued lease are included. Where the lease relates to land or assets that are not plant or machinery, the present value of the lease is so much of the present value of the amounts above, as is attributable to the plant and machinery on a just and reasonable apportionment.

The present value is calculated using the interest rate implicit in the lease, which is the rate that would, in accordance with normal commercial criteria including GAAP, apply. Where a rate cannot be determined then it is taken as the incremental borrowing rate (as defined for accounting purposes) or, where the relevant time is before 1 January 2022, LIBOR plus 1%.

Qualifying change of ownership

There is a '*qualifying change of ownership*' in relation to a company (A) on any day if there is 'a relevant change in the relationship' on that day between A and a 'principal company' of A.

Leaving aside consortium relationships, a company (B) is a '*principal company*' of A if A is its 'qualifying 75% subsidiary' (broadly as defined for group relief purposes) and B is not itself a qualifying 75% subsidiary of another company. There is a '*relevant change in the relationship*' between A and B on any day on which A ceases to be a qualifying 75% subsidiary of B. The same applies in the case of a chain of companies where the principal company is at the top of the chain, the '*relevant change in the relationship*' occurring whenever any of the links in the 75% chain are broken. There is also a *relevant change in the relationship*' between A and B on any day (under *CTA 2010, s 394ZA*) if either (i) A becomes a member of a tonnage tax group without itself entering tonnage tax; or (ii) the day immediately precedes a day on which A both becomes a member of a tonnage tax group and itself enters tonnage tax.

In the case of consortium relationships, a company (E) is the principal company of A if it is itself not a qualifying 75% subsidiary of any company and A is owned by a consortium, or is a 'qualifying 75% subsidiary' (broadly as defined for group relief purposes) of a company owned by a consortium, of which E is a member.

There is a '*relevant change in the relationship*' between A and E on any day if the 'ownership proportion' at the end of the day is less than it was at the start of the day.

The '*ownership proportion*' is whichever of these is the lowest: the percentage of A's ordinary share capital owned by E, the percentage to which E is beneficially entitled of profits available for distribution to equity holders of A and the percentage to which E would be entitled of any assets of A available for distribution to equity holders on a winding-up. But if A is a qualifying 90% subsidiary of a company, these three alternatives must be read as if references to that company were substituted for references to A. If E is a qualifying 75% subsidiary of another company (F), F would then be the principal company of A provided that F is not itself a qualifying 75% subsidiary of another company.

There is a '*relevant change in the relationship*' between A and F on any day if the ownership proportion at the end of the day is less than it was at the start of the day or if E ceases to be a qualifying 75% subsidiary of F. The same applies if F is a qualifying 75% subsidiary of another company and so on; the principal company of A is the company at the top of the chain and a '*relevant change in the relationship*' occurs whenever the ownership proportion falls or any of the links in the 75% chain are broken.

There is an exception to change of ownership rules in certain intra-group reorganisations (see *CTA 2010, s 395*) or if a principal company's interest in a consortium company remains unchanged despite a relevant change in the relationship (see *CTA 2010, s 396*).

Computing the amount of the taxable receipt

The basic amount of the taxable receipt is given by the formula PM – TWDV, which is broadly the net book value of the plant or machinery less its tax written-down value for capital allowances purposes. PM and TWDV are defined in more detail below. The basic amount may then be subject to adjustment as described. If the basic amount given by the formula is a negative amount, the basic amount is taken instead to be nil.

PM is the aggregate of (i) amounts (if any) which would be shown in respect of plant and machinery in the company's balance sheet as at the start of the relevant day and (ii) any amount which would be shown in the company's balance sheet drawn up at the end of the relevant day and would also have been shown in the balance sheet of an 'associated company' (as defined by *CTA 2010, s 408*) drawn up at the start of that day.

For this purpose, the amounts shown in a company's balance sheet in respect of any plant or machinery are the amounts shown as the net book value (or carrying amount) in respect of the plant or machinery and the amounts shown in that balance sheet as the net investment in respect of 'finance leases' of the plant or machinery. Where any of the plant or machinery is a fixture in land the amount of the net book value (or carrying amount) in respect of the fixture is determined on a just and reasonable basis. Where any of the plant or machinery, together with any other land or asset, is subject to a finance lease, the amount of the net investment in respect of the finance lease of that plant or machinery is similarly determined.

A lease is a '*finance lease*' in relation to a particular person if it falls (or would fall), in accordance with generally accepted accounting practice ('GAAP'), to be treated as a finance lease or loan in that person's accounts. For periods of account beginning on or after 1 January 2019, in relation to a lessee, a right-to-use lease (see **10.49**(5) CAPITAL ALLOWANCES ON PLANT AND MACHINERY) is a finance lease for this purpose if it would have been accounted for as such had the lessee been required, in accordance with GAAP, to determine whether or not it was a finance lease.

All amounts must be determined on the assumptions that balance sheets are drawn up in accordance with GAAP and that, broadly if any plant or machinery has been acquired from connected parties, it was acquired at its ascribed value on the relevant day. A special rule applies if, at the start of the relevant day, the company is the lessee of plant or machinery under a long funding lease (see **10.47** CAPITAL ALLOWANCES ON PLANT AND MACHINERY) or is treated as its owner under *CAA 2001, s 67* (hire-purchase and similar contracts — see **10.57** CAPITAL ALLOWANCES ON PLANT AND MACHINERY). This rule also applies if the company acquired the plant or machinery from an associated company on the relevant day and either of those conditions are met at the end of that day. Under this rule, the amount included in the total in respect of the plant and machinery is replaced with ascribed value.

'*Plant or machinery*' for the purpose of computing PM above means any plant or machinery (whether or not subject to a lease) apart from plant or machinery (i) on which the company has not incurred expenditure that is qualifying expenditure for capital allowances purposes; or (ii) of which the company is a lessor under a long funding lease; or (iii) treated as owned by other persons under *CAA 2001, s 67*; or (iv) which is to be ignored under the migration rule described below.

TWDV is the total amount of unrelieved qualifying expenditure on plant or machinery in single asset pools, class pools and the main pool carried forward under normal capital allowances rules (see **10.26** CAPITAL ALLOWANCES ON PLANT AND MACHINERY) to the start of the new accounting period that begins the day after the relevant day (see above). Any expenditure incurred by the company on plant or machinery on the relevant day itself is to be left out of account unless it was acquired from an associated company. In addition any expenditure incurred on the relevant day but attributable to plant and machinery acquired by a company before that day is also left out of account.

An *adjustment* may fall to be made to the basic amount calculated above to reflect the degree to which the economic control of the company has changed. The adjustment is made where, on a company (A) ceasing to be a qualifying 75% subsidiary of another company (B) (the qualifying change of ownership referred to above), A becomes instead owned by a consortium (or a qualifying 90% subsidiary of a company owned by a consortium) of which B is a member. The taxable receipt is then limited to the 'appropriate percentage' of the basic amount.

The '*appropriate percentage*' is found by subtracting the 'ownership percentage' at the end of the relevant day from 100%.

The '*ownership percentage*' is whichever of these is the lowest: the percentage of A's ordinary share capital owned by B, the percentage to which B is beneficially entitled of profits available for distribution to equity holders of A and the percentage to which B would be entitled of any assets of A available for distribution to equity holders on a winding-up. But if A becomes a qualifying 90% subsidiary of a company, these three alternatives must be read as if references to that company were substituted for references to A.

Where the qualifying change of ownership arises from a change in a consortium relationship the adjustment is calculated as follows. If the change arises only because the 'ownership proportion' (see above) at the end of the day on which the change occurs is less than it was at the start of the day, the taxable receipt is limited to the 'appropriate proportion' of the basic amount. The '*appropriate proportion*' is found by subtracting the ownership proportion at the end of the day from the ownership proportion at the start of the day. In any other case, the taxable receipt is found by taking the ownership proportion at the start of the day on which the change occurs and applying it to the basic amount.

Migration to UK

If a company comes within the charge to corporation tax on any day as a result of migration into the UK and there is a qualifying change of ownership on that day in relation to that company, plant or machinery is to be ignored in calculating the amount of the taxable receipt if an amount would be shown in respect of it in a balance sheet of the company drawn up immediately before that day in accordance with GAAP.

[*CTA 2010, ss 382–385, 387–408, 437, 437A–437C, Sch 2 para 68(2)–(5); F(No 2)A 2017, Sch 4 paras 164, 165; FA 2019, Sch 14 paras 4(7), 6(1); FA 2021, s 132(3)96)*].

Leasing business carried on by a company in partnership

[49.11] If on any day (the '*relevant day*'):

- a company carries on a 'business of leasing plant or machinery' in partnership;
- the partner company is within the charge to corporation tax in respect of the business; and
- there is a qualifying change in the partner company's interest in the business,

the partner company is treated as receiving a taxable business receipt and any other company which carries on the business on that day and which is within the charge to corporation tax in respect of the business is treated as incurring a deductible business expense. See below as to the amount of the taxable receipt and deductible expense. Each such receipt is brought into account as a receipt of the notional business of the partner company in the accounting period in which it is treated as received. If, at the end of the relevant day, the other company is carrying on the business alone, the expense is treated as an expense of that company in its actual business and is allowed as a deduction for corporation tax purposes for the accounting period in which the expense is incurred.

This expense potentially qualifies for the relief at **49.12** below. In any other case, the expense is brought into account as a deductible expense of the notional business of the other company in the accounting period in which it is treated as incurred; the expense does not qualify for the relief at **49.12** below. A company's '*notional business*' is the business the profits or losses of which are determined, in relation to the company, under *CTA 2009, s 1259* (see **56.3** PARTNERSHIPS). The above does not apply where:

- at the end of the relevant day none of the companies that carried on the business any longer has a share in the profits or loss of the business;
- as a result of what happens on the relevant day, the disposal value of all the business plant and machinery on which capital allowances were claimed is to be brought into account as in **10.27** CAPITAL ALLOWANCES ON PLANT AND MACHINERY; and
- the disposal value is the open market value of the plant and machinery.

Business of leasing plant or machinery

The question of whether a partnership is carrying on a '*business of leasing plant or machinery*' is determined as for a company in **49.10** above, but with the appropriate modifications. 'Associate' in this case means a person who is a partner in the partnership or connected with a partner in the partnership. A 'qualifying associate' is a person who is an associate at the start of the relevant day or at any earlier time in the prior twelve months.

Qualifying change in a partner company's interest in a business

There is a 'qualifying change in a partner company's interest in a business' if there is a fall on any day of its percentage share in the profits or loss of the business. The percentage share for this purpose is to be determined on a just and reasonable basis and with regard, in particular, to any matter that would be taken into account in determining the company's share of partnership profits or losses (see **56.3** PARTNERSHIPS, but disregard for this purpose **56.6** PARTNERSHIPS). 'Profits' for this purpose do not include chargeable gains or capital losses.

Computing the amount of the taxable receipt

The basic amount of the taxable receipt is given by the formula PM – TWDV where these have the meaning below. The basic amount may then be subject to adjustment as described further below. If the basic amount given by the formula is a negative amount, the basic amount is taken instead to be nil.

PM has the meaning given in **49.10** above but references to the company are to be read as references to the partnership and references to an associated company are to be read as references to a 'qualifying company'. '*Qualifying company*' means:

(a) the partner company or a company which is an 'associated company' (as defined by *CTA 2010, s 430*) of the partner company on the relevant day;
(b) any other partner company in relation to whose interest in the business there is a qualifying change on the relevant day;
(c) any other partner company in relation to which there is a qualifying change of ownership (as in **49.10** above) on the relevant day; any
(d) any company which is an associated company on the relevant day of any partner company mentioned in (b) or (c) above.

References in (b) and (c) to another partner company are to a company which carries on the business at the start of the relevant day and is within the charge to corporation tax in respect of it.

TWDV is the total amount of unrelieved qualifying expenditure on plant or machinery in single asset pools, class pools and the main pool that would be carried forward under normal capital allowances rules (see **10.26** CAPITAL ALLOWANCES ON PLANT AND MACHINERY) if a new chargeable period of the partnership began on the day after the relevant day. Any expenditure incurred by the partnership on plant or machinery on the relevant day itself is to be left out of account unless it was acquired from a qualifying company (as defined above). Expenditure incurred on the relevant day but attributable to plant and machinery acquired by the partnership before that day is also left out of account.

An adjustment is made to the basic amount calculated above to reflect the fall in the partner company's percentage share in the profits or loss of the business. This is achieved by limiting the amount of the taxable receipt of the partner company to the appropriate percentage of the basic amount. The appropriate percentage is found by subtracting the company's percentage share at the end of the day on which the taxable receipt arises from its percentage share at the start of that day.

If another company's percentage share in the profits or loss of the business is greater at the end than at the start of the relevant day and the increase (or any part of it) is wholly attributable to the change in the partner company's interest in the business, the amount of the deductible expense it is treated as incurring is limited to the appropriate percentage of the amount of the taxable business receipt.

The appropriate percentage is found by the formula OCI/PCD, where OCI is the increase in that company's percentage share that is wholly attributable to the said change and PCD is the decrease in the partner company's percentage share. If, however, at the end of the relevant day the other company is carrying on the business alone, the deductible expense is equal to the amount of taxable business receipt.

Qualifying change of ownership of a corporate partner

If on any day (the '*relevant day*'):

- a company carries on a 'business of leasing plant or machinery' (as defined above) in partnership;
- the partner company is within the charge to corporation tax in respect of the business; and
- there is a 'qualifying change of ownership' (as in **49.10** above) in relation to the partner company,

the accounting period of the partner company ends on the relevant day and a new accounting period begins on the following day. Also, the partner company is treated as receiving a taxable business receipt (of its notional business) in the accounting period ending on the relevant day and as incurring a deductible business expense (of its notional business) of an equal amount in the new accounting period. See below as to the amount of the taxable receipt. The expense potentially qualifies for the relief at **49.12** below. A company's '*notional business*' is the business the profits or losses of which are determined, in relation to the company, under *CTA 2009, s 1259* (see **56.3** PARTNERSHIPS).

No part of any loss can be deducted under *CTA 2010, s 37(3)(b)* (relief for trade losses against total profits of earlier accounting periods) or *s 45F* (terminal loss relief for carried-forward losses) from so much of the company's total profits as derive from the taxable receipt. In determining how much of the profits derive from the receipt, profits are to be calculated on the basis that the receipt is the final amount to be added.

The amount of the taxable business receipt is calculated by first applying the formula above (PM – TWDV) to give the basic amount. This is then adjusted as described in **49.10** above. The taxable business receipt is then limited to the appropriate percentage' of this adjusted amount. If there is no qualifying change in the company's interest in the business on the relevant day, the appropriate percentage is the company's percentage share in the profits or loss of the business on the relevant day. If there is such a change, the appropriate percentage is the company's percentage share in the profits or loss of the business at the end of the relevant day.

[*CTA 2010, ss 409–418, 420–427, 429–431, 437; F(No 2)A 2017, Sch 4 para 166*].

Relief for expense in subsequent accounting period

[49.12] A special provision applies where:

(a) a company is treated under the provisions at **49.10** or **49.11** above as incurring an expense in an accounting period;

(b) the company also makes a loss in that accounting period or in a later accounting period;

(c) some or all of that loss would be carried forward to the accounting period after that in which the loss is made (the '*subsequent period*');

(d) some or all of that carried forward loss derives from the expense in (a) or from a notional expense (as below) which is allowed as a deduction for the accounting period in which the loss is made; and

(e) the subsequent period begins within the period of five years beginning immediately after the 'relevant day' (as in **49.10** or **49.11** above) and does not begin as a result of a subsequent application of **49.10** or **49.11** above.

To the extent that the loss derives from the expense, it is not carried forward but is instead treated as giving rise to a notional expense of an amount equal to:

$$DL + \frac{DL \times D \times R}{365}$$

where:

DL = the amount of the loss deriving from the expense;

D = the number of days in the accounting period in which the loss is incurred; and

R = the rate of INTEREST ON OVERPAID TAX (**43**).

The amount of that notional expense is allowed as a deduction in calculating profits for corporation tax purposes for the subsequent period. The extent to which a loss derives from an expense is determined on the basis that the expense is the final amount to be deducted.

[*CTA 2010, ss 386, 419, 428*].

Anti-avoidance

[49.13] Where a company enters into any 'arrangements' (as widely defined), a main purpose of which is to secure that it is treated as incurring an expense under **49.10** or **49.11** above, so much of any loss it incurs that derives from the expense may be carried forward but can only be set against 'relevant leasing income'. It is not available for group relief or group relief for carried-forward losses or for relief against total profits of the company. '*Relevant leasing income*' is income deriving from any plant or machinery lease which was entered into before the day on which the company is treated as incurring the expense and which is not an excluded lease of background plant or machinery for a building (see **10.49**(1)(B) CAPITAL ALLOWANCES ON PLANT AND MACHINERY). The extent to which a loss derives from the expense is to be determined on the basis that the expense is the final amount to be deducted. A loss carried forward and set off against relevant leasing income is ignored for the purposes of the restriction on the deduction of carried-forward losses at **51.13** LOSSES.

Anti avoidance provisions restrict certain deductible amounts claimed by a company where there has been a qualifying change in relation to the ownership of a company. A '*qualifying change*' is defined as for the capital allowance buying provisions at *CAA 2001, s 212C*, and is aimed at changes in ownership of a company, or changes in profit ratios of a partnership or changes in ownership ratios for a consortium. Where an expense (or part of an expense) is disallowed under these provisions for profit transfers at *CTA 2010, s 730D(2)*, then such expense is disregarded (to that extent) for the purposes of the restrictions imposed under the sale of lessors provisions, and therefore is disregarded for the purposes of *CTA 2010, s 432(1)*. For further details see **51.23** LOSSES.

The following rules apply in relation to any qualifying change of ownership (**49.10** above) or qualifying change in a company's interest in a business (**49.11** above). They potentially apply where there is a question:

(a) as to whether a company is carrying on a business of leasing plant or machinery (whether alone or in partnership);
(b) as to the amount of the taxable receipt under **49.10** or **49.11** above; or
(c) as to the amount of any disposal value to be substituted by *s 398G(3)*.

The first of these rules (*CTA 2010, s 435*) applies if:

(i) in determining the question at (a), (b) or (c) above, regard must be had to listed in below;
(ii) there would be a reduction or increase in any such amount; and
(iii) the reduction or increase would arise in any way from any arrangements (as widely defined) a main purpose of which is to secure a 'relevant tax advantage'.

The amounts to be considered are:

(a) the relevant plant or machinery value;
(b) the value of plant or machinery falling within *s 387(7)* (for companies) or *s 410(6)* (for partnerships);
(c) the relevant company's or partnership's income in the period of twelve months ending with the relevant day;
(d) the amount of the PM;
(e) the amount of the TWDV;
(f) the amount of any disposal value to be substituted by *s 398G(3)*; and
(g) any underlying amount required to calculate or verify an amount mentioned above.

A '*relevant tax advantage*' arises if, disregarding this anti-avoidance rule:

- any company would not be regarded as carrying on a business of leasing of plant or machinery; or
- any taxable receipt of any company under **49.10** or **49.11** above is reduced; or
- any expense that any company is treated as incurring under **49.10** or **49.11** above is increased; or
- the amount of any disposal value to be substituted by *s 398G(3)* would be reduced.

The rule is that, for the purpose of determining the question at (a), (b) or (c) above, the reduction or increase in the amounts to be ascertained in respect of the plant or machinery, referred to at (ii) above must be ignored.

Secondly, (under *CTA 2010, s 436*), if a company owns any plant or machinery at any time on any day and, in determining the question at (a) or (b) above, regard must be had to the amount (if any) which would fall to be shown in its balance sheet in respect of that plant or machinery, the rule below applies if, disregarding this anti-avoidance rule:

(I) no amount would appear in the company's balance sheet in respect of that plant or machinery; or
(II) the amount which would appear is less than the amount which would appear on the assumption that the company had no liabilities of any kind (including share capital) in its balance sheet on the day in question.

The rule is that, for the purpose of determining the question at (a) or (b) above, the assumption referred to at (II) above must be made. This rule applies equally to partnerships as it applies to companies.

[*CTA 2010, ss 432–437; F(No 2)A 2017, Sch 4 paras 166, 167*].

Reconstructions of companies with leasing trades

[49.14] An anti-avoidance measure at *CTA 2010, s 950* applies to counter the use of reconstructions of companies with leasing trades to avoid tax.

It applies only where the trade is part of a 'business of leasing plant or machinery' as in **49.10** above which the predecessor or the successor carries on on the day of transfer. Provided the business is carried on other than in partnership, the parties are not treated as the successor and predecessor.

Where the parties are carrying on the leasing trade in partnership the predecessor has to stop trading on the date of transfer for *CTA 2010, s 948* to apply.

The effect of these provisions is that the provisions of *CTA 2010, s 948* do not apply unless the companies share the same principal company or companies for the purposes of **49.9–49.13** above.

For the above purpose, the principal company or companies of the predecessor are not regarded as the same as the principal company or companies of the successor (where this would otherwise be the case) if, on or before the transfer day, there is a relevant change in the relationship between the successor and a principal company of the successor within *CTA 2010, s 394ZA* (company joining tonnage tax group — see **49.10** above).

If *CTA 2010, s 948* does not apply to a transfer, for capital allowances purposes there is deemed to be a disposal by the predecessor of the leasing assets at the higher of its 'ascribed value' immediately before transfer of the trade and the disposal value that the predecessor would be required to bring into account under *CAA 2001, Pt 2* and an acquisition by the successor at the same value on the date of cessation of the trade.

'Ascribed value' is as defined in **49.10** above, but with reference to predecessor instead of company or partnership.

[*CTA 2010, s 950*].

50

Loan Relationships

Cross-references. See 3 ALTERNATIVE FINANCE ARRANGEMENTS; 4.26 ANTI-AVOIDANCE for restrictions on the carry forward of non-trading loan relationship debits and deficits after a change of ownership of a shell company; 25 CORPORATE INTEREST RESTRICTION; 41.11 INCOME TAX IN RELATION TO A COMPANY; 64.6 RESIDENCE for the charge to corporation tax on non-UK resident companies in respect of loan relationships to which a company is a party for the purposes of a UK property business or to generate other UK property income.

Simon's Taxes. See D1.7.

Introduction to loan relationships

[50.1] Under the loan relationships provisions, all income, gains, profits and losses made by companies on money debts which arise from transactions for the lending of money (i.e. loans) are treated as income items. Interest and certain other amounts arising in respect of money debts which do not arise from the lending of money (such as trade debts) are also taxed under the loan relationship rules.

Loan relationship debits and credits are based on the profits and losses that are reflected in a company's accounts in respect of its loan relationships as items of profit or loss where its accounts are prepared in accordance with UK generally accepted accounting practice or international accounting standards.

Trading items are dealt with as trading receipts or deductions and non-trading items are within the charge to corporation tax on income from non-trading loan relationships). Whether a company is treated as being a party to a debtor relationship for trading or non-trading purposes depends on the purposes for which it is a party to the loan relationship. In the case of a creditor relationship a company will only be treated as being a party to the loan relationship for the purposes of its trade where it is a party to the loan relationship in the course of activities forming an integral part of its trade. In practice this means that such treatment normally only applies where the company is carrying on a financial trade.

See also 27 DERIVATIVE CONTRACTS. The current provisions generally take priority over the derivative contracts provisions.

The deduction of debits in respect of certain loan relationships may be subject to restriction by the CORPORATE INTEREST RESTRICTION (24).

Other sources. See HMRC Company Taxation Manual, CTM50000 *et seq*. and HMRC Corporate Finance Manual.

Meaning of 'loan relationship'

[50.2] A company has a '*loan relationship*' wherever it is a creditor or debtor as respects any 'money debt' which arises from a transaction for the lending of money, i.e. any debt which is, under general law, a loan. A debt is not taken to arise from such a transaction to the extent that it arises from rights conferred by 'shares' in a company. For this purpose, a 'share' is any share in a company under which an entitlement to receive distributions may arise, but does not include a share in a building society. Subject to this, a money debt is taken to arise from such a transaction where an instrument is issued by any person for the purpose of representing security for, or the rights of a creditor in respect of, the debt. Where a company is a party to a loan relationship as a debtor it is a party to a debtor relationship and where it is a party to a loan relationship as a creditor it is a party to a creditor relationship.

A '*money debt*' is a debt falling to be settled by:

(a) payment of money;
(b) the transfer of a right to settlement under a debt falling to be so settled; or
(c) in relation to loan relationships to which a company is a party, the issue or transfer of any shares in any company (mandatory convertibles).

The settlement as above may be at the option of the debtor or creditor and any other option exercisable by either party is to be disregarded. This reverses the decision in *HSBC Life (UK) Ltd v Stubbs and related appeals* (Sp C 295) 2001, [2002] SSCD 9 in which certain financial futures contracts entered into with derivatives dealers, involving both an option for cash settlement and one for settlement in a non-cash form, were held not to constitute loan relationships.

In *Stagecoach Group plc v HMRC* FTT, [2016] SFTD 982 it was held that debits claimed by the taxpayer related to a recapitalisation scheme using forward subscription agreements, which were not loan relationships, and therefore no debits were allowable.

Certain types of interest and other amounts arising from a money debt which is not a loan relationship are treated as if they did so arise as regards credits and debits relating to those amounts (see **50.3** below). In addition, there are a number of provisions treating certain transactions or amounts as loan relationships or as rights, payments or profits under loan relationships. For details see:

- **50.49** below (holdings in OEICS, unit trusts and offshore funds);
- **22** CO-OPERATIVE AND COMMUNITY BENEFIT SOCIETIES;
- **3** ALTERNATIVE FINANCE ARRANGEMENTS;
- **50.47** below (shares treated as liabilities);
- **50.39** below (disguised interest).

[*CTA 2009, ss 294, 302, 303, 476(1)*].

Any payment or interest paid or payable in pursuance of any of the rights or liabilities under a loan relationship, or under the arrangement(s) by virtue of which the relationship exists (including a security representing the relationship), are treated as made or payable under that relationship. [*CTA 2009, s 305*].

Money debts etc. not arising from the lending of money

[50.3] Certain money debts which do not arise from a loan relationship (such as trade debts, unpaid or overpaid tax) are nevertheless effectively treated as payable under a loan relationship. This applies where the money debt is one of the following (referred to in *CTA 2009* as '*relevant non-lending relationships*').

(a) A debt on which interest is payable by or to a company. Where a company has such a relevant non-lending relationship and it enters into a related transaction in respect of the right to receive interest, and as a result interest is no longer payable to the company, the company nevertheless continues to be treated as having a relevant non-lending relationship.

(b) A debt in relation to which exchange gains or losses arise to a company.

(c) A debt in relation to which an impairment loss (or credit in respect of a reversal of an impairment loss) arises in relation to a trading receipt or a receipt of a UK or overseas property business (this means that where the creditor is connected with the debtor (see 50.23) the creditor will be denied relief for any impairment loss).

(d) A debt in respect of which a company has been entitled to relief for the underlying expense represented by the debt in calculating the profits of a trade, UK property business, or overseas property business. This provision was designed to ensure that the release of the debt would not give rise to a taxable profit where the debtor was connected with the creditor for the purposes of the loan relationships legislation. This is because the creditor was already denied relief for any impairment provisions or release debits arising in respect of such debts.

(e) A debt from which a discount (of an income or capital nature) arises to a creditor company in respect of a money debt to which the company is party where:
   - the money debt would not be treated as a trading receipt if it is consideration (or part-consideration) for the disposal a disposal of property;
   - the money debt arises from the disposal of property which is not an asset representing a loan relationship or derivative contract the disposal of which is a 'relevant disposal'; and
   - the discounts would be accounted for as an alternative finance return (see 3 ALTERNATIVE FINANCE ARRANGEMENTS).

   A discount will arise, in particular, where the company disposes of a property for consideration which is wholly or partly deferred, the amount of the total consideration is greater than that which the purchaser would have paid if payment was required in full at the time of the disposal and some or all of the excess can reasonably be regarded as being a return on an investment of money at interest (and, thus, as being a discount arising from the money debt).

In relation to the disposal of property which is a loan relationship or a derivative contract, a *'relevant disposal'* is one as respects which the whole consideration is brought into account under the loan relationship or derivative contract rules or it is one to which the group provisions at **50.40** below, or at **27.24** DERIVATIVE CONTRACTS, apply or would apply but for the use of fair value accounting. Note that where a disposal of a loan relationship or derivative is a 'relevant disposal' the above provision is applied where the payment of the transfer consideration is deferred and the conditions above are satisfied (see *CTA 2009, s 340(5)* and *s 341(7)* — the equivalent provisions that apply for the purposes of the derivative contracts legislation are discussed in **27.24** DERIVATIVE CONTRACTS).

Interest payable on a money debt includes payments which fall under *TIOPA 2010, Pt 4* (see **70** TRANSFER PRICING) to be treated as interest on a money debt or an amount treated as a money debt.

Where a company has a relevant non-lending relationship, the loan relationship provisions apply to the matters listed below as they apply to such matters in relation to actual loan relationships but the only debits or credits to be brought into account under these provisions in respect of the relationship are those relating to those matters and any references in other provisions to loan relationships is taken to include a relevant non-lending relationship. For relationships within (a)–(c) above, the matters in relation to which this applies are:

(A) the interest, exchange gains or losses, impairment or reversal as appropriate; and

(B) with effect for money debts which are assets and in respect of which interest is payable to the company, profits (but not losses) arising to the company from any 'related transaction' (see **50.8** below) in respect of the right to receive interest (i.e. where the company disposes of the rights without disposing of the associated asset).

For relationships within (d) above, the matters in relation to which the above rules apply are:

(I) matters within (A) or (B) above;

(II) the discount arising from the debt;

(III) profits (but not losses) arising from any related transaction; and

(IV) any impairment, or reversal of an impairment, in respect of the discount.

Credits in respect of a discount are determined using an amortised cost basis of accounting.

These provisions do not apply to profits, gains or losses arising on money debts, which fall within the derivative contracts regime or the intangible assets regime.

See **50.4** below with respect to the determination of the trading or non-trading nature of the associated debits.

Any debits or credits which relate to INTEREST ON OVERPAID TAX (**43**) or INTEREST ON OVERDUE TAX (**42**) are treated as non-trading debits or credits.

Exchange gains and losses arising on money debts are not to be taken into account under this provision where they relate to:

(i) UK tax; or
(ii) foreign tax (unless deductible under *TIOPA 2010, s 112*;
(iii) amounts which would, but for any statutory provision (other than *CTA 2009, s 53*), which relates to capital expenditure) or rule of law prohibiting such deduction, be deductible in computing trading profits, or as a management expense; or
(iv) ordinary basic life and general annuity business management expenses within the meaning of *FA 2012, s 77*.

The money debts owed to a company on which exchange gains and losses arising are taken into account by virtue of this provision include any currency held by the company and certain deferred acquisition costs of an insurance company. The money debts owed by a company to which this applies include any provision for future liabilities in the company's statutory accounts which would be incurred and fall to be taken into account in computing the profits or losses of a trade, a UK property business or an overseas property business and, in the case of an insurance company, certain provisions for unearned premiums and unexpired risks.

[*CTA 2009, ss 478–486, Sch 2 para 72; SI 2007 No 2483, Art 3*].

In *Amalgamated Metal Corporation plc v HMRC* FTT, [2018] SFTD 410, advance corporation tax (ACT) paid by the company to HMRC which was subsequently determined to have been charged unlawfully was held to have given rise to a money debt within these provisions. Compensation was paid by the company's accountants for settling the company's claim to interest from HMRC on the ACT for a lower amount than would otherwise have been due. As the compensation related to the interest, it was liable to tax under the loan relationship rules.

Simon's Taxes. See **D1.743.**

Taxation of loan relationships

[50.4] Profits arising to a company from 'loan relationships are (subject to the exception for certain distributions at **50.45** below) chargeable to corporation tax as income.

The credits or debits for an accounting period in respect of any loan relationship (including interest, discount, impairment and foreign exchange movements arising on a money debt not resulting from a transaction for the lending of money — see **50.3**) (computed as described at **50.8** onwards below) are brought into account as follows.

(a) Where the loan relationship is for trading purposes, they are treated as receipts or expenses of the trade for that period (in the case of expenses, notwithstanding *CTA 2009, ss 53, 54* or *59*). (This does not affect any requirement for deduction of tax by the payer from payments of yearly interest (see **41.2**(b) INCOME TAX IN RELATION TO A COMPANY).

(b) Where there are credits and/or debits in respect of a non-trading relationship (i.e. '*non-trading credits*' and/or '*non-trading debits*'), they are aggregated, and the net amount is chargeable to corporation tax on income or relievable as a non-trading deficit (see below) as the case may be.

For a creditor company, a loan relationship is taken to be for trade purposes only if it is a party to the relationship in the course of activities forming an integral part of that trade. Mutual trading, mutual insurance or other mutual business which is not life assurance business and any basic life assurance and general annuity business are treated for this purpose as not constituting the whole or any part of a trade.

A non-UK resident company carrying on a trade in the UK through a permanent establishment must bring into account debits and credits to the extent they are attributable to the permanent establishment, in accordance with the rules at **64.6** RESIDENCE. With effect from 6 April 2020 (subject to the transitional provisions at **64.7** RESIDENCE), non-resident companies must also bring into account non-trading debits and credits from loan relationships to which the company is a party for the purposes of a UK property business or to enable it to generate other UK property income.

[*CTA 2009, ss 295–301; FA 2019, Sch 5 paras 15, 35; FA 2020, Sch 6 paras 1, 10*].

Unless otherwise specified, a charge or relief under the loan relationship provisions precludes any other charge to or relief from corporation tax in respect of the same matter.

[*CTA 2009, s 464*].

Non-trading deficits

[50.5] A company has a non-trading deficit from its loan relationships for an accounting period if the non-trading debits for the period exceed any non-trading credits. [*CTA 2009, s 301(6)*].

The provisions which provide relief for loan relationships non-trading deficits were substantially revised by *F(No 2)A 2017*. Subject to transitional rules, the changes apply to deficits for accounting periods beginning on or after 1 April 2017. The previous rules continue to apply, however, where the company is a charity.

For these purposes, an accounting period which straddles 1 April 2017 is treated as if it were two separate accounting periods, the first ending on 31 March 2017 and the second beginning on 1 April 2017. Any necessary apportionments between the two periods must be made on a time basis unless that would produce an unjust or unreasonable result, in which case a just and reasonable basis must be used. Special rules apply, however, where the amount to be apportioned is either an amount chargeable to corporation tax which would have been less but for the CORPORATE INTEREST RESTRICTION (**25**) provisions or an amount for which relief is available which would have been greater but for the restriction. An amount chargeable to corporation tax which would not have arisen at all but for the restriction provisions is apportioned entirely to the second period.

[F(No 2)A 2017, Sch 4 paras 190–192].

For the provisions applicable to post-1 April 2017 deficits see **50.6** below. The old rules are described at **50.7** below.

Post-1 April 2017 deficits

[50.6] Subject to the transitional rules for straddling periods at **50.5** above, the following applies where a company other than a charity has a non-trading deficit from its loan relationships for an accounting period (the '*deficit period*') beginning on or after 1 April 2017. The whole or part of the deficit may be claimed, to the extent not already surrendered as group relief (under *CTA 2010, s 99*, see **35.2** onwards GROUP RELIEF):

(A) by set-off against profits of the deficit period;
(B) by carry-back and set-off against profits of earlier accounting periods arising from non-trading loan relationships; or
(C) where the conditions below are satisfied, by carry-forward and set-off against total profits of the next accounting period.

Claims under (A) and (B) above must be made within two years of the end of the deficit period or within such further period as HMRC may allow. Different claims may be made for different parts of a non-trading deficit, but not so as to give relief more than once. A claim under (C) above must be made within two years of the end of the first accounting period after the deficit period.

A claim under (A) above is given effect by setting off the deficit against profits for the period identified in the claim and is given before relief under *CTA 2010, s 37* or *s 62* (losses relieved against profits of current or earlier accounting periods, see **51.3**, **51.4** LOSSES, **60** PROPERTY INCOME) or under (B) above. Relief against oil companies' ring-fenced profits is prohibited.

A claim under (B) above must exclude any amount claimed under (A) above or surrendered as group relief. Only profits for the accounting periods (or parts) falling within a 12-month period immediately preceding the deficit period may be relieved and relief is given for later accounting periods before earlier ones. Profits of an accounting period straddling the start of the 12-month period are apportioned for this purpose on a time basis. Relief is given after any relief under (A) above and after any relief for losses or deficits of accounting periods before the deficit period, for qualifying charitable donations made for the purposes of a trade, for trading losses of the same or subsequent periods, or, for companies with investment business (**45** INVESTMENT COMPANIES AND INVESTMENT BUSINESS), for plant and machinery capital allowances, management expenses or qualifying charitable donations made for the purposes of the business.

A claim under (C) above may be made for so much of a deficit as has not been set off against profits under (A) or (B) above and has not been surrendered as group relief or as group relief for carried-forward losses (see **35.24** GROUP RELIEF). The company must not cease to be a company with investment business in the deficit period and, if it were such a company immediately before the beginning of the deficit period, the business must not become small or negligible in that period. Relief against oil companies' ring-fenced profits is prohibited.

Where, under (C) above, a deficit is carried forward to an accounting period (the '*later accounting period*') but is not fully relieved (and is not fully surrendered as group relief for carried-forward losses) the unrelieved deficit can be carried forward to the next period for a further claim under (C) above to be made as if it were a deficit of that later period. This does not apply if the company ceased to be a company with investment business in the later accounting period or, if it were such a company immediately before the beginning of that period, if the business became small or negligible in the period. This rule can then be reapplied where the deficit is not fully relieved in the period following the later accounting period.

Where a company cannot make a claim under (C) above only because its investment business became small or negligible in the deficit period, so much of the deficit as it not claimed under (A) or (B) above is carried forward and set against non-trading profits (i.e. so much of the company's profits as does not consist of trading income for the purposes of *CTA 2010, s 37*) for succeeding accounting periods. The carried forward non-trading deficit is set against the non-trading profits of the accounting period immediately following the deficit period ('period 2'). This is subject to a claim for any amount of that deficit to be excepted from being set against non-trading profits of period 2 (to allow, for example, for any double taxation relief to be used that would otherwise be wasted). Where such a claim is made, or where there are insufficient non-trading profits in period 2 for the whole of the deficit to be set off in that period, the amount not set off in that period is treated as a non-trading deficit of that period to be carried forward for offset against non-trading profits of succeeding accounting periods, provided that the company continues to be a company with investment business throughout period 2 (or, where this rule applies to carry forward an amount from period 3, throughout period 3 (and so on)). This provision applies equally where a further claim cannot be made under (C) above for an unrelieved deficit carried forward from a later accounting period because its investment business became small or negligible in the later period. A claim for relief not to be given for a period must be made within two years after the end of that period or within such further period as HMRC allow.

[*CTA 2009, ss 463A–463I; F(No 2)A 2017, Sch 4 para 4*].

See also **51.23** LOSSES for anti-avoidance provisions which restrict amounts of loss relief and group relief claims available to a company where there has been a qualifying change in relation to the company.

Pre-1 April 2017 deficits

[50.7] Subject to the transitional rules at **50.5** above, a non-trading deficit of an accounting period beginning before 1 April 2017, (the '*deficit period*') may be claimed, to the extent not already surrendered as group relief (under *CTA 2010, s 99*, see **35.2** onwards GROUP RELIEF), either:

(A) by set-off against profits of the deficit period; or
(B) by carry-back and set-off against profits of earlier accounting periods arising from non-trading loan relationships.

Relief under (A) or (B) above is not available if the company is a charity. The following provisions do apply to charities, however, and continue to do so for accounting periods beginning on or after 1 April 2017.

Any non-trading deficit for which relief is not claimed under (A) or (B) above, or surrendered as group relief, is carried forward and set against non-trading profits (i.e. so much of the company's profits as does not consist of trading income for the purposes of *CTA 2010, s 37*) for succeeding accounting periods.

The carried forward non-trading deficit is set against the non-trading profits of the accounting period immediately following the deficit period (the 'first later period'). This is subject to a claim for any amount of that deficit to be excepted from being set against non-trading profits of the first later period (to allow, for example, for any double taxation relief to be used that would otherwise be wasted). Where such a claim is made, or where there are insufficient non-trading profits in the first later period for the whole of the deficit to be set off in that period, the amount not set off in that period is treated as a non-trading deficit of that period to be carried forward for offset against non-trading profits of succeeding accounting periods.

Claims under (A) and (B) above must be made within two years of the end of the deficit period or within such further period as HMRC may allow. A claim for a part or the whole of the deficit to be treated as a non-trading deficit of the first later period, to be carried forward for offset against non-trading profits of succeeding accounting periods, must be made within two years of the end of that first later period.

A claim under (A) above is given effect after relief for brought forward trading losses, but before relief under *CTA 2010, ss 37* or *62* (losses relieved against profits of current or earlier accounting periods, see **51.3**, **51.4** LOSSES, **59** PROPERTY INCOME) or under (B) above. Relief against oil companies' ring-fenced profits is prohibited. Different claims may be made as respects different parts of a non-trading deficit, but not so as to give relief more than once.

A claim under (B) above must exclude any amount claimed under (A) above or surrendered as group relief. Only profits for the accounting periods (or parts) falling within a twelve-month period immediately preceding the deficit period may be relieved and relief is given for later accounting periods before earlier ones. Profits of an accounting period straddling the start of the twelve-month period are apportioned for this purpose on a time basis. Relief is given after any relief under (A) above and after any relief for losses or deficits of accounting periods before the deficit period, for qualifying charitable donations made for the purposes of a trade, for trading losses of the same or subsequent periods, or, for companies with investment business (**44** INVESTMENT COMPANIES AND INVESTMENT BUSINESS), for plant and machinery capital allowances, management expenses or qualifying charitable donations made for the purposes of the business.

[*CTA 2009, ss 456–463; F(No 2)A 2017, Sch 4 para 3*].

See also **51.23** LOSSES for anti-avoidance provisions which restrict amounts of loss relief and group relief claims available to a company where there has been a qualifying change in relation to the company.

Simon's Taxes. See **D1.739, D1.739A, D1.740.**

Example

Sigma Ltd, which is not part of a group, has non-trading deficits of £8,400 for the year ended 31 March 2017 and £8,500 for the year ended 31 March 2021.

Sigma Ltd's computations for relevant years are as follows.

	Year ended 31.3.16	Year ended 31.3.17	Year ended 31.3.18	Year ended 31.3.19	Year ended 31.3.20	Year ended 31.3.21	Year ended 31.3.22
	£	£	£	£	£	£	£
Trading income	11,000	800	12,000	10,000	11,000	800	2,500
Non-trading loan relationship income/(deficit)	2,000	(8,400)	400	2,000	1,000	(8,500)	2,000

The deficit of £8,400 for the year ended 31 March 2017 (a pre-1 April 2017 deficit) may be relieved as follows (group relief not being available).

		£
Non-trading deficit		8,400
1. Set off against total profits of the year ended 31 March 2017		(800)
2. Carry back against profits from non-trading loan relationships of the preceding accounting period		(2,000)
3. Carry forward against non-trading profits of the company for year ended:	31 March 2018	(400)
	31 March 2019	(2,000)
	31 March 2020	(1,000)
	31 March 2022	(2,000)
Net deficit to carry forward against subsequent non-trading profits		£200

The deficit of £8,500 for the year ended 31 March 2021 (a post-1 April 2017 deficit) may be relieved as follows (group relief not being available).

		£
Non-trading deficit		8,500
1. Set off against total profits of the year ended 31 March 2021		(800)
2. Carry forward against total profits of the company for year ended:	31 March 2022	(2,500)
Net deficit to carry forward against subsequent non-trading profits		£5,200

Note to the example

(a) It is assumed that the company will seek to utilise the carried-forward deficit from the year ended 31 March 2017 in priority to that from the year ended 31 March 2021 as the latter can be set off against the company's trading profits as well as non-trading loan relationship profits.

Computation of debits and credits

[50.8] The amounts that must be brought into account in respect of a company's loan relationships are:

(a) profits and losses of the company that arise to it from its loan relationships and related transactions (excluding interest or expenses);
(b) interest under those relationships; and
(c) expenses incurred by the company under or for the purposes of those relationships and related transactions.

[*CTA 2009, s 306A*].

Subject to the exception at **50.45** below, a '*related transaction*' is any disposal or acquisition (in whole or part) of rights or liabilities under a relationship. This includes the transfer or extinguishment of any such rights or liabilities by any sale, gift, exchange, surrender, redemption or release. Certain transfers under *Proceeds of Crime Act 2002, Part 5*, known as 'Part 5 transfers' (by which property obtained through unlawful conduct is vested in an appointed trustee for civil recovery), which would otherwise be 'related transactions', are, however, disregarded for this purpose except for the purpose of identifying the person for whom debits or credits not related to the transfer are to be brought into account.

See **50.17** below with regard to exchange gains and losses.

Expenses within (c) above include only those incurred directly:

(i) in bringing any of the loan relationships into existence;
(ii) in entering into or giving effect to any of the related transactions;
(iii) in making payments under any of the relationships or in pursuance of any of the related transactions; or
(iv) in taking steps for ensuring the receipt of payments under any of the relationships or in pursuance of any of the related transactions.

They do, however, include expenses connected with entering into, or giving effect to any obligation under, a prospective loan relationship or related transaction into which the company has not entered at the time they are incurred. See HMRC Corporate Finance Manual, at CFM33060 for examples of the expenses allowed.

[*CTA 2009, ss 293, 304, 306A, 329*].

HMRC have previously confirmed that costs directly incurred in varying the terms of a loan relationship may be brought into account as a debit under the above provisions (HMRC Tax Bulletin, Issue 25). Guarantee fees payable by a borrower are normally allowed as an expense (HMRC Corporate Finance Manual CFM31100). It should be noted that HMRC do not consider that premiums payable for key person insurance are deductible (see HMRC Corporate Finance Manual at CFM33060).

There is a special relief for debits which are pre-trading expenditure. A company can elect for a non-trading debit not to be brought into account in the period in which it arises, within two years of the end of that period. If the company then begins to carry on a trade within seven years after the end of that period, and the debit would have been a trading debit if it had been given in the accounting period in which the trade commenced, it is brought into account as a trading debit in that period. [*CTA 2009, s 330*].

A similar rule applies with effect from 6 April 2020 where a non-UK resident company has debits under a loan relationship to which it is party for the purposes of its UK property business which are referable to any time within the seven years before commencement of the business. Such debits (net of certain credits) can be brought into account in the first accounting period in which the company carries on the business, provided that they have not otherwise been brought into account for tax purposes. It is a further requirement that the debits would have been brought into account in computing the profits or losses of the company if it had been carrying on the business at the time to which the debits are referable. The credits which must be set off against the debits are those which would have been brought into account at any time in the seven-year period if the company had then been carrying on the business and which would not otherwise have been brought into account. This rule applies subject to the anti-avoidance provisions relating to imported losses (see **50.30** below).

The above rule applies also to a non-UK resident company which is party to a loan relationship for the purpose of enabling it to generate other UK property income (i.e. rent receivable in connection with a *CTA 2009, s 39* concern (mines, quarries etc. — see **60.18** PROPERTY INCOME), rent receivable for electric-line wayleaves (see **60.18**) or post-cessation receipts from a UK property business (see **60.4**)).

[*CTA 2009, s 330ZA; FA 2020, Sch 6 paras 3, 10*].

Simon's Taxes. See **D1.715**.

Imputed interest and other amounts

[50.9] Where, under the TRANSFER PRICING (70) rules, any amount falls to be treated as interest payable under a loan relationship of a company, the loan relationship provisions have effect as if the amounts were actual interest.

No credit is to be brought into account to the extent that it corresponds to an amount which has not previously been brought into account as a debit as a result of the above rule.

[*CTA 2009, s 446*].

Recognition of profit — generally accepted accounting practice

[50.10] The amounts to be brought into account as credits and debits in computing a company's loan relationship profits are amounts that, in accordance with generally accepted accounting practice, are recognised in the company accounts for the relevant period as an item of profit or loss. This includes amounts that were previously recognised as an item of other comprehensive income and have been transferred to become an item of profit or loss in determining the company's profit or loss for the relevant accounting period. The terms 'item of profit or loss' and 'item of other comprehensive income' each has the meaning that it has for accounting purposes.

Transitional rules apply where amounts that were recognised in other comprehensive income for accounting periods beginning before 1 January 2016 were taken into account under previous rules in computing a company's loan relationship profits for such accounting periods. An amount equal and opposite to the net debits or credits that have been so recognised (and have not been reversed to profit or loss before the start of the company's first accounting period beginning on or after 1 January 2016) is brought into account in computing the company's loan relationship profits over a five year period (with a percentage of the overall transitional adjustment allocated as follows: year 1 — 40%; year 2 — 25%; year 3 — 15%; year 4 — 10%; year 5 — 10%) (see *F(No 2)A 2015, Sch 7 paras 115–119*).

Where an accounting period does not coincide with a company's period of account (statutory accounting period) the company is deemed to have two accounting periods, the first ending 12 months after the start of its period of account and the second starting with the end of the first period and ending with the end of the period of account. The company's loan relationship profits are normally apportioned between these two deemed accounting periods on a time basis unless such apportionment would work unreasonably or unjustly. In this latter case the company's loan relationship profits that are attributable to the two accounting periods are determined by reference to the amounts that would have been recognised in determining the company's accounting profit or loss for each period, if it had drawn up accounts for each of the two accounting periods.

Amounts arising in respect of a loan relationship that, in accordance with generally accepted accounting practice, have been recognised in other comprehensive income, and which have not been recycled to profit or loss, are deemed to be recycled to profit or loss at the time that a company ceases to recognise the loan relationship in its accounts, or at a later time, if at such time it is not expected that such amounts will subsequently be recycled to profit or loss. The rules apply in the same way where a company ceases to recognise part of an asset or a liability representing a loan relationship in its accounts, see **50.13** below.

[*CTA 2009, ss 307, 308, 320A*].

For cases in which the Tribunal ruled on whether a particular way of accounting was compliant with the relevant accounting standards see *Greene King plc v HMRC* CA 2016, [2017] STC 615 and *Fidex Ltd v HMRC* CA, [2016] STC 1920.

Generally, credits and debits may be determined on any accounting basis that is in accordance with generally accepted accounting practice. [*CTA 2009, s 313(1)*]. In a number of specified cases, however, the legislation requires that an amortised cost basis of accounting or a fair value basis must be used.

Amortised cost accounting basis

'*Amortised cost basis of accounting*' means a basis under which an asset or liability representing the loan relationship is measured in the balance sheet of the company at its 'amortised cost' using the effective interest method, adjusted as necessary where the loan relationship is the 'hedged item' under a 'designated fair value hedge'. 'Amortised cost', 'effective interest method', 'hedge item' and 'designated fair value hedge' are all defined as for accounting purposes. [*CTA 2009, s 313(4)(4A)(7)*].

IFRS 9, IAS 39 and FRS 102 define the amortised cost of a financial asset or a financial liability (which will include creditor and debtor loan relationships respectively) as the amount at which the financial asset or financial liability is measured at initial recognition plus or minus principal repayments, plus or minus the cumulative amortisation using the effective interest method of any difference between that initial amount and the maturity amount, and (under IFRS 9) in the case of financial assets adjusted for any loss allowance (or under IAS 39 or FRS 102, minus any reduction for impairment or uncollectibility). The effective interest rate is the rate of interest which exactly discounts the estimated future cash payments or receipts through the expected life of the financial asset or financial liability to the gross carrying amount (or, in the case of a financial liability, its amortised cost) or, under IAS 39 and FRS 102, to its initial carrying value. Under the accounting standards, where a company accounts for a creditor or debtor loan relationship on an amortised cost basis, any expenses incurred in connection with the acquisition or issue of that loan relationship are generally required to be added to (or in the case of a debtor loan relationship, deducted from) the initial carrying value of the loan relationship and will be taken into account in determining the effective interest rate.

See **50.12** below for the treatment where a company accounts for a creditor loan relationship using an amortised cost basis of accounting and an asset representing a loan relationship is revalued, and for a discussion of revaluations under *CTA 2009, s 324*.

Fair value basis

'*Fair value accounting*' means a basis under which assets and liabilities are measured in the company's balance sheet at their fair value and changes in the fair value are recognised as items of profit or loss. 'Fair value' is defined as for accounting purposes. [*CTA 2009, ss 313(5)(6), 476(1)*].

The accounting standards define 'fair value' as the amount for which an asset could be exchanged, or a liability settled, between knowledgeable, willing parties in an arm's length transaction.

Interest paid late

[50.11] In certain circumstances, where:

(a) interest payable under a relationship is not paid within 12 months of the end of the accounting period (the '*actual accrual period*') in which it would otherwise be treated as accruing; and

(b) credits representing the full amount of the interest are not brought into account for any accounting period in respect of the corresponding creditor relationship,

debits relating to interest payable under the relationship are not brought into account until the interest is paid. This restriction applies in the following cases.

(i) At any time in the actual accrual period, the debtor company is a 'close company' and the creditor is either:
   - a 'participator' in the debtor company or a person who controls a company which is such a participator (a 'participator company');
   - an 'associate' of a person who is a participator in the debtor company at that time or an associate of a person who controls a participator company at that time;
   - a company controlled by a participator in the debtor company or a person who controls a participator company; or
   - a company in which a participator in the debtor company has a 'major interest'.

   In addition, where the creditor is a company, the restriction only applies if it is resident in a non-qualifying territory (within *TIOPA 2010, s 173*; broadly, a tax haven) or is effectively managed in a non-qualifying territory in which companies are not taxable by reason of domicile, residence or place of management.

   However, the restriction does not apply where:
   - either:
     - the debtor company is a 'CIS-based close company' and a 'small or medium-sized enterprise' (as defined by *TIOPA 2010, s 172*), and the creditor is not 'resident' (as defined by *TIOPA 2010, s 172*) in a 'non-qualifying territory' (as defined by *TIOPA 2010, s 173*); or
     - the debt is owed to (or to persons acting for) a 'CIS limited partnership' no member of which is resident in a non-qualifying territory (this to be confirmed in writing by the partnership to the debtor company) and the debtor company is a small or medium-sized enterprise;

(ii) the loan is made by the trustees of a occupational pension scheme (within *FA 2004, s 150(5)*) and, at any time in the actual accrual period, the debtor company is the employer operating the scheme, or is connected with the employer (see **50.23** above), or the employer is a company in which the debtor company has a 'major interest' or which itself has a major interest in the debtor company.

This provision also applies to indirect creditors where there is a series of loan relationships, or money debts which would be loan relationships if a company directly stood in the position of creditor or debtor. In this case, the reference to the corresponding creditor relationship in (b) above includes a person who indirectly stands in the position of a creditor.

A '*CIS-based close company*' is a company that would not be close apart from the attribution under *CTA 2010, s 451(4)–(6)* of the rights and powers of a partner in a 'CIS limited partnership' to other partners by virtue of *CTA 2010, s 448(1)(a)*. A '*CIS limited partnership*' is a limited partnership which is a collective investment scheme or would be a collective investment scheme if not a body corporate, within the meaning of the *Financial Services and Markets Act 2000, s 235* (see **50.49** below).

For these purposes, a '*close company*' is as defined at **16.2** CLOSE COMPANIES but, notwithstanding **16.3**, includes non-resident companies. An '*associate*' is as defined at **16.9** CLOSE COMPANIES. '*Control*' is as defined in *CTA 2009, s 472* (see **50.24** above). A '*participator*' in relation to a company is a person who, by virtue of **16.7** CLOSE COMPANIES, is treated as such for the purposes of the close company legislation other than by reason only of being a loan creditor. A person who is a participator in a company which controls another company is treated as also being a participator in that other company.

A company ('company A') has a '*major interest*' in another company ('company B') if company A and one other person ('C') together control (within *CTA 2009, s 472*, see **50.24** below) company B, and each of C and company A have at least 40% of the total interests, rights and powers subsisting in company B giving that control. Connected companies' interests, rights and powers are attributed to company A and (if it is a company) C for this purpose (companies being connected if one controls the other or they are under common control). Where interests, rights or powers are held in partnership, these are apportioned to company partners in proportion to their share in partnership profits. Where a partnership which carries on a trade or a business stands as debtor or creditor in relation to a money debt, each company partner is for the purposes of this test treated as holding a separate money debt corresponding to their share in partnership profits. A general partner of a limited partnership which is a collective investment scheme within the meaning of the *Financial Services and Markets Act 2000, s 235* is disregarded for these purposes.

[*CTA 2009, ss 372–379, 473, 474, 476(1)*].

For a discussion of when interest can be treated as paid (under (a) above), see HMRC Corporate Finance Manual, CFM35830. See also CFM35840 for HMRC's view of when credits (under (b) above) should be treated as being 'brought into account' by the creditor.

Revaluation of debts

[50.12] Where a creditor company does not use fair value accounting and revalues an asset representing a loan relationship:

(a) no debits can be brought into account for loan relationship purposes except an impairment loss or a debit resulting from the release of any liability under the relationship; and
(b) no credits can be brought into account in respect of a reversal of any debits disallowed under (a) above.

A '*revaluation*' of an asset for these purposes includes any provision or allowance made by the company reducing the carrying value of the asset (or group of assets including the asset in question).

This provision does not affect debits to be brought into account in respect of exchange gains and losses or debits or credits to be brought into account where the creditor relationship is the hedged item under a designated fair value hedge.

[*CTA 2009, ss 324, 325*].

Company is not or has ceased to be a party to a loan relationship

[50.13] Where a company is not, or has ceased to be, party to a loan relationship, special rules apply to prevent debits/credits being accounted for where the following conditions are met:

(a) in accordance with generally accepted accounting practice, amounts in respect of a qualifying relationship (defined as a loan relationship or a relationship that would be a loan relationship if a company were a party to it) as are recognised in a company's accounts as an item of profit or loss even though during all or part of the period the company is not a party to the qualifying relationship;

(b) any of conditions A–D (see below) is met; and

(c) in the absence of this provision the credits and debits brought into account by the company for the purposes of the loan relationships legislation or the derivative contracts legislation for the relevant accounting period would not include the credits or debits representing the whole of such amounts.

Condition A is that: the company was a party to the qualifying relationship; amounts in respect of the qualifying relationship were recognised in the company's accounts as an item of profit or loss when it was a party to the relationship; and any such amounts continue to be recognised in those accounts as an item of profit or loss.

Condition B is that the amounts recognised in the company's accounts as an item of profit or loss in respect of the qualifying relationship are recognised as a result of a transaction which has the effect of transferring to the company all or part of the risks or reward relating to the qualifying relationship without a corresponding transfer of rights or obligations under the relationship.

Condition C is that the amounts recognised in the company's accounts as an item of profit or loss are recognised as a result of a related transaction in relation to a qualifying relationship to which the company was, but has ceased to be, a party.

Condition D is that: the amounts recognised as an item of profit or loss are recognised because the company may enter into a qualifying relationship or related transaction but has not yet done so; and the amounts are not expected to be amounts to which *CTA 2009, s 329* (pre-loan relationship and abortive expenses) applies.

If the conditions at (a)–(c) above are met, where a debit/credit arises a company is not permitted to bring the debit/credit into account in computing its loan relationship profits to the extent that the amount is:

(i) brought into account as a debit/credit for the purposes of the loan relationships legislation by another company;

(ii) brought into account so as to determine the assumed taxable total profits another company for the purposes of the controlled foreign companies legislation (see **21** CONTROLLED FOREIGN COMPANIES); or

(iii) allowable as a deduction or recognised as income by a person of the purposes of income tax.

In the case of a credit, in order to avoid a double charge to tax in respect of the same amount a company has to make a claim for a consequential adjustment to be made in respect of the amount which would otherwise be brought into account as a credit. When such a claim is made HMRC must make such of the consequential adjustments claimed as are just and reasonable. Such adjustments may be made in respect of any period, by way of an assessment, the modification of an assessment, the amendment of a claim, or otherwise and despite any time limit imposed by or under any enactment.

[*CTA 2009, ss 330A–330C*].

Amounts not fully recognised for accounting purposes

[50.14] An anti-avoidance provision applies where a company is, or is treated as being, a party to a creditor relationship in an accounting period and as a result of tax avoidance arrangements to which the company is at any time a party, in accordance with generally accepted accounting practice, an amount is not fully recognised for the period in respect of the creditor relationship in the company's accounts. Arrangements are tax avoidance arrangements if the main purpose, or one of the main purposes, of any party to the arrangements, in entering into them is to obtain a tax advantage (the *CTA 2010, s 1139* definition applies). Arrangements in turn are defined as including any arrangements, scheme or understanding of any kind, whether or not legally enforceable, involving a single transaction or two or more transactions.

For the purposes of this provision an amount is regarded as not being fully recognised in a company's accounts where either no amount is recognised in respect of the creditor relationship or an amount is only recognised in respect of part of the relationship. Under this provision a company is treated as remaining a party to a creditor relationship in cases where the company has disposed of its rights under the creditor relationship under a repo or stock lending transaction, or under a transaction which is treated as not involving any disposal by virtue of *TCGA 1992, s 26*.

Where the above conditions are satisfied the company is required to recognise the full amount of the credits arising in respect of the creditor relationship during the accounting period. Where a company partially recognises credits arising in respect of the creditor relationship in its accounts, the credits that are recognised under this provision have to be determined using the same basis of accounting. In other cases an amortised cost basis of accounting has to be used to determine the credits to be brought into account under this provision. Where this provision applies, however, a company is not permitted to bring any debits into account in respect of the creditor relationship where the company became a party to the tax avoidance arrangements in question on or after 23 March 2011.

Where pursuant to the tax avoidance arrangements the company becomes, or is treated as becoming, a party to a debtor relationship and in accordance with generally accepted accounting practice an amount is not fully recognised in respect of the debtor relationship, the company is required to recognise the full amount of any credits arising on the debtor relationship. The debits that it is permitted to recognise under this provision may not exceed the credits that are brought into account under this provision in respect of the creditor relationship. Again, where the debtor relationship is partially recognised in the company's accounts the accounting treatment adopted in its accounts will be used to determine the credits and debits to be brought into account under this provision. In other cases an amortised cost basis of accounting has to be used.

[*CTA 2009, ss 311, 312*].

Debits arising from the derecognition of a creditor relationship

[50.15] A company is denied relief under the loan relationships legislation (and cannot otherwise obtain relief for tax purposes) for any debits arising from the derecognition in whole or in part of a creditor relationship where:

(a) the company continues to be a party to the creditor relationship; and
(b) the derecognition results from tax avoidance arrangements to which the company is a party at any time.

Arrangements are tax avoidance arrangements if the main purpose, or one of the main purposes, of any party to the arrangements, in entering into them, is to obtain a tax advantage (the *CTA 2010, s 1139* definition applies). Arrangements in turn are defined as including any arrangements, scheme or understanding of any kind, whether or not legally enforceable, involving a single transaction or two or more transactions.

A company is treated as continuing to be a party to a creditor relationship where it has disposed of the loan relationship under a repo or stock lending transaction or under a transaction which is treated as not involving any disposal as a result of *TCGA 1992, s 26* (mortgages and charges not to be treated as disposals).

[*CTA 2009, s 455A*].

Change of accounting policy

[50.16] The following provisions apply where a company changes the basis of accounting on which credits or debits are calculated from one period (the '*earlier period*') to the next (the '*later period*') if the basis in each period is in accordance with the law and practice applicable to that period and the change is not made to comply with amending legislation not applicable to the earlier period. The change in basis may result from a change in accounting policy (such as the company switching from UK generally accepted accounting practice to international accounting standards or vice versa) or made to comply with a requirement under the loan relationship provisions for credits and debits to be determined on a particular basis (such as where a company has accounted for a creditor loan relationship using a fair value basis and the loan relationship becomes a connected companies relationship so that the company is required to determine the profits or losses using an amortised cost basis).

(a) Any difference between the closing 'tax-adjusted carrying value' of an asset or liability representing a loan relationship in the earlier period and the opening 'tax-adjusted carrying value' in the later period, is treated as a debit or credit (as the case may be).

Where the change in basis is to comply with a requirement for credits and debits to be determined on a particular basis, the debit or credit is brought into account in the later period. Where the change in basis results from a change in accounting policy, the debit or credit is spread over a ten-year period beginning with the later period. One-tenth of the debit or credit is brought into account in each year, but if the company ceases to be within the charge to corporation tax before the end of the ten-year period, any remaining amount is brought into account in the final accounting period.

Where the debit or credit relates to 'own credit risk' (as defined for accounting purposes) which would be recognised in the company's accounts as an item of other comprehensive income under IFRS 9, it is spread over a five-year period as follows starting with the later period: year 1 — 40%; year 2 — 25%; year 3 — 15%; year 4 — 10%; and year 5 — 10%.

Spreading does not apply to debits and credits in relation to loan relationship assets or liabilities falling to be fully discharged at the latest on a date within the later period, so that the debit or credit is brought into account in the later period. This exception is disapplied in respect of a change in basis to adopt IFRS 9 (so that the adjustment is spread even if the loan relationship falls to be discharged in the later period).

Special rules apply to debits and credits in respect of dormant accounts of banks and building societies (see *SI 2004 No 3271, Reg 3B*).

No amount is to be brought into account under the above provisions where a company holds a debtor loan relationship which is the subject of a substantial modification or replacement, and it is reasonable to assume that without the changes to the loan relationship, there would be a material risk that within 12 months, the company would be unable to pay its debts. In addition, no debits will be brought into account that represent the reversal of the excluded credit.

No debits or credits are brought into account if they were recognised in other comprehensive income for accounting periods beginning before 1 January 2016 and were not subsequently transferred to become items of profit or loss in an accounting period beginning before that date.

The above provisions also do not apply to debits and credits where the loan relationship was brought into account in the earlier period at a contract rate and in the later period at a spot rate of exchange, to the extent that those debits and credits are attributable to the different rates of exchange. Also excluded are debits and credits under a loan relationship denominated in a currency other than the company's functional currency, to the extent that they represent the reversal of exchange gains and losses arising to the company in an accounting period before the later period and where those gains and losses have not been brought into account for corporation tax purposes. See also **50.17** below for exchange movements on permanent-as-equity creditor loan relationships.

(b) Where the company ceases to be party to a loan relationship in an accounting period (the '*cessation period*') and *CTA 2009, s 330A* (see **50.13** above) provides for debits and credits to be accounted for as though the relationship had not ceased, then any difference between 'the amount outstanding' in respect of the loan relationship at the end of the earlier period and 'the amount outstanding' at the beginning of the later period is treated as a debit or credit (as the case may be) in the later period.

In (a) above, the '*tax-adjusted carrying value*' means the carrying value of the assets or liabilities recognised for accounting purposes and includes accruals, prepayments and impairment losses (including provisions for bad and doubtful debts), as adjusted for certain provisions (for example, the use of the amortised cost basis where parties are connected as required by *CTA 2009, s 349(2)*) as they apply for the purpose of determining loan relationship debits and credits.

As regards (b) above, '*the amount outstanding*' means so much of the amount recognised in the company's balance sheet as deferred income or loss arising in the cessation period as has not yet brought into account.

These provisions do not apply if the differences as detailed above are otherwise brought into account in computing a company's loan relationship profits.

[*CTA 2009, ss 315, 316, 318, 319, 465B; FA 2019, Sch 12 para 2; SI 2004 No 3271*].

Change in accounting policy where loan relationship as permanent-as-equity

Special transitional provisions apply where a permanent as equity loan had been advanced before the start of a company's first accounting period beginning on or after 1 January 2015 and exchange movements were not brought into account for accounting periods beginning before that date in respect of the loan, either because the exchange movements were recognised in reserves, or the loans were translated using an historic exchange rate (i.e. where the company prepared its accounts in accordance with UK generally accepted accounting practice and did not adopt FRS 26 (and thus FRS 23)). Any transitional adjustments arising on the adoption of FRS 101 or FRS 102 on such a creditor loan relationship in respect of exchange movements are disregarded for the purposes of the above provisions and instead are normally brought into account (under *SI 2002 No 1970, Reg 13*) when the company ceases to be a party to the creditor loan relationship in question.

[*SI 2002 No 1970, Reg 13; SI 2004 No 3256 Reg 12A*].

Exchange gains and losses

[50.17] The general rule is that exchange movements that are recognised as an item of profit or loss in a company's accounts in accordance with generally accepted accounting practice are brought into account in computing its loan relationship profits in the accounting period in which they are so recognised. However, certain movements are expressly excluded as follows:

(1) any exchange gain or loss that arises as a result of the translation of the assets, liabilities, income and expenses of all or part of a company's business from the functional currency of the business, or part of the business, into another currency and that has been recognised as an item of other comprehensive income. The effect of this exclusion is that such amounts will not be taken into account in computing the company's loan relationship profits to the extent that they are recycled from other comprehensive income to profit or loss;

(2) any exchange movements that arise as a result of the change to the functional currency of an investment company. This exclusion does not apply, however, where an investment company has elected to use a designated currency under *CTA 2010, s 9A*; and

(3) any exchange gain or loss arising in respect of a loan relationship which is a designated hedge of a net investment in a foreign operation of the company (e.g. a branch) where amounts representing exchange gains or losses in respect of the loan relationship have, in accordance with generally accepted accounting practice, been recognised in the company's accounts as items of other comprehensive income.

The Treasury has the power, by regulation, to prescribe that exchange gains or losses arising on a company's loan relationships are not to be brought into account on the basis in which they are recognised in a company's accounts in accordance with generally accepted accounting practice but are to be brought into account on some other basis. See **50.18** below for the 'disregard regulations' which permit loan relationships and other money debts to be treated as matched against certain assets.

[*CTA 2009, s 328; SI 2004 No 3256, Reg 5A*].

Matching of exchange gains and losses (the 'Disregard Regulations')

[50.18] There are provisions which enable companies to bring into (or leave out of) account foreign exchange movements which are matched with certain items in computing its loan relationship profits. The provisions are contained in *SI 2004 No 3256*, usually known as the 'Disregard Regulations'.

Matching shares, ships or aircraft

Exchange movements arising on a debtor relationship (including a relevant non-lending relationship within **50.3** above) that is used to hedge exchange movements on shares, ships or aircraft are disregarded in computing loan relationship profits where certain conditions are satisfied. This rule does not apply, however, to the extent that movements in the fair value of, or in profits or losses arising on the disposal of the shares, ships, or aircraft are taken into account in computing the company's profits for the purposes of a trade carried on by it where this trade consists of, or includes, dealing in shares, ships or aircraft.

Where a company acquires the shares, ship or aircraft after it has become a party to the debtor relationship, exchange movements arising on the debtor relationship in the accounting period in which the asset is acquired are only treated as matched to the extent that the exchange movements are attributable, on a just and reasonable basis, to the period for which the company held the asset (and if appropriate, to the extent that the debtor relationship is treated as matched against the asset).

Shares, ships or aircraft are treated as matched to the greatest possible extent first with debtor loan relationships which have been designated as a hedge of that asset (see condition 1 below) and then with debtor loan relationships within condition 2 below.

Condition 1 is satisfied if, for the accounting period in question, the shares, ships or aircraft are a hedged item under a designated hedge of exchange rate risk in which the debtor relationship is the hedging instrument. This is designed to cover cases where a debtor relationship is designed as a fair value hedge of the relevant asset in the company's individual (as opposed to consolidated) accounts.

Condition 2 is that the currency in which the liability is expressed is such that the company intends, by entering into and continuing to be a party to that liability, to eliminate or substantially reduce the economic risk of holding the asset, or part of the asset, which is attributable to fluctuations in exchange rates. In this case a debtor relationship is treated as matched with an asset only to the extent that the carrying value of the debtor relationship does not exceed the unmatched carrying value of the asset at the time at which the company becomes a party to the debtor relationship or, if later, the time at which the asset is acquired. The carrying value of the liability is its value as shown in the company's accounts. The unmatched carrying value of the asset is normally its 'relevant value' to the extent that it has not previously been matched. The 'relevant value' of an asset is the value shown in the company's accounts. In the case of shares this is subject to the election below.

Where a debtor relationship is treated as matched by virtue of condition 2 and only part of the debtor relationship could be regarded as matching an investment in shares, ships or aircraft, matching treatment will only apply to the relevant portion of the debtor relationship.

[*SI 2004 No 3256, Regs 3(1)–(4)(7), 4A(1), 4B, 5(2)*].

Election to match net asset value of shares

A company can make an election at any time for shares held by it to be treated as being matched at the higher of the carrying value of the shares in its accounts and the net asset value underlying such shares (as defined). An election is made by notice in writing to HMRC, and has effect from a date specified in the notice. The election can be revoked before it has taken effect, or from a date specified in the revocation notice, which must be at least 12 months after the election was made. The election has effect for all shares of the company which are matched under condition 2 above or the equivalent rule for matching of derivative contracts. A review period (see below) must be specified. Where the date specified for the election to take effect is not the first day of an accounting period, then the accounting period is split into separate periods falling before and after the date the election takes effect.

Where a company makes such an election, it has to designate a review period. The company may choose the length of its review periods provided that a review period starts with the start of an accounting period (or if later the date when a liability (or derivative contract) is first matched with shares) and a review period ends with the end of an accounting period. The company is required to determine the net asset value underlying the shares in question at the start of each review period and this becomes the value which is eligible to be treated as matched during that period. Where during a review period (current review period) there is an increase or decrease of 10% or more in the net asset value underlying any shares that the company is matching, a new review period is deemed to start in respect of those shares at that time and will end at the end of the current review period. This is to permit a company to vary its hedging in respect of the shares in question at the time that the variation in the net asset value occurs.

[*SI 2004 No 3256, Regs 4A, 4B, 4C*].

Creditor relationship matched with share capital

Provision is also made for exchange movements arising on a creditor relationship which is matched with the whole or part of a company's share capital that is denominated in a foreign currency to be disregarded in computing loan relationships profits. Exchange movements on creditor relationships are also disregarded where matched with the whole or part of any hybrid capital instrument (previously any regulatory capital security — see 50.28 below) issued by the company or, in the case of a building society, any deferred shares issued by the society. In the latter two cases, the disregard applies only to the extent that the instrument or shares are accounted for as equity instruments in accordance with GAAP. The regulations do not specify any other conditions which have to be satisfied in order for such treatment to apply. HMRC provide guidance in the Corporate Finance Manual at CFM62850 as to the circumstances in which they consider that this provision will apply. They suggest that this is most likely where share capital is treated as a financial liability in a company's accounts.

[*SI 2004 No 3256, Reg 3(5)(6); FA 2019, Sch 20 para 9(3)*].

Identification rules

Where a company holds a number of assets in the same currency and has debtor relationships or derivative contracts which are eligible to be treated as matched against such assets, identification rules apply to determine the extent to which an asset is to be treated as matched.

The extent to which an asset is matched is determined in accordance with the following rules:

- Rule 1: Debtor relationships and currency contracts are regarded as matched to the greatest extent possible with assets which are ships or aircraft;
- Rule 2: Subject to Rule 1, debtor relationships and currency contracts are regarded as matched to the greatest possible extent with assets on the disposal of which a chargeable gain would accrue if a disposal were

made on a date falling more than twelve months after the date of acquisition of the asset. This is designed to exclude shares and assets related to shares which are eligible for substantial shareholding relief (*TCGA 1992, Sch 7AC*);

- Rule 3: Subject to Rules 1 and 2, debtor relationships and currency contracts are regarded as matched with assets on the disposal of which no chargeable gain would be treated as accruing by virtue of the substantial shareholding legislation.

[*SI 2004 No 3256, Reg 5*].

Bringing into account of matched exchange gains and losses

[50.19] Any matched exchange gains and losses are only brought into account for tax purposes when a company ceases to own the matched asset. The treatment that applies depends on the nature of the asset.

Shares

In the case of shares the matched exchange movement is dealt with under capital gains rules.

The consideration for the disposal of the shares is increased where a net gain has arisen and is reduced where a net loss has arisen. If the amount of the net loss exceeds the consideration (before adjustment under these provisions) the excess is treated as additional consideration for the acquisition of the shares. The net forex gain or loss must be calculated using the company's 'relevant currency' (see **34.6** FOREIGN CURRENCY) at the time of the disposal. Where there has been a change in the relevant currency, the net gain or loss is re-translated from the previous currency into the new currency based on the spot rate of exchange for the day of the change in currency.

[*SI 2002 No 1970, Regs 2, 4, 5*].

It is possible for the time of recognition of the matched exchange movements to be deferred where a company disposes of shares and the disposal is treated as a no gain no loss disposal for the purposes of *TCGA 1992*.

[*SI 2002 No 1970, Reg 8*].

Loan relationships, ships and aircraft

Where the matched asset is a ship or an aircraft, the matched exchange gain or loss will be brought into account as a loan relationship debit or credit when the company disposes of the asset in question. Where a debtor loan relationship is matched with a creditor loan relationship any exchange gains or losses arising on the debtor relationship are brought into account as a credit or debit under the loan relationship legislation in the accounting period in which the company ceases to be a party to the creditor loan relationship. It is possible for the exchange movements on a creditor loan relationship to be left out of account for tax purposes. In such cases the net exchange movement that has been so disregarded is included in computing the company's loan relationship profits for the accounting period in which it disposes of that creditor loan relationship.

[*SI 2002 No 1970, Regs 6, 13*].

Net investment in a branch

Where the matched asset is a net investment in a branch the matched exchange movement is not brought into account for tax purposes. This is because there is no provision to bring such deferred exchange movements within the charge to tax.

Risk transfer schemes

[50.20] Anti-avoidance legislation applies to counter so-called risk transfer or over hedging transactions. The scheme typically involved one company in a group entering into a cross currency swap in order to hedge exchange exposure arising on an asset owned by another group company. As exchange movements on the cross currency swap were not left out of account for tax purposes, the amount of the swap was grossed up so that, on an after-tax basis, exchange movements on the swap would be equal to exchange movements on the asset. For example, where the rate of corporation tax was 30% and the asset had a cost of US$100, the amount of the US dollar leg of the swap would be $143. The arrangements are called risk transfer schemes as the effect of the over hedging is that the risk of loss is transferred to the Exchequer through tax relief being available for the grossed up loss.

The effect of the legislation is that where a company or a group (an extended definition applies — see *CTA 2010, s 937K*) enters into a risk transfer or over hedging scheme, any exchange losses arising on a loan relationship or derivative contract that forms part of the scheme will be ring fenced to the extent that the loss exceeds the economic loss suffered by the group. Such ring fence losses can only be relieved against future gains which arise to the same company on loan relationships or derivative contracts that form part of the scheme and then only to the extent that the exchange gains exceed the economic profit realised by the group. The economic profit or loss is, in effect, the amount by which the exchange movement on the loan relationship or derivative contract exceed the exchange movement on the asset which is being hedged as part of the scheme.

Whilst the transactions undertaken were transactions to hedge foreign exchange risk, the anti-avoidance legislation will also catch transactions which are 'grossed up' to hedge the RPI or other index or any price or other value.

[*CTA 2010, ss 937A–937O; F(No 2)A 2017, Sch 5 para 7*].

Debt releases and impairment losses

[50.21] Where a company accounts for a loan relationship on an amortised cost basis and it is not connected with the other party to the loan relationship (see **50.23** below), it is able to claim relief for any impairment provision or any impairment losses or losses arising from the release of all or part of the debtor company's obligations under a loan relationship on the basis in which these are reflected in its accounts. If a debtor company accounts for a loan relationship on an amortised cost basis and the debt is released (i.e. the creditor formally waives the obligation to pay), the amount released will normally be included as a credit in the debtor company's loan relationship tax computation. The following paragraphs consider exceptions to these general rules.

Debt releases where credit need not be brought into account

Where a liability under a debtor relationship is released in an accounting period for which the debtor company uses an amortised cost basis of accounting as respects the relationship in question, no credit is required to be brought into account in respect of the release in any of the following circumstances.

(i) The release is part of a statutory insolvency arrangement (see **76.5** WINDING UP).
(ii) Where the release is not a release of 'relevant rights' (i.e. rights within **50.25**(ii) below) and is in consideration of shares (or an entitlement to shares) forming part of the ordinary share capital of the debtor company.
(iii) Where the debtor company is in one of the forms of insolvency procedure noted at **50.25** below and the debtor relationship is not a 'connected companies relationship' (see **50.23** below).
(iv) The relationship is a connected companies relationship. However, this does not apply in the case where a credit is required to be brought into account on a deemed release within **50.25**(i) below. This provision does not affect any credits or debits to be brought into account in respect of exchange gains or losses arising from a debt.
(v) Where the creditor company is in one of the forms of insolvency procedure noted at **50.25** below and the relationship between the parties immediately before but not immediately after the company enters into the insolvency procedure, is a connected companies relationship.
(vi) Where the release occurs as a result of the making of a mandatory reduction instrument or a third country instrument or the application of any of the stabilisation powers contained in the *Banking Act 2009, Pt 1*.
(vii) For releases which are neither deemed releases nor a release of relevant rights (see **50.25**(ii) below), where immediately before the release it is reasonable to assume that, without the release and any arrangements of which the release forms part, there would be a material risk that at some time in the next 12 months, the company would be unable to pay its debts. A company is regarded as being unable to pay its debts if it is unable to pay its debts as they fall due or the value of its assets is less than the amount of its liabilities, taking into account its contingent and prospective liabilities.
(viii) Where a government investment in a company is written off (within the meaning of *CTA 2010, s 92*).

Credits are not prevented from being brought into account under (iv) or (v) above where the debtor relationship has been revalued as a result of it being the hedged item under a designated fair value hedge, to the extent that the credits represent the reversal of revaluation adjustments.

In addition, a company is not required to recognise any credits arising where a debtor loan relationship of the company is modified or replaced by another where:

(a) immediately before the modification or replacement it is reasonable to assume that, without the modification or replacement and any arrangements of which the modification or replacement forms part, there would be a material risk that at some time within the next 12 months, the company would be unable to pay its debts (as defined in (vii) above); and

(b) the modification or replacement is treated for accounting purposes as a substantial modification of the terms of a loan relationship of the company.

Where credits have been excluded under this provision, no debits may be recognised for the purposes of the loan relationships legislation in subsequent accounting periods, to the extent that such debits represent the reversal of credits that have been excluded.

[*CTA 2009, ss 322, 323, 323A, 326, 358, 359*].

Connected companies creditor relationships

See **50.25** below for the denial of relief for impairment losses and release debits arising on a connected companies creditor relationship.

Release of loans to participators

Where a loan to a participator, which has given rise to a charge under *CTA 2010, s 455*, is released or written off in whole or in part, the amount written off may not be treated as a loan relationship debit for loan relationship purposes. [*CTA 2009, s 321A*].

Impairment losses, debt releases and consortium relief

[50.22] The following provision applies to restrict relief where an impairment loss or a debit in respect of a release of liability, has been brought into account in respect of a 'relevant consortium creditor relationship'. For this purpose, a '*relevant consortium creditor relationship*' is a creditor relationship of a company which is a member of a consortium (the '*member company*'), or of any fellow group member (not being a member of the consortium), where a company owned by the consortium (the '*consortium company*') or, where it is a holding company, a consortium company which is its subsidiary, is the debtor. Membership of a group is determined for these purposes as under *CTA 2010, Pt 5* (see **35.3** GROUP RELIEF) and ownership of the consortium company as under *CTA 2010, s 153* (see **35.19** GROUP RELIEF). (Note that this provision does not affect ordinary group relief, since impairment relief is restricted where the parties to the loan relationship are connected under *CTA 2009, s 354* as detailed in **50.25** below.)

The restriction of relief (which effectively allows for relief to be given to the higher of the impairment provision or the group relief claim) works as follows. 'Group relief' for the purposes of these provisions includes group relief for carried-forward losses.

(a) **Restriction of impairment loss debits.** The 'net consortium debit' is reduced (but not below nil) by the amount of any group relief which may be surrendered by the consortium company and which is claimed in the same 'group accounting period' by the member company or by any fellow group member. Where a reduction is to be made to more than one debit (where impairment relief is claimed by more than one company), it is to be apportioned between the debits in proportion to their respective amounts.

The '*net consortium debit*' is the excess of the total impairment losses and release debits brought into account for that accounting period by the member company or by any fellow group members in respect of relevant consortium creditor relationships over the total of any credits so brought into account in that period in respect of debt recoveries from consortium companies in respect of those relationships.

A '*group accounting period*' means any accounting period of the member company or any accounting period of a fellow group member 'corresponding' to such a member company accounting period. Such periods are regarded as the same accounting period for the purposes of this provision. An accounting period of a group member '*corresponds*' to an accounting period of a member company if:

(i) the two accounting periods coincide;
(ii) the accounting period of the member company includes more than half of the accounting period of the group member; or
(iii) the accounting period of the member company includes part of the accounting period of the group member, but the remainder of that period does not fall within any accounting period of the member company.

(b) **Reduction of credits exceeding impairment losses.** Where, in any group accounting period, the total credits brought into account by the member company and any fellow group member in respect of relevant consortium creditor relationships exceed the impairment losses and release debits brought into account by those companies for that period under the relevant relationships, the credits are reduced (but not below nil) as follows. The total cumulative reduction made in earlier group accounting periods to the debits in (a) above (so far as not previously apportioned under this provision) is apportioned between the credits in proportion to their respective amounts.

(c) **Restriction of group relief based on earlier debits.** Any claim for group relief for a group accounting period by the member company or a fellow group member, in respect of amounts available for surrender by debtor consortium companies, is to be reduced (but not below nil) by the cumulative net amount of the net consortium debits for earlier group accounting periods (as reduced under (a) above) in respect of the relevant consortium creditor relationships (i.e. the claim for group relief is to be reduced by the actual amount of debt relief claimed). If there is more than one such group relief claim, the reduction is to be apportioned between them in proportion to their respective amounts.

(d) **Group relief claim to restrict future impairment loss.** Where there is a claim for group relief as in (c) above, but there is no net consortium debit in the same group accounting period in respect of the relevant consortium creditor relationships, the amount of the claim is taken into account when considering restrictions under (a) above in subsequent accounting periods. Thus, the claim for group relief is treated as carried forward for the purposes of this provision to the next accounting period, and, in addition to any actual claim for that period, is used to restrict impairment losses and release debits as under (a) above.

Where any credit is brought into account by the consortium company in respect of the release of a debt owed to the member company, the released amount is not to be treated as a debit by the member company for the purposes of these provisions.

When determining the amount of group relief or group relief for carried forward losses which can be claimed, *CTA 2010, ss 143, 144, 188DH* have priority over this provision. See generally **35.19** onwards GROUP RELIEF for consortium and group relief claims and **35.24** onwards for group relief for carried-forward losses.

[*CTA 2009, ss 364–371; F(No 2)A 2017, Sch 4 paras 130, 131*].

See also HMRC Corporate Finance Manual, CFM35610–CFM35710.

Connected parties

[50.23] If a loan relationship is a 'connected companies relationship' (see **50.24** below), the debits and credits brought into account must be determined on an amortised cost basis of accounting. [*CTA 2009, s 349(2)*].

Where in accordance with generally accepted accounting practice, a creditor company does not accrue interest or discount on a connected companies creditor relationship in its accounts, it will not be required to recognise such interest or discount in computing its loan relationship profits. This is because there is nothing in the definition of an amortised cost accounting treatment that requires interest or discount to be recognised (see *CTA 2009, s 313(4)*).

Adjustments may arise under the provisions for changes in accounting policy at **50.16** above, where a loan relationship either becomes or ceases to be connected, to deal with the move to or from the amortised cost basis.

Where in any period a related transaction (see **50.8** above) takes place in relation to a creditor relationship which is a connected companies relationship, the debits in respect of the relationship for that period shall be no more, and the credits no less, than they would have been had the transaction not taken place (disregarding any amounts which would have accrued after the transaction took place). This does not, however, affect any debits or credits in respect of any changes in the fair value of the asset which are attributable to movements in market interest rates. No amounts are to be brought into account for the purposes of the loan relationships legislation to the extent that these represent the reversal of a debit for which relief has been denied under this provision. These provisions do not affect the debits and credits to be brought into account in respect of exchange gains and losses arising from the debt. [*CTA 2009, ss 352, 352A*].

Loan relationships with a qualifying link

For accounting periods beginning on or after 1 January 2019 (and subject to the transitional rules below), a special rule applies where a company has a connected companies loan relationship subject to the above provisions and is a party to another loan relationship the '*external loan relationship*') which is not a connected companies loan relationship but is a debtor relationship dealt with in its accounts on the basis of fair value accounting. If there is a 'qualifying link' with one or more connected companies relationships, the credits and debits to be brought into account in respect of the external loan relationship must be determined on an amortised cost basis of accounting.

For this purpose, an external loan relationship has a '*qualifying link*' with one or more connected companies loan relationships if, taking the connected companies relationships together, the money received by the company under the external loan relationship is wholly or mainly used to lend money under the connected companies relationships.

Where there is a hedging relationship between a derivative contract and the liability representing the external loan relationship, in applying the amortised cost basis of accounting to that relationship it must be assumed that the derivative has where possible been designated for accounting purposes as a fair value hedge of the loan relationship.

These provisions are subject to the following transitional rules. An accounting period which straddles 1 January 2019 is treated as two separate periods, the second of which begins on that date. If there is a difference between the tax-adjusted carrying value (see **50.16** above) of the liability representing the external loan relationship at the end of the accounting period ending on 31 December 2018 (whether that is a notional or actual accounting period) and its tax-adjusted carrying value at the beginning of the following period (using the amortised cost basis of accounting), a credit or debit of an amount equal to the difference is treated as arising in the later period.

The Treasury can amend the above provisions, and make consequential amendments to other provisions, by regulations made by statutory instrument at any time up to 31 December 2019.

[*CTA 2009, s 352B; FA 2019, Sch 12 paras 1, 3–5*].

Hedging relationship between a derivative contract and a connected companies loan relationship

Where there is a hedging relationship between a derivative contract and a debtor or creditor loan relationship and the loan relationship is carried at fair value in the company's accounts, in applying an amortised cost basis of accounting it is to be assumed that, as far as possible, the derivative contract had been designated as a fair value hedge of the loan relationship. In effect, this means that the loan relationship can be revalued by reference to movements in the risk (normally interest rates) that is being hedged by the derivative contract. For these purposes, there is a hedging relationship if:

(a) the derivative contract is designated as a hedge in the company's accounts; or
(b) in other cases if: the derivative contract is intended to act as a hedge of the exposure to changes in fair value of the loan relationship which is attributable to particular risk and could affect the profit or loss of the company; and, the hedged item (i.e. loan relationship) is an asset or liability recognised for accounting purposes or is an identified portion of such an asset or liability.

[*CTA 2009, ss 349(2A), 475A*].

Meaning of 'connected companies relationship'

[50.24] For this purpose, there is a '*connected companies relationship*' for an accounting period if there is a 'connection' at any time in that period between the company and a company which is a party to the relationship (including any company standing indirectly in that position by reference to a series of loan relationships, or money debts which would be loan relationships were the company a debtor or creditor).

Subject to the exception below, there is a '*connection*' between two companies for an accounting period if at any time in the period one company controls the other or both are under the control of the same person (other than the Crown, a Minister of the Crown, a government or NI department, a foreign sovereign power or an organisation of which two or more sovereign powers, or their governments, are members).

Where a partnership which carries on a trade or a business has a loan relationship with a company, any connection between companies, and the effect of any such connection, is to be determined as though each of the partners (excluding the general partner of a limited partnership which is a collective investment scheme within *Financial Services and Markets Act 2000, s 235*) holds a separate loan relationship with the company equivalent to that partner's share of the partnership's loan relationship. The partner's share is that corresponding to its share in partnership profits.

'*Control*' in relation to a company means the power of a person to secure:

(i) by means of the holding of shares or possession of voting power in, or in relation to, the company or any other company; or
(ii) by virtue of any powers conferred by the articles of association or other document regulating the company or any other company,

that the affairs of the company are conducted in accordance with his wishes.

'*Shares*' for this purpose do not include those held by companies where a profit on sale would be a trading receipt (e.g. banks or financial traders), and powers arising from such shares are similarly excluded. This does not apply where such shares are assets of an insurance company's long-term insurance fund.

Where a partnership has property, rights or powers in a company, these are attributed to company partners in proportion to their share in the partnership profits. This excludes a general partner of a limited partnership which is a collective investment scheme within *Financial Services and Markets Act 2000, s 235* (so that it cannot be regarded as controlling the partnership for the purposes of this provision).

Connection ignored in certain cases

Where a company is party to a creditor relationship, any connection in an accounting period with another company which (directly or indirectly) stands in the position of the debtor is disregarded where the conditions below are met. This does not apply in relation to the other company in relation to its debtor relationship. The conditions are that:

(A) in the course of carrying on activities forming an integral part of a trade carried on in that period the creditor company disposes of or acquires assets representing creditor relationships;

(B) the asset representing the creditor relationship in question was acquired in the course of those activities and is either listed on a recognised stock exchange at the end of that period or a security which must be redeemed within 12 months of issue;

(C) at some time in that period, assets of the same kind as the asset representing the creditor relationship in question are in the beneficial ownership of persons other than the company; and

(D) in not more than three months (in aggregate) in that period is the equivalent of 30% or more of the assets of that kind in the beneficial ownership of connected companies (and a connected company is taken as having beneficial ownership of an asset wherever there is (apart from the current exemption) a connection between the company having beneficial ownership of the asset and a company which (directly or indirectly) stands in the position of debtor as respects the debt by reference to which any loan relationship represented by that asset exists).

As regards (C) and (D) above, assets are taken to be of the same kind where they are so treated by the practice of any recognised stock exchange (or would be if dealt with on such an exchange).

See *CTA 2009, s 471* for the operation of the exemption in the case of an insurance company carrying on basic life and general annuity business.

[*CTA 2009, ss 348, 466–472*].

Simon's Taxes. See D1.720.

Connected companies relationships — impairment losses and release of debts

[50.25] Where *CTA 2009, s 349* (parties to relationship having connection, see 50.23 above) requires an amortised cost basis of accounting to be applied for an accounting period as regards a creditor relationship of a company, no 'impairment loss' or 'release debit' may be recognised except in one of the following circumstances:

(a) where the creditor company is in insolvent liquidation, insolvent administration or insolvent administrative receivership, or a provisional liquidator has been appointed under *Insolvency Act 1986* or NI equivalent, or corresponding processes under non-UK law are in place and the amount in question accrues to the company at any time in the course of the winding up or administration, or when the appointment of the administrative receivership or appointment of the provisional liquidator is in force, or at a corresponding time under the foreign process; or

(b) where the company treats the liability as discharged in consideration of shares (or an entitlement to shares) forming part of the ordinary share capital of the debtor company, and was no connection between the companies before the shares (or entitlement) were acquired.

Where the carrying value of a loan relationship has been adjusted as a result of the asset being the hedged item under a designated fair value hedge (see **50.23** above), any credits or debits are not prevented by the above provisions from being brought into account to the extent that they represent the reversal of such adjustments.

If an impairment loss is not allowed under the above provisions, no credit is to be brought into account for the reversal of the impairment.

These provisions do not affect the debits and credits to be brought into account in respect of exchange gains and losses arising from the debt.

An '*impairment loss*' is a debit relating to an uncollectable amount of the loan or financial asset (i.e. a bad debt). A '*release debit*' is a debit in respect of a release by a company of liability under a creditor relationship.

[*CTA 2009, ss 354, 356, 357, 360, 476(1)*].

Cessation of connection

Where relief for an impairment loss or release debit has been denied in an accounting period due to a connection between the parties as above, and the connection ceases in a subsequent accounting period, no debits are to be brought into account in that or any later accounting period to the extent that they represent the loss or release debit.

[*CTA 2009, s 355*].

Exclusion of credits on release of debt

Where a liability to pay an amount under a debtor relationship is released in an accounting period in which an which an amortised cost basis of accounting is used because the loan relationship is a connected companies relationship, the debtor is not required to bring a credit into account in respect of the release unless:

(i) the release is deemed to occur because of the anti-avoidance rules below; or
(ii) the release is a release of rights of a company (C) that were acquired by C before 18 November 2015 in circumstances that would have been a deemed release but for the application of certain exemptions which applied before that date or were acquired by another company in such circumstances before that day and transferred to C by assignment.

Where (ii) above applies, the amount of the credit to be brought into account is the amount that would have been treated as a release but for the exemption, less any actual credits brought into account in respect of that amount (by C or another company).

Where the carrying value of a loan relationship has been adjusted as a result of the asset being the hedged item under a designated fair value hedge (see **50.23** above), any credits or debits are not prevented by the above provisions from being brought into account to the extent that they represent the reversal of such adjustments.

These provisions do not affect the debits and credits to be brought into account in respect of exchange gains and losses arising from the debt.

[*CTA 2009, s 358*].

Where the release takes place in circumstances where (a) above applies, the debtor is not required to bring a credit into account in respect of the release even if the loan relationship ceased to be a connected companies relationship as a result of the insolvency etc. Again, this rule does not prevent the bringing into account of a credit which represents the reversal of adjustments resulting from the asset being the hedged item under a designated fair value hedge. [*CTA 2009, s 359*].

Anti-avoidance—loan relationship purchased at a discount

An anti-avoidance provision applies to prevent a group of companies from avoiding a tax charge arising on the release of an unconnected party loan relationship by first arranging for the loan relationship to be acquired by a connected company and then arranging for it to be released. The provision applies where the purchaser is connected with the borrower or becomes connected with the borrower in the accounting period of the borrower in which the purchase takes place.

In such cases where the purchase price of the creditor relationship is less than the carrying value of the corresponding debtor relationship, there is deemed to be a release of an amount owed in respect of the debtor relationship equal to that difference and the debtor company is required to include the amount of the deemed release in computing its loan relationship profits. The carrying value of the debtor relationship is determined on the assumption that an accounting period of the debtor company had ended immediately before the time at which the creditor relationship was acquired and in determining the carrying value of the debtor relationship, any accrued amounts or amounts that have been paid or received in advance are ignored.

No charge will arise under this provision where either of the following applies:

(a) the **equity-for-debt exception** which applies where the following two conditions are satisfied:
  (1) the acquisition is an arm's-length transaction; and
  (2) the consideration given by the purchaser for the acquisition consists only of:
    - shares forming part of the ordinary share capital of the purchaser or of a company connected with the purchaser; or
    - an entitlement to ordinary shares in the purchaser or a company connected with the purchaser.

(b) the **corporate rescue conditions** are satisfied and the debt is released by the connected purchaser (or a company that with it) within 60 days after the time that the connected purchaser becomes a party to the creditor loan relationship. Where only part of the debtor loan relationship is released the amount of the deemed release that would otherwise arise is reduced (but not below nil) by the amount that is actually released.

The corporate rescue conditions are that:

(i) the acquisition by the purchaser of its rights under the creditor loan relationship is an arm's-length transaction;
(ii) immediately before the purchaser became a party to the creditor loan relationship, it was reasonable to assume that, without the release and any arrangements of which the release forms part, there would be a material risk that at some time within the next 12 months, the debtor would have been unable to pay his debts. For these purposes, a company is unable to pay its debts if it is unable to pay its debts as they fall due, or the value of its assets is less than the amount of its liabilities, taking into account is contingent and prospective liabilities.

[*CTA 2009, ss 361, 361C, 361D*].

Anti-avoidance—parties becoming connected

A similar anti-avoidance provision applies where a creditor company becomes connected with the company that is a party to the loan relationship as debtor. The creditor company is treated as releasing its rights under the loan relationship when the two companies become connected. A charge will arise in such cases on the difference (if any) between the pre-connection carrying value of the creditor loan relationship in the creditor's accounts and the pre-connection carrying value of the debtor loan relationship in the debtor's accounts.

The pre-connection value of the creditor loan relationship is:

- the value at which the creditor relationship would have been carried in the creditor company's accounts in accordance with an amortised cost basis of accounting on the last day of the period of account preceding that in which it became connected with the debtor company, disregarding accrued amounts and amounts paid or received in advance; or
- where the creditor company only became a party to the creditor relationship in the period of account in which it became connected with the debtor company, the consideration for which the creditor company acquired the creditor relationship.

The pre-connection value of the debtor relationship is the value at which it would have been carried in the debtor company's accounts in accordance with an amortised cost basis of accounting (disregarding accrued amounts and amounts paid or received in advance) had a period of account of the debtor company ended immediately before it became connected with the creditor company and accounts had been drawn up for that period.

Where the corporate rescue conditions are satisfied, no charge arises where the creditor releases the debtor from its obligations in respect of the debtor loan relationship within 60 days of becoming connected. Where the creditor releases the debtor from part of its obligations in respect of the debtor loan relationship, the amount of the deemed release is reduced (but not below nil) by the amount that is released. The corporate rescue conditions are:

(i) the debtor and creditor became connected as a result of an arm's length transaction; and
(ii) immediately before the two companies became connected, it was reasonable to assume that, without the connection and any arrangements of which the connection forms part, there would have been a material risk

that at some time within the next 12 months, the debtor would have been unable to pay its debts. For these purposes, the debtor is treated as being unable to pay its debts if it is unable to pay its debts as they fall due or the value of its assets is less than the amount of its liabilities, taking into account its contingent and prospective liabilities.

[*CTA 2009, s 362, 362A*].

Arrangements for avoiding the anti-avoidance provisions

A further anti-avoidance rule applies where arrangements are entered into and the main purpose, or one of the main purposes, of any party in entering into them (or any part of them) is to avoid a deemed release arising under either of the above anti-avoidance provisions, or to reduce the amount that is treated as released under either of those provisions. Where this rule applies, the arrangements are treated as not having effect so that an amount, or a greater amount, falls to be treated as released under the anti-avoidance provision in question. [*CTA 2009, s 363A*].

For HMRC guidance setting out some of the circumstances in which this rule will or will not apply, see CFM35590–CFM35595. It is understood that HMRC will be prepared to give an advance clearance as to whether or not *CTA 2009, s 363A* will apply to a proposed transaction.

Particular types of loan relationship

Funding bonds issued in respect of interest on certain debts

[50.26] Funding Bonds etc. issued in respect of a liability to pay interest on a debt incurred by any government, public authority or institution, or company are treated as income, the payment of interest equal to the bonds' value when issued; but their eventual redemption is not treated as a payment of the interest. '*Funding bonds*' include 'stocks, shares, securities or certificates of indebtedness' and do not include any instrument providing for payment in the form of goods or services or a voucher.

[*CTA 2009, ss 413, 414*].

Deeply discounted securities

[50.27] A restriction deferring relief for discount applies where:

(I) a debtor relationship of a close company is represented by a 'deeply discounted security' issued by the company;

(II) at any time in the accounting period in question (the 'relevant period'), the creditor as respects that security was either:
   - (i) a 'participator' in the issuing company (within **16.7** CLOSE COMPANIES but see also below) or a person who controls a company which is such a participator (a 'participator company'); or
   - (ii) an 'associate' (within **16.9** CLOSE COMPANIES) of a participator in the debtor company or an associate of a person who controls a participator company; or

(iii) a company 'controlled' by a participator in the debtor company or by a person who controls a participator company. '*Control*' is as defined in *CTA 2009, s 472* (see **50.24** above).

However, the restriction does not apply in relation to the debtor relationship in the case of the following exceptions.

- The discounted security is held by a creditor which is a company and brings into account credits representing the full amount of the discount referable to the period in respect of the corresponding creditor relationship.
- The discounted security is held by a company that is not resident for tax purposes in a non-qualifying territory within the meaning of *TIOPA 2010, s 173* or is effectively managed in a non-qualifying territory under whose laws companies are not liable to tax by reason of domicile, residence or place of management at any time in the accounting period in which the discount accrued.
- The issuing company is a 'CIS-based close company' and is a small- or medium-sized enterprise (as defined by *TIOPA 2010, s 172*), and the creditor is not 'resident' (as defined by *TIOPA 2010, s 172*) in a 'non-qualifying territory' (as defined by *TIOPA 2010, s 173*).
- The debt is owed to (or to persons acting for) a 'CIS limited partnership' no member of which is resident in a non-qualifying territory at any time in the period where the creditor is connected with the debtor (this to be confirmed in writing by the partnership to the debtor company) and the issuing company is a small or medium-sized enterprise.

A '*CIS-based close company*' is a company that would not be close apart from the attribution under *CTA 2010, s 451(4)–(6)* of the rights and powers of a partner in a 'CIS limited partnership' to other partners by virtue of *CTA 2010, s 448(1)(a)*. A '*CIS limited partnership*' is a partnership which is a collective investment scheme or would be if not a body corporate.

'*Participator*' excludes a person who is such by reason only of being a loan creditor of the company, and in the case of a banking business, securities acquired in the ordinary course of the business are disregarded. A participator in a company which controls another company is treated for this purpose as a participator in that other company.

The restriction also applies to a company which indirectly stands in the position of a creditor by reference to a series of loan relationships or money debts which would be loan relationships if a company directly stood in the position of creditor or debtor.

The effect of the restriction is that the debits to be brought into account in respect of the relationship are adjusted so that every debit which relates to the amount of the discount and which is referable to the relevant period is brought into account instead for the accounting period of redemption. The amount of the discount referable to the relevant period for this purpose is the amount which would otherwise be brought into account for the relevant period relating to the difference between the issue price and the amount payable on redemption.

Where the security is held by a person within (II) above for only part of the relevant period, the amount deferred is restricted (on a time basis) to the debit applicable to that part period.

A '*deeply discounted security*' for these purposes is as defined for the purposes of the income tax rules under *ITTOIA 2005, s 430*. It means, broadly, any security which is such that, as at the time of issue, the amount payable on maturity or any other possible occasion of redemption exceeds (or may exceed) the issue price by more than 0.5% of that amount payable on maturity etc. for each year in the 'redemption period' up to a maximum of 30 years. Exclusions include:

(A) shares in a company;
(B) gilt-edged securities which are not strips;
(C) excluded indexed securities (broadly, where the amount payable on redemption is linked to the value of capital gains tax chargeable assets);
(D) life assurance policies and capital redemption policies (see **50.47** below).

[*CTA 2009, ss 406, 409–412, 476(1)*].

Simon's Taxes. See **D1.755**.

Hybrid capital instruments

[50.28] Special rules apply to loan relationships which are 'hybrid capital instruments' with certain limited equity features if the debtor company makes an election to that effect. The provisions apply for accounting periods beginning on or after 1 January 2019, subject to transitional rules which apply to 'transitional qualifying instruments' (see below). For this purpose, accounting periods straddling 1 January 2019 are treated as two separate periods, the second of which begins on that date. [*FA 2019, Sch 20 paras 10, 11*]. The rules replace and expand on those for regulatory capital securities issued by banks and other financial institutions (see further below).

Any 'qualifying amount' payable in respect of a loan relationship which is hybrid capital instrument for an accounting period of the debtor is treated for corporation tax purposes as not being a distribution (and so is not prevented from being treated as interest). A '*qualifying amount*' is an amount that would not be regarded as a distribution if the instrument did not entitle the debtor to defer or cancel a payment of interest. [*CTA 2009, s 420A; FA 2019, Sch 20 para* 2]. A hybrid capital instrument is not a special security by virtue of being an equity note within **29.5**(e) DISTRIBUTIONS, so that amounts payable cannot be treated as distributions on that basis. [*CTA 2010, s 1015(1A); FA 2019, Sch 20 para* 4].

An amount within **50.8**(a)–(c) above in respect of a hybrid capital instrument which, in accordance with GAAP, is recognised in equity or shareholders' funds for a period and is not recognised as an item of profit or loss or of other comprehensive income is nevertheless brought into account as a credit or debit for loan relationships purposes for the period. This rule does not, however, apply to bring into account any exchange gain or loss recognised in the company's statement of total recognised gains and losses, statement of recognised income and expense, statement of change in equity or statement of income and retained earnings. [*CTA 2009, s 320B; FA 2019, Sch 20 para 5*].

Meaning of 'hybrid capital instrument'

A loan relationship is a '*hybrid capital instrument*' for an accounting period of the debtor if the debtor is entitled to defer or cancel a payment of interest under its terms and it has no other significant equity features.

For the above provisions to apply, the debtor company must make an election for hybrid capital instrument treatment. The election is irrevocable and must be made within six months of the day on which the debtor becomes a party to the loan relationship or, if later, the first day of the accounting period following that in which the loan relationship is amended so as to become a hybrid capital instrument. Where the debtor became a party before 1 January 2019, the election must be made no later than 30 September 2019. Where a loan relationship becomes a hybrid capital instrument as a result only of the change made to the meaning of 'conversion event' mentioned below, the election must be made no later than 3 May 2020. Once made, an election has effect for the accounting period in which the debtor becomes a party to the loan relationship or the accounting period following the amendment of the loan relationship and subsequent accounting periods. An election is of no effect, however, if the debtor becomes a party to the loan relationship as a result of, or in connection with, any arrangements with a main purpose of securing a tax advantage for any person.

A loan relationship has no other significant equity features if under it:

(i) there are no voting rights in the debtor (ignoring voting rights of a creditor which are limited to one vote exercisable on matters generally affecting the debtor without conferring any special advantage or other right on the creditor);
(ii) there is no right to give directions on the debtor's operating and financial policies with which it is obliged to comply (even if they are not for the debtor's benefit)
(iii) any provision for altering the amount of the debt is limited to 'write-down events' or 'conversion events' in 'qualifying cases'; and
(iv) any provision for the creditor to receive anything other than interest or repayment of the debt is limited to conversion events in qualifying cases.

A '*write-down event*' is a permanent release of some or all of the debt or a temporary reduction in the amount of the debt, including to nil, whether triggered by the meeting of conditions, the exercise of a right or otherwise. A provision is not treated as failing to meet (iii) above if it provides for an increase in the amount of the debt (but not above the original amount) following a write-down event involving the temporary reduction in the amount of the debt. A '*conversion event*' is the conversion of the loan relationship into shares forming part of the ordinary share capital of the debtor or a company ('C') which, after the conversion, has control of the debtor or would have control of the debtor if C were taken to have all the rights and interests in the debtor of any company connected with C. Note that this definition was amended by *SI 2019 No 1250*, but the revised definition is deemed to have always applied. The original definition was that a conversion event was the conversion of the loan relationship into shares forming part of the ordinary share capital of the debtor or its quoted parent company (defined as at **35.4** GROUP RELIEF). A loan relationship provides for a '*qualifying case*' if either the provision applies only where there is a material risk of the debtor becoming unable to pay its debts on time or the value of the debtor's assets is less than its liabilities (including contingent and prospective liabilities or the provision is included only due to a regulatory or other legal requirement.

The Treasury may amend the above definition by statutory instrument, including with retrospective effect.

[*CTA 2009, s 475C; FA 2019, Sch 20 paras 3, 19; SI 2019 No 1250*].

Regulatory capital securities

For accounting periods beginning before 1 January 2019 and subject to the transitional provisions for transitional qualifying instruments below, a company has a loan relationship if it is an issuer or holder of a regulatory capital security. For this purpose, accounting periods straddling 1 January 2019 are treated as two separate periods, the second of which begins on that date.

A regulatory capital security is broadly defined as a security which qualifies as an Additional Tier 1 instrument or a Tier 2 instrument for the purposes of the Commission Regulation (EU) No 575/20135 (which imposes prudential requirements on financial institutions). For accounting periods commencing on or after 1 January 2016, the definition also includes insurers' Tier 1 and Tier 2 compliant Solvency II instruments issued in the form of debt. Special rules apply though for the issuer of such securities and, in the case of a connected company, the holder of the security. In those cases, the corporation tax provisions treating an embedded derivative or equity instrument as a separate contract are disapplied (see **50.48** below), fair value accounting of the security is not permitted for tax purposes (see **50.10** above) and no credits or debits are brought into account in relation to certain conversions, write-downs and subsequent write-ups of the security. These rules do not apply, however, where the main purpose (or one of the main purposes) of the arrangements is to obtain a tax advantage).

[*SI 2013 No 3209; SI 2015 No 2056; FA 2019, Sch 20 paras 1, 10, 11*].

Transitional rules

A '*transitional qualifying instrument*' is a security which was a regulatory capital security immediately before 1 January 2019. Certain provisions under the regulatory capital security regime continue to apply to such instruments for accounting periods ending on or before 31 December 2023. For this purpose, accounting periods straddling 1 January 2024 are treated as two separate periods, the second of which begins on that date. The provisions in question include the disapplication of the rules treating an embedded derivative or equity instrument as a separate contract and the prohibition on fair value accounting of the security.

Where this transitional rule applies and there is a difference between the tax-adjusted carrying value (see **50.16** above) of the liability representing the external loan relationship at the end of the accounting period ending on 31 December 2023 (whether that is a notional or actual accounting period) and its tax-adjusted carrying value at the beginning of the following period (the

'2024 period'), a credit or debit of an amount equal to the difference is treated as arising in the 2024 period. If the instrument is divided in the 2024 period between a loan relationship and one or more derivative financial instruments or equity instruments, the tax-adjusted carrying value is the sum of the tax-adjusted carrying values of each component.

If a transitional qualifying instrument is a Tier 1 or Tier 2 compliant Solvency II instrument, the provisions relating to write-downs or conversions continue to apply where the writing down or conversion takes place before 1 July 2019.

Where the principal amount of a transitional qualifying security has been temporarily written down and no credit has been brought into account because of the regulatory capital security provisions, no debit is to be brought into account in respect of the writing up of the principal amount in accordance with a regulatory requirement or the provisions governing the security.

[*FA 2019, Sch 20 paras 12–15*].

Gilt-edged securities

Index-linked

[50.29] Where a loan relationship is represented by an index-linked gilt-edged security, the debits and credits brought into account for this purpose must be determined using fair value accounting and an adjustment is to be made wherever the fair value of the security is to be found at two different times, and there is a change in the index of prices by reference to which payments under the security are determined (the 'relevant prices index' (RPI)) between those times. The carrying value of the security is to be increased or decreased, as the case may be, at the earlier time by the same percentage as the percentage increase or reduction in the RPI between the earlier and later time. (Thus, any increase or reduction in value attributable to a change in the RPI is left out of account in computing the loan relationship debit or credit.)

The Treasury may, by order, disapply this provision, or specify a different basis of adjustment, in relation to any description of index-linked gilt (but not with retrospective effect).

Hedging

Where a company acquires index linked gilt-edged securities and the inflation risk is hedged, any increase in carrying value to give relief for the inflation gain will be reduced to the extent of the hedge. This provision prevents the investor from obtaining double relief for the inflationary gain. It applies where there is between two times:

(a) a 'relevant hedging scheme';
(b) an increase in RPI; and
(c) part or all of the 'index-linked capital return' is hedged.

A '*relevant hedging scheme*' is a scheme with the purpose, or one of the main purposes, of any party on entering the scheme is to hedge part or all of the indexed-linked capital return on the security.

The '*index-linked capital return*' is that part of the return which would increase the carrying value of the security and is attributable to the RPI.

The return is hedged if the pre-tax economic profit or loss by the company or group is unaffected by movements in the RPI.

A group is the investing company and all its associates. To be associated, one of five conditions must be met:

(i) the financial results of the companies must meet the consolidation requirement;
(ii) there must be a connection between the companies for the accounting period;
(iii) company A must have a major interest in B or B in A;
(iv) the financial results of A and a third company meet the consolidation requirement and at the relevant time the third company has a major interest in B;
(v) there is a connection between A and a third company and the third company has a major interest in B.

The consolidation requirement is met if consolidated accounts are required under *Companies Act 2006* or exemption applies.

[*CTA 2009, ss 399–400C*].

Strips

Where a gilt is exchanged for strips of the same security, it is treated as redeemed at market value and the strips as acquired at that value in total, apportioned by reference to their own market values. Similarly, where strips are consolidated into a gilt, each strip is treated as redeemed at market value and the gilt as acquired at the sum of those values. The Treasury may make regulations for determining market value for these purposes.

[*CTA 2009, ss 401–403*].

FOTRA securities

A company which is the beneficial owner of a FOTRA security (within *CTA 2009, s 1280(1)*) must not bring into account for loan relationship purposes any amount relating to changes in the value of the security or any debit in respect of the loan relationship represented by the security (including expenses related to holding the security or any transaction concerning it). This provision applies only if the company would be exempt from corporation tax on the security under *CTA 2009, s 1279*.

[*CTA 2009, s 404*].

Simon's Taxes. See D1.755.

Anti-avoidance provisions

Imported losses

[50.30] Special rules apply for an accounting period (the '*loss period*') of a company (the '*chargeable company*') where:

(a) there is a loss arising in connection with a loan relationship of the company which would fall to be brought into account under the loan relationship provisions; and
(b) that loss is wholly or partly referable to a time when the chargeable company (or any predecessor in the same position as respects the loan relationship at that time) would not have been liable to UK tax on any profits arising from the relationship.

In those circumstances, the amounts brought into account in the loss period in respect of that relationship are adjusted to ensure that no part of the loss referable to such a time is treated for the purposes of the current provisions as arising in any accounting period of the chargeable company or as otherwise available to be brought into account for corporation tax purposes.

This provision does not apply where a fair value basis of accounting is used.

[*CTA 2009, s 327*].

Simon's Taxes. See **D1.790.**

Transactions not at arm's length

[50.31] Where debits or credits falling to be brought into account in respect of a loan relationship relate to amounts arising from a non-arm's length 'related transaction' (as in **50.8** above), they are determined on the assumption that the transaction was entered into on the same terms it would have been if at arm's length between knowledgeable and willing independent persons. This does not, however, apply to:

(A) debits arising from the acquisition of rights under a loan relationship for less than market value; or
(B) any related transaction where the transaction is one, or part of a series of transactions, to which **50.40** (continuity of treatment to provide for tax neutral intra-group transactions) below applies or would apply but for the fact that the transferor uses fair value accounting; or
(C) any of a series of transactions by a member of a group which together have the same effect as a related transaction between members of a group; or
(D) exchange gains or losses (but see further below); or
(E) amounts falling within the scope of *TIOPA 2010, Pt 4* (see **72** TRANSFER PRICING) whether or not the amounts fall to be adjusted.

The exclusion at (C) above applies only if both group members are within the charge to corporation tax in respect of the transaction. See **12.2** CAPITAL GAINS — GROUPS with regard to the residence requirements for groups of companies.

[*CTA 2009, ss 444, 445*].

Transactions not at arm's length — Exchange gains and losses

[50.32] Where a company has a debtor relationship in an accounting period, and either:

(i) the whole or part of any interest or other distribution paid in respect of securities of the company representing that relationship falls to be regarded as a distribution under *CTA 2010, s 1015(6)* (see **29.5**, **29.6** DISTRIBUTIONS); or

(ii) the profits and losses of the company fall by virtue of *TIOPA 2010, s 147(3) or (5)* (transactions not made at arm's length) to be computed as if the loan had not, or had not in part, been made,

the whole, or a proportionate part, of any exchange gains or losses arising in respect of a liability representing the debtor relationship are to be left out of account in determining the loan relationship debits and credits.

Where a company has a creditor relationship in an accounting period, and, had the parties been dealing at arm's length, either the transaction giving rise to the loan would not have been entered into at all or the loan would have been smaller, any exchange gains or losses arising in respect of an asset representing the relationship, or in the case of a reduced arm's length loan the non-arm's length proportion thereof, are to be ignored in determining the loan relationship debits and credits. This does not, however, apply to the extent that the same amount of exchange gains or losses is brought into account (or would be brought into account apart from *CTA 2009, s 328(3)–(7)* by a person having a corresponding debtor relationship.

Where the relationship in question is to any extent 'matched', the above provisions apply to leave out of account exchange gains or losses only to the extent that they are unmatched. Where the rule in (i) above or the exception to the creditor relationship rule above applies, the amount left out of account is, if less, the amount which would have been left out of account but for the application of the rule.

A loan relationship is '*matched*' for this purpose if and to the extent that it is in a matching relationship with another loan relationship or derivative contract (i.e. one is intended to eliminate or substantially reduce the risk of the other from exchange rate fluctuations) or exchange gains or losses arising in relation to an asset or liability representing the loan relationship are excluded from being brought into account under the Disregard Regulations (see **50.18** above).

Where a company would be treated as having a debtor relationship if a claim were made under *TIOPA 2010, s 192(1)(2)(4)* (see **72.7** TRANSFER PRICING) and the company is 'connected' (see **50.24** above) with the company which would have the corresponding creditor relationship, in determining the exchange gains and losses to be brought into account in respect of the debtor relationship, it is assumed that such a claim has been made. Where, because of such a claim (whether an actual claim or one deemed to be made under these provisions) one company is treated as having a debtor relationship or more than one company is treated as having a debtor relationship in respect of the same liability, the total credits in respect of exchange gains from the relationships must not exceed the total exchange gains or the proportion of the exchange gains left out of account under (i) above by the issuing company (defined as in *TIOPA 2010, s 191(1)*), and the total debits in respect of exchange losses from the relationships must not exceed the total exchange losses or the proportion of them left out of account under (i) above by the issuing company.

[*CTA 2009, ss 447–452, 475B*].

Countering the effect of avoidance arrangements

[50.33] An anti-avoidance provision applies to counteract the effect of avoidance arrangements. It applies to counter any loan-related tax advantages that would, in the absence of the provision, arise from relevant avoidance arrangements. Where the provision applies the arrangements are counteracted by the making of such adjustments as are just and reasonable in relation to the debits and credits that would otherwise be brought into account for the purposes of the loan relationships legislation. Such adjustments may be made (whether or not by HMRC) by way of an assessment, the modification of an assessment, amendment or disallowance of a claim or otherwise.

A company will obtain a loan-related tax advantage if:

(a) it brings a debit to which it would not otherwise be entitled into account in computing its profits for the purposes of the loan relationships legislation;
(b) it brings a debit into account in computing its profits for the purposes of the loan relationships legislation which exceeds that to which it would otherwise be entitled;
(c) it avoids having to bring a credit into account in computing its profits for the purposes of the loan relationships legislation;
(d) the amount of any credit brought into account by the company in computing its profits for the purposes of the loan relationships legislation is less than it would otherwise be; or
(e) it brings a debit or credit into account in computing its profits for the purposes of the loan relationships legislation earlier or later than it otherwise would.

Arrangements include any agreement, understanding, scheme, transaction or series of transactions (whether or not legally enforceable). Arrangements are relevant avoidance arrangements if their main purpose, or one of their main purposes, is to enable a company to obtain a loan-related tax advantage. Arrangements will not be treated as being relevant avoidance arrangements if the obtaining of any loan-related tax advantages that would, in the absence of this anti-avoidance provision, arise from them can reasonably be regarded as consistent with the principles on which the provisions of the loan relationships legislation that are relevant to the arrangements are based (whether expressed or implied) and the policy objectives of those provisions.

The legislation provides examples of results that may indicate that this exclusion is not applicable. These examples are:

(i) the elimination or reduction, for the purposes of corporation tax, of the profits of a company arising from any of its loan relationships, where for economic purposes profits, or greater profits, arise to the company from that relationship;
(ii) the creation or increase, for the purposes of corporation tax, of a loss or expense arising from a loan relationship, where for economic purposes no loss or expense, or a smaller loss or expense, arises from that relationship;

(iii) preventing or delaying the recognition as an item of profit or loss of an amount that would apart from the arrangements be recognised in the company's accounts as an item of profit or loss, or be so recognised earlier;

(iv) ensuring that a loan relationship is treated for accounting purposes in a way in which it would not have been treated in the absence of some other transaction forming part of the arrangements;

(v) enabling a company to bring into account for the purposes of the loan relationships legislation a debit in respect of an exchange boss, in circumstances where a corresponding exchange gain would not give rise to a credit, or would give rise to a credit of a smaller amount;

(vi) enabling a company to bring into account for the purposes of the loan relationships legislation a debit in respect of a fair value loss in circumstances where a corresponding fair value gain would not give rise to a credit, or would give rise to a credit of a smaller amount;

(vii) ensuring that the effect of the provisions of *CTA 2009, Pt 5 Ch 4* (continuity of treatment of transfers within groups or on reorganisations, *CTA 2009, ss 335–347*) is to produce an overall reduction in the credits brought into account for the purposes of the loan relationships legislation, or an overall increase in the debits brought into account for the purposes of the loan relationships legislation;

(viii) bringing into account for the purposes of the loan relationships legislation an impairment loss or release debit in a case where, but for the arrangements, this would have been prevented by the rules dealing with impairment losses and release debits on connected companies loan relationships (*CTA 2009, ss 353–363A*).

It is provided that in each case the result is only capable of indicating that the exclusion is not available if it is reasonable to assume that such a result was not the anticipated result when the provisions of the loan relationships legislation that are relevant to the arrangements were enacted.

[*CTA 2009, ss 455B–455D*].

Loan relationships for unallowable purposes

[50.34] Any debits which, on a just and reasonable apportionment, are attributable to an 'unallowable purpose' of a loan relationship in an accounting period are not to be brought into account for that period as loan relationship debits or for any other corporation tax purposes. This also applies to both debits and credits in respect of exchange gains and losses. Amounts so excluded are not to be brought into account for corporation tax purposes under any other provision.

A company will be regarded as being a party to a loan relationship for an unallowable purpose where it is a party to the loan relationship at any time during an accounting period, or enters into a related transaction in respect of that loan relationship (essentially an acquisition or disposal of that loan relationship in whole or in part):

(a) otherwise than for its business or other commercial purposes; or

(b) in respect of activities for which it is not within the charge to corporation tax; or

(c) for a tax avoidance purpose.

Paragraph (b) would, for example, catch a loan relationship entered into by a UK permanent establishment of a non-resident company where the loan relates to the company's non-UK operations or a mutual trading company borrowing money to finance its non-taxable mutual activities. Note that it is the company's purpose in being a party to a loan relationship in the accounting period in question only that is taken into consideration for this purpose — see *Fidex Ltd v HMRC* FTT, [2013] SFTD 964. The Upper Tribunal in *Fidex* confirmed the First-tier Tribunal finding that having an unallowable purpose for only a brief period (a 'scintilla' of time) was enough to establish an unallowable purpose for the taxable period in question [2014] UKUT 454.

In the case of (c), a company will be regarded as being a party to a loan relationship or a related transaction for a tax avoidance purpose where the main purpose or one of the main purposes for which it was a party to the loan relationship at that time or for which it entered into the related transaction was to secure a tax advantage, whether for itself or for any other person. '*Tax advantage*' is as widely defined in *CTA 2010, s 1139*.

The definition of a 'related transaction' for these purposes is extended to include anything which equates in substance to a related transaction.

Where the amount of a debit which would otherwise have fallen to be disallowed has been reduced by set off against a credit arising for the purposes of the loan relationships legislation the amount that is to be disallowed is required to be increased by the amount that has been so set off.

[*CTA 2009, ss 441, 442*].

In *Versteegh Ltd v HMRC* FTT 2013, [2014] SFTD 547, the unallowable purpose provisions were held not to apply to the borrower in a case in which a group of companies entered into a tax avoidance scheme designed to achieve a loan relationship debit in the borrowing company (N) without incurring a tax charge in any other group company.

In *Blackrock Holdco 5 LLC v HMRC* FTT 2020, [2021] SFTD 267, the FTT held that the unallowable provisions did not apply in circumstances in which the company had both a commercial purpose and the purpose of securing a tax advantage. Since the securing of the tax advantage had not changed the amount of the debits incurred, all of the debits in question could be allocated to the commercial purpose rather than the tax advantage purpose.

The Court of Appeal considered the 'main purpose' test in *HMRC v Lloyds TSB Equipment Leasing (No 1) Ltd* [2014] EWCA Civ 1062. The decision was in the context of the capital allowance legislation, and notes that the test of 'main objects or one of the main objects' test is different to the test of 'sole or main benefit'. Evidence, such as contemporaneous documents, or witness evidence, is key to the determination. In this case the Court overturned a tribunal decision allowing capital allowances in a leasing structure and held that the tribunal's approach to the 'main object' test appeared to be flawed, and so the Court required the tribunal to reconsider their decision on this point (see FTT, [2015] SFTD 1012).

In *Travel Document Service v HMRC* CA, [2018] STC 723, the court upheld the Tribunal's ruling that the unallowable purpose rules applied to disallow the debits attributable to a deemed loan relationship which was part of a tax avoidance scheme.

For guidance on the application of the unallowable purposes rule see HMRC Corporate Finance Manual CFM38110 onwards.

Simon's Taxes. See **D1.787**.

Company ceasing to be UK-resident etc.

[50.35] Where a company ceases to be UK-resident, it will be deemed to have assigned the assets and liabilities representing its loan relationships immediately before and to have reacquired them immediately after it ceased to be UK-resident, at their fair value. (Thus, any profit or loss on an asset or liability will be brought into account as a loan relationship credit or debit.)

This does not apply, however, if the provisions in **50.40** below apply (application of degrouping charge where a transferee company leaves the group within six years) and the company leaves the group under those provisions at the same time as it ceases to be UK-resident.

It also does not apply if, immediately after the company ceases to be UK-resident, the asset or liability is held for the purposes of the company's UK permanent establishment, its trade of dealing in or developing UK land, or (with effect from 6 April 2020, subject to the transitional provisions at **64.7** RESIDENCE) its UK property business or (with effect from 6 April 2020, subject to those transitional provisions) for the purpose of enabling the company to generate other UK property income.

If an asset or liability held by a non-UK resident company ceases to be held for one of the above purposes (and does not then become held for any other of those purposes), it is treated as if the company had assigned, and immediately reacquired, it immediately before the cessation for its fair value at that time. This does not apply, however, if the provisions in **50.40** below apply and the company leaves the group under those provisions at the same time as it ceases to hold the asset for any of the above purposes.

[*CTA 2009, ss 333, 334; FA 2019, Sch 5 paras 16, 17, 35*].

See **58.19** PAYMENT OF TAX for exit charge payment plans under which a company may pay corporation tax under these provisions by instalments or defer payment.

Group mismatch schemes

[50.36] Legislation applies to counter transactions that seek to exploit an asymmetry in the accounting (and hence tax) treatment of transactions involving loan relationships or derivatives in order for a group (see below) to obtain a tax advantage. Where this legislation applies any profits or losses arising on loan relationships or derivative contracts that form part of the scheme are disregarded for tax purposes. The legislation also applies to transactions that are deemed to be loan relationships for tax purposes including repos and quasi repos and transactions treated as financing arrangements under *CTA 2010, ss 758, 763 and 767* (see *CTA 2010, ss 938I, 938J*).

Scheme profit or loss

The legislation applies to a scheme profit or a scheme loss. This is a profit or loss that forms part of the group mismatch scheme, which, but for this legislation, would be brought into account as a debit or credit for the purposes of the loan relationships or derivative contracts legislation and meets the first or second asymmetry condition.

The first asymmetry condition is that the loss or profit affects the amount of any relevant tax advantage secured by the scheme. Where at the end of an accounting period it is not certain whether the scheme will secure a relevant tax advantage or what the amount of the relevant tax advantage secured by the scheme will be, the first asymmetry condition is regarded as being met if there is a chance that the scheme will secure a relevant tax advantage and the loss or profit will affect its amount.

The second asymmetry condition applies where the loss or profit does not meet the first asymmetry condition but arises from a transaction, or series of transactions, that might (if events had turned out differently) have given rise to a loss or profit that would have met the first asymmetry condition.

[*CTA 2010, s 938C*].

Meaning of group mismatch scheme

A '*scheme*' is defined as including any scheme, arrangements or understanding of any kind whatever, whether or not legally enforceable, involving a single transaction or two or more transactions. [*CTA 2010, s 938H*]. A scheme is a group mismatch scheme if the parties to the scheme are, or include, members of the same group (see below) and condition A or condition B is met.

Condition A is that at the time that the scheme is entered into there is no practical likelihood that the scheme will fail to secure a relevant tax advantage (see below) of £2 million or more.

Condition B is that:

(a) the purpose, or one of the main purposes, of any member of the scheme group in entering into the scheme is to obtain the chance of securing a relevant tax advantage (of any amount); and
(b) at the time the scheme is entered into:
  (i) there is no chance that the scheme will secure a relevant tax disadvantage (see below); or
  (ii) there is such a chance but the expected value of the scheme is nevertheless a positive amount.

If at the time the company enters into the scheme, there are chances that the scheme would, if carried out, secure different relevant tax advantages or disadvantages in different circumstances, the amount and probabilities of each must be taken into account in determining the expected value of the scheme. Where at the time that the scheme is entered into the length of the scheme is uncertain condition A or condition B will be regarded as being met where they would be met on any reasonable assumption as to the length of the scheme period.

[*CTA 2010, s 938B*].

Relevant tax advantage and relevant tax disadvantage

A relevant tax advantage is defined in relation to a scheme as an economic profit:

(a) that is made by the scheme group over the scheme period (defined as the period over which the scheme has effect) which arises as a result of asymmetries in the way different members of the group bring, or do not bring, amounts into account as debits and credits for the purposes of *CTA 2009, Pt 5* or *7* (or for the purposes of *CTA 2009, Pt 3*, where the relevant member of the group is a party to the loan relationship or derivative for the purposes of its trade); and
(b) is not negligible.

A relevant tax disadvantage is in turn defined in relation to a scheme as an economic loss that:

(a) is made by the scheme group over the scheme period and arises as a result of asymmetries in the way different members of the scheme group bring, or do not bring, amounts into account as debits and credits for the purposes of *CTA 2009, Pt 5* or *7* (or for the purposes of *CTA 2009, Pt 3*, where the relevant member of the group is a party to the loan relationship or derivative for the purposes of its trade); and
(b) is not negligible.

Asymmetries are defined as including, in particular, asymmetries relating to quantification and asymmetries relating to timing.

The reference to an economic profit includes an increase in an economic profit and a decrease in an economic loss. Similarly the reference to an economic loss includes an increase in an economic loss and a decrease in an economic profit.

[*CTA 2010, ss 938D, 938K*].

The reference to amounts being not brought into account for the purposes of the loan relationships legislation or the derivative contracts legislation do not include:

(a) a company not bringing amounts into account because the company is not UK resident and the amounts are not attributable to a permanent establishment that the company has in the UK; or
(b) amounts attributable to an overseas permanent establishment of a UK resident company that has made an election to exclude the profits of its foreign permanent establishments from tax under *CTA 2009, s 18A*.

[*CTA 2010, s 938L*].

Economic profit or loss

Whether an economic profit or loss arises to the scheme group as a whole for the purposes of the group mismatch scheme legislation is to be determined by taking into account, in particular:

(a) profits and losses made as a result of the operation of the Corporation Tax Acts; and
(b) any adjustments required to reflect the time value of money.

For these purposes any profits or losses made by a member of the scheme group are only to be taken into account to the extent that they are attributable to times at which the member is a party to the scheme.

In determining the economic profits and losses made by the scheme group as a whole over the scheme period it is to be assumed that each company that is a party to the scheme:

(1) is in a position to fully relieve any losses; and
(2) incurs the full tax cost of any profit made by that company,

where such losses or profits arise in respect of loan relationships or derivative contracts. The full tax cost is defined as the profit that would be brought into account as a credit (or as a reduction of a debit) if the company had no other profits for the period.

[*CTA 2010, ss 938, 938G*].

Priority over other anti-avoidance measures

The group mismatch scheme legislation takes precedence over the following anti-avoidance provisions that are treated as having no effect:

- *CTA 2009, s 441* (loan relationships for unallowable purposes);
- *CTA 2009, 690* (derivative contract unallowable purposes);
- *TIOPA 2010, Pt 4* (transfer pricing);
- *TIOPA 2010, Pt 6* (tax arbitrage — repealed for accounting periods beginning on or after 1 January 2017);
- *TIOPA 2010, ss 259A–259NE* (hybrid mismatches — accounting periods beginning on or after 1 January 2017)
- *TIOPA 2010, Pt 7* (worldwide debt cap legislation — repealed from 1 April 2017); and
- *TIOPA 2010, Pt 10* (25 CORPORATE INTEREST RESTRICTION — from 1 April 2017).

[*CTA 2010, s 938N; F(No 2)A 2017, Sch 5 para 8*].

Meaning of group

For the purposes of the group mismatch legislation a company (company A) is treated as being a member of a group in relation to a scheme if any other company is associated with company A at any time during which the scheme has effect. The group consists of company A and each company with which it is associated. For these purposes another company (company B) is associated with company A at a time (the relevant time) if any of the following conditions is met:

(1) the first condition is that the financial results of company A and company B for a period that includes the relevant time:
  (a) are required to be comprised in group accounts;
  (b) would be required to be comprised in such accounts but for the application of an exemption; or
  (c) are included in group accounts;

(2) the second condition is that there is a connection between company A and company B for the accounting period of company A in which the relevant time falls. There will be a connection for these purposes where one company controls the other or both companies are under the control of the same person (the *CTA 2009, s 472* definition of 'control' applies — see **50.24** above);

(3) the third condition is that at the relevant time company A has a major interest in company B or company B has a major interest in company A ('major interest' has the meaning of *CTA 2009, ss 473, 474* — see **50.11** above);

(4) the fourth condition is that:
  (a) the financial results of company A and a third company, for a period that includes the relevant time:
    (i) are required to be comprised in group accounts;
    (ii) would be required to be comprised in such accounts but for the application of an exemption; or
    (iii) are comprised in such accounts; and
  (b) at the relevant time the third company has a major interest in company B (within the meaning of *CTA 2009, ss 473, 474*);

(5) the fifth condition is that:
  (a) there is a connection between company A and a third company for the accounting period of company A in which the relevant time falls; and
  (b) at the relevant time the third company has a major interest in company B (within the meaning of *CTA 2009, ss 473, 474*).

[*CTA 2010, s 938E*].

Tax mismatch schemes

[50.37] The tax mismatch scheme legislation was introduced by counter avoidance schemes intended to defeat the group mismatch scheme legislation at 50.36 above.

Disregard of scheme profits and losses

Where a company is at any time a party to a 'tax mismatch scheme', any 'scheme loss' or 'scheme profit' cannot be brought into account as a debit or credit under the loan relationships or the DERIVATIVE CONTRACTS (27) regimes and is disregarded for all other corporation tax purposes. [*CTA 2010, s 938O*].

Definitions

A 'scheme' is a '*tax mismatch scheme*' if either:

(1) at the time it is entered into there is no practical likelihood (disregarding the current provisions) that the scheme will fail to secure a 'relevant tax advantage' of £2 million or more; or

(2) a main purpose of the company in entering into the scheme is to obtain the change of securing a relevant tax advantage (of any amount) and, when the company enters into the scheme, there is no chance that it will secure a 'relevant tax disadvantage' or, if there is such a chance, the expected value of the scheme is nevertheless a positive amount.

In determining whether these conditions are met it must be assumed that the parties actually carry out the scheme. If, when the company enters into the scheme, there are chances that the scheme might secure different relevant tax advantages or disadvantages in different circumstances, the amounts and probabilities of each must be taken into account in determining the expected value in (2) above. If the length of the 'scheme period' is uncertain, each of the above conditions is treated as met if it would be met on any reasonable assumption about the length of that period.

'*Scheme*' includes any scheme, arrangements of understanding of any kind whatever, whether or not legally enforceable, involving a single transaction or two or more transactions. The '*scheme period*' is the period in which the scheme has effect.

The amount in (1) above may be increased by Treasury order.

A '*relevant tax advantage*', is a non-negligible 'economic profit' (or increase in an economic profit) arising over the scheme period from asymmetries in the way the company brings, or does not bring, amounts into account as debits and credits under the loan relationship or derivative contracts regimes. '*Relevant tax disadvantage*' is defined in the same way but by reference to an economic loss (or increase in an economic loss). Asymmetries include in particular asymmetries relating to quantification and timing.

An '*economic profit*' or '*economic loss*' is computed taking into account, in particular, profits and losses made as a result of the operation of corporation tax law and any adjustments required to reflect the time value of money. Profits or losses are only taken into account to the extent that they are attributable to times when the company is a party to the scheme.

The economic profits and losses made by the company over the scheme period are calculated on the assumption that the company:

(1) is in a position to fully relieve any losses; and
(2) incurs the 'full tax cost' of any profit made by that company,

where such losses or profits arise in respect of loan relationships or derivative contracts. The '*full tax cost*' is the increase in the company's corporation tax liability that would result if the profit were brought into account as a credit (or as a reduction of a debit) and the company had no other profits for the period.

A profit or loss is a '*scheme profit*' or '*scheme loss*' if:

- it arises from a transaction or transactions forming part of the scheme;
- it is, or is part of, a debit or credit which, but for the current provisions, would be brought into account as a debit or credit under the loan relationship or derivative contract regimes; and
- it meets one of the two asymmetry conditions.

The first asymmetry condition is that the profit or loss affects the amount of any relevant tax advantage secured by the scheme. Where at the end of an accounting period it is not certain whether the scheme will secure a relevant tax advantage or what the amount of the relevant tax advantage secured by the scheme will be, the first asymmetry condition is regarded as being met if there is a chance that the scheme will secure a relevant tax advantage and the profit or loss will affect its amount. If only part of a profit or loss meets the condition, only that part is a scheme profit or scheme loss.

The second asymmetry condition is that the profit or loss does not meet the first asymmetry condition but arises from a transaction, or series of transactions, that might (if events had turned out differently) have given rise to a loss or profit that would have done so.

The terms 'profit' and 'loss' include profits or losses arising in respect of interest or expenses.

[*CTA 2010, ss 938P–938U*].

Priority over other anti-avoidance provisions

The tax mismatch scheme legislation takes precedence over the following anti-avoidance provisions that are treated as having no effect:

- *CTA 2009, s 441* (loan relationships for unallowable purposes; see **50.34** above);
- *CTA 2009, 690* (derivative contracts for unallowable purposes; see **27.19** DERIVATIVE CONTRACTS);
- *TIOPA 2010, Pt 6* (tax arbitrage — repealed for accounting periods beginning on or after 1 January 2017);
- *TIOPA 2010, ss 259A–259NE* (hybrid mismatches — accounting periods beginning on or after 1 January 2017);
- *TIOPA 2010, Pt 7* (worldwide debt cap legislation — before 1 April 2017); and
- *TIOPA 2010, Pt 10* (**25** CORPORATE INTEREST RESTRICTION — from 1 April 2017).

[*CTA 2010, s 938V; F(No 2)A 2017, Sch 5 para 9*].

Non-market loans

[50.38] There are anti-avoidance provisions intended to prevent a debit arising to a borrower from a discount on a non-market loan where there is no corresponding credit arising to the lender. The provisions apply for an accounting period if a company has a debtor relationship in the period and:

(1) the amount recognised in the company's accounts in respect of the debt at the time the company became party to the debtor relationship was less than the transaction price;
(2) credits in respect of the whole or part of the discount (i.e. the difference between the two amounts in (1) above) were not brought into account under the loan relationship rules; and
(3) where the creditor is a company, it is liable, under the law of a non-qualifying territory (within *TIOPA 2010, s 173*), to tax there by reason of domicile, residence or place of management at any time in the

accounting period or it is effectively managed at any such time in a non-qualifying territory under the law of which companies are not liable to tax by reason of domicile, residence or place of management.

Where these conditions are satisfied, no debit is to be brought into account for the accounting period in respect of the discount or the part of the discount not brought into account by the creditor.

[*CTA 2009, s 446A*].

Disguised interest

[50.39] There are provisions which seek to ensure that the return on a transaction which is designed to produce an interest-like return and which has a tax avoidance purpose (see below) is taxed under the loan relationships legislation.

The legislation applies, subject to a number of exclusions (see below), where:

(a) a company is a party to an arrangement which produces a return for the company on any amount which is economically equivalent to interest (see below). An arrangement is defined as including any agreement, understanding, scheme, transaction or series of transactions (whether or not legally enforceable), other than one which constitutes a finance lease within the meaning of *CAA 2001, s 219; CTA 2009, s 486B(9)*; or

(b) two or more persons are party to an arrangement which produces a return which is economically equivalent to interest for the persons taken together but not for either of them individually. Where a company is a party to such arrangements, its share of the return, determined on a just and reasonable basis, is treated as a profit arising from a loan relationship.

Note, it is possible for a company that is not a party to an arrangement for a tax avoidance purpose to elect that the disguised interest legislation apply to the return. Such an election must be made no later than the time at which the arrangement begins to produce a return for the company and is irrevocable. No election may be made, however, where the arrangement would only be within the disguised interest legislation by virtue of *CTA 2009, s 486B(6)* (return arising to two or more persons — see (b) above). The purpose of this election is to enable a lender under a structured finance arrangement to elect to be taxed under this regime where it might otherwise be taxed on a greater amount than under the disguised interest rules.

[*CTA 2009, ss 486A–486E*].

Tax avoidance purpose

An arrangement will be seen as having a '*tax avoidance purpose*' if it is reasonable to assume that the main purpose or one of the main purposes of the company being a party to the arrangement is to obtain a relevant tax advantage. '*Obtain a relevant tax advantage*' means to secure that the return (or any part of it) is produced in such a way that its treatment for corporation tax purposes is more advantageous to the company than it would be if it were:

(a) charged to corporation tax as income of the company; or
(b) brought into account as income of the company for corporation tax purposes,

at the time at which the amounts would be brought into charge to tax under the disguised interest legislation.

[*CTA 2009, s 486D*].

Return that is economically equivalent to interest

A return will be treated as economically equivalent to interest if (and only if):

(a) it is reasonable to assume that it is a return by reference to the time value of that amount of money;
(b) it is at a rate reasonably comparable to what is (in all the circumstances) a commercial rate of interest; and
(c) at the time when the company becomes party to the arrangement, or if later, when the arrangement begins to produce a return for the company, there is no practical likelihood that the return will cease to be produced in accordance with the arrangement, unless the person making the payment is prevented from producing it by reason of insolvency or otherwise.

Where this provision applies, the debits and credits arising to the company in respect of the return, whether or not recognised in arriving at its accounting profit or loss for the period, have to be determined for the purposes of the loan relationships legislation using an amortised cost basis of accounting. The definition of debits and credits includes exchange gains and losses arising as a result of translating at different times the carrying value of the return or the amount by reference to which the return falls to be produced (i.e. the notional principal).

[*CTA 2009, s 486B*].

Exclusions

The disguised interest rules do not apply to the extent that the return arising to a company:

(a) is charged to, or is brought into account as, income of the company for corporation tax purposes, no later than the time when the amounts are brought into account under the disguised interest rules;
(b) would be included in computing the company's profits for the purposes of the derivative contracts legislation or the intangible fixed assets legislation, but for any exception relating to particular credits or debits. This exclusion does not prevent the disguised interest rules from applying where the profits or losses arising to a company on a derivative are treated as chargeable gains or allowable losses under *CTA 2009, s 641* (see **27.40** DERIVATIVE CONTRACTS);
(c) would be taken into account in computing the company's loan relationship profits under the loan relationship rules (in *CTA 2009, Pt 5*), otherwise than as a result of the disguised interest provisions, but for any exemption relating to particular debits or credits; or

(d) is from an arrangement which only involves relevant shares (see below).

[*CTA 2009, ss 486C, 486E*].

Relevant shares

The disguised interest legislation also does not apply for an accounting period (relevant accounting period) to an arrangement which produces a return for the company (holding company) if the arrangement only involves relevant shares (see below) held by the holding company throughout the relevant period (see below). This thus means that the return must be solely derived from the shares. Where the shares are combined with some other transaction, for example a derivative (e.g. an option or forward over the shares), the legislation is capable of applying.

An arrangement is regarded as only involving relevant shares if and only if the return produced reflects only an increase in the fair value of the shares. This is defined as an amount which the company would obtain from a knowledgeable and willing purchaser of the shares dealing at arm's length [*CTA 2009, s 486E(4)(a)*]. For these purposes, there is an increase in the fair value of the shares even if the increase is realised by the payment of a distribution in respect of the shares.

The relevant period is defined as the period beginning with the later of the time when the company becomes a party to the arrangement and the time when the arrangement begins to produce a return for the company and ending with the earliest of the:

(a) end of the relevant accounting period (see above);
(b) time the company ceases to be party to the arrangement; and
(c) time when the arrangement ceases to produce a return for the company.

Shares are treated as relevant shares if, throughout the relevant period, they are:

(a) fully paid-up shares of a relevant company (see below);
(b) shares of a company, other than a relevant company, which would be accounted for by the issuer as a liability in accordance with generally accepted accounting practice and which produce for the holding company a return in relation to any amount which is economically equivalent to interest. The reason for this exclusion is because such shares could fall to be treated as if they were a loan relationship of the holding company by virtue of the shares accounted as liabilities rules.

For these purposes, shares are treated as being fully paid-up if there are no actual or contingent obligations to meet unpaid calls on the shares or to make a contribution to the capital of the issuer which could affect the value of the shares.

A company is a relevant company if:

(a) it and the holding company are connected companies. The *CTA 2009, s 466* definition of connection applies for these purposes (i.e. one company controls the other or both companies are under the control of the same person);

(b) it is a relevant joint venture company. A company is a relevant joint venture company if: (i) the holding company is one of two persons who, taken together, control the company and the holding company has interests, rights and powers representing at least 40% of the holdings, rights and powers in respect of which the holding company and the second person fall to be treated as controlling the company: and (ii) the second person has interests, rights and powers representing at least 40% but no more than 55% of the holdings, rights and powers in respect of which the holding company and the second person fall to be treated as controlling the company.

(c) it is a controlled foreign company.

[*CTA 2009, s 486E*].

Transfers of loan relationships between members of a group

[50.40] The following provisions apply to ensure that intra-group transactions are tax neutral under the loan relationships regime. The provisions apply where:

(i) as a result of a 'related transaction' (as in **50.8** above) between two members of a group (both being within the charge to corporation tax in respect of the transaction), one of those companies (the '*transferee*') directly or indirectly replaces the other (the 'transferor') as a party to a loan relationship or becomes party to a loan relationship which is 'equivalent' (for which see *CTA 2009, s 338*) to a loan relationship to which the other company has ceased to be a party;

(ii) a series of transactions, having the same effect as a related transaction between two companies each of which has been a member of the same group at some time in the course of those transactions (and would be within the charge to corporation tax in respect of such a related transaction), results in such a replacement; or

(iii) *TCGA 1992, ss 127–130* (equation of original shares and new holding — reorganisation of share capital; see Tolley's Capital Gains Tax) apply (or would apply but for *TCGA 1992, s 116(5)*) as a result of *TCGA 1992, s 135(3)* (which permits an exchange of securities to be treated as a reorganisation) to an exchange and the 'original shares' consist of or include an asset representing a loan relationship. The two companies involved must be resident in different EU member states and the provisions at **50.41** and **50.42** below must not apply to the exchange.

A company is resident in a member state for this purpose if it is within a charge to tax under the law of the State as being resident for that purpose and it is not regarded, for the purposes of any DOUBLE TAX RELIEF (**31**) arrangements to which the State is a party, as resident in a territory not within a member state.

The provisions also apply to certain transfers between insurance companies which result in one replacing the other as a party to a loan relationship (and (i) and (ii) above are correspondingly disapplied to certain such transfers). See *CTA 2009, s 337*.

Where (i) or (ii) above apply, the transferor company is treated as having entered into the transaction (or the first of the series of transactions, as the case may be) in the accounting period in which the transaction takes place for a consideration equal to the 'notional carrying value' of the loan relationship asset or liability. The transferee is treated as having acquired the loan relationship asset or liability for a consideration equal to that amount for any accounting period in which it is party to the relationship.

The '*notional carrying value*' is the amount that would have been the tax-adjusted carrying value of the asset or liability in the transferor's accounts had a period of account ended immediately before the company ceased to be party to the loan relationship. Where a discount arises (see further below) in respect of the transaction (or series of transactions or transfer), the consideration treated as receivable by the transferor company is to be increased by the amount of the discount (but the consideration treated as payable by the transferee is not increased). See **50.16** for the meaning of 'tax-adjusted carrying value'.

A '*relevant transaction*' is a related transaction (as in **50.8** above) or the first of a series of related transactions or a transfer by virtue of which these provisions apply or would apply but for the transferor company using fair value accounting (see below).

A discount arises, in particular, where the payment of the transfer consideration is deferred, the amount of the consideration exceeds what the purchaser would have paid if payment had been required in full at the time of sale and it is reasonable to regard some or all of the excess as representing a return on an investment of money at interest.

The transfer pricing provisions of *TIOPA 2010, Pt 4* (see **72** TRANSFER PRICING) do not apply to amounts so determined as above.

'Group' for these purposes is as under *TCGA 1992, s 170* (see **12.2** CAPITAL GAINS — GROUPS).

Where (iii) above applies, debits and credits are brought into account as if the transaction had been a disposal of the loan relationship constituting or included in the original shares at its notional carrying value.

See **58.20** PAYMENT OF TAX for CT payment plans which allow for payment by instalments where a transaction (or the first in a series of transactions) results in a company being directly or indirectly replaced as a party to a loan relationship by a company resident outside the UK in an EEA state, and the transaction would have been within the above provisions if the transferee were UK-resident. Plans can be entered into in respect of transactions occurring in accounting periods ending on or after 10 October 2018.

Fair value accounting

The above provisions do not apply where the transferor uses fair value accounting in respect of the loan relationship. Instead, where (i) or (ii) above applies, the amount to be brought into account by the transferor company is the fair value of the asset (or rights under or interest in the asset) or liability as at the date on which the transferee becomes a party to the loan relationship. Where the payment of the transfer consideration is deferred, the amount of the consideration exceeds what the purchaser would have paid if payment had been required in full at the time of sale and it is reasonable to regard some or all of the excess as representing a return on an investment of money at interest, this element of the purchase price will be included in computing the transferor's profits but the transferee will be unable to obtain relief for this amount.

The transferee is treated as acquiring the asset or liability for a consideration equal to the same amount as that brought into account by the transferor company ignoring any deemed interest element of the consideration that is required to be brought into account by the transferor.

Where (iii) above applies, the amount to be brought into account by the transferor is the fair value of the asset (or rights under or interest in the asset) as at the date of the exchange. The company acquiring the loan relationship is treated as acquiring it for the same amount as that brought into account by the transferor.

For these purposes, a company is regarded as using fair value accounting as respects a loan relationship only if the debits and credits brought into account in respect of the relationship are determined for the purposes of the loan relationships legislation on a fair value basis, whether or not it otherwise uses fair value accounting as respects the relationship.

[*CTA 2009, ss 335–343, 480(5)*].

Degrouping charge

A degrouping charge applies where, after replacing the transferor as party to a loan relationship as in (i) or (ii) above, the transferee ceases within the 'relevant six-year period' to be a member of the group. The '*relevant six-year period*' is the period of six years following the related transaction or the last of the series of transactions.

In this case, the transferee company is treated (subject to the conditions below) as having assigned the loan relationship asset or liability immediately before the cessation for consideration equal to its fair value at that time and as having immediately reacquired it for the same amount where a gain or loss would arise. (Thus, any gain, or loss as applicable, is brought into charge to tax under the loan relationship provisions immediately before the transferee leaves the group.)

Where an asset or liability is transferred in the course of a transfer or merger to which **50.41** or **50.42** below applies and as a result the transferee leaves a group, the transferee is not treated for these purposes as leaving the group. If the transferee becomes the member of another group, it is treated for the purposes of these provisions as if that group and the original group were the same.

The degrouping charge does not apply where the transferee company ceases to be a member of the group by reason only of an exempt distribution within *CTA 2010, s 1075*. However, if there is a chargeable payment (within the meaning of *CTA 2010, s 1088(1)*) within five years after making the exempt distribution, a degrouping charge arises as above but the transferee company is treated as having assigned the loan relationship asset or liability immediately before making the chargeable payment for a consideration equal to its fair value at the time the company left the group.

[*CTA 2009, ss 344–346*].

European cross-border mergers

[50.41] The following provisions apply to:

(a) (before Brexit IP completion day (11pm on 31 December 2020)) the formation of an SE by the merger of two or more companies in accordance with *Council Regulation (EC) No 2157/2001, Arts 2(1), 17(2)*;

(b) (before Brexit IP completion day) the formation of an SCE by the merger of two or more 'co-operative societies', at least one of which is a society registered under *Co-operative and Community Benefit Societies Act 2014*, in accordance with *Council Regulation (EC) No 1435/2003*;

(c) a merger effected by the transfer by one or more companies of all their assets and liabilities to a single existing company or co-operative society; and

(d) a merger effected by the transfer by two or more companies of all their assets to a single new company (which is not an SE or SCE) in exchange for the issue by the transferee company of shares or debentures to each person holding shares in or debentures of a transferee company.

From Brexit IP completion day, no new SEs or SCEs can be formed in the UK.

Each of the merging companies must be resident in a relevant state, but not all can be resident in the same state. A company is resident in a relevant state for this purpose if it is within a charge to tax under the law of the State as being resident for that purpose and it is not regarded, for the purposes of any DOUBLE TAX RELIEF (**31**) arrangements to which the State is a party, as resident in a territory not within a relevant state.

A '*relevant state*' is an EU member state or, after the end of the Brexit implementation period, the UK or an EU member state.

For the purposes of (b) above, a '*co-operative society*' is a society registered under *Co-operative and Community Benefit Societies Act 2014* or a similar society established under the law of a relevant state other than the UK.

Where:

(i) immediately after the merger the transferee is within the charge to corporation tax; and

(ii) for mergers within (a), (b) or (c) above, the transfer of assets and liabilities is made in exchange for the issue of shares in or debentures of the transferee to the holders of shares in or debentures of a transferor, except where, and to the extent that, the transferee is prevented from meeting this requirement by reason only of *Companies Act 2006, s 658* (rule against limited company acquiring its own shares) or a corresponding provision in another relevant state,

then, in determining the debits and credits to be brought into account in respect of a loan relationship, if an asset or liability representing the loan relationship is transferred in the course of the merger, the transfer is treated as having been made for a consideration equal to the notional carrying value (see **50.40** above). For mergers falling within (d) above, and in the case of mergers falling within (c) above where the transfer is not made in exchange for shares in the transferee, in the course of the merger the transferor must cease to exist without being liquidated. Where the transferor's profits and losses arising on loan relationships that are transferred are determined for the purposes of the loan relationship legislation using a fair value basis of accounting. Instead, the amount to be brought into account by the transferor is the fair value of the asset (or rights under or interest in the asset) or liability as at the date on which the transferee becomes a party to the loan relationship. The transferee is treated as acquiring the asset or liability for a consideration equal to the amount brought into account by the transferor.

[*CTA 2009, ss 431–434, 439, Sch 2 para 70; egs 1, 16(6)(7)(9); European Union (Withdrawal Agreement) Act 2020, Sch 5 para 1(1)*].

Reorganisations involving loan relationships

Where *TCGA 1992, ss 127–130* (equation of original shares and new holding — reorganisation of share capital; see Tolley's Capital Gains Tax) apply, or would apply but for *s 116(5)* (reorganisations involving a qualifying corporate bond), to a reorganisation taking place on or after 1 January 2007 and the 'original shares' consist of or include an asset representing a loan relationship, then, if the above provisions apply to a transfer in the course of the merger in which the reorganisation occurs, debits and credits are brought into account as if the reorganisation had been a disposal of the asset representing the loan relationship at its notional carrying value (see **50.40** above).

This rule also applies if the above provisions do not apply only because (i) above is not satisfied if in the course of the merger a UK-resident company transfers to a company resident in another member state all assets and liabilities relating to a business which it carried on in a member state other than the UK through a permanent establishment and the transfer includes the transfer of an asset or liability representing a loan relationship.

Where the original holder of the original shares is regarded (as above) as using fair value accounting in respect of the loan relationship constituting or included in the original shares, the above rule does not apply. Instead, the amount to be brought into account by the original holder is the fair value of the asset (or rights under or interest in the asset) representing the loan relationship as at the date of the reorganisation. The successor creditor company (i.e. the company which holds the creditor relationship immediately after the reorganisation) is treated as acquiring the asset for a consideration equal to the amount brought into account by the original holder.

[*CTA 2009, ss 435, 436*].

Anti-avoidance

The above provisions do not apply unless the merger is effected for genuine commercial reasons and is not part of a scheme or arrangements of which the main purpose or one of the main purposes is avoiding a liability to tax. Advance clearance can be obtained that this condition is met.

[*CTA 2009, s 437*].

Transparent entities

The above provisions do not apply to a transfer, resulting from a merger, of the assets and liabilities of a 'transparent entity' to another company. The reorganisation provisions above do not apply to the new holding if as a result of a merger the assets and liabilities of one or more other companies are transferred to a transparent entity. as a result of a merger.

A '*transparent entity*' for this purpose is an entity which is resident in a relevant state other than the UK and is listed as a company in the Annex to the Mergers Directive, but which does not have an ordinary share capital.

[*CTA 2009, s 438; SI 2019 No 689, Reg 16(8)*].

Cross-border transfers of business within the EC

Transfer of UK business

[50.42] Special provisions apply where:

(i) a company resident in one relevant state transfers the whole or part of a business carried on in the UK to a company resident in another relevant state in exchange for shares or debentures issued by the latter company, and both companies make a claim; or

(ii) a company resident in a relevant state transfers part of a business that is carried on in the UK to one or more companies all of which are resident in relevant states and at least one transferee is resident in a relevant state other than that in which the transferor is resident, the transferor continues to carry on a business after the transfer, and either the transfer is made in exchange for an issue of shares or debentures of the transferees to the holders of shares and debentures in the transferor, or the only reason that this is not done is a legal prohibition on acquisition of own shares.

A '*relevant state*' is an EU member state or, after the end of the Brexit implementation period (11pm on 31 December 2020), the UK or an EU member state.

In either case, the transferee, or each of the transferees must be within the charge to corporation tax immediately after the transfer.

Where the above conditions are satisfied, a claim is made by all the parties and an asset or liability representing a loan relationship is transferred during the transfer, that asset or liability is treated as transferred at its notional carrying value (see 50.40 above).

This does not apply where the transferor is regarded as using fair value accounting in respect of the loan relationship. Instead, the amount to be brought into account by the transferor is the fair value of the asset (or rights under or interest in the asset) or liability as at the date on which the transferee becomes a party to the loan relationship. The transferee is treated as acquiring the asset or liability for a consideration equal to the amount brought into account by the transferor. For this purpose, a company is regarded as using fair value accounting as respects a loan relationship only if the debits and credits brought into account in respect of the relationship for the purposes of the loan relationships legislation are determined on a fair value basis, whether or not it otherwise uses fair value accounting as respects the relationship.

A company is resident in a member state for the above purpose if it is within a charge to tax under the law of the State as being resident for that purpose and it is not regarded, for the purposes of any DOUBLE TAX RELIEF (**31**) arrangements to which the State is a party, as resident in a territory not within a member state.

[*CTA 2009, ss 421–423, 430, Sch 2 para 70; SI 2019 No 689, Regs 1, 16(4); European Union (Withdrawal Agreement) Act 2020, Sch 5 para 1(1)*].

Reorganisations involving loan relationships

Where *TCGA 1992, ss 127–130* (equation of original shares and new holding — reorganisation of share capital; see Tolley's Capital Gains Tax) apply, or would apply but for *s 116(5)* (reorganisations involving a qualifying corporate bond), to a reorganisation and the 'original shares' consist of or include an asset representing a loan relationship, then, if (ii) above applies to the transfer in the course of which the reorganisation occurs, debits and credits are brought into account as if the reorgansiation had been a disposal of the asset representing the loan relationship at its notional carrying value (see **50.40** above).

This rule also applies if a UK-resident company transfers part of its business which is carried on in a member state other than the UK through a permanent establishment to one or more companies, all of which are resident in member states, if at least one transferee is resident in a member state other than that in which the transferor is resident, the transferor continues to carry on a business after the transfer, and either the transfer is made in exchange for an issue of shares or debentures of the transferees to the holders of shares and debentures in the transferor, or the only reason that this is not done is a legal prohibition on acquisition of own shares.

Where the original holder of the original shares is regarded (as above) as using fair value accounting in respect of the loan relationship constituting or included in the original shares, the above rule does not apply. Instead, the amount to be brought into account by the original holder is the fair value of the asset (or rights under or interest in the asset) representing the loan relationship as at the date of the reorganisation. The successor creditor company (i.e. the company which holds the creditor relationship immediately after the reorganisation) is treated as acquiring the asset for a consideration equal to the amount brought into account by the original holder.

[*CTA 2009, ss 424, 425*].

Anti-avoidance

The above provisions do not apply if the transfers are not executed for genuine commercial reasons or if they form part of a scheme or arrangements a main purpose of which is to avoid income tax, corporation tax or capital gains tax. However, if advance clearance has been sought and given, these exclusions will not apply. See *CTA 2009, ss 427, 428* for the clearance procedures.

[*CTA 2009, s 426*].

Transparent entities

The above provisions do not apply if the transferor is a 'transparent entity'. In addition, the reorganisation provisions above do not apply if the transferee is a transparent entity.

A '*transparent entity*' for this purpose is an entity which is resident in a relevant state other than the UK and is listed as a company in the Annex to the Mergers Directive, but which does not have an ordinary share capital.

[*CTA 2009, s 429; SI 2019 No 689, Reg 16(5)*].

Transfer of non-UK business

See **31** DOUBLE TAX RELIEF.

Miscellaneous provisions concerning loan relationships

Partnerships involving companies

[50.43] Where any of the partners in a firm (i.e. a partnership which carries on a trade or business) is a company, and a money debt is owed to or by the firm, no account is taken of debits or credits in relation to the money debt, or any loan relationship arising from it, in calculating the profits of the firm for corporation tax purposes. Each company partner is instead required to bring into account a share of those debits and credits as follows. The credits and debits are determined separately for each company partner as if the money debt were owed to or by the company for the purposes of its trade or business, and as if anything done by or in relation to the firm in connection with the money debt were done by or in relation to the company. The company must then bring into account a share of those debits and credits corresponding to its share in partnership profits.

Where the company's accounting date or functional currency differs from that of the partnership, HMRC consider that the company is not required to substitute its own accounting date or functional currency for that of the partnership in computing the company partner's credits and debits. (HMRC Corporate Finance Manual CFM36100).

Where a company partner uses fair value accounting for its interest in the partnership, it must use fair value accounting in determining those debits and credits.

Credits and debits relating to exchange gains or losses are generally included in the determination of credits and debits (as in **50.17** above) but may be excluded to the extent that they are recognised in the firm's statement of recognised gains or losses, statement of recognised income and expense, statement of changes in equity or statement of income and retained earnings, to the extent they are carried to and sustained by partnership reserves.

Where the firm holds a deeply discounted security (within the meaning of *ITTOIA 2005, s 430* — see **50.27** above) each partner is treated as beneficially entitled to a separate share of the security corresponding to their share in partnership profits.

Where a company partner is a debtor or creditor in relation to money lent by or to the firm, and the company controls the firm (see **50.24** above), there is deemed to be a connection between the company and any other partner companies which are treated under the above provisions as having a corresponding creditor or debtor relationship, and the connected companies rules apply accordingly (see **50.23** above). Control of the firm may, for this purpose, be by the company alone or by the company together with other company partners which it controls or is controlled by or which are under common control.

[*CTA 2009, ss 380–385, Sch 2 para 71*].

Options etc.

[50.44] Where the amortised cost basis of accounting applies for an accounting period, and the question of an amount becoming due under a loan relationship after the end of the period (or of its amount or timing) depends on the exercise of an option by a party to the relationship, it is assumed that the option will be exercised in the manner which, as at the end of the period, appears most advantageous to that party (disregarding taxation). This applies equally where the option is exercisable by an associate of a party to the relationship (within **16.9** CLOSE COMPANIES), and where a similar power is exercisable other than under an option.

[*CTA 2009, s 420*].

Distributions

[50.45] Except where the distribution arises as a result of or in connection with arrangements one of the main purposes of which is securing a tax advantage (within *CTA 2010, s 1139*), credits relating to any amounts treated as DISTRIBUTIONS (**29**) are excluded from these provisions, but this does not prevent them from being brought into charge to corporation tax for other purposes. Certain amounts are prevented from being distributions for corporation tax purposes and are therefore within the loan relationship provisions: distributions from holdings in OEICs, unit trusts and offshore funds which are treated as rights under creditor relationships (*CTA 2009, s 490(2)*); for accounting periods beginning on or after 1 January 2019, amounts relating to hybrid capital instruments recognised in equity (*CTA 2009, s 320B*); shares subject to outstanding third party obligations and non-qualifying shares (*CTA 2009, s 523(2)(b)*); relevant alternative finance return (*CTA 2010, s 1019*); building society dividends etc. (*CTA 2010, s 1054*); and, dividends, bonuses and other sums payable to shareholders in registered industrial and provident societies and UK agricultural or fishing co-operatives (*CTA 2010, ss 1055, 1057*). Debits relating to any amounts treated as DISTRIBUTIONS (**29**) are excluded from these provisions, but this does not prevent them from being brought into charge to corporation tax for other purposes.

[*CTA 2009, s 465; FA 2019, Sch 20 paras 7, 10, 11*].

Credits and debits relating to capital expenditure

[50.46] A relieving provision applies where debits or credits in respect of a loan relationship are, in accordance with generally accepted accounting practice, included in determining the carrying value of an asset or a liability. In such cases where the profits or losses arising on the asset or liability for corporation tax purposes are not determined by reference to the basis on which they are recognised in the company's accounts in accordance with generally accepted accounting practice the debits and credits that have been so included are brought into account in computing the company's loan relationship profits in the same way as if they had been recognised as an item of profit or loss for the accounting period in which they are so included. Such treatment does not apply in respect of amounts that are capitalised in respect of an intangible fixed asset where an election has been made under *CTA 2009, s 730* to write down the intangible fixed asset on a fixed-rate basis.

Where relief has been claimed under this provision in respect of debits that have been capitalised no debit in respect of the writing down, amortisation, or depreciation may be claimed in respect of the asset or liability under the loan relationship legislation to the extent that such amount is attributable to the debit for which relief has been obtained under the above rules.

[*CTA 2009, s 320*].

In *Stagecoach Group plc v HMRC* FTT, [2016] SFTD 982, a debit in respect of forward subscription agreements made under a scheme for the recapitalisation of two group companies was held not to fall within the above provisions.

Shares accounted for as liabilities

[50.47] Where certain conditions are satisfied a company (investing company) that holds shares in another company is required to treat the shares for tax purposes as if they were a creditor relationship. For this purpose, a share is not defined other than that it excludes a share in a building society.

Where the conditions are met, any distributions received by the investing company in respect of the share are not treated as distributions and thus have to be included in computing the profits arising in respect of the deemed creditor relationship. This does not prevent the dividend from being treated as a dividend for the purposes of determining whether the requirements of the CFC acceptable distribution policy have been satisfied.

Further, the investing company is not permitted to claim relief for any debit arising in respect of the share except in the case of a foreign exchange loss.

There is no requirement that the investing company should follow a particular accounting treatment in respect of the share.

The provisions of *CTA 2009, s 550(3)* (repos: ignoring effect on the borrower of sale of securities) do not apply for the purposes of the shares as liability provisions. The result of this is that where a company sells shares under the terms of a repo, it will not be treated as continuing to own the shares for the purposes of the shares as liabilities provisions. In such cases the return that the company receives from the repo of the shares might be taxable under the disguised interest provisions, where the necessary conditions are satisfied, as it will no longer be derived wholly from share ownership.

[*CTA 2009, ss 521A, 521B*].

Conditions

Such treatment applies where the following conditions are satisfied:

(a) the share would be accounted for by the issuing company as a liability in accordance with generally accepted accounting practice. Note that this condition does not require that the issuing company actually accounts for the share as a liability;
(b) the share produces for the investing company a return on any amount which is economically equivalent to interest. This would cover, for example, a preference share which carries a dividend linked to a rate of interest or a fixed rate preference share;
(c) the issuing company and the investing company are not connected companies. The *CTA 2009, s 466* definition of connection applies;
(d) the share does not fall to be treated for the accounting period in question as if it were a creditor relationship of the investing company because of *CTA 2009, s 490* (holdings in OEICs, unit trusts and offshore funds treated as creditor relationships);
(e) the share is not an excepted share (see below); and
(f) the investing company holds the share for an unallowable purpose (see below).

[*CTA 2009, s 521C*].

Excepted shares

A share will be treated as being an excepted share where it is a qualifying publicly-issued share or it is a share which mirrors a qualifying public issue.

Qualifying publicly-issued share

A share is treated as being a qualifying publicly-issued share if it was issued by a company as part of an issue of shares to persons not connected with the company and less than 10% of the shares in issue are held by the investing company or persons connected with it. The *CTA 2010, s 1122* definition of connection applies for these purposes. This is because this is the 'default' definition of connection for the purposes of the *CTA 2009*.

Mirroring a public issue

A share is treated as mirroring a public issue where it is a first-level or a second-level mirroring share. The legislation refers to what is termed here as a first-level mirroring share as 'mirroring shares'.

A share is treated as a first-level mirroring share where the following conditions are satisfied:

(a) a company (company A) issues shares (the public issue) to persons not connected with the company;

(b) within seven days of that issue, one or more other companies (companies BB) issue the first-level mirroring shares to company A on the same, or substantially the same, terms as the public issue;
(c) company A and companies BB are members of the same group relief group of companies. This is defined as a group of companies for the purposes of *CTA 2010, Pt 5 (group relief)*; and
(d) the total nominal value of the first level mirroring shares does not exceed the nominal value of the public issue.

A share is treated as a second-level mirroring share where:

(a) the share is issued within seven days of the public issue by one or more other companies (companies CC) to one or more of companies BB on the same, or substantially the same, terms as the public issue;
(b) company A, companies BB and companies CC are each members of the same group relief group of companies (within the meaning of *CTA 2010, Pt 5*); and
(c) the total nominal value of the second-level mirroring shares does not exceed the nominal value of the public issue.

The exceptions for first-level and second-level mirroring shares are a little unusual given that the shares as liability provisions do not apply where the investing company is connected with the issuing company for the purposes of *CTA 2009, s 466*. Under this definition one company is connected with the other where one company controls the other or both companies are under the control of the same company. The cases in which company A, companies BB and companies CC will be members of the same group relief group of companies and yet not connected with each other for the purposes of *CTA 2009, s 466* will be very rare. However, there is nothing which requires the first-level mirroring shares or the second-level mirroring shares to continue to be held by company A and companies BB respectively in order for such shares to be treated as being excepted in shares, and thus, the exception will continue to apply where such shares are sold to unconnected companies.

The reason for the inclusion of an exception for first-level and second-level mirroring shares is because the shares as liability provisions were introduced as part of a consultation exercise and there was a request to preserve the provisions for first-level and second-level mirroring shares that were contained in the former *FA 1996, s 91D*.

[*CTA 2009, s 521D*].

Unallowable purpose

An investing company will be treated as holding a share for an unallowable purpose if the main purpose or one of the main purposes for which it holds the share is to obtain a relevant tax advantage. (Note though that even if a share is not held for an unallowable purpose, an investing company may elect for the shares as liabilities rules to apply in relation to the share.)

A relevant tax advantage is where the return produced by the share (or any part of it) is received in a way that means its treatment for corporation tax purposes is more advantageous to the investing company than it would be if the return were:

(a) charged to corporation tax as income of the investing company; or
(b) brought into account as income of the investing company for corporation tax purposes,

at the time when the amount would be brought into account for the purposes of *CTA 2009, s 521B* (i.e. the time that the return would be recognised were the investment in the share treated as an investment in a creditor relationship).

[*CTA 2009, s 521E*].

Beginning or ceasing to fall within the shares as liability provisions

Where a share begins or ceases to fall within the shares as liability provisions, the investing company is treated for the purposes of the loan relationships legislation as having disposed of the share immediately before that time for a consideration equal to the notional carrying value of the shares at that time and as having immediately reacquired the share for the same consideration. The notional carrying value of the share is the amount which would be its tax-adjusted carrying value had a period of account ended immediately before the time that the share began or ceased to fall within the shares as liability provisions.

For capital gains purposes immediately before a share becomes subject to the shares as liability provisions, the investing company is deemed to have disposed of it for a consideration equal to its notional carrying value, and where a share ceases to become subject to the provisions, the investing company is deemed to have acquired the share for its notional carrying value immediately before the shares ceased to be subject to the shares as liability provisions. The definition of notional carrying value is as set out above.

[*TCGA 1992, s 116B; CTA 2009, s 521F*].

Loan relationships with embedded derivatives

[50.48] Special provisions apply where a company, in accordance with generally accepted accounting practice, splits (or 'bifurcates') the rights and liabilities under a loan relationship into those under the loan relationship (the 'host contract') and '*embedded derivatives*' which are those under one or more derivative financial instruments or equity instruments.

In this case, the host contract falls, for corporation tax purposes, within the loan relationship rules and the embedded derivative is treated as a relevant contract under the derivative contracts rules under *CTA 2009, s 585* (see **27** DERIVATIVE CONTRACTS). Note that where the embedded derivative is an equity instrument, it is treated as a relevant contract but, because it will not be treated as a derivative for accounting purposes, it will not meet the accounting test at **27.2** and will therefore not be a derivative contract.

[*CTA 2009, ss 415*].

Under current generally accepted accounting practice, however, bifurcation is less common than in the past. In particular, a company is not permitted to bifurcate an embedded derivative in the following circumstances.

- It adopts FRS102 and accounts for the instrument in accordance with section 12 of FRS102 (and has not chosen to apply the recognition and measurement provisions of IAS39 or IFRS9). The instrument will be carried at fair value through profit or loss.
- It adopts IFRS9 (including through the option under FRS102) in respect of a financial asset. The instrument will typically be carried at fair value through profit or loss.
- It is a micro-entity and adopts FRS105 (although it would be unusual for a micro-entity to hold such instruments). An amortised cost basis will apply under which interest and costs are allocated over the life of the instrument and provision is made for impairment, where appropriate.
- The whole instrument is accounted for at fair value through profit or loss under IAS39 or IFRS9.

Where the instrument is accounted for at fair value through profit or loss, then the fair value movements will typically be brought into account under the loan relationship rules on normal principles.

(HMRC Corporate Finance Manual CFM37780).

Collective investment schemes

[50.49] Special provisions apply in relation to such schemes. Broadly, these are as follows.

Investment trusts and venture capital trusts

Any capital profits or losses arising to an investment trust or a venture capital trust from a creditor relationship must not be brought into account in determining loan relationship credits or debits. Capital profits or losses in this case are those which are accounted for through the capital column of the income statement in accordance with the relevant Statement of Recommended Practice (SORP) (or which would have been so carried had the relevant SORP been correctly applied). The relevant SORP is that relating to the Financial Statements of Investment Trust Companies issued by the Association of Investment Trust Companies in January 2003 and revised in December 2005 (as modified, amended or revised) or any subsequent SORP replacing it.

[*CTA 2009, ss 395, 396*].

See generally **47.2** INVESTMENT TRUSTS and **74** VENTURE CAPITAL TRUSTS.

Authorised unit trusts and open-ended investment companies

'Capital profits, gains or losses' arising to an authorised unit trust or an open-ended investment company on a creditor relationship must not be brought into account as loan relationship debits or credits. '*Capital profits, gains or losses*' in this case are those which, in preparing accounts in accordance with UK generally accepted accounting practice, fall to be dealt with in the statement of total return (under the heading of 'net gains/losses') in accordance with the relevant Statement of Recommended Practice (SORP). The relevant SORP in the case of an authorised unit trust or an open-ended investment company, is that relating to authorised investment funds, issued by the Investment Management Association in November 2008.

[*SI 2006 No 964, Regs 8, 12*].

See generally **45** INVESTMENT FUNDS.

Corporate holdings in authorised unit trusts, open-ended investment companies, and offshore funds

Holdings of rights under a unit trust scheme (other than a non-exempt unauthorised unit trust within **46.22** INVESTMENT FUNDS), shares in an open-ended investment company or an interest in an offshore fund, termed a '*relevant holding*', which fail to satisfy the 'qualifying investments test', are treated for the purposes of the loan relationships provisions as rights under creditor relationships, in relation to which a fair value basis of accounting must be used. A relevant holding does not include arrangements which are investment bond arrangements under the alternative finance arrangement provisions, or holdings in an offshore fund if the income arising to the fund is treated as income of the company. Any distribution in respect of such holdings are not treated as distributions and are taxable within the loan relationship provisions.

Anti-avoidance provisions apply where a company has a relevant holding, and the 'relevant fund' enters into any arrangements, or arrangements are entered into that in whole or in part relate to a relevant fund, the main purpose of which arrangements, or one of the main purposes of which, is to obtain a tax advantage for any person (whether identified when the arrangements are entered into, or not). This includes arrangements entered into at a time when the company does not hold a relevant holding. In such an instance, the company with the relevant holding must make adjustments (as are just and reasonable) to counteract any tax advantage connected in any way with the holding that would be obtained either by the company, or any other person, directly or indirectly as a consequence of such arrangements.

'*Arrangements*' is widely drafted and includes any scheme, arrangement or understanding of any kind, whether or not legally enforceable, involving single or two or more transactions. '*Relevant fund*' means the open-ended investment company, unit trust scheme or offshore fund in which the relevant holding is held, or the same in which a relevant fund has a holding.

The '*qualifying investments test*' requires that not more than 60% of the market value of scheme or fund investments is represented by 'qualifying investments' (defined, broadly, as at **46.6** INVESTMENT FUNDS).

[*CTA 2009, ss 490–497; SI 2006 No 964, Regs 90, 95, 96A*].

Simon's Taxes. See **D1.765**.

Key points on loan relationships

[50.50] Points to consider are as follows.

- Under the loan relationships provisions, all income, gains, profits and losses made by companies on money debts which arise from transactions for the lending of money (i.e. loans) are treated as income items. Interest and certain other amounts arising in respect of money debts which do not arise from the lending of money (such as trade debts) are also taxed under the loan relationship rules. See **50.2** and **50.3** above.

- The credits or debits for an accounting period are brought into account as follows.
  - Where the loan relationship is for trading purposes, they are treated as receipts or expenses of the trade for that period.
  - Where there are credits and/or debits in respect of a non-trading relationship (i.e. '*non-trading credits*' and/or '*non-trading debits*'), they are aggregated, and the net amount is chargeable to corporation tax on income or relievable as a non-trading deficit (see below) as the case may be.
- The provisions which provide relief for loan relationships non-trading deficits were substantially revised by *F(No 2)A 2017*. Where a company has unrelieved deficits for accounting periods beginning before 1 April 2017, the previous rules continue to apply to those deficits. Consequently, records must be maintained to separate such deficits from subsequent deficits carried forward. See **50.5** above.
- The amounts to be brought into account as credits and debits in computing a company's loan relationship profits are amounts that, in accordance with generally accepted accounting practice, are recognised in the company accounts for the relevant period as an item of profit or loss. See **50.10** above.
- Subject to exceptions, exchange movements that are recognised as an item of profit or loss in a company's accounts in accordance with generally accepted accounting practice are brought into account in computing its loan relationship profits in the accounting period in which they are so recognised. See **50.17** above. There are provisions which enable companies to bring into (or leave out of) account foreign exchange movements which are matched with certain items in computing its loan relationship profits. See **50.18** above.
- Where a company is connected with the other party to a loan relationship, it is required to use an amortised cost basis of accounting for that loan relationship and where the loan relationship is a creditor relationship, the company is unable to obtain relief for any impairment losses or any losses arising from a release of all or part of the debt represented by the creditor relationship. Correspondingly, however, a debtor company is generally not liable to tax on the release of a debtor relationship that is a connected companies relationship. Two companies are connected with each other where one controls the other or both are under common control. See **50.23**, **50.24**, **50.25** above.
- Where profits and losses arising on a loan relationship are determined for tax purposes using an amortised cost basis of accounting, it is possible for the loan relationship to be transferred at its

tax-adjusted carrying value to another company in the same group. A degrouping charge may arise where the transferee company leaves the group within six years of the transfer. See 50.40 above.

- There are a number of anti-avoidance rules applicable to the loan relationships provisions. These include the unallowable purpose rule which applies where a company is a party to a loan relationship or enters into a related transaction otherwise than for its business or other commercial purposes, in respect of activities for which it is not within the charge to corporation tax or for a tax avoidance purpose. See 50.34 above.
- The deduction of debits in respect of certain loan relationships may be subject to restriction by the CORPORATE INTEREST RESTRICTION (24).

51

Losses

Cross-reference. See **35.2–35.18** GROUP RELIEF.

Simon's Taxes. See **D1.11**.

See **11.3** CAPITAL GAINS for the treatment of capital.

Introduction to losses

[51.1] There are several ways of obtaining relief for losses of a company, depending on the source of them. The following table illustrates the various reliefs available:

Source of loss	Relief available			
	Current year	Carry back	Carry forward	Paragraph
Trading	y	y	y	51.3, 51.4, 51.7
UK Property	y	n	y	51.10
Overseas income	n	n	y	51.11
Miscellaneous income	y	n	y	51.12
Qualifying charitable donations	y	n	n	51.16

In addition, terminal loss relief may be available on cessation of trading, and under this losses may be carried back up to three years.

Loss relief must generally be claimed. The claim must normally be made in the company's corporation tax return.

However, in *Bloomsbury Verlag Gmbh v HMRC* [2015] UKFTT 660, it is notable that in the unusual circumstance that a company had not filed a return in the year of the losses (because it had not known that it had become UK resident), the First-tier Tribunal found that the losses were available for set-off against profits assessed in later years.

[*CTA 2010, s 37(7)*].

In *English Holdings (BVI) Ltd v HMRC* UT 2017, [2018] STC 220, a non-UK resident company was able to set off against its profits subject to income tax a loss incurred in a trade which, if profitable, would have been subject to corporation tax. (For the charge to corporation tax and income tax on non-resident companies generally see **64.5** RESIDENCE.)

For commentary on devolution of the power to set the corporation tax rate in Northern Ireland to the Stormont Assembly and consequential modification of the treatment of losses, see **1.1** INTRODUCTION: CHARGE TO TAX, RATES AND PROFIT COMPUTATIONS.

Trading losses eligible for relief

[51.2] A loss is not available for relief as a trading loss under **51.3** (current year relief) or **51.4** (carry back relief) below unless:

(a) the trade is carried on in the exercise of functions conferred by or under any enactment (normally any public sector body); or

(b) for the accounting period in question, the trade was carried on on a commercial basis and with a view to the making of a profit either in the trade itself or in any larger undertaking of which it formed part.

A trade carried on so as to afford a 'reasonable expectation of profit' is treated as carried on with a view to making a profit. For a case where the First-tier Tribunal upheld HMRC's contention that the company's trade was not being undertaken with a reasonable expectation of profit and so did not qualify for loss relief see *Glapwell Football Club Ltd v HMRC* [2013] UKFTT 516 (TC).

The questions of commerciality and profit generation were considered by the First-tier tribunal in the similar context of income tax loss relief. In *McMorris v HMRC* [2014] UKFTT 1116 the fact that an activity was carried out with the hope of profit was not sufficient to establish a trade, and in *Dipak Patel v HMRC* [2015] UKFTT 0013 it was held that the business was not being conducted on a commercial basis as the motivation was not to generate profits. In *Akhtar Ali v HMRC* [2016] UKFTT 8 it was found that an activity consisting in the buying and selling of publicly listed shares undertaken by a pharmacist constituted a trade. Mr Ali did have a business plan and the First-tier Tribunal accepted that, particularly 'in the age of the internet', a share trading activity could be operated 'on a shoe string'. However in *Anthony and Julia Rowbottom v HMRC* [2016] UKFTT 9 it was found that the trade carried out by a boat chartering partnership had not been commercial. The tribunal noted this was an objective test, with a distinction being drawn between the serious trader who, whatever his shortcomings in skill or experience, is seriously interested in profit, and the amateur or dilettante. Similarly in *C Lucy v HMRC* [2016] UKFTT 85 the First-tier Tribunal found that the taxpayer had not carried on a trade on a commercial basis, with an important factor being the taxpayer's casual attitude, which suggested he had undertaken his activities as hobbies rather than as commercial ventures.

If there is a change in the manner of carrying on the trade in an accounting period, it is treated as having throughout that period been carried on in the same manner as at the end of that period.

Relief is only allowable for trading losses if the company is carrying on the trade so as to be within the charge to corporation tax in respect of it; for example, a non-resident company carrying on a trade in the UK through a permanent establishment can only get relief for losses incurred by that permanent establishment. If a non-resident company trading abroad becomes UK resident and chargeable to corporation tax in respect of its trade on a particular date, no relief is available for losses incurred before that date.

Trades carried on wholly outside the UK are similarly excluded from current year and carry back loss relief.

With regard to the above restrictions, relief is, however, available to be set off against future income of the same trade under *CTA 2010, s 45*.

[*CTA 2010, ss 36(3), 37, 44, 45*].

See also HMRC Company Taxation Manual CTM4020.

These provisions are without prejudice to those in **51.32** below.

For the determination of the amount of losses see **65.7** RETURNS.

Simon's Taxes. See **D1.1110.**

Trading losses — current year relief

[51.3] A company which 'carries on a trade' may claim that a loss incurred in that trade be set off against total profits (including chargeable gains) of the same accounting period. [*CTA 2010, s 37(1)(2)(3)(a)*]. The claim may also require that any unrelieved balance of the loss be carried back against total profits of the previous accounting period or periods so far as they fall (wholly or partly) within the period of 12 months ending with the start of the loss making period — see **51.4** below.

A trading loss is computed in the same way as trading income.

[*CTA 2009, s 47; CTA 2010, s 35(3)*].

A company '*carries on a trade*' if it is within the charge to corporation tax in respect of that trade. 'Trade' includes, for this purpose, an office. [*CTA 2010, s 36(3)(4)*]. As noted above, no claim under *CTA 2010, s 37* can, however, be made if in the loss-making accounting period the trade is carried on wholly outside the UK.

[*CTA 2010, s 37(5)(6)*].

See also **51.2, 51.33** below for restrictions on this relief.

Note that *capital losses* cannot generally be set off against trading profits (but see **51.27** below regarding certain losses of investment companies on unquoted shares).

See **15.3** CLAIMS. See also generally HMRC Company Taxation Manual, CTM04580 and CTM04590.

Simon's Taxes. See **D1.1104.**

Example

A Ltd is a trading company. Its results for the year ended 31 March 2022 show:

	£
Trading loss	(100,000)
Property income	30,000
Income from non-trading loan relationships	40,000
Chargeable gains	72,000
Management expenses	(20,000)
Qualifying charitable donations	(10,000)

The loss may be relieved as follows:

	£
Property income	30,000
Income from non-trading loan relationships	40,000
Chargeable gains	72,000
	142,000
Deduct Management expenses	(20,000)
	122,000
Deduct Trading loss	(100,000)
	22,000

Deduct Qualifying charitable donations	(10,000)
Taxable Total Profits	£12,000

Trading losses — carry-back relief

[51.4] Where a company incurs a trading loss in an accounting period and makes a claim to set the loss against other profits of that accounting period (see **51.3** above), the claim can also require that the balance of the loss not so relieved be carried back. Thus a claim for current year relief must be made first, where possible. [*CTA 2010, s 37(4)*].

The loss is then set against the profits (including chargeable gains) of preceding accounting periods falling wholly or partly within a specified period immediately preceding the accounting period in which the loss is incurred. The specified period is normally twelve months but has been extended temporarily to three years for losses incurred in accounting periods ending between 1 April 2020 and 31 March 2022 inclusive, subject to certain restrictions (for which see further below). Profits of an accounting period beginning before, and ending within, the specified period are apportioned on a time basis. No relief is available for accounting periods ending earlier. A three-year carry-back period also applies to terminal losses (see **51.8** below). The company must have been carrying on the same trade in the accounting period to which the loss is carried back, and must have done so not wholly outside the UK.

The profits of each accounting period are treated as reduced by losses so carried back. Partial relief claims are not allowed, i.e. if carry-back of a loss is claimed, any part of the loss not relieved in the immediately preceding accounting period must be carried back to the period before that and so on, and losses arising in earlier accounting periods are relieved in priority to those of later periods.

If, for a single accounting period, losses of two or more different accounting periods are to be deducted under these provisions and those at **51.3** above, the deduction is made in the order in which the losses were made, earliest first.

Excess qualifying charitable donations may not be carried back.

See **51.1** above for the time limits for making a claim.

[*CTA 2010, ss 37(3)(b)(4)(6)(8), 38, 40, 42, Sch 2 para 18; FA 2021, Sch 2 para 4*].

See also **51.2** above and **51.32** below.

Temporary extension of carry-back period

As indicated above, the specified carry-back period is extended from twelve months to three years for losses incurred in accounting periods ending between 1 April 2020 and 31 March 2022 inclusive. A number of further rules and restrictions apply to the extension. In applying the rules and restrictions, claims for losses arising in accounting periods ending in the period 1 April 2020 to 31 March 2021 ('2020 claims') are dealt with separately from losses arising in accounting periods ending in the period 1 April 2021 to 31 March 2022 ('2021 claims').

The following rules and restrictions apply (separately to 2020 claims and 2021 claims).

- The total relief for losses carried back by a company which is not a member of a group beyond the normal twelve-month period must be less than £2 million. If there is more than one accounting period ending in the period in question (e.g. for 2020 claims, the year ended 31 March 2021), the limit applies to the total relief for all of the accounting periods. There is no restriction on the loss that can be carried back within the normal twelve-month period.
- A claim which is below a de minimis limit of £200,000 (see further below) may be made outside of the company's tax return. This allows claims, and any resulting repayment, to be made earlier than would otherwise be the case. Claims above the limit ('*non de minimis claims*') must be made in the tax return for the accounting period in which the loss is incurred. A 2020 claim that is not a de minimis claim cannot be made before 31 March 2021. Similarly, a 2021 non de minimis claim cannot be made before 31 March 2022.
- Companies which are members of a group can only make claims for amounts equal to or above the de minimis limit to the extent that relief given beyond the normal twelve-month period in respect of any other claims by the company or other group members (including de minimis claims) total less than £2 million. Such non de minimis claims can only be made if an allocation statement (see further below) has been submitted by the group and the claim is for the amount specified in the statement. If only de minimis claims are made by members of the group, then it appears that the £2 million group cap does not apply. See further below for the effect of making a de minimis claim after an allocation statement has been submitted.
- Whether a company is a member of a group is determined by applying the definition in *CTA 2010, s 269ZZB* (see **51.15** below) at the end of 31 March 2021 for 2020 claims and the end of 31 March 2022 for 2021 claims.

De minimis claims

The following rules apply separately to 2020 claims and 2021 claims determine whether the claim is a de minimis claim. A claim is a de minimis claim only if the relief given in respect of the loss beyond the normal twelve-month period is under £200,000. If there is more than one accounting period ending in the period in question (e.g. for 2020 claims the year ended 31 March 2021), the limit applies to the total relief for all of the accounting periods. It is a further requirement that this condition would still be met if:

- the company had made all capital allowances or other claims which would have increased the amount of the loss;
- it did not surrender any amount as group relief; and
- the claim is for the maximum possible relief.

HMRC can amend the provisions relating to de minimis claims by statutory instrument but not with retrospective effect.

Group allocation statements

A non de minimis claim can only be made by a company which is a member of a group if an allocation statement has been submitted by the group and the claim is for the amount specified in the statement. The following rules regarding allocation statements apply separately to 2020 claims and 2021 claims.

An allocation statement must be submitted by the nominated company (see further below) in writing and received by HMRC before 31 March 2023 in respect of 2020 claims or 31 March 2024 in respect of 2021 claims. It must be signed by an appropriate person on behalf of the nominated company. It must identify the group's ultimate parent and all of its members and list the following:

- the name of any companies which have made de minimis claims and the amount of those claims;
- the total amount of relief given as a result of the de minimis claims; and
- the non de minimis claims that may be made by any group members, specifying the name of each company and the amount of the claim.

The total amounts claimed (including both de minimis and non de minimis claims) must be less than £2 million.

The nominated company may, by notice in writing, amend the statement to change the specification of non de minimis claims at any time within the time limit for making the original statement.

Where a group company makes a de minimis claim after the allocation statement has been submitted, the nominated company must amend the statement by notice within 30 days to include the new claim. If the effect is that the total group claims are £2 million or more, the notice must also amend the non de minimis claims so that the limit is no longer breached. If the nominated company fails to do so, HMRC may amend the non de minimis claims by notice to the nominated company or the ultimate parent company (or both).

Amendments to group companies' tax returns required as a result of the submission or amendment of an allocation statement can be made even if the normal time limits for such amendments have expired.

Only one company can be the nominated company at any time (although different companies can be nominated for 2020 claims and 2021 claims). Nominations must be made in writing and signed by an appropriate person on behalf of the companies making it. The nomination can be made by the ultimate parent, all group members together or by two or more group members with the authorisation of the ultimate parent. A nomination has effect until a new one is made.

If HMRC consider that a company has received an overpayment of relief, they can make an assessment in the amount they consider should be recovered. The amount assessed is treated as if it were an amount assessed under the provisions at **58.24** PAYMENT OF TAX (recovery of excessive repayments).

Anti-avoidance

A company cannot make a 2020 claim if at any time in the period 1 April 2020 to 31 March 2021 it ceases to be a member of a group (within the meaning of *CTA 2010, s 269ZZB* (see **51.15** below)) and a main purpose of its so ceasing is to increase the total relief given as a result of a 2020 claim. An equivalent rule applies to 2021 claims by reference to the period 1 April 2021 to 31 March 2022.

[*FA 2021, Sch 2 paras 4–14; SI 2021 No 704*].

Simon's Taxes. See **D1.1104**.

Trading losses — carry-forward relief

[51.5] The provisions which provide relief for trading losses carried forward were substantially revised by *F(No 2)A 2017*. Subject to transitional rules, different rules apply to losses for accounting periods beginning before 1 April 2017 from those applying to accounting periods beginning on or after that date.

For these purposes, an accounting period which straddles 1 April 2017 is treated as if it were two separate accounting periods, the first ending on 31 March 2017 and the second beginning on 1 April 2017. Any necessary apportionments between the two periods must be made on a time basis unless that would produce an unjust or unreasonable result, in which case a just and reasonable basis must be used. Special rules apply, however, where the amount to be apportioned is either an amount chargeable to corporation tax which would have been less but for the CORPORATE INTEREST RESTRICTION (**25**) provisions or an amount for which relief is available which would have been greater but for the restriction. An amount chargeable to corporation tax which would not have arisen at all but for the restriction provisions is apportioned entirely to the second period.

[*F(No 2)A 2017, Sch 4 paras 190–192*].

For the provisions applicable to post-1 April 2017 losses see **51.6** below. The rules for pre-1 April 2017 are described at **50.7** below, including new rules for carry forward of such losses after 1 April 2017. Note that the pre-1 April 2017 rules continue to apply to losses of furnished holiday lettings businesses (see **60.7** PROPERTY INCOME).

Post-1 April 2017 losses

[51.6] If a company makes a loss in its trade for an accounting period beginning on or after 1 April 2017 (applying the transitional rule at **51.5** above if the period straddles that date), and relief is not given for any amount of the loss under **51.3** or **51.4** above or as GROUP RELIEF (**35**) then the unrelieved amount is carried forward to the next accounting period, provided that the trade continues in that period and that:

(i) the trade did not become small or negligible in the loss-making period;

(ii) relief under **51.3** or **51.4** above was not unavailable because the trade was carried on outside the UK; the trade did not meet the conditions at **51.2**(a)(b) above; one of the restrictions at **51.32** or **51.35** below applied or the loss was that of a separate trade under any of the CREATIVE INDUSTRIES RELIEFS (**26**); and

(iii) relief under **51.3** or **51.4** above would not be unavailable for a loss arising in the next accounting period.

The company may claim for all or part of the unrelieved loss to be deducted from its *total profits* for the next accounting period. Such a claim must be made within two years after the end of the later period or within such further time as HMRC allow. Relief against oil companies' ring-fenced profits is prohibited.

If any amount of the loss remains unrelieved after set off against the total profits of the next accounting period then, if it is not surrendered as group relief for carried forward losses (see **35.24** GROUP RELIEF), the amount may be carried forward to the following accounting period and a further claim made under the above provisions accordingly (and so on for subsequent periods). The company must continue to carry on the trade in the following accounting period. The trade must meet the conditions at **51.2**(a)(b) above in that accounting period and it must not have become small or negligible in the accounting period from which the loss is carried forward.

[*CTA 2010, ss 45A, 45C; F(No 2)A 2017, Sch 4 para 11*].

Where a loss cannot be carried forward as above because any of (i)–(iii) is not met or because of the post-completion losses restriction for film, television and video production companies (see **26.7, 26.13, 26.24** CREATIVE INDUSTRIES RELIEFS), it is nevertheless carried forward and set against any *profits of the same trade* of the next accounting period. This is subject to a claim for any amount of that loss to be excepted from being set against trade profits of the next period (to allow, for example, for any double taxation relief to be used that would otherwise be wasted). Where such a claim is made, or where there are insufficient trade profits in the next period for the whole of the loss to be set off in that period, the amount not set off in that period is carried forward for offset against trade profits of succeeding accounting periods. See **51.7** below for whether the same trade is carried on in subsequent accounting periods. A claim must be made within two years after the end of the later period or within such further time as HMRC allow.

The profits of the trade against which a carried-forward loss can be set are those profits which are chargeable to corporation tax. Where a loss is carried forward to a later accounting period the trading profits for which are insufficient to absorb it, interest and dividends which would be trading receipts but for having been otherwise subjected to tax (as in the case of banks, share dealers, and other companies carrying on financial business) are to be treated as profits of the trade.

[*CTA 2010, ss 45(5), 45B, 45E, 46; F(No 2)A 2017, Sch 4 paras 11, 148*].

If a carried forward loss initially qualifies for set off against total profits but ceases to do so before being fully relieved because the trade fails to meet the conditions at **51.2**(a)(b) above or becomes small or negligible, the remaining amount is instead set off against profits of the trade. This is subject to the same right to make a claim for exception from set off as above. [*CTA 2010, s 45D; F(No 2)A 2017, Sch 4 para 11*].

Pre-1 April 2017 losses

[51.7] Where a company which carries on a trade (see 51.3 above) suffers a loss in that trade in an accounting period beginning before 1 April 2017 (applying the transitional rule at 51.5 above if the period straddles that date), the default position is that those losses may be carried forward and set off against any 'profits of the trade' in succeeding accounting periods. So long as the company carries on the same trade, its trading profits from it are treated as reduced by the losses carried forward (or the balance of such losses not relieved in an earlier accounting period).

Note that these provisions continue to apply after 1 April 2017 to losses of furnished holiday lettings businesses (see 60.7 PROPERTY INCOME).

Where such a loss is carried forward *to* an accounting period beginning on or after 1 April 2017 (again applying he transitional rule at 51.5 above for straddling periods), a claim can be made for any amount of that loss to be excepted from being set against trade profits of that period (to allow, for example, for any double taxation relief to be used that would otherwise be wasted). A claim must be made within two years after the end of the period or within such further time as HMRC allow.

Whether the same trade is being carried on in subsequent accounting periods is a question of fact with each situation being decided on its own facts.

For example, in the case of *Kawthar Consulting Ltd* before the Special Commissioners', a company's activities were described in its accounts as being:

- 'manufacturers, designers, importers, exporters and dealers in computers' for the years ended 31 December 1984 to 1987;
- 'manufacturers, designers, importers, exporters and dealers in computers and computer software' for the years from 1988 to 1997; and
- 'computer consultancy and the provision of management services' for the years from 1998 to 2001.

From 1987 to 1990 the company was mainly concerned with a large project for one client. After 1990, when the client went into administration, the company's turnover flagged until 1997 when another major contract was secured. (The project was run through another group company which provided the necessary software).

The company wanted to carry forward the losses arising in the earlier years to the 1998 accounting period, maintaining that it had throughout carried on the same trade, described as 'IT consultancy': it had never ceased trading nor changed from carrying on one trade to carrying on another.

It was held that there had been a change in the trade in the period after 1997 because:

- the involvement of the other group company constituted a major change in the manner in which company was carrying on its trading activities; and

- there had been an overall change in emphasis of activities towards consultancy services (as opposed to providing computer software etc.).

It was held, the earlier changes prior to 1997 simply amounted to organic developments in the nature of the activities over the years to 1997 and did not amount to a change in the trade of providing computer systems. *Kawthar Consulting Ltd v HMRC* [2005] SSCD 524 (SpC 477).

In *Rolls-Royce Motors Ltd*, a company (run as six divisions) ran into financial difficulties. As part of its recovery plan, the assets and undertakings of four of the divisions were transferred to a Government owned company, with the remaining two being transferred to a subsidiary of the original company. It was held that the subsidiary was not carrying on the same trade as the company before the transfer (as four of the six divisions were now in Government ownership) and therefore losses incurred before the transfer could not be offset against subsequent profits. *Rolls-Royce Motors Ltd v Bamford* Ch D 1976, 51 TC 319.

[*CTA 2010, s 45(1)–(4), Sch 2 para 17; F(No 2)A 2017, Sch 4 para 10*].

For this purpose, a loss is computed in the same way as trading income.

[*CTA 2009, s 47; CTA 2010, s 35(3)*].

See **51.2** above as regards determination of losses, and **35.5** GROUP RELIEF for group relief interaction.

'*Profits of the trade*' means the profits of the trade which are chargeable to corporation tax. Where a loss is carried forward to a later accounting period the trading profits for which are insufficient to absorb it, interest and dividends which would be trading receipts but for having been otherwise subjected to tax (as in the case of banks, share dealers, and other companies carrying on financial business) are to be treated as profits of the trade.

[*CTA 2010, ss 45(5), 46; F(No 2)A 2017, Sch 4 para 148*].

It was held that for interest etc to constitute trading receipts it must arise from capital actively employed in the trade and, in a real and practical sense, at risk in the ordinary course of current trading. Interest etc. received on reserve funds was therefore excluded *Bank Line Ltd v CIR* CS 1974, 49 TC 307.

Similarly it was also held in another case that, when establishing whether interest etc constituted trading income, the crucial test was whether the investments were employed in the business in the year in question. The Court of Appeal, whose judgment was approved, considered decisive the facts that the liabilities against which the investments were provided were liabilities to third parties rather than customers, and that, in view of the long-term nature of the liabilities, the business could be carried on for a long period without maintaining a fund of investments at all. *Nuclear Electric plc v Bradley* HL 1996, 68 TC 670.

(HMRC Business Income Manual, BIM40801, 40805). For the general inclusion of trade interest in trading profits, see **49** LOAN RELATIONSHIPS.

As to whether the successor into which the trade was hived down before sale to the eventual claimant was trading see *Barkers of Malton Ltd v HMRC* [2008] SSCD 884 (Sp C 689).

See **51.26** below for the carry forward of losses in a currency other than sterling where the company prepares its accounts in the foreign currency.

Simon's Taxes. See **D1.1102, D1.1106.**

Examples (A) Carry forward

Z Ltd has been trading for many years and draws up accounts to 31 March each year. For the year ended 31 March 2022, it has trading profits of £75,000 and property income of £130,000. It has trading losses brought forward as follows:

	£
Pre-1 April 2017 losses	100,000
Post-1 April 2017 losses	100,000

The losses can be set off as follows

Y/e 31.3.22		
	£	£
Trading income	75,000	
Deduct pre-1 April 2017 losses brought forward	(75,000)	—
Property income		130,000
		130,000
Deduct post-1 April 2017 losses brought forward		(100,000)
Carried forward trading losses		£30,000
Loss memorandum		
Pre-1 April 2007 loss brought forward		100,000
Relieved in y/e 31.3.22		(75,000)
Pre-1 April 2017 loss carried forward		£25,000

(B) Same year and carry back

For the years ending 31 March 2019 and 31 March 2020, X Ltd has the following results.

	2019	2020
	£	£
Trading profit/(loss)	60,000	(200,000)
Property income	25,000	30,000
Income from non-trading loan relationships	15,000	10,000
Chargeable gains	15,000	45,000
Management expenses	(40,000)	(40,000)

The loss can be relieved as follows.

	£	Loss memorandum £
Year ended 31 March 2020		
Trading loss		(200,000)
Property income	30,000	
Income from non-trading loan relationships	10,000	
Chargeable gains	45,000	
	85,000	
Deduct Management expenses	(40,000)	
	45,000	
Deduct Trading loss	(45,000)	45,000
Taxable total profits	—	
		(155,000)
Year ended 31 December 2019		
Trading income	60,000	
Property income	25,000	
Income from non-trading loan relationships	15,000	
Chargeable gains	15,000	
	115,000	
Deduct Management expenses	(40,000)	
	75,000	
Deduct Loss carried back	(75,000)	75,000
Taxable total profits	—	
Loss carried forward		(£80,000)

(C) Temporary extension of loss carry back period

K Ltd's recent results were as follows:

	12 months 30.11.17 £	12 months 30.11.18 £	12 months 30.11.19 £	8 months 31.7.20 £	12 months 31.7.21 £
Trading income	199,500	150,000	100,000	(250,000)	(450,000)
Property income	10,125	10,125	10,250	6,000	—
Chargeable gain	—	70,000	—	—	20,500

The trading losses can be relieved as follows:

	12 months 30.11.17	12 months 30.11.18	12 months 30.11.19	8 months 31.7.20	12 months 31.7.21
	£	£	£	£	£
Trading profit	199,500	150,000	100,000	—	—
Property income	10,125	10,125	10,250	6,000	—
Chargeable gain	—	70,000	—	—	20,500
	209,625	230,125	110,250	6,000	20,500
Less: Loss relief					
Current period				(6,000)	(20,500)
Carried back from p/e 31.7.20		(133,750)	(110,250)		
Carried back from y/e 31.7.21	(69,875)				
Taxable total profits	139,750	Nil	Nil	Nil	Nil

Loss memorandum		8 months 31.7.20	12 months 31.7.21
		£	£
Loss for period		250,000	450,000
Set against:	Profits of same period *s 37(3)(a)*	(6,000)	(2,500)
	Profits of previous 12 months *s 37(3)(b)*	(110,250)	—
	Extended carry-back *FA 2021, Sch 2*	(133,750)	(69,875)
Unrelieved (for carry-forward)		Nil	£377,625

Note

The 'specified period' for carry-back of the loss of the year ended 31 July 2021 is the three years from 1 August 2017 to 31 July 2020. Thus, only one-third (£69,875) of the profits of the year ended 30 November 2017 are available for offset against the loss of the year ended 31 July 2021.

(D) Accounting periods of different lengths

Y Ltd, which previously made up accounts to 31 December, changes its accounting date after the year ended 31 December 2018 to 30 September. Its results for the accounting periods to 31 December 2017, 30 September 2018 and 30 September 2019 are as follows.

	12 months 31.12.17	9 months 30.9.18	12 months 30.9.19
	£	£	£
Trading profit/(loss)	255,000	(90,000)	(420,000)
Income from non-trading loan relationships	25,000	30,000	—
Chargeable gains	40,000	—	20,000

Y Ltd makes all available loss relief claims so as to obtain relief against the earliest possible profits.

The computations are summarised as follows.

	12 months 31.12.17	**9 months 30.9.18**	**12 months 30.9.19**
	£	£	£
Trading income	255,000	—	—
Income from non-trading loan relationships	25,000	30,000	—
Chargeable gains	40,000	—	20,000
	320,000	30,000	20,000
Loss relief			
CTA 2010, s 37(3)(a)		(30,000)	(20,000)
CTA 2010, s 37(3)(b)	(140,000)		
Taxable total profits	£180,000	—	—

Loss memoranda

	9 months 30.9.18	12 months 30.9.19	Total
	£	£	£
Trading loss	90,000	420,000	510,000
Relieved against current year profits	(30,000)	(20,000)	(50,000)
Relieved by carry-back to y/e 31.12.17	(60,000)	(80,000)	(140,000)
Carried forward	Nil	£320,000	£320,000

Note

The 'specified period' for carry-back of the loss of the year ended 30 September 2019 is the 12 months from 1 October 2017 to 30 September 2018. Thus, only one-quarter (£80,000) of the profits of the year ended 31 December 2017 are available for offset against the loss of the year ended 30 September 2019.

Terminal losses — carry-back relief

[51.8] The relief described at **51.4** above (which permits the carry back of trading losses) also applies where a loss is incurred in the accounting period in which the trade ceases, except that losses incurred in the twelve months prior to cessation may be carried back to accounting periods ending within the three years preceding the start of the accounting period in which the loss is incurred (with losses of any accounting period falling partly within and partly outside that twelve-month period being apportioned on a time basis).

Where the final twelve months straddles two accounting periods this means the part of the terminal loss which arises in the earlier accounting period may be carried back to accounting periods which end more than three years prior to the start of the twelve month terminal loss period.

Claims to relief must be made within two years of the end of the accounting period in which the loss is incurred, or within such further period as HMRC may allow (for which see **51.1** above).

The enhanced carry back of losses does not apply if, when a company ceases to carry on a trade, any of the activities of the trade continue to be carried on by a person or persons not within the charge to corporation tax and the cessation of trade is part of a scheme or arrangement with a main purpose of securing the enhanced carry-back.

[*CTA 2010, ss 39, 41, Sch 2 para 20*].

See also HMRC Manual CTM04520 and CTM04530.

Example

A Ltd ceased to trade on 31 July. Recent results were as follows:

	12 months to 30 Nov Year 1	12 months to 30 Nov Year 2	12 months to 30 Nov Year 3	12 months to 30 Nov Year 4	8 months to 31 July Year 5
	£	£	£	£	£
Trading income	19,500	15,000	10,000	(15,000)	(40,000)
Property income	1,125	1,125	1,250	600	—
Chargeable gain	—	7,000	—	—	2,500

The maximum amount of the loss which can be treated as a terminal loss is the loss for the 12 months to 31 July: Year 5, as follows:

	£
8 months to 31 July: Year 5	40,000
4 months to 30 November: Year 4 (4/12 × 15,000)	5,000
Available for terminal loss relief	45,000

However, part of the loss will be relieved against general profits of the current accounting period, or previous accounting period (as the first prior year of the claim), in this case, leaving a balance of £40,650 (see loss memo below) available for offset against the earlier two prior years as a terminal loss.

The loss arising in the four months to 30 November: Year 4 which forms part of the terminal loss may be carried back to accounting periods ending within the three years preceding the start of this accounting period (1 December: Year 3). Thus this part of the terminal loss may be carried back to the period ending 30 November: Year 1. However, the loss should be set off against profits arising in later periods first (on a LIFO basis).

The terminal loss arising in the 8 month period to 31 July: Year 5 may be carried back to accounting periods preceding the start of this loss making period (1 December: Year 4). Thus this loss may be carried back to the accounting period ending 30 November: Year 2.

The earlier part of the terminal loss is used first as losses of earlier accounting periods are relieved before the losses of later periods.

Therefore, the losses will be relieved as follows:

	12 months to 30 Nov Year 1	12 months to 30 Nov Year 2	12 months to 30 Nov Year 3	12 months to 30 Nov Year 4	8 months to 31 July Year 5
	£	£	£	£	£
Trading result	19,500	15,000	10,000	—	—
Property income	1,125	1,125	1,250	600	—
Chargeable gain	—	7,000	—	—	2,500
	20,625	23,125	11,250	600	2,500
Less: Loss relief					
Current period				(600)	(2,500)
Carried back			(11,250)		
Terminal		(3,150)			
		(19,975)			
Taxable total profits	20,625	Nil	Nil	Nil	Nil

Loss memorandum		12 months to 30 Nov Year 4	8 months to 31 July Year 5
		£	£
Loss for period		15,000	40,000
Set against:	Profits of same period *s 37(3)(a)*	(600)	(2,500)
	Profits of previous period *s 37(3)(b)/ s 39*	(11,250)	—
Balance available as terminal loss (total £40,650)		3,150	37,500
Terminal loss relief (balance) *s 39*		(3,150)	(19,975)
Unrelieved		Nil	19,975

In *Electronics Ltd v HM Inspector of Taxes* [2005] SSCD 512 (Sp C 476), a claim for terminal loss relief on the closure of two of the company's six divisions was denied on the basis that the trade of all six divisions was a single trade. The

Special Commissioners considered the trade of all divisions to be too similar to be broken down into discrete categories and that the place of operational management was not decisive in determining whether there was more than one trade.

HMRC may allow a claim for carry-back of losses from the final period of account of a company which has collapsed despite no formal accounts having been prepared for the period if it is apparent from all the facts that the claimed losses will be significantly less than the losses actually suffered by the company, even after any possible adjustment of the computations for capital items, disallowable expenditure, balancing charges, etc. See HMRC Company Taxation Manual, CTM04570.

Simon's Taxes. See **D1.1110.**

Terminal loss relief for carried forward losses

[51.9] Where a company carries forward a trade loss under the provisions at **51.6** or **51.7** above to the accounting period in which the trade ceases (the '*terminal period*) ') but relief in that period cannot be given under any of those provisions for the whole of the unrelieved loss, the company may make a claim for the unrelieved part of the loss to be set off against the 'relevant profits' of the terminal period and previous accounting periods so far as they fall wholly or partly within the three-year period ending with the end of the terminal period. Profits of an accounting period beginning before, and ending within, that period are apportioned on a time basis. Relief is given for later accounting periods first. A loss cannot be carried back to the accounting period in which it arose or to an earlier accounting period. Nor can it be carried back to a period beginning before 1 April 2017 (applying the transitional rules at **51.5** above to periods straddling that date).

Where the loss carried forward is available for relief against total profits as in **51.6** above, the '*relevant profits*' are the company's total profits. Otherwise, the 'relevant profits' are the profits of the trade.

A claim must be made within two years after the end of the terminal period or within such further period as HMRC allow.

Relief is not available if the company ceases to trade and any of the activities of the trade begin to be carried on by a person or persons outside the charge to corporation tax if the cessation is part of a scheme or arrangements a main purpose of which is to obtain the relief.

[*CTA 2010, ss 45F–45H; F(No 2)A 2017, Sch 4 para 11; FA 2019, Sch 10 para 21*].

Property business losses

UK property businesses

[51.10] Losses incurred in a property income business are:

(i) automatically set against total profits of the same accounting period. (Total profits means profits from any source, including chargeable gains); or

(ii) carried forward, if they cannot be used against total profits. Such losses become a property income business loss of the subsequent period and are available for offset against total profits or further carried forward if not utilised, for so long as the company continues to carry on the property business. Relief is, however, denied for non-commercial losses in the same circumstances as apply in the case of trading losses — see **51.2** above.

For accounting periods beginning on or after 1 April 2017 (subject to the transitional provisions at **51.5** above), relief under (ii) above must be claimed. A claim may be made for all or part of the unrelieved loss and must be made within two years after the end of the accounting period to which the loss is carried forward or within such later period as HMRC allow. Previously, relief was automatic.

There are no rules covering the interaction of property income business losses and trading losses carried forward. The order of offset will therefore be decided by the company and based on its individual circumstances.

See also **35.5** and **35.24** GROUP RELIEF for the surrender of UK property business losses as group relief or group relief for carried-forward losses.

See **64.7** RESIDENCE for relief for income tax losses incurred by non-UK resident companies and carried forward to accounting periods for which the company's property income is subject to corporation tax (i.e. for accounting periods beginning on or after 6 April 2020, subject to transitional provisions).

UK furnished holiday lettings

Lettings treated as a trade under the provisions for UK furnished holiday lettings (see **60.7** PROPERTY INCOME) are excluded from the company's UK property business for the purposes of the above provisions. Losses from such lettings are instead dealt with under the trade loss provisions (see **51.3** onwards above). However, the loss relief allowed for furnished holiday lettings is restricted — the relief for losses against total profits (under *CTA 2010, ss 37–44*, and *ss 48–54*) is not available. Losses can be carried forward under *CTA 2010, s 45* and set against profits of the same trade.

[*CTA 2010, ss 62, 65; F(No 2)A 2017, Sch 4 para 13*].

See also **45.6** INVESTMENT COMPANIES AND INVESTMENT BUSINESS for the conversion of UK property business losses to management expenses where an investment company ceases to carry on a UK business, and also **45.9** for restrictions applying to property business losses on the change of ownership of an investment company or a company with investment business.

Overseas property businesses

Losses from overseas property businesses (see **60** PROPERTY INCOME) are available for carry forward against future profits from the same business. This provision is, however, subject to the same commerciality test as applies to UK property business losses (see above).

See also the provisions with regard to losses of an EEA furnished holiday lettings business which is treated as a trade and has similar restrictions as to trade loss relief as outlined for a UK furnished holiday lettings business.

[*CTA 2010, ss 66, 67, 67A*].

See generally **60** PROPERTY INCOME.

Simon's Taxes. See **B6.203**.

Overseas income losses

[51.11] Losses from overseas trades can only be carried forward and set against future profits of the same trade. See **51.3–51.6** above.

Relief is not available for losses arising on other overseas sources, apart from overseas property businesses — see **51.10** above.

Miscellaneous losses

[51.12] Losses on transactions within the charge to corporation tax under any of the miscellaneous income provisions listed at *CTA 2010, s 1173* may be set off against income from such transactions in the same or any subsequent accounting period. Such income is then treated as reduced by so much of the loss as has not been relieved in an earlier accounting period.

Losses must be set against the first arising profits. No claims are required in this respect.

These provisions do not apply to losses in relation to:

- premiums, leases at an undervalue etc. (see **60.10–60.13** PROPERTY INCOME);
- certain exchange losses (see **27.23** DERIVATIVE CONTRACTS); and
- miscellaneous profits of non-distributing offshore funds.

[*CTA 2010, s 91*].

Subject to any express provision to the contrary, the same rules apply in calculating miscellaneous losses as apply in calculating the corresponding miscellaneous income. [*CTA 2009, s 1306*].

Companies in partnership

Where tax in respect of any of the profits of a partnership of which a company is a member (and to which arrangements as outlined in **51.34** below apply) is chargeable on miscellaneous income, the company's share is treated as arising from a trade carried on by the partnership and any allowance under *CAA 2001, s 19* or *CAA 1990, s 61(1)* is treated as made in taxing that trade.

Restrictions are applicable to the loss relief available to a corporate limited partner or a corporate partner of an LLP. See further *CTA 2010, ss 55–61*, also **56.10** and **56.11** PARTNERSHIPS.

[*CAA 2001, Sch 2 para 21; CTA 2010, ss 55–61*].

Simon's Taxes. See **D1.1114**.

Restriction on deduction of carried-forward losses

[51.13] *F(No 2)A 2017* introduced a restriction on the amount of carried-forward losses which can be deducted in an accounting period. Broadly, the restriction limits the amount of post-1 April 2017 profits against which any carried-forward losses can be relieved to 50% of profits over an annual 'deductions allowance' of £5 million. A single £5 million limit is shared between all of the members of a group, but can be allocated to each company as the group sees fit.

The provisions apply for accounting periods beginning on or after 1 April 2017. For this purpose, an accounting period which straddles 1 April 2017 is treated as if it were two separate accounting periods, the first ending on 31 March 2017 and the second beginning on 1 April 2017. Any necessary apportionments between the two periods must be made on a time basis unless that would produce an unjust or unreasonable result, in which case a just and reasonable basis must be used. Special rules apply, however, where the amount to be apportioned is either an amount chargeable to corporation tax which would have been less but for the CORPORATE INTEREST RESTRICTION (25) provisions or an amount for which relief is available which would have been greater but for the restriction. An amount chargeable to corporation tax which would not have arisen at all but for the restriction provisions is apportioned entirely to the second period.

[*F(No 2)A 2017, Sch 4 paras 190–192*].

For accounting periods beginning on or after 1 April 2020, the provisions extend to carried-forward capital losses. For this purpose, an accounting period which straddles 1 April 2020 is treated as if it were two separate accounting periods, the first ending on 31 March 2020 and the second beginning on 1 April 2020. See below for the calculation of the restriction for such periods.

Note that the provisions apply with certain modifications to oil industry ring-fence trades, oil contractors and insurance companies which are outside the scope of this publication.

The provisions operate by separating carried-forward losses between those which can be set off against total profits, profits of the same trade, non-trading income profits or chargeable gains and applying a maximum deduction in each case. A company can choose how to allocate its deductions allowance to each category by specifying the amount of a trading profits deductions allowance, a chargeable gains deductions allowance and so on.

Losses of furnished holiday lettings businesses carried forward are excluded from these provisions (see **60.7** PROPERTY INCOME) as are losses carried forward and set off against relevant leasing income under the anti-avoidance rules at **49.13** LEASING.

Deductions from trading profits

In calculating a company's taxable total profits for an accounting period, the total deductions for losses brought forward for set-off against profits of the same trade is restricted to the sum of:

- 50% of the company's 'relevant trading profits' (see **51.14** below) for the period; and
- the company's 'trading profits deductions allowance' for the period.

The losses in question are trade losses brought forward under *CTA 2010, s 45* or *s 45B* (which cannot be set off against total profits — see **51.6, 51.7** above). A company's '*trading profits deductions allowance*' for an accounting period is so much of its 'deductions allowance' (see **51.15** below) as is specified in the company tax return for the period (and is therefore nil if no amount is specified). The amount specified may not be greater than the difference between the deductions allowance and the company's total non-trading profits deduction allowance (see below) specified in the return. For accounting periods beginning before 1 April 2020 (subject to the transitional rules above for deductions from chargeable gains), the amount specified could not be greater than the difference between the deductions allowance and the company's non-trading profits deduction allowance specified in the return.

This restriction does not apply if the company's modified total profits (see **51.14** below) are not greater than nil.

[*CTA 2010, s 269ZB; F(No 2)A 2017, Sch 4 para 16; FA 2019, Sch 10 para 4; FA 2020, Sch 4 paras 25, 42–46*].

Deductions from chargeable gains

In calculating a company's taxable total profits for an accounting period beginning on or after 1 April 2020 (and see below for transitional provisions), the total deductions for allowable capital losses (see **11.3** CAPITAL GAINS) brought forward for set-off against chargeable gains is restricted to the sum of:

- 50% of the company's 'relevant chargeable gains' (see **51.14** below) for the period; and
- the company's 'chargeable gains deductions allowance' for the period.

A company's '*chargeable gains deductions allowance*' for an accounting period is so much of its deductions allowance as is specified in the company tax return for the period (and is therefore nil if no amount is specified). The amount specified may not be greater than the difference between the deductions allowance and the total of any trading profits deduction allowance and non-trading income profits deduction allowance (see below) specified in the return.

This restriction does not apply if the company's modified total profits (see **51.14** below) are not greater than nil.

[*CTA 2010, s 269ZBA; FA 2020, Sch 4 paras 2, 42*].

Pre-entry losses are not treated as brought forward losses for these purposes, but see **12.27** CAPITAL GAINS — GROUPS for the effect of these provisions for such losses. See also **11.3** CAPITAL GAINS — GROUPS for the exclusion of certain losses carried forward to an accounting period falling wholly within the same financial year as that in which they arose.

Transitional rules

A company's chargeable gains for an accounting period which straddles 1 April 2020 are calculated as if the period were two separate accounting periods, the first ending on 31 March 2020 and the second beginning on 1 April 2020.

Chargeable gains and allowable losses are allocated to each of those notional periods according to the time at which they arise. If allowable losses in one of the notional periods exceed the gains in that period, the excess is treated as a loss arising in the other period (and not as a loss carried forward or back to that period). Losses brought forward from previous accounting periods can be set off against gains arising in the first notional period without restriction. Any remaining brought forward losses are carried forward to the second notional period and are subject to the restriction. In applying the restriction to the second period, in step (3) at **51.14** below, the chargeable gains included in the modified total profits are taken to be the total of the gains of the first notional period (after deducting losses arising in that period and brought forward losses) and the gains of the second notional period (after deducting losses arising in that period).

Special transitional rules apply to a non-UK resident company which carries on a UK property business or which has other UK property income if:

(i) it is within the charge to income tax for 2019/20 and within the charge to corporation tax on income for an accounting period beginning on 6 April 2020 (see **64.6**(4), (5), **64.7** RESIDENCE); and

(ii) it is chargeable to corporation tax for one or more accounting periods falling wholly within the period 1 April 2020 to 5 April 2020 (inclusive) because of a chargeable gain arising on the disposal of an asset (see **64.6**(3)).

In such circumstances, losses arising in any of the accounting periods in (i) or (ii) above are treated as losses arising in the other period or periods, so far as they are not otherwise relieved, so that no restriction applies to such losses in those periods. The company is treated as if it had made a claim under CTA 2010, s 269ZYA(3) (see **51.15** below) for all of the periods in (i) and (ii) and the company's deductions allowance for the accounting period in (i) is reduced by the amount of any deductions allowance for each accounting period in (ii). The company can elect for these rules not to apply.

An anti-forestalling rule applies where a company would otherwise obtain a tax advantage as a result of a deduction, or increased deduction, of a carried-forward allowable loss in an accounting period ending before 1 April 2020 as a result of arrangements entered into on or after 29 October 2018 (when the extension of the restriction to capital losses was first announced), which have, as a main purpose, securing a tax advantage resulting from the fact that the restriction does not apply to that period. In such a case, losses carried forward can be deducted only up to a maximum of 50% of the qualifying chargeable gains (see **51.14** below) for the period. For this purpose, an accounting period straddling 1 April 2020 is treated as two accounting periods, the first of which ends on 31 March 2020 (so that this rule may apply to that first period). For examples of when the anti-forestalling rule may apply see HMRC Capital Gains Manual CGAPP17.

[*FA 2020, Sch 4 paras 42–46*].

Deductions from non-trading profits

In calculating a company's taxable total profits for an accounting period, the total deductions for non-trading loan relationship deficits (see **50.5** LOAN RELATIONSHIPS) brought forward for set-off against non-trading profits is restricted to the difference between:

- the sum of 50% of the company's 'total relevant non-trading profits' (see **51.14** below) for the period and the company's 'total non-trading profits deductions allowance' for the period; and
- any deductions made for the period in respect of allowable capital losses brought forward from an earlier accounting period.

For accounting periods beginning before 1 April 2020 (subject to the transitional rules above for deductions from chargeable gains), the maximum set-off was the sum of 50% of the company's 'relevant non-trading profits' (see **51.14** below) for the period and the company's 'non-trading profits deductions allowance' for the period.

A company's '*total non-trading profits deductions allowance*' for an accounting period is the sum of its 'non-trading income profits deductions allowance' and its chargeable gains deductions allowance (as above).

A company's '*non-trading income profits deductions allowance*' for an accounting period is so much of its deductions allowance as is specified in the company tax return for the period (and is therefore nil if no amount is specified). The amount specified may not be greater than the difference between the deductions allowance and the sum of any trading profits deduction allowance and chargeable gains deductions allowance specified in the return. For accounting periods beginning before 1 April 2020 (subject to the transitional rules above for deductions from chargeable gains), a company's '*non-trading profits deductions allowance*' for an accounting period is so much of its deductions allowance as is specified in the company tax return for the period (and is therefore nil if no amount is specified). The amount specified may not be greater than the difference between the deductions allowance and any trading profits deduction allowance specified in the return.

This restriction does not apply if the company's modified total profits (see **51.14** below) are not greater than nil.

[*CTA 2010, s 269ZC; F(No 2)A 2017, Sch 4 para 16; FA 2019, Sch 10 para 5; FA 2020, Sch 4 paras 3, 26, 42–46*].

Deductions from total profits

In calculating a company's taxable total profits for an accounting period, the total deductions for losses brought forward for set-off against total profits is restricted to the difference between:

(a) the '*relevant maximum*', i.e. the sum of 50% of the company's 'relevant profits' for the period and the company's deductions allowance for the period; and

(b) the sum of any deductions made for the period in respect of trade losses brought forward for set-off against profits of the same trade, allowable capital losses brought forward for set off against chargeable gains and non-trading loan relationship deficits brought for set-off against non-trading profits.

For accounting periods beginning before 1 April 2020 (subject to the transitional rules above for deductions from chargeable gains), the amount in (b) was simply the sum of the deductions in respect of trade losses brought forward for set-off against profits of the same trade and non-trading loan relationship deficits brought for set-off against non-trading profits.

The losses in question are:

(1) non-trading loan relationship deficits carried forward against total profits (see **50.6** LOAN RELATIONSHIPS);
(2) non-trading losses on intangible fixed assets (see **42.9** INTANGIBLE ASSETS);
(3) management expenses carried forward and treated as management expenses of the accounting period (see **45.3** INVESTMENT COMPANIES AND INVESTMENT BUSINESS);
(4) UK property business losses carried forward and treated as management expenses of the accounting period (see **45.6** INVESTMENT COMPANIES AND INVESTMENT BUSINESS);
(5) trade losses arising to a production company under one of the CREATIVE INDUSTRIES RELIEFS (26) carried forward and treated as a loss of a later period for set-off against profits of that or earlier periods;
(6) trade losses carried forward for set-off against total profits (see **51.6** above);
(7) UK property business losses carried forward and treated as a loss of the period (see **51.10** above);
(8) group relief in respect of a loss surrendered by a production company under one of the CREATIVE INDUSTRIES RELIEFS (26) in respect of brought forward treated as losses of a later period; and
(9) group relief for carried-forward losses (see **35.24** GROUP RELIEF).

A company's '*relevant profits*' for an accounting period are its 'qualifying profits' less its deductions allowance (see **51.15** below). For accounting periods beginning before 6 July 2018, a company's relevant profits are the sum of its relevant trading profits and its relevant non-trading profits. For this purpose, accounting periods straddling 6 July 2018 are treated as two separate accounting periods, the second of which begins on that date. Any necessary apportionments between the two notional periods must be made on a time basis or, if that basis would be unjust or unreasonable, on a just and reasonable basis. The relevant profits cannot be a negative amount. A company's '*qualifying profits*' are its modified total profits (see **51.14** below) less the amount calculated at **51.14**(2) below.

This restriction does not apply if the company's modified total profits are not greater than nil.

[*CTA 2010, ss 269ZD, 269ZFA; F(No 2)A 2017, Sch 4 para 16; FA 2019, Sch 10 paras 6, 8, 32; FA 2020, Sch 4 paras 4, 27, 30, 42–46; FA 2021, Sch 8 paras 10, 19*].

Relevant profits

[51.14] The following applies for the purposes of the restriction on deduction of carried-forward losses. Note that transitional rules apply to accounting periods straddling 1 April 2020 (see **51.13** above under 'Deductions from chargeable gains').

Accounting periods beginning on or after 1 April 2020

A company's '*relevant trading profits*' for an accounting period are its 'qualifying trading profits' for the period less its trading profits deductions allowance (see **51.13** above) for the period. '*Relevant non-trading income profits*' are the 'qualifying non-trading income profits' less the non-trading income profits deductions allowance (see **51.13** above) for the period. '*Relevant chargeable gains*' are the 'qualifying chargeable gains' less the chargeable gains deductions allowance (see **51.13** above) for the period. In each case, a negative amount is taken to be nil.

A company's '*total relevant non-trading profits*' for a period are the sum of its qualifying non-trading income profits and is qualifying chargeable gains less the total non-trading profits deductions allowance for the period.

The '*qualifying trading profits*', '*qualifying non-trading income profits*' and '*qualifying chargeable gains*' are calculated by taking the following steps.

(1) Calculate the company's 'modified total profits' for the period. If the modified total profits are not greater than nil, then both the qualifying trading profits, qualifying non-trading income profits and qualifying chargeable gains are taken to be nil. The '*modified total profits*' are the total profits for the period modified by:
   - ignoring income consisting of distributions;
   - making no deductions for trade losses brought forward for deduction against profits of the same trade other than deductions that would be ignored for the purposes of the restriction under *CTA 2010, s 269ZB* (see **51.13** above) by reason of the CREATIVE INDUSTRIES RELIEFS (**26**) provisions or the provisions for UK and EEA furnished holiday lettings;
   - making no deductions for non-trading loan relationship deficits carried forward for set-off against non-trading profits; and
   - making no deductions for allowable capital losses brought forward.

(2) Calculate the sum of any amounts which could be relieved against the company's total profits (as modified in (1) above) of the period, ignoring any amounts which require a claim if a claim is not in fact made and any 'excluded deductions'. If the amount in (1) above does not exceed the amount given by this step, then the qualifying trading profits, qualifying non-trading income profits and qualifying chargeable gains are each taken to be nil. The following are '*excluded deductions*':
   - deductions within **51.13**(1)–(9) above;
   - a deduction for a trade loss carried back from a later accounting period;
   - a deduction in respect of a terminal loss for carried-forward losses (see **51.9** above);

- a deduction for excess special leasing capital allowances carried back (see **10.54** CAPITAL ALLOWANCES ON PLANT AND MACHINERY); and
- a deduction for a non-trading loan relationship deficit carried back from a later accounting period.

(3) Divide the modified total profits into trade profits (i.e. the profits of a trade of the company), non-trade income profits (the remaining profits other than any chargeable gains) and chargeable gains.

(4) Allocate the whole of the amount found in (2) above to one or more of the amounts found in (3) above and reduce each of those amounts by the amount so allocated. The company can allocate the reliefs within (2) above to the amounts in (3) above as it wishes but the trade profits, non-trade income profits and chargeable gains cannot be reduced below nil.

(5) The amounts found in (4) above are the company's qualifying trading profits, qualifying non-trading income profits and qualifying chargeable gains.

Accounting periods beginning before 1 April 2020

A company's '*relevant trading profits*' for an accounting period are its 'qualifying trading profits' for the period less its trading profits deductions allowance (see **51.13** above) for the period. '*Relevant non-trading profits*' are the 'qualifying non-trading profits' less the non-trading profits deductions allowance (see **51.13** above) for the period. In either case, a negative amount is taken to be nil.

The '*qualifying trading profits*' and '*qualifying non-trading profits*' are calculated by taking the following steps.

(1) Calculate the company's 'modified total profits' for the period. If the modified total profits are not greater than nil, then both the qualifying trading profits and qualifying non-trading profits are taken to be nil. The '*modified total profits*' are the total profits for the period modified by:
- ignoring income consisting of distributions;
- making no deductions for trade losses brought forward for deduction against profits of the same trade other than deductions that would be ignored for the purposes of the restriction under *CTA 2010, s 269ZB* (see **51.13** above) by reason of the CREATIVE INDUSTRIES RELIEFS (**26**) provisions or the provisions for UK and EEA furnished holiday lettings; and
- making no deductions for non-trading loan relationship deficits carried forward for set-off against non-trading profits.

(2) Calculate the sum of any amounts which could be relieved against the company's total profits (as modified in (1) above) of the period, ignoring any amounts which require a claim if a claim is not in fact made and any 'excluded deductions'. If the amount in (1) above does not exceed the amount given by this step, then both the qualifying trading profits and qualifying non-trading profits are taken to be nil. The following are '*excluded deductions*':
- current period deductions within **51.13**(1)–(9) above;
- a deduction for a trade loss carried back from a later accounting period;

- a deduction in respect of a terminal loss for carried-forward losses (see **51.9** above);
- a deduction for excess special leasing capital allowances carried back (see **10.54** CAPITAL ALLOWANCES ON PLANT AND MACHINERY); and
- a deduction for a non-trading loan relationship deficit carried back from a later accounting period.

(3) Divide the modified total profits into trade profits (i.e. the profits of a trade of the company) and non-trade profits (the remaining profits).

(4) Take the amount found in (2) above and either reduce the trade profits found in (3) above by the whole of that amount, reduce the non-trade profits by the whole of the amount or reduce the trade profits by part of that amount and the non-trade profits by the remainder. In each case, the trade profits and the non-trade profits cannot be reduced below nil.

(5) The amounts found in (4) above are the company's qualifying trading profits and qualifying non-trading profits.

[*CTA 2010, s 269ZF; F(No 2)A 2017, Sch 4 para 16; FA 2020, Sch 4 paras 5–7, 29, 42–46; FA 2021, Sch 8 paras 9, 19*].

Deductions allowance

[51.15] Subject to the claim for an alternative calculation available to companies without a source of chargeable income (see below), the '*deductions allowance*' for a company which is not a member of a group for an accounting period is £5 million. If the period is less than 12 months long, the deductions allowance is proportionately reduced.

Where a company is a member of a group (and at least one other member is within the charge to corporation tax), its deduction allowance is the part of the 'group deductions allowance' allocated to it. Where the company joins or leaves the group during an accounting period, it is also entitled to a proportionate part of the £5 million limit for any part of the period for which it is not a member of a group. The company's overall deductions allowance cannot exceed £5 million (reduced proportionately for a period of less than 12 months).

Where two or more members of a group are within the charge to corporation tax, all of them need jointly to nominate one of their number to be responsible for allocating the group deductions allowance. The '*group deductions allowance*' is £5 million for each accounting period of the nominated company throughout which the group allowance nomination has effect (reduced proportionately for periods of less than 12 months). If a nomination takes effect, or ceases to take effect part way through an accounting period, the two parts must be dealt with separately — the nominated company can only allocate a proportionate part of the allowance for the whole period. There are provisions which allow a group allowance nomination to be made after the date a group has ceased to exist (for example because of an acquisition or demerger) to cover the period up to that date. The provisions were introduced by *FA 2021* but apply retrospectively from the introduction of the restriction on deductions of carried-forward losses (see **51.13** above). There are transitional rules to deal with nominations and allowance statements for earlier periods which only became possible on the enactment of the provisions. See further below.

The amount of a company's deductions allowance is increased in certain circumstances where a credit or other income is brought into account in respect of the reversal of an onerous lease provision in calculating the company's modified total profits (see **51.14** above) for the accounting period. The allowance is increased by the amount of the credit or income (or, if lower, the amount of the modified total profits).

For accounting periods beginning on or after 1 April 2020 (subject to the transitional rules for periods straddling that date at **51.13** above under 'Deductions from chargeable gains'), a company's deductions allowance is increased where it is in insolvent liquidation (i.e. where its assets are insufficient to pay its debts, liabilities and the expenses of the winding up). For each accounting period during the winding-up, the deductions allowance is increased by the lower of the chargeable gains arising the period after deducting allowable losses arising in the period and the total allowable losses brought forward to that period. For this purpose, gains (but not losses) are ignored if the asset was acquired by the company by intra-group transfer during the winding-up and the transfer was treated as no gain/no loss (under *TCGA 1992, s 171* — see **12.4** CAPITAL GAINS — GROUPS), provided that the transferor was not itself in insolvent liquidation at the time of the transfer. Gains (but not losses) are also ignored if they were transferred to the company by way of a *TCGA 1992, s 171A* election (see **12.6** CAPITAL GAINS — GROUPS) during the winding-up from a company which was not itself in insolvent liquidation at the time the election was made.

If a company makes any of the deductions which may be restricted by these provisions for an accounting period it must state the amount of its deductions allowance for the period in its company tax return. If the allowance is increased because of the reversal of an onerous lease provision or because the company is in insolvent liquidation, it must also state what the allowance would have been without the increase. If a company's tax return specifies an excessive amount as its deductions allowance, its trading profits deduction allowance, its chargeable gains deductions allowance or its non-trading income profits deductions allowance (previously its non-trading profits deduction allowance), it must amend the return so that the amounts are not excessive. If an HMRC officer considers that an undue amount of relief has been given because of the inclusion of an excessive amount, he may make an assessment in the amount which in his opinion ought to be charged. If the amount became excessive because of a change in the amount of group deductions allowance allocated to the company and the company fails, or is unable to amend its return accordingly, an HMRC assessment is not out of time if made within 12 months of the date on which the change took place.

[*CTA 2010, ss 269ZDA, 269ZR, 269ZS(1)–(4), 269ZW–269ZY, 269ZZ–269ZZA; F(No 2)A 2017, Sch 4 para 16; FA 2020, Sch 4 paras 8, 9, 28, 32–35, 42–46*].

Companies without a source of chargeable income

Where a company has no source of chargeable income throughout a financial year, it can make a claim for its deductions allowance to be calculated in a different way for an accounting periods falling wholly within that year if it is chargeable to corporation tax for the period only because of a chargeable gain arising on the disposal of an asset. A claim can be made for accounting periods beginning on or after 1 April 2020 (subject to the transitional rules for periods straddling that date at **51.13** above under 'Deductions from chargeable gains').

The company must, at all times in the financial year, either be outside the charge to corporation tax or be chargeable to corporation tax only because of a chargeable gain arising on the disposal of an asset. If the company is a member of a group, every other group member must also satisfy this requirement.

A claim is made for a specific accounting period, but a company may have more than one accounting period falling wholly within a financial year. A period for which a claim is made is referred to below as a 'claim AP'. An accounting period falling wholly within the same financial year as a claim AP but for which no claim is made is an 'alternative AP'.

A company's deductions allowance for a claim AP is the lower of:

- the 'available deductions allowance amount';
- the total allowable capital losses carried forward to the period; or
- the chargeable gains arising in the period.

A company's deductions amount for an alternative AP is the lower of the deductions amount that would be found using the normal rules and the available deductions allowance amount.

The '*available deductions allowance amount*' for an accounting period is £5 million less the total of any deductions allowances already claimed by the company (or any other group member) for any claim APs and alternative APs falling wholly within the financial year. For this purpose, the deductions allowance already claimed in respect of an alternative AP is taken to be the amount specified in the company's return for the period as its chargeable gains deduction allowance. Deductions allowances are treated as claimed in the order shown in the following table.

Case	Rule
1. There is a claim AP and another claim AP starting on the same or a different day	The order in which the claims are made.
2. there is an alternative AP (AP1) and another alternative AP (AP2) starting on a later day.	AP1 before AP2.
3. There is an alternative AP and another alternative AP starting on the same day.	The order in which the tax returns for the alternative APs are delivered.
4. There is a claim AP and an alternative AP starting on the same day, earlier day or a later day.	The claim AP before the alternative AP.

A claim must be made within two years after the end of the accounting period but cannot be made before the end of the financial year. If a company files its tax return for an accounting period before the end of the financial year, it can, however, include a declaration that the requirements for a claim are met and that it intends to make a claim. If it does so, it is treated as if it had made a claim until either the declaration is withdrawn or an actual claim is made. A declaration also ceases to have effect if the company, or a group member, comes within the charge to corporation tax before the end of the financial year otherwise than as a result of a chargeable gain arising on the disposal of an asset. If it has not otherwise ceased to have effect, a declaration ceases to have effect two years after the end of the accounting period. Any adjustments to returns, assessments etc. required when a determination ceases to have effect can be made regardless of any time limits.

[*CTA 2010, ss 269ZYA, 269ZYB; FA 2020, Sch 4 paras 10, 42–46*].

See also **11.3** CAPITAL GAINS for losses arising in different accounting periods within the same financial year to a company within the charge to corporation tax only because of chargeable gains.

Group allowance nomination

A group allowance nomination must be signed by an appropriate representative of each member which is within the charge to corporation tax and must state the date on which it takes effect (which may be before the nomination is actually made). A nomination ceases to have effect when a new nomination is made, when an appropriate representative of one of the companies notifies HMRC in writing to that effect or when the nominated company ceases to be a member of the group or within the charge to corporation tax.

The nominated company must submit a group allowance allocation statement to HMRC for each accounting period before the latest of:

- the first anniversary of the filing date for the company tax return for the period;
- 30 days after the completion of an enquiry into a return of any of the group companies to which an allocation is, or could be, made in the statement;
- 30 days after an HMRC amendment to such a return following the completion of an enquiry into it;
- 30 days after the date on which an appeal against such an amendment is finally determined; and
- such later time as HMRC allow.

For accounting periods beginning before 1 April 2021, the statement must be submitted before the first anniversary of the filing date for the company tax return for the period, or by such later time as HMRC allow.

If a new nomination takes effect before the statement for an accounting period is submitted, it is the new nominated company which must make the submission. This rule does not, however, affect the validity of a statement submitted before the new nomination is made. For accounting periods beginning on or after 1 April 2021, there is no requirement to submit a statement if it would make no allocation of the group deduction allowance.

A statement must be signed by an appropriate representative of the nominated company and must allocate amounts of the group deductions allowance to one or more group members. For each amount allocated it must specify the accounting period of the member company to which it is allocated. Where a company's accounting period does not coincide exactly with that of the nominated company, only part of the group deductions allowance can be allocated to that accounting period, proportionate to the part of the period which overlaps with the nominated company's accounting period. The total allocations must not exceed the group deductions allowance. If the allocations exceed the maximum for a particular company or the overall maximum the nominated company must submit a revised statement within 30 days of the original submission or within such period as HMRC allow. If the allocations in a statement subsequently become excessive, a revised statement must be submitted within 30 days of the date the allocations became excessive or within such period as HMRC allow. If a company fails to submit a revised statement HMRC may amend the original statement as they think fit by notice in writing to the company (and must send a copy of the amended statement to each company to which an allocation is made). The normal time limits for amending company tax returns are disapplied to amendments made as a result of the submission of a statement.

A nominated company may submit a revised statement at any time before the latest of: the first anniversary of the filing date for the company's accounting period; 30 days after the completion of an enquiry into a return of any of the group companies to which an allocation was, or could have been, made in the original return; 30 days after an HMRC amendment to such a return following an enquiry; 30 days after any appeal against such an amendment is finally determined and any later time allowed by HMRC.

HMRC have the power to make regulations relating to administrative requirements for nominations and group allowance allocation statements.

Former groups

Where a group (see below) ceases to be a group (because the companies no longer meet the necessary conditions) and immediately before it ceased to be a group, two or more members were within the charge to corporation tax but no group allocation nomination had effect, all of the companies that were then members of the group and within the charge to corporation tax may together make a group allocation nomination. The nomination applies from the date on which it is stated to take effect until immediately before the group ceased to be a group. It is not necessary for any of the companies (including the nominated company) to be within the charge to corporation tax when the nomination is made, but the nominated company must have been within the charge to corporation tax immediately before the group ceased to be a group. Only one nomination for a group can be made under these provisions.

Where a group ceases to be a group (because the companies no longer meet the necessary conditions) and immediately before it ceased to be a group, a group allocation nomination is in effect (whether as a result of the above rule for former groups or otherwise), the provisions relating to group allowance allocation statements above apply with necessary modifications. In particular, the company that is the nominated company immediately before the group ceased to be a group is treated throughout as if it continued to be the nominated company.

The provisions for former groups were introduced by *FA 2021* but apply retrospectively from the introduction of the restriction on deductions of carried-forward losses (see **51.13** above).

Where a group ceased to be a group before 10 June 2021 (the date of Royal Assent to *FA 2021*) and some of the group companies no longer exist, a group allocation nomination can be made by the companies which still exist. If only one company still exists, it can nominate itself.

The time limit for making a group allowance allocation statement in respect of a group which has ceased to be a group is extended to 31 March 2022 if it would otherwise be before that date.

[*CTA 2010, ss 269ZS(5)–(10),269ZSA–269ZVA; F(No 2)A 2017, Sch 4 para 16; FA 2019, Sch 10 para 12; FA 2021, Sch 8 paras 2, 3, 11, 12, 16, 17, 20, 22, 23*].

Meaning of 'group'

A '*group*' consists of two or more companies, one of which is the 'ultimate parent' of the others but is not the ultimate parent of any other companies. A company is the '*ultimate parent*' of another company if it is the parent of the other company and no company is the parent of both of them. A company (A) is the parent of another company (B) if B is a 75% subsidiary of A, if A is beneficially entitled to at least 75% of any profits available for distribution to equity holders of B or A would be so entitled to at least 75% of any assets of B available to equity holders on a winding up. '75% subsidiary' and 'equity holder' are defined as for GROUP RELIEF (**35.3**, **35.4**) but extended to apply to companies without ordinary share capital, unincorporated associations, and to ownership through entities other than companies, trusts or other arrangements.

For accounting periods beginning on or after 1 April 2020 (subject to the transitional rules for periods straddling that date at **51.13** above under 'Deductions from chargeable gains'), an offshore collective investment vehicle (see **11.27** CAPITAL GAINS) which is neither a company nor a partnership is treated for these purposes as if it were a company and as if the rights of the participants were shares in that company.

[*CTA 2010, s 269ZZB; F(No 2)A 2017, Sch 4 para 16; FA 2020, Sch 4 paras 11, 42–46*].

Example

Stephenson Ltd, which is not a member of a group, begins to trade on 1 April 2020. It has the following results for the two years ending 31 March 2021 and 2022.

	y/e 31.3.21	y/e 31.3.22
	£	£
Trading profit/(loss)	(9,000,000)	8,000,000
Property income	—	2,000,000

Taxable profits for the two years are computed as follows

	y/e 31.3.21	y/e 31.3.22
	£	£
Trading profit	—	8,000,000
Property income	—	2,000,000
	—	10,000,000
Less loss brought forward from y/e 31.3.21 (restricted)		(7,500,000)
Taxable profits	—	£2,500,000

The restriction on the set-off of the carried-forward loss against profits for the year ending 31 March 2022 is calculated as follows.

	£
Qualifying profits	10,000,000
Less deductions allowance	(5,000,000)
Relevant profits	5,000,000
Relevant profits x 50%	2,500,000
Add deductions allowance	5,000,000
Maximum set-off	£7,500,000

Loss memorandum

	£
Loss y/e 31.3.21	9,000,000
Less relieved y/e 31.3.22	(7,500,000)
Carried forward to y/e 31.3.23	£1,500,000

Special situations

Company reconstructions — common ownership

[51.16] The following provisions apply where, on a company ('the predecessor') ceasing to carry on a trade, another company ('the successor') begins to carry it on, and:

(a) on, or within two years after, the cessation, the trade is at least 75% 'owned' by the same persons as owned a similar interest within a year before the cessation; and
(b) throughout the periods referred to above, the trade is carried on by a company which is within the charge to tax in respect of it.

References to 'the trade' include any other trade comprising the activities of the original trade.

'*Ownership*'. A trade carried on by two or more persons is treated as owned by them in the shares in which they are entitled to the profits.

A trade or an interest therein belonging to trustees (other than for charitable or public purposes) is treated as owned by the persons entitled to the trust's income for the time being.

A trade or an interest therein belonging to a company is (if necessary to bring these provisions into effect) treated as owned by:

- the beneficial owners of the 'ordinary share capital' of the company in proportion to their holdings; or
- the company's 'parent company'; or
- the beneficial owners of the 'ordinary share capital' of the parent company in proportion to their holdings; or
- the person or body of persons controlling a corporate shareholder within the previous three categories.

'*Ordinary share capital*' is as defined in *CTA 2010, s 1119*.

A '*parent company*' is one owning, directly or indirectly, 75% of the ordinary share capital of the company (determined in accordance with *CTA 2010, ss 1155–1157*) and which is not also a subsidiary of a third company.

In determining for the purposes of (a) and (b) above to what extent a trade belongs to the same persons, persons who are 'relatives' and the persons from time to time entitled to the income under a trust are respectively treated as a single person. '*Relative*' means spouse, civil partner, ancestor, lineal descendant, brother or sister. There is no requirement that the interest of the members of a group of persons in the predecessor and successor companies should be in the same proportions, so long as the same persons meet the requisite 75% ownership test.

[*CTA 2010, ss 940A–943; F(No 2)A 2017, Sch 4 para 62*].

The following modifications are made to the general loss relief provisions:

(1) (subject to the exception below) the special reliefs for terminal losses (see **51.8** and **51.9** above) are not available to the predecessor;

(2) terminal losses for carried-forward losses (see **51.9** above) is available to the successor as if losses of the predecessor were incurred in the accounting period in which the successor began carrying on the trade;

(3) pre-1 April 2017 trading losses may be carried forward (see **51.7** above) against income arising from the same trade to the successor, as if there had been no succession;

(4) post-1 April 2017 trading losses meeting the necessary conditions (see **51.6** above) may be carried forward against total profits of the successor as if there had been no succession;

(5) post-1 April 2017 trading losses not meeting the necessary conditions (see **51.6** above) may be carried forward against income arising from the same trade to the successor as if there had been no succession;

(6) losses of the trade transferred arising in subsequent periods cannot be carried back to a period before the transfer of the trade.

The exception to (1) above is that the predecessor may claim terminal loss relief for carried-forward losses under **51.9** above where the transfer is before 13 July 2017 and the losses were all carried forward to the accounting period in which the transfer took place under *CTA 2010, s 45* (carry-forward of pre-1 April 2017 losses — see **51.7** above).

As noted, where the conditions are met, the successor company may claim to set off against the income of the trade to which it has succeeded or, where applicable, against total profits any losses that: (i) were incurred in the predecessor's trade for which the predecessor has not claimed relief under *CTA 2010, s 37* or (for pre-13 July 2017 transfers) *s 45F*; and (ii) would have been relievable if the predecessor had continued to carry on the trade.

This procedure is known as loss streaming. It is important to note that, to the extent that (4) above does not apply, the losses are only relievable against future profits of the trade transferred. Consequently until the losses are utilised any trade transferred is treated as a separate notional trade. See *Leekes Ltd v HMRC*, CA, [2018] STC 1245.

[*CTA 2010, ss 943A–944C, 951; F(No 2)A 2017, Sch 4 paras 63–65, 67*].

See also HMRC Company Taxation Manual CTM06110 and CTM06120.

In addition the carry forward of losses to the successor is subject to a restriction. Where the amount of the 'relevant liabilities' immediately before a transfer exceeds the open market value of 'relevant assets' at that time, the losses which may be carried forward are reduced or extinguished by the amount of that excess.

'*Relevant assets*' are:

- assets which were vested in the predecessor immediately before the transfer, and which were not transferred to the successor; and
- consideration given to the predecessor by the successor in respect of the change of company carrying on the trade (but the assumption by the successor of any liabilities of the predecessor is not treated as consideration for this purpose).

'*Relevant liabilities*' are liabilities outstanding and vested in the predecessor immediately before the transfer, and not transferred to the successor. However, the following are excluded:

- share capital;
- share premium account;
- reserves; or
- 'relevant loan stock' of the predecessor unless such liability arose on a conversion of a liability not representing any such item within one year before the transfer.

As an anti-avoidance measure, where a liability was transferred to the successor, but the creditor agreed to accept part payment in settlement of the whole, the balance of the liability is treated as not having been transferred to the successor.

Any assets or liabilities apportioned to a successor on a previous application of these provisions (see below) are excluded.

In a First-tier Tribunal case it was held that the successor company must assume legal responsibility for the liabilities of the predecessor, otherwise such liabilities will be taken as remaining with the predecessor, which will reduce the loss available to the successor company. In this instance the successor company had merely loaned the predecessor funds to discharge its liabilities, instead of assuming responsibility for them, and therefore the successor was not able to use the trading losses post the transfer of trade. *Houston Cox Interiors Ltd v HMRC* FTT, [2010] UKFTT 510 (TC).

'*Relevant loan stock*' is any loan stock or similar security, secured or unsecured, but excluding any in respect of which, at the time the liability giving rise to it was incurred, the creditor was carrying on a trade of lending money. The amount of a liability representing relevant loan stock which is not a relevant liability, but which is secured on a relevant asset, is deducted from the value of the asset for the purposes of this provision.

[*CTA 2010, s 945; F(No 2)A 2017, Sch 4 para 66*].

Capital allowances are given to, and balancing charges made on, the successor as if there had been no succession (and losses are calculated accordingly unless the successor is a 'dual resident investing company' (see **35.23** GROUP RELIEF)). [*CTA 2010, s 948*]. Where the trade is transferred during the currency of accounting periods of the companies concerned:

(i) writing-down allowances are calculated on the 'pool' at the end of the transferee's accounting period, and apportioned on a time basis between the periods in which each company carried on the trade;
(ii) annual investment allowance and first-year allowances are given to the company incurring the expenditure; and
(iii) balancing adjustments are made on the company carrying on the trade at the relevant time.

(CCAB Guidance Notes TR 500, 10 March 1983). See also HMRC Capital Allowances Manual, CA 15400.

An anti-avoidance measure counters the use of reconstructions of companies carrying on a 'business of leasing plant and machinery' (see **49.9** LEASING) to avoid tax. Where the predecessor and successor companies carry on the business otherwise than in partnership, for capital allowances purposes, they are not treated as the same person under *CTA 2010, s 948* unless the principal company of the group is the same before and after the change, or, in the case of a consortium, the percentage of the successor held by the principal company is the same before and after the reconstruction. Where the parties are carrying on the leasing business in partnership, the predecessor has to stop trading on the date of transfer for *CTA 2010, s 948* to apply. The effect of this is to ensure that the companies share the same principal company for the purposes of *CTA 2010, Pt 9* (sale of lessor company carrying on business of leasing plant or machinery — see **49.9** *et seq.* LEASING).

If *CTA 2010, s 948* does not apply to a transfer, for capital allowances purposes there is deemed to be a disposal by the predecessor of the leasing assets at market value and an acquisition by the successor at that value on the date of cessation of the trade.

The plant or machinery belonging to the trade is treated as sold by the predecessor to the successor at the ascribed value on the day of cessation. The ascribed value is, broadly, the higher of the market value of the plant or machinery and the present value of the lease, although for certain equipment lessors the ascribed value is the present value.

[*CTA 2010, ss 437A, 950, 950(5)*].

The carry over of capital allowances does not apply if the successor is a dual resident investing company.

[*CTA 2010, s 949*].

Repeated successions are each treated in accordance with the above provisions, provided that the conditions in (a) and (b) above are satisfied on each occasion.

Where the successor takes over part of the predecessor's trade, or where the activities to which it succeeds are carried on as part only of the successor's existing trade, the transferred activities are treated as a separate trade and receipts, expenses, etc. are apportioned as may be just. See *Falmer Jeans Ltd v Rodin* Ch D, 1990, 63 TC 55 for a case in which this provision was held to apply.

See also **51.17** below.

Simon's Taxes. See **D6.315–D6.332.**

Example

A Ltd and B Ltd are two wholly-owned subsidiaries of X Ltd. All are within the charge to corporation tax, although A Ltd has accumulated trading losses brought forward and unrelieved of £200,000 and has not paid tax for several years. As part of a group reorganisation, A Ltd's trade is transferred to B Ltd on 31 October 2021.

A Ltd's balance sheet immediately before the transfer is as follows.

	£		£
Share capital	100,000	Property	90,000
Debenture secured		Plant	20,000
on property	50,000	Stock	130,000
Group loan	10,000	Trade debtors	120,000
Trade creditors	300,000		
Bank overdraft	60,000		
	520,000		
Deficit on reserves	(160,000)		
	£360,000		£360,000

Book values represent the approximate open market values of assets. B Ltd takes over the stock and plant to continue the trade, paying £150,000 to A Ltd and taking over £15,000 of trade creditors relating to stock. A Ltd is to collect outstanding debts and pay remaining creditors.

A Ltd's 'relevant assets' are:

	£
Freehold property (£90,000 – £50,000)	40,000
Trade debtors	120,000
Consideration from B Ltd	150,000
	£310,000

A Ltd's 'relevant liabilities' are:

	£
Bank overdraft	60,000
Group loan	10,000
Trade creditors (£300,000 – £15,000)	285,000
	£355,000

Tax losses transferable with trade:
£200,000 – £(355,000 – 310,000) = £155,000

Change in ownership of a company

[51.17] Special rules apply if there is a 'change in the ownership of a company' and:

(a) within any period beginning no more than three years before the change in ownership which is a period of five years in which that change occurs there is a 'major change in the nature or conduct of a trade' carried on by the company; or

(b) the change in ownership occurs at any time after the scale of activities in a trade carried on by the company has become small or negligible and before any considerable revival in the trade.

Where either the change in ownership or the major change in the nature or conduct of the trade occurred before 1 April 2017, the requirement in (a) above was that the major change had to take place within any period of three years in which the change in ownership occurred.

[*CTA 2010, s 673(1)–(3); F(No 2)A 2017, Sch 4 para 72*].

There is a '*change in the ownership of a company*' if:

(i) a single person acquires as beneficial owner more than half the ordinary share capital (see *CTA 2010, s 1119*) of the company; or

(ii) two or more persons each acquire as beneficial owner a holding of at least 5% (or an addition to their existing holding sufficient to raise it to 5%) of the company's ordinary share capital, and the combined holdings exceed half that capital. Acquisitions by, and holdings of, CONNECTED PERSONS (**19**) are treated as a single acquisition or holding.

See, however, **29.20** DISTRIBUTIONS for the interaction of these provisions and the demerger provisions of *CTA 2010, ss 1073–1099*.

In comparing a person's holdings at any two dates, he is to be treated at the later date as having acquired whatever he did not hold at the earlier date, irrespective of intervening acquisitions and disposals. Comparisons are made in percentage terms throughout.

Acquisitions of shares on death are left out of account as is any gift which was unsolicited and made without regard to these provisions.

The date of any acquisition corresponds with the date of the contract of sale, or with the assignment of the benefit of that contract, or with the acquisition of the option to acquire, as the case may be.

Where the existence of extraordinary rights or powers renders ownership of the ordinary share capital an inappropriate test of change of ownership, holdings of all kinds, or of any particular kind, of share capital, voting power or any other special kind of power may be taken into account instead.

A change in the direct ownership of a company is ignored if, immediately before and after the change, it continues to be a 'qualifying 75% subsidiary' of the same company.

A '*qualifying 75% subsidiary*' is a '*75% subsidiary*' (defined under *CTA 2010, s 1154* by reference to direct or indirect ownership of at least 75% of ordinary share capital), with an additional requirement that the parent company would be beneficially entitled to at least 75% of any profits available for distribution to equity holders and of any assets so available on a winding-up (see **35.4** GROUP RELIEF).

This allows for a new holding company to be inserted beneath a parent company of a group without triggering the loss restriction provisions.

A change in ownership is also disregarded where a new company (N) acquires all the issued share capital of another company (C) if immediately afterwards N:

(i) possesses all the voting power in C;
(ii) is beneficially entitled to 100% of any profits available for distribution to equity holders and of any assets so available on a winding up (as for equity holders under *CTA 2010, Pt 5 Ch 6* per the group relief provisions, as above); and
(iii) meets certain requirements as to continuity (see below).

This allows for a new holding company to be inserted above the parent company of a group.

A company is classified as '*new*' if, before the acquisition, it has not issued any shares other than subscriber shares and has not begun to carry on a trade or business.

The continuity requirements broadly ensure that the acquisition has been undertaken by way of a share for share exchange. Specifically the requirements are met by N if, and only if, the consideration for the acquisition consists only of the issue of shares in N to the shareholders of C and immediately after the acquisition:

- each person who was a shareholder of C immediately before the acquisition is a shareholder of N;

- the shares in N are of the same classes as those in C were immediately before the acquisition;
- the number of shares of any particular class in N bears to all the shares in N the same proportion as the number of that shares in C did to all its shares immediately before the acquisition; and
- the proportion of shares of any particular class in N held by any shareholder is the same as the proportion of shares of that class held by that shareholder in C immediately before the acquisition.

N is also treated as acquiring all the issue share capital of C for consideration only of the issue of shares in N to shareholders in C, if, pursuant to a scheme of reconstruction, the original shares in C were cancelled, new shares in C were issued only to N, and only shares in N were issued to the persons who were shareholders in C immediately before the cancellation. The continuity conditions then apply on the basis of the position immediately before the shares in C were cancelled, instead of immediately before the acquisition, as appropriate.

A '*scheme of reconstruction*' means a scheme carried out in pursuance of a compromise or arrangement to which *Companies Act 2006, Pt 26* applies, or under any corresponding law of a country or territory outside the UK.

No event or situation preceding a change of ownership to which these provisions have applied is to be taken into account in ascertaining whether a subsequent change has taken place.

Within the change of ownership provisions, '*ownership*' means beneficial ownership, and references to acquisition and to shareholder are construed accordingly.

HMRC may consider that the ordinary share capital test is not appropriate where persons have extraordinary rights. In this situation, an alternative basis for quantifying ownership may be proposed.

For the interaction of these provisions and the demergers provisions see **29.26** DISTRIBUTIONS.

[*CTA 2010, ss 719–721, 723–726; F(No 2)A 2017, Sch 4 paras 89, 90; FA 2021, Sch 8 paras 14, 15, 21*].

Major change

[51.18] A '*major change in the nature or conduct of a trade*' includes a major change in the type of property dealt in, or the services or facilities provided, in the trade, or in customers, outlets or markets, even if that change is the result of a gradual process which began outside the five-year or three-year period. A '*change*' for these purposes is to be decided by a qualitative test but in determining whether a change is '*major*' the change should not be viewed in isolation but a quantitative test of fact and degree should be applied (*Willis v Peeters Picture Frames Ltd* CA (NI) 1982, 56 TC 436). [*CTA 2010, s 673(4); F(No 2)A 2017, Sch 4 para 72(3)*]. The cessation of a trade is unlikely to be regarded as a major change in the nature or conduct of the trade, although the events leading up to it may be so; the interposition of a holding company between a company and its shareholders usually represents a change in ownership, but does not represent a major change in the nature or conduct of a trade carried on by the company.

HMRC Statement of Practice, SP 10/91 (as revised) sets out other factors to which HMRC will have regard in considering whether there has been a major change in the nature or conduct of a trade or business. This applies for the purposes of these provisions and for the purposes of *CTA 2010, ss 706–712* (company purchase schemes, see **58.14** PAYMENT OF TAX), *CTA 2010, ss 677–691* (change in ownership of investment companies, see **45.9** INVESTMENT COMPANIES AND INVESTMENT BUSINESS), *TCGA 1992, Sch 7A* and *SI 1999 No 358* (carry forward of shadow ACT, see **29.36** DISTRIBUTIONS).

These would include changes in factors such as location of the business premises, identity of suppliers, management or staff, methods of manufacture, or pricing or purchasing policies, in so far as they are indicative of a major change. It will not be regarded as a major change in the nature or conduct of a trade where all that has happened is that changes have been made to increase efficiency, or to keep pace with developing technology in the industry concerned or with developing management techniques, or to rationalise the product range by withdrawing unprofitable items and, possibly, replacing them with new items of a related kind. Although it is acknowledged that every case rests on its own facts, examples are cited where a change would *not* be regarded as major.

The following examples are cited by HMRC, although they do acknowledge that every case will be decided on its particular facts.

Major change	**No major change**
A company operating a dealership in saloon cars switches to operating a dealership in tractors (a major change in the type of property dealt in).	A company manufacturing kitchen fitments in three obsolescent factories moves production to one new factory (increasing efficiency).
A company owning a public house switches to operating a discotheque in the same, but converted, premises (a major change in the services or facilities provided).	A company manufacturing kitchen utensils replaces enamel with plastic, or a company manufacturing time pieces replaces mechanical with electronic components (keeping pace with developing technology).
A company fattening pigs for their owners switches to buying pigs for fattening and resale (a major change in the nature of the trade, being a change from providing a service to being a primary producer).	A company manufacturing both filament and fluorescent lamps (of which filament lamps form the greater part of the output) concentrates solely on filament lamps (a rationalisation of product range without a major change in the type of property dealt in).
A company switches from investing in quoted shares to investing in real property for rent (a change in the nature of investments held).	A company whose business consists of making and holding investments in UK quoted shares and securities makes changes to its portfolio of quoted shares and securities (not a change in the nature of investments held).

Where these provisions have to be considered in relation to the transfer of part of a trade which is to be treated as the transfer of a separate trade under *CTA 2010, s 951* (see **51.16** above), SP 10/91 indicates that the transfer of the part-trade will not of itself be regarded as a major change in the nature or conduct of either the part-trade transferred or that retained. Instead, each of the trades (or the relevant part of a combined trade) after the transfer will be compared with the equivalent part of the combined trade before the transfer. In cases where the transfer occurs *after* the relevant change of ownership, however, it may be necessary to consider whether it involves a major change in the nature or conduct of the undivided trade as it subsisted at the date of the change in ownership, and in such cases it may be appropriate to regard the transfer as constituting a major change, depending on the surrounding circumstances. HMRC will not, however, take this point if there was no other major change in either the original trade, or the parts into which it was divided, in the relevant period.

Effect of provisions

[51.19] Where these provisions apply, no relief may be claimed under *CTA 2010, ss 45, 45A* or *45B* against the trade profits or total profits of an accounting period ending after the change of ownership for losses incurred in an accounting period beginning before the change. This provision applies equally to UK property business losses.

Relief may similarly not be claimed under *CTA 2010, ss 37, 42* for a loss incurred in an accounting period ending after the change to be set against profits of an accounting period beginning before the change.

For these purposes only, the accounting period in which the change takes place is treated as two separate accounting periods, ending with the date of the change and beginning with the following date respectively. The profits or losses of the whole period are apportioned to each on a time basis, or by such other method as is just and reasonable.

[*CTA 2010, s 674; F(No 2)A 2017, Sch 4 para 73*].

Where a pre-change of ownership loss includes unrelieved capital allowances, those capital allowances are treated as not having been given when calculating any balancing charges on an asset owned at the date of the change in ownership and sold later. (In determining whether a capital allowance could have been relieved it is to be assumed that relief would have been given for the capital allowance in priority to any loss.)

This provision is necessary because the cancellation of losses does not affect underlying computations of capital allowances. This is because the trade itself does not cease. Without this provision a company which, at the time of the change of ownership, owns assets on which capital allowances have been given could effectively be penalised twice by:

- disallowance of any unused capital allowances included in the losses disallowed; and
- a balancing charge when the assets are disposed of.

See CTM06430.

[*CTA 2010, s 675*].

There are provisions with regard to restrictions on the loss carry forward of non-trading losses where there is a change in ownership of a 'shell' company, see **4.26** ANTI-AVOIDANCE for details of these provisions.

Company reconstructions

Where the change in ownership takes place after a company reconstruction under *CTA 2010, s 940A* onwards (see **51.16** above), for the purposes of determining any relief available to the company under those provisions, references to the trade in the above provisions *include* the trade as carried on by the predecessor, and relief for losses incurred before the company reconstruction are restricted in the same way as losses incurred after the company reconstruction.

Where the change in ownership takes place before the company reconstruction, for the purposes of determining the amount of any trading losses available to be carried forward by the company (under *CTA 2010, ss 45–45B* — see **51.5–51.7** above) or by the successor company or its successor companies (under *CTA 2010, s 940A* onwards), references to the trade in the above provisions include the trade as carried on by the successor company or any of its successor companies.

For accounting periods beginning before 1 April 2019, these provisions apply only to relief under *CTA 2010, s 944(3)* and trading losses carried forward under *CTA 2010, s 45*. For this purpose, accounting periods straddling 1 April 2019 are treated as two separate accounting periods, the second of which begins on that date. Any necessary apportionments between the two notional periods must be made on a time basis unless to do so would be unjust or unreasonable, in which case a just and reasonable basis must be used.

[*CTA 2010, s 676; FA 2019, Sch 2 paras 28, 32*].

Assessment

As the operation of these provisions can depend on events occurring after the change of ownership, the time limit for making assessments is extended (where relevant) to six years after the latest relevant event (being an event occurring not later than five years after the change of ownership (three years for changes before 1 April 2017)).

[*CTA 2010, s 727; F(No 2)A 2017, Sch 4 para 91*].

Property business losses

Where either (a) or (b) above applies in relation to a company carrying on a UK property business or an overseas property business (see **60** PROPERTY INCOME), so that the provisions described apply, or would apply, in relation to trading losses, a similar restriction applies to prevent property business losses incurred before the change being set against profits arising after the change.

[*CTA 2010, ss 704, 705; F(No 2)A 2017, Sch 4 paras 87, 88*].

General

These provisions are intended to prevent the purchase of companies with accumulated trading or property losses, in order to claim relief against the purchaser's trading profits and vice versa.

See also 29.36 ADVANCE CORPORATION TAX — SHADOW ACT, 45.9 INVESTMENT COMPANIES AND INVESTMENT BUSINESS and 58.14 PAYMENT OF TAX.

Further restrictions for cases involving a change in activities

[51.20] If the provisions at 51.19 above and 45.9 INVESTMENT COMPANIES AND INVESTMENT BUSINESS do not apply, the following provisions apply where:

- on or after 1 April 2017 there is a 'change in ownership' of a company (the '*transferred company*'); and
- a major change in the business of the company or a co-transferred company occurs within the required period but not before 1 April 2017. For the purposes of the restriction on the use of carried-forward post-1 April 2017 trade losses below, the '*required period*' is any period beginning no more than three years before the change in ownership which is a period of five years in which that change occurs. For the purposes of the other restrictions below, the required period is the period of eight years beginning three years before the change in ownership.

There is a '*change in ownership*' of a company (C) for this purpose in the circumstances described at 51.17(i)(ii) above and also where, as a result of the acquisition by a person of a holding of the ordinary share capital of C, the group condition in 35.26 GROUP RELIEF is met in relation to C and another company which was not a member of the same group as C before the acquisition.

A '*co-transferred company*' is any company which is 'related' to the transferred company both immediately before and after the change in ownership. Two companies are '*related*' if, assuming either was the claimant company and the other the surrendering company, the group condition or any of the consortium conditions at 35.26 GROUP RELIEF are satisfied.

A major change in a business includes a major change in the nature, conduct or scale of any trade or business carried on by the company and beginning or ceasing to carry on a particular trade or business. A major change in the nature or conduct of a trade or business includes a major change in the type of property dealt in, or the services or facilities provided, in the trade or business, or in customers, outlets or markets or a major change in the nature or the investments held by the company for the purposes of an investment business, even if that change is the result of a gradual process which began outside the five-year or eight-year period. See further 51.18 above. The transfer of a trade, business or property between two companies is disregarded in determining whether there is a major change in the business of either company if the companies were related immediately before the change in ownership and at the time of the transfer.

The accounting period in which the change of ownership takes place is treated as two separate accounting periods, ending with the date of the change and beginning with the following date respectively. The profits or losses of the whole period are apportioned to each period on the same basis as in **45.9** INVESTMENT COMPANIES AND INVESTMENT BUSINESS.

The provisions generally restrict the use of pre-change losses and other amounts against profits arising in accounting periods ending after the change in ownership ('*affected profits*') so far as they arise within five years of the end of the accounting period of the transferred company in which the change in ownership occurred and they can fairly and reasonably be attributed to activities or other sources of income as a result of which (or partly as a result of which) the major change has occurred. Accounting periods which straddle the end of the five-year period are treated for this purpose as two separate notional accounting periods, ending with the end of the five-year period and beginning with the following date respectively. Apportionments between the two notional periods are made on a time basis unless that would be inequitable, in which case a just and reasonable basis is used.

The effect of the provisions is as follows:

(1) **Post-1 April 2017 trade losses.** A trade loss of the transferred company for an accounting period beginning before the change in ownership may not be deducted from affected profits of an accounting period ending after the change under *CTA 2010, s 45A* (post-1 April 2017 trade loss carried forward and deducted from total profits — see **51.6** above) or *s 45F* (terminal loss relief for carried-forward losses — see **51.9** above). For accounting periods beginning on or after 1 April 2019, a loss made by another company (the 'predecessor company') in an accounting period beginning before the change in ownership may not be deducted from affected profits of an accounting period ending after the change in ownership under either *CTA 2010, s 45A* or *s 45F* as applied by *CTA 2010, s 940A* onwards (transfer of trades — see **51.16** above).

(2) **Loan relationship debits.** 'Relevant non-trading debits' may not be brought into account for the accounting period beginning immediately after the change of ownership or any subsequent accounting period to the extent to which the aggregate of those debits (including any amounts brought into account for any previous period ending after the change in ownership) exceed the total taxable profits for the accounting period ending with the change in ownership.

'*Relevant non-trading debits*' are non-trading debits which are determined on an amortised cost basis of accounting (see **50.1** LOAN RELATIONSHIPS) where:

(I) *CTA 2009, s 409* (postponement until redemption of debits for close companies' deeply discounted securities — see **50.27** LOAN RELATIONSHIPS) applies and, were it not for those sections, the debit would have been brought into account for an accounting period ending before or with the change in ownership; or

(II) *CTA 2009, s 373* (late interest not treated as accruing until paid — see **50.11** LOAN RELATIONSHIPS) applies and, were it not for that section, the debit would have been brought into account for an accounting period ending before or with the change in ownership: or

(III) the debit is not within (I) or (II) above but is in respect of a debtor relationship and relates to an amount which accrued before the change in ownership.

(3) **Non-trading loan relationship deficits.** A brought-forward non-trading loan relationship deficit which is apportioned to the notional accounting period ending at the time of the change in ownership cannot be deducted from affected profits of an accounting period ending after the change.

(4) **Post-1 April 2017 non-trading loss on intangible fixed assets.** Relief for such a loss (see **42.9** INTANGIBLE ASSETS) against the total profits of the same accounting period is available only in relation to each of the notional accounting periods considered separately. A loss for an accounting period beginning on or after 1 April 2017 and before the change in ownership cannot be deducted from affected profits of an accounting period ending after the change.

(5) **Post-1 April 2017 management expenses.** 'Relevant management expenses' and 'relevant capital allowances' which are apportioned to either of the notional accounting periods are treated as referable to, or falling to be made, in that notional period. In computing the taxable total profits of the company for an accounting period ending after the change, no deduction can be made from affected profits for relevant management expenses or allowances. '*Relevant management expenses*' are those first deductible for an accounting period beginning on or after 1 April 2017 and before the change in ownership. '*Relevant capital allowances*' are those falling to be made for an accounting period beginning on or after 1 April 2017 and before the change in ownership.

(6) **Post-1 April 2017 UK property business losses.** Relief for 'relevant losses' under *CTA 2010, s 62* (relief for loss against total profits of accounting period of loss — see **51.10** above) is available only in relation to each of the notional accounting periods considered separately. A relevant loss may not be deducted from affected profits of an accounting period ending after the change in ownership. '*Relevant losses*' are those made in an accounting period beginning on or after 1 April 2017 and before the change in ownership.

For these purposes, an accounting period which straddles 1 April 2017 is treated as if it were two separate accounting periods, the first ending on 31 March 2017 and the second beginning on 1 April 2017. Any necessary apportionments between the two periods must be made on a time basis unless that would produce an unjust or unreasonable result, in which case a just and reasonable basis must be used. Special rules apply, however, where the amount to be apportioned is either an amount chargeable to corporation tax which would have been less but for the CORPORATE INTEREST RESTRICTION (**25**) provisions or an amount for which relief is available which would have been greater but for the restriction. An amount chargeable to corporation tax which would not have arisen at all but for the restriction provisions is apportioned entirely to the second period. Similar rules apply by reference to 1 April 2019 for the purposes of (1) above.

[*CTA 2010, ss 676AA–676AL, 719; F(No 2)A 2017, Sch 4 paras 75, 89; FA 2019, Sch 10 paras 29, 32*].

Restriction on relief for post-1 April 2017 trade losses where asset transferred within group

[51.21] Restrictions on the use of post-1 April 2017 carried-forward trade losses where, on or after 1 April 2017, there is a 'change in ownership' of a company; and either:

(1) after the change the company acquires an asset from another group company so that either *TCGA 1992, s 171* (no gain/no loss transfer; see **12.4** CAPITAL GAINS — GROUPS) or *CTA 2009, s 775* (tax-neutral transfer of INTANGIBLE ASSETS (see **42.13**)) applies and the company realises a chargeable gain or non-trading chargeable realisation gain on the same asset within five years of the change; or
(2) a chargeable gain (or part of such a gain) on a disposal of an asset within five years of the change is treated as arising under *TCGA 1992, s 171A* (notional transfers within a group; see **12.6** CAPITAL GAINS — GROUPS).

The gain, or part, in (1) or (2) is the '***relevant gain***' for the purposes of these provisions.

There is a '*change in ownership*' of a company (C) for this purpose in the circumstances described at **51.17**(i)(ii) above and also where, as a result of the acquisition by a person of a holding of the ordinary share capital of C, the group condition in **35.26** GROUP RELIEF is met in relation to C and another company which was not a member of the same group as C before the acquisition.

In (1) above, an asset acquired by the company is treated as the same as an asset owned by it at a later time if the value of the latter is derived in whole or part from the former. In particular a leasehold is treated as the same asset as a freehold where the lessee has acquired the reversion.

The accounting period in which the change of ownership takes place is treated as two separate accounting periods, ending with the date of the change and beginning with the following date respectively. The profits or losses of the whole period are generally apportioned to each notional period on the same basis as in **45.9** INVESTMENT COMPANIES AND INVESTMENT BUSINESS. In addition, the chargeable gains and the non-trading chargeable realisation gains included, in accordance with *TCGA 1992, s 8(1)* and *Sch 7A* (see **11.3** CAPITAL GAINS, **12.25** CAPITAL GAINS — GROUPS) and *CTA 2009, Pt 8 Ch 6* (see **42.10** INTANGIBLE ASSETS), in the total profits for the period being divided are also apportioned. The total of those amounts, in so far as it exceeds the relevant gain, is apportioned to the pre-change part of the divided period, and an amount equivalent to the relevant gain (or, if less, the total itself) is apportioned to the post-change part of the divided period.

If the total profits of the company for the accounting period in which the relevant gain accrues include, in accordance with *TCGA 1992, s 8(1)* and *Sch 7A* and *CTA 2009, Pt 8 Ch 6*, an amount in respect of chargeable gains or non-trading chargeable realisation gains, the following restrictions apply:

(a) relief under *CTA 2010, s 45A* (post-1 April 2017 trade loss carried forward and deducted from total profits — see **51.6** above) for a loss made by the company is only available for each of the notional accounting periods considered separately;

(b) a trade loss of the company for an accounting period beginning before the change in ownership may not be deducted under *CTA 2010, s 45A* or *s 45F* (terminal loss relief for carried-forward losses — see **51.9** above) from so much of the total profits of an accounting period ending after the change as represent the relevant gain; and

(c) for accounting periods beginning on or after 1 April 2019, a loss made by another company (the 'predecessor company') in an accounting period beginning before the change in ownership may not be deducted under either *CTA 2010, s 45A* or *s 45F* as applied by *CTA 2010, s 940A* onwards (transfer of trades — see **51.16** above) from so much of the total profits of an accounting period of the company ending after the change in ownership as represents the relevant gain.

In (b) and (c) above, the profits which represent a gain for this purpose are found by comparing the amount of the gain (Y) and the amount included in total profits in respect of chargeable gains or non-trading chargeable realisation gains (Z). If Y does not exceed Z, the amount of the profits which represent the gain is equal to Y; otherwise it is Z. For the purposes of (c) above, an accounting period which straddles 1 April 2019 is treated as if it were two separate accounting periods, the first ending on 31 March 2019 and the second beginning on 1 April 2019. Any necessary apportionments between the two periods must be made on a time basis unless that would produce an unjust or unreasonable result, in which case a just and reasonable basis must be used.

[*CTA 2010, ss 676BA–676BE; F(No 2)A 2017, Sch 4 para 76; FA 2019, Sch 10 paras 30, 32*].

Cases involving the transfer of a trade

[51.22] The following restriction applies where on or after 1 April 2017 there is a change in ownership of a company (the '*transferred company*') and the transferred company transfers a trade (in circumstances within **51.16** above) to a successor company within the period of eight years beginning three years before the change. The transferred company and successor company must not be 'related' to one another both immediately before the change and at the time of the transfer.

There is a '*change in ownership*' of a company (C) for this purpose in the circumstances described at **51.17**(i)(ii) above and also where, as a result of the acquisition on or after 1 April 2021 by a person of a holding of the ordinary share capital of C, the group condition in **35.26** GROUP RELIEF is met in relation to C and another company which was not a member of the same group as C before the acquisition.

A loss made by the transferred company in the transferred trade in an accounting period beginning before the change cannot be deducted under *CTA 2010, s 45A* from profits of an accounting period of the successor company ending after the change so far as those profits arise within the period ending five years after the end of the accounting period of the transferred company in which the change occurred and cannot fairly and reasonably be attributed to the carrying on by the successor company of the transferred trade.

Accounting periods of the transferred company which straddle the date of the change and accounting periods of the successor company which straddle the end of the five-year period are treated for this purpose as two separate notional accounting periods, ending with the change or the end of the five-year period and beginning with the following date respectively. Apportionments between the two notional periods are made on a time basis unless that would be inequitable, in which case a just and reasonable basis is used.

Two companies are '*related*' if, assuming either was the claimant company and the other the surrendering company, the group condition or any of the consortium conditions at **35.26** GROUP RELIEF are satisfied.

See also **35.32** GROUP RELIEF for the restriction on group relief for carried-forward losses.

If a trade transferred by the transferred company or co-transferred company is subsequently transferred to another company, that subsequent transfer is treated for the purposes of these provisions as having been made by the transferred company or co-transferred company (rather than the successor company) at the time of the actual transfer. If the actual transfer was within **51.16** above, then the deemed transfer is so treated. These rules apply also where, following the original transfer, the original trade was included in the activities of another composite trade carried on by the successor trade and it is that composite trade that is subsequently transferred.

[*CTA 2010, ss 676EA, 676EB, 676ED, 676EE; F(No 2)A 2017, Sch 4 para 79*].

Transfer of deductions

[51.23] There are provisions which restrict the circumstances in which deductions may be claimed by a company where there has been a qualifying change in relation to the company. A '*qualifying change*' is defined as for the capital allowance buying provisions at *CAA 2001, s 212C*, and is aimed at certain changes in ownership of a company, or changes in profit ratios of a partnership or changes in ownership ratios for a consortium. See further details at **10.66** CAPITAL ALLOWANCES ON PLANT AND MACHINERY.

The deductible amounts are those which, at the date of the qualifying change (the '*relevant day*'), are regarded as highly likely to arise as deductions for an accounting period ending on or after that day. The term '*deductible amount*' refers to any expense of a trade or property business, an expense of management of an investment business and non-trading loan relationship, derivatives, and intangible fixed asset debits (within *CTA 2009, Pts 5, 6, 8*). It does not include any amount which has already been taken into account in determining the RTWDV under the capital allowance buying provisions highlighted above.

The deductible amount with regard to expenses of a trade does not include an amount which is a research and development allowance treated as an expense of the trade by virtue of the capital allowance provisions found at *CAA 2001, s 450(a)* (see **9.20** CAPITAL ALLOWANCES).

Disallowance of deductible amounts

Where a company, or any company connected with it, makes a claim (a '*relevant claim*') for losses to be relieved by way of set off against total profits (for trade losses, under *CTA 2010, s 37* or, for accounting periods beginning before 1 April 2019, *s 45A*), or as group relief (*CTA 2010, Pt 5 Ch 4*) or group relief for carried-forward losses (*CTA 2010, Pt 5A*), and the deductible amount meets the two conditions below, then such amount is a '*restricted deductible amount*' and is not allowed to be part of the claim, or be brought into account as a deduction by the company. For the purposes of the exclusion of claims under *CTA 2010, s 45A* from these provisions, an accounting period which straddles 1 April 2019 is treated as if it were two separate accounting periods, the first ending on 31 March 2019 and the second beginning on 1 April 2019. Any necessary apportionments between the two periods must be made on a time basis unless that would produce an unjust or unreasonable result, in which case a just and reasonable basis must be used.

The two conditions are:

(A) on the relevant day it is highly likely that the deductible amount would be the subject of, or brought into account as a deduction under a claim for, such relief for an accounting period ending on or after the relevant day. In considering whether this is '*highly likely*' any arrangements made or events that take place on or before the qualifying change are taken into account; and

(B) the purpose or one of the main purposes of any 'change arrangements' is for the deductible amount to be the subject of a claim, or brought into account as part of such a relief claim.

An amount is brought into account '*as a deduction*' where in any period it is used as a deduction in calculating the profits, losses or other amounts for corporation tax purposes, or as a deduction from profits or other amounts chargeable to corporation tax. '*Change arrangements*' are arrangements made to bring about, or otherwise connected to, a qualifying change. '*Arrangements*' are broadly defined to cover any agreement, understanding, scheme, transaction or series of transactions, regardless of whether they are legally enforceable.

Where the relevant day is on or after 1 April 2017, a claim for group relief for carried-forward losses cannot be made in respect of any amount so far as it was, in a previous accounting period, a restricted deductible amount. For this purpose it is assumed that amounts were brought into account in previous accounting periods in the order resulting in the greatest amount being excluded from the claim.

However this restriction does not apply to any amount that could have been claimed or brought into account as a deduction if there had not been a qualifying change — therefore the restriction is aimed at deductions which have been brought about by the qualifying change. In addition the restriction under this section does not apply to a deductible amount where such amount is disallowed under the profit transfer provisions at *CTA 2010, s 730D(2)* (see below), or where such amount gives rise to a restricted loss, or part of a loss, under the sale of lessor provisions at *CTA 2010, s 433(2)*.

[*CTA 2010, ss 730A–730C; F(No 2)A 2017, Sch 4 paras 92, 172; FA 2019, Sch 10 paras 31, 32*].

Profit transfers

A deductible amount is similarly not brought into account for a company, nor for any company connected with it, where '*profit transfer arrangements*' are made, being arrangements which result in an increase in the total profits of a company, or any company connected with it, or a reduction in any loss (or other amount which relieves corporation tax) of the company, or any company connected with it, in any accounting period ending on or after the relevant day (i.e. the date of the qualifying change, as noted above). The deductible amount must meet the following two conditions:

(a) on the relevant day it is highly likely that the deductible amount would (ignoring this provision) be brought into account as a deduction by the company, or any company connected with it, for any accounting period ending on or after the relevant day. In considering whether this is '*highly likely*' any arrangements made or events that take place on or before the qualifying change are taken into account; and
(b) the purpose or one of the main purposes of the profit transfer arrangements is to bring the amount (whether or not together with other deductible amounts) into account as a deduction in any accounting period ending on or after the relevant day.

However, where the company would have had profits in that accounting period in the absence of any profit transfer arrangements, and disregarding any deductible amounts, then only a just and reasonable proportion of the deductible amount is disallowed.

[*CTA 2010, s 730D*].

A company is connected with another company as defined under the provisions of *CTA 2010, s 1122*.

Tax avoidance involving losses

[51.24] For accounting periods beginning on or after 1 April 2017 there are provisions which counteract 'loss-related' tax advantages arising from 'tax arrangements'. Where the tax advantage would otherwise relate to an accounting period beginning before 1 April 2017 and ending on or after that date, the period is treated as two separate periods, the second beginning on 1 April 2017. Any necessary apportionments are made on a time basis or, if such a basis would be inequitable, on a just and reasonable basis. The provisions apply by reference to 13 July 2017 rather than 1 April where the loss in question is a post-1 April 2017 non-trading loan relationship deficit which can only be carried forward against non-trading profits or a UK property business loss.

'*Tax arrangements*' are arrangements (as widely defined) with a main purpose of obtaining a loss-related tax advantage if it is reasonable to regard them as circumventing the intended limits of relief under the provisions in question or otherwise exploiting shortcomings in those provisions. All relevant circumstances must be taken into account, including whether there are any steps which are contrived or abnormal or lack a genuine commercial purpose.

A tax advantage (within *CTA 2010, s 1139*) is '*loss-related*' if it arises as a result of a deduction (or increased deduction) in respect of trade losses, non-trading loan relationship deficits, non-trading losses on intangible assets, management expenses, UK property business losses, group relief, group relief for carried-forward losses or, for accounting periods beginning on or after 1 April 2020, allowable capital losses. For the purpose of adding capital losses to this list, the above transitional rules for accounting periods straddling 1 April 2017 apply by reference to 1 April 2020.

Counteraction is made by the making of just and reasonable adjustments (by HMRC or the company) by way of an assessment, the modification of an assessment, amendment or disallowance of a claim or otherwise.

[*F(No 2)A 2017, s 19; FA 2020, Sch 4 para 23*].

Tax avoidance involving carried-forward losses

[51.25] Anti-avoidance provisions apply to prevent companies converting brought forward losses and other amounts into in-year deductions (known as the 'corporate loss refresh prevention'). Essentially, the provisions operate to prevent a company from utilising brought forward losses against profits created as a result of an arrangement entered into the main purpose of which was to utilise the brought forward losses.

The provisions apply to 'relevant carried forward losses' which are defined as:

(a) trading losses which have been carried forward from a previous accounting period (under *CTA 2010, ss 45, 45A, 45B*) (see **51.5** above);
(b) non-trading loan relationship deficits which have been carried forward from a previous accounting period (under *CTA 2009, ss 457, 463G, 463H*) (see **50.5** LOAN RELATIONSHIPS);
(c) management expenses which have been carried forward from a previous accounting period which are treated as expenses of management deductible for the period (under *CTA 2009, s 1223*) (see **45.3** INVESTMENT COMPANIES AND INVESTMENT BUSINESS); or any amounts treated as management expenses deductible for the next accounting period under *CTA 2010, s 63*, with regard to a company with investment business which ceases to carry on UK property business;
(d) for accounting periods beginning on or after 1 April 2017, UK property business losses carried forward from a previous accounting period (under *CTA 2010, s 62* — see **51.10** above); and
(e) for accounting periods beginning on or after 1 April 2017, non-trading losses on intangible fixed assets carried forward from a previous accounting period (under *CTA 2009, s 753* — see **42.9** INTANGIBLE ASSETS).

For the purposes of (d) and (e) above, where an accounting period straddles 1 April 2017, it is split into two notional periods with amounts apportioned between the two periods on a time basis, or if that produces an inequitable result, a just and reasonable basis.

The restriction applies if all the following conditions are met:

(i) because of the tax arrangements, relevant profits arise to the company against which one or more relevant carried-forward losses would otherwise be available, and the relevant company, or a company connected with it, will bring a deductible amount into account;
(ii) the main purpose, or one of the main purposes, of the tax arrangements was to secure a corporation tax or CFC charge advantage for the company, or the company taken with any other connected companies, involving both the entitlement to the deductible amount and the use of relevant carried-forward losses;
(iii) it is reasonable to assume that when the tax arrangements were entered into the tax value of the arrangements it was expected to be greater than the non-tax value. The tax value is defined as both the corporation tax advantage, any other economic benefits derived from the corporation tax advantage, and any CFC charge advantage. The non-tax value is defined as any other economic value derived from the arrangements. This an objective test to ensure that the rules will only apply to arrangements entered into predominantly for their tax value; and
(iv) the rules restricting certain deductions by banking companies do not apply—see further **7.2** BANKS.

Where the restriction applies the company is not entitled to deduct any amount in respect of the relevant carried forward losses from relevant profits arising from the tax arrangements.

Certain terms are defined in *CTA 2010, s 730H*:

'*arrangements*' includes any agreement, understanding, scheme, transaction or series of transactions (whether or not legally enforceable);
'*corporation tax advantage*' means any relief from (or increased relief), any deferral of, any repayment of, or avoidance or reduction of, corporation tax;
'*CFC charge advantage*' means the avoidance or reduction of a CFC charge or assessment to such charge, under *TIOPA 2010, Pt 9A*;
'*deductible amount*' means an expense of a trade (apart from certain R&D allowances under *CAA 2001, s 450(a)*), an expense of a UK or overseas property business, an expense of management of a company's investment business, a non-trading loan relation or derivative contract debit, or a non-trading IFA debt. It does not include any amount which has already been taken into account in determining the RTWDV under the capital allowance buying provisions (see *CAA 2001, s 212K*), see further **10.66** CAPITAL ALLOWANCES ON PLANT AND MACHINERY.

References to bringing a deductible amount into account may be taken to mean that the deduction reduces a profit, relieves a profit or increases a loss.

[*CTA 2010, ss 730E–730H; F(No 2)A 2017, Sch 4 paras 69, 190*].

Companies accounting in foreign currency

[51.26] There are provisions which aim to ensure that, where a company has had a functional currency other than sterling in a period in which a loss was incurred, or in a period against the profits of which a loss is to be relieved, the loss and the profits are translated at the same rate of exchange.

The general rule is that, in computing the profits or losses of a company which prepares accounts in a foreign currency, translation into sterling is to be made at:

- the average exchange rate for the accounting period concerned;
- at the appropriate spot rate; or
- on a just and reasonable basis derived from a number of spot rates.

See **34.5** FOREIGN CURRENCY. This rule is subject to the provisions below.

[*CTA 2010, s 11*].

UK resident investment companies

A UK resident investment company can elect for a currency to be its designated currency for tax purposes. See **34.4** FOREIGN CURRENCY.

Thus where the company has prepared its accounts in a currency other than sterling and has elected for sterling to be its designated currency, or (where no election has been made) has identified sterling as its functional currency in its accounts, then the profits or losses for the period are calculated in sterling (see *CTA 2010, s 6(2)*).

Where the company has prepared its accounts in one currency and has elected for a different non-sterling currency to be its designated currency, or (where no election has been made) has identified such different non-sterling currency as its functional currency in its accounts, then the profits or losses for the period are first calculated in the designated or identified currency and the sterling equivalent then taken (see *CTA 2010, s 7(2)*).

If neither of the above applies, and the UK resident investment company prepares its accounts in a currency other than sterling then the profits or losses for the period are calculated in the accounts currency and the sterling equivalent then taken (see *CTA 2010, s 8(2)*).

Therefore the rules that are discussed below in the case of UK resident companies equally apply with regard to the translation of the UK resident investment company's losses that are being carried forward and back.

[*CTA 2010, ss 6(1A)(2), 7(1A)(2), 8(2)*].

Losses carried back

Where a loss has to be translated into its sterling equivalent in order to calculate a 'carried-back amount' (i.e. a trading loss carried back under *CTA 2010, s 37* or *s 45F*, a deficit of an insurance company carried back under *CTA 2009, s 389(2)* or a non-trading loan relationship deficit carried back under *CTA 2009, s 459(1)(b)* or *s 463B(1)(b)*), under the provisions of *CTA 2010, ss 7(2), 8(2)* or *9(2)* (see **34.3** and **34.4** FOREIGN CURRENCY with regard to when these sections apply), then one of three rules applies.

- If the tax calculation currencies (i.e. the currencies used to calculate the company's profits or losses before translation into sterling) are the same in the accounting period of loss or deficit and the period to which the carried-back amount is to be carried back, the same rate of exchange is used as that required under *CTA 2010, s 11* to be used in calculating the profit against which the amount is to be set off.
- If the later tax calculation currency is not the same as that for the earlier period, and the earlier currency is sterling, the rate to be used is the spot exchange for the last day of the 'relevant accounting period'.
- If the two currencies are different and neither is sterling, the carried-back amount must be converted into the tax calculation currency for the earlier period at the spot rate of exchange for the last day of the relevant account period before being translated into sterling at the same rate as the profits against which the loss is to be set are required to be translated under *CTA 2010, s 11*.

For this purpose, the '*relevant accounting period*' is the most recent accounting period of the company before that in which the carried-back amount arises in which the tax calculation currency is the same as the tax calculation currency of the period to which the amount is to be carried back.

[*CTA 2010, ss 12, 17(2)(5); F(No 2)A 2017, Sch 4 para 147*].

Where a UK resident company prepares its accounts in accordance with generally accepted accounting practice ('GAAP') in sterling or in another currency, but identifies its functional currency as sterling; and

- a loss arises on a generally accepted accounting practice basis for corporation tax, which is to be a carried-back amount; and
- the tax calculation currency for the period to which the loss is to be carried back is not sterling; then

the loss must first be translated into that earlier tax calculation currency at spot rate for the last day of the relevant accounting period before being translated into sterling at the rate required under *CTA 2010, s 11* to be used to convert the profits against which the loss is to be set.

[*CTA 2010, s 14*].

Losses carried forward

For 'carried-forward amounts' (as defined below), where a loss has to be translated into its sterling equivalent in order to calculate a 'carried-forward amount' under the provisions of *CTA 2010, ss 7(2), 8(2) or 9(2)* (see **34.3** and **34.4** FOREIGN CURRENCY with regard to when these sections apply), then one of three rules for translation applies.

- Where the tax calculation currency is the same in the period in which the amount arises and the period to which it is carried forward, the amount must be translated at the same rate as applies under *CTA 2010, s 11* to the profits against which it is to be set off.
- Where the earlier tax calculation currency is not the same as the later currency and the later currency is sterling, the spot rate for the first day of the 'relevant accounting period' must be used.

- Where the earlier tax calculation currency is not the same as the later currency and the later currency is not sterling, the carried-forward amount must first be translated into the later currency at the spot rate of exchange for the first day of the relevant accounting period, and then into sterling at the same rate as that applied to the profits against which the amount is to be set off.

For this purpose, the '*relevant accounting period*' means the first accounting period after the period in which the carried-forward amount arose when the tax calculation currency became the tax calculation currency of the period to which the amount is to be carried forward.

'*Carried-forward amounts*' are trade losses carried forward under *CTA 2010, ss 45, 45A, 45B*; UK property business losses carried forward under *CTA 2010, s 62(5)* or *s 63(3)*; overseas property losses carried forward under *CTA 2010, s 66(3)*; losses from miscellaneous transactions carried forward under *CTA 2010, s 91(6)*; expenses and other losses of insurance companies carried forward; non-trading loan relationship deficits carried forward under *CTA 2009, ss 457(3), 463G(6), 463H(4)*; non-trading losses on intangible fixed assets carried forward under *CTA 2009, 753(3)*; expenses relating to patent income carried forward under *CTA 2009, s 925(3)*; and management expenses carried forward under *CTA 2009, s 1223*.

[*CTA 2010, ss 13, 17(3); F(No 2)A 2017, Sch 4 para 147*].

Where a UK resident company prepares its accounts in accordance with generally accepted accounting practice ('GAAP') in sterling or in another currency, but identifies its functional currency as sterling, the position is as follows. Where:

- a loss arises on a generally accepted accounting practice basis for corporation tax, which is to be carried-forward; and
- the tax calculation currency for the period to which the loss is to be carried forward is not sterling; then

the loss must first be translated into that later tax calculation currency at spot rate for the first day of the relevant accounting period before being translated into sterling at the rate required under *CTA 2010, s 11* to be used to convert the profits against which the loss is to be set.

[*CTA 2010, s 15*].

Simon's Taxes. See **D4.202, D4.202A.**

Losses on unlisted shares

[51.27] Certain companies may claim relief against income for losses arising on the disposal of unlisted shares for which they have 'subscribed' and which are ordinary share capital of 'qualifying trading companies'. To be eligible to claim relief, a company must meet the following conditions:

- it must have been an 'investment company' on the date of disposal;
- it must have been an investment company throughout the six years prior to the disposal or for a shorter period ending with disposal and has not before the beginning of that period been a 'qualifying trading company' or an 'excluded company'; and

- it must not have been associated with, or a member of the same group as, the 'qualifying trading company' during its ownership of the shares.

For this purpose, an '*investment company*' is a company whose business consists wholly or mainly in the making of investments and which derives the principal part of its income from the making of investments. 'Holding companies' of a 'trading group' are, however, excluded.

A '*holding company*' is a company whose business consists mainly in the holding of shares or securities of 51% subsidiaries.

A '*trading group*' is a 'group' (i.e. a company and its 51% subsidiaries) the business of the members of which, taken together, consists wholly or mainly in the carrying on of a trade or trades (disregarding any trade carried on by a subsidiary which is an excluded company or, as regards shares issued before 6 April 1998, which is non-UK resident).

Companies are '*associated*' where one controls the other or both are under common control, control being as defined in **16.6** CLOSE COMPANIES.

A claim is available only if:

- the disposal is at arm's length; or
- the disposal is by way of a distribution in a dissolution or winding-up; or
- the value of the shares has become negligible and a claim to that effect made under *TCGA 1992, s 24(2)*; or
- the disposal consists of the entire loss, destruction, dissipation or extinction of an asset (within *TCGA 1992, s 24(1)*).

No relief is available where, under *TCGA 1992, s 127*, shares are deemed to have been disposed of on a share exchange or reorganisation, etc. within *TCGA 1992, ss 135* or *136*.

The allowable loss is as calculated for the purposes of corporation tax on chargeable gains. The normal rules for the substitution of market value for consideration apply (see *TCGA 1992, s 17*), but the allowable loss may not exceed the actual loss incurred.

[*CTA 2010, ss 68, 69, 90(1)(6)*].

The shares disposed of must be:

- unquoted at the time of issue;
- originally 'subscribed for' by the company and issued in consideration for money, or money's worth; and
- ordinary share capital.

A company '*subscribes for*' shares in another company if they are issued to it by the other company in consideration of money (or money's worth). If a company has subscribed for shares, it is treated as having subscribed for any bonus shares subsequently issued to it in respect of those shares, provided that the bonus shares are in the same company, of the same class and carry the same rights as the original shares. The bonus shares are treated as issued at the time the original shares were issued. For this purpose, shares are treated as being of the same class only if they would be so treated if they were listed in the UK and traded on the London Stock Exchange. [*CTA 2010, ss 73, 89, 90(1)(2); FA 2020, s 38(2)*].

A '*qualifying trading company*' is defined as a company which:

(a) for disposals before 24 January 2019, has carried on its business wholly or mainly in the UK throughout the period ending on the date of disposal and beginning with the incorporation of the company (or, if later, one year before the date on which the shares were issued);

(b) has met the gross asset condition immediately before and after the issue of the shares; and

(c) for a continuous period of six years ending on the date of disposal/date of cessation either:
   - meets all the trading, control and independence conditions; or
   - has ceased to meet the trading etc conditions in the three years before the date of disposal and has not, since the date of cessation been an excluded company, investment company, trading company or holding company of a trading group.

The requirement in (a) above has been abolished following a formal challenge by the European Commission.

The six year period can be shorter, provided that before the start of the shorter period the company had not met the trading etc requirements or was not an excluded company.

An '*excluded company*' is a company whose trade consists mainly of dealing in land, in commodities or futures or in shares, securities or other financial instruments (as regards shares issued before 6 April 1998 — dealing in shares, securities, land, trades or commodity futures) or which is not carried on a commercial basis with a reasonable expectation of profit, or a company which is the holding company of a group other than a trading group, or which is a building society (see 8 BUILDING SOCIETIES) or a registered society within **22.1** CO-OPERATIVE AND COMMUNITY BENEFIT SOCIETIES.

As to condition (a), in a case regarding share loss relief for individuals, *Professor Sir P Lachmann v HMRC (and related appeal)* [2010] UKFTT 560 (TC), TC00811, a couple claimed loss relief in respect of the disposal of shares in a Canadian company. HMRC rejected the claim on the grounds that what is now *ITA 2007, s 134* stipulated that the company must have 'carried on its business wholly or mainly in the United Kingdom'. The First-Tier Tribunal dismissed the couple's appeal against this decision.

As regards shares issued before 6 April 1998, a '*qualifying trading company*' is a company none of whose shares have been listed on a recognised stock exchange at any time in the period ending with the date of disposal of the shares and beginning with the incorporation of the company, or, if later, one year before the date on which the shares were subscribed for, and which:

(1) either (i) is a trading company on the date of the disposal, or (ii) has ceased to be a trading company within the previous three years and has not since that time been an investment company or an 'excluded company'; and

(2) either (i) has been a trading company for a continuous period of six years ending on the date of disposal of the shares or the time it ceased to be a trading company, or (ii) if shorter, a continuous period ending on that date or that time and had not before the beginning of that period been an excluded company or an investment company; and

(3) for disposals before 24 January 2019, has been resident in the UK since incorporation until the date of disposal.

Securities on the Alternative Investment Market ('AIM') are treated as unlisted for these purposes. (Revenue Press Release 20 February 1995 — see also HMRC Capital Gains Manual CG50255).

[*CTA 2010, ss 78, 90(1); FA 2020, s 38*].

The conditions

[51.28] The conditions which must be met are as follows.

The trading condition

The company must either:

(i) exist wholly for the purpose of carrying on one or more 'qualifying trades' (as defined within *ITA 2007, s 189* with regard to the Enterprise Investment Scheme; or

(ii) be a '*parent company*' (i.e. a company that has one or more 'qualifying subsidiaries' (as defined)) and the business of the '*group*' (i.e. the company and its qualifying subsidiaries) must not consist wholly or as to a substantial part in the carrying on of 'non-qualifying activities'.

Where the company intends that one or more other companies should become its qualifying subsidiaries with a view to their carrying on one or more qualifying trades, then, until any time after which the intention is abandoned, the company is treated as a parent company and those other companies are included in the group for the purposes of (ii) above.

For the purpose of (ii) above, the business of the group means what would be the business of the group if the activities of the group companies taken together were regarded as one business. Activities are for this purpose disregarded to the extent that they consist in:

- holding shares in or securities of any of the company's qualifying subsidiaries;
- making loans to another group company;
- holding and managing property used by a group company for the purposes of a qualifying trade or trades carried on by any group company;
- holding and managing property used by a group company for the purposes of research and development from which it is intended either that a qualifying trade to be carried on by a 'group company' will be derived or, for shares issued after 5 April 2007, a qualifying trade carried on or to be carried on by a group company will benefit. '*Group company*' includes, for this purpose, any existing or future company which will be a group company at any future time; or

- any activities that are not part of the company's main purpose.

Activities are similarly disregarded to the extent that they consist, in the case of a subsidiary whose main purpose is the carrying on of qualifying trade(s) and whose other purposes have no significant effect on the extent of its activities (other than in relation to incidental matters), in activities not in pursuance of its main purpose.

'*Non-qualifying activities*' are:

- excluded activities within *ITA 2007, s 192* (with regard to the Enterprise Investment Scheme); and
- non-trading activities (other than research and development (as defined in *CTA 2010, s 1138*)).

For the ascertainment of the purposes for which a company exists, see HMRC Venture Capital Schemes Manual VCM15070.

A company ceases to meet the trading requirement if, before the time that is relevant for the purposes of (a) above, a resolution is passed or an order is made for the winding-up of the company or if the company is dissolved without winding-up. This does not, however, apply if the winding-up is for genuine commercial reasons and not part of a scheme a main purpose of which is tax avoidance and the company continues, during the winding-up, to be a trading company. (Note that the continuation of trading condition now applies in relation to shares issued after 5 April 2001 but did originally apply up to and including 20 March 2000, after which a drafting error inadvertently altered the law.) For shares issued after 20 March 2000, a company does not cease to meet the trading requirement by reason of anything done as a consequence of its being in administration or receivership (both as defined by *ITA 2007, s 252*), provided everything so done and the entry into administration or receivership are for genuine commercial (and not tax avoidance) reasons. For shares issued after 16 March 2004, these provisions are extended to refer also to the winding-up, dissolution, administration or receivership of any of the company's subsidiaries.

[*CTA 2010, ss 79, 80*].

The control and independence condition

The issuing company must not:

(I) control another company other than a qualifying subsidiary (as defined) or, for shares issued before 21 March 2000, have a 51% subsidiary other than a qualifying subsidiary, 'control' being construed in accordance with *CTA 2010, ss 450, 451* and being considered with or without connected persons within **19** CONNECTED PERSONS;

(II) be a 51% subsidiary of another company or otherwise under the control of another company, 'control' being construed in accordance with *CTA 2010, s 1124* and again being considered with or without connected persons; or

(III) be capable of falling within (I) or (II) by virtue of any arrangements (as very broadly defined).

[*CTA 2010, s 81, Sch 2 para 31*].

The qualifying subsidiaries condition

The company must not have any subsidiaries other than qualifying subsidiaries (as defined in accordance with *ITA 2007, s 191*).

[*CTA 2010, s 82, Sch 2 para 32*].

The property managing subsidiaries condition

For shares issued on or after 17 March 2004, any 'property managing subsidiary' (as defined in *ITA 2007, s 188(2)*) that the company has must be a 'qualifying 90% subsidiary' (as defined in *ITA 2007, s 190*).

[*CTA 2010, s 83, Sch 2 paras 33, 41*].

The gross assets condition

The value of the company's gross assets must not exceed £7 million immediately before the issue of the shares in respect of which relief is claimed and must not exceed £8 million immediately afterwards. In relation to shares issued before 6 April 2006, these limits were £15 million and £16 million respectively; the higher limits continue to apply in relation to shares issued after 5 April 2006 to a person who subscribed for them before 22 March 2006. If the issuing company is a parent company, the gross assets test applies by reference to the aggregate gross assets of the company and all its qualifying subsidiaries (disregarding certain assets held by any such company which correspond to liabilities of another).

[*CTA 2010, s 84, Sch 2 para 34*].

The general approach of HMRC to the gross assets requirement is that the value of a company's gross assets is the sum of the value of all of the balance sheet assets. Where accounts are actually drawn up to a date immediately before or after the issue, the balance sheet values are taken provided that they reflect usual accounting standards and the company's normal accounting practice, consistently applied. Where accounts are not drawn up to such a date, such values will be taken from the most recent balance sheet, updated as precisely as is practicable on the basis of all the relevant information available to the company. Values so arrived at may need to be reviewed in the light of information contained in the accounts for the period in which the issue was made, and, if they were not available at the time of the issue, those for the preceding period, when they become available. The company's assets immediately before the issue do not include any advance payment received in respect of the issue. Where shares are issued partly paid, the right to the balance is an asset, and, notwithstanding the above, will be taken into account in valuing the assets immediately after the issue regardless of whether it is shown in the balance sheet.

(SP2/06).

The unquoted status condition

For shares issued on or after 7 March 2001, the company must be 'unquoted' at the time (the '*relevant time*') at which the shares are issued and no arrangements must then exist for it to cease to be unquoted. If, at the time of issue, arrangements exist for the company to become a wholly-owned subsidiary of a new holding company by means of a share exchange within the provisions below, no arrangements must exist for the new company to cease to be unquoted. A company is '*unquoted*' if none of its shares etc. are listed on a recognised stock exchange or on a foreign exchange designated for the purpose, or dealt in on the Unlisted Securities Market (now closed) or outside the UK by such means as may be designated for the purpose. Securities on the Alternative Investment Market ('AIM') are treated as unquoted for these purposes. (Revenue Press Release 20 February 1995). If the company is unquoted at the time of the share issue, it does not cease to be unquoted in relation to those shares solely because they are listed on an exchange which becomes a recognised stock exchange or is designated by an order made after the date of the issue (see HMRC Venture Capital Schemes Manual VCM15020).

[*CTA 2010, s 85, Sch 2 para 35; ITA 2007, s 184(2)*].

Treasury power to amend conditions

The Treasury may amend the above requirements by order.

[*CTA 2010, s 86, Sch 2 para 36*].

Operation of and claims for relief

[51.29] Relief is given after calculating the loss (in accordance with the chargeable gains rules but is not offset against the total chargeable gains for the period). This loss is then deducted from the total income of the accounting period in which the loss arises in priority to expenses such as management expenses and charges on income, but after any CVS loss relief claim (25 CORPORATE VENTURING SCHEME — it is notable this scheme only applies to shares issued before 1 April 2010).

If the loss cannot be fully utilised in this way, the excess may be carried back and set against income of the previous twelve months. Where an accounting period falls partly within the twelve month period, the loss can only be set against income attributable to the specified period (**47.14** INVESTMENT TRUSTS) and therefore the profits of such an accounting period must be apportioned on a time basis. There is no facility to carry forward any element of the loss, and therefore if the loss cannot be utilised within the specified period, a claim should not be made.

Any earlier loss is relieved in priority to a later one.

Relief must be claimed within two years of the end of the accounting period in which the loss was incurred.

Where relief is claimed under these provisions, no relief may be claimed against chargeable gains in respect of the loss so relieved, but this does not preclude such relief for any part of the loss not relieved under these provisions.

[*CTA 2010, ss 70–72*].

Limits on relief

Where a company claims relief under these provisions for a loss on the disposal of shares which form part of a 'section 104 holding' or a '1982 holding' (i.e. holdings of shares which are pooled for chargeable gains purposes) either at the time of the disposal or an earlier time, the relief is restricted to the sums that would have been allowable as deductions in computing the loss if the qualifying shares had not formed part of the holding.

Where the qualifying shares were acquired on the same day as other shares that are not capable of being qualifying shares (see below), so that under *TCGA 1992, s 105(1)(a)* all the shares are treated as acquired by a single transaction, the amount of relief is restricted to the sums that would have been allowable as deductions in computing the loss if the qualifying shares and the other shares were not so treated.

Where the qualifying shares, taken as a single asset, and other shares or debentures in the same company which are not capable of being qualifying shares, also taken as a single asset, are treated for chargeable gains purposes as the same asset under *TCGA 1992, s 127*, the relief is restricted to the sums that would have been allowable as deductions in computing the loss if the qualifying shares and the other shares or debentures were not to be treated as the same asset.

For these purposes, shares are not capable of being qualifying shares at any time if they were not acquired by subscription or if the gross assets condition would not be met if the shares were disposed of at that time. Additionally, for the purposes only of the 'same asset' restriction above, shares are not capable of being qualifying shares at any time if they are shares of a different class from the qualifying shares concerned.

[*CTA 2010, s 75; FA 2020, s 38(2)*].

Identification

[51.30] The following provisions apply to identify whether a disposal of shares forming part of a mixed holding (i.e. a 'holding' of shares including shares that are not capable of being qualifying shares and other shares) is a disposal of qualifying shares and, if so, to which of any qualifying shares acquired at different times the disposal relates.

Except as noted below, the normal chargeable gains identification rules apply and where shares are thereby identified with the whole or any part of a *section 104* holding or a 1982 holding, they are further identified on a last in/first out (LIFO) basis. This does not apply where the holding includes shares issued on or after 1 April 2000 to which investment relief under the Corporate Venturing Scheme is attributable and which have been held continuously (see 25.5(a) CORPORATE VENTURING SCHEME) by the company; the identification rules at 25.3 CORPORATE VENTURING SCHEME (generally first in/first out) apply instead.

Where the above rules cannot identify the shares disposed of, the identification is to be made on a just and reasonable basis.

A '*holding*' of shares for these purposes is any number of shares of the same class held by one company in the same capacity, growing or diminishing as shares of that class are acquired or disposed of. Shares comprised in a 'new holding' following a reorganisation to which *TCGA 1992, s 127* applies are treated as having been acquired when the original shares were acquired. Any shares held or disposed of by a nominee or bare trustee for a company are treated as held or disposed of by the company.

[*CTA 2010, ss 76, 77*].

Company reconstructions etc.

[51.31] On a **reorganisation** of share capital, new shares may be acquired in exchange for the original holding, and the general rule for capital gains tax purposes is that a disposal will not arise in these cases.

If the new shares are later sold, loss relief may be available if either:

- at the date of the reorganisation the old shares met all of the qualifying conditions; or
- the new shares were acquired for new consideration. Loss relief in this case will be restricted to the amount of that consideration used in the computation of the disposal of the new shares.

'*New consideration*' is money or money's worth excluding any surrender or alteration to the original shares (or rights attached thereto), and excluding the application of assets of the company or of distributions declared but not made out of those assets.

[*CTA 2010, s 74*].

Where, by means of an **exchange of shares**, all of the shares (the old shares) of a company (the old company) are acquired by a company (the new company) in which the only previously issued shares are subscriber shares, then, subject to the further conditions below being satisfied, the exchange is not regarded as involving a disposal of the old shares and an acquisition of the new company shares (the new shares).

Where old shares held by a company were subscribed for by it, the new shares stand in the shoes of the old shares, e.g. as if they had been subscribed for and issued at the time the old shares were subscribed for and issued and as if any requirements under the above provisions met at any time before the exchange by the old company had been met at that time by the new company.

The further conditions are as follows.

(a) The shares must be issued after 5 April 1998.
(b) The consideration for the old shares must consist entirely of the issue of the new shares.
(c) The consideration for old shares of each description must consist entirely of new shares of the 'corresponding description'.
(d) New shares of each description must be issued to holders of old shares of the 'corresponding description' in respect of and in proportion to their holdings.
(e) For new shares issued on or after 6 April 2007, the exchange of shares is not treated for chargeable gains purposes as involving a disposal of the old shares or an acquisition of the new shares by virtue of *TCGA 1992, s 127*.
(f) For new shares issued before 6 April 2007, before the issue of the new shares, on the written application of either the old or new company, HMRC must have notified to that company their satisfaction that the exchange:

(i) is for genuine commercial reasons; and
(ii) does not form part of a scheme or arrangements to which *TCGA 1992, s 137(1) applies*.

HMRC may, within 30 days of an application, request further particulars, which must then be supplied within 30 days of the request (or such longer period as they may allow in any particular case).

For these purposes, old and new shares are of a '*corresponding description*' if, assuming they were shares in the same company, they would be of the same class and carry the same rights.

An exchange within these provisions, or arrangements for such an exchange do not breach the control and independence requirement above.

[*CTA 2010, ss 87, 88, Sch 2 para 37*].

Simon's Taxes. See **D7.312**.

Example

Z Ltd has been an investment company since its incorporation in 1972. It is not part of a trading group and has no associated companies. It makes up accounts to 31 December. On 6 February 2021, Z Ltd disposed of part of its holding of shares in T Ltd for full market value. Z Ltd makes no global re-basing election under *TCGA 1992, s 35(5)*.

Details of disposal	
Contract date	6.2.21
Shares sold	2,000 Ord
Proceeds (after expenses)	£4,500

Z acquired its shares in T Ltd as follows.

				£
6.4.81 subscribed for	1,000	shares	cost (with expenses)	5,000
6.4.91 acquired	1,500	shares	cost (with expenses)	4,000
	2,500			£9,000

T Ltd shares were valued at £3 per share at 31 March 1982. T Ltd has been a UK resident trading company since 1980. Its shares are not quoted on a recognised stock exchange.

Z Ltd may claim that part of the loss incurred be set off against its income as follows.

Identification of the shares in the pool which are sold takes place on a last in, first out basis.

(i) Shares acquired 6.4.91 (not subscribed for)

		£
Proceeds of 1,500 shares $\frac{1,500}{2,000} \times £\ 4,500$		3,375
Cost of 1,500 shares		(4,000)
Capital loss *not* available for set-off against income		£(625)

(ii) Shares acquired 6.4.81 (subscribed for)

	Cost basis	31.3.82 value basis
	£	£
Proceeds of 500 shares $\frac{500}{2,000} \times £\ 4,500$	1,125	1,125
Cost of 500 shares	(2,500)	
31.3.82 value		(1,500)
	£(1,375)	£(375)
Capital loss available for set-off against income		£(375)

The loss of £375 is available primarily against income of the year ended 31 December 2021, with any balance being available against, broadly speaking, income of the 12 months ended 31 December 2020 (see **51.29** above).

Certain business activities

Farming and market gardening

[51.32] A loss incurred in any accounting period in a trade of farming or market gardening cannot be relieved against other income or gains or carried back if a loss, ignoring capital allowances, has been incurred in that period and in each accounting period falling wholly or partly within the five years up to the beginning of the accounting period in question.

This provision does not deny relief where:

(i) the farming, etc. is part of, and ancillary to, a larger trading undertaking; or

(ii) a competent person carrying on the farming, etc. activities in the year in question would reasonably expect to produce profits in the future, but such a person carrying on the activities at the start of the 'prior period of loss' could not reasonably have expected the activities to become profitable until after the end of the year in question; or

(iii) the trade was started or treated as started (see *CTA 2010, s 50*) during the preceding five years.

The prior period of loss in (ii) above is the previous five years or, if longer, all of the successive years prior to the year in question in which a loss was incurred (ignoring capital allowances).

[*CTA 2010, ss 48–51*].

In a case dealing with the equivalent income tax provisions, the rule that is equivalent to (ii) above was considered. The UT held that the second part of the test operated as follows. First, the activities actually carried on in each year for which a claim was made (in that case 2007/08 to 2011/12) had to be determined. Second, it then had to be assumed that *those* activities were being carried on at the beginning of the loss period (in 1995). Having made that assumption, the question was how long a competent farmer in 1995 would have expected it would take for those activities to become profitable. See *HMRC v A Naghshineh* UT, [2020] STC 480.

Simon's Taxes. See **B5.175**.

Leasing contracts for plant and machinery

[51.33] There is a restriction on the offset of 'losses incurred on a leasing contract' if:

- a company incurs capital expenditure on plant or machinery which it leases out to a third party;
- in the accounting period in which annual investment allowance or first-year allowances (see **10.12**, **10.14** CAPITAL ALLOWANCES ON PLANT AND MACHINERY) are available (if at all), there are arrangements for either a successor company or a company connected with the first company, to take over all or part of the first company's obligations under the leasing contract.

The restriction operates by treating any 'losses incurred on a leasing contract' as if they arose on a separate 'leasing contract trade' and they are therefore only available for offset against future profits arising on the same leasing contract.

Anti-avoidance provisions restrict the offset of losses where there is a change in the ownership (or corporate partnership interest) of a company carrying on the business of leasing plant or machinery (**49.3** LEASING).

'*Losses incurred on a leasing contract*' (and profits arising) are computed, and are treated for relief purposes, as if the performance of the leasing contract constituted a separate trade, begun at the commencement of the letting. Loss relief is thus restricted to future profits on the leasing contract.

'*Successor company*' is as defined in **51.16** above or a company connected (see **19** CONNECTED PERSONS) with the first company.

[*CTA 2010, s 53; F(No 2)A 2017, Sch 4 para 150*].

Sale of lessors

For restriction of relief for losses in the case where there is a change in the ownership of a company carrying on a business of leasing plant or machinery, see **49.9** onwards LEASING.

Leasing partnerships

For restriction of relief for losses in the case where there is a change in the interest of a company in a business, carried on in partnership, of leasing plant or machinery, see **49.3** and **49.9** LEASING. For restrictions on the set-off against an individual's total income of certain losses arising from first-year allowances incurred by the individual in partnership with a company, see Tolley's Income Tax under Losses.

Companies trading in partnership

[51.34] There is a restriction on loss relief where a company ('the partner company') is a member of a trading partnership and arrangements exist whereby another partner (or a person connected with him, see **19** CONNECTED PERSONS) receives any payment or enjoys any benefit in money's worth in respect of the partner company's 'share in the profits or losses' of the partnership or whereby the partner company (or a person connected with it) receives any payment or enjoys any such benefit in respect of its share of losses (other than a payment for group relief, see **35.2–35.18** GROUP RELIEF).

If the above conditions are satisfied for any accounting period, the company's share of partnership losses and qualifying charitable donations (see *CTA 2010, s 189*) may be set off only against its share of profits from the partnership's trade, and no other loss incurred by the company in that period may be set against such profits.

[*CTA 2010, ss 958–962*].

The company's '*share in the profits or losses*' of the partnership is determined under *CTA 2009, s 1262* (see **56.3** PARTNERSHIPS).

See also **51.12, 51.33** above and **51.36** below and **56.10** PARTNERSHIPS.

Dealings in commodity futures

[51.35] Special rules apply to **restrict loss relief** when a company deals in commodity futures, as follows:

Transaction	Restriction
Participates in a trade of dealing in commodity futures in partnership (where one of the partners is a company) and arrangements are made with the sole or main benefit being to reduce a tax liability by making a loss relief claim against general income of the current or previous year. [*CTA 2010, s 52(1)–(4)*.	Loss relief claim under *CTA 2010, s 37* is denied. If relief has already been given, it will be withdrawn by an assessment on overseas income or miscellaneous income.

Write-off of government investment

[51.36] Where any amount of Government investment in a company is written-off, an equal amount is set against the company's 'carry-forward losses' as at the end of the accounting period before that in which the investment was written-off, and against such losses of subsequent accounting periods until the amount written-off is extinguished.

[*CTA 2010, s 92*].

This does not prevent a company from deducting a sum in calculating its profits, and in particular, expenditure is not treated as met by a public body for capital allowances or chargeable gains purposes by reason only that an amount of government investment has been written off.

[*CTA 2010, s 96(1)–(3)*].

'*Carry-forward losses*' at the end of an accounting period are any trading losses, losses from a UK property or overseas property business, management expenses, capital allowances or allowable capital losses available for carry-forward at the end of the period, and any unused qualifying charitable donations for the period.

[*CTA 2010, s 95(1); F(No 2)A 2017, Sch 4 para 156(2)*].

The set-off is made against allowable capital losses of a period only after all other carry-forward losses of the period have been exhausted.

[*CTA 2010, s 95(4)*].

In determining the carry-forward losses at the end of the accounting period before that of the write-off, valid claims for group relief or group relief for carried-forward losses, or for relief of trading losses or capital allowances against profits generally and/or of earlier accounting periods, are effective provided that they are made before the write-off date. Such claims made on or after that date are ineffective until the amount written-off has been set off in full.

[*CTA 2010, s 95(2)(3); F(No 2)A 2017, Sch 4 para 156(3)*].

Where the company concerned is a member of a group (i.e. a parent company and its 51% subsidiaries), the set-off for an accounting period may be made against carry-forward losses of any other company which is a group member at the end of the accounting period, any allocation between group companies being on a 'reasonable and just' basis.

[*CTA 2010, s 93*].

An amount of Government investment in a company is treated as written off if:

(a) its liability to repay money lent out of public funds by a Minister of the Crown, the Scottish Ministers or a Northern Ireland department is extinguished; or
(b) any of its shares subscribed for out of public funds by a Minister etc. are cancelled; or

(c) any 'commencing capital debt' (i.e. any debt to a Minister etc. assumed as such under an enactment) is reduced otherwise than by being paid off; or

(d) any 'public dividend capital' (i.e. any amount paid by a Minister etc. under an enactment which so describes it or which corresponds with enactments relating to similar payments so described) is reduced otherwise than by being repaid.

The amount and date of the write-off are determined accordingly. No restriction is, however, made under these provisions if, and to the extent that, the amount written-off is replaced in some other form by money provided out of public funds by a Minister etc.

[*CTA 2010, s 94*].

There is no write-off if the amount written off is replaced in some other form by money provided out of public funds by a Minister, etc. notwithstanding *CTA 2009, s 464(1)* (matters to be brought into account in the case of loan relationships only under the loan relationship provisions, see 50.2 LOAN RELATIONSHIPS).

[*CTA 2010, s 96(4)*].

These provisions apply in priority to the loan relationship rules.

[*CTA 2010, s 96(4)*].

Simon's Taxes. See **D1.1114**.

Double taxation

[51.37] Where:

- interest, dividends or royalties accrue to a non-resident company carrying on a business in the UK;
- which have been treated as tax-exempt under double taxation arrangements (*TIOPA 2010, s 2*);

then they are not to be excluded from trading income or profits of the business so as to give rise to losses to be set off against income or profits.

[*CTA 2010, s 54; F(No 2)A 2017, Sch 4 para 151*].

Key points on losses

[51.38] Points to consider are as follows.

- Losses arising from different sources of income are subject to different rules regarding utilisation, including the types of profits against which the losses may be offset, the periods in which they may be offset and the order in which they are required to be relieved. For example, only trading losses may be carried back to offset profits arising in the twelve months prior to the period in which the loss arose.

- The specified carry-back period for trading losses has been temporarily extended from twelve months to three years for losses incurred in accounting periods ending between 1 April 2020 and 31 March 2022 inclusive. A number of further rules and restrictions apply to the extension. In applying the rules and restrictions, claims for losses arising in accounting periods ending in the period 1 April 2020 to 31 March 2021 ('2020 claims') are dealt with separately from losses arising in accounting periods ending in the period 1 April 2021 to 31 March 2022 ('2021 claims'). The total relief for losses carried back by a company which is not a member of a group beyond the normal twelve-month period must be less than £2 million each for 2020 claims and 2021 claims. The £2 million limit is, broadly, shared between the members of a group.
- The rules for carry-forward of losses have been substantially revised with effect, broadly, from 1 April 2017. Trade losses and non-trading loan relationship deficits carried forward are, subject to certain exceptions, available for set-off against total profits. See **50.6** LOAN RELATIONSHIPS and **51.6** above. A new form of group relief, group relief for carried-forward losses is introduced: see **35.24** GROUP RELIEF. A restriction on the amount of carried-forward amounts which may be deducted is introduced and limits the profits against which any carried-forward amounts can be relieved to 50% of profits over an annual allowance of £5 million. See **51.13** above.
- Any qualifying charitable donations which cannot be offset against other income of the company arising in the same period or, in the event that the company is a member of a group, surrendered as group relief, will be lost as it is not possible to carry them forward for future offset.
- Where a company transfers part or all of its trade to another company within the same 75% ownership, any trading losses of the company are automatically transferred to the successor company. However, there is a restriction of the losses transferred to the extent that liabilities of the trade not transferred exceed the assets of the trade that are not transferred.
- Given the broad application of the loss restriction provisions on a change of ownership of a company (see **51.17**), in most cases it is unlikely that a purchaser would ascribe value to tax losses in the target company.
- Restrictions apply where deductible amounts are claimed by a company (including loss relief and group relief) where there has been a qualifying change in the ownership of a company, and where arrangements are in place with regard to certain relevant claims or profit transfers.
- Anti-avoidance provisions apply for accounting periods beginning on or after 1 April 2017 to prevent companies using artificial arrangements to obtain relief for losses.

- Restrictions apply to prevent companies from using certain brought forward losses against profits created by arrangements entered into with a main purpose of using such losses.
- Where a company has a functional currency other than sterling and seeks to offset losses arising against prior year or future profits, care is needed to ensure that the appropriate exchange rate is used to convert the losses into sterling (see **51.35**).
- Losses arising on a disposal of shares are generally treated as capital losses. However, where the company making the disposal is an investment company, provided certain conditions are met (see **51.27**), it may be able to claim a deduction for the loss against income profits. A claim should only be made in respect of such part of any loss that can be used to shelter income profits arising in the period in which the loss arises, or in the prior twelve months, as any loss that cannot be so used cannot be carried forward.

52

Manufactured Payments

Introduction to manufactured payments

[52.1] There are special provisions which apply to certain arrangements for the transfers of securities under which a person is required to pay to the other party an amount representing a dividend or interest.

The intention of the provisions is for both payer and recipient of the amount in question to be in the same position, for tax purposes, as if the payment had in fact been a dividend or interest.

For the rules for manufactured dividends, see 52.2 below. For the rules applicable to manufactured interest, see 52.3 below.

Manufactured dividends

[52.2] For the purposes of the rules described below, a company has a manufactured dividend relationship if the following three conditions are met:

(a) under any arrangements either an amount is payable by or to the company or any other benefit is given by or to the company (including the release of the whole or part of any liability to pay an amount);

(b) the arrangements relate to the transfer of shares in a company; and

(c) the amount or value of the other benefit is either representative of a real dividend on the shares or will fall to be treated as representative of such a dividend when it is paid or given.

In (a) above, the reference to an amount being payable, or other benefit being given, by the company includes an amount payable, or other benefit given, by another person on behalf of the company. A '*manufactured dividend*' is an amount, or the value of a benefit, within (a) above.

[*CTA 2010, s 814B*].

Treatment of recipient

Where a company has a manufactured dividend relationship under which a manufactured dividend is payable to it, the company (and any company claiming title through it) is treated for corporation tax purposes as if the manufactured dividend was a dividend on the shares in question. The normal tax treatment for dividends then applies (see **29.16** DISTRIBUTIONS). For the purposes of that treatment, the 'payer' of the dividend is the company that pays the real dividend in (c) above.

This treatment does not apply to a company where the manufactured dividend is brought into account as a trading receipt in calculating the profits of a trade carried on by the company.

In addition the manufactured dividend is not treated as a dividend on the shares for the purposes of determining entitlement to DOUBLE TAX RELIEF (**31**).

[*CTA 2010, s 814D*].

Treatment of payer

Where a company has a manufactured dividend relationship under which a manufactured dividend is paid by the company or on its behalf, no deduction is allowed in respect of the manufactured dividend. However, this treatment does not apply where the dividend is brought into account as a deduction in calculating the profits of a trade carried on by the company.

Where the manufactured dividend relates to investment business of the company, the company received the real dividend in (c) above (or a manufactured dividend treated as a real dividend as above) in the accounting period, and the real dividend is taxed as a distribution from a real estate investment trust (see **47.11** INVESTMENT TRUSTS), the manufactured dividend is treated as management expenses of the company's investment business for the accounting period.

[*CTA 2010, s 814C*].

Manufactured interest

[52.3] A company has a manufactured interest relationship if the following conditions are met:

(a) under any arrangements an amount is payable by or on behalf of or to the company;
(b) the arrangements relate to the transfer of an asset representing a loan relationship; and
(c) the amount is either representative of real interest under the loan relationship or will be treated as representative of such interest when it is paid.

'*Manufactured interest*' is an amount within (a) above. It will most commonly arise in connection with repo transactions and stock lending.

Manufactured interest payable by a company under a manufactured interest relationship is treated as if the manufactured interest was interest payable on a loan to the company. The manufactured interest relationship is therefore treated as a loan relationship to which the company is a party.

Similarly, manufactured interest payable to a company under a manufactured interest relationship is treated as if the manufactured interest was interest payable on a loan by the company. The manufactured interest relationship is treated as if it was the loan relationship under which the real interest is payable.

Where a company disposes of its right to receive manufactured interest, the company is treated as if it was still entitled to receive the payments and so continues to be liable to tax on the manufactured interest.

See **50.4** LOAN RELATIONSHIPS for the taxation of interest and for the determination of the trading or non-trading nature of the associated debits and credits.

[*CTA 2009, ss 539–541*].

Simon's Taxes. See **D1.745**.

53

Miscellaneous Income

Introduction to miscellaneous income

[53.1] *CTA 2009, Pt 10* contains provisions relating to miscellaneous income, not chargeable under any other provisions, within the following categories:

(i) estate income (see **53.2** below);
(ii) income from holding an office (see **53.12** below);
(iii) sale of foreign dividend coupons (see **53.13** below);
(iv) annual payments not otherwise charged (see **53.14** below); and
(v) income not otherwise charged (see **53.15** below).

Income which is within (iii) above and also within the profits of a trade or a UK property business is charged to corporation tax under the provisions for trade profits or UK business property business profits as appropriate.

[*CTA 2009, ss 932, 982*].

For relief for miscellaneous losses see **51.12** LOSSES.

Estate income

[53.2] Corporate beneficiaries of deceased person's estates in administration are within the charge to corporation tax on income treated as arising from their interest in the estate (referred to in *CTA 2009* as '*estate income*'). Where a company has an interest in different parts of an estate, each interest is treated as a separate estate.

[*CTA 2009, s 934*].

Liability under these provisions depends on the type of interest that the company has (an 'absolute interest' (53.5 below), a 'limited interest' (53.6 below) or a 'discretionary interest' (53.7 below)) and whether the estate is a 'UK estate' or a 'foreign estate' (as defined at 53.3 below).

Definitions

[53.3] The following definitions apply for the purposes of these provisions.

The '*personal representatives*' of a deceased person mean, in the UK, the persons responsible for administering his estate and, outside the UK, the persons having equivalent functions under the law of the territory concerned.

[*CTA 2010, s 1119*].

A person has an '*absolute interest*' in the whole or part of the residue of an estate if the capital of the residue (or part) is properly payable to that person or would be so payable if the residue had been ascertained.

A person has a '*limited interest*' in the whole or part of the residue of an estate during any period if the person does not have an absolute interest and the income from the residue (or part) would be properly payable to the person if it had been ascertained at the beginning of the period.

A person has a '*discretionary interest*' in the whole or part of an estate if a discretion may be exercised in the person's favour so that any income of the residue during the whole or part of the administration period would be properly payable to the person if the residue had been ascertained at the beginning of that period. For this purpose, an amount is only treated as properly payable to a person (A) if it is properly payable to A, or to another person in A's right, for A's benefit (whether directly or through a trustee or other person). The personal representatives of a deceased person (B) are treated as having an absolute or limited interest in the whole or part of the estate of another deceased person (C) if they have a right in their capacity as B's personal representatives and, were the right vested in them for their own benefit, they would have that interest in C's estate.

[*CTA 2009, s 935*].

An estate is a '*UK estate*' in relation to a tax year if either:

(a) as regards the income of the estate:
   (i) all of the income of the estate (disregarding any life assurance gains and any sums *treated as* bearing income tax at the dividend ordinary rate) has either borne UK income tax by deduction or is income in respect of which the personal representatives are directly assessable to UK income tax for the year; and
   (ii) none of the income of the estate (disregarding any life assurance gains and any sums *treated as* bearing income tax at the dividend ordinary rate) is income for which the personal representatives are not liable to UK income tax for the year because they are not resident in the UK; or

(b) the income of the estate for the year consists only of life assurance gains and/or sums treated as bearing income tax at the dividend ordinary rate.

If an estate is not a UK estate in relation to a tax year it is a '*foreign estate*' in relation to that year.

[*CTA 2009, s 936*].

The '*aggregate income*' of an estate for a tax year is the total of:

(i) the income of the personal representatives in that capacity which is charged to income tax for the year, less any allowable deductions;
(ii) the income of the personal representatives in that capacity which would have been chargeable to income tax if it were income from a UK source of a person resident in the UK, less any deductions which would have been allowable;
(iii) any stock dividends that would be chargeable on the personal representatives if such income were so chargeable;
(iv) any amount that would be chargeable on the personal representatives on release of a loan to a participator in a close company if such amounts were so chargeable; and
(v) any gain from a life insurance contract that would have been treated as income of the personal representatives in that capacity if the condition for such gains to be so treated were met.

Income from property devolving on the personal representatives otherwise than as assets for payment of the deceased's debts and income to which any person is or may become entitled under a specific disposition (as defined) is, however, excluded.

[*CTA 2009, s 947*].

The '*residuary income*' of an estate for a tax year is the aggregate income of the estate for the year less deductions for:

(a) all interest paid in the year by the personal representatives in that capacity (other than interest on unpaid inheritance tax under *IHTA 1984, s 233*);
(b) all annual payments for the year which are properly payable out of residue;
(c) all expenses of management of the estate paid in the year (but only where, ignoring any specific direction in a will, properly chargeable to income); and
(d) any excess of allowable deductions for the previous year over the aggregate income of the estate for that year.

No deduction is allowed for any amount allowable in calculating the aggregate income of the estate.

[*CTA 2009, s 949*].

A transfer of assets or the appropriation of assets by personal representatives to themselves is treated as the payment of an amount equal to the assets' value at the date of the transfer or appropriation.

The set off or release of a debt is treated as the payment of amount equal to it. If at the end of the administration period there is an obligation to transfer assets to any person or the personal representatives are entitled to appropriate assets to themselves, an amount equal to the assets' value at that time is treated as payable then. If at that time there is an obligation to release or set off a debt owed by any person or the personal representatives are entitled to release or set off a debt in their own favour, a sum equal to the debt is treated as payable then.

[*CTA 2009, s 964*].

Grossing-up of estate income

[53.4] In arriving at the amount of estate income (for a UK estate), the basic amounts treated as income of the beneficiary are 'grossed up' by the basic rate of tax or the dividend ordinary rate, depending on the type of income and the tax year in which it arose. The estate income is then treated as having borne income tax at that rate or rates.

In determining the rate applicable, it is assumed:

(a) firstly that amounts are paid to beneficiaries out of the different parts of the aggregate income of the estate in such proportions as are just and reasonable for their different interests; and
(b) secondly that payments are made from those parts bearing tax at the basic rate before they are made from those parts bearing tax at the dividend ordinary rate.

If some of the aggregate income of the estate is income *treated as* having suffered tax at source, e.g. life assurance gains and UK stock dividends, it is assumed that an amount is paid from other income in priority to that income. The above assumptions are then made in relation to each part of the payment.

Foreign estates

Grossing up is applicable to payments out of a foreign estate only in respect of certain sums *treated as* having suffered tax at source, so that, for example, UK stock dividends are grossed up at the dividend ordinary rate. No repayment of such notional tax can be made.

See Tolley's Income Tax for the rates of income tax applicable to different types of income.

[*CTA 2009, ss 941, 942, 946, 962, 963*].

Simon's Taxes. See **I4.540, I4.541.**

Absolute interests

[53.5] A corporate beneficiary with an absolute interest is chargeable to corporation tax on income treated as arising in an accounting period from the interest if:

(a) it has an 'assumed income entitlement' for that accounting period; and
(b) a payment is made in respect of the interest in the accounting period and before the end of the administration period.

For the accounting period in which the administration period ends (the '*final accounting period*'), income is treated as arising if the company has an assumed income entitlement for that accounting period (whether or not any payments are made).

Subject to the grossing-up provisions in 53.4 above, the amount so treated as income for an accounting period is the lower of the:

(i) total amount of all sums paid in the accounting period in respect of the interest; and
(ii) company's assumed income entitlement for the accounting period.

For the final accounting period, the amount is the company's assumed income entitlement for that accounting period. Where, however, the residuary income of the estate for the '*final tax year*' (i.e. the tax year in which the administration period ends) is nil as a result of the allowable deductions exceeding the aggregate income of the estate, the amount for the final accounting period is reduced by the excess (or, where the interest is in part of the residue only, a just and reasonable part of that excess).

A company's '*assumed income entitlement*' for an accounting period is the excess of the total of the company's share of the residuary income of the estate (less, in the case of a UK estate, income tax on that amount at the appropriate rate) for that accounting period and for each previous accounting period for which it held the interest over the total of the amounts (before grossing-up) relating to the interest in respect of which the company was liable to tax for all previous accounting periods (or would have been liable had it been within the charge to corporation tax).

A company's share of the residuary income of an estate is determined firstly by reference to a tax year and then apportioned to the accounting periods (if more than one) coinciding with that tax year.

If the total of all sums paid during or payable at the end of the administration period in respect of the interest (grossed-up, in the case of a UK estate, at the basic rate for the tax year of payment or, where applicable, the final tax year) are less than the total of the company's shares of the residuary income for all tax years, the deficiency is applied to reduce its share of the residuary income, firstly for the final accounting period, then for the previous accounting period and so on.

[*CTA 2009, ss 937, 938, 943, 948, 950–952*].

Simon's Taxes. See **I4.546, I4.547.**

Limited interests

[53.6] Subject to the grossing-up provisions in 53.4 above, sums paid (including assets transferred, debts released etc.) to a corporate beneficiary with a limited interest *during administration* are treated as its income for the accounting period of payment and are chargeable to corporation tax accordingly. Any amount which remains payable in respect of the limited interest *on completion of administration* is treated as income of the company for the accounting period in which the administration period ends. If the interest ceases earlier, any amount then remaining payable is treated as income for the accounting period in which the interest ceased.

[*CTA 2009, ss 939, 944*].

Simon's Taxes. See I4.549.

Discretionary interests

[53.7] The company in whose favour the discretion is exercised is charged to corporation tax on the total payments made in an accounting period in exercise of the discretion, grossed up, where appropriate, as indicated at **53.4** above.

[*CTA 2009, ss 940, 945*].

This applies whether the payments are out of income as it arises, or out of income arising to the personal representatives in earlier years and retained pending exercise of the discretion. See HMRC SP 4/93. For HMRC guidance on discretionary interests see HMRC Trusts, Settlements and Estates Manual TSEM7660.

Simon's Taxes. See I4.550.

Foreign estates

[53.8] Where UK corporation tax is charged for an accounting period on estate income from a foreign estate and UK income tax has already been borne by part of the aggregate income of the estate for the 'relevant tax year', the company may make a claim for the corporation tax charged to be reduced in accordance with the formulae in *CTA 2009, ss 960, 961*. The '*relevant tax year*' is the tax year in which the estate income would be treated as arising if the company were within the charge to income tax rather than corporation tax.

For grossing-up provisions in relation to foreign estates see **53.4**.

[*CTA 2009, ss 946(5), 960, 961*].

Simon's Taxes. See I4.545.

Successive interests

[53.9] Special rules apply to the calculation of estate income where there are two or more successive absolute or limited interests during the period of administration.

[*CTA 2009, ss 953–959*].

Simon's Taxes. See I4.551.

Adjustments etc. after administration period

[53.10] If, after the administration period ends, it is clear that a company's liability under the above provisions for an accounting period is greater or less than previously appeared, all necessary assessments, adjustments etc. can be made. Assessments may be made or adjusted, and relief may be claimed, at any time on or before the third anniversary of 31 January following the accounting period in which the administration period ended.

[*CTA 2009, s 965*].

Simon's Taxes. See **I4.554.**

Information

[53.11] A personal representative has a duty to supply a corporate beneficiary, on request, with a statement of income and tax borne for an accounting period.

[*CTA 2009, s 967*].

Simon's Taxes. See **I4.555.**

Income from holding an office

[53.12] The charge to corporation tax on income applies to income from the holding of an office, computed in accordance with income tax law (in particular *ITEPA 2003, Pt 2* — see Tolley's Income Tax under Employment Income) for the tax year in which the company's accounting period ends. [*CTA 2009, s 969*].

In computing such income, no deduction is allowed in respect of a debt owed to the company except:

- by way of 'impairment loss' (see **69.5** TRADING INCOME—DEDUCTIONS); or
- so far as the debt is released wholly and exclusively for the purposes of the office as part of a 'statutory insolvency arrangement' (see **69.5** TRADING INCOME—DEDUCTIONS).

This does not apply in relation to a debt falling with the regime for LOAN RELATIONSHIPS (**49**). For the purposes of these provisions, 'debt' includes an obligation or liability which falls to be met otherwise than by the payment of money.

[*CTA 2009, s 970*].

Simon's Taxes. See **B2.410.**

Sale of foreign dividend coupons

[53.13] The charge to corporation tax on income applies to income which is treated as arising from '*foreign holdings*' (i.e. shares outside the UK that are issued by or on behalf of a non-UK resident body of persons).

With regard to banks and persons dealing in coupons, income is treated as arising from such holdings in two cases:

(i) where a bank's office in the UK either pays over, or carries into an account, the proceeds of a sale or other realisation of 'dividend coupons' in respect of the holdings;
(ii) where proceeds arise from a sale of 'dividend coupons' in respect of the holdings to a person dealing in coupons in the UK and the seller is neither a bank (as defined) nor a dealer in coupons.

The provisions at (i) apply in any case where a bank's office is in the UK, whether or not the bank is resident in the UK. The provisions at (ii) apply in any case where a person is dealing in coupons in the UK whether or not that person is resident in the UK.

The amount of income treated as arising is the proceeds of sale or realisation. '*Dividend coupons*' means coupons (as defined) for dividends payable in respect of foreign holdings.

[*CTA 2009, ss 974, 975*].

Simon's Taxes. See **D7.726**.

Annual payments not otherwise charged

[53.14] There is a residual charge to corporation tax on income in respect of annual payments not charged to corporation tax under any other provision (other than any such payments not so charged only because of an exemption). In determining whether payments are annual payments, the frequency with which they are made is irrelevant. [*CTA 2009, ss 976, 977*].

The phrase 'annual payment' derives its meaning from an extensive body of case law for which see Tolley's Tax Cases.

[*CTA 2009, s 978*].

Restriction of deductions for annual payments

In calculating a company's income from any source, no deduction is allowed for an annual payment to which the following apply.

- The payment is charged to income tax under *ITTOIA 2005, Pt V* (miscellaneous income) (otherwise than as relevant foreign income — see Tolley's Income Tax under Foreign Income) or is charged to corporation tax under *CTA 2009, ss 976, 977*.
- The payment is made under a liability incurred for consideration in money or money's worth, all or any of which either (a) consists of, or of the right to receive, a dividend, or (b) is not required to be brought into account in calculating for corporation tax purposes the income of the company making the annual payment.
- The payment is not a payment of income which arises under a settlement made on divorce, annulment or separation and payable by one party to the marriage or civil partnership to or for the benefit of the other party.
- The payment is not made to an individual under a liability incurred in consideration of his surrendering, assigning or releasing in interest in settled property to, or in favour of, a person with a subsequent interest.
- The payment is not an annuity granted in the ordinary course of a business of granting annuities.

In calculating a company's income from any source for corporation tax purposes no deduction is allowed for interest except under the loan relationship provisions at *CTA 2009, Pt 5*.

In relation to Scotland, the reference to settled property is to property held in trust.

[*CTA 2009, ss 1301, 1301A*].

Annual payments as above are made without deduction of tax at source.

Income not otherwise charged

[53.15] There is a residual charge to corporation tax on income in relation to income not charged to corporation tax under any other provision. This does not apply to annual payments (for which see the similar residual charge at **53.14** above, income not charged to corporation tax because of an exemption (see, for example, below), and deemed income. [*CTA 2009, s 979*].

Any gain arising in the course of dealing in financial futures or in traded or financial options, other than in the course of a trade, is dealt with under the chargeable gains rules and is not within the charge to corporation tax on income under the above provisions. [*CTA 2009, s 981; TCGA 1992, s 143*].

Exemptions from the charge

Income arising from the commercial occupation of woodlands in the UK is also excluded from the charge to corporation tax under the above provisions. For this purpose, the occupation of woodlands is commercial if the woodlands are managed on a commercial basis and with a view to the realisation of profits. [*CTA 2009, s 980*].

See **68.30**(h) TRADING INCOME as regards short rotation coppice being treated as farming and not as woodlands.

In *Jaggers (trading as Shide Trees) v Ellis* Ch D 1997, 71 TC 164, land on which trees were planted and cultivated in a manner normally associated with Christmas tree production was held not to be woodland, rather they are nurseries and as such comprise market gardening.

54
Mutual Companies

Cross-references. See **8** BUILDING SOCIETIES; **60.18**(b) PROPERTY INCOME; **75** VOLUNTARY ASSOCIATIONS.

Simon's Taxes. See **B1.436–B1.440, D7.509, D7.644.**

Introduction to mutual companies

[54.1] A person cannot derive a taxable profit from trading with himself except in certain cases of self-supply by a trader of trading stock, see *FA 2008, s 37* which gives statutory effect to *Sharkey v Wernher* (1955) 36 TC 275, HL. This principle is extended to a group of persons engaged in mutual activities of a trading nature, if there is:

- an identifiable 'fund' for the common purpose with complete identity between contributors; and
- participators in, the fund (the 'mutuality principle').

Transactions with non-members

[54.2] A body not liable to tax as regards transactions with members may nevertheless be treated as generating taxable trading income from transactions with non-members and is liable in the ordinary way on any investment etc. income. Whether the mutuality principle applies depends on the facts.

See *Liverpool Corn Trade Association Ltd v Monks* (1926) 10 TC 442 (trade association providing corn exchange etc. held to be trading and not 'mutual' — but see **69.64** TRADING INCOME—DEDUCTIONS for special arrangements available for trade associations); *English & Scottish Joint CWS Ltd v Assam Agricultural IT Commr* (1948) 27 ATC 332, PC (wholesale co-operative with two members held to be trading and not mutual — there was no 'common fund').

A members' club does not trade and is not liable on its surplus from the provision of facilities for members (*Eccentric Club Ltd* [1924] 1 KB 390, 12 TC 657, CA), but it is liable on the surplus attributable to non-members (*Carlisle & Silloth Golf Club v Smith* (1913) 6 TC 48, CA). For further cases, see Tolley's Income Tax under Mutual Trading.

Payments on liquidation etc.

[54.3] For distribution of assets by a mutual concern to a trading company, see 68.47 TRADING INCOME.

Credit unions

[54.4] In making loans to its members or investing its surplus funds (e.g. by placing them on deposit), a credit union (within *Co-operative and Community Benefit Societies Act 2014* or *Credit Unions (Northern Ireland) Order 1985*) is not regarded as trading. No loan relationship credits are brought into account where a member of the union is the debtor under the loan relationship. Likewise, no debits are brought into account where a member is the creditor. Annual payments are not deductible in computing the profits of a trade carried on by a credit union.

[*CTA 2009, ss 40, 133, 397, 1319*].

Transfers of business

[54.5] The Treasury are given wide powers to regulate, by statutory instrument, the tax consequences of the transfer of a 'mutual society'. For this purpose a '*mutual society*' is defined as an incorporated building society, a registered friendly society or a registered society within **22.1** CO-OPERATIVE AND COMMUNITY BENEFIT SOCIETIES (previously an industrial and provident society), registered or deemed to be registered.

[*FA 2009, s 124*].

Mutual life assurance companies

[54.6] Payments made to persons participating in the mutual activities of a company carrying on mutual life assurance business are not treated as DISTRIBUTIONS (29).

[*CTA 2010, s 1070*].

55

Offshore Funds

Simon's Taxes. See B5.701–B5.727.

Introduction to offshore funds

[55.1] The current statutory regime for offshore funds operates under legislation now in *TIOPA 2010* and *SI 2009 No 3001* (the *Offshore Funds (Tax) Regulations 2009*). For official guidance on the current regime, see HMRC Investment Funds Manual at IFM12000 onwards.

An eligible offshore fund may apply to HMRC for approval as a 'reporting fund'. It must then comply with various duties as to the preparation of accounts, the computation of its reportable income and the provision of reports to participants and information to HMRC. Generally UK resident investors in reporting funds are taxable on their share of the fund's reported income each year, irrespective of whether such income is actually distributed to them. Any gain or loss on disposal of an interest in the fund is treated as a chargeable gain or allowable loss.

Any fund which is not a reporting fund is a 'non-reporting fund'. UK resident investors are generally taxable on distributions received from the fund (subject to any applicable exemptions). If a non-reporting fund which is a transparent fund has an interest in a reporting fund any excess of reported income treated as made to the non-reporting fund as above is additional income of the participants in the non-reporting fund calculated in proportion to their rights. It is treated as miscellaneous income of a participant chargeable to corporation tax. Subject to certain exceptions, there is a charge to corporation tax on income if a person disposes of an interest (i.e. an investment) in a non-reporting fund and an offshore income gain arises on the disposal. The offshore income gain is treated for corporation tax purposes as miscellaneous income which arises at the time of the disposal.

Definition of offshore fund, etc.

[55.2] To be an '*offshore fund*' an entity must fall into one of the following categories:

(a) a mutual fund, constituted as a company (not including an LLP) resident outside the UK;
(b) a mutual fund where the property is held on trust for the participants and the trustees are not UK resident; or
(c) a mutual fund constituted by other arrangements that create co-ownership rights and are governed by the law of a territory outside the UK (but not including a trading or business partnership).

A '*mutual fund*' is an arrangement affecting any type of property, including money, provided that the purpose of the arrangements is to participate in the acquisition, holding, management or disposal of property or the receipt of income or other payments arising from property so held. Participants must not have day to day control of the management of the property (not including the right to be consulted or give directions) and a reasonable investor would be able to realise his investment for an amount calculated entirely or almost entirely by reference to the net asset value of the property or calculated by reference to an index of any description (the Treasury have power to amend this condition by statutory instrument).

This definition is subject to qualifications for umbrella arrangements and arrangements where there is more than one class of interest. In these cases, each part or class of the arrangements are to be looked at separately, and the umbrella or main arrangements are disregarded. Arrangements are not a mutual fund where they allow a participant to realise all or part of the investments for net asset value or in accordance with an index, or only to do so on a winding up and either the arrangement is not designed to wind up etc. on a specified date or one which is determinable or there is a definite time for winding up etc., the return is not designed to be equivalent to interest and:

- none of the assets are 'relevant income-producing assets'; or
- under the terms of the arrangements, the participants are not entitled to the income or other benefit from the assets or from the income from the assets; or under the terms of the arrangements, any income, net of reasonable expenses, must be paid or credited to the participants and any UK resident individual participant is chargeable to income tax on it.

A '*relevant income-producing asset*' is an asset which produces income which would be subject to UK income tax if it were held directly by an individual resident in the UK. Hedged assets are not relevant income producing assets if no income is expected to arise from the hedged asset or any product of the hedging.

These provisions may be amended by statutory instrument.

Where umbrella arrangements are in place, each part of the asset is treated as separate arrangements, and the umbrella arrangement is disregarded.

Where there is more than one class of arrangement, each class is treated separately and the main arrangements are disregarded.

'*Umbrella arrangements*' means arrangements providing for separate pooling of each participant's contributions and the profits or income attaching to them, out of which payments may be made.

[*TIOPA 2010, ss 354–363*].

See further HMRC Investment Funds Manual IFM12200 et seq.

Where:

- a fund is a body corporate authorised in a foreign country or territory as an UCITS, or is an AIF which is authorised or registered, or has its registered office, in a foreign country or territory, and is not an excluded entity; and
- where the fund would be treated as resident in the UK for the purposes of any enactment relating to income tax, corporation tax or capital gains tax;

then the fund will instead be treated as if it were not resident in the UK.

An excluded entity is an UCITS or AIF which is:

(a) a unit trust scheme with UK resident trustees;
(b) UK resident by virtue of being incorporated in the UK;
(c) is, or has been, an investment trust; or
(d) is, or has been, either a company UK REIT or a member of a group UK REIT (see **47** INVESTMENT TRUSTS).

In addition, if, under *TCGA 1992, ss 99* or *103A*, the UCITS or AIF is treated as if it were a company, then for the purposes of *TCGA 1992*, the company is treated as not resident in the UK.

[*TIOPA 2010, s 363A; SI 2017 No 1204, Reg 14*].

Reporting and non-reporting funds

Offshore funds are allocated into reporting and non-reporting funds. A 'non-reporting fund' is any offshore fund which is not a reporting fund. A 'reporting fund' is an offshore fund to which *SI 2009 No 3001, Pt 3* applies (see below).

The application process is as detailed at **55.3** below.

As noted above, an offshore fund is defined at *TIOPA 2010, ss 355, 356* and may take one of several forms e.g. a company with share capital, a unit trust or a contractual arrangement such as a Fonds Commun de Placement. Partnerships are specifically excluded from the definition of an offshore fund found at *TIOPA 2010, s 355(1)(c)* (mutual fund arrangements) and in addition limited liability partnerships (LLPs) are excluded from the definition of body corporate.

However, it is notable that HMRC's guidance comments that this exclusion relates to UK LLPs; a LLP formed under the law of any other territory could still be an offshore fund if it is a body corporate (and opaque for capital gains purposes) and a mutual fund.

Other arrangements, e.g. certain unit trusts which are transparent for income tax but not capital gains tax, are within the definition of an offshore fund.

[*TIOPA 2010, ss 355, 356; SI 2009 No 3001*].

Simon's Taxes. See **B5.701–B5.703**.

Reporting funds

[55.3] The manager of an eligible offshore fund (or prospective manager of a new fund) may make an application for the fund to be a reporting fund. The manager of a non-reporting fund may apply, provided that the fund is an eligible offshore fund, and has never been a reporting fund or has been such a fund but ceased to be such a fund by giving notice under *Reg 116* (i.e. where notice of termination is given).

The contents of an application are set out in *Reg 53*. Under the amended provisions a fund must apply for reporting status before the later of: the end of the first period of account for which reporting status is required; and the expiry of three months beginning with the first day on which interests are made available to UK resident investors.

An application may be withdrawn at any time after the application has been made and before the end of 28 days after notice has been received from HMRC either accepting or rejecting the application; or at any later time before the end of the first reporting period. Previously the application would need to have been made in writing to HMRC within three months of the first day of the fund's first accounting period as a reporting fund.

HMRC are required within 28 days of receipt to give notice of acceptance or of rejection of the application, or issue a request for further information. [*SI 2009 No 3001, Reg 54*]. The applicant has a right of appeal against rejection within 42 days of the notice. An appeal will normally be heard by the First-tier Tribunal. If an application is accepted, the fund becomes a reporting fund of the later of:

- the first day of the first period of account;
- the day on which the fund is established.

A reporting fund must: prepare accounts in accordance with *Chapter 4* of the Regulations (*Regs 59–61*); provide a computation of reportable income in accordance with *Chapter 5* (*Regs 62–72*) or *Chapter 6A* as applicable to transparent reporting funds (*Regs 89A–89E*); provide reports to participants in accordance with *Chapter 7* (*Regs 90–93*); and provide information to HMRC in accordance with *Chapter 9* (*Regs 106, 107*).

With regard to participants, the reporting fund must make a report available (in one of four specified ways) to each relevant participant for each reporting period within six months of the end of that period. *Regulation 92* gives the contents to be included in the report. See **55.9** for details.

[*SI 2009 No 3001, Regs 54, 55, 56, 58*].

Computing reportable income

[55.4] A reporting fund needs to provide a computation of reportable income for a period of account, based on the 'total comprehensive income for the period' where international accounting standards are used, or the equivalent entries to this where it is not.

Thus, accounts must be prepared using either international accounting standards (IAS) or generally accepted accounting practice (GAAP). The basis to be used must be shown in the application for reporting status. If neither IAS nor an acceptable GAAP is being used then a statement must be provided showing which entries equate to 'total comprehensive income' per IAS, and what adjustments will be used to calculate the effective interest income and comparables required. Where there is a change in accounting policy, an adjustment is required. Where there is a change in accounting practice to GAAP, the fund must apply to give notice to HMRC that the accounts do not comply with IAS. If the new basis uses IAS, the fund must give notice to HMRC. HMRC must accept or reject the application within 28 days. If the application is rejected, there is a right of appeal to the Tribunal.

Adjustments to the income statement are required for:

- capital items and miscellaneous items;
- special classes of income e.g. group income from wholly-owned subsidiaries, income from other reporting funds, income from certain non-reporting funds, interest income computed in an unacceptable way;
- equalisation arrangements operated by the fund when a participator disposes of an interest in it (see below);
- wholly-owned subsidiaries (95% or 100% subsidiaries — see further below), the receipts, expenditure, assets and liabilities of which are attributed to the fund;
- Interests in other offshore funds — where a reporting fund (A) invests in another reporting fund (B) then the excess of income reported by B over what was distributed by B to A must be added to fund A's reportable income; where the investment is in a non-reporting fund then (if certain conditions are met) the fund undertakes its own calculation of the income from the non-reporting fund and includes this in its reportable income. The addition is made in the period of account in which B's fund distribution date falls, or if earlier, the period of account in which the reported income from B in respect of that reporting period is recognised in A's accounts. The fund distribution date is the date six months following the last day of the reporting period.

A company is a wholly-owned subsidiary of an offshore fund if the whole of its issued share capital:

(i) where the fund is a body corporate, is owned directly or indirectly by the fund;

(ii) where the fund is a trust, is owned directly or indirectly by the trustees of the fund for the benefit of the fund; or

(iii) where the fund is a mutual fund constituted under other arrangements, as per *TIOPA 2010 s 355(1)(c)* is owned in a manner corresponding as near as possible with (a) or (b) above.

If the fund in (a) has only one class of issued share capital, a holding of 95% of that capital is treated as a holding of the whole of it.

As noted above, the receipts, expenditure, assets and liabilities of the subsidiary are attributed to the fund itself, but if the fund has a holding of between 95 and 100% of the share capital of the subsidiary, the attribution is restricted to the percentage of share capital held. The fund's interest in the subsidiary and distributions or other payments between the fund and the subsidiary are left out of account. Adjustments must be made to the amounts treated as arising to the fund for capital items as described above.

See below for the rules with regard to transparent funds.

[*SI 2009 No 3001, Regs 59–71, 94; SI 2017 No 240*].

Simon's Taxes. See **B5.716, B5.717.**

Equalisation

Adjustments must be made to reportable income if a reporting fund operates equalisation arrangements. When an interest is acquired by initial purchase (i.e by subscription or allotment of new shares, units, etc issued or created by the fund, or by direct purchase from the fund), the reportable income must be increased by an amount equal to the part of the acquisition price attributable to undistributed income accrued in the period of account up to acquisition and taken into account in determining the acquisition price. This is the equalisation amount. If the participant disposes of an interest in a fund by way of redemption (i.e. when the shares, units, etc are cancelled or sold direct to the fund), the reportable income is reduced by an amount equal to the part of the redemption price attributed to undistributed income accrued in the period of account up to the time of redemption and taken into account in determining the redemption price.

Where a reporting fund does not operate equalisation arrangements and it intends to, or must (see below), make income adjustments on the basis of reportable income, the reportable income of the fund is the sum of the reportable income per unit for a reporting period for all computation periods in the reporting period multiplied by the number of units in the fund in issue at the end of the reporting period. The reportable income per unit for a computation period is calculated by dividing the reportable income of the fund for that period by the average number of units in issue during the period. Where a period of account consists of two reporting periods, the reportable income for the period of account is the sum of the reportable income for both those reporting periods.

Where a fund does not operate equalisation arrangements and it intends to make income adjustments on the basis of accounting income, the reportable income per unit for a reporting fund is calculated as follows:

$$AIU \times \frac{RI}{AI}$$

where:

AIU is the sum of the accounting income per unit for all the computation periods in the reporting period;

RI is the reportable income for the reporting period (computed ignoring this regulation); and

AI is the sum of the accounting income for all the computation periods in the reporting period.

To get the reportable income of the fund the result of this calculation is multiplied by 'U' (the number of units in the fund in issue at the end of the reporting period).

Accounting income means an amount proportionally related to the fund's reportable income determined from the interim or management accounts. It cannot be less than zero.

The computation period is as determined by the fund pursuant to certain rules (see *Reg 72C*).

Where the difference in the amount of reportable) income per unit calculated using the accounting income method and the amount of reportable income per unit using the reportable income method (above) is, or is likely to be, more than 10% of the latter, then the fund must make income adjustments in that and future reporting periods on the basis of reportable income, and the manager must give notice to HMRC of the change in method.

[*SI 2009 No 3001, Regs 72–72C*].

Where a participant has acquired an interest in a reporting fund by way of initial purchase and the fund operates full equalisation arrangements then the distributions are **reduced** in accordance with either of two options:

(1) the amount of any actual distributions to the participant in respect of the reporting period is reduced by the equalisation amount; and the amount of any excess treated as additional distributions made to the participant is reduced by the amount, if any, by which the equalisation amount exceeds the amount of any actual distributions to the participant; or
(2) the amount of any excess treated as additional distributions made to the participant is reduced by the equalisation amount; and the amount of any actual distributions to the participant in respect of the reporting period is reduced by the amount, if any, by which the equalisation amount exceeds the excess.

[*SI 2009 No 3001, Reg 94A*].

Simon's Taxes. See B5.717.

Disposals

A charge to tax arises if a company disposes of an asset. An offshore income gain arises to the disposing company where either the asset is an interest in a non-reporting fund at the time of the disposal or the following are met:

- the reporting fund was previously a non-reporting fund;
- the interest was an interest in a non-reporting fund during some or all of the material period;
- an election was not prevented by *Reg 48(5)* (conversion of a non-reporting fund to a reporting fund);
- no election was made under *Reg 48(2)*.

Non-trading funds

Where the following two conditions are satisfied, a reporting fund is not treated as trading:

- the equivalence condition; and
- the diversity of ownership condition.

These provisions give certainty to these types of funds ('diversely owned funds') that transactions undertaken will be treated as disposals giving rise to capital gains as opposed to 'trading' profits (reportable income). See further HMRC Investment Funds Manual IFM12553.

[*SI 2009 No 3001, Regs 73, 80*].

Thus an investment transaction carried out by a diversely owned fund is a non-trading transaction. An investment transaction is any:

- transactions in stocks and shares;
- transaction in a relevant contract;
- transaction which results in a diversely owned fund becoming a party to a loan relationship or a related transaction in respect of a loan relationship;
- transactions in units in a collective investment scheme;
- transactions in securities of any description not falling within the categories above;
- transactions in the buying or selling of any foreign currency;
- transactions in a carbon emission trading product;
- transactions in rights under a life insurance policy.

The '*equivalence condition*' requires the fund to meet one of three conditions throughout the period of account. These are that the fund is recognised by FSA under *Financial Services and Markets Act 2000, s 272* or, before Brexit IP completion day (11pm on 31 December 2020) *s 264*; that the fund is an Undertaking for Collective Investments in Transferrable Securities (UCITS) fund (as defined); or the fund is a fund constituted in another EEA state which is authorised in that State to market to retail or professional investors and is required to limit its borrowing and exposure under derivative contracts and forward transactions to 100% of its net asset value.

[*SI 2009 No 3001, Regs 74, 80, 81; SI 2019 No 689, Reg 30*].

A '*diversely owned fund*' is one fulfilling the conditions in *SI 2009 No 3001, Regs 75* and *76*. The conditions for the genuine diversity of ownership condition per *Reg 75* are that throughout the period of account:

(A) the fund produces documents, available to investors and to HMRC, which contain:

- a statement specifying the intended categories of investor;
- an undertaking that interests in the fund will be widely available; and
- an undertaking that interests in the fund will be marketed and made available per condition (C);

(B) the specification of the intended categories of investor do not have a limiting or deterrent effect, and, any other terms or conditions governing participation in the fund do not have a limiting or deterrent effect; and

(C) the interests in the fund must be marketed and made available: sufficiently widely to reach the intended categories of investors, and in a manner appropriate to attract those categories of investors; and a person who falls within one of the intended categories of investors can, upon request to the manager of this fund, obtain information about the fund and acquire units in it.

A fund is also a diversely owned fund if an investor is: an offshore fund, an OEIC or an authorised unit trust scheme, ('the feeder fund'); with the same manager as the fund, and where the conditions A to C above are met in relation to the fund when considering in addition the position with regard to the feeder fund, its documents and intended investors.

The manager of an existing eligible offshore fund or the manager of a non-reporting fund may make an application to convert from a non-reporting to a non-trading reporting fund where the equivalence and diversity of ownership conditions are met. The procedure and when clearance may not be relied on are laid out in detail in *Regs 78* and *79* respectively. Where a diversely owned fund carries out an investment transaction (as defined in *Regs 81–89*) in an accounting period, the investment transaction is treated as a non-trading transaction.

There are special rules for financial traders in vesting in diversely owned funds, see *SI 2009 No 3001, Regs 102, 104, 105*, also **Simon's Taxes B5.722.**

Simon's Taxes. See **B5.718.**

Index tracking funds

Where a reporting fund has an interest in a non-reporting fund, and:

- the aim of the fund's investment policy is to replicate the composition of a qualifying index;
- the main purpose of the investment in the non-reporting fund was to represent the composition of the qualifying index; and
- the capital and income of the fund replicate the returns of the investments comprised in the qualifying index;

then the adjustments identified at *SI 2009 No 3001, Regs 69–71* do not apply in respect of the interest in the non-reporting fund.

Transparent funds

Simplified rules for computing reportable income apply to reporting funds that are fiscally transparent, for example certain unit trusts. The rules in *Chapters 4–6* of the 2009 regulations do not apply to such funds. The funds do not therefore have to prepare accounts or computations of reportable income as outlined above and the rules regarding transactions which are not treated as trading transactions (non-trading funds) do not apply.

Chapter 6A of the 2009 Regulations deals with the reportable income for a transparent reporting fund.

A transparent fund must provide a computation of its reportable income for a period of account. This is comprised of:

- each of the separate sums of income for the period which fall within (a) or (b) of *Reg 11*, that is, income which would be chargeable on individual investors resident in the UK as 'relevant foreign income' under *ITTOIA 2005, s 830(2)*, such as trading income, property business income, interest, royalties, etc. (or where the income is from an asset is in the UK, would be so chargeable if the asset were not in the UK); and
- the adjustments made to those sums in accordance with *Regs 89C–89E.*

The adjustments to be made include:

- where the transparent fund has invested in a reporting fund, the excess of the income reported by such fund in respect of its interest, over the amount distributed by the reporting fund (or its best estimate in the absence of a report from the reporting fund);
- where the transparent fund has invested in non-reporting funds (first case), the treatment above for investment in a reporting fund applies, if the following conditions apply:
  - (a) the transparent fund has access to the accounts of the non-reporting fund;
  - (b) the transparent fund has sufficient information to enable it to prepare a computation of reportable income for the non-reporting fund; and
  - (c) the transparent fund can reasonably expect to rely on continued access to the information;
- where the transparent fund has invested in non-reporting funds (second case), but the conditions in the first case (above) are not met, then the reportable income of the transparent fund shall include an amount equal to the increase in fair value of the interest in the non-reporting fund (as reduced by any decrease in fair value in an earlier period, under certain conditions).

Regulation 92D applies for transparent reporting funds stating that the report to participants for a reporting period must contain sufficient information to enable those participants to meet their tax obligations in the UK with respect to their interest in the fund, and include a statement whether or not the fund remains a reporting fund at the date the fund makes the report available.

[*SI 2009 No 3001, Regs 89A–89E*].

Simon's Taxes. See B5.718A.

Tax treatment of participants

[55.5] In a non-transparent fund, the excess of reported income over distributions is treated as additional distributions made to the participants in proportion to their rights, such distributions being made on the fund distribution date (see below), or on such earlier date as the reported income in respect of that reporting period is recognised in the participant's accounts.

For a participant chargeable to corporation tax such distribution is exempt if an actual distribution would normally be treated as exempt, otherwise it will be chargeable to corporation tax under general principles.

Where the fund is transparent, any excess of reported income over the fund's income for the period is treated as additional (notional) income of the participants in proportion to their rights. The notional income is treated as a distribution to participants at the end of the reporting period on the 'fund distribution date'. The latter date is, where the fund reports to participants within six months of the end of the reporting period, the day the report is issued. In any other case, it is the last day of the reporting period.

Where the participant is chargeable to corporation tax, the notional distribution is exempt if an actual distribution would have been exempt. When a company disposes of an interest in the fund, any notional distributions on which it has borne tax is added to the acquisition costs for the purpose of calculating the chargeable gain or allowable loss.

See also **50.49** LOAN RELATIONSHIPS.

Interaction with *TCGA 1992, s 106A*

With regard to the general provisions as to reported income, *para 3A* of *Reg 94* applies. Therefore when a participant disposes of an interest in a reporting fund, and *TCGA 1992, s 106A* (identification of securities for capital gains tax) applies to that disposal, then the disposal is ignored when considering the calculation of the excess of reported income over distributed income and the participant treated as holding the interest at the end of the reporting period.

This closes a loophole which enabled an investor to redeem a holding shortly before the end of a reporting period when the price reflected accrued income for almost a year, and subscribe for the units again in the following period but within 30 days of disposal. As a result the investor could create a small capital loss on the disposal if the only price movement during the period between disposal and subscription related to accrued income, and he would avoid any income tax liability for the reporting period.

[*SI 2009 No 3001, Regs 94, 95, 97, 98*].

Simon's Taxes. See B5.720.

Reporting fund becoming non-reporting fund

[55.6] Where a reporting fund becomes a non-reporting fund, the participant may elect to be treated as making a deemed disposal at the end of the fund's final period of account as a reporting fund and to acquire an interest in the non-reporting fund on the first day of that fund's first period of account.

Offshore income gains

[55.7] Subject to the exceptions below, there is a charge to corporation tax on income if a company disposes of an interest (i.e. an investment) in a non-reporting fund and an offshore income gain (see **55.8** below) arises on the disposal. The gain is treated for tax purposes as miscellaneous income arising at the time of the disposal to the company making the disposal, and tax is charged on that person. The charge may also arise if the interest disposed of is an interest in a reporting fund which has been a non-reporting fund at some time since the interest was acquired. [*SI 2009 No 3001, Regs 17, 18*].

However, no charge to tax under these provisions arises if any of the following apply:

- the interest in the fund falls within the loan relationship rules;
- the derivative contract rules apply to the interest in the fund;
- the intangible asset rules apply to the interest in the fund;
- the asset is a right under a policy of insurance;
- the interest in the fund is held as trading stock;
- the disposal is taken into account in computing trading profits;
- the asset is a loan which is not a 'participating loan';
- they are certain interests in 'transparent funds' (conditions apply);
- they are rights in an offshore fund acquired before 1 December 2009 and those rights did not constitute a material interest in an offshore fund on acquisition;
- they are offshore income gains of charitable trusts, which are exempt when the gains are applicable and applied for charitable purposes (but there is a deemed disposal if the charitable trust ceases).

[*SI 2009 No 3001, Regs 25–31*].

A reporting fund must provide details, to both HMRC and UK investors, of investors' shares of reported income. HMRC may require a fund to provide further information.

In most cases, if a fund has been a reporting fund throughout the period a UK investor has held the investment, any profit on disposal of the holding is taxed as a capital gain. However, this is subject to transitional provisions.

If the fund has been a non-reporting fund then any profit on disposal is charged to income as an offshore income gain.

Unlisted trading company exception: no liability to tax arises under *Reg 17* if:

- the disposal is a disposal of an interest in an offshore fund;
- the sole or main purpose of the fund is to invest in qualifying companies;
- throughout the period starting with the date on which the interest was acquired and ending 12 months before the date of the disposal the fund met the investment condition (see below); and
- participants in the fund have access to, and are able to obtain copies of, sufficient information to demonstrate that the fund intends to dispose of any holdings of shares or securities as required to satisfy the investment condition.

The 'investment condition' is that at least 90% of the value of the assets of the fund consists of: direct or indirect holdings in qualifying companies; or holdings of shares or securities which are listed (on a recognised stock exchange or regulated market) and which the fund is going to dispose of as soon as reasonably practicable; or which the fund believes will cease to be listed (or admitted) within 12 months. Cash holdings are disregarded.

A '*qualifying company*' means a trading company or the holding company of a trading group or a trading subgroup, where: the shares of the company are not listed on a recognised stock exchange or admitted to trading on a regulated market; and the activities of the trading company or, in the case of a holding company, the activities of the members of the group or subgroup taken together, do not include to a substantial extent the carrying out of investment transactions undertaken in the course of a trade.

Reference is made to *TCGA 1992, Sch 7AC* (with regard to substantial shareholdings) for the definitions of 'qualifying company', 'trading company', 'trading group' and 'trading subgroup'.

[*SI 2009 No 3001, Regs 31A–31C*].

Simon's Taxes. See **B5.706**.

Computation of offshore income gains

[55.8] An offshore income gain is the 'basic gain' arising on a disposal.

The 'basic gain' is the gain computed using capital gains tax rules, but ignoring any corporation tax arising under the regulations or any indexation allowance available under capital gains tax rules and subject to the following:

- share for share exchange under *TCGA 1992, s 135*;
- share for share exchange under *TCGA 1992, s 136*;
- exchange of interests of different classes;
- earlier disposal to which no gain/no loss disposal applies;
- where there has been a previous no gain/no loss disposal;
- where a rollover relief claim or a claim for gift relief (check) for capital gains tax is made in respect of a transaction otherwise than at arm's length, the claims do not affect the computation of the basic gain;
- where the basic gain computation produces a loss, the basic gain is nil.

See also **46.26** INVESTMENT FUNDS with regard to regulations in respect of mergers and exchanges of fund interests.

[*SI 2009 No 3001, Regs 34–37*].

Simon's Taxes. See **B5.707**, **B5.708**.

Reporting requirements

[55.9] A company must send or otherwise make available a report for each 'reporting period' to each relevant participant, within six months of the end of the period. There are a number of methods of reporting (see *SI 2009 No 3001, Reg 90*).

A 'reporting period' is the same as the fund's period of account, where that is twelve months or less. Where the period of account exceeds twelve months, there are two reporting periods, the first being the first twelve months and the second the remainder. *Regulation 92* sets out the contents of the report.

A relevant participant is a participant who is UK resident or is a reporting fund.

The report in relation to a non-transparent fund must include the following for the reporting period:

(i) the amount distributed to participants per unit of interest in the fund;
(ii) the excess, if any, of the amount of reported income per unit (see below) over the amount in (i) above;
(iii) the date distributions were made;
(iv) the fund distribution date;
(v) a statement of whether or not the fund remains a reporting fund on the date the report is made available;
(vi) if the fund operates full equalisation arrangements and has not given, in relation to an initial purchase, a statement to the participant regarding the equalisation amount included in the purchase consideration, details of the equalisation amount per unit.

In the case of transparent reporting funds, the report must contain sufficient information to enable the participant to meet their UK tax obligations in respect of their interest in the fund, and must include a statement of whether or not the fund remains a reporting fund at the date the report is made available.

A reporting fund must also provide HMRC with information for each period of account, within six months of the end of that account. The information required is: audited accounts; computation of reportable income; copy of participant's report; the reported income within each reporting period within the period of account; the amount distributed to participants; number of units in issue at the end of each reporting period falling within the period of account; the amount of reported income per such unit; a declaration that the fund has complied with its obligations under the regime (as per the application procedure) (see *Reg 106*).

A reporting fund can provide unaudited accounts if HMRC are satisfied that it would be impossible or unreasonable to expect them to be provided and there is no reason to believe that the unaudited accounts cannot be relied upon for the purpose of calculating reportable income.

[*SI 2009 No 3001, Regs 90, 92, 106*].

Simon's Taxes. See **B5.719, B5.723.**

Offshore income gains and capital gains

[55.10] The offshore income gain on disposal is deducted from consideration used in the capital gains disposal. However, where the disposal is a part disposal and apportionment is required, this rule does not apply. There are consequential adjustments to the calculation of rollover relief and in the case of reconstructions involving the exchange of shares or issue of securities.

Disposals of interest — capital gains implications

[55.11] A disposal of an interest in a reporting fund is a disposal for capital gains tax purposes and the accumulated undistributed income is taken into account as a cost of acquisition and disposal, but excluding an equalisation amount used to reduce the amount of actual distributions. Each undistributed amount is treated as incurred on the fund distribution date for the reporting period for which it is treated as a distribution.

[*SI 2009 No 3001, Regs 94, 99; SI 2017 No 1204, Reg 16*].

For disposals on or after 1 January 2018, disposals of interests in an offshore fund which is a 'transparent fund' are dealt with under the same provisions as apply to authorised contractual schemes which are co-ownership schemes — see **46.25** INVESTMENT FUNDS.

Simon's Taxes. See B5.721.

Breaching the reporting fund requirements

[55.12] A breach may either be minor or serious. A minor breach is one:

- for which there is a reasonable excuse; or
- which is inadvertent and remedied as soon as reasonably possible.

Provided that, if the reporting fund corrects a minor breach without HMRC intervention (as defined in *Reg 108*), it is not regarded as a breach for these purposes. A serious breach is one which is designated as serious or which is not minor.

If a fund is in serious breach of a reporting fund requirement and HMRC notify the fund of that fact and specify the breach (an exclusion notice), the fund is treated as a non-reporting fund for the reporting period in which the notice is given, and for all subsequent reporting periods.

[*SI 2009 No 3001, Reg 108*].

Simon's Taxes. See **B5.724**.

Leaving the reporting fund regime

[55.13] There are two ways of leaving the reporting fund regime:

- giving notice of termination;
- failing to comply with requirements.

[*SI 2009 No 3001, Regs 116, 117*].

Simon's Taxes. See B5.725.

Non-reporting funds

[55.14] Subject to the exceptions above, there is a disposal of an interest in a non-reporting fund where there would be a capital gains tax disposal. However, where *TCGA 1992, ss 135, 136* (reorganisation and reconstruction provisions) would otherwise apply, the company is treated as disposing of an interest in a non-reporting fund for market value at the time of the exchange or deemed exchange.

[*SI 2009 No 3001, Regs 35, 36*].

If a participant disposes of an interest in a non-reporting fund then this will give rise to an offshore income gain which is charged to tax on income. There is similarly a charge to tax with regard to an offshore income gain where the asset disposed of is an interest in a reporting fund at the time of the disposal; the reporting fund was previously a non-reporting fund (which then applied for reporting status); the interest was in a non-reporting fund at the time of acquisition; the participant was not prevented from making an election to be treated as if they had disposed of their interest and reacquired it (see **55.15**); and no such election was made.

Where a disposal gives rise to an offshore income gain and is also a disposal for capital gains tax purposes, the amount of the offshore income gain is deducted from the consideration for capital gains purposes, except in the case of a part disposal where a fraction is applied before the deduction is made. Adjustments are also required where the disposal falls within the reorganisation and reconstruction relief provisions at *TCGA 1992, ss 135, 136*. In such cases the amount of the offshore income gain is treated as additional consideration given for the new holding. Adjustments are also required where *TCGA 1992, s 162* applies.

[*SI 2009 No 3001, Regs 45, 46, 47*].

When a non-reporting fund which is a transparent fund has an interest in a reporting fund, it is taxed on its proportionate share of the reporting fund's income as if it were its miscellaneous income arising on the same date as the reporting funds excess is treated as made.

Simon's Taxes. See **B5.705, B5.709.**

Conversion to a reporting fund

[55.15] Where an offshore fund stops being a non-reporting fund and becomes a reporting fund, a participant in the fund may make an election to be treated as disposing of its interest in the non-reporting fund on the disposal date (i.e. the final day of the last period of account before the fund becomes a reporting fund) and acquiring an interest in the reporting fund at the start of its first period of account. There must be a positive gain for this election to be available. A company must make the election in its corporation tax return for the accounting period that includes the disposal date. [*SI 2009 No 3001, Reg 48*].

A participant in a reporting fund when it becomes a non-reporting fund may elect to make a deemed disposal of the interest at the end of the reporting fund's final period and acquire an interest in a non-reporting fund at the start of that fund's first period of account. This election is conditional on the reporting fund having made a report to the participant for the final period. The deemed disposal and acquisition are treated as made for an amount equal to the net asset value of the participant's interest in the fund at the end of the period of account for which the fund's income is reported. The election should be included in the company participant corporation tax return for the accounting period in which the disposal falls. [*SI 2009 No 3001, Reg 100*].

Information requirements

[55.16] As highlighted at 55.9 above, *SI 2009 No 3001, Reg 106* lays down the information to be provided annually to HMRC within six months of the end of a period of account. In addition, HMRC may notify a fund to provide such information as they may require for the purpose. The fund must be given not less than 42 days to produce the information.

Key points on offshore funds

[55.17] Points to consider are as follows.

- Interests in offshore funds may give rise to a capital disposal in certain circumstances. If the fund does not qualify then the 'gain' is subject to income tax. Funds that do not qualify for capital treatment are often referred to as Roll-up Funds with any gain arising on the ultimate disposal of units in such funds being subject to income tax at the UK resident taxpayer's top rate of tax, without any relief for underlying taxes suffered within the fund.
- A 'reporting fund' has to report its income to HMRC. Shareholders are subject to income tax on distributions received, but in addition they are also liable to income tax on their share of the reported undistributed income.
- Where a UK resident taxpayer is subject to income tax on reported but undistributed income they can treat the 'deemed' distributions as additional costs of acquisition for capital gains tax purposes. This ensures that the taxpayer does not suffer double tax on the ultimate disposal of the units in the fund, as the element of growth that is represented by retained income in the fund is accounted for by these additional acquisition costs.
- If a reporting fund becomes a non-reporting fund the 'shareholder' has the right to elect for a deemed disposal of their interest to crystallise the capital gain. Going forward they will subjected to the tax regime applicable to non-reporting funds such that a future actual disposal of their interest in the fund will give rise to an income gain.
- If a non-reporting fund becomes a reporting fund then the 'shareholder' has the right to elect for a deemed disposal of their interest to crystallise an income gain. Going forward they will be subject to the normal annual charge and a capital gain on ultimate disposal.
- On a practical level, the rules require detailed record keeping by the taxpayer in order to ensure that disposals of units in reporting funds are not unduly overtaxed.

56
Partnerships

Cross-references. See also **50.43** LOAN RELATIONSHIPS; **51.34**, **51.12** LOSSES.

See HMRC Company Taxation Manual CTM36500 *et seq*.

Simon's Taxes. See **B7.510**, **B7.515**.

Introduction to partnerships

[56.1] Companies can form partnerships with individuals, other companies and trustees. Persons carrying on a trade in partnership are referred to collectively as a '*firm*'. A '*company partnership*' is a partnership in which at least one partner is a company. A company member of a partnership is liable to pay corporation tax on its profits. [*CTA 2009, s 1257*].

With effect for accounting periods beginning on or after 1 April 2018, where a partner in a firm is partner as trustee for a beneficiary who is absolutely entitled to the partner's share of the firm's profits and is chargeable to tax on those profits, the beneficiary is itself treated as a partner or member of the firm. [*CTA 2009, s 1258A; FA 2018, Sch 6 paras 2, 4(2)*].

This chapter looks at the tax treatment of companies in partnership. Further guidance can be found in HMRC's Company Tax Manual at CTM36505 onwards. The legislation is contained in the main in *CTA 2009, Pt 17*.

Tax treatment of a company partner's partnership profits and losses

Overview

[56.2] A company that is a member of a partnership is liable to pay corporation tax on its share of partnership profits whereas a partner who is an individual is charged to income tax on his or her share of partnership profits. The following paragraphs look at the tax treatment of a company partner's partnership profits and losses.

Trading profits and losses

[56.3] A partnership is not generally treated for corporation tax purposes as an entity which is separate and distinct from its members.

To assess the amount charged to corporation tax (if any) in respect of a company partner's share of partnership profits, the following approach is adopted.

Step 1 — compute profits of partnership as if the partnership were a company

For any accounting period (see below) of a partnership carrying on a trade for which there is at least one partner who is a UK resident company (a company partner), the trading profits or losses are computed for corporation tax purposes as if the partnership were a UK resident company.

Similarly, for any accounting period for which there is at least one partner who is a non-UK resident company, the profits or losses are similarly computed as if the partnership were a non-UK resident company. For such companies, the computation will cover only those profits in respect of which the company is within the charge to UK corporation tax, generally those arising from a permanent establishment within the UK.

Thus, two separate computations of profits/losses are needed if the partnership includes both resident and non-resident companies (and a third computation is needed if it also includes one or more individuals — see the corresponding chapter of Tolley's Income Tax). See also HMRC Company Taxation Manual CTM36510, 36520.

In computing the profit or loss for the accounting period in question, no account is taken of any losses for any other accounting period, e.g. losses brought forward. Any interest paid or other distribution made by the partnership is not regarded as a distribution, and may therefore be deductible in computing profits.

Step 2 — apportion profits (or losses) to company partner

The taxable profits or allowable losses of the partnership for the accounting period (as adjusted for corporation tax purposes) are apportioned in accordance with the partnership's profit-sharing arrangements during that accounting period (subject to 56.4 below).

Step 3 — assess company partner to corporation tax on its share of partnership profits

The company partner is assessed to corporation tax on its share of the partnership profits. The share of partnership profits are treated as if they were a separate trade carried on by the company, distinct from any other trade that may be carried on alone by the company.

These rules apply equally where the partnership carries on a business other than a trade.

[*CTA 2009, ss 1256–1260, 1262; FA 2018, Sch 6 para* 12].

Accounting periods

[56.4] In order to work out the company partner's share of partnership profits and losses, it is first necessary to work out the notional profits as if the partnership were a company. The profits are computed for an accounting period which is the period that would be an accounting period if the partnership were a company (see 2 ACCOUNTING PERIODS).

For the purposes of the computation, the following assumptions are made as regards this notional company:

- the company is UK resident;
- it acquires a source of income when the trade begins to be carried on by a partnership that includes a company;
- it ceases to trade when the trade ceases to be carried on by a partnership that includes a company; and
- it ceases to trade and immediately afterwards starts to trade if there is a change of partners such that both before and after the change the partnership includes a company but no company that carried on the trade before the change continues to carry it on after the change.

It follows that changes of partners are disregarded for corporation tax purposes so long as a company that carried on the trade in partnership before the change continues to carry it on in partnership after the change.

For the sole purpose of determining, in relation to a company partner, the accounting periods by reference to which profits are to be calculated, the residence of the notional company at any time is taken to be the same as the company partner's.

If the accounting period of the partnership does not coincide with the company partner's own accounting period, the company's share of profit or loss must be apportioned between the company's accounting periods with which the partnership accounting period partially coincides.

[*CTA 2009, ss 1261, 1265*].

The company tax return of a company in a partnership is required to include details from the partnership return (for which see Tolley's Income Tax under Returns).

Simon's Taxes. See **B7.401, B7.520.**

Example

X Ltd and Mr Brown have been in partnership for many years and share profits in the ratio 2:1. The partnership's trading results for the year ended 30 September 2021 are as follows.

	Trading profits (before capital allowances)	Capital allowances
	£	£
Year ended 30 September 2021	72,000	33,000

X Ltd's chargeable profits in respect of the partnership are as follows.

	£
Year ended 30.9.21	
Trading profits	48,000
Deduct Capital allowances	22,000
Chargeable profits	£26,000

Mr Brown's trading income for tax purposes is £13,000.

Note

Capital allowances are a deduction in arriving at profits for both income and corporation taxes.

Losses

[56.5] Partnership losses are computed in the same way as profits. Losses are then apportioned between the individual partners in accordance with the partnership profit-sharing arrangements. It is for each corporate partner to choose how to utilise its own share of losses and to make its own claim(s) for loss relief (see 50 LOSSES).

Where the partnership as a whole makes a profit (as adjusted for tax purposes) but, after the allocation of prior shares (e.g. salaries and interest on capital) the result is that a company partner makes a loss, the loss-making partner cannot claim tax relief for its loss. Instead, the company is treated as making neither profit nor loss, and its 'loss' is reallocated to the profit-making partners in accordance with the profit sharing arrangements in proportion to the profits already allocated to them. The effect of this reallocation to reduce the profit-making partners' profits for tax purposes.

In the situation where *the partnership as a whole makes a profit*, the company partner's share (in accordance with the profit sharing ratios) is a profit but one of the other partner's makes a loss, that loss is reallocated to the partners showing a profit in accordance with the profit sharing arrangements. The effect of the reallocation is to reduce the profits for tax purposes of the company partner (and also any other partners who have made a profit). The formula at *CTA 2009, s 1263(3)* sets out the calculation of the company partner's profits in this situation where the loss of the loss-making partner is reallocated in accordance with the steps set out at *CTA 2009, s 1263(4)*.

In a case *where there is an overall partnership loss*, the aggregate losses allocated to loss-making partners cannot exceed the overall loss and no partner is taxed on a share of profit. Instead, a profit-making company partner is treated as making neither profit nor loss, and its 'profit' is reallocated to the loss-making partners inaccordance with the profit-sharing arrangements.

Likewise, if there is *an overall partnership loss*, the company partner's share is a loss, but the comparable amount for at least one other partner is a profit, the profits of the profit-making partners are reallocated to those showing a loss, thereby reducing the company partner's loss (and that of any other loss-making partners). The formula at *CTA 2009, s 1264(3)* sets out the calculation of the company's partner's loss in this situation. The profit of the profit-making partners is reallocated in accordance with the steps set out at *CTA 2009, s 1264(4)*.

[*CTA 2009, ss 1259(5), 1263, 1264*].

Interest paid

[56.6] A payment of yearly interest chargeable to tax under *ITTOIA 2005* or *CTA 2009* by a partnership of which a company is a member must be paid under deduction of income tax at the basic rate in force for the tax year in which the payment is made. [*ITA 2007, s 874*]. See, however, **41.2** INCOME TAX IN RELATION TO A COMPANY for relief from deduction of tax from certain payments to companies within the charge to corporation tax and **41.5** INCOME TAX IN RELATION TO A COMPANY for relief on certain payments made between associated companies of different EU member states.

Partnership liabilities

[56.7] Partners are jointly and severally liable. Partnership liabilities include the whole of the income tax liability of the individual partners, notwithstanding that a company partner's profit share is liable only to corporation tax.

A partnership which is an Alternative Investment Fund Manager (AIFM) partnership (as defined by *SI 2013 No 1773*), with an AIFM trade (which involves the activities of managing one or more AIFs, or of acting as a delegate to such a manager), is able to elect to pay the income tax liability instead of an individual member of the partnership. If the partnership so elects then the charge to tax will be imposed at the additional rate of tax (45% for 2019/20) with no reliefs or allowances. Any such election must be made by the AIFM partnership to HMRC within six months after the end of the period of account for which the election is to have effect.

Regulations made pursuant to the EU *AIFM Directive No 2011/61/EU* require AIFM partnerships to impose performance conditions as part of the 'remuneration' for key individuals and to defer when those individuals can access such payments. When the AIF manager is a member of a partnership this means access to their share of the partnership profits may be deferred. However for tax purposes such profits are taxed as they arise, so there is a mismatch which means such members are required to pay tax on profits that they do not have access to at the time when the charge arises. This election mechanism allows the partnership to pay the tax charge as it arises, and the individual member will then receive a corresponding tax credit when the remuneration is received, or vests. In addition, the liability to Class 4 NICs is also deferred until the remuneration vests with the individual member. See further Tolley's Income Tax for details.

[*ITTOIA 2005, ss 863H–863L*].

Patent box

[56.8] The patent box regime applies to a corporate partner in a similar way as it applies to a single company carrying on a trade, with modifications. See 57 PATENT INCOME.

Special types of partnership

Members of non-UK resident partnership or partnerships controlled abroad

[56.9] Where a UK resident company is:

- a member of a partnership which is non-UK resident; or
- which carries on any trade or business the control and management of which is outside the UK,

any relief given under a double taxation agreement relieving partnership income from UK corporation tax does not affect the UK tax liability of the UK-resident company in respects of its share of the partnership income. For these purposes, the members of a partnership include any company which is entitled to a share of the income of the partnership. Similar provisions apply to capital gains.

[*CTA 2009, s 1266; TCGA 1992, s 59(2); FA 2019, Sch 1 para 28*].

Limited partnerships

[56.10] The amount of relief that is given for loss made by a company in a trade carried on by that company as a limited partner may be restricted in certain circumstances.

For these purposes, a '*limited partner*' is a company carrying on a trade:

(a) as a limited partner in a limited partnership registered under the *Limited Partnerships Act 1907*;
(b) as a general partner in a partnership, but which is not entitled to take part in the management of the trade, and which is entitled to have its liabilities for debts or obligations incurred for the trade discharged or reimbursed by some other person, in whole or beyond a certain limit; or
(c) who, under the law of any territory outside the UK, is not entitled to take part in the management of the trade, and is not liable beyond a certain limit for debts or obligations incurred for the trade.

The amount of relief is restricted if at any time in an accounting period the company carries on a trade as a limited partner and the company makes a loss in that trade in that period. The restriction operates by capping the relief given for the loss and any relief against total profits (under *CTA 2010, s 37* or *s 45A*) or under group relief or group relief for carried-forward losses (under *CTA 2010, Pt 5, Pt 5A*) for the accounting period in question, and for any other accounting period at any time in which the company carries on the trade as a limited partner at the level of the company's 'contribution to the firm' at the end of the loss-making period. If the company ceases to carry on the partnership trade during that period, the restriction is applied by reference to the company's contribution to the firm at the time of the cessation.

If the partnership is carrying on more than one trade, relief given under *CTA 2010, s 37, 45A* or *Pts 5, 5A* given in respect of each trade is taken into account for the purposes of applying the restriction.

A company's '*contribution to the firm*' at any time is the aggregate of:

(A) capital contributed *less* any capital directly or indirectly withdrawn, any capital the company is or may be entitled to withdraw at any time it carries on the trade as a limited partner, and any capital which it is or may be entitled to require another person to reimburse to it; and
(B) any of the company's share of the profits of the trade to which the company is entitled but which have not been added to the partnership's capital or which the company has not received in money or money's worth.

[*CTA 2010, ss 56–58, Sch 2 para 23; F(No 2)A 2017, Sch 4, para 152*].

Limited liability partnerships

[56.11] For corporation tax purposes, where a trade or other business is carried on by a limited liability partnership (an 'LLP') within *Limited Liability Partnerships Act 2000, s 1* with a view to profit, the activities of the LLP (i.e. anything it does) are treated as carried on in partnership by its members, rather than by the LLP as such. Consequently, anything done by or to the LLP for the purposes of, or in connection with, its activities is treated as done by to or in relation to the members as partners. Property of the LLP is treated as held by the members as partnership property.

This remains the case where an LLP no longer carries on any trade, profession or other business with a view to profit, if the cessation is only temporary and during a winding up following a permanent cessation, provided that the winding up did not occur for reasons wholly or in part connected with tax avoidance and it was no unreasonably prolonged. However, this rule ceases to apply on the appointment of a liquidator or (if earlier) on the making of a winding-up order by the court, or on the occurrence of any corresponding event under the law of a country or territory outside the UK.

Similar provisions apply for capital gains tax purposes (see *TCGA 1992, ss 59A, 156A* and *169A*). See Tolley's Capital Gains Tax under Partnerships and Hold-Over Reliefs.

A return made on the basis that the activities of an LLP are treated as carried on in partnership by its members (because it carries on a business with a view to profit) is treated as a valid partnership return even if in fact, the LLP does not carry on a business with a view to profit. Accordingly, HMRC may open an enquiry into the return under the provisions at **59.18** below or issue a follower notice or partnership payment notice as if it were a partnership return. This rule was introduced to reverse the effect of a number of FTT decisions (although the UT overturned the FTT decision in one of the cases, *Inverclyde Property Renovation LLP v HMRC* UT, [2020] STC 1348). Although it was enacted by *FA 2020*, the rule is treated as always having been in force. It does not apply, however, to a return if a court or tribunal determined before 11 March 2020 that the return in question was not a valid partnership return (provided that the court or tribunal's decision had not been set aside or overturned on appeal before 11 March 2020).

Similar provisions to those at **56.10** above apply to restrict loss relief available to company members of LLPs. The restriction applies where a company carries on a trade as a member of a LLP at any time in an accounting period and the company makes a loss in that period. The sum of the relief and any relief under *CTA 2010, s 37* or *s 45A* (against total profits) or under *CTA 2010, Pts 5, 5A* (group relief and group relief for carried-forward losses) in an accounting period during which the company carries on a trade as a member of a LLP is limited to the company's contribution to the LLP at the end of the loss-making period or, if the company ceases to carry on the trade as a member of the LLP during the period, at the time of cessation.

A member's contribution to the firm at any time (a 'relevant time') is the greater of the 'amount subscribed' by the member and the amount of its liability on a winding up (see below). The 'amount subscribed' by a member is the amount contributed to the LLP as capital, less so much of that amount (if any) as:

(a) it has previously, directly or indirectly, drawn out or received back;
(b) it so draws out or receives back during the five years beginning with the relevant time;
(c) it is or may be entitled so to draw out or receive back at any time when it is a member of the LLP; or
(d) it is or may be entitled to require another person to reimburse to it.

The amount of the liability of a member on a winding up is the amount which it is liable to contribute to the assets of the LLP in the event of its being wound up, and which it remains liable so to contribute for at least the period of five years beginning with the relevant time (or until the partnership is wound up if that happens before the end of that period).

Where as a result of the operation of the restriction, relief has not been given under *CTA 2010, ss 37, 45A* or *Pts 5, 5A* for a loss made by the member company as a member of the LLP in a previous accounting period, the unrelieved loss is treated as having been relieved under *CTA 2010, ss 37, 45A* or *Pts 5, 5A* in the current period for the purposes of determining the amount of the restriction, if any, for the current period. However, no account is taken on the unrelieved loss if it has been treated as being made under a previous period and as result relief would have been given under *CTA 2010, ss 37, 45A* or *Pts 5, 5A* if claimed. Further, no account is taken of a loss for which relief has been given other than under *CTA 2010, s 59*.

In *HMRC v Hamilton & Kinneil (Archerfield) Ltd* [2015] UKUT 130 the Upper Tribunal dismissed a claim for loss relief by a member of a LLP on the basis the company has made no capital contribution to the LLP. The case considered the earlier *ICTA 1988* provisions (*s 118ZC*), but the same principles were in point.

Where the provisions of *ITTOIA 2005, s 863A(2)* (LLPs: salaried members) apply with respect to an individual who is a member of an LLP (see further Tolley's Income Tax with regard to these provisions and the applicable conditions) then, in relation to the charge to corporation tax on income, that individual (the 'salaried member') is treated as being employed by the LLP under a service contract and not as a member of the LLP. Such individual's rights and duties as a member of the LLP are thus treated as rights and duties under that contract. The LLP will be treated as the employer and secondary contributor for employer NICs and statutory payments.

The costs of employing such an individual are expenses of earning profits and are allowable deductions in the same way and the same period as expenses in respect of any other employee. If no deduction is made under normal accounting practice for the expenses paid in respect of the salaried member's employment, then a specific statutory deduction is allowed in arriving at the profits of the LLP (for trade, property businesses) in the period when such employment expenses are paid. Similarly, with regard to an investment business, where such employment costs are expenses of management, but are not referable to an accounting period, then they are treated as referable to the accounting period in which they are paid. The availability of a deduction is then subject to the normal rules for such trade deductions (such as being wholly and exclusively for the purposes of the trade etc.), or for management expenses (such as the restriction for capital expenditure etc.).

As a salaried member is not treated as a partner for tax purposes they are not included on the partnership return for the period in which they are a salaried member. If they are treated as a partner for part of a period then they would be included in the return for that period.

[*CTA 2009, ss 92A, 1227A, 1273, 1273A; CTA 2010, ss 59–61; Limited Liability Partnerships Act 2000, s 10(1); ITTOIA 2005, s 863A; F(No 2)A 2017, Sch 4, paras 153, 154; FA 2020, s 104*].

Investment LLPs and property investment LLPs

[56.12] A number of tax exemptions for income and gains do not apply where the income and gains are received by a member of a 'property investment LLP'. Interest relief under *ITA 2007, ss 383, 398, 399* (see Tolley's Income Tax under Interest Payable) is denied where the partnership is an 'investment LLP'.

An '*investment LLP*' is an LLP whose business consists wholly or mainly in the making of investments and the principal part of whose income is derived therefrom, and a '*property investment LLP*' is similarly defined by reference to investments in land. The status of an LLP in this respect is determined for each period for which partnership accounts are drawn up. [*ITA 2007, s 399; CTA 2010, s 1135*].

The following exemptions do not apply to property investment LLPs:

(i) Exemptions under *ICTA 1988, ss 613(4), 614(3)–(5)* (see Tolley's Income Tax under Pension Provision).

(ii) Corresponding exemption from the trusts rate of income tax under *ITA 2007, s 479* (accumulation and discretionary trusts, see Tolley's Income Tax under Settlements). [*ITA 2007, s 480(1)(4)*].

(iii) Corresponding exemptions under *TCGA 1992, s 271(1)* (see **33.15** EXEMPT ORGANISATIONS). [*TCGA 1992, s 271(12)*].

Anti-avoidance

Leasing partnerships

[56.13] For restriction of relief for losses in the case where there is a change in the interest of a company in a business, carried on in partnership, of leasing plant or machinery, see **49.5** and **49.11** LEASING.

Mixed membership partnerships

[56.14] There are provisions which seek to counteract tax motivated arrangements involving partnerships and LLPs which allow individual members of the partnership to allocate profits and losses to another non-individual member to reduce their tax liabilities. The provisions consider the position with regard to excess profit and excess loss allocation and are aimed at arrangements involving mixed membership partnerships (with individual and non-individual members) that reduce income tax payable by individuals (whether they are partners in the partnership, or in some cases, not).

As the rules apply where a partnership involves non-individuals, which includes corporate partners, they have an effect on the corporation tax position of such a company. The rules focus on the income tax position of the individual, and are outlined in brief here. The corporation tax impact on the corporate member is then highlighted. A more detailed analysis of the income tax position can be found in Tolley's Income Tax.

The rules were applied in *Walewski v HMRC* UT, [2021] UKUT 133 (TC).

See also HMRC Business Income Manual BIM82700 onwards.

Excess profit allocation

[56.15] The rules on excess profit allocation (found at *ITTOIA 2005, s 850C*) apply to arrangements where an individual partner(s) in a partnership diverts all or part of their profit share to a non-individual partner(s), such as a company, so as to reduce tax on their profit share. The legislation counteracts this by overriding the agreed profit sharing arrangements and taxing that individual partner(s) on the diverted profits. The legislation does not apply where the partners are genuinely acting at arm's length and not intending to secure a tax advantage.

The excess profit allocation rules apply where:

- in a period of account ('*the relevant period of account*'), a partnership has a taxable profit (and the individual partner 'A' has a share of that profit);
- a share of the profit is allocated to a non-individual partner 'B' ('B's profit share'); and
- either Condition X or Y (see below) is met.

A '*non-individual partner*' is any person other than an individual and includes companies and individuals acting as trustees. For the purpose of calculating the non-individual B's profit share within these provisions, income tax rules are applied to the calculation of the B's profit share even if it is a company.

Condition X

Condition X is that it is reasonable to suppose that amounts representing A's deferred profits are included in B's profit share and in consequence both A's profit share and the relevant tax amount are lower than they would otherwise have been.

'*Deferred profits*' means any profits (being remuneration, or other benefits or returns) of the individual partner A (or A's share of any such amounts, as provided to A and one or more others, as determined on a just and reasonable basis) that are held back for whatever reason. This includes arrangements where it is possible events may mean that the individual may not actually receive the profits.

Relevant tax amount: as noted in both Conditions X and Y (below), the profit allocation legislation only applies where it is reasonable to suppose that the relevant tax amount is lower than it would have been had the profit shares not been diverted from the individual A to the non-individual partner B. The '*relevant tax amount*' is the tax that would have been payable by both the individual A and the non-individual B on their income as partners in the firm (their profit share) as allocated (ignoring these provisions).

Condition Y

Condition Y is that:

- the non-individual partner B's profit share exceeds the '*appropriate notional profit*';
- the individual partner A has the '*power to enjoy*' B's profit share; and

- it is reasonable to suppose that the whole or any part of B's profit share is attributable to A's power to enjoy, and both A's profit share and the relevant tax amount are lower than they would have been in the absence of A's power to enjoy (with regard to this latter point on the relevant tax amount, see above).

[*ITTOIA 2005, s 850C(1)–(4)(6)(7)(8)(9)*].

The appropriate notional profit

The '*appropriate notional profit*' is the sum of two amounts: the appropriate notional return on capital; and the appropriate notional consideration for services.

The '*appropriate notional return on capital*' is the rate of return which, in all the circumstances, is reasonably comparable to a commercial rate of interest, applied to the non-individual B's contribution to the firm, less any return actually received for the relevant period of account (other than profit share) in respect of B's contribution (for example, this might include a fee). The amount of B's contribution is based on the amount that B has invested in the partnership as capital at that time (less any amounts drawn out, or received back, or which B is entitled to so draw out or receive) as determined under the rules at *ITA 2007, s 108* (for amount A).

The '*appropriate notional consideration for services*' is the arm's length value of any services provided by B for the period, less any other amount received for those services (for example, a service fee) that is not part of the profit share. If any services provided involve other members of the partnership, then the value of these services is not included in arriving at the notional return. It is indicated in the technical note that in most cases, this notional consideration should be no more than the cost to the company B in providing the services plus a modest mark-up.

[*ITTOIA 2005, s 850C(10)–(17)*].

The power to enjoy

In addition, the individual A must meet the 'power to enjoy' requirement in relation to the profit that has been allocated to the non-individual partner B. This test is widely drawn and does not depend upon A deriving any direct benefit from the profits allocated to B, nor does it require A to have any actual connection to B. A has the '*power to enjoy*' B's profits if any of the following apply:

- A and B are connected; or
- A is party to arrangements a main purpose of which is to secure that B's profit share is subject to the corporation tax rules rather than the income tax provisions; or
- any of the enjoyment conditions is met in relation to all or any part of B's profit share.

Connected persons: A and B are 'connected' if they fall within the definition found at *ITA 2007, s 993*, other than simply being connected through being partners.

Arrangements to secure corporation tax rather than income tax treatment: The legislation applies where the individual A is party to arrangements, one of the main purposes of which is to ensure that an amount is included in the non-individual B's profit share and is: subject to corporation tax instead of income tax; or otherwise subject to the provisions of the Corporation Tax Acts rather than the provisions of the Income Tax Acts. For example, where the intention is to ensure that the sum is taxed at corporation tax rates (rather than income tax rates) or where the aim is to access a relief that is only available for corporation tax payers.

Enjoyment conditions: These conditions look at whether the individual, or a person connected to the individual, is in a position to enjoy the benefit of the profit share allocated to the non-individual B.

B's profit share influenced by the power to enjoy

Where the power to enjoy requirement is met, then for Condition Y to be met it must also be reasonable to suppose that B's profits are higher than they would otherwise have been because of A's power to enjoy them, and that both A's profit share and the relevant tax amount (see above) are lower than they would have been in the absence of A's power to enjoy. As highlighted in the technical note, it is possible that individual A may have an interest in the non-individual partner but this may be so small that it is clear that the profit share has not been affected.

[ITTOIA 2005, s 850C(18)–(21)].

Reallocating the excess profits

[56.16] If the provisions apply then the profit shares of A and B are adjusted for tax purposes such that:

- Individual A is taxed on the profits that would have been allocated to A had the deferral arrangements not been entered into (under Condition X), or that reflect A's power to enjoy (under Condition Y), as determined on a just and reasonable basis.
- The non-individual B is taxed on a smaller share to reflect the amount on which the individual is taxed.

In deferred remuneration cases under Condition X, the amount to be reallocated is simply the amount of the deferred profit, so far as is just and reasonable.

Where Condition Y applies, the maximum additional profit that the individual can be taxed on is the difference between the appropriate notional profit for the non-individual and the profit allocated to that non-individual (the non-individual B's 'excess profit'). In addition, the increase must be reduced by any increase that has been made in the case of that individual in respect of any reallocation of deferred profit.

As noted above, for the purpose of these provisions income tax rules are applied in the calculation of the B's profit share (including excess profit share) even if it is a company.

Interaction with the AIFM rules (see **56.7** above): under the legislation dealing with the tax treatment of remuneration of members of AIFM firms, a partnership may elect to be treated as a partner itself, in order to pay tax on a member's remuneration on behalf of the member. If it does so, the AIFM firm is treated as an individual partner of the partnership, not as a non-individual partner for the purposes of the mixed membership rules.

[*ITTOIA 2005, s 850C(4)(6)(7)(8)*].

Adjustments to non-individual's corporate profits

[56.17] As the individual A is being taxed on part of the profit share allocated to the non-individual partner B, the taxable profit share of B has to be reduced (to take account of this increase), so that the profits are taxed only once. Rather than simply reducing the profit share of the non-individual partner B by the amount by which the individual partner A's profit share is increased, the legislation takes account of the possible differences in computational provisions between individuals and corporates.

There is a rule for corporate partners (B) which applies for the accounting period of the firm which coincides with the relevant period of account (or if there is no such accounting period, for the accounting period of the firm in which the relevant period of account falls) such that any adjustments to B's profit calculation under the allocation of a firm's profit or loss provisions at *CTA 2009, ss 1262–1264* should be made on a just and reasonable basis, when taking account of the increase in A's profits.

With regard to an AIFM re-allocation under *ITTOIA 2005, s 863I* (see **56.7** above) any payment by B to the firm representing any income tax for which the firm is liable under the said AIFM rules, is not treated as income of any partner, nor taken into account in calculating the profits or losses of B (or otherwise deducted from any income of B).

[*ITTOIA 2005, s 350C(22)(23); CTA 2009, s 1264A*].

Payments by the non-individual B out of its reallocated profit share

The above provisions reallocate the profits to the individual for tax purposes. However, the reality is that the relevant profit share was allocated to the non-individual member B. It is possible that B may decide to actually pass such profit to another person. Provisions limit the tax which may be chargeable on such payment.

If as a result of an agreement in place in relation to B's excess profit share, B makes a payment to another person out of such excess profit, then the payment:

- is not treated as income of the recipient;
- is not taken into account in calculating the profits or losses of B or otherwise allowed as a deduction against B's income;
- is not treated as a distribution.

This applies for both income tax and corporation tax purposes (per *CTA 2009, s 1264A(3)*). The excess profit share is so much of B's profit share as is represented by the increase in individual A's profit under these rules (*s 850C(4)*) or the anti-avoidance provisions outlined at s *850D(4)* below. This rule does not apply if the payment is part of a scheme or arrangement with a main purpose of obtaining a tax advantage.

[*ITTOIA 2005, s 850E; CTA 2009, s 1264A(3)*].

Anti-avoidance provisions

[56.18] Anti-avoidance provisions, found at *ITTOIA 2005, s 850D*, apply where an individual, who is not a partner, carries out work for a partnership or LLP and their role looks like the role that you would expect a partner to have.

Irrespective of the complexity of the structure, the legislation will apply if:

- the individual (A) personally performs services for the partnership or LLP;
- at that time A is not a partner;
- if A had been a partner then the partnership profit calculation for A for the relevant period of account would have produced a profit for the firm;
- a non-individual B is a partner and receives a share of that profit;
- it is reasonable to suppose that A would have been a partner in the absence of the mixed membership excess profit allocation rules; and
- it is reasonable to suppose that the profit share includes deferred profits in relation to A (another Condition X, as above for *s 850C(2)*) or that A has 'the power to enjoy' the profit share allocated to the non-individual B (another Condition Y, as above for *s 850C(3)*) (in both cases ignoring the requirements in those conditions at *s 850C* that both A's profit share and the relevant tax amount are lower than they would have otherwise been).

The provisions of *s 850D* cross refer for the details to the relevant sections of *s 850C*.

The 'reasonable to suppose' test (that A would have been a partner but for the excess profit allocation rules) is treated as met if A is a member of another partnership which is associated with the firm. A partnership is associated with the firm if: it is a member of the firm; or it is a member of a separate partnership that is associated with the firm.

If the legislation applies, then the individual is treated as if they were a member of the partnership or LLP. The mixed membership partnership rules apply and the individual is taxed on the appropriate amount of the profits reallocated to them. For the non-individual partner B, the adjustment to their corporate profits is made in the same way as for the application of excess profit allocation rules at *s 850C*.

[*ITTOIA 2005, s 850D; CTA 2009, s 1264A(1)*].

Excess loss allocation

[56.19] The provisions also consider the position of excess loss allocation between individual and non-individual members of a partnership, such as a company. The rules deal with arrangements entered into with a view to an individual member(s) being allocated losses of the partnership, instead of a non-individual, in order for them to be able to claim loss relief. The rules ensure that the relief for the losses will be restricted in such cases.

These restrictions apply when:

- an individual makes a trading or property business loss as a partner in a firm;
- which arises, wholly or partly, as a consequence or in connection with relevant tax avoidance arrangements to which the individual is a party, a main purpose of which is to secure that losses are allocated or arise to the individual, rather than a non-individual; and
- with a view to the individual obtaining relief for the loss.

The restriction applies to relief for trade or property business losses and also to claims to use trading losses as relief for capital gains. Where the restrictions apply, no loss relief is available to the individual for their losses from the partnership. The fact that the non-individual is not a partner in the firm or is unknown or does not exist at the time does not prevent the restriction applying.

A relevant tax avoidance arrangement can be any agreement, understanding or any form of arrangement for the loss to be allocated to one or more individuals rather than a non-individual. The allocation of the losses does not have to be the main purpose of the arrangements, only one of the main purposes.

See further Tolley's Income Tax.

[*ITA 2007, ss 116A, 127C*].

Administration of partnerships

Returns and filing dates

[56.20] Where a partnership includes one or more companies and one or more individuals, the filing date of the partnership return cannot be earlier than the filing date for the individuals' personal returns and may be later depending on the companies' accounting periods.

> *Example*
>
> A partnership between A, an individual, and B Ltd has an accounting date of 31 December. A is required to include the partnership income for the year ended 31 December 2021 in his tax return 2021/22, online filing date 31 January 2023. B Ltd's accounting period is the year to 31 July 2021, its corporation tax return being due on 31 July 2022. This is the date for filing the partnership returns.

The period of return will be the same as the tax year:

- where the partnership makes up accounts to 5 April;
- where there are no partnership accounts ending in the tax year; or
- for investment partnerships which do not carry on a trade or profession.

The filing date cannot be earlier than the end of the period of nine months beginning at the end of the relevant period. The filing date for an electronic return cannot be earlier than the first anniversary of the end of the relevant period and at least three months after the date of the notice to file. Where a partnership consists wholly of companies, HMRC normally set the filing date on the same basis as partnerships with individual and company members.

See also **56.11** above with regard to returns made on the basis that the activities of an LLP are treated as carried on in partnership by its members where they are not in fact so carried on and for the position of Salaried Members of LLPs.

European Economic Interest Groupings

[56.21] There are special provisions governing the tax treatment of European Economic Interest Groupings (EEIGs), wherever registered, within *EEC Council Regulation No 2137/85* dated 25 July 1985. Following Brexit, from IP completion day (11pm on 31 December 2020), the ability to form an EEIG within the UK has been removed. Any EEIGs that were registered in the UK immediately before IP completion day were automatically converted into 'UK Economic Interest Groupings' or 'UKEIGs'. The UKEIG structure is expected to be a temporary structure, allowing entities more time to take more appropriate action, rather than a long term corporate choice. Without the European features, it is not believed that the structure will be an attractive long term corporate vehicle.

An EEIG or UKEIG, wherever it is registered, is regarded as acting as the agent of its members. Its activities are regarded as those of its members acting jointly, each member being regarded as having a share of EEIG or UKEIG property, rights and liabilities. The loan relationship rules have effect in relation to a grouping as if it were a partnership (in particular in the application of *CTA 2009, ss 380–385, 467, 472–474*, see **50.23, 50.11, 50.43** LOAN RELATIONSHIPS). A person is regarded as acquiring or disposing of a share of the EEIG or UKEIG assets not only where there is an acquisition or disposal by the EEIG or UKEIG while he is a member but also where he becomes or ceases to be a member or there is a change in his share of EEIG or UKEIG property.

A member's share in EEIG or UKEIG property, rights or liabilities is that determined under the contract establishing the EEIG or UKEIG or, if there is no provision determining such shares, it will correspond to the profit share to which he is entitled under the provisions of the contract. If the contract makes no such provision, members are regarded as having equal shares.

Where the EEIG or UKEIG carries on a trade or profession, the members are regarded for the purposes of tax on income and gains as carrying on that trade or profession in partnership.

[*CTA 2010, s 990*].

For the purposes of making assessments to income tax, corporation tax or capital gains tax on members of EEIGs or UKEIG (or of securing that members are so assessed), an inspector may, in the case of an EEIG which is registered, or has an establishment registered, in Great Britain or Northern Ireland, by notice require the EEIG or UKEIG to make a return containing such information as the notice may require, accompanied by such accounts and statements as the notice may require, within a specified time. In any other case, he may issue a similar notice to any UK resident member(s) of the EEIG or UKEIG (or if none is so resident, to any member(s)). Notices may differ from one period to another and by reference to the person on whom they are served or the description of EEIG or UKEIG to which they refer. Where a notice is given to an EEIG or UKEIG registered in Great Britain or Northern Ireland (or having an establishment registered there), the EEIG or UKEIG must act through a manager, except that if there is no manager who is an individual, the EEIG or UKEIG must act through an individual designated as a representative of the manager under the Directive. The return must in all cases include a declaration that, to the best of the maker's knowledge, it is correct and complete, and where the contract establishing the EEIG or UKEIG requires two or more managers to act jointly for the EEIG or UKEIG to be validly bound, the declaration must be given by the appropriate number of managers. [*TMA 1970, s 12A*].

A penalty not exceeding £300 (and £60 per day for continued failure) may be imposed in the case of failure to comply with a notice under the above provisions. The penalties are multiplied by the number of members of the EEIG or UKEIG at the time of the failure or at the end of the day for which a continuing penalty is imposed. No penalty may be imposed after the failure has been remedied, and if it is proved that there was no income or chargeable gain to be included in the return, the maximum penalty is £100. Fraudulent or negligent delivery of an incorrect return, etc. or of an incorrect declaration may result in a penalty not exceeding £3,000 for each member of the EEIG or UKEIG at the time of delivery, and the act or omission giving rise to the penalty is treated as the act or omission of each member of the EEIG or UKEIG for the purposes of extended time limits for assessments and consequential claims. [*TMA 1970, ss 36(4), 98B; FA 1998, Sch 18 para 91*].

[*TMA 1970, ss 12A, 98B; FA 1998, Sch 18 para 91; ITA 2007, s 842; CTA 2010, s 990, SI 2019 No 689, Regs 1, 2, 8, 15(9), 17(11); European Union (Withdrawal Agreement) Act 2020, Sch 5 para 1(1)*].

Simon's Taxes. See **D4.501–D4.503.**

Key points on partnerships

[56.22] Points to consider are as follows.

- The starting point is to establish whether a partnership exists. The mere existence of a partnership agreement is not sufficient. The partners should be carrying on a business together with a view to making a profit.
- Where there is a corporate member in the partnership it is still treated as transparent for tax purposes with the corporate being charged to corporation tax on its share of the profits. In determining its share of taxable profits the profits must be calculated in accordance with corporation tax principles.
- Where there are losses in an LLP the sideways relief which can be claimed by the corporate partner is restricted to the amount of the capital contribution. The contribution made to the LLP is made up of two parts: Part 1 — any amounts contributed to the LLP less any repayments (this includes repayments in the five years following the use of the loss). Also less amounts the partner is entitled to

draw back while a member of the LLP. Part 2 — the amount of the company's liability on a winding up of the LLP where that is not part of the capital in Part 1. The liability on a winding up is the amount the company must contribute if the LLP is wound up and the company must remain liable to contribute it for a period of five years beginning with the time the loss is used.

- For corporates wishing to accelerate the use of losses terms should be included in the members' agreement to make the company liable on a winding up for an amount equal to the loss used.
- For other partnerships the losses are restricted to the capital plus the partner's share of profits. However the amounts unused as a result of the restriction are treated as being made in the current period so can be eligible for group relief.
- In addition, sideways loss relief for non-active individual partners is restricted to an annual maximum of £25,000.
- Where there are corporate members in a partnership the filing deadline will not always be 31 January.
- Anti-avoidance rules for mixed membership partnerships may give rise to an adjustment for tax purposes in a corporate partner's profit share.

57

Patent Income

Simon's Taxes. See **D1.1202A–D1.1203D**.

Introduction to patent income

[57.1] *CTA 2010, Pt 8A* provides for an elective regime for intellectual property held by UK companies — termed the 'patent box' regime. These provisions allow qualifying companies to elect to effectively apply a 10% rate of corporation tax to all profits attributable to qualifying patents, whether paid separately as royalties or embedded in the sales price of products.

The patent box rate is not given as a reduced rate of tax on eligible profits, instead a deduction is given from trading profits of an amount that has the same effect as reducing the main rate of corporation tax on eligible profits to the special IP rate of 10%.

The regime also applies to other qualifying intellectual property rights such as regulatory data protection (also called 'data exclusivity'), supplementary protection certificates (SPCs) and plant variety rights. Other non-qualifying profits in these companies continue to be taxed at the main rate as normal.

An election for the patent box must be made in writing, specifying the first accounting period to which the rules apply and must be made within twelve months of the fixed filing date of the return for the first accounting period for which the company wishes to elect into the regime. The election can be made in the computations accompanying a tax return, or separate from the return in writing, no set format is required.

An election will apply equally to all trades of the company and for all subsequent accounting periods until it is revoked by notice in writing. Once an election has been revoked, a fresh election normally has no effect for five years following the accounting period of revocation. This is to prevent companies dipping in and out of the regime for purposes which would amount to an abuse of the regime, for example to exclude periods when a company would be required to register a set-off amount that would affect the relief available to other group companies. However, there is an exception to the five-year waiting period where a company has revoked an election with effect for the accounting period ending on 30 June 2016 (which may be a notional accounting period) or an earlier accounting period. In such a case, a new election may have effect for the accounting period ending on 30 June 2016 or any subsequent accounting period. Accounting periods which straddle 1 July 2016 are treated for this purpose only as two separate accounting periods, the first of which ends on 30 June 2016.

[*CTA 2010, ss 357G, 357GA*].

The regime applies equally to corporate partners, with necessary modifications. [*CTA 2010, s 357GB*].

Major changes to the patent box regime were made by *FA 2016* to bring it into line with the outcome of the OECD Base Erosion and Profit Shifting project. Revised rules for calculating the qualifying profits, broadly, apply to new entrants to the patent box on or after 1 July 2016, and also to some assets acquired on or after 2 January 2016. Assets not covered by the revised rules continue to receive the benefit of the existing regime until 30 June 2021, except that some assets acquired on or after 2 January 2016 may only receive the benefit of the existing regime until 31 December 2016. In particular, the changes remove the proportional profit split option so that streaming applies in all cases at the level of an asset, product or process. As an additional step in the calculation, an adjustment is required to reflect the proportion of the development activity on the asset, product or process category undertaken by the company itself. See **57.6** onwards below.

For HMRC guidance, see the Corporate Intangibles Research and Development Manual CIRD200000 onwards.

Qualifying company

[57.2] In order to elect into the regime, the company must, for each relevant accounting period, be a qualifying company. The conditions for single companies and companies that are members of groups differ slightly in that group companies must meet one further condition in order to qualify for the patent box.

Single Companies — generally a qualifying company will be one which either:

(a) currently holds qualifying IP rights (see below) or an exclusive licence in respect of qualifying IP rights; or

(b) has held such rights mentioned in (a), and is taxable in the current accounting period on income in respect of that right. That income must be attributable to events occurring wholly or partly during a period when the company was a qualifying company and had made a patent box election.

This latter condition allows a company to apply the patent box rules to income received when it would not otherwise be a qualifying company. For example, where damages for infringement of patent rights is received after the expiry of a patent, but where the company had made a patent box election at the time of the infringement.

The exclusive licence provision is likely to be particularly helpful to UK subsidiaries of foreign owned groups. The rules also widely define exclusivity, enabling a variety of arrangements to satisfy the definition.

[*CTA 2010, ss 357B, 357BA*].

Group Companies — where a company is a member of a group, in addition to the conditions detailed above for a single company, it must meet the 'active ownership' condition for the relevant accounting period. This condition is deemed to have been met if the company satisfies the development condition (see **57.3** below) on its own account. Alternatively, the company must show that it has, during the accounting period in question, performed a significant amount of management activity in relation to the qualifying IP rights (or licence).

The definition of group is widely drawn so that it will allow joint venture entities and smaller groups that might not be required to be fully consolidated in group accounts under the *Companies Act* to fall within the definition.

[*CTA 2010, ss 357B, 357BE, 357GD*].

Corporate partners. The patent box regime applies to a corporate partner in a similar way as it applies to a single company carrying on a trade, with the following modifications:

(i) a corporate partner may choose to make or revoke a patent box election. That partner's share in the profits/losses of the partnership is computed as if the election had been made or revoked by the partnership. This has no effect on the shares of the other partners;
(ii) any company which is a corporate partner in a partnership must meet the active ownership condition whether or not it is a member of a group;
(iii) a partnership meets the development condition in respect of an IP right where either the partnership itself, or a corporate partner with at least a 40% share in the partnership, has carried out qualifying development in relation to that right;
(iv) any corporate partner who is party to an arrangement designed to secure a return from the partnership that is economically equivalent to the receipt of interest is treated as if they had not made a patent box election.

[*CTA 2010, s 357GB*].

Qualifying IP right

[57.3] A right is a qualifying IP right if it is:

(a) a UK patent granted under the *Patents Act 1977*;

(b) a patent granted under the European Patent Convention;
(c) a right which corresponds with one in (a) or (b) above granted under the law of an EEA state and specified in *SI 2013 No 420*;
(d) a supplementary protection certificate;
(e) any plant breeders' rights granted under *Plant Varieties Act 1997*; or
(f) any Community plant variety rights granted under Council Regulation (EC) No 2100/94,

and the company meets the development condition in relation to the right.

[*CTA 2010, ss 357B, 357BB, 357BC; SI 2013 No 420*].

The 'development condition' broadly requires that the company claiming patent box benefits, or a member of its group, either creates or significantly contributes to the creation of the patented innovation or, that the company, or group member, performs a significant amount of activity to develop the patented innovation, its use or the product it is used in.

The rules set out ways in which the condition may be satisfied. It is notable that the condition itself does not impose a strict self-development requirement. In other words, companies acquiring patents may also meet the development condition.

The four conditions, one of which must be met for the development condition to be satisfied, are as follows:

(i) the company has at any time carried out qualifying development in relation to the right and has not become or ceased to be a controlled member of a group since that time;
(ii) the company has at any time carried out qualifying development in relation to the right and has become or ceased to be a controlled member of a group since that time. The development condition will still be satisfied however if for a period of twelve months beginning with the day on which it left or joined the group it performed activities of the same description (although not necessarily in respect of the same protected item or right) as those that constituted the qualifying development provided that during those twelve months it does not cease to be a member of that group or become a controlled member of any other group;
(iii) the company (Co A) is a member of a group, another company (Co B) that is or has been a member of the group has carried out qualifying development in relation to the right, and Co B was a member of the group at the time it carried out the qualifying development. The company undertaking the qualifying development must have been a member of the relevant group when the qualifying development was carried out (even if the company that holds the right was not). However it is not necessary that the company holding the rights was a member of the group at the time the development occurred; it is only necessary that it is currently a member of the group;
(iv) where a company (Co T), holding IP rights in respect of which it meets the development condition (as in (ii) above), joins a new group and then transfers the IP rights to another company in the new group. The development condition will still be satisfied where the transferee either:

- remains a member of the group or transfers its trade to another member of the group; and
- taken together Co T and/or the transferee company continue to undertake activities of the same nature as those that amounted to the qualifying development for twelve months after Co T joined the group.

[*CTA 2010, ss 357BC, 357BD*].

For the development conditions (i) and (ii) above a company is treated as becoming a controlled member of a group where a company that was not previously associated with the company acquires control of the company or acquires a major interest in the company. A company is treated as ceasing to be a controlled member of a group where each company which previously controlled or held a major interest in a company ceases to do so, and the company is no longer associated with those companies. Where a company ceases to be a controlled member of the group, any company that it controls, and any company in which it holds a major interest is also treated as ceasing to be a controlled member of the original group.

Where a company meets the development condition under (ii) or (iv) it is regarded as meeting that condition from the date that either it or the other company respectively joined the group, rather than on the expiry of the twelve month period.

[*CTA 2010, s 357BC(11)*].

Cost-sharing arrangements

[57.4] Often companies enter into cost-sharing arrangements ('CSAs') to share the costs and risks of developing, producing or obtaining assets, services, or rights. There are special rules to enable such companies to take advantage of the patent box. Revised provisions were introduced by *F(No 2)A 2017* and apply for accounting periods beginning on or after 1 April 2017. For the purposes of the revised provisions, a '*cost-sharing arrangement*' is defined as an arrangement under which:

(a) each of the parties is required either to contribute to the cost of creating or developing an item or process (an '*invention*') or to undertake activities for the purpose of creating or developing an invention;

(b) each party is entitled to a share in any income attributable to the invention or has one or more rights in respect of it; and

(c) any income received by each party is proportionate to its participation in the arrangement (as in (a) above).

A company which is a party to a CSA is treated as if it held any qualifying IP right granted in respect of the invention which is held by another party to the CSA. This does not apply if the company holds an exclusive licence in respect of that right or if the CSA produces a return for the company which is economically equivalent to interest. The right is treated as a 'new qualifying IP right' of the company for the purposes of **57.8** and **57.9** below only if either the company or the other party became a party to the CSA on or after 1 April 2017 or the right is a new qualifying IP right of the other party (or would be if it were a company). It is not so treated as a new qualifying IP right if the company held an exclusive licence in respect of the right immediately before joining the CSA which was granted before 1 July 2016 (or in certain circumstances 2 January 2016 (see below)).

Similarly, a company is treated as if it held any exclusive licence in respect of a qualifying IP right granted in respect of the invention which is held by another party to the CSA. This does not apply if the company itself holds the right or another exclusive licence in respect of it or if the CSA produces a return for the company which is economically equivalent to interest. The right is treated as a new qualifying IP right of the company for the purposes of **57.8** and **57.9** below only if either the company or the other party became a party to the CSA on or after 1 April 2017 or the right is a new qualifying IP right of the other party (or would be if it were a company). It is not so treated as a new qualifying IP right if the company held the right immediately before joining the CSA and the right was granted or issued to the company under an application filed before 1 July 2016 or was assigned to the company before 1 July 2016 (or, in certain circumstances, 2 January 2016). It is also not treated as a new qualifying IP right if the company held an exclusive licence in respect of the right immediately before joining the CSA which was granted before 1 July 2016 (or 2 January 2016).

The circumstances in which the above references to 1 July 2016 are replaced by 2 January 2016 are where the person who assigned the right or granted the licence is not within the charge to corporation tax or a designated foreign tax, the person and the company are connected and a main purpose of the assignment or grant was the avoidance of a foreign tax. For the list of designated foreign taxes, see *SI 2016 No 1181*.

Research and development undertaken by a party to a CSA for the purpose of creating or developing an invention is treated as having been contracted out to that party by each company which is a party to the CSA for the purpose of determining, for each company, the amount of S1 and S2 at **57.7**(6) below. Where the research and development is contracted out by a party to the CSA ('P') to another person ('A'), any company which makes a payment under the CSA in respect of the research and development (whether to P or to A) is treated as having contracted out the research and development to P, and the payment is treated as having been made to P in respect of it.

Where a person ('B') assigns a qualifying IP right in respect of an invention to a party to a CSA ('Q'), any company which is a party to the CSA which makes a payment in respect of the assignment (whether to B or to Q) is treated for the purpose of determining the amount of A at **57.7**(6) below as if the payment were a payment to B for the assignment of the right to the company. A similar rule applies where B grants or transfers an exclusive licence in respect of a qualifying IP right granted in respect of the invention to Q.

Where a company makes a payment to a person for entering into a CSA with it and the person holds a qualifying IPT right in respect of the invention or an exclusive licence in respect of such a right, a just and reasonable part of the payment is treated for the purpose of determining the amount of A at **57.7**(6) below as if it were an amount paid for the assignment or transfer to the company of that right or licence. Similar provisions apply to a payment by a company to a party to a CSA for agreeing to the company becoming a party to the CSA where an existing party holds the qualifying IPT right or exclusive licence, and to a payment by a company which is a party to a CSA to another party for agreeing to the company becoming entitled to a greater share of the income from the invention or acquiring additional rights.

Where a company which holds a qualifying IPT right in respect of an invention or an exclusive licence in respect of such a right receives a payment for entering into a CSA, a just and reasonable part of the payment is treated as relevant IP income (see 57.7 below) of the company. Similar provisions apply where a company which is a party to a CSA receives a payment from a person for agreeing to that person becoming a party to the CSA and an existing party holds the qualifying IPT right or exclusive licence, and where a company receives a payment from another party to the CSA for agreeing to that party becoming entitled to a greater share of the income from the invention or acquiring additional rights.

Previous rules

For accounting periods beginning before 1 April 2017, a CSA was defined as above but it was an additional requirement that one of the parties held a qualifying IP right or an exclusive licence in respect of such a right. A company which was a party to a CSA is treated as if it held the qualifying IP right or exclusive licence. This did not apply where the company's return was no more than economically equivalent to interest.

[*CTA 2010, ss 357GC–357GCZF; F(No 2)A 2017, s 23(3)(5)*].

Calculation of deduction

[57.5] Where an election is made, rather than applying a reduced rate of tax to eligible profits, a deduction is given from trading profits of an amount that has the same effect as reducing the main rate of corporation tax on eligible profits to the special IP rate.

[*CTA 2010, s 357A(2)*].

The deduction is calculated using the formula:

$$RP \times \frac{(MR - IPR)}{MR}$$

where:

- RP is the relevant IP profits of the trade of the company;
- MR is the main rate of corporation tax; and
- IPR is the special IP rate of corporation tax — set at 10%.

In some circumstances there may be relevant IP losses (see **57.11** below).

[*CTA 2010, s 357A(2)–(4)*].

Relevant IP profits

[57.6] Following the amendments to the patent box regime by *FA 2016* (see 57.1 above), there are three sets of rules which may apply to determine the relevant IP profits of a company for an accounting period, depending on when the accounting period begins, whether or not the company is a 'new entrant' and whether or not it obtains new IP rights. The method in 57.7 below will apply in all cases from July 2021.

Transferred trades

The following rules apply in determining how the three sets of rules apply to a company (the 'transferee') if another company (the 'transferor') ceases to carry on a trade (or part of a trade) involving the exploitation of a qualifying IP right and assigns the right to the transferee or grants or transfers and exclusive licence in respect of the right to the transferee and the transferee begins to carry on the trade (or part).

The transferee is treated as not being a new entrant if the patent box regime applied to the transferor on the transfer date (i.e. the date of the assignment, grant or transfer), and the first accounting period for which the regime applied began before 1 July 2016.

The qualifying IP right is treated as an old qualifying IP right (see 57.8 below) in relation to the transferee if it was so treated in relation to the transferor.

Expenditure incurred by the transferor before the transfer date is treated as incurred by the transferee for the purposes of calculating amounts D, S1, S2 and A at step 6 in 57.7 below. Any payment made to the transferor by the transferee for the assignment, grant or transfer is ignored in calculating amount A.

[*CTA 2010, s 357GCA*].

Relevant IP profits — new entrants and accounting periods beginning on or after 1 July 2021

[57.7] The following rules apply to determine the '*relevant IP profits*' of a trade for an accounting period where either the accounting period begins on or after 1 July 2021 or the company is a 'new entrant'.

For this purpose, a company is a '*new entrant*' if the first accounting period for which its election into the regime (see 57.1 above), or its most recent such election, has effect begins on or after 1 July 2016. Accounting periods which straddle 1 July 2021 or 1 July 2016 are treated for this purpose only as two separate accounting periods, the second of which starts on whichever of those date is relevant. Any necessary apportionments are made on a just and reasonable basis.

Alternatively, a company may make an election to be treated as a new entrant. An election must be made in writing, specifying the first accounting period to which it applies and must be made within 12 months of the fixed filing date of the return for that accounting period. An election will apply equally to all trades of the company and for all subsequent accounting periods.

[*CTA 2010, ss 357A(11), 357BF(1), 357G*].

The relevant IP profits of a trade for an accounting period are determined by the following eight-step process.

(1) Amounts which are brought into account as credits in calculating the trade profits for the period are divided into two streams, the '*relevant IP income stream*' consisting of amounts of 'relevant IP income' (see below) and the '*standard income stream*' consisting of amounts of income which are not relevant IP income. Any 'finance income' is excluded before making the division. '*Finance income*' for this purpose means trade credits under the loan relationships or derivative contracts regimes, any amounts which are recognised under generally accepted accounting practice as arising from a financial asset, and any return (as defined) under an arrangement which is economically equivalent to interest.

(2) The relevant IP income stream is divided into '*relevant IP sub-streams*' so that each sub-stream is an '*individual IP right sub-stream*' consisting of income properly attributable to a particular qualifying IP right (see **57.3** above), a '*product sub-stream*' consisting of income properly attributable to a particular kind of 'IP item' or a '*process sub-stream*' consisting or income properly attributable to a particular kind of 'IP process'. Income may be allocated to a product sub-stream or a process sub-stream only if it would not be reasonably practicable to apportion it between individual IP right sub-streams or if to do so would result in it not being reasonably practicable to apply any of the remaining steps.
An '*IP item*' is an item in respect of which a qualifying IP right held by the company has been granted or an item incorporating one or more such items. An '*IP process*' is a process in respect of which a qualifying IP right held by the company has been granted or a process incorporating one or more such processes. Two or more IP items or two or more IP processes may be treated as of a particular kind if they are intended to be, or are capable of being, used for the same or substantially the same purposes.

(3) Amounts which are brought into account as debits in calculating the trade profits for the period, other than 'excluded debits', are allocated on a just and reasonable basis between the standard income stream and each of the relevant IP income sub-streams. '*Excluded debits*' are trade debits under the loan relationships or derivative contracts regimes and additional deductions for RESEARCH AND DEVELOPMENT EXPENDITURE (**63**), or under the television, video games or theatrical production regimes (see **26** CREATIVE INDUSTRIES RELIEFS).

(4) The following amounts are deducted from each relevant IP sub-stream: the amount allocated at step 3 to the sub-stream and the 'routine return figure' for the sub-stream.
If, however, under an arrangement a person has assigned to the company a qualifying IP right or has granted or transferred to the company an exclusive licence in respect of such a right and the company makes an 'income-related payment' to that person, the amount of that payment may not be deducted if it was allocated to the sub-stream at step 3. This does not apply if the payment does not affect the R&D fraction for the

sub-stream (see step 6). A payment is an '*income-related payment*' if the obligation to make it arises under the arrangement by reason of the amount of the company's income which is properly attributable to the right or licence or if the amount of the payment is determined by the arrangement by reference to such income.

The '*routine return figure*' for a sub-stream is 10% of any 'routine deductions' made by the company in calculating the trade profits for the period and allocated to the sub-stream at step 3. Expenses incurred on behalf of C by another group company which would have been routine deductions of the sub-stream had they been incurred by the company are treated as routine deductions made by C and allocated to the sub-stream. Expenses incurred by another group company on behalf of the company and another company are apportioned for this purpose on a just and reasonable basis. '*Routine deductions*' are:

(a) capital allowances;
(b) premises costs;
(c) personnel costs (including for externally provided workers);
(d) plant and machinery costs;
(e) professional services (i.e. legal services, other than IP-related services, financial services, services provided in management or administration of employees and other consultancy services);
(f) deductions for the following services: water, fuel, telecommunications, computers, postal services, transport and refuse collection.

Loan relationship or derivative contract trade debits and capital allowances for expenditure on research and development or patents are not routine deductions. Also excluded are expenditure in respect of which an additional deduction for RESEARCH AND DEVELOPMENT EXPENDITURE(**63**) or under the television or video games regimes (see **26** CREATIVE INDUSTRIES RELIEFS), or an R&D expenditure credit, has been obtained. Deductions in respect of employee share acquisitions (see **69.31** TRADING INCOME — DEDUCTIONS) are also not routine deductions to the extent that the employee in question is engaged in research and development.

(5) The 'marketing assets return figure' for each relevant IP income sub-stream which is greater than nil following step 4 is deducted from the sub-stream.

The '*marketing assets return figure*' is the 'notional marketing royalty' for the sub-stream less the 'actual marketing royalty' for the sub-steam. If the actual marketing royalty is greater than the notional marketing royalty or if the difference between the two is less than 10% of the amount of the sub-stream after making the step 4 deductions, the marketing assets return figure is nil.

The '*notional marketing royalty*' for a sub-stream is the percentage of the income allocated to the sub-stream at step 2 above which the company would pay to another person for the right to exploit any relevant 'marketing assets' in the accounting period if the company were not otherwise able to exploit them. A number of assumptions are to be made for this purpose, including that the company and the other person are dealing at arm's length — see *CTA 2010, s 357BLA(4)*. In determining the percentage the company must act in accordance with Article 9 of the OECD Model Tax Convention and the OECD transfer pricing guidelines. A marketing asset is taken into account for this purpose if the sub-stream includes any income arising from things done by the company involving the exploitation of the asset. A '*marketing asset*' is:

(i) anything in respect of which proceeding for passing off could be brought, including a trademark;

(ii) anything corresponding to an asset within (i) above under the law of a territory outside the UK;

(iii) signs or indications designating geographical origin of goods and services; and

(iv) information about actual or potential customers intended for use for marketing purposes.

The '*actual marketing royalty*' is the total sums paid in acquiring any marketing assets taken into account in computing the notional marketing royalty or in acquiring the right to exploit any such assets.

(6) The amount of each relevant IP income sub-stream is multiplied by the R&D fraction for the sub-stream. The R&D fraction is the lesser of 1 and:

$$\frac{(D + S1) \times 1.3}{D + S1 + S2 + A}$$

where the following definitions apply.

(i) D is the company's qualifying expenditure on relevant R&D expenditure (ie expenditure on research and development which relates (as defined) to a qualifying IP right to which income in the sub-stream is attributable or which is incorporated in an item or process to which such income is attributable) undertaken in-house during the 'relevant period'. The expenditure must be incurred on staffing costs, software, consumable items, externally provided workers or on payments to the subject of clinical trials.

(ii) S1 is the expenditure incurred by the company during the relevant period in making payments to an unconnected person in respect of relevant R&D contracted out to that person.

(iii) S2 is the expenditure incurred by the company during the relevant period in making payments to a connected person in respect of relevant R&D contracted out to that person.

(iv) A is the expenditure incurred by the company during the relevant period in making payments on the acquisition (by assignment, by grant or transfer of an exclusive licence, or by disclosure of an item or process) of a qualifying IP right to which income in the sub-stream is attributable or which is incorporated in an item or process to which such income is attributable. For this purpose, each payment in a series of payments in respect of a single acquisition is treated as made when the first payment in the series is made.

For accounting periods beginning on or after 1 April 2017, where, during the relevant period, the company is party to a cost-sharing agreement ('CSA') (see **57.4** above) and it incurs expenditure in making payments which fall within (ii) above as a result of the provisions at **57.4** above, the expenditure is disregarded in determining the R&D fraction to the extent that it does not exceed the amount of any payments to the company under the CSA in respect of relevant research and development undertaken or contracted out by it. Similarly, payments within (iii) or (iv) above as a result of the provisions at **57.4** above (other than payments in respect of disclosure of an item or process) are disregarded to the extent that they do not exceed the amount of any payments to the company under the CSA either by connected persons in respect of relevant research and development undertaken or contracted out by the company or in respect of an assignment to the company of a qualifying IP right to which the sub-stream is attributable or a grant or transfer to the company of an exclusive licence in respect of such a right.

If the company has made an election for exemption of profits from its foreign permanent establishments (see **31.15** DOUBLE TAX RELIEF), expenditure brought into account in calculating the foreign permanent establishments amount during the period which would otherwise qualify to be included in D or S1 is not so included. It is instead treated as expenditure to be taken into account in calculating S2.

If the company is a new entrant and the accounting period begins before 1 July 2021, the '*relevant period*' is the period beginning on 1 July 2013 and ending on the last day of the accounting period. The company may, however, elect for the relevant period to start on an earlier date, although not a date more than 20 years before the last day of the accounting period. If the company has insufficient information about its expenditure in the period 1 July 2013–30 June 2016 to be able to calculate the R&D fraction, it may elect for the relevant period to start on the date three years before the last day of the accounting period, in which case the R&D fraction is calculated by reference to the company's global research and development expenditure rather than that relating to the particular IP right. For accounting periods beginning on or after 1 July 2019, the effect of the election is that the relevant period starts on 1 July 2016.

Subject to below, in any other case the '*relevant period*' is the period beginning on 1 July 2016 and ending on the last day of the accounting period. The company may elect, as above, for any earlier start date for the relevant period, subject to the 20-year maximum.

For accounting periods ending on or after 1 July 2036, the '*relevant period*' is the 20 years ending with the last day of the accounting period.

Expenditure within (i)–(iii) above is treated as incurred during the relevant period only if it is allowable as a trade deduction for an accounting period falling wholly or partly within the relevant period.

A company may elect to increase the R&D fraction for the sub-stream if otherwise it would be at least 0.325 and it would, due to special circumstances, be less than the fraction which, on a just and reasonable basis, represents the proportion of the value of the qualifying IP rights for the sub-stream which is properly attributable to research and development undertaken by the company itself or on behalf of the company by unconnected persons. Where an election is made, the R&D fraction is increased to that greater fraction. An election must be made by notice to HMRC within the time limit for amending the company's return for the period.

(7) The amounts of each relevant IP income sub-stream following step 6 are added together.

(8) If the company makes an election, the 'additional amount' is added to the amount found in step 7.

A company can make an election if it holds a qualifying IP right within **57.3**(a)–(c) above or an exclusive licence in respect of such a right or would do so but for having disposed of any rights in the invention or licence before the right was granted. The '*additional amount*' is the difference between the aggregate of the relevant IP profits of the trade for each 'relevant accounting period' and what that aggregate would have been if the right had been granted on the '*relevant day*', i.e. the later of: the first day of the period of six years ending with the day on which the right was granted; or either the day on which the application for the grant of the right was filed or the day on which the licence was granted. Relevant IP profits against which relevant IP losses have been set off (see **57.11** below) are excluded in making the calculation. '*Relevant accounting periods*' are the accounting period in which the right is granted and any earlier accounting periods ending on or after the relevant day for which the company was a qualifying company (or would be but for the right not having been granted) and its patent box election was in force. If the company would be a qualifying company for the accounting period in which the right was granted but for its disposal of the rights in the invention or licence before the right was granted, it is treated for patent box purposes generally as if it were a qualifying company for that accounting period.

If the amount found in step 8 is greater than nil, that amount is the relevant IP profits of the trade for the accounting period. A negative amount is the relevant IP losses.

References above to a qualifying IP right held by the company include a reference to a qualifying IP right in respect of which the company holds an exclusive licence.

[*CTA 2010, ss 357BF, 357BG, 357BI–357BM; F(No 2)A 2017, s 23(2)(5)*].

Small claims treatment

A company which carries on only one trade during an accounting period can make any of the following elections where the 'qualifying residual profit' of the trade for the period does not exceed the greater of £1 million and the 'maximum amount'. The elections are: a notional royalty election, a small claims figure election and a global streaming election.

The '*maximum amount*' is £3 million, reduced where the company has related 51% group companies (see **10.34** CAPITAL ALLOWANCES ON PLANT AND MACHINERY) by dividing the figure by one plus the number of such companies which have been elected into the patent box regime. For accounting periods beginning on or after 1 April 2023, the reduction is made by reference to associated companies (defined as at **1.3** INTRODUCTION) rather than related 51% group companies. In many cases, this change will be no more than a change in terminology, but there are differences in the meaning of the two expressions. The maximum amount is also reduced proportionately for accounting periods of less than 12 months.

Where the qualifying residual profit exceeds £1 million, the company cannot make any of the elections for an accounting period if the above provisions applied to determine the relevant IP profits for any accounting period beginning in the four years before the period in question and the company did not make such an election for that previous accounting period. A company cannot make a small claims figure election for an accounting period in which the qualifying residual profit exceeds £1 million if the provisions at **57.9** or **57.10** below applied to determine the relevant IP profits for any accounting period beginning in the four years before the period in question and the company did not make such an election for that previous accounting period.

The '*qualifying residual profit*' is the amount which, in the absence of the election, would be the aggregate of the relevant IP sub-streams established at step 2 above after making the deductions required at step 4 above, ignoring the amount of any sub-streams that are not greater than nil (after making the deductions).

No formal election procedures are stipulated, and a company may simply include an election by way of a note to the computations in its corporation tax return (or an amended return) for the period. The rules are intended to relieve companies with smaller profits from administrative burdens.

Notional royalty election

The effect of a notional royalty election is that, if the company makes an election to treat a proportion of income from the exploitation of a right as relevant IP income (see below under 'Notional royalties'), that proportion is taken to be 75% of that income.

Small claims figure election

The effect of a small claims figure election is that step 5 above applies as if it required the deduction of the 'small claims figure' for each sub-stream and not the deduction of the 'marketing assets return figure'.

If 75% of the qualifying residual profit is lower than £1 million, the '*small claims figure*' is 25% of the amount of the sub-stream following step 4. Otherwise the small claims figure is:

$$A - (\frac{A}{QRP} \times £1\ million)$$

where A is the amount of the sub-stream following step 4 and QRP is the qualifying residual profit.

The £1 million threshold is reduced where the company has related 51% group companies by dividing the figure by one plus the number of such companies which have elected into the patent box regime. For accounting periods beginning on or after 1 April 2023, the adjustment is made by reference to associated companies (as above) rather than related 51% group companies. The £1 million is also reduced proportionately for accounting periods of less than 12 months.

Global streaming election

The effect of a global streaming election is that the division of the relevant IP income stream into separate sub-streams at step 2 above is not made, so that the remaining steps apply to the relevant IP income stream as a whole (and step 7 is not needed). If a small claims figure election is also made, it applies by reference to the relevant IP income stream as a whole.

[*CTA 2010, ss 357BN–357BND; FA 2021, Sch 1 paras 20, 21, 33*].

Relevant IP income

For the purposes of (1) above, '*relevant IP income*' means income within any of the following Heads:

- **Head 1: sales income.** Income from the sale of '*qualifying items*' (i.e. any items protected by a qualifying IP right held by the company), items incorporating a qualifying item and items wholly or mainly designed to be incorporated into a qualifying item or an item incorporating a qualifying item. An item and its packaging are not treated as a single item unless the packaging performs an essential function in the item's use.
- **Head 2: licence fees.** Income consisting of a licence fee or royalties for granting: (i) rights over qualifying IP rights held by the company; (ii) rights over a qualifying item or a process in respect of which a qualifying IP right held by the company has been granted; or (iii) a further right granted for the same purposes as those for which the rights in (i) or (ii) were granted.
- **Head 3: proceeds of sale.** Income arising from the sale or other disposal of a qualifying IP right or an exclusive licence in respect of such a right;
- **Head 4: damages for infringement.** Any amount received in respect of an infringement, or alleged infringement, of a qualifying IP right held by the company.
- **Head 5: other compensation.** Any damages, insurance proceeds or compensation not within Head 4 above which arise in respect of an event and are paid in respect of items within Head 1 above or represent a loss of income which would have been relevant IP income (for example, insurance proceeds received in respect of stocks of qualifying items lost or destroyed by fire).

Income within Head 4 or 5 is only relevant IP income if the event in respect of which it is received took place while the company's election into the patent box regime is in force. If only part of the event happened at such a time, the income is apportioned on a just and reasonable basis.

Income from oil extraction activities or oil rights and income which is on a just and reasonable apportionment attributable to a non-exclusive licence is not relevant IP income. Where a licence is exclusive but also confers any non-exclusive right in respect of the invention concerned, it is treated for this purpose as two licences, one exclusive and one non-exclusive.

For the purposes of the above rules, a qualifying IP right held by a company includes a qualifying IP right in respect of which the company holds an exclusive licence.

Notional royalties

Where a company holds a qualifying IP right within 57.3(a)–(c) above or an exclusive licence in respect of such a right and the company's trading income for an accounting period includes income arising from things done by the company which involve the exploitation of the right which is not otherwise relevant IP income, the company may elect to treat a proportion of the income (other than any finance income or income excluded from being relevant IP income as above) as relevant IP income. The proportion is that which the company would pay another person for the right to exploit the qualifying IP right in the accounting period if the company were not otherwise able to exploit it. A number of assumptions are to be made for this purpose, including that the company and the other person are dealing at arm's length — see *CTA 2010, s 357BHA(4)*. In determining the proportion the company must act in accordance with Article 9 of the OECD Model Tax Convention and the OECD transfer pricing guidelines.

Mixed sources of income

Where an item within Head 1 above is sold together with another item as part of a single unit for a single price, the income is apportioned between relevant IP income and other income on a just and reasonable basis. A similar apportionment is made of income paid under a mixed agreement (as defined).

[*CTA 2010, ss 357BH–357BHC*].

Relevant IP profits—company not new entrant, new qualifying IP rights for accounting periods beginning before 1 July 2021

[57.8] The following rules apply to determine the '*relevant IP profits*' of a trade for an accounting period beginning on or after 1 July 2016 and before 1 July 2021 where the company is not a new entrant (see 57.7 above) and any amount of relevant IP income (see 57.7 above) brought into account in calculating the trade profits for the period is properly attributable to a 'new qualifying IP right'. Accounting periods which straddle 1 July 2021 or 1 July 2016 are treated for this purpose only as two separate accounting periods, the second of which starts on whichever of those date is relevant.

Income which is properly attributable to a new qualifying IP right assigned to the company during the period 2 January 2016 to 1 July 2016 inclusive is treated as properly attributable to an 'old qualifying IP right' if it accrues in the period 1 July 2016 to 1 January 2017 inclusive. This rule applies also to income in respect of which an exclusive licence was granted to the company during the period 2 January 2016 to 1 July 2016 inclusive.

A global streaming election (see 57.7 above) cannot be made where these rules apply.

[*CTA 2010, s 357BO(1)(3)*].

A '*new qualifying IP right*' is a qualifying IP right where:

(i) the right was granted or issued to the company under an application filed on or after 1 July 2016; or
(ii) the right was assigned to the company on or after 1 July 2016; or
(iii) an exclusive licence in respect of the right was granted to the company on or after 1 July 2016.

The conditions in (ii) and (iii) above operate by reference to 2 January 2016 rather than 1 July 2016 where the person who assigned the right or granted the licence is not within the charge to corporation tax or a designated foreign tax, the person and the company are connected and a main purpose of the assignment or grant was the avoidance of a foreign tax. For the list of designated foreign taxes see *SI 2016 No 1181*.

An '*old qualifying IP right*' is a qualifying IP right which is not a new qualifying IP right. See 57.4 above for certain deemed rights treated as new qualifying IP rights in relation to cost-sharing arrangements.

[*CTA 2010, s 357BP; F(No 2)A 2017, s 23(4)*].

The relevant IP profits of a trade for an accounting period are determined by the following eight-step process.

(1) Amounts which are brought into account as credits in calculating the trade profits for the period are divided into two streams, the '*relevant IP income stream*' consisting of amounts of 'relevant IP income' (see 57.7 above) and the '*standard income stream*' consisting of amounts of income which are not relevant IP income. Any 'finance income' (see 57.7 above) is excluded before making the division.
(2) The relevant IP income stream is divided into '*relevant IP sub-streams*' so that each sub-stream is an '*old IP rights sub-stream*' consisting of income properly attributable to old qualifying IP rights, an '*individual IP right sub-stream*' consisting of income properly attributable to a particular new qualifying IP right (see 57.3 above), a '*product sub-stream*' consisting of income properly attributable to a particular kind of 'IP item' (see 57.7 above) or a '*process sub-stream*' consisting or income properly attributable to a particular kind of 'IP process' (see 57.7 above). Income may be allocated to a product sub-stream or a process sub-stream only if it would not be reasonably practicable to apportion it between individual IP right sub-streams or between individual IP right sub-streams and an old IP rights sub-stream or if to do so would result in it not being reasonably practicable to apply any of the remaining steps. Where an IP item or IP process incorporates both items or processes in respect of which an old qualifying IP right is held by the company and items or processes in respect of which a new qualifying IP right is held, the income properly attributable to the IP item or IP process may be treated as properly attributable to an old qualifying IP right only, and the income allocated to an old IP rights sub-stream, if either:

- the value of the IP item or IP process is wholly or mainly attributable to items or processes in respect of which an old qualifying IP right is held by the company; or
- the 'old IP percentage' for the IP item or IP process is at least 80%.

If the old IP percentage is less than 80% but at least 20%, that percentage of the income may be treated as properly attributable to an old qualifying IP right and so allocated to an old IP rights sub-stream. The remainder is allocated to a product sub-stream or a process sub-stream and, in calculating the R&D fraction for that sub-stream (see step 6 below), the IP item or IP process is treated as not incorporating the items or processes in respect of which an old qualifying IP right is held. The '*old IP percentage*' is found by dividing the number of items or processes incorporated in the IP item or IP process in respect of which the company holds an old qualifying IP right divided by the number of items or processes so incorporated in respect of which the company holds any qualifying IP right.

(3) Amounts which are brought into account as debits in calculating the trade profits for the period, other than 'excluded debits' (see 57.7 above), are allocated on a just and reasonable basis between the standard income stream and each of the relevant IP income sub-streams.

(4) The following amounts are deducted from each relevant IP sub-stream: the amount allocated at step 3 to the sub-stream and the 'routine return figure' for the sub-stream (see 57.7 above).

(5) The 'marketing assets return figure' (see 57.7 above) for each relevant IP income sub-stream which is greater than nil following step 4 is deducted from the sub-stream.

(6) The amount of each individual IP right income sub-stream, each product sub-stream and each process sub-stream is multiplied by the R&D fraction for the sub-stream (see 57.7 above).

(7) The amounts of any old IP rights sub-stream following step 5 and any individual IP right income sub-streams, product sub-streams and process sub-streams following step 6 are added together.

(8) If the company makes an election, the 'additional amount' is added to the amount found in step 7. See 57.7 above.

If the amount found in step 8 is greater than nil, that amount is the relevant IP profits of the trade for the accounting period. A negative amount is the relevant IP losses.

[*CTA 2010, s 357BQ*].

Relevant IP profits — company not new entrant, no new qualifying IP rights for accounting periods beginning before 1 July 2021

[57.9] The following rules apply to determine the '*relevant IP profits*' of a trade for an accounting period beginning before 1 July 2021 where the company is not a new entrant (see 57.7 above) and none of the relevant IP income (see 57.7 above) brought into account in calculating the trade profits for the period is properly attributable to a 'new qualifying IP right' (see 57.8 above). Accounting periods which straddle 1 July 2021 are treated for this purpose only as two separate accounting periods, the second of which starts on that date.

Note that as an alternative, the company can elect to allocate profits to relevant IP income using the streaming rules set out in the legislation (see 57.10 below). In some circumstances the company has to use this approach.

Subject to the above, there are three stages to calculate the relevant IP profits (although these are broken down in the legislation into several steps) as follows:

(a) stage 1: identify qualifying trading income and associated trading profits attaching to qualifying IP (there are three steps to this stage);
(b) stage 2: extract a routine profit element from associated trading profits to arrive at qualifying residual IP profit (there is just one step to this stage);
(c) stage 3: extract brand value from the residual IP profit to arrive at patent profits, i.e. relevant IP profits (there are two steps to this stage, although a further step may apply if profits were made previously from inventions awaiting grant of a patent).

[*CTA 2010, s 357C*].

The key features of the process can be summarised in the following diagram.

	Stage 1 Identify qualifying trade income and associated profit attaching to qualifying IP			Stage 2 Extract routine profit element to get qualifying residual IP position	Stage 3 Extract 'brand' value from residual IP profits to get patent profits – RIPP		
STEP	1	2	3	4	5	6	7
calculations	Gross trade income figure – TI *s 357CA*	RIPI as a percentage of TI	Percentage of trade profits attaching to RIPI	Deduct routine return *s 357CI* from step 3 RIPI trade profits to get QRP	Determine whether to opt for small claims treatment	Deduct marketing asset return from QRP *s 357CN*	Add to the post step 6 figure any determined additional amount *s 357CQ*

Stage 1, Step 1

Identify the total gross income of the trade of the company

Total gross income of the trade is defined in the legislation and is made up of income falling within the following heads:

Head 1: trading revenues, credits brought into account for tax purposes on realisation of intangible assets;

Head 2: damages, proceeds of insurance or other compensation which (so far as not falling within Head 1) are brought into account as credits in calculating the profits of the trade;

Head 3: any amounts which (so far as not falling within Head 1) are brought into account as adjustment income receipts (*CTA 2009, s 181*), in calculating the profits of the trade;

Head 4: any amounts which (so far as not falling within Head 1) are brought into account as credits on the realisation of IFA assets, see *CTA 2009, Pt 8 Ch 4*, in calculating the profits of the trade for the accounting period;

Head 5: profits from the sale of pre-2002 patent rights.

Income streams arising from lending activity and financial assets are specifically excluded under *CTA 2010, ss 357CA(2), 357CB*.

Stage 1, Step 2

Identify the proportion of relevant IP income as a percentage of gross income of the trade

This step requires companies to identify relevant RPI income ('RIPI' — see 57.7 above) and determine this amount as a percentage of the gross trading income figure arrived at Step 1.

[*CTA 2010, ss 357CC–357CF*].

Stage 1, Step 3

Apportion the relevant proportion of the profits of the trade to RIPI

Prior to any profit apportionment, the rules require a number of adjustments to be made to a company's taxable profits. In particular an add-back of any R&D tax credit relief super deduction is required. (This works in the taxpayer's favour as it increases the amount of profit benefitting from a 10% rate). Trading loan relationship/derivative debits or credits are also stripped out of the trading profits figure as is any other financial return economically equivalent to interest. In addition the amount of any above the line R&D expenditure credits brought into account (with regard to expenditure incurred on or after 1 April 2013) in calculating the profits of the trade for the accounting period are deducted. Similarly any additional deduction obtained under the television and video games reliefs, and theatrical productions relief (for accounting periods beginning: on or after 1 April 2013 for television relief; on or after 1 April 2014 (applicable as from a specified date) for video games relief; on or after 1 September 2014 for theatrical productions relief) at *CTA 2009, Pts 15A, 15B* and *15C* are added back.

Provisions also apply to increase R&D expenditure and qualifying expenditure for separate programme or video game trades where there is a shortfall in such expenditure (arising from the adjustments above), as described at *ss 357CH, 357CHA* respectively.

Subject to application of the streaming rules (see below) the percentage as calculated at Step 2 is applied to the adjusted taxable profits of the company to arrive at the proportion of trading profits associated with the company's RIPI.

[*CTA 2010, ss 357CG, 357CH, 357CHA*].

Stage 2, Step 4

Remove routine return to determine the qualifying residual profit ('QRP')

Profits attributable to routine activities are calculated by taking 10% of the aggregate of certain 'routine deductions' (see 57.7(4) above).

[*CTA 2010, ss 357CI–357CK*].

Stage 3, Steps 5 and 6

Removal of marketing assets return

The final stage of the calculation is to remove any profits relating to marketing assets.

Step 5

A company can opt to elect for small claims treatment (Step 5) which deems 25% of QRP as a deemed marketing return, leaving the remaining 75% (up to a maximum of £1 million) of QRP inside the patent box. The £1 million threshold is reduced proportionately where a company has one or more 'related 51% group companies' (for accounting periods beginning before 1 April 2015, one or more associated companies) and where an accounting period is less than twelve months long.

See **10.34** CAPITAL ALLOWANCES ON PLANT AND MACHINERY for the meaning of 'related 51% group company'.

A company can elect for small claims treatment where either the total amount of QRP of all of the company's trades taken together does not exceed £1 million or the total amount of QRP of all of the company's trades taken together does not exceed £3 million (reduced proportionately where a company has one or more associated companies and where an accounting period is less than twelve months long).

[*CTA 2010, ss 357CL, 357CM*].

No formal election procedure is stipulated, and a company may simply include the election for small claims treatment by way of a note to the computations in its corporation tax return (or an amended return) for the period. The rule is intended to relieve companies with smaller profits from the administrative burden of carrying out a full analysis of its marketing assets return as is required under Step 6.

Step 6

Alternatively, an arm's-length return on marketing assets must be determined to arrive at a notional marketing royalty amount to be deducted from QRP. Marketing assets are defined in the rules as being:

(i) any trademark (registered or unregistered);
(ii) signs or indications of geographical origin of goods and services; and

(iii) information about actual or potential customers.

The calculation allows a deduction for any actual marketing royalty paid from the notional figure.

[*CTA 2010, ss 357CN–357CP, 357CO(7)*].

Stage 3, Step 7

Identify any profits arising before grant of right

Patent box benefits may only be enjoyed once a patent has been granted. However, the rules recognise that patent profits may be generated between application and grant. Therefore, subject to certain conditions (including a six year look back cap) the rules allow any such profits to be given relief in the period in which the patent is granted. Under Step 7 this amount is added to the profit figure arrived at having worked through Steps 1 to 6. The final figure forms the company's relevant IP profits of the trade for the relevant period which benefit from a 10% tax rate.

[*CTA 2010, s 357CQ*].

Streaming

[57.10] The following alternative rules may apply to determine the '*relevant IP profits*' of a trade for an accounting period beginning before 1 July 2021 where the company is not a new entrant (see **57.7** above) and none of the relevant IP income (see **57.7** above) brought into account in calculating the trade profits for the period is properly attributable to a 'new qualifying IP right' (see **57.8** above). Accounting periods which straddle 1 July 2021 are treated for this purpose only as two separate accounting periods, the second of which starts on that date.

Subject to the above, the legislation provides an alternative method of calculating relevant IP profits (referred to as streaming) to that in **57.9** above; see *CTA 2010, ss 357D–357DC*. Broadly, streaming requires a just and reasonable apportionment of a company's expenses rather than adopting a simple pro rata approach as described above. Depending on the profitability of the company's patented products (or licensing arrangements) this may increase or decrease the amount of trading profits which are further adjusted through Stages 2 and 3 of the calculation to arrive at a relevant IP profits figure.

The streaming method is available if a company so elects or, in certain circumstances, it is mandatory, as follows:

(a) *Election* — a streaming election applies for each of the company's trades and all subsequent accounting periods, unless there is a change of circumstances that make the method inappropriate. In this case, the company can choose to use a different method that does produce a just and reasonable result, or to exit from streaming and use the simple apportionment formula;
(b) *Mandatory* — streaming is mandatory for each accounting period where:
    (1) any amount brought into account as a credit in calculating the profits of the trade for the accounting period is not fully recognised as revenue for the accounting period and that amount is

substantial. Income is 'substantial' if it is more than the lower of £2 million or 20% of the total gross income of the trade for the accounting period. However, if the lower of these two amounts is £50,000 or less then the income is not 'substantial' for these purposes;

(2) the total gross income of the trade for the accounting period includes relevant IP income and a substantial amount of licensing income that is not relevant IP income; or

(3) the total gross income of the trade for the accounting period includes income that is not relevant IP income and a substantial amount of relevant IP income in the form of licence fees or royalties received under an agreement granting rights to another person over IP rights, where the company itself only holds an exclusive license in respect those IP rights. The reason for this is that the licence income received and the royalties paid would result in very little profit. An apportionment process to determine relevant IP profits would not be appropriate in these circumstances. Where a company's income does not meet all these requirements, a just and reasonable apportionment must be made.

HMRC provide the following example as to when a streaming election might be beneficial.

> *Example*
>
> A company that manufactures and sells a range of established products, none of which incorporate items protected by qualifying IP. Turnover from this activity is £900,000 but its net profits are only £50,000. The company also owns qualifying IP which it developed many years previously and has licensed out to another business which takes care of manufacturing, marketing, distribution and sales. It receives an annual licence fee of £100,000.
>
> If the trade profits of £150,000 are apportioned by the ratio of RIPI to total gross income the result will be: £100,000/£1,000,000 × £150,000 = £15,000, but clearly in this example the company will want profits of £100,000 to qualify for the patent box.

The streaming method works by replacing steps 1–4 at **57.9** above with the following steps:

(i) Step 1: The total gross income of the trade is divided into two 'streams' of income consisting of relevant IP income (this will include any notional royalty allowed) and non-relevant IP income;

(ii) Step 2: The debits deducted from total gross income in arriving at taxable trading profit (excluding any additional deduction under the rules for R&D expenditure (see above) and any deduction for trading loan relationship debits) are then allocated against the stream to which they relate on a just and reasonable basis. The aim is that debits that arise in generating the relevant IP income are allocated against the relevant IP income stream and debits that arise in generating the non-relevant IP income stream are allocated against the non-relevant IP income stream.

Clearly, what is just and reasonable will depend on the specific circumstances. However all expenses must be allocated, and so for instance R&D (but not the additional Part 13 deduction), which may of course relate to future income, must still be fairly allocated to the current income streams;

(iii) Step 3: The debits allocated against the relevant IP income stream must be deducted from that income stream to give a figure to carry forward to Step 4;

(iv) Step 4: The 10% routine return percentage is applied to any routine expenses included in the debits allocated against the relevant IP income stream (other than R&D expenses) and the resulting figure is deducted from the figure produced by step 3 to give the figure of QRP.

Steps 5 and 6 follow the same approach as the same as for the normal calculation above, other than in step 6 where it is the aggregate of any actual marketing royalty allocated to the relevant IP stream that is deducted from the notional royalty in calculating what should be deducted from QRP.

[*CTA 2010, ss 357D–357DC*].

Relevant IP losses

[57.11] Where a company would be entitled to make a patent box deduction in calculating the profits of a trade but for the fact there are relevant IP losses, a set-off is allowed of those losses (the set-off amount) against the relevant IP profits:

(a) of other trades of the company for that accounting period;

(b) (any remaining amount after (a)) arising in trades of other group members which have elected into the regime, for that accounting period;

(c) (any remaining amount after (a) and (b)) of the company for the following accounting period (where it is treated as arising in that period).

Where a company ceases to trade, is no longer within the charge to corporation tax, or falls out of the patent box regime, then 'set-off amount' (i.e., the loss) can be set off against the relevant IP profits of other continuing trades of the company for that period, and where there is any remaining it is added to any relevant IP loss of the trades of other group members (who are within the regime).

Where a company transfers its IP trade to another group member, which carries on that trade, then the set-off amount is transferred to the new owner and is added to, or becomes, the set-off amount of the transferee.

Any payment between group members in respect of the set-off amount is not taken into account for corporation tax purposes, so far as the payment does not exceed the reduction in the relevant IP profits of the group company(ies).

[*CTA 2010, ss 357E–357EF*].

Anti-avoidance

[57.12] The rules include three anti-avoidance provisions, which are briefly outlined below.

The first counters the conferment of irrelevant exclusivity under an agreement. It is not intended to apply if there is a commercially reasonable choice about exclusivity, and the two parties agree to opt for one because the licensee recognises that it will qualify for the patent box.

The second counters qualifying items being incorporated into a product with the main intent of generating relevant IP income. Again it is intended to apply where a choice is made for tax purposes when there is no, or insignificant, commercial rationale. It is not intended to affect any reasonable commercial transactions.

The third and main rule applies where a main purpose of a scheme is to secure a relevant tax advantage from the patent box. A relevant tax advantage arises where relevant IP profits are increased as a result of the scheme and the increase would arise from:

(a) schemes designed to avoid the application of any provision in the patent box rules themselves;
(b) not fully recognising as revenue for the accounting period any amount brought into account as a credit in calculating those profits;
(c) a mismatch between relevant IP income and expenditure; or
(d) for accounting periods beginning on or after 1 July 2016 (treating, for this purpose, accounting periods straddling that date as two separate accounting periods, the second of which begins on that date) an R&D fraction being greater than it would otherwise be.

[*CTA 2010, ss 357F–357FB*].

Key points on patent income

[57.13] Points to consider are as follows.

- The patent box regime allows, in effect, a 10% CT rate on certain IP profits.
- Any UK company holding interest in qualifying patents (or certain other rights) may elect into the regime.
- Qualifying profits are calculated by reference to qualifying product sales and (actual or deemed) licence fee income. *Finance Act 2016* dramatically altered the rules for calculating qualifying profits to bring the regime into line with the outcome of the OECD Base Erosion and Profit Shifting project. The changes have been phased in between 2016 and 2021.
- Relevant IP losses can be set off against relevant IP profits in other trades of the company, or against relevant IP profits of other group members that have elected into the regime.

58

Payment of Tax

Cross-references. See 29 DISTRIBUTIONS for shadow advance corporation tax; 41 INCOME TAX IN RELATION TO A COMPANY; 43 INTEREST ON OVERDUE TAX; 64.6 RESIDENCE.

Introduction to payment of tax

[58.1] The dates for payment of tax differ for small and large companies within the UK tax regime. In addition there are provisions which allow for special arrangements to be entered into by groups of companies, and which also allow for tax to be recovered from other parties, in lieu of the company taxpayer. Certain 'exit charges' and tax in respect of transactions by companies with group members in EEA states may be paid by instalments where the company enters into a payment plan.

This chapter considers these and other matters concerned with the payment of tax by a company, including enforcement procedures.

Due dates for payment

[58.2] The general rules is that corporation tax is due and payable on the day following the expiry of nine months from the end of the accounting period, on the basis of the amount computed in the company tax return for the period (see 65.7 RETURNS). This is subject to the provisions described at 58.3 below which require large companies to pay corporation tax by instalments.

Any excess over the tax payable of 'relevant amounts' stated in the company tax return is repaid.

'*Relevant amounts*' are corporation tax paid and not repaid, corporation tax refunds surrendered to the company intra-group (see **58.21** GROUP RELIEF), certain income tax suffered and CONSTRUCTION INDUSTRY SCHEME (20) deductions.

[*TMA 1970, s 59D*].

A company may claim repayment of corporation tax paid for an accounting period where the company's circumstances change so that it has grounds for believing that the amount paid exceeds its probable (although not yet finally established) liability. No claim may be made before the 'material date' in relation to the tax being the later of: the date the tax was paid or the date it became due and payable (see further **44.2** INTEREST ON OVERPAID TAX).

If the tax is the subject of an outstanding appeal, the company may apply to the Tribunal for a determination of the amount to be repaid (and the application may be combined with a postponement application under *TMA 1970, s 55*, see 58.13 below). If the company tax return (see **65.4** RETURNS) has not been made, CONSTRUCTION INDUSTRY SCHEME (20) deductions are ignored for these purposes.

[*TMA 1970, s 59DA*].

'Large' companies to which instalment payments apply are precluded from making a claim under *section 59DA* where a claim for repayment of instalment payments is made (see 58.3 below).

[*SI 1998 No 3175, Reg 6(8)*].

Restitution interest

Special rules apply to companies awarded restitution interest as a result of a mistake in law or following unlawful collection of tax by HMRC, as a result of a judgment or an agreement which became final on or after 21 October 2015. Such interest is chargeable to corporation tax at a special rate of 45%, generally deducted at source by HMRC. Where restitution interest is chargeable to tax under these rules and an assessment is raised by HMRC (with the amount of tax withheld credited against the liability), the company must pay the amount assessed within 30 days of the date of the assessment. See further **1.7** INTRODUCTION: CHARGE TO TAX, RATES AND PROFIT COMPUTATIONS.

Instalment payments

[58.3] A system of quarterly accounting for corporation tax applies for 'large companies'. For accounting periods beginning on or after 1 April 2019, the timing of instalment payments depends on whether or not the company is a 'very large' company.

Corporation tax for this purpose includes any liability under *CTA 2010, s 455 or 464A* (loans to participators, and arrangements conferring benefit on participator, see **16.12** CLOSE COMPANIES) any sum chargeable under *CTA 2010, s 269DA* (bank surcharge — see **7.3** BANKS) and any sum charged under the CFC rules (see **21.5** CONTROLLED FOREIGN COMPANIES). [*TMA 1970, s 59E; SI 1998 No 3175*]. However, corporation tax on restitution interest payments is disregarded for the purposes of the instalment payments regime (*CTA 2010, s 357YT*, see further **1.7** INTRODUCTION: CHARGE TO TAX, RATES AND PROFIT COMPUTATIONS).

The self-assessment company tax return (see **65.4** RETURNS) requires the company to state whether it is liable to make instalment payments on account of its corporation tax liabilities. Although HMRC will at some stage check the position, initial payment applications, interest calculations, etc. will be based on the company's statement of its position. (HMRC Company Taxation Manual CTM92690). For entries required on form CT600, see Revenue Tax Bulletin April 2001 pp 831–833.

Large and very large companies

'Large' companies are those with profits (including UK dividend income, other than intra-group dividends, plus tax credits) exceeding £1.5 million in an accounting period, divided by one plus the number of 'related 51% group companies' (see below) if any. For accounting periods beginning on or after 1 April 2023, the adjustment is made by reference to associated companies (defined as at **1.3** INTRODUCTION: CHARGE TO TAX, RATES AND PROFIT COMPUTATIONS) rather than related 51% group companies. In many cases, this change will be no more than a change in terminology, but there are differences in the meaning of the two expressions. (References below to associated companies apply for accounting periods on or after 1 April 2023.)

'Very large' companies are those with profits (as above) exceeding £20,000,000 in an accounting period, divided by one plus the number of related 51% group companies (or associated companies).

In each instance the thresholds are proportionately reduced for periods of less than 12 months.

The number of related 51% group companies (or associated companies) is determined by reference to the number of such companies existing at the end of the immediately preceding accounting period, or at the commencement of the accounting period concerned if there was no immediately preceding accounting period or there was a gap between the two accounting periods.

A company is neither large nor very large as respects an accounting period for which:

(a) its total corporation tax liability, reduced by any deductions under the CONSTRUCTION INDUSTRY SCHEME (20) from payments in the period, does not exceed £10,000, proportionately reduced for accounting periods of less than twelve months; or

(b) its profits do not exceed £10 million provided that it was not a large or very large company (disregarding the £10 million exclusion) in the 12 months preceding the period.

As regards (b) above, the £10 million limit is reduced proportionately for short accounting periods or where there are related 51% group companies (or associated companies). For this purpose, the number of related 51% group companies (or associated companies) required to be taken into account is determined as at the end of the immediately preceding accounting period, or at the commencement of the accounting period concerned if there was no immediately preceding accounting period or there was a gap between the two accounting periods.

In addition, as regards (b) above, a company is treated as not having been large in the 12 months preceding the period in question where either:

(i) during any part of the 12 months it did not exist or did not have an accounting period; or

(ii) an accounting period during which it was not a large company (other than by virtue of (b) above) either falls within or ends in the 12 months.

'*Profits*' of an accounting period for these purposes are 'augmented profits' being the assessable profits on which corporation tax finally falls to be charged for the period plus 'exempt ABGH distributions' of the period other than any such distributions received from fellow group members (and distributions are treated as coming from within the group as within the meaning of *CTA 2010, s 279G*. For accounting periods beginning on or after 1 April 2023, the definition of 'augmented profits' at **1.3** INTRODUCTION: CHARGE TO TAX, RATES AND PROFIT COMPUTATIONS) is used instead.

A company ('B') is a '*related 51% group company*' of another company ('A') in an accounting period if for any part of that period A is a '51% subsidiary' of B or vice versa, or both A and B are 51% subsidiaries of the same company. This rule applies even if the two companies are related 51% group companies for different parts of the period. However, a company which has not carried on any trade or business at any time in that accounting period (or the part when it was a related 51% group company) is disregarded. A '*51% subsidiary*' is a body corporate more than 50% of the ordinary share capital of which is beneficially owned directly or indirectly by another.

For this purpose, a non-trading 'passive company' which has one or more 51% subsidiaries and which carries on a business of making investments is treated as not carrying on a business (and so is disregarded as above).

A company is a '*passive company*' if it has no assets other than shares in 51% subsidiaries; has no income other than dividends which are exempt ABGH distributions; has no chargeable gains; incurs no management expenses and makes no qualifying charitable donations (see **14.11** CHARITIES). If the company receives dividends in an accounting period it must itself pay dividends in that period of an amount at least equal to the dividends received.

'*Exempt ABGH distributions*' are distributions within **29.2**(a), (b), (f) or (g) DISTRIBUTIONS which are exempt from corporation tax.

[*CTA 2010, s 279F; FA 2021, Sch 1 paras 11, 13, 33; SI 1998 No 3175, Regs 1(2), 2(2)(2A)(3), 3; SI 2017 No 1072*].

Instalments

For accounting periods beginning on or after 1 April 2019, where the company is very large, the first instalment is due two months and 13 days after the first day of the accounting period. The second, third and final instalments are then due at three-monthly intervals. If the accounting period is less than 12 months, the final instalment is generally due 14 days after the date falling one month before the end of the period. Earlier instalments are required only if they fall due before the final instalment date. If the accounting period does not end on the last day of the month and there is no day in the previous month with the same date, the final instalment is due 14 days after the last day of the previous month.

In all other cases, the amounts in respect of a large company's total corporation tax liability for an accounting period (as reduced by any deductions under the CONSTRUCTION INDUSTRY SCHEME (**20**) from payments in the period) become due and payable in up to four instalments as follows.

(1) The first instalment is due six months and thirteen days from the start of the accounting period, and the last instalment is due three months and fourteen days from the end of the accounting period, except that if the latter date precedes the former (i.e. where the accounting period is less than three months), a single instalment equal to the total corporation tax liability is due and payable on the latter date.

(2) Where there is a gap of more than three months between the two dates referred to in (1) above (i.e. where the accounting period is longer than six months), a second instalment is due and payable three months after the first, and if the gap exceeds six months, a third instalment is due and payable three months after the second. Thus for the year ending 31 December 2019, instalments will be due on 14 July 2019, 14 October 2019, 14 January 2020 and 14 April 2020. The four instalments are each of one-quarter of the final corporation tax liability. For an accounting period of eight months ending 31 August 2020, instalments are due on 14 July 2020, 14 October 2020 and 14 December 2020, the first two being of three-eighths of the total corporation tax liability and the final one of the balance of one-quarter.

Where the company's estimate of the amount of its total corporation tax liability for the period is revised, subsequent instalment payments are recalculated accordingly, and top-up payments may be made at any time. The due and payable amount of each instalment for the purposes of interest on over- or under-payments (see below) is that based on the total corporation tax liability as returned by the company (or as determined by the inspector where the normal due date has passed).

[*SI 1998 No 3175, Regs 5, 5AZA; SI 2017 No 1072, Regs 1, 5*].

Although HMRC will send a reminder to those companies which it appears likely will be required to make instalment payments, or to the nominated company within a group payment arrangement (see below), it is in any event the company's responsibility to make such payments if they are due.

A *repayment* may be claimed where the company has grounds for believing that changed circumstances since an instalment or instalments were paid has rendered its earlier calculation of its total corporation tax liability excessive, so that the aggregate amount of the instalments paid exceeds what would have been payable by the date of the claim based on the new figure for that liability. Repayment of that excess may be claimed, and the claim must state the amount to be repaid and the grounds for the company's belief that its earlier calculation was excessive. HMRC will accept claims for repayment that are dependent on events in subsequent accounting periods only in exceptional circumstances; for example, where the losses in the subsequent accounting period are so large they will comfortably exceed the profits in the previous accounting period. Full supporting evidence will be required from the company to confirm the exceptional circumstances. (HMRC Company Taxation Manual CTM92650).

If an appeal against an assessment, or an amendment of a self-assessment, in respect of the total liability for the accounting period concerned is outstanding, the company may apply to the Tribunal for a determination of the amount to be repaid pending determination of the appeal. Such claims and applications are treated in the same way as appeals, and an application for determination of a repayment may be combined with an application for postponement of payment of tax under *TMA 1970, s 55* (see **58.13** below).

Alternatively, the provisions of *CTA 2010, s 963* (surrender of tax refund within group, see **58.21** GROUP RELIEF) are applied to allow the surrender of excess instalment payments intra-group.

[*SI 1998 No 3175, Regs 6, 9, 14; SI 2017 No 1072, Regs 8, 11*].

Companies chargeable to corporation tax only because of chargeable gains

If a company is chargeable to corporation tax for an accounting period beginning on or after 11 March 2020 only because of a chargeable gain and would otherwise be very large for that period, it is instead treated as only large.

Such companies are likely to have short accounting periods, in some cases, of only one day. For a one-day accounting period, this rule may apply to relatively small gains, owing to the requirement to reduce the relevant thresholds on a time basis. The effect for such a period is that the tax is due three months and 14 days after the one-day accounting period instead of on the day itself. This rule affects, in particular, non-resident companies which dispose of direct or indirect interests in UK land. It replaces a previous HMRC concessionary treatment for one-day accounting periods with the same effect which has applied since April 2019. See www.gov.uk/guidance/register-a-non-resident-company-for-corporation-tax.

[*SI 1998 No 3175, Reg 3(11); FA 2020, s 26*].

Interest on unpaid instalments

Unpaid instalment payments (tax which is overdue) carry interest at a special rate from the instalment due date to the date of payment during the period until nine months after the end of the accounting period concerned (whereafter the normal interest rate provisions apply). See **43.2** INTEREST ON OVERDUE TAX for the rates.

Interest on overpaid instalments

Similarly, excess payments in respect of instalments carry interest at a special rate (which also applies to early payments by companies not liable to pay by instalments) from the date the excess arises (but not earlier than the due date of the first instalment) until it is extinguished (but not later than nine months after the end of the accounting period concerned, from when the normal interest rate provisions apply). See **44.2** INTEREST ON OVERPAID TAX for the rates.

Information etc. powers

HMRC have powers to require the production of a wide range of information and records relating to instalment payments once the filing date for the return for the accounting period (normally twelve months after the end of the period, see **65.8** RETURNS) has passed. [*SI 1998 No 3175, Regs 10–12; SI 2017 No 1072, Regs 12–14*].

HMRC have issued guidance (in their enquiry manual) that they will seek to make use of these powers only where a penalty may be imposed (see below). Thus only where there are indications that a company may have deliberately or recklessly failed to comply with its instalment payment obligations, or fraudulently or negligently made a repayment claim (see HMRC Company Taxation Manual, CTM92770 and HMRC Enquiry Manual, EM8320).

There are additional information powers with regard to instalment payments that include the bank levy. The company making the instalments (or the responsible member, within a group payment arrangement) must issue a 'quantification notice' to HMRC which identifies the amount of the instalment which is in respect of the bank levy. [*SI 1998 No 3175, Reg 10A; SI 2017 No 1072, Reg 13*].

Penalties

Where interest is charged on unpaid instalments as above, and the company, or a person acting on its behalf, either:

(I) deliberately or recklessly failed to make an instalment payment; or
(II) fraudulently or negligently made a claim for repayment of an excess amount of instalment payments,

the company is liable to a penalty of up to twice the amount of the interest. [*TMA 1970, s 59E; SI 1998 No 3175, Reg 13*]. HMRC will seek a penalty under these provisions only in the most serious cases involving flagrant abuse of the regulations (see HMRC Enquiry Manual EM8330, Revenue Tax Bulletin August 1999 pp 683, 684, and further guidance published on HMRC's website (at www.hmrc.gov.uk/ctsa/penpowers.htm).

Generally, penalties under *TMA 1970, s 98* apply for any failure to provide information, produce documents, etc. as required under these provisions.

Group payment arrangements

Any group of companies with instalment payment liabilities which wishes to do so may make arrangements with HMRC to account for corporation tax on a group basis rather than company by company. This will enable profit forecasts to be made at group level and mitigate the interest differential on over- and under-paid tax.

[*TMA 1970, s 59F*].

Groups wishing to take part in such arrangements should contact the Group Payment Team at the Cumbernauld Corporation Tax Unit (Tel. 03000 583947, Fax. 03000 583902). (HMRC Company Taxation Manual, CTM97410.)

Broadly, a nominated company may contract with HMRC to make instalment payments on behalf of group companies covered by the arrangements ('participating companies') on the due dates on the basis of the most recent forecast of group profits. Once all the participating companies have either filed their returns or had their corporation tax liabilities determined by HMRC (the 'closing date', which cannot be earlier than the normal due date nine months after the end of the accounting period), the nominated company will be issued with a notice showing what it has paid and the liability at the closing date. It will then be invited to make good any shortfall, or allocate it to any company whose liability it has reason to believe will decrease after the closing date, and to apportion payments to the participating companies. It may allocate any surplus to participating companies or require its repayment.

The arrangements need not apply to all group members, and separate arrangements may be entered into for different sub-sets within a group. Not all companies covered by the arrangements need be UK resident, although the nominated company must be. All companies must have filed returns and paid the due tax in respect of their last but one accounting period. They must have a common accounting period (subject to special arrangements for companies joining the group and aligning their accounting date). There is provision for either the nominated company or HMRC to remove a company from the arrangements in specified circumstances where the rules regarding eligibility to enter the arrangements would no longer be met.

Any group wishing to take part in the arrangements must normally deliver its signed contract to the appropriate Accounts Office (as above) at least two months prior to the first instalment payment due date. All payments must be made by electronic funds transfer.

For detailed requirements, see HMRC Company Taxation Manual, CTM97400 *et seq* which also includes the group payment arrangement contract and the administrative and guidance notes. Guidance is also provided in Revenue Tax Bulletins April 1999 pp 647–650 and April 2001 pp 831–836. These include the entries required on return form CT600, the effect of arrangements on tax repayments and group surrenders thereof, the allocation of payments under an arrangement, the departure from a group of a participating company and the treatment of long periods of account.

HMRC guidance

See generally HMRC Company Taxation Manual, CTM92500 *et seq*. See also Revenue Tax Bulletins April 1999 pp 645–650, February 2000 pp 723–726 and April 2001 pp 831–836.

Simon's Taxes. See **D1.1320–D1.1328**.

Payment

Electronic payment

[58.4] All payments of corporation tax must be made electronically. [*SI 2003 No 282, Reg 3*]. HMRC are not obliged to accept other payment. For payment methods see **43.7** INTEREST ON OVERDUE TAX.

Charges

[58.5] HMRC charge a fee for payment of tax by certain payment methods.

With effect from 1 November 2020, where a payment is made using a business credit card or business debit card, the fee is the sum of the merchant acquirer fee (i.e the fee for processing the payment charged to the payee by the merchant acquirer), the interchange fee (i.e. the fee charged to the merchant acquirer by the issuer of the card and recharged to the payee) and the scheme fee (i.e. the fee charged to the merchant acquirer by the person responsible for the card scheme applying to the card and recharged to the payee) for the payment. Previously, where a payment was made using a credit card, the fee was the percentage of the payment given by the following table. There was no fee in respect of payments by debit card. Tax cannot be paid by personal credit card after 12 January 2018.

	Rate %	
	13.1.18–31.10.20	1.4.16–12.1.18
Personal credit cards		
Visa Personal	n/a	0.415
Mastercard Personal	n/a	0.386
Mastercard World Premium	n/a	0.374
Mastercard Signia Premium	n/a	0.606
Mastercard Elite Premium	n/a	0.606
Corporate credit cards		
Visa Business	1.70	1.508
Visa Commerce	2.80	n/a
Visa Corporate	1.94	1.744
Visa Purchasing	1.92	1.755
Visa Commercial	1.94	n/a
Mastercard Business	1.80	1.973
Mastercard Corporate	1.98	2.248
Mastercard Purchasing	2.20	2.406
Mastercard Fleet	1.97	2.134

Mastercard Commercial	1.98	n/a

[*FA 2008, s 136; SI 2016 No 333; SI 2017 No 1262; SI 2020 No 657*].

Set-off

[58.6] Except in an insolvency (see below), where a company owes money to HMRC but is also due a repayment, the credit may be set off against the debit, subject to any right of HMRC to set the credit against any other sum. Any transfer of the right to the tax repayment due to the company is disregarded. Where there is such a transfer of a right to a repayment to another person, HMRC must use the power of set-off notwithstanding the transfer if they are obliged to do so under legislation in respect of the original creditor and may do so if they had the power of set-off had the creditor retained the right to the repayment.

HMRC have the right of set-off whether the tax in question became due before or after the transfer, but not if repayment has already been made. These provisions take priority where the transferee wishes to set off the repayment against tax due by him — i.e. the set-off against the original creditor's tax debt is effected first. Where the repayment is contingent on the original creditor making a claim, these set-off provisions apply only if a claim is made. References to sums payable to and by a person are to a sum to be paid, repaid or credited to that person. In determining the repayment to be set off, HMRC may make any deduction they could have made if the original creditor had retained the right to the repayment, including a deduction arising from any defence to a claim for the sum.

Following set-off, both HMRC and the original creditor are treated as having discharged their obligations up to the amount of the tax covered by the repayment. These set-off provisions take priority over those in any other legislation.

Where a company is insolvent, but a post-insolvency credit arises (i.e. after the insolvency procedure has commenced) the power of set-off may not be used by HMRC against pre-insolvency debits in relation to the person.

[*FA 2008, ss 130, 131, 133*].

Enforcement

[58.7] The procedure in *TCEA 2007, Sch 12* (taking control of goods) is used by HMRC in England and Wales to recover unpaid sums. In Scotland, HMRC can apply to the sheriff for a summary warrant authorising the recovery of unpaid sums. In Northern Ireland, HMRC may distrain. [*TMA 1970, s 61; FA 2008, ss 127–129*]. See also *Herbert Berry Associates Ltd v CIR* HL 1977, 52 TC 113.

Where an amount of corporation tax due is less than £2,000, HMRC may, within one year after the due date, take summary magistrates' court proceedings. HMRC may also recover tax by proceedings in the county court. [*TMA*

1970, ss 65, 66; CRCA 2005, s 25(1A)(6)]. But for limitations in Scotland and NI see *TMA 1970, ss 65(4), 66(3)(4), 67*, and see *Mann v Cleaver* KB 1930, 15 TC 367.

Unpaid tax (and arrears) may also be recovered (with full costs) as a Crown debt in the High Court. [*TMA 1970, s 68*].

The amount of an assessment which has become final cannot be re-opened in proceedings to collect the tax (*CIR v Pearlberg* CA 1953, 34 TC 57; *CIR v Soul* CA 1976, 51 TC 86), and it is not open to the taxpayer to raise the defence that the Revenue acted *ultra vires* in raising the assessment (*CIR v Aken* CA 1990, 63 TC 395).

For whether unpaid tax is a business liability for commercial etc. purposes, see *Conway v Wingate* CA, [1952] 1 All ER 782; *Stevens v Britten* CA, [1954] 3 All ER 385; *R v Vaccari* CA, [1958] 1 All ER 468; *In re Hollebone's Agreement* CA, [1959] 2 All ER 152.

HMRC can apply to the High Court for a freezing order where there is a risk of the dissipation of assets to avoid compliance with an assessment in the period before the tax is due and payable: *HMRC v Ali* Ch D 2011, [2012] STC 42.

Security for payments of corporation tax and construction industry scheme deductions

[58.8] With effect from 6 April 2019, where an HMRC officer considers it necessary for the protection of the revenue, he may require certain persons to give security for the payment of corporation tax or of amounts payable to HMRC under the CONSTRUCTION INDUSTRY SCHEME (**20**) which it is or may become liable to pay. In the case of corporation tax the persons are the company or its officers. For this purpose, company officers are directors, company secretary, any similar officer or any person purporting to act in such a capacity. In the case of the construction industry scheme, the persons are the contractor and, if the contractor is a company, its officers, If the contractor is a partnership, the persons also include the partners. The persons also include any scheme representative, a personal representative of the contractor or any person purporting to act in such a capacity. Security of a specified value may be required from one or more person and each is jointly and severally liable to give the security.

HMRC must give a notice to each person from whom security is required specifying the value of, the manner in which and the date on which, security is to be given and the period of time for which it is required. The date specified must not be earlier than the thirtieth day after the date the notice is given. Where, in a construction industry scheme case, the contractor makes a request for the suspension of a late payment penalty during the currency of an agreement for deferred payment (see **59.7** PENALTIES) before the date on which security would otherwise be required to be given, the requirement to give security on or before that date does not apply. If HMRC do not agree to the contractor's request, security must be given by the thirtieth day after the day on which HMRC notifies the contractor of their decision.

A person who has given security can apply to HMRC to reduce the value of security held by HMRC (i.e. to seek a repayment) if either his circumstances have changed because of hardship or having ceased to be a person who can be required to give security or there has been a significant change in the company or contractor's circumstances so that either security is no longer needed to protect the revenue or a smaller value is so needed. A person who is jointly and severally liable for the security but has not made a payment cannot make such an application. If an application is made by a person who is jointly and severally liable on the grounds of a change in his circumstances, HMRC may notify the company, contractor or any other person to provide security in substitution for the original security.

A person given a notice requiring security can appeal against it or against any requirement in it. A person who has made an application to reduce the value of security given may appeal against HMRC's decision not to reduce the value or to make a smaller reduction than the application requested. A contractor who has made a request for suspension of a late payment penalty may appeal against HMRC's decision to reject it. Notice of appeal must be given within 30 days of the day on which the notice was given or HMRC notifies their decision and must state the grounds of appeal. On appeal against a notice requiring security, the Tribunal may confirm or vary the requirement or set aside the notice. On appeal against an HMRC decision on an application to reduce security, the Tribunal may confirm or vary the decision. On the final determination of an appeal, any security to be given is due by the thirtieth day after the determination.

Failure to comply with a requirement to give security by the due date is an offence punishable, on summary conviction, to a fine.

[*FA 1998, Sch 18 para 88A; FA 2004, s 70A; FA 2019, s 82(2); SI 2005 No 2045, Regs 17A–17K; SI 2019 No 384*].

Security may in particular be required where a company has a poor compliance record or in cases of phoenixism (i.e. where a company accrues a tax debt, goes into liquidation or administration and the person responsible for running the business sets up again). See Treasury Explanatory Notes to the Finance (No 3) Bill 2018.

Enforcement by deduction from accounts

[58.9] HMRC have the power in England, Wales and Northern Ireland to enforce certain debts by direct recovery from the bank etc. account of the debtor. HMRC may issue a hold notice (see **58.11** below) to 'deposit-takers' effectively freezing the funds needed to pay the debt and giving the taxpayer company and certain other interested parties an opportunity to object to HMRC against the issuing of the notice. If HMRC dismiss any objections there is a right of appeal to the county court. If there is no objection or appeal or if they are unsuccessful HMRC may issue a deduction notice (see **58.12** below) requiring the deposit-taker to deduct specified amounts from the taxpayer's accounts and pay them over to HMRC. Before issuing a hold notice HMRC may, but are not required to, issue an information notice (see **58.10** below) to ascertain which accounts are held by the taxpayer with a particular deposit-taker. All notices must be given in writing.

The power can be used to collect sums which are due and payable by a person to HMRC under or by virtue of an enactment or under a contract settlement where the following conditions are met:

(1) the sum is at least £1,000;
(2) the sum is an 'established debt' or is due under (or is the disputed tax specified in) an accelerated payment notice or partner payment notice (see **4.33** ANTI-AVOIDANCE onwards); and
(3) HMRC are satisfied that the taxpayer is aware that the sum is due and payable to them.

A sum is an '*established debt*' if there is no possibility that it, or any part of it, will cease to be due and payable to HMRC. This will be the case where there is no right of appeal, where the period for making an appeal has expired without an appeal having been made or where an appeal has been finally determined or withdrawn. Powers to grant permission to make a late appeal are disregarded for this purpose.

Before issuing an information notice or hold notice HMRC must consider whether, to the best of their knowledge, there are any matters as a result of which the taxpayer is, or may be, at a particular disadvantage in dealing with HMRC in relation to the unpaid sum. Any such matters must be taken into account in deciding whether or not to issue a notice. HMRC have published guidance on the factors which they consider to be relevant to deciding whether a person is at a particular disadvantage. The guidance sets out four indicators which HMRC will consider: a disability or long-term health condition; a temporary illness, physical or mental health condition; personal issues (such as redundancy, bereavement or trauma) and lower levels of literacy, numeracy and/or education. See www.gov.uk/government/publications/direct-recovery-of-debts-and-vulnerable-customers/direct-recovery-of-debts-vulnerable-customers.

A '*deposit-taker*' is, broadly, a person who may lawfully accept deposits in the UK in the course of a business. A deposit-taker is not liable for damages for anything done in good faith to comply with these provisions.

A deposit-taker may, in certain specified circumstances, charge an administration fee to an account holder for costs incurred in complying with its obligations under the direct recovery provisions. A fee may be charged only where it has agreed with the account holder (or account holders) that a fee can be charged, the direct recovery of debts process has concluded, and the deposit-taker has not previously imposed a fee in respect of those costs. The fee is limited to the lower of the costs reasonably incurred by the deposit-taker and £55, and applies per account holder, not per account (thus where a taxpayer has multiple accounts with the same deposit-taker the fee cap allows only one £55 fee to be charged).

Joint accounts

References below to an account held by a person include a joint account held by that person and one or more others.

[*F(No 2)A 2015, s 51, Sch 8 paras 2, 5, 18, 22–24; SI 2016 No 44*].

Tax charged in a determination

Where HMRC are taking action under these provisions in respect of tax charged by a determination within **65.18 RETURNS** and the determination is superseded by a self-assessment, the action may be continued as if it were an action to recover so much of the tax charged by the self-assessment as is due and payable, has not been paid and does not exceed the amount charged in the determination. [*FA 1998, Sch 18 para 40(5)*].

Regulations

The Treasury has wide powers to make regulations for supplementary provisions and to amend, revoke or repeal enactments in connection with these provisions. HMRC may make regulations to alter various amounts, thresholds and time limits, to exclude certain types of account or amount from the provisions and to prescribe the information which can be required by notices. [*F(No 2)A 2015, s 51, Sch 8 paras 19–21*].

Penalties

Penalties apply to deposit-takers for various failures to comply with the provisions and for disclosures likely to prejudice HMRC's ability to recover an unpaid sum using the provisions. See **59.16 PENALTIES**.

Information notice

[58.10] If it appears to HMRC that a person has failed to pay a sum meeting the above conditions and that the person holds one or more accounts with a deposit-taker, they may give the deposit-taker an information notice. Such a notice requires the deposit-taker to provide HMRC with the following information:

(1) the taxpayer's name and address, national insurance number, email addresses and phone numbers and, in respect of any joint accounts, the proportion of the balance to which the taxpayer is entitled; and
(2) for each account held by the taxpayer, any account number, roll number and sort code, the type of account (including whether it is a joint account), the account balance (in the currency in which it is held), whether, and what rate of, interest is payable, any minimum balance required to keep the account open, any contractual terms under which the taxpayer or any '*interested third parties*' (i.e. persons with a beneficial interest in an amount in the account) may suffer economic loss as a result of a hold notice or deduction notice, and, for each joint account holder, interested third party or person with power of attorney in respect of the account, the information specified in (1) above.

Information must be provided only if it is in the possession of, or immediately available to, the deposit-taker at the time the notice is given.

A notice must explain the time limit for complying with it and the penalties for non-compliance (see **59.16 PENALTIES**). HMRC may issue a notice only for the purpose of determining whether to give the deposit-taker a hold notice (see below) in respect of the taxpayer concerned. The recipient of a notice must comply with it as soon as reasonably practicable and, in any event, within ten working days beginning with the day on which the notice was given.

[*F(No 2)A 2015, Sch 8 paras 3, 8(11); SI 2015 No 1986, Regs 2–4*].

Hold notice

[58.11] If it appears to HMRC that a person has failed to pay a sum meeting the conditions at 58.9 above and that the person holds one or more accounts with a deposit-taker, they may give the deposit-taker a hold notice. The notice must:

(a) specify the taxpayer's name and last known address;
(b) specify a 'specified amount';
(c) specify a 'safeguarded amount';
(d) set out any rules which are to decide the priority order to be used to determine the held amount for each account (see Step 3 below);
(e) explain the effects of the notice, the penalties for non-compliance and any provisions made by regulation excluding certain types of account and amounts from inclusion in a hold notice; and
(f) contain a statement about HMRC's compliance with the requirement to consider whether a taxpayer is at a particular disadvantage in dealing with HMRC (see above).

The notice may also specify any additional information which HMRC considers might assist the deposit-taker in identifying accounts. It may also exclude an account, type of account or specified amount from the notice.

In (b) above, the '*specified amount*' must not exceed what is left of the 'notified sum' after deducting the specified amounts in any other hold notices which relate to the same debts and which were either given on the same day to other deposit-takers or given on an earlier day to either the same or another deposit-taker. The specified amount of an earlier hold notice is not deducted if HMRC has received a notification from the deposit-taker that there are no affected accounts as a result of that notice (see further below). For this purpose, two hold notices relate to the same debts if at least one of the unpaid sums in respect of which they are issued is the same.

The '*safeguarded amount*' must, in general, be at least £5,000 but HMRC may specify a smaller amount (including nil) if they consider it appropriate to do so having regard to the value in sterling (determined in a manner prescribed by regulations) of any amounts in a non-sterling account which would be a 'relevant account' (see below) in relation to the notice if it were denominated in sterling. The safeguarded amount must be nil if HMRC have previously given a hold notice relating to the same debts and, within the 30 days ending with the date the current hold notice is given, HMRC have been notified that there is a held amount as a result of the earlier notice.

HMRC may not give more than one hold notice relating to the same debts to a single deposit-taker on the same day.

Effect of notice

A deposit-taker to whom a hold notice is given must, for each 'relevant account' determine whether or not there is a 'held amount' (greater than nil) for that account and if so must either:

(1) put in place arrangements to ensure that it does not do anything, or permit anything to be done, which would reduce the amount in the account below the held amount; or
(2) transfer an amount equal to the held amount into a specially-created 'suspense account' and put in place arrangements to ensure that it does not do anything, or permit anything to be done, which would reduce the amount in the suspense account below the held amount.

The deposit-taker must comply with these requirements as soon as reasonably practicable and, in any event, within five working days beginning with the day on which the notice is given and must maintain any arrangements made under (1) or (2) above until the notice ceases to be in force.

All accounts held by the taxpayer with the deposit-taker are '*relevant accounts*' unless they are not denominated in sterling or are suspense accounts or they have been excluded from the hold notice by HMRC or excluded from such notices generally by regulations. A relevant account is an '*affected account*' if as a result of the notice there is a held amount in relation to it.

A hold notice ceases to be in force when either HMRC cancel it or a deduction notice is given.

If the deposit-taker determines that there are one or more affected accounts it must give HMRC a notice setting out prescribed information about each account (and in the case of a joint account, about the other account holders) and the held amount for each account. The prescribed information is:

- the information within **58.10**(1) and (2) above;
- confirmation of which accounts are affected accounts;
- the date on which the deposit-taker complied with the requirements above;
- confirmation that the deposit-taker understands the penalties for making a disclosure likely to prejudice HMRC's ability to use these provisions to recover the unpaid tax (see **59.16** PENALTIES);
- the total of all held amounts;
- for each account, the amount not subject to action within (1) or (2) above; and
- a description of any economic loss suffered by an account holder or interested third party under any contractual term as a result of the hold notice.

Information must be provided only if it is the possession of, or immediately available to, the deposit-taker at the time the hold notice is given.

The notice must be given within five working days beginning with the day on which the deposit-taker complies with the hold notice. HMRC must then, as soon as reasonably practicable, give a copy of the hold notice to the taxpayer together with a notice which:

(A) specifies and states the amounts of the unpaid sums to which the hold notice relates;
(B) states the total of the unpaid amounts to which the notice relates; and
(C) states the 'notified sum' for the hold notice, i.e. the total in (B) above.

HMRC must also give a notice to any joint account holders other than the taxpayer and to any 'interested third parties' (see **58.10** above) in respect of whom information has been provided in the deposit-taker's notice. The notice must explain that a hold notice has been given in respect of the account concerned and explaining the effects of the notice and the objection and appeal provisions below.

Once it has complied with the hold notice, the deposit-taker may (but is not required to) notify the taxpayer, any joint account holders and any interested third parties stating that a hold notice has been received and the effect of the notice on the account concerned.

If the deposit-taker determines that there are no affected accounts as a result of the hold notice it must notify HMRC accordingly, including in the notice any information which it has taken into account to determine that there are no affected accounts. The notice must be given within five working days beginning with the day on which it makes the determination.

Held amounts

If there is only one relevant account, the '*held amount*' for that account is, if the 'available amount' exceeds the safeguarded amount, the excess up to the specified amount. If the available amount is not more than the safeguarded amount then the held amount is nil. If there is more than one relevant account, the held amount for each such account is found using the following steps.

Step 1. Determine the available amount for each relevant account.

Step 2. Add the available amounts together to determine the total of those amounts for all such accounts. If the total is no more than the safeguarded amount then the held amount for all of the accounts is nil.

Step 3. If the total in Step 2 is more than the safeguarded amount, the safeguarded amount is matched against the available amounts in the relevant accounts, taking the accounts in reverse priority order. The priority order is determined by the deposit-taker, but joint accounts must have a lower priority than other accounts and any rules included in the hold notice (see (d) above) must be followed. Note that it is the reverse of the priority order that is used in this Step.

Step 4. Match the specified amount against what remains of the available amounts by taking each account in priority order. The held amount for each account is then so much of the account balance as is so matched; if no part of an account balance is so matched, the held amount for that account is nil. Balances which are excluded from the effect of the hold notice by regulations are not matched.

The '*available amount*' is the amount standing to the credit of the account at the time the deposit-taker complies with the hold notice. In the case of a joint account, the available amount is restricted to the appropriate fraction of that amount, according to the number of account holders.

Cancellation or variation

HMRC may cancel or vary a hold notice by notifying the deposit-taker. Variation may take the form of cancelling the effect of the notice in relation to one or more accounts or in relation to part of the held amount for an account or accounts. HMRC must give a copy of the notice of cancellation or variation to the taxpayer and any other person HMRC consider is affected by it and who is a joint account holder or an interested third party.

On receipt of a notice the deposit-taker must cancel or adjust the arrangements made to comply with the hold notice as soon as reasonably practicable and, in any event, within five working days beginning with the day the notice of cancellation or variation was given.

Objections and appeals

The taxpayer, an interested third party or a joint account holder may notify HMRC of an objection to a hold notice on the grounds that:

(i) the debts have been wholly or partly paid;
(ii) at the time the hold notice was given there was no unpaid sum or the taxpayer did not hold an account with the deposit-taker;
(iii) the notice is causing or will cause exceptional hardship to the person making the objection or another person; or
(iv) there is an interested third party in relation to one or more of the affected accounts.

The objection notice must state the grounds of objection and must normally be made within 30 days beginning with the day on which a copy of the hold notice was given to the taxpayer. A joint account holder or independent third party who has received a notice from HMRC explaining that a hold notice has been issued may make an objection within 30 days beginning with the day on which that notice was given. HMRC may, however, agree to the making of a late objection and must do so if they are satisfied that there was reasonable excuse for not making the objection in time and that the person making the objection had sent a written request for agreement to the making of a late objection without unreasonable delay after the reasonable excuse ceased.

HMRC must consider any objections within 30 days of being given the objection notice. They must then decide whether to cancel or vary the hold notice (as above) or to dismiss the objection and must notify their decision to the taxpayer, any other person who objected and any other joint account holder or interested third party who HMRC consider to be affected. HMRC must also notify the deposit-taker if it has decided to cancel or vary the hold notice. A copy of HMRC's notice to the deposit-taker must be given to each of the persons to whom HMRC notified their decision.

The taxpayer, any joint account holder or any interested third party may appeal against HMRC's decision, but only on grounds within (i)–(iv) above. The appeal must state the grounds and must normally be made within 30 days beginning with the day on which the appellant was given notice of HMRC's decision. A joint account holder or independent third party who has not received a notice of HMRC's decision may appeal within 30 days beginning with the day on which the taxpayer was given notice of HMRC's decision. The appeal is to the county court which may cancel or vary the notice or dismiss the appeal.

Where an appeal is on the grounds of exceptional hardship (see (iii) above), the appellant may apply to the court to suspend the effect of the hold notice in full or in relation to a particular account or amount while the appeal is pending. Adequate security must be provided.

If the deposit-taker is served with a court order to cancel or vary the hold notice, it must make any necessary resulting arrangements as soon as reasonably practicable and, in any event, within five working days beginning with the day the order was given.

The normal provisions governing APPEALS (5) do not apply to objections or appeals under these provisions.

[*F(No 2)A 2015, Sch 8 paras 4, 6–12; SI 2015 No 1986, Regs 3, 5, 6*].

Deduction notice

[58.12] If it appears to HMRC that a person in respect of whom a hold notice given to a deposit-taker is in force has failed to pay a sum meeting the conditions at **58.9** above and that the person holds one or more accounts with the deposit-taker in respect of which there is a held amount relating to the unpaid sum, they may give the deposit-taker a deduction notice. The notice will specify one or more affected accounts (see **58.11** above) and require the deposit-taker to deduct and pay a 'qualifying amount' from each account to HMRC by the day specified in the notice. If a held amount for a particular account has been transferred to a suspense account (see **58.11** above), the deduction must be made from the suspense account. HMRC may amend or cancel the notice by notifying the deposit-taker.

A '*qualifying amount*' in an affected account is an amount not exceeding the held amount for that account. The total qualifying amounts specified in a deduction notice must not exceed the unpaid sum. The deposit-taker must not, while a deduction notice is in force, do anything or permit anything to be done that would reduce the amount in a specified account (or a suspense account) to fall below the amount required to make the deduction. A deduction notice must explain this provision and the penalties for non-compliance. A deduction notice comes into force when it is given to the deposit-taker and ceases to be in force when the deposit-taker is given a notice cancelling it or when the final required payment is made.

A deduction notice cannot be given in respect of an account unless the period for making an objection has passed and either no objections were made or any objections have been decided or withdrawn and, if objections were made and decided, unless the period for making an appeal has passed and any appeal or further appeal has been finally determined.

HMRC must give a copy of a deduction notice to the taxpayer and, for each account, must give a notice explaining that a notice has been given and its effect to any joint account holders other than the taxpayer and to any interested third parties about whom HMRC have sufficient information to do so. Similar copies and notices must be given where HMRC cancel or amend a deduction notice.

[*F(No 2)A 2015, Sch 8 para 13*].

Payment of tax pending appeal

[58.13] Where there is an appeal against an amendment of a self-assessment, an assessment to corporation tax other than a self-assessment or an assessment to income tax on company payments (but excluding income tax accountable by quarterly etc. returns, see **43.8** INTEREST ON OVERDUE TAX), the full amount charged will be due and payable (as if there had been no appeal) unless the appellant applies for payment of part of the tax assessed to be postponed.

The application must in the first instance be made in writing to HMRC within 30 days after the date of the issue of the notice of assessment, stating the amount of tax believed to be overcharged (and payment of which is to be postponed), and the grounds for that belief.

Application may be made outside the normal 30-day time limit if there is a change in circumstances giving grounds for belief that the appellant is overcharged. In HMRC's view, this condition requires a change in the circumstances in which the original decision not to apply for postponement was made, not just a change of mind, e.g. further accounts work indicating a substantially excessive assessment, or further reliefs becoming due. (Notes of CCAB meeting with Revenue on the 1982 Finance Bill TR 477, 22 June 1982.)

The appellant and an HMRC officer may agree the amount of tax to be postponed and written confirmation of such agreement shall be treated as if the tribunal had determined it. Failing such agreement an appeal can be made to the tribunal (within 30 days of HMRC's decision) to determine the amount, in the same way as an appeal. A decision of the tribunal is final and conclusive; however, in *Dong v National Crime Agency (No 2)* FTT, [2014] UKFTT 369 (TC) the First-tier Tribunal held that this provision was ultra vires and unlawful, and declined to apply it.

Any tax which is the subject of such an application and which is not postponed by agreement or by the tribunal shall be due and payable as if charged by an assessment issued on the date of the tribunal's determination (or of written confirmation of the agreement with HMRC's officer) and against which no appeal is pending. If circumstances change, a further application may be made by either the appellant or HMRC's officer giving notice to the other to vary the amount postponed.

On determination of the appeal, any tax overpaid is repaid and any postponed tax then becoming collectable or not previously charged becomes due and payable as if charged under an assessment issued when the inspector issues to the appellant notice of the total amount payable.

[*TMA 1970, s 55*].

Numerous issues surrounding postponement of tax have been considered by the courts. For example, in the recent case of *Revenue and Customs Commissioners v Rogers* [2009] EWHC 3433 (Ch), [2010] STC 236 the High Court allowed the taxpayer's application for stay of enforcement action. Before the main appeal in this case came before the tribunal, HMRC had applied for enforcement of the debt. The taxpayer sought stay of enforcement action on grounds that there had been a change of circumstances. The High Court allowed the taxpayer's application for stay of action and dismissed HMRC's application for summary judgment. The Court held that summary judgment should only be granted where the taxpayer's main appeal had 'no real prospect of success' and that this was not the case in the current application. Refusal to grant the stay of action would risk greater harm to the taxpayer than granting the stay would have on HMRC. The first tier tribunal allowed an application in *Blunts Farm Estate Ltd v HMRC* (TC00731) [2010] UKFTT 469 (TC), where the appellant company contended that it had received certain payments as an agent of an associated partnership. In *Patel v HMRC* (TC00980) [2011] UKFTT 104 (TC), the Tribunal allowed a postponement application for 1989/90 to 1995/96, but dismissed it for 1996/97 to 2007/08.

See also **65.7** RETURNS.

For discussion of other cases see **Simon's Taxes** at **A4.609**. Also **D1.1345**.

Recovery of tax from third parties

Change in ownership of company — corporation tax

[58.14] Where an HMRC officer considers that:

(a) there has been a change in ownership of a company (see **51.17** LOSSES);
(b) any corporation tax assessed on the company for an accounting period beginning before the date of the change remains unpaid at any time after the '*relevant date*' (i.e. the date six months after the date of the corporation tax assessment); and
(c) any of the three conditions referred to below is fulfilled,

any of the following persons ('linked' to the company per *CTA 2010*) may be assessed and charged in the name of the company to an amount of corporation tax as below:

(i) any person who at any time during the '*relevant period*' (i.e. the period of three years before the change in ownership, but not so as to include any period before a previous change in ownership) had 'control' of the company; and
(ii) any company of which a person within (i) has at any time in the three years before the change in ownership had 'control'.

For this purpose, a person has '*control*' of a company if he exercises, is able to exercise, or is entitled to acquire direct or indirect control over the company's affairs. In particular, he has control if he possesses or is entitled to acquire 50% of the company's share capital, issued share capital or voting power. He also has control if he possesses or is entitled to acquire so much of the issued share capital as would give the right to receive the greater part of the company's income, were all that income distributed, or rights to the greater part of the company's assets in a distribution on a winding-up or in other circumstances. Future rights and rights of nominees are included.

There may be attributed to a person the rights and powers of any associate (see **16.9** CLOSE COMPANIES) or associates of his, or of any company or companies controlled by him (with or without his associates), together with any nominee of such company or associate. However, the rights and powers of associates' associates and of companies controlled only by associates are disregarded. Where two or more persons together satisfy any of the conditions for control, control will only be imputed to each of them where they have acted together to put themselves in a position where they will in fact satisfy the condition in question.

The three alternative conditions referred to at (c) above are as follows.

(A) At any time during the three years before the change in ownership the activities of a trade or business of the company cease or the scale of those activities become small or negligible, and there is no significant revival of those activities before the change occurs.

(B) At any time after the change in ownership, but under arrangements made before that change, the activities of a trade or business of the company cease or the scale of those activities become small or negligible.

(a) At any time during the six years beginning three years before the change in ownership, there is a '*major change in the nature or conduct of a trade or business*' of the company;

(b) assets of the company are transferred (including any disposal, letting or hiring of an asset, and any grant or transfer of any right, interest or licence in or over it, or the giving of any business facilities with respect to it) to a person within (i) above (or to a person connected with such a person within *CTA 2010, ss 1122, 1123*), or under arrangements which enable any of those assets (or assets representing those assets) to be transferred to such a person, during the three years before the change in ownership (or after the change but under arrangements made before the change); and

(c) the major change in the nature or conduct of the trade or business of the company is attributable to the transfer(s) of the company's assets.

For the purposes of (C)(a) above, a '*major change in the nature or conduct of a trade or business*' includes:

- a major change in the type of property dealt in, or services or facilities provided;
- a major change in customers, outlets or markets;
- a change by which the company ceases to be a trading company (i.e. one whose business is wholly or mainly a trade or trades) and becomes an investment company (i.e. one whose business consists wholly or mainly in the making of investments and the principal part of whose income is derived from investments, but excluding a company whose business consists wholly or mainly in holding shares or securities of 90% subsidiaries which are trading companies);
- a change by which the company ceases to be an investment company and becomes a trading company; and
- if the company is an investment company, a major change in the nature of its investments.

A change includes a change achieved gradually through a series of transfers. See further HMRC Statement of Practice 10/91.

The tax charged in an assessment under these provisions must not exceed the amount of the tax which, at the time of the assessment, remains unpaid by the company, and the assessment is not out of time if made within three years of the final determination of the liability of the company for the accounting period concerned.

TMA 1970, s 87A (see **43.2** interest on overdue tax) applies in relation to tax so assessed by reference to the company's due and payable date. The tax (and any interest) paid is not an allowable deduction for any tax purposes, but the payer is entitled to recover an amount equal to the tax (and any interest) from the company. An amount so recovered (or received under an indemnity in this respect) is not chargeable to tax on the recipient. (Revenue Tax Bulletin April 1995 p 208).

[*CTA 2010, ss 706–712, 716, 717*].

See also **11.10** CAPITAL GAINS; **12.11**, **12.15** CAPITAL GAINS — GROUPS; **38.12** HMRC INVESTIGATORY POWERS and **62.15** REORGANISATIONS AND RECONSTRUCTIONS; **64.10** RESIDENCE.

Simon's Taxes. See **D6.463**.

Change in ownership of company — postponed corporation tax

[58.15] Provisions supplementing the above deal with cases where a corporation tax liability has been postponed to a period commencing after a change in ownership within **51.17** LOSSES.

Where an HMRC officer considers that there has been a change in the ownership of a company, and that any corporation tax for an accounting period ending on or after the change which has been assessed on that company or an 'associated' company remains unpaid at any time more than six months after it was assessed, then (subject to the further 'expectation' condition referred to below) any one of the persons listed below may be assessed and charged (in the name of the company in default) to an amount of corporation tax not exceeding the amount remaining unpaid. Such persons referred to as 'linked' to the company per the legislation found in *CTA 2010, s 713*.

Such an assessment is not out of time if made within three years of the date of final determination of the liability of the company in default for the accounting period for which the tax was assessed. INTEREST ON OVERDUE TAX (**43**) then runs by reference to the date of the original liability of that company.

A company is '*associated*' with another for these purposes if, at the time of the assessment (or at an earlier time before the change in ownership), it has control of or is controlled by the other or they are under common control. 'Control' is defined as for **58.14** above.

The 'expectation' condition

The further condition referred to above is that it would be reasonable (apart from these provisions) to infer, from either or both of the terms of any transactions entered into in connection with the change (for which see below) and the other circumstances of the change and of any such transactions, that at least one of those transactions was entered into by one or more of the parties to it on the assumption that a 'potential tax liability' would be unlikely to be met, or met in full, were it to arise.

A '*potential tax liability*' is a corporation tax liability which, in circumstances reasonably foreseeable at the time of change in ownership (or in circumstances the occurrence of which is something of which there was at that time a reasonably foreseeable risk), would or might arise from an assessment made, after the change in ownership, on the company transferred or an associated company, whether or not a particular associated company.

A transaction is for these purposes entered into in connection with a change in ownership if the change is effected by the transaction (with or without other transactions) or by other transactions forming part of the same series of transactions or scheme (by whomsoever entered into). A 'scheme' is any scheme, arrangements or understanding of any kind, and the cases in which transactions form part of a scheme or series include cases in which it would be reasonable to assume that one or more of them would not have been entered into independently of the other(s), or that if entered into independently it would not have taken the same form or been on the same terms.

Persons assessable

The persons who may be assessed and charged are any person 'linked' to the company, that is any person who at any time during the 'relevant period' before the change had control of the transferred company, and any company of which such a person has at any time had control within the period of three years before the change in ownership. The '*relevant period*' is the period of three years before the change in ownership, or if, during that three years, there was an earlier change in ownership of the transferred company, the period between those changes.

Tax paid under these provisions is not an allowable deduction for tax purposes, but the payer is entitled to recover an amount equal to the tax (and any interest thereon) from the transferred (or associated) company.

[*CTA 2010, ss 706–709, 713–718*].

Simon's Taxes. See **D6.463**, **D6.464**.

Recovery of tax payable by non-resident company

[58.16] Where corporation tax assessed on a non-UK resident company (i.e. in respect of UK branch profits) remains in whole or part unpaid six months after the due date, the following companies may be served notice by HMRC requiring them to pay the tax.

(1) Any company which was, at any time in the 'relevant period', a 51% subsidiary (by reference to ordinary share capital) of the non-resident company, or of which the non-resident company was a 51% subsidiary, or where both were 51% subsidiaries of a third company.

(2) Any company which was, at any time during the 'relevant period', a member of a consortium which owned (see **35.19** GROUP RELIEF) the non-resident company at that time.

(3) Any company which was, at any time during the 'relevant period', a member of the same group (as for group relief purposes, see **35.3** GROUP RELIEF) as a company which was at that time a member of a consortium which owned (see **35.19** GROUP RELIEF) the non-resident company.

The '*relevant period*' is the period beginning twelve months before the start of the accounting period in question and ending when the unpaid tax first became payable.

The notice may require payment, within 30 days of service, of the overdue tax or (in the case of a company within either or both of (2) and (3) above but not within (1) above) of an appropriate proportion thereof (see *CTA 2010, ss 977–979*). A payment made in pursuance of a notice is not an allowable deduction in computing profits, but the paying company may recover the amount from the non-resident company. The notice must state the amount of the unpaid tax, the date it first became payable and the amount required to be paid by the recipient. For recovery and appeals purposes, it has effect as if it were a notice of assessment of an amount of tax due from the recipient. INTEREST ON OVERDUE TAX (**43**) runs from the original due date.

HMRC have three years from the date on which the liability of the non-resident company is finally determined (including a determination under *FA 1998, Sch 18 para 36* or *37* in the absence of a full return, see **65.18** RETURNS) in which to serve notice under these provisions. In the case of a self-assessed liability, including one superseding a determination, the date of determination of the liability is taken as the last date on which notice of an enquiry into the return may be given (see **65.14** RETURNS), or, if such notice is given, 30 days after the action which concludes the enquiry process. In the case of a discovery assessment (see **6.3** ASSESSMENTS), it is the due and payable date or (if there is an appeal against the assessment) the date the appeal is finally determined.

[*CTA 2010, ss 973–980*].

Simon's Taxes. See **D2.245**.

See also **12.11** CAPITAL GAINS — GROUPS and **Simon's Taxes** at **D2.345** with regard to similar provisions in respect of recovery of corporation tax on chargeable gains from other group members. Similar provisions also apply for the purposes of DIVERTED PROFITS TAX (see **30.18**).

Recovery from officers of the company

[58.17] Tax which has fallen due may be recovered from the treasurer or acting treasurer (the 'proper officer') of a company which is not a body corporate or not incorporated under a UK enactment or by charter. That officer then has a right of reimbursement out of moneys coming into his hands on behalf of that company, and to be indemnified by the company for any balance. [*TMA 1970, s 108(2)(3)*].

Joint and several liability of company directors etc.

[58.18] HMRC can issue a notice (a '*joint liability notice*') to individual directors or shadow directors of a company or to individual participators in a company making them jointly and severally liable for the company's tax liabilities or penalties. Such a notice can apply to any amount payable to HMRC by the company under any enactment and includes liabilities under a contract settlement. It is therefore not restricted to corporation tax. A notice can only be given in cases of insolvency or potential insolvency where stringent conditions are satisfied under one of three categories: tax avoidance or evasion; repeated insolvency and non-payment; and penalties for facilitation of tax avoidance or evasion.

The provisions apply to tax liabilities for periods ending on or after 22 July 2020 and to tax liabilities not related to a period arising from an event or default occurring on or after that date.

See also **23.6** CORONAVIRUS for joint and several liability of individuals to income tax charged to recover coronavirus support payments.

[*FA 2020, s 100, Sch 13 paras 1, 19*].

A company is subject to an insolvency procedure if, broadly, it is undergoing, or has undergone, a winding up, it is in administration or receivership, it has moved from administration to dissolution, it is subject to a compromise or arrangement under *Companies Act 2006, Pt 26* or NI or overseas equivalent, or it has been struck off the register under *Companies Act 2006, ss 1000* or *1003*. See *FA 2020, Sch 13 para 8*.

Where a company has ceased to exist, the effect of a joint liability notice is to make the individual solely liable for the amount specified in the notice or, where a notice is given to more than one individual in respect of the same liability, jointly and severally liable with the other individuals. The tax liability of such a company is taken, for the purposes of these provisions, to be whatever it was immediately before the company ceased to exist. [*FA 2020, Sch 13 para 17*].

The provisions apply also to liabilities of limited liability partnerships. References below to directors and shadow directors include members and shadow members of such partnerships. A shadow member is, broadly, a person in accordance with whose instructions the members of the partnership are accustomed to act. [*FA 2020, Sch 13 paras 18, 19*].

Tax avoidance and evasion

An authorised HMRC officer may issue a joint liability notice to an individual if it appears that:

(1) a company has entered into 'tax avoidance arrangements' or has engaged in 'tax-evasive conduct';
(2) the company is subject to an insolvency procedure or there is a serious possibility that it will be;
(3) either:
    (i) at a time when the individual was a director, shadow director or participator, the individual was responsible (alone or with others) for the company entering into the arrangements or engaging in the conduct or the individual received a benefit which, to his knowledge, arose (at least partly) from the arrangements or conduct; or

(ii) at a time when the individual was a director or shadow director or was otherwise concerned or taking part in the management of the company (directly or indirectly) the individual took part in, assisted with or facilitated the arrangements or conduct;

(4) there is, or is likely to be, a tax liability referable to the arrangements or conduct;

(5) there is a serious possibility that some or all of that tax liability will not be paid.

In (3)(i) above, an individual is taken to know anything that he could reasonably be expected to know. Benefits received by a connected person are treated as received by the individual.

The notice makes the individual jointly and severally liable with the company, and any other individuals to whom a notice is given, for the tax liability in (4) above. The amount for which an individual is so liable is reduced by any penalty paid by that individual in relation to that liability.

A notice under these provisions must specify the company to which it relates and set out the reasons why it appears to the officer that the above conditions are met. It must state the effect of the notice and explain the individual's right of review and appeal. It must also specify the amount of the tax liability, but if this is not yet known, the amount can be specified in a further notice.

'*Tax avoidance arrangements*' are:

- arrangements in respect of which a final notice has been given under the general anti-abuse rule (see **4.3** ANTI-AVOIDANCE) stating that a tax advantage is to be counteracted under the rule;
- arrangements in respect of which a follower notice (see **4.29**) has been given and not withdrawn;
- 'DOTAS arrangements' within **4.34**;
- arrangements to which HMRC have allocated a reference number or in respect of which a promoter must provide information under the disclosure of tax avoidance schemes rules for VAT and other indirect taxes;
- arrangements in relation to which a Tribunal has made an order that they are notifiable under the disclosure of tax avoidance schemes rules for direct taxes or VAT etc.; or
- arrangements that are substantially the same as arrangements (involving the same or different parties) in respect of which such an order has been made and which have the same promoter.

'*Tax-evasive conduct*' means giving HMRC any deliberately inaccurate return, claim, document or information or deliberately failing to comply with an obligation to notify etc. within the Table in *FA 2008, Sch 41 para 1.*

[*FA 2020, Sch 13 paras 2, 6, 7, 9*].

Repeated insolvency and non-payment

An authorised HMRC officer may issue a joint liability notice to an individual if it appears that:

(a) the individual had a 'connection' with at least two companies (the old companies) at any time during the five years ending with the day the notice is given and each of those companies became subject to an insolvency procedure during those five years at a time when:
- it had a tax liability; or
- it had failed to submit a return or other document or to make a declaration or application that it was required to and which was relevant to the question whether the company had a tax liability or how much its tax liability was; or
- it had submitted such a return or other document or made such a declaration or application but an act or omission on its part had prevented HMRC from dealing with it;

(b) another company (the new company) is or has been carrying on a trade or activity that is the same as, or similar to, that carried on previously by each of the old companies (or at least two of them if there are more than two);

(c) the individual has had a connection with the new company at any time in the five-year period in (a) above; and

(d) at the time the notice is given, at least one of the old companies has a tax liability and the total tax liabilities of all of the old companies within (b) above is more than £10,000 and is more than 50% of the total of those companies' liabilities to unsecured creditors.

For these purposes, an individual has a connection with an old company if that individual is a director, shadow director or participator. An individual has a connection with the new company if that individual is a director, shadow director or participator or is otherwise concerned, or takes part, in the management of the company (directly or indirectly).

The notice makes the individual jointly and severally liable with the new company and any other individuals to whom a notice is given for any tax liability which the new company has on the day the notice is issued or which arises during the following five years (or while the notice continues in effect if that is less than five years). The individual is also made jointly and severally liable with any old company within (b) above and any other individuals to whom a notice is given for any liability which that company has on the day the notice is given. The amount for which an individual is so liable in respect of any liability is reduced by any penalty paid by that individual in relation to that liability.

A notice must be issued within the two years beginning with the day on which HMRC first become aware of sufficient facts for them reasonably to conclude that the above conditions are met. It must set out the reasons why it appears to the officer that the above conditions are met and specify any amounts for which the individual is liable. It must also state the effect of the notice and explain the individual's right of review and appeal.

The Treasury has a power amend the amount and percentage in (d) above by statutory instrument.

[*FA 2020, Sch 13 paras 3, 4, 9*].

HMRC have indicated that the power to issue a joint liability notice under this provision will not be used in respect of those such as 'turnaround specialists' whose connection with companies is part of a genuine attempt to save the company from failing. When a person falls within the above conditions solely by virtue of being a participator in the company, HMRC will not issue a notice to that person where it is satisfied the person acted in good faith and had no material influence over the company's affairs. (Treasury Explanatory Notes to the 2020 Finance Bill).

Penalty for facilitating avoidance or evasion

An authorised HMRC officer may issue a joint liability notice to an individual if it appears that:

(I) HMRC have imposed a penalty under one of the following provisions on a company or proceedings have commenced before the First-tier Tribunal for the imposition of such a penalty. Penalties imposed, or in respect of which proceedings commenced, before 22 July 2020 are excluded. The provisions are:
- *TMA 1970, s 98C* (failure to disclose tax avoidance scheme; see **59.10** PENALTIES);
- *FA 2014, Sch 35 paras 2, 3* (high-risk promoters of avoidance schemes; see **59.13**);
- *FA 2016, Sch 20 para 1* (enabling offshore tax evasion; see **59.20**);
- *F(No 2)A 2017, Sch 16 Pt 1* (enablers of defeated abusive tax arrangements; see **59.21**);
- *F(No 2)A 2017, Sch 17 Pt 2* (disclosure of tax avoidance schemes (VAT etc.));

(II) the company is subject to an insolvency procedure or there is a serious possibility that it will be;

(III) the individual was a director or shadow director of, or participator in, the company at the time of any act or omission in respect of which the penalty was imposed or proceedings commenced; and

(IV) there is a serious possibility that some or all of the penalty will not be paid.

The notice makes the individual jointly and severally liable for the penalty with the company and any other individuals to whom a notice is given.

A notice under these provisions must specify the company to which it relates and set out the reasons why it appears to the officer that the above conditions are met. It must state the effect of the notice and explain the individual's right of review and appeal. It must also specify the amount of the penalty but if this is not yet known because proceedings before the Tribunal have not concluded, the amount can be specified in a further notice.

[*FA 2020, s 100(4), Sch 13 para 5*].

Withdrawal or modification of notice

HMRC must withdraw a joint liability notice if any of the conditions were not in fact met when the notice was given or if it is not necessary for the protection of the revenue for the notice to continue in effect. They must also withdraw a notice in a repeated insolvency and non-payment case if any of the old companies was being wound up by way of a members' voluntary winding-up and it pays its debts in full, together with interest at the official rate, before the end of the winding-up and condition (a) above would not have been met if that company (or each of them) had not been subject to an insolvency procedure.

HMRC may withdraw a notice if they think it appropriate to do so. They may also issue a further notice varying the amount to which the individual is liable if it seems to them that the amount specified in the notice is too much or not enough.

Withdrawal of a joint liability notice is by HMRC giving a further notice. A withdrawn notice is of no effect but does not give the individual any right to repayment of any amount paid under it, except where the notice is withdrawn because the conditions were not met when the notice was given.

Reviews and appeals

An individual who is given a joint liability notice (or a further notice specifying the amount to which he is liable) can request a review of HMRC's decision to give the notice. A request must be in writing and made within the 'permitted period', i.e. normally the period ending on the 30th day after the day the notice was given. HMRC can allow an extended period by notice given before the end of what would otherwise be the permitted period. It must specify a date at least 30 days after the date of the extension notice. The permitted period can be extended more than once. HMRC must accept a late request for a review if they are satisfied that the individual had a reasonable excuse for the late request and that there was no unreasonable delay after the excuse ceased to apply.

HMRC can conduct their review in a way that appears appropriate in the circumstances, but they must have regard to steps taken before the review by HMRC in reaching their decision to issue the notice, or by an other person in seeking to resolve disagreement about the decision. They must take account of any representations by the individual but the individual cannot challenge the existence or amount of the tax liability to which the notice relates.

HMRC must set aside the notice if it appears on review that any of the conditions were not met when the notice was given or that it is not necessary for the protection of the revenue for it to continue in effect. They must set aside the notice or vary the amount of the liability specified in it if it appears to them that the amount specified is incorrect. Otherwise, HMRC must uphold the notice. If a notice is set aside on the basis that it is not necessary for the protection of the revenue for it to continue, in effect, the individual does not have a right to recover any amounts already paid.

They must normally notify the individual of their conclusions and reasoning in writing within 45 days of the date the review request was received or, in the case of a late request, within 45 days of their decision to undertake the review. HMRC may agree a later date with the individual. If HMRC fail to meet the deadline, the notice is nevertheless upheld, and HMRC must notify the individual accordingly.

HMRC are not required to conduct or continue a review if the individual appeals against the notice.

An individual may appeal to the First-tier Tribunal against a joint liability notice (or a further notice specifying the amount to which he is liable) within the permitted period, i.e. normally the 30 days beginning with the day on which the notice is given. HMRC can allow an extended period by notice given before the end of what would otherwise be the permitted period. It must specify a date at least 30 days after the date of the extension notice. The permitted period can be extended more than once.

If a review has been conducted by HMRC, an appeal can be made within 30 days beginning with the date of the notice of HMRC's conclusions. Where a late request for a review has been made, no appeal can be made unless HMRC have notified the individual as to whether or not a review will be conducted. If HMRC do conduct a review, an appeal must be made within the 30 days beginning with the date of the notice of HMRC's conclusions. If HMRC do not conduct a review, an appeal can only be made with the Tribunal's permission. If HMRC have failed to notify their conclusions following a review within the time limit, an appeal can be made within the 30 days beginning with the date of HMRC's notice that the joint liability notice is upheld.

Late appeals may be made with the Tribunal's permission.

The Tribunal must set aside the notice if it appears that any of the conditions were not met when the notice was given, or that it is not necessary for the protection of the revenue for it to continue in effect. It must set aside the notice or vary the amount of the liability specified in it if it appears that the amount specified is incorrect. Otherwise, the Tribunal must uphold the notice. If a notice is set aside on the basis that it is not necessary for the protection of the revenue for it to continue, in effect, the individual does not have a right to recover any amounts already paid.

An individual cannot challenge the existence or amount of any tax liability of a company on appeal against a joint liability notice. An individual subject to such a notice is, however, entitled to be a party to any ongoing appeal by the company in respect of the liability to which the notice relates if the company is subject to an insolvency procedure. If the company is unwilling or unable to continue the appeal, the individual may do so. If the company has not appealed (but is subject to an insolvency procedure), an appeal may be made in the name of the individual. Such an appeal must be made within the 30 days beginning with day on which the joint liability notice was given and may be made even if the time limit for the company to appeal has expired.

In a penalty for facilitating avoidance or evasion case where penalty proceedings were commenced before the joint liability notice was issued but the penalty had not then been imposed, the individual to whom the notice was issued is entitled to be a party to those proceedings.

[*FA 2020, Sch 13 paras 11–16*].

Exit charge payment plans

[58.19] There is a facility for a company which ceases to be resident in the UK to enter into a CT exit charge payment plan with HMRC to defer payment of the exit charges which arise under a number of corporation tax provisions, including the chargeable gains provisions. The facility can also be used by certain non-resident companies which cease to carry on all or part of a trade in the UK through a permanent establishment. The facility is intended to ensure that the UK's exit charges comply with EU law.

See also **11.22** CAPITAL GAINS and **42.40** INTANGIBLE ASSETS for the treatment of assets subject to EU exit charges.

Company ceasing to be UK resident

An 'eligible company' which ceases to be resident in the UK can enter into an exit charge payment plan if it becomes resident in another European Economic Area (EEA) state and is liable to pay 'qualifying corporation tax' in respect of the 'migration accounting period'. The following further conditions must be satisfied:

(i) on ceasing to be UK resident the company must carry on a business in an EEA state; and
(ii) on becoming resident in the other EEA state, the company must not be treated as resident in a non-EEA territory for the purposes of any double tax arrangements.

For accounting periods ending on or after 1 January 2020, the EEA state must either be a member of the EU or must be party to a mutual assistance agreement with the UK equivalent to the EU's Directive on mutual assistance (*Directive 2010/24/EU*) (a '*relevant EEA state*').

The company must apply to HMRC to enter into the plan before the end of the nine-month period following the migration accounting period and must include in the application all the required information (see below).

An '*eligible company*' is one that has a right to freedom of establishment under EU law or under the Agreement on the EEA. The 'migration accounting period' is, if an accounting period comes to an end on the company ceasing to be UK resident, that accounting period. In any other case, the migration accounting period is the accounting period during which the company ceases to be UK resident.

A company is liable to pay '*qualifying corporation tax*' in respect of the migration accounting period if the corporation tax it is liable to pay for the period (CT1) is greater than the amount of corporation tax it would be liable to pay if any income, profits, gains, losses or debits arising only under the exit charge provisions listed below were ignored (CT2). The amount of the qualifying corporation tax is the difference between CT1 and CT2. The exit charge provisions are:

(a) *TCGA 1992, s 185* (deemed disposal of assets on company ceasing to be UK resident; see **64.9** RESIDENCE);
(b) (before repeal for companies ceasing to be UK-resident on or after 1 January 2020) *TCGA 1992, s 187(4)(c)* (postponed gains charged when principal company ceases to be UK resident; see **64.9** RESIDENCE);
(c) *CTA 2009, s 162* as applied by *CTA 2009, s 41(2)(b)* (valuation of trading stock on ceasing to be within the charge to corporation tax; see **69.63** TRADING INCOME—DEDUCTIONS);

(d) *CTA 2009, s 333* (deemed assignment of loan relationships on company ceasing to be UK resident; see **50.35** LOAN RELATIONSHIPS);
(e) *CTA 2009, s 609* (deemed assignment of derivative contract rights and liabilities on company ceasing to be UK resident; see **27.26** DERIVATIVE CONTRACTS);
(f) *CTA 2009, s 859(2)(a)* (deemed realisation of intangible fixed asset on it ceasing to be chargeable intangible asset when company ceases to be UK resident; see **42.40** INTANGIBLE ASSETS);
(g) (before repeal for companies ceasing to be UK-resident on or after 1 January 2020) *CTA 2009, s 862(1)(c)* (postponed gains on intangible fixed assets charged when parent company ceases to be UK resident; see **42.40** INTANGIBLE ASSETS).

For the purposes of these provisions, '*exit charge assets*' and '*exit charge liabilities*' are assets or liabilities in respect of which income, profits or gains arise in the migration accounting period under the exit charge provisions above. '*TCGA or trading stock exit charge assets*' are exit charge assets in respect of which income, profits or gains arise under (a)–(c) above, other than any intangible fixed assets excluded from the intangible assets regime by that regime's commencement rules (see **42.42** INTANGIBLE ASSETS). '*Financial exit charge assets or liabilities*' are exit charge assets or liabilities in respect of which income, profits or gains arise under (d) or (e) above. '*Intangible exit charge assets*' means exit charge assets in respect of which income, profits or gains arise under (f) or (g) above together with intangible assets excluded from being 'TCGA or trading stock exit charge assets' as above.

[*TMA 1970, s 59FA, Sch 3ZB paras 1–3; FA 2019, Sch 7 para 6, Sch 8 paras 2, 8, 9(4), 10(4)*].

Non-UK resident company with UK permanent establishment

An eligible company (defined as above) which is not resident in the UK but carries on a trade there through a permanent establishment in an accounting period (the 'migration accounting period') can enter into an exit charge payment plan if one or more 'PE qualifying events' occurs and the company is liable to pay 'qualifying corporation tax' in respect of the migration accounting period.

The company must apply to HMRC to enter into the plan before the end of the nine-month period following the migration accounting period and must include in the application all the required information (see below).

A '*PE qualifying event*' occurs in relation to an asset or liability of the company (a PE qualifying asset or liability) if:

- an event occurs which triggers a deemed disposal and reacquisition of the asset or liability, or a valuation of the asset, under one of the exit charge provisions listed below;
- the event occurs during the migration accounting period or causes that period to end;
- at the time of the event, the company is not treated as resident in a non-EEA territory for the purposes of any double tax arrangements; and

- for accounting periods ending on or after 1 January 2020, immediately after the event, the asset or liability is held or owed by the company for the purposes of a permanent establishment in a relevant EEA state or, where the company is resident in a relevant EEA state, is held or owed by the company otherwise than for the purposes of a permanent establishment.

A company is liable to pay '*qualifying corporation tax*' in respect of the migration accounting period if the corporation tax it is liable to pay for the period (CT1) is greater than the amount of corporation tax it would be liable to pay if any income, profits, gains, losses or debits arising only under the exit charge provisions listed below were ignored (CT2). The amount of the qualifying corporation tax is the difference between CT1 and CT2. The exit charge provisions are:

(A) *TCGA 1992, s 25* (deemed disposal of assets leaving UK);
(B) *CTA 2009, s 162* as applied by *CTA 2009, s 41(2)(b)* (valuation of trading stock on ceasing to be within the charge to corporation tax; see **69.63** TRADING INCOME—DEDUCTIONS);
(C) *CTA 2009, s 334* (deemed assignment of loan relationship on company ceasing to hold relationship for UK permanent establishment; see **50.35** LOAN RELATIONSHIPS);
(D) *CTA 2009, s 610* (deemed assignment of derivative contract rights and liabilities on company ceasing to hold contract for UK permanent establishment; see **27.26** DERIVATIVE CONTRACTS);
(E) *CTA 2009, s 859(2)(b)* (deemed realisation of intangible fixed asset on asset ceasing to be a chargeable intangible asset; see **42.40** INTANGIBLE ASSETS).

For the purposes of these provisions, '*exit charge assets*' and '*exit charge liabilities*' are PE qualifying assets or liabilities in respect of which income, profits or gains arise in the migration accounting period under the exit charge provisions above. '*TCGA or trading stock exit charge assets*' are exit charge assets in respect of which income, profits or gains arise under (A) or (B) above, other than any intangible fixed assets excluded from the intangible assets regime by that regime's commencement rules (see **42.42** INTANGIBLE ASSETS). '*Financial exit charge assets or liabilities*' are exit charge assets or liabilities in respect of which income, profits or gains arise under (C) or (D) above. '*Intangible exit charge assets*' means exit charge assets in respect of which income, profits or gains arise under (E) above together with intangible assets excluded from being 'TCGA or trading stock exit charge assets' as above.

[*TMA 1970, s 59FA, Sch 3ZB paras 4–6; FA 2019, Sch 7 para 6, Sch 8 paras 3, 8*].

Entering into a payment plan

An exit charge payment plan takes effect where the company agrees to pay, and HMRC agree to accept payment of, all or part of the qualifying corporation tax in accordance with the payment method below or, for accounting periods ending before 1 January 2020, in accordance with the 'standard instalment method', the 'realisation method' or a combination of both. The company must also agree to pay interest on the tax as described below. The plan must specify the following:

(1) where the company ceases to be UK-resident, the date on which it so ceases and the EEA state in which the company has become resident;
(2) where the company has a UK permanent establishment, the EEA state in which it is resident and, if the PE qualifying event is the company ceasing to trade in the UK through a permanent establishment, the date of cessation;
(3) the amount of qualifying corporation tax which the company considers is payable for the migration accounting period and the amount to be postponed;
(4) for accounting periods ending before 1 January 2020, whether that tax is to be paid using the standard instalment method, the realisation method or a combination of both;
(5) for accounting periods ending before 1 January 2020, if the tax is to be paid by a combination of the methods, the method to be used for each of the company's exit charge assets or liabilities and the amount of tax to be paid under each method;
(6) for accounting periods ending on or after 1 January 2020, the amount of postponed tax attributable to each exit charge asset or liability;
(7) for accounting periods ending on or after 1 January 2020, requirements for ongoing provision of information by the company to HMRC about the exit charge assets and liabilities.

Where tax attributable to an exit charge asset or liability is to be paid using the realisation method (for accounting periods ending before 1 January 2020), the plan must also specify:

- each such asset or liability (so far as not already specified under (5) above) and the amount of tax attributable to it;
- requirements for ongoing provision of information to HMRC in relation to the asset or liability;
- in the case of a financial exit charge asset or liability the remaining term of which is less than ten years, the number of years in the remaining term (rounded up to the nearest whole year); and
- in the case of an intangible exit charge asset the remaining useful life of which is less than ten years, how many years of the useful life remain (rounded up to the nearest whole year).

The amount of tax attributable to each exit charge asset or liability for this purpose is the proportion of the tax postponed under the plan that the income, profits or gains arising in respect of that asset or liability under the exit charge concerned bears to the total income, profits or gains arising in respect of all the exit charges or liabilities under the exit charge provisions.

Where HMRC consider that entering into a plan would otherwise present a serious risk to collection of the tax, the plan may include provision for HMRC to take security for the tax. This would usually be in the form of a bank guarantee.

A payment plan is void if any information provided by the company does not fully and accurately disclose all facts and considerations material to HMRC's decision to enter into it.

[*TMA 1970, s 59FA, Sch 3ZB paras 7, 8, 10–12; FA 2019, Sch 7 para 6, Sch 8 paras 4–6, 8*].

Effect of payment plan

An exit charge payment plan does not prevent the tax included in it from becoming due and payable in the normal way, but HMRC may not seek payment otherwise than in accordance with the plan. HMRC may, however, make repayments of any amount of the tax paid, or amount paid on account of the tax, before the plan is entered into.

The tax deferred under the plan carries interest as if the plan had not been entered into. Each payment under the plan must include any interest on the tax.

A late payment penalty (when in force: see **59.7** PENALTIES) will only be payable if the company fails to make payments in accordance with the plan.

There is nothing to prevent a company paying any of the tax before the time it becomes payable under the plan.

[*TMA 1970, s 59FA, Sch 3ZB para 9; FA 2019, Sch 7 para 6*].

Payment method — accounting periods ending on or after 1 January 2020

The tax postponed under the plan is due in six equal annual instalments starting nine months and one day after the end of the migration accounting period.

Where the company becomes insolvent, enters administration or a liquidator is appointed, the balance of the tax is payable in full on the date on which the next instalment would otherwise be due. This applies also where the company becomes insolvent etc. under a corresponding law of a country or territory outside the UK, where the company ceases to be resident in an EEA state without becoming resident in another relevant EEA state and where the company fails to pay an amount due under the plan within twelve months of it becoming due.

A proportion of the postponed tax becomes due immediately if a 'trigger event' occurs in relation to an exit charge asset or liability before the final instalment becomes due (provided that there has been no previous trigger event in relation to that asset or liability). The amount due is:

$$(A - B) \times \frac{O}{T}$$

where:

A = the amount of postponed tax attributable to the asset or liability;
B = the amount of postponed tax that has previously become chargeable because of a 'partial trigger event' (see below);
O = the outstanding postponed tax at the time of the trigger event; and

T = the total postponed tax.

Where the asset is a TCGA or trading stock exit charge asset or an intangible exit charge, a '*trigger event*' occurs when the company disposes of it or ceases to hold it for the purposes of a business carried on by the company in a relevant EEA state without it then becoming held for the purposes of another such business. A trigger event in relation to a financial exit charge asset or liability occurs if the company ceases to be a party to the loan relationship or derivative contract or ceases to be a party to it for the purposes of a business carried on by the company in a relevant EEA state without it then becoming held for the purposes of another such business.

Part of the postponed tax also becomes due immediately if a 'partial trigger event' occurs in relation to an exit charge asset or liability before the final instalment becomes due (provided that there has been no previous trigger event in relation to that asset or liability). The amount that becomes due immediately must be calculated on a just and reasonable basis, taking account of the amount that would have been due if a trigger event had occurred. Where the asset is a TCGA or trading stock exit charge asset, a '*partial trigger event*' occurs if the company disposes of part (but not all) of it. In relation to a financial exit charge asset or liability, a partial trigger event occurs if there is a disposal of a right or liability under the loan relationship or derivative contract which amounts to a related transaction (within *CTA 2009, s 304* or *s 596*; see **50.8** LOAN RELATIONSHIPS and **27.6** DERIVATIVE CONTRACTS). Where the asset is an intangible exit charge asset, a partial trigger event occurs if there is a transaction resulting in a reduction in the accounting value of the asset but not resulting in the asset ceasing to be recognised on the company's balance sheet.

[*TMA 1970, Sch 3ZB paras 11–14; FA 2019, Sch 8 paras 6, 8*].

Standard instalment method — accounting periods ending before 1 January 2020

A payment plan may specify that the tax is to be paid under the standard instalment method only if:

- in the case of a company ceasing to be UK resident, the company's ceasing to be so resident is not part of arrangements with a main purpose of deferring the payment of any of the qualifying corporation tax; or
- in the case of a company with a UK permanent establishment, none of the PE qualifying events are part of such arrangements.

Where the standard instalment method is used, the tax is payable in six equal instalments. The first instalment is due nine months and one day after the end of the migration accounting period. The remaining instalments are due on each of the first five anniversaries of that date.

Where the company becomes insolvent, enters administration or a liquidator is appointed, the balance of the tax is payable in full on the date on which the next instalment would otherwise be due. This applies also where the company becomes insolvent etc. under a corresponding law of an EEA state and where the company ceases to be resident in an EEA state without becoming resident in another EEA state.

[*TMA 1970, s 59FA, Sch 3ZB paras 10(5), 13 (as originally enacted); FA 2019, Sch 7 para 6, Sch 8 paras 6, 8*].

Realisation method — accounting periods ending before 1 January 2020

Where the realisation method is used for a TCGA or trading stock exit charge asset, the tax becomes payable on the occurrence of the first of the following events:

(I) the disposal or part disposal of the asset at any time after the company becomes non-UK resident or the PE qualifying event occurs;
(II) the tenth anniversary of the end of the migration accounting period;
(III) the company becoming insolvent or entering administration or liquidation under UK or a corresponding EEA state law; and
(IV) the company ceasing to be resident in an EEA state without becoming resident in another EEA state.

Where (I) or (II) apply, the tax is payable on the date of disposal or on the tenth anniversary. Where (III) or (IV) apply the tax is due nine months and one day after the end of the migration accounting period or, if that date has already passed, the next anniversary of that date.

Where part of an asset is disposed of after an event within (I) above, the tax attributable to it is apportioned on a just and reasonable basis.

Where the realisation method is used for a financial exit charge asset or liability or for an intangible exit charge asset, the tax is payable in ten equal annual instalments, unless the remaining term of the loan relationship or derivative contract, or the remaining useful life of the intangible asset, is specified in the plan as fewer than ten years. In the latter case, the number of instalments is the specified number. The first instalment is due nine months and one day after the end of the migration accounting period. The remaining instalments are due on each of the subsequent anniversaries of that date.

All of the outstanding tax attributable to an asset or liability is payable on the date the company ceases to be a party to the loan relationship or derivative contract or disposes of the intangible asset. All of the outstanding balance is also payable if an event within (III) or (IV) above occurs, the tax becoming due on the date of the next instalment.

Where there is a disposal of rights or liabilities under the loan relationship or derivative contract which amounts to a related transaction (within *CTA 2009, s 304* or *s 596*; see **50.8** LOAN RELATIONSHIPS and **27.6** DERIVATIVE CONTRACTS) but the company does not cease to be party to the relationship or contract, so much of the outstanding tax as is attributable, on a just and reasonable basis, to the transaction is payable immediately. The remainder of the outstanding tax continues to be payable by instalments under the plan. This rule applies also where there is a transaction which results in a reduction in the accounting value of an intangible exit charge asset but does not result in the asset ceasing to be recognised in the company's balance sheet. If the asset has no balance sheet value already, it is treated for this purpose only as if it did have such a value.

[*TMA 1970, s 59FA, Sch 3ZB paras 14–17 (as originally enacted); FA 2019, Sch 7 para 6, Sch 8 paras 6, 8*].

Payment plans for transactions with EEA residents

[58.20] Companies liable to pay corporation tax on certain transactions with an EEA resident can defer payment by entering into a CT payment plan with HMRC. Although introduced by *FA 2020*, plans can be entered into in respect of transactions occurring in accounting periods ending on or after 10 October 2018. [*FA 2020, Sch 7 para 4(1)*]. The facility is intended to ensure that the UK's rules for tax neutral transfers within groups of companies comply with EU law following the decision in *Gallaher Ltd v HMRC* FTT, [2019] UKFTT 207 (TC) (see **12.4** CAPITAL GAINS — GROUPS and note that the Upper Tribunal ([2021] STC 247) has referred the compatibility of the relevant UK legislation with EU law to the CJEU).

Given the UK's departure from the EU, the legislation providing for CT payment plans includes provisions for the rules to be repealed by statutory instrument. [*FA 2020, Sch 7 para 5*].

Qualifying transactions

A CT payment plan for an accounting period can be entered into in respect of corporation tax ('qualifying corporation tax') due as a result of any of the following 'qualifying transactions':

(i) a disposal of an asset to a non-UK resident company which is resident in an EEA state where the disposal would have been a no gain/no loss disposal within *TCGA 1992, s 139* (reconstructions involving transfer of business — see **62.15** REORGANISATIONS AND RECONSTRUCTIONS) or *TCGA 1992, s 171* (intra-group transfers — see **12.4** CAPITAL GAINS — GROUPS) if the transferee were UK-resident;

(ii) a transaction (or the first in a series of transactions) which results in the company being directly or indirectly replaced as a party to a loan relationship by a company resident outside the UK in an EEA state, where the transaction would have been within *CTA 2009, s 340(3)* (intra-group transfer at notional carrying value — see **50.40** LOAN RELATIONSHIPS) if the transferee were UK-resident;

(iii) a transaction (or the first in a series of transactions) which results in the company being directly or indirectly replaced as a party to a derivative contract by a company resident outside the UK in an EEA state, where the transaction would have been within *CTA 2009, s 625(3)* (intra-group transfer at notional carrying value — see **50.40** DERIVATIVE CONTRACTS) if the transferee were UK-resident;

(iv) a transfer of an intangible asset to a non-UK resident company which is resident in an EEA state where the transfer would have been tax-neutral under *CTA 2009, s 775(1)* (transfers within a group — see **42.13** INTANGIBLE ASSETS) if the transferee were UK-resident.

The amount of '*qualifying corporation tax*' for an accounting period is the excess of the corporation tax it is liable to pay for the period over the corporation tax it would be liable to pay if any gains, credits, losses or debits for qualifying transactions were ignored. A plan may include all or part of the qualifying corporation tax for the period.

Entering into a payment plan

The company must apply to HMRC to enter into the plan within nine months after the end of the accounting period or by 30 June 2020, if later. The application must include all of the required details of the plan. The plan must:

(a) specify the accounting period to which it relates;
(b) specify the amount of the qualifying corporation tax and the amount to be deferred under the plan;
(c) identify each qualifying transaction and, for each such transaction, the name of the transferee, the EEA state in which it is resident and the amount of tax to be deferred which is attributable to it.

In (c) above, the proportion of the deferred tax attributable to a transaction is equal to the proportion that the gain or credit on the transaction bears to the total gains or credits from all qualifying transactions in the period.

If HMRC consider that there would otherwise be a serious risk to collection of the tax, the plan may include provision for HMRC to take security for the tax.

A payment plan is void if any information provided by the company does not fully and accurately disclose all facts and considerations material to HMRC's decision to enter into it.

Effect of payment plan

A CT payment plan does not prevent the tax included in it from becoming due and payable in the normal way, but HMRC may not seek payment otherwise than in accordance with the plan. HMRC may, however, make repayments of any amount of the tax paid, or amount paid on account of the tax, before the plan is entered into.

The tax deferred under the plan carries interest as if the plan had not been entered into. Each payment under the plan must include any interest on the tax. A late payment penalty (when in force: see **59.7** PENALTIES) will only be payable if the company fails to make payments in accordance with the plan.

There is nothing to prevent a company paying any of the tax (plus interest) before the time it becomes payable under the plan.

The tax postponed under the plan is due in six equal annual instalments starting nine months and one day after the end of the accounting period.

Where the company becomes insolvent, enters administration or a liquidator is appointed, the balance of the tax is payable in full on the date on which the next instalment would otherwise be due. This applies also where the company becomes insolvent etc. under a corresponding law of a country or territory outside the UK, where the company ceases to be within the charge to corporation tax and where the company fails to pay an amount due under the plan within 12 months of it becoming due.

A proportion of the postponed tax becomes due immediately if a 'trigger event' occurs in relation to a qualifying transaction included in the plan before the final instalment becomes due (provided that there has been no previous trigger event in relation to that transaction). The amount due is:

$$(A - B) \times \frac{O}{T}$$

where:

A = the amount of postponed tax attributable to the transaction;
B = the amount of postponed tax that has previously become chargeable because of a 'partial trigger event' (see below);
O = the outstanding postponed tax at the time of the trigger event; and
T = the total postponed tax.

A '*trigger event*' occurs when the transferee disposes of the asset which is the subject of the transaction or ceases to be a party to the loan relationship or derivative contract. A trigger also occurs if the transferee ceases to be resident in an EEA state without becoming resident in another EEA state or if the company and the transferee cease to be members of the same group.

Part of the postponed tax also becomes due immediately if a 'partial trigger event' occurs in relation to a qualifying transaction before the final instalment becomes due (provided that there has been no previous trigger event in relation to that transaction). The amount that becomes due immediately must be calculated on a just and reasonable basis, taking account of the amount that would have been due if a trigger event had occurred. Where the qualifying transaction was within (i) above, a '*partial trigger event*' occurs if the transferee disposes of part (but not all) of the asset. Where the transaction was within (ii) or (iii) above, a partial trigger event occurs if there is a disposal by the transferee of a right or liability under the loan relationship or derivative contract which amounts to a related transaction (within *CTA 2009, s 304* (see **50.8** LOAN RELATIONSHIPS) or *CTA 2009, s 596* (see **27.6** DERIVATIVE CONTRACTS)). Where the qualifying transaction was within (iv) above, a partial trigger event occurs if the transferee enters into a subsequent transaction resulting in a reduction in the accounting value of the asset but not resulting in the asset ceasing to be recognised on the company's balance sheet. If the asset has no balance sheet value this rule applies as if, immediately before the subsequent transaction, it did have such a value.

[*TMA 1970, s 59FB, Sch 3ZC; FA 2020, Sch 7 paras 2, 4*].

Surrender of tax refund, etc. within group

[58.21] Where two companies within a group (defined as for group relief purposes—see **35.3** GROUP RELIEF) jointly give notice to an HMRC officer, a corporation or income tax refund relating to an accounting period which falls to be made to one of them may be surrendered in whole or part to the other. The companies must be members of the same group throughout the period starting with the date the accounting period for which the refund arises and ending with the date the election is made. The notice must be made before the refund is made and must specify the amount to be surrendered. It must be in such form as is specified by HMRC.

The surrendering company is then treated as having received on the 'relevant date' a payment equal to the refund (or part), and the recipient company as having paid on that date corporation tax equal to the amount of the refund (or part) (except that in relation to tax-based penalties under *TMA 1970, s 94(6)* or *FA 1998, Sch 18, para 18* for excessive delay in rendering corporation tax returns (see **59.3** PENALTIES, **65.6** RETURNS) the corporation tax is treated as having been paid on the date of the notice referred to above). If the refund is of corporation tax and interest relating to that tax has been paid by the surrendering company, it is treated as having been paid by the recipient company.

Where the repayment to the surrendering company would not have carried interest ('*the interest-free period*') for part of the period, so that interest on tax repaid to the surrendering company would have been restricted (see **44.2** INTEREST ON OVERPAID TAX), a corresponding restriction applies in relation to the deemed payment by the claimant company.

The surrendering company accounting period to which the refund relates must also be an accounting period of the recipient company. Both companies must be members of the group from the beginning of the relevant accounting period until the date of the notice referred to above.

The '*relevant date*' is the date on which corporation tax for the relevant accounting period became due and payable or, if later and if the refund is of corporation tax, the date on which the corporation tax was paid.

Any agreed payment by the recipient company to the surrendering company for a surrender as above (not exceeding the amount of the refund) is disregarded for tax purposes and is not treated as a distribution.

[*CTA 2010, ss 183, 963–966*].

For the effect on these provisions of group payment arrangements (see **58.3** PAYMENT OF TAX), see HMRC Tax Bulletin April 2001, pp 834, 835 and also HMRC Company Taxation Manual, CTM97400 *et seq*.

Example

[58.22]

V Ltd has had, for some years, a 75% subsidiary, W Ltd, and both prepare accounts to 30 April. On 1 February 2020 (the due date), both companies make payments on account of their CT liabilities for the year ended 30 April 2019, V Ltd pays £250,000 and W Ltd pays £150,000. In January 2021, the liabilities are eventually agreed at £200,000 and £180,000 respectively.

Before any tax repayment is made to V Ltd, the two companies jointly give notice that £30,000 of the £50,000 tax repayment due to V Ltd is to be surrendered to W Ltd. W Ltd makes a payment of £20,000 to V Ltd in consideration for the tax refund surrendered.

It is assumed for illustrative purposes that the rates of interest on overdue tax and overpaid tax are, respectively, 3.5% and 1% throughout.

If no surrender had been made, and all outstanding tax payments/repayments made on, say, 1 February 2021, the interest position would have been as follows.

		£
V Ltd		
Interest on CT repayment of £50,000 for the period 1.2.20 to 1.2.21	£50,000 × 1% =	500
W Ltd		
Interest on late paid CT of £30,000 for the period 1.2.20 to 1.2.21	£30,000 × 3.5% =	1,050
Net interest payable by the group		£550

The surrender has the following consequences.

(i) Only £20,000 of the repayment (the unsurrendered amount) is actually made, and is made to V Ltd together with interest of £200 (at 1% for one year).

(ii) V Ltd, the surrendering company, is treated as having received a CT repayment of £30,000 (the surrendered amount) on the 'relevant date' which in this case is the normal due date of 1.2.20 V Ltd having made its CT payment on time. V Ltd is thus not entitled to any interest on this amount.

(iii) W Ltd, the recipient company, is deemed to have paid CT of £30,000 on the 'relevant date', 1.2.20 as above. It thus incurs no interest charge.

(iv) The group has turned a net interest charge of £550 into a net interest receipt of £200, a saving of £750. This arises from the differential in the rates of interest charged on unpaid and overpaid tax. (The surrendered amount £30,000 × 2.5% (3.5 – 1) × 1 year = £750.)

(v) The payment of £20,000 by W Ltd to V Ltd, not being a payment in excess of the surrendered refund, has no tax effect on either company.

V Ltd could have given notice to surrender its full refund of £50,000 to W Ltd, instead of just £30,000. There would, in fact, have been no point in doing so, but if W Ltd had made its original CT payment later than the due date, so as to incur an interest charge on the £150,000 originally paid, a full surrender would have produced a saving as the amount surrendered would be treated as having been paid on the due date.

Special cases

Partnership liabilities

[58.23] See 56.7 PARTNERSHIPS.

Over-repayments

[58.24] Corporation tax over-repaid and not assessable under *FA 1998, Sch 18 para 41* may be assessed for that period as if it were unpaid tax. Any associated excess INTEREST ON OVERPAID TAX (43) may be included in the assessment. The time limit for such assessments is extended to the end of the accounting period following that of the repayment if it would otherwise be out of time, subject to the usual provisions where loss of tax was brought about carelessly or deliberately by the taxpayer.

Similar provisions apply to enable excess set-offs or payments of tax credit to be recovered, including any INTEREST ON OVERPAID TAX (43) in respect of tax credits.

Where the assessment is to recover a repayment of tax paid for an accounting period, or a repayment of tax on a payment received in an accounting period, the assessment is treated as being for that accounting period, and the sum assessed carries interest under *TMA 1970, s 87A* (see **43.2** INTEREST ON OVERDUE TAX) from the date the repayment being recovered was made until payment.

These provisions also apply the discovery assessment rules of *FA 1998, Sch 18 paras 41–48* to recovery assessments, and extend the period during which assessments may be made to the completion of enquiries in certain cases, in particular where the excessive payment arose as a result of the taxpayer's careless or deliberate actions. See **65.18** RETURNS.

[*FA 1998, Sch 18 paras 52, 53*].

Simon's Taxes. See **A4.333.**

Certificates of tax deposit

[58.25] Before 23 November 2017, companies could make deposits, evidenced by Certificates of Tax Deposit, with HMRC for the subsequent payment of tax, and any liability met by the tendering of such a deposit (and accrued interest) is treated as paid on the normal due date, or on the date of the deposit if later. Petroleum royalties may also be paid in this way. The minimum initial deposit was £500 with minimum additions of £250 subject to a continuing minimum of £500. Deposits of £100,000 or over had to be made by direct remittance to the Bank of England. It is not possible to purchase certificates after 22 November 2017, although existing certificates will continue to be honoured until 23 November 2023. Any certificates remaining after the latter date should be promptly submitted to HMRC for refund.

It should be noted that the taxes which can be paid using certificates of tax deposit are:

- Income Tax;
- Class 4 National Insurance contributions (NICs);
- Capital Gains Tax;
- Petroleum Revenue Tax;
- Petroleum Royalty;
- Inheritance Tax.

Certificates may not be used against corporation tax liabilities, income tax liabilities under PAYE or the construction industry tax deduction scheme, or VAT liabilities.

Interest, which is payable gross but taxable, will accrue for a maximum of six years from the date of deposit to the date of payment of tax (or, if earlier, the normal due date for payment of tax, i.e. disregarding the fact that the payment date may be later due to late issue of the assessment in question or to an appeal having been made against the assessment). A deposit may be withdrawn for cash at any time but will then receive a reduced rate of interest. From 5 December 2008 interest is only paid on deposits of £100,000 or more.

Where a certificate is used in settlement of a tax liability, interest at the higher rate up to the normal due date may be less than interest at the encashment rate up to the reckonable date. In such circumstances the taxpayer may instruct the Collector to calculate interest on the latter basis. The rates of interest, published by the Treasury, and calculated by reference to the rate on comparable investment with the Government, vary with the size and period of the deposit, and the rate payable on a deposit is adjusted to the current rate on each anniversary of the deposit.

Deposits are not transferable except in settlement of tax payable by the depositor's holding company, subsidiary company, or fellow-subsidiary.

See www.gov.uk/guidance/certificate-of-tax-deposit-scheme.

Profits or gains on certificates of deposit issued after 31 March 1996 are chargeable to tax within the loan relationship provisions (see **50.3** LOAN RELATIONSHIPS). See HMRC Inspector's Manual, IM4602.

For rates of interest, see Tolley's Income Tax under Certificates of Deposit. Information on current rates may be obtained from www.hmrc.gov.uk/paying hmrc/cert-tax-deposit.htm.

Simon's Taxes. See **A4.635**.

Date of payment for interest purposes

[58.26] As to the date on which tax is treated as having been paid, see **43.7** INTEREST ON OVERDUE TAX.

59

Penalties

Cross-references. See also **38.18** HMRC INVESTIGATORY POWERS for penalties under the dishonest tax agents provisions; **64.9** RESIDENCE and **73.5** VALUE ADDED TAX.

Simon's Taxes. See **A4.5, D1.1320.**

Introduction to penalties

[59.1] Financial penalties can be charged or sought by HMRC for a substantial number of offences by companies or their agents. The current penalties relevant to corporation tax are summarised in the table below and are described in detail in the paragraphs of this chapter or where indicated in the table.

Offence	Penalty		Para
1. Failure to notify chargeability to tax. Failure to comply with the obligation to notify chargeability to CT within one year of accounting period. *FA 2008, Sch 41.*	Deliberate and concealed failure: 100% of potential lost revenue. Deliberate but unconcealed failure: 70% of potential lost revenue. Any other case: 30% of potential lost revenue. A statutory reduction in the amount of the penalty is made for disclosure of a failure. HMRC can also reduce a penalty in special circumstances.		**59.2**
2. Failure to deliver corporation tax return on time. *TMA 1970, s 7; FA 1998, Sch 18 paras 17, 18.*	(i)	£100 if up to three months late (£500 if previous two returns also delivered late); and	**59.3**
	(ii)	£200 if over three months late (£1,000 if previous two returns also late).	
Failure continuing at later of final day for delivery of return and 18 months after return period.		Further penalty of 10% of tax unpaid 18 months after return period (20% of tax unpaid at that date if return not made within two years of return period)	
3. Error in company's document. Careless or deliberate error in document amounting to or leading to understatement of liability, overstatement or loss or false or inflated claim to repayment of tax. *FA 2007, Sch 24, para 1.*	Deliberate and concealed error: 100% of potential lost revenue. Deliberate but unconcealed error: 70% of potential lost revenue. Any other case: 30% of potential lost revenue. A statutory reduction in the amount of the penalty is made for disclosure of an error. HMRC can also reduce a penalty in special circumstances. Where the error is linked to an offshore matter relating to certain categorised territories the amount of the penalty is increased by 50% or 100%.		**59.4**

Offence	Penalty	Para
4. Error in company's document attributable to another person. Deliberately supplying false information to, or deliberately withholding information from, a person giving a document to HMRC resulting in document containing an inaccuracy amounting to or leading to understatement of liability, overstatement of loss or false or inflated claim to repayment of tax. *FA 2007, Sch 24, para 1A.*	100% of potential lost revenue subject to statutory reduction for disclosure or in special circumstances.	59.5
5. Failure to notify HMRC of error in assessment. Failure to take reasonable steps to notify HMRC of an under-assessment within the 30 days beginning with the date of the assessment. *FA 2007, Sch 24, para 2.*	30% of potential lost revenue subject to statutory reduction for disclosure or in special circumstances.	59.6
6. Failure to make payment of CT on time. *FA 2009, Sch 56.*	(With effect from a date to be appointed) a 5% penalty applies if full amount not paid within 30 days of due date. If amount remains unpaid six months after due date a penalty of 5% applies; a further 5% penalty applies if amount is still unpaid after a further six months.	59.7
7. Special returns etc. Failure to comply with a notice to deliver any return or other document, to furnish any particulars, to produce any document or record, to make anything available for inspection or give any certificate under specified provisions. *TMA 1970, s 98.*	Up to £300 (£3,000 in specified cases).	59.8
8. Failure to keep records. Failure to keep and preserve appropriate records supporting company tax returns. *FA 1998, Sch 18, para 23.*	Up to £3,000.	59.9

Offence		Penalty	Para
9. Failure to disclose tax avoidance scheme. Failure to comply with any of a number of requirements under the disclosure of tax avoidance schemes rules. *TMA 1970, s 98C.*	(i)	Initial penalty of £5,000.	**59.10**
	(ii)	Continuing daily penalty of £600 (£5,000 in specified cases) after penalty in (i) has been imposed.	
	(iii)	Penalty of £100 for failure of party to notifiable arrangements to notify HMRC of scheme reference number. Increased to £500 for second failure in three-year period and £1,000 for third failure.	
10. Failure to comply with HMRC investigatory powers. Failure to comply with an information notice within *FA 2008, Sch 36 Pt 1* or deliberately obstructing an HMRC officer in the course of an inspection of business premises under *FA 2008, Sch 36, Pt 2* which has been approved by the First-tier Tribunal. *FA 2008, Sch 36.*	(i)	Initial penalty of £300.	**59.11**
	(ii)	If failure/obstruction continues, a further penalty up to £60 per day.	
	(iii)	If failure/obstruction continues after penalty under (i) imposed, a tax-related amount determined by the Upper Tribunal.	
11. Disclosure of a third party notice or a financial institution notice. Failure to comply with requirement in a third party notice or a financial institution notice not to disclose notice to taxpayer or other person *FA 2008, Sch 36.*		£1,000	**59.11**
12. HMRC investigatory powers: inaccurate information and documents *FA 2008, Sch 36.*	Up to £3,000.		**59.11**
13. HMRC data-gathering powers: failure to comply *FA 2011, Sch 23.*	(i)	Initial penalty of £300.	**59.12**
	(ii)	If failure continues, a further penalty up to £60 per day.	
	(iii)	If failure continues for more than 30 days after penalty under (ii) imposed, a further daily penalty determined by the Upper Tribunal up to £1,000 per day.	

Offence	Penalty	Para
14. HMRC data-gathering powers: inaccurate data *FA 2011, Sch 23*.	Up to £3,000.	**59.12**
15. High-risk promoters of avoidance schemes. Failure to comply with any of a number of requirements under the high-risk promoters of avoidance schemes rules. Provision of inaccurate information or documents in compliance with such a requirement. *FA 2014, Sch 35*.	Various	**59.13**
16. Follower notices. [*FA 2014, ss 208, 208A*].	Up to 30% of the value of the denied tax advantage or 12% in partnership cases for failure to comply with the notice. An additional penalty of up to 20% (8% in partnership cases) where there is an unreasonable appeal.	**59.14**
17. Failure to make accelerated payment. [*FA 2014, s 226*].	A 5% penalty applies if full amount not paid by due date. If amount remains unpaid five months after due date a penalty of 5% applies; a further 5% penalty applies if amount is still unpaid after a further six months.	**59.15**
18. Dishonest conduct by tax agents *FA 2012, Sch 38 para 26*.	Up to £50,000 (minimum £5,000).	**38.18** HMRC INVESTIGATORY POWERS
19. Tax agents: failure to comply with file access notice *FA 2012, Sch 38 paras 22, 23*.	(i) Initial penalty of £300.	**38.18** HMRC INVESTIGATORY POWERS
	(ii) If failure continues, a further penalty up to £60 per day.	
20. Powers of enforcement by deduction from accounts. [*F(No 2)A 2015, Sch 8*]. Various compliance failures or making disclosure likely to prejudice HMRC's ability to use the powers to recover the sum in question.	(i) Initial penalty of £300.	**59.16**

Offence	Penalty		Para
	(ii)	If failure continues, a further penalty up to £60 per day.	
21. Arrangments counteracted under the GAAR. A person is liable to a penalty if HMRC counteract a tax advantage by making adjustments under the general anti-abuse rule ('GAAR'). *FA 2013, ss 212A, 212B.*	60% of the counteracted advantage.		**59.17**
22. Penalties under the serial avoiders regime. [*FA 2016, Sch 18*]. Where a person suffers a defeat of an avoidance scheme used whilst in a warning period.	Penalty of 20% of the value of the counteracted advantage. If, before the relevant defeat is incurred, the person was liable to be given prior warning notices, the penalty is increased. It is increased to 40% where there has been a single prior warning notice, and to 60% where there has been more than one such notice.		**59.18**
23. Failure to comply with requirement to publish tax strategy. [*FA 2016, Sch 19*].	(i)	Initial penalty of £7,500.	**59.19**
	(ii)	If failure continues for six months, a further penalty of £7,500.	
	(iii)	If failure continues, a further penalty of £7,500 at the end of each subsequent month.	
24. Enabling offshore tax evasion *FA 2016, s 162, Sch 20*	Higher of 100% of the potential lost revenue and £3,000. If the original tax non-compliance resulted in a penalty under *FA 2015, Sch 21* (offshore asset moves), higher of 50% of the potential lost revenue in respect of the original tax non-compliance and £3,000.		**59.20**
25. Enablers of defeated abusive tax arrangements *F(No 2)A 2017, s 65, Sch 16*	The total amount or value of the consideration received or receivable by the enabler for anything done by him which enabled the arrangements.		**59.21**
26. Corporate interest restriction. Various penalties apply, including for failure to make a return, inaccurate returns and failure to keep and preserve records. *TIOPA 2010, Sch 7A*	Various		**59.22**, see also **65.21** RETURNS

Offence	Penalty		Para
27. Country-by-country reporting. Failure to file a report or provide additional supporting information after a request by HMRC or knowingly providing inaccurate information when filing a report or providing additional supporting information. *SI 2016 No 237*	Various		**72.13** TRANSFER PRICING
28. Failure to comply with EU disclosure rules for cross-border tax arrangements. Failure to comply with requirements under the rules. *SI 2020 No 25, Reg 14.*	(i)	Initial penalty of £5,000.	**36.15** HMRC — ADMINISTRATION
	(ii)	daily penalty of £600 (£5,000 in specified cases) during 'initial period' and continuing after penalty in (i) has been imposed.	
Failure by UK relevant taxpayer to make annual return		£5,000; increased to £7,500 for second such failure during the 36 months ending with date on which current failure began; increased to £10,000 for third or subsequent failure in 36-month period.	

Superseded penalties which are still relevant to the last five years are also described in this chapter.

For the procedure for charging penalties see **59.23** onwards below. See **59.31** below for potential liability under the criminal law.

Late submission and late payment penalties reform

FA 2021 introduced new penalty provisions for income tax, capital gains tax and VAT for late filing of return and late payment. Although the Government has indicated that it intends to extend the penalties to corporation tax 'at a later date', corporation tax is not included in the legislation introduced. Partnership returns are, however, included in the legislation.

For late filing, the basic framework of the new regime depends on a points system. Points will be accumulated for each return failure, but a penalty will only be charged once the total number of points reaches a threshold. Once a taxpayer has exceeded the threshold, penalties will continue to be charged until all outstanding returns are submitted and the taxpayer has not missed any further filing dates for a specified period.

For late payment, there will be a two-tiered penalty structure, with an initial penalty applying when payments are made within 15 days of the due date and a further penalty where payments are made 30 days or more after the due date. Penalties will not be charged where time to pay arrangements are in place.

See *FA 2021, ss 116, 117, Schs 24–26* and Tolley's Income Tax for details.

Situations giving rise to penalties

Failure to notify chargeability

[59.2] A penalty is chargeable for non-compliance with the requirement to notify HMRC of chargeability for an accounting period (see **65.4** RETURNS) under a unified penalty code for failures relating to a range of taxes. The code is described below, but only to the extent that it relates to corporation tax. The code also applies to failures by a company to notify HMRC that it is within the scope of DIVERTED PROFITS TAX (**30.14**).

A person is not liable to a penalty for a failure in respect of which he has been convicted of an offence.

Amount of penalty

The amount of the penalty depends on whether or not the failure is deliberate and is subject to reduction as detailed below.

For a deliberate and concealed failure (i.e. where the failure was deliberate and the taxpayer made arrangements to conceal the situation giving rise to the obligation), the penalty is 100% of the 'potential lost revenue' (see below).

For deliberate but not concealed failure (i.e. where the failure was deliberate but the taxpayer did not make arrangements to conceal the situation giving rise to the obligation), the penalty is 70% of the potential lost revenue.

For any other case, the penalty is 30% of the potential lost revenue.

Note that the increases to penalties relating to offshore matters which apply for income tax and capital gains tax purposes do not apply for corporation tax purposes.

The '*potential lost revenue*' is equal to the amount of tax payable for the accounting period that, by reason of the failure, remains unpaid 12 months after the end of the period. Tax payable is computed disregarding any deferred relief arising from the repayment of loans made to close company participators. The fact that potential lost revenue may be balanced by a potential overpayment by another person is ignored, except to the extent that that person's tax liability is required or permitted to be adjusted by reference to the taxpayer's.

No penalty is due in relation to a failure that is not deliberate if the taxpayer satisfies HMRC or, on appeal, the tribunal, that there is a reasonable excuse for the failure. Insufficiency of funds is not a reasonable excuse for this purpose and neither is the taxpayer's reliance on another person to do anything, unless he took reasonable care to avoid the failure. If the taxpayer had a reasonable excuse, he is treated as continuing to have a reasonable excuse after the excuse has ceased if the failure is remedied without unreasonable delay.

Reduction for disclosure

A reduction in a penalty will be given where the taxpayer discloses a failure to notify. The penalty will be reduced to a percentage which reflects the quality of the disclosure and the amount of the reduction will depend on whether the disclosure is 'prompted' or 'unprompted'.

In the case of an unprompted disclosure, a 100% penalty may not be reduced to a percentage below 30%, and a 70% penalty may not be reduced to a percentage below 20%. A 30% penalty may be reduced to any percentage, including 0%, unless HMRC do not become aware of the failure until 12 months after the time tax first becomes unpaid by reason of the failure, in which case the penalty may not be reduced below 10%.

In the case of a prompted disclosure, a 100% penalty may not be reduced to a percentage below 50%, a 70% penalty may not be reduced to a percentage below 35%, and a 30% penalty may not be reduced to a percentage below 10% (20% where HMRC do not become aware of the failure until 12 months after the time tax first becomes unpaid by reason of the failure).

A person is treated as making a disclosure for these purposes only if he tells HMRC about the failure, gives them reasonable help in quantifying the tax unpaid and allows them access to records for the purpose of checking how much tax is unpaid. A disclosure is '*unprompted*' if made when the taxpayer has no reason to believe HMRC have discovered or are about to discover the failure. In all other cases, disclosures are '*prompted*'.

Reduction in special circumstances

HMRC can also reduce, stay or agree a compromise in relation to proceedings for a penalty if they think it is right to do so because of special circumstances. Ability to pay and the fact that a potential loss of revenue from one taxpayer is balanced by a potential overpayment by another are not special circumstances for this purpose.

The power to further reduce a penalty in special circumstances can also be exercised by the First-tier Tribunal on appeal against a penalty [*FA 2008, Sch 41 para 19(3)*].

Reduction for other penalty or surcharge

The amount of a penalty in respect of a failure is reduced by the amount of any other penalty (see **42** INTEREST ON OVERDUE TAX), the amount of which is determined by reference to the same tax liability. No reduction is made for a penalty within **59.7** below, a tax-related penalty within **59.11** below or a penalty within **59.14** or **59.15** below.

Agents

A person is liable to a penalty under the above provisions where the failure is by a person acting on his behalf. He is not, however, liable to a penalty in respect of anything done or omitted by his agent, if he satisfies HMRC or, on appeal, the tribunal, that he took reasonable care to avoid the failure.

Company officers

Where a company is liable to a penalty under the above provisions for a deliberate failure and the failure was attributable to a company 'officer', the officer as well as the company is liable to pay the penalty (but not so that HMRC can claim more than 100% of the penalty).

HMRC can pursue the officer for such part (including all) of the penalty as they specify by written notice. That portion of the penalty is treated as a penalty for the purpose of these provisions. A further notice may be issued specifying an additional portion of the penalty. In relation to a body corporate, a director, shadow director or secretary of the company is an '*officer*'; in any other case, a director, manager, secretary or any other person managing or purporting to manage any of the company's affairs is an '*officer*'.

[*FA 2008, s 123, Sch 41 paras 1, 5–7, 11–15, 20–24; FA 2009, Sch 56 para 9A*].

See **59.26** below as regards reasonable excuse for failure.

Simon's Taxes. See **A4.540–A4.543, A6.202, D1.1301.**

Failure to make a return

[59.3] A company which fails to deliver to HMRC a company tax return for an accounting period on or before the filing date is liable to a penalty. A new unified penalty code for failures to make returns was introduced across a range of taxes from 2009 but has not been applied to company tax returns. It was originally expected that the code would be extended to such returns in 2015, but as the Government now intends to apply the *FA 2021* late filing penalty provisions (see **59.1** above) to corporation tax at a later date, it is unlikely that the unified code will come into force for corporation tax purposes. Both the existing code and the unified code are described below. Note that the unified code applies to returns under the construction industry scheme and annual tax on enveloped dwellings returns.

Current penalties

A company which fails to make a return for any period, when required to do so by notice (see **65.6** RETURNS), is liable to a penalty of £200 (£100 if the return is delivered within three months of the final day for delivery).

If the return period is one for which accounts are required under *Companies Act 2006*, penalties do not apply provided that the return is delivered by the last day for delivery of those accounts.

The penalties are increased to £1,000 and £500 respectively for failure in relation to a return for an accounting period where a penalty under these provisions was incurred for each of the two immediately preceding accounting periods, and the company was within the charge to corporation tax for the whole of the three accounting periods. (See *Lessex Ltd v Spence* [2004] STC (SCD) 79 where three successive defaults straddled the introduction of the self-assessment system applying to accounting periods ending on or after 1 July 1999 and a drafting error in *FA 1998, Sch 18 para 17(3)* was not considered to prevent the higher penalty from applying.)

An additional penalty is imposed, where the return is still outstanding at the later of the end of the final day for delivery of the return and 18 months after the end of the return period. The additional penalty is 10% of the tax unpaid at the time the penalty arises if the return is delivered within two years after the end of the return period, otherwise 20%. The tax taken into account for this purpose under self-assessment is the tax payable for the return period, disregarding any relief deferred under *CTA 2010, ss 458(5), 464B(5)* in respect of the repayment etc. of a loan to, or a benefit conferred on, a participator (see **16.15** CLOSE COMPANIES).

[*FA 1998, Sch 18 paras 17–19*].

By concession, for returns submitted before 1 April 2011, no flat-rate penalty is charged if the return is received by HMRC no later than the last business day within the seven days following the filing date. The concession is withdrawn for returns submitted after 31 March 2011. (HMRC Extra-Statutory Concession B46; HMRC Brief 24/10.)

Any extension of the time limit for making a return under *TMA 1970, s 118(2)* (see **59.26** below) must be agreed with HMRC in advance. (HMRC Company Tax Manual, CTM94130.)

See **59.26** below as regards reasonable excuse for failure.

In *Codu Computer Ltd v HMRC* [2011] UKFTT 186 (TC), a company (C) submitted two CT returns which HMRC rejected on the grounds that they were incomplete because the accounts and directors' report had not been signed. C subsequently submitted the returns online, after the prescribed filing dates. HMRC imposed penalties of £100 for each return under *FA 1998, Sch 18 para 17(2)*. C appealed, contending firstly that no penalty was due because it had originally submitted the returns within the statutory time limits (and alternatively that it had a reasonable excuse because it had not been aware that HMRC would reject the returns). The First-tier Tribunal accepted C's first contention and allowed the appeal. Judge Staker held that: 'in the absence of any evidence or authority having been submitted by HMRC in support of the contention that the appellant was required specifically to submit the relevant documents in signed format, the tribunal finds that HMRC have failed to discharge the burden of proving that the appellant did not submit valid returns within the applicable deadline'.

In *GV Cox Ltd v HMRC* [2011] UKFTT 311 (TC), a company did not post its corporation tax return for the year ending 31 May 2009 until 27 August 2010. HMRC did not receive the return until 6 September 2010. HMRC imposed a penalty of £200 under *FA 1998, Sch 18 para 17(2)(b)*. The company appealed, contending that the return had been submitted within three months of the filing date, so that the penalty should only be £100 (under *FA 1998, Sch 18 para 17(2)(a)*). The First-tier Tribunal rejected this contention and dismissed the appeal, observing that the effect of *Sch 18 para 17(2)(a)* was that the penalty was only £100 provided that the return was delivered within three months of the filing date. Judge Brooks held that, since the return had not been posted until Friday 27, August 2010, and the following Monday had been a bank holiday, the company could not have a reasonable expectation that HMRC would receive the return by Tuesday 31, August 2010.

In *AEI Group Ltd v HMRC*, [2015] UKFTT 290 (TC) the First-tier Tribunal partially allowed appeals against penalties for failure to file company tax returns. It is notable that the request to file was for the period prior to incorporation, and the Tribunal held that returns were not required to be filed for such periods. However, it also held that penalty notices were validly served even though they did not go to the company's place of business or registered office, and that there was no breach of human rights or reasonable excuse based on HMRC's request for returns from both the company and the company's UK agent.

Simon's Taxes. See **A4.557**.

Unified code

The penalties under the unified code are described below, but only to the extent that they would (if introduced) relate to corporation tax.

Where a return is required under *FA 1998, Sch 18 para 3* (corporation tax return — see **65.4** RETURNS), a penalty under the code is payable if the taxpayer fails to make or deliver the return to HMRC on or before the 'filing date'. For this purpose a requirement to make a return includes the requirement to deliver any accounts, statement or document which must be delivered with the return.

The '*filing date*' is the last day of whichever of the periods at **65.4**(a)–(c) RETURNS is the last to end. In the straightforward case, it will be the last day of the 12 months following the accounting period in question.

If a failure to make a return falls within the terms of more than one of the following penalties, the company is liable to each of those penalties (subject to the overall limit for tax-geared penalties below). A taxpayer is not liable to a penalty for a failure or action in respect of which he has been convicted of an offence.

Initial penalty

An initial penalty of £100 is payable for failure to make a return on or before the filing date.

Daily penalty

HMRC can impose a daily penalty where the company's failure to make the return continues after the end of three months beginning with the day after the filing date (the '*penalty date*').

The amount of the penalty is £10 for each day that the failure continues during the period of 90 days starting with a date specified by HMRC. HMRC must notify the company of the starting date, which date cannot be earlier than the end of the three months beginning with the penalty date. The date can, however, be earlier than the date of the notice.

First tax-geared penalty

If the failure continues after the end of six months starting with the penalty date the company is liable to a penalty equal to the greater of £300 and 5% of any tax liability which would have been shown in the return.

For this purpose (and that of the second tax-geared penalty below), the tax liability which would have been shown in a return is the amount which, had a correct and complete return been delivered on the filing date, would have been shown to be due and payable in respect of the tax for the period concerned. If a penalty is assessed before the return is made, HMRC must determine the tax liability to the best of their information and belief. Then, when the return is subsequently made, the penalty must be re-assessed by reference to the amount of tax shown in the return to be due and payable (but subject to any amendments or corrections to the return). Any deferred relief arising from the repayment of loans made to close company participators is disregarded.

Second tax-geared penalty

A further tax-geared penalty is payable if the failure continues to the end of 12 months starting with the penalty date. The amount of the penalty depends on whether or not, by failing to make the return, the taxpayer deliberately withholds information which would enable or assist HMRC to assess the tax liability. If there is deliberate withholding of information, the amount of the penalty further depends on whether the withholding is concealed.

The amount of the penalty is the greater of £300 and the percentage of the tax liability which would be shown in the return found using the table below.

	Percentage of tax liability
deliberate and concealed withholding of information	100
deliberate but not concealed withholding of information	70
any other	5

For this purpose, the withholding of information by a company is concealed if the company makes arrangements to conceal that it has been withheld.

Note that the increases to penalties relating to offshore matters which apply for income tax and capital gains tax purposes do not apply for corporation tax purposes.

Maximum tax-geared penalty

Where both the first and second tax-geared penalties are due in relation to the same tax liability, the total of those penalties cannot exceed the 100% limit.

Reasonable excuse

None of the above penalties are due in respect of a failure to make a return if the company satisfies HMRC or, on appeal, the Tribunal, that there is a reasonable excuse for the failure. Insufficiency of funds is not a reasonable excuse for this purpose and neither is the company's reliance on another person to do anything, unless it took reasonable care to avoid the failure. If the company had a reasonable excuse, it is treated as continuing to have a reasonable excuse after the excuse has ceased if the failure is remedied without unreasonable delay.

Reduction for disclosure

A reduction in the second tax-geared penalty above will be given where the company discloses information which has been withheld by a failure to make a return. The penalty will be reduced to a percentage which reflects the quality of the disclosure (including its timing, nature and extent) and the amount of the reduction will depend on whether the disclosure is 'prompted' or 'unprompted' and is subject to a minimum percentage. The minimum percentage (i.e. the percentage below which a penalty may not be reduced) is as follows. In all cases the amount of the penalty cannot be reduced below £300.

Standard percentage	Minimum percentage for prompted disclosure	Minimum percentage for unprompted disclosure
70	35	20
100	50	30

A company is treated as making a disclosure for these purposes only if it tells HMRC about the information, gives them reasonable help in quantifying the tax unpaid and allows them access to records for the purpose of checking how much tax is unpaid. A disclosure is '*unprompted*' if made when the company has no reason to believe HMRC have discovered or are about to discover the information. In all other cases, disclosures are '*prompted*'.

Reduction in special circumstances

HMRC can also reduce, stay or agree a compromise in relation to proceedings for a penalty if they think it is right to do so because of special circumstances. Ability to pay and the fact that a potential loss or revenue from one taxpayer is balanced by a potential overpayment by another are not special circumstances for this purpose.

Reduction for other penalty

The amount of a tax-geared penalty is reduced by the amount of any other penalty the amount of which is determined by reference to the same tax liability. No such reduction is made for another penalty under the above provisions (but see above for the maximum tax-geared penalty under these provisions), for a tax-related penalty for late payment of tax within **59.7** below or for a penalty within **59.14** or **59.15** below.

[*FA 2009, s 106, Sch 55 paras 1–6A, 14–17, 23–27*].

Careless or deliberate errors in documents

[59.4] The following provisions apply to a wide range of documents relating to both direct and indirect taxes which may be given by a taxpayer to HMRC, including the following which are relevant for the purposes of corporation tax:

- a company tax return under *FA 1998, Sch 18 para 3* (see **65.4** RETURNS);
- a return, statement or declaration in connection with a claim for an allowance, deduction or relief;
- accounts in connection with ascertaining liability to tax; and
- any other document (other than one in respect of which a penalty is payable under *TMA 1970, s 98* — see **59.8** below) likely to be relied on by HMRC to determine, without further inquiry, a question about the company's liability to tax, its payments by way of or in connection with tax, other payments (such as penalties) by the company or repayments or any other kind of payment or credit to it.

A penalty is payable by a company which gives HMRC such a document if it contains a careless or deliberate inaccuracy which amounts to, or leads to, an understatement of its, or another person's, tax liability or a false or inflated statement of a 'loss' or claim to 'repayment of tax'. If there is more than one inaccuracy in the document a penalty is payable for each inaccuracy. See **59.5** below for the penalty payable where an inaccuracy in a document is attributable to the supply of false information or the withholding of information by another person.

For this purpose, giving HMRC a document includes making a statement or declaration in a document and giving HMRC information in any form and by any method (including post, fax, e-mail or telephone). A '*loss*' includes a charge, expense, deficit or any other amount which may be available for, or relied on to claim, a deduction or relief. '*Repayment of tax*' includes allowing a credit against tax and payment of a 'corporation tax credit'. A '*corporation tax credit*' is a research and development tax credit (see **63.7** RESEARCH AND DEVELOPMENT EXPENDITURE), a research and development expenditure credit (see **63.10** RESEARCH AND DEVELOPMENT EXPENDITURE), a film, television, video game, theatre, orchestra or exhibition tax credit (see **26**, CREATIVE INDUSTRIES RELIEFS) or a first-year tax credit (see **10.25** CAPITAL ALLOWANCES ON PLANT AND MACHINERY).

A company is not liable to a penalty for an inaccuracy in respect of which it has been convicted of an offence.

Amount of penalty

The amount of the penalty depends on whether the inaccuracy is careless or deliberate and is subject to reduction as detailed below. For this purpose, an inaccuracy in a document which was neither careless nor deliberate is treated as careless if the company or a person acting on its behalf discovered the inaccuracy after giving HMRC the document but did not take reasonable steps to inform them. Reasonable steps to inform HMRC would, in their view, include consulting with an accountant or agent to discuss the position so that they can inform HMRC, or contacting HMRC directly to discuss the inaccuracy (HMRC Guidance Note, 1 April 2008).

The amount of the penalty (subject to the reductions below) is the percentage of the potential lost revenue found using the table below.

Type of action	Percentage of potential lost revenue
careless	30
deliberate but not concealed	70
deliberate and concealed	100

For this purpose, careless action occurs where the company or a person acting on its behalf failed to take reasonable care. HMRC consider that what constitutes 'reasonable care' has to be viewed in the light of each person's abilities and circumstances. They do not expect the same level of knowledge or expertise from an unrepresented self-employed individual as from a large multinational company. They expect a higher degree of care to be taken over large and complex matters than simple straightforward ones. In HMRC's view, it is reasonable to expect a person encountering a transaction or other event with which they are not familiar to take care to check the correct tax treatment or to seek suitable advice. (HMRC Brief 19/2008). In *Mariner v HMRC* FTT 2013; [2014] SFTD 504, a taxpayer who had relied on the professional advice of an accountant was held not to have been careless.

With effect in relation to documents given to HMRC on or after 16 November 2017 and relating to a tax period beginning on or after 6 April 2017 and ending on or after 16 November 2017, there is a presumption of carelessness where a document contains a non-deliberate inaccuracy as a result of its being submitted on the basis that particular 'avoidance arrangements' had an effect which in fact they did not have. The presumption is disapplied if the company satisfies HMRC or the Tribunal that it took reasonable care to avoid inaccuracy, but neither HMRC nor the Tribunal can take any account of any evidence of any reliance by the company on 'disqualified' advice.

Arrangements (as widely defined) are '*avoidance arrangements*' for this purpose if it would be reasonable to conclude that the obtaining of a tax advantage (also widely defined) was a main purpose of them. There is a let-out for arrangements which accord with established practice accepted by HMRC. Where arrangements are caught by specified anti-avoidance or anti-abuse legislation, they are automatically avoidance arrangements for this purpose, and the let-out does not apply.

Advice is '*disqualified*' if it: (i) was given to the company by an 'interested person'; or (ii) was given to the company as a result of arrangements between an interested person and the person who gave the advice; or (iii) was given by a person without the appropriate expertise; or (iv) did not take account of all the company's individual circumstances (so far as relevant); or (v) was addressed to, or given to, a person other than the company. However, the advice is not disqualified if, when the document is given to HMRC, the company has taken reasonable steps to find out whether or not the advice falls within any of (i) to (iii) and reasonably believes that it does not. There is a limited exemption for certain advice received in connection with 'avoidance-related rules' (as in **4.41** ANTI-AVOIDANCE). The question of whether the company has taken reasonable steps to find out whether or not advice is disqualified, and believes it not to be so, is judged as at the time when the document containing the inaccuracy is given to HMRC.

An '*interested person*' is one who participated in the avoidance arrangements or any transaction forming part of them, or one who, for consideration, facilitated the company's entering into the arrangements.

Prior to the above rules coming into effect, reliance on legal advice was disregarded in determining whether or not an inaccuracy was careless if the advice was given or procured by a monitored promoter (see **28.18** DISCLOSURE OF TAX AVOIDANCE SCHEMES onwards) and related to arrangements of which the monitored promoter was a promoter.

Deliberate but not concealed action occurs where the inaccuracy was deliberate but the company did not make arrangements to conceal it. Deliberate and concealed action occurs where the inaccuracy was deliberate and the company made arrangements to conceal it (for example, by submitting false evidence in support of an inaccurate figure).

It is important to ensure the penalty is determined under the appropriate category. In *Servbet v HMRC* [2015] UKFTT 130 the First-tier Tribunal reduced a penalty imposed under *FA 2007, Sch 24* on the basis that the error had been careless, rather than deliberate and concealed (as contended by HMRC). In addition the tribunal held the company had assisted HMRC and a further reduction was given.

Note that the increases to penalties relating to offshore matters which apply for income tax and capital gains tax purposes do not apply for corporation tax purposes.

Reduction for disclosure

A reduction in a penalty will be given where the company discloses an inaccuracy in a document. The penalty will be reduced to a percentage which reflects the quality of the disclosure and the amount of the reduction will depend on whether the disclosure is 'prompted' or 'unprompted' and is subject to a minimum percentage. The minimum percentage (i.e. the percentage below which a penalty may not be reduced) for each level of penalty is as follows.

Standard percentage	Minimum percentage for prompted disclosure	Minimum percentage for unprompted disclosure
30	15	0
70	35	20
100	50	30

A company is treated as making a disclosure for these purposes only if it tells HMRC about the inaccuracy, gives them reasonable help in quantifying the inaccuracy and allows them access to records for the purpose of ensuring that the inaccuracy is fully corrected. A disclosure is '*unprompted*' if made when the company has no reason to believe HMRC have discovered or are about to discover the inaccuracy. In all other cases, disclosures are '*prompted*'.

Reduction in special circumstances

HMRC can also reduce, stay or agree a compromise in relation to proceedings for a penalty if they think it is right to do so because of special circumstances. Ability to pay and the fact that a potential loss of revenue from one taxpayer is balanced by a potential overpayment by another are not special circumstances for this purpose. It is expected that this power will be used only in rare cases (see Treasury Explanatory Notes to the 2007 Finance Bill). See *Roche v HMRC* FTT, [2012] UKFTT 333 (TC); 2012 STI 2364 in which the Tribunal granted a reduction due to special circumstances where the taxpayer was suffering stress at the time of completing her return.

Reduction for other penalty or surcharge

The amount of a penalty in respect of a document relating to a particular tax year or accounting period is reduced by the amount of any other penalty, the amount of which is determined by reference to the same tax liability. Where a penalty is imposed under these provisions and those at **59.5** below in respect of the same inaccuracy, the aggregate of the penalties cannot exceed 100% of the potential lost revenue. No reduction is made for a tax-related penalty within **59.11** below or for a penalty within **59.14** or **59.15** below.

No reduction is made for a penalty within **59.7** below.

Potential lost revenue

The '*potential lost revenue*' is the additional tax due or payable as a result of correcting the inaccuracy in the document. This includes any amount payable to HMRC having been previously repaid in error and any amount which would have been repayable by HMRC had the inaccuracy not been corrected. Relief under *CTA 2010, s 458* (close company loans) and group relief are ignored (but this does not prevent a penalty being charged for an inaccurate claim for relief).

Where the amount of potential lost revenue depends on the order in which inaccuracies are corrected, careless inaccuracies are taken to be corrected before deliberate inaccuracies, and deliberate but not concealed inaccuracies are taken to be corrected before deliberate and concealed inaccuracies. Where there are inaccuracies in one or more documents relating to a particular accounting period and those inaccuracies include both understatements and overstatements, the overstatements are taken into account in calculating the potential lost revenue and are set off against understatements in the order which reduces the level of penalties the least (i.e. against understatements not liable to a penalty first, then against careless understatements, and so on). The fact that potential lost revenue may be balanced by a potential overpayment by another person is also ignored.

Special rules apply where an inaccuracy leads to there being a wrongly recorded loss which has not been wholly used to reduce a tax liability. The potential lost revenue in respect of that part of the loss which has not been so used is restricted to 10% of the unused part. Where, however, there is no reasonable prospect of a loss being used to support a claim to reduce a tax liability (of any person) because of the taxpayer's circumstances or the nature of the loss, the potential lost revenue is nil.

Where an inaccuracy results in an amount of tax being declared later than it would have been (otherwise than because of a wrongly recorded loss), the potential lost revenue is 5% of the delayed tax for each year of delay (applied pro rata for periods of less than a year).

Suspension of penalty

HMRC can suspend all or part of a penalty for a careless inaccuracy. A notice in writing must be given to the company setting out what part of the penalty is to be suspended, the period of suspension (maximum two years) and the conditions of suspension with which the company must comply. The conditions can specify an action to be taken and a period within which it must be taken. A penalty can be suspended only if compliance with a condition of suspension will help the company to avoid further penalties under these provisions.

A suspended penalty will become payable:

- at the end of the suspension period, if the company does not satisfy HMRC that the conditions have been complied with; and

- if, during the suspension period, the company incurs another penalty under these provisions.

Otherwise, the penalty is cancelled at the end of the suspension period.

Agents

A company is liable to a penalty under the above provisions where a document containing a *careless* inaccuracy is given to HMRC on its behalf. It is not, however, liable to a penalty in respect of anything done or omitted by its agent, if it satisfies HMRC that it took reasonable care to avoid inaccuracy.

Company officers

Where a company is liable to a penalty under the above provisions for a deliberate inaccuracy and the inaccuracy was attributable to a company 'officer', the officer is liable to pay such part (including all) of the penalty as HMRC specify by written notice. In relation to a body corporate (other than a limited liability partnership), a director, shadow director, manager or secretary of the company is an '*officer*'; in relation to a limited liability partnership, a member is an '*officer*'; and in any other case, a director, manager, secretary or any other person managing or purporting to manage any of the company's affairs is an '*officer*'. The procedures for charging penalties apply as if the part payable by the officer were itself a penalty.

Powers to amend provisions

The Treasury may by order make any incidental, supplemental, consequential, transitional, transitory or saving provision in connection with these provisions and those at **59.5** and **59.6** below.

[*FA 2007, s 97, Sch 24 paras 1, 3–12, 14, 18–28; FA 2009, Sch 56 para 9A; F(No 2)A 2017, s 64, Sch 6 para 8; SI 2011 No 976*].

Error in document attributable to another person

[59.5] Where a document (of a type listed at *FA 2007, Sch 24 para 1* (including those at **59.4** above)) given to HMRC contains an inaccuracy which amounts to, or leads to, an understatement of a tax liability or a false or inflated statement of a 'loss' or claim to 'repayment of tax', and the inaccuracy is attributable to a person deliberately supplying false information to the person giving the document to HMRC (whether directly or indirectly) or deliberately withholding information from that person, with the intention of the document containing the inaccuracy, a penalty is payable by the person supplying or withholding the information. See **59.4** above for the meaning of 'loss' and 'repayment of tax'.

The penalty is 100% of the potential lost revenue (defined as at **59.4** above, with the necessary modifications), subject to the same reductions that apply under the provisions at **59.4** above for special circumstances or disclosure. Where a penalty is imposed under these provisions and those at **51.19** above in respect of the same inaccuracy, see **59.4** above for the maximum aggregate of the penalties.

A person is not liable to a penalty for an inaccuracy in respect of which he has been convicted of an offence.

[*FA 2007, Sch 24 paras 1A, 4, 4B, 5, 7–12, 21*].

Failure to notify HMRC of error in assessment

[59.6] A penalty is payable by a company if an assessment issued to it by HMRC understates its liability to tax and the company or a person acting on its behalf has failed to take reasonable steps to notify HMRC of the under-assessment, within the 30 days beginning with the date of the assessment. This penalty applies also to determinations.

The penalty is 30% of the potential lost revenue (defined as at **59.4** above, with the necessary modifications), subject to the same reductions that apply under the provisions at **59.4** above for special circumstances or disclosure. HMRC must consider whether the company or a person acting on its behalf knew, or should have known, about the under-assessment and what steps would have been reasonable to take to notify HMRC.

A company is not liable to a penalty under this provision in respect of anything done or omitted by its agent, if it satisfies HMRC that it took reasonable care to avoid unreasonable failure to notify HMRC.

The amount of a penalty under this provision in respect of a document relating to a particular accounting period is reduced by the amount of any other penalty the amount of which is determined by reference to tax liability for the period (but see **59.4** above for exclusions from this rule).

A company is not liable to a penalty for a failure in respect of which it has been convicted of an offence.

[*FA 2007, s 97, Sch 24 paras 2, 4–12, 18, 21, 28*].

Failure to pay on time

[59.7] With two exceptions, there is in general currently no penalty for a failure to pay corporation tax on time (although interest on unpaid tax will be due (see **42** INTEREST ON OVERDUE TAX)). A unified penalty code for failures to pay tax on time has, however, been introduced in relation to a number of other taxes and was originally intended to be extended to corporation tax. As the Government now intends to apply the FA 2021 late payment penalty provisions (see **59.1** above) to corporation tax at a later date, it is unlikely that the unified code will come into force for corporation tax purposes generally. The code does, however, apply to corporation tax due under an exit charge payment plan, with effect where the first day after the period of nine months beginning immediately after the accounting period in question falls on or after 11 December 2012. The code also applies to DIVERTED PROFITS TAX (**30.18**). Corporation tax payable at the restitution interest rate was added to the code in 2015 but has not taken effect (as *Sch 56 para 4* is not yet in force). For details of the restitution interest rate regime, see further **1.7** INTRODUCTION: CHARGE TO TAX, RATE AND PROFIT COMPUTATIONS. A separate penalty may be charged in certain cases where a company fails to make a quarterly instalment payment of corporation tax on time (see further below).

A penalty is payable under the unified code if a taxpayer fails to make a payment of tax on or before the date specified in the table below. For the purposes of the following provisions, the 'penalty date' is the day after the table date.

	Amount of tax payable	Date after which penalty is incurred
1	Amount shown in company tax return.	The filing date for the tax return for the accounting period for which the tax is due (see **65.4** RETURNS).
2	Amount payable under quarterly accounting rules (see **58.3** PAYMENT OF TAX).	The filing date for the tax return for the accounting period for which the tax is due (see **65.4** RETURNS).
3	Amount payable under a determination of tax where no return is made on time.	The filing date for the tax return for the accounting period for which the tax is due (see **65.4** RETURNS).
4	Amount shown in an amendment or correction of a return.	30 days after the later of the due date and the date on which the amendment or correction is made.
5	Amount shown in an assessment or determination made by HMRC in circumstances other than where the taxpayer was required to make a return but failed to do so on time and that return, had it been made, would have shown an amount of tax payable.	30 days after the later of the due date and the date on which the assessment or determination is made.
6	Amount payable under a CT exit charge payment plan (see **58.19** PAYMENT OF TAX).	The later of the first day after the 12-month period beginning immediately after the migration accounting period and the date on which the amount is payable under the plan.
7	Amount of diverted profits tax payable under *FA 2015, Pt 3*, see further **30.18** DIVERTED PROFITS TAX.	The date when, in accordance with *FA 2015, s 98(2)* the amount must be paid (as charged by notice it must be paid within 30 days after the day the notice is issued).
8	Amount of corporation tax on restitution interest payable under *CTA 2010, s 357YQ*, on assessment by an officer of HMRC, see further **1.7** INTRODUCTION: CHARGE TO TAX, RATE AND PROFIT COMPUTATIONS.	By the end of the period of 30 days beginning with the date on which the company is given notice of assessment.

If a failure is within more than one of the above categories, a penalty is payable in respect of each such category.

Amount of penalty

Where a failure to pay tax on or before the relevant specified date occurs, the company is liable to an initial penalty of 5% of the unpaid tax.

If any of the tax remains unpaid after the end of the five months beginning with the penalty date (three months where the tax is within 1 or 2 above), the company is liable to an additional penalty of 5% of the amount remaining unpaid at that time. A further additional penalty becomes due if any of the tax is unpaid after the end of the 11 months (nine months where the tax is within 1 or 2 above) beginning with the penalty date, again equal to 5% of the amount remaining unpaid.

Reduction in special circumstances

HMRC can reduce, stay or agree a compromise in relation to proceedings for a penalty if they think it is right to do so because of special circumstances. Ability to pay and the fact that a potential loss of revenue from one taxpayer is balanced by a potential overpayment by another are not special circumstances for this purpose.

Suspension of penalty during time to pay agreement

A company is not liable to a penalty under the above provisions if, before the penalty arises, it makes a request to HMRC for the deferral of the tax concerned and HMRC agree (whether before or after the penalty date) to the deferral.

The company remains liable, however, for any penalty which arises after the end of the agreed deferral period. If the company breaks the agreement then it becomes liable to any penalty to which it would have been liable but for the agreement, provided that HMRC notify it to that effect. For this purpose, a company breaks an agreement if it fails to pay the tax when the deferral period ends or if it fails to comply with a condition forming part of the agreement.

Where a deferral agreement is varied, the above rules apply to the agreement as varied from the time of the variation.

Reasonable excuse

None of the above penalties are due in respect of a failure to make a payment if the company satisfies HMRC or, on appeal, the Tribunal, that there is a reasonable excuse for the failure. Insufficiency of funds is not a reasonable excuse for this purpose and neither is the company's reliance on another person to do anything, unless it took reasonable care to avoid the failure. If the company had a reasonable excuse, it is treated as continuing to have a reasonable excuse after the excuse has ceased if the failure is remedied without unreasonable delay.

In *Rodney Warren & Co v HMRC* (TC01754) [2012] UKFTT 57 (TC) a solicitor contended that he had a reasonable excuse because the Legal Services Commission had consistently paid his invoices late. The First-tier Tribunal rejected this contention and upheld the penalty.

In *PSC Photography v HMRC* [2014] UKFTT 926 it was held that the cancellation of a major contract and the subsequent change in banking arrangements were the direct causes of the company's cash flow problems, and this was a reasonable excuse for the late payment of PAYE.

In *The Bunker Secure Hosting v HMRC* [2015] UKFTT 146 the First-tier Tribunal found that being unaware of the penalty regime was not a reasonable excuse for late payment of PAYE and NIC. In *Sudar Shini Mahendran v HMRC*

[2015] UKFTT 278 the Tribunal accepted the taxpayer's arguments for reasonable excuse for late payment of CGT, where it was noted the taxpayer had taken reasonable care to avoid the failure by relying upon accountants and by providing them with any information requested and by chasing them on several occasions (the taxpayer had kept records of communications with her tax advisers).

Double jeopardy

No penalty arises for a failure or action in respect of which the company has been convicted of an offence.

[*FA 2009, Sch 56 paras 1–4, 9, 10, 16, 17; FA 2019, Sch 8 para 7*].

Quarterly instalment payments

Where a charge to interest arises as a result of a failure to pay a quarterly instalment payment of corporation tax and the company (or a person acting on its behalf) has deliberately or recklessly failed to make the payment, a penalty is imposed not exceeding twice the amount of the interest charge.

A similar penalty is imposed where a fraudulent or negligent claim is made for repayment of an instalment payment.

[*TMA 1970, s 59E(4); SI 1998 No 3175, Reg 13*].

Simon's Taxes. See **A4.560–A4.564.**

Special returns etc.

[59.8] Failure to render any information or particulars or any return, certificate, statement or other document which is required, whether by notice or otherwise, under the provisions listed in *TMA 1970, s 98* is the subject of a maximum penalty of £300, plus £60 for each day the failure continues after that penalty is imposed (but not for any day for which such a daily penalty has already been imposed). The maximum penalty for an incorrect return etc. given fraudulently or negligently is £3,000. Penalties for failure to render information etc. required by notice cannot be imposed after the failure is rectified, and daily penalties can similarly not be imposed where the information etc. was required other than by notice. [*TMA 1970, s 98*].

Failure to allow access to computers renders a person liable to a maximum £300 penalty. [*FA 2008, s 114*].

See **56.21** PARTNERSHIPS as regards penalties under *TMA 1970, s 98B* in relation to European Economic Interest Groupings.

See **20.5** CONSTRUCTION INDUSTRY SCHEME for penalties relating to sub-contractors in the construction industry.

See **59.26** below as regards reasonable excuse for failure.

Penalties for failure to keep records as required under *FA 1998, Sch 18 para 21* (see **65.13** RETURNS) apply of up to £3,000. [*FA 1998, Sch 18 para 23*].

Failure to keep records

[59.9] Penalties for failure to keep records as required under *FA 1998, Sch 18 para 21* (see **65.13** RETURNS) apply of up to £3,000. [*FA 1998, Sch 18 para 23*].

Failure to disclose tax avoidance schemes

[59.10] Penalties are chargeable for failures to comply with the following requirements under the disclosure provisions at **28.2–28.16** DISCLOSURE OF TAX AVOIDANCE SCHEMES:

(a) duty of promoter to notify HMRC of notifiable proposals or arrangements (*FA 2004, s 308(1)(3)*);
(b) duty of taxpayer to notify where the promoter is not UK-resident (*FA 2004, s 309(1)*);
(c) duty of parties to arrangements to notify where there is no promoter (*FA 2004, s 310*);
(d) duty of promoter to notify parties of the scheme reference number (*FA 2004, s 312(2)(2A)*);
(e) duty of client to notify parties (and, from 26 March 2015, employees) of the reference number (*FA 2004, s 312A(2)(2A)*);
(f) duty of client to provide information to promoter (*FA 2004, s 312B*);
(g) duty of promoter to provide details of clients (*FA 2004, s 313ZA*);
(h) enquiry following disclosure of client details (*FA 2004, s 313ZB*);
(i) duty of promoter to respond to enquiry (*FA 2004, ss 313A, 313B*);
(j) duty of introducer to give details of persons who have provided information or been provided with, information, (*FA 2004, s 313C*);
(k) duty to provide further information requested by HMRC (*FA 2004, s 310A*);
(l) duty to provide updated information (*FA 2004, s 310C*);
(m) duty to provide additional information with reference number (*FA 2004, s 316A*);
(n) duty or employer to notify HMRC of details of employees (*FA 2004, s 313ZC*);
(o) duty to provide further information requested by HMRC (*FA 2004, s 311C*); and
(p) duty to notify client of scheme reference number (*FA 2004, s 312ZA(2)*).

An initial penalty of up to £5,000 can be determined by the First-tier Tribunal for any failure to comply with one of the above duties. Where, however, the failure relates to (a)–(c), (k) or (o) above, the initial penalty is up to £600 per day during the period beginning with the day after that on which the time limit for complying with the requirement expires and ending with the earlier of the day on which the penalty is determined or the last day before the failure ceases. If the failure relates to (a)–(c) above, and a scheme reference number is subsequently allocated under **28.11**(b) DISCLOSURE OF TAX AVOIDANCE SCHEMES, the failure is treated as ceasing on the day before the number is allocated (if it has not already done so). The amount of the daily penalty must be arrived at after taking account of all relevant considerations, including the desirability of deterring repeated failures and having regard to the amount of fees likely to be received or the tax saving sought by the taxpayer. If the daily penalty appears to the

Tribunal to be inappropriately low, it can be increased to an amount not exceeding £1 million. Where HMRC consider that a daily penalty has been determined to run from a date later than it should, they can commence proceedings for a redetermination of the penalty. This could happen where the failure was in response to an order under *FA 2004, s 306A* for a proposal or arrangements to be treated as notifiable (see **28.15** DISCLOSURE OF TAX AVOIDANCE SCHEMES), so that the initial time limit for compliance was ten days after the giving of the order. If it subsequently becomes clear that the proposal or arrangements were notifiable from the outset, the date by reference to which the penalty should have applied would be considerably earlier.

A further penalty or penalties of up to £600 applies for each day on which the failure continues after the initial penalty is imposed.

Higher maximum daily penalties of up to £5,000 apply where:

(i) an order has been made under *FA 2004, s 306A* (order by Tribunal to treat proposal or arrangements as notifiable); or

(ii) there is a failure to comply with an order made under *FA 2004, s 314A* (order by the Tribunal to make a disclosure).

The increased maximum only applies to days falling after the period of ten days beginning with the date of the order.

Where an order is made under *FA 2004, s 314A* or *FA 2004, s 306A*, the person mentioned in the order cannot rely on doubt as to notifiability as a reasonable excuse after the period of ten days beginning with the date of the order and any delay in compliance after that time is unreasonable unless there is another excuse.

Parties to notifiable arrangements who fail to notify HMRC of the scheme reference number etc. are liable to a penalty of up to £5,000 in respect of each scheme to which the failure relates. The penalty is increased for a second failure, occurring within three years from the date on which the first failure began, to up to £7,500 in respect of each scheme to which the failure relates (whether or not the same as the scheme to which the first failure relates). Any further such failures occurring within three years from the date on which the previous failure began, result in a penalty of up to £10,000 in respect of each scheme to which the failure relates (whether or not the same as the schemes to which any of the previous failures relates).

Where a person fails to comply with a duty within (b) above and the promoter is a 'monitored promoter' for the purposes of the high-risk promoter provisions at **28.18** DISCLOSURE OF TAX AVOIDANCE SCHEMES onwards or with a duty within (c) above where the arrangements concerned are arrangements of a monitored promoter, then legal advice which the person took into account is disregarded in determining whether he has a reasonable excuse if the advice was given or procured by that monitored promoter. In determining whether a monitored promoter has a reasonable excuse for a failure to comply with a duty within (a) to (j) above, reliance on legal advice is taken automatically not to be a reasonable excuse if either the advice was not based on a full and accurate description of the fact or the conclusions in the advice were unreasonable.

The Treasury has the power to amend the £5,000, £600 and £1 million limits above by statutory instrument.

Interest on penalties

With effect from 1 June 2019, interest on a penalty under the above provisions is charged in accordance with *FA 2009, s 101*. Previously, interest was charged at the rate applicable under *FA 1989, s 178*, from the date on which the penalty is determined until payment.

[*TMA 1970, s 98C; FA 2021, Sch 31 para 42; SI 2004 No 1864, Reg 8B; SI 2012 No 1836, Reg 16; SI 2019 No 918*].

Penalties in respect of investigatory powers under FA 2008, Sch 36

[59.11] The penalties below apply to offences under the investigatory powers of *FA 2008, Sch 36* (see **38.3** HMRC INVESTIGATORY POWERS).

Failure to comply — fixed and daily penalties

Where a person (P) fails to comply with an information notice within *FA 2008, Sch 36 Pt 1* (see **38.4 HMRC** INVESTIGATORY POWERS) P is liable to a fixed penalty of £300 and, for each subsequent day of continuing failure, a further penalty not exceeding £60. If the failure continues for more than 30 days beginning with the date on which notice of an assessment to a daily penalty is given, an HMRC officer may make an application to the Tribunal for an increased daily penalty. Such an application can only be made if P has been told that it may be made. If the Tribunal decides that an increased daily penalty should apply, it must also determine the day from which it will apply. Subject to a maximum of £1,000 per day the Tribunal, in determining the amount of the increased penalty, must have regard to the likely cost to P of complying with the notice and any benefits to P or anyone else of non-compliance. Before 10 June 2021, the procedure for imposing an increased daily penalty was slightly different. The Tribunal imposed the increased penalty directly by way of an HMRC notice (rather than HMRC assessing the increased penalty determined by the Tribunal) and the day on which the increase took effect was determined by HMRC in that notice.

For this purpose, failing to comply with a notice includes concealing, destroying or otherwise disposing of, or arranging for the concealment, destruction or disposal of, a document in breach of *FA 2008, Sch 36 paras 42, 43* (see **38.9** HMRC INVESTIGATORY POWERS).

Where a person deliberately obstructs an HMRC officer in the course of an inspection of business premises under *FA 2008, Sch 36 Pt 2* (see **38.10** HMRC INVESTIGATORY POWERS) which has been approved by the First-tier Tribunal he is liable to a fixed penalty of £300 and, for each subsequent day of continuing obstruction, a further penalty not exceeding £60.

No penalty is due where a person fails to do anything required to be done within a limited time period if he does it within such further time as an HMRC officer allows. A person is not liable to a penalty if he satisfies HMRC or (on appeal) the First-tier Tribunal that there is a reasonable excuse for the failure or obstruction. An insufficiency of funds is not a reasonable excuse for this purpose unless it is attributable to events outside the person's control. Where a person relies on another person to do anything, that is not a reasonable excuse unless the first person took reasonable care to avoid the failure or obstruction. Where a person has a reasonable excuse which ceases, he is treated as continuing to have a reasonable excuse if the failure is remedied or the obstruction stops without unreasonable delay.

The Treasury can make regulations amending the amounts of the above penalties.

[*FA 2008, s 108, Sch 36 paras 39–41, 44, 45, 49A, 49B; FA 2021, Sch 34 paras 5, 6*].

In *Qubic Tax Ltd v HMRC*, FTT [2020] SFTD 769, a company appealed against an information notice given during enquiries into its corporation tax returns. The FTT rejected the appeal but allowed the company's appeal against initial and daily penalties for failure to comply with an information notice. The penalties had been issued after the company had appealed against the information notice but before it had received HMRC's review conclusion letter and before the hearing into its appeal against the notice. The FTT held that it must be reasonable not to comply with a notice while it is being challenged in the Tribunal or in the courts. Otherwise, any such appeals would be 'rendered nugatory'. The company therefore had a reasonable excuse for not complying and the appeal was upheld.

The FTT also upheld an appeal against a penalty for failure to comply with an information notice in *Ahmed v HMRC* FTT, [2020] UKFTT 337 (TC); 2020 SWTI 1900. The information required under the notice merely repeated that required by two earlier notices in respect of which the time limit for issuing a penalty had expired. It was not possible for HMRC to refresh the time limit by issuing a new notice.

Failure to comply—tax-related penalty

A tax-related penalty may be imposed by the Upper Tribunal where a person's failure or obstruction continues after a fixed penalty has been imposed under the above provisions. An HMRC officer must have reason to believe that the amount of tax that that person has paid, or is likely to pay is significantly less than it would otherwise have been as a result of the failure or obstruction, and the officer must make an application to the Upper Tribunal before the end of the 12 months beginning with the 'relevant date'. In deciding the amount of the penalty (if any), the Upper Tribunal must have regard to the amount of tax which has not been, or is likely not to be, paid by the person.

The '*relevant date*' is the date on which the person became liable to the penalty. Where, however, the penalty is for a failure relating to an information notice against which a person can appeal, the relevant date is the later of the end of the period in which notice of such appeal could have been given and, where an appeal is made, the date on which the appeal is determined or withdrawn.

A tax-related penalty is in addition to the fixed penalty and any daily penalties under the above provisions. No account is taken of a tax-related penalty for the purposes of **59.27** below and no reduction in a penalty charged under *FA 2007, Sch 24* (see **51.19–51.26** above) or *FA 2008, Sch 41* (see **51.3** above) is to be made in respect of a penalty under these provisions.

A penalty under these provisions was imposed in *HMRC v Tager* CA, [2018] STC 1755.

[*FA 2008, Sch 36 para 50*].

Failure to comply with requirement not to disclose third party notice or financial institution notice

A penalty of £1,000 applies for failure to comply with a requirement in a third party notice or financial institution notice not to disclose the notice or anything related to it to the taxpayer or any other person. The Treasury can make regulations amending the amounts of the penalty. [*FA 2008, Sch 36 paras 41, 51B(1)(4); FA 2021, Sch 34 para 2*].

Inaccurate information or documents

A penalty not exceeding £3,000 applies if, in complying with an information notice, a person provides inaccurate information or produces a document that contains an inaccuracy. The penalty is due if the inaccuracy is careless (i.e. due to a failure to take reasonable care) or deliberate; or the person complying with the notice later discovers the inaccuracy and fails to take reasonable steps to inform HMRC; or, for inaccuracies in information or documents provided on or after 1 April 2012, knows of the inaccuracy at the time the information or document is provided but does not inform HMRC at that time. If the information or document contains more than one inaccuracy, a penalty is payable for each of them.

The Treasury can make regulations amending the amounts of the above penalties.

[*FA 2008, Sch 36 paras 40A, 41*].

A person is not liable to a penalty under any of the above provisions in respect of anything for which he has been convicted of an offence. [*FA 2008, Sch 36 para 52*].

Simon's Taxes. See A6.316.

Penalties in respect of data-gathering powers under FA 2011, Sch 23

[59.12] The penalties below apply to offences under the data-gathering powers of *FA 2011, Sch 23* (see **38.12** HMRC INVESTIGATORY POWERS).

Failure to comply

Where a person fails to comply with a data-holder notice he is liable to a fixed penalty of £300. If the failure continues after the data-holder has been notified of the assessment of the penalty he is liable, for each subsequent day of continuing failure, to a further penalty not exceeding £60. If the failure continues for more than 30 days beginning with the date on which notice of an assessment to a daily penalty is given, an HMRC officer may make an application to the Tribunal for an increased daily penalty. Such an application can only be made if the data-holder has been told that it may be made. If the Tribunal decides to impose an increased daily penalty, that penalty replaces the £60 daily penalty with effect for the day determined by the Tribunal and specified in HMRC's notice to the data-holder of the increased penalty and each subsequent day of continuing failure. Subject to a maximum of £1,000 per day the Tribunal, in determining the amount of the increased penalty, must have regard to the likely cost to the data-holder of complying with the notice and any benefits to the data-holder or anyone else of the data-holder not complying.

For this purpose, failing to comply with a notice includes concealing, destroying or otherwise disposing of, or arranging for the concealment, destruction or disposal of, a 'material document'. A document is a '*material document*' if a data-holder notice has been given in respect of it or of data contained in it or if an HMRC officer has informed the data-holder that such a notice will be or is likely to be given. Once a notice has been complied with, the documents concerned are no longer material documents unless HMRC notify the data-holder in writing that the document must be preserved; in such circumstances the document continues to be a material document until HMRC's notification is withdrawn. If no data-holder notice is made within six months after the data-holder was last informed that a data-holder notice was to be made, any relevant documents cease to be material documents.

No penalty is due where a person fails to do anything required to be done within a limited time period if he does it within such further time as an HMRC officer allows. A person is not liable to a penalty if he satisfies HMRC or (on appeal) the First-tier Tribunal that there is a reasonable excuse for the failure. An insufficiency of funds is not a reasonable excuse for this purpose unless it is attributable to events outside the person's control. Where a person relies on another person to do anything, that is not a reasonable excuse unless the first person took reasonable care to avoid the failure. Where a person has a reasonable excuse which ceases, he is treated as continuing to have a reasonable excuse if the failure is remedied without unreasonable delay.

The Treasury can make regulations amending the amounts of the above penalties.

[*FA 2011, s 86, Sch 23 paras 30, 31, 33, 34, 38, 39, 41, 65; FA 2016, s 177(2)(3)*].

Inaccurate data

A penalty not exceeding £3,000 applies if, in complying with a data-holder notice, a person provides inaccurate data. The penalty is due if either the inaccuracy is due to a failure to take reasonable care or is deliberate, if the data-holder knows of the inaccuracy at the time the data is provided but does not inform HMRC at that time, or he later discovers the inaccuracy and fails to take reasonable steps to inform HMRC.

The Treasury can make regulations amending the amounts of the above penalty.

[*FA 2011, Sch 23 paras 32, 41, 65*].

A person is not liable to a penalty under any of the above provisions in respect of anything for which he has been convicted of an offence. [*FA 2011, Sch 23 para 42*].

Simon's Taxes. See A6.330–A6.337.

High-risk promoters of avoidance schemes

[59.13] Penalties are chargeable for failure to comply with any duty imposed under the high-risk promoters of avoidance schemes provisions at 28.18–28.31 DISCLOSURE OF TAX AVOIDANCE SCHEMES. The maximum penalty for failure to comply with each duty is set out in the table below.

	Provision or duty	Maximum penalty
1	Promotion of arrangements or proposal of a type specified in a stop notice issued on or after 10 June 2021 (*FA 2014, s 236B(1)*)	The sum of £100,000 per stop notice plus £5,000 for each person to whom arrangements or proposal were promoted (and see further below)
2	Requirement to notify persons who are subject to a stop notice issued on or after 10 June 2021 (*FA 2014, s 236B(3)(a)(4)(a)(5(a)*)	£10,000
3	Requirement to notify HMRC of persons who are subject to a stop notice issued on or after 10 June 2021 (*FA 2014, s 236B(3)(b)(4)(b)(5(b)*)	£25,000
4	Duty to make quarterly return to HMRC (*FA 2014, s 236C(1)*)	£5,000
5	Requirement to notify clients and intermediaries of stop notice issued on or after 10 June 2021 (*FA 2014, s 236J(1)*)	£5,000
6	Duty to notify clients of monitoring notice (*FA 2014, s 249(1)*)	£5,000
7	Duty to publicise monitoring notice (*FA 2014, s 249(3)*)	£1,000,000
8	Duty to include information in correspondence etc. (*FA 2014, s 249(10)*)	£1,000,000
9	Duty of promoter to notify client of reference number (*FA 2014, s 251*)	£5,000
10	Duty of others to notify clients and intermediaries of reference number (*FA 2014, s 252*)	£5,000
11	Duty to notify HMRC of reference number (*FA 2014, s 253*)	(a) £5,000 unless (b) or (c) apply;
		(b) £7,500 where the person has previously failed to comply with the duty once during the 36 months before the current failure;
		(c) £10,000 where the person has previously failed to comply with the duty two or more times during the 36 months before the current failure.
12	Duty to provide information or produce document (*FA 2014, s 255*)	£1,000,000

	Provision or duty	Maximum penalty
13	Ongoing duty to provide information or produce document (*FA 2014, s 257*)	£1,000,000
14	Duty of person dealing with non-resident promoter (*FA 2014, s 258*)	£1,000,000
15	Duty of monitored promoter to provide information about clients (*FA 2014, s 259*)	£5,000
16	Duty of intermediary to provide information about clients (*FA 2014, s 260*)	£5,000
17	Duty to provide information about clients following enquiry (*FA 2014, s 261*)	£10,000
18	Duty to provide information required to monitor conduct notice (now repealed) (*FA 2014, s 262*)	£5,000
19	Duty to provide information about address (*FA 2014, s 263*)	£5,000
20	Duty to provide information to promoter (*FA 2014, s 265*)	£5,000
21	Duty to comply with an information notice under *FA 2008, Sch 36 para 1* (as it applies as a result of *FA 2014, s 272A*)	£5,000 or, where the failure is by a person subject to a monitoring notice or a person who controls or has significant influence over such a person, £1,000,000
22	Duty to comply with a notice under *FA 2008, Sch 36 paras 2, 5* or *5A* (as they apply as a result of *FA 2014, s 272A*)	£300

A penalty is also chargeable for deliberately obstructing an HMRC officer carrying out an inspection under *FA 2008, Sch 36 para 10* (as it applies as a result of *FA 2014, s 272A*) which has been approved by the Tribunal. The maximum penalty is £5,000 or, where the obstruction is by a person subject to a monitoring notice or a person who controls or has significant influence over such a person, £1,000,000.

For failures within 1 above, the amounts by reference to which the maximum penalty is calculated are increased to £250,000 and £10,000 where the failure is by a person who is subject to a monitoring notice or by a person who controls, or has significant influence over, a person subject to a monitoring notice. If the maximum penalty so calculated appears inappropriately low (taking into account all relevant considerations (see below)), the maximum is calculated using an amount of £1,000,000 instead of £250,000.

For failures within 4 above, the maximum penalty specified is a maximum which may be imposed for each failure to provide the required information about a client and for each day on which a complete return is not provided after the time limit for doing so.

For failures within 2, 3, 5, 6, 9, 10, 15 or 16 above, the maximum penalty specified is a maximum which may be imposed on each person to whom the failure relates.

The amount of the penalty actually imposed must be arrived at after taking account of all relevant considerations, including the desirability of setting it at a level which appears appropriate for deferring the person on whom it is imposed, or other persons, from similar future failures. In particular, regard must be had to the amount of fees received and the tax advantage gained or sought.

If the failure to comply with a duty within 12–19, 21 or 22 above continues after a penalty has been imposed, a further daily penalty not exceeding £600 or, where the initial maximum penalty was £1,000,000, £10,000 may be imposed for each day on which the failure continues after the day on which the initial penalty was imposed.

A failure to do anything required to be done within a limited time period does not give rise to a penalty under these provisions if the duty is complied with within such further time as HMRC or the Tribunal have allowed.

Reasonable excuse

No penalty arises under the above provisions if there is a reasonable excuse for the failure. Insufficiency of funds is not a reasonable excuse for this purpose unless attributable to events outside the control of the person who failed to comply with the duty, and neither is that person's reliance on another person to do anything, unless he took reasonable care to avoid the failure. If the person had a reasonable excuse, he is treated as continuing to have a reasonable excuse after the excuse has ceased if the failure is remedied without unreasonable delay. Reliance by a monitored promoter on legal advice is automatically taken not to constitute a reasonable excuse if either it was not based on a full and accurate description of the facts or the conclusions in the advice that the promoter relied on were unreasonable. Reliance on legal advice is also automatically taken not to constitute a reasonable excuse for failure to comply with a duty within 9 above if the advice was given or procured by the monitored promoter.

Inaccurate information and documents

Where a person provides inaccurate information or produces a document which contains an inaccuracy in complying with a duty within 4, 12–19, 21 or 22 above or a requirement to provide evidence under *FA 2014, s 236D(2)(d)* or *s 236F(3)(c)* (see **28.22** DISCLOSURE OF TAX AVOIDANCE SCHEMES), the person is liable to a penalty if:

(a) the inaccuracy is careless or deliberate; or
(b) the person knows of the inaccuracy at the time of providing the information or producing the document but does not inform HMRC at that time; or
(c) the person subsequently discovers the inaccuracy and fails to take reasonable steps to inform HMRC.

In (a) above, an inaccuracy is careless if it is due to a failure by the person to take reasonable care. In determining whether or not a monitored promoter took reasonable care, reliance on legal advice is disregarded if either it was not based on a full and accurate description of the facts or the conclusions in the advice that the promoter relied on were unreasonable. Reliance on legal advice is disregarded in determining whether or not a person complying with a duty within 14 above took reasonable care if the advice was given or procured by the monitored promoter.

The maximum penalty is:

- £1,000,000 where the duty is within 12–14 above or is within 21 or 22 above and falls on a person subject to a monitoring notice;
- £10,000 where the duty is within 17 above; or
- £5,000 where the duty is within 4, 15, 16 or 18–19 above, where the duty is within 21 or 22 above and falls on a person not subject to a monitoring notice or where the penalty relates to the provision of evidence under *FA 2014, s 236D(2)(d)* or *s 236F(3)(c)*.

If the information or document contains more than one inaccuracy, only one penalty is payable.

Interaction with other penalties etc.

A person is not liable to a penalty under these provisions for anything in respect of which he has been convicted of an offence.

A person is not liable to a penalty under the provisions at **59.4** and **59.10** above or under any other provision prescribed by statutory instrument by reason of any failure to include in any return or account a reference number required by *FA 2014, s 253* (see 6 above).

Procedure

Penalties under the above provisions are imposed by the Tribunal, using the procedure in **59.23** below. This does not apply, however, to the following penalties; such penalties are instead imposed by HMRC using the procedure at **59.23** below:

- daily penalties for continuing failure to comply with a duty where the maximum penalty is £600;
- a penalty for a failure within 1 above, except where HMRC seek to apply a maximum penalty calculated by reference to £1,000,000;
- a penalty for a failure within 2–5 or 22 above;
- a penalty for a failure within 21 above, except where the maximum penalty is £1,000,000.

Interest on penalties

Interest on a penalty under the above provisions is charged in accordance with *FA 2009, s 101*. Before 1 June 2019, interest was charged at the rate applicable under *FA 1989, s 178*, from the date on which the penalty is determined until payment.

Power to change amount of penalties

The Treasury may, by statutory instrument, change the maximum penalties under the above provisions.

[FA 2014, Sch 35 paras 1–5, 8–13; FA 2019, s 88(3); FA 2021, Sch 30 para 8; SI 2019 No 921].

Follower notices

[59.14] HMRC may charge a penalty where a person fails to take corrective action under a follower notice (see **4.29** ANTI-AVOIDANCE). The maximum penalty is now 30% of the value of the denied tax advantage but for penalties assessed before 10 June 2021, the maximum was 50%. Where such a penalty is assessed on or after 10 June 2021, an additional penalty of up to 20% of the value of the denied tax advantage may be charged where the taxpayer or their representative is found to have acted unreasonably in bringing or conducting an appeal to the tribunal relating to the arrangements which are the subject of the follower notice.

Failure to comply with a follower notice

Where a person who has been given a follower notice fails to take the necessary corrective action before the specified time, that person is liable to a penalty of 30% of the value of the denied tax advantage. If, before the specified time, the person takes the necessary corrective action in respect only of part of the denied tax advantage, the penalty is 50% of the value of the remainder of the advantage. In the case of a partnership follower notice, each person who was a partner during the period for which the return in question was required is liable to the penalty, but the maximum is only 12% of the value of the advantage (or remainder). Each partner is only liable for a share of the penalty in proportion to the profit-sharing arrangements for the period or, if HMRC do not have sufficient information to make such an apportionment, as determined by HMRC.

For penalties assessed before 10 June 2021, the penalty was 50% of the value of the denied tax advantage (or remainder) or 20% in the case of a partnership follower notice.

The value of the denied tax advantage for this purpose is the additional amount of tax due or payable as a result of counteracting the advantage, including any amount payable having been erroneously repaid by HMRC and any amount which would have been repayable by HMRC if the advantage were not counteracted. Relief under *CTA 2010, s 458* (repayment of loan etc. by participator in a close company) and group relief are ignored (subject to the exception below).

Where the denied tax advantage resulted in a wrongly recorded loss which has been partly used to reduce the tax due or payable, the value of the denied advantage is increased by 10% of the part of the loss not so used. This rule applies both where the entire loss is attributable to the denied advantage and where only part of the loss is so attributable (but in the latter case, the rule applies only to that part). Where a denied advantage creates or increases an aggregate loss recorded for a group of companies group relief may be taken into account. To the extent that, because of its nature or the taxpayer's circumstances, there is no reasonable prospect of a loss resulting from a denied advantage being used to reduce a tax liability of any person, the value of the denied advantage is nil.

To the extent that the denied advantage is a deferral of tax (other than one resulting from a loss), the value of it is 25% of the amount of deferred tax for each year of deferral and a proportion of 25% for any separate period of deferral which is less than a year. The value cannot exceed 100% of the deferred tax.

HMRC may reduce the amount of a penalty to reflect the quality (including the timing, nature and extent) of any co-operation by the taxpayer. The maximum reduction is to 10% of the value of the denied advantage, or 4% in the case of a partnership notice. A taxpayer co-operates only if he does one or more of the following:

- providing HMRC with reasonable assistance in quantifying the tax advantage;
- counteracting the denied tax advantage;
- providing HMRC with information enabling corrective action to be taken by HMRC;
- providing HMRC with information enabling them to enter an agreement with the taxpayer for the purpose of counteracting the denied advantage; and
- allowing HMRC to access tax records to ensure that the denied advantage is fully counteracted.

A penalty was set aside in *Corrado v HMRC* FTT, [2019] UKFTT 275 (TC); 2019 SWTI 1129 on the grounds that the taxpayer had a reasonable belief that he had taken corrective action.

Additional penalty for unreasonable appeal

Where a person (P) has been assessed, on or after 10 June 2021, to a penalty for failure to comply with a follower notice, P is liable to an additional penalty if P or P's representative is found to have acted unreasonably in bringing or conducting appeal proceedings which relate to the arrangements which are the subject of the follower notice. The proceedings in question may be before the First-tier Tribunal or, on further appeal, the Upper Tribunal.

P or P's representative is treated as being found to have acted unreasonably only if either:

- the proceedings are struck out because there is no reasonable prospect of the appeal succeeding or because of something that P or P's representative has done or not done; or
- the Tribunal, on HMRC's application, makes a declaration that P or P's representative acted unreasonably in bringing or conducting the proceedings.

The finding of unreasonableness is treated as made when either the time limit for making an appeal against the striking out or declaration expires or, if such an appeal has been made, when the appeal is finally determined, withdrawn or otherwise disposed of.

The amount of the penalty is 20% of the value of the denied advantage (defined as above) or, if P takes the necessary corrective action in respect of part of the denied tax advantage before the finding of unreasonableness is treated as made,

20% of the value of the remainder of the advantage. In the case of a partnership follower notice, each person who was a partner during the period for which the return in question was required is liable to the penalty, but the amount of the penalty is only 8% of the value of the advantage (or remainder). Each partner is only liable for a share of the penalty in proportion to the profit-sharing arrangements for the period or, if HMRC do not have sufficient information to make such an apportionment, as determined by HMRC. HMRC cannot reduce the penalty for co-operation.

Interaction with other penalties

Where a taxpayer incurs a penalty for failure to take corrective action and a penalty under *FA 2007, Sch 24* (see **59.4** above), *FA 2008, Sch 41* (see **59.2** above), *FA 2009, Sch 55* (see **59.3** above), *FA 2013, s 212A* (see **59.17** below) or *FA 2016, Sch 18* (see **59.18** below) in respect of the same amount of tax, the aggregate amount of those penalties, together with the amount of any additional penalty for an unreasonable appeal, is restricted to a maximum of the highest percentage of the amount of tax chargeable under any of the provisions (subject to a minimum limit of 100%). Where one of the penalties is a penalty of £300 under *FA 2009, Sch 55*, the maximum aggregate penalty is £300 if that is greater.

[*FA 2014, ss 208(2), 208A, 209, 210, 212, Sch 30, Sch 31 paras 4(2), 4A, 5(2)–(6); FA 2021, Sch 28 paras 2, 3, 5, 10–12, 14–16*].

Failure to make accelerated payment

[59.15] Where a person who has been given an accelerated payment notice or partner payment notice (see **4.33** ANTI-AVOIDANCE) fails to pay any amount of the accelerated payment within the time limit (see **4.35** ANTI-AVOIDANCE) an initial penalty of 5% of that amount is chargeable. If any amount is still unpaid at the end of the period of five months beginning with the day after the day on which the time limit expired (the '*penalty day*'), a further penalty of 5% of that amount is chargeable. A further 5% penalty applies to any amount remaining unpaid after the end of the eleven months beginning with the penalty day.

Any additional tax arising from the amendment of an accelerated payment notice as a result of the amendment of a partnership return under *TMA 1970, s 12ABZB* (amendment following tribunal determination of partners' shares) is ignored for these purposes (and for the purposes of any other penalty for non-payment or late payment of tax).

Reduction in special circumstances

HMRC can reduce, stay or agree a compromise in relation to proceedings for a penalty if they think it right to do so because of special circumstances. Ability to pay and the fact that a potential loss of revenue from one taxpayer is balanced by a potential overpayment by another are not special circumstances for this purpose.

Suspension of penalty during time to pay agreement

A taxpayer is not liable to a penalty under the above provisions if, before the penalty arises, he makes a request to HMRC for the deferral of the payment concerned and HMRC agree (whether before or after the penalty date) to the deferral.

The taxpayer remains liable, however, for any penalty which arises after the end of the agreed deferral period. If the taxpayer breaks the agreement then he becomes liable to any penalty to which he would have been liable but for the agreement, provided that HMRC notify him to that effect. For this purpose, a taxpayer breaks an agreement if he fails to pay the accelerated payment when the deferral period ends or if he fails to comply with a condition forming part of the agreement.

Where a deferral agreement is varied, the above rules apply to the agreement as varied from the time of the variation.

Reasonable excuse

None of the above penalties are due in respect of a failure to make a payment if the taxpayer satisfies HMRC or, on appeal, the Tribunal, that there is a reasonable excuse for the failure. Insufficiency of funds is not a reasonable excuse for this purpose and neither is the taxpayer's reliance on another person to do anything, unless he took reasonable care to avoid the failure. If the taxpayer had a reasonable excuse, he is treated as continuing to have a reasonable excuse after the excuse has ceased if the failure is remedied without unreasonable delay.

Double jeopardy

No penalty arises for a failure or action in respect of which the taxpayer has been convicted of an offence.

[*FA 2009, Sch 56 paras 9–10, 16, 17; FA 2014, s 226, Sch 32 para 7; FA 2018, Sch 6 para 13(3)*].

Penalties in respect of powers of enforcement by deduction from accounts

[59.16] Under the powers of HMRC to enforce collection of unpaid tax by deduction from the taxpayer's account (see 58.9 PAYMENT OF TAX), a deposit-taker is liable to a penalty of £300 if it:

(a) fails to comply with an information notice;
(b) fails to comply with a hold notice or deduction notice;
(c) fails to comply with an obligation to notify HMRC of the effects of a hold notice;
(d) fails to comply with an obligation to cancel or modify the effect of a hold notice;
(e) fails to comply with an obligation to cancel or adjust arrangements to give effect to HMRC's decision about an objection to a hold notice; or
(f) after receiving an information or hold notice, makes a disclosure of information (other than the required notice) to the taxpayer or any other person which is likely to prejudice HMRC's ability to use their powers to deduct the unpaid tax.

If a failure within (a)–(e) above continues after the day on which notice of a penalty is given, the deposit-taker is liable to a further penalty or penalties of up to £60 per day on which the failure continues.

A failure to comply does not give rise to a penalty if the deposit-taker complies within such further time as HMRC allow. No penalty applies if the deposit-taker satisfies HMRC or the Tribunal that there is a reasonable excuse for the failure or disclosure. Relying on another person to do something is not, for this purpose, a reasonable excuse unless the deposit-taker took reasonable care to avoid the failure or disclosure. Where a reasonable excuse ceases, the deposit-taker is treated as continuing to have the excuse if the failure is remedied without unreasonable delay.

[*F(No 2)A 2015, Sch 8 para 14*].

Arrangements counteracted by the general anti-abuse rule

[59.17] A person (P) is liable to a penalty if:

- P has been given a final counteraction notice stating that a tax advantage arising from tax arrangements is to be counteracted under the general anti-abuse rule ('GAAR'; see **4.3** ANTI-AVOIDANCE) and the advantage has been counteracted by the making of adjustments under the GAAR;
- a tax document has been given to HMRC on the basis that the tax advantage arises to P from the arrangements; and
- the document was given to HMRC by P or by another person and P knew, or ought to have known, that the document was given on the basis that the tax advantage arises to P from the arrangements.

With effect from 10 June 2021, in relation to tax arrangements entered into at any time, a partner (P) in a partnership is liable to a penalty if the partnership's responsible partner (see **4.7** ANTI-AVOIDANCE) has been given a final counteraction notice stating that a tax advantage is to be counteracted and the advantage, so far as arising to P, has been counteracted by the making of adjustments under the GAAR.

The penalty is 60% of the 'value of the counteracted advantage'. For this purpose, a '*tax document*' means a return, claim or other document submitted in compliance (or purported compliance) with any provision of an Act.

See **4.4–4.7** ANTI-AVOIDANCE for certain circumstances in which a penalty cannot be charged.

The '*value of the counteracted advantage*' is the additional amount due or payable in respect of tax as a result of the counteraction. This includes any amount previously repaid by HMRC which is now payable, together with any amount which would be repayable by HMRC if the counteraction were not made and any consequential adjustments. If the counteraction affects P's liability to more than one tax, each of the taxes is considered together in determining the value of the counteracted advantage. Group relief and relief in connection with loans to participators (under *CTA 2010, s 458*) are ignored in the calculation of the additional amount. Where the tax advantage counteracted under the GAAR created or increased a 'loss', and the loss was used to reduce the amount of tax payable, the additional amount due or payable can be ascertained, and the penalty calculated, in the normal way. However, where the loss has not been wholly used in this way, the value of the counteracted advantage is deemed to be 10% of any part of the loss not so used. In the case of an aggregate loss recorded for a group of companies, group relief may be taken into account. The value of the counteracted advantage in respect of a loss is nil where there is no prospect of the loss being used to support a claim to reduce a tax liability (of any person). To the extent that the tax advantage is a deferral of tax, the value of the counteracted advantage is the lower of:

(a) 25% of the deferred tax for each year of deferral (or a proportionate amount for part years); and
(b) 100% of the deferred tax.

For these purposes, a '*loss*' includes a charge, expense, deficit or other amount which may be available for, or relied on to claim, a deduction or relief. A repayment of tax includes a reference to allowing a credit against tax or to a payment of certain corporation tax credits. Giving a document to HMRC includes communicating information in any form and by any method (post, fax, email, telephone or otherwise).

Interaction with other penalties

The following applies where more than one penalty arises in respect of the same amount, one of those penalties is a GAAR penalty, and one or more of the others is incurred under *FA 2007, Sch 24* (errors; see **59.4–59.6** above), *FA 2008, Sch 41* (failure to notify; see **59.2** above), *FA 2009, Sch 55* (failure to make return; see **59.3** above) or *FA 2016, Sch 18* (serial avoiders; see **59.18** below). The general rule is that the aggregate penalty must not exceed 100% of the amount in question or, if at least one of the penalties is a £300 penalty under *FA 2009, Sch 55*, £300 (if greater). Where the maximum penalty under one of the other provisions is more than 100% because of the rules for offshore matters and offshore transfers, the aggregate penalty must not exceed that higher maximum percentage. See **59.14** above for the maximum aggregate penalties where a GAAR penalty and a penalty under *FA 2014, s 212* (follower notices) is incurred in respect of the same tax.

[*FA 2013, ss 212A, 212B, Sch 43C paras 1–4, 8; FA 2021, Sch 32 paras 7, 8, 13*].

Penalties under the serial avoiders regime

[59.18] A person is liable to a penalty if he incurs a relevant defeat (see **4.39** ANTI-AVOIDANCE) in relation to any arrangements which he has used whilst in a warning period (see **4.38** ANTI-AVOIDANCE). The time at which a person has 'used' arrangements is determined by *FA 2016, Sch 18 para 55* (see **4.41** ANTI-AVOIDANCE). The standard penalty is 20% of the 'value of the counteracted advantage'. If, before the relevant defeat is incurred, the person has been given (or become liable to be given) 'prior warning notices', the penalty is increased. It is increased to 40% where there has been a single prior warning notice, and to 60% where there has been more than one such notice. A '*prior warning notice*' is a warning notice in relation to the defeat of arrangements which the person has used in the warning period.

If a person incurs simultaneously two or more relevant defeats in relation to different arrangements, then for the purpose of determining the penalty those defeats are placed in order of value, the defeat of greatest value being deemed to be the first incurred; the value of a defeat is the value of the counteracted advantage. If a person has been given a single warning notice in relation to two or more relevant defeats, he is treated for penalty purposes as having been given a separate warning notice in relation to each defeat.

The Commissioners for HMRC have discretion to mitigate a penalty under these provisions, or stay or compound any proceedings for such a penalty. They may also, after judgment, further mitigate or entirely remit the penalty.

Value of the counteracted advantage

The '*value of the counteracted advantage*' is the additional amount of tax due or payable as a result of the counteraction or corrective action. To the extent that the counteracted advantage has resulted in a loss being wrongly recorded or increased but the counteracted loss has not been wholly used to reduce tax payable, the value of the counteracted advantage is increased by 10% of the part of the counteracted loss not so used. However, the value of a counteracted loss is nil if, due to the nature of the loss or the person's circumstances, there is no reasonable prospect of the loss ever being used to reduce the tax liability of any person. To the extent that the counteracted advantage is a deferral of tax, the value of the advantage is 25% of the amount of deferred tax for each year of the deferral, but not so as to exceed 100% of the total amount of deferred tax.

Interaction with other penalties

The amount of a penalty is to be reduced by any other penalty incurred by the person if the amount of that other penalty is determined by reference to the same tax liability. Other penalties do not for this purpose include the GAAR penalty at **59.17** above and the penalties at **59.14** and **59.15** above (follower notices and accelerated payments notices).

Reasonable excuse

A person is not liable to a penalty in respect of a relevant defeat if he satisfies HMRC or, on appeal, the Tribunal that he had a reasonable excuse for the failures or inaccuracies in question. In determining the rate of penalty an earlier warning notice is disregarded if it relates to a relevant defeat in respect of which the person had a reasonable excuse. Otherwise, the same comments apply regarding 'reasonable excuse' as in **4.41** ANTI-AVOIDANCE.

[*FA 2016, Sch 18 paras 30–35, 40, 42–44*].

Failure to comply with requirement to publish tax strategy

[59.19] A company or partnership is liable to a penalty if it is responsible for ensuring that a tax strategy is published as in **36.19** HMRC — ADMINISTRATION and either:

(i) there is a failure to publish the tax strategy; or
(ii) the tax strategy is published but the requirement for it to remain available to public view free of charge until the next year's strategy is published or (if no such strategy need be published) for at least one year, is not met.

The amount of the penalty is £7,500. Only one penalty can be charged where both (i) and (ii) above apply in respect of a tax strategy for a particular financial year.

A further penalty of £7,500 is chargeable where a failure within (i) above continues for six months and further penalties of £7,500 are chargeable at the end of each subsequent month of continued failure.

A company or partnership is not liable to a penalty for failure to do something within a limited period of time it is done within such further time as HMRC may have allowed.

The Treasury may, by regulations, adjust the £7,500 figure above for inflation.

Reasonable excuse

A company or partnership is not liable to a penalty if it satisfies HMRC or, on appeal, the Tribunal that it had a reasonable excuse for the failure in question. Reasonable excuse does not include insufficiency of funds (unless attributable to events outside the taxpayer's control) or reliance on another person to do anything (unless the taxpayer took reasonable care to avoid the failure or inaccuracy in question or, in the case of a UK group or UK sub-group, where the person relied on is another member of the group or sub-group). A company or partnership with a reasonable excuse is treated as having continued to have it if the failure or inaccuracy in question was remedied without unreasonable delay after the excuse ceased.

[*FA 2016, Sch 19 paras 18, 21, 24, 25, 27, 28, 32*].

Enabling offshore tax evasion

[59.20] With effect for acts or omissions occurring on or after 1 January 2017, a penalty is payable by a person (P) who has 'enabled' another person (Q) to carry out offshore tax evasion or non-compliance if:

(a) P knew when his actions were carried out that they enabled, or were likely to enable, Q to carry out such evasion or non-compliance; and
(b) either:
   (i) Q has been convicted of one of the offences listed below and the conviction is final; or
   (ii) Q has been found to be liable to one of the penalties listed below and either the penalty is final or a contract settlement with HMRC has been agreed under which HMRC undertake not to assess the penalty or to take proceedings to recover it.

For these purposes Q carries out offshore tax evasion or non-compliance by committing an offence within (1)–(3) below or engaging in conduct that makes him liable (if the applicable conditions are met) to a civil penalty within (A)–(D) below, where in either case the tax at stake is income tax, capital gains tax or inheritance tax. Nothing in (b) above affects the law of evidence as to the relevance of the conviction, penalty or contract settlement in proving that (a) above applies. For the purposes of these provisions, '*conduct*' includes a failure to act.

P has '*enabled*' Q to carry out offshore tax evasion or non-compliance if he has encouraged, assisted or otherwise facilitated such conduct. Where (b)(i) above applies, Q must have been convicted of the full offence and not, for example, an attempt. A conviction or a penalty becomes final when the time allowed for any appeal against it expires or, if later, when any appeal has been determined.

The offences referred to in (b)(i) above are:

(1) an offence of cheating the public revenue involving 'offshore activity';
(2) an offence under *TMA 1970, s 106A* (fraudulent evasion of income tax) involving offshore activity; and
(3) an offence under *TMA 1970, ss 106B, 106C* or *106D* (offences relating to offshore income, assets or activities).

The penalties referred to in (b)(ii) above are:

(A) a penalty under *FA 2007, Sch 24 para 1* (error in document — see **59.4** above) involving an offshore matter or offshore transfer (as defined for the purposes of that penalty as it applies to income tax, capital gains tax or inheritance tax);
(B) a penalty under *FA 2008, Sch 41 para 1* (failure to notify — see **59.2** above) for a failure to notify chargeability involving offshore activity;
(C) a second tax-geared penalty under *FA 2009, Sch 55 para 6* (failure to make return — see **59.3** above) involving offshore activity; and
(D) a penalty under *FA 2015, Sch 21 para 1* (offshore asset moves).

It is immaterial that any offence or penalty may also relate to conduct by Q other than offshore tax evasion or non-compliance. Conduct involves '*offshore activity*' if it involves an offshore matter, an offshore transfer or an offshore asset move.

Amount of penalty

Except where (D) above applies, the amount of the penalty is the higher of 100% of the 'potential lost revenue' and £3,000.

Where (D) above applies, the amount of the penalty is the higher of 50% of the potential lost revenue in respect of the original tax non-compliance and £3,000. For this purpose, the potential lost revenue in respect of the original tax non-compliance is the potential lost revenue under *FA 2007, Sch 24* (see **59.4** above) or *FA 2008, Sch 41* (see **59.2** above) or the tax liability which would have been shown on the return (see **59.3** above) according to which provision the original penalty was incurred under.

Where (1), (2) or (3) above apply, the '*potential lost revenue*' is the same amount as the potential lost revenue applicable for the purposes of the corresponding civil penalty (determined as below). For offences within (1) or (2) above, the corresponding civil penalty is that to which Q is liable as a result of the offending conduct. For offences within (3) above, the corresponding civil penalty is *FA 2008, Sch 41* where the offence is under *TMA 1970, s 106B*; *FA 2009, Sch 55* where the offence is under *TMA 1970, s 106C*; and *FA 2007, Sch 24* where the offence is under *TMA 1970, s 106D*. The fact that Q has been prosecuted for the offending conduct is disregarded for this purpose.

Where (A) or (B) above apply, the '*potential lost revenue*' is the amount that is the potential lost revenue under *FA 2007, Sch 24* or *FA 2008, Sch 41*. Where (C) above applies, the '*potential lost revenue*' is the tax liability that would have been shown on the return.

Where any amount of potential lost revenue is only partly attributable to offshore tax evasion or non-compliance, a just and reasonable apportionment is made.

Reduction for disclosure

A reduction in the amount of a penalty will be given where P makes a disclosure to HMRC of a matter relating to an inaccuracy in a document, a supply of false information or a failure to disclose an under-assessment, a disclosure of P's enabling of Q's actions or a disclosure of any other information HMRC regard as assisting them in relation to the assessment of the penalty. A person is treated as making a disclosure of a matter for these purposes only if he tells HMRC about it, gives them reasonable help in relation to it and allows them access to records for any reasonable purpose connected with resolving it.

A reduction will also be given if P assists HMRC in any investigation leading to Q being charged with an offence or found liable to a penalty. A person is treated as assisting HMRC for this purpose only by assisting or encouraging Q to disclose all relevant facts to HMRC, allowing HMRC access to records or any other conduct which HMRC consider assists them in investigating Q.

The penalty will be reduced to an amount that reflects the quality of the disclosure or assistance (including its timing, nature and extent). The amount of the reduction will depend on whether the disclosure or assistance is 'prompted' or 'unprompted'. The penalty may not be reduced below the higher of 10% of the potential lost revenue and £1,000 for unprompted disclosure or assistance and not below the higher of 30% of the potential lost revenue and £3,000 for prompted disclosure or assistance. Disclosure or assistance is '*unprompted*' if made at a time when P has no reason to believe that HMRC have discovered or are about to discover Q's offshore tax evasion or non-compliance. In all other cases, disclosure or assistance is '*prompted*'.

Reduction in special circumstances

HMRC can also reduce, stay or agree a compromise in relation to proceedings for a penalty if they think it right to do so because of special circumstances. Ability to pay and the fact that a potential loss of revenue from one taxpayer is balanced by a potential overpayment by another are not special circumstances for this purpose.

Double jeopardy

A person is not liable to a penalty under these provisions in respect of conduct for which he has been convicted of an offence or has been assessed to another penalty.

[*FA 2016, s 162, Sch 20 paras 1–9, 15*].

Interest on penalties

Late payment interest on a penalty under the above provisions is charged in accordance with *FA 2009, s 101* where the late payment interest start date is on or after 6 September 2019. Repayment interest under *FA 2009, s 102* on an overpaid penalty is similarly available where the repayment date is on or after that date. [*SI 2019 No 1238*].

Information powers

The information and inspection powers of *FA 2008, Sch 36* (see **38.3** HMRC INVESTIGATORY POWERS) apply, with necessary modifications, for the purpose of checking the penalty position of a person whom an HMRC officer has reason to suspect may have enabled offshore tax evasion or non-compliance. The modifications include, in particular, that the exclusions from information notices for auditors and tax advisers (see **38.6** HMRC INVESTIGATORY POWERS) do not apply and that there is no tax-related penalty for failure to comply (see **59.11** above). [*FA 2016, Sch 20 paras 18–21*].

Publishing details of enablers

HMRC may publish information about a person who has been found to have incurred one or more penalties under these provisions (and has been assessed or entered into a contract settlement) if the total potential lost revenue exceeds £25,000 or if that person has been found to be liable to five or more such penalties in any five-year period. Information cannot be published if the maximum reduction of the penalty has been given for disclosure or if the penalty has been reduced to nil or stayed as a result of special circumstances. The Treasury may vary the £25,000 threshold by statutory instrument.

Before publishing any information HMRC must notify the person and give an opportunity to make representations. No information may be published before the day on which the penalty becomes final or, where there is more than one penalty, before the latest day on which any of them becomes final. Information may not be published for the first time more than one year after that day. For this purpose, a penalty becomes final when no further appeal can be made, any appeal is finally determined or when a contract settlement is made.

The information which can be published is the person's name (including trading name, previous name or pseudonym), address, the nature of the person's business, the amount of the penalties and the periods or times to which they relate and any other information HMRC consider appropriate to make the person's identity clear. HMRC may publish the information in any way they think appropriate.

[*FA 2016, Sch 20 paras 22, 23*].

Enablers of defeated abusive tax arrangements

[59.21] With effect for arrangements entered into on or after 16 November 2017, a penalty is payable by a person who has 'enabled' 'abusive tax arrangements' entered into by another person (T) if T incurs a 'defeat' in respect of them. Any actions carried out by a person before 16 November 2017 are disregarded in determining whether that person enabled arrangements. The penalty applies to a number of taxes, including corporation tax and diverted profits tax.

HMRC have published guidance on the provisions: see www.gov.uk/government/collections/tax-avoidance-enablers. See also HMRC Factsheets CC/FS43 — Guidance — Compliance checks — penalties for enablers of defeated tax avoidance and CC/FS45 — Guidance — Compliance checks — The Human Rights Act and penalties for enablers of defeated tax avoidance.

Definitions

Arrangements are '*tax arrangements*' if, taking into account all the circumstances, it would be reasonable to conclude that the obtaining of a tax advantage was the main purpose, or one of the main purposes, of the arrangements. For this purpose, '*arrangements*' include any agreement, understanding, scheme, transaction or series of transactions, whether or not legally enforceable.

Tax arrangements are '*abusive*' if entering into them or carrying them out cannot reasonably be regarded as a reasonable course of action in relation to the tax provisions in question, having regard to all the circumstances. Those circumstances include:

- whether the substantive results of the arrangements are consistent with any express or implied principles on which the provisions are based and their policy objectives;
- whether the means of achieving the results of the arrangements involve one or more contrived or abnormal steps; and
- whether the arrangements are intended to exploit any shortcomings in the provisions.

Where the tax arrangements form part of other arrangements, regard must be had to those other arrangements.

The legislation gives the following non-exhaustive examples of what might indicate that tax arrangements are abusive (assuming that the result was not anticipated when the relevant provisions were enacted).

- The arrangements result in taxable income, profits or gains significantly less than the economic amount.
- The arrangements result in a tax deduction or loss significantly greater than the economic amount.
- The arrangements result in a claim for repayment or crediting of tax, including foreign tax, that has not been, and is unlikely to be, paid.

The legislation also gives an example of what might indicate that arrangements are not abusive: the arrangements accord with established practice accepted by HMRC.

A '*tax advantage*' includes relief or increased relief from tax, repayment or increased repayment of tax, receipt or advancement of receipt of a tax credit, avoidance or reduction of a charge or assessment to tax or a liability to pay tax, avoidance of a possible assessment to tax or liability to pay tax or of an obligation to deduct or account for tax, deferral of a payment of tax, and advancement of a repayment tax.

T incurs a '*defeat*' in respect of arrangements if T, or a person on his behalf, has given HMRC a document on the basis that a tax advantage arose from the arrangements and that tax advantage has been counteracted, with the counteraction having become final. The document must be of a kind listed in *FA 2007, Sch 24, para 1* (penalty for errors in documents—see **59.4** above) or a document amending such a document. A tax advantage is counteracted for this purpose if adjustments have been made to T's tax position (by assessment, modification of an assessment or return, amendment or disallowance of a claim, payment or entering into a contract settlement) on the basis that all or part of the tax advantage does not arise. Counteraction is final when the adjustments and any amounts arising from them can no longer be varied.

T also incurs a '*defeat*' in respect of arrangements if HMRC have made an assessment which counteracts (i.e. prevents T from obtaining all or part of) a tax advantage which it is reasonable to assume T expected to obtain from the arrangements and the counteraction is final. A counteraction is final for this purpose when either a contract settlement which prevents T from obtaining all or part of the tax advantage is made or the assessment and any amounts arising from it can no longer be varied.

A person has '*enabled*' arrangements if he falls within any of the following categories. In the case of (a)–(c) or (e) below, the person must be acting in the course of a business carried on by him. Note that it is possible for there to be more than one enabler of particular arrangements.

(a) **A designer of the arrangements.** A person who was to any extent responsible for the design of the arrangements or a proposal implemented by them. Providing advice which is taken account of in the design of the arrangements does not make a person a designer of the arrangements unless:
   (i) any of the advice suggested arrangements or an alteration of proposed arrangements (or a proposal for arrangements or an alteration of such a proposal) and it is reasonable to assume that the suggestion was made with a view to arrangements being designed so that a tax advantage or greater tax advantage might be expected to arise from them; and
   (ii) when the advice was given, the person providing it knew, or could reasonably be expected to know, that the advice would be taken account of in designing abusive tax arrangements or a proposal for such arrangements or that it was likely that the advice would be so taken account of.

   In (i) above, advice does not suggest anything which was put forward for consideration if the advice can be reasonably read as advising against it. '*Advice*', for these purposes, includes giving an opinion.
(b) **A manager of the arrangements.** A person who was to any extent responsible for organising or managing the arrangements and who, when carrying out functions relating to such organising or managing, knew or could reasonably be expected to know that the arrangements

were abusive tax arrangements. Facilitating T's withdrawal from the arrangements is not organising or managing the arrangements for this purpose if it is reasonable to assume that T's purpose in withdrawing is not to obtain a tax advantage.

(c) **A person who marketed the arrangements.** A person who made available for implementation by T a proposal subsequently implemented by the arrangements or who informed T or another person about a proposal subsequently implemented by the arrangements with a view to T entering into the arrangements or transactions forming part of them.

(d) **An enabling participant.** A person, other than T, who enters into the arrangements or a transaction forming part of them where, without that participation (or the participation of another person in the same capacity), the arrangements would not be expected to result in a tax advantage for T. The person must have known or have been reasonably expected to know, when entering into the arrangements or transaction, that what was being entered into was abusive tax arrangements or a transaction forming part of such arrangements.

(e) **A financial enabler.** A person who provided a financial product directly or indirectly to T or an enabling participant within (d) above where it is reasonable to assume that a purpose of T or the other participant in obtaining the product was to participate in the arrangements. The person must have known or have been reasonably expected to know, when providing the product, that a purpose of obtaining it was to participate in abusive tax arrangements. Financial products include loans, shares, derivative contracts, repos, stock lending arrangements, alternative finance arrangements and contracts which would be required to be treated under generally accepted accounting practice as a loan, deposit or other financial asset or obligation. The Treasury may amend the list of financial products by statutory instrument.

T and, if T is a company, any member of the same group, cannot be treated as an enabler of the arrangements even if they fall within any of the above categories. Two companies are members of a group, for this purpose, if one is a 75% subsidiary of the other or both are 75% subsidiaries of a third company. The Treasury can add to the categories of enabler or provide that a person who would otherwise be an enabler is not to be treated as such in specified circumstances by statutory instrument.

Amount of penalty

The amount of the penalty for each enabler of the arrangements is the total amount or value of the consideration received or receivable by that person for anything done by him which enabled the arrangements. VAT and any consideration previously taken into account in calculating a penalty under these provisions are excluded. Consideration paid (or payable), under arrangements, to a person other than the enabler is treated for this purpose as paid (or payable) to the enabler. If consideration is attributable to more than one transaction, it must be apportioned on a just and reasonable basis. Where consideration is given for what is in substance one bargain, the consideration must be treated as attributable to all elements of the bargain even if separate consideration is given for, or there are separate transactions in respect of, different elements.

Reduction and mitigation of penalty

The amount of the penalty is reduced by the amount of any other penalty incurred by, and assessed on, the enabler in respect of the same conduct.

HMRC have discretion to reduce a penalty, entirely remit a penalty or to stay or agree a compromise in respect of proceedings for the recovery of a penalty.

Assessment of penalty

For the general provisions relating to the assessment of a penalty under these provisions see **59.23** below. The decision to make an assessment must be taken by an HMRC officer designated by the Commissioners for HMRC for the purposes of these provisions (a '*designated HMRC officer*'). If HMRC do not have all the information needed to determine the amount of the consideration on which the penalty is based, they may make an assessment on the basis of a reasonable estimate, provided that they have taken all reasonable steps to obtain the information.

If a proposal for arrangements has been implemented more than once and all of the arrangements are substantially the same, HMRC cannot assess any penalty until

(I) where the penalty results at least in part from actions of the enabler carried out on or after 10 June 2021, at least one implementation has incurred a defeat (whether before or after 10 June 2021) as a result of proceedings before a tribunal or court;

(II) where the penalty results at least in part from actions of the enabler carried out on or after 10 June 2021 and (I) above does not apply, the required number of implementations has incurred a defeat (whether before or after 10 June 2021), as follows:
- where there have been fewer than 21 implementations, at least 50% of them;
- for 21 to 43 implementations, 11 or more;
- for 44 to 199 implementations, at least 25%;
- for 200 or more implementations, at least 50; or

(III) where the penalty results wholly from actions of the enabler carried out before 10 June 2021, more than 50% of the implementations have incurred a defeat (whether before or after 10 June 2021).

Any person liable to a penalty may, however, request that an assessment be made sooner.

Notification of a penalty assessment must be accompanied by a report of the opinion of the GAAR Advisory Panel (see **4.3** ANTI-AVOIDANCE) on which HMRC relied in making the assessment (see below).

GAAR Advisory Panel opinion

A penalty assessment cannot be made unless either of the following applies.

(A) A 'GAAR final decision notice' has been given in relation to the arrangements or other 'equivalent' arrangements and a designated HMRC officer has considered the opinion of the GAAR Advisory Panel which was considered by HMRC in preparing that notice. If the final decision notice related to equivalent arrangements only, a designated HMRC officer must first give the person liable to the penalty a notice in writing explaining HMRC's view, specifying the arrangements concerned and describing the material characteristics of the equivalent arrangements. The notice must also include a report by HMRC of the opinion of the Panel and must explain the right of the person liable to the penalty to make representations. Representations as to why the arrangements under consideration are not equivalent to those considered by the Panel can be made in writing within 30 days beginning with the day the notice is given. HMRC may, on written request, extend the deadline (but are not required to do so). A penalty assessment cannot be made unless a notice has been given, the time allowed for representations has expired and the officer has considered any representations made.

A '*GAAR final decision notice*' is a notice of HMRC's final decision on whether arrangements are to be counteracted under the GAAR after considering the Panel's decision (see **4.4**(10), **4.7**(11) and **4.6** ANTI-AVOIDANCE). Arrangements are '*equivalent*' to one another if they are substantially the same with regard to their results or intended results, the means of achieving those results and the characteristics making them abusive tax arrangements.

(B) A designated HMRC officer has referred the arrangements to the GAAR Advisory Panel. An assessment cannot be made until the officer has considered the opinion of the Panel. See below for the procedure for referring arrangements. If the officer considers that a person is liable to a penalty in relation to particular arrangements on the basis that the opinion of the Panel 'applies' to the arrangements but that person was not notified of the referral to the Panel, then before making an assessment the officer must give that person a notice in writing explaining HMRC's view and specifying the arrangements concerned. The notice must also include a report by HMRC of the opinion of the Panel and must explain the right to make representations. Representations as to why the opinion does not apply to the arrangements in question can be made in writing within 30 days beginning with the day the notice is given. HMRC may, on written request, extend the deadline (but are not required to do so). A penalty assessment cannot be made unless a notice has been given, the time allowed for representations has expired and the officer has considered any representations made.

An opinion of the Panel '*applies*' to the arrangements in respect of which the referral was made and any equivalent arrangements.

The procedure for referring arrangements to the Panel is as follows.

(1) A designated HMRC officer may make a referral if he considers that a person is liable to a penalty in respect of particular arrangements. A referral may not be made if a GAAR final decision notice has already given in relation to the arrangements in question or equivalent arrangements. Before making a referral, the officer must give a notice to each person who he then considers to be liable to a penalty in respect of the arrangements giving his view and explaining why he considers the arrangements to be abusive tax arrangements. The notice must also state

that HMRC are considering making a referral and must explain the right to make representations. Representations can be made in writing within 45 days beginning with the day the notice is given. HMRC may, on written request, extend the deadline (but are not required to do so). A referral is of the question whether the entering into and carrying out of the tax arrangements described in the 'referral statement' is a reasonable course of action in relation to the tax provisions concerned. The '*referral statement*' must accompany the referral and is a general statement of the material characteristics of the arrangements including a factual description of them, HMRC's view as to whether they accord with established practice, why HMRC consider that the tax advantage arises from abusive arrangements, any matters of which HMRC are aware that may suggest that their view is not correct and any other matters which HMRC consider to be required for the purposes of the Panel's functions.

(2) Where a designated HMRC officer decides whether to make a referral he must, as soon as reasonably practicable, give written notice of that decision to each person to whom a notice within (1) above was given.

(3) A referral must be accompanied by the referral statement, a declaration that, as far as HMRC are aware, nothing material has been omitted from the statement, a copy of each notice within (1) above and (4) below and of any representations received, together with any comments on the representations.

(4) At the same time as the referral is made, a designated HMRC officer must give each person to whom a notice within (1) above was given a written notice confirming that the referral has been made and including a copy of the referral statement and of any comments on representations made by that person. It must also explain the right to make representations to the Panel and the requirement to send a copy of any representations to HMRC.

(5) A person who has received a notice under (4) above has 21 days beginning with the day on which the notice was given to send written representations to the Panel about the notice in (1) above or any comments made by HMRC on representations made by him in response to that notice. The Panel may, on written request, extend the deadline (but are not required to do so). A copy of the representations must be sent to HMRC. If no representations had been made in response to the notice in (1) above, HMRC may provide the Panel with comments on the representations now made, and must send a copy of any such comments to the person to who the notice was given.

(6) The Chair of the Panel must arrange for a sub-panel of three members to consider the referral. The sub-panel may invite any person to whom a notice was given under (1) above or the designated HMRC officer (or both) to supply further information within a specified time period. A copy of any information must be given to the designated HMRC officer or to each of the notice recipients.

(7) The sub-panel must produce an opinion notice stating their joint opinion as to whether or not the entering into and carrying out of the tax arrangements was a reasonable course of action in relation to the tax provisions concerned, having regard to the referral statement and the meaning of 'abusive'. An opinion notice may indicate that the sub-panel

consider that it is not possible to reach a view on the information available. Alternatively, the sub-panel may produce two or three opinion notices which taken together state the opinions of all the members. An opinion notice must include the reasons for the opinion and is given to the designated HMRC officer.

In any court or Tribunal proceedings in connection with a penalty under these provisions, any question as to whether the arrangements were abusive must be determined taking account of the Panel's opinion on which HMRC relied in assessing the penalty. The court or Tribunal may also take into account any guidance, statements or other material (of HMRC, a government minster or anyone else) in the public domain when the arrangements were entered into and any evidence of established practice at that time.

Double jeopardy

A person is not liable to a penalty under these provisions in respect of conduct for which he has been convicted of an offence.

[*F(No 2)A 2017, s 65, Sch 16 paras 1–19, 21, 23–36, 52–56; FA 2021, s 123(2)(9)–(11)*].

Information powers

The information and inspection powers of *FA 2008, Sch 36* (see **38.3** HMRC INVESTIGATORY POWERS) apply, with necessary modifications, for the purpose of checking the penalty position of a person whom an HMRC officer has reason to suspect may be liable to a penalty under these provisions. With effect from 10 June 2021 (in relation to arrangements whenever entered into), the powers also apply for the purpose of ascertaining the identity of any other person who has or may have enabled the arrangements in question. [*F(No 2)A 2017, Sch 16 paras 40–43; FA 2021, s 123(4)–(7)(12)*].

Privileged communications

Where a person cannot provide information to demonstrate that he is not liable to a penalty because communications by a lawyer are subject to legal professional privilege (or in Scotland, protected from disclosure in legal proceedings on grounds of confidentiality of communication), that lawyer or another lawyer can make a declaration that the person is not liable to the penalty. Such a declaration must be treated by HMRC, a court or tribunal as conclusive evidence of the things stated in it unless HMRC, the court or tribunal is satisfied that it contains incorrect information. The Treasury may impose requirements as to the form and content of such declarations by statutory instrument. Lawyers, for this purpose, are barristers, advocates, solicitors and other legal representatives communications with whom may be subject to legal professional privilege (or Scottish equivalent). A penalty not exceeding £5,000 applies for carelessly or deliberately giving incorrect information in a declaration. A declaration can also be made, where relevant, in respect of such a penalty. An assessment to such a penalty must be made within the 12 months beginning with the date on which sufficient facts came to HMRC's knowledge to indicate that a penalty is due. Subject to this, the rules for making assessments and appeals are the same as for the main penalty under these provisions (see **59.23** and **59.24** below). [*F(No 2)A 2017, Sch 16 paras 44, 45*].

Publishing details of enablers

HMRC may publish information about a person who has been found to have incurred one or more penalties under these provisions (and has been assessed or entered into a contract settlement) if the total amount of the penalty or penalties exceeds £25,000 or if that person has been found to be liable to 50 or more other such penalties. Penalties and their amounts are only aggregated for this purpose if the 'entry dates' of the penalties fall within a period of 12 months. For this purpose, the '*entry date*' of a penalty is the date (or latest date) on which the arrangements or any agreement or transaction forming part of them was entered into by the person whose defeat resulted in the penalty arising. Penalties which have been reduced to nil or stayed are disregarded as are penalties by reference to which information has already been published and penalties where the arrangements concerned are related to other arrangements in respect of which a penalty has been charged and information published. Penalties incurred solely due to actions carried out before 10 June 2021 are also disregarded if the arrangements are related to other arrangements and it is not the case that HMRC reasonably believe that defeats have been incurred in all of the related arrangements and that each penalty in relation to those arrangements has become final. Arrangements are related to each other if they implement the same proposal for tax arrangements and are substantially the same.

The Treasury may vary the £25,000 and 50 penalties thresholds by statutory instrument.

Before publishing any information, HMRC must notify the person and give an opportunity to make representations. No information may be published before the day on which the penalty becomes final or, where there is more than one penalty, before the latest day on which any of them becomes final. Information may not be published for the first time more than one year after that day. For this purpose, a penalty becomes final when no further appeal can be made, any appeal is finally determined or when a contract settlement is made. Information cannot be republished or continue to be published after the 12 months beginning with the date of first publication.

The information which can be published is the person's name (including trading name, previous name or pseudonym), address, the nature of the person's business, the number and amount of the penalties and any other information HMRC consider appropriate to make the person's identity clear. HMRC may publish the information in any way they think appropriate.

[*F(No 2)A 2017, Sch 16 paras 46–51; FA 2021, s 123(8)(13)*].

Penalties under the corporate interest restriction

[59.22] Under the separate compliance regime (see **65.21** RETURNS) for the CORPORATE INTEREST RESTRICTION (**25**), the following penalties may be charged.

(i) A company which is required to submit an interest restriction return for a period of account and fails to do so by the filing date is liable to a penalty of £500. If the return is not submitted within three months after the filing date, the amount of the penalty is increased to £1,000.

(ii) A company is liable to a penalty if it (or a person acting on its behalf) submits an interest restriction return which contains an inaccuracy which consists of understating the total disallowed amount (see **24.3** CORPORATE INTEREST RESTRICTION) or overstating the interest reactivation cap (see **24.4**). The inaccuracy must either be made deliberately or be due to a failure by the company (or a person acting on its behalf) to take reasonable care. The amount of the penalty is 30% of the 'notional tax' for a careless inaccuracy; 70% for a deliberate inaccuracy which is not concealed; or 100% for a concealed deliberate inaccuracy. The '*notional tax*' is found by applying the average rate of the main corporation tax rate applicable on each day in the period of account to the total amount of the understatement or overstatement. A company is not liable to a penalty for anything done or omitted by its agent if the company took reasonable care to avoid the inaccuracy. An inaccuracy which is not initially a careless or deliberate inaccuracy is nevertheless treated as careless if the company (or a person acting on its behalf) later discovers the inaccuracy and does not take reasonable steps to inform HMRC.

(iii) A company (C) is liable to a penalty if another company submits an interest restriction return which contains an inaccuracy which consists of understating the total disallowed amount or overstating the interest reactivation cap and the inaccuracy is attributable to C deliberately supplying false information to the other company or deliberately withholding information from it, with the intention that the return should contain the inaccuracy. The amount of the penalty is equal to the notional tax. A penalty may be due regardless of whether or not the other company is liable to a penalty under (ii) above in respect of the same inaccuracy.

(iv) A company which fails to fulfil its duty to keep and preserve records (see **65.21** RETURNS) is liable to a penalty not exceeding £3,000.

(v) Where a return includes estimated amounts, the return must identify that information. If the information is not finalised before the end of the period of 36 months beginning with the end of the period of account, a company which fails to must notify HMRC that estimated amounts in a return are not final (see **65.21** RETURNS) is liable to a penalty of £500.

No liability to a penalty under (i) above arises if the company has a reasonable excuse for failing to submit the return by the filing date. If a reasonable excuse has ceased, the company is treated as continuing to have the excuse if the return is submitted without unreasonable delay.

Penalties under (ii) and (iii) above are reduced where the company liable to the penalty discloses the inaccuracy. The reduction must reflect the quality of the disclosure, including its timing, nature and extent but the penalty cannot be reduced below the following minimum amounts. For a careless inaccuracy within (ii) above the minimum is 0% of the notional tax where the disclosure is unprompted and 15% otherwise. For a deliberate but unconcealed inaccuracy within (ii) above the minimum is 30% for an unprompted disclosure and 45% otherwise. For a concealed deliberate inaccuracy within (ii) above the minimum is 40% for an unprompted disclosure and 60% otherwise. For a penalty within (iii) above, the minimum is 40% for an unprompted disclosure and 60% otherwise. A company makes a disclosure for this purpose by telling HMRC about the inaccuracy, giving HMRC reasonable help in quantifying it and allowing them access to records to ensure it is fully corrected. A disclosure is unprompted if the company has no reason at the time it is made to believe that HMRC have discovered or are about to discover the inaccuracy.

HMRC may also reduce the amount of a penalty within (ii) or (iii) above or to stay the penalty or agree a compromise in proceedings relating to the penalty, if they think it right to do so because of special circumstances (other than an inability to pay).

A company is not liable to any of the above penalties in respect of anything in respect of which it has been convicted of an offence.

A payment received by a company liable to a penalty from another company within the charge to corporation tax which is made under an agreement in respect of the penalty and does not exceed the amount of the penalty is not taken into account in calculating the profits of either company for corporation tax purposes and is not a distribution.

[*TIOPA 2010, Sch 7A, paras 27(5), 29(1)(2), 30–33, 37, 39(1), 74; F(No 2)A 2017, Sch 5, para 2; FA 2021, s 38(4)(5)*].

Procedure for penalties

[59.23] Where a penalty is due HMRC may in certain cases seek to negotiate a contract settlement with the taxpayer (see **59.27** below). In the absence of such a settlement, the following formal procedures apply to impose penalties.

Assessment

The following penalties are charged by HMRC assessment:

(1) failure to notify chargeability (*FA 2008, Sch 41* — see **59.2** above);
(2) failure to deliver corporation tax return on time (new code under *FA 2009, Sch 55* (not yet in force) — see **59.3** above);
(3) error in document (*FA 2007, Sch 24 para 1* — see **59.4** above);
(4) error attributable to other person (*FA 2007, Sch 24 para 1A* — see **59.5** above);
(5) failure to notify HMRC of error in assessment (*FA 2007, Sch 24 para 2* — see **59.6** above);
(6) failure to pay on time (*FA 2009, Sch 56* (not generally yet in force) — see **59.7** above);
(7) HMRC investigatory powers: fixed and daily penalties (other than increased daily penalties and tax-related penalties imposed by the Tribunal before 10 June 2021 — see below) for failure to comply or obstruction, penalties for failure to comply with requirement not to disclose a third party notice or financial institution notice and penalties for inaccuracies (*FA 2008, Sch 36* — see **59.11** above);
(8) HMRC data-gathering powers: fixed and daily penalties (other than increased daily penalties imposed by the Tribunal before 15 September 2016 — see below) for failure to comply and penalties for inaccuracies (*FA 2011, Sch 23* — see **59.12** above);

(9) penalties in respect of follower notices (*FA 2014, ss 208, 208A* — see **59.14** above);
(10) failure to make accelerated payment (*FA 2014, s 226* — see **59.15** above);
(11) fixed and daily penalties under the enforcement of tax debts by deduction from accounts provisions (*F(No 2)A 2015, Sch 8* — see **59.16** above);
(12) penalties in respect of arrangements counteracted by the general anti-abuse rule (*FA 2013, ss 212A, 212B* — see **59.17** above);
(13) penalties under the serial avoiders regime (*FA 2016, Sch 18* — see **59.18** above);
(14) penalties for failure to comply with requirement to publish tax strategy (*FA 2016, Sch 19* — see **59.19** above);
(15) penalties for enablers of offshore tax evasion (*FA 2016, Sch 20* — see **59.20** above);
(16) penalties for enablers of abusive tax arrangements (*F(No 2)A 2017, Sch 16*—see **59.21** above); and
(17) penalties under the corporate interest restriction regime (*TIOPA 2010, Sch 7A*—see **59.22** above).

A penalty assessment under (1)–(6), (9), (10), (12), (13) or (15) above is treated in the same way as an assessment to tax and can be enforced accordingly. It may also be combined with a tax assessment. The notice of assessment must state the accounting period in respect of which the penalty is assessed. Where the person liable to a penalty under (12) above is a partner and the final counteraction notice was given to the partnership's responsible partner (see **4.7** ANTI-AVOIDANCE), a notice of assessment must also be sent to the responsible partner. Subject to the time limits at **59.29** below, HMRC can make a supplementary assessment if an existing assessment operates by reference to an underestimate (of the 'potential lost revenue' etc.). Where an assessment of a penalty within (2), (6) or (15) above is excessive, HMRC may issue an amendment. Such an amendment does not affect when the penalty must be paid, and can be made even if the time limit for making the assessment has passed. An assessment of a penalty within (12) or (13) above may be revised if it overestimates the value of the counteracted advantage. Where, following the making of a penalty assessment under (12) above, consequential adjustments are made (see **4.3** ANTI-AVOIDANCE under 'Effect of the GAAR'), HMRC must make any just and reasonable alterations to the penalty assessment to take account of those adjustments, and may do so regardless of any time limits which would otherwise prevent them. Penalties must be paid before the end of the period of 30 days beginning with the day on which the notification of the penalty is issued.

Penalties within (7), (8) and (11) above can be enforced as if they were income tax charged in an assessment. A penalty must be paid within the 30-day period beginning with the date on which HMRC issue notification of the penalty assessment or, if an appeal against the penalty is made, within the 30-day period beginning with the date on which the appeal is determined or withdrawn.

Penalties within (14) above can be enforced as if they were corporation tax charged in an assessment. The penalty must be paid within the 30 days beginning with the date of issue of the notice of assessment or, if an appeal is made, within the 30 days beginning with the day on which the appeal is determined or withdrawn.

A penalty assessment within (16) above is treated in the same way as an assessment to tax and can be enforced accordingly. A penalty must be paid within the 30-day period beginning with the date on which HMRC issue notification of the assessment.

A penalty within (17) above must be paid within the 30-day period beginning with the date on which the company was notified of the penalty or, if an appeal against the penalty is made, within the 30-day period beginning with the date on which the appeal is determined or withdrawn. Penalties within **59.22**(ii) or (iii) above can be enforced as if they were corporation tax charged in an assessment and as if that assessment was also an assessment to corporation tax of any UK group company.

[*FA 2007, Sch 24 para 13; FA 2008, Sch 36 paras 46, 49, 49A, 51B; Sch 41 para 16; FA 2009, Sch 55 para 18, Sch 56 para 11; TIOPA 2010, Sch 7A paras 29(3)(7), 34, 39(2)(6); FA 2011, Sch 23 paras 35, 40; FA 2013, Sch 43C paras 5–7, Sch 50 paras 1, 7, 10, 14; FA 2014, ss 211(1)–(4), 211A(1)–(3), 226(7); F(No 2)A 2015, Sch 8 paras 15(1), 17; FA 2016, ss 158(3), 177(4), Sch 18 paras 38, 39, Sch 19 paras 29, 31, Sch 20 paras 10, 11; F(No 2)A 2017, Sch 5 para 2, Sch 16 paras 19(1), 20; FA 2021, Sch 28 para 4, Sch 32 para 13(7), Sch 34 paras 2, 5*].

Determination

The following penalties are imposed by an authorised HMRC officer making a determination imposing a penalty of an amount which he considers correct or appropriate:

(a) failure to deliver corporation tax return on time (old code under *FA 1998, Sch 18 paras 17, 18* — see **59.2** above);
(b) penalties in respect of special returns (other than the initial penalty for failure to comply) (*TMA 1970, s 98* — see **59.8** above);
(c) failure to keep records (*FA 1998, Sch 18 para 23* — see **59.9** above);
(d) penalties in respect of the disclosure of avoidance schemes (other than an initial penalty or initial daily penalty for failure to comply with any of **59.10**(a)–(n) above) (*TMA 1970, s 98C* — see **59.10** above); and
(e) daily penalties for promoters of avoidance schemes under *FA 2014, Sch 35* (see **59.13** above) where the maximum amount is £600.

See **36.4** HMRC—ADMINISTRATION for the exercise of functions of an HMRC officer by automated process.

The notice of determination must state the date of issue and the time within which an appeal can be made. It cannot be altered unless:

(i) there is an appeal;
(ii) an authorised officer discovers that the penalty is or has become insufficient (in which case he may make a further determination); or

(iii) the penalty arises under *FA 1998, Sch 18 para 18(2)*, and an authorised officer subsequently discovers that the amount of tax is or has become excessive (in which case it is to be revised accordingly).

A penalty under these provisions is due 30 days after the date of issue of the notice of determination, and is treated as tax charged under an assessment and due and payable.

[*TMA 1970, ss 100, 100A; FA 2014, Sch 35 para 10*].

In *Partito Media Services Ltd v HMRC* (TC01949) [2012] UKFTT 256 (TC), 30 April 2012, it was held that a penalty notice had not been validly served because it had been sent to the company's old registered office (notwithstanding that the company had failed to inform HMRC of the change of registered office). Judge Redston rejected HMRC's contention that the effect of *TMA 1970, s 115(2)(a)* was that the notice had been validly served by being sent to P's last known registered office, and held that the phrase 'usual or last known place of residence' was only applicable to sole traders and partners, and did not include companies.

Proceedings before the First-tier Tribunal

The following penalties are imposed using the procedure described below:

(A) initial penalty for failure to file special return (*TMA 1970, s 98(1)(i)* — see **59.8** above); and

(B) initial penalty or initial daily penalty for failure to comply with any of the disclosure requirements at **59.10**(a)–(n) above) (*TMA 1970, s 98C(1)(a)* — see **59.10** above);

An authorised HMRC officer may commence proceedings before the First-tier Tribunal. The proceedings are by way of information in writing to the First-tier Tribunal, and upon summons issued by them to the defendant (or defender), and are heard and decided in a summary way. An appeal lies to the Upper Tribunal on a question of law or, by the defendant (defender), against the amount. The court can confirm, set aside or vary the determination as seems appropriate. The penalty is treated as tax charged in an assessment and due and payable.

[*TMA 1970, s 100C*].

The following penalties are also imposed by the First-tier Tribunal:

(1) increased daily penalties for failure to comply with HMRC investigatory powers (*FA 2008, Sch 36* — see **59.11** above); and

(2) increased daily penalties for failure to comply with HMRC's data-gathering powers (*FA 2011, Sch 23* — see **59.12** above).

Penalties under (2) above and, with effect from 10 June 2021, penalties under (1) above are nevertheless charged by HMRC assessment (see above) and HMRC must notify the person assessed.

Penalty imposed by Upper Tribunal

A tax-related penalty for failure or obstruction under HMRC's investigatory powers must be imposed by the Upper Tribunal — see **59.11** above.

Proceedings before court

If HMRC consider that liability arises from fraud by any person, proceedings can be brought in the High Court (or Court of Session). If the Court does not find fraud proved, it can nevertheless impose a penalty to which it considers the person liable.

[*TMA 1970, s 100D*].

General matters

Statements made or documents produced by or on behalf of a company are admissible evidence in proceedings against it, notwithstanding that reliance on HMRC's practice in cases of full disclosure may have induced it to make or produce them. [*TMA 1970, s 105*].

The imposition of penalties calculated as a percentage of unpaid tax was held to be in the nature of 'criminal' (rather than 'civil') proceedings for the purposes of the European Convention on Human Rights in *King v United Kingdom (Nos 1 & 2): 18881/02*, [2004] STC 911, ECHR.

In *P&H Cleaning Company v HMRC*, [2013] UKFTT 669 (TC), the First-tier tribunal (following *HMRC v Hok* [2012] UKUT 363) confirmed that it is not within its jurisdiction to set aside penalties for the late payment of PAYE on the ground of unfairness and disproportionality. Outside of VAT (which comes within EU law principles) the doctrine of proportionality can affect penalties only through the door of the *Human Rights Act 1998*. In *HMRC v Anthony Bosher*, [2013] UKUT 579 (TCC), with regard to Construction Industry Scheme penalties, the Upper Tribunal stressed that the legislation does not provide a right of appeal against a decision on the mitigation of a penalty, this required an application for judicial review.

For relevant cases, see Tolley's Income Tax and/or Tolley's Tax Cases.

Appeals

[59.24] Procedures for appealing against penalties are described below.

Penalty imposed by assessment

Assessments of penalties under 59.23(1)–(6), (9)–(17) above are subject to specific appeal provisions. An appeal can be made against an HMRC decision that a penalty is payable or against a decision as to the amount of a penalty. Where relevant, an appeal can be made against a decision not to suspend a penalty or against conditions of suspension. In general, an appeal is treated in the same way as an appeal against an assessment to the tax concerned (but not so as to require payment of the penalty before the appeal is determined). An appeal must be made within the 30-day period beginning with the date on which HMRC notification of the penalty assessment is issued.

The powers of the Tribunal are restricted in certain cases, to where it thinks that HMRC's decision was flawed when considered in the light of principles applicable in proceedings for judicial review. The decisions concerned are as follows:

- a decision as to the extent to which the provisions for reduction of a penalty in special circumstances apply;
- (where relevant) a decision not to suspend a penalty; and
- a decision as to the conditions of suspension.

Where the Tribunal orders HMRC to suspend a penalty, there is a further right of appeal against the provisions of HMRC's notice of suspension.

In partnership cases, an appeal against a penalty under *FA 2009, Sch 55* can be brought only by the partner required to make the return or his successor. Such an appeal is treated as an appeal against every penalty payable by any partner in respect of the failure concerned. This provision was applied in *Dyson v HMRC* FTT [2015] SFTD 529, despite the Tribunal holding that it contravened the European Convention on Human Rights.

***Penalty under** FA 2013, ss 212A, 212B*

The following further provisions apply. An appeal against the imposition of a penalty can only be made on the grounds that the arrangements concerned were not abusive or that there was no tax advantage to be counteracted (see **4.3** ANTI-AVOIDANCE). An appeal against the amount of a penalty can only be made on the grounds that the penalty is based on an overestimate of the counteracted advantage (see **59.17** above). Where the person liable to the penalty is a partner and the final counteraction notice was given to the partnership's responsible partner (see **4.7** ANTI-AVOIDANCE), an appeal can only be made by the responsible partner.

If the appeal is against the amount of a penalty and it is heard by the Tribunal, the Tribunal may affirm the amount charged or substitute its own amount (but only an amount that HMRC could have chosen to charge). Payment of the penalty is not required before any appeal is determined.

Penalty under FA 2014, ss 208, 208A

The following further provisions apply to an appeal against an assessment to a penalty under *FA 2014, s 208* (failure to comply with follower notice) or *FA 2014, s 208A* (additional penalty for an unreasonable appeal) (see **59.23**(9) and **59.14** above). The grounds on which an appeal against a penalty under *s 208* can be made include in particular that the conditions for giving the follower notice at **4.30**(a), (b) or (d) ANTI-AVOIDANCE were not satisfied; that the judicial ruling is not relevant to the arrangements which are the subject of the notice; that the notice was given outside the time limit; and that it was reasonable in all the circumstances not to take the necessary corrective action (see **4.31** ANTI-AVOIDANCE).

An appeal against a decision to impose a penalty under *s 208A* can only be made on the grounds that *s 208A* did not apply when the decision was made or no longer applies; that the taxpayer or their representative had not acted unreasonably in bringing or conducting the appeal proceedings; or that the penalty was assessed outside the time limit.

The cancellation of HMRC's decision to impose a penalty under *s 208* on the grounds that it was reasonable not to take the corrective action does not affect the validity of the follower notice nor of any accelerated payment notice or partner payment notice (see **4.33** ANTI-AVOIDANCE) related to the follower notice. If the Tribunal cancels HMRC's decision to impose a penalty under *s 208*, any additional penalty for an unreasonable appeal under *FA 2014, s 208A* is also cancelled.

No appeal can be made against the apportionment of a penalty between partners.

Penalty under FA 2008, Sch 36 or FA 2011, Sch 23

Appeals can be brought to the First-tier Tribunal against an HMRC decision that a penalty other than a tax-related penalty (see **59.11, 59.12** above) is payable or against a decision as to the amount of such a penalty (other than the amount of an increased daily penalty for failure to comply with an information notice and a £1,000 penalty for failure to comply with a requirement not to disclose a third party notice or financial institution notice). Notice of appeal must be given in writing within the 30-day period beginning with the date on which HMRC notification of the penalty assessment is issued, and must state the grounds of appeal. Subject to this, the general APPEALS (5) provisions apply as they apply to income tax assessments.

Penalty under F(No 2)A 2017, Sch 16

If the appeal is against the amount of a penalty and it is heard by the Tribunal, the Tribunal may affirm the amount charged or substitute its own amount (but only an amount that HMRC could have chosen to charge). If the Tribunal substitutes its own amount, it must rely on the provision to mitigate the penalty to the same extent as HMRC unless it thinks that HMRC's decision on mitigation was flawed when considered in the light of judicial review principles.

[*FA 2007, Sch 24 paras 15–17; FA 2008, Sch 36 paras 47, 48, 51C(1)(2); FA 2008, Sch 41 paras 17–19; FA 2009, Sch 55 paras 20–22, 25(4)(5), Sch 56 paras 13–15; TIOPA 2010, Sch 7A paras 29(5)(6), 35, 36, 39(4)(5); FA 2011, Sch 23 paras 36, 37; FA 2013, Sch 43C para 9; FA 2014, ss 214, 214A, 226(7), Sch 31 para 5(7)–(10); F(No 2)A 2015, Sch 8 para 16; FA 2016, ss 158(3), 177(5), Sch 18 para 41, Sch 19 para 30, Sch 20 paras 12–14; F(No 2)A 2017, Sch 5 para 2, Sch 16 paras 37–39; FA 2021, Sch 28 paras 7, 8, 12, Sch 32 para 13(9), Sch 34 paras 2–4*].

Penalty imposed by determination

Subject to the following points, the general APPEALS (5) provisions apply to an appeal against a determination of a penalty as in **59.23**(a)–(e) above.

TMA 1970, s 50(6)–(8) (see **5.24** APPEALS) do not apply. Instead (subject to below), on appeal the First-tier Tribunal can:

- in the case of a penalty which is required to be of a particular amount, set the determination aside, confirm it, or alter it to the correct amount; and
- in any other case, set the determination aside, confirm it if it seems appropriate, or reduce it (including to nil) or increase it as seems appropriate (but not beyond the permitted maximum).

In addition to the right to appeal to the Upper Tribunal on a point of law, the taxpayer can so appeal (with permission) against the amount of a penalty determined by the First-tier Tribunal.

[*TMA 1970, ss 100B, 103ZA*].

In *ASI Properties Ltd v HMRC* (TC00981) [2011] UKFTT 105 (TC) a company failed to submit its CT return for the period ending 31 July 2006 until 25 March 2009. The return showed CT due of £430,850. HMRC imposed a penalty of £82,940 under *FA 1998, Sch 18 para 18(2)*. The First-tier Tribunal dismissed the company's appeal. Judge Trigger held that the company had not demonstrated a responsible attitude to the requirement placed upon it by the legislation to submit a return on time and that there was no reasonable excuse for the long delay in filing the return.

With regard to the standard of proof required, it was held by the High Court in the long running case of *TI Khawaja v HMRC (No 2)* [2008] EWHC 1687 (Ch), [2009] 1 WLR 398, [2008] STC 2880 that the civil standard of proof, on the balance of probabilities, was appropriate with regard to penalties imposed on a company director for understatement of income which represented undisclosed remuneration from the company. The appeals against the penalties were then re-heard by the First-tier tribunal (judgment March 2012). The Court of Appeal had rejected an application by the director to appeal against this decision, suggesting that they agreed that the standard of proof with regard to penalties is the civil standard rather than the criminal standard. In the most recent instalment the decision of the First-tier tribunal as to the imposition of a penalty at 40% of the evaded tax was appealed to the Upper Tribunal, which reduced the penalty to 35%, with a further reduction of 10% to reflect that the matter had not been heard 'within a reasonable time' (at [2013] UKUT 353 (TCC)).

Miscellaneous issues concerning penalties

Interest on penalties

[59.25] Penalties imposed under *FA 1998, Sch 18* (see **59.3** above) in connection with the company tax return, carry interest calculated from the due date (broadly, 30 days after issue of a notice of determination by an officer of HMRC or immediately upon determination by the Tribunal or Court — see **58.24** below) to the date of payment. [*TMA 1970, s 103A; SI 2019 No 918*]. Rates of interest on penalties are synonymous with those on unpaid tax — see **43.2** INTEREST ON OVERDUE TAX.

See also **59.10** above for interest on penalties imposed under *TMA 1970, s 98C*, **59.13** above for interest on penalties imposed under *FA 2014, Sch 35* and **59.20** above for interest on penalties imposed under *FA 2016, Sch 20*.

Reasonable excuse for failure

[59.26] It is generally provided that a person is deemed not to have failed to do anything required to be done where there was a reasonable excuse for the failure and, if the reasonable excuse ceased, provided that the failure was remedied without unreasonable delay after the excuse had ceased. Similarly, a person is deemed not to have failed to do anything required to be done within a limited time if he did it within such further time as HMRC or the Tribunal may have allowed. [*TMA 1970, s 118(2)*].

In *Creedplan Ltd v Winter* [1995] STC (SCD) 352, the Special Commissioner, in confirming a penalty under *TMA 1970, s 94(1)(a)* (before its repeal on the introduction of self-assessment), considered that 'there is no reasonable excuse . . . for sending in a return which was less than was required' (but cf. *Akarimsons Ltd v Chapman* [1997] STC (SCD) 140 in which a penalty under *s 94(1)(b)* was quashed). See also *Steeden v Carver* [1999] STC (SCD) 283, in which reliance on HMRC's advice as to the practical extension of a deadline, unequivocally given, was held to be 'as reasonable an excuse as could be found'. In *David Wake-Walker v HMRC* [2013] UKFTT 717 (TC) it was held that an honest belief on the part of the taxpayer can constitute a reasonable excuse, whether or not it is reasonable. In *Zoltan Hegedus v HMRC* [2014] UKFTT 1049 it was held that a delay in receiving an HMRC authorisation code, due to the taxpayer instructing accountants late, was not a reasonable excuse for the late filing of a return. However HMRC error may give rise to a reasonable excuse being accepted. In *Perfect Permit v HMRC* [2015] UKFTT 171 it was held that the late registration of an agent by HMRC did constitute a reasonable excuse for the late submission of employer annual returns. In *Joanna L Porter t/a Crafty Creations v HMRC* [2015] UKFTT 170 Ms Porter attempted to file her return and pay the tax due online but had access issues and was informed by HMRC that this was due to an IT failure which would be remedied. The IT difficulties encountered were unexpected and were eventually solved when HMRC issued her with a new ID number. It was held the taxpayer had established a reasonable excuse. In *Ann Hauser v HMRC* [2015] UKFTT 682 it was found that in circumstances where HMRC had not received a return even though the taxpayer had clicked 'submit', the taxpayer had a reasonable excuse for late filing. In *Sowinski v HMRC* [2015] UKFTT 636 the First-tier Tribunal held that while the taxpayer had a reasonable excuse for failure to file monthly CIS returns, the penalty should stand as he did not remedy the failure within a reasonable time of the excuse ceasing. In *Dhiren Doshi v HMRC* [2016] UKFTT 5 it was held that the daily penalties imposed for non-compliance with an information notice should not apply as the taxpayer had a reasonable excuse in that he had a serious heart condition during the period and had been in no fit state to deal with such matters.

See HMRC Company Taxation Manual, CTM94140 for HMRC's approach to 'reasonable excuse'.

Mitigation or limitation of penalties

[59.27] The following mitigation rules do not apply to penalties under *FA 2007, Sch 24* or *FA 2008, Schs 36, 41*, *FA 2009, Schs 55, 56*, *FA 2013, s 212A*, *FA 2014, s 208* and *s 226* and *FA 2016, Sch 18*. For the separate rules applicable to those penalties see the relevant paragraphs above.

HMRC may mitigate penalties before or after judgment [*TMA 1970, s 102*]. See Tolley's Tax Cases generally.

Where two or more tax-geared penalties relate to the same liability, the aggregate amount of the penalties is limited to the greater or greatest penalty applicable. [*TMA 1970, s 97A; FA 1998, Sch 18 para 90*].

Contract settlements

A taxpayer may be invited to offer a sum in full settlement of liability for tax, interest and penalties (a 'contract settlement') and such offers are often accepted by HMRC without assessment of all the tax. A binding agreement so made cannot be repudiated afterwards by the taxpayer or his executors.

Contract settlements may also be used to bring an enquiry (or compliance check) to a close, instead of a closure notice.

See *CIR v Nuttall* (1989) 63 TC 148, CA, for confirmation of power to enter into such agreements. Amounts due under such an agreement which are unpaid may be pursued by an action for a debt, but the Crown does not rank as a preferential creditor in respect of the sums due (*Nuttall* above; *CIR v Woollen* [1992] STC 944, 65 TC 229, CA).

Delay

[59.28] In *King v UK (No 3)* (2004) 76 TC 699 it was found that an 'unreasonable delay' by HMRC in bringing penalty proceedings could infringe the taxpayer's human rights, even if there had also been delay by the taxpayer. The implications of the case extend to voluntary contract settlements as well as to formal penalty proceedings. See Special Criminal Investigation Manual, SCIG14320.

Time limits

[59.29] A penalty assessment (see **59.23** above) is treated as, and enforced as, an assessment to tax and must be issued within certain time limits.

The time limits are:

(a) Incorrect returns — *FA 2007, Sch 24*.
   - (i) If the penalty is payable under *FA 2007, Sch 24 paras 1, 1A*, the assessment must be made within twelve months from the end of the appeal period for the decision correcting the inaccuracy. If there was no assessment, the twelve-month period runs from the date on which the inaccuracy was corrected.
   - (ii) If the penalty is payable under *FA 2007, Sch 24 para 2*, the time is twelve months from the end of the appeal period for the amended assessment which corrected the understatement.

   [*FA 2007, Sch 24 para 13*].

(b) Failure to notify chargeability — *FA 2008, Sch 41*.
   - (i) Where an assessment to recover the tax arising from the failure for the year in question has been issued, the penalty assessment must be made within twelve months of the earlier of: expiry of the thirty-day appeal period for the assessment of the unpaid tax; and the determination or withdrawal of an appeal against that assessment.
   - (ii) Where such an assessment has not been issued, the penalty assessment must to be made within twelve months of the date that the amount of tax unpaid as a result of the failure is ascertained.

Further penalty assessments may be made in cases where the potential lost revenue increases after an initial penalty assessment has been made. [*FA 2008, Sch 41 para 16*].

(c) Failure to deliver a return (not yet applicable to corporation tax) — *FA 2009, Sch 55*:
Time limit is the latest of:
  (i) the last day of the period of two years beginning with the filing date;
  (ii) where an assessment to recover the tax arising from the failure for the year in question has been issued, twelve months from the earlier of expiry of the thirty-day appeal period for the assessment or the determination or withdrawal of an appeal; and
  (iii) where an assessment to recover the tax has not been issued, twelve months from the date that the tax liability in the return is ascertained or the liability is found to be nil.

[*FA 2009, Sch 55 para 19*].

(d) Late payment of tax (not yet applicable to corporation tax) — *FA 2009, Sch 56*:
Time limit is the later of:
  (i) the last day of the period of two years beginning with the due date for payment of the tax in question (i.e. the day before the penalty date); or
  (ii) the last day of the period of twelve months beginning with:
    (A) where an assessment has been issued to recover the tax in respect of which the penalty has been charged, the end of the appeal period for the assessment or the determination or withdrawal of an appeal; or
    (B) where no such assessment has been issued, the date that the amount of tax unpaid as a result of the failure is ascertained.

[*FA 2009, Sch 56 para 12*].

The above provisions apply, with any necessary modifications, to penalties for a failure to make an accelerated payment. [*FA 2014, s 226(7)*].

(e) HMRC investigatory powers — *FA 2008, Sch 36*.
An assessment to a fixed or daily penalty must be made within 12 months of the date on which the liability arose. Where, however, the penalty is for a failure relating to an information notice against which a person can appeal, the assessment must be made within 12 months of the later of the end of the period in which notice of such appeal could have been given and, where an appeal is made, the date on which the appeal is determined or withdrawn. An assessment to a penalty for an inaccuracy must be made within 12 months of HMRC first becoming aware of the inaccuracy and within six years of the person becoming liable to the penalty. An assessment for a failure to comply with a requirement not to disclose a third party notice or financial institution notice must be made within twelve months of HMRC first becoming aware of the breach of the requirement.

[*FA 2008, Sch 36 paras 46, 51B(3); FA 2021, Sch 34 para 2*].

(f) HMRC data-gathering powers — *FA 2011, Sch 23*.

An assessment to a fixed or daily penalty must be made within 12 months of the date on which the liability arose. Where, however, the penalty is for a failure relating to a data-holder notice against which a person can appeal, the assessment must be made within 12 months of the later of the end of the period in which notice of such appeal could have been given and, where an appeal is made, the date on which the appeal is determined or withdrawn (if that date is later than the date on which the liability arose). An assessment to a penalty for an inaccuracy must be made within 12 months of HMRC first becoming aware of the inaccuracy and within six years of the person becoming liable to the penalty. [*FA 2011, Sch 23 para 35*].

(g) Follower notices — *FA 2014, ss 208, 208A*.
Where the follower notice was given whilst an enquiry was in progress, an assessment of a penalty under *s 208* for failure to comply must be made before the end of the period of 90 days beginning with the day the enquiry is completed. Where the follower notice was given whilst an appeal was open, an assessment of a penalty must be made before the end of the period of 90 days beginning with the earliest of the day on which the taxpayer takes the necessary corrective action, the day on which a ruling is made on the appeal or further appeal which is a final ruling and the day on which the appeal, or further appeal, is abandoned or otherwise disposed of before being finally determined. An assessment of a penalty under *s 208A* for an unreasonable appeal must be made before the end of the period of 90 days beginning on the day after the day on which the time limit for making an appeal against the striking out of the appeal or declaration that the appeal was unreasonable expires or, where such an appeal has been made, the day on which the appeal is finally determined, withdrawn or otherwise disposed of. [*FA 2014, ss 211, 211A(4), 213; FA 2021, Sch 28 paras 4, 6*].

(h) Fixed and daily penalties under the enforcement of tax debts by deduction from accounts provisions — *F(No 2)A 2015, Sch 8*.
An assessment to a penalty within **59.16**(a) above must be made within 12 months beginning with the date on which the liability to the penalty arose. An assessment to a penalty within **59.16**(b)–(f) above must be made within 12 months beginning with the latest of the date on which the liability to the penalty arose, the end of the period in which an appeal against the hold notice could have been made and, if such an appeal is made, the date on which the appeal is finally determined or withdrawn. [*F(No 2)A 2015, Sch 8 para 15(2)(3)*].

(i) Penalty in respect of arrangements counteracted under the general anti-avoidance rule — *FA 2013, s 212A*.
An assessment to a penalty (see **59.17** above) must be made within the 12 months beginning with the latest of the dates on which the counteraction under the GAAR (see **4.3** ANTI-AVOIDANCE) becomes final. Where a person becomes liable to a penalty before 22 July 2020, the assessment must be made within the 12 months beginning with the end of the appeal period for the assessment giving effect to the counteraction or, if there is no such assessment, the 12 months beginning with the latest of the dates on which the counteraction becomes final. For this purpose, counterac-

tion becomes final when the adjustments made, and any amounts resulting from them, can no longer be varied, on appeal or otherwise. [*FA 2013, Sch 43C para 5; FA 2020, Sch 14 paras 9, 14, 15*].

(j) Penalty under the serial avoiders regime — *FA 2016, Sch 18.*
An assessment to a penalty under *FA 2016, Sch 18* (see **59.18** above) must be made within the 12 months beginning with the date of the relevant defeat in question. [*FA 2016, Sch 18 para 38*].

(k) Penalty for failure to comply with requirement to publish tax strategy — *FA 2016, Sch 19.*
An assessment to a penalty under *FA 2016, Sch 19* (see **59.19** above) must be made within the six months after the failure first comes to the attention of an HMRC officer and cannot be made more than six years after the end of the financial year to which the failure relates. [*FA 2016, Sch 19 para 29*].

(l) Penalty for enabler of offshore tax evasion — *FA 2016, Sch 20.*
An assessment to a penalty under *FA 2016, Sch 20* (see **59.20** above) must be made no more than two years after the fulfilment of the conditions at **59.20**(a) and (b) above first came to the attention of an HMRC officer. [*FA 2016, Sch 20 para 11*].

(m) Penalty for enabler of abusive tax arrangements— *F(No 2)A 2017, Sch 16.*
An assessment to a penalty under *F(No 2)A 2017, Sch 16* (see **59.21** above) may not be made after whichever of the following times applies:
  (i) where a GAAR final decision notice has been given in relation to the arrangements in question (see **59.21**(A) above), the end of 12 months beginning with the date on which T incurs the defeat;
  (ii) where a GAAR final decision notice has been given in relation to equivalent arrangements and HMRC have given a notice stating their view that it is relevant to the arrangements in question (see **59.21**(A) above), the end of 12 months beginning with the end of the time allowed for representations in respect of that notice;
  (iii) where HMRC have made a referral to the GAAR Advisory Panel (see **59.21**(B) above) in respect of the arrangements in question and (iv) below does not apply, the end of 12 months beginning with the date on which the Panel's opinion is given;
  (iv) where the taxpayer was not given a notice within **59.21**(1) above before the referral of arrangements to the GAAR Advisory Panel but HMRC have given a notice stating their view that its opinion applies to the arrangements in question (see **59.21**(B) above), the end of 12 months beginning with the end of the time allowed for representations in respect of that notice.

If HMRC cannot assess a penalty until one of the conditions at **59.21**(I)–(III) above is met, the time limit is extended to the end of the 12 months beginning with the date on which the condition is met. If, in such a case, a person requests assessment of the penalty before any conditions are met, the assessment must be made before the end of the 12 months beginning with the date of the request. If a declaration that a person is not liable to a penalty has been made by a lawyer under the provisions for privileged communications and facts then come to HMRC's knowledge that in their opinion are sufficient to indicate that

the declaration contained a material inaccuracy, the deadline for assessing the penalty is extended to the end of the 12 months beginning with the date on which the facts come to HMRC's knowledge.
[*F(No 2)A 2017, Sch 16 para 22; FA 2021, s 123(3)*].

(n) Penalty under the corporate interest restriction provisions— *TIOPA 2010, Sch 7A*.
An assessment to a penalty under *TIOPA 2010, Sch 7A* (see **59.22** above) must be made within the 12 months:
- (where the penalty is within **59.22**(i) above) beginning with the filing date;
- (where the penalty is within **59.22**(ii) or (iii) above) beginning with the day on which the inaccuracy is corrected;
- (where the penalty is within **59.22**(iv) above) beginning with the day on which HMRC first become away that the company has failed to comply with its record-keeping obligations.

[*TIOPA 2010, Sch 7A paras 29(4), 34(2), 39(3); F(No 2)A 2017, Sch 5 para* 2].

Where a penalty is not imposed by assessment, the time within which it can be determined, or proceedings commenced, is as follows.

(a) If the penalty is ascertainable by reference to tax payable, the time is the later of six years after the penalty was incurred and three years after the determination of the amount of the tax.
(b) In any other case, the time is six years from the time when the penalty was, or began to be, incurred.

[*TMA 1970, s 103*].

Provisional agreement of the amount due subject to HMRC's being satisfied with statements of assets, etc. is not final determination for these purposes (*Carco Accessories Ltd v CIR* CS 1985, 59 TC 45).

Failure to state tax credit etc.

[59.30] Failure to provide the required written statement of the amount of dividend or interest paid and the amount of the related tax credit etc. (see **28.18** DISTRIBUTIONS) carries a penalty of £60 for each offence with a maximum of £600 in respect of any one distribution etc. [*CTA 2010, s 1107*].

Liability under criminal law

[59.31] 'False statements to the prejudice of the Crown and public revenue' are criminal offences (*R v Hudson* CCA 1956, 36 TC 561) as they constitute a fraud on Crown and the public, which is indictable as a common law offence of cheating the public revenue. False statements in tax returns, or for obtaining any allowance, reduction or repayment may involve liability to imprisonment for up to two years, under *Perjury Act 1911, s 5*, for 'knowingly and wilfully' making materially false statements or returns for tax purposes. Also, in Scotland, summary proceedings may be taken under *TMA 1970, s 107*.

Criminal prosecutions for tax fraud in England and Wales are conducted by the Crown Prosecution Service. For HMRC practice in considering whether to accept a money settlement or institute criminal proceedings for fraud, see **38.16** HMRC INVESTIGATORY POWERS.

For criminal offences relating to HMRC INVESTIGATORY POWERS see **38.11** and **38.18**.

The fraudulent evasion of *income tax* (not corporation tax) on behalf of oneself or another person is itself a criminal offence. [*TMA 1970, s 106A*].

Many of the civil penalties described in this chapter specifically include a 'double jeopardy' rule, under which a person is not liable to a penalty for a failure or action in respect of which he has been convicted of an offence.

The Government intends to introduce legislation providing for a new criminal offence for corporations who fail to stop their staff facilitating tax evasion before 2020. See Treasury Notice 11 April 2016.

Simon's Taxes A6.11.

Failure to prevent facilitation of tax evasion

[59.32] With effect from 30 September 2017, a company is guilty of an offence if an employee or agent of the company or any other person performing services for the company commits a 'UK tax evasion facilitation offence' or a 'foreign tax evasion facilitation offence' when acting in the capacity of employee, agent etc. In the case of a foreign tax evasion facilitation offence, the company must be UK incorporated, carry on a business in the UK and any conduct forming part of the facilitation offence must take place in the UK.

It is a defence for the company to prove either that, when the facilitation offence was committed, it had in place procedures designed to prevent employees etc. from committing facilitation offences which it was reasonable to expect it to have in place, or that it was not reasonable to expect the company to have such procedures in place. The Government have published guidance on such procedures. See 'Tackling tax evasion: Government guidance for the corporate offence of failure to prevent the criminal facilitation of tax evasion' dated 1 September 2017.

A '*UK tax evasion facilitation offence*' is an offence under UK law consisting of:

(a) being knowingly concerned in, or in taking steps with a view to, the fraudulent evasion of tax by another person;
(b) aiding, abetting, counselling or procuring the commission of a 'UK tax evasion offence'; or
(c) being involved art and part in the commission of an offence within (a) above.

Conduct within (a) above is not a UK tax evasion facilitation offence unless the other person has committed a UK tax evasion offence facilitated by that conduct. A '*UK tax evasion offence*' is an offence of cheating the public revenue or an offence under UK law consisting of being knowingly concerned in, or in taking steps with a view to, the fraudulent evasion of tax. '*Tax*' includes any UK tax or National Insurance contributions.

A '*foreign tax evasion facilitation offence*' is conduct which amounts to an offence under the law of a foreign country, relates to the commission by another person of a 'foreign tax evasion offence' under that country's law and would be a UK tax evasion facilitation offence if the foreign tax evasion offence were a UK tax evasion offence. A '*foreign tax evasion offence*' is conduct which amounts to an offence under the law of a foreign country, relates to a breach of a duty relating to a tax of that country and would by regarded by UK courts as amounting to being knowingly concerned in, or in taking steps with a view to, the fraudulent evasion of that tax.

A company guilty of an offence under these provisions is liable to a fine. The provisions apply equally to partnerships.

[*Criminal Finances Act 2017, ss 44–52, 58(5); SI 2017 Nos 739, 876*].

HMRC have published guidance for authorised representatives of companies on the procedure for notifying HMRC of a failure by the company to prevent the facilitation of UK tax evasion. HMRC consider that self-reporting does not guarantee that the company will not be prosecuted, but could form part of its defence. See www.gov.uk/guidance/tell-hmrc-about-a-company-helping-people-to-evade-tax.

60

Property Income

Cross references. See **9.22** onwards CAPITAL ALLOWANCES for allowances available in respect of structures and buildings.

Introduction to property income

[60.1] The charge to corporation tax on income (see **1.7** INTRODUCTION) applies to the profits of a 'property business', whether the profits are from property in the UK or overseas. [*CTA 2009, s 209*]. Profits (and losses) are computed broadly in the same way as profits and losses of a trade, i.e. in accordance with generally accepted accounting practice (GAAP) and subject to the exclusion of capital receipts and expenditure and the prohibition on deductions for expenditure not incurred wholly and exclusively for the purposes of the business.

With effect from 6 April 2020 (subject to the transitional rules at **64.7** RESIDENCE), the charge to corporation tax also applies to a non-UK resident company which carries on a UK property business or has other UK property income (i.e. rent receivable in connection with a *CTA 2009, s 39* concern (mines, quarries etc. — see **60.18** below), rent receivable for electric-line wayleaves (see **60.18** below) and post-cessation receipts from a UK property business (see **60.4** below)). Previously such income was within the charge to income tax (see **64.8** RESIDENCE).

Relevant definitions

Where this work refers simply to a '*property business*', then unless the context clearly suggests otherwise, it means either a UK property business or an overseas property business (see in both cases **60.2** below).

In this chapter, '*lease*' includes an agreement for a lease (in so far as the context permits) and any tenancy, but not a mortgage over the property.

'*Premises*' includes land. [*CTA 2009, s 291*].

'*Land*' includes an estate or interest in land. Where the business is an overseas property business, the legislation is to be read so as to produce an effect most closely corresponding with that produced on a UK property. [*CTA 2009, s 290*].

CTA 2009, ss 287, 288 set out certain priority rules where a receipt or other credit item could be dealt with either as trading income or property income (*s 287*); or, either as property income within **60.18** below (electric-line way-leaves or mines, quarries etc.) or as other property income (*s 288*).

See **68.44** TRADING INCOME as regards the inclusion in trading profits of receipts from, and expenses of letting of, surplus business accommodation.

See **69.7** TRADING INCOME — DEDUCTIONS as regards the inclusion in trading profits of receipts and expenses in respect of tied premises (breweries etc), which would otherwise be brought into account in calculating profits of a property business.

[*CTA 2009, ss 287, 288*].

Charge to tax

[60.2] Corporation tax is chargeable on the profits of a property business, whether it is a 'UK property business' or an 'overseas property business'.

See **60.4** below as regards the computation of the profits of a property business. The person liable to pay the tax is the person in receipt of, or entitled to, the profits.

For these purposes, a person's 'UK property business' consists of every business which he carries on for 'generating income from land' (see below) in the UK and any other transactions which he enters into for that purpose. A company's UK property business is separate from any property business carried on by a partnership of which it is a member. An 'overseas property business' is similarly defined.

Where this chapter refers simply to a 'property business' it means either a UK or an overseas property business (unless the context clearly suggests otherwise). Any reference to something being charged to tax as property income or within the charge to tax on property income is a reference to its having to be brought into account in computing the profits of a property business.

'*Generating income from land*' means exploiting an estate, interest or right in or over land as a source of rent or other receipts. Expenditure by a tenant on maintenance and repairs which the lease does not require him to carry out counts as rent in the landlord's hands. The reference above to 'any other transaction' brings into charge, for example, one-off or casual lettings. 'Other receipts' include:

- payments in respect of a licence to occupy or otherwise use land or in respect of the exercise of any other right over land; and
- rentcharges and any other annual payments reserved in respect of, or charged on or issuing out of, land.

For the above purposes, the following activities are *not* treated as carried on for generating income from land:

- farming or market gardening in the UK, which is instead treated as a trade — see **68.30** TRADING INCOME;
- any other *occupation* of land, but commercial occupation of land is treated as a trade (with the exception for woodlands) — see **68.2** TRADING INCOME; and
- activities for the purposes of a concern within *CTA 2009, s 39* (mines, quarries etc.) — see **68.46** TRADING INCOME and **65.11** RETURNS.

[*CTA 2009, ss 204–208, 1270(2)(3)*].

See also *J Nott v HMRC* [2016] UKFTT 106 where the First-tier Tribunal held that an individual was deriving income from property and was not trading. A key consideration was the 'profit derivation' test, in particular where additional services were being provided.

Receipts from furnished lettings in most cases are charged as income from a property business, unless the lettings fall within trading income (such as furnished holiday lettings, see below) and casual lettings.

Annual Tax on Enveloped Dwellings

For a detailed overview of the Annual Tax on Enveloped Dwellings see **Simon's Taxes Division B6.7**.

Companies, partnerships with at least one company member and collective investment schemes (including unit trusts) who own residential dwellings situated in the UK are chargeable to an annual residential property tax, the Annual Tax on Enveloped Dwellings (ATED), if the value of the dwellings on relevant dates exceeds a specified threshold. The charge is payable annually, with the chargeable period running for 12 months from 1 April each year. The value threshold, for chargeable periods beginning on or after 1 April 2016, is £500,000. Genuine property rental businesses and taxpayers holding properties for charitable purposes or properties run as a commercial business can claim a relief from the tax on an annual basis. The tax is administered by HMRC and requires those within the scope of the tax to make annual ATED returns.

See also www.gov.uk/guidance/annual-tax-on-enveloped-dwellings-the-basics. [*FA 2013, ss 94–174; FA 2016, ss 134–136*].

Caravans and caravan sites

Receipts from furnished lettings also includes lettings from caravans which are at a fixed location.

However, if a company carries on material activities connected with the operation of a caravan site and those activities themselves constitute a trade or a part of a trade, the income and expenses of letting the caravans and/or pitches can be included in computing the profits of that trade instead of being treated as property income. See **60.3** (B) below as regards furnished holiday lettings.

A '*caravan*' for this purpose is a structure designed or adapted for living in and which is capable of being moved or towed or transported on a motor vehicle or trailer or a motor vehicle designed or adapted for living in. Railway rolling stock on rails and tents are not included. The definition may include a structure of two sections, separately constructed but designed to be bolted together on site, even though it cannot be legally moved in its assembled condition.

[*CTA 2009, ss 43, 213*].

Exclusions

[60.3] The following items are excluded from the computation of property income for corporation tax purposes, as they are taxed under distinct regimes:

(i) interest payable, and other amounts falling within the LOAN RELATIONSHIPS (50) legislation;
(ii) profits and losses on DERIVATIVE CONTRACTS (27); and
(iii) foreign exchange gains and losses falling within (i) or (ii) above.

[*CTA 2009, s 211*].

In addition, property income does not include:

- profits from occupying land (e.g. from woodlands) (see **68.2** TRADING INCOME);
- profits chargeable to corporation tax as trading income from farming and market gardening (for which see **68.30** TRADING INCOME);
- profits chargeable to corporation tax as trading income from mining, quarrying and other such concerns (for which see **68.2** TRADING INCOME);
- trading receipts and expenses from tied premises (for which see **69.7** TRADING INCOME — DEDUCTIONS);
- rent charged to corporation tax as trading income in connection with mines, quarries, etc. [*CTA 2009, s 271*]; or
- rent charged to corporation tax as trading income in connection with electric line wayleaves (see **60.18** below).

The letting of all property in the UK by the same person is to be treated as a single business, except in the case of the following. (See **60.18** below for rental income from land outside the UK.) [*CTA 2009, s 205*].

(A) *Companies not resident in the UK*. In the case of a non-resident company trading in the UK through a permanent establishment (see **64.6** RESIDENCE), a property business within the charge to corporation tax is treated as a separate business from any UK property business chargeable to income tax before 6 April 2020. See **64.5** *et seq.* RESIDENCE.
(B) *Furnished holiday lettings*. Income from the commercial letting of furnished holiday accommodation which does not amount to the carrying on of a trade is taxed as income from a property business. However, separate calculations are required of holiday letting profits and other profits for the purposes of capital allowances and loss relief. See **60.7** below. [*CTA 2009, s 269*].

Flat management companies

Residential service charges received by an occupier-controlled flat management company are normally received as capital by the landlord in his capacity as trustee. See HMRC Property Income Manual, PIM1075. For a general article on the trust implications of flat management companies, service charge funds and sinking funds, see HMRC Tax Bulletin August 2000 pp 770–774.

Miscellaneous

Receipts from sales of turf have been held to be taxable as property income although they may alternatively be taxed as trading income (*Lowe v J W Ashmore Ltd* (1970) 46 TC 597); but receipts from sale of colliery dross bings were held to be capital (*Roberts (Inspector of Taxes) v Lord Belhaven and Stenton's Executors* (1925) 9 TC 501, 1925 SC 635, Ct of Sess). Sums received for licence to tip soil on land were held to be capital (*McClure v Petre* (1988) 61 TC 226). Note that these cases were decided under the pre-1 April 1998 regime, which differed in a number of material respects from the current rules.

Computing the profits of a property business

[60.4] The profits or losses of a property business are to be computed in accordance with the principles applicable to the computation of trading profits (see 68 TRADING INCOME). These include the fundamental rules that profits or losses be computed in accordance with generally accepted accounting practice (GAAP), that capital receipts and expenditure be excluded and that, subject to any specific rule to the contrary, expenditure is not deductible unless incurred wholly and exclusively for the purposes of the business.

Profits are calculated on an accruals (arising) basis rather than a cash basis.

Account must also be taken of: the capital allowances rules, which in particular override the rules against the inclusion of capital receipts; and the rules relating to credits and debits in respect of intangible fixed assets held for the purposes of a property. Thus capital allowances are treated as deductions and balancing charges as receipts of the business and debits and credits in respect of intangible assets are treated similarly.

Only the following specific trading income equivalents apply to the computation of property business profits or losses:

CTA 2009	**Brief description**	**See main coverage at**
s 46	Use of generally accepted accounting practice	**68.19** TRADING INCOME
s 47	Losses computed on same basis as profits	**51.3** LOSSES
s 48	Receipts and expenses	**69.2** TRADING INCOME — DEDUCTIONS
s 49A	Money's worth	**68.48** TRADING INCOME
s 52	Apportionment of profits and losses to accounting periods	**2.3** ACCOUNTING PERIODS
s 53	Capital expenditure non-deductible	**69.8** TRADING INCOME — DEDUCTIONS

CTA 2009	Brief description	See main coverage at
s 54	'Wholly and exclusively' rule for expenditure	**69.74** TRADING INCOME — DEDUCTIONS
s 55	Bad and doubtful debts	**69.5** TRADING INCOME — DEDUCTIONS
ss 56–58B	Car or motor cycle hire	**69.9** TRADING INCOME — DEDUCTIONS
s 59	Patent royalties paid	**68.49** TRADING INCOME
s 61	Pre-trading expenses	**69.57** TRADING INCOME — DEDUCTIONS
s 68	Replacement and alteration of trade tools (expenditure incurred before 1 April 2016)	**69.60** TRADING INCOME — DEDUCTIONS
s 69	Payments for restrictive undertakings	**69.22** TRADING INCOME — DEDUCTIONS
ss 70, 71	Employees seconded to charities or educational bodies	**69.18** TRADING INCOME — DEDUCTIONS
s 72	Payroll deduction schemes: contributions to agent's administrative costs	**69.29** TRADING INCOME — DEDUCTIONS
ss 73–75	Counselling and retraining services for employees	**69.16** TRADING INCOME — DEDUCTIONS
ss 76–81	Redundancy payments etc	**69.23** TRADING INCOME — DEDUCTIONS
ss 82–86	Contributions of local enterprise organisations or urban regeneration companies	**45.4** INVESTMENT COMPANIES AND INVESTMENT BUSINESS
ss 86A, 86B	Contributions to flood and coastal erosion risk management projects	**69.45** TRADING INCOME — DEDUCTIONS
ss 87, 88	Scientific research	**63** RESEARCH AND DEVELOPMENT EXPENDITURE
ss 89, 90	Expenditure in connection with patents, designs or trade marks	**68.49** TRADING INCOME
s 91	Payments to Export Credits Guarantee Department	**68.47** TRADING INCOME
s 92	Levies under *FISMA 2000*	**45.4** INVESTMENT COMPANIES AND INVESTMENT BUSINESS
s 92A	Deductions in relation to salaried members of limited liability partnerships	**69.26** TRADING INCOME — DEDUCTIONS
s 93	Capital receipts excluded from profits	**69.74** TRADING INCOME — DEDUCTIONS
s 94	Debts incurred and later released	**68.22** TRADING INCOME and **49** LOAN RELATIONSHIPS
s 101	Distribution of assets of mutual concerns	**29.17** DISTRIBUTIONS
s 102	Industrial development grants	**68.64** TRADING INCOME
s 103	Sums recovered under insurance policies	**68.64** TRADING INCOME
s 104	Repayments under *FISMA 2000*	**44** INVESTMENT COMPANIES AND INVESTMENT BUSINESS
s 108	Receipts of benefits by donor or connected persons	**69.46** TRADING INCOME — DEDUCTIONS

CTA 2009	**Brief description**	**See main coverage at**
s 131	Incidental costs of issuing qualifying shares of Building Societies	**8.2** BUILDING SOCIETIES
s 133	Annual payments by a credit union	**54.4** MUTUAL COMPANIES
ss 172–175	Unremittable amounts	**69.70** TRADING INCOME — DEDUCTIONS

[*CTA 2009, ss 210, 212*].

The following further provisions apply in calculating profits from a property business:

(i) the computational provisions relating to the charge on trading profits (see **68** TRADING INCOME) apply generally to the computation of profits from a property business as if the property business were a trade, except in the case of the treatment of premiums paid as a revenue expense under *CTA 2009, ss 62–67* (see **60.14** below) and the treatment of receipts and expenses relating to tied premises as those of a trade (see **69.7** TRADING INCOME — DEDUCTIONS);

(ii) the provisions relating to post-cessation receipts and expenses, etc.(see below);

(iii) the provisions for the treatment of a company commencing or ceasing to carry on a trade [*CTA 2009, s 41, Sch 1 para 519*];

(iv) change of accounting basis (see **68.20** TRADING INCOME); and

(v) any rule permitting a deduction takes priority over a rule prohibiting a deduction, except in relation to car or motor cycle hire, unpaid remuneration, employee benefit contributions and crime-related payments, and cases involving 'relevant tax avoidance arrangements'. [*CTA 2009, s 214*].

'*Relevant tax avoidance arrangements*' are arrangements (being any agreement, understanding, scheme, transaction or series of transactions, whether or not legally enforceable) to which the company carrying on the property business is a party, and whose main purpose, or one of whose main purposes, is the obtaining of a tax advantage. '*Tax advantage*' is as defined in *CTA 2010, s 1139* (broadly, any relief, repayment, avoidance, reduction of tax, or any increase in such amounts).

[*CTA 2009, s 214(1A)(3A)*].

In the case of *Kato Kagaku Co Ltd v Revenue and Customs Comrs* [2007] STC (SCD) 412 a deduction from property income was claimed for an indemnity payment paid in respect of a swap contract entered into in connection with obtaining finance for the purpose of purchasing the rented property. The appeal was allowed in part. The indemnity payment was a capital payment, but a deduction was available as the payment was an incidental cost of finance. However, no deduction was allowed in respect of that part of the payment which arose due to exchange rate fluctuations. The indemnity was not a premium.

CTA 2009, s 215 et seq. provide for the treatment of premiums on the grant of leases or subleases of less than 50 years. See further **60.10** with regard to the treatment of lease premiums etc.

[*CTA 2009, s 210*].

Miscellaneous restrictions, use of cash basis etc.

The following provisions apply in calculating income from *any* source (thus including a property business):

- no deductions for employees' Class 1 NICs (see **69.21** TRADING INCOME — DEDUCTIONS);
- restriction of, or no deduction for business entertainment and gifts (see **69.40**);
- timing of deductions for employees' remuneration (see **69.27**);
- no deductions for illegal payments (see **69.49**);
- no deductions for tax penalties, interest and surcharges (see **69.55**); and
- restriction of deductions for annual payments.

For a general article on what constitutes an allowable *repair* calculating the profits of a property business, see HMRC Tax Bulletin June 2002, pp 935, 936.

See also **59.14** PENALTIES as regards reliefs for certain expenditure on remediation of contaminated land.

See generally the HMRC Property Income Manual.

Profits or losses on contracts taken out to hedge interest payments deductible in computing profits or losses of the property business will normally be taxed or relieved as receipts or deductions of that business. Such profits or losses would generally be computed on an accruals basis in accordance with normal accountancy practice. For corporation tax purposes where these fall within the loan relationship or derivative contracts rules then these will apply.

Similarly deposits paid to landlords by tenants or licensees will ordinarily be receipts of the business, to be recognised in accordance with generally accepted accountancy practice, normally by being deferred and matched with the related costs. Excess deposits which are refunded should be excluded from the business receipts. (See HMRC Property Income Manual, PIM1051 and PIM2105).

As regards allowable legal and professional and other costs, see HMRC Property Income Manual, PIM2120.

Apportionment of profits

Per the table above, *CTA 2009, s 210* provides that certain provisions applying to the computation of trading are to apply for the computation of a property business. These include *CTA 2009, s 52* which deals with apportionment etc. of profits and losses to accounting periods. Where a period of account of a property business does not coincide with an accounting period, profits must be apportioned to accounting periods. This must normally be done by reference to the number of days in the periods concerned [*CTA 2009, s 52*].

In practice, the company may choose any other method, e.g. months and part-months, if it is reasonable to do so and so long as the chosen method is applied consistently.

Simon's Taxes. See **B6.202.**

Change of accounting basis

If a company changes the basis on which it calculates profits from a property business, both bases being in accordance with the law or practice in the periods before and after the change respectively, the provisions dealing with change of basis for trading profits purpose broadly apply also to property income. (See **68.20** TRADING INCOME.)

A positive or negative adjustment is to be calculated as if the property business were a trade. Subject to the exception for depreciation adjustments (see below) in the former case (positive adjustment), the amount is treated as a receipt of the property business on the first day of the first period for which the new basis is used. In the case of a negative adjustment, the treatment is the same for a deduction as for a receipt. Where the adjustment affects the depreciation charge, the adjustment is not made until the asset is sold or written off. These provisions take effect for periods of account ending after 31 March 2009.

[*CTA 2009, ss 180–183, 261–262, 1267, 1269, Sch 2 para 51*].

See **49.2** LEASING for the transitional rule allowing for spreading of adjustment amounts where a lessee adopts IFRS 16 and treats a lease as a right-of-use asset having not previously accounted for the lease as a finance lease.

Simon's Taxes. See **B6.212.**

Commencement and discontinuance

Where a company starts or ceases to be within the charge to corporation tax in respect of an overseas property business, it is treated as starting or ceasing to carry on the business at that time. Before 6 April 2020, this rule applied to all property businesses. With effect from that date, however, UK property businesses are within the charge to corporation tax whether or not the company is UK resident, so that a change in residence status will not result in the company starting or ceasing to be within the charge. Only UK resident companies are within the charge to corporation tax in respect of an overseas property business, so that a change in residence status will result in the company starting or ceasing to be within the charge.

[*CTA 2009, s 289; FA 2019, Sch 5 paras 14, 35*].

Simon's Taxes. See **B6.215.**

Post-cessation receipts

Corporation tax is charged on any 'post-cessation receipts' of a UK property business by adapting the rules applicable to trades under *CTA 2009, ss 188–201* (see **68.16** TRADING INCOME).

A '*post-cessation receipt*' is a sum which is received after a company permanently ceases to carry on a UK property business and which arises from the carrying on of the business before cessation.

'*Cessation*' includes permanently ceasing the property business, ceasing to be within the charge to corporation tax or ceasing to be a partner in a continuing property business. Where a trade ceases on the sale of the right to receive property income, but the transferee does not carry on that business, the amount received is treated as a post-cessation receipt. If the transfer is not at arm's length, the amount brought into account is the value of the rights were the transfer at arm's length.

The charge for any accounting period is on the full amount of post-cessation receipts for that period. The charge does not apply in relation to an overseas property business.

[*CTA 2009, ss 249, 280–286; ITTOIA 2005, s 353, 362*].

Simon's Taxes. See **B6.213**.

Integral features

Where capital allowances are available on expenditure on the repair or replacement of an integral feature, no relief is to be given for the same expenditure in computing the profits of the property business. (See **10.10** CAPITAL ALLOWANCES ON PLANT AND MACHINERY).

[*CTA 2009, s 263; CAA 2001, s 33A*].

Replacement domestic items relief

[60.5] Replacement domestic items relief enables companies which are landlords of residential property to deduct capital expenditure on domestic items, e.g. furniture, furnishings, appliances (including white goods) and kitchenware, where the expenditure is on a replacement item provided for use in the property. The relief applies to both furnished and unfurnished lettings, but not to furnished holiday lettings (within **60.7** below) where the property constitutes some or all of the furnished holiday accommodation for the tax year. A fixture is not a domestic item for this purpose, and '*fixture*' is defined as plant or machinery that is so installed, or otherwise fixed in or to, a property as to become, in law, part of that property; the definition specifically includes any boiler or water-filled radiator installed as part of a space or water heating system.

The relief is available where all the following conditions are met:

- a company (C) carries on a property business in relation to land which consists of or includes a dwelling-house;
- C incurs expenditure on replacing a domestic item; the new item must be provided solely for the 'lessee' for use in the dwelling-house, and the old item must no longer be available for such use following its replacement; a '*lessee*' for this purpose is a person who is entitled upon payment to the use of the dwelling-house, whether or not a formal lease exists;
- the expenditure is of a capital nature and is incurred wholly and exclusively for the purposes of the business; and
- no capital allowances are available on the expenditure.

The deduction is made in computing the profits of the property business, and does not require the making of a claim. The amount of the deduction is the cost of the replacement item, but is limited to the cost of an equivalent item if the new item is not the same, or substantially the same, as the old . If C incurs incidental capital expenditure in connection with the disposal of the old item or the purchase of the new, the deduction is increased by the amount of that expenditure. If the old item is disposed of for consideration, the deduction is reduced by the amount or value (in money or money's worth) to which C, or a person connected with it (within **19** CONNECTED PERSONS), is thus entitled. If the disposal is in part-exchange for the new item, the part-exchange value is treated as expenditure incurred on the new item but the deduction is then reduced by the same amount.

[*CTA 2009, s 250A*].

Furnished lettings

[60.6] Furnished lettings are taxable as, or as part of, a property business (and the computational rules at **60.4** above thus apply). See **60.7** below for special rules for furnished holiday lettings.

A '*furnished letting*' is a lease or other arrangement to which a company is party for 'generating income from land' (including a caravan or houseboat) and the person entitled to the use of the premises is also entitled to the use of furniture. Any consideration receivable for the use of furniture is chargeable as property income in the same way as rent (and expenditure incurred in providing furniture is treated accordingly). This does not apply to any amount taken into account in computing profits of a trade involving the making available of furniture for use in premises.

[*CTA 2009, ss 205, 207, 209, 248, 249*].

Dependent on the nature of the lettings, including their frequency and the extent to which the landlord provides services, e.g. cleaning, laundry and meals, the letting may amount to a trade of providing serviced accommodation and be taxed as trading income rather than property income.

Alternatively, the provision of services may amount to a trade separate to the letting (cf. *Salisbury House Estate Ltd v Fry* (1930) 15 TC 266, HL). In *Gittos v Barclay* (1982) 55 TC 633, the letting of two villas in a holiday village was held not to amount to trading. A similar decision was reached in *Griffiths v Jackson*; *Griffiths v Pearman* (1982) 56 TC 583 in relation to the extensive letting of furnished rooms to students. Note that all the decisions cited were made before 1 April 1998 when non-trading furnished lettings were within *Schedule D, Case VI* rather than *Schedule A* (as was).

Where a company carries on a furnished holiday letting business and other property businesses or transactions, separate computations are needed, with such allocations as are just and reasonable for each part where there are capital allowances claims or a loss claim. [*CAA 2009, s 269*].

Prohibition of capital allowances

Capital allowances are not due on plant or machinery let for use in a dwelling-house (see *CAA 2001, s 35* and **10.4** CAPITAL ALLOWANCES ON PLANT AND MACHINERY) (but see **60.7** below as regards furnished holiday lettings).

Furnished holiday lettings

[60.7] In so far as a property business consists in the 'commercial letting' of 'furnished holiday accommodation' (a 'furnished holiday lettings (FHL) business') for an accounting period, it is treated as a trade for the purposes of the carry forward of losses against profits of the same trade (see below).

In addition, a furnished holiday lettings business is a qualifying activity for the purposes of capital allowances on plant and machinery (see **10.4** CAPITAL ALLOWANCES ON PLANT AND MACHINERY).

In contrast to furnished lettings generally, it is possible to claim capital allowances on plant or machinery provided for use in a dwelling-house, but neither the replacement domestic items relief at **60.5** above nor its predecessor the 10% wear and tear allowance in **60.6** above can be claimed as an alternative.

All commercial lettings of furnished holiday accommodation by a particular company (or partnership) are treated as a single trade or, for capital allowances purposes, as a single qualifying activity, separate from any other trade or other qualifying activity carried on by that company. The same applies (though separately) to all such lettings outside the UK but in the EEA (see below).

If a UK property business consists only partly of the commercial letting of furnished holiday accommodation, the profits and losses of the separate parts of the business must be separately calculated. If there is a letting of accommodation only part of which is holiday accommodation, such apportionments are to be made as are just and reasonable. The same rules apply to an overseas property business by reference to accommodation outside the UK but in the EEA (see below).

Relief for losses

An FHL business is treated as a trade for the purpose of loss relief, but losses may only be relieved by carry-forward under *CTA 2010, s 45* (see **51.7** LOSSES) against profits of the same trade in subsequent accounting periods. Note that *s 45* continues to apply to post-1 April 2017 FHL losses despite its repeal for most other trade losses. A UK business and an overseas business are treated separately for this purpose.

A loss carried forward under these provisions is ignored for the purposes of the restriction on deduction of carried-forward amounts at **51.13** LOSSES.

There is nothing to prevent losses of a UK property business (whether in the same accounting period or brought forward from earlier periods) from being set against profits of a UK FHL business as the latter is part of the UK property business. The same applies as regards losses of an overseas property business against profits of an EEA (excluding the UK) FHL business. However, losses of an FHL business cannot be set against profits of an ordinary rental business.

Property outside the UK

The special treatment of furnished holiday lettings described above applies also to the commercial letting of qualifying furnished holiday accommodation outside the UK but in the European Economic Area (EEA). It does not to apply to furnished holiday accommodation outside the EEA. The EEA consists of: Austria, Belgium, Bulgaria, Cyprus, Czech Republic, Denmark, Estonia, Finland, France, Germany, Gibraltar, Greece, Hungary, Iceland, Ireland, Italy, Latvia, Liechtenstein, Lithuania, Luxembourg, Malta, Netherlands, Norway, Poland, Portugal, Romania, Slovakia, Slovenia, Spain, Sweden, Switzerland and (until the end of the Brexit implementation period (11pm on 31 December 2020)) the UK.

Meaning of 'commercial letting'

'*Commercial letting*' is letting (whether or not under a lease) on a commercial basis and with a view to the realisation of profits. For a case in which the 'commercial letting' test was satisfied despite a significant excess of interest over letting income, see *Walls v Livesey* (Sp C 4), [1995] SSCD 12, but see also *Brown v Richardson* (Sp C 129), [1997] SSCD 233 in which the opposite conclusion was reached. See Revenue Tax Bulletin October 1997 pp 472, 473 for HMRC's view of the requirements in this respect.

Meaning of 'furnished holiday accommodation'

For any tax year, '*holiday accommodation*' is accommodation which:

(a) is available for commercial letting to the public generally as holiday accommodation for at least 210 days in the 12-month period referred to below; and
(b) is so let for at least 105 such days (but see below as regards the possibility of averaging).

See also the 'period of grace' rule described below.

Any period of more than 31 consecutive days during which the accommodation is in the same occupation (otherwise than because of abnormal circumstances) does not count towards fulfilling the number of days required in (b) above. Any such period is known as a '*period of longer-term occupation*', and if, during the 12-month period referred to below, more than 155 days fall during periods of longer-term occupation, the accommodation is *not* '*holiday accommodation*'.

The 12-month period referred to above is the 12 months ending with the last day of the accounting period in question, unless:

(1) the accommodation was not let by the person concerned as furnished accommodation in the 12 months immediately preceding the accounting period, in which case the 12-month period runs from the date such letting commenced in the accounting period in question; or
(2) the accommodation was let by the person concerned as furnished accommodation in the 12 months immediately preceding the accounting period but is not so let in the 12 months immediately after the accounting period, in which case the 12-month period is the 12 months ending with the date such letting ceased in the accounting period in question.

Holiday accommodation is '*furnished holiday accommodation*' if the tenant is entitled to use of the furniture.

Averaging

In satisfying the test in (b) above, averaging may be applied to the number of let days of any or all of the accommodation let by the same company which either is holiday accommodation or would be holiday accommodation if it satisfied the test on its own. An election for averaging must be made within two years beginning at the end of the accounting period to which it is to apply. It must specify the accommodation to be included in the averaging calculation. Holiday accommodation cannot be included in more than one averaging election for an accounting period. See below for an example of how averaging works.

An averaging election has to be made separately for properties in the UK and for properties in the EEA. A single election cannot cover both.

Period of grace

A period of grace is allowed if:

- during an accounting period (Period 1), a company lets furnished holiday accommodation that qualifies for the special treatment (whether on its own or as a result of averaging but other than as a result of this 'period of grace' rule);
- it continues to let the accommodation during the following accounting period (Period 2) or the following two accounting periods (Periods Years 2 and 3);
- it does not qualify for the special treatment for Period 2 (or Periods 2 and 3) purely because the letting condition in (b) above is not met; and
- there was a genuine intention to meet that letting condition for Period 2 (or for each of Periods 2 and 3).

If the company so elects for either Period 2 or each of Periods 2 and 3, the accommodation is treated as qualifying for the special treatment for the accounting period or periods in question. Holiday accommodation that qualifies for the special treatment by virtue only of this rule cannot be included in an averaging claim. If an election is not made for Period 2, no election can be made for Period 3. Any election must be made within two years beginning at the end of the accounting period to which it is to apply.

[*CTA 2009, ss 264–269A; CTA 2010, ss 65, 67A; F(No 2)A 2017, Sch 4 para 155; SI 2019 No 689, Reg 16(3)*].

See Tolley's Capital Gains Tax as regards relief from capital gains tax in respect of furnished holiday lettings.

Simon's Taxes. See **B6.401–B6.405**.

Example

X Ltd owns and lets out furnished holiday cottages. None is ever let to the same person for more than 31 consecutive days. Three cottages have been owned for many years but Rose Cottage was acquired on 1 April 2021 (and first let on that day) while Ivy Cottage was sold on 30 April 2021 (and last let on that day).

In B Ltd's accounting period ending 31 December 2021, days available for letting and days let are as follows.

	Days available	Days let
Honeysuckle Cottage	230	160
Primrose Cottage	150	110
Bluebell Cottage	215	90
Rose Cottage	220	70
Ivy Cottage	60	15

Additional information

Rose Cottage was let for 40 days between 1 January 2022 and 31 March 2022.

Ivy Cottage was let for 60 days in the period 1 May 2020 to 31 December 2020 but was available for letting for 160 days in that period.

Qualification as 'furnished holiday accommodation'

Honeysuckle Cottage qualifies as it meets both the 210-day availability test and the 105-day letting test.

Primrose Cottage does *not* qualify although it is let for more than 105 days as it fails to satisfy the 210-day test. Averaging (see below) is only possible where it is the 105-day test which is not satisfied.

Bluebell Cottage does not qualify by itself as it fails the 105-day test. However it may be included in an averaging election.

Rose Cottage qualifies as furnished holiday accommodation. It was acquired on 1 April 2021 so qualification in the accounting period ending 31 December 2021 is determined by reference to the period of twelve months beginning on the day it was first let, in which it was let for a total of 110 days.

Ivy Cottage was sold on 30 April 2021 so qualification is determined by reference to the period from 1 May 2020 to 30 April 2021 (the last day of letting). It does not qualify by itself as it was let for only 75 days in this period but it may be included in an averaging election.

Averaging election for accounting period ending 31 December 2021

	Days let
Honeysuckle Cottage	160
Bluebell Cottage	90
Rose Cottage	110
Ivy Cottage	75

$$\frac{160 + 90 + 110 + 75}{4} = 108.75 \text{ days}$$

All four cottages included in the averaging election now qualify as furnished holiday accommodation as each is deemed to have been let for 108.75 days in the accounting period ending 31 December 2021.

If the average had been less than 105, the two cottages which qualify in any case could have been included in an averaging election together with one of the non-qualifying cottages (leaving the other as non-qualifying). If averaging three cottages still did not improve the position, an average of just two could be tried.

See **60.6** for position where a furnished holiday business is carried on and there is also another property business or transaction.

Distributions from REITs

[60.8] A distribution received from a Real Estate Investment Trust (REIT) by a shareholder within the charge to corporation tax is treated in the shareholder's hands as profits of a UK property business to the extent that it is paid out of the tax-exempt profits (including tax-exempt chargeable gains) of the REIT. For distributions from a UK REIT to another UK REIT, see further **47.24** INVESTMENT TRUSTS [*CTA 2010, s 548*].

Deduction of tax at source

Generally, basic rate tax is deducted at source from distributions by the REIT; the shareholder remains liable for any excess liability, i.e. excess of the higher rate of tax over the basic rate (where the distribution is subject to income tax in the hands of the recipient). [*CTA 2010, s 549(2); ITA 2007, ss 973, 974*]. However, certain distributions are made without deduction of tax at source, for example, distributions to companies resident in the UK and within the charge to UK corporation tax, or non UK resident companies carrying on a trade in the UK through a permanent establishment where such distribution is taken into account in computing the chargeable profits for UK corporation tax purposes. [*SI 2006 No 2867, Reg 7*].

A distribution made by a company that has ceased to be a REIT is subject to the above treatment to the extent that it is paid out of tax-exempt profits made while the company was a REIT.

Profits of a single property business

Distributions subject to this treatment (known as property income distributions or PIDs) are treated in the shareholder's hands as profits of a single business, regardless of the fact that they may come from different REITs or be received by the shareholder in different capacities. The single business is separate from any UK or overseas property business carried on by the shareholder. Thus the losses on other property business of a shareholder cannot be set off against PIDs from a REIT.

These rules apply to a corporate partner's share of any such distributions received by a partnership as if it were received by it as a direct shareholder.

[*CTA 2010, ss 548, 549*].

If the shareholder is non-UK resident, a distribution out of tax-exempt profits is again treated as profits of a UK property business, but this does not preclude its being dealt with under the relevant dividend article of a double tax agreement (Treasury Explanatory Notes to Finance Bill 2006). Such distributions are outside the non-resident landlords regime at **60.17** below.

The treatment above does not apply to distributions falling to be taken into account in computing the recipient's trading profits (see **68.57** TRADING INCOME under Dealers in securities).

The requirements concerning deduction of basic rate tax at source are set out at *ITA 2007, ss 973, 974* and in regulations (see *SI 2006 No 2867* as amended). These inter alia specify classes of shareholder to whom distributions out of tax-exempt profits can be made without deduction of tax (such as UK resident corporate shareholders, see further above), and require REITs to provide shareholders with deduction certificates containing specified information and also provide for returns and payment of tax deducted to HMRC.

There are rules to determine the extent to which a distribution of a REIT is made out of its tax-exempt profits. It is one of the conditions of tax-exempt status that at least 90% of the profits of a REIT's property rental business is paid out as dividends within a specified time, and where a UK REIT invests in another UK REIT then 100% of profits derived from that investment must be distributed (see **47.20** INVESTMENT TRUSTS for how the distributions are attributed firstly to the tax-exempt profits and then to other profits).

REITs can offer investors a stock dividend as an alternative, or in combination with, a cash dividend, in meeting the 90% profit distribution requirements.

[*CTA 2010, Pt 12, ss 518 et seq*].

Holders of excessive rights

CTA 2010, ss 551–554 imposes a tax charge on a REIT if it makes a distribution to a shareholder with a 10% interest or more in the company or its dividends. The issue is that such a shareholder, if they were resident in a territory with an appropriate treaty, would be able to make a claim for a repayment of withholding tax deducted, thereby removing the REIT profits from the UK tax net.

Therefore provisions were introduced to counter this, now found at *CTA 2010, ss 551–554*. A tax penalty may be levied on the REIT if it pays out a dividend to any corporate shareholder (as defined for treaty purposes) with an entitlement to 10% or more of the dividends, share capital or voting rights in the company (referred to as 'holders of excessive rights'). Regulations may provide that a charge does not arise or is reduced if the company takes certain action, and may require certain information to be provided to HMRC in relation to any distribution.

Prior to the rewrite to *CTA 2010*, the Treasury was provided with powers to make regulations for such a penalty to be levied unless reasonable specified steps were taken — such reasonable steps are set out in the HMRC REIT Manuals and include: a mechanism that can identify holders of excessive rights; a prohibition on the payment of dividends on shares that form part of the shareholding of a holder of excessive rights unless certain conditions are met; a mechanism to allow dividends to be paid on shares that form part of the shareholding of a holder of excessive rights where the shareholder has disposed of their rights to dividends on their shares; and a mechanism that is designed to prevent a holder of excessive rights being beneficially entitled to dividends on their shareholding.

In addition, in order for a holder of excessive rights to receive a distribution without the REIT incurring such a tax charge, it would have to enter into a dividend strip or share repurchase arrangement. The manufactured dividend provisions as set out in *CTA 2010, ss 785, 786* deal with this latter case.

The provisions as rewritten in *CTA 2010* do not reproduce the same broad powers for the Treasury to make regulations because a number of those regulations have actually been included in the rewrite, including a key regulation dealing with the tax consequences of a distribution to a holder of excessive rights. The power to make regulations is restricted in that such regulations may now only provide that a charge does not arise or is reduced if the company takes certain action, and for the collection of information.

[*CTA 2010, ss 518 et seq, 785, 786*].

See generally **47.11** *et seq.* INVESTMENT TRUSTS.

Simon's Taxes. See **D7.1116, D7.1127.**

Treatment of losses

[60.9] The treatment of losses from both a UK and overseas property business are now dealt with under the provisions found in *CTA 2010, ss 62 et seq.*

Losses from a UK property business

Where a company carrying on a UK property business makes a loss in that business then it may be set off against the company's total profits for the same accounting period. Any unrelieved part of the loss may be treated as a UK property business loss of succeeding periods, for set-off against total profits of such periods, provided that the company continues to carry on the property business in the period concerned.

Where the company is a company with investment business (see **45.6** INVESTMENT COMPANIES AND INVESTMENT BUSINESS), and the UK property business ceases, unrelieved losses can be carried forward and treated as excess management expenses in the subsequent and later periods, provided that the company continues to be a company with investment business. These reliefs are available only where the UK property business is carried on on a commercial basis or in the exercise of statutory functions (see **51.2** LOSSES).

Lettings treated as a trade under the provisions for UK furnished holiday lettings (see **60.7** above) are excluded from the company's UK property business for the purposes of the above provisions. See **60.7** above for the treatment of furnished holiday lettings losses.

[*CTA 2010, ss 62–65*].

Where a claim is made to set off a non-trade loan relationship deficit against the gross profits for the deficit period, that deficit is set off before relief for UK property business losses.

[*CTA 2009, s 461*].

See **50.4** LOAN RELATIONSHIPS.

Losses from an overseas property business

Losses from overseas property businesses are available for carry forward against future profits from the same business. This provision is, however, subject to the same commerciality test as applies to UK property business losses (see above).

These provisions do not apply to the losses of an EEA furnished holiday lettings business, which are treated as trade losses. See further **60.7** above.

[*CTA 2010, ss 66, 67*].

Group relief

Group relief is available for UK property business losses excluding losses brought forward from earlier periods and losses incurred in a UK property business which was not carried on either on a commercial basis or in the exercise of statutory functions.

[*CTA 2010, ss 99(1)(e), 102;*]. See **35.5** GROUP RELIEF.

Change of ownership of company

The carry forward of UK property business losses, and overseas property business losses, is restricted on the change of ownership of a company in a similar manner as applies to trading losses and excess management expenses.

[*CTA 2010, ss 683, 684, 700, 701, 704, 705*]. See **45.9** INVESTMENT COMPANIES AND INVESTMENT BUSINESS, **51.17** LOSSES.

Simon's Taxes. See B6.203.

Lease premiums etc.

[60.10] The provisions treating certain lease premiums and related items as property business profits for corporation tax purposes are found in *CTA 2009, ss 215–247*.

The types of receipt within these provisions are:

(a) premiums payable under a '*short lease*' (i.e. a lease with an effective duration of 50 years or less);
(b) work done by a tenant, treated as a lease premium, in addition to any actual premium.
The amount of the premium is the excess of the value of the landlord's interest immediately after the lease is entered into, over what it would have been had the lease not included the obligation to carry out work. 'Excepted work' is left out of account.
'*Excepted work*' is work which, if the landlord and not the tenant were obliged to carry it out, would be an allowable deduction in calculating the profits from the landlord's property business;
(c) payments for surrender of a lease;
(d) amounts received for assignment of a lease granted at an undervalue;
(e) sums payable instead of rent;
(f) sums payable for variation or waiver of terms of lease;
(g) sales with the right to re-conveyance; and
(h) sale and lease back transactions where the term of the leaseback is 50 years or less and the sale price exceeds the total of any premium and the value of the right to receive conveyance of the reversion immediately after the lease begins. However, these provisions do not apply if the lease is granted and begins to run within one month of the sale.

(d)–(h) are anti-avoidance provisions.

Simon's Taxes. See B6.3.

Short-term lease — receipt of income

In the case of (a) above, if a premium is payable under a '*short-term lease*' (i.e. lease whose effective duration, see below, is 50 years or less), or under the terms on which such a lease is granted, the company to which it is due (whether or not the landlord) is treated as entering into a transaction for the purpose of generating income from land. An amount must be brought into account as a receipt in computing the profits of the property business which consists of or includes that transaction for the tax year in which the lease is granted. The amount to be brought into account is:

$$P \times \frac{50 - Y}{50}$$

where:

P = the amount of the premium, and

Y = the number of *complete* periods of twelve months (*other than the first*) comprised in the effective duration of the lease.

Example

A Ltd grants a 14-year lease of premises for a premium of £50,000 in its accounting period ended 30 June 2021. The amount to be included as a receipt in computing the profits of its property business for that period is as follows.

$$£50{,}000 \times \frac{50 - 13}{50} = £37{,}000$$

Note that these provisions refer to leases granted and not to leases assigned.

Duration of a lease

There are rules contained within *CTA 2009, ss 243–244* for ascertaining the effective duration of a lease, which is not necessarily the same as its contractual duration. In particular, any rights the tenant has to extend the lease, or any entitlement of the tenant to a further lease of the same premises, may possibly be taken into account.

Information relevant to the duration of the lease can be obtained by HMRC under the provisions relating to their information gathering powers (found at *FA 2008, Sch 36*). See **38** HMRC INVESTIGATORY POWERS.

A lease's term is not treated as ending later than a date which the terms of the lease etc. (including the amount of the premium) make it unlikely it will continue beyond.

Work carried out by tenant

If the terms on which a lease is granted oblige the tenant to carry out work on the premises (see (b) above) (other than work such as normal repairs or maintenance which, if incurred by the landlord, would be deductible expenditure in computing the profits of his property business), the lease is treated as requiring the payment of a premium (or additional premium) to the landlord of the amount by which the value of the landlord's interest increases as a result of the obligation.

Sum in lieu of rent

If the terms on which a lease is granted require the tenant to pay a sum in lieu of rent for a period (and that period is less than 50 years) the company to whom the sum is due (whether or not the landlord) is treated as if it were entitled to a premium equal to that sum. It is treated as a receipt of a property business.

CTA 2009 makes it explicit that this applies irrespective of the duration of the lease itself, and in particular whether or not it is a short-term lease.

The charge to corporation tax is made for the accounting period in which the sum becomes payable. The value of Y in the above formula is the number of complete periods of twelve months (other than the first) comprised in the period in relation to which the sum is payable (but excluding any part of the period other than that in relation to which the sum is payable) and P becomes S, the sum payable instead of rent.

'*Premium*' is widely interpreted for the above purposes by *CTA 2009, ss 246, 247* and, in particular, includes payments to a person connected with the landlord (as in **19** CONNECTED PERSONS).

See generally HMRC Property Income Manual PIM1200–1232.

Payment by instalments

Where any premium etc. is payable by instalments, the tax thereon may itself be paid by such instalments as HMRC may allow in the particular case; the tax instalment period cannot exceed eight years or, if less, the period during which the premium instalments are payable. See HMRC Property Income Manual PIM1220.

This applies to receipts taxable under the following provisions: *CTA 2009, s 217* (lease premium on a short-term lease); *CTA 2009, s 219* (sum paid on a lease instead of rent); *CTA 2009, s 220* (sum paid for the surrender of a lease); and *CTA 2009, s 221* (sum paid for the variation or waiver of a lease term).

[*CTA 2009, ss 236, 243–247*].

Capital gains tax

See Tolley's Capital Gains Tax for the treatment of chargeable gains arising from disposals by way of a lease.

Note particularly that the part of the premium chargeable to income tax is omitted from the computation of the chargeable gain.

Surrender under the terms of a lease

If, under the terms on which a short-term lease is granted, a sum becomes payable by the tenant as consideration for the surrender of the lease, consequences ensue as above as if that sum were a premium (and the calculation above would apply, suitably amended, see *CTA 2010, s 220*).

See HMRC Property Income Manual PIM1214. [*CTA 2009, s 220*].

Variation or waiver of term of lease

If a sum becomes payable by a tenant otherwise than by way of rent as consideration for the variation or waiver of the terms of a lease, and the sum is due to the landlord or to a company connected with the landlord (within **19** CONNECTED PERSONS) (and the period for which the variation or waiver has effect is 50 years or less) consequences ensue as above as if that sum were a premium (the calculation above would apply, suitably amended, see *CTA 2010, s 221*).

The charge to corporation tax is made for the accounting period in which the contract for the variation or waiver is entered into. The value of Y in the above formula is the number of complete periods of twelve months (other than the first) comprised in the period for which the variation or waiver has effect (but excluding any part of that period preceding the time at which the variation or waiver takes effect or falling after the time at which it ceases to have effect).

[*CTA 2009, ss 215–221*].

CTA 2009 makes it explicit that this applies irrespective of the duration of the lease itself. See HMRC Property Income Manual PIM1216.

Anti-avoidance — leases granted at undervalue etc.

[60.11] If a short-term lease (as in **60.10** above) was granted at an undervalue and is assigned at a profit, similar consequences ensue as in **60.10** above as regards the assignor as if the assignor had received a premium (except that the opportunity to pay the tax by instalments is not available).

The charge to corporation tax is made for the accounting period in which the consideration for the assignment becomes payable. The value of P in the formula in **60.10** above is the lesser of the profit on the assignment and the amount of the undervalue (adjusted to take account of any profits on earlier assignments of the same lease).

This does not apply in relation to a lease granted before 6 April 1963 or arising from a contract entered into before that date. If the landlord, a company which assigned the lease or the assignee provides HMRC with a statement showing that there is or may be an amount taxable under these provisions, the HMRC officer musts certify the accuracy of the statement provided that he is satisfied that it is accurate.

[*CTA 2009, ss 222, 223, 237*].

Simon's Taxes. See **B6.306**.

Anti-avoidance — sale of land with right to reconveyance

[60.12] If land is sold subject to terms requiring it to be reconveyed on a future date to the vendor or a person connected with the vendor (within **19** CONNECTED PERSONS) for a price lower than the sale price, similar consequences ensue as in

60.10 above as regards the vendor as if the vendor had received a premium. This applies only if the period beginning with the sale and ending with the earliest date on which, under the said terms, the land could fall to be reconveyed is 50 years or less. The charge to corporation tax is made for the accounting period in which the sale occurs.

The value of P in the formula in **60.10** above is the excess of the sale price over the price at which the land is to be reconveyed. The value of Y is the number of complete periods of twelve months (other than the first) comprised in the period of 50 years or less referred to above.

Similar provisions apply (with appropriate modifications) if, instead of being reconveyed, the land is to be leased back to the vendor or to a person connected with the vendor. (They do not, however, apply if the lease is granted and begins to run within one month after the sale.) In this case, the sale price is compared to the total of (i) any premium payable for the lease and (ii) the value on the date of sale of the right to lease back the land.

If the date for the reconveyance (or leaseback) is not fixed under the terms of the sale and the reconveyance price (or the total of (i) and (ii) above) varies dependent upon that date, the price (or total) is taken to be the lowest possible under the terms of the sale. There is provision for any overpaid tax to be repaid if the actual date of reconveyance (or of the grant of the lease) turns out to be different to the date by reference to which the tax charge was calculated; a claim for repayment must be made within four years after the reconveyance (or the grant of the lease).

[*CTA 2009, ss 224, 225, 238, 239, Sch 2 para 42*].

See HMRC Property Income Manual PIM1222, 1224, 1226. For the so-called 'treasury arrangement' to avoid a charge under these provisions where there is a genuine commercial reason for the owner of mineral-bearing land to sell with a right to repurchase, see HMRC Property Income Manual PIM1228. See **4.8**, **4.9** ANTI-AVOIDANCE for other provisions concerning the sale and leaseback of land.

Simon's Taxes. See **B6.307, B6.308.**

Sub-leases etc.

[60.13] Relief is due with regard to these charges, where any of the charges at **60.10** above apply, or the charge on assignment at **60.11** above applies, and the grant of the lease in question is out of a 'taxed lease' (or a head lease) or, as the case may be, the assignment in question is of a 'taxed lease' (or a head lease).

A '*taxed lease*' is one in respect of which there has already been such a charge (or there would have been a charge but for the availability of this relief).

Thus, in broad terms, the relief applies where the taxable company is itself a tenant and its own landlord has received a premium or other taxable sum in respect of the same property.

The amount given by the formula in **60.10** above is reduced by the proportion of amount previously charged which the duration of the sub-lease bears to the duration of the head lease. The amount of the reduction can be found by the formula:

$$\frac{A \times LRP}{TRP}$$

where:

A = the amount given by the formula in **60.10** above in respect of the previous charge;

LRP = the length of the 'receipt period' of the receipt under calculation; and

TRP = the total 'receipt period' of the receipt by reference to which the previous charge was made.

The '*receipt period*' is:

- in the case of a premium (or similar sum) or a sum payable for the surrender of a lease, the effective duration of the lease (see **60.10** above);
- in the case of a sum payable in lieu of rent, the period for which it is payable;
- in the case of a sum payable for variation or waiver, the period for which the variation or waiver has effect; and
- in the case of an assignment, the effective duration of the lease remaining at the date of the assignment.

If the current charge is under **60.10** above and the sub-lease relates to only part of the premises subject to the head-lease, the relief is reduced proportionately on a just and reasonable basis.

Example

A Ltd grants a 14-year lease of premises to B Ltd for a premium of £50,000 in June 2021. The amount to be included as a receipt in computing the profits of A Ltd's property business in its accounting period ending 31 December 2021 is £37,000 as computed in the Example in **60.10** above.

After 4 years, i.e. in June 2025, B Ltd grants a 10-year sub-lease for which it receives a premium of £60,000. The amount to be included as a receipt in computing the profits of B Ltd's property business for its accounting period ending 31 December 2025 is as follows.

		£
Normal calculation	$£60{,}000 \times \dfrac{50-9}{50}$	49,200
Less relief as above	$\dfrac{£37{,}000 \times 10}{14}$	26,429
		£22,771

The relief is restricted to the 'unrelieved balance' of the value of A in the above formula ('A' being the previous charge).

The '*unrelieved balance*' is found by deducting the following from the value of A:

- any relief previously given under these provisions;
- any deductions allowed under **60.14** below; and
- any deductions allowed under *CTA 2009, ss 62–67* (deductions allowed where the land is used for the purposes of a trade etc. — see **68.53** TRADING INCOME),

so far as attributable to the charge to which A relates.

If there is more than one previous charge in relation to which there is an unrelieved balance, an amount of relief is computed separately for each previous charge and then aggregated, but the total relief cannot exceed the total of the unrelieved balances.

For these purposes, in a case where the previous charge resulted from the tenant's obligation to carry out work on the premises (see **60.10** above), the value of A in the above formula is recomputed as if that obligation had not included the carrying out of any work that results in expenditure qualifying for capital allowances.

If the relief would otherwise exceed the amount from which it is deductible, it is restricted to that amount.

[*CTA 2009, ss 66, 228, 229*].

Simon's Taxes. See **B6.309**.

Interaction of income tax and corporation tax rules

The income tax rules with regard to leases are in *ITTOIA 2005, ss 287–290* (the above narrative being largely based on these provisions) and the equivalent corporation tax rules are in *CTA 2009, ss 215–247*.

The provisions of *ITTOIA 2005, ss 296–298* and *CTA 2009, ss 227–233*, seek to ensure that the two sets of rules interact, for example where the landlord is an individual and the tenant is a company. The tenant remains entitled to the above relief even though the previous charge, i.e. the charge on the landlord etc., is a charge to income tax rather than corporation tax.

Other deductions available to tenant

[60.14] A tenant is allowed a deduction, in computing the profits of the tenant's property business, by reference to a premium etc. charged on the landlord. The deduction is available to a tenant under a 'taxed lease' (or head lease).

A '*taxed lease*' is a lease by reference to which:

- any of the charges at **60.10** have arisen, or the charge on assignment at **60.11** above has arisen (or would have done so but for the availability of the relief at **60.13** above); or
- any charges have arisen (or would have done so but for the availability of relief) under the equivalent income tax provisions.

The deduction is available for any 'qualifying day' on which the whole or part of the premises subject to the taxed lease is either occupied by the tenant for the purposes of carrying on a property business or sub-let. It is given by treating an amount calculated as below as a revenue expense of the tenant's property business, but *not* so as to override any statutory rule governing deductible expenditure generally (see **60.4** above).

A '*qualifying day*' is a day that falls within the 'receipt period' (as defined in **60.13** above) of the receipt charged under **60.10** or **60.11** above).

The amount of the expense for *each* qualifying day is the amount given by the formula in **60.10** above in respect of the charge under **60.10** or **60.11** above

Examples

(A)

A Ltd grants a 14-year lease of premises to B Ltd for a premium of £50,000 on 1 June 2021. The amount to be included as a receipt in computing the profits of A Ltd's property business for its accounting period ending 31 December 2021 is £37,000 as computed in the Example in **60.10** above. B Ltd immediately sub-lets the premises but does not receive any premium.

The number of days in the 14-year receipt period is 5,113. The deduction due to B Ltd in calculating the profits of its property business for any one qualifying day is £37,000 divided by 5,113 = £7.24.

For the accounting period ending 31 December 2021, the available deduction is £7.24 × 214 (1.6.20 to 31.12.20) = £1,549.

If, however, the tenant is also entitled to relief under **60.13** above, the tenant is treated as incurring a revenue expense for a qualifying day only to the extent (if any) that the daily amount computed as above exceeds the daily amount of the relief under **60.13**.

(B)

The sub-letting in Example (A) above ceases in the accounting period ending 31 December 2024. On 1 January 2025, B Ltd again grants a sub-lease of the premises but this time for a period of 11 years at a premium of £70,000. The amount to be included as a receipt in computing the profits of B Ltd's property business for the year ending 31 December 2025 is as follows.

		£
Normal calculation as in 60.10	$£70{,}000 \times \frac{50-10}{50}$	56,000
Less relief as **60.13**	$\frac{£37{,}000 \times 11}{14}$	29,071
		£26,929

The number of days in the 11-year receipt period of the sub-lease is 4,018. The daily amount of the relief given is therefore £29,071 divided by 4,018 = £7.24.

This equals the daily expense computed in Example (A); as there is no excess, B Ltd is not entitled to any deduction for a revenue expense under these provisions for any of the 4,018 qualifying days covered by the sub-lease.

Supposing B Ltd had been able to obtain a premium of only £30,000 for the 11-year sub-lease. The amount to be included as a receipt in computing the profits of B Ltd's property business for the year ending 31 December 2025 would then be as follows.

		£
Normal calculation as in **60.10**	$£30{,}000 \times \frac{50-10}{50}$	24,000
Less $\frac{£37{,}000 \times 11}{14}$ = £29,071 but restricted to		24,000
		Nil

The daily amount of the relief given is now £24,000 divided by 4,018 = £5.97. This is less than the daily expense of £7.24 computed in Example (A), the deficit being £1.27.

B Ltd would be entitled to a deduction of £1.27 as a revenue expense for each of the 4,018 qualifying days covered by the sub-lease.

If a sub-lease relates to only part of the premises covered by the main lease, the above rules are applied separately to the different parts of the premises, the premium under the main lease being apportioned between those parts on a just and reasonable basis.

If the premises subject to the taxed lease (or head lease) are used for the purposes of a trade instead of for those of a property business, very similar rules apply under *CTA 2009, ss 62–67*, with the deduction being given as an expense in computing the profits of the trade etc. See **68.53** TRADING INCOME.

The total of the deductions allowed under these provisions, any deductions allowed under *CTA 2009, ss 62–67* referred to above and any relief given under **60.13** above cannot exceed the amount charged under **60.10** or, where appropriate, **60.11** above.

No deduction under these provisions is allowed if the lease is a taxed lease only because of the application of the first rule (rule 1) in *CTA 2009, s 243* or *ITTOIA 2005, s 303*. Rule 1 applies where:

(a) the terms of the lease, or any other circumstances, make it unlikely that the lease will continue beyond a date before the end of the term for which the lease was granted; and

(b) the premium was not substantially greater than it would have been had the term been one ending on that date.

In these circumstances the lease is treated as ending on the earlier date.

[*CTA 2009, ss 231–235*].

Simon's Taxes. See **B6.309** *et seq.*

Reverse premiums

[60.15] There are provisions to ensure that reverse premiums are taxable as revenue receipts.

They apply in relation to any 'reverse premium' (which is broadly a payment made, or benefit provided, by a landlord to a prospective tenant as an inducement to enter into a lease).

Other than in cases where the transaction is entered into for the purposes of the recipient's trade, or prospective trade (where it is treated as the receipt of a trade), a reverse premium is to be treated as a receipt of a UK property business or an overseas property business carried on by the recipient (even if the recipient is not otherwise carrying on a property business).

Normally, under generally accepted accounting principles, such a payment is spread over the period of the lease, or, if shorter, the period to the first rent review. However there are specific anti-avoidance provisions that apply where the parties are connected and the arrangements entered into are not such as would have been agreed at arm's length. In such an instance the entire value of the premium is taxed in the tax year in which the transaction is entered into.

[*CTA 2009, s 250*].

Capital gains

[60.16] Any UK property business consisting of the letting of furnished holiday accommodation is treated as a trade for the purposes of replacement of business assets relief, relief for loans to traders, retirement relief and substantial shareholdings exemption. Similarly with regard to an EEA furnished holiday lettings business.

See **13** CAPITAL GAINS — SUBSTANTIAL SHAREHOLDINGS and Tolley's Capital Gains Tax under Furnished Holiday Accommodation, Losses and Rollover Relief.

[*TGCA 1992, ss 241, 241A; SI 2019 No 689, Reg 6(14)*].

Non-resident landlords scheme

[60.17] Where a landlord is non-UK resident and is chargeable on the profits of a UK property business under *ITTOIA 2005, Ch 2 Pt 3* or *CTA 2009, Ch 2 Pt 4*, then tax is deductible from the profits of the business at the basic rate. Such tax is to be deducted at source by the agent for the property or, where there is no agent, the tenant.

Deduction of income tax may therefore apply to non-resident company landlords. Where the profits are chargeable to corporation tax (with effect from 6 April 2020), relief for income tax suffered is obtained under the rules at **41.9** INCOME TAX IN RELATION TO A COMPANY. If the income tax suffered is not sufficient to cover the company's corporation tax liability for an accounting period, it must register with HMRC and give notice that it is chargeable to corporation tax.

The regulations giving effect to these requirements provide broadly as follows.

(i) Letting agents who receive or have control over UK property income of a non-resident must operate the scheme.

(ii) Where there is no letting agent acting, tenants of a non-resident must operate the scheme.

(iii) Tenants who pay less than £100 per week do not have to operate the scheme unless asked to do so by HMRC.

(iv) Letting agents and tenants who have to operate the scheme must pay tax at the basic rate each quarter on the non-resident's UK property income less certain allowable expenses and deductions, and must give the non-resident an annual certificate showing details of tax deducted.

(v) Non-residents whose property income is subject to deduction of tax may set the tax deducted against their UK tax liability through their self-assessment.

(vi) Non-residents may apply to HMRC for approval to receive their UK property income without deduction of tax provided that:
  (a) their UK tax affairs are up to date;
  (b) they have never had any obligations in relation to UK tax; or
  (c) they do not expect to be liable to UK income tax,

  and that they undertake to comply with all their UK tax obligations in the future. An appeal may be made against refusal or withdrawal of approval.

The regulations also make provision for interest on unpaid tax and for payments on account under self-assessment, and set out details of the annual information requirements on those operating the scheme, and of other information to be supplied on request.

Penalties apply under *TMA 1970, s 98* for non-compliance with these return and information provisions.

HMRC publish detailed guidance notes for those required to operate the scheme (see www.gov.uk/government/publications/non-resident-landord-guidance-notes-for-letting-agents-and-tenants-non-resident-landlords-scheme-guidance-notes.

Simon's Taxes. See **B6.217**.

Corporate interest restriction

With effect from 6 April 2020, non-resident company landlords are potentially subject to the CORPORATE INTEREST RESTRICTION (**24**) in respect of financing costs. The restriction may affect the amount of the allowable deductions in (iv) above and so require agents to apply the restriction before deducting income tax. As an alternative, agents may make an irrevocable election to calculate the financing cost deduction using a fixed allowance, 30% of the rental income net of deductible expenses other than financing cist. Any unused allowance may be carried forward from one quarter period to the next and any unused financing costs may also be carried forward. See *SI 1995 No 2902, Regs 9, 9A*.

See also www.gov.uk/government/publications/income-tax-changes-to-the-regulations-for-the-non-residents-landlord-scheme/guidance-note.

[*ITA 2007, s 972; SI 1995 No 2902; SI 2020 No 151*].

Miscellaneous provisions regarding property income

Capital allowances on plant and machinery

[60.18] A property business is a qualifying activity for the purposes of such allowances (see **10.4** CAPITAL ALLOWANCES ON PLANT AND MACHINERY).

Allowances are thus given as expenses, and charges treated as receipts, of the business. Plant or machinery provided for use in a dwelling-house is excluded (with a just and reasonable apportionment of expenditure where such use is partial).

[*CAA 2001, ss 15, 16, 35*].

Overseas property business

An 'overseas property business' is defined in the same way as a 'UK property business' (see **60.2** above) except that the source of the income is outside the UK. Before *CTA 2009* took effect, rental income from land situated outside the UK was chargeable under *Schedule D Case V*.

The overseas letting is treated as a separate business and the same computational rules (including the lease premium rules) apply in determining the receipts and expenses to be included in computing the profits of overseas property business as if the property were situated in the UK. Where a business falls within the property income provisions and those for trading income, the trading income provisions take priority.

[*CTA 2009, ss 206, 209*].

The special rules governing the tax treatment of furnished holiday lettings do not apply to an overseas property business, save the rules with regard to an EEA furnished holiday lettings business, see **60.7** above. [*CTA 2009, s 210(2)*].

Overseas property business losses may be carried forward and set off against overseas property business profits from the same business in subsequent accounting periods, provided that the business is carried on on a commercial basis or in the exercise of statutory functions.

[*CTA 2009, s 287*].

Non-resident companies are within the charge to income tax (not corporation tax) in certain circumstances (see **63** RESIDENCE).

Where a company starts or ceases an overseas property business or to be within the charge to corporation tax in respect of an overseas property business, it is treated as starting or ceasing to carry on the business at that time.

[*CTA 2009, s 289*].

Mutual businesses

The normal exemption for mutual companies (**54** MUTUAL COMPANIES) does not extend to property businesses, the transactions and relationships involved in mutual business being instead treated as if they were between persons between whom no relationship of mutuality existed. Any surplus is chargeable on the company to which the profits arise or which is entitled to the profits. (This does not affect the treatment of Co-operative Housing Associations — see 40 HOUSING ASSOCIATIONS.)

[*CTA 2009, s 260*].

Simon's Taxes. See **B6.211**.

Items apportioned on sale of land

If on a sale of land, receipts and outgoings due to be received or paid by the buyer are apportioned to the seller, then, in computing the profits of the seller's property business, the part apportioned to it is treated as being of the same nature, i.e. revenue or capital, as the transaction itself.

So, for example, if rent is receivable in arrears and the sale price includes an accrual for rent receivable up to date of sale, the amount of that accrual is income in the hands of the vendor and not capital.

[*CTA 2009, s 259*].

Simon's Taxes. See **B6.210**.

Sea walls

For allowances for expenditure on making sea walls, see *CTA 2009, ss 254–257*; and *Hesketh v Bray* (1888) 2 TC 380.

Simon's Taxes. See **B6.208**.

Electric-line wayleaves

Where rent is receivable for a UK electric-line wayleave, it is chargeable to corporation tax as property income. If a company carries on a UK property business in relation to some or all of the land to which the wayleave relates and the business has other receipts for the accounting period in question, the rent receivable for the wayleave is brought into account as profits from a property business. Otherwise, it is taxed as a separate item; the charge is on the full amount of the profits arising in the accounting period.

Rent is receivable for a UK electric-line wayleave if it is receivable in respect of an easement enjoyed in the UK, which includes any right, privilege or benefit in, over or derived from land in connection with any electric, telegraph or telephone wire or cable, including supporting poles or pylons and related apparatus. All references above to 'rent' include any other receipt in the nature of rent.

[*CTA 2009, ss 277–279, 287, 288*].

However, if a company carries on a trade, profession or vocation on some or all of the land to which the wayleave relates and (apart from rent receivable, or expenses incurred, in respect of the wayleave) no other receipts or expenses in respect of any of the land are included in computing the profits of any property business of the company, then the rent receivable, or expenses incurred, in respect of the wayleave may be brought into account (at the company's option) in computing the profits of the trade etc. instead of being charged as above.

[*CTA 2009, s 45*].

Simon's Taxes. See **B6.502**.

Mines, quarries etc.

Profits of mines, quarries, gravel pits, sand pits, brickfields, ironworks, gas works, canals, railways, rights of fishing, rights of markets, fairs and tolls and like concerns (as specified in *CTA 2009, s 39*) are computed and charged to corporation tax trading income where they are carried on on a commercial basis. (see **68.46** TRADING INCOME).

Where no trade is carried on, or the trade is not carried on by the owner of the mine etc. income other than mineral royalties is taxable as income of a property business. If a company lets the right to work mineral deposits in the UK and it pays an amount wholly and exclusively as management expenses in that period, a deduction for the paid amount is against income for the accounting period, subject to the reduction of one half mentioned below. If the rent is received in kind, it is chargeable in the same way as rent received in cash: this is a change from the previous treatment.

[*CTA 2009, ss 39, 258, 270–272*].

Key points on property income

[60.19] Points to consider are as follows.

- Distributions of income and gains deriving from a REIT's property rental business are treated as property income in the hands of shareholders and are generally subject to a deduction of 20% tax at source. UK resident corporate shareholders can receive the distributions without suffering deduction at source. Where the REIT's shareholders are non-UK resident, the dividend article of any relevant tax treaty applies to the distribution and as a result, for shareholders that can benefit from tax treaties, the rate of withholding may be lower than 20%. In these cases, the REIT is still required to withhold tax at a rate of 20%. The shareholder may then make a claim to HMRC for a refund. There are new rules with regard to distributions paid from a UK REIT to another UK REIT.
- Where a corporate shareholder holds 10% or more shares in a REIT, it may be possible to ensure that the shareholder is not treated as a 'holder of excessive rights' by fragmenting its holding across a number of sister subsidiaries, each holding less than 10%, provided the parent company itself does not hold any shares in the REIT.
- Care is needed when considering how unrelieved property losses for an accounting period can be utilised. It is not possible to carry back property losses to a prior period. Property losses can be set off against the company's total profits for the accounting period in

which the loss arises. They may only be group relieved to the extent that current period property losses exceed current period profits of the surrendering company (i.e. profits before offset of losses (current year or brought forward), charges on income and management expenses).

- Property losses carried forward are treated as property losses arising in the subsequent period and may be offset against total profits arising in that period. UK property business losses of accounting periods beginning on or after 1 April 2017 so carried forward can be surrendered as group relief for carried-forward losses.
- If a company with both an investment business and a property business ceases to carry on its property business but continues to have investment business, any unrelieved property losses may be carried forward and treated as management expenses deductible in later periods. UK property business losses of accounting periods beginning on or after 1 April 2017 so carried forward can be surrendered as group relief for carried-forward losses.
- If a company with a property business ceases that business, any property losses will lapse unless the company also has an investment business (see above). In the event that the company has sold all of its properties, but fully intends to acquire further assets in the future, it may be possible to treat the dormant period as a temporary break in business, with the effect that the losses should be available for use on recommencement of that business. The question as to whether a property business has ceased is a question of fact.
- Given the broad application of the loss restriction provisions on a change of ownership of a company (see **60.9**), in most cases it is unlikely that a purchaser would ascribe value to tax losses in the target company.
- A lease premium receivable in respect of a lease with a term of less than 50 years are treated as part income and part capital in the hands of the landlord. The shorter the term of the lease, the greater the proportion of the premium treated as income. A revenue tax deduction is available to the payer of the premium over the term of the lease for the element of the premium that is treated as income in the hands of the landlord, provided that the tenant remains in occupation (where the tenant is a trader) or the property is sub-let (where the tenant has a property business).
- Where the provisions of a lease do not provide for it to be surrendered in return for the payment of a premium, any such premium received for a surrender of the lease will be treated as a capital receipt in the hands of the landlord. This results in a beneficial tax treatment for landlords with capital losses or those that are non-UK resident.
- A reverse premium is generally treated as an income receipt in the hands of an incoming tenant. Consideration could be given to structuring the incentive as a contribution by the landlord to tenant's fixtures and fittings that qualify for capital allowances, in

which case the tenant loses the right to claim capital allowances, but is not taxed on the contribution. The tax position for the landlord is also likely to be improved as the landlord will be able to claim capital allowances on the contribution made towards qualifying assets, rather than relief for the premium being deferred until the property is sold (since it will otherwise generally be treated as enhancement spend).

- Non-UK resident corporate owners of UK property are chargeable to corporation tax with effect from 6 April 2020. Such owners may suffer deduction of income tax under the non-resident landlords' scheme. Relief for income tax suffered is obtained under the rules at **41.9** INCOME TAX IN RELATION TO A COMPANY.

61

Purchase by a Company of its Own Shares

Introduction to purchase by a company of its own shares

[61.1] *Companies Act 2006, Pt 18* provides the authority for a company to buy back its own shares from its shareholders, subject to various conditions. This facility can be useful in providing an exit route for investors where an external buyer for shares is not available. A company can buy back its own shares out of distributable profits or proceeds from a new share issue. Normally, the repurchased shares are cancelled but a company may purchase and hold its own shares (known as treasury shares) — see **61.10** below.

A purchase of own shares may be taxed either as:

(1) a DISTRIBUTION (**29**) to the extent that the proceeds exceed the amount originally subscribed for the shares (although the purchase by the company is still treated as a disposal by the shareholder concerned) — see **61.2** below; or

(2) a capital receipt in the hands of the shareholder (for purchases by unquoted companies only and where certain conditions are satisfied) — see **61.3** onwards below.

In either case, the purchasing company is not treated as acquiring an asset, even where it retains the shares as treasury shares. See HMRC Capital Gains Manual CG58600.

Where a company purchases its own shares from a dealer, the purchase price is a trading receipt of the trader and no part of it is chargeable on the dealer as a distribution. See HMRC Company Taxation Manual CTM17640.

In a case where the repurchase did not comply with the provisions of the *Companies Act 2006* and the transaction was void, an attempt by HMRC to tax the distribution was not accepted by the tribunal in *Baker v HMRC* FTT, [2013] UKFTT 394 TC.

Simon's Taxes. See **D6.605–D6.618.**

Legal costs

Legal and other expenditure incurred by a trading company on the redemption, repayment or purchase of its own shares is generally regarded by HMRC as capital expenditure on the grounds that it is part of the cost of changing the share capital of the company and it is a sum in respect of capital withdrawn from the trade. It is therefore not deductible in computing trading profits. HMRC consider that the expenditure is also likely to fail the wholly and exclusively test. (HMRC Company Taxation Manual CTM17600).

Distribution treatment

[61.2] A purchase of shares by a company is treated as a distribution to the extent that it exceeds the amount originally subscribed for the shares (i.e. to the extent that it represents a repayment of share capital — see **29.2, 29.10** DISTRIBUTIONS) unless:

(1) it meets the necessary conditions to be treated as a capital payment (see **61.3** onwards below); or
(2) it is in exchange for new consideration (see **29.11** DISTRIBUTIONS).

The purchase by the company is nevertheless still a disposal by the shareholder concerned for capital gains purposes, but, for a non-corporate shareholder, the element of the consideration representing a distribution is excluded in the computation under *TCGA 1992, s 37*, as it is taken into account for the purposes of computing income. See the example at **61.3** below.

For a corporate shareholder, it is likely that the distribution will be treated as exempt from corporation tax (see **29.16** DISTRIBUTIONS). Consequently, the whole of the purchase price must be brought into account in the calculation of any chargeable gain on the disposal. Only if a company receives a non-exempt distribution will the element of the consideration representing a distribution be excluded in the computation.

The purchasing company is not treated as acquiring an asset, even where it retains the shares as treasury shares. See **61.1** above.

See also **61.1** above as regards dealers in securities and **29.9** DISTRIBUTIONS as regards certain subsequent bonus issues.

Capital treatment

[61.3] Where the conditions at **61.4–61.7** below are satisfied, a payment (or anything else which is a distribution or would be but for these provisions) made by a company for the purchase, redemption or repayment of its own shares is not treated as a distribution. [*CTA 2010, s 1033(1), (6)*]. Such a payment in the hands of the vendor is brought into account for capital gains purposes only (but see **61.1** above as regards dealers in securities).

The purchasing company is not treated as acquiring an asset, even where it retains the shares as treasury shares. See **61.1** above.

Example

In June 2021, A Ltd, an unquoted trading company, is planning to re-purchase the shares of Mr X, a 20% shareholder, for £100,000. Mr X owns 30,000 ordinary shares in A Ltd which he acquired from a third party in September 2004 for £50,000. The third party subscribed for the shares at par for £30,000 in May 2002.

Income treatment:	£	Capital treatment:	£
Income tax:		Capital gains tax:	
Proceeds	100,000	Proceeds	100,000
Less: original subscription cost	(30,000)	Less: cost of shares	(50,000)
Taxable as a distribution	70,000	Capital gain	50,000
		Less: annual exemption	(12,300)
Tax on the distribution:		Taxable gain	37,700
£70,000 × 32.5% (assuming a 40%		Tax on the gain:	
tax rate payer)	£22,750	£37,700 × 20%	£7,540

Capital loss	£
Original subscription cost	30,000
Less: price paid	(50,000)
Capital loss	(20,000)

The tax under the capital route will be even lower at £3,770 if business asset disposal relief (formerly entrepreneurs' relief) is available to Mr X. That would require Mr X to have been an officer or employee of the company throughout the two years ending with the disposal.

Conditions to be satisfied by the company

[61.4] For the capital treatment in **61.3** above to apply, the following conditions must be satisfied.

- The company must be an 'unquoted company', i.e. neither the company, nor any company of which it is a '51% subsidiary' may have any class of shares listed in the official list of a stock exchange.
  Securities on the Alternative Investment Market ('AIM') are treated as unquoted for these purposes. (HMRC Share Valuation Manual, SVM09070.)
  A company is a '*51% subsidiary*' of another if more than 50% of its ordinary share capital is beneficially owned directly or indirectly by the other company.
- The company must be either a 'trading company' or the 'holding company of a trading group'.

A '*trading company*' is a company whose business consists wholly or mainly of carrying on a trade or trades. '*Trade*' does not include dealing in shares, securities, land or futures. A '*trading group*' is a group the business of whose members, taken together, consists wholly or mainly of carrying on a trade or trades. A '*group*', for this purpose only, is a company and its 75% subsidiaries. A '*holding company*' is a company whose business (ignoring any trade carried on by it) consists wholly or mainly of holding shares or securities in 75% subsidiaries. A company is a '*75% subsidiary*' of another if not less than 75% of its ordinary share capital is beneficially owned directly or indirectly by the other company.

[*CTA 2010, ss 1033(1)(a), 1047, 1048(1), (2), 1154*].

Conditions regarding the reason for the purchase

[61.5] Either Condition A or Condition B must be met to enable the payment etc. to qualify for capital treatment as in **61.3** above.

Condition A — Payment made for the benefit of the trade

Where Condition B does not apply, the following requirements must be satisfied:

- the purchase etc. of the shares must be made wholly or mainly to benefit a trade carried on by the company or by any '75% subsidiary' (see **61.4** above);
- the purchase must not form part of a scheme or arrangement the main, or one such, purpose of which is either the obtaining by the vendor of a share in the company's profits without receiving a dividend, or the avoidance of tax; and
- the requirements at **61.6** and **61.7** below must be met.

[*CTA 2010, s 1033(1), (2)*].

As regards whether a purchase etc. is for the benefit of the trade, HMRC have given their interpretation in HMRC Statement of Practice, SP 2/82. This emphasises that the purpose must be the benefit of a trade and not, for example, the benefit of the vending shareholder (although he will usually also benefit), or of some wider commercial purpose to which the payment etc. may be put, or of a non-trading activity of the trading company. Generally, the condition will be satisfied where (after taking into account any associate's interests) the vending shareholder is genuinely giving up his entire interest of all kinds in the company. Four examples are cited.

(1) The withdrawal of his investment by an outside shareholder providing equity finance.
(2) The retirement of the proprietor of a company to make way for new management.
(3) The death of a shareholder, on which his personal representatives or the beneficiaries do not wish to keep the shares.
(4) A disagreement over the management of the company.

In the last example, however, the condition would only be satisfied if the disagreement would, as will usually be the case, have an adverse effect on the running of the trade. It would not be satisfied if the disagreement were, for example, over whether the company should discontinue trading and become an investment company, and the vending shareholder advocated the continuance of trading.

It may happen that the company wants, but cannot afford, to buy out a shareholder completely. In these circumstances, it is acceptable for the repurchase to proceed and for the shareholder to lend part of the consideration back to the company immediately after the purchase. Where the shares are of high market value and the issued capital is relatively small, this could result in the shareholder continuing to be 'connected with' the company (see below). To prevent this, it is acceptable for the company to make a bonus issue to increase its issued capital before the repurchase. (Revenue Tax Bulletin February 1996 p 281).

Where a shareholder is only 'substantially reducing' his interest (see **61.7** below), the only situations in which HMRC envisage the condition being satisfied are where a complete disinvestment is to be achieved in a number of transactions, or where a small shareholding (not exceeding 5% of issued share capital) is retained for sentimental reasons.

Condition B — Discharge of inheritance tax liability

Substantially the whole of the payment etc. (apart from any sum applied in paying capital gains tax on the disposal) must be used to meet the payee's inheritance tax liability on a death, within two years of that death, being a liability he could not have met without undue hardship other than through the purchase etc. of the shares or the purchase etc. of its own shares by another company within **61.4** above. Where Condition B is satisfied, there is no requirement to meet the conditions at **61.6** and **61.7** below.

[*CTA 2010, s 1033(1), (3), (4)*].

Conditions to be satisfied by the vendor

[61.6] Where Condition A at **61.5** above is relied on to obtain the capital treatment in **61.3** above, the following conditions must be satisfied by the vendor.

- The vendor (and any nominee holder) must be resident in the UK in the tax year of the purchase etc. The residence of trustees is determined as under *TCGA 1992, s 69* (see Tolley's Capital Gains Tax under Settlements), and that of personal representatives follows that of the deceased immediately before his death.
- The vendor must have held the shares for the five years ending with the date of purchase. If he acquired them under a will or intestacy, or as a personal representative, ownership by the deceased person (and, in the former case, by his personal representative) counts as ownership by the vendor, and the qualifying period is reduced to three years.

Similarly, where the shares were transferred to the vendor by his spouse or civil partner living with him at the time of transfer, the spouse's or partner's ownership counts as ownership by the vendor provided that the transferor either is still his spouse or partner living with him or is deceased at the time of the purchase etc. Where identification of different holdings of shares of the same class is necessary, earlier acquisitions are taken into account before later ones, and previous disposals identified with later acquisitions before earlier ones, for this purpose.

[*CTA 2010, ss 1034–1036*].

Except in the case of certain shares allotted as stock dividends and falling within *CTA 2010, ss 1049–1051* (see Tolley's Income Tax under Savings and Investment Income), the time of acquisition of shares acquired through a reorganisation of share capital or conversion of securities etc. is that determined under *TCGA 1992, Pt IV, Ch II* (i.e. generally the date of acquisition of the original shares) (see Tolley's Capital Gains Tax under Shares and Securities).

Other conditions to be satisfied

[61.7] Where Condition A at **61.5** above is relied on to obtain the capital treatment in **61.3** above, the following further conditions must be satisfied.

Required reduction in the vendor's interest

The vendor's shareholding must be substantially reduced or eliminated by the purchase. Where associates of the vendor are shareholders and the associate owns shares immediately after the purchase, the combined shareholdings of the vendor and his associates must be substantially reduced. However, this condition is relaxed if the vendor has agreed to the purchase in order for another vendor to satisfy the substantial reduction condition.

'*Associate*' includes spouse or civil partner and minor children, and a broad range of relationships whereby an individual or company may be able to influence the actions of another, or to benefit from the co-ordination of their actions.

A shareholding is '*substantially reduced*' if the proportion of the company's issued share capital held by him immediately after the purchase does not exceed 75% of that immediately before the purchase.

It is not regarded as so reduced if the share of profits to which the vendor would be entitled (beneficially except in the case of trustees or personal representatives) on a distribution of available profits by the company immediately after the purchase etc. exceeds 75% of the corresponding share immediately before the purchase etc.

Profits available for distribution by a company are as defined in *Companies Act 2006, s 830(2)* (broadly, accumulated realised profits not distributed or capitalised less accumulated realised losses not written off) plus £100 plus, where any person is entitled to periodic distributions calculated by reference to fixed rates or amounts, the amount required to make the maximum distribution to which he would be entitled for a year.

[*CTA 2010, ss 1037, 1038, 1043, 1059, 1060*].

See **61.5** above for HMRC's view on the circumstances in which the requirement for the purchase to be for the benefit of the trade can be satisfied where the vendor's shareholding is not completely eliminated.

For a case where the requirements for capital treatment, and in particular this condition, were not met, see *Preston Meats Ltd v Hammond* Sp C, [2005] SSCD 90.

Reduction of a vendor's interest in a group situation

If the company making the purchase etc. is, immediately before that purchase etc., a member of a 'group of companies', and, immediately after the purchase etc., either:

- the vendor owns shares in other group member(s); or
- still owns shares in the company making the purchase etc. *and* had immediately before the purchase owned shares in other group member(s),

then the vendor's holding must be substantially reduced in relation to his interest in the group as a whole, taken as the average of his proportionate holdings of the issued share capital of the company purchasing the shares and of all other group members in which he holds shares immediately before or after the purchase. This includes, for averaging purposes, companies in which he held shares immediately before or after the purchase but in which he holds no shares when the average is to be determined.

A '*group of companies*' for this purpose is a company (not a 51% subsidiary of any other company) and its 51% subsidiaries, except that a company which ceased to be a 51% subsidiary of another before the time of purchase of the shares is treated as continuing to be such a subsidiary if at that time there were arrangements in existence under which it could again become such a subsidiary.

Where the whole or a significant part of the business first carried on within three years before the purchase etc. by an unquoted company (see **61.4** above), the 'successor company', was previously carried on by the company purchasing the shares (or by a member of the same group), the successor company and any company of which it is a 51% subsidiary are treated as being members of the same group as the company purchasing the shares.

Where an associate of the vendor owns shares in any company in the same group as the company purchasing the shares immediately before the purchase, the combined interests of vendor and associate(s) must satisfy the substantial reduction test. However, this condition is relaxed if the vendor has agreed to the purchase in order for another vendor to satisfy the substantial reduction condition.

[*CTA 2010, ss 1039, 1043, 1047*].

Where a vendor is connected with the company following the purchase

The vendor must not, immediately after the purchase, be 'connected with' the company purchasing the shares or any company in the same group.

He is so 'connected with' a company if, together with his associates, he directly or indirectly possesses or is (or will be) entitled to acquire:

- more than 30% of its voting power, its issued ordinary share capital, or its issued share capital and loan capital (i.e. any debt incurred by the company for money borrowed, for capital assets acquired, for any right to income created in its favour or for insufficient consideration); or

- rights enabling him to more than 30% of its assets available for distribution to the company's equity holders (see **35.4** GROUP RELIEF),

or if he has 'control' of it.

'*Control*' for this purpose means the power of a person by shareholding or voting power (whether directly or through another company), or under Articles of Association, to secure that the company's affairs are conducted according to his wishes.

[*CTA 2010, ss 1042(1), 1062, 1063, 1124*].

Rights of the vendor after the purchase

The purchase must not be part of a scheme or arrangement the likely result of which is the acquiring by the vendor of rights such that, had he had them immediately after the purchase the above conditions could not have been satisfied. Any transaction within one year of the purchase is deemed to be part of a scheme of which the purchase is also a part.

[*CTA 2010, ss 1042(2)–(5)*].

Returns

[61.8] Within 60 days of making a payment treated by the company as not being a distribution under the provisions at **61.3–61.7** above, the company must notify HMRC of the particulars of the payment, and why it is regarded as falling within those provisions. If within **61.5** above, any person connected with the company who knows of any scheme or arrangement within the provisions under the heading 'Rights of the vendor after the purchase' in **61.7** must give details thereof to HMRC within 60 days of his coming to know of both the payment etc. and the scheme etc.

[*CTA 2010, s 1046*].

Clearance procedure

[61.9] A company may apply in writing for clearance from HMRC that a proposed transaction falls or, as the case may be, does not fall within the provisions at **61.3** to **61.7** above. HMRC must notify its decision within 30 days of receiving the application or, if further particulars are requested, within 30 days of the furnishing of the last such particulars. Such particulars must be requested within 30 days of the application (or of the furnishing of particulars previously requested), and must be supplied by the company within 30 days (or such longer period as HMRC may allow). Failure to supply full and accurate information voids any clearance. [*CTA 2010, ss 1044, 1045*].

Applications for clearance should be addressed to BAI Clearance, HMRC, BX9 1JL (or, if market-sensitive information is included, to Team Leader at that address). Applications may be emailed to reconstructions@hmrc.gsi.gov.uk (after advising Team Leader if market-sensitive information is included). Application may be made in a single letter to the same address for clearance under

CTA 2010, s 1044 and under any one or more of *CTA 2010, s 1075* (demergers, see **29.29** DISTRIBUTIONS), *CTA 2010, s 748* (transactions in securities, see **70.1** TRANSACTIONS IN SECURITIES), *TCGA 1992, s 138(1)* (share exchanges, see Tolley's Capital Gains Tax under Anti-Avoidance), *TCGA 1992, s 139(5)* (reconstructions involving the transfer of a business, see **62.15** REORGANISATIONS AND RECONSTRUCTIONS), *TCGA 1992, s 140B* (transfer of a UK trade between EU member states), *TCGA 1992, s 140D* (transfer of non-UK trade between EU member states) and *CTA 2009, s 832* (see **42.30** INTANGIBLE ASSETS).

The application should state whether the purchase, etc. is regarded as falling within *CTA 2010, s 1033* (see **61.5**), and give details of any earlier clearance applications (by the company or by a fellow group member). If the purchase etc. is regarded as within *CTA 2010, s 1033(2)*, (see **61.5** above) the application must be in writing and should include:

(i) the name, reference number and status (e.g. whether a trading company, etc) of the purchasing (etc.) company, and confirmation that it is unquoted;
(ii) full details of any group of which it is a member, and of company and (if appropriate) group shareholdings;
(iii) details of the proposed share purchase and of any other transactions between the company and vendor at or about the same time, and confirmation that the purchase is permitted by the company's Articles;
(iv) full details of any prior transactions and of the reasons for, and the benefits expected from, the purchase, etc.;
(v) confirmation, with any necessary calculations, etc., that the other conditions outlined in **61.7** above are satisfied; and
(vi) the company's latest available balance sheet and profit and loss account (and, in the case of a member of a group, those of any fellow group members and, if appropriate, of the group as a whole) together with a note of any later relevant and material changes.

However, if the purchase is regarded as within *CTA 2010, s 1033(3)*, (see **61.5** above). The application should include the information as at (i) to (iv) and (vi) above, together with full details of the inheritance tax liability concerned and of the circumstances in which 'undue hardship' would arise.

An application for clearance that a proposed purchase, etc. does not fall within the provisions at **61.3** to **61.7** above should give full details of the purchasing company and of the proposed purchaser and be accompanied by a statement of the grounds on which clearance is sought.

If all details are not fully and accurately disclosed, the clearance will be void.

(HMRC Statement of Practice, SP 2/82).

[*CTA 2010, ss 1044, 1045*].

'Treasury shares'

[61.10] The tax consequences of the acquisition by a company with share capital of its own shares are set out above. However companies may purchase and *hold* their own shares. These shares are known as 'treasury shares'. In these circumstances:

(a) The acquisition by the company of its own shares is not treated as the acquisition of an asset.

(b) The company is not treated as a member of itself by reason of the acquisition or holding of its own shares.

(c) (Subject to (f) below) the company's issued share capital is treated as reduced by the nominal value of the shares acquired.

(d) (Subject to (f) below) such of those shares as are not cancelled on acquisition are treated as if they had been so cancelled.

(e) Any subsequent cancellation of the shares by the company is disregarded (and so is not treated as a disposal of an asset and does not give rise to an allowable capital loss).

(f) Where the shares are issued to the company as bonus shares, i.e. as paid up otherwise than by the receipt of 'new consideration' (within *CTA 2010, s 1115*, see **29.11** DISTRIBUTIONS), (c) and (d) above do not apply, and the shares are treated as not having been issued.

(g) Where, disregarding (a)–(f) above, a company holds any of its own shares and issues bonus shares in respect of any of those shares, these provisions do not prevent the existing shares from being the company's holding for the purposes of *TCGA 1992, s 126* (company reorganisations etc., see Tolley's Capital Gains Tax under Shares and Securities), although this does not apply where *s 126* is applied in a modified form by virtue of any other enactment.

(h) Where a company disposes of its own shares and, but for (a)–(f) above, would be regarded as holding the shares immediately before the disposal, (d), (e) and (f) above cease to apply in relation to the shares disposed of (the '*relevant shares*'), and:

   (i) the relevant shares are treated as having been issued by the company as new shares to the acquirer at the time of the disposal (and not as having been disposed of by the company at that time);

   (ii) the acquirer is treated as having subscribed for the shares an amount equal to the amount or value of the consideration (if any) payable for the disposal;

   (iii) if the amount or value of that consideration does not exceed the nominal value of the shares, the share capital of those shares is to be treated for the purposes of *CTA, Pt 23* (company distributions, etc.) as if it were an amount equal to the amount or value of the consideration; and

   (iv) if the amount or value of that consideration exceeds their nominal value, the shares are treated as if they had been issued at a premium representing that excess.

(i) Where a company purchases its own shares and the price payable is a trading expense (i.e. the company is a share dealer), (a)–(g) above do not apply, and (h) above does not apply to the disposal by the company of any of the shares.

It is notable that in *Biffa (Jersey) v HMRC* [2014] UKFTT 982 the Tribunal found that whilst *FA 2003, s 195* applied such that the acquisition of own shares is not to be treated as an asset of the company, this did not mean that the company was to be treated as not having acquired shares, and so in this case the application of *ICTA 1988, s 730A* was not prevented.

[*FA 2003, s 195*].

62

Reorganisations and Reconstructions

Introduction to reorganisations and reconstructions

[62.1] There are a number of common transactions carried out by companies and groups that do not necessarily involve any element of cash consideration passing and generally do not involve any real changes of ownership. In such cases, there are special rules to ensure that no immediate tax charge arises on these cashless transactions. Instead, the tax charge arises on the disposal of the new securities received in the transactions.

The main transactions concerned are:

- Reorganisations of shares capital.
- Share-for-share or share-for-debenture exchanges.
- Schemes of reconstruction.

Reorganisation of share capital

[62.2] The simplest transaction to which these rules apply is a reorganisation of a company's share capital, where there is no change of ownership of the company.

Basic principles

[62.3] Where a company reorganises its share capital, the reorganisation does not normally constitute a disposal. Instead, the 'new holding' is treated as the same asset, acquired at the same date, as the 'original shares'.

For this purpose:

- '*original shares*' means shares held before, and concerned in, the reorganisation, and
- '*new holding*' means, in relation to any original shares, the shares in and debentures of the company which, following the reorganisation, represent the original shares, and any remaining original shares.

In effect, the new holding stands in the shoes of the original shares, so it has the same base cost and is treated as having been acquired at the same time (e.g. for indexation purposes, where relevant).

[*TCGA 1992, ss 126(1), 127*].

Simon's Taxes. See **D6.103.**

> *Example*
>
> Jeff and Jill own all the shares of JJ Ltd between them, 50 £1 shares each. All the shares are converted into 10p shares, so that they now own 500 10p shares each.
>
> This is a reorganisation of share capital within *TCGA 1992, s 126(1)* and the shareholdings have the same base cost and are deemed to have been acquired at the same time as the original shares.

Scope of provisions

[62.4] A 'reorganisation' is defined as a '*reorganisation or reduction of a company's share capital*', although there is no actual definition of what is meant by a 'reorganisation'. '*Reorganisation of a company's share capital*' includes the making of bonus and rights issues of shares or debentures in proportion to the original holdings (see **62.8** below), the reduction of share capital and the alteration of rights attaching to the original shares. '*Reduction of share capital*' does not include the paying off of redeemable share capital, and where shares in a company are redeemed by the company otherwise than by the issue of shares or debentures (with or without other consideration) and otherwise than in a liquidation, the shareholder is treated as disposing of the shares at the time of the redemption.

[*TCGA 1992, s 126*].

The legislation states that the alteration of rights attaching to any one class of shares is a reorganisation, where there is already more than one class of shares in issue. However, it is generally accepted that, where a company has only one class of shares, a reorganisation into more than one class also qualifies as a reorganisation for the purposes of this legislation on first principles, i.e. such a transaction is a reorganisation of share capital (and a common transaction preparatory to many schemes of reconstruction). (HMRC Capital Gains Manual CG51780).

[*TCGA 1992, s 126(2)(b)*].

Example

Jeff and Jill now own each 500 10p shares of JJ Ltd. Jill's shares are converted to A preference shares.

This is a reorganisation of share capital within *TCGA 1992, s 126(1)* and the Jill's shareholding still has the same base cost and is deemed to have been acquired at the same time as the original 50 £1 shares.

Example

Jeff now owns 500 10p shares of JJ Ltd and Jill owns 500 10p A preference shares. Jeff's shares are converted to non-voting shares.

This is a reorganisation of share capital within *TCGA 1992, s 126(2)(a)*. Jeff's shareholding still has the same base cost and is deemed to have been acquired at the same time as the original 50 £1 shares.

In *Dunstan v Young Austen Young Ltd* [1989] STC 69, 61 TC 448, CA, the Court of Appeal held that an increase in share capital can be a reorganisation even if it is not a conventional bonus or rights issue, 'provided that the new shares are acquired by existing shareholders because they are existing shareholders and in proportion to their existing beneficial holdings'. In essence, again, the point is that the transaction was a reorganisation on first principles.

See also *Unilever (UK) Holdings Ltd v Smith* [2002] EWCA Civ 1787, [2003] STC 15, 76 TC 300 and *Fletcher v HMRC* [2008] STC (SCD) 1219.

[*TCGA 1992, s 126*].

Simon's Taxes. See **D6.101**.

HMRC will treat any subscription for shares under an 'open offer', which is equal to or less than the shareholder's minimum entitlement under the offer, as a share reorganisation. Any shares subscribed for in excess of the minimum entitlement will be treated as a separate acquisition. (An 'open offer' is where a company invites its shareholders to subscribe for shares subject to a minimum entitlement based on their existing holdings, and possibly enabling them to subscribe also for shares which other shareholders do not want.) (HMRC Capital Gains Manual CG51756).

No part of any acquisition of shares by existing shareholders under a 'vendor placing' can be treated as a share reorganisation. For this purpose, a '*vendor placing*' takes place where a company wishes to pay for the purchase of an asset by issuing its own shares and, with the vendors not wanting the shares, the company makes arrangements to sell the shares on the vendors' behalf to its existing shareholders. (HMRC Capital Gains Manual CG51763).

For HMRC's views on the treatment of rights to acquire shares in other companies, see HMRC Capital Gains Manual CG52065.

Consideration given by shareholder

[62.5] Any additional consideration given by the shareholder at the time of reorganisation (e.g. as a subscription for a rights issue — see **62.8** below) is added to the cost of the original holding for the purpose of computing the unindexed gain on a subsequent disposal.

The surrender, cancellation or alteration of the original holding or the rights attached thereto, and any consideration met out of the assets of the company (e.g. on a bonus issue) or represented by a dividend or other distribution declared but not paid are not regarded as 'additional consideration'. Similarly, in the case of a reorganisation occurring after 9 March 1981, any consideration given, otherwise than by way of a bargain made at arm's length, for part or all of the new holding will be disregarded, to the extent that its amount or value exceeds the amount by which the market value of the new holding, immediately after the reorganisation, exceeds the market value of the original shares immediately before the reorganisation. (See also *CIR v Burmah Oil Co. Ltd* [1982] STC 30, 54 TC 200, HL.)

[*TCGA 1992, s 128(1)(2)*].

Example

Gavin and Gail own all the shares of GG Ltd between them, 50 £1 shares each. They decide to increase the capital of the company and arrange for an issue of another 950 £1 shares each, which they each subscribe for at par.

This is a reorganisation of share capital within *TCGA 1992, s 126(2)(a)* and *TCGA 1992, s 129* applies, so that Gavin and Gail have a base cost of £1,000 for their shareholding of 1,000 £1 shares.

Consideration received by shareholder

[62.6] Where, on a reorganisation, a person receives (or is deemed to receive), or becomes entitled to receive, any consideration, other than the new holding, for the disposal of an interest in the original shares, and in particular:

(i) where under *TCGA 1992, s 122* he is to be treated as if he had in consideration of a capital distribution disposed of an interest in the original shares; or

(ii) where he receives (or is deemed to receive) consideration from other shareholders in respect of a surrender of rights derived from the original shares,

he is treated as if the new holding resulted from his having for that consideration disposed of an interest (but without prejudice to the original shares and the new holding being treated in accordance with *TCGA 1992, s 127* above as the same asset).

[*TCGA 1992, s 128(3)*].

Simon's Taxes. See D6.103.

Valuation of different classes of share on subsequent disposal

[62.7] Where the new holding consists of more than one class of share, security, debenture, etc., none of which is quoted on a recognised stock exchange within three months of the reorganisation, the allowable acquisition cost is arrived at on the basis of the market value of the various classes at the date of a chargeable disposal of the new holding or part thereof. This also applies where consideration, other than the new holding, is received as in *TCGA 1992, s 128(3)* above.

[*TCGA 1992, ss 128(4), 129*].

Simon's Taxes. See D6.224.

Example

Harry and Henrietta own 1,000 £1 shares each of GG Ltd. The shares are reorganised so that they each have 500 ordinary shares and 500 A preference shares. This is a reorganisation within *TCGA 1992, s 126*), so the shares still have the original base cost of £1,000. Harry then sells 250 preference shares to Helga for £10,000. The market value of Harry's ordinary shares at that time is £25,000.

The market value of Harry's shares after the disposal is £25,000 (the ordinary shares) plus £10,000 (the other 250 preference shares), a total of £35,000. Applying the normal A/(A+B) formula for a part-disposal, we have £10,000 / £10,000 + £35,000 = 0.222. so the base cost of the shares Harry sells is 0.222 × £1,000, i.e. £222.

The capital gain is therefore the consideration, £10,000, less base cost, £222, giving a gain of £978.

However, in the case of shares and securities any one class or more of which is or are listed on a recognised stock exchange (or, in the case of unit trust rights, of which the prices were published daily by the managers) within three months after the reorganisation takes effect (or such longer time as HMRC may allow), the base value is determined *once and for all* by reference to the respective market value, on the first day on which the market values or prices of the shares are quoted or published (whether published before or after the actual reorganisation).

[*TCGA 1992, ss 130*].

Bonus and rights issues

[62.8] A bonus issue (often called a scrip issue) is a reorganisation within **62.4** above, as is a rights issue, which involves paying for the new shares, although the allocation is on the basis of current shareholdings.

Where a company has acquired its own shares and holds them as treasury shares a bonus issue in respect of shares of the same class can be a reorganisation whether or not bonus shares are issued in respect of the treasury shares (HMRC Capital Gains Manual CG51750).

In practice, where a bonus issue follows a repayment of share capital (e.g. under *CTA 2010, s 1022*), and is treated as income of the recipient, the net amount of the distribution is treated as the acquisition cost of the new shares (HMRC Capital Gains Manual CG51825).

Example

X plc, a quoted company, makes a bonus issue in September 2021 of one preference share for every eight ordinary shares held. On first trading after issue, the preference shares were valued at £10 and the ordinary shares at £6.

Mr A had purchased 1,000 ordinary shares in December 2014 for £7,000. After the issue of preference shares, the allowable expenditure on a subsequent disposal of the ordinary and preference shares is computed as follows.

	£
Initial value of preference shares (125 × £10)	1,250
Initial value of ordinary shares (1,000 × £6)	6,000
Total	£7,250

Allowable cost of 1,000 ordinary shares $\frac{6{,}000}{7{,}250} \times 7{,}000$ = £5,790

Allowable cost of 125 preference shares $\frac{1{,}250}{7{,}250} \times 7{,}000$ = £1,210

A rights issue of shares or debentures in respect of shares already held in a company is a reorganisation within **62.4** above. A company cannot grant rights in respect of treasury shares, but this will not in itself prevent the rights issue being a reorganisation (HMRC Capital Gains Manual CG51750).

A rights issue requires the shares to be paid for, so the provisions relating to consideration given for the new holding will apply.

[*TCGA 1992, s 126(2)(a)*].

Simon's Taxes. See **D6.102**.

Disposal of rights

[62.9] Where a person receives or becomes entitled to receive in respect of any shares in a company a provisional allotment of shares in or debentures of the company and he disposes of his rights, *TCGA 1992, s 122* applies as if the amount of consideration for the disposal were a capital distribution received by him from the company in respect of the first-mentioned shares, and as if he had, instead of disposing of the rights, disposed of an interest in those shares. This rule also applies to rights obtained in respect of any debentures of a company.

[*TCGA 1992, s 123*].

Simon's Taxes. See **D6.233**.

Exchange of securities for those in another company

[62.10] The share reorganisation provisions at 62.3 above apply with appropriate modifications where a company (company B) issues shares or debentures in exchange for the shares or debentures of another company (company A), provided that one of the following conditions is satisfied. The conditions are that:

- company B holds, or in consequence of the exchange will hold, more than 25% of company A's 'ordinary share capital';
- company B holds, or in consequence of the exchange will hold, more than 50% of the voting power in company A; or
- company B issues the shares etc. as the result of a general offer made to the members of company A (or any class of them) and the offer is initially made on a condition which, if satisfied, would give company B control of company A. (This covers abortive takeover bids which become unconditional, but which do not succeed.)

In applying the share reorganisation provisions, company A and company B are treated as if they were the same company. Following the exchange, therefore, the shares etc. in company B (which form the 'new holding' for the purposes of the reorganisation provisions) are treated, in the hands of the original holders of the exchanged company A shares etc., as the same asset, acquired at the same date, as the exchanged shares etc. (which form the 'original shares').

For this purpose, the '*ordinary share capital*' of a company is all its issued share capital (by whatever name called), other than shares carrying only a right to fixed rate dividends and no other right to participate in profits and also includes units in a unit trust and, in relation to a company with no share capital, interests in the company possessed by its members. In relation to such a company, references above to shares or debentures include any such interests. For HMRC's interpretation of 'ordinary share capital', see Appendix 11 to the CGT Manual.

These provisions are subject to the anti-avoidance rule below.

Example

Bertram and Bertha own all the shares of BB Ltd, which cost them £1,000 each when they subscribed 15 years ago. The company is now worth £750,000. Benjamin Plc offers to buy their shares and to pay them by issuing them new shares, which they accept. They sell BB Ltd to Benjamin Plc and receive 25,000 shares each of Benjamin Plc as consideration.

This is an exchange to which *TCGA 1992, s 135* applies, as Benjamin Plc has acquired all the shares and voting power of BB Ltd (and, arguably, the offer was made to all the members on appropriate terms). Therefore, Bertram and Bertha have £1,000 each base cost in the shares of Benjamin Plc which have been issued to them.

The above provisions can apply in several different commercial situations, including straightforward takeovers, reverse takeovers, forming groups out of associated companies and buy-outs. See HMRC Capital Gains Manual CG52570. Where the conditions are satisfied, the provisions apply automatically, without claim.

[*TCGA 1992, s 135; CTA 2010, s 1119*].

In certain cases involving business asset disposal relief (formerly entrepreneurs' relief), an election may be made for the reorganisation to be treated as an actual disposal and reacquisition.

[*TCGA 1992, s 169Q*].

Simon's Taxes. See **C3.1308.**

Treasury shares

Where company A has acquired its own shares and is holding them as treasury shares at the time of the exchange, no issue of shares by Company B can be made in respect of the treasury shares. The treasury shares do not count as issued share capital in determining whether the conditions for the above treatment are met. A disposal of its treasury shares by Company B is treated as the company issuing those shares. (HMRC Capital Gains Manual CG52521, 52523).

Anti-avoidance, disapplication of relief and advance clearance

[62.11] The reorganisation provisions for the shareholder reliefs for share-for-share exchanges and schemes of reconstruction (*TCGA 1992, ss 135 and 136*), and for the corporate relief (*TCGA 1992, s 139*) do not apply unless the transactions are for *bona fide* commercial reasons and not to avoid corporation tax or capital gains tax (*TCGA 1992, ss 135 and 136 by s137(1)*) or corporation tax, capital gains tax or income tax (*TCGA 1992, s 139*), or where HMRC, on written application by the acquiring company, has notified its satisfaction with the scheme before the transfer is made.

For the purposes of *TCGA 1992, S 137(1)* only, these restrictions do not apply where a person to whom the new shares or debentures are issued owns (or he and persons connected with him together own) less than 5% of, or any class of, the shares or debentures of company A.

There are provisions for advance clearance of an exchange by HMRC. Applications for such clearance should be addressed to BAI Clearance, HMRC, BX9 1JL (or, if market-sensitive information is included, to the Team Leader, at that address). Applications may be emailed to reconstructions@hmrc.gov.uk.

Application may be made in a single letter to the same address for clearance under *TCGA 1992, ss 138 and 139* and under any one or more of *CTA 2010, ss 1091, 1092* (demergers, see **29.29**), *CTA 2010, ss 1044, 1045* (see **61.9** PURCHASE BY A COMPANY OF ITS OWN SHARES), *CTA 2010, ss 748, 749* (transactions in securities, see **70.1** TRANSACTIONS IN SECURITIES), *TCGA 1992, s 140B* (transfer of a UK trade between EU member states, see **11.18** CAPITAL GAINS), *TCGA 1992, s 140D* (transfer of non-UK trade between EU member states, see **11.25** CAPITAL GAINS) and *CTA 2009, ss 831, 832* (see **42.30** INTANGIBLE ASSETS).

The application should give full details of the transactions and of all the companies directly involved, their tax districts and references. Copies of accounts for the last two years for which accounts have been prepared should accompany the application. HMRC may, within 30 days of receipt, call for further particulars (to be supplied within 30 days, or longer if HMRC allows; if the information is not supplied, the application lapses). Subject to this, HMRC must notify its decision within a further 30 days. If not so notified, or if dissatisfied with the decision, the applicant may within a further 30 days require HMRC to refer the application to the tribunal for their decision. All material facts and considerations must be disclosed, otherwise any decision is void.

[*TCGA 1992, ss 137(1), 138, 139(5)*].

In *Euromoney Institutional Investor plc v HMRC* FTT, [2021] UKFTT 61 (TC), the above provisions were held not to apply even though one of the taxpayer's purposes was the avoidance of a tax liability. That purpose was not one of the taxpayer's main purposes; its main purposes were commercial and it considered the tax advantage to be no more than a bonus.

Simon's Taxes. See **D6.202, D6.204, D6.450.**

See also HMRC Statement of Practice 13/80.

Where the provisions are disapplied, then under general principles the disposal proceeds will be the value in money's worth of the shares or debentures issued by the acquiring company or, if the transaction is not a bargain made at arm's length, the market value of the shares or debentures sold (if different).

TCGA 1992, s 135 is disapplied in certain circumstances (with the result that an exchange of securities is treated as a disposal of the original holding and an acquisition of a new holding) in relation to shares and securities that have qualified for tax relief under one of the various venture capital tax schemes or the community investment tax credit scheme.

Reconstructions

[62.12] There are two reliefs applicable to schemes of reconstruction, which is broadly where companies and groups are reconstructed and there is an issue of shares by a company to the shareholders of another company as part of the transaction (see **62.13** below). Firstly, the shareholders of a company subject to a scheme of reconstruction are treated as if the transaction were a reorganisation of share capital; secondly, any transfer of assets by a company in a scheme of reconstruction may be at a consideration that gives rise to no gain and no loss for capital gains purposes.

One particular scheme of reconstruction is the demerger, where a company or group is split into 2 groups, each carrying on part of the business of the original company or group. See, for example, **29.29** DISTRIBUTIONS and **11** CAPITAL GAINS.

Definition — scheme of reconstruction

[62.13] A '*scheme of reconstruction*' is a scheme of merger, division or other restructuring meeting both of conditions (a) and (b) below and either condition (c) or condition (d) below.

(a) **Issue of ordinary share capital.** The scheme must involve the issue of 'ordinary share capital' of a company or companies (the 'successor company' or 'successor companies') to holders of ordinary share capital of another company or companies (the 'original company' or 'original companies'). Or, if the original company or any of the original companies has more than one class of ordinary shares, the issue to holders of one or more classes of ordinary share capital of any such company. The scheme must not involve the issue of ordinary share capital of the successor company or companies to anyone else.
'*Ordinary share capital*' of a company is all the issued share capital of the company other than capital the holders of which have a right to a dividend at a fixed rate but no other right to share in company profits. It also includes interests possessed by members in a company which has no share capital, and rights in unit trust schemes which are treated as shares under *TCGA 1992, s 99(1)(b)*.

(b) **Equal entitlement to new shares.** The entitlement of any person to acquire ordinary share capital of the successor company or companies by virtue of holding ordinary share capital (or any class of such capital) of the original company or companies which is involved in the scheme (as in (a) above) must be the same as that of any other person holding such shares (or shares of that class). (See the example in HMRC's Capital Gains Manual at CG52707b.)

Where a reorganisation (within *TCGA 1992, s 126*) of the share capital of the original company, or of any of the original companies, is carried out for the purposes of the scheme, (a) and (b) above apply in relation to the position after the reorganisation.

An issue of shares in or debentures of the successor company, or any of the successor companies, after the latest date on which any ordinary share capital of the successor company, or of any of them, is issued in consideration of the transfer of any business (or part) under the scheme, or in pursuance of the compromise or arrangement referred to in (d) below, is disregarded for the purposes of (a) and (b) above.

As referred to above, both (a) and (b) above and either (c) or (d) below must be satisfied.

(c) **Continuity of business.** The effect of the restructuring must be either:
   (i) if there is one original company, that the business or substantially the whole of the business carried on by the original company is carried on by a successor company (which must not be the original company) or successor companies (which may include the original company); or
   (ii) if there is more than one original company, that all or part of the business(es) carried on by one or more of the original companies is carried on by a different company, and the whole or substan-

tially the whole of the business(es) carried on by the original companies are carried on by the successor company (which may be one of the original companies) or successor companies (which may be the same as or include the original companies).

The requirement in (i) and (ii) above that the whole or substantially the whole of a business or businesses be carried on by two or more companies is satisfied where the activities of those companies taken together embrace the whole or substantially the whole of the business or businesses concerned. See HMRC Capital Gains Manual, CG52709 as regards the meaning of 'business' for these purposes.

A business carried on by a company under the control (within *CTA 2010, s 1124*) of another company is for these purpose treated as carried on by both the controlling and the controlled company.

The holding and management of assets retained by the original company (or by one of the original companies) for the purpose of making a capital distribution (within *TCGA 1992, s 122*) in respect of shares in the company is disregarded for these purposes.

(d) **Compromise or arrangement with members**. The scheme must be carried out in pursuance of a compromise or arrangement under *Companies Act 2006* (or NI or foreign equivalent), and no part of the business of the original company, or any of the original companies, must be transferred under the scheme to any other person.

[*TCGA 1992, s 139(1)(1A)(2)(9), Sch 5AA*].

Simon's Taxes. See **D6.450.**

For practical illustrations of 'schemes of reconstruction', see HMRC Capital Gains Manual, CG52720–52728.

Scheme of reconstruction and shareholders

[62.14] The share reorganisation provisions at **62.3** above apply where certain arrangements between a company (company A) and its share- or debenture-holders (or any class of them) are entered into for the purposes of, or in connection with, a 'scheme of reconstruction'. Under the arrangement, another company (company B) must issue shares or debentures to those holders in respect of, or in proportion to (or as nearly as may be in proportion to), their original holdings, which latter are then retained, cancelled or otherwise extinguished.

In such a case, the holders are treated as exchanging their holdings in company A for the shares or debentures held by them as a consequence of the arrangement and the share reorganisation provisions apply as if company A and company B were the same company and the exchange were a reorganisation of its share capital. Any shares in or debentures of company A that are of a class involved in the scheme and that are retained are treated as if they had been cancelled and replaced by a new issue.

Where company A carries out an actual reorganisation of its share capital as a prelude to a scheme of reconstruction the above provisions apply to the position after the preliminary reorganisation has been carried out.

References above to shares or debentures being retained include their being retained in altered form, whether as a result of reduction, consolidation, division or otherwise. In relation to a company with no share capital, references to shares or debentures include any interests in the company possessed by its members.

[*TCGA 1992, s 136*].

> *Example*
>
> Oliver bought 1,000 £1 shares of Olga Plc on the London Stock Exchange for £2,300. Olga Plc is the subject of a takeover bid by Orville Plc, another UK-listed company. The offer is that Orville Plc will issue 1 share to shareholders of Olga Plc for every 2 Olga Plc shares held. The Olga Plc shares will be cancelled and reissued to Orville Plc under a scheme of reconstruction.
>
> As this is a scheme of reconstruction, *TCGA 1992, s 136* applies. Oliver will receive 500 shares of Orville Plc and his base cost will be the same £2,300 that he paid for the shares of Olga Plc.

TCGA 1992, s 136 is disapplied in certain circumstances (with the result that a scheme of reconstruction is treated as a disposal of the original holding and an acquisition of a new holding) in relation to shares and securities that have qualified for tax relief under one of the various venture capital tax schemes or the community investment tax credit scheme.

Reconstructions involving transfer of business

[62.15] The provisions found at *TCGA 1992, s 139* allow for the deferral of the capital gains charge where two companies are involved in a reconstruction which includes the transfer of a business, in specific circumstances, and where the transaction has been undertaken for bona fide commercial reasons.

Under these provisions (and subject to the following conditions) where a 'scheme of reconstruction' takes place which involves the transfer of a company's business to another company for no consideration (other than the assumption of liabilities of the business), the capital assets (not used as trading stock by either company) are regarded as being transferred at a 'no gain, no loss' price, and the acquiring company takes over the disposing company's acquisition date.

Thus no gain or loss arises at the time of the reconstruction – a gain (or loss) only arises when the acquiring company subsequently disposes of any capital assets transferred with the business (such gain or loss being the 'full' amount – calculated with a base cost as at the original acquisition date of the disposing company).

The provisions *TCGA 1992, s 139* apply where:

(i) any scheme of reconstruction involves the transfer of the whole or part of a company's business to another company; and
(ii) the conditions at (A) and (B) below are met in relation to the assets included in the transfer; and

(iii) the first-mentioned company receives no part of the consideration for the transfer (otherwise than by the acquiring company taking over the whole or part of the liabilities of the business).

The degrouping charge rules may apply to deem a degrouping charge to be added to the consideration for the main disposal on such a business transfer (see **12.15** CAPITAL GAINS — GROUPS). Where this is so, *TCGA 1992, s 139(1B)* operates so that this deemed consideration is ignored for the purposes of *TCGA 1992, s 139(1)*.

The application of these provisions is conditional on:

(A) either the transferee company being UK resident at the time of acquisition or the assets being 'chargeable assets' or, for disposals before 6 April 2019, 'NRCGT assets' in relation to that company immediately after that time; and

(B) either the transferor company being UK resident at that time or the assets being 'chargeable assets' or, for disposals before 6 April 2019, 'NRCGT assets' in relation to that company immediately before that time.

For these purposes, an asset is a '*chargeable asset*' in relation to a company at a particular time if, on a disposal by the company at that time, any gain would be a chargeable gain chargeable to corporation tax. An asset is an '*NRCGT asset*' at a particular time if a disposal of the asset would be a non-resident CGT disposal (see **11.24** CAPITAL GAINS) and the company would not be within one of the categories of persons not chargeable to non-resident CGT.

See **58.20** PAYMENT OF TAX for CT payment plans for transactions with EEA resident group members which allow for payment by instalments where *s 139* does not apply because the conditions in (A) and (B) above are not met. The facility for such plans was introduced to prevent the disapplication of a tax charge in accordance with the decision in *Gallaher Ltd v HMRC* [2019] UKFTT 207 (TC) (see **12.4** CAPITAL GAINS — GROUPS and note that the Upper Tribunal ([2021] STC 247) has referred the compatibility of the relevant UK legislation with EU law to the CJEU). Plans can be entered into in respect of transactions occurring in accounting periods ending on or after 10 October 2018.

[*TCGA 1992, s 139(1)–(1AA); FA 2019, Sch 1 paras 49, 120*].

Simon's Taxes. See **D6.450.**

Example

William owns William Ltd but, for various reasons, wants to start running the business of William Ltd from a new company, William (2020) Ltd. He incorporates the new company, William (2020) Ltd, and a scheme of reconstruction is carried out whereby William Ltd transfers all its assets to William (2019) Ltd for no consideration and William (2020) Ltd issues shares to William.

From William's perspective this is a scheme of reconstruction to which *TCGA 1992, s 136* applies, so his base cost in the new shares issued by William (2020) Ltd is the same as the original price he paid for the shares in William Ltd.

For the companies *TCGA 1992, s 139* applies, so that the assets are deemed to be transferred from William Ltd to William (2020) Ltd at no gain and no loss for corporation tax purposes. So no chargeable gain arises in William Ltd and William (2020) Ltd inherits the same base cost in the assets as William Ltd had.

If any tax arises on a transfer, i.e. the relief does not apply, and that tax is not paid by the disposing company within six months of a specified date, then, within two years of that date, the tax may be assessed on any person who:

(a) holds all or any of the assets to which the tax relates; and
(b) is either the acquiring company or any other group member to which the assets have been subsequently transferred.

The date specified (as above) is the date the tax became payable by the company or, if later, the date the assessment was made on the company.

The tax charge will be proportionate to the assets held and the paying company has the right of recovery against the original disposing company of the tax charged and any interest thereon under *TMA 1970, s 87A* (see **43.2** INTEREST ON OVERDUE TAX). Where the disposing company has been wound up, any tax due from it may be recovered from the acquiring company.

[*TCGA 1992, s 139(5)–(8)*].

The provisions of *TCGA 1992, s 139* do not apply to the transfer of the whole or part of a company's business to a unit trust scheme (where it is either within *TCGA 1992, s 100(2)* or an authorised unit trust, see **46.3** INVESTMENT FUNDS), to an investment trust (see **47.2** INVESTMENT TRUSTS) or to a venture capital trust (see **74.2** VENTURE CAPITAL TRUSTS).

[*TCGA 1992, s 139(4)*].

Where *s 139* has applied in relation to a transfer to a company which was not then an investment trust but which subsequently becomes one for an accounting period, then any assets of the business transferred which are still owned by the company at the beginning of that accounting period are deemed to have been sold and immediately reacquired by the transferee company, immediately after the transfer, at their market value at that time. The resulting chargeable gain or allowable loss is deemed to accrue to the transferee company immediately before the end of the accounting period preceding that in which the company becomes an investment trust. Notwithstanding normal time limits, a corporation tax assessment in respect of any resulting liability can be made within six years after the end of the accounting period in which the company becomes an investment trust.

Similar provisions apply where, after a transfer to which *s 139* applied, the transferee company becomes a venture capital trust (within *ITA 2007, Pt 6*, see **74.2** VENTURE CAPITAL TRUSTS). They apply by reference to the time at which HMRC's approval for the purposes of the VCT legislation comes into effect, and the resulting gain or loss is deemed to accrue immediately before that time rather than at the time of the deemed disposal. In a case in which HMRC's approval has effect as from the beginning of an accounting period, any consequential corporation tax assessment can be made, notwithstanding normal time limits, within six years after the end of that accounting period. These provisions do not apply if those above relating to investment trusts have already applied (in relation to the same transfer of assets) and *vice versa.*

[*TCGA 1992, ss 101, 101B*].

The provisions of *TCGA 1992, s 139* are adapted for certain transfers of an insurance company's long-term business.

Other transactions treated like reorganisations

[62.16] The reorganisations provisions are applied to a number of other transactions that are similar in nature.

Conversion of securities

[62.17] The share reorganisation provisions at **62.3** above apply also to the '*conversion of securities*', which phrase includes:

(a) a conversion of securities of a company into shares in that company;
(b) a conversion of a security which is not a qualifying corporate bond (QCB) (see **62.20**) into a security of the same company which is a QCB;
(c) a conversion of a QCB into a security of the same company which is not a QCB;
(d) a conversion in lieu of redemption at the option of the holder of the securities; and
(e) any exchange of securities in pursuance of compulsory purchase powers.

Any of the above is a conversion of securities regardless of whether effected by a transaction or occurring as a result of the operation of the terms of any security or debenture.

'*Security*' includes any loan stock or similar security issued by national or local government or public authority in the UK or elsewhere, or by a company, and whether secured or unsecured. Certain company debentures are deemed under *TCGA 1992, s 251* to be securities for the purposes of that section. There are provisions to ensure that (b) and (c) above operate in relation to such debentures.

[*TCGA 1992, s 132*].

An amendment to the terms of loan notes which was intended to transform the notes into a QCB by removing the right to redeem them in dollars was held to be a conversion of the notes within the above provisions in *Klincke v HMRC* [2010] UKUT 230 (TCC), [2010] STC 2032.

A premium in money (in addition to a new holding) on a conversion of securities is treated in virtually identical terms as under *TCGA 1992, s 122* for a capital distribution. (It would appear that the case of *O'Rourke v Binks* [1992] STC 703, 65 TC 165, CA mentioned therein applies equally to premiums on conversion within this provision as it does to capital distributions within *TCGA 1992, s 122*.) Similar rules as in *s 122* apply if the premium is 'small'.

[*TCGA 1992, s 133*].

Simon's Taxes. See D6.211.

Compensation stock

[62.18] Instead of *TCGA 1992, s 132* above applying, where gilt-edged securities are issued on the compulsory acquisition of shares or securities the gain that would have accrued had the shares or securities been disposed of at their value at that time is not treated as arising until the gilt-edged securities are disposed of. However, for corporation tax purposes where the gilt-edged securities received are disposed of after 5 April 1988 no gain arises under this provision if its application would be directly attributable to the disposal of an asset before 1 April 1982.

Disposals are, so far as possible, identified with gilts issued under the above provisions rather than with other gilts of the same kind and subject to this, with gilts issued at an earlier time rather than with those issued at a later time.

The deferment of the gain otherwise arising on the issue of the gilt-edged securities is extended to the recipient where their later disposal is within *TCGA 1992, s 58(1)* (spouses or civil partners), *s 62(4)* (legatee acquiring asset from personal representatives) and *s 171(1)* (groups of companies).

[*TCGA 1992, s 134, Sch 4 paras A1, 4(5)*].

Simon's Taxes. See C2.826.

Euroconversion of securities

[62.19] A 'small' cash payment received on a 'euroconversion' of a security, not involving a disposal of the security and therefore not within *TCGA 1992, s 132* (see above), is treated in virtually identical terms as a 'small' capital distribution under*TCGA 1992, s 122*. '*Euroconversion*' for these purposes refers to the redenomination into euros of a security expressed in the currency of an EU member state participating in the European single currency.

[*TCGA 1992, s 133A*].

Qualifying corporate bonds

[62.20] Gains on qualifying corporate bonds (QCBs) are exempt from tax on chargeable gains but there are special provisions which apply to reorganisations of share capital where either the original shares or the new shares are QCBs.

Different rules apply for corporation tax and capital gains tax purposes. For corporation tax purposes, any asset representing a loan relationship of a company is a qualifying corporate bond. For capital gains tax, broadly, a qualifying corporate bond is a security on which the debt is a normal commercial loan and which is expressed in sterling with no provision for its conversion into, or redemption in, another currency. See 62.21 below for the detailed provisions.

Definitions of QCBs

[62.21] Different definitions apply for the purposes of corporation tax and capital gains tax.

For corporation tax purposes a 'qualifying corporate bond' is any asset representing a loan relationship of a company.

[*TCGA 1992, s 117(A1)*].

Simon's Taxes. See **C2.820.**

For income tax purposes, the definition requires firstly the identification of a corporate bond, then a determination as to whether it is a qualifying corporate bond.

Definition of corporate bond

[62.22] Before defining a 'qualifying corporate bond', it is first necessary to define a 'corporate bond'. Subject to the specific inclusion of certain securities within this definition (see below) and the exclusion of some (again, see below), a '*corporate bond*' is a 'security' which fulfils both the following conditions.

(a) The debt on the security represents, and has at all times represented, a 'normal commercial loan'.
'*Normal commercial loan*' is as would be defined by *CTA 2010, s 162* if, for *subsection (2)(a)–(c)* of that section, there were substituted the words 'corporate bonds (within the meaning of *TCGA 1992, s 117*)'. The broad effect of the modification is that securities can be treated as corporate bonds if they carry conversion rights into other corporate bonds but not if the conversion rights relate to securities other than corporate bonds. Securities carrying an indirect right of conversion into ordinary shares were held not to be corporate bonds in *Weston v Garnett* CA, [2005] STC 1134.
(b) The security is expressed in sterling and no provision is made for its conversion into, or redemption in, a currency other than sterling.
A security is *not* treated as expressed in sterling if the amount of sterling falls to be determined by reference to the value at any time of any other currency or asset. A provision for redemption in a currency other than sterling is disregarded provided the rate of exchange to be used is that prevailing at redemption.
Securities carrying an option for redemption in a foreign currency do not become corporate bonds when the option lapses (*Harding v HMRC* [2008] EWCA Civ 1164, [2008] STC 3499, 79 TC 885). In *Trigg v HMRC* CA, [2018] EWCA Civ 17, [2018] SWTI 257, the court held that bonds which according to their terms would be redeemed in euros if the UK joined the Euro, were qualifying corporate bonds.

'*Security*' includes any loan stock or similar security of any government or public or local authority in the UK or elsewhere, or of any company, and whether secured or unsecured.

[*TCGA 1992, ss 117(1), 132(3)(b)*].

Simon's Taxes. See **C2.820.**

For more information, see Tolley's Capital Gains Tax SHARES AND SECURITIES

Definition of qualifying corporate bond

[62.23] A corporate bond:

(A) is a '*qualifying corporate bond*' if it is issued after 13 March 1984; and
(B) becomes a '*qualifying corporate bond*' if, having been issued before 14 March 1984, it is acquired by any person after 13 March 1984 unless
  (i) the acquisition is as the result of *any* disposal treated as a no gain/no loss transaction or a disposal where the consideration is reduced by an amount of held-over gain under *TCGA 1992, s 165* or *s 260*; and
  (ii) the bond was not a qualifying corporate bond before the disposal.

[*TCGA 1992, s 117(7)(8)*].

Simon's Taxes. See **C2.820.**

Where a right to a security is comprised in a provisional letter of allotment or similar instrument, the security is not deemed to be issued until acceptance has been made. [*TCGA 1992, s 117(11)(a)*].

A security which is a corporate bond due to its being a deeply discounted security (see above) is a qualifying corporate bond whatever its date of issue. [*TCGA 1992, s 117(8A)*].

Reorganisations involving QCBs

[62.24] Special provisions apply to a transaction ('*relevant transaction*') where otherwise *TCGA 1992, ss 127–130* (share reorganisation rules for 'original shares' and 'new holding' would apply under any provision contained in *TCGA 1992, Pt IV Ch II* (reorganisation of share capital, conversion of securities etc.), and either the original shares would consist of or include a qualifying corporate bond and the new holding would not, or the original shares would not and the new holding would consist of or include such a bond.

The provisions apply equally to a conversion of securities effected other than by means of a transaction, for example in consequence of the terms of the security. Where the qualifying corporate bond would constitute the original shares it is referred to as '*the old asset*', the shares and securities constituting the new holding being referred to as '*the new asset*'. Where the qualifying corporate bond would constitute the new holding it is referred to as '*the new asset*', the shares and securities constituting the original shares being referred to as '*the old asset*'.

TCGA 1992, ss 127–130 do not apply to the relevant transaction so far as it relates to the old asset and the new asset. (HMRC has stated that where shares (or other chargeable securities) are exchanged, converted etc. for a new holding consisting partly of qualifying corporate bonds and partly of shares etc., then *TCGA 1992, ss 127–130* are only disapplied to the extent that the consideration takes the form of qualifying corporate bonds, any apportionment of the base cost of the original shares being on a just and reasonable basis under *TCGA 1992, s 52(4)* by reference to the respective market values at the time of exchange etc. of the shares etc. and qualifying corporate bonds received in exchange etc. (Revenue Tax Bulletin February 1993 p 57).

Where the qualifying corporate bond would constitute the old asset, the shares or securities which constitute the new asset are to be treated as being acquired on the date of the relevant transaction and for a consideration of the market value of the old asset immediately before the relevant transaction. Similar provisions apply where the qualifying corporate bond constitutes the new asset. Where a sum of money by way of consideration for the old asset is received, in addition to the new asset, that sum is to be deducted from the deemed market value consideration and where a sum of money is paid by way of consideration, in addition to the old asset, that sum is to be added to the deemed market value consideration. See also (ii) below.

Old asset consisting of qualifying corporate bond

[62.25] Where the old asset consists of a qualifying corporate bond, then so far as it relates to the old and the new asset, the relevant transaction is to be treated as a disposal of the old asset and an acquisition of the new asset.

[*TCGA 1992, s 116(9)*].

Simon's Taxes. See **D6.110.**

New asset consisting of qualifying corporate bond

[62.26] In all other cases (e.g. where the new asset consists of a qualifying corporate bond) then so far as it relates to the old asset and to the new asset the relevant transaction is *not* to be treated as a disposal of the old asset but:

(a) the chargeable gain or allowable loss is calculated that would have accrued had the old asset been disposed of at the time of the relevant transaction at its market value immediately before that time, and

(b) subject to the exclusions below, the whole or a corresponding part of the calculated chargeable gain or allowable loss at (a) above is to be deemed to accrue on a subsequent disposal of the whole or part of the new asset. The exemption provided by *TCGA 1992, s 115* applies only to the gain or loss that actually accrues on that disposal and not to the gain or loss that is deemed to accrue.

[*TCGA 1992, s 116(10)*].

Simon's Taxes. See **D6.110.**

Where a chargeable gain arises when the computation is made under (a) above, and part of the consideration for the old asset is received as money, a proportion of the chargeable gain is deemed to accrue at that time. The proportion is the ratio which the sum of money bears to the market value of the old asset immediately before the relevant transaction. On a later disposal of a part or the whole of the new asset, the proportion already deemed to have accrued is to be deducted from the gain accruing under (b) above. However, if the sum of money is 'small' in comparison with the market value of the old asset immediately before the relevant transaction, HMRC may direct that no chargeable gain accrues at that time. The money consideration is then deducted from allowable expenditure on any subsequent disposal.

For the purpose of the above, HMRC regard 'small' as meaning 5% or less (see HMRC Capital Gains Manual CG53717, 57836) and also regard an amount of £3,000 or less as 'small', regardless of whether or not it would pass the 5% test (Revenue Tax Bulletin February 1997 p 397).

[*TCGA 1992, s 116(12)*].

Simon's Taxes. See **D6.110.**

Example

Alfred set up Albatross Ltd in 2008 and subscribed for 10,000 shares for £125,000. Skua Plc offers to buy the company for £2,250,000, to be settled by the issue of debentures by Skua Plc, which will be redeemable over a period of 10 years from the date of the transaction, at £225,000 a year.

Under *TCGA 1992, s 116(10)* Alfred's gain is computed as if he had sold the shares for cash. The gain is £2,250,000 – £125,000 = £2,125,000.

This gain is then held over until the debentures are redeemed. Each time a tranche of £225,000 of debentures is redeemed, £212,500 of the gain is deemed to crystallise (i.e. 10% of the gain each year in line with the redemption being 10% of the debentures each year).

The computation and hold-over of the gain (*TCGA 1992, s 116(10)*) do not apply to disposals falling within: *TCGA 1992, s 58(1)* (married persons and civil partners); *s 62(4)* (death); *s 139* in respect of disposals after 13 March 1989; *s 140A, s 140E* (see **11.17** onwards CAPITAL GAINS); or *s 171(1)* (**12.4** CAPITAL GAINS — GROUPS). Where there is such a disposal (and without there having been a previous disposal other than such a disposal or a devolution on death) the person who has acquired the new asset is treated for the purposes of (b) above as if the new asset had been acquired by him at the same time and for the same consideration as it was acquired by the person making the disposal.

[*TCGA 1992, s 116(11)*].

Simon's Taxes. See **D6.110.**

Key points on reorganisations and reconstructions

[62.27] Points to consider are as follows.

- A reorganisation is effectively treated as a non-transaction. Any new shares or securities held after the reorganisation effectively 'stand in the shoes' of the original shares, being treated as having been acquired at the same price and time as those original shares.

- A bonus issue of shares and a rights issue are both forms of reorganisation.
- A reduction of capital is also a reorganisation as long as it is not a redemption of redeemable shares.
- If any further consideration is given by the shareholder in the reorganisation, that consideration is added to the base cost.
- But only to the extent that the consideration is reflected in the increased value of the shares.
- Any apportionment of base cost between different classes of share or security is determined at the time of disposal of part of the new holding, based on the market value of the holding retained.
- Unless the new holding is listed shares or securities, in which case the apportionment of base cost is on the basis of the relative dealing prices on the first day of listing.
- A share-for-share exchange is treated as a reorganisation, so far as possible, so the shares issued by the acquiring company stand in the shoes of the target company shares, so long as the transaction is carried out for commercial reasons and not to avoid tax.
- A scheme of reconstruction is also treated as a reorganisation, so far as possible, so the shares held after the transaction – which may be just shares issued by the acquiring company and may also include shares of the original target company – stand in the shoes of the target company, so long as the transaction is carried out for commercial reasons and not to avoid tax.
- If a business is transferred in a scheme of reconstruction, the assets pass at non gain / no loss, so long as the transaction is carried out for commercial reasons and not to avoid tax.
- Pre-transaction clearance is available from HMRC regarding the commercial reasons and lack of tax avoidance motive.
- A share-for-debenture exchange is treated as not involving a disposal. Instead, the gain that would have accrued is computed and held over until the debentures are redeemed or otherwise disposed of.

63

Research and Development Expenditure

Simon's Taxes. See **D1.4**.

Introduction to research and development expenditure

[63.1] Relief is available for expenditure of a revenue nature on 'research and development' ('R&D'). There are two schemes:

- the small and medium-sized enterprise (SME) scheme (see **63.5** and **63.8** below); and
- research and development expenditure credit ('RDEC') or above the line tax credit scheme for large companies and SMEs (see **63.9** below).

SMEs incurring qualifying R&D expenditure can obtain relief for 230% of the expenditure. SMEs not in profit or not yet trading can claim relief upfront as a cash payment, R&D tax credit, equal to 14.5% of their surrenderable loss (subject to the application of a cap for accounting periods beginning on or after 1 April 2021). Where SME relief is not available because the work is subcontracted to it or the expenditure is subsidised or SME relief or relief is restricted by the cap on relief (see **63.8** below), the company may be able to claim relief under the RDEC regime.

The RDEC scheme allows companies to claim R&D relief as a taxable above the line R&D credit, as a percentage of their qualifying R&D expenditure. The credit is fully payable to companies with no corporation tax liability, once the relevant set off steps outlined at **63.11** below have been considered.

A company may be eligible for relief under more than one type of relief in respect of the same expenditure. For provisions relevant to two or more categories of relief, see **63.2** below. See **63.12** below for claims procedures.

For reliefs for research and development expenditure of a capital nature, see **9.20** CAPITAL ALLOWANCES.

For the restrictions on claiming enhanced R&D relief, or the RDEC, and creative industries reliefs see **26** CREATIVE INDUSTRIES RELIEFS.

For commentary on devolution of the power to set the corporation tax rate in Northern Ireland to the Stormont Assembly and consequential modification of the R&D relief regime, see **1.5** INTRODUCTION: CHARGE TO TAX, RATES AND PROFIT COMPUTATIONS.

HMRC guidance

HMRC publish guidance on research and development corporation tax relief. See HMRC's Corporate Intangibles Research and Development Manual at CIRD80000 onwards (for R&D) and CIRD89700 onwards (RDEC). The guidance covers all aspects of the scheme and includes an interactive calculator for working out R&D relief for SMEs.

Advance assurance

HMRC offer an advance assurance process for small companies (ie those with less than 50 employees and with turnover of £2m or less) making their first R&D relief claims. Once HMRC have accepted a company's application, they will allow R&D relief claims for the first three accounting periods without further enquiries. This advance assurance process is only available to companies that haven't claimed R&D tax relief before. The stated purpose of this advance assurance process is to enable small companies to concentrate on their business, rather than focussing on their R&D tax claim. See www.gov.uk/guidance/research-and-development-tax-relief-advance-assurance.

Meaning of research and development

[63.2] For the purpose of the reliefs, the term '*research and development*' ('*R&D*') means activities treated as such under generally accepted accounting practice (see **68.18** TRADING INCOME) [*CTA 2009, s 1041; CTA 2010, s 1138*]. The definition also includes activities specified by Treasury regulations made under *ITA 2007, s 1006*. However, oil and gas exploration and appraisal (within *CTA 2010, s 1134*) are expressly excluded [*CTA 2010, s 1138(5)*].

The accounting standards that deal with R&D are FRS 102, section 18, FRS 105, section 13 and IAS 38.

Reference should also be made to the 2004 BEIS guidelines, as referred to by HMRC, with regard to the definition of R&D which develops the definition found under GAAP. These can be found at HMRC Corporate Intangibles Research and Development Manual CIRD81900.

Relevant research and development

'*Relevant research and development*' in relation to a company is research and development either related to a trade carried on by the company or from which it is intended that such a trade will be derived. Research and development which may lead to or facilitate an extension of the trade and of a medical nature which has a special relation to the welfare of the workers employed in the trade are specifically included. [*CTA 2009, s 1042*].

Simon's Taxes. See D1.402A–D1.403A.

'Small or medium-sized enterprise (SME)'

[63.3] The R&D tax relief available to a company is dependent on whether the company is an SME or a large company. The definition of SME for this purpose is taken from *Commission Recommendation 2003/361/EC* of 6 May 2003 defining a micro, small or medium-sized enterprise, as adapted. For a company to be an SME for R&D tax reliefs purposes, it must not exceed the limits below.

Number of employees	500
Annual turnover	€100 million
Balance sheet value	€86 million

In determining whether a company qualifies as an SME, its employee and financial figures must be aggregated with 100% of the figures for any 'linked enterprise' and with the amount of the figures for any 'partner enterprise' situated immediately 'upstream' or 'downstream' from it, proportionate to the percentage interest in the capital or voting rights (whichever is greater).

A '*linked enterprise*' is widely defined by the *Recommendation* but broadly covers enterprises where one has a majority of the voting rights in the other, has the right to appoint or remove the majority of the management of the other and has the right to exercise a dominant influence over the other. '*Partner enterprises*' are enterprises, other than linked enterprises, one of which (the '*upstream enterprise*') holds (solely or jointly with one or more linked enterprises) at least 25% of the capital or voting rights of the other (the '*downstream enterprise*').

A company will not qualify as an SME if at least 25% of its capital or voting rights are controlled by one or more public bodies. A company will still qualify as an SME if the 25% threshold is reached or exceeded by enterprises which are public investment corporations, venture capital companies, institutional investors (including regional development funds), universities or non-profit research centres, autonomous local authorities with an annual budget of less than €10 million and fewer than 5,000 inhabitants, or groups of individuals with regular venture capital investment activity who invest equity capital in unquoted businesses ('business angels'), provided the total investment of those investors in the same enterprise is less than €1,250,000.

In *Pyreos v HMRC* FTT, [2015] UKFTT 123 (TC) a substantial shareholder was held to be a venture capital company. In *Monitor Audio Ltd v HMRC* FTT, [2015] UKFTT 357 (TC), 2015 SWTI 3174 a subsidiary of a bank was held to be an institutional investor.

A company is not an SME until it has satisfied these criteria over two consecutive accounting periods, and similarly does not cease to be one until it has ceased to fulfil the criteria over two accounting periods. However, this condition is disregarded in determining whether a company qualifies as an SME in an accounting period in which the limits for the employee or financial figures are exceeded where the company on its own does not exceed the limits but would do so if its figures were added to those of a partner or linked enterprise and the partner or linked enterprise would on its own exceed the limits. In determining whether a company qualifies as an SME in its first accounting period, the above provisions are treated as applying to the immediately preceding accounting period.

[*CTA 2009, ss 104Y, 1119–1121*].

Simon's Taxes. See **D1.404**.

'Large company'

[63.4] A '*large company*' is a company which does not qualify as a small or medium-sized enterprise (as above). [*CTA 2009, s 1122*].

Simon's Taxes. See **D1.404B**.

R&D relief for SMEs

[63.5] An SME (see **63.3** above) which meets the necessary conditions is entitled to claim R&D tax relief as described at **63.6** below for an accounting period in respect of 'qualifying Chapter 2 expenditure'.

Qualifying Chapter 2 expenditure

'*Qualifying Chapter 2 expenditure*' consists of 'qualifying expenditure on in-house direct R&D development' and 'qualifying expenditure on contracted out R&D'.

Expenditure incurred by a company is '*qualifying expenditure on in-house direct R&D*' if:

(1) it is:
- incurred on 'staffing costs';
- 'qualifying expenditure on externally provided workers';
- incurred on computer software or 'consumable items'; or
- incurred on 'relevant payments' to subjects of a 'clinical trial';

(2) it is attributable to relevant R&D (see **63.1** above) undertaken by the company itself;
(3) the expenditure is not incurred in carrying on activities contracted out to the company by any other person (and see HMRC CIRD Manual at CIRD84250 for what is considered to be subcontracting); and
(4) it is not subsidised.

A company's '*qualifying expenditure on contracted out R&D*' is expenditure incurred by it in making the 'qualifying element' of a 'subcontractor payment'. The expenditure must be attributable to relevant R&D undertaken on behalf of the company and must meet conditions (3) and (4) above.

[*CTA 2009, ss 1051–1053*].

Where expenditure is excluded from relief by (3) or (4) above or by the cap on relief at **63.8** below, the company may instead be able to claim relief under the RDEC regime at **63.9** onwards below, subject to meeting the necessary conditions.

Staffing costs

For the purposes of (1) above, '*staffing costs*' are all employment earnings (other than benefits in kind), amounts (other than benefits in kind) paid to employees in respect of expenses, employer NICs (and equivalent contributions under the legislation of an EEA State or Switzerland), and employer pension contributions. Staffing costs are attributable to relevant R&D (and therefore meet condition (2) above) if paid to, or in respect of, directors or employees directly and actively engaged in the relevant R&D.

The appropriate proportion of the staffing cost is allowable where the director or employee is only partly directly and actively involved in relevant R&D.

Staff providing support services (e.g. secretarial or administrative services) are not thereby treated as engaged in the activities they support, although ancillary staff employed in a dedicated R&D facility (e.g. technicians, maintenance, clerical and security staff) may qualify.

[*CTA 2009, ss 1123, 1124; SI 2019 No 689, Reg 16(21); SI 2020 No 1499*].

HMRC consider that reimbursed expenses, such as travel and subsistence, do not generally fall within the meaning of 'staffing costs'. (HMRC Notice 29 January 2015).

HMRC consider that, where employees have been furloughed as a result of the coronavirus (COVID-19) pandemic and ceased all work, those employees cannot be regarded as being directly or actively engaged in relevant R&D. To the extent that furlough payments are met by the Government under the CJRS, the general rules for subsidised expenditure (see below) apply so that the staffing costs covered will not qualify for relief in any event. See further HMRC Corporate Intangibles Research and Development Manual CIRD83200.

Qualifying expenditure on externally provided workers

A company incurs expenditure on externally provided workers if it makes a payment (a '*staff provision payment*') to another person (the '*staff provider*') in respect of the supply to the company, by or through the staff provider, of the services of externally provided workers. A person is an '*externally provided worker*' in relation to the company if:

(a) he is an individual;
(b) he is not a director or employee of the company;
(c) he personally provides, or is under an obligation personally to provide, services to the company under the terms of a contract between the worker and a person other than the company (the 'staff controller');
(d) his services are supplied to the company through a staff provider (whether or not he is a director or employee of the staff provider or any other person);

(e) he is subject to (or to the right of) supervision, direction or control by the company as to the manner in which those services are provided; and
(f) the provision of the services to the company does not constitute the carrying on of activities contracted out by the company.

Such expenditure is attributable to relevant R&D (and therefore meets condition (2) above) to the extent that the externally provided workers are directly and actively engaged in such R&D. Services supplied in support of such activities carried on by others (e.g. secretarial or administrative services) are excluded.

Unless the company and the staff provider or, if different, the staff controller are (or elect to be) connected persons (see below), the company's qualifying expenditure on externally provided workers is 65% of the staff provision payment.

Where the company, the staff provider and, if different, the staff controller(s) are all connected persons (within *CTA 2010, s 1122*), the amount of the company's qualifying expenditure on externally provided workers is the lower of the amount of the particular staff provision payment in question and the aggregate of the 'relevant expenditure' of each staff controller. The staff provider must have brought the whole of the staff provision payment into account in determining its profit or loss for a 'relevant period' in accordance with normal accounting principles, and the staff controller must also have brought all of its 'relevant expenditure' into account in determining its profit or loss for a relevant period in accordance with normal accounting principles.

The '*relevant expenditure*' for this purpose is the revenue expenditure incurred by the staff controller on staffing costs (as above) or 'agency workers' remuneration' in providing to the company the externally provided workers to which the staff provision payment relates. A '*relevant period*' is a period for which the person draws up accounts, that ends not more than 12 months after the end of the accounting period of the company in which the company recognises the staff provision payment as a deduction in accordance with normal accounting principles. '*Agency workers' remuneration*' is remuneration receivable by an externally provided worker which is not employment income of that worker except under *ITEPA 2003, Pt 2 Ch 7* (agency workers).

Any necessary apportionment of expenditure for these purposes is made on a just and reasonable basis.

The company and the staff provider and the staff controller (if different), may, in any case, jointly and irrevocably elect to be treated as connected for these purposes in relation to all staff provision payments paid under the same contract or other arrangement, such election to be made by written notice to HMRC within two years after the end of the company accounting period in which the contract or arrangement is entered into.

[*CTA 2009, ss 1127–1132*].

Software and consumable items

'*Consumable items*' are defined as consumable or transformable materials including water, fuel and power. Computer software and consumable items are attributable to relevant R&D (and therefore meet condition (2) above) if they are employed directly in relevant R&D. An appropriate portion of the costs are allowed if the software or consumable items are only partly so employed. Software or consumable items employed in the provision of secretarial, administration or other support services, in the support of other activities, are not to be treated as directly employed in those activities.

Where a company sells or otherwise transfers ownership of the products of its R&D activity as part of its ordinary business, then the cost of consumable items that go to make up those products is excluded from expenditure qualifying for relief. This applies where the R&D relates to an item that is produced in the course of the R&D, and also where the R&D relates to a process of producing an item. Thus, where items such as materials, components or machine parts making up a finished product are both used in the development of the product and are also part of the product that is then transferred for consideration in the ordinary course of business, the costs of those items included in the transferred product are **not** qualifying expenditure for R&D purposes. Where not all of the product(s) is sold or transferred, an apportionment must be made between non-qualifying and qualifying expenditure. The effect of this provision is that if some of the products are retained for additional trials, or discarded as substandard, the costs of the consumable items in the retained or discarded products will remain qualifying expenditure and will not be excluded.

Producing an item for these purposes also includes preparing an item for transfer, which would include the use of ancillaries, such as packaging, that might be required before transfer. The reference to 'transfer' includes the transfer of ownership of an item to another person (whether by sale or otherwise) and the transfer of possession of an item (whether by letting or hire or otherwise), and also includes, where the item is incorporated into another item, the transfer of that other item. A transfer is within these provisions when it is made by: the company which incurs the cost of the R&D; the company to which the R&D is contracted out; the person (other than a company) who contracts out the R&D to a company and incurs the cost of the R&D; the person (other than a company) to whom the R&D is contracted out; or, a person who is connected to such a company or person as described.

If an item is transferred to another party for testing and that party supplies the results of the tests to the original company, the provision of the information on the results is not deemed to be consideration for the purposes of these exclusions. Where an item produced in the course of R&D is transferred as waste relief for any consumable items in the waste item will not be restricted because the transfer is not made in the ordinary course of business.

The legislation on consumable items may be amended by Treasury regulations.

[*CTA 2009, ss 1125–1126B*].

Relevant payments to subjects in a clinical trial

'*Relevant payments*' to subjects in a '*clinical trial*' are payments to those participating in an investigation in human subjects undertaken in connection with the development of a health care treatment or procedure. [*CTA 2009, s 1140*].

Subsidised expenditure

For the purposes of (4) above, expenditure is subsidised if a State aid notified to and approved by the European Commission is or has been obtained in respect of all or part of it (or if such aid is or has been obtained for any other expenditure attributable to the same R&D project). To the extent that some other grant or subsidy is obtained in respect of expenditure, or it is otherwise met directly or indirectly by any person other than the company, it is similarly excluded. Aid, grants, etc. not allocated to particular expenditure are for this purpose allocated in a just and reasonable manner. R&D tax reliefs within this chapter, and ATL R&D credits under *CTA 2009, Pt 3 Ch 6A* (below), are not State aid for this purpose. [*CTA 2009, s 1138*].

Subcontractor payment

A '*subcontractor payment*' is a payment by a company to another person (the '*subcontractor*') in respect of R&D contracted out by the company to that person. Except where the company and the subcontractor are, or elect to be treated as if they were, connected persons (see below), the '*qualifying element*' of such a payment is 65% of it.

Special provision is made where the company and the subcontractor are connected persons within *CTA 2010, s 1122*. Provided that, in accordance with generally accepted accounting practice, the whole of the subcontractor payment and all of the subcontractor's 'relevant expenditure' has been brought into account in determining the subcontractor's profit or loss for a 'relevant period', the whole of the subcontractor payment is the qualifying element (up to the amount of the subcontractor's 'relevant expenditure'). Any necessary apportionment of expenditure for these purposes is made on a just and reasonable basis.

'*Relevant expenditure*' is expenditure on staffing costs, or software or consumable items, or payments to subjects of a clinical trial, or externally provided workers, not of a capital nature, which is incurred by the subcontractor in carrying on, on behalf of the company, the activities to which the subcontractor payment relates, and is not subsidised (as above). A '*relevant period*' is a period of account ending not more than twelve months after the end of the period of account of the company in which, in accordance with generally accepted accounting practice, the subcontractor payment is brought into account in determining the company's profit or loss.

The company and the subcontractor may, in any case, jointly and irrevocably elect to be treated as connected for these purposes in relation to all subcontractor payments paid under the same contract or other arrangement, such election to be made by written notice to HMRC within two years after the end of the company accounting period in which the contract or arrangement is entered into.

[*CTA 2009, ss 1133–1136*].

Providing of State aid information

A claim made on or after 1 July 2016 for relief under the above provisions must include any information required by HMRC for the purpose of complying with certain EU State aid obligations. This may include information about the claimant (or his activities), information about the subject-matter of the claim and other information relating to the grant of State aid through the provision of the FYAs. See **36.13** HMRC — ADMINISTRATION as regards the publishing by HMRC of State aid information. [*FA 2016, s 180(1)–(4)(10), Sch 24 Pt 1*].

Simon's Taxes. See **D1.409–D1.414**.

Types of R&D reliefs available to SMEs

[63.6] The R&D reliefs available to an SME in respect of qualifying Chapter 2 expenditure (see **63.5** above) take the form of:

- an additional deduction in calculating the profits of the trade; or
- a deemed trading loss.

Where expenditure is excluded from relief under these provisions because the work is subcontracted to it or the expenditure is subsidised or because of the cap on relief at **63.8** below, the company may instead be able to claim relief under the RDEC regime at **63.9** onwards below, subject to meeting the necessary conditions.

Additional deduction in calculating profits

A company is entitled to corporation tax relief for an accounting period if it meets each of the following conditions.

- It is an SME in the period.
- It carries on a trade for the period.
- It has qualifying Chapter 2 expenditure which is allowable as a deduction in calculating the profits of the trade for the period for corporation tax purposes.

The relief, which must be claimed, is given in the form of an additional deduction in calculating the profits of the trade for the period. The additional deduction is 130% of the qualifying Chapter 2 expenditure for expenditure. However, this is subject to the cap on R&D aid (see **63.8** below).

Deemed trading loss

As an alternative to claiming a deduction for pre-trading expenditure, a company can elect for the relief to be given in the form of a deemed trading loss. However, it should be noted that an election cannot be made if the company is not a going concern (see below). Where an election is made, relief for pre-trading expenditure is given in this way instead of as a deduction under *CTA 2009, s 61*.

For the company to be entitled to relief in this manner for an accounting period, it must be an SME in the period and must have incurred qualifying Chapter 2 expenditure which is not allowable as a deduction in calculating for corporation tax purposes the profits of a trade carried on by it at the time that the expenditure was incurred, but would have been so allowable had it been carrying on a trade consisting of the activities in respect of which the expenditure was incurred.

The relief takes the form of a trading loss for the accounting period (the 'deemed loss-making period') equal to 230% of the qualifying R&D expenditure.

Unless the company is entitled to relief under these provisions for the preceding period, the trading loss cannot be set against the profits of that period under *CTA 2010, ss 37(3)(b)* or *42*.

Where the deemed loss-making period begins on or after 1 April 2017 and the company begins to carry on a trade in that period and continues to do so in the next accounting period or it begins to carry on a trade in a later period, and the trade is derived from the research and development activities in respect of which the relief was obtained, the loss can be carried forward to the 'relevant period' to the extent that relief has not otherwise been given for the loss and it has not been surrendered as group relief. The carry-forward will usually be under *CTA 2010, s 45A* (for set off against total profits — see **51.6** LOSSES) but if the conditions at **51.2**(a)(b) are not met, the carry-forward will be under *CTA 2010, s 45B* (for set off against profits of the trade — see **51.6**). The '*relevant period*' is the accounting period after the deemed loss-making period or the later period in which the trade commenced.

Previously, if the company began in the deemed loss-making period or a later period to carry on a trade and the trade was derived from the research and development activities in respect of which the relief was obtained, the loss could be carried forward and set against future trading profits (under *CTA 2010, s 45*) to the extent that relief has not otherwise been given for the loss and it has not been surrendered as group relief.

Restrictions apply where tax credit is claimed (see **63.7** below).

Where an election is made for relief to be given as a deemed trading loss, the election must specify the accounting period for which it is made. The election, which must be in writing, must be made within two years of the end of the accounting period to which it relates.

Going concern condition

Relief is only available as an additional deduction or as a deemed trading loss if the going concern condition is met. For these purposes, a company is a going concern if:

- its latest accounts were published on a going concern basis; and
- there is nothing in the accounts to indicate that they were only published on a going concern basis because the company would receive relief as outlined above or tax credits as described at **63.7** below.

A company is not a going concern if it is in administration or liquidation.

Restriction on consortium relief

Where relief is claimed for qualifying Chapter 2 expenditure, either as an additional deduction in computing profits or as deemed trading loss, and at any time during the period the company is owned by a consortium of which at least one of the members is a large company (see **63.4** above), relief obtained for the R&D expenditure can only be surrendered to a member of the consortium for the purposes of a consortium group relief claim (under *CTA 2010, ss 132, 133*) if that company is an SME.

[*CTA 2009, ss 1044–1049; F(No 2)A 2017, Sch 4 para 133*].

Simon's Taxes. See **D1.420, D1.422.**

R&D tax credits for SMEs

[63.7] A company is entitled to an R&D tax credit for an accounting period in which it has a 'Chapter 2 surrenderable loss'. The tax credit must be claimed, but can only be claimed if the company is a going concern (see below). Where a claim is made, HMRC must pay the company the amount of the credit.

Relief is subject to the R&D cap (see **63.8** below).

Chapter 2 surrenderable loss

A company has a '*Chapter 2 surrenderable loss*' if in an accounting period it obtains an additional deduction under *CTA 2009, s 1044* (see **63.6**) and makes a trading loss for that period or has a deemed loss under *CTA 2009, s 1045* (see **63.6** above).

Where relief for qualifying Chapter 2 expenditure is obtained by means of an additional deduction, the Chapter 2 surrenderable loss is so much of the trading loss as is unrelieved or, if less, 230% of the qualifying Chapter 2 expenditure in respect of which the relief was obtained.

Where relief is given for pre-trading expenditure by means of a deemed loss, the surrenderable Chapter 2 loss is so much of that deemed loss as is unrelieved.

The amount of the trading loss that is unrelieved is the amount of the loss as reduced by:

- any relief that was or could have been obtained by making a claim to deduct the loss from the profits of the accounting period under *CTA 2010, s 37(3)(a)*; or
- any other relief obtained by the company in respect of the loss, including relief under *CTA 2010, ss 37(3)(b)* or *42* against losses of an earlier accounting period; and
- any loss surrendered to members of a group or consortium as group relief or group relief for carried-forward losses.

In determining the unrelieved amount of the loss, no account is taken of losses carried forward from an earlier accounting period (under *CTA 2010, ss 45, 45A, 45B*) or carried back from a later accounting period (under *CTA 2010, s 37(3)(b)*).

Going concern condition

A claim for an R&D tax credit can only be made by a company at a time when it is a going concern. A company is a going concern for these purposes if its latest published accounts were prepared on a going concern basis and nothing in those accounts indicates that they were only prepared on a going concern basis on the expectation that a company would receive relief for Chapter 2 qualifying expenditure or R&D credits.

A company is not a going concern if it is in administration or liquidation.

Amount of tax credit

For accounting periods beginning on or after 1 April 2021, the R&D tax credit to which a company is entitled is the lower of:

(i) 14.5% of the *Chapter 2 surrenderable loss* for the period, as defined above; and
(ii) (except where the exception below applies) the sum of £20,000 plus three times the company's expenditure on workers for payment periods ending in the accounting period (see further below).

If the accounting period is less than 12 months, the £20,000 figure in (ii) above is reduced proportionately.

For earlier accounting periods, the R&D tax credit is 14.5% of the *Chapter 2 surrenderable loss* for the period.

The percentage of the surrenderable loss, the £20,000 amount and the multiplier in (ii) above can be changed by Treasury order.

Expenditure on workers

A company's expenditure on workers for a payment period is the total of the following amounts:

(1) The company's PAYE and NIC liabilities for the period less any amount to be deducted to avoid double counting.
A company's PAYE and NIC liabilities for a payment period are the sum of the amount of income tax it is required to account for under PAYE to HMRC (disregarding any deductions for child tax credit or working tax credit) and the amount of Class 1 NICs it is required to account for to HMRC (disregarding any deductions for statutory maternity, adoption, paternity, shared parental or parental bereavement pay or child tax credit or working tax credit).
The amounts to be deducted to avoid double counting are a proportion of any staffing costs (see **63.5** above) incurred for the period by the company in providing externally provided workers for a connected company (calculated as in (2) below, treating the company as CC) and any staffing costs incurred for the period in undertaking contracted out R&D on behalf of a connected company (as in (3) below).
(2) If the company is connected with another company (CC) and has incurred qualifying expenditure on externally provided workers (see **63.5** above), part of the staffing costs for the payment period incurred by CC in providing any of those workers for the company. This is the total of the amounts calculated for each provided worker using the following steps.
Step 1. Calculate the part of CC's PAYE and NIC liabilities (as in (1) above) for the period which are staffing costs of CC incurred in providing the worker to the company.
Step 2. Find the part of the company's qualifying expenditure on the worker for the period that has been taken into account in calculating its qualifying Chapter 2 expenditure (see **63.5** above) and express that part

as a percentage of the total qualifying expenditure on the worker for the period. If all of the qualifying expenditure on the worker has been taken into account in calculating the company's Chapter 2 expenditure the percentage will be 100%.
Step 3. Take the percentage found in Step 2 of the amount found in Step 1.

(3) If the company is connected with another company and has incurred qualifying expenditure on contracted out R&D (see **63.5** above), any staffing costs (see **63.5** above) for the payment period which are incurred by the connected company in undertaking any of that contracted out R&D for the company and which form part of the connected company's PAYE and NIC liabilities for the payment period (calculated as in (1) above).

Where a connected company's PAYE and NIC liabilities have to be calculated for the purposes of (2) or (3) above for a period that is only part of that company's payment period, the liabilities must be proportionately reduced.

Exceptions to tax credit cap

The tax credit cap applied by (ii) above does not apply if the company meets both conditions A and B below for the accounting period in question.

- Condition A is that during the accounting period in the company is engaged in:
  - taking (or preparing to take) steps so that intellectual property will be created by it;
  - creating intellectual property; or
  - performing a significant amount of activity consisting of formulating plans and making decisions in relation to the development or exploitation of intellectual property it holds.

  In each case, the whole or greater part (by value) of the intellectual property must be, or have been, created by the company and the activities must be wholly or mainly undertaken by employees of the company. Intellectual property is treated as created by a company if it is created in circumstances in which the right to exploit it vests in the company (alone or jointly). '*Intellectual property*' means any patent, trade mark, registered design, design right or plant breeder's right or non-UK equivalent and any other information or technique not protected by such rights but having industrial, commercial or other economic value.
- Condition B is that the sum of the following amounts does not exceed 15% of the company's qualifying Chapter 2 expenditure for the period. The amounts are:
  - the company's qualifying expenditure on externally provided workers where the company, staff provider and staff controller are all connected or have jointly elected to be treated as connected (see **63.5** above); and
  - the company's qualifying expenditure on contracted out R&D (see **63.5** above) where the company are connected or have jointly elected to be treated as connected.

  The Treasury has the power to amend the 15% above by statutory instrument.

Example

SME Ltd, which is not connected with any other companies and does not qualify for the exception to the tax credit cap, has the following results for the year ended 31 March 2022:

Trading loss	£170,000
Qualifying R&D	£45,000
PAYE and NIC liabilities for payment periods ending in the year	£100,000

The surrenderable loss is the lower of:

(i) £170,000

(ii) £45,000 × 230% = £103,500

(iii) £20,000 + (3 × £100,000) = £320,000

i.e. £103,500

The tax credit given is thus 14.5% × £103,500 = £15,007.

This tax credit of £15,007 will either be used to reduce SME Ltd's tax bill, if it has other sources of income or will be received as a tax free refund.

The trading loss of the company carried forward is now:

£170,000 – £103,500 = £66,500

For expenditure of £45,000 the company has received a refund of £15,007 which equates to 33.35% (15,007/45,000) or 230% × 14.5% = 33.35%.

Payment of tax credit

A payment in respect of an R&D credit is not treated as income of the company for any tax purpose.

The R&D tax credit and any associated interest thereon may be applied in discharging any liability of the company to corporation tax.

In the event that there is an enquiry by HMRC into the company's tax return for the accounting period, the R&D credit need not be paid by HMRC until the enquiries are complete, although a provisional payment can be made if the HMRC officer thinks fit. Likewise, no R&D credit need be paid if the company has outstanding PAYE and NIC liabilities for the period. PAYE and NIC liabilities are regarded as outstanding for the period if the company has not paid to HMRC any amount that it is required to pay under the PAYE regulations (*SI 2003 No 2682*) or in respect of Class 1 National Insurance contributions for any payment period ending in the accounting period.

Restriction on losses carried forward

Where a company claims an R&D credit for an accounting period, the amount of the loss that is available to carry forward for relief against future profits (under *CTA 2010, ss 45, 45A, 45B*) is treated as reduced by the amount of the surrenderable loss for the period. This is the amount of the Chapter 2 surrenderable loss in respect of which the company claims an R&D tax credit for the period.

[*CTA 2009, ss 1054–1062; F(No 2)A 2017, Sch 4 paras 134,135; FA 2021, Sch 3*].

Simon's Taxes. See **D1.420**.

Cap on SME relief for R&D

[63.8] SME R&D tax relief is state aid under EU rules and to be compatible with European Commission state aid rules, a cap of €7.5 million applies on the amount of total R&D aid that can be given in respect of a particular project.

The restriction is applied to qualifying R&D reliefs, i.e. any relief or tax credit within **63.6** and **63.7** above.

The total R&D aid (which is subject to the cap) in respect of expenditure by a company attributable to an R&D project is given by the formula:

$TC + R + (P \times CT) - N$

where:

'TC' — is the tax credits (i.e. the total credits paid to the company in respect of expenditure attributable to the R&D project. A credit which has been claimed but not paid is treated as having been paid, unless HMRC has informed the company that it will not be paid);

'R' — is the actual reduction in tax liability. This is the sum of:

(a) the reduction in the company's corporation tax liability in any accounting period in consequence of qualifying R&D relief attributable to the R&D project; and
(b) the amounts by which the corporation tax liability of any other company has been reduced in consequence of a loss arising in respect of qualifying R&D relief surrendered as group relief, consortium relief or group relief for carried-forward losses;

'P' — is the potential relief (i.e. the total amount of any qualifying R&D relief (other than an R&D tax credit) for which the company has made a claim or election which has not been brought into account at the time of calculating the total R&D aid. This does not include any item in respect of which HMRC has advised the company that the relief will not be given).

'N' — is the notional R&D expenditure credit (i.e. the credit which the SME could have claimed if it had been a large company).

'CT' — is the main rate of corporation tax at the time when the total aid is calculated.

[*CTA 2009, ss 1113–1118; F(No 2)A 2017, Sch 4, para 136*].

Simon's Taxes. See **D1.402A**.

Research and development expenditure credit (RDEC)

[63.9] A company which carries on a trade may make a claim for an amount, an 'R&D expenditure credit' ('RDEC') to be brought into account as a receipt in calculating its trade profits for an accounting period if it has 'qualifying R&D

expenditure' (see **63.10** below) which is allowable as a deduction in computing the taxable profits of the trade for that period. The RDEC is sometimes referred to as an 'above the line credit' as it is a taxable receipt. The amount of the credit is then used to discharge the company's tax liabilities, according to a seven-step process (see **63.11** below).

The amount of the credit is **13%** of the qualifying R&D expenditure for the period (12% for expenditure incurred before 1 April 2020; 11% for expenditure incurred before 1 January 2018). In the case of a ring fence trade, this percentage is 49%. These percentages may be altered by regulation.

No claim for an R&D expenditure credit may be made by an 'ineligible company', being an institution of higher education (as defined by *CTA 2009, s 1142(1)(b)*), a charity, or any company prescribed by Treasury regulations.

A company may not make a claim under the provisions for R&D reliefs at **63.5–63.8** above in respect of the same expenditure for which RDEC is claimed.

See **63.12** below for the making of claims.

[*CTA 2009, ss 104A(1)(2), 104B, 104M, 104WA; FA 2018, s 19; FA 2020, s 28*].

Anti-avoidance

To the extent a transaction is attributable to arrangements entered into wholly or mainly for a disqualifying purpose, it is to be disregarded for the purpose of determining the RDEC to which a company is entitled under these provisions.

Arrangements (which includes any scheme, agreement or understanding, whether legally enforceable or not) are entered into wholly or mainly for a disqualifying purpose if their main object, or one of their main objects, is to enable the company to obtain:

- an RDEC to which it would not otherwise be entitled; or
- an RDEC under this regime of a greater amount than that to which it would otherwise be entitled.

[*CTA 2009, s 104X*].

See **Simon's Taxes D1.435A, D1.435B.**

Expenditure qualifying for RDEC

[63.10] For a company which is an SME (see **63.3** above) in an accounting period, 'its *qualifying R&D expenditure*' for the period for the purposes of RDEC is:

- its qualifying expenditure on sub-contracted R&D;
- its subsidised qualifying expenditure; and
- its capped R&D expenditure.

For a company that is a large company throughout an accounting period, the '*qualifying R&D expenditure*' for the period is its qualifying expenditure on:

- in-house direct R&D;

- contracted out R&D; and
- contributions to independent R&D.

[*CTA 2009, ss 104A(3)(4)*].

SMEs — qualifying expenditure on sub-contracted R&D

A SME company's qualifying expenditure on sub-contracted R&D means expenditure that:

- is incurred on research and development contracted out to the company by a large company or by any person otherwise than in the course of carrying on a chargeable trade (which is a trade, profession or vocation carried on wholly or partly in the UK whose profits are chargeable to income tax under *ITTOIA 2005* or to corporation tax under *CTA 2009*); and
- the expenditure is expenditure which is on sub-contracted R&D (either undertaken in-house, or not, see below).

Sub-contracted R&D undertaken in-house

Expenditure falls within this category where:

(A) it is undertaken by the company itself;
(B) it is expenditure incurred on staffing costs, software and consumable items, qualifying expenditure on externally provided workers or on relevant payments to the subjects of a clinical trial; and
(C) the expenditure is attributable to relevant research and development of the company.

The expressions used in (B) and (C) above have the same meanings as for the purposes of R&D tax reliefs for SMEs at **63.5** above. See **63.2** above for the meaning of 'relevant research and development'.

Sub-contracted R&D not undertaken in-house

Expenditure falls within this category where it is:

- incurred in making payments to: a qualifying body; an individual; or a firm, each member of which is an individual; in respect of R&D contracted out by the company to the body, individual or firm;
- undertaken by the body, individual or firm itself; and
- attributable to relevant R&D in relation to the company.

[*CTA 2009, ss 104C–104E*].

SMEs — subsidised qualifying expenditure

A SME company's subsidised qualifying expenditure means its subsidised qualifying expenditure on in-house direct R&D and its subsidised qualifying expenditure on contracted out R&D.

Subsidised qualifying expenditure on in-house direct R&D

Expenditure falls within this category where:

- it is expenditure which is subsidised;
- it is expenditure incurred on staffing costs, software and consumable items, qualifying expenditure on externally provided workers or on relevant payments to the subjects of a clinical trial;
- the expenditure is attributable to relevant research and development of the company; and
- the expenditure is not incurred by the company in carrying on activities which are contracted out to the company by any person.

Subsidised qualifying expenditure on contracted out R&D

Expenditure falls within this category where it is incurred in making the qualifying element of a sub-contractor payment (see **63.5** above)) and each of the following conditions is met:

- the expenditure is subsidised;
- the sub-contractor is: a qualifying body; an individual; or a firm, each member of which is an individual;
- the body, individual or firm undertakes the contracted out R&D itself;
- it is attributable to relevant R&D in relation to the company; and
- the expenditure is not incurred by the company in carrying on activities which are contracted out to the company by any person.

[*CTA 2009, ss 104C–104E*].

SME — capped R&D expenditure

A SME company's capped R&D expenditure means any expenditure: in respect of which the company is not entitled to relief under the R&D relief provisions at **63.5** above merely because of the cap on R&D aid (see **63.8** above) which is not qualifying expenditure on sub-contracted R&D and which would have been qualifying expenditure had the company been a large company throughout the accounting period in question.

[*CTA 2009, s 104I*].

Large companies—expenditure on in-house direct R&D

Expenditure falls within this category where:

- it is expenditure incurred on staffing costs, software and consumable items, qualifying expenditure on externally provided workers or on relevant payments to the subjects of a clinical trial;
- it is attributable to relevant R&D undertaken by the company itself; and
- if it is incurred on research and development contracted out to the company, it is so contracted out either by a large company; or by any person otherwise than in the course of carrying on a chargeable trade (which is a trade, profession or vocation carried on wholly or partly in the UK whose profits are chargeable to income tax under *ITTOIA 2005* or to corporation tax under *CTA 2009*).

Large companies—expenditure on contracted out R&D

Expenditure falls within this category where it is:

- incurred in making payments to: a qualifying body; an individual; or a firm, each member of which is an individual; in respect of R&D contracted out by the company to the body, individual or firm;
- undertaken by the body, individual or firm itself;
- attributable to relevant R&D in relation to the company; and
- if the contracted out R&D is itself contracted out to the company, it is so contracted out either by a large company or by any person otherwise than in the course of carrying on a chargeable trade (which is a trade, profession or vocation carried on wholly or partly in the UK whose profits are chargeable to income tax under *ITTOIA 2005* or to corporation tax under *CTA 2009*).

Large companies—expenditure on contributions to independent R&D

Expenditure falls within this category where:

- it is incurred in making payments to: a qualifying body; an individual; or a firm, each member of which is an individual; for the purpose of funding R&D carried on by the body, individual or firm (the '*funded R&D*');
- the funded R&D is relevant research and development in relation to the company;
- the funded R&D is not contracted out to the qualifying body, individual or firm by another person;
- if the payment is made to an individual the company is not connected with the individual when the payment is made; and
- if the payment is made to a firm (other than a qualifying body) the company is not connected with any member of the firm when the payment is made.

[*CTA 2009, ss 104J–104L*].

R&D expenditure of group companies

Where a company (A) incurs expenditure on making payments to another company within the same group (B) in respect of activities contracted out by A to B, and those activities would, if they were carried out by A be research and development of A, then:

- if B carries out the activities itself the expenditure is treated for the purposes of the RDEC regime as research and development undertaken by B itself; or
- where B contracts the activities out to a third party (C), and the activities are undertaken by C itself, then the expenditure is treated as research and development contracted out by B to C.

Two companies are members of the same group if they are members of the same group of companies for the purposes of group relief (see 35.3 GROUP RELIEF).

[*CTA 2009, s 104W*].

Payment of RDEC

[63.11] Where a company is entitled to an RDEC for an accounting period, as noted above, it is taken into account as a receipt of the company, before being set off in the first instance against the company's tax liability, with any excess remaining being dealt with in a specific order. The amount of set off in relation to such credit (the '*set-off amount*') is determined by following the seven steps set out at *CTA 2009, s 104N*. These are outlined below.

Step 1

The set-off amount is used to discharge any liability of the company to pay corporation tax for the accounting period. If there is any amount unused then step two is applied.

Step 2

If the amount remaining after step one is greater than the net value of the set-off amount (being the amount net of corporation tax chargeable on it) then that amount is reduced to the net value of the set-off amount. The difference (being the amount of the reduction) is termed the '*Step 2 amount*' and is carried forward and used to discharge any liability of the company to pay corporation tax for any subsequent accounting period.

However, if the company is a member of a group then it may surrender the whole or any part of the Step 2 amount to any other member of the group (a '*relevant group member*') to be used to discharge their liability to pay corporation tax, as detailed in Step 5 below. If any amount so surrendered is not set off and remains, then it is treated as not having been surrendered and so will be dealt with under the subsequent steps below.

Any amounts set off against corporation tax under the carry forward provisions, or group surrender provisions, at step 2 are applied before any amounts which may be set off under the operation of steps 1 (current tax charge set off), 4 (set off for any other period) or 5 (group surrender) herein. The surrender of the step 2 amount to a group company is neither taxable, nor deductible, for corporation tax purposes, in any company, nor does it give rise to a distribution.

The '*net value of the set-off amount*' is determined by reducing the set-off amount by the corporation tax which would be chargeable on the amount, on the assumption that no brought forward amounts (per step 3) are included in it, and that the main rate of corporation tax for that period applies.

For a ring fence trade the '*net value of the set-off amount*' is determined by reducing the set-off amount by the supplementary charge which would be chargeable on the amount, on the assumption that no brought forward amounts (per step 3) are included in it, and that it was an amount of adjusted ring fence profits for the accounting period (see *CTA 2010, ss 276, 277, 330(2)* with regard to ring fence trades).

Any remaining amount is dealt with under step 3.

Step 3

If the amount remaining after step 2 is greater than the company's total expenditure on workers for the accounting period, then: firstly, that amount is to be reduced to the amount of that total expenditure; and the amount so deducted is treated as an amount of R&D expenditure credit of the company for the next accounting period.

The amount of a company's total expenditure on workers for an accounting period is the sum of:

(i) the relevant portion of the company's staffing costs for the period, which are those costs that are paid to, or in respect of, directors or employees who are directly and actively engaged (wholly or in part) in relevant R&D, and which costs are part of the company's total amount of PAYE and NIC liabilities for the period. A company's total amount of PAYE and NIC liabilities is the total amount of income tax accounted for under the PAYE regulations for the period (ignoring child tax and working tax credits), together with the total amount of Class 1 national insurance contributions accounted for, ignoring deductions for statutory sick pay, maternity pay, child tax and working tax credits. Where the payment period does not fall wholly within the accounting period a just and reasonable apportionment is made; and

(ii) if the company is a member of a group and has incurred expenditure on any externally provided workers, the relevant portion of any staffing costs for the period incurred by another group member (the 'relevant group company') in providing any of those workers for the company.

With regard to the amounts at point (ii) above, the relevant portion of any staffing costs for the period incurred by the relevant group company is determined for each of those workers as follows:

- calculate the expenditure incurred by the relevant group company in providing the externally provided worker, and on staffing costs, and which forms part of the total amount of the relevant group company's PAYE and NIC liabilities for the period;
- calculate the '*appropriate percentage*' given by:
  R / T x 100
  where: R is the amount of the company's qualifying expenditure on the externally provided worker which has been taken into account in the company's qualifying R&D expenditure for the period; and T is the total amount of the company's qualifying expenditure on the externally provided worker;
- multiply the amount from bullet point one by the appropriate percentage to give the amount incurred by the company on externally provided workers.

If any of the set-off amount is remaining then step 4 applies.

Step 4

The amount remaining after step 3 is used to discharge any liability of the company to pay corporation tax for any other accounting period. If any set-off amount remains then step 5 applies.

Step 5

Where the company is a member of a group it may surrender the whole or any part of the amount remaining after step 4 to any other member of the group (the '*relevant group member*'). The principles applied with regard to overlapping periods of the companies are similar to those applied in respect of group relief.

The surrender amount is then used to discharge the corporation tax liability of the relevant group member. The amount to be discharged is determined as follows.

— Firstly an 'overlapping period' in respect of the accounting periods of the companies is determined. This is the period which is common to both the relevant group member and the company making the surrender. The proportion of the relevant group member's accounting period which is included in the overlapping period is taken, and that proportion is applied to the amount of corporation tax payable by the relevant group member for that accounting period.
— Secondly, the proportion of the surrender period of the company which is in the overlapping period is determined, and that proportion is applied to the amount surrendered to the relevant group member.
— The second amount with regard to the proportion surrendered is used to discharge the amount of corporation tax payable for the overlapping period.

Any amounts surrendered which are not used to discharge such a corporation tax liability are treated as if they had not been surrendered under this step. As above for step 2, any amount so surrendered is neither taxable, nor deductible, for corporation tax purposes, in either company, nor does it give rise to a distribution.

If no such surrender is made, or any of the set-off amount is otherwise remaining then step 6 applies.

Step 6

The amount remaining after step 5 is used to discharge any other liability of the company to pay a sum to HMRC under or by virtue of any enactment or under a contract settlement (being an agreement made in connection with any persons's liability to make a payment to HMRC under any enactment).

If any set-off amount remains then step 7 applies.

Step 7

The amount remaining after step 6 is payable to the company by HMRC. However this is subject to the following restrictions:

(i) The company is not entitled to be paid the amount if it was not a going concern at the time of claiming the credit, and the amount is then extinguished. A company is a 'going concern' if its latest published accounts were prepared on an on-going basis and nothing in those accounts indicates that they were only prepared on that basis because of an expectation that the company would receive R&D expenditure credits. A company is not a going concern at any time if it is in administration (under *Part 2* of the *Insolvency Act 1986*, or *Part 3* of the *Insolvency (Northern Ireland) Order 1989 (SI 1989 No 2405)*, or overseas equivalent) or liquidation (under *s 247* of the *Insolvency Act 1986*, or *Article 6* of the *Insolvency (Northern Ireland) Order 1989 (SI 1989 No 2405)*, or overseas equivalent). However, if the company becomes a going concern on or before the last day on which an amendment to the company's tax return for the period could be made (see **65.8** RETURNS) then the company is entitled to be paid that amount.

(ii) Where the company's tax return is enquired into by HMRC then no payment of that amount need be made before the enquiries are completed, however, an officer may make a payment on a provisional basis in such amount as thought fit.

(iii) If the company has outstanding PAYE and NIC liabilities for the period then no payment of that amount need be made. Such liabilities are outstanding if the company has not paid to HMRC amounts it is required to pay under PAYE regulations or in respect of Class 1 national insurance contributions for the period.

[*CTA 2009, ss 104N–104T*].

Example

The following provides an example of how a claim under RDEC regime works, and compares this with the position of a company that does not make such a claim.

	Claim under RDEC Regime	No claim
	£'000	£'000
Turnover	6,000	6,000
Qualifying R&D expenditure	(2,000)	(2,000)
R&D expenditure credit	260	—
Additional R&D expenditure relief	—	—
Other expenditure	(1,000)	(1,000)
Profits	3,260	3,000
CT at 19%	619	570
Deduct R&D expenditure credit	(260)	—
CT payable	359	570

Claims for R&D reliefs and RDEC

[63.12] A claim for R&D tax relief or RDEC must be made in a company tax return (or amended return) (see **65.4** RETURNS) for the accounting period for which the claim is made, within one year of the filing date for that return (see **65.8** RETURNS) or by such later time as HMRC may allow. It can similarly only be amended or withdrawn by amendment of the company tax return within the same time limit. It must specify the quantum of the amount claimed.

Penalties may apply where an incorrect claim is made (see **59.4** PENALTIES).

[*FA 1998, Sch 18 paras 83A–83E*].

For recovery of overpayments of tax credits, see **6.4** ASSESSMENTS.

Late claims should be dealt with in accordance with HMRC Statement of Practice 5/01 (HMRC CIRD Manual CIRD81800).

HMRC operate an online service allowing SMEs to send HMRC details to support claims to R&D tax relief in respect of up to ten R&D projects. The service can only be used once the company tax return has been submitted. See www.gov.uk/guidance/corporation-tax-research-and-development-tax-relief-for-small-and-medium-sized-enterprises#support-claim.

Key points on research and development expenditure

[63.13] Points to consider are as follows.

- There are two schemes which provide tax relief to companies for expenditure of a revenue nature on 'research and development' ('R&D'):
  - the small and medium-sized enterprise (SME) scheme; and
  - the research and development expenditure credit ('RDEC') for large companies and for certain expenditure by SMEs which is not eligible for relief under the SME scheme.
- The SME scheme provides for an additional deduction equal to 130% of the expenditure. Alternatively, a company can elect to have a deemed trading loss equal to 230% of the expenditure, which can be relieved in the normal way. SMEs not in profit or not yet trading can claim relief upfront as a cash payment, R&D tax credit, equal to 14.5% of their surrenderable loss, subject to the tax credit cap which has been introduced for accounting periods beginning on or after 1 April 2021.
- Under the RDEC scheme, a company which carries on a trade may make a claim for an RDEC to be brought into account as a receipt in calculating its trade profits for an accounting period if it has qualifying R&D expenditure which is allowable as a deduction in computing the taxable profits of the trade for that period, equal to 13% of the expenditure. The amount of the credit is then used to discharge the company's tax liabilities, according to a seven-step process.
- In order to claim relief under either regime, a company needs, first of all, to identify qualifying R&D projects. These are projects that extend the bounds of scientific or technological understanding within the wider relevant community, and not projects that seek to expand the company's own knowledge in the area concerned.
- Scientific or technological research must be carried out on a systematic basis by staff that have requisite knowledge and expertise.
- The development of a new product may involve a number of R&D projects that qualify for enhanced relief as well as projects that do not have sufficient innovation to qualify. However, it is possible that the development of a prototype can be regarded as an R&D project that can qualify for the enhanced relief.

- Only certain categories of expenditure can qualify for relief, principally staff costs and consumables. Subcontracted R&D costs are subject to special rules, and often only 65% of such costs can be used in a claim for enhanced relief.
- Certain types of expenditure on consumable items are excluded: where a company sells or transfers the products of its R&D activity as part of its ordinary business, then the cost of materials that go to make up those products is excluded from being expenditure qualifying for relief.
- Proper presentation of a claim, including the provisions of all relevant information, is essential to maximise the chances of acceptance. HMRC are likely to ask for timesheets or similar time recording to establish what proportion of employment costs are eligible for the enhanced relief, by looking at the time spent on qualifying R&D projects. SMEs can use HMRC's online service to provide information in support of claims.
- Capitalised revenue expenditure that falls within one of the allowable categories can be claimed when incurred, rather than when it is released to Profit & Loss Account.
- Capital expenditure in connection with R&D may qualify for 100% capital allowances.
- The rules which apply to determine which regime of relief applies depend in part on whether the claimant company is a small or medium sized entity or a large entity. The rules for establishing the size of a company for this purpose are complex, based on the Commission Recommendation 2003/361/EC of 6 May 2003. Linked and partner enterprises must be taken into account to determine the size of a company, which gives rise to difficulties where, for example, the claimant company has a bank or venture capital fund as a shareholder. What may look like an SME could turn out to be large.
- A claim for relief by an SME will not be accepted if a company was not a going concern when the claim was made, or if it ceases to be a going concern before the claim is processed.

64

Residence

Cross-references. See **4.12**, ANTI-AVOIDANCE; **7.6** BANKS; **11.16** CAPITAL GAINS; **21** CONTROLLED FOREIGN COMPANIES; **29.5** DISTRIBUTIONS; **31** DOUBLE TAX RELIEF; **34** FOREIGN CURRENCY; **35.23** GROUP RELIEF; **72** TRANSFER PRICING. For special rules concerning disposals of certain interests in offshore funds, see **55** OFFSHORE FUNDS.

Simon's Taxes. See D4.1.

Introduction to residence

[64.1] The question of a company's residence is important in that it determines the extent to which the company is within the charge to UK corporation tax. UK resident companies are taxable on their worldwide income. A non-resident company is charged to corporation tax only if:

(1) it carries on a trade of dealing in or developing UK land (see **71.2** TRANSACTIONS IN UK LAND);
(2) it carries on a trade (other than a trade within (1) above) in the UK through a permanent establishment (see **64.6** below);
(3) (for disposals on or after 6 April 2019) it disposes of any interests in UK land (see **11.25** CAPITAL GAINS) or assets deriving at least 75% of their value from UK land where the company has a substantial indirect interest in that land (see **11.26**);
(4) with effect from 6 April 2020 (subject to the transitional provisions at **64.7** below) it carries on a UK property business; or
(5) with effect from 6 April 2020 (subject to the transitional provisions at **64.7**) it has other UK property income.

See **64.6** below. Special rules apply to European Companies, see **64.2** below.

The residence of companies in the UK was historically decided by case law (based on the concept of management and control of the company) until legislation was introduced to apply a test of residence for tax purposes based on incorporation which took effect in 1988.

This chapter considers the tests for residence within UK tax law, and includes an examination of the position of non-resident companies with UK permanent establishments, UK representatives of such non-resident companies, and migration of companies from the UK.

Residence

The incorporation test

[64.2] A company incorporated in the UK is regarded for the purposes of the *Corporation Tax Acts* as resident there, irrespective of any rule of law giving a different place of residence [*CTA 2009, s 14*].

A company which is no longer carrying on any business, or is being wound up outside the UK, is treated as continuing to be resident in the UK if it was regarded as so resident immediately before it ceased business or any of its activities came under the control of the foreign equivalent of a liquidator. [*CTA 2009, s 15*].

Companies becoming resident under the above provisions are under an obligation to notify chargeability (see **59.2** PENALTIES) where appropriate, whether or not notice has been served requiring a return (see **65.4** RETURNS).

Interaction with Double Tax Arrangements

It is possible for a company to be treated as dual resident for tax purposes. For example, a company might be incorporated within the UK, and so be UK resident, but also resident outside the UK under the rule of law of a foreign territory. In such a case UK tax law states that the company continues to be treated as UK resident, save where the provisions of an applicable double tax arrangement are in point.

Double tax arrangements generally have a tie-breaker rule to resolve issues of dual residence of companies. Where a company which would otherwise be regarded as UK-resident (whether under *CTA 2009, s 14, 15, 16* or *17* or by virtue of some other rule of law), is regarded for the purposes of any double taxation arrangements under *TIOPA 2010, s 2, s 6* as resident in a territory outside the UK (and as not UK-resident), then it is treated for UK tax purposes as resident outside the UK and as not UK-resident, per *CTA 2009, s 18*.

See further Revenue Tax Bulletin December 1994 p 179 for a list of double tax agreements to which this is applicable. It is assumed for this purpose that the company has made a claim for relief under the arrangements, in consequence of which a decision falls to be made as to its residence status thereunder.

The above rules for determining the residence of companies, also applies for the purposes of *TMA 1970 and TCGA 1992*. [*TMA 1970, s 109A*].

[*CTA 2009, s 18*].

See generally Revenue Tax Bulletin December 1994 pp 179–181 for the application in practice of the above rule and HMRC International Manual INTM120070, 120080.

European Companies (SEs)

An SE (a European Company — see **32.6** EUROPEAN UNION LEGISLATION) which transfers its registered office to the UK in accordance with *Council Regulation (EC) 2157/2001, Art 8* is regarded upon registration in the UK as resident in the UK for tax purposes. Notwithstanding that a different place of residence may be given by any rule of law, the SE is not considered resident in that place for UK corporation tax purposes. However, the tie-breaker test outlined above with regard to double tax arrangements does apply to SE's and SCEs [*CTA 2009, s 18(3)*].

Under these provisions the SE will not lose its UK residence status by reason only of a later transfer from the UK of its registered office. Identical rules apply to an SCE (European Co-operative Society) which transfers its registered office in accordance with *Council Regulation (EC) 1435/2003, Art 7*. [*CTA 2009, ss 16, 17; SI 2007 No 3186*]. These provisions are subject to *CTA 2009, s 18* above.

From Brexit IP completion day (11pm on 31 December 2020), no new SEs or SCEs can be formed in the UK. From IP completion day, every SE that is registered in the United Kingdom immediately before that day is automatically converted into a 'UK Societas'.

Note

For DOUBLE TAX RELIEF (**31**) purposes, the definition of residence will often be affected by the terms of the relevant agreement. For the circumstances in which HMRC will certify that a company is UK resident for the purposes of double tax agreements, see Revenue Tax Bulletin December 2002 pp 989–991.

Simon's Taxes. See **D4.102, D4.103** and also INTM162031.

Central management and control

[64.3] There is no general statutory definition of residence, and before the enactment of the deeming provisions described in **64.2** above the courts had determined that a company resides where its real business is carried on, i.e. *where its central management and control actually abide*. This test was set down in the case of *De Beers Consolidated Mines Ltd v Howe* (1906) 5 TC 198, HL, which involved a company established, and operating its business, in South Africa but whose important affairs were controlled from the UK, where the majority of the directors resided.

This criterion continues to apply for companies incorporated outside the UK and for companies covered by the transitional provisions.

In the following cases, the company was held to be managed and controlled from, and hence resident in, the UK: *Calcutta Jute Mills Co Ltd v Nicholson Ex D* (1876) 1 TC 83 (UK company operating abroad but directors and shareholders meeting in UK); *New Zealand Shipping Co Ltd v Thew* (1922) 8 TC 208, HL (New Zealand company with New Zealand directors, but overall control lay with separate London board); *American Thread Co v Joyce* (1913) 6 TC 163, HL (UK company operating in USA with US directors in charge of current business, but overall control in London); *John Hood & Co Ltd v Magee* (1918) 7 TC 327 (company registered in both UK and USA, with the only director resident in USA, but general meetings and material trading activities in UK). But in *A-G v Alexander Ex D* (1874) LR 10 Ex 20, a foreign state bank with a UK branch was held resident abroad, notwithstanding that shareholders' meetings were held in London.

The case *Unit Construction Co Ltd v Bullock (Inspector of Taxes)* [1960] AC 351, [1959] 3 All ER 831, HL, involved companies operating in South Africa. The constitution of each company gave control to the board of directors who had to hold their meetings outside the UK. However, as a question of fact, it was found that real control was being exercised by the directors of the parent company in the UK, even though this was unconstitutional.

However see also *Untelrab Ltd v McGregor*; *Unigate Guernsey Ltd v McGregor* [1996] STC (SCD) 1, in which subsidiaries of a UK-resident parent were held to be resident where their boards met (in Bermuda) and their business was transacted, as they did 'function in giving effect to [the] parent's wishes', notwithstanding that they were 'complaisant to do [the parent company's] will'. The directors were able to show that whilst no request from the parent had to date been improper or unreasonable, if it had been it would have been refused — the directors would not have carried out directions from the parent if they considered that such instructions were to the subsidiary's detriment. The Special Commissioners also held that the burden of proving residence on an appeal lies on the Crown.

A contrasting decision was reached in *Development Securities plc v HMRC* CA 2020, [2021] STC 84, in which Jersey-registered companies were held to be resident in the UK. The companies were set up solely to implement a tax avoidance scheme. The court upheld the FTT's decision that the Jersey directors had merely formally approved what the UK parent had already decided so that central management and control was in the UK.

An important case is *Wood and another v Holden* [2006] STC 443, CA, in which a married couple who were resident in the UK entered into a sophisticated scheme involving non-UK resident companies, a key part of which involved transferring shares to a Dutch resident company Eulalia BV. The Revenue issued assessments on the basis that the 'central management and control' of the Dutch company was exercised in the UK, by or on behalf of the husband, and that the company was therefore UK resident.

The Court of Appeal held that the company in question was resident in the Netherlands as contended by the taxpayers. It argued that, in determining where central management and control was exercised, a distinction had to be made 'between cases where control of the company is exercised through its own constitutional organs (the board of directors or the general meeting) and cases where the functions of those constitutional organs are "usurped" – in the sense that management and control is exercised independently of, or without regard to, those constitutional organs.'

In the former case, it was important to recognise whether outside advisors dictated or merely influenced the decisions to be taken. The fact that the board may not have taken due care and consideration in making their decisions was not considered relevant in establishing the place of management and control. It was further held that, in appealing against an adjustment to a self-assessment, although the statutory burden of proof falls on the taxpayer, if the taxpayer produces evidence which suggests the assessment is wrong, 'the evidential basis must pass to the Revenue'.

More recently HMRC were successful in arguing that a Dutch company was being managed and controlled in the UK, through a former director who had not, as a matter of fact, relinquished his involvement with the company — *Laerstate BV v HMRC* FTT (TC 162), [2009] SFTD 551. The First-Tier Tax Tribunal found that the relevant decisions in relation to the BV were primarily taken by one of its directors, Mr Bock, in the UK. Whilst the BV did hold board meetings outside the UK, Mr Bock was not in regular attendance, although he was the driving force behind the company. As a director he was authorised to represent the BV and create legally binding obligations, and the minutes of the board meetings provided little evidence that there was any real consideration of matters by the board.

Even after Mr Bock had resigned as a director he continued to wield his influence and the Tribunal concluded that throughout the relevant period the BV's 'course of business and trading' was being undertaken largely by Mr Bock, in the UK, through his extensive involvement in '... policy, strategic and management matters...' The case highlights the importance of factual evidence. In addition it is interesting to note that the Tribunal considered the Netherlands-UK treaty test of effective management, and held that on the facts such effective management also took place in the UK. An appeal to the Upper Tribunal was withdrawn.

Statement of Practice SP 1/90

HMRC's approach to applying the basic test can be found in SP1/90. The first step is to ascertain whether the directors in fact themselves exercise central management and control; if so, to then determine where that central management and control is exercised (not necessarily where they meet); if not, to establish where and by whom it is exercised.

The concept of the place of central management and control is directed at the highest level of control of the company's business, rather than the place where the main business operations are to be found. This must always be a question of fact in any particular case, but the place of directors' meetings will usually be of significance if they are the medium through which central management and control is exercised. If, however, central management and control is in reality exercised by, for example, a single individual, the company's residence will be where that individual exercises his powers.

With regard to the particular problem of residence of a subsidiary, HMRC would not normally seek to impute to the subsidiary the residence of its parent unless the parent in effect usurps the functions of the Board of the subsidiary. Matters taken into account would include the extent to which the directors of the subsidiary take decisions on their own authority as to investment, production, marketing and procurement without reference to the parent (and see below).

In all cases, HMRC will seek to determine whether a major objective of the existence of any particular factors bearing on residence is the obtaining of tax benefits from residence or non-residence, and to establish the reality of the central management and control.

See **64.2** above as regards deemed residence for tax purposes of companies incorporated in the UK. Before 15 March 1988 under the general law, incorporation in the UK and compliance with the requirements of the *Companies Acts* did not in themselves render a company tax resident here. See *Egyptian Delta Land and Investment Co Ltd v Todd (Inspector of Taxes)* [1929] AC 1, 14 TC 119, HL, and cf *Eccott v Aramayo Francke Mines Ltd* (1925) 9 TC 445, HL. A company may be resident in more than one country. See *Swedish Central Railway Co Ltd v Thompson* (1925) 9 TC 342, HL, and for an authoritative discussion of dual residence, *Union Corporation Ltd v CIR* (1953) 34 TC 207, HL.

As regards companies in liquidation, the appointment of a UK liquidator of a non-UK resident company may result in the company's becoming UK resident. The exercise of central management and control remains, however, a question of fact, and if it is exercised overseas by the liquidator, or if the liquidator acts in accordance with the wishes of non-resident shareholders so that it is not in fact exercised in the UK, the company will not become UK resident.

A company may have a domicile (see *Gasque v CIR* (1940) 23 TC 210), but it would seem from the *Union Corporation* case above that, for a company, ordinary residence and residence are synonymous. Similar rules apply for ascertaining the residence of PARTNERSHIPS (**55**).

Note

For DOUBLE TAX RELIEF (**31**) purposes, the definition of residence will often be affected by the terms of the relevant agreement. For the circumstances in which HMRC will certify that a company is UK resident for the purposes of double tax agreements, see Revenue Tax Bulletin December 2002 pp 989–991 and also INTM162031.

See **35.23** GROUP RELIEF as regards certain 'dual resident investing companies'.

Simon's Taxes. See **D4.104**.

Overseas income and chargeable gains

[64.4] A UK resident company is chargeable to corporation tax on its overseas profits, and income, whether remitted to the UK or not, although an election can be made for the profits from an overseas PE to be exempt (see **31.15** DOUBLE TAX RELIEF).

Where control of a UK resident company's trade rests abroad, the trade is a foreign possession, income from which is overseas income (*Mitchell (Surveyor of Taxes) v Egyptian Hotels Ltd* [1915] AC 1022, 6 TC 542, HL).

Where overseas income cannot be remitted to the UK, by reason of the laws or executive action of the government, or the impossibility of obtaining foreign currency in the territory that could be transferred to the UK (and where the income has not been realised outside that territory for sterling or an unblocked currency) then that income may be disregarded if the company so claims before any assessment by reference to that income becomes final.

The claim must be made within two years of the end of the accounting period in which the income arises.

No claim may be made under these provisions if an Export Credit Guarantee Department (ECGD) payment has been made in respect of it.

When the income ceases to be unremittable or an ECGD payment is made in respect of it, then the relief claimed above will be withdrawn, either in whole or in part. The income is valued as at the date it ceases to be unremittable or the ECGD payment is made, taking into account foreign taxes chargeable on it in the territory concerned. Disputes are to be settled by the tribunal.

Where relief falls to be withdrawn, but the company has permanently ceased to carry on the trade or property business or the source of other income no longer belongs to it, the following applies:

- for trading income, the income is treated as a post-cessation receipt (see **68.16** TRADING INCOME); and
- for a property business, the income is treated as a post-cessation receipt of a UK property business (see **60.4** PROPERTY INCOME).

If no claim is made under these provisions, the unremittable income to be taken into account for corporation tax purposes is valued at its normal sterling exchange rate, if available, and in other cases, the official rate of exchange of the territory in which the income arises.

[*CTA 2009, ss 1274–1278*].

Where tax on overseas income or chargeable gains has been assessed, HMRC may allow that tax to remain uncollected, without payment of interest, if they are satisfied that the income etc. cannot be remitted due to government action in the country of origin and that it is otherwise reasonable to do so. Interest then ceases to run from the date on which HMRC were first in possession of information necessary to enable them to agree to deferment. If that date is three months or less from the due and payable date, no interest is payable. But where a demand is later made for payment of the deferred tax, interest is exigible if the tax is not paid within three months of that demand. [*TMA 1970, s 92*]. HMRC may defer collection indefinitely.

Non-resident companies

[64.5] A non-UK resident company is liable to corporation tax in the circumstances set out at **64.6**(1)–(5) below.

Where there is a non-discrimination clause in the relevant double tax treaty, an overseas company was able to benefit from the reduced rates of corporation tax available for companies with small profits (governed by world-wide company profits) for financial year 2014 and earlier years as if the overseas company were UK resident. Associated companies were taken into account wherever resident. (CCAB Guidance Notes TR 500, 10 March 1983). If there is no such clause in the applicable treaty then the main rate of corporation tax applied.

See Revenue Tax Bulletin August 1995 pp 237–239 as regards application of the arm's length principle in measuring the profits chargeable on a non-resident in respect of UK trading. See generally, HMRC International Manual, INTM260000 *et seq.*

Where a non-resident company suffers income tax by deduction at source on income which is also subject to corporation tax then the income tax is set off against the corporation tax chargeable. If the income tax exceeds the corporation tax liability for the relevant accounting period, repayment of the excess may be claimed.

[*CTA 2010, s 968; FA 1998, Sch 18 para 10*].

A non-resident company is not liable to UK income tax on its income which is chargeable to corporation tax as in **64.6** below (or would be but for an exemption). [*CTA 2009, s 3; FA 2019, Sch 5 para 11*]. It is liable to UK income tax on income from other sources in the UK (excluding income specifically exempt in the hands of a non-resident).

Where a non-resident company is within the charge to corporation tax in respect of one source of income and is assessable to income tax on another source of income, capital allowances related to each source are given against income from that source only according to the rules of the tax involved. [*CAA 2001, s 566*].

Where a company becomes UK resident during a year of assessment, it is liable to capital gains tax on gains arising during that year prior to its becoming resident. Similarly, on a company's ceasing to be UK resident during a year of assessment, it is liable to capital gains tax on gains arising during that year after it ceases to be resident, where any such gains are not within the charge to corporation tax under *TCGA 1992, ss 2B(3), 2C* (previously *TCGA 1992, s 10B*; assets used in a trade carried on through a permanent establishment). (HMRC Capital Gains Manual CG42360–42411).

See **21** CONTROLLED FOREIGN COMPANIES as regards special rules applying to those with an interest in such companies. See **35.23** GROUP RELIEF as regards certain 'dual resident investing companies'.

Simon's Taxes. See **D4.115–D4.123**.

The charge to corporation tax

[64.6] A non-resident company is within the charge to corporation tax only if:

(1) it carries on a trade of dealing in or developing UK land (see **71.2** TRANSACTIONS IN UK LAND);

(2) it carries on a trade (other than a trade within (1) above) in the UK through a permanent establishment;
(3) (for disposals on or after 6 April 2019) it disposes of any interests in UK land (see **11.25** CAPITAL GAINS) or assets deriving at least 75% of their value from UK land where the company has a substantial indirect interest in that land (see **11.26**);
(4) with effect from 6 April 2020 (subject to the transitional provisions at **64.7** below) it carries on a UK property business; or
(5) with effect from 6 April 2020 (subject to the transitional provisions at **64.7** below) it has other UK property income.

Where (1) above applies, the company is chargeable to corporation tax on all its profits from the trade wherever arising. Where (2) above applies, the company is liable to corporation tax on the income and gains of the permanent establishment. Where (3) above applies, the company is chargeable to corporation tax on gains from such disposals.

Where (4) above applies, the company is chargeable to corporation tax on all its profits from the business and from loan relationships or derivative contracts that the company is a party to for the purposes of the business. Where (5) above applies, the company is chargeable to corporation tax on all it profits that consist of that income and any profits arising from loan relationships or derivative contracts to which the company is a party for the purposes of enabling it to generate the income. Other UK property income is rent receivable in connection with a *CTA 2009, s 39* concern (mines, quarries etc. — see **60.18** PROPERTY INCOME), rent receivable for electric-line wayleaves (see **60.18**) and post-cessation receipts from a UK property business (see **60.4**).

[*CTA 2009, ss 2(1), 5; TCGA 1992, ss 2B, 10B; FA 2019, Sch 1 paras 2, 110, 120, Sch 5 paras 2–5, 35*].

Permanent establishments

The rules described below relate to permanent establishments within (2) above, but will not apply if different rules are included in the relevant double taxation agreement; in such a case the rules in the agreement take precedence.

The profits within the charge to corporation tax are those which are attributable to the permanent establishment, as follows:

- trading income arising directly or indirectly through or from the establishment;
- income from property or rights used by, or held by or for, the establishment; or
- chargeable gains within *TCGA 1992, s 2B(3)* (previously *TCGA 1992, s 10B*) from assets used for the permanent establishment or for the trade carried on by the company through it (see Tolley's Capital Gains Tax under Overseas Matters).

The profits attributable to the permanent establishment are determined as if the permanent establishment were a distinct and separate enterprise, engaged in the same or similar activities under the same or similar conditions, dealing wholly independently with the non-UK resident company (the '*separate enterprise principle*'). Profits within (1), (4) or (5) above are excluded.

It is assumed for this purpose that the establishment has the same credit rating as the non-resident company and has such equity and loan capital as it could reasonably be expected to have in these circumstances. No deduction may be made for tax purposes for costs in excess of those that would have been incurred on those assumptions. In *Irish Bank Resolution Corpn Ltd v HMRC* CA, [2020] STC 1946, the company's contention that the double tax treaty between the UK and Ireland precluded the application of this rule to disallow interest deductions was unsuccessful.

In accordance with the separate enterprise principle, transactions between the permanent establishment and any other part of the non-UK resident company are treated as taking place on arm's length terms. If the non-resident company supplies the establishment with goods or services, then if they are of a kind which the company supplies on arm's length terms to third parties in the ordinary course of its business, the separate enterprise principle is applied to the transactions; if not, the matter is dealt with as an expense incurred by the company for the purposes of the permanent establishment.

Expenses, including executive and general administrative expenses, incurred for the purposes of the permanent establishment, whether incurred in the UK or elsewhere and whether or not incurred or reimbursed by the establishment, are deductible, at the actual cost to the non-UK resident company, if they are of a kind that would have been deductible if incurred by a UK resident company.

There are prohibitions on deductions for certain payments in respect of intangible assets, and for certain payments of interest and other financing costs, where such payments are made by the permanent establishment to any other part of the non-UK resident company.

CTA 2009, ss 25–28 make special provision applicable only to non-UK resident banks. (See also HMRC Banking Manual at BAM32000 *et seq.*). HMRC may make special provision (by regulations) in relation to insurance companies (for which see *SI 2003 No 2714*) in respect of the application of *CTA 2009, s 21(1)*.

Special rules apply to interest and royalties paid by the UK permanent establishment of an EU company (i.e. one resident in an EU member state other than the UK) to another EU company — see **41.5** and **41.6** INCOME TAX IN RELATION TO A COMPANY.

[*CTA 2009, ss 19–32; FA 2019, Sch 5 para 13*].

The meaning of 'permanent establishment'

The following definition of a permanent establishment applies for UK tax purposes. It is to a large extent based on the meaning in the OECD Model Tax Convention (and thus the meaning which may be found in many double tax arrangements based on the Convention), but is not identical in all respects. In addition, other forms of double taxation may have slightly different definitions. In such cases, the interpretation in the particular agreement will prevail, although such interpretation cannot create a charge to UK tax which is not within the provisions described below.

A company has a '*permanent establishment*' in a territory if (and only if):

(a) it has a 'fixed place of business' there through which its business is wholly or partly carried on, or
(b) it has an agent acting on its behalf there and this agent has and habitually exercises there authority to do business on its behalf.

A '*fixed place of business*' includes a place of management; a branch; an office, factory or workshop; an installation or structure for the exploration of natural resources; a mine or quarry, oil or gas well or any other place of extraction of natural resources; and a building site or construction or installation project.

There are three specific exclusions in that a company is *not* regarded as having a permanent establishment in a territory by reason of the fact that:

(i) it carries on business there through an agent of independent status acting in the ordinary course of his business (and see below the conditions with regard to the 'independent status'); or
(ii) a fixed place of business is maintained there for the purpose of carrying on company activities, or such activities are carried on there for or on behalf of the company by an agent, and those activities are, in relation to the company's business as a whole, only of a 'preparatory or auxiliary character' and, for accounting periods beginning on or after 1 January 2019 (see further below), are not part of a 'fragmented business operation'; or
(iii) the company is party to ALTERNATIVE FINANCE ARRANGEMENTS (3) in relation to an arrangement giving rise to an alternative finance return under *CTA 2009, ss 511–513, Sch 1 para 653; ITA 2007 ss 564I, 564K or 564L.*

Reference to activities of a 'preparatory or auxiliary character' include:

- the use of facilities for the purpose of storage, display or delivery of goods or merchandise belonging to the company;
- the maintenance of a stock of goods or merchandise belonging to the company for that purpose or for the purpose of processing by another person; and
- purchasing goods or merchandise, or collecting information, for the company.

Activities are part of a '*fragmented business operation*' if they are carried on, either in the same place or in different places in the same territory, by the company or a person closely related to it, they constitute complementary functions that are part of a cohesive business operation and either:

- the overall activity resulting from the combination of the complementary functions is not of a preparatory or auxiliary character; or
- the company or a person closely related to it has a permanent establishment in the territory by reason of carrying on any of those functions. A person which is not a company is treated for this purpose as having a permanent establishment in the territory if it would be so treated if it were a company.

One person is '*closely related*' to another person if one is able to secure that the other acts in accordance with its wishes; if one can reasonably be expected to act, or typically acts, in accordance with the other's wishes; a third person is able to secure that both act in accordance with its wishes; both can be reasonably expected to act, or typically act, in accordance with a third person's wishes; or the 50% investment condition is met. The 50% investment condition is met if one person has a 50% investment (as defined at *TIOPA 2010, s 259ND*) in the other or a third person has a 50% investment in both.

For the purpose only of the change in the above provisions taking effect for accounting periods beginning on or after 1 January 2019, accounting periods straddling that date are treated as two separate accounting period, the second of which begins on 1 January 2019. Any necessary apportionments between the two notional periods must be made on a time basis or, if a time basis would be unjust or unreasonable, on a just and reasonable basis.

Agents of independent status

Three particular types of agent are given specific exemptions under the legislation, which provide certain conditions to be met in order for such UK persons to be treated as independent agents in respect of services provided to non-resident companies: a broker; an investment manager and a Lloyd's member's agent or syndicate managing agent for the company.

For the purpose of these rules, a person is regarded as carrying out a transaction on behalf of another where he undertakes it himself or gives instructions for it to be carried out by another person. A person is not regarded as acting in an independent capacity on behalf of a company unless the relationship between them (legal, financial and commercial) is between independent businesses dealing at arm's length.

Where the non-resident company is a corporate member of Lloyd's, a person who acts on behalf of the company in relation to a transaction in the course of its underwriting business is regarded as an independent agent acting in the ordinary course of his business if he acts as members' agent or as managing agent of the syndicate concerned.

The independent broker conditions

A *broker* is regarded as an agent of independent status in respect of a transaction carried out on behalf of a non-resident company only if each of the following conditions is met:

(a) at the time of the transaction he is carrying on the business of broker;
(b) the transaction is carried out in the ordinary course of that business;
(c) his remuneration in respect of the transaction is not less than is customary for that class of business; and
(d) he does not fall to be treated as a permanent establishment of the non-resident company in relation to any other transaction in the same accounting period.

The independent investment manager conditions

An *investment manager* is regarded as an agent of independent status in respect of an investment transaction carried out on behalf of a non-resident company only if each of the following conditions is met:

(a) he is carrying on the business of providing investment management services, at the time of the transaction;

(b) the transaction is carried out in the ordinary course of that business;
(c) he acts on behalf of the non-resident company in an independent capacity;
(d) he meets the requirements of the '20% rule' (see below);
(e) his remuneration in respect of the transaction is not less than is customary for that class of business.

An '*investment transaction*' is defined for these purposes as at **47.7** INVESTMENT TRUSTS.

The requirements of the '*20% rule*' are broadly that the interests of the investment manager and CONNECTED PERSONS (**19**) in the '*relevant disregarded income*' (i.e. profits, see below) of the non-resident company's investment transactions in a qualifying period do not, or are not intended to, amount to 20% or more, with special provisions applying in relation to the non-resident company's participation in collective investment schemes (see *CTA 2010, ss 1147, 1148, 1152*). If that intention is not fulfilled, the failure must be attributable to matters outside their control and must not result from a failure to take reasonable steps to mitigate the effect of such matters.

Where the 20% rule is not satisfied, the investment manager will still be regarded as an agent of independent status except in relation to relevant disregarded income in which he and connected persons have or have had any beneficial entitlement.

The *relevant disregarded income* means profits derived from transactions carried out by the investment manager on behalf of the non-resident company in respect of which the manager is *not* treated as a permanent establishment (other than under the requirements of the 20% rule). This definition is important when the interaction with a possible income tax charge (see **64.8** below) is being considered.

A qualifying period is the accounting period in which the transaction is carried out or a period of up to five years comprising two or more complete accounting periods including the one in which the transaction was carried out.

There are certain further requirements with regard to the application of the 20% rule to collective investment schemes, see further *CTA 2010, s 1149.*

[*CTA 2010, ss 1141–1153; FA 2019, s 21*].

Assessment, collection and recovery of corporation tax

Obligations and liabilities in relation to corporation tax which are imposed on a non-resident company are also imposed on its 'UK representative'. This applies to the assessment, collection and recovery of tax, or of interest on tax.

A UK 'permanent establishment' (see above) through which the non-resident company carries on a trade is the company's '*UK representative*' in relation to the 'chargeable profits' attributable to that establishment (see above) and within the charge to corporation tax. The permanent establishment continues to be the UK representative even after it ceases to be a permanent establishment through which the company carries on a trade. It is treated as a person separate and distinct from the company for these purposes.

Either the company itself or its UK representative may satisfy any such obligation or liability, and the company is bound by the acts or omissions of its UK representative. Formal notices, demands, etc. must, where relevant, be given or notified to, or served on, the UK representative for these provisions to apply to it. The company is not bound by a mistake in information provided by its UK representative in pursuance of such an obligation unless it resulted from an act or omission of the company, or from one to which the company consented or in which it connived.

Similarly the UK representative is not by virtue of these provisions liable to be proceeded against for a criminal offence in relation to any of the above unless it committed the offence itself or consented to, or connived in, its commission.

[*CTA 2010, ss 969–972*].

See **30.18** DIVERTED PROFITS TAX for the application of these provisions to that tax.

See also **Simon's Taxes**. See **D4.116–D4.121**. CTM34210 and 34220.

UK property income: transitional provisions

[64.7] The charge to corporation tax on certain property and related income of non-UK resident companies within **64.6**(4) and (5) above applies with effect from 6 April 2020 (the 'commencement date') subject to the following transitional rules. Previously such income was within the charge to income tax (see **64.8** below).

Where a period of account of a company straddles the commencement date, it is treated as two separate periods, the first ending on 5 April 2020 and the second beginning on the commencement date. It must be assumed that the company has drawn up accounts for each of the notional periods in accordance with GAAP. The profits or losses of the first notional period remain within the charge to income tax, and the profits or losses for the second period are chargeable to corporation tax.

Where a company is a partner in a partnership which carries on a trade and has untaxed income or relievable losses from a UK property business and the company is accordingly treated as carrying on a notional business under *ITTOIA 2005, s 854*, the company's basis period of that business for 2019/20 is taken to end on 5 April 2020 if it would not otherwise do so.

Unrelieved income tax losses of a UK property business can be carried forward as corporation tax losses and relieved in accounting periods ending after the commencement date against profits of the UK property business and profits arising from loan relationships or derivative contracts to which the company is a party for the purposes of that business. Such losses must be used in priority to any losses made on or after 6 April 2020 under the corporation tax regime but are not subject to the restriction on deduction of carried-forward losses at **51.13** LOSSES (HMRC Property Income Manual PIM4230).

[*FA 2019, Sch 5 paras 35–38*]

Loan relationships and derivative contracts

The following transitional rules apply to loan relationships and derivative contracts of a non-resident company to which the company is a party for the purposes of a UK property business or to generate UK property income.

Where a loss arises in connection with a loan relationship on or after the commencement date and all or part of the loss relates to a time before that date, that part is not disallowed by *CTA 2009, s 327* (see **50.30** LOAN RELATIONSHIPS) if it would have been allowable for income tax purposes in computing the company's UK property business profits if the loss had arisen before the commencement date.

Where a loss arises in connection with a derivative contract in an accounting period beginning on or after the commencement date and all or part of the loss relates to a time before that date when the contract was not subject to corporation tax, none of the loss relating to that time is treated as arising in the accounting period if it would not have been allowable for income tax purposes in computing the company's UK property business profits if the loss had arisen before the commencement date. For this purpose, a contract is not subject to corporation tax at a particular time if the company (or whoever was then in the same position under the contract as the company would subsequently hold) would not then have been chargeable to corporation tax on any profits arising from it. Any amount disallowed under this rule is excluded from being otherwise brought into account for corporation tax purposes. This rule takes priority over that in *CTA 2010, s 607ZA* (debits referable to times before UK property business was carried on — see **27.6** DERIVATIVE CONTRACTS).

Where a profit arises in connection with a loan relationship or derivative contract in an accounting period beginning on or after the commencement date and all or part of the profit (the 'profit amount') relates to a time before the commencement date when the instrument was not subject to corporation tax, then the following applies if:

(i) had the profit arisen before the commencement date it would not have been allowable for income tax purposes in computing the company's UK property business profits;

(ii) at that time the instrument is in a hedging relationship with another loan relationship or derivative contract (the 'second instrument'); and

(iii) an amount of a loss would otherwise be disallowed (either under the above rule for derivative contract losses or under *CTA 2009, s 327*).

Where these conditions are met, the loss in (iii) above may be brought into account to the extent that it does not exceed the profit amount. If the two instruments are in a hedging relationship only to a limited extent, this rule applies only to a just and reasonable proportion of the loss. For this purpose, two instruments are in a hedging relationship to the extent that one of them is intended to act as a hedge of the company's exposure to changes in the fair value of the other. An instrument is not subject to corporation tax at a particular time if the company (or whoever was then in the same position under the instrument as the company would subsequently hold) would not then have been chargeable to corporation tax on any profits arising from it.

Where a company is within the charge to income tax on the profits of a UK property business before the commencement date and becomes chargeable on that date to corporation tax in respect of a derivative contract to which it is a party for the purposes of that business, then, if there is a 'tax asymmetry' in the treatment of the contract, the credits and debits to be brought into account in respect of it must be adjusted on a just and reasonable basis. There is a '*tax asymmetry*' for this purpose if 'fair value amounts' were brought into account in calculating the company's income tax profits or losses from the business but such amounts are not brought into account for corporation tax purposes after the commencement date as a result of *SI 2004 No 3256, Reg 9* (the Disregard Regulations — see **27.13, 27.14** DERIVATIVE CONTRACTS). '*Fair value amounts*' are amounts representing a change in the fair value of a contract which is recognised in determining the company's profit or loss in accordance with GAAP.

If an amount representing a change in the fair value of a derivative contract is disallowed for income tax purposes for a tax year beginning before the commencement date because it is capital in nature, for corporation tax purposes the company is treated as having made an election under *SI 2004 No 3256, Reg 6A* (election to apply *Reg 7, 8*, or *9*). If, as a result, *Reg 7* or *8* apply to the contract for corporation tax purposes, the amount disallowed for income tax purposes is treated for the purposes of *Reg 10* as if it had been disallowed by *Reg 7* or *8*, as appropriate.

If a company measures a 'relevant derivative contract' at fair value before 1 January 2015 and on the commencement date it comes within the charge to corporation tax as a result of the introduction of the charge on UK property income of non-residents, then if the first 'relevant period' of the company begins on or after the commencement date, the company is treated for the purposes of *SI 2004 No 3256, Reg 6A* as if it were a 'new adopter'. The expressions 'relevant derivative contract', 'relevant period' and 'new adopter' are all defined as in *Reg 6A(5)* (see **27.12** DERIVATIVE CONTRACTS). In determining whether a company comes within the charge to corporation tax as a result of the introduction of the charge on UK property income of non-residents, for this purpose, no account is taken of any direct or indirect disposal of UK land before the commencement date which is within **11.25, 11.26** CAPITAL GAINS.

[*FA 2019, Sch 5 paras 39–44; FA 2020, Sch 6 paras 5, 9, 11*]

Intangible assets

If an asset held for the purposes of a UK property business or the purposes of enabling the company to generate other UK property income becomes a chargeable intangible asset (see **42.11** INTANGIBLE ASSETS) as a result of the business or income coming within the charge to corporation tax, the intangible assets provisions apply as if the company had acquired the asset on the commencement date for its accounting value.

An election cannot be made to reallocate a degrouping charge (see **42.23** INTANGIBLE ASSETS) if company Y is a non-resident company and the time of the event triggering the degrouping charge was before 5 July 2016 where company Y carries on a trade of dealing in or developing UK land or before the commencement date where company Y carries on a UK property business.

[*FA 2019, Sch 5 paras 45, 46*]

Contaminated land

LAND REMEDIATION (**48**) relief is not available for capital expenditure incurred by a company before the commencement date for the purposes of a UK property business which it is about to carry on if it begins to carry on the business on or after that date at a time when it is non-UK resident. The normal rule (see **48.3**) treating expenditure incurred for the purpose of a business about to be carried on as incurred on the first day of business is disapplied.

[*FA 2019, Sch 5 para 47*]

Instalment payments

Where a company ceases to be within the charge to income tax and comes within the charge to corporation tax on the commencement date as a result of the introduction of the corporation tax charge on UK property income and an accounting period begins on that date, the instalment payment provisions (see **58.3** PAYMENT OF TAX) do not apply to that period.

[*FA 2019, Sch 5 para 48*]

Anti-avoidance

If a company enters into arrangements on or after 29 October 2018 and the arrangements have a main purpose of securing a tax advantage for any person as a result of the introduction of the corporation tax charge on UK property income of non-resident companies, the tax advantage can be counteracted by the making of adjustments by way of assessment, modification of an assessment, amendment or disallowance of a claim or otherwise. Such an arrangement is not, however, counteracted if the arrangements take only ordinary commercial steps in accordance with a generally prevailing commercial practice if the tax advantage is a relief expressly conferred in respect of the CORPORATE INTEREST RESTRICTION (**24**) and securing the advantage is wholly consistent with the policy objectives of the restriction. The advantage is also not counteracted under the provisions at **24.11** CORPORATE INTEREST RESTRICTION, regardless of when the arrangements were entered into.

[*FA 2019, Sch 5 paras 49, 50*]

The charge to income tax

[64.8] A non-resident company is chargeable to income tax on income arising within the UK which is not chargeable to corporation tax. [*ITA 2007, s 5; FA 2019, Sch 5 para 9*]. Subject to the transitional rules at **64.7** above, before 6 April 2020, this included UK property income (not connected with a permanent establishment) payable to a non-resident company. Such income is chargeable to corporation tax with effect from 6 April 2020 (see **64.6** above). See **42.44** INTANGIBLE ASSETS for the income tax charge on offshore receipts in respect of intangible property, which applies in particular to non-resident companies.

There is a limit to the liability to income tax of non-resident companies. The limit is linked with the provisions in respect of the activities of an independent broker or investment manager, and the conditions outlined above with regard to such independent persons apply equally here. The limit does not apply to the charge on offshore receipts in respect of intangible property

In *English Holdings (BVI) Ltd v HMRC* UT 2017, [2018] STC 220, a non-UK resident company carried on a trade in the UK through a permanent establishment (so that the profits would be chargeable to corporation tax) and also carried on a UK property business (the profits of which were chargeable to income tax). The Tribunal held that the company could set off losses from the UK trade against profits from the UK property business under *ITA 2007, s 64*.

Limit on liability to income tax

The limit on the liability to income tax of non-resident companies is given by the sum of two amounts, which are termed 'Amount A' and 'Amount B'.

Amount A is the total of amounts deducted, or treated as deducted from 'disregarded company income' (see below) together with, for distributions before 6 April 2016, associated tax credits. Amount B is the non-resident company's liability to income tax for the tax year if disregarded company income were to be ignored.

'Disregarded company income' (prior to *ITA 2007* this was referred to as 'excluded income') is made up of the following:

(a) disregarded savings and investment income;
(b) disregarded annual payments;
(c) income on transactions through a broker in the UK provided the independent broker conditions are satisfied;
(d) income on transactions through an investment manager in the UK provided the independent investment manager conditions are satisfied;
(e) any other description of income which the Treasury designate by regulations.

The independent broker and independent investment manager conditions are those described in **64.5** above.

Income may still fall to be disregarded even if the independent investment manager conditions are not met. This rule will apply if an investment manager (who, for whatever reason, is not regarded as an 'agent of independent status') carries out one or more transactions on behalf of a non-resident company; and either:

(i) the investment transaction meets all the investment manager conditions (outlined above); or
(ii) the investment transaction meets all the those conditions with the exception of the 20% rule. Where the 20% rule is not satisfied, profits are to be disregarded only if they do not represent relevant excluded income in which the investment manager and connected persons have or have had any beneficial entitlement.

An EU company is not liable to income tax on interest and royalty payments from an associated UK company or from the UK permanent establishment of another EU company provided that certain conditions are satisfied.

For a non-resident company which does not undertake a business (including a trade, profession or vocation) in the UK the charge to income tax is therefore limited to that deducted at source.

[*ITA 2007, ss 815–828*].

The above limit does not apply to the income tax charge on offshore receipts in respect of intangible property (see **42.44** INTANGIBLE ASSETS. Where that charge applies, therefore, the non-resident company's income tax liability is the sum of the liability under that charge (with the limit not applying) plus the liability in respect of anything else (subject to the application of the limit). [*ITTOIA 2005, s 608X(3); FA 2019, Sch 3 paras 4, 7*].

Assessment, collection and recovery of income tax

As noted above the charge to income tax for a non-resident company arises only in limited circumstances and is limited in scope.

The UK representative provisions in respect of income tax do not apply to income tax chargeable on income of a non resident company otherwise than as a trustee (*ITA 2007, s 835D*, as inserted by *TIOPA 2010*).

The obligations and liabilities in relation to income tax which are imposed on a non-resident company ***as a trustee*** are also imposed on a branch or agency which is the company's 'UK representative' in relation to the amounts giving rise to the tax.

The following are, however, excluded from being a 'UK representative':

(1) an agent acting other than in the course of carrying on a regular agency for the company;
(2) a broker;
(3) an investment manager acting in an independent capacity through whom certain investment transactions (see *ITA 2007, s 835M–Q*) are carried out;
(4) a Lloyd's member's agent or syndicate managing agent for the company;
(5) any party to, or person acting for a non-resident person who is party to, ALTERNATIVE FINANCE ARRANGEMENTS (3) within *CTA 2009, s 504*.

With regard to (2) and (3) reference should be made to the conditions for independent brokers and investment managers described above at **64.5**.

As regards (3) above, see further HMRC Statement of Practice 1/01 which clarifies the requirements for the exclusion to apply. This statement of practice examines further the conditions for the investment manager exemption to apply, and considers the nature of 'independence'. The original statement applied from February 2001. On 20 July 2007, a revised statement was issued. This applies from the date of issue, except where the non-resident or his investment manager needs to make changes to current circumstances or contractual arrangements in order to comply with the revised statement, in which case the original statement may be applied until 31 December 2009.

This applies to the assessment, collection and recovery of tax, or of interest on tax. Either the company itself or its 'UK representative' may satisfy such obligations and liabilities, and the company is bound by the acts or omissions of its 'UK representative'.

A person is, however, guilty of a criminal offence in relation to any of the above only where he committed the offence himself or consented to, or connived in, its commission.

Formal notices, etc., where relevant, must be notified to the 'UK representative' for these provisions to apply. The 'UK representative' is treated as a person separate and distinct from the company for these purposes.

[*ITA 2007, ss 835G–835Y*].

Simon's Taxes. See **D4.122, D4.123.**

The effect of double taxation agreements

Most double taxation agreements lay down rules to determine in which country a particular source of income is to be taxed, ie in the country in which the income arises or the country in which the recipient of the income is resident. Such rules take precedence over the internal tax legislation of the countries concerned. This means that a non-resident company cannot be required to pay tax in the UK in excess of that stipulated in the double taxation agreement, but subject to that may be taxed in accordance with the provisions outlined above.

Company becoming non-resident

[64.9] A company may cease to be UK resident, even if it is incorporated it the UK, if it changes its central management and control, or effective management, and, for UK incorporated companies, the terms of an applicable double tax treaty apply such that the company is considered resident in the other contracting state.

There are various migration provisions that apply in such circumstances with regard to capital gains, loan relationships, derivative contracts, and intangible fixed assets. In essence these are anti-avoidance provisions and provide for a charge to tax to arise on migration, save in certain circumstances, such as where a permanent establishment of the company continues to exist in the UK post migration.

Chargeable gains

If, at any time (the '*relevant time*'), a company ceases to be resident in the UK, and does not cease to exist, then:

(a) it is deemed to dispose of, and immediately re-acquire, all its assets at their market value at that time, and
(b) rollover relief under *TCGA 1992, s 152* is not subsequently available by reference to disposals of old assets made before that time.

If at any later time the company carries on a trade in the UK through a permanent establishment (see **64.6** above — previously a branch or agency), (a) above does not apply to any assets which, immediately after the relevant time, are situated in the UK and are used in or for a trade, or are used or held for the permanent establishment. Similarly (b) above does not apply to new assets acquired after the relevant time which are so situated and used or held. For this purpose assets situated in the UK include various assets and rights relating to exploration or exploitation activities in the UK or designated areas of the sea within *TCGA 1992, s 276*.

[*TCGA 1992, s 185; FA 2019, Sch 8 para 9(3)*].

Where the company ceases to be UK-resident before 1 January 2020 and the deemed disposal in (a) above includes any '*foreign assets*' (i.e. assets situated, and used in or for a trade carried on, outside the UK), postponement of tax will be available, as described below, if:

(i) immediately after the relevant time the company was a 75% subsidiary of a company (the '*principal company*') which was resident in the UK (i.e. not less than 75% of its ordinary share capital was owned directly by the principal company); and
(ii) both companies so elect in writing within two years after that time.

Any excess of gains over losses arising on the foreign assets included in the deemed disposal is treated as a single chargeable gain not accruing to the company on that disposal. An equal amount (the '*postponed gain*') is instead treated as follows.

If, within six years after the relevant time, the company disposes of any assets (the '*relevant assets*') chargeable gains on which were taken into account in arriving at the postponed gain, a chargeable gain equal to the whole, or the 'appropriate proportion', of the postponed gain, so far as this has not already been treated as a chargeable gain under these provisions, is deemed to accrue to the principal company. The '*appropriate proportion*' is the proportion which the chargeable gain taken into account in arriving at the postponed gain in respect of the part of the relevant assets disposed of bears to the aggregate of the chargeable gains so taken into account in respect of the relevant assets held immediately before the time of the disposal.

If at any time:

(a) the company ceases to be a 75% subsidiary of the principal company on a disposal by the principal company of ordinary shares in it; or
(b) after the company otherwise ceases to be a 75% subsidiary, the principal company disposes of ordinary shares in it; or
(c) the principal company ceases to be resident in the UK,

a chargeable gain equal to so much of the postponed gain as has not previously been charged under these provisions is deemed to arise to the principal company. The deemed gain can itself be further postponed by way of a CT exit charge payment plan (see **58.19** PAYMENT OF TAX).

If any part of the postponed gain becomes chargeable on the principal company, and the subsidiary has unrelieved capital losses, the companies may jointly elect, in writing within two years, for part or all of the losses to be set against the amount so chargeable.

The facility to postpone a charge under *TCGA 1992, s 185* under this provision is no longer available where a company ceases to be UK-resident on or after 1 January 2020. The charge can, however, still be postponed by way of a CT exit charge payment plan.

[*TCGA 1992, s 187; FA 2019, Sch 8 para 9(1)(5)*].

Postponement of the tax also applies to a deemed gain or loss arising before 6 April 2019 as a result of (a) above that is an ATED-related gain or loss chargeable to, or allowable for the purposes of, capital gains tax (see **11.23**

CAPITAL GAINS). The gain or loss is treated as accruing to the company on a subsequent disposal of the asset (in addition to any gain or loss actually accruing on the disposal). [*TCGA 1992, s 187A; FA 2019, Sch 1 paras 66, 120*].

Similar provisions in respect of a company ceasing to be UK resident apply with regard to loan relationships (*CTA 2009, s 333*), derivative contracts (*CTA 2009, s 609*) and intangible fixed assets (*CTA 2009, ss 859–862*).

See **58.19** PAYMENT OF TAX for exit charge payment plans under which a company may pay corporation tax under these provisions by instalments or defer payment.

Simon's Taxes. See **D4.131**.

Notification and arrangements to pay tax

[64.10] There are certain administrative requirements which must be fulfilled before the company ceases to be UK resident. These are found in *TMA 1970, ss109B–109F*, for corporation tax purposes.

A company must, before ceasing to be resident in the UK, give to HMRC:

(a) notice of its intention to cease to be UK resident, specifying the time when it intends so to cease;
(b) a statement of the amount of tax which it considers payable for periods beginning before that time; and
(c) particulars of the arrangements which it proposes to make to secure payment of that tax.

It must also make arrangements to secure the payment of that tax, and the arrangements must be approved by HMRC. Guidance notes regarding the giving of notice and the making of arrangements have been published by HMRC. (HMRC Statement of Practice, SP 2/90 as revised). See also HMRC manual guidance at CTM34195.

Any reference to tax payable includes the following (and tax under corresponding earlier legislation):

(i) tax under PAYE regulations;
(ii) income tax payable under *ITA 2007, ss 946, 962* (company payments which are not distributions, see **41.2** INCOME TAX IN RELATION TO A COMPANY and **8.2** BUILDING SOCIETIES);
(iii) income tax payable under *ITA 2007, ss 965–970* as amended by *CTA 2009, Sch 1 para 715* (entertainers and sportsmen);
(iv) any amount payable under *FA 2004, ss 61, 62* (see **20.3** CONSTRUCTION INDUSTRY SCHEME);
(v) any amount payable under *TMA 1970, s 77C* (territorial extension of charge to tax, see **64.13** below);
(vi) interest on tax within (i)–(v) (whether or not the tax is paid).

Any question as to the amount of tax payable is to be determined by the First-tier Tribunal, or the Upper Tribunal as applicable. If any information provided by the company does not fully and accurately disclose all the material facts and considerations, any resulting approval is void. [*TMA 1970, ss 109B–109F*].

A person who is, or who is deemed to be, involved in a failure to comply with the foregoing provisions is liable to a penalty not exceeding the amount of unpaid tax for periods beginning before the failure occurred.

Any tax not paid within six months of becoming payable can, within the three years following determination of the amount, be recovered from a person who is, or who was so in the year before residence ceased, a member of the same group or a controlling director. See **12.2** CAPITAL GAINS — GROUPS with regard to the definition of a group which applies also in the twelve-month period before residence ceases.

[*TMA 1970, ss 109B–109F*].

Simon's Taxes. See D4.131.

Banks, insurance companies and dealers in securities

[64.11] In contrast to other non-resident companies, banks, insurance companies and dealers in securities which are non-resident but carrying on business in the UK are not exempt on income from overseas securities, stocks and shares by reason of non-residence.

Certain income such as that deriving from foreign state securities, foreign dividends and interest on quoted Eurobonds, are included in computing the profits and losses of the UK trade of the non resident company (notwithstanding that for other non residents such income would be exempt). [*See the computation of profits of a permanent establishment per CTA 2009, ss 25–28*, and the application of the loan relationship provisions in such instances]. See also *Owen v Sassoon* (1950) 32 TC 101 in which funds deposited against default by a Lloyd's underwriter were held to be within the underwriters profits chargeable to tax.

See Tolley's Income Tax under Life Assurance Policies for special treatment of policies issued by non-UK resident companies outside the scope of UK tax.

Non-resident performers

[64.12] *ITA 2007, s 966* requires deduction of tax from certain payments and transfers to entertainers and sportsmen and women in relation to activities performed in the UK in a tax year for which the performer is non-UK resident.

That legislation also applies in some cases to payments made to a person other than the performer (typically to a company controlled by the performer). In those cases, the payments are generally treated as made instead to the performer. See Tolley's Income Tax under Non-Residents for full coverage.

Where a payment or transfer made to a company is treated as above as made to a performer, the company is treated for corporation tax purposes as if the payment or transfer had not been made to it.

[*CTA 2009, s 1309*].

United Kingdom

[64.13] The United Kingdom for tax purposes comprises England, Scotland, Wales and Northern Ireland. The Channel Islands (Jersey, Guernsey, Alderney, Sark, Herm and Jethou) and the Isle of Man are not included. Great Britain comprises England, Scotland and Wales only.

Territorial extension of tax area

The territorial sea of the UK is regarded as part of the UK for tax purposes. Earnings, profits and gains from exploration or exploitation activities in a designated area (under *Continental Shelf Act 1964, s 1(7)*) (and unlisted shares deriving most of their value from assets used for such activities) are treated as arising in the UK. Transfers of exploration or exploitation rights by a company not resident in the UK to a company which is so resident or which is resident in the same territory, are brought within the provisions relating to intra-group transfers. See **12** CAPITAL GAINS — GROUPS.

A resident licence-holder under *Petroleum (Production) Act 1934* may be held accountable for the liability of a non-resident and may be required by the inspector to provide information concerning transactions with other persons and emoluments or other payments made. [*TMA 1970, Pt 7A; CTA 2009, s 1313; TCGA 1992, s 276*].

The case *Clark v Oceanic Contractors Incorporated* (1982) 56 TC 183, HL, considers the liability of a non-resident company engaged in exploration and exploitation activities to apply PAYE to its employees subject to tax on employment income,

For the liability to tax on profits or gains of non-resident lessors of mobile drilling rigs, vessels or equipment used in connection with exploration or exploitation activities, see HMRC Statement of Practice, SP 6/84.

Key points on residence

[64.14] Points to consider are as follows.

- Most residence issues arise for UK tax purposes where a company is incorporated outside the UK and is intended to be resident outside the UK for tax purposes. The following bullet points may be used as an initial checklist to establish and maintain the non-UK residence of such a company.
  (a) It is generally preferable for the board of directors to exercise central management and control of the company — i.e. taking its strategic and policy decisions.
  (b) The board should comprise appropriately senior and competent individuals with relevant experience. Corporate directors should be avoided.
  (c) UK resident individuals should not be directors of the company unless it is necessary. Such individuals should not comprise a majority of the board, be able to form a quorum for a board meeting or pass a resolution.

(d) Where the board is influenced by others in the UK, the level of influence must be kept in check to avoid assertions that the board's powers are being usurped by persons in the UK.
(e) A board meeting should be held at least once each calendar quarter. Board meetings should be held in person outside the UK. Participation in board meetings by telephone and written resolutions of the board should be avoided, particularly if one or more of the directors are resident or present in the UK.
(f) Where possible, focus on a particular jurisdiction as the place of residence of the company rather than having board meetings in a variety of different jurisdictions. That jurisdiction should have appropriate infrastructure (i.e. an office and personnel) for the company and the company books should be kept there.
(g) The board should avoid delegating its strategic powers to persons who are based or tax resident in the UK.
(h) Keep good written records of board proceedings, including notes of where the meetings are held and minutes which reflect discussions at the meetings.
(i) Documents relating to key decisions should be executed outside the UK and correspondence to which the company is a party should clearly show the company's address outside the UK. Care should be taken to ensure that informal correspondence does not imply that persons in the UK have the power to make decisions on behalf of the company.

- Where it appears that a company incorporated outside the UK may be resident in the UK for UK tax purposes, the terms of any applicable double tax treaty should be reviewed. This may rule out UK residence and/or dual residence.

- Bear in mind that treaty residence tests may focus on the test of effective management; this concept is broader and focuses more on day-to-day management of the business than on strategic and policy decisions of the business.

- As well as the compliance burden suffered by dual resident companies, such companies are unable to claim the benefit of certain UK tax reliefs (for example, group relief and intra-group 'no gain/no loss' transfers for the purposes of corporation tax on chargeable gains).

- Although a company may not be tax resident in the UK, it may still be carrying on a business in the UK through a permanent establishment. Where this is the case, an analysis of the UK business should be carried out to establish whether it constitutes a trade, which will bring the company within the charge to corporation tax to the extent that profits are attributable to the UK trade.

- Where a non-UK resident company is trading in the UK through a UK permanent establishment, consider whether it would be prudent to establish a UK subsidiary to ring fence UK tax liabilities, perhaps further safeguard the non-UK residence of the company and avoid complicated attribution of profits calculations.

65

Returns

Simon's Taxes. See **D1.1301–D1.1308**.

Introduction to returns

[65.1] This chapter details the provisions with regard to returns to be made by a company. It provides an outline of the procedures for submission and amendment of such returns, an overview of the enquiry process, and the position when no return is delivered.

Penalties with regard to matters such as late submission of returns, or submission of incorrect returns are considered in brief, the full details in this regard can be found at 59 PENALTIES.

Returns of profits etc.

[65.2] The company tax return must include a self-assessment by the company of its corporation tax liability on the basis of the information contained in the return, and taking account of reliefs or allowances claimed in the return. See 65.4 *et seq.* below.

Notification of coming within charge to corporation tax

A company (but not an unincorporated association or partnership) must give notice to HMRC of when its first accounting period begins (e.g. when the company starts its business) and of when any subsequent accounting period begins that does not follow on immediately from the end of a previous accounting period (e.g. when the company restarts its business after a period of dormancy). The notice stating when the accounting period began must be given to any HMRC officer within three months after the beginning of the accounting period in question. It must be in writing and contain other information as prescribed by regulation.

The information required by *SI 2004 No 2502* includes the name, address of the registered office and registered number of the company, the nature and principal place of business, the accounting date, details of the directors, details of any former business taken over, details of the parent company if part of a group, and the date on which there was an obligation (if any) to operate PAYE.

[*FA 2004, s 55; SI 2004 No 2502*].

With effect from 6 April 2020, notice need not be given if the company reasonably expects that all of its income for the period on which it is chargeable to tax will consist of payments on which income tax is deducted at source, the company will have no chargeable gains for the period and (as a result of deducting the income tax from any corporation tax liability), the corporation tax payable for the period will be nil. If this exception ceases to apply, notice under the above provisions must be given within three months after the date of it so ceasing. If an accounting period to which the exception applies is immediately followed by another accounting period, the above rules apply to the second period as if it did not immediately follow a previous accounting period (so that notice must be given to HMRC where the conditions are met). [*FA 2004, s 55A; FA 2019, Sch 5 paras 7, 35; FA 2020, Sch 6 paras 7, 10*].

Notification of chargeability

[65.3] A company chargeable to corporation tax which has not already made a company tax return for an accounting period, and has not received a notice requiring such a return (see **65.4** below), must give notice of its chargeability to HMRC within twelve months from the end of the period. With effect from 6 April 2020, notice need not be given if all of the company's income for the period on which it is chargeable to tax consists of payments on which income tax is deducted at source, the company has no chargeable gains for the period and (after deducting the income tax) the corporation tax payable for the period is nil. [*FA 1998, Sch 18 para 2; FA 2019, Sch 5 paras 6, 35; FA 2020, Sch 6 paras 6, 10*].

See **59.2** PENALTIES for the penalties charged for failure to notify chargeability in accordance with the above provisions.

Simon's Taxes. See **D1.1301.**

Self-assessment returns

[65.4] If so required by notice given by an HMRC officer (Form CT603), a company must make a 'company tax return' (CT600) of such information, relevant to its corporation tax liabilities, as is reasonably required under the notice. Supporting accounts, statements and reports may similarly be required. [*FA 1998, Sch 18 para 3*]. Generally, all corporation tax returns must be filed online, see below.

See **36.4** HMRC—ADMINISTRATION for the exercise of functions of an HMRC officer by automated process.

For HMRC guidance on corporation tax self-assessment (CTSA), see their Company Taxation Manual at CTM90000 onwards.

Voluntary returns

Where a company makes a return for a period without having been given a notice to do so (i.e. the return is made voluntarily), then for all tax purposes the return is treated as made pursuant to such a notice issued on the date the return was made (and therefore as a return to which the self-assessment provisions apply), provided that HMRC decide to treat it in that way. This rule in effect overturns the decision in *Patel v HMRC* FTT, [2018] SFTD 1000, where it was held that a voluntary return was not a return and therefore HMRC could not open an enquiry into it. The rule applies with retrospective effect to any voluntary return, whenever made, but it does not apply to a return if, before 29 October 2018, the company made an appeal or a claim for judicial review and one of the grounds for the appeal or claim was that the voluntary return was not a return because no notice to make a return was given. [*FA 1998, Sch 18 para 20A; FA 2019, s 87(2)–(4)*].

Simon's Taxes. See **D1.1308.**

Filing online

Self-assessment corporation tax returns must be filed online in a format approved by HMRC, which is iXBRL. Supporting accounts and other documents must also be filed online as attachments. If the attachments are not sent, the filing obligation is not satisfied. Supplementary pages CT600A–CT600K may also be required.

These must be completed either on the HMRC downloadable online templates or can be company prepared returns attached to the HMRC online filing software CT600 return form.

The online filing requirement does not apply to:

(a) amendments of such returns;
(b) returns required by a company being wound up, in administrative receivership or having its affairs managed by an administrator. Note this exemption does not apply to companies moving towards informal striking off or during a solvent Members' Voluntary Liquidation; see HMRC guidance on this particular situation (www.gov.uk/government/publications/corporation-tax-mandatory-online-filing-and-the-end-of-a-companys-life);

(c) returns required by a company which: has a liquidator appointed for the purposes of a creditors' voluntary winding up; has a liquidator provisionally appointed by a court; has a supervisor carrying out functions in relation to a company voluntary arrangement; has a compromise or arrangement in effect; or, is a limited liability partnership and is being wound up.

[*SI 2003 No 282, Reg 3(2A), (10), (10A)*].

The return

Most company tax returns will be by companies resident in the UK throughout the return period, and required to prepare accounts under *Companies Act 2006 or 1985* (or NI equivalent) for a period consisting of, or including, the return period, and in such cases the accounts required are only those it is required to prepare under the *Companies Acts*, and any attachments required under the *Companies Acts* must also accompany the company tax return.

In *Slater Ltd v Beacontree General Commrs* (2001) 74 TC 471 (and also the subsequent case of *Slater Ltd v CIR* [2002] EWHC 2676 (Ch), [2004] STC 1342, [2002] All ER (D) 275 (Nov)), it was, however, held that that restriction on the accounts which may be required did not restrict the information which may be required in support of those accounts. In the case of a non-resident company trading through a UK permanent establishment (or branch or agency), the accounts required are (English language) trading and profit and loss accounts of both the company and the UK permanent establishment together with the balance sheet of the company and (if prepared) of the UK permanent establishment. Other companies are required to deliver the accounts they are required to prepare by law or under their constitution. (HMRC Company Taxation Manual, CTM93180).

HMRC point out in Working Together issue 27 – June 2007 that it is the full accounts which must accompany the CTSA return, not abbreviated accounts.

For most companies, accounts forming part of their online tax return (i.e. returns filed on or after 1 April 2011) must be delivered to HMRC in iXBRL format. HMRC have published a list setting out the format requirements for the accounts of particular types of companies, including those organisations which may instead submit the required information in PDF format. This can be found at www.gov.uk/government/publications/company-tax-returns-format-for-accounts-forming-part-of-an-online-return.

HMRC had adopted the practice that such accounts should be signed. However, In *Codu Computer Ltd v HMRC* (TC01055) [2011] UKFTT 186 (TC), the First-tier Tribunal found that there was no legal justification for HMRC requiring that accounts were required to be submitted in signed format.

In *Goodtime Print & Design Ltd v HMRC*, [2012] UKFTT 609 (TC), TC02286, the First-tier Tribunal upheld HMRC's view that a company was required to submit a directors' report with the accounts when submitting its return, and upheld penalties imposed on a company which had failed to do this.

Forms CT603 are usually issued to all active companies between three and seven weeks after the end of the period specified in them, which is usually a period thought to be an accounting period of the company. In a continuing case this will be based on the company's history. In the case of a new, or newly active, company, it will be based on information provided by the company in Form CT41G (new company details), which is issued to all such companies. If the company does not reply to such enquiries, it is assumed that the first accounting period runs for twelve months from the date of incorporation (see **65.2** above on the duty to give notice on coming within charge to corporation tax). (Revenue Guide to Self-Assessment, paras 2.2, 2.3.1).

As regards dormant companies, Forms CT204 are sent at intervals of not more than five years to check whether the company has traded or carried on any other activity, received any income or disposed of any assets in the review period, and to enquire about its future intentions. (Revenue Guide to Self-Assessment, para 2.4). See below as regards discretionary treatment as dormant of certain members' clubs etc.

The return must include a declaration to the effect that, to the best of the knowledge of the person making it, it is correct and complete, and must be delivered (together with all the supplementary information, etc. required) by the 'filing date', i.e. the later of:

(a) twelve months after the end of the period to which it relates;
(b) twelve months after the end of the period of account in which falls the last day of the accounting period to which it relates (except that periods of account in excess of 18 months are treated as ending after 18 months for this purpose, thus the deadline is 30 months from the beginning of that period); and
(c) three months after service of the notice requiring the return,

(and see HMRC Company Taxation Manual, CTM93040 for detailed application of these dates).

[*FA 1998, Sch 18 paras 3, 4, 11, 13, 14*].

Before making their returns, companies may ask their Tax Office (on Form CG34) to check their valuations used for capital gains purposes in completing their returns. (HMRC Share Valuation Manual, SVM24041).

As regards (c) above, the date of service of the notice is the fourth working day after the date of posting unless the company proves otherwise. (HMRC Company Taxation Manual, CTM93040, CTM93080). HMRC usually issue an acknowledgement of receipt of every company tax return (HMRC Company Taxation Manual, CTM93270).

The notice requiring the return specifies the period to which it relates. A return is required for any accounting period which ends during or at the end of that period (separate returns being required if there is more than one such accounting period). If no accounting period ends during or at the end of the specified period, but there is an accounting period which commences during that period, then a return is required for the part of the specified period which falls before the start of that accounting period. If the company was outside the corporation tax charge throughout the specified period a return is required for the whole of the period. If none of the above applies, no return is required in response to the notice. [*FA 1998, Sch 18 para 5*].

In the absence of a return, HMRC have power to determine the corporation tax liability. [*FA 1998, s 117, Sch 18 paras 36–40*].

Where the company carries on a trade, profession or business in partnership, the return must include its share of any income, loss, consideration, tax, credit or charge stated in the partnership return under *TMA 1970, s 12AB* for any period including, or including any part of, the company tax return period. [*FA 1998, Sch 18 para 12*].

See **32.6** EUROPEAN UNION LEGISLATION regarding the application of the corporation tax provisions where a company ceases to be UK-resident in the course of the formation of an SE or where an SE becomes non-UK resident.

Simon's Taxes. See **D1.1308.**

Estimates

[65.5] Where, despite the company's best efforts, a figure cannot be finalised by the filing date, the company may make its best estimate of the figure, tell HMRC that the figure is estimated and say when a final figure is expected. Provided that the company has taken all reasonable steps, a return so completed is not incomplete. If the company subsequently becomes aware that the estimate is no longer a 'best estimate', or that it can be replaced by an accurate figure, this information should be sent to HMRC without unreasonable delay. If estimates are submitted which prove not to be reasonable, the return is not thereby rendered incomplete, although penalties may arise if information in the return was incorrect as a result of careless or deliberate behaviour. (HMRC Company Taxation Manual, CTM93280).

Failure to make return

[65.6] See 59.3 PENALTIES for the penalties charged where a company fails to deliver a return to HMRC by the filing date.

Self-assessment and payment of tax

[65.7] The company tax return must include a self-assessment by the company of its corporation tax liability on the basis of the information contained in the return, and taking account of reliefs or allowances claimed in the return. For this purpose a return is regarded as a return for an accounting period if the period is so treated in the return and is not longer than twelve months, whether or not it is in fact an accounting period. The self-assessment is required even if no tax is payable or a repayment due.

The calculation proceeds in five steps.

- *Step 1* The corporation tax chargeable on the company's profits (including its share(s) of any partnership profits) is calculated by applying the applicable rate or rates of corporation tax to those profits for that period (apart from the restitution interest rate).
- *Step 2* Effect is given to any available set-offs or reliefs under:
  - (i) *CTA 2010, Pt 7* (COMMUNITY INVESTMENT TAX RELIEF (**17**));
  - (ii) any double tax relief under *TIOPA 2010, ss 2 and 6, or s 18(1)(b)(2)* (double taxation relief, see **31.2, 31.3** DOUBLE TAX RELIEF); or

(iii) *SI 1999 No 358* (surplus ACT under the shadow ACT system, see **29.33** DISTRIBUTIONS).

- *Step 3* Add any amounts assessable or chargeable as if they were corporation tax under: *CTA 2010, s 455 or s 464A* (loans to and benefits conferred on close company participators — see **16.12** CLOSE COMPANIES); *CTA 2010, s 269DA* (bank surcharge — see **7.3** BANKS); *CTA 2010, s 330(1)* in respect of ring fence trades; *TIOPA 2010, s 371BC(1)* step 5 (controlled foreign companies); or *FA 2011, Sch 19* (bank levy).
- *Step 4* Deduct any amounts to be set off against the overall corporation tax liability under: *CTA 2010, ss 967, 968* (income tax borne by deduction, see **41.9** INCOME TAX IN RELATION TO A COMPANY, **64.5** RESIDENCE), deducting such amounts from the bank levy addition at Step 3 in the last instance.
- *Step 5* Calculate any corporation tax due on restitution interest and add that to the amounts from Steps 1 to 4 above to give the total corporation tax liability for the period. A special regime applies to companies awarded restitution interest as a result of a judgment or an agreement which became final on or after 21 October 2015. See further below, and **1.7** INTRODUCTION: CHARGE TO TAX, RATES AND PROFIT COMPUTATIONS. [*CTA 2010, ss 357YA–357YW*].

[*FA 1998, Sch 18 paras 7, 8*].

Subject to the instalment provisions applicable to 'large' companies (see below and **58.3** PAYMENT OF TAX), corporation tax is due and payable on the day following the expiry of nine months from the end of the accounting period, on the basis of the amount computed (as above) in the company tax return for the period. Any excess over the tax payable of 'relevant amounts' stated in the company tax return is repaid.

'*Relevant amounts*' are corporation tax paid and not repaid, corporation tax refunds surrendered to the company intra-group (see **58.21** GROUP RELIEF), income tax as described in *Step 4* above (so far as not set off under that calculation) and CONSTRUCTION INDUSTRY SCHEME (**20**) deductions. [*TMA 1970, s 59D*].

A company may claim repayment of corporation tax paid for an accounting period where the company's circumstances change so that it has grounds for believing that the amount paid exceeds its probable (although not yet finally established) liability. The claim must state the amount the company considers has been overpaid and the grounds for believing the payment to have become excessive. No claim may be made before the 'material date' in relation to the tax (see **44.2** INTEREST ON OVERPAID TAX). If the tax is the subject of an outstanding appeal, the company may apply to the tribunal for a determination of the amount to be repaid (and the application may be combined with a postponement application under *TMA 1970, s 55*, see **58.13** PAYMENT OF TAX).

If the company tax return has not been made, CONSTRUCTION INDUSTRY SCHEME (**20**) deductions are ignored for these purposes. [*TMA 1970, s 59DA*]. 'Large' companies to which instalment payments apply are precluded from making a claim under *section 59DA* where a claim for repayment of instalment payments is made (see **58.3** PAYMENT OF TAX). [*SI 1998 No 3175, Reg 6(8)*].

See generally 44.2 INTEREST ON OVERPAID TAX, 43.2 INTEREST ON OVERDUE TAX.

The company tax return requires the company to state whether it is liable to make instalment payments on account of its corporation tax liabilities (see 58.3 PAYMENT OF TAX). Although HMRC will at some stage check the position, initial payment applications, interest calculations, etc. will be based on the company's statement of its position. (HMRC Company Taxation Manual, CTM92550, CTM92690).

Restitution interest

As noted above, special rules apply to companies awarded restitution interest as a result of a mistake in law or following unlawful collection of tax by HMRC, as a result of a judgment or an agreement which became final on or after 21 October 2015. Such interest is chargeable to corporation tax at a special rate of 45%, generally deducted at source by HMRC for interest paid on or after 26 October 2015 (which is then set off against the company's liability to tax on restitution interest when it is formally assessed). See further 1.6 INTRODUCTION: CHARGE TO TAX, RATES AND PROFITS. [*CTA 2010, ss 357YA–357YW*].

Losses, etc.

It should be noted that losses and other negative amounts also have to be included in the return and become final in the same way as the assessment itself, and are similarly subject to enquiry, although this would not apply to, for example, a loss in a self-assessment return brought forward from a pre-self-assessment period. The same figure must be used for a negative amount which becomes final in any other return affected by it. (HMRC Company Taxation Manual, CTM95440, CTM95430). The use of the figure in another return does not give HMRC an opportunity to enquire into the figure by means of an enquiry into that return (although this does not prevent an enquiry into the use of the negative amount in that return). (HMRC Company Taxation Manual, CTM04150).

Where the loss relief restriction rules at *CTA 2010, Pt 7A* apply to a building society, and losses are designated as unrestricted, then they must be identified in a company tax return for the period a deduction is claimed, either in the original return or an amended return. A designation can be amended or withdrawn by an amended return. Where the loss allowance under these provisions for such societies is allocated to other group companies then a statement of allocation must be submitted at or before the time when a company submits a tax return, or amends a tax return, making a designation. (*FA 1998, Sch 18 paras 83Y–83YC*).

Amendments to returns

[65.8] The company may, by notice to HMRC within twelve months of the filing date (see above), amend its own return. A return made for the wrong period must be amended within twelve months of what would have been the final date for delivery of a return for the period if it had been an accounting period.

HMRC may, by notice to the company, amend the return to correct obvious errors or mistakes (including arithmetical errors and errors of principle, but *not* where any judgment as to the accuracy of figures in the return is involved) up to nine months after the date of delivery of the return (or after the date of the amendment if the correction relates to a company amendment).

HMRC may also amend a return for anything else they have reason to believe is incorrect, in the light of information held by them. An HMRC correction is, however, of no effect if the company amends the return so as to reject the correction or, if the time limit for an amendment has passed, gives written notice rejecting it to the officer of HMRC by whom the notice of correction was issued within three months of the date of issue.

[*FA 1998, Sch 18 paras 15(1)(4), 16*].

Amendments to returns must be in such form, and accompanied by such information, etc., as HMRC may require. [*FA 1998, Sch 18 para 15(2)(3)*]. No official form is prescribed for this purpose, and amendments may be made using an unofficial form or by correspondence. (HMRC Company Taxation Manual, CTM93300).

With regard to a restriction in respect of relief from a charge to tax under *CTA 2010, ss 455, 464A* (close companies, loans to and benefits conferred on participators) if a person who has made a return becomes aware that, after making it, it has become incorrect because of the operation of *s 464C(1) or (3)*, then the person must give notice to an officer of HMRC specifying how the return needs to be amended. Such notice must be given within three months beginning with the day on which the person became aware that anything in the return had become incorrect because of the operation of that section.

[*CTA 2010, s 464D*].

See **30.16** DIVERTED PROFITS TAX for circumstances in which a return may be amended during the review period following the issue of a charging notice.

Simon's Taxes. See **D1.1308**.

Returns of income tax deducted by a company

[65.9] Under *ITA 2007, Pt 15 Ch 15, ss 945–962*, the company must make returns of payments made under deduction of income tax for payments specified under *ITA 2007, s 946* (such as yearly interest, patent rights and annuities). In practice this requirement is satisfied by the completion of forms CT61.

Returns must be made by reference to 'return periods'. A '*return period*' ends on 31 March, 30 June, 30 September and 31 December and at the end of a company's accounting period.

[*ITA 2007, Pt 15 Chs 15, 16, 17*].

For details, see **41.8** INCOME TAX IN RELATION TO A COMPANY.

Simon's Taxes. See **D5.510**.

Returns of distributions

[65.10] The recipient of a distribution other than one within **29.2**(c) DISTRIBUTIONS, is entitled to ask the distributing company for a written statement showing the amount or value of the distribution.

The right to this statement is distinct from the duty on the distributing company to provide a tax certificate to the recipient of the distribution.

[*CTA 2010, ss 1100, 1104*].

Where a company makes a distribution other than one to which the above provisions apply it must make a return to HMRC: (a) within 14 days of the end of the accounting period in which the distribution is made; or (b) if the distribution is not made in any accounting period, within 14 days of when it is made. The return must show particulars of the transaction, the name and address of the person(s) receiving the distribution and the amount or value received by each.

This is done on forms CT61.

[*CTA 2010, ss 1101–1103*].

Simon's Taxes. See **D5.505**.

Returns of stock dividends issued

[65.11] Where a company issues stock dividends (see **29.15**(g) DISTRIBUTIONS), it must make a return to the inspector within 30 days of the end of the return period as specified in **65.9** above. The return must show the first date on which the company was required to issue the shares, particulars of terms of issue and the cash equivalent of the share capital in accordance with *ITTOIA 2005, s 412*. See Tolley's Income Tax under Savings and Investment Income.

[*CTA 2010, ss 1052, 1053*].

Simon's Taxes. See **D5.506**.

Other returns

[65.12] For returns by employers and partnerships, see Tolley's Income Tax under Returns. For returns by companies purchasing own shares, see **61.4** PURCHASE BY A COMPANY OF ITS OWN SHARES. For returns in respect of exempt distributions and chargeable payments in connection with a demerger (*CTA 2010, ss 1095, 1096*), see **29.28** DISTRIBUTIONS.

Record keeping

[65.13] A company which may be required to deliver a company tax return (see **65.4** above) for any period must preserve for at least six years after the end of the return period the records required to enable it to make a complete and correct return for the period. HMRC may specify, in writing, an earlier date.

This includes records and 'supporting documents' (e.g. accounts, books, deeds, contracts, vouchers and receipts) of all receipts and expenses, and the matters in respect of which they arise, and, in the case of a trade involving dealing in goods, of all trade sales and purchases. The obligation to keep records permits keeping them in any form or keeping the information in them in any form, subject to any exceptions specified by HMRC in writing. HMRC is given power to amend these provisions by statutory order, and different provisions may be made for different cases.

If the company is required by notice to deliver a return for the period, the records must be preserved until the later of the end of the six years and either:

(a) the date on which any enquiry into the return is completed (see **65.8** above); or
(b) if there is no enquiry, the date on which HMRC no longer have power to enquire into the return (see **65.14** below).

If the notice requiring the return is given after the expiry of the six years, the records which must be preserved are any which the company still has in its possession at the time the notice is given.

The duty to preserve records may generally be satisfied by the preservation of the information contained in them (e.g. in electronic form), and a copy of any document forming part of the records is admissible in evidence before the Commissioners to the same extent as the records themselves. This does not, however, apply to vouchers, certificates etc. which show distributions or deductions at source of UK or foreign tax, e.g. dividend vouchers, interest vouchers (including those issued by banks and building societies), which must be preserved in their original form.

The maximum penalty for failure to preserve records as above is £3,000 in relation to any one accounting period. No penalty is incurred where the records not preserved are such as might have been needed only for the purposes of claims, elections or notices not included in the return, or where they are vouchers, certificates, etc. showing distributions or deductions at source (e.g. dividend vouchers and interest certificates) and HMRC are satisfied that other documentary evidence supplied to them proves any facts they reasonably require to be proved and which the voucher, etc. would have proved. HMRC will seek such penalties only in the more serious cases where, for example, records have been destroyed deliberately to obstruct an enquiry or there has been a history of serious record-keeping failures (see HMRC Enquiry Manual EM4650).

[*FA 1998, Sch 18 paras 21–23*].

See also HMRC Compliance Handbook CH11000, CH13000, CH14000 *et seq*.

Simon's Taxes. See **D1.1301.**

Enquiries into returns

[65.14] HMRC may begin an enquiry into a return within twelve months after the date the return was filed with HMRC unless the return was filed late (see below). Notice of intention to open an enquiry must first be given. In *Dock and*

Let Ltd v HMRC [2014] UKFTT 943 (TC) the tribunal upheld HMRC's contention that the word 'from' excluded the day when the return was filed, so that a notice of enquiry which HMRC had delivered exactly 12 months after the submission of the return was within the time limit.

However, where the company is a member of a group (other than a small group), the enquiry window continues to run until twelve months from the filing date. A group is defined as 'a parent undertaking and its subsidiary undertakings' and a group broadly qualifies as 'small' for a year if two or more of the qualifying conditions are met in that year and the preceding financial year. The qualifying conditions are met by a group in a year in which it satisfies two or more of the following requirements (per *Companies Act 2006, s 383* as amended by *SI 2008 No 393*):

1 Aggregate turnover	Not more than £6.5 million net (or £7.8 million gross)
2 Aggregate balance sheet total	Not more than £3.26 million net (or £3.9 million gross)
3 Aggregate number of employees	Not more than 50

'Net' means after any set-offs and other adjustments made to eliminate group transactions and 'gross' means without those set-offs and other adjustments. A company may satisfy any relevant requirement on the basis of either the net or the gross figure.

If the return is delivered late (after the filing date), HMRC may enquire into the return if they give notice of their intention to do so by the quarter day (31 January, 30 April, 31 July or 31 October) next following the first anniversary of the day on which the return was delivered. HMRC consider that notice is 'given' when the notice is issued, which, in the case of notice by post, means the date of posting (see HMRC Enquiry Manual, EM1506, EM1510, EM1525), but in a Special Commissioner's decision on the similar provisions for individual self-assessment, it was held that service of the notice is treated as effected at the time at which the letter would be delivered in the ordinary course of post, i.e. on the second working day after posting for first class mail or on the fourth working day after posting for second class mail (*Wing Hung Lai v Bale* [1999] STC (SCD) 238). It was held in the case of *R (oao Spring Salmon and Seafood Ltd) v CIR* [2004] STC 444, Ct of Sess, that a notice of enquiry made under *FA 1998, Sch 18 para 24* was not required to be made in writing.

An enquiry following an amendment to a return must be notified by the quarter day next following the first anniversary of the making of the amendment, and if it is given at a time when notice of an enquiry could no longer have been given had the return not been amended, is limited to matters to which the amendment relates or which are affected by it. (In practice, except where an amendment relates to or affects matters fundamental to the whole return, HMRC enquiries will normally be limited to the area of the return that was amended, regardless of whether a full enquiry would still be in time (see HMRC Enquiry Manual, EM1520)).

Only one notice of enquiry may be given in respect of a return, except one given in consequence of an amendment (or further amendment(s)) by the company of the return.

HMRC does not have to justify an enquiry, by stating dissatisfaction with the return or identifying particular aspects giving cause for concern, and will not give reasons (although they may identify particular areas on which the enquiry will focus). Enquiries will range from questioning simple errors not identified during initial processing of the return through to full in-depth reviews of companies' affairs, including the underlying records. Business documents and records will commonly be requested. Although random selection will play a part, most enquiry cases will continue to be selected on the basis of a judgment, informed by all the information in HMRC's possession, of the risk of tax loss. (HMRC Enquiry Manual, EM1503, EM1550–EM1581).

In *Tinkler v HMRC* CA, [2019] STC 1685, a copy of an income tax enquiry notice purportedly sent to the taxpayer's agent was held not to be a valid notice of enquiry in itself. (HMRC sent the original of the notice to the taxpayer's former address, so that it was never received by the taxpayer.)

An appeal against a closure notice was upheld on the grounds that no valid notice of enquiry had been given in *Credit Suisse Securities (Europe) Ltd v HMRC* FTT, [2020] UKFTT 86 (TC); 2020 SWTI 403.

Large companies

Where it is practical to do so, HMRC will aim to open all enquiries into a group's returns by the 'group anniversary target'. The '*group anniversary target*' is twelve months after the last company files its return. However, while HMRC say that enquiries will be opened as early as possible, if it is not possible to open an enquiry within the group anniversary target, they will continue to open them up to the statutory deadline (twelve months after the filing date). There will be liaison through customer relationship managers and customer managers. Where there is no agreement to meet the group anniversary target, the statutory deadline will apply. See HMRC Enquiry Manual, EIM1514, 1515.

Conduct of enquiry

HMRC have published a series of factsheets about their investigation and compliance check processes. The following factsheets are appropriate for companies:

COP 8	HMRC fraud investigation service (February 2018).
COP 9 (2014)	HMRC investigations where we suspect tax fraud (June 2014).
CC/FS1a	General information about compliance checks (October 2020).
CC/FS1b	General information about checks by Campaigns and Projects (November 2019).
CC/FS1c	General information about compliance checks into large businesses (April 2020).

CC/FS2	Compliance checks — checking a customer's tax position (February 2020).
CC/FS3	Compliance checks — visits by agreement or with advance notice (December 2017).
CC/FS4	Compliance checks — unannounced visits for inspections (December 2017).
CC/FS5	Compliance checks — unannounced visits for inspections approved by the tribunal (January 2020).
CC/FS7a	Compliance checks series — penalties for inaccuracies in returns or documents (April 2020).
CC/FS7b	Compliance checks series — penalties for not telling us about an under-assessment (December 2017).
CC/FS7c	Compliance checks — penalties for careless inaccuracies relating to tax avoidance (October 2019)
CC/FS9	Compliance checks — Human Rights Act and penalties (April 2018).
CC/FS10	Compliance checks — suspending penalties for careless inaccuracies in returns or documents (February 2020).
CC/FS11	Compliance checks — penalties for failure to notify (April 2020).
CC/FS13	Compliance checks — publishing details of deliberate defaulters (April 2020).
CC/FS14	Compliance checks — managing serious defaulters (February 2020).
CC/FS15	Compliance checks — self assessment and old penalty rules (May 2019).
CC/FS17	Compliance checks — higher penalties for income tax and CGT involving offshore matters (February 2020).
CC/FS17a	Compliance checks — penalties for enablers of offshore tax evation or non-compliance (March 2020).
CC/FS18a	Compliance checks — late filing penalties (February 2020)
CC/FS21	Compliance checks — alternative dispute resolution (March 2021)
CC/FS22	Compliance checks — sending electronic records to HMRC (February 2020)
CC/FS23	Compliance checks — third party information notices (April 2017)
CC/FS24	Tax avoidance schemes — accelerated payments (March 2017)
CC/FS25a	Tax avoidance schemes — follower notices (May 2018)
CC/FS28	Tax avoidance schemes — accelerated payments for corporation tax and group relief (June 2017)
CC/FS30a	Tax avoidance schemes — penalties for follower notices (May 2020)
CC/FS34a	Compliance checks — information about the general anti-abuse rule (July 2020)
CC/FS35	Compliance checks — general anti-abuse rule and pooling notices (September 2020)

CC/FS36	Compliance checks — provisional counteraction notices given under the GAAR (March 2018)
CC/FS37	Compliance checks — general anti-abuse rule and notices of binding (June 2021)
CC/FS38a	Compliance checks — serial tax avoidance regime — general information (September 2018)

When the time limit for opening an enquiry into a return has passed, HMRC can still ask questions about the return, but further action can only be taken in cases of deliberate or careless errors or failure to disclose all relevant information (see **6.3** ASSESSMENTS). (HMRC Enquiry Manual, EM1053, EM3250 *et seq.*).

Subject to the limitation referred to above in the case of enquiries into amendments to returns, an enquiry extends to anything contained (or required to be contained) in the return, including any claim or election and any amount that affects or may affect the tax liability of another accounting period or another company.

If it appears to HMRC that the return is, or may be, for the wrong period, or has become for the wrong period as a result of a direction from HMRC under *CTA 2009, s 11* (see **2.5** ACCOUNTING PERIODS), the enquiry may extend to the period for which the return should have been made. A return is for this purpose made for the wrong period if either it is made for a period treated as, but not in fact, an accounting period, or it is made on the basis that there is no accounting period ending in or at the end of the period specified in the notice requiring the return but there is in fact such an accounting period. The time limits for notice of enquiry into a return for the wrong period are by reference to the date by which the return would have been required to be delivered had the period for which the return was made not been the wrong period.

An enquiry may also extend to consideration of whether to give a company, which is a medium-sized enterprise, a transfer pricing notice under *ITIOPA 2010, s168(1)* (see **72.6** TRANSFER PRICING). An enquiry may also extend to a notice under *TIOPA 2010, ss 81, 82* in respect of schemes and arrangements designed to increase double taxation relief or *TCGA 1992, s 184G* or *s 184H* (avoidance utilising losses — see **11.4** CAPITAL GAINS).

These provisions are amended to provide for extended time limits in the cases of non-annual accounting of general insurance business and of insurance companies and friendly societies with non-annual actuarial investigations.

[*FA 1998, Sch 18; paras 24–26, 85–87*].

Where an enquiry remains open after expiry of the period within which a notice of enquiry may be issued solely because of an unagreed valuation for the purpose of computing chargeable gains of a company or other body within the charge to corporation tax, HMRC will not raise further enquiries into unrelated matters unless, had the enquiry already been completed, a discovery could have been made (see **6.3** ASSESSMENTS). This does not inhibit HMRC from enquiring into matters relating to the valuation which were not raised on first reference. (HMRC Statement of Practice, SP 1/02).

Simon's Taxes. See A6.4.

Amendments during enquiry

[65.15] If during the course of an enquiry into a particular matter HMRC form the opinion that the company's self-assessed tax is insufficient and that unless the assessment is immediately amended there is likely to be a loss of tax, they may by notice to the company amend its self-assessment to make good the deficiency so far as it relates to that matter. An appeal in writing may be made against such an amendment within 30 days of the notice, but will not be heard and determined before completion of the enquiry (although application for postponement may be made under *TMA 1970, s 55*, see **58.13** PAYMENT OF TAX).

If the enquiry is limited to matters arising from an earlier amendment by the company of its self-assessment (as above), the notice may only apply to a deficiency attributable to that amendment. In practice, HMRC normally ask the company to make an additional payment on account to cover any deficiency identified during an enquiry, and only make an amendment as above where the company refuses to make such a payment and they believe that tax is at risk, e.g. where the company might dispose of its assets or go into liquidation (see HMRC Enquiry Manual, EM1936, EM1951).

If a company amends its return during an enquiry, the amendment does not restrict the scope of the enquiry, but may be taken into account in the enquiry. So far as the amendment affects the self-assessed tax, or any amount that affects or may affect the tax payable for another accounting period or by another company, it does not take effect while the enquiry is in progress in relation to any matter affected by the amendment (without prejudice to any claim for repayment of tax under *TMA 1970, s 59DA*, see **65.7** above). For this purpose, an enquiry into a particular matter is in progress until a partial closure notice is issued in relation to it, or if no such notice is issued, when a final closure notice is issued.

When the enquiry into the matter in question is completed, if the conclusions in the partial or final closure notice state that the amendment to the return was not taken into account or that no amendment to the return is required, the company's amendment takes effect on the day the notice is issued. Otherwise, it takes effect as part of the conclusions stated in the partial or final closure notice.

[*FA 1998, Sch 18 paras 30, 31; F(No 2)A 2017, Sch 15 paras 24, 25*].

Simon's Taxes. See A6.413.

Referral of questions to the tribunal

[65.16] Any question arising in connection with the subject matter of the enquiry while it is in progress in relation to that question may be referred to the tribunal for its determination. For this purpose, an enquiry is in progress in relation to a particular matter until a partial closure notice is issued in relation to it or, if no such notice is issued, a final closure notice is issued.

Written notice of referral must be given to the tribunal jointly by HMRC and the company, specifying the question(s) being referred, and more than one such referral may be made during the course of an enquiry. Either side may withdraw the notice at any time up to the first hearing by the tribunal by written notice to the other party and to the tribunal.

While proceedings on such a referral are in progress, no partial closure notice relating to the question referred may be given and no final closure notice may be given. No application may be made for a direction to issue a partial closure notice relating to the question referred or a final closure notice (see **65.17** below). Proceedings are for this purpose treated as still in progress until the question(s) is (are) determined by the tribunal and there is no further possibility of the determination(s) being varied or set aside (other than by virtue of an out-of-time appeal for which permission could be granted).

The tribunal's determination is binding on the parties as if it were a decision on a preliminary issue on an appeal (and similar rights of appeal against the determination apply), and must be taken into account by HMRC in reaching their conclusions on the enquiry.

[*FA 1998, Sch 18 paras 31A–31D; F(No 2)A 2017, Sch 15 paras 26, 27; SI 2001 No 4024*].

Simon's Taxes. See **A6.414**.

Completion or partial completion of enquiry

[65.17] An enquiry is completed when an officer of HMRC gives the company notice (a final closure notice) that he has completed his enquiries. As regards enquiries commenced on or after 16 November 2017, or in progress on that date, an HMRC officer can issue a partial closure notice, which completes the enquiry insofar as it concerns the matters specified in the notice.

The enquiry is not fully completed until a final closure notice has been issued to inform the taxpayer that the officer has completed his remaining enquiries. A partial or final closure notice takes effect when it is issued and must state the officer's conclusions and make the necessary amendments to the return and any other returns to give effect to those conclusions or state that no amendment is required. An enquiry may also be settled by entering into a contract settlement.

HMRC will make use of partial closure notices where the company's affairs are complex or where there is tax avoidance or large amounts of tax at risk; HMRC officers may issue a partial closure notice at their own discretion by agreement with the company (www.gov.uk/government/publications/tax-enquiries-closure-rules).

In *HMRC v Embiricos* UT, [2020] UKUT 370 (TCC), the Upper Tribunal held that HMRC could not issue a partial closure notice denying the taxpayer's claim to the remittance basis without specifying the amount of tax due. A similar decision was reached in *Executors of Levy (decd) v HMRC* FTT, [2019] SFTD 1045. That case also concerned an application for a direction to be made for a partial closure notice in relation to a taxpayer's domicile status, and it was held that there was no power to issue a partial closure notice in respect of a matter at a time when the tax effect of the determination is unknown.

With regard to partial or final closure notices, if the return was for the wrong period, the notice must designate the accounting period for which a return should have been made. If there is more than one accounting period ending in or at the end of the period specified in the notice requiring a return, the closure notice may only designate the first of those accounting periods for which no return has been delivered. If there is then another period for which a return should have been made under the original notice, and which no other return by the company can be amended to refer to, the original notice is taken to require the company to deliver a return in respect of the outstanding period. The filing date for the return for that period is the later of the original filing date and the thirtieth day after it is finally determined that the outstanding return is required.

During the course of an enquiry, the company may apply to the Tribunal for a direction requiring HMRC to issue a partial or final closure notice within a specified period, such application to be heard and determined in similar manner to an appeal. The Tribunal must give the direction unless satisfied that there are reasonable grounds for not issuing the partial or final closure notice within a specified period. Such a direction does not require HMRC to confirm that the company's return and self-assessment are correct, and the closure notice will include HMRC's conclusions based on the information available at the time of completion and representing what they believe to be the correct amounts to be included in the return on the basis of that information (see HMRC Enquiry Manual, EM1975). See *Jade Palace Ltd v HMRC* [2006] STC (SCD) 419 in which such a direction was given.

In *Eastern Power Networks plc v HMRC* CA, [2021] EWCA Civ 283, 2021 SWTI 1145, the Court of Appeal criticised the approach of four companies in using an application for a closure notice to avoid providing information to HMRC. HMRC opened enquiries into the consortium relief claims made by the companies. The companies provided much, but not all, of the information requested by HMRC and applied to the FTT for a direction for closure notices. HMRC considered that an anti-avoidance rule might apply and so opposed the application, arguing that they required the outstanding information to determine the purpose of the 'arrangements'. The companies contended that HMRC did not need the information because, as a matter of law, there were no arrangements and therefore no need to consider their purpose. The FTT considered that it had jurisdiction to decide the point of law, on the authority of *Vodafone 2 v HMRC* [2006] EWCA Civ 1132, as to do so would determine the application for the closure notices. It held that there were arrangements but that the anti-avoidance rule did not apply and therefore directed HMRC to issue closure notices. The Court of Appeal was highly critical of the approach taken by the taxpayers and the FTT. It would often be the case, as here, that a statutory provision set a number of cumulative conditions. Those conditions could require varying amounts of information to determine and 'taxpayers should not be encouraged to pick and choose which information they provide and then ask the tribunal to decide the applicability of one element in the hope that a "quick win" will bring the rest of the enquiry to a halt.' The approach adopted by the FTT required the tribunals to apply the statute without any clear findings of fact or agreed statement of facts. The jurisdiction to decide an incidental point of law in a closure notice application was useful, as in *Vodafone*, but only if used sparingly; applications for closure notices were not generally a suitable vehicle for deciding points of law.

See **5.3** APPEALS for right of appeal against any conclusion stated or amendment made by a partial or final closure notice.

Recent case law has reinforced the principle that enquiries should not be used as a method of obtaining information as to a third party's tax affairs. In *Estate 4 Ltd v HMRC* (TC01131) [2011] UKFTT 269 (TC), HMRC began an enquiry in December 2009 into a return submitted by a company (E), whose accounts showed a turnover of £187,000 and directors' salaries of £116,500. A meeting took place in May 2010, and the officer responsible for the enquiry formed the opinion that the salaries shown in E's accounts were insufficient to meet its directors' living expenses. E applied for a closure notice, contending that it had already supplied information about its own income and could not be required to provide information about its directors' personal affairs. The company considered that HMRC was using the enquiry as a 'bridge' to other issues unrelated to the tax affairs of the company itself. The First-Tier Tribunal agreed and granted the application. Judge Clark held that there was no basis for continuing to make further enquiries into the level of the remuneration.

In *Finnforest UK Ltd v HMRC* (TC01202 – June 2011) HMRC began enquiries into the returns submitted by a company claiming cross border group loss relief. The companies applied for closure notices in May 2010. The Tribunal rejected the applications on the basis that HMRC had reasonable grounds for not giving a closure notice as the group structure was complicated and it was reasonable for HMRC to want to gather detailed information on specific points which required clarification.

In *Spring Salmon and Seafood v HMRC* [2015] UKFTT 616 the First-tier Tribunal found that the company had made a valid claim in its tax return, so that the closure notice issued by HMRC was valid, and was therefore effective in denying the claim (as the notice disallowed the terminal loss relief claimed).

An application for judicial review of a closure notice was unsuccessful in *R (oao Archer) v HMRC* CA 2017, [2018] STC 38. The notice did not state the tax due and was therefore defective but the defect in the notice could be rectified by applying *TMA 1970, s 114(1)* (see **6.2** ASSESSMENTS).

[*FA 1998, Sch 18 paras 32–35; F(No 2)A 2017, Sch 15 paras 28–30, 44*].

Simon's Taxes. See **A6.418A.**

Determinations where no return delivered

[65.18] If no return is delivered, in response to a notice requiring one, on or before the filing date for the return required by the notice (see **65.4** above) (or, if no such date can be ascertained, by the later of 18 months from the end of the period specified in the notice and three months from the date of service of the notice (which is assumed to be four working days after its issue), (see HMRC Company Taxation Manual, CTM95350)), HMRC have power to determine, to the best of their information and belief, the tax payable by the company for the accounting period or periods ending in or at the end of the period specified in the notice. They may also determine what those accounting periods are if they have insufficient information to identify the company's accounting periods.

Notice of a determination under these provisions must be served on the company, stating the date of issue, but no determination may be made more than three years after the first day on which the power of determination could have been exercised. The determination is of no effect if the company shows that it has no accounting period ending in or at the end of the period specified in the notice requiring the return, or that it has delivered the return(s) for that accounting period or each of those accounting periods, or that no return is yet due for any such period. An effective determination is superseded where, before the expiry of three years from the day on which the power of determination first became exercisable (or, if later, the expiry of twelve months from the date of the determination), the company delivers a return for an accounting period ending in or at the end of the period specified in the notice requiring a return. If there is more than one determination in relation to the notice concerned, the determination superseded is that for the period which is, or most closely approximates to, the period for which the return is made.

In practice, HMRC normally review cases for determination 18 months after the end of what is assumed or believed to be the company's accounting period. If the filing date is believed to be later than that, they will wait until after the presumed filing date before making a determination. Where, for example, they believe there would be a risk of loss of tax if no immediate action was taken, or the absence of a return prevents a proper review of other companies in the same group, an earlier review may be made of the need for a determination. (HMRC Company Taxation Manual, CTM95340).

If a return is delivered, in response to a notice requiring one, for an accounting period ending in or at the end of the period specified in the notice, but it appears to HMRC that there is another ('outstanding') period so ending which is or may be an accounting period, they have power to determine, to the best of their information and belief, the corporation tax payable by the company for the outstanding period. The power becomes exercisable once the filing date for the outstanding period has passed without a return being delivered, or, if no such filing date can be ascertained, once the later of 30 months from the end of the period specified in the notice and three months from the date of service of the notice has passed without a return for the outstanding period being delivered.

Notice of a determination under these provisions must be served on the company, stating the date of issue, but no determination may be made more than three years after the first day on which the power of determination could have been exercised. The determination is of no effect if the company shows that the outstanding period is not an accounting period or that it has delivered a return for that period. An effective determination is superseded where, before the expiry of three years from the day on which the power of determination first became exercisable (or, if later, the expiry of 12 months from the date of the determination), the company delivers a further return for an accounting period ending in or at the end of the period specified in the notice requiring a return.

The power to make a determination in the circumstances described above includes power to determine any of the constituent amounts required to calculate the amount of tax payable. The notice of determination may be accompanied by a notice of any determination by HMRC of the due and payable dates under *TMA 1970, s 59D* or *s 59E* (see **58.2** PAYMENT OF TAX). For enforcement purposes (i.e. payment, collection and recovery, interest, penalties, etc.) the determination has effect as if it were a self-assessment, and is treated as made for an accounting period where HMRC had insufficient information to determine whether a period was an accounting period (see above). Where any proceedings have been begun for the recovery of tax charged by a determination, and before the proceedings are concluded the determination is superseded (as above), the proceedings may be continued as if they were for the recovery of so much of the tax charged by the self-assessment as is due and payable but unpaid.

[*FA 1998, Sch 18 paras 36–40*].

Simon's Taxes. See **A6.508–A6.509.**

Examples of return periods

[65.19]

(A)

Aquarius Ltd has always prepared its accounts to 31 October. In 2021, it changes its accounting date, preparing accounts for the nine months to 31 July 2021. On 31 January 2021, HMRC issue a notice specifying a return period of 1 November 2019 to 31 October 2020. On 31 January 2022, they issue a notice specifying a return period of 1 November 2020 to 31 October 2021.

In respect of the first-mentioned notice, Aquarius Ltd is required to make a return for the period 1.11.19 to 31.10.20.

In respect of the second of the above-mentioned notices, the company is required to make a return for the period 1.11.20 to 31.7.21.

(B)

Pisces Ltd has always prepared its accounts to 31 December. In 2021, it changes its accounting date, preparing accounts for the nine months to 30 September 2021. On 15 December 2021, HMRC issue a notice specifying a return period of 1 October 2020 to 30 September 2021.

Pisces Ltd is required to make returns both for the period 1.1.20 to 31.12.20 and for the period 1.1.21 to 30.9.21.

(C)

Aries Ltd has always prepared accounts to 31 October. After 2020, it changes its accounting date, preparing accounts for the fifteen months to 31 January 2022. On 21 August 2021, HMRC issue a notice specifying a return period of 1 November 2019 to 31 October 2020. On 31 January 2022, they issue a notice specifying a return period of 1 November 2020 to 31 October 2021.

In respect of the first-mentioned notice, Aries Ltd is required to make a return for the period 1.11.19 to 31.10.20 accompanied by accounts and tax computations for that period.

In respect of the second of the above-mentioned notices, the company is required to make a return for the accounting period 1.11.20 to 31.10.21 accompanied by accounts and tax computations for the period of account 1.11.20 to 31.1.22.

(D)

Taurus Ltd has always prepared accounts to 31 October. After 2020, it changes its accounting date, preparing accounts for the fifteen months to 31 January 2022. On 31 January 2021, HMRC issue a notice specifying a return period of 1 November 2019 to 31 October 2020. On 1 April 2021, they issue a notice specifying a return period of 1 November 2020 to 31 January 2021.

In respect of the first-mentioned notice, the position is as in (C) above.

In respect of the second of the above-mentioned notices, Taurus Ltd is not required to make a return, but should notify HMRC of the correct accounting dates and periods.

(E)

Gemini Ltd was incorporated on 1 July 2018 but remained dormant until 1 April 2020 when it began to trade. The first trading accounts were prepared for the year to 31 March 2021 and the company retains that accounting date. On 1 May 2022, HMRC issue notices specifying return periods of 1 July 2018 to 30 June 2019, 1 July 2019 to 30 June 2020, 1 July 2020 to 30 June 2021 and 1 July 2021 to 31 March 2022.

In respect of the notice for the period 1.7.18 to 30.6.19, Gemini Ltd is required to make a return for that period.

In respect of the notice for the period 1.7.19 to 30.6.20, the company is required to make a return for the period 1.7.19 to 31.3.20.

In respect of the notice for the period 1.7.20 to 30.6.21, the company is required to make a return for the period 1.4.20 to 31.3.21 accompanied by accounts and tax computations for that period.

In respect of the notice for the period 1.7.21 to 31.3.22, the company is required to make a return for the period 1.4.21 to 31.3.22 accompanied by accounts and tax computations for that period.

(F)

The final dates for the filing with HMRC of the returns in (A)–(E) above, and for the payment of corporation tax (assuming none of the companies concerned fall within the definition of a 'large company', see **58.3** PAYMENT OF TAX), are as follows.

Return period	*Filing date*	*Payment date*
(A) above		
1.11.19 – 31.10.20	31.10.21	1.8.21
1.11.20 – 31.7.21	31.7.22	1.5.22
(B) above		
1.1.20 – 31.12.20	15.3.22	1.10.21
1.1.21 – 30.9.21	·30.9.22	1.7.22
(C) above		
1.11.19 – 31.10.20	21.11.21	1.8.21
1.11.20 – 31.10.21	31.1.23	1.8.22
(D) above		
1.11.19– 31.10.20	31.10.21	1.8.21

Return period	*Filing date*	*Payment date*
(E) above		
1.7.18 – 30.6.19	1.8.22	—
1.7.19 – 31.3.20	1.8.22	—
1.4.20 – 31.3.21	1.8.22	1.1.22
1.4.21 – 31.3.22	31.3.23	1.1.23

Notes

(a) The time allowed for filing returns is effectively extended to the time allowed under the *Companies Act 2006* if this would give a later filing date. This will not be so in the majority of cases.

(b) HMRC may grant an extension, on an application by the company, if satisfied that the company has a 'reasonable excuse' (see **59.26** PENALTIES) for not being able to meet the filing date as above.

Rounding of tax computations

[65.20] To reduce the compliance burden on large companies whose statutory accounts are produced in round thousands, HMRC are generally prepared to accept profit computations for tax purposes in figures rounded to the nearest £1,000 from single companies with an annual turnover of at least £5 million (including investment and estate income) in the accounts in question or in the preceding year, where rounding at least to that extent has been used in preparing the accounts. (Turnover of groups of companies is not aggregated for this purpose.) Companies should continue to state amounts of group relief or relief for losses from other accounting periods in the actual sums surrendered, brought forward or carried back.

Such computations must be accompanied by a certificate by the person preparing the computations stating the basis of rounding, and confirming that it is unbiased, has been applied consistently and produces a fair result for tax purposes. It must also give the program or software used where relevant), or, if there have been no changes from the previous year in these respects, confirming the unchanged basis.

The rounding may not extend to the tax payable or other relevant figures of tax. Rounding is not acceptable where it would impede the application of the legislation, or where recourse to the underlying records would normally be necessary to do the computation. Thus it is not acceptable e.g. in computations of chargeable gains (except in relation to the incidental costs of acquisition and disposal), in accrued income scheme computations, in computations of tax credit relief or in certain capital allowance computations. HMRC may exceptionally insist that roundings are not used in other circumstances.

(See HMRC Statement of Practice, SP 15/93; also HMRC Manuals: CTM 93220, BIM31047).

Interest restriction returns

[65.21] Under the CORPORATE INTEREST RESTRICTION (**24**) provisions, the 'reporting company' for a worldwide group must submit a return (an '*interest restriction return*') to HMRC for each period of account of the group. A copy of the return must also be sent to each of the group's UK group companies.

With effect from 12 February 2019, the return must be received by HMRC before the end of the period of 12 months beginning with the end of the period of account. If the reporting company for the period of account was appointed by HMRC (see below), then the filing date is, if later than the normal date, the end of the period of three months beginning with the day on which the reporting company was appointed. The filing date is not extended where the group appoints a reporting company more than nine months after the end of the period.

Before 12 February 2019, the time limits were as follows: the return had to be received by HMRC before the latest of 31 June 2018, the end of the period of 12 months beginning with the end of the period of account and the end of the period of three months beginning with the day on which the reporting company was appointed (whether by the group or HMRC).

If a period of account ends on or after 29 October 2018 solely because the ultimate parent of the group becomes a member of another group, and the period is twelve months or less, the filing date is the end of the period of 24 months beginning with the affected period, if this is later than the normal filing date.

Returns are of no effect if received later than 36 months from the end of the period of account or, if later, three months from the day on which the reporting company was appointed. A return may be amended by submission of a revised return within that 36- or three-month period.

A revised return must be submitted where a group member amends its company tax return to alter the amount to be disallowed or reactivated under the restriction provisions. Such a revised return must be received by HMRC within the three months beginning with the day on which the amended company tax return was received by HMRC or the day as from which the company tax return was treated as amended.

If a group which is not subject to any interest restrictions for a period of account submits a return (which may be a full return or an abbreviated return — see below), it may submit a full return within 60 months of the end of the period.

A reporting company must keep such records as enable it to submit a correct and complete return and preserve those records for six years after the end of the period of account. The six-year period may be reduced or extended in certain circumstances.

The reporting company

A group may appoint any '*eligible company*' (i.e. any UK group company (see **24.2** CORPORATE INTEREST RESTRICTION) which is not dormant) as the group's '*reporting company*'. The appointment is made by notice to HMRC, specifying the first period of account for which the appointment has effect. The notice must be given within twelve months of the end of that period and must be authorised by at least 50% of the group's eligible companies. Before 12 February 2019, the time limit was six months from the end of the period (or 31 March 2018 if later). The notice must be accompanied by a list of the authorising companies and a statement that those companies constitute at least 50% of the eligible companies. The notice may be accompanied by a list of companies which do not wish to be consenting companies (see below). A newly appointed reporting company must notify all of the eligible companies and the ultimate parent of the group of its status as soon as reasonably practical. The company must inform any company which becomes an eligible company in the group during a period of account of its status within six months from the end of the period.

The appointment continues in effect for subsequent periods but may be revoked by notice to HMRC authorised by at least 50% of the eligible companies. The revocation applies from the period of account specified in the notice and the notice must be given within twelve months of the end of that period. Before 12 February 2019, the time limit was six months from the end of the period (or 31 March 2018 if later). A new appointment may be made at the same time (or later).

If a group fails to appoint a reporting company for a period of account and the time limit for doing so has passed, HMRC may appoint an eligible company as the reporting company for that period only. The appointment is made by notice to the company concerned and may be made at any time within 36 months of the end of the period of account or at any later time when any amount in a company tax return of a group company for an accounting period falling wholly or partly in the period of account can still be altered.

If HMRC consider that an appointed reporting company has not complied with its responsibilities, or will not do so, they may revoke the appointment and appoint another eligible company as the reporting company for the group. Notice must be given to both the outgoing and incoming reporting companies. The appointment of the new reporting company has effect only for a single period of account (after which a new reporting company will need to be appointed). HMRC may also exercise this power on a request by a reporting company.

[*TIOPA 2010, Sch 7A paras 1, 2, 4–9, 38, 60(4); F(No 2)A 2017, Sch 5 paras 2, 28; FA 2018, Sch 8 para 14; FA 2019, Sch 11 paras 15–17, 25*].

Contents of the return

If a group is subject to an interest restriction for a period of account, or if it is not so subject but the reporting company has not made an abbreviated return election (see below), a full return must be made. It must include the names and (where they have them) unique taxpayer references of the ultimate parent and any UK group companies and must contain a statement of calculations and details of any disallowed amount and reactivated interest amount for the period, together with a statement of how the amounts are allocated between companies. It must also contain a declaration by the person making the return that it is correct and complete to the best of their knowledge.

If the group is not subject to an interest restriction for a period of account it may include within the return a revocable abbreviated return election. If such an election is made, the return needs to contain only the names and unique taxpayer references and the declaration referred to above.

The statement of calculations in a full return must include details of all of the amounts needed to calculate the total disallowed amount or reactiviated interest. The statement of allocated interest restrictions must specify an allocated disallowance for the period for each UK group company which has net tax-interest expense, and allocate each company's disallowed amount between its accounting periods which wholly or partly overlap the period of account. See **24.3** CORPORATE INTEREST RESTRICTION. The statement of allocated interest reactivations must specify an allocated reactivation for the period to one or more UK group companies and allocate the allocated amount to the company's first accounting period which overlaps the period of account. If the company joined the group during the period of account, it must bring the reactivation into account for the first accounting period in which it is a member. See **24.4** CORPORATE INTEREST RESTRICTION.

A group ratio election (see **24.4** CORPORATE INTEREST RESTRICTION), an abbreviated return election and any of the elections at **24.8** must be made or (where possible) revoked in an interest restriction return for the period of account (or the first period of account) to which it relates. See *TIOPA 2010, Sch 7A paras 12–18*.

A return (whether full or abbreviated) submitted on or after 1 April 2019 must also include information specified by HMRC (in a published notice).

[*TIOPA 2010, Sch 7A paras 19, 20; F(No 2)A 2017, Sch 5 para 2; FA 2019, Sch 11 paras 18, 26*].

Where a return includes estimated amounts, the return must identify that information. If the information is not finalised before the end of the period of 36 months beginning with the end of the period of account, the reporting company must notify HMRC within the next 30 days. The notice must identify the information which is not final and must indicate when the company expects it to be finalised. A reporting company which fails to give such notice is liable to a penalty of £500. HMRC may accept a late revised return if the revisions are limited to those needed to finalise estimated amounts if HMRC consider that it was not possible to make those changes in time. [*TIOPA 2010, Sch 7A para 27; F(No 2)A 2017, Sch 5 para 2*].

HMRC powers

Provisions similar to those which apply to company tax returns enable HMRC to correct errors or omissions in a return and to conduct enquiries into returns. Although in general only one enquiry may be opened into a return, where a revised return replaces an original return, an enquiry may be made into the revised return even if an enquiry was made into the original. An enquiry may extend to anything contained, or required to be contained, in the return but may not extend to anything contained, or required to be contained, in a company tax return of a UK group company which is taken into account in any calculation required for the purposes of the interest restriction return. Notice of enquiry into a return must be given before the latest of: 39 months from the end of the period of account; six months from the day the reporting company for the period was appointed; and, in the case of a revised return, 31 January, 30 April, 31 July or 31 October next following the first anniversary of the day on which HMRC received the revised return. The time limit is extended where the return contains estimated information not finalised within 36 months after the end of the period of account. In such circumstances an enquiry may be opened within the 12 months following the end of the 36-month period.

HMRC also have the power to make a determination of each UK group company's pro rata share of the total disallowed amount for the period of account and for each of the company's accounting period which overlap the period of account in the absence of a return or where a return fails to meet the statutory requirements (for example by including inaccurate figures). Where such a determination is made each company must leave out of account the amounts so determined. Where a determination notice has been issued, the time limit for making a return, or a revised return, is extended to 12 months after the date the notice was given. A determination may also be made following an enquiry where a company fails to make a return required under the enquiry closure notice.

[*TIOPA 2010, Sch 7A paras 28, 40–59; F(No 2)A 2017, Sch 5 para 2*].

HMRC's enquiry powers are supplemented by additional powers enabling them to obtain information and documents from the members of a group. The powers are separate to those in *FA 2008, Sch 36* (see **38.3** HMRC INVESTIGATORY POWERS). See *TIOPA 2010, Sch 7A paras 62–67.*

Penalties

Penalties apply for failure to make a return, incorrect or uncorrected returns, for companies which supply false information to the group's reporting company and for failure to keep and preserve records. See **59.22** PENALTIES. See below for the penalty for failing to make consequential amendments to company tax returns.

Company tax returns

A company must make or revoke the following elections in its company tax return (whether as originally made or by amendment):

(i) where the company is a non-consenting company, an election to leave out of account its pro rata share of the total disallowed amount (see **24.3** CORPORATE INTEREST RESTRICTION);

(ii) an election to specify which tax-interest expense amounts are to be left out of account (see **24.3**); and

(iii) an election to specify which tax-interest expense amounts are to be reactivated (see **24.4**).

A company may amend its return to make or revoke an election within (i) above at any time before the filing date for the interest restriction return or if later three months from the day on which that return is received by HMRC. The return must also be amended within that time limit to take account of the election.

A company may amend its return to make or revoke an election within (ii) or (iii) above at any time before the end of the period of 36 months from the day after the end of the accounting period or if later three months from the day on which an interest restriction return for a period of account which overlaps the accounting period is received by HMRC. The return must also be amended within that time limit to take account of the election.

If a company is required to leave an amount out of account under the corporate interest restriction but has already delivered a return of the period in question, it may amend the return within three months after the filing date for the interest restriction return or, where no reporting company has been appointed, within 12 months after the end of the period of account. If, as a result of the submission of an interest restriction return or an HMRC determination, a company's tax return is made incorrect, the company must amend it to make the necessary corrections within three months of the date the interest restriction return was submitted or, if later, within the normal time limit for amending a return.

Where a company fails to make a required amendment to its return for an accounting period by the 'amendment deadline' (i.e. the date by which the amendment is required to be made), it is liable to a penalty of £500. HMRC may make the required amendments, to the best of their information and belief, within the 12 months beginning with the amendment deadline. The company may then amend the return to correct HMRC's amendment within three months of the date of HMRC's amendment. A penalty is charged by HMRC assessment, applying the same provisions as for a penalty within **59.23**(17) PENALTIES. No penalty can apply where a company's tax return is amended before 15 March 2018.

If the effect of an amendment or deemed amendment made to a return following an enquiry or HMRC determination is to increase the corporation tax payable, any 'qualifying claim' can be made within one year beginning with the day on which the company receives the enquiry closure notice or determination notice. Any such claim previously made which is not irrevocable can be revoked or varied within the same period. A '*qualifying claim*' is one whose making, revocation or variation reduced the corporation tax liability (but not so as to exceed the additional tax due under the amendment). Claims which alter the tax liability of another person are excluded. '*Claims*' include elections, applications and notices.

[*TIOPA 2010, Sch 7A paras 68–70A, 72, 73; F(No 2)A 2017, Sch 5 para 2; FA 2018, Sch 8 paras 15, 16, 25, 26*].

66
Statutory Bodies

Introduction to statutory bodies

[66.1] For corporation tax purposes, many statutory bodies are treated as if they were companies, with the result that they are charged to corporation tax on their profits and gains.

However, special rules apply to certain statutory bodies. Including:

- marketing boards;
- harbour reorganisation schemes;
- local authorities; and
- the Nuclear Decommissioning Authority.

This chapter looks at the provisions specific to these bodies and also at treatment of statutory bodies generally. It also considers the position of a statutory corporation borrowing in a foreign currency.

Marketing Boards

[66.2] Certain statutory bodies are required by the Government to pay all or part of their trading surplus into a reserve fund. A statutory body whose objects include:

- marketing an agricultural product; or
- stabilising the price of an agricultural product,

and which is obliged by or under a government-approved scheme to pay all or part of any trading surplus into a reserve fund may deduct such payments in computing the profits of the trade carried on by them, provided that the reserve fund meets the conditions set out below.

The first condition is that no sum can be withdrawn from the fund without the authority of a Minister or Department.

The second condition is that if money has been paid to the body by a minister or department in connection with arrangements for maintaining guaranteed prices or in connection with the body's trading arrangements and that money is repayable to the Minister or department, sums standing to the credit of the fund are required to be applied in repaying the money.

The third condition is that the fund is reviewed by a Minister at fixed intervals and if it appears to the Minister that the fund exceeds what is reasonably required by the body, the excess is withdrawn.

Any withdrawal from the fund which is not required to be passed on to a Minister or Government Department, producers, or persons paying levies or duties, is treated as a trading receipt.

The definition of Minister includes Ministers of the Crown, Scottish Ministers, Welsh Ministers or a Minister of Northern Ireland, to take account of the devolved powers given to the national parliaments.

[*CTA 2009, ss 153–155, Sch 2 para 33*].

Simon's Taxes. See B5.647.

Local authorities etc. and health service bodies

[66.3] Local authorities and health service bodies are exempt from corporation tax.

A '*local authority*' is any incorporated or unincorporated association:

- of which all the constituent members are local authorities, groups of local authorities or local authority associations; and
- which has as its object or primary object the protection and furtherance of the interests in general of local authorities or any description of local authorities.

The Police and Crime Commissioners and the London Mayor's Office for Policing and Crime fall within the definition of 'local authority', as did their predecessor bodies, the Police Authorities.

A '*health service body*' is a body that is:

- a Strategic Health Authority or Health Authority;
- a Special Health Authority;
- a Primary Care Trust;
- a Local Health Board or Board;
- (in Wales) a National Health Service trust;
- an NHS foundation trust;
- (in Scotland) a Health Board or Special Health Board, the Common Services Agency for the Scottish Heath Service or a State Hospital Management Committee;
- in Northern Ireland, a special health and social services agency, a Health and Social Care trust, a Health and Social Services Board, or the Northern Ireland Central Services Agency;
- the Scottish Dental Practice Board;

- the Public Health Laboratory Service Board;
- a clinical commissioning group;
- the Health and Social Care Information Centre;
- the National Health Service Commissioning Board; and
- the National Institute for Health and Clinical Excellence.

The Treasury may also make an order that an NHS foundation trust is liable to corporation tax in relation to a specified activity, which appears to the Treasury to be of a commercial nature and such order is necessary to avoid any differences in treatment between such trust and any other commercial body undertaking the same or similar activity.

[*CTA 2010, ss 984, 985, 986, 987; TCGA 1992, ss 271(3), 288(1)*].

See **33.11** EXEMPT ORGANISATIONS.

Simon's Taxes. See **D1.201A, D1.203**.

Chief constables etc. in England and Wales

[66.4] The following are not liable to corporation tax:

- a chief constable of a police force maintained under *Police Act 1996, s 2*; and
- the Commissioner of Police of the Metropolis.

[*CTA 2010, s 987A*].

Education Authority of Northern Ireland

[66.5] The Education Authority of Northern Ireland is not liable to corporation tax with effect from its inception on 1 April 2015. [*CTA 2010, s 987B; FA 2018, s 25*].

Northern Ireland Housing Executive

[66.6] The Northern Ireland Housing Executive is not liable to corporation tax with effect for accounting periods beginning on or after 1 April 2020. [*CTA 2010, s 987C; FA 2021, s 39*].

Nuclear Decommissioning Authority

[66.7] The Nuclear Decommissioning Authority ('NDA') is exempt from tax on trading income arising or accruing to it or to an 'NDA company' from the carrying on of exempt activities. An '*NDA company*' is defined as a 'relevant site licensee' (as defined) or a company of which the ordinary share capital is owned directly or indirectly by the NDA.

Exempt activities are specified by regulation (for which see *SI 2005 No 644* which also provides further conditions to be satisfied by a site licensee for it to qualify as an NDA company). They are defined as the operation of designated facilities for the treatment, storage transportation or disposal of hazardous material, carried on for the purpose of thermal oxide reprocessing or mixed oxide manufacture at Sellafield in Cumbria.

[*Energy Act 2004, ss 27–30, 47, Sch 4; FA 2006, ss 99, 100; F(No 2)A 2017, Sch 4 para 127*].

Simon's Taxes. See **D1.234**.

Other statutory bodies

[66.8] Subject to the special provisions above and, where appropriate, to the Crown exemption (see 33.6 EXEMPT ORGANISATIONS), statutory bodies are liable in the ordinary way to corporation tax on their income and capital gains. Whether their activities amount to trading depends on the facts.

There is a wealth of case law on the subject. See *Mersey Docks and Harbour Board v Lucas* HL 1883, 2 TC 25 (trading surplus held chargeable notwithstanding that it had to be applied in reducing debt), *Port of London Authority v CIR* CA 1920, 12 TC 122, and *Forth Conservancy Board cases*, HL 1928, 14 TC 709, and HL 1931, 16 TC 103 (liable under Schedule D Case VI on surplus from shipping dues) and *British Broadcasting Corporation v Johns* CA 1964, 41 TC 471 (liable on trading profits from publications etc. but not on rest of surplus; not entitled to Crown exemption). For further cases, see Tolley's Tax Cases.

Statutory corporation borrowing in foreign currency

[66.9] Interest on securities issued after 5 April 1982 by, or on a loan to, a local authority or a statutory corporation (as defined) in a currency other than sterling shall be paid without deduction of income tax and be exempt from income tax (but not corporation tax) in the hands of a non-UK resident beneficial owner of such securities or, in the case of a loan, in the hands of the non-UK resident person for the time being entitled to repayment or eventual repayment of the loan.

[*ITTOIA 2005, ss 755, 756*].

Key points on statutory bodies

[66.10] The key points are as follows:

- Subject to special provisions to the contrary, statutory bodies are taxable to corporation tax on their income and gains.
- Special provisions apply which amend the rules in relation to certain statutory bodies.
- Local authorities and health service bodies are exempt from tax.
- Payments by agricultural marketing boards into Government reserve funds are deducted in computing taxable profits.

- Nuclear Decommissioning Authority is exempt from tax arising on trading income derived from exempt activities.

67

Time Limits

Introduction to time limits

[67.1] Where no special provision is made, the normal time limit for claims and elections is four years from the end of the accounting period to which they relate.

[*FA 1998, Sch 18 para 55*].

Many provisions do, however, include a specific time limit. This chapter outlines important time limits which apply to different provisions within UK tax law which are relevant to companies.

Simon's Taxes. See **A4.204, D1.1345**.

Accounting principles

[67.2] Limits with regard to certain accounting principles are as follows:

On a change of accounting basis, election to spread the adjustment income equally over six periods of account beginning with the first period to which the new basis applies. Election to be made within twelve months after the end of the first accounting period to which the new basis applies. [*CTA 2009, s 186*]. See **68.20** TRADING INCOME.

Appeals

[67.3] Limits with regard to appeals are as follows:

(a) Formal notice of appeal against an amendment to a corporation tax return following an enquiry or against an assessment which is not a self-assessment, must be lodged within **30 days** after the date of issue of the notice of amendment or assessment. See **5.1** APPEALS.

(b) For appeals from the First-tier Tribunal to the Upper Tribunal, written applications must be made to the First-tier Tribunal within **56 days** of the later of: the tribunal sending out full written reasons for the decision; notification of amended reasons following a review of a decision; or, notification that the application to set aside a decision has been unsuccessful. Appeals from the Upper Tribunal to the Court of Appeal are governed by the *Civil Procedures Rules 1998 (SI 1998 No 3132)*. See **5.26, 5.36** APPEALS.

(c) Except as indicated above, appeals against amendments to claims etc. must be made within **30 days** of the receipt of the decision on a claim or of an amendment of a claim, as the case may be. See **15.9** CLAIMS.

Capital allowances

[67.4] Capital allowances are claimed in the tax return of the company for the accounting period in question and can be amended within the usual time limits for amending such a return. However, certain claims relating to capital allowances are treated as follows:

(a) With regard to the Special Leasing provisions, claims for machinery or plant allowances to be set off against income other than that against which they are primarily given must be made within **two years** of the end of the accounting period for which the allowances are made. [*CAA 2001, s 260(6)*].

(b) With regard to Overseas Leasing in *CAA 2001, Ch 11*, a notice that machinery or plant on which allowances have been given has ceased, during the 'designated period', to be used for a 'qualifying purpose' (no longer used for 'protected leasing') must be given within **three months** of the end of the accounting period in which the non-qualifying use takes place, or within **30 days** of the cessation's coming to the notice of the lessor, whichever is the later. A notice with regard to the provision of plant and machinery leased to joint lessees under the provisions of *s 116(1)* must be given within three months of the end of the accounting period in which the plant and machinery is first leased; or within 30 days of such use coming to the notice of the lessor. Note that these provisions apply only to leases finalised before 1 April 2006. [*CAA 2001, ss 119, 120*].

See generally **9** CAPITAL ALLOWANCES, **10** CAPITAL ALLOWANCES ON PLANT AND MACHINERY.

Capital gains

[67.5] Time limits in respect of certain capital gains provisions are as follows:

(a) **Assets held on 6 April 1965**. An election for such assets to be valued at 6 April 1965 must be made within **two years** after the end of the accounting period in which the relevant disposal was made. [*TCGA 1992, Sch 2 para 17*]. For certain concessional treatment on a company's leaving a group see **12.15** CAPITAL GAINS — GROUPS.

(b) **Assets held on 31 March 1982**. An irrevocable election for assets to be valued at 31 March 1982 must be made within **two years** of the end of the accounting period in which the first relevant disposal occurs (or such longer time as HMRC may allow).

(c) **Assets of negligible value.** A claim must be made within **two years** after the end of the accounting period in which the relevant date falls. See Tolley's Capital Gains Tax.

(d) **Groups of companies.** A company leaving a group remains liable for unpaid corporation tax on chargeable gains arising from the disposal of any asset formerly owned by that company while it was a member of the group where the disposal occurs within **twelve months** following its departure from the group. [*TCGA 1992, s 190*].

(e) **Know-how.** Joint election for so much of the consideration for the sale of know-how of a trade (or part of a trade) **not** to be treated as a payment for goodwill must be made within **two years** of the disposal. [*CTA 2009, s 178*]. See **68.45** TRADING INCOME.

(f) **Residence.** An election for a net gain to be postponed when a company ceases to be resident before 1 January 2020 must be made within two years of the cessation of residence. A subsequent claim for any part of such 'postponed gain' which becomes chargeable to be offset by capital losses of the subsidiary concerned must be made within **two years** of accrual of that part of the postponed gain. [*TCGA 1992, s 187; FA 2019, Sch 8 para 9(1)(5)*]. See **64.9** RESIDENCE.

(g) **Rollover relief** is only available if the acquisition of the new assets is made within **three years** after the disposal of the old or within **twelve months** before. See **12.8** CAPITAL GAINS — GROUPS.

For further details of the above and other time limits, see Tolley's Capital Gains Tax under the appropriate heading.

Chargeability to tax

[67.6] A company chargeable to corporation tax for any accounting period which has not received notice requiring a return for that period must notify HMRC that it is so chargeable within **one year** of the end of that period. [*FA 1998, Sch 18 para 2, Sch 19 para 1*].

Simon's Taxes. See **D1.1301**.

Coming within charge to corporation tax

[67.7] A company must give notice to HMRC of when its first accounting period begins and of when any subsequent accounting period begins that does not follow on immediately from the end of a previous accounting period. The notice must be given within three months after the beginning of the accounting period in question. See **65.2** RETURNS. [*FA 2004, s 55*].

Construction industry scheme

[67.8] The requirements are as follows:

(a) Remittances must be made to HMRC within **14 days** after the end of the tax month (ending on the fifth of the calendar month) or in certain cases the tax quarter (ending on 5 July etc.). Where the payment is made by an approved method of electronic communication, the time limit is extended to **17 days** in both cases.

(b) Monthly returns must be made to HMRC within **14 days** after the end of the tax month.

[*FA 2004, s 61; SI 2005 No 2045*].

Contaminated land remediation expenditure

[67.9] Contaminated land remediation expenditure is treated as follows:

(a) Election for 'qualifying land remediation expenditure' of a capital nature to be allowed as a deduction from trade or property business profits must be made within **two years** after the end of the accounting period in respect of which it is made. [*CTA 2009, ss 1147, 1148*].

(b) Claims for 'land remediation tax credit' must be included in the company tax return (or amended return) and must be made within **one year** of the filing date for that return or by such later time as HMRC may allow.

[*CTA 2009, s 1151*].

Double taxation

[67.10] Relief by way of credit for foreign tax in respect of any income must be claimed within four years after the end of the accounting period for which the income is chargeable or, if later, within one year after the end of the accounting period in which the foreign tax is paid. [*TIOPA 2010, s 19*].

See 31.6 DOUBLE TAX RELIEF.

Employees' remuneration

[67.11] A claim for the computation for a period of account to be adjusted for employees' remuneration paid after the computation has been made, but within nine months after the end of the period, is made by amendment to the tax return, and the normal time limits for such amendment apply.

See 69.27 TRADING INCOME — DEDUCTIONS.

Film and other creative industries reliefs

[67.12] A claim for film tax relief, for television, video games or theatrical production tax relief or for orchestra tax relief or museums and galleries relief must be made in a company tax return (or amended return) for the accounting period for which the claim is made, within one year of the filing date for that return or by such later time as HMRC may allow. It can similarly only be amended or withdrawn by amendment of the company tax return within the same time limit. See 26 CREATIVE INDUSTRIES RELIEFS. [*FA 1998, Sch 18 para 83W*].

Group relief

[67.13] See *FA 1998, Sch 18 Pt VIII* and further 15.2 CLAIMS.

Herd basis

[67.14] An election by a farming company for the herd basis must be made within **two years** of the end of the first accounting period during which a production herd of the class concerned was kept or in which compensation is received for compulsory slaughter. See 68.33 TRADING INCOME.

[*CTA 2009, s 122*].

Housing associations

[67.15] Exemption from corporation tax on rents and chargeable gains must be claimed within two years of the end of the relevant accounting period. The same applies to self-build societies. See 40 HOUSING ASSOCIATIONS.

Income tax

[67.16] Returns of income tax deducted from payments made by a company are due within **14 days** of the end of the return period. See 41 INCOME TAX IN RELATION TO A COMPANY.

Intangible assets

[67.17] Intangible assets claims are treated as follows:

(a) An election to replace accounts depreciation with a fixed writing-down allowance of 4% must be made within **two years** after the end of the accounting period in which the asset was created or acquired. [*CTA 2009, s 730*]. See **42.5** INTANGIBLE ASSETS.

(b) An election to exclude from the intangible assets provisions certain expenditure on computer software must be made within **two years** after the end of the accounting period in which the expenditure was incurred. [*CTA 2009, s 815*]. See **42.4** INTANGIBLE ASSETS.

Loan relationships

[67.18] Relief for a non-trading deficit of an accounting period may be claimed by set-off against other profits of the period or by carry back within **two years** of the end of the accounting period (or within such longer time as HMRC may allow). A claim for a post-1 April 2017 deficit to be carried forward and set off against total profits of the next period must be made within **two years** of the end of that next accounting period. A claim for part or all of a pre-1 April 2017 deficit to be excepted from being set against non-trading profits of the accounting period immediately following the deficit period and treated as a non-trading deficit of that period to be carried forward for offset against non-trading profits of succeeding accounting periods, must be made within **two years** of the end of that period. [*CTA 2009, ss 458–460*]. See **50.4** LOAN RELATIONSHIPS.

Loans to participators

[67.19] The time limit for claiming repayment of tax paid on a loan by a close company to certain participators is **four years** after the end of the **financial year** in which the loan is repaid. See *CTA 2010, s 458(3)* and further **16.15** CLOSE COMPANIES.

Overpayment of tax

[67.20] Relief for overpayment of tax must be claimed within four years after the end of the relevant accounting period.

[*FA 1998, Sch 18 para 51B, Sch 19 para 15*].

See **15.10** CLAIMS.

Over-repaid tax

[67.21] Assessments to recover tax over-repaid may, if otherwise out of time, be made up to the end of the accounting period following that of the repayment or, if later, within **three months** of the closure of an HMRC enquiry into a self-assessment return. [*FA 1998, Sch 18 para 53, Sch 19 para 13*].

Overseas PE election

[67.22] An election for all a company's overseas permanent establishments ('PEs') to fall within the exemption regime at *CTA 2009, Pt 2, Ch 3A* is effective for the accounting period following the period in which the election is made. The election becomes irrevocable at the start of the first period to which the exemption regime applies.

An election for territorial 'streaming' of losses for the overseas PEs takes effect for the accounting period after that in which the election is made. The streaming election must be made at the same time as the main election into the regime.

[*CTA 2009, ss 18F, 18L*].

See **31.15** DOUBLE TAX RELIEF — overseas PE.

Patents

[67.23] Patents excluded from the intangible assets regime are treated as follows:

(a) Where a company resident in the UK sells patent rights wholly or partly for a capital sum, and does not wish that sum to be spread over six years, an election to have the entire sum charged to tax for the accounting period in which it was received must be made within **two years** of the end of that period.

(b) A non-resident company selling UK patent rights wholly or partly for a capital sum may claim to have that sum spread over six years (and not treated as a single lump sum) within **two years** of the end of the accounting period in which it was received.

[*CTA 2009, ss 914, 916*].

See **42.43** INTANGIBLE ASSETS.

Patent Box election

[67.24] A company may make an election for an accounting period (and all subsequent periods) to fall within the patent box regime. Such an election must be made on or before the last day on which an amendment of a company's tax return for that period could be made under *FA 1998, Sch 18 para 15*. Generally this is two years after the end of the accounting period in question (see further 65.8 RETURNS).

An election to be within the regime can be revoked for an accounting period within similar time limits, and will apply to that accounting period and subsequent accounting periods. However, once revoked a new election for the regime to apply will not be effective for a period of 5 years after the end of the accounting period for which the revocation notice was made.

[*CTA 2010, ss 357A, 357G, 357GA*].

Payment of tax

[67.25] Corporation tax is generally payable **nine months** after the end of the accounting period (subject to any requirement for instalment payment). See 58 PAYMENT OF TAX.

Pre-trading expenditure

[67.26] An election for a pre-trading debit on a loan relationship to be deferred to the period in which the trade commences must be made within **two years** of the end of the accounting period in which the debit arose. [*CTA 2009, ss 330(1)–(3)*].

Research and development expenditure

[67.27] Research and development expenditure is treated as follows:

(a) A claim for R&D tax relief, or for the RDEC under *CTA 2009, Pt 3 Ch 6A*, for an accounting period must be made, amended or withdrawn in the company tax return (or amended return) for which the claim is made, within **one year** of the filing date for that return (see **65.8** RETURNS) or by such later time as HMRC may allow.
[*FA 1998, Sch 18 paras, 83A–83F, 83LA–83LE, 83M–83R*].

(b) An election for 'connected person's treatment' to be applied to all sub-contractor payments made under the same contract or arrangement must be made within **two years** after the end of the accounting period in which the contract or arrangement is entered into.
[*CTA 2009, ss 1131, 1135*].
The similar election in relation to staff provision payments must be made within a similar time limit.

(c) An election for the alternative treatment of pre-trading expenditure in an accounting period must be made within **two years** after the end of the accounting period to which the election relates.
[*CTA 2009, s 1047*].

See **63** RESEARCH AND DEVELOPMENT EXPENDITURE.

Returns

[67.28] Returns time limits are as follows:

(a) Company tax returns must be made within **one year** of the end of the accounting period (or of the period of account in which falls the last day of the accounting period) or, if later, within **three months** of the date of the notice requiring the return. [*FA 1998, Sch 18 para 14*]. See **65.4** RETURNS.

(b) *Certain distributions* must be returned within **14 days** of the end of the accounting period in which they were made or within **14 days** of their having been made (if they were not made in an accounting period).

(c) *Stock dividends* must be returned within **30 days** of the end of the return period.

See 65.9 *et seq.* RETURNS.

Trading losses

[67.29] A claim for trading losses to be set off against profits of the same or an earlier accounting period must be made within **two years** of the end of the accounting period in which the losses were incurred, or within such further period as HMRC may allow. A claim for post-1 April 2017 carried-forward losses to be set off against profits of a subsequent accounting period must be made within **two years** of the subsequent period or within such further period as HMRC may allow. A claim to except a carried-forward loss from set off against trade profits of a subsequent post-1 April 2017 accounting period must be made within two years of the subsequent period or within such further period as HMRC may allow.

[*CTA 2010, ss 37(7), 45(4C), 45A(7), 45B(6), 45C(3), 45D(2)*]. See **51** LOSSES.

Unlisted shares

[67.30] Claims for relief of losses on such shares by investment companies must be made within **two years** of the end of the accounting period in which the loss was incurred.

[*CTA 2010, ss 70, 71*]. See **51.27** LOSSES.

Unremittable income

[67.31] A claim for unremittable income to be left out of account must be made within **two years** after the end of the accounting period in which the income arose.

[*CTA 2009, s 1275*].

See **64.4** RESIDENCE.

68
Trading Income

Cross-references. See **4** ANTI-AVOIDANCE; **21** CONTROLLED FOREIGN COMPANIES; **31** DOUBLE TAX RELIEF; **35** GROUP RELIEF; **42** INTANGIBLE ASSETS; **45** INVESTMENT COMPANIES AND INVESTMENT BUSINESS; **51** LOSSES; **63** RESEARCH AND DEVELOPMENT EXPENDITURE; **64.4** RESIDENCE; **72** TRANSFER PRICING.

Introduction to trading income

[68.1] This chapter describes the provisions which charge corporation tax on trading income. For this purpose, trading income comprises the profits of a trade (see **68.2** below) and post-cessation receipts arising from a trade (see **68.16** below). [*CTA 2009, s 34*]. For whether a trade is carried on see **68.3** onwards below. For the calculation of taxable trade profits see **68.18** onwards below. For tax treatment of specific items of income and specific trades see **68.21** onwards. For ease of use, a separate chapter **69** TRADING INCOME — DEDUCTIONS describes the rules determining whether and to what extend particular types of expenditure are allowed as deductions in computing trade profits.

See also **1.5** INTRODUCTION: CHARGE TO TAX, RATES AND PROFITS for the power for the Northern Ireland Assembly to set the corporation tax rate on trade profits of certain companies in Northern Ireland and consequential modifications to the provisions for the calculation of trade profit.

Crisis-driven changes to trading activities

HMRC have published guidance on the possible implications for the taxation of trading income arising from changes in normal business activities caused by crisis situations such as coronavirus. The guidance does not introduce any relaxations to the rules but summaries existing law and practices that might be relevant to affected companies. These include consideration of whether changes result in a new trade being carried on, the effect of temporary breaks in trading activity, donations and other income and expenditure. See HMRC Business Income Manual BIM48000.

Charge to tax on profits of a trade

[68.2] Corporation tax is charged on the profits of a trade. [*CTA 2009, s 35*]. For whether a trade is carried on see **68.3** onwards below and for the calculation of taxable trade profits see **68.18** onwards below.

See also **2.7** ACCOUNTING PERIODS for the apportionment of profits to an accounting period where accounts are drawn up for a period of more than 12 months.

Whether a trade carried on

[68.3] Trade 'includes any venture in the nature of trade' [*CTA 2010, s 1120*]. For a discussion on the *scope* of a trade, see HMRC Business Income Manual BIM21000–21040. Whether a trade is being carried on is normally a question of fact but a trade can be deemed to exist (or not exist) by statute. See also **54** MUTUAL COMPANIES and **66** STATUTORY BODIES. Special types of activity are dealt with below in alphabetical order.

Simon's Taxes. See **B1.4**.

Avoidance schemes

[68.4] A line is drawn between transactions of a trading nature which remain trading even though entered into to secure tax advantages and transactions so remote from ordinary trading as to be explicable only as fiscal devices and hence not trading.

In *Ransom v Higgs and Kilmorie (Aldridge) Ltd v Dickinson etc.* (1974) 50 TC 1, HL, the taxpayers entered into complex arrangements to siphon development profits into the hands of trustees. They succeeded, the Crown failing to establish that, looked at as a whole, the arrangements constituted trading.

In *Johnson v Jewitt* (1961) 40 TC 231, CA, an elaborate and artificial device to manufacture trading losses was held not to amount to trading, but see *Ensign Tankers (Leasing) Ltd v Stokes* (1992) 64 TC 617, HL, where the company's investment in two film production partnerships was entered into with a view to obtaining first-year capital allowances. In *Eclipse Film Partners (No 35) LLP v HMRC* CA 2015, [2015] STC 1429 a film partnership offered investors substantial current year interest deductions, which depended on whether the partnership was trading. The CA upheld the FTT's decision that Eclipse's involvement lacked commercial substance and that 'an adventure in the nature of trade' required an element of speculation which was not present. In addition whilst it noted that fiscal considerations naturally affect the taxpayer's evaluation of a venture, such motivations can alter the trading character of the activities in question if they affect the commerciality of the transaction. See also *Ingenious Games LLP v HMRC* UT, [2019] STC 1851.

In *Flanagan v HMRC* FTT, [2014] SFTD 881, an individual (F) entered into a tax avoidance scheme. In his tax return he claimed that he had begun self-employment as a car dealer, with no turnover and a tax loss of £5,000,284, largely attributable to finance charges. The First-tier Tribunal held that this was not 'a trade seriously pursued with a view to profit', since 'the supposed traders care nothing about the profit and, moreover, have not in reality put any money at risk'. From F's perspective, 'this was not a trade but a means of securing tax relief'.

In *Investec Asset Finance plc v HMRC* CA, [2020] STC 1293, two financial dealing companies acquired interests in partnerships as part of a scheme to avoid being taxed on lease rental income. Both companies were held to be carrying on two trades, one being their sole financial trades and the other being their share of the partnership profits treated as the profits of a separate trade. The costs of purchasing the partnership interests were deductible revenue expenses in the sole trades, but the costs of making further contributions to the partnerships were disallowed as not incurred wholly and exclusively for the purposes of the financial trades.

See also *Black Nominees Ltd v Nicol* (1975) 50 TC 229 and *Newstead v Frost* (1980) 53 TC 525, HL. See generally **4** ANTI-AVOIDANCE.

Betting

[68.5] Betting by professional bookmakers is assessable (*Partridge v Mallandaine* (1886) 2 TC 179) even if carried on in an unlawful way (*Southern v A B* (1933) 18 TC 59)). Winnings from betting (including pool betting) or lotteries are exempt from CGT. [*TCGA 1992, s 51(1)*]. Receipts from newspaper articles based on betting system held assessable in *Graham v Arnott* (1941) 24 TC 157.

Lotteries and football pools promotion constitutes trading, but where a pool or small lottery is run by a supporters club or other society on terms that a specified part of the cost of the ticket is to be donated to a club or body within the purposes in *Lotteries and Amusements Act 1976, s 5(1)*, the donation element is not treated as a trading receipt (HMRC Statement of Practice, SP/C1). For further detail, see HMRC Business Income Manual BIM61600–61615. See **14.6** CHARITIES as regards charitable lotteries.

Horse racing etc.

[68.6] Racing and selling the progeny of a brood mare was held to constitute trading in *Dawson v Counsell* (1938) 22 TC 149, CA. In *Norman v Evans* (1964) 42 TC 188 the share of prize monies for letting racehorses was held to be assessable (under the old *Sch D, Case VI*). Profits from stallion fees are assessable (assessments upheld in case law under both old *Sch D, Case I* and *Case VI*) (*Malcolm v Lockhart* (1919) 7 TC 99, HL; *McLaughlin v Bailey* (1920) 7 TC 508; *Derby (Lord) v Bassom (Inspector of Taxes)* (1926) 10 TC 357, 135 LT 274; *Wernher v CIR* (1942) 29 TC 20; *Benson v Counsel (Inspector of Taxes)* (1942) 1 KB 364, [1942] 1 All ER 435) but wear and tear allowances (the forerunner of modern capital allowances on plant etc.) for stallions was refused in *Derby v Aylmer* (1915) 6 TC 665. Profits from greyhound breeding were held to be trading in *Hawes v Gardiner* (1957) 37 TC 671. 'Private' horse racing and training is not normally trading (cf *Sharkey v Wernher* (1955) 36 TC 275, HL).

Illegal trading

[68.7] Crime, e.g. burglary, is not trading but the profits of a commercial business are assessable notwithstanding the business may be carried on in an unlawful way, e.g. 'bootlegging' (*Canadian Minister of Finance v Smith* (1926) 5 ATC 621, PC, and cf *Lindsay Woodward & Hiscox v CIR* (1932) 18 TC 43, Ct of Sess), operating 'fruit machines' illegal at the time (*Mann v Nash* (1932) 16 TC 523), street bookmaking illegal at the time (*Southern v A B* (1933) 18 TC 59) and prostitution (*CIR v Aken* (1990) 63 TC 395, CA). But penalties for trading contrary to war-time regulations held not deductible (*CIR v E C Warnes & Co* (1919) 12 TC 227; *CIR v Alexander von Glehn & Co* (1920) 12 TC 232). See also **68.5** above. See **69** TRADING INCOME — DEDUCTIONS as regards prohibition on deduction of expenditure involving crime.

Simon's Taxes. See **B1.420.**

Income from land

[68.8] Rents and other income derived from the exploitation of proprietary interests in land are taxed as profits from a property business (see **60** PROPERTY INCOME) and not treated as income derived from a trade. [*CTA 2009, s 201(1)*]. The leading case is *Salisbury House Estate Ltd v Fry* (1930) 15 TC 266, HL, and see also *Sywell Aerodrome Ltd v Croft* (1941) 24 TC 126, CA; *Webb v Conelee Properties Ltd* (1982) 56 TC 149. For relaxations to this rule, see **68.23** below (tied premises), **68.44** below (surplus business accommodation), **60.2** PROPERTY INCOME (caravan sites) and **60.18** PROPERTY INCOME (electric-line wayleaves).

The commercial occupation of woodlands in the UK with a view to the realisation of profits is not a trade or part of a trade (and is also not within the charge on property income or on income not otherwise charged (see **53.15** MISCELLANEOUS INCOME). Otherwise, the commercial occupation of UK land with a view to realisation of profits is treated as the carrying on of a trade (though this does not apply if the land in question is being prepared for forestry purposes). [*CTA 2009, ss 37, 38*]. See **68.30** below as regards farming and market gardening and for a general exemption for woodlands.

Mines, quarries etc. Profits of mines, quarries, gravel pits, sand pits, brickfields, ironworks, gas works, canals, railways, rights of fishing, rights of markets, fairs and tolls and like concerns are computed and charged to corporation tax *as if* the concern were a trade, and losses are relieved as if it were a trade carried on in the UK. This applies only where the concern is not, in fact, a trade on first principles and is not treated as such under the commercial occupation rule above. [*CTA 2009, s 39; F(No 2)A 2017, Sch 4 para 129*]. As regards rent received in connection with such concerns, see **60.18** PROPERTY INCOME.

Isolated or speculative transactions — badges of trade

[68.9] For property transactions and share dealing see **68.13** and **68.14** respectively.

Whether the surplus on the purchase and resale of assets, otherwise than in the course of an established commercial enterprise, is derived from an 'adventure or concern in the nature of trade' depends on the facts. Para 116 of the Final Report of the Royal Commission on the Taxation of Profits and Income (1955 HMSO Cmd. 9474) lists six 'badges of trade':

(i) the subject matter of the realisation;
(ii) length of period of ownership;
(iii) frequency or number of similar transactions;
(iv) supplementary work on assets sold;
(v) reason for sale;
(vi) motive.

Other relevant factors may be the degree of organisation, whether the taxpayer is or has been associated with a recognised business dealing in similar assets and how the purchases were financed. For a review of the factors to be considered, see *Marson v Morton* (1986) 59 TC 381. In that case the court emphasised that the badges were not a comprehensive list and no single item is in any way decisive. At most they provide common sense guidance as to whether a trade is being carried on.

HMRC's summary of each badge of trade (HMRC Business Income Manual BIM20205) with a brief pointer as to its meaning, is as follows:

(1) Profit seeking motive. An intention to make a profit supports trading, but by itself is not conclusive.
(2) The number of transactions. Systematic and repeated transactions will support 'trade'.
(3) The nature of the asset. Is the asset of such a type or amount that it can only be turned to advantage by a sale? Or did it yield an income or give 'pride of possession', for example, a picture for personal enjoyment?
(4) Existence of similar trading transactions or interests. Transactions which are similar to those of an existing trade may themselves be trading.
(5) Changes to the asset. Was the asset repaired, modified or improved to make it more easily saleable or saleable at a greater profit?
(6) The way the sale was carried out. Was the asset sold in a way that was typical of trading organisations? Alternatively, did it have to be sold to raise cash for an emergency?
(7) The source of finance. Was money borrowed to buy the asset? Could the funds only be repaid by selling the asset?

(8) Interval of time between purchase and sale. Assets which are the subject of trade will normally, but not always, be sold quickly. Therefore, an intention to resell an asset shortly after purchase will support trading. However, an asset which is to be held indefinitely is much less likely to be a subject of trade.

(9) Method of acquisition. An asset which is acquired by inheritance, or as a gift, is less likely to be the subject of trade.

Tax cases where found trading:

- *Martin v Lowry* (1926) 11 TC 297, HL (a leading case) — on a purchase and resale of war surplus linen;
- *CIR v Livingston* (1926) 11 TC 538, Ct of Sess — a purchase, conversion and resale of a ship;
- *Cape Brandy Syndicate v CIR* (1921) 12 TC 358, CA — transactions in brandy;
- *Lindsay Woodward* at **68.7** above — whisky;
- *P J McCall decd v CIR* (1923) 4 ATC 522; *CIR v Fraser* (1942) 24 TC 498, Ct of Sess — whisky in bond;
- *Pickford v Quirke* (1927) 13 TC 251, CA — 'turning over' cotton mills;
- *Edwards v Bairstow & Harrison* (1955) 36 TC 207, HL — purchase and resale of cotton spinning plant;
- *Rutledge v CIR* (1929) 14 TC 490, Ct of Sess — purchase and resale of toilet rolls.

Tax cases where found not trading:

- *Jenkinson v Freedland* (1961) 39 TC 636, CA — the Commissioners' finding that a profit on the purchase, repair and sale (to associated companies) of stills was not assessable, was upheld;
- *Kirkham v Williams* (1991) 64 TC 253, CA — the Commissioners' decision that the sale of a dwelling house built on land partly acquired for storage etc. was an adventure in the nature of trade was reversed in the CA;
- *Rosemoor Investments v Insp of Taxes* [2002] STC (SCD) 325 — where it was decided that an investment company's participation in a property refinance scheme was by way of investment, not by way of trade, see **68.13** below;
- *Ms P Azam v Revenue and Customs Comrs* (No 2) [2011] UKFTT 50 — where the Tribunal was not satisfied on a balance of probabilities that the appellant was engaged in a trade in property. See **68.13** below.
- *Samarkand Film Partnership No 3 v HMRC* CA [2017] STC 926 — where it was decided that the two film leasing partnerships in question were not trading and so were not entitled to sideways loss relief. Similarly, in *Patrick Degorce v HMRC* [2015] UKUT 447 (TCC), [2013] UKFTT 178 (TC), the Upper Tribunal confirmed the First-tier Tribunal's finding that the purchase of film rights, followed immediately by their assignment so as to generate a loss, had not been a trading transaction. The loss was therefore not allowable as a trading loss.

Simon's Taxes. See **B1.405–B1.407, B1.447.**

Liquidators or receivers

[68.10] Whether a liquidator or receiver is continuing the company's trade or merely realising its assets as best he can, is a question of fact. For liquidators or receivers see *Armitage v Moore* (1900) 4 TC 199; *CIR v 'Old Bushmills' Distillery* (1927) 12 TC 1148; *CIR v Thompson* (1936) 20 TC 422; *Wilson Box v Brice* (1936) 20 TC 736, CA; *Baker v Cook* (1937) 21 TC 337.

Miscellaneous

[68.11] Assessments were upheld on a committee operating golf links owned by a Town Council (*Carnoustie Golf Course Committee v CIR* (1929) 14 TC 498, Ct of Sess); trustees under a private Act managing a recreation ground (*CIR v Stonehaven Recreation Ground Trustees* (1929) 15 TC 419, Ct of Sess); temporary joint coal merchanting (*Gardner and Bowring Hardy & Co v CIR* (1930) 15 TC 602, Ct of Sess); promotion of mining companies to exploit mines (*Murphy v Australian Machinery etc. Co Ltd* (1948) 30 TC 244, CA, and cf *Rhodesia Metals v Commr of Taxes* (1940) 19 ATC 472, PC); purchase and resale of amusement equipment (*Crole v Lloyd* (1950) 31 TC 338).

A company which made loans to another company to finance a trading venture was held not to be trading itself (*Stone & Temple Ltd v Waters*; *Astrawall (UK) Ltd v Waters* (1995) 67 TC 145).

The activities of the British Olympic Association (which included the raising of funds through commercial sponsorship and the exploitation of its logo, but many of which were non-commercial) were held as a whole to be uncommercial and not to constitute a trade (*British Olympic Association v Winter* [1995] STC (SCD) 85).

For whether *ostrich farming* (i.e. the ownership of ostriches which are looked after on the owner's behalf by others) amounts to trading, and for the consequences of such trading, see Revenue Tax Bulletin June 1996 pp 318, 319, issue 23.

See also *J Bolson & Son Ltd v Farrelly* (1953) 34 TC 161, CA (deals in vessels by company operating boat services held a separate adventure), and *Torbell Investments Ltd v Williams* (1986) 59 TC 357 (dormant company revived for purpose of acquiring certain loans held to have acquired them as trading stock). But a company formed to administer a holidays with pay scheme for the building etc. industry was held not trading (*Building & Civil Engineering etc Ltd v Clark* (1960) 39 TC 12). Assessments on profits from promoting a series of driving schools were upheld in *Leach v Pogson* (1962) 40 TC 585; in concluding that the profit from *first* sale was assessable, Commissioners were entitled to take into account the subsequent transactions.

Oil-related activities

[68.12] The carrying on of oil-related activities (i.e. oil extraction activities within *CTA 2010, s 272* for corporation tax or *TIOPA 2010, Sch 1* for income tax and any activities consisting of the acquisition, enjoyment or exploitation of oil rights) as part of a trade is treated for corporation tax purposes as a separate trade in itself. [*CTA 2010, ss 274, 279*].

The carrying on of 'oil contractor activities' as part of a trade is similarly treated for corporation tax purposes as a separate trade in itself. '*Oil contractor activities*' are activities carried on by a company which are not oil-related activities but are either exploration or exploitation activities in, or in connection with, which the company provides, operates or uses a relevant asset in an offshore service, or are activities otherwise carried on in, or in connection with, the provision by the contractor of an offshore service. For this purpose, a company provides an '*offshore service*' if it provides, operates or uses a relevant asset in, or in connection with, the carrying on of exploration or exploitation activities in UK territorial waters or the Continental shelf by the company or any other associated person. A '*relevant asset*' is, broadly, a moveable structure for use in drilling for oil or for housing individuals who work on or from another structure used for exploration or exploitation activities. The asset must have a market value of £2 million or more and must be leased (whether by the company or not) from an associated person other than the company. [*CTA 2010, ss 256L, 256LA, 256M*].

Property transactions

[68.13] This part relates to transactions in land and buildings otherwise than in the course of an established business of property development, building etc. For HMRC's view, see HMRC Business Income Manual BIM60000–60165. For other sales of property see **68.52** below.

A line is drawn between realisations of property held as an investment or as a residence and transactions amounting to an adventure or concern in the nature of trade. The principles at **68.9** above apply suitably adapted.

In *Leeming v Jones* (1930) 15 TC 333, HL, an assessment on the acquisitions and disposal of options over rubber estates was confirmed by Commissioners. In a Supplementary Case the Commissioners found there had been no concern in the nature of the trade. The Court held there was no liability. Per Lawrence LJ 'in the case of an isolated transaction ... there is really no middle course open. It is either an adventure in the nature of trade, or else it is simply a case of sale and resale of property.' See also *Pearn v Miller* (1927) 11 TC 610.

Property transactions were held to be trading in:

- *Californian Copper Syndicate v Harris* (1904) 5 TC 159 — purchase of copper bearing land shortly afterwards resold;
- *Thew v South West Africa Co* (1924) 9 TC 141, CA — numerous sales of land acquired by concession for exploitation;
- *Cayzer, Irvine & Co v CIR* (1942) 24 TC 491, Ct of Sess — exploitation of landed estate acquired by shipping company;
- *Emro Investments v Aller* and *Lance Webb Estates v Aller* (1954) 35 TC 305 — profits carried to capital reserve on numerous purchases and sales;
- *Orchard Parks v Pogson* (1964) 42 TC 442 — land compulsorily purchased after development plan dropped;
- *Parkstone Estates v Blair* (1966) 43 TC 246 — industrial estate developed: land disposed of by sub-leases for premiums;

- *Eames v Stepnell Properties Ltd* (1966) 43 TC 678, CA — sale of land acquired from associated company while resale being negotiated. See also *Bath & West Counties Property Trust Ltd v Thomas* (1977) 52 TC 20.

Property transactions held to be non-trading in:

- *Hudson's Bay v Stevens* 1909, 5 TC 424, CA — numerous sales of land acquired under Royal Charter: contrast *South West Africa Co* above;
- *Tebrau (Johore) Rubber Syndicate v Farmer* (1910) 5 TC 658 — purchase and resale of rubber estates: contrast *Californian Copper* above.
- *Rand v Alberni Land Co Ltd* (1920) 7 TC 629 — sales of land held in trust were held not trading but contrast *Alabama Coal Iron Land v Mylam* (1926) 11 TC 232; *Balgownie Land Trust v CIR* (1929) 14 TC 684, Ct of Sess; *St Aubyn Estates v Strick* (1932) 17 TC 412; *Tempest Estates v Walmsley* (1975) 51 TC 305.
- *CIR v Hyndland Investment Co Ltd* (1929) 14 TC 694, Ct of Sess; *Glasgow Heritable Trust v CIR* (1954) 35 TC 196, Ct of Sess; *Lucy & Sunderland Ltd v Hunt* (1961) 40 TC 132 — sales of property after a period of letting held realisations of investments or not trading. Contrast held trading in *Rellim Ltd v Vise* (1951) 32 TC 254, CA (notwithstanding that company previously admitted as investment company); *CIR v Toll Property Co* (1952) 34 TC 13, Ct of Sess; *Forest Side Properties (Chingford) v CIR* (1961) 39 TC 665, 40 ATC 155, CA.
- *Simmons v CIR* (1980) 53 TC 461, HL (reversing Commissioners' decision) — sales by liquidator of property owned by companies following abandonment of plan for their public flotation held not trading.
- *Rosemoor Investments v Inspector of Taxes* [2002] STC (SCD) 325 — it was not open to the Commissioners to recharacterise as trading a complex transaction routed via an investment company subsidiary and structured to produce capital.
- In *Ms P Azam* [2011] UKFTT 50 (TC) the Tribunal found, on the balance of probabilities, that the appellant was not engaged in a trade in property. The appellant purchased eleven properties and although she claimed that it had always been her intention to sell each of the properties within a period of six months of their purchase, she had in fact not sold any of them. She claimed she had to rent the properties as she was waiting for an improvement in the property market. However, notwithstanding this, she continued to buy properties and thus repeat her mistake. The Tribunal was therefore satisfied on the balance of probabilities that at the time of purchasing subsequent properties, she was aware that she would have to rent the properties for some years, and indeed this could even have been the intention from the outset. Furthermore, the nature of the appellant's activities in relation to the properties were consistent with those of a landlord.

Simon's Taxes. See **B1.406, B5.213, B5.216–B5.222.**

Share dealing

[68.14] Share dealing with the public is strictly controlled by the *Financial Services and Markets Act 2000*. This paragraph is concerned with share transactions entered into (generally through the Stock Exchange) by persons not authorised to deal under that Act and the question arises whether they amount to an adventure or concern in the nature of trade. The principles of **68.9** above apply suitably adapted. The prudent management of an investment portfolio may necessitate changes in the holdings but this is not normally trading. Stock Exchange speculation, particularly by individuals, may be quasi-gambling and not trading — see Pennycuick J in *Lewis Emanuel & Son Ltd v White* (1965) 42 TC 369 in which, reversing the Commissioners' finding, he held that the Stock Exchange losses of a fruit etc. merchanting company were from a separate trade of share dealing but observed that gambling by the company would have been *ultra vires*. Subsequent *Companies Act* changes have, however, removed any such restriction on the activities of most companies (see HMRC Inspector' Manual IM 129a). In *Cooper v C & J Clark Ltd* (1982) 54 TC 670, the losses of a manufacturing company on its sale of gilts, in which it had invested temporarily surplus cash, were allowed as a set-off against its general trading profits. An individual speculating in stocks and shares and commodity futures was held to be trading in *Wannell v Rothwell* (1996) 68 TC 719 (although loss relief was refused on the grounds that the trading was 'uncommercial', see **51.8**(a) LOSSES), but the opposite conclusion was reached in *Salt v Chamberlain* (1979) 53 TC 143.

For share dealing by investment companies see *Scottish Investment Trust Co v Forbes* (1893) 3 TC 231 and *Halefield Securities Ltd v Thorpe* (1967) 44 TC 154. For trading in secured loans, see *Torbell Investments Ltd v Williams* (1986) 59 TC 357.

For share sales connected with an existing business see **68.55** below.

Commencement or cessation

[68.15] Where a company starts or ceases to be within the charge to corporation tax in respect of a trade, it is treated as starting or permanently ceasing to carry on the trade at that time. [*CTA 2009, s 41*].

For a short article on the distinction between succession to a trade, extension of an existing trade and commencement of a new trade, see HMRC Tax Bulletin February 1996 pp 285, 286, issue 21. See also HMRC Business Income Manual BIM38300 *et seq*.

Simon's Taxes. See **B1.6**.

Post-cessation receipts

[68.16] Corporation tax is charged on 'post-cessation receipts' arising from a trade to the extent that they have not been brought into account in computing trading profits or the profits of a property business for any period and that they are not otherwise chargeable to tax. However, a post-cessation receipt is not within this charge if it is received by or on behalf of a non UK resident which is beneficially entitled to it and it represents income arising outside the UK or if it derives from a trade carried on wholly outside the UK (other than a trade of dealing in or developing UK land (see **71.2** TRANSACTIONS IN UK LAND)). The charge is made on the full amount of post-cessation receipts received in the accounting period subject to the allowable deductions set out below.

For these purposes, a '*post-cessation receipt*' is a sum which a company receives after permanently discontinuing a trade (including on a change of ownership which, under *CTA 2009, s 41* (company beginning or ceasing to carry on a trade, see above), is treated as a permanent discontinuance) but which arises from the carrying on of the trade before cessation. Certain sums as below are specifically treated as being, or as not being (as the case may be), post-cessation receipts.

Where the trade is carried on in partnership, the person treated as permanently discontinuing the trade is the partner. Receipts within the legislation will include, *inter alia*, royalties and similar amounts which under decisions such as *Carson v Cheyney's Exor* (1958) 38 TC 240, HL, prior to the original legislation being enacted, had been held not to be taxable.

Debts

To the extent that a deduction has been made, in computing the profits of the trade, for an impaired loss or a release of liability (see **69.5** TRADING INCOME — DEDUCTIONS), any amount received after cessation in settlement of that debt is a post-cessation receipt. If an amount owed *by* the trader is released, in whole or in part, after cessation, the amount released is a post-cessation receipt; this applies only if a trading deduction was allowed for the expense giving rise to the debt and does not apply if the release of the debt is part of a statutory insolvency arrangement (as defined in **69.5** TRADING INCOME — DEDUCTIONS).

Transfers of rights

If a company permanently ceases to carry on a trade and the right to receive a post-cessation receipt is transferred for value to another person (other than one who succeeds to the trade), the transferor is treated as receiving at that point a post-cessation receipt equal to the consideration for the transfer or, if the transfer is not at arm's length, the value of the rights transferred. The post-cessation receipts themselves are not then charged when received by the transferee. This paragraph is subject to the provision that a sum received for the transfer of trading stock on a cessation is not a post-cessation receipt if the stock has been brought into account in the accounts to cessation.

If, however, the right to receive any sums arising from the transferor's trade are transferred to a company which does succeed to the trade, then, to the extent (if any) that they were not brought into account in computing the transferor's profits for any pre-cessation period, those sums are treated as trading receipts of the transferee as and when received. They are not post-cessation receipts.

Allowable deductions

A deduction from post-cessation receipts is allowed for any loss, expense or debit or capital allowance that would have been deductible if the trade had not ceased, has not been relieved in any other way and which does not arise directly or indirectly from the cessation itself. A deduction may not be given more than once. In the case of a loss, relief is given against the first available post-cessation receipts, i.e. receipts for an earlier accounting period in priority to those for a later one, but not so as give relief for a loss against receipts charged for an accounting period before that in which the loss is made.

Election to carry back

A company may elect to carry back a post-cessation receipt received in an accounting period beginning not later than six years after cessation of trade. The election allows for the receipt to be taxed as if it had arisen on the date of cessation. The election must be made within two years after the end of the accounting period in which the amount is received. Where loss relief has been given for the year of cessation by carry-back from a later period, this relief is not disturbed by an election. The '*additional tax*' (i.e. the recalculated liability to corporation tax for the accounting period in which cessation occurred less what it would have been without the election) is payable for the accounting period in which the receipt is received; if previous elections under these provisions have been made, these are taken into account in arriving at the additional tax.

[*CTA 2009, ss 95, 188–201*].

Simon's Taxes. See B2.8.

Case law

[68.17] Whether or not a company has commenced/ceased trading and, if so, the date, are questions of fact.

- Preliminary activities in setting up a business do not amount to trading (*Birmingham & District Cattle By-Products Co Ltd v CIR* (1919) 12 TC 92). Carrying on negotiations to enter into contracts which, when formed, constitute operational activity, does not amount to trading (*Mansell v Revenue and Customs Comrs* [2006] STC (SCD) 605).
- For whether the sale of a business can be effective for tax purposes before the vending agreement, see *Todd v Jones Bros Ltd* (1930) 15 TC 396 and contrast *Angel v Hollingworth & Co* (1958) 37 TC 714.
- 'Permanent discontinuance' does not mean a discontinuance which is everlasting (see *Ingram v Callaghan* (1968) 45 TC 151, CA) but a trade may continue notwithstanding a lengthy break in active trading (*Kirk & Randall Ltd v Dunn* (1924) 8 TC 663 but contrast *Goff v Osborne & Co (Sheffield) Ltd* (1953) 34 TC 441).
- The trade was held to have been continuous when the owner of a drifter continued to manage it after its war-time requisition (*Sutherland v CIR* (1918) 12 TC 63, Ct of Sess); when a flour miller and baker gave up a mill (*Bolands Ltd v Davis* (1925) 4 ATC 532); when a barrister took silk (*Seldon v Croom-Johnson* (1932) 16 TC 740); when a building partner-

ship transferred construction activities to a company but retained building land and continued to sell land with houses built thereon by the company (*Watts v Hart* (1984) 58 TC 209).

- A new trade was held to have commenced when the vendor of a business retained the benefit of outstanding hire-purchase agreements (*Parker v Batty* (1941) 23 TC 739) and when the vendor of a business got commission on open contracts completed by the purchaser (*Southern v Cohen's Exors* (1940), 23 TC 566).

It is similarly a question of fact whether a trader expanding by taking over an existing business and operating it as a branch has succeeded to the trade. See e.g. *Bell v National Provincial Bank of England Ltd* (1903) 5 TC 1, CA (bank succeeded to trade of single-branch bank taken over); *Laycock v Freeman Hardy & Willis Ltd CA* (1938) 22 TC 288 (shoe retailer did not succeed to trade of manufacturing subsidiaries taken over); *Briton Ferry Steel Co Ltd v Barry* (1939) 23 TC 414, CA (steel manufacturer succeeded to trade of tinplate manufacturing subsidiaries taken over); and *Maidment v Kibby* (1993) 66 TC 137 (fish and chip shop proprietor did not succeed to trade of existing business taken over). See also *H & G Kinemas Ltd* (1933) 18 TC 116 (cinema company disposed of existing cinemas and opened new one, held to commence new trade).

More recently with regard to sole traders and whether there was a discontinuance of trade, in *T J Moore v HMRC* [2011] UKFTT 526 (TC) it was held that a self-employed musician, who had begun working as a peripatetic music teacher when his income from work as a touring musician declined, was continuing to trade as a musician despite the fact that, in the year in question, 94% of his trading income derived from his work as a music teacher.

However, in *Admirals Locums and Bhadra v HMRC* [2011] UKFTT 573 (TC), [2011] SWTI 2929 where a doctor had been erased from the register of medical practitioners, the First-Tier Tribunal held that he had ceased to carry on a trade or profession as a doctor, even though he had taken court proceedings against the General Medical Council in an attempt to be restored to the register.

Whether or not there has been a commencement etc. has arisen in a number of cases where the activities of a company have altered on e.g. a change of shareholdings or a group reconstruction or on its absorption of another trade or part-trade. See:

- *Robroyston Brickworks Ltd v CIR* [1976] STC 329, 51 TC 230, Ct of Sess — trade of a brick-manufacturing company treated as continuous despite closure of works and their re-opening five months later, following the acquisition of its shares by another company, at different premises and with different staff;
- *Howden Boiler & Armaments Co Ltd v Stewart* (1924) 9 TC 205 — shell-making considered an extension of the existing business as boilermakers;
- *Gordon & Blair Ltd v CIR* (1962) 40 TC 358, Ct of Sess — brewing company treated as ceasing the trade of brewing and beginning a new trade of beer selling when it ceased brewing but continued to sell beer supplied to its specification by another company;

- *Cannon Industries Ltd v Edwards* (1965) 42 TC 625 — assembly of electric food mixers for retail sale treated as extension of existing trade of manufacture of gas cookers.

Calculation of trade profits

Generally accepted accounting practice

[68.18] Trading profits must be computed in accordance with 'generally accepted accounting practice' (GAAP) (see also **68.19** below). GAAP is defined by reference to the practice adopted in UK company accounts that are drawn up to give a true and fair view, but in relation to the affairs of a company or other entity that prepares accounts using international accounting standards ('IAS'), GAAP means generally accepted accounting practice in relation to IAS accounts. The requirement is subject to any adjustment required or authorised by law; see, for example, the prohibition at **69.8** TRADING INCOME — DEDUCTIONS on deducting capital expenditure. [*CTA 2009, s 46; CTA 2010, s 1127*].

Where one company within a group of companies (as defined in *TCGA 1992, s 170(3)–(6)* — broadly, a parent and its 75% subsidiaries) prepares accounts in accordance with international accounting standards and another company in the same group prepares accounts in accordance with UK generally accepted accounting practice and, as a result, a tax advantage is gained in relation to a transaction or a series of transactions, the profits will be computed for tax purposes as though both companies prepared accounts in accordance with UK generally accepted accounting practice. '*Tax advantage*' is as defined in *CTA 2010, s 1139* (see **70.1** TRANSACTIONS IN SECURITIES) and '*series of transactions*' is as defined by *TIOPA 2010, s 147* — see **72.2** TRANSFER PRICING. [*CTA 2010, s 996*].

For HMRC's view on the relationship between accounting profits and taxable profits, see HMRC Business Income Manual BIM31000–31115 and for generally accepted accounting practice and accounting standards, see BIM31020–31065.

See **68.19** below for the application of accounting principles generally, and **68.20** below for the tax treatment where there is, from one period of account of a trade etc. to the next, a 'change of basis' in computing trading profits. [*CTA 2009, ss 180–187*].

Simon's Taxes. See **B2.101, B2.101A, B2.102.**

Application of accountancy principles

[68.19] Although *CTA 2009, s 46* requires profits to be computed in accordance with GAAP (see **68.18**), accountancy principles cannot override established income tax principles (*Heather v P-E Consulting Group Ltd* (1972) 48 TC 293, CA; *Willingale v International Commercial Bank Ltd* (1977) 52 TC 242, HL; but see *Threlfall v Jones* (1993) 66 TC 77, CA; *Johnston v Britannia Airways Ltd* (1994) 67 TC 99). See also *RTZ Oil & Gas Ltd v Elliss* (1987) 61 TC 132. Other examples include:

- *Meat Traders Ltd v Cushing* [1997] STC (SCD) 245 — a 'provision for a future operating loss', whose inclusion could not be said to have 'violated existing accounting principles', was disallowed).
- *Robertson v CIR* [1997] STC (SCD) 282 — regards timing of inclusion of insurance agents' advance commission.
- *Herbert Smith v Honour* (1999) 72 TC 130 — timing of deductions in respect of future rents under leases of premises ceasing to be used for business purposes, and Revenue Press Release 20 July 1999 for Revenue practice following that decision.

Per Sir Thomas Bingham MR in *Threlfall v Jones*: '... I find it hard to understand how any judge-made rule could override the application of a generally accepted rule of commercial accountancy which:

(a) applied to the situation in question;
(b) was not one of two or more rules applicable to the situation in question; and
(c) was not shown to be inconsistent with the true facts or otherwise inapt to determine the true profits or losses of the business'. FRS 18 now requires companies to choose accounting policies that are most appropriate to their particular circumstances (see Revenue Tax Bulletin April 2002 p 923 to 924, issue 58).

In *L Smith v HMRC*, UT May 2011, FTC/47/2010, the First-tier Tribunal considered that accounts not prepared in accordance with GAAP which therefore understated the value of a trader's work in progress amounted to negligent conduct.

In *Ball UK Holdings Ltd v HMRC* UT 2018, [2019] STC 193, the Upper Tribunal held that, 'the question of what is generally accepted accounting practice, as well as the question whether a particular set of accounts are prepared in accordance with it, is a question of fact to be determined with the assistance of expert evidence'. The Court or Tribunal's role was 'the proper assessment of expert evidence'. A judge could prefer the evidence of one expert to that of another, but should not 'develop his own theory'.

For HMRC's view on the timing of deductions where an expense is taken to the balance sheet rather than charged immediately against profits, i.e. *deferred revenue expenditure*, see HMRC Business Income Manual BIM42215. For a case in which HMRC sought unsuccessfully to disallow deferred revenue expenditure on maintenance of a property when that property was sold, see *West Burton Property Ltd v HMRC* FTT, [2021] UKFTT 160 (TC). For *provisions*, see HMRC Business Income Manual BIM46500 *et seq.* and HMRC Press Release 20 July 1999, HMRC Business Income Manual BIM31000 onwards.

Simon's Taxes. See **B2.104, B2.106.**

Adjustments on change of basis

[68.20] The adjustment described below is required where:

- there is, from one period of account of a trade to the next, a 'change of basis' in computing taxable profits;

- the old basis accorded with the law or practice applicable in relation to the period of account before the change; and
- the new basis accords with the law and practice applicable in relation to the period of account following the change.

A '*change of basis*' for this purpose is:

- a change of accounting policy; or
- a change in the statutory tax adjustments applied (including a change resulting from a change of view as to application of the statute but excluding a change made to comply with an amendment to the statute which was not applicable to the earlier period of account).

A change of accounting policy can include, but is not limited to, a change from using UK GAAP (see **68.18** above) to using international accounting standards and vice versa.

Subject to the special cases referred to below, the adjustment required is calculated as follows.

(i) Taxable receipts and allowable expenses of the trade etc. for periods of account before the change are determined on the old and new bases, and the net understatement of profits (or overstatement of losses) on the old basis compared with that on the new basis (a negative figure indicating a net overstatement of profits (or understatement of losses)).
(ii) That figure is then adjusted for any difference between the closing stock or work in progress for the last period of account before the change and the opening stock or work in progress for the first period of account after the change, also taking account of any change in the basis of calculating those amounts.
(iii) Finally an adjustment is made for depreciation to the extent that it was not the subject of an adjustment for corporation tax purposes in the last period of account before the change but would be the subject of such an adjustment on the new basis.

No further deduction is allowed for amounts taken into account in calculating the adjustment. A positive adjustment is treated as a receipt of the trade on the first day of the first period to use the new basis. A negative adjustment is treated as an expense of the trade arising on the first day of the first period of account for which the new basis is used.

Special rules modify the above in a number of cases.

(A) **Expenses spread over more than one period of account after the change** on the new basis which were brought into account before the change on the old basis are excluded from the calculation at (i) above, but may not be deducted for any period of account after the change.
(B) **Adjustment not required until asset realised or written off.** Where the change of basis results from a tax adjustment affecting the calculation of amounts relating to trading stock or depreciation, the adjustment required by is brought into account only when the asset concerned is realised or written off.
(C) **Change from realisation basis to mark to market,** i.e. from recognition of a profit or loss on an asset only when it is realised to bringing assets into account in each period of account at fair value. Any adjustment

required by the above for an understatement of profit (or overstatement of loss) or under or overstatement of a expense in relation to an asset that is trading stock within *CTA 2009, s 163* is not given effect until the period of account in which the value of the asset is realised. An election may, however, be made for the adjustment receipt to be spread equally over six periods of account beginning with the first period after the change. The election must be within twelve months after the end of the first accounting period to which the new basis applies. If the trade etc. is permanently discontinued before the whole of the adjustment charge has been brought into charge, the uncharged balance is charged as if it arose immediately before the discontinuance. Special provision is made for the application of this rule in the case of insurance business transfers.

[*CTA 2009, ss 180–187*].

Partnerships

In the case of trades carried on by a company in partnership, the adjustment (as above) is calculated as if the partnership were a company resident in the UK. Each partner's share is determined according to the profit-sharing arrangements for the twelve months immediately before the first day of the first period of account for which the new basis was adopted. Changes in the members of a partnership are disregarded so long as a company carrying on the trade in partnership immediately beforehand continues to carry it on in partnership immediately afterwards (see **56.3** PARTNERSHIPS). An election for spreading of an adjustment under (C) above must be made jointly by all persons who were partners in the afore-mentioned twelve-month period.

[*CTA 2009, ss 1267–1269*].

Simon's Taxes. See B2.619.

Tax treatment of income and specific types of trade

[68.21] The following paragraphs refer to matters of relevance to companies in computing trading profits. See **1** INTRODUCTION for the general principles in computing profits chargeable to corporation tax. See also **9** CAPITAL ALLOWANCES; **10** CAPITAL ALLOWANCES ON PLANT AND MACHINERY; **27** DERIVATIVE CONTRACTS; **41** INTANGIBLE ASSETS; **49** LOAN RELATIONSHIPS; **60** PROPERTY INCOME; **63** RESEARCH AND DEVELOPMENT EXPENDITURE and **69** TRADING INCOME — DEDUCTIONS.

See HMRC Business Income Manual BIM50000 onwards for HMRC guidance on measuring the profits of a wide range of particular trades.

See **68.18** for the requirement to adhere to generally accepted accounting practice (GAAP), **68.19** above for the application of accountancy principles generally and **68.20** above for adjustments required on a change of basis.

The provisions for computing trading profits are in *CTA 2009, Pt 3*. Wherever they appear in corporation tax legislation in the context of computing trading profits, the words 'receipts' and 'expenses' refer generally to items brought into account as credits or debits in computing those profits, and contain no implication that an amount has actually been received or paid. [*CTA 2009, s 48*].

Bad debts — Recovery of impairment losses

[68.22] (The tax treatment of impairment provisions is dealt with at 69.5 TRADING INCOME — DEDUCTIONS.)

If a debt owed to a company by a trader is released (otherwise than as part of a statutory insolvency arrangement — see **69** TRADING INCOME — DEDUCTIONS), and the expense giving rise to the debt has been allowed as a deduction for corporation tax purposes, the amount released is treated as a trading receipt arising in the accounting period in which the release is effected. [*CTA 2009, s 94*]. HMRC take the view that the modern accountancy practice requires such write-backs to be taxed, subject only to the exception provided for releases under statutory insolvency arrangements (HMRC Business Income Manual BIM40265). See generally Business Income Manual BIM40201 *et seq*.

Where a company is a debtor in respect of a debt for the purposes of its trade, UK or overseas property business, the loss arising from the release of that debt falls to be dealt with under the loan relationships legislation. As a result, where the debtor and the creditor are connected the release is treated as tax free in the hands of the debtor. [*CTA 2009, ss 479(2)(d), (3A), 481(3)(f), (4A)*].

For debt recoveries and releases after the cessation of a trade, see **68.16** above. For VAT on bad debts, see **73.2** VALUE ADDED TAX.

Where an asset accepted in satisfaction of a trading debt is of market value (as at the date of acceptance) less than the outstanding debt, the deficit may be allowed as a deduction, provided the trader agrees that, on a disposal of the asset, any excess of disposal proceeds over that value (up to the amount by which the debt exceeds that value) will be brought in as a trading receipt (such receipt being excluded from any chargeable gain computation on the disposal) (HMRC Business Income Manual BIM42735).

Breweries, distilleries, licensed premises

Tied premises

[68.23] Receipts in respect of 'tied premises' which would otherwise be brought into account in calculating profits of a property business (see **60.2** PROPERTY INCOME) are instead brought into account as trading receipts. For treatment of expenses see **69** TRADING INCOME — DEDUCTIONS. Any necessary apportionment (e.g. where only part of the premises qualifies) is on a just and reasonable basis. '*Tied premises*' are premises through which goods supplied by a trader are sold or used by another person, where the trader has an estate or interest in the premises which he treats as property employed for trade purposes. [*CTA 2009, s 42*]. (*Note*. These rules are of general application, although of most common application in the licensed trade.)

Simon's Taxes. See **B5.611**.

Capital receipts

[68.24] In computing trading profits, capital receipts are not brought into account; this is made explicit for accounting periods ending on or after 1 April 2009 (and see **68.2** above) but was already a long-established principle. [*CTA 2009, s 93*].

As to the distinction between capital and income receipts, 'no part of our law of taxation presents such almost insoluble conundrums as the decision whether a receipt or outgoing is capital or income for tax purposes' (Lord Upjohn in *Regent Oil Co Ltd v Strick (Inspector of Taxes)* [1966] AC 295, [1965] 3 All ER 174, HL, qv for a comprehensive review of the law). A widely used test is the 'enduring benefit' one given by Viscount Cave in *British Insulated and Helsby Cables Ltd v Atherton (Inspector of Taxes)* [1926] AC 205, 10 TC 155, HL. For other cases involving expenses see **69** TRADING INCOME — DEDUCTIONS.

A gain or loss on the sale of a capital asset not included in trading profits is dealt with according to the provisions relating to capital gains tax. A sale of a fixed asset on which capital allowances have been claimed may result in a balancing charge or allowance, see **9** CAPITAL ALLOWANCES, **10** CAPITAL ALLOWANCES ON PLANT AND MACHINERY.

The revenue or capital nature of a payment is fixed at the time of its receipt (*Tapemaze Ltd v Melluish* (2000) 73 TC 167, following *Morley (Inspector of Taxes) v Tattersall* [1938] 3 All ER 296, 22 TC 51, CA).

For a brief note on HMRC's approach to challenging schemes or arrangements designed to turn income into capital (or capital expenditure into a revenue deduction), see Revenue Tax Bulletin June 1997 p 438, issue 29.

For HMRC's own guidance on capital *v* income, see HMRC Business Income Manual BIM35000–35910.

For case law on the difference between capital and revenue see **Simon's Taxes** B2.202–B2.204.

Car hire rebate

[68.25] Where the rental payments for hiring a car have been restricted see **69.9** TRADING INCOME — DEDUCTIONS, any subsequent rental rebate (or debt release other than as part of a statutory insolvency arrangement — see **69.5** TRADING INCOME — DEDUCTIONS) is reduced for tax purposes in the same proportion as the hire charge restriction. This treatment extends to amounts brought in as post-cessation receipts (see **68.16** above) after the trade has ceased.

Commission, cashbacks and discounts

[68.26] HMRC Statement of Practice SP 4/97 sets out HMRC's views on the tax treatment of commissions, cashbacks and discounts. The types of payment with which the Statement is concerned are as follows.

Commissions

Sums paid by the providers of goods, investments or services to agents or intermediaries as reward for the introduction of business, or in some cases paid directly by the provider to the customer. Sums paid to an agent or intermediary may be passed on to the customer or to some other person.

Cashbacks

Lump sums received by a customer as an inducement for entering into a transaction for the purchase of goods, investments or services and received as a direct consequence of having entered into that transaction. The payer may be either the provider or another party with an interest in ensuring that the transaction takes place.

Discounts, i.e. where the purchaser's obligation to pay for goods, investments or services is less than the full purchase price, other than as a result of commissions or cashbacks.

The Statement also deals with commissions or cashbacks which are netted off, or invested or otherwise applied for the benefit of the purchaser, or where extra value is added to the goods, investments or services supplied (e.g. the allocation of bonus units in an investment) (although in the case of the addition of value to investments this may represent a return on the investment, which is outside the scope of the Statement).

The Statement provides detailed guidance on the circumstances in which liability may arise either as trading income or as miscellaneous income on receipts of commission etc. It also considers deductibility of commission etc. passed on to customers.

Generally, ordinary retail arm's length customers will not be liable to income tax or capital gains tax. The Statement outlines the circumstances in which receipts are treated as tax-free, or payments qualify for tax relief, and contains an element of concession for those who, in the ordinary course of their business, earn commission relating to their own transactions. It contains a warning that the principles outlined may not be followed where tax avoidance schemes are involved, or where the arrangements for the commission etc. include an increase in the purchase price of the goods etc. involved. The tax treatment of the payer and the recipient are in all cases considered independently of one another.

For an article explaining the legal basis of this approach, see HMRC Business Income Manual BIM40650–40690.

Whilst SP 4/97 is couched in terms of *Sch D Cases I, II* and *VI*, which schedule no longer applies for corporation tax purposes post 1 April 2009, the principles relating to the nature of the income are still relevant.

See also HMRC manual guidance at BIM100210 with regard to the provisions in respect of miscellaneous income under *CTA 2009, Ch 8, Pt 10.*

Company directors and professionals in practice

[68.27] In certain circumstances, where a company makes a payment to, or for the benefit of, a director in respect of his employment as a director and the director was or is a member of a partnership or was appointed by another company, then, if the payment would otherwise be taxable employment income of the director, it is treated for corporation tax as a trading receipt of the partnership or appointing company. Where the director is a member of a partnership, this treatment applies only where the director carries on a profession. Being a director is a normal incident of that profession and of membership of the partnership, the director is required under the partnership agreement to account to the partnership for the payment and the amount of the payment is insubstantial compared with the partnership's total trading receipts. Where the director is appointed by a company, the treatment applies if the appointing company's profits are within the charge to corporation tax and the director is required to account for the payment to that company. The appointing company must either have the right to appoint a director to the board of the paying company because of its shareholding in, or an agreement with, the paying company or not be a company over which the director has control. In determining whether the director has control of the company the rights and powers of his spouse, civil partner, his children and their spouses and his parents, will also be taken into account.

A payment received by an individual who carries on a profession in partnership and paid in his capacity as an employee or office-holder (other than as a director) which would otherwise be taxable employment income, is treated for corporation tax purposes as a trade receipt of the partnership if the individual is required to account for the payment to the partnership and actually does so. The time spent by the individual on the office or employment must be insubstantial compared with the time spent on the profession, the office or employment must be related to the profession and the amount of the payment must be insubstantial compared with so much of the partnership's trading receipts as are attributable to the individual.

[*CTA 2009, ss 40A, 40B; SI 2018 No 282*].

Note that, before 6 April 2018, these provisions applied only by concession — see HMRC Extra-statutory Concession A37.

Compensation, damages etc. — receipts

[68.28] Compensation and damages receipts are treated as follows:

(a) **Capital sums** (i.e. sums not taken into account in computing income) received as compensation for damage, injury, destruction or depreciation of assets are subject to corporation tax on capital gains [*TCGA 1992, s 22(1)*] (but this does not apply to compensation or damages to an individual for wrong or injury to his person or in his profession or vocation). [*TCGA 1992, s 51(2)*]. See Tolley's Capital Gains Tax.

(b) **Cancellation or variation of trading contracts and arrangements**. An important case is *Van den Berghs Ltd v Clark* (1935) 19 TC 390, HL, in which a receipt on the termination of a profit-sharing arrangement was held to be capital. The arrangement related to the whole structure of the recipient's trade, forming the fixed framework within which its circulating capital operated.

Compensation etc. receipts were also held to be capital in:

- *Sabine v Lookers Ltd* (1958) 38 TC 120, CA — varying car distributor's agreement;
- *British-Borneo Petroleum v Cropper* (1968) 45 TC 201 — cancelling a royalty agreement;
- *Barr Crombie & Co Ltd v CIR* (1945) 26 TC 406, Ct of Sess — terminating agreement as ship-managers.

Other relevant cases:

- *Consultant v Inspector of Taxes* [1999] STC (SCD) 63 — termination of profit participation agreement. Receipts held not to be capital.
- *Chibbett v Robinson & Sons* (1924) 9 TC 48 — a payment by the liquidator of a shipping company to its managers as authorised by the shareholders held not assessable.

Compensation etc. receipts on the cancellation of contracts receipts from which, if completed, would have been trading receipts are normally themselves trading receipts, to be credited in the computations for the period in which cancelled. See:

- *Short Bros Ltd v CIR* and *Sunderland Shipbuilding Co Ltd v CIR* (1927) 12 TC 955, CA — cancellation of order for ships;
- *CIR v Northfleet Coal Co* (1927) 12 TC 1102; *Jesse Robinson & Sons v CIR* (1929) 12 TC 1241 — cancellation of contracts for sale of goods etc.;
- *Greyhound Racing Assn v Cooper* (1936) 20 TC 373 — cancellation of agreement to hire greyhound track;
- *Shove v Dura Mfg Co Ltd* (1941) 23 TC 779 — cancellation of commission agreement.

Similarly compensation to a merchanting company on cancellation of a contract to supply goods to it was held a trading receipt (*Bush, Beach & Gent Ltd v Road* (1939) 22 TC 519). See also *United Steel v Cullington (No 1)* (1939) 23 TC 71, CA; *Shadbolt v Salmon Estates* (1943) 25 TC 52; *Sommerfelds Ltd v Freeman* (1966) 44 TC 43; *Creed v H & M Levinson Ltd* (1981) 54 TC 477.

Compensation received on the termination of agencies is a trading receipt unless the agency, by reason of its relative size etc., is part of the 'fixed framework' (see *Van den Berghs* above) of the agent's business. See *Kelsall Parsons* (1938) 21 TC 608, Ct of Sess; *CIR v Fleming & Co* (1951) 33 TC 57, Ct of Sess; *CIR v David MacDonald & Co* (1955) 36 TC 388, Ct of Sess; *Wiseburgh v Domville* (1956) 36 TC 527, CA; *Fleming v Bellow Machine Co* (1965) 42 TC 308; *Elson v James G Johnston Ltd* (1965) 42 TC 545 (in all of which the compensation etc. was held to be a trading receipt). See also *Anglo-French Exploration Co Ltd v Clayson* (1956) 36 TC 545, CA.

For payments received on termination of building society agencies, see HMRC Capital Gains Tax Manual CG13050 *et seq*.

More recently, in *Countrywide Estate Agents FS Ltd v HMRC* (TC00557) [2011] UKUT 470 (TCC), [2012] STC 511, a company carried on business as a financial intermediary and received £25 million from a life insurance company in return for entering into an exclusivity agreement. In its corporation tax return, this was treated as a capital receipt. HMRC issued an amendment charging corporation tax on the basis that it was a trading receipt. On appeal, the First-Tier Tribunal applied the principles laid down in *British Dyestuffs Corporation (Blackley) Ltd v CIR*, CA 1924, 12 TC 586, and on the evidence that the taxpayer company had not disposed of 'anything in the nature of a capital asset', dismissed the appeal. In October 2011 the upper tribunal dismissed Countrywide's appeal and decided that HMRC was correct in ruling that the £25 million payment was a revenue receipt and not a capital receipt.

(c) **Compensation etc. relating to capital assets.** The courts have been concerned with a number of cases of compensation for sterilisation of an asset used in a trade. Most frequently cited relates to compensation to a company making fireclay goods for refraining from working a fireclay bed under a railway line — it was held to be capital (*Glenboig Union Fireclay Co Ltd v CIR* (1922) 12 TC 427, HL, and cf *Thomas McGhie & Sons v BTC* (1962) 41 ATC 144 and *Bradbury v United Glass Bottle* (1959) 38 TC 369, CA), but compensation to a colliery from the Government for requisition of part of its mining area was held to be a trading receipt (*Waterloo Main Colliery v CIR (No 1)* (1947) 29 TC 235). Compensation to a shipping company for delay in the overhaul of a ship was held to be a trading receipt (*Burmah Steam Ship Co v CIR* (1930) 16 TC 67, Ct of Sess) as was compensation to a jetty owner for loss of its use after damage by a ship (*London & Thames Haven v Attwooll* (1966) 43 TC 491, CA) and compensation for the detention of a ship (*Ensign Shipping Co v CIR* (1928) 12 TC 1169, CA, but contrast *CIR v Francis West* (1950) 31 TC 402, Ct of Sess). Compensation to a company for temporary loss of use of part of a landfill site was held to be a trading receipt (*Able (UK) Ltd v Revenue and Customs Comrs* [2008] STC 136, CA).

(d) **Compensation on compulsory acquisition etc.** Where compensation is paid for the acquisition of business property by an authority possessing powers of compulsory acquisition, any amounts included as compensation for temporary loss of profits or losses on trading stock or to reimburse revenue expenditure, such as removal expenses and interest, are treated as trading receipts. (See HMRC Statement of Practice, SP 8/79 and HMRC Business Income Bulletin BIM40115. This Statement of Practice was originally issued as consequence of *Stoke-on-Trent City Council v Wood Mitchell & Co Ltd* [1979] STC 197, CA.)

More recently this has been seen in the privy council case of *Lutchmumun v Director General of the Mauritius Revenue Authority* [2008] UKPC 53, [2009] STC 444. The issue before the Privy Council was whether a compensation sum payable in respect of a compulsory purchase order was taxable as income, as part of the taxpayers' business, or as capital, which would be a tax-free payment. In that case, part of the taxpayers' land was subject to a compulsory purchase order. The compensation received by was more than had originally been paid on acquisition. The Mauritius tax authorities treated the compensation as taxable income in the hands of the taxpayers on the basis that property had been acquired in the course of a business, the main purpose of which was the acquisition and sale of immovable property. The Privy Council found that the compensation sum was taxable as income and that the original assessments should stand.

(e) **Other compensation etc. receipts.** Voluntary payments to an insurance broker on the loss of an important client company (made by its parent company) were held, approving *Chibbett v Robinson* and *Carnaby Harrower* (see (b) above), not to be assessable (*Simpson v John Reynolds & Co* (1975) 49 TC 693, CA) and similarly for voluntary payments from a brewer to a firm of caterers for the surrender of the leases of tied premises (*Murray v Goodhews* (1977) 52 TC 86, CA) but *ex gratia* payments to an estate agent who had not been given an agency he expected were held, on the facts, to be additional remuneration for work already done and assessable. (*McGowan v Brown & Cousins (Stuart Edwards)* (1977) 52 TC 8). A payment to a diamond broker under informal and non-binding arbitration as damages for the loss of a prospective client was held assessable (*Rolfe v Nagel* (1981) 55 TC 585, CA). Compensation for 'loss of profits' following the destruction of the premises of a business not recommenced was held to be of a revenue nature in *Lang v Rice* (1983) 57 TC 80. For compensation receipts relating to the terms on which business premises are tenanted, see **68.53** below.

For the treatment of compensation received by businesses as customers of e.g. utility companies for interruptions and other service deficiencies, see HMRC Business Income Manual BIM40101.

Damages awarded to a theatrical company for breach of a licence it had, were held to be assessable (*Vaughan v Parnell & Zeitlin* (1940) 23 TC 505) as was compensation received by a development company under legislation for restricting development (*Johnson v W S Try Ltd* (1946) 27 TC 167, CA). A retrospective award for a war-time requisition of trading stock was held to be a trading receipt of the year of requisition (*CIR v Newcastle Breweries Ltd* (1927) 12 TC 927, HL).

Simon's Taxes. See **B2.417**.

Embezzlement etc.

[68.29] Where defalcations of employees of a company were made good by the auditor, who admitted negligence, a refund was held to be a trading receipt for the year in which it was made (*Gray v Penrhyn* (1937) 21 TC 252). This should be contrasted with *North v Spencer's Exors* (1956) 36 TC 668, 35 ATC 264, where a lump sum award paid to a doctor was held to be income of his practice in the years to which the award related.

Farming and market gardening

[68.30] Farming or market gardening in the UK is treated for corporation tax purposes as trading. All the UK farming carried on by a particular company (other than as part of a different trade) is treated as a single trade. Farming carried on by a partnership in which a company is partner is, however, separate from any farming carried on by the partner company itself. This does not apply to the woodlands or to land being prepared for forestry use. *CTA 2010, s 1125* (and previously *CTA 2009, s 1317*) defines farming as 'the occupation of land wholly or mainly for the purposes of husbandry'. The earlier definition referred only to the occupation of farm land. Market gardening is defined as 'the occupation of land as a garden or nursery for the purpose of growing produce for sale'.

[*CTA 2009, ss 36, 1270(1)*]. See *Bispham v Eardiston Farming Co* (1962) 40 TC 322 and *Sargent v Eayrs* (1972) 48 TC 573. The matters listed below are of particular application to farming or (where relevant) market gardening.

(a) **Compensation for compulsory slaughter.** Where compensation is received for compulsory slaughter of animals to which the herd basis (see **68.34–68.42** below) does not and could not apply, any excess of the amount received over the book value or cost of those animals may be excluded from the accounting period of slaughter and treated, by equal instalments, as profits of the next three accounting periods. The profit on an animal born in the year of slaughter is deemed to be 25% of the compensation received. The relief must be claimed on or before the first anniversary of the filing date for the company's return for the period of slaughter. [*CTA 2009, ss 127A–127G*].
For a worked example of this spreading relief, see HMRC Business Income Manual BIM55185.

(b) **Grants and subsidies.** As regards the time at which a receipt should be brought in for tax purposes the starting point is to identify the precise purpose of the grant or subsidy. A distinction should be drawn between grants to meet particular costs and those subsidising the sale proceeds of a specific crop. The former should reduce the costs in question (and if those costs are included in the closing stock valuation, the net cost should be used), whereas the latter should be recognised as income of the year in which the crop is sold. (Revenue Tax Bulletin February 1993 p 53 issue 6). A grant subsidising trading income generally is a trading receipt of the period when the entitlement to the grant was established, provided that it can be quantified with reasonable accuracy. As regards instalments of grant, the tax treatment should follow accounting practice, which provides that information available before accounts are completed and signed should be taken into account as regards those to which entitlement arose in the period of account. (Revenue Tax Bulletin February 1994 p 108 issue 10).
As regards animal grants and subsidies, these are generally recognised either at the end of the retention period or on receipt. Either of these bases will be accepted for tax purposes provided that it is consistently applied, as will any other basis which reflects generally accepted accounting practice provided that it does not conflict with tax law. A change of basis should be made only where the need for change outweighs the requirement for accounts to be prepared on a consistent basis, and will be dealt with in accordance with HMRC Statement of Practice SP 3/90 (see **69.63** TRADING INCOME — DEDUCTIONS). (Revenue Tax Bulletin December 1994 p 182 issue 14). SP3/90 has been superseded by HMRC manual guidance found at BIM34000 onwards.
The following relate to specific types of farm support payment.

(i) *Advances under British Sugar Industry (Assistance) Act 1931*, linked with sugar production and prices, were held to be assessable as trading receipts (*Smart v Lincolnshire Sugar Co Ltd* (1937) 20 TC 643, HL).

(ii) *Arable area payments*. Payments under the 1992 scheme for land set aside may be treated as sales subsidies, and hence recognised when the crops are sold. Valuations based on 75% of market value should include the same proportion of the related arable area payments. (Revenue Tax Bulletin February 1994 p 109). See (v) below for specific comment on oilseed support payments.

(iii) *Dairy herd conversion scheme*. Grants for changing from dairying to meat production were held to be assessable as trading receipts (*White v G & M Davis* (1979) 52 TC 597; *CIR v Biggar* (1982) 56 TC 254, Ct of Sess).

(iv) *Flood rehabilitation grants* in excess of rehabilitation costs (admitted to be capital) were held to be capital receipts (*Watson v Samson Bros* (1959) 38 TC 346).

(v) *Oilseed support scheme*. Payments of aid under the 1992 scheme are a subsidy towards the selling price, and as such should be recognised as income at the time of sale. If the final amount is not known when the accounts are prepared, but it is reasonably certain that a further payment will be received, the tax computations should be kept open to admit the final figure. If a reasonable estimate is included in the accounts and the difference when the final amount is known has only a small effect on the overall tax liability, the inspector may agree to recognise the difference in arriving at profits of the following year. (Revenue Tax Bulletin February 1993 p 53 issue 6).

(vi) *Ploughing subsidies* were held to be assessable as trading receipts (*Higgs v Wrightson* (1944) 26 TC 73).

(c) **Share farming.** HMRC consider that both parties to a share farming agreement based on the Country Landowners Association model may be considered to be carrying on a farming trade for tax purposes. In the case of the landowner, he must take an active part in the share farming venture, at least to the extent of concerning himself with details of farming policy and exercising his right to enter onto his land for some material purpose, even if only for the purposes of inspection and policy-making. (Country Landowners Association Press Release 19 December 1991).

(d) **Short rotation coppice.** This is a way of producing renewable fuel for certain power stations. The cultivation of 'short rotation coppice' (i.e. a perennial crop of tree species planted at high density, the stems of which are harvested above ground level at intervals of less than ten years) is treated for tax purposes as farming and not as forestry, so that UK land under such cultivation is farm or agricultural land and not woodlands (which is exempt from tax). [*FA 1995, s 154*]. For HMRC's view of the taxation implications of short rotation coppice, see HMRC Business Income Manual BIM55120. For the exemption for woodlands, see **68.8** above.

(e) **Sugar beet outgoers scheme.** Receipts and payments derived from the disposal of contract tonneage entitlement under contracts between farmers and British Sugar are to be dealt with on revenue and not capital account, i.e. as taxable receipts and allowable deductions in computing profits. Payments for entitlement which are amortised in the accounts over the period for which the entitlement may reasonably be expected to be of value to the business are similarly allowed for tax purposes. (See Revenue Interpretation 236; HMRC Tax Bulletin October 2001 pp 891, 892 issue 55). The Sugar Beet Quota system ended from 1 October 2017.

(f) **Trading profits.** Proceeds from the sale of trees (mostly willows planted by the taxpayer) were held to be farming receipts (*Elmes v Trembath* (1934) 19 TC 72), but no part of the cost of an orchard with nearly ripe fruit purchased by a fruit grower was an allowable deduction in computing his profits, which included receipts from the sale of the fruit (*CIR v Pilcher* (1949) 31 TC 314, CA). Proceeds from sales of turf were held to be trading receipts from farming (*Lowe v J W Ashmore Ltd* (1970) 46 TC 597).

(g) **Woodlands grants.** Under the Farm Woodland Premium Scheme and its predecessor, the Farm Woodland Scheme, farmers receive annual payments to compensate for lost farming profits. Such payments are taxable as part of the farming profits. If a person buys the woodland attracting such annual payments, they may continue to receive these payments. The payments are received as the owner of commercial woodlands rather than as a farmer whose land has been turned to woodland. Such receipts are not taxable, because they are receipts from commercial woodlands. (HMRC Business Income Manual BIM55165).

For these and other aspects of farming taxation, see HMRC Business Income Manual BIM55000–55730, 84000–84185 and 85600–85650.

Simon's Taxes. See **B5.1** onwards.

Creative industries reliefs

[68.31] See 26 CREATIVE INDUSTRIES RELIEFS.

Gifts and donations received

[68.32] The fact that a receipt is gratuitous is not in itself a reason for its not being a trading receipt. See *Severne v Dadswell* (1954) 35 TC 649 (payments under war-time arrangements held trading receipts although *ex gratia*); *CIR v Falkirk Ice Rink* (1975) 51 TC 42, Ct of Sess (donation to ice rink from associated curling club held taxable); *Wing v O'Connell* [1927] IR 84 (gift to professional jockey on winning race taxable).

Cremation fees (often known as 'ash cash') assigned in advance, and paid directly, to a medical charity may escape liability to tax on miscellaneous income where the doctor entitled to them is not chargeable to tax on trading income, but liability to tax on trading income is not affected by such assignment. See HMRC Business Income Manual BIM54015.

Gifts to charities and educational establishments

A relief is available for certain gifts by trading companies for the purposes of a charity (within **14** CHARITIES), any of the similar bodies listed in *CTA 2009, s 105(4)*, a 'designated educational establishment' or a registered community amateur sports club.

Where the gift is of an article manufactured by the company, or of a type sold by the company, in its trade, it is not required to bring in any amount as a trading receipt in respect of the disposal of the article.

Where the gift is of an item of plant or machinery used in the course of the company's trade, its disposal value for capital allowances purposes (see **10.27** CAPITAL ALLOWANCES ON PLANT AND MACHINERY) is nil.

The value of any benefit received by the company or by a person connected with the company (within **19** CONNECTED PERSONS), which is in any way attributable to the making of a gift for which relief has been given as above, must be brought into account as a trading receipt in the accounting period in which the benefit arises or, if the company has ceased to carry on the trade by then, as a post-cessation receipt (within **68.16** above).

See also **14.10** CHARITIES for anti-avoidance provisions which apply where donors receive benefits from a charity.

'*Designated educational establishment*' means any educational establishment designated (or of a category designated) in regulations, broadly all UK universities, public or private schools and further and higher educational institutions (see *SI 1992 No 42*).

[*CTA 2009, ss 105, 106, 108, Sch 2 paras 26, 27; 84; CAA 2001, s 63(2)–(4), Sch 2 paras 16, 17*].

Gifts of medical supplies and equipment

Where, for humanitarian purposes, a company makes a gift from trading stock of medical supplies or medical equipment for human use, no amount is required to be brought into account for tax purposes in respect of the donated items as a trading receipt. Transportation, delivery or distribution costs incurred by the company in making the gift are deductible in computing trading profits for the accounting period in which those costs are incurred.

The value of any benefit received by the company or by a person connected with the company (within **19** CONNECTED PERSONS) which is in any way attributable to a gift (or to ancillary costs) for which relief has been given as above must be brought into account as a trading receipt in the accounting period in which the benefit arises or, if the company has ceased to carry on the trade by then, as a post-cessation receipt (within **68.16** above).

The Treasury may by order exclude from the relief medical supplies or medical equipment of any specified description.

[*CTA 2009, ss 107, 108*].

No claim form or entry on the CT600 tax return is required for operation of this relief. For this and for the 'humanitarian purposes' requirement, and the broad scope of 'medical supplies and equipment', see the article on the operation of the scheme in the HMRC Tax Bulletin October 2002, pp 975–977 issue 61 & 62.

Simon's Taxes. See B2.441, B2.442, D1.353.

Herd basis

[68.33] See generally HMRC Business Income Manual BIM55501–55640.

Animals kept for the purposes of a trade

[68.34] Animals and other living creatures kept for the purposes of farming or similar trades (e.g. animal or fish breeding) are generally treated as trading stock (see 69.63 TRADING INCOME — DEDUCTIONS) unless:

- they are part of a herd in relation to which an election is made under *CTA 2009, s 109/122* for the 'herd basis' to apply; or
- the animals etc. are kept wholly or mainly for the work they do in connection with the trade or for public exhibition or racing or other competitive purposes.

[*CTA 2009, ss 50, 109(1)*].

Once an election is made the animals in the herd from part of the farmer's fixed capital for tax purposes, much like plant and machinery (although the herd does not qualify for capital allowances). Animals etc. are exempt from capital gains tax as wasting assets within *TCGA 1992, s 45*.

Herd basis — definitions

[68.35] For the purposes of the herd basis rules, an '*animal*' means any living creature, a '*herd*' includes a flock and any other collection of animals, and a '*production herd*' means a herd of animals of the same species, irrespective of breed, kept by a farmer or other trader wholly or mainly for the saleable produce obtainable from the living animal, which includes the young of the animal and any other product obtainable from it without slaughtering it. The herd basis provisions apply equally to animals kept singly and to shares in animals.

Immature animals kept in a production herd are generally not regarded as part of the herd for these purposes, but if:

- the nature of the land on which the herd is kept is such that replacement animals have to be bred and reared on that land (e.g. acclimatised hill sheep);
- the immature animals in question are bred and maintained in the herd for the purpose of replacing animals in the herd;
- it is necessary to maintain the immature animals for that purpose,

the immature animals are regarded as part of the herd in so far as they are required to prevent a fall in numbers.

An immature animal which is not regarded as part of the herd is regarded as added to the herd when it reaches maturity. Female animals are treated as becoming mature when they produce their first young or, in the case of laying birds, when they first lay (but see below as regards temporary concession during the 2001 foot and mouth outbreak).

[*CTA 2009, ss 110, 111(5), 122*].

Herd basis elections

[68.36] An election for the herd basis to have effect must specify the class of production herd to which it relates and must be made not later than two years after the end of the first accounting period during the whole or part of which a production herd of the class specified was first kept by the company. The election is irrevocable, and has effect in relation to all the production herds of the class to which it relates, including any which the farmer has ceased to keep before making the election or starts to keep after making the election. The election cannot relate to more than one class of production herd, but separate elections can be made for different classes. Two or more production herds are of the same class if the animals kept in those herds are of the same species (irrespective of breed) and the saleable produce for which the herds are wholly or mainly kept is of the same kind. An election has effect for every accounting period in which the farmer carries on the trade and keeps a production herd of the relevant class.

If the farmer is a partnership of which the company is a member, it is the partnership that has the right to elect for the herd basis to apply. In this case, the election must be made not later than the first anniversary of 31 January following the tax year in which ends the first period of account during the whole or part of which a production herd of the class specified was first kept by the partnership. Where there is a change in the persons carrying on a trade in partnership, a further election is required if the herd basis is to continue to apply. The further election must be made not later than the first anniversary of 31 January following the tax year in which ends the first period of account during the whole or part of which the 'new' firm keeps a production herd of the class to which the election relates.

[*CTA 2009, ss 111(2), 122, 1319*].

See below as regards a further opportunity to make an election in a case of compulsory slaughter.

Further assessments may be made for any accounting period as necessary, and repayments may be made (on a claim), to give effect to a herd basis election. [*CTA 2009, s 127*].

Five-year gap between keeping herds

[68.37] If a farmer has kept a production herd of a particular class, ceases to keep herds of that class for at least five years and then does so once more:

- any herd basis election previously made in relation to herds of that class ceases to have effect; but
- the farmer may make a further election by reference to the first accounting period (or period of account in the case of a partnership) in which the farmer again keeps a production herd of that class.

[*CTA 2009, s 123*].

Consequences of herd basis election

[68.38] Where a herd basis election is in force, the animals in the herd are in effect treated as capital assets instead of as trading stock. The initial cost of the herd is not deductible in computing trading profits, and its value is not brought into account. No deduction is allowed for additions to the herd (as opposed to replacement animals — see below). If the additional animal was previously part of trading stock, a receipt must be brought into account equal to the cost of breeding it, or acquiring it, and rearing it to maturity. If it is not possible to ascertain actual costs of breeding and rearing, an alternative deemed cost method may be used (HMRC Business Income Manual BIM55410, 55530). [*CTA 2009, ss 112, 113*].

Replacement animals

The replacement of an animal dying or ceasing to be a member of a herd gives rise to a trading receipt equal to the disposal proceeds (if any) of the animal replaced, and a trading deduction equal to the cost of the replacement animal (so far as not otherwise allowable) but limited to the cost of an animal of similar quality to that replaced (for which see Revenue Tax Bulletin October 2001 pp 890, 891). See below for meaning of disposal proceeds. Where the animal replaced was compulsorily slaughtered, and the replacement animal is of inferior quality, the trading receipt is restricted to the amount allowable as a deduction in respect of the new animal. [*CTA 2009, ss 111(3), 114, 115*].

Whether a particular animal brought into the herd replaces an animal disposed of is a question of fact, requiring a direct connection between the disposal and the later addition rather than a simple restoration of numbers. As a practical matter, HMRC will accept that replacement treatment is appropriate where animals are brought into the herd within twelve months of the corresponding disposal. Where disposal and replacement are in different accounting periods, the overall profit or loss may either be brought in the first period and any necessary adjustment made in the second, or the profit or loss arising in the first period may be held over to the second period. Where the interval is more than twelve months, there is unlikely to be sufficient evidence to support the necessary connection where the new animal is bought in. Where animals are home bred, however, a longer interval may be reasonable where e.g. there is insufficient young stock to replace unexpected disposals. (See HMRC Business Income Manual BIM55520 and Revenue Tax Bulletin February 1997 p 396, issue 27).

Disposal of animals from the herd

[68.39] Where an animal is disposed of from the herd, any profit is brought into account as a trading receipt and any loss is deductible as an expense. This does not apply if the animal is replaced (for which see above) or on a disposal of the whole or a substantial part of the herd within a 12-month period (for which see below). The profit or loss is computed by reference to disposal proceeds and the cost of breeding the animal, or acquiring it, and rearing it to maturity. Market value is substituted for acquisition cost if the animal was acquired other than for valuable consideration. [*CTA 2009, s 116*]. For HMRC's interpretation of this provision, including a change of view on how the profit on such disposals is to be computed, see Revenue Tax Bulletin April 2003 pp 1024, 1025.

For the purposes of the herd basis rules, the disposal of an animal includes its death or destruction as well as its sale, and disposal proceeds include sale proceeds and, in the case of death or destruction, insurance or compensation money received and proceeds of carcass sales. [*CTA 2009, s 111(3)(4)*].

On the disposal of the whole or a substantial part of the herd, either all at once or over a period of twelve months or less, any profit is not brought into account as a receipt and any loss is not deductible as an expense. (20% or more of the herd is regarded as a 'substantial' part of it (but this does not prevent a smaller percentage from being regarded as 'substantial' in any particular case). If, however, the disposal is of *the whole herd* and the farmer acquires, or starts to acquire, a new production herd of the same class within 5 years of the disposal, the following rules apply.

(i) The replacement rules above apply as if a number of animals, equal to the smaller of the number in the old herd and the number in the new, had been disposed of in the old herd and replaced in that herd. Disposal proceeds of any animal are brought into account when the 'replacement' animal is acquired.
(ii) If the number of animals in the new herd is smaller than that in the old by an insubstantial margin (i.e. normally less than 20% — see above), the difference is subject to the normal disposal rules in *CTA 2009, s 116* above.
(iii) If the number of animals in the new herd is smaller than that in the old by a substantial margin (i.e. normally 20% or more — see above), the difference is treated as a disposal of a substantial part of the herd.
(iv) If the number of animals in the new herd is greater than that in the old, the difference is treated as additions to the herd.

If the disposal is of *a substantial part of the herd* and the farmer acquires, or starts to acquire, a new production herd of the same class within 5 years of the disposal, the following rules apply.

(1) The replacement rules above apply insofar as the animals included in the part disposed of are replaced. Disposal proceeds of an animal included in the part sold are brought into account when the replacement animal is acquired.
(2) If some of the animals included in the part disposed of are not replaced, any profit on their disposal is not brought into account as a receipt and any loss is not deductible as an expense.

Where the disposal of all or a substantial part of a herd is for reasons wholly outside the farmer's control and a 'replacement' animal is of inferior quality to the old, the replacement rules above apply as they do when animals are slaughtered under a disease control order (whether or not that is indeed the case).

[*CTA 2009, ss 111(6), 117–121*].

Elections following compulsory slaughter

[68.40] Where compensation is receivable in respect of the whole, or a substantial part (normally 20% or more), of a production herd slaughtered by order under animal diseases laws, the farmer may, notwithstanding the time limits above, elect for the herd basis to apply. The election must be made not later than two years after the end of the first accounting period in which the compensation falls (or would otherwise fall) to be taken into account as a trading receipt. The election has effect for that accounting period and each subsequent accounting period of account in which the farmer carries on the trade and keeps a production herd of that class. (There are appropriate modifications where the farmer is a partnership rather than a company.) [*CTA 2009, s 124*].

Anti-avoidance

[68.41] There are provisions for the prevention of avoidance of tax in the case of a non-arm's length transfer of all or part of a production herd where either transferor and transferee are bodies of persons under common control or the sole or main benefit of the transfer relates to its effect on a herd basis election. [*CTA 2009, s 125*].

Information etc.

[68.42] Where an election has effect, HMRC may by notice require the farmer to make returns of information as to the animals kept and their produce. As from August 2009 see the information provisions provided for by *FA 2008, Sch 36* at *para 37A*.

[*FA 2008, Sch 36, para 37A; CTA 2009, s 126*].

Example

A farming company acquires a dairy herd and elects for the herd basis to apply. The movements in the herd and the tax treatment are as follows.

Year 1	No	Value
		£
Mature		
Bought @ £150	70	10,500
Bought in calves @ £180		
(Market value of calves £35)	5	900
Immature		
Bought @ £75	15	1,125
Herd Account		
Friesians	70	10,500
Friesians in calf (5 × £(180 – 35))	5	725
Closing balance	75	£11,225

Year 1	No	Value
Trading Account		£
Calves (5 × £35)	5	175
Immature Friesians	15	1,125
Debit to profit and loss account		£1,300

Year 2	No	Value £
Mature		
Bought @ £185	15	2,775
Sold @ £200	10	2,000
Died	3	—
Immature		
Born	52	—
Matured @ 60% of market value of £200 (note (a))	12	1,440
Herd Account		£
Opening balance	75	11,225
Increase in herd		
Purchases	15	2,775
Transferred from trading stock	12	1,440
	27	4,215
Replacement cost £4,215 × 13/27	(13)	2,029
Non-replacement animals cost	14	2,186
Closing balance	89	£13,411
Trading Account		£
Sale of 10 mature cows replaced		(2,000)
Transfer to herd — 14 animals		(1,440)
Cost of 13 mature cows purchased to replace those sold/deceased (13/15 × £2,775)		2,405
Net credit to profit and loss account (note (b))		£(1,035)

Year 3	No	Value £
Mature		
Jerseys bought @ £250	70	17,500
Friesians slaughtered @ £175 (market value £185)	52	9,100
Immature		
Friesians born	20	—

	No	£	£
Matured			
Friesians @ 60% of market value of £190 (note (a))		15	1,710
Herd Account	No	£	£
Opening balance	89		13,411
Increase in herd			
Jerseys	18		4,500
52 Improvement Jerseys @		250	
less Market value of Friesians		185	
52 @		65	3,380
Transfer from trading stock			
Friesians	15		1,710
Closing balance	122		£23,001

Trading Account	£
Compensation	(9,100)
Transfer to herd	(1,710)
Purchase of replacements (note (c)) (52 × £185)	9,620
Net credit to profit and loss account	£(1,190)

Year 4

The farmer ceases dairy farming and sells the whole herd.

		No	Value £
Mature			
Jerseys sold @ £320		70	22,400
Friesians sold @ £200		52	10,400
Immature			
Friesians sold @ £100		65	6,500
Herd Account			£
Opening balance		122	23,001
Friesians	52		
Jerseys	70		
Sales		(122)	(32,800)
Profit on sale (note (d))			£(9,799)

Trading Account	£
Sale of 65 immature Friesians	(6,500)
Credit to profit and loss account	£(6,500)

Notes

(a) The use of 60% of market value was originally by agreement between the National Farmers' Union and HMRC (see now HMRC manual BIM55410). Alternatively, the actual cost of breeding or purchase and rearing could be used.

(b) As the cost of rearing the 12 cows to maturity will already have been debited to the profit and loss account, no additional entry is required to reflect that cost. Due to the fact that the animals were in opening stock at valuation and will not be in closing stock, the trading account will in effect be debited with that valuation.

(c) The cost of the replacements is restricted to the cost of replacing like with like.

(d) Provided these animals are not replaced by a herd of the same class within five years, the proceeds will be tax-free.

Insurance received

[68.43] Premiums paid for business purposes are normally allowable (see 69.50 TRADING INCOME — DEDUCTIONS) and any corresponding recoveries are normally trading receipts (or set off against trading expenses or capital, according to the nature of the policy). Where a deduction was allowed for a loss or expense and the company trader recovers a capital sum under an insurance policy or contract of indemnity in respect of that loss or expense, the sum must be brought into account, up to the amount of the deduction, as a trading receipt. [*CTA 2009, s 103, Sch 2 para 25*]. Otherwise, if capital, the recovery may be taken into account, where appropriate, for the purposes of capital allowances or CAPITAL GAINS (11).

The whole of a recovery in respect of the destruction of trading stock was held to be a trading receipt of the year of destruction, notwithstanding that it exceeded the market value of the stock lost or not all the stock was replaced (*J Gliksten & Son Ltd v Green (Inspector of Taxes)* [1929] AC 381, 14 TC 364, HL; *Rownson Drew & Clydesdale Ltd v CIR* (1931) 16 TC 595). The total recovery under a loss of profits was held a trading receipt although in excess of the loss suffered (*R v British Columbia Fir & Cedar* (1932) 15 ATC 624, PC). See also *Mallandain Investments Ltd v Shadbolt* (1940) 23 TC 367. For recoveries under accidents to employees see *Gray & Co v Murphy* (1940) 23 TC 225; *Keir & Cawder Ltd v CIR* (1958) 38 TC 23, Ct of Sess. Where a shipping company insured against late delivery of ships being built for it, both premiums and recoveries held capital (*Crabb v Blue Star Line Ltd* (1961) 39 TC 482).

For premiums on policies insuring against death or critical illness of key employees see 69.50 TRADING INCOME — DEDUCTIONS.

Simon's Taxes. See **B2.211**.

Commissions

HMRC Statement of Practice SP 4/97 (see 68.26 above) deals widely with commissions, cashbacks and discounts.

See also *Robertson v CIR* [1997] STC (SCD) 282 as regards timing of inclusion of insurance agents' advance commission.

Investment income (including letting income)

[68.44] Investment income may be treated as a trading receipt where it is the fruit derived from a fund employed and risked in the business (see *Liverpool and London and Globe Insurance Co v Bennett* (1913) 6 TC 327, HL). This treatment is not confined to financial trades, but the making and holding of investments at interest must be an integral part of the trade. See *Nuclear Electric plc v Bradley* (1996) 68 TC 670, HL, in which (in refusing the company's claim that interest on investments to meet possible long term future liabilities was trading income) the crucial test was considered to be whether the investments were employed in the business (of producing electricity) in the accounting period in question. The Court of Appeal, whose judgment was approved, considered decisive the facts that the liabilities against which the investments were provided were liabilities to third parties, not to customers, and that, in view of the long-term nature of the liabilities, the business could be carried on for a long period without maintaining any fund of investments at all. See also *Bank Line Ltd v CIR* (below).

See **51.27** LOSSES as regards relief available to investment companies for losses on shares subscribed for in certain unlisted trading companies.

Payments received in lieu of dividends in contango operations were held to be trading receipts in *Multipar Syndicate Ltd v Devitt* (1945) 26 TC 359; also co-operative society 'dividends' on trading purchases (*Pope v Beaumont* (1941) 24 TC 78). For interest received by underwriters on securities deposited with Lloyd's see *Owen v Sassoon* (1950) 32 TC 101 and for discount receivable on bills see *Willingale v International Commercial Bank Ltd* (1978) 52 TC 242, HL.

In *Rosemoor Investments v Insp of Taxes* [2002] STC (SCD) 325, it was decided that an investment company's participation in a property refinance scheme was by way of investment, not by way of trade. That case involved a complex transaction routed via an investment company subsidiary. The transaction was structured to produce capital. The main issue in the appeal was whether Rosemoor's participation in the transactions was by way of trade (as argued by HMRC) or by way of investment (as argued by Rosemoor). That issue raised the following points: whether the transaction was the provision of short-term finance by Rosemoor's parent company, for whom the transaction was a trading transaction; or, if the transaction was that of Rosemoor, whether its participation was by way of trade or investment. The Commissioners decided that, in reality, the transaction was not the provision of short-term finance by Rosemoor's parent company. The transaction was Rosemoor's, and having regard to the 'badges of trade' and considering the whole picture, it was clear Rosemoor had invested its money and was not dealing in land as a trade. Accordingly, the appeal was allowed.

In certain cases income received under deduction of tax was unable to be included in a trading assessment (*Sch D, Case I or II*) (cf. *F S Securities Ltd v CIR* (1964) 41 TC 666, HL; *Bucks v Bowers* (1969) 46 TC 267; *Bank Line Ltd v CIR* (1974) 49 TC 307, Ct of Sess), and nor, subject to the Crown option between Cases could income received gross from sources within *Sch D, Cases III, IV* or *V* (cf. *Northend v White & Leonard & Corbin Greener* (1975) 50 TC 121) and also from sources *explicitly* within *Sch D, Case VI.*

Rents receivable

Rents receivable and other letting income are within the charge to tax on property income as opposed to trading income (see **68.2** above).

If, however, a company lets **surplus business accommodation** and the conditions below are satisfied, it may choose to include the receipts and expenses of the letting in computing its trading profits instead of treating them as receipts and expenses of a property business. The conditions are that the let accommodation must be 'temporarily surplus to requirements', it must not be part of trading stock, it must be part of a building of which another part is used to carry on the trade, and the letting receipts must be relatively small. For these purposes, 'letting' includes a licence to occupy. Once the receipts and expenses of a letting are included in trading profits, all subsequent receipts and expenses of the letting must similarly be so included. Accommodation is '*temporarily surplus to requirements*'. It must have been used for trading within the last three years or acquired within that period; the company must intend to use it for trading in future; and the letting itself must be for a term of no more than three years. The position is judged as at the beginning of a period of account. [*CTA 2009, s 44*].

See **60.2** PROPERTY INCOME for a further relaxation of the main rule above, this time in relation to caravan site operators.

Know-how

[68.45] For corporation tax purposes, 'know-how' created or acquired from an unrelated party on or after 1 April 2002 or acquired from any party (related or otherwise) on or after 1 July 2020 generally falls within the intangible assets regime. See in particular the commencement and transitional rules for that regime at **42.42** INTANGIBLE ASSETS. The following applies where know-how does not fall within that regime.

'*Know-how*' is any industrial information and techniques likely to assist in (a) manufacturing or processing goods or materials, (b) working, or searching for etc., mineral deposits, or (c) agricultural, forestry or fishing operations. For capital allowances on purchases of know-how, see **9.8** CAPITAL ALLOWANCES.

Where know-how used in the vendor's trade is disposed of, with the trade thereafter continuing, the consideration received is treated as a trading receipt, except to the extent that it is brought into account as a disposal value for capital allowances purposes (see **9.8** CAPITAL ALLOWANCES). This does not apply to a sale between bodies of persons (which includes partnerships) under the same control.

If the know-how is disposed of as part of the disposal of all or part of the trade, both vendor and purchaser are treated for corporation tax purposes as if the consideration for the know-how were a payment for goodwill. They may, however, jointly elect to disapply this treatment (within two years of the disposal, and provided they are not bodies under common control), and it is disapplied in any event in relation to the purchaser if, prior to his acquiring it, the trade was carried on wholly outside the UK. In either case, the purchaser may then claim capital allowances on the expenditure (see **9.8** CAPITAL ALLOWANCES).

Any consideration received for a restrictive covenant in connection with a disposal of know-how is treated as consideration received for the disposal of the know-how. An exchange of know-how is treated as a sale of know-how.

[*CTA 2009, ss 176–179, 907–910*].

For patents, see **68.49** below.

Simon's Taxes. See **B5.343–B5.348.**

Mines, quarries etc.

[68.46] A key issue with regard to the profits from this business is whether any expenditure is capital or revenue in nature, and there is a considerable body of case law that considers this in respect of various items of expenditure. See **9.9** onwards CAPITAL ALLOWANCES for mining etc. expenditure allowable. The relevant legislation which applied before 1 April 1986 originated from 1945 and may therefore affect any pre-1945 decisions below.

The cost of sinking (*Coltness Iron Co v Black* (1881) 1 TC 287, HL), deepening (*Bonner v Basset Mines* (1912) 6 TC 146) or 'de-watering' (*United Collieries v CIR* (1929) 12 TC 1248, Ct of Sess) a pit is capital.

A lump sum paid at the end of a mining lease for surface damage was held capital (*Robert Addie & Sons v CIR* (1924) 8 TC 671, Ct of Sess) but not periodic payments during the currency of the lease based on acreage worked (*O'Grady v Bullcroft Main Collieries* (1932) 17 TC 93). *Bullcroft* was decided before the enactment of what was *ICTA 1988, s 119* and is now *CTA 2009, s 270* and rents and tonnage payments for the right to withdraw surface support are easements within *s 119* (*CIR v New Sharlston Collieries Co Ltd* [1937] 1 KB 583, [1937] 1 All ER 86, 21 TC 69), CA. For shortworkings, see *Broughton & Plas Power v Kirkpatrick* (1884) 2 TC 69; *CIR v Cranford Ironstone* (1942) 29 TC 113. Provision for the future costs of abandoning an oil field and of restoring hired equipment used therein to its original state held capital (*RTZ Oil and Gas Ltd v Elliss* (1987) 61 TC 132).

For HMRC's view of the treatment of payments by mining concerns to landowners for restoration for surface damage, see HMRC Business Income Manual BIM62025. In particular, a payment of compensation for ascertained past damage is allowable, as is a provision for such expenditure where made in accordance with generally accepted accounting practice and accurately quantified.

Purchase of unworked deposits by sand and gravel merchant held capital (*Stow Bardolph Gravel Co Ltd v Poole* (1954) 35 TC 459, CA) as was purchase of land with nitrate deposits by chemical manufacturer (*Alianza Co v Bell* (1905)

5 TC 172, HL) and payment by oil company for unwon oil in wells it took over (*Hughes v British Burmah Petroleum* (1932) 17 TC 286). See also *Golden Horse Shoe v Thurgood* (1933) 18 TC 280, CA (purchase of tailings for gold extraction, allowable), and *CIR v Broomhouse Brick* (1952) 34 TC 1, Ct of Sess (purchase of blaes for brick manufacture, allowable).

See generally HMRC Business Income Manual BIM62000–62085.

Production wells etc.

The costs of drilling the second and subsequent production wells in an area are not generally allowable. [*CTA 2009, s 137*]. Although not specifically stated in the statute, this prohibition applies particularly to intangible drilling costs. For a discussion of this, see HMRC Oil Taxation Manual OT26237. Such costs may attract mineral extraction capital allowances (see **9.9** onwards CAPITAL ALLOWANCES).

Simon's Taxes. See **B5.651–B5.653**.

Miscellaneous receipts

[68.47] **Card winnings** of club proprietor, trading receipts (*Burdge v Pyne* (1968) 45 TC 320). For lotteries and football pools, see **68.5** above.

Mutual concerns, distribution of assets from

If a deduction has been allowed (in computing trading profits) for a payment to a corporate mutual concern for the purposes of its mutual business and the company receives a distribution in money or money's worth upon the winding-up or dissolution of the mutual concern, the amount or value received is a trading receipt. This applies only if the assets being distributed represent profits of the mutual concern. It does not apply to distributions of chargeable gains. If the trade has ceased by the time of the distribution, the amount or value received is a post-cessation receipt (within **68.16** above). [*CTA 2009, s 101*]. See generally **54** MUTUAL COMPANIES.

Simon's Taxes. See **B1.439**.

Overpayments received, due to errors by customers or their banks which the taxpayer neither caused nor facilitated, held not to be trading receipts (*Anise Ltd v Hammond* [2003] STC (SCD) 258).

Sales of assets

See *T Beynon & Co v Ogg* (1918) 7 TC 125(profits of colliery agent from deals in wagons held trading receipts); *Gloucester Railway Carriage v CIR* (1925) 12 TC 720, HL (sale by wagon manufacturer of wagons previously let, held trading receipts); *Bonner v Frood* (1934) 18 TC 488 (sale of rounds by credit trader, held trading receipts).

Timber purchases and sales

For purchases and sales of standing timber by timber merchants see *Murray v CIR* (1951) 32 TC 238, Ct of Sess; *McLellan, Rawson & Co v Newall* (1955) 36 TC 117; *Hood Barrs v CIR (No 2)* (1957) 37 TC 188, HL; *Hopwood v C N Spencer Ltd* (1964) 42 TC 169; *Russell v Hird and Mercer* (1983) 57 TC 127. For sales of trees by farmer see *Elmes v Trembath* (1934) 19 TC 72.

VAT repayment

Repayments of VAT held not to be due were held to be trading receipts in *Shop Direct Group v HMRC* SC, [2016] STC 747. In *Coin-a-Drink v HMRC* UT, [2017] STC 1351 the Upper Tribunal dismissed an appeal against an assessment to corporation tax on a VAT repayment.

General

See also *Thompson v Magnesium Elektron* (1943) 26 TC 1, CA (payments based on purchases, held trading receipts); *British Commonwealth International Newsfilm v Mahany* (1962) 40 TC 550, HL (payments to meet operating expenses, trading receipts).

Simon's Taxes. See **B1.431**.

Money's worth

[68.48] For transactions entered into in the course of a trade involving money's worth, there is a specific statutory rule that an amount equal to the value of the money's worth must be brought into account as a trading receipt if, had the transaction involved money, an amount would have been so brought into account. The rule is disapplied if there is another statutory rule which provides expressly for an amount in respect of the money's worth to be brought into account as a trading receipt. [*CTA 2009, s 49A*].

HMRC consider that this rule simply confirms previous law and practice following *Gold Coast Selection Trust v Humphrey* (1948) 30 TC 209, HL (Treasury Explanatory Notes to the 2016 Finance Bill).

Patents

[68.49] For corporation tax purposes, expenditure and receipts in respect of intellectual property created or acquired from an unrelated party on or after 1 April 2002 or acquired from any party (related or otherwise) on or after 1 July 2020 falls within the intangible assets regime. See in particular the commencement and transitional rules for that regime at **42.42** INTANGIBLE ASSETS.

Sums received on the sale of patent rights may, dependent on the facts, be trading receipts (*Rees Roturbo Development v Ducker* [1928] 1 KB 506, 13 TC 366, CA; *Brandwood v Banker* (1928) 14 TC 44; *CIR v Rustproof Metal Window* (1947) 29 TC 243, CA, and cf *Harry Ferguson (Motors) v CIR* (1951) 33 TC 15). Other sums are taxable under *CTA 2009, ss 912–920*, see **42.43** INTANGIBLE ASSETS.

Where a company held a patent for renovating car tyres, lump sums received by it under arrangements for giving the payer a *de facto* franchise in his area, were held to be capital receipts (*Margerison v Tyresoles Ltd* (1942) 25 TC 59).

For know-how and trade marks, see **68.45** and **69.68** respectively.

See also 56 PATENT INCOME for the 'Patent Box' regime. This allows companies to elect to apply a 10% corporation tax rate (as phased in from 1 April 2013) to profits attributable to qualifying intellectual property, which includes patents granted by the UK Intellectual Property Office and the European Patent Office, as well as supplementary protection certificates, regulatory data protection and plant variety rights.

However, where companies do not elect into the new regime the existing provisions will continue to apply.

Simon's Taxes. See **B2.456.**

Pooling of profits

[68.50] Where traders pool profits or act together in consortia but so as not to form PARTNERSHIPS (55) or trade jointly (cf *Gardner and Bowring Hardy v CIR* (1930) 15 TC 602, Ct of Sess; *Geo Hall & Son v Platt* (1954) 35 TC 440) each trader's share of the pooled profits will normally be treated as a receipt of his main trade and any payment under the arrangement by one trader to another will be deductible in computing his profits (*Moore v Stewarts & Lloyds Ltd* (1905) 6 TC 501, Ct of Sess, and cf *United Steel v Cullington (No 1)* (1939) 23 TC 71, CA). In *Utol Ltd v CIR* (1943) 25 TC 517 payments by one company to another under a profit sharing arrangement were held to be dividends payable less tax under the law then in force. For compensation received on the termination of a profit sharing arrangement see *Van den Berghs* at **68.28**(b) above.

For the tax treatment of consortium losses and relief, see **35** GROUP RELIEF.

Private Finance Initiative ('PFI') projects

[68.51] For a series of articles on the tax aspects of PFI projects (dealing with the introduction by the public sector body of surplus land, or cash derived there from, with stamp duty considerations, with income arising from leases of fully serviced accommodation and with the scope of a PFI operator's trade), see Revenue Tax Bulletin April 1999 pp 642–645 issue 40, October 1999 pp 694–697 issue 43, August 2002 p 950 issue 60. See also HMRC Business Income Manual BIM64000–64400.

Property sales and other property receipts

[68.52] As to whether a trade of property dealing is carried on, see **68.13** above; for rents receivable, see **68.44** above. For builders and property developers generally, see HMRC Business Income Manual BIM51500–51665. The trade of furnished holiday lettings is considered at **60.7** PROPERTY INCOME. See also **71** TRANSACTIONS IN **UK** LAND for trades of developing or dealing in UK land.

Sales of property by builders in special circumstances have been considered in a number of cases. Profits held trading receipts:

- *Spiers & Son v Ogden* (1932) 17 TC 117 — building activities extended;

- *Sharpless v Rees* (1940) 23 TC 361 — sale of land acquired for hobby abandoned for health reasons;
- *Shadford v H Fairweather & Co* (1966) 43 TC 291 — sale of site after development plan dropped;
- *Snell v Rosser, Thomas & Co* (1967) 44 TC 343 — sale of land surplus to requirements;
- *Bowie v Reg Dunn (Builders)* (1974) 49 TC 469 — sale of land acquired with business;
- *Smart v Lowndes* (1978) 52 TC 436 — sale of land in wife's name.

Sales of property built but let meanwhile held trading in *J & C Oliver v Farnsworth* (1956) 37 TC 51; *James Hobson & Sons v Newall* (1957) 37 TC 609; *W M Robb Ltd v Page* (1971) 47 TC 465 and this notwithstanding active building given up (*Speck v Morton* (1972) 48 TC 476; *Granville Building Co v Oxby* (1954) 35 TC 245). But in *Harvey v Caulcott* (1952) 33 TC 159 the sales were held realisations of investments and in *West v Phillips* (1958) 38 TC 203 some houses were treated as investments and others as trading stock. See also *Andrew v Taylor* (1965) 42 TC 557, CA. Sales of houses retained after business *transferred* held sales of investments in *Bradshaw v Blunden (No 1)* (1956) 36 TC 397; *Seaward v Varty* (1962) 40 TC 523, CA. See also *Hesketh Estates v Craddock* (1942) 25 TC 1 (profit on sale of brine baths held trading receipt of mixed business including land development).

For house sales subject to ground rents etc, see *CIR v John Emery & Sons* [1937] AC 91, 20 TC 213, HL; *B G Utting & Co Ltd v Hughes* (1940) 23 TC 174, HL; *McMillan v CIR* (1942) 24 TC 417, Ct of Sess; *Heather v Redfern & Sons* (1944) 26 TC 119. For ground rents (England) and feu duties (Scotland) there should be credited the lower of their market value and cost, the cost being taken as the proportion of the cost of the land and building in the ratio of the market value to the sum of the market value and the sale price. For ground annuals (Scotland) which are perpetual the realisable value is brought in. The right to receive the rent then becomes part of the fixed capital of the trade, whose subsequent sale is not taken into account for corporation tax purposes. Any premiums on the grant of leases are part of the sale proceeds.

Turf sales by a farmer were held to be farming receipts in *Lowe v J W Ashmore Ltd* (1970) 46 TC 597. For timber sales see **68.47** above.

A lump sum received by a property investment company in return for the assignment for a five-year term of a stream of rental income was held to be a capital receipt for part disposal of the company's interest (*CIR v John Lewis Properties plc* [2003] STC 117, CA).

Any excess of allowable deductions over rent received by a builder from property held as trading stock may be allowed as a trading expense (HMRC Business Income Manual BIM51555).

In *Rosemoor Investments v Insp of Taxes*, [2002] STC (SCD) 325, it was decided that an investment company's participation in a property refinance scheme was by way of investment, not by way of trade; for further details, see **68.44** investment income, above.

More recently, in a case concerning an individual, *Ms P Azam* [2011] UKFTT 50 (TC), the Tribunal found, on the balance of probabilities, that the appellant was not engaged in a trade in property, but was rather engaged in a property rental business. Although the appellant stated her intention was to sell the purchased properties, she did not sell any and rented them all. Her activities were consistent with those of a landlord. See **68.13** above.

Annuities under *Agriculture Act 1967* for giving up (after attaining age of 55) uncommercial agricultural land are treated as earned income and receipts of grants under the same *Act* for the same reason are exempt from capital gains tax. [*TCGA 1992, s 249*].

Where sales of land etc., are capital, the profits on assets disposed of are liable to capital gains tax.

For transactions not at market value see **69.63** TRADING INCOME — DEDUCTIONS.

Rents etc. for business premises

Reverse premiums

[68.53] See also **60** PROPERTY INCOME. In *New Zealand Commissioner of Inland Revenue v Wattie and another* (1998) 72 TC 639, PC, a decision which has persuasive authority in the UK, it was held that a lump sum paid by a landlord to a prospective tenant as an inducement to enter into a lease at an above-market rental (generally known as a reverse premium) was a receipt of a capital nature. Legislation was introduced to counter this decision, and it applies in relation to any 'reverse premium' received broadly after 9 March 1999. For these purposes, a '*reverse premium*' is a payment or other benefit received by way of inducement in connection with a transaction (the '*property transaction*') entered into by the company or a person 'connected' with the company (see below), where:

(a) the property transaction is one under which the company or connected person becomes entitled to an estate or interest in, or a right in or over, land; and
(b) the payment (or other benefit) is made (or provided) by:
    (i) the person (the '*grantor*') by whom that estate, interest or right is granted, or was granted at an earlier time; or
    (ii) a person 'connected' with the grantor; or
    (iii) a nominee of (or a person acting on the directions of) the grantor or a person connected with the grantor.

As regards (b)(i) above, the use of the word 'grantor' means that the provisions do not apply when a freehold is conveyed. The most common occasion on which the provisions will apply will be a payment by a landlord as an inducement to a tenant to take a new lease, but they may apply where an existing tenant pays a new tenant an inducement to take over the remaining term of a lease if (and only if) (b)(ii) or (iii) applies to the existing tenant (Revenue Tax Bulletin December 1999 pp 711–713 issue 44).

For the purposes of these provisions, persons are '*connected*' with each other if they are connected within *CTA 2010, s 1122* (see **19** CONNECTED PERSONS) at any time during the period when the 'property arrangements' are entered into. The '*property arrangements*' comprise the property transaction and any arrangements entered into in connection with it (whether earlier, simultaneously or later).

A reverse premium is treated as a receipt of a revenue nature. Where the property transaction is entered into by the recipient of the reverse premium for the purposes of a trade carried on (or to be carried on), the reverse premium must be taken into account in computing the trading profits. In any other case, the reverse premium is to be treated as a receipt of a UK property business, or (as the case may be) an overseas property business (see **60** PROPERTY INCOME), carried on by the recipient.

It is understood that accountancy principles require the receipt to be brought into account by spreading over the period of the lease or, if shorter, to the first rent review. This treatment must normally be followed for tax purposes (see **68.19** above) but, as an anti-avoidance measure, is overridden where:

(A) two or more parties to the property arrangements (see above) are connected persons (see above); and
(B) the terms of the those arrangements differ significantly from those which, at that time and under prevailing market conditions, would be regarded as reasonable and normal between persons dealing at arm's length in the open market.

In such case, the full amount or value of the reverse premium must be brought into account in the period of account in which the property transaction (see above) is entered into or, where applicable, the first period of account of the trade which the recipient subsequently begins to carry on.

None of these provisions apply to the extent that the payment or benefit is consideration for the first leg of a sale and leaseback arrangement within **4.8** or **4.9** ANTI-AVOIDANCE) or is taken into account under *CAA 2001, s 532* (contributions to expenditure) to reduce the recipient's expenditure qualifying for capital allowances (see **9.2** CAPITAL ALLOWANCES).

[*CTA 2009, ss 96–100, Sch 2 para 24*].

It will be seen that a reverse premium within the above provisions is not confined to a lump sum payment and that 'other benefit' may include, for example, a contribution to the tenant's costs or an assumption of the recipient's liabilities under an existing lease. 'Other benefit' must, however, represent money or something capable of being turned into money. It does not include a sum foregone or deferred by the provider, rather than actually expended, such as a rent free period. See the article in the Revenue Tax Bulletin December 1999 pp 711–713 issue 44, in particular in relation to the meeting of the tenant's costs.

For HMRC approach to these rules, see HMRC Business Income Manual BIM41050–BIM41140.

Simon's Taxes. See **B2.208.**

General

[68.54] See **4.8** ANTI-AVOIDANCE [*CTA 2010, ss 834–848*] regarding restrictions where there is a lease-back at a non-commercial rent and **4.9** ANTI-AVOIDANCE [*CTA 2010, ss 849–862*] for taxation of capital sums received on certain lease-backs.

Simon's Taxes. See B2.465.

Shares and securities

[68.55] For whether a trade of 'share dealing' carried on see **68.14** above. For transactions not at market value see **69.63** TRADING INCOME — DEDUCTIONS.

Profits and losses on realisations of investments by a bank in the course of its business enter into its trade (*Case I*) profits (*Punjab Co-operative Bank v Lahore IT Commr* (1940) 19 ATC 533, PC, and see *Frasers (Glasgow) Bank v CIR* (1963) 40 TC 698, HL) and similarly for insurance companies (*Northern Assce Co v Russell* (1889) 2 TC 551; *General Reinsurance Co v Tomlinson* (1970) 48 TC 81 and contrast *CIR v Scottish Automobile* (1931) 16 TC 381, Ct of Sess). Profits/losses held capital in *Stott v Hoddinott* (1916) 7 TC 85 (investments acquired by architect to secure contracts); *Jacobs Young & Co v Harris* (1926) 11 TC 221 (shares held by merchanting company in subsidiary wound up); *Alliance & Dublin Consumers' Gas Co v Davis* (1926) 5 ATC 717 (investments of gas company earmarked for reserve fund). A profit by a property dealing company on the sale of shares acquired in connection with a property transaction was held a trading receipt (*Associated London Properties v Henriksen* (1944) 26 TC 46, CA) but contrast *Fundfarms Developments v Parsons* (1969) 45 TC 707 and see now **4** ANTI-AVOIDANCE.

Shares allotted for mining concessions granted by company dealing in concessions held trading receipts at market value (*Gold Coast Selection Trust v Humphrey* (1948) 30 TC 209, HL). See also *Murphy v Australian Machinery & Investment Co* (1948) 30 TC 244, CA, and *Scottish & Canadian Investment Co v Easson* (1922) 8 TC 265, Ct of Sess.

For options, see *Varty v British South Africa Co* (1965) 42 TC 406, HL (no profits or loss until shares sold). See also *Walker v Cater Securities* (1974) 49 TC 625.

Conversion etc. of shares and securities held as circulating capital

[68.56] Where a new holding of shares or securities (as defined) is issued in exchange for an original holding a profit on sale of which would fall to be treated as part of trading profits of a banking, insurance or share dealing business, the transaction is treated as not involving any disposal of the original holding, the new holding being treated as the same asset as the original holding. This applies only to transactions which result in the new holding being equated with the original holding under *TCGA 1992, ss 132–136* (capital gains rollover in cases of conversion etc.) or *TCGA 1992, s 134* (compensation stock).

The above rules do not apply to shares or securities for which unrealised profits or losses (computed on a mark to market basis by reference to fair value) are brought into account in the period of account in which the transaction takes place. Where consideration is receivable in addition to the new holding, the above rule apply only to a proportion of the original holding, computed by reference to the market value of the new holding and the other consideration received.

[*CTA 2009, s 129*].

Dealers in securities etc.

[68.57] Where, in accordance with generally accepted accounting practice (see 68.18 above), profits and losses on the sale of securities by a bank, insurance company or other dealer in securities are calculated by reference to the fair value of the securities and taken to reserves rather than profit or loss account, they are nevertheless brought into account in computing trading profits. [*CTA 2009, s 128*].

FISMA levies

[68.58] In computing the profits of a trade carried on by a company authorised for the purposes of *Financial Services and Markets Act 2000* ('FISMA'), a deduction is available for certain levies payable under that Act, so far as not otherwise deductible. A deduction is similarly available for sums paid by a company as a result of an award of costs under costs rules within the ambit of that Act. Certain repayments under that Act must be brought into account as a trading receipt. [*CTA 2009, ss 92, 104; Financial Services and Markets Act 2000, s 411*].

Simon's Taxes. See B5.632.

Extra return on new issues of securities

[68.59] Where:

(a) securities of a particular kind are issued (being the original issue of securities of that kind);
(b) new securities of the same kind are issued subsequently;
(c) a sum (the 'extra return') is payable by the issuer in respect of the new securities, to reflect the fact that interest is accruing on the old securities and calculated accordingly; and
(d) the issue price of the new securities includes an element (separately identified or not) representing payment for the extra return,

the extra return is treated for all tax purposes (except corporation tax) as a payment of interest, but the issuer is not entitled to tax relief, either as a deduction in computing profits or otherwise as a deduction or set-off, for the payment. [*ITA 2007, s 845*].

Euroconversion of shares

[68.60] Costs incurred in respect of the conversion of a trading company's shares or other securities from the currency of a State which has adopted the euro into euro (a 'euroconversion', see *SI 1998 No 3177, Reg 3*) which is effected solely by the issue of replacement shares and other securities are allowable as a trading deduction. In the case of a company with investment business (or, subject to special provisions, a company carrying on life assurance business), such costs are treated as management expenses (see **45.4** INVESTMENT COMPANIES AND INVESTMENT BUSINESS). [*SI 1998 No 3177, Pt II*].

General

[68.61] See also **69** TRANSACTIONS IN SECURITIES, including transactions in securities to obtain tax advantage [*CTA 2010, s 731*].

For share transactions entered into to secure tax advantages see **68.4** above.

Sound recordings income

[68.62] Receipts from disposal of the original master version of the sound recording are treated as revenue receipts in the period of account (or if no accounts are made up, accounting period) in which they are received. An '*original master version*' is a master tape or master audio disc and the term '*sound recording*' does not include a film soundtrack. Such receipts can include amounts received from the disposal of any interest or rights in or over the original master version (including those created by the disposal), and insurance, compensation or similar money derived from the original master version.

[*CTA 2009, ss 150, 151*].

Subscriptions and contributions

[68.63] For any receipts from trade and professional associations see **69.64** TRADING INCOME — DEDUCTIONS.

Subsidies, grants etc.

Farming support payments

[68.64] See 68.30 above.

Fishing grants

For the tax treatment of decommissioning grants and laying-up grants, see HMRC Business Income Manual BIM57001.

Football pools promoters

See **69** TRADING INCOME — DEDUCTIONS.

Industrial development grants

Grants to a company under *Industrial Development Act 1982, s 7* or *s 8* (or corresponding NI legislation) are trading receipts, unless the grant is designated as made towards the cost of specified capital expenditure or as compensation for loss of capital assets or, is made towards the meeting of a corporation tax liability. [*CTA 2009, s 102*].

An earlier interest relief grant under *Industry Act 1972* was held to be assessable in *Burman v Thorn Domestic Appliances (Electrical) Ltd* (1981) 55 TC 493, as was a similar grant undifferentiated between revenue and capital in *Ryan v Crabtree Denims Ltd* (1987) 60 TC 183, applying *Gayjon Processes Ltd* (below) and distinguishing *Seaham Harbour* (below).

Research grant by trading company to medical practitioner held assessable (*Duff v Williamson* (1973) 49 TC 1). For research grants and fellowships generally, see HMRC Business Income Manual BIM65151.

Temporary employment subsidy was paid under *Employment and Training Act 1973, s 5* (as amended by *Employment Protection Act 1975, Sch 14 para 2*) as a flat-rate weekly payment or (in the textile, clothing and footwear industries) by way of reimbursement of payments made to workers on short time.

Such payments were held to be taxable as trading receipts in *Poulter v Gayjon Processes Ltd* (1985) 58 TC 350, distinguishing the grants made by the Unemployment Grants Committee in *Seaham Harbour* (below).

Simon's Taxes. See **B2.210.**

Unemployment grants

Subsidy to dock company (from Unemployment Grants Committee) for extension work to keep men in employment held, although the grant was made in terms of interest, not to be a 'trade receipt' for tax purposes (*Seaham Harbour v Crook* (1931) 16 TC 333, HL).

See **9.2** CAPITAL ALLOWANCES for effect of grants and subsidies on capital allowances.

Tied petrol stations receipts

[68.65] For tied licensed premises see **68.23** above.

In the hands of the retailer, exclusivity payments from the oil companies were held to be capital, when in respect of capital expenditure incurred by the retailer (*CIR v Coia* (1959) 38 TC 334, Ct of Sess; *McLaren v Needham* (1960) 39 TC 37; *Walter W Saunders Ltd v Dixon* (1962) 40 TC 329; *McClymont v Glover (Inspector of Taxes)* [2004] STC (SCD) 54) but revenue, when in respect of repairs etc. (*McLaren v Needham* above) or sales promotion (*Evans v Wheatley* (1958) 38 TC 216) or where petrol sales were a relatively small part (some 30%) of the company's turnover (*Tanfield Ltd v Carr* [1999] STC (SCD) 213).

For a summary of HMRC's view of such arrangements, see HMRC Business Income Manual BIM40300.

Tonnage tax

[68.66] Tonnage tax is an alternative charge to corporation tax in respect of certain shipping profits. 'Qualifying companies', or groups of companies of which at least one member is a 'qualifying company', may elect for their corporation tax profits from the activities of 'qualifying ships' to be calculated by reference to the net tonnage of each of those ships, and for losses to be left out of account for corporation tax purposes. All 'qualifying companies' within a group must be taxed on the same basis.

A '*qualifying company*' is a company within the charge to corporation tax which operates 'qualifying ships' which are strategically and commercially managed in the UK (for which see Revenue Tax Bulletin October 2000 p 787, issue 48). Certain temporary cessations from operating any 'qualifying ships' may be disregarded.

'*Qualifying ships*' are broadly ships carrying on certain activities which are of at least 100 tons gross tonnage, but excluding fishing and factory support vessels, pleasure craft, harbour and river ferries, offshore installations (within *CTA 2010, s 1132*), existing dedicated shuttle tankers subject to the petroleum revenue tax regime, dredgers (other than certain 'qualifying dredgers' as defined), and any vessel whose main purpose is the provision of goods or services normally provided on land. Other types of vessel may be added to or removed from the excluded categories by Treasury order.

The activities in which they must be engaged are transportation by sea, the provision of marine assistance or the provision of transport for services necessarily provided at sea. They may also, to a limited extent, include certain secondary and incidental activities (see *SI 2000 No 2303, Reg 3*).

Flagging rules apply for qualifying dredgers and tugs which must be registered in the UK, Gibraltar or an EU member state to qualify for tonnage tax (or other state aids). Other ships may be registered under any flag but where the relevant conditions are met, operators bringing 'new' ships within tonnage tax will have to do so under a UKE, Gibraltar or EU member state registration. Otherwise, ships can still qualify if they are re-registered to a Community flag within three months of first operation. A '*new*' ship for these purposes is, broadly, one which is brought within tonnage tax (in a financial year which is not excepted by Treasury Order) after the later of 1 July 2005 or the end of the first accounting period in which the company (or group) became a tonnage tax company but the financial years 2005, 2006, 2007, 2018 and 2019 are excepted (see *SI 2005 No 1480; SI 2006 No 333; SI 2018 No 421; SI 2019 No 658*).

Foreign dividends from non-UK resident shipping companies are (subject to conditions) also included in the profits covered by an election, as is any loan relationship credit (see **50.8** LOAN RELATIONSHIPS), and any derivative contract credit. Otherwise, investment income is excluded.

Profits within the tonnage tax regime are 'ring-fenced', with appropriate anti-avoidance measures to prevent exploitation of the regime, and there are similarly capital allowance 'ring-fencing' provisions (see also *SI 2000 No 2303, regs 4–8* as regards machinery and plant written-down values on exit from the regime or on transfer to use for offshore activities). No chargeable gains will arise during the currency of the election in relation to assets used for the qualifying activities, and balancing charges (on the disposal of assets for which capital allowances had previously been given) will be phased out using a sliding scale.

Capital allowances to lessors leasing to companies within the tonnage tax regime are similarly 'ring-fenced' and restricted.

However, with regard to lessors, there are rules which equalise the capital writing down allowances for ships leased to a company which has elected into the tonnage tax regime, with assets held outside the regime. A lessor can claim writing down allowances at the main rate for capital allowances (for expenditure which is not special rate expenditure, otherwise at the special rate (now 6%)), on the first £40 million of expenditure, and at the special rate (6%) on the second £40 million of expenditure.

See also **49.10** LEASING for the 'trigger' event in the sale of lessor company legislation, which will bring the deferred tax profits of a lessor company into charge immediately before a lessor company comes within the charge to tonnage tax.

Special provisions apply to the chartering in of qualifying ships and joint charters and to the chartering out of short-term over-capacity. There are also special rules for offshore activities in the UK sector of the continental shelf, and for group mergers and demergers.

Companies participating in the tonnage tax regime must also meet a minimum training obligation (for which see also *SI 2000 No 2129* as amended).

For existing qualifying companies, the *election* initially had to be made within twelve months from 28 July 2000. If the company was not a qualifying company on that date, it may have been made up to twelve months after its first becoming a qualifying company.

In the case of a group no member of which was a qualifying company on 28 July 2000, it may have been made within twelve months of a group company first becoming a qualifying company, provided that the group is not substantially the same as a group which at any earlier time had a member which was a qualifying company.

The election generally had effect from the beginning of the accounting period in which it was made (or, where that accounting period began before 1 January 2000, from the beginning of the following accounting period), subject to earlier or later effect in certain cases with HMRC agreement.

Special provisions apply in relation to mergers and demergers.

The election normally remains in effect for ten years for so long as the company (or group) qualifies and is not excluded, and (subject to the training requirements having been met) may at any time be renewed (such renewal being treated in effect as a valid new election).

There is provision for exit charges on a company leaving the tonnage tax regime, and a bar on re-entry to the regime within ten years.

The Treasury may make provision by regulations for the application of the above provisions to activities carried on by a company in partnership. See now *SI 2000 No 2303, Regs 8–13*.

[*FA 2000, s 82, Sch 22; CAA 2001, Sch 2 para 108; SI 2005 No 1449; SI 2005 No 1480; SI 2018 No 238; SI 2019 No 398; SI 2020 No 332*].

A very lengthy and detailed Statement of Practice, setting out administrative practice for the operation of the entire regime and structured in the same order as the legislation, is contained in HMRC Statement of Practice, SP 4/00. See also HMRC's Tonnage Tax Manual TTM00100.

Unclaimed balances

[68.67] Unclaimed balances for which a firm was liable to account were held not assessable despite their being distributed to partners (*Morley v Tattersall* (1938) 22 TC 51, CA). Such balances held by a pawnbroker are, however, assessable when claimants' rights expire (*Jay's, the Jewellers v CIR* (1947) 29 TC 274), and deposits on garments not collected were held trade receipts assessable when received (*Elson v Prices Tailors* (1962) 40 TC 671). The fact that trading receipts were subsequently, and correctly, treated for accountancy purposes as an element in a sale of fixed assets did not alter their nature for tax purposes (*Tapemaze Ltd v Melluish* (2000) 73 TC 167). In *Anise Ltd and ors v Hammond* [2003] STC (SCD) 258, it was decided that overpayments received from customers were not trading receipts of the taxpayer. The Special Commissioners decided that the issue to be determined was whether the overpayments were trading receipts at the time they were received. They found as a fact that the overpayments were not received as part of the trading activities of the companies and therefore the sums were not received as trading receipts.

See 69.5 TRADING INCOME — DEDUCTIONS for releases of debts owing.

Unremittable amounts

[68.68] See 69.70 TRADING INCOME — DEDUCTIONS.

Key points on trading income

[68.69] The two key points for this chapter in practice are often whether activities amount to a 'trade' and whether all income is assessable as part of a trade. Whether activities amount to trading is considered in detail at 68.3. It is principally a question of fact but in the words of Lord Wilberforce 'trade cannot be precisely defined'. Case law provides a vast volume of factors to consider which are summarised above. In general it is necessary to look at all relevant factors, particular circumstances, characteristics indicative of trading and assess whether looked at as a whole the company's activities amount to a trade. For whether a source of income is assessable see below to find the detailed guidance above.

Source of income	See above at
Bad debt —recoveries	68.22
Capital receipts	68.24
Car hire rebates	68.25

Cash back	68.26
Commission	68.26
Compensation	68.28
Damages	68.28
Discounts	68.26
Donations received	68.32
Embezzlement	68.29
Farming compensation	68.30
Farming grants and subsidies	68.30
Farming support payments	68.30
Gifts received	68.32
Grants	68.64
Impairment losses — recoveries	68.22
Insurance received	68.43
Investment income	68.44
Letting income	68.44
Miscellaneous receipts	68.47
Patents income	68.49
Property sales	68.52
Rents received	68.53
Reverse premiums	68.53
Shares and securities	68.55
Sound recording income	68.62
Subscriptions	68.63
Subsidies	68.64
Unremittable amounts	68.68
Woodlands	68.30

69

Trading Income — Deductions

Cross-references. See 4 ANTI-AVOIDANCE; 9 CAPITAL ALLOWANCES; 10 CAPITAL ALLOWANCES ON PLANT AND MACHINERY; 21 CONTROLLED FOREIGN COMPANIES; 31 DOUBLE TAX RELIEF; 35 GROUP RELIEF; 41 INTANGIBLE ASSETS; 44 INVESTMENT COMPANIES AND INVESTMENT BUSINESS; 50 LOSSES; 63 RESEARCH AND DEVELOPMENT EXPENDITURE; 64.4 RESIDENCE; 68 TRADING INCOME; 72 TRANSFER PRICING.

Introduction to trading income — deductions

[69.1] Trading profits must, for corporation tax purposes, be computed in accordance with 'generally accepted accounting practice' (GAAP) (see 68.19 TRADING INCOME). GAAP is defined by reference to the practice adopted in UK company accounts that are drawn up to give a true and fair view, but in relation to the affairs of a company or other entity that prepares accounts using international accounting standards ('IAS'), GAAP means generally accepted accounting practice in relation to IAS accounts. The requirement is subject to any adjustment required or authorised by law. [*CTA 2009, s 46; CTA 2010, s 1127*].

Deductions made in accordance with GAAP are therefore allowable if they are not prohibited by a general or specific tax rule. There are a number of specified rules, but the two most important general rules are that:

(a) the expenditure must be incurred wholly and exclusively for the purposes of the trade (*CTA 2009, s 54*) — see **69.74** below; and
(b) the expenditure must be of a revenue rather than a capital nature (*CTA 2009, s 53*) — see **69.8** below.

This chapter considers the main general and specific rules determine whether or not an expense is allowed as a deduction. Some less common deductions specific to particular trades or activities are also covered such as herd basis, taxation of films, tonnage tax, know how, mines and quarries, pooling of profits, shares and securities, telecommunications rights and unclaimed balances etc.

The chapter concludes with a table that briefly summarises the tax treatment of items of expenditure in calculating trading profits. This is referenced to the detailed explanations below, statute and HMRC manuals.

Allowable deductions

[69.2] The following paragraphs refer to matters of relevance to companies in computing trading profits. See **1** INTRODUCTION and **68** TRADING INCOME for the general principles in computing profits chargeable to corporation tax. See also **9** CAPITAL ALLOWANCES, **10** CAPITAL ALLOWANCES ON PLANT AND MACHINERY, **33** FOREIGN CURRENCY, **27** DERIVATIVE CONTRACTS, **41** INTANGIBLE ASSETS, **49** LOAN RELATIONSHIPS, **59** PROPERTY INCOME, **62** RESEARCH AND DEVELOPMENT EXPENDITURE.

See HMRC Business Income Manual BIM50000 et seq. for HMRC guidance on measuring the profits of a wide range of particular trades.

See **68.18** TRADING INCOME re the requirement to adhere to generally accepted accounting practice (GAAP), **68.19** TRADING INCOME re the application of accountancy principles generally and **68.20** TRADING INCOME re adjustments required on a change of basis.

The provisions for computing trading profits are in *CTA 2009, Pt 3*. It has been clarified that, wherever they appear in corporation tax legislation in the context of computing trading profits, the words 'receipts' and 'expenses' refer generally to items brought into account as credits or debits in computing those profits, and contain no implication that an amount has actually been received or paid. [*CTA 2009, s 48*]. See also *HMRC v NCL Investments Ltd* CA, [2020] STC 1201 in which a debit required under IFRS 2 was held to be an allowable expense even though the company did not incur any 'actual expenditure'.

CTA 2009, s 51 contains a rule intended to resolve any conflict between statutory rules prohibiting a deduction in computing trading profits and statutory rules permitting such a deduction. It does so by giving priority, with specified exceptions, to the rule permitting the deduction. In practice, such conflict should rarely occur. The order of priority is reversed in cases where a deduction would otherwise be given for an amount which arises directly or indirectly in consequence of, or in connection with, tax avoidance arrangements. [*CTA 2009, s 51*].

There are provisions which restrict the circumstances in which deductions may be claimed by a company where there has been a qualifying change (in respect of ownership) in relation to the company. See **51.23** LOSSES.

Simon's Taxes. See **B2.3–B2.4.**

Advertising

[69.3] Expenditure generally is allowable (but not capital outlay such as fixed signs (but see *Leeds Permanent Building Society v Proctor* (1982) 56 TC 293), nor initial costs etc. of new business). Where the promotion of the business and improvement not merely changes its structure or secures its outlets but represents an expansion of the trade, whether in the same or a new area, the expenditure will often be capital expenditure. In *United Steel Co Ltd v Cullington* [1940] AC 812, 23 TC 71, HL, two steel companies entered into an agreement with the London, Midland and Scottish Railway Co under which the railway company agreed to close certain parts of its steel works and to refrain from operating the works for ten years or from selling them except on terms that a purchaser complied with its agreement. The steel companies paid for that obligation and the railway company also agreed that for ten years it would purchase specified steel products from the steel companies. The sum paid by the steel companies was held to be a capital sum and not deductible.

Contribution to campaign for Sunday opening held allowable (*Rhymney Breweries* (1965) 42 TC 509). As to political campaign see *Tate & Lyle* (1954) 35 TC 367, HL, contrasted with *Boarland v Kramat Pulai* (1953) 35 TC 1.

In the case of *Interfish Ltd v Revenue and Customs Comrs* CA, [2014] EWCA Civ 876; 2014 STI 2286 the deduction of sums laid out for the purpose of promoting the trade of someone other than the taxpayer, in circumstances where the 'knock-on' benefits to the taxpayer's trade, while real, were intangible and hard to quantify, were not allowable.

See HMRC Business Income Manual BIM42550–42565.

Simon's Taxes. See **B2.462.**

Application of profits

[69.4] No deduction is available in respect of expenditure which represents the application of the profits earned. Such expenditure is not incurred for the purposes of the trade but for the purpose of enabling the profits of the trade to be distributed or applied for a particular purpose. No deduction may be claimed, therefore, by a company in respect of its dividends or other distributions. In *Thomson (Archibald) Black & Co Ltd v Batty* (1919) 7 TC 158, 56 SLR 185 the company incurred expenditure in applying to the court to have its capital reduced, so enabling it to pay a dividend. Although the expenditure was held to have been quite properly incurred and the company's action to have been in its own interest, the expenditure was incurred to enable it to distribute its profits more advantageously and accordingly was not a proper deduction in arriving at the balance of the profits available for distribution.

A requirement that a trading surplus is to be applied in a particular way does not remove the trade from assessment (under old *Schedule D Case I*) (*Mersey Docks and Harbour Board v Lucas* (1883) 2 TC 25, HL) and applications of the profits under the requirement are not allowable deductions (*City of Dublin Steam Packet Co v O'Brien* (1912) 6 TC 101; *Hutchinson & Co v Turner* (1950) 31 TC 495; *Racecourse Betting Control Board v Young (Inspector of Taxes)* [1959] 3 All ER 215, [1959] 1 WLR 813, HL, and cf *Pondicherry Rly Co Ltd v Madras Income Tax Comrs* (1931) LR 58 Ind App 239, 10 ATC 365, PC; *Tata Hydro-Electric Agencies* (1937) 16 ATC 54, PC; *India Radio & Cable Communication Co* (1937) 16 ATC 333, PC).

For circumstances in which the profits of a trade may not accrue to the proprietor, see *Alongi v CIR* (1991) 64 TC 304, Ct of Sess.

Simon's Taxes. See **B2.324**.

Bad debts — impairment losses

[69.5] For the purposes of these provisions, '*debt*' includes an obligation or liability which may be met otherwise than by the payment of money. International Accounting Standards refer to debtors as receivables.

Under *CTA 2009, s 55* in the case of debts not falling with the regimes for LOAN RELATIONSHIPS (**49**), DERIVATIVE CONTRACTS (**27**) INTANGIBLE ASSETS (**41**), a deduction is allowed in respect of a debt owed to the company for:

(a) an impairment loss (previously known as 'bad' and 'doubtful debts'); or
(b) a debt release to the extent the debt is released wholly and exclusively for the purposes of that trade as part of a 'statutory insolvency arrangement'.

A '*statutory insolvency arrangement*' is defined in *ITTOIA 2005, s 259* as a voluntary arrangement under, or by virtue of, *Insolvency Act 1986* (or Scottish or NI equivalents) or a compromise or arrangement under *Companies Act 2006, s 895* (or NI equivalent) or any corresponding arrangement or compromise under, or by virtue of, the law of a non-UK jurisdiction.

There is a corresponding rule for bad debts incurred in relation to a company's income from holding an office at *CTA 2009, s 970*. A company can hold an office, for example, as a company secretary, and the charge to tax on income from holding an office is to be calculated in accordance with income tax principles; see *CTA 2009, s 969*. A separate provision is therefore required for the treatment of bad debts in these circumstances.

[*CTA 2009, ss 55, 970*].

The above rules apply where a trade is treated as notionally discontinued (see **68.15** TRADING INCOME). (See Change 8 listed in Annex 1 to the Explanatory Notes to *CTA 2009*).

For release of a debt owed to a company by a trader see **68.22** TRADING INCOME.

Simon's Taxes. See B2.410.

Bank Levy

[69.6] The Bank Levy applies to: the consolidated balance sheet of UK banking groups and building societies; the aggregated subsidiary and branch balance sheets of foreign banks and banking groups operating in the UK; and the balance sheets of UK banks in non-banking groups. These institutions and groups are liable for the levy where their relevant aggregate liabilities amount to £20 billion or more and the levy is charged as if it were an amount of corporation tax chargeable on the relevant entity, and all provisions applying to the collection and payment of corporation tax apply equally to it. The levy is not deductible for corporation tax purposes. [*FA 2011, Sch 19 para 46*].

Foreign bank levies are also not an allowable deduction for corporation tax purposes.

[*FA 2011, Sch 19 para 69A*].

See further 7 BANKS.

Simon's Taxes. See D7.707.

Breweries, distilleries, licensed premises

Tied premises

[69.7] Expenses in respect of 'tied premises' which would otherwise be brought into account in calculating profits of a property business (see **60.2** PROPERTY INCOME) are instead brought into account as trading expenses. Any necessary apportionment (e.g. where rents etc. relate only in part to the tied premises or where only part of the premises qualifies) is on a just and reasonable basis. '*Tied premises*' are premises through which goods supplied by a trader are sold or used by another person, where the trader has an estate or interest in the premises which he treats as property employed for trade purposes. [*CTA 2009, s 42*]. (*Note.* These rules are of general application, although of most common application in the licensed trade.)

Case law

Repairs, rates, insurance premiums paid on behalf of tied tenants allowable (*Usher's Wiltshire Brewery v Bruce* (1914) 6 TC 399, HL) but not extra expenditure incurred to keep licensed houses open while undergoing rehabilitation (*Mann Crossman & Paulin Ltd v Compton* (1947) 28 TC 410) or compensation to a tenant displaced on a licence transfer (*Morse v Stedeford* (1934) 18 TC 457). For compensation paid on the termination of tenancies of tied houses, see *Watneys (London) Ltd v Pike* (1982) 57 TC 372. Losses on advances to 'customers and connections' held allowable (*Reid's Brewery v Male* (1891) 3 TC 279).

The expenses of an unsuccessful application for licences were held not allowable (*Southwell v Savill Bros* (1901) 4 TC 430 — it was conceded that expenses of successful applications are capital) nor expenses of applying for licence transfers (*Morse v Stedeford* above; *Pendleton v Mitchells & Butlers* (1968) 45 TC 341). Contributions by a brewer to a trade association to promote Sunday opening in Wales allowed in *Cooper v Rhymney Breweries* (1965) 42 TC 509. Compensation Fund levies deductible (*Smith v Lion Brewery* (1910) 5 TC 568, HL) but not monopoly value payments (*Kneeshaw v Albertolli* (1940) 23 TC 462; *Henriksen v Grafton Hotels Ltd* (1942) 24 TC 453, CA).

Damages paid to hotel guest injured by falling chimney held not allowable — see *Strong & Co v Woodifield* at **69.11** below. For accrued whisky storage rents see *Dailuaine-Talisker Distilleries v CIR* (1930) 15 TC 613, Ct of Sess; *CIR v Oban Distillery Co* (1932) 18 TC 33, Ct of Sess, and *CIR v Arthur Bell & Sons* (1932) 22 TC 315, Ct of Sess.

Where a brewery company ceased brewing but continued to sell beer brewed for it by another company it was held to have discontinued its old trade and commenced a new one (*Gordon & Blair Ltd v CIR* (1962) 40 TC 358, Ct of Sess).

Simon's Taxes. See **B5.611–B5.614.**

Capital expenditure

[69.8] In computing trading profits, no deduction is allowed for items of a capital nature unless it is specifically provided otherwise. [*CTA 2009, s 53*].

As to the distinction between capital and revenue expenditure and between capital and income receipts, 'no part of our law of taxation presents such almost insoluble conundrums as the decision whether a receipt or outgoing is capital or income for tax purposes' (Lord Upjohn in *Regent Oil Co Ltd v Strick (Inspector of Taxes)* [1966] AC 295, [1965] 3 All ER 174, HL, qv for a comprehensive review of the law). A widely used test is the 'enduring benefit' one given by Viscount Cave in *British Insulated and Helsby Cables Ltd v Atherton (Inspector of Taxes)* [1926] AC 205, 10 TC 155, HL. For recent reviews of the cases, see:

- *Lawson v Johnson Matthey plc* (1992) 65 TC 39, HL — cash injection into subsidiary deemed revenue expenditure.
- *Halifax plc v Davidson* [2000] STC (SCD) 251 — costs incurred by a building society on conversion to a public limited company were disallowed as capital expenditure to the extent that they related to payment of statutory cash bonuses to non-voting members of the society, but otherwise allowed.
- *Dass v Special Commissioner and others* [2006] EWHC 2491 (Ch), [2007] STC 187 — the High Court held that an examination fee under consideration was incurred 'with a view to bringing into existence an asset or advantage for the enduring benefit of a trade' and was attributable to capital.
- *Ingenious Games LLP v HMRC* FTT, [2017] SFTD 1443 — provisions for impairment of film rights deemed capital expenditure.

It is by virtue of the rule in *CTA 2009, s 53* above that depreciation of fixed assets is not allowable in computing profits (*In re Robert Addie & Sons* CES 1875, 1 TC 1). Where the depreciation charge in the accounts was reduced by capitalising part of it and including that part in the balance sheet value of stock (i.e. as an overhead cost), it was held by the House of Lords that net depreciation (i.e. the amount after deduction of depreciation included in stock) had to be added back in arriving at taxable profits on the basis that if the profit or loss was arrived at by deducting the net figure, the gross figure could not be adjusted for in the tax computation. Accounting principles stated that the profit or loss for a period of account had to take into account only revenue and expenditure relating to that year. (*Revenue and Customs Comrs v William Grant & Sons Distillers Ltd; Small (Inspector of Taxes) v Mars UK Ltd* [2007] UKHL 15).

No deduction is allowed for expenditure on the provision or replacement of integral features (whether capital or revenue) which qualifies for special rate capital allowances. [*CTA 2009, s 60*].

A gain or loss on the sale of a capital asset not included in trading profits is dealt with according to the provisions relating to capital gains tax. A sale of a fixed asset on which capital allowances have been claimed may result in a balancing charge or allowance, see **9** CAPITAL ALLOWANCES, **10** CAPITAL ALLOWANCES ON PLANT AND MACHINERY.

The revenue or capital nature of a payment is fixed at the time of its receipt (*Tapemaze Ltd v Melluish* (2000) 73 TC 167, following *Morley (Inspector of Taxes) v Tattersall* [1938] 3 All ER 296, 22 TC 51, CA).

For a brief note on HMRC's approach to challenging schemes or arrangements designed to turn income into capital (or capital expenditure into a revenue deduction), see Revenue Tax Bulletin June 1997 p 438, issue 29.

For HMRC's own guidance on capital *v* revenue, see HMRC Business Income Manual BIM35000–35910.

Generally see **Simon's Taxes B2.304–B2.309**.

For case law on the difference between capital and revenue see **Simon's Taxes B2.306**.

Car hire

[69.9] Where a car, not falling into one of the following categories is hired, the hire charges are restricted by 15%. The excepted categories are:

(a) a car first registered before 1 March 2001;
(b) a car with low carbon dioxide emissions (from 1 April 2021, not more than 50 g/km driven);
(c) an electrically propelled car; or
(d) a qualifying hire car.

(b) and (c) are defined as for capital allowances.

For contracts entered into before 1 April 2021, the threshold for low carbon dioxide emissions is not more than 110 g/km if the hire period begins before that date. For contracts entered into before 1 April 2018, the threshold for low carbon dioxide emissions is not more than 130 g/km if the hire period begins before that date.

The restriction does not apply if A or B applies:

(A) —
- (i) the hire period does not exceed 45 consecutive days; and
- (ii) the hire period and any linked period do not together exceed 45 days 'the sub-hire period',

or if:

(B) —
- (i) the company makes the car available to a customer for more than 45 days; or
- (ii) a car is so made available and the linked periods exceed 45 days.

Condition B does not apply if the customer is an employee of the taxpayer company, or connected with it and there must be no reciprocal arrangements. The exceptions do not apply if there is an avoidance motive. Where there is a sub-hire period, expenditure must be apportioned between it and the remainder of the period on a time basis. If the contract provides for a replacement car in the event of the original car being unavailable, both cars are treated as if they were the same car. Where connected persons (whether both or all companies or not) incur hire charges in respect of the same vehicle for the same period, and one or more of them incur the expenses under commercial arrangements, the provisions will apply only to the commercial lessee or by the first commercial lessee in a chain.

If the rental agreement separately identifies charges for costs such as maintenance, those costs are not subject to the 15% restriction. However, the lease costs subject to restriction do include any unrelievable VAT (normally 50%).

'Hire charges' for these purposes were held to include payments under a finance lease providing a revolving facility for the purchase of vehicles for use in a contract hire operation (*Lloyds UDT Finance Ltd and Another v Britax International GmBH and Another* (2002) 74 TC 662, CA).

Where the above restrictions have applied, any subsequent rental rebate (or debt release other than as part of a statutory insolvency arrangement — see **69.5** above) is reduced for tax purposes in the same proportion as the hire charge restriction. This treatment extends to amounts brought in as post-cessation receipts (see **68.16** TRADING INCOME) after the trade has ceased).

[*CTA 2009, ss 56–58; SI 2017 No 740; SI 2021 No 120*].

See HMRC Business Income Manual BIM47714–47785.

Simon's Taxes. See **B2.413**.

Cemeteries and crematoria

[69.10] In computing profits of a trade consisting of, or including, the carrying on of a cemetery or the carrying on of a crematorium (and, in connection therewith, the maintenance of memorial garden plots), a deduction as a trading expense for any period of account is allowed for:

- the capital cost of purchasing and preparing land (including cost of levelling, draining or otherwise making suitable) sold for interments or memorial garden plots *in that period*; and

- a *proportion* (based on the ratio of number of grave-spaces/garden plots sold in the period to that number plus those still available — see Example below) of 'residual capital expenditure'.

'*Residual capital expenditure*' is the total 'ancillary capital expenditure' incurred before the end of the period of account in question after subtracting (i) amounts previously deducted under these provisions, any sale, insurance or compensation receipts for assets representing ancillary capital expenditure and sold or destroyed, and (ii) certain expenditure before the basis period for the tax year 1954/55. '*Ancillary capital expenditure*' is capital expenditure incurred on any building or structure (other than a dwelling-house), or on the purchase or preparation of other land not suitable or adaptable for interments or garden plots, which is in the cemetery or memorial garden and is likely to have little or no value when the cemetery or garden is full; it also includes capital expenditure on the purchase or preparation of land taken up by said buildings and structures.

For these purposes, sales of land in a cemetery include sales of interment rights, and sales of land in a memorial garden include appropriations of part of the garden in return for dedication fees etc. Expenditure met by subsidies cannot be deducted as above (the detailed rules being similar to those at **9.2** CAPITAL ALLOWANCES).

Any change in the persons carrying on the trade is ignored; allowances continue as they would to the original trader, disregarding any purchase price paid in connection with the change itself.

Where, in the case of a crematorium, the trade includes the sale of niches or memorials and/or the making of inscriptions, certain deductions are available. For niches, two-thirds of both revenue and capital costs are allowable. For memorials and inscriptions, the whole of the revenue costs and two-thirds of the capital costs are allowable. Capital costs are an appropriate proportion of the associated building costs or, for inscriptions, the associated framework costs. [*ITTOIA 2005, ss 172ZA–172ZE*]. See HMRC Business Income Manual BIM52520–52530.

As regards crematoria, see also *Bourne v Norwich Crematorium* (1967) 44 TC 164.

[*CTA 2009, ss 146–149E*].

Simon's Taxes. See **B5.620**.

Example

GE Ltd, which operates a funeral service, owns a cemetery for which accounts to 31 December are prepared. The accounts to 31 December 2021 reveal the following.

(i)	Cost of land representing 110 grave spaces sold in period	£3,400
(ii)	Number of grave spaces remaining	275

(iii)	Residual capital expenditure on buildings and other land unsuitable for interments	£18,250
	The allowances available are	£
(a)	Item (i)	3,400
(b)	$\frac{110}{110+275} \times £18,250$	5,214

Note

(a) £8,614 will be allowed as a deduction in computing GE Ltd's trading profits for the period of account ending on 31 December 2021.

Compensation, damages etc. — payments

[69.11] For compensation and redundancy payments to directors or employees see **69.26** below. An important case is *Anglo-Persian Oil Co Ltd v Dale* (1931) 16 TC 253, CA, in which a substantial payment by a company for the cancellation of its principal agency, with ten years to run, was held to be allowable. It was not for a capital asset nor to get rid of an onerous contract (cf *Mallett (or Mallet) (Inspector of Taxes) v Staveley Coal and Iron Co Ltd* [1928] 2 KB 405, 13 TC 772, CA) but to enable it to rationalise its working arrangements. The decision was applied in *Croydon Hotel & Leisure Co Ltd v Bowen* [1996] STC (SCD) 466, in which a payment for the termination of a hotel management agreement was held to be allowable. See also *Vodafone Cellular Ltd v Shaw* (1997) 69 TC 376, CA (payment for release from onerous agreement), in which the principle underlying the decision in *Van den Berghs Ltd v Clark* (see **68.28**(b) TRADING INCOME) was applied, but cf *Tucker v Granada Motorway Services Ltd* (1979) 53 TC 92, HL, where a payment to modify the method of calculating the rent was held to be capital, and *Whitehead v Tubbs (Elastics) Ltd* (1983) 57 TC 472, CA, where a payment to alter the terms of a capital loan by removing borrowing restrictions on the borrower was held to be capital.

A payment by a shipping company for cancelling an order it had placed for a ship was held capital (*'Countess Warwick' SS Co Ltd v Ogg* (1924) 8 TC 652 and contrast *Devon Mutual Steamship Insce v Ogg* (1927) 13 TC 184). A payment to an associated company in return for its temporarily ceasing production held allowable (*Commr of Taxes v Nchanga Consolidated Copper Mines* (1964) 43 ATC 20, PC) as were statutory levies on a brewery for a Compensation Fund where a licence is not renewed (*Smith v Lion Brewery Co Ltd* (1910) 5 TC 568, HL) and a payment to secure the closure of a rival concern (*Walker v The Joint Credit Card Co Ltd* (1982) 55 TC 617). Payments by a steel company to secure the closure of railway steel works were held capital (*United Steels v Cullington (No 1)* (1939) 23 TC 71, CA) as were payments to safeguard against subsidence on a factory site (*Bradbury v United Glass Bottle Mfrs* (1959) 38 TC 369; compare *Glenboig Union Fireclay* at **68.28**(c) TRADING INCOME and a payment for cancelling electricity agreement on closure of a quarry (*CIR v William Sharp & Son* (1959) 38 TC 341, 38 ATC 18, Ct of Sess). For compensation paid on the termination of tied houses of breweries, see *Watneys (London) Ltd v Pike* (1982) 57 TC 372.

Where damages awarded by a Court against a solicitor were later compounded, the compounded amount (accepted as allowable) was held to be an expense of the year in which the Court award was made (*Simpson v Jones* (1968) 44 TC 599). See also *CIR v Hugh T Barrie Ltd* (1928) 12 TC 1223.

Damages paid by a brewery to a hotel guest injured by a falling chimney were held to have been incurred by it *qua* property owner and not *qua* trader and not deductible (*Strong & Co of Romsey Ltd v Woodifield* (1906) 5 TC 215, HL). Penalties for breach of war-time regulations and defence costs not allowed (*CIR v Warnes & Co* (1919) 12 TC 227, HL; *CIR v Alexander von Glehn & Co Ltd* (1920) 12 TC 232, CA), nor fines imposed by professional regulatory body (*McKnight v Sheppard* (1996) 71 TC 419), nor damages for breach of American 'anti-trust' law (*Cattermole v Borax & Chemicals Ltd* (1949) 31 TC 202). In *HMRC v McLaren Racing Ltd* UT, [2014] UKUT 269 (TCC); 2014 STI 2288, the UT held that a substantial fine imposed by the FIA, the governing body of Formula 1 motor racing, for a serious breach of rules was not deductible since the activities which gave rise to the fine were not carried out in the course of the company's trade. See also *G Scammell & Nephew v Rowles* (1939) 22 TC 479; *Fairrie v Hall* (1947) 28 TC 200; *Golder v Great Boulder Proprietary* (1952) 33 TC 75; *Knight v Parry* (1972) 48 TC 580; *Hammond Engineering v CIR* (1975) 50 TC 313.

Simon's Taxes. See **B2.417, B2.419, B2.455.**

Computer software

[69.12] Subject to the application of the INTANGIBLE ASSETS (**41**) regime, HMRC's views on the treatment of expenditure on computer software are summarised as follows.

Software acquired under licence

Regular payments akin to a rental are allowable revenue expenditure, the timing of deductions being governed by correct accountancy practice (see **68.19** TRADING INCOME). A lump sum payment is capital if the licence is of a sufficiently enduring nature to be considered a capital asset in the context of the licencee's trade, e.g. where it may be expected to function as a tool of the trade for several years. Equally the benefit may be transitory (and the expenditure revenue) even though the licence is for an indefinite period. Officers will in any event accept that expenditure is revenue expenditure where the software has a useful economic life of less than two years. Timing of the deduction in these circumstances will again depend on correct accountancy practice.

Where the licence is a capital asset, capital allowances are available.

Expenditure on a package containing both hardware and a licence to use software must be apportioned before the above principles are applied.

Software owned outright

The treatment of expenditure on such software (including any in-house costs) follows the same principles as are described above in relation to licensed software.

(HMRC Business Income Manual BIM35800 *et seq*).

For the treatment of expenditure on systems modification work relating to the Year 2000 problem and to EMU conversion, see Revenue Tax Bulletin April 1998 p 531 issue 34. Broadly, such work will always be a revenue matter unless it is carried out as part of a major new project instituting changes on such a scale as to be of a capital nature in relation to the business.

See HMRC Business Income Manual BIM35800–35865 for a detailed analysis of HMRC's views generally.

Simon's Taxes. See **B2.418.**

Contracts

[69.13] For compensation etc. on the cancellation or variation of contracts see **69.11** above and **68.28** TRADING INCOME. For work in progress under contracts see **69.63** below.

Where a taxpayer took over a coal merchanting business on the death of his father, an amount paid for the benefit of contracts between his father and suppliers was held capital (*John Smith & Son v Moore* (1921) 12 TC 266, HL, and see *City of London Contract Corpn v Styles* (1887) 2 TC 239, CA). The completion of outstanding contracts following a partnership dissolution (*Hillerns & Fowler v Murray* (1932) 17 TC 77, CA) and on a company going into liquidation (*Baker v Cook* (1937) 21 TC 337) held to be trading.

Where under a long-term contract goods were invoiced as delivered, the sale proceeds are receipts of the year of delivery (*J P Hall & Co Ltd v CIR* (1921) 12 TC 382, CA). If contract prices are varied retrospectively the resultant further sums are assessable or deductible for the years applicable to the sums at the original prices (*Frodingham Ironstone Mines Ltd v Stewart* (1932) 16 TC 728; *New Conveyor Co Ltd v Dodd* (1945) 27 TC 11). Compare *English Dairies Ltd v Phillips* (1927) 11 TC 597; *Isaac Holden & Sons Ltd v CIR* (1924) 12 TC 768 and contrast *Rownson Drew & Clydesdale Ltd v CIR* (1931) 16 TC 595.

Losses because of a fall in prices fixed under forward contracts etc. cannot be anticipated (*Edward Collins & Sons Ltd v CIR* (1924) 12 TC 773, Ct of Sess; *Whimster & Co v CIR* (1925) 12 TC 813, Ct of Sess) and cf *Wright Sutcliffe Ltd v CIR* (1929) 8 ATC 168, Ct of Sess; *J H Young & Co v CIR* (1926) 12 TC 827, 4 ATC 579, Ct of Sess; *CIR v Hugh T Barrie Ltd* (1928) 12 TC 1223.

Simon's Taxes. See **B2.419, B2.455.**

Embezzlement etc.

[69.14] Losses arising from theft or misappropriation by an employee are normally allowable, but not misappropriation by partner or director. See *Bamford v ATA Advertising* (1972) 48 TC 359 and cf *Curtis v J & G Oldfield Ltd* (1925) 9 TC 319. See BIM45855.

Where defalcations were made good by the auditor who admitted negligence, a refund held to be a trading receipt for the year in which made (*Gray v Penrhyn* (1937) 21 TC 252).

See **69.49** below as regards prohibition on deduction of expenditure involving crime.

Simon's Taxes. See **B2.429**.

Employees (and directors) — benefits

[69.15] See **69.27** below as regards timing of benefits.

Counselling services etc.

[69.16] Expenditure on counselling and other outplacement services which falls within the earnings exemption of *ITEPA 2003, s 310* (see Tolley's Income Tax under Employment Income) is deductible in computing the profits of the employer company's trade. [*CTA 2009, ss 54, 73, 74*].

Simon's Taxes. See **B2.428**.

Council tax

[69.17] An employer who pays the council tax for an employee will normally be able to claim a deduction for it. If such payments are also made on behalf of members of the employee's family, they too are deductible if they are part of the employee's remuneration package (which would normally mean they were paid under the contract of employment). (HMRC Business Income Manual BIM46820).

Employees seconded to charities or educational bodies

[69.18] If an employer seconds an employee temporarily to a charity (as defined for charitable companies in *CTA 2010, s 467* and other bodies in *ITA 2007, s 519*) — see **14** CHARITIES), any expenditure of the employer which is attributable to the employment is deductible in computing the employer's profits regardless as to whether such expenditure would have been deductible if the employee's services had continued to be available to the employer. This relief is extended to secondments to educational establishments (as defined and including education authorities, educational institutions maintained by such authorities, and certain other educational bodies). See also **68.2** TRADING INCOME. [*CTA 2009, ss 70, 71*].

Simon's Taxes. See B2.430.

Interest on director's property loan

[69.19] Where interest is paid by a company on a loan (other than an overdraft) taken out by a director to purchase land (including buildings etc.) occupied rent-free by the company and used for business purposes, it is considered that the company may obtain relief as a trading expense for the interest in the normal way and that the payments would not normally constitute either remuneration or a benefit of the director.

See HMRC Business Income Manual BIM45755–45765.

Key employee insurance

[69.20] Premiums on policies in favour of the employer insuring against death or critical illness of key employees are generally allowable, and the proceeds of any such policies are treated as trading receipts. However, in *Beauty Consultants Ltd v Inspector of Taxes* [2002] STC (SCD) 352, premiums on a policy insuring a company against the death of either of its controlling shareholder-directors were disallowed, in that the premiums benefited the shareholders personally by improving the value of their shares. In *Greycon Ltd v Klaentschi* [2003] STC (SCD) 370, it was held that the company's sole purpose in taking out key man policies was to meet a requirement of an agreement under which funding and other benefits were obtained from another company, that the policies had a capital purpose and that, consequently, the proceeds of those policies were not trading receipts. See generally HMRC Business Income Manual BIM45525, 45530.

Simon's Taxes. See B2.425.

National insurance contributions ('NICs')

[69.21] Secondary (i.e. employers') Class 1 NICs are deductible in computing profits. Relief is similarly available for Class 1A NICs (payable by an employer where benefits-in-kind are provided to employees) and for Class 1B NICs (payable in respect of PAYE settlement agreements — see Tolley's Income Tax under Pay As You Earn). No deduction is allowed for employees' Class 1 NICs for any corporation tax purposes. [*CTA 2009, s 1302*].

Simon's Taxes. See B2.425.

Payments for restrictive undertakings

[69.22] Payments to employees for restrictive undertakings, falling to be treated as earnings of the employee under *ITEPA 2003, s 225*, are deductible in computing profits. [*CTA 2009, s 69*].

In *First De Sales Ltd Partnership v HMRC* UT 2018, [2019] STC 805, the partnership's appeals against HMRC's decision to disallow payments in respect of restrictive undertakings entered into by two non-UK resident employees were struck out. The payments totalled £970 million and were paid to a third party. The Upper Tribunal agreed with the First-tier Tribunal that the payments were not in respect of restrictive undertakings but were in respect of a tax avoidance arrangement.

Simon's Taxes. See **B2.426**.

Redundancy payments

[69.23] Redundancy payments, or other employer's payments, under *Employment Rights Act 1996* (or NI equivalent) are allowable. Rebates recoverable are trading receipts. [*CTA 2009, ss 76–78, 81*].

Non-statutory redundancy and similar payments are normally deductible unless made on the cessation of trading (but see following paragraphs) (*CIR v Anglo-Brewing Co Ltd* (1925) 12 TC 803; *Godden v Wilson's Stores* (1962) 40 TC 161, CA; *Geo Peters & Co v Smith* (1963) 41 TC 264) or as part of the bargain for the sale of shares of the company carrying on the business (*Bassett Enterprise Ltd v Petty* (1938) 21 TC 730, CA; *James Snook & Co Ltd v Blasdale* (1952) 33 TC 244, CA). See also *Overy v Ashford Dunn & Co* (1933) 17 TC 497 and contrast *CIR v Patrick Thomson Ltd* (1956) 37 TC 145, Ct of Sess. A payment to secure the resignation of a life-director who had fallen out with his co-directors was allowed in *Mitchell v B W Noble Ltd* (1927) 11 TC 372, CA. See also *O'Keeffe v Southport Printers Ltd* (1984) 58 TC 88. For provisions for future leaving payments see **69.58**.

Payments in addition to the statutory payment made on cessation of trading are allowable deductions if they would have been allowable had there been no cessation. Allowance is up to three times the statutory payment. For these purposes, a partnership change is treated as a cessation unless a company carrying on the trade in partnership immediately before the change continues to carry it on in partnership after the change. [*CTA 2009, ss 79, 80*]. Relief is similarly given under *s 79* for such payments made on cessation of *part* of a trade.

A gratuitous payment made on partial cessation of a company's trade to a managing director who nevertheless continued thereafter to be a director was held non-deductible in *Relkobrook Ltd v Mapstone (Inspector of Taxes)* [2005] STC (SCD) 272, [2005] SWTI 158.

Relief under *CTA 2009, ss 76–81* above is given for the accounting period in which the payment is made (or, if paid after cessation, for the accounting period in which falls the last day on which the trade is carried on). Where, instead, relief is due under general principles, a provision for future payments may be allowed as a deduction for a period of account provided that:

(a) it appears in the commercial accounts in accordance with generally accepted accounting principles; and
(b) payment was made within nine months of the end of the period.

(HMRC Business Income Manual BIM47215).

See generally HMRC Business Income Manual BIM47200–47215.

Simon's Taxes. See B2.426.

Retirement provision

[69.24] See Tolley's Income Tax under Pension Provision for the tax treatment of such schemes generally.

Contributions made by an employer to a registered pension scheme in respect of an individual are deductible in computing profits for the period of account in which they are made (subject to the spreading provisions below). The contributions must meet the normal conditions for expenditure deductible in computing trading profits, in particular the 'wholly and exclusively' rule (see **69.74** below), but it is specifically provided that they are not treated as capital expenditure even if they would fall to be so treated under general principles.

Certain payments an employer may make to discharge its statutory obligations in relation to an under-funded defined benefits scheme are treated as contributions to the scheme for the above purposes and, if made after cessation of the employer's business, are treated as if made immediately before cessation. Otherwise, no sums other than contributions are deductible in connection with the cost of providing benefits under the registered pension scheme.

The deductibility of contributions to a registered scheme is restricted in respect of an individual if the individual's benefits from the scheme are dependent on the non-payment of benefits from an employer pension scheme which is not a registered scheme or if the transfer value of the individual's rights under the registered scheme is reduced by virtue of benefits being payable out of the non-registered scheme.

Where the contributions paid by an employer in a period of account exceed 210% of the contributions paid in the previous period of account, relief for the excess contributions may fall to be spread over more than one period of account as follows. Firstly, identify the amount of current period contributions that exceeds 110% of previous period contributions (the '*relevant excess contributions*'). If this amount is less than £500,000, spreading does not apply. Otherwise, relief for the relevant excess contributions is spread over the current and following periods of account as follows.

Amount of relevant excess contributions	*Spread equally over*
£500,000 to £999,999 inclusive	2 periods of account
£1,000,000 to £1,999,999 inclusive	3 periods of account
£2,000,000 or more	4 periods of account

If the current and previous periods of account are unequal in length, the amount of the previous period contributions is adjusted proportionately in order to determine the excess (if any). Any contributions paid in the current period to fund cost of living increases in current pensions are disregarded in determining any excess, as are any contributions to fund a future service liability for employees joining the scheme in the current period. If the employer ceases business, such that some of the excess contributions would otherwise remain unrelieved, the otherwise unrelieved amount is relieved in the period of account which ends with the date of cessation or, at the employer's option, is apportioned on a daily basis over the whole of the spreading period up to the date of cessation.

[*FA 2004, ss 196, 196A, 197–199, 200; SI 2005 No 3458*].

Indirect contributions

Where a pension contribution is made in a chargeable period and, in the next period, an indirect payment is made to a registered pension scheme by the employer and the 'avoidance condition' is satisfied, relief for the payment is spread (see below). A payment is within this provision if all of part of it is intended to enable the payment of pension contributions under the original or a substitute scheme by a person other than the employer. The employer is '*entitled*' to relief if it would be entitled to a deduction as a trading expense or as management expenses. The '*avoidance condition*' is that spreading of relief would apply had the payment been made by the employer under the original scheme and the purpose, or one of the purposes, of the arrangement was to avoid spreading the relief.

The 'relevant relief' is treated as if it were paid by the employer, so that spreading of relief applies. The '*relevant relief*' is the relief to which the employer would be entitled in respect of the payment, or of that part of the payment intended to facilitate the payment of pension contributions. The payment may be to the original pension scheme, or to a '*substitute scheme*', which is any scheme to which there is a relevant transfer within two years ending with the day the payment is made or to which it is envisaged a transfer may or will be made after that day. A '*relevant transfer*' is a transfer of more than 30% of the aggregate of:

- where there is a relevant transfer within two years, the market value of the assets and money in the scheme immediately before the transfer; and
- where the transfer is envisaged, the market value of those assets and that money on the day the payment is made.

[*FA 2004, s 199A*].

See HMRC guidance on employers' contributions to registered pension schemes in the HMRC Business Income Manual at BIM46001 *et seq* and also at RPSM510200.

Asset-backed pension contributions

There are provisions to ensure that the amount of tax relief given to employers using asset-backed contribution (ABC) arrangements to fund their registered pension schemes accurately reflects, but does not exceed, the total amount of payments the employer makes to the scheme. An ABC arrangement involves offsetting an employer's legal obligation to pay a pension contribution against the registered pension scheme's legal obligation to purchase an asset from the employer, directly or indirectly, using the contribution. There are also ABC arrangements that involve an upfront monetary contribution. Without the legislation it was possible for an employer to obtain both an upfront deduction for the pension contribution and another deduction for income payments derived from the asset. It is understood that, due to the complexity and transaction costs involved, these arrangements tend to be used only by very large companies. The Government expected about a dozen large employers with (predominantly defined benefit) pension schemes to be affected by the provisions. The legislation is not intended to apply to any straightforward monetary sum that an employer pays to a registered pension scheme as a pension contribution or any transfer of an asset by an employer to a pension scheme which is unconditional or outright so that the scheme gains full and irrevocable ownership of the asset. The types of arrangement within the ambit of the legislation enable an employer, or a person connected with him, to provide for payments over a period of time (an 'income stream') to the pension scheme. A more complex ABC arrangement typically involves a special purpose vehicle (for example, a partnership of which the employer is a member), in which case the employer provides the pension scheme with the income stream indirectly through the vehicle. The income stream is derived from assets of the employer or a connected party such as a partnership as mentioned above. Under the legislation, a key factor in determining whether an employer can claim upfront relief for an ABC is whether the structured finance arrangement legislation would apply to the ABC arrangement. This legislation is covered at **4.11** ANTI-AVOIDANCE.

[*FA 2004, ss 196A–196L*].

Simon's Taxes. See **B2.427**.

Training costs

[69.25] Costs incurred by an employer in respect of employee training are generally allowable as a trading expense. For HMRC view of the circumstances in which such relief may be prohibited (including training for those with a proprietary stake in the business), see HMRC Business Income Manual BIM47080.

Retraining course expenses paid or reimbursed by an employer and satisfying the conditions of the earnings exemption in *ITEPA 2003, s 311* (see Tolley's Income Tax under Employment Income) are deductible in computing the profits of the employer's trade (or as a management expense). Similar provisions relating to recovery of tax, information and penalties as apply in relation to the earnings exemption apply in relation to this deduction. [*CTA 2009, ss 74, 75*]. See **69.69** below as regards contributions to training and enterprise councils.

Simon's Taxes. See **B2.428**.

Employees (and directors) — remuneration

[69.26] **Bona fide remuneration** is normally deductible including bonuses, commissions, tax deducted under PAYE and the cost of board, lodging, uniforms and benefits provided. The deduction is for the remuneration etc. payable; future payments cannot be anticipated (*Albion Rovers Football Club v CIR* (1952) 33 TC 331, HL). The remuneration etc. must be shown to be wholly and exclusively for the purposes of the trade. In *Stott & Ingham v Trehearne* (1924) 9 TC 69 an increase in the rate of commission payable to the trader's sons was disallowed as not on a commercial footing. See also *Johnson Bros & Co v CIR* (1919) 12 TC 147, *Copeman v William Flood & Sons Ltd* (1940), 24 TC 53 and *Earlspring Properties Ltd v Guest* (1995) 67 TC 259, CA. Payments by a farming couple to their young children for help on the farm were disallowed in *Dollar v Lyon* (1981) 54 TC 459. For excessive payments to 'service company' see *Payne, Stone Fraser* at **69.53** below. For wife's wages see *Thompson v Bruce* (1927) 11 TC 607; *Moschi v Kelly* (1952) 33 TC 442, CA. The salary etc. of an employee for service in an overseas subsidiary was allowed in computing the profits of the parent in *Robinson v Scott Bader & Co Ltd* (1981) 54 TC 757, CA. The secondment was wholly and exclusively for the purposes of the parent's business, notwithstanding the benefit to the subsidiary's business.

Any excess of the market value over the par value of shares issued to employees at par is not deductible (*Lowry v Consolidated African Selection Trust Ltd* (1940) 23 TC 259, HL). For payments to trustees to acquire shares for the benefit of employees, see *Heather v P-E Consulting Group* (1972) 48 TC 293, CA, *Jeffs v Ringtons Ltd* (1985) 58 TC 680 and *E Bott Ltd v Price* (1985) 59 TC 437, and contrast *Rutter v Charles Sharpe & Co Ltd* (1979) 53 TC 163 and *Mawsley Machinery Ltd v Robinson* 1998] STC (SCD) 236. See also **69.28** and **69.31** below.

Where an individual who is a member of an LLP is treated as an employee under *ITTOIA 2005, s 863A(2)* (a Salaried Member) then the costs of employing such a Salaried Member are expenses of earning profits and are allowable deductions in the same way and the same period as expenses in respect of any other employee. If no deduction is made under normal accounting practice for the expenses paid in respect of the Salaried Member's employment, then a specific statutory deduction is allowed in arriving at the profits of the LLP for trade purposes in the period when such employment expenses are paid. The availability of a deduction is then subject to the normal rules for such trade deductions (such as being wholly and exclusively for the purposes of the trade, restriction for capital expenditure etc.). See further **56.11** PARTNERSHIPS.

[*CTA 2009, s 92A*].

Simon's Taxes. See **B2.421**.

Timing of deductions

[69.27] In calculating trading profits for a period of account, no deduction is allowed for an amount charged in the accounts in respect of employees' remuneration unless it is paid no later than nine months after the end of the period of account. Remuneration paid at a later time (and otherwise deductible) is deductible for the period of account *in which* it is paid. For these purposes, 'remuneration' includes any amount which is, or falls to be treated as, earnings for income tax purposes, and includes remuneration of office holders as well as other employees. Remuneration is treated as paid when it falls to be treated for income tax purposes as received by the employee (see Tolley's Income Tax under Employment Income). These provisions apply whether the amount charged is in respect of particular employments or employments generally and apply equally to remuneration for which provision is made in the accounts with a view to its becoming employees' remuneration. Computations prepared before the end of the said nine-month period must be prepared on the basis that any still unpaid remuneration will not be paid before the expiry of that nine-month period and thus will not be deductible for the period of account in question. If, in fact, such remuneration *is* paid by the end of the nine-month period, the matter may be dealt with by way of amendment to the tax return.

These provisions apply in calculating income for corporation tax purposes from any source, e.g. PROPERTY INCOME (59), and not just trading profits.

[*CTA 2009, ss 1288, 1289*].

Similar provisions apply in relation to companies with investment business (*CTA 2009, ss 1249, 1250*) and insurance companies.

Payments to an employee benefit trust were held to fall within these restrictions in *Dextra Accessories Ltd and Others v Macdonald* [2005] UKHL 47 (and see now below under Employee benefit contributions). See also *Sempra Metals Ltd v HMRC* [2008] STC 1062.

Simon's Taxes. See B2.422.

Employee benefit contributions

[69.28] There are statutory rules for the timing of deductions for 'employee benefit contributions' (EBCs). They apply instead of the more general rules at 69.27 above. For these purposes, an '*employee benefit contribution*' is made if, as a result of any act or omission, property is held, or may be used, under an 'employee benefit scheme' or there is an increase in the total net value of any such property. An '*employee benefit scheme*' is a trust, scheme or other arrangement for the benefit of persons who are, or include, present or former employees of the employer or persons linked with present or former employees. The definition also includes, insofar as it would not otherwise come within the definition, a relevant arrangement under the income tax disguised remuneration provisions (i.e. a relevant arrangement within *ITEPA 2003, s 554A(1)(b)* to which *s 554A(1)(c)* applies) and any other arrangement connected (directly or indirectly) with that relevant arrangement. The question of whether a person is linked with another is determined as for the purposes of the disguised remuneration provisions (see *ITEPA 2003, s 554Z1*).

A deduction is allowed only to the extent that, during the period in question or within nine months after the end of it, 'qualifying benefits' are provided, or 'qualifying expenses' are paid, out of the contributions. (If the employer's contribution is itself a qualifying benefit, it is sufficient that the contribution be made during the period or within those ensuing nine months.) Subject to what is said below, any amount thus disallowed remains available for deduction in any subsequent period during which it is used to provide qualifying benefits. For these purposes, qualifying benefits are treated as provided, and expenses are treated as paid, as far as possible out of EBCs, with no account being taken of any other receipts or expenses of the scheme manager.

Computations prepared before the end of the said nine-month period must be prepared by reference to the facts at the time of computation. If any contributions are used for qualifying purposes after that time, but within the nine months, the computation may be adjusted accordingly (subject to the normal time limits for amending company tax returns).

These restrictions do not apply to disallow deductions for consideration given for goods or services provided in the course of a trade or profession or for contributions to a registered pension scheme, qualifying overseas pension scheme (if the employee is a relevant migrant member) or accident benefit scheme (as defined). They also do not apply to any deductions that are allowable under **69.31–69.36** (employee share acquisitions), **69.37** (share incentive plans) or **69.38** (qualifying employee share ownership trusts) below.

The above is subject to an overriding rule preventing any deduction of EBCs for a period of account beginning more than five years after the end of the period of account in which the contributions were made. Also in relation to EBCs made on or after that date, where the provision of qualifying benefits out of (or by way of) the contributions gives rise to both a charge to employment income tax and a charge to NICs, a deduction is denied for the EBCs, for any period of account for which it would otherwise be available, unless the tax and NICs are paid no later than 12 months after the end of that period of account. It is also specified that where a deduction would otherwise be allowable for an amount of employees' remuneration in respect of which EBCs are made (or are to be made), the deduction is to be treated as a deduction in respect of EBCs and not as a deduction in respect of remuneration, thus bringing it within the restrictions.

A '*qualifying benefit*' is a payment of money or transfer of assets (other than by way of loan) that:

(a) gives rise to *both* a charge to income tax on employment income and a charge to NICs (or would do so but for available exemptions for duties performed outside the UK); or
(b) is made in connection with termination of employment; or
(c) is made under an employer-financed retirement benefits scheme.

However, a payment or transfer within (c) above is a qualifying benefit only if it gives rise to an income tax charge under *ITEPA 2003, Pt 6 Ch 2* or *Pt 9* or is an excluded benefit (within *ITEPA 2003, s 393B(3)*).

A 'chargeable relevant step' is also the provision of a qualifying benefit. A '*chargeable relevant step*' is a relevant step within the income tax disguised remuneration provisions which gives rise to a charge under *ITEPA 2003, Pt 7A Ch 2*.

'*Qualifying expenses*' are those expenses (if any) of the scheme manager in operating the scheme that would have been deductible in computing profits if incurred by the employer.

Money benefits are treated for the above purposes as provided at the time the money is treated as received for the purposes of income tax on employment income.

To the extent that the provision of a qualifying benefit is a chargeable relevant step (see above), the benefit is treated as provided when the relevant step is taken or, if later, when the emloyee begins his employment with the employer.

Where a qualifying benefit takes the form of the transfer of an asset which meets a condition at (a) to (c) above, the amount provided is the aggregate of:

(i) the amount that would otherwise be deductible by the employer (in a case where the scheme manager acquired the asset from the employer);
(ii) the amount expended on the asset by the scheme manager; and
(iii) (in a case where the transfer is a chargeable relevant step and so far as not already taken into account under (i) or (ii)) the cost of the relevant step.

If, however, the amount charged to income tax under *ITEPA 2003* (or which would be so charged if the duties of employment were performed in the UK) is lower than that aggregate, any amount deductible under these provisions at any time is limited to that lower amount; this rule is aimed at a situation where the asset falls in value after its acquisition by the scheme manager but before its transfer to the employee (Treasury Explanatory Notes to the 2003 Finance Bill).

If the provision of a qualifying benefit is a chargeable relevant step which is not covered by the above and does not involve a sum of money, the amount provided is the cost of the relevant step. However, the amount provided cannot exceed the amount that is charged to tax under *ITEPA 2003* in relation to the relevant step or would be so charged if the employee had not been non-UK resident in any tax year. This limit applies equally if the chargeable relevant step does involve a sum of money.

[*CTA 2009, ss 1290–1297; FA 2017, s 12(4); F(No 2)A 2017, s 37*].

Payments to a trust the beneficiaries of which were members of employees' families were held to fall within these restrictions in *Sempra Metals Ltd v HMRC* (Sp C 698), [2008] SSCD 1062. If a contrived scheme is effected to achieve the opposite result to that intended by Parliament, it fails if only because for that very reason the contributions then have a duality of purpose (see **69.74** below) that itself undermines a deduction (*Scotts Atlantic Management Ltd v HMRC* UT, [2015] STC 1321). Payments to an employee benefit trust to provide funds which could be placed at the disposal of directors were held not to be allowable in *Alway Sheet Metal Ltd v HMRC* FTT, [2017] SFTD 719. However, payments were held to be allowable where the amounts were used to make outright payments to employees and consultants.

Simon's Taxes. See **B2.422.**

Payroll deduction schemes — agents' expenses

[69.29] Voluntary contributions made by an employer company to assist an approved agent with its costs in managing a payroll deduction scheme on the employer's behalf are deductible in computing the profits of the employer's trade. [*CTA 2009, s 72*].

Personal service companies and managed service companies

[69.30] There are provisions designed to prevent the avoidance of tax and Class 1 National Insurance contributions by the use of intermediaries such as personal service companies. The rules (commonly known as IR35 after the

Revenue Budget press release which announced them in 1999) apply where the worker would otherwise be an employee of the client or the income would be income from an office held by the worker. For 2017/18 onwards, separate rules apply where the end client is a public authority and these rules are extended to medium-sized and large businesses with effect from 6 April 2021.

See Tolley's Income Tax and Tolley's National Insurance Contributions for the detailed provisions

Except where the separate rules for services provided to public authority rules for 2017/18 onwards or medium-sized and large business for 2021/22 onwards apply (see further below), a personal service company which is within IR35 can make an adjustment in its corporation tax computation. The deemed employment payment, and associated National Insurance contributions, are treated as an allowable expense in computing the trade profits (or losses) of the intermediary for the period of account in which the payment is made (but for no other period of account).

[*CTA 2009, s 139*].

Similar provisions apply to managed service companies (also known as composite companies). [*CTA 2009, s 141*].

Where the separate rules for services provided to a public authority or a medium-sized and large business apply, payments made to a personal service company in respect of services provided to the public authority are not brought into account in calculating the trading profits to the extent that a payment has been treated as made directly to the worker under *ITEPA 2003, s 61N* in respect of the same services.

[*CTA 2009, s 141A*].

Simon's Taxes. See **B9.128.**

Employee share schemes

[69.31] As described at **69.32–69.36** below, corporation tax relief is available to a company where, by reason of an employment with that company (whether it is his own or another person's employment), a person either acquires shares or obtains an option in pursuance of which he acquires shares. 'Employment' for this purpose includes a former or a prospective employment, the holding of an office, and being a member of a company whose affairs are managed by its members. 'Shares' includes stock and an interest in shares or stock. Shares are acquired by a person when he acquires a beneficial interest in them. [*CTA 2009, ss 1002, 1003*].

For the provisions of *ITEPA 2003* pertaining to the employee, see Tolley's Income Tax under Share-Related Employment Income and Exemptions.

Simon's Taxes. See **D1.330–D1.338.**

Transfer pricing

For an article on the interaction of these provisions with the TRANSFER PRICING (70) rules, see Revenue Tax Bulletin February 2003 pp 1002–1007.

Relief if shares acquired

[69.32] Relief is available to a company (the '*employing company*') if:

(i) a person has an employment with the company in relation to a business carried on by the company the profits of which are within the charge to corporation tax (or would be, but for the operation of a foreign PE exemption election — see **31.15** DOUBLE TAX RELIEF);
(ii) the employee or another person acquires shares because of the employment;
(iii) the conditions below relating to the shares acquired are met; and
(iv) the conditions below relating to the employee's income tax position are all met.

This relief is not available if the employing company is entitled to the relief at **69.33** below (relief if option obtained) in relation to the acquisition of the shares.

Relief is also available where a person has an employment (the '*actual employment*') with a non-UK resident company not within the charge to corporation tax (an '*overseas employer*') and as part of the duties of that employment works in the UK for (but is not employed by) a 'host' employer (for example under secondment or similar arrangements) which is within the charge to corporation tax. In such circumstances, the employee is deemed for the purposes of the above provisions to have an employment with the host employer, the duties of which consist of the work done for the host employer. If shares are acquired because of the actual employment and, because of the employee's work for the host employer, the employee is charged to tax under *ITEPA 2003* in respect of the acquisition, the shares are treated as if they are acquired because of the deemed employment.

The shares

The conditions relating to the shares acquired are as follows.

(a) They must be irredeemable, ordinary, fully paid-up shares and either:
  - shares of a class listed on a recognised stock exchange (see **16.4** CLOSE COMPANIES); or
  - shares in a company not under the control (within *CTA 2010, s 1124*) of another company; or
  - shares in a company under the control of a company whose shares are listed on a recognised stock exchange and which is neither a close company (see **16** CLOSE COMPANIES) nor a company which would be a close company if it were UK resident.

(b) The company whose shares are acquired must be:
  (i) the employing company (or, where relevant, the overseas employer); or
  (ii) a company of which the employing company or overseas employer is a 51% subsidiary; or
  (iii) a company which is a member of a consortium which owns the employing company, overseas employer or a company within (ii) above; or

(iv) a company which is a member of a consortium of which the employing company, overseas employer or a company within (ii) above is also a member, and is also a member of the same 'commercial association of companies' as another company owned by the consortium; or

(v) a company which has a 51% subsidiary within (iv) above.

Conditions (b)(ii) to (iv) above must be met at the time the shares are acquired. For the purposes of (b)(iii) and (iv) above, a company is a member of a consortium owning another company if it is one of five or fewer companies which between them beneficially own at least 75% of that company's ordinary share capital, with each of them so owning at least 10%. In (b)(iv) above, a '*commercial association of companies*' means a company together with such of its associated companies (within **16.10** CLOSE COMPANIES) as carry on businesses that are of such a nature that the businesses of the company and those associated companies, taken together, may be reasonably considered to make up a single composite undertaking.

The employee's income tax position

If the shares are not restricted shares, the employee must be subject to an income tax charge under *ITEPA 2003* on the acquisition of the shares and *ITEPA 2003, s 446UA* (pre-acquisition avoidance) must not apply in relation to the shares.

If, however, the shares are 'restricted shares' (see **69.34** below), the condition is instead that the employee either has earnings subject to an income tax charge under *ITEPA 2003, Pt 2* in respect of the acquisition or has no such earnings but will be subject to a charge by virtue of *ITEPA 2003, s 426* if a chargeable event occurs. For this purpose, earnings include amounts treated as earnings under *ITEPA 2003, s 226A* (employee shareholder shares — now repealed).

In either case, if the condition is not met but would have been met if, at all material times, the employee had been UK resident and the duties of the employment had been performed in the UK, the condition is treated as if met.

The relief

If the shares are neither 'restricted shares' nor 'convertible shares' (see, respectively, **69.34** and **69.35** below), the amount of relief is equal to the excess of the market value of the shares at the time they are acquired over the total amount or value of any consideration given in respect of the acquisition, by whomsoever given, with just and reasonable apportionment of any consideration given only partly in respect of the acquisition. The consideration excludes the performance of any duties of, or in connection with, the employment. Where relief is available in respect of employees of overseas companies who work in the UK, the amount of the relief is limited to the total amount of employment income of the person charged to tax under *ITEPA 2003* (and only one company may be given relief). Any £2,000 payment deemed to have been made by an employee shareholder (under *ITEPA 2003, s 226B* — now repealed) is ignored for the purposes of establishing whether a person is subject to income tax, the amount that counts as employment income and the consideration given by a person in relation to the acquisition of shares.

If the shares are 'restricted shares', the amount of relief is equal to the amount chargeable as earnings of the employee as a result of the acquisition. If the shares are 'convertible shares', the amount of relief is similarly computed, except that in calculating earnings for this purpose the market value of the shares is determined as if they were not convertible shares (and disregarding *ITEPA 2003, s 437(2)(3)*). If the shares are both restricted and convertible, the amount of relief is equal to the greater of the two amounts so given (or, if the two amounts are the same, that amount). See, respectively, **69.34** and **69.35** below for additional corporation tax relief in certain circumstances in cases involving restricted or convertible shares.

In any case, the relief is given by way of deduction in computing the profits of the qualifying business for corporation tax purposes for the accounting period in which the shares are acquired. If the company is one with investment business, then unless the qualifying business is a property business (in which case the foregoing applies), the amount of relief is treated as management expenses. The relief is scaled down on a just and reasonable basis if the employment relates to both a qualifying business and another business. The relief is apportioned between qualifying businesses on a just and reasonable basis if the employment relates to more than one such business.

[*CTA 2009, ss 1004–1013, 1038B; CTA 2010, s 1124*].

Relief if option obtained

[69.33] Relief is available to a company (the '*employing company*') if:

(i) a person has an employment with the company in relation to a business carried on by the company the profits of which are within the charge to corporation tax (or would be but for the operation of a foreign PE exemption election — see **31.15** DOUBLE TAX RELIEF);
(ii) an option to acquire shares is obtained by an employee or another person because of the employment;
(iii) the person who obtained the option (the '*recipient*') acquires shares pursuant to it;
(iv) the conditions below relating to the shares acquired are met; and
(v) the condition below relating to the employee's income tax position are all met.

Relief is also available where a person has an employment (the '*actual employment*') with a non-UK resident company not within the charge to corporation tax (an '*overseas employer*') and as part of the duties of that employment works in the UK for (but is not employed by) a 'host' employer (for example under secondment or similar arrangements) which is within the charge to corporation tax. In such circumstances, the employee is deemed for the purposes of the above provisions to have an employment with the host employer, the duties of which consist of the work done for the host employer. If shares are acquired under an option obtained because of the actual employment and, because of the employee's work for the host employer, the employee is charged to income tax under *ITEPA 2003* in respect of the acquisition, the option treated as if it is obtained because of the deemed employment.

Relief is available where a person (E) has or had an employment (the '*overseas employment*') with a non-UK resident company not within the charge to corporation tax (an '*overseas employer*') and E or another person obtains an option to acquire shares because of that employment if the following applies:

- E has an employment (the '*UK employment*') with a company which is within the charge to corporation tax;
- the person who obtained the option acquires shares under it; and
- either E is charged to income tax under *ITEPA 2003* in respect of the acquisition or the acquisition is able to take place only because of the UK employment.

In such circumstances, the option is treated as if it were obtained because of the UK employment.

In *Metso Paper Bender Forrest Ltd v HMRC* FTT 2013, [2014] STFD 529 the Tribunal refused to allow relief where options were granted to a director who had no employment contract.

If the recipient dies and the shares are subsequently acquired by someone else under the option, the relief continues to be available as if the recipient had lived and had acquired the shares.

The shares

The conditions relating to the shares acquired are as follows.

(a) They must be irredeemable, ordinary, fully paid-up shares and either:
  (I) shares of a class listed on a recognised stock exchange (see **16.4** CLOSE COMPANIES); or
  (II) shares in a company not under the control (within *CTA 2010, s 1124*) of another company; or
  (III) shares in a company under the control of a company whose shares are listed on a recognised stock exchange and which is neither a close company (see **16** CLOSE COMPANIES) nor a company which would be a close company if it were UK resident; or
  (IV) shares which were within any of (I)–(III) above when the option was obtained but have ceased to be so as a result of a company takeover.

  Where (IV) above applies, the shares must be acquired within 90 days of the takeover. The avoidance of tax must not be a main purpose of the takeover.

(b) The company whose shares are acquired must be:
  (i) the employing company (or, where relevant, the overseas employer); or
  (ii) a company of which the employing company or overseas employer is a 51% subsidiary; or
  (iii) a company which is a member of a consortium which owns the employing company, overseas employer or a company within (ii) above; or

(iv) a company which is a member of a consortium of which the employing company, overseas employer or a company within (ii) above is also a member, and is also a member of the same 'commercial association of companies' as another company owned by the consortium; or

(v) a company which has a 51% subsidiary within (iv) above; or

(vi) a 'qualifying successor company' (see further below).

Conditions (b)(ii)–(iv) above must be met at the time the option is obtained. For the purposes of (b)(iii) and (iv) above, a company is a member of a consortium owning another company if it is one of five or fewer companies which between them beneficially own at least 75% of that company's ordinary share capital, with each of them so owning at least 10%. In (b)(iv) above, a '*commercial association of companies*' means a company together with such of its associated companies (within **16.10** CLOSE COMPANIES) as carry on businesses that are of such a nature that the businesses of the company and those associated companies, taken together, may be reasonably considered to make up a single composite undertaking.

The employee's income tax position

The acquisition of the shares must be a chargeable event under *ITEPA 2003, s 476* in relation to the employee (whether or not an amount counts as employment income because of that event). If the shares are acquired under the option after the death of the employee, the condition is treated as met if it would have been met had the employee been still alive.

Takeovers

Where another company obtains control (within *CTA 2010, s 1124*) of a company whose shares are the subject of an option within these provisions, and the option holder and the acquiring company agree to roll over the rights into a new option relating to shares in a 'qualifying company' (the '*qualifying successor company*'), the new option stands in the shoes of the old for the purposes of these provisions. A '*qualifying company*' is a company which is within any of (b)(i)–(v) above when the takeover occurs, substituting references to the acquiring company for references to the employing company etc.

The relief

If the shares are neither 'restricted shares' nor 'convertible shares' (see, respectively, **69.34** and **69.35** below), the amount of relief is equal to the excess of the market value of the shares at the time they are acquired over the total amount or value of any consideration given in respect of the obtaining of the option or the acquisition of the shares, by whomsoever given, with just and reasonable apportionment of any consideration given only partly in respect of these matters. The consideration excludes (i) the performance of any duties of, or in connection with, the employment and (ii) certain employer national insurance contributions which the employee may have elected to pay. Where relief is available in respect of employees of overseas companies, the amount of the relief is limited to the total amount of employment income of the person charged to tax under *ITEPA 2003* (and only one company may be given relief).

Any £2,000 payment deemed to have been made by an employee shareholder (under *ITEPA 2003, s 226B* — now repealed) is ignored for the purposes of establishing whether a person is subject to income tax, the amount that counts as employment income and the consideration given by a person in relation to the acquisition of shares.

If the shares are 'restricted shares' or 'convertible shares', the amount of relief is equal to the amount that counts as employment income of the employee under *ITEPA 2003, s 476* or, if the option is a qualifying option under the Enterprise Management Incentive provisions, the amount that would have so counted apart from those provisions. In the case of convertible shares, the amount that counts as employment income is determined for this purpose as if the shares were not convertible shares (disregarding *ITEPA 2003, s 437(2)* and *(3)*). In either case, no account is taken if any relief due under *ITEPA 2003, s 481* or *482* (relief for certain national insurance contributions). No account is taken of the death of the employee before the shares are acquired, if such is the case. If the shares are both restricted and convertible, the amount of relief is equal to the greater of the two amounts so given (or, if the two amounts are the same, that amount). See, respectively, **69.34** and **69.35** below for additional corporation tax relief in certain circumstances in cases involving restricted or convertible shares.

In any case, the relief is given by way of deduction in computing the profits of the qualifying business for corporation tax purposes for the accounting period in which the shares are acquired. If the company is one with investment business, then unless the qualifying business is a property business (in which case the foregoing applies), the amount of relief is treated as management expenses. The relief is scaled down on a just and reasonable basis if the employment relates to both a qualifying business and another business. The relief is apportioned between qualifying businesses on a just and reasonable basis if the employment relates to more than one such business.

Transfer of business within a group

There is special provision for the relief to be given to a successor company (or companies) where, between the grant of the option, and the acquisition of the shares, the whole, or substantially the whole, of the qualifying business is transferred intra-group to the successor company (or companies). Companies are for this purpose members of the same group if one is a 51% subsidiary of the other or both are 51% subsidiaries of a third company.

Shares not acquired

Where:

(1) a person obtains an option to acquire shares and (a) above applies; or
(2) a person obtains an option to acquire shares and the obtaining of the option is connected to a previously obtained option either within (1) above or covered by this rule,

no deduction is allowed in relation to the option or any matter connected with it unless the shares are actually acquired. If the shares would have been acquired under an employee share scheme, the amounts so disallowed include, in particular, amounts paid by the employing company in relation to the participation of the employee in the scheme.

However, this does *not* exclude relief for the expenses of setting up the share scheme or of meeting, or contributing to, its administration costs, or for costs of borrowing for the purposes of the scheme, or for fees, commission, stamp duty, stamp duty reserve tax or similar incidental expenses of acquiring the shares. Deductions are not disallowed for amounts on which the employee is chargeable to income tax under *ITEPA 2003* or would have been so chargeable had he been a UK employee at all relevant times or, where he has died, had he been alive.

[*CTA 2009, ss 1004, 1005, 1014–1024, 1038A, 1038B; CTA 2010, s 1124; FA 2017, s 12(4)*].

Additional relief for restricted shares

[69.34] Shares are '*restricted shares*' if they are restricted securities (or a restricted interest in securities) within *ITEPA 2003, ss 423, 424*.

If relief is potentially available under **69.32** or **69.33** above on acquisition, relief is also available to the employing company on a subsequent chargeable event under *ITEPA 2003, s 426* in relation to the restricted shares or if *ITEPA 2003, Pt 7 Ch 2* ceases to apply to the shares because the employee dies. If the original acquisition was made pursuant to an option and, because of the death of the recipient of the option the shares were acquired by someone else, the additional relief applies as if the recipient were still alive and had acquired the shares.

Where the original relief was given under **69.32** or **69.33** above and there is an overseas employer, additional relief is available on a chargeable event, but not on the employee's death. The amount of the relief is limited to the total amount of employment income of the person charged to tax under *ITEPA 2003* (and only one company may be given relief). Any £2,000 payment deemed to have been made by an employee shareholder (under *ITEPA 2003, s 226B* — now repealed) is ignored for the purposes of establishing the amount that counts as employment income.

Relief is also available (to the 'UK company' below) where a person (E) has or had an employment (the '*overseas employment*') with a non-UK resident company not within the charge to corporation tax (an '*overseas employer*') and E or another person acquires restricted shares because of that employment (whether or not under an option) if the following applies:

- relief under **69.32** or **69.33** above would have been available to the overseas employer if at all material times the company had carried on a business the profits of which were within the charge to corporation tax (or would have been, but for the operation of a foreign PE exemption election — see **31.15** DOUBLE TAX RELIEF);
- E has a 'UK employment' with a company (the '*UK company*') which is within the charge to corporation tax;
- the UK employment is in relation to a business carried on by the UK company the profits of which are within the charge to corporation tax (or would be, but for the operation of a foreign PE exemption election);
- a chargeable event under *ITEPA 2003, s 426* occurs in relation to the restricted shares; and

- E is charged to income tax under *ITEPA 2003* in respect of the chargeable event because of the UK employment.

For these purposes, E has a '*UK employment*' with a company if E is employed by it or otherwise works for it in the course of performing the duties of the overseas employment.

The relief is given for the accounting period in which the chargeable event occurs or the employee dies, whichever is applicable. It is given in the same manner as in **69.32** and **69.33** above. The quantum of relief is given by *CTA 2009, s 1026(3), (4)* (chargeable events) or *CTA 2009, s 1027(3), (4)* (death of employee).

Provisions similar to those at **69.33** above apply on a transfer of the qualifying business within a group in the period between the acquisition of the shares or the obtaining of the option and the chargeable event or employee's death. These enable the additional relief to be given to the successor company (or companies).

[*CTA 2009, ss 1004, 1005, 1025–1029, 1038B; FA 2017, s 12(4)*].

Additional relief for convertible shares

[69.35] Shares are '*convertible shares*' if they are convertible securities (or an interest in convertible securities) within *ITEPA 2003, s 436*. The First-tier Tribunal confirmed in *Michael Bruce-Mitford v HMRC* [2014] UKFTT 954 that this definition of 'convertible securities' is very wide (and includes a redesignation in the articles of the company).

If relief is potentially available under **69.32** or **69.33** above on acquisition, relief is also available to the employing company on a subsequent 'chargeable event' or on a 'relief event'.

If there has been an acquisition of convertible securities that are not shares and relief would have been potentially available under **69.32** or **69.33** above if they had been shares and had satisfied the conditions relating to shares acquired, this 'additional' relief is nevertheless available.

For these purposes, '*chargeable event*' means an event that is a chargeable event under *ITEPA 2003, s 438* in relation to the convertible securities and is a conversion of the securities into shares satisfying the conditions in **69.32** or **69.33** above (whichever is applicable) relating to shares acquired (disregarding the extension to these conditions referred to in **69.33**).

A '*relief event*' is the first event to occur after the death of the employee that would have been a 'chargeable event' (as above) if the employee had lived.

If the original acquisition was made pursuant to an option and, because of the death of the recipient of the option the shares were acquired by someone else, the additional relief applies as if the recipient were still alive and had acquired the shares.

Where the original relief was under **69.32** or **69.33** above and there is an overseas employer, additional relief is available on a chargeable event, but not as a result of the employee's death. The amount of the relief is limited to the total amount of employment income of the person charged to tax under *ITEPA 2003* (and only one company may be given relief). Any £2,000 payment deemed to have been made by an employee shareholder (under *ITEPA 2003, s 226B* — now repealed) is ignored for the purposes of establishing the amount that counts as employment income.

Relief is also available (to the 'UK company' below) where a person (E) has or had an employment (the '*overseas employment*') with a non-UK resident company not within the charge to corporation tax (an '*overseas employer*') and E or another person acquires convertible securities because of that employment (whether or not under an option) if the following applies:

- relief under **69.32** or **69.33** above would have been available to the overseas employer if the convertible securities had been shares and at all material times the company had carried on a business the profits of which were within the charge to corporation tax (or would have been but for the operation of a foreign PE exemption election — see **31.15** DOUBLE TAX RELIEF);
- E has a 'UK employment' with a company (the '*UK company*') which is within the charge to corporation tax;
- the UK employment is in relation to a business carried on by the UK company the profits of which are within the charge to corporation tax (or would be but for the operation of a foreign PE exemption election);
- a chargeable event occurs in relation to the restricted shares; and
- E is charged to income tax under *ITEPA 2003* in respect of the chargeable event because of the UK employment.

For these purposes, E has a '*UK employment*' with a company if E is employed by it or otherwise works for it in the course of performing the duties of the overseas employment.

The relief is given for the accounting period in which the chargeable event occurs or the relief event occurs, whichever is applicable. It is given in the same manner as in **69.32** and **69.33** above. The quantum of relief is given by *CTA 2009, s 1033(3), (4)* (chargeable events) or *CTA 2009, s 1034(3), (4)* (relief events).

Provisions similar to those at **69.33** above apply on a transfer of the qualifying business within a group in the period between the acquisition of the shares or the obtaining of the option and the chargeable event or relief event. These enable the additional relief to be given to the successor company (or companies).

[*CTA 2009, ss 1004, 1005, 1030–1036, 1038B; FA 2017, s 12(4)*].

Relationship with other reliefs

[69.36] A deduction under *CTA 2009, ss 983–998* in relation to a share incentive plan (see **69.37** below) is given priority over relief under **69.32–69.35** above, and no relief is available under **69.32–69.35** in respect of shares in relation to which a deduction is allowable, or has been made, under **69.37**.

Where relief under **69.32–69.35** above is available (or would be available were it not for the further condition in **69.32** concerning *ITEPA 2003, s 446UA*), the following applies.

(1) No other corporation tax deduction is allowed to any company in respect of expenses directly related to the provision of the shares, including any amount paid or payable by the employing company in respect of the employee's participation in an employee share scheme.

(2) So far as not covered by (1) above, no other corporation tax deduction is allowed to a company, in a case in which shares are acquired under an option, of expenses in relation to the option or any matter connected with the option. This applies to both the old and new options in the event of a company takeover (see **69.33** above).

However, the above provisions do *not* exclude relief for the expenses of setting up an employee share scheme under which the shares are acquired, or of meeting, or contributing to, its administration costs, or for costs of borrowing for the purposes of the scheme, or for fees, commission, stamp duty, stamp duty reserve tax or similar incidental expenses of acquiring the shares.

[*CTA 2009, ss 1037, 1038*].

Share incentive plans

[69.37] Subject to the exceptions below, the items at (a)–(d) below are allowable deductions in computing company trading profits in connection with a share incentive plan within *ITEPA 2003, Sch 2* (see Tolley's Income Tax under Share-Related Employment Income and Exemptions). If the company is carrying on a property business (as in **59** PROPERTY INCOME), the items are similarly treated as allowable deductions in computing the profits. If the company is one with investment business (other than a property business) they are treated as management expenses.

(a) The market value (at time of acquisition by the plan trustees, and see below) of free and matching shares awarded to employees under the plan (the deduction being given *to the employer company* for the period of account in which the shares are awarded);

(b) Any excess of the market value (at time of acquisition by the plan trustees, and determined as for capital gains tax purposes) of partnership shares over the amounts paid by participating employees to acquire them (the deduction being given *to the employer company* for the period of account in which the shares are acquired on participants' behalf);

(c) Expenditure on setting up the plan, which is self certified as a 'Schedule 2 SIP'. The deduction is given for the period of account in which the expenditure is incurred if the relevant date falls within nine months after the end of that period; otherwise it is given for the period of account in which the relevant date falls. The relevant date is the date the self certification declaration is made;

(d) Contributions by the company to the expenses of plan trustees in operating a plan, *excluding* expenses in acquiring shares (other than incidental costs such as fees, commission, stamp duty etc.) but *including* interest on money borrowed to acquire shares.

Once a deduction is made under (a) or (b) above, no other deduction (other than any within (c) or (d) above) may be made by the employer company or any associated company (as defined) in respect of the provision of the shares, and no deduction within (a) or (b) above may then be made by any other company in that respect. Once a deduction is made under (c) above, no other deduction may be made in respect of the costs of setting up the plan.

For the purposes of (a) above, market value is determined as for capital gains tax purposes, and, for the purposes of that determination (and also for those of (iii) below), shares acquired by the trustees on different days are deemed to be awarded under the plan on a first in/first out basis. In the case of a group plan (i.e. a plan established by a parent company and extending to one or more companies under its control), the total market value of the shares awarded is apportioned between the relevant employer companies by reference to the number of shares awarded to the employees of each company.

No deduction is allowed under (a) or (b) above:

(i) in respect of shares awarded to an individual whose earnings from the eligible employment are not, at the time of the award, taxable earnings (whether or not subject to the remittance basis as regards overseas earnings);
(ii) in respect of shares that are liable to depreciate substantially in value for reasons that do not apply generally to shares in the company;
(iii) if a deduction has been made (on whatever basis), by the company, or an associated company (as defined) in respect of providing the same shares for the plan trust or for another trust (whatever its nature or purpose); or
(iv) in respect of the subsequent award of shares previously forfeited by participants (such shares being treated as acquired by the trustees at time of forfeit for no consideration).

No deduction is allowed under (c) above if any employee acquires rights under the plan, or the trustees acquire any shares, before the plan receives HMRC approval. Subject to (d) above, no deduction is allowed for expenses in providing dividend shares.

If the SIP ceases to be a 'Schedule 2 SIP' because the necessary requirements are not met then the deductions made under (a), (b), (c) and (d) above may be withdrawn (although transitional rules apply to SIPs established prior to that date, such that the set up costs will not be withdrawn).

The notional receipt is treated as a receipt of the company's trade or property business if applicable. If the business has ceased, it is treated as a post-cessation receipt (see **68.16** TRADING INCOME). In any other case, it is treated as a receipt within the charge to corporation tax on income.

A payment made by the employer company to the trustees sufficient to enable them to acquire (other than from a company) a significant block of shares (at least 10% of the employer company's ordinary share capital) normally (see below for anti-avoidance) attracts a deduction (in computing trading profits etc.) which, in contrast to the above, is not deferred until the shares are awarded to employees. The deduction normally falls to be given for the period of account in which falls the first anniversary of the date of acquisition, provided the 10% requirement is then met. The deduction will, however, be clawed back unless at least 30% of those shares are awarded within five years of acquisition by the trustees and all of the shares are awarded within ten years. On clawback, the company is deemed to have received an amount equal to the deduction at the time that HMRC direct that the deduction be withdrawn, the notional receipt being treated as above. If all the shares are subsequently awarded, the deduction is reinstated at that later time. An appropriate proportion of the original deduction is also subject to clawback if the plan terminates before all the shares have been awarded or if shares are awarded to an individual within (i) above. In the event of HMRC withdrawing their approval to the plan, the same provisions apply as above as regards potential withdrawal of deductions.

No deduction is given for a payment to trustees above where the main purpose or one of the main purposes was tax avoidance arrangements. Arrangements are widely defined to include arrangements, a scheme of any kind, whether or not legally enforceable involving a single transaction or two or more transactions.

[*CTA 2009, ss 983–998*].

Employee share ownership trusts

[69.38] Expenditure incurred in setting up a qualifying employee share ownership trust (QUEST) (within *FA 1989, Sch 5*) is deductible in computing the company's trading profits. If the company is carrying on a property business (as in 59 PROPERTY INCOME), the expenditure is similarly deductible in computing the profits. If the company is one with investment business (other than a property business) the expenditure is treated as management expenses.

If the deed establishing the trust is executed more than nine months after the end of the period of account in which the expenditure is incurred, the deduction is made for the period of account in which the deed is executed. (In the case of a company with investment business (other than a property business) the expenditure is treated as referable to the accounting period in which the deed is executed.)

[*CTA 2009, s 1000*].

See Tolley's Income Tax under Qualifying Employee Share Ownership Trusts for the definition of a QUEST, for the charge on trustees and for certain information requirements relating to trustees. See Tolley's Capital Gains Tax under Shares and Securities for details of a limited rollover relief on sale of shares to the trustees of such a trust in *TCGA 1992, ss 227–235*.

Non-qualifying employee share ownership trusts

For the treatment of contributions to employee share ownership trusts not within the above provisions which are not capital expenditure on general principles but which are required under UITF 13 to be treated as giving rise to an asset in the employer's accounts, see Revenue Tax Bulletin February 1997 pp 399, 400 issue 27. Broadly, relief for the contributions is deferred until the rights in the shares are transferred to employees, although this would not prevent a deduction for a properly calculated provision reflecting employees' accruing entitlement to such benefits.

Tax-advantaged share option schemes

[69.39] Expenditure on establishing an SAYE option scheme or CSOP scheme (see Tolley's Income Tax under Share-Related Employment Income and Exemptions) is deductible in computing the company's trading profits. If the company is carrying on a property business (as in 60 PROPERTY INCOME), the expenditure is similarly deductible in computing the profits. If the company is one with investment business (other than a property business) the expenditure is treated as management expenses.

The deduction is given for the period of account in which the expenditure is incurred if the relevant date falls within nine months after the end of that period; otherwise it is given for a period of account in which the relevant date falls. The relevant date is the date the self certification declaration is made (or the first grant date if earlier).

[*CTA 2009, s 999*].

Entertainment and gifts

[69.40] Subject to the exceptions below, no deduction is allowed, in computing income from any source, for expenses incurred in providing entertainment (including hospitality of any kind) or gifts. This includes sums paid to or on behalf of an employee (including a director), or put at the employee's disposal, *exclusively* for meeting expenses incurred, or to be incurred, by the employee in providing the entertainment or gift. (See Tolley's Income Tax under Employment Income for the employee's position.) It also includes expenses incidental to providing entertainment or gifts.

Entertainment expenditure is not within the above prohibition if:

- the entertainment is of a kind which it is the company's business to provide and it is provided in the ordinary course of that business either for payment or free of charge for advertising purposes; or
- the entertainment is provided for the company's employees (except where such entertainment is incidental to the entertainment of non-employees).

Gifts are not within the above prohibition if:

- they are of an item which it is the company's business to provide and are made for advertising purposes; or
- they incorporate a conspicuous advertisement for the company *and* do not consist of food, drink, tobacco or a token or voucher exchangeable for goods *and* the cost to the company of all such gifts to the same person in the same accounting period does not exceed £50; or
- they are provided for the company's employees (except where such gifts are incidental to the providing of gifts for non-employees); or
- they are made to a charity or to either of the similar organisations specified in *CTA 2009, s 1300(5)*.

[*CTA 2009, ss 1298–1300*].

By Extra Statutory Concession, B7, other gifts are allowed as deductions provided that they are:

(i) wholly and exclusively for the purposes of the business;
(ii) made for the benefit of a body or association established for educational, cultural, religious, recreational or benevolent purposes which is local to the donor's business activities and not restricted to persons connected with the donor; and
(iii) reasonably small in relation to the scale of the donor's business In *Bourne & Hollingsworth v Ogden* (1929) 14 TC 349 an abnormally large donation was disallowed. See also **69.46** below.

Deductions were allowed for items provided in the ordinary course of a trade of providing entertainment (see *Fleming v Associated Newspapers Ltd* (1972) 48 TC 382, HL). See also the VAT cases of *C & E Commissioners v Shaklee International and Another CA*, [1981] STC 776 and *Celtic Football and Athletic Co Ltd v C & E Commissioners CS*, [1983] STC 470. There is also a restriction on capital allowances where plant or machinery is used to provide entertainment, with similar exceptions as above where relevant (see **10.4** CAPITAL ALLOWANCES ON PLANT AND MACHINERY).

For an article on the scope and application of these rules, see Revenue Tax Bulletin August 1999 pp 679–682 issue 42 as supplemented by Revenue Tax Bulletin February 2000 p 729 issue 45. For further comprehensive guidance on business entertainment, see HMRC Business Income Manual BIM45000–45090.

Simon's Taxes. See **B2.432.**

Farming and market gardening

[69.41] Farming or market gardening in the UK is treated for corporation tax purposes as trading. All the UK farming carried on by a particular company (other than as part of a different trade) is treated as a single trade. Farming carried on by a partnership in which a company is partner is, however, separate from any farming carried on by the partner company itself. This does not apply to the woodlands or to land being prepared for forestry use. [*CTA 2009, ss 36, 1270(1); ITTOIA 2005, Sch 1 para 32*]. See *Bispham v Eardiston Farming Co* (1962) 40 TC 322 and *Sargent v Eayrs* (1972) 48 TC 573. The matters listed below are of particular application to farming or (where relevant) market gardening.

(a) **Compensation for compulsory slaughter.** See **68.30** TRADING INCOME.
(b) **Drainage.** Where land is made re-available for cultivation by the restoration of drainage or by re-draining, the net expenditure incurred (after crediting any grants receivable) will be allowed as revenue expenditure in farm accounts provided it excludes (i) any substantial element of improvement (e.g. the substitution of tile drainage for mole drainage) and (ii) the capital element in cases in which the present owner is known to have acquired the land at a depressed price because of its swampy condition (HMRC Statement of Practice, SP 5/81). See also HMRC Business Income Manual BIM55270.

(c) **Farmhouses.** The apportionment of the running costs of a farmhouse between business and private use should be based on the facts of the case for the year of account in question (HMRC Business Income Manual BIM55250).

(d) **Grants and subsidies.** See **68.30** TRADING INCOME.

(e) **Share farming.** See **68.30** TRADING INCOME.

(f) **Short rotation coppice.** See **68.30** TRADING INCOME.

(g) **Stock valuations.** See **68.33** TRADING INCOME for the herd basis, and, for trading stock generally, **69.63**. In general, livestock is treated as trading stock unless the herd basis applies, and home-bred animals may be valued, if there is no adequate record of cost, at 75% for sheep and pigs (60% for cattle) of open market value. Dead stock may be taken at 75% of market value.

Where an animal grant or subsidy for which application has been made has not been taken into account for a particular period but has been applied for, and that application materially affects the value of the animal, the grant or subsidy should be taken into account as a supplement to the market value when deemed cost is computed. Grants or subsidies applied for but not recognised as income in the period concerned should also be taken into account in arriving at net realisable value for stock valuation purposes. (HMRC Tax Bulletin December 1994 p 182 issue 14).

(h) **Subscriptions** to the **National Farmers Union** are allowable in full. HMRC also allow deductions for annual subscriptions paid by farmers to an agricultural society or to a breed society. For this purpose, an agricultural society is one whose main aim is the raising of the standard of livestock, produce etc. and the dissemination of relevant information among farmers. A breed society is a society established mainly for the purpose of improving or maintaining the purity of different breeds of livestock and of registering pedigrees. See HMRC Business Income Manual BIM55280.

(i) **Sugar beet outgoers scheme.** See **68.30** TRADING INCOME.

(j) **Trading profits.** See trade profits **68.30** TRADING INCOME.

(k) **Woodlands grants.** See trade profits **68.30** TRADING INCOME.

For these and other aspects of farming taxation, see HMRC Business Income Manual BIM55000–55730, 84000–84185 and 85600–85650.

Simon's Taxes. See **Division B5.1**.

Finance leasing

[69.42] The rules on leasing of *plant or machinery* under long funding leases are described at **10.47** CAPITAL ALLOWANCES ON PLANT AND MACHINERY. See also **69.52** below. The Statement of Practice described below has no application to such a long-funding lease. The *CTA 2010, Pt 21* provisions at **69.43, 69.44** below are specifically disapplied in relation to such leases.

See **49.2** LEASING for tax provisions relating to leases accounted for under IFRS 16, including transitional rules and the previous tax rules relating to changes in accounting basis for leases.

Statement of Practice

In relation to finance leases entered into after 11 April 1991, HMRC practice described below applies to rentals payable by a lessee under a finance lease, i.e. a lease which transfers substantially all the risks and rewards of ownership of an asset to the lessee while maintaining the lessor's legal ownership of the asset. The treatment of such rentals depends upon whether or not GAAP has been applied. This practice has no implications for the tax treatment of rentals receivable by the lessor, nor for the availability of capital allowances to the lessor. (HMRC Statement of Practice, SP 3/91 and Revenue Press Release 11 April 1991). HMRC have confirmed that the Statement of Practice applies to GAAP (not just SSAP 21 as stated in the Statement) so the same principles apply to entities accounting under IFRS, and presumably now FRS 102 (HMRC Business Leasing Manual BLM32215).

Finance lease rentals are revenue payments for the use of the asset, and, both under normal accounting principles and for tax purposes, should be allocated to the periods of account for which the asset is leased in accordance with the accruals concept. Where there is an option for the lessee to continue to lease the asset after expiry of the primary period under the lease, regard should be had, in allocating rentals to periods of account, to the economic life of the asset and its likely period of use by the lessee, as well as to the primary period.

Where GAAP has not been applied, the lessee's accounting treatment of rental payments is normally accepted for tax purposes, provided that it is consistent with the principles described above. If not, computational adjustments are made to secure the proper spreading of the rental payments.

Where GAAP has been applied, the finance charge element of the rental payments for a period of account is normally accepted as a revenue deduction for that period. In determining the appropriate proportion of the capital repayment element to be deducted for tax purposes, a properly computed commercial depreciation charge to profit and loss account will normally be accepted. Where, however, the depreciation charge is not so computed, the appropriate proportion for tax purposes will be determined in accordance with the principles described above.

For comment on the principles set out in SP 3/91, and on their application to particular arrangements, see Revenue Tax Bulletin February 1995 pp 189–193, issue 15. This considers in particular: sums paid before the asset comes into use; depreciation of leased assets; long-life assets; termination adjustments; fixtures leases; and the interaction of SP 3/91 with statutory restrictions on relief for rental payments.

Rental rebates

Some short term finance leases contain no provision for a secondary period and provide for rentals over the term of the lease, which allow the lessor to recoup in full its expenditure in acquiring the asset plus interest. In these circumstances the lessee will probably secure the right to be paid what the asset is worth at the end of the short lease term (the rental rebate).

Rental rebates should be taken into account in the computation of trading profits for the period in which they are recognised in the lessee's accounts under correct accounting practice. Any rebate or further rebate arising on the substitution of one finance lease for another in respect of the same asset will also be a revenue item for tax purposes.

Where the correct accounting treatment is to regard the sum in question as an adjustment of the finance charge element of the rentals under the replacement lease, that treatment may be followed for tax purposes.

A premature termination payment which represents a charge imposed on the lessee for being freed early from his obligations under the lease is capital expenditure, particularly where the payment equals total undiscounted future rentals.

See HMRC Business Leasing Manual BLM32330.

Anti-avoidance provisions apply to tackle an avoidance scheme involving the leasing of plant and machinery in relation to which HMRC received a disclosure. The scheme involves arrangements intended to create a company that is taxed on very little income from the leasing of the asset but which is potentially able to claim capital allowances on the full cost of the asset, creating tax losses where there is a commercial profit. The lessor may, alternatively or additionally, rely on obtaining a deduction for a rebate of rentals to generate a tax loss where there is a commercial profit.

The legislation addresses the avoidance in two ways, by restricting the amount on which capital allowances are available and by restricting the amount allowed as a deduction for rental rebates as outlined below.

Where plant or machinery (the asset) is leased (other than by a long funding lease) and a rental rebate is payable by the lessor, the amount of deduction in respect of the rebate is limited to the amount of the lessor's income from the lease. In calculating that amount, the finance charge element of the rental paid under a finance lease is excluded, as are any disposal receipts to be brought in for capital allowances purposes (under *CAA 2001, s 60(1)*), any service charges or any UK or foreign tax to be paid by the lessor.

The rental rebate is any sum payable to the lessee calculated by reference to the termination value of the asset, and the termination value is generally the value of the asset at or about the time when the lease terminates. It can be calculated by reference to any one or more of: the sale proceeds if the asset is sold; any insurance proceeds, compensation or similar sums in respect of the assets; and an estimate of the market value of the asset.

Other calculations which provide broadly similar results are permitted.

Where the asset is acquired by the lessor in a transaction to which, for corporation tax purposes, the transfer of trade without change of ownership provisions apply (*CTA 2010, s 948*), or in relation to which a connected persons election under *CAA 2001, s 266* applies, then the provisions apply as if the successor had done everything done by the predecessor.

The amount of the disallowed rebate, or, if less, the amount by which the rental rebate exceeds the capital expenditure incurred by the lessor, is treated as an allowable loss for capital gains tax purposes accruing to the lessor on the termination of the lease. The loss may only be deducted from chargeable gains accruing on the disposal of the asset.

[*CTA 2009, s 60A*].

See also HMRC Technical Note 'Plant and machinery leasing: anti-avoidance' dated 9 December 2009; see *Simon's Weekly Tax Intelligence*, 2009, Issue 50, p 3260.

See also **49** LEASING.

See also above under Long funding leases of plant or machinery.

General

See **10.47** onwards CAPITAL ALLOWANCES ON PLANT AND MACHINERY for other finance lease capital allowance restrictions. It was held in *Caledonian Paper plc v CIR* [1998] STC (SCD) 129 that annual or semi-annual payments of commitment fees, guarantee fees and agency fees relating to guarantees required in relation to finance leasing arrangements were deductible in computing profits, but that a one-off management fee was not.

Simon's Taxes. See **B5.404, B5.405.**

Finance leases — return in capital form

[69.43] *CTA 2010, Pt 21 Ch 2 (ss 899–924)* (the 'Chapter 2 provisions') apply in relation to asset leasing arrangements which fall to be treated under generally accepted accounting practice (GAAP) (see **68.19** TRADING INCOME) as finance leases or loans, and whose effect is that some or all of the investment return is or may be in the form of a sum that is not rent and would not, apart from these provisions, be wholly taxed as lease rental. The principal purposes of the Chapter 2 provisions are to charge any person entitled to the lessor's interest to tax by reference to the income return for accounting purposes (taking into account the substance of the matter as a whole, e.g. as regards connected persons or groups of companies); and to recover reliefs etc. for capital and other expenditure as appropriate by reference to sums received which fall within the provisions.

The Chapter 2 provisions apply where an asset lease (as widely defined) is or has at any time been granted in the case of which the conditions at (a)–(e) below are or have been met at some time (the '*relevant time*') in a period of account of the current lessor. Where the conditions have been met at a relevant time, they are treated as continuing to be met unless and until the asset ceases to be leased under the lease or the lessor's interest is assigned to a person not connected with any of the following:

(i) the assignor,
(ii) any other person who was the lessor at some time before the assignment, and

(iii) any person who at some time after the assignment becomes the lessor under arrangements made by a person who was the lessor (or was connected with the lessor) at some time before the assignment.

A lease to which the Chapter 2 provisions cease to apply can come within those provisions again if the conditions for their application are again met.

For the purposes of these provisions generally, and those at **69.44** below, **19** CONNECTED PERSONS applies initially to determine if persons are connected. But persons who are thus connected at any time in the 'relevant period' are then treated as being connected throughout that period. The '*relevant period*' runs from the earliest time at which any of the leasing arrangements were made to the time when the current lessor finally ceases to have an interest in the asset or any arrangements relating to it.

The Chapter 2 provisions do *not* apply if (or to the extent that), as regards the current lessor, the lease falls to be regarded as a long funding lease (within **10.47** CAPITAL ALLOWANCES ON PLANT AND MACHINERY) of plant or machinery.

The conditions referred to above are as follows.

(a) At the 'relevant time' (see above), and in accordance with GAAP, the leasing arrangements fall to be treated as a finance lease or loan, and either:
 (i) the lessor (or a connected person) is the finance lessor in relation to the finance lease or loan; or
 (ii) the lessor is a member of a group of companies for the purposes of whose consolidated accounts the finance lease or loan is treated as subsisting.
(b) under the leasing arrangements, there is or may be payable to the lessor (or to a connected person), a sum (a '*major lump sum*') that is not rent but falls to be treated, in accordance with GAAP, partly as a repayment of some or all of the investment in respect of the finance lease or loan and partly as a return on that investment.
(c) Not all of the part of the major lump sum which is treated as a return on the investment (as in (b) above) would, apart from these provisions, be brought into account for corporation tax purposes, as 'normal rent' (see below) from the lease for periods of account of the lessor, in accounting periods of the lessor ending with the 'relevant accounting period'. The '*relevant accounting period*' is the accounting period (or latest accounting period) consisting of or including all or part of the period of account in which the major lump sum is or may be payable under the arrangements.
(d) The period of account of the lessor in which the relevant time falls (or an earlier period during which he was the lessor) is one for which the 'accountancy rental earnings' in respect of the lease exceed the normal rent. The normal rent is determined by treating rent as accruing and falling due evenly over the period to which it relates (unless a payment falls due more than twelve months after any of the rent to which it relates is so treated as accruing).
(e) At the relevant time, either:

(i) arrangements exist under which the lessee (or a person connected with the lessee) may directly or indirectly acquire the leased asset (or an asset representing it — see *CTA 2010, s 934*) from the lessor (or a person connected with the lessor), and in connection with that acquisition the lessor (or connected person) may directly or indirectly receive a 'qualifying lump sum' from the lessee (or connected person); or

(ii) in the absence of such arrangements, it is in any event more likely that the acquisition and receipt described in (i) above will take place than that, before any such acquisition, the leased asset (or the asset representing it) will have been acquired in an open market sale by a person who is neither the lessor nor the lessee nor a person connected with either of them.

In (i) above, a '*qualifying lump sum*' is a sum which is not rent but at least part of which would be treated under GAAP as a return on investment in respect of a finance lease or loan.

For the purposes of the Chapter 2 provisions (and also the provisions at **69.44** below):

- a '*normal rent*' for a period of account of a lessor is the amount which (apart from these provisions) the lessor would bring in for corporation tax purposes in the period as rent arising from the lease;
- '*rental earnings*' for any period is the amount that falls for accounting purposes to be treated, in accordance with GAAP, as the gross return for that period on investment in respect of a finance lease or loan in respect of the leasing arrangements; and
- the '*accountancy rental earnings*' in respect of a lease for a period of account of the lessor is the greatest of the following amounts of rental earnings for that period in respect of the lease:
  (i) the rental earnings of the lessor;
  (ii) the rental earnings of any person connected with the lessor;
  (iii) the rental earnings for the purposes of consolidated group accounts of a group of which the lessor is a member.

  Where (ii) or (iii) applies and the lessor's period of account does not coincide with that of the connected person or the consolidated group accounts, amounts in the periods of account of the latter are apportioned as necessary by reference to the number of days in the common periods.

Current lessor to be taxed by reference to accountancy rental earnings. If for any period of account of the current lessor (L):

- the Chapter 2 provisions apply to the lease; and
- the accountancy rental earnings exceed the normal rent.

L is treated for corporation tax purposes as if in that period of account L had been entitled to, and there had arisen to L, rent from the lease of an amount equal to those accountancy rental earnings (instead of the normal rent). That rent is deemed to have accrued at an even rate throughout the period of account (or so much of the it as corresponds to the period for which the asset is leased).

Reduction of taxable rent by cumulative rental excesses

If a period of account of the current lessor is one in which the normal rent in respect of the lease exceeds the accountancy rental earnings, and there is a 'cumulative accountancy rental excess', the rent otherwise taxable for the period (the '*taxable rent*') is reduced by setting that excess against it. It cannot be reduced to less than the accountancy rental earnings.

There is an '*accountancy rental excess*' for a period if the period is one in which the current lessor is taxed by reference to accountancy rental earnings as above; it is the excess of the accountancy rental earnings over the normal rent. If, however, the taxable rent for that period is reduced by a 'cumulative normal rental excess' (see below), the accountancy rental excess for the period is limited to the excess (if any) of the accountancy rental earnings, reduced by the same amount as the taxable rent, over the normal rent. A '*cumulative accountancy rental excess*' is so much of the aggregate of accountancy rental excesses of previous periods of account as has not already been used, whether under these rules, the bad debt rules below or the rules below on disposals.

If a period of account of the current lessor is one in which the current lessor is taxed by reference to accountancy rental earnings, and there is a 'cumulative normal rental excess', the taxable rent is reduced by setting that excess against it. It cannot be reduced to less than the normal rent.

The '*normal rental excess*' for a period of account is the excess (if any) of normal rent over accountancy rental earnings. If, however, the taxable rent for that period is reduced by a cumulative accountancy rental excess (as above), the normal rental excess for the period is limited to the excess (if any) of the normal rent, reduced by the same amount as the taxable rent, over accountancy rental earnings. A '*cumulative normal rental excess*' is so much of the aggregate of normal rental excesses of previous periods of account as has not already been used, whether under these rules or the bad debt rules below.

Bad debts

Where accountancy rental earnings for a period of account are substituted for normal rent for corporation tax purposes (as above), and a 'bad debt deduction' in excess of the accountancy rental earnings falls to be made for the period, any cumulative accountancy rental excess for the period is reduced (but not below nil) by that excess. If the accountancy rental earnings do not exceed the normal rent, any bad debt deduction acts to reduce the amount of the normal rent against which a cumulative accountancy rental excess may be set, and the cumulative accountancy rental excess is reduced (but not below nil) by any excess of the bad debt deduction over the normal rent. There is provision for such reductions in the cumulative accountancy rental excess to be reversed in the event of subsequent bad debt recoveries or reinstatements. A '*bad debt deduction*', in relation to a period of account of the lessor, means the total of the deductions (if any) falling to be made for accounting purposes for that period by way of impairment loss in respect of rents from the lease of the asset.

There are similar provisions relating to the effect of bad debt deductions on cumulative normal rental excesses.

Effect of disposals

If the current lessor (or a connected person) disposes of its interest under the lease or the leased asset or an asset representing the leased asset (see *CTA 2010, s 934*), the Chapter 2 provisions have effect as if immediately before the disposal (or simultaneous such disposals) a period of account of the current lessor ended and another began.

In determining the amount of any chargeable gain on the disposal, the disposal consideration is reduced by setting against it any cumulative accountancy rental excess (as above) for the period of account in which the disposal occurs. *TCGA 1992, s 37* does not exclude any money or money's worth from the disposal consideration so far as it is represented by any cumulative accountancy rental excess set off under this rule (whether on the current disposal or previously). On a part disposal, the cumulative accountancy rental excess is apportioned in the same manner as the associated acquisition costs. Where there are simultaneous disposals, the cumulative accountancy rental excess is apportioned between them on a just and reasonable basis.

On an assignment of the current lessor's interest under the lease treated under *TCGA 1992* as a no gain/no loss disposal (see *TCGA 1992, s 288(3A)*), a period of account of the assignor is treated as ending, and a period of account of the assignee as beginning, with the assignment. Any unused cumulative accountancy rental excess or cumulative normal rental excess at the time of the assignment is transferred to the assignee.

Capital allowances etc.

Where an occasion occurs on which a major lump sum (as in (b) above) falls to be paid, there are provisions (see *CTA 2010, ss 917–922*) for the withdrawal of earlier reliefs for expenditure incurred by the current lessor in respect of the leased asset. This applies to capital allowances (**9**) and to reliefs for capital expenditure under **69.10** above (cemeteries and crematoria) and **69.72** below (waste disposal). The earlier reliefs are withdrawn either by the bringing in of a disposal value or by the imposition of a balancing charge or, in the case of expenditure allowed in respect of cemeteries etc., waste disposal or films etc., by the bringing in of a countervailing receipt. These provisions apply equally to capital allowances for contributors to capital expenditure under *CAA 2001, ss 537–542*.

Schemes to which Chapter 3 provisions applied first

If the Chapter 2 provisions come to apply to a lease to which the Chapter 3 provisions at **69.44** below applied immediately beforehand, the cumulative accountancy rental excess and the cumulative normal rental excess are determined as if the Chapter 2 provisions had applied throughout the period for which the Chapter 3 conditions in fact applied.

[*TIOPA 2010, Sch 3 para 7, CTA 2010, ss 895–924, 930–937; TCGA 1992, s 37A*].

For HMRC's views on various points of interpretation regarding the Chapter 2 provisions, see HMRC Business Leasing Manual BLM70005 onwards.

Simon's Taxes. See B3.340D, B5.416.

See also **49** LEASING — finance leasing with regard to further anti-avoidance provisions in respect of a leasing business and the treatment of lessors.

Finance leases not within the above provisions

[69.44] *CTA 2010, Pt 21 Ch 3 (ss 925–929)* (the Chapter 3 provisions) apply to arrangements, not within the Chapter 2 provisions at **69.43** above, which involve the lease of an asset and would fall to be treated under generally accepted accounting practice (GAAP) as finance leases or loans. The main purpose of the Chapter 3 provisions is to charge tax on amounts falling to be treated under GAAP as the income return on investment in respect of the finance lease or loan (taking into account the substance of the matter as a whole, e.g. as regards connected persons or groups of companies). The Chapter 3 provisions accordingly apply where:

- a lease of an asset is granted which forms part of a scheme;
- condition (a) at **69.43** above (or its income tax equivalent) is met at some time in a period of account of the current lessor; and
- the Chapter 2 provisions described at **69.43** above do not apply because not all of conditions (b)–(e) at **69.43** above (or their income tax equivalents) have been met at that time.

Where condition (a) at **69.43** above is met, it is treated as continuing to be met until either the asset ceases to be leased under the lease or the lessor's interest is assigned to a person not connected with any of the following:

(i) the assignor;
(ii) any other person who was the lessor at some time before the assignment, and
(iii) any person who at some time after the assignment becomes the lessor under arrangements made by a person who was the lessor (or was connected with the lessor) at some time before the assignment.

A lease to which the Chapter 3 provisions cease to apply can come within those provisions again if the conditions for their application are again met.

If for any period of account of the current lessor (L):

- the Chapter 3 provisions apply to the lease, and
- the 'accountancy rental earnings' (**69.43** above) exceed the 'normal rent' (**69.43** above),

L is treated for corporation tax purposes as if in that period of account L had been entitled to, and there had arisen to L, rent from the lease of an amount equal to those accountancy rental earnings (instead of the normal rent). That rent is deemed to have accrued at an even rate throughout the period of account (or so much of the it as corresponds to the period for which the asset is leased).

The provisions at **69.43** above relating to reduction of taxable rent by cumulative rental excesses, bad debt relief and the effect of disposals apply equally for the purposes of the Chapter 3 provisions.

The Chapter 3 provisions do *not* apply if (or to the extent that), as regards the current lessor, the lease falls to be regarded as a long funding lease (within **10.47** CAPITAL ALLOWANCES ON PLANT AND MACHINERY) of plant or machinery.

[*CTA 2010, ss 925–937; TIOPA 2010, Sch 3*].

For HMRC's views on various points of interpretation regarding the Chapter 3 provisions, see HMRC Business Leasing Manual BLM74600 onwards.

Simon's Taxes. See **B5.416**.

Flooding

[69.45] A specific deduction is allowable for qualifying contributions to a qualifying flood or coastal erosion risk management project where a deduction would not otherwise be available (and, in this regard, the relief takes priority over capital allowances). A flood or coastal erosion risk management project is qualifying if an English risk management authority (within the meaning of *s 6(14)* of the *Flood and Water Management Act 2010*) has applied to the Environment Agency for a grant under *s 16* of that Act, in order to fund the project, or the Environment Agency has determined that it will carry out the project, and the Environment Agency has allocated funding by way of grant-in-aid to the project.

A contribution to such a project is a qualifying contribution if it is made for the purposes of the project under an agreement between the person making the contribution, and the applicant authority or (as the case may be) the Environment Agency, or between those two persons and other persons. Relief is not available if the person making the contribution, or a person connected with them, receives or is entitled to receive a 'disqualifying benefit', either from carrying out the project or from any other person. If, after having made the contribution either as a sum of money or as a provision of services, the contributor or a connected person receives a refund of any part of the contribution in money or money's worth, the amount, or an amount of equal value, is brought into account in calculating the profits of the trade (so far as not already done so), either as a receipt arising on the date on which the refund or compensation is received, or as a post-cessation receipt if there has been a permanent cessation of the trade before that date.

A '*disqualifying benefit*' is a benefit consisting of money or other property, but it does **not** include the following:

(a) a refund of the contribution, if the contribution is a sum of money;
(b) compensation for the contribution, if the contribution is the provision of services;
(c) a structure, or an addition to a structure, that is or is to be used for the purposes of flood or coastal erosion risk management, and is put in place in carrying out the project ('structure' includes a road, path, pipe, earthwork, and plant and machinery);
(d) land, plant or machinery that is or is to be used, in the realisation of the project, for the purposes of flood or coastal erosion risk management; and

(e) a right over land that is or is to be used, in the realisation of the project, for the purposes of flood or coastal erosion risk management.

[*CTA 2009, ss 86A, 86B*].

Gifts and donations etc.

[69.46] See also **69.40** above (entertainment and gifts), **68.32** TRADING INCOME for gifts received, disposals of assets and inventory, and **14.11** for gift aid donations.

In relation to *ex gratia* payments on the termination of long-standing business arrangements, a distinction is drawn between parting gifts as personal testimonials (not taxable as business receipts) and payments which, on the facts, can be seen as additional rewards for services already rendered or compensation for a loss of future profits (taxable). For cases see **68.28**(e) TRADING INCOME.

A relief is available for certain gifts by trading companies for the purposes of a charity see **68.32** TRADING INCOME. Relief is also available for gifts for humanitarian purposes of medical supplies or medical equipment again see **69.40**.

An ordinary annual subscription by a trading company to a charity, made for the benefit of its employees, may be allowed as a trade expense where the availability of the charity to the employees can reasonably be regarded as a direct and valuable advantage to the employer's business and the amount is not unreasonably high (see *Bourne & Hollingsworth v Ogden* (1929) 14 TC 349). This would include reasonable annual subscriptions made to, for example, a general hospital in the locality of the employer's place of business, or to a trade charity maintained primarily for the benefit of employees in the type of trade in question. It can also include subscriptions made to charities of benefit to a specific category of the employees. See HMRC Business Income Manual BIM37510.

For donations of part of cost of ticket in football pools and lotteries, see **68.5** TRADING INCOME.

Companies which gift pre-eminent objects to the nation can obtain a reduction in their UK tax liability of 20% of the value of the object they are donating. See **14.17** CHARITIES.

Simon's Taxes. See **B2.441.**

Guarantees

[69.47] Losses under guarantees of the indebtedness of another are analogous to impairment losses (see **69.5** above) and similar principles apply.

Cases where losses were allowed as a deduction include:

- *Jennings v Barfield* (1962) 40 TC 365 — to a solicitor under the guarantee of a client's overdraft.
- *Lunt v Wellesley* (1945) 27 TC 78 — to a film-writer under guarantee of loans to a film company with which he was associated.

Cases where losses were refused include

- *Milnes v J Beam Group Ltd* (1975) 50 TC 675 — a company under a guarantee of loans to an associated company with which it had close trading connections.
- *Redkite Ltd v Inspector of Taxes* [1996] STC (SCD) 501 — a guarantee of loans to a subsidiary.

Also see *Bolton v Halpern & Woolf* (1980) 53 TC 445, CA, and *Garforth v Tankard Carpets Ltd* (1980) 53 TC 342.

A loss by an asphalt contractor under a guarantee to an exhibition (for which he hoped but, in the event, failed to work) allowed (*Morley v Lawford & Co* (1928) 14 TC 229, CA).

Payments under guarantees made to a trader for the setting up or the purposes of the trade and irrecoverable are in certain circumstances allowable as a capital loss for corporation tax. For loans made before 24 January 2019, it was a requirement that the borrower must be UK-resident. A claim under these provisions must be made not more than four years from the end of the accounting period in which the payment is made. [*TCGA 1992, s 253; FA 2020, s 27*]. See Tolley's Capital Gains Tax.

Simon's Taxes. See **B2.453.**

Hire-purchase

[69.48] Where assets are purchased under hire-purchase agreements, the charges (the excess of the hire-purchase price over the cash price, sometimes called interest but not true interest) are, appropriately spread, allowable deductions (*Darngavil Coal Co Ltd v Francis* (1913) 7 TC 1, Ct of Sess). See **69.5** for the bad debt etc. provisions of hire-purchase traders. For relief on capital element, see **10.57** CAPITAL ALLOWANCES ON PLANT AND MACHINERY.

For whether goods sold under hire-purchase are trading stock, see *Lions Ltd v Gosford Furnishing Co Ltd & CIR* (1961) 40 TC 256, Ct of Sess, and cf *Drages Ltd v CIR* (1927) 46 TC 389.

See generally HMRC Business Income Manual BIM40550–40551 (hire-purchase receipts) and BIM45350–45365 (hire-purchase payments).

Simon's Taxes. See **B2.406, B5.640–B5.642.**

Illegal payments etc.

[69.49] In computing income from any source for corporation tax purposes, no deduction may be made in respect of expenditure incurred:

(a) in making a payment the making of which constitutes a criminal offence; or
(b) in making a payment outside the UK where the making of a corresponding payment in any part of the UK would constitute a criminal offence there.

A deduction is similarly denied for any payment induced by a demand constituting blackmail or extortion. [*CTA 2009, s 1304*].

For a discussion of the circumstances in which the above may apply, see HMRC Business Income Manual BIM43100–43185.

Simon's Taxes. See **B2.420**.

Insurance paid

[69.50] Premiums for business purposes are normally allowable including insurance of assets, insurance against accidents to employees, insurance against loss of profits and premiums under mutual insurance schemes (cf. *Thomas v Richard Evans & Co* (1927) 11 TC 790, HL; for trade associations, see **69.64**).

For any recoveries on insurance policies see **67** TRADING INCOME.

Premiums on policies in favour of the employer insuring against death or critical illness of key employees are generally allowable, and the proceeds of any such policies trading receipts. However, in *Beauty Consultants Ltd v Inspector of Taxes* [2002] STC (SCD) 352, premiums on a policy insuring a company against the death of either of its controlling shareholder-directors were not allowed as deductions; the 'dual purpose rule' at **69.74** applied, in that the premiums benefited the shareholders personally by improving the value of their shares. In *Greycon Ltd v Klaentschi* [2003] STC (SCD) 370, it was held that the company's sole purpose in taking out key man policies was to meet a requirement of an agreement under which funding and other benefits were obtained from another company, that the policies had a capital purpose and that, consequently, the proceeds were not trading receipts.

Simon's Taxes. See **B2.425, B2.445**.

Legal and professional expenses

[69.51] The costs of forming a company are capital but in so far as they relate to loan capital may qualify for relief by virtue of *CTA 2009, s 61* (pre-trading expenditure — see **69.57** below).

The expenses of a company incorporated by charter in obtaining a variation of its charter etc. were allowed (*CIR v Carron Co* (1968) 45 TC 18, HL). See also *McGarry v Limerick Gas HC* [1932] IR 125 and contrast *A & G Moore & Co v Hare* (1914) 6 TC 572, Ct of Sess. In general, the costs of maintaining existing trading rights and assets are revenue expenses (*Southern v Borax Consolidated* (1940) 23 TC 597; *Bihar etc IT Commr v Maharaja of Dharbanga* (1941) 20 ATC 337, PC, and compare *Morgan v Tate & Lyle Ltd* (1954) 35 TC 367, HL). But the incidental costs of acquiring new assets etc. are part of their capital cost. The expenses of obtaining or renewing a lease of business premises are strictly capital but, in practice, the expenses of renewing leases under 50 years are generally deductible (although a proportionate disallowance may apply where a lease premium is involved — see HMRC Business Income Manual BIM46420). The cost of an unsuccessful application to vary a carrier's licence was disallowed (*Pyrah v Annis & Co* (1956) 37 TC 163, CA) as was the cost of an unsuccessful application for planning permission (*ECC Quarries Ltd v Watkis* (1975) 51 TC 153.

Legal expenses in defending charges brought by a professional regulatory body were allowed as deductions on the grounds that they were incurred to prevent suspension or expulsion and thus to protect the taxpayer's business (applying *Tate & Lyle Ltd* (above)), although the fines imposed were disallowed (see **69.11** above) (*McKnight v Sheppard* (1999) 71 TC 419, HL).

Costs incurred by a partner in connection with the dissolution of the partnership were disallowed in *C Connelly & Co v Wilbey* (1992) 65 TC 208.

The cost of tax appeals even though successful is not deductible (*Allen v Farquharson Bros & Co* (1932) 17 TC 59; *Smith's Potato Estates v Bolland* (1948) 30 TC 267, HL; *Rushden Heel Co v Keene* (1948) 30 TC 298, HL). Where an accountant etc. agrees the tax liabilities based on the accounts he prepares, normal annual fees are allowed as a deduction but not fees for a special review of settled years (*Worsley Brewery Co v CIR* (1932) 17 TC 349, CA).

In the case of *Market South West (Holdings) Ltd v HMRC*, [2011] UKUT 257 (TCC), [2011] STC 1469, a company operated an indoor market at a site in Cornwall. The relevant planning permission only allowed it to trade at weekends. They applied for planning permission to trade on weekdays. The council granted planning permission to trade on ten weekdays. The company subsequently breached the terms of this permission. The council issued an enforcement notice, against which the company appealed. The QB dismissed this appeal. In its tax return, the company claimed a deduction for the legal and professional fees incurred in applying for planning permission and in appealing against the enforcement notice issued by the council. HMRC issued an amendment disallowing the deduction on the basis that this was capital expenditure. The First-Tier Tribunal dismissed the company's appeal but the Upper Tribunal remitted the case for rehearing. Judge Avery Jones held that 'there should be an apportionment on the analogy of expenditure on a building that is partly an improvement and partly repairs'.

In *Duckmanton v Revenue and Customs Comrs* UT, [2013] STC 2379 the costs of defending a sole trader against a manslaughter charge, after a lorry which he owned had killed a pedestrian were not deductible; and in *Raynor v Revenue and Customs Comrs* [2011] UKFTT 813 (TC), [2012] SWTI 166 the costs of defending a partner who was charged with polluting a river with insecticide were also not deductible.

Additional accountancy expenses incurred as a result of an enquiry by HMRC into a return will normally be allowed as a deduction if the investigation results in no addition to profits, or an adjustment to the profits for the year of enquiry only and that adjustment does not arise as a result of careless or deliberate behaviour. Where the enquiry reveals discrepancies and additional liabilities for the year of enquiry or any earlier year which arise as a result of careless or deliberate behaviour, the expenses will be disallowed. (HMRC Enquiry Manual EM3981).

It is HMRC's view that premiums for a fee protection insurance policy, which entitles the policy holder to claim for the cost of accountancy fees incurred in negotiating additional tax liabilities resulting from careless or deliberate conduct, are not allowable. Even if the policy covers other risks as well, the premiums cannot be apportioned between allowable and non-allowable elements. (HMRC Business Income Manual BIM46452).

Simon's Taxes. See **B2.449**.

Long funding leases of plant or machinery

[69.52] The rules on leasing of plant and machinery are in *CTA 2010, ss 359–381, Sch 2 paras 61–64*. For 'long funding leases', the current regime grants entitlement to capital allowances to the lessee rather than to the lessor as previously (see **10.47** CAPITAL ALLOWANCES ON PLANT AND MACHINERY). There were corresponding changes to the tax treatment of lease rentals, to ensure that the lessor is no longer taxed on, and the lessee does not obtain a deduction for, the capital element of rentals (see below). The regime applies only to leases which are essentially financing transactions, known as '*funding leases*', comprising mainly finance leases but also some operating leases.

The coverage below considers firstly the lessor's position and then the lessee's. The provisions differ in each case according to whether the lease is a long funding operating lease or a long funding finance lease.

See HMRC Business Leasing Manual BLM40000 *et seq*.

As regards finance leases that fall outside the definition of a long funding lease or preceded its introduction, see **69.42–69.44** above.

Lessors

Long funding operating leases

For any period of account for the whole or any part of which the company is the lessor of plant or machinery under a 'long funding operating lease' (see **10.49**(4) CAPITAL ALLOWANCES ON PLANT AND MACHINERY), it is entitled to a deduction as follows in computing its profits (so as to compensate it for non-entitlement to capital allowances). Firstly, determine the 'starting value' in accordance with *CTA 2010, ss 364, 365*. This varies depending on whether or not there has been any previous use of the plant or machinery by the lessor and on the nature of any such previous use. In the most straightforward case where the sole use has been leasing under the long funding operating lease, the starting value is equal to cost. Secondly, deduct from the starting value the amount that is expected (at the commencement of the term of the lease — see *CAA 2001, s 70YI(1)*) to be the 'residual value' of the plant or machinery (i.e. its estimated market value assuming a disposal at the end of the term of the lease, less the estimated costs of that disposal). This gives the expected gross reduction in value over the term of the lease. Next, time-apportion that figure between all periods of account that coincide wholly or partly with the term of the lease. The resulting figure for each period of account is the amount deductible for that period.

Where the lessor (as above) incurs additional capital expenditure on the plant or machinery that is not reflected in its market value at the commencement of the term of the lease, an additional deduction is due as follows. Determine the amount which, at the time the additional expenditure is incurred, is expected to be the residual value of the plant or machinery. Deduct the amount previously expected to be the residual value. If this produces a positive amount, determine how much of that amount is attributable to the additional expenditure. Next, deduct the attributable amount from the amount of the additional expenditure. This gives the expected reduction in value of the additional expenditure over the remainder of the term of the lease. Time-apportion that figure between all periods of account that coincide wholly or partly with the term of the lease and which end after the additional expenditure is incurred. The resulting figure for each such period of account is the additional amount deductible for that period.

In the period of account in which a long funding operating lease *terminates*, any profit arising to the lessor from the termination must be brought into account as trading income and any loss so arising must be brought into account as a revenue expense. The profit or loss is computed as follows.

(1) Determine the 'termination amount' (for which see **10.50** CAPITAL ALLOWANCES ON PLANT AND MACHINERY) and subtract from it any sums paid to the lessee that are calculated by reference to the 'termination value' (as defined by *CAA 2001, s 70YH*), e.g. lease rental refunds.
(2) Determine the 'starting value' as above and subtract from it all deductions (other than additional deductions) allowable as above to that same lessor up to the date of termination.
(3) If any additional capital expenditure has been incurred as above, determine the total amount thereof and subtract from it all additional deductions allowable as above to that same lessor up to the date of termination.
(4) If the total in (1) above exceeds the aggregate of the totals in (2) and (3), a profit arises equal to the excess.
(5) If the total in (1) above falls short of the aggregate of the totals in (2) and (3), a loss arises equal to the deficit.

In computing the lessor's profits for the period of account in which termination occurs, no trading deduction is allowed for any sums paid to the lessee that are calculated by reference to the 'termination value' (as these are brought into account in (1) above).

[*CTA 2010, ss 363–369, 381; FA 2019, Sch 14 para 4(6)*].

Long funding finance leases

For any period of account in which the company is the lessor of plant or machinery under a 'long funding finance lease' (see **10.49**(4) CAPITAL ALLOWANCES ON PLANT AND MACHINERY), the amount to be brought into account as his taxable income from the lease is the amount of the 'rental earnings' in respect of the lease. The '*rental earnings*' for any period is the amount that, in accordance with generally accepted accounting practice (GAAP), falls to be treated as the gross return on investment for that period in respect of the lease. If, in accordance with GAAP, the lease falls to be treated as a loan in the accounts in question, so much of the lease rentals as fall to be treated as interest are treated for these purposes as rental earnings. There is also provision for exceptional profits or losses (including capital items) arising from the lease to be brought into account for tax purposes, as trading income or as revenue expenditure, if they fall to be brought into account under GAAP in the period of account in question but otherwise than as part of the profits calculation.

Where the lease *terminates* and any sum calculated by reference to 'termination value' (as defined by *CAA 2001, s 70YH*) is paid to the lessee, e.g. lease rental refunds, no deduction is allowed for that sum in computing the lessor's trading profits, except to the extent (if any) that it is brought into account in determining rental earnings.

[*CTA 2010, ss 360–362, 381; FA 2019, Sch 14 para 4(6)*].

Anti-avoidance legislation disapplies *CTA 2010, ss 360–369* above where:

(a) expenditure incurred on the leased plant or machinery is (apart from anything in *CTA 2010, ss 360–369*) allowable as a deduction in computing the lessor's trading profits because the plant or machinery is held, or comes to be held, as trading stock; or

(b) the long funding lease is part of an arrangement, including one or more other transactions, entered into by the lessor a main purpose of which is to secure that, over the term of the lease, there is a substantial difference between the amounts brought into account under GAAP and the amounts brought into account in computing taxable profits, such difference being at least partly attributable to the application of any of *CTA 2010, ss 360–369*.

There is also anti-avoidance legislation designed to counter a scheme involving a mismatch in the treatment of lease rentals under a head lease and a sub-lease of the same plant or machinery. Under a typical scheme, the head lease from A to B will not be a long funding lease from B's (the lessee's) point of view but the sub-lease from B to C will be a long funding lease from B's (the lessor's) point of view. The result is that B would be entitled to tax relief on the full amount of the lease rentals under the head lease (i.e. including the capital element) but would not be chargeable to tax on the capital element of the sub-lease rentals. The legislation seeks to ensure that B is taxed on the full amount of the sub-lease rentals by disapplying *CTA 2010, ss 360–369* above in these circumstances in relation to the sub-lease.

See further **10.47** onwards CAPITAL ALLOWANCES ON PLANT AND MACHINERY.

[*CTA 2010, ss 370–375*].

Film lessors

CTA 2010, ss 360–369 above are disapplied where the subject of the long funding lease is a film. [*CTA 2010, s 376*].

Lessees

Long funding operating leases

In computing the profits of a company for any period of account in which it is the lessee of plant or machinery under a 'long funding operating lease' (see **10.49**(4) CAPITAL ALLOWANCES ON PLANT AND MACHINERY), the otherwise allowable deductions in respect of amounts payable under the lease must be reduced as follows.

Firstly, determine the 'starting value' in accordance with *CTA 2010, s 380*. In the straightforward case where the sole use of the plant or machinery has been in a qualifying activity (within **10.4** CAPITAL ALLOWANCES ON PLANT AND MACHINERY) carried on by the lessee, the starting value is equal to the market value of the plant or machinery at the commencement (see *CAA 2001, s 70YI(1)*) of the term of the lease. Secondly, deduct from the starting value the amount that is expected (at the commencement of the term of the lease) to be the market value of the plant or machinery at the end of the term of the lease. This gives the expected gross reduction over the term of the lease. Next, time-apportion that figure between all periods of account that coincide wholly or partly with the term of the lease. The resulting figure for each period of account is the amount of the reduction for that period.

[*CTA 2010, ss 379–381; FA 2019, Sch 14 para 4(6)*].

Long funding finance leases

In computing the profits of a company for any period of account in which it is the lessee of plant or machinery under a long funding finance lease, the amount deducted in respect of amounts payable under the lease must not exceed the amount that, in accordance with GAAP, falls to be shown in the lessee's accounts as finance charges or interest expenses in respect of the lease. If, in accordance with GAAP, the lease falls to be accounted for as a loan, it is for this purpose treated as if it fell to be accounted for as a finance lease.

Where the lease *terminates* and a sum calculated by reference to 'termination value' (as defined by *CAA 2001, s 70YH*) is paid to the lessee, e.g. lease rental refunds, that sum is not brought into account in computing the lessee's profits for any period. (It is, however, brought into account in calculating the disposal value of the plant or machinery for capital allowances purposes — see **10.27** CAPITAL ALLOWANCES ON PLANT AND MACHINERY under Lessees: Disposal events and values).

[*CTA 2010, ss 377, 378, 381; FA 2019, Sch 14 para 4(4)(6)*].

Where a company is, for any part of a period of account beginning on or after 1 January 2019, the lessee of plant or machinery under a 'right-to-use lease' (where the lessee applies IFRS 16 — see **10.49**(5) CAPITAL ALLOWANCES ON PLANT AND MACHINERY) which is a long funding finance lease, the following applies if there is a change in the amounts payable under the lease as a result of which (and in accordance with GAAP) either a remeasurement of the lease liability is shown in the company's accounts or a deduction is shown in the accounts (other than an interest expense or depreciation or impairment of the right-of-use asset arising from the lease). In computing the profits for the period, the deduction in respect of amounts payable under the lease is, after taking account of any limitation under the above provisions, increased or decreased to take account of the remeasurement or deduction resulting from the change. This does not apply if the remeasurement or deduction results in the lessee being treated as incurring further capital expenditure on plant or machinery under *CAA 2001, s 70D* (see **10.48** CAPITAL ALLOWANCES ON PLANT AND MACHINERY). [*CTA 2010, s 377A; FA 2019, Sch 14 paras 4(5), 6(1)*].

See also **10.47** onwards CAPITAL ALLOWANCES ON PLANT AND MACHINERY.

Simon's Taxes. See B5.405–B5.409A.

Miscellaneous expenses

[69.53] Export Credits Guarantee Department A deduction is allowed for amounts payable by a trading company to that Department under an agreement entered into by virtue of arrangements made under Export and *Investment Guarantees Act 1991, s 2* or with a view to entering into such an agreement. [*CTA 2009, s 91*].

Distribution of assets from mutual concerns see **68.47** TRADING INCOME.

Reimbursements of capital expenditure spread over 30 years held capital as regards both payer and recipient (*Boyce v Whitwick Colliery* (1934) 18 TC 655, CA). For allowances from railway in respect of traffic on sidings paid for by trader see *Westcombe v Hadnock Quarries* (1931) 16 TC 137; *Legge v Flettons Ltd* (1939) 22 TC 455.

Excessive payments to **service company** of professional firm held not deductible (*Stephenson v Payne, Stone Fraser & Co* (1967) 44 TC 507).

For purchases and sales of standing timber see **68.47** TRADING INCOME.

DVD rental

Relief for the cost of acquiring DVDs, or similar items, for hire may be obtained by way of either:

(i) capital allowances (provided the useful economic life is at least two years);
(ii) valuation basis (where the useful economic life is two years or less); or
(iii) renewals basis.

See Revenue Tax Bulletin October 1995 pp 254, 255 issue 19 for a discussion of each of these methods in this context. See also HMRC Business Income Manual BIM67200–67220.

See also *CIR v Pattison* (1959) 38 TC 617, Ct of Sess (weekly instalments for business, capital).

Simon's Taxes. See B2.454.

Patents

[69.54] For corporation tax purposes, expenditure and receipts in respect of intellectual property created or acquired from an unrelated party on or after 1 April 2002 or acquired (from any party) on or after 1 July 2020 falls within the intangible assets regime. See in particular the commencement and transitional rules for that regime at **42.42** INTANGIBLE ASSETS.

Expenses (agent's charges, patent office fees etc.) are deductible if incurred in obtaining, for the purposes of a trade, the grant of a patent or the extension of its term. Expenses are also deductible in connection with a rejected or abandoned application for a patent made for the purposes of the trade. [*CTA 2009, s 89, Sch 2 para 22*].

For capital expenditure on the purchase of patent rights see **10.36** CAPITAL ALLOWANCES ON PLANT AND MACHINERY.

For sums received on the sale of patent rights see **68.49** TRADING INCOME.

Royalties and other sums paid for the use of patents are not deductible in computing trading profits. [*CTA 2009, s 59*]. For spreading of patent royalties received, see **42.43** INTANGIBLE ASSETS.

For know-how and trade marks, see **68.45** and **69.53** respectively.

See also **56** PATENT INCOME for the patent box regime.

However, where companies do not elect into the new regime the existing provisions will continue to apply.

Simon's Taxes. See **B2.456.**

Penalties, interest and surcharges

[69.55] Generally, tax penalties, interest and surcharges are not allowable deductions in computing profits for any corporation tax purpose. This applies to interest and certain penalties and surcharges in respect of late paid or unpaid or under-declared value added tax, insurance premium tax, landfill tax, climate change levy, aggregates levy, stamp duty land tax, excise duties, customs, excise or import duties, and income tax payable under the CONSTRUCTION INDUSTRY SCHEME (**20**); for a list of the specific charges to which this prohibition applies, see *CTA 2009, s 1303*. It does *not* apply to interest on late paid or unpaid corporation tax, which is dealt with under the loan relationships rules — see **43.2** INTEREST ON UNPAID TAX. [*CTA 2009, s 1303*].

See also BIM45740 and 31610.

Post cessation receipts (allowable deductions from)

[69.56] A deduction from post-cessation receipts is allowed for any loss, expense or debit or capital allowance that would have been deductible if the trade had not ceased, has not been relieved in any other way and which does not arise directly or indirectly from the cessation itself. A deduction may not be given more than once. In the case of a loss, relief is given against the first available post-cessation receipts, i.e. receipts for an earlier accounting period in priority to those for a later one, but not so as give relief for a loss against receipts charged for an accounting period before that in which the loss is made.

See further **68.16** TRADING INCOME.

Pre-trading expenditure

[69.57] The general rule is that trading expenditure is deductible when incurred and hence is not allowable if incurred before trading commenced (cf. *Birmingham & District Cattle By-Products Ltd v CIR* (1919) 12 TC 92). The rule is modified for certain pre-trading capital expenditure, including research and development expenditure and abortive exploration expenditure by mining concerns (see **9** CAPITAL ALLOWANCES).

There is also a special relief for expenditure incurred by a company within the seven years before it commences to carry on a trade which, had it been incurred on the first day of trading, would have been deductible in computing the trading profit. The expenditure is treated as if it was incurred on the on the first day of trading and is thus deductible. Expenditure otherwise deductible, e.g. pre-trading purchases of stock or advance payments of rent, is not within this special relief.

See also **50.8** LOAN RELATIONSHIPS for the election available to treat pre-trading debits as trading debits of the accounting period in which the trade commences.

[*CTA 2009, s 61*].

The above provisions apply equally to a property business carried on by a company (see **59** PROPERTY INCOME).

Simon's Taxes. See **B2.460**.

Provisions for contingent and future liabilities

[69.58] For forward contracts see **69.13** above.

Where a company is required under overseas legislation to make leaving payments to its employees, a provision in its accounts for its prospective liability is permissible if capable of sufficiently accurate calculation (*Owen v Southern Railway of Peru* [1957] AC 334, [1956] 2 All ER 728, HL). The allowance each year is the actual payments as adjusted for any variation between the opening and closing provisions but the deductible provision for the year in which the legislation was enacted may include an amount in respect of previous services of the employees (*CIR v Titaghur Jute Factory Ltd* CS 1978, 53 TC 675).

No deduction is normally permissible for future repairs or renewals (*Clayton v Newcastle-under-Lyme Corpn* QB 1888, 2 TC 416; *Naval Colliery Co Ltd v CIR* HL 1928, 12 TC 1017; *Peter Merchant Ltd v Stedeford* CA 1948, 30 TC 496). However, this rule is now subject to Financial Reporting Standard FRS 12 (see **69.60** below), which considers further provisions for repairs and renewals). More recently, following the decision in *Herbert Smith (a firm) v Honour* [1999] STC 173, [1999] 11 LS Gaz R 70 which concerned a provision for future rent payable on surplus business premises, HMRC now accept that there is no tax rule that denies a deduction for provisions made for 'anticipated losses'. Accurate provisions for foreseen losses on long-term contracts made in line with correct accounting practice are deductible. No deduction is permissible for the future cost of collecting debts (*Monthly Salaries Loan Co v Furlong* Ch D 1962, 40 TC 313) or for future payments of damages in respect of accidents to employees unless liability has been admitted or established (*James Spencer & Co v CIR* CS 1950, 32 TC 111). See also *Albion Rovers Football Club v CIR* HL 1952, 33 TC 331 (wages deductible when paid). A provision for regular major overhaul work accrued due on aircraft engines was allowed in *Johnston v Britannia Airways Ltd* Ch D 1994, 67 TC 99 (but see Revenue Tax Bulletin February 1999 p 624 issue 39 and further below as regards changes in accounting practice superseding this decision).

For provisions by insurance companies for unexpired risks etc., see *Sun Insurance Office v Clark* HL 1912, 6 TC 59. For the liability of cemetery companies in receipt of lump sums for the future maintenance of graves, see *Paisley Cemetery Co v Reith* CES 1898, 4 TC 1 and *London Cemetery Co v Barnes* KB 1917, 7 TC 92.

A provision by a company engaged in the exploitation of a North Sea oil field, for anticipated future expenditure on the completion of the exploitation, in dismantling installations used and (as required under its licence) in 'cleaning up' the sea bed, was disallowed as capital when incurred in *RTZ Oil & Gas Ltd v Elliss* Ch D 1987, 61 TC 132.

See generally HMRC Business Income Manual BIM42201, 46500–46565. See also Revenue Press Release 20 July 1999, and FRS 12 and articles in the Revenue Tax Bulletin April 1999 pp 636–639 issue 40 and December 1999 pp 707–709 issue 44 commenting on its implications for the treatment of provisions in tax computations.

Simon's Taxes. See **B2.504, B2.505.**

Rents etc. for business premises

[69.59] Rents paid for business premises are deductible in computing profits. For repairs, see **69.60** below. As regards rents receivable, see **68.44** TRADING INCOME.

Where premises partly used privately (e.g. shop with residential accommodation above), *CTA 2009, s 54* gives the specific power to apportion dual purpose expenditure; see **69.74** under the 'wholly and exclusively' rule and see the note on *s 54* in the Explanatory Notes to *CTA 2009*. For allowance for use of home for business, see *Thomas v Ingram* Ch D 1979, 52 TC 428. See also *Mason v Tyson* Ch D 1980, 53 TC 333 (expenses of flat used occasionally to enable professional man to work late not allowed as a deduction).

Additional rent liability incurred to obtain the freehold reversion to premises already rented held capital (*Littlewoods Mail Order v McGregor* CA 1969, 45 TC 519 following *CIR v Land Securities* HL 1969, 45 TC 495), as were periodical payments to reimburse capital expenditure incurred by landlord (*Ainley v Edens* KB 1935, 19 TC 303) and payments based on production for grant of sisal estates (*Ralli Estates v East Africa IT Commr* PC 1961, 40 ATC 9). But payments for the use of a totalisator calculated by reference to its cost were allowed (*Racecourse Betting Control Board v Wild* KB 1938, 22 TC 182) as were rents subject to abatement dependent on profits (*Union Cold Storage v Adamson* HL 1931, 16 TC 293). For Scottish duplicands see *Dow v Merchiston Castle School* CS 1921, 8 TC 149. Rent paid by partnership to partner owning business premises allowed (*Heastie v Veitch & Co* CA 1933, 18 TC 305). For excessive payments to professional 'service company' see *Payne, Stone Fraser* at **69.53** above.

Property no longer required

Where premises became redundant or were closed down, continuing rents (less sub-letting receipts) were allowed as a deduction (*CIR v Falkirk Iron* CS 1933, 17 TC 625; *Hyett v Lennard* KB 1940, 23 TC 346) but not payments to secure the cancellation of leases no longer required (*Mallett v Staveley Coal & Iron* CA 1928, 13 TC 772 (the leading case here); *Cowcher v Richard Mills & Co* KB 1927, 13 TC 216; *Union Cold Storage v Ellerker* KB 1939, 22 TC 547; *Dain v Auto Speedways* Ch D 1959, 38 TC 525; *Bullrun Inc v Inspector of Taxes* (Sp C 248), [2000] SSCD 384). See also *West African Drug Co v Lilley* KB 1947, 28 TC 140. Where the rent of a motorway service station was calculated by reference to takings, a lump sum payment for the exclusion of tobacco duty from takings was held capital (*Tucker v Granada Motorway Services* HL 1979, 53 TC 92), but, distinguishing *Granada Motorways*, an amount received by a company in respect of its agent's negligent failure to serve its landlord with counter-notice of a notice of an increase in its rent, was held to be a trading receipt in *Donald Fisher (Ealing) Ltd v Spencer* CA 1989, 63 TC 168. Rent for a building not required for occupation for business purposes but to control access to the lessee's works was held deductible (less sub-let rents) in *Allied Newspapers v Hindsley* CA 1937, 21 TC 422.

For allowance of a provision in respect of future rents under leases of premises ceasing to be used for business purposes, see *Herbert Smith v Honour* Ch D 1999, 72 TC 130. Following that decision, HMRC accept that there is no longer a tax rule which denies provisions for anticipated losses or expenses (see HMRC Press Release 20 July 1999). See the article in the HMRC Tax Bulletin December 1999 pp 707–709 issue 44 summarising HMRC's view.

Rates and council tax

Business rates are deductible in the same way as rent. Council tax may similarly be deducted where it is attributable to premises (or part) used for trade purposes. (Revenue Press Release 16 March 1993).

Coronavirus (COVID-19))

Many companies claimed the relief from business rates introduced by the Government during the coronavirus pandemic, anticipating that their business would suffer severe adverse consequences from the impact of the pandemic. Some later found they were not as badly affected as they expected, and decided to repay the business rates waived. This repayment is not in itself a payment of business rates and would not have been an allowable deduction under ordinary principles. *FA 2021, s 33* provides that a deduction should be allowable. It has effect regardless of when the repayment is made. The deduction is allowed for the accounting period in which the original business rates liability was due and payable, overriding generally accepted accounting practice (GAAP).

Premiums

Certain lease premiums etc. in relation to leases not exceeding 50 years are chargeable on the landlord to an extent which varies with the length of the lease (see **60.10** PROPERTY INCOME). For any part of the 'relevant period' (as defined in *CTA 2009, s 228(6)* — generally the duration of the lease) during which the company occupies the premises for the purposes of a trade or (with certain limitations) deals with its interest therein as property employed for the purposes of a trade, the company is treated as incurring expenditure of a revenue nature. This is deductible in computing the company's trading profits, subject to any rule that might prohibit such deduction in a particular case (e.g. the 'wholly and exclusively' rule). For each day of the relevant period on which the above conditions are satisfied, the amount of additional rent treated as incurred is the amount which falls to be included in computing the landlord's property income divided by the total number of days in the relevant period. If only part of the leased land is used for trading purposes, the amount is proportionately reduced. The amount is also proportionately reduced to the extent, if any, to which the company is entitled to an allowance under *CAA 2001, s 403* (mineral asset expenditure — see **9.10** CAPITAL ALLOWANCES).

If the company itself grants a sublease out of the leased property at a taxable premium, it is treated as paying a revenue expense only to the extent, if any, that the daily amount computed above exceeds the daily reduction in its own taxable premium. For more detail of how this rule operates, see **60.13** PROPERTY INCOME. If the sublease relates to only part of the premises covered by the main lease, the above rules are applied separately to the different parts of the premises, the premium under the main lease being apportioned between those parts on a just and reasonable basis.

The above rules apply whether the premium is chargeable to income tax or corporation tax in the hands of the landlord. They also apply in relation to leases of property *outside* the UK where the landlord's property business is an overseas property business.

No deduction under these provisions is allowed if the lease is a taxed lease only because of the application of the first rule (rule 1) in *CTA 2009, s 243* or *ITTOIA 2005, s 303*. Rule 1 applies where:

(a) the terms of the lease, or any other circumstances, make it unlikely that the lease will continue beyond a date before the end of the term for which the lease was granted; and
(b) the premium was not substantially greater than it would have been had the term been one ending on that date.

In these circumstances the lease is treated as ending on the earlier date.

[*CTA 2009, ss 62–67*].

Except to the extent that the above provisions apply, lease premiums are not deductible in computing trading profits (see *MacTaggart v Strump* CS 1925, 10 TC 17).

In the case of a company dealing in land, there is provision to prevent a lease premium or similar sum being taxed as both (i) a trading receipt and (ii) a receipt of a property business (as in **60.10** onwards. PROPERTY INCOME). This is achieved by reducing the amount at (i) by the amount at (ii). [*CTA 2009, s 136*].

Reverse premiums

See **68.53** TRADING INCOME for treatment of reverse premiums received.

The payment of a reverse premium by a company to achieve the assignment of a lease which had become disadvantageous (due to the company's failure to meet its obligations under a repairing covenant) was held to be on capital account (*Southern Counties Agricultural Trading Society Ltd v Blackler* (Sp C 198), [1999] SSCD 200). HMRC take the view that where a reverse premium is paid by a developer trading in property, it is deductible in computing his trading profits (Revenue Press Release 9 March 1999).

For HMRC approach to these rules, see HMRC Business Income Manual BIM41050–41140.

General

See **4.8** ANTI-AVOIDANCE [*CTA 2010, ss 834–848*] regarding restrictions where there is a lease-back at a non-commercial rent and **4.9** -AVOIDANCE *CTA 2010, ss 849–862*] for taxation of capital sums received on certain lease-backs.

Simon's Taxes. See B2.465.

Repairs and renewals

General

[69.60] Any allowable expenditure is deductible in the period when incurred and not when the repairs etc. accrued (*Naval Colliery Co Ltd v CIR* HL 1928, 12 TC 1017). Provisions for future repairs and renewals were held not allowable in *Clayton v Newcastle-under-Lyme Corpn* QB 1888, 2 TC 416 and *Peter Merchant Ltd v Stedeford* CA 1948, 30 TC 496, but see now **68.19** TRADING INCOME, and HMRC Business Income Manual BIM46515, 46901, for the requirement for the application of generally accepted accountancy principles in this context. Hence a provision for regular major overhaul work accrued due on aircraft engines was allowed as a deduction in *Johnston v Britannia Airways Ltd* Ch D 1994, 67 TC 99 (but see Revenue Tax Bulletin February 1999 p 624 issue 39 as regards changes in accounting practice superseding this decision).

No deduction is available for expenditure on providing or replacing an integral feature of a building or structure if the expenditure is a qualifying expenditure for plant and machinery capital allowances purposes. [*CAA 2001, s 33A(3); CTA 2009, s 60*]. See **10.10** CAPITAL ALLOWANCES ON PLANT AND MACHINERY.

See also **9.23** CAPITAL ALLOWANCES for allowances in respect of the cost of renovation or conversion of a part of a building or structure.

Business premises

The general rule is that expenditure on additions, alterations, expansions or improvements is capital but the cost of repairs, i.e. restoring a building to its original condition, is allowable. However, the use of modern materials in repairing an old building does not make the expenditure capital (*Conn v Robins Bros Ltd* Ch D 1966, 43 TC 266), and HMRC now consider that this applies to the replacement of single-glazed windows by double-glazed equivalents (see Revenue Tax Bulletin June 2002 p 936 issue 59). If the expenditure is capital, the estimated cost of 'notional repairs' obviated by the work is not allowable (see *Wm P Lawrie* and *Thomas Wilson (Keighley)* below).

HMRC accept that provisions properly made under GAAP are tax deductible if they are estimated with sufficient accuracy except where there is an express rule to the contrary (e.g. provisions for capital expenditure). FRS 102 imposes a requirement that for a provision to be allowable it must be a present obligation (either legal or constructive) as a result of a past event; it must be probable that a transfer of economic benefits will be required to settle the obligation; and it must be possible to make a reliable estimate of the amount of that obligation. See HMRC Business Income Manual BIM46500 onwards.

Summary of cases:

- *Fitzgerald v CIR Supreme Court (IFS)* 1925, 5 ATC 414; *Wm P Lawrie v CIR* CS 1952, 34 TC 20A — renewal of a building, i.e. a complete re-construction, is capital.
- *O'Grady v Bullcroft Main Collieries* KB 1932, 17 TC 93 — the cost of rebuilding a factory chimney was held capital.
- Contrast *Samuel Jones & Co v CIR* CS 1951, 32 TC 513 — where the chimney was an integral part of the building and allowed.
- *Wm P Lawrie* (above) and *Thos Wilson (Keighley) v Emmerson* Ch D 1960, 39 TC 360 — roof replacements.
- *Wynne-Jones v Bedale Auction Ltd* Ch D 1976, 51 TC 426 and *Brown v Burnley Football Co Ltd* Ch D 1980, 53 TC 357 — the replacement of the ring in a cattle auction mart and of a stand in a football ground were held not to be repairs respectively in which the problem is reviewed.
- *Avon Beach & Cafe v Stewart* HC 1950, 31 TC 487 — cost of barrier against coastal erosion held capital.
- *Phillips v Whieldon Sanitary Potteries* HC 1952, 33 TC 213 — replacing a canal embankment was capital.
- *Pitt v Castle Hill Warehousing* Ch D 1974, 49 TC 638 — building new access road was capital.
- *Auckland Gas Co Ltd v CIR* PC, [2000] STC 527 — involving the insertion of plastic pipes within dilapidated metal ones over substantial lengths of a gas pipe network, held to be capital.
- *Transco plc v Dyall* (Sp C 310), [2002] SSCD 199 — Auckland Gas was considered but distinguished in case involving the insertion of plastic pipes in cast iron ones on a selective basis that had not changed the character of the pipeline system as a whole.
- *Jackson v Laskers Home Furnishers* Ch D 1956, 37 TC 69 — where on taking a lease of dilapidated property the dilapidations were made good under a covenant in the lease, the cost was held disallowable as attributable to the previous use of the premises.
- *Odeon Associated Theatres Ltd v Jones* CA 1971, 48 TC 257 — however, in this case, where cinemas were acquired in a state of disrepair (but still fit for public showings) because of war-time restrictions on building work, the cost of the repairs was allowed.

In practice, expenditure on repairing and redecorating newly acquired premises is allowed unless the premises could not be used, or could only be used in the short term, without the repairs or the need for the repairs is reflected in the purchase price or rent payable. See generally HMRC Business Income Manual BIM46935.

Dilapidations of a repair nature on the termination of a lease are generally deductible.

For repairs to tied premises see **69.7**.

Plant and other business assets etc.

The general rules for premises above apply to plant.

Under what is known as the **valuation basis**, a class of assets, for example spare parts for plant and machinery, are dealt with in a similar way to trading stock, involving opening and closing valuations. For further detail, and for change from capital allowances to valuation basis, see HMRC Business Income Manual BIM46970, 46975.

For repairs soon after the acquisition of an asset see *Law Shipping v CIR* CS 1923, 12 TC 621 and *CIR v Granite City SS Co* CS 1927, 13 TC 1 in which the cost of repairs to ships attributable to their use before acquisition, was held capital. But see *Odeon Associated Theatres* above in which *Law Shipping* was distinguished. See also *Bidwell v Gardiner* Ch D 1960, 39 TC 31 in which the replacement of the furnishings of a newly acquired hotel was held capital.

Expenditure on renewal of railway tracks was allowed in *Rhodesia Railways v Bechuanaland Collector* PC 1933, 12 ATC 223, distinguishing *Highland Railway v Balderston* CES 1889, 2 TC 485 in which held capital. Abnormal expenditure on dredging a channel to a shipyard was held capital in *Ounsworth v Vickers Ltd* KB 1915, 6 TC 671 but the cost to a Harbour Board of removing a wreck (*Whelan v Dover Harbour Board* CA 1934, 18 TC 555) and of renewing moorings (*In re King's Lynn Harbour* CES 1875, 1 TC 23) was allowed. For shop fittings see *Eastmans Ltd v Shaw* HL 1928, 14 TC 218; *Hyam v CIR* CS 1929, 14 TC 479. See also *Lothian Chemical v Rogers* CS 1926, 11 TC 508.

Assets held under an operating lease

A deduction may be allowed for a provision to cover future repairs of assets held under an operating lease which contains a repairing obligation (for example, tenants' repairing leases of property). The obligation, required under FRS 12 (see above), subsists from the signing of the lease. (HMRC Business Income Manual BIM46550).

See generally HMRC Business Income Manual BIM46900–46965.

Simon's Taxes. See **B2.404, B2.409, B2.466.**

Research and development and scientific research

[69.61] For enhanced tax reliefs for research and development expenditure see 63 RESEARCH AND DEVELOPMENT EXPENDITURE.

Revenue expenditure incurred by a company on 'research and development' (within *CTA 2010, s 1138*) related to its trade, whether undertaken directly or on its behalf, is allowable as a deduction in computing profits. Expenditure incurred in the acquisition of rights in, or arising out of, the research and development is excluded, but the allowable expenditure otherwise includes all expenditure incurred in, or providing facilities for, carrying it out. Research and development 'related' to a trade includes any which may lead to or facilitate an extension of the trade, or which is of a medical nature and has a special relation to the welfare of workers employed in the trade. These provisions apply equally to expenditure on oil and gas exploration and appraisal (within *CTA 2010, s 1134*).

Expenditure by a company on research and development is not precluded from deduction under these provisions by reason only of the fact that it is brought into account in determining the value of an intangible asset, but there are rules to prevent double relief in respect of the same expenditure. See also **42.40** INTANGIBLE ASSETS.

Scientific research associations

Relief is similarly given for any sum paid to an Association within **33.13** EXEMPT ORGANISATIONS which has as its object the undertaking of research and development which may lead to or facilitate an extension of the class of trade to which the company's trade belongs.

Relief is also given for any sum paid to an approved university, college research institute etc. to be used for 'scientific research' 'related' to that class of trade.

'*Scientific research*' means any activities in the fields of natural or applied science for the extension of knowledge. Scientific research 'related' to a class of trade includes any which may lead to or facilitate an extension of trades of that class, or which is of a medical nature and has a special relation to the welfare of workers employed in trades of that class. Any question as to what constitutes scientific research is to be referred by HMRC to the Secretary of State, whose decision is final.

[*CTA 2009, ss 87, 88, 1308*].

For *capital expenditure* on research and development, see **9.20** CAPITAL ALLOWANCES.

For the definition of 'research and development', see **63.1** RESEARCH AND DEVELOPMENT EXPENDITURE.

Simon's Taxes. See **B2.467**.

Sound recordings expenses

[69.62] See **68.62** TRADING INCOME for sound recording income.

Expenditure on the production or acquisition of the 'original master version' of a sound recording (including any rights held or acquired in it) is treated as expenditure of a revenue nature. An '*original master version*' is a master tape or master audio disc and the term '*sound recording*' does not include a film soundtrack.

Where the company's trade consists of, or includes, the exploitation of original master versions of sound recordings and these are not trading stock of that trade, the expenditure which is incurred on the production or acquisition of the original master version of a sound recording is revenue expenditure (whether incurred as above or otherwise). It is allocated to periods of account (or if no accounts are made up, to accounting periods) using an 'income matching' rule. So much of the expenditure as is just and reasonable is allocated to the relevant period having regard to:

- the amount of the expenditure that remains unallocated at the beginning of the period;
- the proportion which the estimated value of the original master version realised in the period (by way of income or otherwise) bears to the sum of the value so realised and the estimated remaining value at the end of the period; and
- the need to bring the whole expenditure into account over the time during which the original master version is expected to be realised.

Additional amounts can be allocated to a period provided the amount so allocated does not exceed the value of the original master version realised in that period (by way of income or otherwise).

[*CTA 2009, ss 150, 151*].

Stock (inventory) and work in progress

[69.63] The general rule is that stock is to be valued at the lower of cost and net realisable value. Leading cases are *Minister of National Revenue v Anaconda American Brass Co* (1955) 34 ATC 330, PC, and *BSC Footwear v Ridgway* (1971) 47 TC 495, HL. Market value held to be replacement price for a merchant (*Brigg Neumann & Co v CIR* (1928) 12 TC 1191) and retail price for a retailer in *BSC Footwear* above (HMRC prepared to take price net of any selling commission). Stock may be valued partly at cost and partly at market value where lower (*CIR v Cock Russell & Co* (1949) 29 TC 387). The base stock method is not permissible (*Patrick v Broadstone Mills* (1953) 35 TC 44, CA) nor is 'LIFO' (*Anaconda American Brass* above). See also *Asia Mill Ltd v Ryan (Inspector of Taxes)* [1951] WN 390, 32 TC 275, HL. The cost should include as a minimum the cost of materials and direct labour but the accounts treatment of overheads is normally accepted (*Ostime (Inspector of Taxes) v Duple Motor Bodies Ltd* [1961] 2 All ER 167, [1961] 1 WLR 739, HL).

HMRC take the view that any valuation of stock included in financial statements prepared in accordance with generally accepted accounting practice (see **68.19** TRADING INCOME) should be accepted provided that:

- it reflects the correct application of generally accepted accounting practice;
- the method pays sufficient regard to the facts; and
- the basis does not violate the taxing statutes as interpreted by the courts.

(HMRC Business Income Manual BIM33115).

A mark to market basis of valuation, used mainly by financial institutions and commodity dealers and under which stock is valued at market value, may also be acceptable (HMRC Business Income Manual BIM33160).

For the use of formulae in computing stock provisions and write-downs, see HMRC Tax Bulletin December 1994 p 184 issue 14. Broadly, Officers will accept formulae which reflect a realistic appraisal of future income from the particular category of stock and which result in the stock being included at a reasonable estimate of net realisable value (under IAS now fair value less costs to sell). Where computations are accepted without enquiry, it is on the assumption that profits are arrived at in accordance with such principles.

For the treatment of depreciation taken into account in arriving at stock valuations, see HMRC Business Income Manual BIM33190.

For motor dealer stock valuations, see HMRC Tax Bulletin August 1994 p 156 issue 12.

HMRC consider that the proper valuation of professional work in progress depends on the correct application of GAAP to the facts. Under FRS 102 section 23, revenue for uncompleted service contracts is to be accounted for under the 'percentage of completion' method. This means that if a contract is in progress at the year end, then the supplier of services would include the proportion of the contract undertaken to that date in its accounts. (HMRC Business Income Manual BIM33165).

Changes in basis of valuation

Where the stock was found to be grossly undervalued it was held that an assessment to rectify the closing undervaluation must be reduced by the opening undervaluation to bring out the true profits (*Bombay IT Commr v Ahmedabad New Cotton Mills Co* (1929) 9 ATC 574, PC). But where a company altered its method of dealing with accrued profits on long-term contracts and the closing work in progress in the year 1 accounts on the old basis was substantially below the opening figure in the year 2 accounts on the new basis, held, distinguishing *Ahmedabad*, the difference must be included in the year 2 profits (*Pearce v Woodall-Duckham Ltd* (1978) 51 TC 271, CA).

Where there is a change in the basis of valuation, the following practice is applied for tax purposes. If the bases of valuation both before and after the change are valid bases, the change is dealt with under the provisions at **68.20** TRADING INCOME. If the change is from an invalid basis to a valid one, the opening figure for the period of change must be arrived at on the same basis as the closing figure for that period, and liabilities for earlier years will be reviewed where it is possible to do so. (HMRC Business Income Manual BIM33199). See, however, *Woodall-Duckham Ltd* (above) as regards long-term contracts.

See **68.20** for spreading of the tax charge in relation to adjustments on a change of accounting basis arising from the interpretation of UITF 40.

Long-term contracts

HMRC accept that accurate provisions for foreseen losses on long-term contracts (e.g. in the construction industry) made in accordance with correct accounting practice are tax deductible. (HMRC Business Income Manual BIM33025).

In *Symons v Weeks and Others* (1982) 56 TC 630, it was held that progress payments under the long-term contracts of a firm of architects did not fall to be brought into account for tax before the relevant contract was completed, notwithstanding that they exceeded the figure brought in for work in progress, calculated on the correct principles of commercial accounting.

See above for changes of basis.

Goods sold subject to reservation of title

Where the supplier of goods reserves the title in them until payment is made (as a protection should the buyer become insolvent) and meanwhile the goods are treated by both parties for accountancy purposes as having been sold/purchased, HMRC will follow the accounts treatment (HMRC Statement of Practice, B6). See Note A of Financial Reporting Standard No 5 and HMRC Business Income Manual BIM33375.

Goods on consignment stock are normally treated as stock in the hands of the supplier until disposed of by the consignee (e.g. sale or return) (HMRC Statement of Practice, B6).

For **forward contracts**, see **69.13** above.

Trading stock acquired or disposed of other than in the course of trade

The following provisions apply to changes in trading stock.

(a) Where trading stock is appropriated by the trader for another purpose (e.g. his own consumption), market value is brought into account as a receipt on the date of appropriation and any actual consideration received for it is left out of account for corporation tax.

(b) Where an item owned by the trader otherwise than as trading stock is appropriated to trading stock, for corporation tax purposes, the cost (treated as incurred at the time it became trading stock) to be brought into account on the date the item became trading stock is open market value of the item on the day it became trading stock, any actual value passing being left out of account.

(c) Where trading stock is disposed of otherwise than in the course of trade and (a) above does not apply, market value at the date of disposal is brought into account as a receipt at the date of disposal and any actual consideration is left out of account.

(d) Where trading stock is acquired other than in the course of a trade and (b) above does not apply, open market value on the date it became stock has to be brought into the accounts as a cost arising at the date of acquisition. Any consideration passing is left out of account.

The rules at (c) and (d) above and the TRANSFER PRICING rules (**72**) both apply so as to bring into overall charge an amount not less than the market value of the stock.

For these purposes only, '*trading stock*' is defined as stock held for sale in the course of a trade, or partially completed or immature items which are intended for sale when complete or mature. It does not include materials used for manufacture etc, services carried out in the course of a trade or materials used in the performance of these services.

[*CTA 2009, ss 156–161; TIOPA 2010, s 147; FA 2019, Sch 1 para 54*].

The above provisions give statutory effect to pre-existing rules established by case law. In *Sharkey v Wernher* (1955) 36 TC 275, HL, it was established that where trading stock was disposed of otherwise than by way of trade, the realisable value was to be credited for tax purposes. The rule applied, *inter alia*, to goods taken out of stock by a retailer for his own use (see below). It was applied in *Petrotim Securities Ltd v Ayres* (1963) 41 TC 389, CA, to a disposal of shares at gross under-value as part of a tax avoidance scheme, but in *Ridge Securities Ltd v CIR* (1963) 44 TC 373, dealing with the other end of the same scheme, it was held that the same principle applied to acquisitions of trading stock otherwise than by way of trade, market price being substituted for the actual purchase price. But the principle was not applicable to sales or purchases by way of trade notwithstanding not at arm's length. Hence when a share dealing company acquired shares at substantial overvalue from an associated company, the claim by the Revenue for market value failed (*Craddock v Zevo Finance Co* (1946) 27 TC 267, HL), and when a property dealing company acquired property from its controlling shareholder at substantial undervalue, its claim to substitute market value failed (*Jacgilden (Weston Hall) v Castle* (1969) 45 TC 685). See also *Skinner v Berry Head Lands* (1970) 46 TC 377 and *Kilmorie (Aldridge) v Dickinson* (1974) 50 TC 1, HL.

Appropriations to trading stock

Appropriations to trading stock of assets held in another capacity are generally treated as a disposal and reacquisition at market value. Where a chargeable gain or allowable loss would otherwise arise for capital gains tax purposes under *TCGA 1992, s 161(1)*, the company may elect for the market value to be reduced for these purposes by the amount of the chargeable gain (or, before 8 March 2017, increased by the amount of the allowable loss), the trading profits being computed accordingly and the appropriation being disregarded for capital gains tax purposes. The election must be made within two years after the end of the accounting period in which the asset is appropriated. With effect for appropriations of assets to trading stock made on or after 8 March 2017, the election is permitted only where appropriation at market value would give rise to a chargeable gain and not where it would give rise to an allowable loss. [*TCGA 1992, s 161(3)(3A); F(No 2)A 2017, s 26*].

For purposes other than those of the provisions above for trading stock acquired or disposed of other than in the course of trade, case law applies as follows. Greyhounds kept by greyhound racing company were not trading stock (*Abbot v Albion Greyhounds (Salford)* (1945) 26 TC 390). Payments by cigarette manufacturer for cropping trees (not owned by it) for leaves used in manufacture, held to be for materials (*Mohanlal Hargovind of Jubbulpore v IT Commr* (1949) 28 ATC 287, PC). For payments for unworked minerals, sand and gravel etc, (including tailings etc) by mines, quarries etc. see **68.46** TRADING INCOME. For payments for oil by oil companies, see *Hughes v British Burmah Petroleum* (1932) 17 TC 286; *CIR v Europa Oil (NZ) Ltd* [1971] AC 760, [1971] 2 WLR 55, PC; *Europa Oil (NZ) v New Zealand Commr* [1976] STC 37, PC. For timber see **69.53** above and *Coates v Holker Estates Co* (1961) 40 TC 75.

Valuation on cessation of trade

Unless the transfer pricing provisions apply (see further below), trading stock at cessation must be valued as follows. These rules apply to partnerships, unless a company carrying on the trade in partnership immediately before the change continues to do so after the change. For these provisions, 'trading stock' means any property sold in the ordinary course of the trade, or which would be sold if mature or manufacture etc were complete, or materials used in such manufacture etc. Trading stock also includes services performed in the ordinary course of the trade which are wholly or partly completed at cessation and for which it would be reasonable to invoice were there no cessation (or where the services are partly completed, when they are fully completed) and any item produced and material used in the performance of the services. Sale or transfer of trading stock includes sale or transfer of any benefits accruing, or which might reasonably be expected to accrue, from those services.

(1) If the trading stock at cessation is sold to a person carrying on (or intending to carry on) a trade in the UK who can deduct the cost as an expense for corporation tax purposes, the stock is valued at the amount realised on the sale. If, however, the two parties to the sale are connected persons (defined more broadly than by *CTA 2010, s 1122 see below*), arm's length value is to be taken instead unless an election is made under *CTA 2009, s 167* (see below). (Neither rule applies to a transfer of farm animals where the anti-avoidance rules for the herd basis (at **68.43** TRADING INCOME) apply.) If the stock is sold with 'other assets', the amount realised is arrived at on a just and reasonable apportionment; For the purposes of these rules, a 'sale' includes a transfer for valuable consideration, with related expressions then being defined accordingly. Where arm's length value exceeds both (i) actual sale price and (ii) 'acquisition value', connected persons may jointly elect to substitute the greater of (i) and (ii) for the arm's length value. The election must be made within two years after the end of the accounting period in which cessation occurred. '*Acquisition value*' for this purpose is the amount which would have been deductible in calculation profits assuming that the stock had been sold in the course of trade immediately before cessation for a price equal to the value determined on a sale between 'connected persons' (see below) and the accounting period began immediately before the sale.

For the purpose of these provisions, parties are 'connected' if any of the following are met:

(a) they are connected under *CTA 2010, s 1122*;
(b) one is a partnership and the other has a right to share in the partnership's profits;
(c) one is a company and is controlled by the other;
(d) both are partnerships and another party has a right to share in the income or assets of both of them; or
(e) both are companies, or one is a partnership and the other a company and, in either case, another party has control over both of them.

The cost of the trading stock to the buyer is taken to be the value determined under the above rules (or the corresponding income tax rules) in relation to the seller.

Any question as to the application of these rules is to be determined by the Tribunal in the same way as an appeal. See *Bradshaw v Blunden (No 2)* (1960) 39 TC 73; *CIR v Barr (No 2)* (1955) 36 TC 455, Ct of Sess. These rules are not applicable to woodlands managed on a commercial basis (*Coates v Holker Estates* above). For their application to 'hire-purchase debts' see *Lions Ltd v Gosford Furnishing Co Ltd & CIR* (1961) 40 TC 256, Ct of Sess. A contention by HMRC that the rules did not apply to a transfer of closing stock simultaneous to a cessation was rejected in *Moore v Mackenzie* (1971) 48 TC 196.

(2) In all cases not within (1) above, trading stock is to be valued at the price it would have realised if sold in the open market at the time of the cessation.

If the market value of the stock is greater than the amount brought into account under the TRANSFER PRICING (**72**) rules at *TIOPA 2010, Pt 4*. In that case the market value less the transfer pricing amount is brought into account in calculating the trading profits, in addition to the transfer pricing amount.

Similar rules as above apply in relation to '*work in progress*' (as defined in *CTA 2009, s 163*) on cessation of a profession, except that there is no special rule for a transfer of work in progress to a connected person. Additionally, an election is available to the effect that, in computing profits to the date of cessation, closing work in progress is valued at cost and any realised excess over cost is then treated as a post-cessation receipt (see **68.16** TRADING INCOME); the election must be made no later than two years after the end of the accounting period in which the cessation occurred.

[*CTA 2009, ss 162–171*].

See **58.19** PAYMENT OF TAX for exit charge payment plans, which a company may enter into when the above provisions apply on the company ceasing to be within the charge to corporation tax.

Recovery of assets under Proceeds of Crime Act 2002, Pt 5

Where the transfer of trading stock is a *Pt 5* transfer under *Proceeds of Crime Act 2002* (as in **9.2** CAPITAL ALLOWANCES) and the stock is to be treated, as a result of the transfer, as if sold in the course of the trade, it is treated, for the purpose of computing taxable profits and notwithstanding *CTA 2009, ss 162–171* above (if applicable), as sold at cost price. [*Proceeds of Crime Act 2002, Sch 10 para 11; ITTOIA 2005, Sch 1 para 583(6)*].

Simon's Taxes. See **B2.205, B2.617, D2.313.**

Subscriptions and contributions

Trade and professional associations

[69.64] Ordinary annual subscriptions to local associations, including Chambers of Commerce, are normally allowed as deductions in computing profits. Subscriptions to larger associations are deductible, and receipts therefrom chargeable, if the association has entered into an arrangement with HMRC under which it is assessed on any surplus of receipts over allowable expenditure (the association should be asked). Most associations enter into the arrangement but if not the deduction is restricted to the proportion applied by the association for purposes such that it would have been deductible if so applied by the subscriber (*Lochgelly Iron & Coal Co Ltd v Crawford* (1913) 6 TC 267, Ct of Sess). For other cases see Tolley's Tax Cases. Subscriptions to the Economic League are not deductible (*Joseph L Thompson & Sons Ltd v Chamberlain* (1962) 40 TC 657).

Contributions to mutual insurance associations are deductible even though used to create a reserve fund (*Thomas v Richard Evans & Co Ltd* (1927) 11 TC 790, HL). See also **53** MUTUAL COMPANIES.

Local enterprise organisations

Expenditure incurred by a company in making any contribution (whether in cash or kind) to a 'local enterprise organisation' is specifically allowed as deduction in computing trading profits if it would not otherwise be deductible. If, however, in connection with the making of the contribution, the trader or a person connected with him (see **19** CONNECTED PERSONS) receives (or is entitled to receive) a 'disqualifying benefit' of any kind, whether or not from the organisation itself, the value of the benefit is subtracted from the deduction otherwise available. Any such benefit received after such a deduction has been given is recovered by treating its value as a trading receipt for the period of account in which it is received. If received after the trade has permanently ceased, it is treated as a post-cessation receipt (within **68.16** TRADING INCOME). A '*disqualifying benefit*' is a benefit the expenses of obtaining which would not be deductible if incurred directly by the trader in an arm's length transaction.

For these purposes, a '*local enterprise organisation*' means any of the following.

- A local enterprise agency, i.e. a body for the time being approved as such by the relevant national authority (e.g. for England and NI, by the Secretary of State). Various conditions are prescribed for approval. In particular, the body's sole aim must be the promotion or encouragement of industrial and commercial activity or enterprise in a particular area of the UK, with particular reference to small businesses. If that is only one of its main aims, it must maintain a separate fund for the sole purpose of pursuing that aim and the above relief applies only to contributions to that fund. Also, the body must be precluded from transferring its income or profits to its members or its managers, other than as a reasonable return for goods, labour or services provided, money lent or premises occupied. Approval may be conditional and may be withdrawn retrospectively.
- A training and enterprise council, i.e. a body which has an agreement with the Secretary of State to act as such.
- A Scottish local enterprise company, i.e. a company which has an agreement with Scottish Enterprise or Highlands and Islands Enterprise to act as such.
- A business link organisation, i.e. a person authorised by the Secretary of State to use a trade mark designated for these purposes.

[*CTA 2009, ss 82–85*].

Urban regeneration companies

Identical provisions to those described above in relation to local enterprise organisations apply to a contribution made to an urban regeneration company designated as such by Treasury order. A body may be so designated only if its sole or main function is to co-ordinate the regeneration of a specific urban area in the UK in association with public and local authorities. Designation orders may be backdated by up to three months or, in the case of the first such order, to 1 April 2003. [*CTA 2009, ss 82, 86*]. The first designations are made by *SI 2004 No 439*.

Simon's Taxes. See B2.474.

Subsidies, grants etc.

[69.65] See **68.64** TRADING INCOME.

Taxation

[69.66] Income tax and corporation tax are not deductible in computing profits (cf *Allen v Farquharson Bros & Co* (1932) 17 TC 59). Overseas taxes may be subject to DOUBLE TAX RELIEF (**30**) but any such tax not relieved by credit on overseas income included in the profits may generally be deducted [*TIOPA 2010, s 112; ICTA 1988, s 811*] but not on UK income, e.g. profits of UK branches (*CIR v Dowdall O'Mahoney & Co Ltd* (1952) 33 TC 259, HL). See HMRC Business Income Manual BIM45901.

In *Harrods (Buenos Aires) v Taylor-Gooby* (1964) 41 TC 450, CA, an annual capital tax imposed by the Argentine on foreign companies trading there was not a tax on the profits and was allowable.

As regards relief for national insurance contributions by employers in respect of employees, see **69.21** above.

For taxation appeals see **69.51** above. For VAT, see **72** VALUE ADDED TAX.

Simon's Taxes. See B2.472.

Tied petrol stations payments

[69.67] For tied licensed premises see **69.7** above.

'Exclusivity payments' by petrol company to retailers undertaking to sell only its goods were allowed in computing its profits in *Bolam v Regent Oil Co Ltd* (1956) 37 TC 56 (payments for repairs carried out by retailer), *BP Australia Ltd* (1965) 44 ATC 312, PC (lump sums paid for sales promotion), and *Mobil Oil Australia Ltd* (1965) 44 ATC 323, PC, but held capital in *Regent Oil Co Ltd v Strick (Inspector of Taxes)* [1966] AC 295, [1965] 3 All ER 174, HL, where the payment took the form of a premium to the retailer for a lease of his premises (immediately sub-let to him).

Trade marks or designs

[69.68] Expenses are deductible if incurred in obtaining, for the purposes of a trade, the registration of a trade mark or design, the renewal of registration of a trade mark or the extension of the period for which the right in a registered design subsists. [*CTA 2009, s 90, Sch 2 para 22; Copyright, Designs and Patents Act 1988, Sch 7 para 36(1)(2); Trade Marks Act 1994, s 106(2), Sch 5*]. For corporation tax purposes expenditure and receipts in respect of intellectual property acquired or created or acquired from an unrelated party on or after 1 April 2002 or acquired (from any party) on or after 1 July 2020 falls within the intangible assets regime. See in particular the commencement and transitional rules for that regime at **42.42** INTANGIBLE ASSETS.

Training

[69.69] Costs incurred by an employer in respect of employee training are generally allowable as a trade expense. See **69.25** above for this and as regards certain other allowable employee training costs, and **69.64** above as regards contributions to training and enterprise councils.

Unremittable amounts

[69.70] Where a trade is carried on partly in the UK and partly overseas, so that liability to UK corporation tax arises on trading profits, amounts received or receivable overseas (e.g. from export sales) which cannot be brought to the UK because of foreign exchange restrictions would nevertheless fall to be included in computing profits. No relief would be available under *CTA 2009, ss 1274–1275* (unremittable overseas income — see **64.4** RESIDENCE), because the overall profits of the trade do not arise outside the UK, or under *CTA 2009, ss 55, 970* in respect of impairment losses. A debt is not impaired or bad merely because it is unremittable. The provisions described below are designed to give relief in such circumstances.

Where amounts cannot be remitted solely as a result of local foreign exchange control restrictions, relief may be claimed, provided that:

(a) an amount received by, or owed to, a trading company is included in arriving at the trading profit of the company;
(b) it is paid or owned outside the UK
(c) some or all of it is unremittable.

An amount received is unremittable if it cannot be received in the UK due to foreign exchange restrictions. An amount owed (e.g. a trade debt) is unremittable if it temporarily cannot be paid due to exchange control restrictions or it can be paid in the overseas territory but could not then be transferred to the UK only due to foreign exchange restrictions. '*Foreign exchange restrictions*' are imposed by the law of the other country where the amount is paid or owed, by executive action of its government or the impossibility of obtaining, in that country, currency which could be remitted.

Relief is given for the amount in question by deducting it from profits but not so as to create a trading loss. Any excess of unremittable amounts over profits for any period of account is carried forward to the next period of account, aggregated with any unremittable amounts for that period, and used to reduce or extinguish trading profits for that period, and so on *ad infinitum*. If no trading profit has been made for a period of account, any unremittable amounts are similarly carried forward.

However, no such deduction is allowed to the extent that:

- the amount in question is used to finance expenditure or investment outside the UK or is otherwise applied outside the UK; or
- a deduction is allowed under *CTA 2009, s 1275*; or
- it is an amount owed and an insurance recovery is received in respect of it.

Relief is withdrawn for an unremittable amount or any part of it if, subsequently, the amount (or part) ceases to be unremittable or is exchanged for (or discharged by) a remittable amount, or is used to finance overseas expenditure etc., or an 'allowable provision for impairment loss' is made in respect of it, or, in the case of an amount owed, is the subject of an insurance recovery, or the amount or part of it is applied outside the UK or is exchanged for or discharged by a remittable amount. The amount (or part) is treated as a trading receipt for the period of account in which the said event occurs, but only to the extent it has been deducted from profits. An 'allowable provision for impairment loss is either a debit in respect of impairment or a financial asset is brought into account under the loan relationship provisions. See **49** LOAN RELATIONSHIPS.

These provisions also apply to unremittable bank interest in appropriate circumstances (see **7.5** BANKS).

[*CTA 2009, ss 172–175, 1274–1278*].

Simon's Taxes. See **B2.702.**

Valuation fees

[69.71] Property valuation fees incurred in order to comply with *Companies Act 2006* are allowable as trading or management expenses. (HMRC Statement of Practice, C10). It is understood that regular property valuation fees (other than in connection with property acquisitions or sales) are similarly allowable.

Waste disposal

[69.72] Expenditure on purchase and reclamation of tipping sites by a company carrying on a waste disposal business was held to be capital in *Rolfe v Wimpey Waste Management Ltd* (1989) 62 TC 399, CA, as were instalment payments for the right to deposit waste material in *CIR v Adam* (1928) 14 TC 34, Ct of Sess. See also *McClure v Petre* (1988) 61 TC 226, where the receipt of sum for licence to tip soil was also held to be capital.

Site preparation and restoration expenditure

A deduction is allowed as below in computing profits where a company incurs, in the course of a trade, 'site preparation expenditure' in relation to a 'waste disposal site', and, at the time when the company first deposits waste materials on the site in question, it holds a current 'waste disposal licence'. Expenditure incurred for trade purposes by a company about to carry on the trade is for this purpose treated as incurred on the first day of trading. The deduction is not available where the company incurring the expenditure recharges it to another person who holds the licence when first depositing waste (see HMRC Business Income Manual, BIM67465). No claim is required but any supporting documentation should be retained in case of an HMRC enquiry into a return.

A '*waste disposal site*' is a site used (or to be used) for the disposal of waste materials by their deposit on the site, and in relation to such a site, '*site preparation expenditure*' is expenditure on preparing the site for the deposit of waste materials. This includes expenditure incurred before the relevant licence is granted, and in particular expenses associated with obtaining the licence itself (HMRC Business Income Manual BIM67455). A '*waste disposal licence*' is a disposal licence under *Control of Pollution Act 1974, Pt 1* (or NI equivalent), a waste management licence under *Environmental Protection Act 1990, Pt 2* (or NI equivalent), a permit under regulations under *Pollution Prevention and Control Act 1999, s 2* (or NI equivalent), an authorisation for the disposal of radioactive waste, or a nuclear site licence.

The deductible amount of site preparation expenditure for a period of account is the amount allocated to that period, which itself is given by the formula:

$$RE \times \frac{WD}{SV + WD}$$

where:

RE = residual expenditure (see below);
WD = volume of waste materials deposited on the site during the period; and
SV = volume of the site not used up for the deposit of waste materials at the end of the period.

The residual expenditure for a period of account is the site preparation expenditure incurred by the company at any time before and up to the end of that period, less any expenditure which either has been allowed as a trading deduction for a prior period or is capital expenditure qualifying for capital allowances. If the trade commenced before 6 April 1989, a proportion of the expenditure incurred before that date (OE) is excluded, such proportion being calculated by reference to the volume of materials deposited before that date (OWD) and the unused volume of the site immediately before that date (OSV). The reduction is the amount given by the formula:

$$OE \times \frac{OWD}{OSV + OWD}$$

Any site preparation expenditure incurred by a predecessor of the company is brought into account above as if it had been incurred by the company. For this purpose, a predecessor of the company is a person who, on or after that date, has ceased to carry on the trade carried on by the company or has ceased to carry on a trade so far as relating to the site in question and who, in either case, has transferred the whole of the site to the company (though not necessarily the same estate or interest in the site).

A company making a 'site restoration payment', in the course of carrying on a trade, may deduct the payment in computing profits for the period of account (i.e. a period for which an account is drawn up) in which the payment is made. A payment will not qualify for relief to the extent that it represents either expenditure allowed as a trading deduction for prior periods or capital expenditure qualifying for capital allowances.

However, where the site restoration payment is made directly or indirectly to a connected person the deduction is given for the period of account in which the work for which the payment is made is completed. No deduction is allowed if the payment arises from arrangements to which the person carrying on the trade is a party and the main purpose of which is to obtain a deduction.

A '*site restoration payment*' is a payment made:

(a) in connection with the restoration of a site (or part thereof); and
(b) in order to comply with any condition of a 'relevant licence', or any condition imposed on the grant of planning permission to use the site for the carrying out of 'waste disposal activities', or any term of a 'relevant planning obligation'.

'*Waste disposal activities*' are the collection, treatment, conversion and final depositing of waste materials, or any of those activities.

A 'relevant planning obligation' is defined by *CTA 2009, s 145(6)* by reference to *Town and Country Planning Act 1990* and Scottish and NI equivalents.

[*CTA 2009, ss 142–145, Sch 2 paras 30–32*].

See generally HMRC Business Income Manual BIM67405–67550.

Leasing. See **69.43** above as regards restrictions on relief under the above provisions where finance leasing arrangements are involved.

Simon's Taxes. See **B5.672.**

Landfill tax

HMRC's views on the deductibility of landfill tax in computing trading income are as follows.

Site operators

Treatment of landfill tax charged on to customers will follow the generally accepted accounting practice. As regards self-generated waste, landfill tax (net of any credit following a contribution to an environmental trust) will be allowed as a deduction so long as the other costs incurred in disposing of the waste are deductible.

Customers of site operators

The landfill tax element of the global charge does not need to be separately invoiced, and deductibility of the landfill tax element will follow that of the non-landfill tax element of the charge.

Environmental trust contributions

Site operators may obtain relief from landfill tax by making such contributions, the deductibility of which is to be determined in the circumstances of each particular case under the normal test of whether the expenditure is incurred wholly and exclusively for trade purposes. In the case of an unconnected trust engaged in projects of possible use to the operator, the payment would *prima facie* be deductible. If the operator has some degree of control over the trust, or the income of the trust is ultimately received by a person connected with the operator, it might be less clear that the payment was for the purposes of the operator's own trade. Similarly if the trust's objects were insufficiently related to the operator's trade, it might be considered that contributions were for a general philanthropic, and hence non-trade, purpose.

(HMRC Business Income Manual, BIM67525 and BIM67530).

Websites

[69.73] The cost of setting up a website is likely to be capital expenditure; the regular update costs are likely to be revenue expenses (see HMRC Business Income Manual BIM35815).

Wholly and exclusively rule

[69.74] For an expense to be deductible, it must, *inter alia*, have been incurred 'wholly and exclusively for the purposes of the trade'. If an expense is incurred for a *dual purpose*, this rule does not prohibit a deduction for any *identifiable* part or *identifiable* proportion of the expense which is incurred wholly and exclusively for the purposes of the trade. [*CTA 2009, s 54*].

For a review of the leading cases on the 'wholly and exclusively' rule, see *Harrods (Buenos Aires) Ltd v Taylor-Gooby* (1964) 41 TC 450, CA, and for a frequently quoted analysis of the words see *Bentleys, Stokes & Lowless v Beeson* (1952) 33 TC 491, CA. Following that case the dual purpose rule (now in *ITTOIA 2005, s 34*) has figured prominently in Court decisions. 'Dual expenditure is expenditure that is incurred for more than one reason. If one of the reasons is not for business purposes, the expenditure fails the statutory test and there is no provision that allows a "business" proportion' (HMRC Business Income Manual BIM37007). *However*, in practice, where an identifiable part or proportion of an expense has been laid out wholly and exclusively for the purposes of the trade, HMRC do not disallow that part or proportion on the grounds that the expense is not *as a whole* laid out wholly and exclusively for the purposes of the trade (BIM37007); and see now *CTA 2009, s 54* above. See Tolley's Income Tax under Trading Income.

The dual purpose nature of expenditure was considered in the case of *Interfish Ltd v Revenue and Customs Comrs* CA, [2014] EWCA Civ 876; 2014 STI 2286, see also **69.3** above. In that case a company in the fishing industry made substantial sponsorship payments to a rugby club, which had been used to assist the club financially and then to purchase players. The claims for deduction of these payments were rejected by HMRC on the grounds the payments were not made wholly and exclusively for the purpose of the business as they were partly made because the director was very keen on rugby and wanted to strengthen the club. The First-tier Tribunal dismissed the company's appeal and found the payments had been made with a dual purpose. The Upper Tribunal upheld this decision.

A purely incidental consequence of a business expense does not, however, preclude its being wholly and exclusively for business purposes (HMRC Business Income Manual BIM37007, 37400). See, for example, *Robinson v Scott Bader Ltd*, **69.26** above.

It should be borne in mind that the trade for whose purposes the expenditure is incurred must be that in which the expense arose. For a successful appeal against a decision in favour of HMRC on this point, see *Vodafone Cellular Ltd v Shaw* (1997) 69 TC 376, CA. In *Icebreaker 1 LLP v Revenue and Customs Commissioners* [2010] UKUT 477 (TCC), [2011] STC 1078 it was held that a payment of £1.064 million (as part of a larger global payment of £1.273 million) by the appellant to a film distribution company was not expended wholly and exclusively for the purposes of the appellant's trade. It was not a matter of looking at what the recipient company did with the money, but of looking at what the appellant paid the money for. The wording in *ICTA 1988, s 74(1)(a)* (now *CTA 2009, s 54*) focuses on the taxpayer's trade and not on the use of the money by the recipient. The payment was made so that the appellant could be assured that it would recover the loans its members had borrowed from the bank and was therefore expended and disbursed for the sole purpose of investment and security. The appellant never expected or intended that it would be used for any film production or distribution trading purpose.

Two recent cases examine the question of the incidental non-business benefit. In *McQueen v Revenue and Customs Comrs* [2007] STC (SCD) 457 the taxpayer was the proprietor of a coach business and was also an amateur rally driver. He decided to use motor rallying as a way of advertising his business. He purchased a new rally car for this purpose and competed in several events. He claimed capital allowances on the car and claimed related expenditure as advertising expenses. HMRC issued discovery assessments on the basis that the expenditure had not been wholly and exclusively incurred for the purposes of the business. The Special Commissioner decided that the taxpayer's expenditure on motor rallying was incurred for the purposes of promoting his coach business and getting the names and liveries into the public awareness. Although the taxpayer gained some personal satisfaction from competing in rallies, his preferred leisure activity was sailing rather than rallying, and the private satisfaction of success on the rally circuit was an incidental benefit of the expenditure, rather than its purpose.

This can be contrasted with the case *Protec International Ltd v HMRC* [2010] UKFTT 628 in which the company carried on business in the construction industry and claimed deductions for significant payments to another company (M) which took part in motor rallies. The appellant's controlling director was an experienced rally driver who had driven for M. The Tribunal distinguished the McQueen case on the basis that there was no evidence from the appellant of any preferred leisure activity other than rallying and no evidence before it upon which to conclude that the director's private satisfaction was an incidental benefit of the expenditure. The Tribunal found the demonstrable lack of formal commerciality in the transaction inferred non-trade purpose and therefore there was a duality of purpose in the expenditure. See also *Tim Healy v HMRC* [2015] UKFTT 233 where the Tribunal dismissed the taxpayer's claim to deduct expenditure incurred renting a flat near the theatre where he was performing. It was held there was a dual purpose: to enable him to perform but also to receive visitors while he was in London, and therefore the expenditure was not wholly and exclusively for the purposes of the trade.

In *HMRC v P Vaines* [2016] UKUT 2 Mr Vaines, a partner in a law firm, had made a payment to a bank in order to avoid personal bankruptcy as this would have resulted in his loss of partnership interest. The Upper Tribunal accepted that a payment to preserve the trade from destruction can properly be treated as wholly and exclusively for the purpose of the trade. However the fact that a payment is made to preserve the trade from destruction does not necessarily mean it has been incurred wholly and exclusively for that trade. In this instance, Mr Vaines payment inevitably resolved what was a personal matter and this was not just an incidental effect of his decision to protect his professional career. The payment was therefore not incurred wholly and exclusively for the purposes of his trade. The Upper Tribunal, in disagreement with the First-tier Tribunal, held that the 'trade' in this context is the partnership trade conducted collectively by the partners.

For HMRC's own guidance on the 'wholly and exclusively' rule, see HMRC Business Income Manual BIM37000–38600.

Simon's Taxes. See **B2.315–B2.324.**

Key points on trading income — deductions

[69.75] The table below contains a brief summary of the tax treatment of common expenses and deductions. Please refer to the sections above for full explanations of the relevant points.

Expenditure/ item	Tax treatment in calculating trading profits	Reference
Accountancy fees	Normal recurring legal and accountancy fees in preparing accounts and or agreeing tax liabilities are allowed. Accountancy costs relating to an enquiry are not allowable if enquiry reveals discrepancies resulting from negligent (careless) or fraudulent (deliberate) conduct.	69.51
Acquisition of company; costs	Normally capital and hence disallowed.	69.51
Advertising	Generally allowed provided not capital.	69.3
Asset in satisfaction of trading debt	Where MV less than outstanding debt, deficit may be allowed as deduction provided trader agrees that on disposal of asset any excess proceeds treated as trading receipt.	69.5

Expenditure/ item	Tax treatment in calculating trading profits	Reference
Bad debts / impairment losses	Relief normally available for impairment losses and statutory insolvency arrangements.	69.5 *CTA 2009, s 55*
Capital expenditure	Normally disallowed in calculating trading profits.	69.8 *CTA 2009, s 53*
Car hire	Part of hire cost frequently disallowed. Disallowance = 15% of hire cost although rules on type of car and length of hire.	69.9 *CTA 2009, s 56*
Compensation and damages payments	Whether allowable depends upon the specific circumstances and whether capital or outside trading activities.	**69.11**
Computer hardware	Normally capital (see **10** CAPITAL ALLOWANCES ON PLANT AND MACHINERY). Where package consists of both hardware and licence HMRC accept apportionment.	**69.12**
Computer software	Expenditure normally accepted as revenue (hence allowable) where useful economic life less than two years.	**69.12**
Contributions to local enterprise organisations	Contributions in cash or kind normally allowed as a deduction in computing profits.	**69.64** *CTA 2009, s 82*
Crime related expenses	Not allowed for tax purposes.	**69.49** *CTA 2009, s 1304*
Embezzlement	Losses generally allowed as deductions but not misappropriations by directors.	**69.14**
Employee benefits	Generally allowable but see specific types of benefits discussed above. For employee benefit trusts see **69.28**.	**69.15** and **43** INTEREST ON OVERPAID TAX
Employee remuneration	Remuneration meeting the wholly and exclusively test is normally allowable. Payments to connected parties can be disallowed where not commercial. Also see above regarding timing of deductions where paid later than nine months after end of period of account.	**69.26**
Employee share schemes	Corporation tax relief is specifically available for certain qualifying types of employee share schemes.	**69.31–69.39** *CTA 2009, Pt 11 and 12, s 983* onwards
Entertainment	Generally disallowed.	**69.40** *CTA 2009, s 1298*
Entertainment exceptions	Entertainment may be allowable where provision is part of company's trade and or where it relates to employees.	**69.40** *CTA 2009, s 1299*

Expenditure/ item	Tax treatment in calculating trading profits	Reference
Expenses not wholly & exclusively for trade purposes	Normally disallowed in calculating trading profits. However where for dual purposes it may be possible to apportion.	69.74 *CTA 2009, s 54*
Fee protection insurance	Allowable only to extent costs insured against would themselves have been allowable. Premiums disallowed in full if cover negligent (careless) or fraudulent (deliberate) conduct.	69.51 BIM46452
Finance leases	Finance lease rentals are normally revenue payments for the use of the asset and hence allowable. The accounting and tax treatment of finance leases can be different see above.	69.42–69.44 HMRC Business Leasing Manual
Fines	Not normally deductible as not wholly and exclusively for purpose of trade.	69.11
Fines (parking)	Tax treatment depends; if fine is the liability of the employee, the company can claim tax relief although the employee will be chargeable on the emolument; If company car and paid as registered owner the employee is not taxable on an emolument and company cannot claim tax relief in calculating its profits.	69.11
Formation of company; costs	Normally capital and hence disallowed although costs relating to loan capital may qualify for relief.	69.51
Gifts	Generally disallowed but four exceptions; where part of trade, advertisement (limits), to employees and to certain bodies (charities).	69.40 *CTA 2009, s 1300*
Gift aid donations	Not allowed in calculating trading profits but see 14.11 for relief calculating total taxable profits.	14.11 CHARITIES
Guarantees	After regard to the loan relationship rules, it is necessary to consider whether incurred 'wholly and exclusively' and or capital expenditure.	69.47
Hire purchase	The payments made need to be split between revenue (allowable) and capital (see 10 CAPITAL ALLOWANCES ON PLANT AND MACHINERY).	69.48
Illegal payments	Not allowed for tax purposes.	69.49 *CTA 2009, s 1304*

Expenditure/ item	Tax treatment in calculating trading profits	Reference
In house professional fees	In house professional fees not allowed where capital in character eg purchase and sale of capital assets.	**69.51**
Insurance	Premiums for business purposes are normally allowable.	Policies with a dual purpose (benefit shareholders personally) disallowed. **69.50, 69.20** *Beauty Consultants Ltd v Inspector of Taxes* [2002] STC (SCD) 352
Interest on director's property loan	Allowable provided relevant conditions (see above) met.	**69.19**
Key employee insurance	Polices insuring against death or critical illness of key employees generally allowable. See insurance above for case involving dual purpose.	**69.20**
Lease premiums	Not normally deductible as capital. However part of certain lease premiums are taxed on the landlord as income. That part can be deducted over the period of the lease in calculating trading profits.	**69.59** *CTA 2009, ss 217–220*
Legal and professional expenses	Not allowable if capital or excluded by statute.	**69.51**
National Insurance Contributions	Employers' Class 1, 1A and 1B NIC contributions are allowable.	**69.21** *CTA 2009, s 1302*
Onerous contract	Expenditure on the cancellation of a trade agreement normally allowable unless circumstances capital.	**69.11**
Onerous lease	Lump sum to vary terms held to be capital.	**69.59, 69.11** *Tucker v Granada Motorway Services Ltd* BIM46810
Overseas taxation	Relief may be obtained through double tax relief see 24 but any not relieved may generally be deducted.	**69.66**

Expenditure/ item	Tax treatment in calculating trading profits	Reference
Patents	No deduction allowed for royalties paid for use of patents. Expenses incurred in obtaining grant of patent may be allowable.	**69.54**, **42.42** INTANGIBLE ASSETS *CTA 2009, s 59*
Penalties interest surcharges	Generally not allowable. Interest on corporation tax paid late/early is dealt with under **43.2** LOAN RELATIONSHIPS where it is included as an allowable debit/credit.	**69.55**
Pre-trading expenditure	Expenditure incurred in the prior seven years which would have been deductible in computing profits if the trade had commenced is allowed.	**69.57** *CTA 2009, s 61*
Provisions	May be allowable if (1) it relates to allowable revenue not capital expenditure, (2) It is in accordance with UK GAAP and FRS 12, (3) it does not conflict with any statutory rule, and (4) it is estimated with sufficient accuracy.	**69.58**
Rent business premises	Costs for rent, rates insurance and repairs normally allowable. For partial private use see above.	**69.59**
Rent premises no longer required	Continuing rents have been allowed as a deduction but not payments to secure the cancellation of the lease.	**69.59** *CIR v Falkirk Iron CS* (1933) 17 TC 625 *Cowcher v Richard Milss and Co KB* (1927) 13 TC 216
Repairs	Provided revenue and not capital nature normally allowable. The distinction between revenue and capital (repairs vs improvements / replacement of entirety) can cause problems in practice see above.	**69.60**
Research and development	Specific tax reliefs exist see **62** RESEARCH AND DEVELOPMENT EXPENDITURE.	**62** RESEARCH AND DEVELOPMENT EXPENDITURE, **69.61**
Reverse premiums (rent)	Depends upon particular circumstances. For a developer trading in property normally allowable in other circumstances the payment may be capital.	**69.59**
Stock / inventory / WIP	The cost of stock is allowed in accordance with GAAP. For the definitions, recognition and valuation of these items see above.	**69.63**
Subscriptions	To associations are normally allowable, see above regarding checking status of the association.	**69.64**

Expenditure/ item	Tax treatment in calculating trading profits	Reference
Tax appeals	Costs not allowable however see BIM46455 for VAT and business rate appeals.	69.51
Taxation	Income tax and corporation tax are not deductible in computing profits.	69.66
Trade marks	Deduction allowed for expenses incurred in registration, extension and or renewal of trade mark for the purpose of the company's trade.	**69.68 41** INTANGIBLE ASSETS, *CTA 2009, s 90*
Unremittable (from overseas) amounts	Relief via a deduction from profits is available in certain circumstances.	69.70
Valuation fees	Those incurred to comply with *Companies Act 2006* are allowable.	69.71
Website	Depends on exact circumstances but the initial cost of creation is likely to be capital whilst subsequent updates revenue.	69.73
Wholly and exclusively	To be deductible an expense needs to be incurred wholly and exclusively for the purpose of the trade. Where dual purpose may be possible to apportion.	69.74

70

Transactions in Securities

Transactions in securities

[70.1] There are provisions for counteracting corporation tax advantages obtained or obtainable by companies in specified circumstances in respect of a transaction or transactions in securities. These rules were originally introduced in *FA 1960, s 28* to counter tax avoidance arrangements where, in essence, the Inland Revenue perceived that corporate profits were being extracted in capital form, simply because capital profits were not chargeable to tax and dividends were (capital gains tax was not introduced until *FA 1965*, preceded by the taxation of short-term gains legislation in *FA 1962*). While the arrangements that were targeted were often described as dividend stripping or bond washing, the rules were deliberately very wide-ranging in their scope and were not restricted to those specific arrangements. The current rules for corporation tax are at *CTA 2010, Pt 15, Sch 2 para 84*. Originally the rules applied in 5 Circumstances, although Circumstances A and B have now been repealed.

There is a generally held view that the rules are of limited application to corporation tax payers and HMRC has publicly mooted the idea that they may be repealed, although there is no sign of this actually happening.

Subject to the exception below, the provisions apply where, in consequence of 'transaction(s) in securities', combined with any of the circumstances listed at (A)–(C) below, a company (or any body corporate) is able to obtain a 'corporation tax advantage'. 'Securities' includes shares and stock, and, in the case of a company not limited by shares, includes an interest of a member of the company in whatever form. (The provisions apply equally where the advantage is obtainable due to the combined effect of the transaction(s) and the liquidation of the company.) HMRC may make adjustments to counteract the tax advantage (see further below).

The provisions do *not* apply if the company shows that the transaction or transactions are made:

(i) for genuine commercial reasons or in the ordinary course of investment management, and

(ii) that enabling corporation tax advantages to be obtained is not a main object of the transaction or, as the case may be, any of the transactions.

[*CTA 2010, ss 733, 734, 751(1)*].

Simon's Taxes. See **D9.102A, D9.104, D9.116.**

For 'transactions in securities' see *CIR v Joiner* (1975) 50 TC 449, HL (in which a variation of rights prior to a liquidation was held to be such a transaction), and *CIR v Laird Group plc* [2003] STC 1349, HL (in which the payment of a dividend representing previously undistributed profits was held not to be).

For 'genuine commercial reasons' see *Laird Group* in the Ch D ([2001] STC 689) and *CIR v Brebner* (1967) 43 TC 705, HL; *Clark v CIR* [1979] 1 All ER 385, [1979] 1 WLR 416, HL, and *Marwood Homes Ltd v CIR* [1999] STC (SCD) 44. In *Lewis (trustee of Redrow Staff Pension Scheme) v CIR* [1999] STC (SCD) 349, a distribution by way of purchase of its own shares by a company from the trustees of its pension scheme, pursuant to legislation requiring the trustees to reduce their holding, was held to be a transaction carried out by the trustees both for genuine commercial reasons and in the ordinary course of investment management.

Specified circumstances

[70.2] The circumstances mentioned above, only one of which needs to be met, are as follows.

(A) In consequence of a transaction whereby (see *CIR v Garvin* [1981] 1 WLR 793, 55 TC 24, HL, and *Bird v CIR* [1989] AC 300, 61 TC 238, HL, and contrast *Emery v CIR* [1981] STC 150, 54 TC 607) another person has received or subsequently receives 'an abnormal amount by way of dividend', the company receives consideration which:
- is not otherwise taxable as income; and
- represents the value of:
  (i) a company's trading stock or future receipts; or
  (ii) assets which are, or would otherwise have been, available for distribution (see *CIR v Brown* [1971] 3 All ER 502, 47 TC 217, CA) by a company as dividend, and which, in the case of a company incorporated abroad, do not represent a return of capital to subscribers.

(B) In connection with the distribution, transfer or realisation of assets of a 'relevant company', or the application of such assets in discharge of liabilities, the company potentially within these provisions receives consideration which represents the value of:
  (i) the relevant company's trading stock or future receipts, or
  (ii) assets which are, or would otherwise have been, available for distribution (see *CIR v Brown* (1971) 47 TC 217, CA) by the relevant company as dividend, and which, in the case of a company incorporated abroad, do not represent a return of capital to subscribers,

  and receives the consideration in such a way that it is not otherwise taxable as income.

(C) In connection with (i) the transfer of assets of a 'relevant company' to another such company, or (ii) a transaction in securities in which two or more relevant companies are concerned, the company potentially within these provisions receives consideration which:
- consists of any share capital or any security issued by a relevant company;
- is not otherwise taxable as income; and
- represents the value of:
  - (i) a relevant company's trading stock, or
  - (ii) assets which are, or would otherwise have been, available for distribution (see *CIR v Brown* (1971) 47 TC 217, CA) by a relevant company as dividend.

In so far as the consideration consists of non-redeemable share capital, it triggers these provisions only so far as the share capital is repaid (in a winding-up or otherwise, including any distribution made in respect of any shares in a winding-up or dissolution).

In any of (A)–(C) above, references to consideration include money's worth.

[*CTA 2010, ss 735–738, 751(1)*].

Simon's Taxes. See **D9.110–115**.

(A), (B) and (C) above are in practice unlikely to apply unless the company in question has (or has recently had) distributable reserves (HMRC Company Taxation Manual CTM36835–36845). For cases within (A) and (B) above, see *CIR v Cleary* [1968] AC 766, 44 TC 399, HL; *Anysz v CIR* [1977] STC 296, 53 TC 601; *Williams v CIR* [1980] 3 All ER 321, 54 TC 257, HL; *CIR v Wiggins* [1979] 2 All ER 245, 53 TC 639.

Abnormal amount of dividend

[70.3] For the purposes of 70.2(A) above, an '*abnormal amount by way of dividend*' is received if an officer of HMRC, the Commissioners of HMRC or the Tribunal (whichever is determining the question) is satisfied that the condition in (a) below is met and also, in relation to fixed rate dividends only, that the condition in (b) below is met.

(a) This condition is that the dividend substantially exceeds a normal return on the consideration provided by the recipient for the securities (or, if those securities are derived from securities previously acquired by the recipient, those securities). In determining 'normal return', regard must be had to the length of time the securities were held and to dividends paid and other distributions made in respect of them during that time. If the recipient acquired the securities for nil consideration or for greater than market value, the recipient is treated for the purposes of this test as having acquired them at market value.

(b) This condition is that the fixed rate dividend substantially exceeds the amount which the recipient would have received if the dividend had accrued from day to day and the recipient had been entitled to only so much of it as accrued while the recipient held the securities. But this condition is not met if during the six months beginning with the purchase of the securities the recipient does not dispose of them (or dispose of similar securities) or acquire an option to sell them (or to sell similar securities).

'*Dividend*' includes interest and any other distribution other than one within **29.2**(c) DISTRIBUTIONS.

[*CTA 2010, ss 740–742, 751*].

In the case of a purchase by a company of its own shares treated as a distribution under **29.2**(b) DISTRIBUTIONS, it was held that the return was not abnormal (*CIR v Sema Group Pension Scheme Trustees* [2002] EWCA Civ 1857, [2003] STC 95, 74 TC 593).

Simon's Taxes. See D9.113.

Relevant company

[70.4] For the purposes of **70.2**(B) and (C) above, a '*relevant company*' is:

- a company under the control of five or fewer persons; or
- any other company none of whose shares or stocks (disregarding any debenture stock, preferred shares or preferred stock) is included in the Official UK list and dealt in on a recognised stock exchange in the UK.

But a company is not a relevant company if it is under the control of one or more companies which are not themselves relevant companies. 'Control' is defined as in *CTA 2010, s 450* (see **16.6** CLOSE COMPANIES). In determining 'under the control', the relevant date is the date of the dividend (*CIR v Garvin* [1981] 1 WLR 793, 55 TC 24, HL).

During consultation on the transactions in securities legislation, HMRC raised the issue that this provision potentially constitutes unlawful discrimination under the EC Treaty. As a result, when the income tax rules were changed, the new regime was applied to close companies and companies that would be close, were they UK resident. However, no such change has been made or proposed to the corporation tax rules, which therefore remain potentially discriminatory.

[*CTA 2010, s 739*].

Tax advantage

[70.5] For these purposes, a '*corporation tax advantage*' means any of the following:

- a relief (or increased relief) from corporation tax;
- a repayment (or increased repayment) of corporation tax;
- the avoidance or reduction of a charge to corporation tax or an assessment to corporation tax; or
- the avoidance of a possible assessment to corporation tax.

As regards the last two items, it does not matter whether the avoidance or reduction is effected by receipts accruing in such a way that the recipient does not pay corporation tax on them or by a deduction in calculating profits or gains. For distributions made between 8 October 1996 and 31 March 2008 inclusive, it was made clear that, for this purpose, a relief included a dividend tax credit.

[*CTA 2010, s 732*].

Simon's Taxes. See **D9.103**.

For 'tax advantage' see *CIR v Cleary* [1968] AC 766, 44 TC 399, HL (tax advantage obtained where taxpayers' company purchased shares from them), and contrast *CIR v Kleinwort, Benson Ltd* [1969] 2 Ch 221, 45 TC 369 (no tax advantage where merchant bank purchased debentures with interest in arrear shortly before redemption). The decision in *Sheppard and another (Trustees of the Woodland Trust) v CIR (No 2)* [1993] STC 240, 65 TC 724 that no tax advantage could arise where relief was obtained by virtue of charitable exemption was doubted in *CIR v Universities Superannuation Scheme Ltd* [1997] STC 1, 70 TC 193, in which the opposite conclusion was reached.

Prior to the hearing of the latter case, HMRC had, in any event, indicated that they would continue to proceed under the above legislation on the footing that tax-exempt bodies obtain a tax advantage whenever they receive abnormal dividends, since they considered that there would have been good grounds for challenging the earlier decision had it not been for a defect in the assessment under appeal. This continues to be the HMRC approach. (HMRC Tax Bulletin August 1993 p 90, April 1998 p 537, October 1998 pp 590–592). For the quantum of the tax advantage, see *Bird v CIR* [1989] AC 300, 61 TC 238, HL. On the question of whether a tax advantage was a 'main object' of a transaction, see *Marwood Homes Ltd v CIR* [1999] STC (SCD) 44. See also *Laird Group plc v CIR* [2001] STC 689, 75 TC 399; *Snell v Revenue and Customs Comrs* [2008] STC (SCD) 1094.

Transactions in securities — procedure

[70.6] The procedure for raising a counteraction notice is as follows:

(i) An officer of HMRC must notify the company that he has reason to believe that the above provisions may apply to it in respect of transaction(s) specified in the notification. [*CTA 2010, s 743*]. **Simon's Taxes,** see **D9.132**. See *Balen v CIR* (1978) 52 TC 406, CA.

(ii) The company notified may make a statutory declaration that in its opinion the above provisions do not apply, stating supporting facts and circumstances, and send it to the HMRC officer within 30 days. [*CTA 2010, s 744*]. **Simon's Taxes.** See **D9.133**.
For acceptance of late statutory declarations, see HMRC Tax Bulletin April 1999 p 656.

(iii) The HMRC officer must then either take no further action or send the declaration together with a certificate that he sees reason to take further action (and any counter-statement he wishes to submit) to the Tribunal. The Tribunal will consider the declaration and certificate and counter-statement (if any) and decide whether there is a *prima facie* case for proceeding further. Such a determination does not affect the application of these provisions in respect of transactions including not only the ones to which the determination relates but also others. [*CTA 2010, s 745*]. **Simon's Taxes.** See **D9.133.**

HMRC have no right of appeal if the determination goes against them and must take no further action. The taxpayer is not entitled to see HMRC's counter-statement nor to be heard by the Tribunal (*Wiseman v Borneman* [1971] AC 297, 45 TC 540, HL). See also *Howard v Borneman* [1976] AC 301, 50 TC 322, HL, and *Balen v CIR* [1978] 2 All ER 1033, 52 TC 406, CA.

(iv) If the Tribunal decides there is a case, or if no statutory declaration is made under (ii) above by the company, HMRC will make adjustments to counteract the corporation tax advantage. The adjustments required to be made, and the basis on which they are to be made, must be specified in a notice (a '*counteraction notice*') served on the company by an HMRC officer. The adjustments may take the form of an assessment, the cancellation of a tax repayment and/or a recalculation of profits or gains or liability to corporation tax. No assessment may be made later than six years after the accounting period to which the tax advantage relates. [*CTA 2010, s 746*]. If (E) above is in point, and is triggered by the repayment of share capital, the assessment must be for the accounting period in which that repayment occurs. [*CTA 2010, s 747*]. **Simon's Taxes.** See **D9.134.**

(v) A company on which a counteraction notice has been served may appeal, by giving notice to the Commissioners for HMRC within 30 days of the service of the notice, on the grounds that the provisions do not apply to the company in respect of the transaction(s) in question or that the stated adjustments are inappropriate. The Tribunal may then affirm, vary or cancel the counteraction notice or affirm, vary or quash an assessment made in accordance with the notice. [*CTA 2010, s 750*]. **Simon's Taxes.** See **D9.135.**

(vi) HMRC can use its wide powers at *FA 2008, Sch 36* to access information held by the company — **37** HMRC INVESTIGATORY POWERS.

(vii) The application of these provisions is outside self-assessment, so that returns should be made without having regard to a possible charge (although taxpayers may wish to draw the inspector's attention to any correspondence with the Clearance and Counteraction Team (see below) in connection with any particular transaction). Enquiries into the possible application of these provisions will accordingly be carried out independently of any enquiry into the self-assessment return (HMRC Tax Bulletin April 2000 pp 742, 743).

Transactions in securities — clearance

[70.7] Taxpayers may take the initiative by submitting to HMRC particulars of any transaction effected or contemplated; HMRC may, within 30 days of receipt, call for further information (to be supplied within 30 days). Subject to this, they must notify their decision within 30 days of receipt of the particulars or further information, and if they are satisfied that no liability arises the matter is concluded as regards that transaction by itself, provided that all facts and material particulars have been fully and accurately disclosed. [*CTA 2010, ss 748, 749*].

HMRC is not obliged to give reasons for refusal of clearance but where the applicant has given full reasons for his transactions the main grounds for refusing clearance will be indicated. A refusal to give clearance indicates that counteraction would be taken if the transaction were completed. (HMRC Statement of Practice, SP 3/80).

Applications for clearance should be directed to BAI Clearance, HMRC, BX9 1JL (if market-sensitive information is included, to Team Leader at that address). Applications may also be emailed to reconstructions@hmrc.gsi.gov.uk (after advising Team Leader if market-sensitive information is included). A hard copy need not then be sent. Application may be made in a single letter to the same address for clearance under *CTA 2010, ss 748, 749* (transactions in securities, or under any one or more of *TCGA 1992, s 139* (reconstructions — see **61** REORGANISATIONS AND RECONSTRUCTIONS); *CTA 2010, ss 1091, 1092* (demergers, see **29.20** DISTRIBUTIONS), *CTA 2010, ss 1044, 1045* (see **61.9** PURCHASE BY A COMPANY OF ITS OWN SHARES), *TCGA 1992, s 138(1)* (share exchanges, see Tolley's Capital Gains Tax under Anti-Avoidance), *TCGA 1992, s 140B* (transfer of a UK trade between EU member states), *TCGA 1992, s 140D* (transfer of non-UK trade between EU member states, see **11.25** CAPITAL GAINS) and *CTA 2009, ss 831, 832* (see **42.30** INTANGIBLE ASSETS).

HMRC 'Working Together' Bulletin August 2001 pp 8, 9 contain a checklist of the items of information whose omission from clearance applications most commonly causes delay in the processing of applications.

Simon's Taxes. See **D9.120–122**.

71

Transactions in UK Land

Introduction to transactions in UK land

[71.1] There are provisions which seek to ensure that the tax is charged on the full amount of profits from dealing in or developing land in the UK, regardless of whether the company is resident or non-resident in the UK.

The provisions in **71.2** below override the general territorial rule for trading income whereby the charge on profits arising to a non-UK resident company normally depends on the extent to which the trade is carried on in the UK through a permanent establishment (see **1.1** INTRODUCTION).

The provisions in **71.3–71.8** below apply a specific corporation tax charge on profits from dealing in or developing UK land. The charge applies in specified circumstances to profits arising when land is disposed of, and also to disposals of assets deriving their value from land in the UK. There is provision to ensure that the charge applies only to profits not otherwise chargeable to UK tax as income.

For the purposes of these provisions, where any property is disposed of under a contract, the time at which the disposal is made is the time the contract is made and not, if different, the time at which the property is conveyed or transferred. [*FA 2016, s 81(9)*]. This effectively meant that the provisions did not have effect in relation to disposals made on or after 5 July 2016 (when these provisions were introduced) under a pre-5 July 2016 contract. However, *F(No 2)A 2017* provides that all profits recognised in accounts drawn up (in accordance with generally accepted accounting practice) for a period of account beginning on or after 8 March 2017 are to be brought into charge regardless of when the contract was entered into. This also applies for periods of account straddling 8 March 2017, but only by reference to profits that would be so recognised if the period of account began on that date. [*F(No 2)A 2017, s 39*].

See generally the HMRC Technical Note at www.gov.uk/government/publications/profits-from-trading-in-and-developing-uk-land and the guidance at www.gov.uk/government/publications/profits-from-a-trade-of-dealing-in-or-developing-uk-land-guidance.

Simon's Taxes. See B2.255.

Non-resident dealing in or developing UK land

[71.2] Profits of a 'trade of dealing in or developing UK land' arising to a non-UK resident company are chargeable to corporation tax wherever the trade is carried on.

A non-UK resident company's '*trade of dealing in or developing UK land*' consists of any of the following activities: dealing in UK land; developing UK land for the purpose of disposing of it; and any activities the profits from which are treated under **71.3–71.8** below as profits of the company's trade of dealing in or developing UK land. 'Land' includes buildings and structures, any estate, interest or right in or over land, and land under water; 'UK land' means land in the UK. For the meaning of 'disposal', see **71.8** below, which applies for this purpose also.

Pre-trading expenses

Where a non-UK resident company first comes within the charge to corporation tax at a particular time by virtue of carrying on a trade of dealing in or developing UK land having immediately before that time been within the charge by virtue of carrying on the trade in the UK through a UK permanent establishment (see **1.1** INTRODUCTION, *CTA 2009, s 61* (pre-trading expenses — see **69.57** TRADING INCOME — DEDUCTIONS) applies to expenses meeting the conditions below as if the company started to carry on the trade at that time. The conditions are that:

- no deduction would otherwise be allowed for the expenses but a deduction would be allowed for them (in accordance with *CTA 2009, s 41* (trade starting or ceasing to be within charge to corporation tax — see **68.15** TRADING INCOME) or *CTA 2009, s 61*) if the company had not been within the charge to corporation tax immediately before the time it first came within the charge by virtue of carrying on a trade of dealing in or developing UK land; and
- no relief has been obtained for the expenses under any non-UK law.

Anti-avoidance

Where a company has entered into an arrangement of which a main purpose is to obtain a tax advantage in relation to corporation tax to which the company is chargeable (or would otherwise be chargeable) by virtue of the above rule, the tax advantage is to be counteracted by means of adjustments. Such adjustments may be made (whether by an officer of HMRC or by the company) by way of assessment, the modification of an assessment, the amendment or disallowance of a claim, or otherwise. The expressions 'arrangement' and 'tax advantage' are both widely defined for this purpose. If the tax advantage arises by virtue of any provisions of a double tax treaty between the UK and an overseas territory, adjustments fall to be made only if the tax advantage is contrary to the object and purpose of the provisions of the treaty.

[*CTA 2009, ss 5(2A), 5A, 5B*].

Disposals of UK land

[71.3] Subject to the conditions below, a profit from the disposal of land in the UK is treated for corporation tax purposes as profits of a trade carried on by the chargeable company. This applies where the person who realises the profit is:

(a) the person acquiring, holding or developing the land; or
(b) a person who is 'associated' with the person in (a) at a 'relevant time'; or
(c) a person who is a party to, or concerned in, an arrangement which is effected with respect to all or part of the land and enables a profit to be realised by any indirect method or any series of transactions,

and any of the following conditions are met in relation to the land:

(i) a main purpose of acquiring the land was to realise a profit from its disposal;
(ii) a main purpose of acquiring any property deriving its value from the land was to realise a profit from the disposal of the land;
(iii) the land is held as trading stock; or
(iv) in a case where the land has been developed, a main purpose of developing it was to realise a profit from the disposal of the land when developed.

All references to a profit include references to a gain (including a gain which is capital in nature), and see **71.8** below for the meaning of 'disposal'. The provisions apply to losses as they apply to profits. For the purposes of (b) above, a person (A) is '*associated*' with another person (B) if A and B are related parties (within *CTA 2010, s 356OT* — see **71.8** below) or if A is connected with B (within *CTA 2010, s 1122(5)–(7)*). A '*relevant time*' is any time in the period beginning when the activities of the 'project' begin and ending six months after the disposal in question. The '*project*' means all activities carried out for any of the purposes of dealing in or developing the land and any other purposes mentioned in (i)–(iv) above.

For the purposes of (c) above and these provisions generally, 'arrangement' is widely defined, and any number of transactions can be regarded as constituting a single arrangement if a common purpose can be discerned in them or there is other sufficient evidence of a common purpose.

The charge to tax

The profit is treated as profits of a trade carried on by the 'chargeable company' (see below), but only to the extent that it would not otherwise fall to be brought into account as income of any person in calculating profits of any person for UK income tax or corporation tax purposes. The profits are treated as arising in the accounting period in which the profit on the disposal is realised. If the chargeable company is non-UK resident, the trade in question is the company's trade of dealing in or developing UK land, the profits of which are chargeable to corporation tax wherever the trade is carried on (see **71.2** above).

The chargeable company

In most cases the '*chargeable company*' is the company (C) who realises the profit, but this is subject to the following special rules. If all or any part of the profit accruing to C is derived from value provided (directly or indirectly) by another person which is a company (B), whether or not the value is put at C's disposal, B is the chargeable company. If this is not the case but all or any part of the profit accruing to C is derived from an opportunity of realising a profit provided (directly or indirectly) by another person which is a company (D), D is the chargeable company. See also **71.6** below (fragmented activities), which overrides these special rules.

In interpreting the phrase 'another person' in the special rules above:

- a partnership or members of a partnership may be regarded as a person or persons distinct from the individuals or other persons who are for the time being partners;
- the trustees of settled property may be regarded as persons distinct from the individuals or other persons who are for the time being trustees; and
- personal representatives may be regarded as persons distinct from the individuals or other persons who are for the time being personal representatives.

[*CTA 2010, ss 356OB, 356OC, 356OF, 356OG, 356OO, 356OP*].

Where a company is charged to corporation tax under the above provisions on the basis that a main purpose of developing the land was to realise a profit or gain from disposing of it once developed (i.e. where (ii) above applies), that land is also to be treated for chargeable gains purposes (under *TCGA 1992, s 161*) as having been transferred to stock. [*TCGA 1992, s 161(5)(6)*].

Disposals of property deriving its value from UK land

[71.4] A profit from the disposal of property deriving its value from land in the UK is treated for corporation tax purposes as profits of a trade. The charge applies where:

- a person realises a profit from a disposal of any property which (at the time of disposal) derives at least 50% of its value from land in the UK;
- the person is a party to, or concerned in, an arrangement concerning some or all of that land (the '*project land*'); and
- a main purpose of the arrangement is to deal in or develop the project land and realise a profit from a disposal of property deriving the whole or part of its value from that land.

All references to a profit include references to a gain (including a gain which is capital in nature), and see **71.8** below for the meaning of 'disposal'. The provisions apply to losses as they apply to profits. 'Arrangement' is widely defined, and any number of transactions can be regarded as constituting a single arrangement if a common purpose can be discerned in them or there is other sufficient evidence of a common purpose.

The charge to tax

So much of the profit as is attributable, on a just and reasonable apportionment, to the 'relevant UK assets' is treated as profits of a trade carried on by the 'chargeable company' (defined as in **71.3** above), but only to the extent that it would not otherwise fall to be brought into account as income in calculating profits of any person for UK income tax or corporation tax purposes. The '*relevant UK assets*' means any land in the UK from which the property disposed of derives any of its value at the time of disposal. The profits are treated as arising in the accounting period in which the profit on the disposal is realised. If the chargeable company is non-UK resident, the trade in question is the company's trade of dealing in or developing UK land, the profits of which are chargeable to corporation tax wherever the trade is carried on (see **71.2** above).

[*CTA 2010, 356OG, 356OP*].

Exemption for period before intention to develop formed

[71.5] If, in a case in which **71.3**(iv) above (developed land) applies, part of the profit on disposal is fairly attributable to a period before the intention to develop was formed, that part of the profit is exempt from the charge to tax under these provisions. Similarly, in a case in which **71.4** above applies, if part of the profit on disposal is fairly attributable to a period before the person realising the profit was a party to, or concerned in, the arrangement in question, that part of the profit is exempt from the charge under these provisions. [*CTA 2010, s 356OL*].

Fragmented activities

[71.6] The following is intended to prevent profits being fragmented between associated parties with the aim of placing those profits outside the charge to corporation tax, for example by moving some or all of the profit to a person not carrying on a trade of dealing in or developing land in the UK. It applies where a company (C) disposes of UK land in relation to which any of conditions (i)–(iv) in **71.3** above are met, and a person (R) who is 'associated' with C at a 'relevant time' has made a 'relevant contribution' to the development of the land and/or any other activities aimed at realising a profit from its disposal. In any such case any profit realised by C from the disposal is taken to be what it would be if R were not a distinct person from C and, accordingly, as if everything done by or in relation to R had been done by or in relation to C.

If R makes any payment to C for the purpose of meeting or reimbursing the corporation tax which C is liable to pay as a result of the above rule, the payment is not to be taken into account in calculating profits or losses of either R or C for income tax or corporation tax purposes and is not to be treated for corporation tax purposes as a distribution.

For the above purposes, a '*relevant time*' is any time in the period beginning when the activities of the 'project' began and ending six months after the disposal. The '*project*' means all activities carried out for any of the purposes of dealing in or developing the land and any other purposes mentioned in 71.3(i)–(iv) above. Any 'contribution' made by R is a '*relevant contribution*' unless R's profit in respect of the contribution is insignificant having regard to the size of the project. '*Contribution*' means any kind of contribution, including, for example, a financial contribution, the assumption of a financial risk, and the providing of professional or other services. R is '*associated*' with P if R and P are related parties (within *CTA 2010, s 356OT* — see **71.8** below) or if R is connected with P (within *CTA 2010, s 1122(5)–(7)*).

[*CTA 2010, s 356OH*].

Arrangements for avoiding tax

[71.7] Where an arrangement has been entered into of which a main purpose is to enable a company to obtain a 'relevant tax advantage', the tax advantage is to be counteracted by means of adjustments. Such adjustments may be made (whether by an officer of HMRC or by the taxpayer) by way of assessment, the modification of an assessment, the amendment or disallowance of a claim, or otherwise. See **71.3** above as to the meaning of 'arrangement'. A '*relevant tax advantage*' is an advantage (as widely defined) in relation to corporation tax chargeable (or otherwise chargeable) in respect of amounts treated as profits of a trade by virtue of **71.3** or **71.4** above. If the relevant tax advantage arises by virtue of any provisions of a double tax treaty between the UK and an overseas territory, adjustments fall to be made only if the relevant tax advantage is contrary to the object and purpose of the provisions of the treaty. [*CTA 2010, s 356OK*].

Supplementary rules and definitions

[71.8] The following apply for the purposes of **71.3–71.7** above.

Computing a profit

Subject to any modifications that may be appropriate, the profit (if any) on a disposal of any property must be computed in accordance with the principles applicable to the computation of trading profits. The same principles apply in computing losses as apply in computing profits. [*CTA 2010, s 356OI*].

Realising a profit for another person

It does not matter whether the person realising the profit in **71.3** or **71.4** realises it for himself or for another person. If, for example by a premature sale, a person (A) directly or indirectly transmits the opportunity of realising a profit to another person (B), A realises B's profit for B. [*CTA 2010, s 356OS*].

Meaning of disposal

References to a disposal of any property include any case in which the property is effectively disposed of by one or more transactions or by any arrangement. References to a disposal of land or any other property include a part disposal. Where, on a a disposal of an asset, any form of property derived from the asset remains undisposed of (including where an interest or right in or over the asset is created by the disposal as well as where it subsisted before the disposal), the disposal counts as a part disposal. [*CTA 2010, s 356OQ*].

Meaning of 'land' etc.

'Land' includes buildings and structures, any estate, interest or right in or over land, and land under water. References to property deriving its value from land include any shareholding in a company, partnership interest or interest in settled property deriving its value (directly or indirectly) from land, and also include any option, consent or embargo affecting the disposition of land. [*CTA 2010, s 356OR*].

Related parties

Two persons (A and B) are related parties on any particular day if, within the six months beginning with that day, one of the parties directly or indirectly participates in the management, control or capital of the other, or the same person or persons directly or indirectly participate in the management, control or capital of each of A and B. See *CTA 2010, s 356OT(7)* as to interpretation of the reference to direct and indirect participation. A and B are also related parties if one has a 25% investment in the other, or a third person has a 25% investment in each of A and B. The question of whether there is a 25% investment is determined in accordance with *TIOPA 2010, s 259NC*. A and B are also related parties if their financial results are, or are required to be (or would be required to be but for an exemption), comprised in group accounts (i.e. accounts prepared under *Companies Act 2006, s 399* or a non-UK equivalent provision).

[*CTA 2010, s 356OT*].

Value tracing and indirect methods

Where it is necessary to determine the extent to which the value of any property or right is derived from any other property or right, value may be traced through any number of companies, partnerships, trusts and other entities or arrangements, at each stage attributing property held by the company etc. to its shareholders etc. in such manner as is appropriate in the circumstances. In determining whether the charge to tax in **71.3** or **71.4** applies, account may be taken of any method, however indirect, to transfer any property or right, or enhance or diminish its value, e.g. by sales at less, or more, than full consideration, assigning share capital or rights in a company or partnership or an interest in settled property, disposal on the winding-up of any company, partnership or trust etc. Any such transfer or enhancement may give rise to the charge to tax. [*CTA 2010, ss 356OM, 356ON*].

Apportionments

Any apportionment (whether of expenditure, consideration or any other amount) that is required for the purposes of these provisions is to be made on a just and reasonable basis. [*CTA 2010, s 356OJ*].

72

Transfer Pricing

Cross-references. See **29.5** DISTRIBUTIONS; **36.11** HMRC ADMINISTRATION; **59.8–59.25** PENALTIES.

Other sources. See the HMRC International Manual at INTM410000 *et seq*.

Simon's Taxes. See B4.1.

Introduction to transfer pricing

[72.1] Transfer pricing rules seek to stop persons from gaining an advantage in relation to tax by entering into transactions with connected parties using non-arm's length prices. They generally operate to reverse the benefits obtained from such transactions.

The scope of the transfer pricing requirements under UK legislation extend to both UK and cross-border transactions, and the legislation applies to 'persons', so includes individuals and partnerships as well as companies. Dormant companies (see 72.5 below) and small and medium-sized enterprises (see 72.6 below) are, in most circumstances, exempt from applying the transfer pricing and thin capitalisation rules. Where an adjustment is required by the provisions to increase the profits of one party, the corresponding adjustment provisions (see 72.7 below) are extended so that the connected UK party can make a compensating reduction in their taxable profits, and provisions allow for a 'balancing payment' to be made tax-free up to the amount of the compensating adjustment (see 72.8 below).

See generally HMRC International Manual at INTM410000 onwards on a number of transfer pricing issues and at INTM510000 onwards on thin capitalisation.

The transfer pricing provisions must be read in a way consistent with the 'transfer pricing guidelines' and Organisation for Economic Cooperation and Development (OECD) model taxation treaty, whether there is a treaty in force between the UK and any particular country or not.

The '*transfer pricing guidelines*' are the Transfer Pricing Guidelines for Multinational Enterprises and Tax Administrations approved by the OECD in July 2017. The Treasury may by order specify material subsequently published by the OECD to update or supplement the Guidelines. The guidelines are discussed in HMRC's manual with regard to methodologies at INTM421000 onwards. The guidelines are supplemented by 'Transfer Pricing Guidance on Financial Transactions: Inclusive Framework on BEPS: Actions 4, 8–10' published on 11 February 2020. See www.oecd.org/tax/beps/transfer-pricing-guidance-on-financial-transactions-inclusive-framework-on-beps-actions-4-8-10.pdf.

[*TIOPA 2010, s 164; SI 2018 No 266*].

Simon's Taxes. See **B4.120.**

Basic rule

[72.2] The key concept behind transfer pricing rules is that parties who are connected should transact with each other as if they were independent persons. If they do not, and a tax advantage is obtained, then the tax authority has the power to adjust the tax return and put the parties back into the position they would have been in if they had interacted independently.

The basic rule therefore is:

- where a provision has been made other than at an arm's length price (i.e. the price which would apply to a transaction between independent persons);
- with regard to a transaction(s) between persons who are connected (per the legislation where one party is participating in the management or control of the other (see below)); and
- this gives rise to an advantage in relation to UK tax; then
- HMRC is able to make an adjustment (on the basis of what the outcome would have been had an arm's length price been used).

In more detail: *TIOPA 2010, Pt 4* – the UK transfer pricing legislation – applies where provision (the '*actual provision*') has been made or imposed as between two persons (the '*affected persons*') by means of a transaction or series of transactions, and at the time the provision was made or imposed 'the participation condition' was fulfilled.

The '*participation condition*' is that at the time of making or imposing the actual provision or within six months of the date when the actual condition was made or imposed either:

(a) one of the affected persons was directly or indirectly participating in the management, control or capital of the other; or

(b) there was a person who was, or persons who were, directly or indirectly participating in the management, control or capital of each of the affected persons and

at the time the condition was made or imposed either:

(i) one of the parties participated in the management, control or capital of the other, directly or indirectly; or
(ii) the same person was, or persons were, directly or indirectly taking part in the management, control or capital of each affected person.

Subject to the exceptions below (see **72.5** and **72.6**), if:

- the actual provision differs from the provision which would have been made at arm's length as between independent enterprises; or
- if no provision would have been so made; and
- the provision confers a 'potential advantage' (see **72.4** below) in relation to UK taxation on one of the affected persons or (whether or not the same advantage) on each of them;
  then:
- the profits and losses (and certain items treated as losses) of the potentially advantaged person, or of each of them, are computed for tax purposes as if the arm's length provision had been made or imposed (or, as the case may be, no provision made) instead of the actual provision.

See also HMRC International Manual, INTM412050.

[*TIOPA 2010, ss 147–149*].

Simon's Taxes. See **B4.120**.

Definitions

'Transactions' etc. A 'transaction' for these purposes includes schemes or arrangements of any kind, understandings and mutual practices (whether or not legally enforceable), and a 'series' of transactions includes a number of transactions entered into in pursuance of, or in relation to, the same scheme or arrangement.

A series of transactions is not prevented from being regarded as the means by which provision has been made or imposed between two persons by solely because:

- there is no transaction in the series to which both those persons are parties; or
- one or more transactions to which neither of them is a party; or
- that the parties to any scheme or arrangement in pursuance of which the transactions are entered into do not include one or both of them.

[*TIOPA 2010, s 150*].

'Participation in management' etc. A person is for these purposes treated as directly participating in the management, control or capital of another person at a particular time if and only if (but subject to the provisions below on persons acting together in relation to financing arrangements), at that time, the other person is a body corporate or partnership which that person controls (within *CTA 2010, s 1124*, see **61.7** PURCHASE BY A COMPANY OF ITS OWN SHARES).

Similarly indirect participation requires that the person either would be taken to be participating directly if certain rights and powers including future rights and powers, were attributed to him, or is one of a number of 'major participants' in the other person's enterprise.

[*TIOPA 2010, ss 148, 157, 158, 159; F(No 2)A 2017, Sch 5 paras 15, 16; FA 2019, Sch 3 para 6*].

A person is a '*major participant*' in another person's enterprise when the other person (the 'subordinate') is a body corporate or partnership, and he is one of two persons who control (as above) the subordinate, each of whom has at least 40% of the holdings, etc. giving that control (again after attribution of certain rights and powers as above).

This provision is aimed at joint ventures and targets arrangements where participants in such a joint venture could use non-arm's length prices to divert profit overseas for their mutual benefit. It should be noted that the rules only apply to transactions between at least one of the joint venture parties and the joint venture entity, not between the two joint venture parties themselves (unless they are otherwise under common control).

Persons acting together in relation to financing arrangements

There are special rules for financing arrangements. The meaning of 'indirectly participating' above is extended by *TIOPA 2010, ss 161, 162* to include circumstances where a number of parties act together in relation to the 'financing arrangements' of a business and could collectively control the business.

The rules apply where the person for whom the financing arrangements are made (usually, the borrower) is a body corporate or firm. They do not apply to transactions that are not financing arrangements such as the sale of goods, supply of services.

With reference to the 'participation condition' outlined above:

(A) For the purposes of (a) of the condition (determining whether one of the affected persons was participating in the management, etc. of another), a person ('X') is treated as indirectly participating in the management etc. of another ('Y') if:
- the actual provision relates, to any extent, to financing arrangements for Y (where Y is a body corporate or partnership);
- X and other persons acted together in relation to the arrangements; and
- X would be taken to have control of Y if, at any 'relevant time', there were attributed to X the rights and powers of each of those other persons (taking into account any additional rights or powers that would be attributed to any person if *TIOPA 2010, s 157* (see under '*Participation in management etc.*' above) applied in that person's case).

(B) For the purposes of (b) of the condition (determining whether there was a person (or persons) participating in the management, etc. of each of the affected persons), a person ('Z') is treated as indirectly participating in the management etc. of each of the affected persons if:

- the actual provision relates, to any extent, to financing arrangements of one of the affected persons 'A' (where A is a body corporate or partnership);
- Z and other persons acted together in relation to the arrangements; and
- Z would be taken to have control of both A and the other affected person if, at any 'relevant time', there were attributed to Z the rights and powers of each of those other persons (taking into account any additional rights or powers that would be attributed to any person if *TIOPA 2010, s 157* (see under 'Participation in management etc.' above) applied in that person's case).

It is immaterial whether the persons acting together did so at the time the actual provision is made or imposed or did so at some earlier time.

For these purposes, parties are '*connected*' with each other if one of them is an individual and the other is one of the following: the individual's spouse or civil partner; a relative of the individual or spouse or civil partner; or the spouse or civil partner of a relative. Also, two persons are connected if one is a trustee of a settlement and the other is a settlor of that trust or a person connected with him. For this purpose, '*relative*' means brother, sister, ancestor or lineal descendant.

[*TIOPA 2010, s 163*].

'*Financing arrangements*' are arrangements made for providing or guaranteeing, or otherwise in connection with, any debt, capital or other form of finance. A '*relevant time*' is any time when the persons were so acting together and also any time in the six months after they ceased to do so. Where the conditions in (a) or (b) above are satisfied by virtue only of the above rule, a transfer pricing adjustment can be required only to the extent that the actual provision relates to the financing arrangements in question.

As noted above (with reference to the 'relevant time') to the extent that the actual provision relates to financing arrangements, the participation conditions at (a) and (b) above are to be judged not only at the time the provision is made or imposed but at all times within the following six months. Therefore, to this extent transfer pricing adjustments may be triggered by events occurring up to six months before the necessary relationship exists between the parties.

[*TIOPA 2010, s 148*].

In *DSG Retail Ltd v HMRC* SpC [2009] STC (SCD) 397 a company selling electrical goods encouraged customers to take out a warranty, insured with an Isle of Man fellow subsidiary. The Special Commissioners found that the arrangement potentially gave the UK company a tax advantage and a transfer pricing adjustment was imposed using the profit-split methodology. This case highlights various issues such as: the use of comparables; the importance of the concept of bargaining power; the application of the profit split method; and the identification of a provision through a series of transactions. Further discussion of this case can be found at HMRC manuals: INTM412050, 421040, 485050.

Simon's Taxes. See **B4.121–B4.125**.

Thin capitalisation—provision relating to securities

[72.3] A company is thinly capitalised when its level of debt far exceeds its equity. Generally, where a company is thinly capitalised HMRC may not allow a deduction for all the interest payments made with regard to the debt of the company, on the basis that such company would not have been able to borrow that level of funds from a third party when considering the independent position of such company. This is achieved through the transfer pricing legislation with special rules for provision in relation to securities.

HMRC guidance on thin capitalisation is at HMRC International Manual INTM413000 with practical guidance and examples at INTM510000.

See also **25** CORPORATE INTEREST RESTRICTION for the corporation interest restriction provisions and the previous worldwide debt cap.

The transfer pricing rules apply to a provision which differs from an arm's length provision in relation to a 'security' issued by a company ('*the issuing company*') to another company ('*the lending company*'). The effect of the provisions is that the interest attributable to the excessive part of such a loan is disallowed as if the loan was received from a connected party.

In considering whether the provision is at arm's length, account is to be taken of all factors including whether, in the absence of a 'special relationship' (and whether or not it is the business of the lending company to make loans generally):

(a) the loan would have been provided at all;
(b) the amount would have been advanced; and
(c) the rate of interest or other terms of the loan would have been agreed.

A '*security*' can include a loan or advance of money, whether secured or not. A '*special relationship*' in this case means any relationship where the participation is met by the affected person.

In considering whether the provision is made at arm's length, no account is to be taken of any 'guarantee' (or inference drawn from a 'guarantee') provided by a company with which the issuing company has a 'participatory relationship', when determining:

(i) the appropriate level or extent of the issuing company's overall indebtedness;
(ii) whether the issuing company would have issued the security or whether the lending company would have advanced the loan or the particular amount of the loan; and
(iii) the rate of interest and other terms expected in such a transaction.

Where a guarantee is given for the issue of a security, in looking at the arm's length position of the loan, the following must be taken into account:

(A) Whether the guarantee would have been given at all in the absence of the special relationship;
(B) the amount which would have been guaranteed in the absence of the special relationship; and
(C) the consideration for the guarantee and other terms which would have been agreed in the absence of the special relationship.

In considering whether the provision of the guarantee is at arm's length items (i), (ii) and (iii) above are also taken into account.

A '*special relationship*' is any relationship as a result of which the participation condition at **72.2** above is met in the case of the companies concerned.

A company has a '*participatory relationship*' with another in this case where one of them is directly or indirectly participating in the management, control or capital of the other, or the same person or persons is or are directly or indirectly participating in the management, control or capital of each of them.

A '*guarantee*' in this case includes any surety, relationship, arrangement, connection or understanding (whether formal or informal), such that the lending company has a reasonable expectation that the loan will be repaid by the guarantor (or guarantors) in the event of default by the issuing company.

[*TIOPA 2010, ss 152–154*].

Advance thin capitalisation agreements

A company may apply to HMRC for an advance thin capitalisation agreement (ATCA), which is covered by the same legislative rules as for advance pricing agreements (see **72.15** below). HMRC have also published Statement of Practice SP 1/12 on ATCAs and there is guidance at HMRC International Manual INTM512000 onwards.

An ATCA covers the transfer pricing treatment of a particular borrower, interest imputation and the taxation of treasury and finance companies although there are currently no selection criteria for ATCAs applications and none are planned. Situations that are suitable for ATCAs include, but are not limited to the following:

- intra-group loans, quoted Eurobonds, and
- financing arrangements brought into the transfer pricing provisions by the indirect participation rules (see **72.2** above).

HMRC state that the ATCA process is designed to help resolve financial transfer pricing issues which have a significant commercial impact on an enterprise's results, where the issues would be unlikely to be regarded as 'low risk' by HMRC, or where the arm's length provision is a matter of doubt. The potential scope of an ATCA is flexible. They may cover either the treatment of a single applicant's financial instrument, or the treatment of the overall debt position of a group, depending on circumstances.

Potential advantage

[72.4] The actual provision confers a '*potential advantage*' on a person in relation to UK taxation where its effect, compared to that of the corresponding arm's length provision, would be a reduction in chargeable profits or increase in losses (or conversion of profits into losses) of that person for any chargeable period. In determining the chargeable profits or allowable losses for this purpose in the case of a non-UK resident company, no account is to be taken of any income on which the income tax charge is limited under *ITA 2007, s 813* (see **64.6** RESIDENCE).

The CORPORATE INTEREST RESTRICTION (25) and its predecessor the worldwide debt cap and the provisions of *CTA 2010, s 1000(1)* which deem excessive interest to be a distribution are to be disregarded for the purposes of the calculations under *TIOPA 2010, s 155*. Profits include income and losses includes reliefs for pre-trading expenses, carry forward of certain interest, non-trading deficits on loan relationships, excess of management expenses, group relief and group relief for carried-forward losses.

[*TIOPA 2010, ss 155, 156; F(No 2)A 2017, Sch 4 para 178, Sch 5 para 14*].

Exemption for dormant companies

[72.5] The transfer pricing provisions do not apply, when calculating the profits or losses for any chargeable period, to companies which:

(a) are dormant throughout the accounting period ending on 31 March 2004, or if there is no such accounting period, the three-month period ending on that date; and
(b) have continued to be dormant at all times since the end of that period apart from any transfer pricing adjustments.

For these purposes, '*dormant*' has the same meaning as in *Companies Act 2006, s 1169*.

[*TIOPA 2010, s 165*].

Simon's Taxes. See **B4.127**.

Exemption for small and medium-sized enterprises

[72.6] The transfer pricing provisions do not apply, when calculating the profits or losses for any chargeable period, to a company which is a small or medium-sized enterprise. Such companies are as defined in the Annex to the Commission Recommendation *2003/361/EC* of 6 May 2003 with the modifications set out in *TIOPA 2010, s 172*.

Broadly, a small enterprise is defined as a business with less than 50 employees and either turnover or assets of less than €10 million and a small or medium-sized enterprise as a business with less than 250 employees and either turnover of less than €50 million or assets of less than €43 million. Associated enterprises are taken into account in determining whether a company is a small or medium-sized enterprise.

Exceptions

The exemption will not apply where:

(a) a small or medium-sized enterprise elects for the exemption not to apply, such election being irrevocable;
(b) at the time the actual provision was made or imposed, the other affected person or a 'party to the relevant transaction' is resident and liable to tax in a 'non-qualifying territory' (whether or not also resident in a 'qualifying territory');

(c) as respects any provision made or imposed, HMRC gives notice (a '*transfer pricing notice*') to a medium-sized enterprise, which is the advantaged party, requiring that company to increase profits or reduce losses of that chargeable period on an arm's length basis;

(d) as respects the patent box rules, a provision is made or imposed which is taken into account in calculating the relevant IP profits of a trade of a person who is, or was, a party to the transactions, and HMRC gives notice (a 'transfer pricing notice') to a small-sized enterprise, which is the advantaged party, requiring that company to increase profits or reduce losses of that chargeable period on an arm's length basis.

[*TIOPA 2010, ss 167, 167A, 168*].

As regards (b) above, where the actual provision is or was imposed by means of a series of transactions, a '*party to a relevant transaction*' is or was a party to one or more of those transactions. A company is not considered liable to tax in a non-qualifying territory if the liability relates only to income sourced from that territory or capital situated there. A '*non-qualifying territory*' is a territory which is not a qualifying territory. A '*qualifying territory*' is defined as:

(i) the UK;

(ii) a territory with which the UK has a double tax treaty (under *TIOPA 2010, ss 2–6*) containing a non-discrimination article (see *TIOPA 2010, s 173*) unless that territory has been designated as non-qualifying in regulations made by the Treasury; or

(iii) a territory with which the UK has a double tax treaty (under *TIOPA 2010, ss 2–6*) and which is designated as qualifying in regulations made by the Treasury.

[*TIOPA 2010, s 173*].

Transfer pricing notices issued to medium-sized companies

As regards (c) above, a transfer pricing notice given to a medium-sized company, which may only be given following a notice of enquiry, may specify that an arm's length adjustment is to be made in respect of a certain, or certain types of, provision, or in respect of all provisions, which would fall within the transfer pricing rules but for the above exemption. The recipient of a notice may appeal in writing to the officer of HMRC identified for the purpose in the transfer notice, within 30 days from the date the notice is given (see **5.1** APPEALS) but only on the grounds that the company is a small rather than a medium-sized enterprise.

The company receiving the notice may amend the company tax return to which the notice relates at any time within 90 days of the date the notice was given, or if an appeal is made, the day on which the appeal is finally determined or abandoned. HMRC may issue a closure notice once the 90 days have elapsed, or if earlier, once the tax return has been amended for the purpose of complying with the notice. This rule does not prevent HMRC from issuing a partial closure notice which does not relate to any matter to which the transfer pricing notice relates before the expiry of 90 days or before the tax return has been amended.

Where a medium-sized company does not fall within the exceptions to the exemption at (a) or (b) above, there is no need for the company's tax return to take account of the transfer pricing rules. However, this does not prevent the

[*TIOPA 2010, s 180*].

Example

A Ltd provides management and administrative services to a number of its wholly-owned subsidiaries. All companies in the group have accounting periods ending on 31 March and do not qualify as small or medium-sized enterprises for transfer pricing purposes.

For the accounting period ending 31 March 2022, A Ltd makes a charge for its management and administrative services to B Ltd of £450,000. Following an enquiry into A Ltd's return for that period, it is agreed that the arm's length value of the services to A Ltd was £600,000. An adjustment is accordingly made of £150,000 to increase A Ltd's taxable profits by that amount.

B Ltd can claim (within the time limit, see above) to apply a corresponding adjustment to reduce its taxable profits for the same period by £150,000 (increasing its deductible expenses to £600,000). B Ltd may also make a balancing payment to A Ltd of up to £150,000 without it being treated as a distribution or charge on income or otherwise taken into account for tax purposes.

Controlled foreign companies

A special provision applies where a transfer pricing adjustment has been applied to the profits or losses of a controlled foreign company as a result of which the sums charged to chargeable UK companies under *TIOPA 2010, s 371BC* (see **21** CONTROLLED FOREIGN COMPANIES) are more than they would otherwise be. In such cases, the controlled foreign company is treated as an advantaged person such that a compensating adjustment may be claimed (as above) by the disadvantaged party or parties (and references above to an advantaged person include a reference to a controlled foreign company, and to any of the companies who have suffered the CFC charge).

[*TIOPA 2010, s 179*].

Thin capitalisation

Where the thin capitalisation provisions in **72.3** above apply, a compensating adjustment may be claimed (and the claim may be amended) by the disadvantaged person or by the advantaged person on behalf of the disadvantaged person.

Such a claim (a *s 182* claim) may be made before or after the arm's length provision has been applied in the case of the advantaged person (in his return or following a determination, see **72.10** below) but the claim must be consistent with that computation. If the claim is not consistent with the computation, it is treated as if it were amended to make it consistent, allowing for any required adjustments to be made (whether by discharge or repayment of tax, the making of assessments or otherwise).

In making a *s 182* claim before the transfer pricing provision is applied, the lending company is not treated as chargeable to tax on income from non-trading loan relationships with respect to so much of the interest that is subject to the transfer pricing adjustment (see '*Reciprocal treatment*' below). Thus the condition for deducting tax at source under *ITA 2007, Pt 15* is not met. The borrowing company may pay such interest to a non-resident lender without deduction of tax at source.

Claims must be made or amended before the expiry of the time limits noted above and the provisions of *TMA 1970, Sch 1A* (claims made outside a return) apply for this purpose.

If a 'relevant notice' is given by any person, it takes account of a transfer-pricing determination and it appears to an HMRC officer that a person may be disadvantaged he must give the disadvantaged person a notice containing details of the determination. A '*relevant notice*' is a closure notice in respect of a corporation tax or partnership return, a notice of assessment or a notice of discovery assessment or determination. Where the officer issues the notice late, or does not issue a notice at all, so that the disadvantaged person is prejudiced then the Commissioners for HMRC may extend the time limit for making an amendment to a compensating adjustment claim under *TIOPA 2010, s 174*.

[*TIOPA 2010, ss 181–185, 190*].

Thin capitalisation — guarantees

Where a transfer pricing adjustment to disallow interest follows from the provision of a guarantee (see **72.3** above), the guarantor company can claim a compensating adjustment as if it was the borrower (the 'issuing company') and had paid the interest subject to the disallowance. Amounts are brought into account in computing the guarantor company's profits and losses accordingly. Where there is more than one guarantor, the total amount claimed by way of a compensating adjustment must not exceed the amount of interest disallowed. Where, but for the transfer pricing adjustment and the claim, the hybrid mismatch provisions (see **4.13** ANTI-AVOIDANCE) would apply to a payment of interest made on or after 10 June 2021, those provisions apply to the guarantor company.

A claim can also be made by the issuing company on behalf of the guarantor company or companies. Where a claim is made by a guarantor and the lending company subsequently makes a claim for a compensating adjustment in respect of the same loan, the claim made by the lending company must be reduced to the extent of the claim made by the guarantor company.

A claim made by the guarantor company will not be allowed where the lending company has earlier made a compensating adjustment claim for the full amount of the interest disallowance. The provisions above relating to claims and time limits apply equally to claims made by a guarantor company or by the issuing company on behalf of the guarantor company.

[*TIOPA 2010, ss 191–194; FA 2021, Sch 7 paras 31, 37*].

Reciprocal treatment

Where a transfer pricing adjustment applies to disallow interest and the lending company claims a compensating adjustment under either *TIOPA 2010, s 174* or *s 182*, the interest disallowed as a deduction for the borrower is correspondingly not treated as chargeable as income from non-trading loan relationships for the lending company.

The condition for deduction at source in *ITA 2007, Pt 15* is therefore not met. Therefore where a *s 182* claim is made (see above) the borrowing company can pay interest to a non-resident lender without deduction of tax at source.

Where a compensating adjustment to a person (other than a company) is denied under the rules at *TIOPA 2010, s174A*, where the counterparty to the transaction is a company, any interest paid under the actual provision, so far as it exceeds the arm's length, will be treated for income tax purposes as a dividend paid by the company which paid the interest (and, accordingly, as a distribution).

[*TIOPA 2010, ss 187, 187A*].

Foreign taxation

Where a claim for a compensating adjustment is made, it is assumed, as respects any foreign tax credit which has been or may be given to the disadvantaged person, that the foreign tax does not include tax which would not be or have become payable if the arm's length provision had also been substituted for the purposes of that tax, and that the profits from the activities in relation to which the actual provision was made or imposed and in respect of which the tax credit relief arises are reduced to the same extent as they are treated as reduced by virtue of the claim.

Where the application of the arm's length provision in a computation following such a claim involves a reduction in the amount of any income, and that income also falls to be treated as reduced under *TIOPA 2010, s 112* by an amount of foreign tax (where credit relief is not available), the former reduction is treated as made before the latter, and the deductible foreign tax excludes that paid on so much of the income as is represented by the amount of the former reduction.

Any adjustment to double tax reliefs as above may be given effect by set-off against any relief or repayment arising from the claim, and may be made without regard to any time limit on assessments or amendments.

[*TIOPA 2010, ss 188, 189*].

Simon's Taxes. See B4.126.

Balancing payments

[72.8] Where a transfer pricing adjustment applies and there is only one advantaged company, the disadvantaged person is within the charge to income tax or corporation tax, and a claim for a compensating adjustment can be made by the disadvantaged company (see **72.7** above), the disadvantaged company may make a balancing payment to the advantaged company by reason of the transfer pricing adjustment.

Such balancing payments must not in aggregate exceed the amount of the available compensating adjustment. The payments are not taken into account when computing profits or losses for tax purposes and are not regarded as distributions.

The '*available compensating adjustment*' is the difference between the profits and losses of the disadvantaged company computed on the basis of the actual provision and computed for the purposes of making the compensating adjustment under **72.7** above (taking profits as positive amounts and losses as negative amounts) and the profits and losses of the disadvantaged person as calculated for tax purposes on a claim under *TIOPA 2010, s 174*.

[*TIOPA 2010, ss 194–196*].

Balancing payments made by guarantors. Where a transfer pricing adjustment applies in the case of the advantaged company and a claim for a compensating adjustment can be made by a guarantor company (see **72.7** above), the guarantor company may make balancing payments to the issuing company (i.e. the borrower) by reason of the transfer pricing adjustment.

Provided such balancing payments do not in aggregate exceed the amount of the compensating adjustment, the payments are not taken into account for corporation tax purposes when computing profits or losses of the guarantor company (or companies) or of the issuing company and are not regarded as distributions.

The compensating adjustment in this case is the total reductions in interest or other amounts payable under the security subject to the guarantee (and thus treated as paid by the guarantor).

[*TIOPA 2010, ss 197, 198*].

Example

On 1 April 2021, B Ltd is granted a loan of £5,000,000 at 6% interest p.a. from an unassociated bank. The loan is guaranteed by B Ltd's parent company, G plc. Both companies draw up accounts for the year ended 31 March and neither company qualifies as a small or medium-sized enterprise for transfer pricing purposes.

Following an enquiry into B Ltd's return for the accounting period ending 31 March 2022, HMRC successfully maintain that, in the absence of the guarantee from G plc, the bank would not have advanced more than £1,000,000 to B Ltd. Accordingly, an adjustment is made to increase B Ltd's profits for the period by £240,000 in disallowing the interest on £4,000,000 of the loan.

G plc could make a claim (or B Ltd could claim on its behalf) for a corresponding adjustment before or after the transfer pricing adjustment is made in B Ltd's return, or following the determination (but within the time limit, see **72.7** above), so that it is treated as having paid the interest subject to the disallowance. Accordingly, provided the interest in G plc's case would not be subject to a transfer pricing adjustment, G plc could claim a deduction for £240,000 in respect of the interest paid by B Ltd.

G plc can make a balancing payment of up to £240,000 to B Ltd without it being treated as a distribution or otherwise taken into account for corporation tax purposes.

Alternatively, where the conditions (a) and (b) below are met, G plc can elect to pay the tax liability in respect of the interest disallowed, of £45,600. In that case, B Ltd would not have to pay the tax liability arising in respect of the transfer pricing adjustment.

Note

(a) The group would also be subject to the CORPORATE INTEREST RESTRICTION (**24**) rules in *TIOPA 2010, ss 372–498* and *Sch 7A*. Groups with finance costs below £2m per annum are unaffected by CIR. The CIR applies *after* transfer pricing and anti-hybrid rules, etc. but *before* the loss restriction rules. See **51.13** LOSSES for details on loss restriction.

Election to pay tax instead of balancing payment — thin capitalisation

Where both parties are companies, special provisions apply where the actual provision subject to a claim for a compensating adjustment under **72.7** above, is a provision in relation to a security (the 'relevant security') (see **72.3** above on thin capitalisation). In that case, instead of making a balancing payment as above, the disadvantaged company may elect to assume responsibility for the additional tax liability in relation to an accounting period of the advantaged company where the additional liability results from the transfer pricing adjustment in relation to the relevant security (i.e. a disallowance of interest or other amounts).

The tax liability in this case would not be treated as a liability of and recoverable from the advantaged company but would instead be treated as a corporation tax liability of the disadvantaged company.

The disadvantaged company may only make such an election where:

(a) the actual provision relating to the security forms part of a capital market arrangement involving the issue of a capital market investment (as defined in the *Insolvency Act 1986, s 72B(1), Sch 2A paras 1–3*) of a total value of at least £50 million; and
(b) the securities representing the capital market investment are issued wholly or mainly to independent persons (not the disadvantaged company and not persons having a participatory relationship (as defined in **72.3** above) with any of the affected companies).

An election, which is irrevocable, must be made in the disadvantaged company's tax return (whether by amendment or otherwise) for the chargeable period in which the relevant security is issued and has effect for that period and all subsequent chargeable periods (i.e. the lifetime of the loan). HMRC may refuse to accept such an election but only after a notice of enquiry has been issued to the disadvantaged company in respect of the tax return containing the election.

The above provisions relating to an election to pay tax instead of a balancing payment apply equally, with necessary modifications, in cases where a transfer pricing is made in respect of third party loans subject to a guarantee provided by a connected company (see **72.3** above).

[*TIOPA 2010, ss 199–203*].

Simon's Taxes. See **B4.126**.

Capital allowances and capital gains

[72.9] These provisions do not affect the computation of capital allowances or balancing charges under the *Capital Allowances Acts*, or of capital gains or allowable losses under *TCGA 1992*, and do not require any income or losses to be treated as on capital rather than revenue account. However, a compensating adjustment may affect the computation of such allowances, charges, gains or losses.

[*TIOPA 2010, ss 213, 214*].

Determinations requiring the sanction of HMRC

[72.10] A determination of an amount falling to be brought into account under these provisions requires sanction by the Commissioners for HMRC, except in certain cases where an agreement has been reached between HMRC and the person concerned (see *TIOPA 2010, s 208–211*).

Where such a determination is made for the purposes of either:

(i) giving a closure notice; or
(ii) giving a notice amending a partnership statement or return; or
(iii) making a discovery assessment; and
(iv) the notice of the closure, amendment or discovery assessment is given to any person without the determination having been approved by HMRC (or without a copy of HMRC's approval having been served on that person at or before the time the notice was given),

then the closure or amendment notice or discovery assessment is deemed to have been given or made (and in the case of an assessment notified) as if the determination had not been taken into account.

The approval must apply specifically to the case in question and the amount determined, but may otherwise be given (either before or after the making of the determination) in any such form or manner as HMRC may determine. An appeal relating to a determination approved by HMRC may not question HMRC's approval except to the extent that the grounds for questioning the approval are the same as the grounds for questioning the determination itself.

[*TIOPA 2010, ss 208–211*].

For the requirement that HMRC give notice of determinations to persons who it appears to them may be 'disadvantaged persons' (as above) by reference to the subject matter of the determination, see *TIOPA 2010, s 185*.

See also HMRC International Manual, INTM483090.

Simon's Taxes. See B4.180.

Appeals

[72.11] An appeal against an amendment of a return, the refusal of a claim or a discovery assessment or determination involving the application of *TIOPA 2010, Pt 4* lies to the tribunal.

Where the appeal relates to any provision as between two persons each of whom falls within the charge to income or corporation tax in respect of profits arising from relevant activities, either person may be a party to the proceedings and is entitled to appear before and be heard by the tribunal, or to make written representations to them. The tribunal must determine that aspect of the appeal separately from any other, that separate determination being treated as made in an appeal to which each of those persons was a party.

Alternatively, the ultimate parent entity may authorise another UK constituent entity of the group to file the report, provided that it notifies HMRC of that authority in writing before the filing deadline.

If another group member (UK or overseas) has filed a report which satisfies the UK reporting requirements and the UK ultimate parent or group member notifies HMRC accordingly, there is no need for the UK group member to file another report.

The report must be filed, presented and contain certain content as detailed in directions issued by HMRC. The report must be filed via HMRC's online reporting service. See www.gov.uk/guidance/check-if-you-must-send-a-country-by-country-report. The report must show for each country the amount of revenue, profit before income tax, income tax paid and accrued, and total employment, capital, retained earnings and tangible assets. (HMRC International Exchange of Information Manual IEIM300026). HMRC may request further information in order to determine if information contained in a report is accurate. Such information must be provided within 14 days of the request.

In addition to filing a country-by-country report, the entity responsible for filing it must, before the end of the period to which the report relates (or 1 September 2017 if later) notify HMRC of the names and unique taxpayer references of all of the group's entities which are resident in the UK, have a permanent establishment in the UK or are partnerships. In the case of a top UK entity which is not the ultimate parent and which expects another entity to file the country-by-country report, the notification must include the name and unique taxpayer reference (or non-UK equivalent) of that entity. HMRC prefer that the notification be made on a spreadsheet and sent by email to notification.cbcrfiling@hmrc.gov.uk. Alternatively, the notice may be sent by mail, marked 'Country-by-Country Reporting Notification' to HMRC CbCR Notifications, JITSIC - S1715, Business, Assets & International, 9th Floor, Mail Point 3, Central Mail Unit, Newcastle NE98 1ZZ. (HMRC International Exchange of Information Manual IEIM300110).

Penalties apply as follows:

(i) failure to file a report or provide additional supporting information after a request by HMRC: £300 initial penalty plus a daily £60 penalty after the person has been notified of the initial penalty for each day the failure continues. The daily penalty may be increased up to a maximum of £1,000 on determination by a Tribunal if the failure continues for more than 30 days;

(ii) knowingly providing inaccurate information when filing a report or providing additional supporting information after a request by HMRC: £3,000 maximum penalty.

There is a wide ranging anti-avoidance provision to prevent any arrangements from applying where the main purpose of the arrangements is to avoid the reporting requirement obligations.

For OECD guidance on country-by-country reporting internationally, see www.oecd.org/tax/guidance-on-the-implementation-of-country-by-country-reporting-beps-action-13.pdf. See also HMRC International Exchange of Information Manual IEIM300000 onwards.

The UK (along with many other countries) has signed the Multilateral Competent Authority Agreement for the automatic exchange of country-by-country reports. This ensures the timely and consistent implementation of BEPS Action Point 13 across these territories.

[*FA 2015, s 122; FA 2016, Sch 19 para 54; SI 2016 No 237; SI 2017 No 497*].

Enquiries

[72.14] Transfer pricing enquiries into company tax returns are subject to the normal corporation tax enquiry rules found at *FA 1998, Sch 18*, therefore all of the normal rules regarding the opening and conduct of enquiries and the 'enquiry window' apply. See **65.14** RETURNS — enquiries into returns administration.

Transfer pricing enquiries are also subject to special governance rules (see HMRC manual INTM481000 onwards). In their guidance HMRC comment that a transfer pricing enquiry should not be opened without the approval of the Transfer Pricing Panel or Board.

General guidance on the conduct of enquiries is given in HMRC's Enquiry Manual.

See also INTM481000, 482000, 483000 for internal HMRC guidance on transfer pricing enquiries.

Simon's Taxes. See B4.180.

Advance pricing agreements

[72.15] A taxpayer may apply to HMRC for an advance pricing agreement ('APA') (which will always be a written document), on a prospective basis, on the resolution of complex transfer pricing issues relating to any one or more of the following matters which fall, or might fall, to be determined.

(a) Where the taxpayer is not a company, the attribution of income to a branch or agency through which the taxpayer has been carrying on, or is proposing to carry on, a trade in the UK.

(b) Where the taxpayer is a company, the attribution of income to a permanent establishment (see **64.6** RESIDENCE) through which the taxpayer has been carrying on, or is proposing to carry on, a trade in the UK.

(c) The attribution of income to any permanent establishment of the taxpayer (wherever situated) through which he has been carrying on, or is proposing to carry on, any business.

(d) The extent to which income which has arisen or which may arise to the taxpayer is to be taken for any purpose to be income arising outside the UK.

(e) The treatment for tax purposes of any provision operating between the taxpayer and any 'associate' of his. Persons are '*associates*' for this purpose if (as in **72.2**(a) and (b) above in relation to *TIOPA 2010, Pt 4*) one directly or indirectly participates, at the time of the making or imposition of the provision, in the management, control or capital of the other, or the same person or persons so participate in the management, control or capital of each of them (with further special provision in relation to sales of oil).

(f) The treatment for tax purposes of any provision operating between a 'ring fence trade' carried on by the taxpayer and any other activities the taxpayer carries on. A '*ring fence trade*' for this purpose is a trade which is treated as a separate trade under *CTA 2010, ss 274, 279*, or would be so treated if a different trade were also carried on.

[*TIOPA 2010, ss 218, 219*].

The potential scope of an APA is flexible and it may relate to all the transfer pricing issues of the business in question, or it may be limited to one or more specific issues. However, thin capitalisation issues will generally be dealt with via a separate Advance Thin Capitalisation Agreement (see also **72.3** above).

The application must set out the taxpayer's understanding of what would, in their case, be the effect, in the absence of any agreement, of the provisions in relation to which clarification is sought, and in what respects clarification is required. They must also propose how the clarification might be effected in a manner consistent with that understanding.

Per SP 2/10 the APA may be unilateral, bilateral or multilateral, involving multiple jurisdictions (strictly complimentary bilateral APAs). Where a taxpayer is interested in applying for an APA it is recommended by HMRC that it is first contacted on an informal basis to discuss the taxpayer's plans before presenting a formal application — the 'expression of interest process'. This ensures unsuitable applications are taken no further and also allows HMRC to outline a realistic timetable for agreeing the APA.

Where HMRC and the taxpayer have entered into such an agreement (an 'advance pricing agreement' or 'APA') in relation to a chargeable period, then (except as below) any questions relating to those matters are, to the extent provided for in the APA, to be determined in accordance with the APA rather than by reference to the legislative provisions which would otherwise have applied.

However, where the relevant matter falls within (e) or (f) above and not within (a), (b), (c) or (d) above, the only legislative provisions which can be displaced are those contained in *TIOPA 2010, Pt 4 (Transfer Pricing)*.

Where an APA relating to a chargeable period beginning or ending before the date of the APA provides for the manner in which consequent adjustments are to be made, those adjustments are to be made in the manner provided for in the APA.

An APA does not, however, have effect in relation to the determination of any question which relates to:

(i) a time after the revocation of the APA by an officer of HMRC, in accordance with its terms;

(ii) a time after or in relation to which any provision of the APA has not been complied with, where the APA was conditional upon compliance with that provision; or

(iii) any matter as respects which any other essential conditions have not been, or are no longer, satisfied.

The APA must contain a declaration that it is made for the purposes of *TIOPA 2010, s 218*. It is for HMRC to ensure that the APA is modified so as to be consistent with any double taxation arrangements.

Where the APA makes provision for its modification or revocation by HMRC, this may take effect from such time (including a time before the modification or revocation) as HMRC may determine.

An APA does not have effect if a time to which the matter under consideration relates falls after an HMRC officer has recorded the revocation of the agreement under its terms, or falls after a 'significant' provision has been breached, or where a key condition relating to that matter has not been met or is no longer met. A term is '*significant*' or is a '*key condition*' if it is a condition of the agreement having effect.

Any party to an APA must provide HMRC with all such reports and other information as he may be required to provide under the APA or by virtue of any request made by an officer of HMRC in accordance with its terms.

An APA is deemed never to have been made where, before it was made, the taxpayer fraudulently or negligently provided HMRC with false or misleading information in relation to the application for the APA or in connection with its preparation, and HMRC notifies the taxpayer that the APA is nullified by reason of the misrepresentation. A penalty not exceeding £10,000 may apply for so giving such false or misleading information.

For details about the application process see further SP 2/10.

[*TIOPA 2010, ss 218–230*].

HMRC consider that the only way to obtain legal certainty that HMRC will accept the arm's length price of a transaction is through an APA. However, HMRC will provide a 'general opinion' regarding methodology as part of real time working. (HMRC International Manual, INTM480540).

Effect of APA on third parties

Where an APA has effect in relation to any provision between the taxpayer and another person, then in applying the transfer pricing rules under *TIOPA 2010, ss 174–178* and *188–189* (see above) to the other person, the arrangements set out in the APA similarly apply in determining any question as to:

(A) whether the taxpayer is a person on whom a potential advantage in relation to UK taxation is conferred by the actual provision; or
(B) what constitutes the arm's length provision in relation to the actual provision.

This is subject to any APA made between HMRC and the other person. The notice requirements of *TIOPA 2010, s 185* are correspondingly amended.

[*TIOPA 2010, s 222*].

For a detailed explanation of how APAs are administered, see HMRC Statement of Practice, SP 2/10 and HMRC International Manual, INTM422000 onwards.

Simon's Taxes. See B4.181, B4.182.

Transfer pricing, mutual agreement procedure and arbitration

[72.16] The mutual agreement procedure (MAP) is a process which enables double tax treaty partners to interact with the intention to resolve international tax disputes. The MAP found in most of the UK's tax treaties (and also within the EU Arbitration Convention, see further below) provides for the competent authorities of the relevant tax treaty partners to consult each other when a taxpayer enterprise claims that it is being taxed otherwise than in accordance with the treaty/convention, as a result of the actions of one or both of the relevant fiscal authorities.

HMRC's practice in relation to MAP and the use of arbitration where MAP is unsuccessful is set out in Statement of Practice SP 1/18 (replacing SP 1/11). The Statement works in conjunction with the guidance in HMRC's International Manual at INTM423000 onwards.

It should be noted that the MAP is a process of consultation (not litigation) and the taxpayer is not a formal party to those consultations, although they may be invited to participate informally (at the tax authorities' discretion).

With regards to the UK there is no set form of presentation, UK taxpayers may present their cases in writing to HMRC. They should specify the year(s) concerned, the nature of the action giving rise, or expected to give rise, to taxation not in accordance with the treaty/convention, and the full names and addresses of the parties to which the MAP relates, including the UK enterprise's tax office and reference number.

Where a solution or mutual agreement has been reached under the terms of a UK tax treaty, it will be given effect notwithstanding anything in any enactment, in accordance with *TIOPA 2010, s 124(2)*. Where normal time limits may have expired before a solution or mutual agreement is reached, a claim for relief consequential to that solution or mutual agreement, for example to losses, group relief, capital allowances etc., must be made within twelve months following the notification of the solution or mutual agreement per *TIOPA 2010, s 124(4)*.

EU Arbitration Convention

The EU Arbitration Convention (*90/463/EEC*) provides a procedure to resolve disputes between enterprises of different Member States relating to transfer pricing adjustments. Following Brexit, no new UK claims can be accepted under the Convention with effect from IP completion day (11pm GMT on 31 December 2020).

TIOPA 2010, s 127 made provision for domestic legislation and agreements to be over-ridden where necessary under the Convention, and *TIOPA 2010, ss 126, 128* and *FA 1989, s 182A* provided the necessary information powers and confidentiality requirements in relation to disclosures of information to an advisory commission. See also the comments made above with regard to SP1/18, which outlines HMRC's approach to the use of the Convention.

The Convention was supplemented by Council Directive 2017/1852/EU regarding tax dispute resolution mechanisms in the EU. The directive sought to establish an effective regime for the resolution of tax disputes, and to minimise the risk of double taxation for businesses operating across borders. For the UK legislation giving effect to the Directive, see **31.5** double tax relief. The UK legislation is revoked with effect from IP completion day (11pm GMT on 31 December 2020) by *SI 2020 No 1383*.

Code of Conduct

The European Commission has adopted a proposal for a Code of Conduct to ensure a more effective and uniform application of the Convention by EU member states. The Code determines procedural rules covering time limits for dealing with complaints, arrangements concerning the advisory commission that must be established to deal with disputes concerning the elimination of double taxation following transfer-pricing adjustments, and the suspension of tax collection during the dispute resolution period. The Code has recently been revised and updated.

See the Official Journal C176 of 28/07/2006 and the revised code in Official Journal C322 of 30/12/2009.

Simon's Taxes. See B4.183, B4.184.

Key points on transfer pricing

[72.17] Points to consider are as follows.

- Transfer pricing rules apply equally between UK and offshore connected entities as well as UK to UK connected entities. The legislation includes the UK's thin capitalisation rules.
- Where, as a result of a transfer pricing enquiry, UK to UK adjustments are made in one company's corporation tax computation, a corresponding adjustment can be reflected in the other company's tax computation. This means that for UK to UK adjustments the overall corporation tax liability within the group is unlikely to change but will merely be redistributed.
- Where the adjustment is between a UK and offshore entity then similar favourable adjustments do not arise. It may be possible to challenge this where the foreign entity is resident in a jurisdiction with which the UK has a double tax treaty which contains an appropriate non-discrimination clause, but such a challenge would require an application to a fiscal court in that jurisdiction. Practically speaking, such a challenge would not be viable.
- Small and medium enterprises may largely be exempt from the transfer pricing rules, although such entities may be caught in certain circumstances where the listed exceptions apply. For the definition of small and medium reference needs to be made to EU Commissions Recommendation of 2003/361/EC as amended by the UK's taxing statutes.

- A common misconception is that the transfer pricing rules only apply to connected parties which either have a direct controlling relationship or are under common control. In reality, for transfer pricing purposes it is not necessary to have control. A 40% interest between the parties is sufficient to invoke the rules.
- If transactions are sufficiently large then HMRC will expect to see a thorough analysis of the pricing policy between connected parties. Such an analysis needs to be substantiated by appropriate documentation. The EU code of conduct on transfer pricing lays out the recommended documents needed.
- As noted above, the transfer pricing rules also cover thin capitalisation. Where a subsidiary is overly debt laden through connected party debt then the transfer pricing rules can reduce or disallow any interest expense claimed by the paying company. This is particularly the case where the interest payments are to a connected offshore lender.
- A company might also enter into Advanced Pricing Arrangements to give certainty with regard to intra-group cross border transactions (see SP2/10).
- To assist with the resolution of transfer pricing disputes HMRC have issued SP 1/18 which outlines their procedures using the mutual agreement procedure found at *Article 25* of a double tax treaty (per the OECD model) or, prior to Brexit, using the EU Arbitration Convention.

73

Value Added Tax

See HMRC Business Income Manual BIM31500–31625 and, generally, Tolley's Value Added Tax.

Non-taxable persons

[73.1] VAT relating to expenditure that is deductible for corporation tax purposes is also deductible. Capital allowances on any such expenditure are based on the VAT-inclusive cost. See HMRC Statement of Practice, SPB1.

Taxable persons

[73.2] Income and expenditure are taken into account *exclusive* of VAT, and capital allowances are determined accordingly. However, capital allowances on motor cars are computed on the VAT-inclusive cost, as the VAT is not reclaimable. Entertainment expenses *disallowed* for corporation tax purposes include VAT. The full amount of a bad debt (i.e. including irrecoverable VAT) is allowed as a trading expense. See HMRC Statement of Practice, SPB1.

Partly-exempt persons

[73.3] Entertainment expenses and expenditure on motor cars are treated as in 73.2 above. Input VAT on items of expenditure constituting exempt output must be allocated to the categories of such expenditure. It will be treated for corporation tax purposes as part of that expenditure. HMRC is prepared to consider any 'reasonable arrangements' for allocation.

VAT unreclaimed due to the excessive cost of keeping the necessary records may be treated as part of the expenditure to which it relates for corporation tax purposes. See HMRC Statement of Practice, SPB1.

Pre-incorporation expenditure

[73.4] Regulations allow the deduction as input tax of VAT paid on goods acquired before incorporation and services supplied before that time for the business's benefit or in connection with its incorporation.

[*VATA 1994, s 24(6)(c); SI 1995 No 2518, Reg 111(1)*].

Interest, penalties etc. and repayment supplement

[73.5] No deduction is allowed for corporation tax purposes in respect of any payment by way of VAT in relation to:

(a) penalties under *FA 2007, Sch 24, VATA 1994, ss 60–70* (in relation to conduct involving dishonesty which does not relate to an inaccuracy in a document), *FA 2008, Sch 41, F(No 2)A 2017, Sch 16* or *FA 2003, s 25* or *s 26;*
(b) interest under *VATA 1994, s 74*; or
(c) surcharges under *VATA 1994, s 59*.

Similarly any VAT repayment supplement under *VATA 1994, s 79* is disregarded for corporation tax purposes.

[*CTA 2009, ss 1286, 1303*].

Flat rate scheme

[73.6] An optional VAT flat rate scheme is available to all businesses with a VAT-exclusive annual taxable turnover of up to £150,000 in the year of entry to the scheme. A business may opt to leave the flat-rate scheme at any time. It is required to leave the scheme if, on any anniversary of the date on which it was authorised to use the scheme, total income (including VAT) in the previous year exceeded £230,000 or there are reasonable grounds to believe that income for the next 30 days (excluding sales of capital assets) will exceed that amount. The business may be allowed to continue in the scheme, however, if HMRC are satisfied that income in the next year will not exceed £191,500, the increase was the result of unexpected business activity which has not occurred before and is not expected to recur and it arose from genuine commercial activity.

Where the company uses the flat-rate scheme, receipts and expenses to be taken into account are generally *inclusive* of normal output and input VAT (assuming the small business to be a non-taxable person), but the flat-rate VAT itself can either be deducted from turnover or treated as a separate expense and in either case is an allowable deduction for tax purposes. Any irrecoverable VAT on capital items forms part of their cost for the purposes of CAPITAL ALLOWANCES (9).

For HMRC guidance, see www.gov.uk/vat-flat-rate-scheme.

74

Venture Capital Trusts

Cross-references. See **27.35** DERIVATIVE CONTRACTS; **50.49** LOAN RELATIONSHIPS.

Simon's Taxes. See **E3.2**.

Introduction to venture capital trusts

[74.1] The venture capital trust scheme described at **74.2** and onwards was introduced in 1995 to encourage individuals to invest in unquoted trading companies through such trusts by providing reliefs for income tax and capital gains tax (see **74.32** and **74.33** below).

The Treasury has wide powers to make regulations governing all aspects of the reliefs applicable to venture capital trust investments, and for the requirements as regards returns, records and provision of information by the trust. The VCT provisions apply to shares held by nominees on behalf of individuals, and any regulations made as to VCT procedures may apply to nominees as well as to other persons holding VCT shares.

[*ITA 2007, ss 272, 284; SI 1995 No 1979*].

See generally HMRC Venture Capital Schemes Manual VCM50000 onwards.

For company reorganisations involving venture capital trusts, see **62.15** REORGANISATIONS AND RECONSTRUCTIONS. For the transfer of assets within a group of companies to a company which subsequently becomes a venture capital trust, see **12.19** CAPITAL GAINS — GROUPS.

A centralised service is available for companies newly raising money under the venture capital trust scheme. All enquiries about whether a company meets the requirements should be made to the administration team at Venture Capital Reliefs Team, HM Revenue and Customs, WBMC BX9 1BN (enterprise.centre@hmrc.gsi.gov.uk).

Conditions for approval of a venture capital trust

[74.2] A '*venture capital trust*' ('VCT') is a company approved as such by HMRC. The time from which an approval takes effect is specified in the approval, and may not be earlier than the time the application for approval was made.

[*ITA 2007, ss 259, 283*].

Except as detailed further below, approval may not be given unless HMRC are satisfied that the following conditions are met in relation to the most recent complete accounting period of the company and will be met in relation to the accounting period current at the time of the application for approval.

The conditions in more detail:

Close company condition

ITA 2007, s 259 states that the company must not be a close company, in other words it must not be under the control of five or fewer participators or any number of directors who are participators (*CTA 2010, Pt 10*). A company is not a close company if it is controlled by a company which is not a close company, or the public holds 35% or more of the voting share capital of the company and the shares have been subject to dealings on a recognised stock exchange in the preceding twelve months and those shares are listed on such an exchange. However if the voting power held by the principal members exceeds 85%, the public holding test threshold is disregarded and the company may be close.

The listing condition

The company's ordinary shares (or each class thereof) must be admitted to trading on an EU 'regulated market' throughout those periods. '*Regulated market*' is defined for this purpose as in *Directive 2004/39/EC* of the European Parliament and of the Council on markets in financial instruments.

The nature of income condition

The company's income (as defined) in the relevant period must be derived wholly or mainly from shares or 'securities'. HMRC's interpretation of wholly or mainly for the purposes of this test is that at least 70% of the VCT's income must be from shares and securities.

The income retention condition

An amount greater than 15% of its income (as defined) from shares and securities in the period must not be retained by the company.

Only dividends declared for the accounting period in question can be counted for the purposes of this test. Prior period dividends paid in the period in question cannot be counted. This test is relaxed in situations where the company is required to retain income by virtue of a restriction imposed by law, for example in cases where brought forward reserve levels are in deficit and all current period profits are required to make good that deficit. There is also no requirement to retain income where the distributable amount is below a de minimis threshold of £10,000. This threshold is proportionally reduced for a short accounting period. The relaxation does not apply if the distributable amount exceeds the amount restricted by law and the excess is more than the de minimis threshold of £10,000.

The 15% holding limit condition

No 'holding' in any company other than a VCT (or a company which could be a VCT but for the listing condition above) may represent more than 15% of the value of the company's investments at any time in those periods.

Where an addition is made to a holding, the entire holding is revalued to the market value at the time of the latest addition. A holding comprises shares or securities of one or more classes held in the same company and an addition only occurs where the company is liable to give consideration for further investments received. A payment to discharge a liability of the investee which increases the value of the holding will also constitute an addition, for example for partly-paid shares, where a second or subsequent instalment is paid.

'*Holding*' means the shares or securities of whatever class or classes held in any one company. Holdings in associated investee companies must be combined for the purposes of the test, including members of the VCT's own group (taken here to mean 51% subsidiaries) and money owed intra group will be treated as a security. Hence intra group transactions between the VCT and its subsidiaries will constitute an addition for the purposes of revaluing the group holding of the VCT for this test.

Where the VCT is a member of a partnership there are potential pitfalls in meeting the 15% holding limit condition. For the purposes of this condition the underlying holdings of the partnership will count towards the test and not the percentage stake in the partnership itself. Problems can arise for the VCT in obtaining sufficient information from the partnership in respect of its underlying holdings. Similarly in respect of the income retention test, the VCT must be able to determine accurately both the amount and the nature of the income arising to it in respect of its partnership holding for the period in question. Holdings in overseas partnership can also be problematic, in particular where the classification of income differs from that applicable in the UK.

See below for the value of the company's investments.

The 80% qualifying holdings condition

Throughout the accounting periods at least 80% (by value) of the company's investments must be represented by shares or securities in 'qualifying holdings'. Previously, for accounting periods beginning before 6 April 2019, the specified minimum was 70%; all subsequent references to the '80% qualifying holdings condition' should be read accordingly.

The requirements to be satisfied for a holding to be a qualifying holding fall into three groups:

- the form of the investment;
- the type of company invested in; and
- the way in which money raised is to be used.

These conditions are examined in detail below at **74.6** onwards.

For the purpose of this test and for the purpose of the 15% holding limit condition, the company's investments include all money in the company's possession and any sum owned to the company if the company has account-holder's rights over that sum. Examples would be bank accounts, whether interest bearing or not, and accounts held on the company's behalf by third parties such as solicitors or fund managers. However money held for example by the company as trustee for a third party would not usually be included in the company's investments for the purpose of the 80% test.

Where a VCT disposes of a holding that was comprised in its qualifying holdings throughout the six months ending immediately before the disposal, both the fact of the disposal and any monetary consideration for it are disregarded for a period of 12 months beginning with the disposal in determining whether or not the 80% qualifying holdings condition is met. This does not apply if the holding was acquired with money raised by a second or subsequent issue of shares such that the 80% qualifying holdings condition does not for the time being have to be met in relation to that money (see above). It also does not apply if the consideration for the disposal consists entirely of new qualifying holdings. If the consideration for the disposal consists partly of new qualifying holdings, the above treatment applies only to an appropriate proportion of the holding disposed of. The treatment does not apply at all to disposals between companies that are merging. Previously, the period of disregard was six months; the increase to 12 months applies to disposals on or after 6 April 2019.

Where this 80% qualifying holdings condition is breached inadvertently, and the position is corrected without delay after discovery, approval will in practice not be withdrawn on this account. Full details of any such inadvertent breach should be disclosed to HMRC as soon as it is discovered. See also below under 'Withdrawal of approval' as regards the Treasury's power to make regulations.

On a second and subsequent issue of shares by an approved VCT, the 80% qualifying holdings condition and the 30% eligible shares condition below do not have to be met in relation to the money raised by such an issue, in the accounting period of that issue or any later accounting period ending no more than three years after the making of that issue.

See the 15% holding limit condition above for the meaning of 'the company's investments' and see below for the value of investments.

The 70% eligible shares condition

At least 70% of the company's qualifying holdings (by value) must be represented throughout the accounting periods by holdings of 'eligible shares'. For this purpose, '*eligible shares*' are ordinary shares carrying no present or future preferential right to assets on a winding up and no present or future right to redemption; the shares are permitted to carry a present or future preferential right to dividends except in circumstances specified at *ITA 2007, s 285(3B)*.

See the 80% qualifying holdings condition above where a VCT makes a second or subsequent issue of shares and see below for the value of investments.

The non-qualifying investments condition

The condition is that the company has not made and will not make, in the accounting periods, an investment which does not form part of its qualifying holdings and does not come under any of the following descriptions:

(A) shares or units in an alternative investment fund which may be repurchased or redeemed on seven days' notice given by the investor; or
(B) shares or units in a UCITS (an undertaking for collective investment in transferable securities) which may be repurchased or redeemed on seven days' notice given by the investor; or
(C) ordinary shares or securities which are acquired by the company on a regulated market; or
(D) money in the investor's possession; or
(E) a sum owed to the investor over which the investor has the right to require payment, either to the investor or at the investor's direction, on no more than seven days' notice given by the investor.

The investment limits condition

The condition is that the company has not made, and will not make, in the accounting periods, an investment which breaches the permitted investment limits.

An investment breaches the permitted investment limits if:

(i) the 'total annual investment' in the investee company exceeds £5 million; or

(ii) the 'total investment' in the investee company at the date the current investment is made (the '*investment date*' exceeds £12 million or, if the company is a 'knowledge-intensive company' (see **74.18** below) at the investment date, £20 million; or

(iii) the total investment in the investee company at any time during the five-year post-investment period exceeds the limits in (ii) above *and* the company effectively acquires a company or trade after it receives the investment in question. This mirrors the requirement at **74.19** below, which is described there in more detail, and the 'five-year post-investment period' is defined in similar manner.

In (i) above, the '*total annual investment*' in the investee company comprises the investment under review (the '*current investment*') and the total amount of other relevant investments made in the investee company by all investors in the 12 months ending with the day on which the current investment was made. The following also count towards the total annual investment:

- any investment in the said 12-month period in a 51% subsidiary (within *CTA 2010, Pt 24 Ch 3*) of the investee company (including any made before it became a 51% subsidiary but not any made after it last ceased to be one);
- any investment made in any company to the extent that the money raised by the investment has been employed for the purposes of a trade (as widely defined) carried on by another company that has at any time in the said 12-month period been a 51% subsidiary of the investee company (disregarding any money so employed after it last ceased to be such a subsidiary); and
- any other investment made in any company to the extent that the money raised has been employed for the purposes of a trade (as widely defined), and within that 12-month period, but after the investment was made, the trade (or a part of it) was transferred to the investee company, a 51% subsidiary or a partnership of which the investee company or a 51% subsidiary is a member.

In (ii) above, the '*total investment*' in the investee company is defined similarly to 'total annual investment' but disregarding references to a 12-month period and instead taking into account all times before the investment date. In (iii) above, 'total investment' also has a similar meaning but taking into account all times before the time in the five-year post-investment period when (iii) above is being tested.

For the purpose of the conditions for approval of a VCT, a '*relevant investment*' is made in a company if and when:

- an investment (of any kind) in the company is made by a VCT; or
- the company issues shares (for which money has been subscribed) in respect of which it provides a compliance statement under the enterprise investment scheme or seed enterprise investment scheme; or

- an investment is made in the company and (at any time) the company provides a compliance statement under the social investment relief scheme in respect of it; *ITA 2007, s 257KB* applies in determining when such an investment is made; or
- any other investment is made in the company which is aid received by it pursuant to a measure approved by the EC as compatible with Article 107 of the Treaty on the Functioning of the European Union in accordance with the principles laid down in the EC's Guidelines on State aid to promote risk finance investment (previously the Community Guidelines on Risk Capital Investments in Small and Medium-sized Enterprises).

Investments within (A)–(C) above (under the non-qualifying investments condition) are disregarded for the purpose of the investment limits condition.

For the purposes of determining entitlement to VCT income tax relief in respect of investments made on or after 1 December 2017, investments are not prevented from constituting relevant investments by virtue only of their having been made before certain historical dates. Previously, under earlier transitional provisions, certain investments made before 6 April 2012 did not count as relevant investments.

The minimum investment on further issue condition

This condition has effect in relation to money raised by a further issue made in an accounting period beginning on or after 6 April 2018. It must not be breached by the company at any time in the accounting periods. A company breaches the minimum investment on further issue condition where:

- there has been an issue of ordinary share capital of the company;
- the company has been approved as a VCT with effect on or before the date of that issue;
- a further issue of ordinary share capital of the company has since been made; and
- the company does not, on or before the 'relevant deadline', invest at least 30% of the money raised by that further issue in shares or securities which are then comprised in the company's qualifying holdings. The '*relevant deadline*' is the last day of the 12 months immediately following the end of the accounting period in which the further issue is made.

The permitted maximum age condition

The condition is that the company has not made and will not make an investment, in the accounting periods, in a company which breaches the permitted maximum age limit. An investment breaches the limit if it is made after the 'initial investing period' and none of the conditions set out below is met. The '*initial investing period*' is the seven years beginning with the 'relevant first commercial sale' (ten years where the investee company is a 'knowledge-intensive company' (see **74.18** below) when the current investment is made).The conditions are that:

- a 'relevant investment' (as under the investment limits condition above) was made in the investee company before the end of the initial investing period, and some or all of the money raised by that investment was employed for the purposes of the same activities as the money raised by the current investment; or
- the amount of the current investment plus the total amount of any other relevant investments made in the investee company in a period of 30 consecutive days which includes the date of the current investment date is at least 50% of the annual turnover of the investee company averaged over five years (see *ITA 2007, s 280C(8)–(9)*), and the money raised by those investments is employed for the purpose of 'entering a new product or geographical market' (as defined in the General Block Exemption Regulation (Commission Regulation (EU) No 651/2014); or
- the condition immediately above or the equivalent condition for enterprise investment scheme investments was previously met in relation to one or more relevant investments in the investee company, and some or all of the money raised by those investments was employed for the purposes of the same activities as the money raised by the current investment.

'*First commercial sale*' has the same meaning as in the EC's Guidelines on State aid to promote risk finance investments. The '*relevant first commercial sale*' is defined in *ITA 2007, s 280C(7)* by reference to the earliest date of any commercial sale made by (broadly) the investee company or a 51% subsidiary or any other person who has carried on any trade which is carried on by the company or a subsidiary.

With effect for investments made on or after 6 April 2018, an investee company which is a knowledge-intensive company may elect to alter its initial investing period by substituting, for the date of the relevant first commercial sale, the date by reference to which it is treated as reaching an annual turnover of £200,000. That date is normally the last day of the accounting period in which annual turnover first reaches £200,000 or more (with modifications for accounting periods exceeding 12 months). Turnover of other companies in the group (where relevant) must also be taken into account. Any necessary apportionments must be made on a time basis, i.e. in the case of short or long accounting periods or companies joining or leaving the group part way through an accounting period.

Investments made by a company within (A)–(C) above (under the non-qualifying investments condition), and within (D) or (E) above are disregarded for the purpose of the permitted maximum age condition. See **74.31** below as regards modification of the permitted maximum age condition on and after 6 April 2017 in the event of certain company restructuring.

The no business acquisition condition

The condition is that the company has not made and will not make an investment, in the accounting periods, in a company which breaches the prohibition on business acquisitions. An investment breaches the prohibition if any of the money raised by it is employed (whether on its own or with other money) on the acquisition (directly or indirectly) of: an interest in another company such that a company becomes a 51% subsidiary of the investee company; a further interest in a 51% subsidiary of the investee company; a trade (as widely defined); or goodwill or other intangible assets employed for the purposes of a trade.

Investments made by a company within (A)–(E) above (under the non-qualifying investments condition) are disregarded for the purpose of the no business acquisition condition.

Meaning of 'securities'

'*Securities*' for the purposes of the VCT provisions include liabilities in respect of certain loans to the company not repayable within five years, and any stocks or securities relating to which are not re-purchasable or redeemable within five years of issue. Provided that the loan is made on normal commercial terms, HMRC will not regard a standard event of default clause in the loan agreement as disqualifying a loan from being a security for this purpose. If, however, the clause entitled the lender (or a third party) to exercise any action which would cause the borrower to default, the clause would not be regarded as 'standard'. (HMRC SP 8/95).

Any liability in respect of a loan to the company made on or after 15 March 2018 which either carries a return exceeding a commercial rate, or is made on terms enabling a person to acquire any security or preferential rights in relation to assets of the company or the ability to control the company, is excluded from 'securities'. The return on a loan is not to be treated as representing more than a commercial rate if it meets conditions set out in *ITA 2007, s 285(2B)*. Where the return over the term of the loan cannot be determined in advance, best estimates are to be used initially, subject to subsequent adjustment when actual figures are known.

Alternative requirements for the giving of approval

Where any of the above conditions are not met, approval may nevertheless be given where HMRC are satisfied as to the meeting of those conditions (and in some cases other conditions imposed by regulations) in certain future accounting periods.

[*ITA 2007, ss 274–277, 280, 280A–280D, 285, 989, 1005; FA 2018, s 15, Sch 4 paras 7, 10, Sch 5 paras 3, 5–7, 13, 14; SI 2004 No 2199, Reg 14; SI 2018 No 931, Regs 3, 4; SI 2019 No 689, Reg 15(2)*].

Value of investments

The value of any investment for the purposes of the 15% holding limit condition, the 80% qualifying holdings condition and the 70% eligible shares condition above is the value when the investment was acquired. However, where it is added to by a further holding of an investment of the same description (otherwise than for no consideration), or a payment is made in discharge of any obligation attached to it which increases its value, the value of the investment is the value immediately after the most recent such addition or payment.

For this purpose, where, in connection with a 'scheme of reconstruction' (within *TCGA 1992, s 136*; previously a 'scheme of reconstruction or amalgamation'), a company issues shares or securities to persons holding shares or securities in another company in respect of, and in proportion to (or as nearly as may be in proportion to) such holdings, without the recipients' becoming liable for any consideration, the old and the new holdings are treated as the same.

Where:

(i) shares or securities in a company are exchanged for corresponding shares and securities in a new holding company; or
(ii) a VCT exercises conversion rights in respect of certain convertible shares and securities,

then, subject to detailed conditions (see *ITA 2007, ss 326–329*), the value of the new shares is taken to be the same as the value of the old shares when they were last valued for these purposes.

Where, under a company reorganisation or other arrangement:

- a VCT exchanges a qualifying holding for other shares or securities (with or without other consideration); and
- the exchange is for genuine commercial reasons and not part of a tax avoidance scheme or arrangements,

regulations provide a formula which values the new shares or securities by reference to the proportion of the value of the old shares or securities that the market value of the new shares or securities bears to the total consideration receivable. If no other consideration is receivable, the value of the new shares or securities is identical to that of the old shares or securities. The provisions extend to new shares or securities received in pursuance of an earn-out right conferred in exchange for a qualifying holding, in which case an election is available (under *Reg 10*) to modify the formula by effectively disregarding the earn-out right itself.

[*ITA 2007, ss 278, 279; FA 2018, Sch 5 paras 3, 13, 14*].

Withdrawal of approval

[74.3] Approval may be withdrawn where there are reasonable grounds for believing that either:

- the conditions for approval were not satisfied at the time the approval was given;
- in a case where HMRC were satisfied that a condition would be met in relation to any period, that condition has not been, or will not be, met in that period;
- in a case of provisional approval in relation to a second or further issue by an approved VCT, any additional condition included in the approval notice has not been met;
- in a case of full approval, or where provisional approval has become full, a condition was not, or will not be met in relation to the company's last or current accounting period;

- in a case where there has been a further issue of ordinary shares, the conditions for approval will not be met in the first accounting period to which the relaxation, in respect of the additional funds, does not apply; or
- whilst being a VCT the company has issued shares, and within three years from the end of the accounting period in which the shares were issued, the company has:
  (i) made a payment to all or any of its shareholders (other than for redeeming or repurchasing any of those shares) of an amount representing either directly or indirectly a repayment of its share capital (whether made from a reserve arising from a reduction of share capital (as defined in *CTA 2010, s 1027A*) or otherwise);
  (ii) for shares issued at a premium, made a payment to all or any of its shareholders of an amount representing either directly or indirectly that premium (whether made from a share premium reserve, or otherwise); or
  (iii) used an amount which represents (directly or indirectly) the company's share capital, or an amount by which the share capital has been reduced, or share premium, to pay up new shares to be allotted to all or any of its shareholders.

In this final bullet point, 'payment' does not include any distribution of assets made in connection with the winding up of the company, but does include every other description of distribution of the company's assets to its members.

The withdrawal is effective from the time the company is notified of it, except that:

(1) where approval is given on HMRC being satisfied as to the meeting of the relevant conditions in future accounting periods, and is withdrawn before all six of the conditions above have been satisfied in relation to either a complete twelve-month accounting period or successive complete accounting periods constituting a continuous period of twelve months or more, the approval is deemed never to have been given; and
(2) for the purposes of relief for capital gains accruing to a VCT under *TCGA 1992, s 100* withdrawal may be effective from an earlier date, but not before the start of the accounting period in which the failure occurred (or is expected to occur).

Under *ITA 2007, s 270*, where relief is lost on VCT approval being withdrawn, an assessment for withdrawing or reducing VCT relief must be made for the tax year for which the relief was obtained, and may be made at any time within six years from the end of that tax year.

In addition, pursuant to *s 281(5)*, an assessment as a consequence of the withdrawal of approval may, where otherwise out of time, be made within three years from the time the notice of the withdrawal was given.

For the detailed requirements as regards granting of approval, breach of conditions for and refusal (and withdrawal) of approval, and appeals procedures, see *SI 1995 No 1979, Pt II*.

Applications for approval should be made to the Venture Capital Reliefs Team, HMRC, WMBC BX9 1QL.

[*ITA 2007, ss 270, 281, 282*].

There are provisions for the making of Treasury regulations to enable a VCT to apply to HMRC for a determination that they will not exercise, for a certain period, their power to withdraw approval by reason of a specified breach, including a future breach, of the above conditions (see *ITA 2007, s 284(1)(aa)(2)(3)*).

Mergers of VCTs

[74.4] For mergers of two or more VCTs, regulations enable the merging VCTs to retain VCT status and provide for their investors, who continue as investors in the 'successor company', not to lose their tax reliefs. This treatment applies to two types of merger within *SI 2004 No 2199*:

(1) shares in one of the merging companies (company A) are issued to members of the other merging company (or companies) either in exchange for their shares in that other company (or companies) or by way of consideration for a transfer to company A of the whole or part of the business of that other company;
(2) shares in a company (company B), which is not one of the merging companies, are issued to members of the merging companies either in exchange for their shares in those companies or in consideration for the transfer to company B of the whole or part of the businesses of those companies.

Company A or, as appropriate, company B is the '*successor company*'.

For the regulations to apply, a merging company or the successor company must apply to HMRC for approval, and approval must be granted before the merger takes place. For the procedure for obtaining approval see *SI 2004 No 2199, Reg 10*. HMRC will not approve the merger unless they are satisfied that strict conditions are met, including that the merger is for *bona fide* commercial reasons and is not part of a scheme or arrangements with a tax avoidance purpose. For the detailed conditions, see *SI 2004 No 2199, Reg 9(3)*.

Where approval is obtained, the following apply:

- income tax investment relief within **74.32** below cannot be obtained in respect of any shares issued to effect the merger by the successor company, and such shares are ignored in determining whether the 'permitted maximum' has been exceeded;
- the nature of income, income retention, 70% qualifying holdings, 70% eligible shares and 15% holding limit conditions, and the provisions at **74.6** below apply to the successor company:
  (i) as if the property of the merging companies were vested in the successor company (so that transfers between a merging company and the successor company are disregarded);
  (ii) disregarding, in the hands of the successor company, any assets consisting in rights against, or shares or securities of, another company which is a merging company; and
  (iii) disregarding, in the hands of the successor company, the use of any money which, in the hands of another company which is a merging company, would have been disregarded under *ITA*

2007, s 280(2) (use of money raised by further issue of shares to be ignored for certain periods for the purposes of the 70% qualifying holdings and 70% eligible shares conditions — see above), for the same periods as are mentioned in that provision;

- a disposal by a merging company to the successor company after the merger of an asset held by the merging company immediately before, or in the period during which, the merger takes place is not prevented by *TCGA 1992, s 171(2)(cc)* (see **12.4** CAPITAL GAINS — GROUPS) from being treated as a disposal at no gain/no loss;
- for the purposes of the income tax reliefs at **74.32** below and capital gains tax deferral relief at **74.33** below (see Tolley's Capital Gains Tax under Venture Capital Trusts):
  (i) any share for share exchange or share for business transfer is not treated as a disposal of the 'old shares' or as a chargeable event for the purposes of deferral relief;
  (ii) any other act (including the giving of relief) carried out, or failure to act, in relation to the old shares is treated as carried out, or omitted, in relation to the corresponding new shares;
  (iii) references to the company in which the old shares were held are to be read as references to the successor company;
- for the purposes of capital gains tax relief on disposal (see Tolley's Capital Gains Tax under Venture Capital Trusts), if the successor company is not otherwise a VCT at the time the shares issued to effect the merger are acquired but is a VCT at the time of a subsequent disposal of the shares, it is treated as a VCT at and from the time of acquisition;
- where any of the qualifying holding requirements at **74.6** below (other than the qualifying subsidiaries requirement) were satisfied to any extent or for any period in relation to an investment held by a merging company immediately before the merger, they are treated as satisfied to the same extent or for the same period when held by the successor company, as if the two companies were the same company;
- for the purposes of the 15% test above and the qualifying subsidiaries requirement at **74.28** below, the period in which the merger takes place is disregarded and if as a result of the merger that test or requirement is no longer met, it is treated as met for a period of one year;
- for the purposes of the 80% qualifying holdings, 70% eligible shares and 15% holding limit conditions above and the proportion of eligible shares requirement at **74.11** below, the value of investments in the hands of the successor company immediately after the merger is taken to be their value when last valued before the merger in accordance with the rules governing those conditions and that requirement, unless there has been a transaction other than the merger as a result of which the investments would fall to be revalued; and
- where provisional approval of a merging company other than the successor company is withdrawn following the merger, the withdrawal takes effect from the time the company is notified of it (and the approval is not deemed never to have been given).

[*ITA 2007, ss 321–325; SI 2004 No 2199, Regs 1, 9–13*].

Winding-up of a VCT

[74.5] Regulations enable a VCT commencing winding-up to retain its VCT status during a 'prescribed winding-up period', thereby enabling investors' reliefs to continue for that period.

A VCT-in-liquidation can obtain this treatment:

- if it has been approved as a VCT continuously for at least three years ending with the commencement of the winding-up; or
- where the winding-up is by court order, it is approved as a VCT immediately before the commencement.

The winding-up must be for *bona fide* commercial reasons and not part of tax avoidance arrangements and the VCT-in-liquidation must notify HMRC of the commencement. A VCT-in-liquidation which has been at any time a merger company (see above) other than a successor company does not qualify. The '*prescribed winding-up period*' for these purposes is the three years beginning with the commencement of the winding-up, but if the winding-up ends, the company ceases to be wound up or is dissolved, the period comes to an end on the earliest of those events.

Where the VCT-in-liquidation fulfils the above requirements, the following apply:

(I) For the purposes of the income tax relief on investments (see **74.32** below), the commencement of the winding-up does not affect the status of the VCT-in-liquidation as a VCT (i.e. the commencement itself is not treated as an event leading to the withdrawal of approval and the provisions for withdrawal of relief are not triggered by it).

(II) Gains accruing to the VCT-in-liquidation during the prescribed winding-up period on disposal of assets acquired before the commencement of the winding-up are not chargeable gains (and losses are not allowable losses).

(III) Capital gains tax relief on disposal of VCT shares (see **74.33** below) is available (provided that the other conditions for that relief are met) for disposals in the prescribed winding-up period as if the VCT-in-liquidation were a VCT. If, at the end of that period the VCT-in-liquidation still exists and the conditions for approval as a VCT (see above) are not then fulfilled, approval is treated, for the purposes of that relief, as withdrawn at that time.

[*SI 2004 No 2199, Regs 1–7*].

Simon's Taxes. See E3.242.

Qualifying holdings of a VCT

[74.6] A VCT's holding of shares or securities in a company is comprised in its '*qualifying holdings*' at any time if:

- the requirements at **74.7–74.30** below are satisfied at that time in relation to the company and the shares or securities;

- the shares or securities were first issued to the VCT, and have been held by it ever since; and
- the shares or securities were first issued by the company in order to raise money for the purposes of promoting the growth and development of the company or, where the company is a parent company, the group.

If the requirements for the maximum qualifying investment, use of the money raised or relevant company to carry on the relevant qualifying activity requirements would be met by part of the money raised through the issue, and the holding is not otherwise capable of being treated as separate holdings, it is treated as two separate holdings.

These two holdings consist of:

(i) a holding from which that part of the money was raised; and
(ii) a holding from which the remainder was raised,

with the value being apportioned accordingly to each holding. In the case of the use of money raised requirement, this does not require an insignificant amount applied for other purposes to be treated as a separate holding.

[*ITA 2007, ss 286, 293(7); FA 2018, s 14(3)–(5)*].

Risk-to-capital requirement

[74.7] This requirement has effect for shares or securities issued on or after 15 March 2018. The requirement is that, having regard to all existing circumstances at the time of issue to the VCT of the holding in question, it would be reasonable to conclude that:

- the issuing company has objectives to grow and develop its trade in the long term; and
- there is a significant risk that the investing VCT will suffer a loss of capital of an amount greater than its net investment return, i.e. its net return irrespective of whether it takes the form of income, capital growth, fees or other payments or anything else. A loss of capital means a loss of at least part of the amount given by the VCT in consideration for the holding in question.

[*ITA 2007, s 286ZA; FA 2018, s 14(3); SI 2018 No 931, Reg 2*].

The intention is to prevent tax-relieved investment in companies whose activities are geared towards preservation of investors' capital rather than the company's long-term growth and development. *ITA 2007, s 286ZA(3)* provides an illustrative, non-exhaustive list of the types of circumstance that may be taken into account in reaching any conclusion. For draft guidance on the requirement, with examples, see HMRC Venture Capital Schemes Manual VCM8500–8560.

UK permanent establishment requirement

[74.8] The requirement is that the company has a 'permanent establishment' in the UK. The company must have met this requirement at all times from the time of issue to the VCT of the holding in question.

For the above purpose, a company has a '*permanent establishment*' in the UK if (and only if):

- it has a fixed place of business in the UK through which the business of the company is wholly or partly carried on; or
- an agent acting on behalf of the company has the authority to enter into contracts on behalf of the company and habitually exercises that authority in the UK.

The activities carried on at the fixed place of business or carried on in the UK by the agent must, in relation to the company's business as a whole, be more than simply activities of a preparatory or auxiliary character. Examples of such preparatory/auxiliary activities are given at *ITA 2007, s 302A(6)* and include storage.

A company is not regarded as having a permanent establishment in the UK simply because:

- it carries on business in the UK through an independent agent (including a broker or a general commission agent) acting in the ordinary course of his business; or
- it controls a UK resident company or a company carrying on business in the UK (whether or not through a permanent establishment).

[*ITA 2007, ss 286A, 302A*].

Financial health requirement

[74.9] This requirement must have been met at the time of issue to the VCT of the holding in question. The requirement is that the issuing company is not 'in difficulty'. A company is '*in difficulty*' if it is reasonable to assume that it would be regarded as a firm in difficulty for the purposes of the *EU Guidelines on State Aid for Rescuing and Restructuring Firms in Difficulty (2004/C 244/02)*. [*ITA 2007, s 286B*].

No guaranteed loan requirement

[74.10] The holding in question must not include any securities (as defined in 74.2 above) relating to a guaranteed loan. A security relates to a guaranteed loan if there are arrangements entitling the VCT to receive anything (directly or indirectly) from a 'third party' in the event of a failure by any person to comply with the terms of the security or the loan to which it relates. It does not matter whether or not the arrangements apply in all cases of a failure to comply or only in some such cases.

'*Third party*' means any person other than the investee company itself and, if it is a parent company that meets the trading requirement below, its subsidiaries. [*ITA 2007, s 288, Sch 2 para 69; FA 2018, Sch 5 paras 8, 13, 14*].

Proportion of eligible shares requirement

[74.11] At least 10% by value of the VCT's *total* holding of shares in and securities of the company must consist of 'eligible shares' (as defined for the purposes of the 70% eligible shares condition at 74.2 above — broadly, ordinary, non-preferential, shares). For this purpose, the value of shares etc. at any time is taken to be their value immediately after the most recent of the events listed below, except that it cannot thereby be taken to be less than the amount of consideration given by the VCT for the shares etc. The said events are as follows.

- The acquisition of the shares or securities by the investing company.
- The acquisition by the investing company (other than for no consideration) of any other shares or securities of the relevant company which are of the same description as those already held.
- The making of any such payment in discharge (in whole or in part) of any obligation attached to the shares in or securities of the relevant company in a case where such discharge increases the value of the shares or securities.

[*ITA 2007, s 289, Sch 2 para 70; FA 2018, Sch 5 paras 8, 13, 14*].

Trading requirement

[74.12] The company must either:

(a) exist wholly for the purpose of carrying on one or more 'qualifying trades' (disregarding any purpose having no significant effect on the extent of its activities); or

(b) be a '*parent company*' (i.e. a company that has one or more 'qualifying subsidiaries' — see the qualifying subsidiaries requirement below) and the business of the '*group*' (i.e. the company and its qualifying subsidiaries) must not consist wholly or as to a substantial part (i.e. broadly 20% — see HMRC Venture Capital Schemes Manual VCM55090) in the carrying on of 'non-qualifying activities'.

Where the company intends that one or more other companies should become its qualifying subsidiaries with a view to their carrying on one or more qualifying trades, then, until any time after which the intention is abandoned, the company is treated as a parent company and those other companies are included in the group for the purposes of (b) above.

For the purpose of (b) above, the business of the group means that which would be the business of the group if the activities of the group companies taken together were regarded as one business. Activities are for this purpose disregarded to the extent that they consist in:

(i) holding shares in or securities of any of the company's subsidiaries;

(ii) making loans to another group company;

(iii) holding and managing of property used by a group company for the purposes of one of more qualifying trades carried on by any group company; or

(iv) holding and managing of property used by a group company for the purposes of research and development from which it is intended either, that a qualifying trade to be carried on by a group company will be derived or that a qualifying trade carried on or to be carried on by a group company will benefit.

References above to a group company include references to any existing or future company which will be a group company at any future time.

Activities are similarly disregarded to the extent that they consist, in the case of a subsidiary whose main purpose is the carrying on of qualifying trade(s) and whose other purposes have no significant effect on the extent of its activities (other than in relation to incidental matters), in activities not in pursuance of its main purpose.

'*Non-qualifying activities*' are:

(I) excluded activities (as below); and
(II) non-trading activities.

[*ITA 2007, ss 290, 332,*].

A company does not cease to meet this requirement by reason only of anything done as a consequence of its being in administration or receivership (both as defined — see *ITA 2007, s 331*), provided everything so done and the making of the relevant order are for genuine commercial (and not tax avoidance) reasons. [*ITA 2007, s 292, Sch 2 para 73*].

Qualifying trade

[74.13] A trade is a 'qualifying trade' if:

(i) it is conducted on a commercial basis with a view to the realisation of profits; and
(ii) it does not consist wholly or to a substantial extent in the carrying on of 'excluded activities'.

For these purposes, 'trade' (except in relation to the trade mentioned in (t) below) does not include a venture in the nature of trade. '*Excluded activities*' are:

(a) dealing in land, commodities or futures, or in shares, securities or other financial instruments;
(b) dealing in goods otherwise than in an ordinary trade of wholesale or retail distribution (see below);
(c) banking, insurance or any other financial activities;
(d) leasing or letting or receiving royalties or licence fees;
(e) providing legal or accountancy services;
(f) 'property development';
(g) farming or market gardening;
(h) holding, managing or occupying woodlands, any other forestry activities or timber production;
(i) shipbuilding (defined by reference to relevant EU State aid rules);
(j) producing coal or steel (both defined by reference to relevant EU State aid rules and including the extraction of coal);
(k) operating or managing hotels or comparable establishments (i.e. guest houses, hostels and other establishments whose main purpose is to offer overnight accommodation with or without catering) or property used as such;

(l) operating or managing nursing homes or residential care homes (both as defined) or property used as such;
(m) generating or exporting electricity or making electricity generating capacity available;
(n) generating heat;
(o) generating any form of energy not within (m) or (n);
(p) producing gas or fuel;
(q) providing services or facilities for any business consisting of activities within any of (a) to (p) and carried on by another person (other than a parent company), where one person has a 'controlling interest' in both that business and the business carried on by the provider.

HMRC regard as 'substantial' for the above purposes a part of a trade which consists of 20% or more of total activities, judged by any reasonable measure (normally turnover or capital employed) (HMRC Venture Capital Schemes Manual VCM3010). As regards (a) above, dealing in land includes cases where steps are taken, before selling the land, to make it more attractive to a purchaser; such steps might include the refurbishment of existing buildings (HMRC Venture Capital Schemes Manual VCM3020).

As regards (b) above, a trade of wholesale distribution is a trade consisting of the offer of goods for sale either to persons for resale (or processing and resale) (which resale must be to members of the general public for their use or consumption) by them. A trade of retail distribution is a trade in which goods are offered or exposed for sale and sold to members of the general public for their use or consumption. A trade is not an ordinary wholesale or retail trade if it consists to a substantial extent of dealing in goods collected or held as an investment (or of that and any other activity within (a)–(s) above), and a substantial proportion of such goods is held for a significantly longer period than would reasonably be expected for a vendor trying to dispose of them at market value. Whether such trades are 'ordinary' is to be judged having regard to the following features, those under (A) supporting the categorisation as 'ordinary', those under (B) being indicative to the contrary.

(A)
- (i) The breaking of bulk.
- (ii) The purchase and sale of goods in different markets.
- (iii) The employment of staff and incurring of trade expenses other than the cost of goods or of remuneration of persons connected (within **19** CONNECTED PERSONS) with a company carrying on such a trade.

(B)
- (i) The purchase or sale of goods from or to persons connected (within **19** CONNECTED PERSONS) with the trader.
- (ii) The matching of purchases with sales.
- (iii) The holding of goods for longer than would normally be expected.
- (iv) The carrying on of the trade at a place not commonly used for wholesale or retail trading.
- (v) The absence of physical possession of the goods by the trader.

As regards the application of (d) above, a trade is not excluded from being a qualifying trade solely because it consists to a substantial extent in the receiving of royalties or licence fees substantially attributable (in terms of value) to the exploitation of 'relevant intangible assets'. An intangible asset is an asset falling to be treated as such under generally accepted accounting practice, including all intellectual property and also industrial information and techniques (see HMRC Venture Capital Schemes Manual VCM3060). A *'relevant intangible asset'* is an intangible asset, the whole or greater part of which (in terms of value) has been created by the issuing company or by a company which was a 'qualifying subsidiary' (within **74.28** below) of the issuing company throughout the period during which it created the whole or greater part of the asset. The definition also includes an intangible asset the whole or greater part of which was created by a company when it was not a qualifying subsidiary of the issuing company, provided it subsequently became a qualifying subsidiary under a particular type of company reconstruction. Where the asset is 'intellectual property', it is treated as created by a company only if the right to exploit it vests in that company (alone or with others). The term *'intellectual property'* incorporates patents, trade marks, copyrights, design rights, etc. and foreign equivalents.

Also as regards (d) above, a trade will not be excluded by reason only of its consisting of letting ships, other than offshore installations (previously oil rigs) or pleasure craft (as defined), on charter, provided that:

(i) the company beneficially owns all the ships it so lets;
(ii) every ship beneficially owned by the company is UK registered;
(iii) throughout period B, the company is solely responsible for arranging the marketing of the services of its ships; and
(iv) in relation to every letting on charter, certain conditions as to length and terms of charter, and the arm's length character of the transaction, are fulfilled,

and if any of (i)–(iv) above is not fulfilled in relation to certain lettings, the trade is not thereby excluded if those lettings and any other excluded activities taken together do not amount to a substantial part of the trade.

In relation to (d) above, in the Revenue Tax Bulletin August 2001, pp 877, 878, the Inland Revenue set out their views on the scope of the exclusions. The *leasing and letting* exclusion covers all cases where (subject to reasonable conditions imposed by the trader) the customer is free to use the property for the purpose for which it is intended, e.g. television rental, video hire and the provision of self-storage warehousing facilities. In the case of car hire, a distinction has to be drawn between the provision of a *transportation service* and that of a *transportation facility*, only the latter falling within the exclusion. A taxi service would usually fall within the former category, a chauffeured car hire within the latter. *Royalties and licence fees* are received where property rights are exploited by the granting of permission to others to make use of the property. There will, however, be cases (e.g. the retailing of CDs) where, although the sales are made under licence, the receipts are nevertheless consideration for the supply of goods. In the case of *licence fees*, the grant of the right to use the property is often incidental to the supply of services (e.g. a cinema ticket), and the exclusion does not apply in such cases. The principle can be illustrated in relation to sports and leisure facilities provision. Simply making sports facilities available to the general public, with no service provision, would involve the receipt of licence fees. In the more commonly encountered activity of a health club providing a high level of services, including active supervision and advice from qualified staff, the licence to enter the premises and use the equipment would be merely incidental. Similarly where, although there is no direct provision of services, continuous work is required to keep the property in a fit state for use, the question to be considered is the extent to which the fees relate to the cost of such work.

In *Optos plc v HMRC* (Sp C 560), [2006] SSCD 687, the Sp C, in finding for the appellant company on this point, took the view that for these purposes the term 'leasing' should be construed to connote essentially a passive activity where consideration was charged for the use of an asset as opposed to the provision of services.

As regards (e) above, the provision of the services of accountancy personnel is the provision of accountancy services (*Castleton Management Services Ltd v Kirkwood* (Sp C 276), [2001] SSCD 95).

'*Property development*' in (f) above means the development of land by a company, which has (or has had at any time) an 'interest in the land' (as defined), with the sole or main object of realising a gain from the disposal of an interest in the developed land.

Exclusions (k) and (l) above apply only if the person carrying on the activity in question has an estate or interest (e.g. a lease) in the property concerned or occupies that property.

As regards (q) above, a person has a '*controlling interest*' in a trade etc. carried on by a company if he controls (within *CTA 2010, ss 450, 451*) the company; or if the company is a close company and he or an 'associate' is a director of the company and the owner of, or able to control, more than 30% of its ordinary share capital; or if at least half of its ordinary share capital is directly or indirectly owned by him. In any other case it is obtained by his being entitled to at least half of the assets used for, or income arising from, the trade etc. In either case, the rights and powers of a person's 'associates' are attributed to him. An '*associate*' of any person is any 'relative' (i.e. spouse, civil partner, ancestor or linear descendant) of that person, the trustee(s) of any settlement in relation to which that person or any relative (living or dead) is or was a settler and, where that person has an interest in any shares or obligations of a company which are subject to any trust or are part of a deceased estate, the trustee(s) of the settlement or the personal representatives of the deceased and, if that person is a company, any other company which has an interest in those shares or obligations.

[*ITA 2007, ss 300(1)(4), 303–310, 313(4)–(7), Sch 2 paras 81–85; FA 2018, Sch 5 paras 8, 13, 14*].

Research and development

'Research and development' from which it is intended that a qualifying trade carried on 'wholly or mainly in the UK' will either be derived or, for shares issued to the VCT after 5 April 2007, benefit, is treated as the carrying on of a qualifying trade. Preparing to carry on such research and development does not, however, count as preparing to carry on a trade. '*Research and development*' has the meaning given by *ITA 2007, s 1006*.

[*ITA 2007, s 300(2)(3), Sch 2 para 78*].

Carrying on of a qualifying activity requirement

[74.14] A 'qualifying company' (whether or not the same such company at all times) must, when the shares were issued to the VCT and at all times since, have been carrying on one of the following two '*qualifying activities*':

(A) carrying on a 'qualifying trade', 'wholly or mainly in the UK' (see the trading requirement above); or
(B) preparing to carry on a qualifying trade which, at the time the shares were issued, was intended to be carried on wholly or mainly in the UK.

The second of these conditions is, however, relevant only for a period of two years after the issue of the shares, by which time the intended trade must have been commenced by a 'qualifying company', and ceases to be relevant at any time within those two years after the intention is abandoned.

For these purposes, '*qualifying company*' means the relevant company itself or any 'qualifying 90% subsidiary' of that company. In determining the time at which a qualifying trade begins to be carried on by a 'qualifying 90% subsidiary', any carrying on of the trade by the qualifying 90% subsidiary before it became such a subsidiary is disregarded. A qualifying 90% subsidiary includes any existing or future company which will be a qualifying 90% subsidiary at any future time.

A company (the subsidiary) is a '*qualifying 90% subsidiary*' of the relevant company at any time when:

- the relevant company possesses at least 90% of both the issued share capital of, and the voting power in, the subsidiary;
- the relevant company would be beneficially entitled to at least 90% of the assets of the subsidiary available for distribution to equity holders on a winding-up or in any other circumstances;
- the relevant company is beneficially entitled to at least 90% of any profits of the subsidiary available for distribution to equity holders;
- no person other than the relevant company has control (within *ITA 2007, s 995* — see **19** CONNECTED PERSONS) of the subsidiary; and
- no arrangements exist by virtue of which any of the above conditions would cease to be met.

For the above purposes, *CTA 2010, Pt 5 Ch 6* applies, with appropriate modifications, to determine the persons who are equity holders and the percentage of assets available to them.

A subsidiary does not cease to be a qualifying 90% subsidiary by reason only of it or any other company having commenced winding up or by reason only of anything done as a consequence of any such company being in administration or receivership, provided the winding-up, entry into administration or receivership (both as defined) or anything done as a consequence of its being in administration or receivership is for genuine commercial reasons and is not part of a tax avoidance scheme or arrangements.

Also, the listed conditions are not regarded as ceasing to be satisfied by reason only of arrangements being in existence for the disposal of the relevant company's interest in the subsidiary if the disposal is to be for genuine commercial reasons and is not to be part of a tax avoidance scheme or arrangements.

A company (company A) is also a qualifying 90% subsidiary of the relevant company if:

- company A would be a qualifying 90% subsidiary of another company (company B) if that company were the relevant company and company B is a 'qualifying 100% subsidiary' of the relevant company; or
- company A is a qualifying 100% subsidiary of company B and company B is a qualifying 90% subsidiary of the relevant company.

No account is taken for this purpose of any control the relevant company may have of company A.

Maximum amount raised annually through risk finance investments requirement

[74.15] With effect for investments made on or after 6 April 2018, the total amount of 'relevant investments' (see **74.16** below) made in the issuing company in the 12 months ending with the date of issue to the VCT must not exceed:

(i) if the company is a knowledge-intensive company at that date, £10 million; and
(ii) in any other case, £5 million.

See **74.18** below for meaning of knowledge-intensive company, and note the special rule there for companies that have traded for less than three years before issuing the shares etc.

Prior to the above taking effect, the limit is £5 million in all cases.

The following also count towards the above limit:

(a) any relevant investment in a 51% subsidiary (within *CTA 2010, Pt 24 Ch 3*) of the issuing company (including any made before it became a 51% subsidiary but not any made after it last ceased to be one);
(b) any relevant investment made in any company to the extent that the money raised by the investment has been employed for the purposes of a trade (as widely defined) carried on by another company that has at any time in the said 12-month period been a 51% subsidiary of the issuing company (disregarding any money so employed after it last ceased to be such a subsidiary); and
(c) any other relevant investment made in any company to the extent that the money raised has been employed for the purposes of a trade (as widely defined), and within that 12-month period, but after the invest-

ment was made, the trade (or a part of it) was transferred to the issuing company, a 51% subsidiary or a partnership of which the issuing company or a 51% subsidiary is a member (but disregarding trades transferred after a 51% subsidiary in question last ceased to be such a subsidiary).

[*ITA 2007, s 292A(1)–(2B)(7); FA 2018, Sch 4 paras 3(2), 10; SI 2012 No 1901; SI 2018 No 931, Reg 3*].

Relevant investments

[74.16] For the purposes of the VCT qualifying holding requirements, '*relevant investments*' comprise:

(a) investments (of any kind) made by a VCT;
(b) money subscribed for shares issued by the investee company under the enterprise investment scheme (EIS) or the seed enterprise investment scheme (SEIS);
(c) investments made under the social investment relief scheme; and
(d) any other investment made in the company which is aid received by it pursuant to a measure approved by the EC as compatible with Article 107 of the Treaty on the Functioning of the European Union in accordance with the principles laid down in the EC's Guidelines on State aid to promote risk finance investment (previously the Community Guidelines on Risk Capital Investments in Small and Medium-sized Enterprises).

As regards (b) above, shares are treated as having been issued under the EIS or SEIS if at any time the investee company provides an EIS compliance statement or SEIS equivalent in respect of those shares; an investment is regarded as made when the shares are issued. As regards (c) above, an investment is treated as made under the social investment relief scheme if at any time the investee company provides a compliance statement; *ITA 2007, s 257KB* applies in determining when such an investment is made. If the provision of a compliance statement causes this requirement not to be met, the requirement is treated as having been met from the time the shares in question were issued to the VCT to the time the compliance statement was provided.

[*ITA 2007, s 292A(3)–(6)*].

For the purposes of determining entitlement to VCT income tax relief in respect of investments made on or after 1 December 2017, investments are not prevented from constituting relevant investments by virtue only of their having been made before certain historical dates. Previously, under earlier transitional provisions, certain investments made before 6 April 2012 did not count as relevant investments. [*FA 2018, s 15*].

Maximum risk finance investments when holding is issued requirement

[74.17] The total amount of 'relevant investments' (see **74.16** above) made in the issuing company on or before investment date (i.e. the date the holding in question is issued) must not exceed £12 million or, if the company is a 'knowledge-intensive company' (see **74.18** below) at the investment date, £20 million. Relevant investments of the kind in **74.15**(a)–(c) above also count towards these limits, but disregarding references there to a 12-month period and instead taking into account all times before the investment date. If at any time the company provides a compliance statement under the enterprise investment scheme, seed enterprise investment scheme or social investment relief scheme and this requirement ceases to be met as a result, it is nevertheless treated as having been met throughout the period from the investment date until the provision of the compliance statement. [*ITA 2007, s 292AA*].

Knowledge-intensive companies

[74.18] A '*knowledge-intensive company*' is broadly a company whose costs of research and development or innovation are at least 15% of its operating costs in at least one of the years comprising the 'relevant three-year period' or at least 10% of its operating costs in each of those years, and which meets at least one of the two conditions below. The '*relevant three-year period*' is normally the three years ending immediately before the beginning of the last accounts filing period. However, if the last accounts filing period ends more than 12 months before the applicable time, the relevant three-year period is the three years ending 12 months before the applicable time. The applicable time is the date on which the matter of whether a company is a knowledge-intensive company falls to be judged. A company's operating costs are defined by reference to the items recognised as expenses in its profit and loss account. The conditions to be met are that:

- the company has created, is creating or is intending to create, intellectual property (the '*innovation condition*'); or
- the company's full-time employees with a relevant Masters or higher degree who are engaged in research and development or innovation comprise at least 20% of the total of its full-time employees (the '*skilled employee condition*').

In order to meet the innovation condition, the company must be engaged in intellectual property creation at the applicable time, and it must be reasonable to assume that, within ten years after that time, the exploitation of its intellectual property, or business which results from new or improved products, processes or services utilising its intellectual property, will form the greater part of its business. A company is engaged in intellectual property creation if intellectual property is being created by the company, or has been created by it within the previous three years; or the company is taking (or preparing to take) steps in order that intellectual property will be created by it; or the company demonstrates via an independent expert's report that it is reasonable to assume it will create intellectual property in the foreseeable future. Intellectual property is taken into account only if the whole or greater part (in terms of value) of it is created by the company and it is created in circumstances in which the right to exploit it vests in the company (whether alone or jointly with others).

If the company is a parent company, the above rules are appropriately modified to also take account of its 'qualifying subsidiaries' (see **74.28** below).

[*ITA 2007, ss 313(5), 331A*].

Companies that have traded for less than three years

If the company commenced trading less than three years before the date the holding in question is issued, the above definition is modified for the purposes of **74.17**(i) and (ii) above ('maximum amount raised annually through risk finance investments' requirement). The '*relevant three-year period*' is for those purposes the three years *beginning* on the date of issue of the holding. If the company is a parent company, operating costs of a qualifying subsidiary (at time of issue) are not taken into account for any of those three years during any part of which it is not a qualifying subsidiary. [*ITA 2007, s 292A(6A); FA 2018, Sch 4 paras 3(3), 10*].

Maximum risk finance investments in five-year post-investment period requirement

[74.19] This is a requirement which is tested only during a '*five-year post-investment period*', i.e. the period of five years beginning the day after the date the holding in question is issued (the '*investment date*'), and only if the company effectively acquires a company or trade after it receives the investment in question. The requirement is that at any time in the five-year post-investment period the total of the relevant investments (see **74.16** above) so far made must not exceed £12 million or, if the company is a 'knowledge-intensive company' (see **74.18** above) at the investment date, £20 million. Without this requirement, the investment limits in **74.17** above could be sidestepped where the acquired company or trade had already benefited from earlier relevant investments. Relevant investments of the kind in **74.15**(a)–(c) above also count towards these limits, but disregarding references there to a 12-month period and instead taking into account all times before the time in the five-year post-investment period when the requirement is being tested. The requirement applies where:

- a company becomes a 51% subsidiary of the issuing company at a time during the five-year post-investment period;
- all or part of the money raised by the issue of the holding in question is employed for the purposes of a relevant qualifying activity consisting (wholly or partly) of a trade (as widely defined) carried on by that company; and
- the trade (or a part of it) was carried on by that company before that time.

The requirement also applies where all or part of the money raised by the issue of the holding in question is employed for the purposes of a relevant qualifying activity consisting (wholly or partly) of a trade (as widely defined) which, during the five-year post-investment period, is transferred as in **74.15**(c) above.

Similar provision applies as in **74.17** above if at any time the company provides a compliance statement under one of the other venture capital schemes or the social investment relief scheme and this requirement ceases to be met as a result. It is nevertheless treated as having been met throughout the period from the investment date until the provision of the compliance statement.

[*ITA 2007, s 292AB*].

Use of the money raised requirement

[74.20] The money raised by the issue of shares to the VCT must be employed *wholly* (disregarding insignificant amounts) for the purposes of the 'relevant qualifying activity'. Where two or more years have passed since commencement of trading, all the money raised must be applied wholly for the purpose of a relevant qualifying activity.

For these purposes, a qualifying activity is a '*relevant qualifying activity*' if it was a qualifying activity at the time the shares were issued or if it is a qualifying trade and preparing to carry it on was a qualifying activity at that time.

Employing money on the acquisition of shares in a company does not of itself amount to employing it for the purposes of a relevant qualifying activity.

[*ITA 2007, s 293*].

Relevant company to carry on the relevant qualifying activity requirement

[74.21] At all times after the issue of the holding, the relevant qualifying activity by reference to which the use of money raised requirement is satisfied must not be carried on by any person other than the relevant company or a 'qualifying 90% subsidiary'.

This requirement is not treated as not met merely because the trade in question is carried on by a person other than the relevant company or a qualifying subsidiary at any time after the issue of the shares and before the relevant company or a qualifying 90% subsidiary carries on the trade. The carrying on of the trade by a partnership of which the relevant company or a qualifying 90% subsidiary is a member, or by a joint venture to which any such company is a party, is permitted.

The requirement is also not regarded as failing to be met if, by reason only of a company being wound up or dissolved or being in administration or receivership (both as defined), the qualifying trade ceases to be carried on by the relevant company or a qualifying 90% subsidiary and is subsequently carried on by a person who has not been connected (within *ITA 2007, s 993* – see **19 CONNECTED PERSONS** – but with the modifications to the meaning of 'control' that apply for the purposes of the control and independence requirement below) with the relevant company at any time in the period beginning one year before the shares were issued. This let-out applies only if the winding-up, dissolution or entry into administration or receivership (and everything done as a consequence of the company being in administration or receivership) is for genuine commercial reasons and not part of a tax avoidance scheme or arrangements.

[*ITA 2007, s 294, Sch 2 para 75*].

Permitted company age requirement

[74.22] If the holding in question is issued after the 'initial investing period', one of three conditions must be met. These are that:

(a) a 'relevant investment' (see **74.16** above) was made in the issuing company before the end of the initial investing period, and some or all of the money raised by that investment was employed for the purposes of the same qualifying activity as that for which the money raised by the current issue is employed; or

(b) the total amount of relevant investments made in the issuing company in a period of 30 consecutive days which includes the date of issue of the holding in question is at least 50% of the annual turnover of the company averaged over five years (see *ITA 2007, s 294A(7)–(8)*), and the money raised by those investments is employed for the purpose of 'entering a new product or geographical market' (as defined in the General Block Exemption Regulation (Commission Regulation (EU) No 651/2014)); or

(c) the condition in (b) or the equivalent condition for EIS investments (was previously met in relation to one or more relevant investments in the issuing company, and some or all of the money raised by those investments was employed for the purposes of the same qualifying activity as that for which the money raised by the current issue is employed.

The '*initial investing period*' is the seven years beginning with the 'relevant first commercial sale' (ten years where the issuing company is a 'knowledge-intensive company' (see **74.18** above) when the holding in question is issued). '*First commercial sale*' has the same meaning as in the EC's Guidelines on State aid to promote risk finance investments. The '*relevant first commercial sale*' is defined in *ITA 2007, s 294A(6)* by reference to the earliest date of any commercial sale made by (broadly) the company or a 51% subsidiary or any other person who has carried on any trade which is carried on by the company or a subsidiary.

For investments made on or after 6 April 2018, a company which is a knowledge-intensive company may elect to alter its initial investing period by substituting, for the date of the relevant first commercial sale, the date by reference to which it is treated as reaching an annual turnover of £200,000. That date is normally the last day of the accounting period in which annual turnover first reaches £200,000 or more (with modifications for accounting periods exceeding 12 months). Turnover of other companies in the group (where relevant) must also be taken into account. Any necessary apportionments must be made on a time basis, i.e. in the case of short or long accounting periods or companies joining or leaving the group part way through an accounting period.

[*ITA 2007, ss 294A, 331B; FA 2018, Sch 4 paras 8, 9, 10; SI 2018 No 931, Reg* 3].

See **74.31** below as regards modification of the permitted company age requirement on and after 6 April 2017 in the event of certain company restructuring.

Unquoted status requirement

[74.23] The relevant company must be an '*unquoted company*', i.e. none of its shares, stocks, debentures or other securities must be:

- listed on a recognised stock exchange;
- listed on a designated exchange in a country outside the UK; or
- dealt in outside the UK by such means as may be designated for the purpose by order.

The Alternative Investment Market (AIM) and the PLUS Markets (with the exception of PLUS-listed) are not considered to be recognised exchanges for these purposes. The PLUS-listed market is regarded as a recognised stock exchange. (HMRC Venture Capital Schemes Manual VCM55180).

If the relevant company ceases to be an unquoted company at a time when its shares are comprised in the qualifying holdings of the VCT, this requirement is treated as continuing to be met, in relation to shares or securities acquired before that time, for the following five years.

[*ITA 2007, s 295*].

Control and independence requirement

[74.24] The company must not 'control' (with or without 'connected persons') any company other than a 'qualifying subsidiary' (see the qualifying subsidiaries requirement below), nor must another company (or another company and a person connected with it) control it. Neither must arrangements be in existence by virtue of which such control could arise. For these purposes, '*control*' is as under *CTA 2010, s 450*, except that possession of, or entitlement to acquire, fixed-rate preference shares (as defined) of the company which do not, for the time being, carry voting rights are disregarded, as is possession of, or entitlement to acquire, rights as a loan creditor of the company. '*Connected persons*' are as under *ITA 2007, s 993* (see **19** CONNECTED PERSONS) except that the definition of 'control' therein is similarly modified. [*ITA 2007, ss 296, 313(4)–(7)*].

Gross assets requirement

[74.25] The value of the company's gross assets or, where the company is a parent company, the value of the 'group assets', must not have exceeded £15 million immediately before the issue or £16 million immediately thereafter. '*Group assets*' are the gross assets of each of the members of the group, disregarding assets consisting in rights against, or shares in or securities of, another member of the group.

[*ITA 2007, s 297*].

The general approach of HMRC is that the value of a company's gross assets is the aggregate of the company's gross assets as shown in its balance sheet. Where accounts are actually drawn up to a date immediately before or after the issue, the balance sheet values are taken provided that they are in accordance with generally accepted accounting practice. Where accounts are not drawn up to such a date, such values will be taken from the most recent balance sheet, updated as precisely as is practicable taking into account all the relevant information available to the company. Values so arrived at may need to be reviewed in the light of information contained in the accounts for the period in which the issue was made, and, if they were not available at the time of the issue, those for the preceding period, when they become available.

The company's assets immediately before the issue do not include any advance payment received in respect of the issue. Where shares are issued partly paid, the right to the balance is an asset, and, notwithstanding the above, will be taken into account in valuing the assets immediately after the issue regardless of whether it is stated in the balance sheet. (HMRC SP 2/06).

Number of employees requirement

[74.26] The number of 'full-time equivalent employees' for the relevant company must be less than 250 at the time the holding is issued. If the company is a parent company, the sum of the full-time equivalent employees for it and each of its qualifying subsidiaries must be less than 250 at that time. The limit of 250 is doubled to 500 if the company is a 'knowledge-intensive company' (see **74.18** above) at the time the holding in question is issued.

A company's '*full-time equivalent employees*' for this purpose is the number of its full-time employees plus, for each employee who is not full-time, a just and reasonable fraction. Directors are counted as employees for this purpose, but employees on maternity or paternity leave and students on vocational training are excluded.

[*ITA 2007, s 297A*].

The 'proportion of skilled employees' requirement

[74.27] There is a requirement, where the conditions below are met, that at all times in the period of three years beginning with the issue of the holding in question the company's full-time employees with a relevant Masters or higher degree who are engaged in research and development or innovation must comprise at least 20% of the total of its full-time employees. The conditions are that:

- one or more of the requirements in **74.15** (maximum amount raised annually through risk finance investments requirement), **74.17** (maximum risk finance investments when holding is issued requirement), **74.22** (permitted company age requirement) and **74.26** above (number of employees requirement) is or are met only by reason of the company being a knowledge-intensive company at the time the holding in question was issued; and
- the innovation condition in the definition of 'knowledge-intensive company' at **74.18** above was not met by the company at that time.

If the company is a parent company, the above is appropriately modified to also take account of the company's 'qualifying subsidiaries' (see **74.28** below). The requirement is not treated as failing to be met at a time when the company, by virtue of *ITA 2007, s 292* (companies in administration or receivership — see **74.12** above), is not regarded as having ceased to meet the trading requirement.

[*ITA 2007, s 297B; FA 2018, Sch 4 paras 4, 10*].

Qualifying subsidiaries requirement

[74.28] Any subsidiary that the relevant company has must be a 'qualifying subsidiary' of the company.

A subsidiary is a '*qualifying subsidiary*' of the relevant company if the following conditions are satisfied in relation to that subsidiary and every other subsidiary of the relevant company.

The subsidiary must be a **51%** subsidiary (see *CTA 2010, s 1154*) of the relevant company and no person other than the relevant company or another of its subsidiaries may have control (within *CTA 2010, s 1124(1)–(3)* — see **19** CONNECTED PERSONS) of the subsidiary. Furthermore, no arrangements may exist by virtue of which either of these conditions would cease to be satisfied. The conditions are not regarded as ceasing to be satisfied by reason only of the subsidiary or any other company in the process of being wound up or by reason only of anything done as a consequence of its being in administration or receivership, provided the winding-up, entry into administration or receivership or anything done as a consequence of its being in administration or receivership is for genuine commercial reasons and is not part of a tax avoidance scheme or arrangements.

The conditions above are not regarded as ceasing to be satisfied by reason only of arrangements being in existence for the disposal of the interest in the subsidiary held by the relevant company (or, as the case may be, by another of its subsidiaries) if the disposal is to be for genuine commercial reasons and is not part of a tax avoidance scheme or arrangements.

[*ITA 2007, ss 298, 302, 989*].

Property managing subsidiaries requirement

[74.29] The company must not have a 'property managing subsidiary', which is not a 'qualifying 90% subsidiary' (see the carrying on of a qualifying activity requirement above) of the company.

A '*property managing subsidiary*' is a subsidiary whose business consists wholly or mainly in the holding or managing of 'land' or any property deriving its value from land' (as defined).

[*ITA 2007, s 299*].

No disqualifying arrangements requirement

[74.30] The requirement is that the holding in question must not have been issued, nor any money raised by the issue employed, in consequence or anticipation of, or otherwise in connection with, 'disqualifying arrangements'. Arrangements (as broadly defined) are '*disqualifying arrangements*' if a main purpose of them is to ensure that any of the venture capital scheme tax reliefs (see below) are available in respect of the issuing company's business and either or both of conditions A and B below are met. It is immaterial whether the issuing company is a party to the arrangements.

Condition A is that, as a result of the money raised by the issue of the shares to the VCT being employed as required by **74.20** above, an amount representing the whole or most of the amount raised is, in the course of the arrangements, paid to (or for the benefit of) one or more 'relevant persons'. Condition B is that, in the absence of the arrangements, it would have been reasonable to expect that the whole or greater part of the component activities (as defined) of the relevant qualifying activity in **74.20** would have been carried on as part of another business by one or more 'relevant persons'.

A '*relevant person*' is a person who is a party to the arrangements or a person connected with such a party (within **19** CONNECTED PERSONS).

The venture capital scheme tax reliefs comprise:

- enterprise investment scheme income tax and CGT reliefs;
- seed enterprise investment scheme income tax and CGT reliefs;
- qualification as an investee company for VCT purposes (as in **74.6** above); and
- income tax share loss relief.

[*ITA 2007, ss 299A, 313(5)*].

Information powers

If an officer of HMRC has reason to believe that shares or securities have been issued to a VCT in consequence of, or otherwise in connection with, disqualifying arrangements, he may by notice require persons concerned to supply information within a specified time (at least 60 days). The penalty provisions of *TMA 1970, s 98* apply for failure to comply. [*ITA 2007, s 312A*].

Supplementary provisions

Winding up of the relevant company

[74.31] Where the relevant company is being wound up, none of the requirements listed at **74.2** above are regarded on that account as not being satisfied provided that they would be met apart from the winding up, and that the winding up is for genuine commercial reasons and is not part of a scheme or arrangement the main purpose of which is the avoidance of tax.

[*ITA 2007, s 312*].

Power to amend requirements

The Treasury has power by order to modify the trading requirement, the carrying on of a qualifying activity requirement and the qualifying subsidiaries requirement as it considers appropriate, and to substitute the sum referred to in the maximum qualifying investment requirement and the gross assets requirement above.

[*ITA 2007, s 311*].

Restructuring

Where shares or securities in a company are exchanged for corresponding shares and securities in a new holding company, then subject to detailed conditions, including HMRC approval, to the extent that any of the conditions, and any of the requirements, mentioned below was satisfied in relation to the old shares, it will generally be taken to be satisfied in relation to the new shares. The consideration for the old shares must consist wholly of the issue of shares in the new company. Certain deemed securities (see **74.2** above) which are not thus acquired by the new company may be disregarded where these provisions would otherwise be prevented from applying.

The said conditions are the investment limits condition, the permitted maximum age condition and the no business acquisition condition at **74.2** above. The said requirements are those at **74.11, 74.12, 74.14, 74.15, 74.17, 74.19–74.22,** and **74.24–74.27** above.

A new parent company (as above) which has acquired a company that has previously received funding from a VCT can use the funding history of the acquired company when considering if follow-on funding is admissible to fund the continuing activities of that acquired company. The legislation achieves this by effectively treating relevant investments made in the acquired company before the restructuring, and before the end of the initial investing period, as having been made in the new company. This is relevant to the permitted maximum age condition at **74.2** above and the permitted company age requirement at **74.22** above.

[*ITA 2007, ss 326, 326A, 327, 327A, 328, Sch 2 para 87; F(No 2)A 2017, s 12*].

Conversion of shares

Where a VCT exercises conversion rights in respect of certain convertible shares and securities, then subject to detailed conditions, for the purposes of the following requirements, the conversion is treated as an exchange of new shares for old shares to which the restructuring provisions above apply: **74.11, 74.14, 74.20, 74.21** and **74.25** above. [*ITA 2007, s 329, Sch 2 para 87*].

Reorganisations etc.

Where, under a company reorganisation or other arrangement:

- a VCT exchanges a qualifying holding for other shares or securities (with or without other consideration); and
- the exchange is for genuine commercial reasons and not part of a tax avoidance scheme or arrangements,

the new shares or securities may be treated as being qualifying holdings for a specified period even if some or all of the requirements at **74.6** above are not otherwise satisfied. Regulations specify the circumstances in which, and conditions subject to which, they apply and which requirements are to be treated as met.

Where the new shares or securities are those of a different company than before and they do not meet any one or more of the above requirements (disregarding the maximum qualifying investment requirement and the use of the money raised requirement), those requirements are treated as met for, broadly, three years in the case of shares, or five years in the case of securities, reduced in either case to, broadly, two years where the company is not, or ceases to be, an unquoted company as in the unquoted status requirement above.

A formula is provided for valuing the new shares or securities for the purposes of the proportion of eligible shares requirement above. The provisions extend to new shares or securities received in pursuance of an earn-out right conferred in exchange for a qualifying holding, in which case an election is available (under *Reg 10*) to modify the said valuation formula by effectively disregarding the earn-out right itself.

[*ITA 2007, ss 330, 303–311, Sch 2 para 88; SI 2002 No 2661*].

F(No 2)A 2017 gives the Treasury power to make regulations covering cases where, on an exchange of *non-qualifying* shares or securities that otherwise meets the condition in (b) above, a VCT receives other non-qualifying shares or securities. For context, see the non-qualifying investments condition in **74.2** above. The regulations may, inter alia, make provision as to when the new shares or securities are to be regarded as having been acquired.

[*ITA 2007, s 330; F(No 2)A 2017, s 13*].

Linked sales

Where an individual subscribes for shares in a VCT and there is at least one linked sale of other shares by the individual then the amount the individual subscribes for the shares is treated as reduced (but not below nil) by the total consideration given for the linked sale(s). If a sale is linked to more than one subscription for shares then the consideration reduces the subscription amount in the order in which the subscriptions are made.

A sale of shares is 'linked' if:

(i) the shares sold are in the VCT or (but only where Condition X below applies) in a company which is (or later becomes) a successor or predecessor of the VCT as a result of a merger or restructuring; and

(ii) either:
   - the circumstances are such that the purchase of the shares from the individual is conditional upon his making the subscription or *vice versa*; or
   - the subscription and the sale occur within six months of each other (regardless of which occurs first).

The above does not apply if, or to the extent that, the subscription is the result of the individual's electing to reinvest dividends on his VCT shares in acquiring further shares in the VCT. Condition X in (i) above is that the date of the merger or restructuring is no later than two years after the individual subscribes for the VCT shares and either the individual could reasonably be expected to know when subscribing that the merger or restructuring would take place or a main purpose of the merger or restructuring is to enable individuals to obtain a tax advantage in connection with VCT relief. For this purpose the date of the merger or restructuring is generally the date of the issue of shares by means of which it is effected.

[*ITA 2007, s 264A; FA 2018, Sch 5 paras 1, 12*].

Nominees

Shares subscribed for, issued to, held by or disposed of for an individual by a nominee are treated for the purposes of the VCT provisions, as subscribed for, issued to, held by or disposed of by the individual. Therefore an individual will qualify for income tax relief on a subscription of VCT shares if that subscription is made on the individual's behalf by a nominee. Any regulations made as to VCT procedures may apply to nominees as well as to other persons holding VCT shares.

HMRC can request certain information from both nominee and investor in order to identify the beneficial owner of the VCT shares.

[*ITA 2007, s 330A*].

Income tax reliefs

[74.32] Relief from income tax is granted in respect of both investments in VCT share issues (up to £200,000 in a tax year) and distributions from such trusts (in respect of shares acquired up to a 'permitted investment limit' in any tax year; see **74.15**). The rate of relief for investments (given by deduction from the individual's income tax liability) is 30%.

Investment relief applies to shares issued before 6 April 2025 but this date may be amended by the Treasury via statutory instrument.

[*ITTOIA 2005, Pt 6 Ch 5*].

See **74.4** and **74.5** above as regards mergers and winding-up of VCTs. For the detailed conditions for both reliefs, and for the circumstances in which investment relief is withdrawn, see Tolley's Income Tax under Venture Capital Trusts. See also **74.31** above with regard to linked sales and to holding shares via nominees.

Capital gains tax reliefs

[74.33] The capital gains of a VCT are not chargeable gains.

[*TCGA 1992, s 100(1)*].

In addition, individual investors in VCTs are exempt from capital gains on a qualifying disposal of VCT shares (up to the 'annual permitted maximum' acquired in any year of assessment, see **74.32** above). A loss on such a disposal is not an allowable loss.

For shares issued before 6 April 2004 there was a possible deferral of chargeable gains on re-investment in VCT share issue. However, gains so postponed may remain postponed until such time as there is a chargeable event.

[*TCGA 1992, ss 151A, 151B, Sch 5C*].

See **74.4** and **74.5** above as regards mergers and winding-up of VCTs. For the detailed conditions for these reliefs, and for relief on withdrawal of approval, see Tolley's Capital Gains Tax under Venture Capital Trusts.

75
Voluntary Associations

For the special treatment of certain societies, see 8 BUILDING SOCIETIES; 14 CHARITIES; 22 CO-OPERATIVE AND COMMUNITY BENEFIT SOCIETIES; 33 EXEMPT ORGANISATIONS; 40 HOUSING ASSOCIATIONS and 53 MUTUAL COMPANIES. See *Worthing Rugby Football Club Trustees v CIR* [1987] 1 WLR 1057, [1987] STC 273, CA, and *Blackpool Marton Rotary Club v Martin* (1988) 62 TC 686.

Simon's Taxes. See **B1.440, B2.213, C1.211, D1.212.**

Introduction to voluntary associations

[75.1] A club or society may be established as a company or as an unincorporated association of individuals. Whichever form it takes, it is liable to corporation tax on income (other than that generated from members e.g. membership fees or catering income from sales to members) and on capital gains. However, special rules apply to certain types of club, which in some cases offer a number of tax advantages.

This chapter covers the taxation treatment of certain commonly-found clubs and societies.

Community amateur sports clubs

[75.2] Certain tax exemptions can be claimed by sports clubs which are registered with HMRC as community amateur sports clubs (*'registered clubs'*).

For a club to be eligible to register, it must, and its constitution must require it to:

- be 'open to the whole community';
- be 'organised on an amateur basis'; and
- have as its main purpose the provision of facilities for, and promotion of participation in, one or more 'eligible sports'.

The club must also meet the location condition, the management condition and the income condition.

For the above purposes, a club is '*open to the whole community*' if membership is open to all, and the club facilities are available to members, without discrimination (leaving aside necessary differentiation on grounds of age, gender or disability relative to a particular sport). Additionally, fees must be set at a level which does not pose a significant obstacle to membership, use of the facilities or full participation in club activities. Costs are deemed to represent a significant obstacle if the total of the membership fees and sporting activity costs exceed £520 per year and the club has not made arrangements to ensure that the costs do not represent an obstacle to membership. A club is not eligible to register if it receives membership fees exceeding £1,612 in respect of any member for any year. For the meaning of 'membership fees', 'sporting activity costs' and for the increase or decrease of the limits for periods of more than or less than a year see *SI 2015 No 725, Regs 7–9*.

A club is not prevented from being open to the whole community simply because it charges different fees for different descriptions of persons.

A club is '*organised on an amateur basis*' if it meets the following four conditions.

(a) The club must be non-profit making, i.e. its constitution must require surplus income or gains to be reinvested in the club and must not permit the distribution of club assets (whether in cash or in kind) to members or third parties. However, donations by a club to charities or other registered clubs are allowed.

(b) It must provide only the following benefits for members and their guests:
- provision of sporting facilities and suitably qualified coaches;
- reasonable provision and maintenance of club-owned sports equipment;
- provision of, or reimbursement of the costs of, coaching courses;
- provision of insurance cover and medical treatment;
- reimbursement of reasonable and necessary travel or subsistence expenses incurred by players, match officials, coaches, first aiders and accompanying individuals travelling to away matches;
- reasonable provision of post-match refreshments for players and match officials; and
- sale or supply of food or drink as a social adjunct to the sporting purposes of the club.

(c) It does not exceed the limit on paid players. The limit is, broadly, £10,000 per year. For the detailed rules see *SI 2015 No 725, Regs 11–13*.

(d) The club's constitution must provide for any net assets on the dissolution of the club to be applied for the purposes of:
- a charity;
- another registered club; or
- the governing body of an eligible sport for the purposes of which the club existed, for use in related community sport,

as approved by the members of the club in general meeting or by its governing body.

An '*eligible sport*' is one designated as such by Treasury order for the purposes of these provisions. See *SI 2002 No 1966* which designates for these purposes sports appearing on the National Sports Councils list of activities recognised by them.

A club is not regarded as a community amateur sports club if the number of social members within the club exceeds 50% of the total members. For these purposes a social member is defined as a member who either does not participate or only occasionally participates in the sports activities of the club. For the meaning of 'participation' and 'occasional participation' and for the method of calculating the percentage of social members see *SI 2015 No 725, Regs 16–19*.

A club meets the location condition if it is established in the UK, an EU member State or a territory specified in HMRC regulations and its facilities for eligible sports are all in one such State or territory. Iceland, Norway and Liechtenstein have been specified by regulations for these purposes.

A club meets the management condition if its managers are fit and proper persons. For this purpose, the managers are the persons with the general control and management of the administration of the club. If this condition is not met for a period of time it is nevertheless treated as met throughout that period if HMRC consider either that the failure has not prejudiced the purposes of the club or that it is just and reasonable for the condition to be treated as met. The expression 'fit and proper' is not defined and so takes its natural meaning. HMRC consider that the fit and proper person test is the same as that for charities (see **14.1** CHARITIES).

A club meets the income condition if the total of its trading receipts and property receipts does not exceed £100,000 for an accounting period. The limit is reduced proportionately where the accounting period is less than 12 months. The receipts taken into account are those that would be included in computing the club's trading income and property income for corporation tax if the exemptions for such income did not apply.

[*CTA 2010, ss 658(1)–(1C), 659–661CA; SI 2010 No 1904; SI 2015 No 725; SI 2019 No 689, Reg 17(9)*].

For HMRC guidance on eligibility conditions see www.gov.uk/government/publications/community-amateur-sports-clubs-detailed-guidance-notes/community-amateur-sports-clubs-detailed-guidance-notes.

Registration

Applications for registration are made to HMRC. Registration may be backdated (possibly to before the date of the application).

HMRC may terminate a club's registration (possibly with retrospective effect) if it appears to them that the club is not, or is no longer, entitled to be registered.

HMRC must notify a club of a decision to register it, to refuse its application or to terminate its registration. The club may appeal against any such decision by notice in writing to HMRC within 30 days of the date of the notification. The notice of appeal must specify the grounds of appeal. The provisions of *TMA 1970* relating to five APPEALS apply to such an appeal. If not dismissing the appeal, the Tribunal may either remit the matter to HMRC for reconsideration, or, as applicable, direct that the club be registered from a particular date, rescind a termination of registration, or direct that a termination take effect on a particular date.

HMRC publishes the names and addresses of registered clubs. This enables potential donors to confirm that they are donating to a registered club (and, therefore, that the donation may qualify for gift aid relief — see below). For a list of the names of registered clubs see www.gov.uk/government/publications/community-amateur-sports-clubs-casc-registered-with-hmrc--2.

[*CTA 2010, ss 658(2)–(5), 670, 671*].

Tax exemptions

Registered clubs enjoy a number of exemptions from tax.

UK trading income

A club that is a registered club throughout an accounting period can claim for its UK trading income for the period to be exempt from corporation tax if the following two conditions are met.

The first condition is that the receipts that would otherwise be brought into account in calculating the club's UK trading income for the period do not exceed £50,000. The threshold is proportionately reduced for periods of less than 12 months.

The second condition is that the whole of the UK trading income for the period is applied for 'qualifying purposes'. '*Qualifying purposes*' means purposes of providing facilities for, and promoting participation in, one or more eligible sports (and in the following paragraphs, '*non-qualifying purposes*' are to be construed accordingly).

[*CTA 2010, ss 661(3), 662*].

UK property income

A club that is a registered club throughout an accounting period may make a claim for its UK property income to be exempt from corporation tax if both of the following conditions are met

The receipts that would otherwise be brought into account in calculating the club's property income for the period must not exceed £30,000. The threshold is proportionately reduced for accounting periods of less than 12 months.

The second condition is that all of the UK property income for that period is applied for qualifying purposes (as above).

[*CTA 2010, s 662*].

Interest, gift aid income and company gift income

A club that is a registered club throughout an accounting period can make a claim for its interest income, 'gift aid income' and 'company gift income' for the period to be exempt from corporation tax if the whole of the income is applied for qualifying purposes (as above). '*Gift aid income*' for this purpose means gifts to the club made by individuals which are qualifying gift aid donations. 'Company gift income' means gifts of money to the club made by companies which are not charities.

[*CTA 2010, s 664*].

Chargeable gains

A gain accruing to a registered club is not a chargeable gain if it is wholly applied for qualifying purposes (as above) and the club makes a claim to that effect. [*CTA 2010, s 665*].

Where a club holds property and, without disposing of it, ceases at any time to be a registered club or to hold the property for qualifying purposes, it is treated for the purposes of *TCGA 1992* as having disposed of, and immediately reacquired, the property at that time at its then market value. Any gain resulting from the deemed disposal does not attract the above exemption. Additionally, to the extent that any of the property represents, directly or indirectly, the consideration for the disposal of assets by the club, any gain that accrued on that disposal does not attract the exemption. Assessments in respect of resulting chargeable gains can be made at any time not later than three years after the end of the accounting period in which falls the event giving rise to this treatment. [*CTA 2010, s 669*].

Restrictions on exemptions

The above exemptions are restricted where a registered club incurs any expenditure for non-qualifying purposes in an accounting period and any of the club's income or gains for that period are exempted from tax (or would be but for the restriction).

The restriction operates by comparing the amount of the expenditure incurred in the accounting period for non-qualifying purposes ('*the non-qualifying expenditure*') with the aggregate of the club's income (whether or not taxable, and before deducting expenses) and gains (whether chargeable gains or gains exempted as above) for the accounting period ('*the total income and gains*'), as follows:

(1) Where the non-qualifying expenditure is less than the total income and gains, the amount of exempt income and gains is restricted in the proportion that the non-qualifying expenditure bears to the total income and gains.

(2) Where the non-qualifying expenditure equals the total income and gains, the amount of exempt income and gains is reduced to nil.

(3) Where the non-qualifying expenditure exceeds the total income and gains, the amount of exempt income and gains is reduced to nil, and the 'surplus amount' is carried back to previous accounting periods (latest first) ending not more than six years before the end of the current period, and deducted from income and gains exempted for those periods. To the extent that the amount exempted for an accounting period has already been reduced under this provision or (1) or (2) above, it cannot be reduced again by reference to expenditure of a later accounting period. The '*surplus amount*' is the excess of:

(i) an amount equal to the proportion of the originally exempt income and gains that the non-qualifying expenditure bears to the total income and gains, over;

(ii) the amount of the originally exempt income and gains.

Where, as a consequence of this restriction, a registered club has an amount of income and gains for which exemption is not available, the club may, by notice to HMRC, specify which items of income and gains are, in whole or part, to be attributed to that amount. If no such notice is given by the club within 30 days of being required to do so by HMRC, it falls to HMRC to make the attribution.

[*CTA 2010, ss 666–668*].

Reliefs for donations

Gifts to registered clubs by individuals can qualify for relief under the gift aid provisions and gifts by companies can qualify for charitable donations relief (see **14.11** CHARITIES). Gifts received by a registered club which are qualifying gift aid donations are treated as received under deduction of income tax at the basic rate for the tax year in which the gift is made. See *CTA 2010, s 661D*.

Gifts of assets can qualify for relief under *TCGA 1992, s 257* (gifts of assets to charities treated as no gain/no loss).

Mutual trading — members' clubs

[75.3] A club established by its members for its own social and recreational purposes is not carrying on a trade and as such is not liable to tax on its surplus from the provision of facilities for members. Any surplus that arises if subscriptions exceed expenditure is treated as a surplus rather than as a trading profit. However, if the club provides services on a commercial basis to outsiders, such as visitors or temporary members, any surplus arising is taxable as trading income. See **54.1** MUTUAL COMPANIES.

For HMRC's views on the circumstances in which a members' sports club's commercial activities can give rise to taxable trading profits (or to allowable trading losses), see HMRC's Business Income Manual, BIM24215.

VAT repayments

Repayments which are returned to members *pro rata* to the VAT originally paid by them do not give rise to a distribution for tax purposes. VAT repayment supplements under *VATA 1994, s 79* should be disregarded for income and corporation tax purposes pursuant to *CTA 2009, s 1286*. However, interest payable by HMRC in respect of certain cases of official error under *VATA 1994, s 78* is not within this exemption. See further HMRC's Business Income Manual, BIM31610.

Holiday clubs and thrift funds

[75.4] Holiday clubs and thrift funds formed annually for the purpose of saving for holidays are regarded as being outside the scope of corporation tax.

Investment clubs

[75.5] An investment club comprises a group of people who have joined together to invest, primarily on the Stock Exchange. Members are entitled to a share of the income received on the investments and of the gains and losses on the disposal of any shares or other investments. Such clubs are generally unincorporated associations and therefore within the definition of a company for corporation tax purposes. However, HMRC consider that investment clubs generally hold funds in a fiduciary capacity and are therefore outside the scope of corporation tax (HMRC Company Taxation Manual CTM40650).

Members are charged to income tax and capital gains tax on their share of the income and gains. HMRC will accept any reasonable method provided by the rules of the club for dividing gains between members so long as it is based on the proportionate shares of the investments held by members and is consistently applied. See HMRC Capital Gains Manual CG20600.

Lotteries etc.

[75.6] Supporters of a sports club may raise fund for the club by running or promoting a lottery. Any lottery must comply with the terms of the *Lotteries and Amusements Act 1975*. The tax treatment of sports supporters' lotteries is set out in HMRC Statement of Practice C1. This provides that where a football pool or small lottery is run by the supporters of a club or other society on the basis that a stated percentage or fraction of the cost of each ticket will be given to the club, HMRC accept that the donation element can be excluded when computing for tax purposes the profits of the trade promoting the pool or lottery.

[HMRC Statement of Practice C1].

Dissolution

[75.7] An unincorporated association which sells its only fixed asset and closes down is liable to corporation tax on any chargeable gain arising by virtue of being within the definition of a company at *CTA 2010, s 1121*.

The provisions of *CTA 2010, s 1030*, whereby a distribution made in respect of share capital in a winding up is not a distribution of a company, do not apply to the dissolution of most unincorporated associations because these have no share capital. However, by concession (ESC C15) a company which is an unincorporated association has the option of treating distributions on dissolution as chargeable distributions or as capital payments (subject to capital gains tax) provided that:

- it has not carried on an investment trade or business (other than a mutual trade);
- the amount distributed to each member is not large; and
- substantially the whole of its activities have been of a social or recreational nature.

See HMRC's Company Taxation Manual CTM41335.

Key points on voluntary associations

[75.8] The key points are as follows:

- A club may be established as a company or unincorporated society and be liable to corporation tax on income generated other than by members.
- Special rules apply to certain types of clubs.
- Registered community amateur sports clubs enjoy a number of tax advantages, including exemption from tax on UK trading profits and UK property income (up to certain limits) and on interest and gift aid income and chargeable gains. These tax exemptions are contingent on certain conditions being met.
- Clubs established by members for their own social and recreational purposes are not trading and as such are not liable to tax on any surplus of subscriptions over income. However any profit on commercial activities is taxable.
- Holiday clubs and thrift funds are outside the scope to tax.
- Members of investment clubs are taxed on income and gains arising from their investments.
- Where a lottery is run to raise money for a sports club and a percentage of the ticket price is donated to the club, the donation element is excluded from the computation of profits for tax purposes.

76

Winding Up

Cross-reference. See **64.3** RESIDENCE.

Simon's Taxes. See **D6.7**.

Introduction to winding up

[76.1] For most corporation tax purposes, the effect of passing of a resolution to wind up, filing a winding up petition or appointing an administrator is the same. However, there are some differences relating to beneficial ownership of assets and accounting periods.

On the commencement of a winding-up, an accounting period ends and a new one commences. Thereafter an accounting period only ends on the expiration of twelve months from its beginning or by completion of the winding-up.

[*CTA 2009, s 12*].

Where a company enters administration, an accounting period ends immediately before the administration commenced, and another begins immediately thereafter unless the company was being wound up at that time.

[*CTA 2009, s 10*].

Liquidation

[76.2] Corporation tax is charged on the profits of a company arising in the winding-up in the financial year (i.e. a year to 31 March — see **1** INTRODUCTION AND RATES OF TAX) in which the winding-up is completed (the final year) at the rate of corporation tax 'fixed' or 'proposed' for that year. If, however, the rate for the final year has not been proposed or fixed before the winding-up is completed, the rate fixed or proposed for the previous financial year (the penultimate year) applies for the final year. Where the winding-up commenced before the company's final year, the company's profits arising in the penultimate year are charged at the rates applicable to that year.

For the above purposes, the rate of corporation tax means the main rate or, if applicable, the small ring-fence profits rate or, for financial years 2023 onwards, the standard small profits rate. A corporation tax rate is '*fixed*' if it is fixed by an Act passed before the completion of the winding-up. A rate is '*proposed*' if it is proposed by a Budget resolution.

[*CTA 2010, ss 626(2), 627, 628, 632; FA 2021, Sch 1 para 29*].

An assessment on a company's profits for an accounting period falling after the commencement of the winding-up is not invalid because made before the end of the accounting period. The liquidator may determine beforehand an assumed date when the winding-up will be completed for the purpose of making an assessment for a period intended to end with the completion of the winding-up. A date so assumed will not alter the company's final and penultimate years, and if it falls short of the actual completion date, a new accounting period will commence from the assumed date and *CTA 2009, s 12(4)* (length of accounting period after commencement of winding-up, see **76.6** below) will apply as if that new accounting period began with the commencement of the winding-up.

[*CTA 2010, s 629*].

In the company's final accounting period (i.e. the period ending with the completion of the winding-up), any income consisting of INTEREST ON OVERPAID TAX (**43**) is excluded from charge provided that it does not exceed £2,000.

[*CTA 2010, s 633*].

Corporation tax on chargeable gains is a 'necessary expense' of a winding-up within the meaning of *Companies Act 1985, s 560* (*Re Mesco Properties Ltd* CA 1979, 54 TC 238).

The Crown may set off a debt due from one Government Department to the company against a debt due to another Department (or other Departments) under *Bankruptcy Act 1914, s 312*. See *Re Cushla Ltd* Ch D, [1979] STC 615 which involved a VAT repayment and liabilities to HMRC and the DSS (now the Department for Work and Pensions).

Administration

[76.3] Where a company enters administration a new accounting period begins. An accounting period ends when it comes out of administration.

Corporation tax is charged on the profits arising in the administration in the financial year (i.e. a year to 31 March — see **1** INTRODUCTION AND RATES OF TAX) in which the 'dissolution event' occurs (the 'final year') at the rate of corporation tax 'fixed' or 'proposed' for that year. If, however, the rate for the final year has not been proposed or fixed before the dissolution event, the rate fixed or proposed for the previous financial year (the penultimate year) applies for the final year.

The rate of corporation tax for these purposes means the full rate or, if applicable, the small profits rate (for ring-fence profits). A corporation tax rate is '*fixed*' if it is fixed by an Act passed before the dissolution event. A rate is '*proposed*' if it is proposed by a Budget resolution.

The '*dissolution event*' is the sending by the administrator of a notice under *Insolvency Act 1986, Sch B1 para 84(1)* (company moving from administration to dissolution) or, if the company entered administration other than under that Act, anything else done for a like purpose.

An administrator's appointment is normally for twelve months, but this may be extended by six months by creditors or indefinitely by the court.

An assessment on a company's profits for an accounting period in which the company is in administration is not invalid because it is made before the end of the accounting period. In making an assessment after the company enters administration and before the dissolution event, the administrator may act on an assumption as to the date on which an accounting period will end by reason of the occurrence of the dissolution event. A date so assumed will not alter the company's final and penultimate years, and if it falls short of the actual date, a new accounting period will commence from the assumed date, and *CTA 2009, s 10(1)* (see **2.5** ACCOUNTING PERIODS) will apply as if the company entered administration at the start of that new accounting period.

In the accounting period ending with the dissolution event, any INTEREST ON OVERPAID TAX (**43**) is excluded from charge provided that it does not exceed £2,000.

[*CTA 2010, ss 626(3)(4), 630–633*].

Effect on group relationship

[76.4] The passing of a resolution, or the making of an order, or any other act, for the winding-up of a company does not mean that a company (or any of its 75% subsidiaries) ceases to be a member of a group for the purpose of the capital gains provisions in *TCGA 1992, ss 171–181*, regarding which see **12.2** CAPITAL GAINS — GROUPS. [*TCGA 1992, s 170(11)*]. For other group purposes, e.g. group relief, such acts bring about the end of the group relationship, although the making of an administration order would not of itself bring about such a change.

A company in administration does not lose beneficial ownership of its assets. However, where the company in administration is a subsidiary, there may no longer be a group relationship as the subsidiary is under the control of the administrator, not the parent company shareholders.

Release of debts

[76.5] The release does not give rise to a taxable receipt in the debtor company in relation to debts released as part of a statutory insolvency arrangement.

[*CTA 2009, s 94*].

The creditor will obtain relief for a debt so released, provided that it is released wholly and exclusively for trade purposes.

[*CTA 2009, s 55*].

Vesting of company's assets in liquidator

[76.6] The vesting of a company's assets in a liquidator is disregarded for capital gains purposes and all acts of the liquidator in relation to those assets are treated as acts of the company. [*TCGA 1992, s 2G; FA 2019, Sch 1 paras 2, 120*]. Note that the legislation for this provision was previously at *TCGA 1992, s 8(6)*.

Expenses of winding-up

[76.7] All expenses properly incurred in a voluntary winding-up, including the remuneration of the liquidator, are payable out of the company's assets in priority to all other claims.

[*Insolvency Act 1986, s 115*].

Insolvency Rules 1986, Rule 4.218(1) provides that expenses of a liquidation are to be paid out of the assets in the order of priority therein specified, subject to a discretionary power of the court under *Insolvency Act 1986, s 156* to vary the order where assets are insufficient to satisfy liabilities.

[*SI 1986 No 1925, Rules 4.218(1), 4.220*].

Included in the normal order of priority is the amount of any corporation tax on chargeable gains accruing on the realisation of any asset of the company. [*Rule 4.218(1)(p)*]. Notwithstanding the specific inclusion of corporation tax on chargeable gains, corporation tax chargeable on a company's post-liquidation profits is to be treated as a 'necessary disbursement' of the liquidator (within *Insolvency Rules 1986, Rule 4.218(1)(m)*), and thus as an expense requiring priority as above (*Re Toshoku Finance UK plc, Kahn and another v CIR* HL, [2002] STC 368). (See, however, **50.25** LOAN RELATIONSHIPS for provisions which prevent liability arising in the particular circumstances of this case for accounting periods beginning on or after 1 October 2002.)

Legislation is introduced by *FA 2020* to give HMRC priority in the recovery of VAT and other taxes deducted by taxpayers (such as PAYE, NICs and construction industry scheme deductions) with effect for insolvency proceedings beginning on or after 1 December 2020. See *FA 2020, ss 98, 99* and *SI 2020 No 983*.

Profits arising in winding-up

[76.8] A company is chargeable to corporation tax on the profits arising in the winding-up of the company.

[*CTA 2009, s 6(2)*].

Cancellation of tax advantages

[76.9] See *CTA 2010, ss 731–751*, as described at 70.1 TRANSACTIONS IN SECURITIES.

Tax returns during winding-up etc.

[76.10] Where an insolvent company is being wound up, is in administrative receivership or having its affairs, business and property managed by an administrator, the company is not required to file its self-assessment corporation tax return electronically. The exemption extends to equivalent insolvency procedures outside the UK.

[*SI 2003 No 282, Reg 3(10A), (12)*].

See www.gov.uk/government/publications/corporation-tax-mandatory-online-filing-and-the-end-of-a-companys-life.

77

Finance Act 2021 Summary

[77.1]

(Royal Assent 10 June 2021)

Statutory reference	
s 6	**Corporation tax charge.** Corporation tax is charged for 2022 at the rate of 19%. For 2023, the main rate is increased to 25%. See **1.2** INTRODUCTION.
s 7, Sch 1	**Small profits rate.** As a result of the increase in the main rate of corporation tax to 25% for 2023, a small profits rate of 19% is introduced for 2023 onwards. See **1.3** INTRODUCTION.
s 8	**Diverted profits tax.** The 25% rate is to increase to 31% for accounting periods beginning on or after 1 April 2023 (subject to transitional rules for straddling periods). See **30.8** DIVERTED PROFITS TAX.
ss 9–14	**Super-deduction.** Temporary enhanced first-year allowances (FYAs) are available for certain qualifying expenditure incurred by companies in the period 1 April 2021 to 31 March 2023 inclusive. Expenditure on unused (not second-hand) plant and machinery qualifies for an FYA of **130%**. Special rate expenditure, however, qualifies for an FYA of only 50%. A balancing charge arises in an accounting period in which a disposal event occurs to the extent that one of the temporary allowances has been given. See **10.13** CAPITAL ALLOWANCES ON PLANT AND MACHINERY.
s 15	**Annual investment allowance.** The temporary increase from £200,000 to £1,000,000 of the maximum amount of annual investment allowance is extended by twelve months to 31 December 2021. See **10.12** CAPITAL ALLOWANCES ON PLANT AND MACHINERY.
s 17	**Long funding leasing: extensions of plant or machinery leases for reasons related to coronavirus.** Lessors of plant or machinery may have made concessions to allow lessees to defer rental payments during the pandemic. The normal rules on extension of the terms of a lease are temporarily eased in certain circumstances where there is a change in the payments under a lease on a date between 1 January 2020 and 30 June 2021. See **10.52** CAPITAL ALLOWANCES ON PLANT AND MACHINERY.

s 18, Sch 2 **Trade losses carried back.** The period to which trade losses can be carried back to earlier accounting periods is extended from twelve months to three years for losses incurred in accounting periods ending between 1 April 2020 and 31 March 2022 inclusive. A number of further rules and restrictions apply to the extension. In particular, companies which are members of a group can only make claims for amounts equal to or above the de minimis limit of £200,000 to the extent that relief given beyond the normal twelve-month period in respect of any other claims by the company or other group members (including de minimis claims) total less than £2 million. See **51.4** LOSSES.

s 19, Schs 3, 4 **R&D tax credits for SMEs.** For accounting periods beginning on or after 1 April 2021, the R&D tax credit to which a company is entitled is subject to a cap equal to £20,000 plus three times the company's expenditure on workers. There are exceptions to the cap where the company is creating, preparing to create, or managing intellectual property or where no more than 15% of the company's qualifying expenditure is on externally provided workers or contracted out R&D. See **63.7** RESEARCH AND DEVELOPMENT EXPENDITURE.

s 30, Sch 6 **Construction industry scheme (CIS).** The CIS is amended for 2021/22 and subsequent years. The first amendment simplifies the deemed contractor rules, and provides for a period of grace. The second clarifies the rules on deductions for materials purchased by the sub-contractor. The third provides new powers for HMRC to restrict set-off claims for amounts of tax deducted under the CIS. The final amendment expands the scope of current penalties for providing false information for the purpose of becoming a registered sub-contractor. See **20.3–20.5** CONSTRUCTION INDUSTRY SCHEME.

s 33 **Tax deduction for payment of business rates previously waived.** A tax deduction in computing business profits is made available for a payment to a public authority representing business rates previously waived by the authority by way of support to businesses in connection with coronavirus. This has effect regardless of when the payment is made. See **69.59** TRADING INCOME — DEDUCTIONS.

s 34 **Repeal of provisions relating to the Interest and Royalties Directive.** Following Brexit, the provisions which give effect in the UK to the EU Interest and Royalties Directive are repealed. The repeal applies, in most cases, to payments made on or after 1 June 2021. The repeal applies to payments made on or after 3 March 2021, however, if arrangements have been made with a main purpose of securing that the provisions will apply to the payment. See **41.5–41.7** INCOME TAX IN RELATION TO A COMPANY.

s 36, Sch 7 **Hybrid and other mismatches.** Various amendments are made to the rules for hybrid and other mismatches. These include changes to allow certain amounts of taxable income to be treated as dual inclusion income and, in particular, changes to allow groups of companies to allocate dual inclusion income within the group. The latter change applies from 1 January 2021. See **4.13** ANTI-AVOIDANCE onwards and in particular **4.24.**

s 37, Sch 8 **Losses.** A number of changes are made to the provisions which restrict the deduction of carried-forward losses. These include provisions which allow a group allowance nomination to be made after the date a group has ceased to exist (for example because of an acquisition or demerger) to cover the period up to that date. These revised nomination provisions apply retrospectively from the introduction of the restriction on deductions of carried-forward losses. See **51.15** LOSSES.

s 38 **Corporate interest restriction.** Minor technical amendments are made to the rules to ensure that they work as intended. See **24.9** CORPORATE INTEREST RESTRICTION.

s 39 The **Northern Ireland Housing Executive** is exempt from corporation tax with effect from 1 April 2020. See **66.6** STATUTORY BODIES.

s 113 **Designation of freeport tax sites.** This empowers the Treasury to designate by regulations an area in Great Britain as a special area (a 'freeport tax site') for the purposes of, inter alia, the structures and buildings allowance. See **9.23** CAPITAL ALLOWANCES, **10.23** CAPITAL ALLOWANCES ON PLANT AND MACHINERY.

s 114, Sch 22 **Capital allowances and freeport tax sites.** An annual rate of structures and buildings allowance of 10% is available for qualifying expenditure incurred on non-residential structures and buildings situated in freeport tax sites. A 100% first-year allowance is available for expenditure on the provision of unused (not second-hand) plant or machinery for use primarily in an area which (at the time the expenditure is incurred) is in a freeport tax site. These enhanced reliefs are available for expenditure incurred from the date the freeport tax site is designated as such until 30 September 2026. See **9.23** CAPITAL ALLOWANCES, **10.23** CAPITAL ALLOWANCES ON PLANT AND MACHINERY.

s 116, Schs 24, 25 **Late filing penalty.** For income tax self-assessment (ITSA) taxpayers, a new regime will replace the pre-existing late filing penalty regime from 2023. Although it is intended that the new system will eventually apply to corporation tax, the legislation does not include CT at this point. See **59.1** PENALTIES.

s 117, Sch 26 **Late payment penalty.** For income tax self-assessment (ITSA) taxpayers, a new regime will replace the pre-existing late payment penalty regime 2023. Although it is intended that the new system will eventually apply to corporation tax, the legislation does not include CT at this point. See **59.1** PENALTIES.

s 119, Sch 28 **Follower notice penalties.** For penalties assessed on or after date of Royal Assent for failure to take corrective action, the maximum penalty is reduced from 50% to 30% of the value of the denied tax advantage. However, an additional penalty of up to 20% of the value of the denied tax advantage may now be charged where the taxpayer or their representative is found to have acted unreasonably in bringing or conducting an appeal to the Tribunal relating to the tax arrangements in question. See **59.14** PENALTIES.

s 121, Sch 30 **Promoters of tax avoidance schemes.** With effect from Royal Asset, HMRC can issue a 'stop notice' requiring a promoter to stop marketing a particular scheme if it satisfies certain conditions. This power can apply even if the scheme in question has not been defeated before a tribunal or court. Names and other details of promoters subject to such a notice may be published. Other amendments to the regime include widening its scope to include as promoters certain persons involved in promotion structures. See, principally, **28.19, 28.22** DISCLOSURE OF TAX AVOIDANCE SCHEMES.

s 122, Sch 31 **Disclosure of tax avoidance schemes.** This has effect on or after date of Royal Assent, and provides that when HMRC reasonably suspect that a person has failed to disclose arrangements or proposed arrangements which should have been notified to them, they may issue a notice to anyone they reasonably suspect of being a promoter or supplier of the arrangements or proposed arrangements. The notice will explain that, unless the recipient can satisfy HMRC that the arrangements or proposal are not notifiable, HMRC may allocate a scheme reference number to the arrangements or proposal. See, principally, **28.11** DISCLOSURE OF TAX AVOIDANCE SCHEMES.

s 123 **Penalty for enabling defeated tax avoidance.** This makes various amendments to this penalty regime, broadly from date of Royal Assent. In particular, it amends the special provisions for multi-user schemes altering the threshold percentages before a penalty can be issued. It also enables HMRC to use its information powers to check a person's potential liability for a penalty before the arrangements in question are defeated, and to help identify any other person who may have enabled the arrangements. See **59.21** PENALTIES.

s 124, Sch 32 **General anti-abuse rule (GAAR): partnerships.** This makes provision about the operation of the GAAR in relation to partnerships; it provides for the GAAR procedure to work consistently with how HMRC conducts tax enquiries in respect of partnerships. It has effect on and after date of Royal Assent but in relation to tax arrangements entered into at any time (whether before or after that date). See **4.7** ANTI-AVOIDANCE.

s 126 **Financial institution notices.** This allows HMRC to obtain third party information from financial institutions without Tribunal approval. It has effect from date of Royal Assent, but for the purpose of checking the tax position of a taxpayer as regards periods or tax liabilities whenever arising, or for the purpose of collecting a tax debt of a taxpayer whenever arising. See **38.5** HMRC INVESTIGATORY POWERS.

s 127 **Collection of tax debts.** This extends HMRC's information powers to permit information notices, third party notices etc. to be issued for the purpose of collecting a tax debt. It has effect from date of Royal Assent, but for the purpose of collecting a tax debt whenever arising. See **38.3**, **38.4** HMRC INVESTIGATORY POWERS.

s 128, Sch 34 **Miscellaneous amendments to HMRC information powers.** These amendments have effect from date of Royal Assent. In cases where the Tribunal disapplies the requirement to give a copy of a third-party notice or financial institution notice to the taxpayer, the notice can now specifically provide that the third party or financial institution cannot disclose the notice, or anything related to it, to the taxpayer or any other person. See **38.5** HMRC INVESTIGATORY POWERS. Procedural changes are made to the rules governing increased daily penalties for failure to comply with information notices etc. See **59.11** PENALTIES.

s 132 **Replacement of LIBOR.** Minor amendments are made to deal with the withdrawal of the London Interbank Offered Rate (LIBOR) in tax legislation. References in tax legislation to LIBOR are replaced by the 'incremental borrowing rate' defined by GAAP. See **10.49** CAPITAL ALLOWANCES ON PLANT AND MACHINERY and **49.8**, **49.10** LEASING.

78 Table of Statutes

References on the right-hand side of this table are to paragraphs.

79 Table of Statutory Instruments

References on the right-hand side of this table are to paragraphs.

80 Table of Cases

This Table of Cases is referenced to paragraph numbers.

A

B

C

D

E

F

G

H

I

J

K

L

M

N

O

P

Q

R

S

T

U

Decisions of the European Court of Justice are listed below numerically. These decisions are also included in the preceding alphabetical list.

81 Index

This index is referenced to chapter and paragraph number.

B

C

D

E

F

G

H

I

J

M

T

V